Art Sales Index

publications and services for the art world

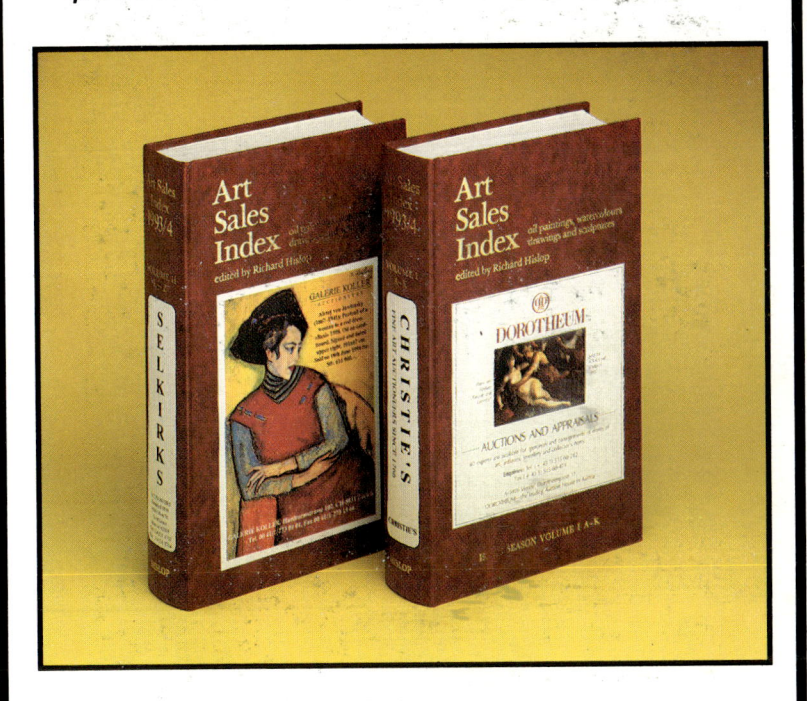

26th Edition of the **Art Sales Index** covering sales up to August 1994. 97,500 works of art by 31,000 artists from over 1900 auctions.

$175 ISBN: 0 903872 49 8

Starting prices:-
   Watercolors $450, Oil paintings $550, Sculpture $750

For orders and further information contact:
   Art Sales Index Ltd., 1 Thames Street, Weybridge, Surrey KT13 8JG UK
   Tel: 011 44 1932 856426   Fax: 011 44 1932 842482

Auction Prices
of
American Artists

Auction Prices
of
American Artists

9th biennial edition

Auction seasons 1992/94

Edited by
Duncan Hislop

Published by

ART SALES INDEX LTD
1 THAMES STREET, WEYBRIDGE, SURREY, ENGLAND

© Art Sales Index Ltd. 1994

All rights reserved. No part of this publication may be reproduced, transmitted or used in any form or by any means - graphic, electronic or mechanical, including photocopying, recording, taping or information storage and retrieval or otherwise - without the prior permission of the Copyright holder.

ISBN 0 903872 50 1

Published, computer composition and typeset by
Art Sales Index Ltd
1, Thames Street, Weybridge, Surrey KT13 8JG UK
Tel: (1932) 856426   Fax: (1932) 842482

Printed and bound by
BPC Wheatons Ltd
Hennock Road, Marsh Barton, Exeter

Whilst every care has been taken in compiling the information in this publication, the Publishers and Copyright holders accept no responsibility for any errors or omissions.

Contents

Introduction 7-9
Million Dollar Club 13-14
Auction season turnover analysis 15

Sale results for the auction seasons 92/93 and 93/94
oil paintings, watercolors and drawings 1-559
sculpture and 3-dimensional works 561-619

INTRODUCTION

The biennial "Auction Prices of American Artists" contains the price and details of Oil Paintings, Watercolors, Drawings, Miniatures and Sculpture of North, South and Central American artists and sculptors sold at public auction, internationally, in the two auction seasons from August 1992 to July 1994. It lists some 22,500 works extracted from the sale results recorded by ASI over that two year period. ASI records nearly 100,000 sale results each season and handles some 2000 sale catalogues from 423 different auctioneers. Items for the different media qualify for entry when they exceed a certain "starting" price. Over the years, starting prices have been raised so as to take inflation into account. The levels for the season are given on the sub-title page of the appropriate section of the book. Artists are shown alphabetically A to Z. Sale prices are listed in ascending order. For each artist, Oil Paintings are given first, followed, in *italics,* by Watercolors and Drawings and Miniatures. Details of Sculpture and three dimensional works are shown at the end of the book.

Sources of information
The index is compiled from catalogues, price lists and other information provided by auctioneers. ASI takes great care in extracting information accurately. However, ASI cannot be held responsible for errors unwittingly made, nor for unknowingly reproducing incorrect information. ASI cannot vouch for the authenticity of pictures recorded. It is the reputation and integrity of the auctioneer which does this.

"Bought-in" pictures
Pictures offered for sale at auction usually have a "reserve" placed on them by the owner in order that they should not be sold at a price which he considers to be below their real value. If the bidding does not reach this reserve, the pictures are deemed to have been unsold. In England, these items are known as "bought-in". ASI DOES NOT RECORD "BOUGHT-IN WORKS". The majority of auctioneer contributors exclude "bought-in" prices from their price lists. However, there might be occasions when a "bought-in" price is inadvertently included. If any price is of particular importance to a subscriber, then he would be advised to check directly with the auctioneers.

Prices, buyer's premium and exchange rates
ASI DOES NOT INCLUDE THE BUYER'S PREMIUM. The price recorded is the "hammer" price, the price which is called out at auction and at which the item is "knocked down" to the bidder. During the course of the auction season, all entries to the ASI Data Bank are made at the EXCHANGE RATE APPLICABLE TO THE DATE OF THE SALE.

Medium and dimensions
All pictures listed are oil on canvas *unless* otherwise stated. Watercolors and Drawings are shown in *italics* and are grouped to follow the Oil Paintings under each artist. Measurements of pictures are "height by width" and measurements of 3-dimensional pieces are "height by width by depth".

Presentation of artists' names

The convention adopted by ASI in the presentation of artists' names is to show the surname first, followed by the forenames, followed by the "de", "de la", "van" and "von" etc. Hence, Sir Anthony van Dyck is listed as "DYCK, Sir Anthony van." Le Corbusier is shown as "CORBUSIER, Le". An exception is made where the "de", etc is embedded in the name, for example: Anne Louis Girodet de Roucy Trioson is shown as : "GIRODET DE ROUCY TRIOSON, Anne Louis". Where the qualifications "after", "circle", "attrib", "studio" and "style" are used, they are shown after the name. A picture catalogued as "Style of Abraham Calraet" is shown as : "CALRAET, Abraham (style)".

Wherever possible, ASI uses the name given by the auctioneer in the sale catalogue. Obvious spelling mistakes are corrected but other changes are kept to a minimum. However, in some instances, and especially with Old Masters, it is necessary to adopt standardisation (there are 15 ways of spelling Bartholomew in European languages!). Also, the presentation of an artist's name is not uniform throughout the world. But there are certain "conventions" which responsible auctioneers follow.

These conventions are best illustrated by quoting directly from a Christie's catalogue:
a) a work catalogued with the name(s) or recognised designation of an artist, without qualification, is in our opinion a work by the artist;
b) in other cases, in our opinion, the following expressions, with the following meanings are used:

- *attributed to*   probably a work by the artist in whole or in part
   (ASI use "attrib");
- *studio of*   a work by an unknown hand in the studio of the artist which may or may not have been executed under the artist's direction
   (ASI use "studio");
- *circle of*   a work by an (as yet) unidentified but distinct hand, closely associated with the named artist but not necessarily his pupil
   (ASI use "circle");
- style or   a work by a painter working in the artist's syle, contemporary or follower of nearly contemporary, but not necessarily his pupil
   (ASI use "style");
- *manner of*   a work executed in the artist's style but of a later date
   (ASI use "style");
- *after*   a copy (of any date) of a known work of the artist
   (ASI use "after").

Note also the views on signatures as recorded in Sotheby's and Christie's catalogues:
a) references to signature, inscription, dates refer to the present state of the work;
b) the term "bears a signature" and/or "date" and/or "inscription" means that in our opinion the artist's name and/or date and/or inscription have been added by another hand;
c) the term "signed" and/or "dated" and/or "inscribed" means that in our opinion the signature and/or date and/or inscription are from the hand of the artist.

Abbreviation
Abbreviations used in the index include:

attrib = attributed to	exec = executed	mono = monogram
bears sig = bears signature	f = foundry	pat = patina
C = Century	fl = flourished	/R = illustrated in catalogue
chk = chalk	htd = heightened	rec = rectangular
chl = charcoal	i = inscribed	s = signed
cm = centimetres	in = inches	snr = senior
col = color	init = initials	st = stamped
d = dated	jnr = junior	W/C = watercolor
dr = drawing	min = miniature	(?) = unknown dimensions
		# = lot number

How to read an entry:
ABBEY, Edwin Austin (1852-1911) American
$17000 £10759   Young woman in the woods (25x30cm-10x12in) s.d.1879 W/C gouache.
           3-Dec-92 Sotheby's, New York #39/R

ABBEY, Edwin Austin	artist's name
(1852-1911) American	artist's dates of birth and death and nationality
$17000 £10759	price realised in $ and £
Young woman in the woods	title or description of picture
(25x30cm-10x12in)	dimensions, height by width in centimetres & inches
s.d.1879 W/C gouache	signed and dated 1879, watercolor gouache
3-Dec-92	date of auction
Sotheby's, New York	Auctioneer and place of sale
#39	lot number of picture
/R	illustrated in the sale catalogue

Sloan's
*Fine Arts Auctioneers - Appraisers
Since 1853*

WILLI BAUMEISTER (German 1889-1955).
<u>Composition</u>. Signed and dated "2.46";
Signed, dated and located
"Stuggart, Germany" on reverse.
Oil on board. 18" x 21" [Sold: 5/1994, $89,000]

NATIONALLY ADVERTISED ESTATE AUCTIONS
Antiques * Fine Art * Silver * Rugs *Jewelry * Porcelain * Libraries

ILLUSTRATED BROCHURES UPON REQUEST

C.G SLOAN & COMPANY
4920 Wyaconda Road, North Bethesda, MD 20852 USA
301 468-4911 Fax 301 468-9182

JOYNER
Auctioneers & Appraisers

CLARENCE ALPHONSE GAGNON, R.C.A. 1881-1942
Midnight Mass, oil on paper, 7¼ x 8½ ins

Pre-auction estimate was $30,000-40,000.
Sold at Joyner's in May 1994 for $110,000.

CANADIAN ART AT AUCTION

Joyner's is the only auction firm specializing exclusively in Canadian Art.

We offer over two decades of expertise and personal service to individuals, corporations and institutions in buying and selling at auction and preparing appraisals for insurance, estate, gift and other purposes.

222 GERRARD STREET EAST, TORONTO, ONTARIO M5A 2E8
TELEPHONE (416) 323-0909   FACSIMILE (416) 323-9249

A Moment for Reflection
J. G. Meyer von Bremen
25 1/2 by 20 inches, sold for
$48,000 on April 17, 1994

Personalized quality service and exposure to international markets

HANZEL GALLERIES • INC

1120 South Michigan Avenue
Chicago, Illinois 60605 USA

Phone: 321-922-6234
Fax: 321-922-6972

THE OVER $1,000,000 CLUB (FROM THE 1992/94 AUCTION SEASONS)

BIERSTADT, Albert
   $1,050,000   Kern's River Valley, California
BOTERO, Fernando
   $1,400,000   La Casa de Las Gemelas Arias
CALDER, Alexander
   $1,650,000   Constellation
CASSATT, Mary
   $2,300,000   Young lady in a loge, gazing to the right
   $1,400,000   Woman in black hat and raspberry pink costume
   $1,000,000   Mother and child
CHASE, William Merritt
   $3,600,000   Peonies
FEININGER, Lyonel
   $1,400,000   Draisinenfahrer
FRANCIS, Sam
   $1,150,000   Red
GORKY, Arshile
   $3,500,000   Year after year
   $3,200,000   Dark green painting
HARTLEY, Marsden
   $1,050,000   Abstraction
HASSAM, Childe
   $5,000,000   Room of flowers
HOMER, Winslow
   $1,100,000   The unruly calf
   $1,000,000   The whittling boy
JOHNS, Jasper
   $2,100,000   O through 9
   $1,300,000   Untitled
LICHTENSTEIN, Roy
   $1,650,000   Girl with piano
NAUMAN, Bruce
   $1,750,000   One hundred Live and Die
O'KEEFFE, Georgia
   $1,100,000   Ritz Tower, night
POLLOCK, Jackson
   $2,200,000   Number 19, 1948
   $1,800,000   Number 6, 1948 - Blue red yellow
   $1,600,000   Number 22, 1949
RAUSCHENBERG, Robert
   $1,000,000   Press
REMINGTON, Frederic
   $1,800,000   'Wounded bunkie' - equestrian group
   $1,100,000   Coming through the rye
ROBINSON, Theodore
   $1,000,000   The gossips

The Over $1,000,000 Club Continued

ROTHKO, Mark
    $1,100,000   Dark over light
    $1,000,000   Untitled
    $1,000,000   Brown, black and blue

SARGENT, John Singer
    $6,900,000   Spanish dancer

SMITH, David
    $3,700,000   Cubi V

TAMAYO, Rufino
    $2,350,000   America
    $2,000,000   Ninos jugando con fuego
    $1,400,000   Mujer con mascara roja
    $1,350,000   Mujer en Extasis
    $1,150,000   Retrato de Olga

TWOMBLY, Cy
    $1,950,000   Untitled
    $1,550,000   Untitled

WARHOL, Andy
    $3,400,000   Marilyn X 100

These sales account for $77,050,000 of the market turnover

TURNOVER AND PRICE ANALYSIS
Price and turnover of the two auction seasons
1992/93 and 1993/94

SALES BY PRINCIPAL CURRENCIES
(Total Turnover $404 million)

Country	Quantity	Currency (m)	UK £(m)	US $(m)
Austria	17	1.17	0.07	0.10
Belgium	36	3.92	0.07	0.11
Canada	2275	13.79	6.96	10.50
Denmark	54	2.92	0.30	0.45
France	656	33.95	4.01	6.07
Germany	289	3.79	1.52	2.30
Holland	74	0.66	0.23	0.36
Italy	71	765.40	0.32	0.48
Mexico	255	280.38	0.94	1.42
Spain	56	47.00	0.24	0.37
Sweden	206	7.95	0.68	1.02
Switzerland	110	2.06	0.94	1.42
United Kingdom	965	12.12	12.12	18.54
USA	17503	360.92	238.26	360.92

NUMBER OF WORKS SOLD BY MEDIUM AND IN US DOLLAR PRICE BANDS

	W/Cs & Drawings	Oils	Sculpture
less than 1,000	1417	2228	32
1,000 - 4,999	2784	6771	685
5,000 - 9,999	906	1761	328
10,000 - 24,999	762	1772	421
25,000 - 49,999	302	763	245
50,000 - 99,999	157	460	124
100,000 - 249,999	81	289	108
250,000 - 499,999	16	74	21
500,000 - 999,999	10	27	7
Over $1million	11	24	5
Total	6446	14169	1976

The Midwest's Leading Fine Art Auctioneers

Albert Bierstadt's *Yosemite Valley Sunset*, oil on paper laid down on board, offered during our May 23, 1994 auction, fetched $162,000.

With an emphasis on personal service,
Leslie Hindman Auctioneers provides a full range
of auction and appraisal services, giving equal attention
to a single object or an entire estate.
Auctions of paintings, drawings and prints,
furniture and decorative arts, Oriental works of art,
silver, porcelain, rugs, and jewelry
are conducted on a regular basis.

For information regarding buying and selling and appraisals
at Leslie Hindman Auctioneers,
please contact our offices at (312) 670-0010.
Please call (312) AUCTION for our upcoming auction schedule.

LESLIE HINDMAN AUCTIONEERS
215 West Ohio Street, Chicago, Illinois 60610 (312) 670-0010

Index

Oil paintings, watercolors and drawings
sold during the auction seasons
1992/93 and 1993/94

STARTING PRICES

Oil Paintings from - $550
Watercolors and drawings from - $450
National or regional "schools" from - $3,000

(sculpture prices are listed in a separate section
at the end of the book)

ABBETT (20th C) American
$3000   £2013   Turkey (46x61cm-18x24in) s. masonite. 5-Aug-93 Eldred, Massachusetts #267/R

ABBEY, Edwin Austin (1852-1911) American
$1800   £1161   Study for Spandrels of Arches over Gallery of Senate Chamber of Harrisburg Capitol (70x52cm-28x20in) s. gouache pencil board. 20-Jan-93 Sotheby's Arcade, New York #413/R
$17000 £10759 Young woman in the woods (25x30cm-10x12in) s.d.1879 W/C gouache. 3-Dec-92 Sotheby's, New York #39/R

ABBEY, Edwin Austin (attrib) (1852-1911) American
$2416   £1600   Study for Joan of Arc (81x147cm-32x58in) 1-Jul-93 Duke & Son, Dorchester #169/R

ABBOTT, Yarnell (1870-1938) American
$850   £578   The switch target (76x91cm-30x36in) s. 14-Apr-94 Freeman Fine Arts, Philadelphia #999

ABELA, Eduardo (1892-1966) Cuban
$6000   £4000   Nina (23x20cm-9x8in) s. tempera panel painted c.1960. 18-May-94 Sotheby's, New York #412/R
$7500   £5068   Retrato de Mini (27x22cm-11x9in) s. panel painted 1957. 23-Nov-93 Christie's, New York #261/R
$8000   £5333   Gallinita (19x31cm-7x12in) s. oil gessoed panel painted c.1960. 18-May-94 Christie's, New York #291/R
$11000 £7333   Pegaso (27x35cm-11x14in) s. panel painted c.1960. 18-May-94 Sotheby's, New York #426/R
$13000 £8784   Nina del sol (30x30cm-12x12in) s. init.i.verso panel. 23-Nov-93 Christie's, New York #260/R
$24000 £15686 Desnudo de mujer (64x50cm-25x20in) s.d.1920. 17-May-93 Christie's, New York #41/R

ABELARD, Gesner (20th C) Haitian
$537   £355   Oiseaux (41x61cm-16x24in) s. panel. 13-Jun-94 Rogeon, Paris #90 (F.FR 3000)

ABERCROMBIE, Gertrude (1909-) American
$1300   £872   Interior with doors and cats (25x28cm-10x11in) s.d.56 masonite. 12-Dec-93 Hindman Galleries, Chicago #287
$1900   £1329   Surrealist composition (20x25cm-8x10in) s.d.54 masonite. 14-Mar-93 Hindman Galleries, Chicago #2/R
$2200   £1438   Interior with still life (10x13cm-4x5in) s. masonite. 16-May-93 Hindman Galleries, Chicago #3/R

ABRAMOVITZ, Albert (1879-?) American/Russian
$800   £552   Street scene with figure in blue (81x64cm-32x25in) s. 17-Feb-93 Doyle, New York #2
$800   £552   Shady canal (76x61cm-30x24in) s.stretcher. 17-Feb-93 Doyle, New York #1

ACCONCI, Vito (1940-) American
$800 *£537* *Untitled (43x56cm-17x22in) marker collage graph paper four parts exec.1982. 5-May-94 Sotheby's, New York #273/R*
$2000 *£1307* *Study for intermediaries (51x72cm-20x28in) s.d.1974 chl. 4-May-93 Sotheby's, New York #153 a/R*
$14000 *£9459* *Jumps (68x356cm-27x140in) s. acrylic col.chk photos 14 foamcore panels. 10-Nov-93 Christie's, New York #200/R*

ACEE BLUE EAGLE (1907-1959) American
$950 *£613* *Buffalo hunt (41x58cm-16x23in) s. gouache. 9-Jan-93 Skinner, Bolton #62/R*
$1000 *£671* *Stylized horses (28x43cm-11x17in) s. gouache. 26-Jun-93 Skinner, Bolton #183/R*
$1500 *£1000* *Stylized horses (28x43cm-11x17in) s. gouache. 29-Jan-94 Skinner, Bolton #202/R*
$1900 *£1226* *Untitled (38x33cm-15x13in) s. gouache art board. 9-Jan-93 Skinner, Bolton #115/R*

ACHENBACH, Anna Thomson (20th C) American
$1250   £735   Saturday fights (56x81cm-22x32in) 8-Oct-92 Freeman Fine Arts, Philadelphia #1038

ACOSTA LEON, Angel (1932-) Cuban
$12000 £8108   Sin titulo (79x148cm-31x58in) s. i.verso. 23-Nov-93 Christie's, New York #152/R
$15000 £9934   Untitled (79x148cm-31x58in) s.d.64. 24-Nov-92 Christie's, New York #163/R
$19000 £12667 Sin titulo (79x148cm-31x58in) s.d.64. 18-May-94 Christie's, New York #119/R
$20000 £13072 Untitled (69x120cm-27x47in) s.d.1963 cardboard. 17-May-93 Christie's, New York #185/R
$22000 £14765 Sin titulo (69x120cm-27x47in) s.i.d.1963 board. 7-Jan-94 Gary Nader, Miami #84/R
$4000 *£2667* *Velocipedo (25x30cm-10x12in) s.i.d.61 W/C ink board. 18-May-94 Sotheby's, New York #229/R*

ACOSTA, Luis (1930-) Mexican?
$3072   £2021   El Valle de Mexico en invierno (68x100cm-27x39in) s.d.1991 canvas on triplay. 4-Nov-92 Mora, Castellort & Quintana, Juarez #132/R (M.P 9700000)

ACS, Joe (1936-) Canadian
$678   £462   Winter hues (76x91cm-30x36in) s. s.i.verso acrylic. 15-Nov-93 Hodgins, Calgary #64 (C.D 900)

ACUNA, Louis Alberto (1905-) Colombian
$1718   £1054   Thunderstorm (91x70cm-36x28in) s.d.1947. 16-Oct-92 Dorotheum, Vienna #296/R (A.S 18000)

ADAM, William (1846-?) American
$800	£506	Fornia sand dunes (30x38cm-12x15in) s. board. 5-Dec-92 Louisiana Auction Exchange #13/R
$1500	£1042	Monterey dunes (25x37cm-10x15in) s. 7-Mar-93 Butterfield & Butterfield, San Francisco #90/R
$1776	£1200	Continental street scene (53x44cm-21x17in) s. 18-Mar-93 Bonhams, London #156/R
$2310	£1500	Morning light, Burnmouth, Berwickshire (92x139cm-36x55in) s. 3-Sep-93 Phillips, Glasgow #162/R

ADAMS, Charles Partridge (1858-1942) American
$1000	£588	Afternoon on Convict Lake (46x36cm-18x14in) s. 4-Oct-92 Butterfield & Butterfield, Los Angeles #196/R
$1500	£882	Moonrise at Laguna Beach (51x61cm-20x24in) s. 4-Oct-92 Butterfield & Butterfield, Los Angeles #175/R
$1700	£1149	Moonrise at Laguna Beach (51x61cm-20x24in) s. 15-Jun-93 John Moran, Pasadena #90a
$2000	£1307	Mountainous landscape (35x46cm-14x18in) s. 4-May-93 Christie's, East, New York #118/R
$2200	£1272	Misty morning (102x154cm-40x61in) s. 25-Sep-92 Sotheby's Arcade, New York #159/R
$2500	£1667	Landscape near Denver (30x46cm-12x18in) indist.s. 15-Mar-94 John Moran, Pasadena #59
$2750	£1809	Sunset behind trees (30x41cm-12x16in) s. 13-Jun-93 Butterfield & Butterfield, San Francisco #3208/R
$3000	£1987	Near the Platte, early spring (36x51cm-14x20in) s. i.stretcher. 15-Jun-93 Butterfield & Butterfield, San Francisco #4544/R
$4000	£2649	Teton Range (51x76cm-20x30in) s. 15-Jun-94 Butterfield & Butterfield, San Francisco #4543/R
$4250	£2815	October Gold, an autumn landscape (23x30cm-9x12in) s. 15-Jun-94 Butterfield & Butterfield, San Francisco #4545/R
$17000	£11333	Chair Mountain, Colorado (102x152cm-40x60in) s. 23-May-94 Hindman Galleries, Chicago #175/R
$450	£302	Haystacks (25x36cm-10x14in) s.d.1896 W/C. 16-Dec-93 Mystic Fine Arts, Connecticut #48
$2000	£1156	Hazy afternoon, Estes Park, Colorado (26x37cm-10x15in) s.i.verso W/C gouache board. 25-Sep-92 Sotheby's Arcade, New York #191/R

ADAMS, Phyllis Kaye (20th C) American
$950	£601	Seated woman (91x61cm-36x24in) s. masonite. 25-Oct-92 Butterfield & Butterfield, San Francisco #2280/R

ADAMS, Wayman (1883-1959) American
$1500	£1007	Virginia Dale (66x51cm-26x20in) 4-Dec-93 Louisiana Auction Exchange #109/R
$3200	£2025	Carriage ride (37x29cm-15x11in) s. indist.i. panel. 2-Dec-92 Christie's, East, New York #115/R
$5500	£3691	Lovitt and son (137x91cm-54x36in) s. 4-Dec-93 Louisiana Auction Exchange #54/R

ADAMS, Willis Seaver (1842-1921) American
$4500	£3000	Morning mist (76x102cm-30x40in) init. s.i.d.1918 verso. 23-May-94 Christie's, East, New York #120/R

ADDAMS, Charles (1912-1988) American
$750	£481	Witches a Go-Go (38x33cm-15x13in) s. pen wash dr executed c.1960. 27-May-93 Swann Galleries, New York #3

ADDISON, Robert (20th C) American
$2200	£1438	Forsaken (41x64cm-16x25in) s.d.56 tempera board. 16-May-93 Hindman Galleries, Chicago #74/R

ADICKES, David (1927-) American
$1000	£680	Portrait of the Confederate officer, Samuel F B Morse (102x76cm-40x30in) s. 20-Nov-93 Hart Gallery, Houston #6
$1000	£680	Portrait of Oliver Wendell Holmes (102x76cm-40x30in) s. panel. 20-Nov-93 Hart Gallery, Houston #7
$1100	£748	Notre Dame, autumn day (114x91cm-45x36in) s. 20-Nov-93 Hart Gallery, Houston #9
$1600	£1074	Conversation (102x76cm-40x30in) s. panel. 6-Mar-94 Hart Gallery, Houston #437
$1600	£1053	Portrait of a bearded man (58x43cm-23x17in) s. panel. 4-Apr-93 Hart Gallery, Houston #1
$3250	£2044	Provincial church (107x71cm-42x28in) s. 23-Apr-93 Hart Gallery, Houston #3

ADOLPHE, Albert Jean (1865-1940) American
$1800	£1208	Artist's studio (43x28cm-17x11in) s. 16-Dec-93 Mystic Fine Arts, Connecticut #295

ADRIANI, Camillo (20th C) American
$700	£490	Cabins in winter (71x76cm-28x30in) s. i.verso. 5-Feb-93 Sloan, North Bethesda #1694
$700	£449	Winter landscape (61x76cm-24x30in) s. 13-Dec-92 Hindman Galleries, Chicago #73
$950	£621	Brook through the field, winter (56x64cm-22x25in) s. 17-Sep-93 Skinner, Bolton #214/R
$1400	£915	Stream in winter, houses in distance (64x76cm-25x30in) s. 17-Sep-93 Skinner, Bolton #211/R

AFRICANO, Nicholas (1948-) American
$4000	£2614	Oysters in vinegar again (38x69cm-15x27in) s.d.1981 verso masonite. 4-May-93 Sotheby's, New York #217/R

AFRICANO, Nicholas (1948-) American-cont.
$9500   £6419   The shadow boxer (113x181cm-44x71in) oil acrylic wax masonite executed 1979.
                       10-Nov-93 Christie's, New York #243/R
*$600   £397   I get hurt (21x28cm-8x11in) pen. 17-Nov-92 Christie's, East, New York #53/R
$3000   £1987   Flesh, Armor (50x43cm-20x17in) init.d.1986verso oil wood collage shaped canvas.
                       17-Nov-92 Christie's, East, New York #131/R*
*$11000   £7190   Let me help you, aren't you the man I love (124x213cm-49x84in) s.d.1981verso oil
                       acrylic magna enamel masonite. 4-May-93 Sotheby's, New York #211/R*

AGROS, Jose (1938-) Mexican
$665   £438   Bugambilias (20x25cm-8x10in) s.d.1992. 4-Nov-92 Mora, Castelltort & Quintana,
                       Juarez #26/R (M.P 2100000)
$4751   £3125   La Malinche (60x80cm-24x31in) s.d.1992. 4-Nov-92 Mora, Castelltort & Quintana,
                       Juarez #149/R (M.P 15000000)

AHN, Miriam (20th C) American
$1100   £696   Flower message (169x165cm-67x65in) 25-Oct-92 Butterfield & Butterfield, San
                       Francisco #2344/R

AHRENDT, William (20th C) American?
$1400   £921   Grand Canyon (79x58cm-31x23in) s. after Thomas Moran. 31-Mar-93 Sotheby's Arcade,
                       New York #193/R

AHRENS, Carl Henry von (1863-1936) Canadian
$610   £407   Sunny glade (51x41cm-20x16in) s.d. i.verso. 30-May-94 Hodgins, Calgary #269/R
                       (C.D 850)

AID, George-Charles (1872-1938) American
$20000   £12821   Bridge players (114x145cm-45x57in) s. 26-May-93 Christie's, New York #85/R

AID, George-Charles (attrib) (1872-1938) American
$786   £498   Julie (69x52cm-27x20in) bears sig. i.d.1904 verso. 1-Dec-92 Ritchie, Toronto
                       #162/R (C.D 1000)

AIZENBERG, Roberto (1928-) Argentinian
$16000   £10596   Torre (151x62cm-59x24in) s.d.1971 i.verso canvas on masonite. 24-Nov-92
                       Christie's, New York #102/R

AKERS, Vivian Milner (1886-1966) American
$750   £490   Clouds at Murren (30x61cm-12x24in) s.d.1937 canvasboard. 18-Sep-93 James Bakker,
                       Cambridge #162/R
$800   £523   Afternoon clouds, Lake of Thun (30x36cm-12x14in) s.d.1937 canvasboard. 18-Sep-93
                       James Bakker, Cambridge #196
$1000   £676   Miss Penly (76x64cm-30x25in) 23-Oct-93 Collins, Maine #187/R
$1100   £719   At Gibson Grove - Maine landscape (20x15cm-8x6in) s.i.d.1948 verso panel.
                       17-Sep-93 Skinner, Bolton #239/R
$2500   £1623   California landscape with mountains (76x86cm-30x34in) s.d.1928. 15-Jan-93 Du
                       Mouchelle, Detroit #2003/R

ALAMON, Gustavo (20th C) South American
*$850   £574   Los notables (118x90cm-46x35in) s. collage fibre. 25-Apr-94 Gomensoro, Montevideo
                       #43/R*

ALBAN, Francisco (18th C) South American
*$1872   £1200   Apparition of Our lady of Aranzazu (29x24cm-11x9in) s.i.d.1747 copper. 27-May-93
                       Christie's, S. Kensington #59/R*

ALBAN, Vicente (18th C) Ecuadorian
$140000   £92715   Castes - Indian from Quito. Yapanga woman and Indian from Quito. Yumbo Indian from
                       Maynas (81x107cm-32x42in) four. 24-Nov-92 Christie's, New York #1/R

ALBEE, Percy F (1883-1959) American
*$650   £428   Free enterprise (56x76cm-22x30in) s. W/C board. 31-Mar-93 Sotheby's Arcade, New
                       York #404/R*

ALBERS, Josef (1888-1976) American
$8500   £5903   Vice versac (37x56cm-15x22in) init.i. executed 1943 paper. 23-Feb-93 Sotheby's,
                       New York #200/R
$12240   £8000   Portal to Green (40x40cm-16x16in) init.d.69 s.i.d.verso masonite. 30-Jun-94
                       Sotheby's, London #144/R
$15000   £9804   Study for 'Homage to the Square' - Heavy and bright under veil (41x41cm-16x16in)
                       mono.d.64 s.i.d.1964verso masonite. 5-May-93 Christie's, New York #266/R
$18000   £12162   Homage to the square (41x41cm-16x16in) init.d.58 s.i.d.58 verso masonite.
                       11-Nov-93 Sotheby's, New York #335/R
$19000   £12583   Homage to square - Neutral Stand (41x41cm-16x16in) init. s.i.d.1969 verso
                       masonite. 18-Nov-92 Sotheby's, New York #110/R
$20860   £14000   Study for Homage to the Square, against a deep sky (41x41cm-16x16in) init.d.64
                       s.i.d.1964verso acrylic masonite. 3-Dec-93 Sotheby's, London #163/R
$20860   £14000   Study for homage to square - Blue Reminder (61x61cm-24x24in) mono.d.64 s.i.d.64
                       verso masonite. 24-Jun-93 Christie's, London #56/R
$22350   £15000   Study for homage to the square-ebbed (46x46cm-18x18in) init.d.67 s.i.d.verso
                       masonite. 23-Mar-94 Sotheby's, London #335/R
$23840   £16000   Study for homage to square - Answer (61x61cm-24x24in) mono.d.61 s.i.d.1961 verso.
                       24-Jun-93 Christie's, London #66/R

ALBERS, Josef (1888-1976) American-cont.

$25500	£17000	Study for Homage to the Square - Wait (76x76cm-30x30in) mono.d.63 s.i.d.1963verso masonite. 26-May-94 Christie's, London #48/R
$26820	£18000	Homage to square - Lone Stele (61x61cm-24x24in) mono.d.62 s.i.d.1962 verso masonite. 24-Jun-93 Christie's, London #64/R
$26860	£17000	Study for homage to square - Evensong (61x61cm-24x24in) init.d.59 s.i.d.1959 verso masonite. 3-Dec-92 Sotheby's, London #15/R
$27808	£17600	Study for hommage to square - Wondering (41x41cm-16x16in) mono.d.60 s.i.d.1960 verso masonite. 3-Dec-92 Christie's, London #47/R
$28000	£18919	Study for homage to square - Adios (61x61cm-24x24in) init.d.64 s.i.d.verso masonite. 11-Nov-93 Sotheby's, New York #318/R
$28310	£19000	Study for homage to square - open look (61x61cm-24x24in) mono.d.66 s.i.d.1966 verso masonite. 24-Jun-93 Christie's, London #45/R
$32000	£21477	Homage to the square, from the soil (81x81cm-32x32in) mono.d.54 s.i.d.verso masonite. 4-May-94 Christie's, New York #107/R
$37250	£25000	Homage to square - Light Shield (61x61cm-24x24in) init.d.57 s.i.d.1957 verso masonite. 24-Jun-93 Christie's, London #77/R
$38740	£26000	Study for homage to square - blond autumn (81x81cm-32x32in) mono.d.64 i.d.1964 verso masonite. 24-Jun-93 Christie's, London #47/R
$40000	£27027	Study for homage to the square, centered yellow (60x60cm-24x24in) mono.d.64 s.i.d.verso masonite. 10-Nov-93 Christie's, New York #151/R
$40500	£27000	Homage to the Square In and Out (102x102cm-40x40in) init.d.59 i.verso masonite. 26-May-94 Christie's, London #46/R
$42000	£27815	Study for Homage to the Square with safron (60x60cm-24x24in) mono.d.62 s.i.d.verso masonite. 19-Nov-92 Christie's, New York #312/R
$44000	£29530	Homage to the square, wondering (75x75cm-30x30in) init.d.57 s.i.d.1957verso. 5-May-94 Sotheby's, New York #119/R
$45000	£30405	Study for homage to square - osmosis (102x102cm-40x40in) init.d.59 s.i.d.59 verso masonite. 11-Nov-93 Sotheby's, New York #265/R
$46000	£31081	Study for homage to square - quiet question (102x102cm-40x40in) init.d.58 s.i.d.58 verso masonite. 11-Nov-93 Sotheby's, New York #323 a/R
$47680	£32000	Wall medium red (60x87cm-24x34in) mono.d.48-55 s.d.48-55 verso masonite. 24-Jun-93 Sotheby's, London #51/R
$55616	£35200	Study for hommage to square - Joy (76x76cm-30x30in) mono.d.64 s.i.d.1964 verso masonite. 3-Dec-92 Christie's, London #45/R
$69520	£44000	Homage to square - slate against sky (102x102cm-40x40in) mono.d.62 s.i.d.1962 verso masonite. 3-Dec-92 Christie's, London #43/R
$70000	£46980	Homage to the square, aphonic (122x122cm-48x48in) init.d.61 s.i.d.verso masonite. 4-May-94 Sotheby's, New York #11/R
$80000	£53691	Study for Homage to the Square, even song (61x61cm-24x24in) mono.d.59 s.i.d.verso masonite. 4-May-94 Christie's, New York #133/R
$90000	£56603	Homage to the square, sudden Yes (122x122cm-48x48in) s.i.d.verso board. 25-Apr-93 Butterfield & Butterfield, San Francisco #2069/R
$4500	*£2980*	*MM-I (46x58cm-18x23in) s.i.d.61 Indian ink. 29-Sep-93 Sotheby's Arcade, New York #234/R*

ALBERT, Ernest (1857-1946) American

$1087	£735	Flowers (70x60cm-28x24in) s. 26-Oct-93 Campo, Vlaamse Kaai #323 (B.FR 40000)
$1200	£816	October landscape (61x61cm-24x24in) i. 17-Nov-93 Doyle, New York #13/R
$1400	£915	Autumn landscape (30x41cm-12x16in) s. 30-Jun-94 Mystic Fine Arts, Connecticut #174
$2500	£1689	Spring tapestry (51x61cm-20x24in) 10-Aug-93 Stonington Fine Arts, Stonington #146/R
$4000	£2614	Golden day (60x76cm-24x30in) s.i. 4-May-93 Christie's, East, New York #90/R
$5000	£3378	Among the hills (51x61cm-20x24in) s. 31-Mar-94 Sotheby's Arcade, New York #209/R
$7500	£4967	Winter eve (64x76cm-25x30in) s. 13-Nov-92 Skinner, Bolton #141/R
$10000	£6536	Evening hour (64x76cm-25x30in) s.i.d.1937. 16-May-93 Hindman Galleries, Chicago #92/R
$750	*£500*	*Antwerp Harbour (24x34cm-9x13in) s. W/C. 12-Mar-94 Kunstgalerij de Vuyst, Lokeren #3 (B.FR 26000)*
$1269	*£846*	*Ponsas (48x57cm-19x22in) s. W/C. 12-Mar-94 Kunstgalerij de Vuyst, Lokeren #2 (B.FR 44000)*

ALBRIGHT, Adam Emory (1862-1957) American

$725	£474	My son (51x38cm-20x15in) s. masonite. 15-May-93 Dunning's, Illinois #1053/R
$5000	£3289	Two boys in meadow (61x41cm-24x16in) s.d.1901. 13-Jun-93 Butterfield & Butterfield, San Francisco #3244/R
$5600	£3733	Summer outing (61x61cm-24x24in) s.d.1903. 23-May-94 Hindman Galleries, Chicago #187/R
$11500	£7616	Children playing on sandy shore (51x76cm-20x30in) s.d.1912. 28-Nov-92 Dunning's, Illinois #1149/R
$13000	£8609	Children picking daisies in meadow (51x66cm-20x26in) s.d.1911 canvas on board. 28-Nov-92 Dunning's, Illinois #1148/R
$24000	£17021	Little fish (122x91cm-48x36in) s.d.1919. 13-Feb-93 Collins, Maine #97/R

ALBRIGHT, Henry James (1887-1951) American

$2500	£1603	Fluteplayer (52x42cm-20x17in) s. 9-Dec-92 Butterfield & Butterfield, San Francisco #3904/R

ALCIBAR, Jose de (1751-1803) Mexican

$14000	£9259	Sor Maria Manuela Margarita (176x103cm-69x41in) s. painted c.1770. 22-Nov-93 Sotheby's, New York #139/R

ALDRICH, George Ames (1872-1941) American

$675	£441	Coastal cliffs (51x61cm-20x24in) s. 16-May-93 Hanzel Galleries, Chicago #20 c

ALDRICH, George Ames (1872-1941) American-cont.
$800	£471	Houses by river (46x56cm-18x22in) s. 3-Oct-92 Weschler, Washington #127/R
$1100	£719	Castle on hillside (76x71cm-30x28in) s. 4-May-93 Christie's, East, New York #92/R
$1300	£818	White house on river (46x51cm-18x20in) s. 22-Apr-93 Freeman Fine Arts, Philadelphia #1327
$1900	£1242	Winter nocturne (79x91cm-31x36in) s. board. 16-May-93 Hanzel Galleries, Chicago #20 b
$2000	£1342	The River Cauche (76x102cm-30x40in) s. 8-Dec-93 Butterfield & Butterfield, San Francisco #3509/R
$2600	£1733	Snowy landscape with figures (61x74cm-24x29in) s. 23-May-94 Hindman Galleries, Chicago #200/R
$3000	£2041	Cottage by a stream, early spring (46x61cm-18x24in) s. 17-Apr-94 Hanzel Galleries, Chicago #6
$3500	£2147	Winter scene with village (79x97cm-31x38in) s. 16-Oct-92 Du Mouchelle, Detroit #2002/R
$3900	£2549	European village, winter (122x102cm-48x40in) s. 16-May-93 Hanzel Galleries, Chicago #20 a
$4600	£3026	Winter landscape (63x76cm-25x30in) s. 31-Mar-93 Sotheby's Arcade, New York #161/R
$5100	£3355	Stream and mill (61x74cm-24x29in) s.d.1911. 4-Jun-93 Dargate Auction Galleries, Pittsburgh #993
$5400	£3553	The creek, winter (76x91cm-30x36in) s. 13-Jun-93 Hindman Galleries, Chicago #230
$5750	£3758	Winter forest with river (91x91cm-36x36in) s. 16-May-93 Hanzel Galleries, Chicago #20 d

ALEXANDER, John (1945-) American
$1950	£1226	Fall landscape (117x117cm-46x46in) s.verso. 23-Apr-93 Hart Gallery, Houston #1
$4000	£2649	Chocolate mousse (96x122cm-38x48in) s. s.i.verso. 29-Sep-93 Sotheby's Arcade, New York #370/R
$8000	£5298	Hiding from hunters (198x213cm-78x84in) painted 1982. 18-Nov-92 Sotheby's, New York #305/R
$11000	£7383	The great horned owl in pursuit of that something special (203x167cm-80x66in) s. s.i.d.verso. 4-May-94 Christie's, New York #332/R

ALEXANDER, John W (1856-1915) American
$1000	*£633*	*Alphonse Daudet, portrait sketch drawn from life (50x46cm-20x18in) s.d.86 chl board. 2-Dec-92 Christie's, East, New York #10*

ALEXANDER, Lady Eveline Marie (fl.1841-1851) Canadian
$3766	£2461	Two-horse sleigh crossing frozen river (25x36cm-10x14in) init.d.1851. 19-May-93 Sotheby's, Toronto #183/R (C.D 4750)

ALEXANDER, Peter (1939-) American
$5000	£3378	Glendora (122x135cm-48x53in) mono. s.i.d.1988verso. 21-Apr-94 Butterfield & Butterfield, San Francisco #1191/R

ALFONZO, Carlos Jose (1950-1991) Cuban
$8000	£5229	Alarma No.1 (77x128cm-30x50in) s.d.90 s.i.d.89-90 verso. 17-May-93 Christie's, New York #168/R
$15000	£9934	Birth (213x153cm-84x60in) s.d.89 s.i.d.1989-1990 verso. 24-Nov-92 Christie's, New York #162/R
$21000	£14189	The artist and the genie (244x183cm-96x72in) s.i.d.1988 verso acrylic canvas. 22-Nov-93 Sotheby's, New York #75/R
$23000	£15333	Thought forms (226x228cm-89x90in) s.d.87 linen. 17-May-94 Sotheby's, New York #83/R
$27000	£17647	Untitled (213x213cm-84x84in) acrylic painted c.1990. 18-May-93 Sotheby's, New York #79/R
$35000	£23649	Wake up story (244x183cm-96x72in) s.d.89 i.verso linen. 23-Nov-93 Christie's, New York #154/R
$4000	*£2685*	*Untitled (75x109cm-30x43in) s.d.88 mixed media. 7-Jan-94 Gary Nader, Miami #51/R*
$4250	*£2852*	*Untitled (75x109cm-30x43in) s.i.d.88 mixed media. 7-Jan-94 Gary Nader, Miami #50/R*
$8000	*£5405*	*Sin titulo (77x112cm-30x44in) s.d.88 gouache. 23-Nov-93 Christie's, New York #217/R*
$8000	*£5333*	*Sin titulo (103x86cm-41x34in) s.d.90 gouache. 18-May-94 Christie's, New York #255/R*

ALICE, Antonio (1886-1943) Argentinian
$1700	£885	Retrato de Fader (18x15cm-7x6in) 4-Aug-92 VerBo, Buenos Aires #2
$2500	£1302	Retrato de Figueroa Alcorta (71x54cm-28x21in) 4-Aug-92 VerBo, Buenos Aires #1
$100000	£57803	Manana en Miramar (33x41cm-13x16in) panel. 23-Sep-92 Roldan & Cia, Buenos Aires #19

ALLAN, William (1936-) American
$600	*£380*	*Unlike the magician (80x75cm-31x30in) s.d.69 s.i.verso W/C graphite. 25-Oct-92 Butterfield & Butterfield, San Francisco #2306/R*

ALLEN, Charles Curtis (1886-1950) American
$1200	£822	Hills in autumn (46x61cm-18x24in) board. 19-Feb-94 Young Fine Arts Auctions, Maine #27/R
$800	*£544*	*Mount Mansfield (36x56cm-14x22in) s. W/C. 16-Apr-94 Young Fine Arts Auctions, Maine #15/R*

ALLEN, Marion Boyd (1862-1941) American
$800	£530	Tumbling glacier, Canadian Rockies (89x71cm-35x28in) s.d.1932. 21-Nov-92 James Bakker, Cambridge #306/R

ALLIS, C Harry (1876-1938) American
$2000 £1325 Covered bridge (102x127cm-40x50in) s.d.1926 s.stretcher. 23-Sep-93 Sotheby's, New York #147/R

ALLSTON, Washington (attrib) (1779-1843) American
$2500 £1712 The Prophetess - study for the painting (46x38cm-18x15in) i.verso oil ink board. 10-Feb-94 Skinner, Bolton #214

ALONSO, Carlos (1929-) Argentinian
$3200 £2133 Payaso (70x50cm-28x20in) 18-May-94 Christie's, New York #264/R
$1000 £662 Campesina (20x30cm-8x12in) mixed media. 11-Nov-92 VerBo, Buenos Aires #2

ALOPEAUS, Kristi (20th C) Mexican?
$863 £583 La pasion contenida (130x90cm-51x35in) 20-Oct-93 Louis Morton, Mexico #167/R (M.P 2700)

ALPUY, Julio (1919-) Uruguayan
$800 £417 Paisaje (43x57cm-17x22in) s. fibre. 12-Aug-92 Castells & Castells, Montevideo #24
$800 £540 Puerto (31x53cm-12x21in) s. board. 25-Apr-94 Gomensoro, Montevideo #74/R
$1200 £706 Ciudad y carro (16x19cm-6x7in) panel. 5-Oct-92 Gomensoro, Montevideo #21/R
$1500 £781 Vagones (39x52cm-15x20in) s. 12-Aug-92 Castells & Castells, Montevideo #25/R
$1500 £980 Constructivo (47x43cm-19x17in) s.d.50 board. 4-Oct-93 Gomensoro, Montevideo #103/R
$1900 £1218 Puerto (45x53cm-18x21in) s.d.57. 7-Dec-92 Gomensoro, Montevideo #65/R
$1928 £1294 Composicion (68x53cm-27x21in) s.d.50. 23-Mar-93 Duran, Madrid #1052/R (S.P 225000)
$2700 £1765 Remolcadores y draga (54x67cm-21x26in) s.d.45 board. 4-Oct-93 Gomensoro, Montevideo #67/R
$3400 £2282 Aborigen y arbol (62x82cm-24x32in) s.d.1978. 29-Nov-93 Gomensoro, Montevideo #83/R
$18000 £12081 Constructivo con figuras (83x121cm-33x48in) s.d.1950 board. 29-Nov-93 Gomensoro, Montevideo #82/R
$2250 £1490 Ciudad (15x18cm-6x7in) s. colour pencil. 23-Nov-92 Sotheby's, New York #192/R

ALTAMIRANO, Arturo Pacheco (1905-) Chilean
$1679 £1190 Taberna (60x73cm-24x29in) s. s.d.1968verso. 10-Feb-93 Ansorena, Madrid #37/R (S.P 200000)
$2600 £1722 La Cosecha (58x70cm-23x28in) s. painted 1958. 24-Nov-92 Christie's, New York #350/R
$3824 £2346 Taberna (60x73cm-24x29in) s. s.d.1968verso. 14-Oct-92 Ansorena, Madrid #116/R (S.P 400000)
$4000 £2649 Escena de Puerto (100x100cm-39x39in) s. 24-Nov-92 Christie's, New York #349/R

ALTOON, John (1925-1969) American
$3250 £2196 Sunset series (168x142cm-66x56in) acrylic painted 1965. 21-Oct-93 Butterfield & Butterfield, San Francisco #2775/R
$550 £372 Hands together (41x33cm-16x13in) s. ink wash pastel board. 21-Oct-93 Butterfield & Butterfield, San Francisco #2774/R
$600 £377 Two women (76x102cm-30x40in) ink board. 25-Apr-93 Butterfield & Butterfield, San Francisco #2131/R
$1400 £886 Study for painting (76x91cm-30x36in) mixed media. 25-Oct-92 Butterfield & Butterfield, San Francisco #2305/R
$2000 £1351 Untitled (76x103cm-30x41in) s.d.66 ink W/C pastel board. 21-Oct-93 Butterfield & Butterfield, San Francisco #2769/R
$2250 £1415 Harper series (75x100cm-30x39in) s.d.66 ink W/C airbrush. 25-Apr-93 Butterfield & Butterfield, San Francisco #2106/R

ALVA DE LA CANAL, Ramon (1899-1985) Mexican
$2104 £1403 Sin titulo , s. mixed media ink W/C five in one frame. 25-May-94 Louis Morton, Mexico #8 (M.P 7000)
$2104 £1403 Sin titulo , s. ink W/C six in one frame. 25-May-94 Louis Morton, Mexico #61 (M.P 7000)

ALVAREZ DIAZ, Emilio (1879-1952) Argentinian
$3867 £2704 Paisaje norteafricano (25x65cm-10x26in) s. panel. 10-Mar-93 Ansorena, Madrid #35/R (S.P 460000)

ALVAREZ, Mabel (1891-1985) American
$750 £507 Fruit stand (30x41cm-12x16in) s. canvasboard. 15-Jun-93 John Moran, Pasadena #175
$1000 £690 Five figures under tree (25x33cm-10x13in) board. 16-Feb-93 John Moran, Pasadena #121
$1000 £658 Hawaiian woman (51x40cm-20x16in) s. canvasboard. 13-Jun-93 Butterfield & Butterfield, San Francisco #941/R
$1700 £1172 Woman at window (33x28cm-13x11in) board. 16-Feb-93 John Moran, Pasadena #99
$2250 £1562 Bouquet in white vase (46x36cm-18x14in) s. board. 7-Mar-93 Butterfield & Butterfield, San Francisco #243/R
$2500 £1656 Portrait of a lady with Spanish Manteka (89x76cm-35x30in) s.d.25 canvas laid down on board. 15-Jun-94 Butterfield & Butterfield, San Francisco #4662/R
$8500 £5629 Dahlias and fruit (63x76cm-25x30in) s. 15-Jun-94 Butterfield & Butterfield, San Francisco #4600/R

ALZIBAR, Jose de (18th C) Latin American
$6000 £4000 El martyr San Felipe de Jesus, patron de la Ciudad de Mexico (94x70cm-37x28in) s.i.d.801. 18-May-94 Sotheby's, New York #155/R

AMADOR, Severo (20th C) Mexican
$1019   £653   Camino al pueblo (23x34cm-9x13in) s.d.1925 W/C. 29-Apr-93 Louis Morton, Mexico #4
                     (M.P 3200)

AMARAL, Antonio Henrique (1935-) Brazilian
$3500   £2349   Fork, knife and banana (69x52cm-27x20in) acrylic paper laid on canvas. 7-Jan-94
                     Gary Nader, Miami #115/R
$7000   £4730   Natureza morta (58x70cm-23x28in) s. painted 1981. 22-Nov-93 Sotheby's, New York
                     #239/R
$10000   £6757   Banana, faca (85x128cm-33x50in) init.d.71 s.d.verso acrylic. 23-Nov-93
                     Christie's, New York #153/R
$12000   £8000   Melancia (121x180cm-48x71in) s.d.80. 18-May-94 Christie's, New York #247/R
$57500   £38591   Bananas and ropes (127x168cm-50x66in) s.i.d.73. 7-Jan-94 Gary Nader, Miami #15/R
$674   £478   Composition (47x41cm-19x16in) s.d.1977 mixed media. 10-Feb-93 Guy Loudmer, Paris
                     #127 (F.FR 3800)
$1250   £839   Untitled (49x68cm-19x27in) s. pencil crayon paper executed 1975. 7-Jan-94 Gary
                     Nader, Miami #116/R
$2250   £1510   Untitled (51x69cm-20x27in) s.d.75 pencil crayon. 7-Jan-94 Gary Nader, Miami
                     #118/R
$2250   £1510   Untitled (51x72cm-20x28in) s.d.75 pencil crayon. 7-Jan-94 Gary Nader, Miami
                     #117/R

AMBELLAN, Harold (1912-) American
$6690   £4582   La danse (130x81cm-51x32in) s. 11-Feb-94 Dumousett-Deburaux, Paris #26/R
                     (F.FR 40000)
$669   £458   Les trois graces (43x31cm-17x12in) s. dr htd. 11-Feb-94 Dumousett-Deburaux, Paris
                     #24 (F.FR 4000)
$669   £458   Femme assise sur colombes (35x26cm-14x10in) s. dr htd.gouache. 11-Feb-94
                     Dumousett-Deburaux, Paris #20/R (F.FR 4000)

AMERICAN PRIMITIVE SCHOOL, 19th C
$7000   £4487   Esther Louisa and Elizabeth Harriet Clay (147x97cm-58x38in) painted c.1845 canvas
                     on board. 11-Dec-92 Du Mouchelle, Detroit #2016/R
$56000   £36364   Father, mother and two children (84x74cm-33x29in) pair. 4-Aug-94 Eldred,
                     Massachusetts #839/R

AMERICAN SCHOOL
$3500   £2333   Personajes (83x100cm-33x39in) s. 25-May-94 Castells & Castells, Montevideo #65/R

AMERICAN SCHOOL, 18th/19th C
$10500   £7000   Ship flying American ensign of 1795 (58x79cm-23x31in) 20-Aug-93 Skinner, Bolton
                     #136/R

AMERICAN SCHOOL, 19th C
$3000   £2055   View of Mount Vernon (48x64cm-19x25in) 12-Feb-94 Boos Gallery, Michigan #530/R
$3000   £2000   Niagara Falls (183x244cm-72x96in) 23-May-94 Christie's, East, New York #49/R
$3000   £2000   USS Chicago off Gravesend, England (41x61cm-16x24in) indist.s. 23-May-94
                     Christie's, East, New York #54/R
$3000   £2013   Portrait of a young gentleman from the Eddy Family of Rhode Island
                     (69x58cm-27x23in) 6-Feb-94 Skinner, Bolton #237/R
$3250   £2226   Portrait of a boy holding a hat (76x61cm-30x24in) canvas on masonite. 12-Feb-94
                     Boos Gallery, Michigan #533/R
$3400   £2297   Boy and girl with dog (99x86cm-39x34in) 31-Oct-93 Hindman Galleries, Chicago #691
$3500   £2303   Niagara Falls (61x76cm-24x30in) 13-Jun-93 Butterfield & Butterfield, San
                     Francisco #3111/R
$3507   £2370   Vapeur aupres d'un trois mats Chesapeake Bay (60x91cm-24x36in) 17-Jun-93 Claude
                     Boisgirard, Paris #30 (F.FR 20000)
$3750   £2568   Portrait of a young man with books (69x56cm-27x22in) 12-Feb-94 Boos Gallery,
                     Michigan #514/R
$3750   £2517   Portrait of young girl with flowers (76x64cm-30x25in) 3-Feb-94 Sloan, North
                     Bethesda #2700/R
$4000   £2703   Portrait of a dog (56x76cm-22x30in) 30-Oct-93 Skinner, Bolton #118/R
$4000   £2614   Portrait of Margaret Pryor (76x64cm-30x25in) 18-Apr-93 Hindman Galleries, Chicago
                     #89/R
$4000   £2632   Portrait of George W King (86x69cm-34x27in) painted c.1838. 31-Mar-93 Sotheby's
                     Arcade, New York #9/R
$4000   £2020   La Grange (56x76cm-22x30in) indis.s.i.d.1842/3verso. 21-Aug-92 Skinner, Bolton
                     #156
$4200   £2819   Landscape with boy and dog (102x74cm-40x29in) 2-Dec-93 Freeman Fine Arts,
                     Philadelphia #804
$4250   £2457   Still life with fruit on ledge (46x61cm-18x24in) 25-Sep-92 Sotheby's Arcade, New
                     York #27/R
$4250   £2778   Portrait of boy in red coat with hoop (45x37cm-18x15in) 31-Oct-92 Skinner, Bolton
                     #132/R
$4750   £3188   View of churchyard (48x51cm-19x20in) 27-Mar-93 Skinner, Bolton #115 a/R
$5000   £3497   Still life with basket of grapes (59x84cm-23x33in) 11-Mar-93 Christie's, New York
                     #27/R
$5000   £3333   Still life of fruit (43x61cm-17x24in) canvas on board painted c.1890. 1-Jun-94
                     Doyle, New York #13/R
$5500   £3667   Portrait of Daniel Webster (69x53cm-27x21in) oval. 12-Jun-94 Skinner, Bolton
                     #143/R
$5500   £3179   Old fashioned family values (51x71cm-20x28in) 23-Sep-92 Christie's, New York
                     #29/R
$6000   £3175   Herder and cows at the Olt Stone Mill, Newport, Rhode Island (74x91cm-29x36in)
                     11-Sep-92 Skinner, Bolton #182/R

AMERICAN SCHOOL, 19th C-cont.

$6000	£4054	Still life with fruit (66x91cm-26x36in) 31-Mar-94 Sotheby's Arcade, New York #14/R
$6000	£3947	Portrait of boy in landscape wearing plaid suit and holding hat (102x83cm-40x33in) 31-Mar-93 Sotheby's Arcade, New York #62/R
$6500	£4276	Portrait of naval captain (84x69cm-33x27in) 2-Jun-93 Doyle, New York #20
$6500	£4248	Portrait of bark Mary E Russell and coastline with fortress beyond (22x33cm-9x13in) 31-Oct-92 Skinner, Bolton #42/R
$6510	£4200	Niagara Falls (53x86cm-21x34in) painted c.1840. 15-Jul-94 Christie's, London #70/R
$7000	£4046	Perils of war (44x73cm-17x29in) s.d.1864. 23-Sep-92 Christie's, New York #11/R
$7500	£5245	Still life with musical instruments (43x54cm-17x21in) panel. 11-Mar-93 Christie's, New York #73/R
$7500	£5137	'The Rand Homestead, Derry, New Hampshire (43x61cm-17x24in) 12-Feb-94 Boos Gallery, Michigan #547/R
$8000	£5479	Three ladies in an extensive landscape with floral wreaths, headdresses and bouquets with doves (36x46cm-14x18in) st. bristol board. 12-Feb-94 Boos Gallery, Michigan #517/R
$9500	£6376	Pair of portraits of Baltimore lady and gentleman (79x66cm-31x26in) panel pair painted c.1830. 3-Feb-94 Sloan, North Bethesda #2896/R
$10000	£6494	Portrait of child in blue holding whip (86x69cm-34x27in) s.i.d.1830 verso. 16-Jan-93 Skinner, Bolton #186/R
$11000	£7383	An ancient port (81x107cm-32x42in) 6-Feb-94 Skinner, Bolton #32/R
$11000	£7237	Still life with fruit, wine glass and bird's nest (58x79cm-23x31in) canvas on panel. 31-Mar-93 Sotheby's Arcade, New York #37/R
$11000	£7333	Mountain panorama (76x147cm-30x58in) 25-May-94 Sotheby's, New York #19/R
$12000	£8392	Autumn in the Catskills (71x101cm-28x40in) bears sig. 11-Mar-93 Christie's, New York #12/R
$12320	£8000	Grey kitten posed before a curtain (48x36cm-19x14in) 20-Jun-94 Christie's, London #1275/R
$13000	£8904	Mourning of a dead Civil War soldier, decorate with lions, eagles, dog and several figures (38x43cm-15x17in) st. bristol board. 12-Feb-94 Boos Gallery, Michigan #516/R
$15000	£10000	Rescue at sea (112x183cm-44x72in) indis.s. 20-Aug-93 Skinner, Bolton #33/R
$2500	£1445	Abundance (67x102cm-26x40in) W/C paper on canvas. 24-Sep-92 Sotheby's, New York #47/R
$3000	£2055	'Ishmael being driven out' (30x38cm-12x15in) i.verso W/C. 12-Feb-94 Boos Gallery, Michigan #551/R
$3250	£2181	Memorial to Eliza and Sarah Little, Newburyport, Mass. (38x53cm-15x21in) W/C. 6-Feb-94 Skinner, Bolton #31/R
$3500	£2333	Portrait of John Quincy Adams (20x15cm-8x6in) i.d.1843 W/C pencil. 12-Jun-94 Skinner, Bolton #3/R
$3750	£2467	Memorial to Amos Tyler (15x20cm-6x8in) i. W/C ink hair. 5-Jun-93 Skinner, Bolton #143/R
$4750	£3167	Portrait of Eliza Fowler of Northbridge, Massachusetts (15x10cm-6x4in) min. sold with tin box haircomb and paper items. 12-Jun-94 Skinner, Bolton #1/R
$7500	£5000	Island of St. Helena (24x30cm-9x12in) W/C ink. 10-Jun-94 Christie's, New York #712/R

AMERICAN SCHOOL, 19th/20th C

$3000	£2027	Portrait of a woman wearing a kimono (38x38cm-15x15in) 20-Apr-94 Doyle, New York #3
$4000	£2632	Gloucester harbour (67x62cm-26x24in) 13-Jun-93 Butterfield & Butterfield, San Francisco #3159/R
$10000	£6494	Deep in thought (63x66cm-25x26in) indis.s. 9-Sep-93 Sotheby's Arcade, New York #250/R

AMERICAN SCHOOL, 20th C

$3750	£2451	Hill and dale (91x127cm-36x50in) indist.s. 17-Sep-93 Skinner, Bolton #204/R
$5000	£3497	Schmaltz Grove (76x107cm-30x42in) tempera masonite. 11-Mar-93 Christie's, New York #231/R
$8500	£4913	Afternoon reflections (71x61cm-28x24in) 23-Sep-92 Christie's, New York #146 a/R
$15000	£8671	Landscape with boats on pond (51x61cm-20x24in) 25-Sep-92 Sotheby's Arcade, New York #232/R
$4000	£2632	New England whale fisheries (51x66cm-20x26in) pen W/C gouache cardboard set of four. 2-Jun-93 Doyle, New York #22

AMES, Ezra (attrib) (1768-1836) American

| $2600 | £1711 | Portrait of young gentleman (89x71cm-35x28in) 2-Jun-93 Doyle, New York #23/R |

AMES, Wally (20th C) American

| $600 | £397 | Summer day (64x76cm-25x30in) s. board. 23-Sep-93 Mystic Fine Arts, Connecticut #78 |
| $750 | £510 | Front garden (64x76cm-25x30in) s. 16-Apr-94 Young Fine Arts Auctions, Maine #21/R |

AMEZAGA, Eduardo (1911-) South American

$900	£469	Tropeando (20x25cm-8x10in) s. panel. 12-Aug-92 Castells & Castells, Montevideo #62
$1200	£784	Disparandole a la tormenta (32x50cm-13x20in) s. board. 4-Oct-93 Gomensoro, Montevideo #62/R
$1450	£954	Playa de los ingleses (40x60cm-16x24in) s. 31-May-93 Gomensoro, Montevideo #30/R
$1500	£980	Puesto y jinetes (53x82cm-21x32in) s. fibre. 4-Oct-93 Gomensoro, Montevideo #61/R
$2200	£1429	Paisaje de campo (50x66cm-20x26in) s. board. 30-Aug-93 Gomensoro, Montevideo #73/R
$900	£604	La carreta (51x65cm-20x26in) s. W/C. 29-Nov-93 Gomensoro, Montevideo #25/R

AMICK, Robert Wesley (1879-1969) American
$800 £544 Railroad workers (34x25cm-13x10in) s. chl ink. 15-Nov-93 Christie's, East, New York #211

AMUCHASTEGUI, Axel (20th C) Argentinian
$5000 £3311 Golden breasted starling (62x44cm-24x17in) acrylic mixed media. 18-Nov-92 Roldan & Cia, Buenos Aires #9

AMYX, Leon Kirkman (1908-) American
$600 £397 Landscape Castroville Area (53x71cm-21x28in) s.i. W/C. 28-Sep-93 John Moran, Pasadena #238

ANASTASI, William (1933-) American
$1500 £993 Two subway drawings (28x29cm-11x11in) s.i.d.1990verso graphite. 17-Nov-92 Christie's, East, New York #22/R

ANDERSON, Doug (1954-) American
$1045 £683 Tape on face (122x244cm-48x96in) s.d.1982 verso diptych. 14-May-93 Skinner, Bolton #185/R

ANDERSON, Karl (1874-1956) American
$2500 £1656 Aesop's garden (66x81cm-26x32in) 23-Sep-93 Sotheby's, New York #141/R

ANDERSON, Stephen Warde (1953-) American
$1450 £960 Madonna Lisa del Giocondo (71x71cm-28x28in) s.d.April 1991 label verso tempera shade cloth. 21-Nov-92 Litchfield Auction Gallery #1

ANDOE, Joe (1955-) American
$1100 £738 Untitled - Wreath (58x61cm-23x24in) s. linen painted 1988. 3-May-94 Christie's, East, New York #190/R
$2000 £1389 Untitled (91x117cm-36x46in) s. painted 1990 oil varnish linen. 22-Feb-93 Christie's, East, New York #245/R
$2000 £1325 Untitled, white wreath (51x61cm-20x24in) painted 1989. 17-Nov-92 Christie's, East, New York #37/R
$2000 £1325 Untitled, olive branch (51x61cm-20x24in) s. oil varnish. 17-Nov-92 Christie's, East, New York #35/R
$2000 £1325 Untitled (51x61cm-20x24in) s. linen painted 1989. 18-Nov-92 Sotheby's, New York #309 a/R
$2500 £1471 Untitled (102x122cm-40x48in) s. linen. 8-Oct-92 Christie's, New York #215/R

ANDRE, Renee (1891-?) American
$2300 £1494 Candida (41x30cm-16x12in) s. s.i.d.1936verso sold with oil by H.V.Poor. 9-Sep-93 Sotheby's Arcade, New York #282/R

ANDREWS, Ambrose (1824-1859) American
$1200 £800 Mountain stream (76x105cm-30x41in) s.d.1857. 23-May-94 Christie's, East, New York #15/R

ANDREWS, Benny (20th C) American
$750 £434 Portrait of Puerto Rican (30x20cm-12x8in) collage board. 24-Sep-92 Mystic Fine Arts, Connecticut #119

ANESI, Carlos (1945-) Argentinian
$3500 £2349 Crijo (86x58cm-34x23in) init. s.i.verso. 7-Jan-94 Gary Nader, Miami #110/R
$7250 £4834 Caballo Corredor (89x133cm-35x52in) init. 9-Jun-94 Sotheby's Arcade, New York #129 a/R
$11500 £7616 Galgo (90x105cm-35x41in) init. s.i.d.1990 verso. 24-Nov-92 Christie's, New York #250/R
$17750 £11913 Caballo (90x130cm-35x51in) init. s.verso acrylic. 7-Jan-94 Gary Nader, Miami #97/R

ANGANUZZI, Mario Nicolas Irineo (1888-1975) Argentinian
$2500 £1471 Nocturno en Chilecito (60x68cm-24x27in) painted 1981. 29-Sep-92 VerBo, Buenos Aires #5

ANGLO-AMERICAN SCHOOL, 19th C
$16000 £10811 Still life with daffodils (65x40cm-26x16in) init.i.d.86 mono.verso. 5-Nov-93 Skinner, Bolton #143/R
$3848 £2600 Colonial estate scene in the West Indies (32x49cm-13x19in) W/C bodycol. 8-Nov-93 Phillips, London #124/R

ANGUIANO, Raul (1915-) Mexican
$2500 £1572 Taxco (41x61cm-16x24in) s. masonite. 25-Apr-93 Butterfield & Butterfield, San Francisco #2075/R
$2500 £1667 Pescadores (50x67cm-20x26in) s.d.Oct.61 gouache. 18-May-94 Christie's, New York #313/R

ANSHUTZ, Thomas Pollock (1851-1912) American
$1500 £943 Grandmother sewing (30x46cm-12x18in) s. 22-Apr-93 Freeman Fine Arts, Philadelphia #1342
$2400 £1600 Cottages Q (20x26cm-8x10in) board. 23-May-94 Christie's, East, New York #171/R
$52000 £34667 Seated woman with bonnet in interior (26x20cm-10x8in) s. board. 25-May-94 Sotheby's, New York #18/R
$900 £520 Horse and boat on the banks of river (25x34cm-10x13in) s.indis.i. W/C paper on board. 25-Sep-92 Sotheby's Arcade, New York #233/R

ANSHUTZ, Thomas Pollock (1851-1912) American-cont.
$2800   £1958   Male nude study (63x47cm-25x19in) s.d.1891 chl paper on paper. 11-Mar-93 Christie's, New York #184/R
$6750   £4272   The summer house (33x50cm-13x20in) W/C. 3-Dec-92 Sotheby's, New York #47/R

ANUSZKIEWICZ, Richard (1930-) American
$1300   £878   Constellation of the figures (61x46cm-24x18in) s.d.1960verso acrylic. 8-Nov-93 Christie's, East, New York #218/R
$2400   £1611   Construction of the portal (102x127cm-40x50in) 3-May-94 Christie's, East, New York #16/R
$2800   £1892   That which is seen (85x86cm-33x34in) s.d.1964verso acrylic masonite. 8-Nov-93 Christie's, East, New York #220/R
$4750   £3146   Burning glass (137x127cm-54x50in) s.d.1961verso. 29-Sep-93 Sotheby's Arcade, New York #315/R
$6000   £3974   Untitled (152x152cm-60x60in) s.d.1972verso acrylic. 17-Nov-92 Christie's, East, New York #181/R
$5000   £3472   Complementary fission (122x122cm-48x48in) s.d.1964verso liquitex masonite. 26-Feb-93 Sotheby's Arcade, New York #313/R

APPEL, Charles P (1857-1936) American
$650   £442   Twilight (35x36cm-14x14in) s.d.1927. 15-Nov-93 Christie's, East, New York #137
$900   £608   Sunset (76x61cm-30x24in) s.d.1927. 31-Mar-94 Sotheby's Arcade, New York #144/R
$1800   £1169   Figure in landscape (46x102cm-18x40in) s.d.1920. 11-Sep-93 Louisiana Auction Exchange #31/R
$2000   £1351   Returning home (51x76cm-20x30in) s. 31-Mar-94 Sotheby's Arcade, New York #48/R

APPLEBY, Theodore (1923-) American
$1743   £1170   Composition (114x86cm-45x34in) s. 27-Mar-94 Perrin, Versailles #179 (F.FR 10000)

AQUINO, Luis (1895-1968) Argentinian
$12000 £6936   Frutas y fuente (70x80cm-28x31in) panel. 23-Sep-92 Roldan & Cia, Buenos Aires #20

ARAGON, Jose (attrib) (19th C) American
$1500   £1007   Our Lady of St. John of the Lakes (38x23cm-15x9in) tempera gesso panel. 26-Jun-93 Skinner, Bolton #135/R
$2500   £1678   Our Lady of Sorrows (23x13cm-9x5in) tempera gesso panel. 26-Jun-93 Skinner, Bolton #230/R
$3250   £2181   Our Lady of Guadalupe (41x25cm-16x10in) tempera gesso panel. 26-Jun-93 Skinner, Bolton #8/R

ARAGON, Rafeal (attrib) (fl.1820-1862) Mexican
$7500   £4870   Holy Child of Prague (33x23cm-13x9in) tempera panel. 25-Jun-94 Skinner, Bolton #33/R
$2250   £1500   The guardian angel (20x15cm-8x6in) tempera gesso panel. 29-Jan-94 Skinner, Bolton #129/R

ARANGO, Alejandro (1950-) Mexican
$4000   £2667   Calzada de los Cipreses (100x100cm-39x39in) s.d.90. 18-May-94 Sotheby's, New York #236/R

ARAUJO, Carlos (1950-) Brazilian
$13000 £8609   Figura (181x160cm-71x63in) s. canvas on panel. 24-Nov-92 Christie's, New York #241/R

ARBUCKLE, George Franklin (1909-) Canadian
$680   £459   Ontario farm, June (45x60cm-18x24in) s. canvas on board. 23-Nov-93 Joyner Fine Art, Toronto #174 (C.D 900)
$755   £510   Afternoon, Rose Blanche, NFL (30x40cm-12x16in) s. canvas on board. 23-Nov-93 Joyner Fine Art, Toronto #160 (C.D 1000)
$775   £524   Tugboats in the inner harbour of Montreal (29x39cm-11x15in) s. board. 3-Nov-93 Sotheby's, Toronto #74/R (C.D 1000)
$793   £518   Winter birch and poplars, Windemere Road (46x61cm-18x24in) s. s.d.1984 verso board. 19-May-93 Sotheby's, Toronto #345/R (C.D 1000)
$872   £570   Norwood, Ontario (30x41cm-12x16in) s. s.d.87 verso board. 19-May-93 Sotheby's, Toronto #275/R (C.D 1100)
$895   £593   Rectory garden, near Fiesole (50x60cm-20x24in) s. board. 24-Nov-92 Joyner Fine Art, Toronto #55/R (C.D 1150)
$1401   £928   Farm scene (62x75cm-24x30in) s. 24-Nov-92 Joyner Fine Art, Toronto #91/R (C.D 1800)
$1427   £933   Quebec village (30x41cm-12x16in) s. board. 19-May-93 Sotheby's, Toronto #257/R (C.D 1800)
$1638   £1092   Charlevoix County (61x81cm-24x32in) s. i.stretcher. 11-May-94 Sotheby's, Toronto #91/R (C.D 2250)
$3285   £2220   Land of the Nootkas (76x102cm-30x40in) s. i.verso. 30-Mar-94 Maynards, Vancouver #68 (C.D 4550)

ARCE Y CEBALLOS, Gregorio Vasquez de (1638-1711) Colombian
$8750   £5872   Mary and Child (157x107cm-62x42in) 24-Mar-94 Mystic Fine Arts, Connecticut #214/R

ARCHE, Jorge (1905-) Cuban
$3000   £2000   Retrato (66x56cm-26x22in) s. painted c.1930. 18-May-94 Sotheby's, New York #405/R

ARCHIPENKO, Alexander (1887-1964) American/Russian
$3500   £2349   Reclining nude (28x38cm-11x15in) s. pencil col.pencil. 24-Feb-94 Sotheby's Arcade, New York #56/R

ARCHIPENKO, Alexander (1887-1964) American/Russian-cont.
$4000	£2703	Standing nude (41x31cm-16x12in) s. pencil executed c.1922-23. 4-Nov-93 Sotheby's, New York #199/R
$5516	£3629	Female nude (43x19cm-17x7in) s. pencil. 10-Jun-93 Hauswedell & Nolte, Hamburg #7/R (DM 9000)
$7000	£4730	Seated woman (42x29cm-17x11in) s. pencil executed c.1921. 4-Nov-93 Sotheby's, New York #195/R
$9000	£6000	Standing nude. Two nudes (51x34cm-20x13in) s. pencil one board executed 1921 pair. 9-Jun-94 Sotheby's Arcade, New York #28/R

ARENO, Joseph R (1950-) American
$1200	£805	Downtown Los Angeles beyond the Broadway Bridge (76x102cm-30x40in) s. s.i.d.93 verso. 8-Dec-93 Butterfield & Butterfield, San Francisco #3534/R
$2500	£1471	Mexican street scene (47x36cm-19x14in) s.i. s.d.91 verso board. 4-Oct-92 Butterfield & Butterfield, Los Angeles #226/R
$2750	£1809	Vineyard, California (56x76cm-22x30in) s. 13-Jun-93 Butterfield & Butterfield, San Francisco #962/R
$1500	£987	Chinatown, Los Angeles (60x46cm-24x18in) s.d.93 pastel. 13-Jun-93 Butterfield & Butterfield, San Francisco #963/R

AREVALO, Xavier (20th C) Mexican
$1273	£816	Sin titulo (56x47cm-22x19in) s.d.1963 ink gouache. 29-Apr-93 Louis Morton, Mexico #20 (M.P 4000)
$2229	£1429	Oaxaca (27x31cm-11x12in) s.i.d.1949 W/C. 29-Apr-93 Louis Morton, Mexico #152 (M.P 7000)

ARIZA, Gonzalo (1912-) Colombian
$12000	£7947	Catleya, Rana y Cardenal (69x43cm-27x17in) s. canvas on panel painted 1969-70. 24-Nov-92 Christie's, New York #232/R

ARMAN, Fernandez (1928-) American/French
$885	£598	Violin (35x34cm-14x13in) s. acrylic air brush. 26-Apr-94 Goteborg Auktionsverk #254 (S.KR 7000)
$936	£632	Violin (35x34cm-14x13in) s. 3-Nov-93 Bukowskis, Stockholm #213/R (S.KR 7600)
$1015	£686	Timbre (5x3cm-2x1in) s.d.1957. 24-Nov-93 Watine-Arnault, Paris #35/R (F.FR 6000)
$1118	£735	Sans titre (65x26cm-26x10in) oil brush pasted on canvas. 4-Nov-92 Francis Briest, Paris #80 (F.FR 6000)
$1638	£1114	Guitar (80x60cm-31x24in) s.d.70 acrylic paper. 13-Apr-94 Bukowskis, Stockholm #300/R (S.KR 13000)
$4031	£2742	Violins with red background (104x74cm-41x29in) s. 13-Apr-94 Bukowskis, Stockholm #298/R (S.KR 32000)
$15037	£9828	Allures d'objets (88x171cm-35x67in) s.d.1957 acrylic panel. 27-Oct-92 Cornette de St.Cyr, Paris #59/R (F.FR 80000)
$544	£367	Long term parking (90x63cm-35x25in) mixed media paper. 16-Jun-93 Watine-Arnault, Paris #52/R (F.FR 3100)
$1197	£814	Saxophone (80x56cm-31x22in) s.d.70 mixed media. 13-Apr-94 Bukowskis, Stockholm #299/R (S.KR 9500)
$2508	£1587	Accumulation of wrenches (72x57cm-28x22in) s. mixed media. 1-Dec-92 AB Stockholms Auktionsverk, Stockholm #6073/R (S.KR 17000)
$2665	£1863	Colere de violon (75x56cm-30x22in) s. ink. 3-Feb-93 Cornette de St.Cyr, Paris #161 (F.FR 15000)
$3800	£2639	Untitled (145x117cm-57x46in) exec.c.1980 collage of cut paperboard on panel. 22-Feb-93 Christie's, East, New York #250/R
$4500	£2647	Fantomatic (127x97cm-50x38in) s. Indian ink cotton fibres acrylic resin. 8-Oct-92 Christie's, New York #150/R
$6057	£4065	Colere de lunettes (35x25cm-14x10in) s. oil collage panel painted 1970. 14-Oct-93 Guy Loudmer, Paris #94/R (F.FR 35000)
$7000	£4636	Plaster violin (97x128cm-38x50in) plaster pigment executed 1987. 18-Nov-92 Sotheby's, New York #193/R
$12217	£7985	Cachets (75x110cm-30x43in) s.d.1962 oil gouache. 28-Oct-92 Guy Loudmer, Paris #14/R (F.FR 65000)
$12225	£7500	Accumulation de tubes de couleurs (92x74cm-36x29in) s. paint tubes canvas on panel. 14-Oct-92 Sotheby's, London #395/R
$28000	£18792	Untitled (101x101cm-40x40in) W/C paint tubes in polyester resin exec.1967. 4-May-94 Christie's, New York #115/R
$37250	£25000	Cachet carmelite (260x150cm-102x59in) oil W/C paper on canvas execute 1957. 2-Dec-93 Christie's, London #138/R

ARMINGTON, Frank Milton (1876-1941) Canadian
$1012	£670	Marly-le-roi (22x27cm-9x11in) s.d.1923 i.verso panel. 18-Nov-92 Sotheby's, Toronto #24 (C.D 1300)
$1451	£980	Untitled - Paris night scene, Notre Dame (38x46cm-15x18in) s.d.1902. 25-Apr-94 Levis, Calgary #5/R (C.D 2000)
$2257	£1495	Boulevard St Michel, Paris (22x27cm-9x11in) s.d.1934 i.verso panel. 18-Nov-92 Sotheby's, Toronto #68 (C.D 2900)
$8173	£5412	Rue Royale, Paris, Pluie d'ete (72x91cm-28x36in) s.d.1923 i.verso. 18-Nov-92 Sotheby's, Toronto #26/R (C.D 10500)
$542	£366	Pont Neuf Paris (24x31cm-9x12in) s.d.1915 pencil W/C. 3-Nov-93 Sotheby's, Toronto #138/R (C.D 700)

ARMSTRONG, Rolf (1881-1960) American
$14000	£7407	Enchantment (213x122cm-84x48in) s.i.d.1921. 11-Sep-92 Skinner, Bolton #273/R

ARMSTRONG, William (1822-1914) Canadian/Irish
$3500	£2333	Mount Shasta (76x127cm-30x50in) s.d.1889 i.verso. 23-May-94 Christie's, East, New York #103/R
$583	£388	Pine tree in a rock cleft, Lake Superior (16x11cm-6x4in) mono.d.06 W/C. 11-May-94 Sotheby's, Toronto #13/R (C.D 800)
$874	£583	River encampment with Indians (16x30cm-6x12in) s.d.06 W/C. 11-May-94 Sotheby's, Toronto #9/R (C.D 1200)
$1472	£995	From Hudson Bay post Red Rock Nipigon (24x36cm-9x14in) s.d.70 i.verso W/C. 3-Nov-93 Sotheby's, Toronto #2/R (C.D 1900)
$2576	£1684	High rock portage - Nipigon (25x36cm-10x14in) s.d.97 W/C. 19-May-93 Sotheby's, Toronto #224/R (C.D 3250)

ARNAUTOFF, Victor Mikhail (1896-1979) American
$1500	£882	City Hall, San Francisco (56x71cm-22x28in) mono. canvasboard. 4-Oct-92 Butterfield & Butterfield, Los Angeles #248/R

ARNESON, Robert (1930-1992) American
$650	£431	Sketch for monument to be erected at 1303 Alice Street (47x66cm-19x26in) s. W/C. 30-Jun-93 Sotheby's Arcade, New York #269/R

ARNOLDI, Charles (1946-) American
$6500	£4392	Untitled (147x122cm-58x48in) acrylic carved wood executed c.1984. 11-Nov-93 Sotheby's, New York #346/R
$1000	£676	Untitled (16x24cm-6x9in) s.d.1978 gouache. 8-Nov-93 Christie's, East, New York #197/R

ARSENIA (19th C) Brazilian
$626	£420	Lima and the River Rimac, Peru (14x23cm-6x9in) pencil wash htd white. 16-Jul-93 Christie's, London #126/R

ARTEAGA, Sebastian de (17/18th C) Mexican
$9540	£6000	Archangel Michael appearing to Bishop of Sipontus (183x151cm-72x59in) s.i. 21-Apr-93 Sotheby's, London #200/R

ARTENS, Peter von (1937-) Colombian
$10000	£6667	Construccion (195x130cm-77x51in) s. s.d.MCMXCIIverso. 18-May-94 Christie's, New York #251/R
$12000	£8000	Dos grandes totumas (162x130cm-64x51in) s. s.d.MCMXCIIIverso. 18-May-94 Sotheby's, New York #263/R

ARTER, John Charles (1860-1923) American
$3250	£2138	Woman with bouquet gazing at harbour, s.d.1895. 11-Jun-93 Du Mouchelle, Detroit #2001

ARTHURS, Stanley Massey (1877-1950) American
$700	£490	Going to church (46x30cm-18x12in) s. 11-Mar-93 Mystic Fine Arts, Connecticut #271

ARTS, Alexis (1940-) Canadian
$755	£510	Montreal, Vue de l'Ile Saint-Helene (45x65cm-18x26in) s. 23-Nov-93 Joyner Fine Art, Toronto #341 (C.D 1000)
$1031	£674	Region Rawdon, Quebec (51x71cm-20x28in) s. 18-May-93 Joyner Fine Art, Toronto #254 (C.D 1300)
$1090	£722	Region Athabask, Alberta (45x55cm-18x22in) s. 24-Nov-92 Joyner Fine Art, Toronto #210 (C.D 1400)

ARTSCHWAGER, Richard (1923-) American
$18000	£12081	T.W.M.D.R.B. - Smoldering (122x124cm-48x49in) s.i.d.1988 verso liquitex on celotex. 23-Feb-94 Christie's, New York #95/R
$30000	£17647	Accelerator II (146x103cm-57x41in) acrylic celotex. 8-Oct-92 Christie's, New York #177/R
$33000	£21854	Untitled (82x37cm-32x15in) acrylic celotex executed c.1967-68. 18-Nov-92 Sotheby's, New York #164/R
$46000	£30872	Untitled (123x82cm-48x32in) s.d.66verso acrylic celotex. 5-May-94 Sotheby's, New York #208/R
$80000	£52980	Double portrait (126x156cm-50x61in) acrylic celotex metal frame. 17-Nov-92 Sotheby's, New York #45/R
$3200	£2148	Untitled (64x48cm-25x19in) i.d.12/22/69 chl. 3-May-94 Christie's, East, New York #27/R
$3250	£1912	Untitled (48x63cm-19x25in) s.d.87 chl. 6-Oct-92 Sotheby's, New York #133/R
$4500	£3041	Tree (63x48cm-25x19in) s.d.68 chl. 8-Nov-93 Christie's, East, New York #211/R
$5000	£3378	Fence (66x61cm-26x24in) s.d.77 i.verso graphite. 8-Nov-93 Christie's, East, New York #14/R
$5500	£3642	Dinner and wait (64x48cm-25x19in) s.d.83 chl. 19-Nov-92 Christie's, New York #378/R
$19000	£12583	Untitled (48x47cm-19x19in) s.d.66 pencil celotex panel. 18-Nov-92 Sotheby's, New York #150/R
$150000	£98039	Mirroir (122x175cm-48x69in) liquitex on celotex painted 1971. 4-May-93 Christie's, New York #18/R
$170000	£114865	Destruction IV (102x122cm-40x48in) liquitex on celotex painted 1972. 10-Nov-93 Christie's, New York #188/R
$200000	£135135	Train wreck (118x109cm-46x43in) i.verso liquitex on Celotex executed 1967. 9-Nov-93 Christie's, New York #34/R

ARZADUN, Carmelo de see CARMELO DE ARZADUN

ASANGER, Jacob (1887-1941) American
$650 £433 Houses in a landscape (46x56cm-18x22in) s.indist.d.1920 board. 15-Mar-94 John Moran, Pasadena #141

ASHLEY, Frank N (1920-) American
$2750 £1821 Supper dance no.1 (61x76cm-24x30in) s.d.1960 s.i.verso masonite. 14-Jun-94 John Moran, Pasadena #62
$4750 £3146 The jazz singer (46x51cm-18x20in) 15-Jun-94 Butterfield & Butterfield, San Francisco #4490/R
$6500 £4305 The party (56x76cm-22x30in) s.d.47. 15-Jun-94 Butterfield & Butterfield, San Francisco #4489/R
$9000 £5960 The jazz musicians (94x117cm-37x46in) s.d.47. 15-Jun-94 Butterfield & Butterfield, San Francisco #4488/R
$3000 *£1923* *Paris, afterhours (71x56cm-28x22in) s. W/C pen. 9-Dec-92 Butterfield & Butterfield, San Francisco #4024/R*

ASKENAZY, Maurice (1888-1961) American
$700 £483 Snow in Venice (48x64cm-19x25in) s. canvas laid down. 16-Feb-93 John Moran, Pasadena #60
$800 £533 Girl with red necklace (30x25cm-12x10in) s. canvas laid on masonite. 15-Mar-94 John Moran, Pasadena #185
$1100 £759 Connie (43x33cm-17x13in) s. 16-Feb-93 John Moran, Pasadena #29 a
$1200 £795 Portrait of 18th century lady (61x51cm-24x20in) s. s.d.1954verso. 28-Sep-93 John Moran, Pasadena #241
$1500 £993 Balenese girl (41x51cm-16x20in) s. 28-Sep-93 John Moran, Pasadena #204
$1500 £987 Portrait of Jenny (81x63cm-32x25in) s. canvas on board. 13-Jun-93 Butterfield & Butterfield, San Francisco #901/R
$1700 £1118 Rooftops (51x61cm-20x24in) s. 13-Jun-93 Butterfield & Butterfield, San Francisco #863/R
$1700 £1076 Seated woman (66x71cm-26x28in) s. 5-Dec-92 Louisiana Auction Exchange #27/R
$2750 £1858 Boats in Venice (81x66cm-32x26in) s. 15-Jun-93 John Moran, Pasadena #113
$3000 £2083 Chioggia, Italy (46x76cm-18x30in) s. s.i.verso. 7-Mar-93 Butterfield & Butterfield, San Francisco #120/R
$3250 £2241 Boats in Venice (91x81cm-36x32in) s. 16-Feb-93 John Moran, Pasadena #47 a
$4000 £2632 Mother and child (107x81cm-42x32in) s. 13-Jun-93 Butterfield & Butterfield, San Francisco #900/R
$4000 £2632 My daughter (102x69cm-40x27in) s. 13-Jun-93 Butterfield & Butterfield, San Francisco #899/R
$4250 £2872 Chavez Ravine-Los Angeles (51x61cm-20x24in) s. 15-Jun-93 John Moran, Pasadena #64
$5500 £3235 House on island (71x86cm-28x34in) s. estate st.stretcher. 4-Oct-92 Butterfield & Butterfield, Los Angeles #193/R
$6000 £4138 Ballerina (81x66cm-32x26in) s. 16-Feb-93 John Moran, Pasadena #49
$7000 £4861 Through window (66x46cm-26x18in) s.d.1930. 7-Mar-93 Butterfield & Butterfield, San Francisco #159/R
$7500 £5208 Interior scene with artist's daughter and friend (43x38cm-17x15in) s.d.1938 board. 7-Mar-93 Butterfield & Butterfield, San Francisco #158/R
$8000 £5263 Japanese sketch book (117x91cm-46x36in) s. 13-Jun-93 Butterfield & Butterfield, San Francisco #857/R
$650 *£430* *Canal (33x38cm-13x15in) s. W/C. 28-Sep-93 John Moran, Pasadena #343*
$1100 *£759* *Figures near house (56x66cm-22x26in) s. W/C double sided. 16-Feb-93 John Moran, Pasadena #101*
$1500 *£1042* *Nude ascending stairwell. Venetian canal scene (65x54cm-26x21in) s. pastel W/C pencil double-sided. 7-Mar-93 Butterfield & Butterfield, San Francisco #235/R*

ATHERTON, John (1900-1952) American
$1500 £1007 Hanging Horn (30x41cm-12x16in) s.d.1942 tempera board. 26-Mar-94 James Bakker, Cambridge #15/R

ATKINS, David (1910-) American
$2400 £1611 Train departure (61x86cm-24x34in) s. i.stretcher. 24-Mar-93 Doyle, New York #4/R

ATKINSON, Howard (19/20th C) American
$700 £455 Spring landscape (51x66cm-20x26in) s. 8-Jul-94 Sloan, North Bethesda #2342

ATL, Dr (1875-1964) Mexican
$185000 £120915 Paisaje con volcanes (81x122cm-32x48in) s. panel. 17-May-93 Christie's, New York #12 a/R
$2000 *£1176* *Paisaje con Volcan (23x28cm-9x11in) s. chl.drawing. 8-Oct-92 Boos Gallery, Michigan #530/R*
$2000 *£1176* *Pasajie con Volcan (23x25cm-9x10in) s. chl.drawing. 8-Oct-92 Boos Gallery, Michigan #531/R*
$2750 *£1858* *Paisaje con volcan (22x26cm-9x10in) s. chl stencil paper on board executed c.1930. 22-Nov-93 Sotheby's, New York #193/R*
$3500 *£2365* *Volcan (27x32cm-11x13in) s. chl stencil paper on board executed c.1930. 22-Nov-93 Sotheby's, New York #191/R*
$4000 *£2649* *Paisaje con volcan (21x23cm-8x9in) chl. 23-Nov-92 Sotheby's, New York #218/R*
$4750 *£3210* *Volcan (32x27cm-13x11in) s.i.d.25-II-29 chl W/C paper on board. 22-Nov-93 Sotheby's, New York #183/R*
$7500 *£5000* *La punta del volcan (51x77cm-20x30in) s.i.d.1956 chl pastel. 18-May-94 Sotheby's, New York #273/R*
$8000 *£5229* *Pedro del Ajusco (32x43cm-13x17in) s.i.d.1942 chl pencil. 17-May-93 Christie's, New York #283/R*
$8750 *£5912* *Iguala (23x31cm-9x12in) s.d.1920 chl chk paper on board. 22-Nov-93 Sotheby's, New York #170/R*

ATL, Dr (1875-1964) Mexican-cont.
$10000	£6623	Paricutin (46x58cm-18x23in) s. chl. graphite. 23-Nov-92 Sotheby's, New York #219/R
$13226	£8818	Paisaje con sol (46x60cm-18x24in) s. mixed media. 25-May-94 Louis Morton, Mexico #72/R (M.P 44000)
$19351	£12987	Paricutin (23x28cm-9x11in) crayon. 1-Dec-93 Louis Morton, Mexico #152/R (M.P 60000)
$30000	£19608	Valle de Mexico (37x61cm-15x24in) s.d.52 atl col.masonite. 17-May-93 Christie's, New York #87/R
$140000	£93333	Paisaje Aero, Valle de Mexico (61x89cm-24x35in) s. atl col.masonite. 17-May-94 Sotheby's, New York #49/R

AUDOBON, Victor Gifford (after) (19/20th C) American?
$2000	£1361	Hawk and heron in flight (66x87cm-26x34in) 15-Nov-93 Christie's, East, New York #78/R

AUDUBON, John James (1785-1851) American/French
$45000	£26012	Eastern grey squirrel in full winter coat (54x44cm-21x17in) pen W/C board. 23-Sep-92 Christie's, New York #1/R
$140000	£93333	Wagtails (53x43cm-21x17in) s.i.d.1826 W/C pencil. 26-May-94 Christie's, New York #4/R

AUDUBON, John Woodhouse (1812-1868) American
$2786	£1400	Scotch highlander (114x78cm-45x31in) i.stretcher. 31-Aug-92 Sotheby's, London #814/R
$27000	£17308	Cat stalking butterfly (63x77cm-25x30in) i. 27-May-93 Sotheby's, New York #142 b/R
$35000	£23490	Mountain brook minks (55x68cm-22x27in) painted c.1848. 2-Dec-93 Sotheby's, New York #11/R

AUERBACH-LEVY, William (1889-1964) American
$900	£577	Three figures waiting (51x61cm-20x24in) s. acrylic. 13-Dec-92 Hindman Galleries, Chicago #69

AULT, George C (1891-1948) American
$16000	£10127	Where the road turns (43x33cm-17x13in) s.d.39 i.stretcher. 3-Dec-92 Sotheby's, New York #150/R
$900	£592	St. Luke's, N.Y (32x20cm-13x8in) s.d.25 graphite. 31-Mar-93 Sotheby's Arcade, New York #372/R
$2400	£1387	Iris (35x25cm-14x10in) s.d.32 pencil. 23-Sep-92 Christie's, New York #214/R
$3000	£1734	Woodstock nocturne (28x52cm-11x20in) s.d.40 gouache. 23-Sep-92 Christie's, New York #240/R
$3250	£2196	House and hill, Bermuda (28x39cm-11x15in) s.d.22 W/C. 31-Mar-94 Sotheby's Arcade, New York #432/R
$8000	£5333	Corn from Iowa (34x50cm-13x20in) s.d.40 gouache. 17-Mar-94 Sotheby's, New York #134/R

AUSTRIAN, Ben (1870-1921) American
$750	£510	Woods in autumn (61x76cm-24x30in) s.d.1921. 16-Apr-94 Young Fine Arts Auctions, Maine #27/R
$2000	£1418	Young chick (25x20cm-10x8in) artist board. 14-Feb-93 Myers, Florida #267
$4000	£2667	Mother hen and her new brood (51x71cm-20x28in) s.d.1911. 1-Jun-94 Doyle, New York #19/R
$6000	£4027	Tabletop still life with curious chick (30x36cm-12x14in) s. 3-Feb-94 Sloan, North Bethesda #2911/R

AVEDISIAN, Edward (1936-) American
$1000	£671	Catskill (93x93cm-37x37in) s.i.d.78 verso enamel panel. 23-Feb-94 Christie's, East, New York #366/R

AVERY, Milton (1885-1965) American
$800	£548	Figures in the fields. Trees in shadow (28x38cm-11x15in) board double-sided. 10-Feb-94 Skinner, Bolton #155
$4500	£2941	Siesta, reclining nude (36x66cm-14x26in) s.i.verso painted 1931 canvasboard. 20-May-93 Boos Gallery, Michigan #470/R
$5750	£3616	Teapot with flowers (18x10cm-7x4in) s.d.1956 paperboard. 23-Apr-93 Hart Gallery, Houston #6
$9000	£6000	Owl (61x45cm-24x18in) s.d.1953 canvasboard. 26-May-94 Christie's, New York #141/R
$9728	£6573	Two pigs (40x51cm-16x20in) s. canvas on board. 21-Apr-94 Germann, Zurich #107/R (S.FR 14000)
$10000	£6623	Vermont hillside (36x46cm-14x18in) s.d.1962 s.i.d.verso canvasboard. 22-Sep-93 Christie's, New York #212/R
$10000	£5780	Strange bird (45x61cm-18x24in) s.d.1953 s.i.d.verso canvas board. 23-Sep-92 Christie's, New York #281/R
$11000	£6258	Sleeping figure (61x46cm-24x18in) s. canvas board. 23-Sep-92 Christie's, New York #279/R
$11000	£7237	Bouquet by sea (23x16cm-9x6in) s.d.1955 board. 13-Jun-93 Butterfield & Butterfield, San Francisco #3187/R
$12000	£7947	Self-portrait (25x21cm-10x8in) s. canvasboard painted c.1930. 23-Sep-93 Sotheby's, New York #285/R
$12000	£8163	Spring trees (30x41cm-12x16in) s.d.1963 i.d.verso canvasboard. 17-Nov-93 Doyle, New York #61/R
$13000	£9091	Portrait of George Constant (76x63cm-30x25in) s. 11-Mar-93 Christie's, New York #244/R

AVERY, Milton (1885-1965) American-cont.
$15000	£9615	Pink turtleneck - self portrait (51x41cm-20x16in) s.d.1963 canvasboard. 26-May-93 Christie's, New York #218/R
$19000	£12025	Pool shark (30x22cm-12x9in) s.d.1955 s.i.d.verso canvasboard. 3-Dec-92 Sotheby's, New York #195/R
$19000	£10983	Lilacs (56x71cm-22x28in) s.d.1961 s.i.d.verso canvas board. 23-Sep-92 Christie's, New York #270/R
$21000	£12139	Orange flowers (28x15cm-11x6in) s.d.1958 s.verso. 24-Sep-92 Sotheby's, New York #219/R
$22000	£13924	Woman in feathered hat (91x61cm-36x24in) s. 3-Dec-92 Sotheby's, New York #196/R
$24000	£15894	Nude reclining (38x76cm-15x30in) s.d.1963 s.i.d.verso canvasboard. 22-Sep-93 Christie's, New York #208/R
$26820	£18000	Birds in blue sea (37x50cm-15x20in) s.d.1963 s.i.d.verso board. 25-Mar-93 Christie's, London #94/R
$32000	£21333	Seated nude (76x46cm-30x18in) s. s.i.verso canvas on board. 16-Mar-94 Christie's, New York #134/R
$90000	£57692	Girl drawing (91x71cm-36x28in) s.d.1951. 27-May-93 Sotheby's, New York #114/R
$160000	£107383	Pine and sea (86x91cm-34x36in) s.d.1952 s.i.d.verso. 2-Dec-93 Sotheby's, New York #141/R
$220000	£141026	Porch sitters - Sally and March (71x107cm-28x42in) s.d.1952. 26-May-93 Christie's, New York #216/R
$1300	*£878*	*Lute player (22x35cm-9x14in) s.d.1950 s.i.d.verso magic marker pen pencil. 31-Mar-94 Sotheby's Arcade, New York #416/R*
$2250	*£1415*	*Life drawing class (36x43cm-14x17in) s. sepia ink. 23-Apr-93 Hart Gallery, Houston #5*
$2800	*£1905*	*Girl with pigtails (28x21cm-11x8in) s. pencil. 15-Nov-93 Christie's, East, New York #217/R*
$3250	*£1879*	*Two seated female nudes (35x43cm-14x17in) s. felt tip pen. 25-Sep-92 Sotheby's Arcade, New York #297 a/R*
$4500	*£3041*	*Woman in a white dress and hat (46x30cm-18x12in) s. gouache. 31-Mar-94 Sotheby's Arcade, New York #415/R*
$7500	*£4717*	*Girl with mandolin (28x43cm-11x17in) s. mixed media. 23-Apr-93 Hart Gallery, Houston #4*
$7633	£5088	Figures on beach. Landscape (55x76cm-22x30in) s.d.1948 s.d.verso W/C double-sided. 25-Aug-93 Joel, Victoria #138 a (A.D 11500)
$9000	£5882	Rainy day (66x51cm-26x20in) s.d.1957 mixed media. 17-Sep-93 Du Mouchelle, Detroit #2046/R
$12355	£8182	Sunbather and seawatcher (56x75cm-22x30in) s.d.1948 W/C. 25-Nov-92 Joel, Victoria #190/R (A.D 18000)
$14000	£9272	Girl with mandolin (30x46cm-12x18in) s. i.verso gouache. 23-Sep-93 Sotheby's, New York #286/R
$16000	£10738	Sails in pale sea (58x78cm-23x31in) s.d.1944 i.verso W/C. 2-Dec-93 Sotheby's, New York #150/R
$18000	£12000	Green hills of Vermont (57x78cm-22x31in) s.d.1943 i.verso W/C. 17-Mar-94 Sotheby's, New York #177/R
$20000	£13333	Stella in red (79x57cm-31x22in) s.d.1945 i.verso W/C pencil. 26-May-94 Christie's, New York #145/R
$26000	£17450	Figures on beach. Landscape (56x74cm-22x29in) s.d.1948 W/C pencil double-sided. 4-May-94 Doyle, New York #53/R
$28000	£17722	The bathers (36x55cm-14x22in) s. W/C. 3-Dec-92 Sotheby's, New York #76/R
$31000	£19620	Pines and meadows (55x78cm-22x31in) s. W/C pencil. 3-Dec-92 Sotheby's, New York #183/R
$35000	£22436	Sun bather and sea watcher (57x78cm-22x31in) s.d.1948 i.verso W/C. 27-May-93 Sotheby's, New York #115/R
$45000	£28846	Green sea (57x78cm-22x31in) s.d.1948 s.i.d.verso gouache pencil. 26-May-93 Christie's, New York #217/R
$120000	£80537	Artist's family by the sea (57x78cm-22x31in) s.d.1944 s.i.d.verso gouache pencil. 3-Dec-93 Christie's, New York #13/R

AYCOCK, Alice (1946-) American
$450	£300	Universal causality (86x112cm-34x44in) s. pencil on mylar. 26-May-94 Freeman Fine Arts, Philadelphia #36
$775	£517	Manufacture ghost (109x140cm-43x55in) s. pencil on mylar. 26-May-94 Freeman Fine Arts, Philadelphia #35
$850	*£567*	*Untitled (74x53cm-29x21in) pencil. 26-May-94 Freeman Fine Arts, Philadelphia #34*
$1000	*£671*	*The First City of the Dead (39x244cm-15x96in) s.i.d.79 pencil vellum. 25-Feb-94 Sotheby's, New York #122/R*
$6000	£3529	The New China Drawing (242x267cm-95x105in) s.i.d.1984 col.pencils mylar. 8-Oct-92 Christie's, New York #194/R

AYOTTE, Leo (1909-1976) Canadian
$1046	£707	Landscape with trees by water (38x46cm-15x18in) s. indist.i.verso paper board. 1-Nov-93 Levis, Calgary #8/R (C.D 1350)
$1510	£1020	Le bateau (40x51cm-16x20in) s.d.72. 23-Nov-93 Fraser Pinneys, Quebec #375/R (C.D 2000)
$2201	£1393	Paysage a Chateauguay (51x61cm-20x24in) s. 1-Dec-92 Fraser Pinneys, Quebec #143 (C.D 2800)

BABBIDGE, James Gardner (1844-1919) American
$3250	£2273	Merchant ship 'Warner Moore' (61x91cm-24x36in) mono. 5-Feb-93 Sloan, North Bethesda #2557

BABBIDGE, James Gardner (1844-1919) American-cont.
$4000 £2632 Merchant ship William H Allison (61x89cm-24x35in) s.i. 2-Apr-93 Sloan, North Bethesda #2469/R

BABER, Alice (1928-) American
$1400 £972 The rain that hears the jaguar (76x127cm-30x50in) s.s.i.d.1977verso. 26-Feb-93 Sotheby's Arcade, New York #393/R

BACKUS, Standish (jnr) (1910-) American
$700 £473 Landscape. Landscape with train (36x53cm-14x21in) s. W/C double-sided. 15-Jun-93 John Moran, Pasadena #70

BACKUS, Standish (jnr-attrib) (1910-) American
$505 £337 Tropical storm (76x91cm-30x36in) s. 31-May-94 Ritchie, Toronto #125/R (C.D 700)

BACON, Charles Roswell (1868-1913) American
$1600 £1074 Roadside conversation (51x61cm-20x24in) s. 24-Mar-94 Mystic Fine Arts, Connecticut #118

BACON, Henry (1839-1912) American
$2640 £1692 Artist painting (41x33cm-16x13in) s. 17-Dec-92 Mystic Fine Arts, Connecticut #252
$4800 £3179 Change of heart - broken engagement (41x30cm-16x12in) s.d.1877 panel. 22-Sep-93 Christie's, New York #56/R
$8000 £5333 At the well (48x71cm-19x28in) s. 25-May-94 Sotheby's, New York #22/R
$17000 £11565 A beauty specialist (34x25cm-13x10in) s.d.1866. 15-Nov-93 Christie's, East, New York #9/R
$29400 £20000 Scottish lady on boat arriving in New York (48x69cm-19x27in) s. 17-Nov-93 Sotheby's, London #176/R
$38000 £24675 Rainy day, artist's tavern at Barbizon (98x131cm-39x52in) s.d.1874. 9-Sep-93 Sotheby's Arcade, New York #4/R
$950 £629 Girl on barge (28x43cm-11x17in) s. W/C. 23-Sep-93 Mystic Fine Arts, Connecticut #183/R
$1100 £714 Cairo (28x30cm-11x12in) s.d.1905 W/C over pencil. 9-Sep-93 Sotheby's Arcade, New York #187/R

BACON, Peggy (1895-1987) American
$748 £499 Dancing party (13x18cm-5x7in) s. pen. 9-Jun-94 Swann Galleries, New York #13/R

BADGER, Samuel Finley Morse (19/20th C) American
$7500 £5068 American bark H G Johnson (91x56cm-36x22in) s.d.98. 30-Jul-93 Eldred, Massachusetts #281/R

BADI, Aquiles (1894-1976) Argentinian
$1800 £938 Moore a Spoleto (28x40cm-11x16in) tempera. 4-Aug-92 VerBo, Buenos Aires #8
$12000 £6936 Iglesia del Tiepolo, Venecia (35x44cm-14x17in) panel. 23-Sep-92 Roldan & Cia, Buenos Aires #49
$15000 £8671 Rio Ognisanti, Venecia (35x44cm-14x17in) panel. 23-Sep-92 Roldan & Cia, Buenos Aires #50

BAECHLER, Donald (1956-) American
$5662 £3800 Two suitcases (50x40cm-20x16in) s.d.88 verso acrylic. 2-Dec-93 Christie's, London #291/R
$18000 £12081 Hommage to Picasso (162x162cm-64x64in) s.i.d.84 verso acrylic canvas collage. 23-Feb-94 Christie's, New York #143/R
$22000 £15278 Untitled Zagreb (282x168cm-111x66in) s.i.d.82verso acrylic. 24-Feb-93 Christie's, New York #145/R
$22350 £15000 Fears of abstraction (190x190cm-75x75in) init.i.d.88 acrylic canvas collage. 25-Mar-93 Christie's, London #168/R
$24000 £15686 Liebespaar (200x200cm-79x79in) init.i.d.87verso oil canvas collage. 5-May-93 Christie's, New York #166/R
$1000 £671 Untitled (28x22cm-11x9in) init.d.89 brush ink gouache paper collage. 23-Feb-94 Christie's, East, New York #264/R
$2500 £1689 Untitled (60x47cm-24x19in) init.d.89 collage gouache graphite. 8-Nov-93 Christie's, East, New York #118/R
$4172 £2800 Horn (30x50cm-12x20in) init.d.88verso oil canvas collaged on canvas. 23-Mar-94 Sotheby's, London #382/R
$4500 £2647 Untitled - head (106x106cm-42x42in) acrylic paper collage canvas. 6-Oct-92 Sotheby's, New York #198/R
$4750 £3210 Untitled (58x39cm-23x15in) init.d.86 ink paper collage. 11-Nov-93 Sotheby's, New York #232/R
$5508 £3600 Untitled composition with standing figures (50x40cm-20x16in) init.i.d.88verso oil canvas collage canvas. 30-Jun-94 Sotheby's, London #259/R
$6500 £4305 Onion eater (107x107cm-42x42in) init.d.88 verso oil canvas collage on canvas. 18-Nov-92 Sotheby's, New York #308/R
$7000 £4730 Abstract picture with tree (107x107cm-42x42in) s.init.i.d.10/85verso acrylic paper collage. 10-Nov-93 Christie's, New York #193/R
$7450 £5000 Black Painting No.10 (60x61cm-24x24in) init.i.d.86 collage fabric acrylic varnish. 25-Mar-93 Christie's, London #193/R
$16000 £10738 Untitled (149x149cm-59x59in) init.d.88 oil cloth collage canvas. 5-May-93 Sotheby's, New York #351/R
$16830 £11000 Abstract painting with tree (147x102cm-58x40in) init.i.d.86verso oil canvas collage canvas. 30-Jun-94 Sotheby's, London #262/R
$17000 £11111 Green carnation (147x102cm-58x40in) s.d.90 verso oil acrylic cloth collage canvas. 4-May-93 Sotheby's, New York #263/R

BAECHLER, Donald (1956-) American-cont.
$22000	£14865	Painting with two balls (190x190cm-75x75in) init.i.d.86verso acrylic fabric collage canvas. 10-Nov-93 Christie's, New York #296/R
$23000	£15541	Untitled - beachball (127x102cm-50x40in) init.i.d.89 verso oil cloth collage canvas. 11-Nov-93 Sotheby's, New York #223/R
$26000	£17568	Dog No.1 (190x190cm-75x75in) init.i.d.91 verso oil cloth collage canvas. 11-Nov-93 Sotheby's, New York #234/R
$50000	£33113	Plague of Responsibility (282x282cm-111x111in) init.d.86 verso acrylic collage canvas. 18-Nov-92 Sotheby's, New York #310/R

BAER, George (20th C) American
$550	£364	Abstract composition (74x56cm-29x22in) s. board. 23-Sep-93 Mystic Fine Arts, Connecticut #135/R

BAER, Jo (1929-) American
$2800	£1944	Untitled (265x183cm-104x72in) s.d.68verso diptych. 22-Feb-93 Christie's, East, New York #158/R
$2800	£1879	Untitled (182x182cm-72x72in) s.i.d.62verso. 4-May-94 Christie's, New York #221/R
$3000	£2083	Untitled (152x218cm-60x86in) s.d.66verso diptych. 22-Feb-93 Christie's, East, New York #159/R
$8000	£5298	Untitled, Korean (183x183cm-72x72in) s.d.62verso. 19-Nov-92 Christie's, New York #386/R

BAER, William Jacob (1860-1941) American
$2200	£1272	Salter's Point, Roundhill, South Dartmouth, Massachusetts (30x51cm-12x20in) 24-Sep-92 Sotheby's, New York #110/R

BAGG, Henry Howard (1852-1928) American
$1000	£671	Valley Vista (56x87cm-22x34in) s.d.1908. 8-Dec-93 Butterfield & Butterfield, San Francisco #3328/R

BAILEY, T (?) American?
$800	£537	American clipper ship (61x81cm-24x32in) s. 25-Mar-94 Eldred, Massachusetts #323/R

BAILEY, Walter Alexander (1894-?) American
$1600	£1067	Taos N.M (51x41cm-20x16in) s.d.1928. 22-May-94 James Bakker, Cambridge #80/R

BAILEY, William (1930-) American
$1500	£1007	Head of girl with long hair (34x25cm-13x10in) s.d.1970 graphite. 3-May-94 Christie's, East, New York #46/R
$2500	£1656	Untitled , s.d.1983 graphite one s. pen two. 17-Nov-92 Christie's, East, New York #71/R
$3000	£1765	Nude in Armchair (38x28cm-15x11in) s.d.1967 graphite. 8-Oct-92 Christie's, New York #132/R
$4000	£2703	Untitled (38x28cm-15x11in) s. one.d.1988 one d.1983 graphite dr two. 8-Nov-93 Christie's, East, New York #150/R

BAIRD, William Baptiste (1847-?) American
$1057	£700	Chickens by step (23x33cm-9x13in) s. s.verso board. 26-Nov-92 Bonhams, London #69/R
$1064	£700	Birch trees (33x46cm-13x18in) s. 8-Jun-93 Sotheby's, London #122
$1079	£701	Grazing sheep (53x81cm-21x32in) s. 21-Jun-94 Fraser Pinneys, Quebec #189 (C.D 1500)
$1200	£759	Marie Antoinette's cottage and cow stable, Park of Versailles and Versailles (21x33cm-8x13in) s. s.i.d.1900verso panel two. 2-Dec-92 Christie's, East, New York #70/R
$1200	£800	The watering place (20x15cm-8x6in) s.d.1877 panel. 8-Mar-94 Sotheby's, Billingshurst #1076
$1355	£909	La Bertran, Seine, France (33x46cm-13x18in) s. i.stretcher. 30-Nov-93 Ritchie, Toronto #67/R (C.D 1800)
$2200	£1447	Mother hen and chicks (25x32cm-10x13in) s. 4-Jun-93 Sotheby's, New York #178/R
$3696	£2400	Hen by watering trough with chicks (23x15cm-9x6in) s.d.1877 panel. 20-Jun-94 Desmond Judd, Cranbrook #654

BAITLER, Zoma (20th C) South American
$700	£458	Redes extendidas, Capetown (50x60cm-20x24in) s. 27-Jun-94 Gomensoro, Montevideo #14
$750	£497	La sinagoga (50x60cm-20x24in) s. 28-Jun-93 Gomensoro, Montevideo #12
$850	£497	Flores (60x50cm-24x20in) s. 16-Sep-92 Castells & Castells, Montevideo #43
$900	£577	Casas municipales, Prado (50x60cm-20x24in) s. 7-Dec-92 Gomensoro, Montevideo #42
$1000	£654	Marina en amarillos (50x60cm-20x24in) s. 27-Jun-94 Gomensoro, Montevideo #23
$1000	£649	Parque, Minas (50x40cm-20x16in) s.d.1935 board. 30-Aug-93 Gomensoro, Montevideo #20
$1050	£705	Aledanos de Amsterdam (50x60cm-20x24in) s. 29-Nov-93 Gomensoro, Montevideo #15
$1100	£738	The Old Beckman, New York (60x50cm-24x20in) s.d.63. 29-Nov-93 Gomensoro, Montevideo #14
$1100	£719	Calle de Paris y panteon (60x50cm-24x20in) s. 26-Oct-92 Gomensoro, Montevideo #67
$1100	£714	Arroyo y puente (60x70cm-24x28in) s. oil. 30-Aug-93 Gomensoro, Montevideo #22
$1400	£909	Paisaje de Paris (46x55cm-18x22in) s. oil. 30-Aug-93 Gomensoro, Montevideo #21
$1800	£1208	Puerto (50x60cm-20x24in) s. s.i.d.89verso. 29-Nov-93 Gomensoro, Montevideo #13
$1800	£1176	Fondo de quinta (66x86cm-26x34in) s. s.i.verso. 4-Oct-93 Gomensoro, Montevideo #50/R
$1800	£1154	Calle y casona (61x71cm-24x28in) s.d.1939. 7-Dec-92 Gomensoro, Montevideo #41
$1900	£1242	Calle Ejido (50x60cm-20x24in) s. 3-May-93 Gomensoro, Montevideo #38

17

BAITLER, Zoma (20th C) South American-cont.
$2000	£1307	Bahia y cerro, puerto de Montevideo (50x70cm-20x28in) s. 26-Oct-92 Gomensoro, Montevideo #64/R
$2000	£1042	Punta del Este (60x76cm-24x30in) s. board. 12-Aug-92 Castells & Castells, Montevideo #53/R
$2000	£1282	Paisaje del Buceo ano 1945 (52x76cm-20x30in) s.d.1945. 7-Dec-92 Gomensoro, Montevideo #40
$2100	£1228	Nueva York (40x50cm-16x20in) s. 16-Sep-92 Castells & Castells, Montevideo #42/R
$2200	£1106	Jovenes en el Parque (50x60cm-20x24in) s. 31-Aug-92 Gomensoro, Montevideo #59/R
$2400	£1611	Playa La Solana (50x63cm-20x25in) s. s.i.verso. 29-Nov-93 Gomensoro, Montevideo #12/R
$2600	£1699	Reflejos de la tarde (70x81cm-28x32in) s.d.1941. 3-May-93 Gomensoro, Montevideo #37/R
$3200	£2092	Demolicion (120x90cm-47x35in) s.d.61. 26-Oct-92 Gomensoro, Montevideo #63/R
$4000	£2010	Otono en el Tigre (66x83cm-26x33in) s. i.d.1948verso. 31-Aug-92 Gomensoro, Montevideo #58/R
$5000	£3356	Paisaje de Cordoba (79x99cm-31x39in) s. s.i.verso. 29-Nov-93 Gomensoro, Montevideo #11/R

BAKER, Bryant see BAKER, Percy Bryant

BAKER, Doris Winchell (1905-1987) American
$850   £567   Mountain stream (64x48cm-25x19in) s. canvasboard. 15-Mar-94 John Moran, Pasadena #57

BAKER, Elisha Taylor (1827-1890) American
$3500   £2318   Safe harbour (76x64cm-30x25in) s. 22-Sep-93 Christie's, New York #29/R
$10000 £6667   Schooner yacht (56x86cm-22x34in) 22-May-94 James Bakker, Cambridge #33/R

BAKER, George A (1821-1880) American
$2500   £1603   Dolly (24x19cm-9x7in) board. 9-Dec-92 Butterfield & Butterfield, San Francisco #3830/R

BAKER, Howard Russell (20th C) American
$560   £373   The Morning Glory Pool - Yellowstone Park (36x51cm-14x20in) s.d.1920 W/C. 23-May-94 Hindman Galleries, Chicago #249

BAKER, Joe (1946-) American
$4000   £2532   Frankie in blue blanket (198x168cm-78x66in) s.i. 25-Oct-92 Butterfield & Butterfield, San Francisco #2399/R

BAKOS, Jozef G (1891-1977) American
$4500   £2601   Western landscape (45x60cm-18x24in) s. 23-Sep-92 Christie's, New York #116/R

BALDAUGH, Anni (1886-1953) American
$5500   £3691   Desert palms (86x93cm-34x37in) s. 8-Dec-93 Butterfield & Butterfield, San Francisco #3504/R

BALFOUR, Helen (1857-1925) American
$1700   £1133   Stream in landscape. Eucalyptus landscape (33x43cm-13x17in) one s. W/C pair. 15-Mar-94 John Moran, Pasadena #56

BALL, Alice W (?-1929) American
$650   £455   Canadian village street (76x61cm-30x24in) s. i.verso. 12-Mar-93 Skinner, Bolton #154/R

BALLAINE, Jerrold (20th C) American
$1100   £743   Sonoma landscape (61x75cm-24x30in) s. acrylic masonite painted 1988. 21-Oct-93 Butterfield & Butterfield, San Francisco #2780/R

BALLIN, Hugo (1879-?) American
$2750   £1809   Mexican party (102x127cm-40x50in) s. 13-Jun-93 Butterfield & Butterfield, San Francisco #945/R

BALMORI, Santos (20th C) Mexican?
$601   £401   Desnudo (21x28cm-8x11in) s.d.1964 ink. 25-May-94 Louis Morton, Mexico #130 (M.P 2000)

BANCROFT, Albert Stokes (1890-1972) American
$750   £510   Crestone Needles, Sangre de Cristo Range, Colorado (16x20cm-6x8in) s. i.verso. 10-Jul-93 Young Fine Arts Auctions, Maine #37/R

BANDEIRA (1922-1967) Brazilian
$805   £537   Le village (10x15cm-4x6in) s.d.1950 W/C ink. 19-Mar-94 Cornette de St.Cyr, Paris #104 (F.FR 4600)

BANDEIRA, Antonio (1922-1967) Brazilian
$4500   £2941   Petite ville (18x26cm-7x10in) s.d.55 s.i.d.1955 verso. 17-May-93 Christie's, New York #217/R
$10000 £6757   Soleil e cabana bleu (20x30cm-8x12in) s.d.1955 s.d.verso. 23-Nov-93 Christie's, New York #186/R
$12000 £8000   Cidade iluminada (55x46cm-22x18in) s.d.58. 18-May-94 Christie's, New York #161/R
$12000 £7947   City in black and red (46x55cm-18x22in) s.d.62. 24-Nov-92 Christie's, New York #262/R

BANDEIRA, Antonio (1922-1967) Brazilian-cont.
$19370   £13000   Blue threes (51x76cm-20x30in) s.d.55 s.i.d.verso. 21-Jun-93 Christie's, S. Kensington #197/R
$35000   £23333   Composition (154x104cm-61x41in) s.d.58 acrylic. 18-May-94 Sotheby's, New York #385/R
$38000   £24837   La grande ville-ville bleu (60x81cm-24x32in) s.d.49. 17-May-93 Christie's, New York #219/R
$1500   £980   Abstract (27x23cm-11x9in) s.d.54 gouache pen col.ink. 17-May-93 Christie's, New York #218/R
$2000   £1325   Abstract in brown (25x39cm-10x15in) s.d.56 gouache pen. 24-Nov-92 Christie's, New York #320/R
$3500   £2318   Abstract in pink (49x35cm-19x14in) s.d.56 gouache brush ink. 24-Nov-92 Christie's, New York #319/R

BANNARD, Walter Darby (1931-) American
$1600   £1111   Grover coast (168x251cm-66x99in) s.on stretcher. 26-Feb-93 Sotheby's Arcade, New York #294/R

BANNISTER, E M (1833-1901) American
$1700   £1090   Moody landscape (28x46cm-11x18in) s. board. 13-Dec-92 Litchfield Auction Gallery #1

BANNISTER, Edward M (1833-1901) American
$16500   £11074   Pastoral scene by the river (76x102cm-30x40in) s.d.97. 6-Dec-93 Grogan, Massachussetts #480/R

BANTING, Sir Frederick Grant (1891-1941) Canadian
$1602   £1068   Caledon, Autumn (21x26cm-8x10in) s. panel. 13-May-94 Joyner Fine Art, Toronto #28/R (C.D 2200)
$1974   £1316   Dundas Harbour inside the Arctic Circle (19x26cm-7x10in) s. i.d.1927 verso panel. 30-May-94 Ritchie, Toronto #224/R (C.D 2750)
$3171   £2143   Village in autumn. Landscape sketch (21x26cm-8x10in) s. panel double-sided. 23-Nov-93 Joyner Fine Art, Toronto #166/R (C.D 4200)
$3503   £2320   Cobalt (22x27cm-9x11in) s. i.d.1932verso panel. 18-Nov-92 Sotheby's, Toronto #61/R (C.D 4500)
$3874   £2618   French River New Brunswick (27x34cm-11x13in) s. i.verso panel. 3-Nov-93 Sotheby's, Toronto #209/R (C.D 5000)
$5286   £3571   Village along the lower St. Lawrence (21x26cm-8x10in) s. panel. 23-Nov-93 Joyner Fine Art, Toronto #30/R (C.D 7000)

BARBEAU, Marcel (1925-) Canadian
$1012   £670   Abstract composition (63x49cm-25x19in) s.d.72 gouache. 18-Nov-92 Sotheby's, Toronto #189/R (C.D 1300)
$1101   £697   Green and navy composition (49x64cm-19x25in) s.d.72 gouache. 30-Nov-92 Ritchie, Toronto #256 (C.D 1400)

BARBER, John (1898-1965) American
$1400   £927   Provincetown scene (38x46cm-15x18in) s. 13-Nov-92 Skinner, Bolton #154/R

BARBOSA, Edilson Elio (1965-) Brazilian
$1200   £789   Shepherd with sheep (40x50cm-16x20in) 5-Apr-93 Ricardo Saba, Sao Paolo #1
$1550   £1099   Still life (50x70cm-20x28in) 10-Feb-93 Ricardo Saba, Sao Paolo #1
$1835   £1199   Searching for pasture (50x60cm-20x24in) 20-May-93 Ricardo Saba, Sao Paolo #1
$2225   £1426   Oriental carpet seller (60x80cm-24x31in) 15-Dec-92 Ricardo Saba, Sao Paolo #1
$2320   £1645   Carpet seller (80x60cm-31x24in) 10-Feb-93 Ricardo Saba, Sao Paolo #2

BARCHUS, Eliza R (1857-1959) American
$700   £449   Mountain lake (76x127cm-30x50in) s. 11-Dec-92 Du Mouchelle, Detroit #2032/R
$1000   £676   Snow capped peak in the Cascades (41x61cm-16x24in) s.d.1890. 27-Nov-93 Young Fine Arts Auctions, Maine #32/R
$1000   £658   Mountain river (41x61cm-16x24in) s. 13-Jun-93 Butterfield & Butterfield, San Francisco #738/R

BARCLAY, McClelland (1891-1943) American
$1000   £654   Horse and rider (89x76cm-35x30in) s.i.d.1933. 4-May-93 Christie's, East, New York #169/R
$1200   £702   Courting couple (56x61cm-22x24in) s. 18-Sep-92 Du Mouchelle, Detroit #1300/R
$1400   £915   Man by roadside asking directions (71x66cm-28x26in) s.i. indist.d. oil en grisaille. 20-May-93 Boos Gallery, Michigan #468/R
$1700   £1141   Woman on sailboat (86x66cm-34x26in) s. 6-Dec-93 Grogan, Massachusetts #554/R
$2100   £1409   Selling raffle tickets (84x64cm-33x25in) s. 6-Dec-93 Grogan, Massachusetts #555

BARD, James (1815-1897) American
$70000   £46667   The paddle steamboat City of Catskill (66x129cm-26x51in) s.d.1880 W/C gouache pencil pen ink. 25-May-94 Sotheby's, New York #26/R

BARILE, Xavier J (1891-?) American
$900   £588   Beyond Artist Drive, Death Valley, California (51x61cm-20x24in) s. s.i.d.verso masonite. 4-May-93 Christie's, East, New York #124/R

BARKER, George (1882-1965) American
$550   £365   Pink Desert (56x71cm-22x28in) 15-Jun-94 Butterfield & Butterfield, San Francisco #4724/R
$1510   £1000   A lady out hunting said to be the Empress of Austria (67x88cm-26x35in) s. framed as an oval. 28-Sep-93 Sotheby's Colonnade, London #470/R

BARKER, Walter (1921-) American
$750 £481 No 11 Persian series (183x132cm-72x52in) s.i.d.1962verso. 24-May-93 Selkirks, St. Louis #171

BARLOW, Myron (1873-1937) American
$650 £445 Landscape (43x56cm-17x22in) s. 18-Feb-94 Du Mouchelle, Detroit #2150/R
$900 £592 French landscape (79x64cm-31x25in) s. 5-Jun-93 Louisiana Auction Exchange #196
$2000 £1351 Cinderella (81x65cm-32x26in) s.d.1914. 31-Mar-94 Sotheby's Arcade, New York #157
$2500 £1656 Interior (91x74cm-36x29in) s.d.1900. 23-Sep-93 Sotheby's, New York #142/R
$2600 £1711 Sisters (81x66cm-32x26in) s.d.1907 canvas on masonite. 31-Mar-93 Sotheby's Arcade, New York #67/R
$3000 £2013 The sisters (81x66cm-32x26in) s.d.1907 canvas laid down on masonite. 15-Dec-93 Boos Gallery, Michigan #552/R
$6000 £4054 Lady with apples seated at table (81x61cm-32x24in) s. 4-Nov-93 Boos Gallery, Michigan #1270 a/R
$7000 £4965 Pink shawl (81x81cm-32x32in) s. 11-Feb-93 Boos Gallery, Michigan #373/R
$7000 £4487 Hospitality (100x100cm-39x39in) s. 27-May-93 Sotheby's, New York #47/R
$7500 £5034 Reverie a young girl seated at a table (76x76cm-30x30in) s. i.stretcher. 15-Dec-93 Boos Gallery, Michigan #546/R
$7500 £4967 Poisson Rose (100x100cm-39x39in) s. 23-Sep-93 Sotheby's, New York #132/R
$8000 £5298 Shepherdess (76x75cm-30x30in) s. i.d.1935 verso. 23-Sep-93 Sotheby's, New York #131/R
$12000 £7692 Cup of tea (100x100cm-39x39in) s. 27-May-93 Sotheby's, New York #48/R

BARNES, E Paul (19/20th C) American?
$550 £377 River landscape (51x76cm-20x30in) s. 19-Feb-94 Young Fine Arts Auctions, Maine #34/R

BARNES, Ernest Harrison (1873-?) American
$3000 £1948 Shady street (63x76cm-25x30in) s. i.stretcher. 9-Sep-93 Sotheby's Arcade, New York #308/R

BARNES, Ernie (20th C) American
$1200 £759 Football players (76x91cm-30x36in) s. 25-Oct-92 Butterfield & Butterfield, San Francisco #2379/R

BARNES, Matthew (1880-1951) American
$1700 £1000 Emerald night (51x61cm-20x24in) s.d.1942 verso. 4-Oct-92 Butterfield & Butterfield, Los Angeles #267/R

BARNET, Will (1911-) American
$3500 £2215 Abstract (114x96cm-45x38in) s. s.i.verso. 2-Dec-92 Christie's, East, New York #404/R
$3750 *£2467* Girl on bicycle (68x70cm-27x28in) s.d.1971 mixed media board. 31-Mar-93 Sotheby's Arcade, New York #484/R

BARNETT, Herbert (1910-1978) American
$2000 £1361 Edge of the woods (30x36cm-12x14in) s. 10-Jul-93 Young Fine Arts Auctions, Maine #38/R

BARNJUM, Frederick S (19th C) Canadian?
$2567 £1735 Gentleman and his lady sleighing in winter (25x35cm-10x14in) s.d.1869 painted oval. 23-Nov-93 Joyner Fine Art, Toronto #53/R (C.D 3400)
$2600 £1745 Roadside picnic (38x53cm-15x21in) s.d.1859. 16-Dec-93 Mystic Fine Arts, Connecticut #128/R
$4551 £3034 Gentleman and lady sleighing in winter (25x36cm-10x14in) s.d.1860 indist.s.i.stretcher oval. 11-May-94 Sotheby's, Toronto #66/R (C.D 6250)

BARNSLEY, James MacDonald (1861-1929) Canadian
$1982 £1295 Autumn, near Dampierre, Normandy (32x20cm-13x8in) s.d.86 panel. 19-May-93 Sotheby's, Toronto #376/R (C.D 2500)
$2220 £1451 Journee d'ete (41x31cm-16x12in) s.d.82. 18-May-93 Joyner Fine Art, Toronto #184/R (C.D 2800)
$6000 £4027 Bridge over Seine at sunset (32x56cm-13x22in) s.d.1883. 13-Oct-93 Sotheby's, New York #99 a/R

BARONE, Antonio (1889-?) American
$7000 £4895 Street vendor (50x60cm-20x24in) s. 11-Mar-93 Christie's, New York #204/R
$6000 *£3797* Beach scene (25x33cm-10x13in) W/C. 3-Dec-92 Sotheby's, New York #35/R

BARR, William (1867-1933) American
$1200 £795 Promenade, Pan Pacific Exhibition, San Francisco (25x36cm-10x14in) s. 15-Jun-94 Butterfield & Butterfield, San Francisco #4581/R
$1377 £900 Fresian and two Ayrshire calves by haystack (46x61cm-18x24in) s. 13-May-93 Christie's, Glasgow #865/R
$5616 £3600 At the end of the day (58x89cm-23x35in) s. 17-Dec-92 John Nicholson, Surrey #773/R

BARRADAS, Rafael (1890-1929) Uruguayan
$2000 £1299 Recuerdos de Barcelona (8x11cm-3x4in) s. panel. 30-Aug-93 Gomensoro, Montevideo #101/R
$2000 £1170 Moises con Las Tablas (41x33cm-16x13in) s. board. 16-Sep-92 Castells & Castells, Montevideo #50/R
$5500 £2865 Figuras de hombres (48x38cm-19x15in) tempera. 4-Aug-92 VerBo, Buenos Aires #11/R

BARRADAS, Rafael (1890-1929) Uruguayan-cont.
$28000	£18182	Serie de los magnificos (81x60cm-32x24in) s. oil. 30-Aug-93 Gomensoro, Montevideo #94/R
$32000	£16080	Paisaje de Hospitalet con Labradores (60x80cm-24x31in) s. 31-Aug-92 Gomensoro, Montevideo #38/R
$32500	£21242	La Fiesta de Los Negros (30x29cm-12x11in) painted 1910. 18-May-93 Sotheby's, New York #22/R
$90000	£60811	Hombre en la taberna, serie Los Magnificos (99x68cm-39x27in) s.d.1925. 23-Nov-93 Christie's, New York #46/R
$1000	£671	Rostro con monoculo (20x14cm-8x6in) s. ink dr. 29-Nov-93 Gomensoro, Montevideo #23
$1000	£654	Plaza y fuente (15x11cm-6x4in) s. pencil W/C. 3-May-93 Gomensoro, Montevideo #55/R
$1000	£671	Matrona (20x14cm-8x6in) s. pencil dr. 29-Nov-93 Gomensoro, Montevideo #24
$1000	£654	Pilar (20x12cm-8x5in) i. ink dr. 4-Oct-93 Gomensoro, Montevideo #92
$1900	£1242	Figura en negro (24x16cm-9x6in) s. ink. 3-May-93 Gomensoro, Montevideo #56
$2000	£1307	Valencia, vibracionista (20x13cm-8x5in) s.d.1921 ink dr. 27-Jun-94 Gomensoro, Montevideo #30/R
$2300	£1503	Paisaje de Sans (26x20cm-10x8in) s. pencil. 3-May-93 Gomensoro, Montevideo #54/R
$3400	£2222	Hombre en el bar. Campesina con chal (20x14cm-8x6in) pencil double-sided. 3-May-93 Gomensoro, Montevideo #99/R
$3500	£2318	Marinero en Libertad (35x26cm-14x10in) s.d.1928 W/C graphite. 23-Nov-92 Sotheby's, New York #153/R
$3600	£2353	Caricatura (40x20cm-16x8in) s. pastel. 26-Oct-92 Gomensoro, Montevideo #62/R
$4000	£2614	Lectura en el bar (23x16cm-9x6in) s. pencil. 3-May-93 Gomensoro, Montevideo #52/R
$4200	£2727	Hospitalet (23x16cm-9x6in) s.i.d.1928 W/C tempera dr. 30-Aug-93 Gomensoro, Montevideo #96/R
$4200	£2745	Catalina Barcena (21x22cm-8x9in) s. Indian ink. 4-Oct-93 Gomensoro, Montevideo #91/R
$4800	£3117	Nina y maniqui (25x16cm-10x6in) s.d.27 col crayon dr. 30-Aug-93 Gomensoro, Montevideo #99/R
$5200	£3467	Marinero (30x22cm-12x9in) s.d.1928 graphite col crayon brown paper. 18-May-94 Sotheby's, New York #300/R

BARREDA, Ernesto (1927-) Chilean
$5000	£3268	Una Mosca (55x130cm-22x51in) s.d.67 s.i.verso. 17-May-93 Christie's, New York #160/R
$10000	£6536	Black clock (109x140cm-43x55in) s.d.91 s.i.d.verso. 17-May-93 Christie's, New York #173/R

BARREL-BOTTI (20th C) American
$1150	£728	Girl in garden (91x91cm-36x36in) s. 30-Nov-92 Selkirks, St. Louis #167

BARRERA, Antonio (1948-) Colombian
$14000	£9333	Platanera (112x145cm-44x57in) s.d.88 acrylic. 18-May-94 Sotheby's, New York #261/R
$20000	£13333	Rio Tropical (119x145cm-47x57in) s.d.89 s.i.d.verso. 18-May-94 Christie's, New York #146/R

BARRERES, Domingo (20th C) American
$880	£575	Costa Brava (102x170cm-40x67in) init.i.d.82 verso mixed media canvas. 14-May-93 Skinner, Bolton #187/R

BARRETT, William S (1854-1927) American
$750	£490	Moonlit waters (20x28cm-8x11in) s. board. 8-May-93 Young Fine Arts Auctions, Maine #37/R

BARRY, Robert (1936-) American
$700	£464	Untitled (16x16cm-6x6in) black ink. 17-Nov-92 Christie's, East, New York #202/R
$885	£590	Sans titre (20x20cm-8x8in) s.d.1979verso ink dr board. 30-May-94 Catherine Charbonneaux, Paris #113 (F.FR 5000)
$2500	£1736	Wire sculpture (24x30cm-9x12in) s.i.d.1968 ink pencil graph paper. 23-Feb-93 Sotheby's, New York #303/R
$2750	£1797	Basic format for hanging string piece (30x24cm-12x9in) s.d.68 ink graph paper. 4-May-93 Sotheby's, New York #122/R

BARSE, George Randolph (jnr) (1861-1938) American
$1700	£1141	Study for Lamar Ceiling (46x76cm-18x30in) s.d.1906. 28-Mar-93 James Bakker, Cambridge #47/R
$16000	£9249	The oasis (67x88cm-26x35in) s. 25-Sep-92 Sotheby's Arcade, New York #184/R

BARTH, Jack (1946-) American
$1900	£1118	Altar of good fortune (226x155cm-89x61in) s.d.82 chl. mounted on canvas. 8-Oct-92 Christie's, New York #234/R

BARTLETT, Dana (1878-1957) American
$800	£556	Sunset on the pacific (61x51cm-24x20in) s. 6-Mar-93 Louisiana Auction Exchange #52/R
$2250	£1520	Ranch Hill (61x76cm-24x30in) s. 15-Jun-93 John Moran, Pasadena #30 a
$2500	£1645	Mountain glacier (86x84cm-34x33in) s. board. 13-Jun-93 Butterfield & Butterfield, San Francisco #864/R
$2750	£1833	Three masted gaff and rigged sailing boats (51x61cm-20x24in) s. 15-Mar-94 John Moran, Pasadena #71
$3000	£2027	Autumn sycamore (51x61cm-20x24in) s. s.i.stretcher. 9-Nov-93 John Moran, Pasadena #934

BARTLETT, Dana (1878-1957) American-cont.
$3250	£2241	California Hills (41x51cm-16x20in) s. sold with book. 16-Feb-93 John Moran, Pasadena #36
$4000	£2759	Laguna Hills (51x61cm-20x24in) s. 16-Feb-93 John Moran, Pasadena #29
$4000	£2778	Rolling hills (51x61cm-20x24in) s. 7-Mar-93 Butterfield & Butterfield, San Francisco #192/R
$5000	£3378	Autumn sycamores (51x61cm-20x24in) s. 15-Jun-93 John Moran, Pasadena #82

BARTLETT, Jennifer (1941-) American
$3500	£2349	Blue House (25x35cm-10x14in) i.stretcher painted 1985. 23-Feb-94 Christie's, New York #100/R
$3500	£2059	Blue House (25x35cm-10x14in) i.stretcher. 8-Oct-92 Christie's, New York #161/R
$30000	£19868	At Sands Point number 25 (122x122cm-48x48in) painted 1985. 19-Nov-92 Christie's, New York #383/R
$30000	£19868	View of Sands Point - no.13 (61x183cm-24x72in) painted 1985-86. 18-Nov-92 Sotheby's, New York #277/R
$45000	£29412	At Sands Point - 31 (152x91cm-60x36in) painted 1985. 4-May-93 Sotheby's, New York #195/R
$3000	£1961	In the garden no.75 (50x66cm-20x26in) chl graphite drawn 1980. 7-May-93 Christie's, East, New York #57/R
$4000	£2614	In the garden (66x49cm-26x19in) ink executed 1980. 4-May-93 Sotheby's, New York #214/R
$7000	£4575	In the garden - 63 (49x66cm-19x26in) pastel executed 1980. 4-May-93 Sotheby's, New York #194/R

BARTON, Donald Blagge (1903-1990) American
$1000	£629	Landscape (91x107cm-36x42in) s. 25-Apr-93 James Bakker, Cambridge #18/R

BASALDUA, Hector (1895-1976) Argentinian
$1000	£578	Flores (45x35cm-18x14in) panel. 23-Sep-92 Roldan & Cia, Buenos Aires #68
$2000	£1176	Naturaleza muerta (80x65cm-31x26in) 29-Sep-92 VerBo, Buenos Aires #8
$2750	£1821	Desnudo de mujer (54x45cm-21x18in) 11-Nov-92 VerBo, Buenos Aires #3
$3500	£1823	Italiana con mandolina (58x47cm-23x19in) 4-Aug-92 VerBo, Buenos Aires #12
$17000	£11258	La plaza (100x150cm-39x59in) 18-Nov-92 Roldan & Cia, Buenos Aires #6

BASCOM, Ruth Henshaw (1772-1848) American
$7500	£4934	Profile protrait of Elizabeth Gates (43x30cm-17x12in) i.verso pastel graphite gold leaf. 5-Jun-93 Skinner, Bolton #160/R
$9500	£6250	Profile portrait of Betsy Wadsworth (43x30cm-17x12in) i. pastel graphite. 5-Jun-93 Skinner, Bolton #158/R
$13000	£8553	Profile portrait of Miss Susan Gates (43x30cm-17x12in) i.verso pastel graphite gold leaf. 5-Jun-93 Skinner, Bolton #159/R

BASING, Charles (1865-1933) American
$1000	£633	Archway into village (46x36cm-18x14in) s.i. canvasboard. 2-Dec-92 Christie's, East, New York #89

BASKE, Yamada (20th C) American
$9000	£5202	Moonlight Shinagawa (76x74cm-30x29in) s. 27-Sep-92 James Bakker, Cambridge #82/R
$450	£302	Swans (43x28cm-17x11in) s.d.1914 W/C. 26-Mar-94 James Bakker, Cambridge #101/R
$475	£319	In the garden (53x36cm-21x14in) s. W/C. 26-Mar-94 James Bakker, Cambridge #118

BASKERVILLE, Charles (1896-) American
$900	£604	Market of Tetouan (76x61cm-30x24in) s.d.1982 i.d.verso. 14-Oct-93 Christie's, New York #343/R
$1700	£1141	Moroccan portrait (55x76cm-22x30in) s.d.36 i.d.July 13-14-15,36verso canvasboard. 14-Oct-93 Christie's, New York #370/R

BASKIN, Leonard (1922-) American
$650	£425	Standing male (54x39cm-21x15in) s.d.1966 ink paper laid down on board. 8-Oct-93 Christie's, East, New York #255
$729	£506	Female nude seated seen from behind (26x23cm-10x9in) s.d.1949 Indian ink brush. 26-Feb-93 Dr Fritz Nagel, Stuttgart #2564/R (DM 1200)
$1200	£805	Eagle (76x58cm-30x23in) s.d.1989 W/C. 24-Mar-93 Grogan, Massachussetts #127/R
$1500	£949	The New Year. The Day of Atonement (77x59cm-30x23in) s.d.1976,1975 W/C ink two. 2-Dec-92 Christie's, East, New York #396/R

BASQUIAT, Jean Michel (1960-1988) American
$3500	£2431	Untitled (50x51cm-20x20in) exec.1981 oilstick panel. 22-Feb-93 Christie's, East, New York #266/R
$4000	£2353	Untitled (46x38cm-18x15in) col.oil sticks paper. 8-Oct-92 Christie's, New York #249/R
$5500	£3642	Did the first man eat pig (76x57cm-30x22in) s.d.1982verso col.oilstick paper. 17-Nov-92 Christie's, East, New York #69/R
$7851	£5269	Untitled (196x60cm-77x24in) acrylic on door double-sided painted 1981-82. 23-Jun-93 Guy Loudmer, Paris #91/R (F.FR 45000)
$8000	£5229	Untitled (36x28cm-14x11in) col.oilstick paper. 7-May-93 Christie's, East, New York #180/R
$8000	£5229	Untitled (36x28cm-14x11in) col.oilstick paper. 7-May-93 Christie's, East, New York #179/R
$10000	£6623	Untitled (93x33cm-37x13in) painted 1981 acrylic tin. 19-Nov-92 Christie's, New York #270/R
$11000	£7383	Untitled (76x56cm-30x22in) oilstick executed 1981. 5-May-94 Sotheby's, New York #293/R

BASQUIAT, Jean Michel (1960-1988) American-cont.

$39211	£26316	Vitaphone (168x150cm-66x59in) s.d.1984verso. 21-Mar-94 Guy Loudmer, Paris #61/R (F.FR 225000)
$43210	£29000	Big snow (168x152cm-66x60in) s.i.d.1984verso. 23-Mar-94 Sotheby's, London #386/R
$45000	£29412	Extra cigarette (84x86cm-33x34in) s.i.d.Sept.1982verso acrylic oilstick window. 5-May-93 Christie's, New York #170/R
$52150	£35000	Pedestrian 2 (152x137cm-60x54in) s.i.d.1984 verso acrylic. 2-Dec-93 Christie's, London #58/R
$52500	£34314	Red rabbit (175x163cm-69x64in) s.d.1982 verso oil acrylic oilstick. 4-May-93 Sotheby's, New York #260/R
$60000	£35294	Figure four (183x183cm-72x72in) s.i.d.1982verso acrylic canvas. 8-Oct-92 Christie's, New York #251/R
$60000	£41667	Untitled (152x102cm-60x40in) s.d.85verso acrylic oilstick. 23-Feb-93 Sotheby's, New York #390/R
$62500	£43403	Untitled (131x188cm-52x74in) painted 1981 acrylic oilstick. 23-Feb-93 Sotheby's, New York #405/R
$69520	£44000	Mississippi (197x108cm-78x43in) s.i.d.82 verso acrylic two joined canvas panels. 3-Dec-92 Christie's, London #61/R
$77480	£52000	Saxophone (168x152cm-66x60in) s.i.d.86 verso. 24-Jun-93 Christie's, London #103/R
$80000	£54054	Carbon dating systems versus scratchproof tape (183x183cm-72x72in) s.i.d.1982verso acrylic oilstick. 10-Nov-93 Christie's, New York #383/R
$80000	£53691	God Monkey (126x100cm-50x39in) s.i.d.86verso acrylic oil. 4-May-94 Christie's, New York #418/R
$80000	£53691	T.V. Star (272x391cm-107x154in) s.d.1988 acrylic oilstick linen. 4-May-94 Christie's, New York #409/R
$90498	£59538	Gin soaked critic (228x142cm-90x56in) s.i.d.1986verso acrylic oil panel. 4-Apr-93 Perrin, Versailles #66/R (F.FR 490000)
$95000	£62914	Untitled (183x122cm-72x48in) s.d.1981verso acrylic col.oilstick masonite. 19-Nov-92 Christie's, New York #443/R
$100000	£66225	Banker (128x127cm-50x50in) s.d.82verso acrylic spray enamel oilstick canvas. 19-Nov-92 Christie's, New York #273/R
$121660	£77000	Jim Crow (206x244cm-81x96in) s.i.d.86 verso oil wooden boards. 3-Dec-92 Christie's, London #65/R
$189873	£126582	Fruits of labor (165x320cm-65x126in) s.d.82verso acrylic oil. 2-Jun-94 AB Stockholms Auktionsverk, Stockholm #7180/R (S.KR 1500000)
$234630	£148500	Everything must go (254x290cm-100x114in) i. s.i.d.84 verso acrylic oil crayon. 3-Dec-92 Christie's, London #63/R
$1500	£993	Untitled (45x30cm-18x12in) blue crayon. 17-Nov-92 Christie's, East, New York #80/R
$2100	£1400	Untitled (35x28cm-14x11in) felt pen col crayons card executed 1980. 26-May-94 Christie's, London #152/R
$3011	£2007	Sans titre (32x28cm-13x11in) pastel dr. 25-May-94 Francis Briest, Paris #9 (F.FR 17000)
$5000	£3311	Untitled (51x61cm-20x24in) acrylic col.xerox collage canvasboard. 17-Nov-92 Christie's, East, New York #84/R
$5000	£3311	Untitled (56x38cm-22x15in) painted 1981 W/C felttip col.crayons. 19-Nov-92 Christie's, New York #275/R
$5500	£3691	Untitled (46x38cm-18x15in) pen oilstick executed c.1982. 25-Feb-94 Sotheby's, New York #160/R
$6000	£4054	Untitledd - achtung (105x75cm-41x30in) crayon col.pencil executed 1987. 11-Nov-93 Sotheby's, New York #185/R
$8000	£5298	Untitled (76x57cm-30x22in) painted 1982 col.oilsticks. 19-Nov-92 Christie's, New York #269/R
$8000	£5405	Untitled (52x37cm-20x15in) crayon executed c.1983. 11-Nov-93 Sotheby's, New York #177/R
$9000	£6000	Untitled (76x56cm-30x22in) oil-stick crayon pencil executed 1988. 26-May-94 Christie's, London #77/R
$14000	£9459	Untitled (56x76cm-22x30in) s.d.83 col.oilstick crayon. 10-Nov-93 Christie's, New York #381/R
$17000	£11409	Untitled (100x70cm-39x28in) s.verso W/C acrylic col.crayons paper collage. 4-May-94 Christie's, New York #401/R
$23840	£16000	Untitled (75x106cm-30x42in) s.d.87 collage acrylic gouache chl graphite. 25-Mar-93 Christie's, London #166/R
$25000	£16892	Untitled (75x57cm-30x22in) pastel oilstick executed 1982. 11-Nov-93 Sotheby's, New York #184/R
$26000	£17568	Untitled (105x75cm-41x30in) s.d.85verso crayons graphite. 10-Nov-93 Christie's, New York #384/R
$30000	£20134	Tuxedo (259x152cm-102x60in) s.i.d.1982 verso polymer silkscreen ink canvas. 23-Feb-94 Christie's, New York #182/R
$31284	£19800	Untitled - slingshot (91x91cm-36x36in) i. oil oilstick acrylic collage canvas. 3-Dec-92 Christie's, London #71/R
$35000	£23179	Untitled (102x128cm-40x50in) s.d.1986 verso pencil col.pencil. 18-Nov-92 Sotheby's, New York #318/R
$40000	£26144	Tuxedo (259x152cm-102x60in) s.i.d.1982verso synthetic polymer silkscreen ink. 5-May-93 Christie's, New York #180/R
$45000	£26471	Untitled (229x117cm-90x46in) s.d.85verso acrylic spray enamel col.oilsticks. 8-Oct-92 Christie's, New York #242/R
$45000	£29412	Untitled head (56x76cm-22x30in) s.d.82verso acrylic col oilsticks felt-tip. 5-May-93 Christie's, New York #165/R
$50000	£33113	Eating birds (153x152cm-60x60in) painted 1984 acrylic oil col.oilsticks canvas. 19-Nov-92 Christie's, New York #276/R
$58000	£38411	Logo (153x122cm-60x48in) s.i.verso acrylic silkscreen oilstick canvas. 19-Nov-92 Christie's, New York #445/R
$59092	£37400	Pimple head - painted with Francesco Clemente and Andy Warhol (180x128cm-71x50in) s.d.85 verso oil acrylic silkscreen canvas. 3-Dec-92 Christie's, London #62/R

BASQUIAT, Jean Michel (1960-1988) American-cont.
$65000	£43919	Toxic (218x172cm-86x68in) s.i.d.1984 verso acrylic xerox collage canvas. 11-Nov-93 Sotheby's, New York #178/R
$68000	£44444	MP (218x173cm-86x68in) s.d.1984 verso acrylic oil xerox collage canvas. 4-May-93 Christie's, New York #38/R
$70000	£45752	Hannibal (152x152cm-60x60in) acrylic col oilsticks collage wood exec.1981. 5-May-93 Christie's, New York #172/R
$72055	£49017	Head of the Mandible (184x184cm-72x72in) s.i.d.1982verso acrylic mixed media canvas. 10-Apr-94 Perrin, Versailles #107/R (F.FR 424000)
$75000	£52083	Number 1 (142x86cm-56x34in) s.i.verso exec.1981 mixed media canvas collage. 23-Feb-93 Sotheby's, New York #382/R
$93852	£59400	Origin of cotton - painted with Francesco Clemente and Andy Warhol (128x181cm-50x71in) s.d.1984 verso oil acrylic silkscreen canvas. 3-Dec-92 Christie's, London #68/R
$120000	£79470	Luna Park (244x370cm-96x146in) mixed media canvas six parts executed 1984. 18-Nov-92 Sotheby's, New York #314/R
$160000	£108108	Potomac (206x244cm-81x96in) s.d.1985verso oil paper collage on wood. 9-Nov-93 Christie's, New York #60/R
$170000	£112583	Jughead (202x425cm-80x167in) s.i.verso acrylic graphite canvas. 18-Nov-92 Christie's, New York #65/R

BASSFORD (20th C) American
$800	£537	Midsummer garden (102x127cm-40x50in) s. s.i.verso. 23-Jun-93 Doyle, New York #3

BASSFORD, Wallace (1900-) American
$1600	£847	Provincetown by moonlight (89x114cm-35x45in) s.i. 11-Sep-92 Skinner, Bolton #245/R

BATCHELDER, John L (jnr) (1907-) American
$1000	£667	Bales of hay in landscape (61x91cm-24x36in) indist.s. 23-May-94 Christie's, East, New York #149

BATCHELLER, Frederick S (1837-1889) American
$600	£403	Forest interior (91x61cm-36x24in) s. 16-Dec-93 Mystic Fine Arts, Connecticut #285
$600	£403	Cows in landscape (30x46cm-12x18in) s. 16-Dec-93 Mystic Fine Arts, Connecticut #93/R
$750	£497	Nasturtium (76x46cm-30x18in) s. 13-Nov-92 Skinner, Bolton #98/R
$900	£604	Cows at the riverbed (36x51cm-14x20in) s. 16-Dec-93 Mystic Fine Arts, Connecticut #148/R
$1600	£1119	Group of pears (25x36cm-10x14in) 11-Mar-93 Mystic Fine Arts, Connecticut #157/R
$2000	£1342	Figures in the shade (36x51cm-14x20in) s. 16-Dec-93 Mystic Fine Arts, Connecticut #147/R

BATEMAN, Charles (1890-?) American
$3500	£2303	Day's catch (46x56cm-18x22in) s. 4-Jun-93 Sotheby's, New York #217/R

BATES, Kenneth (1904-) American
$900	£520	Autumn landscape (91x127cm-36x50in) s. 24-Sep-92 Mystic Fine Arts, Connecticut #248

BATES, Maxwell (1906-1980) Canadian
$758	£480	Classified information (20x24cm-8x9in) s.i.d.1965verso. 21-Oct-92 Maynards, Vancouver #156 (C.D 950)
$1426	£984	Landscape (91x61cm-36x24in) d.1964. 15-Feb-93 Lunds, Victoria #3 (C.D 1800)
$1749	£879	Portrait of woman seated (76x61cm-30x24in) 1-Sep-92 Lunds, Victoria #2 (C.D 2100)
$1937	£1309	Alberta storm (30x41cm-12x16in) s. masonite. 1-Nov-93 Levis, Calgary #11/R (C.D 2500)
$2219	£1530	Near Okotoks (61x76cm-24x30in) 15-Feb-93 Lunds, Victoria #4 (C.D 2800)
$2976	£2011	Woman and child (51x41cm-20x16in) d.1978 board. 14-Jun-93 Lunds, Victoria #6 (C.D 3800)
$3101	£1950	Boulevarde St Michel, Paris (48x58cm-19x23in) d.1962. 19-Apr-93 Lunds, Victoria #7 (C.D 3900)
$3164	£1590	Portrait of Charlotte (91x61cm-36x24in) board. 1-Sep-92 Lunds, Victoria #1 (C.D 3800)
$4005	£2670	Spanish lady (91x61cm-36x24in) s.d.1975 i.stretcher. 11-May-94 Sotheby's, Toronto #208/R (C.D 5500)
$1249	£628	Two figures, animal and house (25x36cm-10x14in) W/C. 1-Sep-92 Lunds, Victoria #3 (C.D 1700)
$1332	£669	Tavern (48x30cm-19x12in) d.1967 W/C chl. 1-Sep-92 Lunds, Victoria #4 (C.D 1600)
$1611	£948	Bathers (38x56cm-15x22in) s.d.1967 W/C. 5-Oct-92 Levis, Calgary #290 (C.D 2000)

BATLLE PLANAS, Juan (1911-1966) Argentinian
$3500	£2059	Untitled (90x70cm-35x28in) 29-Sep-92 VerBo, Buenos Aires #9/R

BAUM, Carl (1812-1877) American
$2355	£1539	Young boy with fruit (102x77cm-40x30in) s. 17-Apr-93 Falkkloos, Malmo #20/R (S.KR 17500)

BAUM, Walter Emerson (1884-1956) American
$700	£440	Spring landscape (41x51cm-16x20in) board. 22-Apr-93 Freeman Fine Arts, Philadelphia #1164
$800	£544	Branch Creek, Sellersville (25x33cm-10x13in) s. s.i.d.1924verso board. 8-Apr-94 Sloan, North Bethesda #2347
$1400	£881	Winter landscape with church and stream (41x51cm-16x20in) s. 22-Apr-93 Freeman Fine Arts, Philadelphia #1180/R

BAUM, Walter Emerson (1884-1956) American-cont.

$1600	£1088	Winter in Manayunk (71x91cm-28x36in) s. 16-Apr-94 Young Fine Arts Auctions, Maine #32/R
$1760	£1128	Winter scene (36x43cm-14x17in) s. board. 17-Dec-92 Mystic Fine Arts, Connecticut #141/R
$2300	£1456	Sellersville Bridge (28x36cm-11x14in) s. board. 3-Dec-92 Freeman Fine Arts, Philadelphia #1826/R
$2500	£1634	Hillside, Point Pleasant (64x76cm-25x30in) s.d.1925 i.d.1925verso. 30-Oct-92 Sloan, North Bethesda #2753/R
$2600	£1699	Winter snow scene (64x76cm-25x30in) s. 30-Jun-94 Mystic Fine Arts, Connecticut #140
$2700	£1765	In the Lehigh Valley (36x43cm-14x17in) s. 22-May-93 Collins, Maine #67/R
$3000	£1899	Emmaus Road - landscape (64x76cm-25x30in) s. 3-Dec-92 Freeman Fine Arts, Philadelphia #1831/R
$6200	£4161	Mother and child on bridge (61x79cm-24x31in) s. 29-Nov-93 Stonington Fine Arts, Stonington #170/R
$8000	£5128	Winter brook (76x91cm-30x36in) s. s.i.d.1925 verso. 26-May-93 Christie's, New York #161/R
$10000	£6667	Rural road in winter (41x51cm-16x20in) s. board. 26-May-94 Christie's, New York #96/R
$11000	£7333	View of Coopersberg, Pennsylvania (76x92cm-30x36in) s. 25-May-94 Sotheby's, New York #91/R
$38000	£25850	Winter landscape with houses and winding stream (101x127cm-40x50in) s. s.d.1931verso board. 15-Nov-93 Christie's, East, New York #133/R
$38000	£25503	View of Allentown, Pennsylvania (81x101cm-32x40in) s. 3-Dec-93 Christie's, New York #49/R

BAUM, Walter Emerson (after) (1884-1956) American

$3250	£2211	Perkiomen Road (64x76cm-25x30in) s. i.verso. 14-Apr-94 Freeman Fine Arts, Philadelphia #1017/R

BAUM, Walter Emerson (attrib) (1884-1956) American

$800	£530	Red house in winter (51x61cm-20x24in) board painted c.1926-1928. 19-Jun-94 Hindman Galleries, Chicago #705/R

BAUMANN, Karl Herman (1911-1984) American

$1850	£1201	Still life with guitar (56x46cm-22x18in) s.verso. 11-Sep-93 Louisiana Auction Exchange #74/R
$550	*£364*	*Abstract no 6 (20x28cm-8x11in) s.d.55 mixed media. 28-Sep-93 John Moran, Pasadena #205*
$650	*£430*	*Sea-star-shells (30x43cm-12x17in) s.d. gouache. 28-Sep-93 John Moran, Pasadena #212*
$900	*£596*	*Across the bay (30x46cm-12x18in) s.d.59 gouache board. 28-Sep-93 John Moran, Pasadena #294*
$1000	*£633*	*Tropical river (41x22cm-16x13in) s.d.40 W/C. 25-Oct-92 Butterfield & Butterfield, San Francisco #2271/R*

BAYLOS, Zelma (?-1950) American/Hungarian

$575	£386	Floral (53x69cm-21x27in) s. 16-Dec-93 Mystic Fine Arts, Connecticut #326

BAZILE, Castera (1923-1965) Haitian

$5000	£3268	Women by river (60x76cm-24x30in) s.d.3-9-56 masonite. 18-May-93 Sotheby's, New York #238/R
$13000	£8784	The Stations of the Cross (91x61cm-36x24in) s.d.55 board four. 21-Apr-94 Butterfield & Butterfield, San Francisco #117/R

BAZIOTES, William (1912-1963) American

$21000	£14094	Figure and mirror (51x63cm-20x25in) s. i.d.1947 verso. 25-Feb-94 Sotheby's, New York #6/R
$25000	£17361	Balcony (90x104cm-35x41in) s. painted c.1943-1944 i.verso. 23-Feb-93 Sotheby's, New York #204/R
$2750	*£1821*	*Abstract composition (20x28cm-8x11in) s.indis.d.1939or40verso W/C. 29-Sep-93 Sotheby's Arcade, New York #242/R*
$6000	*£3529*	*Untitled (33x46cm-13x18in) s. ink. 6-Oct-92 Sotheby's, New York #4/R*
$12000	*£8054*	*Turtle (29x37cm-11x15in) s.i.d.1957verso W/C graphite. 5-May-94 Sotheby's, New York #80/R*

BEAL, Gifford (1879-1956) American

$700	£455	Coastal landscape (23x30cm-9x12in) s. s.verso board. 9-Sep-93 Sotheby's Arcade, New York #421/R
$1200	£759	Ship building at Essex (30x76cm-12x30in) panel. 24-Oct-92 Collins, Maine #102/R
$2100	£1391	Watching the sailboat race (23x33cm-9x13in) s.i.d.11 June 38verso masonite. 2-Oct-93 Weschler, Washington #144/R
$4200	£2937	Circus scene (51x69cm-20x27in) s. 11-Mar-93 Mystic Fine Arts, Connecticut #249/R
$4500	£3147	Beach at Provincetown (15x40cm-6x16in) s.d.20 i.verso board. 11-Mar-93 Christie's, New York #149/R
$6000	£3797	Round up at the circus (30x45cm-12x18in) s. board. 3-Dec-92 Sotheby's, New York #120/R
$25000	£16779	Setting out to sea (46x91cm-18x36in) s.d.21. 2-Dec-93 Sotheby's, New York #127/R
$31000	£19872	Park riders (61x91cm-24x36in) s.d.20 panel double-sided. 27-May-93 Sotheby's, New York #70/R
$70000	£44872	Bass Rocks, Gloucester (51x61cm-20x24in) s. board. 26-May-93 Christie's, New York #162/R
$550	*£353*	*Circus at Newburgh (23x30cm-9x12in) s. W/C. 13-Dec-92 Hindman Galleries, Chicago #53*

BEAL, Gifford (1879-1956) American-cont.
$1300	£823	Old Houses (25x38cm-10x15in) gouache pencil. 2-Dec-92 Christie's, East, New York #306/R
$3000	£2027	Scene from Rosenkavalier - Metropolitan Opera House '35 (51x61cm-20x24in) s. oil mixed media board. 15-Jun-93 John Moran, Pasadena #74

BEAL, Jack (1931-) American
$2400	£1579	The chair (127x132cm-50x52in) s. 4-Nov-92 Doyle, New York #66/R
$5000	£3472	Bouquet of tulips (66x56cm-26x22in) painted 1971. 23-Feb-93 Sotheby's, New York #296/R

BEAL, Reynolds (1867-1951) American
$800	£523	Sailboats (28x38cm-11x15in) s.d.1935 board. 16-May-93 Hindman Galleries, Chicago #78
$1800	£1169	Ada Belle of Noank (76x122cm-30x48in) s.d.1922 i.d.1917 i.stretcher. 9-Sep-93 Sotheby's Arcade, New York #188 a
$19000	£12667	Annapolis (46x61cm-18x24in) d.1924 i.verso. 26-May-94 Christie's, New York #107/R
$21000	£13291	Boat marina at Provincetown (63x86cm-25x34in) s.d.1917 board. 3-Dec-92 Sotheby's, New York #105/R
$28000	£18667	Noank from Mason Island, Connecticut (66x91cm-26x36in) s. painted 1917. 25-May-94 Sotheby's, New York #94/R
$52500	£35000	New York City, lower Manhattan Panorama (91x123cm-36x48in) s.d.1910. 25-May-94 Sotheby's, New York #95/R
$600	£400	Gorman Brothers Circus (21x30cm-8x12in) s.i.d.1936 col.crayon pencil. 23-May-94 Christie's, East, New York #213
$600	£392	Rockport Sept 1941 (20x25cm-8x10in) s.d. ink crayon. 8-May-93 Young Fine Arts Auctions, Maine #39/R
$650	£436	Sandy Bay Yacht club (23x30cm-9x12in) s.i.d.1936 gouache over graphite. 5-Dec-93 James Bakker, Cambridge #14/R
$850	£571	Sells Floto - Lynn - circus scene (29x41cm-11x16in) s.i.d.1929 crayon pencil paperboard. 4-Mar-94 Skinner, Bolton #99/R
$1000	£654	Circus roustabouts (33x38cm-13x15in) s.i.d.1924 col.crayon dr. 16-May-93 Hindman Galleries, Chicago #81
$1100	£728	Downy brothers circus (33x43cm-13x17in) s.d.1934 W/C. 23-Sep-93 Mystic Fine Arts, Connecticut #151
$1100	£738	Sells Floto Circus, 1925 (33x36cm-13x14in) s.i.d. mixed media. 4-Dec-93 Louisiana Auction Exchange #58/R
$1200	£755	Sparks Circus, 1930 (33x41cm-13x16in) s. W/C pastel crayon. 25-Apr-93 James Bakker, Cambridge #172/R
$1200	£755	Circus scene - Salem (30x46cm-12x18in) s.d.1929 crayon. 25-Apr-93 James Bakker, Cambridge #58
$1300	£751	Carnival in Gloucester (29x30cm-11x12in) s.i.d.1948 s.i.verso col.pencil pencil. 25-Sep-92 Sotheby's Arcade, New York #328/R
$1400	£952	Pagliacci circus (25x36cm-10x14in) s.i. col.crayon. 9-Jul-93 Sloan, North Bethesda #2806
$1500	£949	Circus scene, elephants and figures (33x41cm-13x16in) s. crayon. 2-Dec-92 Boos Gallery, Michigan #799/R
$1600	£1060	Circus scene (28x38cm-11x15in) s.d.1934 pastel crayon. 21-Nov-92 James Bakker, Cambridge #61/R
$1600	£925	Sparks Circus , s.i.d.1930 i.verso col.pencil. 25-Sep-92 Sotheby's Arcade, New York #331/R
$1700	£1211	Manzanillo Mexico (20x28cm-8x11in) s. W/C painted 1933. 22-May-93 Collins, Maine #19/R
$1700	£1149	Circus scene (38x46cm-15x18in) s. crayon. 10-Aug-93 Stonington Fine Arts, Stonington #180/R
$1750	£1144	Fishing boats (18x28cm-7x11in) s. W/C. 22-May-93 Collins, Maine #32/R
$1800	£1200	Circus tents (34x46cm-13x19in) s.d.1918 W/C chl col.pencil. 23-May-94 Christie's, East, New York #212/R
$1800	£1184	Circus scene with ferris wheel (34x48cm-13x19in) s. col.pencil. 31-Mar-93 Sotheby's Arcade, New York #399/R
$2000	£1266	Gorman Bros Circus (28x36cm-11x14in) s.i.d.1936 crayon. 2-Dec-92 Boos Gallery, Michigan #798/R
$3250	£1879	Gorham Bros Circus (32x41cm-13x16in) s.i.d.1936 col.pencil. 25-Sep-92 Sotheby's Arcade, New York #332/R
$3250	£1879	Circus scene with camel, lion and elephant (28x36cm-11x14in) s.d.1929 col.crayon W/C pencil. 25-Sep-92 Sotheby's Arcade, New York #327/R

BEAL, S W (19th C) American
$3250	£2226	Portrait of the ship Addie Jordan (56x76cm-22x30in) s. canvas on masonite. 12-Feb-94 Boos Gallery, Michigan #539/R

BEALL, Cecil Calvert (1892-1967) American
$600	£403	The Hold-Up (25x30cm-10x12in) W/C. 27-Mar-94 Myers, Florida #69/R

BEAMENT, Thomas Harold (1898-1984) Canadian
$701	£464	Snowfall across lake, Laurentians (30x40cm-12x16in) s. board. 24-Nov-92 Joyner Fine Arts, Toronto #215/R (C.D 900)
$747	£473	Below boatyard, Portugal (61x81cm-24x32in) s. 30-Nov-92 Ritchie, Toronto #170/R (C.D 950)
$1110	£725	Atlantic Convoy (61x76cm-24x30in) s. 18-May-93 Joyner Fine Art, Toronto #323 (C.D 1400)

BEARD, Alice (19/20th C) American
$2000	£1342	Baby Pan (66x51cm-26x20in) 27-Mar-94 Myers, Florida #37/R

BEARD, Alice (19/20th C) American-cont.
$2300   £1329   The carrousel (81x99cm-32x39in) s.d.1928. 25-Sep-92 Sotheby's Arcade, New York #291/R

BEARD, James Henry (1812-1893) American
$2500   £1634   Resting pups (38x30cm-15x12in) s.d.1872. 5-May-93 Doyle, New York #12/R

BEARD, William Holbrook (1824-1900) American
$70000   £44872   Witches convention (97x149cm-38x59in) s.d.1876. 27-May-93 Sotheby's, New York #159/R
$9000   £5769   Witches' ride (88x119cm-35x47in) s.d.1870 chl. 27-May-93 Sotheby's, New York #160/R

BEARDEN, Romare (1914-1988) American
$3750   £2484   Three figures (50x65cm-20x26in) s. W/C ink. 29-Sep-93 Sotheby's Arcade, New York #234 a/R
$3800   £2639   Northern shore (76x56cm-30x22in) s.i. painted c.1981 W/C. 22-Feb-93 Christie's, East, New York #214/R
$4000   £2685   The soul never dwells in a dry place (63x77cm-25x30in) s. pen black ink W/C. 3-May-94 Christie's, East, New York #48/R
$8000   £4706   Untitled (67x51cm-26x20in) s. W/C ink paper mounted on board. 8-Oct-92 Christie's, New York #108/R
$8000   £4706   Untitled (23x30cm-9x12in) s. mixed media paper collage masonite. 6-Oct-92 Sotheby's, New York #95/R
$8000   £5229   Untitled - church (22x29cm-9x11in) paper collage paperboard executed c.1966. 4-May-93 Sotheby's, New York #343/R
$11000   £7432   Chocolate shake (73x96cm-29x38in) s. W/C painted c.1970. 11-Nov-93 Sotheby's, New York #352/R
$11000   £7285   Untitled (38x22cm-15x9in) s. W/C paper collage board executed c.1988. 18-Nov-92 Sotheby's, New York #172/R
$11000   £7383   Untitled (67x51cm-26x20in) s. W/C gouache executed c.1947-1948. 25-Feb-94 Sotheby's, New York #40/R
$14000   £9396   Untitled (67x52cm-26x20in) s. W/C gouache executed c.1947-48. 25-Feb-94 Sotheby's, New York #41/R
$14000   £9722   Tenement world (48x37cm-19x15in) s. s.i.d.1969verso collage board. 23-Feb-93 Sotheby's, New York #264/R
$22000   £14865   Untitled (53x36cm-21x14in) s. paper fabric collage board executed 1972. 11-Nov-93 Sotheby's, New York #348/R
$29000   £19463   The grey cat (40x61cm-16x24in) collage board executed 1979. 25-Feb-94 Sotheby's, New York #30/R
$38000   £24837   Untitled (76x99cm-30x39in) s. gouache paper collage executed c.1985. 5-May-93 Christie's, New York #231/R
$62500   £43403   Kansas City (113x129cm-44x51in) s. executed 1974 acrylic paper collage on board. 23-Feb-93 Sotheby's, New York #248/R

BEARDY, Jackson (1944-1984) Canadian
$435   £294   Untitled - bird (102x81cm-40x32in) s.d.1967 acrylic gouache on paper board. 25-Apr-94 Levis, Calgary #18/R (C.D 600)

BEATTY, John William (1869-1941) Canadian
$1019   £653   Sunlit landscape (18x20cm-7x8in) s. board. 7-Dec-92 Waddingtons, Toronto #1358 (C.D 1300)
$1100   £697   Canoe Lake (21x26cm-8x10in) s. board. 1-Dec-92 Fraser Pinneys, Quebec #129/R (C.D 1400)
$1133   £765   Autumn landscape (17x24cm-7x9in) s. board. 23-Nov-93 Joyner Fine Art, Toronto #210/R (C.D 1500)
$1168   £773   Forest interior (27x23cm-11x9in) s. panel. 18-Nov-92 Sotheby's, Toronto #272/R (C.D 1500)
$1189   £777   Cottage on lane with trees (23x28cm-9x11in) s. board. 19-May-93 Sotheby's, Toronto #94/R (C.D 1500)
$1359   £918   Rocky landscape (21x26cm-8x10in) s. panel. 23-Nov-93 Joyner Fine Art, Toronto #144/R (C.D 1800)
$1510   £1020   Near Rice Lake, Ontario (26x34cm-10x13in) s.d.29 panel. 23-Nov-93 Joyner Fine Art, Toronto #9/R (C.D 2000)
$1602   £1068   Hills at the water's edge (9x11cm-4x4in) s. board. 13-May-94 Joyner Fine Art, Toronto #143 (C.D 2200)
$1784   £1166   Pickerel Lake, Haliburton (27x35cm-11x14in) s. panel. 19-May-93 Sotheby's, Toronto #118/R (C.D 2250)

BEAU, Henri (1865-1949) Canadian
$852   £576   Interior scene (34x43cm-13x17in) s.d.16. 3-Nov-93 Sotheby's, Toronto #33 (C.D 1100)
$1583   £1028   La Rochelle (38x46cm-15x18in) s. 21-Jun-94 Fraser Pinneys, Quebec #147 (C.D 2200)
$2567   £1735   The Marne (54x72cm-21x28in) s. 23-Nov-93 Joyner Fine Art, Toronto #347 (C.D 3400)

BEAUCHAMP, Robert (1923-) American
$1600   £1053   Rainbow (152x152cm-60x60in) s. 31-Mar-93 Sotheby's Arcade, New York #388/R
$1100   £724   Foot (93x203cm-37x80in) s. graphite. 31-Mar-93 Sotheby's Arcade, New York #389

BEAUGUREAU, Francis Henry (1920-) American
$3200   £2025   Military drill (76x108cm-30x43in) s. acrylic. 2-Dec-92 Christie's, East, New York #49/R

BEAULIEU, Paul Vanier (1910-) Canadian
$2549   £1699   Le compotier rouge (14x18cm-6x7in) s. 11-May-94 Sotheby's, Toronto #146/R (C.D 3500)
$529   £357   Abstract (26x29cm-10x11in) s.d.63 mixe media. 23-Nov-93 Joyner Fine Art, Toronto #293 (C.D 700)

BEAUMONT, Arthur J (1877-1956) American
$650   £430   Pier scene (25x36cm-10x14in) s. board double-sided. 23-Sep-93 Mystic Fine Arts, Connecticut #109/R

BEAUREGARD, Charles G (19th C) Canadian
$624   £410   Portrait of Mrs R B Sheridan (77x64cm-30x25in) s. after Thomas Gainsborough. 8-Jun-93 Ritchie, Toronto #224/R (C.D 800)
$2000   £1333   Reclining putto (58x81cm-23x32in) s. 12-Mar-94 Weschler, Washington #99/R

BEAUX, Cecilia (1855-1942) American
$3500   £2333   Portrait of Robert C Minor (28x20cm-11x8in) s.d.93 panel. 23-May-94 Christie's, East, New York #137/R
$10500 £7143   Portrait of a baby girl in white (53x41cm-21x16in) 14-Apr-94 Freeman Fine Arts, Philadelphia #1070/R
$50000 £34965 Portrait of Mrs Robert Abbe (188x99cm-74x39in) s. painted 1898-99. 10-Mar-93 Sotheby's, New York #102/R
$76000 £53147 Dressing dolls (91x74cm-36x29in) s. 14-Mar-93 Hindman Galleries, Chicago #24/R
$330000 £208861 Portrait of Alice Davison (169x86cm-67x34in) s. 4-Dec-92 Christie's, New York #239/R

BECHTLE, Robert (1932-) American
$3750   £2534   Thelma (114x132cm-45x52in) 21-Oct-93 Butterfield & Butterfield, San Francisco #2825/R

BECK, Otto Walter (1864-?) American
$3000   £1734   Portrait of woman (110x84cm-43x33in) s.d.1916 pastel board. 24-Sep-92 Sotheby's, New York #105 a/R

BECK, Raphael (19/20th C) American
$700   £455   Old Fort Niagra Westside (56x64cm-22x25in) s.i. s.i.d.1900verso. 11-Sep-93 Louisiana Auction Exchange #101/R

BECKER, Maurice (1889-?) American
$750   £434   Bathers (48x57cm-19x22in) sd.38 W/C pencil paper on paper. 25-Sep-92 Sotheby's Arcade, New York #325/R

BECKET, Maria A (?-1904) American
$850   £567   Centaur and priest in forest interior (61x91cm-24x36in) s. 26-May-94 Sloan, North Bethesda #1839
$1200   £784   Sunset through clouds, the sea in distance (51x76cm-20x30in) s. 17-Sep-93 Skinner, Bolton #208/R

BECKMAN, Ford (1952-) American
$1000   £671   Untitled - White painting (223x178cm-88x70in) s.i.d.1990verso acrylic wax varnish panel. 3-May-94 Christie's, East, New York #263/R
$2658   £1772   Untitled - black wall painting (244x244cm-96x96in) s.d.88verso acrylic wax canvas on wood four. 2-Jun-94 AB Stockholms Auktionsverk, Stockholm #7162/R (S.KR 21000)
$11000 £7432   Holy ground (223x518cm-88x204in) acrylic wax varnish canvas on plywood exec.1987. 11-Nov-93 Sotheby's, New York #210/R

BECKMAN, William (20th C) American?
$7000   £4730   Study for Overcoat (37x37cm-15x15in) s.i.d.85verso oil. 8-Nov-93 Christie's, East, New York #151/R

BECKWITH, James Carroll (1852-1917) American
$2500   £1603   Portrait of lady (61x51cm-24x20in) s. 28-Apr-93 Doyle, New York #7
$5500   £3642   Boathouse in Central Park (40x25cm-16x10in) s. panel painted c.1890. 23-Sep-93 Sotheby's, New York #174/R
$7000   £4895   Under the lilacs (61x48cm-24x19in) s.d.1879. 10-Mar-93 Sotheby's, New York #101/R
$1228   £819   Portrait de jeune fille a la chevelure rousse (22x17cm-9x7in) s. pastel crayon dr. 8-Jun-94 Poulain & le Fur, Paris #80/R (F.FR 7000)
$3250   £2153   Woman at a spinet (48x60cm-19x24in) s. chl dr. 15-Jun-94 Butterfield & Butterfield, San Francisco #4405/R

BEDIA, Jose (1959-) Cuban
$12000 £8108   Reflejo Inverso (210x128cm-83x50in) s.i. acrylic painted 1991. 22-Nov-93 Sotheby's, New York #265/R
$7000   £4667   Nsusu que vuela adentro nkunia (236x118cm-93x46in) s.d.92 ink amate paper. 18-May-94 Sotheby's, New York #400/R

BEEB, E (20th C) American?
$750   £524   Girl in riding attire feeding apple to horse, two dogs in foreground (152x107cm-60x42in) s.d.1921. 5-Feb-93 Selkirks, St. Louis #586

BEECHAM, Tom (20th C) American
$675   £441   Prong and stagecoach (53x71cm-21x28in) s. 15-May-93 Dunning's, Illinois #44/R
$850   £556   Mountain rams (53x71cm-21x28in) s. board. 15-May-93 Dunning's, Illinois #40/R

BEECHAM, Tom (20th C) American-cont.
$975   £637   Cougar and wagon train (53x71cm-21x28in) s. board. 15-May-93 Dunning's, Illinois #45/R

BEECHER, William Ward (20th C) American
$900   £529   Trompe L'Oeuil (36x102cm-14x40in) panel. 8-Oct-92 Boos Gallery, Michigan #542/R

BEGAY, Harrison (20th C) American Indian
$1200   £779   The pollen gathers (23x20cm-9x8in) s. gouache. 25-Jun-94 Skinner, Bolton #103/R
$1300   £844   Navajo boy shepherd (25x30cm-10x12in) s. gouache. 25-Jun-94 Skinner, Bolton #7/R

BEIL, Charlie A (1894-1976) Canadian
$2354   £1538   Untitled - Cosgrave Brand (61x91cm-24x36in) s. 10-May-93 Hodgins, Calgary #278/R (C.D 3000)

BELKNAP, Zedekiah (1781-1858) American
$1700   £1111   Portrait of gentleman, possibly painter Cephas Giovanni Thompson (28x23cm-11x9in) inds.i.verso panel. 31-Oct-92 Skinner, Bolton #352/R

BELKNAP, Zedekiah (attrib) (1781-1858) American
$1000   £671   Portrait of a gentleman thought to be Benjamin Allen (84x69cm-33x27in) 1-Dec-93 Doyle, New York #26

BELL, Cecil (1906-1970) American
$2000   £1290   Horses for sale, New York (43x79cm-17x31in) s. st.verso masonite. 13-Jul-94 Boos Gallery, Michigan #567/R
$2000   £1290   Farmer resting (56x76cm-22x30in) s. st.verso painted 1939. 13-Jul-94 Boos Gallery, Michigan #572/R
$4000   £2581   El Station, Turnstile (76x61cm-30x24in) s. st.verso masonite. 13-Jul-94 Boos Gallery, Michigan #570/R
$4750   £3065   Sailor's delight (61x76cm-24x30in) s. painted 1945. 13-Jul-94 Boos Gallery, Michigan #571/R
$10000 £6329   Getting acquainted (76x102cm-30x40in) s. s.i.verso masonite. 4-Dec-92 Christie's, New York #148/R

BELL, Charles (1935-) American
$20000 £13514 Raggedy Ann doll (124x94cm-49x37in) s. painted 1972. 11-Nov-93 Sotheby's, New York #410/R
$52500 £34314 Bunny cycle (127x168cm-50x66in) s. painted 1972. 4-May-93 Sotheby's, New York #417/R
$15000 £9934   Study for the journey (82x102cm-32x40in) s.d.83 gouache col.chk graphite board. 19-Nov-92 Christie's, New York #363/R

BELL, Delos Cline (19th C) Canadian
$1129   £758   Portrait of a child (36x28cm-14x11in) s. panel. 29-Nov-93 Waddingtons, Toronto #1055 (C.D 1500)

BELL, Edward August (1862-1953) American
$16000 £10667 Woman at table (46x29cm-18x11in) s.d.1913 board. 25-May-94 Sotheby's, New York #69/R

BELL, Larry (1939-) American
$1800   £1132   Vapor drawing (132x90cm-52x35in) s.d.82 acrylic vaporized precious metals paper. 25-Apr-93 Butterfield & Butterfield, San Francisco #2171/R
$600   £380   Elipse (128x91cm-50x36in) vaporized metallic powder paper. 25-Oct-92 Butterfield & Butterfield, San Francisco #2370/R

BELL, Leland (1922-1991) American
$1000   £658   Self-portrait (74x39cm-29x15in) oil newsprint board on plywood painted c.1959. 31-Mar-93 Sotheby's Arcade, New York #490/R

BELL-SMITH, Frederick Marlett (1846-1923) Canadian/British
$602   £404   Coastal cliffs (36x61cm-14x24in) s. 29-Nov-93 Waddingtons, Toronto #1066 (C.D 800)
$634   £415   Birches (26x19cm-10x7in) s. paper. 19-May-93 Sotheby's, Toronto #34 (C.D 800)
$856   £567   Yale, B.C. (15x23cm-6x9in) s. i.verso board. 16-Nov-92 Hodgins, Calgary #277 (C.D 1100)
$1012   £670   The gorge, Victoria B.C. (13x25cm-5x10in) s. i.verso board. 16-Nov-92 Hodgins, Calgary #75/R (C.D 1300)
$1019   £680   Coastal cliffs, Nova Scotia (36x58cm-14x23in) s. painted 1880s. 11-May-94 Sotheby's, Toronto #168/R (C.D 1400)
$1245   £825   Boats on Thames (22x35cm-9x14in) s.d.92 board. 24-Nov-92 Joyner Fine Art, Toronto #137/R (C.D 1600)
$1311   £874   Toronto from the Island (21x29cm-8x11in) s. i.verso board. 11-May-94 Sotheby's, Toronto #41/R (C.D 1800)
$1743   £1178   Seascape the sun's last kiss (14x23cm-6x9in) s. s.i.verso panel. 3-Nov-93 Sotheby's, Toronto #337 (C.D 2250)
$1820   £1214   Putney, Coronation Night (11x12cm-4x5in) s. board. 11-May-94 Sotheby's, Toronto #165/R (C.D 2500)
$2114   £1429   Parting day, Selkirk Mountains, B.C (55x80cm-22x31in) s. 23-Nov-93 Joyner Fine Art, Toronto #15/R (C.D 2500)
$2131   £1440   Spot sketch of London (19x14cm-7x6in) s. s.i.verso board. 3-Nov-93 Sotheby's, Toronto #135/R (C.D 2750)
$2576   £1684   Dusk, Westminster Bridge, London (22x27cm-9x11in) s. board. 19-May-93 Sotheby's, Toronto #101/R (C.D 3250)

BELL-SMITH, Frederick Marlett (1846-1923) Canadian/British-cont.

$3425	£2268	Carlton Street. Church Street, Toronto (15x11cm-6x4in) s. i.verso panel pair. 18-Nov-92 Sotheby's, Toronto #256/R (C.D 4400)
$4733	£3155	Parting day, Selkirk Mountains, B.C. (56x81cm-22x32in) s. 11-May-94 Sotheby's, Toronto #170/R (C.D 6500)
$20024	£13350	Old and New London, Staples Inn, Holborn (87x128cm-34x50in) s.d.1910. 11-May-94 Sotheby's, Toronto #82/R (C.D 27500)
$543	£362	Repairing the nets (19x27cm-7x11in) s. W/C. 6-Jun-94 Waddingtons, Toronto #1251 (C.D 750)
$629	£398	Bay of Fundy - gathering seaweed (26x37cm-10x15in) s. W/C. 30-Nov-92 Ritchie, Toronto #158/R (C.D 800)
$653	£441	Sandy cove (21x36cm-8x14in) s. i.verso W/C painted c.1907. 25-Apr-94 Levis, Calgary #20/R (C.D 900)
$655	£437	Tower of London (25x32cm-10x13in) s. i.verso W/C. 11-May-94 Sotheby's, Toronto #197/R (C.D 900)
$697	£471	Boating near a shore (20x34cm-8x13in) s.d.82 W/C. 3-Nov-93 Sotheby's, Toronto #1/R (C.D 900)
$702	£462	Hermit Range from above Lake Marion (23x30cm-9x12in) s. W/C. 7-Jun-93 Waddingtons, Toronto #1137 i (C.D 950)
$741	£487	Rocky Mountain river (34x27cm-13x11in) s. W/C. 7-Jun-93 Waddingtons, Toronto #1133 (C.D 950)
$784	£503	Rocky mountain lake (25x36cm-10x14in) s. W/C. 7-Dec-92 Waddingtons, Toronto #1340 (C.D 1000)
$793	£518	Mountain cabin (25x37cm-10x15in) s. W/C. 19-May-93 Sotheby's, Toronto #4/R (C.D 1000)
$935	£615	Rockies (30x46cm-12x18in) s. W/C. 7-Jun-93 Waddingtons, Toronto #1166 c (C.D 1200)
$951	£622	Fraser Canyon (48x32cm-19x13in) s.d.06 W/C. 19-May-93 Sotheby's, Toronto #45/R (C.D 1200)
$1005	£670	Rocky Mountain lake view (22x35cm-9x14in) s. W/C. 30-May-94 Ritchie, Toronto #285/R (C.D 1400)
$1238	£825	Street scene with figures (32x23cm-13x9in) s. W/C. 13-May-94 Joyner Fine Art, Toronto #154 (C.D 1700)
$1240	£838	Rapids in the gorge (53x36cm-21x14in) s. W/C. 3-Nov-93 Sotheby's, Toronto #350/R (C.D 1600)
$1245	£825	A gorge in the Rockies (59x40cm-23x16in) s. i.verso W/C. 18-Nov-92 Sotheby's, Toronto #269/R (C.D 1600)
$1268	£829	Village scene with figures (20x29cm-8x11in) s.d.1913 s.i.verso W/C. 19-May-93 Sotheby's, Toronto #374/R (C.D 1600)
$1348	£881	Canadian deep sea fishing (46x61cm-18x24in) s.d.04 W/C. 19-May-93 Sotheby's, Toronto #23/R (C.D 1700)
$1395	£942	Hermit Range from above Lake Marion (23x32cm-9x13in) s. i.verso W/C paper laid down on board. 1-Nov-93 Levis, Calgary #16/R (C.D 1800)
$1648	£1077	Lake Louise (25x37cm-10x15in) s. W/C. 10-May-93 Hodgins, Calgary #269/R (C.D 2100)
$1820	£1214	On the St. Lawrence River (22x47cm-9x19in) s.i. W/C. 11-May-94 Sotheby's, Toronto #20/R (C.D 2500)
$1946	£1289	View in the rockies (61x41cm-24x16in) s.i.verso W/C. 18-Nov-92 Sotheby's, Toronto #1/R (C.D 2500)
$2179	£1443	The Strand, London (17x27cm-7x11in) s. i.verso W/C. 18-Nov-92 Sotheby's, Toronto #253/R (C.D 2800)
$2906	£1963	Lake Louise (34x51cm-13x20in) s.d.03 i.verso W/C. 3-Nov-93 Sotheby's, Toronto #12/R (C.D 3750)
$3606	£2312	Cascade in Great Glacier Rocky Mountains (63x46cm-25x18in) s. W/C. 7-Dec-92 Waddingtons, Toronto #1342/R (C.D 4600)

BELLEFLEUR, Leon (1910-) Canadian

$1054	£707	Nearly April (33x41cm-13x16in) s.d.72 s.i.d.verso. 29-Nov-93 Ritchie, Toronto #226/R (C.D 1400)
$1204	£808	Indian scene (33x41cm-13x16in) s.d.72 s.i.d.verso. 29-Nov-93 Ritchie, Toronto #206/R (C.D 1600)
$1472	£995	To starboard (25x29cm-10x11in) s.d.58 i.verso. 3-Nov-93 Sotheby's, Toronto #52/R (C.D 1900)
$1656	£1111	Night visions (27x34cm-11x13in) s.d.71 s.i.d.verso. 29-Nov-93 Ritchie, Toronto #224/R (C.D 2200)
$1937	£1309	Les barques perlee (32x41cm-13x16in) s.d.58 init.i.d.verso. 3-Nov-93 Sotheby's, Toronto #47/R (C.D 2500)
$2333	£1555	Quelques papillons (38x45cm-15x18in) s.d.74. 30-May-94 Ritchie, Toronto #240/R (C.D 3250)
$2643	£1786	Vers l'hiver (41x33cm-16x13in) s.d.61 s.i.verso. 23-Nov-93 Fraser Pinneys, Quebec #384/R (C.D 3500)
$3409	£2273	Retour de peche (66x81cm-26x32in) s.d.88. 30-May-94 Ritchie, Toronto #241/R (C.D 4300)
$3574	£2399	Rediscovered places (51x61cm-20x24in) s.d.71 s.i.d.verso. 29-Nov-93 Ritchie, Toronto #205/R (C.D 4750)
$3947	£2632	Le Coin des Araignees (66x81cm-26x32in) s.d.74. 30-May-94 Ritchie, Toronto #239/R (C.D 5500)
$5549	£3627	Trinidad (51x61cm-20x24in) s.d.69. 19-May-93 Sotheby's, Toronto #285/R (C.D 7000)
$701	£464	Noel (44x34cm-17x13in) s.d.79 gouache collage. 24-Nov-92 Joyner Fine Art, Toronto #141 (C.D 900)
$1012	£670	Vase de chine (38x30cm-15x12in) s.d.79 gouache. 24-Nov-92 Joyner Fine Art, Toronto #109 (C.D 1300)
$1168	£773	Sur l'eau (38x30cm-15x12in) s.d.79 gouache. 24-Nov-92 Joyner Fine Art, Toronto #194 (C.D 1500)

BELLOWS, Albert F (1829-1883) American
$1500	£1000	Picking berries (34x28cm-13x11in) s.indist.d. board painted oval. 23-May-94 Christie's, East, New York #23/R
$2600	£1327	The fisherman (25x20cm-10x8in) s. 18-Aug-92 Richard Bourne, Hyannis #61/R
$13500	£8940	Autumn afternoon (43x71cm-17x28in) s.d.1862. 22-Sep-93 Christie's, New York #24/R
$25000	£16892	Main St, Clinton, Ct (51x76cm-20x30in) s. 10-Aug-93 Stonington Fine Arts, Stonington #55/R
$42000	£26582	Country life (51x77cm-20x30in) s. canvas tacked over panel. 4-Dec-92 Christie's, New York #202/R
$3200	£2119	Afternoon in Surrey (30x50cm-12x20in) s.d.1868 s.i.d.1868 verso W/C paper on board. 22-Sep-93 Christie's, New York #9/R

BELLOWS, George (1882-1925) American
$20000	£13423	The after glow (46x56cm-18x22in) exec.1919 board. 24-Jun-93 Mystic Fine Arts, Connecticut #154
$30000	£18987	Mountain orchard (51x61cm-20x24in) bears sig. s.i.verso panel. 4-Dec-92 Christie's, New York #153/R
$37500	£24038	Trout stream and mountains (51x61cm-20x24in) s. 27-May-93 Sotheby's, New York #78/R
$77500	£49051	West Wind (38x48cm-15x19in) s. i.verso panel. 3-Dec-92 Sotheby's, New York #129/R
$180000	£113924	Sanctuario (51x61cm-20x24in) s.d.1917 panel. 4-Dec-92 Christie's, New York #172/R
$1600	£925	The prisoner (31x24cm-12x9in) s. chl crayon paper on board. 25-Sep-92 Sotheby's Arcade, New York #305/R
$4200	£2857	First aid station (33x34cm-13x13in) s. chl. 15-Nov-93 Christie's, East, New York #110/R
$4200	£2937	Jean (22x14cm-9x6in) init.i. i.verso pencil. 11-Mar-93 Christie's, New York #182/R
$4800	£3038	Nude reclining (28x35cm-11x14in) s. conte crayon paper laid down on board. 2-Dec-92 Christie's, East, New York #372 a/R
$7000	£4636	Family, evening (45x54cm-18x21in) init.i. pencil chl black crayon tissue paper. 22-Sep-93 Christie's, New York #202/R
$11000	£7333	Hand to hand combat (45x58cm-18x23in) s.i. crayon ink wash. 17-Mar-94 Sotheby's, New York #150/R

BELZILE, Louis (1929-) Canadian
$2024	£1340	Philtre d'Orage (87x114cm-34x45in) s.d.64. 24-Nov-92 Joyner Fine Art, Toronto #251/R (C.D 2600)

BEMELMANS, Ludwig (1898-1963) American
$3500	£2303	Sacre Coeur and nun on motorcycle (107x76cm-42x30in) s. 31-Mar-93 Sotheby's Arcade, New York #494/R
$1000	£676	Les six brandies (55x76cm-22x30in) s.i.d.53 gouache Indian ink board. 31-Mar-94 Sotheby's Arcade, New York #361/R

BEN-TRE, Howard (20th C) American
$5000	£3356	Untitled no.28 (183x52cm-72x20in) gesso gouache copper gold leaf wax paste exec.89. 25-Feb-94 Sotheby's, New York #153/R

BENEDETTO, Steve di (1958-) American?
$600	£403	Sofa size painting (76x76cm-30x30in) s.i.d.1989 verso acrylic. 23-Feb-94 Christie's, East, New York #233/R
$750	£507	Cryptic envelopment (76x76cm-30x30in) s.i.d.1990verso acrylic. 8-Nov-93 Christie's, East, New York #100/R
$750	£507	Easy Wind (76x76cm-30x30in) s.i.d.1990verso acrylic. 8-Nov-93 Christie's, East, New York #101/R
$1582	£1055	Lame theme (183x122cm-72x48in) s.d.1987verso acrylic spray paint. 2-Jun-94 AB Stockholms Auktionsverk, Stockholm #7165/R (S.KR 12500)
$1600	£1111	Gary Floyd (183x183cm-72x72in) s.i.d.1990verso acrylic. 22-Feb-93 Christie's, East, New York #257/R
$1900	£1319	Domestic paralysis (152x152cm-60x60in) s.i.d.1988verso acrylic. 22-Feb-93 Christie's, East, New York #219/R

BENEKER, Gerritt Albertus (1882-1934) American
$700	£490	Portrait of artist's daughter (61x51cm-24x20in) 11-Mar-93 Mystic Fine Arts, Connecticut #210
$3000	£2098	Wellfleet in January (30x41cm-12x16in) s. painted 1926 board. 7-Feb-93 James Bakker, Cambridge #54

BENES, Barton Lidice (1942-) American
$480	£322	Reconstruction (57x38cm-22x15in) s.i.d.1983 d.6-18-83 verso acrylic paper. 23-Feb-94 Christie's, East, New York #309/R

BENGSTON, Billy Al (1934-) American
$5500	£3819	Punta entrada Draculas I (112x198cm-44x78in) acrylic. 22-Feb-93 Christie's, East, New York #184/R
$2000	£1266	August watercolour (106x73cm-42x29in) W/C. 3-Dec-92 Sotheby's, New York #79/R
$3500	£2349	Alamo - One Unit , init. lacquer polyester resin on aluminium. 25-Feb-94 Sotheby's, New York #104/R
$5400	£3649	Alamo (91x86cm-36x34in) init. lacquer polyester resin aluminium 4 parts. 11-Nov-93 Sotheby's, New York #347/R

BENITEZ, Enrique (?) Mexican?
$1854	£1253	Los Volcanes (31x40cm-12x16in) s. masonite. 9-Nov-93 Louis Morton, Mexico #141 (M.P 6000)

BENITO, Jean (20th C) Mexican?
$792   £521   Rejoneador (30x40cm-12x16in) W/C. 4-Nov-92 Mora, Castelltort & Quintana, Juarez #144/R (M.P 2500000)

BENJAMIN, Karl (1925-) American
$1000   £676   Untitled, 1984 (76x76cm-30x30in) s.d.1983. 21-Apr-94 Butterfield & Butterfield, San Francisco #1173/R

BENJAMIN, Mario (20th C) Haitian
$1109   £735   Visage eclate (75x91cm-30x36in) s.d.85. 13-Jun-94 Rogeon, Paris #141/R (F.FR 6200)

BENN, Ben (1884-1983) American
$1200   £816   Bananas and grapes (56x76cm-22x30in) s.d.33. 16-Apr-94 Young Fine Arts Auctions, Maine #36/R

BENNETT, Francis I (1876-?) American
$3200   £2092   Boats at Martiques (64x76cm-25x30in) s. 16-May-93 Hindman Galleries, Chicago #2/R

BENNETT, Joseph (1899-?) American
$1500   £882   Ceaseless attack, West coast (76x102cm-30x40in) s. 4-Oct-92 Butterfield & Butterfield, Los Angeles #81/R

BENNETT, William James (1787-1844) American
$900   £577   Landscape with mountain stream (20x28cm-8x11in) s.d.1843 W/C. 27-May-93 Swann Galleries, New York #34/R

BENOIT, Rigaud (1911-1986) Haitian
$11000   £7285   Shipwreck (61x75cm-24x30in) s.d.1/2/74 masonite. 24-Nov-92 Christie's, New York #279/R
$16000   £10596   Sansive Pas Joue (70x83cm-28x33in) s.d.15-8-60 masonite. 23-Nov-92 Sotheby's, New York #176/R
$27000   £17881   La Duchesse Noire (76x61cm-30x24in) s. i.verso masonite. 24-Nov-92 Christie's, New York #269/R

BENSELL, George F (1837-1879) American
$650   £425   Landscape with fisherman (43x33cm-17x13in) s. canvasboard. 7-Oct-93 Freeman Fine Arts, Philadelphia #861
$1100   £733   Landscape with waterfall (38x30cm-15x12in) s. 13-Mar-94 Hindman Galleries, Chicago #752/R
$2800   £1647   River landscape with Indians (61x107cm-24x42in) s. 8-Oct-92 Freeman Fine Arts, Philadelphia #946/R

BENSON, Eugene (1839-1908) American
$3200   £2177   Morning mending (61x51cm-24x20in) s. 15-Nov-93 Christie's, East, New York #151/R

BENSON, Frank W (1862-1951) American
$800   £523   Shore landscape (15x13cm-6x5in) s. panel. 16-May-93 Hanzel Galleries, Chicago #3
$50000   £31646   Portrait of Emily Vanderpoel Binney (74x59cm-29x23in) s.d.1894 i.verso. 3-Dec-92 Sotheby's, New York #88/R
$380000   £255034   Reflections (111x91cm-44x36in) s.d.1921. 2-Dec-93 Sotheby's, New York #119 a/R
$3200   £1850   Flying geese (30x49cm-12x19in) s.d.1903 W/C wash en grisaille. 25-Sep-92 Sotheby's Arcade, New York #140/R
$3500   £2397   Canada geese in flight (30x48cm-12x19in) s.d.1903 W/C. 10-Feb-94 Skinner, Bolton #1/R
$4500   £3020   The Maine Coast (51x36cm-20x14in) s.d.22 W/C pencil paper on board. 4-May-94 Doyle, New York #36/R
$6000   £4196   Camden Hills from North Haven, Maine (51x33cm-20x13in) s.d.23 W/C graphite. 12-Mar-93 Skinner, Bolton #198 a/R

BENSON, John P (1865-1947) American
$2750   £1858   The trapper's return (46x61cm-18x24in) s. canvasboard. 31-Mar-94 Sotheby's Arcade, New York #179/R

BENTLEY, Claude (20th C) American
$600   £400   Untitled (76x107cm-30x42in) s.d.55. 23-May-94 Hindman Galleries, Chicago #275

BENTLEY, John W (1880-?) American
$1200   £779   Farmhouse at dusk (64x76cm-25x30in) s. 9-Sep-93 Sotheby's Arcade, New York #310
$1494   £945   Springtime hickories (61x76cm-24x30in) s. 1-Dec-92 Ritchie, Toronto #182/R (C.D 1900)
$1600   £1053   Early snow and sunlight (61x81cm-24x32in) s. 31-Mar-93 Sotheby's Arcade, New York #238/R
$2100   £1321   Winter symphony (41x51cm-16x20in) s. 22-Apr-93 Freeman Fine Arts, Philadelphia #1308 a
$2201   £1393   Early snow and sunlight reflections (61x92cm-24x36in) s. 1-Dec-92 Ritchie, Toronto #181/R (C.D 2800)
$2500   £1656   Farm, late winter (68x79cm-27x31in) s. 2-Oct-93 Weschler, Washington #150/R
$3000   £1987   Brook in winter (63x76cm-25x30in) s. 15-Jun-94 Butterfield & Butterfield, San Francisco #4439/R
$5250   £3409   Rock City road (76x102cm-30x40in) s. 9-Sep-93 Sotheby's Arcade, New York #311/R
$6000   £4000   The mill, Woodstock, Vermont (82x102cm-32x40in) s. 16-Mar-94 Christie's, New York #99/R
$9000   £6000   La Cumbra Peak, Santa Ynes, Santa Barbara, California (63x76cm-25x30in) s.i.stretcher. 26-May-94 Christie's, New York #76/R

BENTON, Thomas Hart (1889-1975) American

$4000	£2312	King Philip (24x18cm-9x7in) s.verso en grisaille. 23-Sep-92 Christie's, New York #243/R
$8000	£5594	Landscape with trees (25x18cm-10x7in) paper. 10-Mar-93 Sotheby's, New York #149/R
$8000	£5333	Two figures at picnic (18x19cm-7x7in) paper painted c.1920. 25-May-94 Sotheby's, New York #122/R
$9000	£6000	Study for The Butterfly Chaser (20x15cm-8x6in) s. tempera masonite. 25-May-94 Sotheby's, New York #120/R
$24000	£13873	Study for changing west (20x25cm-8x10in) s. canvasboard. 24-Sep-92 Sotheby's, New York #188/R
$26000	£16456	The Crapshooters (40x30cm-16x12in) s. canvas laid down on board. 4-Dec-92 Christie's, New York #145/R
$32500	£21812	Profile of old man (61x46cm-24x18in) s. tempera canvas on board. 2-Dec-93 Sotheby's, New York #142/R
$45000	£28846	Waiting (41x51cm-16x20in) s. 27-May-93 Sotheby's, New York #89/R
$60000	£37975	On Menemsha Pond (46x61cm-18x24in) s.d.71 acrylic on paper. 3-Dec-92 Sotheby's, New York #180/R
$65000	£41139	Loading cotton (30x40cm-12x16in) s.d.44 i.verso board. 3-Dec-92 Sotheby's, New York #171/R
$105000	£70000	Frisky day (52x73cm-20x29in) s. fiber board painted 1939. 25-May-94 Sotheby's, New York #117/R
$190000	£127517	After many springs (76x56cm-30x22in) s.d.40 oil tempera masonite. 2-Dec-93 Sotheby's, New York #82/R
$210000	£140000	The beach (102x127cm-40x50in) s. painted c.1921. 25-May-94 Sotheby's, New York #128/R
$1100	*£719*	*The unsocial socialist (48x33cm-19x13in) s. pencil. 1-Nov-92 Hanzel Galleries, Chicago #201*
$2000	*£1351*	*Studies for Riverclub mural Indians (58x41cm-23x16in) one s.i.d.56 pencil four. 31-Mar-94 Sotheby's Arcade, New York #430/R*
$3000	*£1899*	*Farm scene (19x22cm-7x9in) oil ink gessoed board. 2-Dec-92 Christie's, East, New York #284/R*
$5000	*£2890*	*Pine trees (49x39cm-19x15in) s. W/C pastel. 23-Sep-92 Christie's, New York #230/R*
$5000	*£3333*	*Two mules and wagon (20x26cm-8x10in) s. pen W/C. 16-Mar-94 Christie's, New York #117/R*
$5500	*£3526*	*Study for 'Apple of Discord' and 'Sunday Paper' (52x33cm-20x13in) one s.d.47 one s.i.d.47 pen wash pencil two. 26-May-93 Christie's, New York #192/R*
$6500	*£3757*	*Cotton pickers (26x37cm-10x15in) s. W/C Indian ink pencil. 25-Sep-92 Sotheby's Arcade, New York #323/R*
$8000	*£5063*	*Cotton pickers (37x26cm-15x10in) s. ink W/C pencil. 4-Dec-92 Christie's, New York #150/R*
$12000	*£7595*	*Cotton pickers with windmill (37x26cm-15x10in) s. ink W/C pencil. 4-Dec-92 Christie's, New York #149/R*
$13000	*£8333*	*Sugar Mill A (28x38cm-11x15in) s. pen pencil. 26-May-93 Christie's, New York #193/R*
$20000	*£13333*	*Blast furnace Western Pennsylvania (55x37cm-22x15in) s. i.verso W/C executed c.1928. 17-Mar-94 Sotheby's, New York #144/R*
$28000	*£17722*	*Study for Poker Night (25x34cm-10x13in) s.d.48 pencil. 4-Dec-92 Christie's, New York #146/R*
$50000	*£32051*	*Fishermen's Camp No.1, Buffalo River, Ozarks, North Arkansas (55x67cm-22x26in) s.d.68 W/C pencil board. 26-May-93 Christie's, New York #222/R*

BERDANIER, Paul F (1879-?) American

$1000	£654	Snow Halo - landscape (48x38cm-19x15in) board. 30-Oct-92 Douglas, South Deerfield #10

BERDIA, Norberto (20th C) South American

$1400	£915	Cuzco (55x74cm-22x29in) s. 27-Jun-94 Gomensoro, Montevideo #21/R

BERISSO, Alfredo (1873-1931) Argentinian

$800	£530	Paisaje (20x34cm-8x13in) 11-Nov-92 VerBo, Buenos Aires #4

BERK, Henrietta (20th C) American

$900	£566	Summer landscape (83x96cm-33x38in) s. 25-Apr-93 Butterfield & Butterfield, San Francisco #2149/R

BERKE, Ernest (1921-) American

$750	£493	Reclining nude (30x41cm-12x16in) s.d.81 canvasboard. 31-Mar-93 Sotheby's Arcade, New York #483/R
$2000	£1299	Mourning , s.d.1977 s.i.verso. 9-Sep-93 Sotheby's Arcade, New York #234/R
$4000	£2597	Under the blanket (91x61cm-36x24in) s.d.1976. 9-Sep-93 Sotheby's Arcade, New York #236/R
$4500	£2922	Ceremony of the fastest horse (107x112cm-42x44in) s.d.1976. 9-Sep-93 Sotheby's Arcade, New York #237/R

BERKOWITZ, Leon (20th C) American

$2100	£1419	Circular I (143x189cm-56x74in) s.d.82verso i.d.stretcher acrylic. 20-Mar-93 Weschler, Washington #148/R
$3200	£2162	Untitled (132x152cm-52x60in) i.d.1966verso. 20-Mar-93 Weschler, Washington #143/R
$1600	£1026	Untitled (76x58cm-30x23in) s.d.1984 pastel wove paper. 10-Dec-92 Sloan, North Bethesda #2795

BERLANDINA, Jane (1898-?) American

$1600	£1039	White iris (91x69cm-36x27in) s. 9-Sep-93 Sotheby's Arcade, New York #278/R

33

BERLANT, Tony (1941-) American
$2800	£1854	*Queen of Clubs* (67x67cm-26x26in) executed 1980 baked enamel metal nails panel. 17-Nov-92 Christie's, East, New York #135/R
$5500	£3459	*Steering wheel* (123x154cm-48x61in) metal collage studs panel. 25-Apr-93 Butterfield & Butterfield, San Francisco #2127/R

BERMAN, Eugene (1899-1972) American/Russian
$1600	£1026	*Coucher de soleil* (72x91cm-28x36in) s.d.1931 s.i.d.verso canvas on board. 9-Dec-92 Butterfield & Butterfield, San Francisco #4018/R
$2000	£1389	*Antique fragments in a Roman garden* (46x30cm-18x12in) init.d.1954. 26-Feb-93 Sotheby's Arcade, New York #77/R
$2400	£1558	*Gypsy camp* (71x56cm-28x22in) s.d.1929. 11-Sep-93 Louisiana Auction Exchange #78/R
$2900	£2014	*Trio* (41x30cm-16x12in) init.d.1954. 26-Feb-93 Sotheby's Arcade, New York #78/R
$4000	£2778	*Lady from Parma* (102x71cm-40x28in) init.d.1942. 26-Feb-93 Sotheby's Arcade, New York #79/R
$4750	£3146	*Vue imaginaire* (91x73cm-36x29in) s.d.1928. 30-Jun-93 Sotheby's Arcade, New York #22/R
$12000	£8333	*Souvenir de Padova, l'eglise Santa Giustina* (101x65cm-40x26in) s.d.1931 s.i.d.Oct-Nov.1931verso. 23-Feb-93 Sotheby's, New York #126/R
$17000	£11333	*Souvenir d'Ischia* (100x81cm-39x32in) s.d.1932. 12-May-94 Sotheby's, New York #362/R
$550	£367	*Figures in a classical landscape* (25x33cm-10x13in) pen black ink col wash. 11-May-94 Christie's, New York #481/R
$700	£467	*Figures in a landscape* (28x22cm-11x9in) init.d.1936 s.verso brush ink. 23-May-94 Christie's, East, New York #312/R
$700	£464	*Il Barbiere di Siviglia* (30x22cm-12x9in) init.i.d.1953 Indian ink W/C pastel. 29-Sep-93 Sotheby's Arcade, New York #80/R
$1549	£950	*Du passe de la Meduse* (30x23cm-12x9in) mono. pen W/C htd gouache paper on card. 14-Oct-92 Sotheby's, London #181/R
$1600	£1081	*Stage set for Roma* (41x58cm-16x23in) init.i.d.1955 W/C gouache ink. 2-Nov-93 Christie's, East, New York #91/R
$1600	£1060	*El volcano* (43x35cm-17x14in) init.d.1949 gouache Indian ink board. 30-Jun-93 Sotheby's Arcade, New York #24/R
$1600	£1060	*Decor design for Don Giovanni* (15x20cm-6x8in) s.d.1957 W/C Indian ink htd white. 29-Sep-93 Sotheby's Arcade, New York #85/R
$2000	£1342	*Bella Venezia* (33x25cm-13x10in) init.i.d. Indian ink gouache collage double-side. 24-Feb-94 Sotheby's Arcade, New York #159/R
$2200	£1457	*Decor design for Giselle* (30x53cm-12x21in) init.i.d.1946 Indian ink wash htd double-sided. 29-Sep-93 Sotheby's Arcade, New York #84/R

BERMUDEZ, Cundo (1914-) Cuban
$5250	£3500	*Naturaleza muerta con botella* (108x44cm-43x17in) s.d.55 tempera board. 18-May-94 Sotheby's, New York #407/R
$6500	£4392	*Las Viudas de Yarini* (61x102cm-24x40in) s.d.87 acrylic. 22-Nov-93 Sotheby's, New York #264/R
$26000	£16993	*Jimaguas* (46x36cm-18x14in) s.i. board painted c.1954. 18-May-94 Sotheby's, New York #159/R
$45000	£30000	*Retrato de Enrique Labrador Ruiz* (81x75cm-32x30in) s.d.45. 18-May-94 Christie's, New York #43/R
$2500	£1678	*Musicos* (25x26cm-10x10in) s. W/C pen pencil. 24-Feb-94 Sotheby's Arcade, New York #315/R
$6500	£4333	*Mujer* (102x73cm-40x29in) s.d.71 gouache. 18-May-94 Christie's, New York #283/R
$12000	£8000	*Figura con pina* (76x55cm-30x22in) s.d.60 gouache board. 18-May-94 Sotheby's, New York #355/R
$15000	£9804	*Los danzoneros* (73x57cm-29x22in) s.d.54 graphite oil gouache. 18-May-93 Sotheby's, New York #160/R
$16000	£10458	*Hombre en rojo* (89x64cm-35x25in) s. gouache executed c.1950. 18-May-93 Sotheby's, New York #161/R

BERNATH, Sandor (1897-?) American
$450	£300	*New England dock scene* (33x43cm-13x17in) s. W/C. 26-May-94 Sloan, North Bethesda #1592
$650	£455	*Goose Creek, South Carolina* (33x43cm-13x17in) s.d.37 W/C. 7-Feb-93 James Bakker, Cambridge #110
$1000	£578	*Harbour Motif* (33x41cm-13x16in) s. W/C. 27-Sep-92 James Bakker, Cambridge #163/R
$1100	£582	*Yachting* (38x53cm-15x21in) s. W/C. 11-Sep-92 Skinner, Bolton #252/R

BERNEKER, Louis Frederick (1876-?) American
$800	£533	*Flower seller, Paris* (53x46cm-21x18in) s.i.d.1909. 13-Mar-94 Hindman Galleries, Chicago #818/R
$1600	£1046	*Woman sewing in interior* (61x51cm-24x20in) s. 4-May-93 Christie's, East, New York #173/R
$525	£339	*A woman*, W/C. 16-Jul-94 San Rafael Auction Galleries #376

BERNI, Antonio (1905-1981) Argentinian
$4100	£2412	*Caserio* (33x55cm-13x22in) 29-Sep-92 VerBo, Buenos Aires #13
$7500	£4412	*Mujer pensativa* (54x38cm-21x15in) 29-Sep-92 VerBo, Buenos Aires #12
$9000	£5882	*Paisaje* (61x80cm-24x31in) s. painted 1926. 18-May-93 Sotheby's, New York #118/R
$18000	£11921	*Paisaje con Silos* (80x100cm-31x39in) s.d.53 board. 24-Nov-92 Christie's, New York #152/R
$20000	£11561	*Hay Changa* (100x76cm-39x30in) 23-Sep-92 Roldan & Cia, Buenos Aires #27
$700	£412	*Martin Fierro* (25x22cm-10x9in) ink. 29-Sep-92 VerBo, Buenos Aires #11
$700	£365	*El Ancla* (15x23cm-6x9in) W/C. 4-Aug-92 VerBo, Buenos Aires #16
$750	£497	*Suburbio* (20x38cm-8x15in) W/C. 11-Nov-92 VerBo, Buenos Aires #5
$1000	£662	*Figura* (30x24cm-12x9in) W/C. 11-Nov-92 VerBo, Buenos Aires #6

BERNI, Antonio (1905-1981) Argentinian-cont.
$2500   £1471   Pibe con gorra (63x69cm-25x27in) pastel. 29-Sep-92 VerBo, Buenos Aires #14

BERNINGHAUS, Oscar E (1874-1952) American
$6500   £4545   Resting in the shade (23x33cm-9x13in) s. board. 10-Mar-93 Sotheby's, New York #52/R
$8500   £5667   Moving camp (23x33cm-9x13in) s. canvasboard. 17-Mar-94 Sotheby's, New York #66/R
$13000   £9091   After the storm (41x51cm-16x20in) s. canvasboard. 11-Mar-93 Christie's, New York #121/R
$20000   £12658   On the trail, winter (41x51cm-16x20in) s. 4-Dec-92 Christie's, New York #274/R
$24000   £15894   Group of four Indians and horses by watering hold in desert (56x91cm-22x36in) s. 27-Sep-93 Selkirks, St. Louis #291/R
$28000   £18543   Their Mountain Retreat two Pueblo Indians by a fire (41x51cm-16x20in) sold with embellished letter. 27-Sep-93 Selkirks, St. Louis #292/R
$8500 *£5380* *Hills of Taxco (36x50cm-14x20in) s.i. W/C. 3-Dec-92 Sotheby's, New York #60/R*
$13500 *£9060* *Early industry, transportation, communication, St. Louis riverfront (36x48cm-14x19in) s.i. W/C gouache. 2-May-94 Selkirks, St. Louis #123/R*

BERNSTEIN, Richard (20th C) American
$1600   £1074   Dan Flavin at Max's Kansas City (127x128cm-50x50in) acrylic painted 1974. 23-Feb-94 Christie's, East, New York #365/R

BERNSTEIN, Theresa F (1890-?) American
$850   £571   New York, Red church (15x20cm-6x8in) s.d.12 board. 6-May-94 Skinner, Bolton #136 c/R
$900   £520   Landscape (23x30cm-9x12in) s. board. 27-Sep-92 James Bakker, Cambridge #85
$1000   £671   Sunset - coastal view (13x19cm-5x7in) s. board. 6-May-94 Skinner, Bolton #82 c/R
$1200   £784   Folley Cove Point (30x41cm-12x16in) s.d.16 s.i.d.44 verso board. 4-May-93 Christie's, East, New York #204/R
$1300   £878   Summer at the beach (23x30cm-9x12in) s. board. 31-Mar-94 Sotheby's Arcade, New York #239/R
$1300   £890   Pear orchard (30x41cm-12x16in) s.d.1916 s.i. verso board. 19-Feb-94 Young Fine Arts Auctions, Maine #37/R
$1320   £863   Window shopping (23x18cm-9x7in) s.d.14 board. 14-May-93 Skinner, Bolton #166/R
$1400   £940   Twilight (20x15cm-8x6in) s. i.verso board. 6-May-94 Skinner, Bolton #136 b/R
$1500   £1007   Little boats on the Hudson (20x15cm-8x6in) s.d.1912 i.verso board. 6-May-94 Skinner, Bolton #82 d/R
$1900   £1301   Figures on a New York trolley (53x74cm-21x29in) s.d.1915 verso. 10-Feb-94 Skinner, Bolton #133
$2310   £1510   Looking towards sea, Gloucester, Massachussetts - Norman's Woe (36x51cm-14x20in) s.d.18 with i.verso board. 14-May-93 Skinner, Bolton #131/R
$2500   £1323   Folley Cove sunset, Gloucester, MA (38x51cm-15x20in) s. s.i.d.1920 verso board. 12-Sep-92 Louisiana Auction Exchange #41/R
$2750   £1821   Suffrage Parade (53x64cm-21x25in) i.d.1912. 13-Nov-92 Skinner, Bolton #185/R
$3000   £1734   Spuyten Duyvil (69x90cm-27x35in) s.d.23. 23-Sep-92 Christie's, New York #200/R
$4000   £2649   Coney Island beach scene (48x58cm-19x23in) i.d.15. 13-Nov-92 Skinner, Bolton #180/R
$4950   £3235   Suffrages Parade (56x64cm-22x25in) s.d.12. 14-May-93 Skinner, Bolton #145/R
$8250   £5392   Preparedness Parade (74x99cm-29x39in) s. d.1916 verso. 14-May-93 Skinner, Bolton #142/R
$8500   £5629   Art party (69x89cm-27x35in) s.d.23. 13-Nov-92 Skinner, Bolton #183/R
$12000   £6936   Hawthorne Inn (70x90cm-28x35in) s.d.15. 24-Nov-92 Sotheby's, New York #104/R

BERRIO, Gaspar Miguel de (1700-1786) Bolivian
$13000   £8609   Adoration of shepherds (82x100cm-32x39in) 24-Nov-92 Christie's, New York #69/R
$21000   £13907   Virgen del Carmen (86x68cm-34x27in) s.i.d.1761. 24-Nov-92 Christie's, New York #76/R

BERRUECO, Luis (18th C) Mexican
$17000   £11486   La Virgen del Apocalipsis (41x33cm-16x13in) s. copper painted c.1730. 22-Nov-93 Sotheby's, New York #3/R

BERRY, P V (1843-1914) American
$850   £570   Connecticut Valley (51x30cm-20x12in) 29-Dec-93 Douglas, South Deerfield #3

BERRY, Patrick Vincent (1843-1914) American
$550   £367   Leading the herd home (25x35cm-10x14in) s. canvas on masonite. 17-May-94 Christie's, East, New York #506
$1400   £959   Cattle watering (36x25cm-14x10in) s. 19-Feb-94 Young Fine Arts Auctions, Maine #39/R
$3000   £2013   Summer landscape - cows in meadow (23x36cm-9x14in) s. 11-Dec-93 Sloan, North Bethesda #2538

BERTHELSEN, Johann (1883-1969) American
$754   £493   City bridge in snow (30x41cm-12x16in) s. board. 6-Oct-93 Maynards, Vancouver #330 (C.D 1000)
$850   £545   Fountain, New York (30x23cm-12x9in) s. canvasboard. 24-May-93 Grogan, Massachussetts #359/R
$900   £577   Times Square, New York (41x30cm-16x12in) s. 9-Dec-92 Grogan, Massachussetts #82/R
$1000   £667   Washington Square Park (30x23cm-12x9in) s. 23-May-94 Christie's, East, New York #196
$1000   £658   Winter snow scene (41x30cm-16x12in) s. canvasboard. 31-Mar-93 Sotheby's Arcade, New York #257/R
$1000   £641   New York in winter (30x41cm-12x16in) s. canvasboard. 24-May-93 Grogan, Massachussetts #360/R

BERTHELSEN, Johann (1883-1969) American-cont.

$1000	£662	New York scene in winter (48x38cm-19x15in) s. 28-Nov-92 Dunning's, Illinois #1003
$1049	£704	New York by night (46x77cm-18x30in) s. 9-Dec-93 Sotheby's, Amsterdam #114/R (D.FL 2000)
$1100	£714	Washington Square Park in the snow (30x23cm-12x9in) s. 9-Sep-93 Sotheby's Arcade, New York #216/R
$1200	£784	Little church around the corner (41x30cm-16x12in) s. s.i.d.1945verso canvasboard. 16-Sep-93 Sloan, North Bethesda #3242/R
$1200	£784	Bethesda Fountain, winter (30x41cm-12x16in) s. i.verso. 16-Sep-93 Sloan, North Bethesda #3241/R
$1200	£784	St. Paul's Chapel (30x15cm-12x6in) s. 15-May-93 Dunning's, Illinois #1011
$1300	£855	Lower Manhattan in winter (30x23cm-12x9in) s. canvasboard. 2-Jun-93 Doyle, New York #26
$1300	£872	Fifth Avenue, New York (41x30cm-16x12in) s. st.verso canvasboard. 24-Mar-93 Grogan, Massachussetts #132/R
$1300	£878	Times Square New York in winter (30x23cm-12x9in) s. 9-Nov-93 John Moran, Pasadena #832
$1300	£850	Times Square in snow (30x23cm-12x9in) s. 4-May-93 Christie's, East, New York #251/R
$1300	£878	Upper Fifth Avenue New York in winter (30x23cm-12x9in) s. 9-Nov-93 John Moran, Pasadena #831
$1300	£872	Columbus Circle, New York (30x23cm-12x9in) s. canvasboard. 24-Mar-93 Grogan, Massachussetts #134/R
$1300	£850	View of Brooklyn Bridge, Manhattan skyline beyond (23x30cm-9x12in) s. board. 15-May-93 Dunning's, Illinois #1089/R
$1400	£921	Brooklyn Bridge in the snow (30x23cm-12x9in) s. canvasboard. 2-Jun-93 Doyle, New York #25
$1400	£915	Fifth Avenue, winter, eternal light (41x30cm-16x12in) s. board. 15-May-93 Dunning's, Illinois #1010
$1400	£940	Trinity Church, New York (41x30cm-16x12in) s. st.verso canvasboard. 24-Mar-93 Grogan, Massachussetts #133/R
$1500	£962	Central Park, New York (61x91cm-24x36in) s. 24-May-93 Grogan, Massachussetts #361/R
$1500	£962	23rd Street between Fifth and Sixth Avenue at Madison Square (51x41cm-20x16in) s. i.verso canvasboard. 12-Dec-92 Weschler, Washington #72/R
$1600	£1081	Brooklyn Bridge in winter (41x30cm-16x12in) s. canvasboard. 9-Nov-93 John Moran, Pasadena #830
$1600	£1046	Times Square (41x30cm-16x12in) s. board. 30-Jun-94 Mystic Fine Arts, Connecticut #44 a
$1650	£1146	St Paul's Chapel, New York (41x30cm-16x12in) s. s.i.verso. 6-Mar-93 Louisiana Auction Exchange #28/R
$1700	£1111	Brooklyn Bridge (30x23cm-12x9in) s. 15-May-93 Dunning's, Illinois #1022
$1700	£983	Skating in Central Park (51x62cm-20x24in) s. 25-Sep-92 Sotheby's Arcade, New York #382/R
$1700	£1090	Washington Square, New York (30x41cm-12x16in) s. 9-Dec-92 Grogan, Massachussetts #81/R
$1796	£1151	Manhattan winter (40x30cm-16x12in) s. canvas laid down on board. 27-May-93 Sotheby's, Amsterdam #64/R (D.FL 3200)
$1800	£1224	Grand Central Station (41x30cm-16x12in) s. canvasboard. 15-Nov-93 Christie's, East, New York #175/R
$1800	£1216	Nightime view of Manhattan from under the Brooklyn Bridge (30x41cm-12x16in) s. canvasboard. 31-Mar-94 Sotheby's Arcade, New York #273/R
$2000	£1333	The Brooklyn Bridge (51x41cm-20x16in) s. 1-Jun-94 Doyle, New York #20/R
$2200	£1410	Fifth Avenue, New York (61x51cm-24x20in) s. 9-Dec-92 Grogan, Massachussetts #80/R
$2200	£1294	Fifth Avenue, New York City, St. Patrick's Cathedral (41x30cm-16x12in) s. 3-Oct-92 Weschler, Washington #139/R
$2250	£1442	Snow storm, Wall street (30x23cm-12x9in) i.verso canvasboard. 10-Dec-92 Sloan, North Bethesda #2313/R
$2500	£1656	Central Park in spring (51x61cm-20x24in) s. 15-Jun-94 Butterfield & Butterfield, San Francisco #4467/R
$2700	£1588	Red Cross Building (51x41cm-20x16in) s. canvas on board. 3-Oct-92 Weschler, Washington #147/R
$2750	£1797	Street scene (38x48cm-15x19in) s. board. 15-May-93 Dunning's, Illinois #1000 a
$3500	£2023	Times Square, New York (61x50cm-24x20in) s. canvas board. 23-Sep-92 Christie's, New York #208/R
$4300	£2756	Washington Square Park (61x76cm-24x30in) s. 12-Dec-92 Weschler, Washington #80/R
$5500	£3741	Brooklyn Bridge (61x91cm-24x36in) s.d. 1902. 9-Jul-93 Sloan, North Bethesda #2775/R
$800	*£423*	*City Nocturne (38x28cm-15x11in) s. pastel paperboard. 11-Sep-92 Skinner, Bolton #269/R*

BERTHOT, Jake (1939-) American

$1000	£671	Untitled (76x57cm-30x22in) init.d.87 paper. 3-May-94 Christie's, East, New York #175/R
$2600	£1757	Untitled (76x57cm-30x22in) init.d.87 paper. 8-Nov-93 Christie's, East, New York #56/R
$14000	£9459	Double bar white (188x132cm-74x52in) s. i.d.1977-78stretcher. 10-Nov-93 Christie's, New York #229/R

BESS, Forrest (1911-) American

$15000	£10067	The Golden Mountain (25x36cm-10x14in) s. s.i.d.1966 verso. 25-Feb-94 Sotheby's, New York #37/R

BESSIRE, Dale Phillip (1892-1974) American
$900   £455   Fall landscape (23x30cm-9x12in) s. board. 28-Aug-92 Young Fine Arts Auctions, Maine #46

BEST, Arthur W (1859-1935) American
$1400   £966   Cattle in landscape (30x41cm-12x16in) s. 16-Feb-93 John Moran, Pasadena #55
$1900   £1319   Lake Tahoe (31x41cm-12x16in) s. 7-Mar-93 Butterfield & Butterfield, San Francisco #47/R
$2000   £1325   Pastoral Marin country scene (51x76cm-20x30in) s. 15-Jun-94 Butterfield & Butterfield, San Francisco #4570/R

BEST, Fernando (20th C) Mexican
$3090   £2088   Lago de Chapala (60x82cm-24x32in) s.d.1926. 9-Nov-93 Louis Morton, Mexico #95 (M.P 10000)
$5412   £3469   Los Volcanes (41x58cm-16x23in) s. 29-Apr-93 Louis Morton, Mexico #61 (M.P 17000)
$1545   £1044   Hacienda tanque de los Jimenez (23x33cm-9x13in) s.d.1946 W/C. 9-Nov-93 Louis Morton, Mexico #65/R (M.P 5000)

BEST, Harry Cassie (1863-1936) American
$800   £556   Riders in Yosemite (76x91cm-30x36in) s. 6-Mar-93 Louisiana Auction Exchange #43/R
$2000   £1325   Riders in Yosemite (76x91cm-30x36in) s. 15-Jun-94 Butterfield & Butterfield, San Francisco #4635/R
$2250   £1424   Riders in Yosemite (76x61cm-30x24in) s. 5-Dec-92 Louisiana Auction Exchange #39/R
$3000   £2013   Yosemite Valley (76x61cm-30x24in) s. 8-Dec-93 Butterfield & Butterfield, San Francisco #3332/R

BEST, William Robert (fl.1851-60) Canadian
$2000   £1351   English rural landscape (76x127cm-30x50in) s.d.79. 4-Nov-93 Sloan, North Bethesda #2536/R

BETHERS, Ray (1902-) American
$750   £500   Flowers with ocean (64x76cm-25x30in) s. 15-Mar-94 John Moran, Pasadena #98

BETSBERG, Ernestine (1909-) American
$1100   £714   Dead end (41x91cm-16x36in) s.d.1945 s.i.d.verso. 9-Sep-93 Sotheby's Arcade, New York #223/R

BETTRIDGE and JENNENS (19th C) Canadian
$1200   £805   El Sibah or the Salt Plain, Tunis (54x68cm-21x27in) s.i. oil gold leaf panel. 11-Dec-93 Weschler, Washington #17/R

BETTS, Harold H (1881-?) American
$1050   £665   Taos nights (76x84cm-30x33in) s. i.verso. 5-Dec-92 Louisiana Auction Exchange #41/R

BETTS, Louis (1873-1961) American
$1800   £1176   Seated nude (102x76cm-40x30in) s. 8-May-93 Young Fine Arts Auctions, Maine #43/R
$5750   £3912   After the bath (127x94cm-50x37in) s. 16-Apr-94 Young Fine Arts Auctions, Maine #38/R

BEWLEY, Murray Percival (1884-1964) American
$3400   £2313   Girl with flowers (77x63cm-30x25in) s. 15-Nov-93 Christie's, East, New York #155/R
$15000 £10204 Mother and child (76x64cm-30x25in) s. 17-Apr-94 Hanzel Galleries, Chicago #26

BICKERSTAFF, George (1897-?) American
$750   £497   Southern California mountain scene (61x76cm-24x30in) s. 14-Jun-94 John Moran, Pasadena #95

BICKERTON, Ashley (1959-) American
$3000   £1961   Reg but (244x244cm-96x96in) s.d.83verso acrylic latex masonite two panels. 5-Oct-93 Sotheby's, New York #244/R

BICKNELL, Albion Harris (1837-1915) American
$850   £574   Praying pillar (16x22cm-6x9in) init. i.verso panel. 5-Nov-93 Skinner, Bolton #72/R
$1000   £671   Cows grazing (64x76cm-25x30in) s. 6-Dec-93 Grogan, Massachussetts #493/R
$1900   £1242   Sunset over woodcock cover (64x76cm-25x30in) 22-May-93 Collins, Maine #86/R

BICKNELL, Frank Alfred (1866-1943) American
$1600   £1013   Windy day (25x20cm-10x8in) s. panel. 2-Dec-92 Christie's, East, New York #172/R
$1600   £1074   Autumn landscape (51x61cm-20x24in) s. 24-Jun-93 Mystic Fine Arts, Connecticut #157
$6500   £4362   Auvers sur Oise (81x102cm-32x40in) s.d.1891. 8-Dec-93 Butterfield & Butterfield, San Francisco #3367/R

BICKNELL, William H W (1860-?) American
$4250   £2852   Gloucester, MA (61x71cm-24x28in) 5-Mar-94 San Rafael Auction Galleries #288
$13000 £8497   Portrait of violin maker Jerome Bonaparte Squire in his studio (76x102cm-30x40in) s.i. 16-May-93 Hindman Galleries, Chicago #58/R

BIDLO, Mike (1959-) American
$3800   £2484   Watery Ways, 1950 (131x279cm-52x110in) s.stretcher painted 1983. 7-May-93 Christie's, East, New York #125/R

BIDLO, Mike (1959-) American-cont.
$6200	£4189	Study for no.8 (91x177cm-36x70in) s.verso oil enamel painted 1949. 8-Nov-93 Christie's, East, New York #169/R
$6250	£4195	Untitled (51x41cm-20x16in) s.verso acrylic painted c.1987 pair. 24-Feb-94 Sotheby's Arcade, New York #492/R
$9685	£6500	Not Pollock (92x173cm-36x68in) s.verso s.i.stretcher silver paint oil. 25-Mar-93 Christie's, London #173/R
$12000	*£8333*	*Arabesque (97x276cm-38x109in) s.i.d.1948 painted 1981 oil enamel canvas. 22-Feb-93 Christie's, East, New York #221*

BIDNER, Robert (20th C) American
$1000	£662	Rolls royce DKB 559 (151x122cm-59x48in) s. s.d.76 stretcher acrylic panel. 30-Jun-93 Sotheby's Arcade, New York #337/R

BIEDERMAN, James (1947-) American
$2000	*£1325*	*Storyline (77x227cm-30x89in) s.d.Jan-Feb-March 1984verso oil col.chk wood. 17-Nov-92 Christie's, East, New York #134/R*
$3000	*£1987*	*Roz-ah (134x93cm-53x37in) s.i.d.May 1982verso acrylic chl col.chk. 17-Nov-92 Christie's, East, New York #78/R*

BIELECKY, Stanley (1903-1985) American
$1400	£915	Baskets and sombreros (74x48cm-29x19in) s. board. 15-May-93 Dunning's, Illinois #1001

BIELER, Andre Charles (1896-1989) Canadian
$634	£415	Les Epaves no.2, St. Joseph de la Rive (23x30cm-9x12in) s. canvasboard painted 1979. 18-May-93 Joyner Fine Art, Toronto #179/R (C.D 800)
$951	£622	Dimance a St. Placide, Charlevoix, Quebec (25x36cm-10x14in) s. canvas laid down on board painted 1973. 18-May-93 Joyner Fine Art, Toronto #19/R (C.D 1200)
$1022	£647	Les Epaves, St. Joseph de la Rive (22x26cm-9x10in) s.d.1978 verso panel. 30-Nov-92 Ritchie, Toronto #199/R (C.D 1300)
$1245	£825	Paniers jaunes (35x50cm-14x20in) s. tempera painted 1953. 24-Nov-92 Joyner Fine Art, Toronto #163/R (C.D 1600)
$1268	£829	La Berline (30x41cm-12x16in) s. d.1976 verso acrylic oil. 19-May-93 Sotheby's, Toronto #309/R (C.D 1600)
$1355	£909	The model (76x61cm-30x24in) s. i.d.54 verso board. 29-Nov-93 Waddingtons, Toronto #1087/R (C.D 1800)
$1585	£1036	Evening (41x51cm-16x20in) s. board painted 1976. 18-May-93 Joyner Fine Art, Toronto #98/R (C.D 2000)
$1712	£1134	St. Fidele, Charlevoix (30x40cm-12x16in) s. canvasboard. 24-Nov-92 Joyner Fine Art, Toronto #8/R (C.D 2200)

BIERSTADT, Albert (1830-1902) American/German
$2000	£1333	Trees, rocks and moss (33x30cm-13x12in) paper painted 1857. 23-May-94 Christie's, East, New York #36/R
$2200	£1392	Cloud study over mountains (34x47cm-13x19in) s. masonite. 2-Dec-92 Christie's, East, New York #15
$2400	£1538	Mountainside (28x38cm-11x15in) paper on board. 11-Dec-92 Du Mouchelle, Detroit #2012/R
$2400	£1538	Mountain by the sea (48x33cm-19x13in) paper on board. 11-Dec-92 Du Mouchelle, Detroit #2011/R
$3850	£2516	Moonlight reflections (33x48cm-13x19in) s. board. 14-May-93 Skinner, Bolton #33/R
$4500	£3147	Butterfly (18x27cm-7x11in) s. oil pencil paper on board. 11-Mar-93 Christie's, New York #57/R
$5000	£2890	Ruins in Roman campagna (20x33cm-8x13in) s.i.d.1867 i.verso paper. 24-Sep-92 Sotheby's, New York #53/R
$5250	£3548	A native of the woods (14x25cm-6x10in) s. paper. 31-Mar-94 Sotheby's Arcade, New York #182/R
$5250	£3671	Snow peaked mountains (13x13cm-5x5in) s. board. 11-Mar-93 Mystic Fine Arts, Connecticut #182/R
$6800	£4474	Cows grazing in spring landscape (30x48cm-12x19in) mono. paper on canvas. 4-Nov-92 Doyle, New York #3/R
$7000	£4487	Yellowstone Park (33x48cm-13x19in) paper on board. 11-Dec-92 Du Mouchelle, Detroit #2013/R
$7000	£4667	Sunset (28x39cm-11x15in) init. paper on board. 23-May-94 Christie's, East, New York #104/R
$8000	£5298	Cliff dwellers (33x48cm-13x19in) init. paper on canvas. 22-Sep-93 Christie's, New York #91/R
$9500	£6376	Clam diggers (30x46cm-12x18in) s. paper. 8-Dec-93 Butterfield & Butterfield, San Francisco #3337/R
$9500	£5491	Western mountain lake (35x49cm-14x19in) s. paper on masonite. 24-Sep-92 Sotheby's, New York #11/R
$9500	£6291	Summit of Sierra, California (48x36cm-19x14in) s. i.verso. 23-Sep-93 Sotheby's, New York #87 a/R
$10000	£6993	Campfire, Yosemite Valley (20x38cm-8x15in) init. i.verso paper on board. 11-Mar-93 Christie's, New York #113/R
$10000	£6711	Courtyard of manor house (34x49cm-13x19in) s. paper on canvas. 8-Dec-93 Butterfield & Butterfield, San Francisco #3336/R
$12000	£8054	Head of Indian (14x23cm-6x9in) init. paper on canvas. 3-Dec-93 Christie's, New York #69/R
$12000	£8054	Forest scene (46x35cm-18x14in) board. 11-Dec-93 Weschler, Washington #79/R
$13000	£9091	Grand Tetons (36x49cm-14x19in) init. paper on board. 11-Mar-93 Christie's, New York #115/R
$15000	£8671	Coastal scene (15x23cm-6x9in) init. board. 23-Sep-92 Christie's, New York #42/R

BIERSTADT, Albert (1830-1902) American/German-cont.

$16000	£10256	Wasatch mountains, Utah (34x48cm-13x19in) s. paper. 27-May-93 Sotheby's, New York #200/R
$16000	£10738	Western Trail, the Rockies (37x49cm-15x19in) init. paper on masonite. 3-Dec-93 Christie's, New York #73/R
$18000	£11392	Western landscape (35x45cm-14x18in) mono. paper on board. 3-Dec-92 Sotheby's, New York #51/R
$21000	£14000	Landscape, New Hampshire (28x38cm-11x15in) bears mono. paper on canvas painted c.1857-1859. 25-May-94 Sotheby's, New York #7/R
$22000	£14103	Figure in Hudson River landscape (10x15cm-4x6in) init. board. 27-May-93 Sotheby's, New York #150/R
$22000	£14765	The Columbia River, Oregon (20x30cm-8x12in) init.d.62 paper on canvas. 3-Dec-93 Christie's, New York #63/R
$24000	£16000	Among the Bernese Alps (72x55cm-28x22in) s.init.i. canvas on panel. 16-Mar-94 Christie's, New York #43/R
$24000	£16000	Cowboy and Indian. Buffalo calf. Antelope , bears mono. three. 25-May-94 Sotheby's, New York #36/R
$26000	£17219	Black Point, San Francisco Bay with rower and swimmers (33x48cm-13x19in) s. paper laid down on canvas. 15-Jun-94 Butterfield & Butterfield, San Francisco #4566/R
$26000	£16667	Palm tree, Nassau (48x35cm-19x14in) init. paper on masonite. 26-May-93 Christie's, New York #62/R
$28000	£18667	The fishing fleet (25x35cm-10x14in) init.d.1862 board. 16-Mar-94 Christie's, New York #10/R
$28000	£18667	Bahamian view (48x36cm-19x14in) bears mono. paper. 25-May-94 Sotheby's, New York #3/R
$31000	£19872	View of Grindelwald (76x112cm-30x44in) s. indist.i.verso. 27-May-93 Sotheby's, New York #211/R
$32500	£21812	View in the Bahamas (36x49cm-14x19in) mono. paper. 2-Dec-93 Sotheby's, New York #12/R
$35000	£23490	Men in two canoes (35x49cm-14x19in) init. paper on panel. 3-Dec-93 Christie's, New York #68/R
$38000	£25333	Rocky Mountains (36x48cm-14x19in) mono. paper. 25-May-94 Sotheby's, New York #43/R
$38000	£25503	Fishing from a canoe (37x51cm-15x20in) init. paper on board. 3-Dec-93 Christie's, New York #67/R
$39000	£26000	Studies for the Last of the Buffalo (23x36cm-9x14in) s. paper three. 17-Mar-94 Sotheby's, New York #1/R
$41000	£25949	In the foothills of the Rockies (35x48cm-14x19in) s. paper laid down on canvas. 4-Dec-92 Christie's, New York #249/R
$42500	£28333	Woodward's Garden animal studies, fox, deer and boar, mountain lion (23x36cm-9x14in) s. one i.d.1872 verso one i. paper three. 17-Mar-94 Sotheby's, New York #2/R
$60000	£40000	Sunlit forest, Merced River, Yosemite Valley (65x48cm-26x19in) paper laid down on canvas. 26-May-94 Christie's, New York #56/R
$80000	£53691	California coast (77x113cm-30x44in) init. 3-Dec-93 Christie's, New York #76/R
$90000	£60000	Nature's Paradise (36x51cm-14x20in) s. 17-Mar-94 Sotheby's, New York #51/R
$115000	£77181	Nevada Falls, Yosemite (53x71cm-21x28in) mono. paper on canvas. 2-Dec-93 Sotheby's, New York #43/R
$145000	£96667	Yosemite Valley sunset (33x48cm-13x19in) mono. paper on board. 23-May-94 Hindman Galleries, Chicago #182/R
$240000	£153846	Jenny Lake, Wyoming (76x112cm-30x44in) s. 27-May-93 Sotheby's, New York #226/R
$310000	£206667	Estes Park, Colorado (81x122cm-32x48in) mono.d.1869. 25-May-94 Sotheby's, New York #45/R
$360000	£241611	Western Kansas (71x100cm-28x39in) mono. painted 1875. 2-Dec-93 Sotheby's, New York #41/R
$630000	£403846	Indian encampment (34x48cm-13x19in) s.d.61 i.verso. 27-May-93 Sotheby's, New York #221/R
$1050000	£704698	Kern's River Valley, California (90x132cm-35x52in) s. 2-Dec-93 Sotheby's, New York #46/R
$11000	*£7333*	*Butterfly (20x14cm-8x6in) s. gouache. 26-May-94 Christie's, New York #71/R*

BIERSTADT, Albert (attrib) (1830-1902) American/German

$1000	£654	Alpine scene with red roofs (25x18cm-10x7in) s.d.92 paper on board. 3-May-93 Schrager Galleries, Milwaukee #624
$3002	£1900	Mountain landscape with a pine tree (23x32cm-9x13in) paper laid down on card. 21-Oct-92 Sotheby's, London #279/R
$7000	£4698	Autumn landscape with grazing cattle (18x23cm-7x9in) sig. board. 4-Mar-94 Skinner, Bolton #212/R
$20000	£12658	Indian encampment in the Rockies (51x36cm-20x14in) s. 30-Nov-92 Schrager Galleries, Milwaukee #385

BIERSTADT, Albert (style) (1830-1902) American/German

$1300	£850	By the falls (91x102cm-36x40in) bears sig. 16-May-93 Hanzel Galleries, Chicago #24

BIGAUD, Wilson (1931-) Haitian

$1000	£662	Going to Mass (61x40cm-24x16in) s. masonite. 30-Jun-93 Sotheby's Arcade, New York #236/R
$1000	£676	Noel (51x76cm-20x30in) s.indist.i. masonite. 24-Nov-93 Christie's, New York #15/R
$1300	£861	Festival (74x102cm-29x40in) s. board. 23-Sep-93 Mystic Fine Arts, Connecticut #220/R
$2400	£1600	Le cireur melancolique (60x75cm-24x30in) s.d.1955 masonite. 9-Jun-94 Sotheby's Arcade, New York #132/R
$2400	£1589	Carnival (61x91cm-24x36in) s. masonite. 24-Nov-92 Christie's, New York #274/R

BIGAUD, Wilson (1931-) Haitian-cont.
$2500	£1656	Central market (61x122cm-24x48in) s. masonite. 24-Nov-92 Christie's, New York #273/R
$3000	£1987	Chickens (61x75cm-24x30in) s.d.1965 masonite. 24-Nov-92 Christie's, New York #291/R
$3000	£2000	Le Moulin de Canne a Sucre (60x122cm-24x48in) s. masonite. 18-May-94 Christie's, New York #319/R
$3000	£2027	La Ronde (34x35cm-13x14in) s.d.4/4/56 masonite. 24-Nov-93 Christie's, New York #21/R
$8500	£5667	Fight in the gambling den (50x61cm-20x24in) s.d.17 Nov.1951 masonite. 18-May-94 Christie's, New York #320 a/R

BIGELOW, Daniel Folger (1823-1910) American
$1900	£1258	Town in landscape (61x91cm-24x36in) s. 28-Sep-93 John Moran, Pasadena #347

BILL MELENDEZ STUDIO (20th C) American
$700	£470	What a Nightmare, Charlie Brown, Snoopy asking to let him inside house (27x33cm-11x13in) i. vinyl celluloid multi-cel set up on acrylic. 22-Jun-93 Sotheby's, New York #787/R
$800	£537	A Boy named Charlie Brown, competing in big spelling bee (34x43cm-13x17in) i. vinyl celluloid multi-cel set up on acrylic. 22-Jun-93 Sotheby's, New York #790/R
$900	£604	It's the Easter Beagle, Charlie Brown, Lucy and Linus with basket (27x36cm-11x14in) i.vinyl celluloid multi-cel set up on W/C. 22-Jun-93 Sotheby's, New York #788/R
$900	£604	Charlie Brown's All-Stars, Charlie looking at Linus sucking thumb (28x32cm-11x13in) i. vinyl celluloid on acrylic background. 22-Jun-93 Sotheby's, New York #795/R
$1000	£671	It's a Mystery, Charlie Brown, Snoopy and Woodstock looking at footprints (27x42cm-11x17in) i. vinyl celluloid on W/C background. 22-Jun-93 Sotheby's, New York #794/R
$1000	£671	Charlie Brown's All-Stars, Snoopy and girls reconsider behaviour (27x33cm-11x13in) vinyl celluloid multi-cel on acrylic background. 22-Jun-93 Sotheby's, New York #796/R
$1000	£671	It was a short summer, Charlie Brown, cabin mates look at him walking by (42x55cm-17x22in) i. vinyl celluloid multi-cel on acrylic backg. 22-Jun-93 Sotheby's, New York #797/R
$1000	£671	It was a short summer, Charly Brown, Snoopy bounces coin off bunk bed (27x34cm-11x13in) i. vinyl celluloid on acrylic background. 22-Jun-93 Sotheby's, New York #789/R
$1400	£940	Snnopy the Musical, Snoopy and Lucy share hug as Woodstock looks on (27x30cm-11x12in) i. vinyl celluloid multi-cel on acrylic backg. 22-Jun-93 Sotheby's, New York #792/R
$1500	£1007	Charlie Brown's All-Stars, Linus races after fly ball (28x32cm-11x13in) i. vinyl celluloid on acrylic background. 22-Jun-93 Sotheby's, New York #791/R
$2000	£1342	Charlie Brown racing after fly ball through gate and into the house (27x99cm-11x39in) i. vinyl celluloid on acrylic pan background. 22-Jun-93 Sotheby's, New York #785/R
$2000	£1342	You're in Love, Charlie Brown, Schroeder put Beethoven bust on piano (27x89cm-11x35in) i. vinyl celluloid multi-cel on acrylic backg. 22-Jun-93 Sotheby's, New York #793/R
$2250	£1510	Charlie Brown chasing ball up the stairs and into bedroom (27x116cm-11x46in) i. vinyl celluloid. 22-Jun-93 Sotheby's, New York #786/R
$2500	£1678	Charlie Brown's All-Stars (28x136cm-11x54in) i. vinyl celluloid multi-cel set-up. 22-Jun-93 Sotheby's, New York #784/R
$3750	£2517	It was a short summer, Charlie Brown, Snoopy sleeps atop pitched tent (27x34cm-11x13in) i. vinyl celluloid on acrylic background. 22-Jun-93 Sotheby's, New York #798/R

BILT, Johannes van der (1882-1943) American/Dutch
$787	£532	View of Constantinople (55x85cm-22x33in) s.d.30 init.i.verso. 21-Apr-94 Christie's, Amsterdam #33 (D.FL 1500)

BINFORD, Julien (1908-) American
$3100	£2081	Lake Washington (46x61cm-18x24in) s. 28-Mar-93 James Bakker, Cambridge #55/R

BINGHAM, George Caleb (1811-1879) American
$3750	£2517	Portrait of Vachel Hobbs (69x56cm-27x22in) canvas laid down painted c.1839. 2-May-94 Selkirks, St. Louis #121/R
$8200	£4740	Portrait of Mary Ann Brent Brown and Elisha Warfield Brown (69x56cm-27x22in) oval pair. 21-Sep-92 Selkirks, St. Louis #329/R

BINNING, Bertram Charles (1909-) Canadian
$3322	£2245	Black sun (65x89cm-26x35in) s. canvas on board. 23-Nov-93 Joyner Fine Art, Toronto #91/R (C.D 4400)

BIRCH, Thomas (1779-1851) American
$2000	£1333	Winter sleigh ride (46x66cm-18x26in) s.d.1846. 22-May-94 James Bakker, Cambridge #116/R
$13000	£8667	Steamsailor Benjamin Franklin (51x77cm-20x30in) s. 16-Mar-94 Christie's, New York #13/R
$15000	£9494	The carriage ride home (43x70cm-17x28in) s. 4-Dec-92 Christie's, New York #176/R
$19000	£12583	New York harbour (56x84cm-22x33in) 22-Sep-93 Christie's, New York #6/R
$24000	£16000	Boats navigating the waves (50x82cm-20x32in) 16-Mar-94 Christie's, New York #7/R

BIRCH, Thomas (attrib) (1779-1851) American
$2359 £1492 View of Derby Creek, State of Delaware, New Chester, North America (30x35cm-12x14in) painted c.1820. 1-Dec-92 Ritchie, Toronto #175/R (C.D 3000)

BIRCH, William (1755-1834) American/British
$969 £560 Charles 2nd Marquess of Rockingham (6x?cm-2x?in) min.gold frame after Sir Joshua Reynolds. 22-Sep-92 Sotheby's Colonnade, London #562
$3529 £2262 Portrait of Don Jose Ignacio Viar, Charge d'Affaires of the King of Spain (9x?cm-4x?in) min.init.d.1795 enamel oval. 25-May-93 Sotheby's, Geneva #43/R (S.FR 5000)

BIRD, Cameron (1970-) Canadian
$754 £513 Alpine meadow at sunrise (61x76cm-24x30in) s. s.i. 15-Nov-93 Hodgins, Calgary #303/R (C.D 1000)

BIRDSALL, Amos (1865-?) American
$1250 £850 Ships at sea (33x53cm-13x21in) s. 14-Apr-94 Freeman Fine Arts, Philadelphia #995

BIRNEY, William Verplanck (1858-1909) American
$1000 £641 Recounting the day's hunt (41x30cm-16x12in) s. 28-Apr-93 Doyle, New York #9
$1600 £1074 Smoking a pipe (30x41cm-12x16in) s.i. 13-Jan-94 Christie's, East, New York #270
$2200 £1438 Lighting his pipe (21x25cm-8x10in) s. 4-May-93 Christie's, East, New York #15
$4000 £2597 Smoker (41x31cm-16x12in) s. 9-Sep-93 Sotheby's Arcade, New York #99/R
$6000 £4196 Relaxation (36x30cm-14x12in) s. i.verso. 10-Mar-93 Sotheby's, New York #82/R

BIRREN, Joseph P (1864-?) American
$700 £473 Landscape with poplar and willows (61x71cm-24x28in) s. masonite. 9-Nov-93 John Moran, Pasadena #904

BIRREN, Joseph Pierre (1865-1933) American
$1500 £882 Yosemite (81x96cm-32x38in) s. board. 4-Oct-92 Butterfield & Butterfield, Los Angeles #17/R
$3750 £2206 Rock of ages - Sierra Nevada (61x71cm-24x28in) s. board. 4-Oct-92 Butterfield & Butterfield, Los Angeles #18/R

BISCHOFF, Elmer Nelson (1916-1991) American
$29000 £18954 Landscape with bare tree (119x118cm-47x46in) painted 1958. 4-May-93 Sotheby's, New York #341/R
$75000 £50336 Red house (152x171cm-60x67in) s.i.d.6/61verso. 4-May-94 Christie's, New York #141/R
$85000 £55556 Two women in landscape (150x150cm-59x59in) canvas on board. 4-May-93 Sotheby's, New York #339/R

BISCHOFF, Franz A (1864-1929) American
$1500 £1000 Coastal scene (33x41cm-13x16in) s. canvasboard. 15-Mar-94 John Moran, Pasadena #105
$1600 £1135 Southern california desert scene (41x51cm-16x20in) board. 12-Feb-93 Du Mouchelle, Detroit #2007/R
$1700 £1118 California landscape (20x25cm-8x10in) s. board. 13-Jun-93 Butterfield & Butterfield, San Francisco #883/R
$1900 £1118 California blue bonnets (33x48cm-13x19in) s. board. 4-Oct-92 Butterfield & Butterfield, Los Angeles #119/R
$2500 £1678 Mission Arcade (33x48cm-13x19in) s. board. 8-Dec-93 Butterfield & Butterfield, San Francisco #3418/R
$2700 £1776 Landscape with trees (33x48cm-13x19in) s. board. 31-Mar-93 Sotheby's Arcade, New York #160/R
$2750 £1846 Coastal scene (33x48cm-13x19in) s. board. 8-Dec-93 Butterfield & Butterfield, San Francisco #3402/R
$3000 £2013 Rocky seascape (33x48cm-13x19in) s. board. 8-Dec-93 Butterfield & Butterfield, San Francisco #3403/R
$3000 £2000 Rocky Pacific Coast, California (33x46cm-13x18in) s. board. 15-Mar-94 John Moran, Pasadena #44
$3000 £1765 California coastline (33x41cm-13x16in) s. canvas on board. 4-Oct-92 Butterfield & Butterfield, Los Angeles #163/R
$3750 £2534 River landscape (33x48cm-13x19in) s. board. 9-Nov-93 John Moran, Pasadena #912
$4250 £2853 Old Man Farm, Zion National Park, Utah (33x48cm-13x19in) s.i. s.verso board. 8-Dec-93 Butterfield & Butterfield, San Francisco #3569/R
$4250 £2853 Mount Alice (32x42cm-13x17in) s. board. 8-Dec-93 Butterfield & Butterfield, San Francisco #3430/R
$5500 £3235 Hilltop vista (47x61cm-19x24in) s. 4-Oct-92 Butterfield & Butterfield, Los Angeles #200/R
$7000 £4861 Oak Creek (32x41cm-13x16in) s. paper. 7-Mar-93 Butterfield & Butterfield, San Francisco #147/R
$7500 £5208 At the table (30x38cm-12x15in) s. 7-Mar-93 Butterfield & Butterfield, San Francisco #162/R
$12000 £8333 Dancing reflections (76x102cm-30x40in) s. 7-Mar-93 Butterfield & Butterfield, San Francisco #117/R
$16000 £10738 Peonies (61x88cm-24x35in) s. i.verso. 8-Dec-93 Butterfield & Butterfield, San Francisco #3376/R
$20000 £13158 San Pedro fishing boats (61x87cm-24x34in) s. s.i.verso. 13-Jun-93 Butterfield & Butterfield, San Francisco #835/R
$20000 £13514 Landscape with sycamores and cows (76x102cm-30x40in) s. 15-Jun-93 John Moran, Pasadena #50 a
$52500 £35235 Still life with white and pink roses (76x103cm-30x41in) s. 8-Dec-93 Butterfield & Butterfield, San Francisco #3375/R

BISCHOFF, Franz A (1864-1929) American-cont.
$62500   £41391   Still life with pink and yellow roses (76x107cm-30x42in) s. 15-Jun-94 Butterfield
                    & Butterfield, San Francisco #4598/R

BISHOP, Isabel (1902-1988) American
$3200   £2105   Nude shown from behind (91x76cm-36x30in) 2-Jun-93 Doyle, New York #27
$5000   £3311   Three men in Union Square (61x51cm-24x20in) s. i.stretcher oil tempera. 23-Sep-93
                    Sotheby's, New York #235/R
$10500   £6863   Nude in repose (84x102cm-33x40in) 5-May-93 Doyle, New York #54/R
$700   £452   Snack bar (23x15cm-9x6in) s. pencil pen wash. 13-Jul-94 Doyle, New York #6
$800   £462   Woman with child (15x13cm-6x5in) s. pen wash. 25-Sep-92 Sotheby's Arcade, New
                    York #298/R
$1500   £1000   Seated female nude (11x9cm-4x4in) s. pen wash. 23-May-94 Christie's, East, New
                    York #303
$1700   £1156   Seated nude female (12x13cm-5x5in) s. ink wash. 15-Nov-93 Christie's, East, New
                    York #206/R
$3000   £2000   Mother and child waiting (20x18cm-8x7in) s. pen wash. 23-May-94 Christie's, East,
                    New York #234

BISPHAM, Henry Collins (1841-1882) American
$2000   £1307   Family of deer (51x91cm-20x36in) s.d.1891. 4-May-93 Christie's, East, New York
                    #42/R

BISTTRAM, Emil (1895-1976) American
$3000   £2041   Omnis (56x49cm-22x19in) s.d.52 masonite. 15-Nov-93 Christie's, East, New York
                    #274
$7500   £5034   Heavenly choir (152x124cm-60x49in) s.d. 8-Dec-93 Butterfield & Butterfield, San
                    Francisco #3576/R
$650   £422   Feeding the pigs (36x48cm-14x19in) s. W/C. 11-Sep-93 Louisiana Auction Exchange
                    #15/R
$800   £537   Province Town (51x34cm-20x13in) s. W/C. 8-Dec-93 Butterfield & Butterfield, San
                    Francisco #3590/R
$2000   £1325   Young moon (33x48cm-13x19in) s.d.1928 W/C. 23-Sep-93 Mystic Fine Arts,
                    Connecticut #89
$2300   £1523   Gold and blue (33x48cm-13x19in) s.d.1928 W/C. 23-Sep-93 Mystic Fine Arts,
                    Connecticut #88/R
$2800   £1842   Mother (46x41cm-18x16in) s.d.31 s.i.verso pencil. 31-Mar-93 Sotheby's Arcade, New
                    York #353/R
$11000   £7333   Church at Rancho de Taos (35x51cm-14x20in) s.d.30 W/C pencil double-sided.
                    23-May-94 Christie's, East, New York #228/R
$12000   £7692   Domingo chorus (58x43cm-23x17in) s.d.36 gouache pencil. 26-May-93 Christie's, New
                    York #210/R

BITTAR, Antoine (1957-) Canadian
$510   £340   Vue sur le Fleuve, Que. (45x60cm-18x24in) s. 13-May-94 Joyner Fine Art, Toronto
                    #243/R (C.D 700)
$652   £435   Along the terrace, Quebec (61x46cm-24x18in) s. s.i.verso. 6-Jun-94 Waddingtons,
                    Toronto #1301 (C.D 900)
$674   £440   Printemps d'Europe, France (51x61cm-20x24in) s. 18-May-93 Joyner Fine Art,
                    Toronto #221 (C.D 850)
$1168   £773   View from the harbour front, Toronto (61x76cm-24x30in) s. i.d.1988verso.
                    18-Nov-92 Sotheby's, Toronto #90/R (C.D 1500)

BITTINGER, Charles (1879-?) American
$1200   £694   The old homestead (41x51cm-16x20in) s. 25-Sep-92 Sotheby's Arcade, New York
                    #226/R
$1300   £823   The lamp (77x64cm-30x25in) s.d.1911 masonite. 2-Dec-92 Christie's, East, New York
                    #353/R

BITTNEY, Bye (20th C) American
$900   £588   Tea time (51x61cm-20x24in) s. board. 16-Sep-93 Sloan, North Bethesda #2915/R

BLACK, Harold (1913-) American
$3500   £2233   Express track (101x92cm-40x36in) s.d.1935. 23-May-94 Christie's, East, New York
                    #195/R

BLACK, Laverne Nelson (1887-1938) American
$20000   £13286   Ration days (81x107cm-32x42in) s. 10-Mar-93 Sotheby's, New York #54/R

BLACK, Olive Parker (1868-1948) American
$1300   £884   Summer river landscape (41x61cm-16x24in) s. 15-Nov-93 Christie's, East, New York
                    #62/R
$1800   £1184   Summer landscape with stream (36x51cm-14x20in) s. 31-Mar-93 Sotheby's Arcade, New
                    York #159/R
$2100   £1429   A bend in the river Berkshire (61x76cm-24x30in) s. 17-Nov-93 Doyle, New York
                    #29/R
$2250   £1500   Stream in wooded landscape (41x61cm-16x24in) s. 15-Mar-94 John Moran, Pasadena
                    #153
$3200   £2133   Reflections in a pond (51x76cm-20x30in) s. 23-May-94 Christie's, East, New York
                    #121/R
$3500   £2318   Summer river landscape (51x76cm-20x30in) s. 15-Jun-94 Butterfield & Butterfield,
                    San Francisco #4421/R

BLACKMAN, Walter (1847-1928) American
$3250   £2152   Venetian harbour scene (89x71cm-35x28in) s. 21-Sep-93 Grogan, Massachussetts #716

BLACKMAN, Walter   (1847-1928) American-cont.
$4000   £2649   Venetian scene (41x69cm-16x27in) s. 28-Nov-92 Dunning's, Illinois #1036

BLACKOWL, Archie   (1911-) American
$800   £516   Moving camp (38x38cm-15x15in) s. gouache. 9-Jan-93 Skinner, Bolton #61/R

BLACKTON, James Stuart   (1875-1941) American
$2000   £1325   Early view of San Francisco Bay (38x61cm-15x24in) s. 15-Jun-94 Butterfield &
                         Butterfield, San Francisco #4560/R
$650   £442   A view of the San Maggiore Venice (49x75cm-19x30in) s.d.1913 pastel board.
                         15-Nov-93 Christie's, East, New York #144

BLACKWOOD, David L   (1941-) Canadian
$785   £513   Navigational marine light, Lumsden North (44x61cm-17x24in) s.d.1986 W/C.
                         10-May-93 Hodgins, Calgary #297 (C.D 1000)
$1165   £777   Study for 'The Flora S Nickerson in Labrador Sea' (23x36cm-9x14in) s.d.1981
                         pencil. 13-May-94 Joyner Fine Art, Toronto #113/R (C.D 1600)
$1487   £1005   Red Gate, Templeton (70x106cm-28x42in) s.d.1987 W/C gouache. 25-Apr-94 Levis,
                         Calgary #32/R (C.D 2050)
$2180   £1425   View of Newton from Templeman (69x104cm-27x41in) s.d.1981 d.verso W/C.
                         19-May-93 Sotheby's, Toronto #351/R (C.D 2750)

BLAIR, Lee Everett   (1911-) American
$4000   £2703   Anacostia - W W II snowy reconnaissance (36x56cm-14x22in) s.d.1944 W/C.
                         15-Jun-93 John Moran, Pasadena #135

BLAIR, Mary Robinson   (1911-1979) American
$550   £364   Farm with windmill (43x53cm-17x21in) s.d.41 W/C. 28-Sep-93 John Moran,
                         Pasadena #284

BLAISE, Andre   (1961-) Haitian
$1038   £687   Je suis branche (91x46cm-36x18in) s. 13-Jun-94 Rogeon, Paris #5/R (F.FR 5800)

BLAISE, Serge Moleon   (1954-) Haitian
$537   £355   Dessalines et Christophe (41x51cm-16x20in) s. board. 13-Jun-94 Rogeon, Paris #32
                         (F.FR 3000)
$1091   £723   Deportation de Toussaint en bateau (30x40cm-12x16in) s. board. 13-Jun-94 Rogeon,
                         Paris #6/R (F.FR 6100)

BLAKE, Leo   (1887-1976) American
$700   £467   Woman driving geese in garden (18x23cm-7x9in) s. canvas laid on board. 15-Mar-94
                         John Moran, Pasadena #10

BLAKELOCK, R A   (1847-1919) American
$1500   £993   River scene (30x15cm-12x6in) 30-Dec-92 Douglas, South Deerfield #1

BLAKELOCK, Ralph Albert   (1847-1919) American
$800   £519   River landscape (13x15cm-5x6in) s. panel. 11-Sep-93 Louisiana Auction Exchange
                         #7/R
$1000   £667   Moonlight glow (18x15cm-7x6in) s. canvas on board. 1-Jun-94 Doyle, New York #23
$1100   £643   Landscape (25x10cm-10x4in) 18-Sep-92 Du Mouchelle, Detroit #2013/R
$1100   £738   Moonlight (10x15cm-4x6in) s. panel. 6-Dec-93 Grogan, Massachussetts #498
$1100   £748   River landscape (12x9cm-5x4in) s. 15-Nov-93 Christie's, East, New York #68/R
$1100   £738   Evening glow (30x41cm-12x16in) s. 6-Dec-93 Grogan, Massachussetts #483 a
$1400   £979   Woodland clearing with Indian camp (23x30cm-9x12in) s. 14-Mar-93 Hindman
                         Galleries, Chicago #38/R
$1500   £1020   Forest clearing (23x30cm-9x12in) s. 17-Apr-94 Hanzel Galleries, Chicago #25
$1700   £1076   Indian encampment (15x20cm-6x8in) s. panel. 2-Dec-92 Christie's, East, New York
                         #25/R
$3000   £2098   Landscape with clouds (11x18cm-4x7in) s. panel on panel. 11-Mar-93 Christie's,
                         New York #88/R
$3000   £1587   Moonlight (28x36cm-11x14in) s. 12-Sep-92 Louisiana Auction Exchange #45/R
$3000   £2041   Sunrise. Sunset (51x30cm-20x12in) s. pair. 17-Nov-93 Doyle, New York #4/R
$3200   £1850   Landscape, twilight (11x14cm-4x6in) s. 23-Sep-92 Christie's, New York #86/R
$4000   £2667   Sunrise. Sunset (15x26cm-6x10in) one s. panel one s. canvas on board pair.
                         26-May-94 Christie's, New York #65/R
$5500   £3846   The old mill (46x81cm-18x32in) s. 11-Mar-93 Christie's, New York #63/R
$6500   £4167   Walking along the river (69x89cm-27x35in) s. canvas on canvas. 9-Dec-92
                         Butterfield & Butterfield, San Francisco #3817/R
$9500   £6333   Sunset, Indian encampment (51x76cm-20x30in) s. 26-May-94 Christie's, New York
                         #53/R
$13000   £8228   Mountain watershed (45x81cm-18x32in) s. 3-Dec-92 Sotheby's, New York #23/R
$15000   £10490   Deep woods (94x55cm-37x22in) s. 10-Mar-93 Sotheby's, New York #5/R
$38000   £25333   The canoe builders (34x30cm-13x12in) s. i.d.May 21 1897verso panel. 26-May-94
                         Christie's, New York #66/R
$48000   £30769   Teepees in moonlight (69x58cm-27x23in) s.i. 26-May-93 Christie's, New York #91/R
$67500   £43269   Jamaican coastal scene (89x142cm-35x56in) s.d.1875. 27-May-93 Sotheby's, New York
                         #205/R

BLAKELOCK, Ralph Albert (attrib)   (1847-1919) American
$800   £471   Indian encampment (34x55cm-13x22in) s. panel. 3-Oct-92 Weschler, Washington #103
$900   £604   Indian encampment (38x51cm-15x20in) 3-Feb-94 Sloan, North Bethesda #2650
$1300   £867   Landscape with Indian encampment (40x51cm-16x20in) bears sig.with arrowhead
                         device. 12-Mar-94 Weschler, Washington #153

BLAKELOCK, Ralph Albert (style) (1847-1919) American
$1200 £851 Indian encampment (41x56cm-16x22in) indis.s. panel. 12-Feb-93 Du Mouchelle, Detroit #2199/R

BLANCH, Arnold (1896-1968) American
$1300 £855 Green field (30x91cm-12x36in) s.d.57 board. 13-Jun-93 Butterfield & Butterfield, San Francisco #3270/R

BLANCO, Antonio Maria (20th C) American
$5125 £3416 Profile portrait (47x28cm-19x11in) s. canvas on board. 8-Jun-94 Glerum, Gravenhage #43/R (D.FL 9600)
$3737 £2491 Portrait of a girl (16cm-6in circular) s. W/C. 8-Jun-94 Glerum, Gravenhage #44/R (D.FL 7000)
$4599 £3026 Balinese girl (34x25cm-13x10in) s. st. mixed media. 2-Nov-92 Sotheby's, Amsterdam #680 (D.FL 8200)

BLANCO, Dionisio (1953-) Dominican
$3000 £1987 Fantasias Oniricas de Sembradores (74x101cm-29x40in) s.d.90. 23-Nov-92 Sotheby's, New York #197/R

BLANES VIALE, Pedro (1879-1926) Uruguayan
$2304 £1600 Etoile de cabaret (116x86cm-46x34in) s.d.12-1913 i.stretcher. 2-Mar-93 Sotheby's, Billingshurst #1170
$4400 £2857 Paisaje de Minas (34x55cm-13x22in) s.d.1902 panel. 30-Aug-93 Gomensoro, Montevideo #75/R
$5100 £3269 Paisaje, caballos y tropa (58x73cm-23x29in) s.d.1900. 7-Dec-92 Gomensoro, Montevideo #77/R
$5600 £3660 La espera (38x46cm-15x18in) s. panel. 26-Oct-92 Gomensoro, Montevideo #79/R
$5800 £3791 La garganta del diablo (20x23cm-8x9in) s. panel. 3-May-93 Gomensoro, Montevideo #60/R
$6200 £4079 La terraza de Pocitos (23x16cm-9x6in) s.d.1901 panel. 31-May-93 Gomensoro, Montevideo #53/R
$6500 £4248 Jardines de Villahermosa, Palma de Mallorca (23x27cm-9x11in) s.d.1909 panel. 4-Oct-93 Gomensoro, Montevideo #98/R
$6600 £4430 Ceibos en flor (47x43cm-19x17in) s.d.1912. 29-Nov-93 Gomensoro, Montevideo #35
$9000 £5263 Vista de Montevideo (48x65cm-19x26in) s. 16-Sep-92 Castells & Castells, Montevideo #49/R
$11000 £7190 Almendros en flor (54x45cm-21x18in) s. 26-Oct-92 Gomensoro, Montevideo #78
$12000 £8108 Cataratas del Iguazu (47x56cm-19x22in) s. painted c.1917. 22-Nov-93 Sotheby's, New York #178/R
$13500 £6784 Paisaje de Atlantida 1919 (65x81cm-26x32in) s. 31-Aug-92 Gomensoro, Montevideo #39/R
$16500 £9649 Penon de Mallorca (48x65cm-19x26in) s. 16-Sep-92 Castells & Castells, Montevideo #48/R
$31000 £20395 L'etoile de cabaret, Paris (116x87cm-46x34in) s.d.1913. 31-May-93 Gomensoro, Montevideo #52/R
$42000 £28378 El Sendero (86x100cm-34x39in) s. painted c.1922. 22-Nov-93 Sotheby's, New York #177/R
$75000 £49020 Glicina de la quinta de castro (138x87cm-54x34in) s.d.9-1922. 18-May-93 Sotheby's, New York #29/R
$175000 £115894 Sol Y Sombra (131x114cm-52x45in) s. 23-Nov-92 Sotheby's, New York #39/R
$550 £364 Caballo (25x30cm-10x12in) col dr. 28-Jun-93 Gomensoro, Montevideo #18
$550 £364 Caballo (25x30cm-10x12in) s.d.1924 col dr. 28-Jun-93 Gomensoro, Montevideo #17
$12000 £8054 Dama en la berlina (101x79cm-40x31in) s. pastel. 29-Nov-93 Gomensoro, Montevideo #34/R

BLANES, Juan Manuel (1830-1901) Uruguayan
$1900 £1111 Retrato de Nina (130x100cm-51x39in) 16-Sep-92 Castells & Castells, Montevideo #41
$15000 £9804 Bocoto para el caballo de la revista de santos (35x22cm-14x9in) s.i. oil graphite board executed c.1886. 18-May-93 Sotheby's, New York #115/R
$35000 £23490 En la sierra (44x38cm-17x15in) 29-Nov-93 Gomensoro, Montevideo #44/R

BLANEY, Dwight (1865-1944) American
$700 £458 Ironbound island crevice (30x25cm-12x10in) s. 22-May-93 Collins, Maine #24/R
$3400 £2378 Hollyhocks (33x41cm-13x16in) s.i.d.1890 W/C paperboard. 12-Mar-93 Skinner, Bolton #265 a/R

BLASHFIELD, Edwin Howland (1848-1936) American
$1000 £685 The duel (66x86cm-26x34in) s.i. 15-Feb-94 Christie's, New York #37/R
$1672 £1100 Rescued (45x37cm-18x15in) s.i.d.71. 2-Jun-93 Sotheby's, Billingshurst #460
$4250 £2457 Offering to the gods (86x61cm-34x24in) s. 25-Sep-92 Sotheby's Arcade, New York #107/R

BLASHKI, Miles Evergood (1871-?) American
$1339 £905 St. Ives (29x37cm-11x15in) s.i.d.1911 board. 3-Nov-93 Joel, Victoria #61/R (A.D 2000)

BLASINGAME, Frank Marvin (1903-1967) American
$1900 £1258 Untitled (183x122cm-72x48in) s. 20-Sep-93 Butterfield & Butterfield, Los Angeles #108/R
$2250 £1480 Native dancers (127x96cm-50x38in) s. 31-Mar-93 Butterfield & Butterfield, Los Angeles #5259/R

BLASZKO, Martin (1920-) Argentinian
$20000   £13333   El gran ritmo (93x43cm-37x17in) s.i.verso board painted 1949. 17-May-94 Sotheby's, New York #35/R

BLAUVELT, Charles F (1824-1900) American
$1500   £1020   Tasting broth (76x102cm-30x40in) s.d.50. 9-Jul-93 Sloan, North Bethesda #2837/R
$1900   £1098   The helping hand (25x20cm-10x8in) s. 25-Sep-92 Sotheby's Arcade, New York #103/R

BLECKNER, Ross (1949-) American
$4000   £2703   Untitled (46x36cm-18x14in) s.i.d.8.85verso linen. 8-Nov-93 Christie's, East, New York #131/R
$4000   £2778   Pieces of months (34x34cm-13x13in) s.i.d.1985-1987verso panel. 22-Feb-93 Christie's, East, New York #231/R
$5500   £3642   The sense of ending (46x40cm-18x16in) painted 1983 i.verso linen. 19-Nov-92 Christie's, New York #146/R
$5500   £3642   Untitled (26x20cm-10x8in) s.i.d.1985verso oil varnish. 17-Nov-92 Christie's, East, New York #42/R
$8500   £5629   Untitled (41x51cm-16x20in) s.d.1984verso. 19-Nov-92 Christie's, New York #120/R
$8500   £5705   One part of a recurring triangle (25x20cm-10x8in) init.i.d.87verso. 3-May-94 Christie's, East, New York #168/R
$9000   £5882   Untitled (61x61cm-24x24in) s.d.1986 verso. 4-May-93 Sotheby's, New York #248 a/R
$9000   £6040   Untitled (67x67cm-26x26in) s.verso painted 1986. 4-May-94 Christie's, New York #256/R
$9500   £6419   Untitled (80x70cm-31x28in) s.d.1983verso linen. 10-Nov-93 Christie's, New York #290/R
$22000   £14865   Love's fairytale (122x102cm-48x40in) s.i.d.1992verso linen. 10-Nov-93 Christie's, New York #275/R
$24000   £16107   Untitled (50x41cm-20x16in) s.d.1990verso. 5-May-94 Sotheby's, New York #318 a/R
$25000   £16340   Untitled (259x193cm-102x76in) s.d.81 verso. 4-May-93 Sotheby's, New York #241/R
$40000   £27027   Architecture of the sky III (269x234cm-106x92in) executed 1988. 10-Nov-93 Sotheby's, New York #60/R
$45000   £29412   Burning trees (274x183cm-108x72in) s.d.1986 verso. 4-May-93 Sotheby's, New York #238/R
$47500   £32095   Growing grass (274x213cm-108x84in) s.d.1982/1986 verso. 11-Nov-93 Sotheby's, New York #204/R
$70000   £46358   Ellipse of us (274x183cm-108x72in) painted 1988. 18-Nov-92 Sotheby's, New York #305 b/R
$120000   £79470   Twelve nights (193x157cm-76x62in) s.i.d.1986verso. 19-Nov-92 Christie's, New York #233/R
$5000   *£3378*   *Untitled (41x30cm-16x12in) W/C executed 1987. 11-Nov-93 Sotheby's, New York #203/R*

BLENNER, Carle J (1864-1952) American
$1200   £795   Portrait of young girl (61x51cm-24x20in) s. 3-Oct-93 Hanzel Galleries, Chicago #763
$5500   *£3642*   *Old fashioned bouquet (76x63cm-30x25in) s. 15-Jun-94 Butterfield & Butterfield, San Francisco #4474/R*

BLOCH, Albert (1882-1961) American
$15000   £10417   Eine Gruppe andachtiger Gestalten (137x102cm-54x40in) init.d.Febr'y-March,1914verso. 23-Feb-93 Sotheby's, New York #86/R

BLOCH, Julius Thiengen (1888-1966) American
$1000   £588   Floral still life (61x51cm-24x20in) s.d.1920. 8-Oct-92 Freeman Fine Arts, Philadelphia #1099

BLOCH, Lucienne (1909-) Swiss/American
$5000   £2890   Flint Flood (51x35cm-20x14in) s.d.48 egg tempera masonite. 24-Sep-92 Sotheby's, New York #151/R

BLOIS, Francois B de (1829-1913) Canadian
$850   £567   Winter scene with figures and huts (30x46cm-12x18in) s.d. i.verso. 26-Aug-93 Skinner, Bolton #47

BLOORE, Ronald (1925-) Canadian
$437   £291   *Sunburst (20x14cm-8x6in) mixed media framed as dyptich. 13-May-94 Joyner Fine Art, Toronto #38/R (C.D 600)*
$555   *£363*   *Composition (13x18cm-5x7in) mixed media wood. 19-May-93 Sotheby's, Toronto #208/R (C.D 700)*
$1794   *£1196*   *Chausible Series (123x152cm-48x60in) s.d.1983 verso mixed media panel. 30-May-94 Ritchie, Toronto #220 (C.D 2500)*

BLOSER, Florence Parker (1889-1935) American
$750   £517   Figures, Olvera St. L.A. (61x76cm-24x30in) s. 16-Feb-93 John Moran, Pasadena #16

BLUEMNER, Oscar (1867-1938) American
$16000   £10667   Red building (14x18cm-6x7in) init. s.i.June 34verso tempera board. 16-Mar-94 Christie's, New York #130/R
$575   £383   Oak Pond at Bloomfield (13x15cm-5x6in) mono.bears i.d.Oct.11.16 crayon dr. 12-May-94 Boos Gallery, Michigan #521/R
$900   £520   New York cityscape (12x19cm-5x7in) i.d.Je 29-15 i.d.verso chl. 23-Sep-92 Christie's, New York #222/R
$1600   £1060   Landscape, sunset (15x25cm-6x10in) mono.d.06 W/C paper on board. 22-Sep-93 Christie's, New York #218/R

BLUEMNER, Oscar (1867-1938) American-cont.
$2500	£1445	German valley. California (12x19cm-5x7in) init.d. chl pair. 24-Sep-92 Sotheby's, New York #152/R
$3400	£1965	Bloomfield Lock. Canal Port. River Canal, upper plane. North end of Plane (13x16cm-5x6in) mono.init.d. chl four. 24-Sep-92 Sotheby's, New York #153/R
$3500	£2448	Portland. Little Falls. Delaware River. Herman's Farm. Morning twilight, mono.s.d. W/C crayon set of five. 10-Mar-93 Sotheby's, New York #154/R
$6500	£4333	North Bloomfield (15x18cm-6x7in) s. gouache paper on board. 22-May-94 James Bakker, Cambridge #146
$12000	£8000	Fall River (13x17cm-5x7in) init.i.d.Je 17-22 W/C chl. 25-May-94 Sotheby's, New York #137/R
$22000	£13924	The azure and reflections (13x18cm-5x7in) i. W/C pencil paper laid down on board. 4-Dec-92 Christie's, New York #127/R
$24000	£15894	Study for Montville - Movement of Forms and Space N.J. Town (18x22cm-7x9in) W/C. 22-Sep-93 Christie's, New York #220/R

BLUHM, Norman (1920-) American
$1400	£940	Untitled (39x28cm-15x11in) s.d.61 s.d.1961 verso acrylic paper. 23-Feb-94 Christie's, East, New York #375
$1500	£1007	Untitled (65x90cm-26x35in) s.d.61 board. 3-May-94 Christie's, East, New York #24/R
$2500	£1656	Carry on (61x51cm-24x20in) s.d.60. 30-Jun-93 Sotheby's Arcade, New York #253/R
$3000	£2083	Smuggler's notch (98x164cm-39x65in) s.i.d.62. 26-Feb-93 Sotheby's Arcade, New York #341/R
$3800	£2639	Untitled (91x74cm-36x29in) s.d.53 s.stretcher. 22-Feb-93 Christie's, East, New York #140/R
$16500	£11458	White light (259x218cm-102x86in) s.i.d.1958verso. 22-Feb-93 Christie's, East, New York #170/R
$1500	£1000	Untitled (74x105cm-29x41in) s.d.56 W/C. 26-May-94 Christie's, London #38 a/R
$2900	£1946	Untitled (76x56cm-30x22in) s.d.57 gouache. 24-Feb-94 Sotheby's Arcade, New York #348/R
$6500	£4305	Untitled (91x152cm-36x60in) painted 1957 W/C gouache. 17-Nov-92 Christie's, East, New York #287/R

BLUM, Motke (1925-) American?
$2500	£1678	Jerusalem, Old City Corner (35x33cm-14x13in) s. 23-Feb-94 Christie's, East, New York #149/R

BLUM, Robert Frederick (1857-1903) American
$600	£408	Ladies on a balcony (15x8cm-6x3in) s. W/C. 8-Apr-94 Sloan, North Bethesda #2329/R
$725	£366	Italian village (23x25cm-9x10in) s. W/C. 30-Aug-92 Litchfield Auction Gallery #400
$1000	£658	In cathedral (21x29cm-8x11in) s.d.1882 W/C. 13-Jun-93 Butterfield & Butterfield, San Francisco #3162/R
$2400	£1611	The bridal maidens (18x18cm-7x7in) s. W/C. 4-May-94 Doyle, New York #21/R
$3000	£1899	Portrait of Oriental lady (18x33cm-7x13in) s. W/C. 3-Dec-92 Freeman Fine Arts, Philadelphia #1802/R
$70000	£44304	Filipino woman (44x36cm-17x14in) s.d.89 pastel. 3-Dec-92 Sotheby's, New York #84/R

BLUME, Peter (1906-1992) American/Russian
$2500	£1445	Suburban houses (48x39cm-19x15in) s.d.1926 W/C chl pencil. 25-Sep-92 Sotheby's Arcade, New York #255/R

BLUMENSCHEIN, Ernest L (1874-1960) American
$2600	£1757	Untitled - nude with drapery (38x30cm-15x12in) init. bears i.verso panel. 31-Mar-94 Sotheby's Arcade, New York #155/R

BLUNT, John S (1798-1835) American
$20000	£12821	Niagara Falls, looking down the river (71x91cm-28x36in) s.d.1831 s.i.d.verso. 26-May-93 Christie's, New York #24/R

BOARDMAN, William G (1815-c.1895) American
$2400	£1589	Along Hudson, near Peekskill, New York (83x122cm-33x48in) s.d.69. 22-Sep-93 Christie's, New York #19/R

BOBAK, Bruno (1923-) Canadian
$610	£407	Fredericton Street (30x41cm-12x16in) s. s.i.verso. 30-May-94 Hodgins, Calgary #31 (C.D 850)
$1057	£714	St. John, N.B (40x60cm-16x24in) s. 23-Nov-93 Joyner Fine Art, Toronto #72/R (C.D 1400)
$1092	£728	Windy day (40x60cm-16x24in) s. 13-May-94 Joyner Fine Art, Toronto #4/R (C.D 1500)
$1189	£777	Evening landscape (41x61cm-16x24in) s. 19-May-93 Sotheby's, Toronto #195/R (C.D 1500)
$1348	£881	Flowers (81x61cm-32x24in) s. board. 18-May-93 Joyner Fine Art, Toronto #158 (C.D 1700)
$1602	£1068	St John's River (55x75cm-22x30in) s. 13-May-94 Joyner Fine Art, Toronto #53/R (C.D 2200)
$1903	£1244	Sunset (56x76cm-22x30in) s. 18-May-93 Joyner Fine Art, Toronto #135 (C.D 2400)
$2061	£1347	Vancouver Harbour (102x122cm-40x48in) s. 18-May-93 Joyner Fine Art, Toronto #29/R (C.D 2600)
$2567	£1735	Campbellton in winter (75x100cm-30x39in) s. 23-Nov-93 Joyner Fine Art, Toronto #19/R (C.D 3400)

BOBAK, Molly Lamb (1922-) Canadian
$2854	£1865	Saint John (76x102cm-30x40in) s. 18-May-93 Joyner Fine Art, Toronto #28/R (C.D 3600)
$3892	£2577	Woolastook, The Queen's visit to Fredericton (56x76cm-22x30in) s. i.verso. 18-Nov-92 Sotheby's, Toronto #46/R (C.D 5000)
$634	£415	Fall bouquet (45x59cm-18x23in) s. W/C. 18-May-93 Joyner Fine Art, Toronto #165 (C.D 800)

BOCCHERINI (20th C) American
$522	£350	Landscape with water buffalo watering (28x58cm-11x23in) s.i.d.88 pencil W/C. 19-Jan-94 Christie's, S. Kensington #106

BOCHNER, Mel (1940-) American
$9000	£5294	Implode (231x225cm-91x89in) s.i.d.1984verso shaped canvas. 8-Oct-92 Christie's, New York #216/R
$1300	£903	Untitled (25x61cm-10x24in) s.i.d.1982 graphite pencil. 22-Feb-93 Christie's, East, New York #248/R
$2500	£1656	Axes (26x36cm-10x14in) s.d.1979 W/C. 18-Nov-92 Sotheby's, New York #204/R
$3000	£2083	Second double italic no 3 (51x69cm-20x27in) s.i.d.May 1975 W/C. 23-Feb-93 Sotheby's, New York #306/R
$3000	£2083	First fulcrum study (31x41cm-12x16in) s.d.11 Aug 1975 gouache. 23-Feb-93 Sotheby's, New York #305/R
$8000	£5229	Duple (96x127cm-38x50in) s.d.1975 pastel. 4-May-93 Sotheby's, New York #117/R
$9000	£5960	Three, five, four - step (96x127cm-38x50in) s.d.1973 chl. 18-Nov-92 Sotheby's, New York #203/R

BOESE, Henry (fl.1847-1863) American
$2800	£1854	Hiking in mountains (70x127cm-28x50in) s. 22-Sep-93 Christie's, New York #18/R
$3500	£2288	Cows watering (76x147cm-30x58in) s. 4-May-93 Christie's, East, New York #45/R
$10000	£5780	Scene near Hudson, Duchess County, New York (61x107cm-24x42in) s. 24-Sep-92 Sotheby's, New York #68/R

BOGERT, George H (1864-1944) American
$650	£425	Landscape at dusk (40x91cm-16x36in) s. 4-May-93 Christie's, East, New York #180/R
$800	£533	Seascape (71x91cm-28x36in) s. 23-May-94 Hindman Galleries, Chicago #221
$900	£588	Sunset (36x51cm-14x20in) s.i.verso board. 8-May-93 Young Fine Arts Auctions, Maine #44/R
$900	£588	Afterglow (61x91cm-24x36in) indist.sig. board. 15-May-93 Dunning's, Illinois #1096
$1100	£719	Landscape at sunset (69x99cm-27x39in) s. 19-Sep-93 Hindman Galleries, Chicago #738/R
$1400	£903	Dutch canal scene (71x91cm-28x36in) s. 13-Jul-94 Doyle, New York #7
$1400	£952	Dutch canal scene with windmill (48x71cm-19x28in) s. 14-Apr-94 Freeman Fine Arts, Philadelphia #993/R
$3100	£2039	Dusk in Venice (69x99cm-27x39in) s. 4-Jun-93 Dargate Auction Galleries, Pittsburgh #992
$3200	£2025	Grand Canal at night (72x102cm-28x40in) s. 2-Dec-92 Christie's, East, New York #156/R

BOGGS, Frank Myers (1855-1926) French/American
$750	£500	French harbour scene (40x66cm-16x26in) s. 23-May-94 Christie's, East, New York #179/R
$1100	£719	Brooklyn Bridge from the river (56x41cm-22x16in) s. 5-May-93 Doyle, New York #32/R
$1422	£900	Une barque sur l'estuaire (30x62cm-12x24in) s. 30-Nov-92 Christie's, S. Kensington #14/R
$1800	£1259	View of Seine (38x46cm-15x18in) s. 3-Feb-93 Doyle, New York #10/R
$2885	£1923	Le remorqueur (27x41cm-11x16in) s. canvas laid down on board. 25-Jul-93 Lesieur & Le Bars, Paris #42/R (F.FR 17000)
$3250	£2138	Trafalgar Square (27x41cm-11x16in) s.i. 4-Nov-92 Doyle, New York #87/R
$4117	£2691	La Seine, Paris (29x46cm-11x18in) s. 5-May-93 Galerie Dobiaschofsky, Bern #123/R (S.FR 6000)
$4640	£3200	St Vast La Hougue (53x37cm-21x15in) s.i.d.1882. 28-Jan-93 Lawrence, Crewkerne #386/R
$7278	£4665	La Seine et la cite (38x55cm-15x22in) s.d.1909. 13-Dec-92 Eric Pillon, Calais #85/R (F.FR 39000)
$8768	£5924	Voilier au large de Honfleur (81x53cm-32x21in) s.d.84. 14-Jun-93 Jean Louis Picard, Paris #10/R (F.FR 50000)
$9250	£6126	Paris, rainy day (37x55cm-15x22in) s.i.d.1899. 23-Sep-93 Sotheby's, New York #209/R
$9866	£6325	Rue de Caen (55x46cm-22x18in) s.d.1899. 18-Dec-92 Renaud, Paris #3/R (F.FR 53000)
$10000	£6667	Cathedral spire in Paris (65x51cm-26x20in) s. 17-Mar-94 Sotheby's, New York #114/R
$15000	£9615	Along Seine (65x81cm-26x32in) s.i. 27-May-93 Sotheby's, New York #11/R
$25669	£16888	Dieppe (59x82cm-23x32in) s.i.d.1881. 11-Apr-93 Deauville #106/R (F.FR 140000)
$32500	£21667	Street scene in Paris (96x150cm-38x59in) s.i.d.1878. 25-May-94 Sotheby's, New York #76/R
$831	£565	Market scene and cathedral, Le Mans (32x39cm-13x15in) s. W/C. 16-Nov-93 Vendue Huis, Gravenhage #357 c (D.FL 1600)
$831	£565	Prins Hendrikkade and Nicolaaskerk (37x45cm-15x18in) s. W/C. 16-Nov-93 Vendue Huis, Gravenhage #357 b (D.FL 1600)
$831	£565	Windmills near Delft (27x40cm-11x16in) s. W/C. 16-Nov-93 Vendue Huis, Gravenhage #357 a (D.FL 1600)
$850	£567	Arc de Carrousel (32x40cm-13x16in) s.i. chl W/C. 23-May-94 Christie's, East, New York #148/R

BOGGS, Frank Myers (1855-1926) French/American-cont.
$900	£600	Quai de Tournelle, Paris (29x37cm-11x15in) init. W/C over pencil. 25-May-94 Sotheby's, Billingshurst #162/R
$921	£602	Caudebec (33x25cm-13x10in) s.d.1908 W/C. 18-Apr-93 Lesieur & Le Bars, Paris #3 (F.FR 5000)
$930	£629	Gisors (26x40cm-10x16in) s.i. W/C crayon. 8-Nov-93 Guy Loudmer, Paris #6 (F.FR 5500)
$1103	£721	La cathedrale de Bayeux (34x26cm-13x10in) s. W/C oil crayon. 21-Dec-92 Jean Louis Picard, Paris #18 (F.FR 6000)
$1224	£800	Au bord du lac, Vicq (38x53cm-15x21in) s.i.d.1908 W/C crayon. 27-Jun-94 Christie's, S. Kensington #49/R
$1438	£971	La Tour Saint Jacques Paris (41x33cm-16x13in) s. W/C. 14-Nov-93 Eric Pillon, Calais #125/R (F.FR 8500)
$1586	£1017	Paris, Rue de la Montagne Sainte Genevieve (26x33cm-10x13in) s.d.1913 W/C. 13-Dec-92 Eric Pillon, Calais #92/R (F.FR 8500)
$1636	£946	Cathedrale de Chartres (39x26cm-15x10in) s. W/C chl. 22-Sep-92 Jean Louis Picard, Paris #22/R (F.FR 8000)
$1636	£946	Un canal en Hollande (26x40cm-10x16in) s. W/C chl. 22-Sep-92 Jean Louis Picard, Paris #23 (F.FR 8000)
$1776	£1200	Les quais le Pont des Arts Paris (28x48cm-11x19in) s.i. W/C crayon. 8-Nov-93 Guy Loudmer, Paris #10/R (F.FR 10500)
$1837	£1241	Le port de Trouville (27x40cm-11x16in) s.i. W/C. 2-Apr-94 Deauville #48 (F.FR 10500)
$1876	£1226	Dordrecht (32x44cm-13x17in) s.d.1902 W/C oil crayon. 21-Dec-92 Jean Louis Picard, Paris #19 (F.FR 10200)
$2415	£1600	Marseille (25x39cm-10x15in) s.i. W/C. 17-Jun-94 Claude Boisgirard, Paris #40/R (F.FR 13500)
$2684	£1777	Charenton (23x36cm-9x14in) s.i.d.22 avril 1905 W/C. 17-Jun-94 Claude Boisgirard, Paris #41/R (F.FR 15000)
$3050	£2047	Paris, la Place Blanche (29x71cm-11x28in) s.i. chl W/C. 25-Mar-94 Francis Briest, Paris #82/R (F.FR 17500)
$3353	£2206	Paris, le pont neuf (32x46cm-13x18in) s. W/C. 8-Nov-92 Eric Pillon, Calais #73/R (F.FR 18000)
$3702	£1889	St Yves (36x47cm-14x19in) s. W/C. 21-Aug-92 French Auctioneer #10/R (F.FR 18000)

BOGGS, Frank Myers (attrib) (1855-1926) French/American
$800	£523	Waterfront night labourers (38x46cm-15x18in) indis.s. 30-Oct-92 Sloan, North Bethesda #2189/R

BOHM, C Curry (1894-?) American
$1100	£738	Main street in winter (48x58cm-19x23in) W/C. 27-Mar-94 Myers, Florida #39/R

BOHM, Max (1868-1923) American
$900	£625	Garden of artist's home at Etaples (33x25cm-13x10in) s. studio st.i.verso. 27-Feb-93 Young Fine Arts Auctions, Maine #49/R

BOHROD, Aaron (1907-1992) American
$1200	£851	End of summer (30x41cm-12x16in) s. gessoed panel. 14-Feb-93 Hanzel Galleries, Chicago #42/R
$1300	£867	The bass (25x36cm-10x14in) s. oil gesso board. 13-Mar-94 Hindman Galleries, Chicago #785/R
$1500	£962	Burlesque show (30x41cm-12x16in) s.d.32 tempera. 13-Dec-92 Hindman Galleries, Chicago #3/R
$2500	£1656	The sea (30x23cm-12x9in) s.d.1961 s.i.d.verso oil gesso panel. 15-Jun-94 Butterfield & Butterfield, San Francisco #4497/R
$2800	£1830	The torso (79x58cm-31x23in) s. board. 16-May-93 Hanzel Galleries, Chicago #6/R
$2800	£1830	Chicago alley scene. Chicago street scene (51x69cm-20x27in) s.d.33 s.d.31 double-sided. 19-Sep-93 Hindman Galleries, Chicago #737
$5000	£3378	Evening in Carbondale (36x48cm-14x19in) s. masonite. 31-Mar-94 Sotheby's Arcade, New York #278/R
$9000	£6081	Road through the dunes (63x91cm-25x36in) s. s.d.1941 verso masonite. 31-Mar-94 Sotheby's Arcade, New York #325/R
$700	£470	Breaking the Prairie (15x64cm-6x25in) s.i. pencil. 12-Dec-93 Hindman Galleries, Chicago #333/R
$1600	£1088	The foundry (46x36cm-18x14in) s. gouache. 17-Apr-94 Hanzel Galleries, Chicago #29

BOHROD, Aaron (attrib) (1907-1992) American
$3500	£2318	The green house (76x38cm-30x15in) s. masonite. 26-Sep-93 Schrager Galleries, Milwaukee #492
$5500	£3642	The lake (61x81cm-24x32in) s. panel. 26-Sep-93 Schrager Galleries, Milwaukee #482
$500	£340	City skyline with boats in waterway (25x33cm-10x13in) s.d.31 W/C. 17-Apr-94 Schrager Galleries, Milwaukee #813

BOIT, Edward Darley (1840-c.1915) American
$1200	£800	Pastoral landscape (18x25cm-7x10in) s.indist.d. panel. 22-May-94 James Bakker, Cambridge #5
$1200	£800	Sunset (15x23cm-6x9in) panel. 22-May-94 James Bakker, Cambridge #6
$1400	£933	Sails along the coast (15x23cm-6x9in) panel. 22-May-94 James Bakker, Cambridge #3
$2000	£1333	Strolling at water's edge (15x23cm-6x9in) panel. 22-May-94 James Bakker, Cambridge #1/R
$2900	£1933	View across the water (15x23cm-6x9in) s.d.82 panel. 22-May-94 James Bakker, Cambridge #2/R
$6500	£4333	Mother and child in the park (18x25cm-7x10in) s.d.82 panel. 22-May-94 James Bakker, Cambridge #4
$750	£490	The terrace view (36x51cm-14x20in) W/C. 18-Sep-93 James Bakker, Cambridge #207/R

BOIT, Edward Darley (1840-c.1915) American-cont.
$1000   £654   Pau (28x36cm-11x14in) d.9-Mars-93 W/C. 18-Sep-93 James Bakker, Cambridge #51/R

BOLDUC, Blanche and Yvonne (20th C) Canadian
$943   £597   Baie St-Paul, Quebec (33x58cm-13x23in) s. carved wood. 1-Dec-92 Fraser Pinneys, Quebec #26 (C.D 1200)

BOLDUC, Yvonne (1905-) Canadian
$1100   £697   Baie St.Paul (33x59cm-13x23in) s.i. 1-Dec-92 Fraser Pinneys, Quebec #133 (C.D 1400)

BOLIVIAN COLONIAL SCHOOL, 18th C
$3346   £2053   San Isidro labrador (160x106cm-63x42in) 14-Oct-92 Ansorena, Madrid #67/R (S.P 350000)
$3824   £2346   San Francisco Serafico (106x167cm-42x66in) 14-Oct-92 Ansorena, Madrid #64/R (S.P 400000)
$3824   £2346   Virgen del Rosario con el Nino (110x74cm-43x29in) 14-Oct-92 Ansorena, Madrid #77/R (S.P 400000)
$4302   £2639   La Divina Pastora (93x78cm-37x31in) 14-Oct-92 Ansorena, Madrid #63/R (S.P 450000)
$6214   £3812   Virgen de Aranzazu (129x109cm-51x43in) 14-Oct-92 Ansorena, Madrid #81/R (S.P 650000)
$7648   £4692   Virgen, Padre Eterno y Angeles (127x187cm-50x74in) 14-Oct-92 Ansorena, Madrid #83/R (S.P 800000)

BOLLENDONK, Walter (1897-1977) American
$1050   £705   Morning greetings (61x76cm-24x30in) s. 4-Dec-93 Louisiana Auction Exchange #61/R

BOLOTOWSKY, Ilya (1907-1981) American/Russian
$2800   £1879   Golden Rhomb (40x22cm-16x9in) s.d.75 s.i.d.1975verso acrylic panel. 3-May-94 Christie's, East, New York #78/R
$5100   £3423   Untitled (99cm-39in circular) s.d.1962. 24-Jun-93 Mystic Fine Arts, Connecticut #127
$6500   £4362   Untitled (23x84cm-9x33in) s.d.73 panel. 24-Feb-94 Sotheby's Arcade, New York #368/R
$11000 £7383   Yellow rectangular (77x123cm-30x48in) s.i.d.1975stretcher acrylic. 5-May-94 Sotheby's, New York #139/R
$1800   £1216   Abstract composition (24x35cm-9x14in) s. collage gouache ink pencil. 2-Nov-93 Christie's, East, New York #133/R
$2500   £1736   Untitled (21x29cm-8x11in) s.init. exec.1937 col.crayon collage. 23-Feb-93 Sotheby's, New York #89/R
$3750   £2604   Study for mural (30x46cm-12x18in) gouache pencil executed c.1936. 26-Feb-93 Sotheby's Arcade, New York #260/R

BOLT, Ronald William (1938-) Canadian
$1602   £1068   The subtleties beneath No.2 (83x108cm-33x43in) s.d.75. 13-May-94 Joyner Fine Art, Toronto #229 (C.D 2200)

BOLTON, Hale William (1885-1930) American
$1100   £724   A peaceful forest clearing (76x102cm-30x40in) s. panel. 4-Apr-93 Hart Gallery, Houston #4

BOLTON-JONES, Hugh see JONES, Hugh Bolton

BONATI, Dante (1894-?) Argentinian
$700   £443   At the quarry (58x69cm-23x27in) s.d.1922 board laid down on masonite. 5-Dec-92 Louisiana Auction Exchange #172/R

BONDOIN, Hariette (19/20th C) American
$850   £556   Piazza San Marco (28x36cm-11x14in) canvas on board. 19-Sep-93 Hindman Galleries, Chicago #711/R

BONELLI, James (1916-) American
$1500   £943   Rooftops (76x91cm-30x36in) s. i.verso. 22-Apr-93 Freeman Fine Arts, Philadelphia #1335/R

BONEVARDI, Marcelo (1929-) Argentinian
$9000   £5882   Guard (140x99cm-55x39in) s.i.d.66 verso oil wood. 17-May-93 Christie's, New York #169/R
$564   £379   Veleta - weathervane (33x26cm-13x10in) s.i.d.81 s.i.verso pastel chl conte. 30-Nov-93 Ritchie, Toronto #89/R (C.D 750)
$11000 £7432   Hooked wall (178x122cm-70x48in) s.d.68 i.verso mixed media on wood construction. 23-Nov-93 Christie's, New York #182/R
$16000 £10458 Supreme instrument (178x217cm-70x85in) s.d.65 verso wood twine oil canvas construction. 18-May-93 Sotheby's, New York #77/R

BONFIELD, George R (attrib) (1802-1898) American
$650   £442   Delaware shore (7x10cm-3x4in) i.verso board. 10-Jul-93 Young Fine Arts Auctions, Maine #50/R

BONFIELD, William van de Velde (19th C) American
$800   £544   Man riding a horse in a snowstorm (20x36cm-8x14in) s. 14-Apr-94 Freeman Fine Arts, Philadelphia #964

BONGART, Sergei R (1918-1985) American/Russian
$800	£530	Summer landscape (41x51cm-16x20in) s. board. 15-Jun-94 Butterfield & Butterfield, San Francisco #4746/R
$1000	£671	Spring garden (51x55cm-20x22in) s. board. 8-Dec-93 Butterfield & Butterfield, San Francisco #3532/R
$2750	£1846	A boy and his dog (66x76cm-26x30in) s.d.80 acrylic masonite. 8-Dec-93 Butterfield & Butterfield, San Francisco #3531/R

BONNAR, James King (1885-1961) American
$800	£556	Autumn (51x61cm-20x24in) s. 27-Feb-93 Young Fine Arts Auctions, Maine #50/R
$650	£425	Winter New England village (25x33cm-10x13in) s. W/C gouache. 8-May-93 Young Fine Arts Auctions, Maine #45/R

BONSALL, Elizabeth Fearne (1861-1956) American
$1000	£685	Squalls (15x13cm-6x5in) s. board. 19-Feb-94 Young Fine Arts Auctions, Maine #44/R

BOOG, Carle Michel (1877-?) American
$3500	£2318	Young girl reading in garden (102x76cm-40x30in) s. 23-Sep-93 Mystic Fine Arts, Connecticut #71/R

BOOKBINDER, Jack (1911-) American
$900	£612	Twilight (61x74cm-24x29in) s.d.47 s.verso. 14-Apr-94 Freeman Fine Arts, Philadelphia #1057
$1100	£738	September (46x64cm-18x25in) s. 2-Dec-93 Freeman Fine Arts, Philadelphia #842

BORDUAS, Paul Emile (1905-1960) Canadian
$131068	£87379	Legers Vestiges D'Automne (127x192cm-50x76in) s. 13-May-94 Joyner Fine Art, Toronto #68/R (C.D 180000)

BOREIN, Edward (1872-1945) American
$600	£403	Indians (23x30cm-9x12in) s.i.verso pen. 4-Dec-93 Louisiana Auction Exchange #182/R
$700	£467	Indian on horseback (18x18cm-7x7in) ink. 23-May-94 Hindman Galleries, Chicago #226
$750	£500	Two steers (15x25cm-6x10in) ink. 23-May-94 Hindman Galleries, Chicago #225
$750	£500	Indian on horseback (18x18cm-7x7in) ink. 23-May-94 Hindman Galleries, Chicago #227
$925	£609	Herd of cows (18x33cm-7x13in) ink dr. 5-Jun-93 Louisiana Auction Exchange #173/R
$1200	£795	Indian women with Travois (17x25cm-7x10in) Indian ink. 15-Jun-94 Butterfield & Butterfield, San Francisco #4521/R
$1900	£1275	Four horsemen (22x29cm-9x11in) s. ink vellum on board. 8-Dec-93 Butterfield & Butterfield, San Francisco #3546/R
$2000	£1282	Running Indian (20x16cm-8x6in) pen. 9-Dec-92 Butterfield & Butterfield, San Francisco #3989/R
$2300	£1447	Tied patience , mono. s.i.d.1933verso gouache. 22-Apr-93 Freeman Fine Arts, Philadelphia #1334/R
$2500	£1678	Mounted rurale (38x30cm-15x12in) W/C. 8-Dec-93 Butterfield & Butterfield, San Francisco #3536/R
$4500	£2980	Heading up the herd. Horse and rider followed by cattle (21x27cm-8x11in) s. W/C pastel gouache pencil double-sided. 23-Sep-93 Sotheby's, New York #111/R
$4750	£3146	The Cowboy (18x22cm-7x9in) s. W/C. 15-Jun-94 Butterfield & Butterfield, San Francisco #4517/R
$5500	£3691	The Vaquero (25x25cm-10x10in) s. W/C. 8-Dec-93 Butterfield & Butterfield, San Francisco #3540/R
$6500	£3757	Round up (17x25cm-7x10in) s. W/C. 24-Sep-92 Sotheby's, New York #82/R
$37500	£25168	The long drive (30x51cm-12x20in) s. W/C. 2-Dec-93 Sotheby's, New York #60/R

BOREIN, James (1921-) American
$5000	£3356	Making tracks for home (53x74cm-21x29in) s.d.1983 W/C. 8-Dec-93 Butterfield & Butterfield, San Francisco #3597/R

BORENSTEIN, Samuel (1908-1969) Canadian
$1937	£1309	Still life with flowers (71x56cm-28x22in) s. 3-Nov-93 Sotheby's, Toronto #26/R (C.D 2500)
$2335	£1546	House in country (47x77cm-19x30in) s. 24-Nov-92 Joyner Fine Art, Toronto #43/R (C.D 3000)
$3641	£2427	Wild flowers in a blue vase (76x61cm-30x24in) s.d.58 s.i.d.60stretcher. 11-May-94 Sotheby's, Toronto #206/R (C.D 5000)
$3766	£2461	Near Mount Orford, Eastern townships (61x51cm-24x20in) s. d.1919 verso board. 19-May-93 Sotheby's, Toronto #333/R (C.D 4750)
$500	£333	Early spring (48x66cm-19x26in) s.d.37 i.verso W/C. 23-May-94 Christie's, East, New York #252/R

BORG, Carl Oscar (1879-1947) American
$1140	£750	El Baile Mexicaine (53x36cm-21x14in) s. 3-Jun-93 Christie's, S. Kensington #87
$1400	£972	Doorway, Santa Fe (19x25cm-7x10in) s. canvas on board. 7-Mar-93 Butterfield & Butterfield, San Francisco #225/R
$6500	£4305	Saddling up (41x51cm-16x20in) s. 15-Jun-94 Butterfield & Butterfield, San Francisco #4494/R
$7000	£4730	Padre blessing Indians at Mission (203x226cm-80x89in) s. 15-Jun-93 John Moran, Pasadena #125
$893	£580	El Baile Mexicaine (53x36cm-21x14in) s. pastel. 9-Sep-93 Christie's, S. Kensington #150
$900	£608	Adobe on Plaza, Raffour and harmer (25x32cm-10x13in) s.i.verso pencil. 31-Mar-94 Sotheby's Arcade, New York #200/R

BORG, Carl Oscar (1879-1947) American-cont.
$1000	£676	Harbour entrance (13x18cm-5x7in) s. gouache cardboard. 15-Jun-93 John Moran, Pasadena #68 a
$1177	£790	Pins maritimes (50x65cm-20x26in) s.d.1913 W/C. 25-Mar-93 Beaussant & Lefevre, Paris #13 (F.FR 6500)
$1600	£1013	Western landscape (28x25cm-11x10in) s. W/C. 5-Dec-92 Louisiana Auction Exchange #40/R
$1700	£1118	Rhyolite, Nevada (41x70cm-16x28in) s. W/C graphite htd white. 13-Jun-93 Butterfield & Butterfield, San Francisco #3232/R
$2250	£1552	Indian on horseback (8x13cm-3x5in) s.d.1946 ink W/C. 16-Feb-93 John Moran, Pasadena #120 a
$2250	£1324	Mission San Luis Rey (51x38cm-20x15in) s. W/C. 4-Oct-92 Butterfield & Butterfield, Los Angeles #184/R
$2500	£1678	Morning ride, Hollywood Hills (41x51cm-16x20in) s. gouache. 8-Dec-93 Butterfield & Butterfield, San Francisco #3528/R
$2750	£1897	Hopi Ruins (25x36cm-10x14in) s. gouache pencil. 16-Feb-93 John Moran, Pasadena #113
$7500	£5034	Canyon de Chelly (46x30cm-18x12in) s.i.d.1929 W/C. 8-Dec-93 Butterfield & Butterfield, San Francisco #3582/R
$8500	£5743	Canyon de Chelly-Indian (53x58cm-21x23in) s. W/C. 15-Jun-93 John Moran, Pasadena #63

BORGLUM, John Gutzon (1867-1941) American
$2750   £1809   Sheep in California landscape (41x63cm-16x25in) s.i.d.1891. 13-Jun-93 Butterfield
                      & Butterfield, San Francisco #735/R

BORGORD, Martin (1869-1935) American
$850   £535   Cloisonne vase with apple blossoms (51x41cm-20x16in) s. panel. 22-Apr-93 Freeman
                      Fine Arts, Philadelphia #1300

BORIE, Adolphe (1877-1934) American
$1850   £1209   Man reading in garden (23x28cm-9x11in) s.d.July 1916 board. 1-Nov-92 Hanzel
                      Galleries, Chicago #177

BORISOV, Mick (20th C) American/Russian
$650   £422   Leon Gaspard's Kachina dolls (51x76cm-20x30in) s. 11-Sep-93 Louisiana Auction
                      Exchange #16/R

BOROFSKY, Jonathan (1942-) American
$26000   £17450   Tree head at 2,9,84 (245x155cm-96x61in) acrylic painted 1984. 5-May-94 Sotheby's,
                      New York #334/R

BORONDA, Lester D (1886-1951) American
$625   £409   Autumn scene (36x41cm-14x16in) s. board. 30-Jun-94 Mystic Fine Arts, Connecticut
                      #51

BORRIDGE, Walter (attrib) (19/20th C) American
$4250   £2457   Long's Peak and Mount Meeker, Estes Park. View of Estes Park, Colorado
                      (91x122cm-36x48in) init.d.78 pair. 25-Sep-92 Sotheby's Arcade, New York #53/R

BOSA, Louis (1905-1981) American/Italian
$1100	£764	Rural scene with figures (25x41cm-10x16in) s. 6-Mar-93 Louisiana Auction Exchange #57
$1200	£784	Stroll in country (51x76cm-20x30in) s. 30-Jun-94 Mystic Fine Arts, Connecticut #177/R
$2050	£1424	Central Park (38x64cm-15x25in) s.d.1939 W/C. 6-Mar-93 Louisiana Auction Exchange #56/R

BOSKERCK, R W van (1855-1932) American
$573   £392   Johns Brook, Keene Valley (49x75cm-19x30in) s. 13-Feb-94 Dunbar Sloan, Wellington
                      #48 (NZ.D 1000)

BOSKERCK, Robert Ward van (1855-1932) American
$800	£530	Stream through meadow, early autumn (30x46cm-12x18in) s.d.1879. 13-Nov-92 Skinner, Bolton #62/R
$900	£600	Landscape with cattle and pond (56x89cm-22x35in) s. 13-Mar-94 Hindman Galleries, Chicago #749
$1100	£724	Wooded river view, Fontainbleau (33x46cm-13x18in) s. i.stretcher. 7-Apr-93 Doyle, New York #7
$1500	£949	Springtime stream (61x91cm-24x36in) s. 2-Dec-92 Christie's, East, New York #81/R
$1600	£1046	River scene (66x89cm-26x35in) s. 19-Sep-93 Hindman Galleries, Chicago #720
$1700	£1111	American farm scene (61x84cm-24x33in) s. 16-May-93 Hanzel Galleries, Chicago #1/R
$3200	£2177	A winding river with lily pads (82x61cm-32x24in) s. 15-Nov-93 Christie's, East, New York #124/R

BOSLEY, Frederick Andrew (1881-1941) American
$1500   £1000   Portrait of Lilla Cabot Perry (76x71cm-30x28in) s.d.1931. 17-May-94 Grogan,
                      Massachussetts #356/R

BOSMAN, Richard (1944-) American
$2750   £1858   Man falling out of window (130x106cm-51x42in) s.d.81 verso. 11-Nov-93 Sotheby's,
                      New York #199/R

51

BOSTON, Frederick James (1855-1932) American
$825	£539	New England fall (51x41cm-20x16in) s. board. 15-May-93 Dunning's, Illinois #1184/R
$1200	£800	A Civil War campsight (46x56cm-18x22in) s. oil en grisaille. 23-May-94 Christie's, East, New York #48
$1400	£959	Autumn glow (46x61cm-18x24in) 19-Feb-94 Young Fine Arts Auctions, Maine #45/R
$1400	£909	Girl sitting by the water (46x34cm-18x13in) s. 9-Sep-93 Sotheby's Arcade, New York #95/R
$1700	£1111	Reading under the wisteria (61x51cm-24x20in) s. 5-May-93 Doyle, New York #21/R

BOTERO, Fernando (1932-) Colombian
$100000	£67568	Apotheosis of St. Joan (175x184cm-69x72in) s.d.61. 22-Nov-93 Sotheby's, New York #242/R
$115000	£76667	Sin titulo (104x91cm-41x36in) s.d.68. 18-May-94 Sotheby's, New York #242/R
$120000	£79470	Naturaleza muerta (129x150cm-51x59in) s.d.78. 24-Nov-92 Christie's, New York #92/R
$130000	£86667	Naturaleza muerta con girasoles. Portrait of a boy (113x114cm-44x45in) s.d.68 double-sided. 18-May-94 Christie's, New York #64/R
$150000	£98039	Tribulaciones de Sor Angelica (53x293cm-21x115in) s.d.61 s.i.d.9-61 verso. 17-May-93 Christie's, New York #63/R
$180000	£119205	El Secuestro (41x198cm-16x78in) s.d.66 i.verso. 24-Nov-92 Christie's, New York #61/R
$190000	£124183	Familia de Perros (129x137cm-51x54in) s.d.66. 17-May-93 Christie's, New York #65/R
$200000	£132450	La Madre Superiora (126x93cm-50x37in) s.d.74. 24-Nov-92 Christie's, New York #49/R
$200000	£133333	Monja recien nacida (94x129cm-37x51in) s.d.75. 17-May-94 Sotheby's, New York #24/R
$220000	£148649	Madre Superiora en las Rocas (110x112cm-43x44in) s.d.66 s.d.verso i.stretcher. 23-Nov-93 Christie's, New York #19/R
$320000	£216216	Our lady of Cajica (243x182cm-96x72in) s.d.72 s.i.d.stretcher. 23-Nov-93 Christie's, New York #68/R
$325000	£216667	El Conquistador Espanol (198x126cm-78x50in) s. painted c.1981. 18-May-94 Christie's, New York #49/R
$360000	£240000	Naturaleza muerta en azul (150x187cm-59x74in) s.d.79. 18-May-94 Christie's, New York #26/R
$440000	£287582	Pedro (158x123cm-62x48in) s.i.d.74. 17-May-93 Christie's, New York #60/R
$480000	£317881	Naturaleza Muerta con Sandia y Naranjas (178x183cm-70x72in) s.d.70 s.i.d.verso. 24-Nov-92 Christie's, New York #15/R
$500000	£337838	Frutas (156x190cm-61x75in) s.d.68. 23-Nov-93 Christie's, New York #56/R
$650000	£424837	Cuatro mujeres (206x191cm-81x75in) s.d.87. 18-May-93 Sotheby's, New York #39/R
$1400000	£927152	La Casa de Las Gemelas Arias (228x188cm-90x74in) s.d.73. 23-Nov-93 Sotheby's, New York #44/R
$11062	*£7326*	*La femme aux six doigts (43x34cm-17x13in) s.i.d.81 black crayon. 25-Nov-92 Jean Louis Picard, Paris #13/R (F.FR 60000)*
$12000	*£8108*	*Auttoretrato en el dia de mi primera comunion (42x35cm-17x14in) s.i.d.69 graphite. 22-Nov-93 Sotheby's, New York #241/R*
$12000	*£8000*	*The bedroom (43x35cm-17x14in) s.d.80 pencil paper laid down on board. 18-May-94 Christie's, New York #181/R*
$14000	*£9259*	*Mujer recostada (27x35cm-11x14in) s.d.65 pencil. 23-Nov-93 Christie's, New York #251/R*
$16500	*£10784*	*Femme assise (44x35cm-17x14in) s.d.81 graphite. 18-May-93 Sotheby's, New York #193/R*
$20000	*£13245*	*El Patron (42x35cm-17x14in) s.i.d.1971 pencil. 24-Nov-92 Christie's, New York #212/R*
$21000	*£13725*	*Man with bowler hat (44x36cm-17x14in) s.d.80 ggraphite. 18-May-93 Sotheby's, New York #192/R*
$24000	*£16216*	*Mujer regando (43x35cm-17x14in) s.d.80 pencil chk. 23-Nov-93 Christie's, New York #111/R*
$24000	*£16000*	*Mujer con Paraguas (43x36cm-17x14in) s.i.d.83 pencil paper laid down on board. 18-May-94 Christie's, New York #182/R*
$26000	*£17333*	*Toreador. Female nude (40x46cm-16x18in) s.i.d.90 graphite chl sanguine double-sided. 18-May-94 Sotheby's, New York #313/R*
$26000	*£17568*	*Seated man (43x33cm-17x13in) s.d.80 bistre paper on board. 23-Nov-93 Christie's, New York #110/R*
$32000	*£21192*	*Desnudo Fumando (47x35cm-19x14in) s. sanguine drawn 1986. 24-Nov-92 Christie's, New York #131/R*
$55000	*£36667*	*Nature morte aux fruits (36x51cm-14x20in) s.d.75 W/C pastel. 17-May-94 Sotheby's, New York #43/R*
$57500	*£38333*	*Picador (46x61cm-18x24in) s.i.d.86 graphite grey wash. 18-May-94 Sotheby's, New York #312/R*
$130000	*£84967*	*El Cuarto de Costura (102x81cm-40x32in) s.d.69 pastel Crescent board. 17-May-93 Christie's, New York #62/R*
$140000	*£92715*	*Presidente (181x112cm-71x44in) s.d.81 W/C. 23-Nov-92 Sotheby's, New York #63/R*
$155000	*£102649*	*Primera Dama (181x112cm-71x44in) s.d.1981 W/C. 23-Nov-92 Sotheby's, New York #64/R*

BOTHWELL, Dorr (1902-) American
$3250	£1879	For National Defence (61x60cm-24x24in) s.d.40 board. 24-Sep-92 Sotheby's, New York #221/R

BOTKE, Cornelius (1887-1954) American
$800	£541	Landscape (36x46cm-14x18in) s. plywood. 15-Jun-93 John Moran, Pasadena #25
$2750	£1809	Late afternoon, Santa Paula Canyon (41x51cm-16x20in) s. canvas on board. 13-Jun-93 Butterfield & Butterfield, San Francisco #895/R

BOTKE, Jessie Arms (1883-1971) American
$550	£364	Woman knitting (48x43cm-19x17in) s. 19-Jun-94 Hindman Galleries, Chicago #641
$1200	£795	Swans (20x25cm-8x10in) s. board. 20-Sep-93 Butterfield & Butterfield, Los Angeles #104/R
$8000	£5298	Cockatoos in flowering trees (30x41cm-12x16in) s. oil gold leaf masonite. 14-Jun-94 John Moran, Pasadena #68
$23000	£15232	Egrets by the water (102x86cm-40x34in) s. canvas laid down on masonite. 27-Sep-93 Selkirks, St. Louis #290/R
$45000	£30000	White peacock and solphus-crested cockatoos (102x82cm-40x32in) s. masonite. 26-May-94 Christie's, New York #147/R
$800	*£556*	*San Gabriel (39x30cm-15x12in) s.i.d.06 gouache paper on board. 7-Mar-93 Butterfield & Butterfield, San Francisco #179/R*
$1000	*£662*	*Crown crested cranes (38x33cm-15x13in) s. W/C pencil. 20-Sep-93 Butterfield & Butterfield, Los Angeles #103/R*
$1700	*£1118*	*Flamingos (38x33cm-15x13in) s. gouache. 13-Jun-93 Butterfield & Butterfield, San Francisco #942/R*
$4000	*£2649*	*Flamingos and water lilies (38x33cm-15x13in) s. gouache. 14-Jun-94 John Moran, Pasadena #28*

BOTT, Emil (attrib) (1827-1908) American
$850	£567	Landscape with body of water and hills (58x94cm-23x37in) 21-May-94 Dargate Auction Galleries, Pittsburgh #1

BOTTI, Italo (1889-1974) Argentinian
$900	£529	Riachuelo (14x21cm-6x8in) 29-Sep-92 VerBo, Buenos Aires #17
$1150	£599	El puerto (19x26cm-7x10in) 4-Aug-92 VerBo, Buenos Aires #20

BOUCHARD, Lorne Holland (1913-1978) Canadian
$583	£388	Near Oka (30x40cm-12x16in) s. board. 13-May-94 Joyner Fine Art, Toronto #191 (C.D 800)
$597	£398	Summer camps in winter, Ste. Placide (25x35cm-10x14in) s. board. 13-May-94 Joyner Fine Art, Toronto #120/R (C.D 820)
$775	£524	La Remise St. Placide Quebec (30x51cm-12x20in) s. s.i.d.1968verso masonite. 1-Nov-93 Levis, Calgary #26/R (C.D 1000)
$801	£534	Back of Cripps' Place, Ulverton, Quebec (25x35cm-10x14in) s. canvas on board. 13-May-94 Joyner Fine Art, Toronto #138 (C.D 1100)
$902	£610	Wheat fields (23x46cm-9x18in) s. panel. 30-Mar-94 Maynards, Vancouver #17 (C.D 1250)
$906	£612	Perce, Quebec (30x41cm-12x16in) init. i.d.1936verso board. 23-Nov-93 Fraser Pinneys, Quebec #435 (C.D 1200)
$930	£628	Late April landscape (49x74cm-19x29in) s. i.verso. 3-Nov-93 Sotheby's, Toronto #131/R (C.D 1200)
$936	£607	Village street near Montmorency, Quebec (46x61cm-18x24in) s. s.i.verso. 21-Jun-94 Fraser Pinneys, Quebec #144 (C.D 1500)
$1092	£728	After snowfall, St. Placide, Quebec (41x76cm-16x30in) s. s.i.d.March 12 1962verso board. 11-May-94 Sotheby's, Toronto #47/R (C.D 1500)
$1168	£773	Farm - St Placide - Quebec (30x46cm-12x18in) s. i.d.Sept.24 1969verso masonite board. 18-Nov-92 Sotheby's, Toronto #59/R (C.D 1500)
$1820	£1214	Petit Lac Ha Ha, Parc des Laurentides (71x92cm-28x36in) s. s.i.d.May 6verso board. 11-May-94 Sotheby's, Toronto #240/R (C.D 2500)

BOUCHE, Louis (1896-1969) American
$700	£461	Urban renewal (41x51cm-16x20in) s. 31-Mar-93 Sotheby's Arcade, New York #303/R
$1393	£929	Figures in a surrealist landscape (63x76cm-25x30in) s.d.nov.1918. 31-May-94 Christie's, Amsterdam #68/R (D.FL 2600)

BOUGHTON, George Henry (1834-1905) American
$608	£400	Study for 'Rip van Winkle' (30x61cm-12x24in) paper on board. 8-Jun-93 Sotheby's, London #212
$706	£452	Bright autumn noonday, Pass of Lennie, Pertshire, Scotland (37x46cm-15x18in) s.verso panel. 7-Dec-92 Waddingtons, Toronto #1516 (C.D 900)
$1628	£1100	Girl on bridge (51x30cm-20x12in) init. canvas on board. 18-Mar-93 Bonhams, London #161/G
$2000	£1361	A Pause to Consider a young woman reading (63x53cm-25x21in) s.d.1899 canvas over panel. 15-Nov-93 Christie's, East, New York #149/R
$2200	£1392	Christmas Eve (24x32cm-9x13in) s. panel. 2-Dec-92 Christie's, East, New York #29/R
$2200	£1429	Summer (51x30cm-20x12in) s. s.i.verso. 9-Sep-93 Sotheby's Arcade, New York #119/R
$3000	£1987	In the field (53x35cm-21x14in) init. s.indist.i.verso panel. 23-Sep-93 Sotheby's, New York #134/R
$3648	£2400	Coming from church (52x37cm-20x15in) s.d.1889. 11-Jun-93 Christie's, London #238/R
$18000	£11921	Gathering firewood in winter (76x45cm-30x18in) panel. 22-Sep-93 Christie's, New York #55/R
$20000	£12658	New Year's day in New Amsterdam (101x162cm-40x64in) s.d.1870. 3-Dec-92 Sotheby's, New York #25/R
$1900	*£1203*	*Portrait of woman in white (24x20cm-9x8in) init. W/C gouache. 2-Dec-92 Christie's, East, New York #7/R*

BOUGUEREAU, Elizabeth Gardner (1837-1922) American
$3100	£1950	Philome and Procne (81x61cm-32x24in) 22-Apr-93 Freeman Fine Arts, Philadelphia #1122
$14500	£9732	Philome and Procne (80x62cm-31x24in) after William Adolphe Bourguereau. 19-Jan-94 Sotheby's Arcade, New York #414/R

BOUGUEREAU, Elizabeth Gardner (1837-1922) American-cont.
$14500   £9295   Sketch for portrait of Rudyard Kipling's daughter (91x64cm-36x25in) s. pen.
                 26-May-93 Sotheby's, New York #53/R

BOUNDEY, Burton Shepard (1879-1962) American
$600   £400   Boats in a bay (30x41cm-12x16in) s. board. 15-Mar-94 John Moran, Pasadena #133
$6500   £3824   Bank of my lake (61x76cm-24x30in) s. 4-Oct-92 Butterfield & Butterfield, Los
                 Angeles #99/R

BOURGEOIS, Denis (1938-) Canadian
$678   £462   First snow (51x61cm-20x24in) s. bears i.verso. 15-Nov-93 Hodgins, Calgary #18/R
                 (C.D 900)

BOURGEOIS, Louise (1911-) American/French
$4000   £2353   Untitled (48x31cm-19x12in) s.d.50 pen. 8-Oct-92 Christie's, New York #116/R
$7500   £4902   Figure abstraite (39x24cm-15x9in) s.i. brush ink. 5-May-93 Christie's, New York
                 #101/R
$9000   £6250   Untitled (28x22cm-11x9in) s.d.47 pen graphite. 24-Feb-93 Christie's, New York
                 #23/R
$9000   £6250   Untitled (28x21cm-11x8in) init. exec.1951 brush ink graph paper. 24-Feb-93
                 Christie's, New York #24/R

BOUTELLE, De Witt Clinton (1817-1884) American
$1200   £774   Old Jackson Falls (28x38cm-11x15in) s.d.1872 canvas on board. 6-Jan-93 Doyle, New
                 York #7
$5000   £3333   Catskill grandeur (135x119cm-53x47in) 23-May-94 Christie's, East, New York #14/R
$6000   £3468   Sunset in the Catskills (26x21cm-10x8in) s.d.1871. 23-Sep-92 Christie's, New York
                 #55/R

BOWDOIN, Harriette (19/20th C) American
$750   £507   Sunlit garden path (69x58cm-27x23in) s. 27-Nov-93 Young Fine Arts Auctions, Maine
                 #44/R

BOWEN, John T (1801-1856) American
$3000   £1899   Natural Bridge, Virginia (24x18cm-9x7in) W/C. 3-Dec-92 Sotheby's, New York #2/R

BOWEN, P T (19th C) American
$900   £600   H W Fish, aged 21 years (76x64cm-30x25in) s.d.1836verso panel. 26-Aug-93 Skinner,
                 Bolton #15/R

BOWER, Alexander (1875-1952) American
$800   £523   Seascape (51x91cm-20x36in) s. 18-Sep-93 Young Fine Arts Auctions, Maine #45/R

BOWER, J (attrib) (fl.1850-1855) American
$800   £523   Still life with basket and fruits on marble topped table (20x23cm-8x9in) pastel.
                 31-Oct-92 Skinner, Bolton #113/R

BOWERS, Frank Taylor (1875-1932) American
$1400   £952   Vanquished (36x30cm-14x12in) s.d.27. 10-Jul-93 Young Fine Arts Auctions, Maine
                 #54/R

BOWERS, George Newell (19th C) American
$2600   £1757   Women fetching water (51x66cm-20x26in) s. 10-Aug-93 Stonington Fine Arts,
                 Stonington #157

BOWES, David (20th C) American?
$2000   £1342   Colour combat (154x113cm-61x44in) s.i.d.1982 verso acrylic. 24-Feb-94 Sotheby's
                 Arcade, New York #479/R
$2200   £1477   Hagringen (137x152cm-54x60in) s. mono.d.3/89 verso acrylic. 24-Feb-94 Sotheby's
                 Arcade, New York #485/R
$3100   £2081   Conversation (152x122cm-60x48in) s.d.1983 verso tempera linen. 25-Feb-94
                 Sotheby's, New York #144/R

BOWLER, Joseph (jnr) (1928-) American
$750   £500   Day of always, couple in interior (51x61cm-20x24in) s. board painted 1959.
                 18-Mar-94 Du Mouchelle, Detroit #2220/R

BOWMAN, John (1953-) American
$3800   £2517   Harvest (91x213cm-36x84in) s.i.d.1985-86 panel. 17-Nov-92 Christie's, East, New
                 York #157/R

BOXER, Stanley (1926-) American
$2500   £1572   Slenderfallweepedlackingvale (203x165cm-80x65in) s.d.78verso linen. 25-Apr-93
                 Butterfield & Butterfield, San Francisco #2174/R

BOYD, J Rutherford (1884-1951) American
$1500   £1000   Fields in winter (28x35cm-11x14in) painted between 1908-1910. 23-May-94
                 Christie's, East, New York #153/R

BOYD, Rutherford (?-1951) American
$12000 £8000   In the pantry, Boydsnest (56x72cm-22x25in) s. W/C. 17-Mar-94 Sotheby's, New York
                 #133/R
$21000 £13291 Shanghai Express (44x64cm-17x25in) s. W/C. 3-Dec-92 Sotheby's, New York #67/R

BOYER, Bob (1948-) Canadian
$785   £513   Tom Thompson - Indian summer and tongues of angels (152x122cm-60x48in) s.d.88 verso. 10-May-93 Hodgins, Calgary #248/R (C.D 1000)

BOYNTON, Raymond Sceptre (1883-1951) American
$1200   £789   Ranch near foothills (51x61cm-20x24in) s.d.1947. 13-Jun-93 Butterfield & Butterfield, San Francisco #769/R
$3000   £2083   Manoa Valley, Honolulu (61x46cm-24x18in) s. s.i.d.1938verso. 7-Mar-93 Butterfield & Butterfield, San Francisco #178/R

BRACKETT, Sidney Lawrence (1852-1910) American
$1200   £784   Curious kittens (15x20cm-6x8in) s. board. 18-Sep-93 James Bakker, Cambridge #11/R
$1600   £1081   Boston Harbour - Governor's Island Jetty on Castle Island (25x36cm-10x14in) s.d.1884. 30-Jul-93 Eldred, Massachusetts #265/R
$550   £369   Naughty kittens (38x48cm-15x19in) s. pastel. 28-Mar-93 James Bakker, Cambridge #23/R
$550   £369   Kittens (25x33cm-10x13in) s. W/C. 29-Nov-93 Stonington Fine Arts, Stonington #97/R

BRACKMAN, Robert (1898-1980) American
$1500   £1014   Still life with apples (41x51cm-16x20in) s. 31-Mar-94 Sotheby's Arcade, New York #323/R
$1800   £1176   Still life (41x51cm-16x20in) s. 30-Jun-94 Mystic Fine Arts, Connecticut #121
$1800   £1224   Fruit still life (30x13cm-12x5in) s. 17-Apr-94 Hanzel Galleries, Chicago #22
$2200   £1457   Still life apples and pears (46x56cm-18x22in) s. 3-Oct-93 Hanzel Galleries, Chicago #40
$3200   £2092   Two figure study (51x30cm-20x12in) s. s.i.verso. 4-May-93 Christie's, East, New York #277/R
$6500   £4305   At a table (62x91cm-24x36in) s.i. s.i.d.1932verso. 15-Jun-94 Butterfield & Butterfield, San Francisco #4476/R
$550   £369   Two women (56x76cm-22x30in) s. pastel col.chk. 24-Mar-93 Grogan, Massachussetts #138
$750   £510   Two women (72x43cm-28x17in) s. pastel chl. 15-Nov-93 Christie's, East, New York #190/R
$1100   £724   Two peasant women (46x61cm-18x24in) s. pastel. 4-Nov-92 Doyle, New York #47/R
$1100   £724   Study of two female nudes (50x65cm-20x26in) s. pastel. 31-Mar-93 Sotheby's Arcade, New York #435/R
$1200   £811   Study of a young woman (51x66cm-20x26in) s. pastel. 31-Mar-94 Sotheby's Arcade, New York #379/R
$1300   £878   Reclining nude (50x66cm-20x26in) s. pastel. 31-Mar-94 Sotheby's Arcade, New York #376/R
$1600   £1053   Two figures (69x55cm-27x22in) s. pastel. 31-Mar-93 Sotheby's Arcade, New York #440/R
$1900   £1329   Seated woman with staff (48x64cm-19x25in) s. pastel. 14-Mar-93 Hindman Galleries, Chicago #39/R
$1900   £1203   Washing her hair (76x64cm-30x25in) s. pastel on paperboard. 2-Dec-92 Christie's, East, New York #380/R
$2700   £1765   Two peasant women (61x46cm-24x18in) s. pastel. 5-May-93 Doyle, New York #55/R

BRADFORD, William (1827-1892) American
$1100   £738   Seascape with a ship. Seascape (13x36cm-5x14in) s. one paper on masonite one board pair. 25-Mar-94 Eldred, Massachusetts #717/R
$1350   £900   Coastal view (25x48cm-10x19in) s. board. 22-May-94 James Bakker, Cambridge #90/R
$4500   £2601   Perce Rock, Belle Isle Straits (46x76cm-18x30in) s.i. 24-Sep-92 Sotheby's, New York #15/R
$9000   £6000   Cape Charles, Coast of Labrador (46x76cm-18x30in) s.i.verso board. 23-May-94 Christie's, East, New York #68/R
$14000   £8974   Summer evening in Arctic (46x76cm-18x30in) s.d.75. 26-May-93 Christie's, New York #57/R
$21000   £13462   Fishermen off coast of Labrador (46x77cm-18x30in) i.verso. 27-May-93 Sotheby's, New York #204/R
$28000   £19048   Inbound whaler (41x61cm-16x24in) s.d.1865 canvas laid down on metal. 17-Nov-93 Doyle, New York #15/R
$32000   £18497   Among the icebergs, coast in Labrador (46x76cm-18x30in) s.i. s.i.stretcher. 23-Sep-92 Christie's, New York #41/R
$40000   £26846   Fishermen off the coast of Labrador (52x83cm-20x33in) s.i. 2-Dec-93 Sotheby's, New York #14/R
$600   £400   Fishing boat at low tide (23x33cm-9x13in) s. ink wash. 23-May-94 Hindman Galleries, Chicago #167/R
$1400   £946   End of the day (13x23cm-5x9in) s.d.74 W/C grisaille. 30-Jul-93 Eldred, Massachusetts #310/R
$1600   £1074   The passing front - marine scene (51x77cm-20x30in) s. oil chl en grisaille. 4-Mar-94 Skinner, Bolton #215/R

BRADLEY, Anne Cary (1884-?) American
$3800   £2405   Corner in Albion Perry's garden, Fryeburg Maine (56x51cm-22x20in) s. 2-Dec-92 Christie's, East, New York #136/R

BRADLEY, J (fl.1832-1847) American
$441   £300   A lady in brown dress with white stole and bonnet, tied under chin (7x?cm-3x?in) min. gilt-metal mount rec. 12-Apr-94 Christie's, S. Kensington #78

BRADSHAW, Eva Theresa (?) Canadian?
$700   £490   Still life with yellow roses (30x61cm-12x24in) mono. 12-Mar-93 Skinner, Bolton #165/R

BRADSHAW, Eva Theresa (?) Canadian?-cont.
$1300   £867   Roses (30x61cm-12x24in) s. 26-May-94 Sloan, North Bethesda #2153

BRADSHAW, Nell Mary (1904-) Canadian
$523   £354   Figures in the sun (51x61cm-20x24in) s. board. 30-Mar-94 Maynards, Vancouver #76 (C.D 725)

BRADSTREET, Julie E (19th C) American
$1000   £662   Still life with strawberries (33x51cm-13x20in) s. 21-Nov-92 James Bakker, Cambridge #224/R

BRADY, Michael (1936-) American
$869   £587   To have and have not (50x75cm-20x30in) s. painted c.1990. 29-Mar-94 Campo & Campo, Antwerp #71 (B.FR 30000)
$1159   £783   Afternoon, female nude lying in water (94x60cm-37x24in) s. painted c.1992. 29-Mar-94 Campo & Campo, Antwerp #70/R (B.FR 40000)

BRANDRIFF, George Kennedy (1890-1936) American
$2000   £1176   Children of Mission (46x37cm-18x15in) s. i.verso masonite. 3-Oct-92 Weschler, Washington #119/R
$2750   £1809   Children of Mission (46x36cm-18x14in) s. board. 13-Jun-93 Butterfield & Butterfield, San Francisco #880/R

BRANDT, Carl Ludwig (1831-1905) American
$1310   £873   Female nude reclining in landscape (30x40cm-12x16in) s. 15-Mar-94 Weiner, Munich #167/R (DM 2200)
$3000   £2069   Classical figures (16x42cm-6x17in) one s.i.d. two. 16-Feb-93 Christie's, East, New York #3/R

BRANDT, Rexford Elson (1914-) American
$750   £517   *Morning wave* (28x51cm-11x20in) s.i.d.6.4.60 W/C. 16-Feb-93 John Moran, Pasadena #84
$1800   £1192   *Ensenada Race* (51x66cm-20x26in) s.d.63 W/C mixed media. 14-Jun-94 John Moran, Pasadena #76
$1800   £1200   *Cattle grazing in rolling landscape* (41x58cm-16x23in) s.d.7.12.72 W/C. 15-Mar-94 John Moran, Pasadena #176
$2500   £1736   *Fishing off the point* (37x53cm-15x21in) s. W/C. 7-Mar-93 Butterfield & Butterfield, San Francisco #254/R
$2500   £1471   *Salton Sea State Park* (32x52cm-13x20in) s. W/C. 4-Oct-92 Butterfield & Butterfield, Los Angeles #262/R

BRANDT, Warren (1918-) American
$650   £425   Rose bed (51x41cm-20x16in) s. i.stretcher painted c.1964. 7-Oct-93 Freeman Fine Arts, Philadelphia #982

BRANDTNER, Fritz (1896-1969) Canadian
$1077   £718   Broken Mountains 3 (41x51cm-16x20in) s.i.verso paper on board lucite 44. 30-May-94 Hodgins, Calgary #302 (C.D 1500)
$1982   £1295   No title - no.2 (20x25cm-8x10in) s.d.68 board. 19-May-93 Sotheby's, Toronto #204/R (C.D 2500)
$18932   £12621   Sunflowers (52x62cm-20x24in) s.d.36. 13-May-94 Joyner Fine Art, Toronto #92/R (C.D 26000)
$634   £415   *View of gaspe* (30x41cm-12x16in) s. W/C. 19-May-93 Sotheby's, Toronto #238/R (C.D 800)
$934   £619   Abstract composition (25x34cm-10x13in) s. col.ink. 18-Nov-92 Sotheby's, Toronto #142/R (C.D 1200)
$1284   £851   *City view* (22x20cm-9x8in) s. i.verso mixed media. 18-Nov-92 Sotheby's, Toronto #143 (C.D 1650)
$1348   £881   *Georgian Bay* (43x56cm-17x22in) s.d.1946 col.ink. 19-May-93 Sotheby's, Toronto #197/R (C.D 1700)
$1784   £1166   Abstract composition (25x33cm-10x13in) s. mixed media. 19-May-93 Sotheby's, Toronto #202/R (C.D 2250)

BRASHER, Rex (1869-1960) American
$660   £423   Shore birds on the rocks (38x53cm-15x21in) s.d.1910 W/C. 17-Dec-92 Mystic Fine Arts, Connecticut #56
$660   £423   Shore birds on the rocks (38x53cm-15x21in) s.d.1910 W/C. 17-Dec-92 Mystic Fine Arts, Connecticut #55/R
$1320   £846   Flamingos nesting (38x53cm-15x21in) s.d.1909 W/C. 17-Dec-92 Mystic Fine Arts, Connecticut #57

BRAUGHT, Ross Eugene (1898-) American
$1600   £1026   Winter landscape through the trees (76x91cm-30x36in) s. 13-Dec-92 Litchfield Auction Gallery #2

BRAUN, Maurice (1877-1941) American
$1500   £1007   Autumn (25x25cm-10x10in) s. canvasboard. 8-Dec-93 Butterfield & Butterfield, San Francisco #3440/R
$1600   £941   Sunset (51x66cm-20x26in) s. s.i.verso. 4-Oct-92 Butterfield & Butterfield, Los Angeles #174/R
$2000   £1342   Southern California Hills (20x25cm-8x10in) s. i.verso board. 8-Dec-93 Butterfield & Butterfield, San Francisco #3422/R
$2000   £1299   Summer landscape (41x30cm-16x12in) s. board. 11-Sep-93 Louisiana Auction Exchange #62/R
$2300   £1554   The blue Pacific (63x76cm-25x30in) s. 31-Mar-94 Sotheby's Arcade, New York #250/R

BRAUN, Maurice (1877-1941) American-cont.

$2500	£1689	Autumn landscape (25x36cm-10x14in) s. canvas laid down on board. 9-Nov-93 John Moran, Pasadena #927
$2750	£1821	Western mountains (41x51cm-16x20in) s. 28-Nov-92 Young Fine Arts Auctions, Maine #54
$2750	£1846	Summer (41x51cm-16x20in) s. 8-Dec-93 Butterfield & Butterfield, San Francisco #3443/R
$2750	£1846	Spring (30x41cm-12x16in) s. 8-Dec-93 Butterfield & Butterfield, San Francisco #3421/R
$3250	£2167	Landscape (41x51cm-16x20in) s. canvas laid down on canvas. 15-Mar-94 John Moran, Pasadena #127
$3500	£2318	Begonias (61x51cm-24x20in) s. 15-Jun-94 Butterfield & Butterfield, San Francisco #4669/R
$5000	£3378	Early springtime (91x102cm-36x40in) s. 15-Jun-93 John Moran, Pasadena #100
$5500	£3716	Landscape (15x23cm-6x9in) s. board. 15-Jun-93 John Moran, Pasadena #30
$5500	£3716	Autumn in California (30x41cm-12x16in) s. 9-Nov-93 John Moran, Pasadena #854
$6500	£4514	Hill country (63x76cm-25x30in) bears sig. 7-Mar-93 Butterfield & Butterfield, San Francisco #190/R
$7000	£4698	Mountains in the spring (41x51cm-16x20in) s. 8-Dec-93 Butterfield & Butterfield, San Francisco #3442/R
$7500	£5208	Summer landscape (36x46cm-14x18in) s. 7-Mar-93 Butterfield & Butterfield, San Francisco #180/R
$8000	£5298	In Purple hills (51x61cm-20x24in) s. 22-Sep-93 Christie's, New York #177/R
$9000	£6040	Eucalyptus trees (63x76cm-25x30in) s. 8-Dec-93 Butterfield & Butterfield, San Francisco #3469/R
$9500	£6376	San Diego harbour (51x61cm-20x24in) s. 26-Mar-94 James Bakker, Cambridge #60/R
$11000	£7285	Chula Vista (51x61cm-20x24in) s. 28-Sep-93 John Moran, Pasadena #295
$13000	£8784	Houses in eucalyptus landscape (51x61cm-20x24in) s. 15-Jun-93 John Moran, Pasadena #115 b
$18000	£12162	Eucalyptus landscape (64x76cm-25x30in) s. 15-Jun-93 John Moran, Pasadena #115 a
$25000	£16892	Eucalyptus landscape (64x76cm-25x30in) s. 9-Nov-93 John Moran, Pasadena #836
$750	£507	Eucalyptus landscape (15x10cm-6x4in) s. W/C. 9-Nov-93 John Moran, Pasadena #812 a

BRAUN, Maurice (attrib) (1877-1941) American

$1000	£654	Quiet pool (63x48cm-25x19in) bears sig. 4-May-93 Christie's, East, New York #114
$1100	£738	California landscape (71x81cm-28x32in) bears sig. 4-Dec-93 Louisiana Auction Exchange #115/R

BRAUNTUCH, Troy (1954-) American

$886	£591	Untitled - sled (112x76cm-44x30in) white chk black paper executed 1981. 2-Jun-94 AB Stockholms Auktionsverk, Stockholm #7066/R (S.KR 7000)
$886	£591	Untitled composition (112x76cm-44x30in) white chk black paper executed 1982. 2-Jun-94 AB Stockholms Auktionsverk, Stockholm #7065/R (S.KR 7000)
$2400	£1611	Untitled (112x76cm-44x30in) white pencil. 3-May-94 Christie's, East, New York #128/R
$3000	£1961	Untitled (91x273cm-36x107in) chl cotton three panels executed 1983. 22-Dec-92 Christie's, East, New York #2

BRAVO, Claudio (1936-) Chilean

$14000	£9459	Moroccan landscape (16x22cm-6x9in) s.d.MCMLXXIII painted 1973. 23-Nov-93 Christie's, New York #2/R
$18000	£12000	Manos (33x41cm-13x16in) s.d.MCMLXII. 18-May-94 Sotheby's, New York #264/R
$35000	£23649	Naturaleza muerta (70x50cm-28x20in) s.d.MCMLXV panel painted 1965. 23-Nov-93 Christie's, New York #10/R
$55000	£37162	Cabeza de Marroqui (65x80cm-26x31in) s.d.MCMLXXVII painted 1977. 23-Nov-93 Christie's, New York #4/R
$55000	£36667	Conversation between Clark and Ring (64x92cm-25x36in) s.d.MCMLXX. 17-May-94 Sotheby's, New York #44/R
$65000	£42484	Papel rojo (127x105cm-50x41in) s.d.MCMLXX painted 1970. 17-May-93 Christie's, New York #49/R
$75000	£50000	Bodegon con vela y vasos (75x100cm-30x39in) s.d.MCMLXXXIII. 17-May-94 Sotheby's, New York #55/R
$95000	£64189	Messaoud et son fils (130x97cm-51x38in) s.d.MCMLXXVI painted 1976. 23-Nov-93 Christie's, New York #14/R
$100000	£67568	L'Ami du Gardien (130x98cm-51x39in) s.d.MCMLXXVI painted 1976. 23-Nov-93 Christie's, New York #5/R
$130000	£87838	Noureddine (147x114cm-58x45in) s.d.MCMLXXXIII painted 1983. 23-Nov-93 Christie's, New York #8/R
$160000	£108108	Red package (100x81cm-39x32in) s.d.MCMLXXV painted 1975. 23-Nov-93 Christie's, New York #15/R
$165000	£109272	Requiem for soprano (160x150cm-63x59in) s.d.MCMLXIX. 24-Nov-92 Christie's, New York #38/R
$170000	£114865	Dos Amigas, Marbella (150x199cm-59x78in) s.d.MCMLXXVIII painted 1978. 23-Nov-93 Christie's, New York #11/R
$180000	£121622	Sidi Moktar (150x200cm-59x79in) s.d.MCMLXXVI painted 1976. 23-Nov-93 Christie's, New York #3/R
$330000	£220000	White package (100x150cm-39x59in) s.d.MCMLXVII panel. 18-May-94 Christie's, New York #36/R
$1210	£806	Hedgehog (15x21cm-6x8in) s.d.MCMLXVII chk W/C htd white. 28-May-94 Villa Grisebach, Berlin #452/R (DM 2000)
$1500	£1014	Estudio para retrato de Rudolf Nureyev (20x12cm-8x5in) s.i.d.MCMLXIX red crayon executed 1969. 23-Nov-93 Christie's, New York #12/R
$3250	£2124	Mariposa (8x8cm-3x3in) s.d.MCMLXX pastel oil. 18-May-93 Sotheby's, New York #199/R
$3500	£2381	Trees (32x45cm-13x18in) s.d.MCMLXXXV pencil. 17-Nov-93 Doyle, New York #123/R

BRAVO, Claudio (1936-) Chilean-cont.
$4536   £3024   Stones (24x33cm-9x13in) s.d.MCMLXVII col.chk pastel htd white. 28-May-94 Villa
                      Grisebach, Berlin #451/R (DM 7500)
$6500   £4392   Figure from the ballet 'Stars and Stripes'. Head of Bach, Beethoven andHaydn
                      (25x18cm-10x7in) s.d.1953 pen pencil four. 23-Nov-93 Christie's, New York #13/R
$13000   £8609   Legs and hands (65x50cm-26x20in) s.d.MCMLXXV chl pencil Canson paper. 24-Nov-92
                      Christie's, New York #215/R
$18000   £12162   The seated guardian (70x53cm-28x21in) s.d.MCMLXXVII pen wash conte crayon
                      executed '77. 23-Nov-93 Christie's, New York #9/R
$20000   £13333   Easter lillies (36x50cm-14x20in) s.d.MCMXCI conte crayon. 17-May-94 Sotheby's,
                      New York #53/R
$22000   £14379   Still life with lemons and seashells (72x102cm-28x40in) s.d.MCMLXIII graphite
                      sanguine chl. 18-May-93 Sotheby's, New York #197/R
$22000   £14570   Gato (100x71cm-39x28in) s.d.MCMLXII chl pencil sanguine masonite. 24-Nov-92
                      Christie's, New York #22/R
$25000   £16779   Still life (48x53cm-19x21in) s.d.MCMLXII pastel. 7-Jan-94 Gary Nader, Miami #11/R
$26000   £17333   Madonna (110x65cm-43x26in) s.d.MCMLIX chl gouache brown paper. 18-May-94
                      Christie's, New York #307/R
$26000   £16993   El minotauro (98x62cm-39x24in) s.d.MCMLXVII chl pastel paper on panel drawn 67.
                      17-May-93 Christie's, New York #234/R
$29000   £19205   Tin cans (49x64cm-19x25in) s.d.MCMLXXI pastel graphite. 23-Nov-92 Sotheby's, New
                      York #71/R
$30000   £19868   Gato con Clavel (100x71cm-39x28in) s.d.MCMLXII chl pencil paper on masonite.
                      24-Nov-92 Christie's, New York #21/R
$30000   £20270   La Marcha Verde sobre El Sahara - 27 de Octubre (47x85cm-19x33in) s.i.d.MCMLXXV
                      chl pastel conte crayon exec.1975. 23-Nov-93 Christie's, New York #1/R
$32000   £21622   The Chrysanthemum (57x38cm-22x15in) s.d.MCMLXXIV chl sanguine pencil pastel
                      exec.74. 23-Nov-93 Christie's, New York #7/R
$32000   £21192   Mujer con Rosa (37x32cm-15x13in) s.d.MCMLXV sanguine chl. 24-Nov-92 Christie's,
                      New York #167/R
$32500   £21959   Boots and shoes (75x103cm-30x41in) s.d.MCMLXXII W/C pastel. 22-Nov-93 Sotheby's,
                      New York #258/R
$35000   £23333   Cat's Cradle, Mother and Son (95x70cm-37x28in) s.d.MCMLXVI chl sanguine chk
                      executed 1966. 18-May-94 Christie's, New York #15/R
$38000   £25166   El Enigma (75x110cm-30x43in) s.d.MCMLXVI pastel pencil paper on panel. 24-Nov-92
                      Christie's, New York #213/R
$46000   £31081   Seated male nude (61x48cm-24x19in) s.d.MCMLXXXII pencil chl executed 1982.
                      23-Nov-93 Christie's, New York #6/R
$65000   £43333   Muchacho en el estudio (109x75cm-43x30in) s.d.MCMLXXX pastel paper laid down on
                      panel. 18-May-94 Christie's, New York #16/R

BRECK, John Leslie (1861-1899) American
$26000   £16667   River (46x55cm-18x22in) s. init.stretcher. 26-May-93 Christie's, New York #144/R
$29810   £20142   Hiver a Giverny (34x44cm-13x17in) s.i.d.fev.88. 14-Jun-93 Laurin Guilloux
                      Buffetaud Tailleur, Paris #2/R (F.FR 170000)

BRECKENRIDGE, Hugh Henry (1870-1937) American
$3250   £2211   Summer glow (64x61cm-25x24in) s. 17-Nov-93 Doyle, New York #57/R

BREDIN, Ray Sloan (1881-1933) American
$8000   £5298   Grey day - Delaware Valley scene (30x36cm-12x14in) s. 13-Nov-92 Skinner, Bolton
                      #171/R
$8500   £5629   The Japanese Print (43x33cm-17x13in) s. 15-Jun-94 Butterfield & Butterfield, San
                      Francisco #4407/R

BRENNEMAN, George W (1856-?) American
$4200   £2781   No idea (45x30cm-18x12in) s. s.i.verso cradled panel. 22-Sep-93 Christie's, New
                      York #53/R

BRENNER, Carl Christian (1838-1888) American
$3800   £2550   In the Cumberland Mountains (66x117cm-26x46in) s.d.1882. 11-Dec-93 Weschler,
                      Washington #87/R
$5500   £3595   Tabletop still life of orientalia and peacock feathers (51x36cm-20x14in)
                      s.d.1884. 16-Sep-93 Sloan, North Bethesda #3212/R

BRENT, Adalie Margules (1920-1992) American
$950   £625   Boy peeling corn (61x41cm-24x16in) s.d.1945 egg tempera panel. 5-Jun-93 Louisiana
                      Auction Exchange #98/R

BRETON, Louis le (?) South American
$1467   £965   Promeneurs aux abords de la Mosquee, Ispahan (59x79cm-23x31in) s. 5-Apr-93 Ader
                      Tajan, Paris #168 (F.FR 8000)

BRETT, Harold M (1880-1955) American
$1100   £714   A sailor's return (76x64cm-30x25in) s. 4-Aug-94 Eldred, Massachusetts #622/R
$4300   £2792   The Brewster Church, Cape Cod (76x51cm-30x20in) s. 4-Aug-94 Eldred, Massachusetts
                      #623/R

BREUER, Henri Joseph (1860-1932) American
$3500   £2303   View of Mount Tamalpais (41x51cm-16x20in) s.d.1917. 13-Jun-93 Butterfield &
                      Butterfield, San Francisco #770/R
$20000   £13245   View of the Sierras from Independence, Inyo Country, California
                      (34x244cm-13x96in) s.i.d.1903. 15-Jun-94 Butterfield & Butterfield, San
                      Francisco #4682/R

BREVOORT, James Renwick (1832-1918) American
$2750	£1786	Landscape with figure (83x63cm-33x25in) s. 9-Sep-93 Sotheby's Arcade, New York #18/R
$6000	£3947	Vicinity of Farmington, Connecticut (27x51cm-11x20in) s.d.67. 31-Mar-93 Sotheby's Arcade, New York #32/R
$6000	£3468	Fishing on the pond (37x56cm-15x22in) s. 23-Sep-92 Christie's, New York #69/R
$9000	£5696	Late summer fishing (35x70cm-14x28in) s.d.68. 4-Dec-92 Christie's, New York #191/R

BREVOORT, James Renwick (attrib) (1832-1918) American
$1050	£528	West Point on Hudson (56x91cm-22x36in) init. 6-Sep-92 Litchfield Auction Gallery #141a

BREWER, Adrian (1891-1956) American
$1300	£872	Grove of trees at dawn (91x76cm-36x30in) s.d.25. 3-Feb-94 Sloan, North Bethesda #2038/R

BREWER, Nicholas Richard (1857-1949) American
$550	£369	Winter landscape (30x46cm-12x18in) s. s.d.1912verso panel. 3-Feb-94 Sloan, North Bethesda #1654
$600	£403	Still life (51x41cm-20x16in) s.d.1901. 5-Mar-94 Louisiana Auction Exchange #160/R
$625	£419	Harbour view at dusk (30x46cm-12x18in) s.i.d.9/23/12verso panel. 3-Feb-94 Sloan, North Bethesda #1653
$850	£570	Sunset (46x56cm-18x22in) s.i.d.1913verso. 3-Feb-94 Sloan, North Bethesda #2039/R
$1000	£654	Harvest time (64x76cm-25x30in) s. 30-Oct-92 Sloan, North Bethesda #2171
$1600	£1119	Shadows of Capistrano (91x71cm-36x28in) s. i.stretcher. 5-Feb-93 Sloan, North Bethesda #2208/R

BREWERTON, George Douglas (1820-1901) American
$1400	£940	Scenes and coastal scene (91x38cm-36x15in) s. pastel three. 24-Mar-94 Mystic Fine Arts, Connecticut #83
$2400	£1579	Mountainous river landscape (91x76cm-36x30in) s. pastel paper on canvas. 2-Jun-93 Doyle, New York #33

BREWSTER, Anna Richards (1870-1952) American
$1400	£915	Point Judith Breakwater (36x51cm-14x20in) s. 17-Sep-93 Skinner, Bolton #219/R
$1500	£1007	Sunset at Biskra (15x41cm-6x16in) s. 6-Dec-93 Grogan, Massachussetts #509

BREWSTER, John (jnr) (1766-1854) American
$62000	£41611	Portrait of a young boy (58x48cm-23x19in) 25-Mar-94 Eldred, Massachusetts #923/R

BREWSTER, John (jnr-attrib) (1766-1854) American
$2200	£1447	Portrait of Mrs Lewis (81x66cm-32x26in) 2-Jun-93 Doyle, New York #35
$11000	£7237	Portrait of Captain Lewis (79x66cm-31x26in) 2-Jun-93 Doyle, New York #34/R

BRICHER, Alfred Thompson (1837-1908) American
$1196	£797	The City of Saint Paul, Dubuque (20x36cm-8x14in) 23-May-94 Christie's, East, New York #51/R
$1900	£1098	Ships off rocky coast (23x33cm-9x13in) s. board. 25-Sep-92 Sotheby's Arcade, New York #56/R
$2750	£1833	Landscape with grazing cows by a stream (20x15cm-8x6in) init.d.63 board. 26-May-94 Sloan, North Bethesda #2119/R
$3500	£2244	River landscape (25x20cm-10x8in) s.d.64. 9-Dec-92 Butterfield & Butterfield, San Francisco #3842/R
$5500	£3691	Narragansett Bay (23x46cm-9x18in) s. board. 6-Dec-93 Grogan, Massachussetts #434/R
$6000	£3974	Autumn at Lake George (23x45cm-9x18in) board. 22-Sep-93 Christie's, New York #7/R
$7000	£4698	Forest brook (36x56cm-14x22in) s. painted c.1865. 6-Dec-93 Grogan, Massachussetts #432/R
$7500	£5245	Wintry day (23x18cm-9x7in) init.d.62 board. 11-Mar-93 Christie's, New York #41a/R
$8000	£5128	Autumn on lake (18x31cm-7x12in) init.d.66. 26-May-93 Christie's, New York #7/R
$9000	£5882	Beach at sunset, vessels in distance (25x36cm-10x14in) s. 17-Sep-93 Skinner, Bolton #190/R
$10000	£6536	Grand Manan with sailboat (23x43cm-9x17in) s. canvas on board. 18-Sep-93 Young Fine Arts Auctions, Maine #46/R
$10000	£6623	Low tide (46x99cm-18x39in) s. 23-Sep-93 Sotheby's, New York #177/R
$11000	£7233	Seascape, Newport, Rhode Island (23x46cm-9x18in) s. i.verso board. 17-Mar-94 Sotheby's, New York #41/R
$18000	£11921	Beached rowboat (46x91cm-18x36in) s. 23-Sep-93 Sotheby's, New York #13/R
$20000	£13423	Winter landscape (23x46cm-9x18in) s.d.66 board. 2-Dec-93 Sotheby's, New York #23/R
$31000	£20667	Along the coast (46x99cm-18x39in) mono. painted late 1880s. 25-May-94 Sotheby's, New York #34/R
$32500	£20833	Summer afternoon, Long Island (56x81cm-22x32in) s. painted c.1882. 27-May-93 Sotheby's, New York #190/R
$37000	£24832	Newport Beach (31x61cm-12x24in) s.d.72. 3-Dec-93 Christie's, New York #109/R
$52500	£33654	Evening at Scituate - low tide (38x84cm-15x33in) s. 27-May-93 Sotheby's, New York #158/R
$55000	£36913	Headlands (43x91cm-17x36in) s. 3-Dec-93 Christie's, New York #94/R
$57500	£40210	Afternoon at the shore (30x51cm-12x20in) mono painted early 1880's panel. 10-Mar-93 Sotheby's, New York #19/R
$57500	£36392	New England landscape in autumn (50x106cm-20x42in) s.d.85. 3-Dec-92 Sotheby's, New York #35/R

BRICHER, Alfred Thompson (1837-1908) American-cont.
$750	£504	The Hopper - marine scene (25x59cm-10x23in) sig.i.d.24 W/C graphite paperboard. 4-Mar-94 Skinner, Bolton #213/R
$800	£503	Steamer at sea (23x51cm-9x20in) s. W/C. 22-Apr-93 Freeman Fine Arts, Philadelphia #1296 a
$800	£423	Morning Calm (30x51cm-12x20in) mono. W/C gouache. 11-Sep-92 Skinner, Bolton #148/R
$1300	£878	Rocky beach (25x55cm-10x22in) s. W/C paper on board. 31-Mar-94 Sotheby's Arcade, New York #28/R
$1300	£850	Rocky coastline, lighthouse and vessels in distance (48x86cm-19x34in) s. W/C graphite gouache board. 17-Sep-93 Skinner, Bolton #188/R
$1500	£1027	Summer landscape (13x28cm-5x11in) s.d.1874 W/C gouache. 10-Feb-94 Skinner, Bolton #153
$1800	£1184	On the Esopus Creek (23x33cm-9x13in) mono.d.1875 i.verso W/C paper on board. 2-Jun-93 Doyle, New York #36
$2000	£1299	Seascape (23x46cm-9x18in) s. W/C paper on paper. 9-Sep-93 Sotheby's Arcade, New York #132
$2600	£1711	Rocky coast (25x67cm-10x26in) s. W/C pencil paper on board. 31-Mar-93 Sotheby's Arcade, New York #87/R
$3900	£2468	Seashore with rocky point in background (23x53cm-9x21in) s.W/C. 5-Dec-92 Louisiana Auction Exchange #132/R
$4000	£2649	Boats moored along tidal river (25x53cm-10x21in) s. W/C gouache pencil painted 1880's. 23-Sep-93 Sotheby's, New York #60/R
$4200	£2781	Lighthouse (53x37cm-21x15in) s. W/C. 22-Sep-93 Christie's, New York #37/R
$5000	£3333	The daisy field (37x53cm-15x21in) mono. W/C paper on board. 16-Mar-94 Christie's, New York #44/R
$6000	£4000	A showery day - Narragansett Pier (23x54cm-9x21in) s. execute c.1871. 17-Mar-94 Sotheby's, New York #40/R
$10000	£6410	Far Rockaway Beach (25x53cm-10x21in) init. W/C pencil paper on board. 26-May-93 Christie's, New York #32/R
$20000	£12658	Low tide (36x52cm-14x20in) s.d.1880 W/C gouache. 4-Dec-92 Christie's, New York #220/R

BRIDGES, Charles (attrib) (fl.1730-1750) American
$3250	£2181	Portrait of a lady (76x64cm-30x25in) 6-Feb-94 Skinner, Bolton #194/R

BRIDGES, Fidelia (1834-1923) American
$1900	£1234	Landscape with bird (19x15cm-7x6in) s.d.1872 W/C. 9-Sep-93 Sotheby's Arcade, New York #23/R

BRIDGES, Fidelia (attrib) (1834-1923) American
$660	£431	Blue birds with nest among raspberries and Morning Glories (33x23cm-13x9in) W/C gouache. 14-May-93 Skinner, Bolton #44/R

BRIDGMAN, Frederick Arthur (1847-1928) American
$698	£469	North African bay with sailing boats at evening (27x46cm-11x18in) s. 3-Dec-93 Michael Zeller, Lindau #1476/R (DM 1200)
$800	£471	Caravan a Bou-Saada (29x42cm-11x17in) s.i.d.1920 board. 3-Oct-92 Weschler, Washington #115/R
$800	£526	Brittany peasant (38x33cm-15x13in) s. 5-Jun-93 Louisiana Auction Exchange #113/R
$1328	£885	La lavandiere (40x65cm-16x26in) s. 27-May-94 Ferri, Paris #55 (F.FR 7500)
$4000	£2759	Entrance to mosque (55x46cm-22x18in) s. 17-Feb-93 Sotheby's, New York #152/R
$4250	£2724	Relaxing among trees and flowers (46x89cm-18x35in) s. 9-Dec-92 Butterfield & Butterfield, San Francisco #3899/R
$4430	£2954	Mediterranean bay with sailing boat at anchor (43x65cm-17x26in) s. 31-May-94 AB Stockholms Auktionsverk, Stockholm #5398/R (S.KR 35000)
$4500	£2601	La Cigale (105x55cm-41x2in) s.d.1882. 25-Sep-92 Sotheby's Arcade, New York #110/R
$6000	£3846	Rue Droite, dans le vieux Nice (54x67cm-21x26in) s.i. 26-May-93 Sotheby's, New York #145/R
$6000	£4000	Veiled beauty (35x27cm-14x11in) s.d.1882. 25-May-94 Christie's, New York #54/R
$6055	£4064	Sailing vessel at anchor in Mediterranean bay (43x65cm-17x26in) s. 29-Nov-93 AB Stockholms Auktionsverk, Stockholm #5546/R (S.KR 51000)
$8500	£5862	Arab women at town wall (50x73cm-20x29in) s.d.1925. 17-Feb-93 Sotheby's, New York #155/R
$9000	£5769	At running brook (46x90cm-18x35in) s. 26-May-93 Christie's, New York #76/R
$9500	£6376	Prayer beside tomb (46x55cm-18x22in) s.i. 14-Oct-93 Christie's, New York #376/R
$10000	£6536	Calm coast of Algiers (55x114cm-22x45in) s. 29-Oct-92 Sotheby's, New York #231/R
$10474	£6936	View of town, possibly Tunis (43x77cm-17x30in) s. 29-Sep-93 Dorotheum, Vienna #79/R (A.S 120000)
$13000	£8497	Last glow, Tangiers (54x91cm-21x36in) s. 29-Oct-92 Sotheby's, New York #232/R
$16000	£10267	In the Arab quarter (21x27cm-8x11in) s.d.1885 panel. 26-May-94 Sotheby's, New York #67/R
$16170	£11000	At the oasis (52x74cm-20x29in) s. 19-Nov-93 Christie's, London #117 a/R
$17000	£11409	La Nubie (61x93cm-24x37in) s.i. 14-Oct-93 Christie's, New York #374/R
$18000	£12081	Le bivouac (82x100cm-32x39in) s.i. 14-Oct-93 Christie's, New York #373/R
$20000	£13699	Arab village (46x74cm-18x29in) s.d.79. 15-Feb-94 Christie's, New York #19/R
$20000	£13072	Young Moorish girl in the Algerian countryside (76x49cm-30x19in) s.i.indis.d.188. 30-Oct-92 Christie's, New York #31/R
$30000	£20134	Tete-a-tete (38x48cm-15x19in) s. 14-Oct-93 Christie's, New York #375/R
$35000	£22436	The first steps (39x55cm-15x22in) s.d.1878. 27-May-93 Christie's, New York #44/R
$38000	£24837	Domestic interior scene (60x93cm-24x37in) s. 30-Oct-92 Christie's, New York #28/R
$55000	£35256	In a village at El Biar, Algiers (83x117cm-33x46in) s. 27-May-93 Christie's, New York #41/R

BRIGANTI, Nicholas P (1895-1989) American

$648	£438	Venise la Punta de la Dogana (36x51cm-14x20in) s. 5-Nov-93 Ader Tajan, Paris #110 (F.FR 3800)
$650	£419	Venetian canal scene (51x76cm-20x30in) s. 13-Jul-94 Boos Gallery, Michigan #52/R
$850	£556	Venetian canal (61x46cm-24x18in) s. 16-May-93 Hindman Galleries, Chicago #110
$1000	£667	Venice (61x91cm-24x36in) s. 23-May-94 Christie's, East, New York #72/R
$1000	£633	Venetian canal scene (51x71cm-20x28in) s. 2-Dec-92 Boos Gallery, Michigan #803/R
$1133	£750	Venice (51x76cm-20x30in) s. 26-Nov-92 Christie's, S. Kensington #51
$1200	£789	Venetian canal scene (51x71cm-20x28in) s. 7-Apr-93 Doyle, New York #8
$1300	£855	Venetian canal (61x91cm-24x36in) s. 31-Mar-93 Sotheby's Arcade, New York #79/R
$1750	£1151	Mediterranean coast (61x91cm-24x36in) s. 31-Mar-93 Sotheby's Arcade, New York #72 a/R
$1911	£1300	Venice (52x70cm-20x28in) s. 18-Nov-93 Christie's, S. Kensington #143/R
$2300	£1513	Grand Canal, Venice (46x103cm-18x41in) s. 31-Mar-93 Sotheby's Arcade, New York #80/R
$2400	£1569	View of Doges Palace, Venice (71x102cm-28x40in) s. 4-May-93 Christie's, East, New York #140/R

BRIGDEN, Frederick Henry (1871-1956) Canadian

$1812	£1208	Horseback at Lake Louis (61x71cm-24x28in) s. 6-Jun-94 Waddingtons, Toronto #1287/R (C.D 2500)
$467	£311	Haying scene on an Ontario farm (26x36cm-10x14in) s. W/C. 30-May-94 Ritchie, Toronto #243/R (C.D 650)
$584	£387	Woodland stream (36x30cm-14x12in) s. W/C. 18-Nov-92 Sotheby's, Toronto #286 (C.D 750)
$642	£434	View of a lake (22x31cm-9x12in) s. W/C. 23-Nov-93 Joyner Fine Art, Toronto #168 (C.D 850)
$642	£434	On the Rouge River (24x32cm-9x13in) s. W/C. 23-Nov-93 Joyner Fine Art, Toronto #153 (C.D 850)
$831	£561	Birches by a lake (29x39cm-11x15in) s. W/C. 23-Nov-93 Joyner Fine Art, Toronto #82/R (C.D 1100)
$865	£547	The Haywagon approaching the bridge (38x53cm-15x21in) s. W/C. 1-Dec-92 Fraser Pinneys, Quebec #13/R (C.D 1100)

BRIGGLE, A van (19/20th C) American

$1300	£850	Group of Indians coursing through winter landscape (41x56cm-16x22in) s. 7-Oct-93 Freeman Fine Arts, Philadelphia #984

BRIGGS, C W (19th C) American

$2000	£1361	Still life with playing cards and newspaper (46x61cm-18x24in) s.d.2.88. 14-Apr-94 Freeman Fine Arts, Philadelphia #967/R

BRINLEY, Daniel Putnam (1879-1963) American

$600	£403	On the road through the village (48x61cm-19x24in) s.d.54 masonite. 4-Mar-94 Skinner, Bolton #284/R

BRISCOE, Franklin D (1844-1903) American

$650	£433	Coastal view (61x46cm-24x18in) s. 26-May-94 Sloan, North Bethesda #2139
$700	£455	French sailing ship in choppy seas (36x28cm-14x11in) s.d.95 board on board. 9-Sep-93 Sotheby's Arcade, New York #112/R
$1000	£578	Rough seas (15x20cm-6x8in) s. board. 24-Sep-92 Mystic Fine Arts, Connecticut #141/A
$1100	£705	Ships at sea (18x28cm-7x11in) s. board. 17-Dec-92 Mystic Fine Arts, Connecticut #49/R
$1500	£1027	Rough seas (36x28cm-14x11in) s.d.95 board. 19-Feb-94 Young Fine Arts Auctions, Maine #48/R
$1600	£1067	Rocky seascapes (46x35cm-18x14in) s. one d.76 one indist.d. pair. 21-May-94 Weschler, Washington #82/R
$1800	£1176	View of Grand Canal, Venice (51x91cm-20x36in) s. 4-May-93 Christie's, East, New York #137/R
$2100	£1364	Sunset in the tropics (37x69cm-15x27in) s.d.1870 s.i.d.verso. 9-Sep-93 Sotheby's Arcade, New York #59 a/R
$2250	£1461	Tropical idyll (38x69cm-15x27in) s. s.i.d.1870verso. 9-Sep-93 Sotheby's Arcade, New York #105 a/R
$3000	£1974	Sailors caught in gale (25x51cm-10x20in) s.d.96 canvas on board. 31-Mar-93 Sotheby's Arcade, New York #22/R
$3200	£2119	Drawing in nets - fisherfolk on shore (76x127cm-30x50in) s.d.1894. 13-Nov-92 Skinner, Bolton #54/R
$4000	£2797	Off the wreck (22x33cm-9x13in) s. s.i.verso board. 11-Mar-93 Christie's, New York #66/R
$4200	£2745	On fishing banks. Breezy weather (12x18cm-5x7in) s. s.i.d.1885 verso panel pair. 4-May-93 Christie's, East, New York #48/R
$5000	£3311	Fishing boat run aground (76x127cm-30x50in) s.d.1874. 22-Sep-93 Christie's, New York #31/R
$6000	£3468	Returning with catch in stormy sea (76x128cm-30x50in) s. 24-Sep-92 Sotheby's, New York #31/R

BRISTOL, John Bunyan (1826-1909) American

$970	£660	Lake landscape (45x75cm-18x30in) s. 16-Apr-94 AB Stockholms Auktionsverk (Lilla Kvaliten) #4284 (S.KR 7700)
$1300	£867	Sunset with palm trees (32x52cm-13x20in) s.d.64. 17-May-94 Christie's, East, New York #517
$2000	£1316	Seesaw in the orchard (46x76cm-18x30in) s. 2-Jun-93 Doyle, New York #37
$2400	£1622	Playing seesaw (47x76cm-19x30in) s. 31-Mar-94 Sotheby's Arcade, New York #59/R

BRITO, Carlos de (20th C) Brazilian
$946   £639   Arlequin (120x85cm-47x33in) s.d.88 i.verso. 20-Oct-93 Galerie Dobiaschofsky, Bern #155/R (S.FR 1400)

BRITO, Maria (1947-) Cuban
$4200   £2800   The fool (49x54cm-19x21in) s.d.1991 panel. 18-May-94 Christie's, New York #232/R

BRITTAIN, Miller Gore (1912-1968) Canadian
$1665   £1088   Floating blue figure (61x41cm-24x16in) init.d.54 board. 19-May-93 Sotheby's, Toronto #330/R (C.D 2100)
$935   £615   Portrait of woman (36x23cm-14x9in) init.d.62 conte dr pastel htd white tempera. 7-Jun-93 Ritchie, Toronto #190/R (C.D 1200)

BRODERSON, Morris (1928-) American
$1300   £751   Reimei Kurama Yama (140x183cm-55x72in) s.d.1962-63. 25-Sep-92 Sotheby's Arcade, New York #504/R

BRODIE, Gandy (1924-1975) American
$2400   £1667   Untitled (122x182cm-48x72in) s.i.d.1963verso. 22-Feb-93 Christie's, East, New York #144/R

BROE, Vern (20th C) American
$600   £403   Catboats (51x61cm-20x24in) board. 25-Mar-94 Eldred, Massachusetts #288
$650   £442   Catboats (30x41cm-12x16in) s. board. 19-Nov-93 Eldred, Massachusetts #932
$825   £558   Catboats (28x38cm-11x15in) s. board. 30-Jul-93 Eldred, Massachusetts #261/R
$900   £604   Yachting scene (48x76cm-19x30in) s. masonite. 25-Mar-94 Eldred, Massachusetts #114/R

BROMLEY, Frank C (19th C) American
$1200   £839   Morning L. Is. Sound (36x48cm-14x19in) s. s.i.d.1884verso. 12-Mar-93 Skinner, Bolton #148/R

BROOK, Alexander (1898-1980) American
$650   £428   Figure (28x23cm-11x9in) s.d.40 s.verso. 31-Mar-93 Sotheby's Arcade, New York #427
$1800   £1139   Still life with flowers, fruit and urn (76x61cm-30x24in) s.d.1927. 2-Dec-92 Christie's, East, New York #340/R
$2000   £1156   View of the Savannah River (33x23cm-13x9in) s. 23-Sep-92 Christie's, New York #263/R

BROOKER, Bertram (1888-1955) Canadian
$680   £459   Plante's barn (29x37cm-11x15in) s. board. 23-Nov-93 Joyner Fine Art, Toronto #130 (C.D 900)
$1557   £1031   Muskoka (25x32cm-10x13in) canvasboard painted 1925. 24-Nov-92 Joyner Fine Art, Toronto #187/R (C.D 2000)
$2718   £1837   Vegetables (40x50cm-16x20in) s. 23-Nov-93 Joyner Fine Art, Toronto #180/R (C.D 3600)
$642   £434   Three dancers (37x28cm-15x11in) W/C ink executed c.1948. 23-Nov-93 Joyner Fine Art, Toronto #251 (C.D 850)
$856   £567   Spreading forms (37x27cm-15x11in) s. W/C. 24-Nov-92 Joyner Fine Art, Toronto #15/R (C.D 1100)

BROOKES, Samuel Marsden (1816-1892) American
$950   £642   Still life of birds (35x28cm-14x11in) s.d.1868 board on board oval. 20-Mar-93 Weschler, Washington #83/R
$1800   £1192   Hanging game (46x3cm-18x1in) s. 15-Jun-94 Butterfield & Butterfield, San Francisco #4602/R
$6500   £4392   Still life with fish (51x61cm-20x24in) s. 31-Mar-94 Sotheby's Arcade, New York #44/R
$11000   £7383   Hanging California salmon (81x51cm-32x20in) s. 8-Dec-93 Butterfield & Butterfield, San Francisco #3347/R

BROOKS, Allan (1869-1946) Canadian
$800   £526   Madagascan white backed duck, masked duck (28x36cm-11x14in) s.i.d. gouache paper on board. 4-Nov-92 Doyle, New York #10/R
$850   £559   Bronze winged duck, crested duck (28x36cm-11x14in) s. i.verso gouache paper on board. 4-Nov-92 Doyle, New York #9/R
$1057   £714   Canada geese in flight. Foraging for worms (35x48cm-14x19in) s.d.1936 W/C pair. 23-Nov-93 Fraser Pinneys, Quebec #428 (C.D 1400)
$1057   £714   Ducks in flight. Ducks approaching lake (35x48cm-14x19in) s.d.1936 W/C pair. 23-Nov-93 Fraser Pinneys, Quebec #427 (C.D 1400)
$1100   £724   Falcated teal (25x36cm-10x14in) s. gouache paper on board. 4-Nov-92 Doyle, New York #14/R
$1200   £789   Tuffed duck, New Zealand scaup (25x36cm-10x14in) s. i.verso gouache paper on board. 4-Nov-92 Doyle, New York #11/R
$1300   £855   Garganey teal (28x36cm-11x14in) s. gouache paper on board. 4-Nov-92 Doyle, New York #15/R

BROOKS, Cora S (?-1930) American
$4000   £2597   Afternoon stroll (51x65cm-20x26in) s. painted c.1915. 9-Sep-93 Sotheby's Arcade, New York #126/R

BROOKS, Frank Leonard (1911-) Canadian
$619   £413   Yellow Ascendant (90x75cm-35x30in) s. acrylic collage. 13-May-94 Joyner Fine Art, Toronto #194 (C.D 850)

BROOKS, Frank Leonard (1911-) Canadian-cont.
$1557   £1031   Thema Japones (79x58cm-31x23in) s. i.d.1977verso acrylic collage canvas.
                  18-Nov-92 Sotheby's, Toronto #147/R (C.D 2000)

BROOKS, James (1906-1992) American
$2100   £1409   Newby II (40x53cm-16x21in) s. s.i.verso acrylic. 24-Feb-94 Sotheby's Arcade, New
                  York #363/R
$5000   £3356   Persolis (193x193cm-76x76in) s. s.i.d.1973 verso acrylic. 12-Dec-93 Hindman
                  Galleries, Chicago #326
$5500   £2865   Eames (66x76cm-26x30in) s. s.d.1968 verso. 5-Aug-92 Boos Gallery, Michigan #539/R
$6500   £4362   Noorcon (89x144cm-35x57in) s. s.i.d.1961 verso. 25-Feb-94 Sotheby's, New York
                  #11/R
$9250   £6208   Axiola (91x86cm-36x34in) s. s.i.d.1963verso. 5-May-94 Sotheby's, New York #110/R
$12000   £8333   Ipswich (152x91cm-60x36in) s. s.i.d.80verso acrylic. 23-Feb-93 Sotheby's, New
                  York #234/R
$19000   £13194   Token (152x183cm-60x72in) s. s.i.d.81verso acrylic. 23-Feb-93 Sotheby's, New York
                  #219/R
$2000   £1325   Untitled (39x51cm-15x20in) s.d.64 brush ink crayons acrylic paper on board.
                  17-Nov-92 Christie's, East, New York #266/R

BROOKS, Nicholas Alden (fl.1880-1914) American
$750   £503   Extensive landscape (41x61cm-16x24in) s. 24-Mar-94 Mystic Fine Arts, Connecticut
                  #100 a

BROOKS, Romaine (1874-1970) American
$3500   £2023   Portrait de la Contesse Anna de Noailles (35x27cm-14x11in) s. 23-Sep-92
                  Christie's, New York #192/R

BROWN, Abigail Keyes (1891-?) American
$800   £423   The old timer (76x91cm-30x36in) s. 11-Sep-92 Skinner, Bolton #222/R

BROWN, Benjamin Chambers (1865-1942) American
$1100   £728   Landscape - probably Owens Valley (15x23cm-6x9in) s.i. canvasboard. 14-Jun-94
                  John Moran, Pasadena #5 a
$1700   £1149   Near Arcadia, California (30x41cm-12x16in) s. board. 15-Jun-93 John Moran,
                  Pasadena #35
$3250   £2181   Sunny canal, Venice (51x41cm-20x16in) s. 8-Dec-93 Butterfield & Butterfield, San
                  Francisco #3473/R
$3750   £2604   Near Elsinore, Dark Canyon (30x40cm-12x16in) s. canvasboard. 7-Mar-93 Butterfield
                  & Butterfield, San Francisco #146/R
$4000   £2312   Golden evening (41x51cm-16x20in) s. 21-Sep-92 Selkirks, St. Louis #335/R
$4250   £2872   Foggy morning San Francisco (41x51cm-16x20in) s. i.stretcher. 9-Nov-93 John
                  Moran, Pasadena #876
$7500   £4967   South Fork - San Gabriel (64x76cm-25x30in) s. 14-Jun-94 John Moran, Pasadena #85
$450   £300   A river in California (13x20cm-5x8in) W/C. 15-Mar-94 John Moran, Pasadena #139
$500   £333   Santa Sophia (23x33cm-9x13in) s.d.9.22.37 W/C. 15-Mar-94 John Moran,
                  Pasadena #75
$1100   £764   Venetian scene (23x33cm-9x13in) s. W/C. 7-Mar-93 Butterfield & Butterfield, San
                  Francisco #184/R

BROWN, C Emerson (1869-?) American
$1050   £729   Newburyport marshes (36x51cm-14x20in) s. 27-Feb-93 Young Fine Arts Auctions,
                  Maine #56/R

BROWN, Carlyle (1919-1964) American
$950   £634   Bouquet and candle (81x61cm-32x24in) s.d.62 s.i.d.1962 verso. 23-May-94
                  Christie's, East, New York #240/R

BROWN, Christopher (20th C) American
$2500   £1582   Swimmer (165x203cm-65x80in) 25-Oct-92 Butterfield & Butterfield, San Francisco
                  #2378/R

BROWN, George Loring (1814-1889) American
$1800   £1259   Stormy day (56x91cm-22x36in) s. 11-Mar-93 Mystic Fine Arts, Connecticut #173
$4667   £3153   View of Palermo (48x81cm-19x32in) s.i.d.1856 i.verso. 9-Nov-93 Galerie Fischer,
                  Lucerne #3170/R (S.FR 7000)
$7000   £4965   Roman sunset in July (150x89cm-59x35in) canvas on board. 12-Feb-93 Douglas, South
                  Deerfield #2
$7000   £4667   Bishops homestead, Medford, Massachusetts (27x38cm-11x15in) s.d.1861 paper laid
                  down on canvas. 26-May-94 Christie's, New York #6/R
$450   £302   Farm in a valley (13x15cm-5x6in) s. W/C. 5-Mar-94 Louisiana Auction Exchange
                  #68/R

BROWN, Harley (1939-) Canadian
$528   £359   Indian portrait (55x46cm-22x18in) s. chl. 15-Nov-93 Hodgins, Calgary #49/R (C.D 700)
$1412   £923   Untitled - native portrait (61x46cm-24x18in) s. pastel. 10-May-93 Hodgins,
                  Calgary #325/R (C.D 1800)

BROWN, Harrison B (1831-1915) American
$2200   £1467   Along the coastline (33x61cm-13x24in) init.d.66. 23-May-94 Christie's, East, New
                  York #67/R
$2200   £1497   Man fishing by waterfall (13x17cm-5x7in) s.d.60. 10-Jul-93 Young Fine Arts
                  Auctions, Maine #62/R
$2500   £1634   Crystal Cascade, Pinkham Notch (61x36cm-24x14in) s.indis.d. 18-Sep-93 Young Fine
                  Arts Auctions, Maine #49/R

BROWN, Harrison B (1831-1915) American-cont.
$3750	£2451	Mt. Washington from Conway Meadows (36x61cm-14x24in) painted c.1875. 8-May-93 Young Fine Arts Auctions, Maine #52/R
$6000	£4082	Venice (15x27cm-6x11in) s.d.75. 10-Jul-93 Young Fine Arts Auctions, Maine #61/R
$10000	£6803	View of the White Mountains (25x42cm-10x17in) 10-Jul-93 Young Fine Arts Auctions, Maine #60/R
$14500	£9864	White mountains from the Conway Valley (25x42cm-10x17in) s.d.1863. 10-Jul-93 Young Fine Arts Auctions, Maine #59/R
$15000	£10204	Wagon and oxen crossing the Saco River (25x42cm-10x17in) s.d.1861. 10-Jul-93 Young Fine Arts Auctions, Maine #58/R

BROWN, James (1951-) American
$4470	£3000	Red Salt XIV (84x60cm-33x24in) s.d.1989verso linen laid down on canvas. 3-Dec-93 Sotheby's, London #294/R
$4768	£3200	Red Salt VIII (113x61cm-44x24in) s.d.1989verso linen laid down on canvas. 3-Dec-93 Sotheby's, London #292/R
$5000	£3356	Blue winter salt I (99x79cm-39x31in) s.i.d.1990verso tempera cardboard on canvas. 3-May-94 Christie's, East, New York #192/R
$5500	£3642	Scene from the life of Achilles (102x102cm-40x40in) s.i.d.1985verso. 19-Nov-92 Christie's, New York #221/R
$6718	£4306	Black and blue (106x96cm-42x38in) s.i.d.1991 acrylic panel. 12-Dec-92 Catherine Charbonneaux, Paris #125 (F.FR 36000)
$7000	£4698	White stabat mater (123x108cm-48x43in) dispersion linen painted 1989. 25-Feb-94 Sotheby's, New York #164/R
$20000	£13423	Untitled (244x168cm-96x66in) s.d.1982verso. 4-May-94 Christie's, New York #403/R
$38339	£25731	Masque (150x140cm-59x55in) s.d.1983verso acrylic. 21-Mar-94 Guy Loudmer, Paris #60/R (F.FR 220000)
$557	*£350*	*Composition (56x56cm-22x22in) init. W/C. 20-Apr-93 Bukowskis, Stockholm #282/R (S.KR 4000)*
$804	*£536*	*Pale coral (100x70cm-39x28in) init.d.VIII.VII s.i.d.verso gouache. 31-May-94 Christie's, Amsterdam #193 (D.FL 1500)*
$804	*£536*	*Five sorrowful mysteries V (100x70cm-39x28in) init.d.VIII VII s.i.d.verso W/C. 31-May-94 Christie's, Amsterdam #194 (D.FL 1500)*
$6000	£4027	White Stabat Mater (89x68cm-35x27in) s.d.1989verso dispersion fabric paper collage. 3-May-94 Christie's, East, New York #195/R
$8000	£5369	Stabat mater (130x90cm-51x35in) s.i.d.1988verso lead oil nails panel. 4-May-94 Christie's, New York #413/R
$8500	£5705	Stella Mares I (206x198cm-81x78in) s.i.d.1985 verso enamel stain on canvas. 25-Feb-94 Sotheby's, New York #148/R
$9500	£6376	The five glorious mysteries II (191x134cm-75x53in) s.d.1987verso oil graphite nails copper. 4-May-94 Christie's, New York #399/R
$10493	£7042	Egyptian series (121x91cm-48x36in) s.d.1984 verso pencil col.crayons gouache. 8-Dec-93 Christie's, Amsterdam #372/R (D.FL 20000)
$13751	£9167	Senza titolo (152x137cm-60x54in) enamel pencil canvas executed 1982. 23-May-94 Christie's, Milan #240/R (I.L 22000000)
$17501	£11667	Black man (213x154cm-84x61in) s.d.1980 enamel. 23-May-94 Christie's, Milan #236/R (I.L 28000000)
$21876	£14584	Poison good and the ha ian things (290x167cm-114x66in) oil enamel pencil canvas executed 1982. 23-May-94 Christie's, Milan #228/R (I.L 35000000)
$22000	£14570	Untitled (153x137cm-60x54in) s.d.1983 enamel oil graphite canvas. 19-Nov-92 Christie's, New York #222/R
$24000	£16667	Horse shoes and crosses that's good luck (213x198cm-84x78in) enamel graphite canvas painted 1982. 24-Feb-93 Christie's, New York #138/R

BROWN, James Francis (1862-1935) American
$900	£570	Viewing an auction exhibition (62x46cm-24x18in) s.d.90. 2-Dec-92 Christie's, East, New York #144/R

BROWN, Joan (1938-1990) American
$1700	£1076	Portrait of Modesto (91x76cm-36x30in) s.d.1978 verso. 25-Oct-92 Butterfield & Butterfield, San Francisco #2322/R
$4000	£2564	Reaching for that chicken at Jack's (142x132cm-56x52in) s.i.d.1960verso. 13-Dec-92 Hindman Galleries, Chicago #79/R
$6000	£3797	Figure study (72x114cm-28x45in) init.d.73 acrylic paper. 25-Oct-92 Butterfield & Butterfield, San Francisco #2310/R
$9000	£5696	Running at McAteer Track (197x243cm-78x96in) s.d.1976 verso. 25-Oct-92 Butterfield & Butterfield, San Francisco #2323/R
$25000	£16892	Sun over Contraption (139x135cm-55x53in) s.i.d.4.60verso. 21-Apr-94 Butterfield & Butterfield, San Francisco #1131
$25000	£16340	People and eye-trees in park in Madrid (183x244cm-72x96in) s.d.10/13/61 verso. 4-May-93 Sotheby's, New York #337/R
$31000	£21528	Things in landscape 2 (188x183cm-74x72in) s.i.d.8/10/59verso. 26-Feb-93 Sotheby's Arcade, New York #289/R
$1200	*£759*	*Vandarecca (29x37cm-11x15in) s.i.d.7/11/76 pastel. 25-Oct-92 Butterfield & Butterfield, San Francisco #2311/R*
$3750	*£2358*	*Untitled (101x66cm-40x26in) mixed media paper laid down on board. 25-Apr-93 Butterfield & Butterfield, San Francisco #2111/R*
$22000	£14379	Reclining nude (76x102cm-30x40in) gouache paperboard painted 1961. 4-May-93 Sotheby's, New York #340/R

BROWN, John Appleton (1844-1902) American
$1200	£816	Mist rising from the sea (17x23cm-7x9in) s. 10-Jul-93 Young Fine Arts Auctions, Maine #63
$1600	£1074	Along the lakeshore, sunset (56x82cm-22x32in) s.d.76. 4-Mar-94 Skinner, Bolton #246/R

BROWN, John Appleton (1844-1902) American-cont.
$1900	£1250	Bend in the pasture stream (46x61cm-18x24in) s. 2-Jun-93 Doyle, New York #39
$2400	£1611	Apple blossoms (51x69cm-20x27in) s. 29-Nov-93 Stonington Fine Arts, Stonington #130/R
$2900	£1946	Autumn lake (43x53cm-17x21in) s. 6-Dec-93 Grogan, Massachussetts #505/R
$4750	£2794	Stream through woods (79x107cm-31x42in) s. 5-Oct-92 Grogan, Massachussetts #701/R
$6000	£3947	Old road near Paris (62x88cm-24x35in) s. 13-Jun-93 Butterfield & Butterfield, San Francisco #3145/R
$850	£582	View probably from Joppa Flats across Merrimac River (25x36cm-10x14in) s. pastel. 19-Feb-94 Young Fine Arts Auctions, Maine #49/R
$1500	£1007	Flowering trees (33x43cm-13x17in) s. pastel. 6-Dec-93 Grogan, Massachussetts #508/R
$2750	£1923	Sheep meadow (36x48cm-14x19in) s. pastel paper on board. 12-Mar-93 Skinner, Bolton #167/R

BROWN, John George (1831-1913) American
$1900	£1250	Two children in woods (18x15cm-7x6in) s.verso. 31-Mar-93 Sotheby's Arcade, New York #59/R
$3600	£2400	Seated lady (33x25cm-13x10in) s.d.1864 canvas on masonite. 17-May-94 Grogan, Massachussetts #336/R
$4250	£2500	Self-portrait (64x51cm-25x20in) s.d.1897. 8-Oct-92 Freeman Fine Arts, Philadelphia #951
$4500	£2980	Young girl with flowers (62x41cm-24x16in) s.d.1888. 23-Sep-93 Sotheby's, New York #74/R
$5000	£3311	Lull in business (61x41cm-24x16in) s. 23-Sep-93 Sotheby's, New York #44/R
$5000	£2646	Fishin' (20x15cm-8x6in) s.d.1872 board. 11-Sep-92 Skinner, Bolton #196/R
$7000	£4636	Finishing touch (61x41cm-24x16in) s. i.stretcher. 23-Sep-93 Sotheby's, New York #43/R
$10000	£6329	Have a game (59x39cm-23x15in) s. 4-Dec-92 Christie's, New York #221/R
$10000	£5882	Shoe shine boy (61x46cm-24x18in) s. 3-Oct-92 Weschler, Washington #95/R
$12000	£6936	Only a nickel, Joe (63x51cm-25x20in) s.i.d.1906. 23-Sep-92 Christie's, New York #48/R
$12000	£7692	He toils at eighty (76x51cm-30x20in) s.d.1884. 27-May-93 Sotheby's, New York #206/R
$14000	£8092	Cant't be coaxed (64x51cm-25x20in) s.i. 23-Sep-92 Christie's, New York #45/R
$16000	£10596	Two musicians (46x36cm-18x14in) s.d.1874. 23-Sep-93 Sotheby's, New York #7/R
$17000	£11565	The bully (46x30cm-18x12in) s. 19-Nov-93 Du Mouchelle, Detroit #2024/R
$17000	£11888	Don't move (61x43cm-24x17in) s.d.1904. 11-Mar-93 Christie's, New York #95/R
$18000	£11392	The berry picker (45x30cm-18x12in) s.d.1877. 3-Dec-92 Sotheby's, New York #32/R
$20000	£13245	Thinking it over (61x43cm-24x17in) s.d.1907. 19-Jun-94 Hindman Galleries, Chicago #703/R
$23000	£14557	The study hour (76x63cm-30x25in) s.d.1905. 3-Dec-92 Sotheby's, New York #33/R
$27500	£17628	We can't be caught (63x76cm-25x30in) s. canvas on board. 9-Dec-92 Butterfield & Butterfield, San Francisco #3832/R
$31000	£19872	Blackberry picking (76x63cm-30x25in) s. 27-May-93 Sotheby's, New York #130/R
$70000	£46980	Deerhunter in the woods (107x147cm-42x58in) s.d.1864. 3-Dec-93 Christie's, New York #83/R
$90000	£60811	A sure thing a young boy taking aim with rifle and girl beside (76x64cm-30x25in) s.i.d.1876. 31-Oct-93 Hindman Galleries, Chicago #684/R
$175000	£112179	Heels over head (102x152cm-40x60in) s.d.1894. 27-May-93 Sotheby's, New York #183/R
$550	£364	Young boy holding his baby brother (13x5cm-5x2in) s.d.91 W/C gouache. 3-Jan-93 Litchfield Auction Gallery #1

BROWN, M (?-1831) American
$978	£600	Sailors on shore leave (57x42cm-22x17in) s. 15-Oct-92 Christie's, S. Kensington #472/R

BROWN, Mather (1761-1831) American/British
$1764	£1200	Portrait study of Sir Edward Astley (34x27cm-13x11in) pencil htd.white executed c.1790. 14-Apr-94 Sotheby's, London #53/R

BROWN, Mather (attrib) (1761-1831) American/British
$800	£519	Portrait of dapper gentleman with bamboo cane and hat (74x61cm-29x24in) 16-Jan-93 Skinner, Bolton #98
$1073	£720	Portrait of gentleman wearing grey coat (58x49cm-23x19in) 5-May-94 Sotheby's Colonnade, London #33/R
$1400	£933	Portrait of William Roger jnr holding black hat (76x61cm-30x24in) panel. 20-Aug-93 Skinner, Bolton #128/R
$1800	£1208	Portrait of a lady (72x62cm-28x24in) 19-Jan-94 Sotheby's Arcade, New York #179/R

BROWN, Mather (circle) (1761-1831) American/British
$1341	£900	Portrait of a gentleman wearing military uniform (32x26cm-13x10in) indist.i.verso oval. 14-Dec-93 Phillips, London #5

BROWN, Norman A (1933-) Canadian
$789	£526	Copithorne Farm, Springbank (51x61cm-20x24in) s. board. 30-May-94 Hodgins, Calgary #149/R (C.D 1100)

BROWN, Paul (19/20th C) American
$6000	£4000	Polo matches , s.i.d.31 and 32 W/C pen chl gouache three. 3-Jun-94 Sotheby's, New York #302/R

BROWN, Roger (1941-) American

$2086	£1400	American sycamore (244x183cm-96x72in) i.verso acrylic. 21-Jun-93 Christie's, S. Kensington #212/R
$6000	£4027	Aboretum by flashbulb (183x121cm-72x48in) acrylic painted 1978. 5-May-94 Sotheby's, New York #206/R
$7500	£4902	Trailer park, truck stop (119x150cm-47x59in) painted 1971. 4-May-93 Sotheby's, New York #415/R
$7500	£4412	Land O'Lakes (183x133cm-72x52in) i.overlap. 8-Oct-92 Christie's, New York #164/R
$9000	£6081	The Nose State (183x122cm-72x48in) i.stretcher painted 1991. 8-Nov-93 Christie's, East, New York #106/R
$11000	£7432	Why (183x122cm-72x48in) i.verso acrylic painted 1985. 11-Nov-93 Sotheby's, New York #200/R
$16000	£10811	Renaissance in reverse, a nightmare in the marsh (183x121cm-72x48in) i. painted 1981. 10-Nov-93 Christie's, New York #242/R
$17000	£11111	Interlocken mit clouden (137x183cm-54x72in) i.verso acrylic. 16-May-93 Hindman Galleries, Chicago #30/R
$5800	*£3841*	*Mess is less (127x84cm-50x33in) painted 1985 oil col.chk canvas. 17-Nov-92 Christie's, East, New York #13/R*

BROWN, Roy (1879-1956) American

$1000	£667	Sheltered cottage (53x66cm-21x26in) s. 22-May-94 James Bakker, Cambridge #164/R
$1100	£582	Autumn breeze (53x64cm-21x25in) s.i. 11-Sep-92 Skinner, Bolton #206/R
$1200	£784	New Hampshire valley (51x61cm-20x24in) s. 8-May-93 Young Fine Arts Auctions, Maine #53/R
$800	*£537*	*A day in the park (61x80cm-24x31in) s. W/C graphite paperboard. 4-Mar-94 Skinner, Bolton #282/R*

BROWN, Sam (1907-) American

$800	£544	Hunter and dogs with pups (74x64cm-29x25in) s. 14-Apr-94 Freeman Fine Arts, Philadelphia #1047

BROWN, William Mason (1828-1898) American

$1900	£1234	Autumn in the hills (31x26cm-12x10in) init. 9-Sep-93 Sotheby's Arcade, New York #16/R
$4000	£2721	Early snow (20x30cm-8x12in) mono. i.verso board. 17-Nov-93 Doyle, New York #2/R
$5750	£3808	Landscape with cows in meadow (30x46cm-12x18in) s. 23-Sep-93 Sotheby's, New York #46/R
$6000	£3468	Summer haze (25x30cm-10x12in) init. board on board. 23-Sep-92 Christie's, New York #72/R
$7500	£5245	Hints of autumn (30x27cm-12x11in) mono board. 10-Mar-93 Sotheby's, New York #21/R
$8500	£5944	Strawberries (26x30cm-10x12in) init. 11-Mar-93 Christie's, New York #50/R
$10000	£6803	Pasture stream (56x91cm-22x36in) init. 17-Nov-93 Doyle, New York #24/R
$15000	£7937	Still life with fruits and nuts (36x30cm-14x12in) mono. 11-Sep-92 Skinner, Bolton #174/R
$16000	£10127	October on Great Otter Creek, Vermont (30x46cm-12x18in) s. s.i.stretcher. 4-Dec-92 Christie's, New York #230/R
$32000	£21477	Still life with melon (64x76cm-25x30in) init. 3-Dec-93 Christie's, New York #126/R
$37000	£23718	Still life with fruit and vase (77x63cm-30x25in) s.s. i.verso. 27-May-93 Sotheby's, New York #142 a/R

BROWN, William Theo (1919-) American

$3250	£2044	Masquerade (30x46cm-12x18in) mono. s.d.61verso panel. 25-Apr-93 Butterfield & Butterfield, San Francisco #2103/R

BROWNE, Belmore (1880-1954) Canadian

$861	£574	Untitled - mountain range (41x51cm-16x20in) s. 30-May-94 Hodgins, Calgary #109 a (C.D 1200)
$1206	£821	Valley of the Kicking Horse (41x51cm-16x20in) s. s.i.verso. 15-Nov-93 Hodgins, Calgary #28/R (C.D 1600)

BROWNE, Byron (1907-1961) American

$1100	£719	Provincetown Beach (15x38cm-6x15in) s.d.1958 verso board. 14-May-93 Skinner, Bolton #183/R
$1200	£816	Head of a woman (35x30cm-14x12in) s. s.d.1941verso masonite. 15-Nov-93 Christie's, East, New York #266/R
$1300	£884	Still life with jug of flowers (51x66cm-20x26in) s.d.1958 s.i.d.verso. 15-Nov-93 Christie's, East, New York #267/R
$1700	£1141	Nude (36x46cm-14x18in) s. s.i.d.1959 verso. 4-Mar-94 Skinner, Bolton #308/R
$2000	£1156	Harlequin (66x51cm-26x20in) s. s.i.d.1960verso. 25-Sep-92 Sotheby's Arcade, New York #482/R
$2600	£1699	Head of clown (35x30cm-14x12in) s. s.i.d.1947 verso. 4-May-93 Christie's, East, New York #313 a/R
$4750	£3210	Sea creature (76x96cm-30x38in) s. s.i.d.1948 verso. 31-Mar-94 Sotheby's Arcade, New York #474/R
$8500	£5449	Sword swallower (97x76cm-38x30in) s. s.i.d.1946 verso. 26-May-93 Christie's, New York #226/R
$15000	£9615	Head of woman (71x61cm-28x24in) s.d.1937 s.i.d.verso. 26-May-93 Christie's, New York #215/R
$600	*£400*	*Autumn still life (49x64cm-19x25in) s.d.1959 s.i.d.1959 verso oil ink. 23-May-94 Christie's, East, New York #245*
$800	*£513*	*Docked boats (48x64cm-19x25in) s.d.1953 ink wash W/C gouache. 28-May-93 Sloan, North Bethesda #2397/R*
$850	*£552*	*Three nudes and head of man with head of woman (51x64cm-20x25in) s.d. May 13, 1953 and 1955 pen. 11-Sep-93 Louisiana Auction Exchange #9/R*

BROWNE, Byron (1907-1961) American-cont.
$1000	£680	Jester (65x49cm-26x19in) s.d.July 6 1952 W/C gouache. 15-Nov-93 Christie's, East, New York #268/R
$1100	£636	Acrobat (65x44cm-26x17in) s.d.1948 gouache ink. 25-Sep-92 Sotheby's Arcade, New York #484/R
$1200	£784	Woman in profile (61x46cm-24x18in) s.d.1948 pastel pencil. 17-Sep-93 Skinner, Bolton #301/R
$1300	£751	Beach at night (51x66cm-20x26in) s.d.1954 s.i.d.verso W/C gouache Indian ink. 25-Sep-92 Sotheby's Arcade, New York #492/R
$1500	£987	Cyclops (66x51cm-26x20in) s.d.1950 estate st.verso Indian ink gouache. 31-Mar-93 Sotheby's Arcade, New York #465/R
$1500	£987	Kouros (66x51cm-26x20in) s.d.1950 estate st.verso gouache. 31-Mar-93 Sotheby's Arcade, New York #464/R
$1600	£1053	Moonlight Aura (66x51cm-26x20in) s.d.1954 estate st.verso Indian ink gouache. 31-Mar-93 Sotheby's Arcade, New York #466/R

BROWNE, Charles Francis (1859-1921) American
$2000	£1351	Indiana autumn (41x61cm-16x24in) s.d.1897 canvas laid down on board. 31-Oct-93 Hindman Galleries, Chicago #670/R
$3250	£2153	By the Daisies, summer landscape (41x61cm-16x24in) s.d.1897. 15-Jun-94 Butterfield & Butterfield, San Francisco #4427/R

BROWNE, George (1905-) Canadian
$642	£425	Bow Valley (30x41cm-12x16in) s. painted c.1930 s.i.verso. 16-Nov-92 Hodgins, Calgary #23/R (C.D 825)

BROWNE, George Elmer (1871-1946) American
$1000	£667	Sheep in a village landscape (53x66cm-21x26in) s.d.1900. 17-May-94 Grogan, Massachussetts #364/R
$1100	£738	Brittany scene (25x33cm-10x13in) s. board. 24-Mar-94 Mystic Fine Arts, Connecticut #128
$1400	£940	The ticket line (38x46cm-15x18in) s. board. 26-Mar-94 James Bakker, Cambridge #22/R
$1600	£1060	A Church (65x55cm-26x22in) s. 15-Jun-94 Butterfield & Butterfield, San Francisco #4452/R
$1600	£1081	Bruges Belgium (25x33cm-10x13in) s. panel. 9-Nov-93 John Moran, Pasadena #860
$1600	£1081	Venice (27x35cm-11x14in) board. 31-Mar-94 Sotheby's Arcade, New York #168/R
$1700	£899	Blue water, white sails (36x41cm-14x16in) pressed board. 12-Sep-92 Louisiana Auction Exchange #38/R
$2200	£1486	The slave market (89x91cm-35x36in) s. panel. 31-Mar-94 Sotheby's Arcade, New York #257/R
$2600	£1745	The farm in Provence (46x56cm-18x22in) s. 11-Dec-93 Weschler, Washington #103/R
$5500	£3716	Hovering clouds (135x160cm-53x63in) s. 10-Nov-93 Doyle, New York #23
$500	£336	Market scene (74x53cm-29x21in) s. W/C. 26-Mar-94 James Bakker, Cambridge #177

BROWNE, Joseph Archibald (1862-1948) Canadian
$510	£340	Evening, Toronto Island (18x25cm-7x10in) s. s.i.d.1908verso panel. 11-May-94 Sotheby's, Toronto #30/R (C.D 700)

BROWNE, Matilda (1869-1947) American
$750	£503	Christmas Cheer (91x71cm-36x28in) s. board. 16-Dec-93 Mystic Fine Arts, Connecticut #303
$28000	£19580	Playing in the garden (46x61cm-18x24in) s.d.1914. 12-Mar-93 Skinner, Bolton #268/R
$750	£497	Old Lyme House (36x53cm-14x21in) s. W/C. 3-Jan-93 Litchfield Auction Gallery #2

BROWNELL, Peleg Franklin (1857-1946) Canadian
$1784	£1166	Skiers in snowy landscape (32x39cm-13x15in) init. board. 19-May-93 Sotheby's, Toronto #259/R (C.D 2250)
$2114	£1429	September landscape (45x55cm-18x22in) s. 23-Nov-93 Joyner Fine Art, Toronto #64 (C.D 2800)
$2170	£1400	A salmon river (29x40cm-11x16in) s.d.20. 15-Jul-94 Christie's, London #73/R
$2184	£1456	Evening, Ladysmith (46x66cm-18x26in) s. 11-May-94 Sotheby's, Toronto #76/R (C.D 3000)
$6236	£4103	Beach scene, St.Kitts (23x35cm-9x14in) init. canvas on board painted c.1913. 7-Jun-93 Ritchie, Toronto #157/R (C.D 8000)
$10702	£6995	By Ward market, Ottawa (25x41cm-10x16in) init.d.24 s.d.verso board. 19-May-93 Sotheby's, Toronto #395/R (C.D 13500)
$692	£461	Old lumber camp, Algonquin Park (29x21cm-11x8in) s. 13-May-94 Joyner Fine Art, Toronto #257/R (C.D 950)
$800	£471	Boats on shore (28x38cm-11x15in) mono. pastel. 3-Oct-92 Weschler, Washington #132/R

BROWNSCOMBE, Jennie (1850-1936) American
$1250	£651	Seated young woman reading by fireplace (25x30cm-10x12in) s.d.1881. 5-Aug-92 Boos Gallery, Michigan #533/R
$1500	£1007	Governor Morris addressing assembly (76x102cm-30x40in) s. 5-Aug-93 Eldred, Massachusetts #820/R
$1600	£936	Woman reading (25x30cm-10x12in) s. 18-Sep-92 Du Mouchelle, Detroit #2003/R
$3000	£1974	An unexpected visitor (51x74cm-20x29in) s. i.verso. 4-Nov-92 Doyle, New York #30/R
$850	£594	Young girl (28x20cm-11x8in) s. W/C. 11-Mar-93 Mystic Fine Arts, Connecticut #78/R
$1400	£809	Young woman with bouquet of roses (71x53cm-28x21in) s. W/C oval. 25-Sep-92 Sotheby's Arcade, New York #144/R

BRUCE, Edward (1879-1943) American
$1200	£805	Meadows (74x99cm-29x39in) s. i.verso. 4-May-94 Doyle, New York #32/R
$1300	£850	Deer Hills, Vermont (30x61cm-12x24in) s. s.i.verso canvas on board. 29-Jun-94 Doyle, New York #8
$1600	£1074	Hillside village (74x97cm-29x38in) s. 4-May-94 Doyle, New York #33/R
$3000	£1734	Landscape with corral and barn (61x74cm-24x29in) s. 25-Sep-92 Sotheby's Arcade, New York #196/R

BRUENCHENHEIN, Eugene von (attrib) (1910-1983) American
$1300	£861	Untitled (61x61cm-24x24in) s.d.July 13 1959 board. 26-Sep-93 Schrager Galleries, Milwaukee #500/R
$1300	£861	Wand of the genie (61x61cm-24x24in) s.d.July 27 1959 board. 26-Sep-93 Schrager Galleries, Milwaukee #505 a

BRUESTLE, George M (1871-1939) American
$600	£405	Tonal landscape (30x41cm-12x16in) s. 27-Nov-93 Young Fine Arts Auctions, Maine #55/R
$800	£537	Autumn landscape (38x28cm-15x11in) s. 6-Mar-94 Hart Gallery, Houston #486
$925	£646	CT Farm scene (28x38cm-11x15in) s. board. 11-Mar-93 Mystic Fine Arts, Connecticut #192 a/R
$950	£642	Landscape with stony pasture and red barn (30x41cm-12x16in) s. masonite. 5-Nov-93 Skinner, Bolton #101/R
$1000	£671	Conn. landscape (30x41cm-12x16in) s. board. 24-Mar-94 Mystic Fine Arts, Connecticut #39
$2300	£1513	New England barns (56x76cm-22x30in) s. 31-Mar-93 Sotheby's Arcade, New York #242/R
$2750	£1821	House by the roadside (81x107cm-32x42in) s.d.1922. 15-Jun-94 Butterfield & Butterfield, San Francisco #4424

BRUGHETTI, Faustino (1889-1974) Argentinian
$900	£529	Tarde de otono (33x42cm-13x17in) painted 1924. 29-Sep-92 VerBo, Buenos Aires #19

BRUMBACK, Louise Upton (1872-1929) American
$650	£417	Red boat, Gloucester, Massachusetts (48x39cm-19x15in) s. s.i.verso W/C. 12-Dec-92 Weschler, Washington #68 a

BRUNHOFF, Laurent de (20th C) American
$1500	£1014	Untitled (147x173cm-58x68in) indist.s. i.d.1981verso. 21-Apr-94 Butterfield & Butterfield, San Francisco #1163/R

BRUNI, Umberto (1914-) Canadian
$504	£327	Vue sur le village, Eboulements, Charlevoix (30x40cm-12x16in) s.i.d.1980verso panel. 21-Jun-94 Fraser Pinneys, Quebec #145 (C.D 700)

BRUNONI, Serge (1930-) Canadian
$583	£388	Montreal, sur Sainte Catherine (61x76cm-24x30in) s. s.i.verso acrylic. 11-May-94 Sotheby's, Toronto #154/R (C.D 800)
$610	£407	Seule (61x51cm-24x20in) s.i. acrylic board. 30-May-94 Hodgins, Calgary #352 (C.D 850)
$619	£413	Reve d'Adolescent (60x50cm-24x20in) s. acrylic board. 13-May-94 Joyner Fine Art, Toronto #193/R (C.D 850)
$646	£431	Magasinage, rue-Ste-Anne, Quebec (51x61cm-20x24in) s. s.i.verso. 30-May-94 Hodgins, Calgary #141/R (C.D 900)
$728	£485	Je T'Invite (60x75cm-24x30in) s. acrylic. 13-May-94 Joyner Fine Art, Toronto #212/R (C.D 1000)
$793	£518	Quebec sur Mer (61x91cm-24x36in) s. acrylic. 18-May-93 Joyner Fine Art, Toronto #180/R (C.D 1000)
$1012	£670	Montreal, La Rue Rivard (60x75cm-24x30in) s. 24-Nov-92 Joyner Fine Art, Toronto #204/R (C.D 1300)
$1092	£728	Derby (91x101cm-36x40in) s. s.i.verso acrylic. 11-May-94 Sotheby's, Toronto #156/R (C.D 1500)
$1133	£765	Plus que le poids des ans (75x100cm-30x39in) s. acrylic. 23-Nov-93 Joyner Fine Art, Toronto #222/R (C.D 1500)
$1233	£833	Quebec a la Chateau Frontenac - setting up camp (76x102cm-30x40in) s. s.i.verso. 25-Apr-94 Levis, Calgary #40/R (C.D 1700)
$1323	£876	L'instant D'avant, L'instant D'apres (76x102cm-30x40in) s. i.verso. 18-Nov-92 Sotheby's, Toronto #75/R (C.D 1700)
$1550	£1047	Augusta Avenue Toronto (76x102cm-30x40in) s. s.i.verso acrylic. 3-Nov-93 Sotheby's, Toronto #40/R (C.D 2000)
$2179	£1443	Quebec, Boulevard St. Louis (75x100cm-30x39in) s. 24-Nov-92 Joyner Fine Art, Toronto #217/R (C.D 2800)
$2913	£1942	Le Ritz Carlton, Montreal, Rue Sherbrooke Ouest (75x100cm-30x39in) s. 13-May-94 Joyner Fine Art, Toronto #149/R (C.D 4000)

BRUSH, George de Forest (1855-1941) American
$26000	£16456	Woman in Renaissance dress (26x22cm-10x9in) s.d.1910 canvas laid down on board. 4-Dec-92 Christie's, New York #232/R
$220000	£139261	A family group (79x100cm-31x39in) s.d.1907. 3-Dec-92 Sotheby's, New York #96/R

BRUTON, Margaret (1894-1983) American
$800	£471	New roof, Mexico (42x58cm-17x23in) s. paper. 4-Oct-92 Butterfield & Butterfield, Los Angeles #225/R
$1200	£706	Taxco, Mexico (76x61cm-30x24in) s. 4-Oct-92 Butterfield & Butterfield, Los Angeles #223/R

BRUTON, Margaret (1894-1983) American-cont.
$1300	£765	Taxco Tots - Mexico (61x76cm-24x30in) s. 4-Oct-92 Butterfield & Butterfield, Los Angeles #224/R
$850	*£500*	*Mining mountain landscape (44x48cm-17x19in) s. W/C. 4-Oct-92 Butterfield & Butterfield, Los Angeles #228/R*

BRYANT, Everett L (1864-1945) American
$1000	£654	Floral still life (56x46cm-22x18in) init. masonite. 22-May-93 Weschler, Washington #103/R

BRYMNER, William (1855-1925) Canadian
$1133	£765	Summer landscape (37x46cm-15x18in) s. 23-Nov-93 Joyner Fine Art, Toronto #143/R (C.D 1500)
$1258	£796	Watching the sunset at St Eustache (13x18cm-5x7in) s.i.d.1908verso board. 1-Dec-92 Fraser Pinneys, Quebec #33 (C.D 1600)
$1583	£1028	Figure walking past geese (38x51cm-15x20in) s.d.1919 panel. 21-Jun-94 Fraser Pinneys, Quebec #52 (C.D 2200)
$1743	£1178	Rural landscape (20x30cm-8x12in) s.d.91. 3-Nov-93 Sotheby's, Toronto #208 (C.D 2250)
$1860	£1257	Venetian view (13x16cm-5x6in) s. board. 3-Nov-93 Sotheby's, Toronto #351/R (C.D 2400)
$2039	£1359	Early morning near St Lawrence (30x50cm-12x20in) s. canvas on board. 13-May-94 Joyner Fine Art, Toronto #117/R (C.D 2800)
$2664	£1800	Indian school (25x42cm-10x17in) s. 16-Mar-93 Phillips, London #68/R
$3769	£2564	Rocky mountains (35x51cm-14x20in) s. 15-Nov-93 Hodgins, Calgary #82/R (C.D 5000)
$19026	£12435	St. Eustache (75x102cm-30x40in) s. painted c.1907. 18-May-93 Joyner Fine Art, Toronto #41/R (C.D 24000)
$529	*£357*	*Near St. Eustache, P.Q (21x29cm-8x11in) s. W/C. 23-Nov-93 Joyner Fine Art, Toronto #244 (C.D 700)*
$663	*£436*	*Old barn and trees reflected (24x34cm-9x13in) s.d.1896 i.verso W/C. 7-Jun-93 Ritchie, Toronto #141/R (C.D 850)*
$697	*£471*	*On the steps of a monument (28x38cm-11x15in) init. W/C. 3-Nov-93 Sotheby's, Toronto #28/R (C.D 900)*
$707	*£448*	*Summer cottage by the river (24x34cm-9x13in) s. W/C. 1-Dec-92 Fraser Pinneys, Quebec #184 (C.D 900)*

BUCK, Claude (1890-?) American
$600	£400	Figure in a landscape (20x30cm-8x12in) s. masonite. 15-Mar-94 John Moran, Pasadena #155
$600	£400	Figure in a landscape (20x38cm-8x15in) s. masonite. 15-Mar-94 John Moran, Pasadena #156
$650	£439	Monkey painting (51x41cm-20x16in) s. s.i.verso masonite. 9-Nov-93 John Moran, Pasadena #923
$650	£430	Still life of bread and knife (51x41cm-20x16in) s. masonite. 28-Sep-93 John Moran, Pasadena #265
$750	£507	Paradise (36x46cm-14x18in) s.d.1934 board. 9-Nov-93 John Moran, Pasadena #929 a
$850	£563	Still life with kettle (41x51cm-16x20in) s. board. 28-Sep-93 John Moran, Pasadena #257
$950	£629	Still life of kettle and oyster shell (41x51cm-16x20in) s. board. 28-Sep-93 John Moran, Pasadena #301
$1000	£654	Family (81x114cm-32x45in) s.i. board. 16-May-93 Hindman Galleries, Chicago #117
$1500	£993	Still life of copper pans, gourd and fruit (61x91cm-24x36in) s. d.1948verso masonite. 28-Sep-93 John Moran, Pasadena #287
$1800	£1216	Wave period (76x56cm-30x22in) s.d.1939 board. 15-Jun-93 John Moran, Pasadena #138
$2000	£1389	Boiling clouds (41x51cm-16x20in) s. board. 7-Mar-93 Butterfield & Butterfield, San Francisco #249/R
$2000	£1333	Magdalen (25x20cm-10x8in) s.d.1940 panel. 15-Mar-94 John Moran, Pasadena #158
$2500	£1678	Four labourers (64x84cm-25x33in) s. paper on cradled panel. 4-Dec-93 Louisiana Auction Exchange #31/R
$7000	£4861	Nude with butterfly (36x86cm-14x34in) s. board. 7-Mar-93 Butterfield & Butterfield, San Francisco #160/R

BUCKLER, Charles E (1869-?) Canadian/American
$900	£625	Mountain valley pool (71x97cm-28x38in) s.verso. 6-Mar-93 Louisiana Auction Exchange #21/R

BUCKLEY, J M (1891-1958) American
$700	£470	Winter Rockport Harbour (36x41cm-14x16in) s. board. 29-Nov-93 Stonington Fine Arts, Stonington #88/R

BUEHLER, Lytton Briggs (1888-?) American
$800	£503	Autumn trees (81x66cm-32x26in) s. s.d.1924 verso. 25-Apr-93 James Bakker, Cambridge #21/R

BUEHR, Karl Albert (1866-1952) American
$800	£523	Yosemite (61x112cm-24x44in) s. 19-Sep-93 Hindman Galleries, Chicago #784/R
$850	£559	Landscape (46x56cm-18x22in) s. board. 13-Jun-93 Hindman Galleries, Chicago #285 a
$900	£588	Yosemite (61x112cm-24x44in) s. 8-May-93 Young Fine Arts Auctions, Maine #55/R
$1500	£1020	Spring landscape with tall trees (46x33cm-18x13in) s. 15-Nov-93 Christie's, East, New York #129/R
$130500	£87000	Tea time (76x61cm-30x24in) s. 15-Mar-94 Phillips, London #87/R

BUEL, Hubert (1915-1984) American
$700	*£473*	*Laguna Beach, hotel, coast highway (36x51cm-14x20in) s. W/C. 15-Jun-93 John Moran, Pasadena #15*

BUFF, Conrad (1886-1975) American
$2750   £1897   Desert landscape (25x46cm-10x18in) s. board. 16-Feb-93 John Moran, Pasadena #96
$3250   £2167   Desert landscape (61x76cm-24x30in) s. board double-sided. 15-Mar-94 John Moran, Pasadena #34

BUHLER, Augustus W (1853-1920) American
$1600   £1060   Low tide, moonlight, Gloucester (23x30cm-9x12in) s. board. 28-Nov-92 Young Fine Arts Auctions, Maine #61

BULA, John (1950-) American
$700   £464   Fantastic woman (56x36cm-22x14in) s.i.d.October 1992verso gouache. 21-Nov-92 Litchfield Auction Gallery #2

BULL, William H (1861-1940) American
$4750   £3167   Panoramic view, Mount Lowe, Pacific electric railway (56x58cm-22x23in) s. board. 15-Mar-94 John Moran, Pasadena #52

BULMAN, Orville (20th C) American
$990   £647   Beginner - Caribbean scene (51x46cm-20x18in) s. s.d.1957 verso. 14-May-93 Skinner, Bolton #173/R
$2000   £1325   'Mes Amis' (108x91cm-43x36in) s. s.d.1973 verso. 30-Jun-93 Sotheby's Arcade, New York #202/R

BUNKER, Dennis M (1861-1890) American
$4000   £2685   Marsh with boat (25x36cm-10x14in) 29-Nov-93 Stonington Fine Arts, Stonington #185/R
$7250   £4899   Still life with white roses (38x23cm-15x9in) s. 10-Aug-93 Stonington Fine Arts, Stonington #120/R
$26000   £16667   Portrait of woman (56x46cm-22x18in) 27-May-93 Sotheby's, New York #23/R

BUNNER, Andrew Fisher (1841-1897) American
$1200   £795   Arrival - Venetian canal scene (53x41cm-21x16in) s.i. with i.verso. 13-Nov-92 Skinner, Bolton #107/R
$3000   £2041   Venice (38x76cm-15x30in) s. 16-Apr-94 Young Fine Arts Auctions, Maine #59/R
$4000   £2649   Cows watering by quiet river (51x91cm-20x36in) s.d.73. 2-Oct-93 Weschler, Washington #95/R
$6750   £4411   Casa Dario (81x56cm-32x22in) s.i. i.verso. 15-Sep-93 Doyle, New York #8/R
$700   £461   Lagoon in Venice with San Giorgio Maggiore in evening (20x38cm-8x15in) s. W/C. 31-Mar-93 Sotheby's Arcade, New York #77/R

BURCHFIELD, Charles (1893-1967) American
$2600   £1722   Grey day in March (35x50cm-14x20in) s. i.d.1916 verso W/C pencil. 22-Sep-93 Christie's, New York #197/R
$2750   £1846   Post Office, Washingtonville, Ohio (28x34cm-11x13in) pencil. 8-Dec-93 Butterfield & Butterfield, San Francisco #3379/R
$3000   £2000   Church with poplars (41x35cm-16x14in) s.d.1916 W/C pencil paper on board. 23-May-94 Christie's, East, New York #449/R
$3750   £2534   Sunset (29x22cm-11x9in) d.1916 d.1915 verso W/C paper on board. 31-Mar-94 Sotheby's Arcade, New York #449/R
$6500   £4248   Old cottage in May (46x69cm-18x27in) init.d.1933 i.verso W/C chl. 4-May-93 Christie's, East, New York #219/R
$6500   £4305   Sunlight and wind (50x55cm-20x22in) init.d.1950 pen chl pencil. 22-Sep-93 Christie's, New York #196/R
$7500   £5000   Summer morning - 'Dutchman's' Salem (33x50cm-13x20in) s. gouache W/C pencil executed c.1917. 17-Mar-94 Sotheby's, New York #152/R
$7500   £5034   Ice bound lake boat, foot of Michigan Street, Buffalo (71x52cm-28x20in) s.d.1925 W/C. 6-May-94 Skinner, Bolton #136 a/R
$8000   £4624   Clouds at sunset (37x52cm-15x20in) s.d.1917 i.d.1917 verso W/C paper on board. 24-Sep-92 Sotheby's, New York #161/R
$8000   £5369   December sunlight (44x61cm-17x24in) mono.d.1943 W/C. 6-May-94 Skinner, Bolton #82a/R
$10000   £6993   Winter afternoon, Broadway, Salem (38x53cm-15x21in) s.d.1920 W/C board. 10-Mar-93 Sotheby's, New York #132/R
$12000   £8000   The silver stream (69x102cm-27x40in) init.d.1935-37 W/C board. 17-Mar-94 Sotheby's, New York #154/R
$12000   £8054   Winter sun through poplars (49x34cm-19x13in) s.d.1916 W/C. 6-May-94 Skinner, Bolton #95/R
$18000   £11392   Between two willows (54x43cm-21x17in) s.d.1918 i.verso W/C. 3-Dec-92 Sotheby's, New York #151/R
$31000   £19620   The haymow, Salem (53x76cm-21x30in) s. W/C pencil paper laid down on board. 4-Dec-92 Christie's, New York #152/R
$35000   £22152   Pussywillows in the rain (76x101cm-30x40in) mono. i.verso W/C paper on board. 3-Dec-92 Sotheby's, New York #152/R
$55000   £36667   Sun and wild sweetpeas (69x102cm-27x40in) init.d.1964 i.verso W/C pencil board. 26-May-94 Christie's, New York #144/R
$80000   £50633   Sun setting in a bank of smoke (54x43cm-21x17in) s.d.1917 i.d.verso W/C gouache paper on board. 3-Dec-92 Sotheby's, New York #149/R
$80000   £51282   Cicada song in September (100x83cm-39x33in) init.d.1956 W/C. 27-May-93 Sotheby's, New York #87/R
$85000   £56667   Hot July wind (75x100cm-30x39in) init.d.1955-60 W/C. 26-May-94 Christie's, New York #143/R

BURDEN, Chris (1946-) American
$5000   £3268   full Financial disclosure (76x91cm-30x36in) s.d.1977 ballpoint pen ink bank cheques on board. 7-May-93 Christie's, East, New York #73/R

BURDEN, Chris (1946-) American-cont.
$6000	£4054	Spook planes (76x102cm-30x40in) s.i.d.1979 postcards newspaper clipping board. 10-Nov-93 Christie's, New York #207/R
$6000	£4054	N for Nigger Z for Zorro (81x102cm-32x40in) s.i.d.1979 paper collage wire felt-tip pen board. 10-Nov-93 Christie's, New York #206/R
$10000	£6623	Thank You (81x102cm-32x40in) s.d.1979 paper collage photos ink metal pin. 18-Nov-92 Sotheby's, New York #208/R
$11000	£7190	Who pays for it. Help Ma (81x102cm-32x40in) s.i.d.1979 felt-tip pen pencil acrylic collage. 5-May-93 Christie's, New York #113/R
$11000	£7285	Man of Seventies (76x102cm-30x40in) s.d.1975 collage magazine articles marker board. 18-Nov-92 Sotheby's, New York #207/R
$20000	£13245	Full financial disclosure, June. Full financial disclosure, March (76x91cm-30x36in) s.d.1977 mixed media bank checks board two. 19-Nov-92 Christie's, New York #240/R

BURGDORFF, Ferdinand (1883-1975) American
$650	£442	Nevada Cottonwood in November (61x76cm-24x30in) s. board. 8-Apr-94 Sloan, North Bethesda #2146
$650	£430	California oak tree with bush lupine near Salinas (61x76cm-24x30in) s.d.1948 masonite. 28-Sep-93 John Moran, Pasadena #310
$850	£538	Sanm Francisco peaks near Snow Bowl (51x61cm-20x24in) s. board. 5-Dec-92 Louisiana Auction Exchange #30/R
$2500	£1736	Field of poppies and lupines (61x76cm-24x30in) s.d.1939 board. 7-Mar-93 Butterfield & Butterfield, San Francisco #187/R

BURGESS, George H (after) (1831-1905) American
$7500	£4412	San Francisco in July, 1849 (71x147cm-28x58in) bears sig.d.1849. 4-Oct-92 Butterfield & Butterfield, Los Angeles #55/R

BURKHARD, Henri (1892-?) American
$600	£403	Farm view through trees (38x46cm-15x18in) panel. 27-Mar-94 Myers, Florida #79/R

BURKHARDT, Emerson C (1905-1969) American
$1500	£1007	Fantasy landscape (64x76cm-25x30in) s. board. 16-Dec-93 Mystic Fine Arts, Connecticut #54/R

BURKHARDT, Hans Gustav (1904-1994) American/Swiss
$1600	£1013	Red and white striped barrier (41x51cm-16x20in) s.d.1945. 25-Oct-92 Butterfield & Butterfield, San Francisco #2270/R
$1200	£789	Two female nudes (61x46cm-24x18in) s.d.1940 pastel. 31-Mar-93 Sotheby's Arcade, New York #356/R

BURKO, Diane (1945-) American
$4100	£2733	Reflets - flowers 1990 (185x107cm-73x42in) s.verso. 26-May-94 Freeman Fine Arts, Philadelphia #42

BURLEIGH, Sidney R (1853-1931) American
$550	£385	Cloudy day (18x25cm-7x10in) s. W/C. 11-Mar-93 Mystic Fine Arts, Connecticut #103
$600	£377	Doorway in Old Charleston (15x25cm-6x10in) pastel. 23-Apr-93 Douglas, South Deerfield #2

BURLIN, Paul Harry (1886-1969) American
$1200	£759	Houses in the hills (64x77cm-25x30in) i. 2-Dec-92 Christie's, East, New York #347/R

BURLIUK, David (1882-1967) Russian/American
$600	£405	Mr. Zaro (30x25cm-12x10in) s.d.1944. 31-Mar-94 Sotheby's Arcade, New York #443
$650	£436	Czechoslovakia (23x33cm-9x13in) s.d.1962 board. 12-Dec-93 Hindman Galleries, Chicago #299
$750	£493	Vase of flowers on bench (16x14cm-6x6in) s. board. 31-Mar-93 Sotheby's Arcade, New York #274
$800	£537	A view of Czechoslovakia (25x36cm-10x14in) s.i.d.1962 masonite. 24-Mar-94 Boos Gallery, Michigan #681/R
$800	£541	The horseback rider (30x41cm-12x16in) s. init.d.1961. 31-Mar-94 Sotheby's Arcade, New York #447/R
$800	£541	The tree-lined path (61x46cm-24x18in) s. 31-Mar-94 Sotheby's Arcade, New York #332/R
$850	£552	Poker game (18x25cm-7x10in) s. 9-Sep-93 Sotheby's Arcade, New York #359/R
$875	£596	Man with cows on country road (46x61cm-18x24in) s. 14-Apr-94 Freeman Fine Arts, Philadelphia #1015 b
$900	£577	Village of Memory (30x46cm-12x18in) tempera. 13-Dec-92 Litchfield Auction Gallery #3
$900	£600	After a long day (19x15cm-7x6in) s.d.1949 canvas on board. 23-May-94 Christie's, East, New York #249
$950	£621	Figure at the shore (46x61cm-18x24in) s. 18-Sep-93 Young Fine Arts Auctions, Maine #54/R
$1000	£658	Portugal (30x41cm-12x16in) s.d.1954 canvas on board. 31-Mar-93 Sotheby's Arcade, New York #391/R
$1100	£692	New Mexico (20x25cm-8x10in) s.i. canvasboard. 25-Apr-93 Butterfield & Butterfield, San Francisco #2058/R
$1100	£636	Woman leading cow (30x30cm-12x12in) s. 25-Sep-92 Sotheby's Arcade, New York #512/R
$1200	£694	Card players (33x36cm-13x14in) s. masonite. 25-Sep-92 Sotheby's Arcade, New York #442/R

BURLIUK, David (1882-1967) Russian/American-cont.

$1200	£706	B_ _e chair with Japanese doll (91x74cm-36x29in) s. 5-Oct-92 Grogan, Massachussetts #751/R
$1200	£789	Woman with white goat (21x26cm-8x10in) s. panel. 31-Mar-93 Sotheby's Arcade, New York #492/R
$1250	£845	Landscape and harbour scene (51x61cm-20x24in) s.d.1953. 4-Nov-93 Boos Gallery, Michigan #1279/R
$1300	£751	Friends (16x29cm-6x11in) s. panel. 25-Sep-92 Sotheby's Arcade, New York #441/R
$1300	£855	Winter in Ural Mountain town (27x41cm-11x16in) s. masonite painted late 1930's. 31-Mar-93 Sotheby's Arcade, New York #495/R
$1300	£867	On the farm, California (23x30cm-9x12in) s.i. tempera canvasboard. 23-May-94 Christie's, East, New York #291/R
$1462	£988	Still life of flowers (69x62cm-27x24in) 26-Nov-93 Schloss Ahlden, Ahlden #1969/R (DM 2500)
$1500	£867	New Mexico (30x41cm-12x16in) s.i. 25-Sep-92 Sotheby's Arcade, New York #439/R
$1500	£1014	A summer afternoon in Port Jefferson (33x46cm-13x18in) s.d.1930. 31-Mar-94 Sotheby's Arcade, New York #445/R
$1500	£1014	A stroll toward the village wharf (43x61cm-17x24in) s. 31-Mar-94 Sotheby's Arcade, New York #277/R
$1600	£925	Still life with photograph (69x48cm-27x19in) s.d.1854. 25-Sep-92 Sotheby's Arcade, New York #410/R
$1600	£1053	Capri (34x44cm-13x17in) s.d.1969 board. 31-Mar-93 Sotheby's Arcade, New York #390/R
$1709	£1139	Manor farm (28x40cm-11x16in) s. 30-Jan-94 Bukowskis, Helsinki #12 (F.M 9500)
$1800	£1176	Bradenton Beach, florida (29x39cm-11x15in) s.d.1946 canvasboard. 4-May-93 Christie's, East, New York #299/R
$2000	£1307	Still life with flowers in vase (48x37cm-19x15in) s.d.1907 panel. 4-May-93 Christie's, East, New York #309/R
$2000	£1351	A tropical garden in Florida (93x57cm-37x22in) s.d.1946 s.i.verso. 31-Mar-94 Sotheby's Arcade, New York #446/R
$2100	£1214	Promenade (30x41cm-12x16in) s. canvasboard. 25-Sep-92 Sotheby's Arcade, New York #514/R
$2100	£1214	Positano (59x92cm-23x36in) s.i. 25-Sep-92 Sotheby's Arcade, New York #515/R
$2300	£1329	The duet (46x33cm-18x13in) s. 25-Sep-92 Sotheby's Arcade, New York #440/R
$2500	£1445	Floral still life and strawberries by the sea (51x41cm-20x16in) s. 25-Sep-92 Sotheby's Arcade, New York #411/R
$2500	£1689	Vineyard haven, Massachusetts (55x61cm-22x24in) s.i.d.1929. 31-Mar-94 Sotheby's Arcade, New York #442/R
$2500	£1645	Cafe scene (28x23cm-11x9in) s. painted c.1931. 31-Mar-93 Sotheby's Arcade, New York #493/R
$2500	£1689	The peasant couple (41x51cm-16x20in) s. 31-Mar-94 Sotheby's Arcade, New York #448/R
$2779	£1781	River landscape with barge (23x33cm-9x13in) s.i.d.1921 board. 26-May-93 Lempertz, Cologne #44 (DM 4400)
$4250	£2457	Southampton (43x56cm-17x22in) s. 25-Sep-92 Sotheby's Arcade, New York #510/R
$4250	£2457	Siesta (81x132cm-32x52in) 25-Sep-92 Sotheby's Arcade, New York #509/R
$4500	£2961	Dahlias and mums in autumn (123x92cm-48x36in) s.d.1964. 31-Mar-93 Sotheby's Arcade, New York #442/R
$5250	£3409	East River Drive (63x99cm-25x39in) s. 9-Sep-93 Sotheby's Arcade, New York #358/R
$5987	£4018	House Beckmann, street corner (52x73cm-20x29in) painted c.1910-1912. 23-Jun-93 Galerie Kornfeld, Berne #243/R (S.FR 9000)
$7500	£4934	Mural landscape (98x126cm-39x50in) s. 31-Mar-93 Sotheby's Arcade, New York #393/R
$600	£395	*Farm in Hampton Bays, Long Island (28x39cm-11x15in) s.i. W/C pastel ink. 31-Mar-93 Sotheby's Arcade, New York #446/R*
$800	*£533*	*Gloucester harbour (27x37cm-11x15in) s. W/C. 23-May-94 Christie's, East, New York #261/R*
$1100	*£696*	*Marussia (30x56cm-12x22in) s.d.1951/53 mixed media canvas on panel. 25-Oct-92 Butterfield & Butterfield, San Francisco #2263/R*
$1200	*£694*	*Figures on dock (23x30cm-9x12in) s. gouache masonite. 25-Sep-92 Sotheby's Arcade, New York #511/R*
$1400	*£881*	*Tea time (29x38cm-11x15in) s. mixed media paper laid down on board. 25-Apr-93 Butterfield & Butterfield, San Francisco #2030/R*

BURNHAM, Anita (1880-?) American

$1000	£654	Portrait of woman (46x30cm-18x12in) s.d.1913. 22-May-93 Weschler, Washington #107

BURNHAM, Ruth W (20th C) American

$650	£430	Eucalyptus landscape - view of Altadena, CA (30x41cm-12x16in) s. canvas on masonite. 14-Jun-94 John Moran, Pasadena #36 a

BURNSIDE, Cameron (1887-?) British/American

$1283	*£844*	*Marchands de dromadaires (59x72cm-23x28in) s. gouache htd.white. 5-Apr-93 Ader Tajan, Paris #91 (F.FR 7000)*

BURPEE, William P (1846-?) American

$8000	£5369	Sand dunes (74x71cm-29x28in) s.indist.d.05. 3-Dec-93 Christie's, New York #44/R
$950	*£638*	*Winter afternoon (29x37cm-11x15in) s. pastel. 6-May-94 Skinner, Bolton #98/R*

BURR, George Brainerd (1876-1950) American

$4000	£2703	Notre Dame de Paris, along the Seine and Bridge over the Seine (22x27cm-9x11in) two s. two panel one cradled panel three. 31-Mar-94 Sotheby's Arcade, New York #165/R
$9000	£6294	Story hour (63x48cm-25x19in) s. 11-Mar-93 Christie's, New York #159/R

BURR, George Elbert (1859-1939) American
$1100   £728   Spanish peaks of the Rock mountains (18x25cm-7x10in) s. W/C. 23-Sep-93 Mystic Fine Arts, Connecticut #53

BURR, Lee (1936-) American
$658   £442   Composition (122x152cm-48x60in) s.d.87 st.sig.i.verso. 22-Feb-94 Rasmussen, Vejle #1223 (D.KR 4400)
$658   £442   Composition (122x152cm-48x60in) s.d.87 st.sig.i.verso. 22-Feb-94 Rasmussen, Vejle #1222 (D.KR 4400)

BURRIDGE, Walter Wilcox (1857-?) American
$650   £442   Chicago in winter (51x41cm-20x16in) s.indist.d. 17-Apr-94 Hanzel Galleries, Chicago #15

BURTON, Richmond (1960-) American?
$1500   £1007   Double thought plane no 9 (30x39cm-12x15in) s. oil pencil canvas on paper. 5-May-94 Sotheby's, New York #323/R
$3500   £2288   Untitled (41x51cm-16x20in) paper on canvas executed 1989. 4-May-93 Sotheby's, New York #237/R
$5500   £3595   Untitled (205x61cm-81x24in) s.d.1989 verso linen wood. 4-May-93 Sotheby's, New York #250/R
$13500   £9122   Thought plane 16 (218x160cm-86x63in) s.i.d.1989verso wood oil. 10-Nov-93 Christie's, New York #269/R
$16000   £10738   Untitled (206x152cm-81x60in) s.i.d.1989verso linen on panel. 4-May-94 Christie's, New York #255/R

BURTON, Samuel Chatwood (1881-c.1955) American
$650   £425   Loading the dingies (46x61cm-18x24in) s. W/C. 19-Sep-93 Hindman Galleries, Chicago #684/R

BUSH, Charles (1842-1909) American
$570   £380   View of Collins Street, looking west (46x61cm-18x24in) s. board. 10-May-94 Phillips, London #29/R

BUSH, Jack (1909-1977) Canadian
$1903   £1244   Abstract (60x44cm-24x17in) s.d.50 board. 18-May-93 Joyner Fine Art, Toronto #117/R (C.D 2400)
$2775   £1813   Saturday afternoon on the Don (63x84cm-25x33in) s.d.30 s.verso. 19-May-93 Sotheby's, Toronto #132/R (C.D 3500)
$3113   £2062   La Maison de Mme Robitaille (41x51cm-16x20in) s. i.d.1943verso board. 18-Nov-92 Sotheby's, Toronto #57/R (C.D 4000)
$4228   £2800   Double Mock O (81x54cm-32x21in) s.d.1968 i.verso acrylic polymer. 24-Nov-92 Phillips, London #362/R
$4670   £3093   September 1932 (91x102cm-36x40in) s.d.32 i.verso. 18-Nov-92 Sotheby's, Toronto #274/R (C.D 6000)
$5000   £3356   Green square (79x79cm-31x31in) s.i.d.1963verso. 4-May-94 Christie's, New York #144/R
$7531   £4922   Sketch for banner (112x48cm-44x19in) s.d.1968 verso acrylic. 19-May-93 Sotheby's, Toronto #207/R (C.D 9500)

BUSH, Norton (1834-1894) American
$650   £439   Tropical river scene with boats (23x30cm-9x12in) s. panel. 9-Nov-93 John Moran, Pasadena #875
$2000   £1176   Tropical landscapes (66x27cm-26x11in) s. board pair. 4-Oct-92 Butterfield & Butterfield, Los Angeles #2/R
$3500   £2431   Napa Falls (39x19cm-15x7in) s.d. paper. 7-Mar-93 Butterfield & Butterfield, San Francisco #28/R
$6000   £4000   Tropical landscape (51x90cm-20x35in) s.d.1870. 17-Mar-94 Sotheby's, New York #21/R
$7000   £4487   Boats on river (36x61cm-14x24in) s.d.74. 27-May-93 Sotheby's, New York #182/R
$28000   £17949   Tropical river scene (56x91cm-22x36in) s.d.1891. 27-May-93 Sotheby's, New York #181/R

BUSSELL, Joshua H (attrib) (1816-1900) American
$11000   £7333   Shaker Village at Poland Hills. Barn and buildings (30x38cm-12x15in) i. W/C. pencil double-sided. 12-Jun-94 Skinner, Bolton #97/R

BUTLER, Edward Burgess (1853-1928) American
$1200   £811   Landscape (64x76cm-25x30in) s.d.1907. 15-Jun-93 John Moran, Pasadena #59

BUTLER, Fray Guillermo (1880-1961) Argentinian
$1600   £941   Paisaje (16x22cm-6x9in) painted 1927. 29-Sep-92 VerBo, Buenos Aires #22
$10000   £5780   Capilla de San Antonio (110x145cm-43x57in) 23-Sep-92 Roldan & Cia, Buenos Aires #34
$12000   £6936   Otono (70x100cm-28x39in) tempera. 23-Sep-92 Roldan & Cia, Buenos Aires #35

BUTLER, Horacio (1897-1983) Argentinian
$2650   £1559   Naturaleza muerta (15x20cm-6x8in) 29-Sep-92 VerBo, Buenos Aires #23/R

BUTLER, Howard Russell (1856-1934) American
$1100   £724   Starlight sky above mission (64x74cm-25x29in) s. board. 2-Jun-93 Doyle, New York #40/R
$2250   £1481   Cliffs on coast (36x51cm-14x20in) s. canvas on board. 13-Jun-93 Butterfield & Butterfield, San Francisco #730/R
$14000   £9790   Zion Canyon, Utah (107x132cm-42x52in) s. 10-Mar-93 Sotheby's, New York #49/R

BUTLER, Mary (1865-1946) American
$1000   £588   Harbourside (61x81cm-24x32in) s. 8-Oct-92 Freeman Fine Arts, Philadelphia #1074

BUTLER, Rozel Oertle (20th C) American
$800   £526   Mexican flower market (99x76cm-39x30in) s. 5-Jun-93 Louisiana Auction Exchange #90/R
$2750   £1821   Marketplace (99x76cm-39x30in) s. 28-Sep-93 John Moran, Pasadena #309

BUTLER, Theodore E (1861-1936) American
$7500   £5034   Canal Montreuil (55x46cm-22x18in) s. 6-May-94 Skinner, Bolton #132 a/R
$19289   £13033   Suzanne Hoschede au lapin (34x43cm-13x17in) mono.i.d.1891. 14-Jun-93 Laurin Guilloux Buffetaud Tailleur, Paris #4/R (F.FR 110000)
$25000   £15823   French landscape (60x73cm-24x29in) s.d.06. 4-Dec-92 Christie's, New York #10/R
$33000   £22000   Place du Rome at night (59x73cm-23x29in) s.d.05. 25-May-94 Sotheby's, New York #83/R

BUTLER, Theodore E (attrib) (1861-1936) American
$1500   £1020   East river scene New York (38x48cm-15x19in) s. i.verso. 17-Apr-94 Schrager Galleries, Milwaukee #690 a

BUTMAN, Frederick A (1820-1871) American
$2500   £1471   River bridge (46x76cm-18x30in) s. 4-Oct-92 Butterfield & Butterfield, Los Angeles #7/R
$5500   £3235   Landscape with children (30x51cm-12x20in) s. 4-Oct-92 Butterfield & Butterfield, Los Angeles #3/R

BUTTERSWORTH, J E (1817-1894) American
$6000   £4000   The British battleship Winterton (69x58cm-27x23in) s. 3-Jun-94 Sotheby's, New York #234/R

BUTTERSWORTH, James E (1817-1894) American
$3000   £2027   Untitled (10x20cm-4x8in) s. panel. 10-Aug-93 Stonington Fine Arts, Stonington #65/R
$3400   £1988   Yacht race (20x25cm-8x10in) s. canvas laid on board. 17-Sep-92 Sloan, North Bethesda #3114/R
$3720   £2400   Yachts racing (17x20cm-7x8in) s. panel. 20-Jan-93 Sotheby's, London #61/R
$5425   £3500   Rapid schooner and deal lugger off south foreland (62x75cm-24x30in) 20-Jan-93 Sotheby's, London #54/R
$6500   £4545   New York harbour (20x36cm-8x14in) 11-Mar-93 Christie's, New York #36/R
$7152   £4800   American schooner off Battery, New York harbour (28x45cm-11x18in) s. canvas on board. 16-Jul-93 Sotheby's, London #41/R
$14000   £9333   Two Clipper ships (20x30cm-8x12in) s. board. 26-May-94 Christie's, New York #11/R
$14000   £9333   The Cambria arriving at New York Sound (20x24cm-8x9in) s. i.verso board. 23-May-94 Christie's, East, New York #58/R
$14076   £9200   Arriving in port (30x40cm-12x16in) s. 7-Oct-93 Christie's, S. Kensington #415/R
$14744   £9700   British Man-of-War off coast at Cadiz (45x60cm-18x24in) s. 6-Apr-93 Sotheby's, London #8/R
$15000   £10067   Rival off Bay Ridge (23x31cm-9x12in) s. i.verso. 2-Dec-93 Sotheby's, New York #2/R
$16000   £10127   Clipper ship in heavy seas (50x76cm-20x30in) s. 3-Dec-92 Sotheby's, New York #5/R
$16000   £10127   View of Nassau in the Bahamas, West Indies (20x30cm-8x12in) s. panel. 4-Dec-92 Christie's, New York #189/R
$18000   £11538   Yachting in Baltimore harbour (36x56cm-14x22in) s. i.stretcher. 26-May-93 Christie's, New York #66 a/R
$18000   £11921   The Volunteer rounding Sandy Hook leading The Thistle (15x30cm-6x12in) s. i.verso panel. 22-Sep-93 Christie's, New York #4/R
$20000   £12821   Yacht race (30x51cm-12x20in) s. 26-May-93 Christie's, New York #26/R
$21750   £14500   Cutters racing and other shipping in choppy sea (46x61cm-18x24in) s. 19-Jul-93 Phillips, Tyne and Wear #170/R
$26000   £17450   Yacht under full sail (31x41cm-12x16in) s. 2-Dec-93 Sotheby's, New York #1/R
$35000   £23490   Yacht regatta off New York having eleven sailboats racing and one steamship (41x30cm-16x12in) 16-Jul-93 Douglas, South Deerfield #1
$75000   £47468   Pilot boats (50x76cm-20x30in) s. 3-Dec-92 Sotheby's, New York #8/R
$85000   £56667   Vesta off the Needles (53x84cm-21x33in) s. 26-May-94 Christie's, New York #12/R
$110000   £70513   Picking up pilot-Isle of Shoals, New Hampshire (43x68cm-17x27in) s. 26-May-93 Christie's, New York #4/R

BUTTERSWORTH, James E (attrib) (1817-1894) American
$2250   £1324   Sailing off coast (63x76cm-25x30in) 3-Oct-92 Weschler, Washington #82/R
$100000   £66667   1876 America's Cup Race (76x102cm-30x40in) 25-Sep-94 Sotheby's, New York #25/R

BUTTERSWORTH, James E (style) (1817-1894) American
$1276   £850   American schooner off the Battery, New York Harbour (28x45cm-11x18in) bears sig. canvas laid down on board. 11-May-94 Sotheby's, London #129/R

BUTTNER, Werner (1954-) American
$5000   £3311   Euphoria - machine painting with 5 spare parts (120x300cm-47x118in) init.d.84 six parts. 18-Nov-92 Sotheby's, New York #299/R
$5000   £3356   Shehu's death (190x240cm-75x94in) s. painted 1984. 5-May-94 Sotheby's, New York #307/R

BYARS, James Lee (20th C) American
$2596   £1742   The perfect lover letter (30cm-12in circular) s. typewritten text crayon. 14-Oct-93 Guy Loudmer, Paris #137 (F.FR 15000)

BYGRAVE, W (19th C) American
$4684   £3061   Southern harbour town (53x71cm-21x28in) 29-Jun-94 Neumeister, Munich #485/R (DM 7500)

BYRON, Michael (1954-) American
$800   £537   Insignia (43x36cm-17x14in) s.i.d.3/85verso oil plaster pigment panel. 3-May-94 Christie's, East, New York #205/R
$848   £565   Ishi (96x59cm-38x23in) s.d.9/82verso mixed media panel. 2-Jun-94 AB Stockholms Auktionsverk, Stockholm #7193/R (S.KR 6700)

CABADA, Havier (20th C) American
$1400   £897   Untitled (122x122cm-48x48in) s.d.1971. 10-Dec-92 Sloan, North Bethesda #2711

CABALLERO, Jorge Mantilla (20th C) Latin American
$3750   £2483   Untitled (99x99cm-39x39in) s.d.71. 23-Nov-92 Sotheby's, New York #198/R

CABALLERO, Luis (1943-) Colombian
$15000   £9934   Figura (145x114cm-57x45in) s.d.88. 24-Nov-92 Christie's, New York #249/R
$30000   £19608   Untitled (195x130cm-77x51in) s.s.d.86 verso. 17-May-93 Christie's, New York #242/R
$911   £600   Sans titre (56x75cm-22x30in) s.d.1975 W/C pencil. 11-Jun-93 Poulain & le Fur, Paris #148 (F.FR 5000)
$2187   £1439   Sans titre (56x75cm-22x30in) s.d.1975 W/C pencil. 11-Jun-93 Poulain & le Fur, Paris #151 (F.FR 12000)
$2500   £1678   Untitled, nude figures (28x35cm-11x14in) s.d.87 pastel. 7-Jan-94 Gary Nader, Miami #74/R

CABANAS OTEIZA, Antonio (?) Uruguayan
$1600   £1046   Aldeanos (65x81cm-26x32in) s. 26-Oct-92 Gomensoro, Montevideo #25

CABOT, Channing (1868-1932) American
$750   £514   Peacocks (191x165cm-75x65in) s.d.1926 three panels. 10-Feb-94 Skinner, Bolton #226

CABRE, Manuel (1890-?) Venezuelan
$19000   £12667   Vista del Avila (49x60cm-19x24in) s. 18-May-94 Christie's, New York #88/R

CABRERA MORENO, Servando (1932-) Cuban
$3500   £2288   Figura cubista (100x46cm-39x18in) s.d.59. 17-May-93 Christie's, New York #205/R

CABRERA, Miguel (1695-1768) Mexican
$11000   £7432   Divino pastor (21x16cm-8x6in) s. copper painted c.1750. 22-Nov-93 Sotheby's, New York #140/R
$12000   £7947   San Jose (26x21cm-10x8in) s.d.1737 copper. 23-Nov-92 Sotheby's, New York #114/R
$13000   £8784   Escudo de Monja (19cm-7in circular) s. copper painted c.1750. 22-Nov-93 Sotheby's, New York #145/R
$24000   £15686   La Virgen y el Nino (54x39cm-21x15in) s. linen. 17-May-93 Christie's, New York #80/R
$27000   £17881   San Juan Nepomuceno (74x57cm-29x22in) s.i.d.1766. 24-Nov-92 Christie's, New York #74/R
$30000   £20270   San Jose y el Nino Jesus (50x40cm-20x16in) s.d.1764 copper. 23-Nov-93 Christie's, New York #17/R
$30000   £20000   La Virgen de Guadalupe (74x61cm-29x24in) s.i. copper painted 1766. 18-May-94 Christie's, New York #1/R
$35000   £23333   Nuestra Senora del Rosario (72x55cm-28x22in) s.d.1768. 18-May-94 Christie's, New York #2/R
$42000   £27815   Nuestra Senora del Rosario (72x55cm-28x22in) s.d.1768. 24-Nov-92 Christie's, New York #78/R

CABRERA, Miguel (attrib) (1695-1768) Mexican
$6000   £3947   Virgen de la Paloma (35x25cm-14x10in) bears sig.d.1762 tin. 20-Jul-94 Sotheby's Arcade, New York #52/R
$14000   £9272   Coronacion de la Virgen (17cm-7in circular) copper. 23-Nov-92 Sotheby's, New York #116/R
$110000   £71895   La Vida de la Virgen Maria (114x96cm-45x38in) eight painted c.1759. 18-May-93 Sotheby's, New York #10/R

CABRERA, Miguel (circle) (1695-1768) Mexican
$6000   £4054   Exaltacion de la Compania de Jesus (29x21cm-11x8in) W/C gouache pen vellum. 23-Nov-93 Christie's, New York #74/R

CABRERA, Raul (?) South American
$2000   £1342   Ultima cena (79x98cm-31x39in) s. board. 29-Nov-93 Gomensoro, Montevideo #3

CADDY, John Herbert (19th C) Canadian
$431   £287   Whirlpool, Niagara River (32x46cm-13x18in) sepia ink W/C over graphite. 30-May-94 Ritchie, Toronto #281 (C.D 600)
$666   £427   McKay Mountain up the Kamanastikevea River, head of Lake Superior (22x36cm-9x14in) W/C. 7-Dec-92 Waddingtons, Toronto #1292/R (C.D 850)
$1903   £1244   View of Hamilton (39x60cm-15x24in) W/C. 19-May-93 Sotheby's, Toronto #390/R (C.D 2400)

CADENASSO, Giuseppe (1858-1918) American
$3750	£2517	Roses (51x66cm-20x26in) s.d.96. 8-Dec-93 Butterfield & Butterfield, San Francisco #3306/R
$1700	£1000	Sunset on marsh (27x34cm-11x13in) s. pastel. 4-Oct-92 Butterfield & Butterfield, Los Angeles #40/R

CADET, Gabriel (jnr) (1953-) Haitian
$670	£430	La cueillette (61x51cm-24x20in) s. i.verso. 14-Dec-92 Hoebanx, Paris #85/R (F.FR 3600)

CADMUS, Paul (1904-) American
$21000	£13291	Mask with false noses (20x31cm-8x12in) s. tempera paper. 4-Dec-92 Christie's, New York #138/R
$32000	£18497	Le Ruban Denoue, hommage a Reynaldo Hahn (53x91cm-21x36in) s.i. s.i.verso egg tempera masonite. 23-Sep-92 Christie's, New York #284/R
$1100	£733	Female nude, no.SL2 (13x9cm-5x4in) s. pencil executed c.1937. 23-May-94 Christie's, East, New York #305
$2200	£1392	Male torso (23x18cm-9x7in) s. ink. 2-Dec-92 Christie's, East, New York #355/R
$2400	£1387	Male nude (36x18cm-14x7in) s. graphite. 27-Sep-92 James Bakker, Cambridge #157/R
$2400	£1519	Maggie the Bulldog , s. chl chk five in one mount. 2-Dec-92 Christie's, East, New York #342/R
$3500	£2215	Seated male nude (33x38cm-13x15in) s. W/C pencil htd white. 2-Dec-92 Christie's, East, New York #356/R
$3500	£2333	Female nude RB7 (41x37cm-16x15in) s.i. col.crayon executed c.1965. 23-May-94 Christie's, East, New York #299/R
$4000	£2312	Male nude (33x51cm-13x20in) s.i. col.chk chl. 25-Sep-92 Sotheby's Arcade, New York #299/R
$4500	£2601	Sleeping figure (33x51cm-13x20in) s. col.chk chl. 25-Sep-92 Sotheby's Arcade, New York #300/R
$4500	£2848	Polo spill (13x18cm-5x7in) s. ink wash. 2-Dec-92 Boos Gallery, Michigan #831/R
$6000	£4054	Seated male nude (46x37cm-18x15in) s. col.chk chl htd white executed 1966. 31-Mar-94 Sotheby's Arcade, New York #427/R
$8500	£5743	Reclining male nude (42x51cm-17x20in) s. col.chk chl htd white. 31-Mar-94 Sotheby's Arcade, New York #423/R

CADY, Walter Harrison (1877-1970) American
$750	£490	Painting the Betty Ann, Rockport (51x81cm-20x32in) exec.c.1940. 18-Sep-93 Young Fine Arts Auctions, Maine #58/R
$650	£376	Picnic on beach (41x53cm-16x21in) s.d.1936 W/C graphite. 27-Sep-92 James Bakker, Cambridge #95/R
$1400	£933	Two nuns at fish market (51x46cm-20x18in) W/C. 3-Jun-94 Douglas, South Deerfield #4
$32000	£20513	Moonlight sonata (44x60cm-17x24in) s.d.1962 oil gouache ink board. 27-May-93 Sotheby's, New York #119/R
$45000	£30000	The moonlight symphony (39x61cm-15x24in) s. oil gouache ink masonite. 25-May-94 Sotheby's, New York #155/R

CAGE, John (1912-) American
$5500	£3691	Where R - Ryoanji (26x48cm-10x19in) s.d.9/84 graphite. 23-Feb-94 Christie's, East, New York #324/R
$10000	£6536	Mesostic tribute to Marcel Duchamp (76x107cm-30x42in) chk slate blackboard executed 1973. 4-May-93 Sotheby's, New York #115 a/R

CAHEN, Oscar (1916-1956) Canadian
$965	£610	Self-portrait (30x23cm-12x9in) s. canvasboard. 30-Nov-92 Ritchie, Toronto #250/R (C.D 1227)
$1427	£933	Semaphor (49x40cm-19x16in) s. W/C col chk. 18-May-93 Joyner Fine Art, Toronto #170 (C.D 1800)

CAHILL, William Vincent (1878-1924) American
$5500	£3526	Grandmother, mother and child (71x107cm-28x42in) s. 9-Dec-92 Butterfield & Butterfield, San Francisco #3946/R

CAHOON, C D (1861-1951) American
$1300	£844	Still life with trout, fishing pole and basket on a bank (28x46cm-11x18in) s. 4-Aug-94 Eldred, Massachusetts #884 a/R
$4500	£2922	Autumn pond landscape with figure (43x64cm-17x25in) s. 4-Aug-94 Eldred, Massachusetts #884 b/R

CAHOON, Charles D (1861-1951) American
$900	£604	Cape Cod sand dune (41x56cm-16x22in) s. 25-Mar-94 Eldred, Massachusetts #916/R
$1800	£1208	Sailing vessel underway on a moonlit sea (61x81cm-24x32in) s. 25-Mar-94 Eldred, Massachusetts #294/R
$1900	£1275	Shore scene with marsh and tree (23x41cm-9x16in) s. 25-Mar-94 Eldred, Massachusetts #915/R
$2400	£1611	Autumn landscape with ocean in distance (41x56cm-16x22in) s. board. 25-Mar-94 Eldred, Massachusetts #698/R
$2750	£1403	Title Marsh, Harwich (23x30cm-9x12in) s. board. 18-Aug-92 Richard Bourne, Hyannis #87/R

CAHOON, Charles D (attrib) (1861-1951) American
$800	£537	Landscape with homestead (20x30cm-8x12in) board. 25-Mar-94 Eldred, Massachusetts #697/R

CAHOON, Martha (20th C) American

$600	£403	Winter skaters (23x33cm-9x13in) s. panel. 1-Dec-93 Doyle, New York #32
$1000	£510	The tiger (20x25cm-8x10in) s. board. 18-Aug-92 Richard Bourne, Hyannis #69/R
$1400	£909	Pennsylvania Dutch boy and girl with flower arrangement (30x38cm-12x15in) s. masonite. 4-Aug-94 Eldred, Massachusetts #808/R
$1600	£1039	Mermaid sirens and stranded sailors (36x51cm-14x20in) s. masonite. 4-Aug-94 Eldred, Massachusetts #810/R
$2400	£1611	Narcissus and Echo (41x51cm-16x20in) s. masonite. 25-Mar-94 Eldred, Massachusetts #922/R
$2900	£1883	Rural landscape with figures (41x51cm-16x20in) s. masonite. 4-Aug-94 Eldred, Massachusetts #811/R
$925	£482	Home is the Sailor - Home from the sea (36x25cm-14x10in) s. painted 1894 W/C. 6-Aug-92 Eldred, Massachusetts #833/R

CAHOON, Ralph (1910-1982) American

$2400	£1600	Wife of the mariner, shore scene with sailor and mermaid (25x30cm-10x12in) i.verso masonite. 20-Aug-93 Skinner, Bolton #60/R
$2600	£1688	Girl on the shore. Female acrobat astride two horses (102x229cm-40x90in) panel pair. 4-Aug-94 Eldred, Massachusetts #596/R
$3100	£1615	Ship buildings with mermaids (28x38cm-11x15in) s. 6-Aug-92 Eldred, Massachusetts #837/R
$3600	£2338	Two men in a balloon (30x51cm-12x20in) s. masonite. 4-Aug-94 Eldred, Massachusetts #820/R
$4300	£2886	Sailors watching mermaids scrub the deck (36x36cm-14x14in) s. masonite. 5-Aug-93 Eldred, Massachusetts #946/R
$8000	£5195	Mermaid and sailors by foremast of ship (46x53cm-18x21in) s. 4-Aug-94 Eldred, Massachusetts #817/R
$8500	£4337	Nantucket Fish Co, mermaids and sailor with boatload of fish (46x61cm-18x24in) s.i. board. 18-Aug-92 Richard Bourne, Hyannis #30/R
$9000	£5844	Three mermaids, two sailors and ship (66x51cm-26x20in) s. masonite. 4-Aug-94 Eldred, Massachusetts #816/R
$10000	£5208	Scrimshaw basket with shells (56x76cm-22x30in) s. masonite. 6-Aug-92 Eldred, Massachusetts #839/R
$12000	£7792	Still life with scrimshaw (41x51cm-16x20in) s. masonite oval. 4-Aug-94 Eldred, Massachusetts #818/R
$16000	£10738	Whimiscal theme with mermaids, fisherman, balloon, ship and lighthouse (38x48cm-15x19in) s. masonite. 5-Aug-93 Eldred, Massachusetts #799/R
$18500	£12013	The lady disapproves, man embracing a mermaid (41x51cm-16x20in) s. masonite. 4-Aug-94 Eldred, Massachusetts #821/R
$21000	£13636	Ship, Red Jacket, in Boston Harbour (51x66cm-20x26in) s. masonite. 4-Aug-94 Eldred, Massachusetts #819/R
$750	£497	Mermouse holding fishing rod and fish (20x15cm-8x6in) s.d.1973 W/C. 20-Nov-92 Eldred, Massachusetts #741/R

CAISERMAN-ROTH, Ghitta (1923-) Canadian

$674	£440	Painter (28x36cm-11x14in) s. ink. 19-May-93 Sotheby's, Toronto #51 (C.D 850)

CALDER, Alexander (1898-1976) American

$3492	£2268	Composizione (48x67cm-19x26in) s.d.1967 tempera paper. 21-Jun-94 Finarte, Milan #293/R (I.L 5500000)
$12000	£8054	Untitled (14x34cm-6x13in) canvas on panel. 23-Feb-94 Christie's, New York #4/R
$693	£469	Mobile (8x13cm-3x5in) s.i. verso gouache postcard. 24-Nov-93 Watine-Arnault, Paris #27 (F.FR 4100)
$700	£464	Portrait of man (76x56cm-30x22in) init.d.68 ink. 29-Sep-93 Sotheby's Arcade, New York #297/R
$900	£604	Belinda Brooks with cats (10x15cm-4x6in) pen double-sided. 24-Feb-94 Sotheby's Arcade, New York #63/R
$1150	£767	Harbour scene (23x25cm-9x10in) s. ink brush W/C. 9-Jun-94 Swann Galleries, New York #54/R
$1490	£1000	Rouge et noir (109x75cm-43x30in) s.d.73 gouache. 21-Jun-93 Christie's, S. Kensington #219/R
$1600	£1074	Portraits of Barnett Owen (28x22cm-11x9in) one s.d.67 one mono. ink onion skin paper two. 24-Feb-94 Sotheby's Arcade, New York #334/R
$1600	£1060	Portrait of Barnett Owen (56x76cm-22x30in) s.d.68 brush ink. 29-Sep-93 Sotheby's Arcade, New York #298/R
$1937	£1300	Three dots make a face (109x75cm-43x30in) s.d.69 gouache. 25-Mar-93 Christie's, London #71/R
$2000	£1307	Untitled (110x75cm-43x30in) s.d.64 gouache brush ink. 7-May-93 Christie's, East, New York #37/R
$2086	£1400	The black mouse (109x75cm-43x30in) s.d.72 gouache. 21-Jun-93 Christie's, S. Kensington #218/R
$2086	£1400	Jack's road (75x110cm-30x43in) s.d.73 gouache. 2-Dec-93 Christie's, London #208/R
$2086	£1400	Foret de geysers (75x108cm-30x43in) s.d.70 gouache. 29-Nov-93 Christie's, S. Kensington #251/R
$2132	£1441	Composizione (75x100cm-30x39in) s.d.73 gouache. 22-Nov-93 Christie's, Milan #110/R (I.L 3600000)
$2132	£1367	Orange hand (109x75cm-43x30in) s.d.70 gouache. 26-May-93 Christie's, Amsterdam #403/R (D.FL 3800)
$2132	£1367	Zeus (75x109cm-30x43in) s.d.71 gouache. 26-May-93 Christie's, Amsterdam #402 (D.FL 3800)
$2374	£1522	Untitled (75x109cm-30x43in) s.d.67 gouache. 10-Dec-92 Christie's, Amsterdam #375 (D.FL 4200)
$2374	£1522	Untitled - stop (109x75cm-43x30in) s.d.70 gouache. 10-Dec-92 Christie's, Amsterdam #379 (D.FL 4200)

CALDER, Alexander (1898-1976) American-cont.

$2400	£1667	Untitled (16x26cm-6x10in) init.d.49 gouache. 26-Feb-93 Sotheby's Arcade, New York #265/R
$2500	£1656	Sun and rays (63x50cm-25x20in) s.d.64 gouache. 29-Sep-93 Sotheby's Arcade, New York #249/R
$2500	£1656	Untitled (58x80cm-23x31in) s. gouache. 17-Nov-92 Christie's, East, New York #195/R
$2750	£1821	Untitled (74x109cm-29x43in) s.d.68 gouache. 30-Jun-93 Sotheby's Arcade, New York #297/R
$2750	£1821	49 (16x26cm-6x10in) gouache. 30-Jun-93 Sotheby's Arcade, New York #241/R
$2750	£1910	Untitled (17x26cm-7x10in) s.d.49 gouache pencil. 26-Feb-93 Sotheby's Arcade, New York #274 a/R
$2800	£1830	Untitled (75x110cm-30x43in) s.d.67 gouache brush ink. 7-May-93 Christie's, East, New York #33/R
$2806	£1799	Yellow flower with blue leaves (109x75cm-43x30in) s.d.71 gouache. 26-May-93 Christie's, Amsterdam #332 (D.FL 5000)
$3000	£1765	Untitled (39x29cm-15x11in) s.d.73 gouache. 6-Oct-92 Sotheby's, New York #61/R
$3000	£1961	Christaux (110x75cm-43x30in) s.d.72 gouache brush ink. 7-May-93 Christie's, East, New York #46/R
$3000	£2013	Pyramid with red and blue (75x110cm-30x43in) s.d.67 gouache brush black ink. 3-May-94 Christie's, East, New York #41/R
$3000	£2013	Flag pinwheel (110x75cm-43x30in) s.d.70 gouache brush black ink. 3-May-94 Christie's, East, New York #42/R
$3129	£2100	Untitled (75x110cm-30x43in) s.d.70 gouache. 25-Mar-93 Christie's, London #91/R
$3148	£2113	Fissures (109x75cm-43x30in) s.d.70 gouache. 8-Dec-93 Christie's, Amsterdam #274/R (D.FL 6000)
$3257	£2201	Composizione (75x110cm-30x43in) s.d.70 gouache. 22-Nov-93 Christie's, Milan #114/R (I.L 5500000)
$3278	£2200	Composition III (65x39cm-26x15in) mono.d.68 W/C ink pencil. 3-Dec-93 Sotheby's, London #226/R
$3278	£2200	Volubilis (110x75cm-43x30in) s.d.74 gouache. 2-Dec-93 Christie's, London #216/R
$3292	£2224	Coloured circles (52x74cm-20x29in) s. W/C. 19-Oct-93 Campo & Campo, Antwerp #120/R (B.FR 120000)
$3500	£2365	Swirls (76x56cm-30x22in) s.d.72 gouache. 21-Oct-93 Butterfield & Butterfield, San Francisco #2764/R
$3500	£2365	Untitled (65x48cm-26x19in) s.d.67 ink gouache. 21-Apr-94 Butterfield & Butterfield, San Francisco #1138/R
$3500	£2431	Untitled (74x109cm-29x43in) s.d.67 gouache. 26-Feb-93 Sotheby's Arcade, New York #303/R
$3500	£2365	Untitled (76x56cm-30x22in) s.d.68 gouache. 21-Apr-94 Butterfield & Butterfield, San Francisco #1139/R
$3538	£2390	Untitled (44x64cm-17x25in) s.d.69 gouache Indian ink. 19-Jun-93 Michael Bode, Pforzheim #82/R (DM 6000)
$3673	£2465	Setting sun, black star (75x110cm-30x43in) s.d.71 gouache. 8-Dec-93 Christie's, Amsterdam #272/R (D.FL 7000)
$3700	£2517	White eye, white nose, black eye (56x79cm-22x31in) s.d.73 gouache. 19-Nov-93 Du Mouchelle, Detroit #2043
$3750	£2604	Red and blue wave (110x75cm-43x30in) s.d.73 gouache. 26-Feb-93 Sotheby's Arcade, New York #326/R
$3874	£2600	L'Ideal (75x109cm-30x43in) s.d.70 gouache. 29-Nov-93 Christie's, S. Kensington #250/R
$3874	£2600	Le couple (75x110cm-30x43in) s.d.1970 gouache. 29-Nov-93 Christie's, S. Kensington #252/R
$3957	£2536	Untitled (109x75cm-43x30in) s.d.70 gouache. 10-Dec-92 Christie's, Amsterdam #376/R (D.FL 7000)
$4000	£2649	Tapestry (78x58cm-31x23in) iit.d.74 i.verso brush ink gouache. 17-Nov-92 Christie's, East, New York #194/R
$4000	£2778	Color field - yellow is dominant (74x109cm-29x43in) s.d.69 gouache. 26-Feb-93 Sotheby's Arcade, New York #306/R
$4000	£2703	Untitled (52x69cm-20x27in) s.d.67 ink gouache. 21-Apr-94 Butterfield & Butterfield, San Francisco #1137/R
$4023	£2700	Quadrature (75x109cm-30x43in) s.d.72 gouache. 21-Jun-93 Christie's, S. Kensington #221/R
$4172	£2800	Trefles (75x109cm-30x43in) s.d.70 gouache. 25-Mar-93 Christie's, London #90/R
$4197	£2817	Sun and sprouts (109x75cm-43x30in) s.d.72 gouache. 8-Dec-93 Christie's, Amsterdam #273/R (D.FL 8000)
$4200	£2745	Pavots (110x75cm-43x30in) s.d.71 gouache brush ink. 7-May-93 Christie's, East, New York #48/R
$4200	£2745	Mistral (75x110cm-30x43in) s.d.71 gouache brush ink. 7-May-93 Christie's, East, New York #47/R
$4250	£2815	Untitled (57x16cm-22x6in) s.d.75 gouache. 29-Sep-93 Sotheby's Arcade, New York #302/R
$4500	£2980	Twenty saucers (109x37cm-43x15in) s.d.72 W/C gouache. 29-Sep-93 Sotheby's Arcade, New York #301/R
$4500	£2980	Untitled (107x74cm-42x29in) s.d.65 gouache. 29-Sep-93 Sotheby's Arcade, New York #296/R
$4500	£3020	Les Tropiques (75x110cm-30x43in) s.d.72 gouache brush ink. 23-Feb-94 Christie's, East, New York #344/R
$4500	£3125	Equilibre (75x110cm-30x43in) s.d.73 gouache brush ink. 22-Feb-93 Christie's, East, New York #183/R
$4700	£3154	Untitled (58x79cm-23x31in) s.d.47 gouache. 24-Feb-94 Sotheby's Arcade, New York #385/R
$4722	£3169	Inner Nautilus (75x109cm-30x43in) s.d.71 gouache. 8-Dec-93 Christie's, Amsterdam #271/R (D.FL 9000)

CALDER, Alexander (1898-1976) American-cont.

$4750	£3188	Cross Mountain (109x74cm-43x29in) s.d.72 W/C. 24-Feb-94 Sotheby's Arcade, New York #383/R
$4768	£3200	Red and yellow nautilus (109x75cm-43x30in) s.d.72 gouache. 21-Jun-93 Christie's, S. Kensington #220/R
$4800	£3221	Soucoupes flottantes (110x75cm-43x30in) s.d.70 gouache brush ink. 23-Feb-94 Christie's, East, New York #345/R
$4880	£3275	Visage et main (109x74cm-43x29in) s.d.1970 gouache. 21-Mar-94 Guy Loudmer, Paris #18 b (F.FR 28000)
$4947	£3320	Tadpole (38x55cm-15x22in) mono.d.1961 i.verso gouache Indian ink vellum. 3-Dec-93 Lempertz, Cologne #629/R (DM 8500)
$5000	£3311	Untitled (38x27cm-15x11in) s.i.d.75 gouache. 29-Sep-93 Sotheby's Arcade, New York #248/R
$5000	£3356	Le grand tremblement (53x78cm-21x31in) s.d.70 i.verso gouache. 24-Feb-94 Sotheby's Arcade, New York #386/R
$5000	£3311	Running woman (48x41cm-19x16in) s.d.46 W/C Indian ink. 30-Jun-93 Sotheby's Arcade, New York #238/R
$5000	£3472	Emerging forms (74x105cm-29x41in) s.d.61 W/C gouache. 23-Feb-93 Sotheby's, New York #208/R
$5050	£3237	Le cheval cailloux (75x109cm-30x43in) s.d.71 gouache. 26-May-93 Christie's, Amsterdam #331 b/R (D.FL 9000)
$5100	£3400	Le tourniquet (75x110cm-30x43in) s.d.73 gouache. 26-May-94 Christie's, London #113/R
$5216	£3200	Le Pie de Sache (110x37cm-43x15in) init.i.d.74 gouache. 14-Oct-92 Sotheby's, London #401/R
$5250	£3500	Higgledy-piggledy (73x107cm-29x42in) s.d.69 gouache W/C Indian ink. 25-May-94 Sotheby's Colonnade, London #389/R
$5250	£3524	Hello, hello (74x109cm-29x43in) s.d.67 gouache. 24-Feb-94 Sotheby's Arcade, New York #332/R
$5370	£3442	Untitled (109x75cm-43x30in) s.d.71 gouache. 10-Dec-92 Christie's, Amsterdam #378/R (D.FL 9500)
$5400	£3600	Soucoupes volantes (75x110cm-30x43in) s.d.72 gouache. 26-May-94 Christie's, London #115/R
$5489	£3587	Boomerang and twirling comma (57x78cm-22x31in) s. gouache ink. 8-May-93 Rusterholtz & Low, Basel #59/R (S.FR 8000)
$5500	£3642	Black on black spirals (74x109cm-29x43in) s.d.70 gouache. 29-Sep-93 Sotheby's Arcade, New York #300
$5500	£3819	Untitled (58x78cm-23x31in) s.d.47 gouache. 26-Feb-93 Sotheby's Arcade, New York #274/R
$5500	£3235	Untitled - sunrise (75x104cm-30x41in) s.d.75 gouache. 6-Oct-92 Sotheby's, New York #62/R
$5500	£3819	Untitled (57x77cm-22x30in) s.d.66 gouache brush ink. 22-Feb-93 Christie's, East, New York #152/R
$5500	£3819	Flags (75x110cm-30x43in) s.d.69 gouache brush ink. 22-Feb-93 Christie's, East, New York #150/R
$5500	£3819	Two starfish (110x74cm-43x29in) s.d.72 gouache. 26-Feb-93 Sotheby's Arcade, New York #325/R
$5500	£3235	Untitled (76x112cm-30x44in) s.d.73 gouache. 6-Oct-92 Sotheby's, New York #63/R
$5513	£3700	Tourniquet (109x75cm-43x30in) s.d.69 gouache. 25-Mar-93 Christie's, London #72/R
$5600	£3758	The black mouse (108x73cm-43x29in) s.d.72 gouache. 3-Jan-94 Gordon Galleries, Tel Aviv #452 a/R
$5700	£3800	Luck (110x75cm-43x30in) s.d.73 gouache. 26-May-94 Christie's, London #117/R
$5960	£4000	Untitled (75x105cm-30x41in) s.d.66 gouache. 25-Mar-93 Christie's, London #73/R
$5960	£4000	Soleil rouge (74x104cm-29x41in) s.d.62 ink gouache. 23-Mar-94 Sotheby's, London #362/R
$5960	£4000	Untitled (75x109cm-30x43in) s.d.70 gouache. 2-Dec-93 Christie's, London #209/R
$5960	£4000	Untitled (75x110cm-30x43in) s.d.71 W/C ink. 23-Mar-94 Sotheby's, London #380/R
$5960	£4000	Composition (46x33cm-18x13in) s. gouache executed 1960. 25-Mar-93 Christie's, London #97/R
$5960	£4000	Haute mer (75x109cm-30x43in) s.d.70 gouache. 29-Nov-93 Christie's, S. Kensington #249/R
$6000	£4027	Path through the orbes (57x77cm-22x30in) s.d.73 gouache. 24-Feb-94 Sotheby's Arcade, New York #389/R
$6000	£4167	Untitled (107x74cm-42x29in) s.d.66 gouache. 26-Feb-93 Sotheby's Arcade, New York #304/R
$6156	£4131	Personnage, totem (109x26cm-43x10in) mono.d.71 gouache. 23-Mar-93 Cornette de St.Cyr, Paris #88/R (F.FR 34000)
$6250	£4195	the orange boomerang (109x75cm-43x30in) s.d.73 gouache pencil. 24-Feb-94 Sotheby's Arcade, New York #382/R
$6258	£4200	L'Ange (75x110cm-30x43in) s.d.73 gouache. 2-Dec-93 Christie's, London #211/R
$6258	£4200	Red and black bubbles (109x75cm-43x30in) s.d.69 gouache. 25-Mar-93 Christie's, London #92/R
$6500	£4514	Untitled (75x110cm-30x43in) s.d.70 gouache. 26-Feb-93 Sotheby's Arcade, New York #309/R
$6500	£4305	Untitled (75x111cm-30x44in) s.d.75 gouache. 30-Jun-93 Sotheby's Arcade, New York #301/R
$6500	£4514	Spheres behind the sun (74x110cm-29x43in) s.d.71 gouache. 26-Feb-93 Sotheby's Arcade, New York #308/R
$6750	£4500	Ottoman's dance (75x108cm-30x43in) s.d.70 gouache. 26-May-94 Christie's, London #112/R
$6750	£4500	Andine (75x110cm-30x43in) s.d.72 gouache. 26-May-94 Christie's, London #114/R
$6854	£4600	Untitled (75x110cm-30x43in) s.d.70 W/C ink. 23-Mar-94 Sotheby's, London #383/R
$6854	£4600	Kwai (75x110cm-30x43in) s.d.74 gouache. 2-Dec-93 Christie's, London #210/R
$6971	£4678	Spheres et pyramides (75x109cm-30x43in) s.d.1975 gouache Indian ink. 21-Mar-94 Guy Loudmer, Paris #24/R (F.FR 40000)

CALDER, Alexander (1898-1976) American-cont.
$7000	£4636	Untitled (75x110cm-30x43in) s.d.74 brush ink. 17-Nov-92 Christie's, East, New York #189/R
$7000	£4698	Composition (72x104cm-28x41in) s.d.62 mixed media paperboard. 4-Mar-94 Skinner, Bolton #305/R
$7000	£4636	Loving couples (109x74cm-43x29in) s.i.d.71 W/C. 29-Sep-93 Sotheby's Arcade, New York #295/R
$7500	£4412	The crickets. The ape. The horse , s. Indian ink three. 5-Oct-92 Sotheby's, New York #75/R
$7748	£5200	Untitled (110x75cm-43x30in) s.d.71 W/C ink. 23-Mar-94 Sotheby's, London #350/R
$7783	£5189	Untitled (75x109cm-30x43in) s.d.70 gouache. 4-Jun-94 Aucktionhaus Burkard, Luzern #99/R (S.FR 11000)
$8000	£5442	Composition in red and black (108x73cm-43x29in) s.d.73 gouache Indian ink. 4-Apr-94 Sotheby's, Tel Aviv #140/R
$8000	£5556	Untitled (74x103cm-29x41in) s.d.62 W/C. 23-Feb-93 Sotheby's, New York #214/R
$8000	£5229	Striped face with red nose (74x110cm-29x43in) s.d.69 gouache. 4-May-93 Sotheby's, New York #347/R
$8000	£5229	Untitled - airplane model and study (75x104cm-30x41in) gouache s.d.75 plane init.gouache fibreglass. 4-May-93 Sotheby's, New York #369/R
$8000	£5298	Overlapping spirals (74x107cm-29x42in) s.d.69 gouache. 29-Sep-93 Sotheby's Arcade, New York #299/R
$8855	£5903	Composition (50x65cm-20x26in) s.i.d.Noel 63 gouache. 25-May-94 Francis Briest, Paris #26 a (F.FR 50000)
$9000	£6000	Roustabout with rope (48x35cm-19x14in) s.d.1932 ink. 26-May-94 Christie's, London #125/R
$9000	£6081	Untitled (57x77cm-22x30in) s.i.d.1932 ink. 11-Nov-93 Sotheby's, New York #321/R
$9500	£6597	Untitled (58x78cm-23x31in) s.d.47 gouache. 26-Feb-93 Sotheby's Arcade, New York #276 a/R
$10757	£7171	Composition with toy windmill (75x100cm-30x39in) s.d.1971 gouache. 6-Jun-94 Wolfgang Ketterer, Munich #43/R (DM 18000)
$11000	£7432	Many red loops (75x108cm-30x43in) s.d.69 gouache. 11-Nov-93 Sotheby's, New York #249/R
$11410	£7000	Parallelogram (75x105cm-30x41in) s.d.61 gouache. 15-Oct-92 Christie's, London #51/R
$11500	£7718	Sun, moon and Zephyr (74x109cm-29x43in) s.d.67 W/C. 24-Feb-94 Sotheby's Arcade, New York #387/R
$12178	£8229	Moons jack etc. (108x75cm-43x30in) s.d.65 gouache. 26-Nov-93 Francis Briest, Paris #70/R (F.FR 72000)
$14190	£9524	Circus sun (73x109cm-29x43in) s.d.1967 gouache wash Indian ink. 16-Oct-93 Cornette de St.Cyr, Paris #23/R (F.FR 82000)
$15500	£10265	Bareback riders (55x75cm-22x28in) s.d.1931 pen. 29-Sep-93 Sotheby's Arcade, New York #247/R
$18000	£12500	Untitled (58x79cm-23x31in) s.d.47 gouache. 26-Feb-93 Sotheby's Arcade, New York #276/R
$28000	£18667	Circus lion no.26 (58x78cm-23x31in) s.d.1931 pen black ink. 11-May-94 Christie's, New York #471/R
$28316	£18387	Lune et soleil, fond d'azur (75x110cm-30x43in) init. W/C gouache Indian ink executed c.1960. 21-Jun-94 Francis Briest, Paris #85/R (F.FR 155000)
$29000	£19595	One handed balancing act (48x35cm-19x14in) s.d.1932 pen. 10-Nov-93 Christie's, New York #101/R

CALIFANO, John (1862-1946) Italian/American
$950	£609	Still life with fruit (56x71cm-22x28in) s. 13-Dec-92 Hindman Galleries, Chicago #40/R
$1000	£671	Shepherd playing a horn with dogs and sheep on alpine road (86x132cm-34x52in) s. 15-Dec-93 Boos Gallery, Michigan #448/R
$1200	£789	Mountain landscape with river (35x51cm-14x20in) s. 31-Mar-93 Sotheby's Arcade, New York #35/R
$1200	£816	Bringing in the catch (85x61cm-33x24in) s. canvas laid down on masonite. 15-Nov-93 Christie's, East, New York #18/R
$2100	£1321	Young woman with herd of goats (74x107cm-29x42in) s. 22-Apr-93 Freeman Fine Arts, Philadelphia #1305/R
$7500	£4967	Love letter (76x46cm-30x18in) s. 23-Sep-93 Sotheby's, New York #6/R

CALIGA, Isaac Henry (1857-1940) American
$1300	£909	Profile of a young woman (13x15cm-5x6in) mono.d.1884 panel. 7-Feb-93 James Bakker, Cambridge #23

CALVO, Pilar (?) Mexican?
$637	£408	India (32x24cm-13x9in) s. W/C. 29-Apr-93 Louis Morton, Mexico #59 (M.P 2000)

CAMACHO, Jorge (1934-) Cuban
$1415	£956	Permeabilite reduite (49x64cm-19x25in) s. paper. 20-Mar-93 Kunstgalerij de Vuyst, Lokeren #51 (B.FR 48000)
$1474	£996	Histoire des oiseaux (65x50cm-26x20in) paper. 20-Mar-93 Kunstgalerij de Vuyst, Lokeren #50 (B.FR 50000)
$2032	£1373	Aucun dessein tenebreux (46x110cm-18x43in) s.d.64verso. 3-Nov-93 Bukowskis, Stockholm #221/R (S.KR 16500)
$10000	£6757	Annunciation to myself (143x178cm-56x70in) s.d.58. 23-Nov-93 Christie's, New York #175/R

CAMARENA, Jorge Gonzalez (1918-) Mexican
$15000	£10000	Ante boceto para mural Dn.Venustano Carranza y La Constitucion de 1917 (41x50cm-16x20in) s. s.i.d.1967verso. 18-May-94 Sotheby's, New York #365/R

CAMERON, Robert Hartly (1909-) American
$582	£391	A two master in small English harbour (91x61cm-36x24in) s. 3-Dec-93 Dr Fritz Nagel, Stuttgart #3242 (DM 1000)
$1300	£850	The Punch and Judy show on the beach (61x94cm-24x37in) s. 7-Oct-93 Freeman Fine Arts, Philadelphia #922
$1300	£850	Girl in a flower garden (76x76cm-30x30in) s. 7-Oct-93 Freeman Fine Arts, Philadelphia #921
$1700	£1172	Playtime in garden (76x91cm-30x36in) s. 17-Feb-93 Doyle, New York #15
$1700	£1069	Tea time under the parasols (79x76cm-31x30in) s. 22-Apr-93 Freeman Fine Arts, Philadelphia #1232
$1900	£1118	Children playing in surf (74x99cm-29x39in) s. 8-Oct-92 Freeman Fine Arts, Philadelphia #1009
$1900	£1250	Summer beach outing (74x71cm-29x28in) s. 4-Nov-92 Doyle, New York #52/R

CAMILLE, Fritz (1965-) Haitian
$555	£367	Marche (51x61cm-20x24in) s. 13-Jun-94 Rogeon, Paris #7 (F.FR 3100)

CAMP, Joseph Rodefer de (1858-1923) American
$24000	£15190	La Penserosa (69x61cm-27x24in) s. 4-Dec-92 Christie's, New York #4/R
$48000	£30769	Trees along coast (63x76cm-25x30in) s. 26-May-93 Christie's, New York #115/R

CAMPBELL, Laurence A (20th C) American
$1700	£899	Rose garden (61x51cm-24x20in) s. 12-Sep-92 Louisiana Auction Exchange #95/R
$2000	£1342	Evie reading (61x51cm-24x20in) s. 5-Mar-94 Louisiana Auction Exchange #72/R
$2100	£1409	Evie working in the garden (61x51cm-24x20in) s. 4-Dec-93 Louisiana Auction Exchange #20/R

CAMPBELL, Leyda (1949-) Canadian
$623	£412	Winter river, Yellowhead HWY. (76x91cm-30x36in) s. s.i.verso. 16-Nov-92 Hodgins, Calgary #141/R (C.D 800)

CAMPBELL, Orville A (20th C) American
$950	£609	Blue bonnets (76x102cm-30x40in) s. 13-Dec-92 Hindman Galleries, Chicago #93

CAMPBELL, Steven (1953-) American
$2750	£1821	Chain of events (249x272cm-98x107in) s.d.83. 30-Jun-93 Sotheby's Arcade, New York #359/R
$2800	£1830	Hiker in landscape turned into marsh overnight (284x234cm-112x92in) executed 1983. 22-Dec-92 Christie's, East, New York #7/R
$4000	£2649	Topiary gardeners in forest at Pulsinane (274x267cm-108x105in) paintedd 1985. 30-Jun-93 Sotheby's Arcade, New York #358/R
$8140	£5500	Two hunters immobilised by excessive use of bark camouflage (280x280cm-110x110in) 25-Nov-93 Christie's, London #156/R
$14000	£8235	In pursuit of Mediocrity we present the dream house (226x239cm-89x94in) s.d.1988 verso. 6-Oct-92 Sotheby's, New York #203/R

CAMPECHE, Jose (1751-1809) Puerto Rican
$260000	£173333	Dama a caballo (42x33cm-17x13in) panel painted c.1785. 17-May-94 Sotheby's, New York #4/R

CAMPING, Simon (1928-) Canadian
$542	£366	Ruckle Park Salt Spring Island (37x55cm-15x22in) s. i.verso W/C. 1-Nov-93 Levis, Calgary #36/R (C.D 700)

CAMPO, Federico del (19/20th C) Peruvian
$3525	£2500	Bordighera (20x12cm-8x5in) s.d.1891 panel. 12-Feb-93 Christie's, London #80/R
$5436	£3600	Feeding pigeons before St. Mark's, Venice (28x18cm-11x7in) s. panel. 24-Nov-92 Phillips, London #235/R
$5624	£3800	Capri mountainous path with peasants (36x23cm-14x9in) s.i.d.1885. 2-Nov-93 Rowland Gorringe, Lewes #2701/R
$6000	£4138	Leaving church (36x23cm-14x9in) s.d.1900. 17-Feb-93 Sotheby's, New York #273/R
$11760	£8000	Scampagnata Partenopea (35x56cm-14x22in) s.d.1886. 19-Nov-93 Christie's, London #143/R
$12080	£8000	On the beach, Capri with Vesuvius in the background (36x56cm-14x22in) s.d.1887. 27-Nov-92 Christie's, London #76/R
$14300	£9662	Canal a Venise (60x36cm-24x14in) s.i.d.1896. 15-Mar-93 Ader Tajan, Paris #649 (F.FR 80000)
$16000	£10738	People leaving waterfront church (53x33cm-21x13in) s. 16-Oct-93 Dargate Auction Galleries, Pittsburgh #11
$22000	£14103	Bridge of Sighs, Venice (60x36cm-24x14in) s.d.1896. 27-May-93 Christie's, New York #92/R
$60000	£41096	The Grand Canal, Venice (36x58cm-14x23in) s.i.d.1900. 16-Feb-94 Sotheby's, New York #142/R
$3000	£2055	Venetian canal (24x34cm-9x13in) s. W/C. 15-Feb-94 Christie's, New York #137/R
$4530	£3000	Gondolas on a Venetian canal (39x21cm-15x8in) s. W/C. 14-Jun-94 Phillips, London #53/R
$5285	£3500	La Ca d'Oro, Venice (32x49cm-13x19in) s. W/C paper on card. 17-Jun-94 Christie's, London #241/R
$8400	£5600	Two Venetian canal scenes (40x25cm-16x10in) s. W/C over pencil pair. 16-Mar-94 Sotheby's, London #153/R

CAMPO, Federico del (attrib) (19/20th C) Peruvian
$7550	£5000	The Grand Canal looking towards Santa Maria della Salute, Venice (46x71cm-18x28in) s. 15-Jun-94 Sotheby's, London #195/R

CAMPOREALE, Sergio (1937-) Argentinian
$2522   £1764   Retrato de familia (80x120cm-31x47in) s. W/C crayon. 3-Feb-93 Cornette de St.Cyr, Paris #159/R (F.FR 14200)
$2572   £1726   El hombre del sombrero gris (80x120cm-31x47in) s. W/C crayon painted 1991. 8-Dec-93 Cornette de St.Cyr, Paris #101/R (F.FR 15000)

CAMPOS, Florencio Molina (20th C) South American
$1500   £1014   Late for dinner (41x51cm-16x20in) s.d.1942 board. 21-Oct-93 Butterfield & Butterfield, San Francisco #2744/R
$6000   £3922   La serenata (37x48cm-15x19in) s.d.48. 17-May-93 Christie's, New York #286/R
$6500   £4305   El Cortejo (40x50cm-16x20in) s.d. canvas on board. 24-Nov-92 Christie's, New York #268/R
$1100   £764   Jinete (21x32cm-8x13in) gouache executed c.1940. 26-Feb-93 Sotheby's Arcade, New York #247/R
$4000   £2614   Domador (32x49cm-13x19in) s.d.33 gouache paper on board. 17-May-93 Christie's, New York #287/R
$8000   £5229   La pulperia (31x48cm-12x19in) s.d.932 gouache chl paper on board. 17-May-93 Christie's, New York #252/R

CANAS, Benjamin (1937-) Chilean
$6455   £4332   Untitled (81x113cm-32x44in) s.d.80 pastel. 7-Jan-94 Gary Nader, Miami #29/R

CANCIO, Carlo (1961-) Puerto Rican
$5000   £3333   La Puertorriquena (102x74cm-40x29in) s.i.d.83 acrylic. 18-May-94 Christie's, New York #230/R

CANDIA, Domingo (1896-1976) Argentinian
$900   £596   La mesa (22x27cm-9x11in) pencil dr. 11-Nov-92 VerBo, Buenos Aires #13

CANIFF, Milton (1907-1988) American?
$475   £319   Miss Lace (23x15cm-9x6in) W/C. 27-Mar-94 Myers, Florida #110/R

CANTIENI, Graham (20th C) Canadian
$907   £613   Parergon number 3 (264x170cm-104x67in) s.d.1980 i.verso acrylic. 25-Apr-94 Levis, Calgary #48/R (C.D 1250)

CANTU, Federico (1908-1989) Mexican
$1100   £743   Mujer con unicornio (26x21cm-10x8in) s.d.40. 21-Apr-94 Butterfield & Butterfield, San Francisco #1107/R
$12000   £7947   Harlequin (53x38cm-21x15in) s.d.35. 23-Nov-92 Sotheby's, New York #181/R
$13000   £8667   Ruth (92x66cm-36x26in) s.d.37. 18-May-94 Christie's, New York #215/R
$800   £503   Desert study (49x65cm-19x26in) s.d.48 pastel. 25-Apr-93 Butterfield & Butterfield, San Francisco #2078/R
$1200   £805   Sevilla (22x31cm-9x12in) pen executed c.1932. 24-Feb-94 Sotheby's Arcade, New York #314/R
$1500   £980   Cuatro jinetes del apocalipsis (65x49cm-26x19in) s.d.MCMXLIV graphite ink W/C. 18-May-93 Sotheby's, New York #149/R
$2500   £1582   Desnuda Rosada con Caracoles (48x61cm-19x24in) s.d.45 mixed media. 25-Oct-92 Butterfield & Butterfield, San Francisco #2245/R

CANTWELL, James (1856-1926) American
$1100   £738   View of North Adams, Massachusetts (58x112cm-23x44in) s.d.1880 i.verso. 26-Mar-94 Skinner, Bolton #275

CAPDEVILA, Maria Elena (20th C) Mexican
$895   £605   Pensando en Gaugin (50x75cm-20x30in) s.d.1993 pastel. 20-Oct-93 Louis Morton, Mexico #77 (M.P 2800)

CAPELLAN, Tony (1959-) Dominican
$2500   £1678   Ritos del Caribe (91x99cm-36x39in) s. acrylic. 7-Jan-94 Gary Nader, Miami #103/R

CAPOZZOLI, Glauco (20th C) South American
$850   £570   Musicos (45x70cm-18x28in) s.d.65 mixed media. 29-Nov-93 Gomensoro, Montevideo #20/R

CARDENAS, Augustin (1927-) Cuban
$2263   £1519   Sans titre (45x62cm-18x24in) s.d.80 paper. 23-Mar-93 Cornette de St.Cyr, Paris #45 (F.FR 12500)
$849   £569   Maternite (31x24cm-12x9in) s.d.1958 W/C ink. 6-Feb-94 Guy Loudmer, Paris #117 (F.FR 5000)
$1101   £719   Formes (49x55cm-19x22in) s.d.81 chl ink wash. 12-May-93 Cornette de St.Cyr, Paris #104/R (F.FR 6000)

CARDENAS, David (20th C) Mexican?
$803   £543   Mangana (45x60cm-18x24in) s. 9-Nov-93 Louis Morton, Mexico #31/R (M.P 2600)

CARDENAS, Juan (1939-) Colombian
$13000   £8667   Autorretrato Frente al Espejo (63x51cm-25x20in) s.d.1982. 18-May-94 Christie's, New York #154/R
$14000   £9459   Autoretrato de Pie con Craneo (71x56cm-28x22in) s.d.1980. 23-Nov-93 Christie's, New York #157/R

CARDENAS, Santiago (1937-) Colombian
$6250   £4085   Autorretrato (109x100cm-43x39in) acrylic painted c.1985. 18-May-93 Sotheby's, New York #223/R

CARIANI, Z J (20th C) American
$2600   £1745   Autumn flies her banners (89x76cm-35x30in) s. 12-Dec-93 Hindman Galleries, Chicago #308

CARLES, Arthur B (1882-1952) American
$1300   £751   On the canal, Venice (24x19cm-9x7in) canvasboard. 25-Sep-92 Sotheby's Arcade, New York #223/R
$3600   £2264   Abstract composition (76x76cm-30x30in) i.stretcher. 22-Apr-93 Freeman Fine Arts, Philadelphia #1169/R
$4750   £3146   Reclining nude (33x41cm-13x16in) panel. 23-Sep-93 Sotheby's, New York #265/R
$14000   £9333   Flowers (54x41cm-21x16in) 25-May-94 Sotheby's, New York #136/R
$900   £584   Seated nude with apple (51x63cm-20x25in) pastel. 9-Sep-93 Sotheby's Arcade, New York #295/R

CARLES, Arthur B (attrib) (1882-1952) American
$1000   £654   Venice (18x25cm-7x10in) init. 7-Oct-93 Freeman Fine Arts, Philadelphia #942

CARLIN, James (1909-) American
$550   £364   Beach scene (51x76cm-20x30in) s. 23-Sep-93 Mystic Fine Arts, Connecticut #252/R
$650   £442   Scantily clad girl with red hair and red gloves (20x16cm-8x6in) s. board. 10-Jul-93 Young Fine Arts Auctions, Maine #76/R
$1200   £694   Tavern interior (61x91cm-24x36in) s. 25-Sep-92 Sotheby's Arcade, New York #433/R
$1600   £1039   Jazz band (50x61cm-20x24in) s. canvas on panel. 9-Sep-93 Sotheby's Arcade, New York #340/R
$600   £395   Girl in the middle (56x71cm-22x28in) s. W/C. 11-Jun-93 Freeman Fine Arts, Philadelphia #29

CARLIN, John (attrib) (1813-1891) American
$622   £420   Young child standing holding wooden cart and crop (11x?cm-4x?in) min. gilt wood frame. 8-Nov-93 Bonhams, Chelsea #24/R

CARLISLE, Mary Helen (attrib) (1869-1925) American
$600   £392   Flowering English style garden (44x51cm-17x20in) init. pastel board. 4-May-93 Christie's, East, New York #82/R

CARLSEN, Dines (1901-1966) American
$6000   £4000   The Bronze Bowl (122x89cm-48x35in) s. 23-May-94 Hindman Galleries, Chicago #250/R
$10000   £5780   The black bottle (63x56cm-25x22in) s. 23-Sep-92 Christie's, New York #164/R
$20000   £11561   The Mandarin coat (74x68cm-29x27in) s.d.1932. 23-Sep-92 Christie's, New York #159/R
$23000   £15333   The Canton bowl (63x76cm-25x30in) 16-Mar-94 Christie's, New York #106/R

CARLSEN, Emil (1853-1932) American/Danish
$650   £434   Under the willows (66x48cm-26x19in) s.d.7/8/76. 17-May-94 Christie's, East, New York #510
$1000   £658   Still life of copper pitcher and onions (36x46cm-14x18in) s. 4-Nov-92 Doyle, New York #5/R
$1100   £724   Morning sunlight (20x23cm-8x9in) panel. 31-Mar-93 Sotheby's Arcade, New York #163/R
$1250   £868   Landscape (30x41cm-12x16in) s.d.1931. 6-Mar-93 Louisiana Auction Exchange #2
$1400   £909   Still life with pineapple. Landscape (25x41cm-10x16in) s.d.77 panel. 9-Sep-93 Sotheby's Arcade, New York #57/R
$2100   £1364   Still life with oriental doll and daisies (23x18cm-9x7in) s. 9-Sep-93 Sotheby's Arcade, New York #268/R
$2400   £1678   Sand dunes (14x25cm-6x10in) init.i.verso board. 11-Mar-93 Christie's, New York #134/R
$3200   £2105   Seated woman (36x26cm-14x10in) 31-Mar-93 Sotheby's Arcade, New York #122/R
$3291   £2194   Interior with woman cleaning dead game (116x76cm-46x30in) s.d.1900. 31-May-94 AB Stockholms Auktionsverk, Stockholm #5402/R (S.KR 26000)
$4000   £2532   Still life with Chinese objects (30x25cm-12x10in) s.d.1901 panel. 2-Dec-92 Christie's, East, New York #139/R
$4108   £2600   Still life with cherries, peaches and melon (49x59cm-19x23in) s. 20-Oct-92 Sotheby's, Billingshurst #1275/R
$7000   £4575   Surf breaking on rocks (69x91cm-27x36in) 5-May-93 Doyle, New York #24/R
$7250   £4932   Still life with copper pot (51x41cm-20x16in) s.d.1906. 14-Apr-94 Freeman Fine Arts, Philadelphia #1016/R
$8000   £5063   Still life with teapot and onion (51x61cm-20x24in) s. 4-Dec-92 Christie's, New York #236/R
$9000   £5202   Still life with game (122x137cm-48x54in) s.d.1894. 23-Sep-92 Christie's, New York #138/R
$9000   £5769   French fan (38x46cm-15x18in) s.d.1922 board. 9-Dec-92 Butterfield & Butterfield, San Francisco #3935/R
$9750   £6588   The green pitcher (41x51cm-16x20in) s.d.1905 panel. 31-Mar-94 Sotheby's Arcade, New York #115/R
$12000   £8054   Still life with black bottle, brass basin and white jug (76x71cm-30x28in) s.d.1929 board. 16-Jul-93 Du Mouchelle, Detroit #2009
$12839   £6452   Standing female nude (50x33cm-20x13in) s. board. 5-Sep-92 Helmut Zimmermann, Frankfurt #118 (DM 18000)
$13000   £8333   Still life with fish (75x112cm-30x44in) s.d.1897. 27-May-93 Sotheby's, New York #28/R
$15000   £8671   Still life with squash and pitcher (77x89cm-30x35in) s.d.93. 24-Sep-92 Sotheby's, New York #88/R
$21000   £13907   Still life with mixed fruit (51x61cm-20x24in) s. 23-Sep-93 Sotheby's, New York #144/R
$35000   £22436   Green trees (127x102cm-50x40in) s.d.1928. 27-May-93 Sotheby's, New York #68/R

CARLSEN, Emil (1853-1932) American/Danish-cont.
$45000   £28846   Mums (89x63cm-35x25in) s.d.93. 9-Dec-92 Butterfield & Butterfield, San Francisco #3934/R
$1700   £1076   Still life with green vase, fan and ceramic glass (32x25cm-13x10in) s. W/C. 2-Dec-92 Christie's, East, New York #175/R

CARLSEN, Emil Soren (1848-1932) American
$850   £563   Still life with oriental (74x58cm-29x23in) s. canvas on canvas. 28-Sep-93 John Moran, Pasadena #304

CARLSON, Charles Joseph (1860-?) American/Swedish
$2044   £1336   Panoramic view of Riga (18x34cm-7x13in) s. board. 17-Sep-93 Schloss Ahlden, Ahlden #1847/R (DM 3300)

CARLSON, John F (1875-1947) American
$2000   £1316   Gathering shadows (30x41cm-12x16in) s. 31-Mar-93 Sotheby's Arcade, New York #239/R
$2500   £1701   Mountain Fastness (30x41cm-12x16in) s. s.i.verso board. 16-Apr-94 Young Fine Arts Auctions, Maine #64/R
$2600   £1503   Sunny groves (30x41cm-12x16in) s. s.i.verso s.stretcher board. 25-Sep-92 Sotheby's Arcade, New York #276/R
$8000   £5369   Woodland waters (64x76cm-25x30in) s. s.i.stretcher. 4-May-94 Doyle, New York #29/R
$8500   £5380   Winter in the forest (77x102cm-30x40in) s. s.i.verso canvas on board. 3-Dec-92 Sotheby's, New York #109/R
$9000   £4688   Snowy streamside (64x76cm-25x30in) s. 5-Aug-92 Boos Gallery, Michigan #649/R

CARLYLE, Florence (1864-1923) Canadian
$1500   £1000   Copper cleaning (41x30cm-16x12in) i.d.1916 board. 25-May-94 Phillips, Sevenoaks #922/R

CARMELO DE ARZADUN (1888-1968) Uruguayan
$750   £481   Arbol florido y ciudad (34x40cm-13x16in) s. board. 7-Dec-92 Gomensoro, Montevideo #44
$760   £497   Las Flores (19x24cm-7x9in) s. board. 4-Oct-93 Gomensoro, Montevideo #105/R
$900   £526   Paisaje con Ranchos (44x66cm-17x26in) s. board. 16-Sep-92 Castells & Castells, Montevideo #37
$1000   £641   Joven reclinado a la escalera (175x100cm-69x39in) s. 7-Dec-92 Gomensoro, Montevideo #82
$1000   £662   Parque Rodo (38x45cm-15x18in) s. board. 28-Jun-93 Gomensoro, Montevideo #48
$1200   £784   Casas de Las Flores (33x40cm-13x16in) s. board. 3-May-93 Gomensoro, Montevideo #48
$1300   £872   Casona rosada (35x27cm-14x11in) panel. 29-Nov-93 Gomensoro, Montevideo #33
$1300   £833   Adolescente (60x45cm-24x18in) s.d.42 board. 7-Dec-92 Gomensoro, Montevideo #80
$1300   £760   Roma (33x24cm-13x9in) s. board. 16-Sep-92 Castells & Castells, Montevideo #38
$1300   £688   Casas y mar (26x17cm-10x7in) s. panel. 10-Sep-92 Gomensoro, Montevideo #38/R
$1300   £833   Casas, duna y tormenta (33x55cm-13x22in) s. board. 7-Dec-92 Gomensoro, Montevideo #45
$1400   £819   Rambla (47x38cm-19x15in) s. fibre. 16-Sep-92 Castells & Castells, Montevideo #36/R
$1500   £987   Paisaje de playa con figuras (93x72cm-37x28in) s. 31-May-93 Gomensoro, Montevideo #32
$1600   £1026   Playa con gaviotas (28x48cm-11x19in) s. i.verso board. 7-Dec-92 Gomensoro, Montevideo #81
$1600   £936   Parque Rodo (37x45cm-15x18in) s. fibre. 16-Sep-92 Castells & Castells, Montevideo #39
$1700   £1118   Casa y sierra (50x70cm-20x28in) s.d.45 board. 31-May-93 Gomensoro, Montevideo #31/R
$1800   £905   Tiempo Humedo (46x55cm-18x22in) s.d.56 board. 31-Aug-92 Gomensoro, Montevideo #55
$2000   £1307   Baile y luna (65x52cm-26x20in) s. i.verso. 26-Oct-92 Gomensoro, Montevideo #75/R
$2000   £1005   Playa Ramirez (47x33cm-19x13in) board. 31-Aug-92 Gomensoro, Montevideo #54/R
$2000   £1299   Tamarises y arena (36x60cm-14x24in) s.d.1948 oil. 30-Aug-93 Gomensoro, Montevideo #71
$2100   £1235   Playa Las Flores (55x39cm-22x15in) s. board. 5-Oct-92 Gomensoro, Montevideo #39
$2100   £1419   Paisaje de Playa Las Flores (70x98cm-28x39in) s. board. 25-Apr-94 Gomensoro, Montevideo #52/R
$2100   £1373   Paisaje con sierra oscura (50x70cm-20x28in) s. board. 3-May-93 Gomensoro, Montevideo #49/R
$2200   £1294   Arena rosada (38x46cm-15x18in) s. board. 5-Oct-92 Gomensoro, Montevideo #30/R
$2200   £1410   Pueblo europeo (46x43cm-18x17in) s.d.1939 board. 7-Dec-92 Gomensoro, Montevideo #79/R
$2300   £1544   Techos de zinc (64x80cm-25x31in) s.d.53 board. 29-Nov-93 Gomensoro, Montevideo #32
$2300   £1503   Campo costero (40x57cm-16x22in) s.d.43 board. 4-Oct-93 Gomensoro, Montevideo #64/R
$2400   £1538   Playa Las Flores (55x80cm-22x31in) s.d.1947 board. 7-Dec-92 Gomensoro, Montevideo #78/R
$2600   £1307   Nino jugando (32x36cm-13x14in) s. board. 31-Aug-92 Gomensoro, Montevideo #56/R
$2600   £1745   Paso nivel, carro y vecina (50x60cm-20x24in) s. board. 29-Nov-93 Gomensoro, Montevideo #31/R
$2700   £1731   Barcas del sena (56x46cm-22x18in) s.d.50 board. 7-Dec-92 Gomensoro, Montevideo #43
$2700   £1765   Playa (47x71cm-19x28in) s. board. 4-Oct-93 Gomensoro, Montevideo #65/R
$2800   £1818   Campo (50x68cm-20x27in) s. board. 30-Aug-93 Gomensoro, Montevideo #70/R

CARMELO DE ARZADUN (1888-1968) Uruguayan-cont.
$3000	£2013	La catedral, constructivo (81x64cm-32x25in) s.d. 1958 panel. 29-Nov-93 Gomensoro, Montevideo #28/R
$3000	£1961	Dia nuboso en balneario Las Flores (80x100cm-31x39in) s.d. 1957 board. 26-Oct-92 Gomensoro, Montevideo #74
$3200	£1882	Pescadores en la playa (60x45cm-24x18in) s. board. 5-Oct-92 Gomensoro, Montevideo #28/R
$3200	£2078	Paisaje con ganado (50x73cm-20x29in) s.d. 1952 board. 30-Aug-93 Gomensoro, Montevideo #69
$3400	£2000	Lluvioso (55x80cm-22x31in) s.d. 1946. 5-Oct-92 Gomensoro, Montevideo #29/R
$3800	£2484	Hombre de boina (65x50cm-26x20in) s.d. 1940 board. 26-Oct-92 Gomensoro, Montevideo #76/R
$4400	£2292	El mar y el viento (73x54cm-29x21in) s. board. 12-Aug-92 Castells & Castells, Montevideo #49/R
$4800	£3117	El regalo (86x114cm-34x45in) s.d. 1917 i. verso oil. 30-Aug-93 Gomensoro, Montevideo #68
$6200	£4161	Porton de San Pedro (64x68cm-25x27in) s. 29-Nov-93 Gomensoro, Montevideo #27/R
$6400	£4238	Rue Cujas, Paris (61x50cm-24x20in) s. board. 28-Jun-93 Gomensoro, Montevideo #46/R
$8500	£5519	Durazneros en flor. Joven sentada (114x93cm-45x37in) s.d. 1917 oil double-sided. 30-Aug-93 Gomensoro, Montevideo #67/R

CARMICHAEL, Franklin (1890-1945) Canadian
$7927	£5181	Lake and hills, N. Ontario (25x30cm-10x12in) panel. 18-May-93 Joyner Fine Art, Toronto #62/R (C.D 10000)
$13232	£8763	Autumn in La Cloche Hills, 1921 (29x25cm-11x10in) i.d. 1921verso board. 18-Nov-92 Sotheby's, Toronto #170/R (C.D 17000)
$3874	£2618	Houses in winter (22x27cm-9x11in) s.d. 1925 W/C. 3-Nov-93 Sotheby's, Toronto #303/R (C.D 5000)
$8524	£5759	Northern lake (27x33cm-11x13in) s.d. 34 W/C. 3-Nov-93 Sotheby's, Toronto #213/R (C.D 11000)
$9816	£6633	Landscape with house (27x32cm-11x13in) s. W/C chl. 23-Nov-93 Joyner Fine Art, Toronto #106/R (C.D 13000)
$19459	£12887	Early spring (27x32cm-11x13in) s. W/C chl. 24-Nov-92 Joyner Fine Art, Toronto #117/R (C.D 25000)

CARMIENCKE, Johan-Herman (1810-1867) Danish/American
$770	£520	North Italian mountain landscape (34x53cm-13x21in) indist.s.d. 1846. 15-Jun-93 Rasmussen, Vejle #628/R (D.KR 5000)
$804	£526	Lake surrounded by mountains (42x57cm-17x22in) init. 11-May-93 Rasmussen, Copenhagen #397 (D.KR 5000)
$1125	£735	Mountain landscape with rider on road (31x42cm-12x17in) i.verso. 5-May-93 Kunsthallen, Copenhagen #25 (D.KR 7000)
$1300	£751	Landscape with river and cottage (41x61cm-16x24in) s.d. 1889. 25-Sep-92 Sotheby's Arcade, New York #50/R
$9500	£6090	Mt Vesuvius and Bay of Naples (91x133cm-36x52in) init.d. 1860. 26-May-93 Christie's, New York #14/R
$11000	£6358	View of Castle of Chillon (129x163cm-51x64in) s.d. 1858. 24-Sep-92 Sotheby's, New York #54/R
$16170	£11000	View of Castello Malcesine, Lake Garda, Italy (122x158cm-48x62in) s.d. 1857. 17-Nov-93 Sotheby's, London #59/R

CARNACINI, Ceferino (1888-1964) Argentinian
$1250	£735	Atardecer (15x21cm-6x8in) 29-Sep-92 VerBo, Buenos Aires #26
$1800	£938	Florero (55x55cm-22x22in) 4-Aug-92 VerBo, Buenos Aires #24
$4500	£2601	Viejo Aguaribay (74x101cm-29x40in) 23-Sep-92 Roldan & Cia, Buenos Aires #48

CARNWATH, Squeak (1947-) American
$1700	£1076	Look (57x76cm-22x30in) s.d. 1989 paper. 25-Oct-92 Butterfield & Butterfield, San Francisco #2346/R
$800	£541	Comfort and Loyalty (102x86cm-40x34in) s.d. 1984 chl. 21-Apr-94 Butterfield & Butterfield, San Francisco #1187/R

CARON, Paul Archibald (1874-1941) Canadian
$642	£434	Old pine, Hudson (17x13cm-7x5in) s. s.i.verso board. 23-Nov-93 Fraser Pinneys, Quebec #359 (C.D 850)
$943	£597	Family preparing for sleigh ride (28x36cm-11x14in) s. W/C. 30-Nov-92 Ritchie, Toronto #202/R (C.D 1200)

CARPENTER, Fred Green (1882-1965) American
$1000	£662	Two women (102x84cm-40x33in) s. 28-Sep-93 John Moran, Pasadena #282

CARPINO, Ralph (20th C) American?
$1200	£811	'A piece of steak' (61x45cm-24x18in) panel. 31-Mar-94 Sotheby's Arcade, New York #394/R

CARR, Emily M (1871-1945) Canadian
$7750	£5000	Village track, Brittany (38x46cm-15x18in) studio st. painted 1911. 15-Jul-94 Christie's, London #90/R
$10922	£7282	Driftwood (36x41cm-14x16in) i.verso panel. 11-May-94 Sotheby's, Toronto #54/R (C.D 15000)
$16648	£10881	Spring wave (41x56cm-16x22in) s. 19-May-93 Sotheby's, Toronto #241/R (C.D 21000)
$21015	£13918	The bole of a tree - Autumn (56x41cm-22x16in) s.i.d. 1930verso paper laid down on panel. 18-Nov-92 Sotheby's, Toronto #64/R (C.D 27000)

CARR, Emily M (1871-1945) Canadian-cont.

$21845	£14563	Abandoned house near Metchosin, B.C. (59x88cm-23x35in) s. paper laid on panel. 11-May-94 Sotheby's, Toronto #73/R (C.D 30000)
$35026	£23196	At Nootka, B C (61x46cm-24x18in) s. i.verso. 18-Nov-92 Sotheby's, Toronto #169/R (C.D 45000)
$44394	£29016	Brittany scene (63x44cm-25x17in) estate st. 19-May-93 Sotheby's, Toronto #151/R (C.D 56000)
$70052	£46392	Kispiox (92x44cm-36x17in) s.d.1912. 24-Nov-92 Joyner Fine Art, Toronto #63/R (C.D 90000)
$1729	£1095	From Beacon Hill (23x32cm-9x13in) s. W/C. 30-Nov-92 Ritchie, Toronto #180/R (C.D 2200)
$3113	£2062	Woodland scene (27x26cm-11x10in) init. W/C. 24-Nov-92 Joyner Fine Art, Toronto #24/R (C.D 4000)
$6342	£4145	China boy (36x28cm-14x11in) s. d.c.1907-9 verso W/C. 19-May-93 Sotheby's, Toronto #187/R (C.D 8000)
$14010	£9278	Indian village (37x27cm-15x11in) s. W/C. 24-Nov-92 Joyner Fine Art, Toronto #76/R (C.D 18000)
$17837	£11658	Study of totem figure (62x46cm-24x18in) s. W/C. 19-May-93 Sotheby's, Toronto #127/R (C.D 22500)

CARR, Lyell (19th C?) American?

$3000	£2000	Santiago de Cuba (50x71cm-20x28in) s.i.d.1898 canvas laid down on board. 18-May-94 Sotheby's, New York #179/R

CARR, Samuel S (1837-1908) American

$1600	£1074	Sheep grazing by the river (41x61cm-16x24in) s. 16-Dec-93 Mystic Fine Arts, Connecticut #262/R
$2450	£1612	Sheep grazing (36x51cm-14x20in) s. 5-Jun-93 Louisiana Auction Exchange #66/R
$2500	£1323	Landscape with sheep (41x61cm-16x24in) s. canvas on board. 12-Sep-92 Louisiana Auction Exchange #49/R
$3500	£2333	Young shepherdess feeding sheep (46x61cm-18x24in) s.d.89. 17-Mar-94 Sotheby's, New York #27/R
$4000	£2614	Crossing the river (61x51cm-24x20in) 17-Sep-93 Du Mouchelle, Detroit #2007/R
$6000	£3846	Playing hooky (30x25cm-12x10in) init. 26-May-93 Christie's, New York #30 d/R
$18000	£12081	Westward ho for New York (26x36cm-10x14in) s.i. 2-Dec-93 Sotheby's, New York #17/R
$22000	£12717	School's out (56x91cm-22x36in) s.d.89 i.stretcher. 24-Sep-92 Sotheby's, New York #51/R

CARRENO, Mario (1913-) Cuban

$4750	£3299	Untitled (79x104cm-31x41in) s.d.57. 26-Feb-93 Sotheby's Arcade, New York #258/R
$11000	£7285	La Pescadora Pescada (61x50cm-24x20in) s.d.79 s.i.stretcher. 24-Nov-92 Christie's, New York #224/R
$24000	£16000	Encuentro en el espacio azul (160x119cm-63x47in) s.d.68. 18-May-94 Sotheby's, New York #327/R
$25000	£16340	Geografia de la angustia (118x168cm-46x66in) s.d.77. 18-May-93 Sotheby's, New York #234/R
$30000	£20270	Mujer con guitarra (96x130cm-38x51in) s.d.72. 23-Nov-93 Christie's, New York #133/R
$33000	£21854	Mythological rider (61x50cm-24x20in) s.d.43 canvas on masonite. 23-Nov-92 Sotheby's, New York #49/R
$37500	£25168	Arbol tropical (170x120cm-67x47in) 7-Jan-94 Gary Nader, Miami #80/R
$110000	£71895	La siesta (76x91cm-30x36in) s.d.46. 17-May-93 Christie's, New York #36/R
$125000	£84459	El caballo en el pueblo (76x91cm-30x36in) s.d.46. 22-Nov-93 Sotheby's, New York #24/R
$200000	£132450	Paisaje (104x78cm-41x31in) s.d.43. 23-Nov-92 Sotheby's, New York #56/R
$280000	£186667	Arlequin (80x60cm-31x24in) s.i.d.39. 17-May-94 Sotheby's, New York #18/R
$3200	£2162	Pareja en paisaje desierto (38x28cm-15x11in) s.i.d.1977 pencil. 23-Nov-93 Christie's, New York #258/R
$3500	£2318	Naturaleza Muerta (19x26cm-7x10in) s.d.45 pen. 23-Nov-92 Sotheby's, New York #163/R
$3500	£2288	Untitled (53x76cm-21x30in) s.d.69 gouache. 18-May-93 Sotheby's, New York #249/R
$4000	£2614	Figuras (40x28cm-16x11in) s.d.48 tempera ink scratch board. 18-May-93 Sotheby's, New York #158/R
$4800	£3137	El sueno de la serie 'Un Mundo Petrificado' (48x38cm-19x15in) s.d.66 s.i.d.verso ink W/C. 17-May-93 Christie's, New York #199/R
$4800	£3243	Composicion abstracta (38x27cm-15x11in) s.d.48 gouache pen. 23-Nov-93 Christie's, New York #253/R
$5000	£3268	Los Amantes de la serie 'Un Mundo Petrificado' (49x39cm-19x15in) s.d.65 s.i.d.verso ink W/C. 17-May-93 Christie's, New York #198/R
$8000	£5405	Figura (65x51cm-26x20in) s.d.47 pastel. 23-Nov-93 Christie's, New York #256/R
$8500	£5629	Piedra Magica (27x38cm-11x15in) s.d.48 tempera ink scratch board. 23-Nov-92 Sotheby's, New York #165/R
$8500	£5743	Nocturno (55x42cm-22x17in) s.d.48 tempera ink scratch board. 22-Nov-93 Sotheby's, New York #201/R
$9000	£6081	Composicion (59x38cm-23x15in) s.d.52 gouache. 23-Nov-93 Christie's, New York #254/R
$11000	£7190	Antillas (42x52cm-17x20in) s.d.48 tempera ink scratch board. 18-May-93 Sotheby's, New York #157/R
$15000	£9934	Fondo Marino (41x52cm-16x20in) s.d.48 tempera ink scratch board. 23-Nov-92 Sotheby's, New York #166/R
$28000	£18301	Mulata con Aguacate (78x56cm-31x22in) s.d.43 gouache. 17-May-93 Christie's, New York #110/R
$32000	£20915	La Iniciacion (53x63cm-21x25in) s.d.44 gouache. 18-May-93 Sotheby's, New York #46/R

CARRENO, Mario (1913-) Cuban-cont.
$40000 £26846 La iniciacion (53x63cm-21x25in) s.i.d.44 gouache. 7-Jan-94 Gary Nader, Miami #35/R

CARRILLO, Lilia (1930-1974) Mexican
$2555 £1703 Sin titulo (30x24cm-12x9in) s. paper. 25-May-94 Louis Morton, Mexico #58 (M.P 8500)
$15000 £9804 El ocaso infinito (50x65cm-20x26in) s.d.1963 masonite. 17-May-93 Christie's, New York #132/R
$22244 £15030 En el espacio (60x50cm-24x20in) s.d.1967. 27-Apr-94 Louis Morton, Mexico #490 (M.P 75000)

CARRINO, David (1959-) American
$519 £346 For love's sake only - Browning Sonnet (136x112cm-54x44in) s.d.88verso Indian ink paper on cloth. 2-Jun-94 AB Stockholms Auktionsverk, Stockholm #7214/R (S.KR 4100)
$700 £470 Joseph Conrad autograph letter (193x203cm-76x80in) s.d.1989 brush black ink felt pen paper on linen. 3-May-94 Christie's, East, New York #224/R
$800 £537 Sarah Orne Jewett autograph manuscript (193x203cm-76x80in) s.d.1989verso brush black ink paper on linen. 3-May-94 Christie's, East, New York #222/R

CARROLL, John (1892-1959) American
$1700 £1111 Zabelle (41x36cm-16x14in) s.d.37 canvas on panel. 17-Sep-93 Du Mouchelle, Detroit #2179/R
$4750 £3146 Three figures (53x74cm-21x29in) s. 13-Nov-92 Du Mouchelle, Detroit #2000/R

CARTER, Clarence Holbrook (1904-) American
$1200 £694 Over and above no 19 (91x46cm-36x18in) s.d.65. 25-Sep-92 Sotheby's Arcade, New York #505/R
$1100 £696 Allegory of Church III (56x76cm-22x30in) s.d.62 mixed media. 25-Oct-92 Butterfield & Butterfield, San Francisco #2264/R
$3700 £2569 Cricket in the woodpile (36x53cm-14x21in) s.d.36 mixed media. 6-Mar-93 Louisiana Auction Exchange #134/R

CARTER, Dennis Malone (1827-1881) American
$9000 £6122 Civil War allegory (109x160cm-43x63in) s.d.1865. 8-Apr-94 Sloan, North Bethesda #2527/R

CARTER, F A (20th C) American
$950 £621 Autumn landscape with figures (64x76cm-25x30in) s.d.1918. 7-Oct-93 Freeman Fine Arts, Philadelphia #962

CARTER, Gary (1939-) American
$1400 £940 Stoop philosopher (46x61cm-18x24in) s.d.73 i.verso. 8-Dec-93 Butterfield & Butterfield, San Francisco #3600/R

CARTER, Pruett A (1891-1955) American
$900 £604 The summer wind (51x79cm-20x31in) s. i.d.verso. 6-Dec-93 Grogan, Massachussetts #558/R

CARTLEDGE, William (1916-) American
$625 £414 Patriotism Bull (25x18cm-10x7in) s.i.d.April 1991 paint carved wood. 21-Nov-92 Litchfield Auction Gallery #4

CASE, Edmund E (1840-1919) American
$550 £369 Landscape view with harbour inlet (23x30cm-9x12in) s. 6-May-94 Skinner, Bolton #89/R
$650 £439 Autumn landscape with trees and brook (64x46cm-25x18in) s. 4-Nov-93 Boos Gallery, Michigan #1511/R

CASE, Elizabeth E (1867-?) American
$650 £439 Garden (51x61cm-20x24in) s. 10-Aug-93 Stonington Fine Arts, Stonington #33

CASENELLI, Victor (20th C) American
$1900 £1218 Indian with pack horse (33x46cm-13x18in) s. board. 13-Dec-92 Hindman Galleries, Chicago #30/R

CASILEAR, John W (1811-1893) American
$1200 £795 Edge of a field (25x56cm-10x22in) mono. 28-Nov-92 Young Fine Arts Auctions, Maine #80/R
$2000 £1058 Afternoon near Lake George (30x46cm-12x18in) init.d.82 s.i.verso. 12-Sep-92 Louisiana Auction Exchange #59/R
$3200 £2148 Landscape with cattle, town visible in the distance (30x25cm-12x10in) mono.d.82. 4-Mar-94 Skinner, Bolton #211/R
$3500 £2023 Trees (41x37cm-16x15in) 23-Sep-92 Christie's, New York #23/R
$7500 £4808 Woodland path (51x43cm-20x17in) init.d.59 painted oval. 26-May-93 Christie's, New York #1/R

CASILEAR, John W (attrib) (1811-1893) American
$3000 £2027 Wilderness fishing (94x76cm-37x30in) init.d.80. 4-Nov-93 Sloan, North Bethesda #2744/R

CASIMIR, Laurent (20th C) Haitian
$550 £377 Haitian market (61x76cm-24x30in) s. board. 19-Feb-94 Young Fine Arts Auctions, Maine #54/R

CASS, George Nelson (1831-1882) American

$750	£524	Pastoral landscape (51x76cm-20x30in) s.d.78. 7-Feb-93 James Bakker, Cambridge #29
$900	£604	Cottage by duck pond (35x51cm-14x20in) s. 6-May-94 Skinner, Bolton #73/R
$1800	£1216	Pastoral landscape (51x76cm-20x30in) s. 31-Mar-94 Sotheby's Arcade, New York #57/R
$3520	£2301	River fishing, sunrise (51x76cm-20x30in) s.d.69. 14-May-93 Skinner, Bolton #35/R

CASSATT, Mary (1844-1926) American

$40000	£26144	Portrait de Madame Cordier (48x40cm-19x16in) s.d.1874 panel. 12-May-93 Sotheby's, New York #155/R
$43839	£29621	Portrait d'enfant (24x23cm-9x9in) canvas laid down on board. 16-Jun-93 Francis Briest, Paris #71/R (F.FR 250000)
$74000	£49333	Study for Augusta reading to her daughter (46x38cm-18x15in) s. painted c.1910. 23-May-94 Hindman Galleries, Chicago #195/R
$650	£442	Head of a woman (15x25cm-6x10in) pencil. 15-Nov-93 Christie's, East, New York #199/R
$2000	£1307	Woman sewing (10x20cm-4x8in) pencil. 29-Jun-94 Doyle, New York #10
$2235	£1500	Portrait of a young girl (36x30cm-14x12in) s. pastel. 3-Mar-94 John Nicholson, Surrey #583
$15000	£9615	Portrait of young girl (67x54cm-26x21in) bears sig. pastel. 27-May-93 Sotheby's, New York #4/R
$19000	£12583	Sketch of mother Jeanne, looking down with her baby (23x30cm-9x12in) W/C. 23-Sep-93 Sotheby's, New York #172/R
$58000	£37908	Leontine in pink fluffy hat (38x28cm-15x11in) pastel executed 1898. 13-May-93 Christie's, New York #127/R
$65000	£41667	Portrait of young woman in green (60x47cm-24x19in) s. pastel pencil executed c.1898. 27-May-93 Sotheby's, New York #17/R
$67500	£43269	Drawing for 'Afternoon Tea Party' (36x28cm-14x11in) s. pencil black chk executed c.1891. 27-May-93 Sotheby's, New York #3/R
$80000	£51282	Looking at picture book - no.1 (36x48cm-14x19in) init. pastel. 27-May-93 Sotheby's, New York #18/R
$80000	£53691	Mother and child (68x56cm-27x22in) s. pastel painted c.1908. 2-Dec-93 Sotheby's, New York #103/R
$96850	£65000	Sara regardant vers la droite (47x38cm-19x15in) pastel chl executed c.1901. 22-Jun-93 Sotheby's, London #10/R
$134100	£90000	Portrait de Marie-Louise Durand-Ruel (75x63cm-30x25in) s.d.1911 pastel. 22-Jun-93 Sotheby's, London #22/R
$220000	£146250	Maternite (65x51cm-26x20in) s. pastel executed c.1902. 12-May-94 Sotheby's, New York #162/R
$270000	£182432	Simone in white bonnet seated with clasped hands, no 1 (62x47cm-24x19in) s. pastel painted c.1903. 3-Nov-93 Sotheby's, New York #11/R
$400000	£266667	Mother Louise holding up her blue-eyed child (71x53cm-28x21in) s. pastel. 26-May-94 Christie's, New York #86/R
$1000000	£675676	Mother and child (73x60cm-29x24in) s. pastel. 3-Nov-93 Sotheby's, New York #9/R
$1400000	£945946	Woman in black hat and raspberry pink costume (80x65cm-31x26in) s. pastel paper on canvas executed c.1899. 2-Nov-93 Christie's, New York #27/R
$2300000	£1523179	Young lady in a loge, gazing to the right (65x55cm-26x22in) s. executed c.1880 pastel gouache. 10-Nov-92 Sotheby's, New York #7/R

CASSIDY, Ira Diamond Gerald (1879-1934) American

$2500	£1603	Cliff dwellings (25x43cm-10x17in) s. s.i.d.1914verso. 9-Dec-92 Butterfield & Butterfield, San Francisco #3970/R
$2500	£1603	Rains in Utah (25x43cm-10x17in) s. s.i.d.1914verso. 9-Dec-92 Butterfield & Butterfield, San Francisco #3974/R
$1000	£658	Skiing to campsite (57x47cm-22x19in) s. gouache. 13-Jun-93 Butterfield & Butterfield, San Francisco #3238/R
$4250	£2872	The scout (39x57cm-15x22in) s.d.1910 gouache board. 31-Mar-94 Sotheby's Arcade, New York #178/R

CASSON, Alfred Joseph (1898-1992) Canadian

$969	£650	Norval (20x23cm-8x9in) s.d.1929 panel. 13-Dec-93 Lots Road, London #1
$3623	£2415	Algonquin Park, August 1943 (24x28cm-9x11in) s. i.d.1943 verso board. 6-Jun-94 Waddingtons, Toronto #1297/R (C.D 5000)
$3964	£2591	Island, Oxtongue Lake (30x38cm-12x15in) s. board. 18-May-93 Joyner Fine Art, Toronto #127/R (C.D 5000)
$3964	£2591	Autumn - Grenville, Quebec (30x38cm-12x15in) s. s.d.1968 verso board. 19-May-93 Sotheby's, Toronto #266/R (C.D 5000)
$4005	£2670	Bridge at Myers Cave (23x29cm-9x11in) s. s.i.d.1957verso board. 11-May-94 Sotheby's, Toronto #243/R (C.D 5500)
$4262	£2880	Woodland Oxtongue Lake (30x38cm-12x15in) s. s.i.d.1971verso board. 3-Nov-93 Sotheby's, Toronto #202/R (C.D 5500)
$4649	£3141	York Junction Baptiste Road (23x29cm-9x11in) s. s.i.d.1984 board. 3-Nov-93 Sotheby's, Toronto #357/R (C.D 5500)
$4708	£3077	Buck Hill - Birds Creek (24x29cm-9x11in) s. s.d.1976 verso board. 10-May-93 Hodgins, Calgary #274/R (C.D 6000)
$4716	£2985	Wind after rain (30x38cm-12x15in) s. millboard. 30-Nov-92 Ritchie, Toronto #248/R (C.D 6000)
$4733	£3155	Farm Bridge, Grenville, Quebec (30x38cm-12x15in) s. s.i.d.1971verso board. 11-May-94 Sotheby's, Toronto #242/R (C.D 6500)
$4900	£3333	Below the Falls York River (30x38cm-12x15in) s. s.i.verso board. 15-Nov-93 Hodgins, Calgary #83/R (C.D 6500)
$4908	£3316	Barns at Harrington, Quebec, 1968 (30x37cm-12x15in) s. board. 23-Nov-93 Joyner Fine Art, Toronto #31/R (C.D 6500)
$5097	£3398	Northern Ontario house (24x29cm-9x11in) s. s.i.d.1945verso board. 11-May-94 Sotheby's, Toronto #114/R (C.D 7000)

CASSON, Alfred Joseph (1898-1992) Canadian-cont.

$5153	£3368	Farm on Lake Kamaniskeg (30x38cm-12x15in) s. s.d.1945 verso board. 19-May-93 Sotheby's, Toronto #153/R (C.D 6500)
$5153	£3368	October, Madawaska River (30x38cm-12x15in) s. board. 18-May-93 Joyner Fine Art, Toronto #42/R (C.D 6500)
$5461	£3641	Bay on Baptiste Lake (30x38cm-12x15in) s. board. 11-May-94 Sotheby's, Toronto #121/R (C.D 7500)
$5461	£3641	Morning sky, Birds Creek (30x38cm-12x15in) s. board. 11-May-94 Sotheby's, Toronto #115/R (C.D 7500)
$6227	£4124	Heathcoat road (30x38cm-12x15in) s. i.d.1972verso board. 18-Nov-92 Sotheby's, Toronto #15/R (C.D 8000)
$6371	£4248	The school bus, Grenvill (30x37cm-12x15in) s. board. 13-May-94 Joyner Fine Art, Toronto #39/R (C.D 8750)
$6917	£4612	Birch Island village (30x37cm-12x15in) s. board. 13-May-94 Joyner Fine Art, Toronto #103/R (C.D 9500)
$6917	£4612	Otter Lake (23x28cm-9x11in) s. canvas on board. 13-May-94 Joyner Fine Art, Toronto #83/R (C.D 9500)
$7927	£5181	Glen Williams (24x29cm-9x11in) s. canvas laid down on board painted 1938. 18-May-93 Joyner Fine Art, Toronto #235/R (C.D 10000)
$8562	£5670	Morning on North Channel (30x37cm-12x15in) s. board. 24-Nov-92 Joyner Fine Art, Toronto #15/R (C.D 11000)
$8738	£5825	Humber River - Woodbridge (23x28cm-9x11in) s.d.21 board. 13-May-94 Joyner Fine Art, Toronto #12/R (C.D 12000)
$9340	£6186	Country road (24x29cm-9x11in) s. canvasboard. 24-Nov-92 Joyner Fine Art, Toronto #86/R (C.D 12000)
$9729	£6443	At Parry Sound (25x30cm-10x12in) s. board. 24-Nov-92 Joyner Fine Art, Toronto #12/R (C.D 12500)
$10073	£6806	January morning (32x38cm-13x15in) s. s.i.verso board. 3-Nov-93 Sotheby's, Toronto #190/R (C.D 13000)
$10073	£6806	Afterglow Moose Lake (30x38cm-12x15in) s. s.i.d.1966verso board. 3-Nov-93 Sotheby's, Toronto #106/R (C.D 13000)
$21794	£14433	Blueberry Hill - Lake Baptiste (75x92cm-30x36in) s. 24-Nov-92 Joyner Fine Art, Toronto #73/R (C.D 28000)
$22197	£14508	Snow showers (63x91cm-25x36in) s. 18-May-93 Joyner Fine Art, Toronto #13/R (C.D 28000)
$22197	£14508	Hazy October morning, Madawaska (76x102cm-30x40in) s. painted 1974. 18-May-93 Joyner Fine Art, Toronto #32/R (C.D 28000)
$23782	£15544	Massey Ferguson during World War II (86x102cm-34x40in) s. 19-May-93 Sotheby's, Toronto #325/R (C.D 30000)
$25686	£17010	Summer parade (76x91cm-30x36in) s. i.verso board. 18-Nov-92 Sotheby's, Toronto #95/R (C.D 33000)
$27306	£18204	Summer morning (76x91cm-30x36in) s. board. 11-May-94 Sotheby's, Toronto #110/R (C.D 37500)
$527	£354	Cap on the Magnetawan (22x28cm-9x11in) s.d.1940 pencil. 29-Nov-93 Waddingtons, Toronto #1054 a (C.D 700)
$555	£363	St. John's School, Guelph (23x30cm-9x12in) s.i. pencil. 18-May-93 Joyner Fine Art, Toronto #261 (C.D 700)
$5549	£3627	Summer afternoon, Bon Echo Rock, Lake Mazinaw, Ontario (27x34cm-11x13in) s. s.d.c.1952 verso W/C. 19-May-93 Sotheby's, Toronto #290/R (C.D 7000)

CASTAGNETO, Giovanni (1851-1900) Brazilian

$8000	£5298	Navios de Vela (45x32cm-18x13in) s.d.1897 panel. 24-Nov-92 Christie's, New York #79/R

CASTAGNINO, Juan Carlos (1908-1972) Argentinian

$6000	£3125	En la quemazon (60x90cm-24x35in) 4-Aug-92 VerBo, Buenos Aires #29
$700	£412	La vaca (31x48cm-12x19in) W/C. 29-Sep-92 VerBo, Buenos Aires #27
$1000	£662	Tordillo y azabache (47x46cm-19x18in) ink W/C. 1-Nov-92 VerBo, Buenos Aires #19
$1300	£677	Caballo y recado (32x23cm-13x9in) W/C. 4-Aug-92 VerBo, Buenos Aires #28
$2000	£1176	Viejo criollo (60x48cm-24x19in) pastel. 29-Sep-92 VerBo, Buenos Aires #28

CASTANEDA, Alfredo (1938-) Mexican

$5200	£3514	Uno .. dos .. tres .. (38x38cm-15x15in) s.d.72 oil pencil board. 23-Nov-93 Christie's, New York #227/R
$24000	£16000	Las grandes necesidades (80x80cm-31x31in) s.d.90 i.stretcher. 18-May-94 Sotheby's, New York #265/R
$42000	£27451	Figura en el paisaje (76x102cm-30x40in) s.d.80. 17-May-93 Christie's, New York #44/R
$45000	£30000	La vocacion de Ezequiel (120x120cm-47x47in) s.d.86. 18-May-94 Christie's, New York #61/R
$85000	£56667	Al final o al principio (100x100cm-39x39in) s.d.86 i.stretcher. 17-May-94 Sotheby's, New York #54/R
$4500	£2980	Vidente (24x30cm-9x12in) s.d.84 graphite colour pencil. 23-Nov-92 Sotheby's, New York #247/R
$5000	£3268	La hora del ensayo (35x26cm-14x10in) s.d.1971 acrylic collage panel. 17-May-93 Christie's, New York #244/R
$7500	£5000	Aqui flotando (38x41cm-15x16in) s.d.71 graphite oil ink board. 18-May-93 Sotheby's, New York #266/R
$9000	£5882	Autorretrato con reflecion en burbuja (37x37cm-15x15in) s.d.71 gouache pencil W/C paper on board. 17-May-93 Christie's, New York #230/R
$14000	£9333	Sin titulo (76x51cm-30x20in) s.d.73 acrylic graphite photo collage board. 18-May-94 Sotheby's, New York #322/R
$35000	£23333	El Senor de la Naranjas (80x80cm-31x31in) s.d.71 oil collage panel. 18-May-94 Christie's, New York #147/R

CASTANEDA, Alfredo (1938-) Mexican-cont.
$55000 £37162 Los Ultimos de la Rosita (105x103cm-41x41in) s.d.70 acrylic collage panel. 23-Nov-93 Christie's, New York #127/R

CASTANEDA, Pilar (20th C) Mexican
$4193 £2814 Reunion (170x80cm-67x31in) 1-Dec-93 Louis Morton, Mexico #171/R (M.P 13000)

CASTELLANOS, Carlos Alberto (1881-1945) Uruguayan
$1700 £1126 Arlequin (32x59cm-13x23in) s. board. 28-Jun-93 Gomensoro, Montevideo #63
$3250 £2196 Mujeres con cantaros (20x28cm-8x11in) board painted c.1925. 22-Nov-93 Sotheby's, New York #181/R
$6000 £4000 Personajes en la playa (46x55cm-18x22in) painted c.1930. 18-May-94 Sotheby's, New York #221/R
$6500 £4305 Guaranies en el Bosque (41x32cm-16x13in) board. 23-Nov-92 Sotheby's, New York #230/R
$10000 £6757 Personajes en la playa (81x100cm-32x39in) s. painted c.1930. 22-Nov-93 Sotheby's, New York #217/R

CASTELLANOS, Roberto (20th C) South American
$1500 £1014 Barcas de pesca, puerto de Malaga (60x100cm-24x39in) s.i.d.1924. 25-Apr-94 Gomensoro, Montevideo #51
$1600 £1026 Descanso (64x92cm-25x36in) s.d.1934. 7-Dec-92 Gomensoro, Montevideo #52

CASTELLTORT, Roman (1939-) Mexican
$3167 £2084 Dia de sol..ropa tendida (101x67cm-40x26in) s.d.1985 W/C. 4-Nov-92 Mora, Castelltort & Quintana, Juarez #68/R (M.P 10000000)
$4561 £3000 Puertas y cortinas (67x100cm-26x39in) s.d.1990 W/C. 4-Nov-92 Mora, Castelltort & Quintana, Juarez #91/R (M.P 14400000)
$4909 £3230 Calabazas (100x75cm-39x30in) s.d.1991 W/C. 4-Nov-92 Mora, Castelltort & Quintana, Juarez #110/R (M.P 15500000)

CASTRO, Humberto (20th C) Cuban
$8000 £5369 Mime Tismo (200x140cm-79x55in) s.d.20.5.92 s.i.d.verso. 7-Jan-94 Gary Nader, Miami #61/R

CATALAN, Ramos (20th C) South American
$650 £436 Mountain landscape (41x46cm-16x18in) 27-Mar-93 San Rafael Auction Galleries #311
$1100 £733 Andean mountain village (74x94cm-29x37in) s. 26-May-94 Sloan, North Bethesda #2140/R

CATLIN, George (1794-1872) American
$18000 £12081 Moose at waterhole (48x67cm-19x26in) s.d.54. 2-Dec-93 Sotheby's, New York #10/R
$25000 £15823 Ambush for flamingos in South America (53x67cm-21x26in) i. W/C gouache. 3-Dec-92 Sotheby's, New York #9/R

CAVALCANTI, Emiliano di (1897-1976) Brazilian
$13000 £8497 Duas mulheres (35x24cm-14x9in) s. 17-May-93 Christie's, New York #105/R
$17000 £11258 Mulher Perto do Balcao (71x56cm-28x22in) s. tempera paper painted c.1948. 24-Nov-92 Christie's, New York #137/R
$18000 £12162 Retrato da Noemia Mourao (27x23cm-11x9in) s.d.1929 linen on board. 23-Nov-93 Christie's, New York #116/R
$22000 £14865 Retrato de Noemia (41x33cm-16x13in) painted 1925. 23-Nov-93 Christie's, New York #60 b/R
$22000 £14667 Moca sentada (50x35cm-20x14in) s. panel painted c.1940-42. 18-May-94 Christie's, New York #92/R
$28000 £18543 Casal no paisagem (61x50cm-24x20in) s. painted c.1950-52. 24-Nov-92 Christie's, New York #28/R
$32500 £21667 Natureza morta (73x100cm-29x39in) s.d.63. 17-May-94 Sotheby's, New York #42/R
$50000 £33333 Natureza morta (55x65cm-22x26in) s.d.1933. 18-May-94 Christie's, New York #53/R
$55000 £37162 Natureza morta com frutas (93x73cm-37x29in) s.d.1966. 23-Nov-93 Christie's, New York #52/R
$60000 £40000 Natureza morta com gato branco (81x116cm-32x46in) s.d.69. 18-May-94 Christie's, New York #45/R
$105000 £70946 Duas mulheres (73x54cm-29x21in) s.d.1946. 22-Nov-93 Sotheby's, New York #17/R
$1900 £1258 Luxuria (21x34cm-8x13in) s. ink. 23-Nov-92 Sotheby's, New York #152/R
$29000 £19205 Maternidade (52x74cm-20x29in) s. oil gouache paper on panel. 23-Nov-92 Sotheby's, New York #67/R

CAVALLON, Giorgio (1904-) American
$7000 £4736 Untitled (44x29cm-17x11in) s.d.8.64 s.d.verso canvas on panel. 19-Nov-92 Christie's, New York #349/R
$4000 £2597 Untitled (38x56cm-15x22in) init.d.35 W/C. 9-Sep-93 Sotheby's Arcade, New York #386/R

CAYO, Jean Marc (1958-) Haitian
$1123 £734 Adam et Eve (61x91cm-24x36in) 17-May-93 Hoebanx, Paris #52/R (F.FR 6200)

CEDOR, Dieudonne L (1925-) Haitian
$5000 £3378 Exorcisme (77x63cm-30x25in) s.i.d.3/50 masonite. 24-Nov-93 Christie's, New York #6/R

CEJA, Gonzalo (1936-) Mexican
$1204 £792 De correrias (54x42cm-21x17in) paper. 4-Nov-92 Mora, Castelltort & Quintana, Juarez #92/R (M.P 3800000)

CELENTANO, Daniel Ralph (1902-) American
$1900	£1250	Convalescing (56x58cm-22x23in) s. s.i.verso. 31-Mar-93 Sotheby's Arcade, New York #384/R
$2100	£1364	Harlem looters (41x52cm-16x20in) s. 9-Sep-93 Sotheby's Arcade, New York #352/R
$3000	£1948	Long Island potato pickers (51x63cm-20x25in) s. 9-Sep-93 Sotheby's Arcade, New York #337/R
$10000	£6579	Pitching pennies (61x71cm-24x28in) s.d.48. 31-Mar-93 Sotheby's Arcade, New York #385/R
$10500	£6908	Auto accident. Pleasant Avenue (27x36cm-11x14in) one s. one s.i. chl pair. 31-Mar-93 Sotheby's Arcade, New York #387/R

CELMINS, Vija (1939-) American
$20000	£13423	Long ocean no 3 (76x109cm-30x43in) s.i.d.1973verso graphite acrylic. 5-May-94 Sotheby's, New York #252 a/R

CEMIN, Saint Clair (1951-) American
$800	£556	Candelabro Angelico (42x23cm-17x9in) s.i.d.3/11/84 graphite. 22-Feb-93 Christie's, East, New York #202/R
$1500	£1014	Untitled (56x76cm-22x30in) d.86verso one s.verso one init.verso W/C two. 8-Nov-93 Christie's, East, New York #142/R

CERRA, Mirta (1908-) Cuban
$2000	£1333	Ciudad abstracta (51x24cm-20x9in) s. gouache. 9-Jun-94 Sotheby's Arcade, New York #141/R

CERVANTES, Miguel (20th C) Mexican?
$653	£441	Sin titulo (162x126cm-64x50in) s.d.1987 fibracel. 27-Apr-94 Louis Morton, Mexico #499 (M.P 2200)

CESAR DE PEREZ, Sara (20th C) Mexican
$1279	£864	Alcatraces con talavera y encaje (60x50cm-24x20in) s.d.1993. 20-Oct-93 Louis Morton, Mexico #127/R (M.P 4000)

CHADWICK, William (20th C) American
$1400	£927	Winter snow scene (36x46cm-14x18in) s. board. 23-Sep-93 Mystic Fine Arts, Connecticut #115/R
$8000	£5063	Connecticut autumn (76x76cm-30x30in) s. 4-Dec-92 Christie's, New York #36/R
$12000	£8000	Red roofs, Brandywine (61x76cm-24x30in) s. 25-May-94 Sotheby's, New York #67/R
$15000	£9615	Stream by farm (61x76cm-24x30in) s. 26-May-93 Christie's, New York #160/R
$18000	£11392	Mildred in interior (61x51cm-24x20in) s. 4-Dec-92 Christie's, New York #81/R

CHAFFEE, Oliver N (19/20th C) American
$1800	£1176	Provincetown garden (46x56cm-18x22in) s. 18-Sep-93 James Bakker, Cambridge #154/R

CHAFFEE, S R (19th C) American
$525	£343	Coastal scene (28x51cm-11x20in) s. W/C. 30-Jun-94 Mystic Fine Arts, Connecticut #75 p

CHALE, Gertrudis (19/20th C) Latin American
$3000	£2000	Madre con ninos en el anteplano (46x60cm-18x24in) s. tempera chl painted c.1945. 18-May-94 Sotheby's, New York #301/R

CHALEE, Pop (1907-) American
$1800	£1169	Horses (23x43cm-9x17in) s. tempera board. 25-Jun-94 Skinner, Bolton #221/R
$1600	£1074	Bear cubs (28x41cm-11x16in) s. gouache. 26-Jun-93 Skinner, Bolton #186/R

CHALFANT, Jefferson David (1856-1931) American
$16000	£10256	Clock tinker (38x30cm-15x12in) i. pencil. 27-May-93 Sotheby's, New York #213/R
$23000	£14744	Horn blower (30x24cm-12x9in) s.indist.i. pencil. 27-May-93 Sotheby's, New York #214/R

CHAMBERLAIN, Elwynn (20th C) American
$11000	£7285	Burial of hero (67x36cm-26x14in) s.d.54 tempera paper. 23-Sep-93 Sotheby's, New York #256/R

CHAMBERLAIN, John (1927-) American
$3800	£2550	Untitled (35x43cm-14x17in) s.d.58 paper. 3-May-94 Christie's, East, New York #13/R
$529	£360	Composition (31x24cm-12x9in) s.d.86 chk dr. 13-Apr-94 Bukowskis, Stockholm #355/R (S.KR 4200)
$567	£386	Figure in blue (21x28cm-8x11in) s.d.67 Indian ink. 13-Apr-94 Bukowskis, Stockholm #357 (S.KR 4500)
$655	£446	Heart information (21x27cm-8x11in) s.d.66 Indian ink. 13-Apr-94 Bukowskis, Stockholm #356 (S.KR 5200)
$8000	£5556	Untitled (25x27cm-10x11in) s.d.62verso paper cardboard foil canvas collage. 23-Feb-93 Sotheby's, New York #269/R
$12507	£8451	Untitled, 1962 (30x30cm-12x12in) s.d.verso enamel oil metal collage on panel. 21-Apr-94 Germann, Zurich #21/R (S.FR 18000)

CHAMBERLAIN, Norman Stiles (1887-1961) American
$850	£574	Mission San Gabriel (41x51cm-16x20in) s.d.21. 15-Jun-93 John Moran, Pasadena #26

CHAMBERLIN, Frank Tolles (1873-1961) American
$1800	£1216	Oriental still life - blue jardiniere (61x51cm-24x20in) mono. canvasboard. 15-Jun-93 John Moran, Pasadena #86

CHAMBERS, C Bosseron (1882-?) American
$2300   £1554   Mercury (36x25cm-14x10in) s.i.verso board painted 1926. 31-Mar-94 Sotheby's Arcade, New York #154/R

CHAMBERS, Charles Edward (1883-1942) American
$3000   £1961   Figures beside guitar player (30x30cm-12x12in) s. 14-May-93 Du Mouchelle, Detroit #1036/R

CHAMBERS, John Richard (1931-1978) Canadian
$1162   £785   Portrait of a boy (63x49cm-25x19in) s.d.63 s.i.d.verso pencil dr. 3-Nov-93 Sotheby's, Toronto #259/R (C.D 1500)

CHAMBERS, Richard E E (1863-1944) American
$2000   £1325   Ostrich farm, Norwalk, California (25x36cm-10x14in) init.i.d.1892 W/C paper laid down on board. 15-Jun-94 Butterfield & Butterfield, San Francisco #4621/R

CHAMBERS, Thomas (1808-1866) American
$2700   £1776   Rolling Rapids. Cabin overlooking the falls (46x36cm-18x14in) pair. 5-Jun-93 Skinner, Bolton #194/R

CHAMBERS, Thomas (attrib) (1808-1866) American
$2600   £1769   Hudson River landscape with figures, cattle, buildings (69x89cm-27x35in) rebacked canvas. 17-Apr-94 Schrager Galleries, Milwaukee #775

CHAMPAGNE, Horace (1937-) Canadian
$510   £340   Coming home from school, Cliff St. (43x58cm-17x23in) s. col.chk. 13-May-94 Joyner Fine Art, Toronto #132 (C.D 700)
$510   £340   The Plant Company (43x58cm-17x23in) s. col.chk. 13-May-94 Joyner Fine Art, Toronto #190 (C.D 700)
$574   £383   Ferry crossing at Quebec (30x38cm-12x15in) s. pastel. 30-May-94 Hodgins, Calgary #240 (C.D 800)
$574   £383   White fences - 133 Street N.W (30x38cm-12x15in) s. i.d.verso pastel. 30-May-94 Hodgins, Calgary #335/R (C.D 800)
$583   £388   2113 1 5th St. S W Calgary (43x58cm-17x23in) s. col.chk. 13-May-94 Joyner Fine Art, Toronto #228 (C.D 800)
$610   £407   Untitled - scene of Gibsons Landing, B.C (30x38cm-12x15in) s. pastel. 30-May-94 Hodgins, Calgary #254 (C.D 850)
$642   £434   Lower Town, Quebec City (41x56cm-16x22in) s. col.chk. 23-Nov-93 Joyner Fine Art, Toronto #232 (C.D 850)
$680   £459   Early morning on the farm (57x71cm-22x28in) s. col.chk. 23-Nov-93 Joyner Fine Art, Toronto #179/R (C.D 900)
$680   £459   Ancestral farm, l'Ange-Gardien, P.Q (52x72cm-20x28in) s. col.chk. 23-Nov-93 Joyner Fine Art, Toronto #294 (C.D 900)
$930   £628   Peyto Lake Icefields Parkway (46x61cm-18x24in) s. s.i.d.1984verso pastel. 1-Nov-93 Levis, Calgary #43/R (C.D 1200)
$1057   £714   Coming in to Canmore (69x98cm-27x39in) s. col.chk. 23-Nov-93 Joyner Fine Art, Toronto #255/R (C.D 1400)
$1100   £697   Dufferin Terrace, Quebec (56x74cm-22x29in) s. pastel. 1-Dec-92 Fraser Pinneys, Quebec #14 (C.D 1400)
$1270   £858   Le traversier a levis en mars - ferry crossing in March (46x61cm-18x24in) s. s.i.d.1988 pastel. 25-Apr-94 Levis, Calgary #51/R (C.D 1750)
$1963   £1327   Sunlight and snow, near Beaupre (67x97cm-26x38in) s. col.chk. 23-Nov-93 Joyner Fine Art, Toronto #118/R (C.D 2600)
$3166   £2154   Winter tranquility Sainte Anne de Beaupre (76x102cm-30x40in) s. s.i.verso pastel. 15-Nov-93 Hodgins, Calgary #89/R (C.D 4200)

CHAMPNEY, Benjamin (1817-1907) American
$1100   £719   Rest under birches (46x33cm-18x13in) s. 14-May-93 Skinner, Bolton #39/R
$1300   £861   Cattle and sheep grazing in New Hampshire landscape (30x25cm-12x10in) s. 13-Nov-92 Skinner, Bolton #74/R
$1370   £913   Haywagon and train passing river, mountains beyond (37x24cm-15x9in) s. 31-May-94 Ritchie, Toronto #121/R (C.D 1900)
$1500   £974   Floral still life (53x43cm-21x17in) s. 9-Sep-93 Sotheby's Arcade, New York #70/R
$1500   £1014   Still life with iris geraniums and other flowers (61x74cm-24x29in) s.verso three fold panel. 5-Nov-93 Skinner, Bolton #61/R
$2400   £1611   Autumn day, the White Mountains, New Hampshire (30x51cm-12x20in) s. 4-May-94 Doyle, New York #1/R
$3500   £2318   Figures resting by a river (38x61cm-15x24in) s.d.1863. 28-Nov-92 Young Fine Arts Auctions, Maine #84/R
$3750   £2451   In the White Mountains (76x64cm-30x25in) s.d.1881. 8-May-93 Young Fine Arts Auctions, Maine #62/R
$6000   £4027   Haying (28x48cm-11x19in) s. 6-Dec-93 Grogan, Massachussetts #482/R
$6500   £4362   Still life with Mountain Laurel (54x77cm-21x30in) s.d.1899. 4-Mar-94 Skinner, Bolton #225/R
$7000   £4575   View of Lake George with Black Mountain in the distance (76x122cm-30x48in) s.d.78. 5-May-93 Doyle, New York #9/R

CHAMPNEY, E G (19/20th C) American?
$900   £608   Stroll along the beach (41x61cm-16x24in) s. canvas on board. 31-Mar-94 Sotheby's Arcade, New York #302/R

CHAMPNEY, James Wells (1843-1903) American
$3000   £2041   Happy childhood (30x25cm-12x10in) s.d.70 board. 15-Nov-93 Christie's, East, New York #13/R
$8000   £5063   Sealed with affection (56x46cm-22x18in) 2-Dec-92 Christie's, East, New York #54/R

CHAMPNEY, James Wells (1843-1903) American-cont.
$38000   £25333   Deerfield valley (26x18cm-10x7in) s. 26-May-94 Christie's, New York #28/R

CHAMPNEY, James Wells (attrib) (1843-1903) American
$600   £408   Fidelia (51x43cm-20x17in) s.d.1897 pastel. 17-Apr-94 Schrager Galleries, Milwaukee #602

CHANCE, George Ia (1888-?) American
$950   £601   Ship in harbour (71x81cm-28x32in) s. 30-Nov-92 Selkirks, St. Louis #164/R

CHANDLER, Joseph Goodhue (1813-1880) American
$1300   £867   Reverend Henig H. and Harriet L Woods (76x63cm-30x25in) canvas on masonite pair painted 1853. 12-Mar-94 Weschler, Washington #143/R
$4800   £3179   Portrait of Daniel Webster (91x74cm-36x29in) s. 22-Sep-93 Christie's, New York #61/R

CHANEY, Lester Joseph (1907-) American
$900   £604   Clipper ship on the high seas (71x91cm-28x36in) s. 1-Dec-93 Doyle, New York #34

CHAPIN, Bryant (1859-1927) American
$650   £430   Still life in landscape (25x38cm-10x15in) s.d.1903. 23-Sep-93 Mystic Fine Arts, Connecticut #99 a
$800   £526   Still life with fruit (20x30cm-8x12in) init. 5-Jun-93 Louisiana Auction Exchange #19/R
$1100   £764   Melon and grapes (25x51cm-10x20in) s. 27-Feb-93 Young Fine Arts Auctions, Maine #64/R
$1600   £1081   Still life with apples outdoors (25x36cm-10x14in) s.d.1900. 5-Nov-93 Skinner, Bolton #56/R
$3200   £2148   Still life with apples (33x44cm-13x17in) s.d.1917. 4-Mar-94 Skinner, Bolton #231/R
$3300   £2215   Still life with mixed fruit (32x41cm-13x16in) s.d.1903. 4-Mar-94 Skinner, Bolton #233/R

CHAPIN, C H (19th C) American
$2500   £1656   In the Adirondacks (51x41cm-20x16in) s. 23-Sep-93 Sotheby's, New York #53/R

CHAPIN, Charles H (19th C) American
$1500   £1007   Luminous dawn in the Adirondacks (30x51cm-12x20in) s. 11-Dec-93 Weschler, Washington #77/R

CHAPIN, James Ormsbee (1887-1975) American
$15000   £10000   Street market, New York (69x99cm-27x39in) s.d.1933. 16-Mar-94 Christie's, New York #112/R
$4500   £2601   Musicians (34x24cm-13x9in) s.d.23 W/C. 24-Sep-92 Sotheby's, New York #164/R

CHAPMAN, C W (19th C) American
$2100   £1373   Italian shepherdess with goat (36x48cm-14x19in) s.i.indis.d.186.verso. 16-Sep-93 Sloan, North Bethesda #3221/R

CHAPMAN, Carlton Theodore (1860-1925) American
$1000   £694   Noontime Gloucester Harbour (46x81cm-18x32in) s.d.1884 board. 5-Mar-93 Skinner, Bolton #490 b
$1100   £738   'The Windward Thrash' (56x91cm-22x36in) s. 25-Mar-94 Eldred, Massachusetts #267/R
$1300   £850   Snowy winter stream (36x51cm-14x20in) s. 4-May-93 Christie's, East, New York #109/R
$800   £462   Fishing boats at sea (25x20cm-10x8in) s. W/C. 27-Sep-92 James Bakker, Cambridge #9

CHAPMAN, Charles S (1879-1962) American
$700   £470   California redwoods (61x76cm-24x30in) s. board. 24-Jun-93 Mystic Fine Arts, Connecticut #196 a
$2100   £1364   At the brook (36x36cm-14x14in) s. board. 4-Aug-94 Eldred, Massachusetts #712/R

CHAPMAN, Conrad Wise (1842-1910) American
$10656   £7200   Figures on beach (22x41cm-9x16in) panel. 15-Jun-93 Phillips, London #101/R
$11000   £7432   Valle de Puebla Desde la Piramide de Cholula (13x23cm-5x9in) s.d.1900 panel. 22-Nov-93 Sotheby's, New York #153/R
$11000   £7692   Scene de plage en Normandie (14x22cm-6x9in) mono.d.1880 panel. 10-Mar-93 Sotheby's, New York #18/R
$13860   £9000   Figures on beach (14x22cm-6x9in) s.d.1880 panel. 21-Jun-94 Phillips, London #61/R
$40000   £26144   Valle de Mexico Desde la hacienda de Los Morales (22x47cm-9x19in) s.i.indist.d.1902. 18-May-93 Sotheby's, New York #15/R
$80000   £53333   Mexico from the Hacienda Morales (45x89cm-18x35in) s.i.d.1874verso. 17-May-94 Sotheby's, New York #8/R
$9500   *£6291*   *Campesino (29x20cm-11x8in) s.i. W/C board. 23-Nov-92 Sotheby's, New York #135/R*
$9500   *£6291*   *Campesina (27x19cm-11x7in) s.i. W/C board. 23-Nov-92 Sotheby's, New York #136/R*

CHAPMAN, John Gadsby (1808-1889) American
$15500   £10473   Claudian aqueduct and the Alban Mountains (41x152cm-16x60in) 31-Mar-94 Sotheby's Arcade, New York #96/R

CHAPMAN, John Linton (19th C) American
$775   £520   Ploughing near Loweswater (13x21cm-5x8in) s. i.verso board. 24-Mar-93 Phillips, Chester #254/R

CHAPMAN, John Linton (19th C) American-cont.
$1400	£897	Gleaners of the Campagna (33x25cm-13x10in) mono.i.d.1874 s.i.d.verso board. 24-May-93 Grogan, Massachussetts #296/R
$1900	£1275	Italian peasants with baby (36x25cm-14x10in) mono.i.d.1865 board. 12-Jan-94 Doyle, New York #9/R
$6500	£4333	The Blacksmith Shop, St. Gervasio, Venice (34x73cm-13x29in) s.d.1881. 23-May-94 Christie's, East, New York #74/R

CHAPMAN, Minerva Josephine (1858-1947) American
$619	£405	Beach scene, Calais (15x20cm-6x8in) s.i. panel. 17-Sep-93 Dr Fritz Nagel, Stuttgart #2421 (DM 1000)
$800	£471	Copper kettle (18x28cm-7x11in) s.d.1910. 3-Oct-92 Weschler, Washington #113/R

CHAPPEL, Alonzo (1828-1887) American
$6500	£4545	Frontiersmen (76x63cm-30x25in) s. 11-Mar-93 Christie's, New York #107/R

CHARLESWORTH, Rod (20th C) Canadian?
$510	£340	Winter rollick (30x40cm-12x16in) s. board. 13-May-94 Joyner Fine Art, Toronto #277/R (C.D 700)

CHARLOT, Jean (1898-1979) Mexican/French
$1700	£1141	Musicians (20x25cm-8x10in) s.indist.d. 24-Mar-93 Doyle, New York #15 a
$3500	£2318	Female figure (43x34cm-17x13in) s.d.1966. 29-Sep-93 Sotheby's Arcade, New York #228/R
$3700	£2467	Portrait of Eleanor Freed (51x41cm-20x16in) s.d.1948. 24-Aug-93 Hart Gallery, Houston #2
$4500	£2941	Coiffure (28x20cm-11x8in) s.d.30. 18-May-93 Sotheby's, New York #147/R
$6000	£4027	Dos lavanderas (51x41cm-20x16in) s. painted 1937. 7-Jan-94 Gary Nader, Miami #42/R
$7000	£4667	L'eveil (75x94cm-30x37in) s.d.32 canvas laid down on masonite. 18-May-94 Sotheby's, New York #306/R
$10000	£6757	La Huida a Egipto (51x60cm-20x24in) s.d.45. 23-Nov-93 Christie's, New York #252/R
$15000	£9934	Madre con Hijo (61x50cm-24x20in) s.d.37. 23-Nov-92 Sotheby's, New York #178/R
$3500	*£2349*	*Madre et hija (76x57cm-30x22in) s. W/C gouache painted 1945. 7-Jan-94 Gary Nader, Miami #135 d/R*

CHARTRAND, Augusto (fl.1850-1899) Latin American
$25000	£16667	Efecto de luna en los campos de la Isla de Cuba (43x74cm-17x29in) painted c.1880. 18-May-94 Sotheby's, New York #198/R

CHARTRAND, Esteban (1824-1884) Cuban
$7000	£4636	Paisaje (26x51cm-10x20in) 23-Nov-92 Sotheby's, New York #139/R
$7000	£4636	Paisaje tropical (27x37cm-11x15in) s.d.1878 panel. 23-Nov-92 Sotheby's, New York #140/R
$12000	£7947	La Vallee de Coliseo, Cuba (70x96cm-28x38in) s.d.1865 s.i.stretcher. 24-Nov-92 Christie's, New York #84/R
$18000	£11765	Casa de campo (30x46cm-12x18in) s.d.1882. 17-May-93 Christie's, New York #95/R
$23000	£15541	Paisaje cubano (41x76cm-16x30in) s.d.1877. 22-Nov-93 Sotheby's, New York #150/R
$27000	£18000	La Vallee de Coliseo, Cuba (70x96cm-28x38in) s.d.1865 s.i.verso. 18-May-93 Sotheby's, New York #207/R
$42500	£28333	Paisaje Cubano (50x91cm-20x36in) s.d.Sep.1872. 18-May-94 Sotheby's, New York #206/R
$56000	£37838	Paisaje Cubano (76x121cm-30x48in) s.d.1882. 22-Nov-93 Sotheby's, New York #11/R

CHASE, Adelaide (1869-1944) American
$1250	£839	Woman in a green velvet dress (86x61cm-34x24in) s. 6-Dec-93 Grogan, Massachussetts #530/R

CHASE, Frank Swift (1886-1958) American
$1400	£940	Spring mist (46x61cm-18x24in) s. 26-Mar-94 James Bakker, Cambridge #71/R
$1800	£1053	Spring mist (46x61cm-18x24in) s. i.stretcher. 17-Sep-92 Sloan, North Bethesda #2869

CHASE, Gertrude (20th C) American
$900	£600	Coastal scene (41x51cm-16x20in) s. canvasboard. 15-Mar-94 John Moran, Pasadena #92

CHASE, Henry (1853-1889) American
$900	£577	Figures in sailboat, rough seas (41x25cm-16x10in) s. 26-Apr-93 Selkirks, St. Louis #302/R
$6500	£3757	European coastal scene, figures on beach (41x51cm-16x20in) s.d.1877. 21-Sep-92 Selkirks, St. Louis #331/R
$10000	£6329	European coastline with sailing ships and fishermen unloading nets (51x76cm-20x30in) s.d.1870. 30-Nov-92 Selkirks, St. Louis #255/R

CHASE, Louisa (1951-) American
$750	£497	Untitled (57x76cm-22x30in) paper. 17-Nov-92 Christie's, East, New York #223/R
$1000	£676	Storm (124x124cm-49x49in) s. i.d.1981verso. 4-Nov-93 Boos Gallery, Michigan #233/R
$3000	£1987	Tulip (178x229cm-70x90in) s.d.1980. 30-Jun-93 Sotheby's Arcade, New York #375/R
$7000	£4698	Untitled (213x335cm-84x132in) s. painted 1988. 25-Feb-94 Sotheby's, New York #123/R
$3500	*£2318*	*St Sabastion (183x198cm-72x78in) s.d.79 s.i.d.verso encaustic canvas. 17-Nov-92 Christie's, East, New York #197/R*

CHASE, Susan Miller (20th C) American
$500	£336	A little boy in a blue outfit standing in a field (25x20cm-10x8in) s. board. 24-Mar-94 Boos Gallery, Michigan #555
$650	£425	Young lady in rowing boat (20x25cm-8x10in) s. board. 22-May-93 Collins, Maine #45/R
$750	£500	Woman amongst the flowers (30x25cm-12x10in) s. studio st.verso board. 12-Mar-94 Weschler, Washington #180
$750	£514	Figures at the beach (25x30cm-10x12in) s. board. 19-Feb-94 Young Fine Arts Auctions, Maine #58/R
$800	£523	Nude bather (23x15cm-9x6in) s. board. 18-Sep-93 Young Fine Arts Auctions, Maine #72/R
$800	£530	Day at the beach (20x25cm-8x10in) s. board. 23-Sep-93 Mystic Fine Arts, Connecticut #110/R
$850	£594	Parasol (36x25cm-14x10in) s. board. 12-Mar-93 Skinner, Bolton #269/R
$1000	£671	Two seated girls in white dresses (25x20cm-10x8in) s. board. 24-Jun-93 Boos Gallery, Michigan #595/R
$1000	£633	Woman with parasol (25x36cm-10x14in) s. board. 24-Oct-92 Collins, Maine #47
$1100	£719	Ring around the Rosie (20x25cm-8x10in) s. board. 18-Sep-93 Young Fine Arts Auctions, Maine #71/R
$1300	£861	Beach (25x30cm-10x12in) s. board. 28-Nov-92 Young Fine Arts Auctions, Maine #92/R
$1600	£1046	Figures on beach (25x30cm-10x12in) s. board. 8-May-93 Young Fine Arts Auctions, Maine #65/R
$3250	£2211	Beach scene (20x25cm-8x10in) s. board. 16-Apr-94 Young Fine Arts Auctions, Maine #70/R

CHASE, William Merritt (1849-1916) American
$6500	£4362	Portrait of officer of civic guard of St George at Haarlem (127x61cm-50x24in) s.verso after Frans Hals. 4-May-94 Doyle, New York #24/R
$7000	£4636	Portrait of gentleman (119x96cm-47x38in) s.d.1883. 22-Sep-93 Christie's, New York #135/R
$7500	£4747	Street dancer, Italy (66x39cm-26x15in) s. i.verso. 3-Dec-92 Sotheby's, New York #90/R
$9500	£6013	Portrait of a gentleman (64x53cm-25x21in) s.d.77. 3-Dec-92 Sotheby's, New York #83/R
$10000	£6757	Portrait of a woman (15x15cm-6x6in) canvasboard painted c.1900. 31-Mar-94 Sotheby's Arcade, New York #158/R
$11000	£7051	Miss Mary Margaret Sweeney (62x47cm-24x19in) s. painted c.1910. 27-May-93 Sotheby's, New York #53/R
$14000	£9396	Portrait of young woman holding bouquet (53x36cm-21x14in) s. 4-May-94 Doyle, New York #23/R
$16000	£10256	Still life with fish (72x105cm-28x41in) s. painted c.1910. 27-May-93 Sotheby's, New York #27/R
$20000	£13333	Miss L, Isabella Lathrop (129x96cm-51x38in) s. painted c.1913. 25-May-94 Sotheby's, New York #79/R
$22500	£14706	Shinnicock Bay (20x30cm-8x12in) s. panel. 16-Apr-93 Du Mouchelle, Detroit #2002/R
$26000	£16456	The old book (55x42cm-22x17in) s. 4-Dec-92 Christie's, New York #18/R
$28000	£17949	Portrait of lady in white dress - Miss Edith Newbold (62x47cm-24x19in) s. painted c.1892. 27-May-93 Sotheby's, New York #50/R
$30000	£20000	Bobbie - portrait sketch (41x35cm-16x14in) i. 17-Mar-94 Sotheby's, New York #106/R
$32000	£18497	Gowanus Pier (21x33cm-8x13in) s. panel. 24-Sep-92 Sotheby's, New York #107/R
$37500	£25000	Venice (24x16cm-9x6in) s. panel. 25-May-94 Sotheby's, New York #84/R
$48000	£32000	Sunny Spain (49x74cm-19x29in) s. 26-May-94 Christie's, New York #83/R
$50000	£32051	Jester (38x22cm-15x9in) s.indist.i. panel. 27-May-93 Sotheby's, New York #45/R
$75000	£47468	Shinnecock landscape (16x23cm-6x9in) s. panel. 3-Dec-92 Sotheby's, New York #107/R
$90000	£57692	Portrait of Virginia Gerson (72x60cm-28x24in) s. 27-May-93 Sotheby's, New York #22/R
$120000	£80537	Dorothy (51x41cm-20x16in) s. 3-Dec-93 Christie's, New York #47/R
$125000	£83333	Shinnecock landscape (41x51cm-16x20in) 25-May-94 Sotheby's, New York #87/R
$5000	*£3333*	*Child with prints (56x45cm-22x18in) pastel canvas stretched over board. 26-May-94 Christie's, New York #82/R*
$3600000	*£2307693*	*Peonies (122x122cm-48x48in) s. pastel executed c.1897. 27-May-93 Sotheby's, New York #32/R*

CHASE, William Merritt and RITTENBERG, Henry R (19/20th C) American
$900	£600	Portrait of a woman (51x41cm-20x16in) i.verso. 1-Jun-94 Doyle, New York #56

CHASE, William Merritt and WILES, Irving Ramsey (19th C) American
$25000	£16779	Mrs William Merrit Chase and son Roland Dana Chase (157x128cm-62x50in) s. 2-Dec-93 Sotheby's, New York #125/R

CHATELAIN, James (1947-) American
$650	£433	Bypassing (64x58cm-25x23in) s.i.d.verso. 26-Aug-93 Boos Gallery, Michigan #424/R
$800	£537	Untitled 1977 (91x91cm-36x36in) s.d.77 verso. 25-Mar-94 Boos Gallery, Michigan #419/R

CHATTERTON, Clarence K (1880-1973) American
$850	£571	Ferry boat on the Hudson (30x46cm-12x18in) s. i.d.1912verso board. 1-Dec-93 Doyle, New York #36
$10000	£6410	Regatta at Kennebunkport (30x40cm-12x16in) s. board. 26-May-93 Christie's, New York #146/R
$3000	*£1899*	*Snake Hill (32x47cm-13x19in) s.d.06 gouache pencil paper on board. 3-Dec-92 Sotheby's, New York #22/R*

CHATTERTON, Clarence K (attrib) (1880-1973) American
$1500 £867 Under the old shade tree (29x41cm-11x16in) board. 25-Sep-92 Sotheby's Arcade, New York #224/R

CHAVEZ LOPEZ, Gerardo (1937-) Peruvian
$1542 £988 Titan blasphemateur (130x95cm-51x37in) s. 15-Dec-92 Campo, Vlaamse Kaai #423/R (B.FR 50000)
$1223 £826 The transience of the seas (89x116cm-35x46in) s.d.1975 pastel. 26-Oct-93 Campo, Vlaamse Kaai #210/R (B.FR 45000)

CHAVEZ MORADO, Jose (1909-) Mexican
$6367 £4082 Laureles (47x61cm-19x24in) s.d.1955 canvas on board. 29-Apr-93 Louis Morton, Mexico #56 (M.P 20000)

CHAVIGNAUD, Georges (1865-1944) Canadian
$435 £290 Canal scene (30x46cm-12x18in) s. W/C. 6-Jun-94 Waddingtons, Toronto #1200 (C.D 600)
$549 £352 Unloading day's catch (63x89cm-25x35in) s. W/C. 7-Dec-92 Waddingtons, Toronto #1278 (C.D 700)

CHECCHI, Giuseppe de (1911-) Argentinian
$632 £424 Flower garden (25x34cm-10x13in) canvas on board painted c.1970. 23-Jun-93 Galerie Kornfeld, Berne #273 (S.FR 950)

CHEE, Robert (1938-1971) American
$600 £387 Luring Burro (48x38cm-19x15in) s. gouache board. 9-Jan-93 Skinner, Bolton #224

CHEN, Hilo (1942-) American
$850 £571 Blossom (13x18cm-5x7in) s.i.verso acrylic. 23-Feb-94 Christie's, East, New York #292/R
$1800 £1208 Beach (30x40cm-12x16in) s.i.d.verso acrylic. 23-Feb-94 Christie's, East, New York #293/R
$3000 £2013 Bellies for teeth (102x137cm-40x54in) s.i.verso acrylic. 23-Feb-94 Christie's, East, New York #294/R
$3000 £1987 Bedroom 20 (101x142cm-40x56in) s.i.d.8606verso acrylic. 17-Nov-92 Christie's, East, New York #154/R
$3905 £2552 Beach 61 (77x102cm-30x40in) s.verso painted 1979. 18-Sep-93 Jean Louis Picard, Paris #3/R (F.FR 22000)
$5000 £3311 Ying Yang (137x203cm-54x80in) s.d.74 verso. 30-Jun-93 Sotheby's Arcade, New York #336/R
$6500 £4362 Beach 33 (123x173cm-48x68in) s.i.d.75verso acrylic. 3-May-94 Christie's, East, New York #89/R
$7100 £4640 Beach 64 (97x142cm-38x56in) s.i.verso. 18-Sep-93 Jean Louis Picard, Paris #12/R (F.FR 40000)

CHENEY, Nan Lawson (1897-1985) Canadian
$1085 £733 Drying nets British Columbia (66x72cm-26x28in) s. s.i.d.1936verso. 1-Nov-93 Levis, Calgary #45/R (C.D 1400)

CHERAMI, Gesner (1954-) Haitian
$745 £477 Jungle imaginaire aux elephants (60x50cm-24x20in) 14-Dec-92 Hoebanx, Paris #58/R (F.FR 4000)

CHERRY, Emma Richardson (1859-?) American
$3200 £2092 Hacienda in full bloom (64x76cm-25x30in) s. 22-May-93 Collins, Maine #38/R

CHERRY, Kathryn (1880-1931) American
$950 £664 Rural street scene (28x36cm-11x14in) s. masonite. 5-Feb-93 Selkirks, St. Louis #310/R
$950 £549 Sea beyond (25x38cm-10x15in) s. canvasboard. 21-Sep-92 Selkirks, St. Louis #168
$1150 £665 Still life of fruit on table (46x64cm-18x25in) s. canvasboard. 21-Sep-92 Selkirks, St. Louis #170/R
$3500 £2303 Road to sea (61x56cm-24x22in) s. 13-Jun-93 Butterfield & Butterfield, San Francisco #3202/R

CHEW, Richard (20th C) American
$2800 £1879 Manayunk in winter (76x102cm-30x40in) s. 2-Dec-93 Freeman Fine Arts, Philadelphia #832/R

CHEW, Richard S (jnr) (20th C) American
$1050 £705 Reading R.R. and St.Johns Church (64x76cm-25x30in) s. i.verso. 2-Dec-93 Freeman Fine Arts, Philadelphia #841

CHICHESTER, Cecil (1891-?) American
$1600 £1046 Springtime in Colchester (61x76cm-24x30in) s.d.1915. 30-Jun-94 Mystic Fine Arts, Connecticut #50/R
$1800 £1192 October glory (102x127cm-40x50in) s.d.1913 i.verso. 13-Nov-92 Skinner, Bolton #122/R

CHICHESTER, Cecil (attrib) (1891-?) American
$1000 £680 Landscape, winter with water, figures and buildings (51x61cm-20x24in) s.d.17. 17-Apr-94 Schrager Galleries, Milwaukee #758

CHITTENDEN, Alice B (1860-1934) American
$750	£507	Summer landscape (18x23cm-7x9in) s. canvasboard. 15-Jun-93 John Moran, Pasadena #105
$800	£471	Wild peach blossoms (46x36cm-18x12in) s. paper. 4-Oct-92 Butterfield & Butterfield, Los Angeles #63/R
$3250	£1912	Roses bouquet (46x61cm-18x24in) s. canvas on board. 4-Oct-92 Butterfield & Butterfield, Los Angeles #62/R
$4500	£2647	Roses and daffodils (56x46cm-22x18in) s. 4-Oct-92 Butterfield & Butterfield, Los Angeles #61/R
$10000	£6623	Chrysanthemums in a brass bowl (91x76cm-36x30in) s. 15-Jun-94 Butterfield & Butterfield, San Francisco #4599/R
$15000	£8824	Chrysanthemums (61x102cm-24x40in) s.d.1889. 4-Oct-92 Butterfield & Butterfield, Los Angeles #58/R

CHOUZA, Ileana G de (20th C) Mexican
$1119	£756	Mandarinas (70x90cm-28x35in) 20-Oct-93 Louis Morton, Mexico #53 (M.P 3500)
$1343	£907	Flores silvestres (90x90cm-35x35in) 20-Oct-93 Louis Morton, Mexico #132/R (M.P 4200)

CHRISTENBERRY, William (20th C) American
$3750	£2404	Royal Wall (137x241cm-54x95in) s.i.d.1985verso mixed media wood panel. 10-Dec-92 Sloan, North Bethesda #2681/R
$4250	£2724	Wall construction IV (203x165cm-80x65in) s.i.d.1985 mixed media wood panel. 10-Dec-92 Sloan, North Bethesda #2683/R

CHRISTENSEN, Dan (1942-) American
$1900	£1258	Centerpiece (169x66cm-67x26in) s.i.d.1981verso acrylic. 29-Sep-93 Sotheby's Arcade, New York #293/R
$2100	£1458	Amram (180x203cm-71x80in) i.on stretcher. 26-Feb-93 Sotheby's Arcade, New York #390/R

CHRISTENSEN, Ted (1911-) American?
$1100	£728	Main Street (51x61cm-20x24in) s.d.1947 panel. 15-Jun-94 Butterfield & Butterfield, San Francisco #4743/R

CHRISTO (1935-) American/Bulgarian
$1495	£971	Wrapped statues (89x68cm-35x27in) s. photocollage. 24-Jun-94 Germann, Zurich #132/R (S.FR 2000)
$1558	£999	Sans titre (72x57cm-28x22in) s.i. collage acquatint. 14-Dec-92 Christie's, Rome #23 (I.L 2200000)
$2591	£1728	Wrapped armchair , s. collage serigraph. 15-Mar-94 Rasmussen, Copenhagen #199/R (D.KR 17000)
$4105	£2632	8 barrels, project for Frankfurt (30x45cm-12x18in) s.i.d.1967 pencil crayon two. 27-May-93 Lempertz, Cologne #661/R (DM 6500)
$5000	£3378	Abu Dhabi Mastaba, project for the United Arab Emirates (30x24cm-12x9in) s.i.d.1978 graphite col.crayon board on board. 10-Nov-93 Christie's, New York #171/R
$6000	£3529	Packed Tower (71x56cm-28x22in) s.i.d.1968 graphite col.crayons board. 8-Oct-92 Christie's, New York #137/R
$6200	£4189	Corridor Store Front project (56x35cm-22x14in) s.i.d.66-67 graphite enamel acetate film board. 8-Nov-93 Christie's, East, New York #9/R
$6644	£4343	Package on dolly (55x71cm-22x28in) s.d.1974 collage material string chl. 5-May-93 Ader Tajan, Paris #69/R (F.FR 36000)
$7717	£5179	Wrapped automobile - project for Volvo (55x70cm-22x28in) s.d.1981 mixed media collage. 29-Nov-93 AB Stockholms Auktionsverk, Stockholm #6189/R (S.KR 65000)
$10174	£6522	Pont Neuf (35x56cm-14x22in) s.i.d.1985 collage photo col.chk acrylic. 10-Dec-92 Christie's, Amsterdam #382/R (D.FL 18000)
$11000	£7432	Packed girl University of Pennsylvania project (56x71cm-22x28in) s.i.d.1968 graphite chl tusine plastic board. 8-Nov-93 Christie's, East, New York #30/R
$11410	£7000	Running fence (71x56cm-28x22in) s.i.d.1974 cardboard card. 15-Oct-92 Christie's, London #68/R
$11920	£8000	Package on dolly, project (55x71cm-22x28in) s.i.d.1974 pencil fabric string. 3-Dec-93 Sotheby's, London #175/R
$11920	£8000	The wall, project for wrapped Roman wall (71x56cm-28x22in) s.i.d.1974 pencil pastel felt-tip fabric photo. 3-Dec-93 Sotheby's, London #223/R
$12000	£8000	Wrapped walkways - Two Parks Project (72x56cm-28x22in) s.i.d.1970 graphite col pencil fabric photo. 26-May-94 Christie's, London #131/R
$12665	£8500	Ocean Front/Bay Cover - Project for covering Cove at King's Reach (56x30cm-22x12in) s.i.d.1974 pastel pencil oil. 3-Dec-93 Sotheby's, London #180/R
$12750	£8500	Running Fence (56x71cm-22x28in) s.i.d.1973 pencil col crayon fabric photo card. 26-May-94 Christie's, London #146/R
$13000	£8725	Running fence - project for Sonoma and Marin Counties California (56x71cm-22x28in) s.i.d.1976 fabric chl pastel crayon pencil. 25-Feb-94 Sotheby's, New York #83/R
$13040	£8000	Packed hay wrapped - project for Institute of Contemporary Art (56x71cm-22x28in) s.d.1968 col.crayons staples string fabric card. 14-Oct-92 Sotheby's, London #376/R
$13424	£9070	Ocean Front, project for cove at Kings Beach, New Port, Rhode Island (55x70cm-22x28in) s.i.d.1974 col crayon collage material. 29-Apr-94 Beaussant & Lefeure, Paris #31/R (F.FR 80000)
$13727	£9091	Wrapped Reichstag (84x71cm-33x28in) s.d.1978 collage two parts. 21-Nov-92 Ader Tajan, Paris #367/R (F.FR 75000)
$14459	£9576	The Wall (56x71cm-22x28in) s.d.1973 collage. 21-Nov-92 Ader Tajan, Paris #31/R (F.FR 79000)

CHRISTO (1935-) American/Bulgarian-cont.

$15000	£10135	One million stacked oil drums, project for Houston, Galveston area, Texas (91x126cm-36x50in) s.d.1970 pencil col.pencil oil pastel map. 11-Nov-93 Sotheby's, New York #111/R
$15000	£10067	Running fence project for Marin Counties, California (56x72cm-22x28in) s.i.d.1976 wax crayon pencil paper collage. 5-May-94 Sotheby's, New York #260/R
$15500	£10403	Packed coast - project for Little Bay (71x56cm-28x22in) s.i.d.1969 graphite crayon string collage photo. 23-Feb-94 Christie's, New York #19/R
$15750	£10500	Packed coast/Project for Australia - Little Bay, New South Wales (72x56cm-28x22in) s.i.d.1969 fabric twine pencil collage card. 26-May-94 Christie's, London #74/R
$17000	£11486	Packed coast, project for Little Bay near Sydney, NSW Australia (72x57cm-28x22in) s.i.d.1969 fabric string graphite staples board. 10-Nov-93 Christie's, New York #168/
$17135	£11500	The Umbrellas, joint Project for Japan and USA (98x78cm-39x31in) s.i.d.1989 collage col.crayon graphite enamel. 25-Mar-93 Christie's, London #123/R
$17160	£11916	Emballage de sol, projet pour Chicago (57x72cm-22x28in) s.i.d.1968 collage gouache crayon paper on wood. 3-Mar-93 Guy Loudmer, Paris #83/R (F.FR 97000)
$17930	£11000	The Pont Neuf wrapped (71x56cm-28x22in) s.i.d.1975 collage card. 15-Oct-92 Christie's, London #67/R
$18000	£12081	Two wrapped trees - project for the garden of Pepino Acrati-near Milano (142x180cm-56x71in) s.i.d.71 pencil polyethylene fabric crayon chl. 25-Feb-94 Sotheby's, New York #71/R
$19000	£12752	Wrapped floors and closed windows, project for the Haus Lange Museum (71x56cm-28x22in) s.i.d.1971 graphite fabric glue paper collage. 4-May-94 Christie's, New York #208/R
$19370	£13000	Wrapped walkways (71x55cm-28x22in) s.i.d.1970 pastel pencil fabric collage board. 23-Mar-94 Sotheby's, London #342/R
$19370	£13000	Packed coast, project for Little Bay, N.S.W. (56x71cm-22x28in) s.i.d.1969 pencil pastel fabric string photo map. 3-Dec-93 Sotheby's, London #235/R
$19560	£12000	Wrapped Reichstg (56x72cm-22x28in) s.d.81 collage photographs col.crayon fabric. 15-Oct-92 Christie's, London #66/R
$19560	£12000	The Umbrellas (36x56cm-14x22in) s.i.d.1988 collage card. 15-Oct-92 Christie's, London #69/R
$20375	£12500	Wrapped Reichstag - project for Berlin (57x72cm-22x28in) s.d.1982 col.crayons map string fabric card two. 14-Oct-92 Sotheby's, London #417/R
$20860	£14000	Wrapped reichstag - projekt fur den Deutschen Reichstag (108x56cm-43x22in) s.i.d.1977 fabric graphite col.crayon collage 2. 2-Dec-93 Christie's, London #170/R
$20860	£14000	Empaquetage (85x65cm-33x26in) s.i.d.63 verso plastic string wood canvas. 2-Dec-93 Christie's, London #35/R
$21043	£14218	Valley Curtain, Project for Colorado (72x56cm-28x22in) s.d.1972 crayon dr col.crayons collage. 18-Jun-93 Francis Briest, Paris #59/R (F.FR 120000)
$22000	£14379	Umbrellas - joint project for Japan and USA (77x97cm-30x38in) s.i.d.1988 graphite pastel photo collage. 4-May-93 Sotheby's, New York #226 a/R
$22879	£15152	The Pont Neuf wrapped (71x55cm-28x22in) s.d.1984 collage. 21-Nov-92 Ader Tajan, Paris #39/R (F.FR 125000)
$23000	£15033	Umbrellas - joint project for Japan and USA (77x97cm-30x38in) s.d.1987 graphite pastel photo collage two part. 4-May-93 Sotheby's, New York #157/R
$23700	£15000	Pont Neuf wrapped - project for Paris (98x78cm-39x31in) s.d.1985 crayon pencil thread fabric card. 3-Dec-92 Sotheby's, London #65/R
$23840	£16000	Umbrellas, project for Japan and Western USA (78x67cm-31x26in) s.i.d.1986 col.crayons printed map collage card. 24-Mar-93 Sotheby's, London #333/R
$23840	£16000	Wrapped Reichstag, Project for Berlin (98x78cm-39x31in) s.i.d.1986 collage graphite crayon string card. 25-Mar-93 Christie's, London #122/R
$24000	£16667	Surrounded islands, project for Biscayne Bay, Greater Miami, Florida (?x71cm-?x28in) s.i.d.1982 col.crayon graphite fabric collage. 23-Feb-93 Sotheby's, New York #283/R
$24000	£16107	Running fence, project for Sonoma and Marin County (?x244cm-?x96in) s.i.d.1973 mixed media paperboard two parts. 5-May-94 Sotheby's, New York #231/R
$24000	£16000	The Umbrellas - Joint project for Japan and USA , i.one s.d.1989 pencil crayon gouache collage two. 26-May-94 Christie's, London #78/R
$24450	£15000	Pont Neuf wrapped - project for Paris (56x71cm-22x28in) s.d.1984 col.crayons map pencil thread two. 14-Oct-92 Sotheby's, London #369/R
$24480	£16000	Valley Curtain, project for Colorado (70x5cm-28x2in) s.i.d.1972 pencil pastel gouache fabric collage. 30-Jun-94 Sotheby's, London #188/R
$25265	£15500	Umbrellas - project for Japan and USA (78x68cm-31x27in) s.d.1990 crayon printed map pastel fabric pair. 14-Oct-92 Sotheby's, London #416/R
$26000	£17450	The umbrellas, joint project for Japan and USA (78x98cm-31x39in) s.i.d.1990 crayons chl fabric collage on board. 4-May-94 Christie's, New York #345/R
$26000	£17450	Orange storefront, project (57x76cm-22x30in) s.i.d.1965 enamel chl graphite crayon staples. 4-May-94 Christie's, New York #120/R
$26010	£17000	The Umbrellas, project for Japan and Western USA , one s.i.d.1987 crayon pencil acrylic on map two. 30-Jun-94 Sotheby's, London #180/R
$26010	£17000	The Umbrellas, project for Japan and Western USA , one s.i.d.1986 crayon map pencil fabric two. 30-Jun-94 Sotheby's, London #184/R
$26820	£18000	The Umbrellas - project for Japan and Western USA (98x78cm-39x31in) s.i.d.1987 card graphite col.crayon fabric oil. 2-Dec-93 Christie's, London #171/R
$27000	£17881	Allied chemical tower-packed - project for 1 Times Square (71x56cm-28x22in) s.d.1968 collage board. 18-Nov-92 Sotheby's, New York #151/R
$28310	£19000	Umbrella project for Japan and USA (98x78cm-39x31in) s.i.d.1987 gouache wax crayon pencil fabric card. 2-Dec-93 Christie's, London #120/R
$28440	£18000	Umbrellas - project for Japan and USA (77x97cm-30x38in) s.d.1989 oil crayon pastel fabric paper on card. 3-Dec-92 Sotheby's, London #76/R

CHRISTO (1935-) American/Bulgarian-cont.

$29800	£20000	Running fence, project for Sonoma County and Marin County State (144x244cm-57x96in) s.d.1976 col.crayons map pastel chl dr collage. 3-Dec-93 Sotheby's, London #231/R
$30000	£20134	The Umbrellas - joint project for Japan and U.S.A (78x99cm-31x39in) s.i.d.1990 col.crayon chl collage map two panels. 23-Feb-94 Christie's, New York #41/R
$30000	£20270	Umbrellas, joint project for Japan and USA (78x?cm-31x?in) s.i.d.1989 col.crayons chk graphite two panels. 10-Nov-93 Christie's, New York #143/R
$32500	£21959	Wrapped trees - project for Avenue Champs Elysees in Paris (71x56cm-28x22in) s.d.1969 pencil pastel collage string tape board. 11-Nov-93 Sotheby's, New York #111 a/R
$33000	£21569	Running fence - project for Sonoma County and Marin county, State of California (91x244cm-36x96in) s.d.1974 chl. 4-May-93 Sotheby's, New York #134/R
$33660	£22000	The Mastaba of Abu Dhabi, project for United Arab Emirates , s.i.1980 printed map crayon pencil chl two. 30-Jun-94 Sotheby's, London #218/R
$35000	£23490	The Pont Neuf, wrapped - project for Paris (71x55cm-28x22in) s.i.d.1981 graphite thread fabric paper collage. 4-May-94 Christie's, New York #192/R
$35000	£22876	The umbrellas - joint project for Japan and USA (77x97cm-30x38in) s.i.d.1989 map acrylic crayons fabric board. 5-May-93 Christie's, New York #298/R
$35000	£23179	Wrapped trees, project for Avenue des Champs Elysees in Paris (56x71cm-22x28in) s.i.d.1969 plastic sring col.crayon board. 19-Nov-92 Christie's, New York #412/R
$38000	£25676	Running fence - project for Sonoma County and Marin County, State of California (145x244cm-57x96in) s.i.d.1974 pencil oilstick chl collage two parts. 11-Nov-93 Sotheby's, New York #413/R
$42500	£27778	Wrapped trees - project for Avenue and Rond Point des Champs Elysees in Paris (127x92cm-50x36in) s.d.1969 graphite pencil crayon. 4-May-93 Sotheby's, New York #139/R
$42840	£28000	Wrapped Reichstag, project for Der Deutsche Reichstag, West Berlin (55x70cm-22x28in) s.i.d.77 pencil pastel fabric collage photo map. 30-Jun-94 Sotheby's, London #208/R
$48387	£32258	Wrapped Reichstag (55x71cm-22x28in) s.i.d.1977 col.chk collage board. 27-May-94 Villa Grisebach, Berlin #75/R (DM 80000)
$55300	£35000	Pont Neuf wrapped - Project for Paris (146x244cm-57x96in) s.d.1979 crayon chl pencil paper on board card. 3-Dec-92 Sotheby's, London #68/R
$55300	£35000	Surrounded islands - project for Biscayne Bay, Greater Miami, Florida (144x165cm-57x65in) s.d.1983 map fabric gouache crayons paper card. 3-Dec-92 Sotheby's, London #73/R
$100804	£63800	Umbrellas - joint project for Japan and USA (108x166cm-43x65in) s.i.d.1990 pastel chl photo oil fabric card. 3-Dec-92 Christie's, London #84/R
$160000	£108108	Surrounded Islands - project for Biscayne Bay, Greater Miami, Florida (148x245cm-58x96in) s.i.d.1981 photo acrylic crayon paper on board. 9-Nov-93 Christie's, New York #52/R

CHRISTOPHE, Osmin (1935-) Haitian

$782	£501	Scene de marche (61x51cm-24x20in) s. 14-Dec-92 Hoebanx, Paris #35/R (F.FR 4200)

CHRISTY, Howard Chandler (1872-1952) American

$2250	£1521	Female nude (43x36cm-17x14in) 31-Mar-94 Sotheby's Arcade, New York #337/R
$3500	£2333	Portrait of Mrs Austin (152x101cm-60x40in) s. indist.s.verso. 23-May-94 Christie's, East, New York #199/R
$5500	£3846	Her little red book (51x40cm-20x16in) s. canvasboard. 11-Mar-93 Christie's, New York #215/R
$6600	£4314	Forest interior scene (112x86cm-44x34in) s.d.1944. 14-May-93 Skinner, Bolton #81/R
$8800	£5752	Landscape with woman (109x84cm-43x33in) s. 14-May-93 Skinner, Bolton #84/R
$17000	£9827	Peek-a-boo (50x40cm-20x16in) s.d.1924 canvas board. 23-Sep-92 Christie's, New York #292/R
$850	£590	Woman in red dress (18x51cm-7x20in) s. W/C. 6-Mar-93 Louisiana Auction Exchange #107/R
$1200	£800	Cooking (102x76cm-40x30in) s.d.1924 chl paper on board. 23-May-94 Christie's, East, New York #206/R
$1400	£952	After the match (97x73cm-38x29in) s.d.1929 wash board. 15-Nov-93 Christie's, East, New York #104/R
$1500	£1000	Portrait of Nancy Christy (89x70cm-35x28in) s.d.1920 W/C gouache pastel pencil paper board. 23-May-94 Christie's, East, New York #207/R
$4750	£3085	Suitors (100x74cm-39x29in) s.d.1910 gouache paper on board. 9-Sep-93 Sotheby's Arcade, New York #142/R

CHUMLEY, John (1928-1984) American

$4750	£3125	Kathy (76x101cm-30x40in) s. gouache pencil paper on board. 31-Mar-93 Sotheby's Arcade, New York #487/R

CHURCH, Frederic Edwin (1826-1900) American

$30000	£19231	Winter on Hudson river near Catskill, New York (20x25cm-8x10in) i.verso paper. 27-May-93 Sotheby's, New York #138/R
$37000	£23718	Autumn landscape, Vermont (26x16cm-10x6in) init. paper. 27-May-93 Sotheby's, New York #187/R
$75000	£47468	Twilight in the Adirondacks (27x40cm-11x16in) s. 3-Dec-92 Sotheby's, New York #34/R
$115000	£73718	View from Olana in snow (34x54cm-13x21in) paper. 27-May-93 Sotheby's, New York #137/R
$145000	£91772	Mount Katahdin from Millinocket Camp (68x111cm-27x44in) s.d.1895. 3-Dec-92 Sotheby's, New York #28/R
$1200	£694	Sketch of landscape (14x20cm-6x8in) i. pencil sold with two other W/C. 25-Sep-92 Sotheby's Arcade, New York #134

CHURCH, Frederic Edwin (attrib) (1826-1900) American
$1300   £823   Cattle watering at lake in highland landscape (20x41cm-8x16in) 30-Nov-92
                      Selkirks, St. Louis #247/R

CHURCH, Frederick Stuart (1842-1923) American
$1700   £1090   Young lioness (46x109cm-18x43in) s.i.d.1906. 9-Dec-92 Butterfield & Butterfield,
                      San Francisco #3912/R
$1750   £1159   The fog (56x127cm-22x50in) s.d.89. 23-Sep-93 Sotheby's, New York #119/R
$2000   £1282   Spring song (41x102cm-16x40in) s.i.d.1908. 9-Dec-92 Butterfield & Butterfield,
                      San Francisco #3911/R
$2500   £1603   Nymph and waterlilies (84x100cm-33x39in) s.i.d.84. 9-Dec-92 Butterfield &
                      Butterfield, San Francisco #3901/R
$3000   £1923   Dancing girl (51x76cm-20x30in) s.i.d.1916. 9-Dec-92 Butterfield & Butterfield,
                      San Francisco #3900/R
$12000   £8000   The rites of spring (66x142cm-26x56in) s.d.1905. 16-Mar-94 Christie's, New York
                      #42/R
$500   £333   Three saber-toothed tigers (23x43cm-9x17in) s. ink wash. 12-Mar-94 Weschler,
                      Washington #158/R
$950   £503   The angel and the polar bear (23x36cm-9x14in) s.i.d.92 W/C. 9-Sep-92 Doyle, New
                      York #12
$1200   £769   Jolly time (22x36cm-9x14in) s.i. gouache. 9-Dec-92 Butterfield & Butterfield, San
                      Francisco #3910/R
$1200   £811   Study for careless mother (20x53cm-8x21in) s.i. W/C gouache sketch paperboard.
                      5-Nov-93 Skinner, Bolton #182/R
$1600   £808   Shantytown Trolley (30x46cm-12x18in) s.d.1879 W/C. 30-Aug-92 Litchfield Auction
                      Gallery #218

CHURCH, Frederick Stuart (attrib) (1842-1923) American
$600   £347   Self portrait (22x15cm-9x6in) gouache pencil Indian ink board. 25-Sep-92
                      Sotheby's Arcade, New York #141/R

CHURCHILL, William W (1858-1926) American
$28000   £18667   The painter (109x76cm-43x30in) s.d.1913. 26-May-94 Christie's, New York #88/R

CIKOVSKY, Niccolai (1894-?) American
$700   £467   Lakeside (40x51cm-16x20in) s. 23-May-94 Christie's, East, New York #254/R
$700   £458   Dock workers (41x53cm-16x21in) s.verso. 30-Jun-94 Mystic Fine Arts, Connecticut
                      #163/R
$775   £524   Beaching the skiff (28x38cm-11x15in) s. board. 23-Oct-93 Collins, Maine #137/R
$900   £608   Standing nude (76x61cm-30x24in) s. 23-Oct-93 Collins, Maine #153/R
$1000   £680   Young girl dressing (62x40cm-24x16in) s. 15-Nov-93 Christie's, East, New York
                      #193/R
$1200   £811   Mountain landscape (56x71cm-22x28in) s. canvas on masonite. 31-Mar-94 Sotheby's
                      Arcade, New York #326/R
$1400   £946   Young seated dancer (102x56cm-40x22in) s. 31-Mar-94 Sotheby's Arcade, New York
                      #299/R
$1700   £1133   Dock workers (23x31cm-9x12in) s. 23-May-94 Christie's, East, New York #260/R
$1900   £1234   Artist and model (61x46cm-24x18in) s. 9-Sep-93 Sotheby's Arcade, New York #363/R
$2100   £1264   Wisconsin landscape (62x91cm-24x36in) s. s.indis.i.stretcher. 9-Sep-93 Sotheby's
                      Arcade, New York #303/R

CILFONE, Gianni (1908-) American/Italian
$650   £430   Docking the boat (41x51cm-16x20in) s. canvasboard. 28-Sep-93 John Moran, Pasadena
                      #211
$1100   £728   Busy harbour (71x84cm-28x33in) s. 3-Oct-93 Hanzel Galleries, Chicago #782

CIMIOTTI, Gustave (1875-1969) American
$800   £519   Lake Champlain (33x41cm-13x16in) s.i. s.verso masonite. 11-Sep-93 Louisiana
                      Auction Exchange #85/R
$800   £523   French river boat (18x28cm-7x11in) board. 19-Sep-93 Hindman Galleries, Chicago
                      #778
$950   £621   Ocean Point (41x51cm-16x20in) s. board. 8-May-93 Young Fine Arts Auctions, Maine
                      #68/R
$1300   £903   Stormy sea (41x51cm-16x20in) s. i.verso board. 27-Feb-93 Young Fine Arts
                      Auctions, Maine #72/R

CIRINO, A (20th C) American
$900   £604   Landscape with pines (51x61cm-20x24in) s. 29-Nov-93 Stonington Fine Arts,
                      Stonington #105/R

CIRINO, Antonio (1889-1983) American
$650   £433   Back to the stable (25x30cm-10x12in) s. canvasboard. 22-May-94 James Bakker,
                      Cambridge #151
$770   £503   Yellow house (38x33cm-15x13in) s. canvasboard. 14-May-93 Skinner, Bolton #79/R
$1000   £671   Village Sanctuary (25x30cm-10x12in) s. canvasboard. 5-Dec-93 James Bakker,
                      Cambridge #9/R
$1200   £784   Cape Ann's Littorality (20x25cm-8x10in) s. 17-Sep-93 Skinner, Bolton #216/R
$1300   £867   The lobster boat (20x25cm-8x10in) s. board. 22-May-94 James Bakker, Cambridge
                      #47/R
$1400   £972   Country house (51x61cm-20x24in) s. 27-Feb-93 Young Fine Arts Auctions, Maine
                      #73/R
$1400   £959   Winter in East Providence (30x41cm-12x16in) s. s.i.verso. 19-Feb-94 Young Fine
                      Arts Auctions, Maine #62/R
$1430   £935   Fishing boats, Rockport harbour (20x25cm-8x10in) s. board. 14-May-93 Skinner,
                      Bolton #126/R

CIRINO, Antonio (1889-1983) American-cont.
$1800	£1208	Autumn stroll (64x76cm-25x30in) s. 5-Dec-93 James Bakker, Cambridge #26/R
$2200	£1477	Skiing down a winding road (66x76cm-26x30in) s. 16-Dec-93 Mystic Fine Arts, Connecticut #110 a/R
$3500	£2288	New England harbour scene (64x76cm-25x30in) s. 17-Sep-93 Skinner, Bolton #218/R

CITRON, Minna (1896-?) American
$2000	£1325	Insect carnival (46x61cm-18x24in) s.d.50 board. 30-Jun-93 Sotheby's Arcade, New York #256/R

CLAGHORN, Joseph C (1869-1947) American
$800	£530	American landscape (64x76cm-25x30in) s. 28-Nov-92 Dunning's, Illinois #1009
$1000	£649	Maryland byway (61x51cm-24x20in) s. 9-Sep-93 Sotheby's Arcade, New York #131/R
$870	£580	Mountainside hotel - snow scene with coach and four and passengers (51x79cm-20x31in) s. W/C. 6-Jun-94 Waddingtons, Toronto #1508/R (C.D 1200)

CLAPP, William H (1879-1954) Canadian
$1057	£714	Sunlight and shadows (35x46cm-14x18in) s. board. 23-Nov-93 Fraser Pinneys, Quebec #358/R (C.D 1400)
$1572	£995	Reclining Nude (25x34cm-10x13in) s. board. 1-Dec-92 Fraser Pinneys, Quebec #136 (C.D 2000)
$2500	£1689	Farm in the valley (18x23cm-7x9in) s. masonite. 9-Nov-93 John Moran, Pasadena #827
$2515	£1592	Hayfield (26x35cm-10x14in) s. board. 1-Dec-92 Fraser Pinneys, Quebec #27 (C.D 3200)
$2987	£1891	Fashionable Lady (35x26cm-14x10in) s.d.1907 board. 1-Dec-92 Fraser Pinneys, Quebec #25 (C.D 3800)
$3000	£2027	Abandoned farm and farm in spring (25x30cm-10x12in) s.d.45 panel. 15-Jun-93 John Moran, Pasadena #143
$3113	£2062	Cuban landscape (51x61cm-20x24in) s. i.verso. 18-Nov-92 Sotheby's, Toronto #244/R (C.D 4000)
$17000	£11806	Houses and trees (61x51cm-24x20in) board. 7-Mar-93 Butterfield & Butterfield, San Francisco #198/R
$20000	£11765	Country road (76x91cm-30x36in) s.d.43. 4-Oct-92 Butterfield & Butterfield, Los Angeles #126/R

CLARK, Alson Skinner (1876-1949) American
$850	£579	Evening on the beach at Edisto (56x71cm-22x28in) s. i.verso board. 15-Nov-93 Christie's, East, New York #241/R
$1300	£861	Nude (43x81cm-17x32in) s. board. 14-Jun-94 John Moran, Pasadena #42
$1500	£1042	Autumn landscape near Thermal, California (18x23cm-7x9in) s. canvas on board. 7-Mar-93 Butterfield & Butterfield, San Francisco #167/R
$2250	£1490	Village scene with figures (38x46cm-15x18in) s. board. 14-Jun-94 John Moran, Pasadena #39
$3250	£2138	Church on Seine, Paris (19x24cm-7x9in) s. panel. 13-Jun-93 Butterfield & Butterfield, San Francisco #852/R
$3750	£2534	Fall in Olancha (66x81cm-26x32in) 15-Jun-93 John Moran, Pasadena #24
$3750	£2206	Luxembourg Gardens (65x79cm-26x31in) s. 4-Oct-92 Butterfield & Butterfield, Los Angeles #106/R
$4000	£2353	Luxembourg Gardens (19x24cm-7x9in) s.d.10 s.verso board. 4-Oct-92 Butterfield & Butterfield, Los Angeles #105/R
$4500	£2647	Near Palm Springs, California (66x81cm-26x32in) s. 4-Oct-92 Butterfield & Butterfield, Los Angeles #210/R
$4750	£3146	Indian country (46x56cm-18x22in) indis.s. i.d.1928verso canvas on board. 28-Sep-93 John Moran, Pasadena #297
$4750	£3209	La Jolla Cove (66x81cm-26x32in) 15-Jun-93 John Moran, Pasadena #60
$4750	£2794	Arguello Adobe near San Diego (66x81cm-26x32in) s. 4-Oct-92 Butterfield & Butterfield, Los Angeles #132/R
$5000	£3356	Casa Mexicana - Old Town, San Diego (47x56cm-19x22in) s.d.23 studio st.verso canvas on board. 8-Dec-93 Butterfield & Butterfield, San Francisco #3444/R
$8500	£5000	Salon de l'oeil de boeuf, Versailles (81x66cm-32x26in) s. 4-Oct-92 Butterfield & Butterfield, Los Angeles #107/R
$13000	£8725	La Jolla Cove (66x81cm-26x32in) s. 8-Dec-93 Butterfield & Butterfield, San Francisco #3459/R

CLARK, Benton (1895-1964) American
$900	£570	Sun in west (76x76cm-30x30in) s.d.1938 s.i.verso. 3-Dec-92 Freeman Fine Arts, Philadelphia #1830/R
$1200	£833	Sun in the west (76x76cm-30x30in) s.d.1938. 3-Mar-93 Doyle, New York #14
$1300	£878	Young patriots (76x56cm-30x22in) s.d.1942. 9-Nov-93 John Moran, Pasadena #952 x

CLARK, C Myron (20th C) American
$700	£449	The Lagoon, Venice (51x76cm-20x30in) s. 24-May-93 Grogan, Massachussetts #318/R

CLARK, Eliot (1883-1980) American
$550	£367	New York on a rainy night (51x69cm-20x27in) s. 23-May-94 Christie's, East, New York #198/R
$750	£503	Kent, Connecticut (46x51cm-18x20in) s. s.i.d.1924 verso panel. 4-Dec-93 Louisiana Auction Exchange #3/R
$1000	£654	Creek in spring landscape (41x51cm-16x20in) s. 4-May-93 Christie's, East, New York #216/R
$1200	£805	Winter gleams (51x61cm-20x24in) s. i.verso masonite. 4-Dec-93 Louisiana Auction Exchange #116/R
$1300	£872	Dunes by the sea (51x69cm-20x27in) s. 4-Dec-93 Louisiana Auction Exchange #38/R
$1450	£954	Autumn meadow (51x69cm-20x27in) s. 5-Jun-93 Louisiana Auction Exchange #107/R

CLARK, Eliot (1883-1980) American-cont.
$1500   £794   New Lynchburg (66x66cm-26x26in) s. i.d.1934-35 verso. 12-Sep-92 Louisiana Auction Exchange #54/R

CLARK, Frederick H (?) American
$1300   £833   Evening on the Seine (51x79cm-20x31in) s.d.95. 28-Apr-93 Doyle, New York #15

CLARK, Paraskeva (1898-1986) Canadian
$801   £534   6 a.m. October (41x51cm-16x20in) s. board. 11-May-94 Sotheby's, Toronto #116/R (C.D 1100)
$1784   £1166   Alonquin morning (46x41cm-18x16in) s.d.53 s.verso board. 19-May-93 Sotheby's, Toronto #111/R (C.D 2250)
$2153   £1435   Still life with verandah (50x61cm-20x24in) s.i.indis.d. 30-May-94 Ritchie, Toronto #159/R (C.D 3000)
$1403   £923   Apples. Sketch of seated woman (41x46cm-16x18in) s.d.41 W/C pencil double-sided. 7-Jun-93 Ritchie, Toronto #169/R (C.D 1800)

CLARK, Walter (1848-1917) American
$800   £519   Covered bridge (51x61cm-20x24in) s. s.verso. 11-Sep-93 Louisiana Auction Exchange #104/R
$1500   £1020   Spring landscape (51x61cm-20x24in) s. 17-Nov-93 Doyle, New York #30

CLAUS, May Austin (1882-?) American
$2000   £1342   Impressionate landscape (30x41cm-12x16in) artist's board. 27-Mar-94 Myers, Florida #17/R

CLAUSELL, Joaquin (1886-1935) Mexican
$4509   £3006   Marina (15x9cm-6x4in) s.verso masonite. 25-May-94 Louis Morton, Mexico #68/R (M.P 15000)
$8000   £5229   Paisaje (13x28cm-5x11in) s.d.1916 s.verso board. 17-May-93 Christie's, New York #88/R
$9675   £6494   Paisaje (15x32cm-6x13in) board. 1-Dec-93 Louis Morton, Mexico #44/R (M.P 30000)
$16126 £10823 Tlalpan (31x40cm-12x16in) s.verso. 1-Dec-93 Louis Morton, Mexico #91/R (M.P 50000)
$18000 £12162 Paisaje (23x33cm-9x13in) painted c.1915. 22-Nov-93 Sotheby's, New York #159/R
$21000 £13725 Marina (45x95cm-18x37in) s. canvas on panel painted c.1915. 18-May-93 Sotheby's, New York #21/R
$40000 £26490 Paisaje Marino (35x56cm-14x22in) board. 24-Nov-92 Christie's, New York #4 a/R
$230000 £153333 Marina (70x120cm-28x47in) s. painted c.1915. 17-May-94 Sotheby's, New York #16 a/R

CLAY, Elizabeth C Fisher (fl.1927-1938) American/British
$3000   £2000   Street scene (41x49cm-16x19in) s.verso. 17-Mar-94 Sotheby's, New York #147/R

CLAYES, Alice des (1890-?) Canadian
$1456   £971   Haying (32x41cm-13x16in) s. 13-May-94 Joyner Fine Art, Toronto #216 (C.D 2000)

CLAYES, Berthe des (1877-1968) Canadian
$717   £485   Farms, eastern townships (20x29cm-8x11in) s. board. 23-Nov-93 Fraser Pinneys, Quebec #351 (C.D 950)
$755   £510   Summer landscape (43x33cm-17x13in) s. i.verso. 23-Nov-93 Fraser Pinneys, Quebec #395 (C.D 1000)
$1133   £765   Going to the bush (35x41cm-14x16in) s. board. 23-Nov-93 Fraser Pinneys, Quebec #363/R (C.D 1500)
$1784   £1166   Schooners in harbour, Halifax (25x34cm-10x13in) s. s.i.verso panel. 19-May-93 Sotheby's, Toronto #92/R (C.D 2250)
$2184   £1456   Road in St.Andrews E., autumn (51x63cm-20x25in) s. i.verso. 11-May-94 Sotheby's, Toronto #185 (C.D 3000)
$3099   £2094   Farm scene Eastern townships (51x80cm-20x31in) s. i.verso. 3-Nov-93 Sotheby's, Toronto #64/R (C.D 4000)
$6974   £4712   The red sleigh (36x47cm-14x19in) 3-Nov-93 Sotheby's, Toronto #108/R (C.D 9000)
$620   £419   Maple trees in autumn (25x25cm-10x10in) s. pastel. 3-Nov-93 Sotheby's, Toronto #130 a (C.D 800)
$697   £471   Cloudy day Val Morin (24x29cm-9x11in) s. i.verso pastel. 3-Nov-93 Sotheby's, Toronto #59/R (C.D 900)
$831   £561   Teams of horse-drawn sleighs (22x27cm-9x11in) s. col.chk. 23-Nov-93 Joyner Fine Art, Toronto #231 (C.D 1100)
$888   £600   Horses pulling cart on snow covered road (25x35cm-10x14in) s. pastel. 20-Oct-93 Sotheby's, London #16/R
$1085   £733   Country road in autumn (27x22cm-11x9in) s. pastel. 3-Nov-93 Sotheby's, Toronto #109 (C.D 1400)
$1359   £918   Autumn on the farm (29x33cm-11x13in) s. pastel. 23-Nov-93 Fraser Pinneys, Quebec #442 (C.D 1800)

CLEARY, Manon (20th C) American
$2000   £1351   Menage (213x152cm-84x60in) s.d.76-77. 8-Nov-93 Christie's, East, New York #44/R

CLEGG and GUTTMAN (20th C) American
$2278   £1519   Untitled landscape No.10 (122x184cm-48x72in) y. 2-Jun-94 AB Stockholms Auktionsverk, Stockholm #7091/R (S.KR 18000)

CLEMENS, Paul Lewis (1911-) American
$1300   £850   Two girls in the garden (30x36cm-12x14in) s. 15-Sep-93 Doyle, New York #14
$2500   £1656   Two girls in the garden (30x36cm-12x14in) s. 15-Jun-94 Butterfield & Butterfield, San Francisco #4487/R

CLEMENS, Paul Lewis (1911-) American-cont.
$3500   £2318   Side show barker (66x91cm-26x36in) 15-Jun-94 Butterfield & Butterfield, San Francisco #4485/R
$5500   £3642   Club house argument (56x81cm-22x32in) s.d.34 panel. 15-Jun-94 Butterfield & Butterfield, San Francisco #4486/R

CLEMENTS, Alling (?) American?
$1400   £933   Low tide - Ogynquit (51x61cm-20x24in) s.d.31. 22-May-94 James Bakker, Cambridge #92/R

CLIME, Winfield Scott (1881-1958) American
$825   £539   Valley under blanket of snow (23x30cm-9x12in) s. masonite. 14-May-93 Skinner, Bolton #90/R

CLINEDINST, Benjamin West (1860-1931) American
$5500   £3179   Remedy (114x109cm-45x43in) s.d.1886. 24-Sep-92 Sotheby's, New York #20/R

CLOSE, Chuck (1940-) American
$210000   £139073   Cindy II (183x152cm-72x60in) s.d.1988 verso. 17-Nov-92 Sotheby's, New York #6/R
$20000   £13423   Leslie N (76x57cm-30x22in) s.i.d.1975 s.i.d.verso ink graphite. 5-May-94 Sotheby's, New York #185/R
$38000   £24837   Mark-progression (76x202cm-30x80in) s.i.d.1983 col inks fingerprinted. 5-May-93 Christie's, New York #159/R
$50000   £29412   Linda-Eye Series I-V (76x57cm-30x22in) s.num.1-5 d.1977 W/C five. 6-Oct-92 Sotheby's, New York #105/R
$85000   £56291   Phyllis (146x103cm-57x41in) s.i.d.1981 s.i.d.verso lithographic ink. 19-Nov-92 Christie's, New York #406/R

CLOSSON, William Baxter Palmer (1848-1926) American
$950   £664   Mountain laurel (56x69cm-22x27in) s. s.i.verso board. 5-Feb-93 Sloan, North Bethesda #2204/R
$1300   £823   Buildings in winter (41x51cm-16x20in) s. board. 2-Dec-92 Boos Gallery, Michigan #905/R

CLOUGH, Arthur (20th C) American
$850   *£586*   *Catalina Channel (33x41cm-13x16in) s.d.1934 W/C. 16-Feb-93 John Moran, Pasadena #6*

CLOUGH, George L (1824-1901) American
$1700   £1104   Stag in woods (63x49cm-25x19in) init.d.1870. 9-Sep-93 Sotheby's Arcade, New York #17/R
$3000   £2013   Mill by a river (36x56cm-14x22in) s. 6-Dec-93 Grogan, Massachussetts #438/R
$6500   £3757   Passing shower on the Hudson (61x91cm-24x36in) s. 23-Sep-92 Christie's, New York #54/R

CLOUTIER, Albert Edward (1902-1965) Canadian
$655   £437   August landscape (45x57cm-18x22in) s. 13-May-94 Joyner Fine Art, Toronto #181/R (C.D 900)
$1019   £680   Winter landscape scene (30x41cm-12x16in) s. board sold with oil by K.R.Macpherson. 11-May-94 Sotheby's, Toronto #28/R (C.D 1400)

CLUNIE, Robert (1895-1984) American
$2750   £1858   Mount Sill in the High Sierra (66x76cm-26x30in) s.d.1929. 9-Nov-93 John Moran, Pasadena #896
$4250   £2853   Lake Mary, High Sierras (67x77cm-26x30in) s.d.1929 i.d.verso. 8-Dec-93 Butterfield & Butterfield, San Francisco #3433/R
$6500   £4392   Mt Temple Crags-Contact Pass-5th Lake (107x91cm-42x36in) s.d.1929. 15-Jun-93 John Moran, Pasadena #110 a

CLUSMANN, William (1859-1927) American
$950   £664   Winter landscape with creek (36x51cm-14x20in) s. 14-Mar-93 Hindman Galleries, Chicago #51
$1700   £1156   October morning an autumnal landscape with house (61x76cm-24x30in) s. 19-Nov-93 Eldred, Massachusetts #921/R
$2300   £1503   Lincoln Park Forest (61x76cm-24x30in) s. 15-May-93 Dunning's, Illinois #128/R

CLYMER, James (1893-?) American?
$900   £520   Spanish mountain riders (102x127cm-40x50in) s. 24-Sep-92 Mystic Fine Arts, Connecticut #230

CLYMER, John Ford (1907-1989) American
$1200   £759   Bustling harbour (51x91cm-20x36in) s. 2-Dec-92 Christie's, East, New York #36/R
$1300   £855   Fashion premiere at Court of Lucretia Borgia (71x102cm-28x40in) s. board painted 1959. 31-Mar-93 Sotheby's Arcade, New York #478/R
$1400   £921   Paris-London court fashions meet at Dover, 1670 (74x102cm-29x40in) s. board painted 1961. 31-Mar-93 Sotheby's Arcade, New York #477/R
$3000   £2027   Cavaliers at table (51x91cm-20x36in) s. 31-Mar-94 Sotheby's Arcade, New York #401/R
$4000   £2685   Pack of wolves and sheepdogs fighting, sheep beyond (41x102cm-16x40in) oil en grisaille board. 2-May-94 Selkirks, St. Louis #112/R
$4200   £2781   Snowshoeing in Back Country (66x53cm-26x21in) s. board. 13-Nov-92 Skinner, Bolton #222/R
$21000   £14094   The wolvers (51x76cm-20x30in) s. board painted 1947. 2-May-94 Selkirks, St. Louis #133/R

COARDING, Gerald (20th C) American
$3000　£1923　Egyptians (76x61cm-30x24in) s. 9-Dec-92 Butterfield & Butterfield, San Francisco #4032/R

COATES, Edmund C (1816-1871) American
$3750　£2534　The Indian fisherman a Catskills scene (91x74cm-36x29in) 30-Oct-93 Skinner, Bolton #277/R
$7500　£4967　View of Caldwell's landing (75x91cm-30x36in) s.d.1868. 23-Sep-93 Sotheby's, New York #51/R
$17000　£11888　Sailing off New York Harbour (72x107cm-28x42in) indis.s. 10-Mar-93 Sotheby's, New York #1/R

COBURN, Frank (1866-1931) American
$900　£596　Figures in landscape with barn (15x13cm-6x5in) s. board. 14-Jun-94 John Moran, Pasadena #8 a
$1300　£867　Sunset on the river (20x25cm-8x10in) board. 15-Mar-94 John Moran, Pasadena #31
$1600　£941　Summer landscape (24x34cm-9x13in) s. board. 4-Oct-92 Butterfield & Butterfield, Los Angeles #142/R
$7000　£4828　Rainy Chicago City street, Lafayette St. (43x36cm-17x14in) s. board. 16-Feb-93 John Moran, Pasadena #73
$7500　£4412　Los Angeles park scene, sprinkler action on lawn (51x61cm-20x24in) s. 4-Oct-92 Butterfield & Butterfield, Los Angeles #198/R

COBURN, Frederick Simpson (1871-1960) Canadian
$1722　£1148　Paysage (27x35cm-11x14in) s. board. 30-May-94 Hodgins, Calgary #270/R (C.D 2400)
$1963　£1327　Road through the trees in winter (35x26cm-14x10in) s. board. 23-Nov-93 Joyner Fine Art, Toronto #259/R (C.D 4500)
$3398　£2296　Team of horses (50x67cm-20x26in) s. 23-Nov-93 Joyner Fine Art, Toronto #110/R (C.D 4500)
$6682　£4229　Spring in the woods, Quebec (41x35cm-16x14in) s.d.1924. 1-Dec-92 Fraser Pinneys, Quebec #140 a/R (C.D 8500)
$8010　£5340　Logging (43x57cm-17x22in) s.d.28. 11-May-94 Sotheby's, Toronto #187/R (C.D 11000)
$8524　£5759　A logging sleigh on a snow covered road (36x54cm-14x21in) s.d.22. 3-Nov-93 Sotheby's, Toronto #180/R (C.D 11000)
$9330　£6220　Hauling wood (45x60cm-18x24in) s.d.33. 30-May-94 Ritchie, Toronto #173/R (C.D 13000)
$9466　£6311　Winter landscape with horses (33x55cm-13x22in) s.d.19. 11-May-94 Sotheby's, Toronto #188/R (C.D 13000)
$9513　£6218　Logging team (51x92cm-20x36in) s.d.40. 18-May-93 Joyner Fine Art, Toronto #6/R (C.D 12000)
$10119　£6701　Logging team, winter (56x81cm-22x32in) s.d.45. 18-Nov-92 Sotheby's, Toronto #161/R (C.D 13000)
$10193　£6888　Sunny afternoon (40x60cm-16x24in) s.d.26. 23-Nov-93 Joyner Fine Art, Toronto #36/R (C.D 13500)
$10194　£6796　The logging team (49x63cm-19x25in) s.d.28. 11-May-94 Sotheby's, Toronto #149/R (C.D 14000)
$11623　£7853　Oxen hauling logs (51x63cm-20x25in) s.d.20. 3-Nov-93 Sotheby's, Toronto #99/R (C.D 15000)
$11623　£7853　The logging team (44x60cm-17x24in) s.indist.d. i.verso. 3-Nov-93 Sotheby's, Toronto #110/R (C.D 15000)
$11650　£7767　Team of horses hauling logs (55x70cm-22x28in) s.d.29. 13-May-94 Joyner Fine Art, Toronto #44/R (C.D 16000)
$11675　£7732　Hauling logs, winter (45x60cm-18x24in) s.d.31. 24-Nov-92 Joyner Fine Art, Toronto #32/R (C.D 15000)
$15497　£10471　April morning Melbourne (51x79cm-20x31in) s.d.20. 3-Nov-93 Sotheby's, Toronto #98/R (C.D 20000)

COCHRAN, Allen Dean (1888-1935) American
$600　£411　Red barn, winter (25x20cm-10x8in) board. 18-Feb-94 Douglas, South Deerfield #2
$650　£445　Summer landscape (25x20cm-10x8in) board. 18-Feb-94 Douglas, South Deerfield #3
$750　£514　Spring landscape with birches (20x25cm-8x10in) board. 18-Feb-94 Douglas, South Deerfield #1
$1000　£585　Silent wood (76x104cm-30x41in) s.d.33 board. 16-Sep-92 Butterfield & Butterfield, San Francisco #762/R
$1000　£685　Winter scene of brook (41x28cm-16x11in) board. 18-Feb-94 Douglas, South Deerfield #4

COE, Ethel Louise (1880-1938) American
$700　£470　Tangiers street scene (51x61cm-20x24in) artist's board. 27-Mar-94 Myers, Florida #90/R

COE, Sue (20th C) American
$4000　£2778　Killing fields (334x240cm-131x94in) s.d.87 acrylic paper. 23-Feb-93 Sotheby's, New York #401/R

COE, Theodore Demerest (1866-?) American
$1000　£649　Cows in summer landscape (46x66cm-18x26in) s.d.1892. 9-Sep-93 Sotheby's Arcade, New York #52/R

COFFIN, William A (1855-1926) American
$1200　£811　Johnstown, Pennsylvania (51x61cm-20x24in) s. painted c.1910. 23-Oct-93 Collins, Maine #183/R
$1350　£714　Off New London - early evening (33x48cm-13x19in) s. 13-Sep-92 Dargate Auction Galleries, Pittsburgh #330

COGGESHALL, John I (1856-1927) American
$2200   £1447   Harbour scene (70x102cm-28x40in) s.d.1896. 31-Mar-93 Sotheby's Arcade, New York #82/R

COGGSWELL, Charles (19th C) American
$750   £500   Portrait of a gentleman (8x5cm-3x2in) min. s. in original box oval. 26-May-94 Sloan, North Bethesda #2278/R

COGOLLO, Heriberto (1945-) Colombian
$32500   £21667   The rose terrace (114x146cm-45x57in) s.d.I-91 acrylic sand. 17-May-94 Sotheby's, New York #79/R
$2750   £1846   Untitled (63x48cm-25x19in) s.d.1987 pastel. 7-Jan-94 Gary Nader, Miami #67/R

COGORNO, Santiago (1915-) Argentinian
$2600   £1354   El angel (60x42cm-24x17in) tempera. 4-Aug-92 VerBo, Buenos Aires #31

COHEN, Alfred (1920-) American
$1913   £1250   Green Channel (81x102cm-32x40in) s.i.verso. 19-May-93 Sotheby's, Billingshurst #294/R
$655   £420   Plage (58x71cm-23x28in) s. gouache. 17-Dec-92 Christie's, S. Kensington #282

COLE, Alphaeus P (1876-?) American
$750   £497   Covered bowl and pears (30x41cm-12x16in) s. canvasboard. 21-Nov-92 James Bakker, Cambridge #223
$978   £657   A harvest queen (61x45cm-24x18in) s.d.1921. 29-Nov-93 Waddingtons, Toronto #1412 (C.D 1300)

COLE, Charles Octavius (1814-?) American
$2800   £1867   Young girl holding a dove (112x91cm-44x36in) i. i.d.1854 verso double-sided. 1-Jun-94 Doyle, New York #24

COLE, Joseph Foxcroft (1837-1892) American
$750   £490   Figures in French village (30x46cm-12x18in) s. board. 18-Sep-93 Young Fine Arts Auctions, Maine #77/R
$858   £580   Cow grazing in an open landscape with figures (31x41cm-12x16in) s. panel. 2-Nov-93 Phillips, West Two #137
$1000   £613   Early morning in farmyard (51x41cm-20x16in) s.d.1871. 14-Oct-92 Doyle, New York #10
$1200   £816   On the Rhine (61x91cm-24x36in) s. i.verso. 16-Apr-94 Young Fine Arts Auctions, Maine #77/R

COLE, Joseph Greenleaf (1803-1858) American
$2000   £1316   Gentleman seated by writing table. Lady seated with shawl (91x74cm-36x29in) s.d.Feb.1844verso pair. 5-Jun-93 Skinner, Bolton #165/R

COLE, Joseph Greenleaf (attrib) (1803-1858) American
$3500   £2288   Portraits of Nathaniel March. His wife (86x71cm-34x28in) pair painted c.1829. 16-Sep-93 Sloan, North Bethesda #3210/R

COLE, Thomas (1801-1848) American
$15000   £9615   Waterfall (20x23cm-8x9in) oval. 9-Dec-92 Grogan, Massachussetts #11/R
$15000   £9615   River scene (20x23cm-8x9in) oval. 9-Dec-92 Grogan, Massachussetts #12/R
$18000   £11392   Head of a Roman woman, from nature (62x50cm-24x20in) 3-Dec-92 Sotheby's, New York #18/R
$19000   £12667   Sketch for dream of Arcadia (15x23cm-6x9in) paper laid down on panel. 26-May-94 Christie's, New York #3/R
$230000   £147436   Good shepherd (81x122cm-32x48in) s.d.1848 canvas backed by panel. 27-May-93 Sotheby's, New York #147/R
$390000   £260000   Indian at sunset (36x44cm-14x17in) s. 25-May-94 Sotheby's, New York #11/R
$2500   £1667   Woman with wreath (30x21cm-12x8in) pencil chk executed c.1840's. 16-Mar-94 Christie's, New York #29/R

COLE, Thomas (attrib) (1801-1848) American
$6500   £4248   Figures in Arcadian landscape (71x58cm-28x23in) 30-Oct-92 Sloan, North Bethesda #2780/R

COLE, Thomas (style) (1801-1848) American
$3500   £2288   Figure in landscape (46x38cm-18x15in) i.stretcher. 30-Oct-92 Sloan, North Bethesda #2176

COLE, Thomas C (1888-1976) American
$1100   £728   Portrait of Dorothea Fenwick Cole (46x36cm-18x14in) s. painted 1913. 28-Nov-92 Dunning's, Illinois #1097

COLEMAN, Charles Caryl (1840-1928) American
$1300   £751   Venetian scene (25x41cm-10x16in) s. mono. 24-Sep-92 Mystic Fine Arts, Connecticut #199/R
$2200   £1467   Roman street scene (45x102cm-18x40in) s.i.d.1872. 21-May-94 Weschler, Washington #78/R
$2304   £1600   Mill at Anacapari (28x18cm-11x7in) mono.i.d.1886 i.verso panel. 4-Mar-93 Christie's, S. Kensington #110
$2600   £1722   Capri (44x58cm-17x23in) init.i.d.1906 canvas on panel. 22-Sep-93 Christie's, New York #82/R
$2600   £1503   In the garden of Villa Castello, Isola da Capri (40x25cm-16x10in) mono.i.d.1904 panel. 23-Sep-92 Christie's, New York #93/R

COLEMAN, Charles Caryl (1840-1928) American-cont.
$4000   £2721   Fisherman's Cove Capri (89x41cm-35x16in) mono. i.verso. 17-Nov-93 Doyle, New York #21/R

COLEMAN, Glenn O (1887-1932) American
$3600   £2368   Distant view of New York (45x60cm-18x24in) s. board. 31-Mar-93 Sotheby's Arcade, New York #148/R
$1200   £789   *Patchin Place (42x31cm-17x12in) s. gouache graphite board. 31-Mar-93 Sotheby's Arcade, New York #315/R*

COLEMAN, Michael (1946-) American
$2593   £1641   Desert Indian Encampment Sunset (16x20cm-6x8in) s.d.September 1964 board. 21-Oct-92 Maynards, Vancouver #117 (C.D 3250)
$3500   £2448   *Winter emcampment (26x36cm-10x14in) s.i. gouache board. 11-Mar-93 Christie's, New York #126/R*
$4800   £3357   *Indian encampment (18x27cm-7x11in) s.i.d.1976 gouache. 11-Mar-93 Christie's, New York #127/R*

COLEMAN, R Clarkson (1884-1945) American
$1000   £694   Surf at Arch Beach (71x91cm-28x36in) s. 7-Mar-93 Butterfield & Butterfield, San Francisco #100/R
$1100   £728   Crashing surf on rocks (71x91cm-28x36in) s. 14-Jun-94 John Moran, Pasadena #100 a

COLESCOTT, Robert (1925-) American
$800   £506   *Old crow (58x44cm-23x17in) s.d.78 W/C chl. 25-Oct-92 Butterfield & Butterfield, San Francisco #2330/R*

COLIN, Martinez (20th C) Mexican?
$3484   £2292   Valle de Puebla con volcanes (60x80cm-24x31in) s. 4-Nov-92 Mora, Castelltort & Quintana, Juarez #122/R (M.P 11000000)

COLLAZO Y TEJADA, Guillermo (1850-1896) Cuban
$4500   £2941   En la terraza (23x13cm-9x5in) s.d.1889 panel. 18-May-93 Sotheby's, New York #106/R

COLLIER, Alan Caswell (1911-1990) Canadian
$620   £419   Headland (41x51cm-16x20in) s. i.verso board. 3-Nov-93 Sotheby's, Toronto #189/R (C.D 800)
$641   £436   New Edinburgh Nova Scotia (30x40cm-12x16in) s. s.i.verso board. 15-Nov-93 Hodgins, Calgary #30/R (C.D 850)
$655   £437   Winter fields, King Township (41x51cm-16x20in) s. i.verso board. 11-May-94 Sotheby's, Toronto #92 (C.D 900)
$680   £459   Buckley Valley, S.E. of Hazleton, B.C (30x40cm-12x16in) s. board. 23-Nov-93 Joyner Fine Art, Toronto #87/R (C.D 900)
$728   £485   Autumn leaves, North of Wilno, Ont. (30x40cm-12x16in) s. board. 13-May-94 Joyner Fine Art, Toronto #118/R (C.D 1000)
$728   £485   Neil's Harbour, Cape Breton Island (30x40cm-12x16in) s. board. 13-May-94 Joyner Fine Art, Toronto #188/R (C.D 1000)
$736   £497   Clacial morraine Lake Oesa (30x41cm-12x16in) s.d.c.1972 i.verso canvas laid down on masonite. 1-Nov-93 Levis, Calgary #48 (C.D 950)
$753   £492   Fort Amherst, Newfoundland (30x41cm-12x16in) s. s.i.verso panel. 19-May-93 Sotheby's, Toronto #88/R (C.D 950)
$793   £518   Cloud and thunder, east of High River (61x81cm-24x32in) s. 18-May-93 Joyner Fine Art, Toronto #125 (C.D 1000)
$1177   £769   After many storms (46x61cm-18x24in) s. lucite board. 10-May-93 Hodgins, Calgary #108/R (C.D 1500)
$1378   £931   Off Saglek, Labrador (41x51cm-16x20in) s. i.verso canvas board painted c.1972. 25-Apr-94 Levis, Calgary #55/R (C.D 1900)
$1412   £923   Powder Car (46x61cm-18x24in) s. lucite 44. 10-May-93 Hodgins, Calgary #48 (C.D 1800)
$1456   £971   Last pole at Skidegate (50x90cm-20x35in) s. board. 13-May-94 Joyner Fine Art, Toronto #9/R (C.D 2000)
$1669   £1127   Autumn grey, Kamaniskeg Lake, Ontario (61x81cm-24x32in) s. i.verso masonite painted c.1972. 25-Apr-94 Levis, Calgary #54/R (C.D 2300)
$1748   £1165   Beside Teslin Lake, Yukon (61x81cm-24x32in) s. 11-May-94 Sotheby's, Toronto #52/R (C.D 2200)
$1812   £1224   Brackley Beach, P.E.I (60x80cm-24x31in) s. 23-Nov-93 Joyner Fine Art, Toronto #21/R (C.D 2400)
$1957   £1313   Lonely mountain farm (76x99cm-30x39in) s. i.verso masonite painted 1958. 29-Nov-93 Ritchie, Toronto #187/R (C.D 2600)
$1982   £1295   Morning hush (61x91cm-24x36in) s. i.verso. 19-May-93 Sotheby's, Toronto #322/R (C.D 2500)
$3012   £1969   Towering shore at Bella Coola, B.C. (102x152cm-40x60in) s. 18-May-93 Joyner Fine Art, Toronto #3/R (C.D 3800)
$3020   £2041   Athabasca in March, Athabasca River at Old Fort Crossing, Jasper, Alberta (100x150cm-39x59in) s. 23-Nov-93 Joyner Fine Art, Toronto #41/R (C.D 4000)
$692   £461   *Totem poles at Kispiox, B C (41x17cm-16x7in) s.i. ink gouache. 13-May-94 Joyner Fine Art, Toronto #210 (C.D 950)*
$1245   £825   *Mountain scene I (30x40cm-12x16in) s. W/C. 16-Nov-92 Hodgins, Calgary #98 a (C.D 1600)*
$1245   £825   *Mountain scene II (30x40cm-12x16in) s. W/C. 16-Nov-92 Hodgins, Calgary #98 b (C.D 1600)*

COLLINS, Earl (20th C) American
$900   £608   Portrait of the Bark Kaiulani under sail in choppy seas (61x91cm-24x36in) s. 23-Oct-93 San Rafael Auction Galleries #187
$1500 £1020 Three masted schooner (91x122cm-36x48in) s.d.79. 15-Nov-93 Christie's, East, New York #30/R

COLLIVADINO, Pio (1869-1945) Argentinian
$4500 £2601 Entre arboles (21x29cm-8x11in) 23-Sep-92 Roldan & Cia, Buenos Aires #54

COLLUM, Wendell (20th C) American
$2000 £1299 Cape Cod harbour, shipping and wharves (91x307cm-36x121in) panel pair. 4-Aug-94 Eldred, Massachusetts #597/R

COLLYER, Nora Frances Elisabeth (1889-?) Canadian
$951   £622   Bridge in the country (56x61cm-22x24in) 18-May-93 Joyner Fine Art, Toronto #294 (C.D 1200)
$1557 £1031 Ice storm, Montreal (60x50cm-24x20in) s.d.1962. 24-Nov-92 Joyner Fine Art, Toronto #249/R (C.D 2000)

COLMAN, Rol Clarkson (1884-1945) American
$1200 £755   Monterey Cypress - Pacific Ocean, late afternoon (61x71cm-24x28in) s. 25-Apr-93 James Bakker, Cambridge #26/R

COLMAN, Samuel (1832-1920) American
$900   £616   Mountain town probably in Mexico (18x36cm-7x14in) s.d.68 W/C. 19-Feb-94 Young Fine Arts Auctions, Maine #65/R
$3750 £2373 Puebla, Mexico (19x38cm-7x15in) s.d.Feb 92 W/C gouache. 3-Dec-92 Sotheby's, New York #11/R
$6500 £4333 Yosemite Valley, California (24x38cm-9x15in) W/C pencil executed c.1888. 17-Mar-94 Sotheby's, New York #78/R

COLSON, Jaime Antonio (20th C) Dominican
$1058 £750   Cubist nude with guitar (61x46cm-24x18in) s.d.1925 i.verso. 11-Feb-93 Christie's, S. Kensington #100/R

COLUNGA, Alejandro (1948-) Mexican
$17000 £11333 Musicos fantasmas 4,40 en concierto nocturno (100x129cm-39x51in) s.i.d.1992. 18-May-94 Sotheby's, New York #331/R
$24000 £15686 La llorona con nino, fantasmas y diablos (96x127cm-38x50in) init. s.i.d.1988-92 verso. 17-May-93 Christie's, New York #245/R
$28000 £18667 Mi Corazon es un Chorro de Agua de 3 Pulgadas (166x125cm-65x49in) s.i. s.i.d.1989-91verso linen. 18-May-94 Christie's, New York #224/R
$4000   £2649   El burro (64x48cm-25x19in) s.d.84 s.i.d. oil pastel. 24-Nov-92 Christie's, New York #237/R
$8000   £5333   Nino jugando a la guerra (91x61cm-36x24in) i. mixed media painted 1985. 18-May-94 Christie's, New York #225/R
$8000   £5333   Nino en caballito (102x78cm-40x31in) s.d.1982 s.i.d.verso mixed media. 18-May-94 Christie's, New York #226/R
$18000 £12162 El mago de los ojos (78x102cm-31x40in) s.indis.i.d.1983 mixed media. 23-Nov-93 Christie's, New York #194/R

COLVILLE, Alex (1920-) Canadian
$1585   £1036   Night departure in Mini (10x15cm-4x6in) s.d.12 Dec.70 acrylic pencil. 18-May-93 Joyner Fine Art, Toronto #318 (C.D 2000)
$3736   £2474   Landscape with barn, New Brunswick (30x41cm-12x16in) s.d.46 i.verso board. 18-Nov-92 Sotheby's, Toronto #39/R (C.D 4800)
$98301 £65534 Ocean Limited (68x119cm-27x47in) s.d.1962 s.i.d.verso oil synthetic resin board. 11-May-94 Sotheby's, Toronto #119/R (C.D 135000)
$1638   £1092   Blind man and dog. Study for night walk (22x29cm-9x11in) one d.68 one d.81 col ink mixed media dr pair. 11-May-94 Sotheby's, Toronto #223 (C.D 2250)

COMAN, Charlotte Buell (1833-1925) American
$1000 £649   Mountain hamlet (53x61cm-21x24in) 15-Jan-93 Du Mouchelle, Detroit #2118/R

COMFORT, Charles Fraser (1900-) Canadian
$634   £415   Robert Starr's wood in spring (51x66cm-20x26in) s. 18-May-93 Joyner Fine Art, Toronto #251 (C.D 800)
$856   £567   Nude with Philodendron (90x75cm-35x30in) s. 24-Nov-92 Joyner Fine Art, Toronto #27/R (C.D 1100)
$906   £612   Starr's Channel, go-home (30x40cm-12x16in) s.d.53 board. 23-Nov-93 Joyner Fine Art, Toronto #1/R (C.D 1200)
$934   £619   In-shore wind, Ingonish (30x40cm-12x16in) s. panel. 24-Nov-92 Joyner Fine Art, Toronto #161 (C.D 1200)
$1165 £777   De Guerre's Island (25x30cm-10x12in) s.d.28 board. 13-May-94 Joyner Fine Art, Toronto #16/R (C.D 1600)
$1254 £804   Rain squalls over Cape Smokey (51x66cm-20x26in) s. 7-Dec-92 Waddingtons, Toronto #1319 (C.D 1600)
$1274 £850   Winter landscape (25x30cm-10x12in) st.sig. panel painted 1920s. 11-May-94 Sotheby's, Toronto #139/R (C.D 1750)
$1579 £1053 Pines, Georgian Bay (30x40cm-12x16in) s. masonite. 30-May-94 Ritchie, Toronto #177/R (C.D 1700)
$3371 £2161 Budding oak - Lake Clear, Renfrew County, Ontario (61x81cm-24x32in) s. 7-Dec-92 Waddingtons, Toronto #1336/R (C.D 4300)

COMSTOCK, John (19/20th C) American
$1100   £728   Interior (20x32cm-8x13in) s. W/C. 20-Sep-93 Butterfield & Butterfield, Los Angeles #262/R

COMTOIS, Ulysse (20th C) Canadian
$755   £510   Composition (17x25cm-7x10in) s.d.54 W/C. 23-Nov-93 Joyner Fine Art, Toronto #182 (C.D 1000)

CONANT, Lucy Scarborough (1867-1921) American
$800   £537   the lone pine (36x44cm-14x17in) s. W/C gouache paperboard. 4-Mar-94 Skinner, Bolton #248/R

CONDO, George (1957-) American
$700   £470   The two wear hats (46x35cm-18x14in) s.d.84. 3-May-94 Christie's, East, New York #142/R
$1000   £694   Mouth (22x14cm-9x6in) s.i.d.85verso. 23-Feb-93 Sotheby's, New York #398/R
$1000   £671   The classless man's isolation (35x27cm-14x11in) s.i.d.85.5verso. 3-May-94 Christie's, East, New York #144/R
$1200   £800   Untitled (18x12cm-7x5in) s. executed 1985. 26-May-94 Christie's, London #147/R
$1250   £868   Untitled (18x12cm-7x5in) s.d.85 linen. 23-Feb-93 Sotheby's, New York #389/R
$1490   £1000   Untitled (23x19cm-9x7in) s.d.85 verso. 2-Dec-93 Christie's, London #286/R
$3129   £2100   Frenchman (22x16cm-9x6in) s.i.d.85 verso. 2-Dec-93 Christie's, London #288/R
$3732   £2392   Los mamba (120x80cm-47x31in) acrylic. 12-Dec-92 Catherine Charbonneaux, Paris #105/R (F.FR 20000)
$3797   £2532   Untitled composition (173x173cm-68x68in) s.d.83. 2-Jun-94 AB Stockholms Auktionsverk, Stockholm #7075/R (S.KR 30000)
$4414   £3086   Face in smoke (46x33cm-18x13in) s.d.1985. 10-Mar-93 Watine-Arnault, Paris #60/R (F.FR 25000)
$7000   £4698   White and grey composition (103x91cm-41x36in) s.d.89 s.i.d.verso. 4-May-94 Christie's, New York #404/R
$8000   £5369   Facil forms (183x200cm-72x79in) s.d.87.1. 23-Feb-94 Christie's, New York #148/R
$8000   £5556   Untitled portrait (82x82cm-32x32in) 24-Feb-93 Christie's, New York #150/R
$9000   £6040   Portrait of four powers , s.d.83 verso four panels. 23-Feb-94 Christie's, East, New York #208/R
$12000 £8333   Surrealist landscape (90x121cm-35x48in) s.d.6.83 init.verso. 24-Feb-93 Christie's, New York #163/R
$15000 £10417 Yellow fool (170x129cm-67x51in) s.i.d.86verso. 23-Feb-93 Sotheby's, New York #393/R
$16300 £10000 The Intoxification of Freedom (150x150cm-59x59in) s.d.84. 15-Oct-92 Christie's, London #76/R
$16300 £10000 Blue clown (195x129cm-77x51in) s.d.85 i.verso. 15-Oct-92 Christie's, London #89/R
$19000 £12583 Untitled (152x122cm-60x48in) 19-Nov-92 Christie's, New York #125/R
$25000 £16556 Dream sequence and big sur (160x195cm-63x77in) s.i.d.91verso s.i.stretcher linen. 19-Nov-92 Christie's, New York #447/R
$28880 £18278 Blue painting (150x150cm-59x59in) 6-Dec-92 Binoche et Godeau, Paris #16/R (F.FR 155000)
$40000 £26144 Big reclining nude (249x300cm-98x118in) s.d.88. 5-May-93 Christie's, New York #176/R
$2100   £1409   Untitled (34x23cm-13x9in) two s.d. pencil ballpoint pen four. 24-Feb-94 Sotheby's Arcade, New York #419/R
$2980   £2000   On the corner (41x27cm-16x11in) s.i.d.85 verso oil pastel felt-tip pen canvas. 2-Dec-93 Christie's, London #287/R
$3500   £2431   Untitled (80x58cm-31x23in) exec.1989 col.chk. 22-Feb-93 Christie's, East, New York #279/R
$5960   £4000   Untitled (217x90cm-85x35in) s.d.89 pastel craft paper. 2-Dec-93 Christie's, London #259/R
$8000   £5229   Spotted stain (150x80cm-59x31in) s.d.1989 oil paper collage canvas. 4-May-93 Sotheby's, New York #255/R
$9780   £6000   Condo's comics (203x160cm-80x63in) oil encaustic red pencil canvas. 15-Oct-92 Christie's, London #77/R
$15000 £9804   Chapeau (122x152cm-48x60in) s.d.89-9 oil pastel paper collage canvas. 4-May-93 Sotheby's, New York #268/R
$22000 £14765 American abstract painting (205x300cm-81x118in) oil crayons pencil chl pen paper collage canvas. 5-May-94 Sotheby's, New York #337/R
$42000 £27815 Big white one (249x300cm-98x118in) s.d.87 oil pen paper collage graphite canvas. 19-Nov-92 Christie's, New York #103/R

CONE, Marvin D (1891-1964) American
$6000   £3468   Landscape (46x51cm-18x20in) s. 24-Sep-92 Sotheby's, New York #163/R

CONELY, William B (1830-1911) American
$1100   £719   Portrait of Richard Storrs Willis (30x25cm-12x10in) s.d.1887. 14-May-93 Du Mouchelle, Detroit #79/R

CONGDON, Thomas R (1862-1917) American
$779   £513   Portrait reputedly Mrs. Bond a prominent opera singer (100x80cm-39x31in) s.i.d.1912. 7-Jun-93 Waddingtons, Toronto #1308 (C.D 1000)

CONNAWAY, Jay Hall (1893-1970) American
$750   £503   Farrell's Point-Monhegan, Maine (51x76cm-20x30in) s.i. board. 24-Mar-93 Grogan, Massachussetts #74
$800   £513   Running off the rocks (30x46cm-12x18in) s. masonite. 13-Dec-92 Litchfield Auction Gallery #79/R
$800   £537   Underwater rocks (30x41cm-12x16in) s. i.verso board. 4-Mar-94 Skinner, Bolton #262/R

CONNAWAY, Jay Hall (1893-1970) American-cont.
$1200	£805	Seascape (51x76cm-20x30in) s. 24-Jun-93 Mystic Fine Arts, Connecticut #110 a
$1800	£1208	Green Point, Monhegan, Me (51x76cm-20x30in) s. i.verso masonite. 6-May-94 Skinner, Bolton #112/R

CONNER, John Anthony (1892-1971) American
$550	£364	Coastal - glimpse of the Pacific (33x38cm-13x15in) s. canvasboard. 14-Jun-94 John Moran, Pasadena #9 a
$750	£507	Landscape (23x30cm-9x12in) s. 15-Jun-93 John Moran, Pasadena #14
$950	£629	Landscape (46x91cm-18x36in) s. 28-Sep-93 John Moran, Pasadena #214
$1400	£966	Flowered hillside (23x30cm-9x12in) s. board. 16-Feb-93 John Moran, Pasadena #18

CONNER, John Ramsey (1867-1952) American
$2000	£1342	The fisher (25x30cm-10x12in) s. 26-Mar-94 James Bakker, Cambridge #81 a

CONNER, Paul (1881-1968) American
$950	£625	Desert flowers verbena (58x76cm-23x30in) s. board. 11-Jun-93 Du Mouchelle, Detroit #2140/R

CONSTANTINEAU, Jean (?) Canadian
$707	£448	St-Simon dans la bas St.Laurent (76x91cm-30x36in) s.i.d.88. 1-Dec-92 Fraser Pinneys, Quebec #131 (C.D 900)

CONTE, Guillermo (1956-) Argentinian
$14000	*£9459*	*Te pegaron mucho .. de grande (203x146cm-80x57in) s.d.1991 i.verso mixed media canvas. 23-Nov-93 Christie's, New York #167/R*

CONWAY, Fred (1900-1972) American
$850	£570	St. Louis skyline, figure of St. Louis in the clouds (41x56cm-16x22in) s.d.70 board. 2-May-94 Selkirks, St. Louis #96
$1100	£696	Dancer (122x84cm-48x33in) s.d.54 acrylic masonite. 30-Nov-92 Selkirks, St. Louis #168/R
$1200	£769	Shadynook (102x122cm-40x48in) s.d.1931. 26-Apr-93 Selkirks, St. Louis #293/R

COOK, Gordon (1927-1985) American
$2000	£1266	Large Delta Tower and tree (63x46cm-25x18in) s.verso painted c.1982. 25-Oct-92 Butterfield & Butterfield, San Francisco #2340/R
$4500	£2848	Soft cheese box (39x46cm-15x18in) s.i.verso. 25-Oct-92 Butterfield & Butterfield, San Francisco #2339/R
$1200	*£759*	*Top (22x19cm-9x7in) init. W/C. 25-Oct-92 Butterfield & Butterfield, San Francisco #2320/R*
$1500	*£949*	*Sailboat (21x22cm-8x9in) s. W/C. 25-Oct-92 Butterfield & Butterfield, San Francisco #2318/R*
$1600	*£1013*	*House in trees (23x20cm-9x8in) W/C. 25-Oct-92 Butterfield & Butterfield, San Francisco #2319/R*
$1700	*£1076*	*Watertower (22x24cm-9x9in) s. W/C. 25-Oct-92 Butterfield & Butterfield, San Francisco #2341/R*
$1700	*£1076*	*Sailing (24x34cm-9x13in) init. W/C. 25-Oct-92 Butterfield & Butterfield, San Francisco #2342/R*

COOK, Howard (1901-1980) American
$950	£638	Sangre de Cristos Mountains (41x51cm-16x20in) s. mixed media board. 8-Dec-93 Butterfield & Butterfield, San Francisco #3578/R

COOK, Otis (1900-1980) American
$1400	£979	Winter snow scene (51x61cm-20x24in) s. 11-Mar-93 Mystic Fine Arts, Connecticut #241/R
$2000	£1325	Street in Rockport (51x61cm-20x24in) s. 28-Nov-92 Young Fine Arts Auctions, Maine #101/R

COOLEY, Brian (20th C) American?
$942	£628	Hunting from a canoe (71x91cm-28x36in) s. board. 6-Jun-94 Waddingtons, Toronto #1254 (C.D 1300)

COOLIDGE, Cassius M (1844-1934) American
$1000	£667	The winner, a game of cards (71x56cm-28x22in) mono. 21-May-94 Weschler, Washington #105/R
$1100	£738	Two fishermen (56x72cm-22x28in) s. s.indist.i.verso en grisaille. 11-Dec-93 Weschler, Washington #108/R
$1600	£1067	Your Dad's come home (61x88cm-24x35in) 21-May-94 Weschler, Washington #114/R
$2000	£1176	Monarch (70x86cm-28x34in) s. 3-Oct-92 Weschler, Washington #114/R
$4600	£3007	Sick in bed (56x71cm-22x28in) mono. 22-May-93 Weschler, Washington #91/R
$5700	£3851	Eating his words (51x66cm-20x26in) mono. 20-Mar-93 Weschler, Washington #97/R
$13000	£8784	Summit conference (61x86cm-24x34in) mono. 20-Mar-93 Weschler, Washington #107/R
$16000	£9412	Poker game (58x84cm-23x33in) s. 3-Oct-92 Weschler, Washington #131/R

COOLIDGE, Mary Rosamond (1884-?) American
$770	£503	Lumber yard (41x51cm-16x20in) s. canvasboard. 14-May-93 Skinner, Bolton #94/R
$800	£559	Portrait of Edna Hathaway (81x66cm-32x26in) s. 11-Mar-93 Mystic Fine Arts, Connecticut #149/R

COOMBS, Delbert Dana (1850-1938) American
$650	£439	Cattle grazing (36x64cm-14x25in) s.d.1896. 27-Nov-93 Young Fine Arts Auctions, Maine #96/R

COOPER, A D M (1865-1924) American
$700	£458	Hawaiian landscape (61x46cm-24x18in) board. 18-Sep-93 San Rafael Auction Galleries #339
$800	£516	Portrait of a youth (81x66cm-32x26in) 16-Jul-94 San Rafael Auction Galleries #368
$2000	£1316	Cheyenne autumn (36x43cm-14x17in) s.d.1914. 13-Jun-93 Butterfield & Butterfield, San Francisco #928/R
$5000	£3472	Buffalo with fallen Indian (81x132cm-32x52in) s.d.1888 canvas on board. 7-Mar-93 Butterfield & Butterfield, San Francisco #229/R
$9500	£5588	Indian encampment in Tetons (213x325cm-84x128in) s.d.1905. 4-Oct-92 Butterfield & Butterfield, Los Angeles #46/R

COOPER, Adeline (19th C) American?
$3000	£2013	Baskets of fruit (36x46cm-14x18in) one st.sig. Theorem painting velvet pair. 1-Dec-93 Doyle, New York #41

COOPER, Astley D M (1865-1924) American
$550	£374	Waterfall at dawn (76x46cm-30x18in) s. 16-Apr-94 Young Fine Arts Auctions, Maine #82
$600	£400	View along the river's edge (61x46cm-24x18in) s. 26-May-94 Sloan, North Bethesda #2172/R
$2250	£1490	Indian burial (46x61cm-18x24in) s. 15-Jun-94 Butterfield & Butterfield, San Francisco #4637/R

COOPER, Austin (1890-1964) Canadian
$922	£640	Harrogate British Spa (196x307cm-77x121in) s. W/C gouache. 22-Feb-93 British Auctioneer #34/R

COOPER, Colin Campbell (1856-1937) American
$700	£473	Houses in residential landscape (33x41cm-13x16in) s. board. 9-Nov-93 John Moran, Pasadena #907
$700	£470	Brooklyn Bridge (18x18cm-7x7in) s. board. 4-Dec-93 Louisiana Auction Exchange #94/R
$1000	£667	Balboa Park, San Diego (30x23cm-12x9in) s. canvasboard. 15-Mar-94 John Moran, Pasadena #84
$1100	£728	Church interior (81x48cm-32x19in) 28-Sep-93 John Moran, Pasadena #264
$1400	£881	Church interior (61x51cm-24x20in) s. 22-Apr-93 Freeman Fine Arts, Philadelphia #1320
$1500	£962	Coastal view at dawn (20x33cm-8x13in) s. canvasboard. 28-May-93 Sloan, North Bethesda #2664/R
$1900	£1310	House in summer landscape (30x41cm-12x16in) s. oil masonite. 16-Feb-93 John Moran, Pasadena #93
$2400	£1633	Girl with raquet (24x14cm-9x6in) s.d.1901 panel. 15-Nov-93 Christie's, East, New York #160/R
$2500	£1645	View of Notre Dame (18x30cm-7x12in) s. board. 13-Jun-93 Butterfield & Butterfield, San Francisco #853/R
$3000	£1987	Church interior (99x46cm-39x18in) s. 28-Sep-93 John Moran, Pasadena #263
$3000	£1899	Church at St. Anastasia Verona (61x81cm-24x32in) s. 2-Dec-92 Boos Gallery, Michigan #819/R
$3500	£2215	Nantucket street at night (35x46cm-14x18in) s. canvasboard. 2-Dec-92 Christie's, East, New York #107/R
$3750	£2483	Amsterdam Harbour (56x43cm-22x17in) s.d.1896. 28-Sep-93 John Moran, Pasadena #26
$4000	£2797	Broadway from the post office (35x26cm-14x10in) s. board. 11-Mar-93 Christie's, New York #223/R
$6000	£3974	Michigan Avenue at the Art Institute (51x61cm-20x24in) s. 3-Oct-93 Hanzel Galleries, Chicago #33/R
$6500	£4422	Winter weather by the Plaza (36x51cm-14x20in) s. 17-Nov-93 Doyle, New York #35/R
$7000	£4118	Happy days (58x74cm-23x29in) s.d.1903. 4-Oct-92 Butterfield & Butterfield, Los Angeles #127/R
$9750	£6588	Battery Park (33x25cm-13x10in) s. canvas on board. 31-Mar-94 Sotheby's Arcade, New York #222/R
$10000	£6667	Figures in front of cathedral (92x74cm-36x29in) s. 25-May-94 Sotheby's, New York #75/R
$18000	£11765	Madison Square, Flatiron building (66x51cm-26x20in) s. 5-May-93 Doyle, New York #30/R
$21000	£14000	The 42nd Street library (41x61cm-16x24in) s. 25-May-94 Sotheby's, New York #72/R
$33000	£21854	Southwest corner of Madison Square (56x76cm-22x30in) s. 23-Sep-93 Sotheby's, New York #199/R
$700	£467	Sunday in the gardens (18x10cm-7x4in) s. gouache. 15-Mar-94 John Moran, Pasadena #5
$900	£596	Hacienda garden (38x44cm-15x17in) s. W/C pencil. 15-Jun-94 Butterfield & Butterfield, San Francisco #4653/R
$1300	£867	The Gloria Porch, Santiago de Compostella, Spain (45x36cm-18x14in) s. gouache paper on board. 23-May-94 Christie's, East, New York #135/R
$1300	£922	Mosque (64x76cm-25x30in) s. gouache board. 14-Feb-93 Hanzel Galleries, Chicago #783/R
$1400	£921	California landscape (51x66cm-20x26in) s. pastel. 5-Jun-93 Louisiana Auction Exchange #112/R
$1600	£1013	Manhattan business district (41x33cm-16x13in) s. W/C. 5-Dec-92 Louisiana Auction Exchange #25/R
$1800	£1208	Harbour scene (38x36cm-15x14in) s. W/C. 5-Mar-94 Louisiana Auction Exchange #115/R
$3000	£1974	View of Rochester, New York (18x25cm-7x10in) s. W/C gouache. 13-Jun-93 Butterfield & Butterfield, San Francisco #865/R
$4000	£2685	Sisters in Cloister (37x49cm-15x19in) s.d.1916 gouache. 8-Dec-93 Butterfield & Butterfield, San Francisco #3529/R

COOPER, Colin Campbell (1856-1937) American-cont.
$9500   £5491   Balboa Park, Sand Diego, California (44x55cm-17x22in) s.d.1916 W/C gouache paper on corrugated board. 24-Sep-92 Sotheby's, New York #128/R

COOPER, Emma Lampert (1860-1920) American
$700   £467   Les Martiguia, France (33x25cm-13x10in) s. i.verso board. 26-Aug-93 Skinner, Bolton #76
$900   £604   Delhi fruit stand, India (56x46cm-22x18in) s. 24-Jun-93 Boos Gallery, Michigan #478/R
$1800   £1208   Tropical street scene (46x61cm-18x24in) s. 16-Dec-93 Mystic Fine Arts, Connecticut #79
$4200   £2658   Chickens feeding outside barn (66x81cm-26x32in) s. 2-Dec-92 Christie's, East, New York #73/R
$6500   £4422   Mexican home (46x56cm-18x22in) s. 15-Nov-93 Christie's, East, New York #166/R

COOPER, Virginia S (1875-1940) American
$700   £464   Eucalyptus landscape (64x76cm-25x30in) s. 14-Jun-94 John Moran, Pasadena #101

COPE, George (1855-1929) American
$190000 £120253 The hunter's equipment (129x81cm-51x32in) s. s.d.1891 on stretcher. 3-Dec-92 Sotheby's, New York #40/R

COPE, Gordon Nicholson (1906-1970) American
$650   £430   Stream in landscape (66x91cm-26x36in) s.d.1962 board. 14-Jun-94 John Moran, Pasadena #107

COPELAND, Alfred Bryant (1840-1909) American
$800   £516   Bit of Old Cluny (99x46cm-39x18in) s.i.d.1885 i.d.1885 verso. 6-Jan-93 Doyle, New York #13
$2500   £1678   Still life with green apples, chickens, roast and objects on table (74x103cm-29x41in) s.i.d. after Guillaume-Romain Fouace. 15-Oct-93 Christie's, East, New York #36/R
$13000 £8497   Birth of Venus (68x117cm-27x46in) s.i.d.1887 i.d.1863 after Alexander Cabanel. 29-Oct-92 Christie's, East, New York #30/R

COPELAND, Charles (1858-?) American
$1050   £745   Monarch of the forest (46x71cm-18x28in) s. W/C. 13-Feb-93 Collins, Maine #116/R

COPLEY, John Singleton (1737-1815) American
$14500 £9667   Portrait of man (48x38cm-19x15in) canvas on masonite oval. 16-Mar-94 Christie's, New York #11/R
$80000 £53333 Portrait of a gentleman (76x63cm-30x25in) painted c.1760's or early 1770's. 17-Mar-94 Sotheby's, New York #15/R
$4354   £2846   Portrait of George Washington (11x8cm-4x3in) min.mono.d.1794 oval. 4-May-93 Michael Zeller, Lindau #519/R (DM 7000)
$9000   £6000   Prince Regent, study for Battle of Pyrenees (30x44cm-12x17in) pencil white chk. 26-May-94 Christie's, New York #1/R
$37500 £23734 Portraits of Gregory and Lucretia Hubbard Townsend (59x47cm-23x19in) first s.d.1756 pastel canvas pair. 3-Dec-92 Sotheby's, New York #9/R

COPLEY, John Singleton (attrib) (1737-1815) American
$13090 £8500   Portrait of young girl, seated, holding yellow bird in left hand and landscape beyond (85x74cm-33x29in) 21-Jun-94 Phillips, London #35/R

COPLEY, William Nelson (1919-) American
$3800   £2550   Je m'en fou (46x46cm-18x18in) s.d.62 i.verso acrylic. 3-May-94 Christie's, East, New York #28/R
$3800   £2517   Quatuoir (73x60cm-29x24in) s.d.59-61 s.i.d.verso acrylic sand. 17-Nov-92 Christie's, East, New York #290/R
$4800   £3333   Saysme no 6 (81x65cm-32x26in) s.d.57verso. 22-Feb-93 Christie's, East, New York #281/R
$2506   £1660   Vive la France (61x45cm-24x18in) s.d.1964 Indian ink brush over chl. 28-Nov-92 Villa Grisebach, Berlin #469/R (DM 4000)
$3500   £2431   Untitled (108x63cm-43x25in) s.d.82 acrylic black lace canvas. 22-Feb-93 Christie's, East, New York #282/R

COPPEDGE, Fern Isabel (1888-1951) American
$6000   £3974   Winter scene by river (46x51cm-18x20in) s. 22-Sep-93 Christie's, New York #152/R
$7000   £4667   After glow, Gloucester (63x76cm-25x30in) s. s.i.stretcher. 23-May-94 Christie's, East, New York #180/R
$7500   £4967   Gloucester Harbour (63x76cm-25x30in) s. 2-Oct-93 Weschler, Washington #146/R
$11000 £7285   Swan Creek road (63x76cm-25x30in) s. i.stretcher. 22-Sep-93 Christie's, New York #151/R
$13500 £8544   Mill at Bowman's Hill (61x61cm-24x24in) s. 24-Oct-92 Collins, Maine #86/R

COPPIN, John Stevens (1904-) American
$750   £507   Nude female swimming under the sea (51x46cm-20x18in) s. i.verso. 22-Apr-94 Du Mouchelle, Detroit #2012 a/R
$1300   £850   Uncle Sam (61x56cm-24x22in) s.d.1942. 19-Sep-93 Hindman Galleries, Chicago #743

CORBINO, Jon (1905-1964) American
$775   £513   Dancers (30x15cm-12x6in) s. 3-Oct-93 Hanzel Galleries, Chicago #774
$1700   £1141   Circus performers (25x20cm-10x8in) s. 24-Mar-94 Mystic Fine Arts, Connecticut #100 k

CORBINO, Jon (1905-1964) American-cont.
$1700 £1141 Equestrian performers (20x15cm-8x6in) s. 24-Mar-94 Mystic Fine Arts, Connecticut #100 j
$5500 £3235 Equestrian acrobats in action (25x30cm-10x12in) s. 8-Oct-92 Boos Gallery, Michigan #508/R
$625 £408 Pensive woman (41x30cm-16x12in) s. i.verso pencil ink masonite. 16-May-93 Hanzel Galleries, Chicago #403
$1200 £839 Halloween party (25x20cm-10x8in) s. i.verso oil graphite masonite. 12-Mar-93 Skinner, Bolton #290/R

CORDERO, F (19th C) Mexican
$2200 £1146 Mujeres en el Naranjal (33x46cm-13x18in) s. 12-Aug-92 Castells & Castells, Montevideo #80/R
$2200 £1146 Ciudad (33x46cm-13x18in) s. 12-Aug-92 Castells & Castells, Montevideo #81/R

CORDERO, Francisco (19th C) Mexican
$744 £503 Casas (40x25cm-16x10in) s. panel. 18-Oct-93 Duran, Madrid #1381/R (S.P 100000)
$800 £541 Paisaje con casa (30x56cm-12x22in) s. 20-Oct-93 Castells & Castells, Montevideo#29

CORDIVIOLA, Luis Adolfo (1892-1967) Argentinian
$1000 £521 En el monte (28x24cm-11x9in) 4-Aug-92 VerBo, Buenos Aires #34

CORLEY, Philip (20th C) American
$700 £458 Cafe de Tertre (66x79cm-26x31in) s. panel. 16-May-93 Hanzel Galleries, Chicago#328

CORNE, Michele Felice (attrib) (1752-1832) Italian/American
$1000 £671 Self-portrait (74x61cm-29x24in) i.verso. 26-Mar-94 Skinner, Bolton #237

CORNELL, Joseph (1903-1972) American
$5500 £3691 Untitled (31x27cm-12x11in) s.verso collage cardboard executed c.1962-65. 25-Feb-93 Sotheby's, New York #25/R
$12000 £8333 Untitled (29x37cm-11x15in) s.verso executed c.1966 paint col.pencil collage. 23-Feb-93 Sotheby's, New York #225/R

CORNOYER, Paul (1864-1923) American
$925 £593 Figures in sunlit Italian courtyard (33x41cm-13x16in) s. 26-Apr-93 Selkirks, St. Louis #167/R
$1350 £854 Nocturnal river landscape with light from windows of buildings reflected (30x41cm-12x16in) s. 30-Nov-92 Selkirks, St. Louis #250/R
$2600 £1667 Busy New York street scene, monument beyond (30x41cm-12x16in) s. 26-Apr-93 Selkirks, St. Louis #304/R
$3000 £1923 Venetian street scene, figure beside canal (56x46cm-22x18in) s. 26-Apr-93 Selkirks, St. Louis #305/R
$3000 £1587 Parisian winter (30x41cm-12x16in) s. 12-Sep-92 Louisiana Auction Exchange #112/R
$5000 £3268 Urban nocturne (69x50cm-27x20in) s. 4-May-93 Christie's, East, New York #192/R
$8500 £4913 New England house in moonlight (56x69cm-22x27in) s. 24-Sep-92 Sotheby's, New York #130/R
$23000 £13295 Flatiron building (56x69cm-22x27in) s. 24-Sep-92 Sotheby's, New York #129/R
$25000 £16779 New York City view in winter (61x44cm-24x17in) s. 2-Dec-93 Sotheby's, New York #104/R
$25000 £14451 Street scene (46x61cm-18x24in) s. 23-Sep-92 Christie's, New York #181/R
$31000 £20530 Bryant Park (46x61cm-18x24in) s. 23-Sep-93 Sotheby's, New York #200/R
$80000 £50633 Late afternoon, Washington Square (56x66cm-22x26in) s. 4-Dec-92 Christie's, New York #46/R
$1300 £861 Couple on a park bench (41x48cm-16x19in) s. pastel. 19-Jun-94 Hindman Galleries, Chicago #674/R

CORNOYER, Paul (attrib) (1864-1923) American
$650 £417 Landscape with figures, farm buildings beyond (30x160cm-12x63in) triptych. 26-Apr-93 Selkirks, St. Louis #165
$850 £594 Old mill beside stream and large shade tree, filtering afternoon sun (66x53cm-26x21in) 5-Feb-93 Selkirks, St. Louis #313/R

CORNWELL, Dean (1892-1960) American
$2800 £1892 Study for GM Building 1939 World's Fair (48x38cm-19x15in) panel. 10-Aug-93 Stonington Fine Arts, Stonington #115/R
$3000 £1923 I object, I object...,Illustration for story (74x84cm-29x33in) s.i.d.1938 board sold with copy of story. 24-May-93 Grogan, Massachusetts #365/R
$7800 £5455 Bullet train (53x79cm-21x31in) 14-Mar-93 Hindman Galleries, Chicago #7/R
$9000 £6000 In front of the New York Athletic Club (76x71cm-30x28in) s.d.20. 17-Mar-94 Sotheby's, New York #172/R
$15000 £9934 Washing the Saviour's feet (86x122cm-34x48in) init.d.25 s.i.d.1928 verso. 23-Sep-93 Sotheby's, New York #295/R
$16000 £10596 Bar room scene (71x117cm-28x46in) s.d.22. 23-Sep-93 Sotheby's, New York #297/R
$19000 £13287 Waiting (91x71cm-36x28in) s.d.20. 11-Mar-93 Christie's, New York #138/R
$24000 £13873 The cafe table (76x71cm-30x28in) s.d.20. 23-Sep-92 Christie's, New York #193/R

CORONEL, Pedro (1923-1985) Mexican
$20000 £13514 Ano l luna (116x89cm-46x35in) s.d.69 i.verso. 23-Nov-93 Christie's, New York #174/R
$26000 £17219 La Sonadora (120x80cm-47x31in) s.i.d.1974 verso. 24-Nov-92 Christie's, New York #114/R

CORONEL, Pedro (1923-1985) Mexican-cont.
$26000 £17568 Los arlequines (122x83cm-48x33in) s. masonite painted 1953-54. 23-Nov-93 Christie's, New York #132/R
$34000 £22667 Rencontre (116x89cm-46x35in) s.i.d.67 i.verso. 18-May-94 Christie's, New York #159/R
$3870 £2597 Formas (26x18cm-10x7in) s.verso W/C. 1-Dec-93 Louis Morton, Mexico #64/R (M.P 12000)

CORONEL, Rafael (1932-) Mexican
$4000 £2649 El Payaso (40x55cm-16x22in) s. i.verso masonite. 24-Nov-92 Christie's, New York #307/R
$5500 £3595 Ice cream seller (39x25cm-15x10in) s.d.73. 14-May-93 Du Mouchelle, Detroit #2030/R
$8500 £5629 Dark heads in profile (50x50cm-20x20in) s. board. 30-Jun-93 Sotheby's Arcade, New York #230/R
$8500 £5629 La Pantomima (50x50cm-20x20in) s. board. 30-Jun-93 Sotheby's Arcade, New York #229/R
$9000 £6040 Woman with a bow (65x60cm-26x24in) s.d.64 masonite. 7-Jan-94 Gary Nader, Miami #95/R
$10000 £6757 Tres figuras (60x85cm-24x33in) s.d.62 masonite. 23-Nov-93 Christie's, New York #159/R
$10220 £6814 Desnudo en amarillo (78x60cm-31x24in) s. acrylic paper. 25-May-94 Louis Morton, Mexico #74/R (M.P 34000)
$11143 £7143 Madame (64x48cm-25x19in) s.d.1960 masonite. 29-Apr-93 Louis Morton, Mexico #132 (M.P 35000)
$14000 £8861 El Viejo y la Foca (119x119cm-47x47in) s.d.67. 25-Oct-92 Butterfield & Butterfield, San Francisco #2257/R
$18000 £11765 El viejo y la foca (120x120cm-47x47in) s.d.67 i.verso. 17-May-93 Christie's, New York #128/R
$20000 £13423 Elactor Y Su Hijo (99x124cm-39x49in) s.d.65. 14-Jan-94 Du Mouchelle, Detroit #2007/R
$20000 £13072 Escena del circo (100x120cm-39x47in) s. s.i.verso painted 1965. 18-May-93 Sotheby's, New York #207/R
$30000 £19868 La Ficcion (101x130cm-40x51in) s. 24-Nov-92 Christie's, New York #192/R
$30000 £19868 Personaje (80x100cm-31x39in) s. init.i.verso. 24-Nov-92 Christie's, New York #240/R
$38000 £25676 Anonimo III (126x125cm-50x49in) s. s.i.d.1969verso. 23-Nov-93 Christie's, New York #136/R
$40000 £26667 Caballo II (126x150cm-50x59in) s. init.i.verso. 18-May-94 Christie's, New York #142/R
$42000 £27815 La Espera (127x152cm-50x60in) s. i.stretcher. 24-Nov-92 Christie's, New York #55/R
$45000 £30405 Concilio familiar (200x150cm-79x59in) s. s.i.verso. 23-Nov-93 Christie's, New York #45/R
$50000 £33113 Anciana (150x125cm-59x49in) s. 24-Nov-92 Christie's, New York #32/R
$150000 £100000 Peregrini (226x150cm-89x59in) s. init.i.verso painted 1976. 18-May-94 Christie's, New York #70/R
$1613 £1082 Viejo con abrigo (41x37cm-16x15in) s. pencil drawing. 1-Dec-93 Louis Morton, Mexico #8/R (M.P 5000)
$2500 £1634 Retrato Conyugal (23x33cm-9x13in) s. i.verso pencil. 16-Sep-93 Sloan, North Bethesda #2589/R
$3750 £2500 El mago (36x28cm-14x11in) s. graphite W/C notebook paper exec.c.1965. 18-May-94 Sotheby's, New York #413/R
$4000 £2649 El Buscador (101x75cm-40x30in) s.d.1969 graphite acrylic board. 23-Nov-93 Sotheby's, New York #250/R

CORREA, Juan (1650-1740) Mexican
$25000 £16556 Santa Teresa Y el Nino Jesus (151x196cm-59x77in) s. 23-Nov-92 Sotheby's, New York #26/R
$28000 £18543 Guardian Angel (171x110cm-67x43in) 24-Nov-92 Christie's, New York #63/R

CORTAZAR, Roberto (20th C) Mexican?
$1631 £1102 Rostro Desfigurado (100x70cm-39x28in) s.d.1982 pencil dr. 27-Apr-94 Louis Morton, Mexico #506 (M.P 5500)

CORTEZ DE ALCOCER, Jose (attrib) (18th C) Ecuadorian
$13000 £8609 Apocalyptic Virgin of Quito (105x81cm-41x32in) painted c.1775. 24-Nov-92 Christie's, New York #68/R

CORWIN, Charles Abel (1857-1938) American
$650 £422 Great Falls on the Potomac (41x61cm-16x24in) s. i.stretcher. 8-Jul-94 Sloan, North Bethesda #2367
$6500 £4305 Inner harbour, Gloucester (61x91cm-24x36in) s. i.stretcher. 23-Sep-93 Sotheby's, New York #183/R

CORZAS, Francisco (1936-1983) Mexican
$4500 £3041 Desnudo (41x31cm-16x12in) s.d.65 oil pen. 22-Nov-93 Sotheby's, New York #254/R
$12000 £7843 El Vissione No.2 (102x81cm-40x32in) s.d.69. 17-Sep-93 Skinner, Bolton #302/R
$22000 £14379 Retrato de hombre (99x79cm-39x31in) s.d.1970. 17-May-93 Christie's, New York #127/R
$24000 £16000 El Manco de Mocorito (81x70cm-32x28in) s.d.72 i.verso. 18-May-94 Christie's, New York #145/R
$40000 £26144 Desnudo (135x111cm-53x44in) s.d.76. 18-May-93 Sotheby's, New York #74/R
$50000 £32680 Obstinacion (90x75cm-35x30in) s.d.78. 17-May-93 Christie's, New York #17/R
$50000 £33113 El Burgues (120x100cm-47x39in) s.d.1979. 24-Nov-92 Christie's, New York #33/R

CORZAS, Francisco (1936-1983) Mexican-cont.
$50000	£33333	Perfil de mujer (120x100cm-47x39in) s.d.83. 18-May-94 Sotheby's, New York #314/R
$2500	£1667	Sin titulo, la ofrenda (26x36cm-10x14in) s.d.63 ink W/C. 18-May-94 Sotheby's, New York #417/R
$2600	£1757	El pintor y su modelo (27x34cm-11x13in) s.d.64 W/C pen sepia. 23-Nov-93 Christie's, New York #222/R
$5000	£3333	Contrada della selva (56x41cm-22x16in) s.i.d.73 ink. 18-May-94 Sotheby's, New York #415/R

COSGROVE, Stanley Morel (1911-) Canadian
$1799	£1168	Foret (25x30cm-10x12in) s. panel. 21-Jun-94 Fraser Pinneys, Quebec #167 (C.D 2500)
$1937	£1309	Grove of trees (41x51cm-16x20in) s. masonite. 1-Nov-93 Levis, Calgary #49/R (C.D 2500)
$2735	£1776	Foret (25x30cm-10x12in) s. panel. 21-Jun-94 Fraser Pinneys, Quebec #53 (C.D 3800)
$2807	£1822	Paysage (35x45cm-14x18in) s. panel. 21-Jun-94 Fraser Pinneys, Quebec #148 (C.D 3900)
$2869	£1939	Still life with yellow pears (25x30cm-10x12in) s. canvasboard. 23-Nov-93 Joyner Fine Art, Toronto #25/R (C.D 3800)
$3022	£1963	Foret (30x40cm-12x16in) s. panel. 21-Jun-94 Fraser Pinneys, Quebec #157 (C.D 4200)
$3058	£1986	Nature morte (30x35cm-12x14in) s. panel. 21-Jun-94 Fraser Pinneys, Quebec #56 (C.D 4250)
$3171	£2073	Still life with apples and pitcher (30x41cm-12x16in) s.d.59 board. 19-May-93 Sotheby's, Toronto #304/R (C.D 4000)
$3204	£2136	Raisins bleus (30x40cm-12x16in) s. board. 13-May-94 Joyner Fine Art, Toronto #37/R (C.D 4400)
$3330	£2176	Hiver (36x46cm-14x18in) s. board. 18-May-93 Joyner Fine Art, Toronto #97/R (C.D 4200)
$3350	£2233	Trees in winter (25x30cm-10x12in) s. 13-May-94 Joyner Fine Art, Toronto #85/R (C.D 4600)
$3369	£2202	Landscape (41x30cm-16x12in) s. board. 19-May-93 Sotheby's, Toronto #109/R (C.D 4250)
$3567	£2332	Landscape of trees (30x41cm-12x16in) s. panel. 19-May-93 Sotheby's, Toronto #194/R (C.D 4500)
$3587	£2423	View of the trees and lake (51x40cm-20x16in) s. 23-Nov-93 Fraser Pinneys, Quebec #449 (C.D 4750)
$3624	£2448	Forest (40x50cm-16x20in) s. 23-Nov-93 Joyner Fine Art, Toronto #33/R (C.D 4800)
$3624	£2449	Nature morte (17x22cm-7x9in) init.d.48 paper. 23-Nov-93 Fraser Pinneys, Quebec #370/R (C.D 4800)
$3773	£2388	Paysage d'hiver (40x30cm-16x12in) s. board. 1-Dec-92 Fraser Pinneys, Quebec #36 (C.D 4800)
$3776	£2551	Bol et deux poires (30x40cm-12x16in) s. canvasboard. 23-Nov-93 Joyner Fine Art, Toronto #37/R (C.D 5000)
$3874	£2618	Paysage (51x61cm-20x24in) s. i.verso. 3-Nov-93 Sotheby's, Toronto #276/R (C.D 5000)
$3964	£2591	Road through the trees (41x51cm-16x20in) s. canvasboard. 18-May-93 Joyner Fine Art, Toronto #43/R (C.D 5000)
$4153	£2806	Portrait of lady (45x35cm-18x14in) s.d.68 canvasboard. 23-Nov-93 Joyner Fine Art, Toronto #94/R (C.D 5500)
$4281	£2835	Trees with river, La Tuque, Quebec (41x51cm-16x20in) s. i.verso canvas laid on board. 18-Nov-92 Sotheby's, Toronto #246/R (C.D 5500)
$4306	£2871	Trees near Hudson (40x30cm-16x12in) s. 30-May-94 Ritchie, Toronto #204/R (C.D 6000)
$4360	£2850	Grove of trees (41x62cm-16x24in) s. 19-May-93 Sotheby's, Toronto #336/R (C.D 5500)
$4531	£3061	Forest (50x40cm-20x16in) s. board. 23-Nov-93 Joyner Fine Art, Toronto #125/R (C.D 6000)
$4756	£3109	Anne (51x41cm-20x16in) s. canvasboard. 18-May-93 Joyner Fine Art, Toronto #120/R (C.D 6000)
$5059	£3351	Nature morte sur table brune (20x24cm-8x9in) s.d.53 board. 24-Nov-92 Joyner Fine Art, Toronto #167/R (C.D 6500)
$5059	£3351	River in Latuque (62x80cm-24x31in) s. 24-Nov-92 Joyner Fine Art, Toronto #23/R (C.D 6500)
$5825	£3883	Landscape (51x61cm-20x24in) s. 11-May-94 Sotheby's, Toronto #124/R (C.D 8000)
$6189	£4126	Trees and sand (60x50cm-24x20in) s. 13-May-94 Joyner Fine Art, Toronto #32/R (C.D 8500)
$6418	£4337	La femme en rose (50x40cm-20x16in) s. board. 23-Nov-93 Joyner Fine Art, Toronto #61/R (C.D 8500)
$7005	£4639	Winter Scene (51x61cm-20x24in) s.d.74. 18-Nov-92 Sotheby's, Toronto #66/R (C.D 9000)
$7173	£4847	Lake near La Tuque (62x80cm-24x31in) s. 23-Nov-93 Joyner Fine Art, Toronto #90/R (C.D 9500)
$8010	£5340	Trees under blue sky (70x75cm-28x30in) s. 13-May-94 Joyner Fine Art, Toronto #55/R (C.D 11000)
$9513	£6218	Ombres d'ete (81x65cm-32x26in) s. painted 1954. 18-May-93 Joyner Fine Art, Toronto #83/R (C.D 12000)
$543	£362	Nue assise (18x22cm-7x9in) s. i.verso ink. 6-Jun-94 Waddingtons, Toronto #1241 (C.D 750)
$588	£377	Nude (31x24cm-12x9in) s.d.1976 conte. 26-Apr-93 Levis, Calgary #33 (C.D 750)
$778	£515	Foret (30x25cm-12x10in) s. chl. 24-Nov-92 Joyner Fine Art, Toronto #247 (C.D 1000)
$872	£570	Landscape with trees (32x42cm-13x17in) s. chl. 18-May-93 Joyner Fine Art, Toronto #141 (C.D 1100)

COSTA, Joao Baptista da (1865-1926) Brazilian
$19000   £12838   Paisagem de Petropolis (82x65cm-32x26in) s.d.1916 linen. 23-Nov-93 Christie's, New York #84/R

COSTA, Milton da (1915-1988) Brazilian
$30000   £20000   Menina ajoelhada (65x54cm-26x21in) s. s.i.verso. 18-May-94 Christie's, New York #59/R

COSTIGAN, John E (1888-1972) American
$1200   £811   Winter along the brook (30x41cm-12x16in) s. i.verso canvasboard. 10-Nov-93 Doyle, New York #33
$1400   £946   Mother and child (41x30cm-16x12in) s. canvasboard. 10-Nov-93 Doyle, New York #32
$1500   £1007   Mother and children in autumn landscape (30x41cm-12x16in) s.i.verso board. 23-Jun-93 Doyle, New York #15
$5500   £3716   Springtime (66x91cm-26x36in) s. s.i.verso masonite. 31-Mar-94 Sotheby's Arcade, New York #333/R
$900   £616   The goat girl (46x53cm-18x21in) s. W/C. 10-Feb-94 Skinner, Bolton #20
$2250   £1424   Milking the cow (55x73cm-22x29in) s. i.verso W/C. 3-Dec-92 Sotheby's, New York #68/R

COSTIGLIOLO, Jose P (20th C) Uruguayan?
$650   £428   Naturaleza muerta abstracta (46x38cm-18x15in) s.d.1947 board. 31-May-93 Gomensoro, Montevideo #22
$1600   £1074   Abstraccion (46x33cm-18x13in) s.d.46 s.i.d.verso board. 29-Nov-93 Gomensoro, Montevideo #19
$800   £423   Desnudo (50x81cm-20x32in) s.d.46 ink fibre. 10-Sep-92 Gomensoro, Montevideo #48/R

COTE, Bruno (1940-) Canadian
$563   £380   L'ours (41x51cm-16x20in) s. s.i.verso masonite. 25-Apr-94 Levis, Calgary #59/R (C.D 775)

COTO, Luiz (1830-1891) Mexican
$38614   £25743   Interior de la Hacienda de la Teja, hoy La Colonia Cuauhtemoc (60x80cm-24x31in) s.d.1869. 8-Jun-94 Louis Morton, Mexico #118/R (M.P 130000)
$59406   £39604   Exterior de la Hacienda de la Teja, hoy La Colonia Cuauhtemoc (60x80cm-24x31in) s.d.1869. 8-Jun-94 Louis Morton, Mexico #65/R (M.P 200000)

COTTINGHAM, Robert (1935-) American
$1902   £1112   El toro (27x27cm-11x11in) s.d.74 acrylic paper. 16-Sep-92 Kunsthallen, Copenhagen #22 (D.KR 11000)
$4000   £2685   Jack and Hy (43x43cm-17x17in) s. i.d.1973 verso acrylic paper. 25-Feb-94 Sotheby's, New York #81/R
$15000   £8824   Dr. Gibson (199x199cm-78x78in) s.d.1971 verso. 6-Oct-92 Sotheby's, New York #106/R

COTTON, William (1880-1958) American
$750   £439   Unemployment line (30x23cm-12x9in) s.i.verso pastel drawing over pencil. 17-Sep-92 Sloan, North Bethesda #1785/R

COUGHTRY, John Graham (1931-) Canadian
$4455   £3010   Acrobat (213x137cm-84x54in) s.d. s.i.d.Oct.61verso oil lucite canvas. 3-Nov-93 Sotheby's, Toronto #361/R (C.D 5750)
$1240   £838   Angry head (76x51cm-30x20in) s. s.i.verso ink gouache. 3-Nov-93 Sotheby's, Toronto #251/R (C.D 1600)

COULTER, William Alexander (1849-1936) American
$1500   £1007   Rocky shoreline (51x30cm-20x12in) s. 4-Dec-93 Louisiana Auction Exchange #18/R
$1800   £1059   In tow (30x25cm-12x10in) s. board. 4-Oct-92 Butterfield & Butterfield, Los Angeles #22/R
$2500   £1471   At Angel Island (62x39cm-24x15in) s.d.1889. 4-Oct-92 Butterfield & Butterfield, Los Angeles #21/R
$4500   £3125   Black Ball liner (63x53cm-25x21in) s. 7-Mar-93 Butterfield & Butterfield, San Francisco #53/R
$5500   £3691   Sailing schooner (54x28cm-21x11in) s. canvas on board. 8-Dec-93 Butterfield & Butterfield, San Francisco #3333/R
$2500   £1656   Historic marine scenes, two init. two s. three ink one ink W/C four. 15-Jun-94 Butterfield & Butterfield, San Francisco #4561/R
$2750   £1821   Historic marine scenes, three s. one init. three ink one ink W/C four. 15-Jun-94 Butterfield & Butterfield, San Francisco #4562/R

COUPER, J S (1867-?) American
$1000   £685   Mammy holding baby (51x41cm-20x16in) s. 7-Feb-94 Selkirks, St. Louis #118

COURT, Elizabeth van (20th C) American
$700   £476   Children with flowers in summer meadow (122x79cm-48x31in) s. 8-Apr-94 Sloan, North Bethesda #2126/R

COURTICE, Rody Kenny (1895-?) Canadian
$1268   £829   Mine head (51x41cm-20x16in) s.verso board. 19-May-93 Sotheby's, Toronto #126/R (C.D 1600)

COUSE, E Irving (1866-1936) American
$8500   £5705   Pueblo fireplace (23x30cm-9x12in) s. board. 8-Dec-93 Butterfield & Butterfield, San Francisco #3561/R

COUSE, E Irving (1866-1936) American-cont.
$14000	£9396	Taos Turkey shooters (22x25cm-9x10in) s. board. 2-Dec-93 Sotheby's, New York #35/R
$15000	£8671	Juan, Pueblo Indian (41x30cm-16x12in) s.i. indis.s.i.d.1927verso board. 23-Sep-92 Christie's, New York #109/R
$17000	£11409	The quiver maker (29x39cm-11x15in) s. 2-Dec-93 Sotheby's, New York #34/R
$18000	£12081	By the evening fire (46x38cm-18x15in) s. 2-Dec-93 Sotheby's, New York #39/R
$23000	£13295	Pueblo fireplace (30x41cm-12x16in) s. i.verso board. 24-Sep-92 Sotheby's, New York #81/R
$32000	£21333	An evening reverie (61x74cm-24x29in) s. painted 1911. 17-Mar-94 Sotheby's, New York #63/R
$37500	£23734	The sacred rain bowl (62x74cm-24x29in) s. 3-Dec-92 Sotheby's, New York #67/R
$45000	£30000	Flute song, Moonlight (76x91cm-30x36in) s. painted 1925. 17-Mar-94 Sotheby's, New York #64/R
$50000	£32051	Warming hands by stream (61x73cm-24x29in) s.i. 26-May-93 Christie's, New York #109/R
$90000	£60000	The conjurer (89x117cm-35x46in) s. painted 1909. 25-May-94 Sotheby's, New York #46/R
$115000	£73718	San Juan pottery (89x117cm-35x46in) s. painted 1911. 27-May-93 Sotheby's, New York #230/R
$140000	£93333	Making pottery (90x118cm-35x46in) s. painted 1912. 25-May-94 Sotheby's, New York #54/R
$160000	£102564	Magic flute -flute player at spring (117x89cm-46x35in) s. painted 1918. 27-May-93 Sotheby's, New York #233/R
$750	*£475*	*Adobe House (18x25cm-7x10in) s. W/C. 5-Dec-92 Louisiana Auction Exchange #44/R*

COUSE, E Irving (attrib) (1866-1936) American
$935	£615	Loughridge - Indian Brave (74x53cm-29x21in) i.verso. 8-Jun-93 Ritchie, Toronto #78/R (C.D 1200)

COUSE, William Percy (1898-?) American
$4750	£3045	Boom town (30x76cm-12x30in) s.d.1921. 9-Dec-92 Butterfield & Butterfield, San Francisco #3961/R

COUTARD, Gabriel (1960-) Haitian
$626	£415	Jungle (76x102cm-30x40in) s. 13-Jun-94 Rogeon, Paris #8 (F.FR 3500)

COUTTS, Alice Gray (1880-1973) American
$1400	£940	Song of spring (25x20cm-10x8in) s. 4-Dec-93 Louisiana Auction Exchange #35/R
$1600	£1074	Pink roses (28x23cm-11x9in) s.d.1905. 6-Dec-93 Grogan, Massachussetts #500
$2000	£1418	Indian baby with bird (25x20cm-10x8in) 13-Feb-93 San Rafael Auction Galleries #230

COUTTS, Gordon (1868-1937) British/American
$600	£400	Beach scene, Tangiers (30x41cm-12x16in) s.d.1916 canvas laid down on canvas. 15-Mar-94 John Moran, Pasadena #122
$750	£507	Desert landscape (41x51cm-16x20in) s. board. 9-Nov-93 John Moran, Pasadena #917
$1150	£728	View of Chinatown (41x25cm-16x10in) s. 5-Dec-92 Louisiana Auction Exchange #18/R
$1400	£933	Spanish lady (76x91cm-30x36in) s. 15-Mar-94 John Moran, Pasadena #55
$1500	£993	The oaks (76x102cm-30x40in) s. 28-Sep-93 John Moran, Pasadena #315
$1700	£1149	Tangiers (51x71cm-20x28in) s. canvas on board. 15-Jun-93 John Moran, Pasadena #165
$1800	£1169	Twilight on the lake (76x102cm-30x40in) s. 9-Sep-93 Sotheby's Arcade, New York #259/R
$2250	£1490	Tangiers market place (76x97cm-30x38in) s. 28-Sep-93 John Moran, Pasadena #273
$2500	£1689	La fiesta - old Mexico (91x122cm-36x48in) s. 15-Jun-93 John Moran, Pasadena #130
$2500	£1689	California landscape (76x102cm-30x40in) s. 9-Nov-93 John Moran, Pasadena #845
$3000	£2013	Stagecoach on the Trail (66x93cm-26x37in) s. 8-Dec-93 Butterfield & Butterfield, San Francisco #3580/R
$3250	£2111	Portrait of Indian brave (43x36cm-17x14in) s. 9-Sep-93 Sotheby's Arcade, New York #226/R
$3500	£2349	Prospector near Palm Springs (61x71cm-24x28in) s. 8-Dec-93 Butterfield & Butterfield, San Francisco #3581/R
$6041	£4054	Sydney Harbour from McMahon Point (45x27cm-18x11in) s. linen on board painted 1898. 29-Nov-93 Sotheby's, Paddington #94/R (A.D 9000)
$8000	£5229	Marin County landscape (91x140cm-36x55in) 18-Sep-93 San Rafael Auction Galleries #342
$13000	£8609	Alice and Jeannie in garden (89x74cm-35x29in) s. 28-Sep-93 John Moran, Pasadena #311

COUTTS, Gordon (attrib) (1868-1937) British/American
$4250	£2778	Marin County landscape (91x140cm-36x55in) 18-Sep-93 San Rafael Auction Galleries #343

COVARRUBIAS, Miguel (1904-1957) Mexican
$8000	£5205	Desnudo de Nieves (37x73cm-15x29in) egg tempera gessoedd masonite painted c.1945. 22-Nov-93 Sotheby's, New York #208/R
$16000	£10458	Two Balinese women bathing (67x52cm-26x20in) s. canvas on masonite. 17-May-93 Christie's, New York #175/R
$25000	£16667	The Watering Hole, Bali (39x53cm-15x21in) s. oil paper laid down on board. 18-May-94 Christie's, New York #310/R
$645	*£433*	*Tehuana con jarro (25x15cm-10x6in) pencil dr. 1-Dec-93 Louis Morton, Mexico #174 (M.P 2000)*
$650	*£417*	*Untitled - holiday dance (25x18cm-10x7in) init. pen dr. 27-May-93 Swann Galleries, New York #76/R*

COVARRUBIAS, Miguel (1904-1957) Mexican-cont.
$700	£486	Urchin (28x19cm-11x7in) s. Indian ink pencil htd white. 26-Feb-93 Sotheby's Arcade, New York #251/R
$1000	£662	Indio Chamula (27x21cm-11x8in) s. W/C. 23-Nov-92 Sotheby's, New York #252/R
$1300	£867	Two Highbrow Ladies of Montparnasse discussing James Joyce (23x28cm-9x11in) i. wash black ink painted 1929. 18-May-94 Christie's, New York #309/R
$1800	£1200	Boceto para mules and men (31x25cm-12x10in) init. graphite gouache W/C executed c.1935. 9-Jun-94 Sotheby's Arcade, New York #127/R
$2000	£1325	Mujer sentada (29x22cm-11x9in) s. gouache. 30-Jun-93 Sotheby's Arcade, New York #222/R
$4000	£2667	Cuban Flapper (35x25cm-14x10in) i. black ink gouache painted 1928. 18-May-94 Christie's, New York #308/R
$20000	£13072	Mapa de Mexico (45x69cm-18x27in) s. W/C pencil. 17-May-93 Christie's, New York #271/R

COVERT, John (1882-1960) American
$1900	£1250	Moorish warrior (96x76cm-38x30in) s.d.06. 31-Mar-93 Sotheby's Arcade, New York #68/R

COWELL, W W (1856-?) American
$700	£470	Sunset Sail, a schooner (18x25cm-7x10in) init.d.76 board. 6-Feb-94 Skinner, Bolton #63

COWLEY, Reta (1910-) Canadian
$942	£615	City scene (47x62cm-19x24in) s. W/C. 10-May-93 Hodgins, Calgary #247/R (C.D 1200)

COX, Allyn (1896-?) American
$900	£588	Faggot carrier and woman (132x102cm-52x40in) s.d.1922. 16-May-93 Hindman Galleries, Chicago #198/R
$1000	£654	Seaside (61x343cm-24x135in) s. 29-Jun-94 Doyle, New York #13 a

COX, Charles Hudson (1829-1901) American
$2516	£1700	Springtime in Texas in buffalo clover (49x90cm-19x35in) s.d.93 W/C over pencil. 20-Oct-93 Sotheby's, London #5/R

COX, Kenyon C (1856-1919) American
$15000	£8824	September sunshine , s.i.d.1884 s.i.verso. 8-Oct-92 Freeman Fine Arts, Philadelphia #1128/R

COX, Patrick Douglass (1953-) Canadian
$754	£513	The Ranch Coulee (53x44cm-21x17in) s.d.1992 W/C. 15-Nov-93 Hodgins, Calgary #31/R (C.D 1000)

COZZENS, Frederick Schiller (1846-1928) American
$550	£359	Sailboat on Long Island Sound (18x28cm-7x11in) s.d.1900 W/C. 16-Sep-93 Sloan, North Bethesda #2924
$550	£359	Sailing vessels (41x33cm-16x13in) s.d.1899 W/C. 30-Jun-94 Mystic Fine Arts, Connecticut #45
$650	£430	Beach scene (28x66cm-11x26in) s.d.1910 W/C. 23-Sep-93 Mystic Fine Arts, Connecticut #262
$800	£462	Ships sailing along the coast (36x56cm-14x22in) s.d.1901 W/C pencil on board. 25-Sep-92 Sotheby's Arcade, New York #123/R
$800	£537	Schooners in open water (33x56cm-13x22in) s.d. W/C paperboard. 27-Mar-93 Skinner, Bolton #47/R
$850	£556	Ships off New England Coast (36x53cm-14x21in) s.d.97 W/C. 16-Sep-93 Sloan, North Bethesda #2923/R
$850	£582	Seascape with boats and figures (23x30cm-9x12in) s.d.05 W/C. 19-Feb-94 Young Fine Arts Auctions, Maine #69/R
$1500	£1007	Ship and tugs (36x61cm-14x24in) s.d.15 W/C paperboard. 27-Mar-93 Skinner, Bolton #32/R
$1500	£949	Breakwater at low tide (36x54cm-14x21in) s.i.d.95 W/C. 3-Dec-92 Sotheby's, New York #20/R
$3250	£2138	'Close hauled' (30x26cm-12x10in) s.d.87 sepia ink gouache pencil. 4-Jun-93 Sotheby's, New York #191/R
$3750	£2517	Ships and vessels at New York harbour, sunset (33x61cm-13x24in) s.d.15 W/C paperboard. 27-Mar-93 Skinner, Bolton #4
$3874	£2600	Columbia and Shamrock II believed to be Americas Cup 1901 off Newport (31x56cm-12x22in) s.d.1901 W/C arched top. 13-Jan-94 Bonhams, London #336
$4300	£2905	Morning in N.Y. Bay -upper (27x37cm-11x15in) s.d.83 s.i.verso W/C paper on board. 31-Mar-94 Sotheby's Arcade, New York #26/R

CRAIG, Charles (1846-1931) American
$4250	£2891	Lonely road, dusk (61x89cm-24x35in) s.d.1902. 9-Jul-93 Sloan, North Bethesda #2782/R
$7500	£5068	The scout (56x91cm-22x36in) s.d.1894. 31-Mar-94 Sotheby's Arcade, New York #184/R
$7500	£5068	Responding to the smoke signal (71x91cm-28x36in) s.d.1895. 31-Mar-94 Sotheby's Arcade, New York #189/R
$8000	£5442	River valley, dusk (61x91cm-24x36in) s.d.1902. 9-Jul-93 Sloan, North Bethesda #2781/R
$7500	£5102	Geronimo (58x48cm-23x19in) s. W/C. 9-Jul-93 Sloan, North Bethesda #2783/R

CRAIG, T B (19th C) American
$1900	£1284	Christmas Night (124x84cm-49x33in) s.d.1873 canvas laid down on board. 31-Oct-93 Hindman Galleries, Chicago #808/R

CRAIG, Thomas Bigelow (1849-1924) American

$725	£494	Pompton Lake, New Jersey (46x66cm-18x26in) s. 14-Apr-94 Freeman Fine Arts, Philadelphia #982/R
$750	£521	Cattle on hillside (30x41cm-12x16in) s. s.i.verso. 6-Mar-93 Louisiana Auction Exchange #4/R
$888	£600	Cattle at the brook (25x36cm-10x14in) s.d.89 panel. 26-Nov-93 Tennants, Leyburn #440/R
$1100	£636	Autumn afternoon (76x63cm-30x25in) s. s.i.verso. 25-Sep-92 Sotheby's Arcade, New York #115/R
$1300	£867	In the orchard, meadow view with sheep (25x36cm-10x14in) s.i. 26-Aug-93 Skinner, Bolton #182/R
$1400	£940	A dusty road - landscape with cattle (46x66cm-18x26in) s. s.i.verso. 4-Mar-94 Skinner, Bolton #209/R
$1500	£1014	The homestead (51x76cm-20x30in) s. 31-Mar-94 Sotheby's Arcade, New York #134/R
$1500	£987	Late afternoon sunshine (25x36cm-10x14in) s. 13-Jun-93 Butterfield & Butterfield, San Francisco #3151/R
$1500	£1020	River landscape with cows (46x66cm-18x26in) s. 19-Nov-93 Eldred, Massachusetts #745/R
$1800	£1154	By the riverside (25x36cm-10x14in) s. i.d.1899verso. 9-Dec-92 Grogan, Massachussetts #29/R
$1800	£1184	'Midsummer' - depicting cows in landscape (51x76cm-20x30in) s. i.d.1897 verso. 2-Apr-93 Eldred, Massachusetts #444/R
$2000	£1316	One August morning (41x51cm-16x20in) s. s.i.d.1905verso. 2-Jun-93 Doyle, New York #45/R
$2200	£1447	Cows watering in river (51x76cm-20x30in) s. 31-Mar-93 Sotheby's Arcade, New York #129/R
$2600	£1806	Cows watering in pasture stream (41x51cm-16x20in) bears sig.i. 3-Mar-93 Doyle, New York #17/R
$3000	£2027	Sunshine and shower (25x36cm-10x14in) s. s.i.verso. 27-Nov-93 Young Fine Arts Auctions, Maine #99/R
$3000	£2041	Passing the old homestead (46x66cm-18x26in) s. s.i.verso. 15-Nov-93 Christie's, East, New York #37/R
$3500	£2365	The road near Fordham, New York (51x76cm-20x30in) s. 31-Mar-94 Sotheby's Arcade, New York #67/R
$3500	£2365	Market at 11th and 12th Street, Philadelphia (46x76cm-18x30in) s.d.83. 31-Mar-94 Sotheby's Arcade, New York #112/R
$4750	£2794	Figures ashore watching sailboat , s. canvas on masonite. 8-Oct-92 Freeman Fine Arts, Philadelphia #971/R
$650	£433	Return from the field (23x36cm-9x14in) s. i.verso W/C. 26-May-94 Sloan, North Bethesda #2137/R

CRAIG, William (1829-1875) American

$2600	£1781	Lawrence Creek, KY - landscape with boys fishing beside a stream (25x38cm-10x15in) s.d.1864. 10-Feb-94 Skinner, Bolton #275
$7000	£4667	Along the Ohio River, Maysville, Kentucky (30x51cm-12x20in) s.d.1864. 23-May-94 Christie's, East, New York #33/R

CRAM, Allen G (1886-1947) American

$1700	£1141	Beach scene with figures , s. 26-Mar-94 James Bakker, Cambridge #128 a
$2750	£1797	People at the beach (41x51cm-16x20in) s. board. 30-Jun-94 Mystic Fine Arts, Connecticut #137

CRAM, Edith T (1873-?) American

$1300	£839	At forest's edge (86x61cm-34x24in) mono.d.1877. 6-Jan-93 Doyle, New York #15

CRAMER, Konrad (1888-1965) American

$4750	£3188	Bouquet in white vase (51x41cm-20x16in) s.d.1928 board. 4-May-94 Doyle, New York #68/R
$800	£526	16 4/10 cents a gallon (28x43cm-11x17in) s. Indian ink wash black crayon graphite. 31-Mar-93 Sotheby's Arcade, New York #375

CRANCH, Christopher Pearse (1813-1892) American

$2000	£1379	Boaters on Grand Canal (46x74cm-18x29in) s.d.1862. 17-Feb-93 Doyle, New York #21

CRANDELL, Bradshaw (1896-1966) American

$1300	£833	Seated female bather (102x76cm-40x30in) s. 13-Dec-92 Hindman Galleries, Chicago #78
$1700	£1141	Girl with red umbrella on beach (53x46cm-21x18in) pastel. 27-Mar-94 Myers, Florida #50/R

CRANE, Bruce (1857-1937) American

$1300	£855	Autumn sunset (23x30cm-9x12in) s. 2-Jun-93 Doyle, New York #46
$1400	£940	Brook through meadow, autumn (36x51cm-14x20in) s. 6-May-94 Skinner, Bolton #78/R
$1500	£949	Mohawk Hights (20x25cm-8x10in) s. canvasboard. 2-Dec-92 Christie's, East, New York #189/R
$1600	£1088	Near Hoboken (30x51cm-12x20in) s.i.d.May 80. 15-Nov-93 Christie's, East, New York #65/R
$1900	£1242	River landscape (36x46cm-14x18in) s. 20-May-93 Boos Gallery, Michigan #472/R
$2200	£1467	Path towards town (24x40cm-9x16in) s.i. 23-May-94 Christie's, East, New York #92/R
$2400	£1633	A winter landscape (31x41cm-12x16in) s. 15-Nov-93 Christie's, East, New York #67/R
$2400	£1622	Sunset landscape (46x61cm-18x24in) s. 31-Mar-94 Sotheby's Arcade, New York #146/R
$2400	£1633	A memory (30x50cm-12x20in) s. 15-Nov-93 Christie's, East, New York #70/R

CRANE, Bruce (1857-1937) American-cont.
$3000	£1734	Countryside in autumn (36x51cm-14x20in) s. 25-Sep-92 Sotheby's Arcade, New York #151/R
$3000	£1961	Grey October (35x51cm-14x20in) s. 4-May-93 Christie's, East, New York #57/R
$3500	£2349	Golden fields (56x76cm-22x30in) s.d.1908. 8-Dec-93 Butterfield & Butterfield, San Francisco #3351/R
$4400	£2876	Stream, Indian summer (46x61cm-18x24in) s. 14-May-93 Skinner, Bolton #76/R
$6250	£3613	Harvest (51x76cm-20x30in) s. 25-Sep-92 Sotheby's Arcade, New York #150/R
$7500	£4902	Winter forest scene (71x91cm-28x36in) s. 1-Nov-92 Hanzel Galleries, Chicago #46/R
$9000	£5769	Peace and quiet (63x76cm-25x30in) s. 9-Dec-92 Butterfield & Butterfield, San Francisco #3856/R
$10000	£6329	After the storm (45x61cm-18x24in) s.i. 3-Dec-92 Sotheby's, New York #82/R
$20000	£13986	February thaw (71x91cm-28x36in) s. painted c.1915 i.stretcher. 10-Mar-93 Sotheby's, New York #118/R
$25000	£17483	Hills (117x115cm-46x45in) s. painted c.1910. 10-Mar-93 Sotheby's, New York #116/R
$28000	£17722	Winter on Long Island (63x76cm-25x30in) s. 4-Dec-92 Christie's, New York #237/R

CRARY, Robert Fulton (19th C) American?
$1000	£633	Still life with pipe, tobacco, cigar and matches (25x30cm-10x12in) s.d.1879. 2-Dec-92 Christie's, East, New York #143/R

CRASH (1961-) American
$6500	*£4362*	*That old art pimp (132x107cm-52x42in) s.i.d.8/84verso spray enamel canvas. 3-May-94 Christie's, East, New York #143/R*

CRAWFORD, Ralston (1906-1978) American
$7500	*£4747*	*Tampa - St Petersburg (26x40cm-10x16in) W/C ink pencil. 3-Dec-92 Sotheby's, New York #189/R*
$14000	*£8861*	*Buffalo grain elevators (40x50cm-16x20in) W/C pencil. 3-Dec-92 Sotheby's, New York #191/R*

CRAWLEY, Ida Jolly (1867-?) American
$950	£633	Allegory with sphinx and vulture (43x64cm-17x25in) s.i.d.1912 arched top. 13-Mar-94 Hindman Galleries, Chicago #767

CREIFELDS, Richard (1853-1939) American
$1500	£980	Monk's advice (41x61cm-16x24in) s. 16-Sep-93 Sloan, North Bethesda #3220

CRESSWELL, William Nichol (1822-1888) Canadian
$1100	£697	Boats off Flower Pot Island (54x82cm-21x32in) s.d.1864 paper on canvas. 30-Nov-92 Ritchie, Toronto #166/R (C.D 1400)
$1401	£928	Fishing camp (47x70cm-19x28in) s.d.1859. 24-Nov-92 Joyner Fine Art, Toronto #136/R (C.D 1800)
$1550	£1047	Coast scene (46x76cm-18x30in) s.d.1879 i.stretcher. 3-Nov-93 Sotheby's, Toronto #336/R (C.D 2000)
$2335	£1546	Sheep resting in a landscape (46x77cm-18x30in) s.d.1876. 18-Nov-92 Sotheby's, Toronto #165/R (C.D 3000)
$555	*£363*	*Rocky shore with boats (13x28cm-5x11in) init. W/C. 19-May-93 Sotheby's, Toronto #19/R (C.D 700)*
$706	*£462*	*White mountains (25x36cm-10x14in) s.d.1870 W/C. 10-May-93 Hodgins, Calgary 84/R (C.D 900)*
$784	*£503*	*Coastal scene with fishermen (30x51cm-12x20in) s.d.1867 W/C. 7-Dec-92 Waddingtons, Toronto #1310 (C.D 1000)*
$1268	*£829*	*Thumb Rock (38x52cm-15x20in) s.d.1881 s.i.verso W/C. 19-May-93 Sotheby's, Toronto #22/R (C.D 1600)*

CRILEY, Theodore Morrow (1880-1930) American
$650	£428	Point Aven (46x55cm-18x22in) s. 13-Jun-93 Butterfield & Butterfield, San Francisco #799/R
$1000	£658	Blossoming orchard (61x74cm-24x29in) mono. 13-Jun-93 Butterfield & Butterfield, San Francisco #822/R
$1300	£765	Rocky point from North of Sobrantes (81x102cm-32x40in) mono. bears estate st.verso. 4-Oct-92 Butterfield & Butterfield, Los Angeles #93/R
$1300	£855	Coast hills, Monterey County (66x81cm-26x32in) mono. 13-Jun-93 Butterfield & Butterfield, San Francisco #839/R
$1400	£972	Portrait of John O'Shea (81x66cm-32x26in) mono. 7-Mar-93 Butterfield & Butterfield, San Francisco #237/R
$1600	£941	Oak tree on Spring Hill (81x102cm-32x40in) mono. bears estate st.verso. 4-Oct-92 Butterfield & Butterfield, Los Angeles #83/R
$1600	£1053	Cove at Jamses (76x91cm-30x36in) mono. 13-Jun-93 Butterfield & Butterfield, San Francisco #804/R
$1600	£1053	China Cove, Point Lobos (81x66cm-32x26in) mono. board. 13-Jun-93 Butterfield & Butterfield, San Francisco #811/R
$1900	£1118	Canyon landscape (76x91cm-30x36in) mono. bears estate st.verso. 4-Oct-92 Butterfield & Butterfield, Los Angeles #221/R
$2250	£1481	Weston Beach, South Shore Point (76x91cm-30x36in) mono. 13-Jun-93 Butterfield & Butterfield, San Francisco #810/R
$2250	£1324	Carmel River near Fish Ranch (81x102cm-32x40in) mono. bears estate st.verso. 4-Oct-92 Butterfield & Butterfield, Los Angeles #92/R
$2500	£1645	San Jose Beach near Bay School (66x81cm-26x32in) mono. 13-Jun-93 Butterfield & Butterfield, San Francisco #828/R
$2750	£1618	Arizona Canyon (81x102cm-32x40in) mono. bears estate st.verso. 4-Oct-92 Butterfield & Butterfield, Los Angeles #215/R
$3250	£1912	Jameses Rocks, Bird Island (81x102cm-32x40in) mono. bears estate st.verso. 4-Oct-92 Butterfield & Butterfield, Los Angeles #91/R

CRILEY, Theodore Morrow (1880-1930) American-cont.
$3250	£1912	On Point Lobos North shore, Carmel (77x91cm-30x36in) mono. bears estate st.verso. 4-Oct-92 Butterfield & Butterfield, Los Angeles #94/R
$3750	£2206	Road through Fremont (97x124cm-38x49in) mono. bears estate st.verso. 4-Oct-92 Butterfield & Butterfield, Los Angeles #95/R
$4250	£2500	North shore - Point Lobos (102x122cm-40x48in) mono. bears estate st.verso. 4-Oct-92 Butterfield & Butterfield, Los Angeles #82/R
$5000	£2941	Weston beach, South shore point (102x112cm-40x44in) mono. bears estate st.verso. 4-Oct-92 Butterfield & Butterfield, Los Angeles #90/R

CRISP, Arthur (1881-?) American/Canadian
$677	£455	A beauty in period costume (54x36cm-21x14in) s. board. 29-Nov-93 Waddingtons, Toronto #1405 (C.D 900)

CRISS, Francis (1901-1973) American
$3200	£2177	Romans (61x91cm-24x36in) s. masonite. 15-Nov-93 Christie's, East, New York #106/R

CRITE, Allan Rohan (1910-) American
$900	£520	Young woman (30x23cm-12x9in) s.d.1932 canvasboard. 27-Sep-92 James Bakker, Cambridge #43/R
$900	£520	Boston street scene (41x51cm-16x20in) s.d.1939 s.verso canvasboard. 25-Sep-92 Sotheby's Arcade, New York #278/R
$2500	£1667	Slumber time (20x25cm-8x10in) s.d.34 canvasboard. 22-May-94 James Bakker, Cambridge #9/R

CROCKER, John Denison (1823-?) American
$1600	£1074	Morning mist (46x71cm-18x28in) s. 24-Mar-94 Mystic Fine Arts, Connecticut #155/R
$3800	£2517	Young girl with basket of flowers (51x41cm-20x16in) s.d.1886. 23-Sep-93 Mystic Fine Arts, Connecticut #94/R

CROCKFORD, Duncan (1920-1991) Canadian
$662	£438	Spring break up on the Sheep River, Alberta (30x41cm-12x16in) s.d.80 i.stretcher. 16-Nov-92 Hodgins, Calgary #217/R (C.D 850)
$764	£489	Banff Valley, Alberta (41x51cm-16x20in) s.d.1971 i.stretcher. 26-Apr-93 Levis, Calgary #40 (C.D 974)
$1077	£718	View of the Calling Valley (46x61cm-18x24in) s.d. 30-May-94 Hodgins, Calgary #334/R (C.D 1500)
$1244	£846	Looking east from the Neutral Hills near Consort (41x51cm-16x20in) s. i.stretcher painted 1979. 15-Nov-93 Hodgins, Calgary #234/R (C.D 1650)
$1569	£1026	Mount Eisenhauer - from Bow Valley (56x76cm-22x30in) s. board. 10-May-93 Hodgins, Calgary #307 (C.D 2000)
$1790	£1186	Panther River (46x61cm-18x24in) s.d.1964. 16-Nov-92 Hodgins, Calgary #135 (C.D 2300)
$2040	£1333	View from hilltop house near de Winton (61x76cm-24x30in) s.d.1974. 10-May-93 Hodgins, Calgary #110/R (C.D 2600)
$2111	£1436	Mountain scene (61x76cm-24x30in) s.d.1960. 15-Nov-93 Hodgins, Calgary #69 (C.D 2800)
$3446	£2328	Untitled - Castle Mountain and Bow river (61x76cm-24x30in) s.d.1965. 25-Apr-94 Levis, Calgary #62/R (C.D 4750)
$3580	£2371	Silver city (61x76cm-24x30in) s.d.1970. 16-Nov-92 Hodgins, Calgary #58/R (C.D 4600)

CROPSEY, Jasper Francis (1823-1900) American
$3500	£2288	People fishing on Greenwood Lake (8x13cm-3x5in) s. board. 1-Nov-92 Litchfield Auction Gallery #105
$3750	£2168	Cows watering along river in autumn (21x25cm-8x10in) 25-Sep-92 Sotheby's Arcade, New York #63 a/R
$5000	£2890	Sunset (7x11cm-3x4in) init.d.1875 board. 23-Sep-92 Christie's, New York #14 a/R
$8000	£5594	The brook (20x15cm-8x6in) s.d.1881 s.i.stretcher. 11-Mar-93 Christie's, New York #11/R
$9500	£6250	Anne Hathaway's cottage (46x76cm-18x30in) indist.i. 31-Mar-93 Sotheby's Arcade, New York #48/R
$11000	£6258	Autumn by the brook (25x39cm-10x15in) init.d.1855. 23-Sep-92 Christie's, New York #73/R
$11000	£7333	Italian landscape (30x51cm-12x20in) s.d.1875. 16-Mar-94 Christie's, New York #19/R
$12000	£7692	Autumn on Hudson (36x53cm-14x21in) s.d.1884. 27-May-93 Sotheby's, New York #184/R
$12000	£7595	Rowing at sunset (25x20cm-10x8in) s.d.1873. 4-Dec-92 Christie's, New York #186/R
$16000	£10811	White Mountain autumn landscape with cattle grazing (31x51cm-12x20in) s.d.1875. 5-Nov-93 Skinner, Bolton #46/R
$16000	£10738	Fishing on a lake (31x51cm-12x20in) s.d.1890. 3-Dec-93 Christie's, New York #99/R
$16000	£10127	Pond in springtime (26x20cm-10x8in) s.d.1879. 4-Dec-92 Christie's, New York #219/R
$18000	£12081	Seascape (23x45cm-9x18in) s.d.1882. 3-Dec-93 Christie's, New York #95/R
$25000	£16556	Autumn landscape with boaters on lake (30x51cm-12x20in) s.d.1875. 23-Sep-93 Sotheby's, New York #57/R
$26000	£15029	Winter in Switzerland (38x61cm-15x24in) s.d.1860 canvas on panel. 23-Sep-92 Christie's, New York #18/R
$35000	£22152	View on Hudson River (56x68cm-22x27in) s.d.1852 s.indist.i.stretcher. 4-Dec-92 Christie's, New York #192/R
$41000	£27517	Fisherman in autumn landscape (30x51cm-12x20in) s.d.1879. 2-Dec-93 Sotheby's, New York #4/R
$47500	£30449	Autumn by lake (46x96cm-18x38in) s.d.1890. 27-May-93 Sotheby's, New York #185/R
$70000	£44872	Saw mill river (46x97cm-18x38in) 26-May-93 Christie's, New York #56/R

CROPSEY, Jasper Francis (1823-1900) American-cont.
$170000	£108974	Sunset at Greenwood lake (91x150cm-36x59in) s.d.1888. 27-May-93 Sotheby's, New York #193/R
$1300	*£867*	*The artist sketching (19x28cm-7x11in) init.d.1858 pencil. 23-May-94 Christie's, East, New York #2/R*
$1800	*£1208*	*View of Mount Chocorua (25x41cm-10x16in) init.i.d.1855 graphite. 4-Mar-94 Skinner, Bolton #206/R*
$5500	£3667	An autumnal afternoon, Hastings-on-Hudson (34x51cm-13x20in) s.d.1890 W/C pencil. 23-May-94 Christie's, East, New York #62/R
$5500	£3667	Hudson River landscape (33x52cm-13x20in) s. W/C pencil paper on board. 23-May-94 Christie's, East, New York #65/R
$9500	£6643	On the docks (37x63cm-15x25in) s.d.1886 W/C pencil china paper on board. 11-Mar-93 Christie's, New York #16/R

CROPSEY, Jasper Francis (attrib) (1823-1900) American
$1163	£750	River landscape with cattle at ford (41x61cm-16x24in) 15-Jul-94 Christie's, London #59/R

CROPSEY, Jasper Francis (style) (1823-1900) American
$2534	£1273	Wooded landscape with a heron standing in water (46x66cm-18x26in) panel. 5-Sep-92 AB Stockholms Auktionsverk, Stockholm #4165/R (S.KR 13000)

CROSS, Henry H (1837-1918) American
$950	£638	Moose and hunter in snowy mountain landscape (74x91cm-29x36in) s.d.1899. 2-May-94 Selkirks, St. Louis #107/R
$10000	£6579	Bay pacer, believed to be 'St. Patrick', on race-track (71x107cm-28x42in) 4-Jun-93 Sotheby's, New York #167 a/R

CROWNINSHIELD, Frederic (1845-1918) American
$700	£470	Apple blossoms (46x71cm-18x28in) s. 24-Jun-93 Mystic Fine Arts, Connecticut #135 a

CRUZ-DIEZ, Carlos (1923-) Venezuelan
$3303	£2202	Physichromie n.646 (100x150cm-39x59in) s.i.d.1973verso acrylic panel plastic strips. 15-Mar-94 Finarte, Milan #279/R (I.L 5500000)
$1696	*£1067*	*Physichromie no 1272 (16x19cm-6x7in) d.1990 s.verso mixed media. 21-Apr-93 Germann, Zurich #37 (S.FR 2400)*
$4000	*£2649*	*Physiochromie No. 437 (60x59cm-24x23in) s.i.d.1968 verso mixed media panel. 24-Nov-92 Christie's, New York #264/R*
$17000	*£11333*	*Physiochromie No.336 (61x242cm-24x95in) s.i.d.1967 i.verso mixed media panel diptych. 18-May-94 Christie's, New York #170/R*

CUAIK, Tere (1960-) Mexican
$1108	£729	Gran jarron (100x100cm-39x39in) s.d.1991. 4-Nov-92 Mora, Castelltort & Quintana, Juarez #21/R (M.P 3500000)

CUCUEL, Edward (1879-1951) American
$1875	£1250	Women by the lake (22x33cm-9x13in) s. panel painted 1931. 30-Jan-94 Unicum, Warsaw #3 (P.Z 40000000)
$2175	£1460	View of town (56x76cm-22x30in) s. panel. 13-Oct-93 Vendu Notarishuis, Rotterdam #47 (D.FL 4000)
$8000	£5594	Gitta Cucuel the dancer. Sketch of woman (121x95cm-48x37in) s. double-sided. 11-Mar-93 Christie's, New York #157/R
$9000	£6294	House by the river (63x79cm-25x31in) s. 11-Mar-93 Christie's, New York #160/R
$16490	£11067	Girl in boat (41x52cm-16x20in) s. painted c.1920. 22-Jun-93 Sotheby's, Munich #166/R (DM 28000)
$16733	£11155	La robe bleue (65x80cm-26x31in) s. 6-Jun-94 Wolfgang Ketterer, Munich #58/R (DM 28000)
$19110	£13000	Lady wearing a white dress beside a lake at evening (68x55cm-27x22in) s. i.verso. 16-Nov-93 Phillips, London #78/R
$20613	£13834	Studio visitors (79x64cm-31x25in) s. s.i.stretcher. 22-Jun-93 Sotheby's, Munich #165/R (DM 35000)
$27000	£15607	Woman picking flowers (81x81cm-32x32in) s. painted c.1920's. 24-Sep-92 Sotheby's, New York #118/R
$27545	£17886	Au bord du lac - young lady in summer dress on garden bench (101x91cm-40x36in) s. s.i.verso. 4-Jun-94 Karrenbauer, Konstanz #1617/R (DM 44000)
$34922	£23438	Two young women gathering blossoms by the water (90x80cm-35x31in) s. i.verso. 4-Dec-93 Lempertz, Cologne #106/R (DM 60000)
$39000	£26000	Lady with umbrella by a lake in autumn (120x95cm-47x37in) s. 4-Jun-94 Neumeister, Munich #179/R (DM 65000)
$800	*£519*	*Monte Carlo by moonlight (27x33cm-11x13in) s. gouache paper on board. 9-Sep-93 Sotheby's Arcade, New York #320/R*

CUCUEL, Edward (attrib) (1879-1951) American
$650	*£430*	*Monte Carlo (23x25cm-9x10in) s. gouache. 19-Jun-94 Hindman Galleries, Chicago #320*

CUEVAS, Jose Luis (1934-) Mexican
$593	*£401*	*Dos personajes (14x19cm-6x7in) s.73 ink dr. 27-Apr-94 Louis Morton, Mexico #721 (M.P 2000)*
$1000	*£676*	*La prostituta (45x66cm-18x26in) s.d.1954 ink wash htd.white. 21-Oct-93 Butterfield & Butterfield, San Francisco #2743/R*
$2076	*£1403*	*Augusto Bolte (29x20cm-11x8in) s.d.1980 W/C pencil. 27-Apr-94 Louis Morton, Mexico #389/R (M.P 7000)*

CUEVAS, Jose Luis (1934-) Mexican-cont.
$2076	£1403	La Herida (37x47cm-15x19in) s.i.d.1981 pencil ink dr. 27-Apr-94 Louis Morton, Mexico #509/R (M.P 7000)
$2500	£1678	Untitled (52x70cm-20x28in) s.d.1959 ink W/C. 7-Jan-94 Gary Nader, Miami #89/R
$2903	£1948	Autoretrato con modelo (20x29cm-8x11in) d.1979 W/C pastel pencil. 1-Dec-93 Louis Morton, Mexico #206/R (M.P 9000)
$3263	£2204	Vincent Van Gogh y Paul Gauguin (34x24cm-13x9in) s.d.1968 W/C ink. 27-Apr-94 Louis Morton, Mexico #418/R (M.P 11000)
$3559	£2405	Autorretrato con modelos (38x52cm-15x20in) s.d.1978 W/C ink. 27-Apr-94 Louis Morton, Mexico #630/R (M.P 12000)
$5500	£3716	Autoretrato con prostituta (70x55cm-28x22in) s.i.d.III 1978 brush ink wash. 23-Nov-93 Christie's, New York #205/R
$6500	£4248	Barrio Chino I (48x65cm-19x26in) s.i.d.1981 wash W/C pen. 17-May-93 Christie's, New York #228/R
$8000	£5229	Los Papeles de Salazar No.4 (80x121cm-31x48in) s.i.d.23.II.83 wash W/C pen. 17-May-93 Christie's, New York #227/R
$19102	£12245	Lucrecia y Cesar Borgia (67x101cm-26x40in) s.d.1968 mixed media. 29-Apr-93 Louis Morton, Mexico #67 (M.P 60000)

CUGAT, Delia (1935-) Argentinian
$8000	£5298	Mujer en el Muelle (96x130cm-38x51in) s. 24-Nov-92 Christie's, New York #251/R
$10000	£6667	Sin titulo (73x92cm-29x36in) s.d.1984verso. 18-May-94 Sotheby's, New York #395/R

CULLEN, Maurice Galbraith (1866-1934) Canadian
$3171	£2073	Grand Canal, Venice (25x34cm-10x13in) s. panel. 19-May-93 Sotheby's, Toronto #389/R (C.D 4000)
$3580	£2371	Early spring (27x34cm-11x13in) s. board. 18-Nov-92 Sotheby's, Toronto #126/R (C.D 4600)
$4716	£2985	Moonlight (59x73cm-23x29in) s.d.1902. 1-Dec-92 Fraser Pinneys, Quebec #141 a (C.D 6000)
$5448	£3608	Mediterranean view (44x55cm-17x22in) canvas laid on board. 18-Nov-92 Sotheby's, Toronto #35/R (C.D 7000)
$6485	£4104	Pont St-Michel,Paris (21x25cm-8x10in) s.i. board. 1-Dec-92 Fraser Pinneys, Quebec #38/R (C.D 8250)
$10897	£7216	Venice (44x53cm-17x21in) s.d.1902. 18-Nov-92 Sotheby's, Toronto #51/R (C.D 14000)
$13107	£8738	Autumn near St Jovite (45x60cm-18x24in) s. 13-May-94 Joyner Fine Art, Toronto #99/R (C.D 18000)
$15855	£10363	Au petit matin (43x71cm-17x28in) s. 18-May-93 Joyner Fine Art, Toronto #12/R (C.D 20000)
$17124	£11340	Moonlight landcape (74x168cm-29x66in) mono. canvas laid on board. 18-Nov-92 Sotheby's, Toronto #200/R (C.D 22000)
$24757	£16505	Spring break-up on the North River (60x81cm-24x32in) s. 13-May-94 Joyner Fine Art, Toronto #27/R (C.D 34000)
$58115	£39267	Country road in winter (62x54cm-24x21in) s. 3-Nov-93 Sotheby's, Toronto #134/R (C.D 75000)
$58252	£38835	Hoar frost, Cache River (45x55cm-18x22in) s. 13-May-94 Joyner Fine Art, Toronto #50/R (C.D 80000)
$1090	£722	Stream in winter (15x11cm-6x4in) s. W/C. 16-Nov-92 Hodgins, Calgary #220/R (C.D 1400)
$4670	£3093	Montreal river, early winter (56x46cm-22x18in) s.i.d. January 1925verso pastel paper laid panel. 18-Nov-92 Sotheby's, Toronto #11/R (C.D 6000)

CULLEN, Maurice Galbraith (attrib) (1866-1934) Canadian
$1323	£876	Sugar cabin (61x77cm-24x30in) 18-Nov-92 Sotheby's, Toronto #160/R (C.D 1700)

CULMER, Henry L A (1854-1914) American
$563	£378	River and forest in filtered sunlight (15x25cm-6x10in) s. W/C. 23-Mar-94 Maynards, Vancouver #396 (C.D 775)

CUMING, Frederick (1865-1949) American
$700	£455	New London Harbour (51x61cm-20x24in) s. 9-Sep-93 Sotheby's Arcade, New York #196/R

CUMMING, Arthur (19th C) American
$900	£604	A tree-lined fence (43x76cm-17x30in) s. 25-Mar-94 Eldred, Massachusetts #719/R
$909	£610	Ship in dry dock (76x51cm-30x20in) s. 24-Mar-94 Mystic Fine Arts, Connecticut #184/R
$900	£588	Coastal scene (61x91cm-24x36in) s.d.1905 W/C. 1-Nov-92 Hanzel Galleries, Chicago #34/R

CUNEO, Cyrus (1878-1916) American
$5436	£3600	Giving out matches, Friday Night Supper (39x28cm-15x11in) s. i.verso board. 13-Nov-92 Christie's, London #208/R

CUNEO, Jose (1889-1977) Uruguayan
$2200	£1410	Jarron con flores y libros (65x54cm-26x21in) s. 7-Dec-92 Gomensoro, Montevideo #83/R
$2600	£1667	Paisaje en azul, Versailles (37x46cm-15x18in) s. fibre. 7-Dec-92 Gomensoro, Montevideo #85
$2600	£1699	Jarron con amapolas (80x63cm-31x25in) s.d.1947. 27-Jun-94 Gomensoro, Montevideo #34/R
$3800	£2436	Paisaje Cagnes sur mer (33x40cm-13x16in) s.d.1928 board. 7-Dec-92 Gomensoro, Montevideo #84/R
$5000	£3356	Quinta Capuro en Santa Lucia (48x58cm-19x23in) s.d.1942 s.d.1977verso fibre. 29-Nov-93 Gomensoro, Montevideo #39/R

CUNEO, Jose (1889-1977) Uruguayan-cont.
$5200	£3399	Paisaje lacustre con barcas (50x65cm-20x26in) s.d.1951. 3-May-93 Gomensoro, Montevideo #63/R
$7000	£4667	Corral de Piedra (50x64cm-20x25in) s.d.1945 i.d.verso board. 18-May-94 Sotheby's, New York #303/R
$8000	£5229	Ranchos (54x64cm-21x25in) s.d.1931. 3-May-93 Gomensoro, Montevideo #64/R
$9000	£5882	Casas de Cagnes (73x60cm-29x24in) s. panel. 26-Oct-92 Gomensoro, Montevideo #82/R
$10000	£6711	Isla de Gorriti, Pinares (50x65cm-20x26in) s.d.1951. 29-Nov-93 Gomensoro, Montevideo #38/R
$10500	£6863	La canada (100x101cm-39x40in) s. 26-Oct-92 Gomensoro, Montevideo #81
$12000	£6030	La Casa de los Novios - Punta del Este (60x73cm-24x29in) s.d.1949. 31-Aug-92 Gomensoro, Montevideo #43/R
$12000	£8108	Casas, Florida (54x65cm-21x26in) s.d.1931. 22-Nov-93 Sotheby's, New York #180/R
$13000	£8497	Rancho pobre (65x50cm-26x20in) s.d.1946 board. 4-Oct-93 Gomensoro, Montevideo #94/R
$16500	£10714	Suburbios de Florida (54x66cm-21x26in) s. oil. 30-Aug-93 Gomensoro, Montevideo #85/R
$27500	£18333	Luna (99x70cm-39x28in) s. painted c.1935. 17-May-94 Sotheby's, New York #27/R
$30000	£20134	Luna con rancho (147x97cm-58x38in) s. 29-Nov-93 Gomensoro, Montevideo #104/R
$30000	£19608	Luna del Barranco (100x81cm-39x32in) s.d.1931. 3-May-93 Gomensoro, Montevideo #76/R
$37500	£24834	Luna Menguante (90x90cm-35x35in) s. s.i.d.1931 verso. 23-Nov-92 Sotheby's, New York #40/R
$650	*£422*	*La esquilla (27x20cm-11x8in) s.d.1969 W/C. 30-Aug-93 Gomensoro, Montevideo #87*
$650	*£430*	*Nido y horneros sobre tuna (20x16cm-8x6in) s. pastel. 28-Jun-93 Gomensoro, Montevideo #16*
$800	*£523*	*Jarron con flores (62x46cm-24x18in) s.d.1928 pastel. 4-Oct-93 Gomensoro, Montevideo #96*
$800	*£513*	*Puerto de Salto (63x48cm-25x19in) s.d.1946 ink dr. 7-Dec-92 Gomensoro, Montevideo #87*
$800	*£530*	*Rio y arboleda (65x50cm-26x20in) s.i. W/C. 28-Jun-93 Gomensoro, Montevideo #62*
$1100	*£719*	*Carreta (21x31cm-8x12in) s. pastel. 3-May-93 Gomensoro, Montevideo #61*
$1100	*£719*	*Revoleando porotos (20x32cm-8x13in) s. pastel. 3-May-93 Gomensoro, Montevideo #62*
$1500	*£987*	*Carneando (33x48cm-13x19in) s.d.1952 W/C. 31-May-93 Gomensoro, Montevideo #37*
$1500	*£987*	*Descuartizando (49x33cm-19x13in) s.d.1950 W/C. 31-May-93 Gomensoro, Montevideo #38*
$1700	*£899*	*Carreta de bueyes en el arenal (58x43cm-23x17in) s. W/C. 10-Sep-92 Gomensoro, Montevideo #64*
$2600	*£1529*	*Paisaje serrano con bandada de teros (36x50cm-14x20in) s.d.1953 W/C. 5-Oct-92 Gomensoro, Montevideo #27/R*
$2600	*£1711*	*Estancia (64x49cm-25x19in) s. ink W/C. 31-May-93 Gomensoro, Montevideo #35/R*
$2800	*£1795*	*Paisaje con monte, nandues y teros (61x47cm-24x19in) s. W/C. 7-Dec-92 Gomensoro, Montevideo #86*
$3000	*£1563*	*Paisaje Campero (69x54cm-27x21in) s. W/C ink. 12-Aug-92 Castells & Castells, Montevideo #51/R*

CUNEO, Rinaldo (1877-1935) American
$750	£497	Landscape with houses 'Richmond Dist' (28x30cm-11x12in) s. canvas on board. 14-Jun-94 John Moran, Pasadena #14
$1200	£795	San Francisco Bay. A Landscape (28x30cm-11x12in) s. canvas laid down on board double-sided. 15-Jun-94 Butterfield & Butterfield, San Francisco #4582/R

CUNSOLO, Victor J (1898-1937) Argentinian
$8000	£4624	Riachuelo (32x44cm-13x17in) board. 23-Sep-92 Roldan & Cia, Buenos Aires #30

CUPRIEN, Frank W (1871-1948) American
$1100	£733	The Arch Arch Beach (41x56cm-16x22in) s. i.stretcher. 15-Mar-94 John Moran, Pasadena #89
$2750	£1897	Shadow of the cliff, Cal. (46x71cm-18x28in) s. 16-Feb-93 John Moran, Pasadena #43
$6500	£4362	Song of the pines (63x69cm-25x27in) s. s.i.stretcher. 8-Dec-93 Butterfield & Butterfield, San Francisco #3450/R

CURLEY, Donald (20th C) Canadian
$906	£612	'Gateway', painted Peel Inlet, Queen Charlotte Islands, B.C (60x90cm-24x35in) s. oil acrylic board. 23-Nov-93 Joyner Fine Art, Toronto #286/R (C.D 1200)

CURNOE, Greg (20th C) Canadian
$874	*£583*	*Self-portrait 1981 (30x22cm-12x9in) s.i.d.1981 W/C. 13-May-94 Joyner Fine Art, Toronto #159 (C.D 1200)*

CURRAN, Charles Courtney (1861-1942) American
$1200	£816	Portrait of a girl (30x23cm-12x9in) 14-Apr-94 Freeman Fine Arts, Philadelphia #1035 a/R
$1600	£1081	Landscape with cloudy sky (46x61cm-18x24in) s. masonite. 31-Mar-94 Sotheby's Arcade, New York #269/R
$1900	£1098	On the crest of the mountain (22x30cm-9x12in) s.i. init.i.verso masonite. 23-Sep-92 Christie's, New York #168/R
$2000	£1282	Portrait of young girl (51x30cm-20x12in) s.d.93. 9-Dec-92 Butterfield & Butterfield, San Francisco #3922/R
$2250	£1521	The fox holds his ground (45x55cm-18x22in) s.d.1941 i.verso masonite. 31-Mar-94 Sotheby's Arcade, New York #283/R
$2700	£1765	Pier fisherman on New York Harbour (13x20cm-5x8in) s. wooden cigar box cover. 18-Sep-93 James Bakker, Cambridge #10/R
$5000	£2890	Gathering flowers (41x20cm-16x8in) s.d.94. 23-Sep-92 Christie's, New York #166/R

CURRAN, Charles Courtney (1861-1942) American-cont.

$6500	£4305	Blue Hills and Golden Rod (23x18cm-9x7in) s. 15-Jun-94 Butterfield & Butterfield, San Francisco #4431/R
$10000	£6667	Deep sea fantasy (81x46cm-32x18in) s.i.d.1929 canvas laid down on masonite. 26-May-94 Christie's, New York #105/R
$19000	£12667	The edge of the woods (76x76cm-30x30in) s.d.1912. 16-Mar-94 Christie's, New York #103/R
$21000	£13462	West wind (76x76cm-30x30in) s.d.1918 s.i.verso masonite. 27-May-93 Sotheby's, New York #20/R
$26000	£16456	May afternoon (51x77cm-20x53in) s.d.1916. 4-Dec-92 Christie's, New York #53/R
$35000	£22152	The cabbage field (76x76cm-30x30in) s.d.1914. 4-Dec-92 Christie's, New York #97/R
$47500	£31879	May morning (56x46cm-22x18in) s. i. verso. 2-Dec-93 Sotheby's, New York #116/R
$60000	£39735	Ladies amongst flowers on a hill (56x46cm-22x18in) s.d.1914. 15-Jun-94 Butterfield & Butterfield, San Francisco #4454/R
$1600	£1067	Old garden at Welbord, the home and haunt of Shakepeare (41x30cm-16x12in) s. gouache board. 23-May-94 Christie's, East, New York #138
$2000	£1361	Rhododendrons (56x46cm-22x18in) s.d.1914 pastel paper laid down on canvas. 15-Nov-93 Christie's, East, New York #152
$2600	£1733	The Connoisseur - the artist's father (30x41cm-12x16in) s.d.1911 pastel board. 23-May-94 Christie's, East, New York #84/R

CURRIER, J Frank (1843-1909) American

$2500	£1623	Head of boy (41x37cm-16x15in) panel. 9-Sep-93 Sotheby's Arcade, New York #122/R
$900	£604	Tree by a house (10x20cm-4x8in) s. pastel. 24-Mar-94 Mystic Fine Arts, Connecticut #115

CURRY, John Steuart (1897-1946) American

$950	£629	Landscape (36x28cm-14x11in) s.verso. 2-Oct-93 Boos Gallery, Michigan #274/R
$13000	£7514	Study for the Freeing of the Slaves (37x84cm-15x33in) s.indis.d.193. board on board painted arch. 23-Sep-92 Christie's, New York #245/R
$2000	£1307	Children and school sleigh (20x43cm-8x17in) init. gouache board. 4-May-93 Christie's, East, New York #163/R
$14000	£8861	Study for the Mississippi Flood (34x26cm-13x10in) s.d.1937 W/C gouache pencil. 3-Dec-92 Sotheby's, New York #69/R

CURRY, R F (1872-1945) American

$587	£394	Mountain lake (50x62cm-20x24in) s. i.verso board. 9-Dec-93 Neumeister, Munich #2795 (DM 1000)

CURRY, Robert F (1872-1945) American

$825	£539	Stream in autumn (71x56cm-28x22in) s. 14-May-93 Skinner, Bolton #96/R
$1010	£664	Sunny day in mountains (60x73cm-24x29in) s. canvas on board. 2-Nov-92 Sotheby's, Amsterdam #590 (D.FL 1800)
$1103	£637	Snow covered wooded Alpine landscape (60x75cm-24x30in) s. i.verso. 26-Sep-92 Michael Bode, Pforzheim #686/R (DM 1600)
$1228	£813	Mountain landscape with houses (80x60cm-31x24in) s. 25-Sep-93 Michael Bode, Pforzheim #631/R (DM 2000)
$1548	£1032	Winter mountain landscape (60x80cm-24x31in) s. 15-Mar-94 Weiner, Munich #242 (DM 2600)
$1793	£1195	Encampment houses, Passau (81x100cm-32x39in) s. 7-Jun-94 Karl & Faber, Munich #594/R (DM 3000)
$2053	£1378	Winter in Oberstdorf, Allgau, with sunlit farmhouse (80x100cm-31x39in) s. 8-Dec-93 Neumeister, Munich #586/R (DM 3500)
$2829	£1736	Riverside houses (60x75cm-24x30in) s. 14-Oct-92 Weiner, Munich #245/R (DM 4200)

CURTIS, David (20th C) American

$1100	£692	Pastoral twilight (51x102cm-20x40in) s. 25-Apr-93 James Bakker, Cambridge #148/R

CURTIS, Leland (1897-?) American

$650	£430	Atmospheric landscape (41x51cm-16x20in) s. 14-Jun-94 John Moran, Pasadena #54
$1500	£987	Oasis (46x61cm-18x24in) s. 13-Jun-93 Butterfield & Butterfield, San Francisco #877/R
$2000	£1389	Desert and mountains (76x102cm-30x40in) s. s.i.stretcher. 7-Mar-93 Butterfield & Butterfield, San Francisco #230/R

CURTIS, Ralph W (1854-1902) American

$900	£570	Still life (14x23cm-6x9in) panel. 2-Dec-92 Christie's, East, New York #126

CURTIS, Ralph W (attrib) (1854-1902) American

$900	£604	European harbour, init.d.1906 panel. 24-Jun-93 Mystic Fine Arts, Connecticut #118a

CUSI, Ezio (20th C) Mexican

$639	£432	Paisaje colorido (60x80cm-24x31in) 20-Oct-93 Louis Morton, Mexico #124/R (M.P 2000)

CUSTIS, Eleanor Parke (1897-1983) American

$650	£455	Among the ruins (48x64cm-19x25in) gouache. 7-Feb-93 James Bakker, Cambridge #254
$650	£455	Street scene with figures (38x41cm-15x16in) s. gouache chl. 7-Feb-93 James Bakker, Cambridge #9
$750	£503	At the foot of the Matterhorn (38x33cm-15x13in) s. gouache over chl. 5-Dec-93 James Bakker, Cambridge #31/R
$800	£503	At the well (64x48cm-25x19in) s. chl gouache. 25-Apr-93 James Bakker, Cambridge #73/R

CUSTIS, Eleanor Parke (1897-1983) American-cont.
$1000   £578   Boston street scene (20x23cm-8x9in) gouache. 27-Sep-92 James Bakker, Cambridge #145/R

CUTRONE, Ronnie (1948-) American
$4000   £2649   Beauty is in the eye of the beholder (183x184cm-72x72in) s.init.i.d.1984stretcher acrylic six panels. 17-Nov-92 Christie's, East, New York #59/R

CUTTS, Gertrude Spurr (1858-1941) Canadian
$526   £360   Dead birds by the side of mossy bank (33x43cm-13x17in) s.d.1884 panel. 9-Feb-94 Bonhams, Chelsea #32
$713   £466   Path to farm (18x25cm-7x10in) s. board. 19-May-93 Sotheby's, Toronto #25/R (C.D 900)
$861   £574   Farmscene with woman picking fruit in orchard (52x81cm-20x32in) s.d.96. 30-May-94 Ritchie, Toronto #203/R (C.D 1200)

CUZCO SCHOOL   South American
$3000   £1974   Joseph with the Christ Child (141x108cm-56x43in) 20-Jul-94 Sotheby's Arcade, New York #49/R
$4287   £2877   Portrait d'une Infante sous les traits d'une Sainte peut etre S.Thecle (93x73cm-37x29in) 15-Dec-93 Guy Loudmer, Paris #139/R (F.FR 25000)
$7000   £4575   La Virgen Maria y el Nino Jesus. San Jose y el Nino Jesus (36x31cm-14x12in) two. 17-May-93 Christie's, New York #82/R
$24000   £16216   La Virgen de Pomata y el Nino Jesus (196x135cm-77x53in) i.d.1800. 23-Nov-93 Christie's, New York #71/R

CUZCO SCHOOL, 17th C   South American
$16000   £10667   La Vision de San Antonio de Padua (168x112cm-66x44in) 18-May-94 Sotheby's, New York #166/R

CUZCO SCHOOL, 17th/18th C   South American
$4286   £2857   The Madonna and Child (151x110cm-59x43in) 11-May-94 Christie's, Amsterdam #14/R (D.FL 8000)

CUZCO SCHOOL, 18th C   South American
$3200   £2133   The Annunciation (113x153cm-44x60in) 17-May-94 Christie's, East, New York #668
$4000   £2667   Sacrificio de Manoah (80x108cm-31x43in) i. 18-May-94 Sotheby's, New York #162/R
$4000   £2649   Sagrado Matrimonio (66x81cm-26x32in) 23-Nov-92 Sotheby's, New York #119/R
$5000   £3289   Virgen de Belen (185x123cm-73x48in) 20-Jul-94 Sotheby's Arcade, New York #53/R
$5000   £3333   Arcangel con Arcabuz (85x65cm-33x26in) 18-May-94 Christie's, New York #79/R
$5487   £3682   Archange Rephael (108x78cm-43x31in) 15-Dec-93 Guy Loudmer, Paris #137/R (F.FR 32000)
$5487   £3682   Saint Isidore Le Laboureur (77x61cm-30x24in) 15-Dec-93 Guy Loudmer, Paris #141/R (F.FR 32000)
$6500   £4305   Santiago De Matamoros (62x42cm-24x17in) 23-Nov-92 Sotheby's, New York #107/R
$7000   £4575   Santiago de Matamoros (62x49cm-24x19in) 18-May-93 Sotheby's, New York #85/R
$7000   £4575   La Sagrada Familia (188x119cm-74x47in) 17-May-93 Christie's, New York #83/R
$7500   £5000   Virgen de Pomata (108x83cm-43x33in) 18-May-94 Sotheby's, New York #154/R
$8000   £5405   Nuestro Senor de Los Temblores (157x104cm-62x41in) 22-Nov-93 Sotheby's, New York #136/R
$8000   £5298   Capac Yupamqui, Quinto Rey Inca (45x38cm-18x15in) 23-Nov-92 Sotheby's, New York #113/R
$8000   £5405   La Adoracion de la Eucaristia (180x118cm-71x46in) 22-Nov-93 Sotheby's, New York #135/R
$8500   £5667   Arcangel con Arcabuz y Cuerno de Polvora (85x65cm-33x26in) 18-May-94 Christie's, New York #80/R
$9000   £6000   La Immaculada (191x159cm-75x63in) 18-May-94 Sotheby's, New York #167/R
$9000   £6081   Arcangel Miguel (155x104cm-61x41in) 23-Nov-93 Christie's, New York #76/R
$9430   £6329   Saint Georges terrassant le dragon (68x62cm-27x24in) 15-Dec-93 Guy Loudmer, Paris #143/R (F.FR 55000)
$9500   £6333   Nuestra Senora de Chocharcas (136x93cm-54x37in) 18-May-94 Sotheby's, New York #156/R
$10000   £6536   La Corte Celestial (117x104cm-46x41in) 17-May-93 Christie's, New York #84/R
$11000   £7432   Arcangel (138x107cm-54x42in) 22-Nov-93 Sotheby's, New York #138/R
$11000   £7333   La Virgen de Pomata y el Nino Jesus (121x85cm-48x33in) 18-May-94 Christie's, New York #81/R
$12000   £7947   Archangel Gabriel (132x97cm-52x38in) 24-Nov-92 Christie's, New York #71/R
$12000   £7843   Nuestra Senora Pastora (106x91cm-42x36in) 17-May-93 Christie's, New York #77/R
$12000   £7947   Huida a Egipto (81x125cm-32x49in) 24-Nov-92 Christie's, New York #77/R
$12002   £8055   Archange au mousquet (149x104cm-59x41in) 15-Dec-93 Guy Loudmer, Paris #135/R (F.FR 70000)
$14000   £9272   Arcangel con Arquebus (112x83cm-44x33in) 24-Nov-92 Christie's, New York #72/R
$16000   £10811   Anunciacion (161x118cm-63x46in) 23-Nov-93 Christie's, New York #79/R
$18000   £12162   Virgen de Pomata con Rosario (161x110cm-63x43in) 23-Nov-93 Christie's, New York #81/R
$19000   £12418   San Isidro Labrador (84x60cm-33x24in) 17-May-93 Christie's, New York #81/R
$24000   £16216   Huida a Egipto (81x125cm-32x49in) 23-Nov-93 Christie's, New York #78/R
$28000   £18919   Nuestra Senora del Rosario (234x186cm-92x73in) 23-Nov-93 Christie's, New York #70/R
$30000   £19868   Adoracion de Los Reyes Magos (168x207cm-66x81in) 23-Nov-92 Sotheby's, New York #24/R
$37000   £24183   Nuestra Senora del Lago Titicaca (128x93cm-50x37in) 17-May-93 Christie's, New York #78/R

CUZCO SCHOOL, 18th/19th C   South American
$20120   £13594   Archange de parade en costume bleu. Archange de parade en costume rouge
                            (153x101cm-60x40in) canvas laid on panel two. 5-Nov-93 Cornette de St.Cyr, Paris
                            #38/R (F.FR 118000)

CUZCO SCHOOL, 19th C   South American
$6000   £3922   La Virgen del Rosario de Pomata (105x68cm-41x27in) canvas on masonite. 18-May-93
                            Sotheby's, New York #96/R

CYGNE, E J (1929-) American
$550   £364   Parisian street scene (41x51cm-16x20in) s. 19-Jun-94 Hindman Galleries, Chicago
                            #816

DABO, Leon (1868-1960) American
$1200   £784   Meadow and trees (41x56cm-16x22in) s. 18-Sep-93 Young Fine Arts Auctions, Maine
                            #88/R
$1300   £850   Still life of flowers (50x40cm-20x16in) s. board. 4-May-93 Christie's, East, New
                            York #152/R
$1800   £1184   Shades of fall afternoon (61x76cm-24x30in) 31-Mar-93 Sotheby's Arcade, New York
                            #237/R
$2000   £1266   Trees and rocks , s. canvasboard two. 2-Dec-92 Christie's, East, New York #110/R
$2000   £1282   Landscapes (23x30cm-9x12in) s.d.39 pair. 13-Dec-92 Litchfield Auction Gallery #10
$2250   £1442   Marinescape (30x38cm-12x15in) s. 13-Dec-92 Litchfield Auction Gallery #6
$2250   £1442   Landscape (36x46cm-14x18in) s. painted 1945. 13-Dec-92 Litchfield Auction Gallery
                            #7
$2600   £1667   Provence (33x41cm-13x16in) s.d.39 board. 13-Dec-92 Litchfield Auction Gallery #8
$2750   £1821   Luminous seascape with small boats (38x53cm-15x21in) mono.sig. 13-Nov-92 Skinner,
                            Bolton #162/R
$4200   £2692   Memory of Southern France (58x43cm-23x17in) s.d.54. 13-Dec-92 Litchfield Auction
                            Gallery #9
$4400   £2876   Grey cloud - Hudson River view (86x74cm-34x29in) s.d.1911 verso. 14-May-93
                            Skinner, Bolton #147/R
$11000   £7051   Summer idyll (76x86cm-30x34in) s.d.16. 27-May-93 Sotheby's, New York #106/R

DABO, Theodore Scott (1877-?) American
$2750   £1763   Nocturne (53x72cm-21x28in) s. 9-Dec-92 Butterfield & Butterfield, San Francisco
                            #3896/R

DAHLGREEN, Charles W (1864-1955) American
$750   £524   Creek in autumn (56x66cm-22x26in) s. s.i.verso board. 14-Mar-93 Hindman
                            Galleries, Chicago #4
$850   £556   Autumn in brown county (46x56cm-18x22in) s. board. 16-May-93 Hanzel Galleries,
                            Chicago #20/R
$950   £664   Landscape (56x66cm-22x26in) s. masonite. 14-Mar-93 Hindman Galleries, Chicago #6
$2200   £1538   White River, Ozarks (81x99cm-32x39in) s. board. 14-Mar-93 Hindman Galleries,
                            Chicago #5

DAHLGREN, Carl Christian (1841-1920) American
$950   £660   Resting on the shore (51x36cm-20x14in) s. 7-Mar-93 Butterfield & Butterfield, San
                            Francisco #10/R
$1600   £1053   Wooded passage (51x61cm-20x24in) s. 13-Jun-93 Butterfield & Butterfield, San
                            Francisco #710/R
$550   £362   *California wildflowers (22x29cm-9x11in) s. gouache. 13-Jun-93 Butterfield &
                            Butterfield, San Francisco #757/R*

DAINGERFIELD, Elliott (1859-1932) American
$1300   £872   Wooded landscape at sunset (30x46cm-12x18in) board. 27-Mar-93 San Rafael Auction
                            Galleries #318
$1450   £973   Sunset (20x25cm-8x10in) s. board. 4-Dec-93 Louisiana Auction Exchange #22/R
$4250   £2872   Forest at dusk (76x92cm-30x36in) s. s.d.1905 verso. 31-Mar-94 Sotheby's Arcade,
                            New York #139/R
$5000   £3401   The dancers (27x28cm-11x11in) s. canvas laid down on board. 15-Nov-93 Christie's,
                            East, New York #169/R

DALEE, Justus (fl.1826-1847) American
$1100   £743   *Portrait of a gentleman (8x8cm-3x3in) min. W/C pencil paper painted oval.
                            30-Oct-93 Skinner, Bolton #316/R*

DALEE, Justus (attrib) (fl.1826-1847) American
$1100   £738   *Portrait of a gentleman. Portrait of a lady wearing lace cap (8x8cm-3x3in)
                            min.i.d.Feb.22 1845 W/C graphite ink paper pair. 6-Feb-94 Skinner, Bolton #229
                            b/R*

DALLAIRE, Jean Philippe (1916-1965) Canadian
$6553   £4369   Exotic village (60x73cm-24x29in) s. s.i.d.1964verso. 11-May-94 Sotheby's, Toronto
                            #231/R (C.D 9000)
$4281   £2835   *Autoportrait au drapeau (17x14cm-7x6in) s.d.46 gouache. 24-Nov-92 Joyner Fine
                            Art, Toronto #132/R (C.D 5500)*
$5448   £3608   *Conditional mood (30x22cm-12x9in) s.i. gouache col.pencil. 18-Nov-92 Sotheby's,
                            Toronto #179/R (C.D 7000)*

DALY, Kathleen (1898-) Canadian
$1638	£1092	Portrait of Alphonse L'Abbe (91x79cm-36x31in) s. board. 11-May-94 Sotheby's, Toronto #151/R (C.D 2250)
$2002	£1335	Family reading (91x79cm-36x31in) s.d.40. 11-May-94 Sotheby's, Toronto #65/R (C.D 2750)
$5461	£3641	Interior of fish house, Peggy's Cove (117x132cm-46x52in) s. s.i.stretcher. 11-May-94 Sotheby's, Toronto #228/R (C.D 7500)

DAMROW, Charles (20th C) American
$650	£430	Cattle drive (61x91cm-24x36in) s. 28-Sep-93 John Moran, Pasadena #348
$900	£476	Elk in autumn mountains (61x76cm-24x30in) s. board. 12-Sep-92 Louisiana Auction Exchange #84/R
$2000	£1351	Cowboys and Indians (122x198cm-48x78in) s. 9-Nov-93 John Moran, Pasadena #950

DANA, Charles Edmund (1843-1924) American
$1500	£1007	Sultan Hassan (74x43cm-29x17in) s.i.d.3.20.94 W/C. 14-Oct-93 Christie's, New York #218/R
$1700	£1141	Garneal Arabee (51x38cm-20x15in) s.i.d.Dec.23.93 W/C. 14-Oct-93 Christie's, New York #217/R

DANBY, Ken (1940-) Canadian
$856	£567	Study of Sculler (20x39cm-8x15in) s.d.75 pencil. 24-Nov-92 Joyner Fine Art, Toronto #195 (C.D 1100)
$1189	£777	Blue truck (27x37cm-11x15in) s.d.76 W/C. 19-May-93 Sotheby's, Toronto #316/R (C.D 1500)
$2325	£1571	Across the gorge (34x53cm-13x21in) s.d.80 i.verso W/C. 3-Nov-93 Sotheby's, Toronto #335/R (C.D 3000)
$2354	£1538	The end of the Alora Gorge (8x53cm-3x21in) W/C. 12-May-93 Maynards, Vancouver #261 (C.D 3000)
$2537	£1658	Grand River reflections (51x67cm-20x26in) s.d.79 W/C. 18-May-93 Joyner Fine Art, Toronto #95/R (C.D 3200)
$2621	£1748	Sleeping (51x71cm-20x28in) s.d.70 W/C. 13-May-94 Joyner Fine Art, Toronto #87/R (C.D 3600)
$3099	£2094	The back door (70x48cm-28x19in) s.d.70 i.verso W/C. 3-Nov-93 Sotheby's, Toronto #291/R (C.D 4000)
$3277	£2184	Winter landscape (46x69cm-18x27in) s.d.66 W/C. 11-May-94 Sotheby's, Toronto #219/R (C.D 4500)
$3503	£2320	Old suede (54x69cm-21x27in) s.d.71 W/C. 16-Nov-92 Hodgins, Calgary #36/R (C.D 4500)

DANERI, Eugenio (1881-1970) Argentinian
$1950	£1016	Paisaje (28x36cm-11x14in) 4-Aug-92 VerBo, Buenos Aires #37
$2800	£1458	Naturaleza muerta (35x45cm-14x18in) 4-Aug-92 VerBo, Buenos Aires #536
$4000	£2353	Composicion (55x45cm-22x18in) 29-Sep-92 VerBo, Buenos Aires #40
$4000	£2649	Magnolia II (50x30cm-20x12in) 11-Nov-92 VerBo, Buenos Aires #31/R
$7000	£4636	Barcas (41x50cm-16x20in) 18-Nov-92 Roldan & Cia, Buenos Aires #5
$8600	£4971	Viviendas obreras (80x110cm-31x43in) 23-Sep-92 Roldan & Cia, Buenos Aires #45
$10000	£5780	Bruma (50x92cm-20x36in) 23-Sep-92 Roldan & Cia, Buenos Aires #44

DANGERFIELD, Elliot (19th C) American
$1850	£1312	Christ in the Wilderness (71x61cm-28x24in) s.d.1894. 21-Feb-93 Hart Gallery, Houston #3

DANIEL, William Swift (1865-1933) American
$800	£541	California landscape (41x25cm-16x10in) s.d.1906 W/C. 9-Nov-93 John Moran, Pasadena #926

DANN, Frode N (1892-?) American
$750	£487	California landscape (51x64cm-20x25in) s.d.1940. 11-Sep-93 Louisiana Auction Exchange #22/R

DANNAT, William Turner (1853-?) American
$8200	£5467	Woman with castanets (66x38cm-26x15in) s. 23-May-94 Hindman Galleries, Chicago #194/R

DANNER, Sara Kolb (1894-1969) American
$1200	£795	Street scene with figures-flags-parade (41x51cm-16x20in) s. canvas on board. 14-Jun-94 John Moran, Pasadena #45
$1500	£882	Art fair (71x76cm-28x30in) s. board. 4-Oct-92 Butterfield & Butterfield, Los Angeles #256/R
$1600	£1060	Lambertville (71x76cm-28x30in) s. board. 28-Sep-93 John Moran, Pasadena #248

D'ARCANGELO, Allan (1930-) American
$12000	£8108	Smoke dream (130x112cm-51x44in) s. acrylic painted 1963. 11-Nov-93 Sotheby's, New York #397/R
$900	£625	Constellation No.114 (122x122cm-48x48in) s.i.d.1971verso dry pigment canvas. 26-Feb-93 Sotheby's Arcade, New York #392/R

DARCOVICH, Michael (20th C) American
$2100	£1391	Entertainers (61x147cm-24x58in) s. 3-Oct-93 Hanzel Galleries, Chicago #765/R

DARLEY, Felix O C (1822-1888) American
$550	£369	Lake George, September, 1888 (25x30cm-10x12in) s.i. W/C. 4-Dec-93 Louisiana Auction Exchange #15/R

DARLEY, Felix O C (1822-1888) American-cont.
$1300	£855	Fishing on shore (23x33cm-9x13in) s. pen wash. 13-Jun-93 Butterfield & Butterfield, San Francisco #3132/R
$1800	£1224	Illustration from The Old Curiosity Shop (47x38cm-19x15in) s. ink wash paperboard. 15-Nov-93 Christie's, East, New York #108/R
$1800	£1192	Working mother (35x51cm-14x20in) s. W/C pencil. 22-Sep-93 Christie's, New York #69/R
$3250	£2273	Spirit of 76. Bear attack. Farmer's lunch. Pursuit of knowledge , s.i.W/C en grisaille four. 10-Mar-93 Sotheby's, New York #2/R
$8000	£5369	A day at the beach (26x36cm-10x14in) s. W/C graphite paperboard. 4-Mar-94 Skinner, Bolton #227/R

DARLEY, Felix O C (after) (1822-1888) American
$4500	£3000	The Wyoming Valley Massacre (81x91cm-32x36in) canvas on panel. 16-Mar-94 Christie's, New York #3/R

DARLING, William (1856-1933) American
$1500	£987	June in Palm Springs (61x76cm-24x30in) s. canvas on board. 13-Jun-93 Butterfield & Butterfield, San Francisco #940/R

DARLING, William S (1882-1963) American
$750	£507	Landscape (36x46cm-14x18in) s. masonite. 15-Jun-93 John Moran, Pasadena #22
$850	£563	Landscape - twilight (46x56cm-18x22in) s. masonite. 14-Jun-94 John Moran, Pasadena #80 a
$900	£600	Landscape with two western riders (41x51cm-16x20in) s. canvasboard. 15-Mar-94 John Moran, Pasadena #101
$950	£642	Landscape (30x41cm-12x16in) s. masonite. 9-Nov-93 John Moran, Pasadena #853
$1300	£878	Dunes in bloom (51x76cm-20x30in) s. canvas on masonite. 15-Jun-93 John Moran, Pasadena #176
$1500	£1014	Laguna shores (51x61cm-20x24in) s. canvas laid down on masonite. 9-Nov-93 John Moran, Pasadena #915
$2250	£1520	Landscape cloudy morning (56x71cm-22x28in) s. masonite. 9-Nov-93 John Moran, Pasadena #881

DARRAH, Ann Sophia Towne (1819-1881) American
$2500	£1634	Figures near shore (66x102cm-26x40in) s. 8-May-93 Young Fine Arts Auctions, Maine #80/R

DASBURG, Andrew (1887-1979) American
$2500	£1445	Winter street scene (61x51cm-24x20in) s. 27-Sep-92 James Bakker, Cambridge #32/R
$9500	£6291	Landscape (33x41cm-13x16in) s.d.19 canvas on board. 22-Sep-93 Christie's, New York #199/R
$2200	£1467	Taos Pueblo (45x61cm-18x24in) s. conte crayon. 23-May-94 Christie's, East, New York #217 a

D'ASCENZO, Nicola (1871-?) American
$850	£538	Sketch of fountain (31x20cm-12x8in) inits. 2-Dec-92 Christie's, East, New York #59
$1000	£633	Still life with fish (61x76cm-24x30in) s. 3-Dec-92 Freeman Fine Arts, Philadelphia #1806/R
$1050	£665	Landscape with sailboat (66x86cm-26x34in) s. 3-Dec-92 Freeman Fine Arts, Philadelphia #1809

DASH, Robert (1934-) American
$3400	£2222	Garden path (152x152cm-60x60in) s. 5-May-93 Doyle, New York #57/R

DAUGHERTY, James (1889-1974) American
$1000	£658	Comforter (41x80cm-16x31in) 31-Mar-93 Sotheby's Arcade, New York #364/R
$15000	£8671	The Wilderness Road (92x110cm-36x43in) st.sig. st.studio stretcher. 23-Sep-92 Christie's, New York #244/R
$700	£405	Untitled (60x91cm-24x36in) init.d.71 pastel. 25-Sep-92 Sotheby's Arcade, New York #475/R

DAVENPORT, Carlson (1908-1972) American
$7750	£5099	Century of progress (69x152cm-27x60in) s.d.1939. 4-Nov-92 Doyle, New York #42/R

DAVENPORT, Henry (19/20th C) American
$1000	£671	Entering Mediterranean, depicting passengers on cruise ship (51x61cm-20x24in) s. board. 5-Aug-93 Eldred, Massachusetts #580/R
$1500	£1014	Late afternoon at Old Garden Beach Rockport (61x77cm-24x30in) s. i.verso. 5-Nov-93 Skinner, Bolton #115/R
$3080	£2013	End of summer (66x81cm-26x32in) s. 14-May-93 Skinner, Bolton #124/R

DAVENPORT, Rebecca (1943-) American
$1300	£855	Fragment (46x61cm-18x24in) monoi.d.1983. 2-Apr-93 Sloan, North Bethesda #2333

DAVENPORT, William Slocum (1868-?) American
$526	£351	Bord de mer, Cap d'Antibes (65x54cm-26x21in) s.i. 8-Jun-94 Guy Loudmer, Paris #54 (F.FR 3000)

DAVEY, Randall (1887-1964) American
$700	£467	Mare and foal (30x23cm-12x9in) s. board. 26-Aug-93 Skinner, Bolton #194
$7200	£4865	Still life with flowers in vase (81x66cm-32x26in) s. 31-Oct-93 Hindman Galleries, Chicago #673/R

DAVEY, Randall (1887-1964) American-cont.
$600	£405	Elegant woman in an interior (51x36cm-20x14in) s. pastel board. 10-Nov-93 Doyle, New York #36
$700	£370	Polo Match (20x28cm-8x11in) s. W/C gouache graphite. 11-Sep-92 Skinner, Bolton #271/R
$750	£514	Showing of thoroughbreds before the race (23x28cm-9x11in) s. W/C. 13-Feb-94 Hart Gallery, Houston #413
$1200	£769	Horses and jockeys (43x58cm-17x23in) s. pastel. 13-Dec-92 Hindman Galleries, Chicago #5/R

DAVID, Michael (20th C) American
$1600	£1060	Untitled no 93 (48x56cm-19x22in) init.d.87 acrylic chk paint. 29-Sep-93 Sotheby's Arcade, New York #338/R

DAVID, Stanley S (?) American
$13000	£8609	Hanging apples (31x25cm-12x10in) s. 22-Sep-93 Christie's, New York #27/R
$13000	£8609	Hanging pears (31x25cm-12x10in) s. 22-Sep-93 Christie's, New York #28/R

DAVIDSON, Clara D (1874-) American
$2000	£1342	Sweeping the path, church in background (89x79cm-35x31in) s.d.1916. 4-May-94 Doyle, New York #16/R
$3500	£2349	Still life of books and flowers (89x79cm-35x31in) s. 4-May-94 Doyle, New York #18/R

DAVIES, Albert Webster (1890-?) American
$700	£476	William and Mary College, Version II (51x74cm-20x29in) s. panel. 14-Apr-94 Freeman Fine Arts, Philadelphia #1021

DAVIES, Arthur B (1862-1928) American
$750	£490	Equal measure (15x38cm-6x15in) s. 17-Sep-93 Skinner, Bolton #270/R
$775	£509	California (13x24cm-5x9in) panel. 31-Mar-93 Sotheby's Arcade, New York #202/R
$900	£584	Under the greenwood tree (46x76cm-18x30in) s. i.stretcher. 9-Sep-93 Sotheby's Arcade, New York #266/R
$1200	£789	Dancing bacchantes (25x30cm-10x12in) s. 31-Mar-93 Sotheby's Arcade, New York #289/R
$1400	£886	Two figures by sea (35x29cm-14x11in) 2-Dec-92 Christie's, East, New York #406/R
$1600	£1103	Blue landscape (66x102cm-26x40in) 17-Feb-93 Doyle, New York #22
$1700	£1104	Mountains and sky (67x102cm-26x40in) 9-Sep-93 Sotheby's Arcade, New York #264/R
$2000	£1399	Mermaid on the dunes (56x43cm-22x17in) 14-Mar-93 Hindman Galleries, Chicago #34/R
$2000	£1316	Fleecy arcady (20x41cm-8x16in) s. 31-Mar-93 Sotheby's Arcade, New York #286/R
$2000	£1156	Iris and aeolis bandying showers (66x102cm-26x40in) s. 25-Sep-92 Sotheby's Arcade, New York #214/R
$2900	£1908	Mountain landscape with village (66x102cm-26x40in) 31-Mar-93 Sotheby's Arcade, New York #184/R
$3200	£2119	Fording song (46x76cm-18x30in) studio st.stretcher. 2-Oct-93 Weschler, Washington #133/R
$4250	£2457	Indian enchantment (76x46cm-30x18in) s. i.stretcher. 25-Sep-92 Sotheby's Arcade, New York #212/R
$6000	£3974	Hours and the freedom of the fields (46x76cm-18x30in) s. 22-Sep-93 Christie's, New York #124/R
$6250	£3613	Breathing sacrifice (58x71cm-23x28in) s. 24-Sep-92 Sotheby's, New York #210/R
$6500	£4114	Nymphs and satyrs (55x42cm-22x17in) s. 3-Dec-92 Sotheby's, New York #131/R
$11000	£6962	Protest against violence (101x66cm-40x26in) i.stretcher. 3-Dec-92 Sotheby's, New York #130/R
$600	£397	La Belle Endormita, Carrara (23x30cm-9x12in) s. W/C. 13-Nov-92 Skinner, Bolton #87/R
$600	£397	Country house (23x30cm-9x12in) s. W/C gouache. 13-Nov-92 Skinner, Bolton #89/R
$1000	£641	Day at the beach (30x23cm-12x9in) studio st.gouache paper on board. 9-Dec-92 Butterfield & Butterfield, San Francisco #4020/R
$1000	£671	Forest scene with nude (180x36cm-71x14in) s. gouache W/C board. 4-Dec-93 Louisiana Auction Exchange #83/R
$1300	£823	The dancer (35x28cm-14x11in) s. pastel. 4-Dec-92 Christie's, New York #52/R
$1300	£751	Carrara. Rhone Valley (24x32cm-9x13in) st.sig. s.i.d.1924 pastel pair. 25-Sep-92 Sotheby's Arcade, New York #252/R

DAVIES, Harold Christopher (1891-1976) American
$1500	£949	Third Street Bridge, San Francisco (58x66cm-23x26in) i.d.1930 verso. 25-Oct-92 Butterfield & Butterfield, San Francisco #2208/R

DAVILA, Jose Antonio (1935-) Venezuelan
$8000	£5556	El Decimotercer encuentro (100x121cm-39x48in) s. s.i.d.1984verso acrylic. 26-Feb-93 Sotheby's Arcade, New York #257/R

DAVIS, Ann (19th C) American
$700	£461	Primitive American winter scene (79x56cm-31x22in) s. 2-Apr-93 Eldred, Massachusetts #551/R

DAVIS, Charles Harold (1856-1933) American
$1100	£769	The country road, Amesbury (28x46cm-11x18in) s. i.verso board. 12-Mar-93 Skinner, Bolton #210/R
$2000	£1399	Road (41x33cm-16x13in) s.i. 12-Mar-93 Skinner, Bolton #207/R
$3000	£1887	Passing (64x76cm-25x30in) s. i.verso masonite. 22-Apr-93 Freeman Fine Arts, Philadelphia #1333
$4100	£2169	Afternoon shadows, Mystic, Conn. (43x53cm-17x21in) s. 11-Sep-92 Skinner, Bolton #205/R

DAVIS, Charles Harold (1856-1933) American-cont.
$7250	£4802	Afternoon shade, summer (63x76cm-25x30in) s. i.stretcher. 23-Sep-93 Sotheby's, New York #148/R
$13000	£8176	Summer (64x76cm-25x30in) s. 25-Apr-93 James Bakker, Cambridge #127/R
$1700	£1189	Sheep meadow, late afternoon. Across the field and beyond the river (23x36cm-9x14in) one oil canvasboard, one W/C gouache. 12-Mar-93 Skinner, Bolton #209/R

DAVIS, Gene (1920-1985) American
$5500	£3819	Dolphin (178x229cm-70x90in) s.i.d.1975verso acrylic. 22-Feb-93 Christie's, East, New York #166/R
$6500	£4392	65-2 (148x188cm-58x74in) acrylic painted 1965. 8-Nov-93 Christie's, East, New York #217/R
$700	£467	Untitled (65x51cm-26x20in) s.d.1980 col marker pen. 21-May-94 Weschler, Washington #143/R
$800	£530	Untitled (51x38cm-20x15in) s.d.1980 col.marker. 2-Oct-93 Weschler, Washington #163

DAVIS, Gladys Rockmore (1901-1967) American
$2000	£1156	Portrait of seated female nude (61x51cm-24x20in) s. 25-Sep-92 Sotheby's Arcade, New York #417/R
$5750	£3734	August afternoon (76x102cm-30x40in) init. 9-Sep-93 Sotheby's Arcade, New York #285/R

DAVIS, Joseph H (fl.1832-1837) American
$5000	£3247	Portrait of Eleanor Jane Jones, aged 10 years, 1835 (25x15cm-10x6in) i. W/C ink. 16-Jan-93 Skinner, Bolton #150/R

DAVIS, Joseph H (attrib) (fl.1832-1837) American
$2250	£1136	Portrait of Samson Webb of Stratford, New Hampshire (25x33cm-10x13in) i.d.1836 W/C ink graphite. 21-Aug-92 Skinner, Bolton #1/R

DAVIS, Leonard M (1864-?) American
$3000	£2000	Mountains and valleys in Gramercy Park (46x61cm-18x24in) s.d.1916 s.i.stretcher. 23-May-94 Christie's, East, New York #191/R

DAVIS, Rita Hicks (1956-) American
$650	£430	First date (43x53cm-17x21in) s. i.d.1992verso acrylic board. 21-Nov-92 Litchfield Auction Gallery #7

DAVIS, Roger (1898-1935) American
$750	£532	Head of young girl with red hair (33x28cm-13x11in) s. 12-Feb-93 Du Mouchelle, Detroit #2013/R

DAVIS, Ron (1937-) American
$2500	£1689	Untitled (56x77cm-22x30in) s.d.1979 W/C graphite. 21-Oct-93 Butterfield & Butterfield, San Francisco #2808/R

DAVIS, Samuel (1757-c.1809) American
$2205	£1500	The Fort of Juvinpore, India (34x54cm-13x21in) init.i.d.1797 verso pencil W/C. 12-Apr-94 Christie's, London #160/R
$5880	£4000	Mountain view near Choka in Bhutan (36x48cm-14x19in) mono.i. W/C over pencil. 14-Apr-94 Sotheby's, London #270/R

DAVIS, Stark (1885-?) American
$900	£588	Peacock (30x30cm-12x12in) s. board. 16-May-93 Hindman Galleries, Chicago #107
$1150	£762	Perching parrot (94x94cm-37x37in) s. 3-Oct-93 Hanzel Galleries, Chicago #874

DAVIS, Stuart (1894-1964) American
$52500	£33228	Chinatown (94x76cm-37x30in) s.d.1912. 3-Dec-92 Sotheby's, New York #136/R
$60000	£40000	Artist in search of model (26x46cm-10x18in) s. tempera paper painted 1931. 25-May-94 Sotheby's, New York #113/R
$100000	£63291	Synthetic souvenir (23x31cm-9x12in) s. s.i.d.1941stretcher. 4-Dec-92 Christie's, New York #128/R
$2100	£1409	Railroad station (20x28cm-8x11in) s. W/C ink. 5-Mar-94 Louisiana Auction Exchange #132/R
$2400	£1611	Boating party (25x38cm-10x15in) s.d.1912 W/C pencil. 4-May-94 Doyle, New York #49/R
$7500	£4335	Snowy night (30x23cm-12x9in) s.d.1911 W/C pen gouache. 23-Sep-92 Christie's, New York #21/R
$55000	£34810	Study for Package Deal (33x30cm-13x12in) s. gouache. 3-Dec-92 Sotheby's, New York #188/R

DAVIS, Warren B (1865-1928) American
$850	£556	Female nude in landscape (8x10cm-3x4in) s. canvas laid down on board. 14-May-93 Du Mouchelle, Detroit #120/R
$900	£612	Nude on a rock (20x25cm-8x10in) s. canvasboard. 15-Nov-93 Christie's, East, New York #188
$1200	£779	Dancers (18x13cm-7x5in) s. board. 15-Jan-93 Du Mouchelle, Detroit #2020/R
$1500	£1007	Nude in a landscape (51x36cm-20x14in) s. 11-Dec-93 Weschler, Washington #119/R
$1600	£1046	The bather (25x20cm-10x8in) canvas on board. 18-Sep-93 James Bakker, Cambridge #83/R
$9500	£6090	New York crossing (40x56cm-16x22in) s. 26-May-93 Christie's, New York #154/R

DAVISSON, Homer Gordon (1866-?) American
$800   £537   Autumn landscape (64x76cm-25x30in) s. board. 24-Mar-94 Mystic Fine Arts, Connecticut #73/R

DAWES, Edwin M (1872-1945) American
$700   £458   Landscape (61x76cm-24x30in) s. 16-May-93 Hindman Galleries, Chicago #127

DAWIS, J (20th C) American
$1338   £892   Still life of fruit (25x20cm-10x8in) s. panel. 10-May-94 Galerie Fischer, Lucerne #3457/R (S.FR 1900)

DAWSON, Manierre (1887-1969) American
$13000   £8228   Malta (45x53cm-18x21in) s.d.13. 3-Dec-92 Sotheby's, New York #155/R

DAWSON-WATSON, Dawson see WATSON, Dawson

DAY, James Francis (1863-1942) American
$2400   £1611   A book and a hot cup of coffee (30x46cm-12x18in) s. pastel. 2-Dec-93 Freeman Fine Arts, Philadelphia #778

DEACHMAN, Nelly (1895-) American
$575   £374   Lilacs (56x69cm-22x27in) s. 4-Aug-94 Eldred, Massachusetts #584

DEAKIN, Edwin (1838-1923) American
$1000   £671   Couple by a lake (66x107cm-26x42in) s.d.1870. 8-Dec-93 Butterfield & Butterfield, San Francisco #3345/R
$1100   £728   Eglise de Chelles (61x79cm-24x31in) s. 23-Sep-93 Mystic Fine Arts, Connecticut #217/R
$1700   £1181   Mill near Chillon Castle, Switzerland (76x51cm-30x20in) s.d.1897 s.i.d.verso. 7-Mar-93 Butterfield & Butterfield, San Francisco #29/R
$1700   £1118   Black grapes spilling from basket (36x43cm-14x17in) s. 4-Nov-92 Doyle, New York #6/R
$1800   £1059   St. Etienne du Mont, Paris (92x46cm-36x18in) s. s.i.d.1898 verso. 4-Oct-92 Butterfield & Butterfield, Los Angeles #104/R
$2000   £1282   Eglise de Chelles, le soir (61x79cm-24x31in) s. s.i.d.1879 and 1883verso. 24-May-93 Grogan, Massachussetts #327/R
$2800   £1879   Hanging grapes (23x28cm-9x11in) s.d.1883verso. 1-Dec-93 Doyle, New York #45

DEAN, Ronald (?) American
$450   £304   Ship Antiope and estuary traffic (30x43cm-12x17in) s. W/C. 23-Oct-93 San Rafael Auction Galleries #257

DEAN, Walter Lofthouse (1854-1912) American
$1500   £1049   Silvery day. Sailing out of the harbour (23x33cm-9x13in) s. i.verso pair. 12-Mar-93 Skinner, Bolton #225/R

DEAS, Charles (1818-1867) American
$280000   £185430   Indian warrior on edge of precipice (93x67cm-37x26in) s.d.1847. 22-Sep-93 Christie's, New York #90/R

DECAMP, Joseph Rodefer see CAMP, Joseph Rodefer de

DECKER, Joseph (1853-1924) American
$23000   £15541   Roasting apples by the fire (43x35cm-17x14in) s.d.68. 5-Nov-93 Skinner, Bolton #59/R

DECKER, Robert M (1847-?) American
$1100   £738   Wooded landscape (56x76cm-22x30in) s. 11-Dec-93 Weschler, Washington #86/R
$1900   £1267   Forest stream (31x72cm-12x28in) s. 12-Mar-94 Weschler, Washington #151

DEFOREST, Lockwood (1850-1932) American
$650   £439   Coastal scene (25x36cm-10x14in) init. board. 9-Nov-93 John Moran, Pasadena #908
$1000   £676   Sunset over a field with ruins (56x91cm-22x36in) s.d.1872. 20-Apr-94 Doyle, New York #28
$1500   £993   Near Santa Barbara (61x86cm-24x34in) s.d.1923. 15-Jun-94 Butterfield & Butterfield, San Francisco #4688/R
$1800   £1184   Californian desert with three palms. Indio landscape (25x36cm-10x14in) mono.i.d.09 board pair. 13-Jun-93 Butterfield & Butterfield, San Francisco #936/R
$3000   £2013   Trees and distant hills (61x87cm-24x34in) s.d.1918 boar. 8-Dec-93 Butterfield & Butterfield, San Francisco #3346/R
$6500   £4514   Sunset beyond valley (74x122cm-29x48in) s.d.1878 canvas on board. 7-Mar-93 Butterfield & Butterfield, San Francisco #23/R

DEFOREST, Roy see FOREST, Roy de

DEHAVEN, Franklin see HAVEN, Franklin de

DEHN, Adolf (1895-1968) American
$1200   £789   Haitian gala (81x112cm-32x44in) s. s.d.1956 verso board. 13-Jun-93 Butterfield & Butterfield, San Francisco #3259/R
$1500   £1020   New York, winter (46x81cm-18x32in) s. board. 16-Apr-94 Young Fine Arts Auctions, Maine #92
$3000   £2055   Farm village in the hills (71x107cm-28x42in) board. 19-Feb-94 Young Fine Arts Auctions, Maine #72/R

DEHN, Adolf (1895-1968) American-cont.
$800	£526	Rolling hills in winter (48x71cm-19x28in) s. W/C. 7-Apr-93 Doyle, New York #18
$900	£608	Two farms (48x67cm-19x26in) s. s.i.d.1956 verso W/C. 31-Mar-94 Sotheby's Arcade, New York #383/R
$950	£621	Big barn (36x53cm-14x21in) s.d.52 W/C htd gouache graphite. 17-Sep-93 Skinner, Bolton #244/R
$1100	£769	Inlet (51x71cm-20x28in) s. W/C. 11-Mar-93 Mystic Fine Arts, Connecticut #75
$1200	£759	Strollers (32x52cm-13x20in) s.d.90 W/C. 2-Dec-92 Christie's, East, New York #273/R
$1600	£1053	Breakers, Palm Beach (37x55cm-15x22in) s.d.1951 gouache pencil. 31-Mar-93 Sotheby's Arcade, New York #396/R
$1900	£1234	The fair (41x51cm-16x20in) s. W/C. 11-Sep-93 Louisiana Auction Exchange #29/R
$13000	£7514	My heart belongs to daddy (41x59cm-16x23in) s.d.41 W/C pencil. 23-Sep-92 Christie's, New York #251/R
$13000	£9091	Jazz horns (39x57cm-15x22in) s. W/C. 11-Mar-93 Christie's, New York #258/R

DEHN, Adolph (1895-1968) American
$1100	£738	Native dance (56x86cm-22x34in) s.d.1940 W/C. 24-Mar-94 Mystic Fine Arts, Connecticut #99

DEHOSPODAR, Stephen (1902-1959) American
$700	£473	Winter river (66x48cm-26x19in) s. 15-Jun-93 John Moran, Pasadena #130 a

DELANO, Gerard Curtis (1890-1972) American
$3250	£2196	A break from the hunt (102x76cm-40x30in) s. 31-Mar-94 Sotheby's Arcade, New York #395/R

DELAPP, Terry (1934-) American
$1800	£1250	Orange branch (61x81cm-24x32in) init acrylic. 7-Mar-93 Butterfield & Butterfield, San Francisco #264/R
$2500	£1736	Two palms (61x81cm-24x32in) init. acrylic. 7-Mar-93 Butterfield & Butterfield, San Francisco #263/R
$4000	£2649	Oak Grove, San Simeon (61x81cm-24x32in) init. acrylic. 15-Jun-94 Butterfield & Butterfield, San Francisco #4744/R

DELBOS, Julius (1879-1967) American
$1200	£811	The young shepherd (76x102cm-30x40in) s. 31-Mar-94 Sotheby's Arcade, New York #211/R
$600	£392	Southern street scene with figures (36x38cm-14x15in) s. W/C. 18-Sep-93 James Bakke, Cambridge #197/R

DELFOSSE, Georges Marie Joseph (1869-1939) Canadian
$906	£612	Maison de P. du Calvet, Montreal, Quebec (28x35cm-11x14in) s. 23-Nov-93 Fraser Pinneys, Quebec #439/R (C.D 1200)
$3892	£2577	Vieille maison (69x91cm-27x36in) s. 18-Nov-92 Sotheby's, Toronto #228/R (C.D 5000)

DELIOTTI, Walter (20th C) Uruguayan?
$650	£422	Puente ferroviario (41x52cm-16x20in) s. 30-Aug-93 Gomensoro, Montevideo #24
$720	£474	Calle de la Aguada (24x33cm-9x13in) s. 31-May-93 Gomensoro, Montevideo #18
$800	£523	Constructivo de Montevideo (50x70cm-20x28in) s.d.1985. 3-May-93 Gomensoro, Montevideo #24/R
$1500	£754	Composicion Portuaria (40x57cm-16x22in) s.d.85 board. 31-Aug-92 Gomensoro, Montevideo #61/R
$2000	£1351	Calle (73x88cm-29x35in) s.d.78. 25-Apr-94 Gomensoro, Montevideo #35/R

DELOOPER, William (1932-) American
$750	£487	Untitled (170x203cm-67x80in) s.d.1970verso. 8-Jul-94 Sloan, North Bethesda #2344

DEMETROPOULOS, Charles (1912-1976) American
$600	£420	Boston Garden (51x74cm-20x29in) d.July 1973 W/C. 7-Feb-93 James Bakker, Cambridge #192/R
$950	£664	Boston Garden, Swan boats (46x69cm-18x27in) d.July 27 1054 W/C. 7-Feb-93 James Bakker, Cambridge #134

DEMING, Edwin Willard (1860-1942) American
$1000	£654	Recital of Ancient Myths (30x41cm-12x16in) s. board. 4-May-93 Christie's, East, New York #165
$1400	£921	Heading home from successful hunt (61x122cm-24x48in) s. masonite. 31-Mar-93 Sotheby's Arcade, New York #197/R
$2400	£1558	Indian father and son (72x56cm-28x22in) s. 9-Sep-93 Sotheby's Arcade, New York #235/R
$3500	£2333	Prayer to the sun (71x56cm-28x22in) s. 17-May-94 Grogan, Massachussetts #349/R

DEMUTH, Charles (1883-1935) American
$750000	£474684	Welcome to our city (63x50cm-25x20in) s.d.1921 s.d.verso. 3-Dec-92 Sotheby's, New York #153/R
$2200	£1429	Acrobats (33x20cm-13x8in) pencil crayon. 9-Sep-93 Sotheby's Arcade, New York #371/R
$2400	£1600	Woolworth building roof no.1, Lancaster, Pennsylvania (11x15cm-4x6in) init. W/C executed c.1914. 23-Nov-94 Christie's, East, New York #220/R
$5000	£3311	Coastal scene, Etretat (25x35cm-10x14in) W/C paper on board. 22-Sep-93 Christie's, New York #203/R
$17000	£11409	Abstract landscape (30x41cm-12x16in) s.d.1915 W/C. 2-Dec-93 Sotheby's, New York #139/R

DEMUTH, Charles (1883-1935) American-cont.
$23000	£14557	Floral still life - wild daisies (20x27cm-8x11in) s.d.1915 W/C. 3-Dec-92 Sotheby's, New York #50/R
$25000	£15823	Still life with tulips (35x25cm-14x10in) s.d.1917 W/C. 3-Dec-92 Sotheby's, New York #58/R
$30000	£19231	Man and woman, Provincetown (28x21cm-11x8in) s.d.34 W/C pencil. 26-May-93 Christie's, New York #197/R
$34000	£22667	Three sailors (22x24cm-9x9in) W/C pencil. 26-May-94 Christie's, New York #130/R
$100000	£67114	Roof tops, Provincetown (36x25cm-14x10in) W/C pencil painted c.1917-1918. 3-Dec-93 Christie's, New York #9/R
$100000	£63291	Pears and plate (27x40cm-11x16in) W/C. 3-Dec-92 Sotheby's, New York #147/R

DENNIS, Roger Wilson (1902-) American
$2300	£1513	Morning at Noank (69x84cm-27x33in) s.d.1985 i.stretcher. 4-Nov-92 Doyle, New York #51/R

DENNY, Gideon Jacques (1830-1886) American
$2750	£1910	Square rigger foundering off the coast (30x46cm-12x18in) s.d.1879 board. 7-Mar-93 Butterfield & Butterfield, San Francisco #16/R

DENTON, Troy (20th C) American
$650	£430	Buffalo hunter on horseback (91x61cm-36x24in) s. 27-Sep-93 Selkirks, St. Louis #930

DEROME, Albert Thomas (1885-1959) American
$800	£530	Seascape - February evening, Monterey Coast 1933 (13x18cm-5x7in) s. 14-Jun-94 John Moran, Pasadena #90 a
$1300	£897	Veils of light, Santa Cruz Mountains (25x36cm-10x14in) s. canvas laid down on board. 16-Feb-93 John Moran, Pasadena #107 a
$1600	£941	Monterey Bay (25x36cm-10x14in) s. canvasboard. 4-Oct-92 Butterfield & Butterfield, Los Angeles #74/R
$2500	£1724	Spring flowers near Asilomar, Monterey Bay (46x61cm-18x24in) s. oil masonite. 16-Feb-93 John Moran, Pasadena #107
$550	£362	Bright Angel Canyon, Grand Canyon (29x19cm-11x7in) s. W/C. 13-Jun-93 Butterfield & Butterfield, San Francisco #933/R
$800	£533	Deerheart Mountain near Bonanza (13x20cm-5x8in) s. W/C painted 1918. 15-Mar-94 John Moran, Pasadena #116 c
$850	£567	Old Batchelor's Cabin on Trinity River (20x28cm-8x11in) s. W/C. 15-Mar-94 John Moran, Pasadena #116 b
$850	£567	Mount Whitney from Lone Pine (30x20cm-12x8in) s. W/C painted 1922. 15-Mar-94 John Moran, Pasadena #116
$1000	£690	Lone Pine Peak, Inyo country, Mt. Whitney (20x23cm-8x9in) s. W/C painted 1927. 16-Feb-93 John Moran, Pasadena #117 a
$1200	£828	Gull Lake, No. of Bishop... (30x20cm-12x8in) s. W/C painted 1921. 16-Feb-93 John Moran, Pasadena #117
$1300	£897	Bear Buttes, Eel River, Garberville (20x30cm-8x12in) s. W/C painted 1920. 16-Feb-93 John Moran, Pasadena #117 b
$1300	£897	Half dome, Yosemite, with Hastes (30x20cm-12x8in) s. W/C. 16-Feb-93 John Moran, Pasadena #116

DERRICK, William R (19/20th C) American
$700	£452	Winter woodland stream (91x66cm-36x26in) s. 13-Jul-94 Doyle, New York #15

DESRUISSEAU, Rose-Marie (1933-1988) Haitian
$1163	£770	Erzulie Freda et les anges (72x80cm-28x31in) s.d.81. 13-Jun-94 Rogeon, Paris #83 (F.FR 6500)
$3177	£1949	Fuite en masse des indiens vers la bahoruco (77x92cm-30x36in) s.d.1984. 12-Oct-92 Ader Tajan, Paris #8/R (F.FR 16000)
$3177	£1949	Quatre grnds chefs marrons (102x92cm-40x36in) s.d.1984. 12-Oct-92 Ader Tajan, Paris #28/R (F.FR 16000)
$3177	£1949	Francois Mackandal,le plus Grand Marron Vaudouisant (92x77cm-36x30in) s.d.1983. 12-Oct-92 Ader Tajan, Paris #17/R (F.FR 16000)
$3574	£2192	Lutte des classes (143x107cm-56x42in) painted 1983. 12-Oct-92 Ader Tajan, Paris #22/R (F.FR 18000)
$3574	£2192	Les peres de la Patrie (102x92cm-40x36in) s.d.1984. 12-Oct-92 Ader Tajan, Paris #31/R (F.FR 18000)
$3574	£2192	Repartimientos (91x101cm-36x40in) s.d.1985. 12-Oct-92 Ader Tajan, Paris #6/R (F.FR 18000)
$3574	£2192	Revolte generale des indiens (97x117cm-38x46in) s.d.1983. 12-Oct-92 Ader Tajan, Paris #7/R (F.FR 18000)
$3971	£2436	Salut arbres sacres de la foret (85x90cm-33x35in) s.d.1982. 12-Oct-92 Ader Tajan, Paris #1/R (F.FR 20000)
$3971	£2436	L'execution de Mackandal (91x101cm-36x40in) s.d.1986. 12-Oct-92 Ader Tajan, Paris #20/R (F.FR 20000)
$3971	£2436	Etablissement des Francais (91x101cm-36x40in) s.d.1986. 12-Oct-92 Ader Tajan, Paris #15/R (F.FR 20000)
$4169	£2558	Fuite des esclaves (102x77cm-40x30in) s.d.1986. 12-Oct-92 Ader Tajan, Paris #23/R (F.FR 21000)
$4368	£2680	Nuits orgiaques de Mackandal (92x102cm-36x40in) s.d.1986. 12-Oct-92 Ader Tajan, Paris #18/R (F.FR 22000)
$4368	£2680	Soulevement General des esclaves (92x122cm-36x48in) s.d.1986. 12-Oct-92 Ader Tajan, Paris #26/R (F.FR 22000)
$4963	£3045	Fete au village (76x101cm-30x40in) s.d.1980. 12-Oct-92 Ader Tajan, Paris #3/R (F.FR 25000)

DESRUISSEAU, Rose-Marie (1933-1988) Haitian-cont.
$4963	£3045	massacre des blancs (92x102cm-36x40in) s.d.1983. 12-Oct-92 Ader Tajan, Paris #27/R (F.FR 25000)
$4963	£3045	Caonabo et Anacaona (92x77cm-36x30in) s.d.1985. 12-Oct-92 Ader Tajan, Paris #5/R (F.FR 25000)
$4963	£3045	Debarquement des Laos (92x87cm-36x34in) s.d.1982. 12-Oct-92 Ader Tajan, Paris #11/R (F.FR 25000)
$5559	£3410	Croyances Indiennes (70x81cm-28x32in) s.d.1982. 12-Oct-92 Ader Tajan, Paris #2/R (F.FR 28000)
$5956	£3654	La Creation du drapeau (91x76cm-36x30in) s.d.1983. 12-Oct-92 Ader Tajan, Paris #32/R (F.FR 30000)
$5956	£3654	Le Grand appel de toussaint louverture (121x76cm-48x30in) s.d.1985. 12-Oct-92 Ader Tajan, Paris #29/R (F.FR 30000)
$5956	£3654	L'affaire des poisons (92x77cm-36x30in) s.d.1985. 12-Oct-92 Ader Tajan, Paris #21/R (F.FR 30000)
$6353	£3898	Victoire a vertieres (122x92cm-48x36in) s.d.1974. 12-Oct-92 Ader Tajan, Paris #33/R (F.FR 32000)
$6949	£4263	La ceremonie du Bois-Caimoin (143x214cm-56x84in) s.d.1986. 12-Oct-92 Ader Tajan, Paris #25/R (F.FR 35000)
$7147	£4385	Bacchanales (176x225cm-69x89in) s.d.1972. 12-Oct-92 Ader Tajan, Paris #19/R (F.FR 36000)
$7544	£4629	L'echo du Lambi (92x77cm-36x30in) s.d.1986. 12-Oct-92 Ader Tajan, Paris #24/R (F.FR 38000)
$7942	£4872	Quatre Chefs marrons (75x90cm-30x35in) s.d.1982. 12-Oct-92 Ader Tajan, Paris #16/R (F.FR 40000)
$8339	£5116	Debarquement des esclaves (91x122cm-36x48in) s.d.1985. 12-Oct-92 Ader Tajan, Paris #10/R (F.FR 42000)
$8934	£5481	Le cacique Henri (82x72cm-32x28in) s.d.1981. 12-Oct-92 Ader Tajan, Paris #9/R (F.FR 45000)
$8934	£5481	Oracle du destin - debarquement des Espagnols en 1492 (76x101cm-30x40in) s.d.1980. 12-Oct-92 Ader Tajan, Paris #4/R (F.FR 45000)
$9530	£5847	La Bataille de la Crete-a-Pierrot (107x143cm-42x56in) s.d.1980. 12-Oct-92 Ader Tajan, Paris #30/R (F.FR 48000)
$10324	£6334	Bapteme et danse des esclaves (92x122cm-36x48in) s.d.1983. 12-Oct-92 Ader Tajan, Paris #12/R (F.FR 52000)
$11912	£7308	Refuge des marrons (82x72cm-32x28in) s.d.1982. 12-Oct-92 Ader Tajan, Paris #13/R (F.FR 60000)
$12309	£7552	Nourriture des esclaves (56x77cm-22x30in) s.d.1982. 12-Oct-92 Ader Tajan, Paris #14/R (F.FR 62000)
$12309	£7552	Liberation - Chant d'Allegresse (122x92cm-48x36in) s.d.1974. 12-Oct-92 Ader Tajan, Paris #34/R (F.FR 62000)

DESSAR, Louis Paul (1867-1952) American
$1400	£824	Figure and cart at sunset (61x76cm-24x30in) s. 8-Oct-92 Freeman Fine Arts, Philadelphia #1043

DESVARREUX-LARPENTEUR, James (1847-1937) American
$2280	£1500	Changing pastures (59x80cm-23x31in) s. 2-Jun-93 Sotheby's, Billingshurst #509/R

DEUTSCH, B (1892-1978) American
$1184	£800	Roman maidens at a window (69x56cm-27x22in) s. 25-Nov-93 Christie's, S. Kensington #121

DEUTSCH, Boris (1892-1978) American
$3500	£2318	Draped head (56x71cm-22x28in) s.d.1930. 23-Sep-93 Sotheby's, New York #248/R
$5500	£3642	One world or none (152x114cm-60x45in) s.d.1947. 23-Sep-93 Sotheby's, New York #250/R

DEUTSCH, David (20th C) American?
$5000	£2941	Untitled (214x153cm-84x60in) brush ink paper mounted on canvas. 8-Oct-92 Christie's, New York #235/R

DEVINE, Bernard (1884-?) American
$2800	£1842	Fanueil Hall, Boston (76x91cm-30x36in) s.indist.d. 31-Mar-93 Sotheby's Arcade, New York #262/R

DEVOLL, Frederick Usher (1873-1941) American
$1500	£1049	April showers city scene (30x41cm-12x16in) s. 12-Mar-93 Skinner, Bolton #274/R

DEWEY, Charles Melville (1849-1937) American
$1400	£940	Potatoe farming (41x61cm-16x24in) s.d.83 canvas on board double-sided. 4-Mar-94 Skinner, Bolton #244/R
$2000	£1333	Lowville, New York (84x107cm-33x42in) s. 23-May-94 Christie's, East, New York #194/R
$12000	£8054	Hollyhocks (37x24cm-15x9in) s. board. 4-Mar-94 Skinner, Bolton #221/R

DEWING, Thomas W (1851-1938) American
$85000	£56667	Young woman with violincello (53x41cm-21x16in) s. painted c.1912. 25-May-94 Sotheby's, New York #71/R
$4750	£3084	Seated lady attended by two putti (41x25cm-16x10in) s.d.1889 W/C pastel. 11-Sep-93 Dargate Auction Galleries, Pittsburgh #3
$9000	£5960	Woman in blue (37x28cm-15x11in) s. pastel paper on board. 22-Sep-93 Christie's, New York #125/R

DEWING, Thomas W (attrib) (1851-1938) American
$700 £455 Woman with pearl necklace (51x43cm-20x17in) s. pastel. 11-Sep-93 Louisiana Auction Exchange #84/R

DEXTER, Freeman (19th C) American
$2700 £1800 Portrait of William Alden Dexter holding dog, about age 3 (43x33cm-17x13in) board. 12-Jun-94 Skinner, Bolton #47/R

DEY, John William (1912-1978) American
$1500 £993 Bears with Kitty Trouble (43x56cm-17x22in) s.i. model airplane enamel board. 21-Nov-92 Litchfield Auction Gallery #9
$1650 £1093 Bird Park Commando (30x69cm-12x27in) s.i. painted 1973 model plane enamel cardboard. 21-Nov-92 Litchfield Auction Gallery #10
$2100 £1391 Charlie Chaplin inspecting Country Real Estate (61x76cm-24x30in) s.i. model airplane enamel board. 21-Nov-92 Litchfield Auction Gallery #8

DIAGO, Roberto (1920-1957) Cuban
$1200 £784 Untitled (31x45cm-12x18in) s.d.12-1942 W/C ink. 18-May-93 Sotheby's, New York #164/R
$2500 £1656 Dos musicos (25x25cm-10x10in) s.d.XLV verso gouache. 24-Nov-92 Christie's, New York #342/R
$4000 £2649 Abstracto (28x36cm-11x14in) s.i.d.XLVIII ink. 23-Nov-92 Sotheby's, New York #202/R

DIAMOND, Jessica (1957-) American
$800 £537 Money having sex (124x97cm-49x38in) s.d.1989verso acrylic paper four sheets. 3-May-94 Christie's, East, New York #196/R
$1500 £1042 Those who dream and do, coffee achievers. Jimmy Swaggart shorts are wrong , exec.1984 and 1986 brush ink paper collage two. 22-Feb-93 Christie's, East, New York #259/R

DICKINSON, Edwin (1891-1978) American
$1200 £789 Judith (66x76cm-26x30in) s.d.1937. 31-Mar-93 Sotheby's Arcade, New York #301/R
$7500 £4335 Vuillet's house (20x25cm-8x10in) s.indis.s.d.1946 masonite. 25-Sep-92 Sotheby's Arcade, New York #339/R
$1800 £1040 Concert touche (20x12cm-8x5in) s.i. pencil sold with etching of female nude. 25-Sep-92 Sotheby's Arcade, New York #260/R
$4750 £2746 Counter schooner Levuka. Annapolis. First sight of Greece , one s.i.d.24 one s.i.d.1959 pencil pair. 25-Sep-92 Sotheby's Arcade, New York #254/R

DICKINSON, Preston (1891-1930) American
$11000 £6358 Still life (14x9cm-6x4in) s.d.24 board. 23-Sep-92 Christie's, New York #216/R
$7000 £4046 High bridge (56x24cm-22x9in) s. chl ink. 23-Sep-92 Christie's, New York #221/R

DICKINSON, Sidney Edward (1890-1980) American
$3600 £2400 Unrest - nude (157x117cm-62x46in) s.d.1917. 23-May-94 Hindman Galleries, Chicago #218/R

DIEBENKORN, Richard (1922-1993) American
$46000 £30872 Untitled (41x45cm-16x18in) executed c.1960. 4-May-94 Christie's, New York #140/R
$54000 £36242 Untitled (32x41cm-13x16in) init.d.55 muslin. 5-May-94 Sotheby's, New York #186/R
$75000 £49669 Reclining nude - pink stripe (79x63cm-31x25in) init.d.62 s.d.1962 verso. 18-Nov-92 Sotheby's, New York #117/R
$101320 £68000 Knife in glass (27x37cm-11x15in) init.d.63 d.1963 stretcher board. 23-Mar-93 Phillips, London #49/R
$120000 £81081 No.24 - Albuquerque (169x123cm-67x48in) s.num.d.1952 verso. 9-Nov-93 Christie's, New York #12/R
$600000 £402685 Berkeley no 37 (177x177cm-70x70in) init.d.55 s.i.d.verso. 3-May-94 Christie's, New York #33/R
$8000 £4706 Untitled (32x43cm-13x17in) init.d.65 pencil chl. 6-Oct-92 Sotheby's, New York #17/R
$14000 £9150 Seated nude with necklace (43x35cm-17x14in) init.d.66 conte crayon. 4-May-93 Sotheby's, New York #338/R
$25000 £14706 Untitled (43x35cm-17x14in) init.d.65 ink pencil. 6-Oct-92 Sotheby's, New York #15/R
$40000 £26846 Untitled (89x58cm-35x23in) init.d.80 oil chl crayon. 5-May-94 Sotheby's, New York #278/R
$41000 £24118 Untitled (40x33cm-16x13in) init.d.64 ink. 6-Oct-92 Sotheby's, New York #16/R
$45000 £29412 Sleeping nude (36x42cm-14x17in) init.d.61 ink pencil. 4-May-93 Sotheby's, New York #336/R
$60500 £40878 Untitled - Berkeley (51x46cm-20x18in) init.d.55 oil brush ink graphite. 9-Nov-93 Christie's, New York #3/R
$90000 £58824 Untitled (95x63cm-37x25in) init.d.84 gouache paper collage. 4-May-93 Sotheby's, New York #190/R
$135000 £90604 Ocean Park (61x43cm-24x17in) init.d.77 gouache. 4-May-94 Sotheby's, New York #5/R
$175000 £118243 Untitled No.15 - Ocean Park (94x66cm-37x26in) init.d.83-4 acrylic gouache col.crayons collage. 9-Nov-93 Christie's, New York #40/R

DIEDRICKSEN, Theodore (1884-?) American
$9500 £6250 Egyptian fantasy (112x96cm-44x38in) s.d.1912 st.verso. 31-Mar-93 Sotheby's Arcade, New York #72/R

DIEGO, Paquita de (1937-) Mexican
$1140 £750 Coro de pajaros (60x80cm-24x31in) s.d.1992. 4-Nov-92 Mora, Castelltort & Quintana, Juarez #22/R (M.P 3600000)

DIEGO, Paquita de (1937-) Mexican-cont.
$1520 £1000 Angel de la guarda (100x100cm-39x39in) s.d.1992 mixed media canvas. 4-Nov-92 Mora, Castelltort & Quintana, Juarez #142/R (M.P 4800000)

DIEHL, Arthur (1870-1929) American
$650	£428	Seascape (30x46cm-12x18in) s. 2-Apr-93 Eldred, Massachusetts #553/R
$750	£472	Venetian port (30x46cm-12x18in) s.d.1919. 22-Apr-93 Freeman Fine Arts, Philadelphia #1282 a
$800	£559	Oriental street (48x71cm-19x28in) s.d.1922 i.verso board. 12-Mar-93 Skinner, Bolton #248/R
$800	£530	Fishing boats and figures by shore (43x43cm-17x17in) s. board. 13-Nov-92 Skinner, Bolton #158/R
$990	£647	Dunes, late afternoon (51x102cm-20x40in) s.d.1918 board. 14-May-93 Skinner, Bolton #116/R
$1100	£728	Cape Cod dunes (51x81cm-20x32in) s.d.1928 board. 23-Sep-93 Mystic Fine Arts, Connecticut #143/R
$1200	£635	Dunes at Provincetown (51x102cm-20x40in) s.i.d.1914. 11-Sep-92 Skinner, Bolton #244/R
$1300	£878	Seascape with steamer (38x79cm-15x31in) s.d.1920 board. 22-Apr-94 Du Mouchelle, Detroit #2153/R
$3500	£2303	Trophy fish (28x79cm-11x31in) s.d.1917 card. 4-Jun-93 Sotheby's, New York #215/R
$3800	£2550	Sunny day, Provincetown (30x46cm-12x18in) s.d.1927 board. 5-Aug-93 Eldred, Massachusetts #800/R

DIKE, Philip Latimer (1906-) American
$750 £507 Figure study (51x20cm-20x8in) indist.s. mixed media. 9-Nov-93 John Moran, Pasadena #992

DILBY, B H (19th C) American
$2100 £1419 Still life with strawberries (20x25cm-8x10in) s.d.1867 panel. 31-Mar-94 Sotheby's Arcade, New York #11/R

DILL, Laddie John (1943-) American
$900	£566	Untitled (60x122cm-24x48in) acrylic painted 1985. 25-Apr-93 Butterfield & Butterfield, San Francisco #2123/R
$3000	£1899	Untitled, 1982 (124x216cm-49x85in) 25-Oct-92 Butterfield & Butterfield, San Francisco #2386/R
$1500	£943	Untitled (107x213cm-42x84in) s.d.1977-83verso mixed media wood. 25-Apr-93 Butterfield & Butterfield, San Francisco #2124/R
$2250	£1521	Untitled (93x143cm-37x56in) s.d.1981 mixed media. 21-Oct-93 Butterfield & Butterfield, San Francisco #2811/R
$2250	£1521	Untitled (81x161cm-32x63in) s.d.1988 mixed media. 21-Apr-94 Butterfield & Butterfield, San Francisco #1199/R

DILLER, Burgoyne (1906-1965) American
| $70000 | £47297 | First theme No 46 (122x91cm-48x36in) painted c.1964. 10-Nov-93 Sotheby's, New York #10/R |
| $3500 | £2365 | Untitled (23x20cm-9x8in) init.d.48 pencil col.pencil. 11-Nov-93 Sotheby's, New York #324/R |

DILLON, Julia (1834-1919) American
$600 £405 Watermelon (46x76cm-18x30in) s.d.93. 27-Nov-93 Young Fine Arts Auctions, Maine #108/R

DINCKEL, George W (1890-?) American
$950 £660 Seascape (61x76cm-24x30in) s. canvas on board. 6-Mar-93 Louisiana Auction Exchange #85/R

DINE, Jim (1935-) American
$65000	£43624	The floor of the heart (213x213cm-84x84in) s.i.d.1981verso acrylic resin sand linen. 3-May-94 Christie's, New York #63/R
$95000	£63758	At the wedding (168x305cm-66x120in) canvas in two parts painted 1989. 5-May-94 Sotheby's, New York #228/R
$1200	£805	Untitled (38x23cm-15x9in) s.d.75 pencil paperboard. 25-Feb-94 Sotheby's, New York #59 a/R
$1400	£819	Awl (61x50cm-24x20in) s.d.num.28/200 screenprint wove paper. 19-Sep-92 Christie's, East, New York #93
$6000	£4054	Nancy in the soup (96x77cm-38x30in) s.d.1979 chk pencil ink chl. 11-Nov-93 Sotheby's, New York #401/R
$6500	£4114	Four hearts (33x33cm-13x13in) s.d.1970 W/C. 25-Oct-92 Butterfield & Butterfield, San Francisco #2383/R
$10430	£7000	Bathrobe (104x75cm-41x30in) s.d.1984 oil pastel acrylic ink. 23-Mar-94 Sotheby's, London #355/R
$14000	£9150	Jessie with a shell V (109x77cm-43x30in) s.d.1982 W/C col chk chl. 5-May-93 Christie's, New York #292/R
$20000	£13423	Four palettes (43x130cm-17x51in) s.d.1963 W/C gouache pencil paper collage. 5-May-94 Sotheby's, New York #178/R
$23840	£16000	Pink bathrobe (105x75cm-41x30in) s.d.1984 oil enamel pastel acrylic chl. 3-Dec-93 Sotheby's, London #234/R
$24000	£15686	Robe (160x91cm-63x36in) s.i.d.1983 monotype oil. 11-May-93 Christie's, New York #406/R
$25000	£16340	Untitled (152x90cm-60x35in) s.d.1974 pencil graphite chl. 4-May-93 Sotheby's, New York #401 a/R
$32780	£22000	Four big hearts (75x70cm-30x28in) s.d.1970 spraypaint waxed paper on board. 25-Mar-93 Christie's, London #68/R

DINE, Jim (1935-) American-cont.
$35000	£23490	Untitled (133x100cm-52x39in) s.d.1981 W/C col.chk. 23-Feb-94 Christie's, New York #51/R
$90000	£60403	Untitled (63x244cm-25x96in) s.d.1982 W/C brush paper fabric collage. 25-Feb-94 Sotheby's, New York #106/R
$130000	£87248	Objects in palette landscape (213x152cm-84x60in) s.i.d.1963verso oil doorknob and objects canvas. 3-May-94 Christie's, New York #15/R
$160000	£104575	Heart called 'Rancho Pastel' (263x244cm-104x96in) s.d.1982 verso acrylic resin wood straw ceramic. 4-May-93 Christie's, New York #54/R

DINEEN, Tom (20th C) American
$600	£385	No.25 (142x107cm-56x42in) s.i.d.1977 chl.pastel. 10-Dec-92 Sloan, North Bethesda #2728/R

DINGLE, Adrian (1911-1974) Canadian
$1866	£1244	A frosty frolic (50x60cm-20x24in) s. masonite. 30-May-94 Ritchie, Toronto #161/R (C.D 2600)

DINNERSTEIN, Harvey (1928-) American
$650	£417	Federal court, Chicago (41x38cm-16x15in) init.i. pastel. 8-Dec-92 Swann Galleries, New York #85
$900	£577	Prophet II - proclaiming (43x74cm-17x29in) s.d.1970 pastel. 8-Dec-92 Swann Galleries, New York #87
$950	£609	Prophet I - crying (43x74cm-17x29in) s.d.1970 pastel. 8-Dec-92 Swann Galleries, New York #86

DIOMEDE, Miguel (1902-1974) Argentinian
$6000	£3974	Limones (21x29cm-8x11in) 11-Nov-92 VerBo, Buenos Aires #36
$7000	£3646	Barcazas en el Riachuelo (21x34cm-8x13in) 4-Aug-92 VerBo, Buenos Aires #41

DISNEY, Walt (1901-1966) American
$500	£342	Ariel, the little mermaid, surprised reaction (36x30cm-14x12in) cel. 18-Feb-94 Du Mouchelle, Detroit #1178
$550	£367	Scrooge McDuck, animation cell (23x41cm-9x16in) st.i. cell. 18-Mar-94 Du Mouchelle, Detroit #77/R
$550	£353	Snow white (30x23cm-12x9in) i. pencil. 11-Dec-92 Du Mouchelle, Detroit #1225/R
$1100	£733	Who framed Roger Rabbit, animation cell (20x30cm-8x12in) st.i. cell. 18-Mar-94 Du Mouchelle, Detroit #80/R
$1400	£897	Ariel the little mermaid (25x33cm-10x13in) celluloid painting. 11-Dec-92 Du Mouchelle, Detroit #1217/R
$2500	£1656	Hop-low and the mushrooms dancing from Fantasia Nutcracker Suite (20x25cm-8x10in) studio st. gouache celluloid. 12-Nov-92 Freeman Fine Arts, Philadelphia #15/R
$4000	£2353	Jiminy Cricket (15x15cm-6x6in) i. air brushed W/C. 8-Oct-92 Boos Gallery, Michigan #454
$4256	£2800	Mickey Mouse (10x8cm-4x3in) s. pen. 5-Apr-93 Christie's, S. Kensington #44/R

DIXON, Francis Fitzroy (fl.1890-1904) Canadian
$1635	£1082	La Normandie (23x612cm-9x241in) mono.d.27.8.81 i. ink. 18-Nov-92 Sotheby's, Toronto #3/R (C.D 2100)

DIXON, Francis Stillwell (1872-1967) American
$1000	£654	Summer day (51x66cm-20x26in) s. 15-Sep-93 Doyle, New York #19
$1100	£753	Mountain lake (51x66cm-20x26in) s. 19-Feb-94 Young Fine Arts Auctions, Maine #79/R
$2200	£1438	Sunset after rain - view of Point Lobos, California (51x66cm-20x26in) s. 14-May-93 Skinner, Bolton #138/R

DIXON, Marie R (19th C) American
$1600	£1039	Portrait of lady with ruff collar (102x66cm-40x26in) s. 9-Sep-93 Sotheby's Arcade, New York #120/R
$1818	£1220	'He's out to sea' (48x36cm-19x14in) s. board. 24-Mar-94 Mystic Fine Arts, Connecticut #146/R

DIXON, Maynard (1875-1946) American
$2250	£1510	Desert hills (15x22cm-6x9in) s.d.12 i.verso board. 8-Dec-93 Butterfield & Butterfield, San Francisco #3568/R
$7000	£4118	Skies of New Mexico (25x36cm-10x14in) s.d.1931 board. 4-Oct-92 Butterfield & Butterfield, Los Angeles #213/R
$7000	£4636	On the way to Death Valley, Inyo Country (25x36cm-10x14in) init.i.d.Oct.1919 board. 15-Jun-94 Butterfield & Butterfield, San Francisco #4514/R
$7500	£4967	Indian man wearing a shawl (34x25cm-13x10in) init.i.d.Oct.1923 board. 15-Jun-94 Butterfield & Butterfield, San Francisco #4511/R
$8000	£5298	Lava topped ridge (25x36cm-10x14in) init.i.d.Sept.1933 board. 15-Jun-94 Butterfield & Butterfield, San Francisco #4530/R
$12000	£8054	South Point and junipers (31x42cm-12x17in) s.d.1942 s.i.verso canvasboard. 8-Dec-93 Butterfield & Butterfield, San Francisco #3574/R
$13000	£9028	Promise of spring (30x41cm-12x16in) s.i.d.1942 canvas on board. 7-Mar-93 Butterfield & Butterfield, San Francisco #221/R
$15000	£10490	The lone rider (23x15cm-9x6in) mono.d.15 i.verso canvasboard. 12-Mar-93 Skinner, Bolton #220/R
$15000	£10417	Peak and clouds (30x41cm-12x16in) s.d.1945 canvas on board. 7-Mar-93 Butterfield & Butterfield, San Francisco #220/R
$80000	£53691	Saddlehorses grazing (51x188cm-20x74in) s.d.1922. 2-Dec-93 Sotheby's, New York #55/R

DIXON, Maynard (1875-1946) American-cont.
$750	£487	Bucking bronco (25x18cm-10x7in) init.st.d.1943 pencil. 11-Sep-93 Louisiana Auction Exchange #86/R
$1100	£724	Figures in desert with distant mesas - mural study (7x15cm-3x6in) init.d.1937 pencil. 13-Jun-93 Butterfield & Butterfield, San Francisco #3227/R
$1100	£724	Roundup at Flathead (11x15cm-4x6in) i.d.09 pencil. 13-Jun-93 Butterfield & Butterfield, San Francisco #3229/R
$1200	£789	Indians on horseback (10x11cm-4x4in) init.d.1942 pen pencil. 13-Jun-93 Butterfield & Butterfield, San Francisco #3230/R
$1200	£789	Riders and Burros, Guadalajara (16x12cm-6x5in) init.i.d.05 pastel pencil ink. 13-Jun-93 Butterfield & Butterfield, San Francisco #918/R
$1300	£855	Black bucker (10x9cm-4x4in) init.d.1942 pencil. 13-Jun-93 Butterfield & Butterfield, San Francisco #3236/R
$1700	£1181	Dinner (12x8cm-5x3in) st.d.Apr 04 chl. 7-Mar-93 Butterfield & Butterfield, San Francisco #233/R
$1700	£1181	San Francisco character no 5 (13x11cm-5x4in) st.i.d.1903 pencil. 7-Mar-93 Butterfield & Butterfield, San Francisco #232/R
$2750	£1821	The Indian flute player. A Western Dance (25x20cm-10x8in) init.d.1912 i.verso W/C pencil double-sided. 15-Jun-94 Butterfield & Butterfield, San Francisco #4516/R
$2750	£1821	The Kachina Doll maker (40x28cm-16x11in) init.i.d.Oct.1923 chl dr. 15-Jun-94 Butterfield & Butterfield, San Francisco #4512/R
$3000	£2041	Battle cry (45x31cm-18x12in) s.d.95 ink htd.white gouache board. 15-Nov-93 Christie's, East, New York #101/R
$3100	£2081	Night rider (36x66cm-14x26in) s.i.d.06 pastel paperboard. 5-Mar-94 Louisiana Auction Exchange #144/R
$4000	£2685	Storm clouds and distant mountains (25x32cm-10x13in) s.d.1922 pastel paperboard. 4-Mar-94 Skinner, Bolton #249/R
$5000	£3289	Youapai County, Arizona (20x27cm-8x11in) s.d.1900 pen wash. 13-Jun-93 Butterfield & Butterfield, San Francisco #922/R
$5000	£3356	Buffalo hunt (30x28cm-12x11in) W/C. 27-Mar-94 Myers, Florida #43/R
$5500	£3716	Southern Pacific steam locomotive passing Indians (23x94cm-9x37in) s. gouache board. 9-Nov-93 John Moran, Pasadena #891
$6500	£4276	Saguaro landscape (23x48cm-9x19in) s.i. gouache. 13-Jun-93 Butterfield & Butterfield, San Francisco #872/R
$6500	£4276	Desert clouds (29x25cm-11x10in) s.i. gouache. 13-Jun-93 Butterfield & Butterfield, San Francisco #873/R
$7500	£4967	New Mexican Pueblo (26x35cm-10x14in) s.i.d.Oct.1900 pencil gouache. 15-Jun-94 Butterfield & Butterfield, San Francisco #4513/R
$8500	£5592	Indian encampment (62x35cm-24x14in) s.d.1940 gouache pencil. 31-Mar-93 Sotheby's Arcade, New York #193 a/R
$8500	£5629	A tearful farewell (56x38cm-22x15in). s. i.verso W/C paper laid down on board. 15-Jun-94 Butterfield & Butterfield, San Francisco #4515/R

DIXON, Maynard (attrib) (1875-1946) American
$750	£475	Taos (18x41cm-7x16in) s.i. board. 30-Nov-92 Schrager Galleries, Milwaukee #451

D'LEON, Omar (20th C) South American
$2500	£1645	Still life of melons and pomegranates (51x61cm-20x24in) s.d.1989 oil wax with pencil sketch verso. 4-Nov-92 Doyle, New York #63/R

DODGE, William de Leftwich (1867-1935) American
$5250	£3454	Golden flow (103x61cm-41x24in) s. 31-Mar-93 Sotheby's Arcade, New York #263/R

DOEMING, John Carl (20th C) American
$725	£474	Rockaneck Street, Gloucester (66x81cm-26x32in) s. 16-May-93 Hanzel Galleries, Chicago #417

DOGHERTY, Felix (19th C) American?
$1300	£909	George Washington on horseback (23x29cm-9x11in) s.d.1810 W/C. 10-Mar-93 Sotheby's, New York #2 a/R

DOHANOS, Stevan (1907-) American
$700	£458	Logs in winter (51x61cm-20x24in) s.d.48 masonite. 4-May-93 Christie's, East, New York #170/R
$600	£403	Mail room (33x66cm-13x26in) s. W/C. 16-Dec-93 Mystic Fine Arts, Connecticut #187/R
$700	£458	Steps of New York Public Library, 42nd Street (57x75cm-22x30in) s. W/C. 4-May-93 Christie's, East, New York #161/R
$750	£524	Day at the fair (20x25cm-8x10in) s. oil graphite masonite. 12-Mar-93 Skinner, Bolton #305/R

DOLICE, Leon (20th C) American
$700	£458	New York City scene (61x46cm-24x18in) s. pastel. 30-Jun-94 Mystic Fine Arts, Connecticut #148/R

DOLINSKY, Nathan (1890-?) American
$750	£497	Woman sewing by window (76x64cm-30x25in) s. 28-Sep-93 John Moran, Pasadena #247

DOLPH, John Henry (1835-1903) American
$1300	£884	Among friends (25x36cm-10x14in) s. 16-Apr-94 Young Fine Arts Auctions, Maine #94
$1400	£940	In the artist's studio (13x20cm-5x8in) sig. panel. 4-Mar-94 Skinner, Bolton #202/R
$1500	£993	View of valley (51x76cm-20x30in) init.d.1863. 21-Nov-92 James Bakker, Cambridge #265/R

DOLPH, John Henry (1835-1903) American-cont.
$1700	£1156	The sword maker (112x84cm-44x33in) s. 14-Apr-94 Freeman Fine Arts, Philadelphia #972/R
$1700	£1076	Asleep by the fireplace (23x30cm-9x12in) s. 2-Dec-92 Christie's, East, New York #75 a
$2000	£1282	A curious spool (48x61cm-19x24in) s. 28-Apr-93 Doyle, New York #19/R
$3000	£1923	Mate (23x33cm-9x13in) s. panel. 10-Dec-92 Sloan, North Bethesda #2617/R
$6000	£3922	Baby playing with kittens (56x77cm-22x30in) init. 4-May-93 Christie's, East, New York #172/R
$8500	£5667	Time out for haying, New Haven (55x102cm-22x40in) s.d.1867. 16-Mar-94 Christie's, New York #36/R

DOMELA, Jan Marinus (1894-1973) American
$650	£428	Farm and fields (30x41cm-12x16in) s. board. 13-Jun-93 Butterfield & Butterfield, San Francisco #884/R
$1900	£1319	Old Mammoth Road (41x51cm-16x20in) s. board. 7-Mar-93 Butterfield & Butterfield, San Francisco #141/R

DOMINGUEZ NEIRA, Pedro (1894-1970) Argentinian
$450	£304	Naturaleza muerta (35x52cm-14x20in) s.d.1938 gouache paper laid down on board. 21-Apr-94 Butterfield & Butterfield, San Francisco #111/R

DOMINIQUE, John August (1893-?) American
$3000	£2083	Mountains ner Matilya Dam (71x91cm-28x36in) s.d.1960. 7-Mar-93 Butterfield & Butterfield, San Francisco #202/R

DONAGHY, John (1838-?) American
$3200	£2133	Sailing toy boats (71x50cm-28x20in) s.d.91. 23-May-94 Christie's, East, New York #88/R

DONATI, Enrico (1909-) American/Italian
$850	£571	Red and black (20x25cm-8x10in) oil sand painted 1968. 23-Feb-94 Christie's, East, New York #372/R
$5500	£3642	Fossil series 3000 B.C. (89x114cm-35x45in) s. s.i.d.10/62 oil sand. 17-Nov-92 Christie's, East, New York #238/R
$11000	£7383	The three elders (180x250cm-71x98in) s. painted c.1953-55. 5-May-94 Sotheby's, New York #86/R

DONNA, Porfirio di (1942-1986) American
$900	£604	Centre shift (91x76cm-36x30in) s.d.1977 verso. 25-Mar-93 Boos Gallery, Michigan #435
$1100	£738	Untitled (61x56cm-24x22in) s.d.1977 verso. 25-Mar-93 Boos Gallery, Michigan #431/R

DONNELLY, Thomas (1893-?) American
$1100	£719	Progress of industry (71x91cm-28x36in) s.d.1938 s.d.stretcher. 5-May-93 Doyle, New York #58/R

DORSEY, William (20th C) American
$650	£439	Stream with eucalyptus (51x61cm-20x24in) s. 9-Nov-93 John Moran, Pasadena #969
$650	£430	Coastal 'China Cove' (41x51cm-16x20in) s. 14-Jun-94 John Moran, Pasadena #44
$700	£464	Coastal (46x61cm-18x24in) s. 28-Sep-93 John Moran, Pasadena #366
$750	£497	Coastal landscape (51x61cm-20x24in) 28-Sep-93 John Moran, Pasadena #384
$800	£541	Eucalyptus coastal scene (61x46cm-24x18in) s. masonite. 9-Nov-93 John Moran, Pasadena #798
$850	£563	Ojai oranges (30x46cm-12x18in) s. masonite. 28-Sep-93 John Moran, Pasadena #213
$850	£563	Flowered coastal (58x79cm-23x31in) 28-Sep-93 John Moran, Pasadena #341
$900	£608	Flowered landscape (51x61cm-20x24in) s. 9-Nov-93 John Moran, Pasadena #797
$900	£608	Landscape by stream (102x127cm-40x50in) s. 15-Jun-93 John Moran, Pasadena #85
$1000	£658	Santa Barbara beach (61x91cm-24x36in) s. 13-Jun-93 Butterfield & Butterfield, San Francisco #882/R
$1000	£676	Coastal eucalyptus (76x127cm-30x50in) s. 9-Nov-93 John Moran, Pasadena #967
$1000	£676	Eucalyptus coastal (41x51cm-16x20in) s. 15-Jun-93 John Moran, Pasadena #121
$1000	£676	Eucalyptus pathway with blue iris (122x66cm-48x26in) s. 15-Jun-93 John Moran, Pasadena #147
$1100	£743	Eucalyptus coastal (102x76cm-40x30in) s. 15-Jun-93 John Moran, Pasadena #131
$1100	£728	Coastal view with iris (30x41cm-12x16in) s. 28-Sep-93 John Moran, Pasadena #390
$1200	£795	Coastal (79x56cm-31x22in) s. 28-Sep-93 John Moran, Pasadena #268
$1300	£861	Flowered coastal (86x102cm-34x40in) s. 28-Sep-93 John Moran, Pasadena #267
$1500	£993	Coastal with eucalyptus trees (81x71cm-32x28in) s. 28-Sep-93 John Moran, Pasadena #365
$1500	£993	Landscape (89x102cm-35x40in) s. 28-Sep-93 John Moran, Pasadena #229
$1700	£1126	Flowered coastal (76x81cm-30x32in) s. 28-Sep-93 John Moran, Pasadena #236
$1800	£1250	Big Sur coastline (61x91cm-24x35in) s. 7-Mar-93 Butterfield & Butterfield, San Francisco #93/R
$2000	£1325	Flowered coastal (79x130cm-31x51in) s. 28-Sep-93 John Moran, Pasadena #237
$2750	£1821	Coastal eucalyptus and iris (102x122cm-40x48in) s. 28-Sep-93 John Moran, Pasadena #225
$4000	£2649	View to the coast (74x104cm-29x41in) s. 15-Jun-94 Butterfield & Butterfield, San Francisco #4700/R

DOSAMANTES, Francisco (1911-) Mexican
$4509	£3006	Las Quemas (105x80cm-41x31in) s. 25-May-94 Louis Morton, Mexico #97/R (M.P 15000)

DOUGHERTY, Paul (1877-1947) American
$1200	£795	Rocky seascape (40x56cm-16x22in) s. 2-Oct-93 Weschler, Washington #140/R
$2000	£1351	Calming after a gale (46x61cm-18x24in) s.i.d.1922 stretcher. 31-Mar-94 Sotheby's Arcade, New York #248/R
$3600	£2416	Misty morning Little White Head (91x122cm-36x48in) s.i.stretcher. 2-Dec-93 Freeman Fine Arts, Philadelphia #855 a
$4000	£2703	Waves (91x138cm-36x54in) s. 31-Mar-94 Sotheby's Arcade, New York #249/R
$4750	£3105	Pounding breakers (66x91cm-26x36in) s. 8-May-93 Young Fine Arts Auctions, Maine #91/R
$5500	£3235	Rocky coast (91x86cm-36x34in) s.d.1901. 4-Oct-92 Butterfield & Butterfield, Los Angeles #160/R
$6000	£4027	Off the coast of Maine (53x65cm-21x26in) s. panel. 8-Dec-93 Butterfield & Butterfield, San Francisco #3455/R
$6000	£3529	Rocks and surf (60x73cm-24x29in) s. 4-Oct-92 Butterfield & Butterfield, Los Angeles #159/R
$6000	£3468	Freshening gale (68x92cm-27x36in) 23-Sep-92 Christie's, New York #197/R
$12000	£8333	Crashing surf (66x91cm-26x36in) s. 7-Mar-93 Butterfield & Butterfield, San Francisco #171/R

DOUGHERTY, Paul (attrib) (1877-1947) American
$750	£500	Rocky seascape (40x56cm-16x22in) s. 21-May-94 Weschler, Washington #122/R

DOUGHTY, Thomas (1793-1856) American
$9500	£6090	Southern swamp (51x70cm-20x28in) 26-May-93 Christie's, New York #17/R
$10000	£6329	Landscape by the dam (53x74cm-21x29in) 3-Dec-92 Sotheby's, New York #6/R
$40000	£27972	Early winter (108x142cm-43x56in) canvas on masonite. 11-Mar-93 Christie's, New York #3/R

DOUGHTY, Thomas (attrib) (1793-1856) American
$1100	£733	The trout fisherman (46x33cm-18x13in) panel. 17-May-94 Christie's, East, New York #494

DOUGLAS, Bloomfield (1832-1906) Canadian
$1019	£680	Lake Achigan looking south. Lake Achigan (20x30cm-8x12in) s.i.d.1891 i.verso two. 11-May-94 Sotheby's, Toronto #17 (C.D 1400)

DOUGLAS, Walter (1864-?) American
$1000	£680	New England farm (25x36cm-10x14in) s. board. 19-Nov-93 Du Mouchelle, Detroit #2324/R
$1150	£777	Chickens in barnyard (30x41cm-12x16in) s. panel. 23-Oct-93 Collins, Maine #165/R
$1700	£1164	On his own hill (30x41cm-12x16in) s. 19-Feb-94 Young Fine Arts Auctions, Maine #82/R

DOVE, Arthur G (1880-1946) American
$7000	£4667	Northpoint harbour (35x46cm-14x18in) coppper laid down on board. 26-May-94 Christie's, New York #128/R
$160000	£101266	Barn next door (51x71cm-20x28in) s. 4-Dec-92 Christie's, New York #131/R
$220000	£139241	Brick barge with landscape (76x102cm-30x40in) s. i.d.1930 verso board. 3-Dec-92 Sotheby's, New York #181/R
$2200	£1497	Untitled (10x15cm-4x6in) s. pencil crayon ink paper on board exec.1945. 15-Nov-93 Christie's, East, New York #221/R
$6000	£3974	Beach umbrella (12x18cm-5x7in) s. W/C chl painted 1931. 22-Sep-93 Christie's, New York #195/R
$8000	£4624	Abstraction, autumn leaves (12x17cm-5x7in) s.i. W/C pen paper on board. 23-Sep-92 Christie's, New York #218/R
$9000	£5882	Pier and boathouses (15x23cm-6x9in) s. W/C. 5-May-93 Doyle, New York #43/R
$10000	£6711	Landscape formation (13x18cm-5x7in) W/C painted 1941. 2-Dec-93 Sotheby's, New York #132/R

DOW, Arthur W (1857-1922) American
$3000	£2041	A Maine headland (30x41cm-12x16in) s. canvasboard. 17-Nov-93 Doyle, New York #21 a
$4000	£2614	Distant trees (76x102cm-30x40in) s. 17-Sep-93 Skinner, Bolton #237/R
$8800	£5752	June morning - view of Ipswich (36x51cm-14x20in) s. i.verso canvasboard. 14-May-93 Skinner, Bolton #136/R
$9000	£6000	The hayfields (20x25cm-8x10in) s.d.1899 canvasboard. 22-May-94 James Bakker, Cambridge #41/R

DOWD, Robert (20th C) American
$2500	£1582	Inverted Jenny (81x96cm-32x38in) s. s.d.68 verso. 25-Oct-92 Butterfield & Butterfield, San Francisco #2376/R
$3250	£2044	Twenty Dollar bill (71x102cm-28x40in) s. 25-Apr-93 Butterfield & Butterfield, San Francisco #2125
$11000	£7432	Picasso Lamp (147x112cm-58x44in) s. s.i.d.1968verso. 21-Apr-94 Butterfield & Butterfield, San Francisco #1145/R
$1600	£1013	Mail train (28x41cm-11x16in) s. W/C chl. 25-Oct-92 Butterfield & Butterfield, San Francisco #2375/R

DRAPER, William Franklin (1912-) American
$1300	£833	At the circus (32x37cm-13x15in) s. board. 9-Dec-92 Butterfield & Butterfield, San Francisco #4015/R

DRAYTON, Grace G (1877-1936) American
$900	£566	Tessa (36x36cm-14x14in) s. W/C. 22-Apr-93 Freeman Fine Arts, Philadelphia #1162

DREIER, Katherine Sophie (1877-1952) American
$6000   £3846   Improvisation (41x76cm-16x30in) s.d.1938 verso. 26-May-93 Christie's, New York #224/R

DREIN, Maude (19/20th C) American
$750   £500   Asters and Japanese doll (76x64cm-30x25in) s. 26-May-94 Sloan, North Bethesda #2111

DRESSLER, Edward James (1859-1907) American
$2400   £1579   Summer landscape (76x102cm-30x40in) s.d.1901. 31-Mar-93 Sotheby's Arcade, New York #157/R

DREW, C (1806-1889) American
$1900   £1348   Minot's Light from shore, 1886 (28x18cm-11x7in) 12-Feb-93 Douglas, South Deerfield #3

DREW, Clement (1806-1889) American
$1100   £719   Thacher Island Lights (23x30cm-9x12in) s.i.verso board painted 1883. 8-May-93 Young Fine Arts Auctions, Maine #92/R
$1600   £1060   Ship scudding (18x25cm-7x10in) s.d.1877verso. 23-Sep-93 Mystic Fine Arts, Connecticut #188/R
$3100   £2095   Boston light southeast gale (36x56cm-14x22in) i.d.1879verso. 30-Jul-93 Eldred, Massachusetts #141/R
$3200   £2162   Outward bound off Boston Light (46x66cm-18x26in) s.i.d.1863. 30-Jul-93 Eldred, Massachusetts #350/R

DREW, Clement (attrib) (1806-1889) American
$1000   £676   The red buoy (33x43cm-13x17in) oil metal. 27-Nov-93 Young Fine Arts Auctions, Maine #111/R
$1100   £738   Ship off a rocky coast (56x76cm-22x30in) 6-Feb-94 Skinner, Bolton #69/R

DREW, George W (1875-?) American
$700   £473   Spring cherry blossoms a river landscape (61x92cm-24x36in) s. 5-Nov-93 Skinner, Bolton #35/R
$800   £462   Summer landscape with farmhouse and lake (51x76cm-20x30in) s. s.i.d.Oct.11-1941stretcher. 25-Sep-92 Sotheby's Arcade, New York #205/R
$950   £625   Homestead, mid-summer along the pond, N. E. (61x91cm-24x36in) s. s.i.stretcher. 2-Apr-93 Sloan, North Bethesda #2311
$950   £625   Spring blossoms (51x76cm-20x30in) s. i.d.1940stretcher. 2-Jun-93 Doyle, New York #53/R
$1000   £662   Day of yachting (46x91cm-18x36in) s. d.1938 verso. 13-Nov-92 Skinner, Bolton #160/R
$1500   £794   Peaceful spot (61x91cm-24x36in) s. 9-Sep-92 Doyle, New York #25

DREWES, Werner (1899-1985) American
$900   £608   Olive abstract (19x33cm-7x13in) s. s.d.44 verso. 31-Mar-94 Sotheby's Arcade, New York #476/R
$1076   £717   Starlight (61x92cm-24x36in) s.i.d.77 s.i.verso. 7-Jun-94 Karl & Faber, Munich #629/R (DM 1800)
$1900   £1284   Abstract No.366 (30x56cm-12x22in) s. s.i.d.45 verso. 31-Mar-94 Sotheby's Arcade, New York #470/R
$2000   £1156   Abstract (30x56cm-12x22in) s.d.45. 27-Sep-92 James Bakker, Cambridge #221/R
$3200   £2177   Telegraph pole (46x61cm-18x24in) mono.d.31. 17-Nov-93 Doyle, New York #56/R
$3201   £2148   Landscape with bridge (51x76cm-20x30in) s0.i.d.36 i.d.verso. 4-Dec-93 Lempertz, Cologne #142/R (DM 5500)
$3201   £2148   Town by the river with bridge (73x92cm-29x36in) s. i.d.1956verso. 4-Dec-93 Lempertz, Cologne #144/R (DM 5500)
$3300   £2340   Meteors (81x107cm-32x42in) s. mono.verso. 14-Feb-93 Hanzel Galleries, Chicago #46
$3800   £2695   Abstract figure (97x91cm-38x36in) s. s.d.1959verso. 14-Feb-93 Hanzel Galleries, Chicago #43
$4500   £2922   Untitled (96x91cm-38x36in) s.d.1959. 9-Sep-93 Sotheby's Arcade, New York #448 a/R
$11000   £7383   Vertical, horizontal interchange (51x36cm-20x14in) s.i.d.37 i.d.37verso. 4-May-94 Doyle, New York #63/R
$550   *£390*   *Abstraction (18x15cm-7x6in) s. W/C. 14-Feb-93 Hanzel Galleries, Chicago #44*
$700   *£405*   *Abstraction (20x16cm-8x6in) s. W/C pencil. 23-Sep-92 Christie's, New York #285/R*
$950   *£549*   *Biomorphic abstraction (21x17cm-8x7in) s. W/C pencil. 25-Sep-92 Sotheby's Arcade, New York #463/R*
$1000   *£578*   *Cubist abstraction (21x16cm-8x6in) s. W/C pencil. 25-Sep-92 Sotheby's Arcade, New York #462/R*
$1200   *£694*   *Abstraction (15x23cm-6x9in) s.mono.i.d.35 i.verso W/C. 25-Sep-92 Sotheby's Arcade, New York #464/R*

DREYFOUS, Florence (19/20th C) American
$600   *£385*   *Peony (38x28cm-15x11in) s. i.verso W/C. 8-Dec-92 Swann Galleries, New York #91*

DREYFUS, Bernardo (1940-) Nicaraguan
$4250   £2852   Recuerdo fulminante de sol (100x81cm-39x32in) s.d.92 s.i.d.verso acrylic oil linen. 7-Jun-94 Gary Nader, Miami #53/R
$8000   £5229   Pajaros que en nuestro camino nos servian de pensamiento (114x145cm-45x57in) s.d.92 s.i.d.verso. 17-May-93 Christie's, New York #167/R

DRIGGS (19/20th C) American
$950   £638   Lake at sunset (30x51cm-12x20in) s.indist.d.1886. 12-Jan-94 Doyle, New York #21

DRIGGS, Elsie (1898-) American
$650   £376   The soul selects her own society (43x38cm-17x15in) s.d.1938 W/C pencil. 25-Sep-92
                Sotheby's Arcade, New York #448
$850   £559   Hark, hark, dogs do bark (38x52cm-15x20in) s.d.1937 d.verso W/C pencil
                double-sided. 31-Mar-93 Sotheby's Arcade, New York #413/R

DROGKAMP, Charles (20th C) American
$1100   £743   In the park (53x79cm-21x31in) s. 9-Nov-93 John Moran, Pasadena #941

DRUM, David Clayton (1944-) Canadian
$543   £362   Sumach and maple on the Commanda River chute (36x46cm-14x18in) s. i.verso.
                6-Jun-94 Waddingtons, Toronto #1201 (C.D 750)
$741   £487   Great white trillium and yellow lady's slipper (39x41cm-15x16in) s. i.verso.
                7-Jun-93 Waddingtons, Toronto #1204 b (C.D 950)
$935   £615   Tiger lilies and poppies (51x61cm-20x24in) s. i.verso board. 7-Jun-93
                Waddingtons, Toronto #1204 a (C.D 1200)

DRYER, Moira (1957-1992) American
$2000   £1342   Portrait no.124 (61x65cm-24x26in) s.i.d.1989 verso acrylic panel. 23-Feb-94
                Christie's, East, New York #232/R
$6000   £4027   Captain courageous (198x218cm-78x86in) s.i.d.1990verso acrylic panel. 4-May-94
                Christie's, New York #254/R
$6000   £3974   Box plaid (122x155cm-48x61in) s.i.d.1990verso acrylic panel. 17-Nov-92
                Christie's, East, New York #33/R
$8000   £5405   Stiff sentence (213x274cm-84x108in) s.i.d.1991verso acrylic panel. 10-Nov-93
                Christie's, New York #253/R
*$4430 £2954   Fingerprint No.2645 (122x160cm-48x63in) s.d.1987 casein. 2-Jun-94 AB Stockholms
                Auktionsverk, Stockholm #7117/R (S.KR 35000)*

DRYSDALE, Alexander John (1870-1934) American
$1200   £805   Louisiana Bayou (51x76cm-20x30in) oil wash. 27-Mar-94 Myers, Florida #45/R
$1700   £1181   On the Bayou (56x69cm-22x27in) s.d.1916 oil wash paperboard. 6-Mar-93 Louisiana
                Auction Exchange #119/R
$1800   £1169   Landscape (38x76cm-15x30in) paper. 11-Sep-93 Louisiana Auction Exchange #51/R
*$1000 £658   Southern landscape with willow tree (50x76cm-20x30in) s. gouache. 31-Mar-93
                Sotheby's Arcade, New York #139/R*

DUBOIS, Albert (c.1831-?) American/German
$15000 £10067 The skating party (20x41cm-8x16in) s. panel. 4-May-94 Doyle, New York #8/R

DUCMELIC, Zdravko (1923-) Argentinian
*$800   £471   Mujer joven del pasado (32x23cm-13x9in) mixed media executed 1959. 29-Sep-92
                VerBo, Buenos Aires #46*
$800   £417   Dos figuras (32x25cm-13x10in) ink dr. 4-Aug-92 VerBo, Buenos Aires #45
$900   £596   Musicantes (37x31cm-15x12in) mixed media. 11-Nov-92 VerBo, Buenos Aires #39

DUDLEY, Frank V (1868-1957) American
$800   £523   Landscape with pond (46x61cm-18x24in) s. 19-Sep-93 Hindman Galleries, Chicago
                #731
$1600   £1088   Autumn forest (46x61cm-18x24in) s. 17-Apr-94 Hanzel Galleries, Chicago #13
$2400   £1569   Farm scene with cornshucks (46x61cm-18x24in) s. 19-Sep-93 Hindman Galleries,
                Chicago #732
$2400   £1569   Beach scene (51x56cm-20x22in) s. 19-Sep-93 Hindman Galleries, Chicago #726

DUESSEL, Henry A (19th C) American/German
$1200   £805   Seaton Falls, Winchester County, New York (76x127cm-30x50in) s. i.verso. 4-Dec-93
                Louisiana Auction Exchange #177/R

DUFF, John (1925-) Canadian
*$1100 £764   Untitled (57x47cm-22x19in) s.d.2-81 graphite acrylic. 22-Feb-93 Christie's, East,
                New York #247/R*

DUFFAUT, P (1923-) Haitian
$1500   £993   Haitian city (74x51cm-29x20in) board. 30-Dec-92 Douglas, South Deerfield #8

DUFFAUT, Prefete (1923-) Haitian
$724   £473   Ville imaginaire (40x30cm-16x12in) 17-May-93 Hoebanx, Paris #67 (F.FR 4000)
$1038   £687   Ville imaginaire (81x61cm-32x24in) s. 13-Jun-94 Rogeon, Paris #11/R (F.FR 5800)
$1073   £711   Village fantastique (60x75cm-24x30in) s. 13-Jun-94 Rogeon, Paris #73 (F.FR 6000)
$1177   £769   Ville imaginaire (51x61cm-20x24in) 17-May-93 Hoebanx, Paris #69 (F.FR 6500)
$1195   £781   Ville imaginaire (41x51cm-16x20in) 17-May-93 Hoebanx, Paris #68/R (F.FR 6600)
$1300   £861   Imaginary landscape (61x41cm-24x16in) s. masonite. 30-Jun-93 Sotheby's Arcade,
                New York #235/R
$2143   £1429   Village with figures dancing (35x45cm-14x18in) s.d.82. 31-May-94 Christie's,
                Amsterdam #108/R (D.FL 4000)
$2234   £1432   La montagne magique (45x50cm-18x20in) s. wood. 14-Dec-92 Hoebanx, Paris #169/R
                (F.FR 12000)
$3200   £2162   Jacmel (37x45cm-15x18in) s.d.58 masonite. 24-Nov-93 Christie's, New York #4/R
$3800   £2568   Cite Imaginaire (75x102cm-30x40in) s. masonite painted 1965. 24-Nov-93
                Christie's, New York #14/R
$5200   £3444   Tresors de Reine Herzulie (77x61cm-30x24in) s.i.d.1955 masonite. 24-Nov-92
                Christie's, New York #286/R

DUFNER, Edward (1872-1957) American

$1300	£657	Forest interior with figures (41x61cm-16x24in) s. 30-Aug-92 Litchfield Auction Gallery #197
$2000	£1307	Garden scene (18x23cm-7x9in) s.d.1911 board. 1-Nov-92 Hanzel Galleries, Chicago #8/R
$2500	£1736	Bathers at sunset (41x46cm-16x18in) s. 3-Mar-93 Doyle, New York #21
$4250	£2872	Bathers in the late afternoon (42x46cm-17x18in) s. 5-Nov-93 Skinner, Bolton #146/R
$4500	£2941	Early morning bather (30x41cm-12x16in) s. 30-Jun-94 Mystic Fine Arts, Connecticut #93/R
$6250	£4223	Morning stroll (21x25cm-8x10in) s. i.verso canvas on board. 31-Mar-94 Sotheby's Arcade, New York #218/R
$10000	£6711	Reverie by lake - female nude sitting under willow tree (102x76cm-40x30in) s. 4-May-94 Doyle, New York #30/R
$15000	£10067	Luncheon on the verandah - portrait of the artist and his wife (63x76cm-25x30in) s. 4-Mar-94 Skinner, Bolton #275/R
$19000	£12667	Afternoon by the lake (46x61cm-18x24in) s. i.verso. 26-May-94 Christie's, New York #103/R
$20000	£13245	Lake shore in spring (51x61cm-20x24in) s. 3-Oct-93 Hanzel Galleries, Chicago #29/R
$52000	£32911	Morning sunshine (65x78cm-26x31in) s. canvas laid down on board. 4-Dec-92 Christie's, New York #50/R
$600	*£347*	*Coastal inlet (38x49cm-15x19in) s. W/C paper on board. 25-Sep-92 Sotheby's Arcade, New York #320/R*
$8800	*£5752*	*Summer noon (61x74cm-24x29in) s. i.verso W/C gouache paperboard. 14-May-93 Skinner, Bolton #86/R*

DUMA, William (1936-) Canadian

$641	£436	Near the Leighton Centre (71x91cm-28x36in) s. 15-Nov-93 Hodgins, Calgary #235/R (C.D 850)
$662	£438	Summer clouds (56x71cm-22x28in) s. s.i.verso acrylic. 16-Nov-92 Hodgins, Calgary #218/R (C.D 850)

DUMOND, Frank Vincent (1865-1951) American

$1800	£1259	Lilacs (61x76cm-24x30in) s. studio st.i.verso. 12-Mar-93 Skinner, Bolton #191/R
$2000	£1351	Connecticut river (30x41cm-12x16in) s. 23-Oct-93 Collins, Maine #178/R
$3000	£1987	Margaree River Valley, Cape Breton, Nova Scotia (61x76cm-24x30in) s. 23-Sep-93 Sotheby's, New York #207/R
$4000	£2614	Dancing children , s.i.d.55. 4-May-93 Christie's, East, New York #179
$6000	£4196	Stream, Nova Scotia (63x76cm-25x30in) s. i.d.1933stretcher. 10-Mar-93 Sotheby's, New York #122/R
$6500	£4333	The overgrown fence (30x42cm-12x17in) s.d.08 board. 23-May-94 Christie's, East, New York #122/R

DUNBAR, Harold (1882-?) American

$900	£588	New England brook in springtime. French village (91x86cm-36x34in) s. with i.verso double-sided. 17-Sep-93 Skinner, Bolton #203/R
$2900	£1959	McCoy Farm, Chatham (56x66cm-22x26in) s.d.1922. 23-Oct-93 Collins, Maine #177/R

DUNCAN, James D (1806-1881) Canadian

$2576	*£1684*	*Ottawa River at Les Chats (15x23cm-6x9in) s. W/C. 19-May-93 Sotheby's, Toronto #66/R (C.D 3250)*

DUNCAN, James D (attrib) (1806-1881) Canadian

$11060	*£7000*	*Sleighs in Dalhouse Square, Montreal , W/C over traces pencil htd.bodycol. two. 21-Oct-92 Sotheby's, London #265/R*

DUNCAN, Scott (?) American

$675	*£447*	*A beach fantasy (61x91cm-24x36in) s. 27-Sep-93 Selkirks, St. Louis #89*

DUNCANSON, Robert S (1821-1872) American

$1000	£671	Portrait of seated man holding cane (79x64cm-31x25in) s.verso. 5-Aug-93 Eldred, Massachusetts #942/R
$2500	£1678	Fishing in the wilds (46x61cm-18x24in) 24-Mar-94 Mystic Fine Arts, Connecticut #49/R
$5500	£2865	Seated man holding a cane (79x64cm-31x25in) s.verso painted 1845. 6-Aug-92 Eldred, Massachusetts #816/R
$9000	£6000	Lake Maggiori (84x71cm-33x28in) s.d.1871 indist.s.i.d.1871 verso. 17-Mar-94 Sotheby's, New York #48/R
$9000	£5921	Fisherman (25x41cm-10x16in) s. 31-Mar-93 Sotheby's Arcade, New York #47/R
$20000	£13333	Maya Ruins (36x51cm-14x20in) s.d.1848. 18-May-94 Sotheby's, New York #178/R
$32000	£20253	Vale of Kashmir (66x125cm-26x49in) s.d.1870. 4-Dec-92 Christie's, New York #190/R
$42000	£28188	The Falls of Minnehaha (84x71cm-33x28in) s.d.1870 i.d.verso. 2-Dec-93 Sotheby's, New York #27/R

DUNHAM, Carroll (1949-) American

$11000	£7432	Seven (89x62cm-35x24in) s.i.d.10/5/84 casein flashe chl tape on veneer. 10-Nov-93 Christie's, New York #274/R
$11000	£7285	Secondary (75x52cm-30x20in) s.i.d.Mar-Sept 1986 oil brush graphite ballpoint. 19-Nov-92 Christie's, New York #113/R
$12000	£7947	Untitled (135x48cm-53x19in) s.d.1987 i.verso oil casein ink graphite 2panel. 19-Nov-92 Christie's, New York #121/R
$15000	£10067	Transit (198x99cm-78x39in) s.d.1986-87 s.i.d.verso oil brush ink panel. 4-May-94 Christie's, New York #259/R

DUNHAM, Carroll (1949-) American-cont.
$32000   £22222   American walnut (230x154cm-91x61in) s.i.d. June-Oct.1984 casein dry pigment chl panel. 24-Feb-93 Christie's, New York #106/R

DUNN, Harvey (1884-1952) American
$3400   £2208   Moonlit encounter (96x81cm-38x32in) s.d.1922. 9-Sep-93 Sotheby's Arcade, New York #90/R
$19000   £10983   Woodsman (92x61cm-36x24in) s.d.19-08. 24-Sep-92 Sotheby's, New York #80/R
$28000   £17722   The tea party (77x97cm-30x38in) mono.d.16. 4-Dec-92 Christie's, New York #35/R
$32000   £21477   Chinook wind (76x114cm-30x45in) s. 2-Dec-93 Sotheby's, New York #63/R

DUNNING, Robert Spear (1829-1905) American
$1700   £1090   Fishing the stream (23x33cm-9x13in) s.d.1892 s.d.verso. 9-Dec-92 Butterfield & Butterfield, San Francisco #3821/R
$3500   £2381   Figures by the sea with sailboats beyond (15x28cm-6x11in) s.d.1881. 15-Nov-93 Christie's, East, New York #24
$6000   £4027   Still life with mixed fruit (25x32cm-10x13in) s.d.1904. 4-Mar-94 Skinner, Bolton #226/R

DUNOYER, Pierre (1949-) American?
$1187   £771   Noir et blanc (200x150cm-79x59in) mixed media. 24-Jun-94 Binoche, Paris #37 (F.FR 6500)
$1370   £890   Marron, jaune, noir (130x200cm-51x79in) mixed media. 24-Jun-94 Binoche, Paris #36 (F.FR 7500)
$1644   £1068   Bleu, vert, noir (160x150cm-63x59in) mixed media. 24-Jun-94 Binoche, Paris #35 (F.FR 9000)
$2558   £1661   Vert et blanc (130x180cm-51x71in) mixed media diptych. 24-Jun-94 Binoche, Paris #37 b/R (F.FR 14000)

DUPUIS, David (20th C) American
$2400   £1622   When the Tingle Becomes a Chill (183x152cm-72x60in) s.i.d.90verso acrylic W/C graphite paper canvas. 8-Nov-93 Christie's, East, New York #102/R

DURA, Alberto (1888-1971) Uruguayan
$750   £497   Paisaje con arboles, casas y sierras (34x49cm-13x19in) s. board. 28-Jun-93 Gomensoro, Montevideo #22
$920   £487   Paisaje costero (32x40cm-13x16in) s.i.d.1918 board. 10-Sep-92 Gomensoro, Montevideo #42
$920   £487   Campo y ciudad (38x43cm-15x17in) s.d.1926 board. 10-Sep-92 Gomensoro, Montevideo #41
$1200   £805   Bahia de Pocitos (29x40cm-11x16in) s.d.1930. 29-Nov-93 Gomensoro, Montevideo #26
$1500   £993   Paisaje primaveral con iglesia (35x45cm-14x18in) s.i. canvas laid down on fibre. 28-Jun-93 Gomensoro, Montevideo #20/R
$1500   £980   Parque con rosedal y fuente (85x95cm-33x37in) s.d.47 fibre. 26-Oct-92 Gomensoro, Montevideo #85
$2000   £1316   Gruta de los matreros (45x45cm-18x18in) s. 31-May-93 Gomensoro, Montevideo #25/R
$3200   £1882   Caricia (68x59cm-27x23in) s. 5-Oct-92 Gomensoro, Montevideo #26/R
$6000   £3922   Cascada (61x47cm-24x19in) s.d.1936 masonite. 18-May-93 Sotheby's, New York #119/R
$8000   £5229   Jardin (79x66cm-31x26in) s.d.1920. 18-May-93 Sotheby's, New York #116/R

DURAND, A B (1796-1886) American
$4000   £2667   Forest brook (56x45cm-22x18in) s. 23-May-94 Christie's, East, New York #3/R

DURAND, Asher Brown (1796-1886) American
$10500   £6069   Landscape (55x43cm-22x17in) s.d.1869. 24-Sep-92 Sotheby's, New York #18/R
$16000   £10596   Peaceful glen (49x69cm-19x27in) indist.s. 22-Sep-93 Christie's, New York #12/R
$1500   £980   Green river (20x25cm-8x10in) s. graphite htd white. 17-Sep-93 Skinner, Bolton #163/R

DURAND, Elias W (19th C) American?
$900   £600   Landscape with trees. Mountainous landscape (61x46cm-24x18in) one s.d. one s. pair. 23-May-94 Christie's, East, New York #1/R

DUREN, Terence Romaine (1907-1968) American
$800   £519   The tree (60x75cm-24x30in) s. 9-Sep-93 Sotheby's Arcade, New York #434/R
$900   £520   Terrace (61x76cm-24x30in) s. 25-Sep-92 Sotheby's Arcade, New York #459/R

DURRIE, George Henry (1820-1863) American
$2400   £1600   Basket with strawberries and cherries (21x33cm-8x13in) s. paper on board. 23-May-94 Christie's, East, New York #22/R
$2600   £1733   Self-portrait (30x25cm-12x10in) panel. 23-May-94 Christie's, East, New York #18/R
$28000   £18792   Woodsman in winter (46x61cm-18x24in) painted c.1858. 3-Dec-93 Christie's, New York #120/R

DURRIE, J (1818-?) American
$3400   £2267   Still life of peaches and grapes (25x20cm-10x8in) 27-Aug-93 Douglas, South Deerfield #1

DURRIE, John (1818-?) American
$4800   £3221   Still life with fruit (25x35cm-10x14in) s.verso. 3-Dec-93 Christie's, New York #119/R

DUTCH-AMERICAN SCHOOL, 19th C
$17000   £11111   Bark Tedesco John Higgins Master leaving Port of Antwerp (24x30cm-9x12in) 31-Oct-92 Skinner, Bolton #31/R

DUVAL-CARRIE, Edouard (1954-) Haitian
$2400   £1622   Adi Bobo (58x69cm-23x27in) s.d.89. 24-Nov-93 Christie's, New York #17/R

DUVALL, Fannie Eliza (1861-1934) American
$600   £403   Still life with zinnias (61x74cm-24x29in) s.d.1889. 5-Feb-94 Skinner, Bolton #511/R
$3250   £2257   Still life with bowl of violets (37x48cm-15x19in) s. canvas on board. 7-Mar-93 Butterfield & Butterfield, San Francisco #153/R
$450   £302   Still life with grapes, figurine and copper urn (51x58cm-20x23in) s.d.1929 pastel paperboard. 5-Feb-94 Skinner, Bolton #478/R

DUVENECK, Frank (1848-1919) American
$3000   £1987   William Griffin (55x46cm-22x18in) init. 23-Sep-93 Sotheby's, New York #159/R
$3750   £2484   Head of child (37x30cm-15x12in) 23-Sep-93 Sotheby's, New York #151/R
$5400   £3576   Georg von Hoesslin (41x35cm-16x14in) mono. i.stretcher. 23-Sep-93 Sotheby's, New York #150/R

DUVENECK, Frank (school) (1848-1919) American
$1600   £1074   Head of a boy (43x30cm-17x12in) 1-Dec-93 Doyle, New York #46

DWYER, Nancy (1954-) American
$1400   £946   Out of My Mind (178x229cm-70x90in) s.d.11.88verso. 8-Nov-93 Christie's, East, New York #107/R
$2025   £1350   Zero Foreplay (153x191cm-60x75in) s.d.1987verso acrylic. 2-Jun-94 AB Stockholms Auktionsverk, Stockholm #7071/R (S.KR 16000)
$4500   £2980   Rich (201x229cm-79x90in) painted 1989 acrylic. 17-Nov-92 Christie's, East, New York #60/R

DYCK, Yolanda van (1948-) Canadian
$544   £368   Untitled - Dufy and anenomes (58x43cm-23x17in) s. pastel. 25-Apr-94 Levis, Calgary #338 (C.D 750)

DYE, Charlie (1906-1972) American
$25000   £14451   Open range branding (61x91cm-24x36in) s.d.1960. 24-Sep-92 Sotheby's, New York #73/R

DYER, Nancy A (1903-) American
$650   £425   The young artist (18x28cm-7x11in) s. W/C. 30-Jun-94 Mystic Fine Arts, Connecticut #91/R

DZIGURSKI, A (20th C) American
$1300   £878   Seascape with rocky montainous coastline (61x91cm-24x36in) s. 23-Oct-93 San Rafael Auction Galleries #231

DZIGURSKI, Alex (1910-) American
$700   £455   Shoreline at dusk (61x76cm-24x30in) s. i.verso. 8-Jul-94 Sloan, North Bethesda #2358
$786   £498   California sunset (61x91cm-24x36in) s. d.1956 verso. 1-Dec-92 Ritchie, Toronto #170/R (C.D 1000)
$900   £584   Majestic tetons (61x102cm-24x40in) s. 11-Sep-93 Louisiana Auction Exchange #54/R
$900   £584   Nature's majesty (61x102cm-24x40in) s. 11-Sep-93 Louisiana Auction Exchange #55/R
$1000   £671   Seascape at sunset (61x91cm-24x36in) s. 4-Dec-93 Louisiana Auction Exchange #17/R
$1100   £696   Seascape (61x91cm-24x36in) s. 24-Oct-92 Collins, Maine #82
$1200   £784   Seascape (61x91cm-24x36in) s. 16-May-93 Hindman Galleries, Chicago #122
$1300   £657   California coastline (61x122cm-24x48in) s. 28-Aug-92 Young Fine Arts Auctions, Maine #105
$1500   £1049   Mediterranean sea (58x91cm-23x36in) s. 12-Mar-93 Du Mouchelle, Detroit #2004/R
$1500   £980   Seascape (71x94cm-28x37in) s. 16-Apr-93 Du Mouchelle, Detroit #2025/R
$1600   £1060   Panoramic Monterey coastal (71x97cm-28x38in) s. 14-Jun-94 John Moran, Pasadena #81

DZUBAS, Friedel (1915-) American/German
$4800   £3179   Late fire (91x86cm-36x34in) s.i.d.65verso. 17-Nov-92 Christie's, East, New York #239/R
$9000   £5769   Green Edge (244x244cm-96x96in) s.d.73 i.verso magna canvas. 24-May-93 Grogan, Massachussetts #380/R
$14000   £9150   Hesperus (157x295cm-62x116in) s.i.d.75verso acrylic. 5-May-93 Christie's, New York #317/R
$15000   £10135   Shadows fall (183x183cm-72x72in) s.i.d.1979 verso acrylic. 11-Nov-93 Sotheby's, New York #332/R
$19000   £12583   Cross River (183x183cm-72x72in) s.d.1986 verso acrylic. 18-Nov-92 Sotheby's, New York #132/R
$1900   £1203   Untitled (86x86cm-34x34in) s.d.81 handmade paper. 25-Oct-92 Butterfield & Butterfield, San Francisco #2366/R

EAKINS, Thomas (1844-1916) American
$15000   £9804   Portrait of Dr. Anders. Spinners (36x25cm-14x10in) board double-sided. 7-Oct-93 Freeman Fine Arts, Philadelphia #987/R
$80000   £53333   Portrait of Francesco Romano (51x41cm-20x16in) s.d.1904 i.verso. 26-May-94 Christie's, New York #8/R

EARL, James (1761-1796) American
$8000 £5298 Frances Horton and her sister (61x51cm-24x20in) pair. 22-Sep-93 Christie's, New York #1/R

EARL, Ralph (attrib) (1751-1801) American
$3250 £2138 Portrait of Major John Middleton Lovell of Massachusetts (76x64cm-30x25in) 2-Apr-93 Sloan, North Bethesda #2471/R

EARLE, Lawrence Carmichael (1845-1921) American
$3400 £2378 Still lives of game birds (51x86cm-20x34in) s.d.75 pair. 3-Feb-93 Doyle, New York #20/R
$6000 £4196 Marsh (90x124cm-35x49in) s.d.08. 10-Mar-93 Sotheby's, New York #81/R
$650 £411 Still life with game (41x51cm-16x20in) s. W/C. 5-Dec-92 Louisiana Auction Exchange #64/R

EARLY, Miles J (1886-?) American
$700 £473 Late November (46x61cm-18x24in) s. s.i.verso. 31-Oct-93 Hindman Galleries, Chicago #743

EASTLAKE, Mary Alexandra (1864-1951) Canadian
$755 £510 Mother an child (46x37cm-18x15in) s. col.chk. 23-Nov-93 Joyner Fine Art, Toronto #323/R (C.D 1000)

EASTMAN, Seth (1808-1875) American
$5000 £3165 View in Texas - Miles north of San Antonio (12x19cm-5x7in) s.d.1849 i.verso W/C ink. 3-Dec-92 Sotheby's, New York #6/R
$10000 £6667 Oneota Stone, cemetary in Utica, New York (16x22cm-6x9in) s.i. W/C. 16-Mar-94 Christie's, New York #80/R

EASTMAN, Seth (attrib) (1808-1875) American
$5500 £3595 Sheep grazing, Merrimack River Oxbow and Concord, New Hampshire in distance (64x76cm-25x30in) 17-Sep-93 Skinner, Bolton #167/R

EATON, Charles Harry (1850-1901) American
$735 £500 Summer landscape (41x56cm-16x22in) s.d.86. 16-Nov-93 Rasmussen, Copenhagen #353/R (D.KR 5000)
$1000 £680 Along the river (68x91cm-27x36in) s.i. 15-Nov-93 Christie's, East, New York #45/R
$1900 £1098 Autumn landscape (39x56cm-15x22in) s.d.87 board on board. 25-Sep-92 Sotheby's Arcade, New York #162/R
$9750 £6373 Still life of cherries (30x38cm-12x15in) s.d.82. 29-Jun-94 Doyle, New York #19

EATON, Charles Warren (1857-1937) American
$800 £533 Canal scene (41x30cm-16x12in) s. 23-May-94 Hindman Galleries, Chicago #172
$800 £537 Houses across the field (41x31cm-16x12in) i.verso. 6-May-94 Skinner, Bolton #85/R
$800 £537 On the canal (25x20cm-10x8in) s. i.verso board. 26-Mar-94 James Bakker, Cambridge #14/R
$1000 £671 Landscape (51x61cm-20x24in) s. 4-Dec-93 Louisiana Auction Exchange #52/R
$1400 £921 Sentinel Pines (91x61cm-36x24in) sd.1901 s.i.verso. 2-Jun-93 Doyle, New York #54
$1500 £987 River in the woods (46x41cm-18x16in) s. 13-Jun-93 Hindman Galleries, Chicago #218/R
$1500 £993 The brook. Forest interior , s. one d.1892 pair. 28-Nov-92 Young Fine Arts Auctions, Maine #127/R
$1900 £1293 Spring sunset (61x91cm-24x36in) s. s.i.verso. 17-Nov-93 Doyle, New York #14/R
$2000 £1325 Distant cottages, dusk (30x56cm-12x22in) s. 13-Nov-92 Skinner, Bolton #72/R
$2200 £1429 Misty morning (41x56cm-16x22in) s. 11-Sep-93 Louisiana Auction Exchange #44/R
$2600 £1699 Landscape (51x61cm-20x24in) s. 18-Sep-93 James Bakker, Cambridge #181/R
$700 £405 Snow scene (38x30cm-15x12in) s. W/C. 24-Sep-92 Mystic Fine Arts, Connecticut #63/R

EATON, Charles Warren (attrib) (1857-1937) American
$2200 £1392 The valley (25x20cm-10x8in) s. s.i.verso board. 30-Nov-92 Schrager Galleries, Milwaukee #461

EBERT, Charles H (1873-1959) American
$4500 £2601 Ebert's Pond (91x91cm-36x36in) 23-Sep-92 Christie's, New York #163/R

ECHLIMANN, Y (20th C) American
$2000 £1316 Trompe l'oeil landscape with house, tree and birds (119x119cm-47x47in) s.d.79. 2-Apr-93 Sloan, North Bethesda #2337

EDDY, Don (1944-) American
$8327 £5665 Wrecking II (120x168cm-47x66in) s.i.d.1971verso acrylic. 10-Apr-94 Perrin, Versailles #79/R (F.FR 49000)
$13000 £8609 Private Parking IV (122x168cm-48x66in) s.d.71 overlap acrylic. 18-Nov-92 Sotheby's, New York #169/R

EDE, Frederick Charles Vipond (1865-1907) American
$638 £434 Bergere et son troupeau (50x65cm-20x26in) s. 19-Nov-93 Morelle & Marchandet, Paris #41/R (F.FR 3800)
$800 £491 Woman beside stream (61x74cm-24x29in) s. 14-Oct-92 Doyle, New York #19
$1100 £780 River landscape with fishermen (58x71cm-23x28in) s. 11-Feb-93 Boos Gallery, Michigan #365/R
$1300 £751 Cottage by rushing stream (51x61cm-20x24in) s. 25-Sep-92 Sotheby's Arcade, New York #231/R

EDE, Frederick Charles Vipond (1865-1907) American-cont.
$1705	£1152	Bergere et son troupeau pres d'un pont (197x131cm-78x52in) s.d.1905. 5-Nov-93 Ader Tajan, Paris #147 (F.FR 10000)
$3100	£2039	Summer landscape with stream (38x46cm-15x18in) s. 31-Mar-93 Sotheby's Arcade, New York #156/R
$3500	£2023	Bend in the river (60x81cm-24x32in) s. 25-Sep-92 Sotheby's Arcade, New York #235/R

EDMONDS, Francis William (1806-1863) American
$750	£493	Shearing the lamb (8x13cm-3x5in) s. paper wash en grisaille. 7-Apr-93 Doyle, New York #22
$50000	£33557	The two culprits (63x76cm-25x30in) s.d.1850. 3-Dec-93 Christie's, New York #117/R

EDMONDSON, Edward (19th C) American
$1100	£705	Cherries (41x33cm-16x13in) d.1864's.verso oval. 17-Dec-92 Mystic Fine Arts, Connecticut #100

EDSON, Allan (1846-1888) Canadian
$682	£455	Cows resting by river, early evening (59x87cm-23x34in) s. 30-May-94 Ritchie, Toronto #140/R (C.D 950)
$755	£510	View of church beyond trees (61x40cm-24x16in) s. 23-Nov-93 Fraser Pinneys, Quebec #440/R (C.D 1000)
$1168	£773	The berry picker (56x39cm-22x15in) s. 18-Nov-92 Sotheby's, Toronto #130 (C.D 1500)
$588	£400	A mounted officer and North American Indians in woodland (54x38cm-21x15in) s. W/C htd white. 14-Apr-94 Bonhams, Chelsea #219/R
$634	£415	Piling grass (20x30cm-8x12in) s. W/C. 19-May-93 Sotheby's, Toronto #36/R (C.D 800)
$3095	£2063	Landscape with elk (55x90cm-22x35in) s.d.1872 W/C. 11-May-94 Sotheby's, Toronto #182/R (C.D 4250)

EDWARDS, George Wharton (1869-1950) American
$1320	£846	Old fashioned treasures (61x46cm-24x18in) s. 17-Dec-92 Mystic Fine Arts, Connecticut #240 a/R
$1430	£917	Avila Spain (76x76cm-30x30in) s. 17-Dec-92 Mystic Fine Arts, Connecticut #241
$1600	£1074	Untitled (76x76cm-30x30in) s. 24-Mar-94 Mystic Fine Arts, Connecticut #64
$1650	£1058	The Watch store (76x76cm-30x30in) s. 17-Dec-92 Mystic Fine Arts, Connecticut #240
$2750	£1763	Venetian Cathedral (76x76cm-30x30in) s. 17-Dec-92 Mystic Fine Arts, Connecticut #239
$5000	£3205	Alcazar palace Gardens, Seville, Spain (61x50cm-24x20in) s.i. 26-May-93 Christie's, New York #140/R
$5500	£3691	Brittany fishing village (51x61cm-20x24in) s.i. i.verso. 4-Mar-94 Skinner, Bolton #234/R

EGAN, Eloise (20th C) American
$800	£523	Slave quarters, Charleston, South Carolina (64x76cm-25x30in) s. 4-May-93 Christie's, East, New York #214/R

EGGELING, Viking (20th C) American?
$1700	£1090	Abstract composition (46x33cm-18x13in) i.verso pencil. 24-May-93 Grogan, Massachusetts #379/R

EGGENHOFER, Nick (1897-1985) American
$500	£338	Horsecart and river (18x27cm-7x11in) s. W/C pen pencil board. 31-Mar-94 Sotheby's Arcade, New York #384/R
$1000	£641	Jig time (30x45cm-12x18in) s. pen pencil paperboard. 9-Dec-92 Butterfield & Butterfield, San Francisco #4009/R
$1500	£1014	Rio Grande rebels. The stagecoach (37x51cm-15x20in) s. pen board pair. 31-Mar-94 Sotheby's Arcade, New York #190/R
$2200	£1538	Stagecoach (24x38cm-9x15in) s.d.1981 gouache pen board. 11-Mar-93 Christie's, New York #123/R

EGLAU, Max (1825-?) American?
$750	£497	Twilight at the river's edge (20x30cm-8x12in) s. board. 28-Nov-92 Young Fine Arts Auctions, Maine #129/R
$2100	£1429	Hudson River landscape with train man in boat and cattle (48x84cm-19x33in) s. 19-Nov-93 Eldred, Massachusetts #746/R

EHNINGER, John W (1827-1889) American
$1500	£1000	George Washington on horseback (49x41cm-19x16in) s.i.d.1854. 17-May-94 Christie's, East, New York #495
$4250	£2815	Charles Astor Bristed and horse, Fanny Bee (66x81cm-26x32in) s.d.1853. 23-Sep-93 Mystic Fine Arts, Connecticut #171/R

EHRENBERG, Frederick (?-1910) American
$600	£392	Circus wagons (28x46cm-11x18in) s. board. 30-Jun-94 Mystic Fine Arts, Connecticut #155 a/R

EILSHEMIUS, Louis M (1864-1941) American
$600	£387	Coastal scene (33x53cm-13x21in) s. masonite. 13-Jul-94 Doyle, New York #23
$650	£428	Two nudes dancing in landscape (29x21cm-11x8in) s. printed paper on board. 31-Mar-93 Sotheby's Arcade, New York #287/R
$800	£541	Sailing boat on a lake (30x46cm-12x18in) s. board. 27-Nov-93 Young Fine Arts Auctions, Maine #121/R

147

EILSHEMIUS, Louis M (1864-1941) American-cont.
$850	£559	Bathers (38x61cm-15x24in) s.d.1910 paper on board. 31-Mar-93 Sotheby's Arcade, New York #290/R
$850	£491	Landscape with waterfall (23x45cm-9x18in) s.d.1900 board painted oval. 25-Sep-92 Sotheby's Arcade, New York #438/R
$1000	£645	Hymn to motherhood (66x91cm-26x36in) s. 13-Jul-94 Doyle, New York #19
$1200	£779	Woman with hat (22x22cm-9x9in) s. paper on board painted c.1917-20. 9-Sep-93 Sotheby's Arcade, New York #331/R
$1200	£805	Sailboat on lake (30x46cm-12x18in) s. board. 14-Jan-94 Du Mouchelle, Detroit #2228/R
$1200	£800	The bathers (41x57cm-16x22in) s.d.1889 s.i.stretcher. 23-May-94 Christie's, East, New York #219
$1500	£968	The fisherman (99x71cm-39x28in) s.d.1908 board. 13-Jul-94 Doyle, New York #20
$1500	£1000	Dramatic scene (102x154cm-40x61in) s. board. 23-May-94 Christie's, East, New York #269/R
$1500	£962	Golden bough (31x48cm-12x19in) s. board. 9-Dec-92 Butterfield & Butterfield, San Francisco #3902/R
$1600	£925	Bright shoreline (51x76cm-20x30in) s. i.verso masonite. 25-Sep-92 Sotheby's Arcade, New York #437/R
$1600	£1067	Nymph day-dreaming by a river (102x76cm-40x30in) s. board painted 1908. 23-May-94 Christie's, East, New York #216
$1700	£1149	Figures on a moonlit beach (57x67cm-22x26in) s. board. 31-Mar-94 Sotheby's Arcade, New York #441/R
$1700	£1118	Source (51x37cm-20x15in) s.d.1901 masonite. 31-Mar-93 Sotheby's Arcade, New York #288/R
$2300	£1597	Three water nymphs (112x76cm-44x30in) s. painted c.1898. 6-Mar-93 Louisiana Auction Exchange #126/R
$700	*£455*	*Two nudes on road (35x25cm-14x10in) s. W/C pencil paper on paper painted c.1900. 9-Sep-93 Sotheby's Arcade, New York #345*
$700	*£455*	*Two nudes and waterfall (36x25cm-14x10in) s. W/C pencil painted c.1900. 9-Sep-93 Sotheby's Arcade, New York #344/R*

EISELE, Christian (19th C) American
$800	£513	Mountain lake (56x91cm-22x36in) s. 13-Dec-92 Hindman Galleries, Chicago #2/R

ELDRED, L D (1848-1921) American
$3000	£1974	Moonlit marine scene of Homer's Wharf in New Bedford looking toward Fairhaven (23x36cm-9x14in) s.d.1886. 2-Apr-93 Eldred, Massachusetts #674/R

ELDRED, Lemeul D (1848-1921) American
$1000	£662	Sailing ship (46x79cm-18x31in) s.i.d.83. 13-Nov-92 Skinner, Bolton #59/R
$1100	£561	Sea cliffs, Monhegan Island (30x51cm-12x20in) s.d.01. 18-Aug-92 Richard Bourne, Hyannis #80/R
$1800	£1176	Sea breezes (41x66cm-16x26in) s.d.1880. 17-Sep-93 Skinner, Bolton #189/R
$2750	£1846	Coastal scene with ships (23x36cm-9x14in) s.d.73. 6-Dec-93 Grogan, Massachussetts #433
$5000	£3378	View of coastal shipping (41x66cm-16x26in) s. 30-Jul-93 Eldred, Massachusetts #272/R

ELKINS, Henry Arthur (1847-1884) American
$1500	£1014	Rocky Mountain scene with waterfall (76x64cm-30x25in) s. 31-Oct-93 Hindman Galleries, Chicago #668

ELLENSHAW, Peter (1913-) American/British
$1400	£927	Cottage County Carry (61x91cm-24x36in) s. st.sig.i.verso. 28-Nov-92 Dunning's, Illinois #1111
$1500	£993	Coon Lake, Kerry (76x122cm-30x48in) s.d.79 studio st.verso. 28-Nov-92 Dunning's, Illinois #1114
$2100	£1391	Waterville Lake, County Kerry (61x91cm-24x36in) s.d.79 studio st.verso. 28-Nov-92 Dunning's, Illinois #1115
$3500	£2318	Sheehams Point (112x203cm-44x80in) s.d.74. 28-Nov-92 Dunning's, Illinois #1112
$21000	£13907	South on Lee Street Garden (76x122cm-30x48in) s.d.79 studio st.verso. 28-Nov-92 Dunning's, Illinois #1113

ELLIOT, C L (1812-1868) American
$734	£480	Gentleman wearing black coat (88x71cm-35x28in) i.d.1838. 13-May-93 Christie's, S. Kensington #313

ELLIOT, Charles Loring (1812-1868) American
$4000	£2632	Portrait of Mary and Georgina Allen (117x89cm-46x35in) s. 2-Jun-93 Doyle, New York #55/R

ELLIS, Fremont F (1897-?) American
$8000	£5298	Sunlit poplars, Santa Fe, N.M (61x76cm-24x30in) s. s.i.stretcher. 22-Sep-93 Christie's, New York #180/R
$13000	£8609	El Rancho de San Sebastian, Santa Fe (76x102cm-30x40in) s. s.i.stretcher. 22-Sep-93 Christie's, New York #179/R

ELLIS, Stephen (1951-) American
$4000	*£2778*	*Untitled (137x366cm-54x144in) oil alkyd three panels painted 1990. 24-Feb-93 Christie's, New York #162/R*

ELLSWORTH, Clarence (1885-1961) American
$800	£537	Tibouron Island girl (36x28cm-14x11in) s.d.1955 s.i.verso board. 8-Dec-93 Butterfield & Butterfield, San Francisco #3545/R

ELLSWORTH, Clarence (1885-1961) American-cont.
$2000 £1316 Iron Eye Cody (51x34cm-20x13in) s. canvas on board. 13-Jun-93 Butterfield & Butterfield, San Francisco #3239/R
$4250 £2796 Indians riding (60x91cm-24x36in) s.d.28. 13-Jun-93 Butterfield & Butterfield, San Francisco #3231/R

ELVGREN, Gil (?) American
$4750 £3045 Seated female nude (91x74cm-36x29in) s. 26-Apr-93 Selkirks, St. Louis #290
$14000 £8974 Female nude amongst flowers (91x74cm-36x29in) s. 26-Apr-93 Selkirks, St. Louis #297

ELWELL, D Jerome (1847-1912) American
$1000 £699 Entrance to Forest Fontainbleau, Barbizon, France (117x86cm-46x34in) s.d.65. 7-Feb-93 James Bakker, Cambridge #30

EMERSON, W C (19/20th C) American
$700 £467 Impressionistic landscape with wood nymphs (64x61cm-25x24in) board. 3-Jun-94 Douglas, South Deerfield #6

EMMET, Lydia Field (1866-1952) American
$6250 £4252 Portrait of Julie Gillespie (157x71cm-62x28in) s. painted c.1920. 17-Nov-93 Doyle, New York #46/R
$26000 £17333 Miss Ginny and Polly (127x102cm-50x40in) s. 26-May-94 Christie's, New York #87/R

EMMET, Lydia Field (attrib) (1866-1952) American
$5500 £3571 Portrait of seated lady and young girl (109x152cm-43x60in) 9-Sep-93 Sotheby's Arcade, New York #113/R

ENDARA CROW, Gonzalo (1936-) Ecuadorian
$6000 £4027 Es tiempo (82x90cm-32x35in) painted 1988. 7-Jan-94 Gary Nader, Miami #101/R

ENDRES, Louis John (1896-1989) American
$611 £410 Sur la piste, Chellah (48x64cm-19x25in) s.i. 21-Jun-93 Gros & Delettrez, Paris #98/R (F.FR 3500)
$628 £422 Rochers du Grand Atlas, Toufliat (40x50cm-16x20in) s.i. 21-Jun-93 Gros & Delettrez, Paris #91 (F.FR 3600)
$680 £457 Fantassin marocain (22x28cm-9x11in) s.i. paper. 21-Jun-93 Gros & Delettrez, Paris #82 (F.FR 3900)
$733 £492 Mauresque (50x40cm-20x16in) s. 21-Jun-93 Gros & Delettrez, Paris #90/R (F.FR 4200)
$785 £527 Fantassin (40x30cm-16x12in) s.i. panel. 21-Jun-93 Gros & Delettrez, Paris #86/R (F.FR 4500)
$785 £527 Profil arabe (40x30cm-16x12in) s.i. panel. 21-Jun-93 Gros & Delettrez, Paris #85/R (F.FR 4500)
$785 £527 Le depart du caid (48x64cm-19x25in) s.i. 21-Jun-93 Gros & Delettrez, Paris #92/R (F.FR 4500)
$785 £527 Jeune mauresque (50x40cm-20x16in) s. 21-Jun-93 Gros & Delettrez, Paris #89/R (F.FR 4500)
$960 £644 Jeune homme au poignard (62x48cm-24x19in) s.i. 21-Jun-93 Gros & Delettrez, Paris #100/R (F.FR 5500)
$1047 £703 Homme bleu au soufflet (84x76cm-33x30in) s.i. 21-Jun-93 Gros & Delettrez, Paris #105/R (F.FR 6000)
$1186 £796 Casse croute (84x76cm-33x30in) s.i. 21-Jun-93 Gros & Delettrez, Paris #102/R (F.FR 6800)
$1221 £820 Petite vendeuse de fleurs (80x90cm-31x35in) s.i. 21-Jun-93 Gros & Delettrez, Paris #106 (F.FR 7000)
$1309 £878 La maree (84x76cm-33x30in) s.i. 21-Jun-93 Gros & Delettrez, Paris #93/R (F.FR 7500)
$1400 £897 Pelerin pour Moulay Brahim (86x76cm-34x30in) s. 7-Dec-92 Arcole, Paris #156 (F.FR 7500)
$1431 £960 Les bons compagnons (76x84cm-30x33in) s.i. 21-Jun-93 Gros & Delettrez, Paris #101/R (F.FR 8200)
$3667 £2413 Odalisque aux babouches vertes (90x130cm-35x51in) s.i. panel. 5-Apr-93 Ader Tajan, Paris #156/R (F.FR 20000)
$523 £351 Jeune femme de Tiznit (28x22cm-11x9in) s. pastel. 21-Jun-93 Gros & Delettrez, Paris #80/R (F.FR 3000)
$558 £375 Homme bleu (28x22cm-11x9in) s.i. pastel. 21-Jun-93 Gros & Delettrez, Paris #79 (F.FR 3200)
$558 £375 Jeune marocaine (28x22cm-11x9in) s.i. pastel. 21-Jun-93 Gros & Delettrez, Paris #75 (F.FR 3200)
$558 £375 Jeune marocaine (26x22cm-10x9in) s. pastel. 21-Jun-93 Gros & Delettrez, Paris #74 (F.FR 3200)
$558 £375 Le penseur (28x22cm-11x9in) s.i. pastel. 21-Jun-93 Gros & Delettrez, Paris #77 (F.FR 3200)
$576 £386 Jeune mauresque (33x39cm-13x15in) s. W/C gouache. 21-Jun-93 Gros & Delettrez, Paris #72 (F.FR 3300)
$803 £539 Marocaine au foulard jaune (28x22cm-11x9in) s. pastel. 21-Jun-93 Gros & Delettrez, Paris #78/R (F.FR 4600)

ENGELHARDT, Edna (20th C) American
$900 £612 Icy waters (61x76cm-24x30in) s. s.i.verso. 16-Apr-94 Young Fine Arts Auctions, Maine #101
$900 £588 Sunny day in winter (64x76cm-25x30in) s. 18-Sep-93 Young Fine Arts Auctions, Maine #107/R

149

ENGLEHART, John Joseph (1867-1915) American
$2250 £1490 Lake Tahoe - panoramic landscape with Indians (76x127cm-30x50in) s. 14-Jun-94 John Moran, Pasadena #111

ENGLISH, F F (1854-1922) American
$1128 £800 Village street scene with figures and horse and cart passing blacksmith (49x75cm-19x30in) s. W/C. 11-Feb-93 Christie's, Glasgow #521/R
$1500 £980 Coastal view (53x84cm-21x33in) s. W/C. 1-Nov-92 Litchfield Auction Gallery #175 a

ENGLISH, Frank F (1854-1922) American
$900 £600 A stop along the way (53x77cm-21x30in) s. W/C paper on board. 17-May-94 Christie's, East, New York #525
$1000 £529 Windmill on bay (25x51cm-10x20in) s. W/C. 13-Sep-92 Dargate Auction Galleries, Pittsburgh #325
$1000 £662 Farm girl with geese at sunset (36x51cm-14x20in) s. W/C. 28-Nov-92 Young Fine Arts Auctions, Maine #132/R
$2900 £1824 Harvest at sunset (38x76cm-15x30in) s. W/C gouache. 22-Apr-93 Freeman Fine Arts, Philadelphia #1340/R
$3500 £2215 The return home (39x80cm-15x31in) s. W/C. 2-Dec-92 Christie's, East, New York #84

ENMAN, Thomas K (20th C) American
$700 £464 Victoria Beach, early morning (51x61cm-20x24in) s.d.1986 i.verso. 28-Sep-93 John Moran, Pasadena #367

ENNEKING, J J (1841-1916) American
$950 £638 On the dunes (23x18cm-9x7in) s. panel. 26-Mar-94 James Bakker, Cambridge #10

ENNEKING, John J (1841-1916) American
$650 £425 Paper factory at night (20x30cm-8x12in) canvasboard. 17-Sep-93 Skinner, Bolton #254/R
$700 £467 Black sheep (15x15cm-6x6in) s.i.verso canvasboard. 26-Aug-93 Skinner, Bolton #141
$750 £500 Mountain landscape (23x15cm-9x6in) i.verso board. 26-Aug-93 Skinner, Bolton #205
$850 £570 Moonlit harbour (20x28cm-8x11in) s. panel. 4-Dec-93 Louisiana Auction Exchange #108/R
$1200 £789 Landscape with cottages (41x61cm-16x24in) s. 31-Mar-93 Sotheby's Arcade, New York #154/R
$1300 £909 Wagon road in winter (38x36cm-15x14in) s. i.verso panel. 12-Mar-93 Skinner, Bolton #212/R
$1400 £915 Paris - river scene (25x36cm-10x14in) with i.verso. 17-Sep-93 Skinner, Bolton #255/R
$1400 £915 Autumn foliage (25x36cm-10x14in) s.d.92 with i.verso board. 17-Sep-93 Skinner, Bolton #257/R
$1400 £933 Snowy landscape, dusk (23x30cm-9x12in) s.d.1886 i.verso. 26-Aug-93 Skinner, Bolton #151/R
$1400 £933 Milton Blue Hills (25x36cm-10x14in) s. i.verso canvasboard. 26-Aug-93 Skinner, Bolton #184
$1400 £915 Along the River Hyde Park (20x25cm-8x10in) s. with i.verso board. 17-Sep-93 Skinner, Bolton #253/R
$1500 £1007 Tuckerman's ravine (61x76cm-24x30in) 6-May-94 Skinner, Bolton #75/R
$1540 £1007 Neponset River (13x15cm-5x6in) d.1903 i.verso panel. 14-May-93 Skinner, Bolton #78/R
$1900 £1005 Along the Neponset (30x41cm-12x16in) s. 12-Sep-92 Louisiana Auction Exchange #64/R
$2000 £1325 Twilight landscape (25x30cm-10x12in) i.verso board. 28-Nov-92 Young Fine Arts Auctions, Maine #135/R
$2100 £1373 Stormy skies - Milton Blue Hills (25x25cm-10x10in) i. board. 17-Sep-93 Skinner, Bolton #252/R
$2200 £1497 Woodland stream (16x20cm-6x8in) 10-Jul-93 Young Fine Arts Auctions, Maine #122/R
$2300 £1329 Autumn sunset (30x46cm-12x18in) s. 27-Sep-92 James Bakker, Cambridge #19/R
$2400 £1622 European street scene (41x56cm-16x22in) s.d.85. 20-Mar-93 Weschler, Washington #85/R
$2420 £1582 Stream with wooden bridge, autumn sunset (36x46cm-14x18in) s.d.02. 14-May-93 Skinner, Bolton #107/R
$2700 £1765 Summer in Milton, Fall (46x61cm-18x24in) i. 17-Sep-93 Skinner, Bolton #256/R
$2750 £1590 Autumn pasture with cows (56x76cm-22x30in) s.d.97. 27-Sep-92 James Bakker, Cambridge #18/R
$2750 £1846 Indian summer, sunset (56x76cm-22x30in) s.d.98. 6-Dec-93 Grogan, Massachussetts #489/R
$2900 £1921 Farm scene (41x56cm-16x22in) s.d.1887. 23-Sep-93 Mystic Fine Arts, Connecticut #167/R
$3000 £1987 Blue Mountains (51x61cm-20x24in) i. 13-Nov-92 Skinner, Bolton #132/R
$3000 £1734 Snow scene (30x35cm-12x14in) s. canvas on board on aluminum. 23-Sep-92 Christie's, New York #150/R
$3000 £2013 The cabin (61x76cm-24x30in) s. 6-Dec-93 Grogan, Massachussetts #487/R
$3200 £2148 Landscape at sunset (48x58cm-19x23in) s. 5-Mar-94 Louisiana Auction Exchange #26/R
$3500 £2333 Trout Brook, Fall, New England (61x76cm-24x30in) s. 26-Aug-93 Skinner, Bolton #179
$3500 £2448 Spring lambs (46x61cm-18x24in) s.d.92. 12-Mar-93 Skinner, Bolton #168/R
$3600 £2384 Snow scene, New England (46x61cm-18x24in) s.d.06. 13-Nov-92 Skinner, Bolton #136/R
$4000 £2797 Passing clouds (46x61cm-18x24in) s.d.09. 11-Mar-93 Christie's, New York #142/R
$4000 £2649 Autumn in woods (51x61cm-20x24in) i. 13-Nov-92 Skinner, Bolton #128/R
$4000 £2312 Twilight (18x28cm-7x11in) s.indis.d.7. 23-Sep-92 Christie's, New York #136/R
$4000 £2703 Autumn twilight (46x61cm-18x24in) i. 5-Nov-93 Skinner, Bolton #92/R

ENNEKING, John J (1841-1916) American-cont.
$4000	£2614	Old woman sewing in Eliot Homestead, Hyde Park (61x84cm-24x33in) s. painted 1883. 8-May-93 Young Fine Arts Auctions, Maine #103/R
$4250	£2972	Baker chocolate factory (28x33cm-11x13in) s. i.verso board. 12-Mar-93 Skinner, Bolton #196/R
$4400	£2876	Figures working in fields (36x46cm-14x18in) s.d.83. 14-May-93 Skinner, Bolton #48/R
$6000	£4000	Summer landscape (51x62cm-20x24in) s. 17-Mar-94 Sotheby's, New York #113/R
$6000	£4196	Shady brook (64x76cm-25x30in) s. 12-Mar-93 Skinner, Bolton #188/R
$6500	£4392	Coventry Bridge at twilight (46x61cm-18x24in) i. 5-Nov-93 Skinner, Bolton #97/R
$7250	£4739	Moonlit waters, Marblehead (41x36cm-16x14in) s. 18-Sep-93 Young Fine Arts Auctions, Maine #108/R
$7500	£5000	Fall landscape (62x77cm-24x30in) s.d.13. 17-Mar-94 Sotheby's, New York #112/R
$9350	£6111	Potatoe harvesting (46x66cm-18x26in) s.d.77. 14-May-93 Skinner, Bolton #74/R
$12000	£6936	Mill pond (56x86cm-22x34in) s.d.96. 27-Sep-92 James Bakker, Cambridge #17/R
$13000	£9091	Duck pond, autumn (56x76cm-22x30in) s.d.91. 12-Mar-93 Skinner, Bolton #193/R
$16000	£10884	Trout Brook Maine (61x76cm-24x30in) s. 17-Nov-93 Doyle, New York #44/R
$17000	£11565	Trout pool (81x101cm-32x40in) s. 15-Nov-93 Christie's, East, New York #138/R
$29000	£19205	House by the river (56x86cm-22x34in) s.d.89. 15-Jun-94 Butterfield & Butterfield, San Francisco #4419/R
$60000	£37975	Flowers in garden (77x56cm-30x22in) s.d.97. 4-Dec-92 Christie's, New York #32/R

ENNEKING, Joseph Elliot (1881-1942) American
$700	£464	Mystic bridge (20x25cm-8x10in) s.d.1909 board. 23-Sep-93 Mystic Fine Arts, Connecticut #58
$750	£503	Potters Lane (20x25cm-8x10in) s.d.1912 board. 26-Mar-94 James Bakker, Cambridge #139/R
$900	£588	Sailboat off Gloucester (30x41cm-12x16in) s. i.verso canvasboard. 17-Sep-93 Skinner, Bolton #224/R
$950	£621	Windswept sea (30x41cm-12x16in) s. canvasboard. 17-Sep-93 Skinner, Bolton #226/R
$1000	£671	Autumn (30x36cm-12x14in) s. i.verso board. 6-May-94 Skinner, Bolton #77/R
$1300	£818	The Ledge (30x36cm-12x14in) s. 25-Apr-93 James Bakker, Cambridge #14/R
$1300	£861	Autumn scene (25x30cm-10x12in) s. board. 23-Sep-93 Mystic Fine Arts, Connecticut #112
$1430	£935	Late afternoon, mystic village (25x20cm-10x8in) s. board. 14-May-93 Skinner, Bolton #118/R

ENNIS, George Pearse (1884-1936) American
$800	£513	The ledges (36x36cm-14x14in) s.i.d.1923verso board. 9-Dec-92 Butterfield & Butterfield, San Francisco #3892/R
$1000	£658	End of the fisherman's day (91x76cm-36x30in) s. 4-Nov-92 Doyle, New York #56/R
$1150	£723	End of the fisherman's day (91x76cm-36x30in) s. 22-Apr-93 Freeman Fine Arts, Philadelphia #1163
$1300	£765	Rising fog (61x71cm-24x28in) s. 8-Oct-92 Freeman Fine Arts, Philadelphia #1085 a

ENOTRIO (1920-1989) Argentinian
$1057	£709	Paesaggio calabrese (50x70cm-20x28in) s. s.i.d.verso. 25-Mar-93 Finarte, Rome #144 (I.L 1700000)
$1128	£752	Nudo (70x100cm-28x39in) s. s.i.d.verso. 10-May-94 Finarte, Firenze #117 (I.L 1800000)
$1217	£806	Vagoni in un campo (50x70cm-20x28in) s. studio st.s.i.d.verso. 19-Nov-92 Finarte, Rome #230/R (I.L 1700000)
$1289	£854	Paese in Calabria (50x70cm-20x28in) s. panel. 19-Nov-92 Finarte, Rome #146 (I.L 1800000)
$1312	£880	Paesaggio calabrese (51x70cm-20x28in) s. s.verso board. 30-Nov-93 Finarte, Rome #204 (I.L 2200000)
$1352	£913	Casa a Ischia (60x70cm-24x28in) s. s.i.studio st.verso. 19-Apr-94 Finarte, Rome #115 (I.L 2200000)
$1364	£903	Paesaggio calabrese (60x70cm-24x28in) s. s.i.verso panel. 14-Jun-94 Finarte, Rome #117 (I.L 2200000)
$1432	£949	Il salone del barbiere (60x80cm-24x31in) s. s.i.verso. 19-Nov-92 Finarte, Rome #108/R (I.L 2000000)
$1862	£1233	Binario morto (50x70cm-20x28in) s. s.verso panel. 19-Nov-92 Finarte, Rome #129 (I.L 2600000)

ENRIGHT, Richard D (20th C) American
$1200	£805	Texas landscape (61x76cm-24x30in) s. 5-Mar-94 Louisiana Auction Exchange #95/R

ENRIQUEZ, Carlos (20th C) South American
$7500	£4902	Pelea de gallos (61x50cm-24x20in) s. painted c.1950. 18-May-93 Sotheby's, New York #248/R
$10000	£6536	Nina con pescado (63x46cm-25x18in) s.d.47. 17-May-93 Christie's, New York #186/R
$22000	£14667	Mujer con velo (63x51cm-25x20in) s.d.55. 18-May-94 Christie's, New York #111/R
$22000	£14667	Odile (79x63cm-31x25in) s.d.45 s.i.verso. 18-May-94 Sotheby's, New York #348/R
$3000	*£1987*	*Caballos (39x50cm-15x20in) s.d.55 W/C gouache pen. 24-Nov-92 Christie's, New York #312/R*
$8000	*£5333*	*Dos caballos (39x29cm-15x11in) s.d.56 gouache W/C ink. 18-May-94 Sotheby's, New York #227/R*

ENRIQUEZ, Nicolas (fl.1738-1770) Mexican
$4432	£2995	Immaculada con angelitos y Santo Franciscano arrodillado (48x36cm-19x14in) s. copper. 27-Oct-93 Fernando Duran, Madrid #77/R (S.P 600000)
$90000	£60000	Virgen de Guadalupe (82x60cm-32x24in) s.i.d.1777. 17-May-94 Sotheby's, New York #6/R

ERDELY, Francis de (1904-1959) Hungarian/American
$750	£503	Still life (86x71cm-34x28in) s. 5-Feb-94 Dargate Auction Galleries, Pittsburgh #7
$750	£524	Prone nude (25x36cm-10x14in) s. board. 12-Mar-93 Du Mouchelle, Detroit #2126/R
$600	£392	Seated female nude, back view (69x58cm-27x23in) s. pencil htd.col. 20-May-93 Boos Gallery, Michigan #413/R
$700	£409	Religious meeting (51x43cm-20x17in) s. gouache. 18-Sep-92 Du Mouchelle, Detroit #2042/R
$750	£497	Reclining nude (53x86cm-21x34in) s. chl. 14-Jun-94 John Moran, Pasadena #123 a

ERICSON, David (1869-1946) American
$6500	£4452	Venetian carnival (81x81cm-32x32in) s. 15-Feb-94 Christie's, New York #108/R

ERNST, Jimmy (1920-1984) American/German
$850	£579	S.R.O. no.4 (9x15cm-4x6in) s.d.59 panel. 15-Nov-93 Christie's, East, New York #270
$1000	£667	Abstract in grey (20x25cm-8x10in) s.d.61 masonite. 23-May-94 Christie's, East, New York #224/R
$1700	£1111	Yesterday and tomorrow (33x25cm-13x10in) s.d.1963 masonite. 20-May-93 Boos Gallery, Michigan #408/R
$8500	£5556	The silent place (127x119cm-50x47in) s.d.57. 20-May-93 Boos Gallery, Michigan #405/R
$550	£369	Quasars (30x30cm-12x12in) s.d.68 mixed media assemblage. 11-Dec-93 Weschler, Washington #142/R
$700	£476	Untitled Abstract (46x36cm-18x14in) s.d.49 W/C. 14-Apr-94 Freeman Fine Arts, Philadelphia #1043
$800	£537	Memory of Perelkino (20x25cm-8x10in) s.i.d.62 W/C Indian ink paper on board. 11-Dec-93 Weschler, Washington #140
$1000	£671	Abstract composition (20x28cm-8x11in) s.d.41 gouache. 23-Jun-93 Doyle, New York #28
$1800	£1139	Untitled (56x86cm-22x34in) s.i.d.1954 gouache W/C ink. 2-Dec-92 Christie's, East, New York #393
$2600	£1646	Abstract in greys (58x43cm-23x17in) s.d.51 gouache. 2-Dec-92 Christie's, East, New York #394/R
$3000	£2013	Untitled (46x55cm-18x22in) s.d.68 W/C gouache. 24-Feb-94 Sotheby's Arcade, New York #350/R

ERTZ, Bruno (attrib) (1873-1956) American
$600	£408	Blue jay (43x33cm-17x13in) s. W/C. 17-Apr-94 Schrager Galleries, Milwaukee #740

ERTZ, Edward F (1862-?) American
$1444	£950	Boy in meadow (36x25cm-14x10in) s.d.93 artist's board. 11-Jun-93 Christie's, London #264/R

ESCOBEDO, Eberto (1919-) Cuban
$6500	£4305	Paisaje Cubano (92x107cm-36x42in) s.d.1951 i.verso. 24-Nov-92 Christie's, New York #300/R

ESPOY, Angel (1879-1963) American
$750	£507	Flowery hillside in Southern California (61x76cm-24x30in) s. 9-Nov-93 John Moran, Pasadena #899
$750	£497	Landscape with cowboy on horseback (41x51cm-16x20in) s. 14-Jun-94 John Moran, Pasadena #22
$850	£559	Fisherman's cove (51x41cm-20x16in) s. i.verso. 2-Apr-93 Sloan, North Bethesda #2320/R
$1000	£671	Seascape (61x91cm-24x36in) 27-Mar-94 Myers, Florida #117/R
$1100	£759	Flowered hillside (51x61cm-20x24in) s. 16-Feb-93 John Moran, Pasadena #71
$1200	£795	Seascape (51x76cm-20x30in) s. 28-Sep-93 John Moran, Pasadena #223
$1400	£933	Flowered landscape (23x30cm-9x12in) s. canvas laid on board. 15-Mar-94 John Moran, Pasadena #15
$1500	£968	Extensive desert landscape with blooming flowers (69x97cm-27x38in) s. 6-Jan-93 Doyle, New York #24
$1600	£941	Breaking waves (63x76cm-25x30in) s. 4-Oct-92 Butterfield & Butterfield, Los Angeles #176/R
$1600	£1053	Cattle grazing in field of wildflowers (38x58cm-15x23in) s. 13-Jun-93 Butterfield & Butterfield, San Francisco #892/R
$1600	£1111	Yosemite fisherman (56x41cm-22x16in) s. 7-Mar-93 Butterfield & Butterfield, San Francisco #36/R
$1800	£1192	Landscape with cattle (41x51cm-16x20in) s. 14-Jun-94 John Moran, Pasadena #23
$1800	£1216	Wild flowers on mountains near Bakersfield (41x51cm-16x20in) s. painted 1935. 9-Nov-93 John Moran, Pasadena #850
$1900	£1267	Flowered landscape (23x30cm-9x12in) s. canvas laid on board. 15-Mar-94 John Moran, Pasadena #16
$2000	£1342	Lupine and sand dunes (51x76cm-20x30in) s. 8-Dec-93 Butterfield & Butterfield, San Francisco #3503/R
$2000	£1389	Pacific coast at sunset (61x91cm-24x36in) s. 7-Mar-93 Butterfield & Butterfield, San Francisco #109/R
$2000	£1389	Flowered field (66x91cm-26x36in) s. 7-Mar-93 Butterfield & Butterfield, San Francisco #188/R
$2250	£1480	Mountain landscape with figures and cows (76x102cm-30x40in) s. 5-Jun-93 Louisiana Auction Exchange #44/R
$2500	£1656	Flowered eucalyptus landscape (51x41cm-20x16in) s. 14-Jun-94 John Moran, Pasadena #118
$2500	£1656	Half Dome, Yosemite (30x36cm-12x14in) s. board. 15-Jun-94 Butterfield & Butterfield, San Francisco #4638/R

ESPOY, Angel (1879-1963) American-cont.
$2750   £1821   California wild flowers (63x76cm-25x30in) s. 15-Jun-94 Butterfield & Butterfield, San Francisco #4690/R
$3000   £2083   California wildflowers (51x61cm-20x24in) s. 7-Mar-93 Butterfield & Butterfield, San Francisco #196/R
$4250   £2853   High desert (76x102cm-30x40in) s. 8-Dec-93 Butterfield & Butterfield, San Francisco #3501/R

ESSIG, George E (1838-?) American
$1000   £633   Beached sailboat (28x44cm-11x17in) s. 2-Dec-92 Christie's, East, New York #101

ESTE, Florence (1860-1926) American
$1300   £798   River landscape (102x117cm-40x46in) s. 16-Oct-92 Du Mouchelle, Detroit #2010/R

ESTES, Richard (1936-) American
$25000   £16556   Storelights (122x76cm-48x30in) s. masonite painted 1968. 18-Nov-92 Sotheby's, New York #171/R
$45000   £30405   Flughafen - airport (36x51cm-14x20in) s.d.81 canvasboard. 11-Nov-93 Sotheby's, New York #399/R
$165000   £110738   Revolving doors (76x122cm-30x48in) s. masonite painted 1968. 4-May-94 Sotheby's, New York #33/R
$420000   £283784   Nedick's (122x168cm-48x66in) s. painted 1970. 10-Nov-93 Sotheby's, New York #32/R

ESTOCK, Stephen (20th C) American
$650   £433   Loose seducer (147x142cm-58x56in) s.i.d.1978 verso acrylic. 26-May-94 Freeman Fine Arts, Philadelphia #153

ESTOPINAN, Roberto (1920-) Cuban
$1750   £1174   Woman's torso (123x89cm-48x35in) pencil chl. 7-Jan-94 Gary Nader, Miami #127/R

ETIENNE, Arnold (1942-) Haitian
$652   £418   L'animalerie (61x50cm-24x20in) s. painted 1989. 14-Dec-92 Hoebanx, Paris #20/R (F.FR 3500)

ETIENNE, Charnelus (1966-) Haitian
$942   £615   Le Jardin d'Eden (61x82cm-24x32in) painted 1990. 17-May-93 Hoebanx, Paris #75/R (F.FR 5200)

ETIENNE, Jackson (1961-) Haitian
$1117   £716   Jungle imaginaire (91x61cm-36x24in) s. painted 1986. 14-Dec-92 Hoebanx, Paris #167/R (F.FR 6000)

ETKIN, Susan (1955-) American
$468   £312   Positions III (58x76cm-23x30in) s.d.8/86verso mixed media. 2-Jun-94 AB Stockholms Auktionsverk, Stockholm #7073/R (S.KR 3700)
$504   £343   Untitled (61x45cm-24x18in) mixed media. 13-Apr-94 Bukowskis, Stockholm #365 (S.KR 4000)

ETNIER, Stephen (1903-1984) American
$2800   £1842   New England harbour scene (76x102cm-30x40in) s. 31-Mar-93 Sotheby's Arcade, New York #312/R

ETTINGER, Churchill (1903-) American
$800   £567   Playing four pound brook trout (56x71cm-22x28in) s. 13-Feb-93 Collins, Maine #90/R

EVANS DE SCOTT (1847-1898) American
$3000   £1961   Still life with daffodils in brass urn (109x61cm-43x24in) s.d.1885. 5-May-93 Doyle, New York #2/R
$15000   £10000   Grandfather's clock (115x74cm-45x29in) s.d.1881. 26-May-94 Christie's, New York #5/R

EVEREN, Jay van (20th C) American?
$3500   £2023   Composition (89x142cm-35x56in) s. 24-Sep-92 Sotheby's, New York #201/R

EVERGOOD, Phillip (1901-1973) American
$700   £467   Pier by the sea (43x82cm-17x32in) s. 23-May-94 Christie's, East, New York #253
$1500   £867   Siegfried and the Rhine maidens (36x51cm-14x20in) s. s.i.stretcher. 25-Sep-92 Sotheby's Arcade, New York #435/R
$2600   £1688   Figures in interior (43x74cm-17x29in) s. canvas on masonite. 11-Sep-93 Louisiana Auction Exchange #1/R
$3000   £1961   Sacrifice of the queen (63x46cm-25x18in) i.verso i.d.1969,1970stretcher. 22-May-93 Weschler, Washington #152/R
$4000   £2667   Home (63x51cm-25x20in) s. 23-May-94 Christie's, East, New York #232/R
$6500   £3757   The new birth (77x59cm-30x23in) s.d.43 canvas on panel. 25-Sep-92 Sotheby's Arcade, New York #454/R
$7500   £4335   Success team (53x46cm-21x18in) s. s.i.verso canvasboard. 25-Sep-92 Sotheby's Arcade, New York #452/R
$13000   £8333   Holocaust or It's black outside (76x102cm-30x40in) s.d.LXII s.i.stretcher. 26-May-93 Christie's, New York #227/R
$55000   £36667   The siding (91x69cm-36x27in) s.d.36. 25-May-94 Sotheby's, New York #133/R
$550   £367   Two women (49x44cm-19x17in) s.d.1950 pencil. 23-May-94 Christie's, East, New York #242
$600   £390   Seamstress (36x28cm-14x11in) s.d.53 pencil on paper. 9-Sep-93 Sotheby's Arcade, New York #349/R

EVERGOOD, Phillip (1901-1973) American-cont.
$700	£455	Folkway records (74x58cm-29x23in) s. i.verso pencil India ink wash. 9-Sep-93 Sotheby's Arcade, New York #347/R
$1000	£676	Happy Hour (51x61cm-20x24in) s. oil chl canvasboard. 31-Mar-94 Sotheby's Arcade, New York #346/R
$1800	£1192	Portrait of lady (84x69cm-33x27in) s.d.XLX graphite. 13-Nov-92 Skinner, Bolton #194/R
$2000	£1333	Mining scene (74x56cm-29x22in) ink wash htd white. 23-May-94 Hindman Galleries, Chicago #257
$3100	£2039	Three mythological figures (56x41cm-22x16in) s. init. chl conte crayon W/C. 31-Mar-93 Sotheby's Arcade, New York #473/R

EWART, Peter (1918-) Canadian
$697	£456	Packing near Bow Lake (33x43cm-13x17in) s. board. 6-Oct-93 Maynards, Vancouver #277 (C.D 925)
$941	£631	Fall roundup near Ashcroft British Columbia (41x51cm-16x20in) s. board. 8-Dec-93 Maynards, Vancouver #218 (C.D 1250)
$1117	£707	Church at evening (20x24cm-8x9in) s. board. 21-Oct-92 Maynards, Vancouver #129 (C.D 1400)
$1238	£825	Packing in, Bridge River area (61x76cm-24x30in) s. board. 11-May-94 Sotheby's, Toronto #257/R (C.D 1700)

EXUME, Nesly (1960-) Haitian
$688	£450	Ville imaginaire (61x91cm-24x36in) painted 1991. 17-May-93 Hoebanx, Paris #85/R (F.FR 3800)
$745	£477	Ville imaginaire (91x61cm-36x24in) s. 14-Dec-92 Hoebanx, Paris #98 (F.FR 4000)
$797	£521	Poteau Mitan (56x76cm-22x30in) 17-May-93 Hoebanx, Paris #88 (F.FR 4400)
$905	£592	La bande de Rara (61x86cm-24x34in) 17-May-93 Hoebanx, Paris #86/R (F.FR 5000)
$931	£597	Cascade (91x61cm-36x24in) s. 14-Dec-92 Hoebanx, Paris #100 a (F.FR 5000)
$931	£597	Ville imaginaire (91x61cm-36x24in) s. 14-Dec-92 Hoebanx, Paris #97 (F.FR 5000)
$1042	£668	Les deux enfants (61x51cm-24x20in) s. 14-Dec-92 Hoebanx, Paris #62/R (F.FR 5600)
$1675	£1074	Ville imaginaire (91x61cm-36x24in) s. 14-Dec-92 Hoebanx, Paris #63 (F.FR 9000)

EYDEN, William A (1893-) American
$1050	£700	Looking north from Chinatown (76x102cm-30x40in) s. 13-Mar-94 Hindman Galleries, Chicago #808
$800	£404	Indiana woods (53x71cm-21x28in) s. W/C. 28-Aug-92 Young Fine Arts Auctions, Maine #115

FABLO, Serge (1937-) Canadian
$543	£362	En accord avec les interrogations modernes (91x71cm-36x28in) s. s.i.d.1980 verso board. 6-Jun-94 Waddingtons, Toronto #1308 (C.D 750)
$692	£461	Entre Hyannis et Nantuket (40x50cm-16x20in) s. 13-May-94 Joyner Fine Art, Toronto #284 (C.D 950)

FADER, Fernando (1882-1935) Argentinian
$10000	£5780	La carta (36x26cm-14x10in) tempera. 23-Sep-92 Roldan & Cia, Buenos Aires #17

FAIRLEY, Barker (1887-1986) Canadian
$872	£570	Portrait of Leonard Hutchinson (51x41cm-20x16in) s. s.d.1976 verso board. 19-May-93 Sotheby's, Toronto #48/R (C.D 1100)
$1325	£872	Kitchen window (36x30cm-14x12in) s. s.i.d.1974verso board. 7-Jun-93 Waddingtons, Toronto #1118 (C.D 1700)
$1472	£995	Trent River (29x36cm-11x14in) s. s.i.d.1974verso board. 3-Nov-93 Sotheby's, Toronto #309/R (C.D 1900)
$1506	£984	Hills near Eugenia (28x36cm-11x14in) s. s.d.1975 verso board. 19-May-93 Sotheby's, Toronto #244/R (C.D 1900)

FAIRMAN, George (1859-1926) American
$3400	£2313	View of the Orsini Palace, Venice (41x79cm-16x31in) s. i.verso. 14-Apr-94 Freeman Fine Arts, Philadelphia #988/R

FAIRMAN, James (1826-1904) American
$3200	£2078	Ship in rough seas off coast (81x114cm-32x45in) s. 9-Sep-93 Sotheby's Arcade, New York #103/R
$3500	£2333	Sunset on the coast of Corsica (81x114cm-32x45in) s. 23-May-94 Christie's, East, New York #66/R
$5000	£2890	Sunlight on the coast (58x91cm-23x36in) s. 23-Sep-92 Christie's, New York #75/R
$13000	£8609	View near Gilead Maine (69x122cm-27x48in) init.d.66. 15-Jun-94 Butterfield & Butterfield, San Francisco #4432/R
$24000	£16783	Mrs Madison and Adams near Gorham, New Hampshire (50x91cm-20x36in) s.d.1870 init.i.verso. 11-Mar-93 Christie's, New York #24/R

FAIVRE, Justin (1902-) American
$1000	£662	Abstract Composition (41x51cm-16x20in) s. 15-Jun-94 Butterfield & Butterfield, San Francisco #4758/R
$1200	£795	Mendocino Coast (65x126cm-26x50in) s. s.i.verso. 15-Jun-94 Butterfield & Butterfield, San Francisco #4740/R
$2250	£1510	Natural bridges (66x102cm-26x40in) s. s.i.verso. 8-Dec-93 Butterfield & Butterfield, San Francisco #3475/R

FAIVRE, Justin (1902-) American-cont.
$1000   £662   Van's Boat Wharf (33x41cm-13x16in) s.d.Aug.39 W/C. 28-Sep-93 John Moran, Pasadena #209

FALARDEAU, Antoine Sebastien (1822-1889) Canadian
$2500   £1656   Rubens self-portrait (84x69cm-33x27in) s.verso. 23-Sep-93 Mystic Fine Arts, Connecticut #166

FALCONNER, John M (1820-1903) American
$1700   £1181   The reaper maiden (41x51cm-16x20in) s.i.d.1876verso board. 27-Feb-93 Young Fine Arts Auctions, Maine #102/R

FALTER, John P (1910-1982) American
$5000   £3378   Kitchen hanky-panky (91x81cm-36x32in) s. painted c.1930's. 31-Mar-94 Sotheby's Arcade, New York #396/R

FARINA, Ernesto (1912-) Argentinian
$750   £391   Suburbio (21x28cm-8x11in) W/C. 4-Aug-92 VerBo, Buenos Aires #46

FARLEY, Richard Blossom (1875-1951) American
$850   £500   Nude at sunset (41x30cm-16x12in) s. 8-Oct-92 Freeman Fine Arts, Philadelphia #979
$2200   £1438   Young woman wading in a stream (30x41cm-12x16in) s. 7-Oct-93 Freeman Fine Arts, Philadelphia #954/R

FARNDON, Walter (1876-1964) American
$1500   £794   The morning stroll (36x46cm-14x18in) s. board. 11-Sep-92 Skinner, Bolton #221/R
$1600   £1073   Northern Waters (63x76cm-25x30in) s. s.i.stretcher. 8-Dec-93 Butterfield & Butterfield, San Francisco #3371/R
$1700   £1141   Beached boats (36x46cm-14x18in) s. board. 24-Jun-93 Mystic Fine Arts, Connecticut #198
$3000   £2013   Winter village (64x77cm-25x30in) s. 8-Dec-93 Butterfield & Butterfield, San Francisco #3370/R
$3750   £2517   House beside a river (63x77cm-25x30in) s. 8-Dec-93 Butterfield & Butterfield, San Francisco #3369/R
$7000   £4636   Harbour scene (66x81cm-26x32in) s. 23-Sep-93 Mystic Fine Arts, Connecticut #150 a/R

FARNSWORTH, Alfred Villiers (1858-1908) American
$650   £439   Coastal boats off Rocky Pt (30x51cm-12x20in) s.d.1904 W/C. 15-Jun-93 John Moran, Pasadena #56
$700   £486   Grazing cattle on hillside (24x42cm-9x17in) s.d.1903 W/C gouache. 7-Mar-93 Butterfield & Butterfield, San Francisco #18/R
$2750   £1846   Cattle grazing, Marin County (28x53cm-11x21in) s.d.1904 W/C gouache. 8-Dec-93 Butterfield & Butterfield, San Francisco #3316/R

FARNSWORTH, Jerry (1895-?) American
$900   £588   Nude back (58x41cm-23x16in) s. 19-Sep-93 Hindman Galleries, Chicago #722/R

FARNUM, H Cyrus (1886-?) American
$625   £420   German village scene (33x46cm-13x18in) s. 16-Dec-93 Mystic Fine Arts, Connecticut #124/R
$625   £420   Marsh scene (28x43cm-11x17in) s. 16-Dec-93 Mystic Fine Arts, Connecticut #125
$750   £514   Fishing boats at low tide (38x46cm-15x18in) s. canvas on masonite. 10-Feb-94 Skinner, Bolton #3
$800   £537   Woman resting in the countryside (64x46cm-25x18in) s. 16-Dec-93 Mystic Fine Arts, Connecticut #123/R

FARNY, Henry F (1847-1916) American
$9000   £6081   Portrait of Chief John Williams (41cm-16in circular) s. on leather war drum leopard skin drum stick. 31-Mar-94 Sotheby's Arcade, New York #187/R
$19000   £12667   Chief little bear (23x14cm-9x6in) s.d.1904. 26-May-94 Christie's, New York #52/R
$6500   £4422   Approaching enemy a woman standing in doorway (24x14cm-9x6in) s.d.1903 gouache paper laid down on board. 15-Nov-93 Christie's, East, New York #145/R
$11000   £7333   A Zuni farmhouse (29x42cm-11x17in) s. i.d.1883 verso gouache W/C en grisaille. 17-Mar-94 Sotheby's, New York #60/R
$13000   £8333   Indian brave with rifle (39x23cm-15x9in) s.d.97 pen. 27-May-93 Sotheby's, New York #229/R
$15000   £9494   Ukchekehaskan Minneconjue Sioux (24x15cm-9x6in) init.i. W/C board. 3-Dec-92 Sotheby's, New York #54/R
$29000   £19333   In the pine woods (22x15cm-9x6in) s.d.1900 gouache. 17-Mar-94 Sotheby's, New York #62/R
$35000   £23333   Pueblo water carriers (27x39cm-11x15in) s. W/C gouache board. 25-May-94 Sotheby's, New York #37/R
$50000   £33557   The courtship (23x15cm-9x6in) s.d.90 gouache. 2-Dec-93 Sotheby's, New York #37/R
$65000   £43333   A lucky shot (28x44cm-11x17in) s.d.1903 gouache paper on board. 16-Mar-94 Christie's, New York #82/R

FARR, Ellen B (1840-1907) American
$1600   £1074   Pepper tree (61x41cm-24x16in) s. 8-Dec-93 Butterfield & Butterfield, San Francisco #3305/R

FARRELLY, Joseph (20th C) American
$1755   £1186   Girl playing with bubbles (53x33cm-21x13in) mixed media board. 26-Nov-93 Schloss Ahlden, Ahlden #2002/R (DM 3000)

FARRER, Henry (1843-1903) American
$7500	£4747	Evening sail (46x64cm-18x25in) s.d.1900 W/C. 3-Dec-92 Sotheby's, New York #26/R
$13000	£9091	Close of grey day (61x93cm-24x37in) s.d.1887 W/C. 10-Mar-93 Sotheby's, New York #86/R

FAUSETT, Dean (1913-) American
$750	£487	Rural landscape (56x71cm-22x28in) s. W/C. 11-Sep-93 Louisiana Auction Exchange #68/R

FAUSTIN CELESTIN (1948-1981) Haitian
$4652	£3081	La naissance, Ceremonie vaudou (121x183cm-48x72in) s. 13-Jun-94 Rogeon, Paris #78/R (F.FR 26000)

FAUSTIN, Obes (1959-) Haitian
$745	£477	Demande a Dambalha (35x225cm-14x89in) s. 14-Dec-92 Hoebanx, Paris #132/R (F.FR 4000)
$745	£477	Je crois (35x25cm-14x10in) s. 14-Dec-92 Hoebanx, Paris #133 (F.FR 4000)

FAY, Joe (1950-) American
$600	£377	Red Bear (76x114cm-30x45in) s.i.d.1987 mixed media. 25-Apr-93 Butterfield & Butterfield, San Francisco #2185/R
$600	£377	Grizzly and cowboy (77x113cm-30x44in) s.i.d.1987 mixed media. 25-Apr-93 Butterfield & Butterfield, San Francisco #2186/R
$600	£377	Urban coyote with fish (76x113cm-30x44in) s.i.d.1987 mixed media. 25-Apr-93 Butterfield & Butterfield, San Francisco #2188/R
$700	£440	Gunfight at the O.K. Corral (122x142cm-48x56in) s.i.d.1987verso mixed media panel. 25-Apr-93 Butterfield & Butterfield, San Francisco #2187/R

FECHIN, Nicolai (1881-1955) American/Russian
$50000	£31646	Still life with flowers (50x40cm-20x16in) s.i.d.1945. 3-Dec-92 Sotheby's, New York #70/R
$2600	£1722	Head of woman (42x32cm-17x13in) s.d.26 chl pastel paper on board. 22-Sep-93 Christie's, New York #183/R

FECTEAU, Marcel (1927-) Canadian
$602	£404	Fishermen's homes (38x51cm-15x20in) s. board. 29-Nov-93 Waddingtons, Toronto #1176 (C.D 800)

FEELEY, Paul (1913-1966) American
$12000	£8108	Maia (76x63cm-30x25in) s.i.d.1963stretcher acrylic. 10-Nov-93 Christie's, New York #183/R

FEININGER, Lyonel (1871-1956) American/German
$56846	£37398	The vanishing hour (48x81cm-19x32in) s. i.d.1951-2stretcher. 5-Jun-93 Villa Grisebach, Berlin #319/R (DM 92000)
$91800	£60000	Barque at sea (46x76cm-18x30in) s.d.53 s.i.d.stretcher. 28-Jun-94 Christie's, London #215/R
$100000	£67568	Houses at night (41x61cm-16x24in) s. painted 1951. 4-Nov-93 Sotheby's, New York #202/R
$114919	£76613	Architecture with stars II (48x71cm-19x28in) s. i.d.1945verso. 27-May-94 Villa Grisebach, Berlin #49/R (DM 190000)
$350000	£233333	Die Werbung, the proposal (68x53cm-27x21in) painted 1907. 11-May-94 Sotheby's, New York #45/R
$1400000	£945946	Draisinenfahrer (95x85cm-37x33in) s.d.10. 2-Nov-93 Christie's, New York #37/R
$640	£427	Figure (20x13cm-8x5in) s. ink W/C. 14-Mar-94 Australian Art Auctions, Sydney #59 (A.D 900)
$989	£664	Ives the house opposite amongst the trees (10x16cm-4x6in) i.d.Jan 31 11 pencil sketch. 4-Dec-93 Lempertz, Cologne #174/R (DM 1700)
$1165	£766	House and trees (15x9cm-6x4in) d.09 colour chk. 10-Jun-93 Hauswedell & Nolte, Hamburg #281/R (DM 1900)
$1746	£1172	Clouds over the sea (14x22cm-6x9in) i.d.23.8.24 pencil dr. 4-Dec-93 Lempertz, Cologne #173/R (DM 3000)
$1801	£1193	Baltic Sea with tug boat (13x21cm-5x8in) d.27.7.25 pencil. 21-Nov-92 Aucktionhaus Burkard, Luzern #149/R (S.FR 2600)
$2390	£1594	Man in top hat reading newspaper (14x9cm-6x4in) d.1908 lead col. pencil. 9-Jun-94 Hauswedell & Nolte, Hamburg #233/R (DM 4000)
$2910	£1953	Locomotive (13x20cm-5x8in) i.d.Jan 3 1941 col.grease chk. 4-Dec-93 Galerie Bassenge, Berlin #6213/R (DM 5000)
$2988	£1992	Two people on a beach (13x10cm-5x4in) d.1908 lead col pencil. 9-Jun-94 Hauswedell & Nolte, Hamburg #232/R (DM 5000)
$3000	£2083	Figure study (15x9cm-6x4in) d.17-7-09 col.crayon. 23-Feb-93 Sotheby's, New York #81/R
$3085	£2070	Baltic Sea coast and barge (14x22cm-6x9in) d.1925 pencil. 5-Mar-94 Wolfgang Ketterer, Munich #161/R (DM 5300)
$3250	£2167	Vollersroda (16x20cm-6x8in) s.i.d.1913 col.crayons. 9-Jun-94 Sotheby's Arcade, New York #38/R
$3500	£2431	Steam train (14x22cm-6x9in) exec.c.1908 col.crayon. 23-Feb-93 Sotheby's, New York #82/R
$3750	£2604	Mellingen (23x30cm-9x12in) s.i.d.1934 chl. 26-Feb-93 Sotheby's Arcade, New York #14/R
$3807	£2410	Barge (18x27cm-7x11in) s.d.1910 pen. 30-Nov-92 Wolfgang Ketterer, Munich #101/R (DM 6000)
$4500	£2941	Study for pedestrians (13x10cm-5x4in) col.crayon executed 1908. 12-May-93 Sotheby's, New York #252/R

FEININGER, Lyonel (1871-1956) American/German-cont.

$5000	£3268	Street scene (13x10cm-5x4in) col.crayon Indian ink executed 1908. 12-May-93 Sotheby's, New York #251/R
$5000	£3268	Segelschiff (20x29cm-8x11in) s.d.17 3 34 pen. 12-May-93 Sotheby's, New York #253/R
$5250	£3431	Wartende lokomotive mit schlepptender (16x24cm-6x9in) s.d.08 i.verso Indian ink executed 1908. 12-May-93 Sotheby's, New York #250/R
$5500	£3642	Street scene (20x23cm-8x9in) d.1911 col.crayon ink. 11-Nov-92 Sotheby's, New York #190/R
$6179	£4065	Village (24x32cm-9x13in) s. Indian ink pen chl chk W/C executed 1955. 5-Jun-93 Villa Grisebach, Berlin #321 (DM 10000)
$6604	£4288	Park in Weimar (15x20cm-6x8in) s.d.22.IX.13 pencil. 21-Jun-94 Finarte, Milan #36/R (I.L 10400000)
$7258	£4839	Untitled (18x29cm-7x11in) s.d.1954 W/C Indian ink pen over chk. 28-May-94 Villa Grisebach, Berlin #193/R (DM 12000)
$8000	£5556	Street scene (31x24cm-12x9in) s.indis.d.Donn.2.1.06 col.crayon. 23-Feb-93 Sotheby's, New York #83/R
$8068	£5378	Woman on a beach at Heringsdorf (15x9cm-6x4in) d.09 col.chk. 9-Jun-94 Hauswedell & Nolte, Hamburg #234/R (DM 13500)
$8148	£5469	Skyline (29x48cm-11x19in) s.d.1950 pastel W/C. 4-Dec-93 Galerie Bassenge, Berlin #6212/R (DM 14000)
$8769	£5885	Villaggio (20x16cm-8x6in) s.d.9.8.22 pencil. 12-Oct-93 Finarte, Milan #240/R (I.L 14000000)
$9000	£6000	Ghosties (16x24cm-6x9in) s.d.Dec.22, 55 pen W/C. 12-May-94 Sotheby's, New York #258/R
$9886	£6504	The vanishing hour (32x48cm-13x19in) mono.s.i.d.1952 Indian ink pen chl pastel. 5-Jun-93 Villa Grisebach, Berlin #318/R (DM 16000)
$10000	£6667	Street scene (26x21cm-10x8in) col.crayon Indian ink. 12-May-94 Sotheby's, New York #257/R
$10000	£6536	Harbor scene (19x28cm-7x11in) s.d.1942 ink. 13-May-93 Christie's, New York #247/R
$10163	£6731	Mellingen (21x28cm-8x11in) s.i.d.1934 chl. 16-Jun-94 Galerie Koller, Zurich #3034/R (S.FR 14000)
$10195	£6707	Steamer (16x24cm-6x9in) s.d.1952 i.verso Indian ink W/C over chk. 5-Jun-93 Villa Grisebach, Berlin #315/R (DM 16500)
$10282	£6855	The challenge (20x28cm-8x11in) s.d.1950 W/C Indian ink over chk. 28-May-94 Villa Grisebach, Berlin #194/R (DM 17000)
$11368	£7287	Before the storm (28x41cm-11x16in) s.i.d.23.8.28 Indian ink brush pen wash. 26-May-93 Lempertz, Cologne #153/R (DM 18000)
$11664	£7623	Gestanks in Schoneberg (24x31cm-9x12in) s.d.October 1912 chl. 8-May-93 Finarte, Chiasso #134/R (S.FR 17000)
$11700	£7905	Ships (19x27cm-7x11in) s.d.31.7.38 Indian ink pen. 27-Nov-93 Villa Grisebach, Berlin #240/R (DM 20000)
$12000	£7843	Town gate (31x24cm-12x9in) s.i.d.1955 W/C ink. 13-May-93 Christie's, New York #246/R
$12500	£8681	Panic (41x48cm-16x19in) s.d.1949 executed 1949 pen W/C. 23-Feb-93 Sotheby's, New York #57/R
$12531	£8299	Hottelstedt (27x43cm-11x17in) s.i.d.15.8.27 W/C Indian ink. 27-Nov-92 Sotheby's, Berlin #16/R (DM 20000)
$13593	£8943	Very far north (26x46cm-10x18in) s.i.d.II.VIII.43 Indian ink pen W/C. 5-Jun-93 Villa Grisebach, Berlin #322/R (DM 22000)
$13911	£9274	Neppermin (21x31cm-8x12in) s.i.d.2. Feb. 1924 W/C Indian ink. 28-May-94 Villa Grisebach, Berlin #198/R (DM 23000)
$15000	£8824	Untitled (29x48cm-11x19in) s.d.1950 i.verso pen W/C. 5-Oct-92 Sotheby's, New York #60/R
$15121	£10081	Hunting pheasants (18x26cm-7x10in) s.i.d.1918 W/C over Indian ink. 28-May-94 Villa Grisebach, Berlin #184/R (DM 25000)
$15500	£10473	Windows number I (30x39cm-12x15in) s. W/C pen. 4-Nov-93 Sotheby's, New York #256/R
$16000	£10458	Ship in storm (32x49cm-13x19in) s.d.13.vii.53 W/C pen. 12-May-93 Sotheby's, New York #254/R
$16000	£10811	The Baltic (36x56cm-14x22in) s.i.d.1939 W/C Indian ink chl. 4-Nov-93 Sotheby's, New York #303/R
$16000	£10811	North West (32x48cm-13x19in) s.d.12.IX.44 i.verso W/C wash Indian ink chl. 4-Nov-93 Sotheby's, New York #304/R
$17135	£11500	Segelschiffe (20x27cm-8x11in) s.studio st.d.15.9.34 W/C pen Indian ink. 23-Mar-94 Sotheby's, London #224/R
$17719	£11813	L'Eglise de Heiligenhafen (25x35cm-10x14in) s.i.d.10.2.22 ink W/C. 8-Jun-94 Poulain & le Fur, Paris #87/R (F.FR 101000)
$19125	£12500	Dunung II (27x34cm-11x13in) s.i.d.18.Juli 1924 W/C pen ink. 29-Jun-93 Sotheby's, London #213/R
$19125	£12500	Spazierganger mit kleinem kind in rot (29x39cm-11x15in) s.d.1946 W/C pen. 20-May-93 Christie's, London #576/R
$19355	£12903	Baltic Sea (24x43cm-9x17in) s.i.d.19.8.31 W/C Indian ink. 28-May-94 Villa Grisebach, Berlin #195/R (DM 23000)
$22000	£14379	Muhle (23x26cm-9x10in) s.d.1912 chl. 12-May-93 Sotheby's, New York #202/R
$22000	£14379	Blue Haze (32x48cm-13x19in) s.i.d.27.7.38 W/C ink. 13-May-93 Christie's, New York #168/R
$24715	£16260	Steamer with trailing smoke (20x31cm-8x12in) s.d.1955 W/C over chk. 5-Jun-93 Villa Grisebach, Berlin #317/R (DM 40000)
$25263	£16194	Behind the church (48x32cm-19x13in) s.i.d.19.9.26 W/C Indian ink pen. 26-May-93 Lempertz, Cologne #152/R (DM 40000)
$25403	£16935	San Francisco IV Golden Gate (32x54cm-13x21in) s.i.d.9.9.34 W/C Indian ink. 27-May-94 Villa Grisebach, Berlin #51/R (DM 42000)
$26640	£18000	Marine transportation (12x61cm-5x24in) s.d.1938 W/C over Indian ink pen. 30-Oct-93 Dr Fritz Nagel, Stuttgart #126/R (DM 45000)

FEININGER, Lyonel (1871-1956) American/German-cont.
$26909 £18182 Untitled (32x48cm-13x19in) s.d.1954 W/C Indian ink pen over chk. 27-Nov-93 Villa Grisebach, Berlin #238/R (DM 46000)
$27342 £18107 Town (24x33cm-9x13in) s.i.d.15.IV.1921 W/C pen. 21-Nov-92 Lempertz, Cologne #141/R (DM 44000)
$28822 £19087 Locomotive IV (36x26cm-14x10in) s.i.d.Juni 1933 Indian ink wash. 27-Nov-92 Villa Grisebach, Berlin #39/R (DM 46000)
$29400 £19600 Evening clouds II (30x47cm-12x19in) s.i.d.27/7/34 W/C Indian ink pen wash exec.1934. 4-Jun-94 Lempertz, Cologne #151/R (DM 49000)
$30000 £19868 Ship (28x40cm-11x16in) s.d.1940 i.verso painted 1940 W/C ink. 11-Nov-92 Sotheby's, New York #191/R
$30894 £20325 Ships meeting on high seas (17x32cm-7x13in) s.i.d.II.9.32 W/C Indian ink pen. 4-Jun-93 Villa Grisebach, Berlin #34/R (DM 50000)
$31430 £21094 Drobsdorf (24x32cm-9x13in) s.i.d.September 15.1916 W/C. 4-Dec-93 Galerie Bassenge, Berlin #6210/R (DM 54000)
$31452 £20968 Church of Treptow a.d. Rega I (25x20cm-10x8in) s.i.d.14.8.31 W/C Indian ink pen over chk. 27-May-94 Villa Grisebach, Berlin #47/R (DM 52000)
$32313 £21399 Low tide, Benadet, Brittany Coast (26x39cm-10x15in) s.i.d.24.Juli 1931 pen W/C. 21-Nov-92 Lempertz, Cologne #142/R (DM 52000)
$32759 £22134 Eichelborn II (23x29cm-9x11in) s.i.d.25. September 1916 W/C Indian ink pen. 26-Nov-93 Villa Grisebach, Berlin #29/R (DM 56000)
$33266 £22177 Yellow ship on red sea (22x35cm-9x14in) s.i.d.30.VI.34 W/C Indian ink pen. 27-May-94 Villa Grisebach, Berlin #48/R (DM 55000)
$33871 £22581 Quimper I (24x42cm-9x17in) s.i.d.1931 W/C Indian ink. 27-May-94 Villa Grisebach, Berlin #50/R (DM 56000)
$48309 £32422 Steep street (28x34cm-11x13in) s.i.d.27.IV.20 Indian ink pen W/C. 4-Dec-93 Galerie Bassenge, Berlin #6211/R (DM 83000)
$50000 £33333 Pariser Strasse (25x20cm-10x8in) s.i.d.21.Dez.1915 W/C pen. 12-May-94 Sotheby's, New York #259/R

FEININGER, Theodore Lux (1910-) American
$1500 £980 14th St. Fashions (51x48cm-20x19in) init. s.i.verso. 17-Sep-93 Skinner, Bolton #304/R
$2500 £1445 American landscape I (53x71cm-21x28in) s. s.d.1947 verso. 24-Sep-92 Sotheby's, New York #136/R

FEITELSON, Lorser (1898-1978) American
$20000 £13423 Untitled (152x127cm-60x50in) s.d.1962 verso oil enamel. 25-Feb-94 Sotheby's, New York #46/R

FELDMAN, Deborah (20th C) Mexican?
$1119 £756 Ejercicios matinales (100x100cm-39x39in) 20-Oct-93 Louis Morton, Mexico #43/R (M.P 3500)

FELGUEREZ, Manuel (20th C) South American
$12000 £8000 Poza Rica (120x100cm-47x39in) s.d.65. 18-May-94 Christie's, New York #168/R

FELIX, Franz (1892-?) American
$950 £638 New Orleans (79x53cm-31x21in) s. 5-Dec-93 James Bakker, Cambridge #41/R

FELIX, Karl Eugene (1837-1906) American
$900 £588 Ships off the coast (43x89cm-17x35in) s. 30-Jun-94 Mystic Fine Arts, Connecticut #83

FENN, Harry (1845-1911) American
$1000 £667 Still life with cherries, pears and melon (30x40cm-12x16in) mono. 21-May-94 Weschler, Washington #85/R
$2500 £1634 Busy Oriental market place (69x51cm-27x20in) s.d. W/C paperboard. 4-May-93 Christie's, East, New York #66/R

FERGUSON, Elizabeth (1884-1925) American
$750 £521 Fruit (33x48cm-13x19in) s. 27-Feb-93 Young Fine Arts Auctions, Maine #105/R

FERGUSON, Henri A (1842-1911) American
$2400 £1569 View of San Giorgio Maggiore, Venice (26x43cm-10x17in) s. 4-May-93 Christie's, East, New York #143/R
$4650 £3000 The Peak of Palomar in the Andes, Chile (44x31cm-17x12in) s.stretcher. 15-Jul-94 Christie's, London #24/R

FERGUSON, Nancy Maybin (20th C) American
$2800 £1867 The sailors in town - Provincetown (30x30cm-12x12in) indist.s.verso oil gouache board executed c.19. 22-May-94 James Bakker, Cambridge #115/R

FERNANDEZ, Aristides (1904-1934) Cuban
$15000 £10000 Sin titulo (22x32cm-9x13in) W/C brush pen executed c.1930. 17-May-94 Sotheby's, New York #17/R

FERNANDEZ, Augustin (1928-) Cuban
$5500 £3667 Retrato de una mujer (107x71cm-42x28in) s. painted 1951. 9-Jun-94 Sotheby's Arcade, New York #125/R
$13000 £8667 El cordel (124x127cm-49x50in) s.d.83. 18-May-94 Sotheby's, New York #379/R
$15000 £10135 Tenistas (96x149cm-38x59in) s. painted 1952. 23-Nov-93 Christie's, New York #66/R
$15000 £10067 Venus con Letras (198x94cm-78x37in) s.d.92. 7-Jan-94 Gary Nader, Miami #19/R
$15000 £10000 Pareja (111x88cm-44x35in) indist.i. painted c.1951. 18-May-94 Christie's, New York #108/R

FERNANDEZ, Augustin (1928-) Cuban-cont.
$18000   £11765   La Mesa (118x95cm-46x37in) s.d.52. 17-May-93 Christie's, New York #190/R

FERRARI, Adolfo de (1898-1978) Argentinian
$900   £469   Paisaje (30x40cm-12x16in) 4-Aug-92 VerBo, Buenos Aires #39

FERREIRA, Martha (1953-) Mexican
$950   £625   Alcatraces prado verde (80x80cm-31x31in) s. 4-Nov-92 Mora, Castelltort & Quintana, Juarez #13/R (M.P 3000000)

FERREN, John (1905-1970) American
$1600   £925   Summer III (61x51cm-24x20in) s. s.i.d.58verso. 25-Sep-92 Sotheby's Arcade, New York #496/R
$800   *£541*   *The consoling gesture (48x66cm-19x26in) s.d.47 s.i.d.verso gouache board. 31-Mar-94 Sotheby's Arcade, New York #484/R*
$2000   *£1316*   *Untitled (27x21cm-11x8in) s.d.42 casein board. 31-Mar-93 Sotheby's Arcade, New York #467/R*

FERRER, Yazmin (1957-) Mexican
$607   *£410*   *Nochebuenas (50x67cm-20x26in) s. W/C. 20-Oct-93 Louis Morton, Mexico #144/R (M.P 1900)*

FERRIS, Jean Leon Jerome (1863-1930) American
$3500   £2349   Anticipated shower (61x46cm-24x18in) s.d.1893. 6-Dec-93 Grogan, Massachussetts #468/R
$600   *£397*   *The conference (23x29cm-9x11in) mono.sig.d.90 W/C. 2-Oct-93 Weschler, Washington #99*
$750   *£510*   *Tavern interior with 18th century military figure (28x36cm-11x14in) s.d.1891 W/C. 19-Nov-93 Eldred, Massachusetts #910/R*
$900   *£588*   *Seated woman (30x23cm-12x9in) s. W/C. 30-Jun-94 Mystic Fine Arts, Connecticut #68/R*

FERRY, Isabelle H (?-1930) American
$800   £544   Summer idyl (46x30cm-18x12in) s.verso. 16-Apr-94 Young Fine Arts Auctions, Maine #103
$900   £588   Summer landscape (43x61cm-17x24in) 18-Sep-93 James Bakker, Cambridge #157/R
$1000   £654   Building the boat (43x61cm-17x24in) s.verso. 18-Sep-93 James Bakker, Cambridge #16/R
$1100   £719   Coastal landscape, Bermuda (30x41cm-12x16in) s.verso. 18-Sep-93 James Bakker, Cambridge #161/R
$1700   £1111   Inlet, Bermuda (46x61cm-18x24in) s. 18-Sep-93 James Bakker, Cambridge #155/R

FERTIG, David (20th C) American
$750   £500   Interior (114x155cm-45x61in) s.d.81. 13-Mar-94 Hindman Galleries, Chicago #858

FERY, John (1865-1934) American/Hungarian
$700   £473   Landscape (53x61cm-21x24in) s. 10-Aug-93 Stonington Fine Arts, Stonington #210/R
$800   £523   Mountain landscape with deer (46x76cm-18x30in) s. 16-May-93 Hindman Galleries, Chicago #73/R
$1100   £696   Landscape with mountains and deer (41x61cm-16x24in) s. 2-Dec-92 Boos Gallery, Michigan #809/R
$2500   £1656   Twin mountain lake (91x157cm-36x62in) s. 23-Sep-93 Mystic Fine Arts, Connecticut #277

FERY, John (attrib) (1865-1934) American/Hungarian
$1100   £719   Family of elks in the Rockies (46x76cm-18x30in) s. canvas on masonite. 3-May-93 Schrager Galleries, Milwaukee #660
$1100   £748   Cattle watering near shore of lake (25x43cm-10x17in) s. board. 17-Apr-94 Schrager Galleries, Milwaukee #733
$1100   £748   Landscape summer (41x51cm-16x20in) s. masonite. 17-Apr-94 Schrager Galleries, Milwaukee #751
$1500   £993   Elk and family (36x56cm-14x22in) s. 26-Sep-93 Schrager Galleries, Milwaukee #458/R
$1600   £1088   Elk at water's edge, mountain lake in Tetons (36x51cm-14x20in) s. board. 17-Apr-94 Schrager Galleries, Milwaukee #857
$2300   £1565   Bridge over Slough at Northern Wisconsin Lake (46x76cm-18x30in) s. 17-Apr-94 Schrager Galleries, Milwaukee #843
$2300   £1565   American river canyon, Colorado (41x48cm-16x19in) s. i.verso. 17-Apr-94 Schrager Galleries, Milwaukee #859
$3200   £2177   Mountain lake landscape with elk and ducks (51x69cm-20x27in) s. 17-Apr-94 Schrager Galleries, Milwaukee #711/R
$3600   £2449   The elk at water's edge at mountain stream in Tetons (66x81cm-26x32in) s. 17-Apr-94 Schrager Galleries, Milwaukee #710/R
$3800   £2585   Outlet of Jackson Lake with Teton Mountains (61x81cm-24x32in) s. i.verso. 17-Apr-94 Schrager Galleries, Milwaukee #708/R
$4000   £2721   Blackfoot Glacier, Glacier Park, Montana (56x89cm-22x35in) s. i.verso. 17-Apr-94 Schrager Galleries, Milwaukee #709
$1250   *£850*   *Sheep and shepherdess at water's edge near sunset (36x58cm-14x23in) s. W/C. 17-Apr-94 Schrager Galleries, Milwaukee #842*
$2000   *£1361*   *Minnesota, moose at sunrise (33x53cm-13x21in) s. i.verso W/C. 17-Apr-94 Schrager Galleries, Milwaukee #866*

FETHERSTONHAUGH, Olive Jane Graham (1896-1986) American
$950   *£559*   *Opening day, Belvedere (46x122cm-18x48in) s.d.1981 mixed media board. 4-Oct-92 Butterfield & Butterfield, Los Angeles #236/R*

FEUCHTER, Louis (1885-1957) American?
$750	£524	Seated young black girl (20x15cm-8x6in) mono board. 11-Mar-93 Mystic Fine Arts, Connecticut #106
$750	£524	Harbour scene (25x36cm-10x14in) board. 11-Mar-93 Mystic Fine Arts, Connecticut #107/R
$1100	£769	Harbour scene (28x36cm-11x14in) board. 11-Mar-93 Mystic Fine Arts, Connecticut #105/R
$1600	£1119	Sailing day (23x30cm-9x12in) init. board. 11-Mar-93 Mystic Fine Arts, Connecticut #142/R
$1700	£1189	Race (23x30cm-9x12in) init. board. 11-Mar-93 Mystic Fine Arts, Connecticut #143
$800	£513	Chesapeake Bay Schooner under full sail (20x28cm-8x11in) s.d.37 W/C. 28-May-93 Sloan, North Bethesda #2439/R
$950	£609	LA Forrest L Simmons, two topmast schooner and the Stephen Chase (20x28cm-8x11in) s.d.38 W/C. 28-May-93 Sloan, North Bethesda #2437/R
$1000	£641	Fleet of Chesapeake Bay skipjacks (25x30cm-10x12in) init.d.50 W/C. 28-May-93 Sloan, North Bethesda #2441
$1300	£909	Cheasapeake Bay scene (18x28cm-7x11in) W/C. 11-Mar-93 Mystic Fine Arts, Connecticut #143 a

FEVRET DE ST MEMIN, Charles (1770-1852) American
$750	£504	Portrait of a gentleman wearing white cravat (46x36cm-18x14in) i.verso chl chk oval. 6-Feb-94 Skinner, Bolton #203/R

FEVRET DE ST MEMIN, Charles (attrib) (1770-1852) American
$2750	£1834	Portrait of gentleman (41x56cm-16x22in) pastel. 11-May-94 Butterfield & Butterfield, San Francisco #11/R

FIELD, E Loyal (1856-1914) American
$1071	£728	Autumn landscape with house (76x63cm-30x25in) s. 16-Apr-94 AB Stockholms Auktionsverk (Lilla Kvaliten) #4285 (S.KR 8500)
$1300	£872	Quiet place, landscape (51x61cm-20x24in) s. 6-May-94 Skinner, Bolton #72/R
$1300	£850	Burst of flame (51x61cm-20x24in) s. 18-Sep-93 Young Fine Arts Auctions, Maine #114/R
$1350	£794	September clouds (76x64cm-30x25in) s. 8-Oct-92 Freeman Fine Arts, Philadelphia #996

FIELD, Erastus Salisbury (attrib) (1805-1900) American
$650	£436	Imaginary landscape (66x91cm-26x36in) 3-Feb-94 Sloan, North Bethesda #2033/R
$2000	£1342	Allegorical view of columns and ruins with people in foreground (71x51cm-28x20in) sandpaper. 16-Jul-93 Douglas, South Deerfield #3

FIENE, E (1894-1966) American
$1000	£649	Winter churchyard scene (58x74cm-23x29in) s. 4-Aug-94 Eldred, Massachusetts #587/R

FIENE, Ernest (1894-1966) American
$800	£530	Lobster boxes (33x28cm-13x11in) s.d.50. 28-Nov-92 Young Fine Arts Auctions, Maine #147/R
$800	£537	White rose (41x33cm-16x13in) s. masonite. 4-May-94 Doyle, New York #67
$800	£523	Kitchen table (91x122cm-36x48in) s. 4-May-93 Christie's, East, New York #310/R
$900	£596	Stormy day (23x46cm-9x18in) s. board. 28-Nov-92 Young Fine Arts Auctions, Maine #148/R
$950	£629	Sunset Monhegan (41x51cm-16x20in) s. 28-Nov-92 Young Fine Arts Auctions, Maine #143/R
$1100	£714	Jeannette (56x43cm-22x17in) s. 9-Sep-93 Sotheby's Arcade, New York #362/R
$1200	£694	Dancer (41x28cm-16x11in) s. board. 25-Sep-92 Sotheby's Arcade, New York #366/R
$1200	£795	June morning (56x71cm-22x28in) s. 28-Nov-92 Young Fine Arts Auctions, Maine #144/R
$1300	£878	White lilacs in a Japanese vase (76x56cm-30x22in) s. 31-Mar-94 Sotheby's Arcade, New York #342/R
$1800	£1192	Monhegan harbour (46x71cm-18x28in) s. i.verso. 28-Nov-92 Young Fine Arts Auctions, Maine #140/R
$3000	£2041	Ears of corn (30x48cm-12x19in) s. 16-Apr-94 Young Fine Arts Auctions, Maine #104
$3500	£2318	Study for nocturne (41x51cm-16x20in) s. painted c.1940. 23-Sep-93 Sotheby's, New York #251/R
$12000	£8392	Nocturne (152x102cm-60x40in) s.d.48. 11-Mar-93 Christie's, New York #260/R
$18000	£12000	Night shift Aliquippa Plant (91x122cm-36x48in) s. 25-May-94 Sotheby's, New York #144/R
$600	£408	Incoming fog (36x56cm-14x22in) s.d.49 W/C. 16-Apr-94 Young Fine Arts Auctions, Maine #105/R
$650	£430	Morning light, Maine (38x56cm-15x22in) s.d.48 W/C. 28-Nov-92 Young Fine Arts Auctions, Maine #146/R
$650	£430	Sun Path, Maine (38x56cm-15x22in) s. W/C. 28-Nov-92 Young Fine Arts Auctions, Maine #145/R
$3250	£2138	Deer (71x61cm-28x24in) s.pastel. 4-Nov-92 Doyle, New York #45/R

FIGARI, Juan Carlos (20th C) South American
$4800	£3117	El encuentro (32x39cm-13x15in) s.d.1919 board. 30-Aug-93 Gomensoro, Montevideo #89/R

FIGARI, Pedro (1861-1938) Uruguayan
$2000	£1282	Rincon de la quinta de Castro (26x34cm-10x13in) s. board. 7-Dec-92 Gomensoro, Montevideo #92/R
$2058	£1381	Couple de noirs (23x17cm-9x7in) s. board oval. 10-Dec-93 Claude Boisgirard, Paris #22 (F.FR 12000)

FIGARI, Pedro (1861-1938) Uruguayan-cont.

$2100	£1235	Paisaje (39x40cm-15x16in) s. board. 5-Oct-92 Gomensoro, Montevideo #32/R
$2200	£1146	Pescadores (24x20cm-9x8in) board. 12-Aug-92 Castells & Castells, Montevideo #57/R
$2200	£1146	Regreso de la pesca (24x20cm-9x8in) s.d.1880 board. 12-Aug-92 Castells & Castells, Montevideo #56/R
$3000	£1974	El circo (33x40cm-13x16in) board. 31-May-93 Gomensoro, Montevideo #50/R
$3429	£2301	Evil words (32x23cm-13x9in) s. board. 10-Dec-93 Claude Boisgirard, Paris #21/R (F.FR 20000)
$4000	£2685	Trogloditas (37x75cm-15x30in) 29-Nov-93 Gomensoro, Montevideo #43
$4000	£2010	Negro Candombero (38x25cm-15x10in) board. 31-Aug-92 Gomensoro, Montevideo #42/R
$4000	£2703	De fiesta (19x26cm-7x10in) s. i.verso board. 23-Nov-93 Christie's, New York #125/R
$4000	£2597	Aledanos de Montevideo Chacra de la Flia. Figari (65x101cm-26x40in) oil. 30-Aug-93 Gomensoro, Montevideo #92
$5000	£3268	Deliberando (25x16cm-10x6in) board. 3-May-93 Gomensoro, Montevideo #74/R
$5662	£3800	The picnic (51x69cm-20x27in) s. board on masonite. 16-Jul-93 Christie's, London #142/R
$5800	£3791	Paisaje (32x40cm-13x16in) s. board. 3-May-93 Gomensoro, Montevideo #75
$6000	£3974	Carreta (35x50cm-14x20in) s. i.verso board. 28-Jun-93 Gomensoro, Montevideo #56/R
$6000	£3922	Disciplina (33x40cm-13x16in) s. board. 3-May-93 Gomensoro, Montevideo #73/R
$6000	£4027	Despues de la reprimenda (25x16cm-10x6in) board. 29-Nov-93 Gomensoro, Montevideo #101
$6200	£4161	Tapera (35x50cm-14x20in) s. board. 29-Nov-93 Gomensoro, Montevideo #41/R
$7000	£4605	Soledad (34x50cm-13x20in) s. board. 31-May-93 Gomensoro, Montevideo #49/R
$8000	£5263	La capa (33x35cm-13x14in) board. 3-May-93 Gomensoro, Montevideo #51/R
$8000	£5333	Indios (40x49cm-16x19in) s. i.verso board painted c.1930. 18-May-94 Sotheby's, New York #218/R
$10000	£6494	En intimidad (33x40cm-13x16in) s. i.verso board. 30-Aug-93 Gomensoro, Montevideo #91/R
$10000	£6757	A la sombra o Guitarreo (33x40cm-13x16in) panel. 25-Apr-94 Gomensoro, Montevideo #68/R
$10500	£6731	Bajando la sierra (40x33cm-16x13in) s. s.d.1926verso board. 7-Dec-92 Gomensoro, Montevideo #91/R
$11500	£5779	Saliendo de la Fiesta (35x50cm-14x20in) board. 31-Aug-92 Gomensoro, Montevideo #41/R
$12000	£7018	La Recepcion (35x50cm-14x20in) board. 16-Sep-92 Castells & Castells, Montevideo #47/R
$13000	£8333	En la puerta de la pulperia (33x41cm-13x16in) s.d.1918 board. 7-Dec-92 Gomensoro, Montevideo #89/R
$13152	£8886	El incidente (31x47cm-12x19in) s.d.1933 i.verso board. 14-Jun-93 Jean Louis Picard, Paris #28/R (F.FR 75000)
$13500	£8654	La fiesta (35x50cm-14x20in) s. board. 7-Dec-92 Gomensoro, Montevideo #90/R
$14000	£9091	En la estancia (48x62cm-19x24in) s. i.verso board. 30-Aug-93 Gomensoro, Montevideo #90/R
$15000	£10135	En El Campo (50x69cm-20x27in) s. board on masonite painted c.1930. 22-Nov-93 Sotheby's, New York #182/R
$18000	£11921	Idilio Campero (35x50cm-14x20in) s. i.num.35 Serie XVIII.A.D.verso board. 24-Nov-92 Christie's, New York #169/R
$20000	£10417	Candombe (40x50cm-16x20in) 4-Aug-92 VerBo, Buenos Aires #47/R
$20000	£13423	Mancarrones (48x63cm-19x25in) s. board. 29-Nov-93 Gomensoro, Montevideo #40
$24000	£15894	Baile (39x33cm-15x13in) s. board. 23-Nov-92 Sotheby's, New York #186/R
$25000	£16667	Un pedido a rosas (49x69cm-19x27in) s. i.verso board painted c.1930. 17-May-94 Sotheby's, New York #26/R
$27500	£18333	Baile Criollo (49x69cm-19x27in) s. i.verso board painted c.1930. 18-May-94 Sotheby's, New York #219/R
$32000	£21622	Reunion colonial (48x62cm-19x24in) s. i.verso board. 23-Nov-93 Christie's, New York #98/R
$34000	£22517	Baile en el patio (62x82cm-24x32in) s. i.num.46 verso board. 24-Nov-92 Christie's, New York #19/R
$60000	£40541	Alto en el campo (60x80cm-24x31in) s. i.verso board. 23-Nov-93 Christie's, New York #24/R
$500	*£338*	*Rincon en el patio de la estancia (25x37cm-10x15in) s. ink study. 25-Apr-94 Gomensoro, Montevideo #5*
$650	*£425*	*Platicando (9x20cm-4x8in) pencil. 3-May-93 Gomensoro, Montevideo #11/R*

FIGARI, Pedro (attrib) (1861-1938) Uruguayan

$5800	£3867	Folk dance (36x48cm-14x19in) s. board. 23-May-94 Hindman Galleries, Chicago #386/R

FIGUEROA, Antonieta (20th C) Mexican

$1127	£762	Cuento popular (80x64cm-31x25in) s.d.1979 mixed media fibracel. 27-Apr-94 Louis Morton, Mexico #689 (M.P 3800)

FILIP, Demetrio (1921-) Argentinian

$700	£464	Calle de Montmartre (21x15cm-8x6in) i.verso. 11-Nov-92 VerBo, Buenos Aires #49

FINCK, Hazel (1894-1977) American

$3000	£1734	Callas no 2 (76x63cm-30x25in) s. 23-Sep-92 Christie's, New York #258/R
$5000	£2890	Village on the bay (64x76cm-25x30in) s. 23-Sep-92 Christie's, New York #257/R

FINK, Aaron (20th C) American?

$1200	£805	Dark cup, red, yellow, blue (61x76cm-24x30in) s.d.1983verso. 6-May-94 Skinner, Bolton #161/R

FINK, Don (1923-) American
$573	£387	Composition (136x54cm-54x21in) s.d.February 1956verso. 27-Oct-93 Watine-Arnault, Paris #42 (F.FR 3400)

FINSTER, Howard (1916-) American
$800	£559	Coke bottle (86x?cm-34x?in) s. board. 11-Mar-93 Mystic Fine Arts, Connecticut #211
$900	£596	Coke Bottle (86x25cm-34x10in) s.d.October 15 1989 plywood. 21-Nov-92 Litchfield Auction Gallery #12
$750	£497	Don't be a tail (69x28cm-27x11in) s.d.August 9 1989 paint cut-out wood. 21-Nov-92 Litchfield Auction Gallery #11
$900	£625	City of Salcona (44x56cm-17x22in) s.i.d.Jan.6. 1991 oil col.felt tip pen panel. 22-Feb-93 Christie's, East, New York #224/R
$1000	£671	Coca Cola (86x26cm-34x10in) s.i.d.verso oil col.felt-tip pens shaped panel. 23-Feb-94 Christie's, East, New York #265
$1000	£662	Coca cola (87x26cm-34x10in) s.i.d.verso oil col.felttip pens panel. 17-Nov-92 Christie's, East, New York #213/R
$1000	£662	Angel (30x126cm-12x50in) s.i.d. oil col.felttip pen panel. 17-Nov-92 Christie's, East, New York #216/R
$1200	£795	Howard by Howard (56x28cm-22x11in) s.d.1983 paint cut-out wood. 21-Nov-92 Litchfield Auction Gallery #13
$1300	£850	Audience and entertainers (38x52cm-15x20in) mixed media wood executed 1982. 22-Dec-92 Christie's, East, New York #19/R
$1900	£1242	George Washington in Command (90x16cm-35x6in) mixed media wood. 22-Dec-92 Christie's, East, New York #18
$2100	£1391	George Washington at 23 (132x33cm-52x13in) s.d.December 14 1985 paint cut-out wood. 21-Nov-92 Litchfield Auction Gallery #14

FIRFIRES, Nicholas S (1917-) American
$2000	£1333	Oglala sioux (61x76cm-24x30in) s. 22-May-94 Hindman Galleries, Chicago #52/R

FISCHER, Anton Otto (1882-1962) American
$800	£506	Rescue of crew of sinking Marlina (56x102cm-22x40in) s. 3-Dec-92 Freeman Fine Arts, Philadelphia #1840/R
$1300	£751	The shining road (66x71cm-26x28in) s. 25-Sep-92 Sotheby's Arcade, New York #430/R
$4000	£2685	Spring flowers (61x81cm-24x32in) s. 8-Dec-93 Butterfield & Butterfield, San Francisco #3498/R
$4500	£3041	The sixth day (61x91cm-24x36in) s.d.48. 31-Mar-94 Sotheby's Arcade, New York #399/R

FISCHL, Eric (1948-) American
$20000	£13423	Untitled (61x41cm-24x16in) s.d.85 paper. 5-May-94 Sotheby's, New York #363/R
$20540	£13000	Untitled (55x88cm-22x35in) s.d.85 paper. 3-Dec-92 Sotheby's, London #57/R
$21000	£13907	Untitled (33x39cm-13x15in) s.d.84 paper. 19-Nov-92 Christie's, New York #235/R
$28000	£18919	Untitled (46x36cm-18x14in) s.d.1990verso. 10-Nov-93 Christie's, New York #364/R
$32000	£21192	Bathroom I (187x194cm-74x76in) painted 1980 four sheets of glassine on board. 19-Nov-92 Christie's, New York #231/R
$90000	£59603	Boys at bat (214x176cm-84x69in) s.i.d.79verso. 18-Nov-92 Christie's, New York #57/R
$140000	£92715	The beginning and the end (190x280cm-75x110in) s.i.d.1988verso. 18-Nov-92 Christie's, New York #33/R
$150000	£100671	Far rockaway (279x343cm-110x135in) s.i.d.1986verso two panels. 3-May-94 Christie's, New York #67/R
$3000	£2013	Study for Father and Son Sleeping III (91x98cm-36x39in) s.d.80 chl white chk. 3-May-94 Christie's, East, New York #118/R
$3089	£2033	Two nude figures with dog (143x122cm-56x48in) gouache painted c.1980/85. 5-Jun-93 Villa Grisebach, Berlin #433/R (DM 5000)
$3500	£2365	Untitled (30x24cm-12x9in) s.d.89 W/C. 11-Nov-93 Sotheby's, New York #194 a/R
$7500	£4967	Untitled (61x46cm-24x18in) s.d.86 chl. 19-Nov-92 Christie's, New York #380/R
$8145	£5394	Reclining female nude (149x99cm-59x39in) painted c.1981 gouache. 28-Nov-92 Villa Grisebach, Berlin #309/R (DM 13000)
$11905	£7884	Bad boy (140x198cm-55x78in) painted 1981 gouache. 28-Nov-92 Villa Grisebach, Berlin #310/R (DM 19000)
$20050	£13278	Female nude reading in the sun (107x87cm-42x34in) painted c.1980 gouache board. 28-Nov-92 Villa Grisebach, Berlin #311/R (DM 32000)

FISHER, Alvan (1792-1863) American
$2500	£1678	Hillside conversation (36x43cm-14x17in) init. 16-Dec-93 Mystic Fine Arts, Connecticut #270/R
$9750	£6250	Cattle in a landscape (76x102cm-30x40in) s.d.1816 i.verso panel. 24-May-93 Grogan, Massachussetts #289/R
$15500	£10473	At the harbour front (66x89cm-26x35in) s.d.1843 board. 31-Oct-93 Hindman Galleries, Chicago #683/R
$17000	£11888	View to Bear Island, Maine (56x69cm-22x27in) mono.d.1848. 12-Mar-93 Skinner, Bolton #157/R
$20000	£13423	The white pony (61x74cm-24x29in) s.d.1858. 3-Feb-94 Sloan, North Bethesda #2891/R

FISHER, Alvan (attrib) (1792-1863) American
$800	£530	Spaniel lying beside hunting gear (76x64cm-30x25in) 28-Nov-92 Young Fine Arts Auctions, Maine #151/R
$2200	£1447	Cows watering in river (69x97cm-27x38in) panel. 5-Jun-93 Skinner, Bolton #225/R
$4000	£2703	The Shore Road said to be Jerusalem Road Cohasset Massachusetts (43x53cm-17x21in) 30-Oct-93 Skinner, Bolton #477

FISHER, Harrison (1875-1934) American
$3000   £1923   Carriage ride (9x51cm-27x20in) s.i.d.1904 W/C gouache pencil board. 9-Dec-92
                     Butterfield & Butterfield, San Francisco #3949/R

FISHER, Hugo Antoine (1854-1916) American
$4500   £2647   Cascade Lake (102x152cm-40x60in) s. 4-Oct-92 Butterfield & Butterfield, Los
                     Angeles #34/R
$7000   £4861   Spring runoff (149x99cm-59x39in) s. 7-Mar-93 Butterfield & Butterfield, San
                     Francisco #43/R
$600   £405   Horsecart in winter (53x74cm-21x29in) s. W/C gouache. 4-Nov-93 Sloan, North
                     Bethesda #1563
$800   £567   River landscape (28x53cm-11x21in) W/C. 13-Feb-93 San Rafael Auction Galleries
                     #240
$1000   £505   Gathering faggots (33x64cm-13x25in) s. W/C gouache. 28-Aug-92 Young Fine Arts
                     Auctions, Maine #119/R
$1050   £705   Winter landscape with horses pulling sled, accompanied by farmer
                     (53x76cm-21x30in) s. W/C. 5-Aug-93 Eldred, Massachusetts #808/R

FISHER, Hugo Melville (1878-1946) American
$650   £422   Seascape (36x51cm-14x20in) s. canvas on board. 11-Sep-93 Louisiana Auction
                     Exchange #8/R

FISHER, Leonard Everett (1924-) American
$3250   £1879   All through night (48x94cm-19x37in) s.d.1948 tempera masonite. 24-Sep-92
                     Sotheby's, New York #223/R
$5000   £3247   Kite flying (51x62cm-20x24in) s.d.1952 tempera masonite. 9-Sep-93 Sotheby's
                     Arcade, New York #357/R
$5250   £3035   Curfew shadows (46x69cm-18x27in) s.d.1945 i.verso. 24-Sep-92 Sotheby's, New York
                     #179/R
$7000   £4046   Boxing (65x89cm-26x35in) s.d.1948. 24-Sep-92 Sotheby's, New York #180/R
$8500   £5743   All through the night (48x94cm-19x37in) s.d.1948 s.i.d.verso masonite. 31-Mar-94
                     Sotheby's Arcade, New York #402/R

FISHER, Vernon (1943-) American
$6000   £3922   Bridge (183x350cm-72x138in) acrylic laminated paper canvas painted 1983. 4-May-93
                     Sotheby's, New York #209/R
$3000   £1961   Sign language constellation (89x212cm-35x83in) acrylic metal wood paper three
                     panels. 22-Dec-92 Christie's, East, New York #20/R
$7000   £4730   Mamba (160x320cm-63x126in) s.i.d.1983verso mixed media canvas photograph.
                     21-Oct-93 Butterfield & Butterfield, San Francisco #2787/R

FISHMAN, Louise (1939-) American
$11000   £7432   Bath and mardin (119x104cm-47x41in) s.d.1987 verso i.stretcher. 11-Nov-93
                     Sotheby's, New York #171/R
$650   £451   Untitled (30x46cm-12x18in) s. s.d.1984verso chl graphite. 22-Feb-93 Christie's,
                     East, New York #196/R

FISKE, Gertrude (1879-1961) American
$2500   £1656   Little church (62x77cm-24x30in) s. i.stretcher. 23-Sep-93 Sotheby's, New York
                     #205/R

FITLER, William Crothers (1857-1915) American
$650   £434   October meadows (20x25cm-8x10in) s.i. 17-May-94 Grogan, Massachussetts #355
$900   £629   Sunset scene (41x56cm-16x22in) s. 11-Mar-93 Mystic Fine Arts, Connecticut #63 a/R
$1400   £952   A quiet pool at sunset (30x41cm-12x16in) s.i. 15-Nov-93 Christie's, East, New
                     York #126
$3200   £2092   Figures on riverbank (28x39cm-11x15in) s.d.82. 4-May-93 Christie's, East, New
                     York #52/R

FITZGERALD, Harrington (1847-1930) American
$2100   £1419   Smuggler's cave (41x66cm-16x26in) s. 31-Mar-94 Sotheby's Arcade, New York #105/R

FITZGERALD, Lionel Lemoine (1890-1956) Canadian
$1557   £1031   Birch woods (26x20cm-10x8in) s. i.verso board. 18-Nov-92 Sotheby's, Toronto
                     #271/R (C.D 2000)
$3473   £2347   Barn and lane (55x50cm-22x20in) s. painted 1920. 23-Nov-93 Joyner Fine Art,
                     Toronto #108/R (C.D 4600)
$4670   £3093   Sunlit Forest (28x36cm-11x14in) s. canvas laid down on board. 18-Nov-92
                     Sotheby's, Toronto #63/R (C.D 6000)
$5097   £3398   Green tree (42x50cm-17x20in) s. 13-May-94 Joyner Fine Art, Toronto #72/R
                     (C.D 3100)
$7531   £4922   Women working in field (51x41cm-20x16in) s. board. 19-May-93 Sotheby's, Toronto
                     #246/R (C.D 9500)
$7927   £5181   Working in the fields (56x61cm-22x24in) s. 18-May-93 Joyner Fine Art, Toronto
                     #257/R (C.D 10000)
$8562   £5670   Winter landscape (27x35cm-11x14in) s.d.1921. 24-Nov-92 Joyner Fine Art, Toronto
                     #83/R (C.D 11000)
$545   £361   Female nude (26x17cm-10x7in) pencil. 24-Nov-92 Joyner Fine Art, Toronto #265
                     (C.D 700)
$566   £383   Tulips (40x27cm-16x11in) init. ink. 23-Nov-93 Joyner Fine Art, Toronto #212
                     (C.D 750)
$642   £434   Abstract (31x35cm-12x14in) init. ink. 23-Nov-93 Joyner Fine Art, Toronto #224
                     (C.D 850)
$1133   £765   Tree trunks (23x31cm-9x12in) d.10.38 col.chk. 23-Nov-93 Joyner Fine Art, Toronto
                     #156/R (C.D 1500)

FLAGG, James Montgomery (1877-1960) American
$800	£523	French chef (53x69cm-21x27in) s. W/C. 16-May-93 Hanzel Galleries, Chicago #21/R
$850	£556	Setting off (64x53cm-25x21in) s. i.dr. 18-Sep-93 Young Fine Arts Auctions, Maine #116/R
$2000	£1351	'Fifty-fifty on my last smoke, Bill' (68x50cm-27x20in) s.i. W/C pencil boar. 31-Mar-94 Sotheby's Arcade, New York #397/R
$6500	£4114	Study for a boxing mural (23x74cm-9x29in) init.d.Aug 7 44 W/C gouache pencil board. 3-Dec-92 Sotheby's, New York #70/R

FLAVELLE, Geoff H (19th C) American
$1050	£705	Louisiana swamp at dusk (51x107cm-20x42in) 27-Mar-94 Myers, Florida #118/R

FLAVIN, Dan (1933-) American
$5000	£3472	Untitled (43x56cm-17x22in) s.i.d.1972-1973 ink col.pencil graph paper two. 23-Feb-93 Sotheby's, New York #332/R
$9500	£6376	To Barnett Newman, two and four (42x55cm-17x22in) s.i.d.2/22/71 col.pencil ink graph paper. 5-May-94 Sotheby's, New York #242/R

FLEISCHBEIN, Francois (1804-?) American
$4700	£3197	Little girl in blue dress with toys (64x48cm-25x19in) s.d.1836. 17-Apr-94 Hanzel Galleries, Chicago #1

FLEISCHER STUDIOS (20th C) American
$550	£369	Popeye the Sailor, Popeye out for drive with Olive Oyl at the wheel (20x27cm-8x11in) graphite red pencil. 22-Jun-93 Sotheby's, New York #589/R
$1000	£671	Gulliver's Travels, Princess Glory and Prince David clasping hands (25x33cm-10x13in) gouache celluloid on graphite and pencil dr. 22-Jun-93 Sotheby's, New York #752
$1100	£738	Gulliver's Travels, graphite crayon col.pencil three. 22-Jun-93 Sotheby's, New York #585

FLEMING, Alexander M (1878-1929) Canadian
$1350	£854	Clouds and tideland (61x76cm-24x30in) s.d.1922. 3-Dec-92 Freeman Fine Arts, Philadelphia #1777

FLETCHER, Aaron Dean (1817-1902) American
$1600	£925	Portrait of gentleman. Portrait of lady (70x60cm-28x24in) i.d.May 1841verso s.stretcher pair. 25-Sep-92 Sotheby's Arcade, New York #1/R

FLETCHER, Grace (20th C) American
$814	£550	Fishing boats in Venetian lagoon (46x53cm-18x21in) s.d.1936. 28-Apr-94 Christie's, S. Kensington #110

FLEURY, Albert Francois (1848-1925) American
$16000	£10596	Afternoon tea in garden (69x107cm-27x42in) s. i.verso. 13-Nov-92 Skinner, Bolton #48/R

FLOCH, Josef (1895-1977) American/Austrian
$2205	£1500	Portrait of a seated young girl (82x61cm-32x24in) s. 14-Apr-94 Bonhams, London #24/R
$3000	£1948	Rest (100x90cm-39x35in) s. 9-Sep-93 Sotheby's Arcade, New York #448/R
$3234	£2200	A shepherd before a lake and village with mountains beyond (90x80cm-35x31in) s. 14-Apr-94 Bonhams, London #23/R
$3821	£2235	Naked children (54x50cm-21x20in) 16-Sep-92 Dorotheum, Vienna #469/R (A.S 40000)
$5856	£3957	On the outskirts of the town (51x61cm-20x24in) s. 10-Nov-93 Dorotheum, Vienna #559/R (A.S 70000)
$7534	£5090	Female nude in studio (71x74cm-28x29in) s.d.1962. 20-Apr-94 Wiener Auktionen, Vienna #219/R (A.S 90000)
$8509	£5711	House on the coast (38x55cm-15x22in) s. 4-May-94 Dorotheum, Vienna #133/R (A.S 100000)
$9208	£6222	The artist and his model (81x60cm-32x24in) s. 20-Apr-94 Wiener Auktionen, Vienna #194/R (A.S 110000)
$11557	£7756	Two women in interior (81x67cm-32x26in) s. 2-Dec-93 Wiener Auktionen, Vienna #162/R (A.S 140000)
$700	£440	Standing nudes (36x46cm-14x18in) s. W/C chl. 25-Apr-93 James Bakker, Cambridge #65/R

FLODBERG, Gilbert (1938-) Canadian
$1412	£923	Fish Creek Park West (76x107cm-30x42in) s. 10-May-93 Hodgins, Calgary #160/R (C.D 1800)

FLORES KAPEROTXIPI, Mauricio (20th C) Argentinian
$2938	£2083	Campesino fumando en pipa (30x40cm-12x16in) s. 10-Feb-93 Ansorena, Madrid #34/R (S.P 350000)
$5438	£3650	Campesino (92x73cm-36x29in) s. 21-Mar-94 Duran, Madrid #100/R (S.P 750000)

FLORES O, Pedro (20th C) Mexican
$792	£521	Marina (38x50cm-15x20in) s. W/C. 4-Nov-92 Mora, Castelltort & Quintana, Juarez #52/R (M.P 2500000)

FLORES, Francisco (?) Mexican
$2472	£1670	Toros en el campo bravo (70x40cm-28x16in) s. 9-Nov-93 Louis Morton, Mexico #100/R (M.P 8000)
$3090	£2088	Joselito (79x40cm-31x16in) s. 9-Nov-93 Louis Morton, Mexico #45/R (M.P 10000)

FLORES, Francisco (?) Mexican-cont.
$3090   £2088   Manolo Martinez (60x44cm-24x17in) s. 9-Nov-93 Louis Morton, Mexico #102/R (M.P 10000)
$4635   £3132   Pelea de toros (70x40cm-28x16in) s. 9-Nov-93 Louis Morton, Mexico #130/R (M.P 15000)
$556   *£376*   *El soldado (24x33cm-9x13in) s. pencil dr. 9-Nov-93 Louis Morton, Mexico #9 (M.P 1800)*
$556   *£376*   *Derechazo de frente de Manolo Martinez (31x50cm-12x20in) s. pencil dr. 9-Nov-93 Louis Morton, Mexico #122 (M.P 1800)*

FLORES, Leonardo (17th C) Peruvian
$14000   £9272   El matroimonio del Rey David (77x113cm-30x44in) 24-Nov-92 Christie's, New York #75/R

FLORES, Leonardo (studio) (17th C) Peruvian
$11500   £7516   Virgin of Pomata (117x86cm-46x34in) painted c.1695. 17-May-93 Christie's, New York #76/R

FOLINSBEE, John F (1892-1972) American
$1500   £1007   Shad fishermen (30x41cm-12x16in) s. 24-Jun-93 Mystic Fine Arts, Connecticut #218
$2500   £1689   Lopaus Point Vista (61x41cm-24x16in) s. masonite. 31-Mar-94 Sotheby's Arcade, New York #225/R

FONSECA, Gonzalo (1922-) Uruguayan
$1000   £662   Constructivo tabaco (42x55cm-17x22in) board. 28-Jun-93 Gomensoro, Montevideo #39
$1100   £714   Paisaje de campo (38x50cm-15x20in) s.d.45 board. 30-Aug-93 Gomensoro, Montevideo #61
$1600   £1060   Puerto (24x30cm-9x12in) s. board. 28-Jun-93 Gomensoro, Montevideo #38
$2300   £1494   Ciudad vieja (36x47cm-14x19in) s.d.1944 d.18/9/44verso oil. 30-Aug-93 Gomensoro, Montevideo #62
$2500   £1634   Chacra Mendizabal (50x74cm-20x29in) s. 4-Oct-93 Gomensoro, Montevideo #72/R
$2600   £1757   Naturaleza muerta (31x41cm-12x16in) board. 25-Apr-94 Gomensoro, Montevideo #59
$3000   £1563   Paisaje Urbano (31x42cm-12x17in) s. 12-Aug-92 Castells & Castells, Montevideo #33/R
$3000   £1531   Paisaje de Chacras y Caserio (61x83cm-24x33in) 19-Aug-92 Gomensoro, Montevideo #274/R
$3400   £2282   Paisaje (40x49cm-16x19in) 29-Nov-93 Gomensoro, Montevideo #87/R
$5000   £3378   Naturaleza muerta (80x60cm-31x24in) s. 25-Apr-94 Gomensoro, Montevideo #57/R
$8000   £5229   Constructivo con grafismo (43x35cm-17x14in) s.d.50 board. 18-May-93 Sotheby's, New York #138/R
$14000   £9396   Vista de puerto (49x56cm-19x22in) s. board. 29-Nov-93 Gomensoro, Montevideo #86/R
$14500   £9732   Vapor de la carrera (45x55cm-18x22in) s.d.48 board. 29-Nov-93 Gomensoro, Montevideo #103/R
$560   *£366*   *Casas (19x31cm-7x12in) s.d.46 crayon ink. 4-Oct-93 Gomensoro, Montevideo #102*
$800   *£530*   *Ciudad vieja (18x20cm-7x8in) s. W/C. 28-Jun-93 Gomensoro, Montevideo #40*
$1000 *£654*   *Paisaje de campina italiana (24x35cm-9x14in) s. ink W/C. 4-Oct-93 Gomensoro, Montevideo #74*

FONSECA, Pablo (20th C) South American
$650   £436   Constructivo con arbol (60x73cm-24x29in) s. d.1992verso. 29-Nov-93 Gomensoro, Montevideo #7

FONSECA, Reynaldo (1925-) Brazilian
$6000   £4054   O livro vermelho (81x99cm-32x39in) s.d.1985. 22-Nov-93 Sotheby's, New York #205/R
$8000   £5405   Menina e gato (100x91cm-39x36in) s.d.1985. 23-Nov-93 Christie's, New York #277/R
$11000   £7285   Menina com Cachorro e Mulher (100x80cm-39x31in) s.d.1984. 24-Nov-92 Christie's, New York #225/R
$12000   £7843   Mae e criancas jantando (74x101cm-29x40in) s.d.1976. 18-May-93 Sotheby's, New York #198/R
$12000   £7843   Refeicao-mae e filha (81x100cm-32x39in) s.d.1978. 17-May-93 Christie's, New York #221/R
$6200 *£4133* *Menino (70x49cm-28x19in) s.d.1984 oil pastel paper laid on masonite. 18-May-94 Sotheby's, New York #422/R*

FONTAINE, E Joseph (20th C) American
$650   £433   Artist painting in Boston Public Garden (66x53cm-26x21in) s. i.verso. 26-Aug-93 Skinner, Bolton #11
$850   £556   Morning reflection - Boston Public Garden (81x102cm-32x40in) s. 17-Sep-93 Skinner, Bolton #281/R
$900   £600   Wild flowers by the sea (61x46cm-24x18in) s. i.verso. 26-Aug-93 Skinner, Bolton #12
$1000   £667   Summer beach landscape with flowers and boats (51x71cm-20x28in) s. i.verso. 26-Aug-93 Skinner, Bolton #13
$2200   £1467   Garden by the water (56x76cm-22x30in) s. i.verso. 26-Aug-93 Skinner, Bolton #203
$2300   £1533   Landscape with apple blossoms and sea (51x71cm-20x28in) s. i.verso. 26-Aug-93 Skinner, Bolton #30
$2400   £1600   Spring walk, Boston Public Garden (56x76cm-22x30in) s. i.verso. 26-Aug-93 Skinner, Bolton #31/R
$2640   £1725   Swan boats on pond - view of Public Garden, Boston (61x76cm-24x30in) s. 14-May-93 Skinner, Bolton #169/R
$2640   £1725   Winter walk - view of Public Garden (56x76cm-22x30in) s. i.d.1988 verso. 14-May-93 Skinner, Bolton #171/R

FOO FAT, Dulcie (1946-) Canadian?
$4955   £3238   Pacific wildflower (122x155cm-48x61in) s. d. 1984-5 verso. 19-May-93 Sotheby's, Toronto #326/R (C.D 6250)

FOOTE, Will Howe (1874-1965) American
$1700   £1126   Rowboat under autumn trees (30x38cm-12x15in) s. board. 21-Nov-92 James Bakker, Cambridge #216/R
$5000   £3311   Old Bermuda house (61x62cm-24x24in) s. i.stretcher. 23-Sep-93 Sotheby's, New York #212 b/R
$20000 £13245 Summer (62x51cm-24x20in) s. i.stretcher. 23-Sep-93 Sotheby's, New York #212 a/R

FORBES, Helen K (1891-1945) American
$550   £364   Rolling hills (30x38cm-12x15in) s. W/C. 28-Sep-93 John Moran, Pasadena #374

FORBES, John Colin (1846-1925) Canadian
$604   £408   Hills at sunset (31x51cm-12x20in) s. 23-Nov-93 Joyner Fine Art, Toronto #230/R (C.D 800)
$707   £448   Crossing river (61x38cm-24x15in) with sig. 30-Nov-92 Ritchie, Toronto #213/R (C.D 900)
$865   £547   Ducks in marshland at sunset (46x61cm-18x24in) s. 30-Nov-92 Ritchie, Toronto #212/R (C.D 1100)
$991   £648   Moonlight, Toronto harbour (33x46cm-13x18in) s. 19-May-93 Sotheby's, Toronto #137/R (C.D 1250)
$2039   £1359   Her Majesty Queen Alexandra (75x50cm-30x20in) s. canvas on board. 13-May-94 Joyner Fine Art, Toronto #64/R (C.D 2800)
$2518   £1702   Cattle drinking at the river (53x79cm-21x31in) s. s.i.stretcher. 3-Nov-93 Sotheby's, Toronto #184/R (C.D 3250)
$5461   £3641   His Majesty King Edward VII (75x50cm-30x20in) s. canvas on board. 13-May-94 Joyner Fine Art, Toronto #63/R (C.D 7500)

FORBES, Kenneth (1892-1980) Canadian
$583   £388   Stream in summer (70x82cm-28x32in) s.d.1977. 13-May-94 Joyner Fine Art, Toronto #230 (C.D 800)
$728   £485   Lady at the window (60x47cm-24x19in) s.d.1975 canvas on board. 13-May-94 Joyner Fine Art, Toronto #217 (C.D 1000)
$736   £497   Portrait of a woman, the artist's wife (102x71cm-40x28in) s. 3-Nov-93 Sotheby's, Toronto #290/R (C.D 950)
$801   £534   Woman in front of a mirror (48x33cm-19x13in) s.d.1924 painting verso double-sided. 11-May-94 Sotheby's, Toronto #211/R (C.D 1100)
$1092   £728   The black dress (85x62cm-33x24in) s. 13-May-94 Joyner Fine Art, Toronto #115/R (C.D 1500)
$1748   £1165   Portrait of the Hon Leslie Frost (120x90cm-47x35in) s. 13-May-94 Joyner Fine Art, Toronto #58/R (C.D 2400)
$1982   £1295   Portrait of Eola B. Hammell (129x104cm-51x41in) s. 19-May-93 Sotheby's, Toronto #232/R (C.D 2500)
$2913   £1942   My wife and Velazquez (160x97cm-63x38in) s.d.1940. 13-May-94 Joyner Fine Art, Toronto #17/R (C.D 4000)

FORD, Henry Chapman (1828-1894) American
$28000 £18667 Fairy Arch, Mackinac Island (76x128cm-30x50in) s.d.1874. 25-May-94 Sotheby's, New York #20/R

FORD, Henry O (19/20th C) American
$950   £633   Forest pool (102x152cm-40x60in) 23-May-94 Hindman Galleries, Chicago #192/R

FORD, Ruth Vansickel (1897-1980) American
$1000   £662   Kitchen still life with cabbage, apples, pepper and pottery jug (91x102cm-36x40in) s. 28-Nov-92 Dunning's, Illinois #1017

FOREST, Avril (1959-) Haitian
$626   £415   Mangues (51x61cm-20x24in) s. 13-Jun-94 Rogeon, Paris #12/R (F.FR 3500)

FOREST, Henry J de (1860-1924) Canadian
$1800   £1192   View of the Washington River in the evening (59x91cm-23x36in) s.d.1842. 11-Nov-92 Butterfield & Butterfield, San Francisco #3109/R

FOREST, Roy de (1930-) American
$20000 £12579 Attack of the Big Foot (185x216cm-73x85in) s.i.d.1987 verso vinyl acrylic polymer. 25-Apr-93 Butterfield & Butterfield, San Francisco #2120/R
$950   £601   Untitled (74x58cm-29x23in) s. felt-tip pen. 25-Oct-92 Butterfield & Butterfield, San Francisco #2331/R
$16000 £10063 A thousand miles across the pampas and over the Andes with Freddie (163x175cm-64x69in) mixed media canvas painted 1957. 25-Apr-93 Butterfield & Butterfield, San Francisco #2113/R

FOREST, Wesner la (1927-1965) Haitian
$2800   £1867   Voodoo Drummer (76x20cm-30x8in) s. board painted c.1957. 18-May-94 Christie's, New York #320/R

FORG, Gunther (1952-) American
$4656   £3125   Farbfeld (61x201cm-24x79in) s.i.d.1986 oil acrylic panel. 29-Nov-93 Wolfgang Ketterer, Munich #103/R (DM 8000)
$6705   £4500   Untitled (260x148cm-102x58in) s.d.19/11/89 acrylic paper. 23-Mar-94 Sotheby's, London #354/R

FORG, Gunther (1952-) American-cont.
$8000	£5229	Bleibild 21/88 (122x69cm-48x27in) s.d.88 verso lead. 4-May-93 Sotheby's, New York #179/R
$8000	£5556	Untitled (260x160cm-102x63in) s.d.90verso acrylic. 24-Feb-93 Christie's, New York #86/R
$9942	£6584	Untitled (60x160cm-24x63in) s.i.d.1986 acrylic panel. 20-Nov-92 Lempertz, Cologne #533/R (DM 16000)
$11500	£7616	Untitled (122x69cm-48x27in) s.d.1987verso acrylic lead panel. 19-Nov-92 Christie's, New York #186/R
$12000	£8108	Untitled (91x201cm-36x79in) s.i.d.75/88verso acrylic lead panel. 10-Nov-93 Christie's, New York #336/R
$16000	£10458	Untitled - No.125 (241x161cm-95x63in) s.d.88 acrylic lead on wood. 5-May-93 Christie's, New York #195/R
$18000	£10588	Untitled - No.119-88 (241x161cm-95x63in) s.d.88 verso lead. 6-Oct-92 Sotheby's, New York #189/R
$8965	*£5500*	*Untitled (30x21cm-12x8in) s.d.87 metallic paint W/C twelve. 15-Oct-92 Christie's, London #95/R*
$12258	*£8065*	*Window pictures (29x21cm-11x8in) s.i.d.1985 W/C gouache set of 12. 7-Jun-93 Wolfgang Ketterer, Munich #631/R (DM 20000)*
$13500	*£9375*	*Untitled (31x24cm-12x9in) s.i.d.87 W/C metallic pigment twelve sheets. 24-Feb-93 Christie's, New York #129/R*

FORNER, Raquel (1902-1990) Argentinian
$1500	£781	Dama con sombrero (47x31cm-19x12in) tempera. 4-Aug-92 VerBo, Buenos Aires #49
$1800	*£1059*	*Odalisca (38x48cm-15x19in) mixed media. 29-Sep-92 VerBo, Buenos Aires #51*

FORRESTALL, Thomas de Vany (1936-) Canadian
$1427	£933	Park (66x67cm-26x26in) s.d.1975 tempera rounded corners. 18-May-93 Joyner Fine Art, Toronto #321 (C.D 1800)
$1743	£1178	Crows near our house (50x51cm-20x20in) s. s.i.d.1982 egg tempera. 3-Nov-93 Sotheby's, Toronto #293/R (C.D 2250)
$2335	£1546	The old wing (60x91cm-24x36in) s.d.1965 d.Jan 1965 egg tempera board. 18-Nov-92 Sotheby's, Toronto #102/R (C.D 3000)
$2378	£1554	Dog, girl and beach (110x?cm-43x?in) s. s.d.1979 verso egg tempera panel irregular. 19-May-93 Sotheby's, Toronto #332/R (C.D 3000)
$2621	£1748	The owners (70x105cm-28x41in) s.d.1965 tempera. 13-May-94 Joyner Fine Art, Toronto #114/R (C.D 3600)
$3171	£2073	Holiday , s. s.d.1974 verso egg tempera panel irregular. 19-May-93 Sotheby's, Toronto #302/R (C.D 4000)
$3171	£2073	Public beach , s. s.i.d.1976 verso egg tempera panel irregular. 19-May-93 Sotheby's, Toronto #321/R (C.D 4000)
$5461	£3641	Bay of Fundy (61x122cm-24x48in) s.d.1963 s.i.verso tempera board. 11-May-94 Sotheby's, Toronto #214/R (C.D 7500)
$555	*£363*	*Delap's Cove (37x55cm-15x22in) s.i.d.1984 W/C. 18-May-93 Joyner Fine Art, Toronto #322 (C.D 700)*
$801	*£534*	*Interior with table and bookcase (36x52cm-14x20in) s. W/C. 13-May-94 Joyner Fine Art, Toronto #151/R (C.D 1100)*
$1245	*£825*	*Summer hope,New Brunswick (38x51cm-15x20in) s. W/C. 18-Nov-92 Sotheby's, Toronto #40/R (C.D 1600)*

FORSTER, George (fl.1850-1890) American
$3200	£2065	Still life of peaches, grapes and walnuts (36x43cm-14x17in) s.d.1890. 13-Jul-94 Doyle, New York #28
$3600	£2368	Still life of grapes (30x25cm-12x10in) s.d.1844. 7-Apr-93 Doyle, New York #32
$28000	£17949	Still life with fruit (63x76cm-25x30in) s.d.1886. 27-May-93 Sotheby's, New York #121/R

FORSTER, George (attrib) (fl.1850-1890) American
$5500	£3846	Still life with grape, bird nest and salamander (66x52cm-26x20in) 10-Mar-93 Sotheby's, New York #31/R

FORSTER, John Wycliffe Lowes (1850-1938) Canadian
$775	£524	Boy in a field (22x35cm-9x14in) s. board. 3-Nov-93 Sotheby's, Toronto #311/R (C.D 1000)
$1162	£785	The harvest (25x33cm-10x13in) s. canvas laid on board. 3-Nov-93 Sotheby's, Toronto #143/R (C.D 1500)
$1479	£979	The artist reading (29x39cm-11x15in) 18-Nov-92 Sotheby's, Toronto #193/R (C.D 1900)
$1893	£1262	The cup of tea (80x63cm-31x25in) s.d.188-. 13-May-94 Joyner Fine Art, Toronto #59/R (C.D 2600)

FORSYTH, William (19/20th C) American
$8000	£5298	Women beside pond (61x81cm-24x32in) s. 3-Oct-93 Hanzel Galleries, Chicago #802

FORSYTHE, Victor Clyde (1885-1962) American
$650	£430	Landscape (46x61cm-18x24in) s. masonite. 14-Jun-94 John Moran, Pasadena #53
$2500	£1724	Landscape near Shoshone (48x71cm-19x28in) s.d.1950 oil masonite. 16-Feb-93 John Moran, Pasadena #103
$2500	£1678	China cove (63x81cm-25x32in) s.d.1951. 8-Dec-93 Butterfield & Butterfield, San Francisco #3467/R

FORTE, Vicente (20th C) South American
$800	£471	Musicos (46x30cm-18x12in) tempera painted 1968. 29-Sep-92 VerBo, Buenos Aires #53
$1100	£728	Los musicos (100x55cm-39x22in) 11-Nov-92 VerBo, Buenos Aires #52

FORTIN, Marc-Aurele (1888-1970) Canadian
$982	£663	Les voiliers (30x30cm-12x12in) s.verso board. 23-Nov-93 Fraser Pinneys, Quebec #347 (C.D 1300)
$2987	£1891	Couleurs d'Automne (21x18cm-8x7in) s. i.verso board. 1-Dec-92 Fraser Pinneys, Quebec #147/R (C.D 3800)
$13477	£8808	Automne Canadien Laurentides (55x71cm-22x28in) board. 18-May-93 Joyner Fine Art, Toronto #22/R (C.D 17000)
$19633	£13265	Coucher de soleil (50x66cm-20x26in) s. board painted c.1938. 23-Nov-93 Joyner Fine Art, Toronto #77/R (C.D 26000)
$66160	£43814	Landscape with village in valley (120x150cm-47x59in) s. board. 24-Nov-92 Joyner Fine Art, Toronto #99/R (C.D 85000)
$1284	£867	Barques (26x34cm-10x13in) s. W/C. 23-Nov-93 Fraser Pinneys, Quebec #369/R (C.D 1700)
$5037	£3403	Oxen (76x53cm-30x21in) s. W/C. 3-Nov-93 Sotheby's, Toronto #45/R (C.D 6500)
$7531	£4922	Quebec village (56x72cm-22x28in) s. W/C chl. 18-May-93 Joyner Fine Art, Toronto #54/R (C.D 9500)

FORTUNE, Euphemia Charlton (1885-1969) American
$750	£504	Portrait of James Walsh (66x48cm-26x19in) s.d.1913 pastel. 8-Dec-93 Butterfield & Butterfield, San Francisco #3479/R

FOSDICK, James William (1858-1937) American
$1200	£811	Nymphs playing near waterfalls (76x61cm-30x24in) s. 31-Mar-94 Sotheby's Arcade, New York #261/R

FOSTER, Alan (1892-?) American
$4000	£2312	Dance (66x53cm-26x21in) s. 24-Sep-92 Sotheby's, New York #224/R

FOSTER, Ben (1852-1926) American
$1500	£867	Stream through forest (56x46cm-22x18in) s. 24-Sep-92 Mystic Fine Arts, Connecticut #117/R
$2700	£1765	Pasturelands, late summer (76x91cm-30x36in) s. 15-May-93 Dunning's, Illinois #1085/R
$3000	£2027	Landscape (76x91cm-30x36in) s. 15-Jun-93 John Moran, Pasadena #23
$4250	£2872	Morning, late autumn (107x122cm-42x48in) s. 31-Mar-94 Sotheby's Arcade, New York #140/R
$8000	£5298	Litchfield Hills (107x92cm-42x36in) s. painted c.1912. 23-Sep-93 Sotheby's, New York #191/R

FOSTER, Charles Murray (1919-) American
$625	£425	Suzanna, an allegory (56x71cm-22x28in) s.d.53. 14-Apr-94 Freeman Fine Arts, Philadelphia #1039 a/R
$750	£510	Fish on a table (56x76cm-22x30in) init. 14-Apr-94 Freeman Fine Arts, Philadelphia #1042
$850	£578	Still life with lemon (66x102cm-26x40in) s.d.4.50. 14-Apr-94 Freeman Fine Arts, Philadelphia #1041/R
$2000	£1361	Cubist composition with head (102x56cm-40x22in) mono.i.d.1946-47. 14-Apr-94 Freeman Fine Arts, Philadelphia #1040/R
$2900	£1973	Cockerel (66x48cm-26x19in) mono.d.7.3 board. 14-Apr-94 Freeman Fine Arts, Philadelphia #1039

FOSTER, H K (19th C) American
$1214	£850	Quiet river. River in mountains (30x40cm-12x16in) s. pair. 3-Feb-93 Sotheby's Colonnade, London #426

FOSTER, Will (1882-1953) American
$1300	£844	Seated figures in interior (69x94cm-27x37in) s. en grisaille. 11-Sep-93 Louisiana Auction Exchange #106/R

FOSTER, William Frederick (1883-?) American
$650	£422	His wife's love affair (74x91cm-29x36in) s.i.d.1922 oil en grisaille. 8-Jul-94 Sloan, North Bethesda #2529

FOULKES, Lynn (1934-) American
$4500	£3020	The Hill is Blue (126x104cm-50x41in) s.d.1984 oil acrylic chk board on panel. 23-Feb-94 Christie's, New York #96/R

FOURNIER, Alexis Jean (1865-1948) American
$800	£530	Landscape (25x36cm-10x14in) s. panel. 21-Nov-92 James Bakker, Cambridge #232/R
$2000	£1333	Clearing after rain (51x61cm-20x24in) s.d.09. 23-May-94 Christie's, East, New York #144/R
$2300	£1513	Wooded landscape (16x24cm-6x9in) s. board. 31-Mar-93 Sotheby's Arcade, New York #91/R
$2500	£1656	Late summer landscape (30x51cm-12x20in) s.d.92 canvasboard. 22-Sep-93 Christie's, New York #119/R
$2750	£1763	The turn in the road (56x66cm-22x26in) s. i.verso masonite. 10-Dec-92 Sloan, North Bethesda #2604/R
$5500	£3846	Venice (38x55cm-15x22in) s.i.d.13. 11-Mar-93 Christie's, New York #154/R
$9000	£6000	Peace and Plenty (76x91cm-30x36in) 17-Mar-94 Sotheby's, New York #52/R
$13000	£8667	Morning on the Mississippi (71x152cm-28x60in) s.d.1891 s.i.verso. 17-Mar-94 Sotheby's, New York #53/R
$38000	£21965	Hollyhocks in the garden, The Bungle House (66x102cm-26x40in) s. 23-Sep-92 Christie's, New York #147/R

FOURNIER, Paul (1939-) Canadian
$1012	£670	Blue mushroom (122x168cm-48x66in) s.d.73 i.verso oil acrylic. 18-Nov-92 Sotheby's, Toronto #280 (C.D 1300)
$1456	£971	Ochre Terrain (108x127cm-43x50in) s.i.d.74 verso acrylic. 13-May-94 Joyner Fine Art, Toronto #84/R (C.D 2000)
$2002	£1335	Mid April's dance (122x366cm-48x144in) s. i.d.79-81verso. 11-May-94 Sotheby's, Toronto #147/R (C.D 2750)

FOX, John R (1927-) Canadian
$1348	£881	Cloister, Florence (77x61cm-30x24in) s. 19-May-93 Sotheby's, Toronto #63/R (C.D 1700)

FOX, R Atkinson (1860-?) Canadian
$1200	£795	Road through woods (81x76cm-32x30in) s. 23-Sep-93 Mystic Fine Arts, Connecticut #162/R
$2750	£1797	Cows in a pasture (10x16cm-4x6in) s. 14-May-93 Du Mouchelle, Detroit #2021/R
$5250	£3523	Friends (91x61cm-36x24in) 27-Mar-94 Myers, Florida #89/R

FRANCE, Jesse Leach (1862-1926) American
$1430	£935	Wharf on pond (30x46cm-12x18in) s. with i.verso. 14-May-93 Skinner, Bolton #95/R

FRANCES, Esteban (1912-1976) Spanish/American
$11000	£7483	El Cuadro Pelos Abanicos (91x132cm-36x52in) s.d.1946 s.i.d.verso. 17-Apr-94 Hanzel Galleries, Chicago #112
$4700	£3197	Untitled - surrealistic landscape (36x56cm-14x22in) s.d.49 gouache crayon. 17-Apr-94 Hanzel Galleries, Chicago #111
$5000	£3378	Surrealist figure (59x37cm-23x15in) s. col crayon ink. 2-Nov-93 Christie's, East, New York #111/R
$5000	£3401	Untitled - surrealistic collage (36x53cm-14x21in) s. mixed media collage gouache crayon. 17-Apr-94 Hanzel Galleries, Chicago #113

FRANCHERE, Joseph-Charles (1866-1921) Canadian
$634	£415	Scene Venetienne (20x28cm-8x11in) s. board. 18-May-93 Joyner Fine Art, Toronto #264 (C.D 800)
$680	£459	Elise Gagnon (61x50cm-24x20in) s.d.1897. 23-Nov-93 Fraser Pinneys, Quebec #437 (C.D 900)
$684	£444	Pres d'un village (20x25cm-8x10in) panel. 21-Jun-94 Fraser Pinneys, Quebec #40 (C.D 950)

FRANCIS, John F (1808-1886) American
$900	£612	Portrait of William Pratt (76x64cm-30x25in) s.d.Sept.1833. 8-Apr-94 Sloan, North Bethesda #2498/R
$1500	£1000	Portrait of a young girl (76x63cm-30x25in) 23-May-94 Christie's, East, New York #19/R
$1700	£1156	The pink shawl (76x63cm-30x25in) s.d.1886verso. 15-Nov-93 Christie's, East, New York #7/R
$3000	£1987	Still life with grapes in footed bowl (29x36cm-11x14in) board. 23-Sep-93 Sotheby's, New York #4/R
$3000	£1987	Still life with plums and glass bowl (29x34cm-11x13in) board. 23-Sep-93 Sotheby's, New York #1/R
$3750	£2484	Still life with peaches and plums (29x36cm-11x14in) board. 23-Sep-93 Sotheby's, New York #3/R
$3750	£2484	Still life with cherries, glass and currants (29x34cm-11x13in) board. 23-Sep-93 Sotheby's, New York #2/R
$4006	£2653	Nature morte aux pommes et chataignes (18x22cm-7x9in) s.d.1867 panel. 2-Jul-93 Sotheby's, Monaco #342/R (F.FR 23000)
$24000	£15190	Still life with currants (26x33cm-10x13in) s.d.1866. 3-Dec-92 Sotheby's, New York #1/R

FRANCIS, John F (attrib) (1808-1886) American
$1500	£1007	Apples on stacked plates (23x30cm-9x12in) 16-Dec-93 Mystic Fine Arts, Connecticut #106/R

FRANCIS, Sam (1923-) American
$7982	£5357	Diamond (43x35cm-17x14in) s.d.1978verso acrylic. 23-Jun-93 Galerie Kornfeld, Berne #342/R (S.FR 12000)
$8000	£5369	White ghost flower (31x25cm-12x10in) s.i.d.1989 verso acrylic paper. 23-Feb-94 Christie's, New York #30/R
$8000	£5405	Study for Hilde Kirsch (36x28cm-14x11in) s.i.verso acrylic paper painted 1977. 10-Nov-93 Christie's, New York #169/R
$9000	£5294	Untitled (76x56cm-30x22in) acrylic paper. 6-Oct-92 Sotheby's, New York #44/R
$9500	£6419	Untitled (61x43cm-24x17in) s.i.d.1985 verso acrylic paper. 11-Nov-93 Sotheby's, New York #314/R
$9978	£6696	Blue drops (33x24cm-13x9in) s.d.1960. 23-Jun-93 Galerie Kornfeld, Berne #341 (S.FR 15000)
$10000	£6757	Untitled (11x19cm-4x7in) acrylic paper collage painted c.1957. 11-Nov-93 Sotheby's, New York #293/R
$10000	£6711	Untitled (11x36cm-4x14in) init.d.80 verso pigment acrylic. 24-Feb-94 Sotheby's Arcade, New York #469/R
$11973	£8036	Yellow and blue (19x15cm-7x6in) s.verso paper painted 1959. 23-Jun-93 Galerie Kornfeld, Berne #340/R (S.FR 18000)
$12000	£8108	Untitled (22x16cm-9x6in) s.i.verso acrylic paper painted 1973. 10-Nov-93 Christie's, New York #146/R
$14000	£9396	Untitled (33x41cm-13x16in) s.d.1976verso acrylic. 4-May-94 Christie's, New York #209/R

FRANCIS, Sam (1923-) American-cont.

$14000	£9272	Untitled (49x35cm-19x14in) acrylic paper executed 1979. 18-Nov-92 Sotheby's, New York #128/R
$16830	£11000	Pacific Ring Series (153x114cm-60x45in) acrylic paper on four sheets painted 1986. 30-Jun-94 Sotheby's, London #163/R
$17942	£11650	Down drift (51x35cm-20x14in) s.i.d.1976verso acrylic vellum. 22-Jun-94 Galerie Kornfeld, Berne #427/R (S.FR 24000)
$18360	£12000	Untitled (104x74cm-41x29in) acrylic paper painted 1984. 30-Jun-94 Sotheby's, London #124/R
$20000	£13333	Untitled (35x43cm-14x17in) s.i.d.1973verso acrylic paper. 11-May-94 Christie's, New York #477/R
$21000	£13907	Untitled (57x77cm-22x30in) s.d.1970verso acrylic paper. 19-Nov-92 Christie's, New York #359/R
$21774	£14516	Composition red yellow green (76x63cm-30x25in) acrylic over monotype paper on panel exec.1980. 27-May-94 Villa Grisebach, Berlin #73/R (DM 36000)
$23000	£15436	Untitled (30x45cm-12x18in) s.d.1979verso acrylic paper. 5-May-94 Sotheby's, New York #150/R
$24612	£16518	Red, yellow and blue (33x24cm-13x9in) s.i.d.1963verso paper. 25-Jun-93 Galerie Kornfeld, Berne #34/R (S.FR 37000)
$26000	£17450	Untitled (104x75cm-41x30in) s.d.1985verso acrylic. 4-May-94 Christie's, New York #163/R
$26786	£17857	Untitled (63x47cm-25x19in) s.d.1889verso acrylic paper. 1-Jun-94 Sotheby's, Amsterdam #296/R (D.FL 50000)
$30000	£20134	Untitled (93x95cm-37x37in) s.verso paper on canvas. 4-May-94 Christie's, New York #167/R
$30000	£19868	Untitled (38x46cm-15x18in) acrylic paper executed 1973. 18-Nov-92 Sotheby's, New York #118/R
$30326	£18605	Untitled (48x35cm-19x14in) d.1980 s.verso acrylic. 14-Oct-92 Germann, Zurich #69/R (S.FR 40000)
$32000	£21192	Untitled (121x161cm-48x63in) painted 1970 acrylic paper on canvas. 19-Nov-92 Christie's, New York #411/R
$33000	£21854	Untitled (61x46cm-24x18in) s.d.1973verso acrylic. 19-Nov-92 Christie's, New York #302/R
$34230	£21000	Composition (55x76cm-22x30in) s.d.1973 verso acrylic paper. 14-Oct-92 Sotheby's, London #379/R
$35883	£23301	Red, green and blue (50x35cm-20x14in) s.i.d.1980 verso paper. 24-Jun-94 Galerie Kornfeld, Berne #28/R (S.FR 48000)
$36000	£23529	Untitled (107x86cm-42x34in) s.d.73 verso acrylic oil painted 1987. 4-May-93 Sotheby's, New York #361/R
$36914	£24775	Composition (50x36cm-20x14in) s.d.1973verso acrylic. 3-Dec-93 Germann, Zurich #51/R (S.FR 55000)
$40000	£27027	As for the appearance VIII (33x24cm-13x9in) s. painted 1963-5. 11-Nov-93 Sotheby's, New York #241/R
$50000	£33113	Son of Fire (182x91cm-72x36in) acrylic paper painted 1989. 18-Nov-92 Sotheby's, New York #119/R
$50000	£32680	My fairly furry green angel (69x80cm-27x31in) s.d.1973 verso. 4-May-93 Sotheby's, New York #351/R
$55000	£35948	Untitled (181x93cm-71x37in) acrylic painted 1983. 5-May-93 Christie's, New York #286/R
$55000	£36424	Around us day and night (181x91cm-71x36in) acrylic. 19-Nov-92 Christie's, New York #282/R
$55000	£38194	Untitled (184x94cm-72x37in) s. painted 1987 acrylic. 24-Feb-93 Christie's, New York #47/R
$58536	£39286	The upper red (41x33cm-16x13in) s.d.1956-1960. 25-Jun-93 Galerie Kornfeld, Berne #33/R (S.FR 88000)
$61090	£41000	Untitled (92x29cm-36x11in) s.d.1986verso acrylic. 3-Dec-93 Sotheby's, London #196/R
$62500	£41391	Untitled (66x147cm-26x58in) acrylic paper executed 1979. 18-Nov-92 Sotheby's, New York #130/R
$66000	£44295	Untitled (46x38cm-18x15in) s.d.1955verso. 5-May-94 Sotheby's, New York #98/R
$73833	£48574	Soror (183x91cm-72x36in) acrylic paper painted 1989. 8-Jun-93 Rasmussen, Copenhagen #10/R (D.KR 460000)
$75000	£49669	Having to do with the whale (183x122cm-72x48in) s.d.1986 verso acrylic. 18-Nov-92 Sotheby's, New York #125/R
$76500	£50000	Blue yellow red (41x45cm-16x18in) 30-Jun-94 Christie's, London #31/R
$79948	£50600	Crystal state (228x182cm-90x72in) acrylic executed 1971. 3-Dec-92 Christie's, London #51/R
$80000	£53691	Untitled (239x143cm-94x56in) s.d.1987verso acrylic. 5-May-94 Sotheby's, New York #149/R
$85000	£57432	Untitled - SF77-038A and 038B (105x150cm-41x59in) s.verso acrylic paper two parts painted 1977. 11-Nov-93 Sotheby's, New York #273/R
$90000	£60811	White sites (66x76cm-26x30in) s.verso acrylic painted 1963-65. 10-Nov-93 Sotheby's, New York #39/R
$105000	£68627	Untitled (221x279cm-87x110in) s.d.1974verso acrylic. 16-May-93 Hindman Galleries, Chicago #31/R
$120000	£83333	Untitled no 7 (213x305cm-84x120in) acrylic. 24-Feb-93 Christie's, New York #43/R
$130000	£87248	Tokyo blue (131x81cm-52x32in) s.i.d.1961verso acrylic paper. 3-May-94 Christie's, New York #4/R
$155000	£104027	Untitled (41x34cm-16x13in) s.d.1960verso. 4-May-94 Sotheby's, New York #2/R
$160000	£105960	Untitled (183x214cm-72x84in) acrylic. 18-Nov-92 Christie's, New York #15/R
$172946	£116071	Blue (73x60cm-29x24in) s.d.60verso. 25-Jun-93 Galerie Kornfeld, Berne #35/R (S.FR 260000)
$183600	£120000	Untitled (122x153cm-48x60in) s.d.1964verso acrylic. 30-Jun-94 Sotheby's, London #173/R

FRANCIS, Sam (1923-) American-cont.

$260000	£169935	Silvio set one (121x102cm-48x40in) s.d.1963 verso. 3-May-93 Sotheby's, New York #38/R
$950000	£641892	Middle blue III (183x244cm-72x96in) painted 1959. 10-Nov-93 Sotheby's, New York #9/R
$1150000	£771812	Red (310x190cm-122x75in) painted 1955-1956. 4-May-94 Sotheby's, New York #6/R
$8500	£5556	Meteorite (183x107cm-72x42in) s. col.screenprint executed 1986. 11-May-93 Christie's, New York #420/R
$9500	£6209	Untitled (213x152cm-84x60in) s. col.screenprint. 11-May-93 Christie's, New York #421/R
$11175	£7500	Untitled (130x81cm-51x32in) s.d.1980 verso gouache. 2-Dec-93 Christie's, London #121/R
$14000	£9396	Untitled (38x28cm-15x11in) W/C gouache executed c.1957. 25-Feb-94 Sotheby's, New York #23/R
$16156	£10700	Untitled (24x20cm-9x8in) s.i. painted c.1960 bodycol W/C. 20-Nov-92 Lempertz, Cologne #537/R (DM 26000)
$16447	£10680	Spring in Bern (78x57cm-31x22in) s.i.d.1970verso gouache vellum. 22-Jun-94 Galerie Kornfeld, Berne #426/R (S.FR 22000)
$22120	£14000	Untitled No.54 (102x69cm-40x27in) gouache executed 1972. 3-Dec-92 Sotheby's, London #90/R
$22125	£14652	Sans titre (69x101cm-27x40in) s.d.1975verso mixed media. 26-Nov-92 Francis Briest, Paris #42/R (F.FR 120000)
$30000	£19868	Untitled (25x56cm-10x22in) s.d.1957verso W/C. 19-Nov-92 Christie's, New York #320/R
$33660	£22000	Untitled (24x33cm-9x13in) s.i.d.64verso gouache. 30-Jun-94 Sotheby's, London #171/R
$38740	£26000	Blue balls (102x62cm-40x24in) gouache paper on canvas executed 1961. 24-Jun-93 Christie's, London #48/R
$41720	£28000	Untitled (57x76cm-22x30in) gouache executed 1963. 3-Dec-93 Sotheby's, London #134/R
$41864	£27184	Light violet (44x35cm-17x14in) s.d.52 verso W/C. 24-Jun-94 Galerie Kornfeld, Berne #30/R (S.FR 56000)
$46350	£30097	Light blue (50x65cm-20x26in) s.d.1953 verso W/C. 24-Jun-94 Galerie Kornfeld, Berne #29/R (S.FR 62000)
$50000	£33784	Untitled (47x36cm-19x14in) init.d.57 s.i.d.1957-1960verso gouache. 10-Nov-93 Sotheby's, New York #2/R
$65000	£43624	Untitled red and green (76x56cm-30x22in) s.d.1960verso gouache. 5-May-94 Sotheby's, New York #132 a/R
$70000	£45752	Untitled (180x94cm-71x37in) s.verso gouache painted c.1960. 4-May-93 Sotheby's, New York #328/R
$95000	£63758	Possible pure land emblem (57x76cm-22x30in) s.i.d.Feb.1959verso W/C. 4-May-94 Sotheby's, New York #12/R

FRANCISCO, J Bond (1863-1931) American

$550	£364	House in eucalyptus coastal (23x30cm-9x12in) s. board. 14-Jun-94 John Moran, Pasadena #12
$1100	£743	Landscape (23x33cm-9x13in) s. canvasboard. 9-Nov-93 John Moran, Pasadena #914
$2250	£1562	View near Pasadena (40x50cm-16x20in) s. 7-Mar-93 Butterfield & Butterfield, San Francisco #182/R
$2500	£1471	California mountains (41x51cm-16x20in) s. 4-Oct-92 Butterfield & Butterfield, Los Angeles #195/R

FRANCK, Albert Jacques (1899-1973) Canadian

$906	£612	Elizabeth Street South of Gerrard, 1947 (30x40cm-12x16in) s. canvasboard. 23-Nov-93 Joyner Fine Art, Toronto #2/R (C.D 1200)
$1019	£680	University Ave. before 1948 (25x30cm-10x12in) s.d.58 board. 13-May-94 Joyner Fine Art, Toronto #7/R (C.D 1400)
$1087	£725	Queen's Park West (13x16cm-5x6in) s.d.1963 i.d.verso board. 6-Jun-94 Waddingtons, Toronto #1305 (C.D 1500)
$1481	£974	Wellsley St. E at Parliament (25x30cm-10x12in) s.d.60 i.verso masonite. 7-Jun-93 Ritchie, Toronto #179/R (C.D 1900)
$1559	£1026	Ottawa Street (30x25cm-12x10in) s.d.62 i.verso masonite. 7-Jun-93 Ritchie, Toronto #187/R (C.D 2000)
$1957	£1313	Queens Park East (41x30cm-16x12in) s.d.1959 board. 29-Nov-93 Waddingtons, Toronto #1073/R (C.D 2600)
$2102	£1392	The good old days (48x61cm-19x24in) s.d.35 i.verso panel. 18-Nov-92 Sotheby's, Toronto #215/R (C.D 2700)
$2114	£1429	Seaton Street (30x25cm-12x10in) s.d.63 board. 23-Nov-93 Joyner Fine Art, Toronto #83/R (C.D 2800)
$2179	£1443	Grange Park (30x40cm-12x16in) s.d.62 board. 24-Nov-92 Joyner Fine Art, Toronto #58/R (C.D 2800)
$3487	£2356	Backyard Bishop Street (71x61cm-28x24in) s. board. 3-Nov-92 Sotheby's, Toronto #263/R (C.D 4500)
$8562	£5670	St George Street at Sussex (61x76cm-24x30in) s.d.63 i.verso board. 18-Nov-92 Sotheby's, Toronto #444/R (C.D 11000)
$701	£464	Howard Street (29x24cm-11x9in) s. W/C. 24-Nov-92 Joyner Fine Art, Toronto #34/R (C.D 900)
$934	£619	Behind Berryman Street (30x24cm-12x9in) s. W/C. 24-Nov-92 Joyner Fine Art, Toronto #56/R (C.D 1200)

FRANCO, Siron (20th C) South American

$8000	£5405	Untitled (135x154cm-53x61in) s.d.89-90. 23-Nov-93 Christie's, New York #195/R
$15000	£9804	International Debt (180x189cm-71x74in) s.d.1991. 17-May-93 Christie's, New York #157/R

FRANDZEN, Eugene M (1893-1972) American
$1000   £654   Mountainous landscape (64x76cm-25x30in) s. 16-May-93 Hindman Galleries, Chicago #108

FRANK-BOGGS see BOGGS, Frank Myers

FRANKENTHALER, Helen (1928-) American
$6500   £4305   Emerson series III (46x60cm-18x24in) s. painted 1965 acrylic. 19-Nov-92 Christie's, New York #321/R
$7500   £4412   April 1 (43x36cm-17x14in) s. paper. 6-Oct-92 Sotheby's, New York #38/R
$20000   £11765   Covent Garden Study (44x72cm-17x28in) s.i.d.84verso acrylic. 8-Oct-92 Christie's, New York #153/R
$35000   £22436   April Mood (152x434cm-60x171in) s.d.74 i.d.verso acrylic. 24-May-93 Grogan, Massachussetts #381/R
$40000   £26846   Sea green (113x274cm-44x108in) s.i.d.1977 verso acrylic. 23-Feb-94 Christie's, New York #28/R
$42000   £24706   Dusk (86x69cm-34x27in) s. acrylic. 8-Oct-92 Christie's, New York #111/R
$42500   £28716   Gliding figure (63x76cm-25x30in) s. canvasboard painted 1961. 11-Nov-93 Sotheby's, New York #294/R
$50000   £33784   Myth (140x269cm-55x106in) s.d.73 i.d.stretcher acrylic. 10-Nov-93 Christie's, New York #163/R
$55000   £35948   Copper afternoon II (105x180cm-41x71in) s. acrylic painted 1973. 5-May-93 Christie's, New York #270/R
$55000   £35948   Mozart's birthday (209x165cm-82x65in) init. i.d.1986verso acrylic. 5-May-93 Christie's, New York #282/R
$70000   £47297   Living edge (298x170cm-117x67in) s.d.73 acrylic. 9-Nov-93 Christie's, New York #21/R
$72500   £48013   February's turn (122x277cm-48x109in) s. painted 1979. 18-Nov-92 Sotheby's, New York #98/R
$170000   £114094   Blue caterpillar (297x175cm-117x69in) s. i.stretcher painted 1961. 3-May-94 Christie's, New York #5/R
$180000   £117647   Yellow clearing (136x176cm-54x69in) painted 1963. 3-May-93 Sotheby's, New York #37/R
$220000   £148649   Swan Lake II (236x237cm-93x93in) s. i.d.1961 verso. 9-Nov-93 Christie's, New York #9/R

FRANKL, Walter (20th C) American
$750   £510   The blue sweater (16x20cm-6x8in) s. 10-Jul-93 Young Fine Arts Auctions, Maine #138/R

FRANKLIN, Richard (20th C) American
$1100   £728   Untitled (107x152cm-42x60in) chl conte crayon handmade paper goldleaf. 29-Sep-93 Sotheby's Arcade, New York #235/R

FRANQUINET, Eugene Pierre (1875-1940) American
$750   £500   In the canyon (41x51cm-16x20in) s. board. 15-Mar-94 John Moran, Pasadena #72
$1200   £795   Landscape - afterglow (25x36cm-10x14in) s. s.i.verso board. 14-Jun-94 John Moran, Pasadena #71
$2500   £1645   Yellow canvas (76x63cm-30x25in) s. 13-Jun-93 Butterfield & Butterfield, San Francisco #909/R

FRANSIOLI, Thomas Adrian (1906-) American
$3200   £2148   New York City scene (41x43cm-16x17in) s.d.1949 board. 24-Jun-93 Mystic Fine Arts, Connecticut #94
$4000   £2649   On Brimmer Street (41x51cm-16x20in) init.d.48 panel. 21-Nov-92 James Bakker, Cambridge #310/R

FRASER, John Arthur (1839-1898) Canadian/British
$1776   £1200   Lad with cricket bat (48x40cm-19x16in) s.i.d.1868 W/C htd bodycol. 3-Nov-93 Sotheby's, London #162/R
$2039   £1359   View from Ile d'Orleans (43x65cm-17x26in) s. W/C htd.white. 13-May-94 Joyner Fine Art, Toronto #157/R (C.D 2800)

FRASER, Thomas Douglas (1883-1955) American
$1200   £805   Tamalpais, from the Dipsea Trail (30x62cm-12x24in) s.d.1922. 8-Dec-93 Butterfield & Butterfield, San Francisco #3439/R
$2250   £1520   Cypresses in landscape (30x36cm-12x14in) s.d.1912. 15-Jun-93 John Moran, Pasadena #55
$3500   £2349   Creeping shadows, Vallejo (66x91cm-26x36in) s.d.1925. 8-Dec-93 Butterfield & Butterfield, San Francisco #3438/R

FRAZIER, Kenneth (1867-1949) American
$1500   £1014   Sunlit view of the Adirondacks (51x64cm-20x25in) s.d.1924. 10-Nov-93 Doyle, New York #46

FREDENTHAL, David (1914-1958) American
$600   £390   Farmhouse (28x41cm-11x16in) s. W/C. 11-Sep-93 Louisiana Auction Exchange #109/R
$1000   £629   The wounded bird (150x79cm-59x31in) s. W/C paper laid down on board. 25-Apr-93 Butterfield & Butterfield, San Francisco #2026/R

FREDERICK, Rod (20th C) American
$6459   £4306   Winters warming (61x102cm-24x40in) s.d. 30-May-94 Hodgins, Calgary #316/R (C.D 9000)

FREDERICKS, Ernest (1877-1927) American
$800   £530   Forest scene in winter (64x76cm-25x30in) s. 3-Oct-93 Hanzel Galleries, Chicago #759

FREEDMAN, Maurice (1904-) American
$1600   £1074   Grey sea and dunes (51x61cm-20x24in) s.d.60 board. 5-Dec-93 James Bakker, Cambridge #101/R

FREEMAN, Dick (1932-1991) Canadian
$544   £368   Untitled (30x41cm-12x16in) s. i.verso masonite. 25-Apr-94 Levis, Calgary #85 (C.D 750)
$680   £459   Bringing 'em in (50x75cm-20x30in) s. board. 23-Nov-93 Joyner Fine Art, Toronto #279/R (C.D 900)
$689   £466   Prairie Sentinels (30x41cm-12x16in) s. i.verso masonite. 25-Apr-94 Levis, Calgary #84/R (C.D 950)
$785   £513   Getting moving (41x61cm-16x24in) s. board. 10-May-93 Hodgins, Calgary #318 b (C.D 1000)
$1020   £667   Headwind (46x61cm-18x24in) s. board. 10-May-93 Hodgins, Calgary #158/R (C.D 1300)
$1479   £979   Beer break (46x61cm-18x24in) s. i.verso canvasboard. 16-Nov-92 Hodgins, Calgary #328 (C.D 1900)
$1635   £1082   Summer's end (61x91cm-24x36in) s. i.verso. 16-Nov-92 Hodgins, Calgary #253/R (C.D 2100)
$1960   £1333   The Last Bunch cowboys rounding up cattle (46x61cm-18x24in) s. board. 15-Nov-93 Hodgins, Calgary #237/R (C.D 2600)
$2102   £1392   Morning brew (51x86cm-20x34in) s. board. 16-Nov-92 Hodgins, Calgary #62 (C.D 2700)

FREEMAN, George (1787-1868) American
$1100 *£743* Portrait of a lady (15x10cm-6x4in) min. s.i.verso painted c.1835 case. 30-Oct-93 Skinner, Bolton #393/R
$1314 *£900* William and Frances Harrison Ainsworth (11x?cm-4x?in) min.ornate gesso frames one oval one rec. pair. 8-Feb-94 Sotheby's, Billingshurst #1738

FREER, Frederick W (1849-1908) American
$4500   £3147   The old letter (62x49cm-24x19in) s. 10-Mar-93 Sotheby's, New York #90/R

FREIFELD, Eric (1919-) Canadian
$1395 *£942* Study of pansies (36x52cm-14x20in) s. W/C. 3-Nov-93 Sotheby's, Toronto #23/R (C.D 1800)
$1456 *£971* Field of pansies (43x56cm-17x22in) s.d.1978 W/C. 13-May-94 Joyner Fine Art, Toronto #197 (C.D 2000)
$1602 *£1068* Pansies (53x76cm-21x30in) s.d.1978 W/C. 11-May-94 Sotheby's, Toronto #251/R (C.D 2200)

FREIXAS VIVO, A (1912-) South American?
$1000   £658   Calle (55x45cm-22x18in) s. 31-May-93 Gomensoro, Montevideo #91/R

FRELINGHUYSEN, Suzy (1911-1988) American
$75000 £50336 Compostion with Toreador drinking (132x89cm-52x35in) init. s.i.d.1944verso masonite. 4-May-94 Doyle, New York #61/R
$80000 *£53691* Evian (61x51cm-24x20in) init.i. s.i.verso oil collage gesso panel. 4-May-94 Doyle, New York #62/R

FRENCH, Michael (20th C) Canadian
$874   £583   The visitor (49x41cm-19x16in) s.i.d.1981 acrylic board. 11-May-94 Sotheby's, Toronto #235 (C.D 1200)
$1057   £714   August morning, St. Albans (39x31cm-15x12in) s.d.1979 acrylic paper. 23-Nov-93 Joyner Fine Art, Toronto #117/R (C.D 1400)
$1085   £733   In the Beginning (26x42cm-10x17in) s.i.d.1983 i.d.verso acrylic board. 3-Nov-93 Sotheby's, Toronto #52 a (C.D 1400)
$1965   £1244   We enjoyed a warm spring (56x101cm-22x40in) s.d.1987 acrylic masonite. 30-Nov-92 Ritchie, Toronto #172/R (C.D 2500)

FRENZENY, P (1840-1902) American
$13930 £7000   Stalking scenes (145x61cm-57x24in) s. four in one screen. 31-Aug-92 Sotheby's, London #805/R

FRERICHS, William C A (1829-1905) American
$2500   £1689   Bear traversing a waterfall (63x84cm-25x33in) s. 31-Mar-94 Sotheby's Arcade, New York #41/R
$4000   £2667   Source of the Linnville, North Carolina (30x51cm-12x20in) init. 16-Mar-94 Christie's, New York #33/R
$12000 £7692   Shooting birds in river gorge (75x126cm-30x50in) s.d.1878. 27-May-93 Sotheby's, New York #174/R
$14000 £8861   Skating in winter (76x117cm-30x46in) s. 4-Dec-92 Christie's, New York #225/R

FREUND, Harry Louis (1905-1979) American
$1300   £850   Home Sweet Home - shanty with family and livestock (38x46cm-15x18in) s.d.38 masonite. 17-Sep-93 Skinner, Bolton #245/R

FREY, Joseph (20th C) American
$750   £500   Landscape (64x76cm-25x30in) s. 15-Mar-94 John Moran, Pasadena #97

FRIEDMAN, Arnold (1879-1947) American
$2000   £1042   The polo match (74x89cm-29x35in) s. 12-Aug-92 Doyle, New York #63

FRIES, Charles Arthur (1854-1940) American
$800	£533	Moonlight in Yosemite (25x51cm-10x20in) s. canvasboard. 15-Mar-94 John Moran, Pasadena #88
$950	£655	In the eucalyptus grove (25x36cm-10x14in) s. i.stretcher. 16-Feb-93 John Moran, Pasadena #19
$1200	£706	Green pastures (61x91cm-24x36in) s.d.1937. 4-Oct-92 Butterfield & Butterfield, Los Angeles #120/R
$1200	£805	Windy day (41x51cm-16x20in) s. 8-Dec-93 Butterfield & Butterfield, San Francisco #3499/R
$1700	£1097	Morning without clouds (46x61cm-18x24in) s. i.verso. 13-Jul-94 Doyle, New York #30
$3500	£2318	Afternoon in the desert - Palm Springs (61x91cm-24x36in) s. 14-Jun-94 John Moran, Pasadena #89
$3500	£2414	Afternoon in the desert, Palm Springs (61x91cm-24x36in) s. 16-Feb-93 John Moran, Pasadena #75

FRIESEKE, Frederick Carl (1874-1939) American
$3500	£2318	Bank of the Seine (38x55cm-15x22in) s. painted c.1901. 23-Sep-93 Sotheby's, New York #163/R
$5000	£3333	Goats in an orchard (65x81cm-26x32in) s.d.1924. 23-May-94 Christie's, East, New York #172/R
$7750	£5132	French country landscape (46x61cm-18x24in) s. canvas on board. 2-Oct-93 Boos Gallery, Michigan #290/R
$9000	£5960	Coastal scene with boats (48x61cm-19x24in) s.d.1902 canvas on masonite. 2-Oct-93 Boos Gallery, Michigan #277/R
$9314	£6127	Bouquet de fleurs (49x58cm-19x23in) s. panel. 4-Nov-92 Francis Briest, Paris #152/R (F.FR 50000)
$16000	£10667	Reclining nude (49x61cm-19x24in) s. 25-May-94 Sotheby's, New York #70/R
$20000	£11561	The satin slip (61x50cm-24x20in) s. board. 23-Sep-92 Christie's, New York #139/R
$23000	£14557	Dressing (28x24cm-11x9in) s. board in painted oval. 3-Dec-92 Sotheby's, New York #122/R
$50000	£33333	The pink kimono (81x65cm-32x26in) s. 26-May-94 Christie's, New York #90/R
$100000	£66225	Pet rabbit (79x64cm-31x25in) s.d.21. 23-Sep-93 Sotheby's, New York #185/R
$360000	£227848	On the beach (82x82cm-32x32in) s. 4-Dec-92 Christie's, New York #24/R
$14000	£9272	Cup of tea (39x50cm-15x20in) s. W/C chl. 22-Sep-93 Christie's, New York #143/R

FRIIS, Frederick Trap (1865-1909) American
$550	£377	Palmyra, Bjorn and Jan (51x61cm-20x24in) 10-Feb-94 Skinner, Bolton #73
$550	£377	View of Knocke, Belgium with windmill (30x46cm-12x18in) 10-Feb-94 Skinner, Bolton #68
$550	£377	Landscape overlooking an inlet, with village beyond (30x51cm-12x20in) canvasboard. 10-Feb-94 Skinner, Bolton #88
$600	£411	Ponte Vecchio, Perruggi, Florence (48x51cm-19x20in) mono. 10-Feb-94 Skinner, Bolton #126/R
$600	£411	Profile of Palmyra in green (51x61cm-20x24in) 10-Feb-94 Skinner, Bolton #71/R
$650	£446	Landscape by the water (30x46cm-12x18in) 10-Feb-94 Skinner, Bolton #90
$650	£446	Landscape with green fields and two trees, Knocke, Belgium (28x43cm-11x17in) 10-Feb-94 Skinner, Bolton #100
$750	£514	Antique copper pot (30x25cm-12x10in) 10-Feb-94 Skinner, Bolton #85
$750	£514	Still life with mixed fruit and wine glass (36x51cm-14x20in) 10-Feb-94 Skinner, Bolton #83/R
$950	£651	Dunes, beach and surf (53x81cm-21x32in) 10-Feb-94 Skinner, Bolton #72/R
$1000	£685	Lady with parasol by the edge of the vegetable field, near a Swedish village (23x43cm-9x17in) 10-Feb-94 Skinner, Bolton #87
$1600	£847	Artist in atelier (33x25cm-13x10in) estate st.verso. 12-Sep-92 Louisiana Auction Exchange #88/R
$4000	£2312	Florence, Piazza S.Lorenzo (65x60cm-26x24in) 23-Sep-92 Christie's, New York #154/R
$5500	£3716	Still life with fruit (41x61cm-16x24in) mono. i.verso. 5-Nov-93 Skinner, Bolton #81/R
$500	£342	Red haired nude reclining (46x53cm-18x21in) mono. mixed media. 10-Feb-94 Skinner, Bolton #81/R

FRIPP, Thomas William (20th C) Canadian
$550	£348	Snow-capped mountain (29x23cm-11x9in) s. W/C. 30-Nov-92 Ritchie, Toronto #159/R (C.D 700)

FROMUTH, Charles Henry (1861-1937) American
$1192	£800	Coming storm at sunset Concarneau (44x40cm-17x16in) s. pastel. 3-Dec-93 Phillips, Edinburgh #124/R
$1490	£1000	Late September glow at the Harbour Concarneau (44x40cm-17x16in) s.d.1911 pastel. 3-Dec-93 Phillips, Edinburgh #58
$3903	£2602	Barques sous voiles (31x40cm-12x16in) pastel. 24-Jul-93 Thierry, Brest #59/R (F.FR 23000)

FROST, A B (1851-1928) American
$3100	£1962	Gloucester, Massachussetts, July 1906 (25x36cm-10x14in) s. paperboard. 24-Oct-92 Collins, Maine #104/R
$1000	£662	Plant-cutting in Virginia (43x28cm-17x11in) s. W/C en grisaille. 21-Nov-92 James Bakker, Cambridge #47/R

FROST, Arthur Burdett (1851-1928) American
$850	£556	Storytelling , init.i. W/C. 30-Jun-94 Mystic Fine Arts, Connecticut #54/R
$1000	£654	On the site (51x37cm-20x15in) gouache en grisaille. 4-May-93 Christie's, East, New York #159/R

FROST, Arthur Burdett (1851-1928) American-cont.
$1000	£680	Point of Honour (47x56cm-19x22in) s.i. chl. 15-Nov-93 Christie's, East, New York #111/R
$1200	£811	A strategic movement (52x42cm-20x17in) s.i. Indian ink pencil. 31-Mar-94 Sotheby's Arcade, New York #38/R
$3800	£2517	Misery (66x45cm-26x18in) s. ink wash gouache en grisaille board. 22-Sep-93 Christie's, New York #73/R
$6500	£4167	Political talk (46x65cm-18x26in) s. W/C gouache pencil en grisaille on board. 26-May-93 Christie's, New York #64 b/R
$13500	£8940	Shoot, shoot, man - why don't you shoot (49x55cm-19x22in) s. ink wash gouache en grisaille board. 22-Sep-93 Christie's, New York #93/R
$15000	£10490	Shot at pheasant (65x43cm-26x17in) s.i.d.1901verso W/C gouache en grisaille board. 10-Mar-93 Sotheby's, New York #48/R
$22000	£14667	Mr. Bites goes rabbit shooting. Mr Bites goes rail shooting (60x41cm-24x16in) one s.i. one init. pen pair. 17-Mar-94 Sotheby's, New York #79/R

FROST, George Albert (1843-?) American
$2200	£1560	Shepard River (43x74cm-17x29in) s.d.1891. 13-Feb-93 Collins, Maine #96/R
$2500	£1645	Living in Arctic (71x102cm-28x40in) s.d.1882. 13-Jun-93 Butterfield & Butterfield, San Francisco #721/R

FROST, John (1890-1937) American
$25000	£17361	Pool at sundown (61x71cm-24x28in) s.d.23 i.verso panel. 7-Mar-93 Butterfield & Butterfield, San Francisco #150/R
$32000	£22222	Near Lone Pine, California (76x91cm-30x36in) s.d.1924. 7-Mar-93 Butterfield & Butterfield, San Francisco #138/R

FROST, John Orne Johnson (1852-1928) American
$4200	£2800	Studies of clipper ships and grandbankers (20x76cm-8x30in) paper on board. 12-Jun-94 Skinner, Bolton #60/R

FUCHSEL, Hermann (1833-1915) American
$1400	£809	The cataract (77x56cm-30x22in) s.d.1895. 25-Sep-92 Sotheby's Arcade, New York #48/R
$1700	£1076	On the lake (28x51cm-11x20in) s. 2-Dec-92 Christie's, East, New York #43/R
$7000	£4895	Fishing on the lake (38x76cm-15x30in) s. 11-Mar-93 Christie's, New York #76/R

FUERTES, Louis Agassiz (1874-1927) American
$3600	£2416	Eagle descending (46x36cm-18x14in) s. W/C board. 1-Dec-93 Doyle, New York #49/R
$3750	£2467	White face tree duck, black bellied tree duck, grey breasted tree duck (25x38cm-10x15in) s.i.d.1906verso gouache paper on board. 4-Nov-92 Doyle, New York #16/R
$4500	£2961	Muscovy duck with mate (25x38cm-10x15in) s. i.verso gouache paper on board. 4-Nov-92 Doyle, New York #12/R
$4500	£2961	Lesser whistling teal, wandering tree duck, fulvous tree duck (25x38cm-10x15in) s.i.d.June 16,1903verso gouache paper on board. 4-Nov-92 Doyle, New York #13/R
$8500	£5705	Scaup ducks on Great Pond (39x54cm-15x21in) s.d.1913 i.verso W/C paperboard. 4-Mar-94 Skinner, Bolton #257/R

FULDE, Edward (19/20th C) American
$3899	£2634	Meal time - kitchen interior with two women and dog , s.d.1909. 19-Apr-94 Rasmussen, Vejle #780/R (D.KR 26000)

FULLER, Arthur Davenport (1889-1967) American
$1200	£694	Boy meets girl (76x66cm-30x26in) s. 27-Sep-92 James Bakker, Cambridge #174/R
$450	£298	Ducks in flight (41x53cm-16x21in) s. W/C. 23-Sep-93 Mystic Fine Arts, Connecticut #150

FULLER, George (1822-1884) American
$1200	£694	Dandelion girl (30x23cm-12x9in) s. board. 27-Sep-92 James Bakker, Cambridge #16/R

FULLER, Richard Henry (1822-1871) American
$950	£664	Landcape in Everett, Mass. (23x33cm-9x13in) s. panel. 7-Feb-93 James Bakker, Cambridge #16
$1400	£809	Cottage in landscape (20x30cm-8x12in) s. panel. 25-Sep-92 Sotheby's Arcade, New York #26/R
$2400	£1387	Landscape with fisherman on pond (38x66cm-15x26in) s. 25-Sep-92 Sotheby's Arcade, New York #55/R

FULTON, Fitch Burt (1879-1955) American
$2250	£1324	Grazing in yard (63x76cm-25x30in) s. 4-Oct-92 Butterfield & Butterfield, Los Angeles #144/R

FULTON, John (20th C) American
$700	£470	Entertainment (46x61cm-18x24in) s. i.verso. 4-Dec-93 Louisiana Auction Exchange #50/R

FULWIDER, Edwin (1913-) American
$13000	£7514	Vanishing American (62x77cm-24x30in) s. st.verso painted 1937. 24-Sep-92 Sotheby's, New York #137/R

FUSSELL, Charles Lewis (1840-?) American
$10000	£6410	Spring blossoms (51x61cm-20x24in) s.d.1902 W/C gouache. 27-May-93 Sotheby's, New York #58/R

FUSTER, Alberto (19th C) Mexican
$850   £545   Roses and painted fan (56x33cm-22x13in) s. 24-May-93 Grogan, Massachussetts #341/R

GAGEN, Robert Ford (1847-1926) Canadian
$697   £471   On Monhegan's cliffs (33x48cm-13x19in) s.d.1906 i.verso W/C. 3-Nov-93 Sotheby's, Toronto #101/R (C.D 900)

GAGNON, Clarence A (1882-1942) Canadian
$1585   £1036   La riviere Vefsna - Helgeland - Norvege (12x18cm-5x7in) d.1934 verso panel. 19-May-93 Sotheby's, Toronto #291/R (C.D 2000)
$1864   £1235   Street scene and building with scaffolding and memorial (70x49cm-28x19in) s. panel. 20-Nov-92 Neumeister, Munich #133 (DM 3000)
$3020   £2041   Ranafjord, Helgeland, Norvege, 1934 (12x17cm-5x7in) panel. 23-Nov-93 Joyner Fine Art, Toronto #81/R (C.D 4000)
$3171   £2073   Moonlight (16x23cm-6x9in) d.1946 verso board. 19-May-93 Sotheby's, Toronto #272/R (C.D 4000)
$4005   £2670   Indian summer, Baie St Paul (15x23cm-6x9in) panel. 13-May-94 Joyner Fine Art, Toronto #102/R (C.D 5500)
$4670   £3093   First snow, October, Delan, Telemark, Norway, 1935 (15x22cm-6x9in) panel. 24-Nov-92 Joyner Fine Art, Toronto #144/R (C.D 6000)
$8562   £5670   Winter day in Laurentians, Baie St. Paul (16x23cm-6x9in) num.169 verso panel painted c.1909. 24-Nov-92 Joyner Fine Art, Toronto #118/R (C.D 11000)
$9816   £6633   Moulin a Baie St. Paul (12x17cm-5x7in) panel painted c.1923. 23-Nov-93 Joyner Fine Art, Toronto #76/R (C.D 13000)
$10848 £7330   A walk through the park Paris (15x22cm-6x9in) s. indist.i.verso panel. 3-Nov-93 Sotheby's, Toronto #246/R (C.D 14000)
$14010 £9278   Evening, Piazza San Marco, Venice (16x22cm-6x9in) s.d.06 panel. 24-Nov-92 Joyner Fine Art, Toronto #78/R (C.D 18000)
$14347 £9694   La maison rose de Baie St. Paul (12x17cm-5x7in) panel painted c.1924. 23-Nov-93 Joyner Fine Art, Toronto #27/R (C.D 19000)
$14789 £9794   Clair de Lune d'hiver a Baie St Paul (16x22cm-6x9in) s. panel. 18-Nov-92 Sotheby's, Toronto #213/R (C.D 19000)
$15855 £10363 Shy model (92x62cm-36x24in) s.d.1903. 18-May-93 Joyner Fine Art, Toronto #60/R (C.D 20000)
$38918 £25773 Village in winter, Poully, Switzerland (60x81cm-24x32in) s. 18-Nov-92 Sotheby's, Toronto #52/R (C.D 50000)
$72816 £48544 Midnight mass (18x21cm-7x8in) paper on board. 13-May-94 Joyner Fine Art, Toronto #51/R (C.D 100000)
$613   £420   A huntsman on skis with his alsatian (43x25cm-17x10in) s. pencil W/C htd white. 16-Feb-94 Christie's, S. Kensington #69
$3099   £2094   Study for Le Grand Silence Blanc (15x15cm-6x6in) s. gouache. 3-Nov-93 Sotheby's, Toronto #160/R (C.D 4000)
$10702 £6995   Apres la tempete (63x93cm-25x37in) studio st. W/C pastel. 19-May-93 Sotheby's, Toronto #299/R (C.D 13500)

GAGNON, Clarence A (attrib) (1882-1942) Canadian
$617   £417   Untitled - Lake in mountains (50x66cm-20x26in) s. 25-Apr-94 Levis, Calgary #86/R (C.D 850)

GALAN, Julio (1958-) Mexican
$6500   £4305   El Juego (51x66cm-20x26in) s.i.d.84 oil collage canvas. 24-Nov-92 Christie's, New York #338/R
$9500   £6333   El baile de las 9 (80x60cm-31x24in) oil pastel mica collage canvas painted c.1985. 18-May-94 Sotheby's, New York #333/R

GALE, Dennis (1828-1903) Canadian?
$778   £515   Moonlight sleigh ride (15x23cm-6x9in) s. W/C. 18-Nov-92 Sotheby's, Toronto #295/R (C.D 1000)

GALGIANI, Oscar (1903-) American
$850   £563   Sunburst east of the Sierra Nevada (76x91cm-30x36in) s. 28-Sep-93 John Moran, Pasadena #234
$1500   £1014   Mountain landscape (64x76cm-25x30in) s.d.56. 15-Jun-93 John Moran, Pasadena #124

GALLATIN, Albert E (1881-1952) American
$5000   £3333   No 72 (37x25cm-15x10in) s.d.1943verso canvasboard. 16-Mar-94 Christie's, New York #129/R
$7000   £4046   Composition (41x30cm-16x12in) s.d.1938verso. 23-Sep-92 Christie's, New York #232/R
$9500   £6276   Composition 42 (61x41cm-24x16in) s.d.January 1942verso. 4-May-94 Doyle, New York #77/R

GALLISON, Henry Hammond (1850-1910) American
$3250   £2196   A grey day (89x114cm-35x45in) s. painted c.1898. 31-Mar-94 Sotheby's Arcade, New York #183/R

GALVAN, Jesus Guerrero see GUERRERO GALVAN, Jesus

GAMARRA, Gregorio (c.1570-1642) Bolivian
$14000 £9272   Assumption of Virgin (121x104cm-48x41in) 24-Nov-92 Christie's, New York #65/R

GAMARRA, Gregorio (attrib) (c.1570-1642) Bolivian
$24000   £15894   Saint Sebastian (145x104cm-57x41in) painted c.1620. 24-Nov-92 Christie's, New York #66/R

GAMARRA, Jose (1934-) Uruguayan
$12000   £8000   Pintura P.64114 (202x201cm-80x79in) s.d.1964 s.i.d.verso. 18-May-94 Christie's, New York #259/R

GAMBARTES, Leonidas (1909-1963) Argentinian
$2500   £1302   Figuras en el paisaje (22x31cm-9x12in) tempera. 4-Aug-92 VerBo, Buenos Aires #53/R
$3200   *£2133*   *Las Curanderas (45x32cm-18x13in) s.d.51 gouache gessoed board. 18-May-94 Christie's, New York #265/R*

GAMBLE, John M (1863-1957) American
$1900   £1118   Spring landscape (33x41cm-13x16in) s. board. 4-Oct-92 Butterfield & Butterfield, Los Angeles #121/R
$3250   £1912   California gold (41x61cm-16x24in) s. masonite. 4-Oct-92 Butterfield & Butterfield, Los Angeles #87/R
$7000   £4861   Hillside with lupines (36x25cm-14x10in) s. canvas on board. 7-Mar-93 Butterfield & Butterfield, San Francisco #189/R
$8500   £5903   Wildflowers near Litton Springs (30x41cm-12x16in) s.d.1904 i.verso. 7-Mar-93 Butterfield & Butterfield, San Francisco #194/R
$16000   £10738   Poppy field near Banning (46x62cm-18x24in) s. i.verso. 8-Dec-93 Butterfield & Butterfield, San Francisco #3447/R
$20000   £13889   Morning mists, wild lilac (51x76cm-20x30in) s. s.i.verso. 7-Mar-93 Butterfield & Butterfield, San Francisco #128/R
$2250   *£1562*   *Poppies and lupines (22x23cm-9x9in) s. gouache paperboard. 7-Mar-93 Butterfield & Butterfield, San Francisco #195/R*

GAMBLE, Roy C (1887-1964) American
$1200   £625   Portrait of artist's brother with cat (91x71cm-36x28in) s.d.1911 canvas on masonite. 5-Aug-92 Boos Gallery, Michigan #549/R

GAMMELL, Robert Hale Ives (1893-1981) American
$6000   £3974   Era's End (46x32cm-18x13in) s.d.1967 masonite. 22-Sep-93 Christie's, New York #188/R
$1100   *£769*   *Anthony (64x51cm-25x20in) s.d.1938 chl.crayon. 7-Feb-93 James Bakker, Cambridge #27*

GANDIA, Vicente (?) Mexican
$3820   £2449   Copa de agua (30x38cm-12x15in) s.d.62 fibracel. 29-Apr-93 Louis Morton, Mexico #178 (M.P 12000)
$541   *£361*   *Sandias (60x76cm-24x30in) s. ink wash. 25-May-94 Louis Morton, Mexico #36 (M.P 1800)*
$601   *£401*   *Muchacha (42x29cm-17x11in) s. ink. 25-May-94 Louis Morton, Mexico #131 (M.P 2000)*

GANSO, Emil (1895-1941) American
$900   £604   Rural landscape (61x76cm-24x30in) s.d.34 board. 5-Dec-93 James Bakker, Cambridge #27/R
$1900   £1275   Self portrait (30x23cm-12x9in) s. board. 24-Jun-93 Mystic Fine Arts, Connecticut #117
$3900   £2583   Nude in armchair (43x53cm-17x21in) s. board. 21-Nov-92 James Bakker, Cambridge #314/R
$4750   £2746   Sleeping nude with stockings (36x53cm-14x21in) s. 25-Sep-92 Sotheby's Arcade, New York #294/R
$877   £585   Nu allonge (46x35cm-18x14in) s. black crayon stumping. 8-Jun-94 Poulain & le Fur, Paris #88 (F.FR 5000)
$950   *£549*   *Reclining nude (48x33cm-19x13in) s.d.29 chl pastel. 23-Sep-92 Christie's, New York #261/R*
$1300   *£751*   *Reclining nude (41x58cm-16x23in) s.i. chl col.chk. 25-Sep-92 Sotheby's Arcade, New York #302/R*

GARBER, Daniel (1880-1958) American
$1200   £759   Landscape (33x46cm-13x18in) s. 30-Nov-92 Selkirks, St. Louis #254/R
$10000   £6623   Passing canoe (25x33cm-10x13in) s. i.verso board. 23-Sep-93 Sotheby's, New York #197/R
$11000   £7285   Antonins' (29x34cm-11x13in) s. i.verso panel. 23-Sep-93 Sotheby's, New York #196/R
$22000   £14570   April 30th (46x61cm-18x24in) s.d.1952 i.verso board. 23-Sep-93 Sotheby's, New York #198/R
$65000   £41139   Along the Delaware (72x76cm-28x30in) s. 4-Dec-92 Christie's, New York #48/R
$360000   £240000   Mending (117x107cm-46x42in) s. painted 1918. 25-May-94 Sotheby's, New York #74/R
$450   *£300*   *Profile of a woman (62x46cm-24x18in) s. chl. 17-May-94 Christie's, East, New York #530*

GARCIA AMARO, Cecilia (20th C) Mexican
$1119   £756   Patrones (74x56cm-29x22in) s.d.1993 mixed media. 20-Oct-93 Louis Morton, Mexico #24/R (M.P 3500)

GARCIA CABRAL, Ernesto (20th C) Mexican
$1210   £776   Antonio Rivas Mercado (35x26cm-14x10in) s.d.1911 ink W/C. 29-Apr-93 Louis Morton, Mexico #12 (M.P 3800)

GARCIA DE ARIAS, Pilar (20th C) Mexican
$1023 £691 Sandias (80x90cm-31x35in) s.d.1993. 20-Oct-93 Louis Morton, Mexico #70/R (M.P 3200)

GARCIA SANTA OLALLA, Francisco (19th C) Brazilian
$27000 £18243 Columbus before the Spanish Court after his return from the Americas (71x98cm-28x39in) s.d.1894. 23-Nov-93 Christie's, New York #82/R
$50000 £33113 Columbus before Spanish Court after return from Americas (71x98cm-28x39in) s.d.1894. 24-Nov-92 Christie's, New York #81/R

GARCIA, Juan Gil (1879-?) Cuban
$3000 £2027 Pina, Guanabana y Zapote (34x70cm-13x28in) s.d.1918. 22-Nov-93 Sotheby's, New York #168/R

GARDNER, Elisabeth Jeanne see BOUGUEREAU, Elizabeth Gardner

GARET, Jedd (1955-) American
$1500 £1000 Poisoned gems (185x145cm-73x57in) s.i.d.1985verso. 26-May-94 Christie's, London #161/R
$4000 £2649 She (185x144cm-73x57in) s.d.1987 verso acrylic. 30-Jun-93 Sotheby's Arcade, New York #374/R
$5000 £3356 Slide (186x145cm-73x57in) s.d.1981 verso acrylic. 24-Feb-94 Sotheby's Arcade, New York #473/R
$1400 £946 Interior with spiral rug (36x60cm-14x24in) s.i.d.1978verso pastel pair. 21-Apr-94 Butterfield & Butterfield, San Francisco #1167/R

GARRETT, Edmund (1853-1929) American
$650 £433 Porto Rico, bucayo trees and cocoanut palms (63x76cm-25x30in) s.i. i.verso. 12-Mar-94 Weschler, Washington #157
$1000 £694 Stag hounds, Somerset village (51x61cm-20x24in) s. 27-Feb-93 Young Fine Arts Auctions, Maine #113/R
$3000 £1923 Peacocks in the garden (76x63cm-30x25in) s. 9-Dec-92 Butterfield & Butterfield, San Francisco #3907/R

GARRISON, H (19th C) American
$575 £386 Palisades, N. J. (30x51cm-12x20in) s. W/C. 29-Nov-93 Stonington Fine Arts, Stonington #217/R

GARSIDE, Thomas H (1906-1980) Canadian
$603 £410 Winter river scene (29x39cm-11x15in) s. 15-Nov-93 Hodgins, Calgary #275/R (C.D 800)
$745 £477 Pen-Y-Bryn, Bury, Quebec (46x61cm-18x24in) s. 7-Dec-92 Waddingtons, Toronto #1273 (C.D 950)
$740 £500 Spring Mount Tremblant, Quebec Province (40x50cm-16x20in) s. bears i.verso col pastel. 26-Oct-93 Sotheby's, Billingshurst #40/R
$1019 £680 Spring, Mount Tremblant, P.Q. (41x51cm-16x20in) s. s.i.verso pastel. 11-May-94 Sotheby's, Toronto #48/R (C.D 1400)

GASSER, Henry (1909-1981) American
$1600 £1006 Activity in Gloucester Harbour (51x71cm-20x28in) s. 22-Apr-93 Freeman Fine Arts, Philadelphia #1341/R
$450 £300 Coal mining town (48x59cm-19x23in) s. W/C. 17-May-94 Christie's, East, New York #534
$500 £331 Harbour town (38x56cm-15x22in) s. W/C. 23-Sep-93 Mystic Fine Arts, Connecticut #82/R
$550 £369 Monday morning - Montmartre (20x25cm-8x10in) s.i. W/C. 4-Dec-93 Louisiana Auction Exchange #102/R
$600 £390 Entrance to the ruins (34x55cm-13x22in) s.i. i.verso W/C paper on board. 9-Sep-93 Sotheby's Arcade, New York #385/R
$600 £417 Return to the mines (25x36cm-10x14in) s. W/C. 27-Feb-93 Young Fine Arts Auctions, Maine #114/R
$700 £464 Waterfront (30x48cm-12x19in) s. W/C. 28-Nov-92 Dunning's, Illinois #1026
$700 £405 The walk home (48x60cm-19x24in) s. W/C pencil paper on board. 25-Sep-92 Sotheby's Arcade, New York #399/R
$750 £490 Paris street scene (53x36cm-21x14in) s. W/C. 18-Sep-93 James Bakker, Cambridge #44/R
$750 £472 Valley springtime (74x41cm-29x16in) s. W/C. 22-Apr-93 Freeman Fine Arts, Philadelphia #1255
$850 £575 Winter waterfront (57x76cm-22x30in) s. W/C pencil paper on board. 31-Mar-94 Sotheby's Arcade, New York #409/R
$850 £556 Night market (24x19cm-9x7in) s. W/C. 4-May-93 Christie's, East, New York #295/R
$900 £584 Windy harbour (56x71cm-22x28in) s. i.verso W/C paper on board. 9-Sep-93 Sotheby's Arcade, New York #381/R
$950 £617 Winter home (46x65cm-18x26in) s. W/C board. 9-Sep-93 Sotheby's Arcade, New York #382/R
$1000 £658 Summer afternoon in Rome (56x38cm-22x15in) s.i. W/C pencil paper on board. 31-Mar-93 Sotheby's Arcade, New York #406/R
$1000 £680 Street scene in snow (38x56cm-15x22in) s. W/C. 15-Nov-93 Christie's, East, New York #261/R
$1100 £696 Rural town scene (48x61cm-19x24in) s. W/C. 2-Dec-92 Christie's, East, New York #283
$1100 £733 Newark neighbourhood (36x51cm-14x20in) s. W/C. 22-May-94 James Bakker, Cambridge #36/R
$1200 £694 Winter harbour (56x79cm-22x31in) s. i.verso W/C. 25-Sep-92 Sotheby's Arcade, New York #329/R

GASSER, Henry (1909-1981) American-cont.
$1300	£751	Town covered in snow (57x79cm-22x31in) s. W/C pencil paper on paper. 25-Sep-92 Sotheby's Arcade, New York #334/R
$1500	£1014	Montmartre (28x56cm-11x22in) s.i. W/C. 27-Nov-93 Young Fine Arts Auctions, Maine #139/R
$1500	£1000	Port scene (53x74cm-21x29in) s. W/C. 22-May-94 James Bakker, Cambridge #106/R
$1700	£1111	New England winter (56x71cm-22x28in) s. W/C. 18-Sep-93 James Bakker, Cambridge #37/R
$1800	£1216	First snowfall, Broad Street, Newark (41x57cm-16x22in) s. W/C paper on board executed 1941. 31-Mar-94 Sotheby's Arcade, New York #451/R
$2000	£1316	Houses in country (56x76cm-22x30in) s. W/C graphite. 31-Mar-93 Sotheby's Arcade, New York #402/R
$2200	£1447	Hoffman House (39x57cm-15x22in) s. W/C. 31-Mar-93 Sotheby's Arcade, New York #407/R
$2500	£1689	Engelhorn's bar and grill, Newark Tavern (56x76cm-22x30in) s. W/C board. 31-Mar-94 Sotheby's Arcade, New York #417/R

GATCH, Lee (1902-1968) American
$550	£367	Vacation (36x50cm-14x20in) s. 23-May-94 Christie's, East, New York #265
$950	£634	Self-portrait (41x31cm-16x12in) painted 1925. 23-May-94 Christie's, East, New York #229/R
$1100	£733	Migration (18x81cm-7x32in) s. i.verso canvas on panel painted 1954. 23-May-94 Christie's, East, New York #263/R
$1300	£855	Lamb (18x82cm-7x32in) s. st.verso canvas on panel painted 1954. 31-Mar-93 Sotheby's Arcade, New York #454/R
$1400	£933	Hemlock (43x59cm-17x23in) s. painted 1957. 23-May-94 Christie's, East, New York #237/R
$1400	£909	Basketball (19x15cm-7x6in) s. panel painted 1954. 9-Sep-93 Sotheby's Arcade, New York #444/R
$3000	£2027	Pennsylvania farm (36x114cm-14x45in) s. 31-Mar-94 Sotheby's Arcade, New York #478/R
$1700	£1118	Corridor (98x64cm-39x25in) s.d.60 oil collage canvas. 31-Mar-93 Sotheby's Arcade, New York #457/R

GATTO, Victor Joseph (1893-1965) American
$1400	£927	The Lorelei (41x51cm-16x20in) painted c.1947 canvas board. 21-Nov-92 Litchfield Auction Gallery #15
$2100	£1391	Jungle Scene (61x76cm-24x30in) s.verso d.1942. 21-Nov-92 Litchfield Auction Gallery #17

GATTORNO, Antonio (20th C) South American
$3600	£2384	Agricultores (44x49cm-17x19in) s.d.1935 gouache pen paper on board. 24-Nov-92 Christie's, New York #311/R

GAUCHER, Yves (1933-) Canadian
$1585	£1036	Etude pour progression bi-ascendante (25x51cm-10x20in) painted 1965. 18-May-93 Joyner Fine Art, Toronto #7/R (C.D 2000)
$1946	£1289	Square dance - Zing went the string (76x76cm-30x30in) s.i.d.64 acrylic. 18-Nov-92 Sotheby's, Toronto #178/R (C.D 2500)
$2039	£1359	Square dance - zing went the string (75x75cm-30x30in) s.i.d.64 verso acrylic. 13-May-94 Joyner Fine Art, Toronto #135/R (C.D 2800)

GAUL, Gilbert (1855-1919) American
$1122	£753	Portrait of young woman with fan seated by window (90x68cm-35x27in) s.d.1872. 22-Feb-94 Rasmussen, Vejle #967 (D.KR 7500)
$1500	£1000	Fetching water (39x29cm-15x11in) s. 23-May-94 Christie's, East, New York #201
$4000	£2312	The boatbuilder (30x41cm-12x16in) s. canvas on board. 25-Sep-92 Sotheby's Arcade, New York #155/R
$4000	£2667	Man carrying sticks at dusk (63x76cm-25x30in) s. 16-Mar-94 Christie's, New York #84/R
$4500	£3041	On the Hudson (30x41cm-12x16in) one of pair. 10-Aug-93 Stonington Fine Arts, Stonington #160/R
$8500	£5705	The Indian encampment (57x72cm-22x28in) s. 4-Mar-94 Skinner, Bolton #204/R
$12000	£7692	Meeting of Elders (46x61cm-18x24in) s. 26-May-93 Christie's, New York #113/R
$14000	£9396	Young hunter (63x76cm-25x30in) s. 3-Dec-93 Christie's, New York #70/R
$25000	£15823	Cold comfort on the outpost (63x77cm-25x30in) s. 2-Dec-92 Christie's, East, New York #203/R

GAULEY, Robert David (1875-1943) American
$900	£596	Hillside flowers (56x76cm-22x30in) 28-Nov-92 Young Fine Arts Auctions, Maine #171/R
$1800	£1154	Helene and Blanquito (93x75cm-37x30in) s.d.1917-1920. 9-Dec-92 Butterfield & Butterfield, San Francisco #3927/R

GAUTHIER, Joachim (1897-1988) Canadian
$624	£410	Start of autumn (30x38cm-12x15in) s. i.verso board. 7-Jun-93 Waddingtons, Toronto #1103 (C.D 800)
$641	£434	In Georgian Bay (30x37cm-12x15in) s. canvas on board. 23-Nov-93 Joyner Fine Art, Toronto #247 (C.D 850)
$1019	£680	Coming storm - Haliburton (30x37cm-12x15in) s. board. 13-May-94 Joyner Fine Art, Toronto #178/R (C.D 1400)
$1585	£1036	Cloudy landscape with river (76x91cm-30x36in) s. board. 19-May-93 Sotheby's, Toronto #377/R (C.D 2000)
$2378	£1554	Baie Finn Range (77x92cm-30x36in) s.d.36. 19-May-93 Sotheby's, Toronto #280/R (C.D 3000)

GAUTHIER, Joachim (1897-1988) Canadian-cont.
$555   £363   Northern landscape (29x38cm-11x15in) s. W/C. 19-May-93 Sotheby's, Toronto #28 (C.D 700)

GAW, William Alexander (1891-1973) American
$6500   £4362   Belevedere Lagoon (41x51cm-16x20in) s. s.i.stretcher. 8-Dec-93 Butterfield & Butterfield, San Francisco #3460/R
$2750   £1618   Old wharf, Pittsburg (41x51cm-16x20in) s. W/C. 4-Oct-92 Butterfield & Butterfield, Los Angeles #261/R

GAY, Edward (1837-1928) American
$550   £369   Landscape (84x51cm-33x20in) s.d.1924 board. 29-Nov-93 Stonington Fine Arts, Stonington #81/R
$850   £575   Town dock, East Chester (46x38cm-18x15in) s. canvasboard. 31-Mar-94 Sotheby's Arcade, New York #149/R
$950   £621   Resting by brook (38x53cm-15x21in) s. 4-May-93 Christie's, East, New York #86/R
$1100   £719   November landscape at dusk (46x61cm-18x24in) s. 7-Oct-93 Freeman Fine Arts, Philadelphia #949
$1265   £811   Haying scene (13x36cm-5x14in) s. panel. 17-Dec-92 Mystic Fine Arts, Connecticut #224/R
$1300   £823   Quiet pool (25x35cm-10x14in) s.d.1906 canvasboard. 2-Dec-92 Christie's, East, New York #16
$1700   £1126   Country landscape (46x51cm-18x20in) s. 2-Oct-93 Weschler, Washington #101/R
$1700   £1111   Sheep grazing underneath appleblossoms (43x68cm-17x27in) s. canvas on masonite. 4-May-93 Christie's, East, New York #84/R
$1800   £1200   City Island (112x168cm-44x66in) s. 1-Jun-94 Doyle, New York #30
$2000   £1307   Harvest (51x74cm-20x29in) s. panel. 30-Jun-94 Mystic Fine Arts, Connecticut #50 c
$2600   £1711   Winter scene (51x41cm-20x16in) s.d.1879. 31-Mar-93 Sotheby's Arcade, New York #52/R
$3500   £2381   Glenn Island looking towards Travers Island (51x41cm-20x16in) s. 15-Nov-93 Christie's, East, New York #116/R
$9000   £6122   Gathering bait (51x91cm-20x36in) s. 15-Nov-93 Christie's, East, New York #142/R

GAY, George Howell (1858-1931) American
$450   £298   Seascape with ships on the horizon (33x79cm-13x31in) s. W/C. 17-Jun-94 Du Mouchelle, Detroit #2228/R
$450   £302   Landscape (33x51cm-13x20in) s. W/C gouache. 5-Mar-94 Louisiana Auction Exchange #126/R
$550   £359   Seascape (41x64cm-16x25in) s. W/C. 15-May-93 Dunning's, Illinois #1128
$600   £400   Breaking surf (43x69cm-17x27in) s. W/C. 23-May-94 Hindman Galleries, Chicago #185
$600   £347   Seascape (39x85cm-15x33in) s. W/C paper on board. 25-Sep-92 Sotheby's Arcade, New York #60
$650   £411   Seascape (61x91cm-24x36in) W/C. 24-Oct-92 San Rafael Auction Galleries #229
$800   £537   Seascape (38x61cm-15x24in) s. W/C. 5-Mar-94 Louisiana Auction Exchange #125/R
$850   £563   Surf on the rocks (61x91cm-24x36in) s. W/C. 28-Nov-92 Young Fine Arts Auctions, Maine #172/R
$1000   £529   Landscape with stream (36x69cm-14x27in) s. W/C. 12-Sep-92 Louisiana Auction Exchange #51/R
$1200   £784   Rolling tide (33x79cm-13x31in) s. W/C gouache. 5-May-93 Doyle, New York #15/R
$3500   £2215   Surf at Northampton, Long Island (40x99cm-16x39in) s. W/C. 3-Dec-92 Sotheby's, New York #24/R

GAY, Walter (1856-1937) American
$2500   £1645   Bedroom. Man and machine (92x65cm-36x26in) s. one attrib. pair. 31-Mar-93 Sotheby's Arcade, New York #145/R
$2500   £1689   Sunrise in a Japanese village (41x56cm-16x22in) s. 31-Mar-94 Sotheby's Arcade, New York #161/R
$3800   £2484   Still life with blue and white porcelain (55x46cm-22x18in) s. 4-May-93 Christie's, East, New York #153/R
$4000   £2312   Blue and white wares (55x46cm-22x18in) s. board. 25-Sep-92 Sotheby's Arcade, New York #312/R
$6600   £4400   An interior scene (55x46cm-22x18in) s. 25-May-94 Sotheby's, Billingshurst #447/R
$8000   £5128   Interior, Chateau du Breau (55x45cm-22x18in) s. panel. 26-May-93 Christie's, New York #68/R
$8500   £5667   The chemist (39x28cm-15x11in) s. panel. 17-Mar-94 Sotheby's, New York #10 a/R
$24000   £15385   Charity (244x221cm-96x87in) s.d.1889. 27-May-93 Sotheby's, New York #43/R
$550   £367   Living room interior (41x28cm-16x11in) s.d.1880 i.verso W/C. 26-Aug-93 Skinner, Bolton #71
$950   £642   Quietude an interior scene with young woman reading (39x54cm-15x21in) s.d.1882 W/C. 5-Nov-93 Skinner, Bolton #140/R
$4200   £2428   Interior of the library, Chateau du Breau (37x28cm-15x11in) s. W/C pencil. 23-Sep-92 Christie's, New York #133/R
$7250   £4191   The mantel (37x28cm-15x11in) s. W/C gouache. 25-Sep-92 Sotheby's Arcade, New York #147/R

GAY, Winkworth Allen (1821-1910) American
$750   £490   Tree study (20x30cm-8x12in) board. 30-Oct-92 Sloan, North Bethesda #2172
$836   £550   Shepherd with flock of sheep by farm (17x22cm-7x9in) s. s.indis.i.verso panel. 7-Apr-93 Sotheby's Colonnade, London #8/R
$900   £588   Little valley , 30-Oct-92 Sloan, North Bethesda #2173
$1400   £909   Landscape near Kyoto (43x29cm-17x11in) s.i. canvasboard. 9-Sep-93 Sotheby's Arcade, New York #87/R
$1400   £909   Landscape (29x43cm-11x17in) s. canvasboard. 9-Sep-93 Sotheby's Arcade, New York #86/R

GAY, Winkworth Allen (1821-1910) American-cont.
$2400   £1558   Landscape near Inoshino (28x43cm-11x17in) s.i. canvasboard. 9-Sep-93 Sotheby's Arcade, New York #88/R

GAYLOR, Samuel Wood (1883-?) American
$1200   £839   Central Park, New York (27x41cm-11x16in) s.i.d.1918 W/C pencil. 11-Mar-93 Christie's, New York #187/R

GAZE, Harold (20th C) American
$1600   £1074   Spring fairies with red roses (33x26cm-13x10in) s.d.1956 W/C pen htd white. 8-Dec-93 Butterfield & Butterfield, San Francisco #3378/R
$1600   £1026   Water fairies (34x26cm-13x10in) s.d.1942 W/C pen htd white. 9-Dec-92 Butterfield & Butterfield, San Francisco #3957/R
$1600   £1026   Fairy on swing (36x30cm-14x12in) s.d.1947 pen W/C htd white. 9-Dec-92 Butterfield & Butterfield, San Francisco #3956/R
$1600   £1074   Water babies (33x26cm-13x10in) s.d.1951 W/C pen htd white. 8-Dec-93 Butterfield & Butterfield, San Francisco #3377/R

GAZUL, Xaviar (1783-?) Haitian
$4200   £2897   Children of the Duc de Marmelade (49x39cm-19x15in) i. one d.1817 one d.1819 pair. 27-Jan-93 Christie's, New York #30

GECHTOFF, Leonid (19/20th C) American
$1500   £1049   Western scenery (64x76cm-25x30in) s. s.d.1937 verso. 5-Feb-93 Sloan, North Bethesda #1693
$650   £409   Red Mosque of Prophet Aly, Cairo (61x76cm-24x30in) s.d.40 pastel. 22-Apr-93 Freeman Fine Arts, Philadelphia #1192
$775   £487   Vase of flowers (74x61cm-29x24in) s.d.33 pencil pastel. 22-Apr-93 Freeman Fine Arts, Philadelphia #1310

GECHTOFF, Sonia (1926-) American
$900   £608   Two figures (145x100cm-57x39in) s.d.55verso. 21-Apr-94 Butterfield & Butterfield, San Francisco #1094/R

GEDOVIUS, German (1867-1937) Mexican
$10220   £6814   Retrato de nino (191x91cm-75x36in) s.d.1901. 25-May-94 Louis Morton, Mexico #75/R (M.P 34000)

GEERTS, Casey (20th C) American
$550   £377   Illustration of Classic cars (119x58cm-47x23in) s.d.77 acrylic board. 18-Feb-94 Du Mouchelle, Detroit #1157/R

GEMMA, Joseph P di (1910-) American
$990   £647   View of Rockport harbour (61x91cm-24x36in) s. masonite. 14-May-93 Skinner, Bolton #135/R

GENDRON, Pierre (1934-) Canadian
$1092   £728   Epine (79x69cm-31x27in) s.d.60 i.stretcher. 11-May-94 Sotheby's, Toronto #105/R (C.D 1500)

GENN, Robert (1936-) Canadian
$505   £341   Copse Monument (30x41cm-12x16in) s. 30-Mar-94 Maynards, Vancouver #11 (C.D 700)
$523   £354   Fantasy - Long Harbour, Saltspring Island (28x36cm-11x14in) s. 30-Mar-94 Maynards, Vancouver #12 (C.D 725)
$540   £350   Jasper group (30x25cm-12x10in) s. board. 22-Jun-94 Maynards, Vancouver #673 (C.D 750)
$576   £374   Blown gulf (25x30cm-10x12in) s.d.1977 board. 22-Jun-94 Maynards, Vancouver #674 (C.D 800)
$612   £397   The bridge (20x25cm-8x10in) painted 1971. 22-Jun-94 Maynards, Vancouver #683 (C.D 850)
$1223   £794   Sara sunny spirit in gulf change (51x61cm-20x24in) painted 1986. 22-Jun-94 Maynards, Vancouver #681 (C.D 1700)
$1245   £825   Afternoon Effingham (56x76cm-22x30in) s. s.i.d.1977verso. 16-Nov-92 Hodgins, Calgary #330/R (C.D 1600)
$1362   £902   West boat haven (76x86cm-30x34in) s. i.d.1978verso. 18-Nov-92 Sotheby's, Toronto #89/R (C.D 1750)

GENTH, Lillian (1876-1953) American
$700   £467   Spanish ladies on a balcony (26x21cm-10x8in) s. board. 21-May-94 Weschler, Washington #126/R
$1000   £662   Carmel (25x36cm-10x14in) s. panel. 15-Jun-94 Butterfield & Butterfield, San Francisco #4615 a
$1000   £633   Corner Cafe (20x25cm-8x10in) s. 3-Dec-92 Freeman Fine Arts, Philadelphia #1838/R
$2200   £1392   Looking out of window to flower garden (74x61cm-29x24in) s. 2-Dec-92 Christie's, East, New York #153/R
$2200   £1429   Bull fight (51x38cm-20x15in) s. i.verso. 9-Sep-93 Sotheby's Arcade, New York #329/R
$2600   £1646   Nude wading by stream (58x46cm-23x18in) s. 2-Dec-92 Christie's, East, New York #149/R
$3000   £2013   Grand Canal Venice (51x64cm-20x25in) s.i.d.1903. 2-Dec-93 Freeman Fine Arts, Philadelphia #856/R
$7750   £5033   Springtime (99x76cm-39x30in) s. 9-Sep-93 Sotheby's Arcade, New York #94/R
$8500   £4913   Corner cafe (41x51cm-16x20in) s. 23-Sep-92 Christie's, New York #202/R

GEORGES (20th C) Haitian
$1057   £695   Combat naval (41x65cm-16x26in) s. 9-Jun-93 Lenormand, Paris #209 (F.FR 5800)

GEORGI, Edwin (1896-1964) American
$550   £369   Confidential chat (59x56cm-23x22in) ink gouache illustration board. 6-May-94 Skinner, Bolton #169/R
$725   £487   Lovers (36x38cm-14x15in) gouache. 24-Jun-93 Mystic Fine Arts, Connecticut #247
$770   £503   Illustration for story 'Going Away' in Redbook Magazine, December 1954 (56x76cm-22x30in) W/C gouache illustration board. 14-May-93 Skinner, Bolton #201/R
$1320   £863   Illustration for story 'Intentions Complicated' in Saturday Evening Post (69x53cm-27x21in) W/C gouache illustration board. 14-May-93 Skinner, Bolton #200/R

GERLERO, Renata (20th C) Mexican
$1215   £821   Higos (61x76cm-24x30in) 20-Oct-93 Louis Morton, Mexico #49/R (M.P 3800)

GERRY, Samuel Lancaster (1813-1891) American
$900   £596   Wooded stream (51x36cm-20x14in) s. i.verso. 13-Nov-92 Skinner, Bolton #73/R
$950   £621   Landscape near Medfield (25x41cm-10x16in) mono. 8-May-93 Young Fine Arts Auctions, Maine #120/R
$1100   £743   The shepherdess leading her flock home (56x46cm-22x18in) s. 31-Mar-94 Sotheby's Arcade, New York #56/R
$1200   £805   Harris Grounds, Roxbury (43x53cm-17x21in) s. i.stretcher. 6-Dec-93 Grogan, Massachussetts #496
$6000   £4027   Lake George (41x76cm-16x30in) s. i.verso. 4-Mar-94 Skinner, Bolton #207/R
$10000   £5780   Mt Washington vista (51x76cm-20x30in) s.d.185. 23-Sep-92 Christie's, New York #53/R
$10000   £6993   Road to the mountains (45x87cm-18x34in) s. 11-Mar-93 Christie's, New York #23/R
$700   £370   Lake shore, early autumn (23x30cm-9x12in) s. W/C gouache graphite. 11-Sep-92 Skinner, Bolton #189/R

GERVAIS, Lise (1933-) Canadian
$903   £606   Eroica II (35x41cm-14x16in) s.i.d.1958 verso board. 29-Nov-93 Waddingtons, Toronto #1070 (C.D 1200)
$1204   £808   The Devils Lighthouse (81x91cm-32x36in) s.d.59 s.verso masonite. 29-Nov-93 Ritchie, Toronto #227/R (C.D 1600)
$1820   £1214   Prismes paralleles (61x92cm-24x36in) s.d.79 s.i.d.verso. 11-May-94 Sotheby's, Toronto #107/R (C.D 2500)

GERZSO, Gunther (1915-) Mexican
$22000   £14667   Azul-Verde (25x37cm-10x15in) s.d.70 s.i.d.verso masonite. 18-May-94 Christie's, New York #135/R
$30000   £19868   Naranja-Azul-Verde (70x89cm-28x35in) s. s.d.79 verso acryliuc sand masonite. 23-Nov-92 Sotheby's, New York #68/R
$34102   £22887   Untitled (63x109cm-25x43in) s. panel painted 1957. 8-May-94 Jonquet, Paris #93 (F.FR 195000)
$35000   £23649   Mitologia (54x81cm-21x32in) s.d.61 s.i.d.VIII.61 verso. 22-Nov-93 Sotheby's, New York #228/R
$38000   £25333   Untitled (38x56cm-15x22in) s.d.62 oil sand panel. 18-May-94 Christie's, New York #136/R
$38000   £25166   Rojo, Azul y Amarillo (38x46cm-15x18in) s.d.66 s.i.d.XII-66 verso. 24-Nov-92 Christie's, New York #48/R
$38000   £25166   Personaje - paisaje (72x53cm-28x21in) s.d.64 s.i.d.XII.64 verso. 24-Nov-92 Christie's, New York #112/R
$60000   £39216   Recuerdo de Grecia (94x75cm-37x30in) s.d.59 s.i.d.59 oil sand board. 17-May-93 Christie's, New York #26/R
$5805   £3896   Estructura (34x21cm-13x8in) s. mixed media. 1-Dec-93 Louis Morton, Mexico #25/R (M.P 18000)
$7500   £5000   Puente Dos (43x34cm-17x13in) s.d.72 i.d.verso mixed media. 18-May-94 Christie's, New York #199/R
$9500   £6209   Untitled (52x39cm-20x15in) s.d.V.55 gouache pencil. 17-May-93 Christie's, New York #229/R

GESLIN, Jacques (1954-) Haitian
$905   £592   Jungle domestique (51x41cm-20x16in) painted 1979. 17-May-93 Hoebanx, Paris #99 (F.FR 5000)

GEYER, Herman (19th C) American
$1600   £1074   The passing front - an Adirondack view (56x92cm-22x36in) s. 4-Mar-94 Skinner, Bolton #205/R

GIBBS, Len (1929-) Canadian
$2775   £1813   Distant call (70x43cm-28x17in) s. acrylic board. 19-May-93 Sotheby's, Toronto #359/R (C.D 3500)
$603   £410   Log homestead (20x38cm-8x15in) s. bears i.verso W/C. 15-Nov-93 Hodgins, Calgary #52 (C.D 800)
$778   £515   Laura's summer (56x66cm-22x26in) s.i.d.7/30/91verso W/C. 18-Nov-92 Sotheby's, Toronto #220/R (C.D 1000)
$905   £615   Near Rae's Barn (41x20cm-16x8in) s. bears i.verso drybrush W/C. 15-Nov-93 Hodgins, Calgary #236 (C.D 1200)

GIBBS, T Bunny (19/20th C) American
$1100   £719   Portrait of young girl (121x61cm-48x24in) s. 4-May-93 Christie's, East, New York #174/R

GIBRAN, Kahlil (1883-1931) American/Syrian
$5500   £3741   Head of an Indian mystic (15x13cm-6x5in) init. W/C over pencil. 8-Apr-94 Sloan, North Bethesda #2515/R

GIBSON, C D (1867-1944) American
$650   £422   Portrait of a woman (33x23cm-13x9in) s. dr oval. 4-Aug-94 Eldred, Massachusetts #710/R

GIBSON, Charles Dana (1867-1944) American
$800   £533   A rainy day (51x34cm-20x13in) s. pen board. 23-May-94 Christie's, East, New York #205
$2800   £1772   An air of elegance (58x39cm-23x15in) s. chl board. 2-Dec-92 Christie's, East, New York #154/R

GIES, Joseph W (1860-1935) American
$2600   £1667   Cavaliers rolling dice (53x43cm-21x17in) s.i.d.86. 28-May-93 Christie's, East, New York #99/R

GIFFORD, C H (1839-1904) American
$725   £487   Marine cove (15x30cm-6x12in) s. 29-Nov-93 Stonington Fine Arts, Stonington #102/R

GIFFORD, Charles H (1839-1904) American
$700   £458   Coastal scene (41x25cm-16x10in) s. board. 30-Jun-94 Mystic Fine Arts, Connecticut #75/R
$1000   £510   Sunset off the coast (13x25cm-5x10in) s. board. 18-Aug-92 Richard Bourne, Hyannis #129/R
$1200   £800   Approaching storm (13x23cm-5x9in) s.indist.d. 22-May-94 James Bakker, Cambridge #19/R
$1200   £789   Still life with peaches (22x32cm-9x13in) s.d.1902. 31-Mar-93 Sotheby's Arcade, New York #38/R
$2100   £1419   American steam-sail yacht near shore (28x43cm-11x17in) s. 30-Jul-93 Eldred, Massachusetts #241 o/R
$2200   £1384   Moonlit sail (25x20cm-10x8in) s. panel. 25-Apr-93 James Bakker, Cambridge #123/R
$2300   £1554   Fisherman in small boat working at night (25x20cm-10x8in) s. panel. 30-Jul-93 Eldred, Massachusetts #269/R
$2600   £1699   Sailing along the coast (25x36cm-10x14in) s. canvas on masonite. 18-Sep-93 James Bakker, Cambridge #116/R
$2700   £1888   Sailing off the cliffs (23x36cm-9x14in) s.d.1884. 12-Mar-93 Skinner, Bolton #150/R
$3000   £2013   Lake scene with mountain and fog in background, possibly Lake George (23x36cm-9x14in) s.d.1878. 5-Aug-93 Eldred, Massachusetts #806/R
$4000   £2703   Afternoon calm at sea with sailing vessels and cliffs (23x37cm-9x15in) s.d.72. 5-Nov-93 Skinner, Bolton #31/R
$4500   £2961   March Island, New Bedford harbour (33x46cm-13x18in) s.d.1887. 2-Apr-93 Eldred, Massachusetts #681/R
$4500   £3020   Coastal scene (23x36cm-9x14in) s.d.1872. 24-Jun-93 Mystic Fine Arts, Connecticut #171
$4700   £2398   New Bedford fishermen (18x28cm-7x11in) s.d.86. 18-Aug-92 Richard Bourne, Hyannis #83/R
$5250   £2679   Fishing weirs (18x28cm-7x11in) s.d.85. 18-Aug-92 Richard Bourne, Hyannis #221/R
$6500   £4305   Light through clouds - autumnal view (33x46cm-13x18in) s.d.87. 13-Nov-92 Skinner, Bolton #63/R
$8500   £5592   'When the tide is out' - men repairing sailboat on beach (61x46cm-24x18in) s.d.1886. 2-Apr-93 Eldred, Massachusetts #682/R
$14000   £8092   Returning to port as the storm nears (86x140cm-34x55in) s.d.1877-1878. 23-Sep-92 Christie's, New York #66/R

GIFFORD, R Swain (1840-1905) American
$900   £612   Cloudy day (25x36cm-10x14in) s. 16-Apr-94 Young Fine Arts Auctions, Maine #117/R
$1400   £921   Sunset behind trees (74x61cm-29x24in) s. 13-Jun-93 Butterfield & Butterfield, San Francisco #3101/R
$2250   £1442   Landscape with windblown trees (67x112cm-26x44in) s. canvas on board. 9-Dec-92 Butterfield & Butterfield, San Francisco #3838/R
$2300   £1329   Brown meadows (36x64cm-14x25in) s. 25-Sep-92 Sotheby's Arcade, New York #24/R
$2400   £1579   Two figures with baskets in landscape (38x63cm-15x25in) s.d.1881. 31-Mar-93 Sotheby's Arcade, New York #57/R
$4800   £3200   Evening (76x102cm-30x40in) s. 23-May-94 Christie's, East, New York #185/R
$7000   £4895   Seascape (71x127cm-28x50in) s.d.1872. 10-Mar-93 Sotheby's, New York #37/R
$12000   £7595   The Cove Road, Naushon Island (49x100cm-19x39in) s. 3-Dec-92 Sotheby's, New York #45/R
$800   £544   White Head Moneghan Island Maine (10x18cm-4x7in) s. W/C. 19-Nov-93 Eldred, Massachusetts #749/R
$1100   £738   Fisherman in creek with houses in background (18x43cm-7x17in) s.d.1879 W/C. 5-Aug-93 Eldred, Massachusetts #801/R

GIFFORD, Sanford Robinson (1823-1880) American
$4500   £2261   On Nile (30x46cm-12x18in) s. panel. 6-Sep-92 Litchfield Auction Gallery #121
$5000   £3333   Landscape with village in the distance (36x32cm-14x13in) init.d.1853. 17-Mar-94 Sotheby's, New York #39/R
$8500   £5556   Mountain landscape, autumn (28x46cm-11x18in) s. s.stretcher. 16-Sep-93 Sloan, North Bethesda #3203/R
$11000   £7051   Home in woods (13x20cm-5x8in) init.indist.d. 27-May-93 Sotheby's, New York #198/R
$11000   £6962   North of Saratoga. Near Saratoga (15x12cm-6x5in) s. i.verso board two. 2-Dec-92 Christie's, East, New York #12/R

GIFFORD, Sanford Robinson (1823-1880) American-cont.
$12540	£8038	Rider and horse by a gate (41x30cm-16x12in) s. 17-Dec-92 Mystic Fine Arts, Connecticut #248/R
$15000	£10204	At play in the surf (34x69cm-13x27in) s.d.1879. 15-Nov-93 Christie's, East, New York #36/R
$24000	£15190	Sketch of Mansfield Mountain (21x34cm-8x13in) 4-Dec-92 Christie's, New York #193/R
$25000	£16026	Sunset at Catania, Sicily (19x25cm-7x10in) init.i. 26-May-93 Christie's, New York #22/R
$54000	£36000	Summer idyll (46x41cm-18x16in) s.d.1860. 17-Mar-94 Sotheby's, New York #23/R
$55000	£34810	'Tis the Days when Leaves are Falling, Lake St. George' (64x38cm-25x15in) s.d.76 i.verso. 2-Dec-92 Boos Gallery, Michigan #821/R
$500000	£320513	Morning on the Hudson (36x76cm-14x30in) s.d.1866. 9-Dec-92 Butterfield & Butterfield, San Francisco #3812/R

GIGNOUX, Francois Regis (1816-1882) American/French
$1700	£983	View of the Jungfrau and Lake Thun (27x32cm-11x13in) s. painted oval. 25-Sep-92 Sotheby's Arcade, New York #12/R
$4500	£3020	View of the Jung Frau, Switzerland (75x69cm-30x27in) s. s.i.d.1867 verso. 4-Mar-94 Skinner, Bolton #189/R
$7000	£4667	Spring landscape (53x43cm-21x17in) s. 17-Mar-94 Sotheby's, New York #6/R
$12000	£7595	View of the Hudson River Valley (68x101cm-27x40in) s.d.1849. 3-Dec-92 Sotheby's, New York #42/R
$19500	£13087	Skating pond at Morristown, New Jersey (91x112cm-36x44in) s.d. painted arch. 3-Dec-93 Christie's, New York #103/R
$20000	£12658	Autumn on the Hudson (35x51cm-14x20in) s.d.1858. 4-Dec-92 Christie's, New York #187/R
$1800	*£1192*	*Winter landscape with hunter and dog (12x17cm-5x7in) s. W/C gouache. 23-Sep-93 Sotheby's, New York #26/R*

GIHON, Clarence M (1871-1907) American
$550	£359	Street scene , s. board. 30-Jun-94 Mystic Fine Arts, Connecticut #89/R
$888	£600	Harbour scene - La Rochelle (30x41cm-12x16in) s. panel. 26-Apr-94 Rowland Gorringe, Lewes #2253/R
$1617	£1050	The port of La Rochelle (32x39cm-13x15in) s. board. 7-Sep-93 Phillips, West Two #118
$2018	£1345	Le port de la Rochelle (32x40cm-13x16in) s. board. 10-Jun-94 Lenormand, Paris #41 (F.FR 11500)
$2600	£1699	French village with figures (61x74cm-24x29in) s. 7-Oct-93 Freeman Fine Arts, Philadelphia #914/R
$2422	*£1533*	*Le bord a Nemours (24x33cm-9x13in) s. panel. 6-Dec-92 Lesieur & Le Bars, Paris #71/R (F.FR 13000)*

GILBERT, Arthur Hill (1894-1970) American
$700	£496	Carmel coast (30x41cm-12x16in) s.i. i.verso board. 12-Feb-93 Du Mouchelle, Detroit #109/R
$900	£596	Coastal landscape (30x41cm-12x16in) s. canvasboard. 14-Jun-94 John Moran, Pasadena #79
$1000	£658	Cloudy day (41x51cm-16x20in) s. canvasboard. 13-Jun-93 Butterfield & Butterfield, San Francisco #815/R
$1200	£800	Sand dunes, Monterey coast (36x46cm-14x18in) s. i.stretcher. 15-Mar-94 John Moran, Pasadena #58
$1200	£828	Green pastures (28x36cm-11x14in) s. board. 16-Feb-93 John Moran, Pasadena #45
$1500	£1014	Landscape (48x41cm-19x16in) s. canvas on board. 13-Aug-93 Du Mouchelle, Detroit #2006/R
$1500	£1034	Distant silo (30x41cm-12x16in) s. canvas laid down on board. 16-Feb-93 John Moran, Pasadena #91
$3250	£2124	Rocky shore with cypress - California coastal view (64x76cm-25x30in) s. with i.verso. 17-Sep-93 Skinner, Bolton #236/R
$4250	£2853	California poplars (76x61cm-30x24in) s. 8-Dec-93 Butterfield & Butterfield, San Francisco #3488/R
$4500	£2647	Spring, Monterey (52x61cm-20x24in) s. 4-Oct-92 Butterfield & Butterfield, Los Angeles #77/R
$5500	£3819	Path through the trees (61x76cm-24x30in) s. 7-Mar-93 Butterfield & Butterfield, San Francisco #104/R

GILBERT, C Ivar (20th C) American
$900	£588	Road to the sea (64x79cm-25x31in) s. 30-Jun-94 Mystic Fine Arts, Connecticut #55/R

GILCHRIST, William Wallace (jnr) (20th C) American
$22000	£14765	Gilchrist Family at breakfast (47x62cm-19x24in) s.d.16 board. 3-Dec-93 Christie's, New York #31/R

GILE, Seldon Connor (1877-1947) American
$1000	£588	Marin county mountains (28x36cm-11x14in) canvas on board. 4-Oct-92 Butterfield & Butterfield, Los Angeles #238/R
$1200	£635	Coastal steamer (23x30cm-9x12in) sold with letter. 12-Sep-92 Louisiana Auction Exchange #68/R
$1200	£706	Mount Tamalpais from San Anselmo (30x46cm-12x18in) s.d.13 canvasboard. 4-Oct-92 Butterfield & Butterfield, Los Angeles #27/R
$1600	£1053	High Sierras (23x30cm-9x12in) canvas on board. 13-Jun-93 Butterfield & Butterfield, San Francisco #875/R
$2750	£1821	Changing colours, a landscape (30x38cm-12x15in) canvas laid down on board. 15-Jun-94 Butterfield & Butterfield, San Francisco #4617/R

GILE, Seldon Connor (1877-1947) American-cont.
$3000	£1974	Boats and houses near Benecia (30x41cm-12x16in) canvas on board. 13-Jun-93 Butterfield & Butterfield, San Francisco #749/R
$3500	£2318	Hay wagon and barns in landscape (28x38cm-11x15in) s.d.27 board. 28-Sep-93 John Moran, Pasadena #245
$6000	£3529	South Bay South Bay (44x56cm-17x22in) s. board. 4-Oct-92 Butterfield & Butterfield, Los Angeles #237/R
$6500	£4362	Feather River Gorge, Western Pacific Railroad (132x361cm-52x142in) s.d.46. 8-Dec-93 Butterfield & Butterfield, San Francisco #3492/R
$1200	*£789*	*Working women (22x29cm-9x11in) s.d.32 W/C double-sided. 13-Jun-93 Butterfield & Butterfield, San Francisco #766/R*

GILL, James (1934-) American
$2542	£1706	New York Times (129x99cm-51x39in) s.d.65. 4-May-94 Galerie Dobiaschofsky, Bern #592/R (S.FR 3600)

GILLAM, Victor (19/20th C) American
$797	*£524*	*Strike up the band, here comes a sailor (30x47cm-12x19in) s.d.1903 pen W/C. 2-Nov-92 Stephan Welz, Johannesburg #38 (SA.R 2400)*

GIOBBI, Edward (1926-) American
$1600	*£1053*	*Day after day (152x152cm-60x60in) s.i.d.1967 pencil oil chl masonite. 11-Jun-93 Du Mouchelle, Detroit #2014/R*

GIRARDIN, Frank J (1856-1945) American
$650	£430	Forest interior (51x76cm-20x30in) indist.s. 14-Jun-94 John Moran, Pasadena #83

GIRONELLA, Alberto (1929-) Mexican
$2608	£1716	37 Drottning Mariana, Objekt (215x106cm-85x42in) 4-Nov-92 Francis Briest, Paris #13 (F.FR 14000)

GISSING, Roland (1895-1967) Canadian
$546	£364	Athabaska River, Rocky Mountains (30x40cm-12x16in) s. board. 13-May-94 Joyner Fine Art, Toronto #33/R (C.D 750)
$592	£395	Alberta, valley landscape (25x36cm-10x14in) s. canvas on panel. 30-May-94 Ritchie, Toronto #150/R (C.D 825)
$628	£410	Untitled - mountain scene (30x41cm-12x16in) s. paper. 10-May-93 Hodgins, Calgary #102 (C.D 800)
$677	£455	Kananaskis River (30x40cm-12x16in) s. i.verso board. 29-Nov-93 Ritchie, Toronto #198/R (C.D 900)
$706	£462	Untitled - mountain scene (23x31cm-9x12in) s. board. 10-May-93 Hodgins, Calgary #29 (C.D 900)
$718	£478	Alberta harvest (30x41cm-12x16in) s. 30-May-94 Hodgins, Calgary #301/R (C.D 1000)
$754	£493	Canadian winter landscape (43x61cm-17x24in) s. 6-Oct-93 Maynards, Vancouver #282 (C.D 1000)
$775	£524	Table Mountain Buckhorn Range (41x51cm-16x20in) s. s.i.d.1950verso. 3-Nov-93 Sotheby's, Toronto #176/R (C.D 1000)
$778	£515	Wyndell near Creston (30x41cm-12x16in) s.i.d.1962verso board. 16-Nov-92 Hodgins, Calgary #226 (C.D 1000)
$888	£600	Waterfowl Lake, Canada (41x56cm-16x22in) s. s.d.1954 stretcher. 20-Oct-93 Sotheby's, London #18/R
$981	£641	Untitled - rapids (23x30cm-9x12in) s. board. 10-May-93 Hodgins, Calgary #231/R (C.D 1250)
$1085	£733	Harvest stooks (41x56cm-16x22in) s. 3-Nov-93 Sotheby's, Toronto #146/R (C.D 1400)
$1197	£758	Kicking Horse River (16x22cm-6x9in) s. 21-Oct-92 Maynards, Vancouver #124 (C.D 1500)
$1215	£779	Winter landscape, Ghost River (51x61cm-20x24in) s. 26-Apr-93 Levis, Calgary #67 (C.D 1550)
$1370	£806	Winter mountain landscape (41x51cm-16x20in) s. 5-Oct-92 Levis, Calgary #56 (C.D 1700)
$1395	£942	Ghost lake (41x51cm-16x20in) s. bears.i.verso. 1-Nov-93 Levis, Calgary #76/R (C.D 1800)
$1472	£995	Mountain stream (56x86cm-22x34in) s. 3-Nov-93 Sotheby's, Toronto #172/R (C.D 1900)
$1590	£1000	Summer in the foothills (51x66cm-20x26in) 19-Apr-93 Lunds, Victoria #12 (C.D 2000)
$1635	£1082	Kicking Horse River (41x51cm-16x20in) s. i.verso. 16-Nov-92 Hodgins, Calgary #31/R (C.D 2100)
$1635	£1082	Harvest, Bow Valley (46x61cm-18x24in) s. i.verso. 16-Nov-92 Hodgins, Calgary #254 (C.D 2100)
$1883	£1231	Charm of winter (56x76cm-22x30in) s. d.1955 verso. 10-May-93 Hodgins, Calgary #239/R (C.D 2400)
$1886	£1275	Kananaskis river (41x51cm-16x20in) s. i.verso canvas board. 25-Apr-94 Levis, Calgary #89/R (C.D 2600)
$1886	£1275	Foothills - Ghost river valley (48x74cm-19x29in) s. painting verso painted c.1948. 25-Apr-94 Levis, Calgary #88/R (C.D 2600)
$1934	£1137	Homestead in the foothills (46x61cm-18x24in) s. i.verso. 5-Oct-92 Levis, Calgary #54/R (C.D 2400)
$2256	£1327	Evening shadows (41x51cm-16x20in) s. i.verso. 5-Oct-92 Levis, Calgary #55/R (C.D 2800)
$2262	£1538	The river bank (46x61cm-18x24in) s. bears i.verso. 15-Nov-93 Hodgins, Calgary #68 (C.D 3000)
$2354	£1538	Harvest in Alberta (46x61cm-18x24in) s. 10-May-93 Hodgins, Calgary #340/R (C.D 3000)

GISSING, Roland (1895-1967) Canadian-cont.
$2491	£1649	Landscape with oil rigs (76x112cm-30x44in) s. 16-Nov-92 Hodgins, Calgary #3520 (C.D 3200)
$2958	£1959	Mouth of the North Saskatchewan (56x76cm-22x30in) s. 16-Nov-92 Hodgins, Calgary #20/R (C.D 3800)
$620	*£419*	*Lake Louise (42x58cm-17x23in) s. pastel. 3-Nov-93 Sotheby's, Toronto #70/R (C.D 800)*

GISSON, Andre (20th C) American
$700	£490	Paris street scene (30x61cm-12x24in) s. 14-Mar-93 Hindman Galleries, Chicago #128/R
$750	£503	Mother and child in a landscape (25x38cm-10x15in) s. 12-Dec-93 Hindman Galleries, Chicago #404
$750	£510	Flower vendors by the Seine (9x12cm-4x5in) s. 10-Jul-93 Young Fine Arts Auctions, Maine #152/R
$753	£505	Sunlit terrace (60x28cm-24x11in) s. 29-Nov-93 Waddingtons, Toronto #1411 (C.D 1000)
$800	£559	Floral still life (61x51cm-24x20in) s. 14-Mar-93 Hindman Galleries, Chicago #126
$800	£530	Nude (51x41cm-20x16in) s. 30-Jun-93 Sotheby's Arcade, New York #117/R
$800	£559	Dans le pre (23x30cm-9x12in) s. 14-Mar-93 Hindman Galleries, Chicago #127
$850	£570	A landscape with two children (61x91cm-24x36in) s. 24-Mar-94 Boos Gallery, Michigan #666/R
$900	£604	Le jardin (61x30cm-24x12in) s. 12-Dec-93 Hindman Galleries, Chicago #405
$1000	£671	Paris street scene (61x91cm-24x36in) s. 16-Dec-93 Mystic Fine Arts, Connecticut #300/R
$1000	£633	Young girl in pink bonnet (30x41cm-12x16in) s. 5-Dec-92 Louisiana Auction Exchange #161/R
$1100	£769	Pedestrians on a French boulevard (61x30cm-24x12in) s. 12-Mar-93 Hart Gallery, Houston #3
$1150	£762	Portrait of girl in red beret (30x41cm-12x16in) s. 28-Nov-92 Dunning's, Illinois #1049
$1200	£833	Vase of flowers (61x31cm-24x12in) s. 26-Feb-93 Sotheby's Arcade, New York #175/R
$1200	£784	Floral still life (51x41cm-20x16in) s. 16-May-93 Hanzel Galleries, Chicago #341
$1200	£795	Paris street scene (61x76cm-24x30in) s. 21-Nov-92 James Bakker, Cambridge #295/R
$1200	£833	Still life with white and blue vases (51x41cm-20x16in) s. 26-Feb-93 Sotheby's Arcade, New York #201/R
$1300	£872	Rue de Paris. Marchand de fleurs, Paris (51x41cm-20x16in) s. pair. 23-Feb-94 Christie's, East, New York #34/R
$1300	£903	Little Rose (30x41cm-12x16in) s. 26-Feb-93 Sotheby's Arcade, New York #235/R
$1500	£962	Parisian street scene (61x91cm-24x36in) s. 28-May-93 Sloan, North Bethesda #2671
$1600	£1111	Still life with white vase (61x76cm-24x30in) s. 26-Feb-93 Sotheby's Arcade, New York #197/R
$1600	£1060	Les Champs Elysees (61x76cm-24x30in) s. 10-Nov-92 Christie's, East, New York #26/R
$1700	£1111	Beach scene (61x76cm-24x30in) s. 15-May-93 Dunning's, Illinois #1043/R
$1700	£1126	Rue de Paris (61x91cm-24x36in) s. 10-Nov-92 Christie's, East, New York #23/R
$1750	£1174	Paris street scene (28x36cm-11x14in) s. 16-Jul-93 Du Mouchelle, Detroit #2199/R
$1900	£1319	Mother and child by lake (51x61cm-20x24in) s. 26-Feb-93 Sotheby's Arcade, New York #170/R
$1900	£1275	Paris street scene (61x76cm-24x30in) s. 12-Dec-93 Hindman Galleries, Chicago #406/R
$2000	£1299	Beach scene with figures, sailboats in the distance (41x51cm-16x20in) 15-Jan-93 Du Mouchelle, Detroit #2049/R
$2000	£1325	Paris (51x41cm-20x16in) s. pair. 10-Nov-92 Christie's, East, New York #203/R
$2000	£1307	Park with pond (61x76cm-24x30in) s. 1-Nov-92 Hanzel Galleries, Chicago #198 g
$2000	£1333	Paris, jour de pluie (61x91cm-24x36in) s. 9-May-94 Christie's, East, New York #69/R
$2000	£1342	Parisian street scene (36x46cm-14x18in) s. 24-Feb-94 Sotheby's Arcade, New York #234/R
$2100	£1458	Park with blue and purple flowers (51x41cm-20x16in) s. 26-Feb-93 Sotheby's Arcade, New York #181/R
$2200	£1457	Dans le jardin (51x61cm-20x24in) s. 29-Sep-93 Sotheby's Arcade, New York #195/R
$2370	£1500	Bathing impressions (28x36cm-11x14in) s. 4-Dec-92 Tennants, Leyburn #386/R
$2500	£1689	Summer in the park (51x61cm-20x24in) s. 13-Aug-93 Du Mouchelle, Detroit #2096/R
$2500	£1678	Lake landscape (61x91cm-24x36in) s. 25-Mar-93 Boos Gallery, Michigan #471/R
$3200	£2119	Carousel (41x51cm-16x20in) s. 29-Sep-93 Sotheby's Arcade, New York #196/R
$3500	£2333	Still life with fruit and flowers (76x61cm-30x24in) s. 9-May-94 Christie's, East, New York #73/R
$3600	£2553	Portrait of a young girl in a pink bonnet (30x41cm-12x16in) s. 21-Feb-93 Hart Gallery, Houston #2
$3950	£2500	Riverside morning (30x41cm-12x16in) s. 4-Dec-92 Tennants, Leyburn #387
$4500	£2961	Champs Elysees (51x102cm-20x40in) s. 2-Apr-93 Sloan, North Bethesda #2484/R

GIUDICI, Reinaldo (1853-1921) Argentinian
$10000	£5780	Nevado, Como, Italia (39x69cm-15x27in) 23-Sep-92 Roldan & Cia, Buenos Aires #26

GIUNTA, Joseph (1911-) Canadian
$865	£547	Cold winter day Mt. Tremblant, Quebec (30x40cm-12x16in) s. i.verso board. 1-Dec-92 Fraser Pinneys, Quebec #191 (C.D 1100)

GLACKENS, William (1870-1938) American
$12000	£7947	Garden at 110 Rue de Bac, Paris (33x41cm-13x16in) i.verso canvasboard painted 1929. 22-Sep-93 Christie's, New York #132/R
$13000	£7514	Feressy with Pink House (22x27cm-9x11in) st.init.verso panel. 23-Sep-92 Christie's, New York #143/R

GLACKENS, William (1870-1938) American-cont.
$18000	£10405	Roses and persimmons (33x41cm-13x16in) st.init.verso canvas board. 23-Sep-92 Christie's, New York #140/R
$20000	£12821	Girl in yellow dress (46x38cm-18x15in) init. 27-May-93 Sotheby's, New York #76/R
$26000	£17219	Flowers in Bohemian tumbler (26x20cm-10x8in) s. 23-Sep-93 Sotheby's, New York #187/R
$26000	£17450	Little pavilion (32x41cm-13x16in) init. i.studio st.verso canvasboard. 2-Dec-93 Sotheby's, New York #119/R
$34000	£21795	Canal at bayshore (30x38cm-12x15in) init. 26-May-93 Christie's, New York #128/R
$65000	£41667	Flower study (51x38cm-20x15in) s. 27-May-93 Sotheby's, New York #77/R
$105000	£60694	Stroll in the park (61x46cm-24x18in) 23-Sep-92 Christie's, New York #129/R
$140000	£88608	Outdoor swimming pool (46x61cm-18x24in) 4-Dec-92 Christie's, New York #93/R
$700	£443	A man gesturing (22x19cm-9x7in) s. ink. 2-Dec-92 Christie's, East, New York #166/R
$1000	£505	Good old fellow, you saved my life (23x23cm-9x9in) s. s.i.verso ink. 28-Aug-92 Young Fine Arts Auctions, Maine #130/R
$1000	£633	In the kitchen (25x18cm-10x7in) s. chl paper htd white. 2-Dec-92 Christie's, East, New York #165/R
$1200	£805	Man in top hat (18x13cm-7x5in) s. pencil. 5-Mar-94 Louisiana Auction Exchange #150/R
$1500	£949	The dispute (18x23cm-7x9in) s. chl ink. 2-Dec-92 Christie's, East, New York #163/R
$1500	£949	Soldiers embarking for Cuba (38x56cm-15x22in) s. pencil ink gouache wash. 2-Dec-92 Christie's, East, New York #170
$2200	£1497	An elegant lady (22x16cm-9x6in) s. col chk. 15-Nov-93 Christie's, East, New York #201/R
$2500	£1689	She answered calmly, 'I went up' (35x36cm-14x14in) s. pencil ink wash board. 31-Mar-94 Sotheby's Arcade, New York #428/R
$3800	£2197	The castaway brokers (34x43cm-13x17in) s. brush ink Chinese white. 23-Sep-92 Christie's, New York #211/R
$6000	£4054	Bathers and yellow house (20x30cm-8x12in) W/C pencil. 31-Mar-94 Sotheby's Arcade, New York #419/R
$13000	£9091	Gazebo, Hartford (31x41cm-12x16in) s. pastel paper on board. 11-Mar-93 Christie's, New York #156/R
$22000	£14570	Washington Square. Afternoon in the park (43x53cm-17x21in) s. pastel double-sided executed c.1905-1907. 23-Sep-93 Sotheby's, New York #217/R

GLARNER, Fritz (1899-1972) American/Swiss
$1473	£995	Seated woman wearing yellow jacket (60x40cm-24x16in) s.d.26 board. 24-Nov-93 Sotheby's, Zurich #66/R (S.FR 2200)

GLASCO, Joseph (1925-) American
$1600	£1088	Boy (72x51cm-28x20in) s.d.1950 oil aggregate. 15-Nov-93 Christie's, East, New York #222/R

GLASER, David (20th C) American
$2000	£1156	Pool room (52x61cm-20x24in) s. 24-Sep-92 Sotheby's, New York #178/R

GLASS, James William (1825-1857) American
$11000	£7051	A call at the King's Head (112x152cm-44x60in) s.d.1848 i.verso. 24-May-93 Grogan, Massachussetts #282/R
$62500	£43103	Richard, Coeur de Lion, on way to Jerusalem (176x241cm-69x95in) s.d.1854. 17-Feb-93 Sotheby's, New York #27/R

GLEASON, Joe Duncan (1881-1959) American
$950	£655	Near Lake Arrowhead (30x25cm-12x10in) s. i.verso board. 16-Feb-93 John Moran, Pasadena #24

GLUCK, Walter Carl (1929-1986) American
$2118	£1403	The kiss of death (50x62cm-20x24in) s.d.17 XII 1968verso panel. 22-Sep-93 Kunsthallen, Copenhagen #45/R (D.KR 14000)

GLYDE, Henry George (1906-) Canadian
$628	£410	Farm outside Edmonton (25x30cm-10x12in) s. board. 12-May-93 Maynards, Vancouver #214 (C.D 800)
$863	£564	Old barn - near Wallace road, Saanich B.C (25x30cm-10x12in) s. canvasboard. 10-May-93 Hodgins, Calgary #230 (C.D 1100)
$1125	£760	Low tide near Active Pass, British Colombia (33x41cm-13x16in) s.d.1954 i.d.verso board. 25-Apr-94 Levis, Calgary #90/R (C.D 1550)
$1334	£872	Cascade river (33x40cm-13x16in) s. board. 10-May-93 Hodgins, Calgary #49/R (C.D 1700)
$1432	£974	Icefields Canadian Rockies (41x51cm-16x20in) s. s.i.verso. 15-Nov-93 Hodgins, Calgary #54/R (C.D 1900)
$1705	£1152	Eight miles west of Banff Alberta (41x50cm-16x20in) s.d.1965 s.i.d.verso canvasboard. 1-Nov-93 Levis, Calgary #77/R (C.D 2200)
$1883	£1231	Lighthouse (41x51cm-16x20in) s.d.91. 10-May-93 Hodgins, Calgary #111/R (C.D 2400)
$2537	£1658	Small plots, Saanich B.C. (61x76cm-24x30in) s. 18-May-93 Joyner Fine Art, Toronto #118/R (C.D 3200)
$706	£462	Untitled - fishermen (25x36cm-10x14in) s. W/C. 10-May-93 Hodgins, Calgary #293/R (C.D 900)

GOBER, Robert (1954-) American
$3000	£1899	Untitled, 1984 (43x51cm-17x20in) s.d.85 num.R6540 verso pencil. 25-Oct-92 Butterfield & Butterfield, San Francisco #2382/R

GOBER, Robert (1954-) American-cont.
$5000	£3356	Untitled (35x28cm-14x11in) s.d.1985verso graphite. 4-May-94 Christie's, New York #260/R
$7000	£4118	Untitled (21x27cm-8x11in) s.d.1984verso graphite. 8-Oct-92 Christie's, New York #197/R
$8000	£5229	Untitled (36x28cm-14x11in) pencil executed 1986. 4-May-93 Sotheby's, New York #249/R
$9000	£6040	Untitled (28x35cm-11x14in) s.d.84 verso graphite. 23-Feb-94 Christie's, New York #136/R
$10000	£6623	Untitled 51 D (34x69cm-13x27in) painted 1987 fabric paint cotton. 19-Nov-92 Christie's, New York #104/R
$24000	£16216	Untitled (28x36cm-11x14in) graphite executed 1984. 10-Nov-93 Christie's, New York #266/R

GODFREY, Winifred (20th C) American
$2600   £1733   Pink hollyhocks (127x102cm-50x40in) s.d.1984. 13-Mar-94 Hindman Galleries, Chicago #872/R

GODMAN, A C (19/20th C) American
$1600   £1053   New York Harbour (51x61cm-20x24in) s. canvas board. 2-Apr-93 Sloan, North Bethesda #837

GODWIN, Ted (1933-) Canadian
$1812   £1224   Ophelia No.4 (68x56cm-27x22in) s.i.stretcher. 23-Nov-93 Joyner Fine Art, Toronto #145/R (C.D 2400)

GOERITZ, Mathias (1915-) Mexican
$6049   £3878   Los amantes y la noche (29x48cm-11x19in) s. jute. 29-Apr-93 Louis Morton, Mexico #89 (M.P 19000)

GOINGS, Ralph (1928-) American
$56000	£37333	Tiled lunch counter (122x163cm-48x64in) s.d.79. 23-May-94 Hindman Galleries, Chicago #271/R
$60000	£39735	Yellow Ford Camper (114x131cm-45x52in) s.d.69 verso. 18-Nov-92 Sotheby's, New York #170/R

GOITIA, Francisco (1884-1960) Mexican
$12000	£8108	Naturaleza muerta (60x61cm-24x24in) s. painted c.1905. 22-Nov-93 Sotheby's, New York #212/R
$35000	£22876	Costa de Cataluna (46x56cm-18x22in) s.d.1906. 18-May-93 Sotheby's, New York #20/R

GOLDBECK, Walter Dean (1882-1925) American
$1000	£671	Madame Butterfly (76x51cm-30x20in) indist.i. 11-Dec-93 Weschler, Washington #100/R
$3250	£1901	Abroad in the Chalmer car (71x124cm-28x49in) 18-Sep-92 Du Mouchelle, Detroit #2002/R

GOLDBERG, Michael (1924-) American
$1600	£1039	Spiral forms (114x81cm-45x32in) s. masonite. 11-Sep-93 Louisiana Auction Exchange #83/R
$1900	£1258	Moment (36x28cm-14x11in) s.indist.i. paper. 30-Jun-93 Sotheby's Arcade, New York #340/R
$2400	£1667	Untitled (35x28cm-14x11in) s. painted 1960 board on masonite. 22-Feb-93 Christie's, East, New York #138/R
$9500	£6209	Land's End (188x196cm-74x77in) s.i.d.1959verso. 16-May-93 Hindman Galleries, Chicago #33/R
$17000	£11258	The other Sunday afternoon (121x112cm-48x44in) s.i.d.60verso. 19-Nov-92 Christie's, New York #327/R
$1600	*£1074*	Abstract (69x94cm-27x37in) s. mixed media. 5-Mar-94 Louisiana Auction Exchange #10/R

GOLDSTEIN, Jack (1945-) American
$550	£369	Untitled (213x244cm-84x96in) s.d.1988 verso acrylic. 23-Feb-94 Christie's, East, New York #237/R
$823	£549	Untitled (76x112cm-30x44in) s. acrylic paper painted 1984. 2-Jun-94 AB Stockholms Auktionsverk, Stockholm #7220/R (S.KR 6500)
$1300	£872	Untitled - black (213x366cm-84x144in) s.d.1982stretcher acrylic. 3-May-94 Christie's, East, New York #132/R
$1400	£927	Untitled (213x243cm-84x96in) s.d.86verso acrylic. 19-Nov-92 Christie's, New York #134/R
$1600	£1060	Untitled (213x279cm-84x110in) acrylic. 17-Nov-92 Christie's, East, New York #162/R
$2000	£1307	Untitled (244x91cm-96x36in) acrylic painted 1986. 7-May-93 Christie's, East, New York #133/R
$3000	£2083	Untitled (198x229cm-78x90in) painted 1986 acrylic. 23-Nov-93 Sotheby's, New York #367/R

GOLLINGS, William Elling (1878-1932) American
$4250	£2796	Roundup (31x46cm-12x18in) s.indist.d. board. 13-Jun-93 Butterfield & Butterfield, San Francisco #3218/R
$7750	£4480	Passing of time (75x49cm-30x19in) s.mono.d.1910. 25-Sep-92 Sotheby's Arcade, New York #185/R

GOLUB, Leon Albert (1922-) American
$8000	£5229	Head VI (116x110cm-46x43in) s. d.1964 verso acrylic. 4-May-93 Sotheby's, New York #197/R
$8500	£5000	Assassins II (249x200cm-98x79in) s.i.d.1970 cut 1972 acrylic linen. 8-Oct-92 Christie's, New York #209/R
$12000	£8108	Francisco Franco - 1975 (51x43cm-20x17in) s. s.i.d.1976 verso linen. 11-Nov-93 Sotheby's, New York #213/R
$15000	£9804	Three heads (61x163cm-24x64in) s. d.1988 verso acrylic linen. 4-May-93 Sotheby's, New York #254/R
$16000	£10811	Portraits of Ho Chi Minh (89x66cm-35x26in) s.i.d.1976verso acrylic set of three. 10-Nov-93 Christie's, New York #283/R
$23000	£15232	Horsing around IV (305x216cm-120x85in) painted 1983. 18-Nov-92 Sotheby's, New York #282/R
$45000	£29801	White squad III (308x434cm-121x171in) s. painted 1982 acrylic. 19-Nov-92 Christie's, New York #267/R
$2000	*£1351*	*Untitled (59x49cm-23x19in) s. col crayon vellum. 8-Nov-93 Christie's, East, New York #153/R*

GOMEZ CORNET, Ramon (1898-1964) Argentinian
$25000	£14451	Flores (49x39cm-19x15in) 23-Sep-92 Roldan & Cia, Buenos Aires #9

GOMEZ MAYORGA, Guillermo (20th C) Mexican
$3024	£1939	Marinas (21x13cm-8x5in) panel painted c.1930 two. 29-Apr-93 Louis Morton, Mexico #40 (M.P 9500)

GOMEZ OROPEZA, Alejandro (1963-) Mexican
$703	*£475*	*Anatomia de una seduccion (72x57cm-28x22in) mixed media. 20-Oct-93 Louis Morton, Mexico #63/R (M.P 2200)*

GOMEZ, Emilio (20th C) Mexican?
$3090	£2088	La Valenciana (40x35cm-16x14in) masonite. 9-Nov-93 Louis Morton, Mexico #62/R (M.P 10000)

GONSALVES, Mannie (1926-) Canadian
$662	£438	Fireweed, Roberts Pass (46x61cm-18x24in) s. s.i.verso board. 16-Nov-92 Hodgins, Calgary #243 (C.D 850)

GONZALES, Xavier (1898-?) American
$700	*£357*	*Blessing of the fleet (53x74cm-21x29in) s. i.verso mixed media. 18-Aug-92 Richard Bourne, Hyannis #235/R*

GONZALEZ TAVERA, Rosa M (?) Mexican?
$1545	£1044	Bernal, Queretaro (60x40cm-24x16in) s. 9-Nov-93 Louis Morton, Mexico #64/R (M.P 5000)

GONZALEZ, Gregorio (1938-) Mexican
$2258	*£1515*	*Caballito (80x60cm-31x24in) mixed media. 1-Dec-93 Louis Morton, Mexico #212/R (M.P 7000)*

GONZALEZ, Maximiliano (1926-) Cuban
$1200	£805	Untitled (79x60cm-31x24in) painted c.1960. 24-Feb-94 Sotheby's Arcade, New York #296/R
$1800	£1208	Untitled (76x71cm-30x28in) painted c.1960. 24-Feb-94 Sotheby's Arcade, New York #300/R
$6500	£4305	Mujer abstracta (84x67cm-33x26in) s.d.1949. 23-Nov-92 Sotheby's, New York #167/R

GOOD, Bernard Stafford (1893-?) American
$900	£608	Edward rescues Patience illustration for Children of the New Forest (86x63cm-34x25in) i.verso. 5-Nov-93 Skinner, Bolton #183/R

GOOD, Leonard (1907-) American
$1000	£633	Bathers (51x66cm-20x26in) s.d.31. 5-Dec-92 Louisiana Auction Exchange #114/R

GOODE, Joe (1937-) American
$3800	£2639	Ocean blue no 43 (122x114cm-48x45in) s.d.1989verso gator board. 24-Feb-93 Christie's, New York #88/R
$4000	£2685	Untitled (71x56cm-28x22in) painted 1986 four separate works. 23-Feb-94 Christie's, East, New York #261/R

GOODMAN, Bertram (1904-) American
$22000	£12717	The Evolution of tools (78x?cm-31x?in) s.i.d.1934 tempera three panels. 23-Sep-92 Christie's, New York #256/R
$600	*£395*	*Prodigy (56x38cm-22x15in) s. s.i.verso Indian ink W/C pencil. 31-Mar-93 Sotheby's Arcade, New York #481/R*
$800	*£526*	*Chess players (52x34cm-20x13in) s. s.i.verso Indian ink col.pencil pastel W/C. 31-Mar-93 Sotheby's Arcade, New York #480/R*

GOODMAN, Brenda (1943-) American
$950	*£638*	*Untitled (142x100cm-56x40in) s.d.81 verso. 25-Mar-93 Boos Gallery, Michigan #429/R*
$1200	*£805*	*Untitled no.9 (163x122cm-64x48in) s.d.79 verso. 25-Mar-93 Boos Gallery, Michigan #420/R*
$1000	*£671*	*Heart (104x76cm-41x30in) s.d.76 oil pencil wax. 25-Mar-93 Boos Gallery, Michigan #413/R*

GOODMAN, Brenda (1943-) American-cont.
$1250   £839   Magician, No. 2 (104x76cm-41x30in) s. oil mixed media. 25-Mar-93 Boos Gallery, Michigan #434

GOODMAN, Sydney (1936-) American
$2500   £1701   Woman (185x132cm-73x52in) s. 14-Apr-94 Freeman Fine Arts, Philadelphia #1061
$3000   £2083   Afternoon (91x127cm-36x50in) s.i.d.1971. 23-Feb-93 Sotheby's, New York #294/R

GOODNOUGH, Robert (1917-) American
$650   £437   Wild Horses 6 (51x76cm-20x30in) s.d.65 s.i.d.verso. 3-May-94 Christie's, East, New York #17/R
$1300   £903   Seated girl (81x65cm-32x26in) s.i.verso. 26-Feb-93 Sotheby's Arcade, New York #280/R
$1400   £940   Standing figure (153x47cm-60x19in) s.d.62 s.i.verso. 3-May-94 Christie's, East, New York #20/R
$1500   £1042   Untitled (51x61cm-20x24in) s.d.60. 22-Feb-93 Christie's, East, New York #161/R
$1700   £1149   Crowded boat II (20x25cm-8x10in) 21-Apr-94 Butterfield & Butterfield, San Francisco #1093/R
$1800   £1259   RZY (122x198cm-48x78in) s.i.d.1986 s.i.d.verso. 14-Mar-93 Hindman Galleries, Chicago #31/R
$1800   £1192   Tree (69x86cm-27x34in) painted 1954. 17-Nov-92 Christie's, East, New York #285/R
$3000   £2013   Untitled (122x153cm-48x60in) s.d.61. 3-May-94 Christie's, East, New York #18/R
$3200   £2119   Cowboy (100x44cm-39x17in) s.i. s.i.verso. 17-Nov-92 Christie's, East, New York #286/R
$3250   £2257   Abstraction (145x145cm-57x57in) s.d.61. 26-Feb-93 Sotheby's Arcade, New York #345/R
$3500   £2431   Going ashore X (122x122cm-48x48in) s.d.63 s.i.verso. 22-Feb-93 Christie's, East, New York #157/R
$2500   £1736   Standing figure (83x38cm-33x15in) s. s.i.verso exec.c.1957 painted canvas collage. 23-Feb-93 Sotheby's, New York #239/R

GOODWIN, Arthur C (1866-1929) American
$650   £442   Hillside (8x10cm-3x4in) s. 10-Jul-93 Young Fine Arts Auctions, Maine #155/R
$2500   £1603   Popolopon (64x76cm-25x30in) s.i.d.January 1925verso. 9-Dec-92 Grogan, Massachussetts #64/R
$2500   £1656   Boston harbour scene (86x99cm-34x39in) 19-Jun-94 Hindman Galleries, Chicago #701/R
$3000   £1961   Ship at full sail (96x107cm-38x42in) s. 4-May-93 Christie's, East, New York #194/R
$3000   £2013   Kinderhook river (74x91cm-29x36in) s. init.i.verso. 6-Dec-93 Grogan, Massachussetts #533/R
$4600   £3217   Winter snow scene (81x91cm-32x36in) s. 11-Mar-93 Mystic Fine Arts, Connecticut #95/R
$7000   £4118   Park Street (71x56cm-28x22in) s. 5-Oct-92 Grogan, Massachussetts #729/R
$9000   £5960   Boston Public Garden in spring (46x67cm-18x26in) 22-Sep-93 Christie's, New York #133/R
$11000   £7190   Louis Kronberg in studio (56x71cm-22x28in) s. 14-May-93 Skinner, Bolton #150/R
$15000   £9494   The Mystic River Docks (53x68cm-21x27in) s. 4-Dec-92 Christie's, New York #25/R
$19000   £12179   Fifth Avenue (76x92cm-30x36in) s. 26-May-93 Christie's, New York #152/R
$715   £467   Street scene (28x43cm-11x17in) s. d.c.1895 verso pastel paperboard. 14-May-93 Skinner, Bolton #143/R
$750   £504   Farm in the hills (44x57cm-17x22in) s. pastel paper board. 6-May-94 Skinner, Bolton #87/R
$850   £574   The farm across the river (42x50cm-17x20in) s. pastel. 5-Nov-93 Skinner, Bolton #99/R
$1900   £1275   Landscape with red farmhouse (49x57cm-19x22in) pastel paperboard. 4-Mar-94 Skinner, Bolton #251/R

GOODWIN, Arthur C (attrib) (1866-1929) American
$600   £403   New York Municipal Building (51x41cm-20x16in) s. canvasboard. 26-Mar-94 James Bakker, Cambridge #163
$750   £490   City canyon (20x15cm-8x6in) s. board. 18-Sep-93 Young Fine Arts Auctions, Maine #135/R

GOODWIN, Phillip R (1882-1935) American
$15000   £9804   Predators - sporting scene with huntsmen and bear (61x91cm-24x36in) s. 17-Sep-93 Skinner, Bolton #238/R
$19000   £10983   Their lucky day (61x84cm-24x33in) s. 23-Sep-92 Christie's, New York #111/R

GOODWIN, Richard Labarre (1840-1910) American
$1200   £811   Still life with peaches (23x30cm-9x12in) s. 31-Mar-94 Sotheby's Arcade, New York #12/R
$2000   £1351   Two woodcocks (48x38cm-19x15in) s. 31-Oct-93 Hindman Galleries, Chicago #681/R

GORBELY, Edward (1909-) American
$2500   £1656   The vendor (91x76cm-36x30in) s. 19-Jun-94 Hindman Galleries, Chicago #681/R

GORCHOV, Ron (1930-) American
$800   £533   Chaldean instruments (94x130cm-37x51in) s.d.1960. 17-May-94 Christie's, East, New York #539
$1200   £805   Nostalgia (46x46cm-18x18in) s.d.1978 verso linen. 25-Mar-93 Boos Gallery, Michigan #414/R
$1400   £972   Fifth vision of the Queen (122x197cm-48x78in) s.d.1959 s.i.d.verso. 26-Feb-93 Sotheby's Arcade, New York #288/R

GORCHOV, Ron (1930-) American-cont.
$1500   £1007   Constant (104x99cm-41x39in) s.d.1978 verso linen. 25-Mar-93 Boos Gallery, Michigan #421/R
$3750   £2517   Acrobat (107x76cm-42x30in) s.d.1980 stretcher linen. 25-Mar-93 Boos Gallery, Michigan #425/R

GORDER, Luther Emerson van (1861-1931) American
$3000   £1974   Flower sellers along French Boulevard (46x61cm-18x24in) s. 13-Jun-93 Butterfield & Butterfield, San Francisco #3146/R

GORDILLO, Omar (1942-) Colombian
$500   *£338*   *El Montero (66x52cm-26x20in) s. graphite. 21-Apr-94 Butterfield & Butterfield, San Francisco #1102/R*

GORDIN, Sidney (1918-) American
$1300   *£855*   *Untitled IV. Untitled (22x8cm-9x3in) s.d.1942-43 graphite col.pencil pair. 31-Mar-93 Sotheby's Arcade, New York #373/R*

GORDON, John Sloan (1868-1940) Canadian
$646   £431   The Santa Maria la Salute and the Dogona, Venice (33x26cm-13x10in) i.d.1912 canvas on board. 30-May-94 Ritchie, Toronto #142/R (C.D 900)

GORGUE, Jean E (1930-) Haitian
$2000   £1342   Tropical scene with natives picking fruit (102x51cm-40x20in) s. 12-Dec-93 Hindman Galleries, Chicago #433/R

GORKY, Arshile (1904-1948) American
$20000   £13889   Abstraction (37x19cm-15x7in) painted 1936 canvasboard. 23-Feb-93 Sotheby's, New York #202/R
$22500   £14151   Still life with tablecloth, bowl and goblet (25x35cm-10x14in) s. 25-Apr-93 Butterfield & Butterfield, San Francisco #2034/R
$26000   £16993   Portrait of Vartoosh (62x52cm-24x20in) painted 1930's. 5-May-93 Christie's, New York #258/R
$45000   £30405   Portrait of Vartoosh (30x21cm-12x8in) s. paper on board painted 1933-34. 10-Nov-93 Christie's, New York #106/R
$3200000 £2147650 Dark green painting (111x141cm-44x56in) s. painted 1948. 4-May-94 Sotheby's, New York #20/R
$3500000 £2364865 Year after year (86x104cm-34x41in) s.d.47. 9-Nov-93 Christie's, New York #26/R
$2800   *£1892*   *Seated woman (32x24cm-13x9in) ink dr. 8-Nov-93 Christie's, East, New York #1/R*
$130000 *£87838* *Untitled (48x61cm-19x24in) s.d.46 graphite col.crayon paper on board. 9-Nov-93 Christie's, New York #6/R*
$145000 *£96026* *Untitled (44x58cm-17x23in) pastel ink. 17-Nov-92 Sotheby's, New York #30/R*

GORMAN, Carl Nelson (1907-1966) American
$1600   £1074   Ranchos de Taos Church (61x91cm-24x36in) s. 26-Jun-93 Skinner, Bolton #132/R
$2600   £1745   The third World (36x53cm-14x21in) s. mixed media. 26-Jun-93 Skinner, Bolton #1/R

GORMAN, R C (1933-) American
$1400 *£933*   *Taos Man (41x28cm-16x11in) s.d.1970 pastel. 29-Jan-94 Skinner, Bolton #173/R*
$1800 *£1216* *Indian woman (56x71cm-22x28in) s.d.1973 pastel chl graphite. 31-Oct-93 Hindman Galleries, Chicago #779*
$6500   £4333   The red blanket (53x69cm-21x27in) s.d.1979 pastel. 29-Jan-94 Skinner, Bolton #171

GORNIK, April (1953-) American
$10000   £6711   Still mountain light (152x152cm-60x60in) s.i.d.1982 verso. 25-Feb-94 Sotheby's, New York #146/R

GORSON, Aaron Henry (1872-1933) American
$1729   £1095   Morning - Pittsburgh Mill (89x116cm-35x46in) s. painted c.1915. 1-Dec-92 Ritchie, Toronto #186/R (C.D 2200)
$8500   £5592   Morning, Pittsburgh (89x117cm-35x46in) s. 31-Mar-93 Sotheby's Arcade, New York #244/R

GOTSCHKE, Walter (20th C) American
$1000 *£588*   *Mercedes G T (10x23cm-4x9in) s. mixed media board. 8-Oct-92 Boos Gallery, Michigan #92/R*
$1800 *£1059* *Bill Mitchell driving his Mercedes Benz Roadster (20x30cm-8x12in) s.i. mixed media collage. 8-Oct-92 Boos Gallery, Michigan #91/R*
$4500 *£2647* *Rudy Caracciola, driving the Grand Prix of Switzerland, 1937 (53x99cm-21x39in) s.i. mixed media. 8-Oct-92 Boos Gallery, Michigan #90/R*

GOTTLIEB, Adolph (1903-1974) American
$12000   £8054   Untitled (38x51cm-15x20in) s.d.1967 acrylic. 4-May-94 Christie's, New York #137/R
$12000   £7059   Untitled (48x61cm-19x24in) acrylic paper. 8-Oct-92 Christie's, New York #110/R
$18000   £10588   Untitled (61x48cm-24x19in) s.d.1967 acrylic paper on canvas. 6-Oct-92 Sotheby's, New York #42/R
$18000   £11921   Untitled (48x61cm-19x24in) s.d.1967 acrylic. 19-Nov-92 Christie's, New York #323/R
$24000   £16107   Converging forms (28x34cm-11x13in) init. s.i.d.1952verso masonite. 5-May-94 Sotheby's, New York #95/R
$27000   £18243   Untitled (76x56cm-30x22in) s.d.1967 acrylic paper. 11-Nov-93 Sotheby's, New York #275/R
$32000   £21477   Movement east to west (28x34cm-11x13in) init. s.i.d.152verso masonite. 5-May-94 Sotheby's, New York #103/R

GOTTLIEB, Adolph (1903-1974) American-cont.
$32000	£21477	Untitled (61x48cm-24x19in) s.d.1966 acrylic paper on paper. 4-May-94 Christie's, New York #102/R
$38000	£25166	Orange and lavender number 72 (102x76cm-40x30in) s.i.d.1970-72 acrylic paper on canvas. 19-Nov-92 Christie's, New York #303/R
$45000	£29801	Nocturnal beams (122x152cm-48x60in) s.d.1954 verso. 18-Nov-92 Sotheby's, New York #84/R
$50000	£33113	Grey bars (122x91cm-48x36in) s.d.1973 verso. 18-Nov-92 Sotheby's, New York #108/R
$145000	£97315	Triad (122x152cm-48x60in) s.i.d.1972verso. 4-May-94 Sotheby's, New York #19/R
$172000	£113907	Fringe (122x91cm-48x36in) s.i.d.1967verso. 18-Nov-92 Christie's, New York #4/R
$250000	£168919	Cold Front No.2 (127x152cm-50x60in) s.d.1956 s.i.d.1956 verso. 9-Nov-93 Christie's, New York #8/R
$80000	*£52288*	*Pink, blue, black (213x104cm-84x41in) s. s.d.1957 verso oil enamel canvas. 4-May-93 Sotheby's, New York #307/R*

GOTTWALD, Frederick C (1860-1941) American
$900	£604	Afternoon lessons (46x56cm-18x22in) s. 12-Jan-94 Doyle, New York #42

GOULD, John Howard (1929-) Canadian
$595	*£389*	*Old actor (41x26cm-16x10in) s. i.verso mixed media. 19-May-93 Sotheby's, Toronto #50/R (C.D 750)*
$754	£513	Actress (59x85cm-23x33in) s. mixed media. 15-Nov-93 Hodgins, Calgary #246 (C.D 1000)

GOURGUE, Enguerrand-Jean (1930-) Haitian
$750	£487	Still life (41x61cm-16x24in) s. 11-Sep-93 Louisiana Auction Exchange #115/R
$950	£664	Outside the station (51x58cm-20x23in) s. masonite. 12-Mar-93 Skinner, Bolton #255/R
$1100	£582	Under the cool trees (61x76cm-24x30in) s. masonite. 11-Sep-92 Skinner, Bolton #289
$2100	£1409	Voodoo priestess (76x102cm-30x40in) s. 4-Dec-93 Louisiana Auction Exchange #169/R
$3600	£2384	Sleeper (51x76cm-20x30in) s. masonite. 24-Nov-92 Christie's, New York #271/R
$3750	£2517	'Adam et Eve' (102x51cm-40x20in) s. 24-Mar-94 Boos Gallery, Michigan #683/R
$5500	£3716	Untitled (114x91cm-45x36in) s. painted c.1971. 24-Nov-93 Christie's, New York #27/R
$5500	£3716	Tempete (76x61cm-30x24in) s. masonite painted c.1956. 24-Nov-93 Christie's, New York #19/R
$9500	£6419	Cimetiere (75x60cm-30x24in) s. masonite. 24-Nov-93 Christie's, New York #20/R

GOWLAND MORENO, Luis (1902-1971) Argentinian
$1400	£729	Demolicion I (62x51cm-24x20in) 61. 4-Aug-92 VerBo, Buenos Aires #54

GRABACH, John R (1886-1981) American
$2600	£1711	Mending nets (20x25cm-8x10in) s. panel. 31-Mar-93 Sotheby's Arcade, New York #176/R
$3000	£1899	Snow in the woods (69x84cm-27x33in) s. 2-Dec-92 Christie's, East, New York #300/R
$4500	£3041	The city at work (74x79cm-29x31in) s. 5-Nov-93 Skinner, Bolton #129/R
$5000	£2890	Trolley and clearing snow (91x107cm-36x42in) s. double-sided. 24-Sep-92 Sotheby's, New York #155/R
$16000	£10256	Connecticut river in winter, Deerfield (107x122cm-42x48in) s. 26-May-93 Christie's, New York #151/R

GRAHAM, Colin D (1915-) Canadian
$508	*£343*	*Crosswinds (55x73cm-22x29in) s.d.1991 s.i.d.verso W/C gouache. 25-Apr-94 Levis, Calgary #97/R (C.D 700)*

GRAHAM, Kathleen Margaret D (1913-) Canadian
$2367	£1578	Indian summer (122x366cm-48x144in) s. i.d.81verso. 11-May-94 Sotheby's, Toronto #148/R (C.D 3250)
$2958	£1959	Perennial border (76x152cm-30x60in) s. painted 1980 i.stretcher acrylic. 16-Nov-92 Hodgins, Calgary #280/R (C.D 3800)

GRAHAM, Robert (1938-) American
$1800	*£1250*	*Reclining female nude (29x37cm-11x15in) init.i.d.1989 pencil. 26-Feb-93 Sotheby's Arcade, New York #426/R*

GRAMAJO GUTIERREZ, Alfredo (1893-1961) Argentinian
$2000	£1156	El regreso (23x30cm-9x12in) board. 23-Sep-92 Roldan & Cia, Buenos Aires #47
$8000	£4624	El hachero y su familia (50x70cm-20x28in) hardboard. 23-Sep-92 Roldan & Cia, Buenos Aires #11

GRANDEE, Joe (1929-) American
$2500	£1667	Commanche braves breaking a mustang (66x86cm-26x34in) s.mono.d.1966. 22-May-94 Hindman Galleries, Chicago #50/R

GRANDMAISON, Nickola de (1892-1978) Canadian/Russian
$1131	£769	Native Indian portrait (35x28cm-14x11in) s. 15-Nov-93 Hodgins, Calgary #249/R (C.D 1500)
$3964	£2591	Portrait of Indian (51x41cm-20x16in) s. i.stretcher. 19-May-93 Sotheby's, Toronto #226/R (C.D 5000)
$7902	£5303	Portrait of a warrior (76x61cm-30x24in) s. 29-Nov-93 Waddingtons, Toronto #1092 a (C.D 10500)
$754	£493	Portrait of girl (51x41cm-20x16in) s. pastel. 6-Oct-93 Maynards, Vancouver #276 (C.D 1000)

GRANDMAISON, Nickola de (1892-1978) Canadian/Russian-cont.
$980	£667	Portrait of a young girl (43x32cm-17x13in) s.d.1936 pastel. 15-Nov-93 Hodgins, Calgary #276/R (C.D 1300)
$1334	£872	Untitled - woman and child (44x37cm-17x15in) s. graphite. 10-May-93 Hodgins, Calgary #112/R (C.D 1700)
$1725	£1106	Indian child (28x24cm-11x9in) s. pastel. 7-Dec-92 Waddingtons, Toronto #1332 (C.D 2200)
$2378	£1554	Indian child (29x21cm-11x8in) s. col chk pencil dr verso double-sided. 18-May-93 Joyner Fine Art, Toronto #24/R (C.D 3000)
$3171	£2073	Portrait of a warrior (47x34cm-19x13in) s. col chk. 18-May-93 Joyner Fine Art, Toronto #112/R (C.D 4000)
$5838	£3866	Portrait of an Indian (46x34cm-18x13in) s. pastel. 18-Nov-92 Sotheby's, Toronto #7/R (C.D 7500)

GRANDMAISON, O N (1932-1985) Canadian
$678	£462	Prairie March (30x41cm-12x16in) s. s.i.verso canvasboard. 15-Nov-93 Hodgins, Calgary #215/R (C.D 900)

GRANDMAISON, Oreste de (1932-1985) Canadian
$603	£410	Grey road (35x46cm-14x18in) s.bears indist.i. s.verso board. 15-Nov-93 Hodgins, Calgary #299 f (C.D 800)
$620	£419	Autumn along the Red River (41x51cm-16x20in) s. s.i.verso canvasboard. 1-Nov-93 Levis, Calgary #82/R (C.D 800)
$701	£464	House in the woods (51x61cm-20x24in) s. board. 18-Nov-92 Sotheby's, Toronto #153 (C.D 900)
$784	£503	Elevators at morningside (46x76cm-18x30in) s. masonite. 26-Apr-93 Levis, Calgary #69/R (C.D 1000)
$785	£513	Early morning, July (46x61cm-18x24in) s. canvasboard. 10-May-93 Hodgins, Calgary #120/R (C.D 1000)
$798	£539	Rainy weather in Rockies (36x46cm-14x18in) s. s.i.verso. 25-Apr-94 Levis, Calgary #101 (C.D 1100)
$798	£539	July reflections (36x46cm-14x18in) s. s.i.verso canvas board. 25-Apr-94 Levis, Calgary #100/R (C.D 1100)
$824	£538	Indian encampment (41x51cm-16x20in) s. canvasboard. 10-May-93 Hodgins, Calgary #30/R (C.D 1050)
$1401	£928	Foothills landscape (61x76cm-24x30in) s. 16-Nov-92 Hodgins, Calgary #252/R (C.D 1800)

GRANER, Luis (1867-1929) American
$3000	£1923	Chinese lantern (56x112cm-22x44in) s.d. board. 9-Dec-92 Butterfield & Butterfield, San Francisco #3924/R
$8071	£5381	Escena de interior (79x97cm-31x38in) s. 23-May-94 Duran, Madrid #179/R (S.P 1100000)
$8670	£5858	Contando viejas historias (52x64cm-20x25in) s. 25-Apr-94 Duran, Madrid #77/R (S.P 1200000)

GRANSOW, Helmut (1921-) Canadian
$2114	£1429	Table in my backyard (75x55cm-30x22in) s. board. 23-Nov-93 Joyner Fine Art, Toronto #332/R (C.D 2800)

GRANT, Charles Henry (1866-1939) American
$2000	£1316	No.2 Lake George (79x84cm-31x33in) s. 5-Jun-93 Louisiana Auction Exchange #59/R

GRANT, Clement Rollins (1849-1893) American
$1100	£738	Seated young woman (30x20cm-12x8in) s. panel. 16-Dec-93 Mystic Fine Arts, Connecticut #247/R
$7500	£4335	Fisherman's family (51x76cm-20x30in) s. 23-Sep-92 Christie's, New York #95/R
$17000	£11409	Waiting (51x76cm-20x30in) s.i.d.1885. 3-Dec-93 Christie's, New York #58/R
$1000	£529	Quietude (18x23cm-7x9in) init. W/C gouache graphite. 11-Sep-92 Skinner, Bolton #173/R

GRANT, Duncan Edmond (1846-1924) Canadian
$432	£280	The old homestead (32x52cm-13x20in) s.d.85 W/C. 21-Jun-94 Fraser Pinneys, Quebec #209 (C.D 600)

GRANT, Dwinell (1912-) American
$1200	£694	Contrathemis 2811 (22x28cm-9x11in) init.i.d.41 s.i.d.verso collage. 25-Sep-92 Sotheby's Arcade, New York #468/R
$1500	£987	Contrathemis (22x28cm-9x11in) init.num.d.41 s.num.verso collage tissue pair. 31-Mar-93 Sotheby's Arcade, New York #376/R

GRANT, Frederick M (1886-1959) American
$650	£433	Garden statue with ivy (77x76cm-30x30in) s. 21-May-94 Weschler, Washington #121
$1400	£933	Figures in landscape (79x84cm-31x33in) 29-Jan-94 San Rafael Auction Galleries #322
$1400	£940	Still life with roses (76x71cm-30x28in) s. 28-Mar-93 James Bakker, Cambridge #27/R
$4250	£2796	Garden flowers (76x76cm-30x30in) s. s.num.114 stretcher. 31-Mar-93 Sotheby's Arcade, New York #273/R
$11000	£7432	Blue panels a view of the Chicago World's Fair (92x102cm-36x40in) s. 5-Nov-93 Skinner, Bolton #171/R

GRANT, Gordon (1875-1962) American
$650	£417	Fishing craft, Gloucester (30x41cm-12x16in) s.i.d.1941 i.verso canvasboard. 24-May-93 Grogan, Massachussetts #358

GRANT, Gordon (1875-1962) American-cont.
$1800	£1259	Ships in harbour (64x76cm-25x30in) s. 5-Feb-93 Sloan, North Bethesda #2544/R
$2000	£1307	Morning haze (64x76cm-25x30in) s. i.verso. 16-Sep-93 Sloan, North Bethesda #3201/R
$2000	£1316	U.S.S. Alabama (62x92cm-24x36in) s.d.1944. 13-Jun-93 Butterfield & Butterfield, San Francisco #3248/R
$2500	£1645	Mission accomplished, U.S.S. Saratoga (61x81cm-24x32in) s. 13-Jun-93 Butterfield & Butterfield, San Francisco #3247/R
$2750	£1923	With a good wind (61x91cm-24x36in) s.i. s.verso. 12-Mar-93 Du Mouchelle, Detroit #2005/R
$6250	£4371	Sail and steam (100x126cm-39x50in) s. 10-Mar-93 Sotheby's, New York #120/R
$900	£588	First snow (36x51cm-14x20in) s. W/C. 30-Jun-94 Mystic Fine Arts, Connecticut #265/R
$900	£596	Sailing ships at sea (33x51cm-13x20in) s. W/C. 21-Nov-92 James Bakker, Cambridge #130/R
$1050	£709	Harbour scene with boats and buildings (36x53cm-14x21in) s. W/C. 30-Jul-93 Eldred, Massachusetts #144/R
$1100	£636	Harbour scene (53x36cm-21x14in) W/C. 25-Sep-92 Douglas, South Deerfield #5
$1250	£817	Boats at pier (33x46cm-13x18in) s. W/C. 30-Jun-94 Mystic Fine Arts, Connecticut #266
$4250	£2760	Hereschoff 17's off to Marblehead (37x53cm-15x21in) s. i.verso W/C. 9-Sep-93 Sotheby's Arcade, New York #138/R

GRANT, Gordon (attrib) (1875-1962) American
$600	£392	Schooner in port (25x36cm-10x14in) s. W/C. 8-May-93 Young Fine Arts Auctions, Maine #129

GRANT, J Jeffrey (1883-1960) American
$2100	£1373	Landscape with birches (64x69cm-25x27in) s. board. 1-Nov-92 Hanzel Galleries, Chicago #56/R

GRANT, James (1924-) American
$800	£503	Black dot (142x142cm-56x56in) mixed media canvas. 25-Apr-93 Butterfield & Butterfield, San Francisco #2179/R

GRAU, Enrique (1920-) Colombian
$24000	£15686	La toilette (73x129cm-29x51in) s.d.57 canvas on panel. 17-May-93 Christie's, New York #142/R
$6000	£3922	Boy with bees (96x66cm-38x26in) s.d.67 chl pastel crayon. 22-May-93 Weschler, Washington #71/R
$42500	£28523	Untitled, figures and portraits painted at Jose Gomez Sicres' house (41x34cm-16x13in) W/C painted 1964 eighteen. 7-Jan-94 Gary Nader, Miami #135/R

GRAVES, Abbott Fuller (1859-1936) American
$850	£570	Morning oatmeal (51x61cm-20x24in) s. 24-Mar-93 Doyle, New York #32
$1300	£872	Rural farmyard (33x23cm-13x9in) board. 29-Dec-93 Douglas, South Deerfield #2
$2000	£1282	Gathering flowers (30x41cm-12x16in) s.verso canvasboard. 9-Dec-92 Grogan, Massachussetts #63/R
$2250	£1573	To market, Jamaican village scene (25x36cm-10x14in) s.i. 12-Mar-93 Skinner, Bolton #251/R
$3000	£2098	Home from the market, Jamaican scene (41x51cm-16x20in) s. 12-Mar-93 Skinner, Bolton #249/R
$3250	£2111	Still life with grapes (30x37cm-12x15in) s. 9-Sep-93 Sotheby's Arcade, New York #36/R
$4000	£2649	Bouquet of pink roses (36x51cm-14x20in) s. 13-Nov-92 Skinner, Bolton #168/R
$4000	£2614	Fishermen conversing in rowboat (46x61cm-18x24in) s. 17-Sep-93 Du Mouchelle, Detroit #2036/R
$5000	£3247	Fishermen at sunset (45x69cm-18x27in) s. 9-Sep-93 Sotheby's Arcade, New York #91/R
$5000	£3311	Sunset on yacht (61x51cm-24x20in) s. 13-Nov-92 Skinner, Bolton #168 a/R
$8500	£5944	Summer's grace, pool with swimming swans (30x46cm-14x18in) s. canvasboard. 12-Mar-93 Skinner, Bolton #265/R
$12000	£8392	Roses (35x51cm-14x20in) s. 11-Mar-93 Christie's, New York #130/R
$14000	£9260	Spring blossoms - street scene (33x41cm-13x16in) s. st.verso. 13-Nov-92 Skinner, Bolton #169/R
$15000	£10260	Eastern Point, Gloucester (45x36cm-18x14in) s. i.verso canvasboard. 25-May-94 Sotheby's, New York #65/R
$25000	£16667	Young girl in garden (53x46cm-21x18in) i.stretcher. 25-May-94 Sotheby's, New York #64/R
$25000	£16026	Poppies (51x61cm-20x24in) s. executed c.1905-1910. 26-May-93 Christie's, New York #120/R
$26000	£16456	Poppies (51x61cm-20x24in) s. 4-Dec-92 Christie's, New York #70 a/R

GRAVES, Mary de (20th C) American
$750	£503	Ballet dancer (102x76cm-40x30in) s.d.1932 s.verso. 4-Dec-93 Louisiana Auction Exchange #21/R

GRAVES, Morris (1910-) American
$1500	£943	House in landscape (38x38cm-15x15in) painting verso double-sided. 25-Apr-93 Butterfield & Butterfield, San Francisco #2072/R
$3500	£2303	Flowers in urn (56x51cm-22x20in) s. s.i.d.33verso. 4-Nov-92 Doyle, New York #55/R
$4250	£2796	Peaches (22x41cm-9x16in) s. masonite. 31-Mar-93 Sotheby's Arcade, New York #344/R
$85000	£56291	Red powder of Puja, No.1 (115x60cm-45x24in) s.d.80 s.i.d.1980 verso tempera paper. 22-Sep-93 Christie's, New York #224/R

GRAVES, Morris (1910-) American-cont.
$2000	£1156	Slice of fruit (22x34cm-9x13in) s.d.73 tempera ink. 25-Sep-92 Sotheby's Arcade, New York #487/R
$3000	£1974	Stork (60x37cm-24x15in) s. pen wash. 13-Jun-93 Butterfield & Butterfield, San Francisco #3256/R
$4000	£2649	Untitled (25x48cm-10x19in) s.d.54 sumi ink. 13-Nov-92 Skinner, Bolton #219 a/R
$4000	£2667	Animal (42x60cm-17x24in) s.d.54 pen wash. 23-May-94 Christie's, East, New York #307/R
$4000	£2632	Bird trying to get back into shell (43x60cm-17x24in) s. pencil white chk paper on board. 31-Mar-93 Sotheby's Arcade, New York #345/R
$4200	£2857	Atlantic Plover (38x31cm-15x12in) s.d.55 wash. 15-Nov-93 Christie's, East, New York #192
$6000	£3974	Bird (62x107cm-24x42in) s.d.53 W/C gouache. 23-Sep-93 Sotheby's, New York #280/R

GRAVES, Nancy (1940-) American
$2000	£1342	Back and forth (85x66cm-33x26in) s.i.d.6-82verso oil acrylic glitter canvas. 3-May-94 Christie's, East, New York #162/R
$5000	£3356	Fracture No.6 (188x183cm-74x72in) s.i.d.9-82 verso oil acrylic. 24-Feb-94 Sotheby's Arcade, New York #423/R
$7000	£4861	Calipers, legs, lines (163x224cm-64x88in) s.i.d.10.79verso acrylic oil. 24-Feb-93 Christie's, New York #36/R
$13000	£8725	Defacta (163x193cm-64x76in) s.i.d.77verso. 4-May-94 Christie's, New York #165/R
$17000	£11409	Milaek (163x208cm-64x82in) s.d.1978 verso. 25-Feb-94 Sotheby's, New York #110/R
$18000	£12081	Disclose (163x254cm-64x100in) s.i.d.78verso oil encaustic. 3-May-94 Christie's, East, New York #85/R
$6500	*£4362*	*Xill (164x110cm-65x43in) s.d.1-12-83 W/C. 25-Feb-94 Sotheby's, New York #152/R*
$10000	*£6536*	*Vertigo (163x203cm-64x80in) s.i.d.79verso oil encaustic. 5-May-93 Christie's, New York #321/R*

GRAY, Charles Alden (1858-1933) American
$1750	£1190	Adam and Eve (70x85cm-28x33in) s.i.d.1911. 15-Apr-94 Bolland & Marotz, Bremen #766/R (DM 3000)

GRAY, Cleve (1918-) American
$3000	£1987	Waimea, square (174x170cm-69x67in) s.d.71 i.verso acrylic. 17-Nov-92 Christie's, East, New York #177/R

GRAY, Henry Percy (1869-1952) American
$982	£650	Matterhorn (44x53cm-17x21in) board oval. 26-Nov-92 Christie's, S. Kensington #28/R
$5500	£3235	Pacific lighthouse (25x36cm-10x14in) canvas on board. 4-Oct-92 Butterfield & Butterfield, Los Angeles #32/R
$7500	£4934	Monterey cypress (41x51cm-16x20in) s. 13-Jun-93 Butterfield & Butterfield, San Francisco #794/R
$9000	£5921	Sand dunes along Monterey coast (39x49cm-15x19in) s. canvas on board. 13-Jun-93 Butterfield & Butterfield, San Francisco #795/R
$2750	£1809	Crashing waves (21x27cm-8x11in) s.d.94 pen. 13-Jun-93 Butterfield & Butterfield, San Francisco #756/R
$3250	£1912	Cattle ranch (30x41cm-12x16in) s. W/C. 4-Oct-92 Butterfield & Butterfield, Los Angeles #38/R
$3750	£2604	California poppy field (27x34cm-11x13in) W/C. 7-Mar-93 Butterfield & Butterfield, San Francisco #80/R
$3750	£2467	Bend in river (29x39cm-11x15in) s. W/C. 13-Jun-93 Butterfield & Butterfield, San Francisco #755/R
$4000	£2778	Cypress tree (25x35cm-10x14in) s. W/C. 7-Mar-93 Butterfield & Butterfield, San Francisco #79/R
$4250	£2500	Cypress tree along cliffs (36x24cm-14x9in) s. W/C. 4-Oct-92 Butterfield & Butterfield, Los Angeles #33/R
$4250	£2500	Oaks and clouds (25x36cm-10x14in) s. W/C. 4-Oct-92 Butterfield & Butterfield, Los Angeles #39/R
$4750	£3209	Eucalyptus landscape (23x33cm-9x13in) s. W/C. 9-Nov-93 John Moran, Pasadena #887
$4750	£2794	Old oak tree (25x20cm-10x8in) s.d.1910 W/C. 4-Oct-92 Butterfield & Butterfield, Los Angeles #43/R
$5000	£2941	Green valley (25x36cm-10x14in) s. W/C. 4-Oct-92 Butterfield & Butterfield, Los Angeles #111/R
$5500	£3819	Field of daisies (24x34cm-9x13in) s. W/C. 7-Mar-93 Butterfield & Butterfield, San Francisco #78/R
$5500	£3691	Eucalyptus glade (51x41cm-20x16in) s.d.1918 W/C pencil. 8-Dec-93 Butterfield & Butterfield, San Francisco #3395/R
$6500	£3824	Footpath through oaks (25x36cm-10x14in) s. W/C paperboard. 4-Oct-92 Butterfield & Butterfield, Los Angeles #37/R
$7000	£4118	Rocky coast (39x49cm-15x19in) s. W/C. 4-Oct-92 Butterfield & Butterfield, Los Angeles #31/R
$8500	£5903	California oaks (25x34cm-10x13in) s. W/C. 7-Mar-93 Butterfield & Butterfield, San Francisco #75/R
$14000	£9396	When Monterey was young (36x49cm-14x19in) s. W/C. 8-Dec-93 Butterfield & Butterfield, San Francisco #3372/R
$15000	£10490	Summer pasture (50x69cm-20x27in) s. W/C pencil paper on board. 11-Mar-93 Christie's, New York #145/R
$18000	£11921	View to the Bay (49x69cm-19x27in) s.d.1927 W/C. 15-Jun-94 Butterfield & Butterfield, San Francisco #4586/R

GRAY, Jack L (1927-1981) American
$900	£592	Harbour at twilight (58x46cm-23x18in) s. masonite. 4-Nov-92 Doyle, New York #29

GRAY, Jack L (1927-1981) American-cont.
$1456	£971	Margaree Valley, Cape Breton (56x76cm-22x30in) s. s.i.verso board. 11-May-94 Sotheby's, Toronto #74/R (C.D 2000)
$1500	£1000	Two fishermen in a dory (61x91cm-24x36in) s. 23-May-94 Christie's, East, New York #178/R
$1650	£1058	View of Fishermen on their boat (61x91cm-24x36in) s. 13-Dec-92 Litchfield Auction Gallery #13
$2000	£1316	Fishermen in choppy seas (60x90cm-24x35in) s. 31-Mar-93 Sotheby's Arcade, New York #171/R
$3200	£2133	Pulling in herring net (66x91cm-26x36in) s. init.i.verso. 23-May-94 Christie's, East, New York #163/R
$4000	£2614	Off the Gimlet (76x127cm-30x50in) s.d.56. 4-May-93 Christie's, East, New York #200/R
$6500	£4276	Lobsterman pulling in pots (61x91cm-24x36in) s. 4-Nov-92 Doyle, New York #23/R
$11000	£7333	Brooklyn Bridge with New York skyline (66x91cm-26x36in) s. 16-Mar-94 Christie's, New York #115/R
$30000	£19231	Salt bankers - schooner 'Alcala' (92x152cm-36x60in) s. init.i.stretcher. 26-May-93 Christie's, New York #232/R
$880	£575	Grand Banks Doryman (53x71cm-21x28in) s. W/C gouache graphite. 14-May-93 Skinner, Bolton #120/R

GRAY, Mary (20th C) American
$1000	£641	New England fireplace (51x41cm-20x16in) s. 9-Dec-92 Butterfield & Butterfield, San Francisco #4017/R

GRAZIANO, F (20th C) American?
$1400	£921	Lilies of field (51x41cm-20x16in) s. s.d.1921. 31-Mar-93 Sotheby's Arcade, New York #277/R

GREACEN, Edmund William (1877-1949) American
$2500	£1656	Spirit of chrysanthemum (76x63cm-30x25in) s.indist.d. 23-Sep-93 Sotheby's, New York #215/R
$2800	£1618	New York Harbour (40x30cm-16x12in) s.d.1915 s.i.verso board. 23-Sep-92 Christie's, New York #199/R
$5000	£3497	Spray of flowers in blue vase (64x76cm-25x30in) s.d.1940verso. 11-Mar-93 Mystic Fine Arts, Connecticut #209/R
$800	£526	Flowering trees by lake (25x29cm-10x11in) s. pastel. 31-Mar-93 Sotheby's Arcade, New York #280/R

GREATOREX, Eleanor Elizabeth (1854-?) American
$650	£439	Mere Poulain knitting (27x23cm-11x9in) s.d.1894 s.d.verso i.stretcher. 20-Mar-93 Weschler, Washington #92/R

GREEN, C L (1844-1915) American
$2500	£1667	Rocky coast (25x36cm-10x14in) 22-May-94 James Bakker, Cambridge #63/R

GREEN, Charles Lewis (1844-1915) American
$2400	£1270	Morning's stroll (20x30cm-8x12in) s. 11-Sep-92 Skinner, Bolton #203/R

GREENBAUM, Joseph (1864-1940) American
$700	£467	Atmospheric landscape (20x25cm-8x10in) s. panel. 15-Mar-94 John Moran, Pasadena #80
$800	£541	Atmospheric south west landscape (51x61cm-20x24in) s. 9-Nov-93 John Moran, Pasadena #909

GREENE, Albert van Nesse (1887-?) American
$2200	£1477	Snow scene (61x74cm-24x29in) s. 24-Mar-94 Mystic Fine Arts, Connecticut #98
$2800	£1772	Houses by pond in winter (65x81cm-26x32in) s. 2-Dec-92 Christie's, East, New York #400

GREENE, Art (20th C) American
$3800	£2568	Black ice (236x102cm-93x40in) metal acrylic canvas on panel arched top. 8-Nov-93 Christie's, East, New York #4/R

GREENE, Balcomb (1904-1990) American
$1800	£1208	Naked in the light (91x122cm-36x48in) s. 6-May-94 Skinner, Bolton #158 a/R
$2000	£1266	The Parisians (107x137cm-42x54in) s. 2-Dec-92 Christie's, East, New York #390/R
$4000	£2649	Daybreak (157x142cm-62x56in) s. 30-Jun-93 Sotheby's Arcade, New York #317/R
$650	£433	Abstract figures (52x38cm-20x15in) s.d.56 ink wash crayon. 12-Mar-94 Weschler, Washington #176/R

GREENE, J Barry (1895-1966) American
$700	£473	Quaint houses Beaulieu (71x58cm-28x23in) s.d.1927. 31-Oct-93 Hindman Galleries, Chicago #721
$850	£594	Seated woman (56x46cm-22x18in) s.d.1930. 14-Mar-93 Hindman Galleries, Chicago #64/R

GREENE, Walter L (19/20th C) American
$1100	£743	New England landscape (86x64cm-34x25in) 10-Aug-93 Stonington Fine Arts, Stonington #36

GREENLEAF, Jacob (1887-1968) American
$700	£486	Woodland pond (41x51cm-16x20in) s. 27-Feb-93 Young Fine Arts Auctions, Maine #119/R

GREENLEAF, Jacob (1887-1968) American-cont.
$1700   £1111   View of Gloucester (51x61cm-20x24in) s. 18-Sep-93 Young Fine Arts Auctions, Maine #139/R

GREENWOOD, Ethan Allen (1779-1856) American
$7000   £4545   Portraits of husband and wife (61x46cm-24x18in) s.d.1811 pair. 8-Jul-94 Sloan, North Bethesda #2731/R

GREENWOOD, Ethan Allen (attrib) (1779-1856) American
$750   £504   Portrait of a young gentleman (66x51cm-26x20in) i.verso. 26-Mar-94 Skinner, Bolton #158/R

GREENWOOD, John (attrib) (1727-1792) American
$2229   £1476   View of woodsawing mills at Zaan, City of Zaandam beyond (25x35cm-10x14in) s.i.verso pencil chk wash with drawing Jan Rood. 24-Nov-92 Christie's, Amsterdam #310/R (D.FL 4000)

GREENWOOD, Joseph H (1857-1927) American
$1000   £529   Tree, a touch of autumn (25x15cm-10x6in) s.d.99 panel. 11-Sep-92 Skinner, Bolton #241 b/R
$1000   £529   Field on the ridge, autumn (25x41cm-10x16in) s.d.17 panel. 11-Sep-92 Skinner, Bolton #207/R
$2250   £1490   Autumnal scene (76x107cm-30x42in) s.d.98 i.verso. 13-Nov-92 Skinner, Bolton #84/R

GREGOIRE, Alexandre (1922-) Haitian
$1449   £947   Le marche range (51x61cm-20x24in) painted 1976. 17-May-93 Hoebanx, Paris #103 (F.FR 8000)

GREGOR, Harold (1929-) American
$2800   £1830   Illinois landscape no.43 (152x213cm-60x84in) s.d.1980 verso oil acrylic. 7-May-93 Christie's, East, New York #134/R

GREGORY, E (20th C) American
$2100   £1469   Portrait of a young girl in a pink dress (107x79cm-42x31in) s.d.1843 verso. 12-Mar-93 Hart Gallery, Houston #4
$3184   £2211   Portrait de jeune femme (85x64cm-33x25in) s. 4-Mar-93 Courchet Palloc & Japhet, Paris #9/R (F.FR 18000)

GRETHE, Carlos (1864-1913) South American
$1513   £1016   View of Hamburg harbour at evening (24x30cm-9x12in) mono. canvas laid down on board. 3-Dec-93 Dr Fritz Nagel, Stuttgart #3279 (DM 2600)
$1667   £1111   Hamburg Harbour with threemaster (80x80cm-31x31in) s. 11-Mar-94 Dr Fritz Nagel, Stuttgart #2535 (DM 2800)
$1921   £1289   Seascape with fishing boat (25x34cm-10x13in) mono. hessian. 1-Dec-93 Dorling, Hamburg #2027 (DM 3300)
$2430   £1688   Fishermen seated in rowing boat and other boats in calm sea (33x48cm-13x19in) mono board. 26-Feb-93 Dr Fritz Nagel, Stuttgart #2846/R (DM 4000)
$2910   £1953   View of sailing ship (56x80cm-22x31in) mono.i. 3-Dec-93 Dr Fritz Nagel, Stuttgart #3277 (DM 5000)
$3201   £2148   Beach scene at Nieuport (56x80cm-22x31in) mono. 3-Dec-93 Dr Fritz Nagel, Stuttgart #3278 (DM 5500)

GRETZNER, Harold (1902-1977) American
$650   £430   Chinatown with auto (53x71cm-21x28in) s. W/C. 28-Sep-93 John Moran, Pasadena #256
$700   £464   Chinatown (56x71cm-22x28in) s. W/C. 28-Sep-93 John Moran, Pasadena #307
$700   £473   Rotunda Building San Francisco (53x71cm-21x28in) s. W/C. 9-Nov-93 John Moran, Pasadena #811
$750   £507   Chinatown street scene (51x74cm-20x29in) s. W/C. 15-Jun-93 John Moran, Pasedena #177
$800   £552   Lake Merritt, Oakland (46x64cm-18x25in) s. W/C. 16-Feb-93 John Moran, Pasadena #86
$850   £563   Northern California - Back Bay (51x74cm-20x29in) s. W/C. 14-Jun-94 John Moran, Pasadena #86
$850   £563   Street scene with autos (53x71cm-21x28in) s. W/C. 28-Sep-93 John Moran, Pasadena #255
$1600   £1060   San Francisco from Alameda (46x56cm-18x22in) s. d.1944verso W/C. 28-Sep-93 John Moran, Pasadena #240

GRIFFIN, Charles Gerald (1864-1945) American
$1000   £671   Luminous sunset landscape (25x36cm-10x14in) s. 5-Aug-93 Eldred, Massachusetts #676/R

GRIFFIN, Thomas Bailey (19th C) American
$625   £417   River landscape with mountains beyond (30x46cm-12x18in) s. 21-May-94 Weschler, Washington #90/R
$700   £473   Rushing mountain stream (30x25cm-12x10in) s. 31-Mar-94 Sotheby's Arcade, New York #23/R
$900   £629   Landscape with approaching storm (41x51cm-16x20in) s. 5-Feb-93 Sloan, North Bethesda #1685/R
$950   £638   River landscape (41x61cm-16x24in) s. 2-Dec-93 Freeman Fine Arts, Philadelphia #782
$1100   £738   The passing shower (61x91cm-24x36in) s. i.verso. 1-Dec-93 Doyle, New York #53
$1200   £789   Grey sky, White Waters (76x102cm-30x40in) s. 31-Mar-93 Sotheby's Arcade, New York #92/R

GRIFFIN, Thomas Bailey (19th C) American-cont.
$1200	£635	The Delaware river. View near Bethel, Conn. (25x36cm-10x14in) s. two. 11-Sep-92 Skinner, Bolton #194
$1200	£694	Mt Washington, Mass. seen from the Egremont Road (51x76cm-20x30in) s.d.05 s.i.d.verso. 25-Sep-92 Sotheby's Arcade, New York #21/R
$1500	£794	Morning along the river (51x76cm-20x30in) s. 11-Sep-92 Skinner, Bolton #188/R
$2000	£1418	Landscape with waterfall (76x64cm-30x25in) s. 14-Feb-93 Hanzel Galleries, Chicago #10/R
$2000	£1325	Mountain stream (46x71cm-18x28in) s. 15-Jun-94 Butterfield & Butterfield, San Francisco #4413/R
$2250	£1490	River landscape (76x64cm-30x25in) s.indis.d. 28-Sep-93 John Moran, Pasadena #346

GRIFFIN, Walter (1861-1935) American
$1000	£649	Unloading fish (33x41cm-13x16in) s. board. 4-Aug-94 Eldred, Massachusetts #714/R
$1200	£800	Landscape, Longpre, France (33x41cm-13x16in) s. s.d.1914 verso board. 23-May-94 Christie's, East, New York #145/R
$6000	£4000	Old Church Tower, Contes France (84x91cm-33x36in) s. 23-May-94 Christie's, East, New York #147/R
$7000	£4545	Landscape with farmhouses (25x46cm-10x18in) s.i. painted c.1890. 8-Jul-94 Sloan, North Bethesda #2724/R

GRIFFIN, de Lacy (19/20th C) American
$1550	£1054	Scene near Cresson, PA (46x61cm-18x24in) s. 9-Jul-93 Sloan, North Bethesda #2833/R

GRIFFITH, Grace Allison (1885-1955) American
$1600	£1053	Sunrise, Marin County (48x37cm-19x15in) s.d.23 W/C. 13-Jun-93 Butterfield & Butterfield, San Francisco #763/R

GRIFFITH, William Alexander (1866-1940) American
$650	£430	Landscape (18x23cm-7x9in) s. canvasboard. 14-Jun-94 John Moran, Pasadena #44 a
$1000	£588	At Laguna (30x51cm-12x20in) s.d.1919. 4-Oct-92 Butterfield & Butterfield, Los Angeles #181/R
$2000	£1351	California hills (51x61cm-20x24in) s.d.1936. 15-Jun-93 John Moran, Pasadena #58
$3500	£2318	Desert landscape (64x76cm-25x30in) s.d.1929. 28-Sep-93 John Moran, Pasadena #232
$1400	£972	Laguna landscape (51x41cm-20x16in) s.d.Aug.5'24 pastel linen. 7-Mar-93 Butterfield & Butterfield, San Francisco #215/R

GRIGGS, Samuel W (?-1898) American
$650	£425	Northwest Bay, Lake George (28x46cm-11x18in) s.verso board. 30-Jun-94 Mystic Fine Arts, Connecticut #82/R
$1100	£728	Sea view near Lynn (41x66cm-16x26in) s.d.1874. 28-Nov-92 Young Fine Arts Auctions, Maine #185/R
$1300	£850	In quiet cove - coastal view with figure, vessels and lighthouse (36x61cm-14x24in) s.d.76. 17-Sep-93 Skinner, Bolton #191/R
$1600	£1060	N. Conway, NH (20x25cm-8x10in) s.i. d.Sept 22 1868verso board. 28-Nov-92 Young Fine Arts Auctions, Maine #184/R

GRIMEAU, Bryan de (20th C) American
$1800	£1059	Raymond Mays making fastest time of the day (36x74cm-14x29in) s.i. mixed media. 8-Oct-92 Boos Gallery, Michigan #96/R

GRIMM, Paul (1892-1974) American
$550	£374	Flowers on the desert floor (15x20cm-6x8in) s. board. 16-Apr-94 Young Fine Arts Auctions, Maine #123/R
$700	£473	Landscape (20x25cm-8x10in) s. board. 9-Nov-93 John Moran, Pasadena #870
$700	£483	Mr. Rainier (61x76cm-24x30in) s. 16-Feb-93 John Moran, Pasadena #110 a
$750	£517	California (51x102cm-20x40in) s. 16-Feb-93 John Moran, Pasadena #90
$750	£497	Portrait of Thekla (51x41cm-20x16in) s. canvasboard. 28-Sep-93 John Moran, Pasadena #353
$800	£541	Mountains and desert (61x76cm-24x30in) s. 9-Nov-93 John Moran, Pasadena #829 a
$850	£563	Landscape, peace and quiet (61x91cm-24x36in) s. 28-Sep-93 John Moran, Pasadena #249
$850	£570	Desert scene (46x61cm-18x24in) s. 24-Jun-93 Mystic Fine Arts, Connecticut #100 a
$900	£596	Eucalyptus trees (41x30cm-16x12in) s. masonite. 28-Sep-93 John Moran, Pasadena #221
$900	£608	Landscape (23x30cm-9x12in) s. board. 9-Nov-93 John Moran, Pasadena #871
$950	£642	Colourful desert (71x91cm-28x36in) s. 15-Jun-93 John Moran, Pasadena #81
$950	£629	Lonely road (41x51cm-16x20in) s. s.i.verso canvasboard. 15-Jun-94 Butterfield & Butterfield, San Francisco #4726/R
$1000	£658	Lone smoke tree (66x102cm-26x40in) s. s.d.1962. 13-Jun-93 Butterfield & Butterfield, San Francisco #938/R
$1100	£743	Sierra Grandeur-Palisades Glacier (71x91cm-28x36in) s. 15-Jun-93 John Moran, Pasadena #120
$1200	£759	Box Canyon and Smoke Trees near Palm Springs, Ca. (51x62cm-20x24in) s. s.i.d.1963verso canvasboard. 2-Dec-92 Christie's, East, New York #182/R
$1600	£1081	Mountain landscape (30x41cm-12x16in) s. canvasboard. 15-Jun-94 John Moran, Pasadena #42
$1700	£1141	Under desert sky (61x76cm-24x30in) s. s.i.verso. 8-Dec-93 Butterfield & Butterfield, San Francisco #3571/R
$1700	£1090	Desert colours (46x61cm-18x24in) s. s.i.verso board. 28-May-93 Sloan, North Bethesda #2650/R
$1900	£1319	Under the sun (46x61cm-18x24in) s. s.i.d.1947verso. 7-Mar-93 Butterfield & Butterfield, San Francisco #224/R

GRIMM, Paul (1892-1974) American-cont.
$2000	£1389	Colourful sand dunes (61x76cm-24x30in) s. s.i.d.1961verso. 7-Mar-93 Butterfield & Butterfield, San Francisco #223/R
$2000	£1389	Colourful spring dunes (61x76cm-24x30in) s. s.i.d.1960verso. 7-Mar-93 Butterfield & Butterfield, San Francisco #222/R
$3000	£1974	Los Angeles harbour (51x62cm-20x24in) s. 13-Jun-93 Butterfield & Butterfield, San Francisco #885/R

GROLL, Albert Lorey (1866-1952) American
$1200	£795	Rain clouds, Orizon desert near Tauz, Arizona (30x41cm-12x16in) s. painted 1930 board. 28-Nov-92 Young Fine Arts Auctions, Maine #186/R
$1400	£809	Lava beds, Laguna, New Mexico (30x41cm-12x16in) s. 25-Sep-92 Sotheby's Arcade, New York #190

GROMME, Owen J (attrib) (?-1991) American
$20000	£13605	Pheasants alighting (76x102cm-30x40in) s.d.66. 17-Apr-94 Schrager Galleries, Milwaukee #737/R
$25000	£17007	Eagle and otter (61x91cm-24x36in) s.d.86. 17-Apr-94 Schrager Galleries, Milwaukee #744
$30000	£20408	A bevy of Bobwhites (61x76cm-24x30in) s.d.86. 17-Apr-94 Schrager Galleries, Milwaukee #742
$37000	£25170	Ruffled grouse in snow (71x102cm-28x40in) s.d.83. 17-Apr-94 Schrager Galleries, Milwaukee #736/R

GROOM, Emily (attrib) (1876-1975) American
$1400	£952	Floral still life (?x74cm-?x29in) s.d.35 board. 17-Apr-94 Schrager Galleries, Milwaukee #543
$1600	£1088	Floral still life (?x74cm-?x29in) s.d.35 board. 17-Apr-94 Schrager Galleries, Milwaukee #544
$600	*£397*	*Floral still life (61x46cm-24x18in) s. pastel. 26-Sep-93 Schrager Galleries, Milwaukee #448*

GROOME, Esther M (?-1929) American
$4000	£2312	Summer afternoon (64x69cm-25x27in) s. 27-Sep-92 James Bakker, Cambridge #121/R

GROOMS, Red (1937-) American
$2900	*£2014*	*Black and white Maine cows (27x36cm-11x14in) s.d.77 W/C felt tip. 26-Feb-93 Sotheby's Arcade, New York #380/R*
$4500	*£3125*	*Conch cleaners (61x46cm-24x18in) s.d.83 i.verso W/C. 22-Feb-93 Christie's, East, New York #215/R*
$11000	*£7190*	*Jean Louis Scherrer (74x109cm-29x43in) s.d.77 gouache. 4-May-93 Sotheby's, New York #391 a/R*

GROPPER, William (1897-1977) American
$750	£500	Two men on horseback (40x46cm-16x18in) s. paper on masonite. 23-May-94 Christie's, East, New York #231
$850	£552	The Senator (20x25cm-8x10in) s. masonite. 9-Sep-93 Sotheby's Arcade, New York #325/R
$950	£625	Spotter (51x41cm-20x16in) s. s.d.1942 stretcher. 31-Mar-93 Sotheby's Arcade, New York #370/R
$1000	£578	The jurist (29x24cm-11x9in) s. st.sig.verso tempera panel. 25-Sep-92 Sotheby's Arcade, New York #453/R
$1500	£974	Bataan (46x56cm-18x22in) s. painted 1942. 9-Sep-93 Sotheby's Arcade, New York #332/R
$1600	£1039	Fish tonight (46x61cm-18x24in) s. 9-Sep-93 Sotheby's Arcade, New York #326/R
$2100	£1382	Waiter (30x30cm-12x12in) s. panel. 31-Mar-93 Sotheby's Arcade, New York #367/R
$2250	£1471	The politician (36x46cm-14x18in) s. masonite. 20-May-93 Boos Gallery, Michigan #462/R
$7000	£4636	Villagers (66x76cm-26x30in) s. 23-Sep-93 Sotheby's, New York #261/R
$23000	£15333	The last cow (61x86cm-24x34in) s. 25-May-94 Sotheby's, New York #143/R
$1100	*£724*	*Torch song (35x42cm-14x17in) s. gouache. 31-Mar-93 Sotheby's Arcade, New York #359/R*
$1400	*£886*	*Woman reading (28x42cm-11x17in) s. W/C ink. 2-Dec-92 Christie's, East, New York #366*
$1500	*£987*	*Jurist (52x66cm-20x26in) s. chl pastel. 31-Mar-93 Sotheby's Arcade, New York #362/R*

GROSE, Daniel C (1865-1890) American
$1600	£1067	Autumn riverscape with angler (36x61cm-14x24in) s.d.1873. 1-Jun-94 Doyle, New York #32
$1700	£1133	The Old City of Delhi, India (41x76cm-16x30in) s.d.1887 canvas on panel. 23-May-94 Christie's, East, New York #77

GROSS, Chaim (1904-1991) American
$550	£362	Female nude (50x32cm-20x13in) s. indist.i.verso pencil W/C double-sided. 31-Mar-93 Sotheby's Arcade, New York #438/R
$550	£367	Flatbush (34x55cm-13x22in) s.d.48 W/C pen pencil. 23-May-94 Christie's, East, New York #235/R
$600	£347	The gossips (37x58cm-15x23in) s. s.i.d.1950verso W/C ink pencil. 25-Sep-92 Sotheby's Arcade, New York #488/R
$750	£504	At the beach - a Provincetown scene (29x56cm-11x22in) s. W/C graphite paperboard. 4-Mar-94 Skinner, Bolton #300/R
$750	£434	Three rabbis (36x28cm-14x11in) s.mono pencil W/C. 25-Sep-92 Sotheby's Arcade, New York #450/R

GROSS, Chaim (1904-1991) American-cont.
$800	£523	Acrobats (27x19cm-11x7in) s.d.1949 ink. 4-May-93 Christie's, East, New York #275/R
$950	£549	Bird in flight (37x58cm-15x23in) s.d.1948 W/C pencil. 25-Sep-92 Sotheby's Arcade, New York #319/R
$1300	£818	The music maker (56x34cm-22x13in) s. graphite W/C paper laid down on board. 25-Apr-93 Butterfield & Butterfield, San Francisco #2023/R
$1500	£962	Figure on pier with town beyond (58x86cm-23x34in) s.d.1947 W/C. 13-Dec-92 Hindman Galleries, Chicago #60/R

GROSS, Peter Alfred (1849-1914) American
$600	£392	Puerta de ciudadela (31x41cm-12x16in) s.i.d.1891 panel. 27-Jun-94 Gomensoro, Montevideo #45

GROSSMAN, Edwin Booth (1887-1957) American
$1900	£1329	Still life (69x89cm-27x35in) s.d.13 i.verso. 12-Mar-93 Skinner, Bolton #282/R

GROSSMAN, Nancy (1940-) American
$1000	£662	Tether (102x66cm-40x26in) s.d.73 lithographic crayon wash. 30-Jun-93 Sotheby's Arcade, New York #331/R
$1500	£993	Horinzontal swimming figure. Untitled , s.d.75 and 62 crayon wash col.chk two. 17-Nov-92 Christie's, East, New York #212/R
$3500	£2431	Pastel No.11 (66x51cm-26x20in) s.d.76 pastel W/C collage. 26-Feb-93 Sotheby's Arcade, New York #385/R
$4250	£2951	Formal - blue (91x137cm-36x54in) s.d.76 W/C collage. 26-Feb-93 Sotheby's Arcade, New York #386/R

GROSZ, George (1893-1959) American/German
$4800	£3200	Douglaston - winter village with fir trees (41x36cm-16x14in) s. s.i.d.1938verso. 4-Jun-94 Lempertz, Cologne #187/R (DM 8000)
$12240	£8000	Female nude standing (66x51cm-26x20in) 11-May-93 Galerie Fischer, Lucerne #2138/R (S.FR 18000)
$14294	£9593	Nudo femminile (60x38cm-24x15in) s. thinned oil. 25-Mar-93 Finarte, Rome #256/R (I.L 23000000)
$20327	£13462	Female nude on beach (69x51cm-27x20in) s. 16-Jun-94 Galerie Koller, Zurich #3030/R (S.FR 28000)
$21950	£14932	Female nude on beach (69x51cm-27x20in) s.studio st. 19-Nov-93 Galerie Koller, Zurich #3033/R (S.FR 33000)
$41534	£28063	My dream becomes reality (70x51cm-28x20in) s. s.i.d.1944verso. 26-Nov-93 Schloss Ahlden, Ahlden #2009/R (DM 71000)
$700	£461	Nocturne in minor key (59x46cm-23x18in) s.i. i.d.1937 verso Indian ink chl. 31-Mar-93 Sotheby's Arcade, New York #350/R
$835	£565	Standing female nude (32x10cm-13x4in) s.d.1914 Indian ink brush. 23-Oct-93 Wolfgang Ketterer, Munich #341/R (DM 1400)
$837	£558	Reclining female nude (25x10cm-10x4in) chl. 6-Jun-94 Wolfgang Ketterer, Munich #851/R (DM 1400)
$896	£598	Reclining male nude (16x19cm-6x7in) s. pen wash. 6-Jun-94 Wolfgang Ketterer, Munich #850 a/R (DM 1500)
$950	£633	Study of a seated nude (28x23cm-11x9in) s.d.18 pencil Indian ink. 26-May-94 Sloan, North Bethesda #2127/R
$952	£602	Landscape with bush (18x29cm-7x11in) s.i.d.1948 chl. 30-Nov-92 Wolfgang Ketterer, Munich #126 (DM 1500)
$952	£602	Hilly landscape (21x29cm-8x11in) s.i.d.1951 pencil board. 30-Nov-92 Wolfgang Ketterer, Munich #128/R (DM 1500)
$952	£602	Garnet Lake (39x50cm-15x20in) s.i.d.1943 pencil Indian ink pen over W/C. 30-Nov-92 Wolfgang Ketterer, Munich #125/R (DM 1500)
$1020	£680	Elevated railway line (22x17cm-9x7in) s.i.d.15 i.verso chk. 4-Jun-94 Galerie Bassenge, Berlin #6180 (DM 1700)
$1074	£726	Prostitute with three visitors (16x19cm-6x7in) s. Indian ink pen sepia wash vellum. 23-Oct-93 Wolfgang Ketterer, Munich #342/R (DM 1800)
$1100	£733	Drei soldaten (23x28cm-9x11in) pencil China paper. 26-May-94 Sloan, North Bethesda #2126/R
$1193	£780	Cafe scene. Cafe scene (13x15cm-5x6in) d.25.6.12 ar.verso pencil. 27-Jun-94 Christie's, S. Kensington #91/R
$1200	£789	New England beach (48x38cm-19x15in) s. W/C. 31-Mar-93 Sotheby's Arcade, New York #398/R
$1206	£763	Fisher hut (38x49cm-15x19in) s.i.d.1949 chl. 30-Nov-92 Wolfgang Ketterer, Munich #127/R (DM 1900)
$1224	£800	Stream with bass (49x39cm-19x15in) s. W/C. 27-Jun-94 Christie's, S. Kensington #94/R
$1269	£803	Embankment (12x19cm-5x7in) s.d.1912 chl. 30-Nov-92 Wolfgang Ketterer, Munich #123/R (DM 2000)
$1494	£996	Reclining nude (16x32cm-6x13in) s.d.1915 pen. 9-Jun-94 Hauswedell & Nolte, Hamburg #301/R (DM 2500)
$1639	£1100	Eine Studie von Baumstammen (40x58cm-16x23in) s.i.d.39 chl. 13-Oct-93 Sotheby's, London #282/R
$1655	£1089	Seated woman (65x52cm-26x20in) s.i. ink brush. 10-Jun-93 Hauswedell & Nolte, Hamburg #367/R (DM 2700)
$1673	£1116	Delicatessen scene (46x59cm-18x23in) s. W/C Indian ink pen executed 1933 board. 7-Jun-94 Karl & Faber, Munich #729/R (DM 2800)
$1696	£1146	Girl in street (36x25cm-14x10in) s. col.pencil vellum on paper. 27-Nov-93 Villa Grisebach, Berlin #526/R (DM 2900)
$1800	£1192	Sitzender Akt (29x22cm-11x9in) st.verso pen. 10-Nov-92 Christie's, East, New York #109/R

GROSZ, George (1893-1959) American/German-cont.

$1800	£1208	Bauer mit schwerem fass (46x60cm-18x24in) st.s. Indian ink executed c.1924. 24-Feb-94 Sotheby's Arcade, New York #57/R
$2000	£1351	In the woods (30x23cm-12x9in) s.d.43 W/C. 31-Mar-94 Sotheby's Arcade, New York #289/R
$2000	£1342	Nocturne in Minor Key (59x46cm-23x18in) s.i. Indian ink pencil. 11-Dec-93 Weschler, Washington #122/R
$2160	£1440	Portrait of Walter Mehring (41x26cm-16x10in) i.verso pencil. 4-Jun-94 Galerie Bassenge, Berlin #6184 (DM 3600)
$2300	£1513	Back of woman in long skirt (62x46cm-24x18in) s.d.38 chl. 31-Mar-93 Sotheby's Arcade, New York #361/R
$2359	£1594	Woman at a table (59x46cm-23x18in) s. pen. 19-Jun-93 Henner Wachholtz, Hamburg #148 (DM 4000)
$2370	£1500	Sitzende Frau (65x53cm-26x21in) st.sig. painted c.1929 pen brush ink. 30-Nov-92 Christie's, S. Kensington #26/R
$2400	£1600	Sitzender weiblicher akt (31x33cm-12x13in) s. brush black ink. 9-May-94 Christie's, East, New York #99/R
$2475	£1566	Reclining female nude (38x56cm-15x22in) s.i.d.1951 ochre. 30-Nov-92 Wolfgang Ketterer, Munich #129/R (DM 3900)
$2500	£1656	The Wendelstein (61x51cm-24x20in) s. i.d.1952verso W/C. 10-Nov-92 Christie's, East, New York #187/R
$2510	£1673	Scene in the Circus Medrano (30x24cm-12x9in) s.i. pen. 9-Jun-94 Hauswedell & Nolte, Hamburg #305/R (DM 4200)
$2613	£1814	Dada collage (35x20cm-14x8in) st.sig. 26-Feb-93 Dr Fritz Nagel, Stuttgart #607/R (DM 4300)
$2689	£1793	To the Chief Editor - interior with man reading paper (29x35cm-11x14in) s.d.1911 Indian ink W/C board. 7-Jun-94 Karl & Faber, Munich #727/R (DM 4500)
$2689	£1793	Wounded person (59x46cm-23x18in) pencil pen. 6-Jun-94 Wolfgang Ketterer, Munich #95/R (DM 4500)
$2721	£1802	Pfeifen (50x30cm-20x12in) s. ink cardboard. 19-Nov-92 Finarte, Rome #154/R (I.L 3800000)
$2988	£1992	Unlucky conversion (20x26cm-8x10in) s.i. pen. 6-Jun-94 Wolfgang Ketterer, Munich #93/R (DM 5000)
$3000	£2000	World peace (59x46cm-23x18in) s. ink pencil. 9-Jun-94 Sotheby's Arcade, New York #50/R
$3000	£1765	Untitled (44x29cm-17x11in) s. brush ink. 5-Oct-92 Sotheby's, New York #65/R
$3000	£2000	Crouching female figure (27x32cm-11x13in) s.d.16 pencil part wash vellum. 4-Jun-94 Galerie Bassenge, Berlin #6181 (DM 5000)
$3187	£2097	Nude (61x32cm-24x13in) s.i. chl. 8-Jun-93 Karl & Faber, Munich #811/R (DM 5200)
$3500	£2303	Driftwood on the beach (46x61cm-18x24in) s. W/C. 11-Jun-93 Du Mouchelle, Detroit #2013/R
$3500	£2431	Passers by (59x46cm-23x18in) s. studio st.i.verso executed 1928 pencil. 23-Feb-93 Sotheby's, New York #45/R
$3526	£2351	Sand dunes (17x34cm-7x13in) s. W/C. 6-Jun-94 Wolfgang Ketterer, Munich #103/R (DM 5900)
$3725	£2500	Wandervogel (65x50cm-26x20in) s. brush ink. 23-Jun-93 Sotheby's, London #272/R
$4000	£2649	Bavarian woods (37x55cm-15x22in) s. W/C. 10-Nov-92 Christie's, East, New York #188/R
$4000	£2353	Stehende frau (52x40cm-20x16in) st.sig. brush ink double-sided blk.crayon. 5-Oct-92 Sotheby's, New York #64/R
$4200	£2745	Salesclerk (64x44cm-25x17in) st.sig. pen brush Indian ink over pencil 1931. 13-May-93 Christie's, New York #170/R
$4217	£2756	Gute Zeit (63x48cm-25x19in) s. i.verso W/C over pen. 15-May-93 Kunstgalerij de Vuyst, Lokeren #421/R (B.FR 140000)
$4500	£3020	Driftwood on the beach (48x65cm-19x26in) s.i. W/C. 24-Feb-94 Sotheby's Arcade, New York #65/R
$4583	£3076	Hoch Tartarin (32x31cm-13x12in) s. Indian ink pen felttip pen executed c.1921. 29-Nov-93 Wolfgang Ketterer, Munich #120/R (DM 7875)
$4656	£3125	Unlike couple (38x34cm-15x13in) s. Indian ink brush spray technique exec.1928. 4-Dec-93 Galerie Bassenge, Berlin #6252/R (DM 8000)
$4656	£3125	Elect K.P.D., he wants to wipe it out (65x52cm-26x20in) s. Indian ink brush. 4-Dec-93 Galerie Bassenge, Berlin #6250/R (DM 8000)
$4800	£3200	Party round table (49x37cm-19x15in) s.i. Indian ink vellum executed c.1925. 4-Jun-94 Galerie Bassenge, Berlin #6178/R (DM 8000)
$4976	£3252	Bavarian forest (37x55cm-15x22in) s. W/C. 8-May-93 Schloss Ahlden, Ahlden #1216/R (DM 8000)
$5000	£3333	View of New York from Central Park (49x39cm-19x15in) s.d.34 W/C. 23-May-94 Christie's, East, New York #233/R
$5000	£2941	Lola (28x22cm-11x9in) s.i. ink htd.white gouache. 5-Oct-92 Sotheby's, New York #66/R
$5235	£3313	Female nude with stockings reclining (38x57cm-15x22in) s.d.1939 W/C over sepia pen. 30-Nov-92 Wolfgang Ketterer, Munich #124/R (DM 8250)
$5250	£3088	Sitzende frau. Waffenschieber (56x44cm-22x17in) s. brush ink double-sided. 5-Oct-92 Sotheby's, New York #101/R
$5296	£3555	At the art dealer's (47x54cm-19x21in) s. i.verso pen white. 29-Nov-93 Wolfgang Ketterer, Munich #121/R (DM 9100)
$5500	£3595	Nude with straw hat. Standing nude (56x35cm-22x14in) st. col.chk gouache W/C double-sided. 10-May-93 Christie's, East, New York #143/R
$5662	£3800	Liegender Akt (29x44cm-11x17in) st.sig. st.sig.i.verso W/C. 21-Jun-93 Christie's, S. Kensington #56/R
$5677	£3785	In the circle (43x55cm-17x22in) s.i. pen over pencil. 6-Jun-94 Wolfgang Ketterer, Munich #98/R (DM 9500)
$6000	£3529	Beim Rhein-wein (39x50cm-15x20in) W/C. 5-Oct-92 Sotheby's, New York #67/R
$6000	£4196	Prayer (38x51cm-15x20in) s. W/C. 12-Mar-93 Du Mouchelle, Detroit #2000/R

GROSZ, George (1893-1959) American/German-cont.

$6140	£4094	La danseuse (26x19cm-10x7in) s. studio st.verso ink wash htd.white gouache. 8-Jun-94 Poulain & le Fur, Paris #94/R (F.FR 35000)
$6885	£4500	madchen mit hut (60x46cm-24x18in) st.sig.num.5 126 6 verso soft pencil drawn 1925. 20-May-93 Christie's, London #599/R
$7000	£4762	Entente Cordiale (65x52cm-26x20in) s.i. brush ink executed 1924 sketch verso. 4-Apr-94 Sotheby's, Tel Aviv #98/R
$7106	£4675	Nude on the beach (50x35cm-20x14in) s.i. W/C over pencil painted c.1935. 5-Jun-93 Villa Grisebach, Berlin #333 (DM 11500)
$7171	£4781	Untitled (28x21cm-11x8in) s. collage pen chk. 9-Jun-94 Hauswedell & Nolte, Hamburg #311/R (DM 12000)
$7476	£4854	Femme se coiffant (14x9cm-6x4in) s.i.d.26/2/1923verso collage after Edgar Degas. 22-Jun-94 Galerie Kornfeld, Berne #464/R (S.FR 10000)
$7500	£5068	Der Dank des Vaterlandes (49x37cm-19x15in) st.sig. i.studio st.verso W/C pen. 4-Nov-93 Sotheby's, New York #213/R
$7579	£4858	Maytime (57x46cm-22x18in) s. Indian ink pen brush executed 1924. 26-May-93 Lempertz, Cologne #194/R (DM 12000)
$7800	£5200	Man with head on table in despair. Germanics day - forest gathering (52x41cm-20x16in) one s. pen one pencil pen vellum double-sided. 4-Jun-94 Galerie Bassenge, Berlin #6177/R (DM 13000)
$7986	£5288	Standing female nude (41x29cm-16x11in) st.sig. W/C over chl. 16-Jun-94 Galerie Koller, Zurich #3023/R (S.FR 11000)
$8000	£4706	Deutsches Bordel (64x49cm-25x19in) s. pen Indian ink. 8-Oct-92 Christie's, New York #38/R
$8000	£5229	Madchen-Akt, mit blauem Tuch, in der Dunen (50x39cm-20x15in) s. W/C black chk white chk. 13-May-93 Christie's, New York #324/R
$8415	£5500	Die schlachter (39x50cm-15x20in) s.d.1930 gouache W/C brush ink. 20-May-93 Christie's, London #601/R
$8415	£5500	Hail to the chief (47x62cm-19x24in) s. W/C. 27-Jun-94 Christie's, S. Kensington #95/R
$8500	£5000	Figuren in der Strasse (43x56cm-17x22in) st.sig. pen Indian ink. 8-Oct-92 Christie's, New York #39/R
$8597	£5583	Better people (46x59cm-18x23in) s.i.d.23 Indian ink brush. 22-Jun-94 Galerie Kornfeld, Berne #465/R (S.FR 11500)
$8597	£5583	S.P.D - give the Kaiser what belongs to the Kaiser (59x41cm-23x16in) s.i. st.verso Indian ink brush vellum exec.1923. 22-Jun-94 Galerie Kornfeld, Berne #466/R (S.FR 11500)
$8700	£5761	Seated nude with arms folded behind head. Standing nude (50x39cm-20x15in) painted c.1938/40 W/C pen verso double-sided. 20-Nov-92 Neumeister, Munich #159/R (DM 14000)
$8940	£6000	The girl (59x35cm-23x14in) s. W/C. 29-Nov-93 Christie's, S. Kensington #69/R
$9313	£6250	Story teller (44x58cm-17x23in) s.i. Indian ink pen brush over pencil exec.1932. 25-Jun-93 Galerie Kornfeld, Berne #45/R (S.FR 14000)
$10000	£5882	Spanish Civil War (48x65cm-19x26in) s.i.d.34 W/C paper laid down on board. 5-Oct-92 Sotheby's, New York #102/R
$10676	£7165	Figure (50x36cm-20x14in) s.i. ink. 14-Dec-93 Finarte, Milan #432/R (I.L 18000000)
$10757	£7171	Criminal act (19x30cm-7x12in) s.d.1912 pen wash. 6-Jun-94 Wolfgang Ketterer, Munich #92/R (DM 18000)
$11400	£7600	George Grosz and the editing of Knuppler (52x65cm-20x26in) s.i.d.1927 Indian ink vellum. 4-Jun-94 Galerie Bassenge, Berlin #6179/R (DM 19000)
$12638	£8482	Hard times (26x18cm-10x7in) i. Indian ink pen executed 1919. 23-Jun-93 Galerie Kornfeld, Berne #390/R (S.FR 19000)
$14000	£9250	Stickmen in blue (49x37cm-19x15in) s. estate st.num.VC 133 24 verso W/C. 12-May-93 Sotheby's, New York #203/R
$15000	£9804	Fight (44x56cm-17x22in) s.d.34 estate st.num1-99-4 verso W/C Indian ink. 12-May-93 Sotheby's, New York #206/R
$16000	£10811	Badende (60x46cm-24x18in) s.d.39 gouache W/C paper on board painted 1939. 3-Nov-93 Christie's, New York #371/R
$16181	£10241	Hypochondriac Otto Schmalhausen (58x40cm-23x16in) st.sig.i. drawn 1921 pen. 30-Nov-92 Wolfgang Ketterer, Munich #123 a/R (DM 25500)
$16629	£11161	Union officials working (62x41cm-24x16in) Indian ink pen executed c.1922. 25-Jun-93 Galerie Kornfeld, Berne #44/R (S.FR 25000)
$17000	£11486	Strassenszene (46x60cm-18x24in) s. W/C gouache pen painted c.1930. 3-Nov-93 Christie's, New York #167/R
$18000	£11921	Strassenszene (48x63cm-19x25in) W/C over pencil ink. 12-Nov-92 Christie's, New York #160/R
$21000	£13907	Man with whip (64x45cm-25x18in) s. W/C pencil. 11-Nov-92 Sotheby's, New York #192/R
$21000	£13907	Eingeruckt (38x30cm-15x12in) s. ink. 12-Nov-92 Christie's, New York #155/R
$21000	£14189	Hohere Tochter (61x48cm-24x19in) s.i.d.1922 Indian ink. 4-Nov-93 Sotheby's, New York #212/R
$22000	£14103	Nedicks (61x42cm-24x17in) s. W/C executed 1932-34. 27-May-93 Sotheby's, New York #116/R
$22000	£14570	Street scene (27x41cm-11x16in) s. W/C ink wash. 11-Nov-92 Sotheby's, New York #193/R
$29000	£19333	Garderobe (64x46cm-25x18in) s. W/C pen. 12-May-94 Sotheby's, New York #278/R
$30000	£19608	Street scene in Marseille (33x23cm-13x9in) s.i.d.1929 W/C pen. 12-May-93 Sotheby's, New York #204/R
$32000	£21192	Auf dem Markt (47x63cm-19x25in) s. W/C. 12-Nov-92 Christie's, New York #159/R
$36720	£24000	Frau, Kind und Schwester (62x44cm-24x17in) s. W/C. 29-Jun-94 Sotheby's, London #210/R

GROVER, Oliver Dennett (1861-1927) American

$1000	£654	Hillside village (51x66cm-20x26in) s.d.1926 board. 1-Nov-92 Hanzel Galleries, Chicago #191

GROVER, Oliver Dennett (1861-1927) American-cont.
$2200	£1486	Mountain sea and clouds (61x76cm-24x30in) s.d.1911. 31-Oct-93 Hindman Galleries, Chicago #674/R
$3500	£2215	Serving breakfast on the terrace (61x76cm-24x30in) s.d.1913. 2-Dec-92 Christie's, East, New York #71/R
$5000	£3311	Venice (72x102cm-28x40in) s.d.1907. 15-Jun-94 Butterfield & Butterfield, San Francisco #4418/R
$8000	£5333	River scene (69x99cm-27x39in) s.d.94 canvas on board. 23-May-94 Hindman Galleries, Chicago #174/R

GRUENHAGEN, Leon Lorado Merton (attrib) (19/20th C) American
$2200	£1497	Tired of play (132x74cm-52x29in) s.d.06 i.verso. 17-Apr-94 Schrager Galleries, Milwaukee #468

GRUNSTEN, Harry N (1902-) Canadian
$856	£567	Bridge at Weston (61x71cm-24x28in) s. i.verso board. 18-Nov-92 Sotheby's, Toronto #20/R (C.D 1100)

GRUPPE, Charles Paul (1860-1940) American
$653	£450	The Lily pond (31x23cm-12x9in) 28-Jan-93 Lawrence, Crewkerne #392
$750	£503	Boating scene (25x36cm-10x14in) s. 16-Dec-93 Mystic Fine Arts, Connecticut #97/R
$750	£490	Boathouse (20x28cm-8x11in) s. board. 19-Sep-93 Hindman Galleries, Chicago #675
$800	£537	Landscape with sheep (18x25cm-7x10in) s. board. 12-Dec-93 Hindman Galleries, Chicago #244
$800	£559	Oct Bass Rocks Mass (64x76cm-25x30in) s. i.verso. 12-Mar-93 Skinner, Bolton #233/R
$1100	£719	Windmill in landscape (43x36cm-17x14in) s. board. 30-Jun-94 Mystic Fine Arts, Connecticut #146/R
$1200	£784	The lift bridge (25x30cm-10x12in) s. 30-Jun-94 Mystic Fine Arts, Connecticut #102/R
$1400	£915	Milking time (46x61cm-18x24in) s. 30-Oct-92 Sloan, North Bethesda #2198/R
$1500	£867	Under October skies (61x76cm-24x30in) s. 25-Sep-92 Sotheby's Arcade, New York #135/R
$1500	£1000	Autumn in the woods (30x42cm-12x17in) s. 21-May-94 Weschler, Washington #108/R
$1500	£962	The bath in the Catskills (41x30cm-16x12in) s. board. 11-Dec-92 Du Mouchelle, Detroit #2035/R
$1650	£1044	Beach scene with fisherfolk selling catch (15x31cm-6x12in) s. panel. 2-Dec-92 Dorling, Hamburg #2306/R (DM 2600)
$1700	£1111	Old Mill (61x76cm-24x30in) s. 30-Jun-94 Mystic Fine Arts, Connecticut #194/R
$1800	£1200	Stream in winter (28x38cm-11x15in) s. canvas on board. 26-May-94 Sloan, North Bethesda #2266/R
$2800	£1879	Pastoral landscape (51x61cm-20x24in) s. 5-Dec-93 James Bakker, Cambridge #33/R
$3000	£2098	After the storm, landscape with cow and herder (64x99cm-25x39in) s. i.verso. 12-Mar-93 Skinner, Bolton #177/R
$3250	£2273	Twilight canal view (56x71cm-22x28in) s. i.verso. 12-Mar-93 Skinner, Bolton #189/R
$3300	£2215	Under morning skies - canal view with distant houses and windmill (71x87cm-28x34in) s. 4-Mar-94 Skinner, Bolton #238/R
$3500	£2349	Landscape with road, windmill and houses (64x76cm-25x30in) s. 14-Jan-94 Du Mouchelle, Detroit #2000/R
$4000	£2721	Rockport Wharf (24x30cm-9x12in) s. 10-Jul-93 Young Fine Arts Auctions, Maine #164/R
$4000	£2685	By the canal (81x102cm-32x40in) s. 4-May-94 Doyle, New York #28/R
$4200	£2800	The Meadow Brook (61x81cm-24x32in) s. i.stretcher. 23-May-94 Hindman Galleries, Chicago #169/R
$4250	£2778	Baiting the hooks (46x61cm-18x24in) s. 18-Sep-93 Young Fine Arts Auctions, Maine #144/R
$4500	£2381	Winter dream (64x76cm-25x30in) s. 12-Sep-92 Louisiana Auction Exchange #53/R
$666	£427	Shepherd and flock in autumn landscape (34x50cm-13x20in) s. W/C. 7-Dec-92 Waddingtons, Toronto #1501 (C.D 850)
$1000	*£654*	*Return home (46x35cm-18x14in) s. W/C. 4-May-93 Christie's, East, New York #205*
$1400	*£886*	*Landscape with cows and figure (38x56cm-15x22in) s. W/C gouache. 2-Dec-92 Boos Gallery, Michigan #813/R*

GRUPPE, Emile A (1896-1978) American
$700	£486	River landscape (51x61cm-20x24in) s. canvas on board. 27-Feb-93 Young Fine Arts Auctions, Maine #123/R
$850	£545	The sun bather, Florida (51x61cm-20x24in) s. 10-Dec-92 Sloan, North Bethesda #2281/R
$880	£575	Rocks and surf, Cape ann (51x61cm-20x24in) s. canvasboard. 14-May-93 Skinner, Bolton #112/R
$900	£604	Bass Rocks (41x51cm-16x20in) s. 5-Mar-94 Louisiana Auction Exchange #63/R
$900	£588	Autumn woods (41x30cm-16x12in) s. board. 8-May-93 Young Fine Arts Auctions, Maine #142/R
$900	£596	Bass rocks (30x41cm-12x16in) s. i.verso board. 28-Nov-92 Young Fine Arts Auctions, Maine #192/R
$900	£596	Morning Gloucester (41x30cm-16x12in) s. board. 20-Nov-92 Eldred, Massachusetts #886/R
$950	£625	River's edge, autumn (41x30cm-16x12in) s. board. 4-Nov-92 Doyle, New York #32/R
$1000	£676	Nude bathing (23x19cm-9x7in) s. panel. 20-Mar-93 Weschler, Washington #131/R
$1100	£724	Autumn landscape (30x41cm-12x16in) s.d.1927 canvas on board. 13-Jun-93 Butterfield & Butterfield, San Francisco #3203/R
$1100	£738	Vermont winter scene (30x41cm-12x16in) s. board. 24-Jun-93 Mystic Fine Arts, Connecticut #116
$1300	£850	Bass Rocks (51x61cm-20x24in) s. 30-Jun-94 Mystic Fine Arts, Connecticut #165 a/R

GRUPPE, Emile A (1896-1978) American-cont.

$1300	£861	Bass rocks (41x51cm-16x20in) s. i.verso board. 28-Nov-92 Young Fine Arts Auctions, Maine #191/R
$1400	£952	Brook in winter (46x51cm-18x20in) s. 15-Nov-93 Christie's, East, New York #252
$1400	£741	Gloucester Morning (61x51cm-24x20in) s. i.d.1960verso. 11-Sep-92 Skinner, Bolton #248/R
$1400	£921	Landscape with oak tree (30x41cm-12x16in) s. board. 13-Jun-93 Butterfield & Butterfield, San Francisco #3204/R
$1500	£1049	Birch trees in New England (64x76cm-25x30in) s. 14-Mar-93 Hindman Galleries, Chicago #10/R
$1500	£980	Boathouse (40x51cm-16x20in) s. canvasboard. 4-May-93 Christie's, East, New York #275 a/R
$1600	£1081	Fishing (76x91cm-30x36in) s. 31-Mar-94 Sotheby's Arcade, New York #224/R
$1600	£1074	Boat Dock-Naples, Florida (41x51cm-16x20in) s. canvasboard. 5-Dec-93 James Bakker, Cambridge #4/R
$1600	£925	Winter landscape, New England (30x36cm-12x14in) s. canvasboard. 25-Sep-92 Sotheby's Arcade, New York #277/R
$1600	£1053	Covered bridge, Vermont (51x62cm-20x24in) s. 31-Mar-93 Sotheby's Arcade, New York #306/R
$1625	£1128	Fishing from bass rocks (46x61cm-18x24in) s. 6-Mar-93 Louisiana Auction Exchange #70/R
$1800	£1154	Winter view (30x41cm-12x16in) s. canvas on board. 9-Dec-92 Butterfield & Butterfield, San Francisco #3881/R
$1800	£1208	Spring landscape (64x76cm-25x30in) s. 24-Mar-94 Mystic Fine Arts, Connecticut #232/R
$1800	£1176	Woods in snow (51x46cm-20x18in) s. 8-May-93 Young Fine Arts Auctions, Maine #139
$1900	£1293	A winter stream (63x76cm-25x30in) s. 15-Nov-93 Christie's, East, New York #242
$2000	£1307	Fishermen and seagulls at dock (46x51cm-18x20in) s. 8-May-93 Young Fine Arts Auctions, Maine #140/R
$2000	£1361	Harbour scene (51x61cm-20x24in) s. 15-Nov-93 Christie's, East, New York #249/R
$2000	£1342	Road through the trees (64x76cm-25x30in) s. 12-Dec-93 Hindman Galleries, Chicago #245/R
$2000	£1307	Nymphs (25x25cm-10x10in) s. board. 30-Jun-94 Mystic Fine Arts, Connecticut #212
$2200	£1477	Gloucester harbour in evening light (64x76cm-25x30in) s. with i.verso. 4-Mar-94 Skinner, Bolton #265/R
$2250	£1136	Thatcher's Island (41x51cm-16x20in) s. i.verso board. 28-Aug-92 Young Fine Arts Auctions, Maine #143/R
$2250	£1500	Seascape (51x61cm-20x24in) s. 15-Mar-94 John Moran, Pasadena #73
$2271	£1429	Small harbour (69x95cm-27x37in) s. canvas on panel. 20-Apr-93 Sotheby's, Amsterdam #221/R (D.FL 4000)
$2300	£1554	Ships at harbour (36x36cm-14x14in) s. 31-Mar-94 Sotheby's Arcade, New York #241/R
$2400	£1569	Winter stream (76x81cm-30x32in) s. 4-May-93 Christie's, East, New York #108/R
$2400	£1678	Evening, Gloucester (41x51cm-16x20in) s. 11-Mar-93 Christie's, New York #219/R
$2500	£1667	Harbour scene (76x91cm-30x36in) s. 22-May-94 James Bakker, Cambridge #150
$2500	£1689	At dock (61x51cm-24x20in) s. 31-Oct-93 Hindman Galleries, Chicago #714/R
$2600	£1635	Gloucester Port (41x51cm-16x20in) s. 22-Apr-93 Freeman Fine Arts, Philadelphia #1184
$2700	£1812	Mending nets, Portugal (63x76cm-25x30in) s. i.verso. 4-Mar-94 Skinner, Bolton #261/R
$2750	£1403	Gloucester in winter (51x61cm-20x24in) s. i.stretcher. 18-Aug-92 Richard Bourne, Hyannis #97/R
$2800	£1618	Jeffersonville, Vermont (76x91cm-30x36in) s. i.stretcher. 23-Sep-92 Christie's, New York #189/R
$3000	£1987	Fishing boats in Harbour (46x61cm-18x24in) s. board. 28-Nov-92 Young Fine Arts Auctions, Maine #190
$3100	£2081	Gloucester fishing boats at dock (58x48cm-23x19in) 29-Dec-93 Douglas, South Deerfield #5
$3500	£2023	After the storm (76x91cm-30x36in) s. 27-Sep-92 James Bakker, Cambridge #28/R
$3500	£2318	Gloucester fog (63x76cm-25x30in) s. 15-Jun-94 Butterfield & Butterfield, San Francisco #4450/R
$3500	£2349	Gloucester scene (76x64cm-30x25in) s. 16-Dec-93 Mystic Fine Arts, Connecticut #64/R
$3500	£2365	Clam diggers (77x82cm-30x32in) s. 5-Nov-93 Skinner, Bolton #119/R
$3500	£2333	Gloucester morning (50x60cm-20x24in) s. s.i.d.1959 stretcher. 23-May-94 Christie's, East, New York #167/R
$3600	£1818	Fog, Gloucester (51x61cm-20x24in) s. s.i.verso. 28-Aug-92 Young Fine Arts Auctions, Maine #142/R
$3750	£2483	Sugaring Vermont (76x91cm-30x36in) s. i.verso. 28-Nov-92 Young Fine Arts Auctions, Maine #189/R
$3750	£2451	Early morning Gloucester (64x76cm-25x30in) s. 18-Sep-93 James Bakker, Cambridge #20/R
$4000	£2759	Winter River (64x76cm-25x30in) s. 16-Feb-93 John Moran, Pasadena #13
$4200	£2781	Winter landscape (76x91cm-30x36in) s. 22-Sep-93 Christie's, New York #172/R
$4500	£3125	Vermont covered bridge (64x76cm-25x30in) s. 27-Feb-93 Young Fine Arts Auctions, Maine #122/R
$4500	£2885	Harbour scene at sunset (51x61cm-20x24in) s. 12-Dec-92 Weschler, Washington #87/R
$4500	£2903	Winter sun on birches (76x91cm-30x36in) s. 6-Jan-93 Doyle, New York #32
$4750	£3146	Fishing on the Grand Banks (76x91cm-30x36in) s. i.verso. 28-Nov-92 Young Fine Arts Auctions, Maine #188/R
$5500	£3716	Beech in snow (63x76cm-25x30in) s. 31-Mar-94 Sotheby's Arcade, New York #280/R
$7000	£4636	ON fish, out of Gloucester (76x91cm-30x36in) s. i.verso. 28-Nov-92 Young Fine Arts Auctions, Maine #187/R
$7500	£4747	Motif No.1, Rockport (76x63cm-30x25in) s. 4-Dec-92 Christie's, New York #64/R
$14000	£8861	Spring (64x76cm-25x30in) s. 4-Dec-92 Christie's, New York #66/R

GUAGNINI, Nicolas (1966-) Argentinian
$3500   £2333   El bien y el mal (146x146cm-57x57in) init. i.d.1992verso panel. 18-May-94 Sotheby's, New York #392/R

GUARDIA, Wenceslao de la (1861-?) American
$18000   £12081   Embarquement de Lafayette a passages pour son premier voyage en Amerique (114x163cm-45x64in) s.d.83. 13-Oct-93 Sotheby's, New York #130/R

GUAYASAMIN, Oswaldo (1919-) Ecuadorian
$1738   £1151   Retrato de Julio Cortazar (53x43cm-21x17in) s.d.1962. 29-Jun-93 Fernando Duran, Madrid #149/R (S.P 225000)
$3200   £2162   Marimbas from the series Guacaytan (36x53cm-14x21in) s. paper painted 1948-49. 23-Nov-93 Christie's, New York #255/R
$8250   £5464   Desnudo (55x76cm-22x30in) s. paper. 23-Nov-92 Sotheby's, New York #216/R
$10877   £7300   El grito (116x81cm-46x32in) s. 21-Mar-94 Duran, Madrid #57/R (S.P 1500000)
$12000   £7843   Cabeza (40x60cm-16x24in) s. painted 1971. 18-May-93 Sotheby's, New York #233/R
$14583   £9531   Maternidad India (80x80cm-31x31in) s. 12-May-93 Fernando Duran, Madrid #209/R (S.P 1800000)
$15000   £10000   Cabeza de hombre (97x67cm-38x26in) s. painted c.1965. 18-May-94 Sotheby's, New York #369/R
$16000   £10667   Boceto para el mural Homenaje al Hombre Americano (61x45cm-24x18in) s. masonite painted c.1952 pair. 18-May-94 Christie's, New York #274/R
$16000   £10458   Amantes (142x70cm-56x28in) s. 17-May-93 Christie's, New York #143/R
$18128   £12167   Quito rojo (90x130cm-35x51in) s. 21-May-94 Duran, Madrid #56/R (S.P 2500000)
$26000   £17333   Cabeza de la angustia (104x70cm-41x28in) s. painted c.1965. 18-May-94 Sotheby's, New York #377/R
$27000   £18121   Las beatas (116x75cm-46x30in) s. painted c.1946. 7-Jan-94 Gary Nader, Miami #36/R
$30000   £20270   Rostro y Lagrimas (95x134cm-37x53in) s. painted 1967. 23-Nov-93 Christie's, New York #129/R
$30000   £19868   Violinista (129x50cm-51x20in) s. 23-Nov-92 Sotheby's, New York #195/R
$2400 *£1622* *Retrato de mujer (34x27cm-13x11in) s. marker W/C gouache double-sided. 23-Nov-93 Christie's, New York #262/R*
$2400 *£1569* *Caballos y figuras en la selva (38x56cm-15x22in) init. gouache executed c.1940. 18-May-93 Sotheby's, New York #163/R*
$4279 *£2872* *Cabeza femenina (57x41cm-22x16in) s. ink gouache. 20-Dec-93 Ansorena, Madrid #150/R (S.P 600000)*
$6750 *£4470* *Mujer (61x48cm-24x19in) s. gpuache. 23-Nov-92 Sotheby's, New York #225/R*

GUE, David John (1836-1917) American
$875   £572   Boathouse, South Lake, Catskill Mountains (24x36cm-9x14in) s. grisaille. 22-May-93 Weschler, Washington #92/R

GUERREIRO, Sari (1948-) Mexican
$799   £540   Alhelies (80x60cm-31x24in) s.d.1993. 20-Oct-93 Louis Morton, Mexico #164/R (M.P 2500)
$703   *£475*   *Frutas (70x50cm-28x20in) s.d.1992 pastel. 20-Oct-93 Louis Morton, Mexico #145/R (M.P 2200)*

GUERRERO GALVAN, Jesus (1910-1973) Mexican
$8000   £5298   Murcielago (90x120cm-35x47in) s.d.1963. 24-Nov-92 Christie's, New York #132/R
$40000   £26667   Nina con flor (76x55cm-30x22in) s.d.1948 canvas laid down on board. 18-May-94 Sotheby's, New York #338/R
$55000   £36667   El nido (100x81cm-39x32in) s.d.1956. 18-May-94 Sotheby's, New York #363/R
$60000   £40000   Tamborilero (90x60cm-35x24in) s.d.1943. 18-May-94 Sotheby's, New York #337/R
$65000   £43919   Retrato de nina (76x61cm-30x24in) s.d.1942. 23-Nov-93 Christie's, New York #101/R
$3000 *£2000* *Mujer (28x36cm-11x14in) sanguine dr executed c.1960. 18-May-94 Sotheby's, New York #248/R*
$4000 *£2614* *El Espejo (56x40cm-22x16in) s.d.1942 W/C pencil. 17-May-93 Christie's, New York #284/R*
$8000 *£5031* *Peasant woman with basket (53x37cm-21x15in) s.d.1940 W/C. 25-Apr-93 Butterfield & Butterfield, San Francisco #2085/R*
$9500 *£6291* *Retrato de Annette (78x58cm-31x23in) s.d.1944 chl cardboard. 23-Nov-92 Sotheby's, New York #209/R*

GUERRERO, Jose (1914-1992) Spanish/American
$4155   £2789   Sin titulo (53x64cm-21x25in) s. 29-Nov-93 AB Stockholms Auktionsverk, Stockholm #6208/R (S.KR 35000)
$5136   £3424   Semana santa (51x41cm-20x16in) s. i.d.1965verso. 26-May-94 Sotheby's, Madrid #112/R (S.P 700000)
$13909   £9211   Negro rojo (99x109cm-39x43in) s. s.i.d.1969verso. 26-Nov-92 Sotheby's, Madrid #12/R (S.P 1600000)

GUGLIELMI, O Louis (1906-1956) American
$3000   £1974   Red to black (102x46cm-40x18in) s.d.54. 31-Mar-93 Sotheby's Arcade, New York #455/R
$5000   £3311   Night windows (48x48cm-32x19in) s.d.48. 22-Sep-93 Christie's, New York #223/R
$20000   £13333   St. George's Church, Stuyvesant Square (77x61cm-30x24in) s.i.stretcher painted c.1933. 17-Mar-94 Sotheby's, New York #163/R
$40000   £25641   Persistent sea No.2 (76x60cm-30x24in) s. 26-May-93 Christie's, New York #219/R
$1400 *£886*   *Building (50x45cm-20x18in) s.d.47 mixed media. 25-Oct-92 Butterfield & Butterfield, San Francisco #2275/R*

GUIDO, Alfredo (1892-1967) Argentinian
$1300   £765   En las sierras (54x62cm-21x24in) 29-Sep-92 VerBo, Buenos Aires #60

GUIRALDES, Alberto (1897-1961) Argentinian
$1100   £647   En el palenque (35x50cm-14x20in) ink dr. 29-Sep-92 VerBo, Buenos Aires #61

GULAGER, Charles (fl.1860-1880) American
$15000   £10000   Magic (91x136cm-36x54in) s.d.1860. 3-Jun-94 Sotheby's, New York #233/R

GURTUBAY, Jose Antonio (20th C) Mexican
$511   £341   La fiesta (34x48cm-13x19in) s. mixed media. 25-May-94 Louis Morton, Mexico #123/R (M.P 1700)
$968   £649   Mirando (49x68cm-19x27in) W/C. 1-Dec-93 Louis Morton, Mexico #167/R (M.P 3000)

GUSSOW, Bernard (1881-1957) American
$2250   £1510   The window (76x58cm-30x23in) s. i.verso board. 16-Jul-93 Du Mouchelle, Detroit #2018/R

GUSTON, Philip (1913-1980) American
$23000   £15541 August form (58x72cm-23x28in) s. s.d.1964 verso paper. 11-Nov-93 Sotheby's, New York #304/R
$28000   £18792 Winter flower (79x103cm-31x41in) s. s.i.d.1959verso masonite. 5-May-94 Sotheby's, New York #105/R
$36000   £24161 Warwick I (57x76cm-22x30in) s. s.i.d.1959verso paper on masonite. 5-May-94 Sotheby's, New York #101/R
$38000   £25166 Untitled (50x70cm-20x28in) s.i.d.71 paper. 19-Nov-92 Christie's, New York #294/R
$62500   £41391 Untitled (65x93cm-26x37in) s. paper on masonite painted c.1959. 18-Nov-92 Sotheby's, New York #94/R
$100000 £66225 Stranger (180x198cm-71x78in) s.i.d.1964verso. 18-Nov-92 Christie's, New York #18/R
$400000 £261438 As it goes (193x259cm-76x102in) s.verso painted 1978. 3-May-93 Sotheby's, New York #33/R
$3500   £2365   Sound from Leopardi (33x30cm-13x12in) mono. ink dr. 21-Apr-94 Butterfield & Butterfield, San Francisco #1147/R
$5500   £3716   Don't go away (20x13cm-8x5in) ink. 8-Nov-93 Christie's, East, New York #144/R
$30000   £19868 Alone (34x43cm-13x17in) s.d.70 brush ink. 19-Nov-92 Christie's, New York #236/R
$40000   £26490 Pink light (76x102cm-30x40in) s. s.i.d.1963verso gouache. 19-Nov-92 Christie's, New York #287/R

GUY, James M (1910-1963) American
$600   £400   The Discovery (21x26cm-8x10in) s.d.40 pencil. 23-May-94 Christie's, East, New York #298/R

GWATHMEY, Robert (1903-1988) American
$2200   £1467   Still life with roses (41x30cm-16x12in) s. 23-May-94 Christie's, East, New York #238/R
$3500   £2273   Husband and wife (41x56cm-16x22in) s. painted c.1930. 9-Sep-93 Sotheby's Arcade, New York #339/R
$6000   £3797   Yellow tables (96x76cm-38x30in) s. 2-Dec-92 Christie's, East, New York #386/R
$1700   £1111   Study for Homo Sapines, late 20th Century (42x27cm-17x11in) s. pencil. 4-May-93 Christie's, East, New York #269/R
$4500   £2922   Southern farmer (46x36cm-18x14in) gouache board. 9-Sep-93 Sotheby's Arcade, New York #396/R

HABERLE, John (1856-1933) American
$750   £503   From hotel room window (10x18cm-4x7in) pencil. 24-Jun-93 Mystic Fine Arts, Connecticut #54 c

HADDOCK, Arthur (1895-1980) American
$700   £458   Sante Fe landscape (41x51cm-16x20in) s. 15-May-93 Dunning's, Illinois #1076/R

HADER, Elmer Stanley (1889-1973) American
$5000   £2890   Moonlight, Paris (79x58cm-31x23in) s.d.12. 25-Sep-92 Sotheby's Arcade, New York #221/R

HADFIELD, Scott (20th C) American
$825   £539   Eire - Spirit of War Dead (122x97cm-48x38in) s.d.1983 verso alkyd enamel wood. 14-May-93 Skinner, Bolton #190/R

HAGAN, Frederick (20th C) Canadian
$574   £383   Corner store,grocery store and laundry, Dundas St. (18x22cm-7x9in) s. i.d.1937 verso panel. 30-May-94 Ritchie, Toronto #143/R (C.D 800)
$1729   £1095   Karl in springtime (90x60cm-35x24in) s.d.1957 verso polymer masonite. 30-Nov-92 Ritchie, Toronto #185/R (C.D 2200)

HAGAN, Robert Frederick (1918-) Canadian
$706   £462   Mountain mist - Jasper, July 1953 (41x57cm-16x22in) s.d.53 W/C. 10-May-93 Hodgins, Calgary #283/R (C.D 900)

HAGARTY, Clara (1871-1958) Canadian
$942   £628   Zinneas (30x36cm-12x14in) s. i.verso. 6-Jun-94 Waddingtons, Toronto #1207 (C.D 1300)
$1168   £773   View of Seine River, Paris (28x35cm-11x14in) s.d.26 pastel. 18-Nov-92 Sotheby's, Toronto #94/R (C.D 1500)

HAGERUP, Nels (1864-1922) American
$700	£443	San Francisco Bay (33x76cm-13x30in) s.d.02 canvasboard. 2-Dec-92 Christie's, East, New York #102
$800	£530	Seascape at sunset (46x76cm-18x30in) s. 20-Sep-93 Butterfield & Butterfield, Los Angeles #95/R
$850	£563	Seascape (51x76cm-20x30in) s. 14-Jun-94 John Moran, Pasadena #128
$1000	£694	Sand dunes along the coast (36x61cm-14x24in) s. 7-Mar-93 Butterfield & Butterfield, San Francisco #11/R
$1600	£1067	Sailing boat in harbour (36x56cm-14x22in) s. 15-Mar-94 John Moran, Pasadena #81
$1700	£1181	Seascape and sunset (61x91cm-24x36in) s. 7-Mar-93 Butterfield & Butterfield, San Francisco #12/R
$1900	£1118	High tide (51x76cm-20x30in) s. 4-Oct-92 Butterfield & Butterfield, Los Angeles #20/R

HAHS, Philip B (1853-1882) American
$800	£471	Faggot gatherer in winter landscape (41x30cm-16x12in) s. board. 8-Oct-92 Freeman Fine Arts, Philadelphia #1092
$5750	£3382	First step (25x46cm-10x18in) s.verso board. 8-Oct-92 Freeman Fine Arts, Philadelphia #1102
$7750	£4559	Olden time (30x41cm-12x16in) s.d.1880 canvas on board. 8-Oct-92 Freeman Fine Arts, Philadelphia #1088/R
$700	*£412*	*Seated man with shoe (33x23cm-13x9in) s.d.1882 W/C. 8-Oct-92 Freeman Fine Arts, Philadelphia #1103*

HAINES, Frederick Stanley (1879-1960) Canadian
$555	£363	Bracebridge early spring (22x27cm-9x11in) s. panel. 18-May-93 Joyner Fine Art, Toronto #218 (C.D 700)
$574	£383	Sunlit birches (41x51cm-16x20in) s. i.d.verso canvasboard. 30-May-94 Hodgins, Calgary #256/R (C.D 800)
$778	£515	Autumn landscape (37x30cm-15x12in) s. board. 18-Nov-92 Sotheby's, Toronto #251 (C.D 1000)
$933	£622	Gull River (61x66cm-24x26in) s. i.verso board. 30-May-94 Hodgins, Calgary #71/R (C.D 1300)
$947	£631	Fence by the tree, summer (40x50cm-16x20in) s. 13-May-94 Joyner Fine Art, Toronto #67 (C.D 1300)
$1110	£725	Fall, Creemore (61x81cm-24x32in) s. board. 18-May-93 Joyner Fine Art, Toronto #108/R (C.D 1400)
$1165	£777	Rock and trees overlooking lake (40x50cm-16x20in) board. 13-May-94 Joyner Fine Art, Toronto #196 (C.D 1600)
$1189	£777	Watching flock (39x46cm-15x18in) s. 19-May-93 Sotheby's, Toronto #317/R (C.D 1500)
$1189	£777	Cattle on road (41x51cm-16x20in) s. board. 18-May-93 Joyner Fine Art, Toronto #272 (C.D 1500)
$1208	£816	Simcoe County farm (60x80cm-24x31in) s. board painted 1955. 23-Nov-93 Joyner Fine Art, Toronto #28/R (C.D 1600)
$1359	£918	The Albion Hills (50x60cm-20x24in) s. canvasboard. 23-Nov-93 Joyner Fine Art, Toronto #140/R (C.D 1800)
$1510	£1020	Autumn, Haliburton. Holland Mills (30x36cm-12x14in) s. panel pair. 23-Nov-93 Joyner Fine Art, Toronto #322 (C.D 2000)
$1550	£1047	Swamp elm (61x66cm-24x26in) s. i.verso board. 3-Nov-93 Sotheby's, Toronto #20/R (C.D 2000)
$1712	£1134	Sarah Mulock Farm, Thornhill, Ontario (60x65cm-24x26in) s. board. 24-Nov-92 Joyner Fine Art, Toronto #18/R (C.D 2200)
$1790	£1186	Rapids on South River (30x37cm-12x15in) s. i.verso board. 18-Nov-92 Sotheby's, Toronto #120/R (C.D 2300)
$1903	£1244	Autumn evening (108x91cm-43x36in) s. 18-May-93 Joyner Fine Art, Toronto #139/R (C.D 2400)
$1982	£1295	Winter country road (51x66cm-20x26in) s. board. 19-May-93 Sotheby's, Toronto #169/R (C.D 2500)

HALBERSTADT, Ernst (1910-) American
$800	£544	Woman with yellow apron (81x61cm-32x24in) s. 16-Apr-94 Young Fine Arts Auctions, Maine #126/R

HALE, Ellen Day (1855-1940) American
$2000	£1325	Pinecones (84x104cm-33x41in) s.i.d.97. 23-Sep-93 Sotheby's, New York #164/R
$805	*£537*	*Breakfast reverie (58x46cm-23x18in) s.d.1939 pastel. 9-Jun-94 Swann Galleries, New York #158*

HALE, Gardner (1894-1931) American
$900	£604	People in the park (25x36cm-10x14in) s.d.1914. 24-Mar-94 Mystic Fine Arts, Connecticut #43/R

HALE, Lilian Westcott (1881-1963) American
$42000	£26923	Agnes and cat (76x63cm-30x25in) s. 26-May-93 Christie's, New York #126/R
$15000	*£10067*	*The veil. Sketch of a female (58x36cm-23x14in) s. chl double-sided executed c.1920. 6-Dec-93 Grogan, Massachussetts #529/R*

HALE, Philip L (1865-1931) American
$4000	£2797	At the piano (90x61cm-35x24in) 10-Mar-93 Sotheby's, New York #130/R
$9500	£6209	Red barn (51x76cm-20x30in) 17-Sep-93 Skinner, Bolton #258/R

HALL, Edith Emma Dorothea (1883-?) American
$775	£503	Farm houses (46x56cm-18x22in) s. board. 11-Sep-93 Louisiana Auction Exchange #21/R

HALL, George Edward (19th C) American
$770   £503   Early evening, Peach Point, Massachussetts coast (30x46cm-12x18in) s. with
                i.verso. 14-May-93 Skinner, Bolton #56/R

HALL, George Henry (1825-1913) American
$2200   £1392   Young girl in red cape (61x48cm-24x19in) s.d.1887-9. 2-Dec-92 Christie's, East,
                New York #145/R
$2500   £1678   The flower seller (74x91cm-29x36in) s.d.1861. 6-Dec-93 Grogan, Massachussetts
                #473/R
$3250   £2152   Street scene, Capri 1883 (36x46cm-14x18in) s.i.d. 14-Jun-94 John Moran, Pasadena
                #90
$3996   £2700   Still life with peach and grapes on ledge (20x30cm-8x12in) s.d.1865. 25-Nov-93
                Christie's, S. Kensington #116

HALLETT, Hendricks (1847-1921) American
$1000   £649   Marsh on cloudy day (38x76cm-15x30in) s.d.80. 9-Sep-93 Sotheby's Arcade, New York
                #78/R
$600 *£408* *Sailboats in Cove (14x19cm-6x7in) s. W/C. 10-Jul-93 Young Fine Arts Auctions,
                Maine #166*

HALLEY, Peter (1953-) American
$30000 £20134 Blue cell with smokestack and conduit (161x161cm-63x63in) s.i.d.85verso acrylic
                rollatex. 5-May-94 Sotheby's, New York #324/R
$42000 £28378 Black cell with yellow background (122x164cm-48x65in) s.i.d.1984verso day-glo
                acrylic roll-a-tex. 10-Nov-93 Christie's, New York #265/R
$85000 £55556 Alphaville (175x488cm-69x192in) acrylic day-glo acrylic painted 1987. 4-May-93
                Sotheby's, New York #244/R
$100000 £67568 Two cells with circulating conduit (214x367cm-84x144in) s.i.d.1988verso day-glo
                acrylic roll-a-tex. 10-Nov-93 Christie's, New York #285/R
$38000 £25166 *The light of reason (143x104cm-56x41in) s.i.d.1983 acrylic roll-a-tex canvas
                diptych. 19-Nov-92 Christie's, New York #108/R*
$60000 £39216 *Rectangular prison with smokestack (184x315cm-72x124in) day-glo acrylic
                roll-a-tex painted 1987. 4-May-93 Sotheby's, New York #248/R*
$75000 £49669 *Two cells with circulating conduit (196x350cm-77x138in) acrylic roll-a-tex canvas
                diptych painted 1988. 19-Nov-92 Christie's, New York #142/R*
$120000 £81081 *Two cells with circulating conduit (163x265cm-64x104in) s.i.d.1986verso acrylic
                day-glo roll-a-tex. 10-Nov-93 Sotheby's, New York #59/R*

HALPERT, Samuel (1884-1930) American
$2000   £1325   A summer landscape with distant hills (51x61cm-20x24in) s. 15-Jun-94 Butterfield
                & Butterfield, San Francisco #4422/R
$9000 *£5696* *Fruit bowl (38x27cm-15x11in) s.d.14 W/C. 3-Dec-92 Sotheby's, New York #49/R*

HALSALL, William Formby (1841-1919) American
$900   £452   Fishing pinkie off Maine Coast (38x46cm-15x18in) s. board. 6-Sep-92 Litchfield
                Auction Gallery #51
$900   £616   Moonlight sail (30x51cm-12x20in) 10-Feb-94 Skinner, Bolton #249
$2500   £1736   Golden Gate, Lompoc (56x76cm-22x30in) s.indis.i. 7-Mar-93 Butterfield &
                Butterfield, San Francisco #51/R

HAMBLETON, Richard (1954-) American
$823   £549   Marlboro (86x59cm-34x23in) s.d.83verso metal. 2-Jun-94 AB Stockholms
                Auktionsverk, Stockholm #7143/R (S.KR 6500)
$1000   £671   Beverly Hills (300x147cm-118x58in) s.d.83verso. 3-May-94 Christie's, East, New
                York #141/R
$1500   £980   Snake (244x107cm-96x42in) acrylic executed 1983. 22-Dec-92 Christie's, East, New
                York #24
$2800   £1830   Kubla Khan (168x315cm-66x124in) oil acrylic executed 1987. 22-Dec-92 Christie's,
                East, New York #22
$4800   £3137   Rainscape with three lines (162x427cm-64x168in) acrylic executed 1986. 22-Dec-92
                Christie's, East, New York #23

HAMEL, Theophile (1817-1870) Canadian
$720   £467   Portrait d'homme (33x25cm-13x10in) s. W/C. 21-Jun-94 Fraser Pinneys, Quebec #36
                (C.D 1000)

HAMILTON, Edward Wilbur Dean (1864-?) American
$700   £470   Trees in October (31x46cm-12x18in) s. 6-May-94 Skinner, Bolton #76/R
$3000   £2013   Apple blossoms (77x91cm-30x36in) s. 4-Mar-94 Skinner, Bolton #274/R

HAMILTON, Hamilton (1847-1928) American
$2600   £1529   Mist rising over mountains (51x69cm-20x27in) s.d.1879. 8-Oct-92 Freeman Fine
                Arts, Philadelphia #1010
$2800   £1618   California landscape , s. 24-Sep-92 Mystic Fine Arts, Connecticut #74
$3800   £2405   Woman with fan (76x50cm-30x20in) s. canvas laid down on masonite. 2-Dec-92
                Christie's, East, New York #141/R
$5500   £3667   Picking flowers (20x26cm-8x10in) s. 23-May-94 Christie's, East, New York #133
$21000 £14094 Headwaters of the Rio Grande (45x71cm-18x28in) s.indis.d. 2-Dec-93 Sotheby's, New
                York #54/R
$28000 £16185 Farewell (71x44cm-28x17in) s.d.1887. 24-Sep-92 Sotheby's, New York #50/R

HAMILTON, Hamilton (attrib) (1847-1928) American
$850   £582   Young girl looking in mirror (66x86cm-26x34in) s. 19-Feb-94 Young Fine Arts
                Auctions, Maine #103/R

HAMILTON, James (1819-1878) American

$1000	£671	Sun setting over the ocean (51x76cm-20x30in) s. 24-Jun-93 Mystic Fine Arts, Connecticut #163
$1500	£882	Ship in stormy sea at sunset (23x36cm-9x14in) s. 8-Oct-92 Freeman Fine Arts, Philadelphia #1075/R
$1500	£987	Shipwreck at sunset (51x91cm-20x36in) 4-Nov-92 Doyle, New York #20/R
$2000	£1316	Ships under sunset (23x44cm-9x17in) s. canvas on board. 13-Jun-93 Butterfield & Butterfield, San Francisco #3133/R
$2750	£1871	Steamsailer in rough seas (8x15cm-3x6in) s.i.d.1875verso board. 10-Jul-93 Young Fine Arts Auctions, Maine #168
$3500	£2303	Marshes, Atlantic City (20x36cm-8x14in) s. panel. 13-Jun-93 Butterfield & Butterfield, San Francisco #3124/R
$5000	£2890	Action between the Monitor and the Merrimac, morning (31x51cm-12x20in) s. i.d.1874verso. 25-Sep-92 Sotheby's Arcade, New York #11/R
$7000	£4046	New York tidelands (26x57cm-10x22in) s. 23-Sep-92 Christie's, New York #64/R

HAMILTON, John McLure (1853-1936) American

$800	£503	Man in top hat (191x97cm-75x38in) 22-Apr-93 Freeman Fine Arts, Philadelphia #1319
$800	£471	Portrait of boy (127x102cm-50x40in) 8-Oct-92 Freeman Fine Arts, Philadelphia #1033/R
$850	£500	Portrait of gentleman in top hat (191x97cm-75x38in) 8-Oct-92 Freeman Fine Arts, Philadelphia #1004/R
$1300	£884	Portrait of a little boy (127x102cm-50x40in) 14-Apr-94 Freeman Fine Arts, Philadelphia #987
$1600	£941	My mother (160x124cm-63x49in) 8-Oct-92 Freeman Fine Arts, Philadelphia #968/R
$1700	£1000	Portrait of getnleman (107x145cm-42x57in) 8-Oct-92 Freeman Fine Arts, Philadelphia #972
$2000	£1176	Gentleman seated at desk with globes (91x152cm-36x60in) 8-Oct-92 Freeman Fine Arts, Philadelphia #959/R
$2000	£1176	Young girl with flowers (109x91cm-43x36in) 8-Oct-92 Freeman Fine Arts, Philadelphia #943
$5000	£2941	Woman by window with flowers (89x119cm-35x47in) 8-Oct-92 Freeman Fine Arts, Philadelphia #947/R
$9500	£6333	Mother and child (112x142cm-44x56in) s.verso. 26-May-94 Christie's, New York #99/R
$850	*£535*	*Seated woman (53x46cm-21x18in) s.d.1914 pastel. 22-Apr-93 Freeman Fine Arts, Philadelphia #1318*
$1100	*£748*	*Portrait of a man (61x46cm-24x18in) s.d.1890 pastel. 14-Apr-94 Freeman Fine Arts, Philadelphia #986*
$1600	*£1046*	*Elegant lady (71x53cm-28x21in) s.d.1910 pastel. 30-Oct-92 Sloan, North Bethesda #2170*

HAMILTON, Mary Riter (1873-1954) Canadian

$642	£434	Corner of the Luxembourg Gardens (16x24cm-6x9in) s.i. i.verso board. 23-Nov-93 Fraser Pinneys, Quebec #503 (C.D 850)

HAMMER, Johann-J (1842-1906) German/American

$715	£467	Pier, Gloucester harbour (46x30cm-18x12in) s. 14-May-93 Skinner, Bolton #115/R
$1729	£1176	Alsfeld in Oberhessen (152x100cm-60x39in) rem.sig. i.verso. 7-Jul-93 Weiner, Munich #161/R (DM 3000)

HAMMER, Victor (1882-1968) Austrian/American

$3557	£2356	Female halfnude (53x46cm-21x18in) i.verso canvas on board. 25-Nov-92 Dorotheum, Vienna #514/R (A.S 40000)

HAMMERAS, Ralph (1939-) American

$600	£397	High Sierra landscape (30x41cm-12x16in) s. canvasboard. 14-Jun-94 John Moran, Pasadena #41

HAMMERSLOUGH, Ruth Helprin (1883-?) American

$600	£403	Little Dutch doll (35x25cm-14x10in) s. pastel. 6-May-94 Skinner, Bolton #123/R

HAMMOND, Jane (1950-) American

$2800	£1892	Untitled (193x178cm-76x70in) s. i.d.1991verso. 4-Nov-93 Boos Gallery, Michigan #246/R
$5750	£3859	Untitled (183x137cm-72x54in) s.d.1988 verso. 25-Mar-93 Boos Gallery, Michigan #424/R

HAMMOND, John A (1843-1939) Canadian

$596	£400	Harbour St Johns, New Brunswick, at sunset (44x65cm-17x26in) s. board. 23-Feb-94 Bonhams, Chelsea #125
$655	£437	Sunset by the river (13x21cm-5x8in) board. 13-May-94 Joyner Fine Art, Toronto #211/R (C.D 900)
$933	£622	Sheep returning, France (18x24cm-7x9in) s. s.i.verso board. 30-May-94 Ritchie, Toronto #134/R (C.D 1300)
$934	£619	Birch trees along a country road (36x43cm-14x17in) s.d.1927 board. 18-Nov-92 Sotheby's, Toronto #67/R (C.D 1200)
$1007	£681	Courtnay Bay (23x30cm-9x12in) s.d.1907 i.verso board. 3-Nov-93 Sotheby's, Toronto #100/R (C.D 1300)
$1151	£748	Approaching storm clouds (46x61cm-18x24in) s. 21-Jun-94 Fraser Pinneys, Quebec #54 (C.D 1600)
$1284	£867	Fishing boats, St John, N.B. (30x42cm-12x17in) s. board. 23-Nov-93 Fraser Pinneys, Quebec #397 (C.D 1700)
$1284	£867	Sunset over the river (32x41cm-13x16in) s.d.1890 canvas on board. 23-Nov-93 Joyner Fine Art, Toronto #200 (C.D 1700)

HAMMOND, John A (1843-1939) Canadian-cont.

$1311	£874	Misty morning, Bay of Funday (20x33cm-8x13in) s. panel. 13-May-94 Joyner Fine Art, Toronto #26/R (C.D 1800)
$1370	£806	Cathedral Mountain, Canadian Rockies (20x29cm-8x11in) s. s.i.verso canvasboard. 5-Oct-92 Levis, Calgary #139/R (C.D 1700)
$1748	£1165	Fishing boats off the coast (27x35cm-11x14in) s.indis.d. canvas on board. 13-May-94 Joyner Fine Art, Toronto #160 (C.D 2400)
$1812	£1208	Misty morning (22x29cm-9x11in) s.d.1886 i.verso board. 6-Jun-94 Waddingtons, Toronto #1280 (C.D 2500)
$2519	£1636	Herring fishing (47x76cm-19x30in) s. s.i.verso panel. 21-Jun-94 Fraser Pinneys, Quebec #162 (C.D 3500)
$3641	£2427	Sunrise, St. John N.B. (75x100cm-30x39in) d.c.1905verso board. 11-May-94 Sotheby's, Toronto #40/R (C.D 5000)

HAMMONS, David (20th C) American

$5000	£3268	American costume (63x49cm-25x19in) s. ink. 4-May-93 Sotheby's, New York #265/R

HANCK, Sophie (19/20th C) American

$1350	£780	Still life (76x58cm-30x23in) s. 24-Sep-92 Mystic Fine Arts, Connecticut #90

HANKINS, Abraham (20th C) American

$800	£523	Modern apartment (76x84cm-30x33in) s. 7-Oct-93 Freeman Fine Arts, Philadelphia #935

HANKINS, Cornelius H (1864-1946) American

$2250	£1573	Tabletop still life with basket of green apples (76x97cm-30x38in) s.d.1896. 5-Feb-93 Sloan, North Bethesda #2573/R

HANNA, Thomas King (1872-1951) American

$600	£403	Grandma's house (30x41cm-12x16in) s. board. 16-Dec-93 Mystic Fine Arts, Connecticut #261
$800	£506	Grandma's house (28x38cm-11x15in) s. 5-Dec-92 Louisiana Auction Exchange #135/R

HANNA-BARBERA STUDIO (20th C) American

$700	£470	16 character chorus line (27x41cm-11x16in) gouache celluloid. 22-Jun-93 Sotheby's, New York #654
$1900	£1275	Publicity cel of 46 characters with Bill Hanna and Joe Barbera (57x48cm-22x19in) gouache celluloid on airbrushed background. 22-Jun-93 Sotheby's, New York #850

HANNAH, Duncan (20th C) American?

$2100	£1458	City lights (128x136cm-50x54in) st.init.d.2.84 s.i.d.1984verso. 26-Feb-93 Sotheby's Arcade, New York #414/R

HANSEN, Armin Carl (1886-1957) American

$1400	£921	Pulling rowboat ashore (15x18cm-6x7in) panel. 13-Jun-93 Butterfield & Butterfield, San Francisco #812/R
$2750	£1910	Hauling in the nets (18x17cm-7x7in) board. 7-Mar-93 Butterfield & Butterfield, San Francisco #71/R
$4000	£2632	Fisherman's quay (25x35cm-10x14in) s. s.i.verso board. 13-Jun-93 Butterfield & Butterfield, San Francisco #819/R
$5500	£3235	Man in rowboat. After storm (29x43cm-11x17in) s. masonite double-sided. 4-Oct-92 Butterfield & Butterfield, Los Angeles #80/R
$7000	£4730	Men beaching dory (25x36cm-10x14in) s. board double-sided. 15-Jun-93 John Moran, Pasadena #87 a
$8000	£5556	Winter morning (26x36cm-10x14in) s. board. 7-Mar-93 Butterfield & Butterfield, San Francisco #107/R
$8500	£5592	Conversation. Coastal scene (39x47cm-15x19in) s. board double-sided. 13-Jun-93 Butterfield & Butterfield, San Francisco #806/R
$8500	£5903	Wind in the mast tops. Coastal scene with choppy seas (25x36cm-10x14in) s. board double-sided. 7-Mar-93 Butterfield & Butterfield, San Francisco #106/R
$10000	£5882	Landing of Father Serra (102x137cm-40x54in) s. 4-Oct-92 Butterfield & Butterfield, Los Angeles #66/R
$10000	£6944	Monterey fiesta (26x119cm-10x47in) s. canvas on board. 7-Mar-93 Butterfield & Butterfield, San Francisco #105/R
$11000	£7639	Return of the fishing fleet (45x55cm-18x22in) s. board. 7-Mar-93 Butterfield & Butterfield, San Francisco #68/R
$16000	£9412	Three fishermen hauling in nets (86x102cm-34x40in) 4-Oct-92 Butterfield & Butterfield, Los Angeles #67/R
$20000	£13889	Waiting for the news (51x89cm-20x35in) s. board. 7-Mar-93 Butterfield & Butterfield, San Francisco #66/R
$22000	£15278	Between tides (37x48cm-15x19in) s. canvas on board. 7-Mar-93 Butterfield & Butterfield, San Francisco #67/R
$50000	£33113	Outward bound (46x61cm-18x24in) s. i.verso canvasboard. 15-Jun-94 Butterfield & Butterfield, San Francisco #4609/R
$55000	£32253	Fishing boats (76x102cm-30x40in) s. 4-Oct-92 Butterfield & Butterfield, Los Angeles #65/R
$3000	£2013	Pier at Monterey (38x56cm-15x22in) s.d.16 chl. 8-Dec-93 Butterfield & Butterfield, San Francisco #3391/R
$4750	£3209	Boatyard (33x48cm-13x19in) s. W/C. 15-Jun-93 John Moran, Pasadena #33

HANSEN, Ejnar (1884-1965) Danish/American

$3750	£2604	Vase of roses (56x46cm-22x18in) s. s.verso. 7-Mar-93 Butterfield & Butterfield, San Francisco #242/R

HANSEN, Gaylen (1921-) American
$1500   £1014   Untitled (137x183cm-54x72in) s.d.1979. 8-Nov-93 Christie's, East, New York #167/R

HANSEN, Herman Wendelborg (1854-1924) American
$2500   £1773   Riders of the plains (61x91cm-24x36in) s. 12-Feb-93 Du Mouchelle, Detroit #111/R
$4000   £2685   Portrait of an Indian brave (20x13cm-8x5in) s. W/C. 8-Dec-93 Butterfield & Butterfield, San Francisco #3562/R
$18000 £12081 Shooting a rattlesnake (55x37cm-22x15in) s. W/C. 2-Dec-93 Sotheby's, New York #73/R

HANSON, James (20th C) American
$1650   £1078   Finding myself in unusual situation (152x213cm-60x84in) s.d.1983 verso. 14-May-93 Skinner, Bolton #191/R

HARDING, Chester (1792-1866) American
$2736   £1900   Shipping in stormy seas (66x76cm-26x30in) s.d.1835. 1-Mar-93 Desmond Judd, Cranbrook #718

HARDING, Chester (attrib) (1792-1866) American
$850   £552   Portrait of Daniel Pinckney Parker (71x56cm-28x22in) panel painted c.1823. 16-Jan-93 Skinner, Bolton #158
$1200   £805   Portrait of Daniel Webster (91x74cm-36x29in) oval. 6-Feb-94 Skinner, Bolton #147/R

HARDWICK, Melbourne H (1857-1916) American
$880   £575   Toy boat (64x56cm-25x22in) s.d.1913. 14-May-93 Skinner, Bolton #139/R
$880   £509   Young boy holding toy boat (64x56cm-25x22in) s. 24-Sep-92 Mystic Fine Arts, Connecticut #150/R
$1300   £833   Canal in Venice (51x41cm-20x16in) s. 24-May-93 Grogan, Massachussetts #317/R
$450   £302   Cabbage farmer (33x48cm-13x19in) s. W/C. 24-Mar-94 Mystic Fine Arts, Connecticut #202

HARDY, Anna Eliza (1839-1934) American
$1000   £662   Flowers on a branch (43x25cm-17x10in) s. 28-Nov-92 Young Fine Arts Auctions, Maine #201/R
$1600   £808   Still life (61x46cm-24x18in) s.d.78. 28-Aug-92 Young Fine Arts Auctions, Maine #152/R

HARE, Channing (1899-1976) American
$650   £455   Louis MacNeil (86x61cm-34x24in) s.d.1951 i.verso masonite. 12-Mar-93 Skinner, Bolton #292/R
$1100   £719   Princess Francesca Rospigliosi (102x86cm-40x34in) s.d.1948. 17-Sep-93 Skinner, Bolton #309/R

HARE, John (20th C) American
$725   £474   Highland lighthouse in winter (41x51cm-16x20in) s. 22-May-93 Collins, Maine #99/R
$1000   £671   P. Town dock scene (61x91cm-24x36in) s. 24-Mar-94 Mystic Fine Arts, Connecticut #143/R

HARING, Keith (1958-1990) American
$4000   £2649   Untitled (63x34cm-25x13in) s. i.d.April 12 1985verso acrylic board. 29-Sep-93 Sotheby's Arcade, New York #367 a/R
$4768   £3200   Untitled - Napoli (47x35cm-19x14in) s.i.d.10-83. 2-Dec-93 Christie's, London #262/R
$8500   £5705   Red, yellow, blue no 20 (92x61cm-36x24in) s.i.d.Jan.13/87. 4-May-94 Christie's, New York #420/R
$13000 £7647   Untitled (230x150cm-91x59in) acrylic. 8-Oct-92 Christie's, New York #243/R
$13008 £8233   Untitled (68x68cm-27x27in) s.d.1982 acrylic board. 30-Nov-92 Wolfgang Ketterer, Munich #131/R (DM 20500)
$16390 £11000 Red, yellow, blue 4 (120x80cm-47x31in) acrylic oil canvas painted 1987. 2-Dec-93 Christie's, London #212/R
$20000 £11765 Untitled (114x122cm-45x48in) s.d.8.20.81verso acrylic panel. 8-Oct-92 Christie's, New York #250/R
$22500 £14901 Untitled (76x76cm-30x30in) s.i.d.1984 verso acrylic. 18-Nov-92 Sotheby's, New York #317/R
$30000 £19608 Untitled (136cm-54in circular) s.d.17 oct 85verso oil acrylic. 5-May-93 Christie's, New York #169/R
$32500 £22569 Untitled (185x185cm-73x73in) s.d.84 acrylic plastic tarp. 23-Feb-93 Sotheby's, New York #396/R
$35760 £24000 3 children playing (182x182cm-72x72in) init.d.88 acrylic. 24-Mar-93 Sotheby's, London #350/R
$48000 £31788 Untitled (213x216cm-84x85in) s.d.Nov.17.1983 acrylic plastic tarp grommets. 19-Nov-92 Christie's, New York #450/R
$50000 £33784 Sneeze, via Picasso (152x152cm-60x60in) s.i.d. Oct.14 1984 acrylic. 10-Nov-93 Christie's, New York #392/R
$50000 £33557 Healing hand (305cm-120in circular) acrylic painted 1988. 23-Feb-94 Christie's, New York #144/R
$50000 £32680 Untitled (152x152cm-60x60in) s.i.d.1985 verso acrylic. 4-May-93 Sotheby's, New York #252/R
$53165 £35443 Untitled composition (305x300cm-120x118in) s.d.January 1983 acrylic vinyl tarpaulin. 2-Jun-94 AB Stockholms Auktionsverk, Stockholm #7118/R (S.KR 420000)
$55000 £36424 Untitled (300x305cm-118x120in) s.d.82 verso acrylic plastic tarp. 18-Nov-92 Sotheby's, New York #312/R
$617   £414   Les deux acrobates (30x21cm-12x8in) s.i.d.1989 black felt pen dr. 7-Dec-93 Catherine Charbonneaux, Paris #114 (F.FR 3600)

HARING, Keith (1958-1990) American-cont.

$1164	£781	Slow motion (27x22cm-11x9in) s.d.89 felttip pen. 4-Dec-93 Galerie Bassenge, Berlin #6257 (DM 2000)
$1226	£806	Fish (30x21cm-12x8in) s.i.d.1986 col.chk. 7-Jun-93 Wolfgang Ketterer, Munich #689/R (DM 2000)
$1310	£929	'For Piet' (27x17cm-11x7in) s.d.1989 felt pen. 9-Feb-93 Campo & Campo, Antwerp #192 (B.FR 45000)
$1421	£994	Mans 84 (35x30cm-14x12in) s.d.84 ink. 3-Feb-93 Cornette de St.Cyr, Paris #149/R (F.FR 8000)
$1760	£1181	Dancing figure with pyramid (30x23cm-12x9in) s.d.1989 black felt pen board. 10-Dec-93 Henner Wachholtz, Hamburg #278/R (DM 3000)
$1800	£1208	Piege a image , s.i.d.83 black felt pen. 13-Dec-93 Millon & Robert, Paris #10 (F.FR 10500)
$2000	£1258	Wolf and man (21x21cm-8x8in) s.d.83 metallic paint ink board. 25-Apr-93 Butterfield & Butterfield, San Francisco #2172/R
$2092	£1394	Baby study - night and day (40x40cm-16x16in) mono.i.d.1987 felt tip pair. 6-Jun-94 Wolfgang Ketterer, Munich #865/R (DM 3500)
$2135	£1433	For Claudia (23x29cm-9x11in) s.i.d.1983 ink acrylic cardboard. 14-Dec-93 Finarte, Milan #58 (I.L 3600000)
$2261	£1449	Portrait of bidet (35x28cm-14x11in) s.i.d.86 black red felt-tip pen. 10-Dec-92 Christie's, Amsterdam #465 (D.FL 4000)
$2472	£1626	For Piet (30x16cm-12x6in) s.i.d.1989 felttip pen board. 5-Jun-93 Villa Grisebach, Berlin #240/R (DM 4000)
$2526	£1619	Figure (30x23cm-12x9in) s.d.89 felttip pen. 27-May-93 Lempertz, Cologne #768/R (DM 4000)
$2624	£1761	Head (35x50cm-14x20in) s.d.July 1987verso W/C. 4-Dec-93 Kunstgalerij de Vuyst, Lokeren #392 (B.FR 95000)
$2638	£1736	Self portrait (30x23cm-12x9in) s.d.1989 felttip pen. 2-Apr-93 Bolland & Marotz, Bremen #948/R (DM 4200)
$2704	£1581	Untitled (30x23cm-12x9in) s.d.1989 felttip pen board. 19-Sep-92 Henner Wachholtz, Hamburg #630/R (DM 4000)
$2897	£1971	Crying baby (20x25cm-8x10in) Indian ink. 13-Apr-94 Bukowskis, Stockholm #310/R (S.KR 23000)
$2980	£2000	Elvis (98x68cm-39x27in) s.verso brush ink poster executed c.1981. 25-Mar-93 Christie's, London #162/R
$3184	£2041	Bursting man (27x21cm-11x8in) s.d.1988 felttip pen board. 11-Dec-92 Bolland & Marotz, Bremen #1096/R (DM 5000)
$3200	£2119	Poster for anti-missile demonstration (63x49cm-25x19in) s.d.83 s.i.d.verso brush ink. 17-Nov-92 Christie's, East, New York #86/R
$3200	£2119	Poster for anti-missile demonstration (63x49cm-25x19in) s.d.83 s.i.d.verso brush ink. 17-Nov-92 Christie's, East, New York #88/R
$3500	£2318	Untitled (50x63cm-20x25in) s.d.88 s.i.d.verso gouache brush ink. 17-Nov-92 Christie's, East, New York #87/R
$3799	£2550	Figure composition (73x55cm-29x22in) s.d.nov.7-82 Indian ink. 29-Nov-93 AB Stockholms Auktionsverk, Stockholm #6214/R (S.KR 32000)
$3800	£2550	Untitled (58x74cm-23x29in) s.d.Oct.30 1984verso brush ink acrylic. 4-May-94 Christie's, New York #408/R
$4250	£2853	Untitled (58x74cm-23x29in) d.1983 Sumi ink. 24-Feb-94 Sotheby's Arcade, New York #413/R
$4470	£3000	Untitled - Napoli (47x35cm-19x14in) s.i.d.10-83 black felt-tip pen. 2-Dec-93 Christie's, London #260/R
$4864	£3286	The photographer (42x59cm-17x23in) s.d.1983 felt-tip dr. 21-Apr-94 Germann, Zurich #131/R (S.FR 7000)
$5165	£3513	Computer world (80x170cm-31x67in) mixed media. 13-Apr-94 Bukowskis, Stockholm #311/R (S.KR 41000)
$5412	£3632	Sans titre (56x75cm-22x30in) s.d.27 aout 1982 i.verso marker pen. 29-Nov-93 Francis Briest, Paris #95/R (F.FR 32000)
$5500	£3691	Untitled red hand (58x73cm-23x29in) gouache executed c.1984. 5-May-94 Sotheby's, New York #353/R
$5500	£3642	Marilyn Monroe (99x68cm-39x27in) s. painted 1981 brush ink poster. 19-Nov-92 Christie's, New York #272/R
$6000	£4167	Untitled (58x74cm-23x29in) d.1983 ink. 23-Feb-93 Sotheby's, New York #387/R
$6000	£4027	Untitled (240x47cm-94x19in) brush ink. 23-Feb-94 Christie's, East, New York #267/R
$6500	£3824	Untitled (50x65cm-20x26in) s.d.Mar 15 88verso brush ink. 8-Oct-92 Christie's, New York #253/R
$7000	£4575	Untitled (49x70cm-19x28in) s.d.April 29-1982verso brush ink. 5-May-93 Christie's, New York #173/R
$7000	£4636	Untitled (50x65cm-20x26in) s.d.Mar15-88verso brush ink. 19-Nov-92 Christie's, New York #274/R
$7000	£4575	Untitled (56x76cm-22x30in) s.d.Nov. 24-83verso brush ink. 5-May-93 Christie's, New York #174/R
$7325	£4819	Untitled (305x410cm-120x161in) original poster executed 1984. 3-Jun-93 Christian de Quay, Paris #66/R (F.FR 40000)
$8000	£4706	Untitled (50x65cm-20x26in) s.d.Oct. 18-88 brush ink. 8-Oct-92 Christie's, New York #246/R
$8500	£5556	Untitled - Smurf (70x100cm-28x39in) s.d.Jan 14-84verso brush ink acrylic. 5-May-93 Christie's, New York #178/R
$8505	£5708	Untitled (26x41cm-10x16in) s.d.86 felt pen dr. 23-Mar-94 Dorotheum, Vienna #84/R (A.S 100000)
$10000	£6757	Study for untitled no 4 (76x102cm-30x40in) s.d.May 14 1988verso brush ink. 10-Nov-93 Christie's, New York #390/R
$10000	£6711	Untitled (62x74cm-24x29in) s.i.d.89verso brush col.ink. 4-May-94 Christie's, New York #417/R

HARING, Keith (1958-1990) American-cont.
$10000	£6757	Untitled (97x96cm-38x38in) s.d.Oct.4 89verso brush col.ink paper collage. 10-Nov-93 Christie's, New York #388/R
$10000	£6623	Untitled (130x52cm-51x20in) s.d.84 brush ink. 19-Nov-92 Christie's, New York #444/R
$11000	£7432	60 pigs for the NYC Sanitation Dept (96x63cm-38x25in) s.i.d.May 19 1984 black felt pen paper on board. 8-Nov-93 Christie's, East, New York #124/R
$12000	£7843	Untitled (105x114cm-41x45in) s.st.1981 ink vellum. 4-May-93 Sotheby's, New York #259/R
$13000	£8609	Untitled (121x86cm-48x34in) s.i.d.March 5-84verso brush col.ink. 19-Nov-92 Christie's, New York #448/R
$14000	£9272	Untitled (97x127cm-38x50in) s.d.12/81verso brush ink. 19-Nov-92 Christie's, New York #271/R
$17000	£11409	Drawing for Atomic Book (21x16cm-8x6in) s.i.d.83verso black felt-tip pen set of ten. 3-May-94 Christie's, East, New York #140/R
$18000	£12500	Untitled (114x122cm-45x48in) s.d.8/20/81verso enamel black felt-tip pen panel. 24-Feb-93 Christie's, New York #148/R
$18000	£12500	Untitled (109x109cm-43x43in) s.d.Sept 26-27 1982verso enamel metal. 24-Feb-93 Christie's, New York #155/R
$19000	£12583	Untitled (57x122cm-22x48in) s.d.82 verso enamel marker steel. 18-Nov-92 Sotheby's, New York #313/R
$20000	£13889	Untitled (96x126cm-38x50in) executed 1981 acrylic ink. 23-Feb-93 Sotheby's, New York #385/R
$20253	£13502	Raining men (78x100cm-31x39in) s.d.Sept.6 -81 Indian ink. 2-Jun-94 AB Stockholms Auktionsverk, Stockholm #7010/R (S.KR 160000)
$23000	£15436	Untitled (103x151cm-41x59in) gouache sumi ink executed 1988. 25-Feb-94 Sotheby's, New York #161/R

HARITONOFF, Nicholas B (1880-1944) American
$1100	£714	Around the campfire (18x29cm-7x11in) s. panel. 9-Sep-93 Sotheby's Arcade, New York #231/R

HARLES, Victor Joseph (1894-?) American
$2250	£1521	Composition (30x22cm-12x9in) s. canvasboard. 31-Mar-94 Sotheby's Arcade, New York #475/R

HARMON, Annie (1855-1930) American
$1800	£1250	Illilouette Falls, Yosemite (61x41cm-24x16in) mono. 7-Mar-93 Butterfield & Butterfield, San Francisco #37/R

HARMON, Lily (1913-) American
$550	£374	Girl with compote (46x30cm-18x12in) s. 16-Apr-94 Young Fine Arts Auctions, Maine #129/R

HARNDEN, William (1920-1983) American
$1600	£925	Pink house (76x61cm-30x24in) s. masonite. 25-Sep-92 Sotheby's Arcade, New York #349/R

HARNETT, William Michael (1851-1892) American
$8054	£5405	Still life of pipes (30x49cm-12x19in) s.d.1878. 2-Dec-93 Galerie Fischer, Lucerne #2072/R (S.FR 12000)
$52500	£33228	Still life of jug, bread and newspaper (25x20cm-10x8in) mono.d.1881. 3-Dec-92 Sotheby's, New York #39/R
$1500	£867	Portrait of woman, possibly artist's mother (14x11cm-6x4in) s.d.76 pencil. 23-Sep-92 Christie's, New York #28/R

HARNETT, William Michael (style) (1851-1892) American
$1178	£791	Two dead birds hanging on a wall (29x21cm-11x8in) i. panel. 23-Jun-93 Neumeister, Munich #667/R (DM 2000)

HAROLD, Alexander D (?-1923) Canadian
$775	£523	Friends, a carthorse and dog (23x30cm-9x12in) s. board. 3-Nov-93 Sotheby's, Toronto #43/R (C.D 1000)

HARRIS, Charles X (1856-?) American
$41000	£26282	Decision (20x27cm-8x11in) s.d.1884 i.verso panel. 27-May-93 Sotheby's, New York #177/R

HARRIS, Dan (20th C) American
$600	£405	Glissade, assemble, tombe (12x16cm-5x6in) s.i.d.2.46 ink W/C. 21-Apr-94 Butterfield & Butterfield, San Francisco #1081/R

HARRIS, Juan Eduardo (19/20th C) Chilean
$4200	£2800	A nude (160x100cm-63x39in) s. 25-May-94 Sotheby's Colonnade, London #105/R
$4200	£2800	A young woman by a lake (90x70cm-35x28in) s. 25-May-94 Sotheby's Colonnade, London #175/R

HARRIS, Lawren Stewart (1885-1970) Canadian
$3697	£2448	Untitled landscape (99x127cm-39x50in) painted c.1963. 18-Nov-92 Sotheby's, Toronto #117/R (C.D 4750)
$4756	£3109	Late afternoon, winter (21x16cm-8x6in) init.d.12 s.i.verso panel double-sided. 19-May-93 Sotheby's, Toronto #268 a/R (C.D 6000)
$6974	£4712	Quebec farm house (20x25cm-8x10in) s. s.i.verso board. 3-Nov-93 Sotheby's, Toronto #165/R (C.D 9000)

HARRIS, Lawren Stewart (1885-1970) Canadian-cont.
$7749	£5236	Untitled (66x51cm-26x20in) st.mono.i.d.1936,1938verso board. 3-Nov-93 Sotheby's, Toronto #211/R (C.D 10000)
$17476	£11650	Country north of Lake Superior (26x34cm-10x13in) s.i.verso board. 13-May-94 Joyner Fine Art, Toronto #97/R (C.D 24000)
$20237	£13402	Above Lake Superior, Pic Island (27x34cm-11x13in) panel. 18-Nov-92 Sotheby's, Toronto #141/R (C.D 26000)
$23782	£15544	Lismer Lake, Algoma (27x34cm-11x13in) s. panel. 19-May-93 Sotheby's, Toronto #173/R (C.D 30000)
$25368	£16580	Maligne Lake, Jasper Park (27x36cm-11x14in) s. board. 19-May-93 Sotheby's, Toronto #185/R (C.D 32000)
$27746	£18135	Snow squalls (30x38cm-12x15in) s.verso panel. 19-May-93 Sotheby's, Toronto #294/R (C.D 35000)
$29577	£19588	Afternoon, Lake Superior (30x37cm-12x15in) s. board painted c.1924. 24-Nov-92 Joyner Fine Art, Toronto #60/R (C.D 38000)
$35026	£23196	Mountain form (30x41cm-12x16in) s.i.verso board. 18-Nov-92 Sotheby's, Toronto #96/R (C.D 45000)
$62268	£41237	In the ward, Toronto (27x34cm-11x13in) init. i.d.1917verso board. 18-Nov-92 Sotheby's, Toronto #87/R (C.D 80000)
$62268	£41237	Trees and snow (26x36cm-10x14in) s. i.verso panel. 18-Nov-92 Sotheby's, Toronto #148/R (C.D 80000)
$70995	£47330	House in the Ward, winer, City Painting No.1 (81x96cm-32x38in) s. 11-May-94 Sotheby's, Toronto #102/R (C.D 97500)
$75311	£49223	Mountain form, F71 Mount Ann-Alice (124x124cm-49x49in) s. s.d.1943 verso. 19-May-93 Sotheby's, Toronto #255/R (C.D 95000)
$101186	£67010	Isolation peak (30x37cm-12x15in) s.i.verso board. 18-Nov-92 Sotheby's, Toronto #149/R (C.D 130000)
$181224	£122449	Lake in Algoma, Northern Paintings II (105x125cm-41x49in) s. painted c.1925. 23-Nov-93 Joyner Fine Art, Toronto #92/R (C.D 240000)
$186804	£123711	In Ward I, City Paintings (72x87cm-28x34in) s.d.1918. 24-Nov-92 Joyner Fine Art, Toronto #75/R (C.D 240000)
$189320	£126214	South Shore, Bylot Island (90x125cm-35x49in) s. double sided. 13-May-94 Joyner Fine Art, Toronto #75/R (C.D 260000)
$1585	*£1036*	*Arctic shore - No.2 (19x24cm-7x9in) pencil. 19-May-93 Sotheby's, Toronto #288/R (C.D 2000)*

HARRIS, Robert (1849-1919) Canadian
$680	£459	Boats on a beach (21x14cm-8x6in) init. board painted 1911. 23-Nov-93 Joyner Fine Art, Toronto #305/R (C.D 900)
$856	£567	Landscape with houses and forest (30x39cm-12x15in) s. 18-Nov-92 Sotheby's, Toronto #99 a (C.D 1100)
$1208	£816	Portrait of a young man (45x35cm-18x14in) s. board. 23-Nov-93 Joyner Fine Art, Toronto #205/R (C.D 1600)
$1661	£1122	Portrait of the artist's wife (50x40cm-20x16in) s.d.88. 23-Nov-93 Joyner Fine Art, Toronto #120/R (C.D 2200)
$3171	£2073	Portrait of artist's brother (64x51cm-25x20in) s.d.1884. 19-May-93 Sotheby's, Toronto #229/R (C.D 4000)
$604	*£408*	*Portrait of a young girl (30x23cm-12x9in) s. col.chk framed oval. 23-Nov-93 Joyner Fine Art, Toronto #29/R (C.D 800)*
$1133	*£765*	*Young lady writing (24x14cm-9x6in) init. chl htd white chk. 23-Nov-93 Joyner Fine Art, Toronto #190/R (C.D 1500)*

HARRIS, Sam Hyde (1889-1977) American
$950	£629	Desert foothills (41x51cm-16x20in) s. 15-Jun-94 Butterfield & Butterfield, San Francisco #4725/R
$950	£642	Desert morn (23x30cm-9x12in) s. board. 9-Nov-93 John Moran, Pasadena #894
$1100	£764	Cottonwood tree (41x51cm-16x20in) s. canvas on board. 7-Mar-93 Butterfield & Butterfield, San Francisco #226/R
$1200	£828	Barn in landscape (41x51cm-16x20in) s. canvas laid down on board. 16-Feb-93 John Moran, Pasadena #23
$1900	£1118	Desert sentinels (61x76cm-24x30in) s. 4-Oct-92 Butterfield & Butterfield, Los Angeles #202/R
$2000	£1325	Ranch sheleter (41x51cm-16x20in) estate st. 14-Jun-94 John Moran, Pasadena #52
$2100	£1364	The toilers (61x91cm-24x36in) i.verso painted 1947 masonite. 11-Sep-93 Louisiana Auction Exchange #32/R
$2500	£1471	Desert wash (51x61cm-20x24in) s. canvasboard. 4-Oct-92 Butterfield & Butterfield, Los Angeles #203/R
$2500	£1689	Desert radiance (61x76cm-24x30in) s. 9-Nov-93 John Moran, Pasadena #828
$3250	£1912	At ease (41x51cm-16x20in) s. canvasboard. 4-Oct-92 Butterfield & Butterfield, Los Angeles #143/R
$4000	£2649	The woodland grove (63x76cm-25x30in) s. 15-Jun-94 Butterfield & Butterfield, San Francisco #4704/R
$6000	£3529	Blue shadows (61x76cm-24x30in) s. 4-Oct-92 Butterfield & Butterfield, Los Angeles #130/R
$6000	£4000	Eats (41x51cm-16x20in) canvas laid down on board. 15-Mar-94 John Moran, Pasadena #119 a

HARRISON, Birge (1854-1929) American
$650	£425	Village street at moonlite (35x27cm-14x11in) s.d.1907 canvasboard. 4-May-93 Christie's, East, New York #63
$1200	£759	Trout pool (51x61cm-20x24in) s. 2-Dec-92 Christie's, East, New York #111/R

HARRISON, Mark R (1819-1894) Canadian
$2704	£1803	The Silver Lake in the Valley of the Wisconsin (68x112cm-27x44in) s.d.1860. 31-May-94 Ritchie, Toronto #12/R (C.D 3750)

HARRISON, Mark R (1819-1894) Canadian-cont.
$6043   £4197   The critics (58x77cm-23x30in) s.d.1887. 24-Feb-93 Dorotheum, Vienna #401/R
                      (A.S 70000)

HARRISON, Ted (1926-) Canadian
$1879   £1270   Small hamlet (46x61cm-18x24in) acrylic board. 14-Jun-93 Lunds, Victoria #5
                      (C.D 2400)

HARRISON, Thomas Alexander (1853-1930) American
$634   £420   Sunset (61x91cm-24x36in) s. 28-Sep-93 Sotheby's Colonnade, London #1096/R
$1000   £671   Rose twilight (56x91cm-22x36in) s. 11-Dec-93 Weschler, Washington #105
$1100   £743   Seascape (51x81cm-20x32in) s. 10-Aug-93 Stonington Fine Arts, Stonington #51/R
$1800   £1216   Village outskirts (28x36cm-11x14in) s. board. 20-Apr-94 Doyle, New York #43
$2600   £1699   Falls at Montigny, France (71x100cm-28x39in) s.d.1901. 4-May-93 Christie's, East,
                      New York #142/R

HART, Alfred (1816-?) American
$902   £601   Caserio (42x32cm-17x13in) s. 25-May-94 Louis Morton, Mexico #105/R (M.P 3000)

HART, Claudia (1955-) American
$1709   £1139   Untitled (198x153cm-78x60in) diptych painted 1988. 2-Jun-94 AB Stockholms
                      Auktionsverk, Stockholm #7141/R (S.KR 13500)
$823   *£549*   *Untitled - let him be Jupiter in the ether (82x143cm-32x56in) oil pencil painted
                      1987. 2-Jun-94 AB Stockholms Auktionsverk, Stockholm #7142/R (S.KR 6500)*
$3500   *£2059*   *Untitled (199x142cm-78x56in) oil graphite col.pencils. 8-Oct-92 Christie's, New
                      York #214/R*

HART, George Overbury (1868-1933) American
$700   £473   Mexican farmer leaving town (24x33cm-9x13in) s.d.97 panel. 31-Mar-94 Sotheby's
                      Arcade, New York #351/R
$500   *£331*   *Dominica (30x48cm-12x19in) s. W/C. 23-Sep-93 Mystic Fine Arts, Connecticut #255*
$1700   *£859*   *Ruseau Dominica (30x53cm-12x21in) s.i.d.1917 W/C. 28-Aug-92 Young Fine Arts
                      Auctions, Maine #154/R*

HART, James MacDougal (1828-1901) American
$1400   £915   Farm with field of wheat (25x43cm-10x17in) s. board. 8-May-93 Young Fine Arts
                      Auctions, Maine #145/R
$1550   £820   Watering hole (28x18cm-11x7in) s. 12-Sep-92 Louisiana Auction Exchange #46/R
$1700   £1149   Cows grazing near a pond with ducks (41x53cm-16x21in) s. 31-Mar-94 Sotheby's
                      Arcade, New York #114/R
$1700   £1156   Cattle grazing (30x41cm-12x16in) s. 16-Apr-94 Young Fine Arts Auctions, Maine
                      #130/R
$2000   £1325   Cows in meadow (51x77cm-20x30in) s.d.1872. 23-Sep-93 Sotheby's, New York #45/R
$2500   £1656   Grazing cattle (30x41cm-12x16in) s. 17-Jun-94 Du Mouchelle, Detroit #2217
$2600   £1503   Cows watering (12x20cm-5x8in) init. 23-Sep-92 Christie's, New York #19/R
$2960   £2000   River landscape with cattle watering by bank (42x75cm-17x30in) s. 25-Nov-93
                      Christie's, S. Kensington #108/R
$3000   £1961   Landscape (31x26cm-12x10in) s. 4-May-93 Christie's, East, New York #127 f/R
$3000   £1948   Landscape with deer (41x61cm-16x24in) s.d.1857. 9-Sep-93 Sotheby's Arcade, New
                      York #11/R
$3200   £2133   Leading the herd home (101x66cm-40x26in) s.d.1875. 23-May-94 Christie's, East,
                      New York #17
$3500   £2303   Scene near New Russia, Essex County, New York (23x41cm-9x16in) s. 13-Jun-93
                      Butterfield & Butterfield, San Francisco #3107/R
$8000   £5063   Farmington River, Farmington, Connecticut (34x59cm-13x23in) s. 3-Dec-92
                      Sotheby's, New York #46/R
$12000   £6936   View of Farmington, Connecticut (34x59cm-13x23in) s.i.d.1866. 24-Sep-92
                      Sotheby's, New York #38/R
$1200   *£774*   *Studies of cattle (30x46cm-12x18in) s. one d.Aug 19 1871 pencil htd white pair.
                      13-Jul-94 Doyle, New York #36*

HART, Mary Theresa (1829-1921) American
$4200   £2781   Wildflower bouquet (26x25cm-10x10in) s.d.1870 canvas on board. 22-Sep-93
                      Christie's, New York #17/R

HART, William M (1823-1894) American
$1600   £1053   Cows drinking by river (21x27cm-8x11in) s.d.1887. 31-Mar-93 Sotheby's Arcade, New
                      York #58 a/R
$1700   £1111   Forest landscape (29x41cm-11x16in) s. 22-May-93 Weschler, Washington #85/R
$1800   £1250   Cattle by stream (23x30cm-9x12in) s.verso. 6-Mar-93 Louisiana Auction Exchange
                      #97/R
$1800   £1250   Man with two cows by stream (20x25cm-8x10in) s.d.1872verso. 6-Mar-93 Louisiana
                      Auction Exchange #96/R
$1900   £1267   Esopus Creek, Ulster County, New York (12x33cm-5x13in) s.i.d.Oct.1857verso
                      canvas laid down on board. 21-May-94 Weschler, Washington #73/R
$2400   £1600   Cattle watering (61x51cm-24x20in) s. canvas over panel. 23-May-94 Christie's,
                      East, New York #31/R
$2750   £1833   River landscape at sunset (43x89cm-17x35in) s. 18-Mar-94 Du Mouchelle, Detroit
                      #2153/R
$3000   £1734   Craigy barns (27x37cm-11x15in) s.i.d.1850. 23-Sep-92 Christie's, New York #20/R
$4500   £2961   Cows watering by river (62x52cm-24x20in) s.d.1883. 31-Mar-93 Sotheby's Arcade,
                      New York #53/R
$5500   £3595   Autumn river scene (33x38cm-13x15in) s.d.1867 board. 30-Jun-94 Mystic Fine Arts,
                      Connecticut #50 b
$5960   £4000   Harvest time (102x152cm-40x60in) s.d.1854. 3-Mar-94 Christie's, S. Kensington #72

HART, William M (1823-1894) American-cont.
$7500	£4934	Scene on the Heldenberg mountain (94x71cm-37x28in) s.d.1849 s.i.stretcher. 4-Nov-92 Doyle, New York #1/R
$9000	£5882	In the Berkshires (46x35cm-18x14in) s.d.1873. 4-May-93 Christie's, East, New York #127 g/R
$12000	£7947	Sunset on river bank (51x41cm-20x16in) s.d.70. 22-Sep-93 Christie's, New York #8/R

HARTIGAN, Grace (1922-) American
$2500	£1656	Rain King (53x60cm-21x24in) s.d.65. 17-Nov-92 Christie's, East, New York #224/R
$8500	£5705	Untitled (99x114cm-39x45in) s.d.51. 24-Feb-94 Sotheby's Arcade, New York #354/R

HARTLEY, Marsden (1877-1943) American
$9500	£6013	Fish and lemons (22x26cm-9x10in) 3-Dec-92 Sotheby's, New York #146/R
$13000	£8609	Still life with bread and fruit (36x66cm-14x26in) painted 1919. 23-Sep-93 Sotheby's, New York #236/R
$15000	£10000	Gorges du Loup, Provence (62x50cm-24x20in) s. 25-May-94 Sotheby's, New York #129/R
$20000	£12658	Roofs and woods (49x69cm-19x27in) masonite. 3-Dec-92 Sotheby's, New York #168/R
$23000	£15436	Still life with fruit (33x55cm-13x22in) i.stretcher painted c.1923-24. 2-Dec-93 Sotheby's, New York #143/R
$26000	£16456	Still life - blue bottle, oranges and lemons (61x50cm-24x20in) init. s.d.1928 verso. 3-Dec-92 Sotheby's, New York #159/R
$28000	£17722	Peppers (54x80cm-21x31in) 3-Dec-92 Sotheby's, New York #160/R
$29000	£20280	Seashells on violet cloth (53x33cm-21x13in) s.d.1929verso panel. 10-Mar-93 Sotheby's, New York #141/R
$30000	£19868	Red flowers on pink ground (25x61cm-10x24in) init.d.43 masonite. 23-Sep-93 Sotheby's, New York #238/R
$55000	£34810	Abelhard ascending - a fantasy (71x55cm-28x22in) board. 3-Dec-92 Sotheby's, New York #163/R
$65000	£43333	The fish (40x63cm-16x25in) s.d.1932-33verso cardboard. 25-May-94 Sotheby's, New York #131/R
$190000	£127517	Night - and some flowers (60x45cm-24x18in) s.i.verso canvasboard painted c.1940. 3-Dec-93 Christie's, New York #11/R
$600000	£400000	Madawaska - Acadian Light-Heavy (102x76cm-40x30in) s.d.1940 i.versi masonite. 26-May-94 Christie's, New York #134/R
$1050000	£664557	Abstraction (119x100cm-47x39in) 3-Dec-92 Sotheby's, New York #158/R
$2000	£1351	The lighthouse (15x22cm-6x9in) s.d.41 pencil. 31-Mar-94 Sotheby's Arcade, New York #310/R
$5500	£3642	The Rio Grande River (46x61cm-18x24in) s.i.d.Oct.1919 pastel. 15-Jun-94 Butterfield & Butterfield, San Francisco #4525/R
$10000	£6667	Provence landscape (49x65cm-19x26in) pencil. 26-May-94 Christie's, New York #135/R
$37500	£25000	New Mexico landscape (44x71cm-17x28in) s.d.1918 pastel. 25-May-94 Sotheby's, New York #124/R

HARTLEY, Marsden (attrib) (1877-1943) American
$1600	£1013	Male nude (41x30cm-16x12in) init. i.d.1938verso. 30-Nov-92 Schrager Galleries, Milwaukee #530

HARTLEY, Rachel (1884-?) American
$1500	£1007	South Hampton beach scene (30x41cm-12x16in) artist's board. 27-Mar-94 Myers, Florida #33/R

HARTMANN, Bertram (1882-1960) American
$750	£510	A fishing village (53x62cm-21x24in) s. canvas laid down on board. 15-Nov-93 Christie's, East, New York #238/R
$750	£510	Houses in the hills (73x100cm-29x39in) s. 15-Nov-93 Christie's, East, New York #246/R
$800	£537	Farm scene (74x102cm-29x40in) s. 24-Mar-94 Mystic Fine Arts, Connecticut #101/R
$1400	£921	Connecticut apple tree (81x100cm-32x39in) s.d.1936 s.stretcher painted 1932-36. 31-Mar-93 Sotheby's Arcade, New York #278/R
$1000	£633	New York skyline (53x36cm-21x14in) s. W/C. 2-Dec-92 Christie's, East, New York #258

HARTWICH, Herman (1853-1926) American
$1800	£1216	The field on the hill in late afternoon (27x39cm-11x15in) s.d.Oct 3-77. 5-Nov-93 Skinner, Bolton #98/R
$5554	£3267	Landscape with ducks by stream (36x54cm-14x21in) s. 6-Oct-92 Michael Zeller, Lindau #1289/R (DM 8200)
$7779	£5221	Loading hay in the South Tirol (45x60cm-18x24in) s. 23-Mar-94 Kunsthaus am Museum, Cologne #1250/R (DM 13000)

HARTWICK, George Gunther (19th C) American
$1700	£1141	View of Yosemite (76x127cm-30x50in) s.d.1878. 3-Feb-94 Sloan, North Bethesda #2916/R
$2000	£1325	Yosemite Valley (56x91cm-22x36in) s. 2-Oct-93 Weschler, Washington #121/R
$4500	£3000	In the Catskills (84x122cm-33x48in) s.i. 23-May-94 Christie's, East, New York #16/R

HARTWIG, Heinie (1937-) American
$750	£472	Break in the sky (30x61cm-12x24in) s. masonite. 22-Apr-93 Freeman Fine Arts, Philadelphia #1229
$800	£537	Camp in the Aspens (30x46cm-12x18in) s. i.verso masonite. 5-Mar-94 Louisiana Auction Exchange #21/R

HARTWIG, Heinie (1937-) American-cont.
$900	£588	Indian encampment (30x61cm-12x24in) s. masonite. 22-May-93 Weschler, Washington #156/R
$950	£629	By the lake (30x61cm-12x24in) s. i.verso masonite. 2-Oct-93 Weschler, Washington #164/R
$1000	£671	Cheyenne winter camp (30x61cm-12x24in) s. masonite. 4-Dec-93 Louisiana Auction Exchange #73/R
$1119	£751	Indian tent on the prairie (44x67cm-17x26in) s. panel. 24-Jun-93 Neumeister, Munich #2907 (DM 1900)
$1413	£949	Indian tent on the prairie (60x90cm-24x35in) s. panel. 24-Jun-93 Neumeister, Munich #2906 (DM 2400)
$1700	£899	The Grand Tetons (76x61cm-30x24in) s. i.verso masonite. 9-Sep-92 Doyle, New York #45

HARVEY, Bessie (1929-) American
| $1600 | £1060 | Spirits (107x69cm-42x27in) paint board. 21-Nov-92 Litchfield Auction Gallery #16 |

HARVEY, George (1800-1878) American
| $28000 | £16185 | Autumn (64x49cm-25x19in) s.i.stretcher. 23-Sep-92 Christie's, New York #22/R |
| $5000 | £3333 | Tropical landscape (23x38cm-9x15in) s. W/C pencil. 16-Mar-94 Christie's, New York #26/R |

HARVEY, George W (1855-?) American
| $1800 | £1184 | Haystacks in winter (41x61cm-16x24in) s. 2-Apr-93 Sloan, North Bethesda #2478/R |

HARVEY, Reginald L (1888-1963) Canadian
| $576 | £400 | Over the Plough (44x33cm-17x13in) s. 3-Mar-93 Bonhams, London #157 |

HASBROUCK, Dubois Fenelon (1860-1934) American
| $3250 | £2083 | Apple trees (51x76cm-20x30in) s. 9-Dec-92 Butterfield & Butterfield, San Francisco #3852/R |
| $4500 | £3061 | Twilight winter landscape (41x61cm-16x24in) s.d.87. 17-Nov-93 Doyle, New York #22/R |

HASELTINE, Charles Field (1840-1915) American
| $750 | £493 | Meadow landscape with figures at dusk (36x46cm-14x18in) s.d.1905 board. 2-Apr-93 Sloan, North Bethesda #2064 |

HASELTINE, William Stanley (1835-1900) American
$1000	£667	Bay of Naples, near Sorrento (35x49cm-14x19in) 23-May-94 Christie's, East, New York #70/R
$3000	£1961	Canal at Castel Fusano (63x179cm-25x70in) 4-May-93 Christie's, East, New York #41a
$4500	£2961	Bay at dawn (50x80cm-20x31in) s.d.1869 canvas on board. 31-Mar-93 Sotheby's Arcade, New York #94/R
$7500	£4967	Lago Maggiore (35x57cm-14x22in) 22-Sep-93 Christie's, New York #84/R
$15000	£9615	On beach, Capri (49x76cm-19x30in) init. 26-May-93 Christie's, New York #61/R
$27000	£15607	Temple of Fusano (65x180cm-26x71in) s.d.81. 24-Sep-92 Sotheby's, New York #64/R
$700	£458	Farmhouse in Bavaria (56x73cm-22x29in) init. gouache W/C pen three sheets board. 4-May-93 Christie's, East, New York #39
$2500	£1445	Castel Fusano, Ostia (56x38cm-22x15in) i.verso W/C board. 25-Sep-92 Sotheby's Arcade, New York #128/R

HASELTINE, William Stanley (attrib) (1835-1900) American
| $550 | £364 | Marsh country near Lakein, Switzerland (41x33cm-16x13in) 19-Jun-94 Hindman Galleries, Chicago #648 |

HASSAM, Childe (1859-1935) American
$22000	£14103	Quiet stream (36x41cm-14x16in) s. painted c.1880. 26-May-93 Christie's, New York #90/R
$40000	£25316	Autumn twilight (26x36cm-10x14in) s. 4-Dec-92 Christie's, New York #84/R
$47500	£31879	The Cedar Lot, Old Lyme (36x51cm-14x20in) s.d.1904. 2-Dec-93 Sotheby's, New York #102/R
$52500	£33228	Brook in Branchville, Connecticut (55x61cm-22x24in) s.d.1907. 3-Dec-92 Sotheby's, New York #98/R
$65000	£43333	Old bottle man (41x30cm-16x12in) s.d.1892 init.d.1892 verso paper on canvas. 17-Mar-94 Sotheby's, New York #120/R
$65000	£42763	Moonlight on Isles of Shoals (41x56cm-16x22in) s.i.d.1899. 13-Jun-93 Butterfield & Butterfield, San Francisco #3158/R
$95000	£60897	Across common on winter evening (13x29cm-5x11in) s. i.verso panel. 27-May-93 Sotheby's, New York #56/R
$140000	£93960	Evening, Champs-Elysees - pres du Louvre (34x27cm-13x11in) s. s.d.1898 verso. 3-Dec-93 Christie's, New York #48/R
$145000	£91772	October haze, Manhattan (63x76cm-25x30in) s.d.1910 init.d.verso. 3-Dec-92 Sotheby's, New York #108/R
$150000	£100000	Quai des Tuileries (27x20cm-11x8in) s. panel painted c.1888-89. 17-Mar-94 Sotheby's, New York #107/R
$190000	£127517	Tulip tree in blossom (62x93cm-24x37in) s.i.d.June 19,1932 init.d.verso. 2-Dec-93 Sotheby's, New York #117/R
$200000	£128205	Boys marching by (81x72cm-32x28in) s.d.1918. 26-May-93 Christie's, New York #135/R
$200000	£128205	Moonrise at sunset (69x69cm-27x27in) s.d.1900 i.stretcher. 27-May-93 Sotheby's, New York #60/R
$460000	£294872	Couch on porch, Cos cob (63x79cm-25x31in) s.d.1914. 27-May-93 Sotheby's, New York #29/R

HASSAM, Childe (1859-1935) American-cont.
$500000	£320513	Sunny morning, Villiers-le-Bel (66x51cm-26x20in) s. 26-May-93 Christie's, New York #125/R
$5000000	£3205128	Room of flowers (86x86cm-34x34in) s.d.1894. 27-May-93 Sotheby's, New York #21/R
$4250	£2853	Naples (30x44cm-12x17in) s.i.d.83 W/C. 6-May-94 Skinner, Bolton #132/R
$5500	£3216	The Home Sweet Home (25x30cm-10x12in) s.i. etching wove paper. 19-Sep-92 Christie's, East, New York #20/R
$6000	£3797	European street scene (36x27cm-14x11in) s.d.1883 pen pencil board. 3-Dec-92 Sotheby's, New York #92/R
$7500	£4335	Impression (31x46cm-12x18in) s.i.d.86 W/C paper on board. 23-Sep-92 Christie's, New York #126/R
$15000	£9615	Isles of Shoals Daybook, 1901 (11x13cm-4x5in) s. ink pencil W/C. 27-May-93 Sotheby's, New York #57/R
$16000	£10127	Harper's Ferry 2nd (40x48cm-16x19in) s.d.1926 W/C. 3-Dec-92 Sotheby's, New York #40/R
$19000	£10983	Flags, Columbus Circle (22x17cm-9x7in) s.d.1918 W/C chl paper on board. 23-Sep-92 Christie's, New York #134/R
$35000	£23333	Newfields, New Hampshire (35x50cm-14x20in) s.d.1918 W/C. 25-May-94 Sotheby's, New York #81/R
$50000	£33557	November, Cos Cob (46x56cm-18x22in) s.d.1902 pastel board. 3-Dec-93 Christie's, New York #40/R
$55000	£34810	World's Fair, Chicago (28x35cm-11x14in) s. gouache en grisaille board. 4-Dec-92 Christie's, New York #80/R
$65000	£41139	Venetian regatta (44x30cm-17x12in) s.i.d.1891 W/C pencil. 4-Dec-92 Christie's, New York #77/R
$65000	£41667	Old brush house, Cos Cob (45x56cm-18x22in) s.d.1902 pastel board. 26-May-93 Christie's, New York #131/R
$100000	£64103	Verandah of old house (49x34cm-19x13in) s.d.1912 W/C. 26-May-93 Christie's, New York #139/R
$350000	£224359	Horse drawn cabs, New York (45x55cm-18x22in) s.d.1891 pastel canvas. 26-May-93 Christie's, New York #118/R
$750000	£474684	Horse drawn cabs at evening, New York (35x43cm-14x17in) s.i. W/C gouache. 4-Dec-92 Christie's, New York #75/R

HASSELL, Hilton Macdonald (1910-1980) Canadian
$574	£383	Quiet day - Stonehurst, N.S (30x41cm-12x16in) s. i.verso acrylic canvasboard. 30-May-94 Hodgins, Calgary #226/R (C.D 800)
$634	£415	Port de Grave, Newfoundland (36x51cm-14x20in) s. acrylic canvas laid down on board. 18-May-93 Joyner Fine Art, Toronto #107/R (C.D 800)
$754	£513	Hills of the Fjord Pangnirtung Eastern Arctic (30x41cm-12x16in) s. s.i.d.1977verso board. 15-Nov-93 Hodgins, Calgary #255 (C.D 1000)
$831	£561	Bay Roberts, NFLD (30x50cm-12x20in) s. acrylic canvas on board. 23-Nov-93 Joyner Fine Art, Toronto #312 (C.D 1100)
$982	£663	Gallery visitors (60x105cm-24x41in) s. acrylic canvas on board. 23-Nov-93 Joyner Fine Art, Toronto #225 (C.D 1300)
$1162	£785	Dockside pattern (46x66cm-18x26in) s. i.verso board. 3-Nov-93 Sotheby's, Toronto #332/R (C.D 1500)
$2265	£1531	Cove Road, Conception Bay, NFLD (60x90cm-24x35in) s. acrylic board. 23-Nov-93 Joyner Fine Art, Toronto #54/R (C.D 3000)

HASSLER, Carl von (1887-1962) American?
$2100	£1235	Autumn landscape. Winter landscape (50x65cm-20x26in) s. pair. 3-Oct-92 Weschler, Washington #148/R

HATFIELD, Joseph Henry (1863-?) Canadian
$1900	£1319	Road at sunset (46x61cm-18x24in) s. 27-Feb-93 Young Fine Arts Auctions, Maine #134/R

HAUSER, John (1859-1913) American
$850	£545	Study for the Hostiles (43x30cm-17x12in) gouache. 13-Dec-92 Hindman Galleries, Chicago #29/R
$2400	£1558	Indian warrior (36x26cm-14x10in) s.d.1909 s.indis.i.d.verso gouache board. 9-Sep-93 Sotheby's Arcade, New York #225/R

HAVARD, James (1937-) American
$625	£417	Sequeya letter no.8 (43x112cm-17x44in) s.d.71 i.verso acrylic lacquer paper. 26-May-94 Freeman Fine Arts, Philadelphia #149
$950	£629	Hiding Mimbre (23x30cm-9x12in) s.d.87 acrylic. 29-Sep-93 Sotheby's Arcade, New York #359/R
$1000	£662	Grey chair with backfat (25x20cm-10x8in) acrylic. 29-Sep-93 Sotheby's Arcade, New York #356/R
$2000	£1325	Tableta (46x36cm-18x14in) s.d.88 acrylic. 29-Sep-93 Sotheby's Arcade, New York #355/R
$3918	£2629	Hopi (132x92cm-52x36in) s.d.74verso acrylic. 29-Nov-93 AB Stockholms Auktionsverk, Stockholm #6215/R (S.KR 33000)
$4000	£2685	Untitled (102x91cm-40x36in) s.d.74 acrylic. 23-Feb-94 Christie's, East, New York #291/R
$5500	£3691	Untitled (183x91cm-72x36in) s.d.80 acrylic. 24-Feb-94 Sotheby's Arcade, New York #472/R
$14000	£8235	Drink juice of stone (169x169cm-67x67in) s.d.75 verso acrylic. 6-Oct-92 Sotheby's, New York #58/R
$3291	£2194	Crow (101x81cm-40x32in) s.d.84 mixed media plexiglass. 2-Jun-94 AB Stockholms Auktionsverk, Stockholm #6277/R (S.KR 26000)

HAVEN, Franklin de (1856-1934) American
$600	£403	Autumn trees (76x61cm-30x24in) 27-Mar-94 Myers, Florida #35/R
$675	£433	Spring landscape (20x28cm-8x11in) s. board. 10-Dec-92 Sloan, North Bethesda #1666
$850	£545	Twilight (30x36cm-12x14in) s. 10-Dec-92 Sloan, North Bethesda #1665
$900	£520	Seascape with tornado (61x76cm-24x30in) s. 25-Sep-92 Sotheby's Arcade, New York #89/R
$1000	£676	Grazing sheep on a fall day (61x76cm-24x30in) s. 31-Mar-94 Sotheby's Arcade, New York #135/R
$1200	£811	Moon over the river (63x76cm-25x30in) s.d.1931. 31-Mar-94 Sotheby's Arcade, New York #141/R
$1700	£1133	Spring landscape (64x76cm-25x30in) s. 20-May-94 Du Mouchelle, Detroit #2283/R

HAWORTH, Bobs Cogill (1904-1988) Canadian
$623	£412	Home Sweet Home, Cape Breton, Nova Scotia (52x63cm-20x25in) s.i.d.1960verso gouache W/C. 18-Nov-92 Sotheby's, Toronto #58/R (C.D 800)
$872	£570	Fox River (49x51cm-19x20in) s. W/C. 18-May-93 Joyner Fine Art, Toronto #320 (C.D 1100)

HAWORTH, Peter (1889-1986) Canadian
$555	£363	Orchard in spring (38x55cm-15x22in) s. W/C col chk. 18-May-93 Joyner Fine Art, Toronto #1/R (C.D 700)
$623	£412	Abstract - The kitchen (76x61cm-30x24in) s. gouache board. 18-Nov-92 Sotheby's, Toronto #144 (C.D 800)
$1602	£1068	Village in the valley, Quebec (47x56cm-19x22in) s. W/C. 13-May-94 Joyner Fine Art, Toronto #1/R (C.D 2200)

HAWTHORNE, Charles W (1872-1930) American
$8500	£5556	View from the garden (76x61cm-30x24in) s. board on masonite. 18-Sep-93 James Bakker, Cambridge #61/R
$16000	£10667	The Rose (102x102cm-40x40in) 17-Mar-94 Sotheby's, New York #90/R

HAYAKAWA, Miki (1904-1953) American
$1900	£1258	Portrait of a woman (61x46cm-24x18in) s. canvasboard. 15-Jun-94 Butterfield & Butterfield, San Francisco #4659/R
$3000	£1987	Sleeping boy (41x51cm-16x20in) s. board. 15-Jun-94 Butterfield & Butterfield, San Francisco #4660/R

HAYDEN, Carl (20th C) American?
$800	£530	Gloucester Harbour (61x51cm-24x20in) s. 28-Nov-92 Young Fine Arts Auctions, Maine #208/R

HAYDEN, Charles Henry (1856-1901) American
$600	£400	Gloucester (43x53cm-17x21in) s. 22-May-94 James Bakker, Cambridge #15/R
$1400	£940	Hills above Jerusalem (76x107cm-30x42in) s.d.1884. 14-Jan-94 Du Mouchelle, Detroit #1017/R

HAYDEN, Edward Parker (?-1922) American
$1300	£688	Orchard in bloom (56x74cm-22x29in) s.d.1890. 11-Sep-92 Skinner, Bolton #208/R
$1400	£915	Impressionistic landscape with stream (56x79cm-22x31in) 30-Jun-94 Richard Opfer, Timonium #104

HAYDEN, Palmer (1890-1973) American
$1000	£671	Mt Vernon woman (46x36cm-18x14in) s. W/C. 28-Mar-93 James Bakker, Cambridge #99/R

HAYES, Lee (1854-1946) American
$550	£364	Sierra landscape - lake (36x46cm-14x18in) s. canvas on panel. 14-Jun-94 John Moran, Pasadena #96

HAYS, Barton S (1826-1914) American
$1100	£724	Roses (25x36cm-10x14in) s. 13-Jun-93 Hindman Galleries, Chicago #215
$2300	£1503	Peaches and grapes (20x36cm-8x14in) s. 30-Jun-94 Mystic Fine Arts, Connecticut #72/R

HAYS, George Arthur (1854-?) American
$650	£425	Grassmine N H (23x30cm-9x12in) s. board. 30-Jun-94 Mystic Fine Arts, Connecticut #75 b/R
$700	£458	Cows at dusk (15x23cm-6x9in) s. board. 30-Jun-94 Mystic Fine Arts, Connecticut #75 o/R
$825	£577	Cows by the river (25x30cm-10x12in) s. panel. 11-Mar-93 Mystic Fine Arts, Connecticut #162/R
$850	£571	Watering the cows (28x44cm-11x17in) s. 4-Mar-94 Skinner, Bolton #245/R
$850	£556	Cows coming to water (36x51cm-14x20in) s. 30-Jun-94 Mystic Fine Arts, Connecticut #75 h
$850	£556	Cows in the woods, autumn (28x36cm-11x14in) s. 30-Jun-94 Mystic Fine Arts, Connecticut #75 e/R
$1000	£654	The Holstein cow (46x66cm-18x26in) s. 30-Jun-94 Mystic Fine Arts, Connecticut #75d/R
$1000	£654	The watering hole (30x41cm-12x16in) s. 30-Jun-94 Mystic Fine Arts, Connecticut #75 a/R
$1050	£686	Cows grazing on hill (51x71cm-20x28in) s. 30-Jun-94 Mystic Fine Arts, Connecticut #75l/R
$1100	£719	Cattle on the meadow (41x61cm-16x24in) d.1917 s.verso. 30-Jun-94 Mystic Fine Arts, Connecticut #75 f/R
$1600	£1081	Cows resting (30x41cm-12x16in) s. s.i.d.1915verso. 5-Nov-93 Skinner, Bolton #49/R

HAYS, George Arthur (1854-?) American-cont.
$1800	£1176	Sheep coming through the Bar Way (66x76cm-26x30in) s. 30-Jun-94 Mystic Fine Arts, Connecticut #75 c/R
$1900	£1242	Landscape with cattle (30x46cm-12x18in) s. 30-Jun-94 Mystic Fine Arts, Connecticut #75 k/R
$2800	£1879	Cows in evening (66x91cm-26x36in) s. 29-Nov-93 Stonington Fine Arts, Stonington #56/R

HAYWARD, Alfred (attrib) (1893-1939) American
$900	£612	Trompe l'oeil musical instruments (61x51cm-24x20in) s. 14-Apr-94 Freeman Fine Arts, Philadelphia #1026

HAYWARD, Gerald Sinclair (1845-1926) American
$1961	*£1316*	*Retrato de caballero (8x9cm-3x4in) min. s.d.1886 gilt frame leather case oval. 20-Dec-93 Duran, Madrid #319/R (S.P 275000)*
$1961	*£1316*	*Retrato de caballero (8x7cm-3x3in) min. s.d.1885 gilt frame case oval. 20-Dec-93 Duran, Madrid #320/R (S.P 275000)*

HAYWARD, J Harold (?) American?
$1100	£705	Strawberries spilling out of a basket (30x41cm-12x16in) s. 13-Dec-92 Litchfield Auction Gallery #14

HAZARD, Arthur Merton (1872-1930) American
$2750	£1763	Woman in yellow dress (63x51cm-25x20in) s.d.17. 9-Dec-92 Butterfield & Butterfield, San Francisco #3933/R

HAZARD, William Garnet (1903-) Canadian
$941	£603	Path through woods (61x76cm-24x30in) board. 7-Dec-92 Waddingtons, Toronto #1368 (C.D 1200)
$1176	£754	Sunlit winter wood (61x76cm-24x30in) s. board. 7-Dec-92 Waddingtons, Toronto #1367 (C.D 1500)
$930	*£628*	*Still life (61x46cm-24x18in) s. W/C. 3-Nov-93 Sotheby's, Toronto #152/R (C.D 1200)*
$1268	*£829*	*Winter landscape. Still life with vase (44x55cm-17x22in) s. W/C pair. 19-May-93 Sotheby's, Toronto #38/R (C.D 1600)*

HEADE, Martin Johnson (1819-1904) American
$23000	£14744	Roses in crystal goblet (51x31cm-20x12in) s. 26-May-93 Christie's, New York #43/R
$28000	£18543	New England coastal scene (39x62cm-15x24in) s. canvas on masonite. 22-Sep-93 Christie's, New York #39/R
$32000	£21333	Apple blossoms and hummingbird (30x37cm-12x15in) s.d.1875 board. 16-Mar-94 Christie's, New York #48/R
$35000	£23490	The Queen of Roses (41x26cm-16x10in) s. 3-Dec-93 Christie's, New York #96/R
$40000	£23121	Red roses in transparent vase on yellow velvet (51x31cm-20x12in) s. 23-Sep-92 Christie's, New York #76/R
$44000	£29139	Apple blossoms (20x25cm-8x10in) init.d.1878 board. 22-Sep-93 Christie's, New York #59/R
$47000	£31544	Ponds in a Jersey marsh or marshes near Ipswich (25x56cm-10x22in) s. paper on canvas painted c.1890-1900. 6-Dec-93 Grogan, Massachussetts #484/R
$60000	£41958	Still life with flowers in silver vase (46x38cm-18x15in) s.indis.d.1874. 10-Mar-93 Sotheby's, New York #32/R
$70000	£46267	Two hummingbirds at nest (24x31cm-9x12in) s.d.1863verso. 25-May-94 Sotheby's, New York #28/R
$85000	£59441	Ruby throats with apple blossoms (32x28cm-13x11in) canvas on board. 11-Mar-93 Christie's, New York #58/R
$110000	£72848	Still life with apple blossoms in nautilus shell (53x43cm-21x17in) s.d.1870. 23-Sep-93 Sotheby's, New York #24/R
$200000	£139860	Two hummingbirds guarding egg (31x26cm-12x10in) canvas on board. 11-Mar-93 Christie's, New York #40/R
$320000	£205128	Hummingbird and Passion flowers (41x53cm-16x21in) 27-May-93 Sotheby's, New York #168/R
$24000	*£15385*	*Housley sketchbook (22x29cm-9x11in) s.d.1858 i.d.12-69 other sheet pencil 35 pages. 27-May-93 Sotheby's, New York #202/R*

HEALY, George Peter Alexander (1813-1894) American
$700	£476	Portrait of William Fleetwood (110x81cm-43x32in) s.d.1858. 15-Nov-93 Christie's, East, New York #1/R
$810	£540	Portrait of the honourable Mifa Baring (74x62cm-29x24in) s.i.d.1843 i.verso. 16-Mar-94 Bonhams, Chelsea #48/R
$950	£634	Self-portrait (70x56cm-28x22in) 23-May-94 Christie's, East, New York #5/R
$1200	£774	Portrait of young girl holding roses (79x48cm-31x19in) s.d.July 1882. 13-Jul-94 Doyle, New York #37

HEATH, Howard (1879-?) American
$1550	£896	Day at fair (71x91cm-28x36in) s. 24-Sep-92 Mystic Fine Arts, Connecticut #238/R

HEBERER, Charles (19th C) American
$900	£592	After Rubens (112x81cm-44x32in) s.verso. 31-Mar-93 Sotheby's Arcade, New York #60 a/R

HEBERT, Adrien (1890-1967) Canadian
$1311	£874	Le pecheur (11x53cm-4x21in) s.d.191-. 13-May-94 Joyner Fine Art, Toronto #186 (C.D 1800)
$1557	£1031	Man with a harmonica (109x67cm-43x26in) s.d.1924. 18-Nov-92 Sotheby's, Toronto #194/R (C.D 2000)

HEBERT, Adrien (1890-1967) Canadian-cont.
$3473 £2347 Bonsecours market, winter (57x70cm-22x28in) s. 23-Nov-93 Joyner Fine Art, Toronto #16/R (C.D 4600)

HECHT, Victor David (1873-?) American
$17000 £11486 Woman embroidering (76x61cm-30x24in) s.d.1910 canvas on masonite. 31-Mar-94 Sotheby's Arcade, New York #160/R

HEEKS, Willy (20th C) American
$5500 £3819 Untitled (212x188cm-83x74in) s.d.87verso. 23-Feb-93 Sotheby's, New York #352/R

HEIL, Charles Emile (1870) American
$1300 £890 Winter trees (41x30cm-16x12in) s. 10-Feb-94 Skinner, Bolton #283

HEILMAN, Mary (20th C) American?
$9000 £6040 The Secret (152x107cm-60x42in) painted 1989. 25-Feb-94 Sotheby's, New York #166/R

HEKKING, J Antonio (fl.1859-1885) American
$700 £473 River in autumn with distant mountains (15x20cm-6x8in) s. board. 27-Nov-93 Young Fine Arts Auctions, Maine #161/R
$3000 £1587 Deer by a river, early autumn (25x36cm-10x14in) s. 11-Sep-92 Skinner, Bolton #188 a
$3250 £2152 House by Falls (43x66cm-17x26in) s. 13-Nov-92 Skinner, Bolton #60/R
$4500 £2980 Coast of Maine (56x98cm-22x39in) s. 23-Sep-93 Sotheby's, New York #61/R

HELCK, Peter (1897-) American
$750 £500 Liberty and Indian (49x18cm-19x7in) s. pen ink. 21-May-94 Weschler, Washington #135

HELD, Al (1928-) American
$8000 £5369 Untitled (48x63cm-19x25in) s.d.59verso acrylic paper on masonite. 4-May-94 Christie's, New York #131/R
$10000 £6536 Untitled (46x36cm-18x14in) s.d.4/60 verso acrylic. 4-May-93 Sotheby's, New York #359/R
$28000 £18919 Hadrian's Court III (213x183cm-84x72in) s.d.82 verso acrylic. 11-Nov-93 Sotheby's, New York #341/R
$45000 £29412 Pan North VIII (183x276cm-72x109in) s.d.86 verso acrylic. 4-May-93 Sotheby's, New York #368/R
$52500 £35473 North-Northwest (183x244cm-72x96in) acrylic painted 1973. 10-Nov-93 Sotheby's, New York #28/R
$6000 £4167 Hudson 6 (46x61cm-18x24in) s.i.d.89verso W/C graphite. 24-Feb-93 Christie's, New York #50/R
$6000 £3922 Hudson 15 (43x60cm-17x24in) W/C pencil executed 1989. 4-May-93 Sotheby's, New York #367/R

HELD, John (jnr) (1889-1958) American
$2000 £1299 Visit to Grandma (48x41cm-19x16in) s. W/C Indian ink. 9-Sep-93 Sotheby's Arcade, New York #395/R

HELDNER, Knute (1884-1952) American
$900 £600 Creek in winter (38x48cm-15x19in) s. 13-Mar-94 Hindman Galleries, Chicago #768/R
$1600 £1074 Brittany harbour (61x76cm-24x30in) s. i.verso. 4-Mar-94 Skinner, Bolton #270/R
$2500 £1445 Mining accident (109x121cm-43x48in) s. board. 25-Sep-92 Sotheby's Arcade, New York #434/R

HELIKER, John Edward (1909-) American
$625 £425 Roman still life (71x51cm-28x20in) s. 14-Apr-94 Freeman Fine Arts, Philadelphia #1051a
$900 £584 Still life of fruit and flowers (51x71cm-20x28in) s. 9-Sep-93 Sotheby's Arcade, New York #446/R
$1600 £1081 Acrobats (77x50cm-30x20in) s. masonite painted c.1945 double-sided. 31-Mar-94 Sotheby's Arcade, New York #317/R

HELKE, Peter (20th C) American
$2600 £1529 Old Racer (28x46cm-11x18in) s.i.d.57 mixed media. 8-Oct-92 Boos Gallery, Michigan #94/R

HELMICK, Howard (1845-1907) American
$700 £476 Newspaper boy at a front door (20x15cm-8x6in) s. panel. 14-Apr-94 Freeman Fine Arts, Philadelphia #980/R
$750 £507 Warming her hands (48x46cm-19x18in) s.d.75. 31-Oct-93 Hindman Galleries, Chicago #709
$3040 £2000 Interior with two men drinking and maid (38x30cm-15x12in) s. panel. 31-Mar-93 Phillips, Sevenoaks #707/R
$4139 £2778 Scottish lad lacing his sister's shoe (55x42cm-22x17in) s.d.1876. 29-Nov-93 Waddingtons, Toronto #1414/R (C.D 5500)

HELSBY, Alfredo (1862-1933) Chilean
$765 £500 Road in Penaflur, Chile (26x35cm-10x14in) s.i. board. 29-Jun-94 Phillips, Chester #92
$2128 £1400 Autumn day, Penaflor, Chile (25x36cm-10x14in) s.i. board. 19-Jul-94 Rowland Gorringe, Lewes #2131/R
$8940 £6000 Autumn, Maipo Valley, Chile (85x64cm-33x25in) s. i.stretcher. 16-Jul-93 Christie's, London #141 a/R

HEMBROFF-SCHLEICHER, Edythe (1906-) Canadian
$736   £497   Still life with flowers in vase on table (55x46cm-22x18in) s.d.1936. 1-Nov-93
                       Levis, Calgary #95/R (C.D 950)

HEMING, Arthur (1870-1940) Canadian
$973   £644   A wilderness adventure (37x23cm-15x9in) s.d.04 board. 18-Nov-92 Sotheby's,
                       Toronto #294/R (C.D 1250)

HENDERSEN, Edward (20th C) American
$1600   £1081   Untitled no.3 (104x66cm-41x26in) s.d.90 mixed media paper. 31-Oct-93 Hindman
                       Galleries, Chicago #771/R

HENDERSON, Elyot (1908-1975) American
$850   £429   Model and straw hat (81x91cm-32x36in) s.d.39. 28-Aug-92 Young Fine Arts Auctions,
                       Maine #160/R

HENDERSON, James (1871-1951) Canadian
$680   £459   Prairie home in winter (25x30cm-10x12in) s. board. 23-Nov-93 Joyner Fine Art,
                       Toronto #302 (C.D 900)
$688   £459   Northern sunset (23x30cm-9x12in) s. board. 6-Jun-94 Waddingtons, Toronto #1270
                       (C.D 950)
$753   £505   Lakeshore (30x36cm-12x14in) s. board. 29-Nov-93 Waddingtons, Toronto #1076
                       (C.D 1000)
$1012   £670   Qu'appelle (25x36cm-10x14in) s. painted 1914. 16-Nov-92 Hodgins, Calgary #281
                       (C.D 1300)
$1057   £714   Returning home, Qu'Appelle Valley, Saskatchewan (17x26cm-7x10in) s. canvas on
                       board. 23-Nov-93 Joyner Fine Art, Toronto #219 (C.D 1400)
$1317   £890   Echo Lake Qu'Appelle Valley (36x43cm-14x17in) s. s.i.verso. 3-Nov-93 Sotheby's,
                       Toronto #46 (C.D 1700)

HENDERSON, William Penhallow (1877-1943) American
$1600   £1067   Country path (40x29cm-16x11in) 16-Mar-94 Christie's, New York #100/R
$800   *£506*   Lady in black and an orange cloak (17x11cm-7x4in) pastel. 2-Dec-92 Christie's,
                       East, New York #147

HENDON, Cham (1936-) American
$1900   £1242   Sunday afternoon in garden (173x81cm-68x32in) acrylic rhoplex executed 1983.
                       22-Dec-92 Christie's, East, New York #25
$3275   £2228   The Truman balcony (140x140cm-55x55in) s.d.1982verso. 13-Apr-94 Bukowskis,
                       Stockholm #312/R (S.KR 26000)

HENNINGS, Ernest Martin (1886-1956) American
$7500   £4839   Two men on sailboat tending dinghy (76x64cm-30x25in) s. 13-Jul-94 Boos Gallery,
                       Michigan #673/R
$20000   £13333   Twining canyon (76x64cm-30x25in) s. 16-Mar-94 Christie's, New York #85/R
$24000   £16000   From Cumbres Pass, Taos, New Mexico (76x76cm-30x30in) s. s.i.verso. 16-Mar-94
                       Christie's, New York #83/R
$30000   £19355   Three Indians on horseback in moonlight (30x36cm-12x14in) s. panel. 13-Jul-94
                       Boos Gallery, Michigan #672/R
$62500   £43706   Pueblo village (76x91cm-30x36in) s. 10-Mar-93 Sotheby's, New York #51/R
$160000   £103226   Two Indians on horseback by stream in an arroyo (109x114cm-43x45in) s. 13-Jul-94
                       Boos Gallery, Michigan #671/R

HENRI, Calixte (1933-) Haitian
$1117   £716   Marine (81x61cm-32x24in) s. 14-Dec-92 Hoebanx, Paris #81 (F.FR 6000)

HENRI, Robert (1865-1929) American
$900   £600   Seascape (20x25cm-8x10in) panel. 17-May-94 Christie's, East, New York #499
$3200   £2177   Luxembourg Gardens (10x15cm-4x6in) panel. 15-Nov-93 Christie's, East, New York
                       #171/R
$3250   £2153   Summer storm, Pennsylvania landscape (20x25cm-8x10in) s. s.i.d.1902 verso panel.
                       23-Sep-93 Sotheby's, New York #220/R
$3500   £2244   Old house and woman (9x15cm-4x6in) i. panel. 9-Dec-92 Butterfield & Butterfield,
                       San Francisco #3887/R
$7000   £4487   Grey dunes (51x61cm-20x24in) s. s.num.134F verso. 27-May-93 Sotheby's, New York
                       #73/R
$8500   £5667   Street in Moret (8x14cm-3x6in) s.i. panel. 25-May-94 Sotheby's, New York #105/R
$11000   £7333   Street corner in Paris (11x17cm-4x7in) s.i.d.1896 panel. 25-May-94 Sotheby's, New
                       York #104/R
$18000   £12000   Patience (46x38cm-18x15in) s. s.i.verso. 16-Mar-94 Christie's, New York #87/R
$22000   £13924   Ship in the bay (38x48cm-15x19in) i. 3-Dec-92 Christie's, New York #128/R
$34000   £21519   La Jartigo (81x66cm-32x26in) s. s.i.d.1924 on tacking edge. 3-Dec-92 Sotheby's,
                       New York #134/R
$37500   £24038   Laughing boy - Jobie (61x51cm-24x20in) s. s.d.1910 num.145F verso. 27-May-93
                       Sotheby's, New York #74/R
$50000   £32251   Lillian (81x66cm-32x26in) s. s.i.verso. 9-Dec-92 Butterfield & Butterfield, San
                       Francisco #3930/R
$90000   £60403   Young Anthony (71x51cm-28x20in) s. i.verso. 2-Dec-93 Sotheby's, New York #120/R
$90000   £56962   Mata Moana (81x66cm-32x26in) s. s.i.verso. 4-Dec-92 Christie's, New York #156/R
$90000   £56962   Little girl in red (61x52cm-24x20in) s. i.verso. 4-Dec-92 Christie's, New York
                       #58/R
$105000   £67308   Portrait of Katie McNamara (71x51cm-28x20in) s.num.184 N verso painted 1928.
                       27-May-93 Sotheby's, New York #75/R
$115000   £77181   Sissy in yellow (62x51cm-24x20in) s. 2-Dec-93 Sotheby's, New York #103 a/R

HENRI, Robert (1865-1929) American-cont.

$115000	£76667	Portrait of Mary Ann (61x51cm-24x20in) s. s.i.verso painted 1926. 25-May-94 Sotheby's, New York #101 a/R
$115000	£76667	Segovian girl (61x51cm-24x20in) s. i.verso. 25-May-94 Sotheby's, New York #101 b/R
$120000	£76923	Girl with big hat (60x50cm-24x20in) s. s.i.verso. 26-May-93 Christie's, New York #184/R
$300000	£192308	Failure of Sylvester (104x84cm-41x33in) s. s.i.d.1914 verso. 26-May-93 Christie's, New York #193 a/R
$315000	£199367	Skipper Mick (61x51cm-24x20in) s. i.verso. 4-Dec-92 Christie's, New York #56/R
$600	£395	Mountains and sea (15x23cm-6x9in) studio st. Indian ink wash. 2-Apr-93 Sloan, North Bethesda #1758
$750	£524	Seated woman with raised hand (28x20cm-11x8in) estate st. d.1904 verso Indian ink over pencil. 5-Feb-93 Sloan, North Bethesda #2390
$800	£559	At Jonas Lie's Party (20x30cm-8x12in) estate st. d.1915 verso Indian ink. 5-Feb-93 Sloan, North Bethesda #2389/R
$1200	*£795*	*Woman (13x15cm-5x6in) estate st. pen. 13-Nov-92 Du Mouchelle, Detroit #2012/R*
$1300	*£872*	*Brittany (21x24cm-8x9in) wash over pencil. 8-Dec-93 Butterfield & Butterfield, San Francisco #3358/R*
$2400	*£1622*	*Portrait of Marjorie Organ (50x32cm-20x13in) st.sig. pen crayon pastel. 20-Mar-93 Weschler, Washington #112 a*
$2800	*£1772*	*Seated nude (29x43cm-11x17in) s. W/C. 2-Dec-92 Christie's, East, New York #362*

HENRICI, John H (19/20th C) American

$1000	£658	Two boys (76x51cm-30x20in) s. 13-Jun-93 Butterfield & Butterfield, San Francisco #3118/R
$1200	£800	A boy's best friend (36x46cm-14x18in) s.d.1900. 1-Jun-94 Doyle, New York #34

HENRY, E L (1841-1919) American

$1900	£1218	Small children picking flowers, init. board. 13-Dec-92 Litchfield Auction Gallery #15

HENRY, Edward Lamson (1841-1919) American

$6500	£3757	The china cupboard (16x14cm-6x6in) init.d.73 board. 23-Sep-92 Christie's, New York #30/R
$8000	£5333	A quiet afternoon (20x15cm-8x6in) s.d.74. 23-May-94 Christie's, East, New York #26/R
$8140	£5500	Threshing machine (30x35cm-12x14in) s. 15-Jun-93 Phillips, London #99/R
$11000	£7051	On James River, Virginia (17x28cm-7x11in) s.d.1864 s.i.d.1864 verso. 27-May-93 Sotheby's, New York #151/R
$11000	£6358	In glow, sunset (18x15cm-7x6in) init. s.i.d.1872 verso paper on board. 24-Sep-92 Sotheby's, New York #27/R
$15000	£9494	At the well (21x15cm-8x6in) mono. panel. 3-Dec-92 Sotheby's, New York #16/R
$15000	£9615	At home with good book (22x16cm-9x6in) s.d.72 board. 27-May-93 Sotheby's, New York #152/R
$19000	£10983	Leaving home (25x43cm-10x17in) s. 24-Sep-92 Sotheby's, New York #52/R
$28120	£19000	Summer day (30x49cm-12x19in) s.d.90 i.verso. 15-Jun-93 Phillips, London #100/R
$35000	£22152	Unexpected visitors (44x64cm-17x25in) s.d.1909. 4-Dec-92 Christie's, New York #247/R
$38000	£25503	October Day - Cragsmoor Post Office (31x56cm-12x22in) s.d.1903. 3-Dec-93 Christie's, New York #97/R
$48000	£32000	Early days of rapid transit (51x92cm-20x36in) s. 26-May-94 Christie's, New York #29/R
$2188	*£1459*	*Le relais de chevaux (22x34cm-9x13in) s. W/C gouache. 16-Mar-94 Christian Delorme, Paris #36 (F.FR 12500)*
$2900	*£1895*	*Haying (20x33cm-8x13in) s. W/C. 5-May-93 Doyle, New York #8/R*
$5215	*£3500*	*Receiving guests (34x55cm-13x22in) s.d.98 W/C. 16-Jul-93 Christie's, London #153/R*
$10000	*£6329*	*Preparing for the outing (16x13cm-6x5in) s.d.76 W/C gouache. 3-Dec-92 Sotheby's, New York #15/R*
$11000	*£7051*	*Sunday morning (64x51cm-25x20in) s.d.1886 W/C. 27-May-93 Sotheby's, New York #143/R*

HENRY, Harry Raymond (1882-1974) American

$1500	£882	Evening glow (76x102cm-30x40in) s. 4-Oct-92 Butterfield & Butterfield, Los Angeles #145/R
$3000	£1765	Through trees (41x51cm-16x20in) s. 4-Oct-92 Butterfield & Butterfield, Los Angeles #135/R

HENSCHE, Henry (1901-) American

$700	£490	Seated woman with corsage (102x91cm-40x36in) s. masonite. 7-Feb-93 James Bakker, Cambridge #251/R

HENSEL, Stephen Hopkins (1921-1979) American

$950	£629	Saltimbanque (61x30cm-24x12in) s.d.47 masonite double-sided. 13-Nov-92 Skinner, Bolton #190/R
$1300	£861	Clowns (127x61cm-50x24in) s.d.50 masonite. 13-Nov-92 Skinner, Bolton #192/R
$3250	£1879	Reflection (56x91cm-22x36in) s.d.47 i.frame. 24-Sep-92 Sotheby's, New York #183/R

HENSHAW, Glenn Cooper (1881-1946) American

$600	*£400*	*New York at night (56x33cm-22x13in) s.i. pastel. 13-Mar-94 Hindman Galleries, Chicago #797*

HERGESHEIMER, Ella S (1943-) American
$2000 £1361 Still life with jewellery vase with flowers and Japanese painting (54x57cm-21x22in) s. 15-Nov-93 Christie's, East, New York #159/R

HERGET, Herbert (20th C) American
$3000 £1987 Indian war party (81x102cm-32x40in) s. 15-Jun-94 Butterfield & Butterfield, San Francisco #4531/R
$6500 £4333 Attack on the stagecoach (61x81cm-24x32in) s. 17-Mar-94 Sotheby's, New York #74/R

HERIOT, George (1766-1844) Canadian
$1029 £700 Barton House, Dawlish, Devon (18x26cm-7x10in) s.i.d.1819verso W/C over pencil. 14-Apr-94 Sotheby's, London #216/R
$1057 £700 Procession by Pisa cathedral (20x12cm-8x5in) W/C over pencil htd bodycol. 19-Nov-92 Sotheby's, London #349/R
$1092 £728 Lame man and figures (17x20cm-7x8in) s. W/C graphite. 11-May-94 Sotheby's, Toronto #23 (C.D 1500)
$1240 £838 Woman off to market (23x15cm-9x6in) s. W/C graphite. 3-Nov-93 Sotheby's, Toronto #5/R (C.D 1600)
$1323 £900 Distant view of Edinburgh (17x26cm-7x10in) W/C. 14-Apr-94 Sotheby's, London #124/R
$1435 £969 Lake St. Charles (26x36cm-10x14in) i. W/C executed c.1805. 23-Nov-93 Joyner Fine Art, Toronto #66/R (C.D 1900)

HERMANN, Roger (20th C) American
$2000 £1351 Automobile (89x89cm-35x35in) s.i.d.88verso. 21-Oct-93 Butterfield & Butterfield, San Francisco #2836/R

HERNANDEZ XOCHITIOTZIN, Desidero (1922-) Mexican
$1273 £816 Naturaleza muerta (56x85cm-22x33in) s.d.1950 canvas on panel. 29-Apr-93 Louis Morton, Mexico #116 (M.P 4000)
$2580 £1732 El ultimo globo, Patzcuaro Mich. (103x77cm-41x30in) s.d.1952 masonite. 1-Dec-93 Louis Morton, Mexico #208/R (M.P 8000)

HERNANDEZ, D (1856-1932) Peruvian
$3188 £2125 Le bal masque (36x23cm-14x9in) s. panel. 25-May-94 Marc Kohn, Paris #84 (F.FR 18000)

HERNANDEZ, Daniel (1856-1932) Peruvian
$950 £655 South American landscape (22x30cm-9x12in) s.d.10-23-26 board. 16-Feb-93 Christie's, East, New York #292/R
$1500 £1000 High tide (23x19cm-9x7in) s. panel. 16-Mar-94 Sotheby's, London #222
$9208 £6222 Reclining female nude (93x150cm-37x59in) s.i.d.1899. 19-Apr-94 Dorotheum, Vienna #528/R (A.S 110000)
$12370 £7277 Amusing story (105x76cm-41x30in) s. 8-Oct-92 Sotheby's, New Dehli #79/R (I.R 350000)
$16509 £11006 Ante el espejo (44x30cm-17x12in) s. panel. 23-May-94 Duran, Madrid #87/R (S.P 2250000)
$23856 £14033 Ante el espejo (44x30cm-17x12in) s. panel. 6-Oct-92 Duran, Madrid #42/R (S.P 2500000)

HERNANDEZ, M R (19th C) Mexican?
$14155 £9500 Valley of Mexico with Mexico City - Vera Cruz railway and volcanoes (24x35cm-9x14in) s.d.1871. 16-Jul-93 Christie's, London #151/R

HERNDORFF, Michael (20th C) American
$1400 £897 The meeting (99x89cm-39x35in) tempera board two. 10-Dec-92 Sloan, North Bethesda #2684

HEROLD, Georg (20th C) American?
$5000 £3472 Kathedrale II (205x250cm-81x98in) painted 1987 acrylic. 23-Feb-93 Sotheby's, New York #356/R
$950 £638 Kupfer (24x30cm-9x12in) s.i.d.88stretcher copper canvas rubber band. 3-May-94 Christie's, East, New York #257/R
$1100 £738 2154 (18x24cm-7x9in) init.i.d.87stretcher yarn thread gessoed linen. 3-May-94 Christie's, East, New York #256/R
$7500 £4967 Black Beluga (152x122cm-60x48in) acrylic asphaltum shellac beluga caviar canvas. 18-Nov-92 Sotheby's, New York #290/R

HERRAN, Saturnino (1887-1918) Mexican
$9000 £5882 Estudio figuras y manos (60x45cm-24x18in) s. graphite paper on board. 18-May-93 Sotheby's, New York #114/R

HERRERA TORO, Antonio (1857-1914) Venezuelan
$15000 £10000 La visita al estudio (48x39cm-19x15in) s.d.1902. 18-May-94 Christie's, New York #87 a/R

HERRERA, Carlos Maria (1875-1914) Uruguayan
$1300 £833 En el campo (62x51cm-24x20in) s.d.1909. 7-Dec-92 Gomensoro, Montevideo #76/R
$7200 £3618 Joven con capelina roja (57x45cm-22x18in) s. pastel oval. 31-Aug-92 Gomensoro, Montevideo #52/R
$13000 £8784 Dama con capelina, cabeza de mujer (64x48cm-25x19in) s.d.1906 pastel. 25-Apr-94 Gomensoro, Montevideo #65/R

HERRERA, Telesforo (1931-) Mexican
$4117	£2709	Alacena (122x70cm-48x28in) s.d.1990 acrylic. 4-Nov-92 Mora, Castelltort & Quintana, Juarez #43/R (M.P 13000000)

HERRERA, Velino Shije (1902-1973) American
$1000	£645	Eagle dancers (20x36cm-8x14in) s. gouache. 9-Jan-93 Skinner, Bolton #20/R
$2200	£1419	Sand painting ceremonial (28x43cm-11x17in) s. gouache. 9-Jan-93 Skinner, Bolton #258/R

HERRMANN, Frank S (1866-1942) American
$700	£449	Overlooking Central Park in winter (71x61cm-28x24in) st.sig. gouache painted c.1930. 8-Dec-92 Swann Galleries, New York #136/R

HERSHEY, Samuel Franklin (1904-) American
$1400	£915	Winter marshland in Essex. January Marsh (36x41cm-14x16in) s. board pair. 30-Jun-94 Mystic Fine Arts, Connecticut #156

HERTER, Adele (1869-1946) American
$7000	£4698	Trumpet vine (102x91cm-40x36in) board. 4-May-94 Doyle, New York #41/R

HERTER, Albert (1871-1950) American
$850	£559	Floral still life (38x46cm-15x18in) s.i. 2-Apr-93 Sloan, North Bethesda #2314/R
$1500	£867	Beatrice (61x51cm-24x20in) s.i. 23-Sep-92 Christie's, New York #194/R
$13000	£8333	Portrait of lady in kimono (56x51cm-22x20in) s.d.94. 27-May-93 Sotheby's, New York #33/R
$1700	£1149	Interior with cherry blossoms (52x36cm-20x14in) s. W/C htd.graphite gouache paperboard. 5-Nov-93 Skinner, Bolton #139/R
$10000	£6993	Two women on stairs (46x30cm-18x12in) s. W/C. 10-Mar-93 Sotheby's, New York #97/R

HERZOG, Hermann (1832-1932) American/German
$1500	£1020	Washer women (43x33cm-17x13in) s. 14-Apr-94 Freeman Fine Arts, Philadelphia #971
$1600	£925	Beach fishing boats with figures and distant lighthouse (46x36cm-18x14in) s. 25-Sep-92 Sotheby's Arcade, New York #57/R
$2500	£1689	Norwegian fjord (51x41cm-20x16in) s. 15-Jun-93 John Moran, Pasadena #136
$3080	£2000	Beached fishing boats at dusk (44x62cm-17x24in) s.d.1868. 10-Aug-94 Bonhams, London #235/R
$3500	£2288	Curious about the neighbours - genre scene with rabbit and sheep (43x58cm-17x23in) s. panel. 17-Sep-93 Skinner, Bolton #169/R
$4000	£2667	North Sea fishermen (43x53cm-17x21in) s. 17-Mar-94 Sotheby's, New York #44/R
$4000	£2721	Morning on the lake (66x81cm-26x32in) s. 17-Nov-93 Doyle, New York #11/R
$4000	£2564	Canal leading to Alpine lake (51x71cm-20x28in) s. 27-May-93 Christie's, New York #85/R
$4000	£2703	The mill (45x56cm-18x22in) s. 31-Mar-94 Sotheby's Arcade, New York #98/R
$4080	£2667	North German pond landscape (42x58cm-17x23in) s.d.1858. 11-May-93 Galerie Fischer, Lucerne #2289/R (S.FR 6000)
$4200	£2763	Ploughing (41x56cm-16x22in) s. 31-Mar-93 Sotheby's Arcade, New York #55/R
$4750	£3105	Fishing boats (41x56cm-16x22in) s. 18-May-93 Butterfield & Butterfield, San Francisco #1446/R
$5000	£3356	Waterfall (56x69cm-22x27in) s. masonite. 4-May-94 Doyle, New York #3/R
$5500	£3618	Coast near Portland, Maine (56x76cm-22x30in) s. 13-Jun-93 Butterfield & Butterfield, San Francisco #3148/R
$8500	£5782	The country road (91x107cm-36x42in) s. 17-Nov-93 Doyle, New York #10/R
$9000	£5696	Florida live oaks with deer (36x45cm-14x18in) s. 3-Dec-92 Sotheby's, New York#13/R
$9200	£6216	Rocky Mountain landscape with deer frightened by a bear (23x30cm-9x12in) s.d.68 panel. 31-Oct-93 Hindman Galleries, Chicago #672/R
$9500	£5491	Fishing by the Lumber Mill (27x37cm-11x15in) s.d.1872 panel. 23-Sep-92 Christie's, New York #52/R
$9500	£6291	Mountain landscape (71x102cm-28x40in) s.indist.d. 23-Sep-93 Sotheby's New York #87/R
$10000	£6623	Angler and daughter (94x131cm-37x52in) s.d.1897. 22-Sep-93 Christie's, New York #46/R
$12000	£8000	Deer in a forest haunt (61x76cm-24x30in) s. 17-Mar-94 Sotheby's, New York #50/R
$12000	£8392	Fly fishing (34x43cm-13x17in) s. 11-Mar-93 Christie's, New York #84/R
$13000	£9091	Sunlight reflections (43x33cm-17x13in) s. 11-Mar-93 Christie's, New York #81/R
$21000	£14685	Bears by cataract (43x36cm-17x14in) s.d.1874 board. 10-Mar-93 Sotheby's, New York #41/R
$22000	£13924	Relaxation (61x72cm-24x28in) s. 4-Dec-92 Christie's, New York #210/R
$26000	£16667	Artist in wooded landscape (61x55cm-24x22in) s. 26-May-93 Christie's, New York #77/R
$40000	£25641	Summer afternoon on pond (46x61cm-18x24in) s. 26-May-93 Christie's, New York #50/R
$48000	£32000	Mountain landscape and waterfall (73x112cm-29x44in) s.d.1879. 26-May-94 Christie's, New York #67/R
$2500	£1656	Apple blossom time (25x33cm-10x13in) s.d.1888 W/C. 23-Sep-93 Mystic Fine Arts, Connecticut #123 a/R

HERZOG, Hermann (attrib) (1832-1932) American/German
$800	£537	Cone Creek Gulf Coast (46x56cm-18x22in) s. 24-Jun-93 Mystic Fine Arts, Connecticut #173
$1000	£654	Fishing pier at night (43x53cm-17x21in) bears sig. 7-Oct-93 Freeman Fine Arts, Philadelphia #782 b
$3000	£1987	Western landscape with water and three elk (58x84cm-23x33in) s. 26-Sep-93 Schrager Galleries, Milwaukee #452/R

HESELTINE, Jane (20th C) American
$4000   £2532   Two figures on horseback (142x102cm-56x40in) init. 25-Oct-92 Butterfield & Butterfield, San Francisco #2279/R

HESSE, Eva (1936-1970) American
$10000   £6711   Untitled (56x61cm-22x24in) s.d.1960 stretcher. 23-Feb-94 Christie's, New York #11/R
$13000   £7647   Untitled (112x81cm-44x32in) s.d.1957 s.verso. 6-Oct-92 Sotheby's, New York #11/R
$14000   £9459   Untitled (27x22cm-11x9in) s.d.61 W/C chl brush ink. 10-Nov-93 Christie's, New York #181/R
$15000   £10417   Untitled (57x72cm-22x28in) s.i.d.1963 W/C ink crayons pencil paper collage. 24-Feb-93 Christie's, New York #29/R
$32000   £21622   Right after (56x38cm-22x15in) s.i.d.1969 silver gouache pencil. 10-Nov-93 Sotheby's, New York #17/R
$55000   £36913   Untitled (35x27cm-14x11in) ink wash graphite executed 1966. 4-May-94 Christie's, New York #226/R

HESSELIUS, John (attrib) (1728-1778) American
$1200   £784   Portrait of Elizabeth Johns Tilghman of Talbot County, Maryland (75x62cm-30x24in) canvas on board. 22-May-93 Weschler, Washington #79/R

HESSING, Valjean McCarty (1934-) American
$1100   £710   Stylized horses (25x36cm-10x14in) s.d.69 gouache art board. 9-Jan-93 Skinner, Bolton #112/R

HETZEL, George (1826-1899) American
$850   £559   Landscape (23x30cm-9x12in) painted 1893. 5-Jun-93 San Rafael Auction Galleries #270
$6500   £4305   Country road (56x91cm-22x36in) s.d.1878. 15-Jun-94 Butterfield & Butterfield, San Francisco #4420/R

HEWARD, Prudence (1896-1947) Canadian
$1031   £674   Village church (36x30cm-14x12in) s. i.verso panel. 19-May-93 Sotheby's, Toronto #60/R (C.D 1300)
$1506   £984   Settler's cabin (30x36cm-12x14in) init. s.i.d.1931 verso panel. 19-May-93 Sotheby's, Toronto #98/R (C.D 1900)
$1585   £1036   Near Cowansville (30x36cm-12x14in) init. s.i.d.1944 verso panel. 19-May-93 Sotheby's, Toronto #282/R (C.D 2000)
$2180   £1425   Boy at fence (36x30cm-14x12in) i.verso panel. 19-May-93 Sotheby's, Toronto #186/R (C.D 2750)

HEWETT, John (c.1788-1868) American
$3552   £2400   Fredericton, New Brunswick from road to Ormocto River, South of Fredericton (53x71cm-21x28in) W/C over pencil i.verso. 20-Oct-93 Sotheby's, London #9/R

HEWINS, Philip (1806-1850) American
$800   £408   Jane A Bigelow at 22 years (89x71cm-35x28in) s.i.verso. 18-Aug-92 Richard Bourne, Hyannis #213/R
$1500   £765   Portrait of young lady in room with landscape seen through window (81x64cm-32x25in) s.d.1836verso. 18-Aug-92 Richard Bourne, Hyannis #39/R

HEWTON, Randolph Stanley (1888-1960) Canadian
$1784   £1166   Autumn, eastern townships (51x62cm-20x24in) s. 19-May-93 Sotheby's, Toronto #113/R (C.D 2250)
$2335   £1546   St Lawrence South shore, New Cacouna (51x61cm-20x24in) s.i.d.1928verso. 18-Nov-92 Sotheby's, Toronto #157/R (C.D 3000)
$2731   £1820   Grey skies near Baie St.Paul (51x61cm-20x24in) s. i.verso. 11-May-94 Sotheby's, Toronto #258/R (C.D 3750)
$3269   £2165   Baie St. Paul (21x27cm-8x11in) panel. 24-Nov-92 Joyner Fine Art, Toronto #4/R (C.D 4200)
$4281   £2835   Portrait of Audrey Buller (71x58cm-28x23in) 18-Nov-92 Sotheby's, Toronto #198/R (C.D 5500)

HEYDE, Charles Louis (c.1820-1892) American
$3500   £2318   Saxton River, Vermont (86x122cm-34x48in) s.i. 23-Sep-93 Sotheby's, New York #52/R

HIBBARD, A T (1886-1972) American
$1100   £733   Snow drifts, winter farm scene (64x51cm-25x20in) board. 27-Aug-93 Douglas, South Deerfield #4

HIBBARD, Aldro Thompson (1886-1972) American
$700   £470   Snow drifts, depitcing snow scene with bearded man digging way to mailbox (51x66cm-20x26in) s. masonite. 5-Aug-93 Eldred, Massachusetts #686/R
$800   £537   Farm at Jefferson Vermont, winter (44x64cm-17x25in) s. i.verso canvasboard. 6-May-94 Skinner, Bolton #84/R
$850   £594   Afternoon Monterey, coastal view (46x61cm-18x24in) s. i.verso canvasboard. 12-Mar-93 Skinner, Bolton #215/R
$900   £600   Fish still life (61x71cm-24x28in) s.d.1915 canvasboard. 26-Aug-93 Skinner, Bolton #188
$900   £455   Sea rocks (51x66cm-20x26in) s. board. 28-Aug-92 Young Fine Arts Auctions, Maine #175/R
$1400   £940   Autumn river scene (46x64cm-18x25in) s. board. 24-Jun-93 Mystic Fine Arts, Connecticut #195 a
$1500   £1007   Cabin by the river, winter (20x25cm-8x10in) s. canvasboard. 6-Dec-93 Grogan, Massachussetts #550/R

HIBBARD, Aldro Thompson (1886-1972) American-cont.
$1500	£1007	Winter scene (25x30cm-10x12in) s. board. 24-Jun-93 Mystic Fine Arts, Connecticut #89
$1600	£1074	Winter landscape, Rawsonville, Vermont (37x44cm-15x17in) s. canvasboard. 6-May-94 Skinner, Bolton #97/R
$1700	£1111	Monhegan Island (46x66cm-18x26in) s. i.verso board. 8-May-93 Young Fine Arts Auctions, Maine #167/R
$1800	£1216	Winter landscape up the valley (43x51cm-17x20in) s. canvasboard. 9-Nov-93 John Moran, Pasadena #857
$1800	£1208	Winter up country, depicting winter farm scene (61x76cm-24x30in) s. 5-Aug-93 Eldred, Massachusetts #685/R
$1800	£1154	Rushing winter stream (56x81cm-22x32in) s. estate st.verso. 12-Dec-92 Weschler, Washington #85/R
$1800	£1169	Winter (41x51cm-16x20in) s. masonite. 9-Sep-93 Sotheby's Arcade, New York #438/R
$2100	£1391	Stream in winter (43x51cm-17x20in) s. canvasboard. 13-Nov-92 Skinner, Bolton #138/R
$2100	£1364	Winter landscape with stream (44x62cm-17x24in) s. canvasboard. 9-Sep-93 Sotheby's Arcade, New York #439/R
$2350	£1588	In Weston Vermont (43x53cm-17x21in) s. 23-Oct-93 Collins, Maine #189/R
$2400	£1569	Winter stream (56x81cm-22x32in) s. 18-Sep-93 James Bakker, Cambridge #65/R
$2400	£1569	Winter brook (42x53cm-17x21in) s. 4-May-93 Christie's, East, New York #127/R
$2600	£1722	Mount Mansfield (48x56cm-19x22in) s. canvasboard. 13-Nov-92 Skinner, Bolton #134/R
$2700	£1429	Vermont mountains (43x53cm-17x21in) s. canvasboard. 11-Sep-92 Skinner, Bolton #238/R
$2800	£1618	Winter village scene (43x53cm-17x21in) s. canvasboard. 27-Sep-92 James Bakker, Cambridge #158/R
$2970	£1941	Mountain snow scene (43x51cm-17x20in) s. canvasboard. 14-May-93 Skinner, Bolton #103/R
$3250	£2167	Stream in winter (71x91cm-28x36in) s. 17-May-94 Grogan, Massachussetts #367/R
$3750	£2467	Sugaring shack (71x91cm-28x36in) 5-Jun-93 Louisiana Auction Exchange #48/R
$4000	£2649	Deep snow (62x82cm-24x32in) s. 23-Sep-93 Sotheby's, New York #213/R
$4000	£2703	February (41x51cm-16x20in) s. canvas on board. 31-Mar-94 Sotheby's Arcade, New York #285/R
$4400	£2876	Chocorua Mountain, new England (46x51cm-18x20in) s. canvasboard. 14-May-93 Skinner, Bolton #105/R
$5000	£3356	Winter in the mountains (94x124cm-37x49in) s. 6-Dec-93 Grogan, Massachussetts #552/R
$7500	£5034	The old covered bridge (71x91cm-28x36in) s. 5-Dec-93 James Bakker, Cambridge #7/R
$7500	£4967	Signs of thaw (75x91cm-30x36in) s. 23-Sep-93 Sotheby's, New York #194/R
$9500	£6643	Southern Vermont (76x86cm-30x34in) s.d.24. 10-Mar-93 Sotheby's, New York #113/R
$11000	£7333	Melting snow (92x76cm-36x30in) s. 16-Mar-94 Christie's, New York #107/R
$20500	£13758	Late day (107x91cm-42x36in) s. 6-Dec-93 Grogan, Massachussetts #540/R
$32500	£21667	Return of spring, Shelburne, Vermont (77x102cm-30x40in) s. 17-Mar-94 Sotheby's, New York #131/R

HIBEL, Edna (1917-) American
$1300	£850	Figure with hat (71x15cm-28x6in) s. panel. 17-Sep-93 Du Mouchelle, Detroit #2178
$1400	£946	Young girl (36x28cm-14x11in) s. panel. 13-Aug-93 Du Mouchelle, Detroit #2099/R
$3198	£2146	Japanese mother and child (51x61cm-20x24in) s. silk on millboard. 30-Nov-93 Ritchie, Toronto #55/R (C.D 4250)
$3500	£2288	Girl in field with lamb (76x102cm-30x40in) s. board. 16-May-93 Hanzel Galleries, Chicago #73/R

HICKS, David (20th C) American
$950	£625	Furrowed fields (117x117cm-46x46in) s. 2-Apr-93 Sloan, North Bethesda #2340

HICKS, Thomas (1823-1890) American
$750	£497	Sunset on the Navesink River (20x46cm-8x18in) s.d.1880verso panel. 23-Sep-93 Mystic Fine Arts, Connecticut #189
$2600	£1711	After 20 years (59x73cm-23x29in) s. 31-Mar-93 Sotheby's Arcade, New York #99/R
$4250	£2778	Portrait of James Van Dyke (91x76cm-36x30in) s. 14-May-93 Du Mouchelle, Detroit #78/R
$4500	£3020	Cows in landscape (30x51cm-12x20in) 14-Jan-94 Du Mouchelle, Detroit #2010/R
$7500	£5034	Lady with two gentlemen on seashore (25x43cm-10x17in) s.d.1879. 14-Jan-94 Du Mouchelle, Detroit #2001/R
$8000	£5369	Figures on shore with small boat (33x58cm-13x23in) 14-Jan-94 Du Mouchelle, Detroit #2160/R

HICKS, Thomas (attrib) (1823-1890) American
$650	£430	Rustic farmhouse (24x33cm-9x13in) s. 2-Oct-93 Weschler, Washington #90/R

HICKS, Thomas and KENSETT, John Frederick (19th C) American
$4000	£2649	Italian scene (26x36cm-10x14in) init.d.46 i.verso. 23-Sep-93 Sotheby's, New York #72 a/R

HIDER, Arthur H (1870-1952) Canadian
$930	£628	A seated Indian (56x51cm-22x20in) s. board. 3-Nov-93 Sotheby's, Toronto #248/R (C.D 1200)

HIGGINS, Eugene (1874-1958) American
$700	£470	Figures in alleyway (20x15cm-8x6in) s. board. 24-Jun-93 Mystic Fine Arts, Connecticut #80
$750	£503	Farmer returning home (51x41cm-20x16in) s. 24-Jun-93 Mystic Fine Arts, Connecticut #80 a

HIGGINS, Eugene (1874-1958) American-cont.
$800	£559	Poor fisherman (41x51cm-16x20in) s. 11-Mar-93 Mystic Fine Arts, Connecticut #129
$800	£523	Mississippi Rises (66x53cm-26x21in) s. 30-Jun-94 Mystic Fine Arts, Connecticut #160/R
$850	£594	On the road to North Plains (36x46cm-14x18in) 11-Mar-93 Mystic Fine Arts, Connecticut #130/R
$900	£608	When the Mississippi rises (66x53cm-26x21in) s. s.i.stretcher. 31-Mar-94 Sotheby's Arcade, New York #216/R
$1000	£649	Meager shelter (76x102cm-30x40in) s. s.i.d.1945verso. 9-Sep-93 Sotheby's Arcade, New York #323/R
$2500	£1623	Home from the fields (76x102cm-30x40in) s. 9-Sep-93 Sotheby's Arcade, New York #333 a/R
$3000	£2000	Rustic life (100x131cm-39x52in) s. i.stretcher. 23-May-94 Christie's, East, New York #197/R
$500	£323	Holding fast to the bridle (48x56cm-19x22in) init.i. gouache. 13-Jul-94 Doyle, New York #38
$1400	£940	Captured (28x41cm-11x16in) s. W/C. 6-Dec-93 Grogan, Massachussetts #513

HIGGINS, Victor (1884-1949) American
$14000	£8861	Adobe and windmill (38x53cm-15x21in) s. W/C. 3-Dec-92 Sotheby's, New York #61/R
$16000	£11189	Cottonwood trees in winter (40x58cm-16x23in) s. i.verso W/C. 11-Mar-93 Christie's, New York #128/R
$16000	£11189	Hondo Road, Taos, New Mexico (40x58cm-16x23in) s. s.i.verso W/C. 11-Mar-93 Christie's, New York #129/R

HILDEBRANDT, Howard Logan (1872-1958) American
$950	£617	Lady in landscape (41x30cm-16x12in) s. board. 11-Sep-93 Louisiana Auction Exchange #69/R
$1100	£719	Floral still life (76x61cm-30x24in) s. 8-May-93 Young Fine Arts Auctions, Maine #168/R

HILER, Hilaire (1898-1966) American/French
$1000	£633	Abstract (41x30cm-16x12in) s. W/C. 5-Dec-92 Louisiana Auction Exchange #43/R

HILL, A (19th C) American
$1201	£811	Orange seller taking a nap (75x63cm-30x25in) s.d.1875. 23-Apr-94 Soderkopings #247/R (S.KR 9500)

HILL, Carl G (1884-1973) American?
$1500	£987	Haying (46x61cm-18x24in) s.d.1942. 4-Nov-92 Doyle, New York #35/R

HILL, Charles Emil (attrib) (1870-1953) American
$1000	£662	Mother with children (51x41cm-20x16in) indis.s. 28-Nov-92 Dunning's, Illinois #1077

HILL, Edward (19th C) American
$1000	£676	Hunter and dogs in a wood (16x12cm-6x5in) s.d.99 panel. 5-Nov-93 Skinner, Bolton #51/R
$1500	£1007	The forest in summer (51x36cm-20x14in) s. 8-Dec-93 Butterfield & Butterfield, San Francisco #3324/R

HILL, Edward Rufus (1852-c.1908) American
$1500	£1042	Giant redwoods (122x41cm-48x16in) s. 7-Mar-93 Butterfield & Butterfield, San Francisco #31/R
$1500	£1042	Washing in the river (35x58cm-14x23in) s. 7-Mar-93 Butterfield & Butterfield, San Francisco #33/R

HILL, Howard (19th C) American
$1000	£654	Roosters (25x36cm-10x14in) s. canvasboard. 18-Sep-93 James Bakker, Cambridge #233/R
$2500	£1323	Grouse family (66x97cm-26x38in) s. 11-Sep-92 Skinner, Bolton #195/R
$2700	£1824	A family of pheasants (75x126cm-30x50in) s. 31-Mar-94 Sotheby's Arcade, New York #16/R
$3500	£2365	A family of grouse (76x127cm-30x50in) s. 5-Nov-93 Skinner, Bolton #53/R
$5000	£3401	Family of grouse (81x61cm-32x24in) s. 17-Nov-93 Doyle, New York #7/R

HILL, Howard (attrib) (19th C) American
$1700	£1156	Quail family (24x32cm-9x13in) 10-Jul-93 Young Fine Arts Auctions, Maine #179/R

HILL, J W (1812-1879) American
$482	£330	Still life of grapes and a snail shell (15x15cm-6x6in) s.d.1874 W/C htd bodycol. 9-Feb-94 Sotheby's Colonnade, London #215

HILL, John Henry (1839-1922) American/British
$2200	£1438	Pear tree. Landscape (25x33cm-10x13in) s.d.1895 ink W/C graphite double-sided. 14-May-93 Skinner, Bolton #43/R

HILL, John William (1812-1879) American
$900	£520	Landscape with figure in woodlands (41x36cm-16x14in) s.d.1869 W/C. 25-Sep-92 Sotheby's Arcade, New York #131/R
$1200	£811	Hackinsack River near Noack a fishing scene (10x19cm-4x7in) s.d.1869 i.verso W/C graphite gouache board. 5-Nov-93 Skinner, Bolton #44/R
$1600	£1074	Roadside conversation (33x46cm-13x18in) s. W/C. 24-Mar-94 Mystic Fine Arts, Connecticut #207

HILL, John William (1812-1879) American-cont.
$9000	£6081	Still life with grapes and nectarine outdoors (15x19cm-6x7in) s.d.1874 W/C graphite gouache paperboard. 5-Nov-93 Skinner, Bolton #57/R
$15000	£9494	River landscape with boy fishing (22x34cm-9x13in) s.d.61 W/C. 3-Dec-92 Sotheby's, New York #16/R

HILL, T W (19th C) American
$3000	£1961	Romantic couple in winter landscape (76x64cm-30x25in) s. 7-Oct-93 Freeman Fine Arts, Philadelphia #879/R

HILL, Thomas (1829-1908) American
$1200	£805	Woodland stream (28x25cm-11x10in) s. canvasboard. 6-Dec-93 Grogan, Massachussetts #483/R
$3750	£2206	Cathedral spires, Yosemite (32x53cm-13x21in) s. paper on board. 4-Oct-92 Butterfield & Butterfield, Los Angeles #16/R
$4500	£2922	Yosemite , i.verso panel triptych shaped tops. 9-Sep-93 Sotheby's Arcade, New York #13/R
$7000	£4118	Mount Shasta from Castle Lake (36x53cm-14x21in) s. 4-Oct-92 Butterfield & Butterfield, Los Angeles #6/R
$7000	£4118	Hunter at sunset (20x61cm-8x24in) s. panel. 4-Oct-92 Butterfield & Butterfield, Los Angeles #13/R
$9500	£6597	Mountain scene (36x53cm-14x21in) s. board. 7-Mar-93 Butterfield & Butterfield, San Francisco #35/R
$10000	£6711	Sierra Lake (38x55cm-15x22in) s. board. 8-Dec-93 Butterfield & Butterfield, San Francisco #3320/R
$10000	£5882	Wooded landscape with red fox (55x38cm-22x15in) s.d.1868. 4-Oct-92 Butterfield & Butterfield, Los Angeles #35/R
$12500	£8013	Bald eagles over Lower Falls, Yellowstone Park, Grand Tetons beyond (76x51cm-30x20in) s. 24-May-93 Grogan, Massachussetts #326/R
$13000	£9028	Fremont Grove (117x76cm-46x30in) s. 7-Mar-93 Butterfield & Butterfield, San Francisco #54/R
$14000	£8235	Yosemite Valley from Inspiration Point (61x51cm-24x20in) s.d.1901. 4-Oct-92 Butterfield & Butterfield, Los Angeles #45/R
$16000	£11111	Yosemite landscape (55x38cm-22x15in) s. 7-Mar-93 Butterfield & Butterfield, San Francisco #55/R
$17000	£11806	Yosemite Valley (41x61cm-16x24in) s. canvas on board. 7-Mar-93 Butterfield & Butterfield, San Francisco #34/R
$50000	£35461	Yosemite Valley California, from artist's point (107x178cm-42x70in) s. 11-Feb-93 Boos Gallery, Michigan #359/R

HILL, Tom (20th C) American
$850	£571	Winter morning on the river (53x76cm-21x30in) s. W/C. 8-Dec-93 Butterfield & Butterfield, San Francisco #3596/R
$950	£638	Courtyard (53x74cm-21x29in) s. W/C over pencil. 8-Dec-93 Butterfield & Butterfield, San Francisco #3594/R
$950	£638	Mission in Mexico (53x74cm-21x29in) s. W/C. 8-Dec-93 Butterfield & Butterfield, San Francisco #3595/R

HILL, W F (19th C) American?
$1200	£800	Still life of flowers in a glass compote (36x56cm-14x22in) s.indist.d. 1-Jun-94 Doyle, New York #35

HILLIARD, William Henry (1836-1905) American
$597	£403	River landscape with washerwomen (33x55cm-13x22in) s. panel. 22-Oct-93 Bolland & Marotz, Bremen #2059/R (DM 1000)
$750	£490	Tropical paradise (53x43cm-21x17in) s. 17-Sep-93 Skinner, Bolton #198/R
$800	£537	River landscape (33x46cm-13x18in) s. 24-Jun-93 Mystic Fine Arts, Connecticut #134
$800	£537	Autumn landscape by lake with church beyond (23x41cm-9x16in) st.sig.d.1868. 1-Dec-93 Doyle, New York #57
$950	£651	The rowboat (33x53cm-13x21in) s.i.d.1880 panel. 10-Feb-94 Skinner, Bolton #55
$1406	£950	Bringing in the harvest (39x31cm-15x12in) s.d.1882 canvas on board. 18-Mar-93 Bonhams, London #109
$1700	£1189	Landscape (36x48cm-14x19in) s. 11-Mar-93 Mystic Fine Arts, Connecticut #221
$1700	£1149	Feeding the chickens (74x61cm-29x24in) s.d.1882. 5-Nov-93 Skinner, Bolton #29/R

HILLIARD, William Henry (attrib) (1836-1905) American
$691	£480	Back from the fields (39x31cm-15x12in) bears sig.d.1885 canvas on board. 2-Mar-93 Sotheby's, Billingshurst #1150

HILLS, Anna A (1882-1930) American
$1000	£662	Landscape (13x18cm-5x7in) s.d.1921 board. 14-Jun-94 John Moran, Pasadena #17
$1400	£927	Fisherman's shack, Laguna Beach (23x18cm-9x7in) s. board. 28-Sep-93 John Moran, Pasadena #220 a
$1800	£1250	When the tide is out, St Ives Harbour (25x36cm-10x14in) s.d.10 canvasboard. 7-Mar-93 Butterfield & Butterfield, San Francisco #176/R
$2250	£1510	Sunlit waves (46x61cm-18x24in) s.d.1920 canvasboard. 8-Dec-93 Butterfield & Butterfield, San Francisco #3500/R
$2500	£1471	Old cypress near Carmel (36x53cm-14x21in) s.d.1922 canvasboard. 4-Oct-92 Butterfield & Butterfield, Los Angeles #78/R
$2750	£1897	Live oaks and sycamores (18x25cm-7x10in) s.d.1918 i.indist.verso. 16-Feb-93 John Moran, Pasadena #17 a
$4250	£2872	Desert landscape (51x76cm-20x30in) s.d.1914. 15-Jun-93 John Moran, Pasadena #179
$950	£642	Bridge in wooded landscape (18x25cm-7x10in) s.d.1921 W/C. 9-Nov-93 John Moran, Pasadena #808 a

HILLS, Laura Coombs (1859-1952) American
$800	£533	Goose pond (36x43cm-14x17in) s.verso. 20-Aug-93 Skinner, Bolton #478
$900	£592	Portrait of young boy in sailor suit (61x51cm-24x20in) s. pastel. 7-Apr-93 Doyle, New York #38
$950	£621	Petunias in blue vase (34x27cm-13x11in) s. pastel. 22-May-93 Weschler, Washington #126 a/R
$4250	£2852	Floral still life (46x56cm-18x22in) s. pastel. 6-Dec-93 Grogan, Massachussetts #499/R
$7250	£4866	Bowl of pansies (25x28cm-10x11in) s. i.verso pastel paperboard. 4-Mar-94 Skinner, Bolton #276/R
$7500	£3968	Snow berries (33x28cm-13x11in) s. pastel paperboard. 11-Sep-92 Skinner, Bolton #256/R
$9500	£6333	Nicotiana at night and the luna moth (48x38cm-19x15in) s.verso pastel paper on board. 20-Aug-93 Skinner, Bolton #470/R

HINCKLEY, Thomas H (1813-1896) American
$2400	£1579	Portrait of terrier (63x76cm-25x30in) s.d.1870. 4-Jun-93 Sotheby's, New York #6/R
$3500	£2244	Boy with animals in landscape (74x91cm-29x36in) s.d.1843 canvas on canvas. 9-Dec-92 Butterfield & Butterfield, San Francisco #3814/R
$7000	£4667	Spaniel pointing (99x124cm-39x49in) s.d.1843 canvas on masonite. 3-Jun-94 Sotheby's, New York #82/R

HIND, William George Richardson (1833-1888) Canadian
$2518	£1702	Gathering wood (20x30cm-8x12in) board. 3-Nov-93 Sotheby's, Toronto #44/R (C.D 3250)
$14269	£9266	Self-portrait in landscape (25x32cm-10x13in) paper. 19-May-93 Sotheby's, Toronto #181/R (C.D 18000)
$1162	*£785*	*Study of a rabbit (23x30cm-9x12in) W/C. 3-Nov-93 Sotheby's, Toronto #125/R (C.D 1500)*
$1317	*£890*	*Fishing (37x53cm-15x21in) gouache W/C. 3-Nov-93 Sotheby's, Toronto #159/R (C.D 1700)*

HINDS, Patrick Swazo (1929-) American
$2000	£1290	Abstract (61x76cm-24x30in) s. 9-Jan-93 Skinner, Bolton #5/R

HINES, Richard (?) American
$1500	£1007	Young girl with chickens (91x58cm-36x23in) 14-Jan-94 Du Mouchelle, Detroit #1013/R

HINKLE, Clarence Keiser (1880-1960) American
$1000	£676	Pont Marie, Paris (25x36cm-10x14in) s. canvasboard. 15-Jun-93 John Moran, Pasadena #182
$2250	£1500	Laguna back country (46x56cm-18x22in) s. canvas laid down on masonite painted 1927. 15-Mar-94 John Moran, Pasadena #96
$3000	£1765	Artist's studio, Santa Barbara (76x91cm-30x36in) s. 4-Oct-92 Butterfield & Butterfield, Los Angeles #185/R
$3250	£2152	Girl with yellow flower (76x66cm-30x26in) s. board. 28-Sep-93 John Moran, Pasadena #291
$4250	£2872	Pomagranites (91x76cm-36x30in) s. 15-Jun-93 John Moran, Pasadena #123
$4750	£3146	Girl sewing by window (56x46cm-22x18in) s. 28-Sep-93 John Moran, Pasadena #266
$5000	£3289	Still life with persimmons (51x61cm-20x24in) s. 13-Jun-93 Butterfield & Butterfield, San Francisco #911/R
$650	*£439*	*Day at pier (28x38cm-11x15in) s. W/C. 15-Jun-93 John Moran, Pasadena #43*

HINTERMEISTER, Henry (1897-) American
$2200	£1392	Flying a kite (56x61cm-22x24in) s. 2-Dec-92 Christie's, East, New York #331/R
$3200	£2238	Dog's best friend (66x61cm-26x24in) s. 11-Mar-93 Christie's, New York #261/R

HIRSCH, Joseph (1910-1981) American
$3000	£1948	Francis and bird (69x48cm-27x19in) s.d.79. 9-Sep-93 Sotheby's Arcade, New York #351/R
$3200	£1850	The nickel (64x30cm-25x12in) s. 23-Sep-92 Christie's, New York #253/R
$6500	£4276	Self-portrait (76x61cm-30x24in) s. 31-Mar-93 Sotheby's Arcade, New York #489/R
$15000	£10490	Nude and picture book (60x73cm-24x29in) s. 11-Mar-93 Christie's, New York #267/R
$700	*£455*	*Studio (76x51cm-30x20in) s. chl ink wash board exec.1969. 9-Sep-93 Sotheby's Arcade, New York #393 a/R*
$800	*£462*	*The dispute (30x40cm-12x16in) s. ballpoint pen. 25-Sep-92 Sotheby's Arcade, New York #446/R*
$1000	*£578*	*Studio (76x51cm-30x20in) s. chl ink wash board. 25-Sep-92 Sotheby's Arcade, New York #471/R*

HIRSCH, Stefan (1899-1964) American
$950	£629	Portrait of Aline Meyer Liebman (49x43cm-19x17in) s.d.1927 board. 22-Sep-93 Christie's, New York #192/R

HIRSCHBERG, Carl (1854-1923) American
$6000	£3468	The veteran (112x89cm-44x35in) s.d.1893 s.i.verso. 25-Sep-92 Sotheby's Arcade, New York #97/R
$8085	£5500	Good Morning a mother with child in cot and two dogs beside (73x54cm-29x21in) s.d.10. 16-Nov-93 Phillips, London #77/R
$1500	*£1007*	*Motherhood (36x25cm-14x10in) W/C. 24-Mar-93 Doyle, New York #36/R*

HIRSCHFELD, Al (1903-) American
$1200	£784	Jazz player (33x32cm-13x13in) s. W/C ricepaper. 4-May-93 Christie's, East, New York #276

231

HIRSCHFELD, Al (1903-) American-cont.
$1700   £1118   The wiz (53x74cm-21x29in) s.i. ink. 7-Apr-93 Doyle, New York #38 a

HIRSH, Alice (1888-1935) American
$1700   £1090   Manhattan skyline. Washington Square (21x25cm-8x10in) s. canvas on board pair. 9-Dec-92 Butterfield & Butterfield, San Francisco #4022/R

HIRST, Claude Raguet (1855-1942) American
$5000   £2890   Still life with fruit (23x36cm-9x14in) s.i. i.stretcher. 24-Sep-92 Sotheby's, New York #37/R
$9000   £6000   Still life with books and a vase (25x20cm-10x8in) s. W/C. 17-Mar-94 Sotheby's, New York #7/R
$12500   £7225   Book of poems (21x26cm-8x10in) s.i. W/C board. 23-Sep-92 Christie's, New York #90/R

HITCHCOCK, George (1850-1913) American
$2235   £1500   Dutch girl (38x30cm-15x12in) s. canvas on board. 16-Jul-93 Christie's, London #162
$4200   £2658   Woman in field of flowers (61x62cm-24x24in) s.d.1-89. 2-Dec-92 Christie's, East, New York #148/R
$8305   £5500   Dutch flower girl (54x43cm-21x17in) s. 26-Nov-92 Bonhams, London #152/R
$25000   £16026   Dunes, Holland (69x116cm-27x46in) s.d.1892. 27-May-93 Sotheby's, New York #16/R
$30000   £20134   The Christening (109x89cm-43x35in) s. 3-Dec-93 Christie's, New York #53/R
$900   £592   Sailing in choppy waters (53x36cm-21x14in) s.d.1880 W/C pencil paper on board. 31-Mar-93 Sotheby's Arcade, New York #20/R

HITTELL, Charles Joseph (1861-1938) American
$1400   £824   Grand Canyon of Colorado (27x38cm-11x15in) s. canvas on board. 4-Oct-92 Butterfield & Butterfield, Los Angeles #23/R
$1900   £1319   Piute wickiups (23x38cm-9x15in) s.i.d.1903. 7-Mar-93 Butterfield & Butterfield, San Francisco #231/R
$4000   £2353   Frank Hittell bringing home a buck (30x47cm-12x19in) s.d.1893. 4-Oct-92 Butterfield & Butterfield, Los Angeles #26/R

HLITO, Alfredo (1923-1993) Argentinian
$19000   £12667   Estructura (70x50cm-28x20in) s.d.45verso. 17-May-94 Sotheby's, New York #36/R

HOBART, Clark (1868-1948) American
$5500   £3819   Portrait of Miss Helene Maxwell, San Francisco (127x102cm-50x40in) s. canvas on board. 7-Mar-93 Butterfield & Butterfield, San Francisco #155/R
$10000   £5882   Monterey Bay (52x77cm-20x30in) s. 4-Oct-92 Butterfield & Butterfield, Los Angeles #76/R

HODGDON, Sylvester Phelps (1830-1906) American
$4750   £3146   Mountain lake view (51x76cm-20x30in) s.d.1882. 15-Jun-94 Butterfield & Butterfield, San Francisco #4414/R

HODGSON, Thomas Sherlock (1924-) Canadian
$741   £487   Two nudes (118x127cm-46x50in) s.d.1971 on stretcher verso. 7-Jun-93 Ritchie, Toronto #196/R (C.D 950)

HODICKE, K H (1938-) American/German
$12166   £7700   Ampel spring (200x291cm-79x115in) s.i.d.1985 verso acrylic. 3-Dec-92 Christie's, London #90/R
$19118   £12100   Prometheus (295x201cm-116x79in) s.i.d.84 verso acrylic linen. 3-Dec-92 Christie's, London #87/R

HODICKE, Karl Horst (1938-) American/German
$1590   £1060   Man with outstretched tongue (98x68cm-39x27in) s.d.1983 acrylic paper. 3-Jun-94 Lempertz, Cologne #695/R (DM 2650)
$7800   £5200   Flowers (190x150cm-75x59in) s.i.d.1938verso acrylic cotton. 3-Jun-94 Lempertz, Cologne #694/R (DM 13000)
$2175   £1440   Untitled (100x70cm-39x28in) s.i.d.1984 Indian ink brush. 20-Nov-92 Lempertz, Cologne #589 (DM 3500)
$15846   £10494   Attack (170x230cm-67x91in) s.i.d.1984 resin canvas. 20-Nov-92 Lempertz, Cologne #588/R (DM 25500)
$28195   £18672   Great reflection XII (150x160cm-59x63in) s.verso studio st.i.d.65stretcher resin canvas. 27-Nov-92 Villa Grisebach, Berlin #72/R (DM 45000)

HOEBER, Arthur (1854-1915) American
$1400   £952   Woods in autumn (61x51cm-24x20in) s. s.i.verso. 17-Nov-93 Doyle, New York #20/R
$2000   £1282   Farm scene with pond (53x81cm-21x32in) 13-Dec-92 Hindman Galleries, Chicago #32/R
$2250   £1541   'Oaks' (74x64cm-29x25in) s. 18-Feb-94 Du Mouchelle, Detroit #2006/R
$3200   £2238   Beach at Concarneau (56x81cm-22x32in) s. 11-Mar-93 Christie's, New York #74/R
$4000   £2532   Landscape at twilight (64x102cm-25x40in) s. 2-Dec-92 Christie's, East, New York #41/R

HOFFMAN, Harry Leslie (1874-1966) American
$1200   £805   Start of Bermuda Races - New London (30x41cm-12x16in) s. board. 5-Dec-93 James Bakker, Cambridge #80/R
$1700   £983   Ship at sea (61x66cm-24x26in) s. board. 27-Sep-92 James Bakker, Cambridge #112/R

HOFFMAN, Irwin D (20th C) American
$1500   £1000   Portrait of Aiden Lassell Ripley (51x41cm-20x16in) s.i.d.1923. 26-Aug-93 Skinner, Bolton #56/R

HOFFMAN, John (20th C) American
$9000   £5202   Wagon train (86x54cm-34x21in) s. 23-Sep-92 Christie's, New York #114/R

HOFFMANN, Clara (19/20th C) American
$7000   £4575   Arranging flowers (36x56cm-14x22in) s.i.d.1895. 4-May-93 Christie's, East, New York #249/R

HOFFMANN, Gary David (1947-) American
$650   £451   Woman in long white dress (30x23cm-12x9in) s.verso. 27-Feb-93 Young Fine Arts Auctions, Maine #158/R

HOFMANN, Ansen (20th C) American
$2500   £1678   Untitled (71x99cm-28x39in) s. 25-Mar-93 Boos Gallery, Michigan #544/R

HOFMANN, Hans (1880-1966) American/German
$12000 £7843   Sacrifice (43x36cm-17x14in) s. masonite painted 1954. 4-May-93 Sotheby's, New York #327/R
$20000 £12903 Landscape (76x89cm-30x35in) init.i. board. 13-Jul-94 Boos Gallery, Michigan #558/R
$20000 £13072 Flowering tree (26x22cm-10x9in) i.d.1952verso board. 5-May-93 Christie's, New York #261/R
$20000 £13423 Idyll (29x29cm-11x11in) s.i.d.1955verso panel. 4-May-94 Christie's, New York #101/R
$50000 £32680 Landscape 'Sunrise over the dunes' (63x79cm-25x31in) s.d.40 s.d.1940 verso plywood. 4-May-93 Sotheby's, New York #287/R
$55000 £37162 Foreboding of spring (64x76cm-25x30in) s. s.i.d.1962 verso. 11-Nov-93 Sotheby's, New York #280/R
$70000 £47297 Two pyramids (92x122cm-36x48in) s.d.52. 9-Nov-93 Christie's, New York #11/R
$75000 £49669 Durbilant equilibrium (61x77cm-24x30in) s.i.d.1954verso panel. 19-Nov-92 Christie's, New York #324/R
$85000 £57047 Blue interior (102x127cm-40x50in) s.d.1947. 5-May-94 Sotheby's, New York #85/R
$86000 £56954 Bouquet (64x51cm-25x20in) s.d.51 panel. 19-Nov-92 Christie's, New York #314/R
$90000 £60811 Landscape (89x76cm-35x30in) init.d.VIII 30,42verso panel. 10-Nov-93 Christie's, New York #107/R
$200000 £132450 Flowers of the mind (122x91cm-48x36in) s.d.65 i.verso. 18-Nov-92 Christie's, New York #3/R
$200000 £134228 Jubilant (102x127cm-40x50in) s.d.59 s.i.d.verso. 4-May-94 Sotheby's, New York #13/R
$205000 £138514 Toward harvest (91x121cm-36x48in) s.d.58 s.i.d.58 verso panel. 11-Nov-93 Sotheby's, New York #254/R
$330000 £218543 Exabundantia (213x132cm-84x52in) s.d.64 i.verso. 18-Nov-92 Christie's, New York #19/R
$1000   £654   Abstract figures (36x58cm-14x23in) s.d.1931 ink. 1-Nov-92 Litchfield Auction Gallery #267
$2000   £1342   Seagull (35x43cm-14x17in) init.d.VII 17 43 brush ink crayons pap.on board. 23-Feb-94 Christie's, New York #5/R
$2000   £1325   Untitled (81x66cm-32x26in) drawn c.1932 chl. 17-Nov-92 Christie's, East, New York #279/R
$4000   £2703   Untitled (27x21cm-11x8in) s.d.38 brush ink. 10-Nov-93 Christie's, New York #102/R
$6500   £4305   Untitled (28x36cm-11x14in) init.d.41 col.crayon brush. 17-Nov-92 Christie's, East, New York #282/R
$7000   £4698   Untitled (72x57cm-28x22in) init.d.V 18 44 brush ink col.crayon paperboard. 23-Feb-94 Christie's, New York #1/R
$10500 £6863   Untitled (60x48cm-24x19in) s. ink crayon executed 1954. 4-May-93 Sotheby's, New York #304/R
$11000 £7190   Untitled (60x48cm-24x19in) s. ink crayon executed 1954. 4-May-93 Sotheby's, New York #294 a/R
$12000 £7843   Untitled (60x48cm-24x19in) s. ink crayon executed 1954. 4-May-93 Sotheby's, New York #301 a/R
$13000 £8609   Untitled (35x43cm-14x17in) init.d.42 col.crayon felttip pen. 19-Nov-92 Christie's, New York #309/R
$16000 £10738 Untitled (49x61cm-19x24in) s.d.1944 gouache brush ink. 4-May-94 Christie's, New York #134/R
$32000 £20915 Untitled (44x60cm-17x24in) init.d.43 gouache. 4-May-93 Sotheby's, New York #292/R
$35000 £23490 Landscape (61x76cm-24x30in) casein panel painted 1940. 4-May-94 Christie's, New York #103/R

HOHNSTEDT, Peter Lanz (1872-1957) American
$700   £455   Landscape (46x61cm-18x24in) s. 11-Sep-93 Louisiana Auction Exchange #72/R
$700   £464   Eucalyptus landscape with mountains (48x69cm-19x27in) s. 14-Jun-94 John Moran, Pasadena #19

HOLBERTON, Wakeman (1839-1898) American
$1000   £662   Hanging game (51x43cm-20x17in) s.d.1875. 23-Sep-93 Mystic Fine Arts, Connecticut #172/R

HOLBROOK, Hollis (1909-) American
$3250   £1879   Train station (39x50cm-15x20in) tempera masonite painted 1930's. 24-Sep-92 Sotheby's, New York #174/R

HOLDREDGE, Ransome G (1836-1899) American
$950   £642   River scene (53x86cm-21x34in) 6-Nov-93 San Rafael Auction Galleries #214
$1300   £855   Figures on bank (53x112cm-21x44in) s. 13-Jun-93 Butterfield & Butterfield, San Francisco #703/R

HOLDREDGE, Ransome G (1836-1899) American-cont.
$1400	£909	The village market (36x66cm-14x26in) s.d.79 indis.i. 9-Sep-93 Sotheby's Arcade, New York #53/R
$1800	£1277	Village landscape (56x91cm-22x36in) 13-Feb-93 San Rafael Auction Galleries #238
$2000	£1316	Indian encampment (51x76cm-20x30in) s. 13-Jun-93 Butterfield & Butterfield, San Francisco #702/R
$2500	£1645	Wooded road (43x33cm-17x13in) s. 13-Jun-93 Butterfield & Butterfield, San Francisco #715/R
$2500	£1678	Mount Shasta (76x127cm-30x50in) s. 8-Dec-93 Butterfield & Butterfield, San Francisco #3331/R
$3250	£2241	Mountain Indian encampment (76x127cm-30x50in) indist.s. canvas laid down on canvas. 16-Feb-93 John Moran, Pasadena #95
$3500	£2059	Indian encampment (56x91cm-22x36in) s.d.91. 4-Oct-92 Butterfield & Butterfield, Los Angeles #24/R

HOLDSTOCK, A W (1820-1901) Canadian
$1083	£732	Indian encampment, lake views (51cm-20in circular) col.pastel pair. 30-Mar-94 Maynards, Vancouver #47 (C.D 1500)

HOLDSTOCK, Alfred Worsley (1820-1901) Canadian
$634	£415	Grand Falls, Nameanken River, C.W (34x52cm-13x20in) s. pastel. 19-May-93 Sotheby's, Toronto #44/R (C.D 800)
$650	£439	Riviere aux Sables (28x33cm-11x13in) s.i. pastel. 30-Mar-94 Maynards, Vancouver #43 (C.D 900)
$1090	£722	Indian encampment in Thousand Islands (21x32cm-8x13in) s.i. W/C. 24-Nov-92 Joyner Fine Art, Toronto #36/R (C.D 1400)

HOLGATE, Edwin Headley (1892-1977) Canadian
$3647	£2383	Overlooking the lake, summer (22x27cm-9x11in) init. panel. 18-May-93 Joyner Fine Art, Toronto #11/R (C.D 4600)
$4047	£2680	Winter, Morin Heights (21x26cm-8x10in) init. panel. 24-Nov-92 Joyner Fine Art, Toronto #101/R (C.D 5200)
$5059	£3351	Winter in Laurentians, horse-drawn sleigh rounding bend (21x26cm-8x10in) init. panel. 24-Nov-92 Joyner Fine Art, Toronto #10/R (C.D 6500)
$8995	£5841	Pic a l'Ours (39x46cm-15x18in) init. 21-Jun-94 Fraser Pinneys, Quebec #63 (C.D 12500)
$13232	£8763	Melting snow - Morin Heights (53x65cm-21x26in) s. i.verso. 18-Nov-92 Sotheby's, Toronto #108/R (C.D 17000)
$578	£390	Portrait of a young girl (25x20cm-10x8in) init. col.chk. 30-Mar-94 Maynards, Vancouver #44 (C.D 800)
$831	£561	Kenlay - Spitfire, S/L Magwood's Rita (20x26cm-8x10in) s.i.d.30-45 W/C ink. 23-Nov-93 Joyner Fine Art, Toronto #203 (C.D 1100)
$1092	£728	Officers' quarters (19x25cm-7x10in) init.i.d.april 29 43 ink graphite dr. 11-May-94 Sotheby's, Toronto #254/R (C.D 1500)
$1937	£1309	Seated Nude (58x47cm-23x19in) init. chl dr. 3-Nov-93 Sotheby's, Toronto #285/R (C.D 2500)

HOLLAND, Kiff (?) Canadian
$586	£399	Mount Baker slopes (41x61cm-16x24in) s. W/C. 7-Jul-93 Maynards, Vancouver #213 a (C.D 750)

HOLLAND, Tom (1936-) American
$800	£503	62nd St. Series No.48 (90x117cm-35x46in) s.d.78 mixed media. 25-Apr-93 Butterfield & Butterfield, San Francisco #2121/R
$2000	£1351	Untitled (51x66cm-20x26in) s.d.74 acrylic pastel textured paper. 21-Oct-93 Butterfield & Butterfield, San Francisco #2810/R

HOLLOWAY, Edward Stratton (?-1939) American
$1500	£1007	Seascape with fishing boats (76x127cm-30x50in) s.d.1887 i.verso. 4-Mar-94 Skinner, Bolton #216/R

HOLME, Lucy D (1882-?) American
$1500	£1007	Hibiscus (41x36cm-16x14in) 27-Mar-94 Myers, Florida #2/R

HOLMES, Ralph (1876-1963) American
$550	£367	Zion Camp near entrance (41x46cm-16x18in) s. masonite. 15-Mar-94 John Moran, Pasadena #32
$550	£364	Sycamore trees in summer landscape (23x30cm-9x12in) s. canvasboard. 14-Jun-94 John Moran, Pasadena #16
$650	£439	Landscape (46x51cm-18x20in) s. masonite. 15-Jun-93 John Moran, Pasadena #61
$650	£439	Landscape (71x81cm-28x32in) s. 9-Nov-93 John Moran, Pasadena #847
$700	£473	Green hills (61x71cm-24x28in) s. 15-Jun-93 John Moran, Pasadena #90
$800	£530	Grand Canyon (41x51cm-16x20in) s. canvasboard. 14-Jun-94 John Moran, Pasadena #113
$850	£586	Landscape (43x58cm-17x23in) s. board. 16-Feb-93 John Moran, Pasadena #80
$1000	£676	Houses in hazy landscape (41x51cm-16x20in) s. canvasboard. 15-Jun-93 John Moran, Pasadena #38
$1100	£743	Grand Canyon (76x81cm-30x32in) s. 9-Nov-93 John Moran, Pasadena #829
$1200	£805	California landscape (81x71cm-32x28in) s. 8-Dec-93 Butterfield & Butterfield, San Francisco #3502/R
$1600	£1074	Mountains near Palm Springs (61x71cm-24x28in) s. 8-Dec-93 Butterfield & Butterfield, San Francisco #3567/R

HOLMES, William H (1846-1933) American

$950	£609	Pastoral landscape with figures and cows (41x48cm-16x19in) W/C. 28-May-93 Sloan, North Bethesda #1334/R
$1600	£1074	Untitled (36x74cm-14x29in) s. W/C. 16-Dec-93 Mystic Fine Arts, Connecticut #115/R
$2000	£1325	Riverside (36x55cm-14x22in) s.d.1888 W/C. 23-Sep-93 Sotheby's, New York #33/R
$2400	£1600	Florida (23x36cm-9x14in) s.d.1900 W/C paper on board. 23-May-94 Christie's, East, New York #93/R
$6500	£4167	Playing on hillside (26x38cm-10x15in) s. W/C gouache pencil board. 26-May-93 Christie's, New York #72/R
$7000	£4430	Girl sitting on hillside (38x55cm-15x22in) inits. W/C. 4-Dec-92 Christie's, New York #31/R

HOLTY, Carl (1900-1973) American

$1200	£789	Dunes (76x102cm-30x40in) s. s.d.40 verso masonite. 31-Mar-93 Sotheby's Arcade, New York #462/R
$1500	£867	Duneland (61x76cm-24x30in) s. s.i.d.1947verso. 25-Sep-92 Sotheby's Arcade, New York #497/R
$1600	£1081	Autumn. The park (46x36cm-18x14in) s.i.d.verso s.i.d.stretcher one masonite pair. 31-Mar-94 Sotheby's Arcade, New York #483/R
$1900	£1250	Flamenco (119x91cm-47x36in) s. s.d.1948 verso. 31-Mar-93 Sotheby's Arcade, New York #461/R
$2000	£1266	Abstraction in blue, green and red (91x61cm-36x24in) s. s.i.d.1948 canvas laid down on masonite. 2-Dec-92 Christie's, East, New York #395/R
$2500	£1689	Dusk (76x98cm-30x39in) s. s.i.d.1947 verso. 31-Mar-94 Sotheby's Arcade, New York #471/R
$700	£467	Village abstraction (21x15cm-8x6in) init. W/C pencil executed 1932. 23-May-94 Christie's, East, New York #308
$750	£487	Abstraction (32x48cm-13x19in) init.d.36 pastel paper on board. 9-Sep-93 Sotheby's Arcade, New York #399
$1700	£1141	Untitled (18x28cm-7x11in) s.d.1936 pastel. 4-May-94 Doyle, New York #65
$1800	£1169	Mountain and leaves. Abstract house. Untitled abstractions , init. W/C pen pencil gouache board set of three. 9-Sep-93 Sotheby's Arcade, New York #397/R
$1800	£1200	man and woman (129x107cm-51x42in) s. s.i.d.1953 stretcher oil crayon canvas. 23-May-94 Christie's, East, New York #314/R
$2000	£1333	Abstractions (16x22cm-6x9in) three s. two s.d.36 ink wash pencil board five. 23-May-94 Christie's, East, New York #222
$3500	£2303	817 Variations A-B. 820 Variations A-B (28x36cm-11x14in) gouache ink graphite pair. 31-Mar-93 Sotheby's Arcade, New York #463
$4250	£2872	841, 865, 881 and 885 (36x28cm-14x11in) s.d.36 i.verso Indian ink board four. 31-Mar-94 Sotheby's Arcade, New York #472/R
$4750	£3125	Abstraction. Seated figure. Warrior (30x23cm-12x9in) two s.d.45 W/C graphite wash paper board three. 31-Mar-93 Sotheby's Arcade, New York #460/R

HOLTY, Carl (attrib) (1900-1973) American

$600	£380	Man in boat (48x30cm-19x12in) s. cardboard. 30-Nov-92 Schrager Galleries, Milwaukee #452
$600	£380	One angel (48x30cm-19x12in) s.d.33 pencil. 30-Nov-92 Schrager Galleries, Milwaukee #458
$675	£427	Angels VII (48x30cm-19x12in) s.d.33 pencil cardboard. 30-Nov-92 Schrager Galleries, Milwaukee #371

HOLTZMAN, Harry (1912-) American

$3000	£2013	Composition with blue and yellow (36x13cm-14x5in) s.d.1946verso. 4-May-94 Doyle, New York #64

HOLZER, Jenny (1950-) American

$3500	£2431	Selection from the Living Series (54x58cm-21x23in) exec.1980-1982 enamel sheet metal. 22-Feb-93 Christie's, East, New York #228/R

HOMER, Winslow (1836-1910) American

$220000	£146667	Young farmers, study for Weaning the Calf (30x36cm-12x14in) canvas on board. 25-May-94 Sotheby's, New York #21/R
$460000	£306667	On guard - boy sitting on fallen tree branches (31x23cm-12x9in) s.d.64. 26-May-94 Christie's, New York #31/R
$550000	£352564	Noon recess (23x36cm-9x14in) s.d.1873. 26-May-93 Christie's, New York #36/R
$640000	£410256	Looking out to sea (39x57cm-15x22in) s.d.1872. 27-May-93 Sotheby's, New York #154 a/R
$900000	£576923	Uncle Ned at home (36x56cm-14x22in) s.d.1875. 26-May-93 Christie's, New York #19/R
$1000000	£666667	The whittling boy (39x57cm-15x22in) s.d.1873. 26-May-94 Christie's, New York #19/R
$1100000	£696203	The unruly calf (61x97cm-24x38in) s.d.1875. 3-Dec-92 Sotheby's, New York #36/R
$1200	£694	Study for Gulf Stream sailing vessel (11x17cm-4x7in) i. i.verso pencil. 25-Sep-92 Sotheby's Arcade, New York #122/R
$5500	£3179	Bicycle messenger (21x27cm-8x11in) pencil. 24-Sep-92 Sotheby's, New York #46/R
$15000	£10067	Union Cavalry and artillery starting in pursuit of rebels (22x36cm-9x14in) s.d.May 5th 1862 pencil. 2-Dec-93 Sotheby's, New York #16/R
$35000	£23333	Woman seated on a bench (45x35cm-18x14in) s.d.1880 chl gouache. 17-Mar-94 Sotheby's, New York #16/R
$42000	£28000	Woman reading in a hammock (13x19cm-5x7in) s.verso pencil gouache painted c.1875. 17-Mar-94 Sotheby's, New York #55/R
$60000	£40000	In autumn woods (28x19cm-11x7in) init. W/C pencil. 26-May-94 Christie's, New York #18/R
$60000	£40000	Study for In the Mountains (22x33cm-9x13in) init. chl Chinese white executed c.1877. 25-May-94 Sotheby's, New York #23/R

HOMER, Winslow (1836-1910) American-cont.
$67500	£43269	Girl on swing (42x20cm-17x8in) s.d.79 chl gouache. 27-May-93 Sotheby's, New York #156/R
$145000	£96667	St John's River, Florida (35x51cm-14x20in) s.d.1890 W/C. 26-May-94 Christie's, New York #27/R
$180000	£115385	Daydreaming (34x49cm-13x19in) s.i.d.1880 1882 W/C pencil pen. 26-May-93 Christie's, New York #53/R
$230000	£147436	Deep sea fishing (34x53cm-13x21in) s.d.1894 W/C. 27-May-93 Sotheby's, New York #180/R
$250000	£167785	Children on the beach (33x48cm-13x19in) s.d.1881 W/C pencil. 2-Dec-93 Sotheby's, New York #25/R

HONDO, Arroyo (attrib) (fl.1825-1840) American
$2600	£1745	Our Lady of the Immaculate Conception (43x30cm-17x12in) tempera gesso panel. 26-Jun-93 Skinner, Bolton #229/R

HOOD, Dorothy (20th C) American
$1250	£786	Far Away Forest (127x122cm-50x48in) s. 23-Apr-93 Hart Gallery, Houston #7

HOPKIN, Robert (1832-1909) American
$700	£443	Mountain landscape (56x69cm-22x27in) 2-Dec-92 Boos Gallery, Michigan #887
$700	£496	Stormy seas (25x36cm-10x14in) s. 12-Feb-93 Du Mouchelle, Detroit #2076/R
$700	£496	Dock scene (30x38cm-12x15in) s. board. 12-Feb-93 Du Mouchelle, Detroit #2075/R
$800	£537	Missing vessel (38x61cm-15x24in) s. board. 14-Jan-94 Du Mouchelle, Detroit #2021/R
$900	£604	Sailing ship on choppy water with seagulls (51x41cm-20x16in) s. s.d.1908verso. 16-Jul-93 Du Mouchelle, Detroit #2000
$1000	£667	A stormy sea with a sailing vessel in the distance (36x51cm-14x20in) s. 20-May-94 Du Mouchelle, Detroit #83/R
$1100	£719	Art for the night (36x41cm-14x16in) s. 16-Apr-93 Du Mouchelle, Detroit #2000/R
$1200	£800	Shipping in rough sea (41x51cm-16x20in) s. 26-Aug-93 Boos Gallery, Michigan #476/R
$1800	£1259	Sailing ship (61x41cm-24x16in) s. 12-Mar-93 Du Mouchelle, Detroit #1008/R
$2500	£1623	Mount Marcy, Essex Co, N.Y. (71x132cm-28x52in) s. s.i.d.1877verso. 15-Jan-93 Du Mouchelle, Detroit #2024/R
$2700	£1776	Forest landscape with waterfall, Glen Ellis, New Hampshire (77x64cm-30x25in) s.d.1880 s.i.verso. 31-Mar-93 Sotheby's Arcade, New York #90/R
$3000	£1974	Isle of Arran (70x102cm-28x40in) s.d.1871. 31-Mar-93 Sotheby's Arcade, New York #21/R
$3250	£2167	Sailing ship on rough seas (66x122cm-26x48in) s. 20-May-94 Du Mouchelle, Detroit #2000/R
$450	*£290*	*Seascape with sailboat (36x61cm-14x24in) s. W/C. 15-Jul-94 Du Mouchelle, Detroit #2273/R*
$450	*£300*	*Sailing ship on choppy seas (43x56cm-17x22in) s. gouache board. 18-Mar-94 Du Mouchelle, Detroit #2166/R*
$700	*£467*	*Mountain lake landscape (56x97cm-22x38in) s.d.1884 W/C. 18-Mar-94 Du Mouchelle, Detroit #36/R*
$1100	*£738*	*Ship at sea (61x46cm-24x18in) s. W/C. 14-Jan-94 Du Mouchelle, Detroit #2249/R*

HOPKINS, James R (1877-1967) American
$5500	£3179	Cynthia (77x64cm-30x25in) s. 23-Sep-92 Christie's, New York #167/R

HOPKINS, Peter (1911-) American
$5500	£3642	Bus depot (51x61cm-20x24in) s. 23-Sep-93 Sotheby's, New York #244/R

HOPKINS, Robert (19/20th C) American
$564	£381	Mountain village in Provence (38x33cm-15x13in) s. board. 10-Nov-93 James Adam, Dublin #83 (E.P 400)

HOPKINSON, Charles Sydney (1869-1962) American
$1900	£1275	Working fisherman (36x25cm-14x10in) estate st. 5-Dec-93 James Bakker, Cambridge #93/R
$27000	£18121	Summer days - portrait of Rosamond and Elizabeth Eliot (127x127cm-50x50in) s. 5-Dec-93 James Bakker, Cambridge #87/R

HOPPE, Emiel (19th C) American
$1550	£981	Shepherd with flock (89x150cm-35x59in) s.d.17. 3-Dec-92 Freeman Fine Arts, Philadelphia #1825/R

HOPPER, Edward (1882-1967) American
$20000	£13986	Portrait of artist (46x36cm-18x14in) s.verso. 10-Mar-93 Sotheby's, New York #152/R
$2000	*£1342*	*Trees (33x48cm-13x19in) s.d.1952 W/C. 4-Dec-93 Louisiana Auction Exchange #12/R*
$22000	*£14667*	*Man seated in interior (18x26cm-7x10in) init. conte crayon. 25-May-94 Sotheby's, New York #116/R*
$75000	£50336	Oregon Coast (49x70cm-19x28in) s. W/C painted 1941. 2-Dec-93 Sotheby's, New York #140/R
$110000	£73333	Sierra Madre at Monterrey (54x76cm-21x30in) s. W/C painted 1943. 25-May-94 Sotheby's, New York #111/R
$135000	£85443	Vermont sugar house (35x50cm-14x20in) s. W/C. 3-Dec-92 Sotheby's, New York #57/R
$300000	£189873	Gloucester houses (40x55cm-16x22in) s. W/C. 3-Dec-92 Sotheby's, New York #143/R

HOPPER, Edward (attrib) (1882-1967) American
$1100	£738	Switch Engine train study (25x36cm-10x14in) s. graphite dr executed c.1915. 2-Dec-93 Swann Galleries, New York #145/R

HOPPMANN, Arnold (20th C) American
$800	£523	Still life with Oriental wall hanging (89x58cm-35x23in) s.d.1935. 29-Jun-94 Doyle, New York #43

HORACIO (1912-1972) Mexican
$3800	£2484	Nina con cesta de roses (61x46cm-24x18in) s. 5-May-93 Doyle, New York #109/R
$3800	£2484	Nino con conejo (155x117cm-61x46in) s. 5-May-93 Doyle, New York #110/R
$3900	£2549	Nino con sus gatos y perro (58x46cm-23x18in) s. 5-May-93 Doyle, New York #111/R
$4800	£3179	Nina con Perros (60x46cm-24x18in) s. 24-Nov-92 Christie's, New York #334/R
$4800	£3137	Nina con gato (57x49cm-22x19in) s. 17-May-93 Christie's, New York #290/R
$5000	£3378	Nina con perro (58x49cm-23x19in) s. 23-Nov-93 Christie's, New York #294/R
$5000	£3311	Nina con Canasta de Frutas (60x46cm-24x18in) s. 24-Nov-92 Christie's, New York #332/R
$6000	£4054	Nina con frutas (58x48cm-23x19in) s. 23-Nov-93 Christie's, New York #293/R
$6000	£3974	Retrato del Nino Horacio Rentoria Coronado (60x46cm-24x18in) s.i. 24-Nov-92 Christie's, New York #305/R
$6500	£4305	Portrait of Rocha Galarza holding doll (60x46cm-24x18in) s. 30-Jun-93 Sotheby's Arcade, New York #207/R
$6800	£4503	Young girl with tea tray (60x46cm-24x18in) s. 24-Nov-92 Christie's, New York #306/R
$7000	£4667	Nina en el balcon (60x46cm-24x18in) s. 18-May-94 Christie's, New York #321 a/R

HORN, Roni (1944-) American
$4000	£2685	The XXXVI (46x65cm-18x26in) s.i. pigment varnish paper collage executed 1988. 23-Feb-94 Christie's, New York #137/R
$5250	£3548	The XIII (65x94cm-26x37in) s. powder pigment varnish. 11-Nov-93 Sotheby's, New York #160/R

HORTER, Earl (1881-1940) American
$2600	£1745	Reclining nude (30x43cm-12x17in) 2-Dec-93 Freeman Fine Arts, Philadelphia #786
$625	£417	Boats in port (33x41cm-13x16in) s. pastel pencil. 26-May-94 Freeman Fine Arts, Philadelphia #283
$700	£440	House in landscape (43x58cm-17x23in) s. W/C. 22-Apr-93 Freeman Fine Arts, Philadelphia #1160
$1400	£940	Reclining nude (30x43cm-12x17in) W/C. 2-Dec-93 Freeman Fine Arts, Philadelphia #823
$6500	£4362	Cubist still life with wine glass (36x41cm-14x16in) s.d.39 W/C. 2-Dec-93 Freeman Fine Arts, Philadelphia #785/R

HORTON, William Samuel (1865-1936) American
$850	£570	Church interior (64x76cm-25x30in) 24-Mar-94 Mystic Fine Arts, Connecticut #166
$1100	£719	Bernini Columns, Rome (38x46cm-15x18in) s. st.verso panel. 30-Jun-94 Mystic Fine Arts, Connecticut #204
$1200	£784	Garden in Rome (64x76cm-25x30in) s. 30-Jun-94 Mystic Fine Arts, Connecticut #128
$1300	£850	Channel Port (43x56cm-17x22in) s. panel. 30-Jun-94 Mystic Fine Arts, Connecticut #129
$2000	£1342	Industrial scne on the Seine (36x46cm-14x18in) s. board. 24-Mar-94 Mystic Fine Arts, Connecticut #170/R
$2400	£1569	Beach scene, Biarritz (43x53cm-17x21in) s. board. 30-Jun-94 Mystic Fine Arts, Connecticut #202/R
$2700	£1765	Frozen Lake, Gstaad (64x76cm-25x30in) s. board. 30-Jun-94 Mystic Fine Arts, Connecticut #207
$3200	£2148	Industrial scene on the Seine (64x76cm-25x30in) board. 24-Mar-94 Mystic Fine Arts, Connecticut #164/R
$3250	£2181	Industrial barge on the Seine (64x76cm-25x30in) board. 24-Mar-94 Mystic Fine Arts, Connecticut #172/R
$3250	£2124	Sunflowers (107x89cm-42x35in) s.d.1929. 30-Jun-94 Mystic Fine Arts, Connecticut #131
$3300	£2157	Bridge by Old Town (64x76cm-25x30in) s. board. 30-Jun-94 Mystic Fine Arts, Connecticut #203/R
$3500	£2349	Broadstairs beach (36x46cm-14x18in) panel. 24-Mar-94 Mystic Fine Arts, Connecticut #165
$4000	£2614	Disappearing sun, Gstaad (64x76cm-25x30in) s.d.1924 board. 30-Jun-94 Mystic Fine Arts, Connecticut #206
$4500	£3020	Landscape with waterfall (64x76cm-25x30in) s. board. 24-Mar-94 Mystic Fine Arts, Connecticut #240
$5000	£3356	Snow in the mountains (64x76cm-25x30in) s. board. 24-Mar-94 Mystic Fine Arts, Connecticut #241
$5000	£3356	The silence of daybreak (71x81cm-28x32in) s. 24-Mar-94 Mystic Fine Arts, Connecticut #242
$5000	£3356	Pink haystack (64x76cm-25x30in) s.verso. 24-Mar-94 Mystic Fine Arts, Connecticut #163 a
$5250	£3523	Bernini columns - Rome (64x76cm-25x30in) 24-Mar-94 Mystic Fine Arts, Connecticut #167/R
$6000	£3922	Paysage nightfall, Gstaad (69x79cm-27x31in) s. 30-Jun-94 Mystic Fine Arts, Connecticut #201
$9000	£6000	Peace celebration, Arc de Triomphe (37x46cm-15x18in) s.d.1919 panel laid down on stretcher. 26-May-94 Christie's, New York #100/R
$900	£588	Crossing the bridge (46x61cm-18x24in) s. pastel. 30-Jun-94 Mystic Fine Arts, Connecticut #205
$1000	£671	The village (43x58cm-17x23in) s. pastel. 24-Mar-94 Mystic Fine Arts, Connecticut #171
$1100	£719	Mountain bridge (46x61cm-18x24in) pastel. 30-Jun-94 Mystic Fine Arts, Connecticut #209/R

HORTON, William Samuel (1865-1936) American-cont.
$1200	£805	Chalets in the snow (48x64cm-19x25in) pastel. 24-Mar-94 Mystic Fine Arts, Connecticut #243/R
$1200	£784	Evening Gstaad (43x53cm-17x21in) s.d.1922 pastel. 30-Jun-94 Mystic Fine Arts, Connecticut #132
$1300	£872	Abbey in the trees (47x60cm-19x24in) s. pastel. 8-Dec-93 Butterfield & Butterfield, San Francisco #3357/R

HORVATH, George (1933-) Canadian
$610	£407	Near Raium, B.C (46x61cm-18x24in) s. i.verso. 30-May-94 Hodgins, Calgary #236/R (C.D 850)
$1715	£1121	Group of elderly men gathered around table (58x80cm-23x31in) s. 5-May-93 Galerie Dobiaschofsky, Bern #607/R (S.FR 2500)

HOSMER, Billy Price (?) American
$900	£577	Victorian rose (91x61cm-36x24in) s. 26-Apr-93 Selkirks, St. Louis #296/R

HOUSER, Allan C (1915-) American
$3100	£2000	Apache War Dancer (33x23cm-13x9in) s.d.39 gouache. 9-Jan-93 Skinner, Bolton #45/R

HOUSSER, Bess (1890-1969) Canadian
$578	£390	Opakin Pass (25x33cm-10x13in) s. i.verso panel. 30-Mar-94 Maynards, Vancouver #31 (C.D 800)

HOUSSER, Yvonne McKague (1898-) Canadian
$1007	£681	Sunshine Valley Rocky Mountains (32x40cm-13x16in) s. i.verso. 3-Nov-93 Sotheby's, Toronto #179/R (C.D 1300)
$1812	£1224	House in winter (32x40cm-13x16in) s. board. 23-Nov-93 Joyner Fine Art, Toronto #46/R (C.D 2400)
$2491	£1649	Trilliums (45x75cm-18x30in) s.d.66 board. 24-Nov-92 Joyner Fine Art, Toronto #48/R (C.D 3200)
$5461	£3641	Lake Muskoka, Ontario (60x75cm-24x30in) s. 13-May-94 Joyner Fine Art, Toronto #152/R (C.D 7500)
$5825	£3883	Gaspe (89x102cm-35x40in) s. 11-May-94 Sotheby's, Toronto #213/R (C.D 8000)
$11098	£7254	Spring in the park (62x77cm-24x30in) init. d.1941 verso board. 19-May-93 Sotheby's, Toronto #327/R (C.D 14000)

HOWARD, John Langley (1902-) American
$1600	£941	Gathering wood (51x61cm-20x24in) s.d.56. 4-Oct-92 Butterfield & Butterfield, Los Angeles #242/R
$1700	£1000	Night fishing No.1 (75x61cm-30x24in) s.d.1937 mono. board. 4-Oct-92 Butterfield & Butterfield, Los Angeles #239/R
$1800	£1250	Still life with pomegranates (41x58cm-16x23in) s. s.d.6/1981verso board. 7-Mar-93 Butterfield & Butterfield, San Francisco #260/R
$3000	£1765	Mother and Child - Adelaide Day Howard (51x41cm-20x16in) s.d.1931. 4-Oct-92 Butterfield & Butterfield, Los Angeles #243/R
$7500	£4412	Night fishing No. 2 (51x82cm-20x32in) s.d.1937 egg tempera panel. 4-Oct-92 Butterfield & Butterfield, Los Angeles #240/R
$2500	£1645	Paul Masson Wineery (37x55cm-15x22in) s.d.1946 W/C. 13-Jun-93 Butterfield & Butterfield, San Francisco #955/R

HOWE, William Henry (1846-1929) American
$850	£545	Group of cattle grazing in wooded landscape (51x74cm-20x29in) s.d.82. 26-Apr-93 Selkirks, St. Louis #178
$1000	£667	Cows in landscape (54x70cm-21x28in) s.d.90. 23-May-94 Christie's, East, New York #98/R

HOWELL, Felicie (1897-1968) American
$700	£458	Dock workers (30x36cm-12x14in) s.verso board. 30-Jun-94 Mystic Fine Arts, Connecticut #85
$2300	£1523	Circus parade (32x35cm-13x14in) s. s.i.d.1917 canvas on board. 2-Oct-93 Weschler, Washington #128

HOWLAND, Alfred Cornelius (1838-1909) American
$700	£455	Haystacks (19x30cm-7x12in) i.verso canvas on board. 9-Sep-93 Sotheby's Arcade, New York #80
$800	£537	Plantation sketch (30x33cm-12x13in) panel. 5-Mar-94 Louisiana Auction Exchange #93/R
$3000	£1961	Southampton by the sea (38x48cm-15x19in) s. 30-Jun-94 Mystic Fine Arts, Connecticut #191/R
$19000	£12752	On the bridge (44x59cm-17x23in) s. 3-Dec-93 Christie's, New York #84/R

HOYOS, Anna Mercedes (1942-) Colombian
$13000	£8784	Melon (60x60cm-24x24in) s. painted 1990. 23-Nov-93 Christie's, New York #197/R
$20000	£13514	Patilla (100x100cm-39x39in) s.d.92. 23-Nov-93 Christie's, New York #193/R
$28000	£18543	Bazurto (100x100cm-39x39in) s.d.91 i.verso. 24-Nov-92 Christie's, New York #104/R
$38000	£25166	Mis Americas (198x99cm-78x39in) s.d.91 s.i.d.verso. 24-Nov-92 Christie's, New York #234/R
$40000	£26667	Bazurto (200x150cm-79x59in) s.d.91. 18-May-94 Christie's, New York #68/R
$40000	£26144	Inverapuestas el perro (150x150cm-59x59in) s. painted 1992. 17-May-93 Christie's, New York #52/R
$48000	£32432	Palenquera (200x100cm-79x39in) s.d.91. 23-Nov-93 Christie's, New York #67/R

HUBBARD, Charles (1801-1865) American
$2500 £1678 Bella, the famous champion shorthorned heifer (43x53cm-17x21in) painted c.1840. 3-Feb-94 Sloan, North Bethesda #2793/R

HUBBARD, John (1931-) American
$2431 £1700 Midsummer blue (129x119cm-51x47in) s.i.d.1962verso. 10-Mar-93 Sotheby's, London #233/R

HUBBARD, Richard William (attrib) (1817-1888) American
$800 £548 Idyllic landscape with ruins, shepherdess and mill (25x36cm-10x14in) init.d.46. 19-Feb-94 Young Fine Arts Auctions, Maine #119/R

HUDON, Normand (1929-) Canadian
$982 £663 Village Laurentien, 1890 (30x60cm-12x24in) s.i.d.92 mixed media board. 23-Nov-93 Joyner Fine Art, Toronto #328/R (C.D 1300)
$1031 £674 Fin de siecle sur la glace (46x61cm-18x24in) s.i.d.92 board. 18-May-93 Joyner Fine Art, Toronto #271/R (C.D 1300)
$775 £524 La course (41x51cm-16x20in) s.i.d.1992 mixed media board. 1-Nov-93 Levis, Calgary #105 (C.D 1000)

HUDSON, Charles Bradford (1865-1938) American
$5000 £2941 Sunset San Jaciento (81x137cm-32x54in) s. 4-Oct-92 Butterfield & Butterfield, Los Angeles #216/R

HUDSON, Eric (1864-1932) American
$700 £470 Dories, Monhegan Island (30x46cm-12x18in) 4-Mar-94 Skinner, Bolton #264/R
$2000 £1351 Rockport Harbour (41x51cm-16x20in) s. i.verso. 5-Nov-93 Skinner, Bolton #110/R

HUDSON, Grace Carpenter (1865-1937) American
$650 £437 Indian by a hut (24x22cm-9x9in) i.verso. 8-Dec-93 Butterfield & Butterfield, San Francisco #3317/R
$1000 £658 Russian river (28x24cm-11x9in) s.i. i.verso board. 13-Jun-93 Butterfield & Butterfield, San Francisco #759/R
$1200 £833 Poppies near Ukiah (22x18cm-9x7in) s. board. 7-Mar-93 Butterfield & Butterfield, San Francisco #24/R
$1300 £855 Portrait of dog (11x16cm-4x6in) s.d.1898 board. 13-Jun-93 Butterfield & Butterfield, San Francisco #760/R
$2750 £1618 Plume at Matu. Stream through open field (25x20cm-10x8in) s. i.verso paper board pair. 4-Oct-92 Butterfield & Butterfield, Los Angeles #15/R
$3250 £2257 Near Ukiah (20x18cm-8x7in) s. board. 7-Mar-93 Butterfield & Butterfield, San Francisco #25/R
$13000 £8228 Little Papoose (41x31cm-16x12in) s.i.d.x7. 2-Dec-92 Christie's, East, New York #184/R
$15000 £9268 Thrulow (25x20cm-10x8in) s.d.09 s.i.verso. 13-Jun-93 Butterfield & Butterfield, San Francisco #784/R
$24000 £15190 Chu-Bome - the orphan (49x34cm-19x13in) s.d.17.1.1. 3-Dec-92 Sotheby's, New York #64/R

HUEBLER, Douglas (1924-) American
$4500 £2980 Site sculpture project - Cap Cod Star Shape Exchange , s.d.1968 two maps ink 1 frame six photo 1 frame. 18-Nov-92 Sotheby's, New York #219/R

HUEHL, Bob (20th C) American
$1000 £694 Cowboy's breakfast (51x76cm-20x30in) s. 3-Mar-93 Doyle, New York #37

HUGHES, Edward John (1913-) Canadian
$19026 £12435 Boathouses on beach, Ladysmith, B.C. (63x81cm-25x32in) s.d.1969. 18-May-93 Joyner Fine Art, Toronto #64/R (C.D 24000)
$21845 £14563 The Nanaimo Bastion, B.C. (91x71cm-36x28in) s.d.1951 s.i.d.verso. 11-May-94 Sotheby's, Toronto #101/R (C.D 30000)
$23061 £15073 Malaspina's Gallery, Gabriola Island (63x82cm-25x32in) s.d.1966. 18-May-93 Joyner Fine Art, Toronto #25/R (C.D 29090)
$25485 £16990 Mount Stephen (81x63cm-32x25in) s.d.1963 s.i.d.verso. 11-May-94 Sotheby's, Toronto #118/R (C.D 35000)
$28021 £18557 View of Qualicum Beach (80x112cm-31x44in) s.d.1965. 24-Nov-92 Joyner Fine Art, Toronto #25/R (C.D 36000)
$1311 £874 Ferry at the Wharf, Crofton B.C. (28x34cm-11x13in) s. pencil dr. 11-May-94 Sotheby's, Toronto #241 a (C.D 1800)
$2621 £1748 The cannery at Namu (37x48cm-15x19in) s.i. pencil dr. 11-May-94 Sotheby's, Toronto #44/R (C.D 3600)
$3242 £2119 Parliament Buildings, Ottawa (51x61cm-20x24in) s. W/C. 19-May-93 Sotheby's, Toronto #320/R (C.D 4090)
$5153 £3368 Church at Qualicum Beach (51x61cm-20x24in) s.d.1969 W/C. 18-May-93 Joyner Fine Art, Toronto #94/R (C.D 6500)
$5232 £3420 Old maples, Cowichan Bay road (51x61cm-20x24in) s.d.1973 W/C. 19-May-93 Sotheby's, Toronto #167/R (C.D 6600)

HUGHES, George H (attrib) (fl.1832-1861) Canadian
$1820 £1214 Habitants and horse drawn sleigh in storm (31x26cm-12x10in) bears sig. 11-May-94 Sotheby's, Toronto #4/R (C.D 2500)

HUGHTO, Darryl (1943-) American
$3000 £2083 Slippin' and slidin' (168x251cm-66x99in) s.i.d.1976verso acrylic. 26-Feb-93 Sotheby's Arcade, New York #396/R

HULDAH (20th C) American
$1200   £839   La femme au cafe (79x58cm-31x23in) s. s.d.195. i.verso. 14-Mar-93 Hindman Galleries, Chicago #122/R

HULDAH, Cherry Jeffe (20th C) American
$800   £556   Floral (41x51cm-16x20in) s. 6-Mar-93 Louisiana Auction Exchange #86/R

HULL, Richard (1955-) American
$1000   £671   For an ear (96x119cm-38x47in) s.i.d.11/79verso oil wax. 3-May-94 Christie's, East, New York #61/R
$13000   £8784   Post time (122x107cm-48x42in) s.i.d.3.81verso oil wax. 8-Nov-93 Christie's, East, New York #129/R

HULTBERG, John (1922-) American
$800   £548   Leaving the harbour (102x127cm-40x50in) i.verso. 10-Feb-94 Skinner, Bolton #33
$1600   £1111   Great empty sky (127x173cm-50x68in) s.i.d.1962verso. 26-Feb-93 Sotheby's Arcade, New York #342/R

HUMPHREY, Jack Weldon (1901-1967) Canadian
$1011   £683   Abstract - rose crevasse (122x97cm-48x38in) s. 30-Mar-94 Maynards, Vancouver #23 (C.D 1400)
$1715   £1128   The clay head (76x101cm-30x40in) s. s.i.verso oil over tempera masonite. 7-Jun-93 Ritchie, Toronto #150/R (C.D 2200)
$542   *£366*   *Tug boat in harbour (36x48cm-14x19in) s. W/C. 3-Nov-93 Sotheby's, Toronto #75/R (C.D 700)*
$934   *£619*   *Market slip and Kint Street, Saint John (36x49cm-14x19in) s.i.d.1930 W/C. 18-Nov-92 Sotheby's, Toronto #122 a (C.D 1200)*
$1012   *£670*   *Cargo boat in Indiantown. City Scene, Saint John (38x56cm-15x22in) s.d.1940 W/C double-sided. 18-Nov-92 Sotheby's, Toronto #78 (C.D 1300)*

HUMPHREY, Ralph (1932-1990) American
$1200   £833   Untitled (113x77cm-44x30in) s.d.85 acrylic. 22-Feb-93 Christie's, East, New York #237/R
$1700   £1141   Lexington (123x123cm-48x48in) i.verso acrylic painted c.1970. 24-Feb-94 Sotheby's Arcade, New York #380/R
$2000   £1342   Untitled (89x63cm-35x25in) s.d.60overlap. 3-May-94 Christie's, East, New York #26/R
$3000   £1765   Leo for Beth (153x153cm-60x60in) s.d.1971 stretcher acrylic. 6-Oct-92 Sotheby's, New York #122/R
$3800   £2550   Untitled (122x91cm-48x36in) s.d.60verso. 3-May-94 Christie's, East, New York #25/R
$1000   *£694*   *Untitled (76x56cm-30x22in) exec.1982 chl chk. 22-Feb-93 Christie's, East, New York #235/R*

HUMPHREYS, Malcolm (1894-?) American
$1800   £1208   Winter wood (63x77cm-25x30in) s. 6-May-94 Skinner, Bolton #93/R
$2000   £1342   Light on the sea (64x76cm-25x30in) s. i.verso. 6-May-94 Skinner, Bolton #109/R

HUMPHRIES, Jacqueline (1960-) American
$1200   £805   95 per cent (203x203cm-80x80in) s.i.d.1990verso linen. 3-May-94 Christie's, East, New York #186/R
$1600   £1111   Untitled (41x41cm-16x16in) s.d.1990verso linen. 22-Feb-93 Christie's, East, New York #243/R
$1700   £1181   Untitled (41x41cm-16x16in) painted 1990 s.verso linen. 22-Feb-93 Christie's, East, New York #242/R

HUNT, Bryan (1947-) American
$2500   £1736   The waterfall (75x57cm-30x22in) s. oil stick paper. 26-Feb-93 Sotheby's Arcade, New York #388/R
$1000   *£694*   *Untitled (76x56cm-30x22in) s.d.4-21-88 graphite linseed oil col.oilstick. 22-Feb-93 Christie's, East, New York #197/R*
$1000   *£671*   *Mojocar - Window Series 2 (19x19cm-7x7in) s.d.9-86 W/C oilstick dry pigment pencil linseed. 25-Feb-94 Sotheby's, New York #124/R*
$1500   *£882*   *Bridal veil (215x86cm-85x34in) graphite linseed oil. 6-Oct-92 Sotheby's, New York #155/R*

HUNT, Charles D (1840-1914) American
$700   £458   Twighlight, s. 30-Jun-94 Mystic Fine Arts, Connecticut #230
$750   £500   Cattle grazing by river, sunset (23x46cm-9x18in) s. canvasboard. 26-Aug-93 Skinner, Bolton #208
$1500   £974   Late summer landscape. Stage coach in winter, s. pair. 9-Sep-93 Sotheby's Arcade, New York #56/R

HUNT, Esther (1875-1951) American
$2750   £1821   China Town (129x61cm-51x24in) s. 15-Jun-94 Butterfield & Butterfield, San Francisco #4629/R

HUNT, Lynn Bogue (1878-1960) American
$1300   £861   Geese (66x46cm-26x18in) s. 23-Sep-93 Mystic Fine Arts, Connecticut #213
$2900   £1883   Two dogs and covey of quail. Dog with pheasant (28x20cm-11x8in) s. board pair. 11-Sep-93 Louisiana Auction Exchange #23/R
$875   *£621*   *Mallards (20x23cm-8x9in) s. W/C. 13-Feb-93 Collins, Maine #42/R*

HUNT, Thomas Lorraine (1882-1938) American
$2750 £1910 Boat in harbour (19x24cm-7x9in) s. paper. 7-Mar-93 Butterfield & Butterfield, San Francisco #183/R

HUNT, William Morris (1824-1879) American
$1300 £861 Moonrise over the Ocean (51x76cm-20x30in) mono. board. 28-Nov-92 Young Fine Arts Auctions, Maine #237/R
$1600 £1081 Tom in a felt hat (56x41cm-22x16in) init. 31-Mar-94 Sotheby's Arcade, New York #75/R
$2200 £1429 Portrait of gentleman (77x63cm-30x25in) init.d.55. 9-Sep-93 Sotheby's Arcade, New York #6/R
$4000 £2797 Out in the cold (31x37cm-12x15in) s.d.1864. 11-Mar-93 Christie's, New York #19/R
$11000 £7383 Scene at Fayal (30x22cm-12x9in) mono.d.1864 panel. 6-May-94 Skinner, Bolton #51/R
$900 £592 View of Ipswich, Massachusetts (25x41cm-10x16in) mono. chl. 31-Mar-93 Sotheby's Arcade, New York #142/R

HUNTER, Clementine (1883-1988) American
$850 £567 Ladies in Calico (41x51cm-16x20in) init.i.verso canvaboard. 26-Aug-93 Skinner, Bolton #107
$850 £570 Saturday night (41x61cm-16x24in) init. paper. 24-Jun-93 Mystic Fine Arts, Connecticut #147
$1500 £980 Down home (41x51cm-16x20in) mono. canvasboard. 17-Sep-93 Skinner, Bolton #289/R
$1500 £980 Cane River wedding (41x51cm-16x20in) mono. canvasboard. 17-Sep-93 Skinner, Bolton #290/R
$1800 £952 Nativity scene (43x64cm-17x25in) s. board. 12-Sep-92 Louisiana Auction Exchange #123/R
$2000 £1325 Picnic Scene (48x61cm-19x24in) mono. painted c.1980 board. 21-Nov-92 Litchfield Auction Gallery #18
$2100 £1391 Wash day at Melrose (41x61cm-16x24in) mono. painted c.1970. 21-Nov-92 Litchfield Auction Gallery #19
$2250 £1562 Saturday night at the Honky Tonk (41x61cm-16x24in) mono board. 6-Mar-93 Louisiana Auction Exchange #120/R
$2300 £1329 Baptism (41x51cm-16x20in) mono.init. canvasboard. 24-Sep-92 Sotheby's, New York #199/R
$2500 £1445 Still life with flowers (37x29cm-15x11in) mono.init. i.d.1940's verso paper. 24-Sep-92 Sotheby's, New York #200/R

HUNTER, Fred Leo (1858-1913) American
$700 £458 Ship at full sail (46x64cm-18x25in) s. 30-Jun-94 Mystic Fine Arts, Connecticut #77
$1000 £654 View from Battery Park (51x76cm-20x30in) s. 1-Nov-92 Litchfield Auction Gallery #370

HUNTER, Robert Douglas (1928-) American
$1600 £1074 Still life (97x66cm-38x26in) s. 5-Dec-93 James Bakker, Cambridge #76/R
$2500 £1748 Pewter, copper and shells (41x51cm-16x20in) s. 7-Feb-93 James Bakker, Cambridge #215/R

HUNTINGTON, Daniel (1816-1906) American
$4500 £3000 Portrait of lady (98x75cm-39x30in) s.d.1854 canvas on masonite. 16-Mar-94 Christie's, New York #20/R
$12000 £7692 On the Connecticut River at Dalton, New Hampshire (71x127cm-28x50in) s.d.1870. 9-Dec-92 Butterfield & Butterfield, San Francisco #3815/R

HUNTINGTON, Dwight W (19/20th C) American
$2000 £1342 Indian encampment (13x21cm-5x8in) gouache. 8-Dec-93 Butterfield & Butterfield, San Francisco #3538/R

HUOT, Charles Edouard (1855-1930) Canadian
$1100 £697 Le bateau de L'Ile d'Orleans (16x21cm-6x8in) s. board. 1-Dec-92 Fraser Pinneys, Quebec #138/R (C.D 1400)
$1651 £1045 Autoportrait (23x15cm-9x6in) painted c.1880 board. 1-Dec-92 Fraser Pinneys, Quebec #16/R (C.D 2100)
$786 £498 Paysan Russe (12x7cm-5x3in) s.i.d.1883 pencil board. 1-Dec-92 Fraser Pinneys, Quebec #11 (C.D 1000)

HURD, Peter (1904-1984) American
$1900 £1218 Sketch at Bitter Lake (41x51cm-16x20in) s. s.i.d.1928verso. 9-Dec-92 Butterfield & Butterfield, San Francisco #3969/R
$5500 £3691 The young jockey (96x69cm-38x27in) s.d.1941. 8-Dec-93 Butterfield & Butterfield, San Francisco #3552/R
$1500 £987 Heavy weather (48x74cm-19x29in) s. W/C. 31-Mar-93 Sotheby's Arcade, New York #415/R
$5000 £3378 Landscape (36x52cm-14x20in) s. W/C. 31-Mar-94 Sotheby's Arcade, New York #413/R

HURLEY, Robert Newton (1894-1980) Canadian
$472 £319 Untitled - Prairie dawn (25x32cm-10x13in) s.d.1950 W/C paper board. 25-Apr-94 Levis, Calgary #123/R (C.D 650)

HURLEY, Wilson (1924-) American
$27500 £18456 Twilights last gleaming (102x152cm-40x60in) s. 2-Dec-93 Sotheby's, New York #91/R
$60000 £40268 West from Cedar Ridge, Grand Canyon (127x203cm-50x80in) s. painted c.1980-81. 2-Dec-93 Sotheby's, New York #90/R

HUSTON, William (19th C) American
$3250 £2044 Sailboats off the coast (51x94cm-20x37in) s.d.1874. 22-Apr-93 Freeman Fine Arts, Philadelphia #1159/R

HUTCHENS, Frank Townsend (1869-1937) American
$700 £467 Woman playing piano (20x13cm-8x5in) s. 15-Mar-94 John Moran, Pasadena #169
$750 £503 On the Seine (30x41cm-12x16in) s. 24-Mar-94 Mystic Fine Arts, Connecticut #106/R
$1000 £671 Morning in early spring (68x61cm-27x24in) s. 13-Jan-94 Christie's, East, New York #269

HUTCHISON, Frederick William (1871-1953) Canadian
$702 £462 Les Eboulments (30x41cm-12x16in) s. s.i.d.1926verso. 7-Jun-93 Waddingtons, Toronto #1134 (C.D 900)
$935 £615 Village street, St. Urbain, P.Q. (20x25cm-8x10in) s. s.i.verso board. 7-Jun-93 Waddingtons, Toronto #111 (C.D 1200)
$1245 £825 Landscape with trees (37x50cm-15x20in) s. 24-Nov-92 Joyner Fine Art, Toronto #213 (C.D 1600)
$1481 £974 Working the field (41x51cm-16x20in) s. 7-Jun-93 Waddingtons, Toronto #1146/R (C.D 1900)
$2572 £1692 Village street (30x41cm-12x16in) s. s.i.verso. 7-Jun-93 Waddingtons, Toronto #1119 (C.D 3300)

HUTTY, Alfred (1877-1954) American
$2900 £1933 Spring reveille (64x76cm-25x30in) s.d.1919. 22-May-94 James Bakker, Cambridge #113/R
$700 *£458* *Cypress trees (46x53cm-18x21in) s. W/C board. 18-Sep-93 James Bakker, Cambridge #40/R*
$4900 *£3245* *South Carolina Street scene (38x53cm-15x21in) s. W/C. 21-Nov-92 James Bakker, Cambridge #52*

HYATT, Anna V see HUNTINGTON, Anna Hyatt

HYPPOLITE, Hector (1894-1948) Haitian
$893 £595 Landscape with fruit trees in bloom (24x18cm-9x7in) s. canvasboard. 15-Mar-94 Weiner, Munich #328/R (DM 1500)
$42000 £28000 Portrait of Jean Jacques Dessalines (76x61cm-30x24in) s.i. board painted c.1945-47. 18-May-94 Christie's, New York #222/R

IACCARINO, Ralph (20th C) American
$650 *£425* *Clearing in Tambor (112x170cm-44x67in) s. W/C. 16-May-93 Hindman Galleries, Chicago #40/R*
$1300 *£872* *Clearing in Tanbor (112x170cm-44x67in) s.d.82 W/C. 24-Jun-93 Boos Gallery, Michigan #458*

IANELLI, Arcangelo (1922-) Brazilian
$4000 £2703 Composicao em dois tons, marrom (180x129cm-71x51in) s.d.1976. 22-Nov-93 Sotheby's, New York #235/R
$5000 £3311 Untitled (129x100cm-51x39in) s.d.1980. 24-Nov-92 Christie's, New York #263/R
$7118 £4810 Dialogo (180x130cm-71x51in) s.d.1976 tempera. 27-Apr-94 Louis Morton, Mexico #518/R (M.P 24000)

IBARRA, Jose de (attrib) (1688-1756) Mexican
$15000 £10000 El Jardin del Eden (46x58cm-18x23in) copper painted c.1720-1756 oval. 17-May-94 Sotheby's, New York #1/R

ICAZA, Ernesto (1866-1935) Mexican
$20000 £13072 Soldado herido (31x48cm-12x19in) s.d.1918. 17-May-93 Christie's, New York #94/R
$23878 £15306 Jaripeo (39x43cm-15x17in) 29-Apr-93 Louis Morton, Mexico #103 (M.P 75000)
$24718 £16701 Corrida charra (38x57cm-15x22in) 9-Nov-93 Louis Morton, Mexico #84/R (M.P 80000)
$24718 £16701 Herradero (38x57cm-15x22in) 9-Nov-93 Louis Morton, Mexico #101/R (M.P 80000)
$30000 £19608 Toreando un Toro Embolado (60x96cm-24x38in) s.d.1921. 18-May-93 Sotheby's, New York #19/R
$33987 £22965 Lazando al potro (38x57cm-15x22in) 9-Nov-93 Louis Morton, Mexico #66/R (M.P 110000)
$35000 £23179 El Arreo (40x58cm-16x23in) s.d.1910 canvas on masonite. 24-Nov-92 Christie's, New York #127/R
$49000 £32667 Cortame al Toro Pinto (31x47cm-12x19in) s.d.1912 board. 18-May-94 Christie's, New York #8/R
$55000 £36424 Cola en Campo Abierto (73x100cm-29x39in) s.d.1913. 23-Nov-92 Sotheby's, New York #33/R
$55000 £36424 Manganeando a Cuesta de Corral (74x100cm-29x39in) s.d.1913. 23-Nov-92 Sotheby's, New York #34/R

ICAZA, Francisco (20th C) Mexican
$445 *£301* *Pareja (49x34cm-19x13in) s. W/C ink. 27-Apr-94 Louis Morton, Mexico #569 (M.P 1500)*

IGNATIEFF, Alex (1913-) American
$550 *£364* *Victorian house with teeth, Bunker Hill, LA (53x66cm-21x26in) s. W/C. 28-Sep-93 John Moran, Pasadena #391*

IGNATIEFF, Alex (1913-) American-cont.
$600	£397	My old Chevy, Bunker Hill (51x61cm-20x24in) s. W/C. 28-Sep-93 John Moran, Pasadena #328
$1500	£1014	Commercial fishermen, San Pedro harbour (51x71cm-20x28in) s. W/C gouache. 15-Jun-93 John Moran, Pasadena #111

IMHOF, Joseph A (1871-1955) American
$2000	£1282	Mother with baby in cradle (112x85cm-44x33in) s. canvas on board. 9-Dec-92 Butterfield & Butterfield, San Francisco #3983/R
$2000	£1282	Abiqui (82x65cm-32x26in) s. canvas on board. 9-Dec-92 Butterfield & Butterfield, San Francisco #4005/R
$4750	£3085	The potters (76x91cm-30x36in) s. 9-Sep-93 Sotheby's Arcade, New York #233/R
$14000	£9333	Native American potters (76x91cm-30x36in) s. 17-May-94 Grogan, Massachussetts #343/R
$50000	£31646	The Camoufleurs (78x119cm-31x47in) s. canvas laid down on board. 4-Dec-92 Christie's, New York #271/R
$800	£526	Portrait of Indian (55x47cm-22x19in) s. W/C paper on board. 31-Mar-93 Sotheby's Arcade, New York #211/R
$1700	£1141	Medicine man (56x46cm-22x18in) s. mixed media. 5-Mar-94 Louisiana Auction Exchange #16/R

IMPERIALE, Francisco Jose Osvaldo (1913-1977) Argentinian
$800	£541	Puente Pueyrredon, Avallaneda (90x100cm-35x39in) s. 20-Oct-93 Castells & Castells, Montevideo #6

INDIANA, Robert (1928-) American
$13000	£8609	Grass (25x20cm-10x8in) st.s.d.62 verso. 18-Nov-92 Sotheby's, New York #149 a/R
$18000	£12081	Yield brother (61x61cm-24x24in) s.i.d.1964verso. 4-May-94 Christie's, New York #180/R
$38000	£25503	American Love (30x63cm-12x25in) s. init.d.1968 verso two canvases. 23-Feb-94 Christie's, New York #49/R
$250000	£168919	The black diamond American dream No 2 (216x216cm-85x85in) stencilled oil. 10-Nov-93 Sotheby's, New York #16/R
$2916	£1918	The great American dream, San Francisco (102x66cm-40x26in) s.i.d.27 septembre 1969 dr. 11-Jun-93 Poulain & le Fur, Paris #144/R (F.FR 16000)

INFANTE, Gaston (20th C) Brazilian
$5624	£3800	At dressing table (90x117cm-35x46in) s.d.12. 18-Jun-93 Christie's, London #98 a/R

INGERLE, Rudolph (1879-1950) American
$750	£490	Moonlight Sonata (51x61cm-20x24in) s.d.1950 board. 19-Sep-93 Hindman Galleries, Chicago #669
$1600	£1046	New day (64x76cm-25x30in) s. 19-Sep-93 Hindman Galleries, Chicago #670
$1700	£1126	Harvest moon (51x61cm-20x24in) s. canvasboard. 19-Jun-94 Hindman Galleries, Chicago #702/R
$3000	£1961	Smokey Mountains in fall, rushing rapids (41x51cm-16x20in) s. 15-May-93 Dunning's, Illinois #1086/R

INGHAM, Charles Cromwell (1796-1863) British/American
$3500	£2349	Young girl of the Russell Family (53x43cm-21x17in) 3-Feb-94 Sloan, North Bethesda #2890/R

INGLE, John S (1933-) American
$39000	£24684	Still life with watermelon and palm (152x101cm-60x40in) W/C. 3-Dec-92 Sotheby's, New York #82/R

INMAN, George (1825-1894) American
$850	£500	City coastline (20x30cm-8x12in) s. board. 4-Oct-92 Butterfield & Butterfield, Los Angeles #155/R

INMAN, Henry (1801-1846) American
$4250	£2760	Portraits of Samuel Brown and Maria Crosby Brown, seated, views beyond (84x71cm-33x28in) i.verso pair painted c.1839. 16-Jan-93 Skinner, Bolton #367/R

INNERST, Mark (1957-) American
$8000	£5229	Alpine view (37x32cm-15x13in) acrylic board executed 1986. 22-Dec-92 Christie's, East, New York #27
$20000	£13423	The reservoir (25x52cm-10x20in) oil acrylic board painted 1987. 5-May-94 Sotheby's, New York #296 a/R
$7000	£4676	View of Brooklyn (16x22cm-6x9in) s. s.d.1985verso gouache acrylic. 19-Nov-92 Christie's, New York #145/R

INNES, John (1863-1941) Canadian
$706	£462	Untitled - covered wagon (30x46cm-12x18in) s. 10-May-93 Hodgins, Calgary #279 (C.D 900)
$1007	£681	Indian and sunset (86x61cm-34x24in) s. 1-Nov-93 Levis, Calgary #110 (C.D 1300)
$3580	£2371	Westcoast indians (51x41cm-20x16in) s. board. 16-Nov-92 Hodgins, Calgary #291/R (C.D 4600)
$12379	£8252	Riding herd (64x133cm-25x52in) s.d.1903. 11-May-94 Sotheby's, Toronto #87/R (C.D 17000)
$14563	£9709	How No Name made him a name (102x76cm-40x30in) s.d.1904. 11-May-94 Sotheby's, Toronto #162/R (C.D 20000)
$17476	£11650	In the days that were, Red Indians hunting on horseback (112x206cm-44x81in) s.d.1903. 11-May-94 Sotheby's, Toronto #88/R (C.D 24000)

INNESS, George (1825-1894) American
$1900	£1275	Mountain landscape (23x36cm-9x14in) s. board painted late 1870's. 6-Dec-93 Grogan, Massachussetts #495/R
$2400	£1589	Albano Italy (25x36cm-10x14in) s. 3-Oct-93 Hanzel Galleries, Chicago #34
$3508	£2308	Golden sunset (50x74cm-20x29in) s.d.1892. 7-Jun-93 Waddingtons, Toronto #1312/R (C.D 4500)
$4500	£2601	Impressionistic landscape (43x64cm-17x25in) 25-Sep-92 Douglas, South Deerfield #3
$5000	£3268	Albano, Italy (25x36cm-10x14in) s. 16-May-93 Hanzel Galleries, Chicago #28/R
$9500	£6333	Sunset through the trees (46x61cm-18x24in) s. i.verso panel. 26-May-94 Christie's, New York #32/R
$10000	£6711	Spring storm (41x51cm-16x20in) 4-May-94 Doyle, New York #15/R
$10000	£6667	Sundown near Montclair (56x71cm-22x28in) s.d.1885. 26-May-94 Christie's, New York #33/R
$16000	£10884	Landscape (56x69cm-22x27in) s. 17-Nov-93 Doyle, New York #18/R
$19000	£12025	Visionary landscape (39x66cm-15x26in) s. 3-Dec-92 Sotheby's, New York #47/R
$25000	£17007	Phantom sea (38x51cm-15x20in) mono.i.d.Sept.1856verso. 17-Nov-93 Doyle, New York #16/R
$26000	£17450	Hazy summer afternoon (38x66cm-15x26in) s. 3-Dec-93 Christie's, New York #86/R
$32000	£20513	Campagna,from North (50x76cm-20x30in) s.d.1874. 26-May-93 Christie's, New York #41/R
$35000	£22152	Sunset, golden glow (113x101cm-44x40in) s.d.1893. 3-Dec-92 Sotheby's, New York #41/R
$55000	£35256	George Inness's home, Tarpon Springs, Florida (61x91cm-24x36in) s. painted c.1893. 27-May-93 Sotheby's, New York #210/R
$65000	£41667	Winter evening, Montclair (25x41cm-10x16in) s. painted c.1860. 27-May-93 Sotheby's, New York #175/R
$65000	£41139	Sunset, Etretat (76x114cm-30x45in) s.d.1892. 3-Dec-92 Sotheby's, New York #43/R
$72500	£46474	Shepherd in landscape (30x46cm-12x18in) s. panel painted c.1875. 27-May-93 Sotheby's, New York #154/R
$165000	£105769	Evening (122x199cm-48x78in) s.d.1868. 27-May-93 Sotheby's, New York #208/R

INNESS, George (attrib) (1825-1894) American
$2300	£1554	Storm clouds over the Highlands (24x30cm-9x12in) s. canvasboard. 5-Nov-93 Skinner, Bolton #50/R
$3000	£1987	Afterglow a landscape at sunset (36x58cm-14x23in) s. 27-Sep-93 Selkirks, St. Louis #285/R

INNESS, George (circle) (1825-1894) American
$4500	£2961	Edge of forest, Albano, Italy (104x137cm-41x54in) s.d.1876. 13-Jun-93 Butterfield & Butterfield, San Francisco #3109/R

INNESS, George (jnr) (1853-1926) American
$1700	£1156	Holstein heifer (35x50cm-14x20in) s.d.1875. 15-Nov-93 Christie's, East, New York #79/R
$2250	£1490	Landscape with sheep (41x61cm-16x24in) s. canvas on canvas. 28-Sep-93 John Moran, Pasadena #261
$2250	£1442	Walk in the country (23x20cm-9x8in) s. board. 9-Dec-92 Butterfield & Butterfield, San Francisco #3820/R
$2600	£1646	Marsh scene (31x46cm-12x18in) s. 2-Dec-92 Christie's, East, New York #78/R
$2970	£1941	Walk at sunset (51x61cm-20x24in) s. 14-May-93 Skinner, Bolton #34/R
$3500	£2333	Over the wall (41x61cm-16x24in) s. 3-Jun-94 Sotheby's, New York #208/R
$3750	£2517	Out to pasture (51x71cm-20x28in) s. 6-May-94 Skinner, Bolton #52/R

INNESS, George (style) (1825-1894) American
$900	£588	Early autumn, Montclair (41x51cm-16x20in) bears sig. 16-May-93 Hindman Galleries, Chicago #64/R
$1300	£833	River landscape with lady on road (46x61cm-18x24in) bears sig. 13-Dec-92 Hindman Galleries, Chicago #38/R

INSLEY, Albert (1842-1937) American
$700	£473	Porcupine Island off Bar Harbour (30x46cm-12x18in) s. 27-Nov-93 Young Fine Arts Auctions, Maine #175/R
$700	£473	Summer landscape (30x48cm-12x19in) s. 27-Nov-93 Young Fine Arts Auctions, Maine #176/R
$800	£513	Summer landscape (36x51cm-14x20in) s. 28-May-93 Sloan, North Bethesda #2396/R
$850	£450	Grainstacks (36x51cm-14x20in) s. 11-Sep-92 Skinner, Bolton #209/R
$900	£608	North of Tarrytown Valley New York (30x46cm-12x18in) s.d.1926 board. 10-Nov-93 Doyle, New York #59
$900	£608	East Hampton Long Island New York (36x43cm-14x17in) s. i.verso. 10-Nov-93 Doyle, New York #60
$900	£588	On the Passaic River (30x48cm-12x19in) s. i.stretcher. 15-Sep-93 Doyle, New York #35
$950	£621	Blauvelt's residence (30x48cm-12x19in) s. 15-Sep-93 Doyle, New York #34
$2000	£1282	Afternoon boating (51x81cm-20x32in) s. 9-Dec-92 Grogan, Massachussetts #57/R
$2000	£1325	Autumn landscape (64x76cm-25x30in) s. canvas on canvas. 28-Sep-93 John Moran, Pasadena #349
$2400	£1622	Hunter and dog in landscape (74x125cm-29x49in) s. 31-Mar-94 Sotheby's Arcade, New York #24/R

INUKAI, Kyohei (20th C) American
$2000	£1361	Still life with Oriental figurine and necklace on draped table (68x53cm-27x21in) s.d.36. 15-Nov-93 Christie's, East, New York #158/R

IPSEN, Ernest Ludwig (1869-1951) American
$1500	£1020	South Dartmouth landscape (26x35cm-10x14in) init.d.1907 board. 15-Nov-93 Christie's, East, New York #118/R
$1800	£1259	Still life with teapot (35x51cm-14x20in) s.d.92. 11-Mar-93 Christie's, New York #166/R

IRVINE, Wilson (1869-1936) American
$2000	£1307	New England landscape (30x41cm-12x16in) s. 16-May-93 Hindman Galleries, Chicago #96/R
$3000	£2000	Live oak with Spanish moss (61x76cm-24x30in) s. painted late 1920's or early 1930's. 23-May-94 Hindman Galleries, Chicago #179/R
$4000	£2649	Tinkers Lane, Old Lyme (61x69cm-24x27in) s. 23-Sep-93 Mystic Fine Arts, Connecticut #180/R
$4400	£2876	Spring waves, Monhegan Island (61x69cm-24x27in) s. 16-May-93 Hindman Galleries, Chicago #95/R
$5000	£3378	Landscape with pond (61x69cm-24x27in) s. 31-Oct-93 Hindman Galleries, Chicago #678/R
$5000	£3311	Autumn landscape (71x76cm-28x30in) s. 23-Sep-93 Mystic Fine Arts, Connecticut #48 a/R
$5500	£3642	Morning fog lifting (61x69cm-24x27in) s.d.09. 28-Nov-92 Dunning's, Illinois #1098
$7500	£5034	Blue nets at Concarneau (71x79cm-28x31in) s. 29-Nov-93 Stonington Fine Arts, Stonington #175/R
$7800	£5200	Evening at the pool (91x74cm-36x29in) s. i.stretcher. 23-May-94 Hindman Galleries, Chicago #178/R
$9500	£6291	Morning in harbour (61x69cm-24x27in) s. with i.verso. 13-Nov-92 Skinner, Bolton #161/R
$11000	£6358	Snow bound brook (74x91cm-29x36in) s. 23-Sep-92 Christie's, New York #152/R
$17000	£11888	Gloucester harbour (62x68cm-24x27in) 11-Mar-93 Christie's, New York #168/R

IRWIN, Robert (1928-) American
$55000	£37162	Untitled (135cm-53in circular) acrylic lacquer on formed plastic exec.c.1968. 10-Nov-93 Sotheby's, New York #53/R
$200000	£135135	Untitled (210x215cm-83x85in) canvas on shaped wood veneer painted c.1964-66. 10-Nov-93 Sotheby's, New York #22/R

ISENBURGER, Eric (1902-) American/German
$1400	£915	Anemonies (51x41cm-20x16in) s. 30-Jun-94 Mystic Fine Arts, Connecticut #275/R
$2363	£1545	Portrait of seated woman (70x50cm-28x20in) s.d.32. 8-May-93 Michael Bode, Pforzheim #134/R (DM 3800)

ISKOWITZ, Gershon (1921-1988) Canadian
$3495	£2330	Spring passage (98x79cm-39x31in) s.d.65. 13-May-94 Joyner Fine Art, Toronto #162/R (C.D 4800)
$4756	£3109	Red - C (96x84cm-38x33in) painted 1979. 18-May-93 Joyner Fine Art, Toronto #56/R (C.D 6000)
$7394	£4897	Deep lilac no.2 (107x96cm-42x38in) s.i.d.1977verso. 18-Nov-92 Sotheby's, Toronto #216/R (C.D 9500)
$13835	£9223	Landscape in red (150x120cm-59x47in) 13-May-94 Joyner Fine Art, Toronto #108/R (C.D 19000)
$947	£631	*Head (48x31cm-19x12in) s.d.63 W/C. 13-May-94 Joyner Fine Art, Toronto #195 (C.D 1300)*

ISLAS, Andreas de (18th C) Mexican
$11000	£7432	Sagrada Trinidad (42x32cm-17x13in) s.d.1770 copper. 22-Nov-93 Sotheby's, New York #141/R

ITURRIA, Ignacio de (1949-) Uruguayan
$2400	£1206	Mujer de Cadaques (71x58cm-28x23in) s.d.1981. 31-Aug-92 Gomensoro, Montevideo #60/R
$3100	£1987	Vista de Cadaques (73x60cm-29x24in) s.d.79. 7-Dec-92 Gomensoro, Montevideo #36
$4200	£2800	Moteles de Saratoga (48x100cm-19x39in) s.i. oil corrugated cardboard painted 1991. 18-May-94 Christie's, New York #261/R
$9000	£5960	Rosario oriental (117x127cm-46x50in) s.d.1987 board. 28-Jun-93 Gomensoro, Montevideo #52/R
$9000	£6000	Metegol I (99x81cm-39x32in) painted 1991. 18-May-94 Sotheby's, New York #390/R
$9500	£6291	Cadaques (60x73cm-24x29in) s. 23-Nov-92 Sotheby's, New York #204/R
$10000	£6667	Sin titulo (81x100cm-32x39in) s.d.90. 18-May-94 Sotheby's, New York #262/R
$11000	£7190	Interior (116x89cm-46x35in) s.d.81. 17-May-93 Christie's, New York #174/R
$11000	£7285	Otro Gol (100x120cm-39x47in) s. painted 1989. 24-Nov-92 Christie's, New York #258/R
$12000	£7947	Cutlery (170x195cm-67x77in) s. painted 1990. 24-Nov-92 Christie's, New York #158/R
$14000	£9459	Sin titulo (92x73cm-36x29in) s.d.1990. 23-Nov-93 Christie's, New York #176/R
$28000	£18919	Estructuras (149x190cm-59x75in) s.d.88. 23-Nov-93 Christie's, New York #177/R
$32000	£21233	Compartimiento con elefante (182x227cm-72x89in) s.d.93. 18-May-94 Christie's, New York #117/R
$35000	£22760	El Reloj (194x129cm-76x51in) s.d.88 oil wire staples. 17-May-93 Christie's, New York #163/R

IVES, H S (20th C) American?
$800	*£513*	*Ship Sarah M entering Penobscot Bay (53x38cm-21x15in) s. ink linen. 13-Dec-92 Litchfield Auction Gallery #16*

IVES, Percy (1864-1928) American
$1350	£912	Two elderly gentlemen in conversation (56x69cm-22x27in) s.d.1885. 1-Aug-93 Hart Gallery, Houston #2
$8000	£5369	Girl seated with oranges (81x64cm-32x25in) s.d. 16-Jul-93 Du Mouchelle, Detroit #2012

IZQUIERDO, Maria (1906-1950) Mexican
$60000	£40000	Tony y Teresita en su numero (47x57cm-19x22in) s.d.45 masonite. 17-May-94 Sotheby's, New York #72/R
$75000	£49669	Malabarista (53x43cm-21x17in) s.d.45. 23-Nov-92 Sotheby's, New York #58/R
$75000	£49669	Los Peregrinos (60x75cm-24x30in) s.d.45 s.i.d.verso. 24-Nov-92 Christie's, New York #7/R
$125000	£81699	Autorretrato (91x65cm-36x26in) s.d.VII,40 masonite. 18-May-93 Sotheby's, New York #53/R
$15000	*£10135*	*Esclavas en paisaje mitico (21x27cm-8x11in) s.d.36 W/C rice paper on board. 22-Nov-93 Sotheby's, New York #48/R*

IZZARD, Daniel J (20th C) Canadian
$792	£514	Thieves Bay, Pender harbour, British Caledonia (30x36cm-12x14in) s.d.1989verso panel. 22-Jun-94 Maynards, Vancouver #699 (C.D 1100)
$1336	£902	Early spring morning, Horsehoe Bay (46x61cm-18x24in) s. board. 30-Mar-94 Maynards, Vancouver #2 (C.D 1850)

JACK, R (1866-1952) Canadian/British
$1683	£1100	Young woman reading book in interior (112x86cm-44x34in) s.d.1916. 29-Oct-92 Christie's, S. Kensington #298

JACK, Richard (1866-1952) Canadian/British
$583	£388	Moon over a snowy landscape (41x51cm-16x20in) s. board. 11-May-94 Sotheby's, Toronto #112/R (C.D 800)
$659	£445	Home in winter landscape (41x51cm-16x20in) s. board. 3-Nov-93 Sotheby's, Toronto #354/R (C.D 850)
$715	£480	Conchita Supervia as Carmen (127x102cm-50x40in) s.d.1935. 24-Jun-93 Christie's, Glasgow #575
$1490	£1000	Old Covent Garden market (86x112cm-34x44in) s. canvas on board. 5-May-94 Sotheby's Colonnade, London #503/R

JACKMAN, Reva (1892-1966) American
$800	£541	Summer hills (53x64cm-21x25in) s. 15-Jun-93 John Moran, Pasadena #128

JACKSON, Alexander Young (1882-1974) Canadian
$2695	£1762	At Pilot Harbour, Lake Superior (27x34cm-11x13in) s. panel. 18-May-93 Joyner Fine Art, Toronto #186/R (C.D 3400)
$2822	£1894	Lake on the Kaladar Renfrew Highway (26x33cm-10x13in) s. s.i.d.Oct.1954verso panel. 29-Nov-93 Ritchie, Toronto #221/R (C.D 3750)
$2906	£1963	Mount Rundle at Canmore (27x34cm-11x13in) s. i.verso panel. 3-Nov-93 Sotheby's, Toronto #330/R (C.D 3750)
$3012	£1969	Lake at Clontarf, Ontario (27x34cm-11x13in) s. panel. 18-May-93 Joyner Fine Art, Toronto #174/R (C.D 3800)
$3020	£2041	Gale Mountain, Quebec (17x22cm-7x9in) s. panel. 23-Nov-93 Joyner Fine Art, Toronto #208/R (C.D 4000)
$3171	£2073	Shoreline, Georgian Bay (27x34cm-11x13in) panel. 18-May-93 Joyner Fine Art, Toronto #106/R (C.D 4000)
$3269	£2165	Razor Mountain from South Yellowhead, B.C., 1914 (21x26cm-8x10in) s. panel. 24-Nov-92 Joyner Fine Art, Toronto #221/R (C.D 4200)
$3293	£2225	Range River , s. s.i.d.March 1967verso panel. 3-Nov-93 Sotheby's, Toronto #327/R (C.D 4250)
$3369	£2202	Gargantua Beach, Lake Superior (27x34cm-11x13in) s. s.d.1957 verso panel. 19-May-93 Sotheby's, Toronto #141/R (C.D 4250)
$3409	£2304	Quebec farm (25x34cm-10x13in) s. s.i.d.April 1961verso panel. 3-Nov-93 Sotheby's, Toronto #358/R (C.D 4400)
$3503	£2320	Hills at St Hilarion, Quebec (22x27cm-9x11in) s.i.d.1928verso panel. 18-Nov-92 Sotheby's, Toronto #16/R (C.D 4500)
$3528	£2261	Wind blown pine (27x34cm-11x13in) s. board. 7-Dec-92 Waddingtons, Toronto #1328 (C.D 4500)
$3892	£2577	Street in Coleman, Alberta mining town, 1950 (26x34cm-10x13in) s. panel. 24-Nov-92 Joyner Fine Art, Toronto #102/R (C.D 5000)
$3892	£2577	The yellow house (22x27cm-9x11in) s. i.verso board. 18-Nov-92 Sotheby's, Toronto #33/R (C.D 5000)
$4005	£2670	Depleted iron mine, Knob Lake, Labrador (26x33cm-10x13in) s. panel. 13-May-94 Joyner Fine Art, Toronto #71/R (C.D 5500)
$4078	£2718	Lake above Bear River (26x33cm-10x13in) s. panel. 13-May-94 Joyner Fine Art, Toronto #125/R (C.D 5600)
$4262	£2880	View from Eldorado Mine Great Bear Lake (26x34cm-10x13in) s. i.verso panel. 3-Nov-93 Sotheby's, Toronto #240/R (C.D 5500)
$4360	£2850	Georgian Bay (27x34cm-11x13in) s. panel. 18-May-93 Joyner Fine Art, Toronto #50/R (C.D 5500)
$4360	£2850	Light and snow (22x27cm-9x11in) s. panel. 19-May-93 Sotheby's, Toronto #382/R (C.D 5500)
$4682	£3163	In front of the gates (18x23cm-7x9in) s. board. 23-Nov-93 Fraser Pinneys, Quebec #374/R (C.D 6200)

JACKSON, Alexander Young (1882-1974) Canadian-cont.

$4756	£3109	Eastman, Quebec (27x34cm-11x13in) s. d.1958 verso panel. 19-May-93 Sotheby's, Toronto #253/R (C.D 6000)
$5078	£3431	Autumn Algoma (27x34cm-11x13in) s. panel painted c.1937. 25-Apr-94 Levis, Calgary #133/R (C.D 7000)
$5097	£3398	River in winter (27x34cm-11x13in) s. panel. 11-May-94 Sotheby's, Toronto #122/R (C.D 7000)
$5097	£3398	Islands at Hurontario boy's camp (26x33cm-10x13in) s. panel. 13-May-94 Joyner Fine Art, Toronto #21/R (C.D 7000)
$5097	£3398	Sugar shanty near Brownsburg, Quebec (27x34cm-11x13in) s. s.i.d.May 1964verso panel. 11-May-94 Sotheby's, Toronto #226/R (C.D 7000)
$5153	£3368	Silver Mine, Contact Lake, North West Territories (26x34cm-10x13in) s. s.d.1938 verso panel. 19-May-93 Sotheby's, Toronto #125/R (C.D 6500)
$5243	£3495	Muskoka barns (26x33cm-10x13in) s, panel double-sided. 13-May-94 Joyner Fine Art, Toronto #112/R (C.D 7200)
$5277	£3590	Les Eboulements in summer (27x34cm-11x13in) s. s.i.verso panel painted c.1945. 15-Nov-93 Hodgins, Calgary #248/R (C.D 7000)
$5286	£3571	Winter near Tadoussac (21x27cm-8x11in) s. board painted c.1932 double-sided. 23-Nov-93 Fraser Pinneys, Quebec #386/R (C.D 7000)
$5351	£3497	St. Sauveur (22x27cm-9x11in) s. i.d.1930 verso panel. 19-May-93 Sotheby's, Toronto #124/R (C.D 6750)
$5461	£3641	Indian Head, Lake Superior (26x33cm-10x13in) s. panel. 13-May-94 Joyner Fine Art, Toronto #105/R (C.D 7500)
$5549	£3627	Summer, Georgian Bay (21x27cm-8x11in) s. panel. 19-May-93 Sotheby's, Toronto #136/R (C.D 7000)
$6041	£4082	St. Arsene, village in Quebec, April, 1935 (21x26cm-8x10in) s. panel. 23-Nov-93 Joyner Fine Art, Toronto #14/R (C.D 8000)
$6137	£4146	Indian house, Port Simpson, B.C., 1926 (25x20cm-10x8in) board. 30-Mar-94 Maynards, Vancouver #53/R (C.D 8500)
$6236	£4103	St. Pierre Montmagny (21x27cm-8x11in) s. s.i.d.1942verso panel. 7-Jun-93 Ritchie, Toronto #189/R (C.D 8000)
$6818	£4545	Moose Lake, Mile 25, B.C (22x27cm-9x11in) s.d. s.i.verso board. 30-May-94 Hodgins, Calgary #49/R (C.D 9500)
$7405	£4872	Drizzly day St. Joachim Quebec (21x26cm-8x11in) s. s.i.d.1932verso panel. 7-Jun-93 Ritchie, Toronto #156/R (C.D 9500)
$7927	£5181	Diamond Lake (63x81cm-25x32in) init. d.1964 verso. 19-May-93 Sotheby's, Toronto #379/R (C.D 10000)
$8738	£5825	Lake Superior (21x26cm-8x10in) s. panel. 13-May-94 Joyner Fine Art, Toronto #6/R (C.D 12000)
$9816	£6633	Quebec from Levis (21x26cm-8x10in) s. panel. 23-Nov-93 Joyner Fine Art, Toronto #115/R (C.D 13000)
$10897	£7216	Quebec farm (21x26cm-8x10in) s. panel. 24-Nov-92 Joyner Fine Art, Toronto #21/R (C.D 14000)
$12379	£8252	Early spring, Laurentians (21x26cm-8x10in) s. panel. 13-May-94 Joyner Fine Art, Toronto #43/R (C.D 17000)
$14347	£9694	Farm on the road to Mont Laurier (65x80cm-26x31in) s. 23-Nov-93 Joyner Fine Art, Toronto #51/R (C.D 19000)
$20237	£13402	Islands - Georgian Bay (41x51cm-16x20in) s. i.verso. 18-Nov-92 Sotheby's, Toronto #71/R (C.D 26000)
$40049	£26699	St Irenee (50x65cm-20x26in) s. 13-May-94 Joyner Fine Art, Toronto #89/R (C.D 55000)
$65381	£43299	Winter, St. Hilaire, Quebec (52x65cm-20x26in) s. 24-Nov-92 Joyner Fine Art, Toronto #33/R (C.D 84000)
$71347	£46632	Smoke Fantasy (81x102cm-32x40in) s. i.d.1932 verso. 19-May-93 Sotheby's, Toronto #174/R (C.D 90000)
$145631	£97087	Winter, Georgian Bay (90x125cm-35x49in) s. 13-May-94 Joyner Fine Art, Toronto #57/R (C.D 200000)
$5549	*£3627*	*March in the birch woods (76x102cm-30x40in) i.verso gouache study. 18-May-93 Joyner Fine Art, Toronto #246/R (C.D 7000)*

JACKSON, Alexander Young (attrib) (1882-1974) Canadian

$1572	£995	Dock (22x27cm-9x11in) s. s.num.25 verso panel. 30-Nov-92 Ritchie, Toronto #197/R (C.D 2000)

JACKSON, Everett Gee (1900-) American

$11000	£7285	Tehuantepec women (81x81cm-32x32in) s.d.1927. 28-Sep-93 John Moran, Pasadena #355

JACKSON, Oliver (1935-) American

$2500	*£1582*	*Untitled (122x108cm-48x43in) s.d.6-14-84 acrylic W/C. 25-Oct-92 Butterfield & Butterfield, San Francisco #2345/R*

JACKSON, Ronald (?) Canadian?

$505	£341	Port Neville (30x41cm-12x16in) board. 30-Mar-94 Maynards, Vancouver #41 (C.D 700)
$687	£449	Shelter Bay, Queen Charlotte Islands (46x61cm-18x24in) s. board. 12-May-93 Maynards, Vancouver #194 (C.D 875)
$864	£561	Salmon boats (46x61cm-18x24in) board. 22-Jun-94 Maynards, Vancouver #691 (C.D 1200)

JACKSON, William Franklin (1850-1936) American

$1900	£1319	High Sierra (20x27cm-8x11in) s. canvas on board. 7-Mar-93 Butterfield & Butterfield, San Francisco #133/R
$2250	£1510	Poppies and lupines (23x30cm-9x12in) s. canvasboard. 8-Dec-93 Butterfield & Butterfield, San Francisco #3396/R
$3750	£2467	Hillside with poppies and lupines (30x46cm-12x18in) s. canvas on board. 13-Jun-93 Butterfield & Butterfield, San Francisco #856/R

JACKSON, William H (1843-1942) American
$2250	£1490	High Sierras (28x36cm-11x14in) s. 15-Jun-94 Butterfield & Butterfield, San Francisco #4527/R

JACOBI, Otto Reinhard (1812-1901) German/Canadian
$592	£400	Faggot gatherers at cottage door (25x20cm-10x8in) s. panel. 17-Jun-93 Christie's, S. Kensington #42/R
$874	£583	Millpond (22x37cm-9x15in) s.d.1872. 13-May-94 Joyner Fine Art, Toronto #70/R (C.D 1200)
$934	£619	Along the river (28x22cm-11x9in) s.d.1861 i.verso panel. 18-Nov-92 Sotheby's, Toronto #283 (C.D 1200)
$1079	£701	A bend in the river (23x39cm-9x15in) s. panel. 21-Jun-94 Fraser Pinneys, Quebec #51 (C.D 1500)
$2440	£1627	Mother, children and puppy (25x32cm-10x13in) s.d.1854 panel. 30-May-94 Ritchie, Toronto #136/R (C.D 3400)
$4486	£2990	Silent thoughts - children in snowy landscape (23x35cm-9x14in) s.d.1853 panel. 30-May-94 Ritchie, Toronto #135/R (C.D 6250)
$580	*£386*	*View at a gorge (55x41cm-22x16in) s.d.1883 W/C. 6-Jun-94 Waddingtons, Toronto #1245 (C.D 800)*
$602	*£404*	*View at a gorge (55x41cm-22x16in) s.d.1883 W/C. 29-Nov-93 Waddingtons, Toronto #1083 (C.D 800)*
$614	£415	Family in a landscape (36x53cm-14x21in) s.d.1881 W/C. 30-Mar-94 Maynards, Vancouver #35 (C.D 850)

JACOBI, Rudolf (1889-1972) American
$700	£479	View of a French village and harbour (64x76cm-25x30in) s.d.1927. 10-Feb-94 Skinner, Bolton #202
$2905	£1862	Houses amongst trees (50x65cm-20x26in) s.d.27. 26-May-93 Lempertz, Cologne #231/R (DM 4600)
$3274	£2183	Houses in a Berlin street (82x65cm-32x26in) s.d.31. 15-Mar-94 Weiner, Munich #265/R (DM 5500)
$8148	£5469	Amaryllis in vase (65x54cm-26x21in) s.d.22 board. 30-Nov-93 Karl & Faber, Munich #751/R (DM 14000)
$496	*£337*	*Vietri sul mare, coastal scene with sailing boats (37x46cm-15x18in) s.i.d.1923 W/C. 15-Apr-94 Bolland & Marotz, Bremen #781 (DM 850)*
$2400	*£1538*	*Paris street scene (46x62cm-18x24in) s.i.d.1927 W/C. 26-May-93 Lempertz, Cologne #232/R (DM 3800)*

JACOBS, Hobart B (1851-1935) American
$1000	£662	Marine scene with boats (30x41cm-12x16in) s.d.1913. 28-Nov-92 Dunning's, Illinois #1102

JACOBSEN, Antonio (1850-1921) American
$1224	£800	Steamship Commonwealth (56x91cm-22x36in) s.i.d.1902-31. 7-Oct-93 Christie's, S. Kensington #381
$1500	£980	Screw steamer Evangeline under way (20x35cm-8x14in) s.i.d.1915 board. 31-Oct-92 Skinner, Bolton #60/R
$2646	£1800	The steam ship San Jacinto flying the Stars and Stripes (49x89cm-19x35in) s.i. board. 16-Nov-93 Phillips, London #82/R
$2700	£1800	Ship at twilight (76x55cm-30x22in) s. panel. 3-Jun-94 Sotheby's, New York #246/R
$2700	£1812	El Creole - steam ship on rough sea (51x89cm-20x35in) s.i.d.1912 board. 4-May-94 Doyle, New York #7/R
$2750	£1821	Peninsular (46x76cm-18x30in) painted c.1892. 23-Sep-93 Mystic Fine Arts, Connecticut #95/R
$2992	£2008	Ships portrait - 'United States' (53x90cm-21x35in) with sig.i.d.1912. 22-Feb-94 Rasmussen, Copenhagen #143/R (D.KR 20000)
$3000	£2027	The tanker 'Florida' (49x90cm-19x35in) s.i.d.1915 board. 31-Mar-94 Sotheby's Arcade, New York #131/R
$3113	£2090	Ships portrait of the steamer 'Glenisla' (56x92cm-22x36in) s.d.1885. 2-Feb-94 Kunsthallen, Copenhagen #48/R (D.KR 21000)
$3600	£2353	Tow-masted steam sailer (84x53cm-33x21in) 30-Oct-92 Douglas, South Deerfield #4
$3750	£2517	The Bustamante of San Francisco harbour (28x36cm-11x14in) s.i.d.1882 verso board. 8-Dec-93 Butterfield & Butterfield, San Francisco #3335/R
$4000	£2632	Portrait American ship Roscius (30x51cm-12x20in) s.d.1918 board. 5-Jun-93 Skinner, Bolton #17/R
$4004	£2706	Steamship 'M.G.Melchior' in rough seas (56x91cm-22x36in) s.d.1891. 15-Jun-93 Rasmussen, Vejle #671/R (D.KR 26000)
$4250	£2853	American steamer Aransas (56x91cm-22x36in) s.i.d.1905 board. 6-Feb-94 Skinner, Bolton #98/R
$4500	£3041	Umbria (81x152cm-32x60in) s.indist.i.d.1886. 31-Mar-94 Sotheby's Arcade, New York #133/R
$4500	£3147	Gaff rigged three-masted schooner, 'Warner Moore' (43x74cm-17x29in) s.d.1915 artist's board. 5-Feb-93 Sloan, North Bethesda #2558/R
$4896	£3200	S.S. Alfred Dumois (56x91cm-22x35in) s.d.1891. 15-Apr-93 Christie's, S. Kensington #483/R
$5000	£3356	Steam Yacht Winchester (56x89cm-22x35in) s.d.1910 board. 6-Feb-94 Skinner, Bolton #60/R
$5000	£3546	'Roscious' (30x51cm-12x20in) s.d.1918 panel. 13-Feb-93 Richard Bourne, Hyannis #103/R
$5000	£3333	Great Western (29x49cm-11x19in) s.i.indis.d. 3-Jun-94 Sotheby's, New York #240/R
$5500	£3901	'Lightning' 1854 Don. McKay. 244F Australia Trade (30x51cm-12x20in) s.d.1918 panel. 13-Feb-93 Richard Bourne, Hyannis #102/R
$5500	£3618	'Comanche' (36x56cm-14x22in) s.d.1904. 4-Jun-93 Sotheby's, New York #194/R
$5750	£3616	Steamboat W Whilldin, General Cadwalader (56x91cm-22x36in) s.i.d.1890. 22-Apr-93 Freeman Fine Arts, Philadelphia #1298

247

JACOBSEN, Antonio (1850-1921) American-cont.
$6258	£4200	The steel screw-steamer 'Cearense' (56x91cm-22x36in) s.d.1899. 5-May-94 Christie's, S. Kensington #201/R
$6500	£4422	U.S.S. Constitution (41x61cm-16x24in) s.d.1916 board. 9-Jul-93 Sloan, North Bethesda #2773/R
$6750	£4500	Steamship 'Lydian Monarch' (55x90cm-22x35in) s.i.d.1891. 19-Jul-93 Phillips, Tyne and Wear #95/R
$6885	£4500	Cunard liner Mauritania (41x70cm-16x28in) s.d.1908 board. 7-Oct-93 Christie's, S. Kensington #496/R
$6900	£4600	A trans Atlantic steam ship (56x91cm-22x36in) s.i.d.1878. 11-May-94 Sotheby's, London #91/R
$7009	£4300	S.S. Devon (56x91cm-22x36in) s.i.d.1886. 15-Oct-92 Christie's, S. Kensington #518/R
$7500	£4902	Portrait of ship S P Hitchcock with other shipping (20x30cm-8x12in) s.d.1917. 31-Oct-92 Skinner, Bolton #59/R
$7650	£5000	Steamer Colenso (91x56cm-36x22in) s.d.1901. 7-Oct-93 Christie's, S. Kensington #498/R
$7748	£5200	The American liner 'Ponce', a vanguard in the history of wireless (57x91cm-22x36in) s.d.1907 card. 5-May-94 Christie's, S. Kensington #203/R
$7779	£5221	Shipsportrait - 'Thingvalla' (56x92cm-22x36in) s.d.1880. 22-Feb-94 Rasmussen, Copenhagen #8/R (D.KR 52000)
$8000	£5405	Liner St Paul picking up New York pilot from pilot boat (64x99cm-25x39in) s.d.1898. 30-Jul-93 Eldred, Massachusetts #307/R
$8000	£5333	The Charles H Marshall (30x51cm-12x20in) s.i.d.1916. 3-Jun-94 Sotheby's, New York #241/R
$8525	£5500	Steamship 'Devon' (56x91cm-22x36in) s.i.d.1879. 20-Jan-93 Sotheby's, London #130/R
$8642	£5800	S.S. M.G. Melchior (56x91cm-22x36in) s.i.d.1891. 5-May-94 Christie's, S. Kensington #204/R
$8976	£6024	Ships portrait 'Geiser' (56x92cm-22x36in) s.d.1882. 22-Feb-94 Rasmussen, Copenhagen #10/R (D.KR 60000)
$9685	£6500	The liner 'New York', previoulsy the Inman liner 'City of New York' (56x91cm-22x36in) s.i.d.1905. 5-May-94 Christie's, S. Kensington #202/R
$9685	£6500	S.S. Elysia (56x91cm-22x36in) s.i.d.1876. 5-May-94 Christie's, S. Kensington #200/R
$11400	£7600	The steam ship Oceanic (56x92cm-22x36in) s.i.d.1905. 11-May-94 Sotheby's, London #92/R
$11475	£7500	S.S. Hindoo British screw steamer (56x92cm-22x36in) s.i. painted 1879. 7-Oct-93 Christie's, S. Kensington #497/R
$13000	£8609	The Puritan (81x152cm-32x60in) s.indist.i.d.1896. 23-Sep-93 Sotheby's, New York #70/R
$13708	£9200	Steam ship 'Jan Breydel' (74x124cm-29x49in) s.i.d.1882. 16-Jul-93 Sotheby's, London #51/R
$16000	£10458	Schooner Orlando V Wooten n New York Harbour (71x122cm-28x48in) s.i. board. 5-May-93 Doyle, New York #19/R
$16000	£10738	Ships at sea (25x40cm-10x16in) s.d.1886. 11-Dec-93 Weschler, Washington #90/R
$18000	£11392	City of Rome (76x152cm-30x60in) s.i.d.1881. 3-Dec-92 Freeman Fine Arts, Philadelphia #1792 a/R
$37500	£24038	American leaving New York Harbour (74x150cm-29x59in) s.i.d.1884. 27-May-93 Sotheby's, New York #197/R
$4185	*£2700*	*S.Y. Vanadis (54x89cm-21x35in) s.d.1911 W/C gouache. 20-Jan-93 Sotheby's, London #131/R*

JACOBSHAGEN, Keith (1943-) American
$800	£541	In the late afternoon W. of Pleasant (20x23cm-8x9in) s.i. paper. 4-Nov-93 Boos Gallery, Michigan #241

JACOBSON, O (19th C) American
$750	£490	Winter landscape (64x107cm-25x42in) s. 16-Sep-93 Sloan, North Bethesda #2921

JACOT, Don (1949-) American
$1000	*£671*	*View at Belle Isle (30x41cm-12x16in) s.d.86 gouache rag board. 25-Mar-93 Boos Gallery, Michigan #433/R*
$1100	*£738*	*Looking down Wabash, Chicago (28x30cm-11x12in) s.d.90 gouache rag board. 25-Mar-93 Boos Gallery, Michigan #432/R*

JACQUES, Eddy (1957-) Haitian
$626	£415	Carnaval (76x32cm-30x13in) s. 13-Jun-94 Rogeon, Paris #14 (F.FR 3500)
$626	£415	Scene historique (30x102cm-12x40in) s. acrylic. 13-Jun-94 Rogeon, Paris #58 (F.FR 3500)

JACQUETTE, Yvonne (1934-) American
$1200	*£805*	*Ferry with wake (47x32cm-19x13in) s. i.verso brush black ink graphite. 3-May-94 Christie's, East, New York #127/R*

JAMBOR, Louis (1884-1955) American
$680	£450	Gathering roses (50x34cm-20x13in) s. 16-Jun-94 Christie's, S. Kensington #120/R
$982	£650	Reading news (98x71cm-39x28in) s. 26-Nov-92 Christie's, S. Kensington #100
$1000	£654	Butter churners (61x51cm-24x20in) s. 8-May-93 Young Fine Arts Auctions, Maine #178/R
$1750	£1174	Men and women with basket of fish (76x76cm-30x30in) s. 16-Jul-93 Du Mouchelle, Detroit #2014/R

JAMES, Frederick (1857-1932) American
$2000   £1361   Mapping the Pennsylvania Campaign (69x56cm-27x22in) s.d.1882. 14-Apr-94 Freeman Fine Arts, Philadelphia #979/R

JAMISON, Philip (1925-) American
$900   £588   Early thaw (30x48cm-12x19in) s. W/C. 30-Jun-94 Mystic Fine Arts, Connecticut #104 a/R

JANSSON, Alfred (1863-1931) Swedish/American
$800   £506   Country landscape (69x76cm-27x30in) s.d.1923. 5-Dec-92 Louisiana Auction Exchange #80/R
$900   £596   Extensive landscape (69x76cm-27x30in) s.d.1923. 3-Oct-93 Hanzel Galleries, Chicago #823
$1550   £1013   River landscape (56x69cm-22x27in) s.d.1912. 15-May-93 Dunning's, Illinois #1037

JANVIER, Alex (1935-) Canadian
$603   £410   By Grace (71x56cm-28x22in) s. i.verso acrylic painted c.1977. 15-Nov-93 Hodgins, Calgary #240/R (C.D 800)

JARRY, Gaston (1889-1974) Argentinian
$750   £441   Paisaje urbano (60x50cm-24x20in) 29-Sep-92 VerBo, Buenos Aires #62

JARVIS, Georgia (1944-1990) Canadian
$1790   £1186   Fall birch (51x76cm-20x30in) s. s.i.verso board. 16-Nov-92 Hodgins, Calgary #140/R (C.D 2300)
$1794   £1196   A stone mill (51x76cm-20x30in) s. s.i.verso canvasboard. 30-May-94 Hodgins, Calgary #303 a (C.D 2500)

JAVIER, Maximino (20th C) Mexican
$1503   £1002   Trovador melancolico (40x30cm-16x12in) W/C. 25-May-94 Louis Morton, Mexico #24 (M.P 5000)

JEAN, Baptiste Jean (1953-) Haitian
$537   £355   Bord de mer (51x76cm-20x30in) s. 13-Jun-94 Rogeon, Paris #163 (F.FR 3000)
$626   £415   Carnaval (61x91cm-24x36in) s. 13-Jun-94 Rogeon, Paris #17 (F.FR 3500)

JEAN, Eugene (1905-) Haitian
$2792   £1790   La maisonou l'on dort chacun son tour (45x50cm-18x20in) s. 14-Dec-92 Hoebanx, Paris #40/R (F.FR 15000)

JEAN-GILLES, Joseph (1943-) Haitian
$905   £592   Aux champs (61x45cm-24x18in) painted 1977. 17-May-93 Hoebanx, Paris #123 (F.FR 5000)

JEAN-LOUIS, Eric (20th C) Haitian
$626   £415   Chevaux traversant la riviere (40x50cm-16x20in) s.d.88 panel. 13-Jun-94 Rogeon, Paris #76 (F.FR 3500)

JEFFERY, Richard (1919-) American
$650   £436   Winter afternoon (61x76cm-24x30in) s. 5-Dec-93 James Bakker, Cambridge #89/R

JEFFERYS, Charles William (1869-1951) Canadian
$739   £490   Village by water, December (19x24cm-7x9in) s.d.17 board. 24-Nov-92 Joyner Fine Art, Toronto #226 (C.D 950)
$1387   £907   Village by water (20x25cm-8x10in) s.indist.d. d.verso board. 19-May-93 Sotheby's, Toronto #256/R (C.D 1750)

JENKINS, George Washington Allston (1816-1907) American
$14000 £9150   Before the election. After the election (69x56cm-27x22in) pair painted 1856. 16-Sep-93 Sloan, North Bethesda #3198/R

JENKINS, Paul (1923-) American
$600   £403   Phenomena self portrait as a shaman (47x37cm-19x15in) s. s.i.d.1988 verso acrylic linen. 24-Feb-94 Sotheby's Arcade, New York #481/R
$1372   £921   Phenomena Light Key (75x56cm-30x22in) s. i.verso acrylic paper painted 1987. 19-Dec-93 Perrin, Versailles #173 (F.FR 8000)
$1600   £1074   Phenomena Not Left - Phenomena Off Right (61x93cm-24x37in) s. s.i.d.1960 verso two panels. 23-Feb-94 Christie's, East, New York #373/R
$1800   £1208   Phenomena Shanghai for Scorpio (76x112cm-30x44in) s. s.i.d.1974 verso. 24-Feb-94 Sotheby's Arcade, New York #366/R
$2000   £1325   Phenomena Red Arrested (41x51cm-16x20in) s. s.d.1965 verso acrylic. 30-Jun-93 Sotheby's Arcade, New York #303/R
$2400   £1611   Phenomena mirror shield (99x99cm-39x39in) s. s.i.d.1972 verso. 24-Feb-94 Sotheby's Arcade, New York #379/R
$2500   £1656   Phenomena remember him (91x51cm-36x20in) s. s.i.d.1964verso. 2-Oct-93 Weschler, Washington #158/R
$2715   £1822   For Michele and Michel (69x76cm-27x30in) s.i.d.21 septembre 1957verso. 6-Feb-94 Guy Loudmer, Paris #134/R (F.FR 16000)
$2729   £1795   Composition (111x79cm-44x31in) s. acrylic paper. 8-Jun-93 Rasmussen, Copenhagen #67/R (D.KR 17000)
$2729   £1807   Phenomena Young Winston (71x109cm-28x43in) s. acrylic paper. 28-Sep-93 Rasmussen, Copenhagen #67/R (D.KR 18000)
$2914   £1905   Warlock (120x80cm-47x31in) s.i.d.1957verso. 28-Jun-94 Catherine Charbonneaux, Paris #85 (F.FR 16000)

JENKINS, Paul (1923-) American-cont.

$3000	£2000	Phenomena - Prism Nimbus (126x151cm-50x59in) s. s.i.d.14th June 1982overlap acrylic. 26-May-94 Christie's, London #166/R
$3050	£2006	Composition (111x79cm-44x31in) s. acrylic paper. 8-Jun-93 Rasmussen, Copenhagen #68/R (D.KR 19000)
$3120	£2000	Phenomenon by a Shield of Red (127x61cm-50x24in) s.i.d.1966. 17-Dec-92 Christie's, S. Kensington #287/R
$3576	£2400	Phenomena Kanari , s. s.i.d.1979stretcher acrylic. 21-Jun-93 Christie's, S. Kensington #204/R
$4000	£2649	The riddle (96x46cm-38x18in) s. s.i.d.1958verso. 17-Nov-92 Christie's, East, New York #267/R
$4000	£2685	Phenomena Ahab trace (96x137cm-38x54in) s. s.i.d.1974 verso acrylic. 24-Feb-94 Sotheby's Arcade, New York #365/R
$4482	£2988	Phenomenon - St Elmo's Fire (97x130cm-38x51in) s. acrylic. 6-Jun-94 Wolfgang Ketterer, Munich #139/R (DM 7500)
$4800	£3200	Phenomena earth bound (74x61cm-29x24in) s. s.i.d.July-August 1984verso acrylic. 26-May-94 Christie's, London #116/R
$5328	£3600	Phenomena Big Surrounding (160x130cm-63x51in) s.d.1974 s.i.d.verso acrylic. 14-Nov-93 Eric Pillon, Calais #195/R (F.FR 31500)
$5705	£3500	Phenomena blue and compass (145x97cm-57x38in) s. d.1963 verso acrylic. 14-Oct-92 Sotheby's, London #334/R
$7091	£4545	Phenomena coming from north (117x89cm-46x35in) s. i.verso acrylic. 13-Dec-92 Eric Pillon, Calais #190/R (F.FR 38000)
$7851	£5269	Phenomena to remember (100x80cm-39x31in) s. s.i.verso acrylic. 23-Jun-93 Guy Loudmer, Paris #84/R (F.FR 45000)
$8439	£5664	Phenomena (114x146cm-45x57in) s. acrylic painted 1987. 3-Dec-93 Lempertz, Cologne #791/R (DM 14500)
$8500	£5903	Phenomena southern turn (119x196cm-47x77in) s.s.i.d.1983verso. 26-Feb-93 Sotheby's Arcade, New York #331/R
$12000	£8000	Untitled - abstract composition (128x89cm-50x35in) s.d.53. 3-Jun-94 Lempertz, Cologne #719/R (DM 20000)
$13000	£7647	Phenomena fortune wheel (162x121cm-64x48in) s. s.d.1967 overlap acrylic. 6-Oct-92 Sotheby's, New York #43/R
$13167	£8333	Phenomena (56x40cm-22x16in) s. 4-Dec-92 Germann, Zurich #68/R (S.FR 18500)
$15434	£10359	Phenomena Winter Throne Room (180x195cm-71x77in) s.d.1990-91verso acrylic. 29-Nov-93 AB Stockholms Auktionsverk, Stockholm #6222/R (S.KR 130000)
$40000	£27778	Phenomena Comstock Lode II (196x406cm-77x160in) s. s.i.d.1974stretcher acrylic. 23-Feb-93 Sotheby's, New York #242/R
$656	£429	Composition (53x36cm-21x14in) s.d.1957 Indian ink wash. 28-Jun-94 Catherine Charbonneaux, Paris #45 (F.FR 3600)
$700	£467	Sans titre (105x76cm-41x30in) s. W/C. 11-Mar-94 Cornette de St.Cyr, Paris #136 (F.FR 4000)
$702	£450	Phenomena moving North-East (56x76cm-22x30in) s. W/C. 17-Dec-92 Christie's, S. Kensington #283
$1043	£700	Phenomena with yellow edge (75x55cm-30x22in) s. s.i.d.1962verso W/C. 25-Mar-93 Christie's, London #115
$1100	£728	Phenomenon signing torture (56x78cm-22x31in) s. s.d.1965 verso W/C Indian ink. 30-Jun-93 Sotheby's Arcade, New York #304/R
$1200	£795	Phenomena Jade Pass (76x107cm-30x42in) s. s.d.1975 verso W/C. 30-Jun-93 Sotheby's Arcade, New York #300/R
$1400	£927	Phenomena Cleopatra fan (76x56cm-30x22in) s. s.d.1975 verso W/C. 30-Jun-93 Sotheby's Arcade, New York #299/R
$1455	£977	Phenomena Port Side (57x78cm-22x31in) s. s.i.d.1965verso W/C vellum. 3-Dec-93 Lempertz, Cologne #792 (DM 2500)
$1475	£934	Composition (75x57cm-30x22in) s. W/C. 1-Dec-92 AB Stockholms Auktionsverk, Stockholm #6126/R (S.KR 10000)
$1600	£1006	Phenomena, Stately stance (110x79cm-43x31in) s. W/C. 25-Apr-93 Butterfield & Butterfield, San Francisco #2161/R
$1600	£1074	Phenomena Tibetan Clasp II (76x56cm-30x22in) s. W/C. 24-Feb-94 Sotheby's Arcade, New York #407/R
$1600	£1060	Phenomena W Range (79x109cm-31x43in) s. s.d.1982 verso W/C. 30-Jun-93 Sotheby's Arcade, New York #305/R
$1600	£1067	Phenomena Prism Column (105x76cm-41x30in) s. s.i.d.1975verso W/C. 11-May-94 Christie's, New York #476/R
$1700	£1126	Phenomena prism sentinels (79x109cm-31x43in) s. s.i.d.1985verso W/C. 17-Nov-92 Christie's, East, New York #145/R
$1746	£1172	Phenomena Spectrum Rampant (76x55cm-30x22in) s. s.i.d.1971verso W/C vellum. 3-Dec-93 Lempertz, Cologne #793/R (DM 3000)
$1900	£1275	Phenomena cast by daylight (76x106cm-30x42in) s. s.i.d.1979 W/C. 23-Feb-94 Christie's, East, New York #346/R
$2084	£1336	Phenomena Drade's estuary (55x72cm-22x28in) s. s.i.d.1975verso W/C. 27-May-93 Lempertz, Cologne #824/R (DM 3300)
$2479	£1653	Phenomena, Compton Keep (76x106cm-30x42in) s. W/C painted 1972. 25-May-94 Francis Briest, Paris #90/R (F.FR 14000)
$2500	£1572	Phenomena, Hadrian's Wall (117x117cm-46x46in) s.i.d.1979verso W/C canvas. 25-Apr-93 Butterfield & Butterfield, San Francisco #2159/R
$2500	£1678	Phenomena Royal Violet (79x109cm-31x43in) s.i.d.1977 W/C. 14-Jan-94 Du Mouchelle, Detroit #2019
$2500	£1656	Phenomenon moving north east (56x77cm-22x30in) s. s.i.d.1967 W/C. 29-Sep-93 Sotheby's Arcade, New York #260/R
$2614	£1754	Phenomena Cardinal Irange (185x76cm-73x37in) W/C painted 1973. 21-Mar-94 Guy Loudmer, Paris #27 (F.FR 15000)
$2619	£1758	Amber vessel (61x46cm-24x18in) s.indist.d.58 mixed media canvas. 3-Dec-93 Lempertz, Cologne #790/R (DM 4500)
$2750	£1821	Untitled (107x76cm-42x30in) s. W/C. 29-Sep-93 Sotheby's Arcade, New York #262/R

JENKINS, Paul (1923-) American-cont.
$3000	£2013	Phenomena Royal Violet (76x104cm-30x41in) s. W/C. 14-Jan-94 Du Mouchelle, Detroit #2020
$3000	£2013	Phenomena Blue Ash (79x109cm-31x43in) s. s.i.d.1979 verso W/C. 23-Feb-94 Christie's, East, New York #341/R
$3055	£2050	Phenomena O'Malley's Tent (216x51cm-85x20in) s.i.d.1979 collage acrylic canvas. 24-Mar-93 Dorotheum, Vienna #123/R (A.S 35000)
$3626	£2370	Untitled (78x110cm-31x43in) s. painted c.1980 mixed media. 28-Oct-92 Dorotheum, Vienna #192/R (A.S 40000)
$4105	£2632	Phenomena orange profiel (107x76cm-42x30in) s. i.d.1987verso W/C. 30-May-93 Eric Pillon, Calais #226/R (F.FR 22000)
$8960	£5856	Phenomena crossing the sun's anvil (81x179cm-32x70in) s.d.1990 mixed media triptych. 12-May-93 AB Stockholms Auktionsverk, Stockholm #6030/R (S.KR 66000)

JENNENS and BETTRIDGE (19th C) Canadian
$1200	£805	El Sibah or the Salt Plain, Tunis (54x68cm-21x27in) oil gold leaf panel. 11-Dec-93 Weschler, Washington #17/R

JENNEY, Neil (1945-) American
$75000	£44118	Herd and flock (147x147cm-58x58in) acrylic. 8-Oct-92 Christie's, New York #196/R
$75000	£49669	Plowed and plower (149x194cm-59x76in) acrylic. 18-Nov-92 Christie's, New York #62/R
$105000	£61765	Man and beast (154x216cm-61x85in) painted 1970. 6-Oct-92 Sotheby's, New York #159/R
$125000	£82781	Formation 2 (84x201cm-33x79in) wood. 17-Nov-92 Sotheby's, New York #70/R
$160000	£105960	Stop and spakes (149x211cm-59x83in) s.i.d.1970stretcher acrylic graphite canvas. 18-Nov-92 Christie's, New York #26/R

JENNYS, William (attrib) (18/19th C) American
$8000	£5405	Portraits of John Case, aged 5. Portrait of Chester Case, aged 8 (39x46cm-15x18in) i.d.1795verso pair. 3-Nov-93 Butterfield & Butterfield, San Francisco #266/R

JENSEN, Alfred (1903-1981) American
$900	£596	Untitled (132x117cm-52x46in) s. 23-Sep-93 Mystic Fine Arts, Connecticut #264
$3500	£2349	Colour's golden sect for law (46x30cm-18x12in) s.d.58 paper. 25-Feb-94 Sotheby's, New York #17/R
$8000	£5369	Hommage aux Prix Nobel (76x51cm-30x20in) s. oil brush ink board painted c.1975. 4-May-94 Christie's, New York #132/R
$14000	£9150	Acrobatic rectangle - per eight (176x112cm-69x44in) s.d.1967 verso. 4-May-93 Sotheby's, New York #365/R
$15000	£9934	The Parthenon, Athens (140x278cm-55x109in) s.i.d.1970verso diptych. 19-Nov-92 Christie's, New York #330/R
$23000	£15033	Circular structures male vs. female (127x117cm-50x46in) s.d.1963 verso. 4-May-93 Sotheby's, New York #358/R
$25000	£16779	Electromagnetic charge (218x129cm-86x51in) s.i.d.1975verso. 5-May-94 Sotheby's, New York #141/R
$27500	£18456	The great occupation, Per 2 (122x274cm-48x108in) s.i.d.1973verso three parts. 4-May-94 Sotheby's, New York #47/R
$27793	£18779	Pythagoras VII (81x122cm-32x48in) s.i.d.1963verso. 21-Apr-94 Germann, Zurich #59/R (S.FR 40000)
$28000	£18543	Earth, moon, sun and Venus (127x183cm-50x72in) s.i.d.1968verso two panels. 19-Nov-92 Christie's, New York #408/R
$31290	£21000	The acrobatic rectangle (163x82cm-64x32in) s.d.1967verso. 25-Mar-93 Christie's, London #96/R
$65000	£43046	Mayan Mat Patterns' Number Structure (183x183cm-72x72in) painted 1974. 18-Nov-92 Sotheby's, New York #134/R
$5321	£3571	Arithmetical proportion, ratio and harmony (73x58cm-29x23in) s.d.Oct.1st1965 W/C Indian ink brush over pencil. 23-Jun-93 Galerie Kornfeld, Berne #419/R (S.FR 8000)
$6000	£4027	Sixty-five squares (58x58cm-23x23in) s.d.1957 oil paper collage board. 23-Feb-94 Christie's, New York #8/R
$7317	£4911	The actual male square's progression (74x59cm-29x23in) s.d.March 12/1966 oil over pen. 23-Jun-93 Galerie Kornfeld, Berne #420/R (S.FR 11000)

JENSEN, Bill (1945-) American
$8000	£5369	Drawing for Ribbons for Harriet (60x45cm-24x18in) s.i.d.1983-84 verso pastel gouache chl. 25-Feb-94 Sotheby's, New York #121/R

JENSEN, George (1878-?) American
$900	£588	Winter landscape (76x76cm-30x30in) s. board. 16-Apr-93 Du Mouchelle, Detroit #2246/R

JERZY, Richard (20th C) American
$1000	£667	Floral still life (71x91cm-28x36in) s.d.72 W/C. 12-May-94 Boos Gallery, Michigan #507/R

JESS (20th C) American
$26000	£17450	One way (51x38cm-20x15in) i. paper collage. 5-May-94 Sotheby's, New York #172/R
$50000	£33557	Chiron's souvenir from the Arco's crew (61x71cm-24x28in) s.i.d.60verso paper collage on photograph. 5-May-94 Sotheby's, New York #161/R
$85000	£57432	Picture of flowers near the end of the mantle (88x74cm-35x29in) s.i.d.60verso paper collage board. 10-Nov-93 Sotheby's, New York #12/R

JESSUP, Robert (20th C) American
$1200	£769	Making bread (122x122cm-48x48in) s.d.1983verso. 13-Dec-92 Hindman Galleries, Chicago #83

JIMENEZ, Jose de (18th C) Latin American?
$20000	£13072	Divina Pastora (155x97cm-61x38in) s. painted c.1780. 18-May-93 Sotheby's, New York #6/R

JOHANSEN, John C (1876-1964) American
$540	£360	Wooded landscape , s.verso. 31-May-94 Academy Auctioneers, London #830 c
$7500	£5245	Piazza San Marco, Venice (75x100cm-30x39in) s.d.1908. 10-Mar-93 Sotheby's, New York #92/R

JOHNS, Jasper (1930-) American
$70000	£46980	Figure 7 (25x21cm-10x8in) s.i.d.59verso. 5-May-94 Sotheby's, New York #164/R
$550000	£359477	Untitled (77x138cm-30x54in) s.d.1980 verso acrylic plastic on canvas. 4-May-93 Christie's, New York #22/R
$2100000	£1390729	O through 9 (137x114cm-54x45in) s.d.61verso. 18-Nov-92 Christie's, New York #38/R
$18000	£11765	Usuyuki (131x50cm-52x20in) s.d.1980 col.screenprint. 11-May-93 Christie's, New York #471/R
$351900	£230000	Green Target (21x21cm-8x8in) s.verso encaustic collage panel. 29-Jun-94 Sotheby's, London #31/R
$1300000	£872483	Untitled (122x191cm-48x75in) encaustic collage canvas objects painted 1983. 4-May-94 Sotheby's, New York #52/R

JOHNSON, C Everett (1866-?) American
$2500	£1656	Supper maybe (72x38cm-28x15in) s. paper laid down on canvas. 15-Jun-94 Butterfield & Butterfield, San Francisco #4537/R

JOHNSON, Clarence R (1894-1981) American
$1200	£706	Spring trees (84x99cm-33x39in) s. 8-Oct-92 Freeman Fine Arts, Philadelphia #1097

JOHNSON, David (1827-1908) American
$3800	£2533	Roadside, Shark River, New Jersey (20x27cm-8x11in) mono.d.77 s.i.d.1877 verso board. 23-May-94 Christie's, East, New York #39/R
$5500	£3481	Roadside, New Rochelle, New York (31x42cm-12x17in) mono. s.i.d.1884verso canvas laid down on panel. 2-Dec-92 Christie's, East, New York #35 a/R
$6000	£3974	New Jersey farmstead (22x32cm-9x13in) init. s.indist.i.verso. 23-Sep-93 Sotheby's, New York #47/R
$7000	£4636	Near McComb's Dam, Harlem, New York (18x30cm-7x12in) mono.d.72 i.stretcher. 22-Sep-93 Christie's, New York #22/R
$7000	£4487	Joyceville, Connecticut (48x37cm-19x15in) init. s.i.d.1881 verso. 27-May-93 Sotheby's, New York #166/R
$8500	£5449	New Hampshire, near Mt. Lafayette (30x46cm-12x18in) mono.d.1876 s.i.d.verso. 24-May-93 Grogan, Massachussetts #297/R
$20000	£12658	Warwick, Orange County, New York (30x51cm-12x20in) mono.d.74 s.i.d.verso. 4-Dec-92 Christie's, New York #180/R
$35000	£22436	Lake George (41x66cm-16x26in) init.d.1870 s.i.d.1870 verso. 27-May-93 Sotheby's, New York #146/R
$70000	£46980	Summertime, Warwick, New York (46x66cm-18x26in) s.d.1873 i.d.1873 verso. 6-Dec-93 Grogan, Massachussetts #436/R
$110000	£69520	Upper Twin Lakes in Colorado Rockies (52x77cm-20x30in) inits.d.65. 4-Dec-92 Christie's, New York #218/R

JOHNSON, Eastman (1824-1906) American
$7367	£4815	Portrait of Prof.Hendricksz standing leaning on table by curtain (152x113cm-60x44in) s.d.1853. 28-Oct-92 Christie's, Amsterdam #110/R (D.FL 13000)
$12000	£8000	Marguerite Leiter, aged five years (127x81cm-50x32in) s.d.1884. 17-Mar-94 Sotheby's, New York #54 a/R
$40000	£25316	Study for The Nantucket School of Philosophy (17x27cm-7x11in) inits.d.5-11-76 board. 4-Dec-92 Christie's, New York #209/R
$42000	£28000	Self portrait (25x21cm-10x8in) s. painted c.1865-70. 25-May-94 Sotheby's, New York #13/R
$57500	£36392	Sugar camp (33x55cm-13x22in) init. board. 3-Dec-92 Sotheby's, New York #20/R
$85000	£53797	Boy in the Maine Woods (30x50cm-12x20in) init. 3-Dec-92 Sotheby's, New York #21/R
$130000	£83333	Chimney sweep (31x24cm-12x9in) s.d.1863 board. 26-May-93 Christie's, New York #35/R

JOHNSON, Francis Norton (1878-1931) American
$4000	£2703	Daydreaming in the garden (60x73cm-24x29in) s. 31-Mar-94 Sotheby's Arcade, New York #258/R

JOHNSON, Frank Tenney (1874-1939) American
$2500	£1678	Pack horse (23x28cm-9x11in) s.i. s.verso canvas on board. 11-Dec-93 Weschler, Washington #114/R
$2600	£1745	In Catclaw Country (30x40cm-12x16in) s.d.1933 i.verso canvas on board. 11-Dec-93 Weschler, Washington #116/R
$3500	£2023	Along the yellowstone (30x39cm-12x15in) s. board. 25-Sep-92 Sotheby's Arcade, New York #188/R
$6000	£3922	Canyon Creek (51x40cm-20x16in) s.i.d.1931 canvasboard. 4-May-93 Christie's, East, New York #125/R
$10000	£6757	Cowboy on the hunt (76x46cm-30x18in) s.d.1906. 31-Mar-94 Sotheby's Arcade, New York #185/R

JOHNSON, Frank Tenney (1874-1939) American-cont.
$10000	£6410	Sunset shadows (29x22cm-11x9in) s.d.1933 masonite. 27-May-93 Sotheby's, New York #227/R
$12000	£7692	At evening (29x22cm-11x9in) s.d.1933 masonite. 27-May-93 Sotheby's, New York #228/R
$14000	£9272	Red Indian scouting party (51x61cm-20x24in) 15-Jun-94 Butterfield & Butterfield, San Francisco #4493/R
$18000	£11392	Standing guard (31x24cm-12x9in) s.d.1936 board. 3-Dec-92 Sotheby's, New York #60/R
$35000	£22436	Spring roundup (61x76cm-24x30in) s.d.1938verso board. 9-Dec-92 Butterfield & Butterfield, San Francisco #3997/R
$35000	£22152	An evil omen (63x47cm-25x19in) s.d.1930. 3-Dec-92 Sotheby's, New York #61/R
$50000	£33557	Return from the hunt (63x76cm-25x30in) s.d.1934 i.stretcher. 2-Dec-93 Sotheby's, New York #48/R
$8000	*£5263*	*Rider on horseback (76x53cm-30x21in) s.d.1920 W/C. 13-Jun-93 Butterfield & Butterfield, San Francisco #3212/R*

JOHNSON, Guy (1927-) American
$670	£450	Grandmother's house (26x46cm-10x18in) s. painted 1928. 2-Mar-94 Kunsthallen, Copenhagen #62 (D.KR 4500)

JOHNSON, James Ralph (20th C) American
$650	£428	Boots and saddles (61x122cm-24x48in) s. i.verso board. 2-Jun-93 Doyle, New York #69

JOHNSON, Larry (20th C) American
$1000	£633	Seated woman, 1968 (184x76cm-72x30in) acrylic aluminium. 25-Oct-92 Butterfield & Butterfield, San Francisco #2377/R

JOHNSON, Lester (1919-) American
$1600	£1060	Untitled (51x41cm-20x16in) s.d.1961 canvasboard. 29-Sep-93 Sotheby's Arcade, New York #274/R
$1600	£1060	Head of man (101x68cm-40x27in) paper executed 1961. 30-Jun-93 Sotheby's Arcade, New York #278/R
$1900	£1319	Park scene (56x71cm-22x28in) s. 26-Feb-93 Sotheby's Arcade, New York #374/R
$2000	£1389	Dusk (51x76cm-20x30in) s.d.1962verso. 23-Feb-93 Sotheby's, New York #249/R
$2200	£1528	Figure in silhouette (102x66cm-40x26in) s.d.1960 paper. 26-Feb-93 Sotheby's Arcade, New York #366/R
$3500	£2365	Main Street Strollers (46x36cm-18x14in) s. painted 1976. 4-Nov-93 Boos Gallery, Michigan #232/R
$3750	£2484	City girls (61x46cm-24x18in) s.d.86 board. 29-Sep-93 Sotheby's Arcade, New York #360/R
$4000	£2685	Springs head (91x61cm-36x24in) i.d.1964 verso. 24-Feb-94 Sotheby's Arcade, New York #360/R
$6750	£4688	Four men with hats (71x71cm-28x28in) s.d.1970verso. 26-Feb-93 Sotheby's Arcade, New York #375/R
$9000	£5960	City women, ochre (152x127cm-60x50in) painted c.1973. 17-Nov-92 Christie's, East, New York #198/R
$12000	£7843	Untitled (168x152cm-66x60in) s. painted 1975. 4-May-93 Sotheby's, New York #342/R
$13000	£9028	Emerging crowd (173x152cm-68x60in) s.d.1970. 23-Feb-93 Sotheby's, New York #251/R
$600	£397	Untitled (36x51cm-14x20in) s.d.1961 ink wash. 29-Sep-93 Sotheby's Arcade, New York #270/R
$2500	£1678	Prince Street (56x75cm-22x30in) s. mixed media. 24-Feb-94 Sotheby's Arcade, New York #321/R
$4250	£2815	Seven figures (57x85cm-22x33in) s. gouache silver paint pastel. 29-Sep-93 Sotheby's Arcade, New York #251/R

JOHNSON, Marshall (1850-1915) American
$750	£497	Chinese fishing boats (64x76cm-25x30in) s. 28-Nov-92 Young Fine Arts Auctions, Maine #246/R
$900	£459	Heavy going, fishing schooner plows through rough seas (25x36cm-10x14in) s. 18-Aug-92 Richard Bourne, Hyannis #223/R
$950	£629	Two sailing vessels passing in seaway (46x36cm-18x14in) s. 20-Nov-92 Eldred, Massachusetts #510/R
$1200	£612	Meeting at sea (25x36cm-10x14in) s. 18-Aug-92 Richard Bourne, Hyannis #222/R
$1300	£872	Ships at sea (64x76cm-25x30in) s. 24-Mar-94 Mystic Fine Arts, Connecticut #210/R
$1600	£1074	Boston harbour (28x43cm-11x17in) s.d.81. 4-Mar-94 Skinner, Bolton #214/R
$2200	£1429	Taking tow off shore (30x51cm-12x20in) s.indis.d. s.i.verso. 9-Sep-93 Sotheby's Arcade, New York #62/R
$10500	£6863	Gaff rigged cat boat (64x76cm-25x30in) s. 5-May-93 Doyle, New York #18/R
$675	£433	Sailing ships at sea (46x61cm-18x24in) s. W/C. 24-May-93 Selkirks, St. Louis #157/R

JOHNSON, Martin (1951-) American
$950	£642	Autoartology (136x229cm-54x90in) init.d.1977 acrylic graphite. 8-Nov-93 Christie's, East, New York #6/R

JOHNSON, Ray (1927-) American
$1500	£1007	Ladder whirled (77x77cm-30x30in) s.d.1952-65verso board. 3-May-94 Christie's, East, New York #14/R
$2000	*£1351*	*Cave Man (22x25cm-9x10in) s.d.1982 gesso gouache ink board collage. 8-Nov-93 Christie's, East, New York #18/R*
$2000	*£1351*	*Portrait of Bill Copley (38x32cm-15x13in) s.d.1976 brush ink paper and board collage. 8-Nov-93 Christie's, East, New York #16/R*

JOHNSTON, Frank Hans (1888-1949) Canadian

$713	£466	Country lane (20x25cm-8x10in) s. panel. 18-May-93 Joyner Fine Art, Toronto #126 (C.D 900)
$718	£478	End of the day (20x25cm-8x10in) s. masonite. 30-May-94 Ritchie, Toronto #178 (C.D 1000)
$1005	£670	A welcome gleam (25x29cm-10x11in) s. masonite. 30-May-94 Ritchie, Toronto #242/R (C.D 1400)
$1100	£759	Reflection of a pine (33x25cm-13x10in) s.d.22 board. 17-Feb-93 Doyle, New York #46
$1189	£777	Serenity (30x41cm-12x16in) s. board. 19-May-93 Sotheby's, Toronto #283/R (C.D 1500)
$1245	£825	Winter solitude on a Northern river (30x41cm-12x16in) s. i.verso board. 18-Nov-92 Sotheby's, Toronto #214/R (C.D 1600)
$1311	£874	Spring starlight (48x36cm-19x14in) s. tempera. 13-May-94 Joyner Fine Art, Toronto #166 (C.D 1800)
$1323	£876	Road through forest, Georgian Bay (20x25cm-8x10in) s. board. 24-Nov-92 Joyner Fine Art, Toronto #116/R (C.D 1700)
$1522	£1014	On the trail to Little Longloc (34x41cm-13x16in) s. s.i.verso board. 6-Jun-94 Waddingtons, Toronto #1271 (C.D 2100)
$1585	£1036	Great Bear Lake (30x36cm-12x14in) s. s.i.d.39 verso board. 19-May-93 Sotheby's, Toronto #107 (C.D 2000)
$1602	£1068	Great Bear Lake, N W T (25x30cm-10x12in) s. 13-May-94 Joyner Fine Art, Toronto #187/R (C.D 2200)
$1893	£1262	Figure on country lane (37x45cm-15x18in) s. board. 13-May-94 Joyner Fine Art, Toronto #231 (C.D 2500)
$1893	£1262	Sun ring, Great Bear Lake, N W T (25x30cm-10x12in) s.i. canvas on board. 13-May-94 Joyner Fine Art, Toronto #124/R (C.D 2600)
$2153	£1435	The golden age (50x61cm-20x24in) s. i.verso masonite. 30-May-94 Ritchie, Toronto #175/R (C.D 3000)
$2576	£1684	Early snow (41x51cm-16x20in) s. panel. 19-May-93 Sotheby's, Toronto #85/R (C.D 3250)
$2621	£1748	Eldorado 1939 (40x50cm-16x20in) s. board. 13-May-94 Joyner Fine Art, Toronto #153/R (C.D 3600)
$2718	£1837	Misty morning - South Magnetewan River (40x50cm-16x20in) s. board. 23-Nov-93 Joyner Fine Art, Toronto #193 (C.D 3600)
$2767	£1845	Evening - Les Eboulements, Que. (40x50cm-16x20in) s. board. 13-May-94 Joyner Fine Art, Toronto #201 (C.D 3800)
$3012	£1969	Miracle of morning (41x51cm-16x20in) s. board. 18-May-93 Joyner Fine Art, Toronto #161/R (C.D 3800)
$3113	£2062	A river in spring (62x51cm-24x20in) s.d.11. 18-Nov-92 Sotheby's, Toronto #112/R (C.D 4000)
$3171	£2073	Canyon Wall, Algoma (49x36cm-19x14in) s. tempera painted c.1920. 18-May-93 Joyner Fine Art, Toronto #52/R (C.D 4000)
$3308	£2191	Winter sun on the Wye (44x52cm-17x20in) s. i.verso board. 18-Nov-92 Sotheby's, Toronto #159/R (C.D 4250)
$3330	£2176	Sombre reflections (27x34cm-11x13in) board. 18-May-93 Joyner Fine Art, Toronto #9/R (C.D 4200)
$3386	£2273	Silvered snow a memory of Algoma (49x60cm-19x24in) s. i.verso. 29-Nov-93 Ritchie, Toronto #222/R (C.D 4500)
$3473	£2347	The warm light of spring (50x60cm-20x24in) s. board. 23-Nov-93 Joyner Fine Art, Toronto #26/R (C.D 4600)
$3473	£2347	Spring on the Assiniboine (26x32cm-10x13in) s. board painted c.1922. 23-Nov-93 Joyner Fine Art, Toronto #103/R (C.D 4600)
$3503	£2320	The hour of enchantment (63x76cm-25x30in) s.i.verso board. 18-Nov-92 Sotheby's, Toronto #257 (C.D 4500)
$3964	£2591	Athabaska Falls in moonlight (51x61cm-20x24in) s. board painted c.1935. 18-May-93 Joyner Fine Art, Toronto #252/R (C.D 5000)
$4262	£2880	Winter landscape with mill (41x51cm-16x20in) s. panel. 3-Nov-93 Sotheby's, Toronto #192/R (C.D 5500)
$6041	£4082	View from Banff (50x106cm-20x42in) s. board. 23-Nov-93 Joyner Fine Art, Toronto #93/R (C.D 8000)
$6100	£4067	The singing stream (76x91cm-30x36in) s.i. masonite. 30-May-94 Ritchie, Toronto #160/R (C.D 8500)
$6342	£4145	Open stream, Jasper Park, Alberta (61x76cm-24x30in) s. board. 18-May-93 Joyner Fine Art, Toronto #188/R (C.D 8000)
$6553	£4369	Northern Lake (76x102cm-30x40in) s.d.32 s.verso board. 11-May-94 Sotheby's, Toronto #53/R (C.D 9000)
$6917	£4612	Autumn, Algoma (27x34cm-11x13in) s. d.c.1917verso board. 11-May-94 Sotheby's, Toronto #137/R (C.D 9500)
$8231	£5276	Prospector (66x102cm-26x40in) s. board. 7-Dec-92 Waddingtons, Toronto #1341/R (C.D 10500)
$11675	£7732	Children of the wilds (66x102cm-26x40in) s. i.verso masonite. 18-Nov-92 Sotheby's, Toronto #209/R (C.D 15000)
$620	£419	Bringing home the Christmas tree (13x20cm-5x8in) init.d.c.1928 gouache paperboard. 1-Nov-93 Levis, Calgary #118 (C.D 800)
$634	£415	Poplars (34x27cm-13x11in) s. gouache. 18-May-93 Joyner Fine Art, Toronto #137 (C.D 800)
$655	£437	Skies over Great Bear (25x30cm-10x12in) s. W/C. 11-May-94 Sotheby's, Toronto #198 a (C.D 900)
$680	£459	Clearing after rain (13x24cm-5x9in) s. gouache. 23-Nov-93 Joyner Fine Art, Toronto #154 (C.D 900)
$701	£464	Tree in a landscape (25x35cm-10x14in) s. gouache. 18-Nov-92 Sotheby's, Toronto #116/R (C.D 900)
$778	£515	Moonlight (20x15cm-8x6in) s. i.verso gouache. 18-Nov-92 Sotheby's, Toronto #162 (C.D 1000)

JOHNSTON, Frank Hans (1888-1949) Canadian-cont.
$1255   £821   Timber limit (18x25cm-7x10in) s. gouache. 10-May-93 Hodgins, Calgary #105/R
                  (C.D 1600)
$1784   £1166   Lilloet, E.C (26x36cm-10x14in) s. gouache. 19-May-93 Sotheby's, Toronto #265/R
                  (C.D 2250)
$3874   £2618   Tall trees (102x76cm-40x30in) s.d.30 gouache. 3-Nov-93 Sotheby's, Toronto #132/R
                  (C.D 5000)
$8720   £5699   Autumn landscape (51x38cm-20x15in) s. gouache. 19-May-93 Sotheby's, Toronto
                  #110/R (C.D 11000)

JOHNSTON, John (attrib) (1753-1818) American
$1200   £784   Portrait of Annie Ivers (77x64cm-30x25in) 4-May-93 Christie's, East, New York
                  #4/R

JOHNSTON, Reuben le Grand (1850-1919) American
$600   £403   After the shower (33x48cm-13x19in) s. 16-Dec-93 Mystic Fine Arts, Connecticut
                  #52/R

JOHNSTONE, John Young (1887-1930) Canadian
$1300   £823   Snowy street (12x18cm-5x7in) s. canvasboard. 2-Dec-92 Christie's, East, New York
                  #293
$1559   £1026   Road to Chateau Richer, P.Q. (22x27cm-9x11in) s. i.verso board. 7-Jun-93
                  Waddingtons, Toronto #1147/R (C.D 2000)
$2802   £1856   St. Joachim Road, P.Q (27x51cm-11x20in) s. board. 24-Nov-92 Joyner Fine Art,
                  Toronto #47/R (C.D 3600)

JOINER, Harvey (1852-?) American
$700   £458   Beech trees (30x27cm-12x11in) s. 8-Oct-93 Christie's, East, New York #250

JONES, Amy (1899-?) American
$950   £621   St Marks, Venice (61x76cm-24x30in) s.d.1973. 16-May-93 Hindman Galleries, Chicago
                  #116

JONES, C S (19th C) American
$1100   £738   Yacht race (51x71cm-20x28in) W/C. 27-Mar-94 Myers, Florida #82/R

JONES, Francis Coates (1857-1932) American
$2000   £1316   Mother and child (32x22cm-13x9in) s.d.88 panel. 13-Jun-93 Butterfield &
                  Butterfield, San Francisco #3190/R
$24000   £15894   Exchanging confidences (47x52cm-19x20in) s. i.stretcher. 23-Sep-93 Sotheby's, New
                  York #66/R
$35000   £22152   Friends (91x76cm-36x30in) s. 4-Dec-92 Christie's, New York #20/R
$12000   £8392   Lady with lyre (33x39cm-13x15in) s. pastel paper on board. 11-Mar-93 Christie's,
                  New York #89/R

JONES, Hugh Bolton (1848-1927) American
$1200   £800   Rolling landscape with trees (89x56cm-35x22in) 3-Jun-94 Douglas, South Deerfield
                  #2
$1700   £1149   The watermill (23x33cm-9x13in) s.d.1871 canvas laid down on board. 10-Nov-93
                  Doyle, New York #63
$1900   £1098   Summer landscape (51x62cm-20x24in) 25-Sep-92 Sotheby's Arcade, New York #225/R
$2250   £1136   Trees by river (25x41cm-10x16in) s. board. 28-Aug-92 Young Fine Arts Auctions,
                  Maine #189/R
$2700   £1812   Haystacks in landscape (41x58cm-16x23in) s. board. 3-Feb-94 Sloan, North Bethesda
                  #2703/R
$3190   £2085   Stream - spring landscape (41x56cm-16x22in) s. 14-May-93 Skinner, Bolton #80/R
$3750   £2517   Woodland stream, late autumn (51x61cm-20x24in) s. 3-Feb-94 Sloan, North Bethesda
                  #2704/R
$4000   £2685   Landscape with water and trees (56x81cm-22x32in) s. 17-Dec-93 Du Mouchelle,
                  Detroit #2005/R
$4000   £2614   Sun raked forest path (36x51cm-14x20in) s. 5-May-93 Doyle, New York #11/R
$6750   £4561   Spring time (51x61cm-20x24in) s. 10-Aug-93 Stonington Fine Arts, Stonington
                  #145/R
$8000   £4624   Spring landscape (61x102cm-24x40in) s. 24-Sep-92 Sotheby's, New York #67/R
$9500   £6643   Landscape with cows by stream (30x58cm-12x23in) s. 10-Mar-93 Sotheby's, New York
                  #79/R
$13000   £8667   Autumn landscape (56x81cm-22x32in) s. 17-Mar-94 Sotheby's, New York #47/R
$18000   £11921   Young fisherman by a stream (90x62cm-35x24in) s.d.1879. 15-Jun-94 Butterfield &
                  Butterfield, San Francisco #4444/R
$1000   £658   Quiet stream (29x38cm-11x15in) s. W/C. 13-Jun-93 Butterfield & Butterfield, San
                  Francisco #3152/R
$2700   £1812   Landscape (46x36cm-18x14in) s. W/C. 29-Nov-93 Stonington Fine Arts, Stonington
                  #181/R

JONES, Hugh Bolton and Francis Coates (19/20th C) American
$8000   £5229   Threshing grain (122x244cm-48x96in) s. canvas on board. 16-May-93 Hindman
                  Galleries, Chicago #57/R

JONES, Hugh Griffith (1872-1947) Canadian
$540   £350   The medieval harbour (56x71cm-22x28in) s. i.verso panel. 21-Jun-94 Fraser
                  Pinneys, Quebec #137 (C.D 750)

JONES, Joseph John (1909-1963) American
$2300   £1474   Portrait of seated clown (97x61cm-38x24in) s. 24-May-93 Selkirks, St. Louis
                  #167/R

JONES, Paul (1860-?) American
$1961 £1316 Una tensa espera (20x25cm-8x10in) s.d.1882 panel. 20-Dec-93 Duran, Madrid #172/R (S.P 275000)
$2624 £1544 Una tensa espera (20x25cm-8x10in) s.d.1882 panel. 6-Oct-92 Duran, Madrid #70/R (S.P 275000)

JONES, Shields Landon (1901-) American
$675 £447 Three men with a horse and cart (43x58cm-17x23in) s. ink pastel. 21-Nov-92 Litchfield Auction Gallery #20

JONES, William F (1815-?) American
$700 £458 Young woman with letter (76x64cm-30x25in) s.d.1849verso. 16-May-93 Hindman Galleries, Chicago #69

JONNEVOLD, Carl Henrik (1856-1930) American
$700 £461 Late afternoon (44x55cm-17x22in) s. 13-Jun-93 Butterfield & Butterfield, San Francisco #775/R
$950 £633 Cattle in landscape (20x30cm-8x12in) s. 15-Mar-94 John Moran, Pasadena #39
$1900 £1275 Mountain cabin at sunset (30x41cm-12x16in) s. 8-Dec-93 Butterfield & Butterfield, San Francisco #3397/R

JONSON, Raymond (1891-1982) American
$3200 £2025 Abstract with pink and black (51x40cm-20x16in) s.d.50 board. 2-Dec-92 Christie's, East, New York #389/R
$9000 £6000 Golden Wind (71x111cm-28x44in) s.d.35 s.i.d.1935 verso. 23-May-94 Christie's, East, New York #317/R
$55000 £35256 Canyon de Chelly (58x79cm-23x31in) s.d.1928. 27-May-93 Sotheby's, New York #232/R
$80000 £50633 Cliff dwellings 4 (89x103cm-35x41in) s.d.28. 4-Dec-92 Christie's, New York #270/R

JORGENSEN, Christian (1860-1935) American
$2200 £1429 Snow capped mountains (53x69cm-21x27in) s.d.1918. 9-Sep-93 Sotheby's Arcade, New York #208/R
$2750 £1809 By the bay (38x66cm-15x26in) s.d.1917. 13-Jun-93 Butterfield & Butterfield, San Francisco #728/R
$3190 £2045 San Francisco Bay (38x66cm-15x26in) s. 17-Dec-92 Mystic Fine Arts, Connecticut #184
$4000 £2778 Yosemite Valley (61x112cm-24x44in) s.d.09 canvas on board. 7-Mar-93 Butterfield & Butterfield, San Francisco #96/R
$600 £395 House along cliff's edge (37x26cm-15x10in) s. W/C. 13-Jun-93 Butterfield & Butterfield, San Francisco #752/R
$600 £400 Yosemite landscape (41x30cm-16x12in) s. W/C. 12-Mar-94 Weschler, Washington #159
$900 £520 The California in the Mariposa Grove (38x27cm-15x11in) s. W/C paper on board. 25-Sep-92 Sotheby's Arcade, New York #125/R
$950 £621 Yellowstone Park Scene (33x46cm-13x18in) s. W/C. 30-Jun-94 Mystic Fine Arts, Connecticut #170/R

JORGENSEN, Christian (attrib) (1860-1935) American
$700 £470 Italian coast (61x46cm-24x18in) 7-Aug-93 San Rafael Auction Galleries #273

JOSEPH, Jasmin (20th C) Haitian
$2800 £1892 Famille dans la foret (67x61cm-26x24in) s. masonite painted c.1956. 24-Nov-93 Christie's, New York #11/R

JOULLIN, Amadee (1862-1917) American
$4500 £3125 Marsh at sunset near Mt Tamalpais (41x76cm-16x30in) s. 7-Mar-93 Butterfield & Butterfield, San Francisco #5/R
$5000 £3333 American Indian girl decorating pottery (51x66cm-20x26in) s. 22-May-94 James Bakker, Cambridge #96/R

JUAN, Ronaldo de (1930-) Argentinian
$4500 £3000 Sin titulo (183x183cm-72x72in) s.i.d.84 acrylic pastel canvas. 18-May-94 Sotheby's, New York #402/R

JUAREZ, Jose (attrib) (c.1620-c.1670) Mexican
$18000 £12000 Los desposorios de la Virgen (128x149cm-50x59in) painted c.1660. 18-May-94 Sotheby's, New York #161/R

JUDSON, Alice (?-1948) American
$758 £480 Saturday afternoon (20x24cm-8x9in) s. 21-Oct-92 Maynards, Vancouver #111 (C.D 950)

JUDSON, William Lees (1842-1928) American
$650 £428 Sunset in clearing (46x61cm-18x24in) s. 13-Jun-93 Butterfield & Butterfield, San Francisco #842/R
$850 £574 Low tide (46x76cm-18x30in) s. board. 9-Nov-93 John Moran, Pasadena #842
$900 £608 Morning fog (38x64cm-15x25in) s. board. 9-Nov-93 John Moran, Pasadena #843
$900 £529 Oak glen (38x63cm-15x25in) s. 4-Oct-92 Butterfield & Butterfield, Los Angeles #122/R
$950 £629 Morning mist (51x76cm-20x30in) s. canvas on canvas. 28-Sep-93 John Moran, Pasadena #243
$1000 £676 Live Oaks at sunset (76x127cm-30x50in) s. 15-Jun-93 John Moran, Pasadena #173
$1300 £861 Landscape (41x51cm-16x20in) s. canvas on canvas. 28-Sep-93 John Moran, Pasadena #314
$1400 £927 Morning on the desert (38x64cm-15x25in) s. canvas on canvas. 28-Sep-93 John Moran, Pasadena #352

JUDSON, William Lees (1842-1928) American-cont.
$1700	£1126	Landscape (38x61cm-15x24in) s. canvas on canvas. 28-Sep-93 John Moran, Pasadena #260
$1900	£1258	The Cedar Brook Trail (51x76cm-20x30in) s. canvas on canvas. 28-Sep-93 John Moran, Pasadena #220
$3500	£2303	View of Grand Canyon (76x127cm-30x50in) s. 13-Jun-93 Butterfield & Butterfield, San Francisco #924/R
$3750	£2534	Live Oaks at sunset (76x127cm-30x50in) s. 15-Jun-93 John Moran, Pasadena #83
$16000	£10596	Amy, a table by the sea (71x91cm-28x36in) s. canvas on canvas. 28-Sep-93 John Moran, Pasadena #300
$475	£315	Stream in wooded landscape (25x33cm-10x13in) s. W/C. 14-Jun-94 John Moran, Pasadena #6
$475	£317	Southern Californian coastal scene (25x41cm-10x16in) s. W/C. 15-Mar-94 John Moran, Pasadena #26
$529	£357	River landscape (30x52cm-12x20in) s. W/C. 23-Nov-93 Joyner Fine Art, Toronto #172 (C.D 700)
$650	£430	Skiff on the beach (33x51cm-13x20in) s. W/C. 14-Jun-94 John Moran, Pasadena #34
$739	£490	Harbour view (33x53cm-13x21in) s.d.1878 W/C. 18-Nov-92 Sotheby's, Toronto #92/R (C.D 950)

JUERGENS, Alfred (1842-1924) American
$1400	£940	Summer fishing scene (76x102cm-30x40in) 27-Mar-94 Myers, Florida #6/R
$2500	£1667	Lilacs (64x69cm-25x27in) s. board. 13-Mar-94 Hindman Galleries, Chicago #762/R
$4000	£2614	Tropical nook (81x81cm-32x32in) s. i.stretcher. 19-Sep-93 Hindman Galleries, Chicago #681/R

JUHL, Finn (20th C) American
$850	£567	Design for an armchair (41x60cm-16x24in) W/C board. 11-Jun-94 Christie's, New York #346
$1300	£867	Design for a sofa (47x87cm-19x34in) i. W/C. 11-Jun-94 Christie's, New York #349/R
$1300	£867	Design for working desk (40x58cm-16x23in) W/C. 11-Jun-94 Christie's, New York #347/R
$1800	£1200	Designs for armchair and a sidechair (41x58cm-16x23in) w/c pair. 11-Jun-94 Christie's, New York #350/R

JUSZCZYK, James (1943-) American
$732	£498	Untitled (46x61cm-18x24in) s.i.d.Sept.20 1973verso acrylic paper on canvas. 20-Nov-93 Aucktionhaus Burkard, Luzern #221/R (S.FR 1100)
$2312	£1511	Sun gate (101x80cm-40x31in) s.i.d.1987 acrylic foil on canvas. 15-May-93 Aucktionhaus Burkard, Luzern #193/R (S.FR 3400)

KABER, G Frederick (20th C) American
$900	£588	The Flicker and the Toad (53x33cm-21x13in) s. W/C gouache graphite htd gum arabic. 17-Sep-93 Skinner, Bolton #317/R

KABOTIE, Michael (1946-) American
$1100	£710	Untitled (43x58cm-17x23in) s.d.68 mixed media art board. 9-Jan-93 Skinner, Bolton #132/R

KACERE, John (1920-) American
$2277	£1488	Transition Octobre 1951 (65x123cm-26x48in) s.i.d.1951stretcher board. 28-Jun-94 Catherine Charbonneaux, Paris #181/R (F.FR 12500)
$2800	£1879	Big M Woman (102x168cm-40x66in) s.d.69 verso. 23-Feb-94 Christie's, East, New York #364/R
$3372	£2204	Modele de dos (72x50cm-28x20in) s.d.78 pencil dr. 18-Sep-93 Jean Louis Picard, Paris #10/R (F.FR 19000)
$7455	£4872	Judi (89x56cm-35x22in) s.i.d.79verso. 18-Sep-93 Jean Louis Picard, Paris #17/R (F.FR 42000)
$9940	£6497	Debbie (58x76cm-23x30in) s.i.d.79verso. 18-Sep-93 Jean Louis Picard, Paris #5/R (F.FR 56000)
$11892	£7773	Patricia (151x101cm-59x40in) i.d.1980 s.verso acrylic. 18-Sep-93 Jean Louis Picard, Paris #7/R (F.FR 67000)
$13000	£7647	Allison (96x198cm-38x78in) s.d.S-83 verso. 6-Oct-92 Sotheby's, New York #100/R
$14200	£9281	Linda W II (97x147cm-38x58in) s.i.verso. 18-Sep-93 Jean Louis Picard, Paris #15/R (F.FR 80000)
$18104	£11833	Lauren (127x179cm-50x70in) s.i.d.1980verso. 18-Sep-93 Jean Louis Picard, Paris #6/R (F.FR 102000)
$22187	£14501	Sally T (168x182cm-66x72in) s.i.d.72verso acrylic. 18-Sep-93 Jean Louis Picard, Paris #9/R (F.FR 125000)
$1823	£1199	Lorraine (48x63cm-19x25in) s.d.1983 pencil dr. 11-Jun-93 Poulain & le Fur, Paris #140/R (F.FR 10000)
$2130	£1392	Modele vu de face (48x61cm-19x24in) s.d.78 pencil dr. 18-Sep-93 Jean Louis Picard, Paris #2/R (F.FR 12000)
$3195	£2088	Modele vu de face (52x74cm-20x29in) s.d.78 pencil dr. 18-Sep-93 Jean Louis Picard, Paris #14/R (F.FR 18000)

KAELIN, Charles Salis (1858-1929) American
$1000	£578	Woodland path (28x36cm-11x14in) s. canvasboard. 27-Sep-92 James Bakker, Cambridge #108/R
$1500	£867	Landscape (51x61cm-20x24in) s. 24-Sep-92 Mystic Fine Arts, Connecticut #279
$6100	£4122	Woods in winter (61x76cm-24x30in) s. 20-Mar-93 Weschler, Washington #106/R

KAHN, Wolf (1927-) American
$4500   £2961   Mr Hamilton's heifers (61x76cm-24x30in) s. painted 1970. 31-Mar-93 Sotheby's Arcade, New York #485/R
$1300   *£878*   *Blue wall of trees (58x76cm-23x30in) s. pastel. 31-Mar-94 Sotheby's Arcade, New York #453/R*

KAISER, August (1889-?) American/German
$950   £629   The meadows (41x51cm-16x20in) s. 28-Sep-93 John Moran, Pasadena #219

KALISH, Lionel (20th C) American
$2100   £1382   Along village street (25x36cm-10x14in) s. board. 31-Mar-93 Sotheby's Arcade, New York #317/R

KALLEM, Herb (20th C) American
$550   £369   Reclining nude (38x53cm-15x21in) s.d.74 acrylic paper. 4-Mar-94 Christie's, East, New York #223
$600   £403   Nude (43x61cm-17x24in) s.d.70 acrylic paper on board. 4-Mar-94 Christie's, East, New York #225
$1500   £1007   Two nudes (79x56cm-31x22in) acrylic paper. 4-Mar-94 Christie's, East, New York #224

KALLMEYER, Minnie (?) Canadian
$801   £534   Rural cottage scene (56x72cm-22x28in) s. 11-May-94 Sotheby's, Toronto #246 (C.D 1100)

KALLOS, Arpad (1882-?) American/Hungarian
$575   £371   Portrait of gpsey (81x71cm-32x28in) s.d.1922. 13-Jul-94 Boos Gallery, Michigan #663

KANE, Paul (attrib) (1810-1871) Canadian
$9466   £6311   Portrait of Kee-Akee-Ka-Saa-Ka-Wow - The Man Who Gives The War Whoop (50x38cm-20x15in) 13-May-94 Joyner Fine Art, Toronto #110/R (C.D 13000)

KANOVITZ, Howard (1929-) American
$5000   £3356   Elements of prose (127x81cm-50x32in) s.i.d.1972verso acrylic varnish. 3-May-94 Christie's, East, New York #57/R

KANTOR, Morris (1896-1974) American
$650   £422   Iridescent day (71x56cm-28x22in) s. s.i.stretcher. 9-Sep-93 Sotheby's Arcade, New York #442/R
$1600   £1067   Dark red cubist (56x46cm-22x18in) s.d.1924. 23-May-94 Christie's, East, New York #315/R
$650   *£425*   *The lighthouse (33x43cm-13x17in) gouache. 7-Oct-93 Freeman Fine Arts, Philadelphia #932*
$1150   *£767*   *Lighthouse (33x46cm-13x18in) s. gouache board. 9-Jun-94 Swann Galleries, New York #167*

KARELLA, Marina (1940-) American
$2200   £1486   Bed (183x122cm-72x48in) painted 1982. 8-Nov-93 Christie's, East, New York #42/R

KARFIOL, Bernard (1886-1952) American
$1000   £676   Virginie with rabbit (107x61cm-42x24in) board painted c.1916. 23-Oct-93 Collins, Maine #151/R
$1000   £641   By the shore (99x63cm-39x25in) 27-Apr-93 Christie's, East, New York #278
$800   *£530*   *Two seated women (24x30cm-9x12in) s. W/C ink. 30-Jun-93 Sotheby's Arcade, New York #77/R*

KASS, Deborah (20th C) American
$900   £588   His (160x213cm-63x84in) s.d.1987 verso acrylic. 7-May-93 Christie's, East, New York #153/R

KASYN, John (1926-) Canadian
$789   £526   Backyard on River Street (25x20cm-10x8in) s. masonite. 30-May-94 Ritchie, Toronto #196/R (C.D 1100)
$852   £576   Before demolition Nepean near Bronson (30x25cm-12x10in) s.d.75 i.verso board. 3-Nov-93 Sotheby's, Toronto #41 (C.D 1100)
$862   £553   Near Barlett Ave (25x20cm-10x8in) s. s.i.verso masonite. 26-Apr-93 Levis, Calgary #81/R (C.D 1100)
$874   £583   Lane to Sackville St. (25x19cm-10x7in) s. board. 13-May-94 Joyner Fine Art, Toronto #208/R (C.D 1200)
$907   £613   On Cherry Street (25x20cm-10x8in) s. i.verso masonite. 25-Apr-94 Levis, Calgary #136/R (C.D 1250)
$942   £615   On Bain Avenue (31x25cm-12x10in) s. oil lucite 44 masonite. 10-May-93 Hodgins, Calgary #224/R (C.D 1200)
$973   £644   Old House in Weston (25x20cm-10x8in) s. i.verso board. 18-Nov-92 Sotheby's, Toronto #77/R (C.D 1250)
$1031   £674   Approaching evening, River Street, Toronto (30x25cm-12x10in) s. board. 19-May-93 Sotheby's, Toronto #144/R (C.D 1300)
$1092   £728   Near Percy Street (30x25cm-12x10in) s. s.i.verso board. 11-May-94 Sotheby's, Toronto #89/R (C.D 1500)
$1162   £785   Behind Power Street near King (25x20cm-10x8in) s. s.i.verso board. 3-Nov-93 Sotheby's, Toronto #36/R (C.D 1500)
$1162   £785   Backyard in snow Phoebe Street (25x20cm-10x8in) s. s.i.verso masonite. 1-Nov-93 Levis, Calgary #123/R (C.D 1500)

KASYN, John (1926-) Canadian-cont.
$1165	£777	Behind Vanauley Street (25x20cm-10x8in) s. s.i.verso board. 11-May-94 Sotheby's, Toronto #90/R (C.D 1600)
$1168	£773	On Dundas Street West (25x20cm-10x8in) s. board. 24-Nov-92 Joyner Fine Art, Toronto #151/R (C.D 1500)
$1208	£816	Behind Jarvis Street (25x20cm-10x8in) s. board. 23-Nov-93 Joyner Fine Art, Toronto #218/R (C.D 1600)
$1268	£829	Hazelton St, late March (41x51cm-16x20in) s. board painted 1980. 18-May-93 Joyner Fine Art, Toronto #128/R (C.D 1600)
$1282	£872	Back yard on Simcoe Street (30x25cm-12x10in) s. s.i.verso board. 15-Nov-93 Hodgins, Calgary #268/R (C.D 1700)
$1357	£923	Off Berkeley Street Lane (30x25cm-12x10in) s. s.i.verso board. 15-Nov-93 Hodgins, Calgary #48/R (C.D 1800)
$2695	£1762	Back of Boston Ave. (56x41cm-22x16in) s. board. 18-May-93 Joyner Fine Art, Toronto #269/R (C.D 3400)
$3567	£2332	Near King Street in Parkdale (61x46cm-24x18in) s. board. 19-May-93 Sotheby's, Toronto #149/R (C.D 4500)
$546	£359	Behind Robert St. (21x51cm-8x20in) s. i.verso W/C. 7-Jun-93 Waddingtons, Toronto #1091 (C.D 700)
$549	£352	Dundas and Hickory St (20x15cm-8x6in) s. s.i.verso W/C. 26-Apr-93 Levis, Calgary #82 (C.D 700)
$580	£386	Behind Gerrard Street (20x15cm-8x6in) s. i.verso W/C. 6-Jun-94 Waddingtons, Toronto #1249 (C.D 800)
$580	£392	On Power Street (23x18cm-9x7in) s. i.verso W/C. 25-Apr-94 Levis, Calgary #137/R (C.D 800)
$584	£387	On Sherbourne St. North (18x13cm-7x5in) s. i.verso W/C. 18-Nov-92 Sotheby's, Toronto #76/R (C.D 750)
$623	£412	Off Eastern Avenue (17x12cm-7x5in) s. W/C. 24-Nov-92 Joyner Fine Art, Toronto #227/R (C.D 800)
$628	£410	City lane (18x13cm-7x5in) s. W/C. 10-May-93 Hodgins, Calgary #19/R (C.D 800)
$634	£415	Off Henry St. (20x15cm-8x6in) s. W/C. 18-May-93 Joyner Fine Art, Toronto #880 (C.D 800)
$650	£439	After first snow (20x15cm-8x6in) s. s.i.verso W/C. 30-Mar-94 Maynards, Vancouver #18 (C.D 800)
$739	£490	Before the demolition, Parkdale Toronto (18x13cm-7x5in) s. i.verso W/C. 16-Nov-92 Hodgins, Calgary #38/R (C.D 950)
$801	£534	Behind a small cottage (12x20cm-5x8in) s. W/C. 13-May-94 Joyner Fine Art, Toronto #141/R (C.D 1100)

KATO, Kentaro (1889-1926) American
$602	£404	Horse and carriage departing from the stable (56x67cm-22x26in) s.d.07. 30-Nov-93 Ritchie, Toronto #56/R (C.D 800)
$1400	£897	Tidal pool in Gloucester (61x76cm-24x30in) s.i.d.1920. 9-Dec-92 Butterfield & Butterfield, San Francisco #3894/R

KATZ, Alex (1927-) American
$5000	£3356	Study for peony no 1 (23x30cm-9x12in) s.d.88 masonite. 4-May-94 Christie's, New York #204/R
$7000	£4118	Vincent at window (30x36cm-12x14in) s.d.84 masonite. 6-Oct-92 Sotheby's, New York #104/R
$8500	£5556	Study for Peter and Lauren (33x30cm-13x12in) s.d.88 masonite. 4-May-93 Sotheby's, New York #221/R
$9000	£5294	Alex and Ada (23x30cm-9x12in) s.d.80 masonite. 8-Oct-92 Christie's, New York #167/R
$10000	£6536	Upside down Ada (38x46cm-15x18in) s.d.65 masonite. 5-May-93 Christie's, New York #235/R
$12000	£8054	Salute no 3 (46x51cm-18x20in) s.d.62 i.stretcher acrylic masonite. 5-May-94 Sotheby's, New York #183/R
$12500	£8170	Ada (30x30cm-12x12in) s.d.66 masonite. 4-May-93 Sotheby's, New York #402 a/R
$12500	£7353	Ada in woods (51x41cm-20x16in) s.d.84 masonite. 6-Oct-92 Sotheby's, New York #101/R
$18000	£11765	Beach shoes (122x164cm-48x65in) painted 1987. 5-May-93 Christie's, New York #309/R
$30000	£19608	Salute - 4 (109x119cm-43x47in) s. painted 1962. 4-May-93 Sotheby's, New York #392/R
$45000	£30405	Ursula in white (91x183cm-36x72in) painted 1988. 10-Nov-93 Christie's, New York #236/R
$46000	£30872	Jennifer and Mathieu (244x122cm-96x48in) s.d.86. 4-May-94 Christie's, New York #217/R
$48000	£32432	Lauren and Peter (229x168cm-90x66in) painted 1988. 11-Nov-93 Sotheby's, New York #396/R
$52000	£33987	Blue sweater (178x152cm-70x60in) painted 1988. 5-May-93 Christie's, New York #313/R
$70000	£46358	Ada with glasses (244x183cm-96x72in) painted 1977. 19-Nov-92 Christie's, New York #371/R
$115000	£77181	Summer picnic (198x366cm-78x144in) s.d.7/75. 3-May-94 Christie's, New York #76/R

KAUFFER, Edward McKnight (1890-1954) American
$1144	£800	Towards Battersea (24x19cm-9x7in) s.i.d.1915 chk W/C gouache. 10-Mar-93 Sotheby's, London #183

KAULA, Lee Lufkin (20th C) American
$1200	£839	Still life with gladiolas and lilies (74x61cm-29x24in) s.d.1917. 12-Mar-93 Skinner, Bolton #267/R

KAULA, William J (1871-1952) American

$900	£629	Landscape (25x33cm-10x13in) s. board. 11-Mar-93 Mystic Fine Arts, Connecticut #219
$900	£596	Across meadow, late afternoon (38x46cm-15x18in) s. 13-Nov-92 Skinner, Bolton #125/R
$1100	£738	Near the pond, New Ipswich, New Hampshire (30x38cm-12x15in) s. board. 6-Dec-93 Grogan, Massachussetts #551/R
$1350	£944	Coastal scene (25x33cm-10x13in) s. board. 11-Mar-93 Mystic Fine Arts, Connecticut #218/R
$2500	£1656	Furnace brook (61x74cm-24x29in) s.verso. 23-Sep-93 Mystic Fine Arts, Connecticut #218 a
$2860	£1869	Hill top haying New Ipswich, N.H (46x58cm-18x23in) s. board. 14-May-93 Skinner, Bolton #71/R
$4500	£3020	New Ipswich Hills (61x74cm-24x29in) s. 6-May-94 Skinner, Bolton #79/R
$8500	£5449	Over the pond, New Ipswich, New Hampshire (81x99cm-32x39in) s. 9-Dec-92 Butterfield & Butterfield, San Francisco #3862/R
$600	*£408*	*Landscape with blue sky (51x65cm-20x26in) s. gouache board. 15-Nov-93 Christie's, East, New York #131/R*
$800	*£537*	*Landscape (51x64cm-20x25in) s. W/C. 16-Dec-93 Mystic Fine Arts, Connecticut #163*
$1600	*£1074*	*Winter in hills, late afternoon (37x44cm-15x17in) s.d.1913 W/C gouache paperboard. 6-May-94 Skinner, Bolton #94/R*

KAVANAUGH, Marion see WACHTEL, Marion K

KAY, Helena de (1846-1916) American

$1740	£1152	Arabic town (36x46cm-14x18in) s. 20-Nov-92 Schloss Ahlden, Ahlden #1983/R (DM 2800)

KAYE, Otis (1885-1974) American

$16000	£10596	Money to burn - almost (13x18cm-5x7in) s. panel. 22-Sep-93 Christie's, New York #51/R
$17000	£9827	Pennies make dollars (16x24cm-6x9in) s. panel. 23-Sep-92 Christie's, New York #78/R
$47500	£27457	Gun fight today O. Kaye's Corral (37x49cm-15x19in) s. panel. 24-Sep-92 Sotheby's, New York #60/R
$92000	£53179	U.S. Musical notes (76x63cm-30x25in) s. panel. 24-Sep-92 Sotheby's, New York #57/R
$95000	£62914	Easy come, easy go (53x65cm-21x26in) s. init. panel. 22-Sep-93 Christie's, New York #64/R
$2400	*£1633*	*The four o'clock trolley. 47th and Ashland Chicago (18x25cm-7x10in) s. one i.d.1928 one i. gouache pencil pair. 17-Nov-93 Doyle, New York #58/R*
$2500	*£1445*	*Two dollar bill (6x15cm-2x6in) s.d.1953 pencil. 24-Sep-92 Sotheby's, New York #46 a/R*

KAYN, Hilde (1903-1950) American

$1400	£809	Two girls (91x71cm-36x28in) s. i.verso. 25-Sep-92 Sotheby's Arcade, New York #352/R

KEARFOTT, Robert Ryland (1890-?) American

$3500	£2263	Old Adobe, Monterey (56x56cm-22x22in) s.i. d.1920 stretcher. 13-Jun-93 Butterfield & Butterfield, San Francisco #826/R

KEFFER, Frances (1881-1953) American

$700	£483	Autumn landscape (28x36cm-11x14in) s. board. 16-Feb-93 John Moran, Pasadena #14

KEHOE, Patrice (1952-) American

$700	£461	Overend over (201x239cm-79x94in) s.i.d.1982verso. 2-Apr-93 Sloan, North Bethesda #2338

KEITH, William (1839-1911) American

$550	£367	Opening through the trees (36x46cm-14x18in) s. 18-Mar-94 Du Mouchelle, Detroit #2243/R
$900	£581	Landscape with figures (46x69cm-18x27in) s. 15-Jul-94 Du Mouchelle, Detroit #2143
$1000	£658	Morgan's Hill (33x41cm-13x16in) s.i. i.stretcher. 4-Nov-92 Doyle, New York #4/R
$1100	£743	Cattle in a clearing (36x46cm-14x18in) s. board. 27-Nov-93 Young Fine Arts Auctions, Maine #184/R
$1200	£789	Inlet on cloudy day (13x23cm-5x9in) s. panel. 13-Jun-93 Butterfield & Butterfield, San Francisco #718/R
$1400	£933	Wooded landscape (23x30cm-9x12in) indist.s. canvas laid on panel. 15-Mar-94 John Moran, Pasadena #154
$1500	£1007	Portrait of artist's wife (76x63cm-30x25in) s. 8-Dec-93 Butterfield & Butterfield, San Francisco #3313/R
$2000	£1176	Autumn (47x74cm-19x29in) s. 4-Oct-92 Butterfield & Butterfield, Los Angeles #11/R
$2250	£1562	Pastoral landscape (14x24cm-6x9in) s. panel. 7-Mar-93 Butterfield & Butterfield, San Francisco #26/R
$2400	£1611	Mount Rainier (33x43cm-13x17in) s. 6-Dec-93 Grogan, Massachussetts #486/R
$2600	£1699	Bright sky at sunset (97x97cm-38x38in) s. 16-May-93 Hindman Galleries, Chicago #60/R
$2700	£1709	Forest clearing with buildings (46x61cm-18x24in) s.d.85. 5-Dec-92 Louisiana Auction Exchange #12/R
$2750	£1618	Under oak tree (63x76cm-25x30in) s. 4-Oct-92 Butterfield & Butterfield, Los Angeles #10/R
$3000	£1754	Landscape with trees and women (46x69cm-18x27in) s. 18-Sep-92 Du Mouchelle, Detroit #2189/R

KEITH, William (1839-1911) American-cont.
$3000	£2013	Winter landscape (55x66cm-22x26in) s. 8-Dec-93 Butterfield & Butterfield, San Francisco #3341/R
$3000	£1987	The river path (36x51cm-14x20in) s. 15-Jun-94 Butterfield & Butterfield, San Francisco #4565/R
$3000	£1765	Wooded interior (33x38cm-13x15in) s. i.verso board. 4-Oct-92 Butterfield & Butterfield, Los Angeles #12/R
$3250	£2196	Wooded landscape with cattle (61x91cm-24x36in) s.indist.d. 15-Jun-93 John Moran, Pasadena #141
$3500	£2288	Evening (61x91cm-24x36in) s. 4-May-93 Christie's, East, New York #123/R
$3750	£2483	Figures in landscape (74x122cm-29x48in) s. canvas on canvas. 28-Sep-93 John Moran, Pasadena #345
$3750	£2534	Wooded landscape with cattle (61x91cm-24x36in) s.indist.d.190-. 9-Nov-93 John Moran, Pasadena #925
$4250	£2796	Storm clouds (51x67cm-20x26in) s.i.d.02 panel. 13-Jun-93 Butterfield & Butterfield, San Francisco #706/R
$4250	£2853	Sunset farm scene (36x49cm-14x19in) s. board. 8-Dec-93 Butterfield & Butterfield, San Francisco #3325/R
$4250	£2951	Hiking the trail (51x36cm-20x14in) s. 7-Mar-93 Butterfield & Butterfield, San Francisco #32/R
$4250	£2853	Landscape with cows (51x51cm-20x20in) s. 8-Dec-93 Butterfield & Butterfield, San Francisco #3314/R
$4500	£2647	Golden sunset (56x69cm-22x27in) s.i. 4-Oct-92 Butterfield & Butterfield, Los Angeles #9/R
$5000	£3289	Figures on mountainous path (25x38cm-10x15in) s. 13-Jun-93 Butterfield & Butterfield, San Francisco #708/R
$6000	£3947	Sierra landscape (61x46cm-24x18in) s.d.78. 13-Jun-93 Butterfield & Butterfield, San Francisco #700/R
$7000	£4605	Woodland path (55x66cm-22x26in) s.i. panel. 13-Jun-93 Butterfield & Butterfield, San Francisco #785/R
$8500	£5705	Berkeley Pond (41x62cm-16x24in) s. 8-Dec-93 Butterfield & Butterfield, San Francisco #3340/R
$15000	£10417	Near the Russian River (36x53cm-14x21in) s.d.76. 7-Mar-93 Butterfield & Butterfield, San Francisco #57/R
$15000	£10067	Mount Rainier (77x64cm-30x25in) s.d.78. 8-Dec-93 Butterfield & Butterfield, San Francisco #3350/R
$1200	*£789*	*San Francisco Bay (25x43cm-10x17in) s.d.88 W/C. 13-Jun-93 Butterfield & Butterfield, San Francisco #731/R*
$6500	*£4362*	*Approaching storm with cattle (32x46cm-13x18in) s. gouache. 8-Dec-93 Butterfield & Butterfield, San Francisco #3361/R*

KEITH, William (attrib) (1839-1911) American
$750	£487	Man in forest (36x71cm-14x28in) indis.s. 11-Sep-93 Louisiana Auction Exchange #38/R

KELLER, Edgar Martin (1868-1923) American
$700	£483	In the boat yard (30x41cm-12x16in) s. plywood. 16-Feb-93 John Moran, Pasadena #104

KELLER, Henry George (1870-1949) American
$1400	£927	Make ready for the performance (76x61cm-30x24in) s. 19-Jun-94 Hindman Galleries, Chicago #659

KELLER, J (19th C) American
$1042	£700	Eugene Beauharnais, Duke of Leuchtenberg (29x24cm-11x9in) painted oval. 12-Oct-93 Sotheby's, Munich #3232 (DM 1700)

KELLEY, Mike (1954-) American
$1800	£1250	Garbage drawing no 67 (59x80cm-23x31in) i.verso acrylic paper. 22-Feb-93 Christie's, East, New York #264/R
$3500	£2431	Garbage drawing no 37 (60x80cm-24x31in) i.verso acrylic paper. 22-Feb-93 Christie's, East, New York #262/R
$10000	£6623	Double Hierarchy (124x91cm-49x36in) acrylic paper two parts executed 1988. 18-Nov-92 Sotheby's, New York #302/R
$12665	£8500	Rainbow of death (152x151cm-60x59in) acrylic paper executed 1985. 3-Dec-93 Sotheby's, London #275/R
$2600	*£1745*	*Garbage drawing no.33 (71x104cm-28x41in) acrylic paper executed 1988. 23-Feb-94 Christie's, New York #132/R*
$3500	*£2349*	*The Big Day (60x46cm-24x18in) s.i.d.1980 verso brush ink gouache felt-tip pen. 23-Feb-94 Christie's, East, New York #226/R*
$3600	*£2416*	*Garbage drawing no.43 (76x109cm-30x43in) acrylic paper executed 1988. 23-Feb-94 Christie's, New York #133/R*
$11000	*£7383*	*Untitle (76x169cm-30x67in) s.d.1982 verso gesso brush ink felt-tip 3 sheets. 23-Feb-94 Christie's, New York #139/R*
$14000	*£9396*	*Cool. Neutral. Hot. Perpetual motion machine No.1,2 Pinnacle of Justice - The Tower of Babel, pencil acrylic six. 5-May-94 Sotheby's, New York #351 a/R*

KELLY, Ellsworth (1923-) American
$50000	£34722	Brooklyn Bridge (86x33cm-34x13in) init.d.58verso. 24-Feb-93 Christie's, New York #25/R
$130000	£87838	Wave Motif Relief II (57x91cm-22x36in) init.num.d.1960-61 verso panel. 9-Nov-93 Christie's, New York #4/R
$180000	£121622	Yellow black (244x180cm-96x71in) init.d.1972 verso two panels. 9-Nov-93 Christie's, New York #43/R

KELLY, Ellsworth (1923-) American-cont.

$190000	£125828	Blue white (285x292cm-112x115in) s.d.1980verso. 18-Nov-92 Christie's, New York #30/R
$200000	£130719	Blue red (165x381cm-65x150in) s.d.65 stretcher. 4-May-93 Christie's, New York #27/R
$220000	£148649	Green angle (178x587cm-70x231in) init.d.1970. 10-Nov-93 Sotheby's, New York #45/R
$230000	£154362	Black over white, EK 374 (218x203cm-86x80in) init. s.d.66stretcher two panels. 4-May-94 Sotheby's, New York #35/R
$240000	£162162	Black and white (262x357cm-103x141in) s.d.1988 verso two panels. 9-Nov-93 Christie's, New York #37/R
$2600	£1529	Untitled (113x101cm-44x40in) graphite paper. 8-Oct-92 Christie's, New York #156/R
$4075	£2500	Untitled (72x57cm-28x22in) s.d.60 pencil. 14-Oct-92 Sotheby's, London #375/R
$5000	£2941	Branches of leaves (96x53cm-38x21in) s.d.86 pencil three sheets paper on rag board. 6-Oct-92 Sotheby's, New York #161/R
$5500	£3595	Flower drawings (30x15cm-12x6in) init.d.1989 ink pair. 4-May-93 Sotheby's, New York #212/R
$7500	£4412	Untitled, No. 3,4,5 (53x96cm-21x38in) pencil three sheets paper on rag board. 6-Oct-92 Sotheby's, New York #152/R
$8000	£5229	Sea grapes (30x22cm-12x9in) s.i.d.1988 verso graphite. 4-May-93 Sotheby's, New York #194 a/R
$8000	£5229	Oak (25x33cm-10x13in) s.d.1986 verso pencil pair. 4-May-93 Sotheby's, New York #213/R

KELLY, James Edward (1855-1933) American

$3500	£2023	Needlepoint (43x33cm-17x13in) indis.s.verso board. 23-Sep-92 Christie's, New York #158/R

KELLY, Leon (20th C) American

$1800	£1224	Vase of flowers (61x43cm-24x17in) 14-Apr-94 Freeman Fine Arts, Philadelphia #1034
$450	£306	Dancers (28x41cm-11x16in) s. pencil dr. 14-Apr-94 Freeman Fine Arts, Philadelphia #1033
$500	£340	Vase of flowers (43x30cm-17x12in) s. W/C gouache. 14-Apr-94 Freeman Fine Arts, Philadelphia #1032
$2600	£1733	Cubist composition (42x23cm-17x9in) s. pencil. 23-May-94 Christie's, East, New York #225/R

KENDALL, William Sergeant (1869-1938) American

$900	£592	Tongues of fire (41x32cm-16x13in) s. panel. 31-Mar-93 Sotheby's Arcade, New York #185/R
$4000	£2632	Autumn landscape with tree shadows on grassy meadows (53x53cm-21x21in) s. 31-Mar-93 Sotheby's Arcade, New York #183/R
$4250	£2796	Autumn landscape with grassy meadow and hills in distance (53x53cm-21x21in) s. 31-Mar-93 Sotheby's Arcade, New York #182/R

KENDE, Geza (1889-1952) American

$800	£530	Imaginative landscape (74x56cm-29x22in) s. 14-Jun-94 John Moran, Pasadena #94
$2250	£1510	Still life of flowers (64x76cm-25x30in) s. 5-Mar-94 Louisiana Auction Exchange #118/R
$3000	£1987	Reclining nude (56x81cm-22x32in) s. 15-Jun-94 Butterfield & Butterfield, San Francisco #4608/R

KENDERDINE, Augustus (1870-1947) Canadian

$4000	£2649	On the trail (91x61cm-36x24in) indist.s. 15-Jun-94 Butterfield & Butterfield, San Francisco #4408/R
$1596	£1078	Moon rise (64x43cm-25x17in) s.i. W/C chl painted late 1920s/early 30s. 25-Apr-94 Levis, Calgary #138/R (C.D 2200)

KENNEDY, Charles Anthony (20th C) American

$3800	£2550	Portrait of Barbra Streisand eating cake sitting on canopy bed (34x31cm-13x12in) pen pencil executed c.1960's. 4-Mar-94 Christie's, East, New York #338/R

KENNEDY, John William (1903-) American

$2000	£1156	New York skyline (76x92cm-30x36in) s. 24-Sep-92 Sotheby's, New York #146/R

KENSETT, John Frederick (1816-1872) American

$2069	£1389	Belleville-Passiac river landscape (30x41cm-12x16in) indist.d. with sig.i.stretcher. 30-Nov-93 Ritchie, Toronto #63/R (C.D 2750)
$9500	£6419	Mountain vista (30x41cm-12x16in) mono.indis.d.55. 20-Mar-93 Weschler, Washington #82/R
$11000	£7333	Bashbish Falls (41x36cm-16x16in) 25-May-94 Sotheby's, New York #8/R
$18000	£10405	Mist over the lake (32x41cm-13x16in) init.d.69. 23-Sep-92 Christie's, New York #24/R
$20000	£13986	Late summer (36x61cm-14x24in) 11-Mar-93 Christie's, New York #15/R
$24000	£16107	Landscape (86x68cm-34x27in) 3-Dec-93 Christie's, New York #105/R
$30000	£18987	Along the shore (25x46cm-10x18in) 3-Dec-92 Sotheby's, New York #27/R
$38000	£24359	Passing shower (46x61cm-18x24in) init.d.1848 s.i.stretcher. 26-May-93 Christie's, New York #18/R
$95000	£60127	Beach at Newport (25x43cm-10x17in) init. indis.d. 3-Dec-92 Sotheby's, New York #26/R
$850	£491	Steamship by the shore (12x20cm-5x8in) i.d.May 6,68 pencil. 25-Sep-92 Sotheby's Arcade, New York #65/R
$1100	£636	Lake George (25x36cm-10x14in) i. pencil. 25-Sep-92 Sotheby's Arcade, New York #66/R

KENSETT, John Frederick (attrib) (1816-1872) American
$1254   £804   Falls of Niagara and Terrapin Tower, from Goat Island (30x46cm-12x18in) 7-Dec-92 Waddingtons, Toronto #1507/R (C.D 1600)
$1800   £1200   Landscape with stream (25x30cm-10x12in) 23-May-94 Christie's, East, New York #37/R

KENSETT, John Frederick and HICKS, Thomas (19th C) American
$4000   £2649   Italian scene (26x36cm-10x14in) init.d.46 i.verso. 23-Sep-93 Sotheby's, New York #72 a/R

KENT, Frank W (1912-1977) American
$850   £563   Village under fresh snow (56x72cm-22x28in) s.d.37. 15-Jun-94 Butterfield & Butterfield, San Francisco #4440/R

KENT, Rockwell (1882-1971) American
$5000   £3378   A Northern Exposure the Alaskan coast (30x35cm-12x14in) s.d.1919 panel. 5-Nov-93 Skinner, Bolton #154/R
$16000   £10596   Aasgard farm (51x61cm-20x24in) s. panel. 23-Sep-93 Sotheby's, New York #267/R
$26000   £17333   Silmilik Fjord, West Greenland (86x112cm-34x44in) s. i.d.1929verso canvas over panel. 26-May-94 Christie's, New York #120/R
$95000   £63333   Greenland people (71x86cm-28x34in) s. canvas over panel. 26-May-94 Christie's, New York #121/R
$600   £385   Woodcutter (8x10cm-3x4in) s. brush pen dr. 27-May-93 Swann Galleries, New York #145/R
$1600   £1039   Smoking a cigar. The toy sailboat , studio st. chl htd white Indian ink pencil two. 9-Sep-93 Sotheby's Arcade, New York #145/R
$2700   £1788   Mobey Dick (25x43cm-10x17in) ink dr. 23-Sep-93 Mystic Fine Arts, Connecticut #44/R

KENYON, Henry Rodman (1861-1926) American
$1800   £1192   Venice (30x41cm-12x16in) s. 28-Nov-92 Young Fine Arts Auctions, Maine #254/R

KEPES, Gyorgy (1906-) Hungarian/American
$1800   £1192   Broken light (63x76cm-25x30in) i.d.1959verso. 29-Sep-93 Sotheby's Arcade, New York #271/R

KERNAN, Joseph F (1878-1958) American
$2000   £1333   Suspense, boy fishing with his dog (71x56cm-28x22in) s. 13-Mar-94 Hindman Galleries, Chicago #822/R

KERR, Estelle Muriel (1897-1971) Canadian
$1456   £971   The picnic (35x27cm-14x11in) s. s.i.verso panel sold with oil by Betty Lewis. 11-May-94 Sotheby's, Toronto #207 (C.D 2000)

KERR, Illingsworth Holey (1905-1989) Canadian
$620   £419   Untitled Abstract (51x60cm-20x24in) d.c.1960 canvasboard. 1-Nov-93 Levis, Calgary #127 (C.D 800)
$701   £464   Jack pines, French river (30x41cm-12x16in) mono. i.d.Oct.1975. 18-Nov-92 Sotheby's, Toronto #248/R (C.D 900)
$722   £488   The Porcupine Hills, September (30x41cm-12x16in) mono. i.d.1985 verso. 30-Mar-94 Maynards, Vancouver #15 (C.D 1000)
$775   £524   Spring Jasper Highway (30x41cm-12x16in) mono. s.i.d.1986verso canvasboard. 1-Nov-93 Levis, Calgary #126 (C.D 1000)
$846   £498   Tamarisk in blossom, Mesa, Ariz (30x41cm-12x16in) mono.s.i.d.April 1977verso canvasboard. 5-Oct-92 Levis, Calgary #127/R (C.D 1050)
$1020   £667   West of Okotoks (31x41cm-12x16in) mono. s.d.1979 verso. 10-May-93 Hodgins, Calgary #250/R (C.D 1300)
$1057   £714   Moose, Storm Mountain (40x50cm-16x20in) init. canvasboard painted 1982. 23-Nov-93 Joyner Fine Art, Toronto #252 (C.D 1400)
$1097   £704   Night, Aldersyde, Alta (30x41cm-12x16in) s. s.i.d.1981verso canvasboard. 26-Apr-93 Levis, Calgary #84/R (C.D 1400)
$1131   £769   Beaver Canal Beaver Flats (30x41cm-12x16in) mono. s.i.d.1986verso canvasboard. 15-Nov-93 Hodgins, Calgary #239/R (C.D 1500)
$1137   £729   Mt Rundle from Vermilion Lake (30x41cm-12x16in) mono s.i.d.1980verso masonite. 26-Apr-93 Levis, Calgary #85/R (C.D 1450)
$1220   £813   Study in depth (30x41cm-12x16in) s. i.d.verso artist's board. 30-May-94 Hodgins, Calgary #46/R (C.D 1700)
$1550   £1047   The Creek at John Ware's Millarville Ranch (41x51cm-16x20in) mono. s.i.d.1980verso canvasboard. 1-Nov-93 Levis, Calgary #124 (C.D 2000)
$2040   £1333   Nocturne, back of Rundle (31x41cm-12x16in) mono. s.d.1973 verso. 10-May-93 Hodgins, Calgary #223/R (C.D 2600)
$2040   £1333   House by bridge - Chilliwack, B.C (56x76cm-22x30in) mono. s.verso. 10-May-93 Hodgins, Calgary #126/R (C.D 2600)
$2040   £1333   Ice on Bow River, Louise Bridge (56x76cm-22x30in) mono. s.verso. 10-May-93 Hodgins, Calgary #246/R (C.D 2600)
$2488   £1692   Pond in the foothills in autumn (46x61cm-18x24in) s. s.i.d.1969verso board. 15-Nov-93 Hodgins, Calgary #86/R (C.D 3300)
$3113   £2062   Beaver flats, Elbow River Forest Reserve (71x97cm-28x38in) mono s.i.d.1978stretcher. 16-Nov-92 Hodgins, Calgary #129/R (C.D 4000)
$549   £359   Trek (61x79cm-24x31in) mono. sand drawing W/C. 10-May-93 Hodgins, Calgary #159 (C.D 700)
$620   £419   Red heads and horizontals (39x56cm-15x22in) mono.d.1979 i.d.verso W/C. 1-Nov-93 Levis, Calgary #128/R (C.D 800)
$967   £569   Mountain landscape (39x57cm-15x22in) mono W/C. 5-Oct-92 Levis, Calgary #125/R (C.D 1200)

KERR, Vernon (?-1982) American
$650   £430   Mendocino hideaway (76x61cm-30x24in) s. masonite. 28-Sep-93 John Moran, Pasadena #285

KESZTHELYI, Alexander Samuel (1874-1953) American/Polish
$1100 £719   California valley (46x36cm-18x14in) s. 22-May-93 Collins, Maine #37/R

KETCHUM, Abijah E (19th C) American
$800   £537   Little girl with dog (41x33cm-16x13in) s.d.1885 verso. 14-Jan-94 Du Mouchelle, Detroit #2156/R

KEY, John Ross (1832-1920) American
$1500 £1007 Mountain lake with river boat (33x58cm-13x23in) s. 6-Dec-93 Grogan, Massachussetts #481/R
$3500 £2303 Monteray Bay, California (64x76cm-25x30in) s. 4-Nov-92 Doyle, New York #21/R
$5500 £3642 Hollyhocks (76x38cm-30x15in) s. 15-Jun-94 Butterfield & Butterfield, San Francisco #4664/R
$7500 £3968 Mount Dixville, Franconia Plain (46x97cm-18x38in) s.d.73 i.verso. 11-Sep-92 Skinner, Bolton #191/R
$1000 £658   Mountain road (38x63cm-15x25in) s.d.76 pencil. 13-Jun-93 Butterfield & Butterfield, San Francisco #3139/R

KIENHOLZ, Edward (1927-1994) American
$2123   £1474   Drawing for the middle island no.1 (60x136cm-24x54in) s.d.1973 felt pen crayon serigraph metal panel. 3-Mar-93 Guy Loudmer, Paris #88/R (F.FR 12000)
$11920 £8000   Drawing for the Soup Course at She She Cafe (81x101cm-32x40in) s.i.d.1982 mixed media lead. 3-Dec-93 Sotheby's, London #238/R

KILBERT, Robert P (20th C) American
$800   £548   On the alert (58x71cm-23x28in) s. masonite. 7-Feb-94 Selkirks, St. Louis #123/R

KILBOURNE, Samuel A (attrib) (1836-1881) American
$2800 £1618 Pickerel. Bass (8x13cm-3x5in) i.verso board pair. 23-Sep-92 Christie's, New York #26/R

KILGOUR, Andrew Wilkie (1868-1930) Canadian
$1057 £714   Ready for the party (76x63cm-30x25in) s. 23-Nov-93 Fraser Pinneys, Quebec #372 (C.D 1400)

KILLGORE, Charles P (20th C) American
$750   £524   Western landscape with figures (58x74cm-23x29in) s. 7-Feb-93 James Bakker, Cambridge #187

KILPATRICK, Aaron Edward (1872-1953) American
$2750 £1809 Oaks, Chorro Valley (61x76cm-24x30in) s.d.1926. 13-Jun-93 Butterfield & Butterfield, San Francisco #813/R
$3000 £2083 Near Eagle Rock (51x76cm-20x30in) s.d.1912. 7-Mar-93 Butterfield & Butterfield, San Francisco #191/R

KIM, Tag (fl.1978) Canadian?
$502   £335   Eskimo seal hunter (61x91cm-24x36in) s.d. 30-May-94 Hodgins, Calgary #343/R (C.D 700)

KIMBEL, Richard M (1865-1942) American
$4000 £2685 New York City scene (79x97cm-31x38in) s. 16-Dec-93 Mystic Fine Arts, Connecticut #266

KIMLER, Wesley (1953-) American
$2500 £1582 Untitled, 1987 (147x122cm-58x48in) 25-Oct-92 Butterfield & Butterfield, San Francisco #2401/R

KING FEATURES STUDIO (20th C) American
$1000 £671   Yellow Submarine, Paul and George (23x29cm-9x11in) exec.1968 gouache celluloid. 22-Jun-93 Sotheby's, New York #546/R

KING, Albert F (1854-1945) American
$1300 £688   Autumn landscape (43x99cm-17x39in) s. 13-Sep-92 Dargate Auction Galleries, Pittsburgh #333
$1600 £1046 River landscape, early autumn (51x84cm-20x33in) s. 18-Sep-93 Young Fine Arts Auctions, Maine #176/R
$2000 £1307 Grapes and apples (46x61cm-18x24in) s. 22-May-93 Weschler, Washington #88/R
$2100 £1373 Apples by overturned basket (36x51cm-14x20in) s. 22-May-93 Weschler, Washington #108/R
$2500 £1656 Still life with apples and grapes (46x61cm-18x24in) s. 13-Nov-92 Skinner, Bolton #99/R
$2600 £1757 Still life with melon and pears (31x46cm-12x18in) s. 31-Mar-94 Sotheby's Arcade, New York #111/R
$5500 £2910 Still life with peaches, blueberries and melons (46x61cm-18x24in) s. 11-Sep-92 Skinner, Bolton #180/R
$5750 £3885 Table top with peaches, melon and knife (36x46cm-14x18in) s. 31-Mar-94 Sotheby's Arcade, New York #54/R
$7750 £5237 Geranium and cherries (51x33cm-20x13in) s. 31-Mar-94 Sotheby's Arcade, New York #49/R

KING, Charles Bird (1785-1862) American
$4500   £3000   Peechekir - Buffalo, Chippewa (26x16cm-10x6in) chl pencil white chk. 17-Mar-94 Sotheby's, New York #57/R
$4750   £3167   No-Tin - Wind, Chippewa (26x16cm-10x6in) chl white chk. 17-Mar-94 Sotheby's, New York #56/R

KING, Charles Bird (attrib) (1785-1862) American
$1200   £694   Portrait of lady (76x63cm-30x25in) bears mono.d.1850. 25-Sep-92 Sotheby's Arcade, New York #44/R
$4500   £2961   Tabletop still life of grapes (64x76cm-25x30in) 2-Apr-93 Sloan, North Bethesda #2472/R

KING, George W (1836-1922) American
$800   £526   Homestead mill near Lake George New York (46x76cm-18x30in) s. 5-Jun-93 Louisiana Auction Exchange #87/R

KING, James S (1852-1925) American
$15000 £9934   Summer afternoon (63x76cm-25x30in) s. 23-Sep-93 Sotheby's, New York #157/R

KING, Mark (20th C) American
$1200   £816   Couple on dock (76x102cm-30x40in) s. acrylic. 19-Nov-93 Du Mouchelle, Detroit #2045/R

KING, Paul (1867-1940) American
$800   £533   Autumn in the Adirondacks (41x30cm-16x12in) s. s.i.verso canvasboard. 1-Jun-94 Doyle, New York #40
$1000   £658   Landscape with cabin (43x56cm-17x22in) s. 5-Jun-93 Louisiana Auction Exchange #117/R
$2100   £1391   Harbour scene (41x51cm-16x20in) s. 23-Sep-93 Mystic Fine Arts, Connecticut #87 a/R

KINGMAN, Dong (1911-) American
$850   £559   The parade (48x64cm-19x25in) s. W/C. 4-Nov-92 Doyle, New York #39/R
$1000   £633   Cornfields (51x72cm-20x28in) s.d.40 W/C paperboard. 2-Dec-92 Christie's, East, New York #334/R
$1200   £789   Grant Avenue (29x24cm-11x9in) s. W/C. 13-Jun-93 Butterfield & Butterfield, San Francisco #953/R
$1300   £878   New York Buildings (36x53cm-14x21in) s. W/C. 15-Jun-93 John Moran, Pasadena #79
$1300   £855   Pennsylvania Avenue (39x56cm-15x22in) s.d.45 W/C. 31-Mar-93 Sotheby's Arcade New York #395/R
$1300   £850   Rural landscape with farmhouses (33x51cm-13x20in) s. W/C. 30-Oct-92 Sloan North Bethesda #2212/R
$1500   £980   Western mountain landscape (33x51cm-13x20in) s.d.1943 W/C. 30-Oct-92 Sloan, North Bethesda #2213/R
$1600   £1081   Five storied pagoda in snow (55x37cm-22x15in) s. i.verso W/C. 31-Mar-94 Sotheby's Arcade, New York #414/R
$1600   £1053   Church at 15th Street (39x57cm-15x22in) s.d.47 W/C. 31-Mar-93 Sotheby's Arcade, New York #394/R
$1600   £1060   New York rooftops (37x53cm-15x21in) s. W/C. 15-Jun-94 Butterfield & Butterfield, San Francisco #4754/R
$2250   £1562   Lands End light (55x37cm-22x15in) s.d.36 W/C pencil. 7-Mar-93 Butterfield & Butterfield, San Francisco #262/R
$2500   £1623   New York Harbour (56x76cm-22x30in) s. W/C. 9-Sep-93 Sotheby's Arcade, New York #389/R
$2500   £1736   Figures along beach (36x53cm-14x21in) s.d.40 W/C. 7-Mar-93 Butterfield & Butterfield, San Francisco #252/R
$3250   £2181   A night alley in Kyoto (53x36cm-21x14in) s. W/C. 8-Dec-93 Butterfield & Butterfield, San Francisco #3525/R
$3500   £2349   A long view - San Francisco (48x74cm-19x29in) s. W/C. 8-Dec-93 Butterfield & Butterfield, San Francisco #3524/R
$4000   £2703   View of a Chinese village (57x76cm-22x30in) s. W/C. 31-Mar-94 Sotheby's Arcade, New York #412/R
$4250   £2457   Under the East River Drive (55x75cm-22x30in) s. W/C. 25-Sep-92 Sotheby's Arcade, New York #449/R
$6000   £4196   100 fishermen (77x76cm-30x22in) s.i. exec.c.1961 W/C. 10-Mar-93 Sotheby's, New York #164/R

KINGMAN, Eduardo (20th C) South American
$3000   £2027   Guitarrista (79x99cm-31x39in) s.d.63 s.i.verso. 22-Nov-93 Sotheby's, New York #221/R
$10000 £6757   Pirotecnia (105x80cm-41x31in) s.d.47. 23-Nov-93 Christie's, New York #130/R

KINGSBURY, Edward R (19/20th C) American
$800   £523   California hills (61x76cm-24x30in) s. 18-Sep-93 Young Fine Arts Auctions, Maine #178/R

KINKADE, Thomas (20th C) American
$2750   £1910   Yosemite clearing (61x76cm-24x30in) s.i.d.1982 board. 7-Mar-93 Butterfield & Butterfield, San Francisco #137/R

KINNELL, K (20th C) American
$800   £526   Wild horses fleeing storm (61x91cm-24x36in) s.d.1966. 31-Mar-93 Sotheby's Arcade, New York #207

KINNEY, Charles (1906-1991) American
$1900   £1258   The Pack Peddler (56x71cm-22x28in) s.i. pencil W/C. 21-Nov-92 Litchfield Auction Gallery #21

KINNEY, Margaret West (1872-?) American
$2500   £1645   Paris park scene at night (37x46cm-15x18in) s.d.05 cradled panel. 13-Jun-93 Butterfield & Butterfield, San Francisco #3155/R

KIPNISS, Robert (1931-) American
$1000   £699   Landscape with house (86x91cm-34x36in) s. 14-Mar-93 Hindman Galleries, Chicago #79
$1000   £662   Landscape with barns by a mountain (84x89cm-33x35in) s. 3-Jan-93 Litchfield Auction Gallery #5
$1000   £654   Opposing seasons (99x99cm-39x39in) s. 19-Sep-93 Hindman Galleries, Chicago #785

KIRK, Frank C (1889-1963) American
$1200   £784   Studio corner (77x76cm-30x30in) s. 4-May-93 Christie's, East, New York #283/R

KIRKBY, Ken (1940-) Canadian
$1087   £725   Arctic landscape with Inukshuks (91x122cm-36x48in) s. 6-Jun-94 Waddingtons, Toronto #1281 (C.D 1500)
$1204   £808   Arctic landscape with Inukshuks (91x122cm-36x48in) s. 29-Nov-93 Waddingtons, Toronto #1100/R (C.D 1600)
$1403   £923   Birds on driftwood (51x102cm-20x40in) s.d.82 acrylic board. 7-Jun-93 Waddingtons, Toronto #1084 b (C.D 1800)

KIROUAC, Louise Lecor (20th C) Canadian
$507   £338   St. Urbain in Charlevoix (51x61cm-20x24in) s. i.verso acrylic. 6-Jun-94 Waddingtons, Toronto #1315 (C.D 700)
$510   £340   Une belle promenade (50x60cm-20x24in) s. 13-May-94 Joyner Fine Art, Toronto #213/R (C.D 700)
$538   £359   La levee du courrier (51x61cm-20x24in) s. i.verso acrylic. 30-May-94 Hodgins, Calgary #42/R (C.D 750)
$620   £419   Au paye du Saguenay Quebec (51x61cm-20x24in) s. s.i.verso. 1-Nov-93 Levis, Calgary #132/R (C.D 800)
$655   £437   Les deux amis (40x50cm-16x20in) s. 13-May-94 Joyner Fine Art, Toronto #261/R (C.D 900)
$716   £487   Promenade Quebec (51x61cm-20x24in) s. s.i.verso. 15-Nov-93 Hodgins, Calgary #118 (C.D 950)
$722   £488   Doux printemps (41x51cm-16x20in) s.i.verso. 30-Mar-94 Maynards, Vancouver #8 (C.D 1000)
$907   £613   Entre St Gabriel et Ste Angele de Merici, Baie de Fleuve, Quebec (51x61cm-20x24in) s. s.i.verso. 25-Apr-94 Levis, Calgary #141/R (C.D 1250)
$1133   £765   Aux Eboulements, Charlevoix (60x75cm-24x30in) s. 23-Nov-93 Joyner Fine Art, Toronto #327/R (C.D 1500)

KITAJ, R B (1932-) American
$19560 £12000 This train of though which you blame is the sole consolation that my life contains (76x76cm-30x30in) painted 1962. 14-Oct-92 Sotheby's, London #358/R
$45000 £29412 Little slum picture (76x61cm-30x24in) s.verso painted 1968. 4-May-93 Sotheby's, New York #378/R
$55080 £36000 Sorbonne Hotel SW7 (217x59cm-85x23in) s.i.d.90 on overlap. 29-Jun-94 Sotheby's, London #52/R
$22000 *£14865* *Paris bather - art student (137x58cm-54x23in) s. chl pastel executed 1984-86. 11-Nov-93 Sotheby's, New York #358/R*

KITCHELL, H M (1862-1944) American
$800   £533   Forest interior with canoe (61x46cm-24x18in) 29-Jan-94 San Rafael Auction Galleries #328

KITCHELL, Hudson Mindell (1862-1944) American
$600   £408   Blazing forest (64x76cm-25x30in) s. board. 17-Apr-94 Hanzel Galleries, Chicago #3
$650   £433   Autumn landscape (30x25cm-12x10in) s. 21-May-94 Weschler, Washington #112
$800   £523   Dawn landscape (41x61cm-16x24in) s. 15-May-93 Dunning's, Illinois #1074/R
$850   £556   Moonlight (46x36cm-18x14in) s. 16-May-93 Hanzel Galleries, Chicago #16
$900   £588   Wooded landscape (64x76cm-25x30in) s. 8-May-93 Young Fine Arts Auctions, Maine #187/R
$1000   £699   Autumn sunrise (46x71cm-18x28in) s.d.1931. 5-Feb-93 Sloan, North Bethesda #2205/R
$1100   £764   Golden glow (64x76cm-25x30in) s. i.verso. 27-Feb-93 Young Fine Arts Auctions, Maine #177/R
$1300   £855   River landscape with trees (102x152cm-40x60in) s.d.1917. 31-Mar-93 Sotheby's Arcade, New York #153/R

KITTELL, Nicholas Biddle (1822-1894) American
$3500   £2203   Beardsley Children, Kate 14 Louie 6 Jane 3 seated in landscape (89x91cm-35x36in) i.verso painted 1855. 5-Jun-93 Skinner, Bolton #367/R

KLEEMAN, Ron (1937-) American
$1000   £694   Erection site (229x178cm-90x70in) s. painted 1971 acrylic. 22-Feb-93 Christie's, East, New York #173/R

KLEIN, Pat (20th C) American
$1100   *£692*   *Yellow room (183x244cm-72x96in) s.i.d.1981verso mixed media canvas. 25-Apr-93 Butterfield & Butterfield, San Francisco #2137/R*

KLEITSCH, Joseph (1885-1931) American
$950 £655 Parenting joys, European interior (46x61cm-18x24in) s. 16-Feb-93 John Moran, Pasadena #123
$1100 £728 Portrait of cowboy with Tom Mix style hat (51x38cm-20x15in) s. 14-Jun-94 John Moran, Pasadena #88
$3250 £2152 Balboa Park Trolly Depot (43x48cm-17x19in) s. canvasboard. 28-Sep-93 John Moran, Pasadena #344

KLINE, Franz (1910-1962) American
$4309 £2912 Marionett doll (40x33cm-16x13in) s. 6-Nov-93 Falkkloos, Malmo #215/R (S.KR 35000)
$17000 £11111 Untitled (44x44cm-17x17in) s. panel painted c.1947. 4-May-93 Sotheby's, New York #287 a/R
$43000 £29054 Lehigh yellow sand (35x39cm-14x15in) s. paperboard painted 1959. 11-Nov-93 Sotheby's, New York #253/R
$55000 £35948 Black triangle (33x25cm-13x10in) s. canvasboard painted 1961. 4-May-93 Christie's, New York #2/R
$75000 £50336 Untitled, study for Wanamaker Block (30x28cm-12x11in) paper on board painted c.1955-1956. 3-May-94 Christie's, New York #1/R
$130000 £84967 Warm black and white (60x47cm-24x19in) s.d.57 paper. 3-May-93 Sotheby's, New York #5/R
$750 *£521* *Untitled (39x32cm-15x13in) graphite. 22-Feb-93 Christie's, East, New York #135/R*
$3000 *£1987* *Untitled (28x21cm-11x8in) mono.s. brush ink gouache. 17-Nov-92 Christie's, East, New York #281/R*
$3800 *£2517* *Untitled (25x22cm-10x9in) mono.s.d.46 gouache paper on paper. 17-Nov-92 Christie's, East, New York #278/R*
$8000 *£5369* *Untitled (22x28cm-9x11in) col.chk crayon W/C executed c.1950. 4-May-94 Christie's, New York #104/R*
$22000 *£14570* *Untitled (46x53cm-18x21in) s.d.April 17 painted 1949 brush ink. 19-Nov-92 Christie's, New York #328/R*
$22000 *£14765* *Untitled (23x28cm-9x11in) s. brush ink telephone book page on board. 23-Feb-94 Christie's, New York #7/R*
$30000 *£20833* *Untitled (22x28cm-9x11in) s. executed c.1951-53 ink. 23-Feb-93 Sotheby's, New York #213/R*
$40000 *£26144* *Untitled - study for Leda (24x18cm-9x7in) s. ink painted 1950. 3-May-93 Sotheby's, New York #9/R*
$75000 *£50676* *Untitled (27x31cm-11x12in) s. ink executed c.1955. 11-Nov-93 Sotheby's, New York #260/R*

KLIPPERT, Howard (20th C) American
$2500 £1678 Gloucester (41x51cm-16x20in) s. board painted 1934. 26-Mar-94 James Bakker, Cambridge #122/R

KLOSS, Gene (1903-) American
$3600 £2517 Midwinter moonlight (61x76cm-24x30in) s. 14-Mar-93 Hindman Galleries, Chicago #17/R
$3000 *£1987* *Winter in the Sierras (53x72cm-21x28in) s. W/C. 15-Jun-94 Butterfield & Butterfield, San Francisco #4526/R*

KLOSS, Gene (attrib) (1903-) American
$1400 *£886* *October day, Taos (51x69cm-20x27in) s. W/C. 30-Nov-92 Schrager Galleries, Milwaukee #414*

KLUK, Clara (1947-) Mexican?
$633 £417 Las sombras de enero (72x106cm-28x42in) s. acrylic paper. 4-Nov-92 Mora, Castelltort & Quintana, Juarez #51/R (M.P 2000000)

KNAP, Joseph D (1875-?) American
$600 *£426* *Canada geese (36x53cm-14x21in) s. W/C. 13-Feb-93 Collins, Maine #65/R*

KNAPP, C W (1822-1900) American
$6000 £4027 Mountain river scene (71x127cm-28x50in) 27-Mar-94 Myers, Florida #29/R

KNAPP, Charles W (1822-1900) American
$2200 £1497 A New England landscape (51x91cm-20x36in) s. 15-Nov-93 Christie's, East, New York #60/R
$2700 £1588 River landscape with fisherman (51x91cm-20x36in) s. 8-Oct-92 Freeman Fine Arts, Philadelphia #1091/R
$3000 £1734 Rocky coast (36x56cm-14x22in) s. 23-Sep-92 Christie's, New York #58/R
$3000 £1987 On French Creek (51x91cm-20x36in) s. 22-Sep-93 Christie's, New York #23/R
$3500 £2365 Cows grazing by a stream with hills beyond (51x91cm-20x36in) s. canvas on masonite. 31-Mar-94 Sotheby's Arcade, New York #46/R
$3800 £2533 The Mohawk at Westerville, New York (51x91cm-20x36in) s. 23-May-94 Christie's, East, New York #13/R
$5250 £3409 Figures on rocky coast (51x91cm-20x36in) s. 9-Sep-93 Sotheby's Arcade, New York #59/R
$10000 £6229 Early autumn (71x161cm-28x63in) s. 4-Dec-92 Christie's, New York #229/R

KNATHS, Karl (1891-1971) American
$1000 £671 Rooster and sunflowers (76x91cm-30x36in) s. 24-Jun-93 Mystic Fine Arts, Connecticut #128
$1500 £987 Duck-decoy (76x91cm-30x36in) s. s.d.1970 verso. 31-Mar-93 Sotheby's Arcade, New York #468/R
$1850 £1242 Lilac (61x76cm-24x30in) s. 28-Mar-93 James Bakker, Cambridge #66/R
$4000 £2797 Aboriginal (76x115cm-30x45in) s. 11-Mar-93 Christie's, New York #268/R

KNATHS, Karl (1891-1971) American-cont.
$1300   *£878*   *The harbour, Provincetown (38x50cm-15x20in) s. i.verso W/C chl double-sided.*
                        31-Mar-94 Sotheby's Arcade, New York #296/R

KNIGHT, Charles Robert (1874-1953) American
$5000   £2890   Blackfoot Star Lore - studies for Hayden Planetarium mural (61x165cm-24x65in)
                        three studies. 24-Sep-92 Sotheby's, New York #209/R

KNIGHT, Daniel Ridgway (1839-1924) American
$550   £377   'At the ferry' - a study (25x20cm-10x8in) s.i. i.verso panel. 10-Feb-94 Skinner,
                        Bolton #22
$1600   £1067   Head of girl. Girl in profile , s.d. January 19 1909 two. 13-Mar-94 Hindman
                        Galleries, Chicago #754
$1760   £1128   French woman at the river (23x18cm-9x7in) s.d.1876 panel. 17-Dec-92 Mystic Fine
                        Arts, Connecticut #217
$7000   £3646   Jeunes paysannes (80x101cm-31x40in) 12-Aug-92 Naon & Cia, Buenos Aires #16
$15000   £8671   Apple blossoms in Normandy (83x65cm-33x26in) s.i. 24-Sep-92 Sotheby's, New York
                        #89/R
$19000   £12179   At water's edge (81x66cm-32x26in) s.i. 26-May-93 Christie's, New York #71/R
$21000   £14286   Reverie young woman in rose garden by river (81x66cm-32x26in) s.i. 17-Nov-93
                        Doyle, New York #26/R
$21000   £14000   The flower gatherer (56x46cm-22x18in) s.i. 17-Mar-94 Sotheby's, New York #103/R
$22500   £11719   Two ladies overlooking riverside village (64x81cm-25x32in) s.i. 5-Aug-92 Boos
                        Gallery, Michigan #542/R
$23000   £15232   Pensive moment (58x77cm-23x30in) s.i. 23-Sep-93 Sotheby's, New York #118/R
$27000   £18121   Breezy uplands (81x64cm-32x25in) s.i. 15-Oct-93 Du Mouchelle, Detroit #2050
$28000   £18667   At the well (56x47cm-22x19in) s.i. 25-May-94 Christie's, New York #207/R
$30000   £18987   A lovely thought (56x46cm-22x18in) s.i. 4-Dec-92 Christie's, New York #231/R
$30000   £19231   Brittany girl overlooking stream (56x46cm-22x18in) s.i. 27-May-93 Sotheby's, New
                        York #19/R
$32000   £20513   Gardener's daughter (55x46cm-22x18in) s.i. i.stretcher. 26-May-93 Christie's, New
                        York #65/R
$32500   £21667   Gethering a bouquet (81x66cm-32x26in) s.i. 17-Mar-94 Sotheby's, New York #102/R
$38000   £25333   Gathering roses (131x88cm-52x35in) s.i. 26-May-94 Christie's, New York #79/R
$85000   £58219   Noonday repast (84x105cm-33x41in) s.i. 15-Feb-94 Christie's, New York #77/R
$900   £588   Peasant woman standing (32x16cm-13x6in) s. pen. 29-Oct-92 Christie's, East, New
                        York #181 a/R
$1400   *£909*   *Woman with basket (37x26cm-15x10in) s.d.1885 W/C paper on paper. 9-Sep-93
                        Sotheby's Arcade, New York #41/R*
$5000   *£2890*   *The water carrier (35x25cm-14x10in) s.i. W/C gouache pencil paper on board.
                        25-Sep-92 Sotheby's Arcade, New York #145/R*
$8000   *£4624*   *Laundering by river (62x48cm-24x19in) s.i. W/C. 24-Sep-92 Sotheby's, New York
                        #99/R*

KNIGHT, Jacob (20th C) American
$1700   £1126   California Bound to work in movies (61x46cm-24x18in) s.i. painted c.1986.
                        21-Nov-92 Litchfield Auction Gallery #22

KNOWLES, Dorothy (1927-) Canadian
$775   £524   Moon and a road (42x43cm-17x17in) s.i.d.1982verso acrylic. 1-Nov-93 Levis,
                        Calgary #134/R (C.D 1000)
$804   £515   Landscape with bulrushes (23x30cm-9x12in) s.d.1975 acrylic. 26-Apr-93 Levis,
                        Calgary #91/R (C.D 1025)
$863   £564   Summer landscape (31x46cm-12x18in) s.d.1985 verso. 10-May-93 Hodgins, Calgary #222/R
                        (C.D 1100)
$1131   £769   Island in the North Saskatchewan River (40x51cm-16x20in) s.i.d.Aug 16 1985verso.
                        15-Nov-93 Hodgins, Calgary #106/R (C.D 1500)
$1712   £1134   Landscape (70x91cm-28x36in) s. 18-Nov-92 Sotheby's, Toronto #147 b (C.D 2200)
$2184   £1456   June at Beaver Creek (51x71cm-20x28in) s.d.78 i.d.verso acrylic. 11-May-94
                        Sotheby's, Toronto #50/R (C.D 3000)
$2335   £1546   Storm clouds (93x102cm-37x40in) s.d.64 i.verso. 18-Nov-92 Sotheby's Toronto
                        #121/R (C.D 3000)
$2744   £1759   Grey mountain (88x122cm-35x48in) s.i.d.1981 acrylic. 26-Apr-93 Levis, Calgary
                        #90/R (C.D 3500)
$3482   £2353   Cold day (107x91cm-42x36in) s.i.d.1984verso. 25-Apr-94 Levis, Calgary #143/R
                        (C.D 4800)
$3624   £2449   East of Paddock Wood, 1981 (116x124cm-46x49in) 23-Nov-93 Joyner Fine Art, Toronto
                        #59/R (C.D 4800)
$4281   £2835   Gentle greens (110x120cm-43x47in) s.d.78. 24-Nov-92 Joyner Fine Art, Toronto
                        #169/R (C.D 5500)
$743   £505   Blue spots (56x76cm-22x30in) W/C. 7-Jul-93 Maynards, Vancouver #209 (C.D 950)
$897   £598   Vannet et blatt (56x76cm-22x30in) s.d. W/C. 30-May-94 Hodgins, Calgary #25/R
                        (C.D 1250)
$942   £615   Little mauve clouds (56x76cm-22x30in) s.d.76 W/C. 10-May-93 Hodgins, Calgary
                        #22/R (C.D 1200)
$980   £667   Dense blue shadows (56x76cm-22x30in) s. bears i.verso W/C. 15-Nov-93 Hodgins,
                        Calgary #238 (C.D 1300)
$1165   £777   Moon through evening clouds (53x73cm-21x29in) s.d.80 W/C. 13-May-94 Joyner Fine
                        Art, Toronto #46/R (C.D 1600)
$1255   £821   Untitled - landscape (56x76cm-22x30in) W/C. 10-May-93 Hodgins, Calgary #244/R
                        (C.D 1600)

KNOWLES, Farquhar McGillivray (1859-1932) Canadian
$604   £408   Forest nymph (23x16cm-9x6in) s. canvas on board. 23-Nov-93 Joyner Fine Art,
                        Toronto #272 (C.D 800)

KNOWLES, Farquhar McGillivray (1859-1932) Canadian-cont.
$620	£419	Rocky bay Nova Scotia (22x29cm-9x11in) indist.s. i.stretcher board. 3-Nov-93 Sotheby's, Toronto #187/R (C.D 800)
$652	£435	Coastal scene with sailboats (19x28cm-7x11in) s. board. 6-Jun-94 Waddingtons, Toronto #1247 (C.D 900)
$1323	£876	Hauling wood (51x41cm-20x16in) s. i.verso board. 18-Nov-92 Sotheby's, Toronto #166/R (C.D 1700)

KNUDSON, Robert L (20th C) American
$2000	£1342	Sunrise at Zuni Mission (51x61cm-20x24in) s. i.d.1972 verso. 8-Dec-93 Butterfield & Butterfield, San Francisco #3601/R

KOBAYASHI, Milton (1950-) American
$2900	£1883	The bathers (44x69cm-17x27in) s.d.1979 W/C board. 9-Sep-93 Sotheby's Arcade, New York #353/R
$4500	£2848	The bathers (43x68cm-17x27in) s.d.1979 W/C board. 3-Dec-92 Sotheby's, New York #75/R

KOCH, Henry (1846-1906) American
$1100	£738	View along the Merced (69x109cm-27x43in) s. 8-Dec-93 Butterfield & Butterfield, San Francisco #3329/R

KOCH, John (1909-1978) American
$1400	£940	Portrait of my mother (61x51cm-24x20in) s.d.65. 5-Mar-94 Louisiana Auction Exchange #154/R
$3400	£2222	Eating dinner (47x61cm-19x24in) canvas on masonite. 4-May-93 Christie's, East, New York #171/R
$5750	£3885	Self portrait (61x51cm-24x20in) i.verso. 10-Aug-93 Stonington Fine Arts, Stonington #75/R
$7000	£4698	Summertime (91x102cm-36x40in) s. painted c.1940. 12-Dec-93 Hindman Galleries, Chicago #272/R
$11000	£7051	Mr and Mrs Joseph Lasky at home (61x51cm-24x20in) s.d.53. 27-May-93 Sotheby's, New York #109/R
$15000	£10000	The studio (91x76cm-36x30in) s. 17-Mar-94 Sotheby's, New York #157/R
$45000	£28846	Listerners, Setauket (66x101cm-26x40in) s.d.72. 26-May-93 Christie's, New York #231/R
$115000	£73718	Accident No.2 (63x76cm-25x30in) s.d.68. 26-May-93 Christie's, New York #229/R
$280000	£177215	Still life at dusk (101x127cm-40x50in) s. 3-Dec-92 Sotheby's, New York #194/R

KOCH, Samuel (1887-) American
$650	£425	Ducks at pond (13x18cm-5x7in) s. panel. 17-Sep-93 Schloss Ahlden, Ahlden #1680/R (DM 1050)
$650	£425	Nosy kittens (13x18cm-5x7in) s. panel. 17-Sep-93 Schloss Ahlden, Ahlden #1701/R (DM 1050)
$746	£494	Chicken run (18x24cm-7x9in) s. 20-Nov-92 Schloss Ahlden, Ahlden #1920/R (DM 1200)
$777	£514	Chicken yard (18x24cm-7x9in) s. panel. 20-Nov-92 Schloss Ahlden, Ahlden #2004/R (DM 1250)

KOEHLER, Henry (1927-) American
$755	£500	Studying card (36x26cm-14x10in) s. paper. 24-Nov-92 Phillips, London #356
$1419	£940	Jogging out at Curragh (38x76cm-15x30in) s. s.i.d.1977 verso. 24-Nov-92 Phillips, London #357
$3000	£2000	On the course, Kempton Park (30x66cm-12x26in) s.d.1971. 3-Jun-94 Sotheby's, New York #300 a/R
$8000	£5263	Three jockey studies - red and blue (51x76cm-20x30in) s. s.i.d.1986 verso. 4-Jun-93 Sotheby's, New York #238/R
$15000	£9868	Jockeys going into Belmont Paddock (51x61cm-20x24in) s. s.d.1961 stretcher. 4-Jun-93 Sotheby's, New York #237/R
$634	*£420*	*Approaching post (45x59cm-18x23in) s. mixed media. 24-Nov-92 Phillips, London #355*
$1191	*£805*	*Two jockeys in Curragh dressing room (59x44cm-23x17in) s. mixed media. 2-Aug-93 Stephan Welz, Johannesburg #130/R (SA.R 4000)*

KOEHLER, Paul R (c.1866-1909) American
$700	£357	House by the beach, probably Long Island (18x25cm-7x10in) s. pastel. 18-Aug-92 Richard Bourne, Hyannis #225/R

KOEHLER, Paul R (attrib) (c.1866-1909) American
$1000	£662	Evening glow (41x61cm-16x24in) s.i. board. 26-Sep-93 Schrager Galleries, Milwaukee #477

KOEK-KOEK, Stephen Roberto (1887-1934) Argentinian
$800	£462	Dos veleros (24x30cm-9x12in) panel. 23-Sep-92 Roldan & Cia, Buenos Aires #66
$800	£462	Buque en la rada (24x30cm-9x12in) panel. 23-Sep-92 Roldan & Cia, Buenos Aires #65
$1000	£667	Puerto (46x56cm-18x22in) s. 25-May-94 Castells & Castells, Montevideo #19
$1100	£728	Figuras reclinadas (23x31cm-9x12in) 11-Nov-92 VerBo, Buenos Aires #55
$1100	£743	Molino (50x60cm-20x24in) s. panel. 20-Oct-93 Castells & Castells, Montevideo #25
$1200	£811	Nocturno (41x46cm-16x18in) s. 20-Oct-93 Castells & Castells, Montevideo #22/R
$1700	£1149	Pueblo de pescadores (49x82cm-19x32in) s. 20-Oct-93 Castells & Castells, Montevideo #21/R
$2500	£1689	Marina (90x90cm-35x35in) s. 20-Oct-93 Castells & Castells, Montevideo #20

KOENIG, John Franklin (1924-) American
$745	£477	Composition (81x54cm-32x21in) s.d.1965 mixed media paper laid down on canvas. 20-Dec-92 Perrin, Versailles #93 (F.FR 4000)

KOENIGER, Walter (1881-1945) American
$850	£570	Winter landscape (30x41cm-12x16in) s. board. 24-Mar-94 Mystic Fine Arts, Connecticut #200
$900	£455	Forest stream (41x53cm-16x21in) s. 28-Aug-92 Young Fine Arts Auctions, Maine #195
$1500	£962	Mountain stream in winter (67x77cm-26x30in) s. canvas on board. 9-Dec-92 Butterfield & Butterfield, San Francisco #3882/R
$2000	£1282	River in winter (52x61cm-20x24in) s. 9-Dec-92 Butterfield & Butterfield, San Francisco #3878/R
$3000	£1987	Spring thaw (51x61cm-20x24in) s. 22-Sep-93 Christie's, New York #175/R
$3200	£2177	Stream in winter (61x76cm-24x30in) s. 17-Nov-93 Doyle, New York #41/R
$4500	£2980	Distant hills, winter (89x94cm-35x37in) s.d.28. 22-Sep-93 Christie's, New York #171/R
$11000	£6962	Winter landscape (81x81cm-32x32in) s. 4-Dec-92 Christie's, New York #63/R

KOERNER, Henry (1915-) American
$2500	£1678	The dart throwers (41x23cm-16x9in) s.d.45 gouache board. 16-Oct-93 Dargate Auction Galleries, Pittsburgh #7

KOERNER, William Henry Dethlef (1878-1938) American
$700	£467	Dories (36x41cm-14x16in) init. s.verso canvasboard. 23-May-94 Hindman Galleries, Chicago #168
$1000	£662	The squaw woman (91x76cm-36x30in) s.d.1930. 3-Oct-93 Hanzel Galleries, Chicago #815
$1800	£1184	Masqueraders (70x100cm-28x39in) s.d.1930. 31-Mar-93 Sotheby's Arcade, New York #476/R
$2000	£1333	The Higher Ridge (91x76cm-36x30in) s.d.1930. 23-May-94 Christie's, East, New York #1147

KOHLMEYER, Ida (20th C) American
$1350	£849	Cluster No.1-08 (81x69cm-32x27in) s.d.1974. 23-Apr-93 Hart Gallery, Houston #8
$1750	£1101	Large rectangular abstract shapes (122x122cm-48x48in) s.d.74. 23-Apr-93 Hart Gallery, Houston #9

KOLNER, August (1812-1906) American
$1100	£714	Paoli Monuments to 53 American soldiers killed by British troops, 1777 (36x48cm-14x19in) s.i.d.1884 W/C ink. 16-Jan-93 Skinner, Bolton #252/R

KOMAR and MELAMID (20th C) American/Russian
$14000	£9150	Natasha with bust of Stalin (183x120cm-72x47in) s. painted 1982-83. 7-May-93 Christie's, East, New York #142/R
$18000	£10588	Stalin with Hitler's remains (214x153cm-84x60in) s.i. two attached panels. 8-Oct-92 Christie's, New York #223/R

KOMOSKI, Bill (1954-) American
$1000	£694	Untitled (119x81cm-47x32in) s.d.11/13/86verso acrylic. 22-Feb-93 Christie's, East, New York #272/R
$2000	£1307	Untitled (216x155cm-85x61in) oilstick graphite executed 1982. 22-Dec-92 Christie's, East, New York #29/R
$1203	£802	Untitled (211x152cm-83x60in) s.d.8/30/89verso acrylic model paste. 2-Jun-94 AB Stockholms Auktionsverk, Stockholm #7105/R (S.KR 9500)

KOONING, Elaine de (1920-1989) American
$700	£486	Rio Grande (37x49cm-15x19in) s. s.i.d.1959verso. 26-Feb-93 Sotheby's Arcade, New York #275/R
$5000	£3311	Southwestern landscape (122x152cm-48x60in) d.57 verso board. 30-Jun-93 Sotheby's Arcade, New York #252/R

KOONING, Willem de (1904-) American/Dutch
$28440	£18000	Untitled (75x57cm-30x22in) s. paper on newsprint executed c.1970. 3-Dec-92 Sotheby's, London #67/R
$36340	£23000	Woman (61x48cm-24x19in) s. s.d.1974 verso paper on canvas. 3-Dec-92 Sotheby's, London #50/R
$80513	£53676	Femme dans un paysage de moulin a eau (57x75cm-22x30in) s.i. oil newspaper laid on board. 10-Mar-94 Christian de Quay, Paris #195/R (F.FR 460000)
$105000	£72917	Untitled (74x56cm-29x22in) s. painted 1966 newspaper on masonite. 23-Feb-93 Sotheby's, New York #207/R
$115000	£76159	Two figures in Devon (148x110cm-58x43in) s. d.71 stretcher paper on canvas. 18-Nov-92 Sotheby's, New York #88/R
$115000	£77181	Marilyn Monroe (60x75cm-24x30in) s. oil paper on masonite painted 1965. 5-May-94 Sotheby's, New York #94/R
$175000	£117450	Untitled (73x58cm-29x23in) s. paper on masonite painted c.1967. 25-Feb-94 Sotheby's, New York #39/R
$200000	£135135	Untitled (151x93cm-59x37in) s. paper on canvas painted 1968. 11-Nov-93 Sotheby's, New York #263/R
$200000	£135135	Two figures in dunes (104x92cm-41x36in) s.d.i. paper on canvas. 10-Nov-93 Sotheby's, New York #37/R
$200000	£134228	Untitled (185x94cm-73x37in) s.i. paper on canvas painted 1970. 25-Feb-94 Sotheby's, New York #26/R
$630000	£425676	Untitled XVI (140x150cm-55x59in) s.verso painted 1977. 10-Nov-93 Sotheby's, New York #44/R
$800000	£536893	Untitled XIV (203x178cm-80x70in) s.stretcher painted 1982. 3-May-94 Christie's, New York #66/R
$825000	£546358	Flowers, Mary's table (203x179cm-80x70in) s. 18-Nov-92 Christie's, New York #32/R
$6000	£4054	Untitled (61x48cm-24x19in) s. chl paper laid down. 8-Nov-93 Christie's, East, New York #182/R

KOONING, Willem de (1904-) American/Dutch-cont.
$7500	£4967	Woman (25x20cm-10x8in) s. chl. 19-Nov-92 Christie's, New York #322/R
$8217	£5301	Woman (31x20cm-12x8in) s. painted c.1970 dr. 23-Jan-93 Cornette de St.Cyr, Paris #113 (F.FR 44000)
$8478	£5435	Two women (46x60cm-18x24in) s. chl. 10-Dec-92 Christie's, Amsterdam #381/R (D.FL 15000)
$11000	£7432	Untitled (60x48cm-24x19in) s. chl executed c.1965. 11-Nov-93 Sotheby's, New York #262/R
$18500	£12252	Untitled (61x48cm-24x19in) s. chl paper on paper. 19-Nov-92 Christie's, New York #290/R
$28000	£18919	Two women (22x30cm-9x12in) s. graphite executed c.1949. 10-Nov-93 Christie's, New York #110/R
$35000	£23179	Two women (22x30cm-9x12in) s. graphite drawn c.1952. 18-Nov-92 Sotheby's, New York #85/R
$42000	£28378	Untitled (162x107cm-64x42in) s. chl two layered sheets executed 1963. 10-Nov-93 Christie's, New York #116/R
$47680	£32000	Little figure (45x72cm-18x28in) s. chinese ink. 2-Dec-93 Sotheby's, London #15/R
$50000	£33113	Untitled, two women (22x30cm-9x12in) s. graphite. 19-Nov-92 Christie's, New York #315/R
$60000	£39216	Study for stenographer (61x63cm-24x25in) s. oil wash pencil parchment painted 1948. 3-May-93 Sotheby's, New York #2/R
$95000	£62914	Woman (40x51cm-16x20in) s. pastel. 17-Nov-92 Sotheby's, New York #28/R
$165000	£110738	Untitled (33x25cm-13x10in) s. oil graphite board painted 1951. 3-May-94 Christie's, New York #30/R
$200000	£135135	Woman (41x28cm-16x11in) s. graphite col.chk drawn c.1951. 9-Nov-93 Christie's, New York #7/R
$260000	£174497	Untitled (76x102cm-30x40in) s. sapolin enamel painted c.1949. 4-May-94 Sotheby's, New York #17/R
$400000	£264901	Abstraction (61x91cm-24x36in) s. oil chl.enamel paper collage paper on board. 18-Nov-92 Christie's, New York #11/R
$875000	£571895	Untitled - black and white abstraction (56x76cm-22x30in) s. sapolin enamel double-sided painted c.1949. 3-May-93 Sotheby's, New York #7/R

KOONING, Willem de (attrib) (1904-) American/Dutch
$1300	£878	Abstract composition (21x13cm-8x5in) mixed media chl vellum. 21-Oct-93 Butterfield & Butterfield, San Francisco #2720/R

KOOPMAN, Augustus (1869-1914) American
$3600	£2416	Beach scene (46x38cm-18x15in) s. 24-Mar-94 Mystic Fine Arts, Connecticut #246/R

KOOPS, Harmen C (1898-1957) American
$650	£430	Floral still life (46x56cm-18x22in) s. canvas on canvas. 28-Sep-93 John Moran, Pasadena #376

KOPMAN, Benjamin (1887-1965) American
$3000	£2041	Two clowns (81x59cm-32x23in) s.d.1952. 4-Apr-94 Sotheby's, Tel Aviv #121/R

KORN, Christian (1960-) Argentinian
$592	£400	Three figures (30x42cm-12x17in) s. mixed media executed 1992. 30-Oct-93 Dr Fritz Nagel, Stuttgart #7 (DM 1000)

KOSA, Emil (jnr) (1903-1968) American
$2500	£1689	Land of Plenty a landscape (51x66cm-20x26in) s. masonite. 9-Nov-93 John Moran, Pasadena #897
$2500	£1678	Just like back home (63x76cm-25x30in) s. 8-Dec-93 Butterfield & Butterfield, San Francisco #3445/R
$3000	£1987	Mountain landscape with pink smoke trees (61x91cm-24x36in) s. s.i.verso board. 15-Jun-94 Butterfield & Butterfield, San Francisco #4710/R
$4000	£2312	Sunkist pastures (61x91cm-24x36in) 26-Sep-93 San Rafael Auction Galleries #214
$4000	£2759	Landscape, Cottonwoods (61x91cm-24x36in) s. 16-Feb-93 John Moran, Pasadena #42
$5000	£3378	By river (61x76cm-24x30in) s. 15-Jun-93 John Moran, Pasadena #45
$5500	£3691	Uncle's Hills (63x76cm-25x30in) s. 8-Dec-93 Butterfield & Butterfield, San Francisco #3481/R
$5500	£3179	Frenchman's Creek (69x94cm-27x37in) 26-Sep-92 San Rafael Auction Galleries #215
$6000	£4167	One enchanted evening (63x91cm-25x36in) s. s.i.verso canvas on board. 7-Mar-93 Butterfield & Butterfield, San Francisco #212/R
$7500	£4934	Towards evening (61x91cm-24x36in) s. board. 13-Jun-93 Butterfield & Butterfield, San Francisco #861/R
$14000	£8235	Everlasting hills (66x102cm-26x40in) s. 4-Oct-92 Butterfield & Butterfield, Los Angeles #172/R
$600	£417	Marina scene (28x38cm-11x15in) s. W/C. 6-Mar-93 Louisiana Auction Exchange #53/R
$600	£403	The hill overlooking Laguna beach (33x43cm-13x17in) s. W/C. 4-Dec-93 Louisiana Auction Exchange #8/R
$700	£470	The old mill (66x94cm-26x37in) W/C. 4-Dec-93 Louisiana Auction Exchange #136/R
$1000	£690	California coastal (38x56cm-15x22in) s. W/C. 16-Feb-93 John Moran, Pasadena #94
$1100	£724	Chavez Ravine, LA (33x43cm-13x17in) s. W/C. 7-Nov-92 San Rafael Auction Galleries #239
$1300	£867	The Cathedral of St.Miguel (53x74cm-21x29in) s. W/C. 15-Mar-94 John Moran, Pasadena #77
$1500	£1014	The stray colt San Fernando Valley (56x76cm-22x30in) s. W/C painted c.1940. 9-Nov-93 John Moran, Pasadena #865 a
$1500	£1014	White house of peace (56x76cm-22x30in) s. W/C. 15-Jun-93 John Moran, Pasadena #50
$1500	£1000	California landscape (48x61cm-19x24in) s. W/C. 15-Mar-94 John Moran, Pasadena #76
$1500	£949	California coastal scene with two figures (46x58cm-18x23in) s. W/C. 5-Dec-92 Louisiana Auction Exchange #34/R

KOSA, Emil (jnr) (1903-1968) American-cont.
$1600	£1053	Chavez Ravine, LA (36x48cm-14x19in) W/C. 7-Nov-92 San Rafael Auction Galleries #238
$2000	£1351	Landscape - Hermosa (53x69cm-21x27in) s. W/C. 15-Jun-93 John Moran , Pasadena #159
$2000	£1325	Los Angeles harbour - boats, figures, old automobiles (36x51cm-14x20in) s. W/C paper on cardboard. 14-Jun-94 John Moran, Pasadena #75
$2500	£1667	View of Tasco (53x74cm-21x29in) s. W/C. 15-Mar-94 John Moran, Pasadena #69
$3250	£2257	Ranch near Big Pine (53x69cm-21x27in) s. W/C. 7-Mar-93 Butterfield & Butterfield, San Francisco #245/R
$3750	£2517	Santa Paula Hills (37x55cm-15x22in) s. W/C. 8-Dec-93 Butterfield & Butterfield, San Francisco #3521/R

KOSCIANSKI, Leonard (1952-) American?
| $4000 | £2649 | Head to head (243x111cm-96x44in) init.d.84 s.i.d.verso. 17-Nov-92 Christie's, East, New York #58/R |

KOST, Frederick W (1865-1923) American
| $1800 | £1208 | Harvest scene (69x48cm-27x19in) 16-Jul-93 Douglas, South Deerfield #4 |

KOSTABI, Mark (1961-) American
$1238	£836	Migratory patterns (60x50cm-24x20in) s.i.d.1992verso. 20-Oct-93 Finarte, Firenze #211 (I.L 2000000)
$2000	£1282	Reader and rider (178x178cm-70x70in) s.d.1987 s.i.d.verso. 13-Dec-92 Hindman Galleries, Chicago #85
$2000	£1325	I may be young but I'm not green (183x122cm-72x48in) s.i.d.1988verso. 17-Nov-92 Christie's, East, New York #6/R
$2151	£1453	The eleventh plague (75x60cm-30x24in) s.d.1992 s.i.d.verso acrylic. 19-Apr-94 Finarte, Rome #190/R (I.L 3500000)
$2400	£1611	Moses parting the Red Sea with a plunger (122x178cm-48x70in) s.d.84 s.i.d.1984verso. 3-May-94 Christie's, East, New York #216/R
$2600	£1745	I Made that Mistake before (130x130cm-51x51in) s.d.1989 s.i.d.1989 verso. 23-Feb-94 Christie's, East, New York #296/R
$2600	£1806	Revenge of the deer (102x102cm-40x40in) s.i.d.1986verso. 22-Feb-93 Christie's, East, New York #270/R
$2800	£1892	Loving cup (137x122cm-54x48in) s.d.1988 s.i.d.verso. 8-Nov-93 Christie's, East, New York #109/R
$2800	£1879	Beauty, wit, sensuality, intensity and style (183x122cm-72x48in) s.d.1984 s.i.d.1984 verso. 23-Feb-94 Christie's, East, New York #297/R
$2800	£1854	Globalicious (102x67cm-40x26in) s.i.d.1990verso. 17-Nov-92 Christie's, East, New York #4/R
$2800	£1879	Father figure (213x162cm-84x64in) s.d.1988 s.i.d.1988 verso. 23-Feb-94 Christie's, East, New York #295/R
$2800	£1854	Two cultures, Hojo (122x91cm-48x36in) s.d.1990 s.i.d.verso. 17-Nov-92 Christie's, East, New York #5/R
$3200	£2222	The Balinese 2-Step (137x178cm-54x70in) s.d.1989 s.i.d.verso. 22-Feb-93 Christie's, East, New York #271/R
$3200	£2148	Service (122x183cm-48x72in) s.i.d.1985 verso. 23-Feb-94 Christie's, East, New York #300/R
$3500	£2431	Primary light (122x91cm-48x36in) s.d.1989. 22-Feb-93 Christie's, East, New York#269/R
$4000	£2778	Everymanhole (244x183cm-96x72in) s.d.1985. 22-Feb-93 Christie's, East, New York #265/R
$630	£423	Untitled (44x60cm-17x24in) s.d.1984 ink. 9-Dec-93 Sotheby's, Amsterdam #419/R (D.FL 1200)
$2385	£1600	All aboard for Ararat. Addison , s.d.1991 s.i.d.1992 enamel canvas double-sided. 30-Nov-93 Finarte, Rome #280/R (I.L 4000000)

KOSUTH, Joseph (1945-) American
| $14000 | £9459 | Titled - art as idea as idea (119x119cm-47x47in) photostat board executed 1968. 11-Nov-93 Sotheby's, New York #110/R |
| $15000 | £9804 | One and three frames , photograph wood glass matboard. 5-May-93 Christie's, New York #110/R |

KOVNER, Saul (1904-1982) American
| $700 | £458 | Shoe shine boy (69x48cm-27x19in) s.d.38. 19-Sep-93 Hindman Galleries, Chicago #724/R |
| $1100 | £724 | View from Central Park (51x61cm-20x24in) s.d.1947. 5-Jun-93 Louisiana Auction Exchange #43/R |

KRAFFT, Carl R (1884-1938) American
$750	£490	Feeding ducks (41x51cm-16x20in) s. i.verso. 17-Sep-93 Skinner, Bolton #278/R
$850	£556	Mountain scene with Indian on horseback (30x38cm-12x15in) s. masonite. 19-Sep-93 Hindman Galleries, Chicago #668/R
$1100	£743	Winter landscape with stream (64x76cm-25x30in) s. 9-Nov-93 John Moran, Pasadena #987
$1300	£872	Landscape with lake and snowy mountains (76x102cm-30x40in) s.i. 2-May-94 Selkirks, St. Louis #98
$1400	£915	Haywagon (41x51cm-16x20in) s. 22-May-93 Weschler, Washington #99/R
$1500	£1064	Horseback rider on winter road (46x51cm-18x20in) s.i.d.1937. 14-Feb-93 Hanzel Galleries, Chicago #3/R
$1800	£1208	Clouds at Sundance (63x76cm-25x30in) s. 8-Dec-93 Butterfield & Butterfield, San Francisco #3355/R
$2000	£1307	Fall landscape (71x76cm-28x30in) s. 1-Nov-92 Hanzel Galleries, Chicago #1/R
$4500	£3147	Autumn landscape (102x132cm-40x52in) s. 14-Mar-93 Hindman Galleries, Chicago #9/R

KRAIKE, Jane (20th C) American
$2000 £1316 Awaiting their destination (71x91cm-28x36in) s.d.1946 canvas on board. 13-Jun-93 Butterfield & Butterfield, San Francisco #961/R

KRAJCBERG, Frans (1921-) Brazilian
$1434 £962 Empreinte (129x99cm-51x39in) s. painted 1961. 8-May-94 Jonquet, Paris #96 (F.FR 8200)

KRAMER, Peter (1823-1907) American/German
$900 £600 Spirit of Brooklyn, N.Y (46x91cm-18x36in) s.d.52 i.stretcher. 26-May-94 Sloan, North Bethesda #2115/R
$3287 £2191 Jovial gathering of gentlemen tasting wine in old tavern (22x17cm-9x7in) s.d.1896 W/C. 10-Jun-94 Dr Fritz Nagel, Stuttgart #2447 (DM 5500)

KRASNER, Lee (1908-1984) American
$5000 £3378 Still life (63x48cm-25x19in) s.d.39 chl. 11-Nov-93 Sotheby's, New York #288/R
$5000 £3268 Untitled (40x66cm-16x26in) s.d.75 oil col.crayon paper collage. 7-May-93 Christie's, East, New York #53/R

KRAUSSE, Macrina (?) Mexican
$842 £561 Flores (50x70cm-20x28in) s. fibracel. 25-May-94 Louis Morton, Mexico #59 (M.P 2800)

KRAWIEC, Harriet (1894-) American
$650 £425 Floral still life (76x86cm-30x34in) s. 16-May-93 Hanzel Galleries, Chicago #22/R

KRAWIEC, Walter (1889-?) American
$825 £539 Horse corral in winter (76x102cm-30x40in) s. 16-May-93 Hanzel Galleries, Chicago #19

KRIEGHOFF, Cornelius (1815-1872) Canadian
$947 £631 The drink (25x32cm-10x13in) s.indist.i. board. 11-May-94 Sotheby's, Toronto #12 (C.D 1300)
$3964 £2591 Portrait of young woman (36x30cm-14x12in) s. canvas on panel. 19-May-93 Sotheby's, Toronto #386/R (C.D 5000)
$6298 £4255 A troika in snow (30x40cm-12x16in) s.d.1863 paper laid down on board. 19-Apr-94 Sotheby's, Amsterdam #134 (D.FL 12000)
$6800 £4564 The Falls at St. Memm, Quebec (91x66cm-36x26in) s. 5-Mar-94 Louisiana Auction Exchange #141/R
$9340 £6186 Woman with basket (31x24cm-12x9in) s. board. 18-Nov-92 Sotheby's, Toronto #171/R (C.D 12000)
$10897 £7216 Indian hunter (28x23cm-11x9in) s. 24-Nov-92 Joyner Fine Art, Toronto #71/R (C.D 14000)
$10897 £7216 Basket seller (28x23cm-11x9in) s. 24-Nov-92 Joyner Fine Art, Toronto #70/R (C.D 14000)
$11286 £7524 View of Spencer Grange, Sillery, Quebec (30x46cm-12x18in) s. 11-May-94 Sotheby's, Toronto #58/R (C.D 15500)
$12398 £8377 Spearing salmon by torchlight (23x34cm-9x13in) s .i.verso. 3-Nov-93 Sotheby's, Toronto #127/R (C.D 16000)
$12454 £8247 Indian encampment (35x53cm-14x21in) 18-Nov-92 Sotheby's, Toronto #29/R (C.D 16000)
$12684 £8290 Moonlight - salmon fishing (33x46cm-13x18in) s. 19-May-93 Sotheby's, Toronto #305/R (C.D 16000)
$14347 £9694 Indian hunter (26x19cm-10x7in) s. 23-Nov-93 Joyner Fine Art, Toronto #148/R (C.D 19000)
$16019 £10680 Log jam, autumn (46x61cm-18x24in) s. 11-May-94 Sotheby's, Toronto #161/R (C.D 22000)
$17124 £11340 Indians at Big Rock Portage (32x35cm-13x14in) s. 24-Nov-92 Joyner Fine Art, Toronto #107/R (C.D 22000)
$17902 £11856 River Gorge, Autumn (29x44cm-11x17in) s. 18-Nov-92 Sotheby's, Toronto #192/R (C.D 23000)
$18680 £12371 Night encampment (29x41cm-11x16in) s. 18-Nov-92 Sotheby's, Toronto #191/R (C.D 24000)
$21696 £14660 Wigwam in the forest (30x41cm-12x16in) s. i.stretcher. 3-Nov-93 Sotheby's, Toronto #128/R (C.D 28000)
$23351 £15464 Habitants on horse-drawn sleigh (32x40cm-13x16in) s. 24-Nov-92 Joyner Fine Art, Toronto #59/R (C.D 30000)
$23351 £15464 Indian encampment (29x39cm-11x15in) s. 18-Nov-92 Sotheby's, Toronto #192 a/R (C.D 30000)
$30995 £20942 Bilking the tollgate (34x46cm-13x18in) s.d.1856 canvas laid on panel. 3-Nov-93 Sotheby's, Toronto #112/R (C.D 40000)
$35674 £23316 Gentleman's cutter (36x53cm-14x21in) s. 19-May-93 Sotheby's, Toronto #166/R (C.D 45000)
$40049 £26699 Habitant farm in winter (39x51cm-15x20in) s. 11-May-94 Sotheby's, Toronto #136/R (C.D 55000)
$62268 £41237 Hitching up (33x46cm-13x18in) s. 18-Nov-92 Sotheby's, Toronto #177/R (C.D 80000)
$128428 £85052 Bilking the toll gate (51x61cm-20x24in) s.i.d.1857. 18-Nov-92 Sotheby's, Toronto #156/R (C.D 165000)
$2378 £1554 Habitants driving horse drawn sleigh in blizzard (15x20cm-6x8in) s. W/C arched corners. 18-May-93 Joyner Fine Art, Toronto #116/R (C.D 3000)

KRIEGHOFF, Cornelius (after) (1815-1872) Canadian
$3459 £2306 Place d'Armes a Montreal (37x59cm-15x23in) bears sig. i.verso. 11-May-94 Sotheby's, Toronto #22/R (C.D 4750)

KRIEGHOFF, Cornelius (attrib) (1815-1872) Canadian
$8562   £5670   Habitants crossing the ice at Quebec (32x47cm-13x19in) s. 18-Nov-92 Sotheby's, Toronto #174/R (C.D 11000)

KRIEGHOFF, Cornelius (circle) (1815-1872) Canadian
$1550   £1047   The basket seller (27x22cm-11x9in) s. 3-Nov-93 Sotheby's, Toronto #158/R (C.D 2000)

KROLL, Leon (1884-1974) American
$1600   £1088   The Queensboro Bridge (20x28cm-8x11in) s. board painted 1913. 17-Nov-93 Doyle, New York #54
$1600   £1039   Portrait of woman (28x20cm-11x8in) s.i.d.1923 paper on board. 15-Jan-93 Du Mouchelle, Detroit #2019/R
$2100   £1382   Girl with guitar (51x41cm-20x16in) s. 31-Mar-93 Sotheby's Arcade, New York #425/R
$2600   £1818   Mother, child and nursemaid (69x86cm-27x34in) 11-Mar-93 Mystic Fine Arts, Connecticut #202 a/R
$5000   £3425   Her best dress (91x69cm-36x27in) s. 19-Feb-94 Young Fine Arts Auctions, Maine #133/R
$7000   £4895   Interior with nude, Isabel (41x61cm-16x24in) s.d.1966. 11-Mar-93 Christie's, New York #217/R
$9000   £5960   Girl against sea (107x66cm-42x26in) s. 23-Sep-93 Sotheby's, New York #229/R
$11000 £7333   The inlet (70x91cm-28x36in) s. i.stretcher. 17-Mar-94 Sotheby's, New York #156/R
$19000 £12667 Picnic by the lake (68x91cm-27x36in) s. 16-Mar-94 Christie's, New York #127/R
$19000 £12179 Still life on window ledge (63x76cm-25x30in) s.d.33. 26-May-93 Christie's, New York #200/R
$34000 £22667 A day in June (92x150cm-36x59in) s. canvas on masonite. 16-Mar-94 Christie's, New York #124/R
$550   £353   Draped female placing laurel wreath over head of male (51x61cm-20x24in) s. pencil executed c.1940. 8-Dec-92 Swann Galleries, New York #170
$1100   £743   Figure studies (67x52cm-26x20in) s. pencil chl one gessoed board pair. 31-Mar-94 Sotheby's Arcade, New York #373/R
$1400   £886   Seated nude (42x33cm-17x13in) s. conte crayon. 4-Dec-92 Christie's, New York #60/R

KRONBERG, Louis (1872-1965) American
$800   £537   Woman holding fan (81x64cm-32x25in) s.d.1936. 24-Mar-94 Mystic Fine Arts, Connecticut #269
$1400   £946   Gloucester Harbour (51x61cm-20x24in) s. s.i.verso. 27-Nov-93 Young Fine Arts Auctions, Maine #190/R
$1750   £1144   Ballerina, green tutu, pink slippers, rose fan (46x30cm-18x12in) s.i.d.July 1916 i.verso. 15-May-93 Dunning's, Illinois #1087/R
$2500   £1667   Ballerina (66x56cm-26x22in) s.i. init.d.1940 stretcher. 23-May-94 Christie's, East, New York #285/R
$3300   £2115   Woman with fan (56x30cm-22x12in) s.d.1904. 24-May-93 Grogan, Massachussetts #339/R
$4000   £2614   Young ballerina holding parrot (61x49cm-24x19in) s.d.1901. 4-May-93 Christie's, East, New York #222/R
$8000   £5229   Judith (155x102cm-61x40in) s.d.1906. 29-Oct-92 Sotheby's, New York #228/R
$9000   £5202   Dancer in green with fan (76x56cm-30x22in) s.d.1905. 23-Sep-92 Christie's, New York #195/R
$550   £364   Dancer in pink (66x51cm-26x20in) s. pastel. 23-Sep-93 Mystic Fine Arts, Connecticut #190
$800   £559   Ballet (23x43cm-9x17in) mono. i.verso pastel fan shaped. 12-Mar-93 Skinner, Bolton #258/R
$1500   £1000   Dancers at the bar (51x76cm-20x30in) init. init.d.1948 verso pastel board. 23-May-94 Christie's, East, New York #278/R
$2200   £1467   The blue fan (51x30cm-20x12in) s. s.i.stretcher pastel canvas. 23-May-94 Christie's, East, New York #288

KRONBERG, Louis (attrib) (1872-1965) American
$7250   £4898   At the opera (64x76cm-25x30in) 10-Nov-93 Doyle, New York #68

KUEHNE, Max (1880-c.1968) American
$1300   £765   Front beach and Sandy Bay, Rockport, Massachusetts (30x41cm-12x16in) st.sig. panel. 3-Oct-92 Weschler, Washington #145/R
$1600   £1046   Flowers in ceramic pitcher (38x30cm-15x12in) s. board. 5-May-93 Doyle, New York #34/R
$2000   £1361   Front beach and Sandy Bay Rockport Massachusetts (30x41cm-12x16in) s. i.verso panel. 15-Nov-93 Christie's, East, New York #264/R
$3000   £1734   Still life with flowers in vase (61x51cm-24x20in) s. s.indis.i.d.1919verso canvas on masonite. 25-Sep-92 Sotheby's Arcade, New York #311/R
$3250   £2181   Place de la Concorde (30x41cm-12x16in) s. board. 4-May-94 Doyle, New York #39
$4000   £2649   Blue houses, Granada (46x36cm-18x14in) s. board. 23-Sep-93 Sotheby's, New York #212/R
$4000   £2649   Wall Street ferry and Manhattan (23x30cm-9x12in) s. s.i.d.1910 verso canvas on board. 22-Sep-93 Christie's, New York #144/R
$5000   £3497   Still life with vases of flowers and fruit (51x61cm-20x24in) st.sig. 11-Mar-93 Christie's, New York #220/R
$5500   £3716   Still life with flowers (52x74cm-20x29in) s. gessoed panel. 31-Mar-94 Sotheby's Arcade, New York #298/R
$6250   £4223   Still life (69x57cm-27x22in) s. oil pencil masonite. 31-Mar-94 Sotheby's Arcade, New York #303/R
$6500   £4167   Calle del Angel, Granada (45x37cm-18x15in) s.d.1915 canvas on board. 26-May-93 Christie's, New York #141/R

KUEHNE, Max (1880-c.1968) American-cont.
$7000	£4698	Pheasant, fruit and flowers (43x107cm-17x42in) s.d.23 tempera gessoed panel. 4-May-94 Doyle, New York #38/R
$10000	£6329	View of Gloucester (51x61cm-20x24in) s.d.25. 3-Dec-92 Sotheby's, New York #111/R
$14000	£8974	Interior with flowers and turquoise chair (87x102cm-34x40in) s. oil pencil masonite. 26-May-93 Christie's, New York #201/R
$17000	£10759	Still life before curtain (66x76cm-26x30in) s. masonite. 4-Dec-92 Christie's, New York #68/R
$2100	*£1373*	*Untitled (165x132cm-65x52in) s. silver leaf three panel screen. 18-Sep-93 James Bakker, Cambridge #92*
$6500	*£4248*	*Untitled (183x109cm-72x43in) s. silver leaf three panel screen. 18-Sep-93 James Bakker, Cambridge #86/R*
$6500	*£4248*	*Untitled (183x122cm-72x48in) s. silver leaf three panel double-sided screen. 18-Sep-93 James Bakker, Cambridge #81/R*

KUHLER, Otto (1894-1977) American
$3200	*£2177*	*Yards at night. The yard goats. Oiling up. When ladies meet (30x38cm-12x15in) s. W/C four. 17-Apr-94 Hanzel Galleries, Chicago #20*

KUHN, Bob (1920-) American
$1150	£752	*Polar bear on ice float. Water buffalo and wolves (23x36cm-9x14in) s. gouache board two. 15-May-93 Dunning's, Illinois #60/R*
$1500	£980	*Mountain rams (23x36cm-9x14in) s. gouache board. 15-May-93 Dunning's, Illinois #62/R*
$1900	£1242	*Leopard and dogs (23x36cm-9x14in) s. gouache board. 15-May-93 Dunning's, Illinois #61/R*
$3500	£2288	*Buffalo and wolves (23x36cm-9x14in) s. gouache board. 15-May-93 Dunning's, Illinois #63/R*
$9500	£6250	*Leopard stalking (38x82cm-15x32in) s. casein board. 4-Jun-93 Sotheby's, New York #270/R*

KUHN, Walt (1880-1949) American
$2000	£1342	Road through the pine forest (76x64cm-30x25in) 26-Mar-94 James Bakker, Cambridge #121/R
$3000	£2000	Rock and sea (41x51cm-16x20in) s.d.1944. 17-Mar-94 Sotheby's, New York #158/R
$3750	£2484	Landscape of trees (36x44cm-14x17in) s.d.1928. 15-Jun-94 Butterfield & Butterfield, San Francisco #4446/R
$14000	£8861	Anemone (61x34cm-24x13in) s. s.i. stretcher. 3-Dec-92 Sotheby's, New York #141/R
$19000	£12583	Clown in red and green against blue (27x23cm-11x9in) indist.s. painted c.1947. 23-Sep-93 Sotheby's, New York #225/R
$25000	£14451	Woman reclining on rock (84x102cm-33x40in) 23-Sep-92 Christie's, New York #203/R
$30000	£20134	Summer interlude - figures resting at rocky water's edge (84x102cm-33x40in) 4-May-94 Doyle, New York #25/R
$54000	£34177	Apples with salmon cloth (63x76cm-25x30in) s.d.1935 s.i.d.verso. 3-Dec-92 Sotheby's, New York #156/R
$280000	£177215	Clown with drum (152x101cm-60x40in) s.d.1942 i.stretcher. 3-Dec-92 Sotheby's, New York #148/R
$450	*£300*	*Nude seated on chair (30x18cm-12x7in) s. W/C. 22-May-94 James Bakker, Cambridge #129*
$500	*£336*	*Reclining nude (33x51cm-13x20in) s.d.1930 ink. 4-Mar-94 Skinner, Bolton #301/R*
$600	*£377*	*Figure and animal studies (56x46cm-22x18in) s.d.1931 W/C ink. 25-Apr-93 James Bakker, Cambridge #39/R*
$900	*£584*	*Reclining female nude (27x41cm-11x16in) s.d.1929 Indian ink. 9-Sep-93 Sotheby's Arcade, New York #374/R*
$1000	*£699*	*Showgirl on horseback (20x14cm-8x6in) ink crayon. 10-Mar-93 Sotheby's, New York #136/R*
$1300	*£872*	*Boulders (46x56cm-18x22in) s.d.1931 ink wash. 26-Mar-94 James Bakker, Cambridge #135/R*
$2200	*£1272*	*Carnival girl (37x29cm-15x11in) s.d.1943 gouache Indian ink. 25-Sep-92 Sotheby's Arcade, New York #326/R*
$13000	*£8228*	*Horn of plenty (52x32cm-20x13in) s.i.d.1937 W/C. 3-Dec-92 Sotheby's, New York #66/R*
$28000	*£18667*	*At the beach (27x47cm-11x19in) s.d.1919 pen gouache. 26-May-94 Christie's, New York #102/R*

KUITCA, Guillermo (1961-) Argentinian
$7000	£4730	San titulo, Lida (30x41cm-12x16in) acrylic painted 1989. 23-Nov-93 Christie's, New York #165/R
$9500	£6419	Sin titulo, Minsk (39x48cm-15x19in) acrylic painted 1989. 23-Nov-93 Christie's, New York #164/R
$11000	£7333	Bialystok (41x30cm-16x12in) 18-May-94 Christie's, New York #257/R
$16000	£10596	Un Taller Para el Joven Kuitca (139x139cm-55x55in) init. s.i.d.1985 verso. 23-Nov-92 Sotheby's, New York #78/R
$18000	£11765	La cabeza del amante (122x150cm-48x59in) s. acrylic painted c.1985. 18-May-93 Sotheby's, New York #75/R
$20000	£13333	Planta en la Palma de la Mano (178x122cm-70x48in) s.d.1990 i.verso acrylic. 18-May-94 Christie's, New York #256/R
$22000	£14570	Hamburg (200x200cm-79x79in) acrylic painted 1989. 24-Nov-92 Christie's, New York #253/R
$25000	£16667	Siete ultimas canciones (140x132cm-55x52in) acrylic painted c.1986. 17-May-94 Sotheby's, New York #82/R
$30000	£19608	La boca del tigre (140x156cm-55x61in) init. s.i.d.1985 verso acrylic. 17-May-93 Christie's, New York #164/R
$30000	£19868	Siete Ultimas Canciones (131x201cm-52x79in) init. 23-Nov-92 Sotheby's, New York #233/R

KUITCA, Guillermo (1961-) Argentinian-cont.
$30000   £19608   Man (141x193cm-56x76in) s. acrylic painted c.1986. 18-May-93 Sotheby's, New York #76/R
$32000   £21192   Tres Noches (130x200cm-51x79in) init.i. s.i.d.1985 verso acrylic. 24-Nov-92 Christie's, New York #98/R

KULMALA, George Arthur (1896-1940) Canadian
$3763   £2525   Saw mill, Northern Ontario (102x114cm-40x45in) s. i.verso. 29-Nov-93 Waddingtons, Toronto #1084/R (C.D 5000)

KUNIYOSHI, Yasuo (1893-1953) American
$8000   £4624   Landscape (34x57cm-13x22in) s.d.32. 23-Sep-92 Christie's, New York #259/R
$1200   £784   'Torture' - sketch for war poster (29x19cm-11x7in) s.i.d.42 chl ricepaper. 4-May-93 Christie's, East, New York #268/R
$9000   £5960   Central city, Colorado (29x42cm-11x17in) s.i.d.41 chl. 22-Sep-93 Christie's, New York #219/R
$17000   £10897   Cafe (31x26cm-12x10in) s.d.34 pencil. 26-May-93 Christie's, New York #187/R
$21000   £13291   Maine landscape - Joel's barn (38x29cm-15x11in) s.i.d.23 W/C ink double-sided. 3-Dec-92 Sotheby's, New York #182/R

KUNTZ, Roger (1926-1975) American
$4750   £3188   The Captain's House (84x96cm-33x38in) s. 8-Dec-93 Butterfield & Butterfield, San Francisco #3465/R

KURELEK, William (1927-1977) Canadian
$2767   £1845   Nature is still in travail (25x43cm-10x17in) s.d.1964 board. 13-May-94 Joyner Fine Art, Toronto #123/R (C.D 3800)
$2919   £1933   Alcoholism (51x42cm-20x17in) mono.d.75 i.verso board. 18-Nov-92 Sotheby's, Toronto #150/R (C.D 3750)
$4005   £2670   Listening to telephone poles sing (25x39cm-10x15in) init.d.67 board. 13-May-94 Joyner Fine Art, Toronto #477/R (C.D 5500)
$4086   £2706   Fallen boy in hay rake (49x36cm-19x14in) s. egg tempera board. 18-Nov-92 Sotheby's, Toronto #138/R (C.D 5500)
$11675   £7732   Carrying water to the haying crew (61x76cm-24x30in) s. i.verso egg tempera board. 18-Nov-92 Sotheby's, Toronto #137/R (C.D 15000)
$17476   £11650   Haymaking time in Manitoba (53x76cm-21x30in) init.d.67 board. 13-May-94 Joyner Fine Art, Toronto #90/R (C.D 24000)
$20237   £13402   Plane met by eskimo settlement (37x67cm-15x26in) init.d.68 board. 24-Nov-92 Joyner Fine Art, Toronto #125/R (C.D 26000)
$29126   £19417   Ukrainian children off to school, Stuartburn, Manitoba (51x73cm-20x29in) mono.d.71 i.verso mixed media board. 11-May-94 Sotheby's, Toronto #61/R (C.D 40000)
$1311   £874   Night and the Winnipeg flood, Big Lonely Series (25x25cm-10x10in) mono.d.77 mixed media board. 11-May-94 Sotheby's, Toronto #256/R (C.D 1800)
$2325   £1571   Hornet's nest in snow drift (30x30cm-12x12in) mono.d.74 i.verso mixed media board. 3-Nov-93 Sotheby's, Toronto #129/R (C.D 3000)
$3113   £2062   Divine love and natural love (18x44cm-7x17in) mono. i.d.1964verso mixed media board. 18-Nov-92 Sotheby's, Toronto #136/R (C.D 4000)
$4281   £2835   Our Manitoba Farm today (30x16cm-12x6in) mono.d.73 i.verso mixed media board. 18-Nov-92 Sotheby's, Toronto #23/R (C.D 5500)
$4369   £2913   Darn it, missed 'im (46x27cm-18x11in) mono.d.73 i.d.verso mixed media board. 11-May-94 Sotheby's, Toronto #100/R (C.D 6000)
$5097   £3398   Shall I (15x22cm-6x9in) mono.d.73 i.verso mixed media board. 11-May-94 Sotheby's, Toronto #255/R (C.D 7000)
$5448   £3608   Prairie winter mishap (32x47cm-13x19in) mono.d.70 i.verso mixed media board. 18-Nov-92 Sotheby's, Toronto #19/R (C.D 7000)
$5812   £3927   White washing the barn by hand (47x20cm-19x8in) mono.d.72 i.verso mixed media board. 3-Nov-93 Sotheby's, Toronto #295/R (C.D 7500)
$5825   £3883   Lead Kindly Light (58x122cm-23x48in) mono.d.74 mixed media board. 11-May-94 Sotheby's, Toronto #159/R (C.D 8000)
$6189   £4126   Fetching eggs (28x25cm-11x10in) mono.d.73 mixed media board. 11-May-94 Sotheby's, Toronto #98/R (C.D 8500)
$6553   £4369   An incident in the life of Bishop Marrocco (70x91cm-28x36in) mixed media board. 11-May-94 Sotheby's, Toronto #160/R (C.D 9000)
$6616   £4381   An Irish wake in Montreal (61x61cm-24x24in) mono.d.76 i.verso mixed media. 18-Nov-92 Sotheby's, Toronto #85/R (C.D 8500)
$6974   £4712   Ploughing (36x36cm-14x14in) mono.d.76 i.verso mixed media board. 3-Nov-93 Sotheby's, Toronto #216/R (C.D 9000)
$7135   £4663   Glimpse of Mount Robson (61x76cm-24x30in) mono.d.72 d.1973 verso mixed media board. 19-May-93 Sotheby's, Toronto #158/R (C.D 9000)
$7784   £5155   Prairie boy's summer, thunderstorm approaching (36x36cm-14x14in) init.d.74 i.verso mixed media board. 18-Nov-92 Sotheby's, Toronto #139/R (C.D 10000)
$8562   £5670   It is an enemy of mine (102x71cm-40x28in) mono.i.d.1975 mixed media. 18-Nov-92 Sotheby's, Toronto #154/R (C.D 11000)
$10897   £7216   The cook (58x25cm-23x10in) mono.i.d.1973verso mixed media. 18-Nov-92 Sotheby's, Toronto #82/R (C.D 14000)
$11891   £7772   View from Prarie Strawpile on Ukrainian homestead (122x94cm-48x37in) mono.d.72 s.i.d.verso mixed media board. 19-May-93 Sotheby's, Toronto #235/R (C.D 15000)
$12398   £8377   Prairies the Four Seasons , mono. i.d.1968verso mixed media board four. 3-Nov-93 Sotheby's, Toronto #217/R (C.D 16000)
$13107   £8738   The sliver of ice (61x61cm-24x24in) mono.d.70 i.d.verso mixed media board. 11-May-94 Sotheby's, Toronto #60/R (C.D 18000)
$15855   £10363   After blizzard in Manitoba (51x75cm-20x30in) mono.d.67 s.d.verso mixed media board. 19-May-93 Sotheby's, Toronto #233/R (C.D 20000)

KURELEK, William (1927-1977) Canadian-cont.
$22197	£14508	Russian thistles migrating (100x80cm-39x31in) s. mixed media. 19-May-93 Sotheby's, Toronto #159/R (C.D 28000)
$23351	£15464	Hay raking on the prairies (36x36cm-14x14in) init.d.75 i.verso mixed media. 18-Nov-92 Sotheby's, Toronto #227/R (C.D 30000)
$29126	£19417	It's hard for us to realise (58x120cm-23x47in) init.d.72 mixed media. 13-May-94 Joyner Fine Art, Toronto #116/R (C.D 40000)

KUSHNER, Robert (1949-) American?
$850	£571	Two Tillies (87x114cm-34x45in) s.i. acrylic linen. 3-May-94 Christie's, East, New York #163/R
$1962	£1308	Still life II (67x97cm-26x38in) s.d.83 acrylic paper. 2-Jun-94 AB Stockholms Auktionsverk, Stockholm #7102/R (S.KR 15500)
$1543	£1036	Emerald (94x64cm-37x25in) s.d.82 acrylic collage. 29-Nov-93 AB Stockholms Auktionsverk, Stockholm #6228/R (S.KR 13000)
$2025	£1350	Contemplative (153x110cm-60x43in) s.d.84 oil collage. 2-Jun-94 AB Stockholms Auktionsverk, Stockholm #7101/R (S.KR 16000)
$6000	£3974	Can can (227x56cm-89x22in) s.i. gouache W/C col.crayons four sheets. 17-Nov-92 Christie's, East, New York #46/R

LACAMERA, Fortunato (1887-1951) Argentinian
$4000	£2649	Malvones (29x22cm-11x9in) 11-Nov-92 VerBo, Buenos Aires #60
$5000	£2604	Paisaje (40x50cm-16x20in) 63. 4-Aug-92 VerBo, Buenos Aires #61
$7000	£4636	Marina (28x37cm-11x15in) 11-Nov-92 VerBo, Buenos Aires #59/R
$7500	£4335	Marina (33x49cm-13x19in) 23-Sep-92 Roldan & Cia, Buenos Aires #15
$17000	£11258	Barcos carboneros (47x68cm-19x27in) 18-Nov-92 Roldan & Cia, Buenos Aires #2

LACHMAN, Harry (1886-1974) American/French
$650	£439	Figures near doorway (36x25cm-14x10in) s. board. 9-Nov-93 John Moran, Pasadena #864
$1200	£635	Grey day, Brittany (25x36cm-10x14in) s. panel. 12-Sep-92 Louisiana Auction Exchange #40/R
$3000	£2098	Rougemont, Switzerland (51x61cm-20x24in) s.d.14. 14-Mar-93 Hindman Galleries, Chicago #16/R
$6000	£3947	Chemin Azay Le Rideau (46x55cm-18x22in) s. indist.d.stretcher. 31-Mar-93 Sotheby's Arcade, New York #165 a/R

LAER, Alexander T van (1857-?) American
$1100	£738	Approaching storm (36x51cm-14x20in) s. 24-Mar-94 Mystic Fine Arts, Connecticut #201
$850	£563	Roses (30x48cm-12x19in) s. W/C. 23-Sep-93 Mystic Fine Arts, Connecticut #57/R

LAESSLE, Paul (1908-1988) American
$2800	£1905	Wash day in Old Philadelphia. Flowers around the Read Bridge, s. W/C two. 15-Nov-93 Christie's, East, New York #105

LAFARGE, John (1835-1910) American
$3300	£2157	Portrait of Margaret Mason Perry la Farge (41x30cm-16x12in) s. 14-May-93 Skinner, Bolton #42/R
$5250	£3671	Male figure playing lute (18x23cm-7x9in) init. 11-Mar-93 Mystic Fine Arts, Connecticut #146/R
$21000	£14000	The shepherd and the sea (76x63cm-30x25in) 17-Mar-94 Sotheby's, New York #101/R
$1600	£1046	Study of disciple (18x10cm-7x4in) ink wash over pencil. 30-Oct-92 Sloan, North Bethesda #2783/R
$4250	£2834	Sea and sky, Vaiala, Samoa, looking North (13x23cm-5x9in) W/C gouache. 17-May-94 Grogan, Massachussetts #338/R
$7000	£4430	Study for The Dawn (38x24cm-15x9in) W/C. 3-Dec-92 Sotheby's, New York #29/R
$7500	£4335	Statue of Oya-Jiso (38x27cm-15x11in) i.d.1886 W/C. 24-Sep-92 Sotheby's, New York #85/R
$7750	£5201	Wall of our garden, Nikko (30x23cm-12x9in) s.i. W/C. 6-Dec-93 Grogan, Massachussetts #511/R
$11000	£6962	Fishing party in canoes, Samoa (23x26cm-9x10in) W/C board. 3-Dec-92 Sotheby's, New York #28/R
$16000	£10738	Fortune on wheel, study for the Frick Building window (48x37cm-19x15in) s.d.1902 W/C gouache pencil. 2-Dec-93 Sotheby's, New York #101/R
$17000	£9827	Masked dancer of the No, representing Saki Imp (30x24cm-12x9in) i.d.Aug.1886 i.verso W/C gouache pencil. 23-Sep-93 Christie's, New York #89/R
$39000	£26174	Still life (33x48cm-13x19in) mono. pastel linen. 5-Dec-93 James Bakker, Cambridge #98/R

LAFORTUNE, Felix (1933-) Haitian
$644	£427	Le rhum (61x61cm-24x24in) s.d.82 panel. 13-Jun-94 Rogeon, Paris #87 (F.FR 3600)

LAFUGIE (20th C) American
$1834	£1206	Le bain chinois (32x27cm-13x11in) s.i. W/C gouache. 5-Apr-93 Poulain & le Fur, Paris #52/R (F.FR 10000)

LAITTRE, Elinor de (1911-) American
$4000	£2685	Black Harlequin (124x114cm-49x45in) s.d.45. 4-May-94 Doyle, New York #66/R

LALIBERTE, Alfred (1878-1953) Canadian
$906   £612   Homme au travail (59x46cm-23x18in) s. board. 23-Nov-93 Fraser Pinneys, Quebec #366 (C.D 1200)

LALL, Oscar de (1903-1971) Canadian
$1165   £777   March, Laurentians (71x86cm-28x34in) s. 11-May-94 Sotheby's, Toronto #220/R (C.D 1600)
$1638   £1092   Autumn, Laurentians (80x102cm-31x40in) s. 11-May-94 Sotheby's, Toronto #237/R (C.D 2250)

LAM, Wilfredo (1902-1982) Cuban
$4448   £2985   Totem (70x102cm-28x40in) s. ink acrylic cardboard. 14-Dec-93 Finarte, Milan #414/R (I.L 7500000)
$7095   £4762   Animaux fantastiques (35x45cm-14x18in) s.d.1973verso. 16-Oct-93 Cornette de St.Cyr, Paris #24/R (F.FR 41000)
$8880   £5692   Idolo (45x35cm-18x14in) s. painted 1968. 27-May-93 Christie's, Rome #140/R (I.L 13000000)
$10784 £6913   Oiseau blanc (35x45cm-14x18in) s.d. 30-Apr-93 Drouot Estimations, Paris #94 (F.FR 58000)
$10938 £7292   Composizione (30x40cm-12x16in) s.d.1972 s.d.verso. 24-May-94 Sotheby's, Milan #181/R (I.L 17500000)
$13662 £8758   Idoli (50x40cm-20x16in) s.d.1974 s.d.verso. 25-May-93 Sotheby's, Milan #230/R (I.L 20000000)
$14028 £9479   Composition (35x45cm-14x18in) s.d.1973. 18-Jun-93 Francis Briest, Paris #22/R (F.FR 80000)
$15000 £9934   Sans Titre (34x44cm-13x17in) s.d.1974 verso. 23-Nov-92 Sotheby's, New York #199/R
$18000 £12162 Untitled (30x24cm-12x9in) indist.s.d.1975 s.d.verso. 22-Nov-93 Sotheby's, New York #266/R
$18311 £11738 Bodegon de flores (78x61cm-31x24in) init.d.1938 panel. 25-May-93 Sotheby's, Madrid #61/R (S.P 2300000)
$20000 £13333 Untitled (45x35cm-18x14in) s.d.72verso. 18-May-94 Christie's, New York #287/R
$21251 £14167 Totem (61x50cm-24x20in) s.d.1969. 23-May-94 Christie's, Milan #255/R (I.L 34000000)
$23000 £15541 Untitled (29x36cm-11x14in) s. painted 1970. 22-Nov-93 Sotheby's, New York #236/R
$24058 £15827 Sans titre (60x80cm-24x31in) s.d.1972. 11-Jun-93 Poulain & le Fur, Paris #107/R (F.FR 132000)
$24480 £16000 Untitled (49x39cm-19x15in) s.d.1970. 30-Jun-94 Sotheby's, London #137/R
$26000 £16993 Untitled (50x40cm-20x16in) s.d.1962. 17-May-93 Christie's, New York #136/R
$27012 £18129 Personnage et oiseau (46x60cm-18x24in) s.d.1960. 21-Mar-94 Guy Loudmer, Paris #36/R (F.FR 155000)
$27147 £18098 Salamanca (75x130cm-30x51in) s. painted c.1925-30. 26-May-94 Sotheby's, Madrid #66/R (S.P 3700000)
$27540 £18000 Totem (54x65cm-21x26in) s.d.73 verso. 30-Jun-94 Christie's, London #49/R
$29325 £19167 Oiseau et personnages fantastiques (65x54cm-26x21in) s.d.1970. 29-Jun-94 Guy Loudmer, Paris #234/R (F.FR 161000)
$30000 £20000 Sin titulo (50x40cm-20x16in) s.d.1962. 18-May-94 Christie's, New York #129/R
$30000 £20000 Idoli (50x40cm-20x16in) s.d.1974. 18-May-94 Sotheby's, New York #357/R
$34277 £21694 Composition (80x60cm-31x24in) s.d.1962. 2-Dec-92 Kunsthallen, Copenhagen #198/R (D.KR 210000)
$35000 £23333 Diablos (40x55cm-16x22in) s.d.1970. 18-May-94 Christie's, New York #130/R
$35000 £23333 Sagua la Grande (75x100cm-30x39in) s. i.verso painted 1929. 18-May-94 Christie's, New York #12/R
$37442 £25129 Totem (54x80cm-21x31in) s.d.1959 s.d.verso. 5-May-94 Finarte, Milan #87/R (I.L 60000000)
$50000 £33784 Composition (73x76cm-29x30in) s.i.d.1950. 22-Nov-93 Sotheby's, New York #62/R
$70000 £47297 Albarracin (80x100cm-31x39in) s.d.1929. 22-Nov-93 Sotheby's, New York #20/R
$70000 £46980 Elegua (79x59cm-31x23in) s.d.1962. 7-Jan-94 Gary Nader, Miami #85/R
$71978 £47045 La femme fleurie (91x71cm-36x28in) s.d.1955. 5-May-93 Ader Tajan, Paris #64/R (F.FR 390000)
$95000 £63333 Idoli (80x102cm-31x40in) s.d.1955. 17-May-94 Sotheby's, New York #50/R
$100000 £66667 Entre les palmiers (75x94cm-30x37in) s.d.1944 oil paper on canvas. 17-May-94 Sotheby's, New York #70/R
$104280 £66000 Bonjour Monsieur Lam (74x150cm-29x59in) s.d.1959 d.1959 verso burlap. 3-Dec-92 Sotheby's, London #3/R
$110000 £73826 Composition (125x108cm-49x43in) s.d.1963. 7-Jan-94 Gary Nader, Miami #81/R
$110000 £73333 Sans titre (116x90cm-46x35in) s.d.1961 s.d.verso. 17-May-94 Sotheby's, New York #62/R
$112632 £75088 Chimeres et femme cheval (113x141cm-44x56in) s.d.1964. 9-Jun-94 Christian de Quay, Paris #364/R (F.FR 642000)
$130000 £87838 The fascinated nest (60x78cm-24x31in) s. burlap painted 1944. 23-Nov-93 Christie's, New York #20/R
$130000 £84967 Pomme zombie (41x51cm-16x20in) s.d.1945. 17-May-93 Christie's, New York #40/R
$160000 £105960 Femme cheval (111x82cm-44x32in) s.d.1966 burlap. 24-Nov-92 Christie's, New York #31/R
$180000 £120000 Femme assise avec fleurs (113x82cm-44x32in) s.d.1944 paper laid down on canvas. 18-May-94 Christie's, New York #27/R
$200000 £135235 Pasos mimeticos no 2 (114x140cm-45x55in) s.d.1951. 23-Nov-93 Christie's, New York #50/R
$220000 £145695 Diablos (50x61cm-20x24in) s.d.1945 linen. 24-Nov-92 Christie's, New York #17/R
$260000 £175676 Femme cheval (127x97cm-50x38in) s. linen painted 1954. 23-Nov-93 Christie's, New York #33/R
$1629 *£1093*   *Totem (32x46cm-13x18in) s.d.1961 felttip pen. 12-Oct-93 Finarte, Milan #79 (I.L 2600000)*
$2500 *£1701*   *Cat and mouse (61x41cm-24x16in) s.i.verso chl. 16-Apr-94 Young Fine Arts Auctions, Maine #152/R*

LAM, Wilfredo (1902-1982) Cuban-cont.

$3148	£2018	Las dos caras (31x23cm-12x9in) s.d.1942 ink dr. 17-Dec-92 Fernando Duran, Madrid #183/R (S.P 350000)
$4722	£3027	Demonio y mujer (31x23cm-12x9in) s.d.1942 ink dr. 17-Dec-92 Fernando Duran, Madrid #186/R (S.P 525000)
$4770	£3118	Animal fantastique (40x54cm-16x21in) s. wash ink W/C. 12-May-93 Cornette de St.Cyr, Paris #123 (F.FR 26000)
$4826	£3261	Sin titulo (32x72cm-13x28in) s.d.1976 Indian ink oil paper. 25-Nov-93 Sotheby's, Madrid #53/R (S.P 675000)
$4896	£3200	Untitled (52x71cm-20x28in) chl pastel paper on canvas executed c.1959. 30-Jun-94 Sotheby's, London #100/R
$5489	£3587	Rider on unicorn (48x68cm-19x27in) s.d.1961 W/C over pencil. 5-May-93 Galerie Dobiaschofsky, Bern #737/R (S.FR 8000)
$6061	£4068	Le Veve (51x73cm-20x29in) s.i.d.65 pastel. 20-Dec-93 Ansorena, Madrid #147/R (S.P 850000)
$6203	£4054	Sans titre (24x35cm-9x14in) s.d.1951 W/C ink. 27-Oct-92 Cornette de St.Cyr, Paris #39/R (F.FR 33000)
$6379	£4197	Composition (80x100cm-31x39in) s.d.1973 pastel chl. 13-Jun-93 Lombrail & Teucquam, Paris #93/R (F.FR 35000)
$6417	£4222	Tetes d'animaux (48x48cm-19x19in) s. chl pastel executed 1971. 6-Apr-93 Guy Loudmer, Paris #12/R (F.FR 35000)
$6463	£4309	Untitled (49x62cm-19x24in) s.d.1974 W/C gouache. 28-May-94 Kunstgalerij de Vuyst, Lokeren #539/R (B.FR 220000)
$7286	£4762	Couple d'oiseaux (59x85cm-23x33in) s.d.1957 pastel chl. 29-Jun-94 Guy Loudmer, Paris #10/R (F.FR 40000)
$7301	£4900	Untitled (63x47cm-25x19in) s.d.1959 graphite. 2-Dec-93 Christie's, London #255/R
$8000	£5405	Sin titulo (65x47cm-26x19in) s.d.1969 chl chk. 23-Nov-93 Christie's, New York #215/R
$8439	£5516	Sans titre (56x75cm-22x30in) s. pastel. 12-May-93 Cornette de St.Cyr, Paris #122/R (F.FR 46000)
$10034	£6873	Animaux fantastiques (76x56cm-30x22in) s.d.1963 pastel chl. 10-Feb-94 Cornette de St.Cyr, Paris #54/R (F.FR 60000)
$10500	£7000	Sans titre (69x102cm-27x40in) s. pastel ink executed c.1957. 18-May-94 Sotheby's, New York #288/R
$10703	£7331	Personnages fantastiques (76x56cm-30x22in) s.d.1969 pastel chl. 10-Feb-94 Cornette de St.Cyr, Paris #55/R (F.FR 64000)
$11000	£7333	Diablos (50x70cm-20x28in) s.d.1973 chl pastel. 18-May-94 Christie's, New York #179/R
$12000	£8108	Untitled (69x50cm-27x20in) s.d.1970 s.verso pastel. 22-Nov-93 Sotheby's, New York #267/R
$14155	£9500	Untitled (65x49cm-26x19in) s. chl pastel executed c.1970. 25-Mar-93 Christie's, London #33/R
$16000	£10596	Diablo (70x50cm-28x20in) s.d.1970 chl crayon Fabriano paper. 24-Nov-92 Christie's, New York #118/R
$16000	£10458	Foresta (76x55cm-30x22in) s.d.1962 gouache paper on canvas. 17-May-93 Christie's, New York #239/R
$16000	£10811	Pleniluna (65x50cm-26x20in) s.d.1973 chl pastel. 23-Nov-93 Christie's, New York #202/R
$17000	£11333	Untitled (70x100cm-28x39in) s.d.1959 chl pastel. 18-May-94 Christie's, New York #180/R
$18000	£12081	Femme cheval (56x76cm-22x30in) s.d.1965 pastel chl. 7-Jan-94 Gary Nader, Miami #130/R
$26000	£16993	Le cheval enchante (48x63cm-19x25in) s.d.1945 graphite ink W/C. 18-May-93 Sotheby's, New York #62/R
$26075	£17500	Untitled (60x45cm-24x18in) s.d.39 gouache ink paper on canvas. 23-Mar-94 Sotheby's, London #308/R
$27500	£17974	Untitled (76x54cm-30x21in) s.d.1969 chl pastel. 18-May-93 Sotheby's, New York #67/R
$28000	£18543	Tres figuras (76x56cm-30x22in) s.d.1969 i.verso chl pastel Fabriano paper. 24-Nov-92 Christie's, New York #119/R
$28310	£19000	Untitled (80x59cm-31x23in) s. s.verso oil wax crayons canvas executed 1965. 23-Mar-94 Sotheby's, London #310/R
$31290	£21000	La rencontre (60x50cm-24x20in) s.d.1974 s.verso oil wax crayons canvas. 23-Mar-94 Sotheby's, London #327/R
$38000	£25333	Personages (31x24cm-12x9in) s.i.d.40 col ink wash crayon paper laid down. 18-May-94 Christie's, New York #47/R
$62500	£41667	Untitled (102x76cm-40x30in) gouache executed c.1942. 17-May-94 Sotheby's, New York #20/R

LAMASURE, Edwin (jnr) (1866-1916) American

$750	£490	La Laguna, Venice (44x87cm-17x34in) mono W/C. 22-May-93 Weschler, Washington #97/R

LAMB, F Mortimer (1861-1936) American

$900	£588	Old apple tree (47x61cm-19x24in) s. canvasboard. 4-May-93 Christie's, East, New York #100/R
$1700	£1126	Haunt of Oriole (86x102cm-34x40in) s. 13-Nov-92 Skinner, Bolton #117/R
$500	£327	Winter snow scene (30x43cm-12x17in) s. gouache. 30-Jun-94 Mystic Fine Arts, Connecticut #90
$935	£611	Haying scene in New England (41x56cm-16x22in) s. pastel paperboard. 14-May-93 Skinner, Bolton #72/R

LAMB, Matt (20th C) American

$3400	£2378	Abraham, Martin and John (150x211cm-59x83in) s. i.verso acrylic. 14-Mar-93 Hindman Galleries, Chicago #78

LAMBDIN, George Cochran (1830-1896) American
$1700   £1104   Roses (61x36cm-24x14in) s.d.84 s.verso panel. 9-Sep-93 Sotheby's Arcade, New York #66/R
$3500   £2448   Yellow rose study (41x30cm-16x12in) init.d.77 paper. 10-Mar-93 Sotheby's, New York #39/R
$4000   £2667   Contemplation (79x67cm-31x26in) s.d.59. 12-Mar-94 Weschler, Washington #147/R
$6750   £4470   Flowers in oriental vase (48x23cm-19x9in) s.d.1872 panel. 23-Sep-93 Mystic Fine Arts, Connecticut #106/R
$8000   £5298   Pink and yellow roses (62x46cm-24x18in) s. 22-Sep-93 Christie's, New York #60/R
$10000 £6993   Spring blossoms (51x30cm-20x12in) s.d.1875 panel. 11-Mar-93 Christie's, New York #48/R

LAMBDIN, James Reid (1807-1889) American
$800   £523   Portrait of William M. Swain (92x74cm-36x29in) s.d.1859 i.verso. 8-Oct-93 Christie's, East, New York #230

LAMBERT, Ted R (1905-1960) American
$3500   £2349   Winter on Mount McKinley (30x36cm-12x14in) s.d.1943 mono.i.verso board. 8-Dec-93 Butterfield & Butterfield, San Francisco #3588/R
$11000 £7285   Autumn landscape (46x61cm-18x24in) s.d.1948. 15-Jun-94 Butterfield & Butterfield, San Francisco #4459

LAMOTTE, Daniel (1898-1980) American
$1200   £822   Aristotle contemplating a bust of Homer (150x104cm-59x41in) after Rembrandt. 12-Feb-94 Hart Gallery, Houston #157 r

LANDALUZE, Victor Patricio (1828-1889) Cuban
$7000   £4667   Mujer con Abanico (36x27cm-14x11in) s. 18-May-94 Christie's, New York #82/R
$8500   £5743   Llegando a la Iglesia (41x33cm-16x13in) s. painted c.1880. 22-Nov-93 Sotheby's, New York #149/R
$9500   £6333   Baile en el Patio (20x27cm-8x11in) panel painted 1890. 18-May-94 Christie's, New York #83/R
$12000 £7947   El Encuentro (36x20cm-14x8in) s. 24-Nov-92 Christie's, New York #86/R
$12000 £7947   Nino Con Cabra (55x40cm-22x16in) s.d.1886. 23-Nov-92 Sotheby's, New York #131/R
$14000 £9459   Hombre a caballo (41x33cm-16x13in) s. painted c.1880. 22-Nov-93 Sotheby's, New York #148/R
$23000 £15333 Tipos populares (37x23cm-15x9in) s. panel painted c.1875. 17-May-94 Sotheby's, New York #15/R
$42500 £28716 Cortadores de Cana (22x38cm-9x15in) s.i.verso panel painted c.1880. 22-Nov-93 Sotheby's, New York #12/R
$5000   £3268   Tomando agua (27x20cm-11x8in) s. graphite pen W/C executed c.1885. 18-May-93 Sotheby's, New York #113/R
$12000 £7947   Plaza de la Catedral en el Dia de Reyes. Dia de Reyes (41x35cm-16x14in) s. W/C pencil one paper on board pair. 24-Nov-92 Christie's, New York #85/R

LANDECK, Armin (1905-) American
$1000   *£641*   Manhattan Vista (25x20cm-10x8in) s.i.d.1934 pencil. 10-Dec-92 Sloan, North Bethesda #2695/R
$2600   £1520   Manhattan Canyon (35x17cm-14x7in) s. drypoint laid paper. 19-Sep-92 Christie's, East, New York #32/R

LANE, Fitz Hugh (1804-1865) American
$69000 £46309 Marshes, Annisquam, Mass (51x76cm-20x30in) s.d.1848. 3-Feb-94 Sloan, North Bethesda #2886/R

LANE, Susan Minot (1832-1893) American
$1000   £671   Old houses, Salem St (33x41cm-13x16in) s.i.d.1881 i.verso canvasboard. 27-Mar-93 Skinner, Bolton #194/R

LANG, Annie Traquair (1885-1918) American
$1300   £909   Venetian piazza (15x25cm-6x10in) s. i.verso panel. 12-Mar-93 Skinner, Bolton #239/R

LANGEVIN, Claude (1942-) Canadian
$502   £335   Le Long du Saguenay (41x51cm-16x20in) s. s.i.verso. 30-May-94 Hodgins, Calgary #105/R (C.D 700)
$642   £434   Temps gris (20x25cm-8x10in) s. 23-Nov-93 Joyner Fine Art, Toronto #246 (C.D 850)
$680   £459   Le Plateau, St. Joseph de la Rive (50x60cm-20x24in) s. 23-Nov-93 Joyner Fine Art, Toronto #278/R (C.D 900)
$697   £471   Chapel Arundel Laurentides (41x51cm-16x20in) s. s.i.verso. 1-Nov-93 Levis, Calgary #139 (C.D 900)
$706   £462   Le temps d'une halte - Val David, Laurentiens (51x61cm-20x24in) s. 10-May-93 Hodgins, Calgary #21/R (C.D 900)
$778   £515   Percee de soleil (25x30cm-10x12in) s. 24-Nov-92 Joyner Fine Art, Toronto #254/R (C.D 1000)
$784   £503   Hiver dans Charlevoix (41x51cm-16x20in) s. 7-Dec-92 Waddingtons, Toronto #1298 (C.D 1000)
$856   £567   Marche de Sante (25x30cm-10x12in) s. painted 1992 s.i.verso. 16-Nov-92 Hodgins, Calgary #40 (C.D 1100)
$878   £556   Chersey, Laurentides (20x24cm-8x9in) s. i.verso. 21-Oct-92 Maynards, Vancouver #145 (C.D 1100)
$906   £612   Les Eboulements, Charlevoix (60x75cm-24x30in) s. 23-Nov-93 Joyner Fine Art, Toronto #236/R (C.D 1200)
$907   £613   Souvenir de vacances (30x41cm-12x16in) s. s.i.verso. 25-Apr-94 Levis, Calgary #150 (C.D 1250)

LANGEVIN, Claude (1942-) Canadian-cont.
$921	£590	A l'Abandon (51x61cm-20x24in) s. s.i.verso. 26-Apr-93 Levis, Calgary #95/R (C.D 1175)
$943	£637	Dans la vallee (41x51cm-16x20in) s. s.i.verso. 25-Apr-94 Levis, Calgary #148/R (C.D 1300)
$1016	£686	Randonnee hivernale (41x51cm-16x20in) s. s.i.verso. 25-Apr-94 Levis, Calgary #149 (C.D 1400)
$1110	£725	Rue Principale (51x61cm-20x24in) s. 19-May-93 Sotheby's, Toronto #54/R (C.D 1400)
$1148	£766	Le ciel rouge (51x61cm-20x24in) s. s.i.verso. 30-May-94 Hodgins, Calgary #220/R (C.D 1600)
$1165	£777	Le beau eglise, Petit Saguenay (51x61cm-20x24in) s. i.verso. 11-May-94 Sotheby's, Toronto #79/R (C.D 1600)
$1165	£777	Au Rancart, Petit Saguenay (50x60cm-20x24in) s. 13-May-94 Joyner Fine Art, Toronto #232 (C.D 1600)
$1179	£746	Vue des hauteurs (61x76cm-24x30in) s. 30-Nov-92 Ritchie, Toronto #207/R (C.D 1500)
$1189	£777	Fin de journee (41x51cm-16x20in) s. 18-May-93 Joyner Fine Art, Toronto #247/R (C.D 1500)
$1189	£777	La Basse Cour, Notre Dame des Monts (61x76cm-24x30in) s. 19-May-93 Sotheby's, Toronto #97/R (C.D 1500)
$1245	£825	La rentree a la ferme - St Jean de Matha, Laurentides (41x51cm-16x20in) s. i.d.1982verso. 18-Nov-92 Sotheby's, Toronto #211/R (C.D 1600)
$1323	£876	Rang Ste. Catherine (50x60cm-20x24in) s. 24-Nov-92 Joyner Fine Art, Toronto #19/R (C.D 1700)
$1557	£1031	Hockey dans la cour, Ste-Agathe, Laurentides (75x100cm-30x39in) s. 24-Nov-92 Joyner Fine Art, Toronto #248/R (C.D 2000)
$2015	£1361	La croix du chemin (61x76cm-24x30in) s. s.i.verso. 1-Nov-93 Levis, Calgary #138/R (C.D 2600)

LANGWORTHY, W H (19th C) American
$900	£596	Figures in river landscape (51x81cm-20x32in) s.d.69. 27-Sep-93 Selkirks, St. Louis #922

LANING, Edward (1906-1981) American
$1800	*£1216*	Black Friday. Woman with mole *(41x36cm-16x14in) s.i.ink pencil wash pair sold with W/C J Levine. 31-Mar-94 Sotheby's Arcade, New York #388/R*

LANKFORD, Kenneth (20th C) American
$1150	£762	The Anheuser Busch Budweiser wagon pulled by six Clydesdales (114x386cm-45x152in) s. painted c.1946-48. 27-Sep-93 Selkirks, St. Louis #937/R

LANMAN, Charles (1819-1895) American
$850	£570	Beach scene (25x36cm-10x14in) s. board. 24-Mar-94 Mystic Fine Arts, Connecticut #100 c

LANSDOWNE, James Fenwick (1937-) Canadian
$1355	*£909*	Lake Sparrow *(33x27cm-13x11in) s.d.1958 i.verso W/C. 29-Nov-93 Waddingtons, Toronto #1054 (C.D 1800)*
$2409	*£1478*	American Egret *(64x48cm-25x19in) d.1979 pencil. 17-Oct-92 Lunds, Victoria #2 (C.D 3000)*
$2913	*£1942*	Kildeer - female *(42x43cm-17x17in) s.i.d.1968 W/C. 13-May-94 Joyner Fine Art, Toronto #79/R (C.D 4000)*

LANSIL, Walter Franklin (1846-1925) American
$850	£429	Fishermen off Monhegan Coast of Maine (56x74cm-22x29in) s. s.i.d.1914verso. 28-Aug-92 Young Fine Arts Auctions, Maine #200/R
$1300	£878	The Ducal Palace (15x23cm-6x9in) s. s.i.verso board. 5-Nov-93 Skinner, Bolton #76/R
$2100	£1419	In Dordrecht Harbour Holland (36x61cm-14x24in) s. s.i.d.1900verso. 5-Nov-93 Skinner, Bolton #74/R
$2200	£1486	Venice sunset (30x46cm-12x18in) s.d.1897 s.i.d.verso. 5-Nov-93 Skinner, Bolton #70/R
$4000	£2614	Grand Canal Venice (56x91cm-22x36in) s. s.i.verso painted 1895. 8-May-93 Young Fine Arts Auctions, Maine #196/R

LANSIL, Walter Franklin (attrib) (1846-1925) American
$880	£575	Hauling in nets (36x56cm-14x22in) 14-May-93 Skinner, Bolton #57/R

LANTZ, Walter (20th C) American
$800	*£537*	Two gentlemen in top hats leaning over the desk of a clerk at telegraph office *(25x36cm-10x14in) gouache on celluloid over W/C. 12-Dec-93 Butterfield & Butterfield, Los Angeles #1182/R*
$850	*£571*	Old man smoking a cigar over morse code unit *(25x36cm-10x14in) gouache on celluloid over W/C with pencil. 12-Dec-93 Butterfield & Butterfield, Los Angeles #1183/R*
$1000	*£671*	Woody Woodpecker sits on tree branch eyeing apple *(25x25cm-10x10in) st.sig. gouache celluloid on painted background. 22-Jun-93 Sotheby's, New York #755*

LANYON, Ellen (1926-) American
$1000	*£633*	The clown (51x39cm-20x15in) s. board. 2-Dec-92 Christie's, East, New York #403/R
$800	*£513*	Trapeze artists (61x47cm-24x19in) s.d.1952 oil gouache panel. 27-Apr-93 Christie's, East, New York #277

LAPENSEE, Michel (1947-) Canadian
$655   £437   Soir de neige, Rue St Vincent Vieux Montreal (45x60cm-18x24in) s.d.93. 13-May-94
            Joyner Fine Art, Toronto #182/R (C.D 900)

LAPINE, Andreas Christian Gottfried (1868-1952) Canadian
$779   £513   Late afternoon (104x79cm-41x31in) s. i.verso. 7-Jun-93 Waddingtons, Toronto #1139
            (C.D 1000)
$1743 £1178 Late afternoon landscape (104x39cm-41x15in) s. s.i.verso. 3-Nov-93 Sotheby's,
            Toronto #130/R (C.D 2250)

LAPORTE, Domingo (20th C) Uruguayan
$800   £523   Canal veneciano (70x45cm-28x18in) s.d.1891. 26-Oct-92 Gomensoro, Montevideo #86

LARA, Magali (1956-) Mexican
$21000 £14000 La respiracion de las rosas amarillas (180x180cm-71x71in) s.d.86 acrylic.
            18-May-94 Sotheby's, New York #383/R

LARCO, Jorge (1897-1967) Argentinian
$750   £391   Arboles (32x40cm-13x16in) W/C. 4-Aug-92 VerBo, Buenos Aires #63

LARMON, Kevin (1955-) American
$911   £608   Tired of (46x46cm-18x18in) s.d.1985verso canvas on paper. 2-Jun-94 AB Stockholms
            Auktionsverk, Stockholm #7044/R (S.KR 7200)
$1900 £1242 Subjunctive (46x38cm-18x15in) executed 1987. 22-Dec-92 Christie's, East, New York
            #30
$2400 £1569 Untitled (46x46cm-18x18in) executed 1986. 22-Dec-92 Christie's, East, New York
            #32
$2600 £1699 Permanent red (46x46cm-18x18in) executed 1986. 22-Dec-92 Christie's, East, New
            York #31
$506   £338   Standing behind No.2 (46x45cm-18x18in) s.d.1986verso mixed media. 2-Jun-94 AB
            Stockholms Auktionsverk, Stockholm #7028/R (S.KR 4000)
$532   £354   Number three (46x46cm-18x18in) s.d.1986verso mixed media. 2-Jun-94 AB Stockholms
            Auktionsverk, Stockholm #7045/R (S.KR 4200)
$633   £422   Study for black spot (48x38cm-19x15in) s.d.1987verso mixed media. 2-Jun-94 AB
            Stockholms Auktionsverk, Stockholm #7082/R (S.KR 5000)
$759   £506   Multiplication broken and restored (46x38cm-18x15in) s.d.1987verso mixed media.
            2-Jun-94 AB Stockholms Auktionsverk, Stockholm #7027/R (S.KR 6000)
$1266 £844   Cake (48x41cm-19x16in) s.d.1988verso mixed media. 2-Jun-94 AB Stockholms
            Auktionsverk, Stockholm #7007/R (S.KR 10000)

LAROCHE, Ernesto (1879-1940) Uruguayan
$580   £392   Paisaje (27x35cm-11x14in) s. panel. 25-Apr-94 Gomensoro, Montevideo #50
$650   £417   Cancion nativa (18x28cm-7x11in) s. panel. 7-Dec-92 Gomensoro, Montevideo #74
$650   £422   Cancion nativa (11x15cm-4x6in) s. i.verso panel. 30-Aug-93 Gomensoro, Montevideo
            #19
$1050 £695   Serrania de las animas (18x24cm-7x9in) s. panel. 28-Jun-93 Gomensoro, Montevideo
            #30/R
$1100 £705   Tapera (30x40cm-12x16in) s. 7-Dec-92 Gomensoro, Montevideo #73
$1300 £677   Gaucho con Carreton (72x76cm-28x30in) s. 12-Aug-92 Castells & Castells,
            Montevideo #45/R
$1700 £1118 Paisaje y arroyo en crepusculo (40x50cm-16x20in) s. 31-May-93 Gomensoro,
            Montevideo #28
$1900 £1250 Paisaje (58x49cm-23x19in) s. 31-May-93 Gomensoro, Montevideo #29/R
$2600 £1307 Rio Santa Lucia (40x94cm-16x37in) s. s.i.verso panel. 31-Aug-92 Gomensoro,
            Montevideo #57/R
$4000 £2614 La ventana agreste (80x72cm-31x28in) s. 3-May-93 Gomensoro, Montevideo #77/R
$4400 £2821 Cerro de la frontera (94x94cm-37x37in) s. 7-Dec-92 Gomensoro, Montevideo #72/R
$6000 £3529 Agua quieta (110x150cm-43x59in) s. 5-Oct-92 Gomensoro, Montevideo #12/R

LARRANAGA, Enrique de (1900-1956) Argentinian
$2000 £1176 Payaso (40x30cm-16x12in) 29-Sep-92 VerBo, Buenos Aires #66
$3000 £1765 Paisaje del Tandil (51x66cm-20x26in) 29-Sep-92 VerBo, Buenos Aires #67/R
$3500 £2023 Payaso (51x36cm-20x14in) 23-Sep-92 Roldan & Cia, Buenos Aires #70
$4500 £2601 Viejo Madrid (53x68cm-21x27in) 23-Sep-92 Roldan & Cia, Buenos Aires #58

LARRAVIDE, Manuel (1871-1910) Uruguayan
$2600 £1529 Buques en la bahia (71x111cm-28x44in) s.d.1902. 5-Oct-92 Gomensoro, Montevideo #7

LARRAZ, Julio (1944-) Cuban
$13000 £8609 Sobre la Luna (76x61cm-30x24in) s.d.88. 23-Nov-92 Sotheby's, New York #203/R
$19000 £12838 The couple (59x79cm-23x31in) s.d.83 s.i.d.verso. 23-Nov-93 Christie's, New York
            #219/R
$22000 £14667 The Great American Apple Pie (51x114cm-20x45in) s. s.i.d.Feb.1983verso. 18-May-94
            Christie's, New York #153/R
$40000 £26490 El Cazador - hunter (102x152cm-40x60in) s.d.85. 24-Nov-92 Christie's, New York
            #36/R
$75000 £50000 The courtyard (127x152cm-50x60in) s.d.83. 18-May-94 Christie's, New York #62/R
$10000 £6757 Naturaleza muerta con sandia (79x115cm-31:-45in) s. W/C pencil. 23-Nov-93
            Christie's, New York #221/R
$12000 £8000 Sandia (50x61cm-20x24in) s.d.76 pastel canvas. 18-May-94 Sotheby's, New York
            #244/R

LARRINAGA, Mario (1895-1979) American
$1300 £855   Gilded ghetto - San Francisco (76x61cm-30x24in) s. board. 13-Jun-93 Butterfield &
            Butterfield, San Francisco #982/R

LARSON, Cecil (1908-) American
$1000   £671   Winter in the country (66x91cm-26x36in) s. 4-Dec-93 Louisiana Auction Exchange #9/R

LARVIE, Calvin (1920-) American
$650   £436   Buffalo hunt (23x46cm-9x18in) s. gouache board. 26-Jun-93 Skinner, Bolton #36 g/R

LASALLE, Charles (1893-1958) American
$1400   £952   Branding cattle (76x102cm-30x40in) s. 17-Apr-94 Hanzel Galleries, Chicago #35
$3000   £2000   Ranchers gold (76x61cm-30x24in) s.i. 18-Mar-94 Du Mouchelle, Detroit #2026/R
$3000   £2000   The wrangler (61x76cm-24x30in) s.i. board. 18-Mar-94 Du Mouchelle, Detroit #2027/R

LASCARI, Salvatore (1884-?) American
$1500   £962   Touch of the Southwest (83x96cm-33x38in) canvas on board. 9-Dec-92 Butterfield & Butterfield, San Francisco #3995/R

LASKER, Jonathan (1948-) American
$11000   £7285   Terse Psyche (76x61cm-30x24in) s.d.1989verso. 19-Nov-92 Christie's, New York #116/R
$15000   £10135   Spiller (152x198cm-60x78in) s.i.d.1984verso. 10-Nov-93 Christie's, New York #291/R
$15000   £10417   Time for the world (150x180cm-59x71in) s.i.verso acrylic. 23-Feb-93 Sotheby's, New York #350/R
$1300   *£878*   Untitled (56x76cm-22x30in) s.d.1988verso graphite oilstick. 8-Nov-93 Christie's, East, New York #55/R
$2500   *£1689*   Untitled (76x56cm-30x22in) s.d.1986verso graphite chl. 8-Nov-93 Christie's, East, New York #54/R

LATHROP, Ida Pulis (1859-1937) American
$13000   £8333   Peacock feather, print and photograph (49x58cm-19x23in) s. 26-May-93 Christie's, New York #45/R

LATHROP, William Langson (1859-1938) American
$1200   £839   Marsh grass gatherers (30x41cm-12x16in) s. i.verso. 12-Mar-93 Skinner, Bolton #199/R
$2200   £1438   Rocky shore, Lloyd's Harbour, Long Island (41x51cm-16x20in) s. masonite. 5-May-93 Doyle, New York #28
$3000   £2000   Twilight, Bucks County, Pennsylvania (46x66cm-18x26in) s.indist.d. 23-May-94 Christie's, East, New York #174/R

LATIMER, Lorenzo Palmer (1857-1941) American
$1900   £1258   River in spring time (27x37cm-11x15in) s.d.1886 canvas laid down on board. 15-Jun-94 Butterfield & Butterfield, San Francisco #4573/R
$2500   *£1645*   California redwoods (34x24cm-13x9in) s.d.1904 W/C. 13-Jun-93 Butterfield & Butterfield, San Francisco #753/R

L'AUBINIERE, C A de (19/20th C) Canadian
$2549   *£1699*   Waterfall (76x127cm-30x50in) s.d.1889. 11-May-94 Sotheby's, Toronto #71/R (C.D 3500)

LAUFMAN, Sidney (1891-) American
$1700   £1156   Working in the garden (76x102cm-30x40in) s. 16-Apr-94 Young Fine Arts Auctions, Maine #153/R

LAURENCE, Sydney (1865-1940) American
$1000   £633   Rocky beach scene (20x46cm-8x18in) s. board. 2-Dec-92 Christie's, East, New York #193 a
$1692   £1200   Hauling in lobster pot (46x61cm-18x24in) s.d.1899. 11-Feb-93 David Lay, Penzance #208/R
$3250   £2153   Sunset (30x41cm-12x16in) s. 15-Jun-94 Butterfield & Butterfield, San Francisco #4457/R
$4500   £3020   Alaskan landscape (70x46cm-28x18in) s. 8-Dec-93 Butterfield & Butterfield, San Francisco #3586/R
$6000   £3947   Old cache (25x20cm-10x8in) s. board. 13-Jun-93 Butterfield & Butterfield, San Francisco #3254/R
$6500   £4305   Mountain landscape (41x30cm-16x12in) s. indist.i.stretcher. 23-Sep-93 Sotheby's, New York #96/R
$7000   £4636   Evening tide (41x51cm-16x20in) s. panel. 15-Jun-94 Butterfield & Butterfield, San Francisco #4456/R
$7500   £5245   Safe in Gloucester Harbour (91x132cm-36x52in) s. 14-Mar-93 Hindman Galleries, Chicago #32/R
$9350   £5994   Ship in full sail (41x51cm-16x20in) s. 17-Dec-92 Mystic Fine Arts, Connecticut #183/R
$10000   £5882   Northern Lights, Cape Homer, Alaska (51x61cm-20x24in) s. s.i.stretcher. 3-Oct-92 Weschler, Washington #120/R
$15000   £8671   Early evening, Mt McKinley (54x65cm-21x26in) s. 23-Sep-92 Christie's, New York #124/R
$17000   £11888   Morning sunlight, Mt McKinley (61x51cm-24x20in) s. i.d.1929stretcher. 10-Mar-93 Sotheby's, New York #53/R
$18000   £12081   Autumn day, Mount McKinley (61x41cm-24x16in) s. 3-Dec-93 Christie's, New York #61/R
$715   *£480*   Venetian backwater (31x16cm-12x6in) s.i. pencil W/C. 23-Mar-94 Christie's, S. Kensington #74

283

LAURENCE, Sydney (1865-1940) American-cont.
$790   £500   The breakwater, St Ives (34x24cm-13x9in) s.i. W/C. 21-Oct-92 Sotheby's, London #278
$950   £638   Alaskan Cache (20x18cm-8x7in) s. W/C. 8-Dec-93 Butterfield & Butterfield, San Francisco #3585/R

LAURITZ, Paul (1889-1975) American
$650   £428   High Sierras at Lone Pine (51x61cm-20x24in) s. canvasboard. 13-Jun-93 Butterfield & Butterfield, San Francisco #874/R
$850   £563   Autumn landscape (30x38cm-12x15in) s. canvasboard. 28-Sep-93 John Moran, Pasadena #250
$850   £586   Landscape (51x64cm-20x25in) s. canvas laid down on board. 16-Feb-93 John Moran, Pasadena #74
$1000   £676   Morning surf (41x46cm-16x18in) s. i.verso board. 9-Nov-93 John Moran, Pasadena #858
$1100   £743   Sierra landscape (56x66cm-22x26in) s. 15-Jun-93 John Moran, Pasadena #96
$1200   £779   California landscape (41x51cm-16x20in) s. 11-Sep-93 Louisiana Auction Exchange #27/R
$1200   £811   Crashing surf (51x81cm-20x32in) s. 15-Jun-93 John Moran, Pasadena #153
$1500   £987   Clouds building above desert (71x92cm-28x36in) s. 13-Jun-93 Butterfield & Butterfield, San Francisco #931/R
$1500   £1042   Grant's Pass, Oregon (61x86cm-24x34in) s. canvas on board. 7-Mar-93 Butterfield & Butterfield, San Francisco #217/R
$1800   £1192   Landscape - Golden Day (56x66cm-22x26in) s. 14-Jun-94 John Moran, Pasadena #121
$1800   £1176   Morain Mountain (49x60cm-19x24in) s. 4-May-93 Christie's, East, New York #127 d/R
$2000   £1389   Entrance to Zion National Park (46x66cm-18x26in) s. canvas on board. 7-Mar-93 Butterfield & Butterfield, San Francisco #218/R
$2250   £1520   Landscape (41x51cm-16x20in) s. board. 15-Jun-93 John Moran, Pasadena #21
$650 *£439* *Landscape (36x48cm-14x19in) s. W/C. 15-Jun-93 John Moran, Pasadena #36*
$750 *£507* *Rolling hills (18x20cm-7x8in) s. W/C. 9-Nov-93 John Moran, Pasadena #865*
$900 *£592* *Icy river (51x74cm-20x29in) s. W/C. 13-Jun-93 Butterfield & Butterfield, San Francisco #845/R*
$1000   £662   Moonlight coastal (33x38cm-13x15in) s. mixed media board. 14-Jun-94 John Moran, Pasadena #50
$1100   £724   Mountain stream (53x60cm-21x24in) s. W/C. 13-Jun-93 Butterfield & Butterfield, San Francisco #846/R

LAUX, A (1847-1921) American
$1800   £1200   Still life of raspberries (33x23cm-13x9in) 27-Aug-93 Douglas, South Deerfield #2

LAUX, August (1847-1921) American
$1000   £680   Chickens (35x25cm-14x10in) s. 15-Nov-93 Christie's, East, New York #80/R
$1200   £755   Bouquet of grapes (51x28cm-20x11in) s.d.94. 22-Apr-93 Freeman Fine Arts, Philadelphia #1278
$1300   £823   Chickens, roosters and ducks in farmyard (25x36cm-10x14in) s. 2-Dec-92 Christie's, East, New York #87 a
$1900   £1098   Rooster with chickens (16x22cm-6x9in) s. board. 25-Sep-92 Sotheby's Arcade, New York #116/R
$2000   £1266   Basket of cherries (28x41cm-11x16in) s. 2-Dec-92 Christie's, East, New York #75/R
$2500   £1582   Chickens feeding (25x35cm-10x14in) s. 2-Dec-92 Christie's, East, New York #76
$3500   £2349   Still life with yellow and pink roses (36x46cm-14x18in) s.d.89. 6-Dec-93 Grogan, Massachussetts #467/R
$3600   £2500   Wild berries (28x36cm-11x14in) s. 6-Mar-93 Louisiana Auction Exchange #82/R
$3966   £2644   Apples in a basket (40x50cm-16x20in) s. 31-May-94 Ritchie, Toronto #123/R (C.D 5500)
$4750   £3125   Chickens in barnyard (25x36cm-10x14in) s. 31-Mar-93 Sotheby's Arcade, New York #43/R

LAVALLEY, Jonas Joseph (1858-1930) American
$1100   £719   Autumn stream (51x36cm-20x14in) s. 4-May-93 Christie's, East, New York #78/R
$1600   £1046   Wooded brook (43x56cm-17x22in) s. 4-May-93 Christie's, East, New York #77/R

LAVIN, Robert (1919-) American
$800   £506   Smelting plant against dark blue sky (61x91cm-24x36in) s. 2-Dec-92 Christie's, East, New York #285/R

LAW, Charles Anthony (1916-) Canadian
$680   £459   Jagged ice floes, Dexterity Island, Baffin Island, N.W.T (60x75cm-24x30in) s. 23-Nov-93 Joyner Fine Art, Toronto #285/R (C.D 900)
$1165   £777   Herring Cove in blanket of snow (75x90cm-30x35in) s. 13-May-94 Joyner Fine Art, Toronto #54/R (C.D 1600)

LAW, Margaret M (20th C) American
$1200   £694   Cotton pickers (51x41cm-20x16in) s.d.21 tempera board. 25-Sep-92 Sotheby's Arcade, New York #269/R

LAWLESS, Carl (1894-1934) American
$1200   £784   Glacier Gavarnie (74x74cm-29x29in) 30-Oct-92 Douglas, South Deerfield #1

LAWLEY, Douglas (1906-1971) Canadian
$962   £650   Horse drawn sleds in winter landscape town beyond (71x61cm-28x24in) canvasboard. 26-Nov-93 Tennants, Leyburn #426/R
$1165   £777   Montreal winter, cab stand on Mount Royal (20x25cm-8x10in) s. board pencil dr verso double-sided. 11-May-94 Sotheby's, Toronto #34/R (C.D 1600)

LAWLEY, Douglas (1906-1971) Canadian-cont.
$1572   £995   Montreal from Mount Royal (51x61cm-20x24in) s.i.verso board. 1-Dec-92 Fraser Pinneys, Quebec #148 (C.D 2000)
$1670   £1050   Mount Royal, P Q (51x61cm-20x24in) board. 19-Apr-93 Lunds, Victoria #13 (C.D 2100)

LAWMAN, Jasper Holman (1825-1906) American
$6000   £4000   Artist sketching by a brook (76x109cm-30x43in) s. 17-Mar-94 Sotheby's, New York #5/R

LAWRENCE, Charles B (attrib) (19/20th C) American
$3500   £2288   Extensive river landscape (61x81cm-24x32in) 4-May-93 Christie's, East, New York #31/R

LAWRENCE, Jacob (1917-) American
$62500   £36127 Northbound (61x76cm-24x30in) s.d.62 tempera masonite. 24-Sep-92 Sotheby's, New York #189/R

LAWSON, Ernest (1873-1939) American
$1600   £1039   Country road (13x16cm-5x6in) s. masonite. 9-Sep-93 Sotheby's Arcade, New York #130/R
$4000   £2116   The frozen pool (28x33cm-11x13in) s.i.verso. 11-Sep-92 Skinner, Bolton #239/R
$6500   £4545   Spring planting (23x30cm-9x12in) canvas on board. 11-Mar-93 Christie's, New York #131/R
$8525   £5500   Cripple Creek, Colorado (41x51cm-16x20in) s. canvasboard painted c.1928. 15-Jul-94 Christie's, London #62/R
$9000   £5769   Winter, Spuytin Duyvil (41x51cm-16x20in) 27-May-93 Sotheby's, New York #84/R
$9500   £6333   Last dollar mine, Cripple Creek, Colorado (30x41cm-12x16in) s. i.verso. 17-Mar-94 Sotheby's, New York #118/R
$11000   £6358   Brook, Segovia (30x41cm-12x16in) s. 24-Sep-92 Sotheby's, New York #133/R
$12000   £7595   Boat on a lake (22x40cm-9x16in) s. 3-Dec-92 Sotheby's, New York #114/R
$20000   £13333 Little Ranch, Colorado (41x50cm-16x20in) s. 26-May-94 Christie's, New York #97/R
$24000   £15385 Inwood, Upper Washington Heights (44x53cm-17x21in) 27-May-93 Sotheby's, New York #83/R
$25000   £16779 Greenwich, Connecticut Yacht Club, 4th of July (56x61cm-22x24in) s. painted c.1904. 3-Feb-94 Sloan, North Bethesda #2878/R
$30000   £17341 Reflections of spring (51x61cm-20x24in) s. 23-Sep-92 Christie's, New York #145/R
$75000   £50336 Harbour scene in snow - twilight (51x72cm-20x28in) s. 3-Dec-93 Christie's, New York #51/R

LAWSON, Ernest (attrib) (1873-1939) American
$1400   £915   River in woods (20x28cm-8x11in) s. panel. 3-May-93 Schrager Galleries, Milwaukee #630

LAWSON, Thomas (1951-) American
$2600   £1722   View from the Berghof (168x244cm-66x96in) s.i.d.83verso. 17-Nov-92 Christie's, East, New York #139/R

LAYCOCK, Brent R (1947-) Canadian
$431   £287   Hill to climb (61x86cm-24x34in) s.d. W/C. 30-May-94 Hodgins, Calgary #112 (C.D 600)

LAZARUS, Jacob Hart (1822-1891) American
$900   £600   Portrait of Archibald Durkin (76x64cm-30x25in) s.d.1846 i.d.verso. 12-Jun-94 Skinner, Bolton #315

LAZZELL, Blanche (1878-1956) American
$6000   £4027   Two red petunias (25x30cm-10x12in) s.d.1934 verso board. 5-Dec-93 James Bakker, Cambridge #100/R
$750   £503   A neighbourhood (25x36cm-10x14in) s.d.36 conte crayon pencil. 26-Mar-94 James Bakker, Cambridge #113/R

LEAKE, Eugene (20th C) American
$1300   £867   Black August bridge (107x152cm-42x60in) s. i.d.1980 stretcher. 23-May-94 Christie's, East, New York #257/R

LEAKE, Gerald (1885-1975) American
$550   £369   Road block (77x89cm-30x35in) s. 6-May-94 Skinner, Bolton #166/R

LEAL AUDIRAC, Fernando (20th C) Mexican?
$573   £367   Desnudos (68x97cm-27x38in) s. chl dr executed 1992. 29-Apr-93 Louis Morton, Mexico #185 (M.P 1800)

LEAVITT, Edward C (1842-1904) American
$1300   £872   Single rose and babies breath (20x15cm-8x6in) s. 16-Dec-93 Mystic Fine Arts, Connecticut #75/R
$2000   £1333   Still life with peaches and grapes (38x76cm-15x30in) s.d.1890. 23-May-94 Christie's, East, New York #81/R
$2500   £1603   Blue fish and lobster (51x76cm-20x30in) s.d.1894. 9-Dec-92 Grogan, Massachussetts #34/R
$2700   £1812   Still life with Crab apples (41x51cm-16x20in) s.d.1897. 4-Mar-94 Skinner, Bolton #223/R
$3000   £1765   Roses (66x91cm-26x36in) s.d.1887. 5-Oct-92 Grogan, Massachussetts #702/R
$3500   £2215   Still life with jasperware vase, yellow roses. Still life with copper urn, shell and yellow rose (52x31cm-20x12in) s.d.1876-8 two. 2-Dec-92 Christie's, East, New York #128/R

LEAVITT, Edward C (1842-1904) American-cont.
$4000	£2649	Still life (46x55cm-18x22in) s.d.1885. 22-Sep-93 Christie's, New York #25/R
$4800	£3357	Wedgewood and flowers. Urn, shell and flowers (51x30cm-20x12in) s. pair. 11-Mar-93 Mystic Fine Arts, Connecticut #122/R
$13000	£8228	Pansies (35x45cm-14x18in) s.d.1885. 4-Dec-92 Christie's, New York #27/R

LEAVITT, John Farence (1905-1974) American
$1300	£878	U.S. Clipper Dreadnaught (53x71cm-21x28in) W/C. 30-Jul-93 Eldred, Massachusetts #143/R

LEBDUSKA, Lawrence (1894-1966) American
$650	£433	Four horses (28x23cm-11x9in) panel. 3-Jun-94 Douglas, South Deerfield #7
$700	£470	Fruit on a table , s. board. 16-Dec-93 Mystic Fine Arts, Connecticut #215/R
$1300	£867	Horse, dog, woman and house (61x43cm-24x17in) 3-Jun-94 Douglas, South Deerfield #8
$1600	£925	Prancing horses (51x61cm-20x24in) s.d.56. 25-Sep-92 Sotheby's Arcade, New York #517/R

LEBRUN, Rico (1900-1964) American/Italian
$1300	£878	Familia del Rey da Goya (74x58cm-29x23in) s.i.d.1957 W/C graphite. 21-Oct-93 Butterfield & Butterfield, San Francisco #2726/R
$1600	£1006	Fall of the centurion (44x62cm-17x24in) s.d.1948 ink pastel board. 25-Apr-93 Butterfield & Butterfield, San Francisco #2012/R

LEDESMA, Gabriel Fernandez (1900-1983) Mexican
$23000	£15262	Los Guantes Negros (50x63cm-20x25in) init.d.1940. 23-Nov-92 Sotheby's, New York #52/R

LEDUC, Fernand (1916-) Canadian
$934	£619	Project 10 (35x35cm-14x14in) s.d.73 i.verso gouache board. 18-Nov-92 Sotheby's, Toronto #146/R (C.D 1200)

LEDUC, Ozias (1864-1955) Canadian
$9466	£6311	The Assumption of the Virgin (25x18cm-10x7in) s.d.January 2 1944 board. 11-May-94 Sotheby's, Toronto #135/R (C.D 13000)
$753	£492	Study of contemplative man (40x34cm-16x13in) s. pencil. 19-May-93 Sotheby's, Toronto #52/R (C.D 950)

LEE, Bertha Stringer (1873-1937) American
$750	£507	Moonlight-Golden Gate Park (61x41cm-24x16in) s. 15-Jun-93 John Moran, Pasadena #75

LEE, Catherine (1950-) American
$3000	£2013	Trinity (152x183cm-60x72in) s.i.d.1987verso linen three attached panels. 3-May-94 Christie's, East, New York #184/R

LEE, Henry Charles (1864-1930) American
$600	£408	Spring landscape (89x104cm-35x41in) s. 14-Apr-94 Freeman Fine Arts, Philadelphia #992

LEE, Lowell Merritt (attrib) (1905-) American
$700	£458	Loosening the sheets (91x71cm-36x28in) s.d.37 i.verso. 3-May-93 Schrager Galleries, Milwaukee #562
$800	£523	Coal and coke (71x91cm-28x36in) s.d.1935 i.verso. 3-May-93 Schrager Galleries, Milwaukee #594

LEE, Walt (20th C) American
$600	£397	Landscape - Verdugo Park - Glendale, CA 1946 (64x76cm-25x30in) s. 14-Jun-94 John Moran, Pasadena #108

LEE-SMITH, Hughie (1915-) American
$1400	£819	Deserted beach (28x38cm-11x15in) s. 18-Sep-92 Du Mouchelle, Detroit #1998/R
$1700	£1141	Man sitting in rural landscape (25x36cm-10x14in) s.d.54 board. 17-Dec-93 Du Mouchelle, Detroit #2019/R
$2400	£1589	Landscape (61x74cm-24x29in) board. 13-Nov-92 Du Mouchelle, Detroit #2010/R
$2900	£2057	Portrait of young man with sail boats (20x30cm-8x12in) d.54 masonite. 12-Feb-93 Du Mouchelle, Detroit #2010/R
$3500	£2482	The hill (61x81cm-24x32in) s. painted 1963. 12-Feb-93 Du Mouchelle, Detroit #2012/R
$4750	£3369	Two figures on rooftop overlooking city scene (58x46cm-23x18in) s. 12-Feb-93 Du Mouchelle, Detroit #2011/R
$5000	£3268	Landscape with figure of man (66x91cm-26x36in) 17-Sep-93 Du Mouchelle, Detroit #2033/R

LEES, John (1943-) American
$1500	£1007	Landscape M.S.A.C (46x56cm-18x22in) s.d.78 verso. 25-Mar-93 Boos Gallery, Michigan #417/R
$3500	£2288	Landscape for Carlo Carra (71x56cm-28x22in) executed 1982. 22-Dec-92 Christie's, East, New York #35

LEETEG, Edgar (20th C) American
$1000	£662	Jacquie, female nude (79x69cm-31x27in) s. velvet laid down on panel sold with book. 15-Jun-94 Butterfield & Butterfield, San Francisco #4557/R

LEGARE, Joseph (1795-1855) Canadian
$29058 £19634 Montmorency Falls in winter (36x46cm-14x18in) s.d.1800 board. 3-Nov-93 Sotheby's, Toronto #111/R (C.D 37500)

LEHR, Adam (19/20th C) American
$800 £523 Apples and pitcher (41x58cm-16x23in) s.d.1904. 30-Jun-94 Mystic Fine Arts, Connecticut #72 a/R
$1700 £1104 Still life with pitcher, knife and plums (25x36cm-10x14in) s.d.1903 panel. 8-Jul-94 Sloan, North Bethesda #2362/R

LEIER, Grant (1956-) American
$580 *£392* *Army of New Recession with flair for international politics and out of season fruit (36x102cm-14x40in) s.i.d.1985verso mixed media on illustr. board. 25-Apr-94 Levis, Calgary #202/R (C.D 800)*
$833 *£563* *Regina Cleaners and Tailors (102x76cm-40x30in) s.d.1985 s.i.d.verso mixed media board. 1-Nov-93 Levis, Calgary #141/R (C.D 1075)*

LEIGH, William R (1866-1955) American
$7000 £4667 Western landscape (41x51cm-16x20in) s. 17-May-94 Grogan, Massachussetts #348/R
$7250 £4834 Pueblo Village with dry river bed (15x23cm-6x9in) s.d.1911 board. 17-May-94 Grogan, Massachussetts #347/R
$11000 £7333 Pueblo village (25x30cm-10x12in) s.d.1912 s.i.verso canvas on board. 17-May-94 Grogan, Massachussetts #344/R
$17000 £11333 Cheyenne (36x25cm-14x10in) s. s.i.d.Feb.1906verso canvasboard. 25-May-94 Sotheby's, New York #55/R
$18000 £12081 A Hopi girl at sunset (28x38cm-11x15in) s. board. 25-Mar-94 Eldred, Massachusetts #917/R
$18000 £12000 Storm at trading post, Kayenta, Arizona (33x43cm-13x17in) s. s.d.Aug.1922verso canvasboard. 25-May-94 Sotheby's, New York #56/R
$21000 £14000 Cooking Pu-Vu-Lu (20x25cm-8x10in) s.i.d.1917 s.i.verso canvas on board. 17-May-94 Grogan, Massachussetts #342/R
$24000 £16000 Seated Indian at sunset (30x46cm-12x18in) s.d.1913 board. 17-May-94 Grogan, Massachussetts #345/R
$27500 £18333 Navajo pony, Kayenta, Arizona (34x43cm-13x17in) s. s.d.1922verso canvasboard. 25-May-94 Sotheby's, New York #48/R
$75000 £50000 Voice of the desert (76x102cm-30x40in) s.d.1914 board. 25-May-94 Sotheby's, New York #47/R
$77500 £51667 Bucking horse (102x76cm-40x30in) s.i.d.1915. 17-May-94 Grogan, Massachussetts #341/R
$120000 £80537 The Hopi Indian runners (102x152cm-40x60in) s.d.1913. 2-Dec-93 Sotheby's, New York #64/R
$140000 £93333 The bear tracker (71x56cm-28x22in) s.d.1941. 25-May-94 Sotheby's, New York #49/R
$150000 £94937 Zuni pottery market (63x77cm-25x30in) s.d.1907. 4-Dec-92 Christie's, New York #275/R
$650 *£436* *Smiling cowboy (23x23cm-9x9in) s.d.1937 W/C. 2-Dec-93 Swann Galleries, New York #182/R*

LEIGHTON, F (20th C) American
$950 £549 Harbour scene (20x30cm-8x12in) s. board. 24-Sep-92 Mystic Fine Arts, Connecticut #138/R

LEIGHTON, Scott (1847-1898) American
$1500 £980 Wooded stream. Woodlands (61x41cm-24x16in) s. pair. 17-Sep-93 Skinner, Bolton #160/R
$1800 £1040 Ready for the hunt (61x46cm-24x18in) s. 25-Sep-92 Sotheby's Arcade, New York #112/R
$10000 £6579 'St. Julian' (61x91cm-24x36in) s. 4-Jun-93 Sotheby's, New York #167 b/R
$11000 £7237 Farm and livestock (61x91cm-24x36in) s. 4-Jun-93 Sotheby's, New York #166/R

LEIMANIS, Andris (1938-) Canadian
$1208 £816 Maison Papineau, after snow storm, view of Place Jacques Cartier, Old Montreal (60x75cm-24x30in) s. painted 1986. 23-Nov-93 Joyner Fine Art, Toronto #163/R (C.D 1600)
$1311 £874 Early summer, view of Montreal from Westmount (50x60cm-20x24in) s. 13-May-94 Joyner Fine Art, Toronto #131/R (C.D 1800)

LEITH-ROSS, Harry (1886-1973) American
$850 £563 Spring landscape (20x25cm-8x10in) s. board. 13-Nov-92 Skinner, Bolton #121/R
$2000 £1325 Winter sunlight (37x37cm-15x15in) s. canvas on board. 22-Sep-93 Christie's, New York #174/R
$2400 £1589 Catskill barn (20x25cm-8x10in) s. s.i.verso. 2-Oct-93 Boos Gallery, Michigan #281/R
$5250 £3088 Country house with figures (56x81cm-22x32in) s. 8-Oct-92 Freeman Fine Arts, Philadelphia #1143
$6250 £3676 Spell of spring (61x81cm-24x32in) s. 8-Oct-92 Freeman Fine Arts, Philadelphia #1142

LEIVA, Nicolas (1958-) Argentinian
$6000 £4027 De un lugar tan temido pero tan sonado , s.d.93 s.i.d.verso panel eight. 7-Jan-94 Gary Nader, Miami #14/R
$7500 £5000 De las serie de las Tumbas (109x123cm-43x48in) s. s.i.d.1991verso. 18-May-94 Sotheby's, New York #237/R

LEMBECK, Jack (1942-) American
$1606	£1064	Flat (120x120cm-47x47in) s.d.1986verso. 24-Nov-92 Goteborg Auktionsverk #194 (S.KR 11000)
$3401	£2314	Small orange painting (153x180cm-60x71in) s.d.1983verso. 13-Apr-94 Bukowskis, Stockholm #316/R (S.KR 27000)
$4204	£2765	Lion, lion, lion (174x203cm-69x80in) s.verso. 3-Nov-92 Bukowskis, Stockholm #137/R (S.KR 25000)

LEMIEUX, Annette (1957-) American
$1200	£811	Trying one's virtues (303x153cm-119x60in) acrylic paper on canvas painted 1981. 8-Nov-93 Christie's, East, New York #49/R
$1709	*£1139*	*Life cycle (24x18cm-9x7in) s.d.1989verso ink. 2-Jun-94 AB Stockholms Auktionsverk, Stockholm #7019/R (S.KR 13500)*
$6000	£3974	Finger painting on yellow pages (182x137cm-72x54in) s.i.d.88-89verso oil resin paper collage canvas. 19-Nov-92 Christie's, New York #110/R

LEMIEUX, Jean Paul (1904-1990) Canadian
$6616	£4381	Serenite (46x36cm-18x14in) s. i.verso. 18-Nov-92 Sotheby's, Toronto #53/R (C.D 8500)
$7551	£5102	View of Quebec from Beauport (51x61cm-20x24in) s.i.d.50 verso panel. 23-Nov-93 Joyner Fine Art, Toronto #23/R (C.D 10000)
$14010	£9278	Portrait of a Nun (41x30cm-16x12in) s.d.67 i.verso. 18-Nov-92 Sotheby's, Toronto #54/R (C.D 18000)
$17440	£11399	Portrait of a nun (41x30cm-16x12in) s.d.67. 18-May-93 Joyner Fine Art, Toronto #78/R (C.D 22000)
$37864	£25243	Petite fille dans le noir (65x41cm-26x16in) s. 13-May-94 Joyner Fine Art, Toronto #91/R (C.D 52000)
$5153	*£3368*	*Femme en bleu (60x46cm-24x18in) s. gouache. 18-May-93 Joyner Fine Art, Toronto #111/R (C.D 6500)*

LEON, Omar de (20th C) South American
| $1000 | £662 | Casas (53x43cm-21x17in) s. painted 1950. 2-Oct-93 Weschler, Washington #73 |

LEONARD, Ruth (1955-) American
| $950 | £638 | Slow fires of autumn (66x97cm-26x38in) s.d.1983. 25-Mar-93 Boos Gallery, Michigan #416/R |
| $1000 | £671 | Cliffside Highway (152x183cm-60x72in) s. d.1984 verso. 25-Mar-93 Boos Gallery, Michigan #428/R |

LEONE, John (20th C) American
| $2200 | £1467 | Red Rock Warrior (76x102cm-30x40in) s. panel. 22-May-94 Hindman Galleries, Chicago #49/R |

LEONIDAS, Rony (20th C) Haitian
| $626 | £415 | Bataille de Verpieres (61x91cm-24x36in) s. 13-Jun-94 Rogeon, Paris #22 (F.FR 3500) |

LEONORI, R G L (fl.1847-1848) American
| $3500 | £2023 | Snow scene (34x46cm-13x18in) 23-Sep-92 Christie's, New York #16/R |

LESLIE, Alfred (1927-) American
$2400	£1569	Portrait of Mikey Besch (147x112cm-58x44in) s.d.1990. 7-May-93 Christie's, East, New York #49/R
$12000	£8108	Number 5 (49x75cm-19x30in) oil paper collage canvas painted 1960. 11-Nov-93 Sotheby's, New York #298/R
$1200	*£805*	*Woman (64x48cm-25x19in) s.d.52 oil pastel paper collage. 4-May-94 Doyle, New York #59*

LESLIE, Edward (1891-1960) American
| $1600 | £1053 | Marin landscape (61x76cm-24x30in) s.d.1928. 13-Jun-93 Butterfield & Butterfield, San Francisco #773/R |

LESPINASSE, Herbert (1884-1972) American
| $796 | £553 | L'etang (15x21cm-6x8in) s. 2-Mar-93 Poulain & le Fur, Paris #151/R (F.FR 4500) |

LETENDRE, Rita (1929-) Canadian
| $934 | £619 | Chevauchee 61 (31x36cm-12x14in) s.d.61 i.verso. 18-Nov-92 Sotheby's, Toronto #264/R (C.D 1200) |
| $2378 | £1554 | Lutte, Ramat Gan (65x81cm-26x32in) s.d.63 s.i.d.verso acrylic. 19-May-93 Sotheby's, Toronto #210/R (C.D 3000) |

LETHBRIDGE, Julian (1947-) American
$26000	£17568	Untitled (214x172cm-84x68in) s.i.d.86/87verso. 10-Nov-93 Christie's, New York #275 a/R
$850	*£575*	*Untitled (57x48cm-22x19in) init.d.8.88 acrylic graphite. 8-Nov-93 Christie's, East, New York #58/R*
$1600	£1111	Cobweb (45x30cm-18x12in) init.d.88 graphite gouache. 22-Feb-93 Christie's, East, New York #251/R
$2600	£1806	Untitled (32x25cm-13x10in) init.d.6-89 graphite gouache. 22-Feb-93 Christie's, East, New York #249/R
$5000	£3472	Untitled (69x53cm-27x21in) s.i.d.1988verso acrylic alkyd linen. 22-Feb-93 Christie's, East, New York #244/R

LEUTZE, Emanuel Gottlieb (1816-1868) American/German
$1500	£993	The mournful harpist (29x22cm-11x9in) s.i.d. Jan 28.44 pencil dr. 15-Jun-94 Butterfield & Butterfield, San Francisco #4406/R
$6000	£3468	Portrait of George Washington - study from Washington crossing Delaware (33x25cm-13x10in) s.d.1851 pencil. 24-Sep-92 Sotheby's, New York #45/R

LEVA, Barry (1941-) American
$4200	£2781	Sculpture activities green (153x154cm-60x61in) s.d.1986verso spray enamel paper collage canvas. 19-Nov-92 Christie's, New York #395/R

LEVEE, John (1924-) American
$1132	£755	Composition (14x24cm-6x9in) s.d.5 s.d.verso. 4-Jun-94 Auctionhaus Burkard, Luzern #115/R (S.FR 1600)
$2655	£1782	Composition, April I (81x100cm-32x39in) s.d.59. 1-Dec-93 Kunsthallen, Copenhagen #190/R (D.KR 18000)

LEVER, Richard Hayley (1876-1958) American
$650	£425	Street in St Ives (18x25cm-7x10in) s. panel. 5-May-93 Doyle, New York #31
$858	£600	Sailing off quay at sunset (16x23cm-6x9in) board. 9-Mar-93 Phillips, London #69 a
$1100	£636	View of Sheridan Square (30x41cm-12x16in) s.init. panel. 25-Sep-92 Sotheby's Arcade, New York #336/R
$1100	£738	Still life with fruit (30x38cm-12x15in) s. s.verso board. 1-Dec-93 Doyle, New York #59
$1200	£811	Fishing boat (30x41cm-12x16in) s. masonite. 20-Mar-93 Weschler, Washington #111/R
$1200	£816	Pier Street Cornwall (16x24cm-6x9in) s. panel. 15-Nov-93 Christie's, East, New York #177/R
$1386	£900	Coastal landscape (23x23cm-9x9in) s. canvas laid on board. 23-Jun-94 Christie's, London #175/R
$1400	£933	In the harbour (30x41cm-12x16in) s. board. 22-May-94 James Bakker, Cambridge #73/R
$1500	£1000	Moonrise (25x30cm-10x12in) s. board. 12-Mar-94 Weschler, Washington #169/R
$1500	£974	Sunny morning (25x30cm-10x12in) s. painted 1905. 9-Sep-93 Sotheby's Arcade, New York #189/R
$1600	£1053	Rock by sea (36x46cm-14x18in) s. 31-Mar-93 Sotheby's Arcade, New York #170/R
$1800	£1184	Sailboat at dockside (36x55cm-14x22in) s. 31-Mar-93 Sotheby's Arcade, New York #172/R
$1800	£1169	Queensborough Bridge (25x30cm-10x12in) s. s.i.verso canvasboard. 9-Sep-93 Sotheby's Arcade, New York #222/R
$1870	£1100	Bathing machines at Porthminster. Figures on beach, St. Ives (15x23cm-6x9in) one s. panel pair. 8-Oct-92 David Lay, Penzance #57/R
$1900	£1293	The two quays Concarneau Brittany (26x35cm-10x14in) s. canvasboard. 15-Nov-93 Christie's, East, New York #176/R
$2000	£1342	Summer day, Woodstock (30x41cm-12x16in) s. board. 8-Dec-93 Butterfield & Butterfield, San Francisco #3364/R
$2200	£1392	Early morning, St.Ives (36x46cm-14x18in) s. s.i.stretcher. 2-Dec-92 Christie's, East, New York #176/R
$2400	£1633	Chelsea England (16x24cm-6x9in) s. 15-Nov-93 Christie's, East, New York #179
$2500	£1689	Cape Cod, Massachusetts. River Exe, England. Brittany (41x48cm-16x19in) one s.oil one init.W/C one mono.i.W/C three. 31-Mar-94 Sotheby's Arcade, New York #252/R
$2500	£1689	New York harbour (61x122cm-24x48in) s.i. masonite. 31-Mar-94 Sotheby's Arcade, New York #272/R
$2600	£1688	The apple tree (46x36cm-18x14in) s. panel. 11-Sep-93 Louisiana Auction Exchange #2/R
$2640	£1692	Brittany beach scene (15x23cm-6x9in) s. 17-Dec-92 Mystic Fine Arts, Connecticut #140/R
$2800	£1905	Paris France (18x25cm-7x10in) s. 15-Nov-93 Christie's, East, New York #174
$2800	£1842	Covered bridge leading to Stowe (36x46cm-14x18in) s.d.1933 s.i.verso board. 4-Nov-92 Doyle, New York #48/R
$2900	£1946	Yachting centre, Larchmont, New York (35x46cm-14x18in) s. s.i.d.1947 verso panel. 11-Dec-93 Weschler, Washington #126/R
$3000	£1948	Fishing fleet going out (25x33cm-10x13in) s.d.1910 canvas laid on board. 9-Sep-93 Sotheby's Arcade, New York #190/R
$3000	£2027	Spring (51x61cm-20x24in) board. 27-Nov-93 Young Fine Arts Auctions, Maine #205/R
$3250	£1879	Central Park with bridge and lake (25x33cm-10x13in) s.i. 25-Sep-92 Sotheby's Arcade, New York #337/R
$3250	£2111	Lobster pots, Maine (30x40cm-12x16in) s. canvasboard. 9-Sep-93 Sotheby's Arcade, New York #418/R
$5000	£3289	Harbour with fishing boats (51x61cm-20x24in) s. 31-Mar-93 Sotheby's Arcade, New York #169/R
$5000	£3311	Beach at Cornwall (26x34cm-10x13in) s.d.08 board. 23-Sep-93 Sotheby's, New York #210/R
$5309	£3587	St. Ives, Cornwall (61x92cm-24x36in) 24-Nov-93 Christie's, Victoria #324/R (A.D 8000)
$6500	£4545	St Ives (61x77cm-24x30in) s. 11-Mar-93 Christie's, New York #218/R
$7250	£4802	Fishing town (61x76cm-24x30in) s. 23-Sep-93 Sotheby's, New York #203/R
$8500	£5667	Dockside with gulls (51x61cm-20x24in) s. board. 17-Mar-94 Sotheby's, New York #161/R
$11000	£7383	Main Street, Mt Vernon, New York (61x127cm-24x50in) s. masonite painted c.1930. 2-Dec-93 Sotheby's, New York #156/R
$12500	£8741	Smeaton's Pier, St Ives (46x61cm-18x24in) painted c.1910. 10-Mar-93 Sotheby's, New York #125/R
$13000	£9091	Anchored ships at St Ives, Cornwall (61x76cm-24x30in) s.stretcher. 11-Mar-93 Christie's, New York #230/R
$13000	£7514	View of Gloucester (184x176cm-72x69in) s. 24-Sep-92 Sotheby's, New York #112/R
$30000	£18987	Lower Manhattan (63x76cm-25x30in) s. 4-Dec-92 Christie's, New York #37/R

LEVER, Richard Hayley (1876-1958) American-cont.
$35000	£22436	Summer afternoon, St. Ives harbour, Cornwall (127x152cm-50x60in) s. painted c.1910. 27-May-93 Sotheby's, New York #66/R
$600	£397	Beached boats (35x56cm-14x22in) s. W/C. 2-Oct-93 Weschler, Washington #142
$600	£397	Gloucester harbour (28x36cm-11x14in) s. W/C. 21-Nov-92 James Bakker, Cambridge #68
$600	£377	Still life with pears and grapes (23x33cm-9x13in) init. W/C. 22-Apr-93 Freeman Fine Arts, Philadelphia #1284
$900	£592	Kew Common, London (23x33cm-9x13in) s.i.painted c.1900 i.verso W/C. 2-Apr-93 Sloan, North Bethesda #2065/R
$1200	£800	Newlyn harbour, Penzance, Cornwall (39x46cm-15x18in) s.d.1912 W/C gouache. 23-May-94 Christie's, East, New York #165/R
$1200	£811	Gloucester and regatta at Marblehead (28x38cm-11x15in) one mono. one s. W/C pair one executed 1935. 31-Mar-94 Sotheby's Arcade, New York #312/R
$1700	£1149	Dock with house, boats and two figures (38x43cm-15x17in) s. W/C board. 22-Apr-94 Du Mouchelle, Detroit #2001
$2300	£1608	Shore town (28x39cm-11x15in) s. W/C pencil. 11-Mar-93 Christie's, New York #227/R
$9000	£5696	Gloucester Hills (27x39cm-11x15in) s. W/C. 3-Dec-92 Sotheby's, New York #53/R

LEVESQUE, Isabel (1919-) Canadian
$574	£383	Morning light - three sisters (51x76cm-20x30in) s. i.verso acrylic board. 30-May-94 Hodgins, Calgary #64/R (C.D 800)
$610	£407	Steam engine harvest (41x61cm-16x24in) s.d. s.i.verso acrylic board. 30-May-94 Hodgins, Calgary #283/R (C.D 850)

LEVINE, David (1926-) American
$4500	£2848	Joy ride (31x24cm-12x9in) s.d.82 W/C. 3-Dec-92 Sotheby's, New York #77/R

LEVINE, Jack (1915-) American
$7000	£4046	Girl with red hair (81x66cm-32x26in) s. 23-Sep-92 Christie's, New York #280/R
$9000	£6294	Portrait of Joan (81x66cm-32x26in) s. 11-Mar-93 Christie's, New York #250/R
$10000	£6329	The oath (50x70cm-20x28in) s. 4-Dec-92 Christie's, New York #141/R
$16000	£10127	Woman in green (61x53cm-24x21in) s. 3-Dec-92 Sotheby's, New York #192/R
$24000	£15190	Lady in the woods (66x82cm-26x32in) s. 4-Dec-92 Christie's, New York #142/R
$26000	£18182	David and Goliath (122x107cm-48x42in) s. 11-Mar-93 Christie's, New York #249/R
$30000	£17341	Lolita (71x81cm-28x32in) s. 23-Sep-92 Christie's, New York #272/R
$1400	£921	Study of man's head. Toulouse-Lautrec at Mikado (56x42cm-22x17in) s. conte crayon pencil pair. 31-Mar-93 Sotheby's Arcade, New York #469/R
$4750	£3006	Old City Hall, Boston (27x37cm-11x15in) s. W/C pencil gouache. 3-Dec-92 Sotheby's, New York #78/R

LEVINE, Sherrie (1947-) American
$9000	£6040	Untitle - Mr. Austridge 3 (120x69cm-47x27in) casein executed 1989. 23-Feb-94 Christie's, New York #115/R
$11000	£7639	Gold knot no 1 (53x43cm-21x17in) s.i.d.1985 acrylic panel. 24-Feb-93 Christie's, New York #107/R
$1900	£1275	After Francis Picabia (36x28cm-14x11in) s.i.d.1983 verso W/C graphite. 23-Feb-94 Christie's, East, New York #219/R
$2000	£1389	After Henri Matisse (35x28cm-14x11in) s.i.d.1983verso W/C graphite. 22-Feb-93 Christie's, East, New York #276/R
$11000	£7285	Untitled, Mr. Austridge 2 (120x69cm-47x27in) painted 1989 casein panel. 19-Nov-92 Christie's, New York #143/R
$13000	£8609	Broad stripe no 1 (61x51cm-24x20in) painted 1985 casein wax mahogany. 19-Nov-92 Christie's, New York #132/R
$17500	£11438	Untitled, lead knots 4 (132x107cm-52x42in) s.d.1988verso metallic paint plywood. 5-Oct-93 Sotheby's, New York #223/R
$50000	£33557	Untitled copper knots no 2-5 (116x92cm-46x36in) metallic paint plywood executed 1990. 5-May-94 Sotheby's, New York #316/R

LEVOW, Irving (1902-) American
$1100	£719	Handball players (41x61cm-16x24in) s.d.1939. 4-May-93 Christie's, East, New York #280/R

LEVUS, Jesus (20th C) Mexican
$2100	£1419	Platicando (43x61cm-17x24in) s. d.78 verso mixed media panel. 29-Oct-93 Hart Gallery, Houston #5

LEVY, Beatrice S (1892-1974) American
$800	£526	Back of Guadaloupe Church, Santa Fe (25x36cm-10x14in) s.d.4/29/20. 13-Jun-93 Butterfield & Butterfield, San Francisco #3215/R

LEWANDOWSKI, Edmund D (1914-) American
$3200	£2238	White barn, Wisconsin (43x71cm-17x28in) s.d.1960 gouache pencil board. 11-Mar-93 Christie's, New York #196/R

LEWIS, Betty Y (1909-) Canadian
$1456	£971	The waiting room (44x51cm-17x20in) s.d.46 board sold with oil by Estelle M. Kerr. 11-May-94 Sotheby's, Toronto #207/R (C.D 2000)

LEWIS, C H (19th C) American
$540	£360	Portrait of Mrs Albert Mortimer (58x38cm-23x15in) bears i.d.1840stretcher. 16-Mar-94 Bonhams, Chelsea #158

LEWIS, Edmund Darch (1835-1910) American

$950	£621	Flowering banks near waterfall (89x76cm-35x30in) s.d.1897 canvas laid down on board. 7-Oct-93 Freeman Fine Arts, Philadelphia #896/R
$1500	£1020	Bass Rocks after a storm (76x129cm-30x51in) s.d.Sep 18 1869. 15-Nov-93 Christie's, East, New York #33/R
$2000	£1156	Valley lake with cows (46x76cm-18x30in) s.d.1874. 27-Sep-92 James Bakker, Cambridge #10/R
$2200	£1384	Fishing on the Delaware River (56x91cm-22x36in) s.d.1874. 22-Apr-93 Freeman Fine Arts, Philadelphia #1212 a/R
$2200	£1392	Lighthouse amidst palms (46x76cm-18x30in) s.d.1874. 2-Dec-92 Christie's, East, New York #37/R
$2500	£1603	Cattle by lake (38x65cm-15x26in) s.d.1886. 9-Dec-92 Butterfield & Butterfield, San Francisco #3816/R
$2500	£1582	Fishermen along Chester Creek, Mt.Joy (61x51cm-24x20in) s.d.1867. 2-Dec-92 Christie's, East, New York #39/R
$3000	£2013	Cattle by edge of lake (51x91cm-20x36in) s.d.1873. 6-May-94 Skinner, Bolton #55/R
$3000	£2000	Extensive river landscape (76x127cm-30x50in) s.d.1880. 13-Mar-94 Hindman Galleries, Chicago #755/R
$3500	£2273	Children fishing along riverbank (76x127cm-30x50in) s.d.1891. 9-Sep-93 Sotheby's Arcade, New York #55/R
$3750	£2534	Landscape with falls (71x102cm-28x40in) s. 31-Mar-94 Sotheby's Arcade, New York #45/R
$4000	£2667	The deer run (76x127cm-30x50in) s.d.1872. 23-May-94 Christie's, East, New York #46/R
$4800	£3243	Yachts racing offshore and committee boat (36x56cm-14x22in) s.d.August 2,1875. 30-Jul-93 Eldred, Massachusetts #271
$7000	£4895	By the mill stream (60x107cm-24x42in) s.d.1876. 11-Mar-93 Christie's, New York #64/R
$8000	£5333	Cuban landscape (48x81cm-19x32in) s.d.1860. 16-Mar-94 Christie's, New York #46/R
$11000	£7383	Fort McHenry, Chesapeake Bay (76x127cm-30x50in) s. i.d.1886 verso. 5-Mar-94 Louisiana Auction Exchange #116/R
$13000	£7514	Seascape, Jersey coast (28x49cm-11x19in) s.d.1876 i.stretcher. 24-Sep-92 Sotheby's, New York #13/R
$22000	£14570	Morro Castle, Havana Harbour, Cuba (76x128cm-30x50in) s.d.1869. 23-Nov-92 Sotheby's, New York #31/R
$475	£315	Homestead (25x38cm-10x15in) s.d.1858 W/C gouache. 23-Sep-93 Mystic Fine Arts, Connecticut #119
$650	£433	Boats on the river (51x76cm-20x30in) init. W/C. 26-May-94 Sloan, North Bethesda #2280/R
$650	£430	Narragansett Bay (25x48cm-10x19in) s.d.1883 W/C gouache. 28-Nov-92 Young Fine Arts Auctions, Maine #266/R
$700	£464	Sailing neaar the shore (18x46cm-7x18in) s. indist.d. W/C gouache. 28-Nov-92 Young Fine Arts Auctions, Maine #265/R
$700	£440	Distressed vessel along the coast (18x36cm-7x14in) s.d.1888 W/C gouache board. 22-Apr-93 Freeman Fine Arts, Philadelphia #1310 a
$750	£487	Santiago de Cuba (24x53cm-9x21in) s.d.1892 i.verso gouache paper on board. 9-Sep-93 Sotheby's Arcade, New York #133/R
$750	£500	Boats on the river (51x76cm-20x30in) init. W/C. 26-May-94 Sloan, North Bethesda #2281
$825	£485	Figures walking through surf (18x38cm-7x15in) s.d.1892 W/C. 8-Oct-92 Freeman Fine Arts, Philadelphia #1126
$850	£579	Clearing away Newport (31x60cm-12x24in) s.d.1901 i.verso W/C gouache. 15-Nov-93 Christie's, East, New York #32/R
$850	£556	Sunset on the beach (23x48cm-9x19in) s. W/C. 7-Oct-93 Freeman Fine Arts, Philadelphia #894
$900	£588	Coastal scene (43x71cm-17x28in) s.d.1882 W/C. 30-Jun-94 Mystic Fine Arts, Connecticut #243
$1000	£654	Coastal view (20x23cm-8x9in) s.d.1882 W/C. 7-Oct-93 Freeman Fine Arts, Philadelphia #952
$1500	£758	Betrand's yacht (20x51cm-8x20in) s.i.d.1892 W/C. 30-Aug-92 Litchfield Auction Gallery #183
$1800	£1169	Entrance to Newport of the fleet, Baltimore, New York and Philadelphia (25x53cm-10x21in) s.i.d.1891 gouache over pencil paper on board. 9-Sep-93 Sotheby's Arcade, New York #135/R
$1900	£1195	Casino (18x36cm-7x14in) s.i.d.1888 W/C gouache board. 22-Apr-93 Freeman Fine Arts, Philadelphia #1310 b
$2200	£1447	Sailboats in harbour (55x86cm-22x34in) s.d. gouache. 31-Mar-93 Sotheby's Arcade, New York #89/R
$2200	£1538	Ships off Point Lookout, New Jersey, entering New York harbour (32x60cm-13x24in) s.d.896 gouache paper on board. 11-Mar-93 Christie's, New York #54/R
$2200	£1467	Indian Rock, Narragansett, Rhode Island (42x70cm-17x28in) s.d.1881 W/C gouache board. 23-May-94 Christie's, East, New York #63/R
$2500	£1582	Sailing off the rocks (25x53cm-10x21in) s.d.1903 W/C pencil gouache. 3-Dec-92 Sotheby's, New York #19/R
$2600	£1818	Narragansett Bay (25x53cm-10x21in) sd.1891 gouache paper on board. 11-Mar-93 Christie's, New York #56/R
$3000	£2027	Narragansett Beach, afternoon (18x38cm-7x15in) s.d.1891 gouache board. 31-Mar-94 Sotheby's Arcade, New York #121/R
$3500	£2023	Moored in inlet (25x53cm-10x21in) s.d.1896 W/C gouache pencil. 23-Sep-92 Christie's, New York #38/R

LEWIS, Harry Emerson (1892-1958) American

$800	£541	Old barn and corral (61x76cm-24x30in) s. board. 15-Jun-93 John Moran, Pasadena #11

LEWIS, Laura Craven (1874-?) American
$650	£439	Pennsylvania winter view (61x76cm-24x30in) s. canvas on board. 4-Nov-93 Sloan, North Bethesda #2313

LEWIS, Martin (1881-1962) American
$1200	£759	Brooklyn Bridge from Downtown New York (41x27cm-16x11in) s. W/C pencil. 2-Dec-92 Christie's, East, New York #326

LEWIS, Phillips Frisbee (1892-1930) American
$1300	£855	Green screen and old plants (27x36cm-11x14in) s. canvas on board. 13-Jun-93 Butterfield & Butterfield, San Francisco #827/R
$15000	£9615	Valley of Sweet Peas (51x61cm-20x24in) s. i.stretcher. 26-May-93 Christie's, New York #164/R

LEWIS, Thomas (?) American
$4144	£2800	Insignia of the Household Cavalry (86x68cm-34x27in) s.d.1864 arch topped. 18-Mar-93 Bonhams, London #121/R

LEWITT, Sol (1928-) American
$548	£356	Sans titre (65x30cm-26x12in) s.d.1990 monochrome. 24-Jun-94 Binoche, Paris #65/R (F.FR 3000)
$2500	£1634	Maquette for Chicago Wall Project (61x46cm-24x18in) s.num.14/15 verso acrylic wood executed 1983. 7-May-93 Christie's, East, New York #140/R
$949	£637	15 lines (30x30cm-12x12in) s.i. Indian ink. 14-Dec-93 Finarte, Milan #82 (I.L 1600000)
$1100	£764	Untitled (14x19cm-6x7in) s.d.89 W/C. 22-Feb-93 Christie's, East, New York #211/R
$1342	£901	Wrapped paper (50x70cm-20x28in) s.d.1973verso paper collage. 3-Dec-93 Germann, Zurich #63/R (S.FR 2000)
$1505	£1004	Sans titre (48x48cm-19x19in) s.d.1.6.81 felt pen pencil dr. 25-May-94 Francis Briest, Paris #114 a (F.FR 8500)
$2009	£1305	Sans titre (48x48cm-19x19in) s.d.1.6.81 felt pen pencil dr. 24-Jun-94 Francis Briest, Paris #47 (F.FR 11000)
$2164	£1369	Cube (22x24cm-9x9in) s. painted 1984 W/C over pencil board. 30-Nov-92 Wolfgang Ketterer, Munich #212/R (DM 3410)
$2601	£1700	Untitled (25x25cm-10x10in) ink pencil executed 1972. 30-Jun-94 Sotheby's, London #214/R
$2608	£1600	Location of straight, not straight and broken red, blue and yellow lines (55x55cm-22x22in) s.i.d.1974 pencil felt-tip pen. 14-Oct-92 Sotheby's, London #374/R
$3000	£2027	Untitled (37x56cm-15x22in) s.d.87 gouache. 11-Nov-93 Sotheby's, New York #141/R
$3319	£2198	Forms derived from a rectangle (55x75cm-22x30in) gouache. 26-Nov-92 Francis Briest, Paris #83/R (F.FR 18000)
$3393	£2148	Sans-Titre - geometric shapes (46x55cm-18x22in) s.d.1985 gouache. 1-Dec-92 AB Stockholms Auktionsverk, Stockholm #6149/R (S.KR 23000)
$3553	£2401	Senza titolo (38x56cm-15x22in) s.d.1988 W/C. 22-Nov-93 Christie's, Milan #195/R (I.L 6000000)
$3853	£2551	Location of triangle, not-straight line, parallelogram and yellow circle (37x37cm-15x15in) s.i.d.8.15.75 pencil col.ink board. 20-Nov-92 Lempertz, Cologne #668/R (DM 6200)
$4284	£2800	Untitled (49x49cm-19x19in) s.d.9.12.81 pencil dr. 30-Jun-94 Sotheby's, London #270/R
$4500	£3020	Blue grid, yellow circles, red arcs from four sides and black arcs (33x33cm-13x13in) s.i.d.FEB 7 1972 pen col.inks. 4-May-94 Christie's, New York #245/R
$4530	£3000	Untitled (80x55cm-31x22in) gouache painted 1988. 24-Nov-92 Christie's, Victoria #71/R (A.D 6600)
$4768	£3200	Untitled (38x54cm-15x21in) s.d.87 gouache. 24-Mar-93 Sotheby's, London #365/R
$4800	£3179	Double ink drawing (39x76cm-15x30in) s.d.1982 brush ink. 19-Nov-92 Christie's, New York #260/R
$6000	£4027	Untitled (33x66cm-13x26in) s.d.June 19,1969 pen. 4-May-94 Christie's, New York #224/R
$6500	£3824	Plan for wall drawing-library-Wisconsin state University-River Falls (36x89cm-14x35in) s.d.1970 ink. 6-Oct-92 Sotheby's, New York #118/R
$8000	£4706	Plan for drawing on east wall, Dwan Gallery (48x89cm-19x35in) s.d.1969 ink. 6-Oct-92 Sotheby's, New York #111/R
$8000	£4706	22 pieces in 5 sets in which no.3 cube is predominant (46x61cm-18x24in) s.d.1969-70 ink. 6-Oct-92 Sotheby's, New York #126/R
$8000	£5369	Two part drawing using thre colours in each part (36x41cm-14x16in) s.i.d.March 28,1970 ink. 5-May-94 Sotheby's, New York #237 a/R
$9000	£5294	12345-1 (18x51cm-7x20in) s.d.1979 graphite pen. 8-Oct-92 Christie's, New York #193/R
$10000	£6623	Four colour drawing with error (43x42cm-17x17in) s.i.d.March 24,1971 col.felttip pens. 19-Nov-92 Christie's, New York #375/R
$10000	£6623	Four colour drawing (43x43cm-17x17in) s.i.d.March 23,1971 col.felttip pen. 19-Nov-92 Christie's, New York #376/R
$15000	£10417	Wall drawing no 506 , executed October 1986 col.ink. 23-Feb-93 Sotheby's, New York #315/R
$24000	£16216	Drawings, one inch long lines (131x109cm-52x43in) s.i.d.1970 pen six drawings. 11-Nov-93 Sotheby's, New York #118/R
$24890	£16484	Paravent (183x76cm-72x30in) s.d.1989 mixed media 5 panels double-sided. 26-Nov-92 Francis Briest, Paris #55/R (F.FR 135000)
$30000	£19608	Geometric drawing, LSM00873A-N (51x178cm-20x70in) s. ink 14 parts executed 1981. 4-May-93 Sotheby's, New York #127/R
$70000	£47297	Wall drawing No.273 , col.lines black pencil grid covers seven walls. 11-Nov-93 Sotheby's, New York #114/R

LEWY, James (19th C) American
$650	£425	Peaches (25x36cm-10x14in) s.d.1898. 16-May-93 Hindman Galleries, Chicago #56
$800	£523	Horse fair (91x183cm-36x72in) s.i. after Rosa Bonheur. 19-Sep-93 Hindman Galleries, Chicago #719

LEYENDECKER, Frank Xavier (1877-1924) American
$4500	£3147	Athlete before mosaic (91x66cm-36x26in) s. 10-Mar-93 Sotheby's, New York #175/R

LEYENDECKER, Joseph C (1874-1951) American
$1800	£1184	He giveth his beloved sleep (38x25cm-15x10in) s. i.verso canvas on board. 2-Apr-93 Sloan, North Bethesda #2327/R
$15000	£10067	George Washington (74x53cm-29x21in) mono. 2-Dec-93 Sotheby's, New York #157/R

LEYVA, Alicia (1922-) Mexican
$1299	*£854*	*Dejame mi bosque I (50x35cm-20x14in) s. W/C. 4-Nov-92 Mora, Castelltort & Quintana, Juarez #24/R (M.P 4100000)*
$1330	*£875*	*Por donde el camino va.. (60x40cm-24x16in) s. W/C. 4-Nov-92 Mora, Castelltort & Quintana, Juarez #47/R (M.P 4200000)*

LIBERMAN, Alexander (1912-) American
$3000	£1987	Untitled (154x230cm-61x91in) s.d.82 acrylic. 30-Jun-93 Sotheby's Arcade, New York #348/R
$1500	*£1014*	*Unknown 4 (102x64cm-40x25in) s.d.78 acrylic chl. 10-Nov-93 Doyle, New York #74*

LICHTENSTEIN, Roy (1923-) American
$1400	£946	Brooch (8x8cm-3x3in) st.s. enamel on metal executed 1968. 11-Nov-93 Sotheby's, New York #378/R
$2600	£1757	Brooch (8x6cm-3x2in) st.s. enamel on metal executed 1968. 11-Nov-93 Sotheby's, New York #379/R
$20000	£13423	Modern painting in porcelain (88x114cm-35x45in) s.verso enamel on steel painted 1967. 25-Feb-94 Sotheby's, New York #103/R
$50000	£33784	Eccentric scientist (91x91cm-36x36in) enamel steel executed 1964 1/6. 11-Nov-93 Sotheby's, New York #390/R
$60000	£39735	Mirror (61cm-24in circular) s.d.70 verso magna canvas. 18-Nov-92 Sotheby's, New York #153/R
$65000	£43624	Red tree (51x61cm-20x24in) s.d.79 verso oil magna. 23-Feb-94 Christie's, New York #61/R
$75000	£50676	Studio wall with hanging string (91x76cm-36x30in) s.d.73verso oil magna. 10-Nov-93 Christie's, New York #141/R
$85000	£57047	Abstraction (122x152cm-48x60in) s.d.75verso oil magna. 4-May-94 Christie's, New York #191/R
$90000	£58824	Modern painting with yellow arc (46x61cm-18x24in) s.d.67 verso oil magna canvas. 4-May-93 Sotheby's, New York #385/R
$140000	£94595	Cubist still life (46x61cm-18x24in) s.d.74verso magna oil sand. 10-Nov-93 Christie's, New York #136/R
$150000	£99338	Cubist still life (51x61cm-20x24in) s.d.74 verso oil magna canvas. 18-Nov-92 Sotheby's, New York #162/R
$160000	£104575	Le (137x152cm-54x60in) s.d.75 verso oil magna. 4-May-93 Christie's, New York #55/R
$160000	£104575	Plus and Minus III (102x81cm-40x32in) s.d.83 verso oil magna canvas. 3-May-93 Sotheby's, New York #51/R
$170000	£114094	Woman II (203x142cm-80x56in) s.d.82verso oil magna canvas. 3-May-94 Christie's, New York #64/R
$180000	£121622	Portrait (142x91cm-56x36in) s.d.86 verso oil magna. 9-Nov-93 Christie's, New York #51/R
$190000	£128378	Still life with coffee pot (178x203cm-70x80in) s.d.76 verso oil magna canvas. 9-Nov-93 Christie's, New York #32/R
$220000	£148649	Still life with crystal coblet and lemons (91x102cm-36x40in) s.d.72verso s.i.d.1972 stretcher oil magna. 10-Nov-93 Sotheby's, New York #34/R
$235000	£155629	Trigger finger (91x102cm-36x40in) s.d.63verso oil magna canvas. 18-Nov-92 Christie's, New York #24/R
$250000	£163399	Modular painting with four panels IX (229x305cm-90x120in) s.d.70 num.1-4 oil magna four panels. 4-May-93 Christie's, New York #52/R
$280000	£187919	Landscape with red sky (274x195cm-108x77in) s.d.85verso oil magna canvas. 3-May-94 Christie's, New York #69/R
$290000	£195946	Stretcher frame with vertical bar (91x122cm-36x48in) s.d.63verso oil magna. 10-Nov-93 Sotheby's, New York #46 a/R
$350000	£231788	Woman with flower (273x111cm-107x44in) s.d.78verso oil magna. 18-Nov-92 Christie's, New York #37/R
$420000	£278146	Girl with tear II (127x107cm-50x42in) s.d.77verso oil magna canvas. 17-Nov-92 Sotheby's, New York #48/R
$420000	£281879	Modern paintings with green segment (173x173cm-68x68in) s.d.67verso oil magna canvas. 3-May-94 Christie's, New York #19/R
$660000	£431373	White brushstroke I (122x142cm-48x56in) s.d.65 verso oil magna. 4-May-93 Christie's, New York #31/R
$1650000	£1092715	Girl with piano (173x122cm-68x48in) s.d.63verso magna canvas. 17-Nov-92 Sotheby's, New York #23/R
$8500	*£5705*	*Study for large barn (19x19cm-7x7in) s.i.d.69 crayon. 25-Feb-94 Sotheby's, New York #73/R*
$9000	*£5294*	*Evening sea (48x66cm-19x26in) plastic board. 6-Oct-92 Sotheby's, New York #76/R*
$10000	*£6711*	*Untitled (37x34cm-15x13in) s.d.64-65verso plastic magna offset litho board. 5-May-94 Sotheby's, New York #199/R*
$10000	*£6536*	*The melody haunts my reverie from 11 pop Artists Vol II (76x61cm-30x24in) s.d.1965 col.screenprint. 11-May-93 Christie's, New York #491/R*

LICHTENSTEIN, Roy (1923-) American-cont.
$13000	£9028	Untitled (66x71cm-26x28in) s.d.66verso paper collage on Rowlux elec.light. 23-Feb-93 Sotheby's, New York #265/R
$17000	£11111	Reflections on crash from the reflections series (150x191cm-59x75in) s.d.1990 col.screenprint. 11-May-93 Christie's, New York #496/R
$18000	£12081	Study for interior with swimming pool painting (22x17cm-9x7in) s.d.92 verso graphite col.pencil. 23-Feb-94 Christie's, New York #53/R
$24000	£16667	Modern painting in porcelain (86x114cm-34x45in) s.verso enamel steel. 24-Feb-93 Christie's, New York #17/R
$27000	£18121	Hot dog (61x122cm-24x48in) s.d.1964 num.6/10verso enamel steel. 4-May-94 Christie's, New York #179/R
$28000	£18301	Painting in gold frame (122x93cm-48x37in) s.verso acrylic paper collage board painted 1983. 5-May-93 Christie's, New York #288/R
$35000	£20588	Head V (65x42cm-26x17in) s.d.86 verso acrylic collage paper. 6-Oct-92 Sotheby's, New York #91/R
$36000	£23529	Sunrise (57x91cm-22x36in) s.d.65 verso enamel steel 1/5. 4-May-93 Sotheby's, New York #389/R
$42000	£27451	Study fro Aspen Winter Jazz (20x13cm-8x5in) init.d.feb.26.1967 graphite col pencils. 5-May-93 Christie's, New York #236/R
$220000	£147651	The melody haunts my reverie (82x68cm-32x27in) s.d.65 gouache brush ink paper collage. 3-May-94 Christie's, New York #14/R

LIDOV, Arthur Herschel (1917-) American
$1000	£658	De Glory Road (61x56cm-24x22in) s.d.12-9-36 verso. 13-Jun-93 Butterfield & Butterfield, San Francisco #3260/R

LIE, Jonas (1880-1940) American
$850	£545	Harbour scene (51x41cm-20x16in) s. canvas on board. 12-Dec-92 Weschler, Washington #70/R
$1700	£1149	Windswept birches (76x64cm-30x25in) s. 15-Jun-93 John Moran, Pasadena #148
$3000	£1515	Adirondack stream (64x91cm-25x36in) s. 28-Aug-92 Young Fine Arts Auctions, Maine #206/R
$3200	£2092	Winter stream (109x128cm-43x50in) s. 4-May-93 Christie's, East, New York #110/R
$4000	£2312	Harbour with boats (46x61cm-18x24in) s. 25-Sep-92 Sotheby's Arcade, New York #236/R
$4500	£2601	Rocky harbour (53x81cm-21x32in) s. 24-Sep-92 Sotheby's, New York #109/R
$4800	£3200	Blue sails (53x70cm-21x28in) s. 23-May-94 Christie's, East, New York #166/R
$8000	£5031	In Northern Seas (76x114cm-30x45in) s. 25-Apr-93 James Bakker, Cambridge #32/R
$8000	£5128	After snow fall (89x107cm-35x42in) s.d.08. 26-May-93 Christie's, New York #158/R
$27500	£18212	Gloucester Harbour (86x91cm-34x36in) s. 15-Jun-94 Butterfield & Butterfield, San Francisco #446/R

LIEBERMAN, Harry (1876-1983) American
$1900	£1258	If the judge is rich you will be more likely to get Justice (51x41cm-20x16in) s. acrylic. 21-Nov-92 Litchfield Auction Gallery #23

LIEBMAN, Aline Meyer (1879-1966) American
$900	£600	Paris chimneys (65x81cm-26x32in) s.d.1932 verso. 23-May-94 Christie's, East, New York #267

LIGARE, David (1945-) American
$6000	£3974	Milos, thrown drapery (200x281cm-79x111in) s.i.d.1980verso. 17-Nov-92 Christie's, East, New York #156/R

LILJESTROM, Gustave (1882-?) American
$1000	£658	Superstition Mountain (51x76cm-20x30in) s. 13-Jun-93 Butterfield & Butterfield, San Francisco #772/R

LILLYWHITE, Raphael (1891-1958) American
$1700	£1126	Sunrise at Shiprock (58x76cm-23x30in) s. canvas laid down on board. 15-Jun-94 Butterfield & Butterfield, San Francisco #4532/R

LINCOLN, John (20th C) American?
$2982	£1988	Basket Serie no.2 (69x50cm-27x20in) s. chl black crayon ink white chk executed 1964. 8-Jun-94 Poulain & le Fur, Paris #93/R (F.FR 17000)

LINDBORG, Carl (1903-) American
$800	£523	The white house, Chester Springs, PA (61x76cm-24x30in) s.d.1939. 18-Sep-93 James Bakker, Cambridge #31

LINDENMUTH, Tod (1855-?) American
$800	£559	Fishing village (51x74cm-20x29in) s. 7-Feb-93 James Bakker, Cambridge #206
$800	£537	Provincetown pier (36x43cm-14x17in) s. board. 26-Mar-94 James Bakker, Cambridge #117/R
$1300	£867	Wellfleet Beach (28x36cm-11x14in) s. board. 22-May-94 James Bakker, Cambridge #21/R

LINDER, Harry (1886-1931) American
$600	£395	Meandering brook (62x100cm-24x39in) s. pastel. 13-Jun-93 Butterfield & Butterfield, San Francisco #776/R

LINDNER, Ernest (1897-1988) Canadian
$1176	£754	Bodil, artist's wife (61x50cm-24x20in) s. painted c.1940's canvasboard. 26-Apr-93 Levis, Calgary #100/R (C.D 1500)

295

LINDNER, Ernest (1897-1988) Canadian-cont.
$545	£361	*Intimacy* (54x70cm-21x28in) s.d.1972 pencil. 24-Nov-92 Joyner Fine Art, Toronto #216/R (C.D 700)
$1450	£853	*Light in the forest clearing* (39x56cm-15x22in) s.d.1950 W/C. 5-Oct-92 Levis, Calgary #275/R (C.D 1800)
$1507	£1005	*Jazz* (43x34cm-17x13in) s.d.1934 W/C card. 30-May-94 Hodgins, Calgary #334 e (C.D 2100)
$2413	£1598	*Deadfall* (41x56cm-16x22in) s.d.62 i.verso W/C. 16-Nov-92 Hodgins, Calgary #286/R (C.D 3100)

LINDNER, Richard (1901-1978) American/German
$100000	£67114	*Coney Island* (152x101cm-60x40in) s.d.1961 s.d.verso. 4-May-94 Sotheby's, New York #8/R
$1700	£1141	*Untitled* (34x25cm-13x10in) s.d.1964 pencil col.crayon paper on board. 24-Feb-94 Sotheby's Arcade, New York #319/R
$2000	£1307	*Untitled* (67x50cm-26x20in) W/C painted 1936. 7-May-93 Christie's, East, New York #69/R
$2200	£1477	*Opera Escalier d'Honneur* (63x46cm-25x18in) s.i.d.39 W/C gouache board. 23-Feb-94 Christie's, East, New York #377/R
$4000	£2649	*Untitled* (45x34cm-18x13in) s.d.41 pen gouache. 17-Nov-92 Christie's, East, New York #273/R
$4500	£3000	*Talk to me* (54x40cm-21x16in) s. Indian ink pen pencil W/C htd white c.1970. 4-Jun-94 Galerie Bassenge, Berlin #6402/R (DM 7500)
$18000	£10588	*Jacques* (43x34cm-17x13in) s.d.1965 col.pencil W/C paper collage board. 6-Oct-92 Sotheby's, New York #74/R
$40000	£26144	*Angel in Me* (99x72cm-39x28in) s.d.1966 graphite ink W/C. 5-May-93 Christie's, New York #253/R
$41000	£27517	*Couple No.2* (69x45cm-27x18in) s.d.1961 crayon col.pencil ink W/C. 25-Feb-94 Sotheby's, New York #67/R

LINDNEUX, Robert (1871-1970) American
$1800	£1192	*Race for life, emigrants fleeing prairie fire, Nebraska* (61x97cm-24x38in) s.d.1926-27. 15-Jun-94 Butterfield & Butterfield, San Francisco #4535/R

LINFORD, Charles (1846-1897) American
$1000	£671	*Coastal landscape* (71x91cm-28x36in) s. canvas on board. 24-Jun-93 Boos Gallery, Michigan #464/R

LINKE, Simon (1958-) American
$1200	£805	*Juan Hamilton April 1987* (183x183cm-72x72in) s.i.d.87 1988overlap. 3-May-94 Christie's, East, New York #167/R
$3576	£2400	*George Sugarman, December 85* (152x152cm-60x60in) s.i.d.1986. 25-Mar-93 Christie's, London #184/R
$4051	£2700	*Gene Davis October 1986-1987* (183x183cm-72x72in) 2-Jun-94 AB Stockholms Auktionsverk, Stockholm #7046/R (S.KR 32000)
$5000	£3268	*Gary Stephan, October 1986* (183x183cm-72x72in) linen executed 1987. 4-May-93 Sotheby's, New York #235 a/R

LINSON, Corwin Knapp (1864-1959) American
$950	£638	*Rushing water* (63x76cm-25x30in) s.d.1926. 11-Dec-93 Weschler, Washington #112
$950	£664	*Winter meadows* (30x41cm-12x16in) s.d.1910 panel. 12-Mar-93 Skinner, Bolton #186/R
$1000	£529	*Winter afternoon by the sea* (25x20cm-10x8in) s.d.Mar 1912 board. 11-Sep-92 Skinner, Bolton #215/R
$1600	£1088	*Autumn woods* (46x51cm-18x20in) s.d.1927. 16-Apr-94 Young Fine Arts Auctions, Maine #156/R
$6000	£3468	*Underwoods, winter sunshine* (101x121cm-40x48in) s.d.1923. 24-Sep-92 Sotheby's, New York #123/R

LIPPINCOTT, William H (1849-1920) American
$1300	£890	*Portrait of a woman in pink holding a fan* (41x30cm-16x12in) s.d.1879. 10-Feb-94 Skinner, Bolton #139/R
$1500	£1049	*Just a few puffs* (27x36cm-11x14in) s. panel. 11-Mar-93 Christie's, New York #20/R
$1700	£1111	*Autumn glow* (41x30cm-16x12in) s. 5-May-93 Doyle, New York #22/R
$12000	£7595	*The cliffs at Etretat* (27x35cm-11x14in) s.d.1890. 3-Dec-92 Sotheby's, New York #44/R

LISMER, Arthur (1885-1969) Canadian
$3293	£2225	*Grey house with trees* (30x41cm-12x16in) s. board. 3-Nov-93 Sotheby's, Toronto #356/R (C.D 4250)
$3503	£2320	*Water and rocks* (34x40cm-13x16in) board laid on canvas. 18-Nov-92 Sotheby's, Toronto #36/R (C.D 4500)
$3964	£2591	*Old stump, B.C.* (41x30cm-16x12in) s.d.62 panel. 18-May-93 Joyner Fine Art, Toronto #49/R (C.D 5000)
$4360	£2850	*Rocky shore VI* (41x51cm-16x20in) s.d.61. 19-May-93 Sotheby's, Toronto #367 (C.D 5500)
$4649	£3141	*Georgian Bay* (30x41cm-12x16in) s.d.46 s.i.d.verso panel. 3-Nov-93 Sotheby's, Toronto #244/R (C.D 6000)
$5217	£3478	*B.C. Forest, Vancouver Island* (41x30cm-16x12in) s.d.61 i.verso board. 6-Jun-94 Waddingtons, Toronto #1298/R (C.D 7200)
$5435	£3623	*Rocky cove, Georgian Bay* (30x41cm-12x16in) s.d.47 i.verso board. 6-Jun-94 Waddingtons, Toronto #1294/R (C.D 7500)
$5946	£3886	*Evening sun glow, Georgian Bay* (31x41cm-12x16in) s. panel. 19-May-93 Sotheby's, Toronto #213/R (C.D 7500)
$6227	£4124	*The Sentinel, Canadian Rockies* (32x40cm-13x16in) s.d.22 i.verso board. 18-Nov-92 Sotheby's, Toronto #119/R (C.D 8000)

LISMER, Arthur (1885-1969) Canadian-cont.
$6500	£4305	Pine tree, Georgian Bay (51x56cm-20x22in) s. i.d.1944verso. 3-Oct-93 Hanzel Galleries, Chicago #772
$8720	£5699	Little Lake, Baie Finn (30x41cm-12x16in) s. estate st.verso panel double-sided. 19-May-93 Sotheby's, Toronto #120/R (C.D 11000)
$8720	£5699	Channel, Georgian Bay (30x41cm-12x16in) d.1952 verso panel. 19-May-93 Sotheby's, Toronto #119/R (C.D 11000)
$9340	£6186	Rocks and pines, Georgian Bay (34x42cm-13x17in) board laid on canvas. 18-Nov-92 Sotheby's, Toronto #37/R (C.D 12000)
$11675	£7732	Pine Island, Georgian Bay (22x30cm-9x12in) s.d.26 panel. 24-Nov-92 Joyner Fine Art, Toronto #40/R (C.D 15000)
$12577	£7960	Georgian Bay (48x61cm-19x24in) s.d.47 s.d.46 verso masonite. 30-Nov-92 Ritchie, Toronto #268/R (C.D 16000)
$17476	£11650	Cape Breton Island beach (60x75cm-24x30in) s.indis.d. 13-May-94 Joyner Fine Art, Toronto #14/R (C.D 24000)
$23246	£15707	French River Ontario (41x51cm-16x20in) s.d.43. 3-Nov-93 Sotheby's, Toronto #119/R (C.D 30000)
$546	£359	Milk maid in farmyard (31x47cm-12x19in) s. W/C graphite. 7-Jun-93 Ritchie, Toronto #211 (C.D 700)
$576	£374	Forest growth (25x33cm-10x13in) s. ink. 21-Jun-94 Fraser Pinneys, Quebec #143 (C.D 800)
$583	£388	Georgian Bay, shoreline (21x32cm-8x13in) s.d.59 ink dr. 11-May-94 Sotheby's, Toronto #144/R (C.D 800)
$640	£429	Rocks and shore (26x33cm-10x13in) s. ink. 29-Nov-93 Ritchie, Toronto #269/R (C.D 850)
$947	£631	Windswept pine, Georgian Bay (23x28cm-9x11in) s. ink dr. 11-May-94 Sotheby's, Toronto #224 (C.D 1300)
$982	£663	Pensive - the Lismer babysitter, Thornhill (24x34cm-9x13in) mixed media double-sided executed c.1915. 23-Nov-93 Joyner Fine Art, Toronto #229/R (C.D 1300)
$1031	£674	Tree study (39x29cm-15x11in) s.d.64 ink wash. 19-May-93 Sotheby's, Toronto #15/R (C.D 1300)

LITTERMAN, Anne (1956-) American
$6500	£4305	Lee observes that Marr's unchecked impulses are having effect on Paloma (168x122cm-66x48in) init.d.91 linen. 17-Nov-92 Christie's, East, New York #16/R
$7500	£4967	The healing of Paloma (168x122cm-66x48in) init.d.92 linen. 17-Nov-92 Christie's, East, New York #15/R

LITTLE, John C (1928-) Canadian
$1550	£1047	Une journee ensoleillee de mars Rue Napoleon Quebec (30x41cm-12x16in) s. d.i.d.73verso. 3-Nov-93 Sotheby's, Toronto #39/R (C.D 2000)
$1585	£1036	Rue Marie Anne, Montreal (30x41cm-12x16in) s. s.d.72 stretcher. 19-May-93 Sotheby's, Toronto #215/R (C.D 2000)
$1799	£1168	Rue Panet, Montreal (30x40cm-12x16in) s. i.verso. 21-Jun-94 Fraser Pinneys, Quebec #58 (C.D 2500)
$1868	£1237	Deux fillettes, Baie St. Paul, Quebec (21x26cm-8x10in) s. 24-Nov-92 Joyner Fine Art, Toronto #16/R (C.D 2400)
$2024	£1340	Rue Duluth, Coin Laval, Montreal (31x41cm-12x16in) s. i.d.69verso. 18-Nov-92 Sotheby's, Toronto #107/R (C.D 2600)
$2077	£1403	Rue St Ignace, eglise St Malo, Quebec (30x41cm-12x16in) s. s.i.d.88verso. 23-Nov-93 Fraser Pinneys, Quebec #373 (C.D 2750)
$3171	£2073	Le printemps, rue Bagot vers Victoria, Quebec (61x76cm-24x30in) s. s.d.75 stretcher. 19-May-93 Sotheby's, Toronto #217/R (C.D 4000)
$3171	£2143	Monsieur Poulin, Rue Bedard, d'Autrefois Quebec (60x75cm-24x30in) s. 23-Nov-93 Joyner Fine Art, Toronto #40/R (C.D 4200)
$3171	£2143	Une journee de mars - Rue Chateauguay - Pointe St. Charles - Montreal (60x75cm-24x30in) s. painted 1974. 23-Nov-93 Joyner Fine Art, Toronto #96/R (C.D 4250)
$3369	£2202	Avenue des Pins, Montreal (41x51cm-16x20in) s. d.1968 verso. 19-May-93 Sotheby's, Toronto #219/R (C.D 4250)
$4138	£2687	Une journee humide, Rue Bagot, Quebec (51x61cm-20x24in) s. s.i.d.73verso. 21-Jun-94 Fraser Pinneys, Quebec #165 (C.D 5750)
$4153	£2806	Une journee humide a Notre Dame de la Portage, P.Q, avec deux goelettes (60x75cm-24x30in) s. painted 1974. 23-Nov-93 Joyner Fine Art, Toronto #79/R (C.D 5500)
$4262	£2880	Looking west on St.Paul from St.Nicholas (61x76cm-24x30in) s.d.67 s.i.verso. 3-Nov-93 Sotheby's, Toronto #37/R (C.D 5500)

LITTLE, Philip (1857-1942) American
$1000	£676	Sailboats in a harbour (56x69cm-22x27in) s. 31-Mar-94 Sotheby's Arcade, New York #226/R
$1200	£795	Herring weirs, sunset (91x74cm-36x29in) s.d.1913 i.verso. 13-Nov-92 Skinner, Bolton #166/R
$1300	£861	Old fish weirs (76x127cm-30x50in) s. s.d.1911-1912 verso. 13-Nov-92 Skinner, Bolton #159/R
$2200	£1467	Old fish weirs - Salem harbour (76x127cm-30x50in) s. d.1911-1912 verso. 22-May-94 James Bakker, Cambridge #52/R

LITZGUS, Hazel (1927-) Canadian
$603	£410	Testing the crop (35x54cm-14x21in) s.d. i.verso W/C. 15-Nov-93 Hodgins, Calgary #92 (C.D 800)

LITZINGER, Dorothea M (1889-1925) American
$2420   £1582   Pond lilies and Japanese irises (102x107cm-40x42in) s. 14-May-93 Skinner, Bolton #163/R

LLONA, Ramiro (1947-) Peruvian
$5000   £3378   Un intento de logica en el medio del paisaje (172x203cm-68x80in) s.i.d.83 verso acrylic. 22-Nov-93 Sotheby's, New York #271/R
$16000   £10811   Close up of creativity (172x180cm-68x71in) s. s.i.d.1982verso. 23-Nov-93 Christie's, New York #169/R
$18000   £11921   Arquitectura de Desierto (173x183cm-68x72in) s.i.d.1987 verso. 24-Nov-92 Christie's, New York #159/R

LLOPEZ, J (20th C) South American
$850   £552   La puerta azul (60x73cm-24x29in) s.d.85verso mixed media fibre. 30-Aug-93 Gomensoro, Montevideo #38/R

LOATES, Glen (1945-) Canadian
$1937   £1309   Snowy owl Arctic (51x36cm-20x14in) s.i. W/C. 3-Nov-93 Sotheby's, Toronto #120/R (C.D 2500)

LOBDELL, Frank (1921-) American
$1200   £811   Untitled (23x36cm-9x14in) s.d.58 ink gouache. 21-Oct-93 Butterfield & Butterfield, San Francisco #2768/R

LOCHER, Thomas (1956-) American
$2500   £1634   1-7 (60x60cm-24x24in) s.d.1987 verso acrylic glass. 7-May-93 Christie's, East, New York #182/R
$3278   £2200   1-7 (115x94cm-45x37in) s.i.d.1987verso acrylic glass. 21-Jun-93 Christie's, S. Kensington #160/R
$4500   £3125   1-5 (120x100cm-47x39in) painted 1987 glass. 23-Feb-93 Sotheby's, New York #371 a/R
$4500   £3125   1-5 (120x100cm-47x39in) acrylic glass. 22-Feb-93 Christie's, East, New York #267/R
$5811   £3900   1-5 (115x94cm-45x37in) s.i.d.1987verso acrylic glass. 21-Jun-93 Christie's, S. Kensington #159/R

LOCKMAN, Dewitt (1870-1957) American
$4000   £2532   The Gold Jacket - Mrs. Mary Steel (128x102cm-50x40in) s. 2-Dec-92 Christie's, East, New York #8/R

LODDER, Warren W (19/20th C) American
$850   £570   Portrait of Teddy Roosevelt (91x76cm-36x30in) s. 3-Feb-94 Sloan, North Bethesda #2651/R

LOEMANS, Alexander Francois (19th C) American
$538   £359   Ravine in Colorado (70x43cm-28x17in) s. board. 30-May-94 Ritchie, Toronto #293 (C.D 750)
$1279   £859   Indian encampment near falls in the Rockies (56x91cm-22x36in) s. 29-Nov-93 Ritchie, Toronto #200/R (C.D 1700)
$2100   £1409   Lake view in the Tropics (30x46cm-12x18in) s. board. 6-May-94 Skinner, Bolton #54/R

LOGAN, Maurice (1886-1977) American
$650   £439   Marina (33x48cm-13x19in) s. W/C. 15-Jun-93 John Moran, Pasadena #178
$700   £405   Seascape (30x41cm-12x16in) W/C. 26-Sep-92 San Rafael Auction Galleries #227
$750   £441   Pescadero Coast (57x77cm-22x30in) s. W/C. 4-Oct-92 Butterfield & Butterfield, Los Angeles #264/R
$750   £497   Fishing village (36x48cm-14x19in) s. W/C. 28-Sep-93 John Moran, Pasadena #278
$800   £462   Seascape (36x51cm-14x20in) W/C. 26-Sep-92 San Rafael Auction Galleries #226
$850   £567   Rocky coastal scene (43x58cm-17x23in) s. W/C. 15-Mar-94 John Moran, Pasadena #137a
$850   £563   Northern California harbour (48x69cm-19x27in) s. W/C. 14-Jun-94 John Moran, Pasadena #87
$1000   £662   On the bay (48x66cm-19x26in) s. W/C. 28-Sep-93 John Moran, Pasadena #305
$1200   £795   Storm over rural farm (53x71cm-21x28in) s. W/C double-sided. 28-Sep-93 John Moran, Pasadena #275
$1300   £855   Rocks and quiet surf (53x74cm-21x29in) s. W/C. 13-Jun-93 Butterfield & Butterfield, San Francisco #978/R

LOMBARDO, Spartaco (20th C) Mexican
$1032   £693   Paisaje y flores (50x70cm-20x28in) s. 1-Dec-93 Louis Morton, Mexico #60 (M.P 3200)

LONE WOLF (1882-?) American
$2100   £1419   Contemplation (31x26cm-12x10in) s.d.1923. 31-Mar-94 Sotheby's Arcade, New York #177/R
$2600   £1503   Indian scouts on horseback (56x70cm-22x28in) s.d.21. 25-Sep-92 Sotheby's Arcade, New York #192 a/R

LONECHILD, Michael (1955-) Canadian
$502   £335   Taking some hay along (41x51cm-16x20in) s. acrylic. 30-May-94 Hodgins, Calgary #334 f (C.D 700)

LONGFELLOW, Ernest Wadsworth (1845-1921) American
$850 £563 Workers along Nile (46x38cm-18x15in) init. 21-Nov-92 James Bakker, Cambridge #243/R
$1500 £1000 Beached sailboat (61x41cm-24x16in) s.d.1871. 23-May-94 Christie's, East, New York #59

LONGO, Robert (1953-) American
$1500 £993 Untitled. Black cross on white (58x76cm-23x30in) s.i.d.41 acrylic on newsprint pair. 17-Nov-92 Christie's, East, New York #48/R
$1400 *£940* Untitled - Men, back only (101x129cm-40x51in) s.d.1979verso chl. 3-May-94 Christie's, East, New York #117/R
$12000 *£8054* Study for pressure (100x71cm-39x28in) s.i.d.83 W/C graphite acrylic. 23-Feb-94 Christie's, New York #126/R
$15500 *£10131* Men in the cities (244x152cm-96x60in) chl graphite executed 1981. 5-Oct-93 Sotheby's, New York #159/R
$27500 *£18581* Untitled (244x122cm-96x48in) s.verso chl graphite ink executed 1982. 11-Nov-93 Sotheby's, New York #182/R
$30000 *£20134* Untitled (244x152cm-96x60in) s.i.d.1981verso grphite chl ink paper masonite. 4-May-94 Christie's, New York #248/R

LONGPRE, Paul de (1855-1911) French/American
$900 £600 White lilacs and cherry blossoms (51x71cm-20x28in) s. gouache. 15-Mar-94 John Moran, Pasadena #129
$1500 *£882* Chrysanthemums (24x90cm-9x35in) s. W/C gouache. 4-Oct-92 Butterfield & Butterfield, Los Angeles #59/R
$1800 *£1040* Apple blossoms and bumble bees (30x22cm-12x9in) s. W/C. 25-Sep-92 Sotheby's Arcade, New York #130/R
$2250 *£1461* Still life with violets and white spring blossoms (43x64cm-17x25in) s.d.1897 W/C over pencil board. 9-Sep-93 Sotheby's Arcade, New York #140/R
$3000 *£2069* California poppies in oriental vase (51x38cm-20x15in) s.d.1900 W/C. 16-Feb-93 John Moran, Pasadena #111
$3553 *£2249* Still life of white roses and lilac (68x51cm-27x20in) s. pastel. 4-Dec-92 Dr Fritz Nagel, Stuttgart #3112/R (DM 5600)
$4000 *£2685* Roses and bumblebees (41x30cm-16x12in) s.d.1906 W/C. 8-Dec-93 Butterfield & Butterfield, San Francisco #3308/R
$7000 *£4267* Rhododendron (46x34cm-18x13in) s.d.1895 W/C pencil board. 26-May-93 Christie's, New York #75/R

LONGPRE, Raoul de (19/20th C) American
$1200 £759 Red roses and white lilies (66x51cm-26x20in) s. gouache paperboard. 2-Dec-92 Christie's, East, New York #117/R
$2000 *£1333* White roses and lilacs (67x51cm-26x20in) s. gouache. 21-May-94 Weschler, Washington #94/R
$2075 *£1313* Still life of lilacs (34x21cm-13x8in) s. gouache. 21-Oct-92 Maynards, Vancouver #306 (C.D 2600)
$2554 *£1616* Still life with roses and lilacs (34x21cm-13x8in) s. gouache. 21-Oct-92 Maynards, Vancouver #307/R (C.D 3200)
$8000 *£5556* Lilacs (53x72cm-21x28in) s. W/C gouache. 7-Mar-93 Butterfield & Butterfield, San Francisco #152/R

LONGSTREET, Stephen (20th C) American
$600 £405 Fruit (62x93cm-24x37in) s. board. 21-Apr-94 Butterfield & Butterfield, San Francisco #1092/R

LOOMIS, Chester (1852-1924) American
$1700 £1149 A path in the country (28x41cm-11x16in) s.d.1911 canvas laid down on board. 31-Oct-93 Hindman Galleries, Chicago #669/R

LOOMIS, Osbert Burr (19th C) American
$3000 £1734 Watermelon, cigars and wine (43x53cm-17x21in) s.d.1866. 25-Sep-92 Sotheby's Arcade, New York #34/R

LOPEZ CANALES, Luis (1928-) Mexican
$1438 £972 Nostalgia en el desvan (90x110cm-35x43in) s.d.1993 W/C. 20-Oct-93 Louis Morton, Mexico #47/R (M.P 4500)

LOPEZ PUERTO, Alma Luisa (20th C) Mexican
$799 £540 Fantasias de un nino (90x70cm-35x28in) s.d.1992 acrylic. 20-Oct-93 Louis Morton, Mexico #104/R (M.P 2500)

LOPEZ, Andreas (18th C) Mexican
$18000 £12162 La Inmaculada (83x63cm-33x25in) s.d.1796 copper. 22-Nov-93 Sotheby's, New York #142/R

LOPEZ, Julia (20th C) Mexican
$2258 £1515 Virgen de Guadalupe (110x80cm-43x31in) s.d.1993. 1-Dec-93 Louis Morton, Mexico #105/R (M.P 7000)
$534 *£361* Sin titulo (63x48cm-25x19in) s. gouache. 27-Apr-94 Louis Morton, Mexico #657 (M.P 1800)

LOPEZ, Lauro (20th C) Mexican
$2580 £1732 Rey Alfonso XIII (72x62cm-28x24in) s.d.1957 masonite. 1-Dec-93 Louis Morton, Mexico #106/R (M.P 8000)
$6450 £4329 Bodegon (67x77cm-26x30in) s.d.1983. 1-Dec-93 Louis Morton, Mexico #69/R (M.P 20000)

LOPEZ-LOZA, Luis (1939-) Mexican
$1780   £1202   De Colores (180x120cm-71x47in) s.d.1973 encaustic canvas. 27-Apr-94 Louis Morton, Mexico #415 (M.P 6000)

LORAN, Erle (1905-) American
$1200   £833   Coastal scene (32x49cm-13x19in) s.d.45 board. 7-Mar-93 Butterfield & Butterfield, San Francisco #250/R
$1400   £927   The old Dam-Elk, CA (33x58cm-13x23in) s.d.47 oil tempera board. 14-Jun-94 John Moran, Pasadena #66
$1500   £882   Old dam at Elk (36x61cm-14x24in) s.d.47 tempera masonite. 4-Oct-92 Butterfield & Butterfield, Los Angeles #272/R
$1700   £1181   Self portrait (91x69cm-36x27in) s.d.43. 7-Mar-93 Butterfield & Butterfield, San Francisco #236/R
$3500   £2059   San Francisco docks (46x71cm-18x28in) s.d.46. 4-Oct-92 Butterfield & Butterfield, Los Angeles #251/R
$650   £428   Relics (37x55cm-15x22in) s.d.49 gouache. 13-Jun-93 Butterfield & Butterfield, San Francisco #965/R
$800   £526   Town on shore (37x55cm-15x22in) s.d.46 W/C gouache. 13-Jun-93 Butterfield & Butterfield, San Francisco #949/R
$1000   £588   Jenner (41x57cm-16x22in) s.d.47 W/C. 4-Oct-92 Butterfield & Butterfield, Los Angeles #277/R
$1100   £724   Boatyard (37x55cm-15x22in) s. W/C gouache. 13-Jun-93 Butterfield & Butterfield, San Francisco #971/R
$1200   £706   Telegraph Hill, San Francisco (32x49cm-13x19in) s.d.46 gouache. 4-Oct-92 Butterfield & Butterfield, Los Angeles #252/R
$1200   £833   Under the bridge (37x55cm-15x22in) s.d.48 W/C gouache. 7-Mar-93 Butterfield & Butterfield, San Francisco #255/R
$1300   £903   Red cliffs (37x55cm-15x22in) s.d.45 W/C gouache. 7-Mar-93 Butterfield & Butterfield, San Francisco #257/R
$1300   £855   Houses by pier (37x55cm-15x22in) s.d.46 W/C gouache. 13-Jun-93 Butterfield & Butterfield, San Francisco #948/R
$1400   £824   Red cliffs (38x56cm-15x22in) s.d.48 gouache. 4-Oct-92 Butterfield & Butterfield, Los Angeles #276/R
$1400   £972   Boathouses (36x48cm-14x19in) s.d.40 W/C gouache. 7-Mar-93 Butterfield & Butterfield, San Francisco #251/R
$1500   £987   Houses on bank (37x55cm-15x22in) s.d.46 W/C gouache. 13-Jun-93 Butterfield & Butterfield, San Francisco #970/R
$1500   £882   Bridge at Elks (38x55cm-15x22in) s.d.45 W/C. 4-Oct-92 Butterfield & Butterfield, Los Angeles #274/R
$1600   £1053   Coastal view (37x55cm-15x22in) s.d.46 W/C gouache. 13-Jun-93 Butterfield & Butterfield, San Francisco #979/R
$1700   £1126   The modern billboard (38x48cm-15x19in) s.d.39 W/C gouache. 15-Jun-94 Butterfield & Butterfield, San Francisco #4755/R
$1900   £1118   Dark afternoon, cove at Albion (38x46cm-15x18in) s.d.40 gouache. 4-Oct-92 Butterfield & Butterfield, Los Angeles #275/R
$1900   £1319   Winding road (36x48cm-14x19in) s.d.41 W/C gouache. 7-Mar-93 Butterfield & Butterfield, San Francisco #256/R
$3500   £2303   Caspar, North Coast, 1941 (37x48cm-15x19in) s. W/C gouache. 13-Jun-93 Butterfield & Butterfield, San Francisco #947/R

LORD, Caroline A (1860-1928) American
$850   £559   Cincinnati Street scene (46x48cm-18x19in) s.d.1920. 2-Apr-93 Sloan, North Bethesda #1818

LORING, David (jnr) (?) American
$1000   £629   Dusk on Charles River Basin, Boston (18x25cm-7x10in) s. pastel. 25-Apr-93 James Bakker, Cambridge #1/R

LOSTUTTER, Robert (20th C) American
$800   £533   Untitled, for Spike (8x10cm-3x4in) s.i.d.1987 W/C pencil. 13-Mar-94 Hindman Galleries, Chicago #862/R

LOUDERBACK, Walt (1887-1941) American
$700   £490   Read all about it (30x23cm-12x9in) s. 12-Mar-93 Skinner, Bolton #302/R

LOUGHEED, Robert Elmer (1910-1981) Canadian
$700   £458   Rancher and young colts (20x23cm-8x9in) s. board. 30-Jun-94 Mystic Fine Arts, Connecticut #47/R
$874   £583   Man with team of horses (34x46cm-13x18in) s. canvas laid on panel. 11-May-94 Sotheby's, Toronto #36/R (C.D 1200)
$1100   £719   White and Pinto circus horses (30x40cm-12x16in) s. masonite. 4-May-93 Christie's, East, New York #120/R
$2000   £1307   Feeding time (30x41cm-12x16in) s. board on masonite. 4-May-93 Christie's, East, New York #121
$2378   £1554   Delivering mail (61x74cm-24x29in) s. board. 19-May-93 Sotheby's, Toronto #261/R (C.D 3000)

LOUIS, Morris (1912-1962) American
$70000   £46980   Apex (212x82cm-83x32in) acrylic resin painted 1961-1962. 4-May-94 Sotheby's, New York #18/R
$80000   £53691   Number 5 (208x46cm-82x18in) acrylic painted 1962. 4-May-94 Christie's, New York #156/R
$80000   £54054   Number 1-98 (203x44cm-80x17in) acrylic painted 1962. 10-Nov-93 Christie's, New York #165/R

LOUIS, Morris (1912-1962) American-cont.
$80000	£53691	Number 3-10 (204x41cm-80x16in) s. i.verso acrylic resin. 5-May-94 Sotheby's, New York #133 a/R
$100000	£58824	Kuf (229x350cm-90x138in) acrylic. 8-Oct-92 Christie's, New York #130/R
$170000	£114094	Delta Alpha (260x392cm-102x154in) acrylic painted 1960. 3-May-94 Christie's, New York #28/R
$170000	£112583	Infield (229x60cm-90x24in) i.d.1962verso acrylic. 18-Nov-92 Christie's, New York #8/R
$180000	£120805	Albireo (206x132cm-81x52in) acrylic painted 1962. 3-May-94 Christie's, New York #6/R
$230000	£155405	Number 25 (203x84cm-80x33in) d.1962 verso acrylic. 9-Nov-93 Christie's, New York #16/R
$320000	£216216	Beta Tau (259x487cm-102x192in) acrylic painte 1961. 9-Nov-93 Christie's, New York #22/R
$350000	£231788	Beth Zayin (253x361cm-100x142in) acrylic. 18-Nov-92 Christie's, New York #42/R

LOUREIRO, Rita (1953-) Brazilian
$14000	£9459	Arvore da vida (250x150cm-98x59in) s.d.1991. 23-Nov-93 Christie's, New York #273/R

LOVELL, Tom (1909-) American
$900	£604	The bedside (36x28cm-14x11in) s. board. 6-Dec-93 Grogan, Massachussetts #557/R
$1700	£1133	The rescue (58x94cm-23x37in) s. painted c.1957. 23-May-94 Hindman Galleries, Chicago #256/R
$800	*£537*	*Playing the piano (30x46cm-12x18in) init. gouache. 11-Dec-93 Weschler, Washington #135/R*

LOVELY, Candace (1953-) American
$700	£440	Snowy Dock Square (56x81cm-22x32in) s. 25-Apr-93 James Bakker, Cambridge #209
$700	£440	Monet's Giverny (41x64cm-16x25in) s. 25-Apr-93 James Bakker, Cambridge #199
$700	£440	Water lily - Start (76x51cm-30x20in) s. 25-Apr-93 James Bakker, Cambridge #223
$750	£472	Down by boardwalk (64x76cm-25x30in) s. 25-Apr-93 James Bakker, Cambridge #188
$750	£472	Brothers at beach (25x30cm-10x12in) s. 25-Apr-93 James Bakker, Cambridge #181/R
$750	£472	Candace and Lace (61x51cm-24x20in) s. 25-Apr-93 James Bakker, Cambridge #182
$800	£503	Beach basket (36x51cm-14x20in) s. 25-Apr-93 James Bakker, Cambridge #218
$1000	£629	Capital snow (43x64cm-17x25in) s. 25-Apr-93 James Bakker, Cambridge #184
$1300	£818	Key West Beach (46x69cm-18x27in) s. 25-Apr-93 James Bakker, Cambridge #195/R
$1500	£943	Fair Street, Nantucket (46x41cm-18x16in) s. 25-Apr-93 James Bakker, Cambridge #191/R
$2000	£1258	Seaweed Swing I (71x102cm-28x40in) s. 25-Apr-93 James Bakker, Cambridge #205
$2000	£1258	Garden twilight snow (74x99cm-29x39in) s. 25-Apr-93 James Bakker, Cambridge #193
$2200	£1384	Pinckney Street (30x33cm-12x13in) s. 25-Apr-93 James Bakker, Cambridge #202/R

LOVEN, Frank W (1869-1941) American
$2800	£1842	River landscape in winter (75x100cm-30x39in) s.d.1914. 31-Mar-93 Sotheby's Arcade, New York #162/R

LOVEROFF, Frederick Nicholas (20th C) Canadian?
$1823	£1192	Farm view, winter (31x36cm-12x14in) s. board. 19-May-93 Sotheby's, Toronto #251/R (C.D 2300)

LOVEWELL, R (1853-1932) American
$800	£408	Three-masted bark sailing through green seas (25x36cm-10x14in) s.d.1875verso. 18-Aug-92 Richard Bourne, Hyannis #224/R

LOVING, J (1826-?) American
$900	£629	Light breeze (64x99cm-25x39in) s.d.1879verso. 11-Mar-93 Mystic Fine Arts, Connecticut #269/R

LOVINS, Henry (1883-1960) American
$1200	£795	House in nocturnal landscape - moonlight (36x25cm-14x10in) s.d.1915. 14-Jun-94 John Moran, Pasadena #13

LOW, Mary Fairchild see **MACMONNIES, Mary Fairchild**

LOW, Will Hicock (1853-1932) American
$680	£459	Education and work (53x27cm-21x11in) s.d.1879. 23-Nov-93 Fraser Pinneys, Quebec #89/R (C.D 900)
$9000	£6000	Arcadian pool (50x77cm-20x30in) s.d.1891 pieced panel. 16-Mar-94 Christie's, New York #52/R

LOWD, H R (?) American
$1750	£1108	USS Kearsarge (58x94cm-23x37in) 24-Oct-92 San Rafael Auction Galleries #15

LOWE, Stephen (1938-) Canadian
$2377	*£1639*	*Village beyond blossoms (53x99cm-21x39in) W/C. 15-Feb-93 Lunds, Victoria #5 (C.D 3000)*

LOWELL, M H (1848-1927) American
$1200	£805	Autumn landscape (46x102cm-18x40in) s. 14-Jan-94 Du Mouchele, Detroit #2155/R

LOWELL, Milton H (1848-1927) American
$850	£538	Landscape with red barn (61x91cm-24x36in) s. 3-Dec-92 Freeman Fine Arts, Philadelphia #1796

LOWELL, Orson Byron (1871-1956) American
$900   £592   Dick telling story while Roman eats something at old doctor's table (52x65cm-20x26in) s.i. gouache paperboard. 31-Mar-93 Sotheby's Arcade, New York #103/R

LOZANO, Margarita (1936-) Colombian
$7000   £4636   Florero con Fondo Lila (105x120cm-41x47in) s.d.90. 24-Nov-92 Christie's, New York #227/R

LOZOWICK, Louis (1892-1973) American
$800   £462   Inca Highway (36x41cm-14x16in) s. pencil board. 25-Sep-92 Sotheby's Arcade, New York #401/R

LUCIONI, Luigi (1900-1988) American
$1500   £1007   Vermont landscape (20x25cm-8x10in) s.d. board. 24-Jun-93 Mystic Fine Arts, Connecticut #139
$2500   £1678   Green boat, Newport (18x23cm-7x9in) s.d.28 s.i.verso board. 8-Dec-93 Butterfield & Butterfield, San Francisco #3508/R
$3000   £2098   Vermont farmland (30x46cm-12x18in) s.d.1933. 11-Mar-93 Christie's, New York #234/R
$3100   £2039   Vermont (15x20cm-6x8in) s.d.40 masonite. 31-Mar-93 Sotheby's Arcade, New York #310/R
$3500   £2365   Red barn in Vermont. October shadows (13x18cm-5x7in) s. one d.47 one d.57 masonite pair. 31-Mar-93 Sotheby's Arcade, New York #286/R
$4250   £2834   Still life with shell and Rhododendron leaves in a vase (38x30cm-15x12in) s.d.57. 17-Mar-94 Sotheby's, New York #139/R
$6500   £4248   Classic greys (38x41cm-15x16in) s.d.1969. 5-May-93 Doyle, New York #59/R
$6750   £4530   Still life of pewter and peach (30x38cm-12x15in) s.d.1961 s.i.d.verso. 4-May-94 Doyle, New York #47/R
$7000   £4667   Design in blue (53x61cm-21x24in) s.d.1970 i.stretcher. 25-May-94 Sotheby's, New York #135/R
$8000   £5333   Still life with apple and brass pitcher (25x36cm-10x14in) s.d.1959. 17-Mar-94 Sotheby's, New York #138/R
$9000   £5769   Shell (36x41cm-14x16in) s.d.33. 27-May-93 Sotheby's, New York #95/R
$13000 £8553   Portrait of young man (46x38cm-18x15in) s.d.30. 13-Jun-93 Butterfield & Butterfield, San Francisco #3188/R
$15000 £10000 Still life with fruit and flowers (25x33cm-10x13in) s.d.April 1942. 25-May-94 Sotheby's, New York #132/R
$16000 £10667 View down the fairway, Ekwanok Club, Manchester, Vermont (56x76cm-22x30in) s.d.1957. 17-Mar-94 Sotheby's, New York #137/R
$32500 £21812 Through the birches (76x96cm-30x38in) s.d.1953. 2-Dec-93 Sotheby's, New York #151/R
$2500   £1656   Italian garden (23x29cm-9x11in) s.d.1955 W/C ink. 15-Jun-94 Butterfield & Butterfield, San Francisco #4498/R
$3750   £2534   Sunlight and shadows among the birches (53x37cm-21x15in) s.d.1960 W/C ink. 31-Mar-94 Sotheby's Arcade, New York #290/R
$7000   £4730   View from the woods (38x56cm-15x22in) s.d.1953 W/C. 31-Mar-94 Sotheby's Arcade, New York #291/R

LUKE, Alexandra (20th C) Canadian
$1247   £821   Bouquet (54x41cm-21x16in) s. masonite painted c.1958. 7-Jun-93 Ritchie, Toronto #194/R (C.D 1600)

LUKITS, Theodore Nikolai (1897-?) American
$3500   £2333   Eucalyptus landscape (61x76cm-24x30in) s.d.32 board. 15-Mar-94 John Moran, Pasadena #65

LUKS, George (1867-1933) American
$1750   £1159   The veteran (63x51cm-25x20in) panel. 23-Sep-93 Sotheby's, New York #221/R
$2500   £1689   Near the Pallisades (28x36cm-11x14in) s. 4-Nov-93 Sloan, North Bethesda #2557/R
$4500   £3000   Young athlete (76x53cm-30x21in) indist.d. 23-May-94 Hindman Galleries, Chicago #181/R
$11000 £7285   Shirley Smathers (51x41cm-20x16in) s. 23-Sep-93 Sotheby's, New York #223/R
$92000 £61333 Spring morning, Houston and Division Streets, New York (41x51cm-16x20in) s. i.d.1922verso. 26-May-94 Christie's, New York #142/R
$1100   £728   Sketch for 'The Wrestlers' (25x19cm-10x7in) chl. 22-Sep-93 Christie's, New York #216/R
$1300   £867   Donkey in a barn (25x35cm-10x14in) s. ink W/C. 23-May-94 Christie's, East, New York #209
$5000   £3311   Noon hour, Watts Street (19x25cm-7x10in) s.i. W/C black crayon. 23-Sep-93 Sotheby's, New York #222/R
$7000   £4430   Autumn landscape (35x50cm-14x20in) s. W/C. 3-Dec-92 Sotheby's, New York #54/R
$17000 £10897 Market at dawn (45x73cm-18x29in) s.d.1900 pastel. 26-May-93 Christie's, New York #182/R

LUM, Bertha Boynton (1879-1954) American
$650   £433   The sea of lillies (46x25cm-18x10in) s. gouache. 15-Mar-94 John Moran, Pasadena #2

LUM, Ken (1956-) American
$4051   £2700   Language painting (244x153cm-96x60in) s. d.1987verso panel diptych. 2-Jun-94 AB Stockholms Auktionsverk, Stockholm #7135/R (S.KR 32000)
$4430   £2954   Cloe (86x188cm-34x74in) plastic cibachrome executed 1986. 2-Jun-94 AB Stockholms Auktionsverk, Stockholm #7099/R (S.KR 35000)

LUM, Ken (1956-) American-cont.
$5823   £3882   *Woodcutter and his wife (244x152cm-96x60in) col photo mixed media. 2-Jun-94 AB Stockholms Auktionsverk, Stockholm #7100/R (S.KR 46000)*

LUMIS, Harriet Randall (1870-1953) American
$2700   £1812   Birches - group of trees (71x61cm-28x24in) 26-Mar-93 Douglas, South Deerfield #2
$3100   £1987   Rocks at Gloucester (71x58cm-28x23in) 18-Dec-92 Douglas, South Deerfield #1

LUNDE, Emily (?) American
$700   £464   The Dance (56x71cm-22x28in) s. 21-Nov-92 Litchfield Auction Gallery #24

LUNDGREN, Charles (19/20th C) American?
$650   £455   Sailing (46x61cm-18x24in) s. 11-Mar-93 Mystic Fine Arts, Connecticut #158

LUNDMARK, Leon (1875-?) American
$675   £441   Seascape (64x76cm-25x30in) s. 1-Nov-92 Hanzel Galleries, Chicago #51
$800   £523   Rocky coastal scene (61x91cm-24x36in) s. 1-Nov-92 Hanzel Galleries, Chicago #35
$1800   £1250   Seascape (107x152cm-42x60in) s. 3-Mar-93 Doyle, New York #45

LUNGREN, Fernand Harvey (1859-1932) American
$1500   £987   *Indian boy on cliff (48x32cm-19x13in) s.d.91 W/C htd white. 13-Jun-93 Butterfield & Butterfield, San Francisco #3233/R*

LUTZ, Dan (1906-1978) American
$750   £497   River township (61x91cm-24x36in) s.d.53. 28-Sep-93 John Moran, Pasadena #290
$850   £575   Grand portal (61x45cm-24x18in) s.d.52. 21-Apr-94 Butterfield & Butterfield, San Francisco #1078/R

LYALL, Laura Adeline (1860-1930) Canadian
$1247   £821   Reflections of beauty (91x69cm-36x27in) s.i.verso. 7-Jun-93 Waddingtons, Toronto #1155 (C.D 1600)
$3503   £2320   Portrait of a young girl (52x34cm-20x13in) s. 18-Nov-92 Sotheby's, Toronto #204/R (C.D 4500)
$6616   £4381   Maternite (106x81cm-42x32in) s. 24-Nov-92 Joyner Fine Art, Toronto #121/R (C.D 8500)
$1031   £674   *Portrait of girl (25x18cm-10x7in) s.d.1927 W/C. 19-May-93 Sotheby's, Toronto #387/R (C.D 1300)*
$2179   £1443   *Mother and two children (53x37cm-21x15in) s.d.1908 W/C gouache. 24-Nov-92 Joyner Fine Art, Toronto #130/R (C.D 2800)*

LYMAN, John Goodwin (1886-1967) Canadian
$3500   £2349   Coastal village scene (55x65cm-22x26in) s. 8-Dec-93 Butterfield & Butterfield, San Francisco #3366/R

LYNCH, Albert (1851-?) Peruvian
$1200   £805   Summer sunlight (13x23cm-5x9in) s. board. 12-Jan-94 Doyle, New York #55
$1352   £907   The beach promenade (27x21cm-11x8in) s. 6-Dec-93 Blomquist, Oslo #37/R (N.KR 10000)
$1600   £1074   Portrait of a young woman (56x43cm-22x17in) s. 19-Jan-94 Sotheby's Arcade, New York #399/R
$1742   £1153   Paysage (15x24cm-6x9in) s. panel. 29-Jun-93 Francis Briest, Paris #165 (F.FR 10000)
$3600   £2416   Girl in a bonnet (46x36cm-18x14in) s. 12-Dec-93 Hindman Galleries, Chicago #434/R
$5750   £3783   Young beauty in straw hat (61x51cm-24x20in) s. 4-Nov-92 Doyle, New York #76/R
$7000   £4698   Portrait of auburn haired beauty (61x48cm-24x19in) s. 12-Oct-93 Christie's, New York #35/R
$9000   £6000   Young beauty in black hat (46x36cm-18x14in) s. 25-May-94 Christie's, New York #73/R
$9000   £5769   Young lady preparing vase of flowers (61x46cm-24x18in) s. 26-May-93 Sotheby's, New York #288/R
$15000   £10274   Fancy free, portrait of woman with dark hair (66x54cm-26x21in) s. i.stretcher oval. 16-Feb-94 Sotheby's, New York #403/R
$15000   £10000   Portrait of elegant lady in black hat (78x60cm-31x24in) s. 25-May-94 Christie's, New York #72/R
$16000   £10596   Maiden in boat (74x55cm-29x22in) s. 11-Nov-92 Butterfield & Butterfield, San Francisco #3182/R
$7000   £4828   *Lady with fan (107x86cm-42x34in) s. pastel canvas. 17-Feb-93 Sotheby's, New York #90/R*

LYNCH, Justo (1870-1953) Argentinian
$1300   £861   Puerto (22x20cm-9x8in) 11-Nov-92 VerBo, Buenos Aires #63
$3700   £2139   Impresion, Barracas (25x30cm-10x12in) 23-Sep-92 Roldan & Cia, Buenos Aires #51
$6000   £3468   En el riachuelo (48x59cm-19x23in) 23-Sep-92 Roldan & Cia, Buenos Aires #28
$8000   £4624   Sol en el Riachuelo (49x63cm-19x25in) 23-Sep-92 Roldan & Cia, Buenos Aires #29

LYON, Harold (1930-) Canadian
$856   £567   Oil rig (91x61cm-36x24in) s. painted c.1978. 16-Nov-92 Hodgins, Calgary #163 (C.D 1100)
$1886   £1275   Waitin' warmin' (76x102cm-30x40in) s. i.verso. 25-Apr-94 Levis, Calgary #212/R (C.D 2600)

MABE, Manabu (1924-) Brazilian
$2000	£1342	Untitled (64x48cm-25x19in) s.d.62 acrylic paper. 7-Jan-94 Gary Nader, Miami #125/R
$13000	£8497	Sonho cor de Ouro (130x130cm-51x51in) s.d.1961 s.i.d.1960 verso acrylic. 17-May-93 Christie's, New York #171/R
$16000	£10738	Trabaljo (102x130cm-40x51in) s.d.1979 s.i.d.verso. 7-Jan-94 Gary Nader, Miami #23/R

MACARTNEY, Jack (1893-1976) American
$700	£467	City oil wells (51x61cm-20x24in) s. s.i.verso. 15-Mar-94 John Moran, Pasadena #128

MACCIO, Romulo (1931-) Argentinian
$804	£540	Entre las fichas (27x27cm-11x11in) s.d.1966. 8-May-94 Jonquet, Paris #97/R (F.FR 4600)
$839	£563	Memoria (41x33cm-16x13in) s.d.1980. 8-May-94 Jonquet, Paris #98 (F.FR 4800)
$3000	£1961	Otra vez , s.d.64. 18-May-93 Sotheby's, New York #186/R
$6000	£3922	Al pie de la letra (161x129cm-63x51in) s.d.65. 18-May-93 Sotheby's, New York #187/R
$700	£412	Composicion (59x43cm-23x17in) ink executed 1978. 29-Sep-92 VerBo, Buenos Aires #71

MACCONNEL, Kim (1946-) American
$949	£633	Ad Co (67x125cm-26x49in) gouache collage executed 1982. 2-Jun-94 AB Stockholms Auktionsverk, Stockholm #7223/R (S.KR 7500)
$1323	£900	Speedboat - pink (36x62cm-14x24in) gouache executed 1980. 13-Apr-94 Bukowskis, Stockholm #318/R (S.KR 10500)
$1600	£1060	Night owl (57x76cm-22x30in) s.d.8/84 s.i.d.verso gouache brush ink. 17-Nov-92 Christie's, East, New York #47/R

MACDONALD, James Edward Hervey (1873-1932) Canadian
$2416	£1633	Northern Ontario (21x26cm-8x10in) board. 23-Nov-93 Joyner Fine Art, Toronto #228/R (C.D 3200)
$3473	£2347	Northern lake (13x21cm-5x8in) board. 23-Nov-93 Joyner Fine Art, Toronto #3/R (C.D 4600)
$3555	£2402	Cloudy day, Thornhill (20x25cm-8x10in) init. s.i.d.1914verso paper board. 25-Apr-94 Levis, Calgary #215/R (C.D 4900)
$3624	£2449	September shade (21x26cm-8x10in) s. board. 23-Nov-93 Joyner Fine Art, Toronto #99/R (C.D 4800)
$3805	£2487	Fred Hardy's barn near Oakwood, Thoreau Macdonald on the load (22x27cm-9x11in) studio st.verso board. 18-May-93 Joyner Fine Art, Toronto #202/R (C.D 4800)
$4360	£2850	Thornhill fields (22x27cm-9x11in) init.d.29 s.verso board. 19-May-93 Sotheby's, Toronto #243/R (C.D 5500)
$4531	£3061	Winter night (25x20cm-10x8in) s.d.09. 23-Nov-93 Joyner Fine Art, Toronto #62/R (C.D 6000)
$4649	£3141	Thornhill (22x25cm-9x10in) indist.init.d.26 i.verso board. 3-Nov-93 Sotheby's, Toronto #21/R (C.D 6000)
$5424	£3665	Spirits of Christmas No Man's Land (76x53cm-30x21in) init.d.16 board. 3-Nov-93 Sotheby's board. 11-May-94 Sotheby's, Toronto #182/R (C.D 7000)
$6041	£4082	Lake Macarthur (21x26cm-8x10in) init.d.24 board. 23-Nov-93 Joyner Fine Art, Toronto #34/R (C.D 8000)
$6199	£4188	Rock study Haliburton County (20x25cm-8x10in) init. s.i.d.16verso board. 3-Nov-93 Sotheby's, Toronto #243/R (C.D 8000)
$6738	£4404	Mt Stephens, Rocky Mountains (22x27cm-9x11in) s. board. 18-May-93 Joyner Fine Art, Toronto #10/R (C.D 8500)
$8302	£5610	Muskoka, 1932 (20x25cm-8x10in) init. panel. 30-Mar-94 Maynards, Vancouver #52 (C.D 11500)
$8306	£5612	Sunflower (21x26cm-8x10in) bears init.verso board. 23-Nov-93 Joyner Fine Art, Toronto #49/R (C.D 11000)
$9102	£6068	Evening, Mcleans Island, Sturgeon Bay (22x27cm-9x11in) init. s.i.d.August 1932verso board. 11-May-94 Sotheby's, Toronto #241/R (C.D 12500)
$9340	£6186	From Sperry's Hill, Petite Riviere (21x26cm-8x10in) init.d.22 board. 24-Nov-92 Joyner Fine Art, Toronto #119/R (C.D 12000)
$10119	£6701	Hungabee Mountain, form Old Lake O'Hara Camp, Canadian Rockies, 1926 (19x26cm-7x10in) s. board. 24-Nov-92 Joyner Fine Art, Toronto #41/R (C.D 13000)
$10119	£6701	Sunny corner, Apple orchard, Thornhill (32x41cm-13x16in) s.d.14 i.verso board. 18-Nov-92 Sotheby's, Toronto #184/R (C.D 13000)
$10306	£6736	Nasturtiums (20x25cm-8x10in) init. s.verso board. 19-May-93 Sotheby's, Toronto #143/R (C.D 13000)
$11098	£7254	Mountain cabin (22x27cm-9x11in) board painted 1930. 18-May-93 Joyner Fine Art, Toronto #101/R (C.D 14000)
$11650	£7767	Sturgeon Bay (22x27cm-9x11in) s.i.d.aug.31verso board. 11-May-94 Sotheby's, Toronto #109/R (C.D 16000)
$12684	£8290	Cathedral Mountain (22x27cm-9x11in) s. estate st.verso board. 19-May-93 Sotheby's, Toronto #254/R (C.D 16000)
$15567	£10309	Rapid near Minden, Ontario (20x25cm-8x10in) init.d.17 board. 18-Nov-92 Sotheby's, Toronto #185/R (C.D 20000)
$21794	£14433	Georgian Bay (20x25cm-8x10in) init. s.d.1916 verso board. 24-Nov-92 Joyner Fine Art, Toronto #6/R (C.D 28000)
$3641	£2427	Bronte (21x14cm-8x6in) s.i.d.1901 2 framed as one. 13-May-94 Joyner Fine Art, Toronto #122 (C.D 5000)

MACDONALD, James W G (1897-1960) Canadian
$1893	£1262	Mountain meadows, Near Banff, Alta. (30x40cm-12x16in) s.d.53 board. 13-May-94 Joyner Fine Art, Toronto #74/R (C.D 2600)

MACDONALD, James W G (1897-1960) Canadian-cont.
$1903	£1244	No.14 persimmon tree (60x73cm-24x29in) s. 18-May-93 Joyner Fine Art, Toronto #152/R (C.D 2400)
$2039	£1359	La Place, Tourettes, France (30x40cm-12x16in) s.d.55 canvas on board. 13-May-94 Joyner Fine Art, Toronto #129/R (C.D 2800)
$6738	£4404	Castle Towers, Garibaldi Park B.C. (71x96cm-28x38in) s.d.1943. 18-May-93 Joyner Fine Art, Toronto #96/R (C.D 8500)
$7551	£5102	Chrysanthemum (55x46cm-22x18in) s.d.1938. 23-Nov-93 Joyner Fine Art, Toronto #164/R (C.D 10000)
$10571	£7143	Tantalus Range from Garibaldi Park (71x85cm-28x33in) s.d.39. 23-Nov-93 Joyner Fine Art, Toronto #24/R (C.D 14000)
$11327	£7653	Fall - modality - 16 (70x61cm-28x24in) s.d.37. 23-Nov-93 Joyner Fine Art, Toronto #126/R (C.D 15000)
$2913	*£1942*	*Abstract fantasy (35x43cm-14x17in) s. W/C. 13-May-94 Joyner Fine Art, Toronto #148/R (C.D 4000)*

MACDONALD, Kevin (20th C) American
$800	*£513*	*Psatcbgb (41x58cm-16x23in) s.d.1978 col.pencil. 10-Dec-92 Sloan, North Bethesda #2723/R*

MACDONALD, Manly Edward (1889-1971) Canadian
$861	£574	Summer, Bay of Quinte (50x66cm-20x26in) s. 30-May-94 Ritchie, Toronto #145/R (C.D 1200)
$906	£612	Winter landscape (37x45cm-15x18in) s.indist.d. 23-Nov-93 Joyner Fine Art, Toronto #8/R (C.D 1200)
$930	£628	Late summer landscape (51x61cm-20x24in) s. 3-Nov-93 Sotheby's, Toronto #300/R (C.D 1200)
$934	£619	The open stream, Sunnybrook farm (39x49cm-15x19in) s. i.verso board. 18-Nov-92 Sotheby's, Toronto #17 (C.D 1200)
$942	£628	Port Hope harbour (20x25cm-8x10in) s. board. 6-Jun-94 Waddingtons, Toronto #1240 (C.D 1300)
$1014	£676	Riverside mill (27x33cm-11x13in) s. board. 6-Jun-94 Waddingtons, Toronto #1265/R (C.D 1400)
$1019	£653	Sunlit river (30x41cm-12x16in) s. board. 7-Dec-92 Waddingtons, Toronto #1322 (C.D 1300)
$1097	£704	Red barn (30x41cm-12x16in) s. board. 7-Dec-92 Waddingtons, Toronto #1326 (C.D 1400)
$1304	£870	Ploughing (36x43cm-14x17in) s. 6-Jun-94 Waddingtons, Toronto #1289 (C.D 1800)
$1401	£928	Winter river. View of the University (23x27cm-9x11in) s. board pair. 18-Nov-92 Sotheby's, Toronto #215 a (C.D 1800)
$1489	£955	Sunlit river in winter (36x43cm-14x17in) s. 7-Dec-92 Waddingtons, Toronto #1360 (C.D 1900)
$1725	£1106	North of Unionville (51x66cm-20x26in) s. 7-Dec-92 Waddingtons, Toronto #1355/R (C.D 2200)
$1937	£1309	Winter scene with stream (30x41cm-12x16in) s. board. 3-Nov-93 Sotheby's, Toronto #70 a (C.D 2500)
$1946	£1289	Spring willows by a river (49x64cm-19x25in) s. 18-Nov-92 Sotheby's, Toronto #113 a (C.D 2400)
$2325	£1571	Autumn lane with horse drawn carriage (42x52cm-17x20in) s. 3-Nov-93 Sotheby's, Toronto #196/R (C.D 3000)
$2378	£1554	Autumn landscape with stream (61x81cm-24x32in) 19-May-93 Sotheby's, Toronto #131/R (C.D 3000)
$2491	£1649	Mill in valley (50x65cm-20x26in) s. 24-Nov-92 Joyner Fine Art, Toronto #3/R (C.D 3200)
$3057	£1960	Sunlit farmhouse in winter (51x66cm-20x26in) s. 7-Dec-92 Waddingtons, Toronto #1348/R (C.D 3900)
$3488	£2280	Morning light (71x91cm-28x36in) s. 18-May-93 Joyner Fine Art, Toronto #153/R (C.D 4400)
$3763	£2412	At work in winter forest (51x61cm-20x24in) s. 7-Dec-92 Waddingtons, Toronto #1338/R (C.D 4800)
$5487	£3518	Hauling logs (71x91cm-28x36in) s. 7-Dec-92 Waddingtons, Toronto #1333/R (C.D 7000)

MACDONALD-WRIGHT, Stanton (1890-1973) American
$19000	£13287	Cubist still life (76x61cm-30x24in) s.d.54 s.d.verso. 11-Mar-93 Christie's, New York #253/R
$325000	£216667	Conception synchromy (76x30cm-30x12in) init. canvas mounted on board. 26-May-94 Christie's, New York #137/R
$6500	*£4392*	*Still life with fruits (55x41cm-22x16in) s.d.44 W/C pencil. 31-Mar-94 Sotheby's Arcade, New York #454/R*
$36000	*£23841*	*Study for synchromy in red (49x31cm-19x12in) s.i.d.1914 W/C ink. 23-Sep-93 Sotheby's, New York #272/R*

MACGILVARY, Norwood Hodge (1874-1950) American
$950	£597	Nocturnal nymphs (48x20cm-19x8in) 22-Apr-93 Freeman Fine Arts, Philadelphia #1304/R
$1200	£694	Landscape with seated nude (41x33cm-16x13in) s. 25-Sep-92 Sotheby's Arcade, New York #421/R

MACGREGOR, John (1944-) Canadian
$692	£461	Yellow cat (43x77cm-17x30in) s.d.70. 13-May-94 Joyner Fine Art, Toronto #52/R (C.D 950)

MACHEN, William H (1832-1911) American
$1100	£714	Game birds (76x64cm-30x25in) s. 15-Jan-93 Du Mouchelle, Detroit #53/R

MACHEN, William H (1832-1911) American-cont.
$1250   £828   Game birds (69x56cm-27x22in) s. 13-Nov-92 Du Mouchelle, Detroit #60/R

MACIEL, Leonel (1939-) Mexican
$2419   £1623   Pareja (63x55cm-25x22in) s. W/C. 1-Dec-93 Louis Morton, Mexico #34 (M.P 7500)
$2547   £1633   Boda chatina (77x57cm-30x22in) s.d.1991 W/C. 29-Apr-93 Louis Morton, Mexico #55 (M.P 8000)

MACINTIRE, Kenneth Stevens (1891-1979) American
$2200   £1438   Picnic in forest (84x71cm-33x28in) s. estate st.verso board. 14-May-93 Skinner, Bolton #97/R

MACKAY, Donald Cameron (1906-1979) Canadian
$1937   £1309   Last heat at the races (56x76cm-22x30in) i.verso board. 3-Nov-93 Sotheby's, Toronto #66/R (C.D 2500)

MACKAY, Edwin Murray (1869-1926) American
$850   £556   The cellar door (36x25cm-14x10in) 19-Sep-93 Hindman Galleries, Chicago #714
$5500   £3642   Japanese print (81x65cm-32x26in) s. i.stretcher. 23-Sep-93 Sotheby's, New York #153/R
$10000   £5780   Woman reading tea leaves (89x69cm-35x27in) s. 23-Sep-92 Christie's, New York #176/R

MACKENZIE, Frank J (1865-1939) American
$900   £596   San Francisco coastline (30x41cm-12x16in) s.d.05. 15-Jun-94 Butterfield & Butterfield, San Francisco #4646/R

MACKENZIE, Jim (20th C) Canadian?
$754   £493   Squamish highway (102x152cm-40x60in) d.1979. 6-Oct-93 Maynards, Vancouver #279 (C.D 1000)

MACKNIGHT, Dodge (1860-1950) American
$700   £464   Marsh scene (41x56cm-16x22in) s. W/C. 23-Sep-93 Mystic Fine Arts, Connecticut #198/R
$750   £490   Washerwoman (36x43cm-14x17in) s. W/C. 18-Sep-93 James Bakker, Cambridge #48
$1000   £699   Seated woman (53x38cm-21x15in) s. W/C. 7-Feb-93 James Bakker, Cambridge #20
$1100   £738   Untitled - a fishing scene (41x57cm-16x22in) s. W/C double-sided. 4-Mar-94 Skinner, Bolton #273/R
$1200   £635   Canyon passages (43x53cm-17x21in) s. i.verso W/C. 11-Sep-92 Skinner, Bolton #234/R
$1300   £909   Lake in the Rockies (41x58cm-16x23in) s. W/C. 12-Mar-93 Skinner, Bolton #221/R
$1300   £867   Summer stroll (38x56cm-15x22in) s. W/C. 22-May-94 James Bakker, Cambridge #78/R
$1320   £863   Winter - Cape Cod (41x58cm-16x23in) s. W/C graphite. 14-May-93 Skinner, Bolton #104/R
$1400   £927   Along Nile (33x53cm-13x21in) s. W/C. 13-Nov-92 Skinner, Bolton #103/R
$1500   £1014   The road to market a tropical scene (39x55cm-15x22in) s. W/C. 5-Nov-93 Skinner, Bolton #155/R
$1600   £847   Orizaba Mountains, Mexico (36x51cm-14x20in) s. W/C graphite. 11-Sep-92 Skinner, Bolton #231/R

MACLEOD, Pegi Nichol (1904-1949) Canadian
$603   £410   Portrait of Mrs. Cameron New York (50x32cm-20x13in) s. oil pastel paper painted c.1925. 15-Nov-93 Hodgins, Calgary #247/R (C.D 800)
$610   £407   Jane (62x45cm-24x18in) canvas on panel. 30-May-94 Ritchie, Toronto #164/R (C.D 850)
$1090   £722   Skyscraper construction (38x51cm-15x20in) panel. 18-Nov-92 Sotheby's, Toronto #260/R (C.D 1400)
$2002   £1335   Portrait of a young woman (30x30cm-12x12in) init.verso panel. 11-May-94 Sotheby's, Toronto #63/R (C.D 2750)
$2491   £1649   Canoe in glade, Gatineau Hills (61x43cm-24x17in) panel painted c.1930. 24-Nov-92 Joyner Fine Art, Toronto #115/R (C.D 3200)
$2958   £1959   Winter view, St. John river near Fredericton (61x46cm-24x18in) s. 18-Nov-92 Sotheby's, Toronto #8/R (C.D 3800)
$431   £287   View through window (35x25cm-14x10in) W/C over graphite. 30-May-94 Ritchie, Toronto #163 (C.D 600)
$555   £363   Cityscape (49x40cm-19x16in) W/C. 18-May-93 Joyner Fine Art, Toronto #159 (C.D 700)
$861   £574   Red door on tree lined street (35x24cm-14x9in) W/C over graphite. 30-May-94 Ritchie, Toronto #162/R (C.D 1200)

MACMONNIES, Frederick William (1863-1937) American
$17000   £10897   French nursemaid and baby Berthe (46x33cm-18x13in) 27-May-93 Sotheby's, New York #39/R

MACMONNIES, Mary Fairchild (1858-1946) American
$1200   £784   Dawn at Gloucester (60x45cm-24x18in) s.d.1925 board. 4-May-93 Christie's, East, New York #64/R
$1700   £859   Flowers (76x61cm-30x24in) s.d.1943. 28-Aug-92 Young Fine Arts Auctions, Maine #212/R

MACOMBER, Mary Lizzie (1861-1916) American
$1000   £529   Woman in red (46x36cm-18x14in) s. 12-Sep-92 Louisiana Auction Exchange #103/R
$1900   £1098   Study for pot of basil (32x26cm-13x10in) st.studio board. 23-Sep-92 Christie's, New York #175/R

MACPHERSON, John Havard (1894-?) American
$1700   £1076   Corn shucks (41x51cm-16x20in) s. 2-Dec-92 Christie's, East, New York #254/R

MACPHERSON, Kenneth Ross (1861-1916) Canadian
$1019   £680   The old trout pond (30x41cm-12x16in) s.d.1898 panel sold with oil by A.E.Cloutier. 11-May-94 Sotheby's, Toronto #28/R (C.D 1400)

MACRAE, Elmer (1875-1953) American
$5250   £3454   Girl in white dress (69x56cm-27x22in) s. painted 1906. 31-Mar-93 Sotheby's Arcade, New York #264/R
$6500   £4333   Connecticut Hills (91x122cm-36x48in) s.d.1912 s.i.d.verso. 16-Mar-94 Christie's, New York #108/R
$12000 £8054   Mill Bridge, Cos Cob (56x66cm-22x26in) s.d.1906 i.stretcher. 2-Dec-93 Sotheby's, New York #105/R
$850   *£556*   *Ships off coast (41x51cm-16x20in) s.d.1919 pastel linen. 4-May-93 Christie's, East, New York #202*

MACRAE, Emma Fordyce (1887-1974) American
$800   £533   Gloucester harbour (71x56cm-28x22in) s. 22-May-94 James Bakker, Cambridge #55/R
$1800   £1176   Figures at the beach (36x41cm-14x16in) s. board. 30-Jun-94 Mystic Fine Arts, Connecticut #60 a

MACRUM, George (19/20th C) American
$1450   £973   Market street scene (18x23cm-7x9in) s.d.10 canvas on board. 16-Oct-93 Dargate Auction Galleries, Pittsburgh #5
$3000   £2098   Pile driver (63x76cm-25x30in) s. 10-Mar-93 Sotheby's, New York #126/R

MACY, Wendell Ferdinand (19th C) American
$1500   £980   Dunes and lighthouse under passing storm clouds, Nantucket (20x43cm-8x17in) s.d.1882 panel. 17-Sep-93 Skinner, Bolton #187/R

MACY, William Ferdinand (1852-1901) American
$800   £537   Marsh scene with woodland border (28x64cm-11x25in) s.d.79. 5-Aug-93 Eldred, Massachusetts #677/R

MACY, William Starbuck (1853-1945) American
$2200   £1164   Farmyard scene (23x30cm-9x12in) s. panel. 12-Sep-92 Louisiana Auction Exchange #58/R

MAENTEL, Jacob (1763-1863) American
$13000 £8667   Portrait of a lady holding a book (41x27cm-16x11in) W/C. 10-Jun-94 Christie's, New York #432/R
$16000 £10959 Portraits of Mr Nick Gelwicks, 59 years old and Mary Gelwicks, 54 years old (30x25cm-12x10in) i. W/C pair. 12-Feb-94 Boos Gallery, Michigan #526/R

MAGAFAN, Jennie (1916-c.1950) American
$3000   £1734   Pigs (61x89cm-24x35in) s.d.38 s.d.1938 stretcher. 24-Sep-92 Sotheby's, New York #184/R

MAGANA, Enrique (20th C) Mexican
$4250   £2852   La Sombra (152x122cm-60x48in) s. acrylic painted 1993. 7-Jan-94 Gary Nader, Miami #111/R

MAGEE, John L (attrib) (?) American?
$1300   £861   Boys drinking cider (76x64cm-30x25in) 20-Nov-92 Eldred, Massachusetts #793/R

MAHER, Kate Heath (1860-1946) American
$1800   £1059   Sonoma Valley (36x51cm-14x20in) s. 4-Oct-92 Butterfield & Butterfield, Los Angeles #25/R

MAHOKIAN, Wartan (19th C) American
$1431   £948   Coucher de soleil dans les Calanques (58x73cm-23x29in) s. 21-Sep-93 Galerie Moderne, Brussels #373/R (B.FR 50000)

MAJOR, Ernest (1864-1950) American
$1000   £578   Duck blind on creek (26x32cm-10x13in) s. 25-Sep-92 Sotheby's Arcade, New York #154/R
$2000   £1399   Still afternoon harbour view (30x36cm-12x14in) s. canvasboard. 12-Mar-93 Skinner, Bolton #226/R
$800   *£533*   *Portrait of woman (56x43cm-22x17in) s. pastel. 26-Aug-93 Skinner, Bolton #72*

MALANCA, Jose (1897-1967) Argentinian
$1000   £521   Paisaje (30x37cm-12x15in) 4-Aug-92 VerBo, Buenos Aires #67
$1550   £912   Paisaje urbano (26x34cm-10x13in) 29-Sep-92 VerBo, Buenos Aires #72
$1800   £1040   Casa de Campo (42x44cm-17x17in) 23-Sep-92 Roldan & Cia, Buenos Aires #62
$2350   £1556   Calle de pueblo (34x38cm-13x15in) 11-Nov-92 VerBo, Buenos Aires #67/R
$2700   £1788   Paisaje de La Serranita (45x47cm-18x19in) 11-Nov-92 VerBo, Buenos Aires #66
$3000   £1563   Paisaje de La Serranita (43x46cm-17x18in) 4-Aug-92 VerBo, Buenos Aires #68
$3000   £1563   Esquina nortena (39x47cm-15x19in) 4-Aug-92 VerBo, Buenos Aires #66
$3500   £2318   Paisaje norteno (67x65cm-26x26in) 11-Nov-92 VerBo, Buenos Aires #65/R
$5000   £3268   Paisaje (30x39cm-12x15in) s.d.30 panel. 17-May-93 Christie's, New York #216/R
$6000   £4054   Calle del Puno (50x60cm-20x24in) s.d.37. 23-Nov-93 Christie's, New York #140/R
$18000 £10405 La esquina de la plaza (70x76cm-28x30in) 23-Sep-92 Roldan & Cia, Buenos Aires #46
$22000 £12717 Paisaje Serrano (76x85cm-30x33in) 23-Sep-92 Roldan & Cia, Buenos Aires #22
$30000 £17341 Los pinos, Otono (76x85cm-30x33in) 23-Sep-92 Roldan & Cia, Buenos Aires #16

MALHARRO, Martin (1865-1911) Argentinian

$6000	£3468	Sol en el parque (31x22cm-12x9in) 23-Sep-92 Roldan & Cia, Buenos Aires #36
$9000	£5202	Crepusculo (24x36cm-9x14in) board. 23-Sep-92 Roldan & Cia, Buenos Aires #37
$1800	£938	Paisaje (17x26cm-7x10in) W/C. 4-Aug-92 VerBo, Buenos Aires #69
$2500	£1471	Paisaje (29x23cm-11x9in) W/C. 29-Sep-92 VerBo, Buenos Aires #74
$2500	£1656	El Carmen (24x15cm-9x6in) W/C painted 1890. 11-Nov-92 VerBo, Buenos Aires #69/R
$4500	£2601	Sinfonia en color (35x26cm-14x10in) W/C. 23-Sep-92 Roldan & Cia, Buenos Aires #57
$6100	£3588	Marzo 19 (34x52cm-13x20in) W/C. 29-Sep-92 VerBo, Buenos Aires #75/R

MALICOAT, Philip Cecil (1908-) American

$1000	£690	Mist rolling in along Cape Cod Shore (51x61cm-20x24in) with sig.d.1959. 17-Feb-93 Doyle, New York #53
$1600	£1119	The Trio (51x36cm-20x14in) s.d.1937 gouache. 7-Feb-93 James Bakker, Cambridge #10

MALTAIS, Marcelle (1933-) Canadian

$3277	£2184	Abstract Composition (61x87cm-24x34in) s.d.57. 11-May-94 Sotheby's, Toronto #178/R (C.D 4500)

MAN-RAY (1890-1976) American

$3200	£2162	Sans titre (14x10cm-6x4in) s.d.50 canvasboard. 2-Nov-93 Christie's, East, New York #182/R
$9942	£6584	Untitled (46x37cm-18x15in) s.d.1959 acrylic board. 21-Nov-92 Lempertz, Cologne #256/R (DM 16000)
$1063	£713	Profil et main (18x14cm-7x6in) s.d.1955 col crayon dr. 22-Dec-93 Jean Louis Picard, Paris #127/R (F.FR 6200)
$1260	£840	La Fortune (20x25cm-8x10in) s.i.d.1948 dr. 4-Jun-94 Neumeister, Munich #436 (DM 2100)
$2400	£1622	Sans titre (36x49cm-14x19in) s.d.52 collage paper laid down on board. 2-Nov-93 Christie's, East, New York #152 a/R
$2682	£1800	Paysage avec une vache (49x69cm-19x27in) init.verso leather perspex board. 24-Mar-93 Sotheby's, London #55/R
$3279	£2143	Sans titre (35x47cm-14x19in) s.d.1952 collage. 29-Jun-94 Guy Loudmer, Paris #11/R (F.FR 18000)
$4249	£2724	Perpetual motive (80x60cm-31x24in) s.i. i.d.1971verso acrylic collage canvas. 15-Dec-92 Finarte, Milan #147/R (I.L 6000000)
$6984	£4688	Scene with bathing figures (52x45cm-20x18in) s.d.1915 oil gouache board. 4-Dec-93 Lempertz, Cologne #305 (DM 12000)
$11500	£7770	Study for dance (27x21cm-11x8in) s.d.1914 brush ink wash over pencil. 3-Nov-93 Christie's, New York #187/R

MANDELL, Roy (20th C) Canadian

$865	£547	Nature morte (40x51cm-16x20in) s. 1-Dec-92 Fraser Pinneys, Quebec #125 (C.D 1100)

MANGOLD, Robert (1937-) American

$6000	£3922	Rectangle within three rectangles (159x119cm-63x47in) acrylic graphite three joined sheets executed 80. 7-May-93 Christie's, East, New York #76/R
$6000	£4027	Painting for three walls, brown first version (99x140cm-39x55in) acrylic pencil executed 1979. 5-May-94 Sotheby's, New York #259/R
$7000	£4575	Irregular aqua area with drawn ellipse (72x55cm-28x22in) acrylic pencil executed 1986. 4-May-93 Sotheby's, New York #156 a/R
$16000	£10738	Four triangles within a square (92x92cm-36x36in) s.i.d.1974 acrylic graphite. 23-Feb-94 Christie's, New York #72/R
$50000	£33557	Triangle within circle (122cm-48in circular) s.i.d.1974verso s.d.1974stretcher acrylic. 4-May-94 Christie's, New York #247/R
$135000	£91216	4 colour frame painting no.2 (305x213cm-120x84in) s.d.1983 verso acrylic oilstick four panels. 9-Nov-93 Christie's, New York #38/R
$5500	£3691	Four quarter circles within square (18x18cm-7x7in) s.i.d.1975verso chk oil. 5-May-94 Sotheby's, New York #238/R
$6000	£3922	Octagonal within circle (30x30cm-12x12in) s.d.1974 red crayon pencil. 4-May-93 Sotheby's, New York #141/R
$10000	£6757	Untitled drawing no 1, no 2, no 3 (35x21cm-14x8in) init.d.1968 graphite set of three. 10-Nov-93 Christie's, New York #194/R
$12500	£8681	Grey green ellipse, yellow frame (76x113cm-30x44in) s.i.d.1988 acrylic graphite. 24-Feb-93 Christie's, New York #93/R
$16000	£10596	Two triangles within square number 3 (51x51cm-20x20in) s.i.d.1975verso acrylic graphite masonite. 19-Nov-92 Christie's, New York #388/R
$18000	£10588	Four colour frame painting no.4 variation (112x71cm-44x28in) acrylic chl pencil. 6-Oct-92 Sotheby's, New York #134/R
$22000	£14379	Two triangles within three rectangles (99x262cm-39x103in) acrylic pencil painted 1977. 4-May-93 Sotheby's, New York #153/R
$60000	£40541	Circle painting no 5 (121cm-48in circular) s.i.d.1973verso acrylic col.chk canvas. 10-Nov-93 Christie's, New York #195/R
$82000	£53595	Untitled - blue-grey painting (122x122cm-48x48in) s.i.d.1974 acrylic col chk. 5-May-93 Christie's, New York #112/R

MANGOLD, Sylvia (1938-) American

$4500	£2941	Pink and grey clouds (61x76cm-24x30in) linen executed 1982. 22-Dec-92 Christie's, East, New York #37
$6000	£4027	Summerset (152x203cm-60x80in) painted 1982. 3-May-94 Christie's, East, New York #157/R
$6500	£4248	Absent image (143x112cm-56x44in) acrylic executed 1973. 22-Dec-92 Christie's, East, New York #38/R
$3000	£1987	Test (145x145cm-57x57in) acrylic graphite canvas painted 1977. 17-Nov-92 Christie's, East, New York #200/R

MANGRAVITE, Peppino (1896-?) American
$935	£599	Sonny's dream (97x86cm-38x34in) s. 17-Dec-92 Mystic Fine Arts, Connecticut #106/R
$4000	£2721	A mother's farewell (86x61cm-34x24in) s. 16-Apr-94 Young Fine Arts Auctions, Maine #162/R

MANHEIM, Erwin (20th C) American
$4000	£2632	Coastal town (77x58cm-30x23in) s.d.1960 board. 13-Jun-93 Butterfield & Butterfield, San Francisco #964/R

MANIATTY, S G (1910-) American
$1100	£743	Rural School House, Moores Corner, Leverett, MA (74x61cm-29x24in) 12-Nov-93 Douglas, South Deerfield #3
$1100	£733	Ice bound - Allen House, Old Deerfield (74x64cm-29x25in) 27-Aug-93 Douglas, South Deerfield #5

MANIATTY, Stephen G (1910-) American
$550	£369	Silos (30x20cm-12x8in) 25-Mar-94 Douglas, South Deerfield #1
$700	£470	Ice bound, Allen House, Deerfield, Mass (64x76cm-25x30in) s. 5-Aug-93 Eldred, Massachusetts #943/R
$800	£537	Child's Pocumtuck fram, Deerfield, Mass (74x48cm-29x19in) 16-Jul-93 Douglas, South Deerfield #7
$1000	£671	Workers in field, fall (58x48cm-23x19in) 25-Mar-94 Douglas, South Deerfield #3
$1000	£671	Fall landscape with man on horse (58x48cm-23x19in) 25-Mar-94 Douglas, South Deerfield #2
$1200	£805	'Treasure Gold' - flowers (48x38cm-19x15in) 16-Jul-93 Douglas, South Deerfield #8
$1600	£1074	New England jewel - landscape of house and barns (58x43cm-23x17in) 16-Jul-93 Douglas, South Deerfield #5
$2200	£1477	'Pussy's in a march' - pussy willows (58x38cm-23x15in) 16-Jul-93 Douglas, South Deerfield #6

MANIEVITCH, Abraham (c.1882-?) American
$2879	£1869	Lac Brule (80x85cm-31x33in) s. 21-Jun-94 Fraser Pinneys, Quebec #182 (C.D 4000)

MANIGAULT, Edward Middleton (1887-1922) American
$5500	£3642	Town in France (68x84cm-27x33in) s.d.1916 i.stretcher. 22-Sep-93 Christie's, New York #184/R
$8000	£4624	Windswept forest (84x69cm-33x27in) s. 24-Sep-92 Sotheby's, New York #218/R

MANLY, Charles MacDonald (1855-1924) Canadian
$1240	£838	Summer storm (51x76cm-20x30in) s. 3-Nov-93 Sotheby's, Toronto #325/R (C.D 1600)

MANNHEIM, Jean (1863-1945) German/American
$700	£467	Sand dunes (51x61cm-20x24in) s. canvasboard. 15-Mar-94 John Moran, Pasadena #110
$800	£526	Quince in blue vase (61x51cm-24x20in) s. board. 13-Jun-93 Butterfield & Butterfield, San Francisco #910/R
$1200	£795	Landscape - by the Salton Sea (30x38cm-12x15in) s. masonite. 14-Jun-94 John Moran, Pasadena #49
$1300	£903	View through the trees (30x39cm-12x15in) s. board. 7-Mar-93 Butterfield & Butterfield, San Francisco #113/R
$1400	£927	Coastal - evening symphony (51x61cm-20x24in) s. i.verso board. 14-Jun-94 John Moran, Pasadena #24
$1400	£927	View of river (50x60cm-20x24in) s. 2-Oct-93 Weschler, Washington #134
$1500	£1042	Windy day, Arch Beach (30x39cm-12x15in) s. canvas on board. 7-Mar-93 Butterfield & Butterfield, San Francisco #213/R
$1500	£1042	Eucalyptus trees (39x30cm-15x12in) s. canvas on board. 7-Mar-93 Butterfield & Butterfield, San Francisco #170/R
$1800	£1192	Early morning, Arch Beach (61x91cm-24x36in) s. i.stretcher. 2-Oct-93 Weschler, Washington #131/R
$1800	£1216	Portrait of artist's daughter (51x46cm-20x18in) masonite. 15-Jun-93 John Moran, Pasadena #80 a
$2000	£1333	Landscape, Arch Beach wild oats (51x61cm-20x24in) s. 15-Mar-94 John Moran, Pasadena #64
$2000	£1176	Near La Quinta (51x61cm-20x24in) s. board. 4-Oct-92 Butterfield & Butterfield, Los Angeles #209/R
$2250	£1520	Landscape (30x38cm-12x15in) s. board. 15-Jun-93 John Moran, Pasadena #41
$2250	£1490	Clear lake - 1924 (30x41cm-12x16in) s. board. 14-Jun-94 John Moran, Pasadena #18
$2250	£1500	Houses in eucalyptus landscape (30x38cm-12x15in) s. masonite. 15-Mar-94 John Moran, Pasadena #29
$2500	£1645	Southern California coastal scene (51x63cm-20x25in) s. 13-Jun-93 Butterfield & Butterfield, San Francisco #887/R
$2750	£1858	Stream in mountain landscape (51x61cm-20x24in) s. board. 9-Nov-93 John Moran, Pasadena #855 a
$2750	£1833	Coastal scene beyond the trees (30x41cm-12x16in) s. board. 15-Mar-94 John Moran, Pasadena #108
$3250	£2241	Flintridge (30x38cm-12x15in) s. canvas laid down on board. 16-Feb-93 John Moran, Pasadena #98
$3750	£2206	Mountain river (103x128cm-41x50in) s. 4-Oct-92 Butterfield & Butterfield, Los Angeles #190/R
$3750	£2517	Coastal scenes (49x61cm-19x24in) s. pair. 8-Dec-93 Butterfield & Butterfield, San Francisco #3461/R
$4000	£2759	After the rain, Pasadena (30x41cm-12x16in) s. i.verso oil masonite. 16-Feb-93 John Moran, Pasadena #56
$4250	£2951	Fixing her hair (58x48cm-23x19in) s. 7-Mar-93 Butterfield & Butterfield, San Francisco #234/R

MANRIQUE DE LARA, Gerardo (1963-) Mexican
$1457 £958 Eccus (100x70cm-39x28in) s.d.1991 mixed media. 4-Nov-92 Mora, Castelltort & Quintana, Juarez #70/R (M.P 4600000)

MANTEGANI, Roger (1957-) Argentinian
$7500	£5068	Atras del bastidor (90x100cm-35x39in) s.d.92. 23-Nov-93 Christie's, New York #276/R
$10000	£6536	Objetos en el paisaje (130x140cm-51x55in) s.d.92. 17-May-93 Christie's, New York #263/R
$13000	£8609	Naturaleza muerta con calas (130x140cm-51x55in) s.d.90. 24-Nov-92 Christie's, New York #228/R

MANUEL, Victor (1897-1969) Cuban
$2900	£1921	Mujeres Frente al Rio (37x32cm-15x13in) s. 24-Nov-92 Christie's, New York #295/R
$4000	£2649	Mulatta (31x23cm-12x9in) s. 23-Nov-92 Sotheby's, New York #169/R
$5200	£3514	Gitana (61x51cm-24x20in) s. painted c.1960. 22-Nov-93 Sotheby's, New York #275/R
$6500	£4333	French landscape (60x46cm-24x18in) s. painted c.1920. 18-May-94 Christie's, New York #290/R
$2400	*£1589*	*Mujer con paisaje (27x40cm-11x16in) s. W/C. 24-Nov-92 Christie's, New York #303/R*
$2500	*£1656*	*Cerca de la Casa de Sofia. Estudio interior patio. Casa de Sofia (31x23cm-12x9in) s.i.d.1928 brush wash gouache three. 24-Nov-92 Christie's, New York #340/R*
$5000	*£3333*	*Un dia de playa (56x39cm-22x15in) s. gouache W/C painted c.1950. 18-May-94 Sotheby's, New York #411/R*

MANVILLE, Elsie (20th C) American
$700	£470	Black hat (36x41cm-14x16in) s.d.55. 24-Mar-93 Doyle, New York #47
$800	£526	Corn flowers (43x41cm-17x16in) s.d.56. 7-Apr-93 Doyle, New York #52

MANZANOS, Diana (1941-) Mexican
$863 £583 La carta (130x90cm-51x35in) 20-Oct-93 Louis Morton, Mexico #23/R (M.P 2700)

MANZUR, David (1929-) Colombian
$15000 £9934 San Jorge (50x65cm-20x26in) s.i.d.91 pastel. 24-Nov-92 Christie's, New York #217/R

MAPPLETHORPE, Robert (1946-1989) American
$10500 £6863 Untitled (28x36cm-11x14in) s.d.70 mixed media paperboard. 5-Oct-93 Sotheby's, New York #27/R

MARCA-RELLI, Conrad (1913-) American
$1500	£1007	Man in landscape. Cityscape (30x34cm-12x13in) s. pair. 24-Feb-94 Sotheby's Arcade, New York #253/R
$1000	*£694*	*Untitled (45x40cm-18x16in) collage canvas on canvas over panel. 26-Feb-93 Sotheby's Arcade, New York #292/R*
$2400	*£1589*	*S-5-72 (51x64cm-20x25in) s.i.d.72verso acrylic burlap canvas collage. 17-Nov-92 Christie's, East, New York #233/R*
$3000	*£2013*	*Untitled (60x52cm-24x20in) s. s.d.9-2-64 verso oil fabric collage canvas. 23-Feb-94 Christie's, East, New York #314/R*
$5000	*£3472*	*M-S-7-59 (91x91cm-36x36in) s.verso i.d.written oil canvas collage. 22-Feb-93 Christie's, East, New York #139/R*
$5000	*£3356*	*The Sunday caller (71x86cm-28x34in) s. s.i.d.s-1-82 verso mixed media collage canvas. 24-Feb-94 Sotheby's Arcade, New York #462/R*
$5500	*£3235*	*Untitled (53x71cm-21x28in) s. fabric collage. 6-Oct-92 Sotheby's, New York #52/R*
$23000	*£15541*	*M-S-1-59 (91x102cm-36x40in) s. s.d.59 verso oil canvas collage canvas. 11-Nov-93 Sotheby's, New York #267/R*

MARCHAND, John N (1875-1921) American
$6500 £4392 Bucking bronco (91x61cm-36x24in) s.d.1912. 31-Mar-94 Sotheby's Arcade, New York #186/R

MARCIL, Rene (1917-) Canadian
$682	£455	Abstract in blue and green (60x60cm-24x24in) s. masonite. 30-May-94 Ritchie, Toronto #236/R (C.D 950)
$1110	£725	Reclining nude (37x56cm-15x22in) s.d.67 paper. 19-May-93 Sotheby's, Toronto #331/R (C.D 1400)
$527	£354	Reclining nude (43x60cm-17x24in) s.d.51 pastel dr. 29-Nov-93 Ritchie, Toronto #288/R (C.D 700)

MARDEN, Brice (1938-) American
$9500	£6419	Untitled (27x28cm-11x11in) s.d.74 ink. 11-Nov-93 Sotheby's, New York #107/R
$10000	£6711	Untitled (30x19cm-12x7in) init.d.72/3 ink. 5-May-94 Sotheby's, New York #254/R
$12000	£7947	Card drawing, counting number 6 (15x15cm-6x6in) s.i.d.82verso brush col.ink over silkscreen card. 19-Nov-92 Christie's, New York #247/R
$14000	£9150	Untitled (43x35cm-17x14in) s.d.73 ink. 4-May-93 Sotheby's, New York #155/R
$15000	£10067	Card drawing, counting no 3 (16x16cm-6x6in) s.i.d.76verso brush ink. 4-May-94 Christie's, New York #302/R
$15000	£9804	Houston drawing 3 (104x74cm-41x29in) s.d.73 chl. 4-May-93 Sotheby's, New York #146/R
$19000	£12838	Houston drawing No.2 (105x75cm-41x30in) s.d.73 crayon chl. 11-Nov-93 Sotheby's, New York #104/R

MARGILETH, Lynn (20th C) American
$1000 £641 The Oxbow, View from Mt. Holyoke, Mt. Tom (183x218cm-72x86in) s. s.i.d.1978verso. 24-May-93 Grogan, Massachussetts #355/R

MARGO, Boris (1902-) American
$1300	£751	Untitled (59x50cm-23x20in) s. pencil. 25-Sep-92 Sotheby's Arcade, New York #467/R

MARGULIES, Joseph (1896-1984) American
$700	£458	Fish market (91x71cm-36x28in) s. 8-May-93 Young Fine Arts Auctions, Maine #205/R
$1320	£863	Street scene, Rockport (51x61cm-20x24in) s. 14-May-93 Skinner, Bolton #113/R

MARIN, John (1870-1953) American
$19000	£12025	Pertaining to West New Jersey (30x40cm-12x16in) s.d.50 board. 3-Dec-92 Sotheby's, New York #166/R
$1600	£1081	Sailboat (10x8cm-4x3in) s. mixed media. 31-Mar-94 Sotheby's Arcade, New York #308/R
$2500	£1689	Movement fantasy (20x25cm-8x10in) s.d.43 pencil. 31-Mar-94 Sotheby's Arcade, New York #425/R
$2750	£1846	Santa Fe countryside (17x24cm-7x9in) s. col.pencil. 8-Dec-93 Butterfield & Butterfield, San Francisco #3577/R
$4000	£2649	West Street, New York (20x25cm-8x10in) s.i. pencil col.crayon paper on board. 22-Sep-93 Christie's, New York #200/R
$7000	£4636	Landscape (42x49cm-17x19in) s.d.19 W/C pencil. 22-Sep-93 Christie's, New York #194/R
$9000	£6000	The Grey Sea (49x41cm-19x16in) s.d.17 W/C chl. 17-Mar-94 Sotheby's, New York #141/R
$9000	£5960	Back of the Waters, landscape No.2 (39x51cm-15x20in) s.d.42 W/C chl paper on board. 22-Sep-93 Christie's, New York #198/R
$9000	£5202	Sea and rock, Stonington, Maine (24x31cm-9x12in) s.d.19 i.verso W/C. 23-Sep-92 Christie's, New York #229/R
$11000	£7285	Landscape, Maine (31x24cm-12x9in) s.d.26 W/C. 23-Sep-93 Sotheby's, New York #242/R
$13000	£8609	Landscape, Castorland, New York (41x48cm-16x19in) s.d.13 i.verso W/C. 23-Sep-93 Sotheby's, New York #241/R
$15000	£8671	Castorland landscape (36x42cm-14x17in) s.d.13 W/C pencil paper on board. 23-Sep-92 Christie's, New York #220/R
$15000	£10067	Pine tree, morse mountain (49x39cm-19x15in) s.d.32 W/C pencil. 2-Dec-93 Sotheby's, New York #137/R
$17000	£11409	Fall, vicinity of Stonington, Maine (55x47cm-22x19in) s.d.23 i.verso W/C. 2-Dec-93 Sotheby's, New York #136/R
$17000	£11333	On Morse Mountain no 6, Maine (42x56cm-17x22in) s.d.28 W/C. 25-May-94 Sotheby's, New York #118/R
$20000	£12658	Near Taos, New Mexico (33x47cm-13x19in) s.d.30 i.d.verso W/C. 3-Dec-92 Sotheby's, New York #140/R
$22000	£14570	Fishing boat at Eastport, Maine (36x33cm-14x13in) s.d.33 W/C graphite. 13-Nov-92 Skinner, Bolton #189 a/R
$27500	£18456	View of Taos (51x36cm-20x14in) s.d.29 W/C gouache. 8-Dec-93 Butterfield & Butterfield, San Francisco #3575/R
$33000	£22148	Boats and pertaining thereto - Deer Isle Maine Series, No.11 (35x44cm-14x17in) s.d.27 s.i.d.verso W/C plumbago. 3-Dec-93 Christie's, New York #7/R
$40000	£25316	Sea movement, Maine (43x50cm-17x20in) s.d.23 s.i.verso W/C. 3-Dec-92 Sotheby's, New York #139/R
$55000	£34810	Old church at Ranchos, New Mexico (34x47cm-13x19in) ss.d.30 s.i.d.verso W/C. 3-Dec-92 Sotheby's, New York #59/R

MARINKO, George (1908-1989) American
$850	£556	Constellation (56x109cm-22x43in) s. estate st.verso masonite. 1-Nov-92 Litchfield Auction Gallery #109
$1000	£654	Frack (38x46cm-15x18in) s. estate st.verso masonite. 1-Nov-92 Litchfield Auction Gallery #121
$1100	£719	Hedonist (51x61cm-20x24in) s. estate st.verso masonite. 1-Nov-92 Litchfield Auction Gallery #264

MARKART, Hans (1840-1883) American
$3000	£1563	Standing nudes in garden setting (18x5cm-7x2in) s. set of 3. 7-Aug-92 Du Mouchelle, Detroit #1017/R

MARKHAM, Kyra (1891-?) American
$1200	£805	Black street musicians (38x48cm-15x19in) s. board. 16-Dec-93 Mystic Fine Arts, Connecticut #253
$20000	£11561	Square dance (61x76cm-24x30in) s. tempera masonite. 24-Sep-92 Sotheby's, New York #169/R
$24000	£15894	New Year's Eve in Greenwich Village (81x102cm-32x40in) s.d.37. 23-Sep-93 Sotheby's, New York #231/R

MARKOS, Frank (20th C) American/Rumanian
$3600	£2400	Indians on horseback (61x91cm-24x36in) s. 22-May-94 Hindman Galleries, Chicago #51/R

MARKOS, Lajos (1917-1993) American/Rumanian
$2500	£1701	Adobe farmyard (41x51cm-16x20in) s. 20-Nov-93 Hart Gallery, Houston #2
$3250	£2211	Bodega Cantina (51x61cm-20x24in) s. 20-Nov-93 Hart Gallery, Houston #1

MARLATT, H Irving (1860-1929) American
$2000	£1156	Autumn landscape with stone bridge (77x127cm-30x50in) s.d.1926 st.studio verso. 25-Sep-92 Sotheby's Arcade, New York #136/R

MARPLE, William (1827-1910) American

$800	£526	Waiting for ferry (31x51cm-12x20in) s.d.81. 13-Jun-93 Butterfield & Butterfield, San Francisco #732/R
$1050	£705	Mississippi River (30x61cm-12x24in) s.d.79. 2-May-94 Selkirks, St. Louis #84
$1300	£855	Coming into shore (30x51cm-12x20in) s.d.76. 13-Jun-93 Butterfield & Butterfield, San Francisco #729/R

MARSH, Reginald (1898-1954) American

$2250	£1521	Seated girl (15x13cm-6x5in) s.d.48 oil tempera masonite. 31-Mar-94 Sotheby's Arcade, New York #300/R
$2800	£1618	Woman in yellow dress (25x20cm-10x8in) paper on masonite. 25-Sep-92 Sotheby's Arcade, New York #361/R
$3000	£1899	Walking down the street (24x19cm-9x7in) s.d.1952,1953verso masonite double-sided. 2-Dec-92 Christie's, East, New York #368/R
$3250	£2211	Standing woman (30x18cm-12x7in) s.d.1951 tempera board. 17-Nov-93 Doyle, New York #52/R
$3500	£2365	Luxembourg Gardens, Paris (16x22cm-6x9in) panel painted 1926. 31-Mar-94 Sotheby's Arcade, New York #307/R
$3800	£2585	Reading the paper. Walking (13x10cm-5x4in) s. board two. 15-Nov-93 Christie's, East, New York #198 a
$4500	£3147	Out for a walk (30x23cm-12x9in) s.d.51 masonite. 11-Mar-93 Christie's, New York #238/R
$4800	£2775	Ladies in hats (25x21cm-10x8in) s. masonite. 23-Sep-92 Christie's, New York #262/R
$5000	£3165	Two girls of the night (31x23cm-12x9in) board. 2-Dec-92 Christie's, East, New York #371 a/R
$7000	£4487	Young woman walking by stoop (41x30cm-16x12in) s.d.1951 artist's st.verso masonite. 27-May-93 Sotheby's, New York #92/R
$12000	£8163	Out for a stroll (41x30cm-16x12in) s.d.52 masonite. 17-Nov-93 Doyle, New York #51/R
$14000	£9333	Afternoon stroll (51x41cm-20x16in) s.d.1942-53 masonite. 17-Mar-94 Sotheby's, New York #148/R
$14000	£8861	Girl on carousel horse. Girl by theatre marquee (54x44cm-21x17in) s. board double-sided. 4-Dec-92 Christie's, New York #57/R
$17000	£11409	Bums on a New York Pier (41x50cm-16x20in) s.i.d.45 masonite. 3-Dec-93 Christie's, New York #5/R
$26000	£16456	Coney Island (50x61cm-20x24in) s.d.1951 tempera board. 3-Dec-92 Sotheby's, New York #164/R
$32000	£18497	Palace of wonders (56x76cm-22x30in) s.d.1947 tempera board. 23-Sep-92 Christie's, New York #249/R
$95000	£60897	Band playing by Hudson (61x76cm-24x30in) s.d.32 tempera masonite. 27-May-93 Sotheby's, New York #91/R
$155000	£103333	Park Avenue (60x51cm-24x20in) s.d.1936 board. 25-May-94 Sotheby's, New York #107/R
$550	*£369*	*Street scene, Havana (35x51cm-14x20in) s.i.d.1931 W/C graphite. 4-Mar-94 Skinner, Bolton #290/R*
$600	*£395*	*Woman on the street (23x13cm-9x5in) init.d.1953 pen wash. 2-Jun-93 Doyle, New York #76*
$700	*£490*	*Three young girls (23x30cm-9x12in) d.1929 W/C. 11-Mar-93 Mystic Fine Arts, Connecticut #87/R*
$750	*£504*	*Girl with cigarette (13x8cm-5x3in) s. W/C gouache paper board. 6-May-94 Skinner, Bolton #134/R*
$900	*£520*	*Circus sketches (36x28cm-14x11in) s.i. ink wash. 25-Sep-92 Sotheby's Arcade, New York #308/R*
$950	*£642*	*Woman walking (26x24cm-10x9in) W/C ink. 31-Mar-94 Sotheby's Arcade, New York #355/R*
$1100	*£738*	*Circus - two cartoons on single sheet for 'The New Yorker' magazine (35x25cm-14x10in) s. ink graphite. 4-Mar-94 Skinner, Bolton #324/R*
$1200	*£789*	*Grand Windsor Hotel (78x56cm-31x22in) d.1946 graphite. 31-Mar-93 Sotheby's Arcade, New York #352/R*
$1200	*£811*	*Get up a theatre party. Famous people past and present (22x14cm-9x6in) i.d.1944 Indian wash pen pair. 31-Mar-94 Sotheby's Arcade, New York #378/R*
$1300	*£850*	*Walking woman (25x20cm-10x8in) s.i.d.1951 pen W/C gouache paper on board. 29-Jun-94 Doyle, New York #56*
$1300	*£850*	*Twelve figure studies (22x30cm-9x12in) init. pen Indian ink. 4-May-93 Christie's, East, New York #235/R*
$1500	*£974*	*Honourable discharge. The contortionist (32x33cm-13x13in) s.i.d.45 ink wash double-sided. 9-Sep-93 Sotheby's Arcade, New York #350/R*
$1500	*£980*	*Carousel ride (25x20cm-10x8in) s.i.d.1951 pen wash. 29-Jun-94 Doyle, New York #55*
$1700	*£1111*	*Woman reading the newspaper (20x15cm-8x6in) s.d.48 pen W/C paper on masonite. 29-Jun-94 Doyle, New York #53*
$2400	*£1622*	*Bathing beauties (23x28cm-9x11in) ink wash graphite dr verso double-sided. 5-Nov-93 Skinner, Bolton #159/R*
$2600	*£1733*	*Railroad yard (40x57cm-16x22in) s.d.1940 W/C. 23-May-94 Christie's, East, New York #210*
$2750	*£1846*	*Stop all China trade (25x20cm-10x8in) s.d.53 W/C card. 4-May-94 Doyle, New York #69/R*
$3000	*£2013*	*Manhattan skyline (56x76cm-22x30in) d.1948 W/C pencil en grisaille. 11-Dec-93 Weschler, Washington #130/R*
$3250	*£2196*	*Reclining nude (29x36cm-11x14in) s.d.48 W/C. 31-Mar-94 Sotheby's Arcade, New York #429/R*
$3500	*£2318*	*Locomotive (36x51cm-14x20in) s.d.1929 W/C. 23-Sep-93 Sotheby's, New York #232/R*
$3500	*£2023*	*Ship and scows (35x50cm-14x20in) s.d.1928 W/C pencil. 23-Sep-92 Christie's, New York #273/R*
$4000	*£2532*	*Grain elevator (35x50cm-14x20in) i. W/C. 3-Dec-92 Sotheby's, New York #51/R*

MARSH, Reginald (1898-1954) American-cont.
$4000	£2614	Seated woman (18x13cm-7x5in) i.d.Feb.22.1951verso maroger board. 20-May-93 Boos Gallery, Michigan #475/R
$5500	£3642	Tugboats in harbour, New York (36x51cm-14x20in) s.d.1936 W/C. 23-Sep-93 Sotheby's, New York #233/R
$10000	£6623	Aboard the ferry (69x102cm-27x40in) s.d.1947 W/C gouache paperboard. 23-Sep-93 Sotheby's, New York #234/R
$40000	£26667	Burlesque dancers (58x80cm-23x31in) s.d.1950 s.verso W/C double-sided. 17-Mar-94 Sotheby's, New York #151/R
$45000	£30201	Dali's dream of Venus (67x100cm-26x39in) s.d.1939 W/C. 2-Dec-93 Sotheby's, New York #143 a/R

MARSH, Reginald (attrib) (1898-1954) American
$650	£428	Industrial scene (51x76cm-20x30in) s. W/C. 5-Jun-93 Louisiana Auction Exchange #5/R

MARSHALL, Clark S (19/20th C) American
$800	£559	Canoe (51x61cm-20x24in) s. 5-Feb-93 Sloan, North Bethesda #1656/R

MARSHALL, Thomas William (1850-1874) American
$2500	£1645	Forest scene (51x41cm-20x16in) s.d.1870. 13-Jun-93 Butterfield & Butterfield, San Francisco #3100/R

MARSHALL, William Elstob (1837-1906) American
$1617	£1100	A horse outside a stable (56x69cm-22x27in) s.d.1883. 18-Nov-93 Bonhams, London #86/R
$1639	£1100	Study of a gun dog among heather (58x48cm-23x19in) s.d.1871. 8-Dec-93 Phillips, Exeter #531
$1937	£1300	Head of English setter (61x51cm-24x20in) s. 25-Mar-94 Christie's, London #29/R

MARTIN, Agnes (1912-) American/Canadian
$19000	£12838	Untitled (86x86cm-34x34in) s.d.1960verso. 10-Nov-93 Christie's, New York #182/R
$27000	£17881	David (63x63cm-25x25in) s.d.58 verso. 18-Nov-92 Sotheby's, New York #103/R
$150000	£98039	Untitled no.11 (183x183cm-72x72in) s.d.1989 verso. 3-May-93 Sotheby's, New York #59/R
$9500	£6209	Untitled (30x30cm-12x12in) s.d.77 W/C graphite ink. 4-May-93 Sotheby's, New York #144/R
$10852	£7235	Sans titre (22x22cm-9x9in) W/C ink crayon painted 1978. 17-Mar-94 Catherine Charbonneaux, Paris #33/R (F.FR 62000)
$12000	£7947	Untitled (20x20cm-8x8in) ink. 18-Nov-92 Sotheby's, New York #139/R
$16000	£10811	Untitled (30x30cm-12x12in) s.d.1965 verso col.pencil W/C. 11-Nov-93 Sotheby's, New York #106/R
$170000	£114094	Untitled no 3 (183x183cm-72x72in) s.d.1987verso acrylic graphite canvas. 3-May-94 Christie's, New York #24/R
$220000	£143791	Garden (183x183cm-72x72in) s.d.1967 verso oil pencil canvas. 3-May-93 Sotheby's, New York #48/R
$310000	£208054	The feast (183x183cm-72x72in) s.i.d.1966verso acrylic pencil canvas. 4-May-94 Sotheby's, New York #36/R

MARTIN, Benito Quinquela see QUINQUELA MARTIN, Benito

MARTIN, Eddie Owens (1908-1986) American
$1100	£728	Study of Faces and feathers (46x30cm-18x12in) s.d.1985 W/C. 21-Nov-92 Litchfield Auction Gallery #25

MARTIN, Fletcher (1904-1979) American
$800	£462	Pineapple (23x30cm-9x12in) s. s.i.verso board. 25-Sep-92 Sotheby's Arcade, New York #356/R
$950	£642	The flowered hat (66x41cm-26x16in) s. s.i.stretcher. 31-Mar-94 Sotheby's Arcade, New York #347/R
$1800	£1132	The blossom (51x76cm-20x30in) s. painted 1951. 22-Apr-93 Freeman Fine Arts, Philadelphia #1337/R
$2200	£1272	Woman with hat (76x41cm-30x16in) s.d.1956. 25-Sep-92 Sotheby's Arcade, New York #481/R
$3000	£1734	Small businessman (51x61cm-20x24in) s. 25-Sep-92 Sotheby's Arcade, New York #480/R
$3500	£2365	The cigarette (56x81cm-22x32in) s. 31-Mar-94 Sotheby's Arcade, New York #345/R
$700	£405	Seated nude (55x42cm-22x17in) s.d.39 conte crayon. 25-Sep-92 Sotheby's Arcade, New York #261/R
$4000	£2685	Coaching the champ, boxing scene (37x44cm-15x17in) s. gouache paper board. 6-May-94 Skinner, Bolton #148/R

MARTIN, Homer D (1836-1897) American
$1400	£940	Woodland scene, possibly Lake George (30x25cm-12x10in) s. 5-Aug-93 Eldred, Massachusetts #802/R
$1750	£1136	In the Catskills (36x51cm-14x20in) indis.s. 11-Sep-93 Louisiana Auction Exchange #96/R
$1800	£1208	White water (76x51cm-30x20in) s. 29-Nov-93 Stonington Fine Arts, Stonington #120/R
$3400	£2297	Country landscape with distant valley (36x51cm-14x20in) s. 20-Mar-93 Weschler, Washington #80/R
$4250	£2760	Richmond on Thames (42x76cm-17x30in) 9-Sep-93 Sotheby's Arcade, New York #75/R
$5500	£3179	East Hampton (30x51cm-12x20in) s.i.d.Aug.75. 23-Sep-92 Christie's, New York #83/R
$20000	£11561	Lake George (33x61cm-13x24in) i.stretcher. 24-Sep-92 Sotheby's, New York #56/R

MARTIN, John Knox (20th C) American
$1800   £1059   Untitled (30x24cm-12x9in) s. s.d.1964 verso oil paper collage on wood. 6-Oct-92 Sotheby's, New York #50/R

MARTIN, Knox (1923-) American
$4250   £2951   Woman seated yellow nose (37x32cm-15x13in) s. i.d.1972verso paper on canvas. 26-Feb-93 Sotheby's Arcade, New York #376/R
$1900   £1319   White point (51x44cm-20x17in) s.i.verso executed 1964 magna collage board. 23-Feb-93 Sotheby's, New York #233/R

MARTIN, Thomas Mower (1838-1934) Canadian
$778   £515   Settler's home, Muskoka (30x55cm-12x22in) 24-Nov-92 Joyner Fine Art, Toronto #162/R (C.D 1000)
$779   £513   Farmer and chickens (41x66cm-16x26in) s. 7-Jun-93 Waddingtons, Toronto #1116/R (C.D 1000)
$906   £612   Stone quarry works (43x63cm-17x25in) s. 23-Nov-93 Fraser Pinneys, Quebec #458/R (C.D 1200)
$934   £619   A beach view (36x53cm-14x21in) s. board. 18-Nov-92 Sotheby's, Toronto #124/R (C.D 1200)
$1189   £777   Mountain landscape (76x127cm-30x50in) s. 19-May-93 Sotheby's, Toronto #291 a/R (C.D 1500)
$1456   £971   Summer, Muskoka (77x63cm-30x25in) s. canvas laid down on board. 11-May-94 Sotheby's, Toronto #15/R (C.D 2000)
$545   £361   Lake in the rockies (34x51cm-13x20in) s. W/C. 18-Nov-92 Sotheby's, Toronto #21 (C.D 700)
$617   £417   Untitled - forest clearing in autumn (32x24cm-13x9in) s. W/C on paper laid down on mat board. 25-Apr-94 Levis, Calgary #219/R (C.D 850)
$697   £471   Indians and canoe (26x17cm-10x7in) s.d.1880 W/C. 1-Nov-93 Levis, Calgary #202 (C.D 900)

MARTIN, Vicente (?) Uruguayan
$750   £481   Composicion 546 (72x102cm-28x40in) s.d.63. 7-Dec-92 Gomensoro, Montevideo #29
$820   £536   El rey (72x72cm-28x28in) s. acrylic paper on canvas. 4-Oct-93 Gomensoro, Montevideo #39
$1000   £654   Buho (39x36cm-15x14in) s. acrylic. 3-May-93 Gomensoro, Montevideo #33
$1000   £662   Cardos (60x50cm-24x20in) s.d.59. 28-Jun-93 Gomensoro, Montevideo #7

MARTINEZ BAEZ, Salvador (1896-1987) Mexican
$12000   £7947   Orquideas (51x61cm-20x24in) s.d.1946 board. 24-Nov-92 Christie's, New York #134/R

MARTINEZ PEDRO, Luis (1910-) Cuban
$10000   £6757   Flautista (60x50cm-24x20in) s.d.48 tempera paper. 22-Nov-93 Sotheby's, New York #200/R
$5000   £3333   Mujer con flores (60x46cm-24x18in) s.d.Oct.1948 gouache. 18-May-94 Christie's, New York #294/R
$9000   £5882   Hombres atrapando pajaros (59x43cm-23x17in) s.d.41 pen W/C. 18-May-93 Sotheby's, New York #165/R

MARTINEZ, Alfredo Ramos (1872-1946) Mexican
$35000   £23179   Vendedoras de flores (71x61cm-28x24in) s. 24-Nov-92 Christie's, New York #133/R
$48000   £32000   Naturaleza muerta con flores (87x77cm-34x30in) s. painted c.1930. 18-May-94 Sotheby's, New York #279/R
$1500   £1000   Still life with tomatoes (40x43cm-16x17in) s.d.1917 pastel board. 9-Jun-94 Sotheby's Arcade, New York #122/R
$5500   £3716   Un hombre con sombrero (54x40cm-21x16in) s.i. pastel newsprint. 21-Oct-93 Butterfield & Butterfield, San Francisco #2738/R
$5500   £3595   Chalupas en Xochimilco (50x34cm-20x13in) s.d.1898 W/C. 18-May-93 Sotheby's, New York #132 a/R
$7500   £5068   Choza Mexicana (24x35cm-9x14in) s. W/C executed c.1898. 22-Nov-93 Sotheby's, New York #163/R
$9000   £6081   Personaje con magueyes (24x35cm-9x14in) s.d.1898 W/C. 22-Nov-93 Sotheby's, New York #162/R
$10000   £6623   Campesinos (54x40cm-21x16in) s. gouache chl newsprint on board. 24-Nov-92 Christie's, New York #189/R
$11000   £7333   Paisaje con casa y magueyes (49x71cm-19x28in) s. pastel board executed c.1917. 18-May-94 Sotheby's, New York #280/R
$14000   £9396   The six potters (69x81cm-27x32in) s. ink gouache. 8-Dec-93 Butterfield & Butterfield, San Francisco #3583/R
$14000   £9150   Virgen de Guadalupe (57x43cm-22x17in) s. chl tempera newsprint on paper executed c.37. 18-May-93 Sotheby's, New York #48/R
$21000   £14000   Campesinos (59x91cm-23x36in) s. pastel chl executed c.1935. 18-May-94 Sotheby's, New York #270/R
$23000   £15232   Mujer con flores (76x86cm-30x34in) s. chl tempera paper on board. 23-Nov-93 Sotheby's, New York #160/R

MARTINEZ, Ana Maria de (1937-) Latin American
$10000   £6667   Teatro de Naranjas (102x102cm-40x40in) s.d.5.5.1991. 18-May-94 Christie's, New York #250/R

MARTINEZ, Julian (1897-1943) American
$600   £387   Equestrian figure , s. gouache art board. 9-Jan-93 Skinner, Bolton #166/R
$650   £436   Antelope dancers (23x28cm-9x11in) gouache. 26-Jun-93 Skinner, Bolton #237/R
$750   £487   Bow dancer (33x25cm-13x10in) s. gouache. 25-Jun-94 Skinner, Bolton #18/R
$750   £487   Dancer (33x25cm-13x10in) s. gouache. 25-Jun-94 Skinner, Bolton #14/R
$900   £584   Skunk (28x36cm-11x14in) s. gouache. 25-Jun-94 Skinner, Bolton #16/R

MARTINEZ, Julian (1897-1943) American-cont.
$1100   £710   Untitled (30x53cm-12x21in) s. gouache. 9-Jan-93 Skinner, Bolton #265/R
$2000   £1290   Untitled (46x56cm-18x22in) s. gouache. 9-Jan-93 Skinner, Bolton #168/R

MARTINEZ, Luis (fl.1920-1930) Mexican
$115000   £76667   Musicos (160x180cm-63x71in) s.d.1927 s.d.verso. 17-May-94 Sotheby's, New York #23/R

MARTINEZ, Ricardo (1918-) Mexican
$5000   £3268   Mujer (30x25cm-12x10in) s.d.60. 17-May-93 Christie's, New York #144/R
$6500   £4248   Cabeza de mujer (30x26cm-12x10in) s. painted 1960. 18-May-93 Sotheby's, New York #174/R
$6904   £4542   Mujer acostada II (30x90cm-12x35in) s.d.1985. 4-Nov-92 Mora, Castelltort & Quintana, Juarez #67/R (M.P 21800000)
$8000   £5229   Cabeza en rojo (40x25cm-16x10in) s.d.62. 17-May-93 Christie's, New York #145/R
$14000   £9396   Native smokers (70x39cm-28x15in) s.d.41 linen. 7-Jan-94 Gary Nader, Miami #20/R
$17000   £11333   Toros (30x80cm-12x31in) s.d.58. 18-May-94 Sotheby's, New York #343/R
$30000   £20000   Dos mujeres (68x83cm-27x33in) s.d.66. 18-May-94 Christie's, New York #140/R
$40000   £26144   Amantes (129x150cm-51x59in) s.d.59. 17-May-93 Christie's, New York #147/R
$40000   £26667   Mujer con Palma (160x100cm-63x39in) s.d.66 l.stretcher. 18-May-94 Christie's, New York #69/R
$70000   £47297   Mujeres (175x201cm-69x79in) s.d.59. 23-Nov-93 Christie's, New York #113/R

MARTINEZ, Richard (1904-) American
$900   £581   Bonnet dancer (28x33cm-11x13in) s. gouache. 9-Jan-93 Skinner, Bolton #165/R

MARTINEZ, Xavier (1869-1943) American
$750   £497   Clouds and trees (34x50cm-13x20in) mono W/C gouache. 20-Sep-93 Butterfield & Butterfield, Los Angeles #73/R
$1000   £658   Clouds and trees (34x50cm-13x20in) mono. W/C gouache. 13-Jun-93 Butterfield & Butterfield, San Francisco #767/R

MARTINEZ, Xavier (attrib) (1869-1943) American
$7000   £4636   View of San Francisco Bay (58x66cm-23x26in) 15-Jun-94 Butterfield & Butterfield, San Francisco #4578/R

MARTINI, Felix Lewis (1893-1965) American
$1000   £662   Eucalyptus landscape (51x41cm-20x16in) s. board. 14-Jun-94 John Moran, Pasadena #33
$1600   £1060   Landscape with eucalyptus 'Santa Anita' (51x61cm-20x24in) s. 14-Jun-94 John Moran, Pasadena #32

MARTINI, Joseph de (1896-?) American
$1000   £667   Riva Schiavonia, Venice (82x100cm-32x39in) s. s.i.verso. 23-May-94 Christie's, East, New York #295/R
$3750   £2467   Rockport Quarry (70x95cm-28x37in) s. s.i.d.1939 verso. 31-Mar-93 Sotheby's Arcade, New York #313/R

MARTINO, Antonio Pietro (1902-1989) American
$750   £475   Perce boats (61x91cm-24x36in) s. 3-Dec-92 Freeman Fine Arts, Philadelphia #1873/R
$750   £472   Corner house (61x91cm-24x36in) s. 22-Apr-93 Freeman Fine Arts, Philadelphia #1315
$750   £475   Lobster Cove, Monhegan Island (51x102cm-20x40in) s. 3-Dec-92 Freeman Fine Arts, Philadelphia #1872
$1050   £660   From Cotton Street (41x61cm-16x24in) s. s.i.verso. 22-Apr-93 Freeman Fine Arts, Philadelphia #1196
$1200   £784   Perce, Gaspe Peninsula (71x114cm-28x45in) s. 8-May-93 Young Fine Arts Auctions, Maine #208/R
$1400   £952   Vinalhaven Quarry (69x114cm-27x45in) s. 16-Apr-94 Young Fine Arts Auctions, Maine #165/R
$2900   £1946   Figures and house by river in spring (81x102cm-32x40in) s.d.31. 2-Dec-93 Freeman Fine Arts, Philadelphia #855
$4500   £3041   The Blocks, Summer (76x114cm-30x45in) s. s.i.verso. 31-Mar-94 Sotheby's Arcade, New York #275/R
$1050   £665   Sledding down Manayunk Road (30x41cm-12x16in) s.d.35 pastel. 3-Dec-92 Freeman Fine Arts, Philadelphia #1830

MARTINO, Giovanni (1908-) American
$650   £425   Cresson Street early morning (30x46cm-12x18in) s. i.verso board. 7-Oct-93 Freeman Fine Arts, Philadelphia #920
$800   £537   Conshocken in winter (30x46cm-12x18in) s.d.58 board. 2-Dec-93 Freeman Fine Arts, Philadelphia #811
$900   £570   Snow in Manayunk (30x51cm-12x20in) panel. 3-Dec-92 Freeman Fine Arts, Philadelphia #1849/R
$950   £559   Levering Street, Manayunk (30x46cm-12x18in) s. tempera oil board. 8-Oct-92 Freeman Fine Arts, Philadelphia #1042
$1200   £784   Snowy street (51x61cm-20x24in) s. 7-Oct-93 Freeman Fine Arts, Philadelphia #924
$1400   £946   Snow in Manayunk (30x51cm-12x20in) s. board. 27-Nov-93 Young Fine Arts Auctions, Maine #218/R

MARTINO, Renato de (19/20th C) Argentinian
$1400   £927   Fragata (31x27cm-12x11in) panel. 18-Nov-92 Roldan & Cia, Buenos Aires #8

MARTORI, Patty (20th C) American
$500   £336   Skull (183x85cm-72x33in) init.i.d.1990verso eggshells plaster red dye. 3-May-94 Christie's, East, New York #187/R

MARX, Roberto Burle (1909-1982) Brazilian
$851	£560	Abstract design with fish (83x100cm-33x39in) s.d.1943. 6-Apr-93 Phillips, West Two #168
$8000	£5405	Peixe (81x98cm-32x39in) s.d.1942. 23-Nov-93 Christie's, New York #188/R

MARYAN (1927-1977) American
$1210	£802	Composition (41x34cm-16x13in) s.d.57. 22-Sep-93 Kunsthallen, Copenhagen #141 (D.KR 8000)
$1417	£945	Les roues (33x24cm-13x9in) s.d.1960. 30-May-94 Hoebanx & Coutrier, Paris #13 (F.FR 8000)
$6200	£4161	Head (81x65cm-32x26in) s.d.54. 3-Jan-94 Gordon Galleries, Tel Aviv #375/R
$13441	£9082	Personnage, Paris (146x89cm-57x35in) s.d.58. 3-Nov-93 Kunsthallen, Copenhagen #7/R (D.KR 90000)
$797	£531	Portrait (28x18cm-11x7in) s.d.1961 wash gouache. 30-May-94 Hoebanx & Coutrier, Paris #14 (F.FR 4500)
$885	£590	Les besoins naturels (30x23cm-12x9in) s.d.1970 Indian ink W/C. 30-May-94 Hoebanx & Coutrier, Paris #15 (F.FR 5000)
$1328	£885	Le clown (30x40cm-12x16in) s.d.1970 ink W/C. 30-May-94 Hoebanx & Coutrier, Paris #12 (F.FR 7500)

MARYAN, Burstein Pinchas (1927-1977) American
$1863	£1225	Screaming child, N 7 (75x56cm-30x22in) s.d.71. 4-Nov-92 Francis Briest, Paris #18 (F.FR 10000)
$4548	£3053	Composition (89x116cm-35x46in) s.d.55. 21-Mar-94 Pescheteau & Ferrien, Paris #106 (F.FR 26100)
$491	£327	Personnage (24x16cm-9x6in) s.d.1966 gouache ink. 8-Jun-94 Guy Loudmer, Paris #26 (F.FR 2800)
$697	£468	Personnage (36x51cm-14x20in) s.d.1970 W/C ink. 27-Mar-94 Guy Loudmer, Paris #194 (F.FR 4000)
$697	£468	Personnage (36x51cm-14x20in) s.d.1970 W/C ink. 27-Mar-94 Guy Loudmer, Paris #193 (F.FR 4000)
$838	£493	Composition (53x42cm-21x17in) s.d.1958 ink wash. 28-Sep-92 Catherine Charbonneaux, Paris #144 (F.FR 4000)
$838	£493	Composition (54x42cm-21x17in) s.d.1958 ink wash. 28-Sep-92 Catherine Charbonneaux, Paris #145 (F.FR 4000)

MASON, Roy M (1886-1972) American
$700	£443	Chopping wood (30x41cm-12x16in) s. masonite. 5-Dec-92 Louisiana Auction Exchange #119/R
$716	£450	Delray Beach (30x40cm-12x16in) s.i.d.38. 22-Apr-93 Christie's, S. Kensington #64/R
$800	£537	Northrup Landing landscape scene with cottage (61x74cm-24x29in) s. 17-Dec-93 Du Mouchelle, Detroit #1139/R
$975	£617	Heading out (30x41cm-12x16in) s. panel. 24-Oct-92 Collins, Maine #110
$1100	£714	Western landscape with farmhouse and towering cliffs (51x64cm-20x25in) s. 4-Aug-94 Eldred, Massachusetts #594/R
$1100	£738	Misty morning (51x61cm-20x24in) s. 24-Mar-94 Mystic Fine Arts, Connecticut #156/R
$1100	£748	Dawn (56x72cm-22x28in) s. W/C. 15-Nov-93 Christie's, East, New York #117
$1100	£764	The tile yard (25x36cm-10x14in) s. W/C gouache. 6-Mar-93 Louisiana Auction Exchange #106/R

MASON, William Sanford (1824-1864) American
$8500	£5705	Artist painting a view from Susquehanna river, Pennsylvania (56x76cm-22x30in) s.d.1855 canvas laid down on board. 4-May-94 Doyle, New York #5/R

MASSAD, G Daniel (1946-) American?
$1600	£1074	White bowl (22x65cm-9x26in) s.d.85 col.chk. 23-Feb-94 Christie's, East, New York #287/R
$2800	£1879	Noon (55x75cm-22x30in) s.d.1987 col.chk. 23-Feb-94 Christie's, East, New York #288/R

MASSERIA, Francisco (attrib) (1927-) Argentinian
$1300	£884	Little girl (61x51cm-24x20in) s.d. 17-Apr-94 Schrager Galleries, Milwaukee #689/R

MASSON, Henri L (1907-) Canadian
$640	£429	Wakefield Quebec (20x25cm-8x10in) s. s.i.verso panel painted c.1934-40. 29-Nov-93 Ritchie, Toronto #179/R (C.D 850)
$861	£582	Nova Scotia mood (30x41cm-12x16in) 14-Jun-93 Lunds, Victoria #4 (C.D 1100)
$874	£583	Gatineau Waterfall (46x56cm-18x22in) s. 11-May-94 Sotheby's, Toronto #138/R (C.D 1200)
$1005	£670	Winter landscape (30x40cm-12x16in) s.i. 30-May-94 Ritchie, Toronto #195/R (C.D 1400)
$1204	£808	Coastal view and houses (38x46cm-15x18in) s. 29-Nov-93 Ritchie, Toronto #189/R (C.D 1600)
$1208	£816	Paysage (30x40cm-12x16in) s. 23-Nov-93 Fraser Pinneys, Quebec #368 (C.D 1600)
$1268	£829	Altar boys (30x25cm-12x10in) s. 18-May-93 Joyner Fine Art, Toronto #15/R (C.D 1600)
$1279	£859	Snow covered hills (38x46cm-15x18in) s. 29-Nov-93 Ritchie, Toronto #190/R (C.D 1700)
$1284	£867	Mountain road, Quebec, winter (40x50cm-16x20in) s. 23-Nov-93 Joyner Fine Art, Toronto #5/R (C.D 1700)
$1395	£942	Autumn landscape (46x61cm-18x24in) s.d.60. 3-Nov-93 Sotheby's, Toronto #231 (C.D 1800)
$1456	£971	St. Fabien, Quebec (30x41cm-12x16in) s. s.i.stretcher. 11-May-94 Sotheby's, Toronto #77/R (C.D 2000)

MASSON, Henri L (1907-) Canadian-cont.
$1572	£995	Autumn landscape (46x61cm-18x24in) s. i.verso board. 1-Dec-92 Fraser Pinneys, Quebec #37 (C.D 2000)
$1602	£1068	April, McGregor Lake (30x40cm-12x16in) s. board. 13-May-94 Joyner Fine Art, Toronto #31/R (C.D 2200)
$1700	£1141	Late March (30x66cm-12x26in) s. board. 24-Mar-94 Mystic Fine Arts, Connecticut #181/R
$1840	£1243	Returning from school (30x41cm-12x16in) 14-Jun-93 Lunds, Victoria #3 (C.D 2350)
$1893	£1262	Mountain road, Touraine, Que (30x40cm-12x16in) s. 13-May-94 Joyner Fine Art, Toronto #3/R (C.D 2600)
$2335	£1546	Spring, Farrelton, Quebec (40x50cm-16x20in) s. 24-Nov-92 Joyner Fine Art, Toronto #44/R (C.D 3000)
$2476	£1650	Autumn, Limbour, Que. (50x70cm-20x28in) s. board. 13-May-94 Joyner Fine Art, Toronto #73/R (C.D 3400)
$2621	£1748	Autumn rain (40x50cm-16x20in) s. 13-May-94 Joyner Fine Art, Toronto #78/R (C.D 3600)
$2695	£1762	Givre, Papineauville, Quebec (41x51cm-16x20in) s. painted 1979. 18-May-93 Joyner Fine Art, Toronto #53/R (C.D 3400)
$2913	£1942	Nude (65x40cm-26x16in) s. board. 13-May-94 Joyner Fine Art, Toronto #20/R (C.D 4000)
$3113	£2062	Buckingham, P.Q (45x55cm-18x22in) s. 24-Nov-92 Joyner Fine Art, Toronto #135/R (C.D 4000)
$3209	£2168	Paysage d'hiver, Quebec (41x51cm-16x20in) s. 23-Nov-93 Fraser Pinneys, Quebec #377/R (C.D 4250)
$3419	£2150	Street Hull, Quebec (30x41cm-12x16in) 19-Apr-93 Lunds, Victoria #8 (C.D 4300)
$725	*£490*	*Ice fishing, Gatineau Point, Quebec (23x29cm-9x11in) s. i.verso W/C. 25-Apr-94 Levis, Calgary #220/R (C.D 1000)*
$905	*£615*	*Harness racing (30x38cm-12x15in) s. mixed media. 15-Nov-93 Hodgins, Calgary #56/R (C.D 1200)*

MATA, Carolina (1943-) Mexican
$1055	£713	Mirando hacia adentro (90x180cm-35x71in) s. acrylic diptych. 20-Oct-93 Louis Morton, Mexico #68/R (M.P 3300)

MATHEWS, Arthur F (1860-1945) American
$7500	£4412	Old Dutchman (23x28cm-9x11in) s.d.87 panel. 4-Oct-92 Butterfield & Butterfield, Los Angeles #116/R
$8500	£5000	Dutchwoman (29x24cm-11x9in) s. panel. 4-Oct-92 Butterfield & Butterfield, Los Angeles #115/R
$47500	£27941	Monterey Bay (66x76cm-26x30in) s. 4-Oct-92 Butterfield & Butterfield, Los Angeles #75/R

MATHEWSON, Frank Convers (1862-1941) American
$800	£556	Roses in copper pot (51x66cm-20x26in) s. 27-Feb-93 Young Fine Arts Auctions, Maine #204/R

MATSON, Henry Ellis (1887-1971) American
$725	£493	Moonlit stream (38x51cm-15x20in) s. 16-Apr-94 Young Fine Arts Auctions, Maine #166/R

MATSON, Victor (1898-1972) American
$650	£433	High Sierra, Crystal Crag, Lake George (51x61cm-20x24in) 15-Mar-94 John Moran, Pasadena #24

MATSUBARA, Kazuo (1895-?) American
$1300	£903	Chapel through the trees (46x55cm-18x22in) s.d.1927 board. 7-Mar-93 Butterfield & Butterfield, San Francisco #142/R

MATTA (1911-) Chilean
$846	£571	Sans titre (18x14cm-7x6in) painted 1988. 24-Nov-93 Watine-Arnault, Paris #34/R (F.FR 5000)
$9000	£6040	Untitled (54x41cm-21x16in) s. painted c.1968. 24-Feb-94 Sotheby's Arcade, New York #313/R
$9772	£6603	Senza titolo (50x53cm-20x21in) s. painted 1975. 23-Nov-93 Sotheby's, Milan #141/R (I.L 16500000)
$12279	£8186	Composition (46x46cm-18x18in) 20-May-94 Claude Boisgirard, Paris #132/R (F.FR 69500)
$12435	£7971	Le cerf pend comme tous (68x64cm-27x25in) s.i.verso executed 1987. 10-Dec-93 Christie's, Amsterdam #388/R (D.FL 22000)
$14000	£9396	Abstract composition (61x89cm-24x35in) s. 15-Dec-93 Boos Gallery, Michigan #429/R
$14535	£9500	Mas Ceilin (48x52cm-19x20in) init. painted 1975. 30-Jun-94 Sotheby's, London #148/R
$15420	£10349	Metamorfosi (66x77cm-26x30in) s. painted c.1965. 14-Dec-93 Finarte, Milan #474/R (I.L 26000000)
$16123	£10538	Senza titolo (100x80cm-39x31in) s. 8-May-93 Finarte, Chiasso #128/R (S.FR 23500)
$16297	£10938	Untitled (73x60cm-29x24in) mono. painted 1976. 3-Dec-93 Lempertz, Cologne #873/R (DM 28000)
$16466	£10762	Senza titolo (80x100cm-31x39in) s. 8-May-93 Finarte, Chiasso #108/R (S.FR 24000)
$16583	£11204	Paratif (81x72cm-32x28in) s.i.d.73verso. 23-Nov-93 Sotheby's, Milan #174/R (I.L 18000000)
$16707	£11289	Soli in sole (102x97cm-40x38in) mono.verso painted 1981. 20-Oct-93 Finarte, Firenze #310/R (I.L 27000000)
$17184	£11380	Composizione (74x62cm-29x24in) s. 24-Nov-92 Sotheby's, Milan #200/R (I.L 24000000)

MATTA (1911-) Chilean-cont.

$18000	£12000	The Bider (42x36cm-17x14in) s. paper laid down on canvas painted 1955. 18-May-94 Christie's, New York #176/R
$18360	£12000	Untitled (65x71cm-26x28in) s.i.d.69. 30-Jun-94 Sotheby's, London #138/R
$19830	£12711	Senza titolo (66x78cm-26x31in) s.i.d.28.11.1965. 14-Dec-92 Christie's, Rome #114/R (I.L 28000000)
$20375	£12500	Page de Ferme (90x107cm-35x42in) 15-Oct-92 Christie's, London #37/R
$21328	£14509	Composition (68x67cm-27x26in) painted 1966. 10-Apr-94 Perrin, Versailles #28/R (F.FR 125500)
$22950	£15000	Untitled (73x64cm-29x25in) painted 1960. 30-Jun-94 Sotheby's, London #112/R
$24000	£16000	Untitled (44x49cm-17x19in) s.d.1967 i.verso. 18-May-94 Christie's, New York #166/R
$25330	£17000	Untitled (59x72cm-23x28in) s. painted 1957. 23-Mar-94 Sotheby's, London #311/R
$26000	£17333	Sin titulo (66x68cm-26x27in) painted 1966. 18-May-94 Christie's, New York #132/R
$26080	£16000	Untitled (102x83cm-40x33in) s. 15-Oct-92 Christie's, London #50/R
$26241	£17730	Terre d'Abords (102x94cm-40x37in) s.i.d.1972. 31-Mar-94 Christian de Quay, Paris #16/R (F.FR 150000)
$26820	£18000	Sign of the Times (88x108cm-35x43in) painted c.1967. 25-Mar-93 Christie's, London #36/R
$27540	£18000	Vivre pour son feu (107x100cm-42x39in) s. s.i.verso painted 1973. 30-Jun-94 Sotheby's, London #149/R
$28232	£18452	Sans titre (104x80cm-41x31in) s.d.1956-57verso. 29-Jun-94 Guy Loudmer, Paris #232/R (F.FR 155000)
$30000	£20000	Batisseur de N'ou's (99x91cm-39x36in) s. i.verso painted 1984. 18-May-94 Christie's, New York #131/R
$31778	£22222	Ecrire son cri (87x84cm-34x33in) i.verso painted 1975. 10-Mar-93 Watine-Arnault, Paris #66/R (F.FR 180000)
$35031	£23199	Role renverse (160x230cm-63x91in) s. i.verso. 26-Nov-92 Francis Briest, Paris #38/R (F.FR 190000)
$37250	£25000	Il risveglio della natura (66x84cm-26x33in) s. painted 1953. 2-Dec-93 Sotheby's, London #13/R
$38000	£25333	Untitled (65x67cm-26x26in) painted 1966. 18-May-94 Sotheby's, New York #268/R
$38740	£26000	El Confussor (60x50cm-24x20in) painted 1950. 2-Dec-93 Christie's, London #114/R
$40000	£26667	Volare volta per sempre (104x98cm-41x39in) s. painted 1970. 18-May-94 Sotheby's, New York #323/R
$40230	£27000	Untitled (60x77cm-24x30in) s.verso painted 1958. 24-Jun-93 Christie's, London #15/R
$41080	£26000	L'etre c'est la pierre (100x81cm-39x32in) s.d.55 verso. 3-Dec-92 Sotheby's, London #5/R
$41825	£28070	Composition (86x104cm-34x41in) s.d.1969. 21-Mar-94 Guy Loudmer, Paris #54/R (F.FR 240000)
$42000	£28378	Aftermath of World War II, 1945 (49x66cm-19x26in) s. painted 1953. 22-Nov-93 Sotheby's, New York #222/R
$42000	£28000	Sado Burocrazia (83x100cm-33x39in) s. 26-May-94 Christie's, London #49/R
$43682	£29317	Les orienteur (114x145cm-45x57in) s.i. painted c.1960. 5-May-94 Finarte, Milan #59/R (I.L 70000000)
$45000	£29412	Page du germe (84x103cm-33x41in) painted 1974. 17-May-93 Christie's, New York #137/R
$49065	£32710	Le son du soupcon (198x215cm-78x85in) painted 1985. 1-Jun-94 Marc Kohn, Paris #86/R (F.FR 280000)
$52000	£35135	Elasticite du risible (105x93cm-41x37in) s.i. 23-Nov-93 Christie's, New York #163/R
$53640	£36000	Untitled (114x146cm-45x57in) s. painted c.1962-64. 24-Jun-93 Sotheby's, London #27/R
$55616	£35200	Le meilleur dans l'infini (100x80cm-39x31in) s. s.i.num.251 verso. 3-Dec-92 Christie's, London #24/R
$57500	£38333	Untitled (67x67cm-26x26in) 18-May-94 Sotheby's, New York #269/R
$58000	£38411	Pointe (82x101cm-32x40in) painted 1959. 24-Nov-92 Christie's, New York #94/R
$59600	£40000	Untitled (81x100cm-32x39in) painted 1957. 24-Jun-93 Sotheby's, London #5/R
$64408	£42654	The Boxers (88x116cm-35x46in) painted 1955. 13-Jun-94 Guy Loudmer, Paris #45/R (F.FR 360000)
$65000	£43046	Upon the growing (81x97cm-32x38in) s.num.114 verso painted 1957. 24-Nov-92 Christie's, New York #40/R
$70000	£46358	Ecran de la Memoire (175x204cm-69x80in) s. s.i.num.84/7 verso painted 1984. 24-Nov-92 Christie's, New York #41/R
$85000	£56667	Il Risueglio della Natura (66x84cm-26x33in) s. painted 1953. 18-May-94 Christie's, London #48/R
$90000	£60000	La Belle Helene (178x199cm-70x78in) i. painted 1983. 18-May-94 Christie's, New York #38/R
$100000	£65359	Promenade de Venus (200x200cm-79x79in) s. painted 1966. 17-May-93 Christie's, New York #47/R
$110000	£72848	Composition (105x146cm-41x57in) s.verso. 24-Nov-92 Christie's, New York #93/R
$110000	£73333	Composition (81x100cm-32x39in) painted c.1957. 17-May-94 Christie's, New York #33/R
$120000	£80000	Un Bieenanal (113x146cm-44x57in) painted 1957. 18-May-94 Christie's, New York #60/R
$120000	£80000	Sans titre (203x296cm-80x117in) s. 18-May-94 Sotheby's, New York #214/R
$120000	£81081	Pose etat (143x200cm-56x79in) s.i. painted c.1958-60. 23-Nov-93 Christie's, New York #62/R
$150000	£101351	Je me quitte (114x146cm-45x57in) painted c.1953. 22-Nov-93 Sotheby's, New York #63/R
$160000	£104575	Towards (201x293cm-79x115in) painted 1960. 17-May-93 Christie's, New York #29/R
$170000	£113333	Le coeur d'Helene (120x146cm-47x57in) painted 1957. 18-May-94 Christie's, New York #32/R

MATTA (1911-) Chilean-cont.

$180000	£121622	La Promenade de Venus (200x400cm-79x157in) s. s.verso painted 1954. 23-Nov-93 Christie's, New York #27/R
$230000	£154362	La lumiere noire (45x63cm-18x25in) painted 1943. 7-Jan-94 Gary Nader, Miami #43/R
$500000	£333333	Inscape, psychological morphology no 104 (73x92cm-29x36in) s.d.39. 17-May-94 Sotheby's, New York #19/R
$823	£556	Composition with figures (22x47cm-9x19in) s. ink dr. 19-Oct-93 Campo & Campo, Antwerp #257 (B.FR 30000)
$905	£608	L'oiseau Licq (17x18cm-7x7in) s.i. pastel. 23-Mar-93 Cornette de St.Cyr, Paris #61 (F.FR 5000)
$931	£597	Composition (50x70cm-20x28in) col.crayons pastel. 18-Dec-92 Libert, Castor, Paris #26 (F.FR 5000)
$1839	£1202	L'assassinat de Kennedy (48x63cm-19x25in) i. pastel col.crayons. 23-Dec-92 Binoche et Godeau, Paris #23/R (F.FR 10000)
$1908	£1280	Senza titolo (50x65cm-20x26in) indis.i. pastel graphite. 30-Nov-93 Finarte, Rome #166/R (I.L 3200000)
$2049	£1314	Senza titolo (50x35cm-20x14in) mono mixed media. 27-May-93 Christie's, Rome #19 (I.L 3000000)
$3141	£2108	Gods disengagement from the world. The jump to conclusion (42x56cm-17x22in) s.i. pastel col.crayons. 23-Jun-93 Guy Loudmer, Paris #14/R (F.FR 18000)
$3482	£2321	La Guerre (49x64cm-19x25in) s. pencil col crayon executed c.1969. 31-May-94 Christie's, Amsterdam #402/R (D.FL 6500)
$3664	£2476	Pour traicture,... (50x60cm-20x24in) s.i. pastel crayon. 19-Mar-93 Catherine Charbonneaux, Paris #62/R (F.FR 20500)
$3983	£2673	Monde imaginaire (63x48cm-25x19in) s. crayon pastel dr. 25-Mar-93 Beaussant & Lefevre, Paris #94 (F.FR 22000)
$4559	£3081	Composition (52x71cm-20x28in) s. pastel executed c.1958-1959. 18-Jun-93 Francis Briest, Paris #1/R (F.FR 26000)
$4745	£3206	Les Desastrautaunautes (49x64cm-19x25in) s.d.1966 gouache. 27-Apr-94 Louis Morton, Mexico #402 (M.P 16000)
$4781	£3125	Le Monstre (65x50cm-26x20in) s. pastel. 21-Dec-92 Jean Louis Picard, Paris #142/R (F.FR 26000)
$4782	£3065	Le coeur ecologique (66x49cm-26x19in) i. mono.d.1973verso pastel cardboard. 27-May-93 Christie's, Rome #58/R (I.L 7000000)
$4896	£3200	Untitled (40x53cm-16x21in) s. i.verso oil mixed media paper on canvas. 27-Jun-94 Phillips, London #42/R
$4896	£3200	Untitled (40x53cm-16x21in) s. i.verso oil mixed media paper on canvas. 27-Jun-94 Phillips, London #41/R
$5225	£3349	Heurt des realites (44x74cm-17x29in) s.i.d.63 pastel crayon. 12-Dec-92 Catherine Charbonneaux, Paris #42 (F.FR 28000)
$5261	£3555	Untitled (64x48cm-25x19in) s. col.crayons pencil executed 1969. 18-Jun-93 Francis Briest, Paris #2/R (F.FR 30000)
$5962	£3846	New York (45x69cm-18x27in) s. oil pastel. 12-Jul-94 Guy Loudmer, Paris #170/R (F.FR 32000)
$6000	£4000	Untitled (65x50cm-26x20in) s. gouache crayon pencil. 18-May-94 Christie's, New York #177/R
$6000	£3974	Bigne (99x69cm-39x27in) s. pastel drawn 1974. 24-Nov-92 Christie's, New York #120/R
$6099	£4094	Composition (48x63cm-19x25in) s. pastel. 21-Mar-94 Guy Loudmer, Paris #19/R (F.FR 35000)
$6218	£4202	The bider (41x36cm-16x14in) s.i. mixed media paper on canvas. 23-Nov-93 Sotheby's, Milan #167/R (I.L 10500000)
$6333	£4167	Phenomene de la conscience emue (48x63cm-19x25in) s.i. pastel col.crayons. 4-Nov-92 Francis Briest, Paris #21/R (F.FR 34000)
$6796	£4561	Sans titre (50x65cm-20x26in) s. pastel executed 1983. 21-Mar-94 Guy Loudmer, Paris #13/R (F.FR 39000)
$7000	£4730	Composicion (50x65cm-20x26in) s. pencil wax crayon painted 1961. 23-Nov-93 Christie's, New York #216/R
$7500	£4902	Figura (65x50cm-26x20in) s.d.1970 pastel. 17-May-93 Christie's, New York #240/R
$8880	£5692	Senza titolo (38x42cm-15x17in) s.d.55 mixed media paper on panel. 25-May-93 Sotheby's, Milan #231/R (I.L 13000000)
$9000	£6000	Surrealist composition (26x20cm-10x8in) s. col crayon pencil executed 1938. 26-May-94 Christie's, London #12/R
$9050	£5954	L'orchestre (48x65cm-19x26in) s. pastel gouache. 4-Apr-93 Pescheteau, Paris #83/R (F.FR 49000)
$9364	£6243	La femme pliee , i. col crayon dr executed c.1947. 20-May-94 Claude Boisgirard, Paris #145/R (F.FR 53000)
$15000	£10000	Soif d'Aprobe (49x64cm-19x25in) i. crayon pencil executed 1957. 18-May-94 Christie's, New York #175/R
$18000	£12000	ETC..etres (45x70cm-18x28in) oil wax crayon panel. 26-May-94 Christie's, London #51/R
$20115	£13500	Merde a toi (98x149cm-39x59in) s. s.i.verso chl pastel paper on canvas 1951. 3-Dec-93 Sotheby's, London #113/R
$21605	£14500	Popol vuhelve (200x457cm-79x180in) pastel wax crayon paper on hessian three. 24-Jun-93 Sotheby's, London #99/R
$26000	£17333	Wet sheets (32x50cm-13x20in) s.d.36 W/C gouache pen ink photo collage. 18-May-94 Sotheby's, New York #213/R
$27000	£18000	Give me one (29x37cm-11x15in) s.i.d.47 col.pencil graphite paper on paper. 17-May-94 Sotheby's, New York #32/R
$28000	£18667	Sin titulo (37x51cm-15x20in) crayon pencil executed 1946. 18-May-94 Christie's, New York #31/R
$30000	£20000	Arette l'age d'hemmorrage (37x49cm-15x19in) col crayon graphite executed 1947. 18-May-94 Sotheby's, New York #267/R
$30000	£19608	Dialectique du paysage (25x32cm-10x13in) s.d.39 col.pencil graphite. 18-May-93 Sotheby's, New York #139/R

MATTA (1911-) Chilean-cont.
$30000	£20270	L'Octrui en famille (29x37cm-11x15in) s.i. i.verso col.pencil graphite executed c.1945. 22-Nov-93 Sotheby's, New York #70/R
$40000	£26667	Sans titre (25x32cm-10x13in) s.i. i.verso wax crayon col.pencil tryptich. 17-May-94 Sotheby's, New York #56/R
$47880	£32571	Composition (183x300cm-72x118in) mixed media oil pigment plaster jute painted 62. 17-Nov-93 Ader Tajan, Paris #42/R (F.FR 285000)
$60000	£39216	Untitled (28x38cm-11x15in) s.d.40 col.pencil graphite. 18-May-93 Sotheby's, New York #51/R
$75000	£49669	Femme jouant au Balle devant un Vulcan (27x38cm-11x15in) s.d.40 colour pencil graphite. 23-Nov-92 Sotheby's, New York #46/R
$92500	£60458	Psychological morphology no.14 - personnages et automobile (32x48cm-13x19in) s. graphite crayon col.pencil executed 1939. 18-May-93 Sotheby's, New York #50/R
$100000	£67568	Endless muse (26x33cm-10x13in) ink crayon gouache luminous paint paper on board. 22-Nov-93 Sotheby's, New York #59/R

MATTERN, Alice (1909-1945) American
$850	£570	Allegro (107x99cm-42x39in) s. 29-Nov-93 Stonington Fine Arts, Stonington #126/R

MATTHEWS, Marmaduke (1837-1913) Canadian
$549	£359	Cattle in forest clearing (47x65cm-19x26in) s. W/C. 10-May-93 Hodgins, Calgary #88 (C.D 700)
$779	£513	Finding the lost cow (51x38cm-20x15in) s. W/C. 7-Jun-93 Waddingtons, Toronto #1176 (C.D 1000)
$1451	£980	Untitled - Albert Canyon near glacier, British Colombia (51x38cm-20x15in) S. W/C on paper laid down on mat board. 25-Apr-94 Levis, Calgary #221/R (C.D 2000)
$2724	£1804	Birch tree by lake (104x79cm-41x31in) s. W/C. 18-Nov-92 Sotheby's, Toronto #111/R (C.D 3500)

MATTHEWS, Thomas (20th C) Canadian
$502	£335	School's out (45x60cm-18x24in) s.d.1973 verso acrylic masonite. 30-May-94 Ritchie, Toronto #194/R (C.D 700)

MATTO, Francisco (1911-) Uruguayan
$700	£455	Cannes (30x26cm-12x10in) s.d.1959 board. 30-Aug-93 Gomensoro, Montevideo #64
$900	£584	Bodegon (22x21cm-9x8in) s.d.1972 board. 30-Aug-93 Gomensoro, Montevideo #63/R
$1600	£1046	Constructivo (39x47cm-15x19in) s. board. 4-Oct-93 Gomensoro, Montevideo #79/R
$2200	£1477	Naturaleza muerta constructiva (48x34cm-19x13in) s. board. 29-Nov-93 Gomensoro, Montevideo #80/R
$3000	£2013	Puerto (42x43cm-17x17in) s. board. 29-Nov-93 Gomensoro, Montevideo #81/R
$3500	£2318	Cafe (35x43cm-14x17in) s. tempera board on board. 23-Nov-92 Sotheby's, New York #238/R
$4000	£2685	Constructivo (62x46cm-24x18in) s. board painted 1954. 29-Nov-93 Gomensoro, Montevideo #79/R
$5000	£3311	Construccion en madera (84x48cm-33x19in) d.61. 28-Jun-93 Gomensoro, Montevideo #49/R
$6000	£4000	Constructivo con Paloma (52x40cm-20x16in) s.d.51 tempera board. 18-May-94 Sotheby's, New York #258/R
$7000	£4667	Cafe (35x49cm-14x19in) s.d.52 board. 18-May-94 Christie's, New York #272/R
$7500	£4902	Constructivo ABCDEFG (84x53cm-33x21in) s.d.60 tempera board. 18-May-93 Sotheby's, New York #191 a/R
$8000	£5298	Ada (94x65cm-37x26in) s.d.53. 23-Nov-92 Sotheby's, New York #236/R
$9500	£6419	Paisaje urbano (99x70cm-39x28in) s.d.76 tempera oil board. 22-Nov-93 Sotheby's, New York #252/R
$10000	£6536	Grafismo (100x77cm-39x30in) d.53 s.i.verso board. 17-May-93 Christie's, New York #172/R
$14000	£9396	Construction with Lamb (101x80cm-40x31in) s.d.67 board. 7-Jan-94 Gary Nader, Miami #132/R

MATULKA, Jan (1890-1972) American
$1250	£723	Chinese dolls (61x41cm-24x16in) s. 24-Sep-92 Mystic Fine Arts, Connecticut #192
$8000	£5594	Still life with fruit and pitchers (76x61cm-30x24in) s. 10-Mar-93 Sotheby's, New York #158/R

MAURER, Alfred H (1868-1932) American
$5000	£2890	Portrait of woman in rust coloured dress (55x46cm-22x18in) s. board. 23-Sep-92 Christie's, New York #236/R
$6000	£3468	Quarry, Shadybrook (28x39cm-11x15in) s. paper. 23-Sep-92 Christie's, New York #239/R
$8000	£5298	Girl in green dress (56x34cm-22x13in) s. gessoed board. 22-Sep-93 Christie's, New York #205/R
$10000	£5780	Still life (46x55cm-18x22in) s. board. 23-Sep-92 Christie's, New York #238/R
$17000	£11486	Two heads a portrait of two women (54x45cm-21x18in) 5-Nov-93 Skinner, Bolton #158a/R
$3000	£1961	Still life with flowers and fruit (58x43cm-23x17in) s.d.27 W/C. 15-May-93 Dunning's, Illinois #1080/R
$4750	£3210	Head (54x37cm-21x15in) init. gouache pencil executed c.1925. 31-Mar-94 Sotheby's Arcade, New York #420/R
$5000	£2890	Vase of flowers (55x46cm-22x18in) s.i.d.1926 gouache. 23-Sep-92 Christie's, New York #268/R
$5500	£3179	Flowers in vase (54x46cm-21x18in) s.d.26 gouache chl. 23-Sep-92 Christie's, New York #269/R
$6000	£3974	Landscape (22x27cm-9x11in) indist.s. gessoed panel. 22-Sep-93 Christie's, New York #204/R
$27000	£17089	Head of woman (54x45cm-21x18in) s. gouache. 3-Dec-92 Sotheby's, New York #65/R

MAURER, Alfred H (attrib) (1868-1932) American
$1250   £828   Mandarin lady (41x30cm-16x12in) s. board. 26-Sep-93 Schrager Galleries, Milwaukee #457/R

MAURY, Cornelia Field (1866-?) American
$700   £458   Harem (36x38cm-14x15in) s. board. 16-May-93 Hanzel Galleries, Chicago #322

MAX, Peter (1937-) American
$1800   £1216 Grammy (51x41cm-20x16in) s. acrylic. 31-Oct-93 Hindman Galleries, Chicago #777
$2400   £1569 Zero man (30x30cm-12x12in) s. acrylic. 16-May-93 Hindman Galleries, Chicago #22
$2600   £1699 Untitled (76x101cm-30x40in) s.d. 22-Dec-92 Christie's, East, New York #90
$3500   £2147 Figure holding an umbrella (56x46cm-22x18in) s. i.verso acrylic. 16-Oct-92 Du Mouchelle, Detroit #2004/R
$4240   £2667 Degas man on yellow (103x78cm-41x31in) s.d.1983 acrylic. 21-Apr-93 Germann, Zurich #174/R (S.FR 6000)

MAXFIELD, James E (1848-?) American
$850   £567   Portrait of young woman in ruffled blouse (25x19cm-10x7in) s.d.1881. 12-Mar-94 Weschler, Washington #154

MAY, Henrietta Mabel (1884-1971) Canadian
$906   £612   Village, Laurentians (15x22cm-6x9in) s. panel painted c.1926. 23-Nov-93 Joyner Fine Art, Toronto #84/R (C.D 1200)
$1088   £735   Untitled - Still life with roses (50x41cm-20x16in) s. paper board. 25-Apr-94 Levis, Calgary #222/R (C.D 1500)
$1162   £785   Lake of Two Mountains Ottawa Valley (27x35cm-11x14in) s. s.i.d.1921verso board. 3-Nov-93 Sotheby's, Toronto #16/R (C.D 1500)
$1165   £777   Behind our house (30x40cm-12x16in) board. 13-May-94 Joyner Fine Art, Toronto #223/R (C.D 1600)
$1427   £933   Summer cottage, Hudson Heights (25x34cm-10x13in) s. panel. 18-May-93 Joyner Fine Art, Toronto #169/R (C.D 1800)
$1434   £969   The white house (41x50cm-16x20in) s. paperboard. 1-Nov-93 Levis, Calgary #206/R (C.D 1850)
$1638   £1092 Elmvale, Ottawa (41x51cm-16x20in) s. i.stretcher board. 11-May-94 Sotheby's, Toronto #78/R (C.D 2250)
$1868   £1237 Country house (26x34cm-10x13in) s. panel double-sided. 24-Nov-92 Joyner Fine Art, Toronto #223/R (C.D 2400)
$2179   £1443 Calla lillies (76x58cm-30x23in) i.verso board. 18-Nov-92 Sotheby's, Toronto #13/R (C.D 2800)
$2576   £1684 Daffodils (51x41cm-20x16in) s. board. 19-May-93 Sotheby's, Toronto #160/R (C.D 3250)
$2695   £1762 Artist with friends (91x102cm-36x40in) s. 18-May-93 Joyner Fine Art, Toronto #244/R (C.D 3400)

MAYBELL, Claudius (?) American
$1600   £1032 Joan of Arc (81x102cm-32x40in) 16-Jul-94 San Rafael Auction Galleries #357

MAYER, Peter Bela (1888-?) American
$800   £556   Cabin in the woods (51x61cm-20x24in) s. board. 3-Mar-93 Doyle, New York #46/R

MAYER, Ralph (1895-?) American
$600   £392   Buffalo Canal (51x71cm-20x28in) s. board. 30-Jun-94 Mystic Fine Arts, Connecticut #166/R

MAYERS, A (19th C) American
$1269   £813   Foret des bords du Mississippi (29x45cm-11x18in) W/C two. 27-May-93 Audap Solnet & Godeau, Paris #68 (F.FR 6800)

MAYHEW, Nell Brooker (1876-1940) American
$800   £537   San Francisco Bay from San Rafael (76x102cm-30x40in) s. 4-Dec-93 Louisiana Auction Exchange #26
$1300   £878   Landscape (81x56cm-32x22in) s. 15-Jun-93 John Moran, Pasadena #110
$500   £331   Matillaha Poppies (84x41cm-33x16in) init. gouache panel. 15-Jun-94 Butterfield & Butterfield, San Francisco #4665/R

MAYNARD, George Willoughby (1843-1923) American
$4000   £2797 Reading by the fire (27x22cm-11x9in) s. panel. 11-Mar-93 Christie's, New York #71/R
$7500   £4747 Soldier of the Revolution (130x100cm-51x39in) s.d.1876. 4-Dec-92 Christie's, New York #203/R

MAYORGA, Gomez (?) Mexican?
$6797   £4593 Paisaje con lavanderas (70x50cm-28x20in) s.d.55. 9-Nov-93 Louis Morton, Mexico #68/R (M.P 22000)

MAZON, Rafael (1939-) Mexican
$842   £561   Sandias (30x35cm-12x14in) s.d.1993. 25-May-94 Louis Morton, Mexico #93/R (M.P 2800)
$1613   £1082 Mesa con melones (70x60cm-28x24in) s. 1-Dec-93 Louis Morton, Mexico #9/R (M.P 5000)
$1954   £1303 Bodegon con papaya (80x100cm-31x39in) s.d.1994. 25-May-94 Louis Morton, Mexico #98/R (M.P 6500)

MAZZANOVICH, Lawrence (1872-?) American
$900   £476   Spring reflections (38x46cm-15x18in) s.d.1908. 11-Sep-92 Skinner, Bolton #241 a/R

MAZZANOVICH, Lawrence (1872-?) American-cont.
$1100 £710 West Peak, Pinaleno Mountains, Arizona (41x51cm-16x20in) s. panel. 13-Jul-94 Doyle, New York #55
$1900 £1258 Autumn scene (53x64cm-21x25in) s. 23-Sep-93 Mystic Fine Arts, Connecticut #80/R
$7000 £4487 Poplars (81x100cm-32x39in) s. 9-Dec-92 Butterfield & Butterfield, San Francisco #3860/R

McAULIFFE, James J (1848-1921) American
$650 £425 Ships off rocky coast (56x91cm-22x36in) s.d.1890. 18-Sep-93 Young Fine Arts Auctions, Maine #208/R
$2000 £1316 Bay racehorse in landscape (56x69cm-22x27in) s. 4-Jun-93 Sotheby's, New York #2/R
$11000 £7285 Trotters at races (76x101cm-30x40in) s.d.1871. 22-Sep-93 Christie's, New York #78/R

McCAIN, Buck (20th C) American
$2700 £1812 Monument Valley (61x91cm-24x36in) s. board. 2-May-94 Selkirks, St. Louis #111/R

McCALLION, P (19th C) American?
$5000 £2890 One of the stern realities of war (31x40cm-12x16in) s.d.1899. 23-Sep-92 Christie's, New York #77/R

McCARTER, Henry (1866-1947) American
$1100 £738 Hunting dogs (23x30cm-9x12in) s.d.1914 board. 12-Dec-93 Hindman Galleries, Chicago #265/R
$3000 £2041 Pommes (71x81cm-28x32in) 15-Nov-93 Christie's, East, New York #71

McCARTER, Henry Benbridge (1864-1942) American
$2400 £1412 Spring landscape with rolling hills (71x81cm-28x32in) estate st.verso. 8-Oct-92 Freeman Fine Arts, Philadelphia #1090

McCARTER, Henry Benbridge (attrib) (1864-1942) American
$2000 £1361 Bathers , i.stretcher. 14-Apr-94 Freeman Fine Arts, Philadelphia #996/R

McCARTHY, Doris Jean (1910-) Canadian
$713 £466 Bullrushes in snow, Haliburton (29x34cm-11x13in) s. panel. 19-May-93 Sotheby's, Toronto #82/R (C.D 900)
$1189 £777 Little shack up the hill, Haliburton (29x34cm-11x13in) s. panel. 18-May-93 Joyner Fine Art, Toronto #2/R (C.D 1500)
$1401 £928 Daisy time at Barachois on Gaspe (29x34cm-11x13in) s. panel. 24-Nov-92 Joyner Fine Art, Toronto #42/R (C.D 1800)
$1432 £974 Arctic scene (61x76cm-24x30in) s. 15-Nov-93 Hodgins, Calgary #253/R (C.D 1900)
$717 £485 Beach scene, Barachois harbour (29x34cm-11x13in) s. mixed media board. 23-Nov-93 Joyner Fine Art, Toronto #135 (C.D 950)
$831 *£561* *Barachois - Gaspe Co (38x55cm-15x22in) s. W/C. 23-Nov-93 Joyner Fine Art, Toronto #167 (C.D 1100)*
$2135 £1256 Village of Conche, Newfoundland (60x82cm-24x32in) s. painted 1977 W/C. 5-Oct-92 Levis, Calgary #309/R (C.D 2650)
$2179 £1443 Complete Barachois, panoramic view of fishing village, Gaspe (49x59cm-19x23in) s. W/C. 24-Nov-92 Joyner Fine Art, Toronto #5/R (C.D 2800)

McCARTHY, Justin (1892-1977) American
$850 £563 Herman Riederer, Ice Capades (61x38cm-24x15in) s.d.1962-3 masonite. 21-Nov-92 Litchfield Auction Gallery #28
$1450 £960 Cathy Machado Ice Capades (61x36cm-24x14in) s.d.1962 masonite. 21-Nov-92 Litchfield Auction Gallery #27

McCAY, Winsor (1869-1934) American
$3000 *£2013* *Sinking of the Lusitania (18x23cm-7x9in) i. exec.1918 gouache celluloid. 22-Jun-93 Sotheby's, New York #669/R*

McCHESNEY, Robert Pearson (1913-) American
$1000 £671 Young fish (46x30cm-18x12in) s.d.44 W/C gouache. 26-Mar-94 James Bakker, Cambridge #85
$1100 £692 Arena No.64 (63x114cm-25x45in) s.i.verso enamel sand canvas. 25-Apr-93 Butterfield & Butterfield, San Francisco #2147/R

McCLAIN, Helen Charleton (1887-?) Canadian
$2800 £1854 New York street scene (41x31cm-16x12in) s. 22-Sep-93 Christie's, New York #145/R

McCOMAS, Francis (1874-1938) American
$1100 £728 Landscape (46x56cm-18x22in) W/C. 28-Sep-93 John Moran, Pasadena #258
$1261 £852 Hawaii (69x17cm-27x7in) s.d.1898 W/C htd bodycol. 24-Nov-93 Christie's, Victoria #174/R (A.D 1900)
$2250 £1324 Monterey houses (20x24cm-8x9in) s. W/C. 4-Oct-92 Butterfield & Butterfield, Los Angeles #73/R
$2750 £1618 Monterey Bay (17x76cm-7x30in) s.d.98 W/C. 4-Oct-92 Butterfield & Butterfield, Los Angeles #72 a/R
$3000 £2083 Stevenson House, Monterey (46x61cm-18x24in) s. chl. 7-Mar-93 Butterfield & Butterfield, San Francisco #112/R

McCORD, George (1848-1909) American
$650 £425 Fisherfolk on coast (51x91cm-20x36in) s. 4-May-93 Christie's, East, New York #60
$750 £507 Barbizon landscape (51x61cm-20x24in) rem.sig. board. 10-Aug-93 Stonington Fine Arts, Stonington #56

McCORD, George (1848-1909) American-cont.

$800	£462	Seaside village at sunset (30x41cm-12x16in) s. 25-Sep-92 Sotheby's Arcade, New York #167/R
$850	£570	Cows by the river (46x71cm-18x28in) s. 16-Dec-93 Mystic Fine Arts, Connecticut #171/R
$1000	£578	Winter scene (36x51cm-14x20in) s. 24-Sep-92 Mystic Fine Arts, Connecticut #98/R
$1000	£654	Fishing boats, Venice (28x38cm-11x15in) s.i. board on panel. 17-Sep-93 Skinner, Bolton #192/R
$1100	£743	Fisherfolk with sailships on the beach (51x91cm-20x36in) s. 20-Apr-94 Doyle, New York #51
$1200	£811	Venetian twilight (56x69cm-22x27in) s. 31-Mar-94 Sotheby's Arcade, New York #127/R
$1300	£751	Near Nyack on Hudson (30x51cm-12x20in) s. 24-Sep-92 Mystic Fine Arts, Connecticut #183/R
$1300	£867	Angler on a rocky shore (33x48cm-13x19in) s. 1-Jun-94 Doyle, New York #43
$1500	£1007	Fall landscape with ducks swimming in a small pond (41x36cm-16x14in) s. 25-Mar-94 Eldred, Massachusetts #729/R
$2300	£1217	Cows at the edge of the watermeadow, late afternoon (23x36cm-9x14in) s.d.1874. 11-Sep-92 Skinner, Bolton #192/R
$3000	£2098	Watching the regatta near Newburgh, New York (30x23cm-12x9in) s. board. 11-Mar-93 Christie's, New York #34/R
$3200	£2177	Ilfracombe Coast Devon (112x66cm-44x26in) s.d.90. 15-Nov-93 Christie's, East, New York #31/R
$7500	£4967	Sailboats, Gloucester, Massachusetts (81x109cm-32x43in) s. i.verso. 23-Sep-93 Sotheby's, New York #71/R

McCOY, Wilton Guy (1902-1986) American

$10000	£6711	Breaktime (56x71cm-22x28in) s.d.35. 8-Dec-93 Butterfield & Butterfield, San Francisco #3519/R

McCRACKEN, James (20th C) American

$625	£425	History of California (38x76cm-15x30in) s. masonite. 17-Apr-94 Hanzel Galleries, Chicago #7

McDERMOTT and McGOUGH (20th C) American

$1000	£676	Jesus (89x195cm-35x77in) s.d.1918 oil gold leaf linen. 8-Nov-93 Christie's, East, New York #115/R
$3200	£2148	Fear or faith (180x180cm-71x71in) s.d.1921. 23-Feb-94 Christie's, East, New York #209/R
$5000	£3472	Fear or faith (180x180cm-71x71in) s.d.1921 painted 1987. 22-Feb-93 Christie's, East, New York #283/R
$5000	£3472	The red light (219x108cm-86x43in) s.d.1923 sheet metal. 24-Feb-93 Christie's, New York #156/R
$7500	£5208	The newspaper - 1912 (152x152cm-60x60in) s.d.1912 painted 1987. 24-Feb-93 Christie's, New York #153/R

McDOUGAL, Charles Holmes (20th C) Canadian

$861	£574	Haunted house, Glen Allen (60x81cm-24x32in) s. i.d.1956 verso masonite. 30-May-94 Ritchie, Toronto #235/R (C.D 1200)

McDOUGALL, George F (?-1870) Canadian

$977	£660	Disembarking from H.M.S. Resolute with H.M.S. Intrepid across ice (16x28cm-6x11in) s.i. pen W/C over pencil white. 20-Oct-93 Sotheby's, London #10/R

McENTEE, Jervis (1828-1891) American

$1500	£867	Woodland scene (15x23cm-6x9in) mono. 27-Sep-92 James Bakker, Cambridge #149
$1600	£1074	The sawmill (28x38cm-11x15in) s. board. 24-Mar-94 Mystic Fine Arts, Connecticut #105/R
$2000	£1307	Fall landscape with small pond (36x66cm-14x26in) mono. 16-Apr-93 Du Mouchelle, Detroit #2022/R
$2000	£1156	Sunset (21x34cm-8x13in) d.July 26,1870 canvas on board. 23-Sep-92 Christie's, New York #61/R
$3200	£2025	Rocks in woods (18x30cm-7x12in) 2-Dec-92 Christie's, East, New York #24/R
$4000	£2649	Winter landscape (22x37cm-9x15in) 23-Sep-93 Sotheby's, New York #55/R
$5000	£3333	A Mexican village (28x39cm-11x15in) indist.i.d.89. 17-Mar-94 Sotheby's, New York #61/R
$7000	£4667	Autumn landscape (30x51cm-12x20in) d.82. 17-Mar-94 Sotheby's, New York #11/R
$7500	£4747	Journey's pause in Roman campagna (18x30cm-7x12in) mono. 4-Dec-92 Christie's, New York #195/R
$9000	£5696	Little fisher girl (30x35cm-12x14in) mono.d.1875 board. 4-Dec-92 Christie's, New York #201/R
$10000	£6410	Late autumn landscape (91x76cm-36x30in) init.d.1880. 26-May-93 Christie's, New York #54/R
$17000	£9827	Gathering Christmas finery at Roundout, New Jersey (30x50cm-12x20in) mono.d.1877 board. 23-Sep-92 Christie's, New York #65/R

McENTEE, Jervis (attrib) (1828-1891) American

$2400	£1558	Two figures in landscape (23x39cm-9x15in) 9-Sep-93 Sotheby's Arcade, New York #58

McEWEN, Jean (1923-) Canadian

$755	£510	Untitled (30x27cm-12x11in) s.d.verso. 23-Nov-93 Joyner Fine Art, Toronto #183 (C.D 1000)
$870	£580	Les Iles Reunies, no.8 (76x76cm-30x30in) s. i.d.74 verso. 6-Jun-94 Waddingtons, Toronto #1250 (C.D 1200)

McEWEN, Jean (1923-) Canadian-cont.
$5424   £3665   Das Lied von der Erde (152x152cm-60x60in) s.d.72 s.i.d.verso. 3-Nov-93 Sotheby's, Toronto #261/R (C.D 7000)
$11891   £7772   Elegie criblee de bleu (194x204cm-76x80in) s.d.86 stretcher diptych. 19-May-93 Sotheby's, Toronto #262/R (C.D 15000)
$12843   £8505   Les continents fleuris 18 (127x178cm-50x70in) s.i.d.74verso. 18-Nov-92 Sotheby's, Toronto #163/R (C.D 16500)

McEWEN, Walter (1860-1943) American
$900   £604   A friend of the Court (27x23cm-11x9in) s. board. 4-Mar-94 Skinner, Bolton #281/R
$1200   £694   Two girls netting fish in creek (21x36cm-8x14in) s. canvas on board. 25-Sep-92 Sotheby's Arcade, New York #102/R

McGILLIVRAY, Florence Helena (1864-1938) Canadian
$610   £407   Dawn at Perce, Quebec (46x58cm-18x23in) s. 30-May-94 Ritchie, Toronto #174/R (C.D 850)

McGLYNN, Thomas A (1878-1966) American
$2500   £1678   Sycamores (57x62cm-22x24in) s. 8-Dec-93 Butterfield & Butterfield, San Francisco #3489/R
$2500   £1678   Los Padres (63x69cm-25x27in) s. 8-Dec-93 Butterfield & Butterfield, San Francisco #3490/R
$3000   £2027   Sycamores (48x53cm-19x21in) s. 9-Nov-93 John Moran, Pasadena #936 a
$3250   £2181   Lakeside sycamores (61x76cm-24x30in) s. 8-Dec-93 Butterfield & Butterfield, San Francisco #3446/R
$4000   £2778   View of the coast (48x53cm-19x21in) indis.init. 7-Mar-93 Butterfield & Butterfield, San Francisco #95/R
$5000   £3356   Carmel Valley Cottonwoods (71x76cm-28x30in) s. 8-Dec-93 Butterfield & Butterfield, San Francisco #3496/R

McGOUGH and McDERMOTT see McDERMOTT and McGOUGH

McGREW, Ralph Brownell (1916-1994) American
$650   £430   Stream in landscape - high stream (56x46cm-22x18in) s. 14-Jun-94 John Moran, Pasadena #109

McILHENNY, Charles Morgan (1858-c.1908) American
$30000   £17241   Summer afternoon by shore (36x63cm-14x25in) s. 24-Sep-92 Sotheby's, New York #49/R

McKAIN, Bruce (1900-) American
$1000   £699   Fishermen (66x76cm-26x30in) masonite. 7-Feb-93 James Bakker, Cambridge #53/R

McKENNA, Stephen (20th C) American?
$1074   £726   Portrait of Barbara Steinhauer (55x45cm-22x18in) mono. s.i.d.1971/72verso panel. 23-Oct-93 Wolfgang Ketterer, Munich #559/R (DM 1800)

McKIBBEN, Bill (1932-) Canadian?
$754   £513   Foothills west of Calgary (61x122cm-24x48in) s. i.stretcher. 15-Nov-93 Hodgins, Calgary #17 (C.D 1000)

McLAUGHLIN, Charles J (1888-?) American
$1100   £733   Yosemite (76x91cm-30x36in) init.i. 23-May-94 Hindman Galleries, Chicago #205/R

McLAUGHLIN, Isabel (1903-) Canadian
$2646   £1753   Above rooftops (50x47cm-20x19in) 24-Nov-92 Joyner Fine Art, Toronto #145/R (C.D 3400)

McLAUGHLIN, John (1898-1976) American
$9000   £5882   E-1956 (122x91cm-48x36in) s.verso s.d.1956 stretcher. 4-May-93 Sotheby's, New York #363/R
$15000   £10135   No 6 (122x152cm-48x60in) s.i.d.1973verso. 10-Nov-93 Christie's, New York #179/R
$20000   £13514   No.14, 1974 (152x121cm-60x48in) s.i.d.1974 verso acrylic. 11-Nov-93 Sotheby's, New York #283/R
$22000   £14765   No 21 (86x122cm-34x48in) s.d.1960verso. 4-May-94 Christie's, New York #142/R

McLEAN, A M (19th C) American
$950   £625   Still life with apple knife wineglass (25x30cm-10x12in) s.d.1865 oil tin. 13-Jun-93 Hindman Galleries, Chicago #237

McLEAN, Richard (1934-) American
$16000   £9412   Dixie Coast (137x147cm-54x58in) s.d.74 s.d.1974 verso. 6-Oct-92 Sotheby's, New York #107/R
$34795   £22892   IHLE Country (156x156cm-61x61in) s.i.d.1967verso. 3-Jun-93 Christian de Quay, Paris #65/R (F.FR 190000)

McCLEARY, Dan (20th C) American
$750   £507   Geraniums (41x36cm-16x14in) mono.d.88 s.i.d.verso linen. 21-Apr-94 Butterfield & Butterfield, San Francisco #1189/R

McMANUS, James Goodwin (1882-1958) American
$1100   £753   Autumn scene - New England (51x61cm-20x24in) s.d.1924. 10-Feb-94 Skinner, Bolton #60

McNAIR, William (1867-?) American
$2200	£1287	California landscape (76x102cm-30x40in) s.d.1932. 18-Sep-92 Du Mouchelle, Detroit #2025/R

McNEIL, George (1908-) American
$5500	£3595	Palentown abstractscape (142x172cm-56x68in) s.d.84 s.d.1984 verso acrylic. 7-May-93 Christie's, East, New York #99/R
$4200	*£2838*	*They like to dance (173x142cm-68x56in) s.i.d.83 oil acrylic resin sand string canvas. 8-Nov-93 Christie's, East, New York #165/R*

MEAD, Ray John (20th C) Canadian
$789	£526	Gay child (51x40cm-20x16in) s.d.51 board. 30-May-94 Ritchie, Toronto #237/R (C.D 1100)
$1435	£957	Scented garden (130x170cm-51x67in) s.i.d.87 verso acrylic. 30-May-94 Ritchie, Toronto #216/R (C.D 2000)
$538	*£359*	*Black composition (75x55cm-30x22in) s.d.55 W/C ink. 30-May-94 Ritchie, Toronto #311 (C.D 750)*
$1077	*£718*	*Fantasy landscape (55x75cm-22x30in) s.d.52 W/C pen. 30-May-94 Ritchie, Toronto #238/R (C.D 1500)*

MEAKIN, Lewis Henry (1853-1917) American
$1800	£1184	Mountainous landscape (53x84cm-21x33in) s. 31-Mar-93 Sotheby's Arcade, New York #155/R
$2300	£1523	Coastal view, Gloucester (53x84cm-21x33in) s. 23-Sep-93 Mystic Fine Arts, Connecticut #248/R

MEASELLE, Clarence (20th C) American
$550	£367	Self portrait in head lamp (102x122cm-40x48in) s. 13-Mar-94 Hindman Galleries, Chicago #868
$600	£400	Made in the U.S.A. (91x122cm-36x48in) s. 13-Mar-94 Hindman Galleries, Chicago #867

MEDINA, Domingo Martin (1959-) Mexican
$1119	*£756*	*Forma enamorada (110x92cm-43x36in) s.d.1993 mixed media. 20-Oct-93 Louis Morton, Mexico #28/R (M.P 3500)*

MEEKER, Joseph R (1827-1889) American
$600	£403	Bayou at sunset (18x28cm-7x11in) s. 2-May-94 Selkirks, St. Louis #85
$2400	£1589	Southern swamp (40x25cm-16x10in) s. 22-Sep-93 Christie's, New York #45/R
$2800	£1905	Approaching storm (51x76cm-20x30in) s.d.1878. 15-Nov-93 Christie's, East, New York #55
$3800	£2550	Landscape with figure (30x51cm-12x20in) s.d.1881 masonite. 5-Mar-94 Louisiana Auction Exchange #77/R
$4000	£2649	Mississippi cypress swamp (37x46cm-15x18in) s.d.1872 canvas on board. 22-Sep-93 Christie's, New York #44/R
$10500	£7000	In the bayou (36x46cm-14x18in) s. 16-Mar-94 Christie's, New York #45/R
$18000	£11392	The Bayou at Lake Maurepas, Louisiana (35x61cm-14x24in) s.d.1887 i.verso. 3-Dec-92 Sotheby's, New York #14/R

MEEKS, Eugene (1843-?) American
$1200	£805	Italian woman at the well (61x51cm-24x20in) s.i.d.1877. 3-Feb-94 Sloan, North Bethesda #2766/R

MEGARGEE, Edwin (20th C) American
$1500	£1064	Labrador retriever (25x33cm-10x13in) s. board. 13-Feb-93 Collins, Maine #129/R

MEGARGEE, Lon (1883-1960) American
$1400	£940	Indian chief (66x51cm-26x20in) s. board. 24-Mar-94 Mystic Fine Arts, Connecticut #150

MEHRING, Howard (1931-1978) American
$1400	£897	Untitled (114x94cm-45x37in) s.d.1961verso acrylic. 10-Dec-92 Sloan, North Bethesda #2678
$1700	£1090	Continence (147x137cm-58x54in) s.i.d.1963verso acrylic. 10-Dec-92 Sloan, North Bethesda #2679

MELCHER, George Henry (1881-1975) American
$6000	£3947	Point Dume from Malibu Hills (63x76cm-25x30in) s. 13-Jun-93 Butterfield & Butterfield, San Francisco #836/R

MELCHERS, Gari (1860-1932) American
$1700	£1141	Harbour scene (15x20cm-6x8in) s. panel. 16-Dec-93 Mystic Fine Arts, Connecticut #142/R
$15000	£9804	Portrait of gentleman seated (36x25cm-14x10in) s.d.84 canvas on board. 17-Sep-93 Du Mouchelle, Detroit #2013/R
$16000	£11189	Early morning, North River (46x56cm-18x22in) s. painted c.1907 i.verso. 10-Mar-93 Sotheby's, New York #124/R
$16000	£9249	After the ball (29x20cm-11x8in) s.d.84 panel. 24-Sep-92 Sotheby's, New York #97/R
$22000	£14103	Offertory - interior of church (58x74cm-23x29in) s. painted c.1930. 27-May-93 Sotheby's, New York #44/R
$24000	£15385	Girl knitting (46x37cm-18x15in) s. painted c.1900. 27-May-93 Sotheby's, New York #52/R
$45000	£30201	Rainbow (69x76cm-27x30in) s. painted c.1925. 2-Dec-93 Sotheby's, New York #107/R
$72500	£46474	Child with orange (101x76cm-40x30in) s.d.1918. 27-May-93 Sotheby's, New York #38/R

MELCHERS, Gari (1860-1932) American-cont.
$15000 £9615 Madonna of the fields (77x69cm-30x27in) s. gouache pencil canvas painted c.1895-1900. 26-May-93 Christie's, New York #81/R

MELLEN, Mary (1817-?) American
$2600 £1757 Moonlit seascape (30x46cm-12x18in) 31-Mar-94 Sotheby's Arcade, New York #18/R
$4000 £2312 House portrait (56x69cm-22x27in) painted 1855-1860. 24-Sep-92 Sotheby's, New York #35/R

MELROSE, Andrew (1836-1901) American
$800 £544 Family picnic (30x23cm-12x9in) s. board. 16-Apr-94 Young Fine Arts Auctions, Maine #168/R
$850 £574 A Scottish landscape (16x20cm-6x8in) s. s.i.verso panel. 5-Nov-93 Skinner, Bolton #28/R
$1300 £855 Tyrolean landscape (56x69cm-22x27in) s.d.87. 31-Mar-93 Sotheby's Arcade, New York #49/R
$3000 £1987 Summer morning, Loon Lake (51x41cm-20x16in) s. i.stretcher arched top. 2-Oct-93 Weschler, Washington #94/R
$3200 £1850 The narrows (16x31cm-6x12in) s. panel. 23-Sep-92 Christie's, New York #59/R
$4340 £2800 In the Wind River Mountains, Colorado (61x107cm-24x42in) s. i.verso. 15-Jul-94 Christie's, London #57/R
$10000 £6329 View of Jerusalem (46x81cm-18x32in) s. 20-Oct-92 Sotheby's, Tel Aviv #2/R
$12000 £8054 View of New York from Castle Point, Hoboken (64x117cm-25x46in) s. painted c.1870. 3-Dec-93 Christie's, New York #104/R
$16000 £10738 March of Civilization, St. Louis, Missouri (77x122cm-30x48in) s. i.verso. 3-Dec-93 Christie's, New York #98/R
$16000 £10458 View of Temple Mount, Jerusalem (76x122cm-30x48in) s. 14-Apr-93 Sotheby's, Tel Aviv #2/R
$22500 £14423 Life on the river (76x127cm-30x50in) s. 9-Dec-92 Butterfield & Butterfield, San Francisco #3824/R

MELTSNER, Paul R (1905-1966) American
$800 £530 Woman and child with cat (51x61cm-20x24in) s. 14-Jun-94 John Moran, Pasadena #40 b
$9500 £6419 American landscape (71x56cm-28x22in) s. s.i.verso. 5-Nov-93 Skinner, Bolton #170/R

MELTZER, Anna Elkan (20th C) American
$800 £537 Reflection (76x66cm-30x26in) s.d.40. 5-Dec-93 James Bakker, Cambridge #74/R

MELTZER, Arthur (1893-?) American
$1900 £1195 Verbenas and bit o blue (33x36cm-13x14in) s.d.29 i.verso i.stretcher. 22-Apr-93 Freeman Fine Arts, Philadelphia #1183/R

MENDENHALL, Jack (1937-) American
$1000 £694 Store window dining set (145x213cm-57x84in) 22-Feb-93 Christie's, East, New York #169/R

MENDEZ MAGARINOS, Melchor (1885-1945) South American
$700 £461 Lenadores (48x29cm-19x11in) 31-May-93 Gomensoro, Montevideo #27/R
$1550 £1006 Las tres gracias (83x73cm-33x29in) s.d.1926 oil. 30-Aug-93 Gomensoro, Montevideo #49/R

MENDILAHARZU (19th C) Argentinian
$3250 £2273 Ladies at seaside (38x25cm-15x10in) s. 5-Feb-93 Sloan, North Bethesda #2211/R

MENDILAHARZU, G (19th C) Argentinian
$4000 £2564 Feather duster shop (41x33cm-16x13in) s. 26-May-93 Sotheby's, New York #188/R

MENDOZA, Ariel (20th C) Mexican
$2557 £1728 Los mezcales (79x118cm-31x46in) 20-Oct-93 Louis Morton, Mexico #131/R (M.P 8000)

MENGHI, Jose Luis (1869-?) Argentinian
$1100 £573 Naturaleza muerta (72x105cm-28x41in) 4-Aug-92 VerBo, Buenos Aires #72

MEREDITH, John (1933-) Canadian
$874 £583 Pastorale (122x152cm-48x60in) s. d.May-July 1974verso. 11-May-94 Sotheby's, Toronto #103/R (C.D 1200)
$1005 £670 Sprite IV (22x25cm-9x10in) s.d.62. 30-May-94 Ritchie, Toronto #225/R (C.D 1400)
$2913 £1942 The legend (56x86cm-22x34in) s.d.59. 13-May-94 Joyner Fine Art, Toronto #96/R (C.D 4000)
$3641 £2427 The Bridge no.4 (92x85cm-36x33in) s.d.57. 11-May-94 Sotheby's, Toronto #126/R (C.D 5000)
$4262 £2880 September 57 (163x80cm-64x31in) s.d.57 i.verso. 3-Nov-93 Sotheby's, Toronto #250/R (C.D 5500)
$4262 £2880 Swamp mist (71x91cm-28x36in) s.d.55 board. 3-Nov-93 Sotheby's, Toronto #366/R (C.D 5500)
$4360 £2850 Dragon city (91x61cm-36x24in) s.d.55 s.verso board. 19-May-93 Sotheby's, Toronto #199/R (C.D 5500)
$435 £290 Untitled (20x27cm-8x11in) s.d.75 col.ink. 6-Jun-94 Waddingtons, Toronto #1246 (C.D 600)
$1168 £773 Untitled (50x65cm-20x26in) s.d.88 i.verso col.pencils ink. 18-Nov-92 Sotheby's, Toronto #187/R (C.D 1500)
$1189 £777 Composition in red, yellow, blue and purple (36x43cm-14x17in) s.d.92 col.ink. 19-May-93 Sotheby's, Toronto #237/R (C.D 1500)

MEREDITH, John (1933-) Canadian-cont.
$1635	£1082	Untitled (43x35cm-17x14in) s.d.67 i.verso col.inks. 18-Nov-92 Sotheby's, Toronto #190/R (C.D 2100)

MERIDA, Carlos (1891-1984) Guatemalan
$4000	£2649	Oro Y Rojo (51x37cm-20x15in) s.d.1963 tempera paper. 23-Nov-92 Sotheby's, New York #221/R
$8500	£5629	Composicion Geometrica (41x31cm-16x12in) s.d.1961 tempera board. 23-Nov-92 Sotheby's, New York #220/R
$9018	£6012	Dia eterno (60x40cm-24x16in) s. petroplastico sobre amate. 25-May-94 Louis Morton, Mexico #84 a (M.P 30000)
$11000	£7432	Composition (38x28cm-15x11in) s.d.1977 panel. 29-Oct-93 Hart Gallery, Houston #8
$15000	£10000	Dos danzantes (49x30cm-19x12in) s.d.1953 amate paper. 18-May-94 Sotheby's, New York #373/R
$19000	£12667	Abstraccion (58x38cm-23x15in) s.d.1977 board. 18-May-94 Christie's, New York #263/R
$19000	£12418	Los tres reyes magos (50x62cm-20x24in) s.d.1975 amate paper on masonite. 18-May-93 Sotheby's, New York #185/R
$22000	£14570	Untitled (61x45cm-24x18in) s.d.1966 masonite. 23-Nov-92 Sotheby's, New York #223/R
$27500	£18212	Adriana Y El Laberinto (52x61cm-20x24in) s.d.1975 amate paper on masonite. 23-Nov-92 Sotheby's, New York #213/R
$35000	£23333	Las Suplicantes (78x56cm-31x22in) s.d.1969 oil gesso paper. 18-May-94 Christie's, New York #138/R
$40000	£26144	Tohil (61x49cm-24x19in) s.d.1971 masonite. 17-May-93 Christie's, New York #138/R
$40000	£27027	La tentacion (49x65cm-19x26in) s.d.1940. 23-Nov-93 Christie's, New York #30/R
$3500	£2288	Danza de los fecornates (27x37cm-11x15in) s. i.verso gouache. 17-May-93 Christie's, New York #272/R
$5500	£3716	Untitled (48x30cm-19x12in) s.i.d.1934 graphite W/C. 22-Nov-93 Sotheby's, New York #207/R
$6000	£3922	Costa Verde - a la tercera es la Vencida (38x28cm-15x11in) s.i.d.1944 gouache pencil. 17-May-93 Christie's, New York #224/R
$6500	£4392	Los Hermanos y la flauta (65x50cm-26x20in) s.d.1974 pen W/C. 23-Nov-93 Christie's, New York #247/R
$7000	£4575	Enchanted landscape (38x28cm-15x11in) s.i. gouache painted 1944. 17-May-93 Christie's, New York #223/R
$7000	£4730	Proyecto para un mural en mosaico (27x40cm-11x16in) s.i.d.1960 pencil crayon. 23-Nov-93 Christie's, New York #246/R
$7004	£4490	Boceto (20x14cm-8x6in) s. mixed media. 29-Apr-93 Louis Morton, Mexico #79 (M.P 22000)
$7500	£5068	Mayan abstraction (47x35cm-19x14in) s.d.1943 collage W/C gouache graphite. 22-Nov-93 Sotheby's, New York #231/R
$7750	£4874	Untitled (51x38cm-20x15in) s.d.1966 mixed media composition board. 23-Apr-93 Hart Gallery, Houston #12
$8000	£5229	Construccion en rojo (38x27cm-15x11in) s.d.1968 acrylic sand ink board on masonite. 18-May-93 Sotheby's, New York #184/R
$8500	£5667	Vukub Kame (46x34cm-18x13in) s.d.1961 s.i.d.verso politec amate paper. 18-May-94 Sotheby's, New York #344/R
$9000	£6081	Antigua pastoral (49x37cm-19x15in) s.d.1948 tempera Indian ink. 22-Nov-93 Sotheby's, New York #209/R
$12000	£7827	La Consagracion de la Primavera (29x35cm-11x14in) s.i.d.1953 pencil crayon. 17-May-93 Christie's, New York #225/R
$13000	£8667	El Poema del Tropico II, El Agua (28x38cm-11x15in) s.i.d.24 W/C. 18-May-94 Christie's, New York #211/R
$19000	£12667	Recuerdos del Viejo Oriente (56x81cm-22x32in) s.d.1964 s.i.d.verso gouache pen black ink. 18-May-94 Christie's, New York #160/R
$20000	£13245	Cinco Ideas (26x32cm-10x13in) s.d.1939 tempera ink linen. 23-Nov-92 Sotheby's, New York #212/R
$40000	£26490	El Hombre y Su Morada (56x38cm-22x15in) s.d.1961 politec linen. 24-Nov-92 Christie's, New York #113/R
$55000	£35948	Alba en la esquila (57x70cm-22x28in) s.d.1965 s.i.d.verso politec masonite. 17-May-93 Christie's, New York #38/R

MERISE, Fritz (1946-) Haitian
$797	£521	Jungle (51x61cm-20x24in) 17-May-93 Hoebanx, Paris #144 (F.FR 4400)
$815	£533	Jungle, tigre et lion (40x51cm-16x20in) 17-May-93 Hoebanx, Paris #145 (F.FR 4500)

MERLINO, Silvio (1952-) American
$7000	£4861	Vulcano che dorme (123x185cm-48x73in) i.d.1985verso acrylic sand col.chk pap.on canvas. 24-Feb-93 Christie's, New York #165/R

MERRIAM, James Arthur (1880-1951) American
$650	£448	Early morning on the Colorado Desert (76x102cm-30x40in) s. 16-Feb-93 John Moran, Pasadena #90 a
$700	£461	Palm Springs (76x102cm-30x40in) s. 13-Jun-93 Butterfield & Butterfield, San Francisco #937/R

MERSFELDER, Jules (1865-1937) American
$1000	£658	Grazing cattle in clearing (52x76cm-20x30in) s. 13-Jun-93 Butterfield & Butterfield, San Francisco #737/R

MESSER, Edmund Clarence (1842-?) American
$1800	£1200	January landscape (76x97cm-30x38in) s.d.11. 1-Jun-94 Doyle, New York #46

MESTROVIC, Ivan (1883-1962) American/Yugoslavian
$800	£506	Study of male nude (88x46cm-35x18in) s.d.1942 red black conte. 25-Oct-92 Butterfield & Butterfield, San Francisco #2265/R

METCALF, Conger (20th C) American
$800	£537	Three boys (48x38cm-19x15in) s. W/C pencil. 6-Dec-93 Grogan, Massachussetts #560
$850	£521	The little artist (58x43cm-23x17in) s. conte crayon. 16-Oct-92 Skinner, Bolton #370/R
$1400	£940	Seated lady (69x53cm-27x21in) s. s.i.d.1960 verso mixed media masonite. 6-Dec-93 Grogan, Massachussetts #559/R

METCALF, Willard Leroy (1858-1925) American
$6500	£4545	Landscape (38x46cm-15x18in) s.d.1884 canvas on canvas. 11-Mar-93 Christie's, New York #139/R
$11000	£7432	Landscape at twilight (53x64cm-21x25in) s.d.1906. 31-Oct-93 Hindman Galleries, Chicago #685/R
$11000	£7333	Tea on the porch (46x56cm-18x22in) d.1890 stretcher. 17-Mar-94 Sotheby's, New York #105/R
$14000	£9396	Spring study at Belmont (44x36cm-17x14in) s.i.d.80verso. 6-May-94 Skinner, Bolton #81/R
$21000	£13462	Breton girl (36x28cm-14x11in) s.d.1884 cradled panel. 27-May-93 Sotheby's, New York #15/R
$115000	£72785	The lily pond (30x38cm-12x15in) s.d.87. 3-Dec-92 Sotheby's, New York #99/R
$300000	£189873	East Boothbay Harbour (66x74cm-26x29in) s.d.04. 4-Dec-92 Christie's, New York #3/R
$1000	£578	Dance masks and trophies (24x35cm-9x14in) s.i. pen. 25-Sep-92 Sotheby's Arcade, New York #124/R

METCALF, Willard Leroy (attrib) (1858-1925) American
$1200	£833	Sailboats in inlet (51x41cm-20x16in) indis.s. 27-Feb-93 Young Fine Arts Auctions, Maine #211/R
$700	£443	In the harbour, Tunis c.1895 (30x23cm-12x9in) s. W/C. 30-Nov-92 Schrager Galleries, Milwaukee #465

METEYARD, Thomas B (1865-1928) American
$842	£550	River landscape (13x19cm-5x7in) board. 14-Sep-93 Sotheby's, London #336/R
$1769	£1195	Les brisants, surf at Scitutate, Massachusetts (55x38cm-22x15in) 20-Mar-93 Kunstgalerij de Vuyst, Lokeren #390/R (B.FR 60000)

METHFESSEL, Adolf (1836-1909) Argentinian
$6000	£3974	Los Chorros de Las Escabas en la Provincia de Tucuman (28x38cm-11x15in) s. board. 23-Nov-92 Sotheby's, New York #138/R

METRO GOLDWYN MAYER STUDIOS (20th C) American
$608	£400	Deputy Droopy, Droopy Dog and Cowboy (23x28cm-9x11in) gouache on celluloid on background. 5-Apr-93 Christie's, S. Kensington #175 a
$912	£600	Feedin' the Kiddie, Tom, Jerry and Kiddie Mouse (20x28cm-8x11in) d.1957 gouache on full celluloid. 5-Apr-93 Christie's, S. Kensington #174 a/R
$1368	£900	Pup on Picnic, Spike, Tyke, Tom and Jerry (23x30cm-9x12in) d.1955 gouache on multi-cel set-up on W/C. 5-Apr-93 Christie's, S. Kensington #174/R
$2736	£1800	Fit to be tied, Spike walks Tom on lead as Jerry rings bell (23x28cm-9x11in) d.1950 gouache on multi-cel set up on W/C. 5-Apr-93 Christie's, S. Kensington #173/R

METZGER, Henry (1876-1934) Canadian
$897	£598	Chief Pasqua (51x40cm-20x16in) s.i. 30-May-94 Ritchie, Toronto #124/R (C.D 1250)

MEURER, Charles A (1865-1955) American
$4000	£2667	Comrades (61x45cm-24x18in) init.d.1908. 16-Mar-94 Christie's, New York #38/R
$5000	£3165	Sheep in snowy landscape (39x51cm-15x20in) s. 4-Dec-92 Christie's, New York #9/R
$11000	£7190	Trompe l'oeil painting with letters, money and newspaper clipping (30x41cm-12x16in) s.d.1898. 17-Sep-93 Skinner, Bolton #178/R
$37000	£23418	My passport (95x75cm-37x30in) s.d.1892. 4-Dec-92 Christie's, New York #208/R

MEXIAC, Adolfo (1927-) Mexican
$3801	£2500	Encrucijada (100x80cm-39x31in) s.d.1989 resin canvas. 4-Nov-92 Mora, Castelltort & Quintana, Juarez #57/R (M.P 12000000)

MEXICAN COLONIAL SCHOOL, 18th C
$5722	£3740	Inmaculada Concepcion (163x122cm-64x48in) 28-Jul-94 Fernando Duran, Madrid #768/R (S.P 750000)

MEXICAN SCHOOL
$6797	£4593	Alegorico (100x240cm-39x94in) 9-Nov-93 Louis Morton, Mexico #105 (M.P 22000)
$14155	£9500	The Immaculate Conception (189x129cm-74x51in) painted c.1700. 10-Dec-93 Christie's, London #318/R
$35000	£23333	Retrato del Capitan Pedro Marcos Gutierrez y su familia (141x187cm-56x74in) i.d.1814. 17-May-94 Sotheby's, New York #7/R
$160000	£108108	Paseo de la Viga con la Iglesia de Ixtacalco (143x171cm-56x67in) painted between 1685-1720. 22-Nov-93 Sotheby's, New York #5/R

MEXICAN SCHOOL, 16th C
$3030	£2020	El Descendimiento de la Cruz (174x168cm-69x66in) oil tempera. 10-Mar-94 Louis Morton, Mexico #32/R (M.P 10000)

MEXICAN SCHOOL, 17th C

$80000	£54054	La Virgen de Guadalupe (68x49cm-27x19in) oil mother of pearl panel. 23-Nov-93 Christie's, New York #18/R
$19102	*£12245*	*El nacimiento de la Virgen Maria (45x67cm-18x26in) lacquer tempera col panel. 29-Apr-93 Louis Morton, Mexico #115 (M.P 60000)*
$22286	*£14286*	*Presentacion de la Virgen Maria al templo (43x65cm-17x26in) lacquer tempera col panel. 29-Apr-93 Louis Morton, Mexico #84 (M.P 70000)*

MEXICAN SCHOOL, 18th C

$3000	£2000	Virgen de Guadalupe (22x29cm-9x11in) copper. 18-May-94 Sotheby's, New York #148/R
$3500	£2318	Nuestra Senora de Los Dolores de la Capia de Cantuna (28x20cm-11x8in) oil gold paint ink panel. 23-Nov-92 Sotheby's, New York #109/R
$3820	£2449	Crucifixion (59x37cm-23x15in) 29-Apr-93 Louis Morton, Mexico #64 (M.P 12000)
$4500	£2941	Friar Antonius Bremond (48x65cm-19x26in) s. painted c.1759. 18-May-93 Sotheby's, New York #94/R
$4500	£2980	Cristo de la Columna (73x63cm-29x25in) canvas on panel. 23-Nov-92 Sotheby's, New York #124/R
$5500	£3595	La Sagrada Trinidad - escudo de monja (26cm-10in circular) copper. 18-May-93 Sotheby's, New York #97/R
$6500	£4392	Escudo de Monja-La Inmaculada (18cm-7in circular) copper. 22-Nov-93 Sotheby's, New York #133/R
$7690	£5161	Virgen de Guadalupe (165x101cm-65x40in) 8-Dec-93 Louis Morton, Mexico #38/R (M.P 24000)
$12000	£8000	Real de minas del salto en Guanaxuato de Nueba Espana (63x84cm-25x33in) i. 18-May-94 Sotheby's, New York #170/R
$12000	£7843	Immaculada (60x42cm-24x17in) copper. 18-May-93 Sotheby's, New York #93/R
$13000	£8667	Santiago Matamoros (105x87cm-41x34in) 18-May-94 Sotheby's, New York #169/R
$16000	£10667	Genesis (46x84cm-18x33in) 18-May-94 Sotheby's, New York #149/R
$16000	£10596	Archangel St. Michael (164x104cm-65x41in) 24-Nov-92 Christie's, New York #64/R
$20000	£13245	Virgen de Guadalupe (139x99cm-55x39in) d.1758. 23-Nov-92 Sotheby's, New York #20/R
$25000	£16667	Virgen de Guadalupe (124x82cm-49x32in) panel. 18-May-94 Sotheby's, New York #152/R
$28000	£18543	Virgen de Guadalupe Y Sus Apariciones (67x49cm-26x19in) copper. 23-Nov-92 Sotheby's, New York #106/R
$37500	£25000	Virgen de Guadalupe (209x137cm-82x54in) 18-May-94 Sotheby's, New York #163/R
$60000	£39735	La Annunciacion (45x66cm-18x26in) oil mother of pearl panel. 23-Nov-92 Sotheby's, New York #22/R
$70000	£47297	Virgen de Guadalupe (32x24cm-13x9in) oil mother of pearl panel. 22-Nov-93 Sotheby's, New York #4/R
$75000	£49020	Castas (67x56cm-26x22in) i. 17-May-93 Christie's, New York #66/R
$100000	£66667	Seis castas Mexicanas (42x56cm-17x22in) copper set of six painted c.1750. 17-May-94 Sotheby's, New York #5/R

MEXICAN SCHOOL, 18th/19th C

$26000	£16993	Virgen de Guadalupe (160x101cm-63x40in) canvas on masonite painted c.1790-1820. 18-May-93 Sotheby's, New York #80/R
$47500	£31046	Virgen de Guadalupe Con Nopales (118x83cm-46x33in) painted c.1790-1820. 18-May-93 Sotheby's, New York #1/R
$50000	£33113	Cuatro Bodegones (63x50cm-25x20in) four. 23-Nov-92 Sotheby's, New York #145/R

MEXICAN SCHOOL, 19th C

$2673	£1782	Madera con nino (36x26cm-14x10in) laminated sheet. 8-Jun-94 Louis Morton, Mexico #83 (M.P 9000)
$3250	£2124	Retrato del General Agustin Iturbide (105x83cm-41x33in) painted c.1825. 18-May-93 Sotheby's, New York #100/R
$3250	£2167	Retrato de Antonio Gonzalez de Vergara (25x20cm-10x8in) i.d.1829. 9-Jun-94 Sotheby's Arcade, New York #119/R
$3500	£2333	Bodegon con paisaje (66x85cm-26x33in) indist.s. 18-May-94 Sotheby's, New York #191/R
$3750	£2451	Bodegon (36x51cm-14x20in) panel painted c.1880. 18-May-93 Sotheby's, New York #131/R
$4000	£2667	Plaza con iglesia (37x55cm-15x22in) 18-May-94 Sotheby's, New York #175/R
$4000	£2667	Arreglando la Carreta (95x100cm-37x39in) 18-May-94 Sotheby's, New York #180/R
$5455	£3636	Vista de un Convento (50x87cm-20x34in) 10-Mar-94 Louis Morton, Mexico #25/R (M.P 18000)
$6000	£4054	Paisaje de Oaxaca (37x47cm-15x19in) 22-Nov-93 Sotheby's, New York #160/R
$6500	£4333	Plaza de Santo Domingo (41x51cm-16x20in) 18-May-94 Sotheby's, New York #174/R
$7000	£4667	La Villa de Guadalupe (41x52cm-16x20in) 18-May-94 Sotheby's, New York #186/R
$8000	£5333	Valle de Mexico (47x61cm-19x24in) 18-May-94 Sotheby's, New York #197/R
$10327	£6536	Girl with flowers (66x48cm-26x19in) 30-Nov-92 Rasmussen, Stockholm #84 a/R (S.KR 70000)
$13572	£8590	Girl with bird and flowers (60x40cm-24x16in) 30-Nov-92 Rasmussen, Stockholm #84 b/R (S.KR 92000)
$18000	£12000	Virgen de Guadalupe (56x38cm-22x15in) oil glass. 18-May-94 Sotheby's, New York #185/R
$20000	£13333	El descubrimiento del Pulque (183x323cm-72x127in) painted c.1860. 18-May-94 Sotheby's, New York #177/R
$20000	£13514	Virgen de Guadalupe (42x32cm-17x13in) copper. 22-Nov-93 Sotheby's, New York #137/R
$25000	£16892	Actopan, Hidalgo, Mexico (97x149cm-38x59in) 22-Nov-93 Sotheby's, New York #173/R
$37500	£25000	Bodegon poblano (80x101cm-31x40in) 18-May-94 Sotheby's, New York #194/R

MEXICAN SCHOOL, 20th C
$3250	£2153	Fiesta en el Mercado (103x159cm-41x63in) egg tempera masonite painted c.1935-40. 30-Jun-93 Sotheby's Arcade, New York #234/R
$4000	£2614	China poblana (109x71cm-43x28in) painted c.1925. 18-May-93 Sotheby's, New York #129/R

MEYEROWITZ, William (1889-1981) American
$850	£559	Quintet (43x86cm-17x34in) s. 31-Mar-93 Sotheby's Arcade, New York #365/R
$1200	£805	The musicale (74x61cm-29x24in) s. 12-Dec-93 Hindman Galleries, Chicago #273
$1200	£694	Red buildings, Rocky Neck (51x61cm-20x24in) s. board. 25-Sep-92 Sotheby's Arcade, New York #341/R
$1210	£776	Still life by a window (69x91cm-27x36in) s. 17-Dec-92 Mystic Fine Arts, Connecticut #95/R
$1500	£794	West End, Gloucester (51x61cm-20x24in) s. 12-Sep-92 Louisiana Auction Exchange #42/R

MEYERS, Ralph (1885-1948) American
$600	£400	January Day, Taos, New Mexico (28x38cm-11x15in) s.i. i.stretcher. 23-May-94 Hindman Galleries, Chicago #224

MEZA, Guillermo (1917-) Mexican
$5000	£3356	El Muro (83x86cm-33x34in) s.i.d.1984 i.d.verso. 7-Jan-94 Gary Nader, Miami #98/R
$8000	£5405	Eva y la serpiente (100x81cm-39x32in) mono.s.d.1984 s.i.d.verso. 23-Nov-93 Christie's, New York #287/R
$2400	*£1600*	*Retrato de mujer (71x58cm-28x23in) s.d.1960 gouache. 18-May-94 Christie's, New York #220/R*

MGM STUDIO (20th C) American
$1300	*£872*	*Jerry and Jumbo, Tom, Jerry and Jumbo (21x27cm-8x11in) i. gouache celluloid on background. 22-Jun-93 Sotheby's, New York #705/R*

MICHAELS, Glen (1927-) American
$2500	*£1689*	*Untitled assemblage on two panels (185x46cm-73x18in) mixed media. 4-Nov-93 Boos Gallery, Michigan #81/R*

MICHEL, Alfonso (1897-1957) Mexican
$35000	£23179	La Copa (49x44cm-19x17in) s. painted c.1953. 24-Nov-92 Christie's, New York #135/R

MICHEL, Simeon (1953-) Haitian
$838	£537	Le parasol rouge (61x76cm-24x30in) s. 14-Dec-92 Hoebanx, Paris #156 (F.FR 4500)

MIDDLETON, Sam (1927-) American
$4522	£2899	Untitled (114x53cm-45x21in) s.d.62 oil sand board. 9-Dec-92 Sotheby's, Amsterdam #291/R (D.FL 8000)
$729	£468	June bug (32x24cm-13x9in) s.d.61 s.i.d.verso gouache collage board. 27-May-93 Sotheby's, Amsterdam #127 (D.FL 1300)
$1010	£647	Untitled (63x44cm-25x17in) s.d.62 gouache ink collage. 27-May-93 Sotheby's, Amsterdam #142/R (D.FL 1800)
$1130	£725	Music dust (51x77cm-20x30in) s.d.83 collage mixed media. 10-Dec-92 Christie's, Amsterdam #159 (D.FL 2000)
$1347	£863	Untitled (44x62cm-17x24in) s.d.62 gouache ink collage. 27-May-93 Sotheby's, Amsterdam #152/R (D.FL 2400)
$1635	£1083	Abstract composition (50x37cm-20x15in) s.d.62 gouache collage. 14-Jun-94 Christie's, Amsterdam #389/R (D.FL 3000)
$1683	£1079	Impressions from Holland (103x73cm-41x29in) s.74 collage mixed media. 26-May-93 Christie's, Amsterdam #253 (D.FL 3000)
$2826	*£1812*	*Corporate entity (135x74cm-53x29in) s.d.67 s.d.1967 verso gouache collage board. 9-Dec-92 Sotheby's, Amsterdam #288/R (D.FL 5000)*

MIGNOT, Louis Remy (1831-1870) American
$1800	£1200	City harbour at dusk (11x14cm-4x6in) s. panel. 23-May-94 Christie's, East, New York #78/R
$2850	£1900	Landscape with farmhouse by river (42x61cm-17x24in) s. 15-Mar-94 Phillips, London #84/R
$4250	£2724	Sunset on mountainous landscape (81x107cm-32x42in) s. 9-Dec-92 Butterfield & Butterfield, San Francisco #3810/R
$4500	£2961	Mount Cayambe, Ecuador (61x91cm-24x36in) 13-Jun-93 Butterfield & Butterfield, San Francisco #3134/R
$5500	£3481	Day's departure (29x51cm-11x20in) s.d.60. 2-Dec-92 Christie's, East, New York #23/R
$22000	£14765	Karhuikazo (26x41cm-10x16in) s.d.60. 8-Dec-93 Butterfield & Butterfield, San Francisco #3318/R

MIJARES, Jose M (1921-) Cuban
$2250	£1490	Verticalidad (51x67cm-20x26in) s.d.1953 paper on canvas. 23-Nov-92 Sotheby's, New York #200/R
$3250	£2152	Mujer en el balcon (62x46cm-24x18in) s.d.1948. 23-Nov-92 Sotheby's, New York #161/R
$3750	£2500	Payaso (41x29cm-16x11in) s.d.1950. 18-May-94 Sotheby's, New York #232/R
$5000	£3333	En el bar (72x56cm-28x22in) s.d.1954. 18-May-94 Christie's, New York #293/R
$9000	£5960	Barcas (63x86cm-25x34in) s. linen. 24-Nov-92 Christie's, New York #294/R
$13000	£8609	Arlequins (84x112cm-33x44in) s. 24-Nov-92 Christie's, New York #89/R
$3200	*£2133*	*Untitled (74x54cm-29x21in) s. s.i.verso W/C. 18-May-94 Christie's, New York #286/R*

MILARSKY, A (20th C) American
$5000   £3356   Harbour in summertime (71x61cm-28x24in) s.d.81 masonite. 6-Dec-93 Grogan, Massachussetts #514

MILDER, Jay (20th C) American
$1000   £676   Subway man (121x122cm-48x48in) s.d.63 s.i.d.verso. 21-Apr-94 Butterfield & Butterfield, San Francisco #1133/R

MILES, Donald E (1921-) American
$700   £464   Coastal - Pt Fermin (61x91cm-24x36in) s. masonite. 14-Jun-94 John Moran, Pasadena #116
$900   £608   Women in Taos (46x61cm-18x24in) s. masonite. 15-Jun-93 John Moran, Pasadena #69

MILES, Helen Cabot (20th C) American
$1400   £946   Rainy day (61x76cm-24x30in) s.d.41. 31-Mar-94 Sotheby's Arcade, New York #271/R

MILES, John Christopher (1837-1911) Canadian
$3171   £2073   Gathering Dulce (71x112cm-28x44in) s. 19-May-93 Sotheby's, Toronto #342/R (C.D 4000)

MILLAR, Addison T (1860-1913) American
$700   £458   New Holland (25x36cm-10x14in) s.i. 16-Sep-93 Sloan, North Bethesda #2681
$950   £597   Seascape (15x36cm-6x14in) s. board. 25-Apr-93 James Bakker, Cambridge #120/R
$950   £660   Interior with figures (79x99cm-31x39in) s. 27-Feb-93 Young Fine Arts Auctions, Maine #213/R
$1400   £915   Harem guard (30x15cm-12x6in) s. panel. 29-Jun-94 Doyle, New York #58
$1400   £946   Turkish man (48x79cm-19x31in) 12-Nov-93 Douglas, South Deerfield #2
$1450   £767   Still life with fruit (23x28cm-9x11in) s. 12-Sep-92 Louisiana Auction Exchange #105/R
$1900   £1329   In the barn (41x30cm-16x12in) s. 7-Feb-93 James Bakker, Cambridge #175/R
$3100   £2039   Rug merchant (20x25cm-8x10in) s. panel. 31-Mar-93 Sotheby's Arcade, New York #73/R
$8000   £5128   Rug merchant (46x36cm-18x14in) s. 26-May-93 Sotheby's, New York #284/R
$8500   £5705   Shop of the Orient (20x25cm-8x10in) s. panel. 13-Oct-93 Sotheby's, New York #296/R
$20000   £13072   The Turkish vase (46x62cm-18x24in) s. st.i.verso. 29-Oct-92 Sotheby's, New York #44/R

MILLER, Alfred Jacob (1810-1874) American
$1200   £694   Portrait of young lady (61x51cm-24x20in) mono. 25-Sep-92 Sotheby's Arcade, New York #91/R
$18000   £12081   Indian encampment (20x33cm-8x13in) 3-Dec-93 Christie's, New York #65/R
$30000   £20134   Battle of Ft. McHenry (53x76cm-21x30in) 3-Feb-94 Sloan, North Bethesda #2887/R
$50000   £33113   Warrior and family (31x47cm-12x19in) board. 22-Sep-93 Christie's, New York #85/R
$100000   £64103   Indian scout on horseback (30x25cm-12x10in) 27-May-93 Sotheby's, New York #222/R
$170000   £113333   Indian canoe (34x51cm-13x20in) init. 17-Mar-94 Sotheby's, New York #59/R
$500   £340   *Two boys at a woman's window (23x15cm-9x6in) mono.i. col ink wash gouache. 8-Apr-94 Sloan, North Bethesda #1504*
$600   £408   *Group of figures outside an ale house (15x23cm-6x9in) i. col ink pencil wash. 8-Apr-94 Sloan, North Bethesda #1505*
$1000   £633   Portrait of an Indian (20x15cm-8x6in) s. W/C. 2-Dec-92 Boos Gallery, Michigan #823/R
$6000   £4027   Shim-a-co-che, crow chief (21x17cm-8x7in) s. W/C. 11-Dec-93 Weschler, Washington #85/R
$17000   £11409   *Profile of Sioux Indian (11x9cm-4x4in) W/C painted c.1833. 2-Dec-93 Sotheby's, New York #49/R*
$21000   £13291   *Death of the elk (22x27cm-9x11in) i.d.62 ink pencil. 3-Dec-92 Sotheby's, New York #53/R*
$30000   £18987   *Narrow escape from a grizzly bear (18x26cm-7x10in) i. W/C. 3-Dec-92 Sotheby's, New York #8/R*
$40000   £26667   *Shoshone Chasing wild horses (12x17cm-5x7in) init. W/C gouache paper laid down on board. 26-May-94 Christie's, New York #72/R*

MILLER, Alfred Jacob (attrib) (1810-1874) American
$1800   £1259   Indian princess by pond (30x25cm-12x10in) panel. 5-Feb-93 Sloan, North Bethesda #2548/R

MILLER, Barse (1904-1973) American
$750   £500   In the freight yard (51x76cm-20x30in) s.d.35. 15-Mar-94 John Moran, Pasadena #160 a
$1300   £878   Sunday in Phoenixville (36x51cm-14x20in) s.d.1940 W/C. 15-Jun-93 John Moran, Pasadena #134
$1500   £993   Dredging the Sacramento River (38x56cm-15x22in) s. W/C. 15-Jun-94 Butterfield & Butterfield, San Francisco #4753/R

MILLER, Charles Henry (1842-1922) American
$550   £369   Farm scene (33x38cm-13x15in) 27-Mar-94 Myers, Florida #63/R
$1000   £654   Summer day (56x91cm-22x36in) s. 30-Jun-94 Mystic Fine Arts, Connecticut #274/R

MILLER, Evylena Nunn (1888-1966) American
$950   £642   Hillside with trees and clouds (25x36cm-10x14in) s. board. 15-Jun-93 John Moran, Pasadena #3

MILLER, F (?) American
$550 £359 Still life with grapes and oranges (48cm-19in circular) s. pastel. 7-Oct-93 Freeman Fine Arts, Philadelphia #873

MILLER, F H (19th C) American
$1950 £995 Seascape with large rocks (18x36cm-7x14in) s.d.79. 18-Aug-92 Richard Bourne, Hyannis #78/R
$2300 £1173 Seascape with sails on the horizon (18x36cm-7x14in) s. 18-Aug-92 Richard Bourne, Hyannis #77/R

MILLER, Gustaf (20th C) American
$600 £403 Cafeteria (36x48cm-14x19in) s.d.81 mixed media construction. 6-May-94 Skinner, Bolton #160/R
$1000 £671 Boardwalk orange (56x62cm-22x24in) s.d.81 s.i.d.verso mixed media construction. 6-May-94 Skinner, Bolton #162/R

MILLER, H G (?) American
$1000 £676 The fisherman (58x91cm-23x36in) s. 31-Mar-94 Sotheby's Arcade, New York #60/R

MILLER, Henry (1891-1980) American
$1043 £700 Village by the sea (32x22cm-13x9in) s.d.6/51 s.i.verso gouache W/C. 21-Jun-93 Christie's, S. Kensington #125/R
$1200 £759 Untitled (61x43cm-24x17in) i. W/C. 25-Oct-92 Butterfield & Butterfield, San Francisco #2352/R

MILLER, Leonora (1928-) American
$1400 £819 Sunflower in a glass (23x15cm-9x6in) bears mono. pencil. 16-Sep-92 Butterfield & Butterfield, San Francisco #769/R

MILLER, Lewis (1795-1882) American
$1800 £1200 View of Christiansburg, Montogomery County, Virginia (18x13cm-7x5in) d.1867 W/C ink. 10-Jun-94 Christie's, New York #430/R
$2200 £1467 Apothecary (16x9cm-6x4in) s.i. W/C ink. 10-Jun-94 Christie's, New York #431/R

MILLER, Mildred Bunting (1892-?) American
$2500 £1736 The garden (71x64cm-28x25in) s. 27-Feb-93 Young Fine Arts Auctions, Maine #214/R

MILLER, Oscar (1867-?) American
$1600 £1074 The fortune teller (51x61cm-20x24in) s. 3-Feb-94 Sloan, North Bethesda #2676

MILLER, Ralph Davison (1859-1946) American
$850 £574 Mountain landscape (76x102cm-30x40in) s. 15-Jun-93 John Moran, Pasadena #49

MILLER, Richard E (1875-1943) American
$1000 £654 Canton China (51x61cm-20x24in) board. 4-May-93 Christie's, East, New York #178
$5750 £3885 Nocturne (50x61cm-20x24in) s.i.d.1904. 31-Mar-94 Sotheby's Arcade, New York #162/R
$22000 £14667 Daydream (28x34cm-11x13in) panel. 17-Mar-94 Sotheby's, New York #121/R
$30000 £20134 Portrait of Eva. Selfportrait (86x91cm-34x36in) s. board double-sided. 2-Dec-93 Sotheby's, New York #126/R
$50000 £31646 Bather (91x96cm-36x38in) s. s.i.d.1930 verso board. 3-Dec-92 Sotheby's, New York #123/R
$90000 £60000 Day dreams (56x61cm-22x24in) s. s.i.verso painted 1916. 25-May-94 Sotheby's, New York #89/R
$125000 £80128 In the shadow (81x65cm-32x26in) s. 27-May-93 Sotheby's, New York #40/R
$200000 £126582 The necklace (66x71cm-26x28in) s. 4-Dec-92 Christie's, New York #44/R
$600000 £400000 Spring, the open window (149x114cm-59x45in) s. 25-May-94 Sotheby's, New York #85/R
$2200 £1438 Woman reading (56x48cm-22x19in) tempera gouache board. 4-May-93 Christie's, East, New York #81

MILLER, Steve (1951-) American
$1000 £654 Fare zone (152x132cm-60x52in) oil silkscreen executed 1986. 22-Dec-92 Christie's, East, New York #40

MILLER, William Rickarby (1818-1893) American
$8500 £4913 River walk under Castle Point, Hoboken (43x35cm-17x14in) s.d.1873 i.d.verso. 23-Sep-92 Christie's, New York #63/R
$11000 £7692 House in the country (46x61cm-18x24in) s.d.1858. 10-Mar-93 Sotheby's, New York #7/R
$675 £447 Children fishing (18x25cm-7x10in) s. W/C. 23-Sep-93 Mystic Fine Arts, Connecticut #191/R
$2000 £1399 On the Mohawk river, Little Falls, New York (23x38cm-9x15in) s.d.1880 W/C paper on board. 11-Mar-93 Christie's, New York #8/R
$2200 £1457 Shanty scene 102 8th Ave. N.Y (35x46cm-14x18in) s.i.d.1869 W/C pencil. 22-Sep-93 Christie's, New York #70/R
$6250 £3613 Along river, autumn (21x31cm-8x12in) s.d.1892 W/C. 24-Sep-92 Sotheby's, New York #5/R

MILLESON, Royal Hill (1849-?) American
$1000 £671 Boats in harbour (71x56cm-28x22in) s. 5-Mar-94 Louisiana Auction Exchange #45/R
$1000 £667 Springtime (36x46cm-14x18in) s. 20-May-94 Du Mouchelle, Detroit #2221
$1100 £764 Before the storm (71x56cm-28x22in) s. 6-Mar-93 Louisiana Auction Exchange #25/R
$2900 £1908 Gallinas Canyon (102x137cm-40x54in) s. 31-Mar-93 Sotheby's Arcade, New York #187/R

MILLET, Clarence (1897-1959) American
$650   £436   Sunny gateway (33x28cm-13x11in) s. board. 24-Mar-94 Mystic Fine Arts, Connecticut #186/R

MILMAN, F (19th C) American
$1200   £800   View of the Reedy River, South Carolina (25x36cm-10x14in) s.d.1846 W/C. 23-May-94 Christie's, East, New York #34

MILNE, David Brown (1882-1953) Canadian
$12082 £8163   Fireplace (30x35cm-12x14in) s.d.1935. 23-Nov-93 Joyner Fine Art, Toronto #86/R (C.D 16000)
$14269 £9326   Last snowdrift (29x36cm-11x14in) s.d.1936. 19-May-93 Sotheby's, Toronto #228/R (C.D 18000)
$18600 £12000 Melting snow on the St. Lawrence (30x41cm-12x16in) i. painted 1929. 15-Jul-94 Christie's, London #91/R
$21845 £14563 Six Mile Lake (32x41cm-13x16in) s. board. 13-May-94 Joyner Fine Art, Toronto #34/R (C.D 30000)
$22197 £14508 Earth, sky and water (30x41cm-12x16in) s. painted 1945. 18-May-93 Joyner Fine Art, Toronto #81/R (C.D 28000)
$23782 £15544 Houses in autumn, Weston (30x41cm-12x16in) painted 1929. 18-May-93 Joyner Fine Art, Toronto #67/R (C.D 30000)
$24907 £16495 Lot 2, Concession 2, Weston (31x41cm-12x16in) d.1930. 24-Nov-92 Joyner Fine Art, Toronto #13/R (C.D 32000)
$28021 £18557 Road through Cut, Weston (40x50cm-16x20in) s. painted 1929. 24-Nov-92 Joyner Fine Art, Toronto #74/R (C.D 36000)
$28539 £18653 Leaves in sunlight (51x46cm-20x18in) d.1914 verso. 19-May-93 Sotheby's, Toronto #150/R (C.D 36000)
$34869 £23560 Village and country (41x51cm-16x20in) s. i.verso. 3-Nov-93 Sotheby's, Toronto #163/R (C.D 45000)
$35026 £23196 Village, Palgrave. Dark hills and sunlight (30x41cm-12x16in) s. double-sided. 18-Nov-92 Sotheby's, Toronto #80/R (C.D 45000)
$38918 £25773 Snowy woods, Alander (45x55cm-18x22in) s.d.1921. 24-Nov-92 Joyner Fine Art, Toronto #61/R (C.D 50000)
$59456 £38860 Corner of etching table (41x51cm-16x20in) s.d.1930. 18-May-93 Joyner Fine Art, Toronto #58/R (C.D 75000)
$8720   £5699   Empty box (38x56cm-15x22in) s.d.1938 W/C. 19-May-93 Sotheby's, Toronto #303/R (C.D 11000)
$9466   £6311   Tablecloth (31x33cm-12x13in) W/C. 13-May-94 Joyner Fine Art, Toronto #101/R (C.D 13000)
$9783   £6522   China and glass (36x53cm-14x21in) s.d.1940 i.d.1940 verso W/C. 6-Jun-94 Waddingtons, Toronto #1292/R (C.D 13500)
$11650 £7767   Blue church (25x35cm-10x14in) i.d.1944 verso W/C. 13-May-94 Joyner Fine Art, Toronto #42/R (C.D 16000)
$11759 £7538   Rock in the bay (36x50cm-14x20in) s.d.1938 i.verso W/C. 26-Apr-93 Levis, Calgary #120/R (C.D 15000)
$12837 £8673   Zinnias (36x37cm-14x15in) W/C executed 1940. 23-Nov-93 Joyner Fine Art, Toronto #60/R (C.D 17000)
$13107 £8738   Picture on the wall (36x53cm-14x21in) W/C. 13-May-94 Joyner Fine Art, Toronto #81/R (C.D 18000)
$13232 £8763   Mushrooms in Bush (36x49cm-14x19in) i. W/C. 24-Nov-92 Joyner Fine Art, Toronto #84/R (C.D 17000)
$21404 £13990 Ferris wheel, Coney Island (51x38cm-20x15in) s.d.12 W/C. 19-May-93 Sotheby's, Toronto #263/R (C.D 27000)
$26214 £17476 Wolman cottage - posing (42x53cm-17x21in) s. W/C. 13-May-94 Joyner Fine Art, Toronto #23/R (C.D 36000)

MILROY, Lisa (1959-) Canadian
$1200   £795   Untitled (46x61cm-18x24in) s.d.83stretcher. 17-Nov-92 Christie's, East, New York #132/R
$7500   £5034   Butterflies (183x221cm-72x87in) init.d.86overlap. 3-May-94 Christie's, East, New York #169/R

MINER, Alita G (?) American?
$750   £497   Floral still life (51x61cm-20x24in) s. 2-Oct-93 Boos Gallery, Michigan #280/R

MINOR, Robert Crannell (1840-1904) American
$900   £577   Autumn sunset (20x30cm-8x12in) s. board. 13-Dec-92 Hindman Galleries, Chicago #27
$1100   £728   Sunset landscape (40x30cm-16x12in) s. 2-Oct-93 Weschler, Washington #100/R
$1700   £1156   Near New London (30x40cm-12x16in) s. s.i.verso board. 15-Nov-93 Christie's, East, New York #66

MINTER, Marilyn (1948-) American
$6000   £4027   Nine ways to be a better cook (183x229cm-72x90in) s.i.d.1989 enamel on metal nine panels. 23-Feb-94 Christie's, East, New York #207/R
$5500   £3819   Handroling, cleaning painting (60x90cm-24x35in) s.i.d.1988verso enamel canvas in three parts. 23-Feb-93 Sotheby's, New York #370/R
$5500   £3819   Nine ways to be a better cook (180x225cm-71x89in) s.i.d.1989verso enamel metal nine panels. 22-Feb-93 Christie's, East, New York #255/R

MIRA, Alfred S (20th C) American
$3000   £1734   View of Sheridan Square (31x39cm-12x15in) s. canvas board. 25-Sep-92 Sotheby's Arcade, New York #380/R

MIRAGLIA, Juan Carlos (1900-1983) Argentinian
$1400 £824 Naturaleza muerta (40x50cm-16x20in) painted 1950. 29-Sep-92 VerBo, Buenos Aires #78

MIRANDA, Juan de (17th C) Mexican
$60000 £39735 Virgen de Guadalupe (205x144cm-81x57in) s.i.d.1704. 23-Nov-92 Sotheby's, New York #27/R

MITCHELL, Alfred R (1888-1972) American
$900	£629	Spring landscape (41x51cm-16x20in) s.verso. 11-Mar-93 Christie's, New York #163/R
$1000	£662	Foothills (20x25cm-8x10in) s. board. 20-Sep-93 Butterfield & Butterfield, Los Angeles #87/R
$1600	£1074	Ocotillos (20x25cm-8x10in) s. s.i.verso board. 8-Dec-93 Butterfield & Butterfield, San Francisco #3487/R
$1800	£1216	Coachella Desert (20x25cm-8x10in) s. board. 9-Nov-93 John Moran, Pasadena #867
$1800	£1059	La Jolla Rocks (20x25cm-8x10in) s. board. 4-Oct-92 Butterfield & Butterfield, Los Angeles #177/R
$1900	£1118	Cliffs (20x25cm-8x10in) s. board. 4-Oct-92 Butterfield & Butterfield, Los Angeles #178/R
$2000	£1379	Tree shaded stream. Near Philip's house in Berkeley (20x25cm-8x10in) s. board two. 16-Feb-93 John Moran, Pasadena #15
$2250	£1324	Rocky point (20x25cm-8x10in) s. board. 4-Oct-92 Butterfield & Butterfield, Los Angeles #179/R
$2500	£1667	Coastal scene at sunset (20x25cm-8x10in) s. i.verso board. 15-Mar-94 John Moran, Pasadena #87
$2500	£1678	Sierra Waterfall, Yosemite (51x41cm-20x16in) s. board. 8-Dec-93 Butterfield & Butterfield, San Francisco #3434/R
$2500	£1656	San Diego waterfront (20x25cm-8x10in) s. s.i.verso board. 2-Oct-93 Weschler, Washington #145/R
$2500	£1736	Sierra meadow (20x25cm-8x10in) s. board. 7-Mar-93 Butterfield & Butterfield, San Francisco #135/R
$2750	£1858	Summer landscape (18x25cm-7x10in) s. board. 15-Jun-93 John Moran, Pasadena #35 a
$2750	£1846	The red mansion in Sonora (20x25cm-8x10in) board. 8-Dec-93 Butterfield & Butterfield, San Francisco #3486/R
$3000	£1765	Desert Canyon (41x51cm-16x20in) s. board. 4-Oct-92 Butterfield & Butterfield, Los Angeles #212/R
$3000	£2083	Along Riverbed Creek near June Lake (20x25cm-8x10in) s. board. 7-Mar-93 Butterfield & Butterfield, San Francisco #134/R
$3000	£1765	Mount San Miguel in fall (41x51cm-16x20in) s. board. 4-Oct-92 Butterfield & Butterfield, Los Angeles #187/R
$3000	£2083	Sunset, Shadow Lake, Sierras (20x25cm-8x10in) s. board. 7-Mar-93 Butterfield & Butterfield, San Francisco #136/R
$3000	£1734	Morning (41x51cm-16x20in) s. s.i.verso board. 25-Sep-92 Sotheby's Arcade, New York #283/R
$4500	£3125	Mammoth Lakes (41x51cm-16x20in) s. s.i.verso board. 7-Mar-93 Butterfield & Butterfield, San Francisco #132/R
$5000	£3311	Near San Diego (51x62cm-20x24in) s. 15-Jun-94 Butterfield & Butterfield, San Francisco #4679/R
$5000	£2941	Beach at Torrey Pines (51x41cm-20x16in) estate st. num.337 verso board. 4-Oct-92 Butterfield & Butterfield, Los Angeles #167/R
$6000	£4027	Torrey Pines (41x51cm-16x20in) s. s.i.verso board. 8-Dec-93 Butterfield & Butterfield, San Francisco #3470/R
$7000	£4667	Building the dam (41x51cm-16x20in) s. i.verso board painted c.1932. 15-Mar-94 John Moran, Pasadena #117 a
$9500	£6291	Canyon in autumn (41x51cm-16x20in) board. 28-Sep-93 John Moran, Pasadena #308

MITCHELL, James A (20th C) American
$600 £403 Lifesaving boat 'Nauset' being launched into the surf (61x76cm-24x30in) s. board. 25-Mar-94 Eldred, Massachusetts #117

MITCHELL, Janet (20th C) Canadian
$933	£622	A summer place (46x61cm-18x24in) s.d. s.i.verso acrylic canvasboard. 30-May-94 Hodgins, Calgary #223/R (C.D 1300)
$603	£410	Melody (39x57cm-15x22in) s. W/C. 15-Nov-93 Hodgins, Calgary #228/R (C.D 800)
$754	£502	Our mountain town (38x55cm-15x22in) s. W/C. 30-May-94 Hodgins, Calgary #275 (C.D 1050)
$785	£513	French know how to organise those things (48x69cm-19x27in) s.d.84 W/C. 10-May-93 Hodgins, Calgary #104/R (C.D 1000)
$905	£615	Who turned on the lights (57x76cm-22x30in) s.d.1993 W/C. 15-Nov-93 Hodgins, Calgary #105 (C.D 1200)
$1046	£707	The consequences of small buildings (57x76cm-22x30in) s.d.1982 i.verso W/C. 1-Nov-93 Levis, Calgary #219/R (C.D 1350)
$1077	£718	Settlers Home (55x74cm-22x29in) s.d. W/C. 30-May-94 Hodgins, Calgary #27/R (C.D 1500)
$1334	£872	Windy day P.E.I (53x73cm-21x29in) s.d.84 W/C. 10-May-93 Hodgins, Calgary #242/R (C.D 1700)

MITCHELL, Joan (1926-1992) American
$4000	£2685	Untitled (41x51cm-16x20in) paper painted 1957. 23-Feb-94 Christie's, East, New York #277/R
$22500	£15000	Dyptich (61x100cm-24x39in) s. painted 1987. 26-May-94 Christie's, London #85/R
$24000	£15894	Untitled (55x46cm-22x18in) init. s.d.84verso. 19-Nov-92 Christie's, New York #307/R
$26000	£17450	Untitled (36x56cm-14x22in) s.i. paper painted 1952-1953. 4-May-94 Christie's, New York #128/R

MITCHELL, Joan (1926-1992) American-cont.
$32000	£20915	Untitled (61x50cm-24x20in) painted 1974. 4-May-93 Sotheby's, New York #354 a/R
$35000	£23490	Petit matin (81x65cm-32x26in) s. linen painted 1982. 4-May-94 Christie's, New York #139/R
$35000	£20588	Untitled (91x73cm-36x29in) 6-Oct-92 Sotheby's, New York #40/R
$50000	£33113	Untitled (69x66cm-27x26in) s.indist.d. painted c.1954. 18-Nov-92 Sotheby's, New York #93/R
$84446	£55924	Lille V (196x260cm-77x102in) s. i.verso painted 1987 diptych. 13-Jun-94 Guy Loudmer, Paris #96/R (F.FR 472000)
$89606	£60545	Chord II (162x97cm-64x38in) s. painted 1986. 3-Nov-93 Kunsthallen, Copenhagen #55/R (D.KR 600000)
$110000	£74324	Sunflower IV (260x180cm-102x71in) s. painte 1969. 11-Nov-93 Sotheby's, New York #296/R
$135000	£90604	Untitled (163x97cm-64x38in) s. s.verso painted 1969. 5-May-94 Sotheby's, New York #107/R
$140000	£93960	Untitled (91x208cm-36x82in) s. painted 1959. 3-May-94 Christie's, New York #32/R
$160000	£108108	Before, Again I (279x199cm-110x78in) s. linen painted 1985. 9-Nov-93 Christie's, New York #48/R
$230000	£155405	Aquarium (161x483cm-63x190in) s. oil canvas in four panels painted 1964. 10-Nov-93 Sotheby's, New York #41/R
$13000	*£9028*	*Untitled (32x22cm-13x9in) s. col.chk W/C. 24-Feb-93 Christie's, New York #38/R*

MITCHELL, John Ames (1845-?) American
$784	£529	Travellers resting by river (100x78cm-39x31in) 23-Apr-94 Soderkopings #257/R (S.KR 6200)

MITCHELL, John Campbell (1862-1922) American
$578	£380	Morning in Glentrool, Galloway (30x36cm-12x14in) s. board. 20-Jul-94 Bonhams, London #19
$622	£420	On the Duchray Water, Aberfoyle (30x51cm-12x20in) i.verso. 28-Apr-94 Christie's, S. Kensington #54
$643	£420	Sea Breakers, Kintyre (46x76cm-18x30in) s.d.1907. 6-Oct-93 Christie's, Glasgow #563
$1110	£750	Autumn woodland (61x51cm-24x20in) s.d.05. 28-Apr-94 Christie's, S. Kensington #57
$1416	£950	Woodland in Galloway (31x36cm-12x14in) s. 6-May-94 Phillips, Edinburgh #7
$1416	£950	Ben Lomond from near Aberfoyle (25x35cm-10x14in) s. s.i.d.1919 panel. 6-May-94 Phillips, Edinburgh #37
$1493	£750	Cattle by riverside (25x36cm-10x14in) s.d.1919 board. 31-Aug-92 Sotheby's, London #1091/R
$1520	£1000	Springtime near turnhouse (49x59cm-19x23in) s. i.verso. 2-Jun-93 Sotheby's, Billingshurst #533/R
$1788	£1200	The hills of Appin from Barcaldine Moss (29x34cm-11x13in) s.d.1912. 1-Feb-94 Sotheby's, London #150/R
$2086	£1400	Kintyre coast (44x75cm-17x30in) s. s.i.verso. 6-May-94 Phillips, Edinburgh #3/R

MITCHELL, Thomas Wilberforce (1879-1958) Canadian
$713	£466	Mill Pond, Alton (25x32cm-10x13in) s. board. 18-May-93 Joyner Fine Art, Toronto #201/R (C.D 900)
$872	£570	In rural Quebec (29x36cm-11x14in) s. board. 19-May-93 Sotheby's, Toronto #307/R (C.D 1100)
$951	£622	Quebec farmyard (29x36cm-11x14in) s. board. 19-May-93 Sotheby's, Toronto #274/R (C.D 1200)
$2712	£1832	Masham Valley (61x76cm-24x30in) s. s.i.verso. 3-Nov-93 Sotheby's, Toronto #116/R (C.D 3500)

MIZEN, Frederic Kimball (1888-1964) American
$800	£537	Summer sun (84x64cm-33x25in) s. 24-Mar-93 Doyle, New York #52

MOELLER, Gustave (attrib) (1881-?) American
$2100	£1373	River landscape (86x102cm-34x40in) s. 3-May-93 Schrager Galleries, Milwaukee #563

MOELLER, Louis C (1855-1930) American
$2500	£1667	The magician (20x16cm-8x6in) s. 23-May-94 Christie's, East, New York #140/R
$6000	£4196	The violinist (41x30cm-16x12in) s. 11-Mar-93 Christie's, New York #78/R
$7000	£4762	After dinner cordials (43x58cm-17x23in) s. canvas laid down on masonite. 17-Nov-93 Doyle, New York #23/R
$7000	£4046	Discussion (46x61cm-18x24in) s. 24-Sep-92 Sotheby's, New York #10/R
$8000	£4624	Discussion in library (62x81cm-24x32in) l. 24-Sep-92 Sotheby's, New York #9/R
$9000	£5960	Nosegay (46x61cm-18x24in) s. 3-May-93 Sotheby's, New York #8/R
$10000	£6623	The chemists (46x61cm-18x24in) s. 15-Jun-94 Butterfield & Butterfield, San Francisco #4463/R
$12000	£8000	Scouting the trunk (28x33cm-11x13in) s. 17-Mar-94 Sotheby's, New York #24/R
$17000	£11486	A gathering of friends (46x61cm-18x24in) s. 5-Nov-93 Skinner, Bolton #66/R
$20000	£12658	The art critics (30x25cm-12x10in) s. 3-Dec-92 Sotheby's, New York #24/R
$26000	£16667	Cronies (46x61cm-18x24in) s. 26-May-93 Christie's, New York #64 a/R
$26000	£17450	The Connoisseurs (76x107cm-30x42in) s. 3-Dec-93 Christie's, New York #106/R

MOFFETT, Ross E (1888-1971) American
$700	£464	Cattle on the moors (102x127cm-40x50in) s. 23-Sep-93 Mystic Fine Arts, Connecticut #46/R
$3200	£1850	Ice cutting (61x76cm-24x30in) s. 24-Sep-92 Mystic Fine Arts, Connecticut #224/R
$4200	£2781	Boating party (61x86cm-24x35in) s. 23-Sep-93 Mystic Fine Arts, Connecticut #192/R

MOGENSEN, Paul (1941-) American
$2000   £1307   Untitled (153x203cm-60x80in) executed 1987. 22-Dec-92 Christie's, East, New York #42

MOHOLY-NAGY, Laszlo (1895-1946) Hungarian/American
$3500   £2349   Composition (21x28cm-8x11in) s. init.i.d.41 col.wax crayons pencil. 23-Feb-94 Christie's, East, New York #128/R
$3500   £2365   Portrait of Lajos Thror (46x35cm-18x14in) s.i.d.1920 pastel. 21-Apr-94 Butterfield & Butterfield, San Francisco #1054/R
$9180   £6000   Untitled (46x36cm-18x14in) s.d.42 init.d. oil gouache pencil. 28-Jun-94 Christie's, London #222/R
$12350   £6500   Untitled (46x36cm-18x14in) s.d.42 init.d.42 oil gouache pencil. 22-Jun-93 Christie's, London #164/R
$33466   £22311   Composition (76x56cm-30x22in) s.W/C chk. ink. 9-Jun-94 Hauswedell & Nolte, Hamburg #604/R (DM 56000)

MOHRMANN, J H (1857-1916) American
$2974   £2009   Vapeur, Ville de Montevideo (57x97cm-22x38in) s.d.1897. 2-Apr-94 Deauville #40/R (F.FR 17000)

MOHRMANN, John Henry (1857-1916) American
$3875   £2500   Barque 'Kilmeny' (60x99cm-24x39in) s. 20-Jan-93 Sotheby's, London #104/R
$4768   £3200   The barquentine 'Yucatan' under sail (59x88cm-23x35in) s. 5-May-94 Christie's, S. Kensington #189/R
$6500   £4276   Three masted barque 'Highland Glen' in English Channel (58x99cm-23x39in) s.d.1893. 4-Jun-93 Sotheby's, New York #187/R
$7000   £4762   The three master Louis Pasteur under full sail (60x100cm-24x39in) s.d.1906. 15-Apr-94 Bolland & Marotz, Bremen #683/R (DM 12000)
$8000   £5229   Portrait of ship Snow and Burges flying American flag at dawn (24x35cm-9x14in) s.i.d.26/6/1887. 31-Oct-92 Skinner, Bolton #12/R

MOLARSKY, Maurice (1885-1950) American
$850   £563   Zinnias, carnations and hollyhocks (68x68cm-27x27in) s.d.1930. 2-Oct-93 Weschler, Washington #136
$1100   £748   Lake landscape with sailing boats (64x76cm-25x30in) s. 14-Apr-94 Freeman Fine Arts, Philadelphia #1020

MOLLENO, Antonio (attrib) (fl.1800-1845) American
$1800   £1208   Saint Barbara (28x18cm-11x7in) i. tempera gesso panel. 26-Jun-93 Skinner, Bolton #227/R
$2200   £1429   Saint Joseph (20x15cm-8x6in) tempera gesso panel. 25-Jun-94 Skinner, Bolton #32/R
$3250   £2181   Saint Jerome (28x18cm-11x7in) tempera gesso panel. 26-Jun-93 Skinner, Bolton #228/R

MOLLER, Oscar (20th C) American
$850   £570   Spring landscape with white houses (66x71cm-26x28in) d.1924 s.verso. 2-Dec-93 Freeman Fine Arts, Philadelphia #836

MONDESIR, Leon (1947-) Haitian
$838   £537   Celui-la, c'est pour moi (91x61cm-36x24in) s. 14-Dec-92 Hoebanx, Paris #51/R (F.FR 4500)

MONET, Jason (20th C) American
$600   £403   Portrait of old woman (132x76cm-52x30in) chl col.chk. 4-Mar-94 Christie's, East, New York #218/R

MONGE, Luis (1920-) Ecuadorian
$8000   £5405   Selva y palmeras (100x130cm-39x51in) s.d.73. 23-Nov-93 Christie's, New York #283/R
$13000   £8609   Garza en el Triangulo Amazonico (134x121cm-53x48in) s.d.1976. 24-Nov-92 Christie's, New York #233/R

MONKS, John Austin Sands (1850-1917) American
$1300   £855   Sheep in pasture (46x71cm-18x28in) s. 11-Jun-93 Du Mouchelle, Detroit #2139

MONPREMIER, Madsen (1952-) Haitian
$1252   £829   Mariage d'Agoue (80x60cm-31x24in) s.d.79. 13-Jun-94 Rogeon, Paris #136 (F.FR 7000)

MONREAL, Andres (?) Chilean
$5371   £3629   Commentaires sur une bataille (65x50cm-26x20in) s. s.i.verso. 24-Oct-93 Catherine Charbonneaux, Paris #76/R (F.FR 31500)

MONROY, Jose Atanacio (1912-) Mexican
$3225   £2165   El entierro (57x48cm-22x19in) s.d.1939. 1-Dec-93 Louis Morton, Mexico #207/R (M.P 10000)

MONTEIRO, Vicente do Rego (1899-) Brazilian
$16000   £10458   Tres Reis (46x53cm-18x21in) s. W/C gouache pencil artist's board. 17-May-93 Christie's, New York #220/R

MONTENEGRO, Julio (1867-1932) Ecuadorian
$10000   £6711   Courtyard of the Alhambra (51x45cm-20x18in) s.d.889. 14-Oct-93 Christie's, New York #16/R

MONTENEGRO, Roberto (1881-1968) South American

$5000	£3378	Composicion con sandias (33x41cm-13x16in) s.d.57 masonite. 23-Nov-93 Christie's, New York #292/R
$8000	£5298	Inditas Cantadoras (70x70cm-28x28in) s. i.stretcher. 24-Nov-92 Christie's, New York #178/R
$8500	£5743	Payaso con naranja (80x70cm-31x28in) s. painted c.1955. 22-Nov-93 Sotheby's, New York #164/R
$9000	£5696	Two figurines (60x71cm-24x28in) s.indist.i.d.1947 masonite. 25-Oct-92 Butterfield & Butterfield, San Francisco #2247/R
$9000	£6081	El caballo blanco (30x31cm-12x12in) s. 23-Nov-93 Christie's, New York #135/R
$10000	£6623	Pantera Negra (50x50cm-20x20in) s.d.64 s.i.d.verso. 24-Nov-92 Christie's, New York #179/R
$12000	£8000	Naturaleza muerta (41x51cm-16x20in) s. s.i.d.1965verso. 18-May-94 Sotheby's, New York #374/R
$12000	£8108	Construccion (70x59cm-28x23in) s. 23-Nov-93 Christie's, New York #134/R
$14000	£9150	Dos mujeres (60x70cm-24x28in) painted c.1940. 18-May-93 Sotheby's, New York #156/R
$19000	£12418	Sic transit gloria mundi (100x134cm-39x53in) s.i. masonite. 17-May-93 Christie's, New York #130/R
$22000	£14667	Naturaleza muerta (79x68cm-31x27in) s.d.68 s.i.d.verso. 18-May-94 Christie's, New York #99/R
$24000	£16000	Nina con Muneca (54x44cm-21x17in) s. 18-May-94 Christie's, New York #218/R
$30000	£19608	Naturaleza muerta con frutas (105x151cm-41x59in) s.d.65. 17-May-93 Christie's, New York #131/R
$36612	£23469	La urna de la felicidad (112x129cm-44x51in) s.d.1949. 29-Apr-93 Louis Morton, Mexico #98/R (M.P 115000)
$40000	£26144	Autorretrato (70x70cm-28x28in) s.d.1961. 18-May-93 Sotheby's, New York #60/R
$1052	£701	Escenografia (17x23cm-7x9in) s.d.1958 W/C. 25-May-94 Louis Morton, Mexico #45 (M.P 3500)
$2375	£1563	Ilusion (22x20cm-9x8in) s.d.1959 pencil. 4-Nov-92 Mora, Castelltort & Quintana, Juarez #80/R (M.P 7500000)
$3000	£1961	El deseo de volar (30x25cm-12x10in) s. graphite W/C executed c.1940. 18-May-93 Sotheby's, New York #173/R

MONTIEL, Jonio (?) South American

$1300	£872	Figuras clasicas griegas (54x72cm-21x28in) s. board. 29-Nov-93 Gomensoro, Montevideo #62

MONTOYA, Gustavo (1905-) Mexican

$1900	£1319	Girl and her ukulele (56x46cm-22x18in) s. 26-Feb-93 Sotheby's Arcade, New York #252/R
$1900	£1319	Boy and his toy (56x46cm-22x18in) s. painted 1959. 26-Feb-93 Sotheby's Arcade, New York #255/R
$2250	£1490	Nina con dulce (55x45cm-22x18in) s. 30-Jun-93 Sotheby's Arcade, New York #209/R
$2500	£1689	Nina en azul con flores (56x46cm-22x18in) s. 4-Nov-93 Boos Gallery, Michigan #1272/R
$3000	£2000	Nino sentado (54x46cm-21x18in) s. 18-May-94 Christie's, New York #323/R
$3200	£2148	Nina de Chihuahueno (61x46cm-24x18in) s. s.i.verso. 24-Feb-94 Sotheby's Arcade, New York #295/R
$3250	£2057	Girls on bicycles (85x70cm-33x28in) s. s.d.1965 verso. 25-Oct-92 Butterfield & Butterfield, San Francisco #2249/R
$3500	£2201	La muchacha con vestido de amarillo (55x46cm-22x18in) s. 25-Apr-93 Butterfield & Butterfield, San Francisco #2084/R
$4000	£2649	Nino con Sandia (56x46cm-22x18in) s. 30-Jun-93 Sotheby's Arcade, New York #208/R
$4500	£2848	Portrait of young girl in blue dress (56x45cm-22x18in) s. 25-Oct-92 Butterfield & Butterfield, San Francisco #2248/R

MOON, Carl (1878-1948) American

$1200	£779	The canyon trail (41x30cm-16x12in) s. board. 25-Jun-94 Skinner, Bolton #205/R

MOORE, Benson Bond (1882-1974) American

$1300	£833	Early spring on Anacostia (56x61cm-22x24in) s. 12-Dec-92 Weschler, Washington #82/R
$1600	£1060	Path through country landscape (63x76cm-25x30in) s. 2-Oct-93 Weschler, Washington #161/R

MOORE, Edwin Augustus (1858-1925) American

$600	£400	Man with a rifle, standing by atent near a lake and a homestead (61x91cm-24x36in) 20-May-94 Du Mouchelle, Detroit #1008/R
$1700	£859	Apple, grapes and glass (23x30cm-9x12in) s.d.1876. 28-Aug-92 Young Fine Arts Auctions, Maine #224
$4000	£2312	Still life with fruit and vase of flowers (30x46cm-12x18in) s. 24-Sep-92 Sotheby's, New York #36/R

MOORE, Frank Montague (1877-1967) British/American

$1000	£662	Landscape - river reflections (64x76cm-25x30in) s.i. s.verso masonite. 14-Jun-94 John Moran, Pasadena #59
$1500	£1014	Oaks on flowered hillside (51x66cm-20x26in) s. board. 9-Nov-93 John Moran, Pasadena #901 a
$1500	£993	Oaks and moonrise (71x102cm-28x40in) s. i.verso board. 20-Sep-93 Butterfield & Butterfield, Los Angeles #92
$2250	£1481	Hawaiian coast (51x61cm-20x24in) s.d.1924 board. 13-Jun-93 Butterfield & Butterfield, San Francisco #943/R
$2250	£1520	Monterey coastal (30x38cm-12x15in) board. 15-Jun-93 John Moran, Pasadena #122

MOORE, Frank Montague (1877-1967) British/American-cont.
$2250	£1490	Yucca in moonlight (132x107cm-52x42in) s. canvas on board. 20-Sep-93 Butterfield & Butterfield, Los Angeles #94/R
$2250	£1490	Eucalyptus and sea (51x76cm-20x30in) s. s.i.verso board. 15-Jun-94 Butterfield & Butterfield, San Francisco #4648/R

MOORE, Gerald C (20th C) American
$550	£372	Irises (91x76cm-36x30in) s. 22-Apr-94 Du Mouchelle, Detroit #1183/R

MOORE, Harry Humphrey (1844-1926) American
$681	£460	Young Moroccan woman seated in interior (19x13cm-7x5in) s. panel. 16-Mar-93 Phillips, London #62
$1200	£784	New Orleans street scene (22x15cm-9x6in) s. panel. 4-May-93 Christie's, East, New York #140 a/R
$3676	£2450	Portrait de femme au chale (50x39cm-20x15in) s. 18-Mar-94 Audap Solnet & Godeau, Paris #14/R (F.FR 21000)
$22500	£15000	Best of friends (81x64cm-32x25in) s.i. 18-Mar-94 Christie's, London #125/R
$6000	*£4027*	*Citadel of Cairo. The Nile, Egypt (25x63cm-10x25in) s.d.1912 W/C pair. 14-Oct-93 Christie's, New York #252/R*

MOORE, Nelson Augustus (1823-1902) American
$800	£523	Kensington, Conn (36x61cm-14x24in) s.d.95 s.i.verso. 18-Sep-93 Young Fine Arts Auctions, Maine #220/R
$1000	£662	Lake George (34x36cm-13x14in) mono. mono.i.verso. 2-Oct-93 Weschler, Washington #89/R
$1300	£850	Lake George (34x36cm-13x14in) mono s.i.verso. 22-May-93 Weschler, Washington #84/R

MOOTZKA, Waldo (1903-1940) American
$700	*£470*	*The hair cutter (23x25cm-9x10in) s. gouache. 26-Jun-93 Skinner, Bolton #145/R*

MORA, Francis Luis (1874-1940) American
$1200	£805	Navaho girl (27x23cm-11x9in) indist.s. canvas on board. 8-Dec-93 Butterfield & Butterfield, San Francisco #3548/R
$2100	£1373	Circus performers (28x36cm-11x14in) s. board. 30-Jun-94 Mystic Fine Arts, Connecticut #150/R
$3250	£2196	Roses of Spain (56x81cm-22x32in) s. 15-Jun-93 John Moran, Pasadena #108
$4000	£2312	Children on the beach (46x56cm-18x22in) s.d.1909. 23-Sep-92 Christie's, New York #198/R
$6000	£3468	Juan and Juanita (76x64cm-30x25in) s. s.i.verso. 23-Sep-92 Christie's, New York #188/R
$9000	£5696	Family party, Triana, Sevilla (63x76cm-25x30in) s.d.1908 i.verso. 3-Dec-92 Sotheby's, New York #89/R
$9500	£6643	At the shore (30x41cm-12x16in) s.d.1912 panel. 11-Mar-93 Christie's, New York #147/R
$14000	£9333	The little army (121x85cm-48x33in) s. 16-Mar-94 Christie's, New York #86/R
$15000	£9494	Mercedes (77x64cm-30x25in) s.d.1909. 4-Dec-92 Christie's, New York #26/R
$3000	*£1734*	*View of the courtyard (36x26cm-14x10in) s. W/C pencil paper on canvas on board. 23-Sep-92 Christie's, New York #92/R*

MORA, Raul (1942-) Mexican
$1774	£1190	Soltando (100x100cm-39x39in) s.d.1993. 1-Dec-93 Louis Morton, Mexico #102/R (M.P 5500)
$3040	£2000	Asi lo vieron (100x100cm-39x39in) s.d.1992. 4-Nov-92 Mora, Castelltort & Quintana, Juarez #46/R (M.P 9600000)
$4751	£3125	Gritenme piedras del campo (100x220cm-39x87in) s.d.1992 diptych. 4-Nov-92 Mora, Castelltort & Quintana, Juarez #79/R (M.P 15000000)

MORALES, Armando (1927-) Nicaraguan
$3500	£2288	Paisaje maritimo con barco (39x61cm-15x24in) s.d.63. 18-May-93 Sotheby's, New York #204/R
$4500	£3020	Paisaje de Venecia (13x18cm-5x7in) s.d.88 paper. 7-Jan-94 Gary Nader, Miami #21/R
$5500	£3595	Naturaleza muerta (15x24cm-6x9in) s.d.85 paper. 18-May-93 Sotheby's, New York #171/R
$5600	£3758	Bodegon (17x24cm-7x9in) paper. 7-Jan-94 Gary Nader, Miami #22/R
$18000	£12000	Caballos y barcos (30x39cm-12x15in) s.indis.d.79 masonite. 17-May-94 Sotheby's, New York #63/R
$19102	£12245	Tres banistas y barco (20x14cm-8x6in) s. paper on canvas painted 1991. 29-Apr-93 Louis Morton, Mexico #105 (M.P 60000)
$20000	£13514	Banistas (32x40cm-13x16in) s.d.1989-92. 23-Nov-93 Christie's, New York #155/R
$22000	£14379	Tauromaquia (33x24cm-13x9in) s.d.81 pair. 17-May-93 Christie's, New York #148/R
$28000	£18543	Banistas (58x75cm-23x30in) s.d.81 oil wax varnish paper. 24-Nov-92 Christie's, New York #117 a/R
$30000	£19608	Tauromaquia (33x24cm-13x9in) s.d.81 pair. 17-May-93 Christie's, New York #149/R
$35000	£23649	Figure (127x102cm-50x40in) s.d.69 oil wax. 23-Nov-93 Christie's, New York #128/R
$41000	£27152	Mujer Desvistiendose (54x45cm-21x18in) oil wax varnish. 23-Nov-92 Sotheby's, New York #73/R
$43000	£28105	Naturaleza muerta con mangos (61x51cm-24x20in) s.d.80. 18-May-93 Sotheby's, New York #216/R
$60000	£39735	naturaleza muerta con questo, botella y manzana (66x81cm-26x32in) s.d.76 oil wax. 24-Nov-92 Christie's, New York #91/R
$62500	£41667	Three pears (127x109cm-50x43in) s.d.74. 17-May 94 Sotheby's, New York #76/R
$65000	£43919	Foret tropicale, xerophile I (60x70cm-24x28in) s.d.91. 23-Nov-93 Christie's, New York #41/R

MORALES, Armando (1927-) Nicaraguan-cont.
$65000	£43333	Nature morte, bouteille, pomme rouge, poire, Brie (46x62cm-18x24in) s.d.91 i.d.stretcher oil varnish. 18-May-94 Christie's, New York #65/R
$70000	£46667	Arbol (127x101cm-50x40in) s.d.75 i.d.stretcher oil wax varnish panel. 18-May-94 Christie's, New York #33/R
$80000	£54054	Hombre y mujer III, homenaje a vesalio (101x81cm-40x32in) s. s.i.d.stretcher oil wax. 23-Nov-93 Christie's, New York #55/R
$85000	£56667	Nu abstrait (163x130cm-64x51in) s.d.68. 17-May-94 Sotheby's, New York #69/R
$90000	£59603	Mujer entrando en un Espejo II (125x100cm-49x39in) s.d.82 i.d.stretcher oil wax varnish. 24-Nov-92 Christie's, New York #45/R
$110000	£73333	Woman leaving a room I (128x109cm-50x43in) s.d.72 i.d.stretcher oil wax varnish. 18-May-94 Christie's, New York #40/R
$115000	£75163	Desnudo (168x168cm-66x66in) s.d.70 oil wax varnish. 17-May-93 Christie's, New York #100 b/R
$200000	£132450	Circo (148x183cm-58x72in) s.d.81 i.d.981 stretcher oil wax varnish. 24-Nov-92 Christie's, New York #13/R
$210000	£139073	Foret tropicale (161x130cm-63x51in) 23-Nov-92 Sotheby's, New York #65/R
$340000	£222222	Trois nus et voiture a cheval (162x130cm-64x51in) s.d.85. 18-May-93 Sotheby's, New York #65/R
$9500	£6291	Dos figuras (43x59cm-17x23in) s.d.81 pastel. 23-Nov-92 Sotheby's, New York #184/R
$14000	£9150	Abstract composition (203x147cm-80x58in) cardboard gessoed canvas collage canvas exec.64. 18-May-93 Sotheby's, New York #206/R
$18000	£11765	Naturaleza muerta con humero y guanabana (49x59cm-19x23in) s.d.83 pastel. 18-May-93 Sotheby's, New York #215/R
$22000	£14570	En el Circo (54x68cm-21x27in) s.d.80 chl pastel. 24-Nov-92 Christie's, New York #216/R
$25000	£16892	Sueno en la madrugada (49x61cm-19x24in) s.d.83 pastel. 22-Nov-93 Sotheby's, New York #69/R
$25000	£16556	Mujer Dormida (54x85cm-21x33in) s.d.79 gouache. 23-Nov-92 Sotheby's, New York #74/R
$26000	£17450	Sueno en la Madrugada (49x61cm-19x24in) s.d.83 pastel. 7-Jan-94 Gary Nader, Miami #81 b/R

MORALES, Dario (1944-1988) Colombian
$45000	£30405	Mujer desnuda (195x129cm-77x51in) s.d.86. 23-Nov-93 Christie's, New York #54/R
$4500	£2941	Torso (30x37cm-12x15in) s.d.78 graphite notebook paper. 18-May-93 Sotheby's, New York #225/R
$4750	£3105	Torso (30x37cm-12x15in) s.d.78 graphite notebook paper. 18-May-93 Sotheby's, New York #224/R

MORALES, Eduardo (19/20th C) Cuban
$2500	£1689	Palmeras (50x35cm-20x14in) s.d.1919. 23-Nov-93 Christie's, New York #87/R
$6000	£3974	La Volante (59x79cm-23x31in) s.d.1912. 24-Nov-92 Christie's, New York #87/R

MORALES, Rodolfo (1925-) Mexican
$3184	£2041	Untitled (32x78cm-13x31in) s. 29-Apr-93 Louis Morton, Mexico #182 (M.P 10000)
$5000	£3401	Smokers (61x117cm-24x46in) oil sand board. 16-Apr-94 Young Fine Arts Auctions, Maine #174/R
$7000	£4636	Paisaje y figuras (43x80cm-17x31in) s.d.1966 masonite. 23-Nov-92 Sotheby's, New York #246/R
$11000	£7285	Untitled (60x69cm-24x27in) s. 23-Nov-92 Sotheby's, New York #254/R
$12000	£8108	Con la patria .. alto (100x80cm-39x31in) s. painted 1988. 23-Nov-93 Christie's, New York #198/R
$16000	£10667	Aliento (100x80cm-39x31in) s. painted 1988. 18-May-94 Christie's, New York #227/R
$28000	£18543	Untitled (121x150cm-48x59in) s. 24-Nov-92 Christie's, New York #35/R
$50000	£33784	Piedad (182x229cm-72x90in) s. oil sand painted 1989. 22-Nov-93 Sotheby's, New York #71/R
$65000	£43333	Suenos (148x218cm-58x86in) s. painted 1987. 18-May-94 Christie's, New York #67/R
$450	£304	Oaxacan God (49x34cm-19x13in) s. mixed media. 21-Apr-94 Butterfield & Butterfield, San Francisco #1108/R

MORAN, E Percy (1862-1935) American
$850	£590	Genre scene (56x38cm-22x15in) s. board. 5-Mar-93 Skinner, Bolton #605 a
$1729	£1095	Minuet (52x83cm-20x33in) s. canvas on masonite. 1-Dec-92 Phillips, Toronto #79/R (C.D 2500)
$2200	£1438	Waiting in garden (76x51cm-30x20in) s. 4-May-93 Christie's, East, New York #72
$2500	£1623	Departure of George Washington (51x36cm-20x14in) s. canvas on board. 9-Sep-93 Sotheby's Arcade, New York #248/R
$2800	£1842	Minuet (55x89cm-22x35in) s. canvas on masonite. 31-Mar-93 Sotheby's Arcade, New York #96/R
$4450	£2853	The minuet (56x89cm-22x35in) s. canvas laid on board. 28-May-93 Sloan, North Bethesda #2690/R
$500	£333	No One at Home (43x56cm-17x11in) s. W/C pencil paper on card. 1-Jun-94 Doyle, New York #47

MORAN, Edward (1829-1901) American
$600	£411	Marine scene (28x46cm-11x18in) s. 10-Feb-94 Skinner, Bolton #65
$700	£476	Landscape with rockery (30x25cm-12x10in) s. 17-Apr-94 Hanzel Galleries, Chicago #11
$2000	£1307	Ships on high seas (63x56cm-25x22in) s. 4-May-93 Christie's, East, New York #21
$2000	£1342	Sketch at Greenport (30x46cm-12x18in) s. panel. 15-Dec-93 Boos Gallery, Michigan #446/R
$2400	£1270	Sailing vessels before a storm (30x43cm-12x17in) s. 11-Sep-92 Skinner, Bolton #151/R
$3250	£2138	REsting in field (41x61cm-16x24in) s. 31-Mar-93 Sotheby's Arcade, New York #65/R

MORAN, Edward (1829-1901) American-cont.

$4000	£2703	Twilight at sea (30x41cm-12x16in) s. panel. 31-Mar-94 Sotheby's Arcade, New York #21/R
$5750	£3382	Mid-ocean (58x107cm-23x42in) s. 8-Oct-92 Freeman Fine Arts, Philadelphia #1112/R
$6500	£3757	Ships in harbour (30x51cm-12x20in) s. 24-Sep-92 Sotheby's, New York #16/R
$10000	£6993	Children crabbing (76x127cm-30x50in) s.d.1890. 10-Mar-93 Sotheby's, New York #38/R
$11000	£6962	Off Atlantic Highlands (76x122cm-30x48in) s. 4-Dec-92 Christie's, New York #227/R
$13000	£7514	Cliffs in storm (158x114cm-62x45in) s. 24-Sep-92 Sotheby's, New York #32/R
$15000	£8671	Harbour at sunset (43x61cm-17x24in) s. 24-Sep-92 Sotheby's, New York #30/R
$16000	£10526	Moonlight on Thames (93x71cm-37x28in) s. 13-Jun-93 Butterfield & Butterfield, San Francisco #3147/R
$16000	£10596	Oyster gatherers (56x89cm-22x35in) s.d.1883. 22-Sep-93 Christie's, New York #32/R
$17000	£11333	Sunset on the marsh (61x107cm-24x42in) s. 16-Mar-94 Christie's, New York #9/R
$19000	£12179	Early dawn, New York harbour (36x56cm-14x22in) s. 27-May-93 Sotheby's, New York #161/R
$24000	£15190	Little sailors, Rockaway Beach (70x105cm-28x41in) s. 4-Dec-92 Christie's, New York #224/R
$28000	£18792	Reception of the 'Isere' in New York Bay, June 20, 1885 (47x80cm-19x31in) s.d.1885 s.i.stretcher. 3-Dec-93 Christie's, New York #87/R
$55000	£35256	Shipwreck (104x163cm-41x64in) s.d.1866. 27-May-93 Sotheby's, New York #162/R
$140000	£93960	Madeleine's Victory over Countess of Dufferin, Third America's Cup Challenger, 1876 (61x107cm-24x42in), s.d.1876. 3-Dec-93 Christie's, New York #111/R
$1500	*£949*	*Ships in harbour (20x25cm-8x10in) s. pastel. 5-Dec-92 Louisiana Auction Exchange #74/R*
$3000	*£1987*	*Yachting race (56x48cm-22x19in) s. W/C. 23-Sep-93 Sotheby's, New York #49/R*
$3500	*£2023*	*New York from the Channel (46x60cm-18x24in) s. W/C board. 25-Sep-92 Sotheby's Arcade, New York #120/R*

MORAN, Edward (attrib) (1829-1901) American

$850	£556	Return of the fleet (61x91cm-24x36in) 16-May-93 Hindman Galleries, Chicago #61
$1000	£658	Entering New York Harbour (46x61cm-18x24in) bears sig.d.1891 board. 2-Jun-93 Doyle, New York #77

MORAN, Leon (1864-1941) American

$1600	£1053	Sleigh ride to church. Rainbow over mountainous landscape (23x37cm-9x15in) s.d.87 s.d.74 pair. 31-Mar-93 Sotheby's Arcade, New York #133/R
$1937	£1309	Waiting (77x46cm-30x18in) s.d.86 i.verso. 3-Nov-93 Sotheby's, Toronto #32/R (C.D 2500)
$550	*£364*	*Victorian Beauty (46x30cm-18x12in) s. W/C. 3-Jan-93 Litchfield Auction Gallery #6*

MORAN, Percy (1862-1935) American

$650	£442	A rare vintage (46x61cm-18x24in) s. 14-Apr-94 Freeman Fine Arts, Philadelphia #990/R
$5500	£3716	Young girl in the garden (71x56cm-28x22in) s. 31-Oct-93 Hindman Galleries, Chicago #682/R

MORAN, Peter (1841-1914) American

$650	£425	Sheep in winter landscape (61x51cm-24x20in) s.d.1864. 7-Oct-93 Freeman Fine Arts, Philadelphia #897
$1500	£867	Cows by the shore (31x69cm-12x27in) s. en grisaille board. 25-Sep-92 Sotheby's Arcade, New York #114/R
$1900	£1218	Luminous forest interior with figures (46x36cm-18x14in) s. 28-May-93 Sloan, North Bethesda #2673/R
$2250	£1136	Cattle resting (30x56cm-12x22in) s. 28-Aug-92 Young Fine Arts Auctions, Maine #225/R
$3100	£2026	Landscape with cows (51x71cm-20x28in) s. 7-Oct-93 Freeman Fine Arts, Philadelphia #893/R
$700	*£458*	*Cattle auction (61x43cm-24x17in) s. black white chk gouache. 29-Jun-94 Doyle, New York #59*

MORAN, Thomas (1837-1926) American

$7500	£5000	Golden bough (75x113cm-30x44in) s.i.d.1862 after J.M.W.Turner. 16-Mar-94 Christie's, New York #17/R
$12000	£7947	Mission in Old Mexico (51x41cm-20x16in) mono.d.1921. 22-Sep-93 Christie's, New York #92/R
$22000	£14103	Summer shower (35x50cm-14x20in) init.d.1878 panel. 26-May-93 Christie's, New York #64/R
$22000	£14103	Bathers (52x42cm-20x17in) init. painted c.1879. 27-May-93 Sotheby's, New York #209/R
$28000	£18792	Borda Gardens, Mexico (67x51cm-26x20in) mono.d.1913. 2-Dec-93 Sotheby's, New York #18/R
$31000	£20667	Mexican landscape near Cuernavaca (36x51cm-14x20in) mono.d.1905 panel. 25-May-94 Sotheby's, New York #9/R
$32000	£20513	Rustic bridge - Easthampton (26x36cm-10x14in) s.d.1905 s.i.d.verso. 26-May-93 Christie's, New York #79/R
$32000	£21477	the back of the South dome - Yosemite valley view (25x30cm-10x12in) s.i.d.1916. 4-Mar-94 Skinner, Bolton #247/R
$33000	£21854	Gate of Venice, sunset (36x69cm-14x27in) s.d.1895. 23-Sep-93 Sotheby's, New York #36/R
$35000	£23179	Index Peak, Wyoming (16x28cm-6x11in) s. painted 1911. 15-Jun-94 Butterfield & Butterfield, San Francisco #4491/R
$38000	£25503	The angry river (76x102cm-30x40in) mono.d.1911. 2-Dec-93 Sotheby's, New York #58/R
$39000	£25828	Autumn, Peconic Bay, Long Island (51x76cm-20x30in) s.d.1904. 23-Sep-93 Sotheby's, New York #23/R

340

MORAN, Thomas (1837-1926) American-cont.

$40000	£25316	Entrance to the Grand Canal, Venice (36x51cm-14x20in) s.d.1906 s.i.d.verso. 4-Dec-92 Christie's, New York #243/R
$42000	£27815	Grand Canal, Venice (51x41cm-20x16in) s.d.1903. 23-Sep-93 Sotheby's, New York #37/R
$45000	£28481	Green River, Wyoming at Castle Butte (20x33cm-8x13in) mono. panel. 3-Dec-92 Sotheby's, New York #49/R
$48000	£30380	Bathing hole, Cuernavaca, Mexico (51x63cm-20x25in) s.d.1913 s.i.d.verso. 4-Dec-92 Christie's, New York #250/R
$50000	£31646	Venice - Reminiscence of Vera Cruz, Mexico (44x69cm-17x27in) mono.d.1886 i.stretcher. 3-Dec-92 Sotheby's, New York #48/R
$75000	£52448	Under the Red Wall, Grand Canyon of Arizona (25x30cm-10x12in) s.mono.d.1917 and s.with thumbprint. 11-Mar-93 Christie's, New York #111/R
$80000	£51282	Cloud and sunshine on Montauk, Long Island (79x17cm-31x7in) s.i.d.1898stretcher. 9-Dec-92 Butterfield & Butterfield, San Francisco #3823/R
$140000	£93960	Autumn landscape (51x76cm-20x30in) s. 2-Dec-93 Sotheby's, New York #19/R
$175000	£116667	Autumn on the Wissahickon (76x116cm-30x46in) s.i.d.1864. 25-May-94 Sotheby's, New York #29/R
$200000	£128205	Icebergs in Mid-Atlantic (77x115cm-30x45in) s.d.1909. 27-May-93 Sotheby's, New York #176/R
$260000	£173333	Jupiter Terrace, Yellowstone (51x76cm-20x30in) init.d.1893. 26-May-94 Christie's, New York #73/R
$350000	£234899	Grand Canyon (76x63cm-30x25in) mono.s.d.1912. 2-Dec-93 Sotheby's, New York #65/R
$2500	£1678	Breezing Up - a moonlit scene (33x41cm-13x16in) mono.d.1884 i.verso pastel paperboard. 26-Mar-94 Skinner, Bolton #69/R
$4000	£2685	Coastal scene, California (22x45cm-9x18in) s. pencil W/C. 8-Dec-93 Butterfield & Butterfield, San Francisco #3363/R
$20000	£11561	Green River, Wyoming (22x34cm-9x13in) s.d.79 W/C. 24-Sep-92 Sotheby's, New York #83/R
$70000	£44872	Castle Butte, Green River, Wyoming (38x54cm-15x21in) s.d.1894 W/C pencil. 26-May-93 Christie's, New York #96/R
$130000	£87248	Giant Blue Spring, Yellowstone (25x36cm-10x14in) s.d.1873 W/C. 2-Dec-93 Sotheby's, New York #52/R
$240000	£151899	Castle Butte, Green River, Wyoming (50x39cm-20x15in) mono.d.1900 W/C. 3-Dec-92 Sotheby's, New York #14/R

MORAN, Thomas (after) (1837-1926) American

$3600	£2308	Mt Tamalpais (79x58cm-31x23in) s.d.1883. 13-Dec-92 Hindman Galleries, Chicago #36/R

MORANG, Alfred (1901-1958) American

$1200	£789	Ginger (27x23cm-11x9in) s.d.54 W/C pen. 13-Jun-93 Butterfield & Butterfield, San Francisco #3261/R

MORGAN, Ike (?) American

$1800	£1192	George Washington (91x61cm-36x24in) s. pastel ink. 21-Nov-92 Litchfield Auction Gallery #29

MORGAN, Mary Vernon (19th C) Canadian

$1586	£1050	Rhineland flowers (75x49cm-30x19in) s.i.verso W/C. 29-Jun-93 Bearnes, Torquay #696

MORGAN, Mary de Neale (1868-1948) American

$1000	£662	Monterey coastal (30x30cm-12x12in) s. masonite. 14-Jun-94 John Moran, Pasadena #65 b
$1100	£743	Landscape with hay wagon (30x41cm-12x16in) s. canvas laid down on board. 31-Oct-93 Hindman Galleries, Chicago #681 a/R
$1200	£811	Atmospheric landscape (20x25cm-8x10in) s. board. 15-Jun-93 John Moran, Pasadena #87
$1300	£878	Landscape (30x41cm-12x16in) s. canvas laid down on board. 31-Oct-93 Hindman Galleries, Chicago #682 a
$1300	£903	Carmel garden (20x20cm-8x8in) s. paper on board. 7-Mar-93 Butterfield & Butterfield, San Francisco #88/R
$2250	£1510	Sunny hills, Carmel Valley (41x51cm-16x20in) s. board. 8-Dec-93 Butterfield & Butterfield, San Francisco #3412/R
$2250	£1324	Spring rain (61x61cm-24x24in) s. board. 4-Oct-92 Butterfield & Butterfield, Los Angeles #89/R
$2500	£1689	Atmospheric landscape (51x41cm-20x16in) s. board. 9-Nov-93 John Moran, Pasadena #888
$3500	£2431	Cypress trees on Monterey Coast (55x45cm-22x18in) s. board. 7-Mar-93 Butterfield & Butterfield, San Francisco #89/R
$700	£473	Near Palm Springs, CA (41x51cm-16x20in) s. gouache board. 15-Jun-93 John Moran, Pasadena #168
$700	£473	Monterey Coastal (28x36cm-11x14in) s. pastel. 15-Jun-93 John Moran, Pasadena #32
$750	£507	Monterey coastal (28x38cm-11x15in) s. gouache board. 15-Jun-93 John Moran, Pasadena #169
$950	£629	Desert landscape (38x43cm-15x17in) s. gouache board. 28-Sep-93 John Moran, Pasadena #230
$1800	£1184	Cypress trees on coast (29x24cm-11x9in) s. gouache. 13-Jun-93 Butterfield & Butterfield, San Francisco #841/R
$2750	£1910	Sand dunes near Carmel (36x46cm-14x18in) s. gouache paperboard. 7-Mar-93 Butterfield & Butterfield, San Francisco #87/R
$3000	£1987	Foothills in blossom (32x42cm-13x17in) s. gouache. 15-Jun-94 Butterfield & Butterfield, San Francisco #4649/R

MORGAN, Maud Cabot (1903-) American
$2100   £1409   Mountain (91x229cm-36x90in) s.d.80verso. 6-May-94 Skinner, Bolton #158/R

MORGAN-SNELL (1920-) Brazilian
$1426   £964   La Guerre des Centaures (74x53cm-29x21in) s.d.70 s.i.verso mixed media. 29-Apr-94 Beaussant & Lefevre, Paris #78/R (F.FR 8500)

MORIARTY, David (1957-) American
$1600   £1081   Paul Revere in Green and brown. Corral (88x136cm-35x54in) s.i.verso d.89verso d.90verso panel pair oval. 8-Nov-93 Christie's, East, New York #116/R

MORIN, Arturo (1953-) Mexican
$1534   £1037   Casas en el campo (125x125cm-49x49in) s.d.1993 acrylic oil. 20-Oct-93 Louis Morton, Mexico #13/R (M.P 4800)
$1758   £1188   Sandias blancas (130x150cm-51x59in) s.d.1993 paste acrylic canvas. 20-Oct-93 Louis Morton, Mexico #79 (M.P 5500)

MORLETTE, Juan Patricio (1715-1780) Mexican
$42000   £27451   Triumph of Alexander the Great (82x127cm-32x50in) s.i. 7-Oct-93 Christie's, New York #106/R

MORRICE, James Wilson (1865-1924) Canadian
$3113   £2062   Summer landscape (16x20cm-6x8in) s.d.91 canvas on board. 24-Nov-92 Joyner Fine Art, Toronto #197/R (C.D 4000)
$5812   £3927   Children in a garden (23x30cm-9x12in) s. canvas laid on board. 3-Nov-93 Sotheby's, Toronto #245/R (C.D 7500)
$6917   £4612   A garden scene (11x15cm-4x6in) studio st.verso panel. 11-May-94 Sotheby's, Toronto #38/R (C.D 9500)
$8306   £5612   Ruins of Notre Dame de Lorette (23x32cm-9x13in) panel. 23-Nov-93 Joyner Fine Art, Toronto #52/R (C.D 11000)
$13107   £8738   A cafe scene (15x11cm-6x4in) studio st.verso panel. 11-May-94 Sotheby's, Toronto #37/R (C.D 18000)
$21845   £14563   Cab stand, Paris (15x13cm-6x5in) s. studio st.verso panel. 11-May-94 Sotheby's, Toronto #81/R (C.D 30000)
$23301   £15534   Promenade sur la plage (22x30cm-9x12in) s. canvas on board. 13-May-94 Joyner Fine Art, Toronto #134/R (C.D 32000)
$23782   £15544   Venetian Canal scene with gondolier (12x15cm-5x6in) studio st. panel painted c.1901-02. 18-May-93 Joyner Fine Art, Toronto #33/R (C.D 30000)
$29445   £19895   West Indies mud huts (55x66cm-22x26in) i.verso. 3-Nov-93 Sotheby's, Toronto #164/R (C.D 38000)
$43689   £29126   Red houses, Venice (33x23cm-13x9in) s. panel. 11-May-94 Sotheby's, Toronto #95/R (C.D 60000)
$72816   £48544   Plage, Parame (23x32cm-9x13in) s. panel. 13-May-94 Joyner Fine Art, Toronto #15/R (C.D 100000)
$583   £388   Venice (10x15cm-4x6in) dr. 11-May-94 Sotheby's, Toronto #5 (C.D 800)

MORRIS, A (18-20th C) British/American
$988   £650   Scottish grey faced sheep resting on moor (51x76cm-20x30in) s.d.1890. 21-Jul-94 Heathcote Ball, Leicester #693
$1184   £800   Moorland scene with sheep, rocky heather clas outcrops beyond (74x127cm-29x50in) s.d.1882. 18-Oct-93 Henry Spencer, Retford #326/R

MORRIS, Andrew (19th C) American
$721   £481   Elderly countryman and his wife conversing with man and his dog (66x55cm-26x22in) s.d.1844. 31-May-94 Ritchie, Toronto #113/R (C.D 1000)

MORRIS, C (19/20th C) British/American
$1275   £750   Richmond. Landscape with bridge over the river Swale, castle beyond (75x125cm-30x49in) s.d.1876. 8-Oct-92 Lawrence, Crewkerne #71

MORRIS, George Ford (1873-1960) American
$500   £327   Horse and rider (51x74cm-20x29in) s.d.1919 gouache. 30-Jun-94 Mystic Fine Arts, Connecticut #70 a/R

MORRIS, George L K (1905-1975) American
$3500   £2318   Gyration (46x38cm-18x15in) s. i.d.1961 verso. 23-Sep-93 Sotheby's, New York #271/R
$6000   £4082   Torpedo station (18x26cm-7x10in) s. s.i.d.1945verso fresco relief stone. 15-Nov-93 Christie's, East, New York #276/R

MORRIS, Kathleen (1893-1986) Canadian
$982   £663   Cows in field (30x35cm-12x14in) s. panel. 23-Nov-93 Joyner Fine Art, Toronto #198 (C.D 1300)
$3766   £2461   House by river (30x36cm-12x14in) s. panel. 19-May-93 Sotheby's, Toronto #260/R (C.D 4750)
$6974   £4712   McGill cab stand Montreal (25x34cm-10x13in) s. i.verso panel. 3-Nov-93 Sotheby's, Toronto #109 a/R (C.D 9000)
$8010   £5340   Sunday morning, Old Montreal (30x36cm-12x14in) s. i.verso panel. 11-May-94 Sotheby's, Toronto #163/R (C.D 11000)
$9466   £6311   The Iroquois village of Caughnawaga, Quebec (46x53cm-18x21in) s. 11-May-94 Sotheby's, Toronto #164/R (C.D 13000)

MORRIS, Kathleen (attrib) (1893-1986) Canadian
$950   £621   Covered bridge (46x61cm-18x24in) s. i.verso masonite. 18-May-93 Butterfield & Butterfield, San Francisco #1571/R

MORRIS, Kyle (1918-1979) American
$708 £454 White and green flow (190x100cm-75x39in) mono.s.i. 14-Dec-92 Christie's, Rome #39/R (I.L 1000000)

MORRIS, Robert (1931-) American
$1200 £805 Untitled (95x127cm-37x50in) s.i.d.88 graphite black oilstick. 3-May-94 Christie's, East, New York #173/R
$1600 £1111 Untitled (53x70cm-21x28in) s.d.1966 ink. 23-Feb-93 Sotheby's, New York #329/R
$2831 £1900 Untitled (51x68cm-20x27in) s.d.1966 ink. 23-Mar-94 Sotheby's, London #379/R
$4500 £2647 Untitled - hook, track, memory dents (29x98cm-11x39in) s.d.9/16/63 pencil graph paper 8 bronze plaques. 6-Oct-92 Sotheby's, New York #108/R

MORRISEAU, Norval (1932-) Canadian
$1325 £872 Moose (81x129cm-32x51in) s.i.d.1968 tempera kraft paper. 7-Jun-93 Ritchie, Toronto #106/R (C.D 1700)

MORRISSEAU, Norval (?) Canadian
$725 £483 Bird and serpent cycle with man (102x81cm-40x32in) s. i.d.1973 verso acrylic art board. 6-Jun-94 Waddingtons, Toronto #1267 (C.D 1500)
$789 £526 Beaver (77x118cm-30x46in) s. acrylic on brown paper. 30-May-94 Ritchie, Toronto #105/R (C.D 1100)
$1364 £909 Silent eye (175x94cm-69x37in) s. acrylic. 30-May-94 Ritchie, Toronto #107 (C.D 1700)
$1435 £957 Astral consciousness (128x96cm-50x38in) s. acrylic. 30-May-94 Ritchie, Toronto #108 (C.D 2000)
$1505 £1010 Bird of prey fish and butterfly (120x91cm-47x36in) s. acrylic painted c.1978. 29-Nov-93 Ritchie, Toronto #149/R (C.D 2000)
$1881 £1263 Thunderbird (118x75cm-46x30in) s. acrylic painted c.1978. 29-Nov-93 Ritchie, Toronto #150/R (C.D 2500)
$3144 £1990 Mother and children (127x127cm-50x50in) s.syllabics. 30-Nov-92 Ritchie, Toronto #108/R (C.D 4000)
$3574 £2399 Mother and child (101x81cm-40x32in) s. i.d.1966verso acrylic. 29-Nov-93 Ritchie, Toronto #146/R (C.D 4750)

MORROW, Raymond (19th C) American
$1000 £680 Winter skating scene (66x102cm-26x40in) s. 9-Jul-93 Sloan, North Bethesda #2817/R

MORSE, Henry D (1826-1888) American
$750 £391 Hanging duck and woodcock (51x41cm-20x16in) s. painted 1864. 6-Aug-92 Eldred, Massachusetts #1044
$7500 £5068 Hunting dogs , s. 10-Aug-93 Stonington Fine Arts, Stonington #95

MORSE, J B (19th C) American
$2600 £1757 Country landscape, Morris County, New Jersey (44x71cm-17x28in) s. 20-Mar-93 Weschler, Washington #81/R

MORSE, Samuel F B (1791-1872) American
$1800 £1040 Portrait of man in top hat (13x11cm-5x4in) s.i.d.1840 panel painted oval. 25-Sep-92 Sotheby's Arcade, New York #92/R
$4500 £2941 Junius Brutus Booth as Brutus (61x51cm-24x20in) s. 22-May-93 Weschler, Washington #81/R

MORTON, Geer (20th C) American
$750 £507 The blue bicycle (76x61cm-30x24in) 21-Apr-94 Butterfield & Butterfield, San Francisco #1176/R
$1300 £878 Rutherford Vineyard (95x122cm-37x48in) s. s.i.d.July 1979verso. 21-Apr-94 Butterfield & Butterfield, San Francisco #1177/R
$1400 £946 Still life with yellow lamp no.2 (115x104cm-45x41in) s. s.i.d.79verso. 21-Oct-93 Butterfield & Butterfield, San Francisco #2782/R

MORVILLER, Joseph (1800-1870) American
$2400 £1579 Winter landscape (36x56cm-14x22in) s.d.1864. 31-Mar-93 Sotheby's Arcade, New York #54/R
$4000 £2667 Winter landscape at dusk (30x51cm-12x20in) s.d.1869 panel. 23-May-94 Christie's, East, New York #75/R
$7000 £4237 Skating on pond (35x51cm-14x20in) s.d.66. 26-May-93 Christie's, New York #29/R

MOSCA, August (1909-) American/Russian
$5500 £3459 Boy on bicycle (119x84cm-47x33in) s.d.1957. 22-Apr-93 Freeman Fine Arts, Philadelphia #1063 b

MOSES, Anna Mary Robertson (Grandma) (1860-1961) American
$7000 £4730 The miller in the dell (23x28cm-9x11in) s. tempera board. 31-Mar-94 Sotheby's Arcade, New York #350/R
$9000 £5202 Through the bridge (20x25cm-8x10in) s. i.d.Nov.20,1944verso masonite. 23-Sep-92 Christie's, New York #276/R
$9000 £6000 Country garden and cottage (27x32cm-11x13in) s. masonite. 16-Mar-94 Christie's, New York #141/R
$10500 £6954 Milking (25x38cm-10x15in) s. painted 1955 tempera board. 28-Nov-92 Dunning's, Illinois #1141/R
$13000 £8609 Sleet storm (28x38cm-11x15in) s. d.1957 num.1758 verso oil glitter mica board. 13-Nov-92 Skinner, Bolton #223/R
$14000 £9233 A Hunting (23x30cm-9x12in) s. i.d.1944 verso masonite. 17-Mar-94 Sotheby's, New York #184/R

MOSES, Anna Mary Robertson (Grandma) (1860-1961) American-cont.
$14000	£9333	Uncle John's Home (30x35cm-12x14in) s. i.d.1942 verso board. 17-Mar-94 Sotheby's, New York #183/R
$17000	£11409	Which way (24x37cm-9x15in) s.i. i.d.April 23,1942verso oil tempera board. 2-Dec-93 Sotheby's, New York #160/R
$18000	£12000	King Church (46x61cm-18x24in) s.i. d.Aug 28 1952verso tempera masonite. 26-May-94 Christie's, New York #159/R
$19000	£12179	The Thrashers (46x61cm-18x24in) i.d.verso tempera masonite. 26-May-93 Christie's, New York #238/R
$20000	£13986	Home of John Brown (41x51cm-16x20in) s.d.Jan 25 1943 i.verso masonite. 11-Mar-93 Christie's, New York #263/R
$26000	£18182	Canada (46x61cm-18x24in) s. i.d.Feb.7,1958verso masonite. 10-Mar-93 Sotheby's, New York #165/R
$28000	£18667	The Sycamore Farm (51x66cm-20x26in) s. i.d.July 26 1944 tempera masonite. 26-May-94 Christie's, New York #158/R
$28000	£18792	Sugar house (30x41cm-12x16in) s. i.d.Aug.26,1956verso board. 2-Dec-93 Sotheby's, New York #154/R
$30000	£20134	In maple sugar time (46x51cm-18x20in) s. i.d.Sept.14,1942verso board. 2-Dec-93 Sotheby's, New York #153/R
$32500	£21667	The Train (41x61cm-16x24in) s. i.d.1957 verso board. 17-Mar-94 Sotheby's, New York #181/R
$37500	£25168	Over the bridge (41x61cm-16x24in) s. i.d.Oct.1960verso masonite. 2-Dec-93 Sotheby's, New York #159/R
$37500	£25000	Did You See Uncle John (42x55cm-17x22in) s. i.d.1949 verso masonite. 17-Mar-94 Sotheby's, New York #182/R
$40000	£26490	Maple Orchard (56x66cm-22x26in) s. d.1942 verso masonite. 23-Sep-93 Sotheby's, New York #298/R
$42000	£28000	The Old Red Mill in winter (51x60cm-20x24in) s. i.d.Sep 4 1944verso tempera glitter masonite. 26-May-94 Christie's, New York #156/R
$55000	£36667	Help (41x61cm-16x24in) s. i.d.July 6 1956 masonite. 26-May-94 Christie's, New York #160/R
$70000	£46667	The haunted house (49x59cm-19x23in) s. i.d.Jan 25 1943 tempera masonite. 26-May-94 Christie's, New York #157/R
$70000	£44872	In the springtime (61x76cm-24x30in) s. i.d.1944 verso masonite. 26-May-93 Christie's, New York #239/R
$180000	£120805	Country fair (89x114cm-35x45in) s. i.d.May 9,1950verso. 2-Dec-93 Sotheby's, New York #144/R

MOSES, Ed (1926-) American
$1500	£993	Untitled (37x95cm-15x37in) init.i.d.74 crayon pencil vellum. 29-Sep-93 Sotheby's Arcade, New York #258/R

MOSES, Forrest K (1893-1974) American
$750	£507	Tread power (41x61cm-16x24in) s. masonite painted 1959. 31-Oct-93 Hindman Galleries, Chicago #720/R
$750	£503	Winter village scene (23x30cm-9x12in) s. board. 16-Dec-93 Mystic Fine Arts, Connecticut #117/R
$800	£541	Winter days (41x61cm-16x24in) s. masonite painted 1957. 31-Oct-93 Hindman Galleries, Chicago #719/R

MOSKOWITZ, Robert (1935-) American
$7000	£4575	Untitled (63x63cm-25x25in) s.d.1961 verso rabbit skin glue pigment collage. 4-May-93 Sotheby's, New York #109/R
$7500	£5208	Untitled (129x102cm-51x40in) s.d.1962 oil collage canvas. 23-Feb-93 Sotheby's, New York #328/R
$20000	£13245	Untitled (137x102cm-54x40in) s.d.1962 verso collage aluminium paint canvas. 18-Nov-92 Sotheby's, New York #140/R

MOSLER, Henry (1841-1920) American
$2500	£1645	Requiem (160x236cm-63x93in) s. s.i.stretcher. 2-Apr-93 Sloan, North Bethesda #2477/R

MOSNER, Ricardo (1948-) Argentina
$736	£481	Homme debout (29x20cm-11x8in) painted 1987 acrylic paper. 23-Dec-92 Binoche et Godeau, Paris #21 (F.FR 4000)

MOSTEIRO, Mario (?) Argentinian
$750	£441	Naturaleza muerta (39x49cm-15x19in) 29-Sep-92 VerBo, Buenos Aires #81
$850	£500	Naturaleza muerta (50x40cm-20x15in) 29-Sep-92 VerBo, Buenos Aires #82

MOTHERWELL, Robert (1915-1991) American
$6541	£4248	Beside the sea (53x25cm-21x10in) mono. i.d.1962verso canvas laid down on canvas. 22-Jun-94 Galerie Kornfeld, Berne #738 (S.FR 8750)
$7650	£5134	Red and grey (63x35cm-25x14in) mono painted c.1965. 23-Jun-93 Galerie Kornfeld, Berne #605 (S.FR 11500)
$12000	£8108	Alberta Suite No.1 (91x60cm-36x24in) s. acrylic painted 1971. 11-Nov-93 Sotheby's, New York #307/R
$20000	£13072	Elegy of Night (48x70cm-19x28in) init.d.75 acrylic paper on board. 5-May-93 Christie's, New York #279/R
$22000	£14570	Untitled (67x52cm-26x20in) s.d.75 acrylic paper. 19-Nov-92 Christie's, New York #286/R
$27000	£18121	Blackness of black (28x36cm-11x14in) init. board painted 1958. 4-May-94 Christie's, New York #111/R
$60000	£39735	Spanish elegy (29x37cm-11x15in) s.d.1959verso s.i.d.verso paper. 19-Nov-92 Christie's, New York #313/R

MOTHERWELL, Robert (1915-1991) American-cont.

$65000	£43046	Full tide (198x76cm-78x30in) init. s.d.1976verso. 18-Nov-92 Christie's, New York #40/R
$70000	£46358	Splurge number 2 (198x76cm-78x30in) s.d.74 s.i.d.verso acrylic. 19-Nov-92 Christie's, New York #295/R
$350000	£236486	Elegy to Spanish Republic No.159 (112x182cm-44x72in) init.d.79 s.i.d.1979 verso. 9-Nov-93 Christie's, New York #15/R
$865	£580	Etude de femme (36x27cm-14x11in) mono.d.57 pencil. 23-Jun-93 Galerie Kornfeld, Berne #603 (S.FR 1300)
$1346	£874	Etude de femme (36x27cm-14x11in) mono.d.57 pencil. 22-Jun-94 Galerie Kornfeld, Berne #736 (S.FR 1800)
$1996	£1339	Etude de feuillage (21x27cm-8x11in) mono gouache over chk painted c.1960. 23-Jun-93 Galerie Kornfeld, Berne #604 (S.FR 3000)
$2400	£1611	Untitled (37x29cm-15x11in) init. brush sepia ink paperboard. 23-Feb-94 Christie's, East, New York #278/R
$2729	£1772	Spanish elegy - la Carolina (28x36cm-11x14in) mono. s.i.d.1950verso Indian ink pen. 22-Jun-94 Galerie Kornfeld, Berne #735 (S.FR 3650)
$3289	£2136	Etude de feuillage (21x27cm-8x11in) mono. gouache over chk executed c.1960. 22-Jun-94 Galerie Kornfeld, Berne #737 (S.FR 4400)
$4000	£2685	Untitled (183x61cm-72x24in) init.d.74 oil paper collage tape board. 5-May-94 Sotheby's, New York #126/R
$5500	£3235	Untitled (29x36cm-11x14in) init. ink pencil. 6-Oct-92 Sotheby's, New York #46 a/R
$9000	£6081	Untitled (30x23cm-12x9in) init.d.Aug 76 brush ink graphite. 10-Nov-93 Christie's, New York #153/R
$11000	£7383	Mural sketch (38x51cm-15x20in) init.d.67 acrylic crayon pencil paperboard. 5-May-94 Sotheby's, New York #123/R
$16200	£10800	Samurai (60x45cm-24x18in) s.d.Aug 74 tempera Indian ink acrylic. 3-Jun-94 Lempertz, Cologne #801/R (DM 27000)
$20000	£13245	Scarlet and Gauloises (51x40cm-20x16in) init.d. s.i.d.29 June 1972verso acrylic collage. 19-Nov-92 Christie's, New York #291/R
$21000	£12353	Untitled (56x43cm-22x17in) s. acrylic ink. 6-Oct-92 Sotheby's, New York #47/R
$28000	£18919	Yucatan (86x46cm-34x18in) init.d.80 acrylic ink paper collage masonite. 10-Nov-93 Christie's, New York #158/R
$30000	£19608	Gauloises with red and green (51x41cm-20x16in) init.d.71 oil collage board. 4-May-93 Sotheby's, New York #303/R
$32500	£21523	Splatter (29x37cm-11x15in) init. ink executed 1954. 18-Nov-92 Sotheby's, New York #92/R
$34000	£22819	Arte (91x61cm-36x24in) init.d.76 acrylic paper canvas collage masonite. 4-May-94 Christie's, New York #146/R
$35760	£24000	Guardian 3 (56x36cm-22x14in) s.d.1966 collage newspaper acrylic board. 25-Mar-93 Christie's, London #98/R
$58000	£38411	Die Spinnerin (101x68cm-40x27in) init.d.76 acrylic paper canvas collage on board. 18-Nov-92 Christie's, New York #1/R
$72000	£47059	Black palette (183x61cm-72x24in) s.d.75 acrylic canvas paper collage on board. 4-May-93 Christie's, New York #6/R
$85000	£57432	The Sicilian window (184x245cm-72x96in) init.d.72 s.d.1972 verso acrylic chl canvas. 11-Nov-93 Sotheby's, New York #299/R

MOTLEY, Robert (20th C) American

$829	£560	Evening, Impressionist style summer landscape (61x76cm-24x30in) s. painted 1932. 14-Jun-93 Lawrences, Bletchingley #1970/R

MOTTET, Jeanie Gallup (1864-?) American

$1200	£839	Woman sewing on veranda (69x56cm-27x22in) init. 11-Mar-93 Mystic Fine Arts, Connecticut #113/R

MOUNT, Rita (1888-1967) Canadian

$1367	£888	The weaver (49x61cm-19x24in) s.d.1915. 21-Jun-94 Fraser Pinneys, Quebec #153 (C.D 1900)

MOUNT, William Sidney (1807-1868) American

$610	£407	In the barn (23x31cm-9x12in) board. 30-May-94 Hodgins, Calgary #123 (C.D 850)
$1700	£1133	Figure of a woman (20x17cm-8x7in) d.1847 s.d.47 verso canvas on board. 23-May-94 Christie's, East, New York #9/R
$18000	£12081	Master Harry Russell, age 4 (53x43cm-21x17in) s.d.June 29, 1846verso. 3-Feb-94 Sloan, North Bethesda #2889/R
$29000	£20280	Cracking nuts (23x36cm-9x14in) s.d.1856 board. 11-Mar-93 Christie's, New York #9/R
$13000	£9091	Chopping down the tree (27x39cm-11x15in) s.d.Jan 16th 1844 pen sepia ink wash pencil. 11-Mar-93 Christie's, New York #1/R

MOUNTFORT, Arnold (19/20th C) American

$5508	£3600	Repose (71x91cm-28x36in) s.d.1904. 16-Sep-93 Christie's, S. Kensington #127/R

MOWBRAY, Henry Siddons (1858-1928) American

$10000	£6993	Myth of Proserpine, study for ceiling at Gunn Memorial Library (62x122cm-24x48in) oil gold paint. 10-Mar-93 Sotheby's, New York #94/R
$60000	£40000	The marriage of Persephone (53x86cm-21x34in) s. 26-May-94 Christie's, New York #84/R

MOWER, Martin (1870-?) American

$825	£519	Meeting of the waters (66x48cm-26x19in) s.d.1903 W/C. 22-Apr-93 Freeman Fine Arts, Philadelphia #1155/R

MOYA DEL PINO, Jose (1891-1969) American?
$3000 £2013 Procession (101x119cm-40x47in) s.d.37 board. 8-Dec-93 Butterfield & Butterfield, San Francisco #3518/R

MUELLER, Stephen (1947-) American
$1600 £1046 Performing helping hand (203x223cm-80x88in) acrylic raw pigment executed 1982. 22-Dec-92 Christie's, East, New York #43

MUHLSTOCK, Louis (1904-) Canadian
$674   £440   Autumn, Mount Royal (76x66cm-30x26in) s. 19-May-93 Sotheby's, Toronto #55 (C.D 850)
$680   £459   Sunflowers (71x91cm-28x36in) s. 23-Nov-93 Fraser Pinneys, Quebec #348 (C.D 900)
$674   £440   Reclining female nude (63x100cm-25x39in) s. col chk. 18-May-93 Joyner Fine Art, Toronto #215 (C.D 850)
$831   £561   Reclining nude (61x101cm-24x40in) s. col.crayons. 23-Nov-93 Fraser Pinneys, Quebec #393 (C.D 1100)

MULCASTER, Wynona (20th C) Canadian
$510   £340   Evening (72x52cm-28x20in) s.d.70 acrylic paper. 13-May-94 Joyner Fine Art, Toronto #283 (C.D 700)

MULERTT, Carel Eugene (1869-1915) American
$750   £472   Harvest (46x56cm-18x22in) s.d.1898. 25-Apr-93 James Bakker, Cambridge #101/R
$1200 £811   When the day's work is done (76x63cm-30x25in) s. 31-Mar-94 Sotheby's Arcade, New York #138/R

MULHAUPT, Frederick J (1871-1938) American
$650   £434   Walk through the woods (26x35cm-10x14in) s.d.06 panel. 23-May-94 Christie's, East, New York #156
$800   £541   Sailboats at dock (30x41cm-12x16in) s. 20-Apr-94 Doyle, New York #53
$950   £634   Landscape with haystacks (46x61cm-18x24in) s. 23-May-94 Christie's, East, New York #151/R
$1100 £705   Sailing ship encountering storm (30x41cm-12x16in) s.d.10. 26-Apr-93 Selkirks, St. Louis #162
$1200 £779   View from the town square (46x61cm-18x24in) s. 9-Sep-93 Sotheby's Arcade, New York #125/R
$1300 £850   Country road (46x69cm-18x27in) s.d.95. 15-May-93 Dunning's, Illinois #1194
$2000 £1342 Moonlit farm in the winter (41x51cm-16x20in) s. board. 8-Dec-93 Butterfield & Butterfield, San Francisco #3352/R
$2090 £1366 Evening, Wheeler's Wharf - Gloucester harbour view (20x25cm-8x10in) s. board. 14-May-93 Skinner, Bolton #127/R
$3000 £2000 Barn in moonlight (50x40cm-20x16in) s. canvas on board. 23-May-94 Christie's, East, New York #168/R
$8000 £5333 The morning hour (89x71cm-35x28in) s.d.1911. 26-May-94 Christie's, New York #89/R
$13000 £8667 On the dock (91x91cm-36x36in) s. 17-Mar-94 Sotheby's, New York #128/R
$31000 £20667 Cadiz salt ship, Gloucester harbour (127x152cm-50x60in) s. 17-Mar-94 Sotheby's, New York #128/R

MULLICAN, Matt (1951-) American
$2000 £1325 Untitled (36x61cm-14x24in) paper. 30-Jun-93 Sotheby's Arcade, New York #382/R
$10500 £6176 Untitled (243x122cm-96x48in) acrylic oil. 8-Oct-92 Christie's, New York #213/R
$1519 £1013 Mythological views (96x126cm-38x50in) pencil ink executed 1980. 2-Jun-94 AB Stockholms Auktionsverk, Stockholm #7222/R (S.KR 12000)
$11000 £7432 Untitled posters, gouache graphite 15 sheets of paper painted 1977. 10-Nov-93 Christie's, New York #279/R

MUNGER, Gilbert (1837-1903) American
$900   £588   Mountainous lake scene (36x61cm-14x24in) s. 30-Jun-94 Mystic Fine Arts, Connecticut #81

MUNOZ-VERA, Guillermo (1949-) Chilean
$27000 £18121 Bodegon (68x100cm-27x39in) s. 7-Jan-94 Gary Nader, Miami #131/R
$7000 £4698 Cascanueves (33x51cm-13x20in) pastel. 7-Jan-94 Gary Nader, Miami #54/R

MUNROE, Albert E (19/20th C) American
$2600 £1733 Table top fruit (30x25cm-12x10in) s.d.1871. 23-May-94 Hindman Galleries, Chicago #163

MUNSELL, Albert Henry (1858-?) American
$1800 £1216 Dawn road on the Island of Appledore (76x122cm-30x48in) s.d.91 s.id.stretcher. 31-Mar-94 Sotheby's Arcade, New York #113/R

MUNTZ, Laura Adeline see LYALL, Laura Adeline

MURCH, Walter (1907-1967) American/Canadian
$20000 £12821 Still life with lemons and potatoe (36x36cm-14x14in) s. 27-May-93 Sotheby's, New York #96/R
$26000 £17450 Crystals and electricity (48x48cm-19x19in) s. canvas on masonite. 3-Dec-93 Christie's, New York #15/R
$1000 £578   Beam and tower (27x36cm-11x14in) gouache. 25-Sep-92 Sotheby's Arcade, New York #469/R
$1100 £636   Girders and factory (26x36cm-10x14in) gouache. 25-Sep-92 Sotheby's Arcade, New York #470/R
$2000 £1333 Industrial abstraction. Cargo trailer, gouache pencil two. 16-Mar-94 Christie's, New York #138/R

MURCH, Walter (1907-1967) American/Canadian-cont.
$9000   £5960   Study for 'The Circle' (65x52cm-26x20in) chl pencil chk. 22-Sep-93 Christie's, New York #217/R

MURILLO, Gerardo see ATL, Dr

MURPHY, Herman Dudley (1867-1945) American
$2400   £1519   Seascape with sun behind clouds (26x36cm-10x14in) s. canvasboard laid down on aluminium. 2-Dec-92 Christie's, East, New York #42/R
$2600   £1722   Winter landscape (51x69cm-20x27in) s. 20-Nov-92 Eldred, Massachusetts #877/R
$3000   £1923   Path through landscape (91x122cm-36x48in) mono. 9-Dec-92 Butterfield & Butterfield, San Francisco #3861/R
$7500   £4335   The surf (51x69cm-20x27in) init. 23-Sep-92 Christie's, New York #171/R
$8000   £5594   White roses (76x64cm-30x25in) s.mono s.i.verso. 12-Mar-93 Skinner, Bolton #260/R

MURPHY, J Francis (1853-1921) American
$1300   £867   Trout pool (28x41cm-11x16in) s. i.stretcher. 21-May-94 Weschler, Washington #100/R
$1700   £1090   Twilight (20x26cm-8x10in) s. 9-Dec-92 Butterfield & Butterfield, San Francisco #3840/R
$2000   £1342   Sunset landscape (25x36cm-10x14in) s. 8-Dec-93 Butterfield & Butterfield, San Francisco #3354/R
$2000   £1282   Golden landscape (25x36cm-10x14in) s. 9-Dec-92 Butterfield & Butterfield, San Francisco #3841/R
$2800   £1958   Day in October (41x56cm-16x22in) s.d.1904 studio st.i.d.verso canvas on panel. 11-Mar-93 Christie's, New York #141/R
$2800   £1772   Golden hues of autumn (48x66cm-19x26in) s. 2-Dec-92 Christie's, East, New York #88/R
$3000   £2027   Winter on the marsh (19x29cm-7x11in) s. 31-Mar-94 Sotheby's Arcade, New York #136/R
$3000   £2041   Marsh near a pasture (28x36cm-11x14in) s. painted c.1877. 15-Nov-93 Christie's, East, New York #63/R
$3200   £1850   Woodland interior (9x25cm-4x10in) s. panel. 25-Sep-92 Sotheby's Arcade, New York #161/R
$3500   £2448   Aback from the highway (41x56cm-16x22in) s.d.1891. 10-Mar-93 Sotheby's, New York #80/R
$3500   £2365   A wintry landscape (13x18cm-5x7in) s. panel. 31-Mar-94 Sotheby's Arcade, New York #137/R
$4000   £2312   Landscape with sunset (20x30cm-8x12in) s.d.1904. 23-Sep-92 Christie's, New York #87/R
$4000   £2649   September (33x23cm-13x9in) s.d.1904 init.i.d.verso canvas on panel. 22-Sep-93 Christie's, New York #118/R
$6000   £3175   Late fall landscape (41x56cm-16x22in) s.d.1920 canvas on board. 12-Sep-92 Louisiana Auction Exchange #63/R
$9000   £5960   Fall landscape (61x92cm-24x36in) s.d.99. 22-Sep-93 Christie's, New York #117/R
$3600   £2368   Tonalist landscape (17x36cm-7x14in) s.d.1866 W/C board. 31-Mar-93 Sotheby's Arcade, New York #138/R

MURPHY, J Francis (attrib) (1853-1921) American
$750   £500   Autumn sunset (20x30cm-8x12in) s. 1-Jun-94 Doyle, New York #51
$850   £571   Late autumn (18x20cm-7x8in) bears sig. canvas laid down on board. 1-Dec-93 Doyle, New York #64

MURPHY, Nelly Littlehale (1867-?) American
$1000   £649   A fantasy village (33x23cm-13x9in) mono. 4-Aug-94 Eldred, Massachusetts #631/R
$450   £292   Shou Lao, Chinese God of Longevity (38x41cm-15x16in) 4-Aug-94 Eldred, Massachusetts #632/R

MURRAY, Elizabeth (1940-) American
$9500   £6376   Morning is breaking (86x86cm-34x34in) s.i.d.76 verso. 23-Feb-94 Christie's, New York #111/R
$750   £497   Middle Eastern Genre scene (74x58cm-29x23in) s. W/C gouache. 13-Nov-92 Skinner, Bolton #104/R
$7000   £4118   Wave (36x61cm-14x24in) pastel. 6-Oct-92 Sotheby's, New York #162/R
$9000   £5294   Big and small (105x76cm-41x30in) s.d.75 verso chl. 6-Oct-92 Sotheby's, New York #142/R
$12000 £7843   Which way (72x122cm-28x48in) pastel two parts executed 1984. 4-May-93 Sotheby's, New York #184/R
$16000 £10596 Star cup (55x66cm-22x26in) s.d.Oct.82verso col.chk three sheets. 19-Nov-92 Christie's, New York #50/R
$19000 £12583 Walk (59x76cm-23x30in) s.i.d.1981verso col.chk. 19-Nov-92 Christie's, New York #252/R

MURRAY, George (1822-?) American
$1628   £1100   Outside the cottage (36x46cm-14x18in) s. pair. 18-Mar-93 Bonhams, London #22/R
$6795   £4500   Death of Ladas, Greek runner - died on receiving Crown of Victory (101x127cm-40x50in) s.d.1899. 12-Nov-92 Sotheby's, London #50/R

MUSS-ARNOLT, Gustav (1858-1927) American
$1900   £1005   Portrait of Irish terrier (58x74cm-23x29in) s. 9-Sep-92 Doyle, New York #66
$1950   £1309   Army dog (30x23cm-12x9in) s. 27-Mar-94 Myers, Florida #83/R
$2750   £1797   Woodcote punch (46x58cm-18x23in) s.i. panel. 16-Sep-93 Sloan, North Bethesda #3236/R

MUSSELMAN, Darwin (20th C) American
$1500	£867	Industrial fresno (51x62cm-20x24in) s.d.46 d.0-46-8 stretcher. 24-Sep-92 Sotheby's, New York #150/R

MYERS, Frank Harmon (1899-1956) American
$750	£494	Dyeing nets, Brittany (31x39cm-12x15in) s. canvasboard. 13-Jun-93 Butterfield & Butterfield, San Francisco #809/R
$1000	£662	Evening rollers (41x48cm-16x19in) s. canvasboard. 22-Nov-92 Dargate Auction Galleries, Pittsburgh #197
$1200	£789	Bullfight (51x61cm-20x24in) s. 31-Mar-93 Sotheby's Arcade, New York #392/R
$2000	£1342	Harbour scene (51x61cm-20x24in) s. 24-Jun-93 Mystic Fine Arts, Connecticut #114
$2500	£1471	Coast route (61x81cm-24x32in) s. 4-Oct-92 Butterfield & Butterfield, Los Angeles #164/R
$1800	*£1250*	*Fishing boats (15x20cm-6x8in) s. canvas on board. 7-Mar-93 Butterfield & Butterfield, San Francisco #111/R*

MYERS, Harry (20th C) American
$1500	£987	In the park (41x51cm-16x20in) mono. s.i.verso masonite. 4-Nov-92 Doyle, New York #58/R

MYERS, Jerome (1867-c.1941) American
$2400	£1387	Gathering around street shrine in little Italy (61x41cm-24x16in) s.i. 25-Sep-92 Sotheby's Arcade, New York #289/R
$7500	£4808	Wooded Indian (41x56cm-16x22in) s.d.1918 board. 27-May-93 Sotheby's, New York #88/R
$15000	£8671	In the old quarter (64x76cm-25x30in) s. 23-Sep-92 Christie's, New York #264 b/R
$1200	£789	Orange box (27x22cm-11x9in) s.i. W/C pencil Indian ink. 31-Mar-93 Sotheby's Arcade, New York #227/R

MYGATT, Robertson K (attrib) (?-1919) American
$750	£500	The hill path (30x41cm-12x16in) s.d.08. 23-May-94 Christie's, East, New York #130

NADELMAN, Elie (1885-1946) American
$1200	£789	Standing nude (29x14cm-11x6in) init. pen executed c.1907. 31-Mar-93 Sotheby's Arcade, New York #355/R
$1600	£1067	Three birds. Man and woman in top hats (22x20cm-9x8in) one ink brush one ink brush pencil two. 26-May-94 Christie's, New York #125/R
$4000	£2667	Woman in long sleeved dress. Girl in leotard. Classical nude. Male nude (23x11cm-9x4in) mixed media - pen ink wash pencil gouache four. 26-May-94 Christie's, New York #122/R
$6000	£4000	Study of head. Head of girl. Study of heads. Study of woman, eyes closed (25x20cm-10x8in) one init. mixed media sepia pencil ink four. 26-May-94 Christie's, New York #123/R
$7500	£5000	Dancer. Man and woman. Woman in dress, Woman sitting in chair (25x20cm-10x8in) mixed media pen ink wash set of four. 26-May-94 Christie's, New York #124/R

NADIN, Peter (1954-) American
$1329	£886	Still life (91x122cm-36x48in) s. d.81verso. 2-Jun-94 AB Stockholms Auktionsverk, Stockholm #7055/R (S.KR 10500)
$1329	£886	Views I (183x161cm-72x63in) s. d.1986verso. 2-Jun-94 AB Stockholms Auktionsverk, Stockholm #7056/R (S.KR 10500)

NAEGELE, Charles Frederick (1857-1944) American
$5000	£3497	Prospect Pond, Brooklyn (40x86cm-16x34in) s. 11-Mar-93 Christie's, New York #55/R

NAGY, Peter (1959-) American?
$800	£530	End of whole imaginary (91x91cm-36x36in) s.d.86 verso. 30-Jun-93 Sotheby's Arcade, New York #360/R
$886	£591	Sign of Malignancy (122x122cm-48x48in) s.d.1985verso acrylic. 2-Jun-94 AB Stockholms Auktionsverk, Stockholm #7035/R (S.KR 7000)
$2600	£1699	Leger (122x122cm-48x48in) acrylic executed 1988. 22-Dec-92 Christie's, East, New York #44
$5215	£3500	Abstract schematic (183x183cm-72x72in) s.d.1989verso i.stretcher acrylic. 21-Jun-93 Christie's, S. Kensington #161/R

NAHA, Raymond (1933-) American
$750	*£503*	*Tungwup Whipper Kachinas (28x41cm-11x16in) s. gouache. 26-Jun-93 Skinner, Bolton #20/R*
$1700	*£1097*	*Kachina Ceremony (30x46cm-12x18in) s. gouache art board. 9-Jan-93 Skinner, Bolton #136/R*

NAHL, Charles C (1818-1878) American
$750	£503	Flowers in memorial (41x23cm-16x9in) s.d.1862 panel. 16-Jul-93 Du Mouchelle, Detroit #2323
$2220	£1500	Rafting down Chagres River, Isthmus of Panama (16x20cm-6x8in) s.d.1855 metal. 20-Oct-93 Sotheby's, London #31/R
$6759	£3953	The abduction of the Saxon prince (110x90cm-43x35in) s.d.1843. 18-Sep-92 Schloss Ahlden, Ahlden #1905/R (DM 10000)
$9000	£5294	Chase (56x71cm-22x28in) s. 4-Oct-92 Butterfield & Butterfield, Los Angeles #36/R
$9500	£6333	Boating on the Chagres River (16x20cm-6x8in) s.d.1855 tin. 25-May-94 Sotheby's, New York #4/R

NAHL, Hugo Wilhelm Arthur (?-1889) American
$2000   £1342   Hereford cow (30x36cm-12x14in) s.d.1884. 8-Dec-93 Butterfield & Butterfield, San Francisco #3315/R

NAILOR, Gerald (1917-1952) American
$2500   £1613   Doe feeding (36x30cm-14x12in) s.d.41 gouache. 9-Jan-93 Skinner, Bolton #355/R
$2600   £1688   The stubborn child on a burro, the ruluctant rider (36x25cm-14x10in) i.verso gouache. 25-Jun-94 Skinner, Bolton #107/R
$4000   £2685   Ceremonial (36x48cm-14x19in) s.d.46 gouache. 26-Jun-93 Skinner, Bolton #184/R

NAJAM-ES-SANI, Aref (20th C) Canadian
$789   £526   Toy horse with still life (121x189cm-48x74in) s.d.1984. 30-May-94 Ritchie, Toronto #234/R (C.D 1100)

NAKAMURA, Kazuo (1926-) Japanese/Canadian
$753   £492   Form study (43x61cm-17x24in) s.d.53 board. 18-May-93 Joyner Fine Art, Toronto #160 (C.D 950)
$1903   £1244   Waves no.2 (41x48cm-16x19in) s. 18-May-93 Joyner Fine Art, Toronto #140 (C.D 2400)
$2973   £1943   Blue reflections 2, 1967 (102x127cm-40x50in) s.d.67. 19-May-93 Sotheby's, Toronto #201/R (C.D 3750)

NAKIAN, Reuben (1897-1986) American
$650   £425   Europa and the bull (35x42cm-14x17in) s. Indian ink. 22-May-93 Weschler, Washington #150/R
$700   £449   Europa and the bull (36x41cm-14x16in) s. ink W/C. 10-Dec-92 Sloan, North Bethesda #3036/R
$1200   £805   Leda and the swan (50x67cm-20x26in) s. chl wash pair executed 1980. 24-Feb-94 Sotheby's Arcade, New York #417/R

NANGERONI, Carlo (1922-) American
$592   £400   Composizione (59x59cm-23x23in) s.d.1974verso acrylic. 23-Nov-93 Sotheby's, Milan #9/R (I.L 1000000)

NARDONE, Vincent Joseph (1937-) American
$2100   £1373   Point Judith movement Rhode Island (51x76cm-20x30in) s.d.79 liquified pastel. 7-Oct-93 Freeman Fine Arts, Philadelphia #945/R
$2700   £1812   Rhode Island mystique (53x74cm-21x29in) s. W/C. 24-Jun-93 Mystic Fine Arts, Connecticut #281

NASH, E R (20th C) American
$800   £537   Table top still life with tea service and flowering plant (64x76cm-25x30in) s. 4-Mar-94 Skinner, Bolton #229/R

NASH, Manley Kerchaval (20th C) American?
$2400   £1538   The founding of St. Louis (152x213cm-60x84in) s.d.25. 26-Apr-93 Selkirks, St. Louis #300/R

NASH, Thomas (20th C) American
$1300   £867   The Ridge Route, Los Angeles to Bakersfield (76x102cm-30x40in) s.d.1922. 15-Mar-94 John Moran, Pasadena #47

NASH, Willard Ayer (1898-1943) American
$1600   £1074   Still life with revolver (39x56cm-15x22in) s.d.1930 W/C. 8-Dec-93 Butterfield & Butterfield, San Francisco #3579/R

NASON, Gertrude (1890-1969) American
$1300   £844   Trekking down Bleecker Street (76x79cm-30x31in) s. 9-Sep-93 Sotheby's Arcade, New York #335 a/R

NAST, Thomas (1840-1902) American
$1300   £823   The Robber and The Robbed, stocked and punished together (66x49cm-26x19in) s.i. ink pencil htd gouache paper on board. 2-Dec-92 Christie's, East, New York #66/R

NATKIN, Robert (1930-) American
$800   £530   Untitled (56x67cm-22x26in) s.d.1969 acrylic. 17-Nov-92 Christie's, East, New York #248/R
$800   £530   Untitled (21x69cm-8x27in) s. s.i.d.1976verso acrylic. 17-Nov-92 Christie's, East, New York #180/R
$1200   £805   Untitled (94x70cm-37x28in) s. acrylic paper painted 1966. 23-Feb-94 Christie's, East, New York #358/R
$1300   £855   Apollo with red stripe (122x137cm-48x54in) s. acrylic. 13-Jun-93 Hindman Galleries, Chicago #240/R
$1500   £1007   Bern Series (112x89cm-44x35in) s. acrylic paper. 3-May-94 Christie's, East, New York #45/R
$1600   £1074   Bern 696 (79x58cm-31x23in) s. st.i.d.1979 stretcher acrylic. 24-Feb-94 Sotheby's Arcade, New York #408/R
$1900   £1275   Bath Series - Heelstone for G.N (211x193cm-83x76in) s. i.stretcher acrylic painted 1974. 24-Feb-94 Sotheby's Arcade, New York #381/R
$2200   £1477   Bern Series (74x74cm-29x29in) s. 3-May-94 Christie's, East, New York #83/R
$2286   £1514   Field mouse III (76x56cm-30x22in) s. acrylic paper on board. 21-Nov-92 Aucktionhaus Burkard, Luzern #121/R (S.FR 3300)
$3000   £2013   Bern Series (81x86cm-32x34in) s. i.d.1978 stretcher. 23-Feb-94 Christie's, East, New York #354/R

NATKIN, Robert (1930-) American-cont.

$3250	£2181	Apollo Series (138x163cm-54x64in) s.i.verso. 24-Feb-94 Sotheby's Arcade, New York #391/R
$4500	£3020	Bath Apollo (80x127cm-31x50in) s. acrylic painted 1977. 23-Feb-94 Christie's, East, New York #367/R
$5500	£3691	Untitled (127x124cm-50x49in) s. acrylic. 25-Mar-93 Boos Gallery, Michigan #495/R
$5800	£3893	Apollo series, 1964 (122x183cm-48x72in) acrylic. 5-Mar-94 Louisiana Auction Exchange #99/R
$7000	£4861	Apollo (198x180cm-78x71in) s. s.d.1968verso acrylic. 22-Feb-93 Christie's, East, New York #160/R
$8000	£5298	Field mouse (225x201cm-89x79in) s. s.verso acrylic. 17-Nov-92 Christie's, East, New York #261/R
$9500	£6376	Untitled (183x244cm-72x96in) s. acrylic linen painted 1969. 24-Feb-94 Sotheby's Arcade, New York #390/R
$1000	£676	Untitled (79x58cm-31x23in) s.d.1964 W/C. 21-Oct-93 Butterfield & Butterfield, San Francisco #2772/R

NAUMAN, Bruce (1941-) American

$7000	£4730	Dark and stormy night and laughter, study for video installation (56x77cm-22x30in) init.d.1987 polaroids nylon tape felt-tip pen. 10-Nov-93 Christie's, New York #370/R
$8000	£4706	Concrete chamber with video and audio deep in earth or deep in space (58x74cm-23x29in) s.d.72 pencil W/C. 6-Oct-92 Sotheby's, New York #119/R
$11000	£7383	Double cage (76x102cm-30x40in) s.d.74 W/C pencil pen. 5-May-94 Sotheby's, New York #241/R
$12000	£8054	For dream passage chairs (124x90cm-49x35in) s.d.83 graphite masking tape. 23-Feb-94 Christie's, New York #90/R
$12000	£7843	Diamond mind circle of tears fallen all around me (77x101cm-30x40in) s.d.75 ink pencil. 4-May-93 Sotheby's, New York #133/R
$16000	£10811	Sugar Ragus (44x62cm-17x24in) s.d.72 pencil. 11-Nov-93 Sotheby's, New York #123 a/R
$19207	£12891	Upside down drawings (56x46cm-22x18in) mono.d.1965 chl dr four. 3-Dec-93 Lempertz, Cologne #893/R (DM 33000)
$26000	£18056	Drawing for malice (67x88cm-26x35in) s.d.1980 chl. 24-Feb-93 Christie's, New York #96/R
$36500	£24497	Welcome (189x127cm-74x50in) s.i.d.85 W/C gouache chl graphite. 4-May-94 Christie's, New York #322/R
$55000	£37162	Fox wheel I (159x159cm-63x63in) 9 photographs cellophane tape on board exec.1989. 10-Nov-93 Christie's, New York #369/R
$60000	£40268	Human need desire (164x171cm-65x67in) s.d.83 W/C graphite. 4-May-94 Christie's, New York #312/R
$90000	£59603	Study for Dream Passage (160x203cm-63x80in) s.d.84 chl acrylic col. oilsticks graphite. 19-Nov-92 Christie's, New York #239/R

NAVA, John (1947-) American

$2250	£1521	D.A.K. arms overhead (152x121cm-60x48in) s.d.1984 pencil acrylic collage. 21-Oct-93 Butterfield & Butterfield, San Francisco #2828/R

NAVAL, Andre (1949-) Haitian

$626	£415	Les fleurs (50x55cm-20x22in) s. panel. 13-Jun-94 Rogeon, Paris #84/R (F.FR 3500)
$680	£450	Zebus dans la foret vierge (46x91cm-18x36in) s. panel. 13-Jun-94 Rogeon, Paris #142 (F.FR 3800)

NAVARRETE, Antonio (?) Mexican?

$618	£418	Revolera (30x40cm-12x16in) s. 9-Nov-93 Louis Morton, Mexico #35 (M.P 2000)

NAVARRO, Gilberto Acedes (?) Latin American

$1483	£1002	Fondo Amarillo (49x64cm-19x25in) s.d.69 gouache. 27-Apr-94 Louis Morton, Mexico #377 (M.P 5000)
$1631	£1102	Biafra (50x64cm-20x25in) s.d.1969 gouache. 27-Apr-94 Louis Morton, Mexico #562 (M.P 5500)

NAVAZIO, Walter de (1887-1921) Argentinian

$20000	£11561	Paisaje (50x65cm-20x26in) 23-Sep-92 Roldan & Cia, Buenos Aires #10
$30000	£17341	Nocturno, Los Sauces (56x47cm-22x19in) 23-Sep-92 Roldan & Cia, Buenos Aires #41

NEAGLE, John (1796-1865) American

$1000	£671	Portrait of Mrs. Dale (76x64cm-30x25in) s.d.1844. 5-Aug-93 Eldred, Massachusetts #66/R

NEAGLE, John (attrib) (1796-1865) American

$1900	£1250	Portrait of man (76x63cm-30x25in) canvas on board. 31-Mar-93 Sotheby's Arcade, New York #3/R

NECHVATAL, Joseph (1951-) American

$633	£422	Illuminati (152x234cm-60x92in) s.d.1989verso acrylic computer robot assisted. 2-Jun-94 AB Stockholms Auktionsverk, Stockholm #7058/R (S.KR 5000)
$570	£380	Heavens of fire (28x35cm-11x14in) s.d.1984verso pencil. 2-Jun-94 AB Stockholms Auktionsverk, Stockholm #7126/R (S.KR 4500)
$570	£380	Church of confusion (28x35cm-11x14in) s.d.1984verso pencil. 2-Jun-94 AB Stockholms Auktionsverk, Stockholm #7127/R (S.KR 4500)
$633	£422	Thinking of the children (22x53cm-9x21in) s.d.1983verso pencil diptych. 2-Jun-94 AB Stockholms Auktionsverk, Stockholm #7033/R (S.KR 5000)

NEEBE, Louis Alexander (1873-?) American
$4600 £3007 On the beach (91x102cm-36x40in) s. 16-May-93 Hindman Galleries, Chicago #98/R

NEEDHAM, Charles Austin (1844-1923) American
$4500 £3061 A day at the park (58x79cm-23x31in) s.i.d.1899 canvasboard laid down on board. 15-Nov-93 Christie's, East, New York #58/R

NEEL, Alice (1900-1984) American
$4000 £2685 Portrait of the artist's mother (76x66cm-30x26in) s. s.i.verso painted c.1930. ̈ 3-May-94 Christie's, East, New York #6/R
$15000 £9804 Portrait of Bill White (102x102cm-40x40in) s.d.71. 7-May-93 Christie's, East, New York #51/R

NEHLIG, Victor (1830-1910) American
$600 £403 Guard in armour (36x25cm-14x10in) s. panel. 16-Dec-93 Mystic Fine Arts, Connecticut #141/R
$1100 £748 Meeting at the well (28x15cm-11x6in) s.d.1867 panel. 8-Apr-94 Sloan, North Bethesda #2351
$1395 £900 Street musician, Cuba (42x31cm-17x12in) s.d.59 pencil W/C. 15-Jul-94 Christie's, London #19/R

NEIMAN, Leroy (1926-) American
$600 £397 Nude woman (28x61cm-11x24in) s.d.56 paper. 19-Jun-94 Hindman Galleries, Chicago #746
$550 £364 Dog (61x46cm-24x18in) s.d.69 W/C. 19-Jun-94 Hindman Galleries, Chicago #737
$850 £500 Willis Reed, Madison Square Garden (38x28cm-15x11in) s.i. felt-tip. 11-Oct-92 Litchfield Auction Gallery #164
$5000 £3289 Sammy Davis Jr and Bill cosby Harrah's Tahoe (58x43cm-23x17in) s.i.d.1.28.83 W/C. 5-Jun-93 Louisiana Auction Exchange #174

NEIMEYER, Henry J (?) American
$1800 £1216 Lake landscape (56x66cm-22x26in) s. 10-Aug-93 Stonington Fine Arts, Stonington #161

NELSON, Carl Gustaf (1898-?) American
$900 £566 'Parade' or 'Old Bandstand on Washington Square' New York (46x51cm-18x20in) s. 25-Apr-93 James Bakker, Cambridge #48/R

NELSON, Edward D (19th C) American
$2400 £1600 Landscape with sailboats in the distance (61x45cm-24x18in) s.d.1869 canvas on masonite. 23-May-94 Christie's, East, New York #4/R

NELSON, Ernest Bruce (1888-1952) American
$1300 £878 Evening sky (20x25cm-8x10in) s. canvasboard. 5-Nov-93 Skinner, Bolton #93/R
$2500 £1667 Coastal scene at evening (20x25cm-8x10in) s. canvas laid on board. 15-Mar-94 John Moran, Pasadena #82

NELSON, George Laurence (1887-1978) American
$900 £608 Woodsmock (61x76cm-24x30in) s.d.1907 s.i.d.verso. 31-Mar-94 Sotheby's Arcade, New York #265/R
$1500 £1049 Kent garden. View of Ana Capri (41x30cm-16x12in) one s. s.i.verso one indist.s. board pair. 3-Feb-93 Doyle, New York #47/R
$1500 £1000 Poppies in Colonial Pewter (51x41cm-20x16in) s. 22-May-94 James Bakker, Cambridge #179/R
$1500 £1049 Mother's chair (102x76cm-40x30in) s.d.1925. 3-Feb-93 Doyle, New York #46

NELSON, Joan (1958-) American
$4000 £2649 Untitled (61x66cm-24x26in) s.d.1984 verso egg tempera plaster on masonite. 18-Nov-92 Sotheby's, New York #250 a/R
$7500 £5068 Untitled no 258 (23x23cm-9x9in) s.i.d.1990verso panel. 10-Nov-93 Christie's, New York #376/R
$10000 £6711 Untitled no 229 (76x76cm-30x30in) s.d.1989verso oil wax panel. 5-May-94 Sotheby's, New York #312/R
$11000 £7285 Untitled - 197 (41x41cm-16x16in) s.d.1988 verso wood. 18-Nov-92 Sotheby's, New York #276/R
$7000 £4575 Untitled (102x122cm-40x48in) s.d.1984 verso egg tempera plaster masonite. 4-May-93 Sotheby's, New York #187 a/R
$10000 £6536 Untitled - No.223 (38x38cm-15x15in) s.d.1988 oil encaustic panel. 5-May-93 Christie's, New York #154 a/R

NELSON, Roger Laux (1945-) American
$900 £604 Divider (204x152cm-80x60in) s.i.d.85 verso. 23-Feb-94 Christie's, East, New York #286/R

NEMETHY, Albert (20th C) American
$2700 £1561 Victorian winter (100x75cm-39x30in) mono. 25-Sep-92 Sotheby's Arcade, New York #429/R

NEPOTE, Alexander (1913-1986) American
$1000 £633 Waterfall (178x81cm-70x32in) s. 25-Oct-92 Butterfield & Butterfield, San Francisco #2302/R
$600 £397 Fruit stand (36x53cm-14x21in) s. W/C. 28-Sep-93 John Moran, Pasadena #298

NERI, Manuel (1930-) American
$1700 £1149 Gesture study no.65 (31x24cm-12x9in) s.d.80 mixed media magazine page. 21-Apr-94 Butterfield & Butterfield, San Francisco #1179/R

NESBITT, Lowell (1933-1993) American
$800 £544 Eagle and nude (130x89cm-51x35in) s.verso. 17-Apr-94 Hindman Galleries, Chicago #1000
$1191 £805 Gold iris (102x102cm-40x40in) s.verso acrylic. 23-Nov-93 Goteborg Auktionsverk #241/R (S.KR 10000)
$1200 £833 Three yellow tulips (86x56cm-34x22in) s.i.d.90verso acrylic. 26-Feb-93 Sotheby's Arcade, New York #370/R
$1300 £861 Red Cereus on green (76x66cm-30x26in) s.i.d.81 i.verso acrylic. 29-Sep-93 Sotheby's Arcade, New York #379/R
$4250 £2853 Two pink iris (229x152cm-90x60in) s.i.d.77 verso. 24-Feb-94 Sotheby's Arcade, New York #425/R
$800 *£513* *Water flowers (51x94cm-20x37in) s.d.1952 gouache. 10-Dec-92 Sloan, North Bethesda #2266*

NETO, Manuel Chong (1927-) Panamanian
$4500 £3020 Untitled, bathers (93x122cm-37x48in) s.d.92. 7-Jan-94 Gary Nader, Miami #99/R

NETTO, Gontran (1933-) Brazilian
$665 £446 Paysano goiatins (72x50cm-28x20in) s.d.1984 acrylic. 8-May-94 Jonquet, Paris #102 (F.FR 3800)

NEUHAUS, Eugen (1879-1963) American
$3250 £2138 Cerra Obispo (89x96cm-35x38in) s. 13-Jun-93 Butterfield & Butterfield, San Francisco #748/R

NEUMANN, Robert von (attrib) (1888-1976) American
$600 £408 Gill's rock, Door county (48x41cm-19x16in) s. board. 17-Apr-94 Schrager Galleries, Milwaukee #735
$1250 £828 Loretta Upper Michigan (76x89cm-30x35in) s. 26-Sep-93 Schrager Galleries, Milwaukee #480
$1800 £1139 Paying off the perch nets (66x91cm-26x36in) s. 30-Nov-92 Schrager Galleries, Milwaukee #411

NEVELSON, Louise (1899-1988) American
$1300 £861 Untitled (21x11cm-8x4in) s. pencil pair. 30-Jun-93 Sotheby's Arcade, New York #287/R
$5000 £3356 Untitled (76x51cm-30x20in) s.d.80 painted wood paperboard collage board. 3-May-94 Christie's, East, New York #126/R
$5500 £3716 the Mirror (122x91cm-48x36in) s.d.83 acrylic wood board collage panel. 8-Nov-93 Christie's, East, New York #179/R

NEWCOMB, Marie Guise (1865-?) American
$1025 £670 Beagle pups napping in hay (28x38cm-11x15in) s.d.1893. 1-Nov-92 Litchfield Auction Gallery #232 a

NEWHALL, Harriot B (1874-?) American
$2000 £1307 Park Street Church (102x76cm-40x30in) s. s.i.verso. 18-Sep-93 Young Fine Arts Auctions, Maine #225/R

NEWMAN, Henry Roderick (c.1833-1918) American
$2500 £1678 Abu Simbel (66x43cm-26x17in) s.i.d.1908 W/C paper on linen on panel. 6-Dec-93 Grogan, Massachussetts #510/R
$5500 £3819 La Dogana, Venice (36x51cm-14x20in) s.d.1894 W/C. 27-Feb-93 Young Fine Arts Auctions, Maine #218/R
$7000 £4046 Japanese pagoda in woods (39x30cm-15x12in) s.d.1897 W/C. 24-Sep-92 Sotheby's New York #84/R
$38480 £26000 Ramleh (102x68cm-40x27in) s.i.d.1890 W/C htd bodycol. 30-Mar-94 Sotheby's London #168/R
$42000 £28000 Tuscan almond grove (100x67cm-39x26in) s.d.1887 W/C. 9-Jun-94 Sotheby's London #201/R

NEWMAN, John (1952-) American
$1076 £717 Untitled composition (97x171cm-38x67in) mixed media executed 1985. 2-Jun-94 AB Stockholms Auktionsverk, Stockholm #7023/R (S.KR 8500)
$2250 £1510 Untitled (226x100cm-89x39in) pastel chk pencil linocut linen executed 1985. 5-May-94 Sotheby's, New York #339/R

NEWMAN, Robert Loftin (1827-1912) American
$3250 £2138 Good Samaritan (25x36cm-10x14in) s.d.1886. 13-Jun-93 Butterfield & Butterfield, San Francisco #3131/R

NEY, Aramis (1942-) Uruguayan
$536 £357 Composition (58x82cm-23x32in) s. mixed media. 19-Mar-94 AB Stockholms Auktionsverk (Lilla Kvaliten) #4160 (S.KR 4200)

NEYLAND, Harry A (1877-1958) American
$800 £537 La pianiste (43x36cm-17x14in) s. 5-Aug-93 Eldred, Massachusetts #810/R
$900 £604 Autumn nocturne (46x61cm-18x24in) s. 25-Mar-94 Eldred, Massachusetts #728/R
$1300 £872 Storm King Cornwell on Hudson (30x46cm-12x18in) s. board. 25-Mar-94 Eldred, Massachusetts #718/R

NEYLAND, Harry A (1877-1958) American-cont.
$850	£570	Night, depicting a woman carrying a basket into a house under night skies (43x48cm-17x19in) s. W/C. 25-Mar-94 Eldred, Massachusetts #715/R
$850	£570	Evening, depicting a woman carrying a basket into a house (43x48cm-17x19in) s. i.verso W/C thumbnail sketch verso. 25-Mar-94 Eldred, Massachusetts #716/R

NICARAGUAN SCHOOL, 18th C
$7000	£4667	Fray Andres Quiles Galindo (200x117cm-79x46in) i. 18-May-94 Sotheby's, New York #150/R

NICHOLLS, Burr H (1848-1915) American
$700	£470	Venetian entrance way (15x13cm-6x5in) s. board. 24-Mar-94 Mystic Fine Arts, Connecticut #108
$4500	£3020	Arab street scene with figures, pigeons and donkey (63x76cm-25x30in) s. 14-Oct-93 Christie's, New York #265/R

NICHOLLS, Rhoda Holmes (1854-1938) American
$1000	£671	Young lady in woods (41x51cm-16x20in) 29-Dec-93 Douglas, South Deerfield #1
$1200	£606	Fishing boats at dock (38x28cm-15x11in) s. W/C. 28-Aug-92 Young Fine Arts Auctions, Maine #231/R

NICHOLS, Dale (1904-) American
$2400	£1569	Snowy farm scene (61x91cm-24x36in) s. 1-Nov-92 Hanzel Galleries, Chicago #9
$3000	£1961	Last log (76x101cm-30x40in) s. 4-May-93 Christie's, East, New York #290/R
$7500	£4747	Black birds and the evening star (76x101cm-30x40in) s.i.verso. 2-Dec-92 Christie's, East, New York #398/R
$9500	£6250	Winter landscape with barn (60x76cm-24x30in) s.d.1935. 31-Mar-93 Sotheby's Arcade, New York #304/R
$12000	£8000	Christmas sleigh ride in the country (61x107cm-24x42in) 17-Mar-94 Sotheby's, New York #136/R
$18000	£11538	Death in wheatfields (62x102cm-24x40in) s.d. 1937. 27-May-93 Sotheby's, New York #107/R
$800	£506	Red barn at night (43x66cm-17x26in) s.d.1959 pastel chl. 2-Dec-92 Christie's, East, New York #335

NICHOLS, Edward H (1819-1871) American
$2100	£1214	New England landscape. View of Lake Waramaug (30x?cm-12x?in) two. 25-Sep-92 Sotheby's Arcade, New York #23/R

NICHOLS, Edward H (attrib) (1819-1871) American
$1200	£784	Winooski Valley (61x91cm-24x36in) s. 30-Jun-94 Mystic Fine Arts, Connecticut #237/R

NICHOLS, Henry Hobart (1869-1962) American
$600	£403	Cabin in the mountains - winter landscape (76x63cm-30x25in) s. 4-Mar-94 Skinner, Bolton #252/R
$850	£570	Winter scene (61x76cm-24x30in) s. 24-Mar-94 Mystic Fine Arts, Connecticut #52
$1600	£1026	Rockport winter (32x40cm-13x16in) s. canvasboard. 9-Dec-92 Butterfield & Butterfield, San Francisco #3921/R
$1900	£1234	Seagull and dunes (76x91cm-30x36in) s.d.1944. 9-Sep-93 Sotheby's Arcade, New York #301/R
$2400	£1633	Verdant valley (63x76cm-25x30in) s. 15-Nov-93 Christie's, East, New York #130/R
$1000	£667	Forest clearing (49x34cm-19x13in) s.d.05 pastel. 23-May-94 Christie's, East, New York #157/R

NICHOLSON, Edward H (1901-1966) American
$600	£400	Holiday still life with director chair, wine jug and fishing poles (64x76cm-25x30in) s. 15-Mar-94 John Moran, Pasadena #100 a
$900	£596	Summer morning (51x61cm-20x24in) s. canvasboard. 28-Sep-93 John Moran, Pasadena #235
$1900	£1319	Moonlight in Morro Bay (66x66cm-26x26in) s. 7-Mar-93 Butterfield & Butterfield, San Francisco #205/R
$2000	£1351	Lady with umbrella (61x46cm-24x18in) s. canvasboard. 15-Jun-93 John Moran, Pasadena #119

NICHOLSON, George W (1832-1912) American
$825	£529	Coastal scene (28x36cm-11x14in) s. 17-Dec-92 Mystic Fine Arts, Connecticut #129/R
$850	£567	Ladies picking flowers in a landscape overlooking falls (30x41cm-12x16in) s. panel. 26-May-94 Sloan, North Bethesda #2098/R
$850	£491	Boats and cottages along the coast (23x23cm-9x9in) s. panel. 25-Sep-92 Sotheby's Arcade, New York #26 a/R
$1100	£636	Barnyard in the snow (41x30cm-16x12in) s. panel. 25-Sep-92 Sotheby's Arcade, New York #46/R
$1100	£738	Home before the storm (20x25cm-8x10in) s. panel. 4-Mar-94 Skinner, Bolton #169/R
$1200	£811	Arabian town (58x41cm-23x16in) s. panel. 31-Mar-94 Sotheby's Arcade, New York #52/R
$1500	£993	Winter scene (25x30cm-10x12in) s. panel. 23-Sep-93 Mystic Fine Arts, Connecticut #69
$1800	£1169	Harvesting mussels (25x46cm-10x18in) s. 9-Sep-93 Sotheby's Arcade, New York #61/R
$1800	£1040	Landscapes (23x36cm-9x14in) one s. panel pair. 27-Sep-92 James Bakker, Cambridge #92/R
$1950	£1127	People arriving by boat at villa (61x107cm-24x42in) s. 24-Sep-92 Mystic Fine Arts, Connecticut #220
$2000	£1333	Heading home (51x81cm-20x32in) s. 3-Jun-94 Sotheby's, New York #158/R
$2200	£1438	River barge (31x61cm-12x24in) s. 4-May-93 Christie's, East, New York #50/R

NICHOLSON, George W (1832-1912) American-cont.
$2700	£1709	Two figures in winter landscape (30x41cm-12x16in) s. 3-Dec-92 Freeman Fine Arts, Philadelphia #1801/R
$3000	£1734	On the Delaware water gap (12x23cm-5x9in) s. panel. 23-Sep-92 Christie's, New York #70/R
$9500	£6376	After the day's toil (87x143cm-34x56in) s.i. 3-Dec-93 Christie's, New York #128/R
$9500	£6333	Harbour scene (71x127cm-28x50in) s. 16-Mar-94 Christie's, New York #8/R
$701	£474	Old house at Settington, Yorkshire (33x47cm-13x19in) W/C. 29-Mar-94 Joel, Victoria #896 (A.D 1000)
$2500	£1582	Bahamian scene (27x38cm-11x15in) s. W/C gouache. 3-Dec-92 Sotheby's, New York #21/R

NICKERSON, R E (20th C) American
$2934	£1800	White Wings of Baltimore built in 1889 (66x91cm-26x36in) s.i. 15-Oct-92 Christie's, S. Kensington #525/R
$2934	£1800	The American schooner Nettie Shipman (66x101cm-26x40in) s. 15-Oct-92 Christie's, S. Kensington #526/R

NICKERSON, Reginald E (20th C) American
$775	£520	The American bark 'Harvard' (50x101cm-20x40in) s. 11-Dec-93 Weschler, Washington #149/R
$800	£537	The American schooner 'Anna Pendleton' (58x66cm-23x26in) s. 11-Dec-93 Weschler, Washington #146/R
$1788	£1200	The American schooner 'Princeton' (63x76cm-25x30in) s. 5-May-94 Christie's, S. Kensington #191/R
$1800	£1176	The W C Mershon (56x79cm-22x31in) s. 30-Jun-94 Mystic Fine Arts, Connecticut #187/R
$2000	£1333	The Barkentine 'Tam O'Shanter' (61x91cm-24x36in) s.i. 1-Jun-94 Doyle, New York #52
$2086	£1400	Portrait of the three-masted gaff-rigged schooner 'Ida L Hull' entering Barnstaple harbour (61x94cm-24x37in) s. 5-May-94 Christie's, S. Kensington #190/R
$2500	£1678	The schooner Benjamin Hale (61x86cm-24x34in) s. 3-Feb-94 Sloan, North Bethesda #2775/R
$2600	£1711	Enchantress (61x91cm-24x36in) s. 2-Jun-93 Doyle, New York #78
$2600	£1733	The schooner 'Nettie Shipman' (61x91cm-24x36in) s. 26-May-94 Sloan, North Bethesda #2259/R
$2601	£1700	American schooner May O'Neill (53x86cm-21x34in) s. 7-Oct-93 Christie's, S. Kensington #425/R

NICKERSON, Robert E (1915-) American
$1450	£918	Gloriana and Viatore (51x71cm-20x28in) s. 30-Nov-92 Selkirks, St. Louis #151/R
$2200	£1392	Childe Harold (74x89cm-29x35in) s. i.verso. 30-Nov-92 Selkirks, St. Louis #251/R

NICOLL, James Craig (1847-1918) American
$800	£559	California coast (61x102cm-24x40in) s. i.verso. 12-Mar-93 Skinner, Bolton #152/R
$4000	£2797	On Cape Elizabeth, Maine (44x75cm-17x30in) s. 10-Mar-93 Sotheby's, New York #35/R

NICOLL, James McLaren (1892-1986) Canadian
$934	£619	Cabin and pump (37x54cm-15x21in) s. i.verso W/C. 16-Nov-92 Hodgins, Calgary #334/R (C.D 1200)

NICOLL, Marion Florence (1909-1985) Canadian
$1209	£711	Near Sunshine Lodge (31x38cm-12x15in) s.d.1947 i.verso board. 5-Oct-92 Levis, Calgary #66/R (C.D 1500)
$662	£438	Back road, Canmore (27x36cm-11x14in) s.d.42 i.verso W/C. 16-Nov-92 Hodgins, Calgary #14/R (C.D 850)

NIEMAN, Leroy (1921-) American
$850	£578	Carnivale in Rio (38x61cm-15x24in) oil crayon ink. 17-Apr-94 Hindman Galleries, Chicago #991

NIERMAN, Leonardo (1932-) Mexican
$650	£437	Fury (80x58cm-31x23in) s.d.65 i.verso acrylic masonite. 24-Feb-94 Sotheby's Arcade, New York #305/R
$800	£530	Solar influence (80x60cm-31x24in) s. i.verso masonite. 29-Sep-93 Sotheby's Arcade, New York #291/R
$850	£545	Abstract composition (61x79cm-24x31in) s. acrylic board. 13-Dec-92 Hindman Galleries, Chicago #88
$900	£596	Prehistoric dream (61x81cm-24x32in) s. i.verso acrylic board. 28-Nov-92 Dunning's, Illinois #1090
$900	£596	Birth of light (61x81cm-24x32in) s. i.verso acrylic board. 28-Nov-92 Dunning's, Illinois #1089
$1100	£733	Solar system (122x69cm-48x27in) s.d.64 s.i.d.verso acrylic. 26-Aug-93 Boos Gallery, Michigan #472/R
$1200	£800	Lights of city (61x79cm-24x31in) s.d.65 acrylic masonite. 26-Aug-93 Boos Gallery, Michigan #473/R
$1300	£909	Autumn flight (79x58cm-31x23in) s. board. 14-Mar-93 Hindman Galleries, Chicago #95/R
$2000	£1325	Cosmic abstraction (123x91cm-48x36in) s. board. 30-Jun-93 Sotheby's Arcade, New York #233

NIETO, Rodolfo (1936-1988) Mexican
$4400	£2933	Figura (50x61cm-20x24in) s.i.verso painted c.1963. 18-May-94 Sotheby's, New York #425/R

NIETO, Rodolfo (1936-1988) Mexican-cont.
$6000 £4000   Zoologia colerica (97x130cm-38x51in) s.i.verso painted c.1960. 18-May-94 Sotheby's, New York #388/R
$11000 £7432   Untitled (73x77cm-29x30in) s. s.i.d.1964-25verso. 23-Nov-93 Christie's, New York #189/R
$6000 £4054   Untitled (80x61cm-31x24in) acrylic vinyl paper collage panel executed c.75. 22-Nov-93 Sotheby's, New York #229/R

NIEVES, Ignacio Nefero (1920-) Mexican
$5160 £3463   Autoretrato (80x60cm-31x24in) s.d.1965. 1-Dec-93 Louis Morton, Mexico #199/R (M.P 16000)

NIGRO, Adolfo (1942-) Argentinian
$2000 £1333   La colina y el rio (39x46cm-15x18in) s.d.78 board. 18-May-94 Sotheby's, New York #298/R
$4000 £2667   Memoria del agua (80x100cm-31x39in) s.d.89 s.i.d.verso. 18-May-94 Sotheby's, New York #253/R
$6000 £4054   Raices (100x100cm-39x39in) s.d.87. 22-Nov-93 Sotheby's, New York #249/R
$1500 £1014   Pictografia (29x22cm-11x9in) s. gouache W/C executed c.1960. 22-Nov-93 Sotheby's, New York #250/R

NINO, Carmelo (20th C) South American
$9000 £5882   La nina del traje rojo (120x100cm-47x39in) s.d.91 i.verso. 17-May-93 Christie's, New York #262/R

NIRO, Robert de (20th C) American
$800   £556   Table with roses and eggs (55x76cm-22x30in) s.d.62 paper. 26-Feb-93 Sotheby's Arcade, New York #362/R
$1500 £1014   Nudes on yellow background (91x112cm-36x44in) s.d.75. 21-Apr-94 Butterfield & Butterfield, San Francisco #1164/R
$2750 £1910   Still life with red cloth (117x81cm-46x32in) 26-Feb-93 Sotheby's Arcade, New York #371/R
$600   £417   Portrait of woman (48x63cm-19x25in) s.d.57 chl. 26-Feb-93 Sotheby's Arcade, New York #363/R
$700   £486   Mother and child reading (62x49cm-24x19in) s.d.57 chl. 26-Feb-93 Sotheby's Arcade, New York #359/R

NISBET, Robert H (1879-1961) American
$800   £519   Rushing river (56x51cm-22x20in) s. 8-Jul-94 Sloan, North Bethesda #2757
$975   £637   Grey day, South Kent (30x41cm-12x16in) s. board. 1-Nov-92 Litchfield Auction Gallery #139
$1500 £980   Macedonia Brook (64x76cm-25x30in) s. 30-Jun-94 Mystic Fine Arts, Connecticut #154/R
$5000 £2941   View of Connecticut Valley (76x91cm-30x36in) s. 8-Oct-92 Freeman Fine Arts, Philadelphia #1124/R

NISHISAWA, Luis (1926-) Mexican
$5805 £3896   Despoblado estado de Mexico (50x115cm-20x45in) s.d.1987 W/C. 1-Dec-93 Louis Morton, Mexico #46/R (M.P 18000)
$9000 £5960   Paisajes de la Tarde y de la Lluvia - Tlayacapan and Tepoztlan (61x91cm-24x36in) s.i.d.89 st. col.ink Japanese paper pair. 24-Nov-92 Christie's, New York #298/R

NISHIZAWA, Luis (1926-) Mexican
$7959 £5102   Paisaje de la Tarde (56x86cm-22x34in) s.d.1992 ink. 29-Apr-93 Louis Morton, Mexico #19 (M.P 25000)

NISSEN, Chris (20th C) American
$950   £633   Cadwalder landscape (178x178cm-70x70in) s. 26-May-94 Freeman Fine Arts, Philadelphia #115

NIVERVILLE, Louis de (1933-) Canadian
$1019 £680   Sunset girl in repose (60x60cm-24x24in) i.verso board. 11-May-94 Sotheby's, Toronto #186 (C.D 1400)
$2002 £1335   Still life (43x111cm-17x44in) s. 11-May-94 Sotheby's, Toronto #203/R (C.D 2750)

NOBLE, Thomas Satterwhite (1835-1907) American
$5500 £3667   Library of H.G. Fechheimer, Cincinnati, Ohio (47x62cm-19x24in) board painted c.1892. 23-May-94 Christie's, East, New York #85/R
$21000 £13256 The escape (76x102cm-30x40in) s.d.1869. 9-Sep-93 Sotheby's Arcade, New York #60/R

NOE, Luis Felipe (1933-) Argentinian
$700   £469   Untitled (49x64cm-19x25in) s. board. 8-May-94 Jonquet, Paris #113 (F.FR 4000)
$1224 £822   Paysage amazonien (80x100cm-31x39in) s. painted 1982. 8-May-94 Jonquet, Paris #116 (F.FR 7000)
$1000 £654   Untitled (35x43cm-14x17in) s.d.65 collage col.felt-tip pen. 18-May-93 Sotheby's, New York #196/R

NOEH, Anna T (1926-) Canadian
$642   £434   Mother and child (49x39cm-19x15in) s.d.76 gouache col.crayons. 23-Nov-93 Joyner Fine Art, Toronto #324 (C.D 850)
$717   £485   Fishing in Pangnirtung Fjord (30x40cm-12x16in) s. mixed media. 23-Nov-93 Joyner Fine Art, Toronto #248 (C.D 950)
$874   £583   Children with dog. Mother and child (14x19cm-6x7in) s.d.86 mixed media pair. 13-May-94 Joyner Fine Art, Toronto #184 (C.D 1200)

NOEH, Anna T (1926-) Canadian-cont.
$2869	£1939	Children on the see-saw in Pangnirtung (75x100cm-30x39in) s. mixed media. 23-Nov-93 Joyner Fine Art, Toronto #308/R (C.D 3800)

NOGUCHI, Isamu (1904-1988) American
$4500	£3125	Seated nude (43x27cm-17x11in) s. graphite board on board. 26-Feb-93 Sotheby's Arcade, New York #266 a/R
$8000	£5405	Untitled (114x89cm-45x35in) s.d.30 ink. 11-Nov-93 Sotheby's, New York #257 a/R

NOLAND, Kenneth (1924-) American
$4500	£2980	Composition (71x65cm-28x26in) s. s.d.1957verso. 2-Oct-93 Weschler, Washington #156/R
$4768	£3200	Desert view (37x40cm-15x16in) s.i.d.1967 verso acrylic. 2-Dec-93 Christie's, London #176/R
$8195	£5500	Silent Adios II (43x102cm-17x40in) s.i.d.1970 acrylic. 25-Mar-93 Christie's, London #104/R
$8403	£5457	Awry (43x200cm-17x79in) s.i.d.1976verso. 24-Jun-94 Francis Briest, Paris #41/R (F.FR 46000)
$8940	£6000	Untitled (86x86cm-34x34in) s.d.1959 i.d.stretcher acrylic. 25-Mar-93 Christie's, London #110/R
$9685	£6500	10th of May (85x85cm-33x33in) s.d.1963verso acrylic. 25-Mar-93 Christie's, London #109/R
$9685	£6500	Here-in (250x250cm-98x98in) s.i.d.1975verso acrylic. 25-Mar-93 Christie's, London #100/R
$13000	£8725	Level mode (61x483cm-24x190in) s.i.d.1966verso acrylic. 5-May-94 Sotheby's, New York #156/R
$13000	£8725	Verge (136x340cm-54x134in) s.i.d.1979 verso acrylic shaped canvas. 23-Feb-94 Christie's, New York #27/R
$14000	£9722	Up (244x60cm-96x24in) s.i.d.1967verso acrylic. 24-Feb-93 Christie's, New York #45/R
$14900	£10000	Sun dried - Japanese Space (161x161cm-63x63in) s.i.verso magna painted 1963. 2-Dec-93 Christie's, London #168/R
$17000	£10000	Knit (196x170cm-77x67in) s.d.1978 verso acrylic. 6-Oct-92 Sotheby's, New York #115/R
$20000	£13514	Rutile (274x274cm-108x108in) acrylic painted 1973. 10-Nov-93 Christie's, New York #156/R
$22000	£14765	Cosmic price (168x298cm-66x117in) s.i.d.1969verso acrylic. 4-May-94 Christie's, New York #157/R
$24000	£16107	Sunshine and snow (253x207cm-100x81in) s.i.verso acrylic. 4-May-94 Christie's, New York #148/R
$24000	£15894	April in balance (236x112cm-93x44in) s.i.d.1971stretcher acrylic. 19-Nov-92 Christie's, New York #420/R
$24000	£16107	Warm and cool (240x61cm-94x24in) s.i.d.1966 verso acrylic shaped canvas. 23-Feb-94 Christie's, New York #33/R
$30000	£20000	Inner Dark Outer Light (114x114cm-45x45in) s.i.d.1964overlap acrylic. 26-May-94 Christie's, London #45/R
$32000	£21622	Blue wind (153x238cm-60x94in) s.i.d.1977stretcher acrylic. 10-Nov-93 Christie's, New York #175/R
$32500	£21959	Graded exposure (225x582cm-89x229in) s.i.d.1967 verso acrylic. 11-Nov-93 Sotheby's, New York #325/R
$40000	£26490	Via fall (135x257cm-53x101in) s.i.d.1969verso acrylic. 19-Nov-92 Christie's, New York #301/R
$60000	£40541	Dry choice (217x217cm-85x85in) s.i.d.1965 verso acrylic. 9-Nov-93 Christie's, New York #20/R
$62568	£39600	Inner dark outer light (114x114cm-45x45in) s.i.d.1964 verso acrylic. 3-Dec-92 Christie's, London #42/R
$85000	£56291	Blue horizon (177x177cm-70x70in) s.d.1963verso acrylic. 18-Nov-92 Christie's, New York #9/R

NOLF, John Thomas (1872-1955) American
$700	£458	Boys at swimming hole (51x61cm-20x24in) s. 16-May-93 Hanzel Galleries, Chicago #365 e

NORBURY, George (fl.c.1850) Canadian
$930	£628	Wickes Residence London Ontario (20x30cm-8x12in) indist.s.i. graphite W/C. 3-Nov-93 Sotheby's, Toronto #4/R (C.D 1200)

NORDALM, Federico (1949-) Nicaraguan
$6000	£3974	Calabazas (99x91cm-39x36in) s.d.1991 canvas on panel. 24-Nov-92 Christie's, New York #235/R
$11000	£7432	Naturaleza muerta con naranjas (123x95cm-48x37in) s.d.1989 acrylic. 23-Nov-93 Christie's, New York #271/R

NORDFELDT, B J O (1878-1955) American
$1800	£1192	Figures in landscape (51x66cm-20x26in) s. board. 23-Sep-93 Mystic Fine Arts, Connecticut #267/R

NORDFELDT, Bror Julius Olsson (1878-1955) American
$4000	£2312	Sunflower pods (86x107cm-34x42in) s.d.43 i.verso. 24-Sep-92 Sotheby's, New York #203/R
$5280	£3385	At the swimming hole (66x81cm-26x32in) s. board. 17-Dec-92 Mystic Fine Arts, Connecticut #82/R
$5500	£3642	Santa Fe (84x94cm-33x37in) s. s.i.d.1936-37 verso. 22-Sep-93 Christie's, New York #178/R

NORDFELDT, Bror Julius Olsson (1878-1955) American-cont.
$8000	£5298	Still life with plate of fruit. Landscape with houses (63x81cm-25x32in) double-sided painted 1927. 23-Sep-93 Sotheby's, New York #237/R
$12000	£7595	Low tide, California (56x81cm-22x32in) s.d.45 s.i.d.1945verso board. 4-Dec-92 Christie's, New York #130/R
$15000	£9494	White vase (122x86cm-48x34in) 4-Dec-92 Christie's, New York #134/R
$18000	£12587	New Mexico landscape (66x72cm-26x28in) s. 11-Mar-93 Christie's, New York #259/R
$30000	£18987	Fire lilies in clay pot (96x61cm-38x24in) s. 4-Dec-92 Christie's, New York #126/R
$750	£500	Minnesota (38x58cm-15x23in) s. W/C executed 1952. 23-May-94 Christie's, East, New York #218 a
$2200	*£1272*	High country farm (39x57cm-15x22in) s. W/C pencil. 23-Sep-92 Christie's, New York #122/R
$3200	*£1850*	Mountainside (34x49cm-13x19in) s. W/C paper on board. 23-Sep-92 Christie's, New York #123/R
$4750	*£3006*	Trees and sunlight (38x55cm-15x22in) s. W/C. 3-Dec-92 Sotheby's, New York #56/R

NORDHAUSEN, August Henry (1901-) American
$1200	£702	Dorine daydreaming (51x41cm-20x16in) s.i.verso. 17-Sep-92 Sloan, North Bethesda #2576/R

NORDSTRAND, Nathalie Johnson (20th C) American
$1000	£680	Evening marsh, Kettle Cove (15x23cm-6x9in) s. 10-Jul-93 Young Fine Arts Auctions, Maine #241/R

NORMAN, Irving (20th C) American
$650	*£409*	The Bridge (58x93cm-23x37in) s.i.d.1946 i.verso graphite. 25-Apr-93 Butterfield & Butterfield, San Francisco #2099/R

NORMIL, Andre (1934-) Haitian
$2200	£1486	Adoration (41x51cm-16x20in) s. 24-Nov-93 Christie's, New York #8/R

NORRIS, Thomas Bowler (1866-1927) American?
$850	*£563*	Autumn colours (71x91cm-28x36in) s. 28-Nov-92 Young Fine Arts Auctions, Maine #296/R

NORRIS, Walter S (1868-?) American
$3100	£1950	Harbour groupings (61x76cm-24x30in) s. 22-Apr-93 Freeman Fine Arts, Philadelphia #1309/R

NORTON, C W (19th C) American
$1800	*£1233*	Portrait of the ship 'H C Winslow' (43x51cm-17x20in) s.i. W/C pencil. 12-Feb-94 Boos Gallery, Michigan #548/R

NORTON, Crandall (1920-) American
$475	£315	December sun - figures at tide pools (61x81cm-24x32in) s.d.59 W/C. 14-Jun-94 John Moran, Pasadena #117

NORTON, L D (1867-?) American
$1800	£1040	Young boys by water (25x36cm-10x14in) s. canvasboard. 27-Sep-92 James Bakker, Cambridge #78/R

NORTON, William Edward (1843-1916) American
$575	£384	Breton fishermen on the beach (31x41cm-12x16in) s. 21-May-94 Weschler, Washington #79/R
$700	£470	Ship by the dunes (30x41cm-12x16in) s. 16-Dec-93 Mystic Fine Arts, Connecticut #53
$700	£458	Boatyard by river (23x38cm-9x15in) s. 18-Sep-93 Young Fine Arts Auctions, Maine #228/R
$800	£404	Near French village (28x41cm-11x16in) s. board. 28-Aug-92 Young Fine Arts Auctions, Maine #234
$948	£600	Schooner and other sailing boats off coast (16x24cm-6x9in) s. panel. 3-Dec-92 Christie's, S. Kensington #283
$1200	£789	Leaving the ship behind (44x100cm-17x39in) s. 31-Mar-93 Sotheby's Arcade, New York #26/R
$1200	£816	Sailboat (30x41cm-12x16in) s.i. 15-Nov-93 Christie's, East, New York #237/R
$1400	£933	Summer hillside (30x41cm-12x16in) s.i. 21-May-94 Weschler, Washington #87
$1900	£1242	Brittany coastal scene, figures, cart and horses (51x64cm-20x25in) s. 15-May-93 Dunning's, Illinois #1200/R
$2200	£1467	Scene at Noank, Connecticut (30x40cm-12x16in) s. i.verso sketch canvasboard. 21-May-94 Weschler, Washington #83/R
$2900	£1933	Clamdiggers (41x52cm-16x20in) s. 21-May-94 Weschler, Washington #95/R
$3000	£1974	On dunes - Holland - daydreams (30x41cm-12x16in) s. 31-Mar-93 Sotheby's Arcade, New York #64/R
$3000	£2083	Coastal scene (41x61cm-16x24in) s.d.74. 6-Mar-93 Louisiana Auction Exchange #148/R
$3874	£2600	Gathering seaweed at low tide (57x75cm-22x30in) s. 1-Feb-94 Bristol Auction Rooms #628/R
$4500	£3191	Bark sailing near Thatcher's Island lighthouses (41x61cm-16x24in) s.d.76. 13-Feb-93 Richard Bourne, Hyannis #119/R
$5500	£3595	European beach scene (30x41cm-12x16in) s. 17-Sep-93 Skinner, Bolton #145/R
$6000	£3922	Ships at sea (51x76cm-20x30in) s. 30-Jun-94 Mystic Fine Arts, Connecticut #135
$6500	£4333	Summer afternoon (51x63cm-20x25in) s. panel. 21-May-94 Weschler, Washington #92/R
$19240	£13000	Bon Voyage (119x84cm-47x33in) s.d.88. 16-Jun-93 Sotheby's, London #163 a/R
$550	£372	City port (28x19cm-11x7in) s.d.93 W/C. 5-Nov-93 Skinner, Bolton #105/R

NORWELL, Graham Noble (1901-1967) Canadian
$700	£476	Moonlit lake scene (41x51cm-16x20in) s. board. 17-Apr-94 Hindman Galleries, Chicago #1005/R
$775	£524	Snow flakes (41x51cm-16x20in) s.i.verso board. 3-Nov-93 Sotheby's, Toronto #305/R (C.D 1000)
$831	£561	House in Laurentians (40x50cm-16x20in) s. canvasboard. 23-Nov-93 Joyner Fine Art, Toronto #209/R (C.D 1100)
$1638	£1092	Laurentian landscape, spring (76x102cm-30x40in) s. 11-May-94 Sotheby's, Toronto #49/R (C.D 2250)
$2179	£1443	Winter landscape (51x61cm-20x24in) s. 18-Nov-92 Sotheby's, Toronto #212/R (C.D 2800)
$555	£363	Laurentian village (36x48cm-14x19in) s. W/C. 19-May-93 Sotheby's, Toronto #69 (C.D 700)

NOTT, Raymond (1888-1948) American
$700	£490	Desert landscape (64x76cm-25x30in) s. masonite. 14-Mar-93 Hindman Galleries, Chicago #36
$800	£537	Snow scene landscape (61x76cm-24x30in) 27-Mar-94 Myers, Florida #9/R
$550	£367	Eucalyptus coastal scene (48x53cm-19x21in) s. pastel. 15-Mar-94 John Moran, Pasadena #41

NOURSE, Elizabeth (1859-1938) American
$6596	£4311	Madonna and Child (62x48cm-24x19in) s.i.d.1891. 11-May-93 Rasmussen, Copenhagen #291/R
$11000	£7333	Peasant woman (79x60cm-31x24in) s.i.d.1889 i.verso. 17-Mar-94 Sotheby's, New York #104/R
$12000	£8000	Interieur Breton a Penmarch (46x55cm-18x22in) s.d.1902 i.stretcher. 17-Mar-94 Sotheby's, New York #122/R
$650	£436	Peonies (43x53cm-17x21in) s. W/C pencil cardboard oval. 23-Jun-93 Doyle, New York #67

NOVOA, Gustavo (1939-) Chilean
$700	£473	Leopard (30x25cm-12x10in) s.d.1972 masonite. 20-Apr-94 Doyle, New York #57
$1100	£743	Black panther (36x43cm-14x17in) s.d.1972 masonite. 20-Apr-94 Doyle, New York #56

NOYES, E L (20th C) American
$1240	£780	Winter hillside (20x25cm-8x10in) s. canvasboard. 22-Apr-93 Freeman Fine Arts, Philadelphia #1313

NOYES, George L (19/20th C) Canadian
$650	£439	Arab street scene (23x15cm-9x6in) s.d.92 board. 27-Nov-93 Young Fine Arts Auctions, Maine #241/R
$1100	£738	Venice (51x61cm-20x24in) s. 26-Mar-94 James Bakker, Cambridge #49/R
$1200	£694	Lowland landscape (33x46cm-13x18in) s. 25-Sep-92 Sotheby's Arcade, New York #267/R
$1400	£741	The market square (25x20cm-10x8in) s. board. 11-Sep-92 Skinner, Bolton #201/R
$2000	£1325	New England winter (51x61cm-20x24in) s. canvasboard. 21-Nov-92 James Bakker, Cambridge #297/R
$2400	£1611	Still life with oranges and grapes (36x56cm-14x22in) s.d.89. 6-Dec-93 Grogan, Massachussetts #466/R
$3000	£1987	Charles river (36x41cm-14x16in) s. board. 28-Nov-92 Young Fine Arts Auctions, Maine #298/R
$3520	£2301	Coming into harbour (33x38cm-13x15in) s. i.verso board. 14-May-93 Skinner, Bolton #128/R
$3600	£2416	Boats at the pier (33x38cm-13x15in) s. board. 24-Jun-93 Mystic Fine Arts, Connecticut #201
$3750	£2622	Venetian scene along the Grand Canal (38x33cm-15x13in) s. canvasboard. 12-Mar-93 Skinner, Bolton #240/R
$4500	£3020	Rocky Neck Ferry (41x35cm-16x14in) s. i.verso board. 4-Mar-94 Skinner, Bolton #268/R
$5500	£3667	Winter in the valley (63x76cm-25x30in) s. 23-May-94 Christie's, East, New York #175/R
$8750	£5834	Opalescent fog, Gloucester, Massachusetts (46x56cm-18x22in) s. i.verso canvasboard. 17-May-94 Grogan, Massachussetts #368/R
$20000	£12658	Early spring (64x77cm-25x30in) s. 4-Dec-92 Christie's, New York #47/R

NUDERSCHER, Frank (1880-1959) American
$1900	£1218	The founding of St. Louis, Pierre Laclede and Auguste Chouteau (203x274cm-80x108in) s.d.1937 canvas laid down. 26-Apr-93 Selkirks, St. Louis #301/R
$2000	£1282	St. Louis riverfront, Eads Bridge (213x274cm-84x108in) s. canvas laid down. 26-Apr-93 Selkirks, St. Louis #299/R
$4600	£2659	Sunset in Ozarks (94x76cm-37x30in) s. 21-Sep-92 Selkirks, St. Louis #174/R

NUNAMAKER, Alfred R (20th C) American
$1100	£728	Delaware river winter (41x46cm-16x18in) s. 28-Nov-92 Young Fine Arts Auctions, Maine #299/R
$2600	£1646	Village in New Jersey (41x61cm-16x24in) s. 24-Oct-92 Collins, Maine #95

NUNEZ, Armando Garcia (20th C) Mexican
$1200	£800	Paisajes Mexicanos (11x16cm-4x6in) s. masonite painted c.1912 pair. 9-Jun-94 Sotheby's Arcade, New York #123/R
$1854	£1253	Paisaje (33x26cm-13x10in) s.d.1928 fibracel. 9-Nov-93 Louis Morton, Mexico #93 (M.P 6000)
$2547	£1633	Paisaje (21x18cm-8x7in) s. 29-Apr-93 Louis Morton, Mexico #109 (M.P 8000)

NUNEZ, Armando Garcia (20th C) Mexican-cont.
$5000   £3268   Paisaje con Pocateptl e Ixtahuacatil (31x47cm-12x19in) s.d.1962 masonite. 17-May-93 Christie's, New York #258/R

NUNEZ, Daniel (1906-) Mexican
$2405   £1603   Musicos del Pueblo (62x51cm-24x20in) s. 25-May-94 Louis Morton, Mexico #31/R (M.P 8000)

NUTT, Jim (1938-) American
$13000 £8609   I've seen this before (150x124cm-59x49in) s.i.d.74 verso acrylic. 18-Nov-92 Sotheby's, New York #319/R
$15000 £10135 Not One to Quibble but your wrong (79x77cm-31x30in) s.i.d.1977verso acrylic. 8-Nov-93 Christie's, East, New York #40/R
$4800   £3200   Stop pointing (76x69cm-30x27in) col crayon pencil gouache. 13-Mar-94 Hindman Galleries, Chicago #864/R
$5500   £3716   Whichever is yours. In this case neither one (30x35cm-12x14in) col pencil dr executed 1982 executed 1983 pair. 8-Nov-93 Christie's, East, New York #35/R

NYHOLM, Arvid Frederick (1866-1927) Swedish/American
$900   £570   Portrait of woman seated at table wearing yellow dress and jade necklace (69x56cm-27x22in) s. 30-Nov-92 Selkirks, St. Louis #162/R

OAKES, Mario (19th C) American
$6493   £4300   Still life of dead game heron quinea fowl black cock and other birds (108x148cm-43x58in) s.d.1845 canvas laid down. 22-Sep-93 Phillips, Ipswich #620/R

OAKLEY, Thornton (1881-1953) American
$50000 £31646 News vendor on Broadway (135x74cm-53x29in) s.d.1905. 4-Dec-92 Christie's, New York #157/R
$786   £498   Petroleum (76x102cm-30x40in) s. s.i.verso W/C gouache chl. 1-Dec-92 Ritchie, Toronto #187/R (C.D 1000)
$3500   £2273   Jones and Laughlin Steel Mill, Pittsburgh, Pennsylvania (76x50cm-30x20in) s.d.1919 chl htd white board. 9-Sep-93 Sotheby's Arcade, New York #314/R

OAKLEY, Violet (1874-1961) American
$8150   £5719   The Child and Tradition study for mural (89x64cm-35x25in) s.d.1910. 7-Oct-93 Freeman Fine Arts, Philadelphia #919/R
$800   £526   Study of seated woman for mural in Charleston's Yarnall House (48x33cm-19x13in) s. chl pastel htd white. 11-Jun-93 Freeman Fine Arts, Philadelphia #158
$900   £529   Women playing cello (38x25cm-15x10in) s.d.1924 conte crayon. 8-Oct-92 Freeman Fine Arts, Philadelphia #1125/R

OBERTEUFFER, George (1878-1940) American
$7000   £4430   View of Notre Dame (110x131cm-43x52in) s. 2-Dec-92 Christie's, East, New York #155/R

OBIN, Philome (1892-1986) Haitian
$2000   £1361   Three horsemen Dessalines Toussaint Christophe (41x51cm-16x20in) s.i. masonite. 17-Nov-93 Doyle, New York #143/R
$2600   £1722   Hunter (30x21cm-12x8in) s. masonite. 24-Nov-92 Christie's, New York #280/R
$6000   £3974   Une Haitien au bas du Limbe (51x61cm-20x24in) s.i. masonite. 24-Nov-92 Christie's, New York #293/R
$6000   £4054   Quatre joueurs de besigue (61x76cm-24x30in) s.i.d.1958 board. 4-Nov-93 Boos Gallery, Michigan #1270/R
$7000   £4636   Marriage (61x76cm-24x30in) s. oil pencil masonite. 24-Nov-92 Christie's, New York #272/R
$8057   £5266   Autoportrait (61x51cm-24x20in) painted 1986. 17-May-93 Hoebanx, Paris #168/R (F.FR 44500)
$12000 £8108   Carnaval de 1947 (61x76cm-24x30in) s.i. masonite painted 1978. 24-Nov-93 Christie's, New York #23/R
$16000 £10811 Bourgeois du Cap-Haitien vers l'an 1902 (61x76cm-24x30in) s.i. masonite painted 1967. 24-Nov-93 Christie's, New York #16/R
$23000 £15333 Quelques fruits d'Haiti (51x61cm-20x24in) s.i. tempera masonite painted c.1965. 18-May-94 Sotheby's, New York #289/R
$23000 £15232 Le Marche de Limbe (61x75cm-24x30in) s.d.1957 masonite. 24-Nov-92 Christie's, New York #289/R
$42816 £27446 Jeudi au cap haitien avec le paquebot (76x102cm-30x40in) s.d.1972 wood. 14-Dec-92 Hoebanx, Paris #112/R (F.FR 230000)
$27500 £18581 Fete de la garde (50x60cm-20x24in) s.i.d.1945 graphite oil board. 22-Nov-93 Sotheby's, New York #67/R

OBIN, Pierre Frederic (1952-) Haitian
$1630   £1065   Eglise de Carrefour des Peres (61x51cm-24x20in) 17-May-93 Hoebanx, Paris #170 (F.FR 9000)

OBIN, Seneque (1893-1977) Haitian
$850   £450   On the road to market (61x51cm-24x20in) s.d. 11-Sep-92 Skinner, Bolton #287/R
$2400   £1600   La chasse (60x51cm-24x20in) s.i. board painted c.1960. 18-May-94 Sotheby's, New York #293/R

OBIN, Seneque (1893-1977) Haitian-cont.
$3800	£2517	Way to market (41x45cm-16x18in) s. masonite. 24-Nov-92 Christie's, New York #275/R
$8000	£5229	Funeraille maconnique (61x76cm-24x30in) s.i. masonite painted c.1968. 18-May-93 Sotheby's, New York #236/R
$13000	£8497	L'amour de calvaire (61x77cm-24x30in) s.i.d.63 oil graphite. 18-May-93 Sotheby's, New York #235/R

O'BRADY, Gertrude (1901-) American
$3332	£2251	La comtesse de Toulouse-Lautrec (61x44cm-24x17in) s.i.d.1948 black crayon dr. 14-Jun-93 Jean Louis Picard, Paris #30/R (F.FR 19000)

O'BRIEN, Lucius Richard (1832-1899) Canadian
$652	£435	Rocky lake shore (23x36cm-9x14in) s.d.1875 W/C. 6-Jun-94 Waddingtons, Toronto #1266/R (C.D 900)
$697	£471	Windsor Castle (24x34cm-9x13in) W/C. 3-Nov-93 Sotheby's, Toronto #105 (C.D 900)
$713	£466	Coastal scene (36x51cm-14x20in) init. W/C. 19-May-93 Sotheby's, Toronto #65/R (C.D 900)
$1000	£633	River landscape with three men in boat (30x43cm-12x17in) s.d.1895 W/C. 3-Dec-92 Freeman Fine Arts, Philadelphia #1756/R
$1254	£804	Vase of roses (38x28cm-15x11in) s.d.1897 W/C. 7-Dec-92 Waddingtons, Toronto #1331 (C.D 1600)
$1268	£829	Boating on river (32x44cm-13x17in) s.d.1898 W/C. 19-May-93 Sotheby's, Toronto #100/R (C.D 1600)
$1427	£933	Still life of roses (39x28cm-15x11in) s.d.1896 W/C. 19-May-93 Sotheby's, Toronto #161/R (C.D 1800)
$1982	£1295	Waterfall (38x56cm-15x22in) s.d.73 W/c. 19-May-93 Sotheby's, Toronto #223/R (C.D 2500)
$6199	£4188	Mountain settlement at the river bend (51x36cm-20x14in) s.d.Oct.19 1887 W/C. 3-Nov-93 Sotheby's, Toronto #13/R (C.D 8000)
$9117	£5959	Cove on coast of Gaspe (51x66cm-20x26in) s.d.1883 W/C. 19-May-93 Sotheby's, Toronto #105/R (C.D 11500)

OCAMPO, Isidoro (1902-) Mexican
$962	£641	Lavandera (65x50cm-26x20in) s. 25-May-94 Louis Morton, Mexico #32 (M.P 3200)
$1900	£1195	Figure with baskets (51x36cm-20x14in) s. gouache. 25-Apr-93 Butterfield & Butterfield, San Francisco #2083/R

OCANA, Friar Diego de (style) (17th C) Peruvian
$6000	£4054	Virgen de Toledo (104x84cm-41x33in) painted c.1610. 23-Nov-93 Christie's, New York #77/R

OCHTMAN, Dorothy (1892-1971) American
$650	£417	Day lilies in a bowl (76x64cm-30x25in) s. 13-Dec-92 Litchfield Auction Gallery #19

OCHTMAN, Leonard (1854-1934) American
$850	£567	Forest pool (30x41cm-12x16in) s.i. panel. 13-Mar-94 Hindman Galleries, Chicago #761
$1100	£738	Spring landscape (30x41cm-12x16in) s. board. 14-Jan-94 Du Mouchelle, Detroit #2231/R
$5000	£3311	A day in May (61x76cm-24x30in) s. 28-Nov-92 Young Fine Arts Auctions, Maine #301/R
$12000	£7595	Approaching storm, twilight (76x101cm-30x40in) s.d.1899. 4-Dec-92 Christie's, New York #12/R
$725	£480	Winter landscape with houses, at eventide (38x54cm-15x21in) s.d.1892 W/C. 30-Jun-93 Phillips, Chester #113

ODDIE, Walter M (1808-1865) American
$11000	£7333	River landscape (88x137cm-35x54in) s.d.1856. 16-Mar-94 Christie's, New York #14/R

ODJIG, Daphne (1928-) Canadian
$3313	£2179	The family (101x81cm-40x32in) s.d.75 acrylic. 7-Jun-93 Ritchie, Toronto #107/R (C.D 4250)

OGILVIE, J C (1838-1900) American
$1184	£800	Coastal scene with sailing boat and dinghy with sailors , s. 5-Nov-93 Moore Allen and Innocent, Cirencester #535

OGILVIE, John Clinton (1838-1900) American
$900	£577	View on the Croton River, Carmel Putnam Co.N.Y. (41x30cm-16x12in) s.i. 10-Dec-92 Sloan, North Bethesda #2268
$3200	£2078	Landscape with river (114x183cm-45x72in) s.d.1870. 9-Sep-93 Sotheby's Arcade, New York #49/R

OGILVIE, William Abernethy (1901-1989) Canadian
$906	£612	Winter road (30x40cm-12x16in) s. canvasboard. 23-Nov-93 Joyner Fine Art, Toronto #18/R (C.D 1200)
$542	£366	Fields under evening sky (32x46cm-13x18in) s. W/C. 3-Nov-93 Sotheby's, Toronto #148/R (C.D 700)
$620	£419	Evening sky Georgian Bay (34x51cm-13x20in) s.d.62 s.i.verso pastel ink. 3-Nov-93 Sotheby's, Toronto #79 (C.D 800)
$677	£455	Moonlight, Georgian Bay (38x53cm-15x21in) s.d.73 W/C. 29-Nov-93 Waddingtons, Toronto #1071 (C.D 900)

OGILVIE, William Abernethy (1901-1989) Canadian-cont.
$755   £510   Setting sun over Lake Atillan, Guatemala (26x37cm-10x15in) s. W/C. 23-Nov-93 Joyner Fine Art, Toronto #176 (C.D 1000)
$1057   £714   'A.Y' sketching (37x54cm-15x21in) s. mixed media. 23-Nov-93 Joyner Fine Art, Toronto #192 (C.D 1400)

O'GORMAN, Juan (1905-1982) Mexican
$105000 £70000   Paisaje erosionado (45x60cm-18x24in) s.d.1964 oil board. 17-May-94 Sotheby's, New York #71/R
$190000 £126667 Flores imaginarias (65x51cm-26x20in) s.i.d.1944 s.i.verso tempera masonite. 18-May-94 Christie's, New York #25/R
$1656   £1061   Globo Coronation. Globo Montgolfier (17x12cm-7x5in) s.i. pencil crayon s.i. pencil two. 29-Apr-93 Louis Morton, Mexico #127 (M.P 5200)
$2000   £1333   Trazo Geometrico para el Retrato de la Sra.Beeson Lindau (89x55cm-35x22in) s.i.d.1964 chl crayon. 18-May-94 Christie's, New York #316/R
$3200   £2133   Estudio para el Retablo de la Independencia (96x83cm-38x33in) s.i.d.1961 chl crayon chk brown paper. 18-May-94 Christie's, New York #315/R
$4000   £2649   Cuernavaca (16x24cm-6x9in) s.i.d.1929 W/C graphite. 23-Nov-92 Sotheby's, New York #157/R
$7000   £4667   Boceto para el Reino Mineral (86x70cm-34x28in) s.d.1943 chl graphite. 18-May-94 Sotheby's, New York #421/R

OHASHI, Yutaka (20th C) American
$1300   £872   Rock No.3 (57x75cm-22x30in) s. s.i.d.1960 verso oil collage canvas. 4-Mar-94 Skinner, Bolton #310/R

O'HIGGINS, Pablo (1904-1983) Mexican
$9000   £6081   Minero (77x61cm-30x24in) s. masonite painted c.1947. 22-Nov-93 Sotheby's, New York #225/R
$3250   £2152   Dos mujers (23x34cm-9x13in) s.i.d.1934 gouache. 23-Nov-92 Sotheby's, New York #158/R
$4750   £3188   Dos Picadreros (45x46cm-18x18in) s. W/C paper on board painted 1941. 7-Jan-94 Gary Nader, Miami #72/R
$7500   £5000   Maguey de Oxtotepec (51x62cm-20x24in) s.d.75 graphite W/C. 18-May-94 Sotheby's, New York #307/R

OKADA, Kenzo (1902-) Japanese/American
$12665   £8500   Path to Bamboo Grove (163x130cm-64x51in) s. painted 1981. 2-Dec-93 Christie's, London #134/R
$65000   £43324   Ascent (154x132cm-61x52in) s. painted c.1961. 4-May-94 Sotheby's, New York #10/R

O'KEEFFE, Georgia (1887-1986) American
$110000 £73333   Red pear with fig (17x14cm-7x6in) i.indis.d.verso panel painted 1923. 25-May-94 Sotheby's, New York #112/R
$130000 £82278   Cannas (45x30cm-18x12in) 3-Dec-92 Sotheby's, New York #161/R
$140000 £88608   Red gladiola in white vase (26x18cm-10x7in) s.d.1928verso. 4-Dec-92 Christie's, New York #135/R
$160000 £101286 Three pears (45x30cm-18x12in) s. s.with star i.verso. 3-Dec-92 Sotheby's, New York #138/R
$200000 £134288 Gray Hills, New Mexico (41x76cm-16x30in) s.d.1930verso. 2-Dec-92 Sotheby's, New York #135/R
$1100000 £696203 Ritz Tower, night (102x35cm-40x14in) inits.verso. 4-Dec-92 Christie's, New York #123/R
$70000   £46667   Backyard at 65th Street (63x48cm-25x19in) chl paper on board executed c.1920. 25-May-94 Sotheby's, New York #115/R
$120000 £80537   Pink roses and larkspur (41x30cm-16x12in) init. s.verso pastel painted 1931. 2-Dec-93 Sotheby's, New York #92/R
$260000 £173333 East River, New York, No II (27x71cm-11x28in) pastel. 26-May-94 Christie's, New York #138/R

O'KELLY, Mattie Lou (1907-) American
$2800   £1892   My Georgia (31x41cm-12x16in) s.d.Mar 1973 i.verso paperboard. 5-Nov-93 Skinner, Bolton #174/R
$2800   £1854   Mama knitting (15x15cm-6x6in) s.d. mixed media. 21-Nov-92 Litchfield Auction Gallery #30

OLDENBURG, Claes (1929-) American
$1200   £833   Pulling down banana monument from poster for Artist's Call (55x37cm-22x15in) init.i.d.84 frottage crayon col.chk newsprint. 22-Feb-93 Christie's, East, New York #198/R
$1500   £993   Untitled (13x18cm-5x7in) init.d.Feb.9.1985verso acrylic canvas collage. 17-Nov-92 Christie's, East, New York #66/R
$1746   £1172   Billiard table (37x52cm-15x20in) i. felt pen collage paper board. 3-Dec-93 Lempertz, Cologne #904/R (DM 3000)
$3500   £2349   Pat seated (36x28cm-14x11in) init.d.59 ccrayon. 25-Feb-94 Sotheby's, New York #27/R
$3800   £2550   Knife dog holding bone (46x35cm-18x14in) init.d.86 chl W/C. 23-Feb-94 Christie's, East, New York #204/R
$5000   £2941   Teabag in landscape with waving label (25x24cm-10x9in) iit.d.85 W/C col.crayons. 8-Oct-92 Christie's, New York #139/R
$7000   £4730   Door No.1 (32x13cm-13x5in) init.d.65 pencil W/C. 11-Nov-93 Sotheby's, New York #100/R
$7500   £4412   Drainpipe (38x56cm-15x22in) init.d.66 W/C pencil. 6-Oct-92 Sotheby's, New York #86/R

OLDENBURG, Claes (1929-) American-cont.
$9000	£6040	*Study for colossal sculpture in the form of a man's hat (28x35cm-11x14in)* init.d.73 crayon W/C. 25-Feb-94 Sotheby's, New York #78/R
$9000	£5960	*Cotello ship from above (76x51cm-30x20in)* s.d.85 W/C graphite col.crayon. 19-Nov-92 Christie's, New York #405/R
$11000	£7383	*Sailboat (25x34cm-10x13in)* init.i.d.1962 W/C brush ink graphite col.crayons. 4-May-94 Christie's, New York #176/R
$12665	£8500	*Good humour (76x53cm-30x21in)* init. W/C chl. 23-Mar-94 Sotheby's, London #351/R
$15000	£10067	*Proposed colossal monument for Thames river, Thames ball (67x102cm-26x40in)* init.i.d.67 pencil crayon W/C. 5-May-94 Sotheby's, New York #191/R
$23000	£15232	*Colossal monument for Grant Park, Chicago - windshield wiper, overhead view (43x30cm-17x12in)* init.d.67 crayon W/C. 18-Nov-92 Sotheby's, New York #176/R
$28000	£18792	*Home ray guns (60x45cm-24x18in)* init.i.d.1963 lithogr.crayon W/C pencil pastel. 5-May-94 Sotheby's, New York #175/R

OLDFIELD, Otis (1890-1969) American
$2700	£1561	American river (91x76cm-36x30in) 26-Sep-92 San Rafael Auction Galleries #217
$3000	£1987	The last ferry (76x61cm-30x24in) s. 15-Jun-94 Butterfield & Butterfield, San Francisco #4585/R
$6500	£4305	Theme in Red No.2 (39x31cm-15x12in) s.d.1926 s.i.verso panel. 15-Jun-94 Butterfield & Butterfield, San Francisco #4731/R
$12000	£6936	La penupienne (147x114cm-58x45in) s. i.verso. 24-Sep-92 Sotheby's, New York #193/R

OLIN, Nahui (1893-1978) Mexican
$3607	£2405	Descanso (32x45cm-13x18in) s. masonite. 25-May-94 Louis Morton, Mexico #56/R (M.P 12000)

OLINSKY, Ivan G (1878-1962) American
$2500	£1656	Iris dress (61x49cm-24x19in) s.i.1878. 22-Sep-93 Christie's, New York #140/R
$4500	£2922	Girl reclining on pillow (18x20cm-7x8in) i. board. 15-Jan-93 Du Mouchelle, Detroit #2021/R
$16000	£10884	Motherly love (102x76cm-40x30in) s.d.1913. 17-Nov-93 Doyle, New York #25/R
$26000	£17333	Woman reading (63x76cm-25x30in) s. 16-Mar-94 Christie's, New York #98/R
$32000	£20513	Two young women (91x76cm-36x30in) s.d.1914. 27-May-93 Sotheby's, New York #30/R
$80000	£51282	Old fashioned gown (152x91cm-60x36in) s.d.1913. 27-May-93 Sotheby's, New York #31/R
$650	£428	Seated nude with yellow cloth (56x50cm-22x20in) s. pastel chl. 31-Mar-93 Sotheby's Arcade, New York #441/R

OLITSKI, Jules (1922-) American/Russian
$2600	£1806	Thalass mystery-9 (76x49cm-30x19in) s.i.d.78-10-2verso acrylic. 22-Feb-93 Christie's, East, New York #163/R
$5500	£3235	Grand Universe (77x170cm-30x67in) s.d.83 verso acrylic. 6-Oct-92 Sotheby's, New York #46/R
$7500	£4967	Fourth daughter (241x173cm-95x68in) s.i.d.1973verso acrylic. 17-Nov-92 Christie's, East, New York #184/R
$8500	£5000	Overtone one (249x38cm-98x15in) s.i.d.1970verso acrylic. 8-Oct-92 Christie's, New York #149/R
$16000	£10738	Untitled (107x102cm-42x40in) s.d.1964verso acrylic. 4-May-94 Christie's, New York #153/R
$20000	£11765	Dead ringer (112x91cm-44x36in) s.d.1963 verso acrylic. 6-Oct-92 Sotheby's, New York #37/R
$38000	£25676	Total trend (226x165cm-89x65in) s.i.d.1966verso acrylic. 10-Nov-93 Christie's, New York #161/R
$50000	£33557	Bat (300x203cm-118x80in) s.i.d.1965verso acrylic. 4-May-94 Christie's, New York #158/R
$50000	£33784	Flaubert red (208x272cm-82x107in) s.i.d.1964verso oil-miscible acrylic. 10-Nov-93 Sotheby's, New York #8/R
$75000	£49669	Flaming passion of Beverly Torrid (224x204cm-88x80in) s.i.d.1963verso acrylic. 17-Nov-92 Sotheby's, New York #37/R
$4200	£2745	Halcyon (173x125cm-68x49in) s.d.88-01-5 verso acrylic enamel canvas. 7-May-93 Christie's, East, New York #146/R

OLIVA, Pedro Pablo (1949-) Cuban
$6500	£4248	Serie Navegantes - la Balsa Criolla (146x114cm-57x45in) s.d.91 s.i.d.verso acrylic. 17-May-93 Christie's, New York #206/R
$12000	£8000	Los 15 de Juanela, Serie Balcones de la Habana (213x142cm-84x56in) s.i.d.91 oil over acrylic. 18-May-94 Christie's, New York #223/R
$24000	£16216	Serie, Balcones, imagen para un corto amor en Guatemala (178x140cm-70x55in) s. s.i.d.verso. 23-Nov-93 Christie's, New York #288/R

OLIVEIRA, Nathan (1928-) American
$4250	£2951	Untitled figurative painting 2 (90x70cm-35x28in) painted 1988 acrylic. 23-Feb-93 Sotheby's, New York #252/R
$1300	£878	Summer Blossom. Nude study , s. one d.59 s.i.d.verso one d.65 W/C dr two. 21-Apr-94 Butterfield & Butterfield, San Francisco #1123/R
$2400	£1412	Untitled (44x50cm-17x20in) s.d.64 pencil. 6-Oct-92 Sotheby's, New York #18/R
$3750	£2373	Standing woman (76x56cm-30x22in) s.d.61 W/C. 25-Oct-92 Butterfield & Butterfield, San Francisco #2304/R
$8500	£5743	Woman dancing before mirror (66x54cm-26x21in) s.d.61 gouache paper laid on masonite. 21-Oct-93 Butterfield & Butterfield, San Francisco #2776/R

OLIVER, T Clark (?-1893) American
$1320   £863   Ships at sea - view of Boston harbour (30x46cm-12x18in) s.d.79 with i.verso. 14-May-93 Skinner, Bolton #60/R
$2300   £1329   Coming to shore (30x46cm-12x18in) s. 27-Sep-92 James Bakker, Cambridge #1/R

OLSON, Geo Wallace (19/20th C) American?
$550   £369   Carmel, California coastal scene (61x76cm-24x30in) s.d.1909. 25-Mar-94 Eldred, Massachusetts #707

OLSON, J Olaf (1894-1979) American
$1500   £980   Fisherman from way down (61x76cm-24x30in) s.d.25 with i.verso. 17-Sep-93 Skinner, Bolton #230/R
$1800   £1139   Gloucester Harbour fishing boats (40x47cm-16x19in) s. 2-Dec-92 Christie's, East, New York #278

OMLOR, Pete (1947-) American
$1000   £654   Untitled - Kanji (129x132cm-51x52in) oil plastic screen wood executed 1982. 22-Dec-92 Christie's, East, New York #46
$1400   *£915*   *Greek saint (107x107cm-42x42in) oil enamel wood nylon executed 1987. 22-Dec-92 Christie's, East, New York #47*

ONDERDONK, Julian (1882-1922) American
$900   £608   Autumn afternoon (30x41cm-12x16in) s. 31-Mar-94 Sotheby's Arcade, New York #236 a
$4100   £2752   Early spring morning (20x15cm-8x6in) s. s.d.1909 verso panel. 5-Aug-93 Eldred, Massachusetts #812/R
$16000   £10256   Shinnecock (63x76cm-25x30in) s.d.1906. 26-May-93 Christie's, New York #119/R
$16000   £10811   A sultry August afternoon, Bronx Park, New York City (63x76cm-25x30in) s. s.i.verso. 31-Mar-94 Sotheby's Arcade, New York #234/R
$25000   £16447   Winter morning on Guadaloupe River, southwest Texas (63x76cm-25x30in) s.d.1911. 13-Jun-93 Butterfield & Butterfield, San Francisco #3157/R

O'NEILL, Rose (1875-1944) American
$2500   *£1445* *Mother with babies (48x39cm-19x15in) s.i. Indian ink chl pencil pair. 25-Sep-92 Sotheby's Arcade, New York #259/R*

ONLEY, Toni (1928-) Canadian
$602   £404   Standing stones (51x66cm-20x26in) s. panel painted 1966. 8-Dec-93 Maynards, Vancouver #213 (C.D 800)
$716   £487   Reaching Spotting Moon Orchid (51x61cm-20x24in) s. s.i.d.1988verso. 15-Nov-93 Hodgins, Calgary #266 (C.D 950)
$3192   £2020   Hornby Island (29x40cm-11x16in) s.d.July 82. 21-Oct-92 Maynards, Vancouver #135 (C.D 4000)
$650   £439   South coast Isle of Man (25x36cm-10x14in) s.d.47 W/C. 30-Mar-94 Maynards, Vancouver #30 (C.D 900)
$798   £539   Desadeash Lake, Yukon (27x37cm-11x15in) s.i.d.1990 W/C. 25-Apr-94 Levis, Calgary #245/R (C.D 1100)

OPPENHEIM, Dennis (1938-) American
$3772   £2314   Study for untitled wall piece (97x127cm-38x50in) s.i.d.1990 acrylic paper. 18-Oct-92 Catherine Charbonneaux, Paris #6 (F.FR 19000)
$1500   *£1007* *Study for Rag Head (100x131cm-39x52in) s.i.d.1990 acrylic graphite col chks glitter. 3-May-94 Christie's, East, New York #171/R*
$1639   *£1100* *Diagram for ground mutations - University of Kansas (100x80cm-39x31in) s.d.1970 photo wax crayon paper on cardboard. 3-Dec-93 Sotheby's, London #213/R*
$1705   *£1152* *Shape transmission chamber project for Israel Museum, s.d.1979 mixed media study. 24-Oct-93 Catherine Charbonneaux, Paris #81/R (F.FR 10000)*
$4250   *£2853* *Launching structure no.2 (190x124cm-75x49in) s.i.d.1982 col.chk chl W/C. 24-Feb-94 Sotheby's Arcade, New York #466/R*

OPPER, John (1908-) American
$1200   £795   Colour series 9-72 (142x203cm-56x80in) s.d.9-72verso. 29-Sep-93 Sotheby's Arcade, New York #316/R

ORDONEZ, Sylvia (1956-) Mexican
$17000   £11333   Frutero blanco y cielo (100x140cm-39x55in) s.d.93 s.i.d.verso. 18-May-94 Christie's, New York #240/R

ORDWAY, Alfred (1819-1897) American
$1100   £705   Woodland stream (76x91cm-30x36in) s. 28-May-93 Sloan, North Bethesda #2646/R

ORIHUEL, Juan (1907-) Argentinian
$1200   £706   Manzanas con jarron verde (50x60cm-20x24in) painted 1966. 29-Sep-92 VerBo, Buenos Aires #83

ORLANDO, Felipe (1911-) Cuban
$1300   £878   Woman in yellow dress (56x72cm-22x28in) s. 20-Mar-93 Weschler, Washington #54/R

OROPEZA, Jose (20th C) Mexican?
$1077   £708   En la sombra (40x50cm-16x20in) s. 4-Nov-92 Mora, Castelltort & Quintana, Juarez #102/R (M.P 3400000)

OROZCO, Jose Clemente (1883-1949) Mexican
$7000   £4730   Teul (25x32cm-10x13in) s. tempera executed c.1947. 22-Nov-93 Sotheby's, New York #223/R

OROZCO, Jose Clemente (1883-1949) Mexican-cont.
$15000	£10135	Portrait of a soldier (33x20cm-13x8in) s. 21-Oct-93 Butterfield & Butterfield, San Francisco #2745/R
$25000	£16556	La prostituta (38x35cm-15x14in) s. 23-Nov-92 Sotheby's, New York #180/R
$44000	£29139	El Elveado (50x40cm-20x16in) s. painted 1930. 24-Nov-92 Christie's, New York #139/R
$70000	£46358	Rosana (51x33cm-20x13in) s. paper on panel. 24-Nov-92 Christie's, New York #9/R
$340000	£225166	Acordada - Caballos Y Zapatistas (66x81cm-26x32in) s. 23-Nov-92 Sotheby's, New York #43/R
$2500	£1656	Manos (21x36cm-8x14in) s. graphite. 23-Nov-92 Sotheby's, New York #211/R
$4000	£2614	Figura (65x35cm-26x14in) s. chl executed c.1930. 18-May-93 Sotheby's, New York #122/R
$6000	£4054	Pueblo (35x51cm-14x20in) W/C pen graphite executed c.1930. 22-Nov-93 Sotheby's, New York #166/R
$7000	£4730	Fantastico torso de mujer (35x25cm-14x10in) mixed media painted c.1940. 23-Nov-93 Christie's, New York #204/R
$12000	£7947	Mujer (37x26cm-15x10in) s.d.1946 tempera gouache graphite. 23-Nov-92 Sotheby's, New York #232/R
$16000	£10458	Retrato de mujer (58x41cm-23x16in) s. gouache. 17-May-93 Christie's, New York #119/R
$19000	£12838	Mitin I, neoyorquino (27x37cm-11x15in) brush ink. 23-Nov-93 Christie's, New York #239/R
$60000	£39735	Prometheus (51x42cm-20x17in) s.d.45 oil pen. 23-Nov-92 Sotheby's, New York #50/R

OROZCO, Leonor (1924-) Mexican
$1758	£1188	Calabazas (90x60cm-35x24in) s.d.1992. 20-Oct-93 Louis Morton, Mexico #72/R (M.P 5500)

OROZCO, Raul (20th C) Mexican
$1119	£756	Jardines de mi rancho (37x68cm-15x27in) s.d.1992 pastel. ?0-Oct-93 Louis Morton, Mexico #83/R (M.P 3500)

ORR, Alfred Everitt (1886-?) American
$708	£472	Portrait d'Amundsen (61x51cm-24x20in) s.d.1918. 27-May-94 Ferri, Paris #218 (F.FR 4000)

ORR, Eric (20th C) American
$750	£507	Blind window (40x28cm-16x11in) s.i.d.87 gold leaf blood lead. 21-Apr-94 Butterfield & Butterfield, San Francisco #1174/R

ORR, George P (20th C) American
$700	£440	Lobstermen's huts (28x38cm-11x15in) s.i. i.d.1944verso. 22-Apr-93 Freeman Fine Arts, Philadelphia #1175/R

ORTIZ, Emilio (1936-) Mexican
$949	£641	Torero (11cm-4in circular) s. pastel. 27-Apr-94 Louis Morton, Mexico #644 (M.P 3200)

ORTIZ-ECHAGUE, Antonio (1883-1942) Mexican
$6000	£4110	Portrait of Celeste DeLongpre Hecksher (152x101cm-60x40in) s.i.verso. 15-Feb-94 Christie's, New York #149/R
$7400	£5000	Pierrot (185x145cm-73x57in) s.d.1928. 16-Jun-93 Sotheby's, London #240/R

ORTLIP, H Willard (1886-?) American
$1200	£805	Palisades (53x71cm-21x28in) s.d.1926. 16-Dec-93 Mystic Fine Arts, Connecticut #130/R

O'SHEA, John (1876-1956) American
$800	£526	Arizona desert (63x76cm-25x30in) 13-Jun-93 Butterfield & Butterfield, San Francisco #930/R
$950	£559	Early spring, Arizona (63x76cm-25x30in) s. 4-Oct-92 Butterfield & Butterfield, Los Angeles #218/R
$1200	£706	Hideaway (63x76cm-25x30in) estate sig. i.verso. 4-Oct-92 Butterfield & Butterfield, Los Angeles #100/R
$1200	£789	Violence (81x102cm-32x40in) board. 13-Jun-93 Butterfield & Butterfield, San Francisco #798/R
$1400	£940	Impressionistic garden scene (36x28cm-14x11in) s. board. 8-Dec-93 Butterfield & Butterfield, San Francisco #3483/R
$1500	£882	Lush foliage (63x76cm-25x30in) s. i.verso. 4-Oct-92 Butterfield & Butterfield, Los Angeles #96/R
$1600	£941	Autumn reflections (63x76cm-25x30in) estate st.verso. 4-Oct-92 Butterfield & Butterfield, Los Angeles #146/R
$1700	£1181	Fruit trees (63x76cm-25x30in) s. 7-Mar-93 Butterfield & Butterfield, San Francisco #208/R
$2000	£1316	Flowering orchard (63x76cm-25x30in) 13-Jun-93 Butterfield & Butterfield, San Francisco #821/R
$2250	£1324	Seascape (77x91cm-30x36in) s. 4-Oct-92 Butterfield & Butterfield, Los Angeles #72/R
$2250	£1324	Cypress trees (76x91cm-30x36in) estate sig. 4-Oct-92 Butterfield & Butterfield, Los Angeles #79/R
$2250	£1562	Barren hills (63x76cm-25x30in) studio st. 7-Mar-93 Butterfield & Butterfield, San Francisco #207/R
$2750	£1618	Shadows (63x76cm-25x30in) s. i.verso. 4-Oct-92 Butterfield & Butterfield, Los Angeles #84/R

O'SHEA, John (1876-1956) American-cont.

$3000	£1765	Flowering hills (63x76cm-25x30in) s. i.verso. 4-Oct-92 Butterfield & Butterfield, Los Angeles #85/R
$3000	£1765	Grand Canyon No.2 (63x76cm-25x30in) s. bears estate st. i.verso. 4-Oct-92 Butterfield & Butterfield, Los Angeles #220/R
$3000	£1974	Banana blossoms (91x77cm-36x30in) s. 13-Jun-93 Butterfield & Butterfield, San Francisco #823/R
$3000	£1765	California hills (63x76cm-25x30in) s. bears estate st.verso. 4-Oct-92 Butterfield & Butterfield, Los Angeles #86/R
$3250	£2257	Golden hills (51x61cm-20x24in) studio st. board. 7-Mar-93 Butterfield & Butterfield, San Francisco #206/R
$6000	£3529	Corsair (76x91cm-30x36in) s. i.verso. 4-Oct-92 Butterfield & Butterfield, Los Angeles #97/R
$750	£517	Portrait, red head, blue eyes (30x38cm-12x15in) s. mixed media. 16-Feb-93 John Moran, Pasadena #70 a
$900	£592	Portrait of man (76x56cm-30x22in) W/C. 13-Jun-93 Butterfield & Butterfield, San Francisco #904/R
$1500	£882	Cypress trunks and forest (56x75cm-22x30in) estate sig. W/C. 4-Oct-92 Butterfield & Butterfield, Los Angeles #101/R
$1500	£987	Seascape (56x76cm-22x30in) W/C gouache. 13-Jun-93 Butterfield & Butterfield, San Francisco #783/R
$1700	£1000	Ocean through trees, Point Lobos (58x74cm-23x29in) estate sig. W/C. 4-Oct-92 Butterfield & Butterfield, Los Angeles #69/R

O'SICKEY, Joseph B (20th C) American

$2800	£1892	Summer afternoon (76x122cm-30x48in) s.d.80 i.verso. 10-Nov-93 Doyle, New York #107

OSORIO LUQUE, Antonio (1913-) Argentinian

$700	£412	Camino al ingenio (50x60cm-20x24in) painted 1966. 29-Sep-92 VerBo, Buenos Aires #84

OSSORIO, Alfonso (1916-1990) American

$3800	£2517	Garden (46x26cm-18x10in) s.d.1950 s.d.verso W/C wax board. 17-Nov-92 Christie's, East, New York #232/R
$4750	£3188	Untitled - abstract composition (89x69cm-35x27in) s.d.84 ink crayon gouache pastel. 4-May-94 Doyle, New York #58/R

OSTHAUS, Edmund H (1858-1928) American

$3500	£2303	Portrait of English setter (54x44cm-21x17in) s. 4-Jun-93 Sotheby's, New York #152/R
$9000	£6040	Three Pointers in landscape (61x91cm-24x36in) s. 14-Jan-94 Du Mouchelle, Detroit #2004/R
$11500	£7566	Setters on point (46x56cm-18x22in) s. 4-Jun-93 Sotheby's, New York #219/R
$12500	£8446	Autumn landscape with three setters (46x99cm-18x39in) s. 4-Nov-93 Boos Gallery, Michigan #1274/R
$25000	£17483	Landscape with setter and pointer (61x91cm-24x36in) s. 10-Mar-93 Sotheby's, New York #45/R
$30000	£19608	Three hunting dogs in wooded landscape (86x142cm-34x56in) s. 17-Sep-93 Du Mouchelle, Detroit #2019/R
$30000	£20979	Two pointers (61x91cm-24x36in) s. i.verso. 10-Mar-93 Sotheby's, New York #46/R
$4500	£3020	On the scent (20x28cm-8x11in) s. W/C. 26-Mar-94 James Bakker, Cambridge #72/R
$5000	£2890	Two English setters on point (53x76cm-21x30in) s. W/C paperboard. 24-Sep-92 Sotheby's, New York #40/R
$6500	£4545	King of the game birds (58x79cm-23x31in) s. W/C. 10-Mar-93 Sotheby's, New York #47/R
$7500	£4967	Setters in a field (38x56cm-15x22in) s. W/C. 15-Jun-94 Butterfield & Butterfield, San Francisco #4415/R
$7500	£5000	On point (38x55cm-15x22in) s. W/C gouache board. 3-Jun-94 Sotheby's, New York #161/R

OSTHAUS, Edmund H (attrib) (1858-1928) American

$600	£403	Hunting scene (43x53cm-17x21in) s.verso. 26-Mar-94 James Bakker, Cambridge #179

OTERO, Alejandro (1921-) Venezuelan

$35000	£23649	Coloritmo 8 (200x49cm-79x19in) s.i.d.56 verso duco panel. 22-Nov-93 Sotheby's, New York #73/R

OTIS, Bass (1784-1861) American

$3800	£2235	Portraits of William and Eliza (91x69cm-36x27in) painted c.1820 pair. 8-Oct-92 Freeman Fine Arts, Philadelphia #956

OTIS, George Demont (1877-1962) American

$1200	£811	Palace of Fine Art (61x51cm-24x20in) s. 9-Nov-93 John Moran, Pasadena #834
$2100	£1214	Valley farm (61x76cm-24x30in) 26-Sep-92 San Rafael Auction Galleries #222
$2500	£1689	Inverness no.8 (41x51cm-16x20in) s. board. 15-Jun-93 John Moran, Pasadena #104
$2500	£1667	Truckee River (25x36cm-10x14in) s. i.d.Nov.1932verso board. 15-Mar-94 John Moran, Pasadena #28
$4000	£2353	Noon light (51x66cm-20x26in) s. 4-Oct-92 Butterfield & Butterfield, Los Angeles #171/R
$5000	£3289	Sanchez Adobe Ranch (69x107cm-27x42in) s. 13-Jun-93 Butterfield & Butterfield, San Francisco #927/R
$5000	£2941	Lagunitas (61x76cm-24x30in) s. 4-Oct-92 Butterfield & Butterfield, Los Angeles #134/R

OTIS, George Demont (1877-1962) American-cont.
$6000	£3529	Arroyo (61x76cm-24x30in) s. 4-Oct-92 Butterfield & Butterfield, Los Angeles #199/R
$7500	£4967	Sunland (76x91cm-30x36in) s. s.i.verso. 15-Jun-94 Butterfield & Butterfield, San Francisco #4683/R
$12000	£7947	Ranch near San Luis Obispo (76x91cm-30x36in) s. 15-Jun-94 Butterfield & Butterfield, San Francisco #4684/R
$14000	£8235	Cabin by sea (76x91cm-30x36in) s. 4-Oct-92 Butterfield & Butterfield, Los Angeles #137/R

OTT, Jerry (20th C) American?
$4970	£3248	Judy, Paradise backdrop (195x243cm-77x96in) s.i.d.1977 acrylic. 18-Sep-93 Jean Louis Picard, Paris #13/R (F.FR 28000)
$10650	£6961	Nu Paradis (235x370cm-93x146in) s.d.1973 acrylic. 18-Sep-93 Jean Louis Picard, Paris #11/R (F.FR 60000)

OTT, Philip A (19th C) American
$6000	*£3846*	*General Grant's daughter and son with cousin (76x89cm-30x35in) s. pastel. 10-Dec-92 Sloan, North Bethesda #2613/R*

OTTE, William Louis (1871-1957) American
$9500	£6169	California landscape with eucalyptus (76x102cm-30x40in) s. 15-Jan-93 Du Mouchelle, Detroit #2005/R
$12000	£7059	Coachella Valley (66x91cm-26x36in) s. s.d.1927 verso board. 4-Oct-92 Butterfield & Butterfield, Los Angeles #170/R
$700	£470	Red pine by sea (44x34cm-17x13in) s.d.1915 pastel paper board. 6-May-94 Skinner, Bolton #99/R

OTTO, Daniel (attrib) (1770-1821) American
$7000	*£4667*	*Practice drawing depicting four crowns (16x20cm-6x8in) W/C ink. 10-Jun-94 Christie's, New York #765/R*

OUBRE, Hayward (?) American?
$800	£537	Vibrating jazz (86x66cm-34x26in) s.d.48. 28-Mar-93 James Bakker, Cambridge #100/R

OVIEDO, Ramon (1927-) Dominican
$6500	£4305	Areito (102x127cm-40x50in) s. s.i.verso. 24-Nov-92 Christie's, New York #160/R

OWEN, Robert Emmett (1878-1957) American
$550	£377	New England landscape (41x51cm-16x20in) s. i.verso. 10-Feb-94 Skinner, Bolton #290
$600	£403	Autumn landscape (51x61cm-20x24in) s. 23-Jun-93 Doyle, New York #71
$1200	£811	House in snow (41x51cm-16x20in) s. 27-Nov-93 Young Fine Arts Auctions, Maine #247/R
$1200	£694	Haystacks in winter (36x46cm-14x18in) s. canvasboard. 27-Sep-92 James Bakker, Cambridge #40/R
$1400	£819	House in early spring (41x51cm-16x20in) s. 20-Sep-92 Litchfield Auction Gallery #87
$1500	£1000	Fly fishing (112x127cm-44x50in) s. 17-May-94 Grogan, Massachussetts #369/R
$1600	£1074	Sugar maples (112x86cm-44x34in) 27-Mar-94 Myers, Florida #11/R
$1950	£1354	Landscape (76x91cm-30x36in) s. 6-Mar-93 Louisiana Auction Exchange #24/R
$2000	£1333	Connecticut farmhouse in winter (66x86cm-26x34in) s. i.d.1951 stretcher. 23-May-94 Christie's, East, New York #152/R
$2200	£1410	Snowy village (51x61cm-20x24in) s. 24-May-93 Grogan, Massachussetts #349/R
$3500	£2288	Long shadows of winter (76x102cm-30x40in) s. 5-May-93 Doyle, New York #46/R

OWENS, Edward (20th C) American
$850	£563	High fog over San Francisco (36x46cm-14x18in) s.d.1926. 14-Jun-94 John Moran, Pasadena #30 a

PACENZA, Onofrio (1904-1971) Argentinian
$3000	£1987	Paisaje de Uquia (39x56cm-15x22in) painted 1948. 11-Nov-92 VerBo, Buenos Aires #74/R

PACH, Walter (1883-1958) American
$800	*£462*	*Aquarium (25x36cm-10x14in) s.d.1914 W/C. 24-Sep-92 Sotheby's, New York #185/R*

PACHECO, Ana Maria (1943-) Brazilian
$1950	£1300	You get too anxious.. (182x122cm-72x48in) s.d.82 panel. 25-May-94 Christie's, London #114/R

PACHECO, Fernando Castro (20th C) South American
$9491	£6413	Mujeres conversando (80x112cm-31x44in) s.d.1964. 27-Apr-94 Louis Morton, Mexico #578 (M.P 32000)

PACHECO, Maria Luisa (1919-) Bolivian
$2600	*£1733*	*Cela Je (101x122cm-40x48in) s.d.73 i.verso oil collage canvas. 18-May-94 Christie's, New York #262/R*

PADURA, Miguel (1957-) Cuban
$7500	£4902	Still life with tablecloth (64x61cm-25x24in) s. i.stretcher. 17-May-93 Christie's, New York #158/R
$9500	£6291	Acorn squash (58x81cm-23x32in) s. 24-Nov-92 Christie's, New York #226/R

PAEZ, Jose de (1720-?) Mexican
$3250	£2152	Santa Rosa de Lima (81x63cm-32x25in) s. 23-Nov-92 Sotheby's, New York #118/R
$7387	£4991	San Joaquin y la Virgen Nina (85x63cm-33x25in) s. 27-Oct-93 Fernando Duran, Madrid #191/R (S.P 1000000)
$9603	£6489	Virgen de Guadalupe con apariciones (72x56cm-28x22in) s.d.1756. 27-Oct-93 Fernando Duran, Madrid #192/R (S.P 1300000)
$19000	£12418	Escudo de Monja - Virgen de Guadalupe (21cm-8in circular) indist.s. copper painted c.1776. 18-May-93 Sotheby's, New York #7/R
$21000	£14189	Virgen y el nino con Santos Jesuitas (43x34cm-17x13in) s.d.1756 copper. 22-Nov-93 Sotheby's, New York #2/R
$32000	£21333	Coronacion de la Virgen (97x79cm-38x31in) s.i.d. canvas laid down on board. 18-May-94 Christie's, New York #6/R
$32309	£21684	Francisco Antonio de Larrea y Vitorica y sus dos hijos Miguel y Pedro (206x134cm-81x53in) s.i.d.6 Agosto 1774. 24-Feb-94 Sotheby's, Madrid #26/R (S.P 4500000)

PAEZ, Jose de (attrib) (1720-?) Mexican
$250000	£163399	Castas Mexicanas (35x32cm-14x13in) fifteen painted c.1785. 18-May-93 Sotheby's, New York #3/R

PAGANONI, Gabriela (20th C) Mexican
$1023	£691	Calabaza I (100x80cm-39x31in) s.d.1992. 20-Oct-93 Louis Morton, Mexico #89/R (M.P 3200)

PAGE, Edward A (1850-1928) American
$800	£533	Fog bound (28x33cm-11x13in) s.d.1916. 22-May-94 James Bakker, Cambridge #8/R
$950	£638	Seaside cottages (23x33cm-9x13in) s. 5-Dec-93 James Bakker, Cambridge #79/R
$1000	£671	The shoreline (20x25cm-8x10in) s. canvas on panel. 5-Dec-93 James Bakker, Cambridge #1/R
$1050	£528	Gloucester, Massachusetts scene (43x53cm-17x21in) s. 6-Sep-92 Litchfield Auction Gallery #116
$1100	£728	Fishing boat on shore (36x51cm-14x20in) s. 20-Nov-92 Eldred, Massachusetts #502/R
$1200	£800	The old fence by the sea (51x76cm-20x30in) s. 22-May-94 James Bakker, Cambridge #43/R
$1800	£1176	On the beach (25x36cm-10x14in) s. panel. 18-Sep-93 James Bakker, Cambridge #36/R

PAGE, Walter Gilman (1862-1934) American
$1600	£1074	Mount Monadnock (18x44cm-7x17in) i.verso panel. 4-Mar-94 Skinner, Bolton #237/R

PAGE, William (1811-1885) American
$2664	£1800	Arch in town (20x28cm-8x11in) W/C over pencil. 20-Oct-93 Sotheby's, London #168/R
$3002	£1900	Seated Greek smoking at the coast (24x32cm-9x13in) indist.i. W/C over pencil. 21-Oct-92 Sotheby's, London #24/R

PAGE, William (circle) (1811-1885) American
$1259	£850	Acropolis, Athens (20x35cm-8x14in) W/C over pencil gum arabic. 20-Oct-93 Sotheby's, London #167/R

PAGES, Jules (?) American
$677	£457	Paris le Pont Marie (28x36cm-11x14in) s. panel. 14-Nov-93 Eric Pillon, Calais #95/R (F.FR 4000)
$1900	£1258	Italian landscape (46x61cm-18x24in) s. 15-Jun-94 Butterfield & Butterfield, San Francisco #4605/R
$2231	£1430	Jardin des Tuileries (65x100cm-26x39in) s. 30-Apr-93 Drouot Estimations, Paris #98 (F.FR 12000)
$2250	£1490	Reclining nude (30x51cm-12x20in) s.d.05. 15-Jun-94 Butterfield & Butterfield, San Francisco #4607/R
$7000	£4698	Chinatown, San Francisco (46x34cm-18x13in) s. 8-Dec-93 Butterfield & Butterfield, San Francisco #3374/R

PAGES, Jules Eugene (1867-1946) American
$1900	£1319	End of day in Chinatown (25x18cm-10x7in) s. canvasboard. 7-Mar-93 Butterfield & Butterfield, San Francisco #185/R
$4500	£3000	Paris views, probably the Tuileries Gardens and Luxembourg Gardens (18x30cm-7x12in) s. board pair. 15-Mar-94 John Moran, Pasadena #63

PAHSETOPAH, Loren Louis (1934-) American
$476	£317	Winter storm (33x43cm-13x17in) s.d.75 gouache board. 29-Jan-94 Skinner, Bolton #59

PAIK, Nam June (1932-) American/Korean
$2086	£1400	Transistor necklace (14x11cm-6x4in) s.d.67 verso mixed media. 24-Jun-93 Sotheby's, London #86/R
$2980	£2000	Transistor necklace (14x11cm-6x4in) s. i.d.66 verso mixed media. 24-Jun-93 Sotheby's, London #85/R

PAILOS, Manuel (1918-) Uruguayan
$900	£588	Constructivo pez (25x25cm-10x10in) s. acrylic panel. 27-Jun-94 Gomensoro, Montevideo #29/R
$1000	£658	Paisaje con sierra (22x31cm-9x12in) s. 31-May-93 Gomensoro, Montevideo #13

PAILOS, Manuel (1918-) Uruguayan-cont.

$1050	£686	Rio, barcas y ciudad (34x50cm-13x20in) s. board. 3-May-93 Gomensoro, Montevideo #35
$1050	£686	Aserradero (37x46cm-15x18in) s. board. 3-May-93 Gomensoro, Montevideo #34
$1100	£705	Bar, pescado y ancla (35x40cm-14x16in) s. board. 7-Dec-92 Gomensoro, Montevideo #63/R
$1800	£1208	Constructivo (51x41cm-20x16in) s.d.63 fibre. 29-Nov-93 Gomensoro, Montevideo #73/R
$2000	£1342	Mujer y equino (30x52cm-12x20in) s.d.24.5.60verso board. 29-Nov-93 Gomensoro, Montevideo #77/R
$3000	£2013	Constructivo, febrero (33x41cm-13x16in) s.d.1955 board. 29-Nov-93 Gomensoro, Montevideo #74/R
$3900	£2549	Locomotora (67x78cm-26x31in) s. fibre. 4-Oct-93 Gomensoro, Montevideo #60/R
$4000	£2685	Constructivo (56x41cm-22x16in) s. 29-Nov-93 Gomensoro, Montevideo #72
$5400	£3624	Rostro constructive (51x39cm-20x15in) s.d.Mayo 1959verso panel. 29-Nov-93 Gomensoro, Montevideo #75/R
$800	*£526*	*Constructivo maritimo (25x25cm-10x10in) s. encaustic panel. 31-May-93 Gomensoro, Montevideo #15*
$820	*£526*	*Aventuras - Pez y D (26x30cm-10x12in) s. encaustic fibre. 7-Dec-92 Gomensoro, Montevideo #62*
$980	*£519*	*Composicion (25x25cm-10x10in) s. mixed media. 10-Sep-92 Gomensoro, Montevideo #28/R*
$1000	*£658*	*Banistas (23x23cm-9x9in) s. mixed media fibre. 31-May-93 Gomensoro, Montevideo #14*
$1000	*£588*	*Barco madre (33x28cm-13x11in) s.d.67 W/C ink. 5-Oct-92 Gomensoro, Montevideo #1*
$1100	*£714*	*Constructivo (25x25cm-10x10in) s. 30-Aug-93 Gomensoro, Montevideo #39*
$1500	*£980*	*Composicion con figuras (24x24cm-9x9in) s.d.91 encaustic. 3-May-93 Gomensoro, Montevideo #79*
$2400	*£1250*	*Constructivo (56x46cm-22x18in) s. encaustic. 12-Aug-92 Castells & Castells, Montevideo #28*
$6800	*£4564*	*Constructivo marino (74x84cm-29x33in) s. ink encaustic fibre. 29-Nov-93 Gomensoro, Montevideo #71/R*

PALACIOS, Alirio (1944-) Venezuelan

$11000	£7432	El espiritu magico II (80x109cm-31x43in) s.d.91 casein board. 23-Nov-93 Christie's, New York #218/R
$19000	£12583	Aparicion Magica 1 (182x76cm-72x30in) s.d.1989 s.i.d.verso mixed media paper on panel. 24-Nov-92 Christie's, New York #105/R

PALMA, Brett de (1949-) American

$1200	£784	Cyclops head with still life (193x198cm-76x78in) acrylic collage. 22-Dec-92 Christie's, East, New York #10

PALMER, Adelaide (19/20th C) American

$3600	£2338	White spring blossoms (30x46cm-12x18in) s.d.IX9X. 9-Sep-93 Sotheby's Arcade, New York #73/R

PALMER, Franklin (1912-1990) Canadian

$627	£402	Pool and rocks (61x71cm-24x28in) s. i.verso. 26-Apr-93 Levis, Calgary #134/R (C.D 800)

PALMER, Herbert Sidney (1881-1970) Canadian

$620	£419	October afternoon Mountain Lake Haliburton (20x27cm-8x11in) s. s.i.verso panel. 3-Nov-93 Sotheby's, Toronto #241/R (C.D 800)
$666	£427	Sunshine and shadow (25x32cm-10x13in) s. s.i.verso painted c.1935 paperboard. 26-Apr-93 Levis, Calgary #135/R (C.D 850)
$699	£466	Barn beside the road (21x26cm-8x10in) s. panel. 13-May-94 Joyner Fine Art, Toronto #198 (C.D 960)
$713	£466	Humber Valley (15x22cm-6x9in) s. s.d.1912 verso panel. 19-May-93 Sotheby's, Toronto #381/R (C.D 900)
$793	£518	Sketch for October morning (15x21cm-6x8in) s. board. 19-May-93 Sotheby's, Toronto #170/R (C.D 1000)
$856	£567	Morning on Gatineau (30x40cm-12x16in) s. canvas on board. 24-Nov-92 Joyner Fine Art, Toronto #50 (C.D 1100)
$865	£547	Tranquility (31x42cm-12x17in) s. masonite. 30-Nov-92 Ritchie, Toronto #209/R (C.D 1100)
$951	£622	Rolling country, farmer ploughing (27x34cm-11x13in) s. canvas laid down on board. 18-May-93 Joyner Fine Art, Toronto #232 (C.D 1200)
$1092	£728	Half-Way Lake, Ont. (26x33cm-10x13in) s. convas on board. 13-May-94 Joyner Fine Art, Toronto #121 (C.D 1500)
$1168	£773	October over Carson lake, Ontario (21x26cm-8x10in) s. canvas on board. 24-Nov-92 Joyner Fine Art, Toronto #146/R (C.D 1500)
$1189	£777	Sunshine and shadow (44x36cm-17x14in) s. board. 19-May-93 Sotheby's, Toronto #334/R (C.D 1500)
$1238	£825	Houses overlooking a lake (20x25cm-8x10in) s. panel double sided. 13-May-94 Joyner Fine Art, Toronto #18/R (C.D 1700)
$1240	£838	Quebec farm near Wakefield (26x34cm-10x13in) s. s.i.verso board. 3-Nov-93 Sotheby's, Toronto #54/R (C.D 1600)
$1258	£796	Three bathers on beach (58x91cm-23x36in) s. 30-Nov-92 Ritchie, Toronto #208 a/R (C.D 1600)
$2220	£1451	Above the Falls, Eugenia, Ontario (25x32cm-10x13in) s. canvas laid down on board painted 1912. 18-May-93 Joyner Fine Art, Toronto #200/R (C.D 2800)
$2576	£1684	Road to Haliburton (55x67cm-22x26in) s. 19-May-93 Sotheby's, Toronto #279/R (C.D 3250)

PALMER, Herbert Sidney (1881-1970) Canadian-cont.
$3308	£2191	Haliburton Road, Near Ingoldsby (51x61cm-20x24in) s. i.verso. 18-Nov-92 Sotheby's, Toronto #65/R (C.D 4250)

PALMER, Pauline (1867-1938) American
$1000	£654	Portrait of young boy with violin (99x99cm-39x39in) s. canvas on board. 19-Sep-93 Hindman Galleries, Chicago #674
$1200	£769	The garden gate (48x38cm-19x15in) board. 13-Dec-92 Hindman Galleries, Chicago #7/R
$1600	£1046	Autumn landscape with house (41x51cm-16x20in) 16-May-93 Hindman Galleries, Chicago #62/R
$9250	£6293	Summer garden, Provincetown (58x48cm-23x19in) s. 17-Apr-94 Hanzel Galleries, Chicago #21

PALMER, Walter L (1854-1932) American
$3250	£2196	Sailboats in Venice (41x30cm-16x12in) s.d.1894. 31-Mar-94 Sotheby's Arcade, New York #129/R
$6500	£4305	Gleaming sunset (71x53cm-28x21in) s. i.stretcher. 23-Sep-93 Sotheby's, New York #193/R
$6500	£4362	A brook in winter (91x66cm-36x26in) sold with letter. 4-Dec-93 Louisiana Auction Exchange #103/R
$7000	£4575	Venetian boats (53x71cm-21x28in) s. 4-May-93 Christie's, East, New York #144/R
$7250	£4802	After the storm (51x61cm-20x24in) s. board. 23-Sep-93 Sotheby's, New York #192/R
$12000	£7895	Winter thaw (64x76cm-25x30in) s. 4-Nov-92 Doyle, New York #34/R
$14000	£9396	Farmyard with blue snow at sunset (61x41cm-24x16in) s. 5-Aug-93 Eldred, Massachusetts #819/R
$30000	£20134	A brook in winter - Kinderbrook Creek (81x61cm-32x24in) s. 3-Dec-93 Christie's, New York #39/R
$1000	£709	Coastal scene (38x25cm-15x10in) s. W/C gouache board. 14-Feb-93 Hanzel Galleries, Chicago #1/R
$2000	£1361	An oncoming storm (51x61cm-20x24in) s.d.1884 pastel en grisaille paper on fabric. 15-Nov-93 Christie's, East, New York #115/R
$2000	£1299	Stream in winter (36x25cm-14x10in) s. gouache. 11-Sep-93 Louisiana Auction Exchange #39/R
$3000	£1765	Lake in early Fall (33x46cm-13x18in) mono.d.1884 pastel. 8-Oct-92 Freeman Fine Arts, Philadelphia #974/R
$3100	£2067	Winter stream (51x61cm-20x24in) s. pastel. 21-May-94 Weschler, Washington #98/R
$4000	£2632	September (58x44cm-23x17in) s. gouache W/C pencil. 31-Mar-93 Sotheby's Arcade, New York #143/R

PANABAKER, Frank S (1904-1992) Canadian
$753	£492	October sun, Collingwood, Ontario (35x39cm-14x15in) s. canvas laid down on board. 18-May-93 Joyner Fine Art, Toronto #214 (C.D 950)
$942	£628	Northern lake scene (41x51cm-16x20in) s. board. 6-Jun-94 Waddingtons, Toronto #1268 (C.D 1300)
$1054	£707	Autumn colour (51x61cm-20x24in) s. 29-Nov-93 Waddingtons, Toronto #1099 (C.D 1400)
$1100	£697	Autumn valley (61x51cm-24x20in) s.d.1931 s.stretcher. 30-Nov-92 Ritchie, Toronto #214/R (C.D 1400)
$1585	£1036	Stream in winter, Dundas, Ontario (51x61cm-20x24in) s. board. 19-May-93 Sotheby's, Toronto #84/R (C.D 2000)
$1602	£1068	Georgian Bay (50x65cm-20x26in) s. board. 13-May-94 Joyner Fine Art, Toronto #168 (C.D 2200)
$1751	£1160	Red heads (61x76cm-24x30in) s. i.verso. 18-Nov-92 Sotheby's, Toronto #233/R (C.D 2250)
$2319	£1546	Hauling hay (51x61cm-20x24in) s. i.verso. 6-Jun-94 Waddingtons, Toronto #1295/R (C.D 3200)
$3043	£2029	Hauling logs (76x102cm-30x40in) s. 6-Jun-94 Waddingtons, Toronto #1290/R (C.D 4200)

PANCOAST, Morris Hall (1877-?) American
$900	£604	Rockport Beach, winter (76x91cm-30x36in) s. 5-Dec-93 James Bakker, Cambridge #90/R
$1250	£817	Shore line, Maine (36x46cm-14x18in) s. board. 18-Sep-93 James Bakker, Cambridge #9/R
$2800	£1867	Wet day (56x66cm-22x26in) s. s.i.stretcher. 23-May-94 Christie's, East, New York #170/R
$7500	£4902	When the wind's northwest, winter sports, Lanesville (64x76cm-25x30in) s. 18-Sep-93 James Bakker, Cambridge #148/R

PANOZZI, Americo (1887-?) Argentinian
$4500	£2601	Atardecer en Bariloche (64x86cm-25x34in) 23-Sep-92 Roldan & Cia, Buenos Aires #59

PANSING, Fred (19th C) American
$17880	£12000	The Cunard liner R.M.S.Umbria passing whta is thought to be the Brooklyn Heights, New Yor (81x152cm-32x60in) i.d.1885. 5-May-94 Christie's, S. Kensington #242/R

PANTON, Lawrence Arthur Colley (1894-1954) Canadian
$642	£434	Clouds over Lake Rosseau (22x28cm-9x11in) board. 23-Nov-93 Joyner Fine Art, Toronto #337 (C.D 850)
$779	£513	Haliburton Hills (51x61cm-20x24in) s. i.verso board. 7-Jun-93 Waddingtons, Toronto #1123/R (C.D 1000)
$1395	£942	Atlantic Fugue (39x46cm-15x18in) tempera. 3-Nov-93 Sotheby's, Toronto #227/R (C.D 1800)

PANTON, Lawrence Arthur Colley (1894-1954) Canadian-cont.
$5097	£3398	Cottage in foliage, Lake Rosseau (86x102cm-34x40in) s.d.40 board. 11-May-94 Sotheby's, Toronto #245/R (C.D 7000)
$6796	£4592	Island Caprice, 1935 (85x100cm-33x39in) s. 23-Nov-93 Joyner Fine Art, Toronto #112/R (C.D 9000)
$588	£377	Farm road (38x48cm-15x19in) s. painted c.1937 W/C board. 26-Apr-93 Levis, Calgary #136/R (C.D 750)
$619	£413	Buildings in the rocks (40x53cm-16x21in) s. mixed media. 13-May-94 Joyner Fine Art, Toronto #127 (C.D 850)
$655	£437	Abstract study (38x51cm-15x20in) mixed media. 13-May-94 Joyner Fine Art, Toronto #144 (C.D 900)
$969	£654	Mystic landscape (53x61cm-21x24in) s. mixed media masonite. 1-Nov-93 Levis, Calgary #239/R (C.D 1250)
$2220	£1451	Dark landscape (41x48cm-16x19in) s.d.48 W/C. 18-May-93 Joyner Fine Art, Toronto #199/R (C.D 2800)

PAPE, Eric (1870-1938) American
$600	£411	The vegetable patch (41x51cm-16x20in) canvasboard. 10-Feb-94 Skinner, Bolton #186
$1000	£699	Still life with peppers, onions and white pitcher (43x58cm-17x23in) s.d.1901. 12-Mar-93 Skinner, Bolton #267 a/R
$1500	£993	Sunset over water (13x20cm-5x8in) estate st.verso panel. 13-Nov-92 Skinner, Bolton #163/R
$1500	£1027	Valley of the Nile (28x36cm-11x14in) i.verso panel. 10-Feb-94 Skinner, Bolton #178 a/R
$1600	£1096	Portrait of Ellen Terry in costume (259x163cm-102x64in) s.d.1912. 10-Feb-94 Skinner, Bolton #180/R
$2200	£1438	Sunset at sea (13x20cm-5x8in) estate st.verso panel. 14-May-93 Skinner, Bolton #137/R
$2300	£1554	Camel resting with Pyramids at Giza beyond (31x54cm-12x21in) 5-Nov-93 Skinner, Bolton #73/R
$3000	£2055	The garden by the cottage (33x23cm-13x9in) s.i. init.d.1896 verso panel. 10-Feb-94 Skinner, Bolton #175/R
$3000	£2055	The Shield Maiden-Lysistrata (76x64cm-30x25in) s. 10-Feb-94 Skinner, Bolton #179/R
$3400	£2282	The cabbage patch (56x69cm-22x27in) 4-Mar-94 Skinner, Bolton #253/R
$14000	£8092	Artist's home, Wheeler Point, Gloucester, Massachusetts (91x146cm-36x57in) i.verso painted c.1905. 24-Sep-92 Sotheby's, New York #108/R
$14000	£9150	In the orchard - portrait of Natalie Hayes Hammond (89x64cm-35x25in) 17-Sep-93 Skinner, Bolton #260/R
$500	£342	Sea vultures (79x56cm-31x22in) s.d.1925 i.verso chl chk paperboard. 10-Feb-94 Skinner, Bolton #182
$900	£596	Mexican cowboy (84x48cm-33x19in) estate st.verso chl chk. 13-Nov-92 Skinner, Bolton #145/R
$2500	£1323	The Mexican Dancer (97x66cm-38x26in) s.i.d.1914 pastel paperboard. 11-Sep-92 Skinner, Bolton #168 a/R
$3000	£1961	'Love's young dream'-Thomas Moore (94x66cm-37x26in) s.d.1918 i.verso pastel paperboard. 17-Sep-93 Skinner, Bolton #259/R
$3000	£2013	Allegory of America Victorious (81x67cm-32x26in) s. i.verso gouache graphite paperboard. 6-May-94 Skinner, Bolton #164/R
$8000	£5369	Illustrations with cats (49x35cm-19x14in) s.d. W/C gouache pastel eleven. 6-May-94 Skinner, Bolton #163/R

PAQUIN, Pauline (1952-) Canadian
$834	£564	Le petit cochon rose (36x46cm-14x18in) s. s.i.d.1993verso. 25-Apr-94 Levis, Calgary #248/R (C.D 1150)
$973	£644	Que de belles vacances (36x46cm-14x18in) s. s.i.d.1989 board. 16-Nov-92 Hodgins, Calgary #43/R (C.D 1250)
$981	£641	Pres pour la tempete (51x61cm-20x24in) s.d.1986 verso board. 10-May-93 Hodgins, Calgary #52/R (C.D 1250)
$1148	£766	Jonathan Promense sa petite soeur (41x51cm-16x20in) s. s.i.d.verso. 30-May-94 Hodgins, Calgary #247/R (C.D 1600)
$1255	£821	C'est un depart (51x61cm-20x24in) s. d.1986 verso board. 10-May-93 Hodgins, Calgary #245/R (C.D 1600)

PARADISE, John (1783-1834) American
$1200	£759	Portrait of Philip Arcularius (76x61cm-30x24in) 3-Dec-92 Freeman Fine Arts, Philadelphia #1816

PARADISE, Philip Herschel (1905-) American
$1100	£719	California Coast (53x69cm-21x27in) s. s.i.verso. 16-May-93 Hindman Galleries, Chicago #8/R
$1500	£1014	Casita Vieja (46x69cm-18x27in) s. W/C. 15-Jun-93 John Moran, Pasadena #149

PARC, Julio le (1928-) Argentinian
$1655	£1089	Modulation 731 (80x80cm-31x31in) s.i.d.1985verso acrylic. 7-Jun-93 Wolfgang Ketterer, Munich #803 a/R (DM 2700)
$2268	£1492	Modulation 803 (74x55cm-29x22in) s.i.d.1986verso acrylic. 7-Jun-93 Wolfgang Ketterer, Munich #803 b/R (DM 3700)

PARCELL, Malcolm S (1896-?) American
$1300	£878	Still life with fruit jug and wine glass in the artist's studio (62x51cm-24x20in) s. 5-Nov-93 Skinner, Bolton #60/R

PAREDES, Mariano (1912-1979) Mexican
$4128   £2771   Chapultepec (46x61cm-18x24in) s. pastel. 1-Dec-93 Louis Morton, Mexico #147/R (M.P 12800)

PARIS, Walter (1842-1906) American/British
$900   £588   Figures along the avenue (36x48cm-14x19in) s.d.1901 W/C. 30-Oct-92 Sloan, North Bethesda #2201/R
$3250   £2083   East Gloucester (33x51cm-13x20in) s.d.1885 i.verso W/C. 28-May-93 Sloan, North Bethesda #2685/R

PARK, David (1911-1960) American
$97500   £57353   Tea (102x91cm-40x36in) s.d.56. 6-Oct-92 Sotheby's, New York #19/R
$950   £664   Female nude (18x8cm-7x3in) s. gouache. 11-Mar-93 Mystic Fine Arts, Connecticut #131
$2200   £1528   Untitled (43x36cm-17x14in) executed 1955-59 pencil. 23-Feb-93 Sotheby's, New York #261/R
$2250   £1562   Untitled (43x36cm-17x14in) executed c.1955-59 pencil. 23-Feb-93 Sotheby's, New York #250/R
$2800   £1854   Untitled (22x30cm-9x12in) i.d.verso graphite. 17-Nov-92 Christie's, East, New York #280/R
$4500   £3041   Two figures (30x22cm-12x9in) pencil. 21-Apr-94 Butterfield & Butterfield, San Francisco #1126/R

PARKER, Bill (1922-) American
$1011   £661   Composition no.65 (60x73cm-24x29in) init.d.1958. 21-Dec-92 Jean Louis Picard, Paris #170 (F.FR 5500)

PARKER, Lawton S (1868-1954) American
$1500   £962   Field with trees (41x51cm-16x20in) s. canvasboard. 9-Dec-92 Butterfield & Butterfield, San Francisco #3885/R
$2500   £1678   Summer landscape (38x46cm-15x18in) 8-Dec-93 Butterfield & Butterfield, San Francisco #3415/R
$5500   £3691   Study for 'Preparing for the bath'. Nude figure (15x20cm-6x8in) board double-sided with pencil drawing. 8-Dec-93 Butterfield & Butterfield, San Francisco #3416/R
$8000   £5594   Lady seated in landscape (48x33cm-19x13in) i.verso canvas on board. 14-Mar-93 Hindman Galleries, Chicago #26/R
$700   £473   Reclining nude (18x25cm-7x10in) s. pencil chl. 9-Nov-93 John Moran, Pasadena #837

PARKER, Ray (1922-1990) American
$1500   £993   Untitled (117x124cm-46x49in) acrylic. 29-Sep-93 Sotheby's Arcade, New York #317/R

PARKHURST, Thomas (1853-1923) American
$750   £497   Monterey Sea (66x76cm-26x30in) s. 15-Jun-94 Butterfield & Butterfield, San Francisco #4647/R

PARODI MONTANO, Roberto (20th C) Mexican
$1279   £864   Mujer con nino (70x80cm-28x31in) 20-Oct-93 Louis Morton, Mexico #146/R (M.P 4000)

PARR, James Wingate (20th C) American
$1100   £728   Boston street scene in winter (53x74cm-21x29in) s. W/C. 20-Nov-92 Eldred, Massachusetts #893/R

PARRA, Enrique (?) South American
$900   £452   Naturaleza Muerta y Mariposa (80x55cm-31x22in) s. 31-Aug-92 Gomensoro, Montevideo #11

PARREIRAS, Antonio (1860-1937) Brazilian
$3750   £2500   Coastal landscape (62x88cm-24x35in) s.i.d.1936. 18-May-94 Butterfield & Butterfield, San Francisco #2897/R

PARRINO, Steven (1958-) American
$729   £480   Study for diabolo primo (23x30cm-9x12in) i. s.verso acrylic paper painted 1992. 10-Jun-93 Cornette de St.Cyr, Paris #156 (F.FR 4000)
$1266   £844   Idol/Idiot (183x244cm-72x96in) s.d.1986verso acrylic diptych. 2-Jun-94 AB Stockholms Auktionsverk, Stockholm #7096/R (S.KR 10000)
$1899   £1266   Push in and bite (182x122cm-72x48in) s.d.1987verso. 2-Jun-94 AB Stockholms Auktionsverk, Stockholm #7095/R (S.KR 15000)
$658   £439   Untitled - aids benefit (54x53cm-21x21in) s.d.1987verso acrylic mixed media canvas. 2-Jun-94 AB Stockholms Auktionsverk, Stockholm #7231/R (S.KR 5200)

PARRISH, Maxfield (1870-1966) American
$3200   £1871   Jack Sprat (33x25cm-13x10in) s.d.1919. 18-Sep-92 Du Mouchelle, Detroit #2016/R
$10000   £6667   Mask and pierrot (56x41cm-22x16in) init. s.d.1908 verso paper on panel. 23-May-94 Christie's, East, New York #214/R
$19000   £12667   A house among trees (28x23cm-11x9in) i. board. 17-Mar-94 Sotheby's, New York #93/R
$21000   £12139   Illustrations from Phoebus on Halzaphron - men on sands demanding to see king, one s. one init.d.1901 num 286 paperboard pair. 24-Sep-92 Sotheby's, New York #93/R
$24000   £16000   Dawn (46x35cm-18x14in) init. panel. 16-Mar-94 Christie's, New York #122/R
$38000   £24359   Botanical gardens at Padua (43x29cm-17x11in) init. paper on stretcher. 26-May-93 Christie's, New York #66/R
$50000   £34965   Deep valley (39x34cm-15x13in) s.d.1946 s.i.d.verso masonite. 11-Mar-93 Christie's, New York #245/R

PARRISH, Maxfield (1870-1966) American-cont.
$81000   £51266   The old Glen Mill (58x47cm-23x19in) s.d.1950 s.i.d.verso masonite. 4-Dec-92
                       Christie's, New York #162/R
$170000   £107595   Cinderella (76x61cm-30x24in) s.d.1913 s.i.d.verso panel. 4-Dec-92 Christie's, New
                       York #163/R

PARRISH, Stephen (1846-1938) American
$880   £575   Tide-water landscape (51x71cm-20x28in) s. masonite. 14-May-93 Skinner, Bolton
                       #69/R

PARROT, William Samuel (1844-1915) American
$800   £552   Oregon River, Blue Mountain (20x15cm-8x6in) s.verso board. 16-Feb-93 John Moran,
                       Pasadena #47
$5500   £3691   Mount Shasta, California (91x122cm-36x48in) 8-Dec-93 Butterfield & Butterfield,
                       San Francisco #3319/R

PARSHALL, Dewitt (1864-1956) American
$1000   £662   Grand Canyon Moonlight (41x51cm-16x20in) s. panel. 15-Jun-94 Butterfield &
                       Butterfield, San Francisco #4730/R
$2000   £1325   Grand Canyon (91x102cm-36x40in) s. 23-Sep-93 Sotheby's, New York #92/R

PARSHALL, Douglas (1899-?) American
$800   £533   Race track (38x58cm-15x23in) s. masonite. 15-Mar-94 John Moran, Pasadena #106
$950   £633   Landscape (51x61cm-20x24in) s. board. 23-May-94 Hindman Galleries, Chicago #252
$950   £629   Horse round up (41x60cm-16x24in) s. board. 15-Jun-94 Butterfield & Butterfield,
                       San Francisco #4738/R
$2750   £1821   Ouled nail dancers (91x102cm-36x40in) s. 28-Sep-93 John Moran, Pasadena #244
$1700   £1126   *Horses grazing (36x53cm-14x21in) s. W/C. 14-Jun-94 John Moran, Pasadena #37*

PARSONS, Marion Randall (1878-1953) American
$1500   £1042   Old ranch house (41x51cm-16x20in) mono board. 7-Mar-93 Butterfield & Butterfield,
                       San Francisco #228/R
$2000   £1176   House with cactus (41x51cm-16x20in) init. board. 4-Oct-92 Butterfield &
                       Butterfield, Los Angeles #266/R

PARSONS, O Sheldon (1866-1943) American
$858   £580   Taos, New Mexico (23x30cm-9x12in) s. board. 15-Jun-93 Phillips, London #108/R
$3600   £2353   Adobe houses, outside Sante Fe, New Mexico (41x51cm-16x20in) s. board. 4-May-93
                       Christie's, East, New York #122/R

PARSONS, Philip Brown (20th C) American
$675   £479   Aspiring to hunt (51x66cm-20x26in) s. 13-Feb-93 Collins, Maine #26/R

PARTINGTON, Richard Langtry (1868-1929) American
$3000   £2083   Glimpse of Monterey Bay (61x91cm-24x36in) s.d.1914. 7-Mar-93 Butterfield &
                       Butterfield, San Francisco #73/R
$4000   £2778   Sunset at Point Lobos with distant schooner (76x112cm-30x44in) s. 7-Mar-93
                       Butterfield & Butterfield, San Francisco #72/R

PARTON, Arthur (1842-1914) American
$850   £545   Clearing in landscape, early evening (46x61cm-18x24in) s. 28-May-93 Sloan, North
                       Bethesda #2411/R
$1000   £667   Sheep grazing (43x64cm-17x25in) s. 17-May-94 Grogan, Massachussetts #334/R
$1100   £743   Skiff on wooded marsh lake (41x56cm-16x22in) s. 9-Nov-93 John Moran, Pasadena
                       #957
$1300   £867   Cattle grazing by stream (36x46cm-14x18in) s.d.1885. 26-Aug-93 Skinner, Bolton
                       #212
$1400   £927   Out on pond (36x46cm-14x18in) s.i. 13-Nov-92 Skinner, Bolton #66/R
$1600   £1067   A mountain stream (28x30cm-11x12in) s.d.1881. 26-May-94 Sloan, North Bethesda
                       #2114/R
$2400   £1633   Cows resting by a stream (41x62cm-16x24in) s. 15-Nov-93 Christie's, East, New
                       York #47
$2400   £1569   Haymaking on the Sound (51x76cm-20x30in) s.indis.d. 15-Sep-93 Doyle, New York #50
$2800   £1879   Lake view with cattle at the water's edge (31x51cm-12x20in) s.d.74. 4-Mar-94
                       Skinner, Bolton #210/R

PASCHKE, Ed (1939-) American
$8000   £5229   Red float (67x61cm-26x24in) s.d.71 verso. 4-May-93 Sotheby's, New York #412/R
$9000   £6040   Coquette (61x96cm-24x38in) s.d.89 s.i.d.89 verso linen. 23-Feb-94 Christie's, New
                       York #59/R
$13000   £8725   Brand-Ex (81x183cm-32x72in) s.d.80. 4-May-94 Christie's, New York #325/R
$15000   £9934   Essemia (127x244cm-50x96in) s.d.84 s.i.d.stretcher. 19-Nov-92 Christie's, New
                       York #428/R
$16000   £10811   Icon-Ero (208x208cm-82x82in) s.d.80 s.i.d.stretcher. 10-Nov-93 Christie's, New
                       York #244/R
$17000   £11486   Le Lique (137x203cm-54x80in) s.d.83. 8-Nov-93 Christie's, East, New York #39/R
$18000   £12081   Virideon (137x203cm-54x80in) s.d.84. 5-May-94 Sotheby's, New York #205/R
$20000   £13514   Yin et Yang (203x198cm-80x78in) s.i.d.88 linen. 10-Nov-93 Christie's, New York
                       #219/R

PASCIN (1885-1930) American/Bulgarian
$541   £373   *Sur la plage (19x26cm-7x10in) crayon W/C. 31-Jan-93 Millon & Robert, Paris #227
                       (F.FR 3000)*
$554   £362   *Femmes devant une statue (21x14cm-8x6in) studio st. pencil htd.W/C. 6-May-93
                       Laurin Guilloux Buffetaud Tailleur, Paris #139 (F.FR 3000)*

PASCIN (1885-1930) American/Bulgarian-cont.

$559	£386	La conversation (13x9cm-5x4in) crayon W/C. 31-Jan-93 Millon & Robert, Paris #228 (F.FR 3100)
$589	£385	La fille a la poitrine nue (14x12cm-6x5in) s.studio st. wash. 18-Apr-93 French Auctioneer #51 (F.FR 3200)
$775	£507	Femmes et enfants sur la plage (15x9cm-6x4in) s. ink htd.W/C. 6-May-93 Laurin Guilloux Buffetaud Tailleur, Paris #140 (F.FR 4200)
$3463	£2278	Judith et holopherne (48x63cm-19x25in) st.sig. Indian ink htd. dr. 11-Jun-93 Poulain & le Fur, Paris #75/R (F.FR 19000)
$16078	£10718	La presentation (17x23cm-7x9in) bears st.sig.i. ink dr executed c.1905. 20-May-94 Claude Boisgirard, Paris #139/R (F.FR 91000)

PASCIN, Jules (1885-1930) American/Bulgarian

$5307	£3586	Mme Charlotte, seated female nude (56x45cm-22x18in) s.i. board. 19-Jun-93 Michael Bode, Pforzheim #188/R (DM 9000)
$14361	£9386	La grosse Francoise (52x54cm-20x21in) studio st. 18-Apr-93 Lesieur & Le Bars, Paris #107 (F.FR 78000)
$20000	£13333	Jeune femme assise (49x49cm-19x19in) studio st. painted 1929. 12-May-94 Sotheby's, New York #227/R
$22000	£14865	La grosse Francoise (51x54cm-20x21in) st.sig.i.d.1909 studio st.verso. 4-Nov-93 Sotheby's, New York #288/R
$32000	£21333	Jeune fille allongee (45x53cm-18x21in) s. painted 1914. 12-May-94 Sotheby's, New York #231/R
$35000	£23333	Hermine en bleu (43x27cm-17x11in) s. painted 1916. 11-May-94 Christie's, New York #176/R
$35345	£23253	La conversation ou femme et homme (65x54cm-26x21in) studio st. board painted 1912. 3-Jun-93 Christian de Quay, Paris #12/R (F.FR 193000)
$40000	£26490	Le client indecis (46x55cm-18x22in) s.i. board. 12-Nov-92 Christie's, New York #146/R
$41560	£27523	Louisette (65x38cm-26x15in) s.painted 1923 board on canvas. 13-Nov-92 Galerie Koller, Zurich #5044/R (S.FR 60000)
$44000	£29139	Femme nue dans un fauteuil (60x49cm-24x19in) s. board. 11-Nov-92 Sotheby's, New York #149/R
$44700	£30000	Danseuse du Moulin Rouge (80x64cm-31x25in) s. painted 1913. 1-Dec-93 Sotheby's, London #159/R
$50000	£33784	Jeune fille en chemise (55x46cm-22x18in) painted 1925. 4-Nov-93 Sotheby's, New York #175/R
$50000	£33113	Portrait d'Hermine David (80x64cm-31x25in) s. painted 1916. 11-Nov-92 Sotheby's, New York #148/R
$55000	£35948	Nu sur un lit (60x73cm-24x29in) s. painted 1907-1909. 13-May-93 Christie's, New York #182/R
$60000	£40000	Nu dans un fauteuil (65x54cm-26x21in) s. painted 1912. 12-May-94 Sotheby's, New York #226/R
$60000	£39216	Woman wearing hat with roses (64x54cm-25x21in) st.sig. painted 1909. 4-Oct-93 Sotheby's, Tel Aviv #63/R
$68000	£47222	Deux jeunes filles (80x64cm-31x25in) s. painted c.1927-29. 23-Feb-93 Sotheby's, New York #51/R
$70000	£47297	Rosette et Nana (81x100cm-32x39in) painted 1925. 4-Nov-93 Sotheby's, New York #162/R
$75723	£49818	Deux modeles (80x59cm-31x23in) s. 29-Mar-93 Binoche et Godeau, Paris #29/R (F.FR 410000)
$80000	£52288	Le cirque (74x81cm-29x32in) painted 1910. 12-May-93 Sotheby's, New York #191/R
$92380	£62000	Modele assis (65x54cm-26x21in) s. 23-Jun-93 Christie's, London #309/R
$140600	£74000	Bobette (81x65cm-32x26in) st.sig. painted 1928. 22-Jun-93 Christie's, London #192/R
$481	£325	Nu debout (18x9cm-7x4in) st.sig. crayon htd.W/C dr. 20-Apr-94 Guy Loudmer, Paris #351 (F.FR 2800)
$481	£325	Femmes (19x16cm-7x6in) studio st. W/C. 18-Apr-94 Laurin Guilloux Buffetaud Tailleur, Paris #108 (F.FR 2800)
$515	£348	Nu allonge (10x15cm-4x6in) st.sig.studio st. crayon htd.W/C mixed media dr. 20-Apr-94 Guy Loudmer, Paris #352 (F.FR 3000)
$522	£337	Course de chevaux (20x21cm-8x8in) st.sig.studio st. W/C ink. 12-Jul-94 Guy Loudmer, Paris #196 (F.FR 2800)
$523	£351	Etude de personnages (17x14cm-7x6in) s. ink crayon W/C. 27-Mar-94 Guy Loudmer, Paris #153 (F.FR 3000)
$526	£351	La reunion (18x23cm-7x9in) st.sig.studio st. pencil W/C. 8-Jun-94 Guy Loudmer, Paris #122 (F.FR 3000)
$530	£370	Le marche oriental (21x24cm-8x9in) studio st. pencil W/C. 14-Mar-93 Eric Pillon, Calais #104/R (F.FR 3000)
$558	£374	Promenade en famille (18x12cm-7x5in) ink htd.W/C dr. 21-Mar-94 Ader Tajan, Paris #99 (F.FR 3200)
$567	£356	Personnages sur la jetee (20x24cm-8x9in) st.sig. pencil stumping dr htd.W/C painted 1929. 23-Apr-93 Guy Loudmer, Paris #52 (F.FR 3000)
$577	£380	Personnages, Ostende (16x21cm-6x8in) st. sig. studio st. Indian ink W/C. 8-Nov-92 Eric Pillon, Calais #185/R (F.FR 3100)
$591	£389	Etude de femmes (17x25cm-7x10in) st.sig. pencil W/C. 4-Apr-93 Guy Loudmer, Paris #22 (F.FR 3200)
$600	£417	Figures by rocky cliff. Sketch of four figures (23x30cm-9x12in) i. pen double-sided. 26-Feb-93 Sotheby's Arcade, New York #12/R
$628	£413	Paysans sur la plage (18x11cm-7x4in) st.sig.i. W/C. 4-Apr-93 Guy Loudmer, Paris #20 (F.FR 3400)
$661	£416	Trois femmes (29x36cm-11x14in) st.sig. Indian ink executed 1930. 23-Apr-93 Guy Loudmer, Paris #50 (F.FR 3500)
$662	£444	Jeunes femmes dans un bar (16x24cm-6x9in) studio st.i.d.1911 crayon W/C. 27-Mar-94 Guy Loudmer, Paris #156 (F.FR 3800)

PASCIN, Jules (1885-1930) American/Bulgarian-cont.

$674	£459	L'echoppe du barbier Marseille (20x17cm-8x7in) st.sig.studio st.i.d.1922 pencil W/C. 8-Jul-93 Guy Loudmer, Paris #90 (F.FR 4000)
$679	£456	Cavaliers a Cuba (9x18cm-4x7in) st.sig. d.1916verso ink W/C dr. 6-Feb-94 Guy Loudmer, Paris #40 (F.FR 4000)
$685	£473	Le couple (14x13cm-6x5in) st.sig. lead pencil W/C. 27-Jan-93 Guy Loudmer, Paris #95 (F.FR 3800)
$699	£457	Parc en Louisiane et famille sur la plage, USA (20x16cm-8x6in) bears st.sig. blk.crayon double-sided. 21-Dec-92 Jean Louis Picard, Paris #171 (F.FR 3800)
$709	£503	Fillette accroupie (15x21cm-6x8in) st.sig. ink wash htd.W/C. 10-Feb-93 Guy Loudmer, Paris #34/R (F.FR 4000)
$709	£503	Nu allonge (21x32cm-8x13in) st.sig. studio st. pencil W/C ink sketch verso. 10-Feb-93 Guy Loudmer, Paris #45 (F.FR 4000)
$718	£451	Scene de parc (21x27cm-8x11in) st.sig.i.d.1929 pencil W/C. 23-Apr-93 Guy Loudmer, Paris #53 (F.FR 3800)
$721	£498	Femme et enfant (14x20cm-6x8in) st.sig.studio st.d.1929 lead pencil W/C. 27-Jan-93 Guy Loudmer, Paris #94 (F.FR 4000)
$731	£474	Jeune femme assise en robe verte (31x20cm-12x8in) studio st. pencil W/C. 24-Jun-94 Delorme & Fraysse, Paris #115 (F.FR 4000)
$745	£500	Scene de village (18x24cm-7x9in) studio st. pencil pen wash. 24-Mar-93 Sotheby's, London #154/R
$749	£503	Personnages au bord de la riviere (17x14cm-7x6in) bears st.sig.studio st. pencil W/C dr. 27-Mar-94 Perrin, Versailles #153 (F.FR 4300)
$750	£503	Landscape with donkey and rider (12x17cm-5x7in) st.atelier W/C. 2-Jan-94 Gordon Galleries, Tel Aviv #251/R
$770	£513	Jeune fille (14x8cm-6x3in) st.sig. studio st. W/C crayon. 19-Mar-94 Cornette de St.Cyr, Paris #213 (F.FR 4400)
$784	£526	Scene mexicaine (19x12cm-7x5in) studio st.i.d.1915 crayon W/C. 27-Mar-94 Guy Loudmer, Paris #155 (F.FR 4500)
$817	£556	Southern street scene with donkey pulling carriage, man looking on (39x25cm-15x11in) s. Indian ink dr. 15-Apr-94 Arno Winterberg, Heidelberg #2059/R (DM 1400)
$834	£591	Deux enfants (23x31cm-9x12in) st.sig. pencil W/C painted 1913. 10-Feb-93 Guy Loudmer, Paris #39 (F.FR 4700)
$887	£629	Adolescentes dans l'herbe (24x21cm-9x8in) st.sig. studio st. ink htd.W/C dr painted 1915. 10-Feb-93 Guy Loudmer, Paris #41/R (F.FR 5000)
$887	£629	Supplice (16x23cm-6x9in) st.sig. ink htd.W/C dr. 10-Feb-93 Guy Loudmer, Paris #53/R (F.FR 5000)
$887	£629	Fillette au chapeau jaune (23x24cm-9x9in) st.sig. ink W/C ink sketches verso. 10-Feb-93 Guy Loudmer, Paris #49 (F.FR 5000)
$900	£596	Femme au cafe (17x11cm-7x4in) st.sig. i.d.1910 pen. 29-Sep-93 Sotheby's Arcade, New York #6/R
$911	£600	Le bouquet de fleurs (13x17cm-5x7in) s. W/C. 23-Jul-94 Thierry, Brest #92 (F.FR 5000)
$915	£606	Jeune femme de dos (63x47cm-25x19in) st.sig. drawing. 18-Nov-92 Guy Loudmer, Paris #75/R (F.FR 5000)
$923	£608	Etude de couples (16x14cm-6x6in) st.sig. W/C Indian ink. 4-Apr-93 Guy Loudmer, Paris #23 (F.FR 5000)
$950	£629	Trois musiciens (13x20cm-5x8in) s. studio st. pen W/C. 10-Nov-92 Christie's, East, New York #154/R
$994	£667	La lecture (38x25cm-15x10in) s. pencil dr. 19-Dec-93 Perrin, Versailles #128 (F.FR 5800)
$1006	£662	Le defile de mode (22x31cm-9x12in) studio st. lead pencil. 8-Nov-92 Eric Pillon, Calais #186/R (F.FR 5400)
$1009	£659	Etudes (22x27cm-9x11in) st.sig. ink. 12-May-93 Cornette de St.Cyr, Paris #104 b (F.FR 5500)
$1049	£709	Deux amis (17x10cm-7x4in) s. Indian ink dr executed 1915. 24-Nov-93 Watine-Arnault, Paris #69/R (F.FR 6200)
$1064	£755	Nu assis (22x30cm-9x12in) st.sig.studio st. chl W/C. 10-Feb-93 Guy Loudmer, Paris #38 (F.FR 6000)
$1064	£755	Nu a la chaise (28x22cm-11x9in) st.sig. pencil W/C painted 1923. 10-Feb-93 Guy Loudmer, Paris #56 (F.FR 6000)
$1100	£705	Madame Pieper und Madame Schnieper, illustration for work by Heine (30x23cm-12x9in) ink W/C paper laid down on board. 24-May-93 Grogan, Massachussetts #377/R
$1107	£753	Leprin, je veux le boeuf ecorche (21x32cm-8x13in) s.i. pen brown ink. 13-Apr-94 Ricqles, Paris #17/R (F.FR 6500)
$1120	£732	Horses on beach (24x36cm-9x14in) s.d.07 W/C. 4-May-93 Michael Zeller, Lindau #997/R (DM 1800)
$1120	£718	Groupe de personnages (20x26cm-8x10in) s. studio st. W/C ink. 12-Dec-92 Catherine Charbonneaux, Paris #24 (F.FR 6000)
$1200	£784	Deux femmes (25x24cm-10x9in) st. W/C pen double-sided. 10-May-93 Christie's, East, New York #77/R
$1200	£800	Cuban woman (28x22cm-11x9in) studio st. ink graphite. 18-May-94 Butterfield & Butterfield, San Francisco #2907/R
$1217	£817	Le couple (19x19cm-7x7in) st.sig.studio st. ink dr. 19-Dec-93 Perrin, Versailles #127/R (F.FR 7100)
$1220	£819	La mere et l'enfant (16x10cm-6x4in) s. ink W/C. 27-Mar-94 Guy Loudmer, Paris #154 (F.FR 7000)
$1221	£820	Nus en plein air (28x23cm-11x9in) st.sig. ink dr. 23-Jun-93 Ader Tajan, Paris #130 b (F.FR 7000)
$1242	£881	La robe rouge (25x19cm-10x7in) st.sig. pencil W/C. 10-Feb-93 Guy Loudmer, Paris #50 b (F.FR 7000)
$1286	£863	La sieste sur les fortifs (21x25cm-8x10in) st.sig.studio st. W/C wash chl. 17-Dec-93 Guy Loudmer, Paris #80 (F.FR 7500)

PASCIN, Jules (1885-1930) American/Bulgarian-cont.

$1330	£943	Flaneurs au bord du quai (15x19cm-6x7in) st.sig. W/C pencil. 10-Feb-93 Guy Loudmer, Paris #37 (F.FR 7500)
$1500	£1014	Four negroes (25x35cm-10x14in) s. W/C. 20-Mar-93 Weschler, Washington #46/R
$1500	£993	Dans le parc (20x39cm-8x15in) pen brush ink. 10-Nov-92 Christie's, East, New York #31/R
$1534	£1029	Le repos (33x25cm-13x10in) bears studio st. crayon W/C. 27-Mar-94 Perrin, Versailles #154 (F.FR 8800)
$1595	£922	Au parc (24x19cm-9x7in) s. black crayon htd.W/C. 22-Sep-92 Jean Louis Picard, Paris #144 (F.FR 7800)
$1656	£1111	Deux femmes (13x17cm-5x7in) i.d.1927 crayon W/C. 27-Mar-94 Guy Loudmer, Paris #158 (F.FR 9500)
$1683	£1100	Femme nue (32x19cm-13x7in) st. W/C pencil. 27-Jun-94 Christie's, S. Kensington #77/R
$1685	£1195	Sans titre (17x30cm-7x12in) st.sig. ink htd.W/C. 10-Feb-93 Guy Loudmer, Paris #52/R (F.FR 9500)
$1700	£1149	Jeune fille allongee de profil (23x32cm-9x13in) studio st. ink pencil. 2-Nov-93 Christie's, East, New York #47/R
$1700	£1149	tunis (16x20cm-6x8in) s.studio st. W/C pastel. 21-Oct-93 Butterfield & Butterfield, San Francisco #2730/R
$1700	£1133	Scene de rue (23x21cm-9x8in) pen black ink W/C. 9-May-94 Christie's, East, New York #179/R
$1804	£1211	Reclining female nude (17x21cm-7x8in) s.studio st. W/C over pencil vellum. 5-Mar-94 Wolfgang Ketterer, Munich #457/R (DM 3100)
$1862	£1321	Alberta et Rebecca (53x58cm-21x23in) st.sig. studio st.chl dr. 10-Feb-93 Guy Loudmer, Paris #50 (F.FR 10500)
$1872	£1265	Young girl kneeling, Tanna Jadwiga (16x10cm-6x4in) s.i. pen executed c.1914. 27-Nov-93 Villa Grisebach, Berlin #765/R (DM 3200)
$1900	£1258	Martine (24x30cm-9x12in) st.sig. pencil W/C. 29-Sep-93 Sotheby's Arcade, New York #14/R
$1954	£1329	Trois personnages assis (12x21cm-5x8in) studio st. ink W/C. 6-Apr-94 Chayette & Calmels, Paris #10/R (F.FR 11500)
$1989	£1300	Fin de meeting (19x26cm-7x10in) st. w/c. 27-Jun-94 Christie's, S. Kensington #79/R
$2005	£1319	Mere et enfant (38x31cm-15x12in) s. W/C painted c.1927. 9-Jun-93 Couturier & Nicolay, Paris #62/R (F.FR 11000)
$2100	£1409	La chasse a la femme (16x15cm-6x6in) s. st.sig.verso gouache executed 1913. 24-Feb-94 Sotheby's Arcade, New York #10/R
$2128	£1509	Figures pele-mele, fillettes, enfants, portrait, chevaux (18x26cm-7x10in) st.sig. 10-Feb-93 Guy Loudmer, Paris #42 (F.FR 12000)
$2142	£1400	Femme nue et homme (29x20cm-11x8in) st. W/C. 27-Jun-94 Christie's, S. Kensington #78/R
$2190	£1378	Paysage de Cuba (23x36cm-9x14in) s. W/C. 23-Apr-93 Guy Loudmer, Paris #142 (F.FR 11600)
$2200	£1438	Les mariniers (15x21cm-6x8in) s. pen W/C col.pencil paper on board. 10-May-93 Christie's, East, New York #28/R
$2500	£1645	Nude (25x34cm-10x13in) st. pencil. 7-Jun-93 Gordon Galleries, Tel Aviv #406/R
$2500	£1736	Groupe d'hommes (14x21cm-6x8in) st.sig.studio st. col.pencil. 22-Feb-93 Christie's, East, New York #72/R
$2600	£1699	'La Poivrote' (48x63cm-19x25in) st.sig.d.1928 pen. 30-Jun-94 Gordon Galleries, Tel Aviv #407/R
$2600	£1806	Nu assis (39x30cm-15x12in) studio st. col.chk felt tip pen. 22-Feb-93 Christie's, East, New York #71/R
$2601	£1700	Au salon (15x27cm-6x11in) st. W/C. 27-Jun-94 Christie's, S. Kensington #80/R
$2700	£1812	Au marche (35x50cm-14x20in) st. W/C pencil. 23-Feb-94 Christie's, East, New York #3/R
$2750	£1730	Jeune fille (42x31cm-17x12in) s. i.d.1921verso ink W/C. 25-Apr-93 Butterfield & Butterfield, San Francisco #2004/R
$2980	£2000	Nu allonge. Cafe Bowery (25x32cm-10x13in) s.studio st.i.d.Oct 27 crayon wash double-sided. 13-Oct-93 Sotheby's, London #275/R
$2982	£1988	Deux femmes au jardin, Tunisie (30x31cm-12x12in) s. W/C ink. 8-Jun-94 Guy Loudmer, Paris #121/R (F.FR 17000)
$3000	£2013	Figures in a park (28x36cm-11x14in) artist's st. W/C pencil. 3-Jan-94 Gordon Galleries, Tel Aviv #401/R
$3394	£2278	Depart de l'Enfant Prodigue (31x45cm-12x18in) st.sig.studio st. ink crayon dr. 6-Feb-94 Guy Loudmer, Paris #39/R (F.FR 20000)
$3400	£2361	Triple portrait of Jack Taylor, Ernest Fiene and Emile Ganso (61x91cm-24x36in) s.i. transfer dr. 26-Feb-93 Sotheby's Arcade, New York #8/R
$3576	£2400	Dans la campagne Cubaine (20x35cm-8x14in) s.studio st.i.d.1917verso pen ink W/C. 13-Oct-93 Sotheby's, London #276/R
$3725	£2500	Femme assise (24x18cm-9x7in) s. executed c.1921-22 W/C pen Indian ink card. 24-Mar-93 Sotheby's, London #156/R
$3800	£2550	Bavadages (16x22cm-6x9in) artist's st. oil pen canvas. 3-Jan-94 Gordon Galleries, Tel Aviv #402/R
$3838	£2576	Le petit dejeuner, portrait d'Hermine David (22x14cm-9x6in) W/C. 23-Jun-93 Ader Tajan, Paris #130 (F.FR 22000)
$3934	£2490	In the cafe (15x13cm-6x5in) painted c.1909-12 letter verso pen brush. 1-Dec-92 Karl & Faber, Munich #1077/R (DM 6200)
$4000	£2614	Cafe interior (29x35cm-11x14in) studio st. pencil chl pen card. 14-Apr-93 Sotheby's, Tel Aviv #97/R
$4000	£2721	Figure composition (21x29cm-8x11in) s. W/C gouache pen Indian ink. 4-Apr-94 Sotheby's, Tel Aviv #78/R
$4286	£2857	Seated woman (41x28cm-16x11in) s.studio st. W/C ink. 1-Jun-94 Sotheby's, Amsterdam #251/R (D.FL 8000)

PASCIN, Jules (1885-1930) American/Bulgarian-cont.

$4564	£3002	Trois nus (22x38cm-9x15in) studio st. st.sig. W/C gouache tracing paper. 2-Nov-92 Ader Tajan, Paris #68/R (F.FR 24500)
$4800	£3137	Street scene (20x30cm-8x12in) st. pen Indian ink W/C black crayon. 14-Apr-93 Sotheby's, Tel Aviv #110/R
$5500	£3595	Fete champetre (46x60cm-18x24in) s. transfer drawing. 4-Oct-93 Sotheby's, Tel Aviv #141/R
$5500	£3595	Deux femmes allongees (49x39cm-19x15in) estate st. pencil. 12-May-93 Sotheby's, New York #172/R
$5542	£3400	Portrait de Hemingway dans le Cafe du Dome. Esquisse de Hemingway (21x29cm-8x11in) s. st. pen pastel wash double-sided. 14-Oct-92 Sotheby's, London #238/R
$5750	£3859	Madame Pieper and Madame Schnieper (30x23cm-12x9in) init. W/C ink paper on board executed 1910. 24-Feb-94 Sotheby's Arcade, New York #9/R
$5920	£4000	L'Americaine au grand chapeau, New York (47x61cm-19x24in) chl executed 1928. 25-Nov-93 Christian de Quay, Paris #178 (F.FR 35000)
$6800	£4444	Sailors (15x21cm-6x8in) s. W/C pencil. 4-Oct-93 Sotheby's, Tel Aviv #139/R
$6984	£4688	Quay of harbour, North of France (18x22cm-7x9in) s. W/C over pen vellum executed c.1912. 23-Jun-93 Galerie Kornfeld, Berne #638/R (S.FR 10500)
$7152	£4800	Babette et Rebecca (49x64cm-19x25in) st.sig.studio st. chl wash executed c.1929. 13-Oct-93 Sotheby's, London #274/R
$7152	£4800	Deux jeunes filles a table (18x11cm-7x4in) s. exec.1911-12 W/C gouache. 24-Mar-93 Sotheby's, London #195/R
$8000	£5442	La Jeanette (41x30cm-16x12in) s. W/C pen executed 1921. 4-Apr-94 Sotheby's, Tel Aviv #67/R
$8000	£4706	Jeune femmew sous un parasol (71x56cm-28x22in) pastel chl. paper laid down on board. 5-Oct-92 Sotheby's, New York #69/R
$10000	£6711	Seated woman (32x24cm-13x9in) s. pencil executed 1924. 3-Jan-94 Gordon Galleries, Tel Aviv #452/R
$23715	£15500	Nu assis (65x49cm-26x19in) s. oil gouache over pencil board painted 1911. 29-Jun-94 Sotheby's, London #414/R
$24585	£16500	Six etudes de femme (27x21cm-11x8in) bears sig.studio st. pen ink W/C wash set of six. 23-Mar-94 Sotheby's, London #230/R

PASKELL, William (1866-1951) American

$650	£445	Clipper ship (25x33cm-10x13in) s. board. 19-Feb-94 Young Fine Arts Auctions, Maine #158/R
$800	£537	Harbour scene (61x51cm-24x20in) 27-Mar-94 Myers, Florida #22/R

PATINO, Virgilio (1947-) Colombian

$10000	£6623	La Sabana (200x130cm-79x51in) s. painted 1990. 24-Nov-92 Christie's, New York #231/R

PATKIN, Itzar (1955-) American

$6000	£3974	Southern momento (183x134cm-72x53in) oil wire mesh. 19-Nov-92 Christie's, New York #268/R
$1000	£654	Pictures are nets (122x91cm-48x36in) oil metal leaf screen executed 1987. 22-Dec-92 Christie's, East, New York #49
$2600	£1699	Untitled (102x132cm-40x52in) spray paint collage executed 1981. 22-Dec-92 Christie's, East, New York #50
$3000	£1961	Perfect existance in rose garden - pride (152x102cm-60x40in) oil metal leaf screen executed 1988. 22-Dec-92 Christie's, East, New York #48

PATTEN, James van (20th C) American?

$2800	£1637	Bear mountain for now (122x163cm-48x64in) s.d.1985verso acrylic. 18-Sep-92 Du Mouchelle, Detroit #2019/R
$3500	£2047	Pond (122x163cm-48x64in) s.verso painted 1987 acrylic. 18-Sep-92 Du Mouchelle, Detroit #2018/R

PATTERSON, Margaret Jordan (1867-1950) American

$2200	£1457	Two-part landscape for screen (91x61cm-36x24in) s. two canvas. 21-Nov-92 James Bakker, Cambridge #279/R
$3000	£1961	Daisies in Canton jar (46x38cm-18x15in) studio st. 18-Sep-93 James Bakker, Cambridge #53/R
$550	£369	In the mountains (23x33cm-9x13in) s. W/C. 28-Mar-93 James Bakker, Cambridge #195
$650	£455	Edam Church (38x41cm-15x16in) s.d.1902 gouache over graphite. 7-Feb-93 James Bakker, Cambridge #103
$650	£436	In the hills (23x33cm-9x13in) s. W/C gouache. 26-Mar-94 James Bakker, Cambridge #56
$800	£537	Hillside village (38x43cm-15x17in) estate st. W/C. 28-Mar-93 James Bakker, Cambridge #78
$800	£537	Spanish coastal town (38x46cm-15x18in) s.d.1904 gouache. 28-Mar-93 James Bakker, Cambridge #50/R
$850	£491	Capri coast (23x33cm-9x13in) s. gouache. 27-Sep-92 James Bakker, Cambridge #26/R
$850	£491	Cape Cod inlet (36x46cm-14x18in) s.d.1943 W/C. 27-Sep-92 James Bakker, Cambridge #46
$900	£588	Study for summer flowers (25x18cm-10x7in) studio st. W/C. 18-Sep-93 James Bakker, Cambridge #139/R
$950	£664	Monhegan (25x36cm-10x14in) W/C. 7-Feb-93 James Bakker, Cambridge #124
$950	£664	Edge of the forest (46x38cm-18x15in) W/C gouache. 7-Feb-93 James Bakker, Cambridge #185/R
$1000	£699	Sunset on Capri Cliffs (38x46cm-15x18in) s. painted 1924 W/C over graphite. 7-Feb-93 James Bakker, Cambridge #61
$1100	£769	Coastal inlet (36x43cm-14x17in) s.d.1912 W/C gouache. 7-Feb-93 James Bakker, Cambridge #105

PATTERSON, Margaret Jordan (1867-1950) American-cont.
$1400	£979	Capri House (38x46cm-15x18in) s.d.1925 gouache over chl. 7-Feb-93 James Bakker, Cambridge #147
$1400	£979	From a balcony - Sardinia (36x43cm-14x17in) s.d.1929 gouache chl. 7-Feb-93 James Bakker, Cambridge #12
$1500	£1049	Italian Riveria (38x46cm-15x18in) s. W/C over graphite. 7-Feb-93 James Bakker, Cambridge #208
$1500	£1049	House on a hillside (38x46cm-15x18in) s. painted 1925 gouache over chl. 7-Feb-93 James Bakker, Cambridge #62
$1900	£1242	Alvah's House (25x53cm-10x21in) s.d.1944 W/C board. 18-Sep-93 James Bakker, Cambridge #22
$2300	£1503	High tide (38x46cm-15x18in) s.d.1918 gouache over chl. 18-Sep-93 James Bakker, Cambridge #143/R
$2400	£1387	Coastal village, Spain (43x36cm-17x14in) s. gouache. 27-Sep-92 James Bakker, Cambridge #25/R

PATTERSON, Neil (1947-) Canadian
$718	£478	Cabin in the woods (76x102cm-30x40in) s. 30-May-94 Hodgins, Calgary #26 (C.D 1000)
$933	£622	Pink columbines (122x91cm-48x36in) s. s.i.verso. 30-May-94 Hodgins, Calgary #249/R (C.D 1300)
$1244	£846	Fireweed (91x122cm-36x48in) s. bears i.verso. 15-Nov-93 Hodgins, Calgary #45/R (C.D 1650)

PAULUS, Francis Petrus (1862-1933) American
$1900	£990	Portrait of Robert Hopkin (38x30cm-15x12in) s. panel. 7-Aug-92 Du Mouchelle, Detroit #2017/R

PAUS, Herbert Andrew (1880-1946) American
$450	£302	Canoe scene (33x56cm-13x22in) s. W/C. 24-Mar-94 Mystic Fine Arts, Connecticut #219

PAVLOVSKY, Vladmir (20th C) American
$800	£530	Harbour scene (30x41cm-12x16in) s. board. 21-Nov-92 James Bakker, Cambridge #302/R

PAWLA, Frederick Alexander (1876-1964) American
$2750	£1910	Point Lobos (76x91cm-30x36in) s. 7-Mar-93 Butterfield & Butterfield, San Francisco #97/R

PAXSON, Edgar S (1852-1919) American
$5000	£3497	On Solo Trail, head of Bitter Root River (102x65cm-40x26in) s.d.1917 i.stretcher. 11-Mar-93 Christie's, New York #124/R
$5000	£3356	The trapper (30x46cm-12x18in) s.d.1897. 2-May-94 Selkirks, St. Louis #122/R
$2500	£1603	Portrait of Indian (30x25cm-12x10in) s.d.1908 W/C gouache pencil board oval. 9-Dec-92 Butterfield & Butterfield, San Francisco #3985/R
$14000	£8092	Buffalo hunt (40x51cm-16x20in) s. gouache. 23-Sep-92 Christie's, New York #108/R

PAXTON, Elizabeth Vaughn Okie (1877-1971) American
$8000	£5128	Still life of teapot and lemons (30x36cm-12x14in) s. canvasboard. 9-Dec-92 Grogan, Massachussetts #76/R

PAXTON, William McGregor (1869-1941) American
$19000	£12025	Nellie and Phryne (115x92cm-45x36in) s. 4-Dec-92 Christie's, New York #144/R
$22000	£12717	Together (91x91cm-36x36in) s. 23-Sep-92 Christie's, New York #144/R
$500	£333	Nude with a slipper (58x46cm-23x18in) chl. 17-May-94 Grogan, Massachussetts #339/R
$800	£523	Portrait of Alice Trask (18x14cm-7x6in) s. chl. 4-May-93 Christie's, East, New York #156/R
$900	£596	Lady with pearls (28x23cm-11x9in) s.d.1929 drawing. 28-Nov-92 Young Fine Arts Auctions, Maine #314/R

PAYNE, Edgar (1882-1947) American
$775	£524	Ocean at Laguna (25x20cm-10x8in) s. board. 23-Oct-93 Collins, Maine #198/R
$800	£526	Nude in studio (40x30cm-16x12in) s. canvasboard. 13-Jun-93 Butterfield & Butterfield, San Francisco #897/R
$2000	£1351	Mountain landscape (28x38cm-11x15in) s. canvasboard. 9-Nov-93 John Moran, Pasadena #838
$2000	£1351	Brittany boats (30x23cm-12x9in) s. canvasboard. 9-Nov-93 John Moran, Pasadena #869
$2500	£1678	Lake and trees (24x34cm-9x13in) s. canvas on board. 8-Dec-93 Butterfield & Butterfield, San Francisco #3435/R
$2750	£1821	Sierra landscape (30x46cm-12x18in) s. canvasboard. 14-Jun-94 John Moran, Pasadena #38
$2750	£1821	Sailing boats (27x36cm-11x14in) s. canvasboard. 15-Jun-94 Butterfield & Butterfield, San Francisco #4692/R
$3000	£1987	Boats in dock (27x34cm-11x13in) s. panel. 15-Jun-94 Butterfield & Butterfield, San Francisco #4691/R
$3000	£1765	Brittany boats (30x25cm-12x10in) canvasboard. 4-Oct-92 Butterfield & Butterfield, Los Angeles #152/R
$3000	£1765	Brittany village (32x39cm-13x15in) s. canvasboard. 4-Oct-92 Butterfield & Butterfield, Los Angeles #158/R
$3000	£1987	Oak tree (30x41cm-12x16in) s. board. 15-Jun-94 Butterfield & Butterfield, San Francisco #4689/R

PAYNE, Edgar (1882-1947) American-cont.

$3000	£1765	Village of San Gervais beneath Mont Blanc (18x24cm-7x9in) s. s.d.1922 verso canvasboard. 4-Oct-92 Butterfield & Butterfield, Los Angeles #102/R
$3000	£2000	Monterey, California (61x51cm-24x20in) s. i.d.1931 verso. 23-May-94 Christie's, East, New York #187/R
$3250	£1912	Sierra Lkae (25x36cm-10x14in) s. board. 4-Oct-92 Butterfield & Butterfield, Los Angeles #188/R
$3500	£2349	Sierra landscape (26x32cm-10x13in) s. canvasboard. 8-Dec-93 Butterfield & Butterfield, San Francisco #3432/R
$4000	£2353	Fisherman's return (27x34cm-11x13in) s. canvasboard. 4-Oct-92 Butterfield & Butterfield, Los Angeles #157/R
$4000	£2685	Riders and Mesas (23x18cm-9x7in) s. canvas on board. 8-Dec-93 Butterfield & Butterfield, San Francisco #3591/R
$4000	£2685	Timber line (30x36cm-12x14in) s. board. 8-Dec-93 Butterfield & Butterfield, San Francisco #3431/R
$4250	£2872	Afternoon shadows (25x36cm-10x14in) s. canvasboard. 15-Jun-93 John Moran, Pasadena #48
$4500	£3020	Boats in harbour (33x38cm-13x15in) s. 8-Dec-93 Butterfield & Butterfield, San Francisco #3464/R
$4500	£2980	Trees and shadows (30x41cm-12x16in) s. board. 15-Jun-94 Butterfield & Butterfield, San Francisco #4681/R
$5500	£3618	Palisades glacier (41x30cm-16x12in) s. canvas on board. 13-Jun-93 Butterfield & Butterfield, San Francisco #915/R
$6000	£4027	Adriatic ships (61x71cm-24x28in) s. 8-Dec-93 Butterfield & Butterfield, San Francisco #3453/R
$7200	£4865	Western scene (51x61cm-20x24in) s. 31-Oct-93 Hindman Galleries, Chicago #680/R
$8000	£5369	Rocky coast (30x41cm-12x16in) s. board. 8-Dec-93 Butterfield & Butterfield, San Francisco #3452/R
$8000	£5333	Morning in the harbour (51x61cm-20x24in) s. i.verso. 23-May-94 Christie's, East, New York #159/R
$8200	£5541	Alpine vista (61x71cm-24x28in) s. i.stretcher. 31-Oct-93 Hindman Galleries, Chicago #679/R
$9000	£5960	Inner harbour, Concarneau, Brittany (48x58cm-19x23in) s. i.verso. 15-Jun-94 Butterfield & Butterfield, San Francisco #4696/R
$9000	£6250	On the canal, Chioggia (51x61cm-20x24in) s. i.stretcher. 7-Mar-93 Butterfield & Butterfield, San Francisco #172/R
$9000	£5294	Sailboats (63x76cm-25x30in) s. 4-Oct-92 Butterfield & Butterfield, Los Angeles #156/R
$9000	£5960	Anchorage, Breton tuna boats (51x61cm-20x24in) s. i.verso. 15-Jun-94 Butterfield & Butterfield, San Francisco #4695/R
$9000	£6250	Return of the fishing fleet (41x51cm-16x20in) s. canvas on board. 7-Mar-93 Butterfield & Butterfield, San Francisco #173/R
$9500	£5588	Lowering sails (36x36cm-14x14in) s. 4-Oct-92 Butterfield & Butterfield, Los Angeles #117/R
$9500	£6291	Foothills near Pasadena (61x71cm-24x28in) s. 15-Jun-94 Butterfield & Butterfield, San Francisco #4708/R
$10000	£6711	Across the valley (51x62cm-20x24in) s. 8-Dec-93 Butterfield & Butterfield, San Francisco #3471/R
$10000	£6623	Mountain Pass (61x71cm-24x28in) s. i.stretcher. 23-Sep-93 Sotheby's, New York #108/R
$10000	£6944	Summer landscape (37x119cm-15x47in) s.d.24. 7-Mar-93 Butterfield & Butterfield, San Francisco #197/R
$10000	£5882	High Sierra scene (71x86cm-28x34in) s. 4-Oct-92 Butterfield & Butterfield, Los Angeles #149/R
$11000	£7285	Chioggia boats (51x61cm-20x24in) s. 28-Sep-93 John Moran, Pasadena #269
$11000	£7285	Breton fishing boats (51x61cm-20x24in) s. 15-Jun-94 Butterfield & Butterfield, San Francisco #4698/R
$11000	£7333	Sierra, Jenny Lake (51x61cm-20x24in) s. i.stretcher. 15-Mar-94 John Moran, Pasadena #74
$12000	£8108	Rugged Slopes a Sierra landscape (51x61cm-20x24in) s. i.stretcher. 9-Nov-93 John Moran, Pasadena #898
$12000	£7947	Mountain Pass, near Mammoth (61x71cm-24x28in) s. i.stretcher. 15-Jun-94 Butterfield & Butterfield, San Francisco #4685/R
$12000	£8333	Miner Peaks at Iceberg Lake (51x61cm-20x24in) s. s.i.verso. 7-Mar-93 Butterfield & Butterfield, San Francisco #139/R
$12500	£8333	Purple Mountain (86x86cm-34x34in) s. 17-Mar-94 Sotheby's, New York #82/R
$13000	£8667	Fishing boats (74x74cm-29x29in) s. 17-Mar-94 Sotheby's, New York #127/R
$13000	£8784	Sierra landscape (64x76cm-25x30in) s. 9-Nov-93 John Moran, Pasadena #930 a
$13000	£8609	Big Pine Lake, mountain scene (71x86cm-28x34in) s. s.i.verso. 15-Jun-94 Butterfield & Butterfield, San Francisco #4674/R
$14000	£8974	Mountain solitude - near Mt Whitney (86x86cm-34x34in) s. 26-May-93 Christie's, New York #163/R
$14000	£9272	Swiss Alps village (61x71cm-24x28in) s. 28-Sep-93 John Moran, Pasadena #251
$14000	£9722	Fishermen's holiday (61x71cm-24x28in) s. i.verso. 7-Mar-93 Butterfield & Butterfield, San Francisco #116/R
$15000	£9868	Harbour twilight (51x61cm-20x24in) s. 13-Jun-93 Butterfield & Butterfield, San Francisco #818/R
$16000	£10738	Capristrano Canyon (61x72cm-24x28in) s. 8-Dec-93 Butterfield & Butterfield, San Francisco #3448/R
$16000	£10526	Orange sail (74x74cm-29x29in) s. s.i.verso. 13-Jun-93 Butterfield & Butterfield, San Francisco #807/R
$16000	£10596	Sycamore Canyon (61x71cm-24x28in) s. 23-Sep-93 Sotheby's, New York #106/R
$17000	£11486	Boats in harbour (74x74cm-29x29in) s. 15-Jun-93 John Moran, Pasadena #93
$18000	£12162	Venetian fishing boats Chioggia (74x74cm-29x29in) s. 9-Nov-93 John Moran, Pasadena #859

PAYNE, Edgar (1882-1947) American-cont.

$19000	£12752	Tuna boats, Douarnenez, France (71x81cm-28x32in) s. i.verso. 8-Dec-93 Butterfield & Butterfield, San Francisco #3456/R
$20000	£13245	'Mesaland' three Indian riders in atmospheric south-west landscape (46x71cm-18x28in) s. 14-Jun-94 John Moran, Pasadena #61
$24000	£16107	Harbour scene (74x74cm-29x29in) s. 3-Dec-93 Christie's, New York #52/R
$25000	£14706	Tuna boats (61x71cm-24x28in) s. 4-Oct-92 Butterfield & Butterfield, Los Angeles #161/R
$25000	£14706	Summit lake (76x102cm-30x40in) s. 4-Oct-92 Butterfield & Butterfield, Los Angeles #148/R
$37500	£25168	Sunset at Canyon de Chelly (67x81cm-26x32in) s. 2-Dec-93 Sotheby's, New York #75/R
$45000	£30201	Desert skies (71x86cm-28x34in) s. i.verso. 8-Dec-93 Butterfield & Butterfield, San Francisco #3563/R
$55000	£34810	Navahos (101x127cm-40x50in) s. i.verso. 3-Dec-92 Sotheby's, New York #80/R
$800	*£530*	*Sailing boats (22x28cm-9x11in) pencil dr. 15-Jun-94 Butterfield & Butterfield, San Francisco #4722/R*
$1000	*£662*	*California Oaks (22x28cm-9x11in) s. pencil dr. 15-Jun-94 Butterfield & Butterfield, San Francisco #4721/R*
$1300	*£861*	*High Sierras (22x28cm-9x11in) s. pencil dr. 15-Jun-94 Butterfield & Butterfield, San Francisco #4720/R*
$1500	*£993*	*Canyon de Chelly (22x28cm-9x11in) s. pencil. 15-Jun-94 Butterfield & Butterfield, San Francisco #4719/R*
$9000	*£6040*	*Mount Ritter and Lake Edza (43x53cm-17x21in) s. gouache. 8-Dec-93 Butterfield & Butterfield, San Francisco #3429/R*

PAYNE, Elsie Palmer (1884-1971) American

$850	£563	Roma, portrait of woman (58x46cm-23x18in) s. 28-Sep-93 John Moran, Pasadena #254
$1700	£1118	White flowers (61x51cm-24x20in) s. 13-Jun-93 Butterfield & Butterfield, San Francisco #914/R
$800	*£526*	*Floral still life (51x64cm-20x25in) s. pastel. 5-Jun-93 Louisiana Auction Exchange #124/R*
$1100	*£728*	*Street scene, Douarnenez, Brittany (23x27cm-9x11in) s.i. gouache. 15-Jun-94 Butterfield & Butterfield, San Francisco #4694/R*
$1600	*£1060*	*Los Angeles Street Scene (30x37cm-12x15in) s. gouache. 15-Jun-94 Butterfield & Butterfield, San Francisco #4759/R*
$3000	*£1765*	*Mountains in rain. Sierras. Sierra Nevada (30x36cm-12x14in) s. gouache three. 4-Oct-92 Butterfield & Butterfield, Los Angeles #270/R*

PAYZANT, Charles (1898-1980) American

$1000	*£676*	*Going home (48x64cm-19x25in) s. W/C. 15-Jun-93 John Moran, Pasadena #142*

PEALE (studio) (18/19th C) American

$30000	£18987	Washington at the Battle of Princeton 1779 (101x73cm-40x29in) 3-Dec-92 Sotheby's, New York #19/R

PEALE, Charles Willson (1741-1827) American

$9250	£5441	Portrait of Jane Hunter (91x69cm-36x27in) 8-Oct-92 Freeman Fine Arts, Philadelphia #1106/R
$24000	£15190	Portrait of Colonel John Cox (66x56cm-26x22in) canvas laid down on masonite. 4-Dec-92 Christie's, New York #175/R
$90000	£52941	Maskell Ewing (91x69cm-36x27in) 8-Oct-92 Freeman Fine Arts, Philadelphia #1136/R

PEALE, Charles Willson (attrib) (1741-1827) American

$10000	£6711	Portrait of Sarah Latimer (58x48cm-23x19in) oval. 2-Dec-93 Sotheby's, New York #8/R
$2000	*£1258*	*Portrait of Col John Cox (8x5cm-3x2in) min. oval. 22-Apr-93 Freeman Fine Arts, Philadelphia #521*

PEALE, James (elder) (1749-1831) American

$25000	£16779	Still life of grapes and peaches on table (36x48cm-14x19in) s.i.d.1831verso. 3-Feb-94 Sloan, North Bethesda #2885/R

PEALE, James (elder-attrib) (1749-1831) American

$18000	£10205	Still life with peaches and grapes (34x50cm-13x20in) indis.s. i.verso painted by James or Raphaelle. 23-Sep-92 Christie's, New York #4/R

PEALE, Raphaelle (1774-1825) American

$6500	£3757	Portrait of Artemas Ward (65x56cm-26x22in) s.i.d.1795. 23-Sep-92 Christie's, New York #5/R

PEALE, Rembrandt (1778-1860) American

$4000	£2632	Portrait of lady (61x51cm-24x20in) oval. 2-Apr-93 Sloan, North Bethesda #2473/R
$4000	£2312	Captain Jonathan Allen (62x50cm-24x20in) 25-Sep-92 Sotheby's Arcade, New York #10/R
$6500	£4088	Portrait of Provost Marshall of Pennsylvania (53x43cm-21x17in) board. 22-Apr-93 Freeman Fine Arts, Philadelphia #1326
$8000	£4624	Angel (73x62cm-29x24in) s.i. after Correggio. 23-Sep-92 Christie's, New York #2/R
$20000	£13333	Portrait of James Fennimore Cooper (71x58cm-28x23in) s. 12-Mar-94 Weschler, Washington #145/R
$270000	£173077	George and Martha Washington (92x74cm-36x29in) s.indist.i.verso pair. 27-May-93 Sotheby's, New York #133/R
$850	*£427*	*Portrait of woman (28x28cm-11x11in) s. pencil after Botticelli. 6-Sep-92 Litchfield Auction Gallery #66*

PEALE, Rembrandt (after) (1778-1860) American
$3040   £2000   Portrait of George Washington, First President of America (48x39cm-19x15in) i.
                     10-Jun-93 Sotheby's, London #871/R

PEALE, Sarah Miriam (1800-1885) American
$2300   £1544   Portrait of Mary Schley (76x64cm-30x25in) 26-Mar-94 Skinner, Bolton #115/R

PEALE, Sarah Miriam (attrib) (1800-1885) American
$2250   £1461   Portrait of Mrs. Luther Ratcliffe of Baltimore (76x64cm-30x25in) i.verso.
                     8-Jul-94 Sloan, North Bethesda #2486/R

PEARCE, Charles Sprague (1851-1914) American
$698   £468   Judas (32x26cm-13x10in) s.i. 23-Jun-93 Libert, Castor, Paris #159/R (F.FR 4000)
$1800   £1184   Portrait of lady (33x24cm-13x9in) s.i. 31-Mar-93 Sotheby's Arcade, New York #97/R
$2800   £1892   Portrait of a country woman (36x27cm-14x11in) s.i.d.1877. 31-Mar-94 Sotheby's
                     Arcade, New York #103/R
$3909   £2659   Jeune picarde (55x46cm-22x18in) s. painted 1905. 8-Apr-94 Ader Tajan, Paris #3/R
                     (F.FR 23000)
$6000   £3468   Woman in profile (41x28cm-16x11in) s. 27-Sep-92 James Bakker, Cambridge #76/R
$11000   £6358   The blue umbrella (60x73cm-24x29in) s.d.8.June 1890 and 9 June st.sig.stretcher.
                     23-Sep-92 Christie's, New York #162/R
$13000   £8725   The letter (56x48cm-22x19in) s. init.stretcher. 2-Dec-93 Sotheby's, New York
                     #21/R
$60000   £40000   Evening, Auvers-sur-Oise (103x175cm-41x69in) s.i. painted c.1880s. 25-May-94
                     Sotheby's, New York #63/R
$72000   £48000   Peasant girl with pitch fork (74x58cm-29x23in) s. 13-Mar-94 Hindman Galleries,
                     Chicago #753/R

PEARLMUTTER, Stella (20th C) American
$2800   £1772   Spring flowers (142x213cm-56x84in) s.d.75. 30-Nov-92 Selkirks, St. Louis #681

PEARLSTEIN, Philip (1924-) American
$4000   £2778   The Seven Hills of Rome (109x124cm-43x49in) s. 6-Mar-93 Louisiana Auction
                     Exchange #131/R
$6500   £4305   Reclining nude (66x56cm-26x22in) s.d.65. 17-Nov-92 Christie's, East, New York
                     #219/R
$14000   £9150   Nude with legs crossed (122x102cm-48x40in) s.d.74. 5-May-93 Christie's, New York
                     #301/R
$20000   £13245   Two female models seated in chairs (122x152cm-48x60in) s.d.72. 19-Nov-92
                     Christie's, New York #368/R
$24000   £15686   Two nudes on yellow and blue drapes (183x152cm-72x60in) s.d.70. 5-May-93
                     Christie's, New York #302/R
$28000   £18919   Two female models on Navajo rug (152x183cm-60x72in) s.d.71. 10-Nov-93 Christie's,
                     New York #147/R
$35000   £23490   Models with wooden mannequin (152x183cm-60x72in) painted 1987. 5-May-94
                     Sotheby's, New York #362/R
$42000   £24706   Male and female models with circus poster and bambino (213x152cm-84x60in)
                     8-Oct-92 Christie's, New York #135/R
$1850   £1186   Standing and seated nude (43x36cm-17x14in) s.d.1963 sepia wash. 10-Dec-92 Sloan,
                     North Bethesda #3034/R
$2750   £1846   Model on stool (74x58cm-29x23in) s.d.1984 conte crayon. 25-Feb-94 Sotheby's, New
                     York #127/R
$5000   £3311   Untitled (74x104cm-29x41in) s.d.76 brush sepia ink. 17-Nov-92 Christie's, East,
                     New York #222/R
$7000   £4698   Model with minstrel marionettes (105x76cm-41x30in) s.d.86 W/C. 25-Feb-94
                     Sotheby's, New York #126/R
$9000   £6250   Male and female models on Navajo blanket (74x104cm-29x41in) W/C. 23-Feb-93
                     Sotheby's, New York #299/R

PEARSON, Albert (?) American?
$2000   £1342   Fourth story view - Chicago (56x36cm-22x14in) s.verso W/C. 28-Mar-93 James
                     Bakker, Cambridge #98/R

PEARSON, Marguerite S (1898-1978) American
$600   £400   Spring flowers against rose (30x41cm-12x16in) s. canvasboard. 22-May-94 James
                     Bakker, Cambridge #100
$650   £446   Spring flowers (41x30cm-16x12in) s. i.verso canvasboard. 10-Feb-94 Skinner,
                     Bolton #162
$650   £446   Spring flowers against rose - still life (41x30cm-16x12in) s. i.verso
                     canvasboard. 10-Feb-94 Skinner, Bolton #159
$770   £503   Boats at harbour (41x36cm-16x14in) s. canvasboard. 14-May-93 Skinner, Bolton
                     #110/R
$900   £612   Flowers in bowl (16x12cm-6x5in) s. board. 10-Jul-93 Young Fine Arts Auctions,
                     Maine #251/R
$1000   £671   Lilies in Chinese jar (41x30cm-16x12in) s. canvas on board. 24-Mar-93 Grogan,
                     Massachussetts #63/R
$2000   £1325   Autumn at Rockport (51x61cm-20x24in) s. board. 28-Nov-92 Young Fine Arts
                     Auctions, Maine #317/R
$2500   £1613   Still life of dead game and fruit (51x61cm-20x24in) s. 15-Jul-94 Du Mouchelle,
                     Detroit #2009/R
$2800   £1867   Summer day, boats (30x36cm-12x14in) s. i.verso board exec.c.1930. 26-Aug-93
                     Skinner, Bolton #92
$4200   £2937   Still life with brass bowl (74x90cm-29x35in) s. 11-Mar-93 Christie's, New York
                     #181/R
$6000   £4196   Silver moon roses (64x76cm-25x30in) s. 11-Mar-93 Christie's, New York #225/R

PEARSON, Marguerite S (1898-1978) American-cont.
$15000	£9494	Tapestry and brocade (92x76cm-36x30in) s. 4-Dec-92 Christie's, New York #61/R
$19000	£12025	The punch bowl (64x76cm-25x30in) s. 4-Dec-92 Christie's, New York #49/R

PEDEMONTE, Adan (1896-1976) Argentinian
$700	£412	Paisaje (22x27cm-9x11in) 29-Sep-92 VerBo, Buenos Aires #87
$700	£412	Paisaje (27x33cm-11x13in) 29-Sep-92 VerBo, Buenos Aires #88
$900	£529	Crepusculo (28x38cm-11x15in) 29-Sep-92 VerBo, Buenos Aires #86
$1500	£781	Naturaleza muerta (70x83cm-28x33in) tempera. 4-Aug-92 VerBo, Buenos Aires #75
$2200	£1146	Paisaje serrano (90x110cm-35x43in) 4-Aug-92 VerBo, Buenos Aires #76

PEDIASO, Manuel (19th C) Mexican
$4000	£2614	Retrato de una mujer con canario (84x71cm-33x28in) s.d.1865. 18-May-93 Sotheby's, New York #101/R

PEEL, Paul (1861-1892) Canadian
$4281	£2835	Boats at pier (23x16cm-9x6in) s.d.1887 panel. 24-Nov-92 Joyner Fine Art, Toronto #112/R (C.D 5500)
$21404	£13990	Study of lady in bonnet (39x33cm-15x13in) s. 19-May-93 Sotheby's, Toronto #300/R (C.D 27000)
$28021	£18557	Dejeuner (38x55cm-15x22in) s.d.1884. 18-Nov-92 Sotheby's, Toronto #31/R (C.D 36000)
$38918	£25773	La jeunesse (146x102cm-57x40in) s.d.1891. 18-Nov-92 Sotheby's, Toronto #115/R (C.D 50000)
$42809	£28351	Resting (46x38cm-18x15in) s.d.92. 18-Nov-92 Sotheby's, Toronto #32/R (C.D 55000)
$64214	£42526	Children fishing (61x96cm-24x38in) s.d.1881. 18-Nov-92 Sotheby's, Toronto #114/R (C.D 82500)
$73943	£48969	Madame Peel at easel with daughter (145x114cm-57x45in) s. 24-Nov-92 Joyner Fine Art, Toronto #95/R (C.D 95000)

PEERS, Gordon Franklin (1909-) American
$5250	£3409	Still life with fruit (91x76cm-36x30in) s. 9-Sep-93 Sotheby's Arcade, New York #275/R

PEIRCE, Waldo (1884-1970) American
$850	£491	Beach at Truro, Cape Cod (63x76cm-25x30in) init.d.54 s.i.d.verso. 25-Sep-92 Sotheby's Arcade, New York #516/R
$2000	£1316	Bathers in brook no.2 (57x93cm-22x37in) s.d.66 s.i.d.66 verso. 31-Mar-93 Sotheby's Arcade, New York #295/R
$600	*£390*	*Badminton (38x54cm-15x21in) s.d.39 W/C. 9-Sep-93 Sotheby's Arcade, New York #182/R*

PEIXOTO, Ernest Clifford (1869-1940) American
$2000	£1316	Lake Como, Italy (79x63cm-31x25in) s. 13-Jun-93 Butterfield & Butterfield, San Francisco #3161/R

PELAEZ, Amelia (1897-1968) Cuban
$5500	£3595	Silla (30x36cm-12x14in) init.d.67. 18-May-93 Sotheby's, New York #228/R
$9500	£6291	Florero (68x40cm-27x16in) init.d.61. 24-Nov-92 Christie's, New York #220/R
$11000	£7432	Naturaleza muerta (58x43cm-23x17in) s.d.1964 paper on canvas. 23-Nov-92 Christie's, New York #148/R
$11000	£7333	Naturaleza muerta (80x101cm-31x40in) painted c.1930. 18-May-94 Sotheby's, New York #362/R
$26000	£17568	Flores (80x57cm-31x22in) s. painted 1930. 23-Nov-93 Christie's, New York #59/R
$40000	£27027	Pajaro Amarillo (122x91cm-48x36in) s.d.1945 paper on canvas. 22-Nov-93 Sotheby's, New York #64/R
$1800	*£1208*	*Retrato de una nina (45x30cm-18x12in) init.d.62 gouache. 24-Feb-94 Sotheby's Arcade, New York #310/R*
$2000	*£1307*	*Untitled (37x51cm-15x20in) init. gouache. 18-May-93 Sotheby's, New York #229/R*
$2600	*£1699*	*Perfil y florero (28x43cm-11x17in) s.d.1928 crayon pen. 17-May-93 Christie's, New York #200/R*
$5000	*£3333*	*Retrato de una dama (65x50cm-26x20in) init.d.63 gouache. 18-May-94 Sotheby's, New York #231/R*
$6000	*£4000*	*Nino con Pajaro (67x52cm-26x20in) s.d.1945 gouache paper laid down on masonite. 18-May-94 Christie's, New York #282/R*
$6500	*£4248*	*Frutera con sandias (60x45cm-24x18in) init.d.64 gouache brush ink. 17-May-93 Christie's, New York #192/R*
$12000	*£7843*	*Naturaleza muerta (61x87cm-24x34in) init.d.60 gouache. 18-May-93 Sotheby's, New York #227/R*
$13000	*£8667*	*Naturaleza muerta (102x76cm-40x30in) s.d.64 gouache board. 18-May-94 Christie's, New York #114/R*
$15000	*£10000*	*Autorretrato (77x56cm-30x22in) s.d.1946 gouache W/C. 18-May-94 Sotheby's, New York #347/R*
$17000	*£11258*	*Autorretrato (56x70cm-22x28in) s.d.1935 graphite board. 24-Nov-92 Christie's, New York #219/R*
$40000	*£27027*	*Autorretrato (90x90cm-35x35in) gouache executed 1946. 22-Nov-93 Sotheby's, New York #53/R*

PELAEZ, Antonio (20th C) Mexican?
$2669	£1804	La veta perdida (90x90cm-35x35in) s.d.1966. 27-Apr-94 Louis Morton, Mexico #673/R (M.P 9000)

PELLAN, Alfred (1906-1990) Canadian
$10306	*£6736*	*Type de la Rue St. Laurent (60x42cm-24x17in) s. gouache painted 1943. 18-May-93 Joyner Fine Art, Toronto #79/R (C.D 13000)*

PELLEW, John (1903-) American
$1300	£850	Saturday night in Astoria Queens NYC (86x69cm-34x27in) s.d.1947. 8-May-93 Young Fine Arts Auctions, Maine #232/R

PELLON, Gina (1925-) Cuban
$4750	£3188	Sansa tenir vouex (91x75cm-36x30in) s. painted 1967. 7-Jan-94 Gary Nader, Miami #114/R

PELTON, Agnes (1881-1961) American
$2100	£1382	Desert blossoms (51x61cm-20x24in) s. 31-Mar-93 Sotheby's Arcade, New York #199/R
$6750	£4592	Marion Fox at eleven months (86x97cm-34x38in) s.d.1925 i.verso. 14-Apr-94 Freeman Fine Arts, Philadelphia #977/R

PENA, Alfonso X (1903-) Mexican
$3870	£2597	Paisaje (65x45cm-26x18in) s.d.1962 board. 1-Dec-93 Louis Morton, Mexico #48/R (M.P 12000)

PENA, Feliciano (20th C) Mexican?
$1424	£962	Tronco (49x58cm-19x23in) s.d.1942. 27-Apr-94 Louis Morton, Mexico #420 (M.P 4800)

PENA, Tonita (1895-1949) American
$650	£419	Corn dancer (23x15cm-9x6in) s. gouache. 9-Jan-93 Skinner, Bolton #44
$800	£516	'Koshare Corn Dance' (36x18cm-14x7in) s. gouache. 9-Jan-93 Skinner, Bolton #260/R
$800	£516	Corn dancer (23x15cm-9x6in) s. gouache. 9-Jan-93 Skinner, Bolton #256/R
$2000	£1342	Conquistadors (33x53cm-13x21in) s. gouache. 26-Jun-93 Skinner, Bolton #117/R

PENDLETON, C V (19th C) American
$850	£570	Locomotive (53x86cm-21x34in) s. dr. wash. 29-Nov-93 Stonington Fine Arts, Stonington #1

PENE DU BOIS, Guy (1884-1958) American
$850	£567	Sketch of a young woman (48x32cm-19x13in) paper. 17-May-94 Christie's, East, New York #529
$1000	£680	Woman in blue dress (56x37cm-22x15in) paper. 15-Nov-93 Christie's, East, New York #197/R
$2800	£1618	Burlesque dancer (20x23cm-8x9in) s. board. 24-Sep-92 Mystic Fine Arts, Connecticut #95/R
$3000	£1734	Summer landscape with clothesline (37x56cm-15x22in) s. paper. 25-Sep-92 Sotheby's Arcade, New York #340/R
$4000	£2703	Enjoying the show (138x107cm-54x42in) s.d.34. 31-Mar-94 Sotheby's Arcade, New York #369/R
$8000	£5298	Portrait of young woman (51x41cm-20x16in) s.d.34. 23-Sep-93 Sotheby's, New York #253/R
$19000	£12025	Study for Emancipation Mural (58x38cm-23x15in) s.d.36. 4-Dec-92 Christie's, New York #155/R
$42000	£26923	Race day, Saratoga (76x102cm-30x40in) s. 27-May-93 Sotheby's, New York #86/R
$42500	£27244	Sunday walkers (61x51cm-24x20in) s.d.36. 27-May-93 Sotheby's, New York #85/R
$50000	£31646	Class reunion (90x73cm-35x29in) s.d.1924. 3-Dec-92 Sotheby's, New York #145/R
$62500	£39557	Waiting for the train (65x51cm-26x20in) s.d.1917 board. 3-Dec-92 Sotheby's, New York #135/R
$65000	£43333	Country wedding (92x74cm-36x29in) s.d.29. 25-May-94 Sotheby's, New York #134/R
$700	£443	Wind-blown tree (35x25cm-14x10in) s. ink. 2-Dec-92 Christie's, East, New York #279/R
$1000	£578	In God's country (43x32cm-17x13in) s. W/C ink. 24-Sep-92 Sotheby's, New York #168/R

PENNELL, Joseph (1860-1926) American
$1300	£751	New York skyline (18x25cm-7x10in) s. pencil W/C paper on board. 25-Sep-92 Sotheby's Arcade, New York #76/R
$1500	£987	Cityscape (25x28cm-10x11in) s. W/C. 11-Jun-93 Du Mouchelle, Detroit #2005
$1600	£925	The small dome (32x42cm-13x17in) s.i.d.88 gouache India ink pencil paper on board. 25-Sep-92 Sotheby's Arcade, New York #81/R
$1700	£1118	New York harbour (30x41cm-12x16in) init.verso gouache panel. 31-Mar-93 Sotheby's Arcade, New York #86/R
$1700	£1076	Bringing home the heroes after the zeppelin explosion (18x24cm-7x9in) mono. i.verso W/C. 3-Dec-92 Sotheby's, New York #46/R
$1750	£1151	Cityscape (25x30cm-10x12in) s. W/C. 11-Jun-93 Du Mouchelle, Detroit #2004/R
$2500	£1634	Front of the Whitehouse by night (35x48cm-14x19in) s.i. ink wash gouache paper on board. 4-May-93 Christie's, East, New York #160/R
$5750	£3639	Brooklyn Bridge, lighting up (26x31cm-10x12in) mono. i.verso W/C. 3-Dec-92 Sotheby's, New York #45/R

PENNOYER, Albert Shelton (1888-1957) American
$4200	£2745	From Peaks Down (63x76cm-25x30in) s. s.i.verso. 4-May-93 Christie's, East, New York #186/R
$1600	£1046	Monterey picnic (58x48cm-23x19in) s. pastel. 30-Jun-94 Mystic Fine Arts, Connecticut #59/R

PEPPER, Charles Hovey (1864-1950) American
$2600	£1529	Black veil (61x43cm-24x17in) s. 5-Oct-92 Grogan, Massachussetts #743/R
$1400	£940	Jimmie Coull. John Barter (46x30cm-18x12in) s.d.1919 gouache board pair. 5-Dec-93 James Bakker, Cambridge #57/R

PEPPER, George Douglas (1903-1962) Canadian
$1638	£1092	Pond inlet (71x91cm-28x36in) 11-May-94 Sotheby's, Toronto #111/R (C.D 2250)

PEPPER, George Douglas (1903-1962) Canadian-cont.
$3641	£2427	East End houses, Bright Street, Toronto (91x107cm-36x42in) s. s.i.verso. 11-May-94 Sotheby's, Toronto #93/R (C.D 5000)
$5097	£3398	Fields and farm (79x91cm-31x36in) s. 11-May-94 Sotheby's, Toronto #113/R (C.D 7000)
$5825	£3883	A summer day in the park (112x142cm-44x56in) s. 11-May-94 Sotheby's, Toronto #45/R (C.D 8000)
$10922	£7282	Blue Rocks, Nova Scotia (92x107cm-36x42in) s. s.i.verso. 11-May-94 Sotheby's, Toronto #72/R (C.D 15000)

PEPPER, Kathleen Daly see DALY, Kathleen

PERBANDT, Carl von (1832-1911) American
| $1100 | £738 | Sunset grazing (76x51cm-30x20in) 8-Dec-93 Butterfield & Butterfield, San Francisco #3339/R |
| $9500 | £6597 | Artist's children painting (48x64cm-19x25in) s.i.d.73. 7-Mar-93 Butterfield & Butterfield, San Francisco #46/R |

PEREHUDOFF, William (20th C) Canadian?
$628	£410	ACP 82-28 (56x76cm-22x30in) acrylic paper. 10-May-93 Hodgins, Calgary #31 (C.D 800)
$646	£431	Refinery (28x33cm-11x13in) s. masonite painted c.1950's. 30-May-94 Hodgins, Calgary #334 a (C.D 900)
$1189	£777	Arcturus no.9 (35x44cm-14x17in) s.d.1972 verso acrylic. 19-May-93 Sotheby's, Toronto #372/R (C.D 1500)
$1415	£896	Okema no.6 (81x229cm-32x90in) s.d.1974 verso acrylic. 30-Nov-92 Ritchie, Toronto #255/R (C.D 1800)

PEREIRA, Jose (20th C) Cuban
| $583 | £369 | Composition (66x50cm-26x20in) s. gouache. 5-Dec-92 Kunstgalerij de Vuyst, Lokeren #217 (B.FR 19000) |

PEREYRA, Indalecio (1893-1973) Argentinian
| $900 | £596 | Bariloche (30x40cm-12x16in) 11-Nov-92 VerBo, Buenos Aires #81 |
| $900 | £529 | Ranchos de San Isidro (30x40cm-12x16in) painted 1930. 29-Sep-92 VerBo, Buenos Aires #90 |

PEREZ ALCALA, Ricardo (1939-) Mexican
$1910	£1224	Casa de pueblo (26x36cm-10x14in) s. W/C. 29-Apr-93 Louis Morton, Mexico #139 (M.P 6000)
$1910	£1224	La tarde (38x28cm-15x11in) s. W/C. 29-Apr-93 Louis Morton, Mexico #42 (M.P 6000)
$10320	£6926	Casa azul (75x55cm-30x22in) s.d.1990 W/C. 1-Dec-93 Louis Morton, Mexico #130/R (M.P 32000)
$10965	£7359	El aposento (75x55cm-30x22in) s. W/C. 1-Dec-93 Louis Morton, Mexico #66/R (M.P 34000)

PEREZ BARRADAS, Antonio (?) South American
| $650 | £439 | Naturaleza muerta (45x75cm-18x30in) s. 25-Apr-94 Gomensoro, Montevideo #23 |

PEREZ BARRADAS, Rafael (?) South American
| $700 | £461 | El carro del hortelano (18x27cm-7x11in) s. pencil ink W/C dr. 31-May-93 Gomensoro, Montevideo #42 |

PEREZ DE HOLGUIN, Melchor (1665-c.1724) Bolivian
| $3250 | £2138 | St. Christopher and the Christ Child (122x104cm-48x41in) s.d.1714. 20-Jul-94 Sotheby's Arcade, New York #54/R |
| $7000 | £4575 | San Cristobal (145x98cm-57x39in) painted c.1715. 18-May-93 Sotheby's, New York #83/R |

PERINETTI, Jose C (20th C) South American
| $1200 | £779 | Formas (51x36cm-20x14in) s. mixed media. 30-Aug-93 Gomensoro, Montevideo #88 |

PERKINS, Granville (1830-1895) American
$850	£556	Seascape (46x76cm-18x30in) s.d.1891. 18-Sep-93 Young Fine Arts Auctions, Maine #237/R
$850	£491	Rocky stream (41x51cm-16x20in) s. 25-Sep-92 Sotheby's Arcade, New York #22/R
$1000	£654	Coastal village scene (30x46cm-12x18in) s. 30-Jun-94 Mystic Fine Arts, Connecticut #223/R
$1100	£573	Hilly harbour scene with boats (33x58cm-13x23in) canvas on cardboard. 5-Aug-92 Boos Gallery, Michigan #638
$2500	£1689	Beach scene with sailing ship dismasted and other shipping at night (36x61cm-14x24in) s.d.1889. 23-Oct-93 San Rafael Auction Galleries #230
$1450	£973	Anne of Key Port NJ (38x56cm-15x22in) s.d.1893 W/C. 24-Mar-94 Mystic Fine Arts, Connecticut #123

PERLIN, Bernard (1918-) American
$800	£523	Textile inspection (51x66cm-20x26in) s. tempera. 8-May-93 Young Fine Arts Auctions, Maine #237/R
$1400	£915	Study for criminal court (46x71cm-18x28in) s.d.1961 tempera. 8-May-93 Young Fine Arts Auctions, Maine #236/R
$600	£385	Soldiers and prisoners (41x51cm-16x20in) d.1945 pen pencil wash htd white. 8-Dec-92 Swann Galleries, New York #237/R

PERRE, Henri (?) Canadian?
$674   £440   Figures on country road (30x43cm-12x17in) s.d.78 W/C. 19-May-93 Sotheby's, Toronto #6/R (C.D 850)

PERRON, Louis Paul (1919-) Canadian
$680   £459   Retour a la maison (48x63cm-19x25in) s. pastel. 23-Nov-93 Fraser Pinneys, Quebec #438 (C.D 900)

PERRY, Enoch Wood (1831-1915) American
$1600   £1060   Afternoon repose, a Japanese lady (32x41cm-13x16in) s. board. 15-Jun-94 Butterfield & Butterfield, San Francisco #4436/R
$4750   £3299   Girl carrying water (51x41cm-20x16in) s.d.82. 27-Feb-93 Young Fine Arts Auctions, Maine #229/R
$12000   £8392   Chinese children in garden (32x41cm-13x16in) s.d.63 i.verso board. 10-Mar-93 Sotheby's, New York #29/R
$16000   £11189   Chinese family (31x39cm-12x15in) s.d.63 i.verso board. 10-Mar-93 Sotheby's, New York #28/R

PERRY, Lilla Cabot (1848-1933) American
$5500   £3595   Red tunic - portrait of Edith Perry (46x38cm-18x15in) s.d.88. 14-May-93 Skinner, Bolton #151/R
$26000   £16456   Scent of roses (100x76cm-39x30in) s. 4-Dec-92 Christie's, New York #30/R
$32000   £20253   The pink rose (102x76cm-40x30in) s.d.1910. 4-Dec-92 Christie's, New York #7/R

PERRY, Roland Hinton (1870-1949) American
$650   £439   Autumn flowers (94x76cm-37x30in) s.d.1925. 27-Nov-93 Young Fine Arts Auctions, Maine #259/R

PERUVIAN COLONIAL SCHOOL, 17th C
$5736   £3519   Traicion de Judas, Cristo y centurion (57x75cm-22x30in) 14-Oct-92 Ansorena, Madrid #74/R (S.P 600000)
$9560   £5865   La Ascension de la Virgen (162x110cm-64x43in) 14-Oct-92 Ansorena, Madrid #79/R (S.P 1000000)

PERUVIAN SCHOOL
$13000   £8609   Coronacion de la Virgen (135x105cm-53x41in) 23-Nov-92 Sotheby's, New York #115/R

PETERDI, Gabor (1915-) American/Hungarian
$1600   £1026   Kahulu III (76x102cm-30x40in) W/C painted 1972. 8-Dec-92 Swann Galleries, New York #239/R

PETERS, Carl W (1897-1988) American
$1000   £671   The general store (51x61cm-20x24in) s. 24-Jun-93 Mystic Fine Arts, Connecticut #266
$1200   £784   Gathering outside the church (51x61cm-20x24in) s. 18-Sep-93 James Bakker, Cambridge #178
$1200   £805   The fog (64x76cm-25x30in) s. 5-Dec-93 James Bakker, Cambridge #11/R
$1200   £795   Autumn hunting scene (64x76cm-25x30in) s. 21-Nov-92 James Bakker, Cambridge #301/R
$1200   £784   Village in winter (41x51cm-16x20in) s. 8-May-93 Young Fine Arts Auctions, Maine #246/R
$1200   £694   Torpedoed (102x91cm-40x36in) s.i. i.stretcher. 25-Sep-92 Sotheby's Arcade, New York #426/R
$1300   £818   Beach scene with figures (51x61cm-20x24in) s. 25-Apr-93 James Bakker, Cambridge #124/R
$1400   £979   Rockport Yard (51x61cm-20x24in) s. 7-Feb-93 James Bakker, Cambridge #118
$1400   £915   The willow (51x61cm-20x24in) s. 18-Sep-93 James Bakker, Cambridge #15/R
$1400   £927   Winter scene with figure (51x61cm-20x24in) s. 21-Nov-92 James Bakker, Cambridge #255/R
$1400   £881   On the farm (51x61cm-20x24in) s. 25-Apr-93 James Bakker, Cambridge #153/R
$1500   £758   Girl by stream (61x76cm-24x30in) st.studio verso. 28-Aug-92 Young Fine Arts Auctions, Maine #248/R
$1500   £1007   Gloucester Docks (51x61cm-20x24in) s. 5-Dec-93 James Bakker, Cambridge #12/R
$1600   £1074   Springtime (51x61cm-20x24in) s. 5-Dec-93 James Bakker, Cambridge #10/R
$1600   £1074   Winter landscape (51x61cm-20x24in) s. 5-Dec-93 James Bakker, Cambridge #88/R
$1600   £1067   Winter street scene (51x61cm-20x24in) s. 22-May-94 James Bakker, Cambridge #107
$1700   £1111   Boat painters (51x61cm-20x24in) s. 18-Sep-93 James Bakker, Cambridge #13/R
$1800   £1132   Docks - low tide (51x61cm-20x24in) s. 25-Apr-93 James Bakker, Cambridge #33/R
$1900   £1275   Lanes Cove, Lansville, Gloucester (51x61cm-20x24in) s. i.verso. 6-May-94 Skinner, Bolton #108/R
$1900   £1275   Barn in winter (51x61cm-20x24in) s. 26-Mar-94 James Bakker, Cambridge #13/R
$2000   £1342   Path to the harbour (51x61cm-20x24in) s. 26-Mar-94 James Bakker, Cambridge #33
$2100   £1391   Gloucester harbour scene (51x61cm-20x24in) s. 21-Nov-92 James Bakker, Cambridge #231/R
$2400   £1589   Winter stream (64x76cm-25x30in) s. 21-Nov-92 James Bakker, Cambridge #262/R
$2500   £1678   Low tide - Rockport (64x76cm-25x30in) s. 28-Mar-93 James Bakker, Cambridge #177 a
$2500   £1773   At the Whorf Fairpont (71x64cm-28x25in) s. 12-Feb-93 Du Mouchelle, Detroit #2110/R
$2700   £1888   Dock scene with figures (51x61cm-20x24in) s. 7-Feb-93 James Bakker, Cambridge #28
$3500   £2448   Rockport Docks (51x61cm-20x24in) indist.s. 7-Feb-93 James Bakker, Cambridge #145/R
$3600   £1818   Rockport Harbour, Massachusetts (64x76cm-25x30in) s. 30-Aug-92 Litchfield Auction Gallery #232
$3750   £2517   Fish house (64x76cm-25x30in) s. 28-Mar-93 James Bakker, Cambridge #177 b

PETERS, Charles Rollo (1862-1928) American
$800	£544	Big Anchor (24x46cm-9x18in) s. 15-Nov-93 Christie's, East, New York #114
$1700	£1118	Fishing boats and clam diggers (22x27cm-9x11in) s.i.d.1888 board. 13-Jun-93 Butterfield & Butterfield, San Francisco #786/R
$2250	£1481	Adobe at night (41x61cm-16x24in) s. 13-Jun-93 Butterfield & Butterfield, San Francisco #788/R
$2250	£1490	Nocturnal, 'Santa Paula Mission' (41x51cm-16x20in) s. 14-Jun-94 John Moran, Pasadena #36
$2250	£1481	Fishing boats in creek (27x35cm-11x14in) s.indist.i.d.1894 panel. 13-Jun-93 Butterfield & Butterfield, San Francisco #787/R
$2500	£1678	Nocturne, home of Joachim Murietta (20x30cm-8x12in) s. 8-Dec-93 Butterfield & Butterfield, San Francisco #3419/R
$2500	£1656	Adobe House by moonlight (48x63cm-19x25in) s. 15-Jun-94 Butterfield & Butterfield, San Francisco #4651/R
$2500	£1736	Nocturne (53x63cm-21x25in) s. 7-Mar-93 Butterfield & Butterfield, San Francisco #85/R
$3750	£2206	Crescent moon (41x61cm-16x24in) s. 4-Oct-92 Butterfield & Butterfield, Los Angeles #98/R
$6500	£4514	Evening reflection, Mt Tamalpais, California (48x63cm-19x25in) s. 7-Mar-93 Butterfield & Butterfield, San Francisco #84/R
$6500	£4514	Nocturne on Monterey Coast (25x36cm-10x14in) s. 7-Mar-93 Butterfield & Butterfield, San Francisco #86/R
$8000	£4624	Dusk (89x63cm-35x25in) s. 24-Sep-92 Sotheby's, New York #100/R

PETERSEN, Einar Cortsen (1885-1986) American
$1100	£728	Landscape - Hangman Creek (41x51cm-16x20in) s.d.1914. 14-Jun-94 John Moran, Pasadena #112
$1800	£1059	View from garden (81x66cm-32x26in) s. 4-Oct-92 Butterfield & Butterfield, Los Angeles #147/R

PETERSEN, Roland (1926-) American
$3250	£2057	Figure on beach (36x46cm-14x18in) s.d.1969. 25-Oct-92 Butterfield & Butterfield, San Francisco #2309/R
$4000	£2703	Afternoon picnic (122x183cm-48x72in) s.d.60. 21-Oct-93 Butterfield & Butterfield, San Francisco #2785/R

PETERSON, Jane (1876-1965) American
$700	£467	Spring (25x36cm-10x14in) s. i.verso canvasboard. 26-Aug-93 Skinner, Bolton #170
$850	£570	Tulips (76x61cm-30x24in) s. 5-Dec-93 James Bakker, Cambridge #20/R
$900	£588	Meadows and rolling hills (33x41cm-13x16in) s. board. 17-Sep-93 Skinner, Bolton #277/R
$950	£638	Florida beach scene (51x61cm-20x24in) s.d.1946 canvasboard. 5-Dec-93 James Bakker, Cambridge #5/R
$1200	£784	Evening glow (28x35cm-11x14in) s. i.verso board. 22-May-93 Weschler, Washington #115/R
$1200	£784	Country lane, late afternoon (46x46cm-18x18in) s. i.verso. 17-Sep-93 Skinner, Bolton #279/R
$1350	£854	Stage Fort Beach (46x46cm-18x18in) s. i.verso board. 5-Dec-92 Louisiana Auction Exchange #57/R
$1600	£1081	Pansies (46x61cm-18x24in) 10-Aug-93 Stonington Fine Arts, Stonington #162/R
$1800	£1040	Trade winds (61x61cm-24x24in) 25-Sep-92 Sotheby's Arcade, New York #407/R
$2000	£1399	Bouquet of roses (81x81cm-32x32in) s. 14-Mar-93 Hindman Galleries, Chicago #37/R
$2600	£1757	Sailboats (31x40cm-12x16in) s. board. 31-Mar-94 Sotheby's Arcade, New York #230/R
$2800	£1892	Toucan in a palm tree (43x46cm-17x18in) s. board. 5-Nov-93 Skinner, Bolton #177/R
$2979	£1910	Still life - vase of flowers (61x52cm-24x20in) s. 7-Dec-92 Waddingtons, Toronto #1515/R (C.D 3800)
$3250	£2181	Floral still life (76x61cm-30x24in) s. 8-Dec-93 Butterfield & Butterfield, San Francisco #3515/R
$3500	£2448	Vase of zinnias (76x61cm-30x24in) s. 11-Mar-93 Christie's, New York #205/R
$3800	£2533	Pink roses (81x81cm-32x32in) s. 23-May-94 Christie's, East, New York #190/R
$4250	£2891	Mixed flowers (76x61cm-30x24in) s. 9-Jul-93 Sloan, North Bethesda #2776/R
$4500	£3041	Flowers in a vase (61x51cm-24x20in) s. 31-Mar-94 Sotheby's Arcade, New York #297/R
$5000	£2890	Orchids (76x61cm-30x24in) s. d.1943stretcher. 23-Sep-92 Christie's, New York #207/R
$5500	£3179	Petunias (61x61cm-24x24in) s. painted 1925-35. 23-Sep-92 Christie's, New York #206/R
$6000	£3846	Dock scene (43x43cm-17x17in) 12-Dec-92 Weschler, Washington #79/R
$7000	£4430	Still life with zinnias (61x72cm-24x28in) s. 3-Dec-92 Sotheby's, New York #121/R
$7700	£5033	Florida trees and sand in summertime (61x76cm-24x30in) s. canvasboard. 14-May-93 Skinner, Bolton #175/R
$9000	£6000	The harbour (46x61cm-18x24in) s. i.stretcher painted c.1921. 17-Mar-94 Sotheby's, New York #126/R
$9500	£6291	Floral still life in yellow pot (76x102cm-30x40in) 13-Nov-92 Skinner, Bolton #186/R
$14000	£9333	Road by the waterfront (46x46cm-18x18in) s. canvas on board. 16-Mar-94 Christie's, New York #91/R
$35000	£22152	Quiet harbour, Gloucester (81x81cm-32x32in) s. 4-Dec-92 Christie's, New York #86/R
$42500	£28333	Marche aux fleurs (43x58cm-17x23in) s.i.d.1908. 25-May-94 Sotheby's, New York #88/R
$950	*£638*	*San Giorgio Venice (30x30cm-12x12in) s. gouache board painted 1923 study. 2-Dec-93 Swann Galleries, New York #237*
$1000	£671	Parrots (28x43cm-11x17in) s. W/C. 5-Dec-93 James Bakker, Cambridge #6/R
$1100	£705	*Three parrots (48x74cm-19x29in) s. W/C. 24-May-93 Grogan, Massachussetts #370/R*

PETERSON, Jane (1876-1965) American-cont.
$1250	£833	Parrot (43x58cm-17x23in) s. W/C. 20-May-94 Du Mouchelle, Detroit #2343/R
$1500	£1000	Pelicans (36x56cm-14x22in) s. W/C. 20-May-94 Du Mouchelle, Detroit #2342/R
$1600	£1081	Woodlands (43x58cm-17x23in) s. mixed media. 10-Aug-93 Stonington Fine Arts, Stonington #141
$1980	£1294	Florida beach and palms (36x53cm-14x21in) s. W/C ink paperboard. 14-May-93 Skinner, Bolton #176/R
$2100	£1409	Italian courtyard (36x25cm-14x10in) s. gouache chl. 4-Dec-93 Louisiana Auction Exchange #62/R
$3000	£1987	Apple orchard in bloom (46x61cm-18x24in) s. i.verso gouache chl. 22-Sep-93 Christie's, New York #129/R
$3750	£2451	Gloucester River (46x58cm-18x23in) s. gouache graphite. 15-May-93 Dunning's, Illinois #1093/R
$4000	£2797	Palisades, New York (46x61cm-18x24in) s. i.verso gouache chl. 11-Mar-93 Christie's, New York #228/R
$4000	£2564	Vancouver water front (46x61cm-18x24in) d.verso gouache chl. 12-Dec-92 Weschler, Washington #77/R
$5000	£2890	Low Library at Columbia University, New York (46x61cm-18x24in) s. i.verso gouache W/C chl. 23-Sep-92 Christie's, New York #179/R
$5500	£3571	Road in autumn (46x58cm-18x23in) gouache. 8-Jul-94 Sloan, North Bethesda #2721/R
$8500	£5743	Street in old Constantinople (46x61cm-18x24in) s. i.verso gouache pencil executed c.1924. 31-Mar-94 Sotheby's Arcade, New York #431/R
$14000	£8861	Crowded street in Venice (61x45cm-24x18in) s. gouache chl board. 4-Dec-92 Christie's, New York #41/R
$15000	£9615	Docks at Gloucester (46x61cm-18x24in) s. gouache chl. 12-Dec-92 Weschler, Washington #73/R

PETION, Carlos (1939-) Haitian
$652	£418	Jungle imaginaire (61x51cm-24x20in) s. 14-Dec-92 Hoebanx, Paris #157/R (F.FR 3500)

PETO, John F (1854-1907) American
$11000	£7237	My pipe and mug (20x15cm-8x6in) s.d.84 s.i.d.1894 verso. 13-Jun-93 Butterfield & Butterfield, San Francisco #3115/R
$12000	£7595	Still life of bulletin board (56x41cm-22x16in) 2-Dec-92 Christie's, East, New York #127/R
$16000	£9249	Still life with pipe, book and matches (11x23cm-4x9in) panel. 24-Sep-92 Sotheby's, New York #3/R
$17000	£11333	My pipe and mug (21x16cm-8x6in) s.indis.d. s.i.d.1894verso. 25-May-94 Sotheby's, New York #1/R
$22000	£14667	Artist's palette with pipe and pouch (23x16cm-9x6in) i.verso panel. 17-Mar-94 Sotheby's, New York #12/R
$40000	£25641	Still life with mug, pipe and oyster crackers (15x23cm-6x9in) academy board painted c.1880-90. 27-May-93 Sotheby's, New York #120/R
$65000	£43333	Tabletop with violin (76x114cm-30x45in) 26-May-94 Christie's, New York #30/R

PETTIBONE, Richard (1938-) American
$700	£470	Ingres, the Comtesse d'Haussonville, 1845, blue goblet and self portrait (27x20cm-11x8in) s.i.d.1976 verso. 24-Feb-94 Sotheby's Arcade, New York #461/R
$1000	£671	1938 Mercedes, silver rectangle, Andy Warhol, 19 cents, 1962 and Frank Stella (39x29cm-15x11in) s.i.d.1978 verso four joined parts. 24-Feb-94 Sotheby's Arcade, New York #460/R

PETTIBONE, Shirley (20th C) American?
$1200	£833	Shoreline-Brighton beach (66x86cm-26x34in) s.i.d.1973on overlap acrylic. 26-Feb-93 Sotheby's Arcade, New York #400/R

PETTORUTI, Emilio (1892-1971) Argentinian
$15000	£10067	Interior (18x13cm-7x5in) s.d.1946 board. 7-Jan-94 Gary Nader, Miami #9/R
$16000	£10596	Bodegon (16x22cm-6x9in) s. board. 23-Nov-92 Sotheby's, New York #150/R
$20000	£13245	Verano (86x60cm-34x24in) s.d.69 s.i.d.1969 verso. 24-Nov-92 Christie's, New York #153/R
$40000	£23121	Temporal en Tegernsee , board. 23-Sep-92 Roldan & Cia, Buenos Aires #31
$70000	£46358	Costruzione Antica (28x36cm-11x14in) s.d.916 board. 23-Nov-92 Sotheby's, New York #35/R
$200000	£132450	El Cantante (104x70cm-41x28in) s.d.30 s.i.d.1930 verso panel. 24-Nov-92 Christie's, New York #11/R
$11000	£7285	Cuadernos de musica (20x26cm-8x10in) s.d.1919 brush ink. 24-Nov-92 Christie's, New York #214/R

PEYRAUD, F C (1858-1948) American
$600	£400	Top of the dunes (69x53cm-27x21in) 3-Jun-94 Douglas, South Deerfield #3

PEYRAUD, Frank Charles (1858-1948) American
$1000	£654	River landscape (30x38cm-12x15in) s. i.d.Feb.21,1930verso board. 16-May-93 Hindman Galleries, Chicago #4
$3250	£2152	Pic Nic (91x122cm-36x48in) s.d.1912. 28-Nov-92 Dunning's, Illinois #1010
$4000	£2721	Cattle in pasture (51x61cm-20x24in) s. board. 17-Apr-94 Hanzel Galleries, Chicago #27

PEYTON, Bertha (1871-1950) American
$1800	£1154	Fishermen loading ice (48x58cm-19x23in) s. W/C gouache. 9-Dec-92 Butterfield & Butterfield, San Francisco #3917/R

PEZZINO, Antonio (20th C) South American
$800 £537 Constructivo (81x61cm-32x24in) s. board. 29-Nov-93 Gomensoro, Montevideo #58/R

PFAFF, Judy (1946-) American
$700 £470 Quintana Roo (135x77cm-53x30in) s.i.d.1980verso paper collage. 3-May-94 Christie's, East, New York #160/R
$1600 £1046 Untitled (81x107cm-32x42in) adhesive plastics graph paper executed 1988. 22-Dec-92 Christie's, East, New York #54
$2235 £1500 Magic (226x108cm-89x43in) s. paper collage on mylar executed 1981. 21-Jun-93 Christie's, S. Kensington #149/R

PFEIFFER, Gordon (1899-1983) Canadian
$1311 £874 Roadside flowers (61x76cm-24x30in) s. board. 11-May-94 Sotheby's, Toronto #201/R (C.D 1800)

PHELAN, Charles T (1840-?) American
$650 £445 Shepherd and flock (46x64cm-18x25in) s. board. 19-Feb-94 Young Fine Arts Auctions, Maine #164/R
$675 £472 Sheep in landscape (30x41cm-12x16in) s. 11-Mar-93 Mystic Fine Arts, Connecticut #63/R
$700 £496 Homeward (36x25cm-14x10in) s. 21-Feb-93 Hart Gallery, Houston #1
$700 £467 Sheep grazing (43x67cm-17x26in) s.d.94. 17-May-94 Christie's, East, New York #505
$950 £617 Summer afternoon in the country (25x36cm-10x14in) s. panel. 9-Sep-93 Sotheby's Arcade, New York #107

PHELAN, Ellen (1943-) American
$4800 £3137 Floating world (116x185cm-46x73in) linen executed 1986 after Corot. 22-Dec-92 Christie's, East, New York #55

PHELPS, Edith Catlin (1875-1961) American
$650 £430 The white Madonna (61x76cm-24x30in) s.d.1940 masonite. 28-Sep-93 John Moran, Pasadena #270
$1200 £833 Landscape with carriage (66x48cm-26x19in) s. 6-Mar-93 Louisiana Auction Exchange #18/R

PHELPS, William Preston (1848-1923) American
$1400 £979 Landscape with cows at rest (25x36cm-10x14in) s. i.verso. 12-Mar-93 Skinner, Bolton #173/R
$1600 £1074 A Venetian harbour view (41x61cm-16x24in) s. 4-Mar-94 Skinner, Bolton #218/R

PHILIPP, Robert (1895-1981) American
$650 £434 Dancers (41x61cm-16x24in) s. s.i.verso. 23-May-94 Christie's, East, New York #286
$1000 £658 Black haired girl (51x41cm-20x16in) s. s.d.1965 verso. 13-Jun-93 Butterfield & Butterfield, San Francisco #3263/R
$1000 £654 Young girl in bonnet (44x35cm-17x14in) s. masonite. 4-May-93 Christie's, East, New York #278
$1000 £658 Self-portrait with black hat (36x31cm-14x12in) s. 31-Mar-93 Sotheby's Arcade, New York #431/R
$1000 £658 Friends (77x65cm-30x26in) s. s.d.1960 verso. 13-Jun-93 Butterfield & Butterfield, San Francisco #3262/R
$1200 £811 Rochelle in red kimono (76x63cm-30x25in) s. s.i.d.1966 verso. 31-Mar-94 Sotheby's Arcade, New York #335/R
$1300 £872 At the restaurant (28x36cm-11x14in) s. 5-Mar-94 Louisiana Auction Exchange #11/R
$1400 £809 The white hat (51x30cm-20x12in) s. s.i.verso. 25-Sep-92 Sotheby's Arcade, New York #425/R
$1750 £1108 Vacation time (64x76cm-25x30in) s. 2-Dec-92 Boos Gallery, Michigan #793/R
$1900 £1284 The white hat. Twin sisters (38x25cm-15x10in) s. one s.i.d.1951 verso pair. 31-Mar-94 Sotheby's Arcade, New York #377/R
$2000 £1333 Seated nude (33x25cm-13x10in) s. 26-May-94 Sloan, North Bethesda #2248/R
$2000 £1156 Still lifes of flowers and fruit (114x56cm-45x22in) s. pair. 25-Sep-92 Sotheby's Arcade, New York #412/R
$2200 £1392 Woman in red seated with book (79x62cm-31x24in) s. s.d.1947verso. 2-Dec-92 Christie's, East, New York #352/R
$2200 £1410 Young girl reading (46x38cm-18x15in) s. 17-Dec-92 Mystic Fine Arts, Connecticut #207/R
$2300 £1554 No ice and olives at the cocktail lounge (28x36cm-11x14in) s. 5-Nov-93 Skinner, Bolton #161/R
$2400 £1678 Port of Weehawken (51x77cm-20x30in) s. s.verso. 11-Mar-93 Christie's, New York #208/R
$2400 £1569 Woman in contemplation (63x48cm-25x19in) s. 4-May-93 Christie's, East, New York #248/R
$2500 £1678 Two young girls with vase of flowers (81x66cm-32x26in) s. s.d.1960 verso. 24-Mar-93 Grogan, Massachussetts #140/R
$2750 £1858 Fixing her hair (91x76cm-36x30in) s. 31-Mar-94 Sotheby's Arcade, New York #344/R
$3200 £2025 In Central Park (62x122cm-24x48in) s. s.i.d.1977verso. 2-Dec-92 Christie's, East, New York #260/R
$3250 £2181 Young girl by harbour (64x76cm-25x30in) s. 24-Mar-93 Grogan, Massachussetts #135/R
$3800 £2657 Friends (91x76cm-36x30in) s. s.i.verso. 11-Mar-93 Christie's, New York #216/R
$4000 £2312 Siesta (51x66cm-20x26in) s. 25-Sep-92 Sotheby's Arcade, New York #287/R
$8000 £4624 Olympia (95x127cm-37x50in) s. s.i.verso. 23-Sep-92 Christie's, New York #264/R
$1300 £884 Nightclub interior (46x56cm-18x22in) s. W/C. 16-Apr-94 Young Fine Arts Auctions, Maine #200/R

PHILIPPOTEAUX, Paul Dominique (1846-?) American
$2300	£1544	Snake charmer. Egyptian sunset (26x33cm-10x13in) s. panel pair. 19-Jan-94 Sotheby's Arcade, New York #421/R
$9636	£6600	The Odalisque (28x20cm-11x8in) s. panel. 11-Feb-94 Christie's, London #90 a/R
$10000	£6711	Battle scene (72x100cm-28x39in) s. 19-Jan-94 Sotheby's Arcade, New York #404/R
$28120	£19000	Outside the coffee house (81x68cm-32x27in) s. 19-Mar-93 Christie's, London #60/R

PHILIPS, F A (19th C) American?
$914	£618	Farmyard animals in a landscape (19x26cm-7x10in) s.d.1872 panel. 18-Apr-94 Hotel de Ventes Horta, Brussels #166 (B.FR 32000)
$1372	£927	Farmyard animals in a Romantic landscape (19x26cm-7x10in) s.d.1872 panel. 18-Apr-94 Hotel de Ventes Horta, Brussels #165/R (B.FR 48000)
$2044	£1400	Domestic animals by farmstead. Cattle, sheep and chickens in meadow (20x25cm-8x10in) s.d.1872 panel pair. 10-Feb-94 Christie's, S. Kensington #29

PHILLIPP, Werner (1897-1982) American
$1300	£861	San Francisco rooftops (51x61cm-20x24in) s.d.39. 15-Jun-94 Butterfield & Butterfield, San Francisco #4584/R

PHILLIPS, Ammi (1787-1865) American
$2000	£1351	Portrait of seated gentleman (76x64cm-30x25in) painted c.1830. 30-Oct-93 Skinner, Bolton #270 a/R
$7000	£4575	Portrait of young gentleman holding copy of Milton's Works (30x24cm-12x9in) s.i.d.July 20th,1823verso. 31-Oct-92 Skinner, Bolton #228/R
$20000	£13699	A lady with ruffled muslin bonnet, probably Amenia, NY, 1826 (79x64cm-31x25in) 12-Feb-94 Boos Gallery, Michigan #550/R

PHILLIPS, Ammi (attrib) (1787-1865) American
$1600	£1074	Catherine Douw Hoffman Philip. Martin Hoffman Philip (76x64cm-30x25in) pair. 1-Dec-93 Doyle, New York #67/R

PHILLIPS, Bert G (1868-1956) American
$3250	£2083	Song to the moon (30x39cm-12x15in) s. canvas on board. 9-Dec-92 Butterfield & Butterfield, San Francisco #4003/R
$5500	£3819	Cottonwoods after rain (41x51cm-16x20in) s. board. 27-Feb-93 Young Fine Arts Auctions, Maine #232/R
$12000	£6936	Taos Indian and pony (36x36cm-14x14in) s. board. 24-Sep-92 Sotheby's, New York #75/R
$15000	£9494	Taos Indian with his horse (23x30cm-9x12in) s. canvasboard. 3-Dec-92 Sotheby's, New York #68/R

PHILLIPS, Gordon (1927-) American
$6500	£3757	Sadie's back in town (89x107cm-35x42in) s. 24-Sep-92 Sotheby's, New York #72/R
$7500	£5034	Rise and shine (61x51cm-24x20in) s. 2-Dec-93 Sotheby's, New York #80/R

PHILLIPS, John Campbell (1873-?) American
$650	£436	Moonlight, Dover Plains, New York (33x38cm-13x15in) s.d.1908verso. 26-Mar-94 James Bakker, Cambridge #61/R

PHILLIPS, Walter Joseph (1884-1963) American
$1087	£725	Rocky mountain waterfall (53x36cm-21x14in) s.d.57. 6-Jun-94 Waddingtons, Toronto #1286/R (C.D 1500)
$589	*£380*	*Fishing village (27x39cm-11x15in) s.d.13 W/C. 15-Jul-94 Christie's, London #92/R*
$792	*£546*	*Study of South African tree (33x48cm-13x19in) d.06 W/C. 15-Feb-93 Lunds, Victoria #2 (C.D 1000)*
$905	*£615*	*Morning (18x19cm-7x7in) s.i. W/C. 15-Nov-93 Hodgins, Calgary #252 (C.D 1200)*
$1020	*£667*	*Untitled - English landscape (16x24cm-6x9in) init. W/C. 10-May-93 Hodgins, Calgary #89 (C.D 1300)*
$1311	*£874*	*The garden wall. Country village path , s. one d.1911 W/C two. 11-May-94 Sotheby's, Toronto #252 (C.D 1800)*
$1491	*£974*	*Untitled - landscape (24x20cm-9x8in) s. W/C. 10-May-93 Hodgins, Calgary #277/R (C.D 1900)*
$1505	*£1038*	*Coastal scene (30x51cm-12x20in) W/C. 15-Feb-93 Lunds, Victoria #1 (C.D 1900)*
$1883	*£1231*	*Untitled - Prairie harvest scene (25x36cm-10x14in) s. W/C. 10-May-93 Hodgins, Calgary #51/R (C.D 2400)*
$2040	*£1333*	*San Jose Mission, San Antonio, Texas (39x48cm-15x19in) s.d.1955 W/C. 10-May-93 Hodgins, Calgary #300 (C.D 2600)*
$2638	*£1724*	*Lighthouse at Kincardine (36x46cm-14x18in) s.d.45 W/C. 6-Oct-93 Maynards, Vancouver #320 (C.D 3500)*
$4716	*£3186*	*Untitled - Vermilion Lake and Mount Rundle (34x55cm-13x22in) s.d.1946 W/C. 25-Apr-94 Levis, Calgary #259/R (C.D 6500)*

PHIPPEN, George (1915-1966) American
$4000	£2312	Headed for the trap (61x91cm-24x36in) s.i. i.stretcher. 23-Sep-92 Christie's, New York #112/R

PI, Oqwa (1899-?) American
$1600	£1067	Eagle dancers (20x18cm-8x7in) s. gouache. 29-Jan-94 Skinner, Bolton #199/R

PICILLO, Joseph (20th C) American
$850	£535	Study of horse (88x74cm-35x29in) s.i.d.February 1981 graphite chl. 25-Apr-93 Butterfield & Butterfield, San Francisco #2175/R

PICKENS, Lucien Alton (1917-) American
$1600   £925   Child waving flag on beach (34x23cm-13x9in) init.d.45 tempera masonite. 25-Sep-92 Sotheby's Arcade, New York #348/R

PICKHARDT, Carl E (jnr) (1908-) American
$2500   £1445   Nightclub (81x54cm-32x21in) s. 24-Sep-92 Sotheby's, New York #165/R

PICKNELL, William Lamb (1854-1897) American
$3000   £2013   On the trail (38x53cm-15x21in) s.d.1880. 4-May-94 Doyle, New York #10/R
$3200   £2133   Annisquam, Massachusetts (51x91cm-20x36in) s. 23-May-94 Christie's, East, New York #90/R
$3500   £2365   The Grand Canal Venice (36x70cm-14x28in) s.d.1875. 5-Nov-93 Skinner, Bolton #70 a/R
$18000   £11538   Annisquam landscape (71x91cm-28x36in) s. 27-May-93 Sotheby's, New York #5/R

PIERCE, Charles Franklin (1844-1920) American
$550   £365   New England landscape (21x41cm-8x16in) init. 15-Jun-94 Butterfield & Butterfield, San Francisco #4425/R
$2250   £1510   Sheep and chickens in a barn (51x76cm-20x30in) s. 6-Dec-93 Grogan, Massachussetts #492/R
$4675   £3056   Autumn landscape with cows (36x46cm-14x18in) s. 14-May-93 Skinner, Bolton #40/R

PIERRE, Lesly (1958-) Haitian
$724   £473   Le paradis des oiseaux (76x101cm-30x40in) painted 1990. 17-May-93 Hoebanx, Paris #178/R (F.FR 4000)

PIERRI, Orlando (1913-1992) Argentinian
$1000   £521   Paisaje (48x76cm-19x30in) 4-Aug-92 VerBo, Buenos Aires #77

PIGOTT, Marjorie (1904-1990) Canadian
$595   £389   June blossoms (55x35cm-22x14in) s. W/C. 19-May-93 Sotheby's, Toronto #35 (C.D 750)
$778   £515   Natures rythm (61x41cm-24x16in) s. W/C. 24-Nov-92 Joyner Fine Art, Toronto #153 (C.D 1000)

PIKE, Gordon B (19th C) American?
$900   £608   Central Park (33x42cm-13x17in) s.d.1895 W/C board. 31-Mar-94 Sotheby's Arcade, New York #123/R

PIKE, John (1911-) American
$700   £405   Bahamas (53x71cm-21x28in) s. W/C. 24-Sep-92 Mystic Fine Arts, Connecticut #133/R
$900   £596   Portuguese beach scene (53x74cm-21x29in) s. W/C. 23-Sep-93 Mystic Fine Arts, Connecticut #218/R

PILOT, Robert Wakeham (1898-1967) Canadian
$982   £663   Near Penrihyndidreth Wales (21x26cm-8x10in) s.i.d.1943verso board. 23-Nov-93 Fraser Pinneys, Quebec #356/R (C.D 1300)
$1635   £1082   House sheltered by tree (18x24cm-7x9in) panel. 24-Nov-92 Joyner Fine Art, Toronto #222/R (C.D 2100)
$1635   £1082   Winter harbour scene (13x17cm-5x7in) s.indist.d. panel. 18-Nov-92 Sotheby's, Toronto #151 (C.D 2100)
$1751   £1160   Ottawa River facing Seigneury Club (21x28cm-8x11in) s.i.d.1936verso panel. 18-Nov-92 Sotheby's, Toronto #125/R (C.D 2250)
$1957   £1313   House in Chambly (18x24cm-7x9in) panel. 29-Nov-93 Waddingtons, Toronto #1078/R (C.D 2600)
$2751   £1741   Winter thaw - Piedmont - P.Q. Misty Morning (32x43cm-13x17in) s.d.46 panel. 30-Nov-92 Ritchie, Toronto #194 a (C.D 3500)
$2958   £1959   French-Canadian house by river (17x24cm-7x9in) s. panel. 24-Nov-92 Joyner Fine Art, Toronto #26/R (C.D 3800)
$2987   £1891   Bonsecours Market, winter (20x25cm-8x10in) s. board. 1-Dec-92 Fraser Pinneys, Quebec #37 a/R (C.D 3800)
$3113   £2062   The skating rink, Porte St Louis, Quebec (21x28cm-8x11in) s. i.verso board. 18-Nov-92 Sotheby's, Toronto #10/R (C.D 4000)
$3214   £2060   Kingston from Fort Frederick (30x41cm-12x16in) s. board. 7-Dec-92 Waddingtons, Toronto #1349/R (C.D 4100)
$3734   £2363   Spring ice - Montreal from St. Helens Island (32x43cm-13x17in) s.d.50 s.verso panel. 30-Nov-92 Ritchie, Toronto #194/R (C.D 4750)
$3947   £2632   St Simeon P Q (45x61cm-18x24in) s.i. 30-May-94 Ritchie, Toronto #172/R (C.D 5500)
$4756   £3109   Melting snow (51x61cm-20x24in) s.indist.i.d.38. 19-May-93 Sotheby's, Toronto #380/R (C.D 6000)
$5109   £3234   Wildflowers, Kingston, Ontario (41x51cm-16x20in) s. 1-Dec-92 Fraser Pinneys, Quebec #142 a/R (C.D 6500)
$5812   £3927   Winter landscape with stream (25x33cm-10x13in) s. board. 3-Nov-93 Sotheby's, Toronto #328/R (C.D 7500)
$5946   £3886   Early spring, Val Morin (46x56cm-18x22in) s.d.46. 19-May-93 Sotheby's, Toronto #344/R (C.D 7500)
$5946   £3886   Harbour scene, Newfoundland (46x61cm-18x24in) s. 19-May-93 Sotheby's, Toronto #91/R (C.D 7500)
$6540   £4275   View of Kingston from Fort Henry (32x43cm-13x17in) s. 19-May-93 Sotheby's, Toronto #134/R (C.D 8250)
$6796   £4592   Cap-A-L'Aigle (45x60cm-18x24in) s.d.1928. 23-Nov-93 Joyner Fine Art, Toronto #35/R (C.D 9000)
$7784   £5155   View of Lake Memphremagog showing St. Benoit-du-Lac Monastery to fore (47x60cm-19x24in) s. 24-Nov-92 Joyner Fine Art, Toronto #68/R (C.D 10000)

PILOT, Robert Wakeham (1898-1967) Canadian-cont.
$8010	£5340	Rainy day, Baie St. Paul (30x41cm-12x16in) s. canvas on board. 13-May-94 Joyner Fine Art, Toronto #49/R (C.D 11000)
$10306	£6736	St. Lawrence Valle from Montmorency Falls (32x43cm-13x17in) s. panel. 18-May-93 Joyner Fine Art, Toronto #40/R (C.D 13000)
$10571	£7143	Quebec from Beauport (52x70cm-20x28in) 52x70. 23-Nov-93 Joyner Fine Art, Toronto #6/R (C.D 14000)
$10848	£7330	Late winter Perth Ontario (30x42cm-12x17in) s. i.verso panel. 3-Nov-93 Sotheby's, Toronto #245 a/R (C.D 14000)
$15102	£10204	Falling snow, North River, Piedmont (60x80cm-24x31in) s.d.46. 23-Nov-93 Joyner Fine Art, Toronto #78/R (C.D 20000)
$17476	£11650	Twilight, Place D'Armes, Quebec (47x60cm-19x24in) s. 13-May-94 Joyner Fine Art, Toronto #35/R (C.D 24000)
$32767	£21845	Northeast corner Peel and Sherbrooke Streets, Montreal (102x91cm-40x36in) s. 11-May-94 Sotheby's, Toronto #94/R (C.D 45000)
$39320	£26214	Twilight, Lower Town, Quebec (60x80cm-24x31in) s. 13-May-94 Joyner Fine Art, Toronto #82/R (C.D 54000)
$595	*£389*	*Street scene, Montreal (20x25cm-8x10in) s.d.21 pencil. 19-May-93 Sotheby's, Toronto #16/R (C.D 750)*

PILOT, Robert Wakeham (attrib) (1898-1967) Canadian
$856	£567	River scene with tug boats and barge (21x34cm-8x13in) bears sig.verso board. 18-Nov-92 Sotheby's, Toronto #88/R (C.D 1100)

PIMENTEL, Rodrigo Ramirez (1945-) Mexican
$11000	£7333	Musical (139x199cm-55x78in) s. s.i.d.1990verso. 18-May-94 Christie's, New York #252/R
$12000	£7843	Del Mar (220x100cm-87x39in) s.d.86 s.i.d.verso diptych. 17-May-93 Christie's, New York #159/R

PINCAS, Julius see PASCIN, Jules

PINTO, Angelo (1908-) American
$725	£494	Dock scene (48x64cm-19x25in) indist.s. 14-Apr-94 Freeman Fine Arts, Philadelphia #1052 a/R
$1000	£694	Trapeze performer (30x38cm-12x15in) s.d.34 i.verso. 6-Mar-93 Louisiana Auction Exchange #147/R

PINTO, Octavio (1890-1941) Argentinian
$4600	£2659	Paisaje (42x51cm-17x20in) panel. 23-Sep-92 Roldan & Cia, Buenos Aires #55
$2000	*£1325*	*Carnaval de Rio (35x50cm-14x20in) W/C. 11-Nov-92 VerBo, Buenos Aires #83*

PISSARRO, Victor (1891-1937) Argentinian
$5500	£3642	Roma (23x30cm-9x12in) W/C painted 1931. 11-Nov-92 VerBo, Buenos Aires #85

PITCHER, Charles (20th C) American
$1500	£980	Salvation from peril (218x287cm-86x113in) 17-Apr-93 Dargate Auction Galleries, Pittsburgh #567

PITTMAN, Hobson (1898-?) American
$2300	£1513	Poet (79x63cm-31x25in) s. 31-Mar-93 Sotheby's Arcade, New York #147
$5500	£3691	The model (43x66cm-17x26in) s. masonite. 4-May-94 Doyle, New York #34
$500	£327	Vase of flowers (53x36cm-21x14in) s. W/C. 30-Jun-94 Mystic Fine Arts, Connecticut #189/R
$550	£359	Still life of roses (38x25cm-15x10in) s. W/C. 30-Jun-94 Mystic Fine Arts, Connecticut #189 a/R
$750	£490	Veranda (33x56cm-13x22in) s. pastel chl. 16-Sep-93 Sloan, North Bethesda #2680

PITTS, Elizabeth McCord (1880-1963) American
$900	£584	Maida in our Paris studio (100x73cm-39x29in) 9-Sep-93 Sotheby's Arcade, New York #249/R

PIZA, Arthur (1928-) Brazilian
$1661	*£1115*	*Relief (28x27cm-11x11in) mixed media board. 8-May-94 Jonquet, Paris #122 (F.FR 9500)*
$1661	*£1115*	*Relief (30x28cm-12x11in) mixed media board. 8-May-94 Jonquet, Paris #121 (F.FR 9500)*
$1972	*£1315*	*Composition 104 (61x50cm-24x20in) s. s.i.d.65verso material collage canvas. 7-Jun-94 Karl & Faber, Munich #1100/R (DM 3300)*

PLANTE, Daniel (1958-) Canadian
$1658	£1128	After the bath (51x41cm-20x16in) s. bears i.verso acrylic. 15-Nov-93 Hodgins, Calgary #60/R (C.D 2200)

PLASKETT, Joe (1918-) Canadian
$1311	£874	Still life of fruit in bowl (38x46cm-15x18in) s.d.1979. 11-May-94 Sotheby's, Toronto #205/R (C.D 1800)
$1359	£918	Dahlias on a lace tablecloth (90x59cm-35x23in) s.d.62-78. 23-Nov-93 Joyner Fine Art, Toronto #65 (C.D 1800)
$1510	£1020	Still life with flowers and porcelain birds (60x49cm-24x19in) s.d.73. 23-Nov-93 Joyner Fine Art, Toronto #242 (C.D 2000)
$2150	£1463	Shades of Michelangelo (91x71cm-36x28in) s.d.55 s.i.stretcher. 7-Jul-93 Maynards, Vancouver #215 (C.D 2750)
$2888	£1951	Still life - after lunch (71x53cm-28x21in) s.d.71-76. 30-Mar-94 Maynards, Vancouver #102 (C.D 4000)

PLASKETT, Joe (1918-) Canadian-cont.
$3269	£2165	Bronzes no.1 (113x71cm-44x28in) s. 24-Nov-92 Joyner Fine Art, Toronto #90/R (C.D 4200)
$4389	£2778	Crocus with alarm clock (20x25cm-8x10in) s. 21-Oct-92 Maynards, Vancouver #134 (C.D 5500)
$431	£287	Flag decorated public buildings (48x63cm-19x25in) s.d.63 col.chk. 30-May-94 Ritchie, Toronto #255/R (C.D 600)

PLATT, Charles Adams (1861-1933) American
$5000	£3311	Etcher's studio (46x61cm-18x24in) init.d.87. 22-Sep-93 Christie's, New York #54/R
$8000	£5594	Dutch river (51x62cm-20x24in) s. 10-Mar-93 Sotheby's, New York #77/R

PLEISSNER, Ogden M (1905-1983) American
$2100	£1355	Spring in Vermont (51x61cm-20x24in) s. 13-Jul-94 Doyle, New York #59
$6000	£3974	Town in Tuscany (44x69cm-17x27in) s. 23-Sep-93 Sotheby's, New York #289/R
$7000	£4667	Summer cottage, Tee House (50x81cm-20x32in) s. 16-Mar-94 Christie's, New York #110/R
$10500	£7000	Pont Royale (56x91cm-22x36in) s. 25-May-94 Sotheby's, New York #150/R
$11000	£7285	Rue Rataud (71x91cm-28x36in) s. 23-Sep-93 Sotheby's, New York #277/R
$36000	£25175	Evening on the river (57x61cm-22x24in) s. 11-Mar-93 Christie's, New York #246/R
$800	£404	Workmen constructing telephone line (13x23cm-5x9in) s. W/C gouache. 30-Aug-92 Litchfield Auction Gallery #210
$1400	£940	Torrey Creek (41x61cm-16x24in) s. W/C painted c.1938. 2-Dec-93 Swann Galleries, New York #249/R
$1900	£1275	Railway station (46x61cm-18x24in) s. W/C. 5-Mar-94 Louisiana Auction Exchange #12/R
$3500	£2365	Beach at Boca Grande (18x25cm-7x10in) s. W/C. 31-Mar-94 Sotheby's Arcade, New York #313/R
$3750	£2517	Our camp along the Dinwoodie, Wyoming (36x53cm-14x21in) s. i.verso W/C. 4-May-94 Doyle, New York #42/R
$4000	£2564	Local stores of Bonneville, Wyoming (29x38cm-11x15in) s.i. W/C gouache. 9-Dec-92 Butterfield & Butterfield, San Francisco #3913/R
$4750	£3210	Jardin des Tuileries (18x26cm-7x10in) s. W/C. 31-Mar-94 Sotheby's Arcade, New York #433/R
$5000	£3311	Wyoming landscape (53x74cm-21x29in) s. W/C. 23-Sep-93 Sotheby's, New York #290
$5500	£3642	November snow, Vermont (45x75cm-18x30in) s. W/C board. 23-Sep-93 Sotheby's, New York #266/R
$5750	£3885	Lighthouse, Winter Harbour (37x51cm-15x20in) s. bears i.verso W/C. 31-Mar-94 Sotheby's Arcade, New York #311/R
$6000	£3974	Sunday morning, Venice (52x75cm-20x30in) s. W/C board. 23-Sep-93 Sotheby's, New York #278/R
$6000	£3974	Loches (49x74cm-19x29in) s. W/C. 23-Sep-93 Sotheby's, New York #287/R
$7000	£4667	Venetian doorway (52x74cm-20x29in) s. W/C. 17-Mar-94 Sotheby's, New York #153/R
$8000	£5333	Fishing, Grand Lake Stream, Maine (36x53cm-14x21in) s. W/C. 3-Jun-94 Sotheby's, New York #281/R
$8750	£6119	Woodcock shooting (23x30cm-9x12in) s. bears i.verso W/C. 10-Mar-93 Sotheby's, New York #134/R
$9000	£6000	Out for ducks, Great South Bay (36x62cm-14x24in) s. W/C. 25-May-94 Sotheby's, New York #148/R
$10000	£6329	Gnarled juniper (40x58cm-16x23in) s. W/C. 3-Dec-92 Sotheby's, New York #73/R
$18000	£12081	Hunter by a creek (49x75cm-19x30in) s. W/C. 3-Dec-93 Christie's, New York #2/R
$18000	£12587	Got one (38x56cm-15x22in) s. W/C pencil. 11-Mar-93 Christie's, New York #200/R
$18000	£12081	On the branch - quail shooting (39x58cm-15x23in) s. W/C. 3-Dec-93 Christie's, New York #3/R
$22000	£14667	Carolina quail hunt (49x74cm-19x29in) s. W/C. 17-Mar-94 Sotheby's, New York #155/R
$26000	£17450	Fishing near a cabin (54x79cm-21x31in) s. W/C. 3-Dec-93 Christie's, New York #1/R

PLUMMER, Elmer Ginzel (1910-1987) American
$750	£517	Rail cars in eucalyptus landscape (38x56cm-15x22in) indist.s. W/C. 16-Feb-93 John Moran, Pasadena #88

PLUMMER, W (19/20th C) American
$4250	£2778	Traffic on high seas with screw steamer State of Virginia (18x24cm-7x9in) mono.i.d.1876verso board. 31-Oct-92 Skinner, Bolton #34/R

PLUMMER, William (19/20th C) American
$875	£621	Leaping Brookie (36x56cm-14x22in) s.d.1893. 13-Feb-93 Collins, Maine #84/R

PO-YE-GE (20th C) American
$650	£419	Antelope dancers (23x30cm-9x12in) s.i.verso gouache. 9-Jan-93 Skinner, Bolton #21/R

PODCHERNIKOFF, Alexis M (1886-1933) American/Russian
$550	£372	Cows grazing in a forest clearing (36x61cm-14x24in) s. 31-Mar-94 Sotheby's Arcade, New York #210/R
$600	£400	River landscape (13x20cm-5x8in) s. panel. 15-Mar-94 John Moran, Pasadena #6
$650	£433	Summer landscape (46x61cm-18x24in) s. 13-Mar-94 Hindman Galleries, Chicago #810
$700	£483	Flowered hillside (13x20cm-5x8in) s. panel. 16-Feb-93 John Moran, Pasadena #31
$700	£467	Mountainous landscape (61x91cm-24x36in) s. 17-May-94 Christie's, East, New York #515
$750	£514	The evening cloud (56x71cm-22x28in) s. s.i.d.1917verso. 7-Feb-94 Selkirks, St. Louis #287/R
$750	£497	Mountain river with cattle (30x41cm-12x16in) s. board. 20-Sep-93 Butterfield & Butterfield, Los Angeles #69/R

PODCHERNIKOFF, Alexis M (1886-1933) American/Russian-cont.

$750	£507	Sunset river landscape (25x36cm-10x14in) s. masonite. 9-Nov-93 John Moran, Pasadena #933
$850	£574	Autumn landscape (25x30cm-10x12in) s. 9-Nov-93 John Moran, Pasadena #931
$850	£574	River landscape (10x20cm-4x8in) init. board. 9-Nov-93 John Moran, Pasadena #819 a
$850	£574	Landscape with cattle (51x66cm-20x26in) s. 31-Oct-93 Hindman Galleries, Chicago #718/R
$900	£608	Figures and cattle in wooded landscape (51x71cm-20x28in) s. 15-Jun-93 John Moran, Pasadena #95
$900	£600	Cattle in landscape (41x30cm-16x12in) s. board. 15-Mar-94 John Moran, Pasadena #42
$950	£633	Landscape (23x25cm-9x10in) init. panel. 15-Mar-94 John Moran, Pasadena #46
$950	£633	Figures in wooded landscape (51x38cm-20x15in) s. panel. 15-Mar-94 John Moran, Pasadena #48
$950	£633	Breaking surf - Monterey, California (51x76cm-20x30in) s. 23-May-94 Hindman Galleries, Chicago #212/R
$1000	£671	Moonlight on the Pacific, near Santa Barbara (66x107cm-26x42in) s. 8-Dec-93 Butterfield & Butterfield, San Francisco #3326/R
$1000	£690	Carmel Mission near Monterey (23x30cm-9x12in) s. board. 16-Feb-93 John Moran, Pasadena #105
$1100	£733	Eucalyptus landscape (51x61cm-20x24in) s. canvas laid down on masonite. 15-Mar-94 John Moran, Pasadena #120
$1100	£759	Landscape (41x61cm-16x24in) s. 16-Feb-93 John Moran, Pasadena #44
$1100	£728	Figure in wooded landscape (51x41cm-20x16in) s. 14-Jun-94 John Moran, Pasadena #60
$1300	£897	Figures in wooded landscape (51x61cm-20x24in) s. 16-Feb-93 John Moran, Pasadena #32
$1300	£884	Cattle grazing in mountain landscape (61x91cm-24x36in) s. 15-Nov-93 Christie's, East, New York #141
$1300	£855	Sand dunes (19x28cm-7x11in) init. panel. 13-Jun-93 Butterfield & Butterfield, San Francisco #743/R
$1400	£927	Cattle watering - landscape (30x41cm-12x16in) s. board. 14-Jun-94 John Moran, Pasadena #40
$1600	£1081	Flowered hillside (25x36cm-10x14in) s. 9-Nov-93 John Moran, Pasadena #932
$1600	£1060	Moonlight landscape (20x25cm-8x10in) s. masonite. 14-Jun-94 John Moran, Pasadena #10
$1700	£1181	Woman in pastoral landscape (51x76cm-20x30in) s. 7-Mar-93 Butterfield & Butterfield, San Francisco #64/R
$1700	£1172	Eucalyptus (71x56cm-28x22in) s. 16-Feb-93 John Moran, Pasadena #80 a
$1800	£1250	Path through landscape (76x102cm-30x40in) s. s.verso. 7-Mar-93 Butterfield & Butterfield, San Francisco #60/R
$1800	£1192	Flowered hillside, lupines and poppies (25x38cm-10x15in) s. 28-Sep-93 John Moran, Pasadena #219 a
$1900	£1284	Cattle watering in wooded landscape (25x30cm-10x12in) s. masonite. 15-Jun-93 John Moran, Pasadena #101
$2000	£1325	Cattle grazing by a pond (61x91cm-24x36in) s. 15-Jun-94 Butterfield & Butterfield, San Francisco #4626/R
$2500	£1656	Cattle in wooded landscape (56x76cm-22x30in) s. 14-Jun-94 John Moran, Pasadena #123
$3500	£2431	Cattle grazing beneath Mt Tamalpais (84x66cm-33x26in) s. s.i.d.1933verso. 7-Mar-93 Butterfield & Butterfield, San Francisco #77/R
$3750	£2467	Twilight (102x76cm-40x30in) s.i.d.1926. 13-Jun-93 Butterfield & Butterfield, San Francisco #712/R
$3750	£2534	Eucalyptus landscape (25x30cm-10x12in) s. masonite. 15-Jun-93 John Moran, Pasadena #101 a

POGANY, Willy (1882-1956) American

$691	£480	Portrait of young girl seated in coastal landscape holding book (74x59cm-29x23in) s. 2-Mar-93 Sotheby's, Billingshurst #1166
$800	£541	Portrait profile of a woman (76x51cm-30x20in) s. canvas on board. 20-Apr-94 Doyle, New York #65

POIRIER, Jacques (1942-) Canadian

$507	£338	Au petit matin (51x61cm-20x24in) s. i.verso. 6-Jun-94 Waddingtons, Toronto #1316 (C.D 700)
$610	£407	Rivage Gaspesien (41x51cm-16x20in) s. s.i.verso. 30-May-94 Hodgins, Calgary #221/R (C.D 850)

POIRIER, Narcisse (1883-1983) Canadian

$604	£408	La ferme blanche (46x66cm-18x26in) s. 23-Nov-93 Fraser Pinneys, Quebec #333 (C.D 800)
$642	£434	La ferme en ete (40x51cm-16x20in) s. 23-Nov-93 Fraser Pinneys, Quebec #429 (C.D 850)

POISSON, Louverture (1914-1985) Haitian

$700	£440	Voodoo (51x41cm-20x16in) s.i.d.1958 canvas laid down on board. 25-Apr-93 Butterfield & Butterfield, San Francisco #2096/R
$4000	£2703	Maison de Campagne (43x53cm-17x21in) s. linen on gypsum board. 24-Nov-93 Christie's, New York #2/R
$4500	£2941	Mambo conducting ceremony (78x64cm-31x25in) s.i. masonite painted 1959. 18-May-93 Sotheby's, New York #243/R

POITRAS, Jane Ash (1951-) Canadian

$943	£637	Classical landscape (30x91cm-12x36in) s. i.d.1989verso. 25-Apr-94 Levis, Calgary #267/R (C.D 1300)

POITRAS, Jane Ash (1951-) Canadian-cont.
$871 £588 Buffalo was sacred for the Indian (56x46cm-22x18in) s.d.1992 mixed media and collage on canvas. 25-Apr-94 Levis, Calgary #266/R (C.D 1200)

POLELONEMA, Otis (1902-) American
$2200 £1467 Water drinking dance (30x25cm-12x10in) s. gouache board. 29-Jan-94 Skinner, Bolton #149/R

POLEO, Hector (1918-) Venezuelan
$20000 £13333 La Muraille (100x100cm-39x39in) s. s.i.d.1973stretcher acrylic. 18-May-94 Christie's, New York #148/R
$55000 £37162 Victoria (51x41cm-20x16in) s.d.48 linen. 23-Nov-93 Christie's, New York #37/R
$3000 £1961 Memorias de Juventud (34x28cm-13x11in) s.d.46 pencil pastel. 17-May-93 Christie's, New York #233/R
$17000 £11258 La machine calcinee (38x46cm-15x18in) s. s.i.d.1971 stretcher caseine canvas. 24-Nov-92 Christie's, New York #247/R
$48000 £31788 Prelude (73x92cm-29x36in) s. s.i.d.1966 stretcher caseine canvas. 24-Nov-92 Christie's, New York #128/R

POLICASTRO, Enrique (1898-1971) Argentinian
$1050 £618 Paisaje (34x48cm-13x19in) mixed media executed 1961. 29-Sep-92 VerBo, Buenos Aires #93

POLLOCK, Jackson (1912-1956) American
$3015 £1970 Abstract (61x28cm-24x11in) d.1953. 6-Oct-93 Maynards, Vancouver #328 (C.D 4000)
$1600000 £1073826 Number 22, 1949 (71x58cm-28x23in) s.d.49 oil enamel paper on masonite. 3-May-94 Christie's, New York #10/R
$8772 £5848 Number 76 (17x10cm-7x4in) col crayon dr executed c.1939-40. 8-Jun-94 Poulain & le Fur, Paris #99/R (F.FR 50000)
$16000 £10811 Untitled (36x28cm-14x11in) graphite pen col.crayon double-sided exec.c.1939. 10-Nov-93 Christie's, New York #109/R
$20000 £13514 Untitled (35x28cm-14x11in) i.d.verso graphite col.pencil executed c.1938. 10-Nov-93 Christie's, New York #104/R
$125000 £83893 Untitled (31x41cm-12x16in) s.d.51 ink. 5-May-94 Sotheby's, New York #83/R
$250000 £165563 Untitled - composition with black pouring (44x23cm-17x9in) s. oil enamel canvas mounted on masonite. 18-Nov-92 Christie's, New York #5/R
$750000 £506757 Number 26, 1951 (138x93cm-54x37in) enamel canvas. 9-Nov-93 Christie's, New York #10/R
$1800000 £1192053 Number 6, 1948 - Blue red yellow (57x78cm-22x31in) oil enamel paper mounted on board mounted canvas. 18-Nov-92 Christie's, New York #13/R
$2200000 £1437909 Number 19, 1948 (78x58cm-31x23in) s.d.48 oil enamel paper on canvas. 4-May-93 Christie's, New York #10/R

PONCE DE LEON, Fidelio (1896-1957) Cuban
$5000 £3378 Pescado (37x161cm-15x63in) s.d.55. 21-Apr-94 Butterfield & Butterfield, San Francisco #112/R
$6000 £4000 Mujer (71x66cm-28x26in) s.d.941. 18-May-94 Sotheby's, New York #409/R
$8000 £5369 Untitled, portrait of man smoking pipe. Untitled portrait of woman (32x40cm-13x16in) s.d.928 board pair. 7-Jan-94 Gary Nader, Miami #57/R
$9000 £6000 Dos mujeres (48x58cm-19x23in) s. painted c.1940. 18-May-94 Sotheby's, New York #230/R
$9500 £6333 Dos mujeres (51x60cm-20x24in) s.i. painted c.1940. 18-May-94 Sotheby's, New York #284/R
$18000 £12000 Cristo (61x51cm-24x20in) s. painted c.1940. 18-May-94 Sotheby's, New York #283/R
$75000 £49669 Despues del Ensayo - Tras Bambalinas (102x95cm-40x37in) s. painted c.1944. 24-Nov-92 Christie's, New York #51/R

PONSEN, Tunis (1891-1968) American
$700 £476 Summer landscape (51x64cm-20x25in) s. 16-Apr-94 Young Fine Arts Auctions, Maine #203/R
$1300 £878 Lamplit interior studio (76x61cm-30x24in) s. 31-Oct-93 Hindman Galleries, Chicago #738/R

POOLE, Burnell (1884-1933) American
$3000 £1974 J P Morgan's yacht 'Graviling' (51x44cm-20x17in) s.d.1922. 4-Jun-93 Sotheby's, New York #201/R

POOLE, Eugene Alonzo (1841-1912) American
$750 £490 Autumn landscape (18x38cm-7x15in) s.d.1905 board. 17-Apr-93 Dargate Auction Galleries, Pittsburgh #122
$750 £481 Grazing in the meadow (56x76cm-22x30in) s.d.1912. 9-Dec-92 Butterfield & Butterfield, San Francisco #3836/R
$1200 £811 Watering cattle (56x91cm-22x36in) s.d.1904. 4-Nov-93 Sloan, North Bethesda #2310/R

POOLE, Horatio Nelson (1884-1949) American
$3000 £2083 Castaic Lake (93x109cm-37x43in) s.d.1927. 7-Mar-93 Butterfield & Butterfield, San Francisco #99/R

POONS, Larry (1937-) American
$3378 £2222 Smarting young (215x69cm-85x27in) s.d.1975verso acrylic. 3-Jun-93 Kunsthallen, Copenhagen #132/R (D.KR 21000)
$4427 £2952 81 D 16 (121x36cm-48x14in) s.i.d.1981verso acrylic. 30-May-94 Catherine Charbonneaux, Paris #238/R (F.FR 25000)

POONS, Larry (1937-) American-cont.
$6500	£4248	Broken summer (300x98cm-118x39in) s.d.69 verso acrylic. 4-May-93 Sotheby's, New York #355/R
$7500	£4412	Little Cobalt (103x63cm-41x25in) s.d.1972 verso acrylic. 6-Oct-92 Sotheby's, New York #45/R
$55000	£36913	Richmond Ruckus (153x122cm-60x48in) s.i.d.1964stretcher synthetic polymer canvas. 5-May-94 Sotheby's, New York #135/R

POOR, Henry Varnum (1888-1970) American
$600	£403	Dinner repast (61x46cm-24x18in) s. 24-Mar-94 Mystic Fine Arts, Connecticut #94/R
$600	£403	Little grey girl (51x41cm-20x16in) s. board. 24-Mar-94 Mystic Fine Arts, Connecticut #92/R
$1000	£694	Black walnut tree (61x51cm-24x20in) s. 6-Mar-93 Louisiana Auction Exchange #142/R
$1100	£738	Still life (41x51cm-16x20in) s. 24-Mar-94 Mystic Fine Arts, Connecticut #93/R
$1200	£789	Self-portrait with family (88x94cm-35x37in) s.d.1914. 13-Jun-93 Butterfield & Butterfield, San Francisco #3246/R
$2300	£1494	The disappointed fisherman (76x61cm-30x24in) s. sold with painting by Renee Andre. 9-Sep-93 Sotheby's Arcade, New York #282/R

POORE, Henry Rankin (1859-1940) American
$750	£507	Landscape with cattle and haystacks (36x51cm-14x20in) s. 31-Oct-93 Hindman Galleries, Chicago #665
$850	£500	Cow in winter landscape (36x51cm-14x20in) s. 8-Oct-92 Freeman Fine Arts, Philadelphia #1063
$1100	£724	Long day (71x91cm-28x36in) s.i. 31-Mar-93 Sotheby's Arcade, New York #131/R
$2500	£1773	Watchful eye of retriever (56x86cm-22x34in) s. 13-Feb-93 Collins, Maine #25/R
$2970	£1904	Horses hauling logs (51x76cm-20x30in) s. 17-Dec-92 Mystic Fine Arts, Connecticut #200/R
$4500	£3041	The gleaners (58x79cm-23x31in) s. painted c.1904. 31-Mar-94 Sotheby's Arcade, New York #213/R

POPE, Alexander (1849-1924) American
$950	£664	Jumping small mouth bass (41x51cm-16x20in) s. i.verso. 12-Mar-93 Skinner, Bolton #178/R
$1300	£688	Vera (25x20cm-10x8in) s.d.April 1890. 11-Sep-92 Skinner, Bolton #179/R
$2200	£1447	Thanksgiving still life (51x114cm-20x45in) s.d.83. 4-Nov-92 Doyle, New York #7/R
$3100	£2026	Portrait of setter (91x107cm-36x42in) s. 17-Sep-93 Skinner, Bolton #176/R
$4000	£2667	Highland cattle (56x81cm-22x32in) s.d.04. 3-Jun-94 Sotheby's, New York #159/R

PORAY, Stanislaus (1888-1948) American
$1300	£844	Gothic carving (74x58cm-29x23in) s. s.i.verso. 11-Sep-93 Louisiana Auction Exchange #98/R

PORTER, Charles E (1847-1923) American
$3100	£1792	Still life with fruit, nuts and vessel (51x68cm-20x27in) s. 25-Sep-92 Sotheby's Arcade, New York #35/R

PORTER, Cole (20th C) American
$803	*£550*	Good will card to Fred Terry, theatre manager, i. W/C pencil. 10-Feb-94 Richmond Auctions #124

PORTER, Fairfield (1907-1975) American
$10000	£6667	Easter morning (46x51cm-18x20in) s.d.68 masonite. 25-May-94 Sotheby's, New York #146/R
$21000	£13462	Late afternoon, winter (46x56cm-18x22in) s.d.74 s.d.1974 verso panel. 27-May-93 Sotheby's, New York #98/R
$42500	£28523	House by the woods (94x64cm-37x25in) s.d.54. 2-Dec-93 Sotheby's, New York #152/R
$58000	£37179	Living room window, big house, Great Spruce Head (91x91cm-36x36in) 26-May-93 Christie's, New York #230/R

PORTER, Katherine (1941-) American
$2000	£1307	Evening of the day (185x335cm-73x132in) s.d.1970 verso acrylic. 7-May-93 Christie's, East, New York #45/R
$5000	£2941	Southern Persia II (162x241cm-64x95in) i.d.1970verso. 8-Oct-92 Christie's, New York #162/R
$5500	£3716	Balancing act (170x213cm-67x84in) i. painted 1977. 10-Nov-93 Christie's, New York #228/R
$550	*£369*	Untitled - vortex (35x34cm-14x13in) s.d.1976 mixed media graphite pastel. 6-May-94 Skinner, Bolton #160 a/R
$550	*£369*	Untitled - night and day (37x30cm-15x12in) s.d.1976 mixed media graphite pastel. 6-May-94 Skinner, Bolton #160 b/R
$650	*£437*	Clouds (50x53cm-20x21in) s.i. chl graphite col.pencil oil pastels. 23-Feb-94 Christie's, East, New York #275/R

PORTINARI, Candido (1903-1962) Brazilian
$19000	£12838	Menina (41x32cm-16x13in) s.d.1948 board. 23-Nov-93 Christie's, New York #117/R
$24000	£15894	natureza morta com flores (41x33cm-16x13in) s.d.1941. 24-Nov-92 Christie's, New York #136/R
$60000	£39216	Os Noivos (47x38cm-19x15in) s.d.947 linen. 17-May-93 Christie's, New York #106/R
$115000	£77703	Casamento (65x54cm-26x21in) s.d.59 panel. 23-Nov-93 Christie's, New York #99/R
$150000	£101351	Os musicos (195x130cm-77x51in) s. i.verso. 25-May-94 Christie's, New York #25/R
$1100	*£719*	Rostro (16x12cm-6x5in) s.d.1942 ink. 26-Oct-92 Gomensoro, Montevideo #23
$1100	*£719*	Joven sentada (23x20cm-9x8in) s. ink. 26-Oct-92 Gomensoro, Montevideo #22
$1600	*£804*	Negro (15x17cm-6x7in) s.d.1934 ink dr. 31-Aug-92 Gomensoro, Montevideo #19/R

PORTINARI, Candido (1903-1962) Brazilian-cont.

$2600	£1733	Mascara (25x17cm-10x7in) init.i. gouache black ink. 18-May-94 Christie's, New York #186/R
$17000	£11333	Espantalho e Pipas, designs for the ballet Yara (32x48cm-13x19in) init. gouache pencil executed 1946. 18-May-94 Christie's, New York #18/R

PORTOCARRERO, Rene (1912-1986) Cuban

$3000	£1961	Ciudad (31x49cm-12x19in) s.d.1954 paper on masonite. 18-May-93 Sotheby's, New York #176/R
$4000	£2667	Ciudad (30x34cm-12x13in) s.d.60 paper. 18-May-94 Sotheby's, New York #408/R
$4000	£2667	Catedral (63x37cm-25x15in) s. 9-Jun-94 Sotheby's Arcade, New York #138/R
$4000	£2667	De la serie carnavales (49x65cm-19x26in) s.d.70 tempera paper. 18-May-94 Sotheby's, New York #398/R
$4372	£2876	Mujer en bianco (91x61cm-36x24in) s.d.1964/65. 3-Nov-92 Bukowskis, Stockholm #218/R (S.KR 26000)
$5000	£3378	Diablo (51x41cm-20x16in) s.d.62. 23-Nov-93 Christie's, New York #263/R
$5000	£3378	Retrato de una mujer (51x32cm-20x13in) s.d.59 masonite. 22-Nov-93 Sotheby's, New York #203/R
$5315	£3520	Flores (51x41cm-20x16in) s.d.1958 s.i.d.verso. 1-Oct-93 Guy Loudmer, Paris #109 (F.FR 30200)
$6000	£3974	Catedral (68x51cm-27x20in) s.d.63. 24-Nov-92 Christie's, New York #296/R
$7000	£4667	Paisaje Cubano No.1 (43x53cm-17x21in) s.d.1968 s.i.d.verso. 18-May-94 Christie's, New York #279/R
$7500	£5000	Flores (51x41cm-20x16in) s.d.68 s.i.d.verso. 18-May-94 Christie's, New York #107/R
$8000	£5229	Catedral (60x44cm-24x17in) s.d.66. 17-May-93 Christie's, New York #196/R
$10000	£6711	El Conquistador (25x34cm-10x13in) s.d.1950 panel. 7-Jan-94 Gary Nader, Miami #2/R
$12000	£8108	Catedral (83x57cm-33x22in) s. 23-Nov-93 Christie's, New York #151/R
$14000	£9459	Mujer en bianco (92x61cm-36x24in) s.d.1964/65 i.verso. 23-Nov-93 Christie's, New York #150/R
$14000	£9333	Carnaval (69x89cm-27x35in) s.d.70. 18-May-94 Sotheby's, New York #375/R
$16000	£10596	Catedral (61x51cm-24x20in) s.d.62. 24-Nov-92 Christie's, New York #223/R
$16000	£10596	Catedral (70x46cm-28x18in) s.d.66. 24-Nov-92 Christie's, New York #230/R
$28000	£18919	Ciudad Roja (58x120cm-23x47in) s.d.1956. 23-Nov-93 Christie's, New York #58/R
$45000	£30000	Interior del cerro (107x63cm-42x25in) s.d.1960 s.i.d.verso. 17-May-94 Sotheby's, New York #60/R
$767	£518	Perfil femenino (68x49cm-27x19in) s.d.1961 W/C. 17-Mar-93 Fernando Duran, Madrid #202/R (S.P 90000)
$841	£553	Man and woman (26x23cm-10x9in) s.d.40 Indian ink. 3-Nov-92 Bukowskis, Stockholm #2320/R (S.KR 5000)
$1300	£878	Dos mujeres (28x24cm-11x9in) s.d.40 pen pencil crayon. 23-Nov-93 Christie's, New York #257/R
$1345	£885	Surrealistic composition (75x54cm-30x21in) s.d.63 Indian ink wash. 3-Nov-92 Bukowskis, Stockholm #219/R (S.KR 8000)
$1600	£1081	Untitled (38x28cm-15x11in) s.d.1952 tempera ink board. 22-Nov-93 Sotheby's, New York #198/R
$1600	£1074	Seated figure (56x38cm-22x15in) s.d.1948 bears sig.d. ink. 24-Feb-94 Sotheby's Arcade, New York #291/R
$2000	£1351	Composicion (38x28cm-15x11in) s.d.1952 gouache pen. 22-Nov-93 Sotheby's, New York #194/R
$2085	£1408	Tete surrealiste (75x59cm-30x23in) s.d.1972 mixed media. 21-Apr-94 Germann, Zurich #38/R (S.FR 3000)
$2200	£1457	Composicion Abstracta (38x27cm-15x11in) s.d.1952 W/C gouache ink. 23-Nov-92 Sotheby's, New York #244/R
$2700	£1788	Flores, s.d.1943 W/C. 24-Nov-92 Christie's, New York #314/R
$3000	£2013	Flora para Nicaragua (73x49cm-29x19in) s.d.76 i.verso gouache W/C. 24-Feb-94 Sotheby's Arcade, New York #285/R
$4000	£2614	Mujer en el patio (47x29cm-19x11in) s.d.1944 W/C pen. 17-May-93 Christie's, New York #187/R
$4200	£2838	Cara a Cara (51x73cm-20x29in) s.d.77 gouache brush ink. 23-Nov-93 Christie's, New York #259/R
$4250	£2815	Figura con cetro (41x44cm-16x17in) s.d.1948 pastel. 23-Nov-92 Sotheby's, New York #162/R
$4500	£2941	Figuras - from 'Figuras para una mitologia imaginaria' series (35x28cm-14x11in) s.d.43 brush ink notebook paper. 18-May-93 Sotheby's, New York #177/R
$5000	£3356	Cabezas ornamentadas (76x57cm-30x22in) s.d.63 ink. 7-Jan-94 Gary Nader, Miami #63/R
$5500	£3595	Mujer en un interior (48x29cm-19x11in) s.d.1944 W/C pen. 17-May-93 Christie's, New York #188/R
$6000	£3974	Mujeres (49x39cm-19x15in) s.d.48 oil pastel canvas. 30-Jun-93 Sotheby's Arcade, New York #231/R
$7000	£4636	Arte abstracto (51x61cm-20x24in) s.d.1948 pastel. 23-Nov-92 Sotheby's, New York #201/R
$7500	£4967	Figuras Danzantes (58x39cm-23x15in) s.d.48 pastel paper on board. 24-Nov-92 Christie's, New York #313/R
$10132	£6800	Composition (70x95cm-28x37in) s.d.1945 gouache board. 29-Nov-93 Christie's, S. Kensington #105/R
$18000	£11765	Danza (59x73cm-23x29in) s.d.1944 graphite gouache oil. 18-May-93 Sotheby's, New York #166/R
$20000	£13245	Interior del cerro (50x37cm-20x15in) s.d.43 tempera W/C. 23-Nov-92 Sotheby's, New York #164/R
$22000	£14667	Bailarinas de Carnaval (61x43cm-24x17in) s.d.1947 pastel paper laid down on masonite. 18-May-94 Christie's, New York #287/R
$28000	£18919	Interior con florero (63x45cm-25x18in) pastel. 23-Nov-93 Christie's, New York #147/R

POST, George (1906-) American
$550	£364	Boats in harbour (36x43cm-14x17in) s. W/C. 28-Sep-93 John Moran, Pasadena #329
$600	£405	House on hill-San Francisco (43x58cm-17x23in) s. W/C. 15-Jun-93 John Moran, Pasadena #157
$850	£567	The Old Cannery at Newport Beach (43x58cm-17x23in) s. W/C. 15-Mar-94 John Moran, Pasadena #176 a
$1100	£743	Wharfs (43x58cm-17x23in) s. W/C. 15-Jun-93 John Moran, Pasadena #156

POST, William Merritt (1856-1935) American
$1100	£724	Fall landscape (51x41cm-20x16in) s. 5-Jun-93 Louisiana Auction Exchange #125/R
$1200	£759	Autumn landscape with cows (51x76cm-20x30in) s. paper laid down on canvas. 5-Dec-92 Louisiana Auction Exchange #103/R
$1400	£927	Autumn landscape with stream (46x61cm-18x24in) s. 3-Oct-93 Hanzel Galleries, Chicago #766
$1600	£1013	Sun has gone to rest (64x76cm-25x30in) s. 30-Nov-92 Selkirks, St. Louis #249/R
$1900	£1275	Autumn scene (46x61cm-18x24in) s. 24-Mar-94 Mystic Fine Arts, Connecticut #34/R
$1900	£1275	Ducks beside an autumn river (41x66cm-16x26in) s. 6-Dec-93 Grogan, Massachussetts #490
$2400	£1611	Fall landscape (41x66cm-16x26in) s. 4-Dec-93 Louisiana Auction Exchange #51/R
$3200	£2238	The walk home (41x61cm-16x24in) s.i. 11-Mar-93 Christie's, New York #85/R
$1700	£994	Late autumn landscape with stream (33x51cm-13x20in) s. W/C. 20-Sep-92 Litchfield Auction Gallery #173

POTTER, Agnes (1892-?) American
$700	£458	Potted plant (61x61cm-24x24in) s. 30-Jun-94 Mystic Fine Arts, Connecticut #281

POTTER, W C (19th C) American
$1600	£833	Angling party on Adirondack Lake (61x91cm-24x36in) s. painted 1865. 6-Aug-92 Eldred, Massachusetts #1048/R

POTTHAST, Edward Henry (1857-1927) American
$2000	£1342	Rocky coastline (30x41cm-12x16in) s. artist board. 14-Jan-94 Du Mouchelle, Detroit #2002/R
$2500	£1656	Nude at the beach (23x20cm-9x8in) s. 28-Nov-92 Dunning's, Illinois #1034
$5500	£3642	Washerwoman (61x51cm-24x20in) s. 23-Sep-93 Sotheby's, New York #162/R
$6000	£3922	Gloucester Harbor (41x51cm-16x20in) s. 15-May-93 Dunning's, Illinois #1188/R
$6500	£4545	Gloucester harbour (30x41cm-12x16in) s. s.i.verso. 11-Mar-93 Christie's, New York #148/R
$10000	£6410	Bather (40x30cm-16x12in) s. board. 26-May-93 Christie's, New York #123/R
$12500	£8170	A quiet afternoon (51x38cm-20x15in) s. 1-Nov-92 Hanzel Galleries, Chicago #45/R
$14000	£8861	Waiting for sunrise, Yonkers Yacht Club, the Palisades (30x40cm-12x16in) s. 4-Dec-92 Christie's, New York #96/R
$18000	£12000	Wading in the surf (25x29cm-10x11in) s. board. 25-May-94 Sotheby's, New York #99/R
$25000	£16779	In the summertime (30x41cm-12x16in) s. board. 2-Dec-93 Sotheby's, New York #111/R
$25000	£17730	Mother and two children frolicking in surf (30x41cm-12x16in) s. board. 11-Feb-93 Boos Gallery, Michigan #355/R
$27000	£17089	Landscape by the shore (30x40cm-12x16in) s. board. 3-Dec-92 Sotheby's, New York #97/R
$44000	£29530	The bathers (51x61cm-20x24in) s. 12-Dec-93 Hindman Galleries, Chicago #266/R
$75000	£48077	At the beach (61x76cm-24x30in) s. 26-May-93 Christie's, New York #127/R
$105000	£66456	Children at play on beach (30x40cm-12x16in) s. board. 4-Dec-92 Christie's, New York #71/R
$160000	£107383	At the beach (41x51cm-16x20in) s. 2-Dec-93 Sotheby's, New York #110/R
$170000	£113333	Ring around the rosy (63x77cm-25x30in) s. 25-May-94 Sotheby's, New York #97/R
$1500	£993	Beach scene (24x36cm-9x14in) gouache. 15-Jun-94 Butterfield & Butterfield, San Francisco #4475/R
$1600	£1060	The air show (19x14cm-7x6in) gouache. 15-Jun-94 Butterfield & Butterfield, San Francisco #4473/R

POTTHAST, Edward Henry (attrib) (1857-1927) American
$900	£604	Bathers (69x89cm-27x35in) s. 5-Mar-94 Louisiana Auction Exchange #14/R
$3100	£2000	Gloucester Harbour (76x102cm-30x40in) bears sig. 15-Jul-94 Christie's, London #65/R
$6200	£4000	At the seaside (61x76cm-24x30in) bears sig. 15-Jul-94 Christie's, London #64/R

POTTS, W S (1876-1927) American
$1208	£800	Portrait of Master Robinson (76x63cm-30x25in) s. 24-Nov-92 Sotheby's, Billingshurst #517

POTTS, William Sherman (1876-1927) American
$750	£503	Young girl reading (56x46cm-22x18in) s.d.1910. 24-Jun-93 Mystic Fine Arts, Connecticut #72
$1500	£1049	Newspaper (53x48cm-21x19in) s. 5-Feb-93 Sloan, North Bethesda #1682/R

POUGIALIS, Constantine (1894-?) American
$650	£439	Cubist landscape (61x81cm-24x32in) s.d.73. 31-Oct-93 Hindman Galleries, Chicago #760
$750	£507	Seated woman (89x66cm-35x26in) 31-Oct-93 Hindman Galleries, Chicago #757
$1500	£1014	Two women (127x91cm-50x36in) s. 31-Oct-93 Hindman Galleries, Chicago #758
$2800	£1879	Seated woman with apples (89x69cm-35x27in) s. 12-Dec-93 Hindman Galleries, Chicago #276

POULSEN, Charles (19/20th C) American
$850   £578   Ship on rough sea (46x76cm-18x30in) s. i.verso. 17-Apr-94 Hindman Galleries, Chicago #961/R

POUSETTE-DART, Richard (1916-1992) American
$7500   £4967   Untitled (107x122cm-42x48in) s.d.1950 verso acrylic masonite. 13-Nov-92 Skinner, Bolton #219/R
$34000 £22973 Small spiral by the sea (61x122cm-24x48in) s.d.68 verso. 11-Nov-93 Sotheby's, New York #255/R
$11000 £7432   Untitled (61x49cm-24x19in) s.d.1950 gouache board. 11-Nov-93 Sotheby's, New York #279/R
$15000 £8824   Composition No.3 (45x30cm-18x12in) W/C ink. 6-Oct-92 Sotheby's, New York #6/R

POWELL, Arthur J E (1864-1956) American
$2000   £1316   Clipper at full sail (74x103cm-29x41in) 31-Mar-93 Sotheby's Arcade, New York #83/R

POWELL, Lucien Whiting (1846-1930) American
$1500   £949   View of Grand Canal, Venice (61x92cm-24x36in) s. 2-Dec-92 Christie's, East, New York #60
$3750   £2467   Venetian view (48x51cm-19x20in) s.d.1905. 2-Apr-93 Sloan, North Bethesda #2476/R
$4600   £2706   Grand Canyon (76x102cm-30x40in) s.d.1909. 3-Oct-92 Weschler, Washington #111/R
$600   £405   Sunset over the Coliseum (42x66cm-17x26in) s.d.1910 W/C board. 20-Mar-93 Weschler, Washington #98/R

POWELL, Lucien Whiting (attrib) (1846-1930) American
$550   £367   Eastern market scene (63x48cm-25x19in) bears sig. W/C. 12-Mar-94 Weschler, Washington #155

PRADO, Nadine (20th C) Mexican
$890   £601   Triptico (160x258cm-63x102in) s.verso acrylic linen triptych. 27-Apr-94 Louis Morton, Mexico #528 (M.P 3000)

PRAGNELL, Bartley R (1907-1966) Canadian
$785   £513   Portrait story (39x49cm-15x19in) s.d.47 board. 10-May-93 Hodgins, Calgary #106/R (C.D 1000)
$545   £361   Design (30x38cm-12x15in) painted 1949 W/C tempera. 16-Nov-92 Hodgins, Calgary #322/R (C.D 700)
$624   £367   Calgary, Alta (23x29cm-9x11in) s. i.verso painted c.1941 W/C. 5-Oct-92 Levis, Calgary #277/R (C.D 775)

PRATT, Henry Cheeves (1803-1880) American
$11000 £7383   Evening, scene on the Gila River, Arizona, with flying angel and cherub (76x117cm-30x46in) s.i.d.1862 i.verso. 6-Feb-94 Skinner, Bolton #165/R
$11000 £7383   The deserted Mission of Tumacacori, Estado de Sonona, Mexico (76x117cm-30x46in) s.i.verso. 6-Feb-94 Skinner, Bolton #165 a/R

PRATT, Mary Frances (1935-) Canadian
$1946   £1289   Study of a swan (51x66cm-20x26in) s.d.90 mixed media. 18-Nov-92 Sotheby's, Toronto #98/R (C.D 2500)

PRENDERGAST, Maurice (1861-1924) American
$210000 £140940 Harbour, afternoon (39x53cm-15x21in) s. panel painted c.1903-1906. 2-Dec-93 Sotheby's, New York #124/R
$340000 £228188 Snowy day, Boston (49x67cm-19x26in) s. painted c.1907-1910. 2-Dec-93 Sotheby's, New York #115/R
$18000 £11392 Summer day (25x34cm-10x13in) s. i.verso W/C. 3-Dec-92 Sotheby's, New York #117/R
$25000 £14451 On the beach (23x30cm-9x12in) s. W/C paper on board. 23-Sep-92 Christie's, New York #135/R
$45000 £28846 Dancers (28x21cm-11x8in) s. W/C pencil executed c.1893-94. 27-May-93 Sotheby's, New York #9/R
$70000 £44872 Charles Street, Boston (38x30cm-15x12in) s.i. W/C pencil executed c.1895. 27-May-93 Sotheby's, New York #25/R
$100000 £64103 New England village (39x46cm-15x18in) s. W/C gouache pastel pencil executed c.1916-19. 27-May-93 Sotheby's, New York #10/R
$200000 £126582 New England beach scene (35x50cm-14x20in) s. W/C pencil. 4-Dec-92 Christie's, New York #38/R
$245000 £155063 The porch with the old mosaics, St Marks, Venice (40x29cm-16x11in) s.i. W/C pencil. 3-Dec-92 Sotheby's, New York #42/R
$380000 £240506 May Day - Central Park (33x56cm-13x22in) s. W/C pencil. 3-Dec-92 Sotheby's, New York #104/R

PRENTICE, Levi Wells (1851-1935) American
$2500   £1645   Watering hole (23x38cm-9x15in) s. 4-Nov-92 Doyle, New York #25/R
$4500   £2980   Adirondack view (12x22cm-5x9in) s. board. 23-Sep-93 Sotheby's, New York #21/R
$6000   £4027   Country lane (38x66cm-15x26in) s. 24-Mar-93 Grogan, Massachussetts #37/R
$15000 £10000 Tabletop still life with fruit (17x14cm-7x6in) s. 26-May-94 Christie's, New York #10/R
$16000 £11189 Still life with baskets of plums (30x45cm-12x18in) s. 10-Mar-93 Sotheby's, New York #4/R
$18000 £12081 Deer at lakeside, summer afternoon (51x89cm-20x35in) s.d.1878. 24-Mar-93 Grogan, Massachussetts #40/R
$25000 £16556 Basket of plums (20x25cm-8x10in) s. 22-Sep-93 Christie's, New York #14/R
$26000 £16456 Apples and tree trunk (30x25cm-12x10in) s.d.1891. 4-Dec-92 Christie's, New York #246/R

PRENTICE, Levi Wells (1851-1935) American-cont.
$34000	£21795	Still life of raspberries (23x38cm-9x15in) s. 26-May-93 Christie's, New York #42/R
$37000	£24832	Panoramic view of lake in autumn (76x112cm-30x44in) s. 24-Mar-93 Grogan, Massachussetts #33/R
$39000	£26174	Basket of apples (30x51cm-12x20in) s. 3-Dec-93 Christie's, New York #123/R

PRESAS, Leopoldo (1915-) Argentinian
$612	£411	Untitled (80x100cm-31x39in) s. panel. 8-May-94 Jonquet, Paris #128/R (F.FR 3500)
$612	£411	Untitled (80x100cm-31x39in) s. panel. 8-May-94 Jonquet, Paris #126 (F.FR 3500)

PRESTON, Alice Bolam (1888-1958) American
$600	£403	Vogue illustration (33x25cm-13x10in) s. gouache. 24-Mar-93 Grogan, Massachussetts #119/R
$850	£570	Peggy in blue frock (28x18cm-11x7in) s. s.i.verso gouache. 24-Mar-93 Grogan, Massachussetts #118/R
$1000	£641	Boat of wishes come true (30x18cm-12x7in) s. gouache. 9-Dec-92 Grogan, Massachussetts #89/R
$1300	£833	The Crocus field (30x18cm-12x7in) s.i.d.24 gouache. 9-Dec-92 Grogan, Massachussetts #88/R
$1400	£897	Huja and the rose-coloured spectacles (30x18cm-12x7in) s.i. gouache. 9-Dec-92 Grogan, Massachussetts #91/R

PRESTON, James Moore (1874-1962) American
$900	£592	Industrial landscape. View of town (46x61cm-18x24in) s. double-sided. 31-Mar-93 Sotheby's Arcade, New York #316/R

PRESTON, May Wilson (1873-1949) American
$2000	£1333	Mother and child (44x34cm-17x13in) s. 23-May-94 Christie's, East, New York #139/R
$4500	£2922	Portrait of Ernest Lawson (36x25cm-14x10in) s.verso painted c.1912-14. 8-Jul-94 Sloan, North Bethesda #2730/R
$15000	£10490	Woman with fan (127x91cm-50x36in) s. 10-Mar-93 Sotheby's, New York #111/R

PRESTON, William (20th C) American
$548	£370	Portrait of the steam vessel Albano (43x66cm-17x26in) s. board. 22-Apr-94 Richardson & Smith, Whitby #43
$1490	£1000	Barquentine 'Ellen Holt' (44x70cm-17x28in) s. 16-Jul-93 Sotheby's, London #47/R

PRESTOPINO, Gregorio (1907-) American
$900	£592	Figure - mother (20x15cm-8x6in) masonite painted 1943. 31-Mar-93 Sotheby's Arcade, New York #383/R
$1000	£649	Soliloquy, man resting (34x24cm-13x9in) s. fiberboard painted before 1945. 9-Sep-93 Sotheby's Arcade, New York #354/R
$3000	£1974	Scrub woman (92x63cm-36x25in) s. painted 1943. 31-Mar-93 Sotheby's Arcade, New York #382/R
$600	£408	Bathers (66x94cm-26x37in) s. W/C. 14-Apr-94 Freeman Fine Arts, Philadelphia #1037

PRETE, Juan del (1897-1987) Argentinian
$1400	£927	Untitled (25x21cm-10x8in) painted 1973. 11-Nov-92 VerBo, Buenos Aires #32
$6000	£4000	Pareja bajo la luna (49x60cm-19x24in) s.d.43 board. 18-May-94 Christie's, New York #239/R

PREUSSER, Robert Ormerod (1919-) American
$1000	£654	Triplicity (36x51cm-14x20in) s. canvasboard. 17-Sep-93 Skinner, Bolton #296/R
$1100	£719	Line woven forms (36x58cm-14x23in) s. d.1947 verso board. 17-Sep-93 Skinner, Bolton #294/R
$1200	£784	Untitled (46x36cm-18x14in) s. oil tooling board. 17-Sep-93 Skinner, Bolton #292/R
$2600	£1699	Absolute texture (51x41cm-20x16in) s.d.1938 d.verso acrylic tooling masonite. 17-Sep-93 Skinner, Bolton #297/R
$6000	£3468	Dark and light equivalence (122x86cm-48x34in) s. d.1941 verso. 24-Sep-92 Sotheby's, New York #228/R
$8000	£4624	Circular and angular equivalence (86x122cm-34x48in) s. d.1941 verso. 24-Sep-92 Sotheby's, New York #227/R

PRICE, Addison Winchel (1907-) Canadian
$640	£429	Sunshower (61x76cm-24x30in) s. i.verso board. 29-Nov-93 Waddingtons, Toronto #1102 (C.D 850)

PRICE, Mary Elizabeth (20th C) American
$3200	£2148	Hollyhocks (61x51cm-24x20in) 27-Mar-94 Myers, Florida #73/R

PRICE, Norman Mills (1877-1951) American
$950	£621	Illustration for Liberty Magazine Nov.21 1931, Whistling Cat (36x58cm-14x23in) s. gouache. 22-May-93 Collins, Maine #65/R

PRICE, William Henry (1864-1940) American
$1000	£658	Crashing waves (76x91cm-30x36in) s. 13-Jun-93 Butterfield & Butterfield, San Francisco #777/R

PRIDA, Fernando Ramos (1937-) Mexican
$2373	£1603	Silencio (69x89cm-27x35in) s.d.1965 acrylic. 27-Apr-94 Louis Morton, Mexico #590/R (M.P 8000)

PRINA, Stephen (1954-) American
$1329	£886	Manet Series No.52 - 1989 (188x248cm-74x98in) mixed media sold with lithograph. 2-Jun-94 AB Stockholms Auktionsverk, Stockholm #7054/R (S.KR 10500)
$2236	£1415	Manet series no.31 (66x83cm-26x33in) ink wash rag banier. 6-Dec-92 Binoche et Godeau, Paris #25 (F.FR 12000)
$2795	£1769	Manet series no.36 (147x119cm-58x47in) ink wash rag banier. 6-Dec-92 Binoche et Godeau, Paris #24 (F.FR 15000)

PRINCE, Richard (1949-) Canadian
$25000	£16556	Untitled (142x122cm-56x48in) s.d.88 verso acrylic. 18-Nov-92 Sotheby's, New York #303/R
$800	£530	Joke (18x29cm-7x11in) s.d.86verso pen. 17-Nov-92 Christie's, East, New York #51/R
$11500	£7770	Entertainment series, Russell (251x127cm-99x50in) s.d.1983 col.photograph acrylic masonite. 10-Nov-93 Christie's, New York #273/R
$13000	£8609	The song 2120 South Michigan Ave (178x122cm-70x48in) s.i.d.1989 acrylic graphite silkscreen diptych. 19-Nov-92 Christie's, New York #136/R
$23000	£15033	Two leopard joke (244x190cm-96x75in) acrylic silkscreen canvas executed 1989. 4-May-93 Sotheby's, New York #262/R

PRIOR HAMBLEN SCHOOL, 19th C American
$3400	£2222	Primitive portrait of a lady (36x25cm-14x10in) board. 18-Apr-93 Hindman Galleries, Chicago #902/R

PRIOR, William Matthew (1806-1873) American
$1700	£1164	View of Mount Vernon with Washington's tomb in the foreground (48x64cm-19x25in) 12-Feb-94 Boos Gallery, Michigan #531/R
$1900	£1267	Fantastic landscape with figures and waterfall (76x66cm-30x26in) s.i.d.1871verso. 20-Aug-93 Skinner, Bolton #252/R
$3000	£2055	Winter scene of Mount Vernon with Washington's tomb and a horse and rider to fore (48x66cm-19x26in) 12-Feb-94 Boos Gallery, Michigan #532/R
$3000	£2055	Portraits of George Washington and Martha Washington (61x48cm-24x19in) one i.verso reverse paintings on glass pair. 12-Feb-94 Boos Gallery, Michigan #536/R
$4250	£2872	Portrait of a child in green holding a whip (36x25cm-14x10in) paperboard on masonite. 30-Oct-93 Skinner, Bolton #177/R
$4500	£3041	Portrait of a child in green (36x25cm-14x10in) s.d.1853 board. 30-Oct-93 Skinner, Bolton #170/R
$6500	£4452	Portrait of a gentleman with a sailing vessel in the background (69x56cm-27x22in) s.verso. 12-Feb-94 Boos Gallery, Michigan #528/R
$34000	£22973	Portraits of Joseph Sewell Jr. and his wife Eliza (86x71cm-34x28in) i.d.1838verso pair. 23-Oct-93 Collins, Maine #150/R

PRIOR, William Matthew (attrib) (1806-1873) American
$900	£596	Winter scene (61x81cm-24x32in) 28-Nov-92 Young Fine Arts Auctions, Maine #328/R

PRITCHARD, G Thompson (1878-1962) American
$600	£397	Landscape - High Sierra (64x76cm-25x30in) s. 14-Jun-94 John Moran, Pasadena #65 a
$650	£439	Autumn landscape (64x76cm-25x30in) s. 9-Nov-93 John Moran, Pasadena #937
$750	£521	Quiet stream (53x63cm-21x25in) s. 7-Mar-93 Butterfield & Butterfield, San Francisco #203/R
$850	£574	Sunset on the river (46x62cm-18x24in) s. 20-Mar-93 Weschler, Washington #122
$950	£629	Autumn landscape (63x77cm-25x30in) s. 20-Sep-93 Butterfield & Butterfield, Los Angeles #90/R
$1000	£671	Horse drawn wagon in moonlight (30x41cm-12x16in) 27-Mar-94 Myers, Florida #85/R
$1000	£676	Cattle by stream (64x76cm-25x30in) s. 15-Jun-93 John Moran, Pasadena #150
$1000	£690	Sailboats at rest, Gloucester (51x61cm-20x24in) s. canvas laid down. 16-Feb-93 John Moran, Pasadena #34
$1000	£690	Cottage in eucalyptus landscape (64x76cm-25x30in) s. 16-Feb-93 John Moran, Pasadena #52
$1400	£946	Arab street scene (64x76cm-25x30in) s. 13-Aug-93 Du Mouchelle, Detroit #2097/R
$1500	£962	Canal in Cairo (64x76cm-25x30in) s. 13-Dec-92 Hindman Galleries, Chicago #67/R
$1900	£1242	Arab scene (64x76cm-25x30in) s. 16-Apr-93 Du Mouchelle, Detroit #2238/R
$2750	£1897	Gathering kelp (64x91cm-25x36in) s. 16-Feb-93 John Moran, Pasadena #35

PROBST, Thorwald (1886-1948) American
$6000	£3529	Grand Canyon (76x102cm-30x40in) s. 4-Oct-92 Butterfield & Butterfield, Los Angeles #214/R

PROCTER, Burt (1901-1980) American
$1500	£993	Boy and burro in landscape (58x84cm-23x33in) s. 28-Sep-93 John Moran, Pasadena #280
$3750	£2517	New Mexico (51x61cm-20x24in) s. i.verso board. 8-Dec-93 Butterfield & Butterfield, San Francisco #3593/R

PRONSATO, Domingo (1881-1971) Argentinian
$1200	£625	Paisaje (27x30cm-11x12in) 4-Aug-92 VerBo, Buenos Aires #81

PROOM, Al (1933-) American
$2500	£1603	Lilacs (51x41cm-20x16in) s. board. 9-Dec-92 Butterfield & Butterfield, San Francisco #3936/R

PROUTY, Robert V (20th C) American
$550	£367	Evening snow, Connecticut (48x58cm-19x23in) s. board. 26-May-94 Sloan, North Bethesda #2170

PUENTE, Jose (?) Mexican?
$772	£522	Encierro de noche (48x64cm-19x25in) 9-Nov-93 Louis Morton, Mexico #99 (M.P 2500)
$865	£585	Encierro de dia (60x80cm-24x31in) 9-Nov-93 Louis Morton, Mexico #30/R (M.P 2800)

PUGH, David (1946-) Canadian
$718	£478	Lake Louise (102x122cm-40x48in) s.i.d.verso. 30-May-94 Hodgins, Calgary #107/R (C.D 1000)
$814	£550	Minnewanka shore (56x71cm-22x28in) s. s.i.d.1988verso. 1-Nov-93 Levis, Calgary #260 (C.D 1050)
$1883	£1231	Mount Rundel (86x122cm-34x48in) s. s.d.91 stretcher. 10-May-93 Hodgins, Calgary #341/R (C.D 2400)
$2092	£1414	Canmore dawn (91x122cm-36x48in) s.i.d.1990verso. 1-Nov-93 Levis, Calgary #259/R (C.D 2700)
$2825	£1846	Reflections - three sisters (102x152cm-40x60in) s.d.1991 verso. 10-May-93 Hodgins, Calgary #318 d (C.D 3600)

PURDUM, Rebecca (1959-) American
$5000	£3268	Mailers for Lib, NYC 187 (152x152cm-60x60in) executed 1987. 22-Dec-92 Christie's, East, New York #59

PURDY, Donald (20th C) American
$1700	£1149	A la plage (58x76cm-23x30in) s. masonite. 20-Apr-94 Doyle, New York #66
$2400	£1212	Young girls by the beach (41x51cm-16x20in) s. board. 30-Aug-92 Litchfield Auction Gallery #266

PUSHMAN, Hovsep (1877-1966) American
$1100	£705	Chinese figure (69x53cm-27x21in) s. 17-Dec-92 Mystic Fine Arts, Connecticut #269/R
$4750	£3146	Daughter of sheik (81x63cm-32x25in) s. panel painted c.1921. 23-Sep-93 Sotheby's, New York #227/R
$7000	£4575	Autumn solitude (58x36cm-23x14in) s. panel. 16-May-93 Hindman Galleries, Chicago #75/R
$10000	£6711	Oriental still life with seated Buddha figure and lustre vase (48x36cm-19x14in) s. panel. 16-Jul-93 Du Mouchelle, Detroit #2011/R
$13000	£8725	Oriental still life with seated Buddha figure and lustre pitcher (66x51cm-26x20in) s. 16-Jul-93 Du Mouchelle, Detroit #2010/R
$15000	£8671	Still life, wilted rose (69x53cm-27x21in) s. masonite. 23-Sep-92 Christie's, New York #165/R
$20000	£13986	Music of serenity (88x64cm-35x25in) s. masonite. 11-Mar-93 Christie's, New York #226/R
$26000	£17450	When twilight comes (71x61cm-28x24in) s. painted 1939. 2-Dec-93 Sotheby's, New York #118/R
$35000	£23333	Dancing leaves (55x62cm-22x24in) s. panel. 25-May-94 Sotheby's, New York #57/R

PUTHUFF, Hanson Duvall (1875-1972) American
$1900	£1310	Landscape, Topanga (20x25cm-8x10in) s. board. 16-Feb-93 John Moran, Pasadena #22
$2100	£1214	Grand Canyon (30x41cm-12x16in) 26-Sep-92 San Rafael Auction Galleries #220
$3000	£1974	Rocky landscape (41x51cm-16x20in) s. canvas on board. 13-Jun-93 Butterfield & Butterfield, San Francisco #878/R
$4000	£2667	View of the Grand Canyon (28x38cm-11x15in) s. canvasboard. 15-Mar-94 John Moran, Pasadena #109
$4200	£2781	Mount San Cayteno, Santa Clara Valley, California (61x91cm-24x36in) i.verso painted 1907. 18-Jun-94 Eldred, Massachusetts #1
$4250	£2500	House and fall trees (30x41cm-12x16in) s. canvas on board. 4-Oct-92 Butterfield & Butterfield, Los Angeles #131/R
$5500	£3235	Desert Mountain (30x41cm-12x16in) s. canvas on board. 4-Oct-92 Butterfield & Butterfield, Los Angeles #211/R
$5500	£3716	Open grove (41x51cm-16x20in) s. s.i.verso masonite. 9-Nov-93 John Moran, Pasadena #817a
$6000	£4054	Granite slopes high Sierras (41x51cm-16x20in) s. s.i.verso canvas laid down on board. 9-Nov-93 John Moran, Pasadena #817
$9500	£5588	Oaks and mountain grandeur (46x61cm-18x24in) s. 4-Oct-92 Butterfield & Butterfield, Los Angeles #123/R
$10000	£5882	Breath of Azure (61x76cm-24x30in) s. i.verso. 4-Oct-92 Butterfield & Butterfield, Los Angeles #118/R
$14000	£9272	Eucalyptus landscape - quietude (76x66cm-30x26in) s.i. s.verso. 14-Jun-94 John Moran, Pasadena #77

PUTNAM, Stephen Greeley (1858-?) American
$6750	£4561	Nathalie (107x86cm-42x34in) s.i. 31-Mar-94 Sotheby's Arcade, New York #159/R

PYLER, Boyard H (20th C) American
$700	£470	Portrait of young girl in white lace trimmed dress (69x56cm-27x22in) s.i.d.1910 oval. 15-Jan-94 Weschler, Washington #160/R

PYNE, Robert Lorraine (19th C) American
$800	£544	New York State landscape at twilight (51x76cm-20x30in) s.d.1887. 8-Apr-94 Sloan, North Bethesda #2144

QUACKENBUSH, Ralph (1933-) American
$800	£537	Spring on Grass Mountain (46x61cm-18x24in) s. s.i.verso. 8-Dec-93 Butterfield & Butterfield, San Francisco #3535/R
$1100	£728	Spring on Grass Mountain (61x46cm-24x18in) s. s.i.verso. 15-Jun-94 Butterfield & Butterfield, San Francisco #4745/R

QUARTLEY, Arthur (1839-1886) American
$950	£621	On the Jersey Marshes (18x41cm-7x16in) s.d.1874. 30-Jun-94 Richard Opfer, Timonium #105
$2600	£1757	Sunset glow over Isles of Shoals (30x62cm-12x24in) s. i.verso. 5-Nov-93 Skinner, Bolton #106/R
$2600	£1688	Off Cape Cod (30x62cm-12x24in) s. 9-Sep-93 Sotheby's Arcade, New York #64/R
$2700	£1765	Moonlight sail (51x41cm-20x16in) s.d.1878. 30-Jun-94 Mystic Fine Arts, Connecticut #110/R
$3750	£2500	Trinity from the river, New York (71x103cm-28x41in) s. si.d.1880 verso. 15-Mar-94 Phillips, London #85
$4300	£3007	Morning, Raritan Bay (66x51cm-26x20in) s.init.d.1881. 11-Mar-93 Christie's, New York #68/R
$7000	£4667	View from Cedar Island, Isle of Shoals (47x73cm-19x29in) s.d.1876 s.i.d.1876 verso. 23-May-94 Christie's, East, New York #56/R

QUAYTMAN, Harvey (20th C) American
$2400	£1611	Iron glove velvet glove (94x94cm-37x37in) s.i.d.1986overlap acrylic rust. 3-May-94 Christie's, East, New York #183/R
$6500	£4262	For Sonia Delaunay (102x102cm-40x40in) s.i.d. acrylic glass on canvas. 5-May-94 Sotheby's, New York #332 a/R

QUENTEL, Holt (20th C) American
$3000	£1765	Blue 4 - Selvedge (279x259cm-110x102in) s.d.1988 verso pigment sewn canvas. 6-Oct-92 Sotheby's, New York #169/R

QUEST, Charles F (1904-) American
$814	£557	Still life with a sculpture by Donatello (57x82cm-22x32in) s.d.1963 verso canvas on board. 8-Feb-94 Christie's, Amsterdam #89 (D.FL 1600)

QUIGLEY, Edward B (1895-?) American
$2800	£1879	The Green Hand (71x102cm-28x40in) s.d.38. 2-May-94 Selkirks, St. Louis #108

QUIMBEY, Fred G (1863-1923) American
$750	£503	The rocky inlet (30x41cm-12x16in) s. 15-Oct-93 Skinner, Bolton #205/R

QUINQUELA MARTIN, Benito (1890-1977) Argentinian
$1900	£1258	Marina (12x22cm-5x9in) painted 1917. 11-Nov-92 VerBo, Buenos Aires #91/R
$1900	£1258	Marina de noche (12x22cm-5x9in) painted 1917. 11-Nov-92 VerBo, Buenos Aires #92/R
$8000	£5298	Quietud en el Puerto (37x54cm-15x21in) s. board painted 1924. 24-Nov-92 Christie's, New York #245/R
$10000	£5780	Reflejos plateadus (50x60cm-20x24in) panel. 23-Sep-92 Roldan & Cia, Buenos Aires #25
$12000	£8108	Llegada de pescadores (80x90cm-31x35in) s. i.d.1958verso masonite. 23-Nov-93 Christie's, New York #141/R
$13000	£7514	Dia de Niebla (60x70cm-24x28in) panel. 23-Sep-92 Roldan & Cia, Buenos Aires #13
$13000	£7514	Sol y sombra (60x70cm-24x28in) 23-Sep-92 Roldan & Cia, Buenos Aires #24
$13500	£7031	Rincon de la Boca (60x70cm-24x28in) 4-Aug-92 VerBo, Buenos Aires #85/R
$14000	£9233	Amanecer (60x70cm-24x28in) s. s.i.d.1951verso board. 18-May-94 Christie's, New York #85/R
$16000	£10811	Impresion (50x70cm-20x28in) s.indis.i. s.i.d.1925verso board. 23-Nov-93 Christie's, New York #124/R
$18000	£11765	Descarga de maderas (50x70cm-20x28in) s.d.1925 s.i.d.1925 verso board. 17-May-93 Christie's, New York #100/R
$19000	£12583	Barco iluminado (80x90cm-31x35in) panel. 18-Nov-92 Roldan & Cia, Buenos Aires #3
$19000	£10983	Playa de los Ingleses (60x80cm-24x31in) 23-Sep-92 Roldan & Cia, Buenos Aires #14
$20000	£13245	Tarde en La Boca (50x70cm-20x28in) s. board. 24-Nov-92 Christie's, New York #147/R

QUINTANA, Ben (20th C) American
$600	£390	Untitled (10x15cm-4x6in) s. i.verso gouache. 25-Jun-94 Skinner, Bolton #113/R
$600	£390	Fawn (10x15cm-4x6in) s. i.verso gouache board. 25-Jun-94 Skinner, Bolton #111/R

QUIROS, Cesareo Bernaldo (1881-1968) Argentinian
$15000	£9804	En el jardin (76x71cm-30x28in) s. board on panel. 17-May-93 Christie's, New York #108/R
$19000	£12583	Huerta (61x76cm-24x30in) s. masonite. 24-Nov-92 Christie's, New York #148/R
$55000	£31792	Oros y rosas (61x61cm-24x24in) board. 23-Sep-92 Roldan & Cia, Buenos Aires #21

QUISPE TITO, Diego (attrib) (1611-1681) Peruvian
$12000	£7243	Holy Family in Nazareth (95x82cm-37x32in) painted c.1675. 17-May-93 Christie's, New York #71/R

QUISPE TITO, Diego (studio) (1611-1681) Peruvian
$12000	£8000	La Presentacion de la Virgen (115x157cm-45x62in) 18-May-94 Christie's, New York #71/R
$17000	£11258	Holy Family with St. John the Baptist (123x164cm-48x65in) 24-Nov-92 Christie's, New York #70/R

RAFFAEL, Joseph (1933-) American
$11000 £7432 Self portrait (213x184cm-84x72in) painted 1984. 10-Nov-93 Christie's, New York #245/R
$600 £405 Untitled (51x66cm-20x26in) s. W/C. 21-Oct-93 Butterfield & Butterfield, San Francisco #2770/R

RAGUSA, Giovanni (20th C) American?
$750 £475 Untitled (183x122cm-72x48in) s.d.86 verso. 25-Oct-92 Butterfield & Butterfield, San Francisco #2388/R
$900 £570 Untitled - portrait (157x66cm-62x26in) canvas on board. 25-Oct-92 Butterfield & Butterfield, San Francisco #2389/R
$950 £601 Untitled - portrait (165x104cm-65x41in) canvas on wood. 25-Oct-92 Butterfield & Butterfield, San Francisco #2390/R

RAJADELL, Jorge (1952-) Argentinian
$40000 £23121 Jaguar, felis onca (90x130cm-35x51in) acrylic. 23-Sep-92 Roldan & Cia, Buenos Aires #12

RAKES, Sarah (1955-) American
$650 £430 Feeding birds (81x71cm-32x28in) s.d.1992 acrylic wood. 21-Nov-92 Litchfield Auction Gallery #31

RAKIA, David (1928-) American?
$2500 £1678 Cosmos and Music (89x89cm-35x35in) s. i.verso. 23-Feb-94 Christie's, East, New York #148/R

RAMAGE, John (attrib) (c.1748-1802) American
$604 £400 Naval officer in blue uniform with gold facings and white cravat (4x?cm-2x?in) min. gold frame fitted fishskin case oval. 13-Jun-94 Bonhams, London #95/R

RAMIEZ, Martin (c.1885-?) American?
$7000 £4575 Cowboy no.26 (102x84cm-40x33in) graphite executed 1945-1953. 22-Dec-92 Christie's, East, New York #60

RAMOS MARTINEZ, Alfredo (20th C) Mexican
$7641 £4898 Florero (58x38cm-23x15in) s. pastel. 29-Apr-93 Louis Morton, Mexico #46 (M.P 24000)
$12098 £7755 Mujer con velo (44x34cm-17x13in) s.d.1915. 29-Apr-93 Louis Morton, Mexico #106 (M.P 38000)
$4000 £2667 Magnolias (69x56cm-27x22in) s. gouache board. 18-May-94 Christie's, New York #209/R
$4000 £2667 Gardenias (70x55cm-28x22in) s. gouache board. 18-May-94 Christie's, New York #210/R

RAMOS, Domingo (1894-1967) Cuban
$6000 £3974 Paisaje (39x38cm-15x15in) s.d.1921. 24-Nov-92 Christie's, New York #221/R
$9000 £5960 Paisaje de Vinales (60x75cm-24x30in) s.d.1953. 24-Nov-92 Christie's, New York #222/R
$14000 £9333 Paisaje Cubano (96x105cm-38x41in) s.d.1937. 18-May-94 Christie's, New York #292/R
$25000 £16667 Paisaje cubano (99x123cm-39x48in) s. painted c.1935. 18-May-94 Sotheby's, New York #234/R

RAMOS, Mel (1935-) American
$9500 £6376 Barbara (46x36cm-18x14in) s.i.d.1966 verso. 25-Feb-94 Sotheby's, New York #65/R
$22000 £14379 Leta and the Canadian honker (152x132cm-60x52in) s.i.d.1969verso. 5-May-93 Christie's, New York #289/R
$23000 £15232 Mysta of Moon (127x127cm-50x50in) s.d.1963 verso. 18-Nov-92 Sotheby's, New York #165/R
$30000 £19868 Crime buster (76x66cm-30x26in) painted 1962 s.i.verso. 19-Nov-92 Christie's, New York #344/R
$85000 £57432 Virnaburger (152x127cm-60x50in) s.i.d.1965verso. 10-Nov-93 Christie's, New York #186/R

RAMOS, Sanchez (?) Mexican
$1298 £877 Paisajes (13x18cm-5x7in) s. pair. 9-Nov-93 Louis Morton, Mexico #14/R (M.P 4200)

RAMSEY, Milne (1847-1915) American
$750 £490 Cottages along lakebank (25x33cm-10x13in) s. panel. 30-Oct-92 Sloan, North Bethesda #2037
$3750 £2517 The anatomy lesson (67x117cm-26x46in) s.d.7.81 panel. 4-Mar-94 Skinner, Bolton #201/R
$4000 £2797 Alpine waterfall (80x120cm-31x47in) 11-Mar-93 Christie's, New York #43/R
$9500 £6419 Still life with fruits and glass of cider (28x35cm-11x14in) s.i.d.11.66. 5-Nov-93 Skinner, Bolton #63/R

RAND, J (fl.1820s) American
$550 £369 Portrait of Samuel W Bradlet (66x53cm-26x21in) s. i.d.1830 verso panel. 26-Mar-94 Skinner, Bolton #225/R

RANDOLPH, Lee F (1880-1956) American
$650 £430 Boats at the dock, truck and figures (41x51cm-16x20in) s. canvasboard. 14-Jun-94 John Moran, Pasadena #110 b
$2000 £1333 Boats in harbour (64x76cm-25x30in) s. 15-Mar-94 John Moran, Pasadena #138

RANGEL, Mario (1938-) Mexican
$3820   £2449   Mago de la mancha sensible (40x50cm-16x20in) s. acrylic panel. 29-Apr-93 Louis Morton, Mexico #14 (M.P 12000)

RANGER, Henry Ward (1858-1916) American
$825	£554	Landscape (46x64cm-18x25in) s. 16-Dec-93 Mystic Fine Arts, Connecticut #105/R
$1000	£671	River scene (41x30cm-16x12in) s. board. 24-Mar-94 Mystic Fine Arts, Connecticut #84 a
$1100	£719	Sailboats tied in the bay (30x46cm-12x18in) panel. 15-May-93 Dunning's, Illinois #1092/R
$1900	£1284	Autumn landscape (30x41cm-12x16in) panel. 23-Oct-93 Collins, Maine #163/R
$2000	£1299	Landscape with wagon (47x65cm-19x26in) studio st. 9-Sep-93 Sotheby's Arcade, New York #84/R
$2100	£1214	Landscape near Lyme, Connecticut (30x41cm-12x16in) s.d.1911 board. 25-Sep-92 Sotheby's Arcade, New York #153/R
$2250	£1490	Road into town (46x66cm-18x26in) s. estate st. 13-Nov-92 Skinner, Bolton #76/R
$2700	£1765	End of summer, forest glade with cottage, river, man in skiff (46x64cm-18x25in) s.indist.d.92. 15-May-93 Dunning's, Illinois #1091/R
$3000	£1734	Sailboats in stormy cove (30x46cm-12x18in) st.studio board. 25-Sep-92 Sotheby's Arcade, New York #83/R
$4000	£2614	Cottage in the valley (30x41cm-12x16in) s.d.1907 board. 1-Nov-92 Hanzel Galleries, Chicago #24/R
$14000	£8974	Harbour at sunset, Noank, Connecticut (71x91cm-28x36in) s.d.1907. 27-May-93 Sotheby's, New York #65/R

RANNEY, William T (school) (1813-1857) American
$30000   £20979   Wild duck shooting, on the wing (76x114cm-30x45in) 11-Mar-93 Christie's, New York #114 a/R

RAPHAEL, Joseph (1872-1950) American
$1800	£1208	The orchard (18x28cm-7x11in) s. i.d.1916 verso board. 8-Dec-93 Butterfield & Butterfield, San Francisco #3400/R
$1900	£1275	The Rhine, Leiden (15x24cm-6x9in) s. i.verso board. 8-Dec-93 Butterfield & Butterfield, San Francisco #3401/R
$2500	£1656	House on a hill (76x66cm-30x26in) 15-Jun-94 Butterfield & Butterfield, San Francisco #4592/R
$2750	£1809	80 years old and still on the job (27x35cm-11x14in) init. s.i.d.1932 verso board. 13-Jun-93 Butterfield & Butterfield, San Francisco #765/R
$6000	£3974	A fishing village (70x79cm-28x31in) s. 15-Jun-94 Butterfield & Butterfield, San Francisco #4591/R
$20000	£13158	House in clearing (67x65cm-26x26in) s. 13-Jun-93 Butterfield & Butterfield, San Francisco #837/R
$23000	£15436	Still life with poppies (100x84cm-39x33in) s. masonite. 8-Dec-93 Butterfield & Butterfield, San Francisco #3493/R
$67500	£45000	Summer gardening (70x76cm-28x30in) s. 17-Mar-94 Sotheby's, New York #130/R
$500	£331	Hortus Leiden, Glinko Tree (36x48cm-14x19in) s.i. W/C. 15-Jun-94 Butterfield & Butterfield, San Francisco #4595/R
$750	£497	St.Margherita (46x51cm-18x20in) s.i. W/C pencil. 15-Jun-94 Butterfield & Butterfield, San Francisco #4596/R
$750	£497	Toll Brug (48x63cm-19x25in) s.i. W/C pencil. 15-Jun-94 Butterfield & Butterfield, San Francisco #4593/R

RAPHAEL, William (1833-1914) Prussian/Canadian
$728	£485	Country meadow (40x27cm-16x11in) init.d.85 board. 13-May-94 Joyner Fine Art, Toronto #236 (C.D 1000)
$779	£513	The habitant (25x20cm-10x8in) s. panel. 7-Jun-93 Waddingtons, Toronto #1145 b (C.D 1000)
$1091	£718	Musician (32x25cm-13x10in) s. 7-Jun-93 Waddingtons, Toronto #1145 c (C.D 1400)
$1179	£746	The pensive fishermen (43x69cm-17x27in) s.d.1910. 1-Dec-92 Fraser Pinneys, Quebec #35/R (C.D 1500)
$1200	£784	Old tradesman (38x23cm-15x9in) s.d.1877 board. 19-Sep-93 Hindman Galleries, Chicago #718/R
$1651	£1045	Beaver crossing the lake (34x48cm-13x19in) s.d.1874 board. 1-Dec-92 Fraser Pinneys, Quebec #31 a (C.D 2100)
$1820	£1214	Man with a pipe (37x22cm-15x9in) s.d.1879 board. 11-May-94 Sotheby's, Toronto #83/R (C.D 2500)
$3118	£2051	Portrait of young woman (76x56cm-30x22in) s.d.1901. 7-Jun-93 Waddingtons, Toronto #1137 f (C.D 4000)

RASCHEN, Henry (1854-1937) German/American
$700   £464   Flowering landscape 'The Desert in California' (25x36cm-10x14in) s. W/C. 14-Jun-94 John Moran, Pasadena #65

RASER, J Heyl (1824-1901) American
$3000   £1974   View of small mid-19th century American town, probably Reading, Pennsylvania (46x76cm-18x30in) s. 2-Apr-93 Eldred, Massachusetts #547/R

RASKIN, Joseph (1897-1981) American
$1000	£658	Pulling ashore East Gloucester (51x61cm-20x24in) s. 5-Jun-93 Louisiana Auction Exchange #32/R
$2500	£1689	Apple trees (76x91cm-30x36in) s. 31-Mar-94 Sotheby's Arcade, New York #266/R

RASKIN, Saul (1878-?) American
$4000   £2614   Synagogue in Jerusalem (50x60cm-20x24in) s. canvasboard. 15-Apr-93 Sotheby's, Tel Aviv #95/R

RATTNER, Abraham (1895-1978) American
$1400	£809	Descent from the cross (40x34cm-16x13in) s.i. masonite. 25-Sep-92 Sotheby's Arcade, New York #456/R
$8000	£5594	Temptation of St Anthony (100x81cm-39x32in) s. i.stretcher. 10-Mar-93 Sotheby's, New York #160/R
$600	£385	Woman by table (46x30cm-18x12in) s. gouache. 12-Dec-92 Weschler, Washington #93
$677	£457	Six millions (75x102cm-30x40in) s. mixed media board. 13-Nov-93 Neret-Minet, Paris #70 (F.FR 4000)

RATTRAY, Alexander Wellwood (1849-1902) American
$749	£520	Ellen Terry's orchard in Surrey (28x18cm-11x7in) s. board. 1-Mar-93 Robin Fenner, Tavistock #174

RAUGHT, John Willard (1857-1931) American
$1000	£671	Meadow brook (51x76cm-20x30in) s.d.1909. 5-Dec-93 James Bakker, Cambridge #34/R
$1100	£769	Peasants outside cottage (41x33cm-16x13in) s.d.1887. 5-Feb-93 Sloan, North Bethesda #2188/R

RAUL, Josephine G (20th C) American
$1000	£690	Metal and glass (76x64cm-30x25in) s. 16-Feb-93 John Moran, Pasadena #112

RAUSCHENBERG, Robert (1925-) American
$11000	£6471	Untitled (29x22cm-11x9in) s.d.87 solvent transfer acrylic paper. 8-Oct-92 Christie's, New York #252/R
$20000	£11765	Five Wise men because of one tilted tiger (244x122cm-96x48in) acrylic copper sheet. 8-Oct-92 Christie's, New York #176/R
$30000	£20134	Paddy Cake - Shiner (183x213cm-72x84in) s.d.88 acrylic enamel on stainless steel. 25-Feb-94 Sotheby's, New York #100/R
$35000	£20588	Slipper (226x89cm-89x35in) s.d.84 acrylic solvent transfer. 8-Oct-92 Christie's, New York #172/R
$52500	£34314	Lichen - Salvage Series (205x205cm-81x81in) s.d.1984 acrylic linen. 4-May-93 Sotheby's, New York #229/R
$125771	£73983	Half dime (246x298cm-97x117in) s.d.89 acrylic aluminium two panels. 1-Oct-92 Watine-Arnault, Paris #41/R (F.FR 600000)
$155000	£104730	Untitled - Gold painting (27x26cm-11x10in) s.d.53on stretcher gold leaf. 10-Nov-93 Sotheby's, New York #14/R
$3000	£1987	Bottle Cap from Airport Series (107x168cm-42x66in) s.d.74 col. mixed media collage pen. 13-Nov-92 Du Mouchelle, Detroit #2015/R
$3027	£1991	Samarkand stitches (148x136cm-58x54in) s.d.1988 cloth collage in plexiglass. 3-Nov-92 Bukowskis, Stockholm #226/R (S.KR 18000)
$7500	£5034	Untitled (23x38cm-9x15in) s.d.79 solvent transfer fabric plastic rulers. 4-May-94 Christie's, New York #333/R
$9498	£6375	Foot first (103x68cm-41x27in) s.d.88 mixed media fabric pencil transfer. 29-Nov-93 AB Stockholms Auktionsverk, Stockholm #6262/R (S.KR 80000)
$14000	£9396	Alley, hoarfrost series (168x102cm-66x40in) s.d.75 solvent transfer fabric. 5-May-94 Sotheby's, New York #211/R
$14706	£9427	Sans titre (78x56cm-31x22in) s.d.79 collage mixed media. 17-Dec-92 Arcole, Paris #55/R (F.FR 79000)
$17000	£11111	Cornice (165x100cm-65x39in) s.d.88 acrylic solvent transfer on fabric. 5-May-93 Christie's, New York #306/R
$18000	£11765	Untitled - Hoarfrost Series (168x89cm-66x35in) s.d.75 solvent transfer cardboard fabric. 4-May-93 Sotheby's, New York #227/R
$19370	£13000	Albeit (162x90cm-64x35in) s.d.88 acrylic silkscreen pencil fabric paper. 24-Jun-93 Christie's, London #90/R
$20000	£13423	Blue pike (213x91cm-84x36in) s.d.79 solvent transfer oil fabric paper collage. 5-May-94 Sotheby's, New York #220/R
$20860	£14000	Untitled (102x70cm-40x28in) s.d.72 solvent transfer fabric collage on paper. 2-Dec-93 Sotheby's, London #63/R
$22000	£14379	Untitled (215x94cm-85x37in) s.d.82verso oil transfer collage board. 5-Oct-93 Sotheby's, New York #29/R
$22000	£14865	Riddles and guesses (58x74cm-23x29in) solvent transfer oil W/C tape collage exec.1967. 10-Nov-93 Christie's, New York #135/R
$28000	£18792	Onyx rise - Galvanic suite (122x307cm-48x121in) s.d.89 oil silkscreen polymer on aluminium. 23-Feb-94 Christie's, New York #54/R
$28440	£18000	Turn and questionmark (56x75cm-22x30in) s.d.68 transfer print gouache. 3-Dec-92 Sotheby's, London #51/R
$31290	£21000	Egyptian Series (167x101cm-66x40in) s.d.74 solvent transfer fabric. 25-Mar-93 Christie's, London #99/R
$31785	£19500	Night blind - Urban Bourbon Series (122x184cm-48x72in) transfer print oil enamelled metal sheets. 14-Oct-92 Sotheby's, London #380/R
$33000	£21569	Rush IV - Cloister Series (249x189cm-98x74in) s.d.80 mixed media. 4-May-93 Sotheby's, New York #387/R
$38000	£25166	Mobile crypt (78x116cm-31x46in) s.d.79 solvent transfer fabric paper collage. 19-Nov-92 Christie's, New York #373/R
$38000	£25676	Yellow Aisle (168x102cm-66x40in) s.d.88 acrylic solvent transfer fabric on canvas. 10-Nov-93 Christie's, New York #241/R
$42000	£29167	Garden stretch (345x246cm-136x97in) s.d.88 i.d.verso enamel aluminum diptych. 24-Feb-93 Christie's, New York #169/R
$45000	£30201	Untitled (56x76cm-22x30in) s.d.68 gouache solvent transfer. 5-May-94 Sotheby's, New York #166/R
$55000	£36913	Untitled gold painting (20x20cm-8x8in) s.d.Dec.53stretcher gold leaf paper fabric glue. 4-May-94 Sotheby's, New York #22/R
$60000	£40541	Complete relexation (58x73cm-23x29in) s.d.1958verso solvent transfer gess ink crayon. 10-Nov-93 Christie's, New York #128 a/R

RAUSCHENBERG, Robert (1925-) American-cont.
$105000	£70946	Cage (50x63cm-20x25in) ink pencil W/C gouache crayon collage exec.1958. 10-Nov-93 Sotheby's, New York #19/R
$120000	£80537	Orville Wright in S.C. (27x19cm-11x7in) i. s.d.1959verso oil paper fabric collage panel. 3-May-94 Christie's, New York #8/R
$350000	£234899	Lock (102x76cm-40x30in) s.i.d.1964verso oil silkscreen inks canvas. 3-May-94 Christie's, New York #17/R
$650000	£424837	Nettle (215x100cm-85x39in) oil paper collage canvas chain aluminium steel. 4-May-93 Christie's, New York #40/R
$700000	£463576	Untitled (45x46cm-18x18in) mixed media on silk. 18-Nov-92 Christie's, New York #25/R
$1000000	£662252	Press (213x152cm-84x60in) s.i.d.1964verso oil silkscreen ink canvas. 17-Nov-92 Sotheby's, New York #43/R

RAYO, Omar (1928-) Colombian
$3000	£2013	Astorotsa (66x66cm-26x26in) s.d.1977verso acrylic. 7-Jan-94 Gary Nader, Miami #124/R

READING ARTIST (attrib) (19th C) American
$7000	£4667	Portrait of Edward Loss, dated 1850 (21x16cm-8x6in) d.1850 W/C ink executed mid-19th C. 10-Jun-94 Christie's, New York #433/R

REAM, Carducius Plantagenet (1837-1917) American
$500	£333	Portrait of a lady in a wide brimme hat (69x56cm-27x22in) s. 17-May-94 Christie's, East, New York #526
$3200	£2119	Still life with basket of apples (56x69cm-22x27in) s. 22-Sep-93 Christie's, New York #26/R
$3500	£2365	Still life with peaches outdoors (41x51cm-16x20in) s. board. 5-Nov-93 Skinner, Bolton #58/R
$3800	£2550	Still life with plums (53x84cm-21x33in) 12-Dec-93 Hindman Galleries, Chicago #243/R

REAM, Morston C (1840-1898) American
$1600	£1088	Still life with fruit and flowers (61x46cm-24x18in) s.d.75stretcher. 15-Nov-93 Christie's, East, New York #11/R
$2700	£1776	Still life with fruit (76x63cm-30x25in) s. 31-Mar-93 Sotheby's Arcade, New York #39/R
$4100	£2697	Still life with fruit and fish bowl (69x56cm-27x22in) s. 31-Mar-93 Sotheby's Arcade, New York #36/R
$4250	£2815	Still life with wine glass and fruit (28x38cm-11x15in) s. 15-Jun-94 Butterfield & Butterfield, San Francisco #4441/R

REASER, Wilbur Aaron (1860-1942) American
$4500	£2647	Oakland harbour (58x70cm-23x28in) s.d.1903 board. 4-Oct-92 Butterfield & Butterfield, Los Angeles #56/R
$3000	£1974	Butternut Valley, N.W.N.Y.State (95x169cm-37x67in) s. pastel canvas on board shaped top. 31-Mar-93 Sotheby's Arcade, New York #164/R

REBAY, Hilla (1890-1967) American/French
$1500	£1049	Untitled (58x109cm-23x43in) 11-Mar-93 Christie's, New York #266/R
$3000	£2013	Lyricism (127x99cm-50x39in) 24-Feb-94 Sotheby's Arcade, New York #142/R
$3000	£2013	Vivace (96x96cm-38x38in) s.d.46. 24-Feb-94 Sotheby's Arcade, New York #141/R
$3250	£2257	Andantino (127x94cm-50x37in) s.i.d.1942-1945. 26-Feb-93 Sotheby's Arcade, New York #279/R
$700	£470	Portrait of Dorothea Croasdale (56x46cm-22x18in) pastel. 27-Mar-94 Myers, Florida #56/R
$800	£537	Occult (32x25cm-13x10in) s. W/C paper collage. 24-Feb-94 Sotheby's Arcade, New York #137/R
$800	£556	Composition No.14 (34x28cm-13x11in) s. W/C ink executed c.1944. 26-Feb-93 Sotheby's Arcade, New York #261/R
$1100	£764	Green (30x41cm-12x16in) s.d.44 W/C col pencil graphite. 26-Feb-93 Sotheby's Arcade, New York #266/R
$3250	£2181	Untitled (21x27cm-8x11in) s.d.1916 W/C paper collage. 24-Feb-94 Sotheby's Arcade, New York #136/R

REBOLLEDO CORREA, Benito (1880-1964) Chilean
$1300	£833	El Huaso (44x70cm-17x28in) s. 28-May-93 Christie's, East, New York #363/R
$1800	£1154	Goats grazing on hillside (65x84cm-26x33in) s. 28-May-93 Christie's, East, New York #361
$2000	£1282	Los cabrios (56x46cm-22x18in) s. 28-May-93 Christie's, East, New York #359/R

REBRY, Gaston (1933-) Canadian
$508	£343	Riviere au Degel (36x46cm-14x18in) s.s.i.d.1993verso. 25-Apr-94 Levis, Calgary #271/R (C.D 700)
$583	£388	Dans L'Erabliere (40x50cm-16x20in) s. 13-May-94 Joyner Fine Art, Toronto #222 (C.D 800)
$662	£438	Rose and blue (46x61cm-18x24in) s. s.i.d.1992verso. 16-Nov-92 Hodgins, Calgary #32 (C.D 850)
$666	£427	St Mathieu du Parc (41x51cm-16x20in) s. s.i.d.1992verso. 26-Apr-93 Levis, Calgary #157 (C.D 875)
$728	£485	St Mathieu - Que. (45x60cm-18x24in) s. 13-May-94 Joyner Fine Art, Toronto #142/R (C.D 1000)
$739	£490	Nature morte (35x45cm-14x18in) s. 24-Nov-92 Joyner Fine Art, Toronto #253/R (C.D 950)

REBRY, Gaston (1933-) Canadian-cont.
$874	£583	Automne en plein foret (46x61cm-18x24in) s. s.i.d.1991verso. 11-May-94 Sotheby's, Toronto #120/R (C.D 1200)
$1279	£864	Spectacle de la nature (46x61cm-18x24in) s. s.i.d.1993verso. 1-Nov-93 Levis, Calgary #261/R (C.D 1650)
$1395	£942	By the side of a small lake (46x61cm-18x24in) s. s.i.d.1972verso. 3-Nov-93 Sotheby's, Toronto #113/R (C.D 1800)
$1427	£933	Lake Castor, Quebec (46x61cm-18x24in) s. s.d.1992verso. 19-May-93 Sotheby's, Toronto #152/R (C.D 1800)
$1794	£1196	Gel clair d'hiver (102x76cm-40x30in) s. s.i.d.verso. 30-May-94 Hodgins, Calgary #225/R (C.D 2500)
$1959	£1324	Sous le tapis bleu (122x91cm-48x36in) s. s.i.d.1993verso. 25-Apr-94 Levis, Calgary #270/R (C.D 2700)
$2412	£1641	A la decharge du lac (102x76cm-40x30in) s. s.i.verso. 15-Nov-93 Hodgins, Calgary #47/R (C.D 3200)
$3020	£2041	Lac Wapizagong, Parc National de la Mauricie, automne, 1982 (120x150cm-47x59in) s. 23-Nov-93 Joyner Fine Art, Toronto #89/R (C.D 4000)

RECCHIAN, Russell (1959-) American
$650	£442	Portrait of Ellen (107x91cm-42x36in) s.d.1981. 14-Apr-94 Freeman Fine Arts, Philadelphia #1046

RED STAR, Kevin (1943-) American
$600	£390	Portrait of warrior (91x76cm-36x30in) s. acrylic. 25-Jun-94 Skinner, Bolton #190/R
$1400	£909	Taos pueblo, New Mexico (97x91cm-38x36in) s. s.i.d.1981verso. 25-Jun-94 Skinner, Bolton #201/R
$2600	*£1677*	*Ms Jackrabbit and daughters (112x86cm-44x34in) s. d.1976 verso acrylic mixed media canvas. 9-Jan-93 Skinner, Bolton #82/R*

REDDIE, McIvor (20th C) American
$800	£506	Making ready (51x61cm-20x24in) s. board. 24-Oct-92 Collins, Maine #75/R

REDFIELD, Edward (1869-1965) American
$2600	£1722	French countryside (36x53cm-14x21in) s. 23-Sep-93 Mystic Fine Arts, Connecticut #148 a
$6000	£4000	Snowy woodland scene (66x41cm-26x16in) s. painted c.1900. 23-May-94 Christie's, East, New York #154/R
$7000	£4698	The rocky coast (51x61cm-20x24in) s. 8-Dec-93 Butterfield & Butterfield, San Francisco #3458/R
$19000	£12025	Horse and carriage in winter (59x81cm-23x32in) s. painted c.1899. 2-Dec-92 Christie's, East, New York #261/R
$25000	£16026	Meadow brook (66x81cm-26x32in) s. 27-May-93 Sotheby's, New York #63/R
$50000	£34965	Garden, Boothbay Harbour, Michigan (53x66cm-21x26in) s. painted 1924. 14-Mar-93 Hindman Galleries, Chicago #21/R
$60000	£41958	Toymaker's home (67x82cm-26x32in) s. 11-Mar-93 Christie's, New York #150/R
$60000	£38462	Breeze (81x102cm-32x40in) s.i.stretcher. 26-May-93 Christie's, New York #147/R
$80000	£50633	The grey veil (97x127cm-38x50in) s. 4-Dec-92 Christie's, New York #33/R

REDFIELD, Edward (attrib) (1869-1965) American
$750	£493	Lobster Cove Monhegan 20-28 July 1919 (20x25cm-8x10in) i.verso panel painted 1919. 5-Jun-93 Louisiana Auction Exchange #128/R

REDIN, Carl (20th C) American
$1200	£694	New Mexico landscape with adobe house and cottonwood tree (30x41cm-12x16in) s. canvas on board. 25-Sep-92 Sotheby's Arcade, New York #192/R

REDMOND, Granville (1871-1935) American
$1500	£1007	Campfire on the beach (30x41cm-12x16in) s. board. 8-Dec-93 Butterfield & Butterfield, San Francisco #3420/R
$1800	£1192	Landscape (20x25cm-8x10in) s.d.09. 14-Jun-94 John Moran, Pasadena #80
$2250	£1490	Lake sunset (20x25cm-8x10in) s. 15-Jun-94 Butterfield & Butterfield, San Francisco #4616/R
$2400	£1633	Sunset (30x46cm-12x18in) s.d.02. 15-Nov-93 Christie's, East, New York #42
$2500	£1656	Atmospheric landscape (18x25cm-7x10in) s.d.07 canvas on board. 14-Jun-94 John Moran, Pasadena #25
$3000	£1754	Landscape with woods (36x46cm-14x18in) s. 18-Sep-92 Du Mouchelle, Detroit #2188/R
$3000	£2013	A hazy morning (20x25cm-8x10in) s.d.1918 s.i.d.verso board. 8-Dec-93 Butterfield & Butterfield, San Francisco #3463/R
$3000	£1899	Study by moonlight, Golden Gate Park (23x30cm-9x12in) s.d.1916 board. 2-Dec-92 Christie's, East, New York #159/R
$3250	£2181	Sunset along the California Coast (25x29cm-10x11in) s. s.d.1918 verso board. 8-Dec-93 Butterfield & Butterfield, San Francisco #3462/R
$4500	£3000	Moonlit landscape by a pond (20x25cm-8x10in) s. board. 15-Mar-94 John Moran, Pasadena #70
$4750	£3276	River landscape (30x46cm-12x18in) s.d.08 canvas laid down on canvas. 16-Feb-93 John Moran, Pasadena #46
$4750	£2794	Sunrise (23x30cm-9x12in) s. 4-Oct-92 Butterfield & Butterfield, Los Angeles #169/R
$5500	£3667	Landscape with lupin, poppies and oaks (18x25cm-7x10in) s. board. 15-Mar-94 John Moran, Pasadena #25
$5500	£3793	Landscape (20x30cm-8x12in) s. 16-Feb-93 John Moran, Pasadena #53
$6000	£3529	Sunny lagoon (24x34cm-9x13in) s. board. 4-Oct-92 Butterfield & Butterfield, Los Angeles #168/R

REDMOND, Granville (1871-1935) American-cont.
$6500	£4276	Lion's Head, Cherry cove, Catalina Island (29x36cm-11x14in) s.d.1918 board. 13-Jun-93 Butterfield & Butterfield, San Francisco #855/R
$6500	£4276	Catalina moonlight (28x36cm-11x14in) s. board. 13-Jun-93 Butterfield & Butterfield, San Francisco #854/R
$7000	£4730	Sunset at Menlo and Morning at San Mateo (41x51cm-16x20in) s.d.1912. 15-Jun-93 John Moran, Pasadena #98
$7000	£4730	Oaks in landscape (41x51cm-16x20in) s.d.1911. 9-Nov-93 John Moran, Pasadena #882
$8500	£5705	Distant mountains at sunset (30x41cm-12x16in) s. 8-Dec-93 Butterfield & Butterfield, San Francisco #3387/R
$8500	£5000	Stream and wildflowers (20x25cm-8x10in) s. canvas on board. 4-Oct-92 Butterfield & Butterfield, Los Angeles #124/R
$8500	£5000	In shadow of storm, Menlo Park (61x76cm-24x30in) s.d.1911. 4-Oct-92 Butterfield & Butterfield, Los Angeles #57/R
$12000	£7947	Nocturnal landscape (77x113cm-30x44in) s.d.1918. 15-Jun-94 Butterfield & Butterfield, San Francisco #4589 a/R
$28000	£17722	Bringing the flock home (83x179cm-33x70in) s.d.03. 3-Dec-92 Sotheby's, New York #103/R
$37500	£26042	California wildflowers (41x51cm-16x20in) s. 7-Mar-93 Butterfield & Butterfield, San Francisco #127/R

REED (20th C) American
$600	£403	Cottage in a landscape (30x41cm-12x16in) indist.s. canvas laid down on masonite. 2-May-94 Selkirks, St. Louis #492

REED, David (1946-) American
$4500	£2941	No.172-2 (30x256cm-12x101in) two panels executed 1981-1983. 22-Dec-92 Christie's, East, New York #64
$7500	£4902	No. 226 (66x244cm-26x96in) oil alkyd linen executed 1985-1986. 22-Dec-92 Christie's, East, New York #63
$8000	£5298	Untitled (30x208cm-12x82in) s.d.1979 acrylic. 18-Nov-92 Sotheby's, New York #238/R

REED, Marjorie (1915-) American
$725	£487	Monument Valley (51x76cm-20x30in) s. 4-Dec-93 Louisiana Auction Exchange #24
$950	£642	Autumn trail through the High Country (38x76cm-15x30in) s. i.verso canvasboard. 9-Nov-93 John Moran, Pasadena #855
$950	£629	Moonlight staging in old Arizona (51x61cm-20x24in) s. 28-Sep-93 John Moran, Pasadena #260 b
$1200	£795	Changing horses at stage stop (61x76cm-24x30in) s. 28-Sep-93 John Moran, Pasadena #260 a
$2500	£1724	Back country run-off (61x76cm-24x30in) 16-Feb-93 John Moran, Pasadena #76
$2500	£1724	Vallecito Station, midnite stop, Butterfield Stage (61x91cm-24x36in) s. 16-Feb-93 John Moran, Pasadena #66

REEDY, Leonard Howard (1899-1956) American
$1900	£1250	Battle on plain (63x76cm-25x30in) s. masonite. 31-Mar-93 Sotheby's Arcade, New York #206/R

REEP, Edward (1918-) American
$550	£364	L.A. Industrial scene (51x74cm-20x29in) s. W/C. 14-Jun-94 John Moran, Pasadena #98
$650	£430	Mending the nets (48x66cm-19x26in) s. W/C. 28-Sep-93 John Moran, Pasadena #339

REEVES, Richard Stone (20th C) American
$2831	£1900	Bleu Azur and Altesse Royale in paddock with Colonel Hue-Williams (70x80cm-28x31in) s.i. 6-Dec-93 Sotheby's, London #609/R
$6500	£4333	Bold Ruler (51x76cm-20x30in) s.i.d.1957. 3-Jun-94 Sotheby's, New York #285/R

REHN, Frank Knox Morton (1848-1914) American
$600	£411	Fishing boats at dawn (61x46cm-24x18in) s. 19-Feb-94 Young Fine Arts Auctions, Maine #167/R
$675	£433	Sunset at Crescent Beach, Massachusetts (41x71cm-16x28in) s. 28-May-93 Sloan, North Bethesda #2395/R
$800	£533	Country cottage in a landscape (41x71cm-16x28in) s. canvas laid down. 15-Mar-94 John Moran, Pasadena #174
$1100	£696	Gondola on back canal in Venice (41x61cm-16x24in) s. 2-Dec-92 Christie's, East, New York #69/R
$1300	£909	Sailboats along horizon (51x91cm-20x36in) s.d.1875. 3-Feb-93 Doyle, New York #51
$1400	£927	Beach Road, Magnolia (41x61cm-16x24in) s. 21-Nov-92 James Bakker, Cambridge #268/R
$2000	£1316	Long Beach, New York (41x71cm-16x28in) s.i. 31-Mar-93 Sotheby's Arcade, New York #24/R
$2000	£1361	Manomet Beach, Plymouth (22x34cm-9x13in) s. 10-Jul-93 Young Fine Arts Auctions, Maine #264/R
$2491	£1649	Surf (56x91cm-22x36in) s. i.verso. 16-Nov-92 Hodgins, Calgary #298/R (C.D 3200)
$2500	£1623	Bay of Fundy (76x127cm-30x50in) s. 9-Sep-93 Sotheby's Arcade, New York #63/R

REID, George Agnew (1860-1947) Canadian
$502	£335	Twilight, Algoma (43x61cm-17x24in) s.indis.d. 30-May-94 Ritchie, Toronto #176/R (C.D 700)
$623	£412	Pastoral landscape, Paris (23x34cm-9x13in) s.i.d.1888 board. 16-Nov-92 Hodgins, Calgary #81 (C.D 800)
$624	£410	Autumn landscape (34x46cm-13x18in) s. i.verso. 7-Jun-93 Waddingtons, Toronto #1154 (C.D 800)

REID, George Agnew (1860-1947) Canadian-cont.
$718	£478	Cattle grazing by river (43x61cm-17x24in) s.d.1886. 30-May-94 Ritchie, Toronto #148/R (C.D 1000)
$793	£518	Trees and lake (63x107cm-25x42in) s.d.1922. 19-May-93 Sotheby's, Toronto #53 (C.D 1000)
$900	£588	Sunset river scene with cows (43x61cm-17x24in) s.d.1886. 18-Sep-93 Young Fine Arts Auctions, Maine #246/R
$1435	£957	Black spruce, Algoma Valley (75x62cm-30x24in) s.d.1928. 30-May-94 Ritchie, Toronto #139/R (C.D 2000)
$2250	£1490	Lady seated in Windsor chair (38x30cm-15x12in) s. 2-Oct-93 Boos Gallery, Michigan #286/R

REID, Mary Augusta Hiester (1854-1921) Canadian
$753	£505	Chrysanthemums in Quing blue and white vase (36x46cm-14x18in) s.d.1893. 29-Nov-93 Ritchie, Toronto #174/R (C.D 1000)

REID, Robert (1862-1929) American
$2000	£1325	Willow Castle, the home of S.Russell (28x21cm-11x8in) s.d.1916 i.d.verso panel. 15-Jun-94 Butterfield & Butterfield, San Francisco #4423/R
$2100	£1346	Portrait of Elizabeth Purcell (91x61cm-36x24in) s. 9-Dec-92 Grogan, Massachussetts #67/R
$2500	£1603	Portrait of Margaret Sanger (91x61cm-36x24in) s.d.96. 9-Dec-92 Grogan, Massachussetts #66/R
$8000	£5442	Autumn river landscape (94x86cm-37x34in) s. 17-Nov-93 Doyle, New York #33/R
$9000	£6081	White lilacs (107x112cm-42x44in) 31-Oct-93 Hindman Galleries, Chicago #687
$10000	£6803	Midsummer brook (94x76cm-37x30in) s.i. i.verso. 17-Nov-93 Doyle, New York #32/R
$12000	£7947	Tempting sweets (63x76cm-25x30in) s.i.d.1924 i.stretcher. 23-Sep-93 Sotheby's, New York #179/R
$13000	£8228	The bather (65x50cm-26x20in) s. paper laid down on panel. 4-Dec-92 Christie's, New York #59/R
$15000	£10490	Watching the boats (30x41cm-12x16in) s. 12-Mar-93 Skinner, Bolton #234/R
$40000	£25316	The brook (68x78cm-27x31in) s. 4-Dec-92 Christie's, New York #5/R

REIFFEL, Charles (1862-1942) American
$750	£524	Harbour scene (15x18cm-6x7in) s. board. 11-Mar-93 Mystic Fine Arts, Connecticut #167/R
$3000	£1961	Harbour scene (51x61cm-20x24in) s.verso. 30-Jun-94 Mystic Fine Arts, Connecticut #169
$4000	£2778	Prospectors (30x46cm-12x18in) s. s.i.d.1941verso board. 7-Mar-93 Butterfield & Butterfield, San Francisco #216/R
$4750	£3209	Connecticut street scene -edge of Norwalk (30x41cm-12x16in) s. board. 15-Jun-93 John Moran, Pasadena #102
$6000	£3947	Banner Gorge, 1932 (51x61cm-20x24in) s. s.i.d.1932 verso board. 13-Jun-93 Butterfield & Butterfield, San Francisco #860/R
$8500	£5944	Connecticut landscape (71x81cm-28x32in) s. 11-Mar-93 Mystic Fine Arts, Connecticut #166/R
$17000	£10897	Ballast Point, California (45x50cm-18x20in) s. s.s.i.d.1930 verso board. 26-May-93 Christie's, New York #145/R

REINDEL, Edna (1900-1990) American
$800	£537	Still life with fig and pomegranate (30x48cm-12x19in) s. painted c.1966. 25-Mar-93 Boos Gallery, Michigan #568
$1900	£1284	Still life with snuff bottle and other Oriental objects (41x30cm-16x12in) s.d.36. 31-Mar-94 Sotheby's Arcade, New York #364/R

REINHARDT, Ad (1913-1967) American
$8000	£4040	Homage to Taos (23x30cm-9x12in) i.d.11/53verso board. 30-Aug-92 Litchfield Auction Gallery #252
$20000	£13072	Untitled (91x30cm-36x12in) 5-May-93 Christie's, New York #264/R
$47500	£31046	Untitled (81x102cm-32x40in) s.d.48. 4-May-93 Sotheby's, New York #298/R
$70000	£47297	Abstract painting, 1962 (76x76cm-30x30in) s.i.d.verso. 10-Nov-93 Sotheby's, New York #15/R
$80000	£52288	Painting (102x51cm-40x20in) s.d.1959 verso. 4-May-93 Christie's, New York #4/R
$110000	£73826	Abstract painting (76x76cm-30x30in) s.i.d.1952verso. 4-May-94 Christie's, New York #108/R
$170000	£114094	Untitled (152x102cm-60x40in) painted c.1948. 3-May-94 Christie's, New York #44/R
$21000	*£14189*	*Untitled (15x22cm-6x9in) s.d.1940 s.verso gouache paper collage on board. 11-Nov-93 Sotheby's, New York #266/R*

REINHARDT, Siegfried (1925-) American
$700	£458	Allegory of post-war Germany, elderly woman and young girl , s.d.1950. 20-May-93 Eldred, Massachusetts #163/R
$900	£596	Abstract composition (145x244cm-57x96in) 27-Sep-93 Selkirks, St. Louis #934
$1100	£705	Self portrait (91x61cm-36x24in) s.d.1981 acrylic board. 26-Apr-93 Selkirks, St. Louis #295
$1100	£582	Wash day (28x43cm-11x17in) s.d.1955 i.verso masonite. 11-Sep-92 Skinner, Bolton #277/R
$2700	£1709	Abstract composition (46x183cm-18x72in) s.d.1954 acrylic masonite. 30-Nov-92 Selkirks, St. Louis #288
$750	£503	Creation (28x43cm-11x17in) s.d.1953 mixed media. 2-May-94 Selkirks, St. Louis #526

REISMAN, Philip (1904-1992) American
$1300	£844	Loading iron (50x70cm-20x28in) s. masonite. 9-Sep-93 Sotheby's Arcade, New York #334/R

REISMAN, Philip (1904-1992) American-cont.
$2500	£1623	Demolition (81x65cm-32x26in) s.d.1951 s.i.d.verso masonite. 9-Sep-93 Sotheby's Arcade, New York #214/R
$1000	£680	The Old East Side (39x71cm-15x28in) init. s.i.verso chl. 15-Nov-93 Christie's, East, New York #258

REITZEL, Marques E (1896-1963) American
$3000	£1987	Icy river (97x91cm-38x36in) s. 22-Sep-93 Christie's, New York #173/R

REMINGTON, Frederic (1861-1909) American
$85000	£56667	Mandan initiation ceremony - the Sundance (53x47cm-21x19in) s.d.88 board grisaille. 26-May-94 Christie's, New York #62/R
$1300	£872	At the Front (23x25cm-9x10in) s. ink wash dr. 2-Dec-93 Swann Galleries, New York #263
$1300	£844	Valkyrie on horse (21x15cm-8x6in) s.i. pen. 9-Sep-93 Sotheby's Arcade, New York #227/R
$2000	£1325	Indian axe and arrowhead - illustration from Song of Hiawatha (31x18cm-12x7in) i. pen. 23-Sep-93 Sotheby's, New York #102/R
$3250	£2153	Dinner bell (46x27cm-18x11in) s.i. pen wash gouache. 23-Sep-93 Sotheby's, New York #102/R
$3750	£2484	Richard Mansfield as Richard III (56x37cm-22x15in) s. i.verso pen. 23-Sep-93 Sotheby's, New York #105/R
$5500	£3179	Moose head from Song of Hiawatha (22x28cm-9x11in) s.i. pen. 23-Sep-92 Christie's, New York #104/R
$9500	£6376	German Infantry officer, illustration in Harper's Weekly May 20 1893 (51x30cm-20x12in) s.i. W/C paper board painted c.1892. 2-May-94 Selkirks, St. Louis #131/R
$11000	£7333	Government guide looking for tracks (19x23cm-7x9in) s.i. pen paper on board. 16-Mar-94 Christie's, New York #81/R
$14000	£9396	Prussian Infantry Guard, illustration in Harper's Weekly May 20 1893 (56x30cm-22x12in) s.i. W/C paper board painted c.1892. 2-May-94 Selkirks, St. Louis #132/R
$16000	£11189	Besieged by the Utes (28x30cm-11x12in) s. pen wash board. 11-Mar-93 Christie's, New York #112/R
$21000	£14000	The First City Troop of Philadelphia (39x31cm-15x12in) s. W/C gouache ink en grisaille. 17-Mar-94 Sotheby's, New York #73/R
$30000	£20134	Indian riding down hill, illustration from The Oregon Trail (45x26cm-18x10in) s. pen wash gouache. 2-Dec-93 Sotheby's, New York #51/R
$33000	£21154	Commanche on horseback (46x45cm-18x18in) s.i. ink gouache wash. 27-May-93 Sotheby's, New York #224/R
$34000	£22667	Halt to tighten the packs (34x49cm-13x19in) s. pen. 25-May-94 Sotheby's, New York #52/R
$75000	£47468	The three prospectors (45x58cm-18x23in) s. ink wash gouache paper on board. 3-Dec-92 Sotheby's, New York #12/R

REMMEY, Paul (20th C) American
$650	£428	Sea Isle Dock (56x76cm-22x30in) s.d.46 W/C gouache pencil board. 31-Mar-93 Sotheby's Arcade, New York #408/R

RENDON, Manuel (1894-1980) Ecuadorian/French
$1015	£681	Nu assis (41x33cm-16x13in) s. i.verso. 3-Dec-93 Deurbergue & Delvaux, Paris #73 (F.FR 6000)
$11000	£7190	Visage de femme (92x65cm-36x26in) s. painted c.1930. 18-May-93 Sotheby's, New York #125/R
$16000	£10667	Nu en bleu (100x73cm-39x29in) s. painted c.1918-1921. 17-May-94 Sotheby's, New York #21/R

RENNER, Adelaine (1869-1961) American
$1600	£1088	Tiger and cubs , s.d.1910. 14-Apr-94 Freeman Fine Arts, Philadelphia #998/R

RENZONI, Louis (1952-) American?
$1203	£802	Nurse (127x91cm-50x36in) s.verso painted 1984. 2-Jun-94 AB Stockholms Auktionsverk, Stockholm #7228/R (S.KR 9500)
$5000	£3268	Unimportant detail (244x244cm-96x96in) acrylic executed 1985. 22-Dec-92 Christie's, East, New York #65

REPETTO, Armando E (1893-1968) Argentinian
$2500	£1656	Escena de campo (70x60cm-28x24in) 11-Nov-92 VerBo, Buenos Aires #94

REPPEN, John Richard (1933-1964) Canadian
$507	£338	Mexican head study, no.1 (51x46cm-20x18in) s. i.d.61 verso board. 6-Jun-94 Waddingtons, Toronto #1250 e (C.D 700)
$872	£570	Abstract composition (60x41cm-24x16in) s.d.63 board. 19-May-93 Sotheby's, Toronto #73 (C.D 1100)
$1092	£728	Horse and rider (155x128cm-61x50in) s.d.60. 11-May-94 Sotheby's, Toronto #142/R (C.D 1500)

RESNICK, Milton (1917-) American
$650	£442	Couple in Central Park (38x23cm-15x9in) paper on masonite. 17-Apr-94 Hanzel Galleries, Chicago #993
$1000	£694	Skow (102x76cm-40x30in) s.i.d.1981verso laminated cardboard. 26-Feb-93 Sotheby's Arcade, New York #355/R
$6000	£4054	Composition (54x54cm-21x21in) s.d.1963verso masonite. 10-Nov-93 Christie's, New York #172/R

RESNICK, Milton (1917-) American-cont.
$6500	£3824	Untitled (81x51cm-32x20in) s. paper on masonite. 6-Oct-92 Sotheby's, New York #39/R
$6500	£4248	Time I (112x101cm-44x40in) s.d.1984 verso. 7-May-93 Christie's, East, New York #95/R
$10000	£6944	Untitled (160x94cm-63x37in) s.d.1969verso. 23-Feb-93 Sotheby's, New York #241/R
$10000	£6711	Roswell 14 (203x172cm-80x68in) s.i.d.1971 verso. 23-Feb-94 Christie's, New York #25/R
$13000	£9028	Straw (202x152cm-80x60in) s.i.d.82verso. 24-Feb-93 Christie's, New York #40/R

REUSSWIG, William (1902-) American
$770	£503	Raid to kill Rommel (58x61cm-23x24in) s. i.verso tempera board. 14-May-93 Skinner, Bolton #199/R

REVERON, Armando (1889-1956) Venezuelan
$80000	£52980	Autorretrato (93x63cm-37x25in) s.d. tempera oil board painted 1933. 24-Nov-92 Christie's, New York #39/R
$12000	£7843	Mujer frente al espejo (84x80cm-33x31in) s. chl. 17-May-93 Christie's, New York #107/R
$22500	£14706	Mujer ante el espejo (97x95cm-38x37in) s. chl pastel executed c.1950. 18-May-93 Sotheby's, New York #168/R
$28000	£18301	La enfermera (66x47cm-26x19in) s.d.57 chl chk pastel. 18-May-93 Sotheby's, New York #153/R
$45000	£30000	Autorretrato con Munecas (63x83cm-25x33in) s. chl chk pastel. 18-May-94 Christie's, New York #13/R
$55000	£36486	Retrato de mujer (84x60cm-33x24in) gouache paper on board painted 1934. 24-Nov-92 Christie's, New York #129/R

REYES FERREIRA, Jesus (1882-1977) Mexican
$1500	£1000	Caballo (72x47cm-28x19in) paper laid down on board. 18-May-94 Christie's, New York #312/R
$1804	£1202	Nina (75x50cm-30x20in) s. dye. 25-May-94 Louis Morton, Mexico #26 (M.P 6000)
$2258	£1515	Flores (74x48cm-29x19in) mixed media. 1-Dec-93 Louis Morton, Mexico #156 (M.P 7000)
$2419	£1623	Gallo (95x66cm-37x26in) s. mixed media card. 1-Dec-93 Louis Morton, Mexico #170/R (M.P 7500)
$2700	£1824	Gallo. Naturaleza muerta con fruta (73x46cm-29x18in) gouache gold paint rice paper pair exec.c.1945. 22-Nov-93 Sotheby's, New York #195/R
$2706	£1735	Florero (74x48cm-29x19in) s. W/C. 29-Apr-93 Louis Morton, Mexico #120 (M.P 8500)
$2966	£2004	Cristo atado a la Columna (75x49cm-30x19in) s. gouache. 27-Apr-94 Louis Morton, Mexico #531/R (M.P 10000)
$3064	£2056	Canasto con flores (66x95cm-26x37in) s. mixed media card. 1-Dec-93 Louis Morton, Mexico #33 (M.P 9500)
$3064	£2056	Caballo (74x48cm-29x19in) mixed media. 1-Dec-93 Louis Morton, Mexico #95 (M.P 9500)
$3548	£2381	Gallo (74x48cm-29x19in) mixed media. 1-Dec-93 Louis Morton, Mexico #111 (M.P 11000)
$3870	£2597	Caballo azul y negro (70x50cm-28x20in) s. W/C. 1-Dec-93 Louis Morton, Mexico #193/R (M.P 12000)
$4745	£3206	Payaso (75x48cm-30x19in) gouache. 27-Apr-94 Louis Morton, Mexico #560/R (M.P 16000)

REYNOLDS, Frederick Thomas (1882-?) British/American
$900	£604	Boy fishing (51x41cm-20x16in) s. 2-Dec-93 Freeman Fine Arts, Philadelphia #776

REYNOLDS, W S (19/20th C) American
$982	£650	Still life of correspondance between father and son, with objects on table (30x51cm-12x20in) s. 30-Sep-93 Christie's, S. Kensington #98

REZA, Jorge de la (20th C) Bolivian
$1100	£743	Pequeno Dios (58x48cm-23x19in) tempera. 21-Apr-94 Butterfield & Butterfield, San Francisco #1106/R

RHEAUME, Jeanne (20th C) Canadian
$1295	£841	Piazza Santo Spirito, Florence (35x27cm-14x11in) s.d.51 panel. 21-Jun-94 Fraser Pinneys, Quebec #154 (C.D 1800)

RHEES, Morgan (19/20th C) American
$650	£409	Portrait of young woman with bouquet of pink roses (76x64cm-30x25in) s.d.1888. 23-Apr-93 Skinner, Bolton #353

RHODES, Charles Ward (?-1905) American
$1100	£764	Souvenir d'Ete (51x25cm-20x10in) s.i.d.1894 board. 27-Feb-93 Young Fine Arts Auctions, Maine #237/R

RIBAK, Louis (1902-1979) American
$750	£504	Cart horses (20x35cm-8x14in) s. i.verso panel. 6-May-94 Skinner, Bolton #150/R

RIBCOWSKY, Dey de (1880-1936) Bulgarian/American
$750	£494	Sailing in moonlight (51x61cm-20x24in) s.d.1912. 13-Jun-93 Butterfield & Butterfield, San Francisco #779/R
$800	£530	Under full sail (51x76cm-20x30in) s.d.1911. 3-Oct-93 Hanzel Galleries, Chicago #822
$1200	£795	Venice at sunset (76x101cm-30x40in) s. canvasboard. 2-Oct-93 Weschler, Washington #127/R

RIBCOWSKY, Dey de (1880-1936) Bulgarian/American-cont.
$1400   £921   Sunset, Half Moon Bay (36x91cm-14x36in) s. 13-Jun-93 Butterfield & Butterfield, San Francisco #800/R
$3000   £1734   Sunrise over the shore (61x102cm-24x40in) s. 25-Sep-92 Sotheby's Arcade, New York #271

RIBEIRO, Edgardo (20th C) Uruguayan
$600   £392   Jugadores de cartas (47x56cm-19x22in) s.d.85. 4-Oct-93 Gomensoro, Montevideo #31
$720   £487   Calle de pueblo espanol con vecinos (50x60cm-20x24in) s.d.1959. 25-Apr-94 Gomensoro, Montevideo #31
$850   £574   Paisaje de Castilla (51x61cm-20x24in) s.d.66. 25-Apr-94 Gomensoro, Montevideo #72
$2300   £1544   Naturaleza muerta (76x98cm-30x39in) s. 29-Nov-93 Gomensoro, Montevideo #50/R

RICCIARDI, Caesar A (1892-?) American
$800   £544   Men working on dock (61x91cm-24x36in) s.d.1954. 14-Apr-94 Freeman Fine Arts, Philadelphia #1023
$800   £544   Boats at dock (61x91cm-24x36in) s.d.54. 14-Apr-94 Freeman Fine Arts, Philadelphia #1022

RICE, Anne Estelle (1879-1959) American
$1490   £1000   Still life with wine glass (40x51cm-16x20in) s. 24-Mar-94 Sotheby's, London #56/R
$2980   £2000   Cote d'Azur (30x40cm-12x16in) panel. 6-May-94 Phillips, Edinburgh #84/R

RICE, Henry Webster (?) American
$1500   £1007   Cottage, St Johns Hill-Spanish Point (33x48cm-13x19in) s. W/C. 26-Mar-94 James Bakker, Cambridge #1/R

RICE-PEREIRA, Irene (1907-1971) American
$800   £537   Forms in space (23x10cm-9x4in) s. W/C. 24-Mar-94 Mystic Fine Arts, Connecticut #154
$1000   £654   Descent of dove (100x65cm-39x26in) s.i.d.1965 gouache. 4-May-93 Christie's, East, New York #318/R
$5500   £3716   Untitled (61x58cm-24x23in) s. mixed media. 31-Mar-94 Sotheby's Arcade, New York #469/R

RICH, John Hubbard (1876-1954) American
$3000   £2083   Still life with fruit, wine jug and goblet (41x51cm-16x20in) s. 7-Mar-93 Butterfield & Butterfield, San Francisco #241/R

RICHARD, Rene (1895-1982) Canadian
$775   £524   Landscape with cabin (36x46cm-14x18in) s. masonite. 1-Nov-93 Levis, Calgary #268/R (C.D 1000)
$978   £657   Autumn lake landscape Quebec (30x40cm-12x16in) s. masonite. 29-Nov-93 Ritchie, Toronto #219/R (C.D 1300)
$1189   £777   Lac dans les Laurentides (36x46cm-14x18in) s. board. 19-May-93 Sotheby's, Toronto #61 (C.D 1500)
$1888   £1276   Riviere Malbaie a Laroche (41x51cm-16x20in) s. i.verso board. 23-Nov-93 Fraser Pinneys, Quebec #451 (C.D 2500)
$3508   £2308   Parc des Laurentides (77x93cm-30x37in) s. i.verso board. 7-Jun-93 Ritchie, Toronto #147/R (C.D 4500)
$5097   £3398   The trappers (83x85cm-33x33in) s. board. 11-May-94 Sotheby's, Toronto #153/R (C.D 7000)

RICHARDS, Frederick de Berg (1822-1903) American
$875   £576   On the Juniata (46x76cm-18x30in) s. 2-Apr-93 Eldred, Massachusetts #463/R

RICHARDS, Harriet Roosevelt (20th C) American
$1550   £1084   Nellies's secret mine (56x38cm-22x15in) s.verso. 7-Feb-93 James Bakker, Cambridge #159/R

RICHARDS, Lewis (20th C) American
$1100   £728   Barns in mountainous landscape (56x81cm-22x32in) board. 22-Nov-92 Dargate Auction Galleries, Pittsburgh #228

RICHARDS, Phil (1951-) Canadian
$775   £524   Night rising (71x53cm-28x21in) s.i.d.Dec.1986 i.verso gouache. 3-Nov-93 Sotheby's, Toronto #81 (C.D 1000)

RICHARDS, Thomas Addison (1820-1900) American
$700   £443   Mount Chocorua (23x36cm-9x14in) mono. 24-Oct-92 Collins, Maine #105
$2000   £1333   Woodland stream (31x51cm-12x20in) s. 23-May-94 Christie's, East, New York #35/R

RICHARDS, William Trost (1833-1905) American
$590   £398   Beached fishing boats and boys in rowing boat (31x51cm-12x20in) s. 18-Jun-93 Bolland & Marotz, Bremen #639/R (DM 1000)
$1000   £588   Rocky coast (23x41cm-9x16in) s. board. 3-Oct-92 Weschler, Washington #85/R
$1100   £719   Rough seas (20x15cm-8x6in) s. board. 30-Jun-94 Mystic Fine Arts, Connecticut #141
$1159   £767   Paisaje con rio (51x77cm-20x30in) s. 29-Jun-93 Fernando Duran, Madrid #99/R (S.P 150000)
$2000   £1266   Waves crashing on rocky coast (23x39cm-9x15in) s. canvas laid down on board. 2-Dec-92 Christie's, East, New York #32/R
$2200   £1447   The Birdstacks, Scotland (20x38cm-8x15in) i.verso panel. 4-Nov-92 Doyle, New York #27
$2400   £1622   Wales near Pembroke (23x41cm-9x16in) s. i.verso board. 31-Mar-94 Sotheby's Arcade, New York #22/R

RICHARDS, William Trost (1833-1905) American-cont.

$2500	£1582	The tide comes in (22x41cm-9x16in) canvas laid down on board. 2-Dec-92 Christie's, East, New York #13/R
$3004	£2016	Children collecting shells on the beach (32x49cm-13x19in) s. 6-May-94 Konig, Nurnberg #2612/R (DM 5000)
$3300	£1746	Breaking waves, late afternoon (23x41cm-9x16in) s.d.07 board. 11-Sep-92 Skinner, Bolton #147 a/R
$3750	£2517	The Stacks, Guernsey (23x41cm-9x16in) s. board. 26-Mar-94 James Bakker, Cambridge #78/R
$4000	£2721	Trebarwith Strand Cornwall (22x39cm-9x15in) s. board. 15-Nov-93 Christie's, East, New York #27/R
$5500	£3741	Shady grove (25x50cm-10x20in) i.verso canvas laid down on board. 15-Nov-93 Christie's, East, New York #61/R
$5750	£3859	A Long Island beach (23x33cm-9x13in) s.d.93 panel. 2-Dec-93 Freeman Fine Arts, Philadelphia #783/R
$6000	£4054	Ships on the horizon (63x107cm-25x42in) s.d.1885 canvas on panel. 31-Mar-94 Sotheby's Arcade, New York #93/R
$6500	£4362	Beach at Clovely, Devonshire (41x74cm-16x29in) s. 5-Dec-93 James Bakker, Cambridge #32/R
$6500	£3757	Near Philadelphia (51x76cm-20x30in) s.d.1854. 25-Sep-92 Sotheby's Arcade, New York #19/R
$9000	£6000	Water Gate, Cornwall, England (46x61cm-18x24in) s.d.1902 i.stretcher. 17-Mar-94 Sotheby's, New York #43/R
$10500	£7000	Ebbing of the tide (51x102cm-20x40in) s.d.1884. 23-May-94 Hindman Galleries, Chicago #193/R
$11000	£6962	Waves breaking on rocks (36x74cm-14x29in) s.d.93. 2-Dec-92 Boos Gallery, Michigan #817/R
$15750	£10500	Whiteface Mountain, Lake Placid, New York (25x40cm-10x16in) s.d.04 i.verso board. 15-Mar-94 Phillips, London #88/R
$16000	£10667	Lake George opposite Caldwell (48x69cm-19x27in) s.d.1857. 16-Mar-94 Christie's, New York #40/R
$18000	£12000	St Margaret's Well, Cornwall (51x81cm-20x32in) s.d.04. 16-Mar-94 Christie's, New York #18/R
$18000	£12587	Portsmouth light and Channel buoy (63x107cm-25x42in) s.d.1875. 10-Mar-93 Sotheby's, New York #17/R
$20000	£13245	New England seascape (50x83cm-20x33in) s.d.1877. 23-Sep-93 Sotheby's, New York #31/R
$26000	£18182	Arched bridge (61x51cm-24x20in) s.i.stretcher. 10-Mar-93 Sotheby's, New York #8/R
$26000	£16456	Path through the mountains (104x81cm-41x32in) s.d.1858. 4-Dec-92 Christie's, New York #205/R
$27500	£18456	Fisher village near Land's End, Cornwall, England (58x94cm-23x37in) s.d.1884. 3-Feb-94 Sloan, North Bethesda #2884/R
$35000	£24476	Snow storm, Atlantic City (33x59cm-13x23in) s.d.1872. 11-Mar-93 Christie's, New York #18/R
$37500	£25168	Land of the Lotus (61x91cm-24x36in) s.d.1860. 3-Feb-94 Sloan, North Bethesda #2883/R
$45000	£29801	Seascape at sunset (37x66cm-15x26in) s.d.1870. 23-Sep-93 Sotheby's, New York #14/R
$80000	£51282	Atlantic seascape (58x112cm-23x44in) s.d.1870. 27-May-93 Sotheby's, New York #172/R
$900	*£469*	*Sunset at Atlantic City (18x41cm-7x16in) s.d.1871 W/C. 5-Aug-92 Boos Gallery, Michigan #556/R*
$1000	*£633*	*Rocky stream (35x25cm-14x10in) W/C gouache paper laid down on board. 2-Dec-92 Christie's, East, New York #20/R*
$1200	*£800*	*Sailboat in the mist (28x25cm-11x10in) s. W/C pencil. 23-May-94 Christie's, East, New York #89/R*
$1300	*£765*	*Coast and rocks (25x58cm-10x23in) s. W/C. 8-Oct-92 Freeman Fine Arts, Philadelphia #1145*
$1300	*£872*	*Coast and rocks (48x66cm-19x26in) s. W/C gouache. 5-Mar-94 Louisiana Auction Exchange #146/R*
$1900	*£1218*	*Far rockaway to Long Island Beach (36x66cm-14x26in) s.d.1901 W/C. 13-Dec-92 Hindman Galleries, Chicago #59/R*
$2750	*£1786*	*White Sand Bay. First snow at the farm (8x13cm-3x5in) i.d.1879verso i.d.1884verso W/C htd white pair. 9-Sep-93 Sotheby's Arcade, New York #134/R*
$2800	*£1772*	*Crashing waves on rocks (30x60cm-12x24in) s. W/C. 2-Dec-92 Christie's, East, New York #27/R*
$3000	*£1987*	*Deep in woods - rocky stream (18x14cm-7x6in) init.d.68 W/C. 23-Sep-93 Sotheby's, New York #29/R*
$4000	*£2614*	*Spring (20x15cm-8x6in) s.d.63 graphite. 17-Sep-93 Skinner, Bolton #164/R*
$4500	*£2980*	*Fog on Brentons Reef, Newport, R.I (23x47cm-9x19in) s.d.93 i.verso W/C board. 22-Sep-93 Christie's, New York #38/R*
$7000	*£4046*	*Point Judith (19x32cm-7x13in) s.d.1871 W/C gouache pencil paper on paper. 23-Sep-92 Christie's, New York #40/R*
$7750	*£5167*	*Easton's Pond and beach, spring (20x33cm-8x13in) W/C gouache executed c.1874. 17-May-94 Grogan, Massachussetts #337/R*
$8500	*£5380*	*Along the Jersey Coast (23x39cm-9x15in) s.d.1871 W/C pencil paper laid down on board. 4-Dec-92 Christie's, New York #188/R*
$10000	*£5780*	*Along shore (13x23cm-5x9in) s.d.1873 W/C gouache. 24-Sep-92 Sotheby's, New York #1/R*
$10000	*£6410*	*On beach - moonlight (27x41cm-11x16in) s.d.1875 W/C. 27-May-93 Sotheby's, New York #171/R*
$26000	*£16456*	*Fisherman on the shore, Trebarwith Strand, Cornwall (58x94cm-23x37in) s.d.1879 W/C gouache. 3-Dec-92 Sotheby's, New York #18/R*

411

RICHARDS, William Trost (attrib) (1833-1905) American
$700   £470   Sunlit meadow (11x17cm-4x7in) paper on board. 11-Dec-93 Weschler, Washington #84/R
$750   £503   Extensive river landscape (14x20cm-6x8in) paper on board. 11-Dec-93 Weschler, Washington #89/R
$2000 £1333 Sailing boats on the horizon (41x61cm-16x24in) bears sig. 23-May-94 Christie's, East, New York #57/R

RICHARDSON, Constance Coleman (1905-) American
$1125 £798   East Arlington (43x58cm-17x23in) s.d.37 board. 12-Feb-93 Du Mouchelle, Detroit #2314/R

RICHARDSON, Margaret Foster (1881-?) American
$3100 £2081 A young girl (102x61cm-40x24in) s. s.i.d.1914 verso. 6-Dec-93 Grogan, Massachussetts #531/R

RICHARDSON, Mary Curtis (1848-1931) American
$5000 £3472 Mother and Child (96x67cm-38x26in) s. 7-Mar-93 Butterfield & Butterfield, San Francisco #156/R

RICHARDSON, Sam (20th C) American
$750   £490   Crated II (61x56cm-24x22in) d.1983 board. 16-May-93 Hindman Galleries, Chicago #20

RICHER, Ira (20th C) American
$1500 £993   Bark (136x117cm-54x46in) s.i.d.1982verso enamel col.crayon collage wood. 17-Nov-92 Christie's, East, New York #133/R

RICHMOND, Agnes M (1870-1964) American
$2000 £1258 Young nymph at water's edge (46x61cm-18x24in) s. 22-Apr-93 Freeman Fine Arts, Philadelphia #1330/R

RICHTER, Henry Leopold (1870-1960) American
$1200 £811   Saddleback Mountain-Tustin, CA (51x86cm-20x34in) 15-Jun-93 John Moran, Pasadena #53
$1500 £962   Winter stream (41x51cm-16x20in) s. 9-Dec-92 Butterfield & Butterfield, San Francisco #3883/R

RIDDLES, Leonard (1910-) American
$1000 £645   Warriors (43x48cm-17x19in) s.d.1969 gouache art board. 9-Jan-93 Skinner, Bolton #328/R

RIDER, Arthur G (1886-1975) American
$1000 £694   Near Laguna (41x53cm-16x21in) s. i.verso. 7-Mar-93 Butterfield & Butterfield, San Francisco #186/R
$5000 £3289 Pulling in fishing boats (48x63cm-19x25in) s. 13-Jun-93 Butterfield & Butterfield, San Francisco #851/R
$35000 £23649 Breezy day on beach (74x84cm-29x33in) s. 15-Jun-93 John Moran, Pasadena #47
$1400 £940   Hauling in the boat (25x33cm-10x13in) s. W/C. 8-Dec-93 Butterfield & Butterfield, San Francisco #3405/R
$1600 £941   Balancing sail (20x25cm-8x10in) s. W/C. 4-Oct-92 Butterfield & Butterfield, Los Angeles #154/R
$1800 £1059 Bringing home catch (20x25cm-8x10in) s. W/C paperboard. 4-Oct-92 Butterfield & Butterfield, Los Angeles #153/R

RIESENBERG, Sidney (1885-?) American
$1000 £578   The flight (81x56cm-32x22in) s. i.verso en grisaille. 25-Sep-92 Sotheby's Arcade, New York #427/R

RIESTRA, Adolfo (20th C) Mexican?
$741   £501   Negro (76x56cm-30x22in) s.d.1985 gouache. 27-Apr-94 Louis Morton, Mexico #483 (M.P 2500)

RIGAUX, Jack (1931-) Canadian
$502   £335   Untitle - foothills landscape - Millarville, AB (84x132cm-33x52in) s. 30-May-94 Hodgins, Calgary #257 (C.D 700)

RIGGS, Robert (1896-1970) American
$1200 £811   Riot at Kings College. Quarrels in the cabinet (27x29cm-11x11in) scratch board pair executed 1947. 31-Mar-94 Sotheby's Arcade, New York #392/R

RILEY, Arthur Irwin (1911-) American
$1500 £1014 Surf fisherman on rocky coast (53x69cm-21x27in) s. W/C. 15-Jun-93 John Moran, Pasadena #170

RILEY, Kenneth (1919-) American
$2400 £1633 Soldiers (33x38cm-13x15in) s. board. 15-Nov-93 Christie's, East, New York #112/R

RING, Alice Blair (1869-?) American
$5500 £3642 Woman at desk - sunlit interior (76x102cm-30x40in) s. 14-Jun-94 John Moran, Pasadena #76 a

RINKOVSKY, Margaret (20th C) American
$700   £473   Untitled (121x80cm-48x31in) board painted 1984. 21-Oct-93 Butterfield & Butterfield, San Francisco #2813/R

RIOPELLE, Jean-Paul (1923-) Canadian

$3951	£2652	Austarda (107x75cm-42x30in) s. s.d.85verso acrylic paper on canvas. 29-Nov-93 Ritchie, Toronto #212/R (C.D 5250)
$5402	£3626	Composition (19x24cm-7x9in) init. s.verso painted 1973. 21-Mar-94 Guy Loudmer, Paris #28/R (F.FR 31000)
$8195	£5500	Chaque jour (19x27cm-7x11in) s. painted 1974. 24-Jun-93 Sotheby's, London #91/R
$9500	£6597	Untitled (27x22cm-11x9in) painted 1927 s.verso. 24-Feb-93 Christie's, New York #6/R
$12000	£7059	Untitled (41x24cm-16x9in) init. s.verso. 8-Oct-92 Christie's, New York #113/R
$13500	£9000	Composition (24x35cm-9x14in) init. painted c.1957. 26-May-94 Christie's, London #37/R
$13500	£9000	Composition (65x46cm-26x18in) painted c.1966. 26-May-94 Christie's, London #35/R
$17902	£11856	Untitled (22x26cm-9x10in) init. painted 1954. 24-Nov-92 Joyner Fine Art, Toronto #79/R (C.D 23000)
$19000	£11176	Gerardmer (79x59cm-31x23in) s.d.58 d.58 stretcher paper on canvas. 6-Oct-92 Sotheby's, New York #29/R
$20000	£13245	Sur les graviers (55x46cm-22x18in) s. painted 1974 i.stretcher canvas shaped. 19-Nov-92 Christie's, New York #352/R
$20297	£13714	Sur les graviers (55x48cm-22x19in) s. i.stretcher painted 1974 oval. 24-Nov-93 Watine-Arnault, Paris #151/R (F.FR 120000)
$22820	£14000	Composition (81x60cm-32x24in) painted 1961. 14-Oct-92 Sotheby's, London #308/R
$26075	£17500	Composition (53x64cm-21x25in) s. painted c.1959-60. 3-Dec-93 Sotheby's, London #141/R
$26820	£18000	Untitled (46x61cm-18x24in) s. painted 1962. 23-Mar-94 Sotheby's, London #340/R
$27063	£18286	Les oies (73x92cm-29x36in) s. painted 1967. 24-Nov-93 Watine-Arnault, Paris #150/R (F.FR 160000)
$31000	£20805	Verone (49x72cm-19x28in) s.d.62 i.stretcher. 5-May-94 Sotheby's, New York #90/R
$31290	£21000	Sombre Noir (60x92cm-24x36in) s. s.i.d.59stretcher. 25-Mar-93 Christie's, London #21/R
$33669	£21583	Veronne (81x100cm-32x39in) s. s.i.stretcher. 26-May-93 Christie's, Amsterdam #306/R (D.FL 60000)
$34067	£23175	Le pas (65x81cm-26x32in) s. painted 1957. 11-Apr-94 Ader Tajan, Paris #17/R (F.FR 200000)
$37500	£25168	Untitled (99x99cm-39x39in) s.d.62. 25-Feb-94 Sotheby's, New York #1/R
$40000	£27027	Untitled PN no 13 (75x75cm-30x30in) s. s.d.63stretcher. 10-Nov-93 Christie's, New York #119/R
$42000	£28000	Le canon (71x90cm-28x35in) s. painted c.1957. 26-May-94 Christie's, London #9/R
$45000	£26471	Le Puits Hante (54x65cm-21x26in) s.d.57. 6-Oct-92 Sotheby's, New York #33/R
$50660	£34000	Arthur (81x100cm-32x39in) s.d.58 s.i.verso. 24-Jun-93 Sotheby's, London #8/R
$52020	£34000	Veloute (113x162cm-44x64in) s.d.66 s.d.verso. 30-Jun-94 Christie's, London #35/R
$58110	£39000	Doubs (97x130cm-38x51in) s. s.d.59 stretcher. 2-Dec-93 Christie's, London #37/R
$60040	£38000	Untitled (110x122cm-43x48in) s.d.60. 3-Dec-92 Sotheby's, London #35/R
$63509	£42339	Composition (103x128cm-41x50in) s.d.1960. 9-Jun-94 Christian de Quay, Paris #365/R (F.FR 362000)
$68460	£42000	Arles (73x99cm-29x39in) s. 15-Oct-92 Christie's, London #14/R
$68540	£46000	Untitled (24x63cm-9x25in) s. s.d.1950stretcher. 23-Mar-94 Sotheby's, London #317/R
$84582	£55283	Composition (116x89cm-46x35in) s. 28-Oct-92 Guy Loudmer, Paris #24/R (F.FR 450000)
$92380	£62000	Sous les bois (130x80cm-51x31in) s. painted c.1953-54. 24-Jun-93 Sotheby's, London #29/R
$127880	£86406	Composition (93x130cm-37x51in) s. painted 1954. 21-Oct-93 Christian de Quay, Paris #55/R (F.FR 750000)
$127946	£85298	Sans titre (89x130cm-35x51in) s.d.1953. 10-Mar-94 Christian de Quay, Paris #193/R (F.FR 731000)
$130050	£85000	Verts Ombreux (117x89cm-46x35in) s.d.49 s. verso. 30-Jun-94 Christie's, London #12/R
$136713	£91754	Pleine saison (130x161cm-51x63in) s.d.1954. 14-Oct-93 Guy Loudmer, Paris #33/R (F.FR 790000)
$145350	£95000	Composition (80x100cm-31x39in) s.d.50. 29-Jun-94 Sotheby's, London #16/R
$179598	£120536	Retour de l'Espagne (89x130cm-35x51in) s.verso painted 1952. 25-Jun-93 Galerie Kornfeld, Berne #121/R (S.FR 270000)
$192532	£128255	Bonne Bise (81x100cm-32x39in) s. s.d.50verso. 10-Mar-94 Christian de Quay, Paris #190/R (F.FR 1100000)
$305825	£203884	Tryptique (96x287cm-38x113in) painted c.1954 triptych. 11-May-94 Sotheby's, Toronto #127/R (C.D 420000)
$1729	*£1130*	*Sans titre (46x66cm-18x26in) painted 1985 felt collage. 27-Oct-92 Cornette de St.Cyr, Paris #43/R (F.FR 9200)*
$2980	*£2000*	*Untitled (49x67cm-19x26in) pastel executed 1968. 25-Mar-93 Christie's, London #40/R*
$3938	*£2625*	*Composition (89x59cm-35x23in) s.d.1965 chl pastel. 19-Mar-94 Cornette de St.Cyr, Paris #230/R (F.FR 22500)*
$4284	*£2800*	*Plumeuse (36x45cm-14x18in) s.d.55 ink W/C. 30-Jun-94 Sotheby's, London #105/R*
$4609	*£3053*	*Composition (26x77cm-10x30in) s.d.65 oil gouache triptych. 26-Nov-92 Francis Briest, Paris #20/R (F.FR 25000)*
$5215	*£3500*	*Untitled (41x33cm-16x13in) s.d.65 mixed media. 25-Mar-93 Christie's, London #18/R*
$5298	*£3440*	*Composition (50x62cm-20x24in) s.d.65 W/C. 24-Jun-94 Francis Briest, Paris #2/R (F.FR 29000)*
$6411	*£4303*	*Composition (49x64cm-19x25in) s.d.62 mixed media. 29-Nov-93 AB Stockholms Auktionsverk, Stockholm #6265/R (S.KR 54000)*
$7784	*£5155*	*Untitled (26x36cm-10x14in) ink. 18-Nov-92 Sotheby's, Toronto #55/R (C.D 10000)*

RIORDON, Eric (1906-1948) Canadian

$682	£455	Lombardy poplars and staircase leading to hilltop estate (45x33cm-18x13in) s.d.1934. 30-May-94 Ritchie, Toronto #157 a/R (C.D 950)

RIORDON, Eric (1906-1948) Canadian-cont.
$1012	£670	Sunny valley near Ste Adele (30x40cm-12x16in) s. board. 24-Nov-92 Joyner Fine Art, Toronto #160 (C.D 1300)
$1189	£777	Noon sun in the Alps (30x41cm-12x16in) s.d.35. 18-May-93 Joyner Fine Art, Toronto #143 (C.D 1500)

RIPAMONTE, Carlos Pablo (1874-1968) Argentinian
$4800	£3137	Emboscan en noche (394x193cm-155x76in) s. 5-May-93 Doyle, New York #107/R
$6000	£3468	En reposo (52x73cm-20x29in) 23-Sep-92 Roldan & Cia, Buenos Aires #42
$7750	£5065	Amores (127x178cm-50x70in) s.d.1943 i.stretcher. 5-May-93 Doyle, New York #138/R
$12000	£6936	Tierras Altas (71x71cm-28x28in) 23-Sep-92 Roldan & Cia, Buenos Aires #43

RIPLEY, Aiden Lassell (1896-1969) American
$1100	£753	The railroad crossing (76x91cm-30x36in) 10-Feb-94 Skinner, Bolton #140
$1500	£1000	Portrait of woman (91x76cm-36x30in) i.verso. 26-Aug-93 Skinner, Bolton #69
$2000	£1282	Velasquez's Venus and Cupid (122x175cm-48x69in) s.d.1924 i.stretcher. 24-May-93 Grogan, Massachussetts #346/R
$2300	£1575	Port of call - French harbour with fisherman (76x91cm-30x36in) s.d.1928. 10-Feb-94 Skinner, Bolton #62
$3200	£2092	Bathers by pool (56x74cm-22x29in) s.d.1926. 17-Sep-93 Skinner, Bolton #267/R
$4000	£2614	The Model (122x66cm-48x26in) d.1924 i.verso. 17-Sep-93 Skinner, Bolton #269/R
$15000	£10067	October frost (76x102cm-30x40in) s.d.1945 s.i.verso. 12-Dec-93 Hindman Galleries, Chicago #269/R
$600	£426	Chasing piglet to ground (41x28cm-16x11in) init. pen. 13-Feb-93 Collins, Maine #124/R
$650	£437	Churchyard (37x49cm-15x19in) st.verso W/C. 6-May-94 Skinner, Bolton #83/R
$700	£486	Southern street scene (36x51cm-14x20in) s. W/C. 27-Feb-93 Young Fine Arts Auctions, Maine #241/R
$800	£523	Spring ploughing (35x54cm-14x21in) s.d.49 W/C. 4-May-93 Christie's, East, New York #206
$825	£585	Grouse among wild apples (15x23cm-6x9in) estate st. W/C. 13-Feb-93 Collins, Maine #117a
$850	£594	Italian harbour (33x46cm-13x18in) i.verso W/C graphite gouache. 12-Mar-93 Skinner, Bolton #245/R
$850	£563	Man, woman, and dog hunting birds (18x25cm-7x10in) W/C. 28-Nov-92 Young Fine Arts Auctions, Maine #337/R
$900	£588	Goose hunting (20x33cm-8x13in) s. W/C gouache graphite paperboard. 17-Sep-93 Skinner, Bolton #248/R
$900	£588	Hunters on pier, dawn (18x33cm-7x13in) s. W/C gouache graphite paperboard. 17-Sep-93 Skinner, Bolton #250/R
$900	£604	Spring painting (37x54cm-15x21in) s.d.49 W/C. 6-May-94 Skinner, Bolton #86/R
$950	£621	Winter marshes - hunter and dog in landscape (23x33cm-9x13in) s. W/C gouache graphite paperboard. 17-Sep-93 Skinner, Bolton #247/R
$1100	£719	Geese dropping in - scene with hunter and dog hidden among reeds (20x30cm-8x12in) s. W/C gouache graphite paperboard. 17-Sep-93 Skinner, Bolton #246/R
$1100	£738	Big Horn Rams (56x40cm-22x16in) s.d.29 i.verso chl paperboard. 4-Mar-94 Skinner, Bolton #258/R
$1200	£784	Duck blind (20x33cm-8x13in) s. W/C gouache graphite paperboard. 17-Sep-93 Skinner, Bolton #249/R
$1500	£1049	Guides' cabin (36x51cm-14x20in) s. W/C. 12-Mar-93 Skinner, Bolton #179/R
$2200	£1438	Bass Rocks, Cape Ann (33x48cm-13x19in) s. W/C. 14-May-93 Skinner, Bolton #125/R
$3750	£2500	Shooting in the south (23x36cm-9x14in) studio st. pencil board. 3-Jun-94 Sotheby's, New York #279/R
$5000	£3247	Grouse at sunset (55x68cm-22x27in) s.d.1937 W/C. 9-Sep-93 Sotheby's Arcade, New York #188/R
$18000	£12000	Point near the oak (52x76cm-20x30in) s.d.1947 W/C. 25-May-94 Sotheby's, New York #149/R

RITCHIE, Muriel (?) American
$725	£497	Wet street (58x48cm-23x19in) 11-Feb-94 Douglas, South Deerfield #1
$900	£616	Three boats at dock (74x58cm-29x23in) 11-Feb-94 Douglas, South Deerfield #2

RITMAN, Louis (1889-1963) Russian/American
$1200	£784	Seated woman (32x41cm-13x16in) panel. 4-May-93 Christie's, East, New York #247/R
$1300	£884	The blue blouse (46x38cm-18x15in) s. 15-Nov-93 Christie's, East, New York #184/R
$2000	£1361	Pink flowers in green vase (81x48cm-32x19in) s. 15-Nov-93 Christie's, East, New York #235/R
$2250	£1480	White corsage (46x38cm-18x15in) s. panel. 5-Jun-93 Louisiana Auction Exchange #88
$4000	£2721	The pink robe (101x51cm-40x20in) s. 15-Nov-93 Christie's, East, New York #182/R
$4200	£2692	Landscape with grazing cattle (64x81cm-25x32in) s. 13-Dec-92 Hindman Galleries, Chicago #34/R
$4800	£3221	Floral still life (58x71cm-23x28in) s. 11-Dec-93 Weschler, Washington #113/R
$18000	£12587	Interior (107x130cm-42x51in) s. 14-Mar-93 Hindman Galleries, Chicago #25/R
$42000	£28188	Reminiscence (65x81cm-26x32in) s. 3-Dec-93 Christie's, New York #42/R
$100000	£63291	Garden in Giverny (81x66cm-32x26in) s.d.1914. 4-Dec-92 Christie's, New York #11/R
$120000	£76923	Sunday boating on the Epte River (64x81cm-25x32in) s.d.1917. 13-Dec-92 Hindman Galleries, Chicago #37/R
$140000	£93333	Sunny day in garden (81x81cm-32x32in) 26-May-94 Christie's, New York #94/R

RITSCHEL, William (1864-1949) American
$2750	£1858	Seascape (25x30cm-10x12in) s. board. 9-Nov-93 John Moran, Pasadena #839
$3500	£2349	Cows near the shore (20x25cm-8x10in) s.i. board. 8-Dec-93 Butterfield & Butterfield, San Francisco #3399/R
$4500	£2961	Two boats along bay (53x46cm-21x18in) s. 13-Jun-93 Butterfield & Butterfield, San Francisco #808/R

RITSCHEL, William (1864-1949) American-cont.
$8000	£5369	Rocky seascape (46x62cm-18x24in) s. 8-Dec-93 Butterfield & Butterfield, San Francisco #3457/R
$9000	£6081	Girl from Bali-Java (76x64cm-30x25in) s. panel. 15-Jun-93 John Moran, Pasadena #118
$14000	£8235	Kelp gathering, Maine (81x118cm-32x46in) s. s.i. mono.st.verso. 4-Oct-92 Butterfield & Butterfield, Los Angeles #68/R
$18000	£11921	Wake of ship (76x91cm-30x36in) s. s.i.verso ship study verso double-sided. 15-Jun-94 Butterfield & Butterfield, San Francisco #4610/R
$23000	£16084	Moonbeams (63x76cm-25x30in) s.i. s.verso. 10-Mar-93 Sotheby's, New York #121/R
$75000	£47468	Misty shores, California (101x127cm-40x50in) s. s.i.verso. 3-Dec-92 Sotheby's, New York #115/R
$775	*£507*	*Hauling the fishing boats ashore at Katwyk, Holland (63x74cm-25x29in) s. i.verso W/C board. 22-May-93 Weschler, Washington #117*
$1600	*£1060*	*Horses and rider pulling in ships (49x70cm-19x28in) s.i. gouache. 15-Jun-94 Butterfield & Butterfield, San Francisco #4613/R*
$1900	*£1258*	*Ships on the canal (53x70cm-21x28in) s. W/C gouache. 15-Jun-94 Butterfield & Butterfield, San Francisco #4612/R*
$1900	*£1258*	*Return of the fishing fleet (43x69cm-17x27in) s.i. gouache. 15-Jun-94 Butterfield & Butterfield, San Francisco #4611/R*
$6500	*£4276*	*Return of fishing fleet (65x86cm-26x34in) s. gouache. 13-Jun-93 Butterfield & Butterfield, San Francisco #781/R*

RITTENBERG, Henry R and CHASE, William Merritt (19/20th C) American
$900	£600	Portrait of a woman (51x41cm-20x16in) i. 1-Jun-94 Doyle, New York #56

RIVERA TORRES, Silvia (1945-) Mexican
$2375	£1563	Sandias (80x110cm-31x43in) s.d.1992. 4-Nov-92 Mora, Castelltort & Quintana, Juarez #139/R (M.P 7500000)

RIVERA, Diego (1886-1957) Mexican
$37330	£24887	Nature morte cubiste (35x22cm-14x9in) s.i. d.17 octobre 1917verso board. 20-Aug-93 Deauville #100/R (F.FR 220000)
$55000	£37162	Vista de la Plaza Roja (34x49cm-13x19in) s.d.1954 linen on board. 23-Nov-93 Christie's, New York #64/R
$80000	£52980	Portrait of Helen N Starr (120x88cm-47x35in) s.d.1951 s.i.d.1951 verso. 24-Nov-92 Christie's, New York #141/R
$135000	£89404	Retrato de Maria Felix (76x60cm-30x24in) s.d.1948 i.verso. 24-Nov-92 Christie's, New York #46/R
$350000	£236486	Naturaleza muerta con flores (81x66cm-32x26in) s.d.1916 verso. 22-Nov-93 Sotheby's, New York #14/R
$500000	£333333	Retrato de un Espanol (199x165cm-78x65in) s. painted 1912. 18-May-94 Christie's, New York #7/R
$700000	£463576	Nina en Azul y Blanco (127x91cm-50x36in) s.d.1939. 24-Nov-92 Christie's, New York #10/R
$1300	*£878*	*El Mercado (25x35cm-10x14in) s. graphite. 21-Oct-93 Butterfield & Butterfield, San Francisco #2731/R*
$1500	*£1014*	*Children dancing with arches. Portrait of a man (13x9cm-5x4in) s. one d.1948 graphite two. 21-Oct-93 Butterfield & Butterfield, San Francisco #2732/R*
$1935	*£1299*	*Mujeres en el rio (20x13cm-8x5in) s. pencil dr. 1-Dec-93 Louis Morton, Mexico #210/R (M.P 6000)*
$2000	*£1258*	*Arbol cerca de la casas (20x24cm-8x9in) s. ink wash. 25-Apr-93 Butterfield & Butterfield, San Francisco #2074/R*
$2000	*£1307*	*Cabeza (25x21cm-10x8in) s.d.20 graphite. 18-May-93 Sotheby's, New York #126/R*
$3000	*£2013*	*La comida (27x38cm-11x15in) s.d.1934 brush ink rice paper. 6-May-94 Skinner, Bolton #153 a/R*
$3000	*£2027*	*Portrait of a young girl (37x25cm-15x10in) s. chl. 21-Apr-94 Butterfield & Butterfield, San Francisco #1100/R*
$3200	*£2148*	*Profile of a young boy wearing a cap (48x30cm-19x12in) s.d.1948 chl Japan paper. 2-Dec-93 Swann Galleries, New York #269/R*
$3250	*£2153*	*Head of woman. Standing man. Seated mother with child (21x13cm-8x5in) s. pencil three. 30-Jun-93 Sotheby's Arcade, New York #219/R*
$3607	*£2405*	*Cargador (39x27cm-15x11in) s. pencil dr executed c.1925. 25-May-94 Louis Morton, Mexico #29 (M.P 12000)*
$3700	*£2534*	*Dibujo a lapiz (13x8cm-5x3in) s.d.1950 pencil dr. 13-Feb-94 Hart Gallery, Houston #425*
$4000	*£2614*	*Mercado (38x28cm-15x11in) s.d.42 brush ink rice paper. 17-May-93 Christie's, New York #281/R*
$4000	*£2614*	*Modesta peinandose (36x30cm-14x12in) s.d.40 pencil vellum. 17-May-93 Christie's, New York #280/R*
$4200	*£2838*	*Campesino (39x28cm-15x11in) s.d.1934 graphite rice paper. 22-Nov-93 Sotheby's, New York #220/R*
$4457	*£2857*	*Estudio de una figura equina, pilares de la entrada de la Villa (21x13cm-8x5in) s. pencil dr executed c.1921. 29-Apr-93 Louis Morton, Mexico #57 (M.P 14000)*
$4750	*£3210*	*Cardagor de Alcatrares (38x25cm-15x10in) s.d.1940 graphite. 21-Oct-93 Butterfield & Butterfield, San Francisco #2733/R*
$6000	*£4000*	*El Arado (22x31cm-9x12in) s.d.36 black ink. 18-May-94 Christie's, New York #207/R*
$6000	*£3974*	*Mujer y nino (39x31cm-15x12in) s.d.47 brush ink rice paper. 24-Nov-92 Christie's, New York #195/R*
$6000	*£4000*	*Mujer con Alcatraces (35x25cm-14x10in) s. black ink executed 1936. 18-May-94 Christie's, New York #205/R*
$7000	*£4575*	*El Campesino (28x39cm-11x15in) s. brush ink rice paper. 17-May-93 Christie's, New York #279/R*
$7004	*£4490*	*Hombres con armas (39x28cm-15x11in) s.d.1950 pencil dr. 29-Apr-93 Louis Morton, Mexico #111 (M.P 22000)*

RIVERA, Diego (1886-1957) Mexican-cont.

$8500	£5667	Camino al mercado. Mujer con palma (34x24cm-13x9in) s. one d.36 black ink executed 1936 pair. 18-May-94 Christie's, New York #204/R
$11000	£7285	Nina con canasta (39x27cm-15x11in) s. W/C. 30-Jun-93 Sotheby's Arcade, New York #221/R
$11000	£7333	Obrero (39x28cm-15x11in) s.d.47 ink rice paper. 18-May-94 Sotheby's, New York #210/R
$12000	£8108	Albanil jalando varilla (39x28cm-15x11in) s. brush ink rice paper executed c.1936. 22-Nov-93 Sotheby's, New York #227/R
$15000	£9434	Woman carrying basket (38x27cm-15x11in) s.d.1948 W/C. 25-Apr-93 Butterfield & Butterfield, San Francisco #2092/R
$15000	£9434	Woman carrying basket (38x27cm-15x11in) s.d.48 W/C. 25-Apr-93 Butterfield & Butterfield, San Francisco #2093/R
$15000	£9934	Mujer con Alcatrazes (39x27cm-15x11in) s.i. chl W/C. 23-Nov-92 Sotheby's, New York #159/R
$16000	£10667	Paisaje (31x48cm-12x19in) s.d.27 W/C. 18-May-94 Sotheby's, New York #272/R
$17000	£11486	Vendedor de Pajaros (27x18cm-11x7in) s. W/C brush ink. 23-Nov-93 Christie's, New York #242/R
$18000	£11921	Montanas en Sonora (31x48cm-12x19in) s.d.31 i.verso W/C pencil. 24-Nov-92 Christie's, New York #196/R
$18000	£11321	Mother and child (38x28cm-15x11in) s.d.26 pencil. 25-Apr-93 Butterfield & Butterfield, San Francisco #2086/R
$18000	£12587	Nino (30x23cm-12x9in) s.d.35 sanguine graphite. 12-Mar-93 Skinner, Bolton #224/R
$18000	£12000	Mujer con rebozo y mecate (39x27cm-15x11in) s.d.36 W/C rice paper laid down on board. 18-May-94 Sotheby's, New York #274/R
$19000	£12418	Llendo al mercado (39x28cm-15x11in) s.d.46 W/C rice paper. 18-May-93 Sotheby's, New York #154/R
$20000	£13333	Picapedrero (38x28cm-15x11in) s. W/C. 18-May-94 Christie's, New York #203/R
$22000	£14570	Retrato de Ann Harding (62x48cm-24x19in) s. brush ink pencil. 24-Nov-92 Christie's, New York #140/R
$26000	£16993	Rumbo al mercado (39x30cm-15x12in) s.d.44 W/C brush ink rice paper. 17-May-93 Christie's, New York #114/R
$27500	£17974	Young girl kneeling (16x12cm-6x5in) s.d.49 W/C. 14-May-93 Du Mouchelle, Detroit #2035/R
$28000	£18919	Cabeza de mujer (35x27cm-14x11in) s. chl sanguine vellum. 23-Nov-93 Christie's, New York #225/R
$28000	£18543	El Bocadillo (18x27cm-7x11in) s. W/C black chk rice paper. 24-Nov-92 Christie's, New York #197/R
$28000	£18667	Modesta y su hija (37x27cm-15x11in) s.d.1926 pencil. 18-May-94 Christie's, New York #51/R
$32000	£20915	Cabeza de India (39x28cm-15x11in) s. chl sanguine rice paper drawn c.1938. 17-May-93 Christie's, New York #1/R
$32000	£20915	Jardinero (39x28cm-15x11in) s.d.1937 W/C brush ink rice paper. 17-May-93 Christie's, New York #113/R
$35000	£23179	Mujer Cargando Flores (38x27cm-15x11in) s.d.1954 W/C. 23-Nov-92 Sotheby's, New York #48/R
$35000	£23649	Cabeza de Jovencita (38x28cm-15x11in) s. chl sanguine executed c.1938. 23-Nov-93 Christie's, New York #39/R
$35000	£23333	Nino (29x23cm-11x9in) s.d.35 chl sanguine dr rice paper. 18-May-94 Sotheby's, New York #211/R
$35000	£23649	Mujer Sentada (77x58cm-30x23in) s.i.d.39 pen chl. 23-Nov-93 Christie's, New York #100/R
$38000	£24837	Cabeza de Campesino Viejo (39x28cm-15x11in) s.d.1939 sanguine chl W/C rice paper drawn 1939. 17-May-93 Christie's, New York #190/R
$38000	£25676	Campesino Sembrando (39x28cm-15x11in) s.d.41 W/C rice paper. 22-Nov-93 Sotheby's, New York #190/R
$42000	£28378	Cargadores de Lena (38x27cm-15x11in) s. W/C rice paper executed c.1935. 22-Nov-93 Sotheby's, New York #192/R
$45000	£29801	Arboles (48x56cm-19x22in) s.d.1937 W/C rice paper. 24-Nov-92 Christie's, New York #2/R
$47500	£32095	Dos hombres en cuclillas labrando lozas de piedra (28x39cm-11x15in) s.d.47 W/C rice paper. 22-Nov-93 Sotheby's, New York #68/R
$50000	£33784	Vendedora de flores (39x28cm-15x11in) s.d.54 W/C brush ink. 23-Nov-93 Christie's, New York #65/R
$52000	£34667	Nina con Ramo de Flores (38x31cm-15x12in) s.d.1953 W/C black ink rice paper. 18-May-94 Christie's, New York #50/R
$55000	£35948	Cargador (39x27cm-15x11in) s.d.1956 W/C rice paper. 18-May-93 Sotheby's, New York #36/R
$55000	£36424	Vendedora de Flores (50x37cm-20x15in) s.d.41 W/C rice paper. 24-Nov-92 Christie's, New York #3/R
$65000	£43265	Androcles fleeing the Monster (70x95cm-28x37in) s.d.1949 gouache paper laid down on masonite. 18-May-94 Christie's, New York #11/R

RIVERS, Larry (1923-) American

$20000	£13072	At 'Z' Beach (96x71cm-38x28in) s. i.d.1982verso acrylic oilstick. 5-May-93 Christie's, New York #299/R
$38000	£25676	Drug store (76x76cm-30x30in) s.i.d.59 verso. 11-Nov-93 Sotheby's, New York #353/R
$70000	£47297	King of Hearts (94x71cm-37x28in) painted 1964. 10-Nov-93 Christie's, New York #130/R
$95000	£64189	Queen of Spades (81x61cm-32x24in) s.i.d.1964verso. 10-Nov-93 Christie's, New York #129/R
$1200	£805	Portrait of Merry Abel (35x42cm-14x17in) s. init.i.verso pencil chl. 24-Feb-94 Sotheby's Arcade, New York #318/R
$2900	£1959	Evolution of flower (37x42cm-15x17in) s. oil pencil paper collage executed 1963. 11-Nov-93 Sotheby's, New York #363/R

RIVERS, Larry (1923-) American-cont.
$3200	£2222	Untitled (33x42cm-13x17in) s.d.61 graphite cellophane tape paper collage. 22-Feb-93 Christie's, East, New York #155/R
$3300	£2230	Webster collage (18x18cm-7x7in) s.d.62 pencil crayon collage paper on board. 11-Nov-93 Sotheby's, New York #349/R
$4917	£3300	Sketch for Roots (77x108cm-30x43in) s.d.79 pencil pastel gouache. 3-Dec-93 Sotheby's, London #257/R
$5000	£3268	Jewish banker called Rothschild (87x74cm-34x29in) s.d.83 graphite col.crayon chk linen-back paper. 7-May-93 Christie's, East, New York #117/R
$5500	£3235	Natural camels III (28x28cm-11x11in) s.d.80 i.verson col.crayons graphite. 8-Oct-92 Christie's, New York #136/R
$5500	£3691	In the artist's studio (69x65cm-27x26in) s.i.d.81 verso graphite col.crayons paper board. 23-Feb-94 Christie's, East, New York #282/R
$8400	£5676	Untitle (43x48cm-17x19in) s.d.61 s.i.d.61 verso crayon pencil collage. 11-Nov-93 Sotheby's, New York #351/R
$9000	£6250	Three queens (20x25cm-8x10in) s.d.61 W/C pencil. 23-Feb-93 Sotheby's, New York #268/R
$28000	£18919	Chinese information (188x153cm-74x60in) s.d.80 s.i.d.verso acrylic col.crayon. 10-Nov-93 Christie's, New York #247/R

RIX, Julian (1851-1903) American
$1600	£1026	Sunset (27x20cm-11x8in) s.d.76 panel. 9-Dec-92 Butterfield & Butterfield, San Francisco #3834/R
$1600	£1026	Ship returning at sunset (53x71cm-21x28in) s. 12-Dec-92 Weschler, Washington #58/R
$2000	£1361	Sunlit woodland clearing (48x66cm-19x26in) s. 8-Apr-94 Sloan, North Bethesda #2365/R
$2000	£1316	Road through forest (91x137cm-36x54in) s. 31-Mar-93 Sotheby's Arcade, New York #152/R
$2000	£1389	Autumn scene (63x107cm-25x42in) s.d.78. 7-Mar-93 Butterfield & Butterfield, San Francisco #3/R
$3000	£1987	Road through a field (46x66cm-18x26in) s.d.98. 15-Jun-94 Butterfield & Butterfield, San Francisco #4564/R
$3750	£2467	Wooded path (51x30cm-20x12in) s.d.77. 13-Jun-93 Butterfield & Butterfield, San Francisco #701/R
$4000	£2685	Misty camp (61x41cm-24x16in) s. 8-Dec-93 Butterfield & Butterfield, San Francisco #3334/R
$6000	£4167	High country Indian encampment (76x127cm-30x50in) s.d.83 canvas on board. 7-Mar-93 Butterfield & Butterfield, San Francisco #44/R
$8000	£5556	California oaks (46x71cm-18x28in) s. 7-Mar-93 Butterfield & Butterfield, San Francisco #40/R
$9000	£5294	Mountain lake (74x152cm-29x60in) s. 8-Oct-92 Freeman Fine Arts, Philadelphia #1101/R
$800	£530	Cottages in a landscape (36x63cm-14x25in) s. W/C. 15-Jun-94 Butterfield & Butterfield, San Francisco #4628/R

RIX, Julian (attrib) (1851-1903) American
$950	£625	Wooded path (44x27cm-17x11in) 13-Jun-93 Butterfield & Butterfield, San Francisco #714/R

ROBBINS, Ellen (1828-1905) American
$3250	£2152	Wild flowers (84x30cm-33x12in) s.d.1880 pair. 23-Sep-93 Mystic Fine Arts, Connecticut #232/R
$700	£470	Floral still life (41x58cm-16x23in) s.d.1888 W/C. 26-Mar-94 James Bakker, Cambridge #23/R
$1400	£915	Nasturtiums. Red and white roses (43x61cm-17x24in) s.i.d.1888 pair. 22-May-93 Collins, Maine #44/R
$3500	£2215	Lincoln boat house, Sandy Pond (50x63cm-20x25in) s.i. W/C board. 3-Dec-92 Sotheby's, New York #15/R

ROBBINS, Horace Wolcott (1842-1904) American
$1106	£556	Autumn landscape with river and mountains (24x32cm-9x13in) s.indist.d.April. 2-Sep-92 Rasmussen, Copenhagen #198 (D.KR 6000)

ROBERTS, Helen L (20th C) American
$750	£521	Parking lot (46x61cm-18x24in) s. canvasboard. 3-Mar-93 Doyle, New York #55

ROBERTS, Joe Rader (20th C) American
$1800	£1224	The line shack (61x76cm-24x30in) s. s.i.verso. 15-Nov-93 Christie's, East, New York #97
$1800	£1200	Lone Hunter (51x61cm-20x24in) s. 23-May-94 Christie's, East, New York #108/R
$1800	£1224	Five Indians on horseback (51x61cm-20x24in) s. 15-Nov-93 Christie's, East, New York #96/R

ROBERTS, Nathan B (19th C) American
$3200	£1850	Red Bank, Delaware River, storm coming (30x44cm-12x17in) mono. s.i.verso board. 23-Sep-92 Christie's, New York #67/R

ROBERTS, Thomas Keith (1904-) Canadian
$602	£404	Niagara on the lake (41x56cm-16x22in) s. i.verso board. 29-Nov-93 Waddingtons, Toronto #1094/R (C.D 800)
$674	£440	Partk Street (30x46cm-12x18in) s. board. 19-May-93 Sotheby's, Toronto #71 (C.D 850)
$828	£556	Grain boats, Collingwood (48x61cm-19x24in) s. i.d.1941 verso board. 29-Nov-93 Waddingtons, Toronto #1095 (C.D 1100)

ROBERTS, Thomas Keith (1904-) Canadian-cont.
$874	£583	Road to Lac Gelinas (41x51cm-16x20in) s. i.verso board. 11-May-94 Sotheby's, Toronto #244 (C.D 1200)
$906	£612	Batchawana Bay, Lake Superior (40x50cm-16x20in) s. board. 23-Nov-93 Joyner Fine Art, Toronto #194 (C.D 1200)
$1189	£777	Street in St. Johns, Newfoundland (56x81cm-22x32in) s. board. 18-May-93 Joyner Fine Art, Toronto #31/R (C.D 1500)
$1317	£890	October breeze on the lake (41x66cm-16x26in) s. s.i.verso board. 3-Nov-93 Sotheby's, Toronto #188/R (C.D 1700)
$1401	£928	Fishing below mill (60x75cm-24x30in) s. 24-Nov-92 Joyner Fine Art, Toronto #225 (C.D 1800)
$1585	£1036	Rain reflections - Grand Allee (41x56cm-16x22in) s. board. 19-May-93 Sotheby's, Toronto #218/R (C.D 2000)
$1868	£1237	Late winter, Bowmanville (60x90cm-24x35in) s. board. 24-Nov-92 Joyner Fine Art, Toronto #206 (C.D 2400)

ROBERTS, Tom (1909-) Canadian
$652	£435	Golden maples (61x76cm-24x30in) s. i.verso. 6-Jun-94 Waddingtons, Toronto #1253/R (C.D 900)
$1806	£1212	Midwinter, Eden Mills (61x76cm-24x30in) s. i.verso board. 29-Nov-93 Waddingtons, Toronto #1080 a (C.D 2400)

ROBERTS, William Goodridge (1904-1974) Canadian
$978	£657	Woodland (22x27cm-9x11in) s. board. 29-Nov-93 Waddingtons, Toronto #1103 k (C.D 1300)
$1148	£766	By the river, Port-au-Persil (30x40cm-12x16in) s. board. 30-May-94 Ritchie, Toronto #171/R (C.D 1600)
$1350	£900	The farm (31x41cm-12x16in) s. canvas laid on board. 7-Jun-94 Phillips, London #118/R
$1481	£974	Evening, Georgian Bay (30x41cm-12x16in) i.verso board. 7-Jun-93 Waddingtons, Toronto #1137 g (C.D 1900)
$1638	£1092	Georgian Bay (30x41cm-12x16in) s. board. 11-May-94 Sotheby's, Toronto #141/R (C.D 2250)
$2044	£1294	Paysage d'Automne (30x40cm-12x16in) s. board. 1-Dec-92 Fraser Pinneys, Quebec #146/R (C.D 2600)
$3095	£2063	Orchard in blossom (51x61cm-20x24in) s. board. 11-May-94 Sotheby's, Toronto #123/R (C.D 4250)
$4756	£3109	Country road (56x77cm-22x30in) s. 18-May-93 Joyner Fine Art, Toronto #38/R (C.D 6000)
$5037	£3403	Still life with blue cloth (30x41cm-12x16in) s. i.verso board. 3-Nov-93 Sotheby's, Toronto #154/R (C.D 6500)
$6418	£4337	Rock and pine trees, Georgian Bay (62x80cm-24x31in) s. 23-Nov-93 Joyner Fine Art, Toronto #100/R (C.D 8500)
$7282	£4854	Laurentian landscape (62x80cm-24x31in) s. board. 13-May-94 Joyner Fine Art, Toronto #48/R (C.D 10000)
$10897	£7216	Nature morte au Van Gogh (30x40cm-12x16in) s. board. 24-Nov-92 Joyner Fine Art, Toronto #69/R (C.D 14000)
$15855	£10363	Two bouquets (81x122cm-32x48in) s. board. 18-May-93 Joyner Fine Art, Toronto #20/R (C.D 20000)
$21845	£14563	Still life with wild roses, fruit and books (60x90cm-24x35in) s. board. 13-May-94 Joyner Fine Art, Toronto #104/R (C.D 30000)
$1245	*£825*	*Georgian Bay (22x28cm-9x11in) s.d.62 W/C. 24-Nov-92 Joyner Fine Art, Toronto #174 (C.D 1600)*
$2114	*£1429*	*Georgian Bay landscape (34x49cm-13x19in) s.d.62 W/C. 23-Nov-93 Joyner Fine Art, Toronto #142/R (C.D 2800)*

ROBERTSON, Sarah Margaret (1891-1948) Canadian
$3892	£2577	Landscape (39x45cm-15x18in) board. 24-Nov-92 Joyner Fine Art, Toronto #180/R (C.D 5000)

ROBINSON, Albert Henry (1881-1956) Canadian
$2643	£1786	Unloading coal, St Lawrence (21x26cm-8x10in) s.d.1913 i.verso board. 23-Nov-93 Fraser Pinneys, Quebec #378/R (C.D 3500)
$3322	£2245	Entrance to harbour, St Malo (21x27cm-8x11in) s.d.1911 i.verso board. 23-Nov-93 Fraser Pinneys, Quebec #371 (C.D 4400)
$4865	£3222	Cote des neiges and Queen Mary road (22x27cm-9x11in) indist.s.i.d.c.1930 panel. 18-Nov-92 Sotheby's, Toronto #9/R (C.D 6250)
$5825	£3883	Cacouna 1921 winter (20x26cm-8x10in) init. panel. 13-May-94 Joyner Fine Art, Toronto #40/R (C.D 8000)
$5946	£3886	Victoria Square, Montreal (31x46cm-12x18in) s. d.1909 verso. 19-May-93 Sotheby's, Toronto #373/R (C.D 7500)
$8562	£5670	Sunny day, Cacouna (21x26cm-8x10in) s.d.1912 panel double-sided. 24-Nov-92 Joyner Fine Art, Toronto #126/R (C.D 11000)
$14723	£9948	Skating after school (27x32cm-11x13in) s. i.verso panel. 3-Nov-93 Sotheby's, Toronto #191/R (C.D 19000)
$21845	£14563	Laurentian spring (55x65cm-22x26in) s.d.1927. 13-May-94 Joyner Fine Art, Toronto #88/R (C.D 30000)
$83061	£56122	Baie St. Paul (67x82cm-26x32in) s.d.1928. 23-Nov-93 Joyner Fine Art, Toronto #70/R (C.D 110000)

ROBINSON, Alexander (1867-?) American
$1700	£1141	The table in front of the window (65x81cm-26x32in) s. 24-Feb-94 Sotheby's Arcade, New York #214/R
$566	*£380*	*Venetian fishing boats (37x42cm-15x17in) s.indist.i. W/C. 24-Mar-93 Phillips, Chester #194/R*

ROBINSON, Alexander (1867-?) American-cont.
$834	£560	Venetian fishing boats, buildings beyond (46x61cm-18x24in) s.i. W/C. 24-Mar-93 Phillips, Chester #195/R
$969	£646	The Jerusalem Church in Bruges (66x42cm-26x17in) s.i.d.1903 W/C. 28-May-94 Kunstgalerij de Vuyst, Lokeren #291 (B.FR 33000)

ROBINSON, Chas Dorman (1847-1933) American
$650	£425	Mountainous landscape view (13x20cm-5x8in) init. board. 29-Jun-94 Doyle, New York #68
$850	£574	Atmospheric landscape (15x20cm-6x8in) s. i.verso panel. 9-Nov-93 John Moran, Pasadena #852
$1700	£1118	Wildflowers along coast (13x23cm-5x9in) s. panel. 13-Jun-93 Butterfield & Butterfield, San Francisco #742/R
$2500	£1471	Flowering dunes (41x56cm-16x22in) s. 4-Oct-92 Butterfield & Butterfield, Los Angeles #88/R
$3750	£2467	Mt. Tamalpais (71x96cm-28x38in) s.i. 13-Jun-93 Butterfield & Butterfield, San Francisco #771/R
$4500	£3125	Mt Tamalpais (30x46cm-12x18in) s. 7-Mar-93 Butterfield & Butterfield, San Francisco #52/R
$6500	£4514	Sidewheeler in San Francisco Bay (30x46cm-12x18in) indis.s. 7-Mar-93 Butterfield & Butterfield, San Francisco #15/R

ROBINSON, Florence Vincent (1874-?) American
$650	£433	Walking through fields of flowers (18x25cm-7x10in) s. W/C. 26-Aug-93 Skinner, Bolton #210
$950	£634	View of the Pantheon, Paris (36x26cm-14x10in) s. W/C. 23-May-94 Christie's, East, New York #132/R
$2000	£1361	Sunday afternoon, Place de la Concorde (36x46cm-14x18in) s. W/C. 9-Jul-93 Sloan, North Bethesda #2829/R

ROBINSON, Hal (20th C) American
$600	£403	Mountainous lake scene (64x76cm-25x30in) s. 16-Dec-93 Mystic Fine Arts, Connecticut #298
$1000	£654	Winter scene (61x51cm-24x20in) s. 30-Jun-94 Mystic Fine Arts, Connecticut #120 a
$1200	£795	New England stream (76x91cm-30x36in) s. 21-Nov-92 James Bakker, Cambridge #219/R
$1600	£925	Dunes with ocean beyond (71x89cm-28x35in) s. 25-Sep-92 Sotheby's Arcade, New York #238/R

ROBINSON, Irene (1891-1973) American
$950	£629	Floral still life (61x51cm-24x20in) s. 15-Jun-94 Butterfield & Butterfield, San Francisco #4670/R

ROBINSON, Robert (attrib) (1886-1952) American
$4256	£2800	View of house and garden with gentlemen and ladies promenading (75x121cm-30x48in) 7-Apr-93 Christie's, London #137/R

ROBINSON, Theodore (1852-1896) American
$15000	£10490	Girl in red at the piano (32x21cm-13x8in) 11-Mar-93 Christie's, New York #146/R
$70000	£46667	Giverny (36x60cm-14x24in) s.i.d.1887. 25-May-94 Sotheby's, New York #82/R
$90000	£57692	Girl sewing (55x46cm-22x18in) painted c.1886. 26-May-93 Christie's, New York #134/R
$200000	£133333	Young woman with violin (102x72cm-40x28in) s.i.d.MDCCCLXXXVI. 25-May-94 Sotheby's, New York #100/R
$1000000	£666667	The gossips (46x58cm-18x23in) s.d.1891. 25-May-94 Sotheby's, New York #96/R
$500	£338	Portrait of Theo Wendel (10x16cm-4x6in) i. pencil. 31-Mar-94 Sotheby's Arcade, New York #122/R

ROBINSON, Walter (1950-) American
$1000	£654	White bear (46x36cm-18x14in) acrylic executed 1985. 22-Dec-92 Christie's, East, New York #66
$1200	£784	Annie (46x36cm-18x14in) acrylic executed 1985. 22-Dec-92 Christie's, East, New York #67

ROBINSON, William S (1861-1945) American
$800	£408	Village scene (30x41cm-12x16in) s. board. 18-Aug-92 Richard Bourne, Hyannis #104/R
$1250	£801	French landscape (30x41cm-12x16in) s. i.d.1900verso. 13-Dec-92 Litchfield Auction Gallery #20
$1400	£714	Fishing schooner at anchor (41x30cm-16x12in) s. board. 18-Aug-92 Richard Bourne, Hyannis #103/R

ROBINSON, William T (1852-?) American
$650	£445	Pittsfield, N.H. (30x46cm-12x18in) s. i.verso board. 19-Feb-94 Young Fine Arts Auctions, Maine #171/R
$700	£473	Sailing ship in rough seas (23x33cm-9x13in) s. board. 27-Nov-93 Young Fine Arts Auctions, Maine #275/R
$1250	£817	Feeding chickens (36x51cm-14x20in) s.d.1902. 17-Sep-93 Skinner, Bolton #156/R
$1600	£1081	In the rookery (56x69cm-22x27in) s.d.1907. 30-Oct-93 Skinner, Bolton #59/R

ROCCA BRITO, Luis (1964-) Venezuelan
$8000	£5298	El Estanque (160x200cm-63x79in) s.d.90 s.i.d.1990 verso. 24-Nov-92 Christie's, New York #257/R

ROCHA, Ricardo (20th C) Mexican?
$1631   £1102   Retrato de Pajaron no.8 (102x65cm-40x26in) s.d.1968. 27-Apr-94 Louis Morton, Mexico #679/R (M.P 5500)

ROCHE, Rabel (20th C) Puerto Rican
$9000   £6040   Who, In My Mind (181x122cm-71x48in) s. painted 1991. 7-Jan-94 Gary Nader, Miami #96/R

ROCHER, Camy (20th C) Haitian
$1449   £947   Le mariage (60x50cm-24x20in) 17-May-93 Hoebanx, Paris #189 (F.FR 8000)

ROCK, Geoffrey (1923-) Canadian
$2073   £1355   Branding scene, Douglas Lake Ranch (61x91cm-24x36in) s.i.d.1988verso board. 6-Oct-93 Maynards, Vancouver #271 (C.D 2750)

ROCKBURNE, Dorothea (1934-) Canadian
$8000   £5369   Copal no 8 (73x98cm-29x39in) s.i.d.75 pastel paper collage on paperboard. 5-May-94 Sotheby's, New York #264 a/R
$14000   £9272   Messenger angel, dawn (111x166cm-44x65in) s.i.d.82 W/C spray enamel vellum on board. 19-Nov-92 Christie's, New York #391/R

ROCKENSHAUB, Gerwald (1952-) American?
$1100   £719   Untitled - no.18 (30x25cm-12x10in) executed 1987. 22-Dec-92 Christie's, East, New York #68
$1100   £719   Untitled (30x25cm-12x10in) executed 1987. 22-Dec-92 Christie's, East, New York #69

ROCKEY, A B (1779-1834) American
$950   £621   Portrait of a lady (76x64cm-30x25in) s.d.1865verso. 18-Apr-93 Hindman Galleries, Chicago #893

ROCKLINE, Vera (1896-1934) American
$2229   £1496   Maternite (130x89cm-51x35in) s. 14-Dec-93 Chayette & Calmels, Paris #135 (F.FR 13000)
$739   £486   Le modele nu posant (46x25cm-18x10in) s. pastel. 2-Apr-93 Libert, Castor, Paris #93 (F.FR 4000)

ROCKMAN, Alexis (20th C) American
$22000   £14265   Balance of terror (183x213cm-72x84in) s.i.d.88. 11-Nov-93 Sotheby's, New York #230/R

ROCKWELL, Augustus (1822-1882) American
$1100   £728   Coast of Labrador (41x33cm-16x13in) s. oval. 23-Sep-93 Mystic Fine Arts, Connecticut #149/R

ROCKWELL, Cleveland (1837-1907) American
$6500   £4305   Mount Hood (30x51cm-12x20in) s. 15-Jun-94 Butterfield & Butterfield, San Francisco #4430/R
$8000   £5263   Rowing across river (25x51cm-10x20in) s.d.1877. 13-Jun-93 Butterfield & Butterfield, San Francisco #3103/R

ROCKWELL, Norman (1894-1978) American
$8500   £5743   Study for 'Blood Brothers' (69x114cm-27x45in) s. oil graphite painted 1960's. 31-Mar-94 Sotheby's Arcade, New York #403/R
$8500   £5944   Wolf, the watchdog (59x91cm-23x36in) s.d.1918 en grisaille. 11-Mar-93 Christie's, New York #262/R
$9000   £6000   General Dwight D. Eisenhower (28x20cm-11x8in) init. painted c.1952. 25-May-94 Sotheby's, New York #152/R
$13000   £7514   Wolf, the watchdog (59x91cm-23x36in) s.d.1918 en grisaille. 23-Sep-92 Christie's, New York #290/R
$18000   £12081   The Peace Corps (56x48cm-22x19in) init.i. i.verso oil pencil paper painted 1966. 2-Dec-93 Sotheby's, New York #158/R
$24000   £15894   Hungry buddies (26x20cm-10x8in) s. 22-Sep-93 Christie's, New York #228/R
$27000   £18881   Study for harvest moon (43x28cm-17x11in) mono.init. painted c.1920. 10-Mar-93 Sotheby's, New York #173/R
$35000   £23333   Waiting for the art editor (36x55cm-14x22in) s. 17-Mar-94 Sotheby's, New York #166/R
$47500   £31457   War hero job hunting (76x40cm-30x16in) s. board. 23-Sep-93 Sotheby's, New York #294/R
$50000   £33557   'Shuffleton's Barbershop' - a preliminary study (84x79cm-33x31in) painted 1950. 24-Mar-94 Boos Gallery, Michigan #565/R
$52000   £32911   Gramercy Park (76x48cm-30x19in) s. 4-Dec-92 Christie's, New York #161/R
$55000   £34810   Old man and boy - Halloween (38x33cm-15x13in) s. 3-Dec-92 Sotheby's, New York #202/R
$60000   £41958   Boy and shopkeeper, gone on business (76x79cm-30x31in) s. oil pencil posterboard. 10-Mar-93 Sotheby's, New York #171/R
$90000   £62937   Convention, hat check girl (109x86cm-43x34in) s. 10-Mar-93 Sotheby's, New York #172/R
$95000   £63333   Till the boys come home (75x60cm-30x24in) s. 17-Mar-94 Sotheby's, New York #171/R
$115000   £76667   The billboard painter (74x58cm-29x23in) s. 25-May-94 Sotheby's, New York #153 a/R
$120000   £76923   Happy skiers on train (89x72cm-35x28in) s. 27-May-93 Sotheby's, New York #117/R
$120000   £75949   Jazz it up with a sax (86x68cm-34x27in) s. 3-Dec-92 Sotheby's, New York #201/R
$900   £604   Dog biting man August 1928 Saturday Evening Post Cover (30x23cm-12x9in) pencil. 16-Dec-93 Mystic Fine Arts, Connecticut #188 a/R

ROCKWELL, Norman (1894-1978) American-cont.
$900	£604	Fireman march 1931 Saturday Evening Post Cover (30x23cm-12x9in) pencil. 16-Dec-93 Mystic Fine Arts, Connecticut #188/R
$3000	£2027	Genre scene on the bridge of a sidewheeler (27x40cm-11x16in) init. graphite paperboard. 5-Nov-93 Skinner, Bolton #181/R
$6000	£4054	Snorkler's lunch (42x32cm-17x13in) s. pencil executed c.1960. 31-Mar-94 Sotheby's Arcade, New York #386/R
$6500	£3757	Christmas prayer (42x36cm-17x14in) s.i. pencil. 23-Sep-92 Christie's, New York #289/R
$9200	£5823	At the jewellers (58x73cm-23x29in) oil pencil canvas. 2-Dec-92 Christie's, East, New York #330/R
$10000	£6757	Boy scout's lunch (41x33cm-16x13in) s. pen chl executed c.1960. 31-Mar-94 Sotheby's Arcade, New York #387/R
$18000	£11392	Dance on a music box (31x26cm-12x10in) s. W/C board. 4-Dec-92 Christie's, New York #160 a/R
$24000	£16000	The veterinarian's office (96x103cm-38x41in) s.i. chl pencil executed 1952. 25-May-94 Sotheby's, New York #153/R
$25000	£16667	The Problem We All Live With (33x53cm-13x21in) s. gouache. 17-Mar-94 Sotheby's, New York #167/R

ROCKWELL, Norman (attrib) (1894-1978) American
$2812	£1900	Four American soldiers travelling in French train (61x91cm-24x36in) s. 28-Apr-94 Taylors, Honiton #50/R

ROCKWELL, Norman (circle) (1894-1978) American
$1230	£820	Young girl and doll (53x41cm-21x16in) bears sig. gouache. 26-May-94 Bonhams, Chelsea #150
$2700	£1800	Young girl and grandmother (49x39cm-19x15in) bears sig. gouache pencil board. 22-Jul-93 Bonhams, London #103/R

ROCLE, Marius R (1897-1967) American
$7500	£5172	Shorty shoeing Silver (91x102cm-36x40in) s. 16-Feb-93 John Moran, Pasadena #115

RODA, Antonio (20th C) South American
$12000	£7947	Flores No. 16 - De la Serie de los Jardines (130x195cm-51x77in) s.d.87. 24-Nov-92 Christie's, New York #248/R

RODO-BOULANGER, Graciela (20th C) Bolivian
$4500	£3020	Paysan (89x71cm-35x28in) s.d.1967 i.stretcher. 24-Feb-94 Sotheby's Arcade, New York #261/R

RODON, Francisco (1934-) Puerto Rican
$65000	£43333	Partir antes del dia (147x107cm-58x42in) s.d.68 masonite. 18-May-94 Christie's, New York #39/R

RODRIGUEZ LOZANO, Manuel (1896-1974) Mexican
$10188	£6531	Mujer (50x40cm-20x16in) 29-Apr-93 Louis Morton, Mexico #134 (M.P 32000)
$18000	£12000	El Paraiso (70x95cm-28x37in) s.d.51. 18-May-94 Christie's, New York #97/R
$22000	£14865	El encuentro (95x70cm-37x28in) s.d.52. 23-Nov-93 Christie's, New York #138/R
$42000	£28000	Grupo de mujeres (80x109cm-31x43in) s.d.35. 18-May-94 Sotheby's, New York #339/R
$949	£641	Desnudo (66x49cm-26x19in) s.d.1935 pencil dr. 27-Apr-94 Louis Morton, Mexico #526 (M.P 3200)

RODRIGUEZ MOREY, Antonio (1874-1930) Cuban
$3000	£2027	Paisaje Cubano (41x56cm-16x22in) s. 23-Nov-93 Christie's, New York #284/R

RODRIGUEZ, Guillermo (20th C) Uruguayan?
$600	£392	Molino (58x44cm-23x17in) s.d.1930. 4-Oct-93 Gomensoro, Montevideo #49
$2600	£1354	Canada (82x92cm-32x36in) s. fibre. 12-Aug-92 Castells & Castells, Montevideo #44/R

RODRIGUEZ, Mariano (1912-1990) Cuban
$12000	£8000	El gallo (102x82cm-40x32in) s.d.59. 18-May-94 Sotheby's, New York #358/R
$30000	£20000	Mujer (50x40cm-20x16in) s.d.38. 18-May-94 Christie's, New York #109/R
$65000	£43333	Pareja (73x63cm-29x25in) s.d.41 tempera oil canvas laid down on masonite. 18-May-94 Sotheby's, New York #226/R
$100000	£66667	Tres mujeres (83x90cm-33x35in) s.d.42. 17-May-94 Sotheby's, New York #61/R
$270000	£182432	El Gallo Pintado (65x53cm-26x21in) s.d.41. 22-Nov-93 Sotheby's, New York #23/R
$1500	£1000	Pelea de Gallos (28x38cm-11x15in) s.d.62 W/C board. 9-Jun-94 Sotheby's Arcade, New York #142/R
$2000	£1325	Baile (46x57cm-18x22in) s.d.47 pen. 30-Jun-93 Sotheby's Arcade, New York #216/R
$3000	£2013	Portrait of a woman (35x26cm-14x10in) s.d.43 W/C ink. 24-Feb-94 Sotheby's Arcade, New York #288/R
$4000	£2667	Gallo (52x72cm-20x28in) s.d.78 W/C ink. 18-May-94 Christie's, New York #280/R
$4000	£2667	Desnudo sentado (37x29cm-15x11in) s.d.42 ink W/C. 18-May-94 Sotheby's, New York #228/R
$10000	£6757	Banistas (36x29cm-14x11in) s.d.39 graphite. 22-Nov-93 Sotheby's, New York #21/R

ROE, Christopher (?) American?
$550	£369	Clipper ship 'Hurricane', built by Isaac Smith of Hoboken, NJ (53x69cm-21x27in) 25-Mar-94 Eldred, Massachusetts #122

ROERICH, Nikolai Konstantinovitch (1874-1947) American/Russian
$2250	£1424	Figure in hilly landscape with pan pipes and bears (48x98cm-19x39in) mono.d.1919. 25-Oct-92 Butterfield & Butterfield, San Francisco #2205/R

ROERICH, Nikolai Konstantinovitch (1874-1947) American/Russian-cont.
$3775 £2500 Buddhist cave (41x63cm-16x25in) 24-Nov-92 Phillips, London #348/R
$8140 £5500 Finnish landscape, the Island of Tulolansaari (45x84cm-18x33in) mono.i.d.1918 s.i.verso panel. 17-Jun-93 Sotheby's, London #321/R
$15645 £10500 Stage set for the town of Ledenetz from Tsar Saltan (61x91cm-24x36in) s. 15-Dec-93 Sotheby's, London #30/R
$16390 £11000 St Merkuri of Smolensk (91x91cm-36x36in) s.d.1919 tempera. 15-Dec-93 Sotheby's, London #29/R
$755 £500 Himalayan tale (44x59cm-17x23in) mono. gouache. 24-Nov-92 Phillips, London #349

ROESCH, Kurt (1905-) American
$900 £592 Insects (61x86cm-24x34in) s. 13-Jun-93 Butterfield & Butterfield, San Francisco #3268/R

ROESEN, Severin (fl.1848-1871) German/American
$4000 £2649 Still life (15x23cm-6x9in) s. canvas on board. 13-Nov-92 Du Mouchelle, Detroit #2025/R
$5500 £3642 Still life (15x23cm-6x9in) s. canvas on board. 13-Nov-92 Du Mouchelle, Detroit #2024/R
$6000 £3974 Still life (15x23cm-6x9in) s. canvas on board. 13-Nov-92 Du Mouchelle, Detroit #2023/R
$21000 £14094 Still life with peaches and grapes (40x50cm-16x20in) s. panel. 3-Dec-93 Christie's, New York #121/R
$25000 £16779 Still life with fruit and glass of water (102x127cm-40x50in) s. canvas on masonite. 24-Jun-93 Boos Gallery, Michigan #468/R
$25000 £17483 Still life with fruit (51x40cm-20x16in) mono panel oval. 10-Mar-93 Sotheby's, New York #3/R
$25000 £15823 Still life with strawberry basket (38x51cm-15x20in) s. panel. 4-Dec-92 Christie's, New York #177/R
$28000 £16185 Still life with Pilsner glass (64x76cm-25x30in) 23-Sep-92 Christie's, New York #13/R
$42500 £27244 Floral still life (76x63cm-30x25in) s. 27-May-93 Sotheby's, New York #132/R
$19000 £12179 Still life with fruit, bird's nest and wine glass (56x66cm-22x26in) s. pastel. 27-May-93 Sotheby's, New York #131/R

ROGER, Biron (20th C) American
$900 £608 View of downtown Detroit (58x112cm-23x44in) s.i. panel. 4-Nov-93 Boos Gallery, Michigan #1289/R

ROGERS, Charles B (1911-) American
$450 £302 Peak at evening (30x46cm-12x18in) s.i. s.verso W/C. 5-Mar-94 Louisiana Auction Exchange #67/R
$450 £302 Southwest Ridge (30x46cm-12x18in) s.i. s.verso W/C. 5-Mar-94 Louisiana Auction Exchange #66/R

ROGERS, Frank Whiting (1854-?) American
$1500 £1007 Puppies in stable (51x76cm-20x30in) s. 3-Feb-94 Sloan, North Bethesda #2631/R
$650 £436 Basket of peaches (43x53cm-17x21in) init. pastel. 3-Feb-94 Sloan, North Bethesda #2632

ROGERS, Otto Donald (20th C) Canadian
$610 £407 Heavy rain over lake (122x122cm-48x48in) s.i.d.1984 acrylic. 30-May-94 Ritchie, Toronto #219/R (C.D 850)
$1569 £1026 Wet morning (61x61cm-24x24in) s.verso acrylic. 10-May-93 Hodgins, Calgary #295/R (C.D 2000)
$2104 £1422 Attraction (45x157cm-18x62in) s.i.d.1966 stretcher verso. 25-Apr-94 Levis, Calgary #284/R (C.D 2900)

ROHDE, H (19th C) American
$1200 £789 Catskill mountain landscape (79x65cm-31x26in) s. 31-Mar-93 Sotheby's Arcade, New York #17/R

ROITER, Andrei (1960-) American
$1100 £738 The poets know (188x149cm-74x59in) s.i.d.1989 verso. 23-Feb-94 Christie's, East, New York #210/R

ROJAS, Elmar (1938-) Guatemalan
$20000 £13333 El Gran Paseo de los Espantapajaros (121x131cm-48x52in) s.d.89 s.i.d.verso. 18-May-94 Christie's, New York #249/R
$24000 £16000 Temas marineros-pescadores (177x139cm-70x55in) s.d.92 s.i.d.verso acrylic oil. 17-May-94 Sotheby's, New York #78/R
$26000 £17333 Fiesta magica de animales misticos con el senor del campo (150x205cm-59x81in) s.d.92 s.i.d.verso oil acrylic. 18-May-94 Sotheby's, New York #321/R
$26000 £17568 Grandes fiestas del Torofuego en Atitlan (146x181cm-57x71in) s.d.92 s.i.d.verso acrylic oil. 23-Nov-93 Christie's, New York #190/R
$30000 £19868 Un Dia de Fiesta en el Campo (179x174cm-70x69in) s.d.91 s.i.num.10 verso oil acrylic. 24-Nov-92 Christie's, New York #103/R
$6000 £3922 El paso por la villa Burguesa (71x92cm-28x36in) s. i.d.88 verso oil pastel paper on canvas. 17-May-93 Christie's, New York #166/R

ROJO, Vincente (20th C) Mexican
$3559 £2405 Senal sobre fondo marron (140x100cm-55x39in) s.d.1970. 27-Apr-94 Louis Morton, Mexico #688/R (M.P 12000)
$7118 £4810 Senal con rayas grises (80x60cm-31x24in) s.d.1970. 27-Apr-94 Louis Morton, Mexico #734/R (M.P 24000)

ROJO, Vincente (20th C) Mexican-cont.
$741   £501   Sin titulo (49x63cm-19x25in) s.i.d.1967 ink dr. 27-Apr-94 Louis Morton, Mexico #640 (M.P 2500)

ROLLINS, Tim (1955-) American
$8000   £5298   Nature theatre of Oklahoma VI - for Corazon Aquino (81x81cm-32x32in) oil marker book pages linen painted 1986. 18-Nov-92 Sotheby's, New York #309/R

ROLLINS, Tim and K O S (20th C) American
$1000   £654   Untitled (20x13cm-8x5in) init.i. pencil metallic paint printed paper. 4-May-93 Sotheby's, New York #245 a/R
$7000   £4698   From the animal farm, P W Botha (150x241cm-59x95in) acrylic wash printed pages on linen exec.1984-87. 5-May-94 Sotheby's, New York #298/R
$7595   £5063   X-Men (193x492cm-76x194in) s.d.1990verso collage. 2-Jun-94 AB Stockholms Auktionsverk, Stockholm #7090/R (S.KR 60000)
$8000   £5298   Nature theatre of Oklahoma VII (81x81cm-32x32in) s.i.d.86verso acrylic chk bookpages on canvas. 19-Nov-92 Christie's, New York #266/R
$10000 £6623   F451, the scarlet letter (267x122cm-105x48in) .i.d.87-88verso acrylic ash bookpages on canvas. 19-Nov-92 Christie's, New York #128/R

ROLLINS, Warren E (1861-1962) American
$650   £436   Desert scene with figure approaching adobe hut (30x51cm-12x20in) s. 5-Aug-93 Eldred, Massachusetts #809/R
$1100   £724   Navajo weaver (27x15cm-11x6in) s. canvas on board. 13-Jun-93 Butterfield & Butterfield, San Francisco #3211/R
$1600   £1074   Desert landscape (36x71cm-14x28in) s. 8-Dec-93 Butterfield & Butterfield, San Francisco #3589/R
$1800   £1059   Spirit song (46x36cm-18x14in) s.verso canvas on board. 4-Oct-92 Butterfield & Butterfield, Los Angeles #217/R
$2250   £1510   Desert dawn (51x86cm-20x34in) s. s.i.verso. 8-Dec-93 Butterfield & Butterfield, San Francisco #3566/R
$3750   £2168   Indians and teepee by stream (36x43cm-14x17in) s. 25-Sep-92 Sotheby's Arcade, New York #187/R
$4000   £2564   Indians camping on Prairie near Tacoma (25x36cm-10x14in) s.d.91 s.i.d.1891 stretcher. 26-May-93 Christie's, New York #95/R

ROLSHOVEN, Julius (1858-1930) American
$624   £400   Church interior, Assisi (93x84cm-37x33in) s.d.1903. 29-Apr-93 Christie's, S. Kensington #135/R
$1100   £728   Female nude (41x33cm-16x13in) s. 17-Jun-94 Du Mouchelle, Detroit #2360/R
$1900   £1242   Lady with fan (76x61cm-30x24in) s. 1-Nov-92 Hanzel Galleries, Chicago #53/R
$3500   £2318   Florentine interior (81x63cm-32x25in) s. panel. 23-Sep-93 Sotheby's, New York #130/R
$7500   £4747   Rainmaker (40x30cm-16x12in) s.i. board. 3-Dec-92 Sotheby's, New York #63/R

ROMANACH, Leopoldo (1862-1951) Peruvian
$8000   £5369   Cayo frances (35x66cm-14x26in) s. 7-Jan-94 Gary Nader, Miami #123/R
$10000 £6667   Mujer de las Canas (53x72cm-21x28in) s. painted c.1930. 18-May-94 Sotheby's, New York #281/R
$12000 £8108   La cocinera (53x63cm-21x25in) s. 23-Nov-93 Christie's, New York #97/R
$14000 £9459   Cayo Frances (51x68cm-20x27in) s. painted c.1915. 22-Nov-93 Sotheby's, New York #169/R
$19000 £12583 La Casa de los Amos (66x128cm-26x50in) s. painted c.1930. 24-Nov-92 Christie's, New York #83/R
$30000 £19868 Guajiros (90x122cm-35x48in) s.d.1922. 24-Nov-92 Christie's, New York #52/R

ROMANOVSKY, Dimitri (20th C) American
$950   £621   Floating lilies (51x61cm-20x24in) s. board. 18-Sep-93 Young Fine Arts Auctions, Maine #254/R

ROMERO, Carlos Orozco (1898-1984) Mexican
$4838   £3247   Paisaje montanoso (28x44cm-11x17in) s. 1-Dec-93 Louis Morton, Mexico #148/R (M.P 15000)
$8596   £5510   Paisaje montanoso (30x45cm-12x18in) s. 29-Apr-93 Louis Morton, Mexico #68 (M.P 27000)
$10084 £6814   Figura femenina (41x30cm-16x12in) s.d.1949 masonite. 27-Apr-94 Louis Morton, Mexico #485/R (M.P 34000)
$11610 £7792   Carretera de Acapulco (110x85cm-43x33in) s. 1-Dec-93 Louis Morton, Mexico #45/R (M.P 36000)
$12000 £7843   Caminantes (48x64cm-19x25in) s. painted 1962. 18-May-93 Sotheby's, New York #219/R
$24000 £15894 Valle de Mexico (46x61cm-18x24in) s.d.1944. 23-Nov-92 Sotheby's, New York #53/R
$1700   £1111   Hombre con latigo (33x25cm-13x10in) s. pen executed c.1945. 18-May-93 Sotheby's, New York #150/R
$2000   £1307   Pescador (26x22cm-10x9in) s.d.1929 gouache. 18-May-93 Sotheby's, New York #124/R
$5500   £3642   Mujer (28x25cm-11x10in) s. W/C. 23-Nov-92 Sotheby's, New York #210/R
$5500   £3642   Paisaje Metafisico I (32x25cm-13x10in) s.d.1931 gouache. 24-Nov-92 Christie's, New York #210/R

ROMULO, Teodulo (1943-) Mexican
$6914   £4609   Vaca con gallinas (66x50cm-26x20in) s. paper. 25-May-94 Louis Morton, Mexico #81/R (M.P 23000)

RONALD, William S (1926-) Canadian
$1031	£674	Riobbons, the sunlight fly (63x76cm-25x30in) s.d.54. 18-May-93 Joyner Fine Art, Toronto #216 (C.D 1300)
$1240	£838	Abstract composition (89x74cm-35x29in) s. 3-Nov-93 Sotheby's, Toronto #281/R (C.D 1600)
$1656	£1111	Goddess (60x76cm-24x30in) s.d.57 i.verso. 29-Nov-93 Ritchie, Toronto #211/R (C.D 2200)
$2378	£1554	Black and blue (91x122cm-36x48in) s.d.83. 18-May-93 Joyner Fine Art, Toronto #121/R (C.D 3000)
$3766	£2461	The doctor (198x152cm-78x60in) s. s.d.25/9/74 verso. 19-May-93 Sotheby's, Toronto #313/R (C.D 4750)
$545	£361	Abstract (55x75cm-22x30in) s.d.87 W/C. 24-Nov-92 Joyner Fine Art, Toronto #31/R (C.D 700)
$634	£415	Lilli Palmer (56x76crn-22x30in) s.d.81 W/C. 19-May-93 Sotheby's, Toronto #209/R (C.D 800)
$1092	£728	Abstract composition (55x74cm-22x29in) s.d.63 W/C. 11-May-94 Sotheby's, Toronto #108/R (C.D 1500)
$1240	£838	Sundance (46x61cm-18x24in) s.d.64 i.d.verso W/C. 3-Nov-93 Sotheby's, Toronto #225/R (C.D 1600)
$1323	£876	Abstract composition (43x49cm-17x19in) s.d.56 W/C. 18-Nov-92 Sotheby's, Toronto #182 (C.D 1700)

RONDEL, Frederick (1826-1892) American
$1700	£1118	River landscape in autumn (15x25cm-6x10in) s. 31-Mar-93 Sotheby's Arcade, New York #34/R
$1800	£1200	Portrait of lady with red hair (74x58cm-29x23in) s. 22-Jul-93 Sotheby's Arcade, New York #466/R
$2200	£1272	The unexpected visitor (74x102cm-29x40in) s.d.1859. 25-Sep-92 Sotheby's Arcade, New York #117/R
$2400	£1633	A break from work (46x61cm-18x24in) s. 15-Nov-93 Christie's, East, New York #53/R

ROOK, Edward F (1870-1960) American
$4250	£2815	Red sarape (76x76cm-30x30in) s. 23-Sep-93 Mystic Fine Arts, Connecticut #116/R

ROOT, Robert Marshall (1863-c.1938) American
$850	£545	Shelbyville Park (71x122cm-28x48in) s.d.1929 board. 13-Dec-92 Hindman Galleries, Chicago #19

ROPER, Matilda (1886-1958) American
$1200	£779	Portrait of Mrs Lendall (196x97cm-77x38in) s.d.1912. 9-Sep-93 Sotheby's Arcade, New York #121/R

ROPP, Roy M (1888-?) American
$900	£592	California landscape (46x91cm-18x36in) s. 5-Jun-93 Louisiana Auction Exchange #95/R

ROSAIRE, Arthur Dominique (1879-1922) Canadian
$870	£580	Landscape (63x76cm-25x30in) s. i.verso. 6-Jun-94 Waddingtons, Toronto #1261 (C.D 1200)
$3250	£2153	Quebec barges (63x76cm-25x30in) s. 15-Jun-94 Butterfield & Butterfield, San Francisco #4451/R

ROSE, Guy (1867-1925) American
$18000	£11842	Coarse fishing in France (53x61cm-21x24in) s. 13-Jun-93 Butterfield & Butterfield, San Francisco #850/R
$42500	£27961	Sunrise in early sunlight (51x61cm-20x24in) 13-Jun-93 Butterfield & Butterfield, San Francisco #849/R
$44000	£29530	The Blue Pool near Mount Whitney (86x58cm-34x23in) s. i.verso. 8-Dec-93 Butterfield & Butterfield, San Francisco #3482/R
$70000	£48611	Twin Lake, Eastern Sierras near Bridgeport (60x73cm-24x29in) s. canvas on board. 7-Mar-93 Butterfield & Butterfield, San Francisco #140/R

ROSE, Iver (1899-1972) American
$650	£422	Virgins, St Peter's Fiesta, Gloucester (30x20cm-12x8in) s. masonite. 9-Sep-93 Sotheby's Arcade, New York #327
$700	£464	Workman (61x46cm-24x18in) s. masonite. 28-Sep-93 John Moran, Pasadena #336
$1050	£729	Woman artist in studio (46x61cm-18x24in) s. masonite. 6-Mar-93 Louisiana Auction Exchange #98/R
$1200	£779	Clarinet player (76x56cm-30x22in) s. acrylic board. 11-Sep-93 Louisiana Auction Exchange #49/R

ROSE, Manuel (1887-1961) Uruguayan
$800	£523	Paisaje de Piriapolis (46x78cm-18x31in) s. panel. 4-Oct-93 Gomensoro, Montevideo #88
$1220	£646	Punta Colorada (38x46cm-15x18in) board. 10-Sep-92 Gomensoro, Montevideo #39/R
$2200	£1438	Payaso (53x67cm-21x26in) s.d.1953. 26-Oct-92 Gomensoro, Montevideo #72/R
$2200	£1438	Payaso (66x57cm-26x22in) s. 26-Oct-92 Gomensoro, Montevideo #71/R
$3000	£1961	Juegos en la playa (26x34cm-10x13in) board. 26-Oct-92 Gomensoro, Montevideo #73
$5000	£3356	El Pan de Azucar (72x78cm-28x31in) s.d.1953. 29-Nov-92 Gomensoro, Montevideo #36/R
$7000	£4636	La Paica Y El Garado (80x59cm-31x23in) s. 23-Nov-92 Sotheby's, New York #229/R
$10500	£6863	El bailecito (74x92cm-29x36in) s.d.1954. 4-Oct-93 Gomensoro, Montevideo #87/R
$12000	£8108	Desnudo en el paisaje (93x75cm-37x30in) s.d.50. 22-Nov-93 Sotheby's, New York #215/R

425

ROSE, Manuel (1887-1961) Uruguayan-cont.
$13000	£8725	Casco de estancia y alamos (73x73cm-29x29in) s.d.-917. 29-Nov-93 Gomensoro, Montevideo #37/R
$15000	£9804	Calle de Las Piedras (65x58cm-26x23in) s.d.XVI painted 1916. 17-May-93 Christie's, New York #100 a/R
$40000	£26144	La familia del artista (138x158cm-54x62in) s.d.1936. 18-May-93 Sotheby's, New York #30/R

ROSE, Robin (20th C) American
$750	£481	Untitled (91x76cm-36x30in) s.d.1976verso acrylic plexiglass. 10-Dec-92 Sloan, North Bethesda #2704
$600	*£385*	*Untitled (48x66cm-19x26in) encaustic. 10-Dec-92 Sloan, North Bethesda #2718*
$750	*£481*	*Icarus Stone,Key West (61x74cm-24x29in) encaustic. 10-Dec-92 Sloan, North Bethesda #2719*

ROSELAND, Harry (1868-1950) American
$1000	£680	Reading tea leaves (20x25cm-8x10in) s. canvas laid down on board. 15-Nov-93 Christie's, East, New York #83/R
$1600	£1039	Kitchen interior (31x46cm-12x18in) s.d.1908. 9-Sep-93 Sotheby's Arcade, New York #38/R
$2600	£1376	The fortune teller (25x36cm-10x14in) s. 11-Sep-92 Skinner, Bolton #175/R
$3200	£2133	Still life with roses (30x41cm-12x16in) s. canvasboard. 23-May-94 Hindman Galleries, Chicago #196/R
$3250	£2110	Reading the leaves (20x28cm-8x11in) s. panel. 11-Sep-93 Louisiana Auction Exchange #19/R
$3500	£2023	Her favourite flower (20x28cm-8x11in) s. board. 21-Sep-92 Selkirks, St. Louis #333/R
$3800	£2533	The harvest (25x36cm-10x14in) s.d.98. 23-May-94 Christie's, East, New York #118/R
$4000	£2353	Portrait of blonde beauty in red shawl (51x36cm-20x14in) s. 11-Oct-92 Litchfield Auction Gallery #175
$4000	£2721	By the fire (51x76cm-20x30in) s.d.34. 15-Nov-93 Christie's, East, New York #84/R
$4600	£3217	Mother and child (20x25cm-8x10in) s. board. 14-Mar-93 Hindman Galleries, Chicago #20/R
$7000	£4667	Picnic in the hay (25x35cm-10x14in) s. 16-Mar-94 Christie's, New York #35/R
$7500	£5245	Tending the fire (36x52cm-14x20in) s.d.1906. 11-Mar-93 Christie's, New York #79/R
$8000	£5556	Paying the rent (36x51cm-14x20in) 6-Mar-93 Louisiana Auction Exchange #152/R
$13000	£8667	Reading the cards (63x76cm-25x30in) s.d.99 canvas laid down on masonite. 26-May-94 Christie's, New York #98/R
$14000	£8974	Chess game (56x71cm-22x28in) s. 26-May-93 Christie's, New York #61 a/R
$16000	£9249	Reading the crystal (51x76cm-20x30in) s.d.1906 s.i.d.verso. 23-Sep-92 Christie's, New York #103/R
$19000	£13287	He loves me (56x76cm-22x30in) s. 11-Mar-93 Christie's, New York #80/R
$24000	£15190	An important letter (64x82cm-25x32in) s.d.98. 4-Dec-92 Christie's, New York #244/R
$26000	£16456	Reading the tea leaves (52x77cm-20x30in) s.d.10. 4-Dec-92 Christie's, New York #28/R
$47500	£30063	Coney Island (71x101cm-28x40in) s.d.33. 3-Dec-92 Sotheby's, New York #125/R

ROSENBAUM, Richard (19th C) American
$600	*£368*	*Before hunt (25x75cm-10x30in) s. W/C paperboard. 13-Oct-92 Christie's, East, New York #246*

ROSENBERG, Henry M (1858-?) American
$800	£513	Officer taking a smoke (20x15cm-8x6in) s.i.d.97 i.stretcher. 28-Apr-93 Doyle, New York #57

ROSENQUIST, James (1933-) American
$30000	£19608	At the speed of light (183cm-72in circular) s.d.1988overlap canvas on panel. 5-May-93 Christie's, New York #311/R
$37500	£25168	Eye and flowers (76x77cm-30x30in) s.d.1987. 5-May-94 Sotheby's, New York #225/R
$50000	£32680	Fiery flowers (109x139cm-43x55in) painted 1989. 4-May-93 Sotheby's, New York #233/R
$75000	£50336	Untitled (140x143cm-55x56in) s.d.89 verso. 25-Feb-94 Sotheby's, New York #95/R
$105000	£70946	Untitle (203x203cm-80x80in) s.d.1989 verso. 11-Nov-93 Sotheby's, New York #386/R
$120000	£79470	Win a new house this christmas contest (147x147cm-58x58in) s.d.1964verso. 18-Nov-92 Christie's, New York #29/R
$200000	£135135	Silhouette (106x121cm-42x48in) s.i.d.1964 verso board. 9-Nov-93 Christie's, New York #29/R
$210000	£139073	Untitled (190x289cm-75x114in) s.d.1988 diptych canvas mounted on panel. 18-Nov-92 Christie's, New York #64/R
$220000	£147651	TV boat (152x195cm-60x77in) s.i.d.1966verso. 3-May-93 Christie's, New York #56/R
$290000	£192053	While the earth revolves at night (198x503cm-78x198in) 17-Nov-92 Sotheby's, New York #47/R
$7500	£5034	Water, fire, earth (92x187cm-36x74in) s.i.d.1974 W/C string stone. 5-May-94 Sotheby's, New York #202/R
$9500	£6419	4 coloured mile drive (97x193cm-38x76in) s.i.1974 mixed media. 11-Nov-93 Sotheby's, New York #377/R
$10108	£6784	Four wrinkled handkerchiefs and stars, projet pour sculpture Eye Glass (65x102cm-26x40in) s.i.d.1972 W/C chl crayon collage paper. 21-Mar-94 Guy Loudmer, Paris #101/R (F.FR 58000)
$11000	£6471	Star way (72x188cm-28x74in) s.d.74 mixed media paper collage. 6-Oct-92 Sotheby's, New York #75/R
$12000	£8054	Colour sketch for artist rights (76x56cm-30x22in) s.i.d.1975 acrylic metal leather paper collage. 4-May-94 Christie's, New York #189/R

ROSENQUIST, James (1933-) American-cont.
$76000 £50331 Paint brush (152x90cm-60x35in) s.i.d.1964verso canvas molded plastic chain. 19-Nov-92 Christie's, New York #336/R

ROSENTHAL, Albert (1863-1939) American
$14000 £8861 Portrait of Mrs. H. Bryan Owsley, Philadelphia (26x89cm-10x35in) s.d.1910. 4-Dec-92 Christie's, New York #242/R

ROSENTHAL, Bernard see ROSENTHAL, Tony

ROSENTHAL, Doris (20th C) American
$800 £544 Mexican Indian child (71x53cm-28x21in) s. 16-Apr-94 Young Fine Arts Auctions, Maine #214/R
$600 £390 Woman resting (61x48cm-24x19in) s. pencil pastel. 9-Sep-93 Sotheby's Arcade, New York #348/R

ROSENTHAL, Toby Edward (1849-1917) American
$30000 £19231 Seminary alarmed, Mills College (113x183cm-44x72in) init. 9-Dec-92 Butterfield & Butterfield, San Francisco #3828/R

ROSOFSKY, Seymour (1924-) American
$1100 £733 Lovers statue (48x64cm-19x25in) s. ink W/C. 13-Mar-94 Hindman Galleries, Chicago #839

ROSS, Frederick J (1927-) Canadian
$1602 £1068 Woman sleeping (90x105cm-35x41in) s. tempera board. 13-May-94 Joyner Fine Art, Toronto #77/R (C.D 2200)
$642 £434 Girl with a shell (63x47cm-25x19in) s. col.chk ink. 23-Nov-93 Joyner Fine Art, Toronto #133/R (C.D 850)

ROSS, J McPherson (1850-1924) Canadian
$697 £471 Landscape with sheep (36x51cm-14x20in) s. 3-Nov-93 Sotheby's, Toronto #149 (C.D 900)

ROSSEAU, Percival (c.1859-1937) American
$1600 £1053 On point (33x71cm-13x28in) s. 5-Jun-93 Louisiana Auction Exchange #17/R
$5000 £3289 Best of friends (55x47cm-22x19in) s. 4-Jun-93 Sotheby's, New York #81/R
$23000 £15233 Two pointers in landscape (66x82cm-26x32in) s.d.1909 canvas on masonite. 3-Jun-94 Sotheby's, New York #273/R

ROSSI, Alberto Maria (1879-1965) Argentinian
$1400 £729 El baile (42x34cm-17x13in) 4-Aug-92 VerBo, Buenos Aires #91/R
$3000 £1765 Circo (31x26cm-12x10in) 29-Sep-92 VerBo, Buenos Aires #96
$3500 £2023 Payaso (40x33cm-16x13in) 23-Sep-92 Roldan & Cia, Buenos Aires #60
$7000 £4636 Can Can (50x70cm-20x28in) 18-Nov-92 Roldan & Cia, Buenos Aires #4
$7500 £4335 Despedidos (100x70cm-39x28in) 23-Sep-92 Roldan & Cia, Buenos Aires #18

ROSSITER, Thomas Pritchard (1817-1871) American
$4800 £2775 Muses and graces (43x71cm-17x28in) s.d.1859 s.d.verso. 23-Sep-92 Christie's, New York #3/R

ROSSO, Jose D (1898-1958) Argentinian
$700 £464 Motivo de la Boca (22x30cm-9x12in) 11-Nov-92 VerBo, Buenos Aires #95
$1300 £677 Velero (38x48cm-15x19in) tempera. 4-Aug-92 VerBo, Buenos Aires #93
$1400 £729 Naturaleza muerta (44x46cm-17x18in) tempera. 4-Aug-92 VerBo, Buenos Aires #94/R

ROTH, Ernest David (1879-1964) American
$650 £436 Harbour scene (51x36cm-20x14in) s.d.94. 26-Mar-94 James Bakker, Cambridge #155/R
$1600 £1060 Harbour scene (51x36cm-20x14in) s.d.24. 21-Nov-92 James Bakker, Cambridge #207/R

ROTHBORT, Samuel (1882-1971) American
$1500 £1014 Self-portrait with daughter Jane and green parrot (84x71cm-33x28in) s. board. 31-Mar-94 Sotheby's Arcade, New York #341/R
$1500 £962 Coney Island (20x63cm-8x25in) s. canvas on board. 9-Dec-92 Butterfield & Butterfield, San Francisco #4021/R

ROTHENBERG, Susan (1945-) American
$3800 £2517 Untitled (62x58cm-24x23in) s.d.85verso oil chromecoat paper. 17-Nov-92 Christie's, East, New York #74/R
$12000 £8054 Untitled (46x58cm-18x23in) s.i. acrylic pencil executed 1976. 5-May-94 Sotheby's, New York #361/R
$13000 £8497 Untitled (76x58cm-30x23in) paper executed 1985. 4-May-93 Sotheby's, New York #192/R
$55000 £35948 Quoise (91x74cm-36x29in) s.i.d.1979verso. 5-May-93 Christie's, New York #161/R
$3000 £2013 Untitled (53x44cm-21x17in) s.d.1982verso graphite. 3-May-94 Christie's, East, New York #116/R
$3427 £2300 Untitled (57x39cm-22x15in) chl executed 1986. 25-Mar-93 Christie's, London #172/R
$3500 £2349 Untitled (54x46cm-21x18in) s.d.88-89verso chl col chk. 3-May-94 Christie's, East, New York #166/R
$10000 £6623 Untitled, Mondrian (79x56cm-31x22in) s.d.1985verso chl. 19-Nov-92 Christie's, New York #234/R
$12000 £7843 Untitled (56x76cm-22x30in) s.d.1982verso graphite. 5-May-93 Christie's, New York #158/R
$17000 £11409 Untitled (30x39cm-12x15in) s.i.d.1977 oil crayon lithograph. 5-May-94 Sotheby's, New York #296/R

ROTHERMEL, Peter Frederick (1817-1895) American
$1100	£733	Showing him the way (92x74cm-36x29in) s.d.1848. 23-May-94 Christie's, East, New York #10/R
$3000	£1974	Beggar girl (61x51cm-24x20in) s.indist.d. 31-Mar-93 Sotheby's Arcade, New York #60/R
$3000	£2098	Raphael painting portrait of Beatrice Cenci (99x137cm-39x54in) s. 3-Feb-93 Doyle, New York #53

ROTHKO, Mark (1903-1970) American
$90000	£59603	No.9 (44x38cm-17x15in) 17-Nov-92 Sotheby's, New York #29/R
$110000	£73826	Untitled (61x48cm-24x19in) s.d.1958verso paper on canvas. 3-May-94 Christie's, New York #2/R
$240000	£162162	Untitled (193x123cm-76x48in) acrylic paper on canvas painted 1969. 10-Nov-93 Sotheby's, New York #24/R
$270000	£178808	Untitled (199x149cm-78x59in) s.d.69verso acrylic paper mounted on canvas. 17-Nov-92 Sotheby's, New York #40/R
$300000	£196078	Untitled (178x103cm-70x41in) s.d.1969 verso paper on canvas. 3-May-93 Sotheby's, New York #43/R
$330000	£221477	Red on red (101x64cm-40x25in) paper on canvas painted 1968. 4-May-94 Sotheby's, New York #5 a/R
$800000	£522876	Black stripe (173x97cm-68x38in) s.d.57 verso oil magna canvas. 3-May-93 Sotheby's, New York #35/R
$950000	£637584	Four reds (206x127cm-81x50in) s.d.1957verso. 3-May-94 Christie's, New York #47/R
$1000000	£662252	Untitled (201x175cm-79x69in) s.d.1957verso. 18-Nov-92 Christie's, New York #6/R
$1000000	£662252	Brown, black and blue (176x152cm-69x60in) s.d.1958verso. 17-Nov-92 Sotheby's, New York #33/R
$1100000	£728477	Dark over light (229x148cm-90x58in) s.d.1954verso. 18-Nov-92 Christie's, New York #43/R
$22000	*£14865*	*Untitled (66x51cm-26x20in) s. graphite brush ink gouache painted 1944-45. 10-Nov-93 Christie's, New York #105/R*
$42000	*£28188*	*Ancestral imprint (75x53cm-30x21in) s. W/C pastel chl pencil ink executed 1946. 5-May-94 Sotheby's, New York #82/R*

ROTHWELL, Elizabeth L (19/20th C) American
$1300	£872	New York street scene, 34th Street (66x58cm-26x23in) s. 16-Oct-93 Dargate Auction Galleries, Pittsburgh #4

ROTTERDAM, Paul (1939-) American?
$816	*£533*	*Untitled (101x65cm-40x26in) s.d.78 mixed media collage. 15-May-93 Aucktionhaus Burkard, Luzern #233/R (S.FR 1200)*
$3538	*£2358*	*Substance 307 (99x90cm-39x35in) s.d.1978verso acrylic mixed media canvas. 4-Jun-94 Aucktionhaus Burkard, Luzern #157/R (S.FR 5000)*

ROULAND, Orlando (1871-?) American
$6700	£4497	Race Week at Marblehead (64x76cm-25x30in) s. 2-Dec-93 Freeman Fine Arts, Philadelphia #795

ROUSSEAU, Helen (1898-) American
$2000	£1342	The wharf (55x65cm-22x26in) s. board. 8-Dec-93 Butterfield & Butterfield, San Francisco #3554/R
$3500	£2059	Southern California street scene (62x76cm-24x30in) s. board. 4-Oct-92 Butterfield & Butterfield, Los Angeles #208/R
$4250	£2500	Campground (76x86cm-30x34in) s. board. 4-Oct-92 Butterfield & Butterfield, Los Angeles #206/R
$4500	£2647	Section House (51x61cm-20x24in) s. board. 4-Oct-92 Butterfield & Butterfield, Los Angeles #207/R
$5000	£3356	My old neighbourhood (58x74cm-23x29in) s. i.verso board. 8-Dec-93 Butterfield & Butterfield, San Francisco #3553/R
$7000	£4636	Oil Rigs, Southern California (62x67cm-24x26in) s. board. 15-Jun-94 Butterfield & Butterfield, San Francisco #4711/R

ROW, David (20th C) American?
$1937	£1300	Split branch (152x122cm-60x48in) s.i.d.1987verso oil wax. 21-Jun-93 Christie's, S. Kensington #172/R
$4177	£2785	'Skylla' (153x122cm-60x48in) s.d.1987verso oil wax. 2-Jun-94 AB Stockholms Auktionsverk, Stockholm #7086/R (S.KR 33000)
$570	*£380*	*Study for Isis II (67x49cm-26x19in) chl executed 1987. 2-Jun-94 AB Stockholms Auktionsverk, Stockholm #7026/R (S.KR 4500)*
$759	*£506*	*Study for Axon (67x98cm-26x39in) s.verso chl diptych executed 1987. 2-Jun-94 AB Stockholms Auktionsverk, Stockholm #7087/R (S.KR 6000)*
$2658	*£1772*	*Untitled (75x56cm-30x22in) chl pastel executed 1988. 2-Jun-94 AB Stockholms Auktionsverk, Stockholm #7152/R (S.KR 21000)*

ROWLAND, Benjamin (jnr) (1904-1972) American
$1100	£692	Noon day sun on the delta (51x61cm-20x24in) s. 22-Apr-93 Freeman Fine Arts, Philadelphia #1345/R

ROYBAL, Alfonso (1898-1955) American
$2500	*£1623*	*Eagle dance (23x38cm-9x15in) gouache board. 25-Jun-94 Skinner, Bolton #208/R*

ROYBAL, Jose D (1922-1978) American
$4500	*£2922*	*San Ildefonso corn dance (28x46cm-11x18in) s. gouache. 25-Jun-94 Skinner, Bolton #217/R*

ROZEN, Jerome (20th C) American
$1400   £741   Harbour view late afternoon (30x41cm-12x16in) s. canvasboard. 11-Sep-92 Skinner, Bolton #246/R

RUEL, William H (19th C) Canadian
$1100   £697   British frigate tossed at sea (48x72cm-19x28in) s. s.d.84 W/C htd gouache. 30-Nov-92 Ritchie, Toronto #155/R (C.D 1400)

RUFFALO, Carlos Roberto (?) Uruguayan
$750   £503   Parvas Camino Maldonado (22x30cm-9x12in) s. panel. 29-Nov-93 Gomensoro, Montevideo #9
$1050   £705   Playa Pocitos (18x25cm-7x10in) s. board. 29-Nov-93 Gomensoro, Montevideo #10/R
$1600   £833   Atardecer (53x74cm-21x29in) s. fibre. 12-Aug-92 Castells & Castells, Montevideo #52/R
$1650   £1086   Miguelete (60x47cm-24x19in) s. 31-May-93 Gomensoro, Montevideo #26/R

RUIZ, Antonio (1897-1964) Mexican
$2534   £1667   Casco de hacienda morelense (60x90cm-24x35in) s. 4-Nov-92 Mora, Castelltort & Quintana, Juarez #38/R (M.P 8000000)

RUIZ, Arturo (20th C) Mexican
$2296   £1511   Nino en la charca (60x80cm-24x31in) s.d.1990. 4-Nov-92 Mora, Castelltort & Quintana, Juarez #143/R (M.P 7250000)

RUIZ, Gilberto (1950-) Cuban
$3500   £2333   I can swin, but I should fly (152x122cm-60x48in) s.i.d.1986verso acrylic. 18-May-94 Sotheby's, New York #423/R

RUIZ, Juan Patricio (17th C) Mexican
$5939   £4153   San Ambrosio y San Lucas (165x103cm-65x41in) s. 3-Feb-93 Fernando Duran, Madrid #93 (S.P 700000)

RULE, Nicolas (1956-) American
$2000   £1351   Inbreed Blue and You Breed True (274x183cm-108x72in) s.i.d.1990. 8-Nov-93 Christie's, East, New York #80/R
$950   *£638*   *Summer squall (200x101cm-79x40in) s.i.d.1990verso graphite ink paper linen board. 3-May-94 Christie's, East, New York #261/R*

RUNGIUS, Carl (1869-1959) American/German
$1100   £705   Stag in a forest clearing (46x36cm-18x14in) board. 10-Dec-92 Sloan, North Bethesda #2611/R
$2900   £1835   Two moose on promontory (46x36cm-18x14in) s. en grisaille. 30-Nov-92 Selkirks, St. Louis #253/R
$3892   £2577   Mt Assiniboia (23x28cm-9x11in) s. board. 16-Nov-92 Hodgins, Calgary #24/R (C.D 5000)
$11286   £7474   Lake O'Hara (41x51cm-16x20in) s. 16-Nov-92 Hodgins, Calgary #278/R (C.D 14500)
$12000   £7692   Bear in mountains (61x81cm-24x32in) s. init.i. 26-May-93 Christie's, New York #110/R
$12000   £7692   Bighorn sheep, Nigel Pass, Alberta (31x41cm-12x16in) s. s.i.d.1919 stretcher. 26-May-93 Christie's, New York #111/R
$20000   £13986   Rocky mountain landscape, Green River, Wyoming (76x91cm-30x36in) s. 11-Mar-93 Christie's, New York #116/R
$26000   £16667   Old man of mountains (76x114cm-30x45in) s. 27-May-93 Sotheby's, New York #231/R
$30000   £19868   Last of the herd (76x102cm-30x40in) s. 23-Sep-93 Sotheby's, New York #101/R

RUPPERSBERG, Allen (1944-) American
$20000   *£13514* *The Footnote (127x381cm-50x150in) s.d.1975verso photos graphite three fold panel. 8-Nov-93 Christie's, East, New York #32/R*

RUSCHA, Edward (1937-) American
$7500   £5034   Something that was obviously uncommon (56x74cm-22x29in) s.d.1982 dry pigment paper. 23-Feb-94 Christie's, New York #88/R
$10000   £6757   Nerve increasing activity (58x74cm-23x29in) dry pigment painted 1984. 11-Nov-93 Sotheby's, New York #117/R
$14000   £9150   Wire (50x61cm-20x24in) s.d.1972 verso. 7-May-93 Christie's, East, New York #169/R
$20000   £13423   Canada, Mexico, USA (51x406cm-20x160in) s.d.1980 verso. 25-Feb-94 Sotheby's, New York #107/R
$27500   £18212   True Lady (153x102cm-60x40in) acrylic paper executed 1986. 18-Nov-92 Sotheby's, New York #294/R
$40000   £27027   The eighties (51x403cm-20x159in) s.i.d.1980stretcher acrylic. 10-Nov-93 Christie's, New York #379/R
$65000   £43046   Study of friction and wear on mating surfaces (213x315cm-84x124in) s.d.1983verso. 18-Nov-92 Christie's, New York #71/R
$65000   £43919   Olds (122x122cm-48x48in) s.d.1988-89 verso acrylic. 11-Nov-93 Sotheby's, New York #197/R
$75000   £50336   Light - part 2 (157x350cm-62x138in) acrylic painted 1989-90. 25-Feb-94 Sotheby's, New York #102/R
$100000   £69444   Light, part I (157x350cm-62x138in) painted 1989-90 acrylic. 23-Feb-93 Sotheby's, New York #336/R
$7000   *£4730*   *Other matters (36x58cm-14x23in) pastel executed 1974. 11-Nov-93 Sotheby's, New York #116/R*
$8000   *£5229*   *Act (36x57cm-14x22in) gunpowder executed 1974. 4-May-93 Sotheby's, New York #144a/R*
$8000   *£5369*   *Radar (56x71cm-22x28in) s.d.1976 pastel graphite executed 1976. 5-May-94 Sotheby's, New York #200/R*

RUSCHA, Edward (1937-) American-cont.
$8000	£5369	Murder (58x74cm-23x29in) s.d.1974 s.d.verso spinach graphite. 4-May-94 Christie's, New York #292/R
$8500	£5629	Study for light (43x88cm-17x35in) painted 1989-1990 spray enamel acrylic collage. 19-Nov-92 Christie's, New York #399/R
$9500	£6376	Cheese paper (57x70cm-22x28in) gunpowder col.pencil pencil executed 1975. 5-May-94 Sotheby's, New York #177/R
$11000	£7285	Various things that hurt (55x73cm-22x29in) s.d.1976verso dry pigment. 19-Nov-92 Christie's, New York #379/R
$11000	£7639	Small, medium, large companies (58x74cm-23x29in) s.d.1983 dry pigment. 23-Feb-93 Sotheby's, New York #281/R
$11000	£6471	S-Sea of D-D-Desire (58x74cm-23x29in) s.d.79 pastel. 6-Oct-92 Sotheby's, New York #150/R
$11000	£7285	Study for light (43x88cm-17x35in) painted 1989-1990 spray enamel acrylic collage. 19-Nov-92 Christie's, New York #398/R
$12000	£7059	Do you think she has it (91x102cm-36x40in) s.d.1974 verso equalized egg yolk moire. 6-Oct-92 Sotheby's, New York #109/R
$13000	£8784	Floating paper (36x57cm-14x22in) s.d.1973 gunpowder grass stain. 10-Nov-93 Christie's, New York #190/R
$13000	£9028	1984 (58x36cm-23x14in) s.d.1967 gunpowder. 23-Feb-93 Sotheby's, New York #326/R
$15000	£10135	Annie (24x23cm-9x9in) s.d.1967 graphite. 10-Nov-93 Christie's, New York #185/R
$16000	£10596	You and Me (58x74cm-23x29in) s.d.83 dry pigment. 18-Nov-92 Sotheby's, New York #188/R
$16000	£10738	News (29x74cm-11x29in) s.d.1970 gunpowder on paper. 25-Feb-94 Sotheby's, New York #102 a/R
$18000	£10588	Baby cakes (91x102cm-36x40in) s.d.1974 verso blueberry extract egg yolk moire. 6-Oct-92 Sotheby's, New York #139/R
$21000	£13907	Nice destiny (102x153cm-40x60in) s.d.1989 dry pigment board. 19-Nov-92 Christie's, New York #155/R
$26000	£17568	Very angry people (51x61cm-20x24in) cherry stain on moire painted 1973. 10-Nov-93 Christie's, New York #223/R

RUSSELL, Charles M (1865-1926) American
$70000	£44304	Making of a warrior (47x62cm-19x24in) s.d.1898 en grisaille board. 4-Dec-92 Christie's, New York #261/R
$5500	£3741	Charly Cugar and Now making horse hair bridles (20x13cm-8x5in) autographed page letter with illus.W/C pen. 17-Apr-94 Hanzel Galleries, Chicago #33
$5750	£3912	It was a perilous moment and an unfortunate hour (28x25cm-11x10in) init. W/C en grisaille. 17-Apr-94 Hanzel Galleries, Chicago #34
$7000	£4046	Indian with rifle (18x13cm-7x5in) W/C. 23-Sep-92 Christie's, New York #106/R
$40000	£26667	Illustrated letter to Jim Bollinger (28x21cm-11x8in) s.d.April 24 1923 W/C gouache pen pencil. 26-May-94 Christie's, New York #63/R
$45000	£30201	Hunting big horn sheep (29x38cm-11x15in) s.d.1898 W/C. 2-Dec-93 Sotheby's, New York #36/R
$58000	£38926	Indian hunt (58x84cm-23x33in) s.d.94 W/C board. 3-Dec-93 Christie's, New York #66/R
$62500	£41391	Indian on white horse shooting buffalo (25x38cm-10x15in) s. W/C painted c.1905-1906. 23-Sep-93 Sotheby's, New York #107/R
$95000	£63333	Mandan warrior (43x28cm-17x11in) mono.i.d.1906 W/C cardboard. 25-May-94 Sotheby's, New York #53/R
$140000	£93960	Bucking bronco (36x56cm-14x22in) s.d.1899 W/C. 2-Dec-93 Sotheby's, New York #61

RUSSELL, Charles M (attrib) (1865-1926) American
$1050	£660	Two cowboys riding on canyon rim (15x20cm-6x8in) mono pen. 22-Apr-93 Freeman Fine Arts, Philadelphia #1316

RUSSELL, E J (1835-1906) American
$1800	£1216	Portrait of the schooner Fanny Keating entering St John New Brunswick (66x97cm-26x38in) s. W/C. 23-Oct-93 San Rafael Auction Galleries #219

RUSSELL, Edward J (1835-1906) American
$786	£498	Storm petrel (58x91cm-23x36in) s. i.verso W/C pen. 30-Nov-92 Ritchie, Toronto #156/R (C.D 1000)

RUSSELL, George Horne (1861-1933) Canadian
$634	£415	Fishing village (23x32cm-9x13in) s. canvas laid down on board. 18-May-93 Joyner Fine Art, Toronto #328 (C.D 800)
$782	£532	Lake Louise Alberta (30x38cm-12x15in) painted c.1900. 7-Jul-93 Maynards, Vancouver #194 (C.D 1000)
$1456	£971	Incoming tide, Grand Manan (81x119cm-32x47in) s. 11-May-94 Sotheby's, Toronto #169/R (C.D 2000)
$1748	£1165	Sailing boat in harbour (41x58cm-16x23in) s. 13-May-94 Joyner Fine Art, Toronto #2/R (C.D 2400)
$655	£437	Rocky mountain river (43x26cm-17x10in) s. W/C. 13-May-94 Joyner Fine Art, Toronto #270 (C.D 900)

RUSSELL, Gyrth (1892-1970) Canadian
$580	£400	Sailing boat (29x39cm-11x15in) s. 26-Jan-93 Sotheby's, Billingshurst #273/R
$630	£420	Sailing boats (30x41cm-12x16in) s. 9-Jun-94 Taylors, Honiton #51
$643	£420	Old quay, Brixham, Devon (28x41cm-11x16in) s. canvas laid down on panel. 28-Jul-94 Christie's, S. Kensington #79/R
$2664	£1800	Fishing boats St Ives harbour, Cornwall (56x76cm-22x30in) s. 16-Mar-93 Lane, Penzance #230/R
$2886	£1950	Caravans by sea - cliff top gypsy caravans (48x69cm-19x27in) s. canvasboard. 16-Mar-93 Lane, Penzance #235/R

RUSSELL, Gyrth (1892-1970) Canadian-cont.
$3225   £2150   St Ives Harbour, Cornwall (56x76cm-22x30in) s. 9-Jun-94 Taylors, Honiton #65

RUSSELL, John Wentworth (1879-1959) Canadian
$856   £567   Gathering hay (33x41cm-13x16in) s.d.1910 canvas laid down on board. 18-Nov-92 Sotheby's, Toronto #129 (C.D 1100)

RUSSELL, Morgan (1886-1953) American
$1100   £724   Untitled (42x34cm-17x13in) s. i.verso. 31-Mar-93 Sotheby's Arcade, New York #369/R
$1300   £878   The Muse (64x48cm-25x19in) s.i.d.1916verso. 31-Oct-93 Hindman Galleries, Chicago #712
$1600   £1013   Infantry manoeuvres (51x50cm-20x20in) s. 2-Dec-92 Christie's, East, New York #48/R
$2600   £1769   Paysage (58x74cm-23x29in) s. 15-Nov-93 Christie's, East, New York #240/R
$6000   £4000   Judgement of Paris (114x146cm-45x57in) s. i.stretcher. 26-May-94 Christie's, New York #126/R
$27000   £18121   Synchromy (81x25cm-32x10in) s. painted between 1914-1915. 3-Dec-93 Christie's, New York #14/R
$1100 *£636*   *Three bathers (35x32cm-14x13in) s.d.1940 pencil. 25-Sep-92 Sotheby's Arcade, New York #264/R*

RUSSO, Raul (1912-1984) Argentinian
$1050   £695   Paisaje urbano (33x52cm-13x20in) tempera. 11-Nov-92 VerBo, Buenos Aires #97
$4000   £2083   Paisaje (60x49cm-24x19in) 4-Aug-92 VerBo, Buenos Aires #96

RYAN, Anne (1889-1954) American
$3000 *£2098* *Untitled collage (17x13cm-7x5in) s. collage. 11-Mar-93 Christie's, New York #265/R*
$6500 *£4248* *Grey and white collage (42x35cm-17x14in) s. fabric paper silver leaf collage masonite. 4-May-93 Sotheby's, New York #297/R*
$7000 *£4698* *Collage No.552 - Mallorca (48x60cm-19x24in) s. s.d.53 verso fabric collage board. 23-Feb-94 Christie's, East, New York #318/R*

RYDER, Albert Pinkham (attrib) (1847-1917) American
$1300   £878   Cottage along the shore (30x36cm-12x14in) i.d.1877verso. 4-Nov-93 Sloan, North Bethesda #2560

RYDER, Chauncey F (1868-1949) American
$715   £480   Landscape (30x41cm-12x16in) s. canvas on board. 16-Jul-93 Christie's, London #168
$800   £468   Misty morning (41x51cm-16x20in) s. board. 20-Sep-92 Litchfield Auction Gallery #85
$950   £642   Harbour view (15x21cm-6x8in) s. canvasboard. 5-Nov-93 Skinner, Bolton #120/R
$950   £664   Hilly landscape (18x23cm-7x9in) s. board. 11-Mar-93 Mystic Fine Arts, Connecticut #151/R
$1192   £800   Red House at Attica (30x40cm-12x16in) s. board. 16-Jul-93 Christie's, London #166/R
$1400   £915   Topsfield (15x20cm-6x8in) s. panel. 30-Jun-94 Mystic Fine Arts, Connecticut #52
$1500   £1020   Green landscape. Landscape with trees in the distance (16x21cm-6x8in) s. board two. 15-Nov-93 Christie's, East, New York #128/R
$1788   £1200   Hills of Winsor (63x76cm-25x30in) s. 16-Jul-93 Christie's, London #165/R
$2000   £1342   The river at Ipswich (51x61cm-20x24in) s. 5-Dec-93 James Bakker, Cambridge #81/R
$2012   £1250   Mountain at Hoosatonie (81x112cm-32x44in) s. studio st.verso. 2-Dec-93 Christie's, S. Kensington #2
$2500   £1656   Austerlitz, New York (76x91cm-30x36in) s. 21-Nov-92 James Bakker, Cambridge #298/R
$3000   £1987   On mountain side (61x51cm-24x20in) s. 13-Nov-92 Skinner, Bolton #131/R
$3000   £1961   Extensive mountainous landscape (76x91cm-30x36in) s. 4-May-93 Christie's, East, New York #119/R
$3400   £2313   Dent du Midi a mountain landscape (82x112cm-32x44in) s. s.i.verso canvas laid down on panel. 15-Nov-93 Christie's, East, New York #140/R
$3800   £2533   Keyes farm (30x41cm-12x16in) s. i.stretcher. 23-May-94 Christie's, East, New York #150/R
$5500   £3642   Beach (25x33cm-10x13in) s. panel double-sided. 13-Nov-92 Skinner, Bolton #148/R
$7000   £4667   The mountain at Hoosatonic (81x112cm-32x44in) s. i.verso canvas on panel. 17-Mar-94 Sotheby's, New York #54/R
$12000   £8054   Rochester Road (71x91cm-28x36in) s. 17-Dec-93 Du Mouchelle, Detroit #2012/R
$17000   £11409   Spring landscape, Old Lyme, Connecticut (63x76cm-25x30in) s. 3-Dec-93 Christie's, New York #35/R

RYDER, Platt Powell (1821-1896) American
$850   £567   Wash day (36x51cm-14x20in) s. 23-May-94 Hindman Galleries, Chicago #170
$4900   £3289   Black musician (25x30cm-10x12in) s. board. 24-Mar-94 Mystic Fine Arts, Connecticut #88/R

RYLAND, Robert K (1873-1951) American
$2400   £1569   City harbour (64x76cm-25x30in) s.d.39-46 double-sided. 17-Sep-93 Skinner, Bolton #280/R

RYMAN, Robert (1930-) American
$35000   £22876   Surface vale (49x49cm-19x19in) s. oil fibreglass. 4-May-93 Sotheby's, New York #112/R
$36000   £24161   Untitled (63x63cm-25x25in) s.d.69 acrylic mylar on board on fiberglass. 4-May-94 Christie's, New York #230/R

RYMAN, Robert (1930-) American-cont.
$82000   £53595   Untitled (26x26cm-10x10in) s.d.65 verso linen. 4-May-93 Christie's, New York #15/R
$120000 £81081   Marker (107x107cm-42x42in) s.i.d.88 verso oil linen on fibreglass. 9-Nov-93 Christie's, New York #41/R
$150000 £100671 Rule (106x106cm-42x42in) d.1991 oil paper on fiberglas and wood. 4-May-94 Sotheby's, New York #34/R

SABATINI, Raphael (1898-?) American
$850   £535   Coulter Street (41x51cm-16x20in) 22-Apr-93 Freeman Fine Arts, Philadelphia #1268

SABOIA, Jose (1949-) Brazilian
$2700   £1765   Grupo de musicos (35x27cm-14x11in) s. painted c.1960. 18-May-93 Sotheby's, New York #239/R

SACCARO, John (1913-1981) American
$750   £472   Space continuum (11x25cm-4x10in) s.i.d.59verso board laid down on masonite. 25-Apr-93 Butterfield & Butterfield, San Francisco #2104/R

SACKS, Joseph (1887-1974) American
$900   £588   Boy in overalls (51x41cm-20x16in) board. 7-Oct-93 Freeman Fine Arts, Philadelphia #964
$1400   £940   Countryside walk (51x76cm-20x30in) s. 8-Dec-93 Butterfield & Butterfield, San Francisco #3485/R

SADA, Conchalupe (20th C) Mexican
$653   £441   Banista (20x30cm-8x12in) s.d.1985 masonite. 27-Apr-94 Louis Morton, Mexico #527 (M.P 2200)

SAEZ, Carlos F (?) South American
$3600   £1809   Marina nocturna (18x28cm-7x11in) panel. 31-Aug-92 Gomensoro, Montevideo #53/R
$2600   £1711   Retrato del padre del artista y manos (19x23cm-7x9in) s.d.1900 pencil dr. 31-May-93 Gomensoro, Montevideo #40/R

SAHAGUN, Luis (1900-) Mexican
$1935   £1299   Autoretrato Epoca Azul (90x70cm-35x28in) 1-Dec-93 Louis Morton, Mexico #50/R (M.P 6000)

SPURR, Gertrude E see CUTTS, Gertrude Spurr

ST BRICE, Robert (1898-1973) Haitian
$2750   £1846   Un femme africante (66x48cm-26x19in) i.verso masonite. 7-Jan-94 Gary Nader, Miami #112/R
$10321   £6746   Loa (61x50cm-24x20in) painted 1971. 17-May-93 Hoebanx, Paris #192/R (F.FR 57000)

SAINT CLAIR, Gordon (1885-1966) American
$600   £400   Artist's son at age fourteen (107x81cm-42x32in) s. 23-May-94 Hindman Galleries, Chicago #239
$1600   £1067   Xanadu (137x99cm-54x39in) s. canvas on masonite. 23-May-94 Hindman Galleries, Chicago #236

SAINT CLAIR, Norman (1863-1912) American
$750   £507   Coastal (33x43cm-13x17in) s. W/C. 15-Jun-93 John Moran, Pasadena #62

ST JOHN, Terry (20th C) American?
$650   £409   Santa Cruz beach (30x35cm-12x14in) s.i.d.1987verso masonite. 25-Apr-93 Butterfield & Butterfield, San Francisco #2138/R
$900   £566   Clusters of oaks (27x36cm-11x14in) s.i.d.1980verso masonite. 25-Apr-93 Butterfield & Butterfield, San Francisco #2139/R
$950   £597   Contra Costa Ranch (30x41cm-12x16in) s.i.d.1986verso masonite. 25-Apr-93 Butterfield & Butterfield, San Francisco #2140/R
$1000   £629   Rodeo beach (29x36cm-11x14in) s.i.d.1986verso masonite. 25-Apr-93 Butterfield & Butterfield, San Francisco #2141/R
$1000   £629   Benecia from Martinez (28x36cm-11x14in) s.i.d.1988verso masonite. 25-Apr-93 Butterfield & Butterfield, San Francisco #2143/R
$1200   £755   Point Richmond (31x41cm-12x16in) s.i.d.1987verso masonite. 25-Apr-93 Butterfield & Butterfield, San Francisco #2142/R

SAINT VIL, Murat (1955-) Haitian
$1073   £711   Paysage a l'arbre (41x51cm-16x20in) s. 13-Jun-94 Rogeon, Paris #166 (F.FR 6000)
$1431   £948   Jardin fantastique (59x89cm-23x35in) s. 13-Jun-94 Rogeon, Paris #69/R (F.FR 8000)

SAINT-CHARLES, Camille (1947-) Haitian
$905   £592   Rara a Jeremie 1 (102x77cm-40x30in) 17-May-93 Hoebanx, Paris #199/R (F.FR 5000)

SAINT-FLEURANT, Louisianne (1924-) Haitian
$7062   £4615   Les enfants du peristyle (61x61cm-24x24in) painted 1972. 17-May-93 Hoebanx, Paris #193 (F.FR 39000)

SAINT-SURIN, Adrien (1961-) Haitian
$634   £414   Le notable (61x51cm-24x20in) 17-May-93 Hoebanx, Paris #201 (F.FR 3500)

SAINT-SURIN, Adrien (1961-) Haitian-cont.
$652	£418	Vendeuse de chapeaux (61x91cm-24x36in) s. 14-Dec-92 Hoebanx, Paris #79 (F.FR 3500)
$815	£533	Jour de noces (61x51cm-24x20in) 17-May-93 Hoebanx, Paris #200 (F.FR 4500)

SAINTE CROIX, Jean Claude (20th C) Haitian
$537	£355	Village d'autrefois (36x46cm-14x18in) 13-Jun-94 Rogeon, Paris #222 (F.FR 3000)
$537	£355	Les generaux (61x81cm-24x32in) s. 13-Jun-94 Rogeon, Paris #27/R (F.FR 3000)

SAKAI, Kazuya (c.1927-) Argentinian
$1100	£728	Vajra (99x99cm-39x39in) s. d.1962verso. 23-Sep-93 Mystic Fine Arts, Connecticut #134 a/R
$1928	£1303	Serie II no.10, Homenaje a Korin (160x160cm-63x63in) s.d.1976 acrylic. 27-Apr-94 Louis Morton, Mexico #606/R (M.P 6500)

SALA, Kurt (20th C) American
$1200	*£800*	*Traders (97x145cm-38x57in) s.i.d.87 W/C. 23-May-94 Hindman Galleries, Chicago #279*
$2200	*£1467*	*Street of Dreams (147x94cm-58x37in) s.i.d.89 W/C. 23-May-94 Hindman Galleries, Chicago #278*

SALAS, Antonio (1795-1860) Argentinian
$4500	£2941	Yndio Yumbo (40x36cm-16x14in) s. painted c.1830. 18-May-93 Sotheby's, New York #89/R

SALAZAR, Carlos (1956-) Colombian
$1450	£948	Puerto (60x42cm-24x17in) s. 4-Oct-93 Gomensoro, Montevideo #18
$1500	£980	Toledo (150x100cm-59x39in) s. 4-Oct-93 Gomensoro, Montevideo #17

SALDANA, Mateo (?) Latin American
$4635	£3132	Cholula (21x32cm-8x13in) s.i.d.1945 board. 9-Nov-93 Louis Morton, Mexico #48 (M.P 15000)
$4776	£3061	Iglesia de Cholula (23x33cm-9x13in) board. 29-Apr-93 Louis Morton, Mexico #28 (M.P 15000)

SALDIVAR, Jaime (20th C) Mexican
$4838	£3247	La vista del obispo (30x70cm-12x28in) 1-Dec-93 Louis Morton, Mexico #47/R (M.P 15000)

SALEMME, Attilio (1911-1955) American
$3000	£2027	Echo of a Dream (56x102cm-22x40in) s.d.45 i.d.stretcher. 8-Nov-93 Christie's, East, New York #230/R

SALINAS, Baruj (1935-) Cuban
$5000	£3378	Penca de palma triste VII (91x127cm-36x50in) s.d.June 89 i.verso acrylic. 23-Nov-93 Christie's, New York #192/R
$8000	£5229	Tepetl (137x137cm-54x54in) s. acrylic painted 1991. 17-May-93 Christie's, New York #207/R

SALINAS, Porfirio (1910-1972) American
$1400	£909	Texas bluebonnets (41x51cm-16x20in) s. painted c.1940. 11-Sep-93 Louisiana Auction Exchange #71/R

SALLE, David (1952-) American
$17000	£10000	American glass V (76x112cm-30x44in) acrylic oil two parts painted 1987. 6-Oct-92 Sotheby's, New York #172/R
$17000	£11409	American glass (76x112cm-30x44in) acrylic oil painted 1987. 25-Feb-94 Sotheby's, New York #141/R
$20000	£13423	Untitled (183x335cm-72x132in) acrylic three canvases of photosynthesized linen. 5-May-94 Sotheby's, New York #365/R
$30000	£19608	The highest point in France (267x216cm-105x85in) s.d.1990verso two parts. 5-Oct-93 Sotheby's, New York #170/R
$47468	£31646	I like intransitive verbs (218x427cm-86x168in) oil acrylic diptych executed 1981. 2-Jun-94 AB Stockholms Auktionsverk, Stockholm #7204/R (S.KR 375000)
$95000	£62092	Unexpectedly, I missed my cousin Jasper (122x183cm-48x72in) s.d.1980 verso acrylic canvas two panels. 3-May-93 Sotheby's, New York #58/R
$1000	*£662*	*Untitled (48x68cm-19x27in) init.d.90 graphite. 17-Nov-92 Christie's, East, New York #52/R*
$5000	*£3378*	*Untitled (48x66cm-19x26in) s. acrylic pencil executed 1979. 11-Nov-93 Sotheby's, New York #194/R*
$6500	*£4362*	*Untitled, Pumpkin (127x198cm-50x78in) s.i.d.1978 acrylic graphite diamond dust canvas. 3-May-94 Christie's, East, New York #88/R*
$8000	*£5298*	*Untitled (46x61cm-18x24in) s.d.1987 W/C graphite. 19-Nov-92 Christie's, New York #230/R*
$8000	*£5405*	*Untitled (53x75cm-21x30in) s.d.1986 W/C gaphite. 10-Nov-93 Christie's, New York #292/R*
$11000	£7190	Untitled (46x60cm-18x24in) s.d.84 W/C. 4-May-93 Sotheby's, New York #277/R
$19000	£12583	Untitled (152x107cm-60x42in) s.d.1981 acrylic W/C paper collage. 19-Nov-92 Christie's, New York #112/R
$32000	*£21192*	*Express vague humanism number 3 (117x183cm-46x72in) s.i.d.1980 acrylic col.crayon canvas. 19-Nov-92 Christie's, New York #232/R*
$38000	*£25676*	*Untitled (165x239cm-65x94in) acrylic pencil paper on canvas painted 1980. 10-Nov-93 Sotheby's, New York #62/R*

SALMON, Robert (1775-1844) American

$1197	£700	Moonlit seascape (30x46cm-12x18in) with i.d.1827 verso board. 17-Sep-92 Christie's, S. Kensington #99
$1650	£1100	Coastal scene (27x43cm-11x17in) s.d.1827 verso board. 19-Jul-93 Phillips, Tyne and Wear #69/R
$2700	£1561	Moonlight smugglers (18x26cm-7x10in) init.i.d.June 1840 i.verso. 25-Sep-92 Sotheby's Arcade, New York #18/R
$4500	£3147	View of Holly Head (20x25cm-8x10in) indis.i.verso board. 10-Mar-93 Sotheby's, New York #11/R
$6000	£4000	Landscape with figures (24x31cm-9x12in) s. d.1830 verso panel. 17-Mar-94 Sotheby's, New York #14/R
$6750	£4500	Coastal scene with beached vessel and numerous figures (20x25cm-8x10in) init. s.i.d.1814verso panel. 8-Jun-94 Christie's, Glasgow #598/R
$11000	£7692	Coastal view near Greenock (41x61cm-16x24in) init.d.1825. 10-Mar-93 Sotheby's, New York #12/R
$20000	£13072	Royal navy brig at Liverpool (86x56cm-34x22in) init.d.1813. 5-May-93 Doyle, New York #20/R
$21700	£14000	Lauch at Scott's yard, Greenock, 1822 (42x65cm-17x26in) 20-Jan-93 Sotheby's, London #29/R
$23000	£15333	Boston light (38x46cm-15x18in) s. 17-Mar-94 Sotheby's, New York #13/R
$25000	£15823	Two vessels off Greenock (49x78cm-19x31in) s.d.1820 i.verso panel. 3-Dec-92 Sotheby's, New York #7/R
$30000	£19737	Rough seas (46x61cm-18x24in) s.d.1802. 4-Jun-93 Sotheby's, New York #182/R

SALMON, Robert (attrib) (1775-1844) American

$3000	£2128	Shipping off Liverpool -several figures on shore (33x43cm-13x17in) 13-Feb-93 Richard Bourne, Hyannis #140/R
$5400	£3600	The Bark, Foundling and other shipping (61x82cm-24x32in) 21-May-94 Weschler, Washington #72/R

SALOMON, Raynald (1957-) Haitian

$869	£568	Couple de Aras (61x51cm-24x20in) 17-May-93 Hoebanx, Paris #206 (F.FR 4800)

SAMARAS, Lucas (1936-) American

$4000	£2703	Untitled - July 17, 1962 (30x23cm-12x9in) pastel. 11-Nov-93 Sotheby's, New York #395/R
$5500	£3691	Untitled September 8, 1974 (33x25cm-13x10in) init.d.1974 verso pastel. 25-Feb-94 Sotheby's, New York #66/R
$6000	£4054	Head 195 (44x29cm-17x11in) col chk. 8-Nov-93 Christie's, East, New York #140/R
$6000	£4027	Untitled (30x21cm-12x8in) init.d.May 21 60verso col.chk. 4-May-94 Christie's, New York #184/R
$6000	£3922	Untitled - early November 1961 (30x23cm-12x9in) pastel executed 1961. 4-May-93 Sotheby's, New York #408/R
$6000	£3922	Untitled - August 14, 1961 (30x23cm-12x9in) pastel executed 1961. 4-May-93 Sotheby's, New York #406/R
$7000	£4730	Untitled (30x23cm-12x9in) init.d.Aug.20 60verso col.chk. 10-Nov-93 Christie's, New York #184/R
$7000	£4575	Untitled - February 16, 1961 (30x23cm-12x9in) pastel executed 1961. 4-May-93 Sotheby's, New York #379/R
$7350	£4933	Untitled finger (29x22cm-11x9in) s.d.July 3/65verso pastel. 14-Dec-93 Christie's, Athens #50/R (G.D 1800000)
$10000	£5882	Untitled (33x25cm-13x10in) init.d.Sept 9/74verso col.chks. 8-Oct-92 Christie's, New York #128/R
$13000	£8784	Untitled - July 13, 1962 (30x23cm-12x9in) pastel. 11-Nov-93 Sotheby's, New York #366/R
$14000	£9150	Untitled - August 14, 1961 (30x23cm-12x9in) pastel executed 1961. 4-May-93 Sotheby's, New York #404/R

SAMMONS, Carl (1888-1968) American

$550	£367	Winter in Palm Springs (30x41cm-12x16in) s. canvasboard. 15-Mar-94 John Moran, Pasadena #175
$575	£383	Mountain landscape (28x36cm-11x14in) board. 11-Jun-94 San Rafael Auction Galleries #313
$650	£448	June Lake, High Sierra Calif. (36x51cm-14x20in) s. canvas laid down on board. 16-Feb-93 John Moran, Pasadena #92
$650	£446	Carmel coast (30x41cm-12x16in) s. i.verso board. 10-Feb-94 Skinner, Bolton #156
$650	£430	Desert in bloom (51x66cm-20x26in) s. 14-Jun-94 John Moran, Pasadena #93
$700	£473	Landscape (15x20cm-6x8in) s. canvasboard. 15-Jun-93 John Moran, Pasadena #7
$800	£533	Lake Diaz, Lone Pine, California (30x41cm-12x16in) s. canvasboard. 15-Mar-94 John Moran, Pasadena #36
$850	£586	Point Lobos (28x38cm-11x15in) s. board. 16-Feb-93 John Moran, Pasadena #11
$950	£642	Flowered coastal scene (30x41cm-12x16in) s. canvasboard. 9-Nov-93 John Moran, Pasadena #835
$1200	£789	Laquinta Canyon, Palm Springs (51x66cm-20x26in) s. 13-Jun-93 Butterfield & Butterfield, San Francisco #932/R
$1500	£1042	Mattole River, Humboldt County (30x41cm-12x16in) s. i.d.1953verso. 7-Mar-94 Butterfield & Butterfield, San Francisco #165/R
$1500	£987	Wild flowers, Palm Springs (30x41cm-12x16in) s. canvasboard. 13-Jun-93 Butterfield & Butterfield, San Francisco #935/R
$1600	£1074	Orinda Hills (30x41cm-12x16in) s. canvasboard. 8-Dec-93 Butterfield & Butterfield, San Francisco #3411/R
$1900	£1275	17 Mile Drive (30x41cm-12x16in) s. canvasboard. 8-Dec-93 Butterfield & Butterfield, San Francisco #3410/R
$2000	£1389	San Jacinto (51x61cm-20x24in) s. 7-Mar-93 Butterfield & Butterfield, San Francisco #164/R

SAMMONS, Carl (1888-1968) American-cont.
$2500 £1736 Silver lake (61x76cm-24x30in) s. 7-Mar-93 Butterfield & Butterfield, San Francisco #145/R
$3000 £1765 Smoke trees, Palm Springs (30x41cm-12x16in) s. canvasboard. 4-Oct-92 Butterfield & Butterfield, Los Angeles #204/R
$3250 £1912 Yucca, Palm Springs (30x41cm-12x16in) s. canvasboard. 4-Oct-92 Butterfield & Butterfield, Los Angeles #205/R
$550 *£379* *Landscape (20x30cm-8x12in) s. pastel board. 16-Feb-93 John Moran, Pasadena #100*

SAMMONS, Carl (attrib) (1888-1968) American
$1000 £680 Desert wild flowers, Palm Springs, California (30x41cm-12x16in) s. i.verso board. 17-Apr-94 Schrager Galleries, Milwaukee #729
$1000 £680 Smoke trees, Palm Springs, California (30x41cm-12x16in) s. i.verso board. 17-Apr-94 Schrager Galleries, Milwaukee #728

SAMPLE, Paul (1896-1974) American
$4000 £2797 Community of Newark, Vermont (51x79cm-20x31in) s. i.verso acrylic. 10-Mar-93 Sotheby's, New York #127/R
$500 *£342* *Bullfight (23x30cm-9x12in) s. W/C. 19-Feb-94 Young Fine Arts Auctions, Maine #177/R*
$1100 *£728* *Autumn landscape (29x44cm-11x17in) s. W/C. 2-Oct-93 Weschler, Washington #150 a/R*
$1350 *£912* *Farm with two silos (35x51cm-14x20in) s. W/C. 31-Mar-94 Sotheby's Arcade, New York #406/R*
$1500 *£1007* *Sunday services Beaver Meadow (36x53cm-14x21in) W/C paper laid down on board. 1-Dec-93 Doyle, New York #69*
$1600 *£1060* *A Vermont village in winter (67x57cm-26x22in) s. W/C. 15-Jun-94 Butterfield & Butterfield, San Francisco #4469/R*
$1700 *£1189* *Expedition up River Pinware River Labrador (25x36cm-10x14in) s. i.verso W/C gouache. 12-Mar-93 Skinner, Bolton #219/R*
$2250 *£1481* *Family outing, New Hampshire (34x26cm-13x10in) s. W/C ink. 13-Jun-93 Butterfield & Butterfield, San Francisco #3258/R*

SAMPSON, Joseph Ernest (1887-1946) Canadian
$728 £485 Two childrewn and dog sitting on windowsill (120x120cm-47x47in) s. 13-May-94 Joyner Fine Art, Toronto #221 (C.D 1000)
$1238 £825 Farmer with hayfork (122x97cm-48x38in) s. 13-May-94 Joyner Fine Art, Toronto #164/R (C.D 1700)

SANBORN, Percy A (1849-1929) American
$3100 £2081 'Bark Palestina - A.B.Ford, Master' (51x71cm-20x28in) i. after Jose Pineda painted c.1927. 25-Mar-94 Eldred, Massachusetts #230 b/R

SANCHEZ, Carlos (?) Mexican
$1433 £918 Dulces Mexicanos (40x55cm-16x22in) s. 29-Apr-93 Louis Morton, Mexico #10 (M.P 4500)

SANCHEZ, Edgar (1940-) Venezuelan
$6000 £4000 Rostro, Imagen 30028 (120x120cm-47x47in) s.d.93 i.verso acrylic. 18-May-94 Christie's, New York #246/R
$9500 £6291 Rostro, Imagen 3003 (120x120cm-47x47in) s.i.verso acrylic painted 1989. 24-Nov-92 Christie's, New York #164/R

SANCHEZ, Emilio (1921-) Cuban
$10000 £6536 Large doorway (178x126cm-70x50in) s. painted 1971. 18-May-93 Sotheby's, New York #230/R
$11000 £7333 La casa grande (183x183cm-72x72in) init. painted 1971. 18-May-94 Sotheby's, New York #350/R

SANCHEZ, Enrique (1938-) Colombian
$1250 £839 The aviator (61x51cm-24x20in) 27-Mar-94 Myers, Florida #88/R

SANCHEZ, Tomas (1948-) Cuban
$17000 £11111 Palmar (56x75cm-22x30in) s.d.88 s.i.d.verso tempera. 17-May-93 Christie's, New York #203/R
$18000 £12000 Cortina Rompevientos (73x53cm-29x21in) s.d.86 s.i.verso tempera paper. 18-May-94 Christie's, New York #155/R
$21000 £14000 Tarde en la selva (77x57cm-30x22in) s.d.89 s.i.d.verso tempera paper. 18-May-94 Sotheby's, New York #359/R
$21000 £14189 Paisaje quieto con laguna y nube (57x76cm-22x30in) s.d.90 s.i.d.verso acrylic paper. 22-Nov-93 Sotheby's, New York #259/R
$24000 £16000 Retorno a la Orilla en Noche Clara No.1 (60x81cm-24x32in) s.d.89 s.i.d.verso acrylic paper. 18-May-94 Christie's, New York #156/R
$28000 £18919 Despues de las Lluvias (101x70cm-40x28in) s.d.86 s.i.d.verso acrylic. 23-Nov-93 Christie's, New York #156/R
$35000 £23179 Bosque y Laguna en Noche Clara (80x100cm-31x39in) s.d.88 s.i.d.verso acrylic. 24-Nov-92 Christie's, New York #90/R
$40000 £26267 La selva y la nube (76x101cm-30x40in) s.d.91 s.i.d.verso acrylic. 17-May-94 Sotheby's, New York #77/R
$42000 £28000 La Otra Orilla (75x120cm-30x47in) s.d.1988 s.i.d.verso acrylic. 18-May-94 Christie's, New York #116/R
$55000 £37162 Diptico del Dia y la Noche (80x60cm-31x24in) s.d.89 i.d.verso acrylic two panels. 22-Nov-93 Sotheby's, New York #76/R
$60000 £40541 Meditando en la noche (115x70cm-45x28in) s.d.89 acrylic. 23-Nov-93 Christie's, New York #220/R

SANCHEZ, Tomas (1948-) Cuban-cont.
$60000	£40000	La nube y su sombra (149x109cm-59x43in) s.d.89 s.i.d.verso acrylic. 18-May-94 Sotheby's, New York #233/R
$60000	£39735	Ojo de las Aguas (110x151cm-43x59in) s.d.87 s.i.d.verso acrylic. 24-Nov-92 Christie's, New York #44/R
$65000	£43919	Orilla (110x150cm-43x59in) s.d.88 s.i.d.verso acrylic. 23-Nov-93 Christie's, New York #40
$67000	£44667	Orilla (80x100cm-31x39in) s.d.90 s.i.d.verso acrylic. 18-May-94 Christie's, New York #34
$70000	£45752	Paisaje con nube baja (110x150cm-43x59in) s.d.1987 s.verso acrylic. 17-May-93 Christie's, New York #53/R
$4800	*£3179*	*Paisaje Cubano (19x42cm-7x17in) s.d.80 W/C. 24-Nov-92 Christie's, New York #299/R*
$5160	*£3463*	*Bosque (50x30cm-20x12in) s. W/C. 1-Dec-93 Louis Morton, Mexico #67/R (M.P 16000)*
$8000	*£5229*	*Mar y ricahuelo (34x50cm-13x20in) s.d.83 W/C. 17-May-93 Christie's, New York #202/R*
$10000	*£6667*	*Piedra sobre el trillo (34x51cm-13x20in) s.d.83 gouache. 18-May-94 Sotheby's, New York #235/R*
$16000	*£10738*	*Paisaje (51x72cm-20x28in) s.d.85 W/C. 7-Jan-94 Gary Nader, Miami #38/R*
$18000	*£11765*	*Paisaje nocturno (60x79cm-24x31in) s.d.1990 W/C. 17-May-93 Christie's, New York #248/R*
$22000	*£14667*	*Mirando el paisje (68x50cm-27x20in) s.d.79 gouache. 18-May-94 Sotheby's, New York #360/R*

SANCHEZ-ALDANA, Yolanda (20th C) Mexican
$895   *£605*   *Bodegon (70x90cm-28x35in) s.d.1992 pastel. 20-Oct-93 Louis Morton, Mexico #62/R (M.P 2800)*

SAND, Maximilen E (19th C) American
$1800   £1184   Woman with fan (60x50cm-24x20in) s.d.1883. 31-Mar-93 Sotheby's Arcade, New York #10/R

SANDBACK, Fred (1943-) American
$844	*£566*	*Untitled (50x65cm-20x26in) s.d.1977 pastel dr vellum. 3-Dec-93 Lempertz, Cologne #985 (DM 1450)*
$1074	*£688*	*Untitled (48x57cm-19x22in) s.d.1986 pencil col.oil chk. 27-May-93 Lempertz, Cologne #995 (DM 1700)*
$2452	*£1613*	*Shadowroom (70x100cm-28x39in) s.d.1988 pastel chk graphite. 12-Jun-93 Hauswedell & Nolte, Hamburg #380/R (DM 4000)*

SANDER, Ludwig (1906-1975) American
$3500	£2365	Huron I (152x168cm-60x66in) s.i.d.68 verso acrylic. 11-Nov-93 Sotheby's, New York #338/R
$3750	£2484	Huron II (102x112cm-40x44in) s.i.d.1971 s.verso. 29-Sep-93 Sotheby's Arcade, New York #314/R

SANDERSON, Douglas (1942-) American
$1800   £1176   Geometric rage - dedicated to Hans Hofmann (127x107cm-50x42in) oil on gesso on canvas executed 1984. 22-Dec-92 Christie's, East, New York #70

SANDHAM, Henry (1842-1912) Canadian
$1000	£662	Gathering wood - coastal view (25x36cm-10x14in) s. canvasboard. 13-Nov-92 Skinner, Bolton #38/R
$1189	£777	Man carrying driftwood (30x41cm-12x16in) s. 19-May-93 Sotheby's, Toronto #182/R (C.D 1500)
$1220	£813	Sunset on a winter shoreline (61x86cm-24x34in) init. 30-May-94 Ritchie, Toronto #251/R (C.D 1700)
$5254	£3479	Indian camp on river (46x69cm-18x27in) 18-Nov-92 Sotheby's, Toronto #128/R (C.D 6750)
$747	*£473*	*Watching the fishermen leave the quay (35x51cm-14x20in) s. W/C. 1-Dec-92 Fraser Pinneys, Quebec #31/R (C.D 950)*

SANDOR, Mathias (1857-1920) American
$850   £563   Rock formations - southwestern view (61x51cm-24x20in) s. 13-Nov-92 Skinner, Bolton #144/R

SANDZEN, Birger (1871-1954) American/Swedish
$3750	£2517	Smoky river, Kansas (35x30cm-14x12in) s. s.i.d.1925 verso. 4-Mar-94 Skinner, Bolton #250/R
$5500	£3716	Landscape (36x30cm-14x12in) s. d.1929 verso masonite. 15-Jun-93 John Moran, Pasadena #6
$6500	£4333	Glimpse of Stevenson Lake, Graham County, Kansas (41x51cm-16x20in) s. s.i.d.1948verso board. 15-Mar-94 John Moran, Pasadena #33
$1600	*£1081*	*Hutchinson Bend Hills, Kansas (25x38cm-10x15in) s. s.i.verso W/C. 20-Mar-93 Weschler, Washington #113/R*

SANTA CRUZ PUMACALLAO, Basilio (attrib) (1635-c.1710) Peruvian
$17000   £11258   Annunciation (182x129cm-72x51in) canvas on masonite. 24-Nov-92 Christie's, New York #67/R

SANTERO, Santo Nino (attrib) (fl.1836-1860) Mexican
$2400   *£1600*   *Our Lady of Sorrows (23x15cm-9x6in) tempera gesso panel. 29-Jan-94 Skinner, Bolton #130/R*

SANTORE, Joseph (1945-) American
$1400   £915   Cancer (41x35cm-16x14in) executed 1981. 22-Dec-92 Christie's, East, New York #71

SANTRY, Daniel (1859-1922) American
$950	£549	Mountain landscape (33x46cm-13x18in) s. 27-Sep-92 James Bakker, Cambridge #37/R
$1400	£809	Field in summer (41x51cm-16x20in) s. canvasboard. 27-Sep-92 James Bakker, Cambridge #36/R

SAPIA, Mariano (1964-) Argentinian
$2500	£1667	Santa (100x140cm-39x55in) s.d.89 s.i.d.verso. 18-May-94 Sotheby's, New York #326/R

SAPP, Allen (1929-) Canadian
$682	£455	Going visiting (25x30cm-10x12in) s. 30-May-94 Hodgins, Calgary #334 d (C.D 950)
$725	£490	Grandmother taking walk (30x25cm-12x10in) s. i.d.1977 acrylic. 25-Apr-94 Levis, Calgary #288/R (C.D 1000)
$728	£485	Saddle horse (50x40cm-20x16in) s. acrylic. 13-May-94 Joyner Fine Art, Toronto #133 (C.D 1000)
$846	£498	Esquoio washing clothes (23x30cm-9x12in) s. i.stretcher. 5-Oct-92 Levis, Calgary #120/R (C.D 1050)
$934	£619	Lumberman's return (50x60cm-20x24in) s. canvasboard. 24-Nov-92 Joyner Fine Art, Toronto #96/R (C.D 1200)
$1088	£640	New baby sitter (41x51cm-16x20in) s. i.stretcher acrylic. 5-Oct-92 Levis, Calgary #119/R (C.D 1350)
$1090	£722	Making some wood for tonight (41x51cm-16x20in) s. i.verso acrylic. 16-Nov-92 Hodgins, Calgary #151 (C.D 1400)
$1092	£728	Cows are eating (30x41cm-12x16in) s. i.d.1972verso acrylic. 11-May-94 Sotheby's, Toronto #33 (C.D 1500)
$1100	£697	Having rabbit for supper (30x41cm-12x16in) s. d.1979 verso acrylic. 30-Nov-92 Ritchie, Toronto #111/R (C.D 1400)
$1162	£785	Muddy road at Red Pheasant Reserve (61x94cm-24x37in) s. i.d.1972verso acrylic. 3-Nov-93 Sotheby's, Toronto #77 (C.D 1500)
$1168	£773	Tried to ride cow (41x51cm-16x20in) s. painted 1984 i.verso acrylic. 16-Nov-92 Hodgins, Calgary #282 (C.D 1500)
$1284	£867	Bringing water for the house (50x60cm-20x24in) s. acrylic. 23-Nov-93 Joyner Fine Art, Toronto #199 (C.D 1700)
$1395	£942	A boy and his dad just getting home (41x51cm-16x20in) s. i.verso acrylic. 1-Nov-93 Levis, Calgary #281 (C.D 1800)
$1456	£971	On top of a hay rack (61x76cm-24x30in) s. 11-May-94 Sotheby's, Toronto #35/R (C.D 2000)
$1472	£995	Making a tent (41x50cm-16x20in) s. i.d.1980verso acrylic. 1-Nov-93 Levis, Calgary #280/R (C.D 1900)
$1550	£1047	He just started (51x61cm-20x24in) s. i.verso acrylic. 1-Nov-93 Levis, Calgary #279 (C.D 2000)
$1557	£1031	Got two pails of water (51x41cm-20x16in) s. painted 1978 i.verso acrylic. 16-Nov-92 Hodgins, Calgary #88 (C.D 2000)
$1795	£1136	Wont' take long to get a load (16x20cm-6x8in) s. acrylic. 21-Oct-92 Maynards, Vancouver #125 (C.D 2250)
$2061	£1347	Taking water home on sled (61x91cm-24x36in) s. acrylic. 18-May-93 Joyner Fine Art, Toronto #145/R (C.D 2600)
$2176	£1471	Need more water (61x76cm-24x30in) s. i.d.1977verso acrylic. 25-Apr-94 Levis, Calgary #287/R (C.D 3000)
$2367	£1578	Nice evening, a game of ice hockey (51x61cm-20x24in) s. 11-May-94 Sotheby's, Toronto #238/R (C.D 3250)
$2827	£1923	Cattle feeding in winter (61x86cm-24x34in) s.d. 1968 acrylic. 15-Nov-93 Hodgins, Calgary #87/R (C.D 3750)
$3113	£2062	House far away is burglar's place at Red Pheasant Reserve (76x122cm-30x48in) s. acrylic. 16-Nov-92 Hodgins, Calgary #251/R (C.D 4000)
$5137	£3402	Playing hockey a long time ago (76x122cm-30x48in) s. painted 1976 i.verso acrylic. 16-Nov-92 Hodgins, Calgary #53/R (C.D 6600)

SARET, Alan (1944-) American
$1200	£833	Circle-branch circle (28x54cm-11x21in) s.i.verso col pencil crayon. 26-Feb-93 Sotheby's Arcade, New York #277/R
$1200	£833	New grass ensoulment (77x112cm-30x44in) s.i.d.1988verso graphite col.crayon. 22-Feb-93 Christie's, East, New York #246/R

SARGEANT, Geneve Rixford (1868-?) American
$1700	£1126	Still life with bowl and jug (46x36cm-18x14in) s. 15-Jun-94 Butterfield & Butterfield, San Francisco #4667/R

SARGENT, John Singer (1856-1925) American/British
$22500	£15000	Portrait of Charles Octavius Parsons, the Cardiff surgeon (53x43cm-21x17in) s. 7-Jun-94 Phillips, London #23/R
$27500	£17628	Portrait of Mrs Colin Hunter (94x62cm-37x24in) s.d.1896. 27-May-93 Sotheby's, New York #34/R
$31000	£19872	Backwater at Calcot, near Reading (63x76cm-25x30in) painted 1888. 27-May-93 Sotheby's, New York #55/R
$37000	£25000	Coast of Algiers (27x35cm-11x14in) panel painted 1880. 23-Nov-93 Christie's, London #68/R
$70000	£44872	Portrait of Major George Conrad Roller (42x43cm-17x17in) s.i. canvas on board. 26-May-93 Christie's, New York #70/R
$220000	£139241	Portrait of Teresa Gosse (61x51cm-24x20in) s.i. 4-Dec-92 Christie's, New York #6/R
$270000	£180000	The little fruit seller (36x27cm-14x11in) s.i.d.1879 board. 25-May-94 Sotheby's, New York #90/R
$700000	£469799	Mrs Archibald Douglas Dick (161x93cm-63x37in) s.d.1886. 3-Dec-93 Christie's, New York #46/R

SARGENT, John Singer (1856-1925) American/British-cont.
$750000	£500000	Parisian beggar girl (64x45cm-25x18in) s.i. 25-May-94 Sotheby's, New York #66/R
$6900000	£4600000	Spanish dancer (223x151cm-88x59in) 25-May-94 Sotheby's, New York #93/R
$1190	£700	Study for Gassed (17x25cm-7x10in) s. pencil. 29-Sep-92 Phillips, London #30/R
$2000	£1316	Study of cows and rocks (29x39cm-11x15in) pencil. 31-Mar-93 Sotheby's Arcade, New York #113/R
$2368	£1600	Study of standing female and male nudes. Studies of hands and feet (35x24cm-14x9in) red chk pencil double-sided pair. 23-Nov-93 Phillips, London #83
$4250	£2796	Study of three swans (16x23cm-6x9in) pencil. 31-Mar-93 Sotheby's Arcade, New York #112/R
$5720	£4000	Portrait of Mrs George Anderson (61x47cm-24x19in) s.d.1910 chk. 10-Mar-93 Sotheby's, London #24/R
$6468	£4200	Portrait study of Mrs. Comyns-Carr (11x17cm-4x7in) black ink executed c.1889. 23-Jun-94 Christie's, London #129/R
$8250	£5500	Portrait of a young man. Portrait of a young woman (52x27cm-20x11in) s.d.1924 black chk pair. 7-Jun-94 Phillips, London #74/R
$9500	£6291	Eleutherios Venizelos (62x47cm-24x19in) s.d.1924 chl. 23-Sep-93 Sotheby's, New York #126/R
$12000	£7692	Three nudes with Cupid (49x38cm-19x15in) bears st.verso W/C. 27-May-93 Sotheby's, New York #13/R
$12000	£7692	Jupiter beseeching Eros (49x38cm-19x15in) W/C. 27-May-93 Sotheby's, New York #14/R
$15000	£10067	Bivouac (36x25cm-14x10in) W/C pencil. 2-Dec-93 Sotheby's, New York #100/R
$17000	£10897	Sphinx (35x23cm-14x9in) s. W/C. 27-May-93 Sotheby's, New York #2/R
$50000	£31646	Above Lake Garda at San Vigilio (35x53cm-14x21in) s. W/C gouache. 4-Dec-92 Christie's, New York #15/R
$65000	£43333	Villa Torlonia, Frascati (49x34cm-19x13in) W/C pencil traces. 26-May-94 Christie's, New York #91/R
$93620	£62000	Venice (34x24cm-13x9in) s.i. W/C gouache over pencil. 30-Jun-93 Sotheby's, London #16/R

SARGENT, Margarett McKean (20th C) American
$1300	£844	Puffed sleeves (61x46cm-24x18in) s. canvasboard. 9-Sep-93 Sotheby's Arcade, New York #364/R

SARKA, Charles Nicolas (1879-1960) American
$825	£562	Spring landscape with girl on swing (58x48cm-23x19in) s. 14-Apr-94 Freeman Fine Arts, Philadelphia #1010

SARKISIAN, Sarkis (1909-1977) American
$1100	£738	Portrait of female with carnation (41x51cm-16x20in) s.d.35. 16-Jul-93 Du Mouchelle, Detroit #2/R
$1200	£759	Clown (36x23cm-14x9in) s. board. 2-Dec-92 Boos Gallery, Michigan #790/R
$1500	£920	Oriental boy (86x69cm-34x27in) s.d.34. 16-Oct-92 Du Mouchelle, Detroit #2013/R

SARSONY, Robert (1938-) American
$700	£473	Wild roses (91x61cm-36x24in) s. s.i.d.1974verso. 4-Nov-93 Sloan, North Bethesda #2584/R

SARTAIN, William (1843-1924) American
$700	£476	Trees (41x51cm-16x20in) s. 15-Nov-93 Christie's, East, New York #69/R
$1350	£882	River view at sunset (38x76cm-15x30in) s. 7-Oct-93 Freeman Fine Arts, Philadelphia #901/R
$3000	£2013	The sunset house (56x81cm-22x32in) s. 16-Dec-93 Mystic Fine Arts, Connecticut #70
$4000	£2649	Places which pale passion loves - landscape (64x77cm-25x30in) s. s.i.verso. 22-Sep-93 Christie's, New York #126/R

SARTORE, Hugo (1935-) Uruguayan
$800	£523	Aperitivo al medio dia (54x64cm-21x25in) s.d.1970. 26-Oct-92 Gomensoro, Montevideo #55
$850	£500	Gente en el bar (69x79cm-27x31in) s.d.63 fibre. 5-Oct-92 Gomensoro, Montevideo #6/R

SASTRE, Marcos (1808-1887) Argentinian
$6216	£4200	Portraits of Genara Arambue de Sastre and self-portrait (6x5cm-2x2in) W/C bodycol two one mount. 20-Oct-93 Sotheby's, London #26/R

SAUERWEIN, Frank Paul (1871-1910) American
$1250	£786	Chief red feather (30x23cm-12x9in) s. canvasboard. 22-Apr-93 Freeman Fine Arts, Philadelphia #1317
$2000	£1342	The price of Spanish gold (51x76cm-20x30in) s. 4-Dec-93 Louisiana Auction Exchange #53/R
$3500	£2244	Blizzard (30x46cm-12x18in) s.d.1909. 9-Dec-92 Butterfield & Butterfield, San Francisco #3990/R

SAUL, Charles (1943-) Haitian
$2716	£1775	Le bal des canards (61x51cm-24x20in) painted 1974. 17-May-93 Hoebanx, Paris #208/R (F.FR 15000)

SAUL, Peter (1934-) American
$7000	£4730	Modern Homes 62,000 Dollars (170x203cm-67x80in) s.d.68 oil acrylic marker. 21-Apr-94 Butterfield & Butterfield, San Francisco #1146/R
$8000	£5405	Nude descending a staircase (230x154cm-91x61in) s.d.77 acrylic. 8-Nov-93 Christie's, East, New York #41/R

SAUL, Peter (1934-) American-cont.
| $12000 | £8108 | Ice Box 6 (190x160cm-75x63in) s.d.63 s.i.d.verso. 8-Nov-93 Christie's, East, New York #221/R |
| $4500 | £3041 | Ching Chang (102x135cm-40x53in) s.d.65 pen crayon acrylic board on masonite. 8-Nov-93 Christie's, East, New York #222/R |

SAUNDERS, Raymond (1934-) American
| $1400 | £952 | Something about something (165x94cm-65x37in) 14-Apr-94 Freeman Fine Arts, Philadelphia #1042 b |
| $5500 | £3481 | Valentine (122x112cm-48x44in) mixed media collage artist's board. 25-Oct-92 Butterfield & Butterfield, San Francisco #2391/R |

SAUWIN, P (19th C) American?
| $1700 | £1118 | Still life with peaches (22x27cm-9x11in) s.d.62 board. 31-Mar-93 Sotheby's Arcade, New York #44 |

SAVAGE, Anne (1896-1971) Canadian
$793	£518	Roses at Metis (30x36cm-12x14in) s. panel. 18-May-93 Joyner Fine Art, Toronto #102/R (C.D 1000)
$1506	£984	Early spring, Lake Wonish (23x30cm-9x12in) panel. 18-May-93 Joyner Fine Art, Toronto #35/R (C.D 1900)
$1510	£1020	Hills at Wonish, Laurentians (30x35cm-12x14in) s. panel painted 1939. 23-Nov-93 Joyner Fine Art, Toronto #4/R (C.D 2000)
$1510	£1020	Georgian Bay (22x30cm-9x12in) init. panel. 23-Nov-93 Joyner Fine Art, Toronto #101/R (C.D 2000)
$1675	£1117	Laurentians, Autumn 1935 (21x26cm-8x10in) s. panel. 13-May-94 Joyner Fine Art, Toronto #5/R (C.D 2300)
$2114	£1429	Metis, children playing in the village (30x35cm-12x14in) s. panel. 23-Nov-93 Joyner Fine Art, Toronto #55/R (C.D 2800)
$2333	£1566	Sunlit woods (29x34cm-11x13in) s.verso board. 29-Nov-93 Waddingtons, Toronto #1036 (C.D 3100)
$2378	£1554	Ward's house, 16 Island Lake, winter (30x36cm-12x14in) init. panel. 18-May-93 Joyner Fine Art, Toronto #168/R (C.D 3000)
$2491	£1649	Lake Wonish from artist's studio. Landscape (21x26cm-8x10in) init. panel double-sided painted c.1940. 24-Nov-92 Joyner Fine Art, Toronto #88/R (C.D 3200)
$2491	£1649	Lake Wonish, Thanksgiving (30x35cm-12x14in) init. panel painted c.1945. 24-Nov-92 Joyner Fine Art, Toronto #7/R (C.D 3200)
$4162	£2720	Cottage at St. Hilaire (30x36cm-12x14in) panel. 19-May-93 Sotheby's, Toronto #393/R (C.D 5250)

SAVAIN, Petion (20th C) Haitian
| $550 | £364 | Preparing the meal (61x41cm-24x16in) s.d.1969. 23-Sep-93 Mystic Fine Arts, Connecticut #224 |

SAVIAN, Petion (20th C) Haitian
| $1350 | £877 | Figures in market place (112x91cm-44x36in) s.d.1970. 11-Sep-93 Louisiana Auction Exchange #116/R |

SAVITSKY, Jack (1910-1991) American
| $650 | £430 | Adam and Eve (23x30cm-9x12in) s.d.1985 ink pencil crayon. 21-Nov-92 Litchfield Auction Gallery #2 |
| $725 | £480 | Breaker Boy and dog (28x23cm-11x9in) s.d.1981 crayon felt-tip pen. 21-Nov-92 Litchfield Auction Gallery #1 |

SAWYER, Wells M (1863-1961) American
| $1600 | £1135 | Thirteenth at Sleepy Hollow (41x51cm-16x20in) s. d.1919 stretcher. 13-Feb-93 Collins, Maine #79/R |

SAWYIER, Paul (1865-1917) American
| $6500 | £4305 | Children on country road (32x51cm-13x20in) s. W/C. 23-Sep-93 Sotheby's, New York #39/R |
| $8000 | £4624 | Frankfort Bridge over the Kentucky River (41x67cm-16x26in) s. W/C paper on board. 25-Sep-92 Sotheby's Arcade, New York #126/R |

SAYRE, F Grayson (1879-1938) American
$1500	£993	Landscape (84x112cm-33x44in) s. 14-Jun-94 John Moran, Pasadena #130 a
$1500	£987	California landscape (30x37cm-12x15in) s. s.indist.i.verso masonite. 31-Mar-93 Sotheby's Arcade, New York #200/R
$2000	£1325	Favourite nook (51x61cm-20x24in) s. s.i.stretcher. 28-Sep-93 John Moran, Pasadena #210
$2250	£1490	Dancing girl (51x61cm-20x24in) s. 15-Jun-94 Butterfield & Butterfield, San Francisco #4703/R
$3000	£2000	Desert in bloom (51x61cm-20x24in) s. s.i.stretcher. 15-Mar-94 John Moran, Pasadena #104
$4000	£2797	Dancing girl (51x61cm-20x24in) s. painted c.1926. 10-Mar-93 Sotheby's, New York #68/R
$8500	£5000	California foothills (52x61cm-20x24in) s. 4-Oct-92 Butterfield & Butterfield, Los Angeles #194/R

SCALELLA, Jules (1895-?) American
| $1500 | £962 | Winter day (63x76cm-25x30in) s. 9-Dec-92 Butterfield & Butterfield, San Francisco #3880/R |
| $2400 | £1412 | New Hope canal (76x91cm-30x36in) s. 8-Oct-92 Freeman Fine Arts, Philadelphia #1113/R |

SCARLETT, Rolph (1884-1984) American
$1639	£1100	Allegretto in brown (150x181cm-59x71in) s. 21-Jun-93 Christie's, S. Kensington #201/R
$4250	£2457	Nocturne (122x122cm-48x48in) s. 25-Sep-92 Sotheby's Arcade, New York #494/R
$8000	£4624	Largo (122x142cm-48x56in) s. 25-Sep-92 Sotheby's Arcade, New York #493/R

SCARPITTA, Salvatore (1919-) American
$1490	£1000	Natura morta con bottiglie (50x60cm-20x24in) s.verso. 30-Nov-93 Finarte, Rome #233 (I.L 2500000)
$23000	£15436	Red freight (190x155cm-75x61in) s.i.d.1961 verso oil fibreglass canvas collage. 23-Feb-94 Christie's, New York #62/R

SCARPULLA, Russell (1947-) American
$888	£569	Rosette (60x60cm-24x24in) s.i.d.1993 oil wax lino. 24-May-93 Finarte, Firenze #179/R (I.L 1300000)

SCHAEFER, Carl Fellman (1903-) Canadian
$1110	*£725*	*Rock in the pasture (29x45cm-11x18in) s.d.18.7.48 W/C. 18-May-93 Joyner Fine Art, Toronto #196 (C.D 1400)*
$1317	*£890*	*Fields (28x38cm-11x15in) W/C. 3-Nov-93 Sotheby's, Toronto #144/R (C.D 1700)*

SCHAEFFER, J S (?) American?
$1500	£987	Farmhouse (51x61cm-20x24in) s. 2-Apr-93 Eldred, Massachusetts #548/R

SCHAEFFER, Mead (1898-1980) American
$2000	£1266	Paradise poahers (76x107cm-30x42in) i.verso. 2-Dec-92 Christie's, East, New York #169/R
$5000	£3497	He received two dozen lashes .. from Cruise of the Cachalot (97x79cm-38x31in) s.d.25. 12-Mar-93 Skinner, Bolton #303/R

SCHAFER, Frederick Ferdinand (1839-1927) American
$700	£473	View of Mount Baldy (20x30cm-8x12in) s. board. 9-Nov-93 John Moran, Pasadena #818
$800	£556	Tropical sunset (30x25cm-12x10in) s. 7-Mar-93 Butterfield & Butterfield, San Francisco #13/R
$950	£642	Sunset on a lake (76x51cm-30x20in) s. 9-Nov-93 John Moran, Pasadena #928
$1900	£1118	Olympic mountains, Washington (51x91cm-20x36in) s. 4-Oct-92 Butterfield & Butterfield, Los Angeles #8/R
$2500	£1736	Pastoral landscape (51x91cm-20x36in) s. 7-Mar-93 Butterfield & Butterfield, San Francisco #7/R
$2750	£1618	View of Mount Tamalpais (76x127cm-30x50in) s.d.1880. 4-Oct-92 Butterfield & Butterfield, Los Angeles #30/R
$3000	£2083	Mt Hood from Hood River (76x127cm-30x50in) s. i.verso. 7-Mar-93 Butterfield & Butterfield, San Francisco #8/R
$3000	£1765	Coast near Monterey, California (51x91cm-20x36in) s. i.verso. 4-Oct-92 Butterfield & Butterfield, Los Angeles #29/R
$3000	£1765	Cypress Point, Monteray Bay (30x51cm-12x20in) s. 4-Oct-92 Butterfield & Butterfield, Los Angeles #28/R
$4100	£2680	Morning in the San Rafael Valley (51x91cm-20x36in) 18-Sep-93 San Rafael Auction Galleries #347
$4250	£2796	Bear Lake in Wasatch Mountains, Utah (76x127cm-30x50in) s. 31-Mar-93 Sotheby's Arcade, New York #186/R

SCHALDACH, William J (1896-?) American
$1550	*£1099*	*Ruffed grouse feeding (51x38cm-20x15in) s. W/C. 13-Feb-93 Collins, Maine #126/R*

SCHAMBERG, Morton Livingston (1881-1918) American
$1000	£654	Interior view (33x48cm-13x19in) s. 7-Oct-93 Freeman Fine Arts, Philadelphia #912/R

SCHANKER, Louis (1903-1981) American
$4750	£3210	Men in action (89x110cm-35x43in) painted c.1937. 31-Mar-94 Sotheby's Arcade, New York #473/R
$2300	*£1513*	*North Wall (23x50cm-9x20in) s.d.38 gouache graphite board. 31-Mar-93 Sotheby's Arcade, New York #378/R*
$3800	*£2484*	*Mural study for WNYC, 1937 (17x58cm-7x23in) s.i.verso W/C ink board. 4-May-93 Christie's, East, New York #296/R*

SCHARF, Kenny (1958-) American
$4000	£2649	Greenoright over bluepoint (81x60cm-32x24in) s.d.84 verso. 30-Jun-93 Sotheby's Arcade, New York #373/R
$4470	£3000	Untitled (105cm-41in circular) acrylic painted 1982. 25-Mar-93 Christie's, London #180/R
$7000	£4698	Save the Jungle (220x230cm-87x91in) s.i.d.1987 verso oil acrylic. 23-Feb-94 Christie's, New York #147/R
$7000	£4698	ING (269x226cm-106x89in) s.i.d.88 oil acrylic. 3-May-94 Christie's, East, New York #133/R
$9114	£6076	Mundo Azul (213x223cm-84x88in) s.d.83 oil varnish. 2-Jun-94 AB Stockholms Auktionsverk, Stockholm #7188/R (S.KR 72000)
$11175	£7500	New Frontier (217x221cm-85x87in) s.d.84 acrylic spray paint. 25-Mar-93 Christie's, London #177/R
$14000	£9722	Balanca precoriosex (292x224cm-115x88in) s.i.d.Sept 85verso acrylic oil spray paint. 23-Feb-93 Sotheby's, New York #386/R
$24000	£15894	Tangello purple tempelo (122x125cm-48x49in) s.i.d.Dec.85verso acrylic oil. 19-Nov-92 Christie's, New York #276/R

SCHARF, Kenny (1958-) American-cont.
$36000	£24324	Days of our lives (292x262cm-115x103in) s.i.d.84 verso acrylic. 11-Nov-93 Sotheby's, New York #186/R
$7500	£4967	Retchmess chunky chunky (183x196cm-72x77in) s.d.1985 verso acrylic oil toys feathers canvas. 30-Jun-93 Sotheby's Arcade, New York #372/R
$7607	£5283	Tamisha (120x91cm-47x36in) s.d.1989verso oil ink canvas. 3-Mar-93 Guy Loudmer, Paris #72/R (F.FR 43000)
$14000	£9459	Bali Roma (256x320cm-101x126in) s.i.d.84verso oil acrylic enamel plastic collage. 10-Nov-93 Christie's, New York #389/R

SCHARY, Saul (1904-1978) American
$2500	£1445	Portrait of Arshile Gorky (71x56cm-28x22in) s. 23-Sep-92 Christie's, New York #252/R

SCHEFFLER, Rudolf (1884-1973) American
$18000	£11392	Max Schmeling (213x167cm-84x66in) s.d.1929. 3-Dec-92 Sotheby's, New York #124/R

SCHELL, Susan Gertrude (1891-1970) American
$725	£487	Hilltop a composition in Gaspe Vicinage (30x41cm-12x16in) s. board. 2-Dec-93 Freeman Fine Arts, Philadelphia #816

SCHERG, Jacob (attrib) (19th C) American?
$2000	£1333	Portrait of General Howe (11x6cm-4x2in) W/C ink. 10-Jun-94 Christie's, New York #401/R

SCHERMAN, Tony (1950-) American?
$850	£571	British apple (56x38cm-22x15in) s.i.d.80 encaustic graphite. 23-Feb-94 Christie's, East, New York #311/R
$1800	£1208	Shadow with ginger jar (61x61cm-24x24in) encaustic executed 1980. 23-Feb-94 Christie's, East, New York #312/R
$7929	£5357	Dogs in water (135x150cm-53x59in) s.i.d.89 verso encaustic canvas. 23-Nov-93 Joyner Fine Art, Toronto #56/R (C.D 10500)

SCHEURICH, Paul (1883-1945) American/German
$2411	£1526	Lady in dressing gown reclining on chair (131x168cm-52x66in) s.d.1930. 5-Dec-92 Galerie Bassenge, Berlin #7690/R (DM 3800)

SCHIWETZ, Edward M (1898-1984) American
$900	£566	'Run for It' (36x28cm-14x11in) s. mixed media paperboard. 23-Apr-93 Hart Gallery, Houston #2

SCHMID, Richard (20th C) American
$600	£400	Blue Mountains (36x46cm-14x18in) s. s.i.d.1962verso masonite. 21-May-94 Weschler, Washington #102
$3250	£1879	Manhattan, city dawn (61x92cm-24x36in) s. s.i.verso. 25-Sep-92 Sotheby's Arcade, New York #379/R

SCHMID, Rudolf (1896-?) American
$925	£625	Telephone workers (109x104cm-43x41in) s.d.1929 board painted with V.Bing. 20-Mar-93 Weschler, Washington #121/R
$1300	£878	Construction site (101x115cm-40x45in) s.i.d.1929 board. 20-Mar-93 Weschler, Washington #116/R

SCHMIDT, Karl (1890-1962) American
$700	£470	Rural farm scene at sunset (24x32cm-9x13in) s. gouache pencil. 8-Dec-93 Butterfield & Butterfield, San Francisco #3407/R

SCHMIDT, Katherine (1898-?) American
$800	£519	The rose (33x38cm-13x15in) s.d.39. 9-Sep-93 Sotheby's Arcade, New York #273

SCHNABEL, Julian (1951-) American
$7500	£5068	Surfboard (233x45cm-92x18in) s.verso shaped canvas. 8-Nov-93 Christie's, East, New York #60/R
$7500	£5068	Untitled from the series The Names of our Children (178x155cm-70x61in) s.d.May 6 1980 lithograph oil gesso. 10-Nov-93 Christie's, New York #386/R
$7500	£5068	Saturday a long time ago Jacqueline in beige chair (158x234cm-62x92in) s.i.d.1985 paper. 8-Nov-93 Christie's, East, New York #152/R
$13000	£7647	Untitled (121x97cm-48x38in) map. 8-Oct-92 Christie's, New York #2227/R
$15000	£9934	Christ in the Bay of Naples (62cm-24in circular) s.d.1987verso panel. 19-Nov-92 Christie's, New York #217/R
$16456	£10970	A buen retiro (305x276cm-120x109in) painted 1988. 2-Jun-94 AB Stockholms Auktionsverk, Stockholm #7030/R (S.KR 130000)
$20000	£13423	Rigoletto (274x183cm-108x72in) init.d.85verso oil fiberglass linoleum on panel. 4-May-94 Christie's, New York #405/R
$31646	£21097	Alas (456x334cm-180x131in) oil tempera painted 1987. 2-Jun-94 AB Stockholms Auktionsverk, Stockholm #7211/R (S.KR 250000)
$32000	£21192	Series of small crosses can in no way be ominous (193x159cm-76x63in) s.i.d.77verso oil wax. 19-Nov-92 Christie's, New York #440/R
$35000	£23490	Swamp possum of L.H. (183x152cm-72x60in) velvet painted 1984. 4-May-94 Christie's, New York #370/R
$41922	£26533	Bingo (125x115cm-49x45in) 6-Dec-92 Binoche et Godeau, Paris #14/R (F.FR 225000)
$70000	£47297	Untitled (259x206cm-102x81in) painted 1978. 10-Nov-93 Sotheby's, New York #65/R
$79000	£50000	Untitled - submarine painting (274x213cm-108x84in) s. d.1982-83 stretcher velvet. 3-Dec-92 Sotheby's, London #69/R

441

SCHNABEL, Julian (1951-) American-cont.
$100000	£66225	Some peaches (303x273cm-119x107in) oil bondo on velvet. 18-Nov-92 Christie's, New York #58/R
$170000	£112583	Untitled (274x213cm-108x84in) velvet. 17-Nov-92 Sotheby's, New York #62/R
$5500	£3235	Drawings in rain - Barbados (109x176cm-43x69in) s. W/C painted 1981. 6-Oct-92 Sotheby's, New York #148/R
$7500	£5208	Rhonda (269x169cm-106x67in) oil crayon graphite paper. 24-Feb-93 Christie's, New York #122/R
$7500	£5208	Divan (152x102cm-60x40in) s. executed 1979 oil pencil rice paper collage. 23-Feb-93 Sotheby's, New York #349/R
$9500	£6209	Untitled (139x96cm-55x38in) oil paper collage map. 5-May-93 Christie's, New York #155/R
$14000	£9396	Rome - 4th Italian painting (100x69cm-39x27in) s.stretcher oil plaster canvas collage shaped. 23-Feb-94 Christie's, East, New York #327/R
$26820	£18000	La banana e buona (188x138cm-74x54in) collage gouache oil mud paper fabric exec.1988. 25-Mar-93 Christie's, London #178/R
$65000	£43046	Untitled (152x122cm-60x48in) painted 1985 oil ceramic bondo wood. 19-Nov-92 Christie's, New York #227/R
$70000	£46980	Holy night (305x274cm-120x108in) oil modelling paste on velvet executed 1984. 3-May-94 Christie's, New York #51/R
$110000	£74324	Portrait of Jacqueline (152x122cm-60x48in) oil ceramic bondo wood executed 1984. 9-Nov-93 Christie's, New York #54/R

SCHNAKENBERG, Henry (1892-1970) American
$1000	£658	Place to swim (114x168cm-45x66in) s. 31-Mar-93 Sotheby's Arcade, New York #294/R
$550	£372	Copa D'Oro (38x56cm-15x22in) s. i.d.1965 W/C board. 31-Mar-94 Sotheby's Arcade, New York #437/R

SCHNEIDAU, Christian von (1893-1976) American
$650	£433	Portrait of mother and young girl (97x86cm-38x34in) s.d.1921. 15-Mar-94 John Moran, Pasadena #125
$1200	£811	Inspiration a portrait (71x102cm-28x40in) s.d.1922 i.verso. 9-Nov-93 John Moran, Pasadena #919 a
$3250	£2152	Her fan (86x76cm-34x30in) s.d.1920 canvas on canvas. 28-Sep-93 John Moran, Pasadena #331
$5500	£3618	Summertime (117x102cm-46x40in) s. 13-Jun-93 Butterfield & Butterfield, San Francisco #898/R

SCHNEIDER, Theophile (1872-?) American
$750	£500	Farm in rolling landscape (61x76cm-24x30in) s. 15-Mar-94 John Moran, Pasadena #194

SCHNEIDER-BLUMBERG, Ernst (20th C) American
$650	£409	Two boys, music lesson (33x43cm-13x17in) s. 22-Apr-93 Freeman Fine Arts, Philadelphia #1207

SCHNELLE, William G (1897-?) American
$2400	£1678	Woman in interior (76x99cm-30x39in) s. 11-Mar-93 Christie's, New York #167/R

SCHNIER, Jacques (1898-1988) American
$850	£535	Woman with feline (27x43cm-11x17in) init.d.27 graphite. 25-Apr-93 Butterfield & Butterfield, San Francisco #2108/R

SCHNURRENBERGER, John R (1940-) Canadian
$778	£515	What's happening Mamma (51x61cm-20x24in) s.d.75 init.i.verso. 16-Nov-92 Hodgins, Calgary #324/R (C.D 1000)

SCHOFIELD, Walter E (1867-1944) American
$2200	£1410	Autumn lake scene (41x51cm-16x20in) s. board. 17-Dec-92 Mystic Fine Arts, Connecticut #243
$2500	£1634	Stream in winter (66x71cm-26x28in) s. canvas on board. 16-Sep-93 Sloan, North Bethesda #3205/R
$3750	£2534	White Sand Harbour (30x35cm-12x14in) s. s.i.verso canvasboard. 31-Mar-94 Sotheby's Arcade, New York #223/R
$17000	£10759	The Outer Harbour, Polperro (76x92cm-30x36in) s. 4-Dec-92 Christie's, New York #95/R
$33000	£20886	McLegrenow Farm (76x91cm-30x36in) s.d.20. 4-Dec-92 Christie's, New York #54/R

SCHOLDER, Fritz (1937-) American
$3200	£2065	Portrait head (30x25cm-12x10in) s. d.1985 verso. 9-Jan-93 Skinner, Bolton #276/R
$4750	£3188	Portrait in New York No.2 (102x76cm-40x30in) s. painted 1983. 25-Feb-94 Sotheby's, New York #128/R
$8000	£5298	Monster love number 10 (127x102cm-50x40in) s. i.d.1986stretcher acrylic. 17-Nov-92 Christie's, East, New York #142/R
$12500	£8170	Hollywood Indian - 5 (203x173cm-80x68in) d.73 stretcher acrylic. 4-May-93 Sotheby's, New York #344/R
$13000	£8609	Carnival no 7 (203x173cm-80x68in) s. 29-Sep-93 Sotheby's Arcade, New York #377/R
$16000	£10738	Portrait 1876-1976 (102x76cm-40x30in) s. oil acrylic. 2-Dec-92 Sotheby's, New York #89/R
$3000	£1987	Indian with white feather (37x28cm-15x11in) s. acrylic brush ink. 17-Nov-92 Christie's, East, New York #143/R

SCHOONOVER, Frank E (1877-1972) American
$6000	£3974	'Forward, forward', he cried (91x76cm-36x30in) s.d.21. 23-Sep-93 Sotheby's, New York #293/R

SCHOONOVER, Frank E (1877-1972) American-cont.
$10000	£6667	Bombing (91x69cm-36x27in) s.d.18 s.d.1918 verso. 17-Mar-94 Sotheby's, New York #175/R
$13000	£8228	The trooper shifted both hands (76x96cm-30x38in) s.d.26. 4-Dec-92 Christie's, New York #266/R
$21000	£14000	Contact (91x69cm-36x27in) s.d.18 s.d.1918 verso. 17-Mar-94 Sotheby's, New York #174/R
$700	*£470*	*Battery at New Castle (30x48cm-12x19in) W/C. 27-Mar-94 Myers, Florida #23/R*

SCHORRE, Charles (20th C) American
$2450	£1541	The last cloud (91x122cm-36x48in) s. acrylic. 23-Apr-93 Hart Gallery, Houston #13

SCHREIBER, Georges (1904-1977) American
$1200	£805	Figures by a lake (69x99cm-27x39in) s.d.42 and 42 panel. 4-Dec-93 Louisiana Auction Exchange #88/R
$10000	£6757	Portrait of Tom Benton (62x76cm-24x30in) s.d.1945 s.i.stretcher. 31-Mar-94 Sotheby's Arcade, New York #320/R

SCHREYER, Claudius W (1864-1902) American
$2800	*£1772*	*Musical still life (56x86cm-22x34in) s. 3-Dec-92 Freeman Fine Arts, Philadelphia #1894*

SCHREYVOGEL, Charles (1861-1912) American
$5000	£3247	The teepee (25x20cm-10x8in) s. s.verso board. 9-Sep-93 Sotheby's Arcade, New York #224/R
$140000	£93333	The duel (50x41cm-20x16in) s.d.1912. 26-May-94 Christie's, New York #68/R
$230000	£154362	The messenger (86x61cm-34x24in) s.d.1912. 2-Dec-93 Sotheby's, New York #62/R

SCHULTZ, Charles (20th C) American?
$942	*£620*	*Psychiatric help, the doctor is in (91x76cm-36x30in) s. wax crayon. 5-Apr-93 Christie's, S. Kensington #45/R*

SCHULTZ, George F (1869-?) American
$3000	*£2000*	*Sailing off a rocky coast (49x71cm-19x28in) s. W/C gouache board. 23-May-94 Christie's, East, New York #91/R*

SCHULTZ, George F (attrib) (1869-?) American
$750	£510	Twilight shadows at sea, sails at right/centre (51x61cm-20x24in) s. 17-Apr-94 Schrager Galleries, Milwaukee #757

SCHULTZE, Andreas (1955-) American?
$4000	£2685	Untitled (274x290cm-108x114in) acrylic painted 1985. 25-Feb-94 Sotheby's, New York #163/R

SCHULZ, Ada Walter (1870-1928) American
$7000	£4575	Two sisters (56x46cm-22x18in) s. board. 16-May-93 Hindman Galleries, Chicago #1/R

SCHUMACHER, J (19th C) American
$2700	£1888	Untitled (36x41cm-14x16in) s.verso porcelain oval after Sir Luke Fields. 12-Mar-93 Hart Gallery, Houston #12

SCHUSTER, Donna (1883-1953) American
$1500	£882	Sierra mountain lake (76x71cm-30x28in) s. 4-Oct-92 Butterfield & Butterfield, Los Angeles #191/R
$1900	£1284	Palace of fine arts (41x30cm-16x12in) s. 15-Jun-93 John Moran, Pasadena #44
$2000	£1342	Southern California Hills (41x41cm-16x16in) s. board. 8-Dec-93 Butterfield & Butterfield, San Francisco #3424/R
$2250	£1324	Near Los Feliz, Los Angeles (41x51cm-16x20in) s. board. 4-Oct-92 Butterfield & Butterfield, Los Angeles #269/R
$3000	£1765	Anemones (76x63cm-30x25in) s. 4-Oct-92 Butterfield & Butterfield, Los Angeles #64/R
$3000	£2000	The artist's cottage at Laguna Beach (30x41cm-12x16in) s. board. 15-Mar-94 John Moran, Pasadena #68
$9000	£6040	View of the Hollywood Hills (53x69cm-21x27in) s. 8-Dec-93 Butterfield & Butterfield, San Francisco #3441/R
$600	£395	Mexico (53x37cm-21x15in) s. W/C pencil. 13-Jun-93 Butterfield & Butterfield, San Francisco #867/R
$650	£433	Wash day in Mexico (53x33cm-21x13in) s. W/C. 15-Mar-94 John Moran, Pasadena #78
$900	£596	A day at the Pan Pacific Exhibition (49x34cm-19x13in) s. W/C htd.white. 15-Jun-94 Butterfield & Butterfield, San Francisco #4580/R
$900	£621	Sailboats at Pan Pacific Exhibition (48x36cm-19x14in) s. W/C. 16-Feb-93 John Moran, Pasadena #33
$1200	£811	Boats at harbour (33x46cm-13x18in) s. W/C. 15-Jun-93 John Moran, Pasadena #174
$2750	£1821	Fuchias and columns, Palace of Fine Arts, Pan Pacific Exhibition 1915 (51x36cm-20x14in) s. W/C oil. 15-Jun-94 Butterfield & Butterfield, San Francisco #4579/R

SCHUYLER, Remington (1887-1953) American
$1900	£1250	Fending off enemy (77x63cm-30x25in) s. 31-Mar-93 Sotheby's Arcade, New York #212/R

SCHWARTZ, Andrew T (1867-1942) American
$750	£490	Autumn landscape (48x58cm-19x23in) s. board. 30-Jun-94 Mystic Fine Arts, Connecticut #258/R

SCHWARTZ, Andrew T (1867-1942) American-cont.
$17000   £11888   Landscape with houses by river (102x131cm-40x52in) s.d.1911 masonite. 11-Mar-93
                      Christie's, New York #164/R

SCHWARTZ, Davis F (1879-1969) American
$850   £594   California landscape (81x102cm-32x40in) s. 11-Mar-93 Mystic Fine Arts,
                      Connecticut #165/R

SCHWARTZ, Karl (19/20th C) American
$900   £600   Summer (127x102cm-50x40in) 17-May-94 Christie's, East, New York #508

SCHWARTZ, Manfred (1909-1970) American
$800   £548   Still life with flowers (76x91cm-30x36in) s. 19-Feb-94 Young Fine Arts Auctions,
                      Maine #179/R

SCHWARTZ, Robert (20th C) American
$1900 *£1203*   *Soprano Abbandonato (39x33cm-15x13in) s.d.1979 W/C triptych. 25-Oct-92
                      Butterfield & Butterfield, San Francisco #2384/R*

SCHWARTZ, William S (1896-1977) American
$3000   £2000   My friend the engineer (76x60cm-30x24in) s. s.i.stretcher. 23-May-94 Christie's,
                      East, New York #248/R
$3500   £2318   Portrait of an Afro American man (51x42cm-20x17in) s. i.d.1925verso. 15-Jun-94
                      Butterfield & Butterfield, San Francisco #4472/R
$4500   £3000   Day dreams (24x28cm-9x11in) s. canvas on masonite painted 1926. 23-May-94
                      Christie's, East, New York #250/R
$7000   £4046   Solitude (102x76cm-40x30in) s. s.i.d.1936. 25-Sep-92 Sotheby's Arcade, New York
                      #344/R
$12000   £8000   Making a lithograph (76x102cm-30x40in) s. 16-Mar-94 Christie's, New York #123/R
$16000   £10667   A countryside (71x76cm-28x30in) s. s.i.d.1929 verso. 17-Mar-94 Sotheby's, New
                      York #132/R
$900   *£588*   *Self portrait (25x23cm-10x9in) s.d.1926 pencil. 16-May-93 Hindman Galleries,
                      Chicago #15*
$1500 *£1000*   *Fisherman's cabins (38x53cm-15x21in) s. gouache two. 13-Mar-94 Hindman Galleries,
                      Chicago #834*

SCHWARTZKOPF, Earl (1888-?) American
$900   £592   Landscape with cabin (91x76cm-36x30in) s. 5-Jun-93 Louisiana Auction Exchange
                      #52/R

SCORDIA, Antonio (1918-) Central American
$1066   £720   Sequenza (81x100cm-32x39in) s.d.68 s.i.d.verso. 22-Nov-93 Christie's, Milan #59
                      (I.L 1800000)
$1488   £985   A solo (55x50cm-22x20in) s. s.i.d.68verso. 14-Jun-94 Finarte, Rome #216
                      (I.L 2400000)
$1492   £1001   Barca in secca (50x60cm-20x24in) s. s.i.d.1949verso. 25-Mar-93 Finarte, Rome
                      #130/R (I.L 2400000)
$2125   £1417   Natura morta (34x43cm-13x17in) s.d.42 oil masonite. 23-May-94 Christie's, Milan
                      #126 (I.L 3400000)
$2157   £1419   Finestra a Roma (80x100cm-31x39in) s.d.1952. 3-Jun-93 Finarte, Rome #90/R
                      (I.L 3200000)

SCOTT, Adam Sherriff (1887-1980) Canadian
$674   £440   Women at the bake oven, summer (46x61cm-18x24in) studio st.verso. 18-May-93
                      Joyner Fine Art, Toronto #177 (C.D 850)
$951   £622   Inuit woman (62x51cm-24x20in) s. 19-May-93 Sotheby's, Toronto #225/R (C.D 1200)
$3641   £2427   Lake in autumn (104x127cm-41x50in) s. 11-May-94 Sotheby's, Toronto #140/R
                      (C.D 5000)
$3823   £2549   Montreal (79x240cm-31x94in) s.i.d.1809 board. 11-May-94 Sotheby's, Toronto #200/R
                      (C.D 5250)
$4187   £2791   Gathering kelp, Lower St. Lawrence (74x102cm-29x40in) s. 11-May-94 Sotheby's,
                      Toronto #32/R (C.D 5750)
$13107   £8738   Snow scene, Laurentians (76x102cm-30x40in) s. 11-May-94 Sotheby's, Toronto #221/R
                      (C.D 18000)
$21845   £14563   Old time sugaring party (102x163cm-40x64in) s. 11-May-94 Sotheby's, Toronto #67/R
                      (C.D 30000)
$566   *£383*   *Eskimo hunter (75x60cm-30x24in) s. col.chk canvas. 23-Nov-93 Joyner Fine Art,
                      Toronto #334 (C.D 750)*

SCOTT, Frank Edwin (1862-1929) American
$850   £491   Grey Parisian day (36x27cm-14x11in) s. panel. 25-Sep-92 Sotheby's Arcade, New
                      York #279/R

SCOTT, Julian (1846-1901) American
$700   £467   Portrait of General George Thomas (76x63cm-30x25in) s.d.88. 23-May-94 Christie's,
                      East, New York #50/R
$1300   £878   On patrol a gamekeeper in a wood (61x45cm-24x18in) s.d.1882 d.verso. 5-Nov-93
                      Skinner, Bolton #54/R
$3000   £2000   A welcome pause (47x63cm-19x25in) s.d.1888. 23-May-94 Christie's, East, New York
                      #47/R
$3200   £2025   Major General William F.Smith and his Staff (30x51cm-12x20in) s.d.1882. 2-Dec-92
                      Christie's, East, New York #204/R

SCOTT, Louise (1936-) Canadian
$529   £357   A gentle hug (47x30cm-19x12in) s. pastel. 23-Nov-93 Fraser Pinneys, Quebec #475
                     (C.D 700)

SCOTT, Michael (20th C) American?
$1341   £900   Untitled no 16 (244x121cm-96x48in) acrylic on aluminium executed 1990. 21-Jun-93
                     Christie's, S. Kensington #174/R
$1500   £1007   Untitled (84x84cm-33x33in) s.d.90 versoenamel on aluminium two. 23-Feb-94
                     Christie's, East, New York #215/R
$800   £541   Untitled (244x121cm-96x48in) s.i.d.90verso enamel aluminium. 8-Nov-93 Christie's,
                     East, New York #48/R

SCOTTI, Ernesto Mariano (1901-1957) Argentinian
$3000   £1987   Desnudo (70x116cm-28x46in) painted 1939. 11-Nov-92 VerBo, Buenos Aires #98

SCULLY, Sean (1946-) American/Irish
$26000   £17568   Andoman (51x51cm-20x20in) s.i.d.84verso linen. 10-Nov-93 Christie's, New York
                     #231/R
$50000   £33113   Once over (152x152cm-60x60in) s.d.1986 verso s.stretcher. 18-Nov-92 Sotheby's,
                     New York #261/R
$55000   £36913   In the sun (183x152cm-72x60in) s.i.d.83verso two panels. 3-May-94 Christie's, New
                     York #75/R
$55000   £36424   After life (188x183cm-74x72in) s.d.4.89verso three attached canvases. 19-Nov-92
                     Christie's, New York #390/R
$70000   £45752   Sound (244x244cm-96x96in) s.d.87 verso linen four panels. 3-May-93 Sotheby's, New
                     York #77/R
$70000   £46980   Any questions (260x325cm-102x128in) s.i.d.Dec.1984verso seven attached canvases.
                     4-May-94 Christie's, New York #363/R
$90000   £59603   Now (244x274cm-96x108in) s.i.d.1987verso. 17-Nov-92 Sotheby's, New York #61/R
$95000   £62092   Counting (166x201cm-65x79in) linen two attached canvases painted 1988. 4-May-93
                     Christie's, New York #51/R
$6820   £4577   Sans titre (56x76cm-22x30in) s.d.1984 mixed media. 4-May-94 Watine-Arnault, Paris
                     #74/R (F.FR 39000)
$7000   £4698   8.21.89 no 1 (56x76cm-22x30in) s.i.d.8.21.89 pastel. 5-May-94 Sotheby's, New York
                     #251/R
$8000   £4706   Untitled (77x59cm-30x23in) s.d.84 chl chk. 6-Oct-92 Sotheby's, New York #146/R
$19000   £11176   Untitled (122x153cm-48x60in) s.d.7.9.90 pastel. 6-Oct-92 Sotheby's, New York #156
                     a/R
$19000   £12583   Untitled (74x105cm-29x41in) s.d.11.19.89 col.chk. 19-Nov-92 Christie's, New York
                     #253/R

SEADE, Felipe (1912-1969) South American
$650   £428   Cabeza de campesina (25x44cm-10x17in) s.d.46 sacking. 31-May-93 Gomensoro,
                     Montevideo #20

SEARS, Olga (?) American
$1800   £1176   Boston rooftops (51x41cm-20x16in) s. 18-Sep-93 James Bakker, Cambridge #56/R

SEAVEY, George W (1841-1916) American
$1000   £685   Still life with Mums (66x46cm-26x18in) s. 10-Feb-94 Skinner, Bolton #224
$1184   £800   Still life with pink, yellow and red roses (46x35cm-18x14in) s. 20-Oct-93
                     Sotheby's, London #6/R

SEBOROVSKI, Carole (20th C) American?
$5750   £3859   Removed (61x99cm-24x39in) chl paper collage executed 1987. 5-May-94 Sotheby's,
                     New York #250/R

SEERY, John (1941-) American
$650   £425   Snow in summer (81x170cm-32x67in) s.d.1985verso. 16-May-93 Hindman Galleries,
                     Chicago #37
$700   £458   Summer afternoon (117x145cm-46x57in) s.i.d.1990verso acrylic double-sided.
                     16-May-93 Hindman Galleries, Chicago #38
$800   £537   Snow in summer (81x170cm-32x67in) s.d.verso. 24-Jun-93 Boos Gallery, Michigan
                     #598

SEGAL, George (1924-) American
$2750   £1910   Untitled (46x30cm-18x12in) s.d.64 pastel. 23-Feb-93 Sotheby's, New York #279/R
$4656   £3125   Fragment of female nude seen from behind (63x48cm-25x19in) s.d.72 pastel.
                     23-Jun-93 Galerie Kornfeld, Berne #780 (S.FR 7000)
$6120   £4000   Untitled (45x30cm-18x12in) s.d.65 col.chk. 15-May-93 Aucktionhaus Burkard, Luzern
                     #122/R (S.FR 9000)

SEGAR, Elzie Crisler (1894-1938) American
$1500   £962   Art reacts to life (58x50cm-23x20in) s. 9-Dec-92 Butterfield & Butterfield, San
                     Francisco #3948/R

SEGUI, Antonio (1934-) Argentinian
$3485   £2339   L'homme a la cravate (50x64cm-20x25in) s. canvasboard. 25-Mar-94 Francis Briest,
                     Paris #326/R (F.FR 20000)
$7000   £4730   Alegria-Alegria (65x81cm-26x32in) s. s.i.verso. 23-Nov-93 Christie's, New York
                     #199/R
$7000   £4636   The Christ Child Detail (81x100cm-32x39in) 23-Nov-92 Sotheby's, New York #234/R
$8766   £5963   Sans titre (60x73cm-24x29in) s.d.90. 8-Jul-93 Cornette de St.Cyr, Paris #86/R
                     (F.FR 52000)

SEGUI, Antonio (1934-) Argentinian-cont.

$9813	£6542	Idas y vuetas (100x81cm-39x32in) s.i.d.10.11.83verso. 2-Jun-94 Christian de Quay, Paris #84/R (F.FR 56000)
$17199	£11543	An El Cabezow (200x200cm-79x79in) s.d.1985. 23-Mar-93 Cornette de St.Cyr, Paris #104/R (F.FR 95000)
$21203	£14042	La tour de la defense (195x195cm-77x77in) s.i.d.81verso. 26-Nov-92 Francis Briest, Paris #52/R (F.FR 115000)
$1047	£703	Sans titre (49x64cm-19x25in) s.i.d.63 collage Indian ink dr. 25-Jun-93 Francis Briest, Paris #248 (F.FR 6000)
$1103	£726	Composition (21x15cm-8x6in) s.d.84 mixed media. 8-Jun-93 Karl & Faber, Munich #1308 (DM 1800)
$1171	£802	Les dessous (49x64cm-19x25in) s. pencil. 10-Feb-94 Cornette de St.Cyr, Paris #40 (F.FR 7000)
$1268	£851	Sans titre (62x48cm-24x19in) s.d.67 pencil chl dr. 2-Dec-93 Francis Briest, Paris #292 (F.FR 7500)
$1590	£1060	Untitled (48x63cm-19x25in) s.i.d.1963 Indian ink pen brush. 3-Jun-94 Lempertz, Cologne #940/R (DM 2650)
$1760	£1181	Negro fondo gris (48x64cm-19x25in) s.d.63 gouache pastel. 25-Mar-94 Millon & Robert, Paris #82/R (F.FR 10100)
$3310	£2163	Le visiteur (56x76cm-22x30in) s.d.76 pastel. 21-Dec-92 Jean Louis Picard, Paris #190/R (F.FR 18000)
$3383	£2270	Sans titre (65x50cm-26x20in) s.d.1968 mixed media paper laid on canvas. 5-Dec-93 Perrin, Versailles #69/R (F.FR 20000)
$3971	£2436	Sans titre (77x57cm-30x22in) s. d.1966verso W/C pastel paper laid on canvas. 18-Oct-92 Catherine Charbonneaux, Paris #14 (F.FR 20000)
$4928	£3263	Personnage dans un paysage (65x81cm-26x32in) s.d.1975 col ink canvas. 28-Sep-93 Cornette de St.Cyr, Paris #111/R (F.FR 28000)
$6000	£3922	Elefante (92x73cm-36x29in) s.d.79 chl pastel linen. 17-May-93 Christie's, New York #251/R
$6500	£4333	Untitled (64x50cm-25x20in) s.d.65 mixed media board. 18-May-94 Christie's, New York #297/R
$6673	£4361	Le general (65x50cm-26x20in) s.d.63verso mixed media paper laid down canvas. 27-Oct-92 Cornette de St.Cyr, Paris #27/R (F.FR 35500)
$13000	£8784	De tikal con sol (120x180cm-47x71in) s.d.62 s.i.verso paper oil paper collage canvas. 23-Nov-93 Christie's, New York #180/R
$40000	£26667	Sin titulo (100x100cm-39x39in) s. mixed media collage canvas painted 1989. 18-May-94 Christie's, New York #118/R

SEIDENECK, George (1885-?) American

$2000	£1325	Landscape at dusk (64x77cm-25x30in) s. 20-Sep-93 Butterfield & Butterfield, Los Angeles #81/R

SEITZ, John (19th C) American

$1000	£667	Two spread-wing doves holding a garland (15x20cm-6x8in) s.with i.d.1822 W/C ink. 10-Jun-94 Christie's, New York #510/R

SEJOURNE, Bernard (1945-) Haitian

$7000	£4698	Untitled (98x85cm-39x33in) s.d.92 masonite. 7-Jan-94 Gary Nader, Miami #106/R

SEKULA, Sonja (1918-1963) American

$1292	£844	Untitled (17x11cm-7x4in) s.d.48. 15-May-93 Aucktionhaus Burkard, Luzern #177/R (S.FR 1900)
$522	£350	Untitled (15x12cm-6x5in) s.d.1958 collage. 13-Oct-93 Germann, Zurich #177 (S.FR 750)
$557	£374	Call it influence..I can't (17x12cm-7x5in) mono.i.d.1955 Indian ink W/C dr. 13-Oct-93 Germann, Zurich #564 (S.FR 800)
$898	£611	Music - less (11x16cm-4x6in) s.i.d.61 tempera paper collage. 20-Nov-93 Aucktionhaus Burkard, Luzern #314/R (S.FR 1350)
$975	£654	November and a day (14x20cm-6x8in) s.i.d.1951 Indian ink dr. 13-Oct-93 Germann, Zurich #565 (S.FR 1400)
$1904	£1244	Untitled (27x40cm-11x16in) s.d.X.61 gouache paper collage. 15-May-93 Aucktionhaus Burkard, Luzern #176/R (S.FR 2800)

SELBY, Joe (1893-1960) American

$950	£638	Friendship (30x41cm-12x16in) s. 5-Mar-94 Louisiana Auction Exchange #162/R

SELDEN, Roger (1945-) American

$2345	£1553	La tavola nera (100x150cm-39x59in) s.d.1983verso oil collage canvas. 9-Nov-92 Finarte, Milan #213/R (I.L 3200000)

SELIGER, Charles (1926-) American

$1300	£872	Persian night (28x20cm-11x8in) s.d.77 acrylic linen. 24-Feb-94 Sotheby's Arcade, New York #376/R

SELIGMANN, Kurt (1900-1962) American/Swiss

$3800	£2550	Moon flower (61x51cm-24x20in) s.d.58 i.verso. 23-Feb-94 Christie's, East, New York #165/R
$3800	£2533	L'ecrivain au chapeau rouge (81x71cm-32x28in) 9-May-94 Christie's, East, New York #176/R
$4800	£3221	Abstract composition (88x76cm-35x30in) 23-Feb-94 Christie's, East, New York #147/R
$6652	£4525	Siblings (82x61cm-32x24in) s.d.1925. 19-Nov-93 Galerie Koller, Zurich #3129 (S.FR 10000)
$17000	£11333	Apparition (76x56cm-30x22in) s.d.44 i.stretcher. 11-May-94 Christie's, New York #275/R

SELIGMANN, Kurt (1900-1962) American/Swiss-cont.

$19000	£12838	Untitled (101x101cm-40x40in) s.d.61. 3-Nov-93 Christie's, New York #275/R
$20000	£13514	Saraband (122x188cm-48x74in) s.d.49 s.d.1949 verso. 3-Nov-93 Christie's, New York #273/R
$24000	£16216	Carnival (101x131cm-40x52in) s.d.50 s.d.1950 verso. 3-Nov-93 Christie's, New York #274/R
$26887	£17925	Composition - Aquarium (65x54cm-26x21in) s.i.verso panel. 2-Jun-94 Sotheby's, Zurich #141/R (S.FR 38000)
$27000	£17647	Noctambulation (112x84cm-44x33in) s.d.1942 masonite. 12-May-93 Sotheby's, New York #329/R
$28000	£18667	Le down (92x72cm-36x28in) s.d.1931verso panel. 11-May-94 Christie's, New York #229/R
$35000	£23649	Ne vous en deplaise (92x72cm-36x28in) s.i.d.1929 panel. 3-Nov-93 Christie's, New York #253/R
$38000	£25676	Leda II (82x105cm-32x41in) s.d.1933 s.i.d.1933 verso panel. 3-Nov-93 Christie's, New York #259/R
$39154	£26636	The Vanity of the Ancestors (121x148cm-48x58in) i.d.1940verso pavatex. 11-Apr-94 Christie's, Zurich #127/R (S.FR 57000)
$41215	£28037	Slow Motion (119x99cm-47x39in) s. painted 1955. 11-Apr-94 Christie's, Zurich #126/R (S.FR 60000)
$50000	£33113	Exorcist (121x149cm-48x59in) s.d.54-58. 11-Nov-92 Sotheby's, New York #229/R
$52000	£35135	Acteon (89x76cm-35x30in) s.d.44. 3-Nov-93 Christie's, New York #269/R
$80000	£54054	Game of Chance No.2 (109x104cm-43x41in) s.d.1949. 3-Nov-93 Christie's, New York #268/R
$85000	£57432	Initiation (71x91cm-28x36in) s.d.1946. 3-Nov-93 Christie's, New York #272/R
$800	£541	Figure au fond rose (56x39cm-22x15in) W/C ink. 2-Nov-93 Christie's, East, New York #90/R
$950	£638	L'Ecrivain (74x58cm-29x23in) s.d.54 wax crayon. 23-Feb-94 Christie's, East, New York #136/R
$1100	£738	La machine (32x21cm-13x8in) s. pen Indian ink. 23-Feb-94 Christie's, East, New York #168/R
$1463	£982	Un corsaire (41x53cm-16x21in) W/C painted c.1940. 23-Jun-93 Galerie Kornfeld, Berne #781 (S.FR 2200)
$1800	£1216	Figure in a landscape (57x72cm-22x28in) Indian ink over pencil. 2-Nov-93 Christie's, East, New York #167/R
$2200	£1486	Figure (56x45cm-22x18in) Indian ink over pencil. 2-Nov-93 Christie's, East, New York #168/R
$3600	£2400	Dancers (58x69cm-23x27in) s.d.1950 gouache W/C pen black ink. 9-May-94 Christie's, East, New York #172/R
$4500	£3020	Danse (69x101cm-27x40in) s.d.1959 W/C gouache pen. 23-Feb-94 Christie's, East, New York #164/R
$13738	£9346	The meeting point of the elements (71x87cm-28x34in) oil col ink glass painted 1939. 11-Apr-94 Christie's, Zurich #125/R (S.FR 20000)
$15000	£10135	L'abysse (33x66cm-13x26in) s.d.1940 pen brush col.ink glass. 3-Nov-93 Christie's, New York #265/R
$16000	£10811	La colonne (75x60cm-30x24in) s.d.1940 pen brush col.ink glass. 3-Nov-93 Christie's, New York #266/R
$35000	£23649	Le cocon (79x71cm-31x28in) s.d.1941 oil pen brush col.ink glass. 3-Nov-93 Christie's, New York #262/R
$38000	£25676	La recontre des elements (66x81cm-26x32in) s.d.1940 oil pen brush col.ink glass. 3-Nov-93 Christie's, New York #261/R

SELINGER, Jean Paul (1850-1909) American

$4750	£3188	Portrait of a young woman (18x14cm-7x6in) s.d.1879 panel. 4-Mar-94 Skinner, Bolton #220/R

SELLERS, Anna (1824-1905) American

$1500	£1020	Still life with fruit (30x46cm-12x18in) s.d.1894 board. 14-Apr-94 Freeman Fine Arts, Philadelphia #968

SELLIN, Herbert Otto (1943-) Canadian

$1055	£718	Roche Isles Lake (122x183cm-48x72in) s.d.1984. 15-Nov-93 Hodgins, Calgary #22/R (C.D 1400)

SELTZER, Olaf C (1877-1957) American

$22000	£14765	Three Indians on horseback (36x51cm-14x20in) s. 2-Dec-93 Sotheby's, New York #33 c
$40000	£26667	Warriors leaving camp (52x76cm-20x30in) s. 26-May-94 Christie's, New York #54/R
$4464	£3100	Indian camp near Judith Basin (15x23cm-6x9in) s. W/C. 1-Mar-93 Robin Fenner, Tavistock #149
$5000	£3333	The Lookout (23x15cm-9x6in) s. W/C board. 17-Mar-94 Sotheby's, New York #72/R
$6500	£4167	Portrait of Plains Indian (35x28cm-14x11in) s.d.1906 gouache pencil. 26-May-93 Christie's, New York #108/R
$10000	£6410	Indian brave (31x23cm-12x9in) s. gouache pencil. 26-May-93 Christie's, New York #94/R

SENAT, Prosper L (1852-1925) American

$700	£467	Fishing boats (61x94cm-24x37in) s.i.d.1900 W/C. 23-May-94 Hindman Galleries, Chicago #190
$1000	£671	Bermuda street scene (43x28cm-17x11in) s. W/C. 5-Aug-93 Eldred, Massachusetts #674/R
$1000	£671	Coastal village (91x58cm-36x23in) s.i. W/C. 6-Dec-93 Grogan, Massachussetts #454
$1000	£667	Entrance to the Alhambra (61x41cm-24x16in) s.i.d.99 W/C. 23-May-94 Hindman Galleries, Chicago #203

SENATUS, Jean Louis (20th C) South American
$1163 £770 Silhouette dans l'ile (40x30cm-16x12in) s.d.90. 13-Jun-94 Rogeon, Paris #137/R (F.FR 6500)

SEOANE, Luis (1910-1979) Argentinian
$9000 £5882 De Espaldas al Mar (74x92cm-29x36in) s.d.76 i.stretcher. 17-May-93 Christie's, New York #210/R
$660 £440 Los suenos (36x24cm-14x9in) s.d.44 ink dr. 23-May-94 Duran, Madrid #46/R (S.P 90000)
$677 £455 Julia o Nueva Eloisa (35x24cm-14x9in) s. ink dr. 20-Dec-93 Ansorena, Madrid #2/R (S.P 95000)
$725 £487 Joven escribiendo (35x24cm-14x9in) s. ink dr. 21-Mar-94 Duran, Madrid #29/R (S.P 100000)
$784 £526 Julio o la Nueva Eloisa (36x25cm-14x10in) s. ink dr. 20-Dec-93 Ansorena, Madrid #1/R (S.P 110000)
$928 £631 Figuras (35x23cm-14x9in) s.d.45 W/C ink dr. 12-Apr-94 Ansorena, Madrid #148/R (S.P 130000)
$1088 £730 Mario el Epicureo (36x24cm-14x9in) s.d.45 ink W/C dr. 21-Mar-94 Duran, Madrid #30/R (S.P 150000)

SEPESHY, Zoltan L (1898-1974) American
$2250 £1596 Wake of steamer (58x69cm-23x27in) s. tempera board. 12-Feb-93 Du Mouchelle, Detroit #2016/R
$2250 £1596 Mountain landscape with village and cart (64x76cm-25x30in) s. 12-Feb-93 Du Mouchelle, Detroit #2009/R
$5000 £2924 In the taos desert (91x107cm-36x42in) s.d.1926 i. 18-Sep-92 Du Mouchelle, Detroit #2041/R
$700 £458 Indians at water (13x20cm-5x8in) s. W/C. 14-May-93 Du Mouchelle, Detroit #2005
$800 £567 Landscape dane (38x48cm-15x19in) s. W/C. 12-Feb-93 Du Mouchelle, Detroit #2015
$900 £584 Visitors to yesterday (84x114cm-33x45in) s. d.33-45verso gouache oil masonite. 9-Sep-93 Sotheby's Arcade, New York #219/R
$1500 £962 Idle hours (89x97cm-35x38in) pastel canvas. 11-Dec-92 Du Mouchelle, Detroit #1301/R

SERL, Jon (1894-?) American
$1200 £795 Two faces (46x36cm-18x14in) s. 21-Nov-92 Litchfield Auction Gallery #3

SERNA, Antonio (20th C) Mexican
$890 £601 Sin titulo (71x61cm-28x24in) s.d.73verso acrylic sold with postcard. 27-Apr-94 Louis Morton, Mexico #637/R (M.P 3000)
$4745 £3206 Peregrinaje (60x120cm-24x47in) s.d.1962. 27-Apr-94 Louis Morton, Mexico #603 (M.P 16000)

SERPA, Fernando Claudio (fl.1880s) Latin American
$4500 £3000 Bodegon de frutas (48x63cm-19x25in) s.d.Dcbre.3.81stretcher. 18-May-94 Sotheby's, New York #173/R
$5000 £3333 Bodegon de frutas (47x64cm-19x25in) s.d.Dcbre d3.81stretcher. 18-May-94 Sotheby's, New York #172/R

SERRA, Richard (1939-) American
$19000 £13194 Elevator (95x127cm-37x50in) painted 1980 black oilstick. 24-Feb-93 Christie's, New York #92/R
$21000 £14189 Parallelogram (249x151cm-98x59in) paintstick executed 1974. 11-Nov-93 Sotheby's, New York #125/R
$6129 £4032 Clara, Clara II (92x183cm-36x72in) s.i.d.1985verso oil chk on screen print. 12-Jun-93 Hauswedell & Nolte, Hamburg #388/R (DM 10000)
$6258 £4200 Almeda black (182x182cm-72x72in) s.d.1981 i.verso paintstick steel sheet. 24-Mar-93 Sotheby's, London #346/R
$12000 £8108 Horizontal reaching to the floor (104x518cm-41x204in) paintstick aluminium. 11-Nov-93 Sotheby's, New York #146/R
$30000 £19868 Left corner square to floor (204x204cm-80x80in) paintstick linen executed 1979. 18-Nov-92 Sotheby's, New York #239 b/R
$34000 £20000 Untitled (84x124cm-33x49in) ink rolled Arches paper 14 sheets executed 1973. 6-Oct-92 Sotheby's, New York #113/R

SERRANO, Manuel (1917-1948) Mexican
$70000 £46667 Coleando en campo abierto (42x51cm-17x20in) s. painted c.1870. 17-May-94 Sotheby's, New York #9/R
$76408 £48980 Los Tahures (54x44cm-21x17in) s. 29-Apr-93 Louis Morton, Mexico #91 (M.P 240000)

SESSIONS, James (1882-1962) American
$600 £397 Farm jeeps pulling harvest wwagons (58x84cm-23x33in) s. W/C. 13-Nov-92 Du Mouchelle, Detroit #2036
$850 £567 Tall ship at sea (53x71cm-21x28in) s.d.38 W/C. 13-Mar-94 Hindman Galleries, Chicago #820
$900 £604 High country (48x38cm-19x15in) s. W/C. 28-Mar-93 James Bakker, Cambridge #192
$900 £612 Driving home for Glouster (43x58cm-17x23in) s.d.37 W/C. 20-Nov-93 Dargate Auction Galleries, Pittsburgh #3
$1000 £654 Walking on the beach (36x46cm-14x18in) s. W/C. 16-May-93 Hindman Galleries, Chicago #114
$1200 £759 Drying the sails (60x70cm-24x28in) s. W/C. 2-Dec-92 Christie's, East, New York #280
$1300 £861 Boats in harbour (33x46cm-13x18in) s.d.35 W/C. 28-Sep-93 John Moran, Pasadena #332

SETTERBERG, Carl (1897-?) American
$550 £367 Woman sewing (51x61cm-20x24in) s. canvasboard. 15-Mar-94 John Moran, Pasadena #172

SEUSS, Dr (20th C) American
$750 £481 Animation (28x20cm-11x8in) s. celluloid painting. 11-Dec-92 Du Mouchelle, Detroit #1219/R
$800 £513 Animation (30x20cm-12x8in) s. celluloid painting. 11-Dec-92 Du Mouchelle, Detroit #1218/R

SEVIER, Gerald Leslie (?) Canadian
$717 £485 Landscape with lake and mountains (90x125cm-35x49in) s. acrylic. 23-Nov-93 Joyner Fine Art, Toronto #238 (C.D 950)

SEWELL, Robert (1860-1924) American
$850 £450 Rocky coast (51x86cm-20x34in) s. 11-Sep-92 Skinner, Bolton #242/R
$1800 £1200 Procession of the Bacchantes (48x142cm-19x56in) s.d.1903. 26-Aug-93 Skinner, Bolton #104
$8500 £5743 Psyche's wanderings (81x163cm-32x64in) s.d.1901 arched top. 4-Nov-93 Sloan, North Bethesda #2544/R

SEXTON, Frederick Lester (1889-?) American
$1200 £805 Vacations days (51x62cm-20x24in) s.d.32. 6-May-94 Skinner, Bolton #103/R
$1200 £811 Winter in New England (61x91cm-24x36in) s. 31-Mar-94 Sotheby's Arcade, New York #212/R

SEYFFERT, Leopold Gould (1887-1956) American
$4000 £2632 Mrs Henry Clews (208x102cm-82x40in) mono. 31-Mar-93 Sotheby's Arcade, New York #127/R

SHADBOLT, Jack (1909-) Canadian
$1812 £1208 Water edge near Collioure (33x41cm-13x16in) init.i.d.1961 verso board. 6-Jun-94 Waddingtons, Toronto #1288/R (C.D 2500)
$3269 £2165 Valley behind Patras (33x41cm-13x16in) init. i.d.1961verso board. 18-Nov-92 Sotheby's, Toronto #263/R (C.D 4200)
$3896 £2450 Bird Island (102x64cm-40x25in) d.1969 acrylic paper. 19-Apr-93 Lunds, Victoria #9 (C.D 4900)
$4139 £2778 Memory of Delos no.5 (110x61cm-43x24in) s.d.60 i.verso. 29-Nov-93 Ritchie, Toronto #194/R (C.D 5500)
$5386 £3409 Red palms (35x28cm-14x11in) s.d.1957. 21-Oct-92 Maynards, Vancouver #146 (C.D 6750)
$6616 £4381 Abstract (120x120cm-47x47in) s.d.69 acrylic board. 24-Nov-92 Joyner Fine Art, Toronto #128/R (C.D 8500)
$9298 £6283 Still life on a Chinese table (71x122cm-28x48in) s. st.sig.i.d.1959verso. 3-Nov-93 Sotheby's, Toronto #222/R (C.D 12000)
$861 £582 Poem sketches (30x23cm-12x9in) d.68 ink dr pair. 14-Jun-93 Lunds, Victoria #10 (C.D 1100)
$901 £608 Untitled shapes in brown and white (38x28cm-15x11in) W/C. 14-Jun-93 Lunds, Victoria #7 (C.D 1150)
$1096 £741 Festive costumes (23x28cm-9x11in) d.78 collage. 14-Jun-93 Lunds, Victoria #9 (C.D 1400)
$1227 £829 Script clusters on a pink ground (71x122cm-28x48in) mixed media executed c.1960. 30-Mar-94 Maynards, Vancouver #95 (C.D 1700)
$1550 £1047 Still life with squash (77x56cm-30x22in) s.d.60 i.verso mixed media. 3-Nov-93 Sotheby's, Toronto #319/R (C.D 2000)
$2234 £1414 Still life with lanterns (23x18cm-9x7in) s.d.1941 carbon pencil. 21-Oct-92 Maynards, Vancouver #191 (C.D 2800)
$2257 £1495 Abstract collage (66x71cm-26x28in) s. s.i.d.1966verso mixed media board. 16-Nov-92 Hodgins, Calgary #121/R (C.D 2900)
$2428 £1640 Untitled, soldiers resting (41x51cm-16x20in) d.44 pencil sketch. 14-Jun-93 Lunds, Victoria #8 (C.D 3100)
$2634 £1768 Dock view with boats and sailing vessels (80x57cm-31x22in) s.d.62 ink W/C wove paper on panel. 29-Nov-93 Ritchie, Toronto #204/R (C.D 3500)
$3610 £2439 Abstract composition (48x61cm-19x24in) s.d.1962 mixed media. 30-Mar-94 Maynards, Vancouver #109 (C.D 5000)
$4770 £3000 Skeleton bird (43x36cm-17x14in) d.1948 W/C. 19-Apr-93 Lunds, Victoria #11 (C.D 6000)
$5963 £3750 Birds eye view (56x38cm-22x15in) d.1947 W/C. 19-Apr-93 Lunds, Victoria #10 (C.D 7500)

SHAFER, Catharine (19th C) American
$600 £411 Two gentlemen on horseback (10x13cm-4x5in) i.verso pen W/C. 12-Feb-94 Boos Gallery, Michigan #541/R
$1600 £1096 A couple greeting a gentleman with parrots and a dog in the background (10x15cm-4x6in) i.verso pen W/C. 12-Feb-94 Boos Gallery, Michigan #542/R

SHAHN, Ben (1898-1969) American
$2500 £1645 Still life with flowers and fruit (27x33cm-11x13in) s. paper. 31-Mar-93 Sotheby's Arcade, New York #341/R
$8000 £4624 Picnic, Prospect Park (61x81cm-24x32in) s. 23-Sep-92 Christie's, New York #260/R
$1000 £649 Portrait of man (30x24cm-12x9in) s. W/C. 9-Sep-93 Sotheby's Arcade, New York #376/R
$1200 £759 Figures by river (43x63cm-17x25in) s. W/C. 2-Dec-92 Christie's, East, New York #272/R

SHAHN, Ben (1898-1969) American-cont.
$1200	£789	Landscape with houses and trees (27x34cm-11x13in) s. W/C. 31-Mar-93 Sotheby's Arcade, New York #340/R
$1900	£1250	House in woods (44x58cm-17x23in) s. w/C. 31-Mar-93 Sotheby's Arcade, New York #338/R
$3100	£2067	Portrait of Emile Zola (38x28cm-15x11in) s. gouache. 24-Aug-93 Hart Gallery, Houston #5
$3250	£2196	Oppenheimer (44x29cm-17x11in) s. Indian ink executed 1955 double-sided. 31-Mar-94 Sotheby's Arcade, New York #354/R
$12000	£7595	Brick factory with stacks (74x50cm-29x20in) s. gouache. 3-Dec-92 Sotheby's, New York #63/R
$18000	£12000	The Bowery Clothing Store (25x29cm-10x11in) s. gouache. 25-May-94 Sotheby's, New York #142/R

SHAPIRO, Joel (1941-) American
$1000	£662	Untitled (28cm-11in circular) s.d.67-68verso acrylic. 17-Nov-92 Christie's, East, New York #220/R
$6000	£4054	Untitled (64x96cm-25x38in) chl executed c.1977. 11-Nov-93 Sotheby's, New York #140/R
$8500	£5000	Untitled (52x41cm-20x16in) chl chk executed 1990. 6-Oct-92 Sotheby's, New York #143/R

SHAPIRO, Shmuel (1924-1985) American
$692	£438	Untitled (84x56cm-33x22in) s.d.1968 mixed media. 21-Oct-92 Galerie Dobiaschofsky, Bern #1224 (S.FR 950)

SHAPLEIGH, Frank Henry (1842-1906) American
$650	£446	The City gate, St. Augustine (30x20cm-12x8in) s.d.1890 s.i.verso board. 10-Feb-94 Skinner, Bolton #164
$800	£537	European landscape with church, cattle and river (43x81cm-17x32in) s. 5-Aug-93 Eldred, Massachusetts #813/R
$900	£604	Kenilworth Castle (56x86cm-22x34in) s. sold with slide of artist. 5-Aug-93 Eldred, Massachusetts #814/R
$1400	£952	St Sulpice, Lake Geneva (11x25cm-4x10in) s. s.i.verso. 10-Jul-93 Young Fine Arts Auctions, Maine #288/R
$1900	£1005	Road to the Marshes, Barnstable (25x41cm-10x16in) s.d.1878. 11-Sep-92 Skinner, Bolton #187/R
$2000	£1351	Lake Thun from Spiez, Switzerland (76x122cm-30x48in) s.d.1875 s.i.verso. 23-Oct-93 Skinner, Bolton #295 a
$2970	£1941	Conway Valley from Mt Willard (53x91cm-21x36in) s.d.1877 s.verso. 14-May-93 Skinner, Bolton #32/R
$5000	£3356	In Charlotte Street, St. Augustine, Florida (36x51cm-14x20in) s.d.1887 s.i.verso. 6-Dec-93 Grogan, Massachussetts #437/R
$1700	£1104	Wooded landscape (47x84cm-19x33in) init.d.78 gouache board. 9-Sep-93 Sotheby's Arcade, New York #28 a

SHARE, Henry Pruett (1853-1905) American
$700	£458	Pastoral scene (28x36cm-11x14in) s. 22-May-93 Weschler, Washington #95

SHARP, Joseph Henry (1859-1953) American
$875	£612	Sunset over the marshes (20x33cm-8x13in) s. panel. 11-Mar-93 Mystic Fine Arts, Connecticut #188/R
$2000	£1176	Taos, New Mexico landscape (41x51cm-16x20in) s. 11-Oct-92 Litchfield Auction Gallery #183
$3000	£1923	Bright Angel Creek, Grand Canyon, Arizona (51x41cm-20x16in) s. 9-Dec-92 Butterfield & Butterfield, San Francisco #3976/R
$3500	£2244	Sand dunes near Laguna, New Mexico (30x46cm-12x18in) s. 9-Dec-92 Butterfield & Butterfield, San Francisco #3968/R
$4000	£2564	Waimanalo Bay, Honolulu (41x51cm-16x20in) s. 9-Dec-92 Butterfield & Butterfield, San Francisco #3966/R
$4500	£2961	Valley landscape (20x25cm-8x10in) s. canvas on board. 13-Jun-93 Butterfield & Butterfield, San Francisco #3214/R
$7500	£5034	Taos burial scene (30x41cm-12x16in) board. 4-Dec-93 Louisiana Auction Exchange #123/R
$9500	£6333	Grand Canyon (34x25cm-13x10in) s. painted 1950. 17-Mar-94 Sotheby's, New York #68/R
$11000	£7051	Winter afternoon (51x76cm-20x30in) s. 27-May-93 Sotheby's, New York #236/R
$12000	£7595	Crow Camp (38x50cm-15x20in) init. 3-Dec-92 Sotheby's, New York #74/R
$12000	£8000	Stretching the hide (27x35cm-11x14in) s. painted c.1894-95. 17-Mar-94 Sotheby's, New York #67/R
$12000	£7595	Floral still life (63x76cm-25x30in) s. 3-Dec-92 Sotheby's, New York #69/R
$15000	£10067	Bear goes to the otter ground (41x30cm-16x12in) s.d.1915 i.d.verso. 2-Dec-93 Sotheby's, New York #33 b
$16000	£10256	Desert, Palm Springs, California (41x51cm-16x20in) s. board painted 1923. 27-May-93 Sotheby's, New York #234/R
$17000	£11333	Eagle Star (20x15cm-8x6in) s. i.verso panel painted c.1906. 17-Mar-94 Sotheby's, New York #75/R
$21000	£13907	Aspens at Twining (91x76cm-36x30in) s. 23-Sep-93 Sotheby's, New York #94/R
$21000	£13462	Indian encampment (61x91cm-24x36in) s. canvas on board. 13-Dec-92 Hindman Galleries, Chicago #35/R
$22000	£14103	Palm springs, California (41x51cm-16x20in) s. board painted c.1923. 27-May-93 Sotheby's, New York #235/R
$27000	£17881	Spring, the desert and Mt San Jacinto at Palm Springs, California (40x51cm-16x20in) s. i.d.1938 verso masonite. 23-Sep-93 Sotheby's, New York #99/R

SHARP, Joseph Henry (1859-1953) American-cont.
$32500	£21667	Rabbit hunters in round-up (46x61cm-18x24in) s. s.i.verso painted 1943. 17-Mar-94 Sotheby's, New York #69/R
$33000	£22148	Early winter on Crow Reservation, Montana (44x65cm-17x26in) s. i.d.1908verso. 2-Dec-93 Sotheby's, New York #33 a
$37500	£25000	The Eagle Dance (41x62cm-16x24in) s. s.i.1925 verso. 17-Mar-94 Sotheby's, New York #70/R
$42500	£28523	Taos drummers (51x41cm-20x16in) s. i.stretcher. 2-Dec-93 Sotheby's, New York #40/R
$60000	£38462	Drummer in firelight (51x61cm-20x24in) s. 26-May-93 Christie's, New York #104/R
$65000	£43333	Taos Canyon (76x91cm-30x36in) s. 25-May-94 Sotheby's, New York #50/R
$70000	£44304	Indians returning to winter camp (51x76cm-20x30in) s. 4-Dec-92 Christie's, New York #262/R
$70000	£48951	Big medicine camp (46x66cm-18x26in) s. 11-Mar-93 Christie's, New York #117/R
$75000	£50000	Hunting Son in his teepee (63x76cm-25x30in) s. i.verso. 25-May-94 Sotheby's, New York #51/R
$1301	*£850*	*Temporary lodge (33x23cm-13x9in) s.i.verso W/C. 26-Oct-92 Robin Fenner, Tavistock #104*

SHARP, Louis H (1875-1946) American
$2700	£1765	Oriental garden in California hills (64x76cm-25x30in) s. 1-Nov-92 Hanzel Galleries, Chicago #12/R

SHARPE, David (20th C) American
$800	£541	Reclining nude (61x76cm-24x30in) s. acrylic. 31-Oct-93 Hindman Galleries, Chicago #776
$1300	£878	Easter (152x182cm-60x72in) s.i.d.3.26.78. 21-Apr-94 Butterfield & Butterfield, San Francisco #1166/R

SHARPLES, James (attrib) (1752-1811) American
$1500	£987	Gentleman seated before harbour. Lady seated in landscape (28x23cm-11x9in) board panel oval pair. 5-Jun-93 Skinner, Bolton #342/R

SHATTUCK, Aaron Draper (1832-1928) American
$1200	£811	Early autumn - Salmon Creek, Granby, Connecticut (27x44cm-11x17in) s. 31-Mar-94 Sotheby's Arcade, New York #109/R
$1250	£731	Milk cow (30x46cm-12x18in) academy board painted c.1856. 20-Sep-92 Litchfield Auction Gallery #156
$1300	£884	Edge of the woods (25x41cm-10x16in) s. 16-Apr-94 Young Fine Arts Auctions, Maine #226/R
$3500	£2448	Summer in the meadow with cows and sheep (46x76cm-18x30in) s.d.76. 12-Mar-93 Skinner, Bolton #172/R
$4250	£2457	White mountains, New Hampshire (27x47cm-11x19in) board. 24-Sep-92 Sotheby's, New York #12/R
$4500	£3041	Cows in pasture (25x46cm-10x18in) s.d.66. 4-Nov-93 Sloan, North Bethesda #2741/R
$6500	£4392	Landscape Farmington Valley (76x112cm-30x44in) s. 10-Aug-93 Stonington Fine Arts, Stonington #90 b

SHAVER, Nancy (1946-) American
$658	*£439*	*Stories in 5 pieces (53x222cm-21x87in) s.d.1988verso mixed media. 2-Jun-94 AB Stockholms Auktionsverk, Stockholm #7171/R (S.KR 5200)*

SHAW, Austin (19th C) American?
$800	£523	Portrait of woman (48x61cm-19x24in) s. 16-Apr-93 Du Mouchelle, Detroit #2150/R

SHAW, Charles Green (1892-1974) American
$750	£524	Today is soon ago (38x28cm-15x11in) s. board. 11-Mar-93 Mystic Fine Arts, Connecticut #244
$900	£600	Space dimension (102x127cm-40x50in) s.verso. 23-May-94 Hindman Galleries, Chicago #254/R
$1000	£658	Composition (58x51cm-23x20in) s. board. 13-Jun-93 Hindman Galleries, Chicago #224/R
$1000	£658	Composition (51x46cm-20x18in) s. board. 13-Jun-93 Hindman Galleries, Chicago #225/R
$1200	£811	Untitled (51x41cm-20x16in) s.d.1969 canvasboard. 31-Mar-94 Sotheby's Arcade, New York #480/R
$1300	£861	Up surge (137x183cm-54x72in) s. 19-Jun-94 Hindman Galleries, Chicago #732/R
$1500	£980	Bathers on beach (23x31cm-9x12in) s.verso canvasboard. 4-May-93 Christie's, East, New York #281/R
$4500	£2961	Abstraction (23x30cm-9x12in) s.d.1941 canvasboard. 31-Mar-93 Sotheby's Arcade, New York #452/R
$6500	£4545	Abstraction (71x61cm-28x24in) s. 10-Mar-93 Sotheby's, New York #169/R
$14000	£8092	Composition (51x41cm-20x16in) s.verso board. 25-Sep-92 Sotheby's Arcade, New York #495/R

SHAW, Frederick A (1855-1912) American
$850	£552	Great Boston Fire (25x41cm-10x16in) s.d.75. 16-Jan-93 Skinner, Bolton #144 c

SHAW, Jim (20th C) American
$2000	£1342	Esse (44x37cm-17x15in) painted 1990. 25-Feb-94 Sotheby's, New York #139 a/R
$2800	£1892	Bonne Idee, My Mirage Series (43x36cm-17x14in) painted 1987. 8-Nov-93 Christie's, East, New York #105/R
$2000	*£1325*	*Untitled (36x27cm-14x11in) graphite chk chl ink pair. 17-Nov-92 Christie's, East, New York #72/R*

SHEARER, Christopher H (1840-1926) American
$1200	£706	Deer by stream (56x91cm-22x36in) s.d.1894. 8-Oct-92 Freeman Fine Arts, Philadelphia #1016
$1900	£1242	Sunset along a river (71x97cm-28x38in) s. 7-Oct-93 Freeman Fine Arts, Philadelphia #900/R
$2000	£1342	Winter landscape with sunset (61x114cm-24x45in) s.d.1894. 2-Dec-93 Freeman Fine Arts, Philadelphia #805
$2400	£1600	Woodland path (91x137cm-36x54in) s.d.1898. 1-Jun-94 Doyle, New York #58

SHED, Charles D (1818-1893) American
$2500	£1582	Portrait of ship 'Affghan' under full sail (61x91cm-24x36in) 24-Oct-92 San Rafael Auction Galleries #175

SHEELER, Charles (1883-1965) American
$200000	£126582	California Industrial (63x84cm-25x33in) s.d.1957. 4-Dec-92 Christie's, New York #125/R
$10000	£5780	Yachting (17x28cm-7x11in) pencil crayon. 23-Sep-92 Christie's, New York #231/R
$10000	£6329	Rose (14x12cm-6x5in) s.d.1920 pencil paper laid down on board. 4-Dec-92 Christie's, New York #132/R

SHEETS, Millard (1907-1989) American
$4500	£2961	Fishing boats (39x46cm-15x18in) s.d.1926. 13-Jun-93 Butterfield & Butterfield, San Francisco #870/R
$6000	£3947	Dockworkers (51x56cm-20x22in) s.d.5-26 verso. 13-Jun-93 Butterfield & Butterfield, San Francisco #869/R
$7500	£5208	Bridge of Espalion, France (46x53cm-18x21in) s.d.1929 s.i.d.verso. 7-Mar-93 Butterfield & Butterfield, San Francisco #244/R
$650	*£417*	*Evening Ridge Route (104x56cm-41x22in) s. W/C. 24-May-93 Grogan, Massachussetts #375/R*
$1500	*£980*	*Tropical village (56x76cm-22x30in) s.d.1974 W/C pencil. 4-May-93 Christie's, East, New York #298/R*
$2500	*£1656*	*Horses and colt in orchard (53x74cm-21x29in) s.d.1976 W/C. 14-Jun-94 John Moran, Pasadena #130*
$3000	*£1987*	*San Pedro (25x36cm-10x14in) s. W/C. 15-Jun-94 Butterfield & Butterfield, San Francisco #4749/R*
$3000	*£1987*	*Our garden with lillies (56x76cm-22x30in) s.d.1983 W/C. 15-Jun-94 Butterfield & Butterfield, San Francisco #4752/R*
$3000	*£1987*	*Horses in landscape (51x74cm-20x29in) s. W/C. 28-Sep-93 John Moran, Pasadena #289*
$3000	*£1987*	*Goat Ranch (27x37cm-11x15in) s. W/C. 15-Jun-94 Butterfield & Butterfield, San Francisco #4750/R*
$3000	*£2027*	*Date palms (53x74cm-21x29in) s. W/C. 15-Jun-93 John Moran, Pasadena #155*
$4500	*£3125*	*Horses in landscape (56x76cm-22x30in) s. W/C. 7-Mar-93 Butterfield & Butterfield, San Francisco #248/R*
$5500	*£3793*	*Noonday, San Xavier (53x74cm-21x29in) s. i.verso W/C. 16-Feb-93 John Moran, Pasadena #114*
$7500	*£4967*	*Sea rocks and Island near Anchor Bay (56x76cm-22x30in) s. s.i.d.1970verso W/C. 15-Jun-94 Butterfield & Butterfield, San Francisco #4751/R*
$8500	*£5000*	*Plumeria tree (76x56cm-30x22in) s. W/C. 4-Oct-92 Butterfield & Butterfield, Los Angeles #197/R*
$8500	*£5903*	*Horses at Patzquaro (55x76cm-22x30in) s.d.1965 W/C pencil. 7-Mar-93 Butterfield & Butterfield, San Francisco #247/R*

SHEFFER, Glenn C (1881-?) American
$750	£497	Nude study (41x25cm-16x10in) s. board. 28-Sep-93 John Moran, Pasadena #208

SHEFFIELD, Isaac (1798-1845) American
$5500	£3667	Portrait of Captain Joseph Warren of Preston holding telescope (76x61cm-30x24in) panel. 12-Jun-94 Skinner, Bolton #173/R

SHELTON, Alphonse Joseph (1905-) American
$800	£537	The churn (64x91cm-25x36in) s. i.verso. 4-Dec-93 Louisiana Auction Exchange #41/R

SHEPPARD, Peter Clapham (1882-1965) Canadian
$5838	£3866	Old New York (123x89cm-48x35in) s. i.verso. 18-Nov-92 Sotheby's, Toronto #25/R (C.D 7500)
$507	*£338*	*Sketch book (13x19cm-5x7in) s. graphite W/C. 6-Jun-94 Waddingtons, Toronto #1250 r (C.D 700)*

SHEPPARD, Warren W (1858-1937) American
$750	£497	The Iroquois (30x41cm-12x16in) mono. board. 28-Nov-92 Young Fine Arts Auctions, Maine #353/R
$800	£548	Figures at the gate to the city (30x41cm-12x16in) s.d.1897. 10-Feb-94 Skinner, Bolton #216
$850	£594	Sailing at sunset (30x38cm-12x15in) s. canvas on board. 14-Mar-93 Hindman Galleries, Chicago #48
$1100	£719	The Golden West (66x91cm-26x36in) s. 18-Sep-93 Young Fine Arts Auctions, Maine #269/R
$1200	£779	Seascape (51x76cm-20x30in) s. 9-Sep-93 Sotheby's Arcade, New York #197/R
$1500	£765	Luminous sunset at ocean edge (74x51cm-29x20in) 21-Aug-92 Douglas, South Deerfield #3
$1500	£949	Sailboats in moonlight (46x91cm-18x36in) s.d.1884. 2-Dec-92 Christie's, East, New York #160/R
$1800	£1176	Under full sail, moonlight (76x64cm-30x25in) s.d.1886. 16-Sep-93 Sloan, North Bethesda #3217/R

451

SHEPPARD, Warren W (1858-1937) American-cont.
$1900	£1284	Under full sail, moonlight (76x64cm-30x25in) s.d.1886. 4-Nov-93 Sloan, North Bethesda #2323/R
$2000	£1316	Seascape at sunset (51x76cm-20x30in) s. 31-Mar-93 Sotheby's Arcade, New York #108/R
$2000	£1342	On the Grand Canal, Venice (41x61cm-16x24in) s. 6-May-94 Skinner, Bolton #65/R
$2000	£1351	Ship (36x30cm-14x12in) 10-Aug-93 Stonington Fine Arts, Stonington #97/R
$2500	£1689	A Venetian canal scene (61x40cm-24x16in) s. 5-Nov-93 Skinner, Bolton #75/R
$2900	£1895	Racing boats at full sail (41x56cm-16x22in) mono. 18-Sep-93 James Bakker, Cambridge #118/R
$3250	£2138	Venetian canal (40x66cm-16x26in) s. 31-Mar-93 Sotheby's Arcade, New York #75/R
$4000	£2703	A canal scene Venice (61x40cm-24x16in) s. 5-Nov-93 Skinner, Bolton #68/R
$4500	£2344	Sails in the sunset (51x76cm-20x30in) s. 7-Aug-92 Du Mouchelle, Detroit #2020/R

SHEPPARD, Warren W (attrib) (1858-1937) American
$550	£377	Coastal scene (51x76cm-20x30in) injdist.s.d. 10-Feb-94 Skinner, Bolton #25
$1500	£949	Thru Fisher's Island (46x64cm-18x25in) i.stretcher. 2-Dec-92 Christie's, East, New York #97/R

SHERMAN, Gwen (20th C) American
$1500	£974	Central park (61x91cm-24x36in) s. 11-Sep-93 Louisiana Auction Exchange #57/R

SHERRIFF-SCOTT, Adam (1887-1980) Canadian
$604	£408	Eskimo boy, Frobisher Bay (50x40cm-20x16in) s. canvasboard. 23-Nov-93 Joyner Fine Art, Toronto #214/R (C.D 800)
$1007	£654	Contemplation (51x66cm-20x26in) s. panel. 21-Jun-94 Fraser Pinneys, Quebec #44 (C.D 1400)
$1812	£1224	Summer's day at the beach (32x37cm-13x15in) s. board. 23-Nov-93 Fraser Pinneys, Quebec #448/R (C.D 2400)
$9355	£6075	Maple syrup time (77x96cm-30x38in) s. panel. 21-Jun-94 Fraser Pinneys, Quebec #60 (C.D 13000)

SHERWOOD, Mary Clare (1868-1943) American
$1100	£705	Harvest time (34x29cm-13x11in) s. s.i.verso. 9-Dec-92 Butterfield & Butterfield, San Francisco #4006/R

SHERWOOD, Rosina Emmet (1854-?) American
$8500	£5743	Figures along the wharf (74x103cm-29x41in) s. 5-Nov-93 Skinner, Bolton #104/R
$600	£405	Picking oranges (38x28cm-15x11in) s.i.d.1919 W/C. 10-Nov-93 Doyle, New York #105
$700	£473	On the beach (23x33cm-9x13in) s.d.1929 W/C board. 10-Nov-93 Doyle, New York #106
$1300	£878	Garden scene (38x33cm-15x13in) s.d.1911 W/C board. 10-Nov-93 Doyle, New York #104

SHIELDS, Alan (1944-) American
$4750	£3188	Untitled (183x274cm-72x108in) acrylic duck with wooden beads. 5-May-94 Sotheby's, New York #329/R
$1554	*£1036*	*Red Mutt (52x52cm-20x20in) s.i.d.1973 verso W/C collage. 11-Jun-94 Hauswedell & Nolte, Hamburg #346/R (DM 2600)*

SHILLING, Arthur (1941-1986) Canadian
$906	£612	Ojibway girl (60x50cm-24x20in) s.d.69 board. 23-Nov-93 Joyner Fine Art, Toronto #260 (C.D 1200)
$1100	£697	Portrait of woman (61x51cm-24x20in) s. masonite. 30-Nov-92 Ritchie, Toronto #107/R (C.D 1400)
$1401	£928	Clothesline (46x61cm-18x24in) s. i.verso board. 18-Nov-92 Sotheby's, Toronto #145 (C.D 1800)
$1661	£1122	Child (44x37cm-17x15in) s. board. 23-Nov-93 Joyner Fine Art, Toronto #213/R (C.D 2200)
$1820	£1214	Woodland waterfall (57x61cm-22x24in) s.d.76 board. 11-May-94 Sotheby's, Toronto #181 (C.D 2500)
$2153	£1435	Figures by water (61x72cm-24x28in) s.d.82. 30-May-94 Ritchie, Toronto #223/R (C.D 3000)
$2258	£1515	Portrait of a woman (60x50cm-24x20in) s.d.72 masonite. 29-Nov-93 Ritchie, Toronto #197/R (C.D 3000)
$2515	£1592	Portrait of youth (46x38cm-18x15in) s. s.d.73 verso canvasboard. 30-Nov-92 Ritchie, Toronto #106/R (C.D 3200)
$3010	£2020	Self portrait (64x49cm-25x19in) s.d.72. 29-Nov-93 Ritchie, Toronto #196/R (C.D 4000)
$3099	£2094	Black River children Rama (81x107cm-32x42in) i.verso. 3-Nov-93 Sotheby's, Toronto #218/R (C.D 4000)
$3230	£2153	Triple self-portrait and child in parka (72x100cm-28x39in) s.d.75 masonite. 30-May-94 Ritchie, Toronto #221/R (C.D 4500)
$3574	£2399	Two Rama children seated on a couch (61x76cm-24x30in) s.d.82. 29-Nov-93 Ritchie, Toronto #229/R (C.D 4750)
$3874	£2618	Self portrait (91x71cm-36x28in) s.d.67. 3-Nov-93 Sotheby's, Toronto #220/R (C.D 5000)
$3914	£2626	Reflections a scene at Black River (75x101cm-30x40in) s. i.stretcher painted c.1981. 29-Nov-93 Ritchie, Toronto #230/R (C.D 5200)

SHINN, Everett (1876-1953) American
$18000	£10405	Ballet (41x51cm-16x20in) s.d.1943. 24-Sep-92 Sotheby's, New York #170/R
$22000	£14570	Ballet girls (25x30cm-10x12in) s. canvas on board. 22-Sep-93 Christie's, New York #156/R
$42500	£28333	The performer (61x51cm-24x20in) s. painted c.1910. 25-May-94 Sotheby's, New York #102/R

SHINN, Everett (1876-1953) American-cont.

$700	£461	Lawyer's office (18x23cm-7x9in) s.d.1905 ink. 5-Jun-93 Louisiana Auction Exchange #62/R
$800	£526	Woman in landscape (30x43cm-12x17in) s.d.1907 chl paperboard. 31-Mar-93 Sotheby's Arcade, New York #230/R
$800	£523	Study of head (33x27cm-13x11in) s.d.1909 red conte crayon. 4-May-93 Christie's, East, New York #245/R
$850	£552	Chopin in Paris thinking of Marie (35x23cm-14x9in) s.i.d.1942 W/C board. 9-Sep-93 Sotheby's Arcade, New York #240/R
$900	£526	Magi (38x28cm-15x11in) s.d.1943 W/C. 20-Sep-92 Litchfield Auction Gallery #70
$1300	£850	Woman dressing (32x20cm-13x8in) s. red conte crayon. 4-May-93 Christie's, East, New York #236
$1300	£855	Simeon with Christ Child (29x32cm-11x13in) s.d.1945 W/C pencil. 31-Mar-93 Sotheby's Arcade, New York #232/R
$1600	£1088	Woman in yellow. Reclining woman (27x20cm-11x8in) s.d.1929 W/C gouache pencil two. 15-Nov-93 Christie's, East, New York #198/R
$1600	£1013	Girl with skirt over her head (35x20cm-14x8in) s. conte crayon. 2-Dec-92 Christie's, East, New York #360 a/R
$2000	£1266	Quarrel between Landless and Edwin Drood (43x28cm-17x11in) s.d.1941 W/C. 2-Dec-92 Christie's, East, New York #167/R
$2500	£1645	Golden Lancelet, Act I (44x55cm-17x22in) s.d.1934 s.i.verso W/C ink chl board. 31-Mar-93 Sotheby's Arcade, New York #229/R
$2800	£1618	Village in winter (25x34cm-10x13in) s.d.1940 W/C pencil board. 25-Sep-92 Sotheby's Arcade, New York #309 a/R
$3200	£2119	Nude (34x32cm-13x13in) s.d.1934 pastel. 22-Sep-93 Christie's, New York #155/R
$3500	£2365	Woman undressing (30x19cm-12x7in) s.d.1907 black crayon. 31-Mar-94 Sotheby's Arcade, New York #242/R
$4000	£2532	Woman looking in mirror (30x43cm-12x17in) s.d.1904 red chk. 2-Dec-92 Christie's, East, New York #315/R
$4250	£2834	A blustery day (39x58cm-15x23in) indist.s. pastel. 17-Mar-94 Sotheby's, New York #143/R
$6500	£4333	Study for 'Saturday Night, Ringling Hotel' (19x12cm-7x5in) s.i.d.1949 W/C black crayon gouache. 23-May-94 Christie's, East, New York #208/R
$8000	£5298	Old violinist (32x48cm-13x19in) s.d.1904 pastel. 23-Sep-93 Sotheby's, New York #239/R
$8500	£5667	Illustration for David Copperfield (45x76cm-18x30in) s.d.1947 i.verso W/C board. 16-Mar-94 Christie's, New York #121/R
$9000	£5960	Portrait of Helen Brooks (91x49cm-36x19in) s.i.d.123 pastel board. 2-Oct-93 Weschler, Washington #132 a/R
$18000	£12000	The Vanderbilt House . 1900 (23x35cm-9x14in) s.i.d.1945 W/C gouache. 25-May-94 Sotheby's, New York #106/R
$20000	£13423	Nude with green fan (48x41cm-19x16in) pastel. 3-Dec-93 Christie's, New York #33/R
$22000	£12717	After the performance (46x30cm-18x12in) s.d.1934 s.i.d.verso pastel paper on board. 23-Sep-92 Christie's, New York #213/R
$23000	£14557	Fleishman's bread line (21x34cm-8x13in) s.d.1900 pastel W/C. 3-Dec-92 Sotheby's, New York #48/R
$26000	£16456	Alley cat (49x66cm-19x26in) s.i.d.1933 pastel board. 4-Dec-92 Christie's, New York #147/R
$30000	£19231	Soiree (45x60cm-18x24in) s.d.1905 W/C gouache pencil. 26-May-93 Christie's, New York #183/R
$58000	£37179	Rooftop cafe (28x39cm-11x15in) s.d.1925 pastel paper on board. 26-May-93 Christie's, New York #189/R

SHINN, Everett (attrib) (1876-1953) American

$1200	£805	Cathedral interior (48x36cm-19x14in) s. W/C pencil htd.white painted c.1902. 2-Dec-93 Swann Galleries, New York #281/R

SHINODA, Ryusen (20th C) American

$750	£497	Suikage (47x36cm-19x14in) s. s.i.d.1965verso gouache. 29-Sep-93 Sotheby's Arcade, New York #236/R

SHIRLAW, Walter (1838-1910) American

$818	£549	Girl holding doll (18x10cm-7x4in) s.d.1904 board. 24-Mar-94 Mystic Fine Arts, Connecticut #80
$1200	£816	The sketchbook (46x33cm-18x13in) s. 14-Apr-94 Freeman Fine Arts, Philadelphia #976
$1600	£1081	Young bacchus (49x103cm-19x41in) s. 31-Mar-94 Sotheby's Arcade, New York #108/R
$4500	£3061	Laundry day (91x61cm-36x24in) s. 16-Apr-94 Young Fine Arts Auctions, Maine #228/R
$13500	£8824	Musical appeal (46x36cm-18x14in) s.i.d.1861. 30-Oct-92 Sloan, North Bethesda #2735/R

SHOKLER, Harry (1896-?) American

$2100	£1214	New York 9th Avenue and 17th to 19th (61x102cm-24x40in) s.d.1936 i.verso. 25-Sep-92 Sotheby's Arcade, New York #385/R

SHULL, Della (fl.1920-1930) American

$800	£503	Beach scene with figures (28x41cm-11x16in) s. canvasboard. 25-Apr-93 James Bakker, Cambridge #30/R

SHULZ, Ada Walter (1870-1963) American

$11000	£5820	Return from a visit (61x69cm-24x27in) s. 11-Sep-92 Skinner, Bolton #263/R
$16000	£11189	Washing (61x69cm-24x27in) s. 14-Mar-93 Hindman Galleries, Chicago #1/R
$17000	£10897	Portrait of Francis with Stephen (86x81cm-34x32in) s. 13-Dec-92 Hindman Galleries, Chicago #51/R

SHULZ, Adolph Robert (1869-1963) American
$1600   £1119   Houses in landscape (41x46cm-16x18in) s. board. 11-Mar-93 Mystic Fine Arts, Connecticut #180

SHURTLEFF, Roswell Morse (1838-1915) American
$1200   £779   Landscape (51x64cm-20x25in) s. 11-Sep-93 Louisiana Auction Exchange #87/R
$1300   £867   Mountain stream (97x127cm-38x50in) s. 23-May-94 Christie's, East, New York #43
$2000   £1282   Autumn (30x41cm-12x16in) s. 9-Dec-92 Butterfield & Butterfield, San Francisco #3844/R

SHUSTER, William Howard (1893-1969) American
$3250   £2083   Storm clouds (51x61cm-20x24in) s.d.25 canvas on canvas. 9-Dec-92 Butterfield & Butterfield, San Francisco #3975/R

SHUTTE, Thomas (1954-) American?
$2086   £1400   Untitled, melon (143x109cm-56x43in) s.d.1986 crayon gouache W/C varnish. 25-Mar-93 Christie's, London #196/R

SHUTTLEWORTH, Claire (20th C) American
$600   £403   Shiner's Alley, San Antonio (23x30cm-9x12in) s. W/C over pencil. 4-Dec-93 Louisiana Auction Exchange #2/R

SICHEL, Harold (1881-1948) American
$1600   £1111   Grazing under the trees (41x61cm-16x24in) s.d.46. 7-Mar-93 Butterfield & Butterfield, San Francisco #63/R
$3250   £2257   California Hills (46x61cm-18x24in) s.d.42. 7-Mar-93 Butterfield & Butterfield, San Francisco #62/R

SIEBERT, Edward S (1856-?) American
$950   £638   House in landscape (61x76cm-24x30in) s. 24-Mar-94 Mystic Fine Arts, Connecticut #53

SIEBNER, Herbert Johannes Joseph (1925-) Canadian
$1162   £785   Figure ornament (30x45cm-12x18in) s.d. s.i.d.1961verso oil casein wax masonite. 1-Nov-93 Levis, Calgary #305/R (C.D 1500)

SIEGFRIED, Edwin C (1889-1955) American
$750   £517   Eucalyptus tree in Golden Gate Park (51x30cm-20x12in) s. i.d.Sept.1943verso pastel board. 16-Feb-93 John Moran, Pasadena #70 b
$900   £529   Sunrise on Nevada Desert (51x60cm-20x24in) s. i.verso pastel board. 4-Oct-92 Butterfield & Butterfield, Los Angeles #219/R
$2250   £1562   Stinson's beach (63x94cm-25x37in) s. pastel. 7-Mar-93 Butterfield & Butterfield, San Francisco #48/R

SIEGRIEST, Louis Bassi (1899-1989) American
$1700   £1172   Back of C Street, Virginia City (58x69cm-23x27in) s.d.50 oil masonite. 16-Feb-93 John Moran, Pasadena #57
$900   £529   Aguacaliente (25x36cm-10x14in) s. i.verso mixed media board. 4-Oct-92 Butterfield & Butterfield, Los Angeles #268/R
$1000   £629   Utah landscape (29x41cm-11x16in) s. s.i.verso mixed media masonite. 25-Apr-93 Butterfield & Butterfield, San Francisco #2116/R
$1200   £795   Hard times, migrant workers (22x28cm-9x11in) s. gouache. 20-Sep-93 Butterfield & Butterfield, Los Angeles #107/R

SIEGRIEST, Lundy (1925-1985) American
$1600   £1111   Surf and cliffs (20x25cm-8x10in) studio st.verso. 7-Mar-93 Butterfield & Butterfield, San Francisco #267/R
$1700   £1181   China camp, summer (41x51cm-16x20in) studio st.verso. 7-Mar-93 Butterfield & Butterfield, San Francisco #265/R
$2250   £1562   Bass Run, Martinez (41x51cm-16x20in) s. s.i.d.Winter 1979verso. 7-Mar-93 Butterfield & Butterfield, San Francisco #268/R
$2250   £1521   Five horses (41x51cm-16x20in) 21-Oct-93 Butterfield & Butterfield, San Francisco #2784/R
$2500   £1736   Petaluma breaking cart (41x51cm-16x20in) s. s.i.d.Summer 1977verso. 7-Mar-93 Butterfield & Butterfield, San Francisco #266/R
$1500   £949   Desert cliffs (122x122cm-48x48in) s.d.71 s.i.d.71 verso mixed media panel. 25-Oct-92 Butterfield & Butterfield, San Francisco #2301/R

SIEMER, Christian (1874-1940) American
$850   £586   Sierra landscape (61x76cm-24x30in) s.d.37. 16-Feb-93 John Moran, Pasadena #132

SIERRA, Paul (20th C) Cuban
$4500   £3020   Solitude (128x107cm-50x42in) s. 7-Jan-94 Gary Nader, Miami #104/R

SILSBY, Wilson (1883-1952) American
$2750   £1821   Indian houses at Warner's Hot Springs, San Diego (41x51cm-16x20in) s.d.34 i.verso. 15-Jun-94 Butterfield & Butterfield, San Francisco #4699/R

SILVA, Francis Augustus (1835-1886) American
$14000 £8974   Gloucester dawn (23x46cm-9x18in) s. 26-May-93 Christie's, New York #58/R
$18000 £10405 Beach at Long Branch, New Jersey (20x41cm-8x16in) s. 23-Sep-92 Christie's, New York #60/R
$18000 £11538 Along the shore (51x92cm-20x36in) s. 26-May-93 Christie's, New York #31/R
$19000 £12752 Misty morning in New York Bay (15x31cm-6x12in) s. s.i.verso board. 3-Dec-93 Christie's, New York #108/R

SILVA, Francis Augustus (1835-1886) American-cont.
$21000	£13816	View from Hudson River (23x46cm-9x18in) s.d.70. 13-Jun-93 Butterfield & Butterfield, San Francisco #3102/R
$32000	£20253	Autumn afternoon on New England coast (107x148cm-42x58in) s.d.86. 4-Dec-92 Christie's, New York #228/R
$35000	£23490	An old town by the sea, Gloucester harbour (61x112cm-24x44in) s.d.1880. 3-Dec-93 Christie's, New York #100/R
$38000	£25503	Past Her Glory (46x91cm-18x36in) s.indist.i. 8-Dec-93 Butterfield & Butterfield, San Francisco #3338/R
$48000	£32215	Harbour scene (56x92cm-22x36in) s.d.77. 3-Dec-93 Christie's, New York #110/R
$52500	£33228	Midsummer's twilight (61x111cm-24x44in) s.d.81. 3-Dec-92 Sotheby's, New York #29/R
$70000	£44872	Approaching storm (30x61cm-12x24in) s.d.71. 27-May-93 Sotheby's, New York #157/R
$90000	£57692	October on Hudson (61x112cm-24x44in) s.i. 26-May-93 Christie's, New York #30/R
$165000	£115385	On the Hudson near Haverstraw (46x76cm-18x30in) s.d.72 s.i.stretcher. 10-Mar-93 Sotheby's, New York #23/R
$230000	£152318	Calm at sunset (74x127cm-29x50in) s.d.1873 i.stretcher. 23-Sep-93 Sotheby's, New York #35/R
$3000	*£1887*	*Crashing surf (74x51cm-29x20in) s. W/C. 22-Apr-93 Freeman Fine Arts, Philadelphia #1346*

SILVA, Ramon (1890-1919) Argentinian
$4500	*£2601*	*Arboleda (25x34cm-10x13in) 23-Sep-92 Roldan & Cia, Buenos Aires #53*
$6000	*£3468*	*El campanario (35x27cm-14x11in) panel. 23-Sep-92 Roldan & Cia, Buenos Aires #61*
$4000	*£2312*	*Entrando a la Aldea (31x48cm-12x19in) W/C. 23-Sep-92 Roldan & Cia, Buenos Aires #52*

SILVA, William P (1859-1948) American
$800	£541	The Cliffs of Lobos (25x20cm-10x8in) s. s.i.verso canvas laid down. 9-Nov-93 John Moran, Pasadena #868
$1100	£728	Coastal scene (30x40cm-12x16in) s. board. 2-Oct-93 Weschler, Washington #117/R
$1100	£733	River landscape (46x56cm-18x22in) s. 15-Mar-94 John Moran, Pasadena #100
$1200	£805	Night, Point Lobos (25x30cm-10x12in) s. canvas on board. 8-Dec-93 Butterfield & Butterfield, San Francisco #3404/R
$1300	£850	Sunlight through clouds - beach scene (41x51cm-16x20in) s. 17-Sep-93 Skinner, Bolton #222/R
$1300	£909	Springtime, Carmel shore (28x36cm-11x14in) s. board. 11-Mar-93 Mystic Fine Arts, Connecticut #168 a/R
$1500	£987	Springtime, Carmel Shore (28x36cm-11x14in) s. board. 13-Jun-93 Butterfield & Butterfield, San Francisco #801/R
$2000	£1370	Dunes and glinting sea (41x51cm-16x20in) s. 19-Feb-94 Young Fine Arts Auctions, Maine #182/R
$4000	£2649	Misty coastline and cliffs, Carmel (102x81cm-40x32in) s. 15-Jun-94 Butterfield & Butterfield, San Francisco #4645/R
$4500	£2980	Autumn, Del Monte Lake, Monterey (51x62cm-20x24in) s. 15-Jun-94 Butterfield & Butterfield, San Francisco #4644/R
$6500	£3824	Rocky shore (30x41cm-12x16in) s. board. 4-Oct-92 Butterfield & Butterfield, Los Angeles #70/R

SILVERMAN, Burton (1928-) American
$3500	*£2215*	*Woman in beach hat (59x36cm-23x14in) s.d.82 W/C gouache pencil board. 3-Dec-92 Sotheby's, New York #81/R*

SIMARD, Claude A (1943-) Canadian
$1705	£1152	Kennebec 1 (76x91cm-30x36in) s.d.1989 s.i.d.verso. 1-Nov-93 Levis, Calgary #306/R (C.D 2200)

SIMIL (1944-) Haitian
$1252	£829	Femme en bleu (50x35cm-20x14in) s.d.78 panel. 13-Jun-94 Rogeon, Paris #63 (F.FR 7000)

SIMKINS, Martha (20th C) American
$700	£490	Bay view in summer (51x51cm-20x20in) s. board. 7-Feb-93 James Bakker, Cambridge #117

SIMMONS, Edward Emerson (1852-1932) American
$4228	£2800	Female nude playing piano (50x60cm-20x24in) s. 25-Nov-92 Sotheby's, London #617/R

SIMON, Hermann Gustave (1846-1895) American
$1300	*£855*	*Pointer on point (30x44cm-12x17in) s. W/C. 4-Jun-93 Sotheby's, New York #162/R*

SIMPKINS, Henry J (1906-) Canadian
$604	£408	Montreal from above pine avenue (51x80cm-20x31in) s. W/C. 23-Nov-93 Fraser Pinneys, Quebec #459 (C.D 800)

SIMPSON, Lorna (20th C) American
$17000	£11486	Water bearer (138x206cm-54x81in) gelatin silver print acrylic plexiglass exec.86. 11-Nov-93 Sotheby's, New York #214/R

SIMPSON, Maxwell Stewart (1896-) American
$2100	£1321	Baron Benners (102x66cm-40x26in) s. i.d.1947verso s.stretcher. 22-Apr-93 Freeman Fine Arts, Philadelphia #1221

SINCLAIR, Alfredo (1915-) Central American
$7000	£4698	Mujer con redes y pesces (90x77cm-35x30in) s.d.93 s.verso. 7-Jan-94 Gary Nader, Miami #100/R

SINCLAIR, Deborah Lougheed (1953-) Canadian
$708	£478	Sun up - Vermillion Pass (61x107cm-24x42in) s. s.i.d.1983 acrylic. 25-Apr-94 Levis, Calgary #311/R (C.D 975)
$806	£474	Pilot (91x91cm-36x36in) s. s.i.verso acrylic. 5-Oct-92 Levis, Calgary #136/R (C.D 1000)

SINCLAIR, Irving (1895-1969) American
$1300	£861	Farm scene (76x102cm-30x40in) s. 15-Jun-94 Butterfield & Butterfield, San Francisco #4701/R
$7000	£4046	The poker game (37x198cm-15x78in) s.d.44. 23-Sep-92 Christie's, New York #247/R

SINGER, Gail (c.1924-) American
$525	*£350*	*Sans titre (35x48cm-14x19in) s. gouache. 11-Mar-94 Cornette de St.Cyr, Paris #220 (F.FR 3000)*

SINGER, Michael (20th C) American
$2600	*£1722*	*7 moon ritual series (124x96cm-49x38in) s.i.d.7 30 80 chl chk ink paper collage. 29-Sep-93 Sotheby's Arcade, New York #345/R*

SINGER, William Henry (jnr) (1868-1943) American
$1500	£1000	September morning (54x65cm-21x26in) s. s.i.d.1931verso. 31-May-94 Christie's, Amsterdam #9/R (D.FL 2800)
$2500	£1656	Morning dew (100x105cm-39x41in) s.d.1926. 23-Sep-93 Sotheby's, New York #214/R
$3674	£2355	Pine trees (55x46cm-22x18in) s.d.1936 col.chk card. 9-Dec-92 Sotheby's, Amsterdam #214/R (D.FL 6500)

SIQUEIROS, David (1896-1974) Mexican
$6000	£4027	Grupo , acrylic painted 1964. 7-Jan-94 Gary Nader, Miami #83/R
$11000	£7432	Las Montanas (64x63cm-25x25in) s. burlap. 21-Oct-93 Butterfield & Butterfield, San Francisco #2734/R
$11000	£7285	Tormenta (46x32cm-18x13in) s.d.12-63 board on masonite. 23-Nov-92 Sotheby's, New York #231/R
$14000	£9459	El Barranco (32x26cm-13x10in) s.d.64 acrylic paper on masonite. 22-Nov-93 Sotheby's, New York #263/R
$15282	£9796	Arbol (23x19cm-9x7in) s. acrylic triplay. 29-Apr-93 Louis Morton, Mexico #100 (M.P 48000)
$25000	£16556	La Vie (87x40cm-34x16in) s.d.65 acrylic panel. 23-Nov-92 Sotheby's, New York #228/R
$36000	£24000	Paisaje (51x35cm-20x14in) s.d.12.63 paper laid down on board. 18-May-94 Christie's, New York #216/R
$60000	£40541	Cara de nino (69x61cm-27x24in) s.d.39 pyroxiline masonite. 23-Nov-93 Christie's, New York #112/R
$3006	*£2004*	*Montanas con grietas (12x25cm-5x10in) s. W/C painted c.1967. 25-May-94 Louis Morton, Mexico #103/R (M.P 10000)*
$3750	*£2358*	*Tres danzadoras (33x42cm-13x17in) s.d.5.6.61 Indian ink gouache. 25-Apr-93 Butterfield & Butterfield, San Francisco #2087/R*
$4000	*£2703*	*Cara de Piedra Olmeca y Cascada (34x24cm-13x9in) s. gouache painted c.1940. 23-Nov-93 Christie's, New York #243/R*
$4250	*£2778*	*Boceto para una piscina (76x55cm-30x22in) s.d.2-28-1967 W/C col.pencil. 18-May-93 Sotheby's, New York #183/R*
$4750	*£3188*	*Nina en la crujia (28x20cm-11x8in) s.d.64 ink. 24-Feb-94 Sotheby's Arcade, New York #306/R*
$7500	*£5034*	*Revolucionarios (42x32cm-17x13in) s.d.4.64 gouache. 7-Jan-94 Gary Nader, Miami #82/R*
$8836	*£5813*	*Arbol (32x25cm-13x10in) s. mixed media. 4-Nov-92 Mora, Castelltort & Quintana, Juarez #56/R (M.P 27900000)*
$21000	£13907	Cabeza de mujer (37x50cm-15x20in) s. pyroxylin gouache board on panel. 23-Nov-92 Sotheby's, New York #215/R
$26000	£17219	Relacion entre la Objetividad y la Subjetividad (80x60cm-31x24in) s.d.71 s.i.d.1971 verso pyroxilene plywood. 24-Nov-92 Christie's, New York #156/R
$29000	£19253	Cabeza de aguila (49x62cm-19x24in) s.d.7.1952 pyroxylin ink paper on masonite. 18-May-94 Sotheby's, New York #275/R
$45000	£30405	Nostalgia Escapial (122x81cm-48x32in) s.d.7-69 s.verso pyroxylin particle board. 22-Nov-93 Sotheby's, New York #51/R
$50000	£33333	El nahuatl (80x60cm-31x24in) s. proxylin panel painted c.1965. 17-May-94 Sotheby's, New York #67/R
$60000	£40541	Combustible para pobres (65x50cm-26x20in) s.d.12-63 pyroxylin board on panel. 22-Nov-93 Sotheby's, New York #50/R
$60000	£39216	El Padre de la Primera Victima de la Huelga de Cananea (81x60cm-32x24in) s.d.11-61 s.i.verso pyroxylin panel. 18-May-93 Sotheby's, New York #58/R
$60000	£40541	Cabeza (70x85cm-28x33in) s.d.59 pyroxiline panel. 23-Nov-93 Christie's, New York #61/R
$75000	£50000	Volcanes (68x122cm-27x48in) s.d.8-65 pyroxylin panel. 17-May-94 Sotheby's, New York #48/R
$80000	£52288	Paisaje en verde (63x119cm-25x47in) s.d.8-65 piroxyline masonite painted 1965. 17-May-93 Christie's, New York #6/R
$80000	£54054	Mujer y Gato (91x74cm-36x29in) s.d.1931 pyroxiline masonite. 23-Nov-93 Christie's, New York #22/R
$160000	£106667	El machete, autorretrato (122x115cm-48x45in) s.d.7-68 pyroxylin board. 17-May-94 Sotheby's, New York #40/R

SISSON, Laurence P (1928-) American
$900	£588	Sea rocks (79x41cm-31x16in) s. board. 18-Sep-93 Young Fine Arts Auctions, Maine #274
$3500	£2318	Tide pools (102x152cm-40x60in) s. acrylic board. 28-Nov-92 Young Fine Arts Auctions, Maine #355/R

SIVORI, Edouardo (1847-1918) Argentinian
$750	£391	Paisaje (19x14cm-7x6in) W/C. 4-Aug-92 VerBo, Buenos Aires #99/R

SKILLINGS, A L P (19th C) American
$750	£514	Figures by the shore Lake George (51x76cm-20x30in) s.d.1869 s.i.verso. 19-Feb-94 Young Fine Arts Auctions, Maine #183/R

SKLAR, Dorothy (20th C) American
$750	£494	Blanket sellers (76x91cm-30x36in) s.d.62 board. 13-Jun-93 Butterfield & Butterfield, San Francisco #975/R
$950	£559	Savoy Hotel (63x76cm-25x30in) s. board. 4-Oct-92 Butterfield & Butterfield, Los Angeles #250/R
$550	£372	Los Angeles-Outfit cars (41x56cm-16x22in) s. W/C. 15-Jun-93 John Moran, Pasadena #66/R
$550	£372	Los Angeles-outfit cars and tunnel (38x53cm-15x21in) s.d.50 W/C. 15-Jun-93 John Moran, Pasadena #65
$600	£405	Children in city street scene (33x51cm-13x20in) s.d.44 W/C. 15-Jun-93 John Moran, Pasadena #88
$650	£448	Laguna Shore II (33x48cm-13x19in) s.d.46 W/C. 16-Feb-93 John Moran, Pasedena #84a
$1000	£662	Small town landscape (33x51cm-13x20in) s.d.46 W/C. 28-Sep-93 John Moran, Pasedena #226

SKOU, Sigurd (1878-1929) American
$7500	£5102	Still life with fishbowl (91x91cm-36x36in) s. 15-Nov-93 Christie's, East, New York #231/R

SLIPPER, Gary P (1934-) Canadian
$2728	£1795	Untitled (152x102cm-60x40in) s. i.verso. 7-Jun-93 Waddingtons, Toronto #1137 c (C.D 3350)

SLOAN, John (1871-1951) American
$5500	£3526	Nude on harp chair (51x38cm-20x15in) s. s.i.verso tempera oil board. 26-May-93 Christie's, New York #188/R
$11000	£7051	Grey day - Billings Mansion (22x28cm-9x11in) s.i.d.08. 27-May-93 Sotheby's, New York #72/R
$17000	£10897	Pink and blue (61x51cm-24x20in) s. 27-May-93 Sotheby's, New York #82/R
$22000	£12717	Landscape, Santa Fe (40x51cm-16x20in) s. panel. 23-Sep-92 Christie's, New York #120/R
$700	£458	Mr. Ting Fang (25x25cm-10x10in) s. ink. 1-Nov-92 Hanzel Galleries, Chicago #26
$700	£470	'Savings Bank' - people in bank (18x23cm-7x9in) black crayon. 16-Jul-93 Douglas, South Deerfield #2
$1100	£733	Reclining nude (60x74cm-24x29in) s. chl. 23-May-94 Christie's, East, New York #211
$1200	£816	Various figure studies (14x21cm-6x8in) s. ink paper laid down on board. 15-Nov-93 Christie's, East, New York #208
$2500	£1667	Wellington held forth a wedge of layer cake (38x48cm-15x19in) s.i.d.06 crayon. 17-Mar-94 Sotheby's, New York #149/R
$3250	£2111	Study of seated female nude (36x24cm-14x9in) s.d.May 33 crayon. 9-Sep-93 Sotheby's Arcade, New York #341/R

SLOAN, Junius R (1827-1900) American
$1000	£658	Cows watering in mountain lake (51x91cm-20x36in) s.d.1874. 2-Jun-93 Doyle, New York #86
$1700	£1156	Mountain river landscape with cows watering (51x91cm-20x36in) s.d.1874. 14-Apr-94 Freeman Fine Arts, Philadelphia #970/R
$3000	£2041	Extensive landscape with cattle (51x97cm-20x38in) 17-Apr-94 Hanzel Galleries, Chicago #14

SLOANE, Eric (1910-1985) American
$1000	£649	P47 Republic (63x76cm-25x30in) s.i. canvasboard. 9-Sep-93 Sotheby's Arcade, New York #435/R
$1200	£779	Flying above the clouds (63x76cm-25x30in) s. i.verso canvasboard. 9-Sep-93 Sotheby's Arcade, New York #437/R
$1200	£755	Landing strip through the clouds with plane (64x74cm-25x29in) s. canvasboard. 22-Apr-93 Freeman Fine Arts, Philadelphia #1212
$1320	£846	Planes over the city (66x53cm-26x21in) s. board. 17-Dec-92 Mystic Fine Arts, Connecticut #124/R
$1500	£987	Sailing in bay under stormy skies (41x51cm-16x20in) s. 2-Jun-93 Doyle, New York #85
$1500	£1000	Grand Canyon (61x91cm-24x36in) s. board. 13-Mar-94 Hindman Galleries, Chicago #819
$2300	£1329	Cloud painting (49x69cm-19x27in) s.i. s.i.d.1939verso canvasboard. 25-Sep-92 Sotheby's Arcade, New York #478/R
$2750	£1763	Sailing (64x76cm-25x30in) s. canvasboard. 24-May-93 Grogan, Massachussetts #350/R
$3000	£2027	Buck's County in December (41x56cm-16x22in) s.i. s.i.d.1971 verso oil pencil masonite. 31-Mar-94 Sotheby's Arcade, New York #279/R
$3000	£2098	On the water (52x57cm-20x22in) s. masonite. 11-Mar-93 Christie's, New York #240/R

SLOANE, Eric (1910-1985) American-cont.
$3000	£2013	Canvasbacks flying over a marsh (86x117cm-34x46in) masonite. 1-Dec-93 Doyle, New York #73 a
$3250	£1879	Cumulus clouds at 4500 ft (119x165cm-47x65in) s.i.d.1946. 25-Sep-92 Sotheby's Arcade, New York #477/R
$4000	£2632	Vermont September (61x81cm-24x32in) s. masonite. 31-Mar-93 Sotheby's Arcade, New York #311/R
$4200	£2658	Bittersweet season (60x63cm-24x25in) s.i. board. 2-Dec-92 Christie's, East, New York #333/R
$4500	£3147	Father sky (38x28cm-15x11in) s. s.i.verso masonite. 10-Mar-93 Sotheby's, New York #69/R
$7500	£4808	October barn (51x74cm-20x29in) s. masonite. 27-May-93 Sotheby's, New York #108/R
$8000	£5298	The barn (58x91cm-23x36in) s. masonite. 22-Sep-93 Christie's, New York #227/R
$8000	£5333	Fall sky (98x74cm-39x29in) s.i. i.d.1968 verso masonite. 17-Mar-94 Sotheby's, New York #142/R
$9000	£5921	Pennsylvania barn (56x71cm-22x28in) s. masonite. 31-Mar-93 Sotheby's Arcade, New York #305/R
$9000	£6122	The red bridge, Montgomery Vermont (61x91cm-24x36in) s. board. 16-Apr-94 Young Fine Arts Auctions, Maine #234/R
$10000	£6667	Old Kent Farmstead (50x100cm-20x39in) s.i. masonite. 26-May-94 Christie's, New York #153/R
$17000	£10897	Fishing season (90x116cm-35x46in) s. masonite. 27-May-93 Sotheby's, New York #110/R
$18000	£12000	Autumn (68x55cm-27x22in) s. i.verso masonite. 26-May-94 Christie's, New York #152/R
$32000	£21192	Bringing home the Christmas tree (60x83cm-24x33in) s. masonite. 22-Sep-93 Christie's, New York #226/R
$650	*£409*	*Republic Thunderbolt (30x51cm-12x20in) s.i. pastel. 22-Apr-93 Freeman Fine Arts, Philadelphia #1217*
$650	*£433*	*The stone barn (43x53cm-17x21in) s. W/C ink. 26-Aug-93 Skinner, Bolton #167*
$800	*£519*	*Republic Thunderbolt (39x61cm-15x24in) s.i. pastel chl Indian ink pencil. 9-Sep-93 Sotheby's Arcade, New York #436/R*
$1100	*£692*	*Navy ship (53x41cm-21x16in) s.i.d.1942 pastel. 22-Apr-93 Freeman Fine Arts, Philadelphia #1213/R*
$1300	*£818*	*Night and day (53x41cm-21x16in) s.i.d.1942 pastel. 22-Apr-93 Freeman Fine Arts, Philadelphia #1222/R*

SLOANE, Marian Parkhurst (1875-1955) American
$800	£559	Spring (76x102cm-30x40in) s. i.verso. 12-Mar-93 Skinner, Bolton #204/R

SLOBODKINA, Esphyr (1908-) American
$4000	£2632	Houses (33x41cm-13x16in) s. 31-Mar-93 Sotheby's Arcade, New York #453/R
$5250	£3524	Hellas - abstract composition (20x23cm-8x9in) s.init.i.verso gouache pencil card exec.c.1940-42. 4-May-94 Doyle, New York #79/R

SLOUN, Frank van (1879-1938) American
$3750	£2604	In the park (51x41cm-20x16in) s. 7-Mar-93 Butterfield & Butterfield, San Francisco #102/R

SMALL, Arthur (20th C) American
$750	£507	Four-master Garthpool off Rio (61x112cm-24x44in) s.d.1929. 23-Oct-93 San Rafael Auction Galleries #190

SMIBERT, John (school) (1688-1751) American
$2000	£1333	Portrait of two children with dog (64x76cm-25x30in) 12-Jun-94 Skinner, Bolton #290/R

SMILLIE, George H (1840-1921) American
$950	£609	Young girl in landscape (25x33cm-10x13in) s.d.83 canvas laid down on board. 24-May-93 Grogan, Massachussetts #325/R
$1400	£881	Path to the meadow (23x15cm-9x6in) 22-Apr-93 Freeman Fine Arts, Philadelphia #1299/R
$1900	£1242	Rocky shore with distant sailing boats (23x41cm-9x16in) 30-Jun-94 Richard Opfer, Timonium #124
$2200	£1106	Dockside, Cohasset, Massachusetts (23x41cm-9x16in) s. 6-Sep-92 Litchfield Auction Gallery #135
$3100	£2026	Drink at river (41x61cm-16x24in) s. 30-Jun-94 Mystic Fine Arts, Connecticut #226 a/R
$6000	£3846	Pigeon Cove (23x42cm-9x17in) s.i.d.Sept.1861. 9-Dec-92 Butterfield & Butterfield, San Francisco #3818/R
$1300	*£844*	*Unionville, Connecticut (27x38cm-11x15in) s.i.d.1892 pencil W/C board. 9-Sep-93 Sotheby's Arcade, New York #26/R*

SMIT, Derk (20th C) Dutch/American
$725	£507	Winter scene (51x61cm-20x24in) s. 14-Mar-93 Hindman Galleries, Chicago #87

SMITH, Charles Alexander (1864-1915) Canadian
$793	£518	Farm in springtime (61x76cm-24x30in) s. 19-May-93 Sotheby's, Toronto #30 (C.D 1000)
$934	£619	Man in a field (46x32cm-18x13in) s.d.88. 18-Nov-92 Sotheby's, Toronto #285/R (C.D 1200)
$1189	£777	Shepherd (49x65cm-19x26in) s.d.88. 19-May-93 Sotheby's, Toronto #76/R (C.D 1500)
$1401	£928	Boys in the field (51x61cm-20x24in) s. 18-Nov-92 Sotheby's, Toronto #288/R (C.D 1800)

SMITH, Charles Alexander (1864-1915) Canadian-cont.
$1820	£1214	Man working in the field (46x32cm-18x13in) s.d.88. 11-May-94 Sotheby's, Toronto #14/R (C.D 2500)
$3308	£2191	Lady reading (55x46cm-22x18in) s.d.88. 18-Nov-92 Sotheby's, Toronto #282/R (C.D 4250)

SMITH, Charles L A (1871-1937) American
$850	£563	Lowland pasture (63x76cm-25x30in) s.d.1927. 15-Jun-94 Butterfield & Butterfield, San Francisco #4706/R

SMITH, David (1906-1965) American
$750	£504	Give your money to Jesus this day (25x29cm-10x11in) s. i.verso gouache W/C pencil executed c.1936. 24-Feb-94 Sotheby's Arcade, New York #317/R
$5000	£2941	Sketch for sculpture (45x29cm-18x11in) spary enamel. 8-Oct-92 Christie's, New York #157/R
$6000	£4054	Untitled (27x21cm-11x8in) ball pen col crayon dr executed 1957. 8-Nov-93 Christie's, East, New York #224/R

SMITH, Decost (1864-1939) American
$3200	£2025	Signal (114x86cm-45x34in) s.d.1909. 2-Dec-92 Christie's, East, New York #47/R
$8500	£5556	Shot in the back (76x61cm-30x24in) s.d.1898. 17-Sep-93 Skinner, Bolton #234/R
$17000	£11258	Native American scene (76x61cm-30x24in) s.d.1890. 13-Nov-92 Skinner, Bolton #146/R

SMITH, E Boyd (1860-1943) American
$7149	£4798	Bartering for calf outside Dedit Inn, Paris (131x94cm-52x37in) s.i. 30-Nov-93 Ritchie, Toronto #68/R (C.D 9500)

SMITH, Edward Gregory (1880-1963) American
$1750	£1174	Winter landscape (61x76cm-24x30in) panel. 29-Nov-93 Stonington Fine Arts, Stonington #176/R

SMITH, Ernest Browning (1866-1951) American
$650	£430	Mountain landscape (61x76cm-24x30in) s. 28-Sep-93 John Moran, Pasadena #271
$650	£439	Coastal landscape (30x41cm-12x16in) s. canvasboard. 9-Nov-93 John Moran, Pasadena #886
$650	£430	Coastal (36x61cm-14x24in) 28-Sep-93 John Moran, Pasadena #324
$700	£473	Grey morning - Annandale 1914 (38x51cm-15x20in) canvas on board. 15-Jun-93 John Moran, Pasadena #164
$700	£464	Landscape (61x76cm-24x30in) 28-Sep-93 John Moran, Pasadena #283
$700	£464	Mountain landscape (76x91cm-30x36in) s. 28-Sep-93 John Moran, Pasadena #274
$750	£497	Mountain landscape (64x76cm-25x30in) 28-Sep-93 John Moran, Pasadena #312
$750	£517	Landscape (41x51cm-16x20in) s. 16-Feb-93 John Moran, Pasadena #30 a
$900	£621	Coastal (30x41cm-12x16in) s. canvas laid down on board. 16-Feb-93 John Moran, Pasadena #40
$950	£629	Coastal (51x76cm-20x30in) 28-Sep-93 John Moran, Pasadena #351
$1000	£662	Sailboat at Catalina (81x102cm-32x40in) s.d.1928. 14-Jun-94 John Moran, Pasadena #97
$1000	£676	Coastal landscape (46x61cm-18x24in) s. 15-Jun-93 John Moran, Pasadena #67
$1000	£676	Big sky landscape (76x91cm-30x36in) s. 15-Jun-93 John Moran, Pasadena #77
$1000	£662	Fall landscape (51x76cm-20x30in) s. 14-Jun-94 John Moran, Pasadena #99
$1000	£676	Farm house (71x91cm-28x36in) s.d.1922. 15-Jun-93 John Moran, Pasadena #103
$1100	£733	Eucalyptus landscape (46x61cm-18x24in) s. 15-Mar-94 John Moran, Pasadena #37
$1100	£728	Coastal (61x76cm-24x30in) 28-Sep-93 John Moran, Pasadena #281
$1200	£839	California mountains (61x76cm-24x30in) s. 12-Mar-93 Du Mouchelle, Detroit #2247/R
$1200	£828	Landscape (41x51cm-16x20in) s. board. 16-Feb-93 John Moran, Pasadena #67
$1200	£811	Early moonrise-Mount Cahuenga-1919 (76x91cm-30x36in) s. 15-Jun-93 John Moran, Pasadena #106
$1300	£878	Mountain landscape (91x114cm-36x45in) s. 15-Jun-93 John Moran, Pasadena #132

SMITH, Francis Hopkinson (1838-1915) American
$1200	£789	Coastal village (23x28cm-9x11in) s.d.80 W/C. 5-Jun-93 Louisiana Auction Exchange #36/R
$1200	£789	Street in Marianao (30x45cm-12x18in) s.d.8.81 W/C gouache pencil ink paper on board. 31-Mar-93 Sotheby's Arcade, New York #137/R
$1600	£1026	In the shadow of a palace (58x33cm-23x13in) s. W/C pencil. 9-Dec-92 Butterfield & Butterfield, San Francisco #3863/R
$1700	£1104	Fishing village (33x51cm-13x20in) s. W/C. 11-Sep-93 Louisiana Auction Exchange #36/R
$2700	£1561	Sailboats in calm sea (46x66cm-18x26in) s. W/C gouache paper on board. 25-Sep-92 Sotheby's Arcade, New York #121/R
$2900	£1908	Holland canal scene (46x60cm-18x24in) s. gouache W/C board. 31-Mar-93 Sotheby's Arcade, New York #136/R
$3250	£2083	Dock scene (34x56cm-13x22in) s. gouache pencil. 9-Dec-92 Butterfield & Butterfield, San Francisco #3876/R
$4000	£2632	Venetian piazza (31x54cm-12x21in) s. gouache. 31-Mar-93 Sotheby's Arcade, New York #141/R
$6000	£4000	Venetian lagoon (41x90cm-16x35in) s. W/C gouache. 17-Mar-94 Sotheby's, New York #96/R
$6500	£4114	Canal scene, Venice (50x30cm-20x12in) s. W/C gouache. 3-Dec-92 Sotheby's, New York #30/R
$7000	£4430	River view (46x67cm-18x26in) s. W/C chl. gouache. 3-Dec-92 Sotheby's, New York #32/R
$8000	£5594	Elegant ladies (43x58cm-17x23in) s.d.1906 gouache. 10-Mar-93 Sotheby's, New York #107/R

SMITH, Francis Hopkinson (1838-1915) American-cont.
$10000	£6667	Ponte della Reglia (65x53cm-26x21in) s. W/C gouache graphite. 17-Mar-94 Sotheby's, New York #94/R
$13000	£8667	Porta della Carta (67x46cm-26x18in) s. i.verso W/C gouache. 17-Mar-94 Sotheby's, New York #95/R

SMITH, Frank Vining (1879-1967) American
$900	£600	Harbour with boats (51x56cm-20x22in) s. i.verso masonite. 26-Aug-93 Skinner, Bolton #25/R
$1500	£1007	Sunkissed surf (61x92cm-24x36in) s. i.d.1919verso. 6-May-94 Skinner, Bolton #111/R
$1500	£1007	Hong Kong harbour (51x33cm-20x13in) s. canvasboard. 4-Dec-93 Louisiana Auction Exchange #92/R
$2200	£1477	Great Admiral (51x71cm-20x28in) s. panel. 29-Nov-93 Stonington Fine Arts, Stonington #191/R
$2700	£1812	New Bedford whaler (61x87cm-24x34in) s. s.d.1960verso masonite. 6-May-94 Skinner, Bolton #113/R
$2900	£1908	Ship oh high seas (71x91cm-28x36in) s. 31-Mar-93 Sotheby's Arcade, New York #84/R
$3750	£2435	Through tropic seas (76x102cm-30x40in) s. 9-Sep-93 Sotheby's Arcade, New York #109/R

SMITH, Gean (1851-1928) American
$1700	£1111	Four horses in a pasture Alix Crescesus Star Pointer The Abbott (74x97cm-29x38in) s.i.d.1901. 7-Oct-93 Freeman Fine Arts, Philadelphia #905/R
$2500	£1748	Artful and trainer (41x61cm-16x24in) s.i.d.1904. 11-Mar-93 Christie's, New York #109/R

SMITH, George Melville (1879-?) American
$3000	£1734	Land yields her increase (61x109cm-24x43in) tempera panel. 24-Sep-92 Sotheby's, New York #173/R

SMITH, Gordon (1937-) Canadian
$1055	£690	Canadian water series (46x64cm-18x25in) s. acrylic paper. 6-Oct-93 Maynards, Vancouver #299 (C.D 1400)

SMITH, Gordon Appelby (1919-) Canadian
$738	£467	Abstract SB8 (20x18cm-8x7in) s. acrylic. 21-Oct-92 Maynards, Vancouver #141 (C.D 925)
$774	£524	Still life (58x73cm-23x29in) s. 3-Nov-93 Sotheby's, Toronto #235/R (C.D 1000)
$784	£503	Creek (46x77cm-18x30in) s. i.d.c.1955verso. 26-Apr-93 Levis, Calgary #194/R (C.D 1000)
$1814	£1225	Untitled - bowl of tulips (61x76cm-24x30in) s. 25-Apr-94 Levis, Calgary #312/R (C.D 2500)
$1844	£1237	Carmanan Valley (71x97cm-28x38in) s. 8-Dec-93 Maynards, Vancouver #227 (C.D 2450)
$1083	£732	Untitled (48x66cm-19x26in) W/C. 30-Mar-94 Maynards, Vancouver #98 (C.D 1500)

SMITH, Henry Pember (1854-1907) American
$1900	£1293	Cottage by a lake (35x51cm-14x20in) s. 15-Nov-93 Christie's, East, New York #39/R
$2000	£1333	Old homestead (36x51cm-14x20in) s. 23-May-94 Christie's, East, New York #94/R
$2500	£1701	Cottage by a stream (51x71cm-20x28in) s. 15-Nov-93 Christie's, East, New York #43/R
$2600	£1769	A Spanish villa on a river (51x71cm-20x28in) s. 15-Nov-93 Christie's, East, New York #146/R
$2600	£1667	Summer pond (51x71cm-20x28in) s. 9-Dec-92 Grogan, Massachussetts #54/R
$2750	£1834	Waterfront (30x46cm-12x18in) s.d.1881. 17-May-94 Grogan, Massachussetts #335/R
$2800	£1618	Small New England house on the river (25x38cm-10x15in) s. 23-Sep-92 Christie's, New York #80/R
$3000	£2083	Lakeside cottage (36x51cm-14x20in) s. 6-May-93 Louisiana Auction Exchange #124/R
$3000	£1734	Mid-summer morning (51x71cm-20x28in) s. i.verso. 25-Sep-92 Sotheby's Arcade, New York #210/R
$3250	£1879	Day in September (36x51cm-14x20in) s. i.verso. 25-Sep-92 Sotheby's Arcade, New York #202/R
$3500	£2365	Old willows in mid-summer (36x51cm-14x20in) s. 31-Mar-94 Sotheby's Arcade, New York #237/R
$4300	£2905	Boating on the pond (51x72cm-20x28in) s. 31-Mar-94 Sotheby's Arcade, New York #235/R
$650	£425	Shoreline with sailing vessels (18x28cm-7x11in) s.d.1874 gouache. 30-Jun-94 Richard Opfer, Timonium #123
$700	£464	St Mark's Venice (20x25cm-8x10in) s. W/C. 2-Oct-93 Weschler, Washington #116/R
$1900	£1098	Seascape (29x42cm-11x17in) s.d.1883 gouache pencil paper on board. 25-Sep-92 Sotheby's Arcade, New York #127/R

SMITH, Hope (1879-) American
$1100	£743	A sunny afternoon on the farm (61x69cm-24x27in) s.d.38 double-sided. 31-Mar-94 Sotheby's Arcade, New York #263/R

SMITH, Howard E (1885-?) American
$800	£462	Maine coast (71x97cm-28x38in) s. 27-Sep-92 James Bakker, Cambridge #114/R
$1600	£1074	California coast line (41x41cm-16x16in) s. board. 6-May-94 Skinner, Bolton #101/R

SMITH, J Christopher (1891-1943) American
$600	£397	Spring time, Cambria (61x76cm-24x30in) s. 15-Jun-94 Butterfield & Butterfield, San Francisco #4687/R
$900	£596	Cambria (33x41cm-13x16in) s. panel. 15-Jun-94 Butterfield & Butterfield, San Francisco #4678 a

SMITH, J Christopher (1891-1943) American-cont.
$1400	£824	Landscape near Salinas (33x41cm-13x16in) s. board. 4-Oct-92 Butterfield & Butterfield, Los Angeles #141/R
$1500	£882	Green landscape, near Salinas (61x76cm-24x30in) s. 4-Oct-92 Butterfield & Butterfield, Los Angeles #140/R

SMITH, Jack W (1874-1949) American
$950	£629	Seascape (13x15cm-5x6in) s. canvas on board. 14-Jun-94 John Moran, Pasadena #11
$2100	£1409	Mountain landscape, Carmel Valley, board. 7-May-94 San Rafael Auction Galleries #258
$3250	£2167	Sierra landscape (41x51cm-16x20in) s. 15-Mar-94 John Moran, Pasadena #103
$5000	£3356	Trees in sunlight, High Sierras (41x51cm-16x20in) s. board. 8-Dec-93 Butterfield & Butterfield, San Francisco #3389/R
$18000	£11921	Gathering clouds over the sea (76x117cm-30x46in) s. 15-Jun-94 Butterfield & Butterfield, San Francisco #4589/R
$55000	£36424	In the High Sierras, mountain torrent (71x86cm-28x34in) s.i.d.May 20 1925. 15-Jun-94 Butterfield & Butterfield, San Francisco #4673/R

SMITH, Jerome Howard (1861-1941) American
$1400	£966	Cowboys and horses at the watering hole (76x122cm-30x48in) s. 16-Feb-93 John Moran, Pasadena #126 a

SMITH, Jesse Willcox (1863-1935) American
$5200	*£3444*	*'Twas the Night before Christmas (24x36cm-9x14in) s. pen W/C board. 22-Sep-93 Christie's, New York #229/R*
$16000	*£10256*	*Jack and Jill (48x67cm-19x26in) s. gouache chl board. 26-May-93 Christie's, New York #80/R*

SMITH, Joseph Lindon (1863-1950) American
$1700	£1111	Seti, Father of Ramses - from the Temple of Abydos (64x84cm-25x33in) s. 18-Sep-93 James Bakker, Cambridge #195/R
$2700	£1731	Details from Wall Temple of Luxor, Dynasty 19 (64x56cm-25x22in) s. canvasboard. 24-May-93 Grogan, Massachussetts #363
$15000	£9615	Amenhotep III presenting offerings, Luxor Temple, Dynasty 18 (193x97cm-76x38in) 24-May-93 Grogan, Massachussetts #362/R
$750	*£504*	*At the chapel door (31x12cm-12x5in) s.d.1887 W/C graphite paper board. 6-May-94 Skinner, Bolton #64/R*

SMITH, Keith C (1924-) Canadian
$646	£431	Early sunrise (41x51cm-16x20in) s. s.i.verso. 30-May-94 Hodgins, Calgary #88 (C.D 900)

SMITH, Kimber (1922-) American
$4245	£2830	The piano player (228x81cm-90x32in) mono.i.d.1976 acrylic. 4-Jun-94 Aucktionhaus Burkard, Luzern #109/R (S.FR 6000)

SMITH, Leon Polk (1906-) American
$5000	*£3356*	*Untitled (81x118cm-32x46in) s.d. collage. 5-May-94 Sotheby's, New York #131 a/R*

SMITH, Lowell Ellsworth (20th C) American
$1000	*£671*	*Small chapel at San Miguel, Mexico (25x36cm-10x14in) s.i. s.d.1982 verso W/C. 8-Dec-93 Butterfield & Butterfield, San Francisco #3604/R*

SMITH, Mary (1842-1878) American
$1300	£872	The stump orator (23x30cm-9x12in) board. 27-Mar-94 Myers, Florida #15/R

SMITH, Mary T (1904-) American
$900	*£596*	*Six figures (140x56cm-55x22in) s. paint plywood. 21-Nov-92 Litchfield Auction Gallery #4*

SMITH, Miriam Tindall (20th C) American
$1000	£667	Self-portrait with model (114x91cm-45x36in) s.d.37. 23-May-94 Christie's, East, New York #274/R

SMITH, Ray (1959-) American
$2200	£1477	Untitled (63x79cm-25x31in) s.d.1989 paper. 3-May-94 Christie's, East, New York #201/R
$4658	£2948	Untitled (35x45cm-14x18in) 6-Dec-92 Binoche et Godeau, Paris #28/R (F.FR 25000)
$5000	£3472	Pancho (128x127cm-50x50in) s.d.1986 i.d.verso acrylic. 23-Feb-93 Sotheby's, New York #40/R
$9000	£6040	Untitled (156x110cm-61x43in) s.d.1988. 4-May-94 Christie's, New York #411/R
$10000	£6623	Untitled (91x121cm-36x48in) s.d.1989 panel. 19-Nov-92 Christie's, New York #263/R
$10000	£6711	Maria de la Cruz Como Chocmol (244x488cm-96x192in) s.d.1988 i.d.1988 verso four panels. 23-Feb-94 Christie's, New York #141/R
$28000	£18792	La diplomatica (186x427cm-73x168in) s.d.1990 s.i.d.verso oil encaustic panel. 4-May-94 Christie's, New York #393/R
$6000	*£4027*	*Untitled (168x128cm-66x50in) s.d.1986 oil canvas collage. 4-May-94 Christie's, New York #402/R*

SMITH, Russell (1812-1896) American
$900	£570	Pennypack, 1890 (30x46cm-12x18in) init. 3-Dec-92 Freeman Fine Arts, Philadelphia #1814
$1300	£884	Italian coastal scene (12x18cm-5x7in) init.s.d.1869verso. 10-Jul-93 Young Fine Arts Auctions, Maine #277/R

SMITH, Russell (1812-1896) American-cont.
$3500 £2333 Near Louden, Pennsylvania (30x46cm-12x18in) init. s.i.d. 1840 1844verso. 16-Mar-94 Christie's, New York #6/R
$3500 £2349 Island of Cattawissa (61x91cm-24x36in) s.d. 1871. 24-Jun-93 Mystic Fine Arts, Connecticut #166

SMITH, Russell (attrib) (1812-1896) American
$1600 £1067 Portrait of Captain, maritime battle visible beyond (61x51cm-24x20in) i. oval. 12-Jun-94 Skinner, Bolton #151/R

SMITH, Thomas Henry (attrib) (19th C) American
$1350 £849 Portrait of Mary Diston (64x51cm-25x20in) i.d. 1873 i.verso. 22-Apr-93 Freeman Fine Arts, Philadelphia #1275

SMITH, Thomas Lochlan (1835-1884) American
$2600 £1503 Landscape with fisherman on lake (61x51cm-24x20in) s.indis.d. 25-Sep-92 Sotheby's Arcade, New York #129/R

SMITH, Wallace Herndon (1901-) American
$600 £403 Country lane winding through forest (53x74cm-21x29in) s. masonite. 2-May-94 Selkirks, St. Louis #94
$1400 £886 Notre Dame (69x91cm-27x36in) s. 30-Nov-92 Selkirks, St. Louis #163/R
$2600 £1781 Moonlit Michigan landscape with lake (69x91cm-27x36in) s. 7-Feb-94 Selkirks, St. Louis #288/R
$4000 £2532 Finish (64x76cm-25x30in) s. 30-Nov-92 Selkirks, St. Louis #248/R
$4250 £2911 Harbour spring sailboat race (41x69cm-16x27in) s. 7-Feb-94 Selkirks, St. Louis #285/R

SMITH, Walter Granville (1870-1938) American
$700 £458 Landscape (30x41cm-12x16in) s.d. 1922 board. 19-Sep-93 Hindman Galleries, Chicago #742/R
$1000 £690 Hillside by stream (15x20cm-6x8in) s. board. 16-Feb-93 John Moran, Pasadena #118
$1100 £636 Sunset (30x41cm-12x16in) s.i. 25-Sep-92 Sotheby's Arcade, New York #138/R
$2250 £1562 The hillside (41x51cm-16x20in) s. 27-Feb-93 Young Fine Arts Auctions, Maine #118/R
$2600 £1733 St. Urbain, Canada. Sea and rocks (30x40cm-12x16in) s.d. 1937 and s.d. 1929 canvasboard masonite pair. 23-May-94 Christie's, East, New York #169/R
$5500 £3667 Montauk. On the beach (30x40cm-12x16in) one s.d. 1930 one s. s.i.verso board masonite two. 23-May-94 Christie's, East, New York #176/R
$550 £362 Fly fisherman (25x33cm-10x13in) s.d. 1930 W/C pencil board. 31-Mar-93 Sotheby's Arcade, New York #416/R
$1000 £649 At the water's edge (50x33cm-20x13in) studio st.verso W/C graphite htd white board. 9-Sep-93 Sotheby's Arcade, New York #45/R
$2750 £1797 Resting at the inn (43x74cm-17x29in) s.d. 1896 W/C. 8-May-93 Young Fine Arts Auctions, Maine #130/R

SMITH, William St Thomas (1862-1926) Canadian
$663 £436 Sailing ship in stormy seas (76x53cm-30x21in) W/C. 7-Jun-93 Waddingtons, Toronto #1152 (C.D 850)
$1712 £1134 Farm scene at sunset (63x97cm-25x38in) s. W/C. 24-Nov-92 Joyner Fine Art, Toronto #49/R (C.D 2200)

SMITH, Wuanita (1866-1959) American
$2400 £1611 Girl on rocks overlooking sea Rocky Neck Gloucester Massachusetts, s.d. s.i.d. July 1920verso. 2-Dec-93 Freeman Fine Arts, Philadelphia #784

SMITH, Xanthus (1838-1929) American
$1224 £800 Chalets at Zwing Uri, Switzerland (35x57cm-14x22in) s. i.d. 1882verso. 12-May-93 Sotheby's Colonnade, London #28/R
$1500 £987 Mountainous landscape with cottage and figures herding livestock (37x53cm-15x21in) s.d. 1898 i.verso. 31-Mar-93 Sotheby's Arcade, New York #50/R
$4800 £3179 'Old Man's Basin', Franconia Notch, N.H (30x46cm-12x18in) init.d. 76. 22-Sep-93 Christie's, New York #11/R
$1100 £764 Taking in the sails (28x46cm-11x18in) s.d. 1892 gouache brunaille. 3-Mar-93 Doyle, New York #63/R

SMITHSON, Robert (1938-1973) American
$1500 £1042 Untitled (61x46cm-24x18in) s.d. 62 pen paper on board. 23-Feb-93 Sotheby's, New York #291/R
$3200 £2148 Spiral jetty (48x61cm-19x24in) graphite executed 1970. 4-May-94 Christie's, New York #232/R
$5000 £3268 Floating island, barge to travel around Manhattan Island (48x60cm-19x24in) s.d. 71 pencil. 4-May-93 Sotheby's, New York #138/R
$5500 £3235 Mirror thicket - outdoor version (36x43cm-14x17in) s.d. 69 col. pencil ink. 6-Oct-92 Sotheby's, New York #110/R
$6500 £4248 Earth mirror (61x48cm-24x19in) s.d. 68 pencil. 4-May-93 Sotheby's, New York #135/R
$6500 £3824 Mirror thicket - indoor and outdoor (36x43cm-14x17in) s.d. 69 crayon. 6-Oct-92 Sotheby's, New York #120/R
$12500 £8389 No 4 rock coral mirror (59x48cm-23x19in) s.i.d. 71 pencil col. pencil marker. 5-May-94 Sotheby's, New York #262/R

SNEAD, Louise W (19/20th C) American
$550 £372 Woman in white descending outisde staircase (38x28cm-15x11in) s. 12-Aug-93 Eldred, Massachusetts #868/R

SNELGROVE, Walter (1924-) American
$986   £658   Skyline (139x194cm-55x76in) 26-Jan-94 Dorotheum, Vienna #148/R (A.S 12000)
$2750 £1741 Landscape (137x203cm-54x80in) s. 25-Oct-92 Butterfield & Butterfield, San Francisco #2298/R

SNELL, Henry Bayley (1858-1943) American
$7000 £4762 Gloucester (63x76cm-25x30in) s. 15-Nov-93 Christie's, East, New York #247/R

SNOW, Dora Donaldson (19/20th C) American?
$1300 £909   Bulls in pasture (94x173cm-37x68in) s.d.1910 canvas on masonite. 3-Feb-93 Doyle, New York #57

SNOW, E Taylor (attrib) (1844-1913) American
$6000 £3468 Evening's pleasure (30x42cm-12x17in) bears sig. d.1878. 24-Sep-92 Sotheby's, New York #4/R

SNOW, John (1911-) Canadian
$1883 £1231 Road towards mountains (91x122cm-36x48in) s.d.81. 10-May-93 Hodgins, Calgary #141/R (C.D 2400)

SNYDER, Joan (1940-) American
$650   £431   Untitled (61x81cm-24x32in) s.d.71 oil acrylic pencil spray paint paperboard. 30-Jun-93 Sotheby's Arcade, New York #334
$4800 £3179 Cantana number 2 (91x50cm-36x20in) s.d.88verso oil acrylic nails wire linen panel. 17-Nov-92 Christie's, East, New York #43/R

SNYDER, Peter Etril (1944-) Canadian
$602   £404   Rail fence road (20x25cm-8x10in) s.d.1981 i.verso masonite. 29-Nov-93 Ritchie, Toronto #234/R (C.D 800)
$1005 £670   Sugaring in Bowman's Bush (30x40cm-12x16in) s.d.1980 masonite. 30-May-94 Ritchie, Toronto #180/R (C.D 1400)
$1189 £777   In father's footsteps (30x41cm-12x16in) s.d.1981 board. 19-May-93 Sotheby's, Toronto #311/R (C.D 1500)
$1292 £861   Buggy maker (30x40cm-12x16in) s.d.1980 masonite. 30-May-94 Ritchie, Toronto #170/R (C.D 1800)

SNYDER, William McKinley (19/20th C) American
$650   £425   Beech grove (25x36cm-10x14in) s. 8-May-93 Young Fine Arts Auctions, Maine #274/R

SOCKWELL, Carroll (20th C) American
$1400 £897   Untitled (23x183cm-9x72in) s.d.1978verso acrylic panel. 10-Dec-92 Sloan, North Bethesda #2700
$725   £465   Untitled (43x36cm-17x14in) chl.pastel canvas. 10-Dec-92 Sloan, North Bethesda #2699

SOHIER, Alice Ruggles (1880-?) American
$3200 £2078 Still life with vase of lilies, zinnias and bluebells (64x76cm-25x30in) s. 4-Aug-94 Eldred, Massachusetts #882/R
$6750 £4327 The pewter plate (64x64cm-25x25in) s.d.1923. 9-Dec-92 Grogan, Massachussetts #74/R

SOLARI, Luis A (20th C) Uruguayan
$900   £608   Pareja (44x30cm-17x12in) s. fibre. 25-Apr-94 Gomensoro, Montevideo #73
$1000 £676   Tentaciones del nino Antonio (41x57cm-16x22in) s.d.1977 board. 25-Apr-94 Gomensoro, Montevideo #42
$1900 £1275 Gaucho y china (32x42cm-13x17in) s.d.66. 29-Nov-93 Gomensoro, Montevideo #16
$2900 £1895 Reunion de quimeras y paisanos (50x61cm-20x24in) s. board. 3-May-93 Gomensoro, Montevideo #41/R
$550   £369   Partida de naipes (19x29cm-7x11in) s.d.59 W/C. 29-Nov-93 Gomensoro, Montevideo #18
$650   £436   Mascaras de la flor (39x48cm-15x19in) s.d.58 mixed media. 29-Nov-93 Gomensoro, Montevideo #17
$680   £444   Quimeras (14x17cm-6x7in) s. collage. 4-Oct-93 Gomensoro, Montevideo #43
$950   £621   Tres figuras y un piano (21x24cm-8x9in) s.i.d.1972 collage. 4-Oct-93 Gomensoro, Montevideo #42/R
$2200 £1294 Lobizon carnavalero (67x93cm-26x37in) s.d.65 oil collage hardboard. 5-Oct-92 Gomensoro, Montevideo #16/R

SOLDI, Raul (1905-) Argentinian
$2500 £1656 Paisaje (16x22cm-6x9in) 11-Nov-92 VerBo, Buenos Aires #103
$4000 £2614 Casona y parque (16x23cm-6x9in) s.i.d.93 fibre. 4-Oct-93 Gomensoro, Montevideo #16/R
$8200 £4271 La volanta (25x34cm-10x13in) 4-Aug-92 VerBo, Buenos Aires #103/R
$14000 £8092 La nina del Guante (67x38cm-26x15in) tempera. 23-Sep-92 Roldan & Cia, Buenos Aires #40
$1100 £728   Mujer recostada (23x35cm-9x14in) mixed media. 11-Nov-92 VerBo, Buenos Aires #102
$11000 £7285 Arlequines (102x69cm-40x27in) s.d.52 pastel Fabriano paper. 24-Nov-92 Christie's, New York #218/R

SOLMAN, Joseph (1909-) American
$1400 £909   Interior. Portrait of boy (61x41cm-24x16in) s. board. 9-Sep-93 Sotheby's Arcade, New York #368/R

SOMMER, Charles A (19th C) American
$6500 £4248 Storm moving across river valley (51x91cm-20x36in) s. 5-May-93 Doyle, New York #5/R

SOMMERS, Otto (19th C) American
$962 £650 Cattle on riverbank (46x61cm-18x24in) s.d.1874. 17-Jun-93 Bonhams, London #94
$2700 £1800 An Alpine landscape (70x100cm-28x39in) s.d.1876. 25-May-94 Sotheby's Colonnade, London #111/R
$3000 £1935 Cows in mountainous river landscape (86x123cm-34x48in) s.d.1873. 20-Jan-93 Sotheby's Arcade, New York #364/R

SONNTAG, William L (1822-1900) American
$1100 £724 Mountain sunset (13x8cm-5x3in) s.d.Jan1879 cardboard. 2-Jun-93 Doyle, New York #88
$1800 £1216 Cows in clearing (23x38cm-9x15in) s. 4-Nov-93 Sloan, North Bethesda #2742/R
$2000 £1342 Waterfall (25x30cm-10x12in) s. 6-Dec-93 Grogan, Massachussetts #491/R
$3700 £2176 Landscape with figures working by lake (25x46cm-10x18in) s. 11-Oct-92 Litchfield Auction Gallery #130
$3750 £1953 Landscape (51x61cm-20x24in) 7-Aug-92 Du Mouchelle, Detroit #2033/R
$4000 £2632 Fishing near old mill (36x51cm-14x20in) s. 31-Mar-93 Sotheby's Arcade, New York #29/R
$4500 £2961 River landscape (25x30cm-10x12in) s.i. 31-Mar-93 Sotheby's Arcade, New York #27/R
$4700 £3197 Anglers in a rocky cove (38x56cm-15x22in) s.d.1881. 17-Nov-93 Doyle, New York #5/R
$5000 £2890 View of White Mountains (48x81cm-19x32in) s.d.1866 canvas on masonite. 24-Sep-92 Sotheby's, New York #65/R
$5500 £3595 Adirondak landscape (51x91cm-20x36in) s.d.1868. 4-May-93 Christie's, East, New York #29/R
$5500 £3667 Landscape at sunset (25x31cm-10x12in) s. 17-Mar-94 Sotheby's, New York #18/R
$6000 £4000 Tangled wood, New Hampshire (25x30cm-10x12in) s. i.verso. 23-May-94 Christie's, East, New York #105/R
$6500 £4333 Fishing at sunrise (51x66cm-20x26in) s. double-sided. 17-Mar-94 Sotheby's, New York #17/R
$7000 £4487 Eagle Cliff, New Hampshire (18x27cm-7x11in) s. 27-May-93 Sotheby's, New York #148/R
$7000 £4698 Wooded river landscape with figures on raft (107x155cm-42x61in) s. i.d.1849 verso. 4-May-94 Doyle, New York #4
$7500 £5208 Waterfall near snow covered peak (53x89cm-21x35in) s.indis.d.185. 27-Feb-93 Young Fine Arts Auctions, Maine #253/R
$9000 £5202 River view (30x51cm-12x20in) s. 24-Sep-92 Sotheby's, New York #7/R
$10000 £5780 Fishing on mountain lake (31x51cm-12x20in) s. 24-Sep-92 Sotheby's, New York #66/R
$10000 £6623 At foot of Mt Carter, New Hampshire (102x140cm-40x55in) s. 23-Sep-93 Sotheby's, New York #56/R
$10000 £6536 Mountain landscape with waterfall (21x34cm-8x13in) s. 14-May-93 Du Mouchelle, Detroit #1998/R
$11000 £6358 Conestoga wagon (51x79cm-20x31in) s.i. 23-Sep-92 Christie's, New York #74/R
$15000 £9615 White mountain landscape (100x140cm-39x55in) s.d.1881. 27-May-93 Sotheby's, New York #169/R
$16000 £10256 Early autumn morning, Western Virginia (66x91cm-26x36in) s.d.1856. 27-May-93 Sotheby's, New York #188/R
$19000 £12752 Italian landscape with classical ruins (91x142cm-36x56in) s.d.1860. 16-Dec-93 Mystic Fine Arts, Connecticut #98/R
$19000 £12752 Fishing in the cove (77x127cm-30x50in) s.d.1865. 3-Dec-93 Christie's, New York #90/R
$19000 £13287 Mountain landscape, New York State (51x91cm-20x36in) s.d.69. 11-Mar-93 Christie's, New York #65/R

SONNTAG, William L (attrib) (1822-1900) American
$700 £467 Rushing river, autumn (23x30cm-9x12in) bears init. i.verso. 26-May-94 Sloan, North Bethesda #1606

SONNTAG, William L (jnr) (1870-?) American
$2400 £1589 Low tide (23x50cm-9x20in) s. W/C gouache. 22-Sep-93 Christie's, New York #35/R

SORENSEN, Carl Sophus Vilhelm (1864-1915) American
$1607 £929 Pair of horses with harness, buildings in background (87x117cm-34x46in) s.i.d.1898. 24-Sep-92 Rasmussen, Vejle #797/R (D.KR 9000)

SORENSON, Don (20th C) American
$1500 £1014 Yellow abstract, 1976 (229x199cm-90x78in) s.d.1978verso. 21-Apr-94 Butterfield & Butterfield, San Francisco #1165/R

SORIANO, Juan (1920-) Mexican
$8000 £5333 Untitled (120x170cm-47x67in) s.d.2.1.91. 18-May-94 Christie's, New York #143/R
$20000 £13072 Dos mujeres con escundilla (74x60cm-29x24in) s.d.39. 17-May-93 Christie's, New York #182/R
$22000 £14570 Apolo con peces (131x100cm-52x39in) s.d.87. 24-Nov-92 Christie's, New York #188/R
$1000 £654 Gatos (32x41cm-13x16in) s.d.73 pen. 18-May-93 Sotheby's, New York #200/R
$4000 £2667 Florero (44x34cm-17x13in) s.d.88 W/C. 18-May-94 Sotheby's, New York #416/R
$7500 £5068 Untitled (74x50cm-29x20in) s.d.1932 chl. 23-Nov-93 Christie's, New York #245/R
$11000 £7285 Estudio para mural (55x35cm-22x14in) s.d.49 W/C pencil Arches board. 24-Nov-92 Christie's, New York #339/R
$14000 £9272 Untitled (41x68cm-16x27in) s.d.37 W/C pencil. 24-Nov-92 Christie's, New York #187/R

SORIANO, Juan (1920-) Mexican-cont.
$18000 £11921 Banistas (60x60cm-24x24in) s.d.45 gouache composite board. 24-Nov-92 Christie's, New York #186/R

SORIANO, Rafael (1920-) Cuban
$13000	£8784	Sortilegio (127x127cm-50x50in) s. painted 1985. 22-Nov-93 Sotheby's, New York #243/R
$14000	£9333	Viajando hacia el silencio (127x127cm-50x50in) s. s.i.verso painted 1991. 18-May-94 Sotheby's, New York #328/R
$14000	£9396	Memoria Cosmica (130x131cm-51x52in) s.d.87. 7-Jan-94 Gary Nader, Miami #4/R
$17000	£11258	El Hechizo de la Noche (127x152cm-50x60in) s. s.i.verso painted 1991. 24-Nov-92 Christie's, New York #242/R
$18000	£11765	Calida luz (127x153cm-50x60in) s. s.i.verso. 17-May-93 Christie's, New York #155/R

SOSA, Hermenegildo (1946-) Mexican
$11288 £7576 Del sol glorioso (130x150cm-51x59in) 1-Dec-93 Louis Morton, Mexico #129/R (M.P 35000)

SOTO, Jesus Rafael (1923-) Venezuelan
$34000	£22667	Variations (99x99cm-39x39in) s.d.1960 i.verso oil wire masonite. 18-May-94 Christie's, New York #133/R
$14900	£10000	Rond avec Cobalt (101cm-40in circular) s.i.d.1972 acrylic wood metal nylon thread. 25-Mar-93 Christie's, London #103/R

SOTO, Rosendo (1912-) Mexican
$1592	£1020	Barranca tropical (61x81cm-24x32in) s.d.1989. 29-Apr-93 Louis Morton, Mexico #27 (M.P 5000)
$1935	£1299	Cacalotenango, Gro. (70x92cm-28x36in) s.d.1977. 1-Dec-93 Louis Morton, Mexico #191/R (M.P 6000)
$2229	£1429	Paisaje montanoso (80x100cm-31x39in) s.d.70. 29-Apr-93 Louis Morton, Mexico #43 (M.P 7000)
$3197	£2160	Mi viejo contreras (100x80cm-39x31in) 20-Oct-93 Louis Morton, Mexico #130/R (M.P 10000)

SOTTER, George William (1879-1953) American
$2100	£1409	Incoming tide, Monterey Bay (18x23cm-7x9in) s. board. 16-Oct-93 Dargate Auction Galleries, Pittsburgh #6
$2600	£1529	Massachusetts Coast (25x30cm-10x12in) s. canvasboard. 8-Oct-92 Freeman Fine Arts, Philadelphia #1080/R

SOULEN, Henry James (1888-1965) American
$2000	£1325	Gypsy camp (76x66cm-30x26in) s. 13-Nov-92 Skinner, Bolton #110/R
$2500	£1603	Presentation of the Royal child (71x71cm-28x28in) s. 9-Dec-92 Butterfield & Butterfield, San Francisco #3952/R
$2500	£1603	Bridal procession (71x81cm-28x32in) s. 9-Dec-92 Butterfield & Butterfield, San Francisco #3951/R
$5500	£3481	Chinatown (86x81cm-34x32in) s. 3-Dec-92 Freeman Fine Arts, Philadelphia #1829/R
$5500	£3642	Circus scene (86x76cm-34x30in) s. 23-Sep-93 Sotheby's, New York #262/R

SOUTH AMERICAN SCHOOL
$5000 £3378 Virgen del Rosario (35x26cm-14x10in) sheet metal painted between 1780-1830. 22-Nov-93 Sotheby's, New York #132/R

SOWERS, Robert (20th C) American
$1500 £1042 Picnic in the park (102x127cm-40x50in) init.d.8/19/86verso. 26-Feb-93 Sotheby's Arcade, New York #413/R

SOYER, Isaac (20th C) American
$2200	£1467	Street people (61x46cm-24x18in) s. 23-May-94 Christie's, East, New York #236/R
$2250	£1521	Applying red lipstick (61x41cm-24x16in) s. 31-Mar-94 Sotheby's Arcade, New York #370/R
$13500	£8544	The waitress (75x63cm-30x25in) s. 2-Dec-92 Christie's, East, New York #358/R
$14000	£9333	Working girl (76x91cm-30x36in) s. 25-May-94 Sotheby's, New York #138/R
$650	£442	Studies of a young child (41x54cm-16x21in) s. chl col chk. 15-Nov-93 Christie's, East, New York #210/R

SOYER, Moses (1899-1974) American
$850	£575	Portrait of a woman in red shirt (41x30cm-16x12in) s. canvasboard. 31-Mar-94 Sotheby's Arcade, New York #371/R
$950	£647	A couple (25x35cm-10x14in) s. 15-Nov-93 Christie's, East, New York #186/R
$1000	£641	Female nude (41x30cm-16x12in) s. 26-Apr-93 Selkirks, St. Louis #294
$1100	£719	Half-draped woman (41x30cm-16x12in) s. 4-May-93 Christie's, East, New York #257/R
$1100	£724	Self-portrait (30x23cm-12x9in) s.d.66. 31-Mar-93 Sotheby's Arcade, New York #426/R
$1100	£636	Portrait of woman in red (41x30cm-16x12in) s. 25-Sep-92 Sotheby's Arcade, New York #362/R
$1200	£759	Young man in blue shirt (51x38cm-20x15in) paper laid down on canvas. 2-Dec-92 Christie's, East, New York #375/R
$1600	£1046	Pink ballet dancer (51x25cm-20x10in) s. 4-May-93 Christie's, East, New York #252/R
$1600	£1013	Two standing women (51x26cm-20x10in) s. 2-Dec-92 Christie's, East, New York #364/R
$1700	£983	Dancer in red skirt (51x25cm-20x10in) s.i. 25-Sep-92 Sotheby's Arcade, New York #370/R

SOYER, Moses (1899-1974) American-cont.

$1800	£1169	Portrait of Naomi (91x76cm-36x30in) painted 1959. 9-Sep-93 Sotheby's Arcade, New York #281/R
$1900	£1218	Nude in profile (51x41cm-20x16in) s. 26-Apr-93 Selkirks, St. Louis #303/R
$1900	£1098	Girl in red sweater (61x46cm-24x18in) s. 25-Sep-92 Sotheby's Arcade, New York #369/R
$2050	£1424	Young girl (36x28cm-14x11in) s.d.29. 6-Mar-93 Louisiana Auction Exchange #13/R
$2200	£1467	At the bar (61x46cm-24x18in) s.d.1952 init.i.stretcher. 23-May-94 Christie's, East, New York #289/R
$2800	£1867	Two women (51x41cm-20x16in) s. masonite. 23-May-94 Christie's, East, New York #273
$3000	£2013	Seated Burlesque dancer (79x53cm-31x21in) s.d.1938. 14-Jan-94 Du Mouchelle, Detroit #2009
$3100	£2039	Seated girl reading magazine (51x46cm-20x18in) s. 31-Mar-93 Sotheby's Arcade, New York #432/R
$3100	£2039	Dancer and teacher (51x41cm-20x16in) s.i.d.44. 5-Jun-93 Louisiana Auction Exchange #24/R
$3200	£2092	Seated dancer in red (47x39cm-19x15in) s. canvasboard. 4-May-93 Christie's, East, New York #253/R
$3500	£2288	David Burluik sketching his wife (51x41cm-20x16in) s.d.1944. 20-May-93 Boos Gallery, Michigan #471/R
$4000	£2116	Still life with violin and vase (51x61cm-20x24in) s.d.36. 12-Sep-92 Louisiana Auction Exchange #113/R
$5500	£3481	Burlesque dancer (62x51cm-24x20in) s. 2-Dec-92 Christie's, East, New York #371/R
$6000	£3871	Nude (79x41cm-31x16in) s.d.1952. 4-Jan-93 Gordon Galleries, Tel Aviv #442/R
$8000	£5063	Seamstresses (51x41cm-20x16in) s. 5-Dec-92 Louisiana Auction Exchange #89/R
$12000	£8000	The costume maker (63x76cm-25x30in) s. 25-May-94 Sotheby's, New York #141/R
$650	£434	Nude (65x50cm-26x20in) s. chl paper on board. 23-May-94 Christie's, East, New York #282/R
$1300	*£844*	*Reclining nudes (48x67cm-19x26in) s. pencil sanguine wash paper on board. 9-Sep-93 Sotheby's Arcade, New York #297/R*

SOYER, Raphael (1899-1987) American

$950	£609	Semi-draped nude (35x20cm-14x8in) s. canvasboard. 27-Apr-93 Christie's, East, New York #276
$1500	£987	Reclining female nude (20x25cm-8x10in) s. 31-Mar-93 Sotheby's Arcade, New York #433/R
$1500	£987	Two nudes (33x25cm-13x10in) s. 4-Nov-92 Doyle, New York #46/R
$1500	£962	Woman with long red hair (41x30cm-16x12in) s. canvas on board painted c.1949. 27-May-93 Swann Galleries, New York #259/R
$1900	£1218	Nude studies (25x20cm-10x8in) s. oil pencil. 9-Dec-92 Butterfield & Butterfield, San Francisco #4025/R
$2000	£1156	Still life (51x61cm-20x24in) s. panel. 25-Sep-92 Sotheby's Arcade, New York #354/R
$2000	£1389	Woman in purple (23x30cm-9x12in) s. 6-Mar-93 Louisiana Auction Exchange #113/R
$2200	£1410	Portrait of seated girl (51x41cm-20x16in) s. 26-Apr-93 Selkirks, St. Louis #292
$2500	£1445	Girl in green (41x30cm-16x12in) s. 25-Sep-92 Sotheby's Arcade, New York #422/R
$2500	£1689	Seated girl with blond hair (51x41cm-20x16in) s. 31-Mar-94 Sotheby's Arcade, New York #362/R
$3200	£2092	Undressing (41x30cm-16x12in) s. 4-May-93 Christie's, East, New York #258/R
$3250	£2196	Schary and Broussard (25x20cm-10x8in) s. 31-Mar-94 Sotheby's Arcade, New York #340/R
$3500	£2333	A seated ballerina (46x35cm-18x14in) s. 23-May-94 Christie's, East, New York #279/R
$3750	£2534	Seated woman in blue (51x41cm-20x16in) s. 31-Mar-94 Sotheby's Arcade, New York #321/R
$4500	£3041	Lady wearing red jacket (41x30cm-16x12in) s. 4-Nov-93 Boos Gallery, Michigan #1282/R
$5000	£3289	Seated female nude (36x25cm-14x10in) s. 31-Mar-93 Sotheby's Arcade, New York #423/R
$5500	£3667	Rema in brown sweater (51x41cm-20x16in) s. 16-Mar-94 Christie's, New York #114/R
$6000	£4054	Girl in a black blouse (76x51cm-30x20in) s. 31-Mar-94 Sotheby's Arcade, New York #334/R
$7000	£4545	Self portrait (23x18cm-9x7in) s.i.d.1941 board. 15-Jan-93 Du Mouchelle, Detroit #2004/R
$12000	£6936	Roommates (91x61cm-36x24in) s. 23-Sep-92 Christie's, New York #264/R
$12500	£8741	Sarah Jackson (173x102cm-68x40in) s. painted 1964. 10-Mar-93 Sotheby's, New York #161/R
$13000	£8228	Karen Conrad, ballerina (76x50cm-30x20in) s. 3-Dec-92 Sotheby's, New York #193/R
$14000	£8974	Getting dressed (81x66cm-32x26in) s. 26-May-93 Christie's, New York #228/R
$600	*£347*	*Seated female nude (48x39cm-19x15in) s.d.1972 pastel chl. 25-Sep-92 Sotheby's Arcade, New York #445/R*
$700	*£476*	*Studies of a woman (42x53cm-17x21in) s. pencil. 15-Nov-93 Christie's, East, New York #207*
$800	*£506*	*Artist's model (41x54cm-16x21in) s. W/C pencil. 2-Dec-92 Christie's, East, New York #365/R*
$850	*£559*	*Woman reclining on sofa (47x32cm-19x13in) s. pencil W/C. 31-Mar-93 Sotheby's Arcade, New York #437/R*
$850	*£594*	*Meeting with Zosin in front of library (41x30cm-16x12in) s. i.verso W/C graphite. 12-Mar-93 Skinner, Bolton #281/R*
$900	*£552*	*Female studies, s. ink drawing. 16-Oct-92 Du Mouchelle, Detroit #2395/R*
$900	*£608*	*Self-portrait (26x32cm-10x13in) s. ink white chk. 31-Mar-94 Sotheby's Arcade, New York #375/R*
$950	*£642*	*Standing woman (58x42cm-23x17in) s. pencil W/C. 31-Mar-94 Sotheby's Arcade, New York #374/R*

SOYER, Raphael (1899-1987) American-cont.
$1100	£636	Standing female, view from front and back (34x23cm-13x9in) s. ink wash. 25-Sep-92 Sotheby's Arcade, New York #443/R
$1100	£724	Self-portrait. Rebecca (35x27cm-14x11in) s. pencil col.pencil sepia pair. 31-Mar-93 Sotheby's Arcade, New York #439/R
$1200	£779	Reclining nude. Portrait of young woman (34x27cm-13x11in) s. pencil pair. 9-Sep-93 Sotheby's Arcade, New York #342/R
$1500	£980	Self-portrait (34x26cm-13x10in) s.i.d.1964 pencil paper on board. 4-May-93 Christie's, East, New York #263
$1800	£1184	Seated woman in red (39x28cm-15x11in) s. gouache pencil. 31-Mar-93 Sotheby's Arcade, New York #430/R
$1900	£1250	Female nudes (25x19cm-10x7in) s. W/C ink four. 31-Mar-93 Sotheby's Arcade, New York #434/R

SPADER, William Edgar (1875-?) American
$550	£367	Woman in a red hat (25x33cm-10x13in) s. W/C gouache. 17-May-94 Grogan, Massachussetts #376

SPARKS, Will (1862-1937) American
$700	£464	Adobe at night with palm trees (30x46cm-12x18in) s. 20-Sep-93 Butterfield & Butterfield, Los Angeles #77
$850	£563	Tucson (15x23cm-6x9in) s.d.94. 20-Sep-93 Butterfield & Butterfield, Los Angeles #78/R
$1200	£789	Moonlight, Chinese camp (23x33cm-9x13in) s. panel. 13-Jun-93 Butterfield & Butterfield, San Francisco #793/R
$1700	£1118	Woman in front of Adobe (23x30cm-9x12in) s. panel. 13-Jun-93 Butterfield & Butterfield, San Francisco #792/R
$1700	£1118	House in moonlight (15x23cm-6x9in) s. canvas on board. 13-Jun-93 Butterfield & Butterfield, San Francisco #791/R
$1700	£1118	Interior with fireplace (25x36cm-10x14in) s.d.1916. 13-Jun-93 Butterfield & Butterfield, San Francisco #790/R
$1900	£1293	South-western village at evening (20x25cm-8x10in) s. 17-Apr-94 Hanzel Galleries, Chicago #982
$1900	£1275	California Mission with figures (23x30cm-9x12in) s. 8-Dec-93 Butterfield & Butterfield, San Francisco #3394/R
$2000	£1325	La Purisima Concepcion, near Lompoc (41x57cm-16x22in) s. 15-Jun-94 Butterfield & Butterfield, San Francisco #4641/R
$2250	£1490	A desert castle near Laguna, New Mexico (52x58cm-20x23in) s. i.verso. 15-Jun-94 Butterfield & Butterfield, San Francisco #4640/R
$2500	£1656	Adobe in moonlight (25x36cm-10x14in) s. 15-Jun-94 Butterfield & Butterfield, San Francisco #4639/R
$2500	£1471	Old farmhouse (30x46cm-12x18in) s.d.1908 board. 4-Oct-92 Butterfield & Butterfield, Los Angeles #42/R
$3250	£2257	Adobe at twilight (23x30cm-9x12in) s. board. 7-Mar-93 Butterfield & Butterfield, San Francisco #82/R
$3250	£2257	Nocturne (23x20cm-9x8in) s.d.1911 board. 7-Mar-93 Butterfield & Butterfield, San Francisco #83/R
$3500	£2431	Harbour at dusk (25x36cm-10x14in) s.d.1910. 7-Mar-93 Butterfield & Butterfield, San Francisco #94/R
$3750	£2604	La Purisima Concepcion (41x56cm-16x22in) s. 7-Mar-93 Butterfield & Butterfield, San Francisco #81/R
$5000	£2941	Spanish house (61x91cm-24x36in) s.d.1931. 4-Oct-92 Butterfield & Butterfield, Los Angeles #41/R
$12000	£8054	Pueblo (62x92cm-24x36in) s.d.1930 stretcher. 8-Dec-93 Butterfield & Butterfield, San Francisco #3373/R

SPAULDING, Henry Plympton (1868-?) American
$2860	£1869	March of Red Cross flags (71x48cm-28x19in) s. i.d.1918 verso gouache paperboard. 14-May-93 Skinner, Bolton #146/R

SPEAR, Arthur Prince (1879-1959) American
$2100	£1373	Seated nude (81x66cm-32x26in) 1-Nov-92 Hanzel Galleries, Chicago #117

SPECK, Walt (1895-?) American
$600	£397	Street scene (76x63cm-30x25in) s. 15-Jun-94 Butterfield & Butterfield, San Francisco #4735/R
$1600	£1060	Homage to the modern world, mural study (166x91cm-65x36in) 15-Jun-94 Butterfield & Butterfield, San Francisco #4734/R

SPEICHER, Eugene (1883-1962) American
$650	£434	The river (43x56cm-17x22in) s. 23-May-94 Christie's, East, New York #255/R
$950	£625	Rural landscape (46x56cm-18x22in) s. 5-Jun-93 Louisiana Auction Exchange #42/R
$1100	£748	Still life (36x46cm-14x18in) s. board. 16-Apr-94 Young Fine Arts Auctions, Maine #239/R
$1150	£665	Wildflowers and books on table (58x41cm-23x16in) s. 24-Sep-92 Mystic Fine Arts, Connecticut #214/R
$1500	£794	Rural street (48x61cm-19x24in) s. 12-Sep-92 Louisiana Auction Exchange #97/R
$1600	£1074	View of Kingston (46x56cm-18x22in) s. 8-Dec-93 Butterfield & Butterfield, San Francisco #3368/R
$1800	£1139	Yellow and red tulips (48x36cm-19x14in) s. 5-Dec-92 Louisiana Auction Exchange #56/R
$2600	£1503	Seated nude (95x80cm-37x31in) s. 25-Sep-92 Sotheby's Arcade, New York #419/R
$3800	£2405	Still life with flowers (43x33cm-17x13in) s.i.d.1947. 4-Dec-92 Christie's, New York #67/R

SPEIGHT, Francis (1896-1989) American
$3100 £1824 Factories near Manayunk, PA (64x76cm-25x30in) s. s.d.1927 verso. 8-Oct-92 Freeman Fine Arts, Philadelphia #1117/R

SPELMAN, John A (1880-1941) American
$850 £594 Morning mist (61x69cm-24x27in) s.d.28 i.stretcher. 14-Mar-93 Hindman Galleries, Chicago #13
$1900 £1250 Autumn river landscape with mountains in distance (81x91cm-32x36in) s.d.30. 31-Mar-93 Sotheby's Arcade, New York #243 a/R

SPENCER, Frederick R (1806-1875) American
$900 £581 Portrait of man holding book (86x69cm-34x27in) i.verso. 13-Jul-94 Doyle, New York #73

SPENCER, J C (19/20th C) American
$850 £556 Basket of violets with pink rose (46x30cm-18x12in) s.d.1911. 17-Sep-93 Skinner, Bolton #175/R
$900 £638 Brace of grouse (61x51cm-24x20in) s. 13-Feb-93 Collins, Maine #127/R

SPENCER, John C (19/20th C) American
$750 £507 Fishing still life the Finest Catch (41x66cm-16x26in) s.d.1897. 5-Nov-93 Skinner, Bolton #52/R
$1100 £582 Still life with grapes, peaches and a glass compote (51x41cm-20x16in) s.d.1916. 11-Sep-92 Skinner, Bolton #172/R
$1300 £903 Coastal view (36x56cm-14x22in) s.d.1913. 5-Mar-93 Skinner, Bolton #518

SPENCER, Lilly Martin (1822-1902) American
$650 £436 Gazing at the moon (71x46cm-28x18in) 16-Dec-93 Mystic Fine Arts, Connecticut #272
$7500 £4967 Patty cake (62x46cm-24x18in) s.d.1869 board. 22-Sep-93 Christie's, New York #77/R
$18000 £11538 This little piggy went to market (46x36cm-18x14in) s.indist.d.1857 board painted arch. 27-May-93 Sotheby's, New York #141/R

SPENCER, Niles (1893-1952) American
$600 £400 Chair and pitcher (53x36cm-21x14in) s. wash. 17-May-94 Grogan, Massachussetts #378/R

SPENCER, Robert (1879-1931) American
$9500 £6643 Woman hanging clothes (41x30cm-16x12in) s. 11-Mar-93 Christie's, New York #151/R
$11520 £8000 Misty evening (51x61cm-20x24in) s. 3-Mar-93 Dreweatt Neate, Newbury #156/R
$35000 £22152 Hilltown (77x92cm-30x36in) s. 4-Dec-92 Christie's, New York #39/R

SPERGER, Hugo (1922-) American
$650 £430 St Mark (46x61cm-18x24in) s.i.d.1992 acrylic board. 21-Nov-92 Litchfield Auction Gallery #4 a
$700 £464 Shadrach, Meschack and Abednego (61x76cm-24x30in) s.d.1990 acrylic board. 21-Nov-92 Litchfield Auction Gallery #6
$950 £629 An the winner is . (41x30cm-16x12in) s.d.1992 acrylic board. 21-Nov-92 Litchfield Auction Gallery #5

SPERO, Nancy (1926-) American?
$8000 £5229 Lovers (114x137cm-45x54in) executed 1962. 22-Dec-92 Christie's, East, New York #75

SPICKETT, Ronald (1926-) Canadian
$580 £392 Mountain viewpoint number 1 (37x101cm-15x40in) s.d.1957 masonite. 25-Apr-94 Levis, Calgary #317/R (C.D 800)
$653 £441 Mexico (114x65cm-45x26in) s.i.d.1956 heavy paper. 25-Apr-94 Levis, Calgary #318/R (C.D 900)

SPICUZZA, Francesco J (attrib) (1883-1962) American
$1250 £850 Northern Wisconsin rural landscape with water, summer (66x81cm-26x32in) s. board. 17-Apr-94 Schrager Galleries, Milwaukee #748
$600 *£408* *Moonlit landscape with water and buildings (43x64cm-17x25in) s. pastel. 17-Apr-94 Schrager Galleries, Milwaukee #749*
$900 *£612* *Still life floral (61x41cm-24x16in) s. pastel. 17-Apr-94 Schrager Galleries, Milwaukee #746*
$1000 *£633* *Bathing beauties at Bradford Beach (51x71cm-20x28in) s. pastel. 30-Nov-92 Schrager Galleries, Milwaukee #403*

SPIESS-FERRIS, Eleanor (20th C) American
$900 £600 Untitled (150x183cm-59x72in) s. 23-May-94 Hindman Galleries, Chicago #282 a/R

SPILIMBERGO, Lino Eneas (1896-1964) Argentinian
$120000 £81081 Noche de luna en el bosque, espiritu del bosque (110x56cm-43x22in) s. i.verso panel painted 1930. 23-Nov-93 Christie's, New York #42/R

SPIZZIRRI, Luigi (1898-?) American
$1000 £680 The mother (76x63cm-30x25in) s.d.1916. 15-Nov-93 Christie's, East, New York #191/R

SPRAGUE, Howard F (19th C) American
$6500 £4333 Geo Spencer, a ship at sea (43x76cm-17x30in) s.d.89. 18-Mar-94 Du Mouchelle, Detroit #2004/R

469

SPRINCHORN, Carl (1887-1971) American
$3000 £2041 Trail mark (30x25cm-12x10in) 10-Jul-93 Young Fine Arts Auctions, Maine #300/R

SPRUANCE, Benton (1904-1969) American
$600 £403 Mother and child (84x48cm-33x19in) gouache board painted c.1963. 2-Dec-93 Swann Galleries, New York #297
$1500 £993 Touch-down play (33x51cm-13x20in) s. chl. 12-Nov-92 Freeman Fine Arts, Philadelphia #223/R

SPRUCE, Everett (1908-) American
$1350 £888 Little Canyon (41x51cm-16x20in) s. i.verso board painted c.1940. 5-Jun-93 Louisiana Auction Exchange #172/R

STACEY, John F (1859-?) American
$1700 £1000 Haystacks (63x76cm-25x30in) s. 4-Oct-92 Butterfield & Butterfield, Los Angeles #114/R
$2500 £1471 Footpath through meadow (76x102cm-30x40in) s. 4-Oct-92 Butterfield & Butterfield, Los Angeles #112/R
$2500 £1471 Spring meadow (63x76cm-25x30in) s.d.1927. 4-Oct-92 Butterfield & Butterfield, Los Angeles #113/R

STACKPOLE, Ralph W (1885-1973) American
$1000 £671 Vineyards at Lilienthal Ranch, Cloverdale (34x50cm-13x20in) s. W/C. 8-Dec-93 Butterfield & Butterfield, San Francisco #3522/R

STAMOS, Theodoros (1922-) American
$1200 £833 Untitled (77x56cm-30x22in) s.d.1973 acrylic. 22-Feb-93 Christie's, East, New York #179/R
$1500 £993 Infinity field, Lefkada series (60x46cm-24x18in) 29-Sep-93 Sotheby's Arcade, New York #273/R
$2000 £1389 Delphic sun-box (42x174cm-17x69in) s.i.d.1968on overlap acrylic. 26-Feb-93 Sotheby's Arcade, New York #312/R
$2250 £1490 Infinity field, Lefkada series (61x45cm-24x18in) painted 1970. 29-Sep-93 Sotheby's Arcade, New York #275/R
$2400 £1569 Casablanca (101x76cm-40x30in) s. s.verso i.stretcher. 22-May-93 Weschler, Washington #143/R
$2500 £1656 Long yellow, sun box (36x178cm-14x70in) s. s.i.d.1968stretcher acrylic. 17-Nov-92 Christie's, East, New York #271/R
$2776 £1803 Transparence rouge (76x61cm-30x24in) s. acrylic painted 1968. 5-Jul-94 Jean Louis Picard, Paris #161 (F.FR 15000)
$3100 £2081 Transparent Sun-box (152x122cm-60x48in) s.i.d.1969 stretcher acrylic. 24-Feb-94 Sotheby's Arcade, New York #372/R
$3702 £2404 Infinity field lefkada Series (113x87cm-44x34in) acrylic painted 1980. 5-Jul-94 Jean Louis Picard, Paris #162/R (F.FR 20000)
$6000 £4027 The Chosica Sun Box II (152x173cm-60x68in) s.i.d.1968 verso. 24-Feb-94 Sotheby's Arcade, New York #370/R
$6000 £4000 Infinity Field - Lefkada Series (76x56cm-30x22in) s.i.d.1980 verso acrylic. 4-Jun-94 Neumeister, Munich #493/R (DM 10000)
$6500 £4362 Abstraction (74x55cm-29x22in) s.d.45 masonite. 6-May-94 Skinner, Bolton #157/R
$8500 £5556 Infinity field, Lefkada Series (127x76cm-50x30in) s.d.1982 verso acrylic. 7-May-93 Christie's, East, New York #94/R
$8500 £5903 Channel (46x132cm-18x52in) s. s.d.1958stretcher. 23-Feb-93 Sotheby's, New York #236/R
$9000 £5960 Untitled (142x131cm-56x52in) s. 19-Nov-92 Christie's, New York #348/R
$11000 £7432 Infinity field lefkada series (152x127cm-60x50in) s.d.1978 verso acrylic. 11-Nov-93 Sotheby's, New York #327/R
$12000 £7059 Infinity Field, Lefkada Series (117x72cm-46x28in) s.i.d.1980stretcher acrylic canvas. 8-Oct-92 Christie's, New York #152/R
$13000 £9028 Infinity field Lefkada series (152x152cm-60x60in) s.d.1980 i.verso acrylic. 23-Feb-93 Sotheby's, New York #253/R
$14000 £9396 Puritan (183x152cm-72x60in) s.i.d.1959verso. 5-May-94 Sotheby's, New York #112/R
$15000 £8824 Delphic sunbox No.1 (142x132cm-56x52in) s.d.1968 stretcher. 6-Oct-92 Sotheby's, New York #41/R
$18000 £12081 Infinity field, Lefkada series (203x180cm-80x71in) s. s.i.d.1974stretcher acrylic. 4-May-94 Christie's, New York #119/R
$25000 £16779 Baalbek terrace (178x178cm-70x70in) s.i.d.1959-1960 verso. 25-Feb-94 Sotheby's, New York #22/R
$25000 £16892 Day of three suns no.2 (173x112cm-68x44in) s. s.i.d.63 verso. 11-Nov-93 Sotheby's, New York #277/R
$3000 £1987 Transparent sun box (55x56cm-22x22in) acrylic pencil executed c.1967. 30-Jun-93 Sotheby's Arcade, New York #268/R

STANCLIFF, J W (1814-1879) American
$3500 £2023 Coney Island (28x48cm-11x19in) s.d.76 init.i.verso panel. 23-Sep-92 Christie's, New York #62/R

STANLEY, John Mix (1814-1872) American
$50000 £32051 Scouting party (30x36cm-12x14in) s. s.d.1864 painted oval. 27-May-93 Sotheby's, New York #219/R
$31000 £20805 Shu-Ma-Hici, Painted Shirt (23x16cm-9x6in) i. gouache painted 1847. 2-Dec-93 Sotheby's, New York #31/R
$33000 £22148 Mai-E-Cat, One that Flies (23x16cm-9x6in) i. gouache painted 1847. 2-Dec-93 Sotheby's, New York #32/R

STARK, Jack Gage (1882-1950) American
$1100   £728   Pomegranates and limes (49x63cm-19x25in) s. i.verso board. 15-Jun-94 Butterfield & Butterfield, San Francisco #4737/R

STARK, Melville F (1904-1987) American
$850   £429   Across the harbour, Gloucester, Massachussetts (61x76cm-24x30in) s. board. 30-Aug-92 Litchfield Auction Gallery #298

STARKWEATHER, William Edward (1879-1969) American
$1200   £805   Cottage near Valencia (86x58cm-34x23in) s.d.1904 i.verso. 3-Feb-94 Sloan, North Bethesda #2655
$1700   £1149   Connecticut children (76x94cm-30x37in) s. i.d.1921verso. 20-Mar-93 Weschler, Washington #115/R
$6000   £3468   Old Henri and his grandson (73x91cm-29x36in) s.d.1908 s.i.d.1908verso. 23-Sep-92 Christie's, New York #148/R

STARN TWINS (1961-) American
$1000   £676   Untitled Black Abstract (20x91cm-8x36in) s.d.1987verso silver print cellophane tape. 8-Nov-93 Christie's, East, New York #92/R
$4000   £2703   Yellow square, skull (91x91cm-36x36in) silver print cellphane tape nails glass on wood. 10-Nov-93 Christie's, New York #289/R
$9000   £5882   Yellow Plant No.3 (267x267cm-105x105in) s.d.88-90 verso photo collage tape nails panels. 7-May-93 Christie's, East, New York #122/R
$16000   £10596 The Stark portrait (274x201cm-108x79in) photo collage with celophane tape. 19-Nov-92 Christie's, New York #131/R

STARN, Doug and Mike see   STARN TWINS

STEARNS, Junius Brutus (1810-1885) American
$7000   £4667   Branch of cherries (46x30cm-18x12in) s. 26-May-94 Christie's, New York #16/R

STEARNS, Junius Brutus (attrib) (1810-1885) American
$29000   £19333 Death of Pocahontas (91x107cm-36x42in) 17-Mar-94 Sotheby's, New York #29/R

STEBBINS, Roland Stewart (1883-1974) American
$650   £425   Family on porch (51x61cm-20x24in) s. 16-May-93 Hindman Galleries, Chicago #115

STEELE, Theodore Clement (1847-1926) American
$5000   £2890   Rural landscape (56x81cm-22x32in) s.d.1908. 25-Sep-92 Sotheby's Arcade, New York #228/R
$5250   £3035   Seascape (36x56cm-14x22in) s.d.1903. 25-Sep-92 Sotheby's Arcade, New York #85/R

STEELE, Thomas Sedgewick (1845-1903) American
$700   £473   Still life with oysters and pretzels (41x51cm-16x20in) s.d.1899. 27-Nov-93 Young Fine Arts Auctions, Maine #308/R
$2200   £1467   Tomatoes and cucumbers on a ledge (25x41cm-10x16in) s.d.92. 23-May-94 Christie's, East, New York #82/R

STEENE, William (attrib) (1888-1965) American
$1250   £828   Fishing boat near shore forest beyond (102x81cm-40x32in) s. 26-Sep-93 Schrager Galleries, Milwaukee #415/R

STEENKS, Gerard L (1847-1926) American
$1000   £654   Oriental porcelains and fan (18x23cm-7x9in) s.d.1897. 30-Jun-94 Mystic Fine Arts, Connecticut #228/R
$3750   £2517   Onions and chilli peppers (30x38cm-12x15in) s. 24-Mar-94 Mystic Fine Arts, Connecticut #130/R
$14000   £8974   Lobster salad (46x76cm-18x30in) s. 26-May-93 Christie's, New York #74/R

STEFAN, Ross (1934-) American
$1600   £1074   Old gate (41x56cm-16x22in) s. s.i.verso. 8-Dec-93 Butterfield & Butterfield, San Francisco #3603/R
$2250   £1510   At my leisure (71x91cm-28x36in) s. s.i.verso. 8-Dec-93 Butterfield & Butterfield, San Francisco #3602/R

STEHLIN, Caroline (1879-1954) American
$7000   £4487   Flowered kimono (76x41cm-30x16in) s. 26-May-93 Christie's, New York #86/R

STEINBERG, Saul (1914-) American
$1400   £881   E (30x22cm-12x9in) init.d.60 graphite crayon. 25-Apr-93 Butterfield & Butterfield, San Francisco #2134/R
$2550   £1667   Happy Birthday to Mouche (25x33cm-10x13in) s.d.1951 stopping out Indian ink. 29-Jun-94 Guy Loudmer, Paris #6/R (F.FR 14000)
$5000   £3268   Untitled (58x73cm-23x29in) s.d.1960 ink crayon. 4-May-93 Sotheby's, New York #345/R
$5000   £3472   Authentic certification (50x65cm-20x26in) s. pen rubber stamps embossed seal. 22-Feb-93 Christie's, East, New York #153/R
$5000   £2941   Untitled (29x44cm-11x17in) s. ink graph paper. 6-Oct-92 Sotheby's, New York #71/R
$5500   £3642   Self portrait (31x24cm-12x9in) init.d.1946 pen. 17-Nov-92 Christie's, East, New York #276/R
$6000   £3974   Untitled (36x50cm-14x20in) s. pen. 17-Nov-92 Christie's, East, New York #275/R
$6000   £4167   Lion (30x46cm-12x18in) s.d.1950 pen brush graph paper on board. 22-Feb-93 Christie's, East, New York #154/R
$7000   £4698   The sheriff (37x29cm-15x11in) s.d.1951 ink col.crayons foil collage. 23-Feb-94 Christie's, East, New York #326/R

STEINBERG, Saul (1914-) American-cont.

$11000	£7190	Mombasa (59x74cm-23x29in) s.d.1969 W/C rubber stamps ink crayon paperboard. 5-May-93 Christie's, New York #234/R
$12000	£7059	Techniques (48x63cm-19x25in) s.d.1966 pen col.inks col.crayons. 8-Oct-92 Christie's, New York #140/R
$12000	£7947	Six sunsets (58x71cm-23x28in) s.d.1972 W/C col.ink rubber stamps chl. 19-Nov-92 Christie's, New York #372/R
$13000	£9028	Gallery (57x72cm-22x28in) s.d.1966 ink rubber stamp. 23-Feb-93 Sotheby's, New York #247/R
$16000	£10738	The Vicksburg table (71x58cm-28x23in) s.d.1968-1974 pen rubber stamps acrylic collage. 4-May-94 Christie's, New York #207/R
$16000	£10738	Suez table (58x71cm-23x28in) s.d.1974 acrylic W/C pencil wood relief collage. 5-May-94 Sotheby's, New York #174/R
$16000	£11111	Four tiles (66x51cm-26x20in) init.d.1988 graphite crayons photographs panel. 24-Feb-93 Christie's, New York #32/R
$17000	£11258	Landscapes with palaces (74x58cm-29x23in) s.d.65 acrylic W/C col.pencil ink stamp. 19-Nov-92 Christie's, New York #358/R
$18000	£12081	Buenos Aires table (57x73cm-22x29in) s.d.1969 acrylic W/C rubber stamp paper collage. 4-May-94 Christie's, New York #212/R
$18000	£10588	The Egypt Notebook (51x65cm-20x26in) s.d.1973 tin oil felt-tip col.pencils graphite. 8-Oct-92 Christie's, New York #171/R
$22000	£14570	The sketchbook table (71x58cm-28x23in) s.d.1974 i.d.verso mixed media collage on panel. 19-Nov-92 Christie's, New York #311/R
$32000	£21477	Buffalo's exhibit (62x93cm-24x37in) s.d.1972 mixed media wood. 5-May-94 Sotheby's, New York #203/R
$200000	£135135	View of the world from Ninth Avenue (73x51cm-29x20in) s.d.1976 pen graphite col.pencil W/C board. 10-Nov-93 Christie's, New York #128/R

STEINHARDT, Therese (1896-1948) American

$1600	£1039	Lest we forget (128x95cm-50x37in) s. 9-Sep-93 Sotheby's Arcade, New York #335/R

STEIR, Pat (1940-) American

$7500	£4412	Untitled (92x90cm-36x35in) 8-Oct-92 Christie's, New York #163/R
$12000	£7947	Beautiful painting (61x305cm-24x120in) five parts painted 1978. 18-Nov-92 Sotheby's, New York #255/R
$9500	£6291	Cellar door (183x274cm-72x108in) painted 1972 i.stretcher oil graphite canvas. 19-Nov-92 Christie's, New York #392/R

STELLA, Frank (1936-) American

$13991	£9390	Rayy II (51x200cm-20x79in) s.i.d.1970 paper. 4-May-94 Watine-Arnault, Paris #83/R (F.FR 80000)
$60000	£35294	Flin Flon No. XII (274x274cm-108x108in) s.d.70 acrlylic. 8-Oct-92 Christie's, New York #159/R
$66360	£42000	Maze (91x91cm-36x36in) s.d.66 verso acrylic. 3-Dec-92 Sotheby's, London #74/R
$120000	£81081	Gur Variation I (304x457cm-120x180in) acrylic graphite shaped painted 1969. 9-Nov-93 Christie's, New York #18/R
$130000	£87248	Untitled (200x200cm-79x79in) acrylic painted 1974. 4-May-94 Sotheby's, New York #45/R
$160000	£107383	The pearls (77x15cm-30x6in) painted 1962. 3-May-94 Christie's, New York #20/R
$165000	£111486	Mrs Rabbit's rainbow III (175x175cm-69x69in) acrylic painted 1974. 10-Nov-93 Sotheby's, New York #46/R
$250000	£168919	York factory B (274x823cm-108x324in) acrylic painted 1970. 10-Nov-93 Sotheby's, New York #29/R
$280000	£187919	Green grate (205x215cm-81x85in) painted 1958. 3-May-94 Christie's, New York #9/R
$280000	£183007	Sacramento Mall Proposal no.2 (267x267cm-105x105in) acrylic painted 1978. 3-May-93 Sotheby's, New York #68/R
$600000	£405405	Kingsbury Run - first version (175x181cm-69x71in) s.d.1961 stretcher aluminium oil paint shaped. 9-Nov-93 Christie's, New York #35/R
$6000	£3974	Balboa Island (52x100cm-20x39in) s.i.d.1970 gouache felttip pen. 19-Nov-92 Christie's, New York #419/R
$6676	£4542	Polar Co-ordinates variant IA (96x96cm-38x38in) s.d.80 acrylic serigraph col crayon. 13-Apr-94 Bukowskis, Stockholm #329/R (S.KR 53000)
$8000	£5405	Rzochow (84x76cm-33x30in) s.d.73 mixed media collage paperboard. 11-Nov-93 Sotheby's, New York #131/R
$8500	£5743	Untitled study for Conway (43x53cm-17x21in) s.d.70 gouache pen graph paper. 10-Nov-93 Christie's, New York #152/R
$9000	£5882	York factory (47x113cm-19x44in) s.d.1974 col.screenprint. 11-May-93 Christie's, New York #569/R
$9000	£5882	Nasiek (82x68cm-32x27in) s.d.73 col.crayon acrylic fabric paper on board. 7-May-93 Christie's, East, New York #54/R
$10000	£6536	Last cubist collage (51x51cm-20x20in) s.d.1959 verso asbestos tape collage board. 4-May-93 Sotheby's, New York #108/R
$10000	£6711	Untitled (17x17cm-7x7in) s.d.63verso col.pencil. 5-May-94 Sotheby's, New York #241/R
$11000	£7639	Untitled (43x56cm-17x22in) s.d.66 col.pencil. 23-Feb-93 Sotheby's, New York #322/R
$11000	£7190	Olyka - sketch (80x76cm-31x30in) s.d.73 acrylic fabric felt collage graph board. 4-May-93 Sotheby's, New York #118/R
$14000	£8235	Kozangrodek (83x76cm-33x30in) s.d.73 acrylic felt fabric paperboard masonite. 6-Oct-92 Sotheby's, New York #123/R
$14000	£9396	Polar coordinate (97x97cm-38x38in) s.d.79 crayon gouache glitter over lithograph. 25-Feb-94 Sotheby's, New York #51/R
$16000	£9412	Felsztyn (80x68cm-31x27in) s.d.73 acrylic felt fabric paperboard masonite. 6-Oct-92 Sotheby's, New York #114/R

STELLA, Frank (1936-) American-cont.

$18000	£11765	Double gray scramble (74x129cm-29x51in) s.d.1973 col.screenprint. 11-May-93 Christie's, New York #568/R
$22000	£14379	Rabat sketch (53x53cm-21x21in) s.d.1965 verso fluorescent alkyd canvas. 4-May-93 Sotheby's, New York #125/R
$24000	£16216	Bermuda petrel (152x213cm-60x84in) s.d.80 screenprint acrylic oilstick Tycore panel. 11-Nov-93 Sotheby's, New York #156/R
$36000	£24324	Untitled (61x50cm-24x20in) s.d.59 enamel oil canvasboard on foamcore. 10-Nov-93 Christie's, New York #155/R
$55000	£36424	Kagu (155x223cm-61x88in) s.d.80 ground glass oil crayon collage tycore. 18-Nov-92 Sotheby's, New York #136/R
$75000	£50336	Shards IV, IX-A (102x114cm-40x45in) mixed media aluminum executed 1982. 4-May-94 Sotheby's, New York #43 a/R
$75000	£49020	Tuftonboro III (255x279cm-100x110in) fluorescent alkyd epoxy paint canvas irregular. 3-May-93 Sotheby's, New York #47/R
$80000	£52288	Cato Manor (59x59cm-23x23in) s.d.1965 verso alkyd canvas. 4-May-93 Sotheby's, New York #111/R
$90000	£59603	Window sketch (213x107cm-84x42in) s.d.69 polymer fluorescent polymer canvas. 17-Nov-92 Sotheby's, New York #26/R
$100000	£65359	Window sketch (213x107cm-84x42in) s.d.69 verso polymer canvas. 3-May-93 Sotheby's, New York #52/R
$170000	£114094	Double scramble, descending yellow values. Ascending yellow values (176x351cm-69x138in) s.i.d.78stretcher liquitex canvas. 3-May-94 Christie's, New York #62/R
$170000	£114094	Protractor variation VI (152x305cm-60x120in) s.i.d.68stretcher liquitex canvas. 4-May-94 Christie's, New York #159/R
$180000	£119205	Sketch red lead (140x135cm-55x53in) s.i.d.1964stretcher red lead graphite canvas. 18-Nov-92 Christie's, New York #7/R

STELLA, Joseph (1877-1946) American

$1000	£649	St John (46x37cm-18x15in) s. 9-Sep-93 Sotheby's Arcade, New York #366/R
$1600	£1046	Vesuvius (18x30cm-7x12in) 22-May-93 Weschler, Washington #125/R
$2000	£1325	Still life with iris (28x34cm-11x13in) s. s.i.verso. 23-Sep-93 Sotheby's, New York #269/R
$3250	£2138	Still life with tropical flowers (28x38cm-11x15in) 31-Mar-93 Sotheby's Arcade, New York #336/R
$4250	£2872	The Italian house (28x33cm-11x13in) s.d.1938 verso. 31-Mar-94 Sotheby's Arcade, New York #262/R
$7500	£5245	Diana and the stag (34x26cm-13x10in) s. oil pencil canvas on board. 11-Mar-93 Christie's, New York #190/R
$9000	£6294	Belltower (58x38cm-23x15in) s. canvas on board. 11-Mar-93 Christie's, New York #191/R
$10500	£6069	In the Bronx Zoo (28x34cm-11x13in) s. s.i.verso. 23-Sep-92 Christie's, New York #223/R
$14000	£9211	Profile - portrait of Helen Walser (64x47cm-25x19in) s. s.d.1940 verso. 31-Mar-93 Sotheby's Arcade, New York #335/R
$550	£353	Portrait of a young woman (58x46cm-23x18in) s. pencil. 10-Dec-92 Sloan, North Bethesda #2198
$950	£559	Sunflower in blue vase (18x11cm-7x4in) W/C. 3-Oct-92 Weschler, Washington #121/R
$1000	£654	Back view of man and woman (17x15cm-7x6in) pencil col.chk pair. 4-May-93 Christie's, East, New York #242/R
$1000	£680	Mrs. Stella sewing (29x22cm-11x9in) s. W/C pencil. 15-Nov-93 Christie's, East, New York #227
$1400	£915	Portrait of woman in side profile (37x29cm-15x11in) estate st.verso W/C chl board. 4-May-93 Christie's, East, New York #240/R
$1600	£925	Sleeping cat (23x31cm-9x12in) s. pencil col.crayon. 25-Sep-92 Sotheby's Arcade, New York #404/R
$1600	£1053	Portrait of young woman (36x38cm-14x15in) s. pencil col.pencil board drawn c.1918-23. 31-Mar-93 Sotheby's Arcade, New York #346/R
$1800	£1184	Study of white flower (36x29cm-14x11in) s. silverpoint col.crayon. 31-Mar-93 Sotheby's Arcade, New York #348/R
$1900	£1319	Still life (48x20cm-19x8in) s. pastel. 6-Mar-93 Louisiana Auction Exchange #27/R
$2000	£1299	Study of plant and leaf (15x20cm-6x8in) s. pencil col.pencil card. 9-Sep-93 Sotheby's Arcade, New York #375/R
$2300	£1513	Barbados - tropical trees (47x62cm-19x24in) s.d.1937 W/C gouache W/C. 31-Mar-93 Sotheby's Arcade, New York #339/R
$2600	£1722	Flower study, s. col.crayon. 23-Sep-93 Sotheby's, New York #270/R
$3250	£2273	Bird on rose (35x24cm-14x9in) s. crayon pencil. 10-Mar-93 Sotheby's, New York #137/R
$3500	£2023	Hillside village, Provence (63x48cm-25x19in) s. pastel crayon. 24-Sep-92 Sotheby's, New York #159/R
$3500	£2215	Reading the paper (25x29cm-10x11in) s. W/C. 2-Dec-92 Christie's, East, New York #164/R
$3800	£2533	Flowers in a glass (55x33cm-22x13in) s. silverpoint col.pencil paper on board. 23-May-94 Christie's, East, New York #243/R
$4500	£2601	Flower study (17x11cm-7x4in) s. crayon silverpoint pencil. 23-Sep-92 Christie's, New York #215/R
$4800	£3077	Squash (61x47cm-24x19in) bears estate st. pastel. 26-May-93 Christie's, New York #196/R
$6500	£3757	Lily (22x27cm-9x11in) crayon silverpoint. 23-Sep-92 Christie's, New York #227/R
$6500	£4545	Night (47x63cm-19x25in) s. pastel. 10-Mar-93 Sotheby's, New York #148/R
$7000	£4667	Sunflower (48x61cm-19x24in) silverpoint col.crayon pencil. 16-Mar-94 Christie's, New York #140/R
$10000	£5780	Abstraction (47x63cm-19x25in) s. pastel crayon. 24-Sep-92 Sotheby's, New York #225/R

STELLA, Joseph (1877-1946) American-cont.
$14000	£8861	Abstraction (25x17cm-10x7in) s. W/C. 3-Dec-92 Sotheby's, New York #154/R
$16000	£10738	Lotus floating (20x20cm-8x8in) s.d.1919 crayon silver point. 3-Dec-93 Christie's, New York #10/R
$22000	£14103	Italian scenery (47cm-19in circular) s.d.1910 oil brush ink canvas. 26-May-93 Christie's, New York #207/R

STEPHANE, Micius (1912-) Haitian
$650	£439	Famille (40x46cm-16x18in) s. masonite. 24-Nov-93 Christie's, New York #26/R

STEPHENS, James (1961-) American
$650	£436	Rust Hut (69x64cm-27x25in) s.d.1987. 25-Mar-93 Boos Gallery, Michigan #423/R
$1100	£738	Tyrone - spaghetti eater (142x142cm-56x56in) s.d.1990. 25-Mar-93 Boos Gallery, Michigan #426/R

STEPHENSON, Lionel Macdonald (1854-1907) Canadian
$1204	£808	Indian and dog sled outside Fort Garry in winter (31x47cm-12x19in) s. board. 29-Nov-93 Ritchie, Toronto #169/R (C.D 1600)
$1820	£1214	Indian and dog sled team in winter at Fort Garry (31x47cm-12x19in) s. board. 11-May-94 Sotheby's, Toronto #25/R (C.D 2500)

STEPHENSON, Quinton J (1920-) American
$850	£563	Fish (23x91cm-9x36in) st.sig. mixed media materials wood. 21-Nov-92 Litchfield Auction Gallery #7

STERNE, Maurice (1878-1957) American
$750	£500	Bali (46x58cm-18x23in) 22-May-94 James Bakker, Cambridge #27/R
$850	£491	By the sea, Provincetown (61x82cm-24x32in) s.d.1946 i.verso panel. 25-Sep-92 Sotheby's Arcade, New York #286/R
$1600	£1039	Expression of impression (84x114cm-33x45in) s.d.49. 9-Sep-93 Sotheby's Arcade, New York #199/R
$2200	£1486	Benares rhapsody (76x102cm-30x40in) s. 5-Nov-93 Skinner, Bolton #152/R
$6500	£4545	Taos Indian (42x32cm-17x13in) s. oil tissue paper wrapped around board. 11-Mar-93 Christie's, New York #118/R

STERNER, Albert Edward (1863-1946) American
$600	£408	Standing female nude with purple cloak (61x51cm-24x20in) 14-Apr-94 Freeman Fine Arts, Philadelphia #991/R
$800	£544	Flora reading (51x41cm-20x16in) s.d.45 board. 15-Nov-93 Christie's, East, New York #195/R
$850	£559	Green hat (67x51cm-26x20in) s.d.1918. 31-Mar-93 Sotheby's Arcade, New York #123/R
$1800	£1259	Morning bath (70x49cm-28x19in) s.d.1902. 10-Mar-93 Sotheby's, New York #109/R
$2000	£1399	Harold reading (70x60cm-28x24in) 10-Mar-93 Sotheby's, New York #110/R
$550	£353	Evelyn Nesbit Thaw on a swing (64x61cm-25x24in) s.d.1906 conte chk chl. 8-Dec-92 Swann Galleries, New York #290/R
$650	£417	Evening prayers (25x20cm-10x8in) crayon pencil chk. 8-Dec-92 Swann Galleries, New York #291

STERNER, Harold (1895-?) American
$700	£461	Artist at easel in fantastic architectural setting (38x28cm-15x11in) mono. gouache board. 31-Mar-93 Sotheby's Arcade, New York #405/R

STETSON, Charles Walter (1858-1911) American
$1600	£1074	Moonlight in the Pineta, Viareggio (36x43cm-14x17in) s.i. s.i.d.1904 verso. 6-Dec-93 Grogan, Massachussetts #512/R

STETSON, William D (19th C) American
$1800	£1233	The steamboat 'Margarte' going to Wathehill, Franklin (38x56cm-15x22in) s.i. W/C. 12-Feb-94 Boos Gallery, Michigan #540/R

STETTHEIMER, Florine (1871-1944) American
$60000	£37975	My birthday Eyegay (96x66cm-38x26in) i.d.1929 s.i.d.stretcher. 4-Dec-92 Christie's, New York #132 a/R

STEVENS, Dorothy (1888-1966) Canadian
$542	£366	Seated girl with ringlets (59x46cm-23x18in) s. chl dr. 3-Nov-93 Sotheby's, Toronto #92/R (C.D 700)

STEVENS, J A (19/20th C) American
$550	£367	Moorland (33x61cm-13x24in) s.d.Nov 79 i.verso. 12-Mar-94 Weschler, Washington #152

STEVENS, William Lester (1888-1969) American
$700	£461	Rapids (53x64cm-21x25in) s. canvasboard. 2-Jun-93 Doyle, New York #90
$750	£497	Gloucester (61x76cm-24x30in) s. 3-Jan-93 Litchfield Auction Gallery #8
$800	£404	Bridge in winter (48x58cm-19x23in) s. 28-Aug-92 Young Fine Arts Auctions, Maine #288/R
$900	£604	Village scene (63x76cm-25x30in) s. indist.i.verso. 4-Mar-94 Skinner, Bolton #272/R
$900	£608	Conway Church in early spring (51x61cm-20x24in) s. i.verso. 5-Nov-93 Skinner, Bolton #94/R
$950	£664	Gloucester coastal scene (61x76cm-24x30in) s. 11-Mar-93 Mystic Fine Arts, Connecticut #140 a/R
$950	£621	Boats in repair - Cape Ann view (64x76cm-25x30in) s. 17-Sep-93 Skinner, Bolton #217/R

STEVENS, William Lester (1888-1969) American-cont.

$1000	£671	Under the bridge (61x76cm-24x30in) s. masonite. 26-Mar-94 James Bakker, Cambridge #140
$1000	£676	Apple blossoms (65x76cm-26x30in) s. 5-Nov-93 Skinner, Bolton #100/R
$1000	£662	House in spring (51x61cm-20x24in) s. 15-Jun-94 Butterfield & Butterfield, San Francisco #4437/R
$1100	£769	Country road, winter (51x61cm-20x24in) s.d.1904 canvasboard. 12-Mar-93 Skinner, Bolton #214/R
$1320	£863	Gloucester harbour (28x33cm-11x13in) s. canvasboard. 14-May-93 Skinner, Bolton #117/R
$1400	£946	Village church in winter (41x51cm-16x20in) s. panel. 10-Aug-93 Stonington Fine Arts, Stonington #40/R
$1595	£1022	Old white church (30x36cm-12x14in) s. board. 17-Dec-92 Mystic Fine Arts, Connecticut #258/R
$1600	£1060	Landscape - stone bridge with swift running river (61x76cm-24x30in) s. board. 14-Jun-94 John Moran, Pasadena #35
$1700	£1149	A building in the snow by a stream (107x122cm-42x48in) s. 31-Mar-94 Sotheby's Arcade, New York #282/R
$1800	£1233	Old barn in the snow (91x102cm-36x40in) s. 19-Feb-94 Young Fine Arts Auctions, Maine #190/R
$1800	£1224	Fall landscape with barns (53x43cm-21x17in) 8-Apr-94 Douglas, South Deerfield #1
$1900	£1258	Winter village scene (86x102cm-34x40in) s. 23-Sep-93 Mystic Fine Arts, Connecticut #65/R
$2000	£1282	Vase of orange and yellow flowers (81x51cm-32x20in) s. 9-Dec-92 Grogan, Massachussetts #78/R
$2000	£1010	Stream in winter (46x51cm-18x20in) s. 28-Aug-92 Young Fine Arts Auctions, Maine #287/R
$2100	£1373	Fall landscape (89x74cm-35x29in) 30-Oct-92 Douglas, South Deerfield #2
$2300	£1494	New England autumn scene (89x107cm-35x42in) s. 4-Aug-94 Eldred, Massachusetts #884/R
$2500	£1689	Country road in the Fall (81x91cm-32x36in) s. 31-Mar-94 Sotheby's Arcade, New York #264/R
$2750	£1797	Boats at docks, Gloucester harbour (61x76cm-24x30in) s. 14-May-93 Skinner, Bolton #114/R
$2800	£1481	Rockport Morning, Autumn (91x102cm-36x40in) s. 11-Sep-92 Skinner, Bolton #217/R
$3000	£1887	Maple sugaring w/ tyrees and sugar house (74x89cm-29x35in) 23-Apr-93 Douglas, South Deerfield #11
$3250	£2181	Moored fishing boats, Rockport harbour (63x76cm-25x30in) s. i.verso. 4-Mar-94 Skinner, Bolton #267/R
$4500	£3061	Summer landscape (76x76cm-30x30in) s.d.1916. 15-Nov-93 Christie's, East, New York #120/R
$7000	£4698	Mountain village in winter (107x122cm-42x48in) s. 6-Dec-93 Grogan, Massachussetts #532/R
$8500	£5380	Gloucester Harbour (64x76cm-25x30in) s.d.1923. 24-Oct-92 Collins, Maine #109/R
$476	£319	New England farm (53x71cm-21x28in) s. W/C graphite. 4-Mar-94 Skinner, Bolton #255/R
$500	*£338*	*Springtime on Cricket Hill (76x91cm-30x36in) s. W/C. 27-Nov-93 Young Fine Arts Auctions, Maine #310/R*
$550	*£346*	*Barns and trees (69x51cm-27x20in) W/C. 23-Apr-93 Douglas, South Deerfield #13*
$564	*£379*	*New England winter landscape with homestead (27x35cm-11x14in) s. W/C. 30-Nov-93 Ritchie, Toronto #60/R (C.D 750)*
$700	*£464*	*Farm in winter (51x71cm-20x28in) s.i. W/C. 28-Nov-92 Young Fine Arts Auctions, Maine #367/R*
$1000	*£667*	*Fall landscape of Conway, Mass (74x64cm-29x25in) W/C. 3-Jun-94 Douglas, South Deerfield #5*
$1100	*£636*	*View across the fence (37x45cm-15x18in) s.d.1920 gouache board. 25-Sep-92 Sotheby's Arcade, New York #253/R*
$1700	*£983*	*Snow covered harbour (41x51cm-16x20in) s.indis.d. tempera pastel chl. 25-Sep-92 Sotheby's Arcade, New York #396/R*

STEVENSON, W L (1905-1966) Canadian

$1118	£750	The cockpit (53x77cm-21x30in) s.i.d.1941 W/C gouache pencil. 22-Jun-93 Phillips, London #172/R

STEVENSON, William Leroy (1905-1966) Canadian

$574	£383	Autumn mountain (30x36cm-12x14in) s. plywood. 30-May-94 Hodgins, Calgary #340/R (C.D 800)
$718	£478	Tropical blooms (41x31cm-16x12in) s. i.verso. 30-May-94 Hodgins, Calgary #23/R (C.D 1000)
$798	£505	Hills near Cochrane, Alberta (18x24cm-7x9in) s.i.verso board. 21-Oct-92 Maynards, Vancouver #161 (C.D 1000)
$942	£615	Woman with flowers in background (51x41cm-20x16in) canvas panel. 10-May-93 Hodgins, Calgary #309 (C.D 1200)
$1254	£804	Still life with toby jug (51x65cm-20x26in) s. board. 26-Apr-93 Levis, Calgary #198/R (C.D 1600)
$1255	£821	Last snow, Central Alberta (46x61cm-18x24in) s. s.d.1965 verso panel. 10-May-93 Hodgins, Calgary #107/R (C.D 1500)
$1669	£1127	Valley Farm (61x76cm-24x30in) s. i.verso masonite painted c.1960. 25-Apr-94 Levis, Calgary #322/R (C.D 2300)
$1946	£1289	Fish creek on Burns Ranch near Midnapore, Alta. (61x76cm-24x30in) s. s.i.verso board. 16-Nov-92 Hodgins, Calgary #98 d (C.D 2500)

STEWART, Julius L (1855-1919) American

$5000	£2646	Study from a Chinese temple (66x25cm-26x10in) s.d.72. 11-Sep-92 Skinner, Bolton #165/R

STEWART, Julius L (1855-1919) American-cont.
$6000 £3797 Self-portrait (15x13cm-6x5in) s.i.d.86 panel. 4-Dec-92 Christie's, New York #238/R
$13000 £8609 Lady's pastime (85x53cm-33x21in) s. 22-Sep-93 Christie's, New York #74/R
$14000 £9333 Venetian canal (65x48cm-26x19in) s.i.d.1909. 17-Mar-94 Sotheby's, New York #97/R

STEWART, Ron (20th C) Canadian
$1508 £1026 To the Victor.. (51x76cm-20x30in) s. W/C. 15-Nov-93 Hodgins, Calgary #27/R (C.D 2000)

STICK, Frank (1884-1966) American
$3500 £2482 Buck or catamount (91x69cm-36x27in) s. 13-Feb-93 Collins, Maine #120/R

STIHA, Vladan (20th C) American
$1800 £1208 Blanket makers (46x61cm-18x24in) s.d.1970. 8-Dec-93 Butterfield & Butterfield, San Francisco #3599/R
$2500 £1678 Navajo journey (61x76cm-24x30in) s.d.1970. 8-Dec-93 Butterfield & Butterfield, San Francisco #3598/R

STIKAS, Marianne (20th C) American
$886 £591 Untitled (167x152cm-66x60in) s.d.1980verso oil gold foil. 2-Jun-94 AB Stockholms Auktionsverk, Stockholm #7130/R (S.KR 7000)

STITT, Hobart D (1880-?) American
$1700 £1189 Fishing shacks with artist painting (56x61cm-22x24in) s. 7-Feb-93 James Bakker, Cambridge #47/R

STOCK, Joseph Whiting (1815-1855) American
$75000 £50000 Portrait of child standing on Venetian carpet holding book and rose (117x89cm-46x35in) 12-Jun-94 Skinner, Bolton #128/R

STODDARD, Alice Kent (1893-1976) American
$1900 £1293 Child reading a book (41x58cm-16x23in) s. board. 16-Apr-94 Young Fine Arts Auctions, Maine #245/R

STOLTENBERG, Hans John (1880-1963) American
$1500 £974 Lone cabin (61x70cm-24x28in) s. s.i.verso masonite. 9-Sep-93 Sotheby's Arcade, New York #178/R

STONE, Benjamin (19th C) American
$1650 £1100 Portrait of girl wearing white dress, bird on shoulder (28x23cm-11x9in) s.i.d.1837 board. 25-May-94 Phillips, Sevenoaks #948

STONE, Seymour Millais (1877-?) American
$4000 £2614 Visit (49x38cm-19x15in) s. board. 4-May-93 Christie's, East, New York #175/R

STONE, Thomas Albert (1897-1978) Canadian
$655 £437 Autumn Lane, Lake Joseph (46x61cm-18x24in) s. board. 11-May-94 Sotheby's, Toronto #117 (C.D 900)
$697 £471 Seabreeze Road Lake of Bays (54x74cm-21x29in) s. s.i.verso board. 3-Nov-93 Sotheby's, Toronto #193/R (C.D 900)
$739 £490 Mill pond, near Port Hope. Autumn, Country village , s. one d.1923 board pair. 18-Nov-92 Sotheby's, Toronto #79 (C.D 950)
$801 £534 Heavily laden (56x76cm-22x30in) s. board. 11-May-94 Sotheby's, Toronto #51/R (C.D 1100)
$1268 £829 Pioneer homestead (76x91cm-30x36in) s. 19-May-93 Sotheby's, Toronto #96/R (C.D 1600)

STONEHOUSE, Fred (20th C) American
$1200 £811 Untitled Larva Teterrima, Hideous ghoul (152x168cm-60x66in) s.d.1988verso acrylic. 31-Oct-93 Hindman Galleries, Chicago #774/R

STOOPS, Herbert Morton (1887-1948) American
$1700 £1118 Greeting on plain (61x91cm-24x36in) s. 31-Mar-93 Sotheby's Arcade, New York #204/R

STORER, Charles (1817-1907) American
$1100 £714 Choice orchids (76x58cm-30x23in) s.d.1897. 15-Jan-93 Du Mouchelle, Detroit #1999/R
$1200 £816 Brace of ducks (76x46cm-30x18in) s.d.1882. 8-Apr-94 Sloan, North Bethesda #2364

STOREY, H L (19/20th C) American
$6800 £4533 Sailboats (61x91cm-24x36in) s.d.1907 canvas on board. 23-May-94 Hindman Galleries, Chicago #241/R

STORM, Juan (1927-) Uruguayan
$900 £596 Llegando a la querencia (50x61cm-20x24in) s.d.77. 28-Jun-93 Gomensoro, Montevideo #32
$1200 £789 Aduana constructiva (48x60cm-19x24in) s.d.58 board. 31-May-93 Gomensoro, Montevideo #33/R
$1200 £625 Constructivo (77x99cm-30x39in) s. 12-Aug-92 Castells & Castells, Montevideo #36
$1600 £1060 Naturaleza muerta con mate (81x91cm-32x36in) s.d.58 board. 28-Jun-93 Gomensoro, Montevideo #31/R
$9500 £6419 La estancia de mis recuerdos (100x120cm-39x47in) painted 1990. 23-Nov-93 Christie's, New York #279/R

STORY, George H (1835-1923) American
$1300　£909　The letter (25x20cm-10x8in) s.d.78 board. 12-Mar-93 Skinner, Bolton #166/R

STORY, George H (attrib) (1835-1923) American
$850　£500　Sleeping boy (25x20cm-10x8in) 5-Oct-92 Grogan, Massachussetts #695/R

STOUT, Myron (1908-1987) American
$24000　£16216　Tereisias III (20x15cm-8x6in) s.d.72verso graphite. 10-Nov-93 Christie's, New York #180/R

STOUT, Richard (20th C) American
$800　£503　Abstract (104x91cm-41x36in) s.d.1958. 23-Apr-93 Hart Gallery, Houston #14

STOUT, Wade (1955-) Canadian
$1098　£718　Cooling their heels (118x118cm-46x46in) s.verso. 10-May-93 Hodgins, Calgary #344/R (C.D 1400)

STRAIN, Daniel (fl.1870-1890) American
$1100　£582　Watermaids filling their jugs (64x91cm-25x36in) s.i.d.1883 canvas on masonite. 9-Sep-92 Doyle, New York #86

STRAUS, Meyer (1831-1905) American
$700　£461　After the hunt (76x51cm-30x20in) s.d.1877. 13-Jun-93 Butterfield & Butterfield, San Francisco #716/R
$900　£592　Still life with fruit (51x61cm-20x24in) s.d.1884. 13-Jun-93 Butterfield & Butterfield, San Francisco #717/R

STRAYER, Paul (1885-?) American
$1400　£915　The landing of Columbus (71x94cm-28x37in) s. 1-Nov-92 Hanzel Galleries, Chicago #23/R

STREAN, Maria Judson (20th C) American
$1500　£987　Portrait of Miss Wicks (12x8cm-5x3in) s. gouache ivory. 31-Mar-93 Sotheby's Arcade, New York #349/R

STREET, Frank (20th C) American
$1850　£1242　Pastoral scene (56x71cm-22x28in) s. 4-Dec-93 Louisiana Auction Exchange #4/R

STREET, Robert (1796-1865) American
$800　£523　Portrait of John Sexton, grandfather of R.S. James, Philadelphia (76x63cm-30x25in) s.d.1836 s.i.d.verso. 4-May-93 Christie's, East, New York #6
$1000　£649　Wild flowers (65x79cm-26x31in) s.i.d.1839. 9-Sep-93 Sotheby's Arcade, New York #10/R
$1800　£1176　Portrait of John Sexton (76x64cm-30x25in) s.d.1836 canvas laid down on board. 7-Oct-93 Freeman Fine Arts, Philadelphia #980/R
$2000　£1266　Still life with grapes (38x48cm-15x19in) 3-Dec-92 Freeman Fine Arts, Philadelphia #1749/R
$4750　£3188　Portrait of three children (122x94cm-48x37in) s.d.1845. 23-Jan-94 Hart Gallery, Houston #425 a
$6000　£3846　Portrait of two young boys (152x104cm-60x41in) s.d.1839. 9-Dec-92 Butterfield & Butterfield, San Francisco #3803/R

STRISIK, Paul (1918-) American
$1400　£940　Dory on the bridge (51x76cm-20x30in) s. board. 24-Mar-94 Mystic Fine Arts, Connecticut #44/R
$1500　£980　Evening light - winter landscape (41x61cm-16x24in) s. with i.d.1964 verso. 17-Sep-93 Skinner, Bolton #210/R
$2700　£1812　Gloucester Wharf (51x76cm-20x30in) s. 6-May-94 Skinner, Bolton #107/R

STRONG, Elizabeth (1855-1941) American
$1700　£1118　English setter with roses (152x104cm-60x41in) s. 13-Jun-93 Butterfield & Butterfield, San Francisco #3123/R
$2500　£1736　Tilling the fields (51x76cm-20x30in) s.d.1910. 7-Mar-93 Butterfield & Butterfield, San Francisco #41/R

STRONG, Ray Stanford (1905-) American
$550　£367　John Dot's Oak, Winchester Canyon (46x61cm-18x24in) s. masonite. 15-Mar-94 John Moran, Pasadena #163
$1750　£1136　Tamalpais (58x119cm-23x47in) s. 11-Sep-93 Louisiana Auction Exchange #43/R
$2500　£1656　A bend in the river (46x122cm-18x48in) s. board. 15-Jun-94 Butterfield & Butterfield, San Francisco #4747/R
$6500　£4305　Central Park (42x47cm-17x19in) s. 15-Jun-94 Butterfield & Butterfield, San Francisco #4760/R

STRUCK, Herman (1887-1954) American
$1600　£1081　Farmer and team harvesting wheat (41x51cm-16x20in) s. canvas laid down on panel. 9-Nov-93 John Moran, Pasadena #849

STUART, Alexander Charles (1831-1898) American
$1300　£867　Battle between the Confederate Ram Merrimac and the Cumberland, Virginia (41x71cm-16x28in) mono.d.66 W/C. 12-Jun-94 Skinner, Bolton #82/R

STUART, Gilbert (1755-1828) American
$3822　£2600　Portrait of Sir William Barker BT (46x39cm-18x15in) i.stretcher. 13-Apr-94 Sotheby's, London #64/R

STUART, Gilbert (1755-1828) American-cont.
$6080	£4000	Portrait of Lady Grace Maxwell, seated in landscape (75x62cm-30x24in) 6-Apr-93 Sotheby's, London #53/R
$6500	£4333	Mrs Charles Farran (76x63cm-30x25in) 16-Mar-94 Christie's, New York #12/R
$10000	£6993	Portrait of Sir Edward Thornton (74x60cm-29x24in) panel. 10-Mar-93 Sotheby's, New York #6/R
$17480	£11500	Portrait of General Robert Cunninghame in uniform (76x63cm-30x25in) painted oval. 7-Apr-93 Christie's, London #27/R
$50000	£32051	Moses Wheeler and Elizabeth Porter Wheeler (67x54cm-26x21in) panel pair painted 1823. 27-May-93 Sotheby's, New York #126/R
$50000	£33557	Ann Brewster Stow (74x60cm-29x24in) init. panel. 2-Dec-93 Sotheby's, New York #24/R
$130000	£87248	Portrait of George Washington (66x54cm-26x21in) panel. 3-Dec-93 Christie's, New York #125/R
$280000	£179487	Portrait of George Washington (74x61cm-29x24in) 27-May-93 Sotheby's, New York #130 a/R

STUART, Gilbert (attrib) (1755-1828) American
$2348	£1486	Portrait of Mrs John Murray (96x70cm-38x28in) 4-Dec-92 Dr Fritz Nagel, Stuttgart #3232/R (DM 3700)
$2500	£1678	Portrait of Sir John Boydell (66x56cm-26x22in) oval. 26-Mar-94 Skinner, Bolton #173/R
$4131	£2700	Dr. Fothergill reading 'Prudery and Women' (76x64cm-30x25in) i.verso. 13-Sep-93 Desmond Judd, Cranbrook #725
$5100	£3400	Portrait of George Washington (56x47cm-22x19in) canvas laid down on board. 21-May-94 Weschler, Washington #71/R

STUART, Gilbert (circle) (1755-1828) American
$2266	£1500	Portrait of gentleman with blue coat and of his wife with grey dress (57x42cm-22x17in) pair. 28-Sep-93 Sotheby's Colonnade, London #406/R

STUART, J E (1852-1941) American
$700	£470	Taft Point (61x51cm-24x20in) 4-Dec-93 San Rafael Auction Galleries #195

STUART, James Everett (1852-1941) American
$800	£530	Lower Yosemite Valley (61x51cm-24x20in) s.i.d.Aug.4,1918. 20-Sep-93 Butterfield & Butterfield, Los Angeles #79/R
$1500	£882	Cloudy day, Yosemite Valley (91x132cm-36x52in) s.i.d.1901-1914. 4-Oct-92 Butterfield & Butterfield, Los Angeles #79/R
$1639	£1100	Indian camp near The Dalles on the Columbia River (25x36cm-10x14in) s.d.1893 s.i.d.verso. 16-Jul-93 Christie's, London #164/R
$1800	£1139	Summer fishing camp on the Columbia (46x76cm-18x30in) s.d.1884. 2-Dec-92 Christie's, East, New York #106/R

STUBBS, William P (1842-1909) American
$1100	£733	Schooner flying American flag heading to port (56x84cm-22x33in) s. 20-Aug-93 Skinner, Bolton #47
$2400	£1622	Portrait of the vessel C.L. Jeffery (56x91cm-22x36in) 30-Oct-93 Skinner, Bolton #218/R
$2700	£1824	Portrait of the yacht Carrie E. Phillips (58x91cm-23x36in) s.i. 30-Oct-93 Skinner, Bolton #224/R
$3000	£2013	the Schooner 'Benjamin F Poole' (64x104cm-25x41in) s. masonite. 6-Dec-93 Grogan, Massachusetts #418/R
$3000	£1948	Portrait of schooner 'Edwin Forest' (33x48cm-13x19in) s. 16-Jan-93 Skinner, Bolton #39/R
$3250	£2083	U.S. Steam frigate, Lancaster (56x89cm-22x35in) s. 10-Dec-92 Sloan, North Bethesda #2623/R
$3900	£2635	Bark Penobscot (61x91cm-24x36in) 30-Jul-93 Eldred, Massachusetts #149/R
$5000	£3356	The schooner Commander, distant lighthouse and coastline (61x91cm-24x36in) s.d.1879. 6-Feb-94 Skinner, Bolton #82/R
$5300	£3605	The schooner Venus of Baltimore Maryland (56x86cm-22x34in) s.d.1901. 17-Nov-93 Doyle, New York #8/R
$6600	£4459	Schooner Benjamin Hale passing Thatcher's Island Light (64x102cm-25x40in) s. 30-Jul-93 Eldred, Massachusetts #282/R
$7000	£4667	Nellie F Sawyer (56x91cm-22x36in) s.i. 3-Jun-94 Sotheby's, New York #242/R

STUBBS, William P (attrib) (1842-1909) American
$900	£604	An American three-masted schooner (56x81cm-22x32in) 25-Mar-94 Eldred, Massachusetts #113/R
$2300	£1513	American schooner Charles L. Jeffry (56x91cm-22x36in) 5-Jun-93 Skinner, Bolton #25/R
$6800	£4503	Four-masted schooner 'John Twohy' (66x107cm-26x42in) 20-Nov-92 Eldred, Massachusetts #514/R

STUBER, Dedrick B (1878-1954) American
$1000	£633	Sunrise on California coast (30x41cm-12x16in) canvasboard. 5-Dec-92 San Rafael Auction Galleries #216
$1100	£724	Farmhouse (29x41cm-11x16in) s. board. 13-Jun-93 Butterfield & Butterfield, San Francisco #825/R
$1200	£833	Summer landscape (30x41cm-12x16in) s. board. 7-Mar-93 Butterfield & Butterfield, San Francisco #193/R
$1200	£779	Summer landscape (51x61cm-20x24in) s. 9-Sep-93 Sotheby's Arcade, New York #261/R
$1500	£1042	Field and clouds (41x51cm-16x20in) s. canvas on board. 7-Mar-93 Butterfield & Butterfield, San Francisco #204/R

STUBER, Dedrick B (1878-1954) American-cont.
$1900	£1319	Tujunga hills (41x51cm-16x20in) s. canvas on board. 7-Mar-93 Butterfield & Butterfield, San Francisco #201/R
$2000	£1351	Landscape - gold and jade (23x33cm-9x13in) s. board. 15-Jun-93 John Moran, Pasadena #92 a
$2000	£1325	Misty morning with sailing boats (51x41cm-20x16in) s. board. 15-Jun-94 Butterfield & Butterfield, San Francisco #4732/R
$2300	£1494	Desert clouds (74x91cm-29x36in) s. 11-Sep-93 Dargate Auction Galleries, Pittsburgh #1
$3000	£1974	Silvery bay (51x61cm-20x24in) s. board. 13-Jun-93 Butterfield & Butterfield, San Francisco #782/R
$3250	£2181	Golden dawn (41x51cm-16x20in) s. board. 8-Dec-93 Butterfield & Butterfield, San Francisco #3484/R
$3250	£2152	Boats in harbour, twilight (51x61cm-20x24in) s. masonite. 28-Sep-93 John Moran, Pasadena #253
$4750	£3209	Afterglow (64x76cm-25x30in) s. 15-Jun-93 John Moran, Pasadena #92
$5500	£3235	Quiet morning (41x46cm-16x18in) s. board. 4-Oct-92 Butterfield & Butterfield, Los Angeles #133/R
$7500	£4412	Ships of Sentiment (63x76cm-25x30in) s. 4-Oct-92 Butterfield & Butterfield, Los Angeles #162/R
$8000	£5369	Desert clouds (76x91cm-30x36in) s. 8-Dec-93 Butterfield & Butterfield, San Francisco #3572/R

STUEMPFIG, Walter (1914-1970) American/German
$1500	£867	Two boys (20x25cm-8x10in) init. 25-Sep-92 Sotheby's Arcade, New York #347
$2200	£1438	Man in doorway (76x65cm-30x26in) s. 4-May-93 Christie's, East, New York #279/R
$3000	£1987	Makeshift home (76x91cm-30x36in) s. 22-Sep-93 Christie's, New York #187/R
$4000	£2721	Garden statuary (41x30cm-16x12in) s.i.d.1954 panel. 14-Apr-94 Freeman Fine Arts, Philadelphia #1048 a/R
$4750	£3146	Et in Arcadia Ego (96x114cm-38x45in) s. painted 1956. 23-Sep-93 Sotheby's, New York #276/R

STULL, Henry (1851-1913) American
$1400	£824	Bay in paddock (46x58cm-18x23in) s.d.1889 canvas on board. 3-Oct-92 Weschler, Washington #91/R
$2000	£1342	Friendly enemies (41x56cm-16x22in) s. 15-Oct-93 Du Mouchelle, Detroit #2436/R
$2500	£1748	Heads apart (30x46cm-12x18in) s.d.1893. 12-Mar-93 Skinner, Bolton #182/R
$4250	£2796	Portrait of grey colt (46x61cm-18x24in) s.d.1881. 31-Mar-93 Sotheby's Arcade, New York #41/R
$4500	£3020	Racehorse Ferrier with W.S.Hobart up (64x76cm-25x30in) s.d.1895. 2-May-94 Selkirks, St. Louis #120/R
$4500	£2961	Racehorse with jockey up (41x51cm-16x20in) s.d.1896. 4-Jun-93 Sotheby's, New York #45/R
$6500	£4305	Quaterhorse and jockey (42x53cm-17x21in) s. 22-Sep-93 Christie's, New York #79/R
$7500	£5000	Mirage, bay horse (51x71cm-20x28in) s.d.1889. 16-Mar-94 Christie's, New York #24/R
$18000	£12000	Heads apart (30x43cm-12x17in) s.i.d.1893. 3-Jun-94 Sotheby's, New York #72/R
$25000	£16267	Ahead by a length (61x91cm-24x36in) s.d.1910. 3-Jun-94 Sotheby's, New York #71/R

STURTEVANT, Elaine (1926-) American
$6000	£3922	Lichtenstein modular painting (274x274cm-108x108in) s.i.d.73verso four panels. 5-Oct-93 Sotheby's, New York #222/R
$17000	*£11258*	*Study for Lichtenstein's happy tears (137x133cm-54x52in) s.i.d.1967-8verso oil graphite canvas. 19-Nov-92 Christie's, New York #144/R*

STURTEVANT, Helena (1872-1946) American
$550	£369	On the marsh (28x53cm-11x21in) s.d.1911 pastel. 28-Mar-93 James Bakker, Cambridge #34/R

SUBA, Miklos (1880-1944) American
$650	£376	Dead end (39x47cm-15x19in) s.i.d.1936 chl. 25-Sep-92 Sotheby's Arcade, New York #402

SUDDUTH, Jimmy Lee (1910-) American
$575	£381	Hotel (122x91cm-48x36in) s. mixed media plywood. 21-Nov-92 Litchfield Auction Gallery #9
$675	£447	George Washington (84x56cm-33x22in) mixed media compressed board. 21-Nov-92 Litchfield Auction Gallery #5

SUINA, Theodore (1918-) American
$700	£470	Flute player (56x46cm-22x18in) s.d. acrylic gesso. 26-Jun-93 Skinner, Bolton #16/R

SULLY, Thomas (1783-1872) American/British
$800	£533	Mrs Henry S McConnell and her child (49x62cm-19x24in) oval. 23-May-94 Christie's, East, New York #6/R
$900	£570	Elegant lady in white (23x17cm-9x7in) panel. 2-Dec-92 Christie's, East, New York #3/R
$1800	£1259	Portrait of Master Graham (61x48cm-24x19in) i. 14-Mar-93 Hindman Galleries, Chicago #56/R
$3600	£2416	Portrait of General William Brooke Thomas (112x91cm-44x36in) s.d.1865. 16-Dec-93 Mystic Fine Arts, Connecticut #280/R
$5200	£3467	Peasant children (46x35cm-18x14in) init.d.October 1866 i.verso. 16-Mar-94 Christie's, New York #4/R

SULLY, Thomas (1783-1872) American/British-cont.
$6500	£3757	Portrait of young lady (37x32cm-15x13in) 25-Sep-92 Sotheby's Arcade, New York #7/R
$8000	£5229	Mrs James W Paul of 4th Street Philadelphia (51x43cm-20x17in) init.d.1844. 16-Sep-93 Sloan, North Bethesda #3195/R
$12000	£7692	Mrs. Calem Newbold and son Thomas (88x100cm-35x39in) init.d.1813 arched top. 26-May-93 Christie's, New York #12/R
$13000	£8228	Portrait of Levi Fletcher (76x63cm-30x25in) mono.d.1830. 3-Dec-92 Sotheby's, New York #3/R
$14000	£8974	Girl leaning at window (76x63cm-30x25in) 27-May-93 Sotheby's, New York #140/R
$15000	£10067	The Washington Family. Portrait of young child (36x28cm-14x11in) board double-sided. 2-Dec-93 Sotheby's, New York #7/R
$33000	£21154	Interior of Capuchin Chapel on Piazza Barberini (174x128cm-69x50in) init.i.d.1821. 27-May-93 Sotheby's, New York #139/R
$50000	£33333	Portrait of Mrs James Robb and her three children (143x115cm-56x45in) painted 1844. 25-May-94 Sotheby's, New York #10/R
$3648	£2400	Springfield in Chester County, Pennsylvania (19x33cm-7x13in) i.verso pencil W/C. 30-Mar-93 Christie's, London #63/R
$7500	£4747	Mother with her children (27x27cm-11x11in) mono.d.1831 W/C. 3-Dec-92 Sotheby's, New York #1/R

SULLY, Thomas (attrib) (1783-1872) American/British
$800	£533	Portrait of Mrs Hugh Caperton (61x51cm-24x20in) framed oval. 1-Jun-94 Doyle, New York #61
$2100	£1458	Portrait of woman (76x64cm-30x25in) bears sig. 6-Mar-93 Louisiana Auction Exchange #160/R

SULTAN, Donald (1951-) American
$35000	£24306	Streetlight - blue streetlight March 11, 1982 (247x123cm-97x48in) s.init.i.d.verso oil graphite masonite diptych. 24-Feb-93 Christie's, New York #158/R
$600	£417	Iris (35x27cm-14x11in) init.i.d.March 31,1987 pencil W/C. 23-Feb-93 Sotheby's, New York #376/R
$1400	£940	Iris March 31, 1981 (35x28cm-14x11in) init.i. graphite brush ink. 23-Feb-94 Christie's, East, New York #307/R
$2000	£1389	Three images (38x38cm-15x15in) init.i.d.April 5, 1985 ink. 23-Feb-93 Sotheby's, New York #377 a/R
$2000	£1342	Untitled (108x139cm-43x55in) init.d.1978 tar board. 24-Feb-94 Sotheby's Arcade, New York #375/R
$4000	£2778	Black lemon (127x96cm-50x38in) init.d.Aug 29,1984 chl. 23-Feb-93 Sotheby's, New York #368/R
$7000	£4118	Three lemons, March 10, 1987 (152x122cm-60x48in) init.d.1987 chl. 6-Oct-92 Sotheby's, New York #162 a/R
$10000	£5882	Dominoes Nov 30 1989 (30x30cm-12x12in) init.d.1989 tar spackle latex tile over wood. 6-Oct-92 Sotheby's, New York #160/R
$10000	£6623	Black tulip (127x96cm-50x38in) init.i.d.Nov.8.1983 chl. 19-Nov-92 Christie's, New York #147/R
$14000	£9722	Black lemons (127x96cm-50x38in) init.i.d.April 30 1985 chl. 24-Feb-93 Christie's, New York #87/R
$15000	£10067	One lemon Oct.2, 1989 (32x32cm-13x13in) init.i.d. tar spackle oil tile over wood. 5-May-94 Sotheby's, New York #360/R
$17000	£11486	Cigarette (123x123cm-48x48in) d.1980 s.d.verso oil plaster tiles masonite. 11-Nov-93 Sotheby's, New York #145/R
$18000	£11921	Cherries (32x34cm-13x13in) init.d.1987 oil plaster tar vinyl tile on wood. 18-Nov-92 Sotheby's, New York #286 a/R
$26000	£17219	Three pears (33x33cm-13x13in) init.d.1984 oil plaster tar vinyl tile wood. 18-Nov-92 Sotheby's, New York #275/R
$45000	£26471	Double Chinese vase Aug 14 1990 (244x244cm-96x96in) init.d. tar spackle silkscreen tile on masonite. 6-Oct-92 Sotheby's, New York #147/R
$65000	£43046	Quinces (244x244cm-96x96in) init.d.1989 latex tar vinyl tile over masonite. 18-Nov-92 Sotheby's, New York #257/R
$75000	£50676	Roses in brass vase July 24, 1987 (244x244cm-96x96in) s.i.d.verso tar spackle oil vinyl on masonite. 10-Nov-93 Christie's, New York #378/R
$80000	£53691	Roses August 13, 1986 (244x244cm-96x96in) oil spackle tar tile over masonite. 5-May-94 Sotheby's, New York #314/R

SUMMERS, Ivan (?-1964) American
$1500	£993	Winter landscape (64x76cm-25x30in) s. 28-Sep-93 John Moran, Pasadena #222

SUMMERS, P H (19th C) American
$1700	£1149	River landscape near St John's, Newfoundland (60x107cm-24x42in) s. 20-Mar-93 Weschler, Washington #87/R

SUNDBLOM, Haddon Hubbard (1899-1976) American
$1100	£764	Fisherman in rocking chair (48x33cm-19x13in) s. W/C gouache. 6-Mar-93 Louisiana Auction Exchange #108/R

SURREY, Philip Henry (1910-) Canadian
$3776	£2551	La Gare Windsor (40x30cm-16x12in) s. board. 23-Nov-93 Joyner Fine Art, Toronto #102/R (C.D 5000)
$713	£466	Beach scene, Lake of Two Mountains (20x35cm-8x14in) s. W/C. 18-May-93 Joyner Fine Art, Toronto #239 (C.D 900)
$874	£583	Les Motards (29x44cm-11x17in) s. col.chk. 13-May-94 Joyner Fine Art, Toronto #150 (C.D 1200)

SURREY, Philip Henry (1910-) Canadian-cont.
$934 £619 Figures crossing Sherbrooke and Bishop Street, Montreal (25x38cm-10x15in) s. W/C pastel. 18-Nov-92 Sotheby's, Toronto #145 a (C.D 1200)

SUVERO, Mark di (1933-) American
$600 £403 Dangle twins (34x49cm-13x19in) s.d.Nov 65 felt-tip pen. 3-May-94 Christie's, East, New York #11/R

SUZOR-COTE, Marc-Aurele de Foy (1867-1937) Canadian
$1400 £927 Study of a girl (38x41cm-15x16in) s.i.d.98. 3-Oct-93 Hanzel Galleries, Chicago #21/R
$2367 £1578 Etude, study of a woman (37x40cm-15x16in) s.i.d.98. 11-May-94 Sotheby's, Toronto #85 (C.D 3250)
$24000 £16000 Misty morning, September (65x91cm-26x36in) s. s.i.stretcher. 16-Mar-94 Christie's, New York #109/R
$906 £612 La vieille (48x33cm-19x13in) s. chl. 23-Nov-93 Joyner Fine Art, Toronto #80/R (C.D 1200)
$934 £619 Nude with hand mirror (27x23cm-11x9in) s. red pencil drawing. 18-Nov-92 Sotheby's, Toronto #219/R (C.D 1200)

SUZOR-COTE, Marc-Aurele de Foy (attrib) (1867-1937) Canadian
$2913 £1942 Portrait of Josephine (56x34cm-22x13in) bears sig. i.verso. 11-May-94 Sotheby's, Toronto #84/R (C.D 4000)

SWAIN, R (?) American
$900 £588 Gold panning (183x76cm-72x30in) 18-Sep-93 San Rafael Auction Galleries #346
$1400 £915 Assayer's office (183x81cm-72x32in) 18-Sep-93 San Rafael Auction Galleries #345

SWAIN, William (1803-1847) American
$850 £563 Portrait of girl in yellow silk gown (76x64cm-30x25in) i.d.1837verso. 28-Nov-92 Dunning's, Illinois #1027

SWANSON, Ray (1937-) American
$750 £503 'Autumn mood' (56x71cm-22x28in) s.i. board. 24-Mar-94 Boos Gallery, Michigan #675/R
$750 £503 'Passing storm' (61x91cm-24x36in) s. s.i.stretcher. 24-Mar-94 Boos Gallery, Michigan #676/R

SWIFT, Clement (19/20th C) American?
$800 £423 The garden feast (43x53cm-17x21in) s. board. 11-Sep-92 Skinner, Bolton #176/R

SWINNERTON, James G (1875-1974) American
$650 £431 Midday desert sun (30x41cm-12x16in) s. board. 15-Jun-94 Butterfield & Butterfield, San Francisco #4728/R
$650 £433 Landscape (38x30cm-15x12in) s. canvasboard. 15-Mar-94 John Moran, Pasadena #147
$2000 £1351 Landscape (76x76cm-30x30in) s. 9-Nov-93 John Moran, Pasadena #863
$2750 £1821 Desert Landscape (30x41cm-12x16in) s.i. canvasboard four. 15-Jun-94 Butterfield & Butterfield, San Francisco #4727/R
$3000 £2013 George Black's cabin near Sedona (61x46cm-24x18in) s. i.stretcher. 8-Dec-93 Butterfield & Butterfield, San Francisco #3570/R
$16000 £10738 Sunset in Monument Valley (76x102cm-30x40in) s. 8-Dec-93 Butterfield & Butterfield, San Francisco #3573/R

SWOPE, Kate F (19/20th C) American
$650 £411 Mother and child (74x74cm-29x29in) s. 5-Dec-92 Louisiana Auction Exchange #77/R

SWORD, James Brade (1839-1915) American
$1500 £1007 Landscape with sheep (46x76cm-18x30in) s. 5-Aug-93 Eldred, Massachusetts #811/R
$2800 £1879 Rwoing race on a quiet river (30x50cm-12x20in) s.indist.d. 11-Dec-93 Weschler, Washington #78/R
$4900 £3224 Gypsy encampment (51x91cm-20x36in) s. 31-Mar-93 Sotheby's Arcade, New York #33/R
$8000 £5333 Rowing to shore, Lake George (30x51cm-12x20in) s.d.1874 i.verso. 26-May-94 Christie's, New York #24/R
$16500 £10927 Peep into Lake George (92x152cm-36x60in) s.d.1873. 23-Sep-93 Sotheby's, New York #12/R

SYKES, S D Gilchrist (?) American/British
$800 £537 Rockport quarries (64x76cm-25x30in) s. 26-Mar-94 James Bakker, Cambridge #54/R

SYLVESTER, Frederick Oakes (attrib) (1869-1915) American
$1000 £671 The Heritage of Elsah (99x69cm-39x27in) s.d.1913. 2-May-94 Selkirks, St. Louis #99

SYMONS, George Gardner (1863-1930) American
$800 £533 Swimmers by a waterfall (23x30cm-9x12in) s. board. 21-May-94 Weschler, Washington #106/R
$800 £530 Landscape with distant lake (20x25cm-8x10in) canvasboard. 15-Jun-94 Butterfield & Butterfield, San Francisco #4712/R
$850 £563 The lake by the road (20x25cm-8x10in) canvasboard. 15-Jun-94 Butterfield & Butterfield, San Francisco #4714/R
$850 £552 Marine scene (10x15cm-4x6in) init. board. 9-Sep-93 Sotheby's Arcade, New York #192
$900 £596 Winter landscape (20x25cm-8x10in) canvasboard. 15-Jun-94 Butterfield & Butterfield, San Francisco #4713/R
$1000 £667 The pond (18x20cm-7x8in) s. board. 15-Mar-94 John Moran, Pasadena #150

SYMONS, George Gardner (1863-1930) American-cont.

$1400	£921	Red flowers (46x51cm-18x20in) s.verso. 5-Jun-93 Louisiana Auction Exchange #47/R
$1700	£1111	Van Cortland Park, Bronx (38x53cm-15x21in) s. i.verso. 4-May-93 Christie's, East, New York #148
$2000	£1351	Summer morning (15x23cm-6x9in) s. panel. 15-Jun-93 John Moran, Pasadena #127
$2000	£1299	Winter forest (25x20cm-10x8in) init. canvasboard. 9-Sep-93 Sotheby's Arcade, New York #174/R
$2200	£1497	Stream running among snow covered hilltops (20x25cm-8x10in) s. board. 17-Nov-93 Doyle, New York #43/R
$2250	£1490	Shore and rocky coastline (30x41cm-12x16in) s. panel. 15-Jun-94 Butterfield & Butterfield, San Francisco #4460/R
$2250	£1490	Woodland forest (37x45cm-15x18in) s. canvasboard. 15-Jun-94 Butterfield & Butterfield, San Francisco #4461/R
$2750	£1821	Winter landscape with houses (38x53cm-15x21in) s. i.verso. 23-Sep-93 Sotheby's, New York #195/R
$3000	£2083	Connecticut landscape (28x23cm-11x9in) s. studio st.verso. 7-Mar-93 Butterfield & Butterfield, San Francisco #169/R
$3250	£1912	Winter landscape (18x22cm-7x9in) init. with estate st.verso board. 4-Oct-92 Butterfield & Butterfield, Los Angeles #189/R
$12000	£7947	Brook in summer (76x91cm-30x36in) bears sig. canvas laid down on board. 15-Jun-94 Butterfield & Butterfield, San Francisco #4707/R
$22000	£14667	Opalescent mists in mountain river landscape (64x76cm-25x30in) s. 13-Mar-94 Hindman Galleries, Chicago #758/R
$25000	£16026	Near Springfield, Massachusetts (63x76cm-25x30in) s. 27-May-93 Sotheby's, New York #64/R
$1600	*£1046*	*Winter scene (48x58cm-19x23in) s. W/C gouache. 18-Sep-93 Young Fine Arts Auctions, Maine #283/R*

SYMONS, George Gardner (attrib) (1863-1930) American

$800	£537	Winter landscape (43x58cm-17x23in) s. board. 5-Mar-94 Louisiana Auction Exchange #40/R

SZYSZLO, Fernando de (1925-) Peruvian

$8500	£5667	Punchao (81x100cm-32x39in) s. i.d.83vrso. 18-May-94 Sotheby's, New York #382/R
$10000	£6711	Cuarto de Paso I (100x100cm-39x39in) s. i.d.81verso. 7-Jan-94 Gary Nader, Miami #1/R
$12000	£8108	Ankai (81x100cm-32x39in) s. i.d.62 verso acrylic. 22-Nov-93 Sotheby's, New York #232/R
$13000	£8609	Mesa Ritual - Los Instrumentos (101x101cm-40x40in) s. i.d.1986 verso acrylic. 24-Nov-92 Christie's, New York #158 a/R
$13000	£8725	Travesia (150x120cm-59x47in) s. i.d.73verso acrylic. 7-Jan-94 Gary Nader, Miami #87/R
$16000	£10458	Recinto (150x120cm-59x47in) s. s.d.91 verso. 17-May-93 Christie's, New York #156/R
$16000	£10811	Mar de lurin (149x149cm-59x59in) s. i.d.89verso acrylic. 23-Nov-93 Christie's, New York #160/R
$16000	£10811	Saywa (158x129cm-62x51in) s. i.verso. 23-Nov-93 Christie's, New York #161/R
$16000	£10667	Viento Oscuro, Paraca (119x149cm-47x59in) s.d.92 i.verso acrylic. 18-May-94 Christie's, New York #173/R
$16000	£10458	Love letter (129x161cm-51x63in) s. d.1959 verso acrylic canvas. 18-May-93 Sotheby's, New York #78/R
$17000	£11258	Interior IV (150x120cm-59x47in) s. i.d.72 verso acrylic. 24-Nov-92 Christie's, New York #259/R
$17000	£11111	Mesa ritual (120x150cm-47x59in) s. i.d.86 verso acrylic. 17-May-93 Christie's, New York #150/R
$18000	£12162	Runa Macii (150x121cm-59x48in) s. i.d.71 verso acrylic. 22-Nov-93 Sotheby's, New York #246/R
$18000	£11765	Yawar Mayus - un rio de sangre (162x114cm-64x45in) s. i.d.63 verso acrylic. 18-May-93 Sotheby's, New York #205/R
$19000	£12667	Mesa Ritual (100x120cm-39x47in) s.i.d.86 i.verso. 18-May-94 Christie's, New York #157/R
$19000	£12838	Ciudad prohibida IV (150x122cm-59x48in) s. i.d.76verso acrylic. 23-Nov-93 Christie's, New York #201/R
$19000	£12583	Runa Macii (150x119cm-59x47in) s. i.d.71 verso acrylic. 24-Nov-92 Christie's, New York #101/R
$21000	£14189	Camino a Mendieta V (160x201cm-63x79in) s. i.verso acrylic painted 1978. 22-Nov-93 Sotheby's, New York #72/R
$22000	£14570	Recinto (150x149cm-59x59in) s. i.d.90 verso acrylic. 24-Nov-92 Christie's, New York #96/R
$26000	£17219	Sol Negro (200x200cm-79x79in) s. i.d.91 verso acrylic. 24-Nov-92 Christie's, New York #59/R
$3600	*£2432*	*Untitled (50x64cm-20x25in) s. tempera W/C painted c.1962. 22-Nov-93 Sotheby's, New York #245/R*
$16000	£10667	Mar de Lurin (190x136cm-75x54in) s.i.d.90 acrylic chl canvas. 18-May-94 Sotheby's, New York #380/R

TAAFFE, Philip (1955-) American

$2200	£1486	Untitled (56x86cm-22x34in) s.d.1987 oil enamel. 8-Nov-93 Christie's, East, New York #59/R
$1000	*£654*	*Untitled (56x87cm-22x34in) s.d.1987 oil enamel. 7-May-93 Christie's, East, New York #120/R*

TAAFFE, Philip (1955-) American-cont.
$1200	£795	Untitled (36x42cm-14x17in) s.d.88verso col.crayon W/C pair. 17-Nov-92 Christie's, East, New York #77/R
$2400	£1589	Untitled (42x55cm-17x22in) s.d.1988verso W/C gouache wax. 17-Nov-92 Christie's, East, New York #79/R
$2500	£1678	Untitled (48x60cm-19x24in) wax paper executed 1988. 25-Feb-94 Sotheby's, New York #118/R
$2532	£1688	Untitled (56x86cm-22x34in) s.d.1987 mixed media. 2-Jun-94 AB Stockholms Auktionsverk, Stockholm #7131/R (S.KR 20000)
$3000	£2027	Untitled (47x49cm-19x19in) s.d.86verso crayon ink enamel collage fabric. 8-Nov-93 Christie's, East, New York #61/R
$9000	£6081	Untitled (115x152cm-45x60in) s.stretcher acrylic ink paper collage on linen. 10-Nov-93 Christie's, New York #276/R
$24000	£16667	Untitled (107x119cm-42x47in) exec.1984 s.stretcher acrylic ink paper collage. 24-Feb-93 Christie's, New York #105/R
$28000	£18543	Phantastische Gebete II (208x72cm-82x28in) s.i.d.1987verso acrylic silkscreen paper collage. 19-Nov-92 Christie's, New York #139/R
$30000	£19868	Queen of the Night (244x49cm-96x19in) s.d.1985verso linoprint collage acrylic. 19-Nov-92 Christie's, New York #101/R
$32000	£21477	Christus, fire-eater (110x65cm-43x26in) s.i.d.1990verso oil paper collage canvas. 4-May-94 Christie's, New York #257/R
$38000	£25166	Brest (281x281cm-111x111in) s.i.d.1985verso acrylic ink paper collage linen. 18-Nov-92 Christie's, New York #70/R
$80000	£54054	Metamorphosis, il gatto d'oro (167x129cm-66x51in) s.i.d.1990verso oil paper collage on canvas. 10-Nov-93 Christie's, New York #257/R

TACK, Augustus Vincent (1870-1949) American
$1700	£1189	Girl in fancy bonnet (71x64cm-28x25in) 14-Mar-93 Hindman Galleries, Chicago #61
$2200	£1410	Little Miss Ross (91x74cm-36x29in) s. 13-Dec-92 Hindman Galleries, Chicago #17/R
$29000	£18590	Untitled (112x90cm-44x35in) s. oil gold paint painted c.1930. 27-May-93 Sotheby's, New York #101/R
$6500	£3757	Sketch for The High Command (122x122cm-48x48in) gouache board. 25-Sep-92 Sotheby's Arcade, New York #345/R

TACLA, Jorge (1958-) Chilean
$18000	£12000	Centralized temple (167x155cm-66x61in) s.verso jute painted 1991. 17-May-94 Sotheby's, New York #81/R

TAHOMA, Quincy (1921-1956) American
$800	£533	Buck antelope (23x18cm-9x7in) i.verso gouache. 29-Jan-94 Skinner, Bolton #203/R
$1700	£1133	Untitled (30x56cm-12x22in) s. gouache. 29-Jan-94 Skinner, Bolton #205/R
$2200	£1419	Untitled (36x28cm-14x11in) s.d.51 gouache. 9-Jan-93 Skinner, Bolton #111/R

TAILFEATHERS, Gerald (1925-1975) Canadian
$502	£335	Three travois (24x36cm-9x14in) s.d. ink W/C. 30-May-94 Hodgins, Calgary #326/R (C.D 700)
$538	£359	Three riders (23x33cm-9x13in) s.d. ink W/C. 30-May-94 Hodgins, Calgary #241 (C.D 750)
$1410	£829	Indian on horseback (37x30cm-15x12in) s.d.1960 gouache. 5-Oct-92 Levis, Calgary #53 (C.D 1750)

TAIT, A F (1819-1905) American
$7800	£5200	Visitor from the city, two dogs with five chickens (53x33cm-21x13in) 3-Jun-94 Douglas, South Deerfield #9

TAIT, Arthur Fitzwilliam (1819-1905) American
$1700	£1111	Cow watering (30x25cm-12x10in) s.i.d.79 panel. 4-May-93 Christie's, East, New York #44/R
$2000	£1333	Thoroughbred (51x61cm-20x24in) s.d.1848. 23-May-94 Christie's, East, New York #29/R
$2250	£1490	Sheep in the summer meadow (20x25cm-8x10in) s. s.i.d.1899 panel. 15-Jun-94 Butterfield & Butterfield, San Francisco #4416/R
$2300	£1329	Jealousy, cow and calves (46x61cm-18x24in) s.d.96 i.stretcher. 25-Sep-92 Sotheby's Arcade, New York #118/R
$2400	£1600	The happy mother (45x56cm-18x22in) s.d.94. 23-May-94 Christie's, East, New York #32/R
$2400	£1579	Portrait of black labrador (20x24cm-8x9in) s. s.i.d.1860 board. 4-Jun-93 Sotheby's, New York #69/R
$2500	£1748	Summer day (25x36cm-10x14in) s.d.98 s.i.d.1898verso board. 10-Mar-93 Sotheby's, New York #25/R
$2600	£1733	Sheep and fowl (26x36cm-10x14in) s.d.1868. 23-May-94 Christie's, East, New York #38/R
$3000	£2000	In the pasture (36x56cm-14x22in) s.i.d.96 s.i.d.verso canvas on board. 17-May-94 Grogan, Massachussetts #333/R
$3500	£2333	A young stag (21x21cm-8x8in) s.d.58 s.i.d.1858 verso. 23-May-94 Christie's, East, New York #41/R
$4000	£2667	My country friends (46x68cm-18x27in) s.d.97 s.i.d.1897 verso. 23-May-94 Christie's, East, New York #97/R
$4750	£3299	Sheep and chickens in barn (30x46cm-12x18in) s. 27-Feb-93 Young Fine Arts Auctions, Maine #265/R
$5000	£3165	The barnyard (30x40cm-12x16in) s.d.1871 i.verso panel. 2-Dec-92 Christie's, East, New York #56/R
$5000	£3333	Pointer in field (15x20cm-6x8in) s. s.i.d.1867verso board. 3-Jun-94 Sotheby's, New York #83/R

TAIT, Arthur Fitzwilliam (1819-1905) American-cont.
$5000	£3333	Pointer and quail (20x23cm-8x9in) s.d.63 s.i.d.verso panel oval. 3-Jun-94 Sotheby's, New York #267/R
$5250	£3477	Count Ryan (51x76cm-20x30in) s.d.1886 s.i.d.1886 verso. 23-Sep-93 Sotheby's, New York #114/R
$5750	£4021	Farm yard (36x56cm-14x22in) s.d.1861. 10-Mar-93 Sotheby's, New York #26/R
$6000	£3468	Deer in woods (24x41cm-9x16in) s. 24-Sep-92 Sotheby's, New York #24 a/R
$6250	£4252	Rooster and hens (18x28cm-7x11in) i.d.1872 verso board. 16-Apr-94 Young Fine Arts Auctions, Maine #250/R
$6500	£4362	Hen, quail and chicks (23x30cm-9x12in) s.i.d.1863. 3-Dec-93 Christie's, New York #118/R
$8000	£5128	Cows fording stream (25x36cm-10x14in) s.d.65 canvas on masonite. 26-May-93 Christie's, New York #30 b/R
$8000	£5263	Sheep in barnyard (33x53cm-13x21in) s.d.1900. 11-Jun-93 Du Mouchelle, Detroit #957/R
$8500	£5629	Grouse with chicks surprised by squirrel (36x56cm-14x22in) s.d.77. 28-Nov-92 Dunning's, Illinois #1144/R
$8750	£5795	Dilly (51x76cm-20x30in) s.d.1886 s.i.d.1886 verso. 23-Sep-93 Sotheby's, New York #115/R
$10000	£6993	Spaniel and canvas back duck (18x23cm-7x9in) s.i.d.1864 paper on board painted oval. 17-May-93 Christie's, New York #31/R
$12000	£7843	Six chicks and ladybug (25x35cm-10x14in) s.d.1864 s.i.verso board. 22-May-93 Weschler, Washington #82/R
$12500	£8333	Misty morning (36x56cm-14x22in) s.d.1883. 3-Jun-94 Sotheby's, New York #175/R
$13000	£8553	Two Dogs (46x69cm-18x27in) s.d.1897. 4-Jun-93 Sotheby's, New York #169/R
$15000	£9868	Escaped (46x56cm-18x22in) s.d.1883 s.i.verso. 4-Jun-93 Sotheby's, New York #214/R
$19000	£12583	Three ruffed grouse and a setter (46x36cm-18x14in) s.i. 23-Sep-93 Sotheby's, New York #112/R
$22000	£14103	Trying for meal. Noontime meal (21cm-8in circular) s. board pair. 26-May-93 Christie's, New York #30 c/R
$30000	£18987	The challenge (51x77cm-20x30in) s.d.1877. 4-Dec-92 Christie's, New York #245/R
$120000	£80537	Amos F. Adams shooting over Gus Bondher and son, Count Bondher (51x76cm-20x30in) s.d.87. 3-Dec-93 Christie's, New York #62/R

TAIT, Arthur Fitzwilliam (attrib) (1819-1905) American
$2980	£2000	Stag and hind on shores of lake at dusk (74x125cm-29x49in) i.d.79. 5-May-94 Sotheby's Colonnade, London #320/R

TALBOT, Jesse (1806-1879) American
$10000	£6223	Landscape by river with mountains in distance (91x142cm-36x56in) 23-Sep-93 Sotheby's, New York #54/R

TALCOTT, Allen Butler (1867-1908) American
$2640	£1692	Connecticut landscape (46x61cm-18x24in) s. panel. 17-Dec-92 Mystic Fine Arts, Connecticut #155/R

TAMAYO, Rufino (1899-1991) Mexican
$65000	£43046	Hombre con sombrero (61x46cm-24x18in) s.d.0-65 i.verso oil sand. 24-Nov-92 Christie's, New York #4 b/R
$200000	£132450	Pareja (45x66cm-18x26in) s.d.73 i.verso oil sand. 23-Nov-92 Sotheby's, New York #61/R
$210000	£140000	Constelacion (56x104cm-22x41in) s.d.0-47 oil sand. 17-May-94 Sotheby's, New York #31/R
$230000	£153333	Banista quitandose los lentes (130x97cm-51x38in) s.d.0-89 oil sand. 17-May-94 Sotheby's, New York #58/R
$260000	£173333	El Comensal (60x45cm-24x18in) s.d.38. 18-May-94 Christie's, New York #22/R
$300000	£196078	Torso (79x95cm-31x37in) s.d.O-78 oil sand. 18-May-93 Sotheby's, New York #61/R
$350000	£231788	Dos Cabezas (80x100cm-31x39in) s.d.67 i.verso oil sand. 23-Nov-92 Sotheby's, New York #66/R
$360000	£235294	Hombre (100x95cm-39x37in) s.d.79 acrylic. 17-May-93 Christie's, New York #45/R
$370000	£246667	El vaso azul (100x130cm-39x51in) s.d.40. 18-May-94 Christie's, New York #37/R
$380000	£256757	Bailarina (180x124cm-71x49in) s.d.0-81 i.d.verso. 23-Nov-93 Christie's, New York #37 a/R
$380000	£248366	Hombre con los brazos en alto (97x130cm-38x51in) s.d.O-75 oil sand. 17-May-93 Christie's, New York #54/R
$400000	£270270	Cataclismo (61x51cm-24x20in) s.d.0-46. 23-Nov-93 Christie's, New York #26/R
$450000	£304054	Danzantes (114x89cm-45x35in) s.d.42. 22-Nov-93 Sotheby's, New York #31/R
$450000	£298013	The sleepwalker (65x100cm-26x39in) s.d.54. 23-Nov-92 Sotheby's, New York #47/R
$480000	£320000	Dos mujeres en Rojas (111x145cm-44x57in) s.d.78 i.verso acrylic sand canvas. 18-May-94 Christie's, New York #52/R
$750000	£496689	La Tierra Prometida - Israel De Hoy (200x633cm-79x249in) s.d.63 oil sand. 23-Nov-92 Sotheby's, New York #70/R
$1150000	£766667	Retrato de Olga (121x86cm-48x34in) s.d.41. 17-May-94 Sotheby's, New York #41/R
$1350000	£894040	Mujer en Extasis (130x194cm-51x76in) s.d.73 oil sand. 23-Nov-92 Sotheby's, New York #57/R
$1400000	£915033	Mujer con mascara roja (121x85cm-48x33in) s.d.40. 17-May-93 Christie's, New York #25/R
$2000000	£1333333	Ninos jugando con fuego (127x172cm-50x68in) s.d.47 i.stretcher. 18-May-94 Christie's, New York #19/R
$2350000	£1535948	America , s.d.55 mural - 4.04x13.92m. 17-May-93 Christie's, New York #30/R
$6500	*£4392*	*Personaje de Pie (33x26cm-13x10in) s.d.0-72 pencil W/C. 23-Nov-93 Christie's, New York #240/R*
$7000	*£4575*	*Cabezas de caballo (15x22cm-6x9in) s. pencil crayon drawn 1962. 17-May-93 Christie's, New York #275/R*

TAMAYO, Rufino (1899-1991) Mexican-cont.
$7500	£4902	Perro Colima (33x26cm-13x10in) s.d.O-72 pencil W/C. 17-May-93 Christie's, New York #276/R
$7500	£4967	Mujer sentada (30x22cm-12x9in) s. graphite colour pencil. 23-Nov-92 Sotheby's, New York #177/R
$10000	£6623	Mujer (24x31cm-9x12in) s.d.67 graphite colour pencil board. 23-Nov-92 Sotheby's, New York #226/R
$12000	£8000	Tres caballos (22x32cm-9x13in) s.d.32 gouache W/C. 18-May-94 Sotheby's, New York #371/R
$17000	£11486	Mujer de espaldas (28x21cm-11x8in) s.d.31 gouache rice paper. 22-Nov-93 Sotheby's, New York #206/R
$20000	£13514	Dos sandias (25x33cm-10x13in) s.d.O-68 graphite col.pencil. 22-Nov-93 Sotheby's, New York #230/R
$22000	£14865	Caballo (21x28cm-8x11in) s.i.d.34 gouache. 23-Nov-93 Christie's, New York #143/R
$26000	£17219	Sandias (25x33cm-10x13in) s.d.O-68 graphite crayon. 24-Nov-92 Christie's, New York #207/R
$26000	£16993	Mujeres con Rebozo (25x18cm-10x7in) s.d.27 gouache. 17-May-93 Christie's, New York #118/R
$29659	£20040	Cabeza (37x24cm-15x9in) s.d.1972 synthetic lacquer paper on board. 27-Apr-94 Louis Morton, Mexico #478/R (M.P 100000)
$30000	£19608	Mujer de Espaldas (24x19cm-9x7in) s. W/C graphite executed c.1940. 18-May-93 Sotheby's, New York #32/R
$30000	£20270	Caminantes (27x21cm-11x8in) s.d.39 gouache wash. 23-Nov-93 Christie's, New York #102/R
$35000	£23649	Mujer de Espaldas (26x18cm-10x7in) s. gouache painted late 1930's. 23-Nov-93 Christie's, New York #103/R
$37500	£25000	Dos mujeres (25x21cm-10x8in) s.d.40 gouache W/C. 17-May-94 Sotheby's, New York #30/R
$38000	£25166	Hombre con tronco (27x21cm-11x8in) s.d.34 gouache. 24-Nov-92 Christie's, New York #57/R
$45000	£29801	Banistas (47x32cm-19x13in) s.d.38 gouache. 23-Nov-92 Sotheby's, New York #42/R
$45000	£30000	Mirando al infinito (32x48cm-13x19in) s.d.32 gouache. 17-May-94 Sotheby's, New York #29/R
$45000	£30405	Las Flechadoras (14x32cm-6x13in) s.d.32 gouache tempera. 22-Nov-93 Sotheby's, New York #30/R
$47500	£32095	Dos cabezas (39x75cm-15x30in) s.d.O-62 graphite pastel. 22-Nov-93 Sotheby's, New York #255/R
$60000	£40541	Banistas de Tehuantepec (43x35cm-17x14in) s.d.37 gouache. 23-Nov-93 Christie's, New York #36/R
$77500	£51325	Cabeza en Blanco (50x35cm-20x14in) s.d.70 oil sand chl canvas. 23-Nov-92 Sotheby's, New York #76/R

TAMOTZU, Chuzo (1891-1975) American/Japanese
$500	£331	Picnic (43x33cm-17x13in) s. pastel. 23-Sep-93 Mystic Fine Arts, Connecticut #99

TANABE, Takao (1926-) Canadian
$652	£435	Waterfall (96x65cm-38x26in) s.d.60 i.verso. 6-Jun-94 Waddingtons, Toronto #1307 (C.D 900)
$789	£526	The land (104x76cm-41x30in) s. s.i.d.73 verso acrylic. 30-May-94 Ritchie, Toronto #214/R (C.D 1100)
$1245	£825	More flags (80x163cm-31x64in) s.i.d.1962verso. 18-Nov-92 Sotheby's, Toronto #261/R (C.D 1600)
$1359	£918	Foothills looking west, north of Pincher CR (59x195cm-23x77in) s. acrylic. 23-Nov-93 Joyner Fine Art, Toronto #207 (C.D 1800)
$1812	£1224	The Foothills (137x120cm-54x47in) s. acrylic. 23-Nov-93 Joyner Fine Art, Toronto #73/R (C.D 2400)
$3564	£2408	Gulf of Georgia (91x244cm-36x96in) s.d.86 s.i.d.verso acrylic. 3-Nov-93 Sotheby's, Toronto #360/R (C.D 4600)

TANGUY, Yves (1900-1955) American/French
$52157	£34314	Fumier a gauche et violette a droite (60x29cm-24x11in) s. panel. 6-Nov-92 Beaussant & Lefevre, Paris #131/R (F.FR 280000)
$61090	£41000	La premiere clef (31x28cm-12x11in) s.d.52. 23-Mar-94 Sotheby's, London #35/R
$80118	£50708	Sans titre (13x10cm-5x4in) s.d.31 panel. 4-Dec-92 Sotheby's, Monaco #292/R (F.FR 430000)
$107100	£70000	Composition (27x35cm-11x14in) s.d.38. 27-Jun-94 Christie's, London #31/R
$114750	£75000	Le prodigue (28x23cm-11x9in) s.d.43. 27-Jun-94 Christie's, London #36/R
$220000	£148249	Quelques gestes (33x41cm-13x16in) s.d.37 s.d.1937 verso canvasboard. 3-Nov-93 Christie's, New York #267/R
$223500	£150000	Feu couleur (30x40cm-12x16in) s. painted 1941. 22-Jun-93 Sotheby's, London #80/R
$350000	£228758	Composition (54x45cm-21x18in) s.d.39. 12-May-93 Christie's, New York #35/R
$3721	£2514	Composition surrealiste (29x20cm-11x8in) s.d.1936 black crayon. 8-Nov-93 Guy Loudmer, Paris #122/R (F.FR 22000)
$5216	£3431	Composition (29x20cm-11x8in) s.d.1937 ink dr. 6-Nov-92 Beaussant & Lefevre, Paris #13 (F.FR 28000)
$7698	£5166	Apollinaire, couverture du livre par Nancy Cunard, s.i.d.1930verso ink dr study. 4-Mar-94 Binoche, Paris #108/R (F.FR 45000)
$12000	£8108	Untitled (30x24cm-12x9in) s.i. pen col.pencil paper on board. 3-Nov-93 Christie's, New York #270/R
$12218	£8200	Composition (47x29cm-19x11in) s. pen Indian ink executed c.1927. 23-Jun-93 Sotheby's, London #294/R
$13428	£8952	Photo de Tanguy. Dessin erotique (20x13cm-8x5in) i.verso Indian ink dr verso double-sided. 20-May-94 Claude Boisgirard, Paris #99/R (F.FR 76000)
$17000	£11486	Cadavre exquis, parfum (26x16cm-10x6in) pencil exec.1934 with Brauner, Breton and Herold. 3-Nov-93 Christie's, New York #276/R

TANGUY, Yves (1900-1955) American/French-cont.
$21000	£14189	Corps exquis (27x22cm-11x9in) s.pencil paper collage exec.w.Brauner and Herold. 3-Nov-93 Christie's, New York #277/R
$27656	£18315	Composition (46x30cm-18x12in) s.d.1947. 23-Nov-92 Guy Loudmer, Paris #41/R (F.FR 150000)
$52020	£34000	Composition (49x32cm-19x13in) s.d.1950 gouache card. 29-Jun-94 Sotheby's, London #257/R
$55130	£37000	Composition (9x28cm-4x11in) s.d.36 gouache paper on card. 23-Jun-93 Christie's, London #316/R
$61837	£41225	L'industrie du pays (8x23cm-3x9in) s.i.d.36 gouache board. 20-May-94 Claude Boisgirard, Paris #101/R (F.FR 350000)
$62000	£41060	Sns titre (7x24cm-3x9in) s.indist.d. gouache. 12-Nov-92 Christie's, New York #236/R
$90636	£60424	Feu volant (43x32cm-17x13in) s. gouache paper laid down on canvas. 20-May-94 Claude Boisgirard, Paris #100/R (F.FR 513000)

TANNAHILL, Mary H (20th C) American
$1200	£694	Still life with pears, grapes and plant on table (61x46cm-24x18in) s. 25-Sep-92 Sotheby's Arcade, New York #416/R

TANNING, Dorothea (1910-) American
$1863	£1179	Roses sur un gueridon (24x14cm-9x6in) init.d.53. 4-Dec-92 Sotheby's, Monaco #295/R (F.FR 10000)
$2608	£1600	Un pont jete (22x33cm-9x13in) s. s.i.d.1965 verso. 14-Oct-92 Sotheby's, London #259/R
$5402	£3625	L'amour c'est la foret (46x38cm-18x15in) s.d.65. 7-Dec-93 Rasmussen, Copenhagen #17/R (D.KR 36000)
$6000	£4167	Still in the studio (130x96cm-51x38in) s. s.i.d.1979verso. 26-Feb-93 Sotheby's Arcade, New York #397/R
$900	£608	Echantillonage no.2 (11x12cm-4x5in) s.d.61 ink W/C. 2-Nov-93 Christie's, East, New York #107/R
$1200	£811	Deux femmes (11x14cm-4x6in) oil canvas paper collage laid down on board. 2-Nov-93 Christie's, East, New York #106/R

TANOBE, Miyuki (20th C) Canadian
$2913	£1942	Kensington Market, Toronto (51x61cm-20x24in) s. s.i.d.15.09.86verso acrylic board. 11-May-94 Sotheby's, Toronto #155/R (C.D 4000)

TANSEY, Mark (1949-) American
$22000	£14570	Pleasure of the text (38x30cm-15x12in) s.i.d.1986verso. 19-Nov-92 Christie's, New York #149/R
$80000	£52288	Iconograph I (183x183cm-72x72in) s.d.1984 verso. 4-May-93 Christie's, New York #49/R
$100000	£66225	Action painting (91x198cm-36x78in) s.i.d.June 1981verso. 18-Nov-92 Christie's, New York #60/R
$150000	£99338	Forbidden Senses - taste, sound, smell and touch (147x406cm-58x160in) s.d.1982 verso four panels. 17-Nov-92 Sotheby's, New York #11/R
$27000	£15882	Chess game (30x37cm-12x15in) s.i.d.1982 graphite board. 8-Oct-92 Christie's, New York #236/R

TARBELL, Edmund C (1862-1938) American
$12000	£7692	Study for on Bosn's Hill (63x53cm-25x21in) s. 27-May-93 Sotheby's, New York #67/R
$60000	£40268	Portrait of woman in white (74x61cm-29x24in) s.i. 2-Dec-93 Sotheby's, New York #121/R
$140000	£89744	My daughter Josephine (123x93cm-48x37in) s.d.1915. 12-Dec-92 Weschler, Washington #61/R
$400000	£256410	Mother and child in pine woods (63x76cm-25x30in) s. 26-May-93 Christie's, New York #117/R

TATE, Gayle B (1944-) American
$750	£507	Money to burn a trompe l'oeil (25x20cm-10x8in) mono.i. panel. 5-Nov-93 Skinner, Bolton #67/R
$1800	£1216	Still life with pink ribbon (56x40cm-22x16in) s. panel. 31-Mar-94 Sotheby's Arcade, New York #363/R
$3200	£2238	Money to burn (25x20cm-10x8in) s.init. i.verso panel. 11-Mar-93 Christie's, New York #59/R
$4000	£2797	Time is money (25x35cm-10x14in) s. s.i.verso panel. 11-Mar-93 Christie's, New York #60/R
$4800	£3200	Seven poker faces (28x36cm-11x14in) s. s.i.verso masonite. 23-May-94 Christie's, East, New York #79/R
$7500	£4967	Letter rack with picture of Song-Win (58x52cm-23x20in) s. s.i.verso panel. 22-Sep-93 Christie's, New York #52/R

TATOSSIAN, Armand (20th C) Canadian
$874	£583	Landscape, Orford (50x60cm-20x24in) s. 13-May-94 Joyner Fine Art, Toronto #130/R (C.D 1200)
$1019	£680	Fleurs et plantes (75x60cm-30x24in) s. 13-May-94 Joyner Fine Art, Toronto #161 (C.D 1400)
$1022	£647	Ste-Agathe en Hiver (50x61cm-20x24in) s.i.d.1989verso. 1-Dec-92 Fraser Pinneys, Quebec #151 (C.D 1300)
$1133	£765	Floral still life with oranges (75x60cm-30x24in) s. 23-Nov-93 Joyner Fine Art, Toronto #301 (C.D 1500)

TATTO, Gabriela (1958-) Mexican
$752	£501	La huida (74x64cm-29x25in) s.d.1994. 25-May-94 Louis Morton, Mexico #92/R (M.P 2500)
$2217	£1459	Sevilla en morados (138x113cm-54x44in) s.d.1992 pastel. 4-Nov-92 Mora, Castelltort & Quintana, Juarez #95/R (M.P 7000000)

TAUBES, Frederic (1900-1981) American
$900	£596	A woman artist (76x61cm-30x24in) s. 28-Nov-92 Young Fine Arts Auctions, Maine #371/R
$925	£621	Driftwood and figures (30x43cm-12x17in) s. board. 16-Dec-93 Mystic Fine Arts, Connecticut #217/R
$1000	£671	Woman smelling flowers , s. 24-Jun-93 Mystic Fine Arts, Connecticut #288
$1200	£805	Rearing horse (30x38cm-12x15in) s. board. 16-Dec-93 Mystic Fine Arts, Connecticut #218/R
$1350	£854	Summer (48x64cm-19x25in) s. i.verso. 5-Dec-92 Louisiana Auction Exchange #123/R

TAUSZKY, David Anthony (1878-1972) American
$550	£364	Portrait of a young girl (51x51cm-20x20in) s.i. oval. 14-Jun-94 John Moran, Pasadena #106
$1500	£1034	Nudes in Art Deco setting (76x64cm-30x25in) s. 16-Feb-93 John Moran, Pasadena #102

TAYLOR, Grace Martin Frame (1903-) American
$800	£537	Figure on light planes (43x43cm-17x17in) s. canvasboard. 26-Mar-94 James Bakker, Cambridge #132
$2100	£1400	Miss Le Baron, cellist (76x61cm-30x24in) s. 22-May-94 James Bakker, Cambridge #102/R
$2500	£1445	Still life with music (76x61cm-30x24in) s.d.1938. 27-Sep-92 James Bakker, Cambridge #222/R
$2500	£1748	Torso and Image (51x61cm-20x24in) indist.s. 7-Feb-93 James Bakker, Cambridge #72
$700	£405	Coastal abstract (48x58cm-19x23in) s. W/C. 27-Sep-92 James Bakker, Cambridge #226/R

TAYLOR, Newton (19th C) Canadian?
$1013	£667	Duchess and the music lesson (68x51cm-27x20in) s.d.1874. 8-Jun-93 Ritchie, Toronto #108/R (C.D 1300)

TAYLOR, William (fl.1844-1860) American
$675	£450	Still life of partridge and hare in basket on table (43x58cm-17x23in) s. 26-Aug-93 Christie's, S. Kensington #63
$3750	£2500	Contentment (51x61cm-20x24in) s. 17-Mar-94 Bonhams, London #90/R

TAYLOR, William Francis (1883-1934) American
$1000	£662	Autumn farm scene (51x61cm-20x24in) s. board. 23-Sep-93 Mystic Fine Arts, Connecticut #123/R

TCHELITCHEV, Pavel (1898-1957) American/Russian
$8305	£5500	Portrait of clown (51x81cm-20x32in) s.d.32. 30-Jun-93 Boardman Fine Art, Haverhill #208/R
$9685	£6500	Portrait of pierrot (90x72cm-35x28in) s. oil sand. 13-Oct-93 Sotheby's, London #251/R
$536	£357	Souvenir of Toulon (28x22cm-11x9in) s.i.d.31 black ink dr. 31-May-94 Christie's, Amsterdam #76 (D.FL 1000)
$689	£450	Study of man (27x20cm-11x8in) s.d.30 pen wash. 29-Oct-92 Christie's, S. Kensington #4
$750	£500	Profil de jeune fille (35x37cm-14x15in) brown ink wash. 9-May-94 Christie's, East, New York #102/R
$873	£586	Costume study for Blue Bird (49x34cm-19x13in) s.i.d.1923 gouache over pencil board. 29-Nov-93 Wolfgang Ketterer, Munich #1250/R (DM 1500)
$900	£625	Skull face (43x30cm-17x12in) ink wash. 26-Feb-93 Sotheby's Arcade, New York #81/R
$941	£631	Dessin pour Vogue (40x55cm-16x22in) pastel. 4-Mar-94 Binoche, Paris #109 (F.FR 5500)
$950	£634	Tete de femme (36x22cm-14x9in) W/C gouache board. 9-May-94 Christie's, East, New York #101/R
$969	£650	Etudes d'hommes nus. Etudes de femmes nues (28x22cm-11x9in) s. pen Indian ink double-sided. 23-Mar-94 Sotheby's, London #270
$1060	£650	Serving boy - Christmas Greeting (26x20cm-10x8in) s.d.1935 pen Indian ink htd white gouache. 14-Oct-92 Sotheby's, London #182/R
$1073	£720	Study of figures (44x27cm-17x11in) s.verso pen sepia ink wash. 13-Oct-93 Sotheby's, London #252/R
$1500	£993	Space composition (337x25cm-133x10in) s.d.XII/52N pastel. 30-Jun-93 Sotheby's Arcade, New York #25/R
$1600	£1060	Study of man (27x21cm-11x8in) s.d.30 pen wash. 29-Sep-93 Sotheby's Arcade, New York #9/R
$1800	£1200	Femme au collier (65x50cm-26x20in) s.d.25 gouache black ink. 9-May-94 Christie's, East, New York #97/R
$1900	£1258	On the beach (25x35cm-10x14in) init. ink wash. 30-Jun-93 Sotheby's Arcade, New York #28
$2000	£1342	Male dancer (29x19cm-11x7in) s.d.32 ink wash. 24-Feb-94 Sotheby's Arcade, New York #161/R
$2000	£1325	Portrait of dancer (30x20cm-12x8in) s.d.1931 sepia wash. 30-Jun-93 Sotheby's Arcade, New York #23/R
$2086	£1400	Savonarola, decor design (21x32cm-8x13in) s.verso gouache W/C pencil painted c.1922. 13-Oct-93 Sotheby's, London #256/R

TCHELITCHEV, Pavel (1898-1957) American/Russian-cont.

$2295	£1500	Costume design for Savanarola (49x35cm-19x14in) s. gouache gold paint. 27-Jun-94 Christie's, S. Kensington #176/R
$2400	£1600	Portrait d'homme (65x50cm-26x20in) st.sig.verso col.chk. 9-May-94 Christie's, East, New York #96/R
$2416	£1600	Three figures singing (25x20cm-10x8in) s. one d.39 one d.32 W/C pair. 30-Jun-93 Boardman Fine Art, Haverhill #152
$2445	£1500	Tete d'homme (30x21cm-12x8in) s.d.1949 VIII pastel over pencil. 14-Oct-92 Sotheby's, London #191/R
$2869	£1900	Boy in armour , s.d.32 W/C two. 30-Jun-93 Boardman Fine Art, Haverhill #153/R
$3000	£2000	Femme en rouge (50x40cm-20x16in) s.indis d. gouache paper on board. 9-May-94 Christie's, East, New York #95/R
$3250	£2181	Seated nude (32x25cm-13x10in) red white chk executed 1954. 24-Feb-94 Sotheby's Arcade, New York #162/R
$3750	£2517	Three boys (48x30cm-19x12in) s.d.28 i.verso ink. 24-Feb-94 Sotheby's Arcade, New York #163/R
$4401	£2700	Skull - interior landscape (35x25cm-14x10in) s.d.46 col.chk pen. 14-Oct-92 Sotheby's, London #192/R
$5500	£3642	Skull (36x28cm-14x11in) s.d.44 gouache paper laid down on board. 11-Nov-92 Sotheby's, New York #252/R
$8195	£5500	Harvest (65x49cm-26x19in) s.verso oil gouache sand painted c.1928. 13-Oct-93 Sotheby's, London #253/R

TEAGUE, Donald (1897-1991) American

$1050	£705	Mexican on horseback (18x33cm-7x13in) s.i. paperboard. 5-Mar-94 Louisiana Auction Exchange #15/R
$1500	£962	Illustration for Bois d'Arc (43x71cm-17x28in) init.d.45 board. 13-Dec-92 Hindman Galleries, Chicago #61/R
$1800	£1208	Le Consulate - Montmartre (23x15cm-9x6in) s. W/C. 8-Dec-93 Butterfield & Butterfield, San Francisco #3382/R
$2250	£1324	Siesta time (37x42cm-15x17in) s. W/C. 4-Oct-92 Butterfield & Butterfield, Los Angeles #227/R
$4250	£2853	Quiberon Light, Brittany (15x23cm-6x9in) s. W/C. 8-Dec-93 Butterfield & Butterfield, San Francisco #3383/R
$5500	£3642	Gondolas, Venice (16x23cm-6x9in) s. W/C paper on board. 22-Sep-93 Christie's, New York #215/R
$8500	£4913	Range talk (43x57cm-17x22in) s.i. W/C pencil. 23-Sep-92 Christie's, New York #110/R
$11000	£7639	White walls in Andalusia (49x75cm-19x30in) s. W/C pencil. 7-Mar-93 Butterfield & Butterfield, San Francisco #246/R

TEED, Douglas Arthur (1864-1929) American

$900	£604	Fishing village (46x104cm-18x41in) s.d.1900. 24-Mar-94 Mystic Fine Arts, Connecticut #45/R
$1100	£719	Ship on choppy water (53x64cm-21x25in) s.d.1924. 17-Sep-93 Du Mouchelle, Detroit #2180/R
$1100	£748	Arab market scene (28x36cm-11x14in) s.d.1918. 19-Nov-93 Du Mouchelle, Detroit #2037/R
$1200	£800	Landscape with figure by a stream (56x71cm-22x28in) s.d.1918. 20-May-94 Du Mouchelle, Detroit #2001/R
$1500	£877	Mosque scene (41x51cm-16x20in) s. 18-Sep-92 Du Mouchelle, Detroit #2008/R
$1500	£962	Arab mosque (38x53cm-15x21in) d.1905. 11-Dec-92 Du Mouchelle, Detroit #1300/R
$1500	£993	Landscape with stream (56x66cm-22x26in) s.d.1918. 2-Oct-93 Weschler, Washington #130/R
$1900	£1258	North African courtyard scene (25x33cm-10x13in) s.d.1912. 2-Oct-93 Boos Gallery, Michigan #285/R
$2200	£1477	Seated Arab swordsman (44x54cm-17x21in) s.d.1919. 14-Oct-93 Christie's, New York #369/R
$2800	£1830	Arab scene (97x114cm-38x45in) s.d.1924. 17-Sep-93 Du Mouchelle, Detroit #2004/R
$3000	£1974	Rocky beach landscape (85x182cm-33x72in) s. 31-Mar-93 Sotheby's Arcade, New York #95/R
$3000	£1754	Middle Eastern street scene (107x91cm-42x36in) s. 18-Sep-92 Du Mouchelle, Detroit #2009/R
$3000	£1923	Middle Eastern courtyard scene (71x94cm-28x37in) s.d.1921. 11-Dec-92 Du Mouchelle, Detroit #1996/R
$5500	£3691	Entrance to the walled city (61x84cm-24x33in) s.d.95. 14-Oct-93 Christie's, New York #371/R
$8000	£5369	Old palace with guardian (76x102cm-30x40in) s.d.1911. 14-Oct-93 Christie's, New York #372/R
$8500	£5705	The first Lariat (86x183cm-34x72in) s.d.1925. 17-Dec-93 Du Mouchelle, Detroit #2006/R

TEED, Douglas Arthur (attrib) (1864-1929) American

$1200	£800	Wooded landscape (51x76cm-20x30in) s.indis.d. 26-Aug-93 Skinner, Bolton #32

TEITELBAUM, Mashel Alexander (1921-1985) Canadian

$1162	£785	Landscape autumn colours (48x61cm-19x24in) mixed media. 3-Nov-93 Sotheby's, Toronto #298/R (C.D 1500)

TELEMAQUE, Herve (1937-) Haitian

$2250	£1510	Des fleurs pour la tres douce (66x102cm-26x40in) s.d.58.60 s.i.d.verso. 24-Feb-94 Sotheby's Arcade, New York #304/R
$4531	£3041	Le trou (100x100cm-39x39in) s.i.d.1974verso acrylic. 25-Mar-94 Francis Briest, Paris #330/R (F.FR 26000)

TELEMAQUE, Herve (1937-) Haitian-cont.
$10902	£7317	Ou est la vache (150x150cm-59x59in) s.d.1972verso. 14-Oct-93 Guy Loudmer, Paris #56/R (F.FR 63000)
$12812	£8485	Billets, la part des choses (145x114cm-57x45in) s.i.d.1977verso. 22-Nov-92 Perrin, Versailles #48/R (F.FR 70000)
$14571	£9524	Port au Prince, la rose (200x310cm-79x122in) s.i.d.1988verso acrylic triangular. 29-Jun-94 Guy Loudmer, Paris #241/R (F.FR 80000)
$857	£564	Echo (74x91cm-29x36in) s.d.1976-87 cut paper collage. 10-Jun-93 Cornette de St.Cyr, Paris #84/R (F.FR 4700)
$1276	£839	Nouvelles de France (75x109cm-30x43in) s.i.d.1985 mixed media collage. 11-Jun-93 Poulain & le Fur, Paris #138 (F.FR 7000)

TEMPLE, Ruth Anderson (1884-1939) American
$700	£461	Through the trees (53x43cm-21x17in) s.d.1916. 2-Apr-93 Sloan, North Bethesda #2072

TENG-HIOK CHIU (1903-) Chinese/American
$650	£436	New York roof tops (64x76cm-25x30in) 4-Dec-93 Louisiana Auction Exchange #125/R

TEPPER, Saul (1899-1987) American
$1000	£658	Foreign legion (86x58cm-34x23in) s. 2-Apr-93 Sloan, North Bethesda #2071/R

TER-ARUTUNIAN, Rouben (20th C) American?
$800	£537	Stage design for 'La Fontaine dans le Parc' in Pelleas and Melisande (29x38cm-11x15in) init. s.i.d.1966 verso gouache. 24-Feb-94 Sotheby's Arcade, New York #147/R
$1500	£1007	Costume designs for 'Harlequin' and 'Pierrot' in Harlequinade (33x23cm-13x9in) s.i.d.65 col.felt-tip pen ink wash pair. 24-Feb-94 Sotheby's Arcade, New York #148/R

TERELAK, John (1942-) American
$1200	£805	In the garden (61x91cm-24x36in) s.d.83. 26-Mar-94 James Bakker, Cambridge #144/R
$1600	£1096	At the beach (48x48cm-19x19in) s.d.92. 19-Feb-94 Young Fine Arts Auctions, Maine #193/R
$1700	£1090	Sentinel Bell, Eastern Point Lighthouse, Gloucester (127x127cm-50x50in) s. 24-May-93 Grogan, Massachussetts #353/R
$2300	£1503	Rainy day in the city (61x76cm-24x30in) s.d.86. 18-Sep-93 James Bakker, Cambridge #52/R
$3500	£2244	October rain near Manchester, Vermont (218x188cm-86x74in) s.d.78. 24-May-93 Grogan, Massachussetts #354

TERPNING, Howard A (1927-) American
$9000	£6081	Cliff hanger. Desert storm (86x66cm-34x26in) s. acrylic pencil sand board pair. 31-Mar-94 Sotheby's Arcade, New York #390/R

TERRYTOONS (20th C) American
$1000	£671	Mighty Mouse flies over snow-covered landscape (20x27cm-8x11in) i. gouache trimmed paper on W/C background. 22-Jun-93 Sotheby's, New York #802

TETHEROW, Michael (20th C) American?
$850	£571	Untitled (122x107cm-48x42in) init.d.85 pencil acrylic. 24-Feb-94 Sotheby's Arcade, New York #467/R

THALINGER, E Oscar (1885-?) American
$1300	£878	The lumber mill (55x69cm-22x27in) s. masonite. 31-Mar-94 Sotheby's Arcade, New York #287/R
$1900	£1098	The 10.14 (56x61cm-22x24in) s. masonite. 25-Sep-92 Sotheby's Arcade, New York #335/R
$1900	£1284	Railway station (56x91cm-22x36in) s.d.38 panel. 21-Apr-94 Butterfield & Butterfield, San Francisco #1071/R

THEK, Paul (1933-) American
$7000	£4575	Farewell to Washington Square (244x168cm-96x66in) linen executed 1972. 22-Dec-92 Christie's, East, New York #76
$1200	£795	Snowfall in the city (61x46cm-24x18in) s.d.78 W/C. 29-Sep-93 Sotheby's Arcade, New York #292/R
$2400	£1569	C.D. Fredricks (122x89cm-48x35in) col.chk two sheets executed 1975. 22-Dec-92 Christie's, East, New York #77

THERIAT, Charles James (1860-?) American
$1374	£935	Wearing national costume (46x27cm-18x11in) s. 21-Nov-93 Horhammer, Helsinki #38 (F.M 8000)
$2529	£1653	Young woman (46x38cm-18x15in) s. 18-Apr-93 Horhammer, Helsinki #24 (F.M 14000)
$36240	£24000	Beauty by a river (16x22cm-6x9in) s. panel. 15-Jun-94 Sotheby's, London #132/R

THERRIEN, Robert (1947-) American
$11000	£7432	Untitled (122x183cm-48x72in) canvas on panel painted 1985. 10-Nov-93 Christie's, New York #377/R
$12000	£7947	Untitled - dog dish (122x168cm-48x66in) oil tempera painted 1985-87. 18-Nov-92 Sotheby's, New York #284/R
$25000	£16892	Untitled - blue snowman (244x163cm-96x64in) canvas on wood executed 1985. 11-Nov-93 Sotheby's, New York #224/R
$2200	£1528	No title (50x43cm-20x17in) init.exec.1989 tempera metal screen glass board. 22-Feb-93 Christie's, East, New York #234/R

THEUS, Jeremiah (attrib) (1720-1774) American
$9000   £6294   Portrait of Naval officer Vincent Pearce (89x64cm-35x25in) 3-Feb-93 Doyle, New York #59

THIBON DE LIBIAN, Valentin (1889-1931) Argentinian
$8000   £4624   Primera Leccion (18x21cm-7x8in) 23-Sep-92 Roldan & Cia, Buenos Aires #23
$13200   £7765   Paisaje (30x40cm-12x16in) painted 1916. 29-Sep-92 VerBo, Buenos Aires #108/R
$70000   £40462   Pierrot y Colombina (90x70cm-35x28in) 23-Sep-92 Roldan & Cia, Buenos Aires #8
$81000   £46821   Bailarinas (40x50cm-16x20in) 23-Sep-92 Roldan & Cia, Buenos Aires #7

THIEBAUD, Wayne (1920-) American
$60000   £39216   Hot dog and mustard (43x51cm-17x20in) s.d.61 s.stretcher. 3-May-93 Sotheby's, New York #29/R
$105000 £70470   Club sandwich (30x36cm-12x14in) s.d.61. 5-May-94 Sotheby's, New York #188/R
$2250   £1415   San Francisco Bay (46x61cm-18x24in) s.d. W/C pencil. 25-Apr-93 Butterfield & Butterfield, San Francisco #2117/R
$4000   £2614   Cake (26x25cm-10x10in) brush ink graphite executed c.1965. 7-May-93 Christie's, East, New York #25/R
$12000   £7547   River pond study (53x53cm-21x21in) s.d.1970 col pencil. 25-Apr-93 Butterfield & Butterfield, San Francisco #2118/R
$18000   £11921   Cake slices (17x36cm-7x14in) s. painted c.1965 W/C chl. 19-Nov-92 Christie's, New York #334/R

THIEME, Anthony (1888-1954) American/Dutch
$853   £558   In dinghy (20x25cm-8x10in) s. panel. 14-May-93 Skinner, Bolton #122/R
$1025   £693   Woodlands with stone wall (61x76cm-24x30in) s. 10-Aug-93 Stonington Fine Arts, Stonington #85/R
$1045   £683   Day's end - harbour view (30x41cm-12x16in) s. canvasboard. 14-May-93 Skinner, Bolton #119/R
$1150   £665   Rocky shore (38x28cm-15x11in) board. 25-Sep-92 Douglas, South Deerfield #1
$1200   £795   Mexican landscape (30x41cm-12x16in) s. with i.verso canvasboard. 13-Nov-92 Skinner, Bolton #109/R
$1300   £872   Gondolas by the Doge's Palace, San Marco beyond (33x52cm-13x20in) s. board. 4-Mar-94 Skinner, Bolton #269/R
$1400   £927   Covered bridge - autumn landscape (64x76cm-25x30in) s. with i.verso. 13-Nov-92 Skinner, Bolton #119/R
$1400   £897   Lowering the sails (30x41cm-12x16in) s. canvas on board. 9-Dec-92 Butterfield & Butterfield, San Francisco #3919/R
$1635   £1083   Elephants (51x61cm-20x24in) s. i.verso. 14-Jun-94 Christie's, Amsterdam #279/R (D.FL 3000)
$1700   £1141   Boats in harbour (28x38cm-11x15in) s. board. 6-Dec-93 Grogan, Massachussetts #553/R
$2000   £1307   Docked sailboats (40x50cm-16x20in) s. canvasboards. 4-May-93 Christie's, East, New York #201/R
$2250   £1442   Mexican street (36x46cm-14x18in) s. s.i.verso canvas on board. 9-Dec-92 Butterfield & Butterfield, San Francisco #4004/R
$2250   £1442   Vessels in harbour (41x51cm-16x20in) s. canvasboard. 9-Dec-92 Butterfield & Butterfield, San Francisco #3915/R
$2298   £1197   Harbour scene with figures and boats (51x61cm-20x24in) s. 13-Aug-92 Rasmussen, Vejle #896/R (D.KR 13000)
$2400   £1611   Docked (30x41cm-12x16in) s. board. 6-Dec-93 Grogan, Massachussetts #541/R
$2500   £1634   Morning light (79x64cm-31x25in) s. i.verso. 5-May-93 Doyle, New York #42/R
$3250   £2083   Drying sails (76x91cm-30x36in) s. 9-Dec-92 Butterfield & Butterfield, San Francisco #3914/R
$3500   £2288   New York subway (30x40cm-12x16in) s. canvasboard. 4-May-93 Christie's, East, New York #199/R
$3500   £2244   Gaff-rigged trawler heading out (81x81cm-32x32in) s. 12-Dec-92 Weschler, Washington #74/R
$4300   £2810   Fishermen in Gloucester harbour (64x76cm-25x30in) s. 17-Sep-93 Skinner, Bolton #228/R
$5250   £2652   Taxco scene (76x91cm-30x36in) s. st.studio i.verso. 28-Aug-92 Young Fine Arts Auctions, Maine #292/R
$5500   £3691   Coquina Pit (63x76cm-25x30in) s.verso. 8-Dec-93 Butterfield & Butterfield, San Francisco #3365/R
$5500   £3716   Sunny aternoon at Rockport (76x92cm-30x36in) s. i.verso. 5-Nov-93 Skinner, Bolton #121/R
$6500   £4114   Boats in harbour (64x76cm-25x30in) s. board. 5-Dec-92 Louisiana Auction Exchange #131/R
$7000   £4895   Sails up (51x61cm-20x24in) s. s.i.verso canvasboard. 11-Mar-93 Christie's, New York #229/R
$8000   £5298   Down by docks (64x76cm-25x30in) s. 22-Sep-93 Christie's, New York #167/R
$8000   £4624   Boats at dock, Holland (40x50cm-16x20in) s. canvas board. 23-Sep-92 Christie's, New York #190/R
$10000   £6667   Boats in harbour (76x91cm-30x36in) s. 13-Mar-94 Hindman Galleries, Chicago #769/R
$12000   £8200   Rainy day on Main Street, Rockport (51x61cm-20x24in) s. i.verso. 26-May-94 Christie's, New York #106/R
$12000   £7792   Rockport quarry (74x90cm-29x35in) s. i.verso. 9-Sep-93 Sotheby's Arcade, New York #195/R
$14000   £9333   Mount Pleasant Street, Rockport (51x61cm-20x24in) s. i.stretcher. 16-Mar-94 Christie's, New York #96/R
$15000   £10000   Snow in New Hampshire (77x91cm-30x36in) s. i.verso. 16-Mar-94 Christie's, New York #101/R
$15000   £8671   Rockport landscape (76x91cm-30x36in) s. 23-Sep-92 Christie's, New York #191/R
$16000   £10667   South Street, Rockport (63x76cm-25x30in) s. i.verso. 16-Mar-94 Christie's, New York #102/R

THIEME, Anthony (1888-1954) American/Dutch-cont.
$17000	£10897	Patio Mediterreaneo (76x91cm-30x36in) s.i. i.verso. 26-May-93 Christie's, New York #149/R
$20000	£12658	Rooftops, Gloucester (78x92cm-31x36in) s. st.verso. 4-Dec-92 Christie's, New York #55/R
$38000	£24359	79th street Boat Basin, New York (76x91cm-30x36in) s.d.1935. 26-May-93 Christie's, New York #150/R
$800	*£537*	*Gloucester harbour (53x36cm-21x14in) W/C. 29-Dec-93 Douglas, South Deerfield #6*
$1600	*£1026*	*Flowers by open window (23x33cm-9x13in) s. W/C. 24-May-93 Grogan, Massachussetts #357/R*
$2600	*£1733*	*Boats docked by the Brooklyn Bridge (37x54cm-15x21in) s. W/C gouache. 23-May-94 Christie's, East, New York #193/R*

THOM, James Crawford (1835-1898) American
$900	£604	Children at play (25x43cm-10x17in) s. 24-Mar-94 Mystic Fine Arts, Connecticut #89/R
$1000	£676	Playtime at the stream four chldren and dog (20x28cm-8x11in) s. board. 31-Oct-93 Hindman Galleries, Chicago #664/R
$2200	£1486	Picking flowers (30x41cm-12x16in) s.d.84. 31-Mar-94 Sotheby's Arcade, New York #107/R
$2300	£1544	the bouquets - genre scene with girls by a rowboat (38x61cm-15x24in) s. 4-Mar-94 Skinner, Bolton #170/R
$2750	£1786	Reading the letter to the children (51x76cm-20x30in) s. 9-Sep-93 Sotheby's Arcade, New York #102/R
$3000	£1987	Christmas Eve (99x183cm-39x72in) s. 27-Sep-93 Selkirks, St. Louis #936/R
$3600	£2449	Washerwoman and children by woodland stream (46x81cm-18x32in) s. 17-Nov-93 Doyle, New York #19/R
$11160	£7200	Homeward bound (46x56cm-18x22in) s. panel. 13-Jul-94 Christie's, Glasgow #522/R

THOM, James Crawford (attrib) (1835-1898) American
$900	£604	Spring morning (74x28cm-29x11in) 27-Mar-94 Myers, Florida #55/R

THOMAS, Stephen Seymour (1868-?) American
$750	£494	First studio in Paris (27x35cm-11x14in) s.i.d.1892. 13-Jun-93 Butterfield & Butterfield, San Francisco #3173/R
$800	£526	Self-portrait (51x41cm-20x16in) 13-Jun-93 Butterfield & Butterfield, San Francisco #3174/R
$800	£537	Green surf and towering skies (61x76cm-24x30in) s. board. 4-Dec-93 Louisiana Auction Exchange #117/R
$850	*£571*	*Lady in brown (110x80cm-43x31in) s. pastel paper on canvas. 8-Dec-93 Butterfield & Butterfield, San Francisco #3312/R*

THOMPSON, Albert (1853-?) American
$650	£436	The haywagon (30x38cm-12x15in) s. 5-Dec-93 James Bakker, Cambridge #50/R

THOMPSON, Alfred Wordsworth (1840-1896) American
$3800	£2533	Horse auction (15x22cm-6x9in) s. 23-May-94 Christie's, East, New York #30/R
$3800	£2585	The way stop (46x68cm-18x27in) s.i.d.1893. 15-Nov-93 Christie's, East, New York #59/R
$4200	£2857	Goin home (25x22cm-10x9in) s.d.80 board. 15-Nov-93 Christie's, East, New York #52/R

THOMPSON, Bob (1937-1966) American
$4000	£2778	Golden nude (66x102cm-26x40in) s.d.60 tempera paper. 22-Feb-93 Christie's, East, New York #134/R
$4000	£2778	Provincetown beach scene (66x102cm-26x40in) s.d.60 tempera paper. 22-Feb-93 Christie's, East, New York #132/R
$6000	£4027	Untitled (32x36cm-13x14in) canvas on panel painted 1963. 23-Feb-94 Christie's, New York #56/R
$12000	£8054	Untitled (108x67cm-43x26in) s.d.63 verso. 23-Feb-94 Christie's, New York #57/R
$20000	£13072	Stairway to the Stars (102x152cm-40x60in) s.i.verso oil black white photograph panel. 5-May-93 Christie's, New York #230/R

THOMPSON, Cephas Giovanni (1809-1888) American
$650	£409	Portrait of young woman (61x48cm-24x19in) s.i.d.1838verso. 23-Apr-93 Skinner, Bolton #349
$6000	£4082	Portrait of lady (76x64cm-30x25in) 9-Jul-93 Sloan, North Bethesda #2774/R

THOMPSON, George Albert (1868-1938) American
$750	£503	Mystic harbour (30x41cm-12x16in) s. 29-Nov-93 Stonington Fine Arts, Stonington #59/R

THOMPSON, Jerome (1814-1886) American
$8000	£5333	Land of Beulah (103x77cm-41x30in) s.d.1880. 17-Mar-94 Sotheby's, New York #38/R
$10000	£6711	Children at brook (46x66cm-18x26in) 3-Feb-94 Sloan, North Bethesda #2892/R
$14000	£8974	Old age (90x132cm-35x52in) s.d.1874. 27-May-93 Sotheby's, New York #192/R
$16000	£10256	Youth (90x132cm-35x52in) s.d.1874. 27-May-93 Sotheby's, New York #191/R

THOMPSON, Jerome (attrib) (1814-1886) American
$1500	£993	Country landscape (54x76cm-21x30in) s. panel. 2-Oct-93 Weschler, Washington #88/R

THOMPSON, Leslie P (1880-1963) American
$2420	£1582	Portrait of woman reading book (86x76cm-34x30in) s.d.1916. 14-May-93 Skinner, Bolton #149/R

THOMPSON, Wordsworth see THOMPSON, Alfred Wordsworth

THOMSON, Henry Grinnell (1850-1939) American
$1800   £1224   Red barn by stream (56x69cm-22x27in) s. 15-Nov-93 Christie's, East, New York #74/R

THOMSON, Tom (1877-1917) Canadian
$14269   £9326   Lake Scugog (40x60cm-16x24in) s. canvas on panel. 19-May-93 Sotheby's, Toronto #179/R (C.D 18000)
$54485   £36082   Sunset, Canoe Lake (17x25cm-7x10in) s. canvas on board. 24-Nov-92 Joyner Fine Art, Toronto #39/R (C.D 70000)
$64214   £42526   Giant's Tomb - Georgian Bay (22x27cm-9x11in) s. board. 18-Nov-92 Sotheby's, Toronto #72/R (C.D 82500)
$67383   £44041   In Petawawa Gorges, spring (21x27cm-8x11in) estate st. d.1916 verso panel. 19-May-93 Sotheby's, Toronto #222/R (C.D 85000)

THORNDIKE, Charles Hall (1875-?) American
$550   £369   Bowling green, New York (93x74cm-37x29in) s. panel. 6-May-94 Skinner, Bolton #149/R

THORNE, William (19th C) American
$1400   £927   Portrait of young violinist (142x91cm-56x36in) s.d.1904. 3-Oct-93 Hanzel Galleries, Chicago #844

THORNTON, Mildred Valley (1890-1967) Canadian
$778   £515   Rough hair, blood Indian (51x36cm-20x14in) s. i.verso canvasboard. 16-Nov-92 Hodgins, Calgary #329 (C.D 1000)
$824   £538   Chief Back Fat (41x31cm-16x12in) s.d.1943 verso canvasboard. 10-May-93 Hodgins, Calgary #56 (C.D 1050)
$1245   £825   Ambrose Derrick (51x41cm-20x16in) s. i.d.1943verso board. 18-Nov-92 Sotheby's, Toronto #49/R (C.D 1600)
$2325   £1571   Autumn in the Okanagan (76x91cm-30x36in) s. s.i.d.1952stretcher. 3-Nov-93 Sotheby's, Toronto #329/R (C.D 3000)
$3099   £2094   Haidas British Columbia with slaves on ceremonial journey (76x102cm-30x40in) s.i.d.c.1945 board. 3-Nov-93 Sotheby's, Toronto #247/R (C.D 4000)
$545   *£361*   *Mountain view from Burnaby (24x32cm-9x13in) s.i. W/C. 16-Nov-92 Hodgins, Calgary #7/R (C.D 700)*

THORSEN, Lars (1876-1952) American?
$945   £635   Ship at full sail (76x102cm-30x40in) s. 24-Jun-93 Mystic Fine Arts, Connecticut #83
$1000   £662   Full and By - topsail schooner yacht Gression (61x76cm-24x30in) s. i.verso. 13-Nov-92 Skinner, Bolton #58/R

THULSTRUP, Thure de (1848-1930) American
$1000   £676   Charge of the Union officers (53x46cm-21x18in) s. 31-Mar-94 Sotheby's Arcade, New York #207/R
$1500   £1007   The fisherwoman (91x61cm-36x24in) 27-Mar-94 Myers, Florida #30/R
$6500   £4392   Generals Grant and Lee at Appomattox (43x49cm-17x19in) s. 31-Mar-94 Sotheby's Arcade, New York #188/R
$1000   *£676*   *Queen Victoria parading at Trafalgar Square. The Cavalry inspection (68x49cm-27x19in) s. one gouache en grisaille one W/C board pair. 31-Mar-94 Sotheby's Arcade, New York #203/R*

THURBER, James Grover (1894-1961) American
$3000   *£1948*   *Tennis player (19x16cm-7x6in) init. Indian ink. 9-Sep-93 Sotheby's Arcade, New York #372/R*

TIBON, Cristina Cassy (1937-) Mexican
$1279   £864   Tambien los munecos juegan (45x55cm-18x22in) s.d.1993. 20-Oct-93 Louis Morton, Mexico #26/R (M.P 4000)
$1330   £875   Mercado en Oaxaca (30x40cm-12x16in) s. masonite. 4-Nov-92 Mora, Castelltort & Quintana, Juarez #16/R (M.P 4200000)

TICKNER, Michael (?) Canadian?
$758   £480   False Creek boats (30x24cm-12x9in) s. board. 21-Oct-92 Maynards, Vancouver #155 (C.D 950)

TIFFANY, Louis Comfort (1848-1933) American
$2100   £1419   Staten Islar ' (13x30cm-5x12in) init. 10-Aug-93 Stonington Fine Arts, Stonington #86/R
$11000   £6358   Carriage waiting beside wall (21x64cm-8x25in) init. 23-Sep-92 Christie's, New York #98/R
$22000   £12717   View from mosque (33x29cm-13x11in) s. 23-Sep-92 Christie's, New York #101/R
$55000   £31792   Pushing off the boat, Sea Bright, New Jersey (61x91cm-24x36in) s.d.87. 23-Sep-92 Christie's, New York #96/R
$7000   *£4046*   *Old shops in Geneva (33x37cm-13x15in) s. W/C gouache pencil. 23-Sep-92 Christie's, New York #94/R*
$10500   *£6646*   *Arabian subject (38x25cm-15x10in) s. W/C gouache. 3-Dec-92 Sotheby's, New York #31/R*
$11000   *£6358*   *Aswan, Nile (25x18cm-10x7in) s.i.d.Feb.13.08 W/C pen sepia gouache pencil. 23-Sep-92 Christie's, New York #97/R*
$12000   *£6936*   *Islamic door (33x24cm-13x9in) s. gouache pencil. 23-Sep-92 Christie's, New York #100/R*

TIFFANY, Louis Comfort (1848-1933) American-cont.
$50000   £28902   Family group with cow (51x73cm-20x29in) s. gouache W/C paper on board. 23-Sep-92 Christie's, New York #91/R

TIGLIO, Marcos (1903-1976) Argentinian
$2800   £1854   Magnolias (49x34cm-19x13in) 11-Nov-92 VerBo, Buenos Aires #108

TILTON, John Rollin (1833-1888) American
$1600   £1013   La Ronda, Spain (47x76cm-19x30in) 2-Dec-92 Christie's, East, New York #57/R
$19000   £12500   Ruins of Kom Ombo on the Nile (78x124cm-31x49in) init. 20-Jul-94 Sotheby's Arcade, New York #254/R

TIMMINS, William (20th C) American
$1500   £1042   Gutierrez Adobe, Monterey, California (37x43cm-15x17in) s. W/C gouache pencil. 7-Mar-93 Butterfield & Butterfield, San Francisco #98/R

TIMMONS, E J (1882-?) American
$1500   £1007   Woman on bench in woods (58x76cm-23x30in) s. 29-Nov-93 Stonington Fine Arts, Stonington #86/R

TINGUELY, Jean and SAINT PHALLE, Niki de (20th C) Swiss/American
$2337   £1498   Senza titolo, lettera (21x28cm-8x11in) executed 1970 i.by both artists ink collage. 15-Dec-92 Finarte, Milan #73/R (I.L 3300000)
$5559   £3756   Salut Georges 1975 (24x46cm-9x18in) s. mixed media collage. 21-Apr-94 Germann, Zurich #20/R (S.FR 8000)

TITCOMB, Mary Bradish (1856-1927) American
$16000   £10596   Young woman in garen (74x60cm-29x24in) s. canvasboard. 23-Sep-93 Sotheby's, New York #156/R
$17000   £10897   Marblehead harbour (76x91cm-30x36in) s. 27-May-93 Sotheby's, New York #81/R

TITTLE, Walter (1883-1966) American
$1000   £578   Central Park (51x76cm-20x30in) s. 25-Sep-92 Sotheby's Arcade, New York #381/R
$1700   £1149   Seated nude (91x71cm-36x28in) s. 31-Mar-94 Sotheby's Arcade, New York #318

TOBEY, Mark (1890-1976) American
$1000   £699   Beaver (18x36cm-7x14in) s.d.55 i.verso tempera paper. 12-Mar-93 Skinner, Bolton #299/R
$1600   £1111   Strange cloud (17x12cm-7x5in) tempera paper. 26-Feb-93 Sotheby's Arcade, New York #277 a/R
$2000   £1351   Labyrinth (30x13cm-12x5in) s.d.54 tempera paper on ragboard. 11-Nov-93 Sotheby's, New York #256/R
$2800   £1944   White lights. Bahai figures , one s.d.1936 double-sided. 26-Feb-93 Sotheby's Arcade, New York #262/R
$3500   £2349   On the Ritz (22x16cm-9x6in) s.d.58 s.i.d.58 verso tempera paper paperboard. 25-Feb-94 Sotheby's, New York #15/R
$3500   £2318   Totem No.2 (15x14cm-6x6in) s.d.53 tempera paper. 18-Nov-92 Sotheby's, New York #93 b
$3749   £2500   Composition (35x28cm-14x11in) s.d. tempera board. 12-Mar-94 Kunstgalerij de Vuyst, Lokeren #510/R (B.FR 130000)
$4000   £2649   Radiations (18x27cm-7x11in) s.d.57 tempera board. 18-Nov-92 Sotheby's, New York #93 a/R
$7106   £4675   Baroque (13x18cm-5x7in) s.d.1960 tempera paper on board. 5-Jun-93 Villa Grisebach, Berlin #410/R (DM 11500)
$8000   £5063   Modern saint (58x23cm-23x9in) tempera board. 25-Oct-92 Butterfield & Butterfield, San Francisco #2273/R
$9238   £6200   Wafting memories (99x50cm-39x20in) s.d.1970verso tempera polystyrene. 29-Nov-93 Christie's, S. Kensington #247/R
$14343   £9562   Ancient Caves No.1 (30x45cm-12x18in) s.d.1959 tempera paper on canvas. 11-Jun-94 Hauswedell & Nolte, Hamburg #368/R (DM 24000)
$15699   £10194   Minute world (17x33cm-7x13in) s.d.60 tempera on paper laid on board. 22-Jun-94 Galerie Kornfeld, Berne #935/R (S.FR 21000)
$21000   £13907   White writing (30x21cm-12x8in) s.indist.d. tempera paper on rice paper c.1951. 18-Nov-92 Sotheby's, New York #80/R
$47500   £32095   Enchanted garden (41x62cm-16x24in) s.i.d.50 tempera paper. 10-Nov-93 Sotheby's, New York #1/R
$748   £489   Male nude (70x45cm-28x18in) s.indis.d. sepia paper on fabric. 15-May-93 Aucktionhaus Burkard, Luzern #68/R (S.FR 1100)
$800   £556   Symbolist pictograph letter to Royal Markes from Mark Tobey (28x24cm-11x9in) s.i. ink. 26-Feb-93 Sotheby's Arcade, New York #264/R
$1096   £712   Homme assis (26x19cm-10x7in) s. Indian ink wash. 24-Jun-94 Delorme & Fraysse, Paris #137 (F.FR 6000)
$1500   £1007   Patterns (8x21cm-3x8in) s.d.61 gouache graphite board on board. 3-May-94 Christie's, East, New York #23/R
$1662   £1116   Untitled (46x19cm-2x7in) s.d.61 mixed media. 29-Nov-93 AB Stockholms Auktionsverk, Stockholm #6289/R (S.KR 14000)
$1787   £1096   Composition en bleu, rouge et noir (16x11cm-6x4in) s.i.d.1964 gouache. 18-Oct-92 Catherine Charbonneaux, Paris #9/R (F.FR 9000)
$2015   £1371   Monotype (50x31cm-20x12in) s.d.66 W/C. 13-Apr-94 Bukowskis, Stockholm #330/R (S.KR 16000)
$2092   £1394   Labryinth (17x13cm-7x5in) st.sig. gouache board. 6-Jun-94 Wolfgang Ketterer, Munich #1303/R (DM 3500)
$2100   £1409   Untitled (56x46cm-22x18in) s. pastel board executed c.1940. 24-Feb-94 Sotheby's Arcade, New York #349/R

TOBEY, Mark (1890-1976) American-cont.

$2193	£1462	Homme nu (28x9cm-11x4in) s.d.55 black crayon gouache. 8-Jun-94 Poulain & le Fur, Paris #111 (F.FR 12500)
$2200	£1294	Untitled (10x15cm-4x6in) s.d.63 gouache glue. 8-Oct-92 Christie's, New York #107/R
$2250	£1521	Untitled (30x26cm-12x10in) s.d.59 ink wash paper laid down on board. 21-Apr-94 Butterfield & Butterfield, San Francisco #1096/R
$2472	£1626	Figure (26x21cm-10x8in) s.i.d.March 1957 Indian ink brush. 5-Jun-93 Galerie Bassenge, Berlin #6579/R (DM 4000)
$2838	£1918	Untitled (12x17cm-5x7in) s.d.1964 mixed media. 20-Oct-93 Galerie Dobiaschofsky, Bern #1362/R (S.FR 4200)
$2960	£2000	Forms in progress (48x61cm-19x24in) s.d.1973 i.d.verso W/C. 30-Oct-93 Dr Fritz Nagel, Stuttgart #45 (DM 5000)
$3500	£2349	Purple composition (17x12cm-7x5in) s.d.61 gouache paper on board. 24-Feb-94 Sotheby's Arcade, New York #339/R
$3505	£2336	Sans titre (29x18cm-11x7in) s.d.1961 gouache. 1-Jun-94 Marc Kohn, Paris #93/R (F.FR 20000)
$3725	£2500	Untitled (15x11cm-6x4in) s.d.69 gouache monotype. 23-Jun-93 Christie's, London #336/R
$3750	£2534	Abstract composition (16x14cm-6x6in) s.d.58 W/C gouache board. 21-Oct-93 Butterfield & Butterfield, San Francisco #2716/R
$3772	£2515	Ecriture blanche (27x21cm-11x8in) gouache writing paper. 8-Jun-94 Poulain & le Fur, Paris #112/R (F.FR 21500)
$4000	£2532	Space ritual - 10, 1957 (58x86cm-23x34in) ink. 25-Oct-92 Butterfield & Butterfield, San Francisco #2274/R
$5378	£3586	Gray Spectres (17x17cm-7x7in) s.d.1969 ink htd. white. 6-Jun-94 Wolfgang Ketterer, Munich #301/R (DM 9000)
$5677	£3785	One line (86x15cm-34x6in) s.d.1953 tempera white chk. 11-Jun-94 Hauswedell & Nolte, Hamburg #367/R (DM 9500)
$5960	£4000	Happy blue (52x17cm-20x7in) s.d.65 gouache ink paper on board. 2-Dec-93 Christie's, London #222/R
$7500	£5208	Untitled (15x21cm-6x8in) s.d.54 pen gouache paper on paper. 22-Feb-93 Christie's, East, New York #194/R
$8000	£5369	Oriental garden (30x45cm-12x18in) s.d.56 i.d.1956 verso tempera ink. 23-Feb-94 Christie's, New York #10/R
$8000	£5298	Untitled (20x17cm-8x7in) s.d.66 monotype gouache. 19-Nov-92 Christie's, New York #355/R
$8642	£5800	Untitled (100x51cm-39x20in) s.d.61 W/C monotype. 2-Dec-93 Christie's, London #214/R
$9000	£6081	Untitled (102x53cm-40x21in) s.d.66 monotype W/C paper on Japan paper. 11-Nov-93 Sotheby's, New York #290/R
$11410	£7000	Untitled (102x51cm-40x20in) s.d.65 gouache monotype Japan paper on paper. 15-Oct-92 Christie's, London #23/R
$11475	£7500	Untitled (36x28cm-14x11in) s.d.54 tempera gouache paper on board. 30-Jun-94 Sotheby's, London #109/R
$15485	£9500	Untitled (102x51cm-40x20in) s.d.65 gouache monotype Japan paper on paper. 15-Oct-92 Christie's, London #22/R
$17880	£12000	Circular (29x42cm-11x17in) s.d.65 st.sig. verso W/C gouache paper on board. 24-Jun-93 Sotheby's, London #90/R

TODDY, Jimmy (1928-) American

$1100	£710	Mounted warrior (41x51cm-16x20in) s.d.81 gouache art board. 9-Jan-93 Skinner, Bolton #232/R

TODHUNTER, Francis Augustus (1884-1963) American

$800	£530	Landscape with oak trees (46x56cm-18x22in) s.d.1913. 20-Sep-93 Butterfield & Butterfield, Los Angeles #82/R
$900	£520	Valley design - Mt Tamalpais (61x76cm-24x30in) 26-Sep-92 San Rafael Auction Galleries #224
$950	£629	Cemetery (61x76cm-24x30in) s. 15-Jun-94 Butterfield & Butterfield, San Francisco #4619/R
$1000	£588	Catholic church, Mill Valley (61x76cm-24x30in) s. 4-Oct-92 Butterfield & Butterfield, Los Angeles #51/R
$1300	£861	Marin Farm (46x56cm-18x22in) s. 15-Jun-94 Butterfield & Butterfield, San Francisco #4620/R
$1300	£765	Looking north (61x76cm-24x30in) s. 4-Oct-92 Butterfield & Butterfield, Los Angeles #48/R
$1700	£1118	Mountain farmhouse (61x76cm-24x30in) s. 13-Jun-93 Butterfield & Butterfield, San Francisco #736/R
$1700	£1118	Tom Nune's ranch (61x76cm-24x30in) 13-Jun-93 Butterfield & Butterfield, San Francisco #744/R
$2000	£1316	Approaching fog (61x76cm-24x30in) s. 13-Jun-93 Butterfield & Butterfield, San Francisco #746/R
$2250	£1324	Greenbrae (51x66cm-20x26in) s. 4-Oct-92 Butterfield & Butterfield, Los Angeles #52/R
$2250	£1481	Marin Hills (61x76cm-24x30in) s. 13-Jun-93 Butterfield & Butterfield, San Francisco #745/R
$2500	£1471	Mill Valley composition (61x76cm-24x30in) s. 4-Oct-92 Butterfield & Butterfield, Los Angeles #54/R
$2500	£1645	Old Lyford Place (61x76cm-24x30in) 13-Jun-93 Butterfield & Butterfield, San Francisco #739/R
$3500	£2059	Straits (61x76cm-24x30in) s. 4-Oct-92 Butterfield & Butterfield, Los Angeles #49/R
$3750	£2206	Ignacio Ranch (61x76cm-24x30in) s. 4-Oct-92 Butterfield & Butterfield, Los Angeles #53/R

TODHUNTER, Francis Augustus (1884-1963) American-cont.
$3750	£2467	Boats, Old Sausalito (61x76cm-24x30in) 13-Jun-93 Butterfield & Butterfield, San Francisco #740/R
$3750	£2467	Little church at Tiburon (61x76cm-24x30in) s. 13-Jun-93 Butterfield & Butterfield, San Francisco #747/R
$850	£500	Small house at Martins (46x51cm-18x20in) s. W/C. 4-Oct-92 Butterfield & Butterfield, Los Angeles #110/R
$1200	£706	Tiburon (52x70cm-20x28in) s. W/C. 4-Oct-92 Butterfield & Butterfield, Los Angeles #50/R

TOJETTI, Domenico (1806-1892) American
$700	£464	Pope Pius IX (86x69cm-34x27in) 28-Sep-93 John Moran, Pasadena #299
$1445	£850	Classical figures with chariot (25x39cm-10x15in) s. canvas on board. 1-Oct-92 Christie's, S. Kensington #88/R

TOJETTI, Virgilio (1851-1901) American
$2205	£1500	Children with a lute (24x51cm-9x20in) s.d.99 board. 16-Nov-93 Phillips, London #194/R
$3400	£2329	Cherubs at play (107x41cm-42x16in) s.d.1898. 10-Feb-94 Skinner, Bolton #51
$7000	£4667	Decorated column (107x38cm-42x15in) s.d.98. 25-May-94 Christie's, New York #233/R

TOLEDO, Francisco (1940-) Mexican
$5000	£3333	Figura (46x38cm-18x15in) oil sand canvas painted c.1965. 18-May-94 Sotheby's, New York #317/R
$10068	£6803	Personnage (65x54cm-26x21in) s.verso painted 1963. 29-Apr-94 Binoche, Paris #35/R (F.FR 60000)
$15000	£10000	Composition in red (53x46cm-21x18in) s.verso oil sand burlap painted c.1963. 18-May-94 Christie's, New York #137/R
$65000	£42484	Toro (79x109cm-31x43in) oil sand painted 1969. 18-May-93 Sotheby's, New York #68/R
$85000	£56291	Sapo (97x127cm-38x50in) oil sand. 24-Nov-92 Christie's, New York #42/R
$797	£531	Composition (43x54cm-17x21in) W/C wash dr. 30-May-94 Catherine Charbonneaux, Paris #162 (F.FR 4500)
$1200	£706	Composition (43x66cm-17x26in) s.d.59 W/C double-sided. 3-Oct-92 Weschler, Washington #35/R
$1345	£885	Fantasy figures (31x23cm-12x9in) s. mixed media. 3-Nov-92 Bukowskis, Stockholm #273/R (S.KR 8000)
$2250	£1562	Untitled. Sketch of knight in armour (24x31cm-9x12in) s. gouache ink double-sided. 26-Feb-93 Sotheby's Arcade, New York #249/R
$2567	£1700	Jump (24x33cm-9x13in) s. W/C pen. 24-Nov-92 Phillips, London #335
$3000	£2000	Personnage et singe (24x22cm-9x9in) s. gouache pen black ink. 18-May-94 Christie's, New York #194/R
$3171	£2100	Fish sun, 1965 (48x53cm-19x21in) W/C pen. 24-Nov-92 Phillips, London #336/R
$3366	£2200	La Gente jugando (23x29cm-9x11in) s.d.63 gouache. 27-Jun-94 Christie's, S. Kensington #239/R
$3750	£2484	Visage (58x75cm-23x30in) s. W/C ink. 30-Jun-93 Sotheby's Arcade, New York #215/R
$5500	£3716	Sin titulo (28x22cm-11x9in) s. gouache painted c.1969. 23-Nov-93 Christie's, New York #238/R
$6000	£4027	Mythical animals and figures (21x16cm-8x6in) five s. one i. three pencil two chl one W/C six. 24-Feb-94 Sotheby's Arcade, New York #287/R
$6000	£3974	Composition (79x63cm-31x25in) W/C. 30-Jun-93 Sotheby's Arcade, New York #217/R
$6342	£4200	Self-portrait, 1965 (47x63cm-19x25in) s.i. W/C gouache pen. 24-Nov-92 Phillips, London #337/R
$7000	£4698	Standing woman, standing man, woman with mirror, animal figure and chulambalem (84x65cm-33x26in) four s. one d.82 one i. pencil chl pastel W/C 5. 24-Feb-94 Sotheby's Arcade, New York #307/R
$7500	£5000	El Cazador (25x32cm-10x13in) s. gouache pen ink. 18-May-94 Christie's, New York #190/R
$7500	£4967	Chango III (17x26cm-7x10in) W/C gouache silver leaf. 23-Nov-92 Sotheby's, New York #242/R
$8500	£5705	Golpeando un nino (24x31cm-9x12in) gouache Indian ink W/C. 7-Jan-94 Gary Nader, Miami #7/R
$8500	£5743	Sin titulo (24x31cm-9x12in) s.i. gouache W/C sand pen paper on board. 23-Nov-93 Christie's, New York #235/R
$9500	£6209	Pez (28x38cm-11x15in) s. gouache pen. 17-May-93 Christie's, New York #123/R
$10000	£6667	Mujer (62x47cm-24x19in) s. W/C pen black ink. 18-May-94 Christie's, New York #191/R
$11000	£7432	The monkey ride (25x32cm-10x13in) s.d.63 gouache pen. 23-Nov-93 Christie's, New York #234/R
$12000	£7843	El coyote y el conejo (25x35cm-10x14in) gouache pen. 17-May-93 Christie's, New York #126/R
$12000	£7947	Mujer en un bote (24x33cm-9x13in) s. W/C gouache pen Fabriano paper. 24-Nov-92 Christie's, New York #183/R
$12000	£7947	No Te Metas en Enredos (24x31cm-9x12in) s. W/C graphite. 23-Nov-92 Sotheby's, New York #241/R
$12000	£7843	El cangrejo - femme au crabe, Paris (25x32cm-10x13in) s. W/C executed 1985. 18-May-93 Sotheby's, New York #214/R
$12500	£8170	Iguanas y cactus (29x37cm-11x15in) gouache pen panel executed c.1979. 18-May-93 Sotheby's, New York #213/R
$13000	£8609	Escorpiones y Telas de Arana (28x19cm-11x7in) s. W/C pen brush. 24-Nov-92 Christie's, New York #125/R
$13000	£8497	El coyote y el conejo (28x38cm-11x15in) gouache pen. 17-May-93 Christie's, New York #124/R
$13000	£8784	Sin titulo (24x31cm-9x12in) s. W/C pen. 23-Nov-93 Christie's, New York #237/R

TOLEDO, Francisco (1940-) Mexican-cont.
$14000	£9333	El Frio (25x32cm-10x13in) s. s.i.verso gouache pen black ink painted 1978. 18-May-94 Christie's, New York #196/R
$15000	£9934	El Conejo y el Colibri (25x28cm-10x11in) s. W/C gouache pen painted c.1979. 24-Nov-92 Christie's, New York #124/R
$15000	£10135	Estudio para ganado vacuno (61x48cm-24x19in) pen wash. 23-Nov-93 Christie's, New York #236/R
$15000	£9804	Autorretrato (31x24cm-12x9in) s. gouache pen. 17-May-93 Christie's, New York #122/R
$16000	£10811	Sin titulo (24x33cm-9x13in) s. gouache pen. 23-Nov-93 Christie's, New York #214/R
$16000	£10811	Sin titulo (24x33cm-9x13in) s. gouache pen. 23-Nov-93 Christie's, New York #213/R
$17000	£11333	Hombre y Esqueleto (25x33cm-10x13in) s. gouache pen sepia ink painted 1966-67. 18-May-94 Christie's, New York #193/R
$18000	£11921	Untitled (28x38cm-11x15in) s. gouache W/C Arches paper. 24-Nov-92 Christie's, New York #184/R
$19000	£12838	Pescado (50x64cm-20x25in) s. gouache gold paint pen executed c.1968. 22-Nov-93 Sotheby's, New York #270/R
$19000	£12838	Fish sun (49x56cm-19x22in) s. W/C gouache painted 1965. 23-Nov-93 Christie's, New York #144/R
$20000	£13423	The foot (63x46cm-25x18in) gouache. 7-Jan-94 Gary Nader, Miami #52/R
$22000	£14570	La Ronda (33x24cm-13x9in) s. i.verso gouache. 24-Nov-92 Christie's, New York #56/R
$22000	£14667	Autorretrato con Sombrero (24x33cm-9x13in) s. gouache pen black ink painted 1986-87. 18-May-94 Christie's, New York #195/R
$23221	£15584	Tres hamacas (50x65cm-20x26in) gouache. 1-Dec-93 Louis Morton, Mexico #85/R (M.P 72000)
$24000	£16000	Autorretrato (25x32cm-10x13in) s. gouache pen black ink gessoed paper. 18-May-94 Christie's, New York #197/R
$26693	£18036	Puerco contento (40x30cm-16x12in) s.d.76verso mixed media canvas. 27-Apr-94 Louis Morton, Mexico #458/R (M.P 90000)
$28000	£18543	Pareja y Lobos. Cabra (28x38cm-11x15in) s. W/C gouache pen double-sided. 24-Nov-92 Christie's, New York #185/R
$75000	£49669	Yuze (56x75cm-22x30in) s. gouache ink. 23-Nov-92 Sotheby's, New York #75 a/R
$85000	£57432	Mujer con langostinos (72x106cm-28x42in) s. gouache pen painted 1973. 23-Nov-93 Christie's, New York #35/R
$90000	£60000	Cochino (76x76cm-22x30in) s. gouache W/C pen executed 1974. 17-May-94 Sotheby's, New York #57/R
$90000	£59603	El Cuento del Coyote y el Conejo (24x17cm-9x7in) s.i. gouache W/C pen pencil 23 illustrations. 24-Nov-92 Christie's, New York #123/R
$120000	£80000	El cuento del Conejo y el Coyote, gouache ink one ink dr ten. 18-May-94 Christie's, New York #44/R
$240000	£158940	El Perro Ladra (100x130cm-39x51in) s.d.74 verso oil pen canvas. 24-Nov-92 Christie's, New York #43/R

TOLEDO, Jose Rey (1915-) American
$450	£292	Deer (46x61cm-18x24in) s.d.53 i.verso W/C. 25-Jun-94 Skinner, Bolton #203

TOLLANT, R H (20th C) American
$1450	£929	Mountain landscape, Odessa Lake, Colorado (112x76cm-44x30in) s.d.1912. 26-Apr-93 Selkirks, St. Louis #186/R

TOLLIVER, Mose (1919-) American
$675	£447	Self-Portrait (66x41cm-26x16in) s. house paint hair board. 21-Nov-92 Litchfield Auction Gallery #10

TOLMAN, Stacy (1860-1935) American
$2000	£1351	Cottage garden (43x53cm-17x21in) s. 10-Aug-93 Stonington Fine Arts, Stonington #143/R

TOMANECK, Joseph (1889-?) American
$1300	£850	Reclining nude in the studio (30x41cm-12x16in) s. canvasboard. 19-Sep-93 Hindman Galleries, Chicago #698 a
$11000	£7190	Feeding deer (160x160cm-63x63in) s.d.28. 4-May-93 Christie's, East, New York #76/R

TOMLIN, Bradley Walker (1899-1953) American
$5000	£3205	Man painting (86x56cm-34x22in) s. 9-Dec-92 Butterfield & Butterfield, San Francisco #4029/R
$700	£440	Concarneau (25x41cm-10x16in) i.d.1926 W/C. 22-Apr-93 Freeman Fine Arts, Philadelphia #1194

TOMLINSON, Anna C (20th C) American
$900	£577	Hollyhocks (28x23cm-11x9in) s. pastel board. 9-Dec-92 Grogan, Massachussetts #85/R

TOMPKINS, Alan (1907-) American
$6500	£4362	Bathers (112x134cm-44x53in) s.d.1933 s.i.verso. 6-May-94 Skinner, Bolton #144/R

TOMPKINS, Frank H (1847-1922) American
$1000	£676	A Boston view with skaters (20x25cm-8x10in) s. board. 5-Nov-93 Skinner, Bolton #165/R

TONNANCOUR, Jacques de (1917-) Canadian
$3171	£2073	Rio '46 (66x91cm-26x36in) s.d. 19-May-93 Sotheby's, Toronto #363/R (C.D 4000)

TONNANCOUR, Jacques de (1917-) Canadian-cont.
$3171	£2073	Cibles pour trois mousquetaires (91x91cm-36x36in) s.d.1973 verso oil collage board. 19-May-93 Sotheby's, Toronto #206/R (C.D 4000)
$10119	£6701	Blue lake (60x79cm-24x31in) s.d.63 i.verso board. 18-Nov-92 Sotheby's, Toronto #86/R (C.D 13000)
$18122	£12245	Georgian Bay landscape, 1957 (90x120cm-35x47in) s. board. 23-Nov-93 Joyner Fine Art, Toronto #113/R (C.D 24000)

TONSBERG, Gertrude Martin (1903-1973) American
$990	£647	Marlboro Street, boston (61x51cm-24x20in) s. 14-May-93 Skinner, Bolton #170/R
$1000	£667	Copley Square, Boston (74x61cm-29x24in) s. i.verso. 26-Aug-93 Skinner, Bolton #200/R

TOPPING, James (1879-1949) American
$950	£629	Spring landscape. Landscape scene (61x71cm-24x28in) s. board double-sided. 3-Oct-93 Hanzel Galleries, Chicago #776
$3700	£2450	Morning in the blowout (71x76cm-28x30in) s. 3-Oct-93 Hanzel Galleries, Chicago #756

TORR, Helen (1886-1967) American
$6000	£3797	Still life with mechanical man (61x48cm-24x19in) board. 3-Dec-92 Sotheby's, New York #186/R
$6500	*£4167*	*Flower in landscape (36x25cm-14x10in) bears estate st.verso chl. 26-May-93 Christie's, New York #230/R*

TORRALLARDONA, Carlos (1913-1986) Argentinian
$874	£587	Untitled (59x72cm-23x28in) s. painted 1982. 8-May-94 Jonquet, Paris #135 (F.FR 5000)
$1100	£573	El taller (44x30cm-17x12in) 4-Aug-92 VerBo, Buenos Aires #108

TORRE, Carlos de la (1856-1832) Argentinian
$1200	£625	Paisaje (12x21cm-5x8in) 41. 4-Aug-92 VerBo, Buenos Aires #40
$1800	£1040	El puesto (12x16cm-5x6in) board. 23-Sep-92 Roldan & Cia, Buenos Aires #56
$2000	£1325	En el camino (12x21cm-5x8in) 18-Nov-92 Roldan & Cia, Buenos Aires #7

TORRE, Nicolas Andres (17th C) Mexican
$6500	£4305	Madona del Rosario (21x15cm-8x6in) s. copper. 23-Nov-92 Sotheby's, New York #117/R

TORRES DE URRETA, Maria de los Angeles (1949-) Mexican
$1119	*£756*	*Duraznos (66x102cm-26x40in) s. pastel. 20-Oct-93 Louis Morton, Mexico #22/R (M.P 3500)*

TORRES, Antonio de (1666-c.1754) Mexican
$11560	£7811	Virgen de Guadalupe (205x142cm-81x56in) s.d.1724. 25-Apr-94 Duran, Madrid #59/R (S.P 1600000)

TORRES, Augusto (1913-1992) Uruguayan
$1000	£654	Catedral (33x19cm-13x7in) s.d.69 board. 3-May-93 Gomensoro, Montevideo #45
$1900	£1275	Calle de pueblo (36x47cm-14x19in) s. board. 29-Nov-93 Gomensoro, Montevideo #61/R
$2000	£1176	Buque en puerto (42x52cm-17x20in) s. board. 5-Oct-92 Gomensoro, Montevideo #23/R
$2400	£1538	Constructivo (40x48cm-16x19in) s. board. 7-Dec-92 Gomensoro, Montevideo #69/R
$3600	£2384	Iglesia espanola (54x60cm-21x24in) s. 28-Jun-93 Gomensoro, Montevideo #33
$3600	£2308	Naturaleza muerta (55x64cm-22x25in) s. board. 7-Dec-92 Gomensoro, Montevideo #68/R
$4000	£2614	Constructivo (62x63cm-24x25in) s. painted c.1950. 18-May-93 Sotheby's, New York #141/R
$4200	£2819	Estacion Jose Artigas (43x58cm-17x23in) s. 29-Nov-93 Gomensoro, Montevideo #60/R
$8000	£5298	El Mundo del Hombre (61x79cm-24x31in) s. board on masonite. 23-Nov-92 Sotheby's, New York #237/R
$650	*£422*	*La catedral de Santiago (11x16cm-4x6in) s. W/C dr. 30-Aug-93 Gomensoro, Montevideo #59*

TORRES, Horacio (1924-1976) Uruguayan
$800	£523	Arboles (33x52cm-13x20in) s.d.1950 board. 4-Oct-93 Gomensoro, Montevideo #85
$1400	£915	Locomotora y estacion (51x60cm-20x24in) s. 4-Oct-93 Gomensoro, Montevideo #82
$4600	£3007	Naturaleza muerta (49x69cm-19x27in) s.d.1952. 4-Oct-93 Gomensoro, Montevideo #83/R
$5000	£3268	Paisaje de pueblo, campina francesa (59x74cm-23x29in) s.d.1963. 4-Oct-93 Gomensoro, Montevideo #81/R
$5200	£3399	Catedral de Chartres (85x67cm-33x26in) s.d.1964. 4-Oct-93 Gomensoro, Montevideo #80/R
$5500	£3691	Catedral (93x65cm-37x26in) s.d.1965. 29-Nov-93 Gomensoro, Montevideo #46/R
$12000	£7843	Puerto (43x86cm-17x34in) board painted 1960. 18-May-93 Sotheby's, New York #144/R

TORRES, Reynaldo (20th C) Mexican
$823	£542	Mujer con chal blanco (25x36cm-10x14in) s. 4-Nov-92 Mora, Castelltort & Quintana, Juarez #77/R (M.P 2600000)

TORRES-GARCIA, Joaquin (1874-1949) Uruguayan
$4400	£2857	Casa rosa (14x22cm-6x9in) s.d.1898 canvas laid on board. 30-Aug-93 Gomensoro, Montevideo #102/R
$5348	£3589	Bodegon constructivista (34x24cm-13x9in) s.d.1931 board. 20-Dec-93 Ansorena, Madrid #151/R (S.P 750000)

TORRES-GARCIA, Joaquin (1874-1949) Uruguayan-cont.

$6418	£4307	Locomotora (24x34cm-9x13in) init.d.1943 board. 20-Dec-93 Ansorena, Madrid #152/R (S.P 900000)
$11840	£8000	Le jardin (35x46cm-14x18in) mono.d.1923 panel. 8-Nov-93 Guy Loudmer, Paris #117/R (F.FR 70000)
$13531	£9143	Composition a l'arbre (44x30cm-17x12in) s.d.1924. 22-Nov-93 Guy Loudmer, Paris #50/R (F.FR 80000)
$14028	£9479	Visage (35x27cm-14x11in) s.d.28. 14-Jun-93 Jean Louis Picard, Paris #27/R (F.FR 80000)
$14614	£9490	Nature morte a l'eventail (50x60cm-20x24in) s.d.16. 22-Jun-94 Francis Briest, Paris #37/R (F.FR 80000)
$15000	£10000	Cabeza de hombre (46x38cm-18x15in) s.d.1927. 18-May-94 Christie's, New York #94/R
$16000	£10667	Campanario (34x42cm-13x17in) init. board laid down on panel painted c.1947. 18-May-94 Christie's, New York #93/R
$16000	£10596	El Compadrito (30x48cm-12x19in) s.d.24 board on canvasboard. 24-Nov-92 Christie's, New York #146/R
$16507	£10789	Nature morte au porte-monnaie et eventail (50x61cm-20x24in) s.d.1916. 6-Oct-93 French Auctioneer #103/R (F.FR 93000)
$18000	£12000	Le jardin (35x45cm-14x18in) init.d.23 board. 18-May-94 Sotheby's, New York #294/R
$20000	£13245	Naturaleza muerta (35x50cm-14x20in) s.d.24 board. 24-Nov-92 Christie's, New York #145/R
$22650	£15000	Dos figuras constructivas (31x21cm-12x8in) init. board. 24-Nov-92 Phillips, London #338/R
$24000	£15686	Iglesia (53x64cm-21x25in) s. linen painted c.1916. 17-May-93 Christie's, New York #101/R
$26000	£17568	Paisaje de Menton (55x49cm-22x19in) init.d.48 board. 23-Nov-93 Christie's, New York #121/R
$26624	£17401	Les quais (41x33cm-16x13in) mono.d.1921. 6-Oct-93 French Auctioneer #99/R (F.FR 150000)
$27500	£18333	Promenade sur la Cote d'Azur (54x65cm-21x26in) s.d.28. 18-May-94 Sotheby's, New York #295/R
$29000	£19595	Paisaje de Espana (64x47cm-25x19in) init.d.48 board on panel. 23-Nov-93 Christie's, New York #120/R
$29000	£19595	Dos figuras primitivas (33x24cm-13x9in) init.d.30 panel. 22-Nov-93 Sotheby's, New York #43/R
$32780	£22000	Still life with pitcher and cup (35x28cm-14x11in) init.d.30 s.i.d.verso. 29-Nov-93 Christie's, S. Kensington #89/R
$35000	£22876	Vista de Lugano (45x46cm-18x18in) s. i.verso painted 1933. 17-May-93 Christie's, New York #102/R
$37000	£25000	Puerto - perspectiva (41x48cm-16x19in) init.d.47 board. 22-Nov-93 Sotheby's, New York #216/R
$44000	£29333	Paisaje constructivo (32x41cm-13x16in) s.d.29. 18-May-94 Sotheby's, New York #296/R
$50000	£33784	Puerto constructivo (40x73cm-16x29in) s.d.1920. 23-Nov-93 Sotheby's, New York #33/R
$52500	£35473	Composition portuaire (50x61cm-20x24in) s.d.29. 22-Nov-93 Sotheby's, New York #42/R
$55000	£37162	Composition pictografica (45x36cm-18x14in) indist.s.i.d.1936 verso board on canvas. 22-Nov-93 Sotheby's, New York #40/R
$60000	£40541	Constructivo con reloj (30x35cm-12x14in) init.d.36. 22-Nov-93 Sotheby's, New York #37/R
$61000	£40940	Tres figuras y un paisaje (56x66cm-22x26in) init.d.1927 canvasboard. 29-Nov-93 Gomensoro, Montevideo #98/R
$65000	£43046	Naturaleza muerta (36x32cm-14x13in) s.d.30 board. 24-Nov-92 Christie's, New York #151/R
$75000	£49669	Grafismo Inciso con dos figuras (43x30cm-17x12in) s.d.30 verso oil on incised wood. 23-Nov-92 Sotheby's, New York #17/R
$80000	£52980	Composicion constructiva en madera (23x14cm-9x6in) s.d.32 verso wood. 23-Nov-92 Sotheby's, New York #12/R
$85000	£56291	Naturaleza muerta (46x65cm-18x26in) s.d.41 i.num.38 verso. 24-Nov-92 Christie's, New York #6/R
$135000	£90000	Grafismo constructivo sobre cuatro primarios (55x42cm-22x17in) init.d.1943 board. 17-May-94 Sotheby's, New York #39/R
$155000	£102649	Constructivo con figuras extranas (88x54cm-35x21in) 23-Nov-92 Sotheby's, New York #15/R
$160000	£108108	Grafismo (51x41cm-20x16in) s.d.1936 board. 23-Nov-93 Christie's, New York #32/R
$165000	£109272	Constructivo con Pescado (70x35cm-28x14in) init.d.31 panel. 23-Nov-92 Sotheby's, New York #4/R
$170000	£112583	Artefacto en Blanco y Negro (81x52cm-32x20in) init.d.38 tempera board. 23-Nov-92 Sotheby's, New York #8/R
$175000	£115894	Puerto Constructivo Cielo Azul (51x61cm-20x24in) s.d.30. 23-Nov-92 Sotheby's, New York #11/R
$190000	£124183	Forma, estructura y objetos (84x51cm-33x20in) init.d.43 board on board. 17-May-93 Christie's, New York #37/R
$190000	£125828	Puerto con Cuarto Figuras Universales (78x101cm-31x40in) init.d.42 board on canvas. 23-Nov-92 Sotheby's, New York #18/R
$2400	*£1622*	*Construcciones arquitectonicas (14x22cm-6x9in) pencil. 23-Nov-93 Christie's, New York #231/R*
$2600	*£1699*	*Campesino catalan (26x18cm-10x7in) s.d.1897 W/C. 4-Oct-93 Gomensoro, Montevideo #100/R*
$2600	*£1757*	*Formas constructivas (22x14cm-9x6in) pencil. 23-Nov-93 Christie's, New York #232/R*
$3000	*£2000*	*Naturaleza muerta (12x13cm-5x5in) init. pen ink executed c.1930. 18-May-94 Sotheby's, New York #257/R*

TORRES-GARCIA, Joaquin (1874-1949) Uruguayan-cont.
$4000	£2632	La torre arabe (25x17cm-10x7in) s.d.1925 ink. 31-May-93 Gomensoro, Montevideo #43/R
$4000	£2703	El payaso (18x13cm-7x5in) init.i. brush ink tempera painted 1920. 23-Nov-93 Christie's, New York #229/R
$5500	£3235	Constructivo (20x12cm-8x5in) s.d.36 ink pencil. 5-Oct-92 Gomensoro, Montevideo #35/R
$6000	£3974	Composicion Abnoy (19x15cm-7x6in) init.d.32 pen. 23-Nov-92 Sotheby's, New York #1/R
$6000	£3922	Manoletinas (30x13cm-12x5in) s.d.1920 brush pen W/C gold paper on board. 17-May-93 Christie's, New York #232/R
$6500	£4392	Composicion constructiva (17x13cm-7x5in) init.d.Mai 32 i.verso pen. 23-Nov-93 Christie's, New York #233/R
$8000	£5405	Mujer reposando (27x35cm-11x14in) s.d.1900 pencil brush ink. 23-Nov-93 Christie's, New York #230/R
$9000	£5960	Sin Titulo (17x14cm-7x6in) init.d.33 ink graphite. 23-Nov-92 Sotheby's, New York #19/R
$11000	£7285	Pesca Salada (24x31cm-9x12in) s.d.1919 colour pencil. 23-Nov-92 Sotheby's, New York #149/R
$11500	£6765	Modelo (60x41cm-24x16in) s. chl. 5-Oct-92 Gomensoro, Montevideo #34/R
$16000	£10667	Bodegon de la Tetera (36x42cm-14x17in) init.d.1920 s.i.d.verso gouache board. 18-May-94 Christie's, New York #270/R
$16000	£10596	Rosario-Espana (25x33cm-10x13in) s. d.1918 verso pencil crayon. 24-Nov-92 Christie's, New York #150/R
$22000	£14667	Composicion constructiva (29x20cm-11x8in) init.d.33 gouache pencil brown paper. 18-May-94 Christie's, New York #23/R
$25000	£16892	Torso constructivo (50x34cm-20x13in) s.d.1928 casein board on panel. 22-Nov-93 Sotheby's, New York #35/R
$33000	£21854	Madera con Hombre Universal (29x27cm-11x11in) init.d.38 hot iron engraving on panel. 23-Nov-92 Sotheby's, New York #2/R
$47500	£32095	Constructivo blanco (30x18cm-12x7in) init.d.33 gessoed panel. 22-Nov-93 Sotheby's, New York #38/R
$65000	£43046	Constructivo en madera incisa (43x27cm-17x11in) s.d.32 verso ink on incised wood. 23-Nov-92 Sotheby's, New York #7/R
$70000	£46358	Constructivo con Dibujo Inciso (50x30cm-20x12in) hot iron engraving on panel. 23-Nov-92 Sotheby's, New York #14/R

TORREY, Elliot Bouton (1867-1949) American
$7000	£4667	Orvieto (102x127cm-40x50in) s. painted c.1910. 23-May-94 Hindman Galleries, Chicago #165/R

TOUCHSTONE PICTURES (20th C) American
$1500	£1007	Roger Rabbit hangs from ceiling as Dolores discusses Acme's will (28x43cm-11x17in) studio st. gouache celluloid on photog.print. 22-Jun-93 Sotheby's, New York #736
$4500	£3020	Who framed Roger Rabbit, Roger with hearts in eyes and ears (22x30cm-9x12in) studio st.gouache celluloid on photgraphic back. 22-Jun-93 Sotheby's, New York #811/R
$6000	£4027	Who Framed Roger Rabbit, progression as Toons rejoice, Jessica hugs Roger (22x34cm-9x13in) studio st.gouache three-cel on photographic back. 22-Jun-93 Sotheby's, New York #837

TOVAR, Ivan (1942-) Dominican
$28000	£18301	Untitled (162x130cm-64x51in) s.d.73 s.i.d.1973 verso. 17-May-93 Christie's, New York #154/R

TOWERS, J (19th C) American
$518	£350	Autumnal landscape with sheep and figure , s.d.1884 W/C dr. 28-Apr-94 Locke & England, Leamington Spa #199

TOWN, Harold Barling (1924-1990) Canadian
$1323	£876	Hommage to Turner 4 (74x74cm-29x29in) s.d.60 i.verso oil lucite. 18-Nov-92 Sotheby's, Toronto #252 (C.D 1700)
$2512	£1675	Heart of the matter (167x122cm-66x48in) s.d.59/60 oil lucite on masonite. 30-May-94 Ritchie, Toronto #215/R (C.D 3500)
$3043	£2029	Flower outboard (81x81cm-32x32in) i.verso board. 6-Jun-94 Waddingtons, Toronto #1296/R (C.D 4200)
$3478	£2319	Variation on a variation (122x114cm-48x45in) s.d.57 oil lucite board. 6-Jun-94 Waddingtons, Toronto #1285/R (C.D 4800)
$471	£314	St. Veronica (122x122cm-48x48in) s.i.d.1961 verso ink linen on board. 6-Jun-94 Waddingtons, Toronto #1282 (C.D 650)
$1090	£722	Toy horse No. 230 (71x56cm-28x22in) s.d.May 14-15.79 brush ink pencil paint. 24-Nov-92 Joyner Fine Art, Toronto #30/R (C.D 1400)
$12082	£8163	Monument to C.T. Currelly No.2 (240x120cm-94x47in) s.d.58 mixed media collage. 23-Nov-93 Joyner Fine Art, Toronto #12/R (C.D 16000)

TOWNER, Xarifa Hamilton (19/20th C) American
$850	£570	Early morning, Laguna Beach (48x64cm-19x25in) s. i.d.1915verso pastel board. 3-Feb-94 Sloan, North Bethesda #688

TOWNSEND, Ernest (1893-?) American
$7450	£5000	Gossip (107x81cm-42x32in) s.d.1917. 13-Jul-93 Tennants, Leyburn #409/R

TOWNSEND, Harry Everett (1879-1941) American
$700   £470   Woman at the piano (25x30cm-10x12in) s. board. 24-Mar-94 Mystic Fine Arts, Connecticut #162/R

TOXIC (1965-) American
$2677   £1821   The whole -hole- of peace (100x150cm-39x59in) s.i.d.1990verso paint sprayed on metal. 16-Nov-93 Finarte, Milan #59 (I.L 4500000)

TRABUCCO, Alberto (1899-1990) Argentinian
$16500 £10927 Bodegon (51x62cm-20x24in) panel. 18-Nov-92 Roldan & Cia, Buenos Aires #1
$18000 £10405 Bodegon (64x72cm-25x28in) 23-Sep-92 Roldan & Cia, Buenos Aires #39

TRACY, Glen (1883-?) American
$2500   £1656   Putting up the Big Top in a storm (71x91cm-28x36in) s.d.1941 i.verso panel. 15-Jun-94 Butterfield & Butterfield, San Francisco #4495/R

TRACY, John M (1844-1893) American
$1100   £561   Crusoe searching (33x20cm-13x8in) s. 18-Aug-92 Richard Bourne, Hyannis #159/R
$1700   £1000   Setter (41x61cm-16x24in) s. 8-Oct-92 Freeman Fine Arts, Philadelphia #1081/R
$2750   £1797   At the Point (25x36cm-10x14in) s. 14-May-93 Skinner, Bolton #46
$3250   £2153   Hunting party (38x56cm-15x22in) s. 15-Jun-94 Butterfield & Butterfield, San Francisco #4563/R
$3750   £2500   Three dogs looking out interior window (76x51cm-30x20in) s. 20-May-94 Du Mouchelle, Detroit #2008/R
$4000   £2778   Covered wagon driving through pass (91x152cm-36x60in) s. 7-Mar-93 Butterfield & Butterfield, San Francisco #21/R
$12000 £7895   'Erin II' and 'Biddy' (56x112cm-22x44in) s. 4-Jun-93 Sotheby's, New York #218/R

TRAVIS, Olin Herman (1888-1975) American
$750   £497   Horsehead Creek, Ozarks (76x91cm-30x36in) s. 28-Sep-93 John Moran, Pasadena #354

TRELLES, Rafael (1957-) Puerto Rican
$7500   £5000   El Naufragio (62x81cm-24x32in) s.d.89 acrylic. 18-May-94 Christie's, New York #229/R

TRINIDAD, Jose (20th C) Canadian
$794   £537   Abandoned barn scene (61x91cm-24x36in) s. 30-Mar-94 Maynards, Vancouver #55 (C.D 1100)
$895   £593   Old man and dog (51x61cm-20x24in) s. s.verso. 16-Nov-92 Hodgins, Calgary #126 (C.D 1150)

TRINKA, Randi (20th C) American
$1500   £987   Untitled (142x142cm-56x56in) s.d.77. 2-Apr-93 Sloan, North Bethesda #2339

TRISCOTT, Samuel Peter Rolt (1846-1925) American
$1050   £700   A New England lake scene (42x87cm-17x34in) s.d.1876. 25-May-94 Sotheby's, Billingshurst #325/R

TROMPIZ, Virgilio (20th C) Latin American
$1377   £900   Nude in interior (45x49cm-18x19in) s. 27-Jun-94 Christie's, S. Kensington #236/R

TROTTER, Newbold Hough (1827-1898) American
$850   £570   Horses in pasture (25x41cm-10x16in) s. board. 5-Aug-93 Eldred, Massachusetts #803/R
$1300   £833   Short eared owl (36x46cm-14x18in) s.d.1874 i.verso. 9-Dec-92 Grogan, Massachusetts #39/R
$1500   £1014   Lake Eaglesmere (30x51cm-12x20in) s. s.i.d.188 indist.i.verso. 31-Mar-94 Sotheby's Arcade, New York #99/R
$1600   £1053   Coyote and startled deer (61x91cm-24x36in) s.verso. 2-Apr-93 Eldred, Massachusetts #464/R
$1800   £1154   The lake shore evening (61x102cm-24x40in) s. i.d.1875verso. 9-Dec-92 Grogan, Massachusetts #15/R
$3000   £1923   The confrontation (71x107cm-28x42in) s. 9-Dec-92 Grogan, Massachussetts #30/R
$3000   £1923   The Prairie-herd (25x51cm-10x20in) s. i.d.1895verso canvas laid down on masonite. 9-Dec-92 Grogan, Massachussetts #40/R
$3500   £2244   Doe elk and twins (56x61cm-22x24in) s.d.1881 i.verso. 9-Dec-92 Grogan, Massachusetts #17/R

TROVA, Ernest (1927-) American
$1600   £1074   Study FM (163x163cm-64x64in) s.i.d.66-67verso acrylic. 3-May-94 Christie's, East, New York #19/R
$3300   £2215   New girl (84x64cm-33x25in) board painted November 18 1953. 2-May-94 Selkirks, St. Louis #532/R
$3800   £2639   Study for falling man (170x170cm-67x67in) s.d.62verso acrylic. 22-Feb-93 Christie's, East, New York #145/R
$1250   £828   Study for Falling Man Series no.6 (97x97cm-38x38in) latex graphite canvas painted 1963. 27-Sep-93 Selkirks, St. Louis #95/R

TROYE, Edward (1808-1874) American
$15000 £8671   American eclipse (65x76cm-26x30in) s.d.1834. 23-Sep-92 Christie's, New York #32/R

TRUESDELL, Gaylord Sangston (1850-1899) American
$550   £360   Canal view with windmill (48x41cm-19x16in) s.i.d.1893. 15-Sep-93 Doyle, New York #65

TRUJILLO, Guillermo (1927-) Panamanian
$4000   £2685   Nuchos (76x91cm-30x36in) s.d.81. 7-Jan-94 Gary Nader, Miami #102/R

TRUMBULL, Edward (20th C) American?
$1000   £649   Moorish figures by pool (107x84cm-42x33in) s.d.1917. 9-Sep-93 Sotheby's Arcade, New York #93/R

TRUMBULL, John (1756-1843) American
$36000   £23841   Portrait of General Otho Holland Williams of Maryland, in uniform (10x8cm-4x3in) i.verso panel. 20-Nov-92 Eldred, Massachusetts #872/R

TRYON, D W (1849-1925) American
$3000   *£2128*   Evening view of Paris, 1878 (25x15cm-10x6in) pastel. 12-Feb-93 Douglas, South Deerfield #1

TRYON, Dwight W (1849-1925) American
$1100   £710   Nightfall in Brittany (66x81cm-26x32in) s. 6-Jan-93 Doyle, New York #66
$5500   £3667   Twilight in New England (41x61cm-16x24in) s.d.87 cradled panel. 17-Mar-94 Sotheby's, New York #46/R
$10000   £6993   Chrysanthemums (50x32cm-20x13in) init.d.1890 panel. 11-Mar-93 Christie's, New York #136/R
$16000   £10667   Glastonbury meadows (40x61cm-16x24in) s.d.1881. 26-May-94 Christie's, New York #2/R
$40000   £25316   Evening fog (51x76cm-20x30in) s.d.1905 panel. 4-Dec-92 Christie's, New York #82/R
$1300   *£833*   Trees on hillside in wooded landscape (25x18cm-10x7in) s.d.1913 pastel. 11-Dec-92 Du Mouchelle, Detroit #2003/R

TRYON, Dwight W (attrib) (1849-1925) American
$1000   *£680*   Reflections in a stream (27x48cm-11x19in) bears sig. W/C. 15-Nov-93 Christie's, East, New York #22/R

TSINAJINNIE, Andrew van (20th C) American
$650   *£422*   Untitled (33x20cm-13x8in) s. gouache board. 25-Jun-94 Skinner, Bolton #117/R

TSIREH, Awa (1895-1955) American
$600   *£387*   Uno Matachine (20x13cm-8x5in) s. gouache art board. 9-Jan-93 Skinner, Bolton #38
$800   *£516*   Tablita dancer (18x13cm-7x5in) s. gouache art board. 9-Jan-93 Skinner, Bolton #255/R
$2000   *£1290*   Ceremonial dancers (25x38cm-10x15in) s. gouache. 9-Jan-93 Skinner, Bolton #22/R

TUBACH, Allan K (20th C) American
$770   £503   Reflection in yellow (122x122cm-48x48in) s. s.i.verso acrylic board. 14-May-93 Skinner, Bolton #168/R

TUCKER, Allen (1866-1939) American
$1100   £733   Poplars in summer (81x64cm-32x25in) s. 17-May-94 Grogan, Massachussetts #365/R
$1500   £867   Baker's Island (61x51cm-24x20in) s.d.1913. 25-Sep-92 Sotheby's Arcade, New York #393/R
$1500   £867   The deserted garden (63x86cm-25x34in) s.i.d.1937. 25-Sep-92 Sotheby's Arcade, New York #171/R
$2000   £1316   Foot hills (64x76cm-25x30in) s.d.1913 i.stretcher. 4-Nov-92 Doyle, New York #36/R
$2400   £1611   Barn buildings (61x51cm-24x20in) s. 24-Mar-94 Mystic Fine Arts, Connecticut #60/R
$3100   £2039   Claypit Creek (51x62cm-20x24in) i.verso. 31-Mar-93 Sotheby's Arcade, New York #179/R
$4250   £2852   Mount Chocorua (76x86cm-30x34in) s. 6-Dec-93 Grogan, Massachussetts #497/R
$4800   £3179   Track menders (76x87cm-30x34in) s. i.stretcher. 22-Sep-93 Christie's, New York #159/R
$5000   £3401   Winter cedars (76x91cm-30x36in) s.d.1925 i.stretcher. 17-Nov-93 Doyle, New York #39/R
$8000   £4624   Winter landscape (76x63cm-30x25in) s.d.1911. 25-Sep-92 Sotheby's Arcade, New York #168/R
$11500   £7770   The morning air (63x76cm-25x30in) s.d.1918 s.i.verso board. 31-Mar-94 Sotheby's Arcade, New York #220/R
$16500   £10855   In garden (61x51cm-24x20in) s.d.1909. 31-Mar-93 Sotheby's Arcade, New York #177/R
$19000   £12025   Fir tree shadows on snowy bank (71x86cm-28x34in) s.d.1911. 4-Dec-92 Christie's, New York #65/R
$1000   *£658*   Maple trees (51x36cm-20x14in) s. d.1930 verso W/C chl. 31-Mar-93 Sotheby's Arcade, New York #180/R

TUCKERMAN, Ernest (20th C) American
$4861   £3177   Still life of asiatica (66x53cm-26x21in) mono.d.19 panel. 4-May-93 Dorotheum, Vienna #113/R (A.S 55000)

TULLOCH, William Alexander (1887-?) American
$2200   £1438   Modern Amazons (102x137cm-40x54in) s. 4-May-93 Christie's, East, New York #168/R

TURNER, Charles Henry (1848-?) American
$650   £436   Seated woman with greyhound (30x23cm-12x9in) estate st. 28-Mar-93 James Bakker, Cambridge #173/R
$700   £470   Soldiers on the beach (30x46cm-12x18in) s.d.1893. 5-Dec-93 James Bakker, Cambridge #49
$800   £537   Children at the drinking fountain (71x53cm-28x21in) s.d.96. 5-Dec-93 James Bakker, Cambridge #30/R
$1000   £671   Young gentleman in fur collar (107x76cm-42x30in) s.d.1893. 24-Mar-93 Grogan, Massachussetts #44

TURNER, Charles Yardley (1850-1919) American
$700   £486   Woman in black (43x33cm-17x13in) s. 27-Feb-93 Young Fine Arts Auctions, Maine #314/R
$3750   £2517   The little brown jug (51x76cm-20x30in) s.i.d.1890. 6-Dec-93 Grogan, Massachussetts #435/R

TURNER, Helen M (1858-1958) American
$2000   £1282   Autumn forest (41x61cm-16x24in) s. 9-Dec-92 Butterfield & Butterfield, San Francisco #3890/R

TURNER, Janet (20th C) American
$550   £362   Drift roots (56x36cm-22x14in) s. W/C. 5-Jun-93 Louisiana Auction Exchange #99/R

TURNER, John Davenall (1900-1980) Canadian
$662   £438   Above Jumping Pound Creek (43x58cm-17x23in) s. canvasboard. 16-Nov-92 Hodgins, Calgary #98 c (C.D 850)
$775   £524   Mountain river (77x91cm-30x36in) s. painted c.1950's. 1-Nov-93 Levis, Calgary #321/R (C.D 1000)

TURNER, Kenneth (20th C) American
$2600   £1733   Beans again (76x61cm-30x24in) s. 22-May-94 Hindman Galleries, Chicago #53/R

TURNER, Michael (20th C) American
$1000 £588   Grand Prix - Cooper and Ferrari (53x43cm-21x17in) mixed media. 8-Oct-92 Boos Gallery, Michigan #93

TURNER, Ross Sterling (1847-1915) American
*$550   £385   Le asuncion (46x30cm-18x12in) s.i.d.98 W/C gouache paper on board. 12-Mar-93 Skinner, Bolton #247/R
$750   £487   Bermuda scene (20x33cm-8x13in) s. W/C. 4-Aug-94 Eldred, Massachusetts #589/R
$750   £504   Marche aux fleurs, Paris (69x53cm-27x21in) s.i.d.1915 pastel graphite W/C gouache. 6-May-94 Skinner, Bolton #129/R
$1100   £719   View of Venice (28x46cm-11x18in) s.i.d.83 W/C. 14-May-93 Skinner, Bolton #67/R
$1200   £789*   Seascape (33x48cm-13x19in) s. W/C. 5-Jun-93 Louisiana Auction Exchange #26/R

TURNEY, Winthrop (1884-?) American
$3750   £2168   Barber shop (81x71cm-32x28in) s. 25-Sep-92 Sotheby's Arcade, New York #483/R

TURRELL, James (1943-) American
*$3000 £2013   Roden crater, tunnel alignments and cardinal spaces (95x96cm-37x38in) s. s.i.d.1991verso gouache ink photograph. 4-May-94 Christie's, New York #233/R
$6000   £4054* Roden crater bowl, finished contours (92x92cm-36x36in) s. photo emulsion wax acrylic vellum exec.1990. 10-Nov-93 Christie's, New York #209/R

TUTTLE, Richard (1941-) American
$14535 £9500   Storm (50x48cm-20x19in) s.i.d.1965verso wood in two parts. 30-Jun-94 Sotheby's, London #215/R
$65000 £43919 Dancer, yellow (109x74cm-43x29in) s.i.d.1965 panel. 10-Nov-93 Christie's, New York #187/R
*$1060 £650   Untitled (30x22cm-12x9in) gouache. 15-Oct-92 Sotheby's, London #27/R
$1639   £1100* 5, Ville de Paris (23x16cm-9x6in) executed 1986 pencil W/C. 24-Mar-93 Sotheby's, London #400/R
*$1700 £1111   Portland Works, Group II (31x23cm-12x9in) graphite W/C drawn 1976. 7-May-93 Christie's, East, New York #60/R
$1800   £1176   Portland Works, Group II (31x23cm-12x9in) graphite W/C drawn 1976. 7-May-93 Christie's, East, New York #61/R
$1800   £1176   Portland Works, Group II (31x23cm-12x9in) graphite W/C drawn 1976. 7-May-93 Christie's, East, New York #62/R
$3000   £2083   Untitled (35x28cm-14x11in) s.d.1974verso brush ink graphite gesso two. 22-Feb-93 Christie's, East, New York #213/R
$3000   £1765   Untitled (31x24cm-12x9in) enamel. 8-Oct-92 Christie's, New York #185/R
$3789   £2429   DJ - a drawing book (71x50cm-28x20in) s.i.d.Nov.11.1988 collage. 27-May-93 Lempertz, Cologne #1077/R (DM 6000)
$4000   £2353   Untitled (91x75cm-36x30in) W/C pencil transparent paper executed 1970-72. 6-Oct-92 Sotheby's, New York #125 a/R
$14000 £9459* Painting in Italy III (71x112cm-28x44in) pencil W/C col.pencil four parts executed 1988. 11-Nov-93 Sotheby's, New York #127/R

TWACHTMAN, John Henry (1853-1902) American
$11000 £7692   Venetian canal (20x36cm-8x14in) painted 1878. 14-Mar-93 Hindman Galleries, Chicago #19/R
$26000 £16456 New York Harbour (35x61cm-14x24in) s.indist. d.79. 4-Dec-92 Christie's, New York #83/R
$60000 £38462 Niagara Gorge (76x76cm-30x30in) 26-May-93 Christie's, New York #132/R
*$2700 £1765   River landscape (15x33cm-6x13in) s. W/C. 1-Nov-92 Hanzel Galleries, Chicago #32/R
$18000 £12000* Landscape (30x45cm-12x18in) s. pastel pencil paper laid down on board. 26-May-94 Christie's, New York #81/R

TWACHTMAN, John Henry (attrib) (1853-1902) American
$1700   £1111   Trees by river, probably Mianus in Cos Cob (20x28cm-8x11in) s.verso board. 18-Sep-93 Young Fine Arts Auctions, Maine #291/R

TWOMBLY, Cy (1929-) American
$43618 £29274 Untitled (137x99cm-54x39in) s.d.1971 oil crayon canvas laid down on board. 21-Jun-93 Guy Loudmer, Paris #80/R (F.FR 250000)

TWOMBLY, Cy (1929-) American-cont.
$6426	£4200	Untitled (30x36cm-12x14in) s.d.MCMXXXXXX pencil dr. 30-Jun-94 Sotheby's, London #199/R
$7450	£5000	Galerie J. no 4 (25x29cm-10x11in) s.i.d.Novembre 1961 col.crayons. 24-Mar-93 Sotheby's, London #356/R
$15000	£10135	Untitled (33x35cm-13x14in) s.d.May 1963verso graphite col.pencil. 10-Nov-93 Christie's, New York #177/R
$16000	£10811	Untitled (33x27cm-13x11in) s.d.55 verso pencil tracing paper. 11-Nov-93 Sotheby's, New York #305/R
$18000	£12500	Gladdings, love's infinite causes (100x70cm-39x28in) init.d.73 pencil pastel over lithograph. 23-Feb-93 Sotheby's, New York #321/R
$26000	£17568	Untitled (70x100cm-28x39in) graphite col.crayons executed 1958. 10-Nov-93 Christie's, New York #197/R
$28000	£18792	Untitled (50x70cm-20x28in) graphite gouache col.crayons ball-point pen. 23-Feb-94 Christie's, New York #63/R
$45000	£29801	Protea (76x57cm-30x22in) init.i.d. W/C col.oilstick graphite. 19-Nov-92 Christie's, New York #219/R
$52500	£34314	Untitled - Delian ode Series (33x35cm-13x14in) s.d.1961 col.pencil pen. 4-May-93 Sotheby's, New York #116/R
$55000	£35948	Roman note (70x87cm-28x34in) s.d.1970 verso enamel oilstick. 4-May-93 Sotheby's, New York #242/R
$60000	£40268	Untitled (76x102cm-30x40in) s.d.69verso oil crayon. 5-May-94 Sotheby's, New York #167/R
$73876	£48603	Om ma ni pad me hum (100x71cm-39x28in) s.i.d.1982 oil chk. 4-Apr-93 Perrin, Versailles #24/R (F.FR 400000)
$80000	£53691	Untitled (58x45cm-23x18in) s.d.1969 verso oil crayon. 25-Feb-94 Sotheby's, New York #60/R
$86900	£55000	Untitled (73x102cm-29x40in) i.d.1969 col.crayon pencil pen paper on canvas. 3-Dec-92 Christie's, London #35/R
$100000	£67568	Study for school of Athens (24x35cm-9x14in) s.d.1960 oil pencil col.crayon canvas. 11-Nov-93 Sotheby's, New York #306/R
$100980	£66000	Rome Series (70x86cm-28x34in) s.i.d.July 70verso gouache crayon pencil. 30-Jun-94 Sotheby's, London #249/R
$137700	£90000	10 Day wait at Mugda (100x104cm-39x41in) s.i.d.1963 oil pencil wax crayon canvas. 29-Jun-94 Sotheby's, London #45/R
$145000	£97973	Untitled (76x102cm-30x40in) oil crayon paper executed 1969. 10-Nov-93 Sotheby's, New York #49/R
$170000	£114865	Untitled (168x124cm-66x49in) s.d.1971verso oil crayon pencil. 10-Nov-93 Sotheby's, New York #67/R
$190000	£127517	Untitled (84x76cm-33x30in) sd.1969verso oil pencil. 4-May-94 Sotheby's, New York #24/R
$220000	£147651	Untitled (85x76cm-33x30in) s.d.1969verso gouache graphite paper collage. 3-May-94 Christie's, New York #22/R
$230000	£154362	Untitled, Roma (50x60cm-20x24in) s.i.d.1961stretcher oil graphite crayons canvas. 3-May-94 Christie's, New York #11/R
$275000	£182119	Naxos (175x338cm-69x133in) s.i.d.82 three sheets paint stick col.crayons. 18-Nov-92 Christie's, New York #27/R
$550800	£360000	Untitled (110x129cm-43x51in) house paint pencil canvas. 29-Jun-94 Sotheby's, London #30/R
$1550000	£1047297	Untitled (199x250cm-78x98in) init.d.69 house paint oil crayon pencil. 10-Nov-93 Sotheby's, New York #25/R
$1950000	£1291390	Untitled (117x175cm-46x69in) s.d.1956 oil crayon pencil canvas. 17-Nov-92 Sotheby's, New York #22/R

TYLER, Bayard Henry (1855-1931) American
$900	£592	Mist on the mountain (41x51cm-16x20in) s. 5-Jun-93 Louisiana Auction Exchange #46/R
$1200	£795	Lake reflections (36x46cm-14x18in) s. canvasboard. 21-Nov-92 James Bakker, Cambridge #296/R
$4250	£2852	The Palisades, the Hudson River (107x91cm-42x36in) s.i. 6-Dec-93 Grogan, Massachussetts #507/R

TYLER, James Gale (1855-1931) American
$850	£450	Rounding the point at night (51x76cm-20x30in) s.d.1885. 9-Sep-92 Doyle, New York #91/R
$900	£570	Clipper in moonlight (76x63cm-30x25in) s. 2-Dec-92 Christie's, East, New York #34
$1000	£667	Brigantine bowling along (56x46cm-22x18in) s. i.verso. 26-Aug-93 Skinner, Bolton #112
$1000	£699	Coastal schooner in choppy seas (18x23cm-7x9in) s. board. 5-Feb-93 Sloan, North Bethesda #1690/R
$1000	£671	Clipper ship at sea (51x38cm-20x15in) s. canvas laid down on board. 1-Dec-93 Doyle, New York #77
$1100	£719	Beached Dory (23x46cm-9x18in) s. 30-Jun-94 Mystic Fine Arts, Connecticut #111
$1200	£784	Moonlight sail (76x64cm-30x25in) s. 30-Jun-94 Mystic Fine Arts, Connecticut #218/R
$1300	£850	Ship rounding the point (36x48cm-14x19in) s. 30-Jun-94 Mystic Fine Arts, Connecticut #217/R
$1400	£993	Moonlight sailing (76x64cm-30x25in) s. 12-Feb-93 Du Mouchelle, Detroit #2191/R
$1450	£954	Under sail on a calm sea (51x46cm-20x18in) s. 4-Apr-93 Hart Gallery, Houston #2
$1700	£1090	The bay (61x91cm-24x36in) s. canvas on board. 13-Dec-92 Hindman Galleries, Chicago #33/R
$1700	£1141	Ship in choppy seas (51x76cm-20x30in) s. 16-Dec-93 Mystic Fine Arts, Connecticut #68/R
$1900	£1242	Evening full sail (77x107cm-30x42in) s. 4-May-93 Christie's, East, New York #26/R

TYLER, James Gale (1855-1931) American-cont.
$2000	£1307	Ship at full sail (76x64cm-30x25in) s. 30-Jun-94 Mystic Fine Arts, Connecticut #112/R
$2750	£1809	Under sail by moonlight (76x63cm-30x25in) s.d.1882. 31-Mar-93 Sotheby's Arcade, New York #111/R
$3400	£2282	Sails in the wind (36x25cm-14x10in) s.d. 5-Mar-94 Louisiana Auction Exchange #89/R
$4200	£2857	Schooner Blue Gull (61x51cm-24x20in) s. 15-Nov-93 Christie's, East, New York #23/R
$4250	£2815	Square rigger being guided by tugboat (86x69cm-34x27in) s. 23-Sep-93 Sotheby's, New York #50/R

TYLER, W R (19th C) American
$750	£497	Landscape (94x53cm-37x21in) 30-Dec-92 Douglas, South Deerfield #6
$1350	£906	Returning fishing fleet (56x81cm-22x32in) 27-Mar-94 Myers, Florida #97/R

TYNG, Margaret Fuller (20th C) American
$2400	£1622	Picking blueberries a landscape scene with young woman (76x59cm-30x23in) s. 5-Nov-93 Skinner, Bolton #141/R

TYSON, Carroll (1878-1956) American
$500	*£340*	*Ballet class (46x61cm-18x24in) s.d.1922 pastel. 14-Apr-94 Freeman Fine Arts, Philadelphia #1009*
$1400	*£881*	*Ballet class (61x48cm-24x19in) s.d.1927 pastel. 22-Apr-93 Freeman Fine Arts, Philadelphia #1157*

UFER, Walter (1876-1936) American
$4500	£3147	Portrait of woman (51x41cm-20x16in) s. canvas on masonite. 11-Mar-93 Christie's, New York #120/R
$14000	£9396	Tyrolian girl (55x45cm-22x18in) s.d.1922 s.i.stretcher. 3-Dec-93 Christie's, New York #60/R
$36000	£23077	Noon shadows (64x64cm-25x25in) init. 26-May-93 Christie's, New York #103/R
$220000	£139241	Builders of the desert (128x128cm-50x50in) s. canvas laid down on aluminium. 4-Dec-92 Christie's, New York #264/R

UHTHOFF, Ina D D (1889-1971) Canadian
$1177	£769	Two black cars (51x61cm-20x24in) s. board. 10-May-93 Hodgins, Calgary #60/R (C.D 1500)

ULLOA, Victor (1960-) Dominican
$3500	£2349	Untitled (80x81cm-31x32in) s. 7-Jan-94 Gary Nader, Miami #69/R

UMBSTAETTER, Nelly (20th C) American
$2200	*£1477*	*Old apple orchard. Pussy's dream. Elves in woods (23x30cm-9x12in) W/C three. 5-Aug-93 Eldred, Massachusetts #795*
$2300	*£1544*	*Bridge of stairs. Steps to bubble castle. Street in elf lane. Cloud maker (36x25cm-14x10in) W/C four. 5-Aug-93 Eldred, Massachusetts #793/R*

URBAN, Humberto (1936-) Mexican
$2388	£1531	Dos mujeres con rebozo (60x80cm-24x31in) s.d.1991. 29-Apr-93 Louis Morton, Mexico #30 (M.P 7500)

URBAN, Miguel H (20th C) Mexican?
$1000	£667	Planchadoras (91x69cm-36x27in) s.d.1962 masonite. 24-Aug-93 Hart Gallery, Houston #6

URBIETA, Jesus (1959-) Mexican
$8000	£5233	Una historia de caballo (150x189cm-59x74in) s.d.89 oil sand canvas. 18-May-94 Sotheby's, New York #260/R

URIARTE, Carlos (1910-) Argentinian
$752	£504	Campo verde (81x121cm-32x48in) s. panel. 12-Oct-93 Finarte, Milan #196 (I.L 1200000)
$1500	£882	Composicion (49x64cm-19x25in) 29-Sep-92 VerBo, Buenos Aires #110
$2600	£1354	Playa (60x80cm-24x31in) 4-Aug-92 VerBo, Buenos Aires #110

URIBURU, Nicolas Garcia (1937-) Argentinian
$2100	£1419	Mano (99x101cm-39x40in) s. acrylic painted c.1968. 22-Nov-93 Sotheby's, New York #244/R

URQUHART, Tony (1934-) Canadian
$1268	£829	Landscape on tapestry (122x102cm-48x40in) s.d.12/59. 19-May-93 Sotheby's, Toronto #335/R (C.D 1600)

URUETA, Cordelia (1908-) Mexican
$3500	£2288	Viejo barco (35x43cm-14x17in) s.d.89 i.verso paper. 17-May-93 Christie's, New York #231/R
$18000	£11921	El Barco Perdido (140x120cm-55x47in) s.d.1989 s.i.d.verso. 24-Nov-92 Christie's, New York #144/R
$22000	£14865	Iman (150x110cm-59x43in) s.d.1960. 23-Nov-93 Christie's, New York #187/R

URUETA, Cordelia (1908-) Mexican-cont.
$2044	£1363	Tres mujeres (21x18cm-8x7in) s.d.1956 gouache. 25-May-94 Louis Morton, Mexico #21 (M.P 6800)
$3225	£2165	Abanico rojo (40x50cm-16x20in) s.d.1972 W/C. 1-Dec-93 Louis Morton, Mexico #63/R (M.P 10000)

VA, Barry le (1941-) American
$2500	£1656	Distribution and Density Price (22x28cm-9x11in) s.d.1968 ink graph paper. 18-Nov-92 Sotheby's, New York #220/R
$4000	£2614	Diagram for two separate installations combined into one (122x122cm-48x48in) mixed media executed 1982. 22-Dec-92 Christie's, East, New York #34
$5500	£3595	Tangent to tangent - centres, four circles, four lines (107x209cm-42x82in) ink executed 1974. 22-Dec-92 Christie's, East, New York #33
$7500	£5034	No 9477 (178x132cm-70x52in) col.pencil ink paper with vellum executed 1979. 5-May-94 Sotheby's, New York #266/R

VACA, Maria Dolores (20th C) Mexican
$927	£626	Arrullo en cuetzalan (70x50cm-28x20in) W/C. 20-Oct-93 Louis Morton, Mexico #27/R (M.P 2900)

VALCIN, Gerard (1923-) Haitian
$724	£473	Premiere communion (41x30cm-16x12in) painted 1975. 17-May-93 Hoebanx, Paris #215 (F.FR 4000)
$750	£500	Travrance (37x60cm-15x24in) s.i.d.9/5/67 masonite. 12-Mar-94 Weschler, Washington #139/R
$760	£497	Mariage a la campagne (41x30cm-16x12in) painted 1972. 17-May-93 Hoebanx, Paris #216 (F.FR 4200)
$760	£497	Rara Mardi Gras (30x41cm-12x16in) painted 1975. 17-May-93 Hoebanx, Paris #217 (F.FR 4200)
$984	£652	Ceremonie vaudou (30x40cm-12x16in) s. panel. 13-Jun-94 Rogeon, Paris #75/R (F.FR 5500)
$1489	£955	Marassa (50x40cm-20x16in) s. 14-Dec-92 Hoebanx, Paris #164/R (F.FR 8000)
$1600	£1081	Saint-Jacques (61x46cm-24x18in) s.d.85. 24-Nov-93 Christie's, New York #28/R
$2400	£1622	Coumbite (61x41cm-24x16in) s.d.75. 22-Nov-93 Sotheby's, New York #280/R
$2505	£1659	Au restaurant (60x130cm-24x51in) s.d.22.III.70. 13-Jun-94 Rogeon, Paris #141 a (F.FR 14000)

VALENCIA, Manuel (1856-1935) American
$700	£473	Landscape with cattle (51x76cm-20x30in) s. 9-Nov-93 John Moran, Pasadena #877
$1000	£667	Atmospheric landscape (33x53cm-13x21in) s. 15-Mar-94 John Moran, Pasadena #196
$2250	£1481	Old Customs House, Monterey (51x76cm-20x30in) s. 13-Jun-93 Butterfield & Butterfield, San Francisco #768/R

VALENKAMPH, Theodor Victor Carl (1868-1924) American
$650	£425	Sailing off coast (41x51cm-16x20in) s. 30-Jun-94 Mystic Fine Arts, Connecticut #162/R
$850	£574	Full sail (28x43cm-11x17in) s. 27-Nov-93 Young Fine Arts Auctions, Maine #326/R
$850	£594	Adventure on the high seas (66x56cm-26x22in) s. 12-Mar-93 Skinner, Bolton #151/R
$3100	£2095	Full-rigged ship at twilight (30x46cm-12x18in) s. board. 30-Jul-93 Eldred, Massachusetts #142/R
$3190	£2085	Wind power and steam - marine scene (61x91cm-24x36in) s.d.1907. 14-May-93 Skinner, Bolton #59/R
$3750	£2451	In stormy seas (61x91cm-24x36in) s.d.1901. 18-Sep-93 Young Fine Arts Auctions, Maine #293/R

VALERIO, F F (20th C) American
$900	£596	Winter landscape (51x66cm-20x26in) s. 21-Nov-92 James Bakker, Cambridge #263/R

VALLEY, J J la (1858-?) American
$750	£500	Still life of peeled orange (13x10cm-5x4in) board. 27-Aug-93 Douglas, South Deerfield #3
$1650	£954	Painting of flowers (25x18cm-10x7in) 25-Sep-92 Douglas, South Deerfield #8

VALLEY, Jonas Joseph la (1858-?) American
$900	£600	Still life with raspberries (36x51cm-14x20in) s. 26-Aug-93 Skinner, Bolton #206

VALLEY, William la (20th C) American
$550	£369	Landscape with mountain laurel (51x64cm-20x25in) s. 29-Nov-93 Stonington Fine Arts, Stonington #167

VANDERLYN, John (attrib) (1775-1852) American
$1500	£949	Portrait of Aaron Burr (63x51cm-25x20in) 2-Dec-92 Christie's, East, New York #5/R

VARGAS FIGUEROA, Baltasar de (attrib) (17th C) Columbian
$10000	£6536	Archangel St. Raphael (161x102cm-63x40in) painted c.1665. 17-May-93 Christie's, New York #75/R

VARGAS, A (20th C) Mexican
$743	£495	Retrato de nino marinero (64x50cm-25x20in) s. 8-Jun-94 Louis Morton, Mexico #49 (M.P 2500)

VARGAS, Alberto (20th C) American
$2500 £1634 Portrait of young lady (38x28cm-15x11in) s.d.1927 W/C. 7-Oct-93 Freeman Fine Arts, Philadelphia #979
$4500 £2980 Portrait of Frances Dee (43x28cm-17x11in) s.d.1931 W/C board. 27-Sep-93 Selkirks, St. Louis #99/R

VARGAS, Ismael (1947-) Mexican
$8500 £5667 Nocturno de invierno (101x140cm-40x55in) s. acrylic painted 1987. 18-May-94 Sotheby's, New York #387/R

VARLEY, F H (1881-1969) British/Canadian
$1600 £1060 Landscape near Ohawa (23x30cm-9x12in) s. W/C. 3-Oct-93 Hanzel Galleries, Chicago #775

VARLEY, Frederick Horsman (1881-1969) British/Canadian
$4360 £2850 Low clouds, Kootenay Lake (30x38cm-12x15in) s. board. 19-May-93 Sotheby's, Toronto #264/R (C.D 5500)
$5946 £3886 Portrait of Dr. John Goldie (61x51cm-24x20in) s. 18-May-93 Joyner Fine Art, Toronto #132/R (C.D 7500)
$6041 £4082 Wind blown trees (30x40cm-12x16in) s. board. 23-Nov-93 Joyner Fine Art, Toronto #50/R (C.D 8000)
$7927 £5181 Between Trenton and Belleville (30x38cm-12x15in) s. d.1940 verso panel. 19-May-93 Sotheby's, Toronto #135/R (C.D 10000)
$8000 £5369 Mountaintop landscape (30x38cm-12x15in) s. panel. 24-Jun-93 Mystic Fine Arts, Connecticut #100 b
$585 £385 Pines and mountains (25x41cm-10x16in) s. i.verso chl. 7-Jun-93 Waddingtons, Toronto #1137 a (C.D 750)
$655 £437 Group depicting male and female subjects (33x36cm-13x14in) s.i. collage of drawings. 13-May-94 Joyner Fine Art, Toronto #11 (C.D 900)
$692 £461 Rockies near Fairmont - summer's day (22x30cm-9x12in) s. chl. 13-May-94 Joyner Fine Art, Toronto #206 (C.D 950)
$801 £534 Woodland (25x32cm-10x13in) s. chl dr. 11-May-94 Sotheby's, Toronto #214 a (C.D 1100)
$2179 £1443 Lake and mountain (22x30cm-9x12in) s. W/C chl. 24-Nov-92 Joyner Fine Art, Toronto #89/R (C.D 2800)
$2567 £1735 Nascopie at night, 1939 (20x14cm-8x6in) s. W/C. 23-Nov-93 Joyner Fine Art, Toronto #123/R (C.D 3400)

VASSILIEFF, Nicolai (1892-1970) American/Russian
$1600 £1074 Still life with flowers (107x71cm-42x28in) s. 24-Feb-94 Sotheby's Arcade, New York #196/R
$2200 £1438 Still life with maroon tablecloth (61x51cm-24x20in) s. 4-May-93 Christie's, East, New York #305/R

VASSOS, John (1898-?) American
$2400 £1558 Poster study (114x114cm-45x45in) s. tempera board. 9-Sep-93 Sotheby's Arcade, New York #390/R
$1500 £974 Untitled (51x41cm-20x16in) gouache board. 9-Sep-93 Sotheby's Arcade, New York #391/R
$1600 £1039 Vita Nuova (51x40cm-20x16in) i.d.53 gouache board. 9-Sep-93 Sotheby's Arcade, New York #392/R
$2300 £1494 Roman feast no 8 (51x39cm-20x15in) gouache board. 9-Sep-93 Sotheby's Arcade, New York #393/R

VAZ, Oscar (1909-1987) Argentinian
$2100 £1391 Darsena (24x30cm-9x12in) 11-Nov-92 VerBo, Buenos Aires #113
$2400 £1589 Barcas (25x30cm-10x12in) 11-Nov-92 VerBo, Buenos Aires #112/R
$2600 £1503 Boca del Riachuelo (50x60cm-20x24in) panel. 23-Sep-92 Roldan & Cia, Buenos Aires #67
$4500 £2647 Rincon de puerto (86x70cm-34x28in) 29-Sep-92 VerBo, Buenos Aires #113/R
$8000 £4167 Descarga de la madera (70x90cm-28x35in) 4-Aug-92 VerBo, Buenos Aires #112/R

VAZQUEZ LUNA, Jorge (20th C) Mexican
$4031 £2706 Coles (94x70cm-37x28in) 1-Dec-93 Louis Morton, Mexico #195/R (M.P 12500)

VEDDER, Elihu (1836-1923) American
$3000 £2027 The old well, Bordighera (49x98cm-19x39in) s.d.1899. 31-Mar-94 Sotheby's Arcade, New York #72/R
$3200 £2025 Feeding the pigs (22x23cm-9x9in) s.d.04. 2-Dec-92 Christie's, East, New York #72/R
$3400 £2208 Study of flowers (32x19cm-13x7in) s.i. canvasboard painted c.1876. 9-Sep-93 Sotheby's Arcade, New York #71/R
$4750 £3146 Aesop's Fable, The Miller, his son and the donkey, no.3 (18x30cm-7x12in) init.i. panel. 23-Sep-93 Sotheby's, New York #168/R
$5000 £3333 Artist and students before model (15x30cm-6x12in) s. canvas on panel. 16-Mar-94 Christie's, New York #51/R
$10000 £6667 The music party (28x45cm-11x18in) s.d.1871 board on panel. 16-Mar-94 Christie's, New York #50/R
$10000 £6623 Mediterranean coastal scene (25x41cm-10x16in) init.d.1866 i.d.1866 verso. 23-Sep-93 Sotheby's, New York #167/R
$13000 £8667 The soul between Doubt and Faith (18x27cm-7x11in) s. shaped canvas. 17-Mar-94 Sotheby's, New York #99/R
$15000 £10000 Marsyas enchanting the hares (30x44cm-12x17in) s.d.1899 paper on canvas. 25-May-94 Sotheby's, New York #27/R
$725 £490 View in Egypt (30x18cm-12x7in) s.i.d.16 chl. 20-Mar-93 Weschler, Washington #95

VEDDER, Elihu (1836-1923) American-cont.
$800	£541	Decoration for a bench (20x36cm-8x14in) pastel gouache gold paint. 31-Mar-94 Sotheby's Arcade, New York #124/R
$1500	£1049	Study for government (19x33cm-7x13in) i.verso pastel chk shaped. 10-Mar-93 Sotheby's, New York #95/R
$2600	£1503	Sleep (40x31cm-16x12in) chl chk. 23-Sep-92 Christie's, New York #99/R

VEDDER, Simon Harmon (1866-?) American
| $1607 | £1030 | Pine trees (38x23cm-15x9in) s.i.d.23. 7-Dec-92 Waddingtons, Toronto #1506 (C.D 2050) |

VEGA, Jorge de la (1930-1971) Argentinian
| $2500 | £1634 | La bestia y la bestia (70x60cm-28x24in) s.d.62 plaster oil. 18-May-93 Sotheby's, New York #195/R |

VELARDE, Pablita (1918-) American
| $950 | £617 | Earth painting (28x23cm-11x9in) s. i.verso col.sand mixed media board. 25-Jun-94 Skinner, Bolton #200/R |

VELASCO, Jose Maria (1840-1912) Mexican
$19000	£12583	Paisaje (9x14cm-4x6in) s. postcard. 23-Nov-92 Sotheby's, New York #129/R
$62500	£41391	Paisaje (15x25cm-6x10in) paper. 23-Nov-92 Sotheby's, New York #29/R
$115000	£76159	Platanilla (45x35cm-18x14in) s.d.1883 board. 23-Nov-92 Sotheby's, New York #28/R
$166337	£110891	Paisaje serrano cascada de barrio nuevo (72x57cm-28x22in) s.i.d.1876. 8-Jun-94 Louis Morton, Mexico #66/R (M.P 560000)
$8000	£5405	Pino (28x21cm-11x8in) s.i. pencil. 23-Nov-93 Christie's, New York #93/R
$22000	£14865	Arbol viejo (42x31cm-17x12in) s. pencil chk. 23-Nov-93 Christie's, New York #94/R

VELASCO, Jose Maria (circle) (1840-1912) Mexican
| $7450 | £5000 | Valley of Mexico (34x46cm-13x18in) i. canvas on board. 16-Jul-93 Christie's, London #149/R |

VELASQUEZ, Jose Antonio (1906-) South American
$2800	£1944	San Antonio de Orient (52x72cm-20x28in) s.d.1951. 26-Feb-93 Sotheby's Arcade, New York #253/R
$3000	£2000	Paisaje (53x74cm-21x29in) s.d.1949. 9-Jun-94 Sotheby's Arcade, New York #130/R
$3000	£2000	San Antonio Oriente (55x74cm-22x29in) s.d.1950. 18-May-94 Christie's, New York #318/R
$3000	£1987	San Antonio Oriente (51x69cm-20x27in) s.d.1965. 24-Nov-92 Christie's, New York #351/R
$4200	£2745	San Antonio Oriente (48x61cm-19x24in) s.d.1971. 17-May-93 Christie's, New York #289/R

VENA, Angel Domingo (1888-1963) Argentinian
| $10000 | £5780 | Arroyo Serrano (65x80cm-26x31in) panel. 23-Sep-92 Roldan & Cia, Buenos Aires #69 |

VERNER, Frederick Arthur (1836-1928) Canadian
$1031	£674	Figure on country path at sunset (18x25cm-7x10in) s.d.1890 canvas on board. 19-May-93 Sotheby's, Toronto #64 (C.D 1300)
$2775	£1813	Portrait of Charles Dickens (69x56cm-27x22in) 19-May-93 Sotheby's, Toronto #383/R (C.D 3500)
$2913	£1942	The picnic (51x91cm-20x36in) s.d.1878 canvas laid on board. 11-May-94 Sotheby's, Toronto #55/R (C.D 4000)
$5846	£3846	Grzing buffalo (41x66cm-16x26in) s.d.1891. 7-Jun-93 Waddingtons, Toronto #1148/R (C.D 7500)
$9298	£6283	Buffalo in a blizzard (46x61cm-18x24in) s. i.verso. 3-Nov-93 Sotheby's, Toronto #89/R (C.D 12000)
$11623	£7853	Landscape with Indian at waterfall (36x69cm-14x27in) s.d.1876. 3-Nov-93 Sotheby's, Toronto #90/R (C.D 15000)
$12684	£8290	Bison - morning (41x65cm-16x26in) s.d.1916 init.verso. 19-May-93 Sotheby's, Toronto #175/R (C.D 16000)
$12684	£8290	Buffalo - evening (40x60cm-16x24in) s.d.19 init.verso. 19-May-93 Sotheby's, Toronto #177/R (C.D 16000)
$22197	£14508	Buffalo grazing by water (61x91cm-24x36in) s.d.1912. 18-May-93 Joyner Fine Art, Toronto #82/R (C.D 28000)
$549	£352	Sheep grazing among the heather (33x51cm-13x20in) s. W/C. 7-Dec-92 Waddingtons, Toronto #1329 (C.D 700)
$588	£377	Landscape with hare (51x33cm-20x13in) s.d.1899 W/C. 7-Dec-92 Waddingtons, Toronto #1339 (C.D 750)
$697	£471	Sunset on the marsh (30x60cm-12x24in) s.d.1876 W/C. 3-Nov-93 Sotheby's, Toronto #185/R (C.D 900)
$874	£583	Landscape with sheep (33x49cm-13x19in) s.d.1900 W/C. 11-May-94 Sotheby's, Toronto #59/R (C.D 1200)
$1168	£773	Shepherd's cottage, Dorset (33x51cm-13x20in) s.d.1895 i.verso W/C. 18-Nov-92 Sotheby's, Toronto #167/R (C.D 1500)
$1200	£784	Shoreline with Indians and canoes (9x25cm-4x10in) s. W/C htd white gouache. 4-May-93 Christie's, East, New York #28
$1311	£874	Houses in the country (30x60cm-12x24in) s.d.1895 W/C. 13-May-94 Joyner Fine Art, Toronto #8/R (C.D 1800)
$1401	£928	River and hills (19x35cm-7x14in) s.d.1882 W/C. 24-Nov-92 Joyner Fine Art, Toronto #175 (C.D 1800)
$1427	£933	English cottage landscape (33x51cm-13x20in) s.d.1890 W/C. 19-May-93 Sotheby's, Toronto #26/R (C.D 1800)
$1456	£971	Cottage at Sark. Indian encampment , one d. one s.i.verso W/C two. 11-May-94 Sotheby's, Toronto #11/R (C.D 2000)

VERNER, Frederick Arthur (1836-1928) Canadian-cont.
$1661	£1122	Sunset, Kew Bridge (22x54cm-9x21in) s.d.1906 W/C. 23-Nov-93 Joyner Fine Art, Toronto #71/R (C.D 2200)
$1784	£1166	Buffalo (37x55cm-15x22in) s.d.1900 W/C. 19-May-93 Sotheby's, Toronto #176/R (C.D 2250)
$2335	£1546	Buffalo grazing (30x61cm-12x24in) s.d.1893 W/C. 18-Nov-92 Sotheby's, Toronto #5/R (C.D 3000)
$2335	£1546	Canadian Elk (33x51cm-13x20in) s. i.verso W/C. 18-Nov-92 Sotheby's, Toronto #4/R (C.D 3000)
$2367	£1578	House in the country. Return from church (23x16cm-9x6in) s. one d.1893 one d.1894 W/C pair. 11-May-94 Sotheby's, Toronto #183/R (C.D 3250)
$2942	£1923	Micmac Harvest, Quebec (37x68cm-15x27in) s.d.1878 W/C. 10-May-93 Hodgins, Calgary #272 (C.D 3750)
$3874	£2618	Chaudiere Falls (39x76cm-15x30in) s. W/C. 3-Nov-93 Sotheby's, Toronto #9/R (C.D 5000)
$5097	£3398	Indians on the Ottawa River (31x60cm-12x24in) s.indis.d. W/C. 13-May-94 Joyner Fine Art, Toronto #36/R (C.D 7000)
$5838	£3866	Ojibbawas, North Shore, Lake Huron (30x61cm-12x24in) s. W/C. 18-Nov-92 Sotheby's, Toronto #27/R (C.D 7500)
$8623	£5528	Indians in canoe (35x58cm-14x23in) s.d.1880 i.verso W/C. 26-Apr-93 Levis, Calgary #213/R (C.D 11000)
$9340	£6186	Ojibbawa Wigwams - Rainy Lake (53x74cm-21x29in) s.d.1919 i.verso W/C. 18-Nov-92 Sotheby's, Toronto #123/R (C.D 12000)
$11675	£7732	Ojibway Indians, fog bound (51x101cm-20x40in) s.d.1903 W/C. 24-Nov-92 Joyner Fine Art, Toronto #81/R (C.D 15000)

VERNON, Della (1876-1962) American
$1900	£1319	Ox train (91x61cm-36x24in) s. 7-Mar-93 Butterfield & Butterfield, San Francisco #30/R

VIANDEN, Heinrich (attrib) (1814-1899) American
$700	£464	Rushing forest stream (51x76cm-20x30in) s. 26-Sep-93 Schrager Galleries, Milwaukee #481

VICENTE, Esteban (1906-) American/Spanish
$9000	£5960	Spring (173x143cm-68x56in) s.d.1972 verso. 30-Jun-93 Sotheby's Arcade, New York #318/R
$3250	£2181	Aura (56x38cm-22x15in) s. s.i.d.1962 verso paper collage board. 24-Feb-94 Sotheby's Arcade, New York #355 a/R

VICKREY, Robert (1926-) American
$3500	£2318	Remnants (95x112cm-37x44in) tempera masonite painted 1940's. 23-Sep-93 Sotheby's, New York #275/R
$4500	£2980	Tire shadows (30x41cm-12x16in) s. board. 15-Jun-94 Butterfield & Butterfield, San Francisco #4496/R
$6000	£4054	Nun and poster (61x91cm-24x36in) s. tempera masonite. 31-Mar-94 Sotheby's Arcade, New York #482/R
$11000	£6962	Vaudeville figure (58x45cm-23x18in) s. egg tempera masonite. 4-Dec-92 Christie's, New York #137/R
$1200	£811	Clown with ruff (58x46cm-23x18in) s. ink. 31-Mar-94 Sotheby's Arcade, New York #372/R

VICTORICA, Miguel Carlos (1884-1955) Argentinian
$3500	£1823	Paisaje (20x22cm-8x9in) 4-Aug-92 VerBo, Buenos Aires #114/R
$4800	£2824	Retrato de Gaston Jarry (72x49cm-28x19in) 29-Sep-92 VerBo, Buenos Aires #112
$1000	£588	Paisaje de Paris (20x29cm-8x11in) pencil dr executed 1916. 29-Sep-92 VerBo, Buenos Aires #111

VIERA, Petrona (?) Uruguayan?
$1100	£714	Arbol (18x15cm-7x6in) s. board. 30-Aug-93 Gomensoro, Montevideo #79
$1400	£909	En el parque (21x23cm-8x9in) s. board. 30-Aug-93 Gomensoro, Montevideo #77/R
$1700	£1104	Playa (18x18cm-7x7in) s. board fibre. 30-Aug-93 Gomensoro, Montevideo #78
$3600	£2338	Lavanderas (32x32cm-13x13in) s. oil. 30-Aug-93 Gomensoro, Montevideo #76/R
$10000	£6623	Rincon del parque, ramas (97x88cm-38x35in) s. s.d.1932verso. 28-Jun-93 Gomensoro, Montevideo #60/R
$11000	£7237	Torre del vigia, Maldonado (50x61cm-20x24in) s. panel. 31-May-93 Gomensoro, Montevideo #45/R

VIGIL, Romando (1902-) American
$450	£292	Untitled (28x36cm-11x14in) s. gouache. 25-Jun-94 Skinner, Bolton #128/R
$3100	£2013	Legend of the game (43x58cm-17x23in) s. gouache board. 25-Jun-94 Skinner, Bolton #218/R

VILALLONGA, Jesus Carlos de (1927-) Canadian
$655	£437	L'ingenue (41x30cm-16x12in) s.d.60 board. 11-May-94 Sotheby's, Toronto #64 (C.D 900)

VILLA, Carlos (1936-) American
$700	£443	Bedspread (211x183cm-83x72in) s.d.84 mixed media feathers canvas. 25-Oct-92 Butterfield & Butterfield, San Francisco #2347/R

VILLA, Hernando (20th C) American
$4500	£3020	Oaks and Eucalyptus beneath billowy clouds (102x76cm-40x30in) s. 8-Dec-93 Butterfield & Butterfield, San Francisco #3497/R

VILLA, Hernando (20th C) American-cont.
$700   £470   Tourist and Indian guide at Indian ruins (76x51cm-30x20in) s. chl board. 8-Dec-93 Butterfield & Butterfield, San Francisco #3542/R

VILLACRES, Cesar A (1880-?) Ecuadorian
$1200   £795   Mountainous landscape with shepherdess (56x88cm-22x35in) s.i. 30-Jun-93 Sotheby's Arcade, New York #214/R
$1500   £1007   Place de l'Opera. Booksellers along the Seine (46x55cm-18x22in) s. pair. 24-Feb-94 Sotheby's Arcade, New York #221/R

VILLALPANDO, Cristobal (1649-1714) Mexican
$14000 £9459   San Juan Evangelista (28x21cm-11x8in) s.d.1701 copper. 22-Nov-93 Sotheby's, New York #134/R
$33000 £21854 Sagrada Familia Y Sanata Trinidad (178x110cm-70x43in) s. 23-Nov-92 Sotheby's, New York #25/R

VILLALPANDO, Cristobal (attrib) (1649-1714) Mexican
$24000 £15686 La Coronacion de Cristo con la Corona de Espinas (76x114cm-30x45in) painted c.1685. 18-May-93 Sotheby's, New York #9/R

VILLANUEVA, Leoncio (1936-) Peruvian
$8000   £5369   Composicion en Amarillos (100x130cm-39x51in) s. mixed media canvas painted 1992. 7-Jan-94 Gary Nader, Miami #45/R

VILLENEUVE, Arthur (1910-) Canadian
$793   £518   Le carnaval de Chicoutimi en 1961 (63x79cm-25x31in) s. 18-May-93 Joyner Fine Art, Toronto #105 (C.D 1000)
$906   £612   Le port (52x71cm-20x28in) s. 23-Nov-93 Fraser Pinneys, Quebec #460 (C.D 1200)

VINCELETTE, Romeo (20th C) Canadian
$677   £455   Sleighs in winter (46x56cm-18x22in) s. 29-Nov-93 Waddingtons, Toronto #1067 (C.D 900)

VINCENT, Alexander (19/20th C) Latin American
$2812   £1900   Distant view of Mexico City (29x52cm-11x20in) s.d.1908 canvasboard. 18-Mar-93 Bonhams, London #75/R
$10000 £6757   View of Mexico (29x52cm-11x20in) s.d.1908 canvas on board. 22-Nov-93 Sotheby's, New York #154/R

VINCENT, Harry A (1864-1931) American
$1600   £1096   Harbour with fishing boats (28x36cm-11x14in) s. board. 19-Feb-94 Young Fine Arts Auctions, Maine #199/R
$3000   £2000   Harbour scene at dusk (23x30cm-9x12in) s.d.04 board. 23-May-94 Christie's, East, New York #160/R
$7300   £4679   Early morning Harbour scene (64x76cm-25x30in) s. 13-Dec-92 Litchfield Auction Gallery #23

VINTON, Frederick Porter (1846-1911) American
$800   £423   Gate way in Toledo (38x25cm-15x10in) i.verso. 11-Sep-92 Skinner, Bolton #200/R
$1500   £765   The chicken plucker (41x28cm-16x11in) s. board. 18-Aug-92 Richard Bourne, Hyannis #73/R
$3750   £1984   Portrait of a Spanish woman (76x61cm-30x24in) 11-Sep-92 Skinner, Bolton #167/R
$7000   £3704   Across the hay meadow (36x61cm-14x24in) s.d.1886. 11-Sep-92 Skinner, Bolton #204/R

VIVES-ATSARA, Jose (1919-1988) Mexican
$2200   £1429   Noche en al costa de Texas (76x102cm-30x40in) s. s.i.d.63verso masonite. 11-Sep-93 Louisiana Auction Exchange #162/R

VIVIAN, Calthea (1857-1943) American
$850   £574   No.18 Moonlight-Pacific Grove (53x38cm-21x15in) indist.s. 15-Jun-93 John Moran, Pasadena #71

VLECK, Natalie van (1901-1981) American
$700   £464   Four sheep in snow, Woodbury (64x76cm-25x30in) s. 22-Nov-92 Litchfield Auction Gallery #13
$700   £464   Thunderstorm, Red Barn, Woodbury (64x76cm-25x30in) s. 22-Nov-92 Litchfield Auction Gallery #14
$700   £464   Five woman, half length,Mediterranean (64x56cm-25x22in) s. 22-Nov-92 Litchfield Auction Gallery #9
$725   £480   Seated nude in New York studio (91x66cm-36x26in) s. 22-Nov-92 Litchfield Auction Gallery #7
$750   £497   Foxgloves, Woodbury (64x56cm-25x22in) s. painted 1930. 22-Nov-92 Litchfield Auction Gallery #2
$750   £497   Woman in orange dress (86x64cm-34x25in) s. 22-Nov-92 Litchfield Auction Gallery #15
$825   £546   Chickens, Woodbury (51x66cm-20x26in) s. 22-Nov-92 Litchfield Auction Gallery #1
$1300   £861   Nude, waist length (51x41cm-20x16in) s. 22-Nov-92 Litchfield Auction Gallery #5
$1300   £861   Red houses and barns, Woodbury (91x76cm-36x30in) s. painted 1929. 22-Nov-92 Litchfield Auction Gallery #3
$1800   £1192   Portrait with Persian rug (107x81cm-42x32in) s. 22-Nov-92 Litchfield Auction Gallery #4
$1950   £1291   Abstract city scape, New York (81x56cm-32x22in) s. painted c.1924. 22-Nov-92 Litchfield Auction Gallery #6

VLECK, Natalie van (1901-1981) American-cont.
$2000	£1325	Abstract city scape, New York (91x79cm-36x31in) painted c.1924. 22-Nov-92 Litchfield Auction Gallery #8
$570	£377	Portrait of a woman in a green hat holding a flower (58x43cm-23x17in) s. W/C. 22-Nov-92 Litchfield Auction Gallery #11
$650	£430	Town scape with castle on distant mountains, Mediterranean (20x23cm-8x9in) s. gouache. 22-Nov-92 Litchfield Auction Gallery #12
$1200	£795	Abstract City view, New York (71x53cm-28x21in) s. gouache. 22-Nov-92 Litchfield Auction Gallery #10

VOGT, Louis Charles (1864-?) American
$1400	£915	New York City Dock scenes (25x36cm-10x14in) s. W/C pair. 30-Jun-94 Mystic Fine Arts, Connecticut #91 a/R

VOISARD, J (?) Canadian?
$2032	£1195	Still life of lilac in vase and two roses in glass (39x29cm-15x11in) s. panel. 6-Oct-92 Michael Zeller, Lindau #1525/R (DM 3000)

VOLK, Douglas (1856-1935) American
$2000	£1399	Water lily (36x43cm-14x17in) s.i. 11-Mar-93 Christie's, New York #49/R

VOLKERT, Edward Charles (1871-1935) American
$950	£638	Oxen and farmer (30x38cm-12x15in) s. board. 24-Jun-93 Mystic Fine Arts, Connecticut #224
$1400	£915	Spring ploughing (23x30cm-9x12in) s. board. 4-May-93 Christie's, East, New York #73
$1500	£987	Winter morning (64x76cm-25x30in) s. 5-Jun-93 Louisiana Auction Exchange #178/R
$1600	£1135	Steer-drawn wagon (51x61cm-20x24in) s/. 14-Feb-93 Hanzel Galleries, Chicago #778
$1800	£1192	Spring pasture (20x28cm-8x11in) s. board. 21-Nov-92 James Bakker, Cambridge #267/R

VOLKMAR, Charles (1841-1914) American
$1000	£662	Cattle by a stream (76x117cm-30x46in) s. 28-Nov-92 Young Fine Arts Auctions, Maine #390/R

VOLL, Frederick Usher de see DEVOLL, Frederick Usher

VOLLMERING, Joseph (1810-1887) American
$2000	£1361	Cows grazing in mountain landscape (40x53cm-16x21in) s.d.1849stretcher. 15-Nov-93 Christie's, East, New York #54/R

VONNOH, Robert (1858-1933) American
$750	£460	Portrait of elderly lady with pearls (92x77cm-36x30in) s. 13-Oct-92 Christie's, East, New York #245
$975	£650	The poppyfield (27x34cm-11x13in) s.d.indis.1895 card. 19-May-94 Lawrence, Crewkerne #49
$1500	£1014	Portrait of a lady (107x76cm-42x30in) s.d.1881. 31-Mar-94 Sotheby's Arcade, New York #148/R
$12000	£7895	Monarch of valley (61x76cm-24x30in) s. 13-Jun-93 Butterfield & Butterfield, San Francisco #3156/R
$30000	£18987	The orchard (76x91cm-30x36in) s. 3-Dec-92 Sotheby's, New York #95/R
$30000	£18987	Moist weather, France (64x53cm-25x21in) s.d.1890 canvas laid down on board. 4-Dec-92 Christie's, New York #1/R
$55000	£34810	Early spring, Pleasant Valley, Lyme, Connecticut (61x77cm-24x30in) s. 4-Dec-92 Christie's, New York #23/R

VOORHEES, Clark Greenwood (1871-1933) American
$1100	£728	More snow coming (30x41cm-12x16in) s. board. 21-Nov-92 James Bakker, Cambridge #215/R
$1300	£850	Campfire under trees (58x76cm-23x30in) s. 4-May-93 Christie's, East, New York #93/R

VOS, Hubert (1855-1935) American
$750	£481	Dutch family in interior (102x152cm-40x60in) s.d.91. 12-Dec-92 Weschler, Washington #56 a/R
$1415	£896	Coastal coal mining - coal mining landscape at seaport, northern Europe (76x128cm-30x50in) s.d.87. 1-Dec-92 Ritchie, Toronto #179/R (C.D 1800)

VOSS, Frank B (1880-1953) American
$2000	£1290	Two dogs (23x43cm-9x17in) s. 15-Jul-94 Du Mouchelle, Detroit #2007/R
$2500	£1667	Study depicting horse (43x51cm-17x20in) s. 20-May-94 Du Mouchelle, Detroit #2015/R
$3750	£2467	Bay hunter in stable (36x41cm-14x16in) s.d.1936. 4-Jun-93 Sotheby's, New York #221/R

VU, Michel (1941-) American
$550	£359	Modele pour Poiret (58x30cm-23x12in) s.d.1965. 30-Jun-94 Mystic Fine Arts, Connecticut #219

VYSEKAL, Edouard Antonin (1890-1939) American
$2500	£1445	The back of the house (28x36cm-11x14in) 25-Sep-92 Sotheby's Arcade, New York #273/R
$3250	£2138	Japanese nursery (27x34cm-11x13in) init. canvas on board. 13-Jun-93 Butterfield & Butterfield, San Francisco #944/R

VYTLACIL, Vaclav (1892-1984) American

$750	£475	Beach No.3 (31x42cm-12x17in) s.d.1946 tempera board. 2-Dec-92 Christie's, East, New York #318
$1000	£654	Fishing nook (55x80cm-22x31in) s.d.1947 tempera paper. 4-May-93 Christie's, East, New York #285/R
$1400	£909	Cubist still life (28x36cm-11x14in) s.d.1937 paper on panel. 9-Sep-93 Sotheby's Arcade, New York #430/R
$2200	£1392	Beach and boats (43x68cm-17x27in) s.d.1947 tempera board. 2-Dec-92 Christie's, East, New York #313/R
$2800	£1772	Table top abstraction (61x46cm-24x18in) s.d.1938 tempera board. 2-Dec-92 Christie's, East, New York #319/R
$750	*£490*	*Seaport (55x69cm-22x27in) s.d.1954 tempera col.chk chl board. 4-May-93 Christie's, East, New York #286/R*
$1500	*£1000*	*Still life in red (33x43cm-13x17in) s.d.40 i.verso gouache. 26-Aug-93 Skinner, Bolton #103*
$14000	£9396	Collage construction (33x25cm-13x10in) s.d.1936 mixed media board. 4-May-94 Doyle, New York #74/R

WACHTEL, Elmer (1864-1929) American

$600	£397	Distant houses (20x48cm-8x19in) s.d.Nov.25 92 canvas laid down on board. 15-Jun-94 Butterfield & Butterfield, San Francisco #4657/R
$2750	£1846	Sycamores in landscape (36x25cm-14x10in) s. 8-Dec-93 Butterfield & Butterfield, San Francisco #3423/R
$2750	£1821	Landscape (20x25cm-8x10in) s. 14-Jun-94 John Moran, Pasadena #20
$7000	£4636	Sierra landscape (51x41cm-20x16in) s. 15-Jun-94 Butterfield & Butterfield, San Francisco #4686/R
$13000	£7647	Topanga Canyon (41x51cm-16x20in) s. st.verso. 4-Oct-92 Butterfield & Butterfield, Los Angeles #138/R
$17000	£11806	Mt San Antonio, California (76x102cm-30x40in) s. 7-Mar-93 Butterfield & Butterfield, San Francisco #148/R
$20000	£13333	Mountain landscape (76x102cm-30x40in) s. 15-Mar-94 John Moran, Pasadena #113
$550	*£359*	*Wooded river landscape (28x39cm-11x15in) s. W/C. 4-May-93 Christie's, East, New York #89*

WACHTEL, Elmer (attrib) (1864-1929) American

$1300	£903	Sunset beside eucalyptus grove (35x25cm-14x10in) canvas on board. 7-Mar-93 Butterfield & Butterfield, San Francisco #143/R

WACHTEL, Julie (1956-) American

$1900	£1284	Untitled (297x91cm-117x36in) s.d.1986 init.stretcher acrylic. 8-Nov-93 Christie's, East, New York #112/R

WACHTEL, Marion K (1876-1954) American

$3000	£1987	Stream in High Sierra (25x30cm-10x12in) s. 14-Jun-94 John Moran, Pasadena #57
$3500	£2365	Oaks in rolling landscape (36x43cm-14x17in) mono. 9-Nov-93 John Moran, Pasadena #889
$4750	£3209	Floral still life with green pottery bowl (76x66cm-30x26in) s.d.1938. 9-Nov-93 John Moran, Pasadena #900
$4750	£3146	Eucalyptus trees and foothills (44x34cm-17x13in) s. canvas laid down on board. 15-Jun-94 Butterfield & Butterfield, San Francisco #4718/R
$4750	£3146	Landscape - desert near Big Pine (46x61cm-18x24in) s. W/C. 14-Jun-94 John Moran, Pasadena #102
$5000	£3378	Sycamores in landscape (36x43cm-14x17in) mono. canvas on board. 15-Jun-93 John Moran, Pasadena #107
$7000	£4730	California coastal landscape (30x41cm-12x16in) mono. double-sided. 15-Jun-93 John Moran, Pasadena #160
$7000	£4861	High Sierras (51x41cm-20x16in) bears sig. 7-Mar-93 Butterfield & Butterfield, San Francisco #131/R
$8500	£5862	House in landscape (36x43cm-14x17in) s. 16-Feb-93 John Moran, Pasadena #125
$8500	£5629	Arroyo Sycamores (44x34cm-17x13in) s. canvas laid down on board. 15-Jun-94 Butterfield & Butterfield, San Francisco #4709/R
$15000	£10345	Laguna coastal (51x66cm-20x26in) s. 16-Feb-93 John Moran, Pasadena #108
$16000	£10811	Sycamore and oak near stream (76x102cm-30x40in) s.d.1944. 15-Jun-93 John Moran, Pasadena #50 b
$16000	£10667	Eucalyptus coastal scene (51x66cm-20x26in) s. 15-Mar-94 John Moran, Pasadena #40
$22500	£14901	Late autumn mountain landscape (66x76cm-26x30in) s. 15-Jun-94 Butterfield & Butterfield, San Francisco #4671/R
$22500	£15517	After the storm, Mt. San Antonio (56x71cm-22x28in) indist.sig. i.stretcher. 16-Feb-93 John Moran, Pasadena #68
$25000	£17241	Matilaja Canyon (76x102cm-30x40in) s. 16-Feb-93 John Moran, Pasadena #58
$27500	£18966	Sycamores, Millard Canyon (64x76cm-25x30in) s.d.1943. 16-Feb-93 John Moran, Pasadena #69
$1000	*£676*	*Monterey coast (43x59cm-17x23in) s. gouache board. 20-Mar-93 Weschler, Washington #128/R*
$2750	*£1821*	*Mountain stream (41x30cm-16x12in) s. W/C. 15-Jun-94 Butterfield & Butterfield, San Francisco #4717/R*
$3000	*£2069*	*Still life, yellow roses (20x56cm-8x22in) s. W/C. 16-Feb-93 John Moran, Pasadena #110*
$3500	*£2318*	*Portrait of a young lady (34x25cm-13x10in) mono. W/C. 15-Jun-94 Butterfield & Butterfield, San Francisco #4663/R*

WACHTEL, Marion K (1876-1954) American-cont.
$4000	£2649	Southern California valley landscape (23x30cm-9x12in) s. W/C. 15-Jun-94 Butterfield & Butterfield, San Francisco #4715/R
$10000	£6579	View of Sierras (44x60cm-17x24in) s. W/C. 13-Jun-93 Butterfield & Butterfield, San Francisco #871/R

WAGNER, Fred (1864-1940) American
$536	£357	Winter magic (55x45cm-22x18in) s.i.d.1903. 17-Mar-94 Neumeister, Munich #2804 (DM 900)
$1200	£706	Red barn in Norristown (51x66cm-20x26in) 8-Oct-92 Freeman Fine Arts, Philadelphia #987
$6250	£3676	Philadelphia waterfront in winter (74x91cm-29x36in) s. 8-Oct-92 Freeman Fine Arts, Philadelphia #984
$700	£412	Boats in dry dock, Philadelphia waterfront (25x33cm-10x13in) s. pastel. 8-Oct-92 Freeman Fine Arts, Philadelphia #1027
$850	£500	Tug boat Philadelphia Waterfront (33x43cm-13x17in) pastel. 8-Oct-92 Freeman Fine Arts, Philadelphia #1028

WAGNER, J D L van (19th C) American
$1800	£1233	Winter towing in Boston harbour (30x46cm-12x18in) bears i. W/C. 12-Feb-94 Boos Gallery, Michigan #535/R

WAGNER, Jacob (1852-1898) American
$718	£469	Sailor in rowing boat appoaching sailing vessel (68x56cm-27x22in) s. 14-Sep-93 Christie's, Amsterdam #251 (D.FL 1300)

WAGONER, Harry B (19/20th C) American
$900	£529	Vagabond clouds, Palm Springs (51x76cm-20x30in) s. 3-Oct-92 Weschler, Washington #140/R
$2750	£1821	Paradise Valley (61x76cm-24x30in) s. 15-Jun-94 Butterfield & Butterfield, San Francisco #4539/R

WAH, Bernard (1939-1981) Haitian
$3578	£2370	Couple dans la nuit (60x75cm-24x30in) s.d.80. 13-Jun-94 Rogeon, Paris #138/R (F.FR 20000)

WALCHER, Ferdinand Edward (1895-1955) American
$637	£430	Near Hermann, Missouri, U.S.A (56x71cm-22x28in) s. canvas on board. 19-Oct-93 Christie's, Amsterdam #269/R (D.FL 1200)
$796	£538	Nude at table reading book (76x98cm-30x39in) s. 19-Oct-93 Christie's, Amsterdam #270/R (D.FL 1500)

WALDEN, Lionel (1861-1933) American
$616	£400	Chickens feeding by cottages (40x56cm-16x22in) s. 3-Sep-93 Phillips, Glasgow #158

WALDO, Frank (fl.1910-1930) American
$900	£520	Landscape with Indian encampment (61x107cm-24x42in) 26-Sep-92 San Rafael Auction Galleries #232

WALDO, J Frank (1832-c.1914) American
$26000	£16667	View of Island Park, Lake Winnebago, Wisconsin (51x91cm-20x36in) s.d.1875. 26-May-93 Christie's, New York #49/R

WALDO, Samuel Lovett (1783-1861) American
$3400	£1771	Livingston children (91x71cm-36x28in) i.verso. 6-Aug-92 Eldred, Massachusetts #1042/R

WALDO, Samuel Lovett (attrib) (1783-1861) American
$3000	£1899	Portrait of William Steele (74x62cm-29x24in) 3-Dec-92 Sotheby's, New York #17/R

WALES, Susan Makepeace Larkin (1839-1927) American
$1300	£751	Interior of greenhouse (50x35cm-20x14in) s. W/C pencil paper on board. 25-Sep-92 Sotheby's Arcade, New York #133

WALKER, Darryl (20th C) American
$2122	£1406	Reclining model (77x113cm-30x44in) s.d.74. 28-Sep-93 Rasmussen, Copenhagen #37/R (D.KR 14000)

WALKER, Horatio (1858-1938) Canadian
$1557	£1031	Portrait of a lady (47x37cm-19x15in) s.d.1889 i.verso board. 18-Nov-92 Sotheby's, Toronto #197/R (C.D 2000)
$2358	£1493	Calves, Ile d'Orleans (19x27cm-7x11in) init. board. 1-Dec-92 Fraser Pinneys, Quebec #141/R (C.D 3000)
$3144	£1990	The Woodcutter,Ile de Orleans (21x26cm-8x10in) init. board. 1-Dec-92 Fraser Pinneys, Quebec #32/R (C.D 4000)
$23665	£15777	Turning the harrow, early morning (72x96cm-28x38in) s.d.1898. 11-May-94 Sotheby's, Toronto #150/R (C.D 32500)
$1341	£900	Spring ploughing (43x41cm-17x16in) s. pencil W/C bodycol. 24-Mar-93 Christie's, S. Kensington #219
$1868	£1237	The bee keeper (36x28cm-14x11in) s. W/C. 18-Nov-92 Sotheby's, Toronto #290 (C.D 2400)

WALKER, Inez Nathaniel (1911-1990) American
$550	£364	Orange face woman and black face man (30x46cm-12x18in) s.d.1976 col.pencil. 21-Nov-92 Litchfield Auction Gallery #14

WALKER, Inez Nathaniel (1911-1990) American-cont.
$975	£646	Seated pink face woman and a standing black face man (48x61cm-19x24in) s.d.1976 col.pencil. 21-Nov-92 Litchfield Auction Gallery #13

WALKER, John Law (1899-) American
$800	£523	Slightly metaphysical (56x91cm-22x36in) s. 18-Sep-93 James Bakker, Cambridge #60/R
$850	£545	The Santa Clara in spring (81x86cm-32x34in) s. s.i.d.1958verso. 28-May-93 Sloan, North Bethesda #2648
$1700	£1126	Carmen in blue (102x81cm-40x32in) s. 21-Nov-92 James Bakker, Cambridge #311/R
$2000	£1389	Pima fair, night (66x81cm-26x32in) s. s.i.d.1957verso. 7-Mar-93 Butterfield & Butterfield, San Francisco #261/R

WALKER, Myrtle (20th C) American
$2800	£1854	Argentin Percheron stallion (81x102cm-32x40in) s.i. 28-Nov-92 Dunning's, Illinois #1047

WALKER, Stuart (20th C) American?
$900	£604	Montoya's house (46x61cm-18x24in) s. board. 24-Mar-94 Mystic Fine Arts, Connecticut #254/R

WALKER, William Aiken (1839-1921) American
$3000	£2027	Couple in the cotton fields (16x31cm-6x12in) s. i.verso board. 31-Mar-94 Sotheby's Arcade, New York #71/R
$3000	£2027	Old man picking cotton and smoking a pipe (21x11cm-8x4in) s. board. 31-Mar-94 Sotheby's Arcade, New York #68/R
$3200	£2177	Mangrove snapper fish (47x31cm-19x12in) s.d.Nov.1895 board. 15-Nov-93 Christie's, East, New York #86/R
$3800	£2657	New Smyrna Beach, Florida (17x11cm-7x4in) init. 11-Mar-93 Christie's, New York #35/R
$4000	£2797	Man with pipe (20x10cm-8x4in) init. board. 11-Mar-93 Christie's, New York #93/R
$4000	£2797	Fruit vendor (20x10cm-8x4in) init. board. 11-Mar-93 Christie's, New York #94/R
$4000	£2703	Cotton pickers (31x15cm-12x6in) s. board pair. 31-Mar-94 Sotheby's Arcade, New York #70/R
$4400	£2973	Male and female cotton pickers (20x10cm-8x4in) s. board pair. 31-Oct-93 Hindman Galleries, Chicago #677/R
$4500	£3041	Old woman with a basket and old man with a cane (20x10cm-8x4in) s. board pair. 31-Mar-94 Sotheby's Arcade, New York #62/R
$4600	£3046	Outside the cabin (15x30cm-6x12in) board. 19-Jun-94 Hindman Galleries, Chicago #650
$4800	£3179	Family outside cabin (10x28cm-4x11in) board. 19-Jun-94 Hindman Galleries, Chicago #651
$5000	£3497	Cotton pickers (31x23cm-12x9in) init. board. 11-Mar-93 Christie's, New York #92 a/R
$5100	£3377	Cotton field (23x31cm-9x12in) s. board. 23-Sep-93 Sotheby's, New York #80/R
$5500	£3667	Cotton picker with possum (30x15cm-12x6in) s. board. 12-May-94 Boos Gallery, Michigan #509/R
$5600	£3709	Cabin scene (23x30cm-9x12in) s. board. 19-Jun-94 Hindman Galleries, Chicago #649
$6000	£4196	Wash day (15x30cm-6x12in) mono board. 10-Mar-93 Sotheby's, New York #27/R
$7000	£4698	Cabin scene with figures (15x31cm-6x12in) s. board. 6-May-94 Skinner, Bolton #53/R
$7000	£4545	Cotton pickers (31x15cm-12x6in) s. panel pair. 9-Sep-93 Sotheby's Arcade, New York #100/R
$7500	£4747	Laundry day (23x31cm-9x12in) s. board. 4-Dec-92 Christie's, New York #214/R
$7600	£5000	Old bearded cotton picker. Female cotton picker (29x15cm-11x6in) s. board pair. 7-Jun-93 Waddingtons, Toronto #1307/R (C.D 9750)
$8000	£5128	Southern homestead (24x32cm-9x13in) s. board. 9-Dec-92 Butterfield & Butterfield, San Francisco #3825/R
$9000	£6000	A Southern farmsteed. Cotton pickers (15x30cm-6x12in) s. board pair. 17-Mar-94 Bonhams, London #101/R
$9300	£6000	Cotton pickers (31x16cm-12x6in) s. board pair. 15-Jul-94 Christie's, London #54/R
$9500	£6013	Blue Fish (32x51cm-13x20in) s. 4-Dec-92 Christie's, New York #212/R
$12000	£7947	Common blue Crab (40x30cm-16x12in) s. paper on board. 22-Sep-93 Christie's, New York #33/R
$18000	£12000	Return from the market (23x38cm-9x15in) init. 1-Jun-94 Doyle, New York #65/R
$19000	£12583	Old cotton picker (46x30cm-18x12in) init. 22-Sep-93 Christie's, New York #71/R
$26000	£16456	Bringing in the cotton (30x51cm-12x20in) s. 4-Dec-92 Christie's, New York #213/R
$650	£434	Oak leaves (42x28cm-17x11in) init.d.Sept.4 1905 pencil. 16-Mar-94 Christie's, New York #27/R

WALL, William Allen (1801-1885) American
$2700	£1837	Landscape with rolling hills river cattle and boy (61x91cm-24x36in) s. 19-Nov-93 Eldred, Massachusetts #924/R
$14000	£9396	The nativity of truth (183x150cm-72x59in) s.d.1852. 3-Feb-94 Sloan, North Bethesda #2893/R
$850	*£570*	*Apponagansett harbour through trees from South Dartmouth (30x48cm-12x19in) s.d.52 W/C. 5-Aug-93 Eldred, Massachusetts #963/R*
$1200	*£800*	*On the Clark's Point Road (25x38cm-10x15in) i. W/C gouache painted c.1860. 12-Jun-94 Skinner, Bolton #237*
$1400	*£927*	*Autumn, New Bedford, Massachusetts (25x38cm-10x15in) s. gouache. 23-Sep-93 Sotheby's, New York #27/R*

WALL, William Allen (attrib) (1801-1885) American
$2500	£1445	Portrait of three children (152x117cm-60x46in) 25-Sep-92 Sotheby's Arcade, New York #98/R

WALL, William Guy (1792-c.1864) American/Irish
$8288	£5600	Irish lough (71x107cm-28x42in) s. 30-Mar-94 Sotheby's, London #34/R
$500	£338	Looking across the river to town (11x16cm-4x6in) s.d.1825 ink wash shaped. 31-Mar-94 Sotheby's Arcade, New York #25/R

WALLER, Frank (1842-1923) American
$900	£584	North African coastline (22x47cm-9x19in) s.d.87. 9-Sep-93 Sotheby's Arcade, New York #85/R
$1369	£925	Castel del Ovo, Naples (27x36cm-11x14in) s.i.d.1872 panel. 24-Nov-93 Bukowskis, Stockholm #324/R (S.KR 11500)

WALSH, Richard M L (1848-1908) American
$500	£325	Portrait of a beautiful woman (69x53cm-27x21in) s. pastel. 8-Jul-94 Sloan, North Bethesda #2532

WALT DISNEY STUDIOS (20th C) American
$532	£350	Bambi and Thumper (25x36cm-10x14in) gouache on celluloid on W/C. 5-Apr-93 Christie's, S. Kensington #242 a
$532	£350	Winnie the Pooh and Rabbit watch Christopher Robin playing drum (23x28cm-9x11in) painted c.1970s gouache on celluloid. 5-Apr-93 Christie's, S. Kensington #123/R
$532	£350	Dumbo and friends (33x69cm-13x27in) painted c.1970s W/C board. 5-Apr-93 Christie's, S. Kensington #250/R
$532	£350	Snow White and the Seven Dwarfs, Dopey (25x30cm-10x12in) d.1937 animation dr. graphite col.pencil. 5-Apr-93 Christie's, S. Kensington #316/R
$547	£360	Jungle Book, King Louie with arms open (30x41cm-12x16in) d.1967 gouache on full celluloid. 5-Apr-93 Christie's, S. Kensington #106/R
$547	£360	Trader Mickey, the natives (23x30cm-9x12in) d.1932 scene dr. graphite. 5-Apr-93 Christie's, S. Kensington #347/R
$578	£380	Television production, Mickey, sorcerer's apprentice doffs hat (23x18cm-9x7in) gouache on celluloid. 5-Apr-93 Christie's, S. Kensington #259/R
$600	£403	Donald Duck holding up plane (32x18cm-13x7in) gouache celluloid. 22-Jun-93 Sotheby's, New York #748
$600	£403	Winnie the Pooh and Tigger Too, Rabbit looking as Tigger gestures (27x35cm-11x14in) studio st. gouache two cel set up on orange back. 22-Jun-93 Sotheby's, New York #818
$600	£403	Ferdinand the Bull, Ferdinand's mother eating grass amongst the flowers (21x27cm-8x11in) gouache trimmed celluloid on background. 22-Jun-93 Sotheby's, New York #759
$600	£403	The Three Caballeros, Jose Carioca (23x30cm-9x12in) studio label verso gouache celluloid. 22-Jun-93 Sotheby's, New York #684
$600	£403	Bambi, wintery forest scene (24x28cm-9x11in) exec.1942 W/C. 22-Jun-93 Sotheby's, New York #825
$600	£403	Adventures of Ichabod and Mr Toad, Ichabod Crane leaning over (19x23cm-7x9in) gouache celluloid. 22-Jun-93 Sotheby's, New York #732
$600	£403	Ludwig von Drake plays flamenco (27x22cm-11x9in) exec.c.1960 gouache celluloid on lithograph. 22-Jun-93 Sotheby's, New York #622
$600	£403	Goofy and Wilbur, Wilbur about to be swallowed by frog (17x23cm-7x9in) gouache trimmed celluloid on background. 22-Jun-93 Sotheby's, New York #765
$600	£403	Jungle Book, King Louie dances (23x26cm-9x10in) gouache celluloid. 22-Jun-93 Sotheby's, New York #604
$608	£400	Alice in Wonderland talks to the Mad Hatter (15x23cm-6x9in) d.1951 gouache on full celluloid. 5-Apr-93 Christie's, S. Kensington #207/R
$608	£400	Mickey's Mellerdrammer, Mickey and Minnie dance in black-face (25x30cm-10x12in) d.1933 animation drawing graphite. 5-Apr-93 Christie's, S. Kensington #196/R
$608	£400	Peter Pan, Michael, John and The Lost Boys tied up with rope (30x36cm-12x14in) d.1953 gouache on celluloid. 5-Apr-93 Christie's, S. Kensington #191/R
$638	£420	Peg Leg Pete (18x23cm-7x9in) gouache on partial celluloid on W/C. 5-Apr-93 Christie's, S. Kensington #202/R
$650	£437	On ice, animation drawing of Mickey skating (22x29cm-9x11in) exec.1935 graphite. 22-Jun-93 Sotheby's, New York #528
$684	£450	Three Caballeros, Donald is squashed by Llama (23x28cm-9x11in) s.d.1945 gouache on partial celluloid on W/C. 5-Apr-93 Christie's, S. Kensington #236
$684	£450	Sea scouts - Donald Duck (25x30cm-10x12in) graphite col.pencil. 5-Apr-93 Christie's, S. Kensington #126/R
$699	£460	Jungle Book, Mowgli and Baloo (23x28cm-9x11in) gouache on full celluloid on printed Disneyland. 5-Apr-93 Christie's, S. Kensington #108/R
$699	£460	The Flying Mouse, bat (18x23cm-7x9in) d.1934 gouache on celluloid. 5-Apr-93 Christie's, S. Kensington #343/R
$700	£470	The Jungle Book, Mowgli walking (21x15cm-8x6in) gouache celluloid on lithographic background. 22-Jun-93 Sotheby's, New York #665
$700	£470	Snow White and the Seven Dwarfs, two squirrels on toadstol watch tortoise (16x22cm-6x9in) gouache celluloid on background. 22-Jun-93 Sotheby's, New York #851
$700	£470	Chip 'n' Dale (18x24cm-7x9in) exec.c.1960 gouache celluloid. 22-Jun-93 Sotheby's, New York #717
$700	£470	Sleeping Beauty, Prince Phillip rides Samson (29x18cm-11x7in) gouache celluloid. 22-Jun-93 Sotheby's, New York #722
$730	£480	Mickey's Circus, Mickey and Donald falling , d.1936 graphite col.pencil two dr.in one mount. 5-Apr-93 Christie's, S. Kensington #337/R
$730	£480	101 Dalmations, Pongo walks beside Anita (20x25cm-8x10in) gouache on celluloid on Disneyland background. 5-Apr-93 Christie's, S. Kensington #135/R
$760	£500	Mickey as sorcerer's apprentice (23x18cm-9x7in) gouache on celluloid. 5-Apr-93 Christie's, S. Kensington #260
$760	£500	Mickey in shoot-out (25x30cm-10x12in) d.1934 animation dr. graphite col.pencil. 5-Apr-93 Christie's, S. Kensington #157/R

WALT DISNEY STUDIOS (20th C) American-cont.

$760	£500	Donald Duck with telephone (23x18cm-9x7in) paint.c.1950s publicity cel gouache on celluloid. 5-Apr-93 Christie's, S. Kensington #182/R
$760	£500	Mickey Mouse Club, Ranger Rex and bears (28x23cm-11x9in) painted c.1950s gouache on multi-cel set-up. 5-Apr-93 Christie's, S. Kensington #181/R
$760	£500	Snow White and the Seven Dwarfs, Doc, Bashful and Dopey (23x30cm-9x12in) d.1937 model sheet dr. 5-Apr-93 Christie's, S. Kensington #313/R
$760	£500	Canine Caddy (25x30cm-10x12in) d.1941 model sheet dr. col.pencil. 5-Apr-93 Christie's, S. Kensington #249/R
$760	£500	Snow White and the Seven Dwarfs, three blue birds on branch (13x13cm-5x5in) d.1937 gouache on celluloid on airbrush. 5-Apr-93 Christie's, S. Kensington #308/R
$760	£500	Snow White and the Seven Dwarfs, Grumpy (25x30cm-10x12in) d.1937 model sheet dr. graphite. 5-Apr-93 Christie's, S. Kensington #312/R
$800	£537	The Worm Turns, Mickey playing chemist (25x30cm-10x12in) graphite col.pencil. 22-Jun-93 Sotheby's, New York #775
$800	£537	Lady and the Tramp, tiny figure of Lady with playful expression (5x8cm-2x3in) gouache celluloid. 22-Jun-93 Sotheby's, New York #605
$800	£537	Two-gun Mickey (24x30cm-9x12in) i. exec.1934 graphite col.pencil. 22-Jun-93 Sotheby's, New York #542
$800	£537	The Jungle Book, King Louie waves arms in the air as he dances (20x25cm-8x10in) gouache celluloid on lithographic background. 22-Jun-93 Sotheby's, New York #718
$800	£537	The Black Cauldron, Taran, Gurgi and Eilonwy (32x41cm-13x16in) studio st. gouache celluloid. 22-Jun-93 Sotheby's, New York #613
$800	£530	'Donald and Tootsie' from Donald's Penguin, 1938 (18x20cm-7x8in) gouache celluloid applied to scenic background. 13-Nov-92 Skinner, Bolton #225/R
$800	£537	Sleeping Beauty, three good fairies casting spells (11x8cm-4x3in) gouache celluloid on paper painted with stars. 22-Jun-93 Sotheby's, New York #749
$800	£537	Lady and the Tramp, model sheet of lady (32x39cm-13x15in) s.Bob Carr graphite. 22-Jun-93 Sotheby's, New York #532
$800	£537	Lady and the Tramp, Peg looks saucily over shoulder (23x38cm-9x15in) gouache celluloid on loithographic background. 22-Jun-93 Sotheby's, New York #707
$800	£537	Sleeping Beauty, Prince Phillip and Princess Aurora walking arm in arm (13x13cm-5x5in) d.1959 gouache celluloid two. 22-Jun-93 Sotheby's, New York #522
$800	£537	Peter Pan, animation drawing of Captain Hook (32x39cm-13x15in) exec.1953 graphite. 22-Jun-93 Sotheby's, New York #544
$800	£537	Peter Pan, pirates form line (32x41cm-13x16in) gouache celluloid. 22-Jun-93 Sotheby's, New York #688
$800	£537	Jiminy Cricket seated (23x28cm-9x11in) exec.c.1950 gouache celluloid on lithograph. 22-Jun-93 Sotheby's, New York #680/R
$815	£551	Robin Hood (26x36cm-10x14in) studio st. celluloid. 26-Oct-93 Campo, Vlaamse Kaai #420 (B.FR 30000)
$836	£550	Snow White and the Seven Dwarfs, Five dwarfs march (30x46cm-12x18in) d.1937 animation dr. col.pencil graphite. 5-Apr-93 Christie's, S. Kensington #320/R
$836	£550	Fantasia, Centaurettes and fauns frolick (23x30cm-9x12in) animation dr. graphite col.pencil. 5-Apr-93 Christie's, S. Kensington #269
$836	£550	Dumbo, Straw Hat Crow and Preacher Crow dance (25x30cm-10x12in) gouache on celluloid. 5-Apr-93 Christie's, S. Kensington #254/R
$900	£604	Wynken, Blynken and Nod, Nod dangles by candy cane fish hook (22x18cm-9x7in) gouache celluloid multi-cel set up on background. 22-Jun-93 Sotheby's, New York #738
$900	£604	Grand Canyonscope, Donald clutching camera and mountain lion (19x27cm-7x11in) studio label verso gouache celluloid two cel set. 22-Jun-93 Sotheby's, New York #653/R
$900	£604	Snow White, two squirrels help clean around rabbit stein (16x21cm-6x8in) gouache trimmed celluloid on background. 22-Jun-93 Sotheby's, New York #780
$900	£604	Sleeping Beauty, Flora, Fauna and Merryweather casting spells (14x23cm-6x9in) exec.1959 gouache celluloid on background. 22-Jun-93 Sotheby's, New York #538
$900	£604	Peter Pan, Nana loping to the right with tongue hanging out (32x41cm-13x16in) gouache celluloid. 22-Jun-93 Sotheby's, New York #771
$912	£600	Two Chips and Miss, Chip and Dale look at reward poster (18x23cm-7x9in) d.1952 gouache on partial celluloid. 5-Apr-93 Christie's, S. Kensington #225/R
$912	£600	Variety of characters for Disneyland Magazine (30x66cm-12x26in) W/C board. 5-Apr-93 Christie's, S. Kensington #332/R
$912	£600	Jungle Book, King Louie and Baloo dance (28x33cm-11x13in) d.1967 gouache on celluloid. 5-Apr-93 Christie's, S. Kensington #102/R
$925	£593	Prince John (26x36cm-10x14in) celluloid. 15-Dec-92 Campo, Vlaamse Kaai #166 (B.FR 30000)
$1000	£671	Robin Hood, King John with Robin Hood and Little John disguised as women (23x28cm-9x11in) gouache celluloid. 22-Jun-93 Sotheby's, New York #560/R
$1000	£654	Magic Lamp beginning to shake and spew smoke (32x43cm-13x17in) cel. 9-Oct-93 Sotheby's, New York #182/R
$1000	£671	Winnie the Pooh pulling cart of honey pots to table (28x37cm-11x15in) exec.c.1980's gouache on celluloid multi-cel. 22-Jun-93 Sotheby's, New York #521
$1000	£654	Genie attempting to awaken Aladdin by shaking him (32x43cm-13x17in) cel. 9-Oct-93 Sotheby's, New York #184/R
$1000	£671	101 Dalmatians, Pongo proudly holding master's hat (30x23cm-12x9in) gouache celluloid. 22-Jun-93 Sotheby's, New York #691
$1000	£671	The elephant ladies tumbling downward from their pyramid trick (44x39cm-17x15in) gouache on celluloid executed 1941. 12-Dec-93 Butterfield & Butterfield, Los Angeles #1172/R
$1000	£671	Sleeping Beauty, Maleficent (32x39cm-13x15in) graphite. 22-Jun-93 Sotheby's, New York #676
$1000	£671	Dumbo, clowns in fire engine (24x30cm-9x12in) studio st. gouache celluloid. 22-Jun-93 Sotheby's, New York #668

WALT DISNEY STUDIOS (20th C) American-cont.

$1000	£654	Terrified Gazeem approaches tiger's mouth entrance to Cave of Wonders (32x43cm-13x17in) cel. 9-Oct-93 Sotheby's, New York #7/R
$1000	£671	Goofy speeding down a downhill run (40x36cm-16x14in) gouache on celluloid airbrush W/C background st. 12-Dec-93 Butterfield & Butterfield, Los Angeles #1165
$1000	£671	Fantasia, Baby black Pegasus from Pastorale Symphony (20x16cm-8x6in) studio st. gouache celluloid on background. 22-Jun-93 Sotheby's, New York #693
$1000	£671	Sleeping Beauty, Prince Phillip rides Samson (23x30cm-9x12in) gouache celluloid. 22-Jun-93 Sotheby's, New York #675
$1000	£671	Saludos Amigos, Donald dances a Jose Carioca plays umbrella (18x19cm-7x7in) gouache celluloid on W/C background. 22-Jun-93 Sotheby's, New York #814/R
$1035	£690	Winnie the Pooh and Owl, gouache on celluloid. 9-Jun-94 Swann Galleries, New York #98/R
$1048	£672	Robin Hood (26x36cm-10x14in) celluloid. 15-Dec-92 Campo, Vlaamse Kaai #167 (B.FR 34000)
$1064	£700	Pinocchio, Figaro smiles (25x30cm-10x12in) d.1940 gouache on celluloid. 5-Apr-93 Christie's, S. Kensington #284/R
$1064	£700	Minnie Mouse in mouse nursery (23x53cm-9x21in) W/C board painted c.1970s. 5-Apr-93 Christie's, S. Kensington #90/R
$1094	£720	Lady and the Tramp, Toughy, Boris and Pedro sing (25x30cm-10x12in) d.1955 gouache on celluloid. 5-Apr-93 Christie's, S. Kensington #164/R
$1100	£719	Street vendor and customer (32x43cm-13x17in) cel. 9-Oct-93 Sotheby's, New York #146/R
$1100	£738	Little Hiawatha clutches bow and arrow (15x13cm-6x5in) gouache celluloid on wood veneer background. 22-Jun-93 Sotheby's, New York #695
$1100	£738	Fantasia, the black Pegasus foal flies (15x12cm-6x5in) studio st. gouache celluloid. 22-Jun-93 Sotheby's, New York #612
$1100	£738	Sleeping Beauty, Prince Phillip tells King Hubert he's in love (23x29cm-9x11in) label v.gouache celluloid on lithog.background. 22-Jun-93 Sotheby's, New York #801
$1140	£750	Society Dog Show, Mickey with Pluto (25x30cm-10x12in) d.1939 animation dr. graphite col.pencil. 5-Apr-93 Christie's, S. Kensington #172/R
$1140	£750	Winnie the Pooh, Tigger, Piglet and Owl build Eeyore's house (25x36cm-10x14in) painted c.1980s gouache on celluloid on W/C. 5-Apr-93 Christie's, S. Kensington #116 a/R
$1140	£750	Lady and the Tramp, Peg struts (18x23cm-7x9in) d.1955 gouache on celluloid. 5-Apr-93 Christie's, S. Kensington #167/R
$1200	£805	Cinderella, Madame Tremaine walks to the door (24x18cm-9x7in) gouache celluloid. 22-Jun-93 Sotheby's, New York #559
$1200	£805	Melody time, Joe and Jenny out for winter's sleigh ride (22x27cm-9x11in) gouache trimmed celluloid on background. 22-Jun-93 Sotheby's, New York #629
$1200	£805	Fantasia, autumn leaves from The Nutcracker Suite (23x31cm-9x12in) i.st.d.Jun 9 1939verso W/C pastel. 22-Jun-93 Sotheby's, New York #626
$1200	£784	Smoke pouring out of magic lamp hidden in Ali's turban (32x43cm-13x17in) two cel set-up. 9-Oct-93 Sotheby's, New York #193/R
$1200	£784	Abu digging in snow (27x33cm-11x13in) three cel set-up. 9-Oct-93 Sotheby's, New York #213/R
$1200	£784	Three amused townswomen watch as Aladdin evades the guards (32x43cm-13x17in) cel. 9-Oct-93 Sotheby's, New York #19/R
$1200	£784	Chorus of cooks holding up baked goods (32x43cm-13x17in) two cel set-up. 9-Oct-93 Sotheby's, New York #149/R
$1200	£805	Sleeping Beauty, Briar Rose with berry basket wanders through forest (22x28cm-9x11in) gouache celluloid. 22-Jun-93 Sotheby's, New York #641
$1200	£800	Two vultures perched upon limb, from Snow White and Seven Dwarfs, 1937 (15x15cm-6x6in) gouache on celluloid airbrush wood background. 26-May-94 Freeman Fine Arts, Philadelphia #238
$1200	£805	Mickey Mouse plays the drum in white tie and tails (19x25cm-7x10in) exec.c.1960s gouache celluloid. 22-Jun-93 Sotheby's, New York #580/R
$1200	£805	Three Caballeros Poster Art, design for American Airlines flight to Rio (54x36cm-21x14in) exec.c.1945 pastel. 22-Jun-93 Sotheby's, New York #590/R
$1200	£805	Lady and the Tramp, Tony and Joe serenading. Tramp fending off bad dogs, gouache celluloid one two-cel set up two. 22-Jun-93 Sotheby's, New York #833
$1200	£784	Townspeople laugh at Aladdin who has been kicked into the mud (27x33cm-11x13in) cel. 9-Oct-93 Sotheby's, New York #53/R
$1200	£805	Academy Awards, Mickey stands smiling into the spotlight (25x30cm-10x12in) st.sig. gouache celluloid on printed background. 22-Jun-93 Sotheby's, New York #570/R
$1216	£800	Snow White and the Seven Dwarfs, Sleepy (15x13cm-6x5in) d.1937 gouache multi-cell set-up on wood veneer. 5-Apr-93 Christie's, S. Kensington #314/R
$1216	£800	Don Donald, Don Donald rides donkey while Daisy pedals unicycle (28x38cm-11x15in) d.1937 gouache multi-cel set-up on W/C. 5-Apr-93 Christie's, S. Kensington #334/R
$1216	£800	Mickey leads parade of Disney characters (46x71cm-18x28in) pen W/C board. 5-Apr-93 Christie's, S. Kensington #46/R
$1292	£850	Winnie the Pooh and Tigger (28x36cm-11x14in) painted c.1980s gouache on celluloid on W/C. 5-Apr-93 Christie's, S. Kensington #121 a
$1300	£872	Fantasia, elephants performing bubble dance (25x30cm-10x12in) st.i.d.Jul.11,1939 ink graphite two. 22-Jun-93 Sotheby's, New York #548
$1300	£872	Fantasia, Mickey as Sorcerer's apprentice slipping into dreams (25x30cm-10x12in) s. by Preston Blair graphite. 22-Jun-93 Sotheby's, New York #708
$1300	£872	Fantasia, seven mushrooms dancing, Nutcracker Suite (25x30cm-10x12in) exec.1940 pastel. 22-Jun-93 Sotheby's, New York #524
$1300	£872	Fun and Fancy Free, Singing Harp from Mickey and the Beanstalk (23x18cm-9x7in) exec.1947 gouache celluloid. 22-Jun-93 Sotheby's, New York #530/R

515

WALT DISNEY STUDIOS (20th C) American-cont.

$1300	£872	Pinocchio (18x13cm-7x5in) gouache celluloid. 22-Jun-93 Sotheby's, New York #764
$1300	£872	Fantasia, baby Pegasi from Pastorale Symphony fly in formation (27x31cm-11x12in) gouache celluloid. 22-Jun-93 Sotheby's, New York #848
$1300	£872	Snow white and the Seven Dwarfs, vultures wait for meal (16x15cm-6x6in) studio st. gouache trimmed celluloid on panel. 22-Jun-93 Sotheby's, New York #579
$1300	£872	Chip 'n' Dale (23x22cm-9x9in) s.Bill Justice exec.c.1960s gouache celluloid. 22-Jun-93 Sotheby's, New York #753/R
$1300	£872	101 Dalmatians, Cruella in profile lighting cigarette (30x22cm-12x9in) gouache celluloid. 22-Jun-93 Sotheby's, New York #659
$1368	£900	Winnie the Pooh, Christopher Robin, Kanga and Eeyore pull Pooh from tree (33x41cm-13x16in) d.1966 gouache full celloloid on background. 5-Apr-93 Christie's, S. Kensington #114/R
$1368	£900	Lady and the Tramp, Jock, Trusty and the puppies (41x66cm-16x26in) painted c.1970s W/C board. 5-Apr-93 Christie's, S. Kensington #169/R
$1400	£940	Academy Awards, Minnie, Donald and Daisy seated in row (23x29cm-9x11in) gouache celluloid. 22-Jun-93 Sotheby's, New York #633
$1400	£915	Jasmine peering over the sand coming up around her head (27x33cm-11x13in) two cel set-up. 9-Oct-93 Sotheby's, New York #241/R
$1400	£940	Pinocchio sitting on bird swing in cage in Stromboli's wagon (23x20cm-9x8in) i. graphite col.pencil. 22-Jun-93 Sotheby's, New York #562/R
$1400	£940	Bambi meeting Thumper. Bambi nose-to-nose with Flower (14x?cm-6x?in) exec.c.1942 gouache painted glass two. 22-Jun-93 Sotheby's, New York #739/R
$1400	£940	Fantasia, Mlle Upanova stands in 5th position from Dance of the Hours (22x18cm-9x7in) gouache celluloid on background. 22-Jun-93 Sotheby's, New York #746
$1400	£940	Pinocchio, Figaro looking cross (19x19cm-7x7in) exec.1940 gouache celluloid. 22-Jun-93 Sotheby's, New York #529
$1400	£940	The Jungle Book, King Louie (22x29cm-9x11in) gouache celluloid on publication background. 22-Jun-93 Sotheby's, New York #844/R
$1400	£940	Pinocchio, French marionette dancing Can-Can (19x14cm-7x6in) gouache trimmed celluloid on background two. 22-Jun-93 Sotheby's, New York #578
$1400	£940	Cinderella reads palace's invitation (15x14cm-6x6in) gouache celluloid. 22-Jun-93 Sotheby's, New York #727
$1444	£950	Beach Picnic, Pluto stands at the water's edge (23x25cm-9x10in) d.1939 gouache on multi-cel set up on airbrush. 5-Apr-93 Christie's, S. Kensington #288/R
$1444	£950	Mickey and the Beanstalk, Mickey holds box with magic beans (33x28cm-13x11in) exec.c.1940s graphite col.pencil. 5-Apr-93 Christie's, S. Kensington #231/R
$1444	£950	Fantasia, herd of baby unicorns (25x33cm-10x13in) d.1940 gouache trimmed celluloid. 5-Apr-93 Christie's, S. Kensington #272
$1500	£1007	Lady and the Tramp, Peg giving saucy look over her shoulder (25x30cm-10x12in) gouache celluloid. 22-Jun-93 Sotheby's, New York #568/R
$1500	£980	Guards dancing and singing (32x43cm-13x17in) cel. 9-Oct-93 Sotheby's, New York #148/R
$1500	£980	Aladdin and Abu trying to pull Carpet out from under the tower (32x43cm-13x17in) four cel set-up. 9-Oct-93 Sotheby's, New York #211/R
$1500	£1007	Fantasia, Mother Pegasus flies with pink baby Pegasus (28x37cm-11x15in) st.init. exec.1940 gouache celluloid. 22-Jun-93 Sotheby's, New York #540
$1500	£1007	Peter Pan standing on cloud. Two of the Lost Boys, skunk and rabbit , gouache on celluloid two. 22-Jun-93 Sotheby's, New York #724/R
$1500	£980	Abu comes to Aladdin's rescue and pulls Razoul's turban over his head (32x43cm-13x17in) cel. 9-Oct-93 Sotheby's, New York #23/R
$1500	£1007	Peter Pan, two mermaids cavort (20x28cm-8x11in) gouache celluloid on background. 22-Jun-93 Sotheby's, New York #536/R
$1500	£1007	Four pink elephants clustered in dance from Dumbo's dream (25x33cm-10x13in) st. gouache on celluloid airbrushed background. 12-Dec-93 Butterfield & Butterfield, Los Angeles #1162/R
$1500	£980	Razoul, Fazal and Hakim close in on Aladdin on the rooftop (32x43cm-13x17in) three cel set-up. 9-Oct-93 Sotheby's, New York #10/R
$1500	£1007	Toby Tortoise Returns, Max Hare surprises a prober lady (22x27cm-9x11in) exec.1936 gouache celluloid. 22-Jun-93 Sotheby's, New York #533/R
$1500	£1007	Dumbo's mother and Stork look at bundle (20x27cm-8x11in) studio st. gouache trimmed celluloid. 22-Jun-93 Sotheby's, New York #701
$1500	£1007	Working for peanuts, Donald Duck holding elephant's trunk (25x30cm-10x12in) gouache celluloid two. 22-Jun-93 Sotheby's, New York #586
$1500	£1007	Alice in Wonderland, White Rabbit dressed as Queen of Hearts herald (13cm-5in circular) gouache celluloid. 22-Jun-93 Sotheby's, New York #563/R
$1500	£1007	Mickey Mouse (23x33cm-9x13in) exec.c.1940s gouache celluloid on background. 22-Jun-93 Sotheby's, New York #572/R
$1520	£1000	Snow White and the Seven Dwarfs, thew witch clutches the poisoned apple (30x38cm-12x15in) d.1937 animation dr. graphite col.pencil. 5-Apr-93 Christie's, S. Kensington #331/R
$1520	£1000	Now I know, Mickey, Minnie, Goofy and friends (28x43cm-11x17in) d.May 1972 pen W/C board. 5-Apr-93 Christie's, S. Kensington #67/R
$1600	£1046	Aladdin jumps off the roof and onto laundry hanging out to dry (32x43cm-13x17in) cel. 9-Oct-93 Sotheby's, New York #222/R
$1600	£1046	Aladdin's hand reaching for the lamp (32x43cm-13x17in) two cel set-up. 9-Oct-93 Sotheby's, New York #13/R
$1600	£1046	Aladdin and Abu leap from window onto carpet as guards grab thin air (32x56cm-13x22in) cel. 9-Oct-93 Sotheby's, New York #44/R
$1600	£1046	Aladdin pulls blanket over snoring Abu (27x33cm-11x13in) cel. 9-Oct-93 Sotheby's, New York #61/R
$1600	£1046	Aladdin bound and gagged sinks to the bottom of the sea (32x43cm-13x17in) two cel set-up. 9-Oct-93 Sotheby's, New York #178/R

WALT DISNEY STUDIOS (20th C) American-cont.

$1600	£1046	Aladdin realizing that the Magic Carpet is buried in snow (32x43cm-13x17in) four cel set-up. 9-Oct-93 Sotheby's, New York #212/R
$1600	£1074	Melody Time, Pecos Bill rides Widowmaker. Sluefoot Sue checking makeup (19x?cm-7x?in) studio st. gouache trimmed celluloid two. 22-Jun-93 Sotheby's, New York #728
$1600	£1074	Alice in Wonderland, March Hare holds mallet in the air (29x26cm-11x10in) exec.1951 gouache partial celluloid. 22-Jun-93 Sotheby's, New York #543/R
$1600	£1046	Aladdin bounces off closed shutters and falls down to the street (32x43cm-13x17in) cel. 9-Oct-93 Sotheby's, New York #17/R
$1672	£1100	Snow White and the Seven Dwarfs, Grumpy whittling (18x18cm-7x7in) d.1937 storyboard dr. graphite col.pencil. 5-Apr-93 Christie's, S. Kensington #309/R
$1672	£1100	Fantasia, Mlle Upanova (23x25cm-9x10in) d.1940 gouache on celluloid on W/C. 5-Apr-93 Christie's, S. Kensington #267
$1700	£1141	Snow White and the Seven Dwarfs, Old witch clutches poisoned apple (18cm-7in circular) graphite col.pencil. 22-Jun-93 Sotheby's, New York #566/R
$1700	£1141	Sleeping Beauty, Briar Rose carries basket of berries (25x25cm-10x10in) gouache celluloid on background. 22-Jun-93 Sotheby's, New York #561/R
$1700	£1111	Aladdin digging for Abu in the snow (32x43cm-13x17in) two cel set-up. 9-Oct-93 Sotheby's, New York #208/R
$1700	£1111	Jafar, Gazeem and the horses meet with a dark purpose (32x43cm-13x17in) cel. 9-Oct-93 Sotheby's, New York #3/R
$1700	£1141	Peter Pan wears Indian chief's feathered headdress (27x29cm-11x11in) gouache celluloid. 22-Jun-93 Sotheby's, New York #679
$1700	£1111	Narrator entices us with exceptional tale behind the lamp (31x48cm-12x19in) two cel set-up. 9-Oct-93 Sotheby's, New York #2/R
$1700	£1111	Magic Carpet flies to Aladdin and Abu's rescue dodging falling rocks (32x88cm-13x35in) two cel set-up. 9-Oct-93 Sotheby's, New York #110/R
$1700	£1111	Aladdin bound and gagged sinking to the bottom of the sea (102x32cm-40x13in) two cel set-up. 9-Oct-93 Sotheby's, New York #180/R
$1700	£1141	Mary Poppins, Members of Peraly Band perform at race track to audience (25x38cm-10x15in) i. gouache celluloid on pastel W/C background. 22-Jun-93 Sotheby's, New York #660/R
$1700	£1111	Aladdin with weight tied around ankles sinks to bottom of the sea (43x32cm-17x13in) two cel set-up. 9-Oct-93 Sotheby's, New York #179/R
$1800	£1176	Jafar on horseback follows the scarab to its destination (32x129cm-13x51in) three cel set-up. 9-Oct-93 Sotheby's, New York #4/R
$1800	£1176	Jafar attempting to kill Aladdin (32x43cm-13x17in) two cel set-up. 9-Oct-93 Sotheby's, New York #106/R
$1800	£1208	Peter Pan with outstretched arms (25x30cm-10x12in) gouache celluloid. 22-Jun-93 Sotheby's, New York #729/R
$1800	£1176	Aladdin slides down clothesline with drying laundry (24x63cm-9x25in) two cel set-up. 9-Oct-93 Sotheby's, New York #15/R
$1800	£1176	Aladdin runs after Prince Achmed as he enters palace gates (32x43cm-13x17in) two cel set-up. 9-Oct-93 Sotheby's, New York #57/R
$1800	£1176	Prince Ali discovering that the Magic Lamp is no longer hidden in turban (32x43cm-13x17in) cel. 9-Oct-93 Sotheby's, New York #201/R
$1900	£1275	Peter Pan (30x38cm-12x15in) gouache celluloid. 22-Jun-93 Sotheby's, New York #598/R
$1900	£1242	Abu razzes guard (34x43cm-13x17in) cel. 9-Oct-93 Sotheby's, New York #26
$1900	£1275	Snow White and the Seven Dwarfs, Sleepy looking drowsy (15x14cm-6x6in) gouache trimmed celluloid on wood veneer. 22-Jun-93 Sotheby's, New York #637
$1900	£1275	Ferdinand the Bull as young calf under cork tree looking at mother (20x25cm-8x10in) studio label verso gouache celluloid. 22-Jun-93 Sotheby's, New York #643
$2000	£1307	Abu grabs Aladdin as he is falling trapeze style (49x63cm-19x25in) cel. 9-Oct-93 Sotheby's, New York #32/R
$2000	£1342	Snow White and the Seven Dwarfs, sleepy Dopey clutches pillow (11x15cm-4x6in) exec.1937 gouache celluloid on background. 22-Jun-93 Sotheby's, New York #552
$2000	£1307	Aladdin, firewalker and spectators (32x43cm-13x17in) cel. 9-Oct-93 Sotheby's, New York #40/R
$2000	£1307	Aladdin regaining consciousness and thanks Genie for saving his life (32x43cm-13x17in) two cel set-up. 9-Oct-93 Sotheby's, New York #187/R
$2000	£1307	Assassins gagging Ali (32x43cm-13x17in) cel. 9-Oct-93 Sotheby's, New York #177/R
$2000	£1342	Sleeping Beauty, Flora. Fauna. Merryweather (22x15cm-9x6in) gouache celluloid three framed together. 22-Jun-93 Sotheby's, New York #553/R
$2000	£1342	Sleeping beauty, Maleficent turns to raven perched on her shoulder (20x25cm-8x10in) studio label v.gouache celluloid on lithog. 22-Jun-93 Sotheby's, New York #757
$2000	£1342	Snow White and the Seven Dwarfs, Sneezy looking shyly (17x11cm-7x4in) gouache celluloid on paper with silver stars. 22-Jun-93 Sotheby's, New York #799/R
$2000	£1342	Snow White and the Seven Dwarfs, Happy smiling (15x14cm-6x6in) gouache trimmed celluloid on wood veneer. 22-Jun-93 Sotheby's, New York #816
$2000	£1342	Mickey and Minnie (33x43cm-13x17in) gouache celluloid. 22-Jun-93 Sotheby's, New York #591
$2000	£1342	The Jungle Book, Mowgli smiles and hugs himself (27x25cm-11x10in) gouache celluloid on publication background. 22-Jun-93 Sotheby's, New York #841/R
$2000	£1307	Aladdin pinning Jafar to the ground (27x33cm-11x13in) two cel set-up. 9-Oct-93 Sotheby's, New York #230/R
$2000	£1307	Prince Achmed retorts over his shoulder as he enters palace gates (27x33cm-11x13in) two cel set-up. 9-Oct-93 Sotheby's, New York #56/R
$2000	£1342	Snow White and the Seven Dwarfs, Grumpy raises arms in complaint (15x14cm-6x6in) gouache celluloid on wood veneer background. 22-Jun-93 Sotheby's, New York #681
$2000	£1342	Jiminy in rags peeking out from behind curtain (14x13cm-6x5in) gouache celluloid on background. 22-Jun-93 Sotheby's, New York #644/R

517

WALT DISNEY STUDIOS (20th C) American-cont.

$2100	£1373	Jafar and Iago's eyes meet as they hear conditions by Cave of Wonders (32x43cm-13x17in) cel. 9-Oct-93 Sotheby's, New York #6/R
$2100	£1373	Aladdin trapped in Jafar's coil (32x43cm-13x17in) cel. 9-Oct-93 Sotheby's, New York #237/R
$2100	£1373	Townswoman screams as Aladdin slides towards her open window (49x63cm-19x25in) four cel set-up. 9-Oct-93 Sotheby's, New York #16/R
$2200	£1438	Aladdin looking up in horror (27x33cm-11x13in) two cel set-up. 9-Oct-93 Sotheby's, New York #214/R
$2200	£1438	Assassin tying Magic Carpet to tree (32x60cm-13x24in) two cel set-up. 9-Oct-93 Sotheby's, New York #176/R
$2250	£1510	Winnie the Pooh and Gopher. Kanga smiling, studio label gouache celluloid on litho two. 22-Jun-93 Sotheby's, New York #730
$2250	£1510	Snow White and the Seven Dwarfs, Doc with candle (18x13cm-7x5in) gouache celluloid on background. 22-Jun-93 Sotheby's, New York #672
$2250	£1510	Sleeping Beauty, Maleficent as the dragon (25x41cm-10x16in) gouache celluloid. 22-Jun-93 Sotheby's, New York #810
$2250	£1471	Aladdin and turban with magic lamp behind him at the bottom of the sea (32x43cm-13x17in) two cel set-up. 9-Oct-93 Sotheby's, New York #181/R
$2250	£1510	Snow White and the Seven Dwarfs, Doc raising one hand (15x14cm-6x6in) gouache celluloid on wood veneer background. 22-Jun-93 Sotheby's, New York #663
$2280	£1500	Snow White and the Seven Dwarfs, Dopey carries dustpan full of diamonds (18x18cm-7x7in) d.1937 gouache on celluloid on airbrush. 5-Apr-93 Christie's, S. Kensington #323/R
$2300	£1503	Abu steals melon for breakfast (32x43cm-13x17in) cel. 9-Oct-93 Sotheby's, New York #70/R
$2300	£1503	Aladdin leaps over man on bed of nails as guards follow (32x63cm-13x25in) cel. 9-Oct-93 Sotheby's, New York #37/R
$2400	£1569	Aladdin drops backwards into the cave (32x43cm-13x17in) two cel set-up. 9-Oct-93 Sotheby's, New York #107/R
$2400	£1569	Razoul yanks Aladdin out of his sheet and holds him by his vest (32x43cm-13x17in) cel. 9-Oct-93 Sotheby's, New York #22/R
$2400	£1569	Razoul throws Aladdin into group of guards (32x56cm-13x22in) three cel set-up. 9-Oct-93 Sotheby's, New York #82/R
$2400	£1569	Abu shakes off the mud (27x33cm-11x13in) three cel set-up. 9-Oct-93 Sotheby's, New York #54/R
$2400	£1569	Aladdin surrounded by three dancing girls (32x87cm-13x34in) cel. 9-Oct-93 Sotheby's, New York #125/R
$2400	£1569	Magic Carpet struggles to free itself from under the rock and succeeds (32x44cm-13x17in) four cel set-up. 9-Oct-93 Sotheby's, New York #109/R
$2500	£1678	Cinderella tying hair up in ribbon. Cinderella walking (18x18cm-7x7in) gouache celluloid two. 22-Jun-93 Sotheby's, New York #600/R
$2500	£1678	Alice in Wonderland, Hookah-smoking-caterpillar lounges on leaf (27x31cm-11x12in) gouache celluloid. 22-Jun-93 Sotheby's, New York #554/R
$2500	£1634	Abu has come to Aladdin's rescue who is chained in the dungeon (32x43cm-13x17in) three cel set-up. 9-Oct-93 Sotheby's, New York #87/R
$2500	£1678	Peter Pan executes flying jack-knife over Never-Never-Land (22x25cm-9x10in) exec.1953 gouache celluloid on background. 22-Jun-93 Sotheby's, New York #526/R
$2500	£1634	Sultan on Carpet zips under Iago (32x117cm-13x46in) two cel set-up. 9-Oct-93 Sotheby's, New York #153/R
$2500	£1634	Jafar pushing Prince Ali's entourage out of the palace (32x46cm-13x18in) three cel set-up. 9-Oct-93 Sotheby's, New York #150/R
$2500	£1678	Pinocchio, Jiminy Cricket swinging from umbrella (20x19cm-8x7in) gouache trimmed celluloid on background. 22-Jun-93 Sotheby's, New York #550/R
$2500	£1678	Mickey's Christmas Carol, Mickey Mouse, Scrooge Mc Duck, Jiminy Cricket (29x39cm-11x15in) gouache celluloid three. 22-Jun-93 Sotheby's, New York #619
$2500	£1678	Pinocchio, Jiminy Cricket walking head on smiling (13x11cm-5x4in) gouache trimmed celluloid on background. 22-Jun-93 Sotheby's, New York #703/R
$2500	£1678	Fantasia, lily pond (25x30cm-10x12in) pastel. 22-Jun-93 Sotheby's, New York #632/R
$2500	£1678	Fantasia, Ben Ali Gator and Hyacinth Hippo performing Dance of the Hours (25x30cm-10x12in) studio st.i.d.Jul.5,1939 graphite three. 22-Jun-93 Sotheby's, New York #593
$2500	£1678	Lady and the Tramp, Joe presents Tramp with tray of bones (19x19cm-7x7in) gouache trimmed celluloid. 22-Jun-93 Sotheby's, New York #564/R
$2500	£1634	Guards turn to see Aladdin escaping and chase him (32x77cm-13x30in) cel. 9-Oct-93 Sotheby's, New York #36/R
$2500	£1678	Snow White and the Seven Dwarfs, Bashful tugging shyly at his beard (15x14cm-6x6in) gouache trimmed celluloid on wood veneer. 22-Jun-93 Sotheby's, New York #805
$2500	£1634	Abu as elephant whistling for the Magic Carpet (32x43cm-13x17in) cel. 9-Oct-93 Sotheby's, New York #202/R
$2500	£1634	Jafar dressed in Sultan's robes (32x43cm-13x17in) cel. 9-Oct-93 Sotheby's, New York #204/R
$2500	£1678	Snow White and the Seven Dwarfs, Doc holding candle (18x13cm-7x5in) gouache celluloid. 22-Jun-93 Sotheby's, New York #610
$2500	£1678	The Jungle Book, Shere Khan tries to make way through burning branches (32x41cm-13x16in) i.gouache celluloid two-cel set up on background. 22-Jun-93 Sotheby's, New York #743/R
$2500	£1634	Aladdin tumbles backwards down into the cave (32x43cm-13x17in) three cel set-up. 9-Oct-93 Sotheby's, New York #108/R
$2500	£1634	Aladdin finding Abu in the snow (27x33cm-11x13in) cel. 9-Oct-93 Sotheby's, New York #209/R
$2500	£1634	Jafar growing rapidly and pushing up against the ceiling (32x43cm-13x17in) two cel set-up. 9-Oct-93 Sotheby's, New York #242/R

WALT DISNEY STUDIOS (20th C) American-cont.

$2500	£1678	Snow White and the Seven Dwarfs, Dopey watches fly (23x22cm-9x9in) gouache trimmed celluloid on background. 22-Jun-93 Sotheby's, New York #835
$2500	£1678	Trick or Treat, Huey, Dewey and Louie ride on witch's broom (19x25cm-7x10in) exec.1952 gouache celluloid on photgraphic repro. 22-Jun-93 Sotheby's, New York #547
$2500	£1678	Snow White and the Seven Dwarfs, Dopey hitting cymbal (23x20cm-9x8in) gouache celluloid on wood veneer. 22-Jun-93 Sotheby's, New York #849/R
$2584	£1700	Snow White and the Seven Dwarfs, Grumpy sits on barrel (20x13cm-8x5in) d.1937 gouache partial celluloid on wood veneer. 5-Apr-93 Christie's, S. Kensington #326/R
$2600	£1699	Genie turning into submarine shooting to surface with Aladdin in his arms (102x32cm-40x13in) two cel set-up. 9-Oct-93 Sotheby's, New York #185/R
$2600	£1699	Aladdin and the guards on the rooftop (32x43cm-13x17in) cel. 9-Oct-93 Sotheby's, New York #127/R
$2600	£1699	Iago perched on Jafar's shoulder has one of his outbursts (32x152cm-13x60in) cel. 9-Oct-93 Sotheby's, New York #67/R
$2600	£1699	Aladdin and Abu weave their way through the marketplace (27x33cm-11x13in) cel. 9-Oct-93 Sotheby's, New York #43/R
$2600	£1699	Sultan force feeds Iago cracker (32x43cm-13x17in) cel. 9-Oct-93 Sotheby's, New York #65/R
$2600	£1699	Abu as elephant tied up in net hanging from tree next to two guards (32x43cm-13x17in) three cel set-up. 9-Oct-93 Sotheby's, New York #174/R
$2700	£1765	Woman opens door behind Aladdin and picks him up (27x33cm-11x13in) cel. 9-Oct-93 Sotheby's, New York #38/R
$2700	£1765	Rajah looks sad as Jasmine sneaks away from the palace (32x43cm-13x17in) cel. 9-Oct-93 Sotheby's, New York #68/R
$2700	£1765	Iago runs around treadmill to generate storm for Jafar's evil purpose (32x43cm-13x17in) two cel set-up. 9-Oct-93 Sotheby's, New York #73/R
$2700	£1765	Aladdin stands at the closed gates of the palace (32x43cm-13x17in) cel. 9-Oct-93 Sotheby's, New York #58/R
$2750	£1846	Fantasia, dance of the mushrooms from Nutcracker Suite (16x17cm-6x7in) studio st. gouache celluloid on background. 22-Jun-93 Sotheby's, New York #734/R
$2750	£1798	Prince Ali floating on Magic Carpet with Jasmine and Rajah on balcony (32x43cm-13x17in) two cel set-up. 9-Oct-93 Sotheby's, New York #164/R
$2750	£1798	Jafar extends his hand to Aladdin to close the deal (32x43cm-13x17in) cel. 9-Oct-93 Sotheby's, New York #94/R
$2750	£1798	Sultan being hypnotized by Jafar's staff (32x43cm-13x17in) cel. 9-Oct-93 Sotheby's, New York #142/R
$2750	£1846	Fantasia, dancing blossoms from The Nutcracker Suite (25x30cm-10x12in) pastel set of five. 22-Jun-93 Sotheby's, New York #763
$2750	£1798	Prince Ali going to the Princess to win her heart (32x43cm-13x17in) three cel set-up. 9-Oct-93 Sotheby's, New York #157/R
$2750	£1846	Dumbo asleep cradled by tree branch with Timothy Mouse nestled in trunk (18x25cm-7x10in) studio st. gouache celluloid on background. 22-Jun-93 Sotheby's, New York #779/R
$2750	£1798	Aladdin trying to impress Jasmine with words of advice from buzzing bee (32x43cm-13x17in) two cel set-up. 9-Oct-93 Sotheby's, New York #163/R
$2750	£1798	Jafar grabbing Iago's leg (27x96cm-11x38in) cel. 9-Oct-93 Sotheby's, New York #244/R
$2750	£1846	Bambi stands in the meadow on all fours looking at Thumper (34x37cm-13x15in) gouache on celluloid on W/C col.chk background. 12-Dec-93 Butterfield & Butterfield, Los Angeles #1160/R
$2750	£1846	The Sword and the Stone, Dripping wet Merlin laughs (23x32cm-9x13in) exec.1963 gouache celluloid on W/C background. 22-Jun-93 Sotheby's, New York #527/R
$2750	£1798	Prince Ali onstage in spotlight (32x43cm-13x17in) two cel set-up. 9-Oct-93 Sotheby's, New York #198/R
$2750	£1798	Aladdin on the ground holding sword (27x33cm-11x13in) cel. 9-Oct-93 Sotheby's, New York #235/R
$2750	£1846	Lady and the Tramp (25x16cm-10x6in) gouache celluloid on W/C background. 22-Jun-93 Sotheby's, New York #721/R
$2750	£1798	Aladdin and Abu descending curtain (43x32cm-17x13in) two cel set-up. 9-Oct-93 Sotheby's, New York #221/R
$2750	£1846	Dumbo with Timothy Mouse in hat swoops through the air following crows (20x22cm-8x9in) studio st.gouache celluloid multi-cel set up. 22-Jun-93 Sotheby's, New York #761/R
$2750	£1846	Sleeping Beauty, Maleficent patting raven perched on her staff (18x25cm-7x10in) studio label verso gouache celluloid. 22-Jun-93 Sotheby's, New York #773
$2800	£1830	Iago upset at the turn of events (32x95cm-13x37in) cel. 9-Oct-93 Sotheby's, New York #9/R
$2800	£1830	Aladdin with Abu on his back runs into guard (32x88cm-13x35in) cel. 9-Oct-93 Sotheby's, New York #25/R
$2800	£1830	Abu hitting Iago over the head with fruit bowl (36x52cm-14x20in) cel. 9-Oct-93 Sotheby's, New York #229/R
$2800	£1830	Aladdin sitting in the mud insults Prince Achmed (27x33cm-11x13in) cel. 9-Oct-93 Sotheby's, New York #55/R
$2800	£1830	Aladdin runs down steps which turn into steep slide (57x32cm-22x13in) cel. 9-Oct-93 Sotheby's, New York #100/R
$2800	£1830	Jasmine is thrown to the ground by Razoul (32x43cm-13x17in) cel. 9-Oct-93 Sotheby's, New York #81/R
$2800	£1830	Aladdin balances on top of Column A amidst platters of food (49x63cm-19x25in) cel. 9-Oct-93 Sotheby's, New York #122/R
$2900	£1895	Genie as sheep walking away with a warning (32x43cm-13x17in) cel. 9-Oct-93 Sotheby's, New York #138/R
$2900	£1895	Aladdin stops mid-bite (27x33cm-11x13in) cel. 9-Oct-93 Sotheby's, New York #48/R

WALT DISNEY STUDIOS (20th C) American-cont.

$2900	£1895	Aladdin pulls curtain to look at palace (27x33cm-11x13in) two cel set-up. 9-Oct-93 Sotheby's, New York #62/R
$2900	£1895	Aladdin and Abu look up at the palace after confrontation with Prince (32x43cm-13x17in) cel. 9-Oct-93 Sotheby's, New York #59/R
$3000	£1961	Magic Carpet flying to tower where Aladdin and Abu have been thrown (32x43cm-13x17in) cel. 9-Oct-93 Sotheby's, New York #207/R
$3000	£2013	Alice in Wonderland, colourful chorus of pansies sing (20x24cm-8x9in) gouache celluloid. 22-Jun-93 Sotheby's, New York #569/R
$3000	£1961	Aladdin ducks as sword strikes post next to his head (27x33cm-11x13in) cel. 9-Oct-93 Sotheby's, New York #27/R
$3000	£2013	Winnie the Pooh and Roo outside Piglet's house (33x38cm-13x15in) gouache celluloid two cel-set up on W/C. 22-Jun-93 Sotheby's, New York #756/R
$3000	£1961	Prince Ali flying on the Magic Carpet (32x43cm-13x17in) cel. 9-Oct-93 Sotheby's, New York #151/R
$3000	£2013	The Jungle Book, Mowgli and seated Bagheera. King Louie (25x20cm-10x8in) gouache celluloid one multi-cel set up two. 22-Jun-93 Sotheby's, New York #808
$3000	£2013	Winnie the Pooh dancing. Kanga. Pooh talking to Gopher, gouache celluloid on lithograph three. 22-Jun-93 Sotheby's, New York #595/R
$3000	£1961	Genie swirls up smokily away from Aladdin, Abu and Magic Carpet (32x43cm-13x17in) two cel set-up. 9-Oct-93 Sotheby's, New York #118/R
$3000	£1587	Dance of the mushrooms from Fantasia (28x30cm-11x12in) mono. gouache celluloid air brushed two. 11-Sep-92 Skinner, Bolton #292/R
$3000	£1961	Aladdin and Jafar in disguise (32x102cm-13x40in) cel. 9-Oct-93 Sotheby's, New York #91/R
$3000	£1961	Aladdin appearing on Jasmine's balcony as Prince Ali Ababwa (32x43cm-13x17in) three cel set-up. 9-Oct-93 Sotheby's, New York #158/R
$3000	£1961	Jafar transformed from snake into genie (152x32cm-60x13in) two cel set-up. 9-Oct-93 Sotheby's, New York #240/R
$3000	£1961	Iago perches on the top of Jafar's cobra headed staff (49x152cm-19x60in) cel. 9-Oct-93 Sotheby's, New York #136/R
$3000	£1961	Aladdin draped in borrowed clothes holds his loaf of bread (27x152cm-11x60in) cel. 9-Oct-93 Sotheby's, New York #20/R
$3000	£1961	Ali and Magic Carpet struggle against assassins (32x43cm-13x17in) two cel set-up. 9-Oct-93 Sotheby's, New York #175/R
$3000	£2013	Peter Pan, Captain Hook wrapping himself around snout of crocodile (15x23cm-6x9in) gouache celluloid two-cel set up. 22-Jun-93 Sotheby's, New York #751/R
$3000	£1961	Aladdin staring in awe and Abu cowering with fear (32x43cm-13x17in) cel. 9-Oct-93 Sotheby's, New York #95/R
$3000	£1961	Aladdin and Abu fly over exploding lava on Magic Carpet (32x43cm-13x17in) four cel set-up. 9-Oct-93 Sotheby's, New York #103/R
$3000	£2013	Dumbo gleefully follows mother into tent (22x27cm-9x11in) studio st. gouache celluloid on background. 22-Jun-93 Sotheby's, New York #664/R
$3000	£1961	Aladdin wrestling with Jafar trying to take magical staff (32x43cm-13x17in) two cel set-up. 9-Oct-93 Sotheby's, New York #228/R
$3000	£1961	Iago spits out cracker that Sultan has stuffed into his mouth (27x33cm-11x13in) two cel set-up. 9-Oct-93 Sotheby's, New York #141/R
$3040	£2000	Snow White with the Seven Dwarfs and forest animals (28x38cm-11x15in) graphite col.pencil. 5-Apr-93 Christie's, S. Kensington #317
$3100	£2067	Grumpy playing the organ, from Snow White and Seven Dwarfs, 1937 (15x15cm-6x6in) gouache on celluloid on airbrush wood background. 26-May-94 Freeman Fine Arts, Philadelphia #240
$3100	£2067	Dopey holding a pick in right hand - from Snow White and the Seven Dwarfs (20x20cm-8x8in) gouache on multi-cell set up airbrush background. 26-May-94 Freeman Fine Arts, Philadelphia #237
$3250	£2124	Jafar and Iago (32x46cm-13x18in) two cel set-up. 9-Oct-93 Sotheby's, New York #8/R
$3250	£2124	Aladdin dressed in sheet clutching loaf of bread talks to two townswomen (34x88cm-13x35in) cel. 9-Oct-93 Sotheby's, New York #21/R
$3250	£2181	Goofy demonstrating the Art of Skiing, init. exec.1941 gouache celluloid on cel two. 22-Jun-93 Sotheby's, New York #541/R
$3250	£2124	Aladdin about to wish for something outrageous (27x33cm-11x13in) cel. 9-Oct-93 Sotheby's, New York #252/R
$3250	£2181	Dumbo with Timothy in his hat and five crows sitting on head and ear (20x25cm-8x10in) exec.1941 st.init. gouache celluloid. 22-Jun-93 Sotheby's, New York #531/R
$3250	£2124	Sultan standing on the balcony (32x43cm-13x17in) three cel set-up. 9-Oct-93 Sotheby's, New York #145/R
$3250	£2124	Aladdin talking to Genie on palace balcony (27x33cm-11x13in) cel. 9-Oct-93 Sotheby's, New York #248/R
$3250	£2181	Fantasia, Chinese mushroom dance from Nutcracker Suite (17x20cm-7x8in) studio st. gouache celluloid multi-cel on backg. 22-Jun-93 Sotheby's, New York #804/R
$3250	£2181	Snow White and the Seven Dwarfs, Grumpy, Bashful and Doc in cottage (23x23cm-9x9in) studio st. gouache celluloid muti-cel. 22-Jun-93 Sotheby's, New York #747/R
$3250	£2124	Aladdin and Abu slide down canopy (32x43cm-13x17in) cel. 9-Oct-93 Sotheby's, New York #34/R
$3250	£2124	Jafar as cobra (32x43cm-13x17in) cel. 9-Oct-93 Sotheby's, New York #234/R
$3250	£2124	Abu looks down terrified (32x43cm-13x17in) cel. 9-Oct-93 Sotheby's, New York #102
$3500	£2349	Bambi, Bambi and Flower meet nose to nose (20x27cm-8x11in) gouache multi-cel on background. 22-Jun-93 Sotheby's, New York #649
$3500	£2349	Snow White and the Seven Dwarfs, Bashful and Happy (18x20cm-7x8in) studio st.verso gouache celluloid on background. 22-Jun-93 Sotheby's, New York #583/R

WALT DISNEY STUDIOS (20th C) American-cont.

$3500	£2349	Water Babies go waterskiing on backs of fish (19x27cm-7x11in) gouache celluloid on background. 22-Jun-93 Sotheby's, New York #581/R
$3500	£2333	The Prince leads Snow White, seated upon his horse, towards the horizon (18x23cm-7x9in) gouache on celluloid on W/C background. 26-May-94 Freeman Fine Arts, Philadelphia #239
$3500	£2349	Sleeping beauty, Maleficent and raven plot against Briar Rose (18x24cm-7x9in) gouache celluloid on lithographic background. 22-Jun-93 Sotheby's, New York #638
$3500	£2349	Mickey's Delayed Date, Mickey standing with envelope in hand (25x30cm-10x12in) gouache celluloid on W/C background. 22-Jun-93 Sotheby's, New York #737
$3500	£2288	Prince Ali on balcony (32x43cm-13x17in) two cel set-up. 9-Oct-93 Sotheby's, New York #160/R
$3500	£2349	Snow White and the Seven Dwarfs, Doc, Bashful and Sneezy (19x24cm-7x9in) label verso gouache celluloid on wood veneer. 22-Jun-93 Sotheby's, New York #847/R
$3500	£2288	Abu defiantly starts to eat bread (27x33cm-11x13in) cel. 9-Oct-93 Sotheby's, New York #49/R
$3500	£2349	Snow White and the Seven Dwarfs, model sheet of Snow White's expressions (23x29cm-9x11in) i. graphite orange pencil. 22-Jun-93 Sotheby's, New York #609/R
$3500	£2288	Aladdin and Abu scheme to get out of cave without using up a wish (32x43cm-13x17in) cel. 9-Oct-93 Sotheby's, New York #131/R
$3500	£2288	Aladdin, Abu and snake charmer (32x43cm-13x17in) two cel set-up. 9-Oct-93 Sotheby's, New York #41/R
$3500	£2288	Aladdin's big heart wins over his big hunger (27x33cm-11x13in) cel. 9-Oct-93 Sotheby's, New York #50/R
$3500	£2288	Abu reaches out to grab Aladdin (27x33cm-11x13in) cel. 9-Oct-93 Sotheby's, New York #31/R
$3500	£2288	Genie shrugging shoulders in dismay (32x43cm-13x17in) cel. 9-Oct-93 Sotheby's, New York #238/R
$3648	£2400	Dunbo being pushed off cliff by five crows (51x25cm-20x10in) d.1941 gouache on celluloid on W/C. 5-Apr-93 Christie's, S. Kensington #255/R
$3750	£2451	Jafar in disguise draws Aladdin further into his plan (32x43cm-13x17in) cel. 9-Oct-93 Sotheby's, New York #93/R
$3750	£2451	Guards taking Jafar and Iago away (32x43cm-13x17in) cel. 9-Oct-93 Sotheby's, New York #190/R
$3750	£2517	Dumbo swoops through the air with Timothy Mouse in hat, crows following (18x23cm-7x9in) studio st. gouache celluloid on background. 22-Jun-93 Sotheby's, New York #852/R
$3750	£2451	Abu runs off frantically (32x102cm-13x40in) five cel set-up. 9-Oct-93 Sotheby's, New York #98/R
$3750	£2451	Aladdin stunned (27x33cm-11x13in) cel. 9-Oct-93 Sotheby's, New York #224/R
$3750	£2451	Jafar noticing Aladdin's reflection in Jasmine's crown (27x33cm-11x13in) cel. 9-Oct-93 Sotheby's, New York #225/R
$3750	£2517	Snow White and the Seven Dwarfs, Snow White pets sad blue bird (18x23cm-7x9in) gouache trimmed celluloid on background. 22-Jun-93 Sotheby's, New York #689/R
$3750	£2451	Jasmine, Iago, Sultan and Prince Ali exposing Jafar as traitor (32x43cm-13x17in) cel. 9-Oct-93 Sotheby's, New York #189/R
$3750	£2451	Abu and the Magic Carpet (32x43cm-13x17in) three cel set-up. 9-Oct-93 Sotheby's, New York #99/R
$3750	£2451	Jafar holding lamp (27x33cm-11x13in) cel. 9-Oct-93 Sotheby's, New York #218/R
$4000	£2614	Aladdin, Abu and Magic Carpet make their way to entrance of cave (32x81cm-13x32in) cel. 9-Oct-93 Sotheby's, New York #105/R
$4000	£2685	Snow White and the Seven Dwarfs, Sneezy, Happy and Bashful make music (14x16cm-6x6in) studio label v. gouache celluloid on wood veneer. 22-Jun-93 Sotheby's, New York #741
$4000	£2614	Aladdin explaining to Genie why he can't free him (32x43cm-13x17in) cel. 9-Oct-93 Sotheby's, New York #195/R
$4000	£2614	Prince Ali lying on the Magic Carpet staring up at balcony (27x33cm-11x13in) cel. 9-Oct-93 Sotheby's, New York #173/R
$4000	£2116	Mickey mouse as the sorcerer's apprentice from Fantasia (20x23cm-8x9in) st. gouache celluloid air brushed. 11-Sep-92 Skinner, Bolton #297/R
$4000	£2614	Jasmine throws wine into Jafar's face (32x43cm-13x17in) two cel set-up. 9-Oct-93 Sotheby's, New York #216/R
$4000	£2614	Genie framing hands like television screen and Aladdin walking away (32x43cm-13x17in) cel. 9-Oct-93 Sotheby's, New York #194/R
$4000	£2614	Aladdin is magically lifted into the air and placed onto a rock (32x43cm-13x17in) cel. 9-Oct-93 Sotheby's, New York #115/R
$4000	£2614	Aladdin and Abu scheme to get some food (32x102cm-13x40in) cel. 9-Oct-93 Sotheby's, New York #69/R
$4000	£2614	Genie as bee taking a firey dive (32x43cm-13x17in) cel. 9-Oct-93 Sotheby's, New York #162/R
$4000	£2614	Aladdin and Jafar holding Iagos leg as he is pulled into the lamp (49x63cm-19x25in) cel. 9-Oct-93 Sotheby's, New York #245/R
$4000	£2685	The Little Mermaid, Dolphin swims playfully among sea flora (29x86cm-11x34in) multi-cel set up on pan gouache background. 22-Jun-93 Sotheby's, New York #768/R
$4000	£2685	Merbaby plays on sea horse and another merbaby looks on (25x29cm-10x11in) gouache celluloid two-cel set up W/C background. 22-Jun-93 Sotheby's, New York #715/R
$4000	£2614	Jafar and Iago unhappy with results of meeting with Sultan and Jasmine (32x43cm-13x17in) two cel set-up. 9-Oct-93 Sotheby's, New York #134/R
$4000	£2614	Aladdin stands in spotlight as dancing girl leans over to kiss him (50x102cm-20x40in) cel. 9-Oct-93 Sotheby's, New York #126/R
$4000	£2614	Abu takes jewel of the forbidden treasure (32x43cm-13x17in) three cel set-up. 9-Oct-93 Sotheby's, New York #97/R
$4000	£2614	Jasmine and the Sultan stripped off his robes (32x43cm-13x17in) cel. 9-Oct-93 Sotheby's, New York #203/R

WALT DISNEY STUDIOS (20th C) American-cont.

$4000	£2614	Jafar and Iago in Jafar's lab where artificial storm is generated (32x59cm-13x23in) three cel set-up. 9-Oct-93 Sotheby's, New York #74/R
$4250	£2778	Jafar's spell is broken and the Sultan runs to the balcony (32x43cm-13x17in) cel. 9-Oct-93 Sotheby's, New York #144/R
$4250	£2778	Abu turned into wind-up toy and lamp (32x43cm-13x17in) three cel set-up. 9-Oct-93 Sotheby's, New York #231/R
$4250	£2778	Abu and Aladdin steering the Magic Carpet through the cave (49x109cm-19x43in) cel. 9-Oct-93 Sotheby's, New York #104/R
$4250	£2778	Genie gasping (27x33cm-11x13in) cel. 9-Oct-93 Sotheby's, New York #226/R
$4250	£2778	Jasmine telling off her father, Jafar and Prince Ali (27x33cm-11x13in) two cel set-up. 9-Oct-93 Sotheby's, New York #156/R
$4250	£2778	Aladdin bends over to kiss dancing girls replaced by Genie's big face (49x102cm-19x40in) cel. 9-Oct-93 Sotheby's, New York #127/R
$4250	£2853	Pinocchio with donkey ears under water and exploring (19x25cm-7x10in) graphite W/C double-sided. 22-Jun-93 Sotheby's, New York #651/R
$4250	£2778	Aladdin kicks over barrel to escape with Abu from the guards (32x43cm-13x17in) cel. 9-Oct-93 Sotheby's, New York #28/R
$4250	£2853	Snow white fetching water from the wishing well as birds gather round (23x27cm-9x11in) gouache on celluloid matted with label verso. 12-Dec-93 Butterfield & Butterfield, Los Angeles #1157/R
$4250	£2778	Abu frees Aladdin (32x43cm-13x17in) cel. 9-Oct-93 Sotheby's, New York #90/R
$4250	£2778	Genie in the sea seeing his master in trouble (27x33cm-11x13in) two cel set-up. 9-Oct-93 Sotheby's, New York #183/R
$4256	£2800	Donald's Golf Game, Donald shoos bird off tree (18x25cm-7x10in) d.1938 gouache on partial celluloids on W/C. 5-Apr-93 Christie's, S. Kensington #297/R
$4500	£2941	Jasmine discusses Aladdin's fate with Jafar (32x86cm-13x34in) cel. 9-Oct-93 Sotheby's, New York #84/R
$4500	£2941	Rajah attacking Jafar (32x43cm-13x17in) cel. 9-Oct-93 Sotheby's, New York #205/R
$4500	£2941	Jasmine watching from balcony (32x43cm-13x17in) two cel set-up. 9-Oct-93 Sotheby's, New York #147/R
$4500	£2941	Genie spins around like tornado and sucks back into the lamp (49x63cm-19x25in) two cel set-up. 9-Oct-93 Sotheby's, New York #130/R
$4500	£3020	Snow White and the Seven Dwarfs, dwarfs on way to mine (13x18cm-5x7in) gouache celluloid on wood veneer. 22-Jun-93 Sotheby's, New York #824
$4500	£2942	Abu gives his bread to the children (29x39cm-11x15in) cel. 9-Oct-93 Sotheby's, New York #51/R
$4750	£3105	Aladdin amazed at the trouble stealing a loaf of bread gets him into (32x43cm-13x17in) cel. 9-Oct-93 Sotheby's, New York #11/R
$4750	£3188	Pinocchio skips with school books under arm and apple (18x16cm-7x6in) gouache trimmed celluloid. 22-Jun-93 Sotheby's, New York #742/R
$4750	£3105	Aladdin helps Jasmine up onto the rooftop where he and Abu live (49x84cm-19x33in) cel. 9-Oct-93 Sotheby's, New York #76/R
$4750	£3105	Genie transforms into turkey on platter that he has presented to Aladdin (32x51cm-13x20in) two cel set-up. 9-Oct-93 Sotheby's, New York #121/R
$4750	£3105	Jasmine confronts Jafar (32x43cm-13x17in) cel. 9-Oct-93 Sotheby's, New York #83/R
$4750	£3105	Abu scolds Aladdin about infatuation with Jasmine (32x43cm-13x17in) two cel set-up. 9-Oct-93 Sotheby's, New York #89/R
$4750	£3188	Pinocchio smiles at seahorses underwater (20cm-8in circular) gouache celluloid on background. 22-Jun-93 Sotheby's, New York #666/R
$4750	£3105	Aladdin and Abu land safely with loaf of bread using carpet as parachute (89x49cm-35x19in) three cel set-up. 9-Oct-93 Sotheby's, New York #47/R
$4750	£3105	Aladdin cradling Jasmine after breaking the hourglass (32x43cm-13x17in) three cel set-up. 9-Oct-93 Sotheby's, New York #243/R
$4750	£3105	Aladdin surrounded by Razoul and the guards (32x89cm-13x35in) cel. 9-Oct-93 Sotheby's, New York #39/R
$4750	£3105	Aladdin surrounded by trio of indignant Harem girls (32x116cm-13x46in) two cel set-up. 9-Oct-93 Sotheby's, New York #53/R
$5000	£3268	Aladdin, Jasmine and Abu jump off the roof and into the mill (32x43cm-13x17in) three cel set-up. 9-Oct-93 Sotheby's, New York #80/R
$5000	£3268	Jafar and Iago reprimanded by the Sultan (32x46cm-13x18in) cel. 9-Oct-93 Sotheby's, New York #133/R
$5000	£3268	Genie sings with arms crossed across chest (32x43cm-13x17in) two cel set-up. 9-Oct-93 Sotheby's, New York #119/R
$5000	£3268	Abu hops onto Aladdin's knee and then jumps off (49x63cm-19x25in) cel. 9-Oct-93 Sotheby's, New York #88/R
$5000	£3268	Jafar lies to Jasmine (32x43cm-13x17in) cel. 9-Oct-93 Sotheby's, New York #85/R
$5000	£3268	Aladdin salutes Abu who has come to his rescue (27x32cm-11x13in) cel. 9-Oct-93 Sotheby's, New York #24/R
$5000	£3268	Jasmine takes Aladdin's hand in hopes of escape (32x43cm-13x17in) cel. 9-Oct-93 Sotheby's, New York #79
$5000	£3268	Giant Genie sings and dances (84x49cm-33x19in) two cel set-up. 9-Oct-93 Sotheby's, New York #124/R
$5000	£3268	Genie about to execute final wish for Aladdin (32x43cm-13x17in) two cel set-up. 9-Oct-93 Sotheby's, New York #250/R
$5000	£3268	Genie asked by Aladdin about his three wishes (32x86cm-13x34in) cel. 9-Oct-93 Sotheby's, New York #137/R
$5000	£3268	Jafar walking through wall of flames (34x44cm-13x17in) three cel set-up. 9-Oct-93 Sotheby's, New York #232/R
$5000	£3268	Aladdin and Abu climb up ladder to roof of building where they live (27x33cm-11x13in) two cel set-up. 9-Oct-93 Sotheby's, New York #60/R
$5000	£3268	Aladdin and Abu flying on the Magic Carpet (39x67cm-15x26in) three cel set-up. 9-Oct-93 Sotheby's, New York #210/R

WALT DISNEY STUDIOS (20th C) American-cont.

$5168	£3400	Peter Pan, Wendy prepares to sew Peter Pan's shadow back (25x30cm-10x12in) s.i.d.1953 gouache on celluloid on W/C. 5-Apr-93 Christie's, S. Kensington #189/R
$5500	£3595	Genie demonstrating his cramped living quarters (32x43cm-13x17in) cel. 9-Oct-93 Sotheby's, New York #140/R
$5500	£3595	Reluctant and despondent Genie awaits Jafar's final wish (32x43cm-13x17in) cel. 9-Oct-93 Sotheby's, New York #217/R
$5500	£3595	Aladdin reaching for the lamp and Jasmine distracting Jafar (32x43cm-13x17in) cel. 9-Oct-93 Sotheby's, New York #223/R
$5500	£3691	Jiminy advises Pinocchio (21x24cm-8x9in) gouache trimmed celluloid on background. 22-Jun-93 Sotheby's, New York #827/R
$5500	£3595	Aladdin and Abu amazed by Jasmine's athletic prowess (32x43cm-13x17in) two cel set-up. 9-Oct-93 Sotheby's, New York #78/R
$5500	£3595	Prince Ali and Jasmine flying on Magic Carpet descending (32x152cm-13x60in) two cel set-up. 9-Oct-93 Sotheby's, New York #170/R
$5500	£3595	Aladdin, Abu, body builder and townfolk (32x69cm-13x27in) three cel set-up. 9-Oct-93 Sotheby's, New York #35/R
$5500	£3595	Sultan landing beside Prince Ali and Jafar after ride on Magic Carpet (49x152cm-19x60in) three cel set-up. 9-Oct-93 Sotheby's, New York #154/R
$5500	£3595	Genie retreating to lamp (90x49cm-35x19in) two cel set-up. 9-Oct-93 Sotheby's, New York #196/R
$5500	£3595	Jasmine horrified by final command given to the Genie (32x43cm-13x17in) three cel set-up. 9-Oct-93 Sotheby's, New York #219/R
$5500	£3595	Genie placing Aladdin on the ground (32x43cm-13x17in) two cel set-up. 9-Oct-93 Sotheby's, New York #186/R
$5500	£3595	Aladdin slides down rocks (109x49cm-43x19in) two cel set-up. 9-Oct-93 Sotheby's, New York #101/R
$6000	£3922	Prince Ali, Jasmine and the Sultan (32x43cm-13x17in) cel. 9-Oct-93 Sotheby's, New York #192/R
$6000	£3922	Jafar asserting his power of the Genie (32x43cm-13x17in) two cel set-up. 9-Oct-93 Sotheby's, New York #200/R
$6000	£3922	Jafar and Jasmine sitting down upon hearing bad news regarding Aladdin (32x86cm-13x34in) two cel set-up. 9-Oct-93 Sotheby's, New York #86/R
$6000	£3922	Jasmine pleading with Jafar (32x43cm-13x17in) cel. 9-Oct-93 Sotheby's, New York #215/R
$6000	£4027	The Pointer, Mickey out camping with Pluto (20x27cm-8x11in) gouache celluloid multi-cel set up on background. 22-Jun-93 Sotheby's, New York #682/R
$6000	£3922	Jasmine gasping and moving forward (27x33cm-11x13in) cel. 9-Oct-93 Sotheby's, New York #227/R
$6000	£3922	Jasmine and Ali looking at each other (38x88cm-15x35in) three cel set-up. 9-Oct-93 Sotheby's, New York #167/R
$6000	£3922	Genie and Jafar as cobra (32x43cm-13x17in) cel. 9-Oct-93 Sotheby's, New York #239/R
$6000	£3922	Prince Ali, guards and Jafar throwing down magic pellet creating smoke (32x43cm-13x17in) three cel set-up. 9-Oct-93 Sotheby's, New York #191/R
$6000	£3922	Jafar holds out handful of precious jewels to Aladdin and Abu (32x43cm-13x17in) cel. 9-Oct-93 Sotheby's, New York #92/R
$6000	£3922	Aladdin straightens plank as Jasmine is pole-vaulting over his head (49x63cm-19x25in) cel. 9-Oct-93 Sotheby's, New York #77/R
$6500	£4248	Aladdin and townsfolk as young boy runs out into Prince Achmed's path (32x43cm-13x17in) cel. 9-Oct-93 Sotheby's, New York #52/R
$6500	£4248	Jafar has conjured up power to find Aladdin, the diamond in the rough (32x43cm-13x17in) five cel set-up. 9-Oct-93 Sotheby's, New York #75/R
$6500	£4248	Jafar exposing Prince Ali to Jasmine (32x61cm-13x24in) cel. 9-Oct-93 Sotheby's, New York #206/R
$6500	£4248	Jasmine looking despondent realizing she may be losing Aladdin forever (27x33cm-11x13in) cel. 9-Oct-93 Sotheby's, New York #247/R
$6500	£4248	Genie responding with surprise (32x43cm-13x17in) two cel set-up. 9-Oct-93 Sotheby's, New York #220/R
$6500	£4248	Aladdin and Genie opens mouth rolling out tongue like staircase (32x58cm-13x23in) cel. 9-Oct-93 Sotheby's, New York #123/R
$7000	£4575	Narrator sets up stall and introduces us to the story of the lamp (49x104cm-19x41in) two cel set-up. 9-Oct-93 Sotheby's, New York #1/R
$7000	£4575	Jafar with Iago perched on shoulder attempting to mesmerize the Sultan (32x43cm-13x17in) two cel set-up. 9-Oct-93 Sotheby's, New York #143/R
$7000	£4575	Genie shoots beam of light from finger and Aladdin looking on (49x102cm-19x40in) cel. 9-Oct-93 Sotheby's, New York #128/R
$7500	£4902	Genie and Iago (32x43cm-13x17in) cel. 9-Oct-93 Sotheby's, New York #236/R
$7500	£4902	Aladdin and Genie sending lamp inside Cave of Wonders (32x43cm-13x17in) cel. 9-Oct-93 Sotheby's, New York #246/R
$7500	£4902	Genie's torso seperates from legs as he dances vaudeville style (32x99cm-13x39in) cel. 9-Oct-93 Sotheby's, New York #129/R
$8000	£5229	Jafar mesmerizes Sultan who gives him diamond ring (35x62cm-14x24in) cel. 9-Oct-93 Sotheby's, New York #66/R
$8000	£5229	Jasmine (32x43cm-13x17in) two cel set-up. 9-Oct-93 Sotheby's, New York #166/R
$8000	£5369	Fantasia, Mickey the scorcerer's apprentice carries two buckets of water (20x19cm-8x7in) gouache trimmed celluloid on Courvosier back. 22-Jun-93 Sotheby's, New York #834/R
$8000	£5229	Sultan enters Jasmine's room to find her crying (27x33cm-11x13in) cel. 9-Oct-93 Sotheby's, New York #111/R
$8000	£5229	Jafar approaches Sultan who wishes advice on suitor business (43x32cm-17x13in) two cel set-up. 9-Oct-93 Sotheby's, New York #64/R
$8000	£5229	Genie becomes Aladdin's fight trainer and Abu fans with Magic Carpet (32x90cm-13x35in) two cel set-up. 9-Oct-93 Sotheby's, New York #117/R

WALT DISNEY STUDIOS (20th C) American-cont.

$8000	£5229	Jasmine backs into fire-eater (32x43cm-13x17in) cel. 9-Oct-93 Sotheby's, New York #71/R
$8000	£5229	Jasmine and Prince Ali trying to tell the truth (32x43cm-13x17in) two cel set-up. 9-Oct-93 Sotheby's, New York #197/R
$8000	£5229	Aladdin and Abu fly to safety out of guards reach (32x43cm-13x17in) cel. 9-Oct-93 Sotheby's, New York #45/R
$8000	£5229	Genie and Aladdin expressing sadness in having to make important decision (32x43cm-13x17in) cel. 9-Oct-93 Sotheby's, New York #249/R
$8000	£5369	Prince lifts Snow White onto horse in forest clearing (22x25cm-9x10in) gouache trimmed celluloid on W/C background. 22-Jun-93 Sotheby's, New York #711/R
$8000	£5229	Genie and Magic Carpet making throat-slitting gesture (32x43cm-13x17in) two cel set-up. 9-Oct-93 Sotheby's, New York #159/R
$8500	£5705	Snow White singing leaning over well with pigeons (18x18cm-7x7in) studio label v.gouache multi-cel on background. 22-Jun-93 Sotheby's, New York #823/R
$8500	£5705	Snow White and the Seven Dwarfs, old witch hands Snow White apple (19x24cm-7x9in) studio label verso gouache celluloid multi-cel. 22-Jun-93 Sotheby's, New York #642/
$8500	£5556	Aladdin and Abu sit on the Carpet as Genie pilots it out of the cave (149x32cm-59x13in) cel. 9-Oct-93 Sotheby's, New York #132/R
$8500	£5556	Prince Ali and Sultan mounting the Magic Carpet (32x45cm-13x18in) cel. 9-Oct-93 Sotheby's, New York #152/R
$8500	£5556	Iago and Jafar hypnotizing the Sultan (32x43cm-13x17in) two cel set-up. 9-Oct-93 Sotheby's, New York #188/R
$8500	£5556	Genie turns his tail into microphone and addresses the crowd (32x43cm-13x17in) cel. 9-Oct-93 Sotheby's, New York #113/R
$9000	£6040	Snow White sits on the Prince's steed and dwarfs wave good-bye (25x34cm-10x13in) exec.1937 gouache trimmed celluloid. 22-Jun-93 Sotheby's, New York #535/R
$9000	£5882	Genie in waiter's outfit with pad to take order (32x43cm-13x17in) two cel set-up. 9-Oct-93 Sotheby's, New York #120/R
$9000	£5882	Sultan approaches Jasmine who is sitting by fountain with Rajah (32x43cm-13x17in) three cel set-up. 9-Oct-93 Sotheby's, New York #63/R
$9000	£5882	Jafar and Sultan (51x105cm-20x41in) three cel set-up. 9-Oct-93 Sotheby's, New York #155/R
$9500	£6209	Genie growing in size (98x32cm-39x13in) three set-up. 9-Oct-93 Sotheby's, New York #114/R
$9880	£6500	Snow White and the Seven Dwarfs, dwarfs looking down over bannister (13x18cm-5x7in) d.1937 gouache on celluloid on wood veneer. 5-Apr-93 Christie's, S. Kensington #324/R
$10000	£6711	Pinocchio strolls along happy and carefree (20x27cm-8x11in) gouache trimmed celluloid on background. 22-Jun-93 Sotheby's, New York #616/R
$10000	£6711	Lady and the Tramp happily greet each other next to fence (25x37cm-10x15in) gouache celluloid on W/C background. 22-Jun-93 Sotheby's, New York #769/R
$10000	£6536	Genie spinning off into the sky (32x48cm-13x19in) two cel set-up. 9-Oct-93 Sotheby's, New York #254/R
$10000	£6536	Jasmine walking away from Prince Ali after goodnight kiss (32x43cm-13x17in) three cel set-up. 9-Oct-93 Sotheby's, New York #172/R
$10000	£6711	Mr Mouse Takes a Trip, Black Pete with Pluto growling and Mickey in train (24x41cm-9x16in) st.studio gouache trimmed celluloid on W/C. 22-Jun-93 Sotheby's, New York #806/R
$10000	£6536	Genie radiating in magic swirls from head to tail (32x43cm-13x17in) two cel set-up. 9-Oct-93 Sotheby's, New York #251/R
$11000	£7383	Fantasia, Mickey leads bucket-laden broom (25x34cm-10x13in) gouache celluloid two-cel set up. 22-Jun-93 Sotheby's, New York #845/R
$11000	£7190	Jasmine and Rajah (32x43cm-13x17in) two cel set-up. 9-Oct-93 Sotheby's, New York #161/R
$11000	£7190	Genie transformed into cheerleader (32x51cm-13x20in) cel. 9-Oct-93 Sotheby's, New York #233/R
$11000	£7190	Prince Ali and Jasmine on balcony (32x43cm-13x17in) two cel set-up. 9-Oct-93 Sotheby's, New York #171/R
$11000	£7190	Jafar and Iago plot to put Jafar on the throne (32x43cm-13x17in) two cel set-up. 9-Oct-93 Sotheby's, New York #135/R
$11000	£7190	Genie grows to enormous size and lights up (32x43cm-13x17in) three cel set-up. 9-Oct-93 Sotheby's, New York #116/R
$12000	£7843	Jasmine places scarf back over her head to hide her identity (32x86cm-13x34in) cel. 9-Oct-93 Sotheby's, New York #72/R
$13000	£8497	Jasmine on Magic Carpet reaching out to pat little pony (32x46cm-13x18in) cel. 9-Oct-93 Sotheby's, New York #168/R
$13000	£8497	Ali and Jasmine flying through apple orchard on Magic Carpet (32x152cm-13x60in) three cel set-up. 9-Oct-93 Sotheby's, New York #169/R
$13000	£8725	Snow White and the Seven Dwarfs, dwarfs return to find Snow White asleep (20x29cm-8x11in) i.verso gouache celluloid on W/C background. 22-Jun-93 Sotheby's, New York #645/R
$14000	£9150	Aladdin and Genie confiding that his own wish would be for freedom (32x80cm-13x31in) cel. 9-Oct-93 Sotheby's, New York #139/R
$14000	£9396	Peter Pan, Captain Hook and Mr Smee convene on deck of pirate ship (29x38cm-11x15in) gouache celluloid on background. 22-Jun-93 Sotheby's, New York #655/R
$14000	£9150	Jasmine and Aladdin delighted with Genie's reaction to freedom (27x33cm-11x13in) cel. 9-Oct-93 Sotheby's, New York #253/R
$14896	£9800	Snow White dances with Dopey, Doc, Sneezy and Bashful (25x33cm-10x13in) gouache partial celluloid on wood veneer. 5-Apr-93 Christie's, S. Kensington #328/R
$15000	£9804	Aladdin and Abu in the Cave of Wonders (49x64cm-19x25in) three cel set-up. 9-Oct-93 Sotheby's, New York #96/R

WALT DISNEY STUDIOS (20th C) American-cont.
$15000	£9804	Genie emerging from lamp with Jafar in control (32x43cm-13x17in) two cel set-up. 9-Oct-93 Sotheby's, New York #199/R
$17000	£11409	Cinderella flees castle in carriage (32x79cm-13x31in) gouache trimmed celluloid on background. 22-Jun-93 Sotheby's, New York #822/R
$18000	£11765	Aladdin and Jasmine embracing as Magic Carpet flies them off into sky (32x43cm-13x17in) two cel set-up. 9-Oct-93 Sotheby's, New York #255/R
$20000	£13072	Prince Ali hovering on the Magic Carpet in front of Jasmine (32x43cm-13x17in) three cel set-up. 9-Oct-93 Sotheby's, New York #165/R
$20000	£13423	Snow White sits in dwarfs' cottage (21x29cm-8x11in) gouache celluloid on W/C. 22-Jun-93 Sotheby's, New York #774/R
$22000	£14379	Jafar and Iago watching Aladdin and Jasmine on Magic Carpet over Agrabah (37x51cm-15x20in) artwork for cover of catalogue. 9-Oct-93 Sotheby's, New York #112/R
$26000	£17450	Pinocchio, Gepetto's studio (30x32cm-12x13in) i. W/C. 22-Jun-93 Sotheby's, New York #838/R

WALTENSPERGER, Charles (1870-1931) American
$600	£408	Old wharf in Maine (53x66cm-21x26in) s. 17-Apr-94 Hindman Galleries, Chicago #954
$800	£537	Gypsy girl (36x30cm-14x12in) 27-Mar-94 Myers, Florida #81/R
$1100	£738	Self portrait (51x41cm-20x16in) s. 15-Dec-93 Boos Gallery, Michigan #480/R
$1500	£781	Mother with two children in interior scene (41x51cm-16x20in) s. 5-Aug-92 Boos Gallery, Michigan #537/R
$2000	£1342	Interior scene with lady reading (51x41cm-20x16in) s. 15-Dec-93 Boos Gallery, Michigan #479/R
$2500	£1678	Japanese lantern (51x41cm-20x16in) s. 24-Mar-94 Mystic Fine Arts, Connecticut #258/R

WALTER LANTZ STUDIO (20th C) American
$2500	£1678	Oswald Rabbit strolls along country lane (27x32cm-11x13in) i. gouache celluloid on W/C background. 22-Jun-93 Sotheby's, New York #720/R

WALTER, Christian J (1872-1938) American
$1800	£1169	Summer landscape (63x76cm-25x30in) s. 9-Sep-93 Sotheby's Arcade, New York #267/R

WALTER, Martha (1875-1976) American
$3500	£2349	Evening at the fishing port Brittany (20x28cm-8x11in) s. s.i.verso. 15-Dec-93 Boos Gallery, Michigan #437/R
$4500	£2601	Crab sale (38x46cm-15x18in) s. st.studio verso canvas board. 23-Sep-92 Christie's, New York #205/R
$4500	£2601	Baby in blue dress (46x37cm-18x15in) s. canvasboard. 24-Sep-92 Sotheby's, New York #126/R
$5750	£3783	Italian mother and children (51x41cm-20x16in) s. s.i.verso board. 31-Mar-93 Sotheby's Arcade, New York #267/R
$6500	£3757	Mid-France (37x46cm-15x18in) s. canvasboard. 24-Sep-92 Sotheby's, New York #127/R
$8000	£4624	Seated child in cape (81x60cm-32x24in) s. estate st.stretcher. 24-Sep-92 Sotheby's, New York #122/R
$9000	£6000	Bearritz beach (38x46cm-15x18in) s. i.verso board. 26-May-94 Christie's, New York #101/R
$10000	£6757	Boardwalk and beach (21x27cm-8x11in) s. board. 31-Mar-94 Sotheby's Arcade, New York #238/R
$11000	£7692	French beach scene (37x45cm-15x18in) s. canvasboard. 11-Mar-93 Christie's, New York #221/R
$12000	£6936	Quadro Flamenco (37x46cm-15x18in) st.studio verso canvas board. 23-Sep-92 Christie's, New York #187/R
$16000	£9249	Biarritz beach from terrace (37x46cm-15x18in) s. board. 24-Sep-92 Sotheby's, New York #125/R
$22000	£13924	Crowded beach (35x46cm-14x18in) s. board. 4-Dec-92 Christie's, New York #43/R
$24000	£15190	Chairs at Brighton Beach (35x46cm-14x18in) s. s.i.verso canvasboard. 4-Dec-92 Christie's, New York #91/R
$26000	£16456	Pink and purple group (36x45cm-14x18in) s. s.i.verso board. 4-Dec-92 Christie's, New York #92/R
$40000	£26490	At the beach (36x46cm-14x18in) s. 2-Oct-93 Boos Gallery, Michigan #278/R
$57500	£38079	Tea party (36x46cm-14x18in) s. s.i.verso. 2-Oct-93 Boos Gallery, Michigan #279/R

WALTERS, Emile (1893-?) American
$550	£372	Spring landscape (64x76cm-25x30in) s. 27-Nov-93 Young Fine Arts Auctions, Maine #335/R
$750	£497	Winter landscape (51x61cm-20x24in) s. board. 23-Sep-93 Mystic Fine Arts, Connecticut #256

WALTHER, Charles (1879-1938) American
$1400	£915	Moonrise over hill (56x71cm-22x28in) s. 18-Sep-93 Young Fine Arts Auctions, Maine #299/R

WALTON, Henry (attrib) (18/19th C) British/American
$511	£350	Portrait of lady said to be Sarah Spungeon (26x20cm-10x8in) panel. 8-Feb-94 Phillips, London #12
$7104	£4800	Portrait of lady (75x63cm-30x25in) 10-Nov-93 Sotheby's, London #69/R
$7750	£5000	Portrait of boy in jacket, waistcoat and shirt (25x22cm-10x9in) copper plate for part of map of Ireland. 14-Jul-94 Christie's, London #77/R
$1300	£653	Portrait of young woman, vicinity of Utica, New York , W/C c.1845. 6-Sep-92 Litchfield Auction Gallery #133

WANDESFORDE, Juan B (1817-1902) American
$7500 £5034 Lilies (61x41cm-24x16in) s. 8-Dec-93 Butterfield & Butterfield, San Francisco #3348/R

WARD, Charles Caleb (c.1831-1896) American
$850 £535 Resting by road (18x25cm-7x10in) s. board. 25-Apr-93 James Bakker, Cambridge #121/R
$1000 £505 Pastoral (30x25cm-12x10in) s.d.1896. 28-Aug-92 Young Fine Arts Auctions, Maine #304/R

WARD, Edgar Melville (1839-1915) American
$950 £634 California hills (61x76cm-24x30in) s. 17-May-94 Grogan, Massachussetts #360/R

WARD, Edmund F (1892-1991) American
$750 £524 Reviving fallen man (76x91cm-30x36in) s. 11-Mar-93 Mystic Fine Arts, Connecticut #233
$925 £605 Coach and four (46x76cm-18x30in) s. 22-May-93 Collins, Maine #85/R
$1300 £850 Ballet dancers (51x61cm-20x24in) s. board. 22-May-93 Collins, Maine #84/R
$1500 £980 Boys at the beach (51x86cm-20x34in) s. board. 22-May-93 Collins, Maine #101/R
$1550 £1013 Poolside (51x61cm-20x24in) board. 22-May-93 Collins, Maine #102
$1900 £1284 The Church gathering (86x76cm-34x30in) s.d.42. 31-Mar-94 Sotheby's Arcade, New York #405/R
$9000 £6040 The thundering herd (61x91cm-24x36in) s.d.23. 17-Dec-93 Du Mouchelle, Detroit #2008/R

WARD, J Stephen (1876-?) American
$800 £552 Houses in winter landscape (41x51cm-16x20in) s. 16-Feb-93 John Moran, Pasadena #27

WARD, William (jnr) (20th C) American
$950 £638 Boats on an Italian canal (61x91cm-24x36in) s. 2-Dec-93 Freeman Fine Arts, Philadelphia #766

WARDELL, Lindsay A (?) Canadian
$527 £354 Gathering for church (30x41cm-12x16in) s. W/C. 29-Nov-93 Waddingtons, Toronto #1024 (C.D 700)

WARHOL, Andy (1928-1986) American
$5662 £3800 Untitled - Joseph Beuys (80x59cm-31x23in) acrylic paper executed 1980. 2-Dec-93 Christie's, London #236/R
$7855 £5101 Panda Bear (35x28cm-14x11in) s.d.83verso acrylic serigraph canvas. 24-Jun-94 Francis Briest, Paris #68/R (F.FR 43000)
$8221 £5338 Panda Bear (35x28cm-14x11in) s.d.83verso acrylic serigraph canvas. 24-Jun-94 Francis Briest, Paris #81/R (F.FR 45000)
$8769 £5694 Mouse (28x35cm-11x14in) s.d.83verso acrylic serigraph canvas. 24-Jun-94 Francis Briest, Paris #80/R (F.FR 48000)
$9000 £5960 Self-portrait (28x22cm-11x9in) st.s. estate st.verso acrylic paper painted '67. 18-Nov-92 Sotheby's, New York #161/R
$9000 £5294 Untitled (13x13cm-5x5in) init.d.64 verso acrylic. 6-Oct-92 Sotheby's, New York #80/R
$10805 £7251 Children's painting, monkey (36x28cm-14x11in) s.d.1983verso acrylic silkscreen print. 21-Mar-94 Guy Loudmer, Paris #66/R (F.FR 62000)
$11187 £7508 Flowers (21x21cm-8x8in) s.d.1967verso acrylic. 25-Mar-93 Finarte, Rome #238/R (I.L 18000000)
$45820 £29000 Flowers (61x61cm-24x24in) s.d.64 verso. 3-Dec-92 Sotheby's, London #81/R
$84088 £55687 Hector et Andromaque (127x116cm-50x46in) s.d.1982verso acrylic. 13-Jun-94 Guy Loudmer, Paris #19/R (F.FR 470000)
$600 £397 Times fashion special (74x58cm-29x23in) ink hand-coloured. 30-Jun-93 Sotheby's Arcade, New York #288
$600 £397 Waterzoie recipe (57x72cm-22x28in) ink hand-coloured. 30-Jun-93 Sotheby's Arcade, New York #283/R
$855 £574 Anyone for shoes (23x33cm-9x13in) dr. 4-Mar-94 Binoche, Paris #113 (F.FR 5000)
$885 £590 Andy Warhol's T.V. (28x21cm-11x8in) s.i.d.1.10.83 gouache. 30-May-94 Catherine Charbonneaux, Paris #92/R (F.FR 5000)
$945 £643 Suicide (24x17cm-9x7in) s. hand col after original. 13-Apr-94 Bukowskis, Stockholm #337/R (S.KR 7500)
$1042 £704 Beauty is shoe, shoe beauty (25x28cm-10x11in) bears sig. blotted line print W/C. 21-Apr-94 Germann, Zurich #109/R (S.FR 1500)
$1197 £814 Jackie (24x19cm-9x7in) s. hand col after original. 13-Apr-94 Bukowskis, Stockholm #334/R (S.KR 9500)
$1200 £811 A la recherche du shoe perdue (34x30cm-13x12in) s.i. letterpress ink W/C paper laid on board. 21-Oct-93 Butterfield & Butterfield, San Francisco #2755/R
$1400 £927 Dog and shoe. Sewing (39x?cm-15x?in) s.verso Indian ink wash two. 29-Sep-93 Sotheby's Arcade, New York #279/R
$1500 £993 Woman with roses and cupids (71x57cm-28x22in) col.blotted ink line dr. 29-Sep-93 Sotheby's Arcade, New York #278/R
$1500 £1014 Golden slipper show. Pink shoe and yellow stocking , one s.i.d. letterpress ink W/C paper board two. 21-Oct-93 Butterfield & Butterfield, San Francisco #2753/R
$1700 £1149 Two men in provocative pose (42x35cm-17x14in) ink dr. 21-Oct-93 Butterfield & Butterfield, San Francisco #2756/R
$1701 £1157 Electric chair (19x24cm-7x9in) s. i.verso hand col after original. 13-Apr-94 Bukowskis, Stockholm #336/R (S.KR 13500)
$1800 £1192 Designs for shoes (29x?cm-11x?in) i. s.d.1960verso Inidan ink wash W/C htd two. 29-Sep-93 Sotheby's Arcade, New York #280/R

WARHOL, Andy (1928-1986) American-cont.

$1800	£1192	Red and pink rose garland (57x72cm-22x28in) s. ink. 30-Jun-93 Sotheby's Arcade, New York #282/R
$1800	£1053	Gertrude Stein (102x81cm-40x32in) s.num.188/200 screenprint. 19-Sep-92 Christie's, East, New York #241
$1800	£1208	Honeycomb yellow cake (71x57cm-28x22in) hand-coloured ink line drawing. 24-Feb-94 Sotheby's Arcade, New York #324/R
$1847	£1248	Triple Elvis (23x17cm-9x7in) s. blue yellow crayon handcoloured picture. 3-Nov-93 Bukowskis, Stockholm #268/R (S.KR 15000)
$2000	£1307	Birmingham race riot (51x61cm-20x24in) silkscreen printed in black exec.1964. 5-Oct-93 Sotheby's, New York #98/R
$2000	£1351	I dream of Jeannie with the light brown shoes. Sunset and evening shoe (16x27cm-6x11in) i. letter press ink W/C paper laid on board two. 21-Oct-93 Butterfield & Butterfield, San Francisco #2749/R
$2000	£1325	Young woman with halo of birds (72x57cm-28x22in) ink hand-coloured. 30-Jun-93 Sotheby's Arcade, New York #284/R
$2250	£1490	Chocolate balls a la chambord (57x72cm-22x28in) s. hand-col.blotted ink line dr. 29-Sep-93 Sotheby's Arcade, New York #282/R
$2750	£1858	Reclining male nude (42x35cm-17x14in) ink dr. 21-Oct-93 Butterfield & Butterfield, San Francisco #2754/R
$2750	£1846	A and P surprise (57x71cm-22x28in) blotted ink line drawing. 24-Feb-94 Sotheby's Arcade, New York #327/R
$2750	£1821	There is magic in all things (60x46cm-24x18in) hand-col.blotted ink line dr. 29-Sep-93 Sotheby's Arcade, New York #284/R
$2750	£1821	Tom 'n' Jerry recipe (61x46cm-24x18in) ink hand-coloured. 30-Jun-93 Sotheby's Arcade, New York #285/R
$2800	£1854	A and P surprise (72x57cm-28x22in) s.i. hand-col.blotted ink line dr. 29-Sep-93 Sotheby's Arcade, New York #283/R
$2897	£1971	Marilyn (20x20cm-8x8in) s. hand col after original. 13-Apr-94 Bukowskis, Stockholm #335/R (S.KR 23000)
$3000	£2027	Anna Magnani (41x57cm-16x22in) s.i. mixed media paper laid down on board. 21-Oct-93 Butterfield & Butterfield, San Francisco #2758/R
$3042	£1779	Campbell's soup can, pepper pot (89x59cm-35x23in) s.d.1968 num.238/250 silkscreen. 18-Sep-92 Schloss Ahlden, Ahlden #1079/R (DM 4500)
$3250	£2181	Milk punch (60x46cm-24x18in) hand-coloured ink line drawing. 24-Feb-94 Sotheby's Arcade, New York #326/R
$3357	£2381	Perro (100x65cm-39x26in) s. ink dr. 10-Feb-93 Ansorena, Madrid #96/R (S.P 400000)
$3500	£2318	Two ostriches and two giraffes (33x20cm-13x8in) three init. ink paper collage board four. 30-Jun-93 Sotheby's Arcade, New York #281/R
$3500	£2365	Read Miles (36x48cm-14x19in) s.i. mixed media paper laid down on board. 21-Oct-93 Butterfield & Butterfield, San Francisco #2747/R
$3500	£2349	Hopeful Aries (60x46cm-24x18in) hand-coloured ink line collage. 24-Feb-94 Sotheby's Arcade, New York #331/R
$3750	£2484	Fish on platter (58x74cm-23x29in) s. hand-col.blotted ink line dr. 29-Sep-93 Sotheby's Arcade, New York #285/R
$4000	£2685	Oxidation painting (36x25cm-14x10in) s.i.d.86 verso copper pigment mixed media canvas. 25-Feb-94 Sotheby's, New York #113/R
$4000	£2703	Untitled drawing of handbag and shoe (60x46cm-24x18in) s.d.1962 graphite. 8-Nov-93 Christie's, East, New York #229/R
$4250	£2853	Capricorn sloe whiskey fizz (60x46cm-24x18in) hand-coloured ink line drawing. 24-Feb-94 Sotheby's Arcade, New York #333/R
$4309	£2912	Buttons (35x45cm-14x18in) s.verso silkscreen. 3-Nov-93 Bukowskis, Stockholm #267/R (S.KR 35000)
$4500	£3125	Untitled (58x79cm-23x31in) s.d.81 pencil. 23-Feb-93 Sotheby's, New York #275/R
$4800	£2807	Marilyn Monroe (91x91cm-36x36in) s.num.120/250 screenprint wove paper. 19-Sep-92 Christie's, East, New York #29
$4800	£3179	Caution (28x36cm-11x14in) s.i.d.82verso synth.polymer silkscreen canvas. 17-Nov-92 Christie's, East, New York #64/R
$5000	£3311	Untitled (23x23cm-9x9in) s.i.d.86 silkscreen ink synth.polymer canvas. 19-Nov-92 Christie's, New York #277/R
$5000	£3268	Untitled (45x60cm-18x24in) init.d.1980 silkscreen ink chl. 7-May-93 Christie's, East, New York #187/R
$5162	£3167	Marilyn (91x91cm-36x36in) s.num.138/250verso serigraph. 18-Oct-92 Catherine Charbonneaux, Paris #84 (F.FR 26000)
$5250	£3524	Sagacious Sagittarius (60x46cm-24x18in) hand-coloured ink line collage. 24-Feb-94 Sotheby's Arcade, New York #330/R
$5250	£3432	Cow (116x76cm-46x30in) s.i.d.73verso silkscreen on wallpaper exec.1971. 5-Oct-93 Sotheby's, New York #260/R
$5379	£3300	Shadow (36x28cm-14x11in) s.i.d.78 acrylic silkscreen canvas. 14-Oct-92 Sotheby's, London #412/R
$5500	£3235	Poinsettia (66x51cm-26x20in) s.d.82 synthetic polymer silkscreened paper. 6-Oct-92 Sotheby's, New York #84/R
$6000	£4167	Blue Valentine (28x36cm-11x14in) st.sig.d.1982 synth.polymer silkscreen canvas. 23-Feb-93 Sotheby's, New York #285/R
$6000	£3922	Banana (60x136cm-24x54in) s.d.67verso silkscreen printed on styrene. 5-Oct-93 Sotheby's, New York #24/R
$6000	£3529	Shadows (36x28cm-14x11in) silkscreen inks synthetic polymer canvas. 8-Oct-92 Christie's, New York #247/R
$6500	£3801	Goethe (96x96cm-38x38in) s.i.num.3/5 screenprint. 19-Sep-92 Christie's, East, New York #242/R
$6705	£4500	Untitled, parrot (25x20cm-10x8in) s.d.83 acrylic silkscreen canvas. 25-Mar-93 Christie's, London #70/R
$6714	£4762	Marilyn 1967 (92x29cm-36x11in) st.verso serigraph. 10-Feb-93 Ansorena, Madrid #131/R (S.P 800000)

WARHOL, Andy (1928-1986) American-cont.

$6885	£4500	Clockwork panda drummer (35x28cm-14x11in) s.d.1983 acrylic silkscreen canvas. 30-Jun-94 Sotheby's, London #260/R
$6933	£4444	Flowers (20x20cm-8x8in) s.i. acrylic silkscreen canvas. 15-Dec-92 Rasmussen, Copenhagen #34/R (D.KR 42000)
$7000	£4730	Untitled (36x36cm-14x14in) s.d.82 verso polymer paint diamond dust canvas. 11-Nov-93 Sotheby's, New York #374/R
$7000	£4575	Untitled (36x28cm-14x11in) s.d.83 verso synthetic polymer silkscreened. 4-May-93 Sotheby's, New York #397 a/R
$7299	£4591	Mick Jagger (110x74cm-43x29in) s.num.29/250 silkscreen. 19-Apr-93 Stephan Welz, Johannesburg #339/R (SA.R 23000)
$8000	£5405	Flowers (20x20cm-8x8in) s.i.verso polymer paint silkscreened canvas. 11-Nov-93 Sotheby's, New York #405/R
$8000	£5369	Monkey (36x28cm-14x11in) s.d.83 synthetic polymer silkscreen canvas. 3-May-94 Christie's, East, New York #149/R
$8096	£5361	Emergency (28x36cm-11x14in) s.d.1983verso acrylic serigraph canvas. 28-Sep-93 Cornette de St.Cyr, Paris #130/R (F.FR 46000)
$8195	£5500	Untitled, swinging monkey (35x27cm-14x11in) s.d.83 silkscreen acrylic canvas. 25-Mar-93 Christie's, London #69/R
$8250	£5500	Parrot (25x20cm-10x8in) s.d.83verso acrylic silkscreen canvas. 26-May-94 Christie's, London #133/R
$9200	£6013	Grace Kelly (101x81cm-40x32in) s.d.1984 num.90/225 col.screenprint. 11-May-93 Christie's, New York #603/R
$9500	£6209	Marilyn (91x91cm-36x36in) s.d.1967 num.238/250verso col.screenprint. 11-May-93 Christie's, New York #590/R
$9685	£6500	Untitled, ship (28x35cm-11x14in) s.d.83overlap silkscreen acrylic canvas. 25-Mar-93 Christie's, London #88/R
$10000	£6711	Untitled (25x20cm-10x8in) s.i.d.81 verso synthetic polymer silkscreened. 25-Feb-94 Sotheby's, New York #101/R
$10500	£6863	Flash-November 22, 1963 (53x53cm-21x21in) s.i.verso 11 silkscreens printed in col. 5-Oct-93 Sotheby's, New York #16/R
$11000	£7383	Untitled (80x61cm-31x24in) init. studio st.verso synth.polymer silksreened. 5-May-94 Sotheby's, New York #202 a/R
$11000	£7285	Flowers (13x13cm-5x5in) s.d.64 synthetic polymer silkscreen ink canvas. 19-Nov-92 Christie's, New York #333/R
$11000	£7383	Campbell's chicken rice soup box (35x35cm-14x14in) s.d.86 synth.polymer silkscreen ink canvas. 4-May-94 Christie's, New York #339/R
$11000	£7383	Untitled - Barbara Feldon (55x40cm-22x16in) s. offset lithograph acetate film paper collage. 23-Feb-94 Christie's, New York #47/R
$11175	£7500	Marilyn (91x91cm-36x36in) init.verso col.screenprint executed 1967. 30-Nov-93 Christie's, London #774/R
$12000	£8054	Be a somebody with a body (28x35cm-11x14in) s.i.d.85 verso synthetic polymer silkscreen ink. 23-Feb-94 Christie's, New York #145/R
$12000	£8108	Rorschach (51x41cm-20x16in) s.i.d.82 ink canvas. 8-Nov-93 Christie's, East, New York #31/R
$12000	£8054	Flowers (20x20cm-8x8in) s.d.64 synth.polymer silkscreen ink canvas. 4-May-94 Christie's, New York #174/R
$12000	£7947	Album of a mat queen (25x51cm-10x20in) st.sig. synthetic polymer silkscreen ink canvas. 19-Nov-92 Christie's, New York #331/R
$12000	£8054	US Air Mail (15x15cm-6x6in) s.d.62stretcher synth.polymer silkscr.on canvas. 5-May-94 Sotheby's, New York #179/R
$13000	£8609	Untitled (13x13cm-5x5in) init.d.64 polymer paint silkscreened canvas. 18-Nov-92 Sotheby's, New York #157/R
$13000	£8725	Flowers (20x20cm-8x8in) s.d.1964 synth.polymer silkscreen ink canvas. 4-May-94 Christie's, New York #175/R
$13000	£8609	7c airmail stamp (18x18cm-7x7in) s.d.1962verso synth.polymer silkscreen canvas. 19-Nov-92 Christie's, New York #332/R
$13000	£8497	Roll over mouse (28x35cm-11x14in) s.d.83 verso silkscreen ink synthetic polymer. 7-May-93 Christie's, East, New York #172/R
$14000	£9272	Flowers (13x13cm-5x5in) s.d.64 synth.polymer silkscreen ink canvas. 19-Nov-92 Christie's, New York #339/R
$15000	£8824	Shoe (40x30cm-16x12in) s.verso silkscreen synthetic polymer dust. 8-Oct-92 Christie's, New York #255/R
$15000	£10417	Man Ray (41x41cm-16x16in) s.d.1978 synth.polymer silkscreen canvas. 23-Feb-93 Sotheby's, New York #287/R
$15000	£10000	Dollar sign (51x41cm-20x16in) acrylic silkscreen canvas executed 1981. 26-May-94 Christie's, London #132/R
$16000	£10596	Gun (41x51cm-16x20in) s.d.81 silkscreen ink synthetic polymer canvas. 19-Nov-92 Christie's, New York #278/R
$16000	£10811	Campbell's chicken noodle soup box (50x50cm-20x20in) s.d.86 verso polymer paint silkscreened canvas. 11-Nov-93 Sotheby's, New York #381/R
$16000	£10458	Campbell's chicken rice (50x50cm-20x20in) s.d.1986 verso synthetic polymer silkscreened. 4-May-93 Sotheby's, New York #399/R
$16000	£10738	Untitled (48x38cm-19x15in) s.i.d.77 synthetic polymer silkscreened canvas. 5-May-94 Sotheby's, New York #226/R
$17000	£11111	Electric chair (90x122cm-35x48in) s.d.71 silkscreens printed in col. 10 in box. 5-Oct-93 Sotheby's, New York #97/R
$17000	£11111	Campbell's Soup Can (51x41cm-20x16in) s.d.81 verso synthetic polymer silkscreened. 4-May-93 Sotheby's, New York #381/R
$17000	£11111	Skull (38x48cm-15x19in) s.i.d.1977overlap synthetic polymer silkscreen. 5-May-93 Christie's, New York #224/R
$18000	£11765	Dollar sign (51x41cm-20x16in) s.d.83 verso synthetic polymer paint silkscreen. 4-May-93 Sotheby's, New York #390/R
$18000	£11765	Mickey Mouse (96x96cm-38x38in) s.d.1981 num.2/5 col.screenprint diamond dust. 11-May-93 Christie's, New York #598/R

WARHOL, Andy (1928-1986) American-cont.

$19000	£12418	Two flowers (13x13cm-5x5in) init.d.64overlap polymer silkscreen ink pair. 5-May-93 Christie's, New York #237/R
$19630	£13000	Marily - F and S 24 (91x91cm-36x36in) s.verso num.102/250, screenprint. 1-Jul-93 Christie's, London #871/R
$19789	£13281	Shoes, Christine Jorgenson (33x41cm-13x16in) s.i. Indian ink collage foil gold leaf exec.56. 3-Dec-93 Lempertz, Cologne #1068/R (DM 34000)
$20000	£13072	Marilyn (91x91cm-36x36in) init.d.1967 num.48/250verso col.screenprint. 11-May-93 Christie's, New York #589/R
$21000	£14094	Willie Shoemaker (102x102cm-40x40in) s. synth.polymer silkscr.on canvas painted 1978. 5-May-94 Sotheby's, New York #218/R
$22000	£12941	Truman Capote (38x38cm-15x15in) s.i. ink. 8-Oct-92 Christie's, New York #125/R
$24000	£15686	Mao (30x25cm-12x10in) s.i.d.1973overlap synthetic polymer silkscreen. 5-May-93 Christie's, New York #287/R
$27525	£18598	Portrait of Berrocal (102x102cm-40x40in) s. d.1983verso polymer silkscreen ink canvas. 29-Mar-94 Campo & Campo, Antwerp #307/R (B.FR 950000)
$27540	£18000	Jackie (56x45cm-22x18in) s. synthetic polymer silkscreen canvas 1963. 30-Jun-94 Sotheby's, London #244/R
$30000	£20833	Flowers (56x56cm-22x22in) st.sig.d.1964 synthetic polymer silkscreened. 24-Feb-93 Christie's, New York #22/R
$30000	£20134	Volkswagen yellow sky (56x56cm-22x22in) s.d.85 silkscreen ink synth.polymer on canvas. 4-May-94 Christie's, New York #340/R
$30970	£19000	Flowers (56x56cm-22x22in) s. silkscreen canvas. 15-Oct-92 Christie's, London #61/R
$32500	£21523	Blackglama (56x56cm-22x22in) s.d.85 verso polymer paint silkscreened canvas. 18-Nov-92 Sotheby's, New York #187/R
$35000	£20588	One grey Marilyn (46x35cm-18x14in) st.sig.verso silkscreen ink polymer canvas. 8-Oct-92 Christie's, New York #147/R
$35000	£20588	Jackie (51x41cm-20x16in) s.d.64 silkscreen inks synthetic polymer. 8-Oct-92 Christie's, New York #126/R
$40000	£26490	Jackie (51x41cm-20x16in) s.d.64 silkscreen ink synth.polymer canvas. 19-Nov-92 Christie's, New York #342/R
$47500	£31879	Jackie (51x41cm-20x16in) s.verso synthetic polymer paint silkscreened. 25-Feb-94 Sotheby's, New York #74/R
$50000	£33113	Oxidation painting (122x126cm-48x50in) s.d.1978 verso pigment mixed media canvas. 18-Nov-92 Sotheby's, New York #194/R
$50000	£32680	Portrait of Princess Diana (127x102cm-50x40in) acrylic silkscreened canvas painted 1982. 3-May-93 Sotheby's, New York #25/R
$52000	£34899	Marylin, reversal series (46x36cm-18x14in) s. synthetic polymer silkscreened on canvas. 5-May-94 Sotheby's, New York #215/R
$57500	£38079	Shadow (188x152cm-74x60in) synthetic polymer paint silkscreened canvas. 18-Nov-93 Sotheby's, New York #192/R
$58460	£37000	One green and pink Marilyn - Reversal Series (51x40cm-20x16in) s.verso synthetic polymer silkscreened canvas. 3-Dec-92 Sotheby's, London #77/R
$59092	£37400	Pimple head - painted with Jean Michel Basquiat and Francesco Clemente (180x128cm-71x50in) s.d.85 verso oil acrylic silkscreen canvas. 3-Dec-92 Christie's, London #62/R
$60000	£39735	Round Jackie (46cm-18in circular) st.sig. silkscreen ink synthetic polymer canvas. 17-Nov-92 Sotheby's, New York #46/R
$68000	£45638	The Last Supper (102x102cm-40x40in) st.sig.i.1986 synth.polymer silkscr.on canvas. 5-May-94 Sotheby's, New York #196/R
$70000	£41176	Multicoloured Marilyn (46x35cm-18x14in) s.d.1979-86 verso synthetic polymer silkscreen. 6-Oct-92 Sotheby's, New York #98/R
$75000	£49669	One green Marilyn (41x36cm-16x14in) st.sig.overlap polymer paint silkscreen canvas. 18-Nov-92 Sotheby's, New York #166/R
$75000	£49669	Jackie (51x41cm-20x16in) s.i. synthetic polymer paint silkscreen canvas. 18-Nov-92 Sotheby's, New York #146/R
$90000	£60811	Shadow (193x132cm-76x52in) s.d.1978 synthetic polymer silkscreen canvas. 10-Nov-93 Christie's, New York #380/R
$93852	£59400	Origin of cotton - painted with Jean Michel Basquiat and Francesco Clemente (128x181cm-50x71in) s.d.1984 verso oil acrylic silkscreen canvas. 3-Dec-92 Christie's, London #68/R
$94860	£62000	Last Supper (102x102cm-40x40in) st.sig. synthetic polymer silkscreen canvas. 30-Jun-94 Christie's, London #245/R
$97397	£62434	Four multicoloured Marilyns, reversal series (92x71cm-36x28in) s.d.79/86 acrylic silkscreen canvas. 15-Dec-92 Rasmussen, Copenhagen #33/R (D.KR 590000)
$100000	£66225	Russell Means (213x178cm-84x70in) s.d.1976 verso polymer paint silkscreen canvas. 18-Nov-92 Sotheby's, New York #179/R
$107756	£68200	Four multicoloured Marilyns - Reversal Series (92x71cm-36x28in) s.d.79-86 verso acrylic silkscreen canvas. 3-Dec-92 Christie's, London #76/R
$110000	£64706	Four Marilyns - reversal series (91x71cm-36x28in) synthetic polymer paint silkscreened canvas. 6-Oct-92 Sotheby's, New York #85/R
$110000	£73826	70 S and H stamps (41x51cm-16x20in) s.d.62stretcher rubber stamp acrylic canvas. 3-May-94 Christie's, New York #16/R
$115000	£76159	Mao (127x107cm-50x42in) init.d.73 silkscreen ink synthetic polymer. 17-Nov-92 Sotheby's, New York #56/R
$120000	£81081	Four multicolour Marilyns (92x71cm-36x28in) s.d.1986 verso acrylic silkscreened canvas. 11-Nov-93 Sotheby's, New York #369/R
$120000	£79470	Suicide (102x76cm-40x30in) s.d.1964verso silkscreen paper. 17-Nov-92 Sotheby's, New York #16/R
$160000	£107383	The Last Supper (102x102cm-40x40in) st.sig.i.synthetic polymer silksreened on canvas. 5-May-94 Sotheby's, New York #216/R
$165000	£109272	Four Marilyns (92x71cm-36x28in) s.d.79/86 silkscreen ink synth.polymer canvas. 19-Nov-92 Christie's, New York #284/R

WARHOL, Andy (1928-1986) American-cont.

$197500	£125000	Most wanted man No.4, Redmond C (122x101cm-48x40in) s.verso synthetic polymer silkscreened canvas. 3-Dec-92 Sotheby's, London #30/R
$235000	£155629	Five deaths - red (76x76cm-30x30in) s.verso silkscreen ink synthetic polymer paint. 18-Nov-92 Sotheby's, New York #145/R
$250000	£165563	MMarily (138x108cm-54x43in) s.d.1986overlap silkscreen ink polymer canvas. 18-Nov-92 Christie's, New York #61/R
$320000	£211921	Marilyn (45cm-18in circular) s.i.d.62verso gold paint silkscreen ink canvas. 18-Nov-92 Christie's, New York #23/R
$500000	£326797	Old telephone (177x137cm-70x54in) synthetic polymer paint crayon canvas. 3-May-93 Sotheby's, New York #21/R
$570000	£377483	Race riot (156x172cm-61x68in) s.d.64 silkscreen ink polymer canvas four panels. 18-Nov-92 Christie's, New York #48/R
$850000	£562914	Double Marlon (213x244cm-84x96in) s.d.1966verso silkscreen ink canvas. 17-Nov-92 Sotheby's, New York #59/R
$876900	£555000	4 Marilyns (73x55cm-29x22in) s.verso synthetic polymer ink silkscreen canvas. 3-Dec-92 Sotheby's, London #32/R
$3400000	£2251656	Marilyn X 100 (206x568cm-81x224in) s.d.1962 silkscreen ink synthetic polymer paint. 17-Nov-92 Sotheby's, New York #25/R

WARNER BROS STUDIOS (20th C) American

$578	£380	Daffy Duck (25x30cm-10x12in) painted c.1950s gouache on celluloid. 5-Apr-93 Christie's, S. Kensington #197/R
$600	£403	Bugs Bunny snapping fingers (25x30cm-10x12in) studio st. exec.c.1980 gouache celluloid. 22-Jun-93 Sotheby's, New York #706
$608	£400	Sylvester hangs from wire (25x30cm-10x12in) painted c.1950s gouache full celluloid. 5-Apr-93 Christie's, S. Kensington #177/R
$684	£450	Daffy Duck holds footprint stamp (25x30cm-10x12in) gouache on trimmed celluloid. 5-Apr-93 Christie's, S. Kensington #200/R
$790	£520	Bugs Bunny as Super-Rabbit (23x28cm-9x11in) d.1943 title cel gouache on celluloid. 5-Apr-93 Christie's, S. Kensington #239/R
$988	£650	Bugs Bunny (25x30cm-10x12in) s. gouache on celluloid. 5-Apr-93 Christie's, S. Kensington #152/R
$1000	£671	Ali Baba Bunny. Rabbit's Feat , by Chuck Jones graphite two. 22-Jun-93 Sotheby's, New York #740
$1000	£671	Porky Pig popping through circle (27x30cm-11x12in) gouache celluloid. 22-Jun-93 Sotheby's, New York #714/R
$1500	£1007	Feather Dusted, Foghorn Leghorn waiving tomahawk like Indian (24x32cm-9x13in) i. gouache celluloid. 22-Jun-93 Sotheby's, New York #716
$1600	£1074	Elmer Fudd and Daffy Duck (20x25cm-8x10in) i. gouache celluloid two-cel set up. 22-Jun-93 Sotheby's, New York #630/R
$1900	£1275	Pepe le Pew and Kitty , gouache celluloid two framed together. 22-Jun-93 Sotheby's, New York #640/R
$2000	£1342	Syvester and Tweety (21x27cm-8x11in) gouache celluloid two cel set on W/C background. 22-Jun-93 Sotheby's, New York #685/R
$2000	£1342	Bugs Bunny, Bugs all twisted up at sight of comely nude (29x22cm-11x9in) exec.c.1940s gouache celluloid. 22-Jun-93 Sotheby's, New York #534
$2280	£1500	The roadrunner (23x28cm-9x11in) gouache full celluloid on W/C background. 5-Apr-93 Christie's, S. Kensington #96/R

WARNER, Nell Walker (1891-1970) American

$700	£473	Chrysanthemums (30x41cm-12x16in) s. s.i.verso canvasboard. 9-Nov-93 John Moran, Pasadena #812 b
$1500	£993	Floral still life (76x90cm-30x35in) s. 15-Jun-94 Butterfield & Butterfield, San Francisco #4668/R
$2000	£1389	Gold scarf (76x66cm-30x26in) s. 7-Mar-93 Butterfield & Butterfield, San Francisco #239/R
$3250	£2167	Still life with iris (76x66cm-30x26in) s. board. 15-Mar-94 John Moran, Pasadena #67
$3700	£2434	Echoes from cherry garden (86x102cm-34x40in) s. 31-Mar-93 Sotheby's Arcade, New York #445/R
$1200	£779	The white gown (71x46cm-28x18in) s.d.16 W/C. 11-Sep-93 Louisiana Auction Exchange #102/R

WARREN, Harold Broadfield (1859-1934) American

$1100	£738	Canadian Rockies, Alberta (70x55cm-28x22in) s.d.1911 W/C. 6-May-94 Skinner, Bolton #125/R

WARREN, Melvin C (1920-) American

$1800	£1224	Winter in Frio Canyon (46x61cm-18x24in) s.d.1968 s.i.d.verso. 15-Nov-93 Christie's, East, New York #88/R

WARSHAWSKY, Abel George (1883-1962) American

$850	£563	Mexico street scene with burros (61x51cm-24x20in) 28-Sep-93 John Moran, Pasadena #242
$2100	£1409	Spring day in a Mexican village (61x51cm-24x20in) s. i.verso. 12-Jan-94 Doyle, New York #85
$2250	£1190	Open door (46x56cm-18x22in) s. 12-Sep-92 Louisiana Auction Exchange #99/R
$2250	£1562	Isle aux Mornes (46x55cm-18x22in) s.d.30. 7-Mar-93 Butterfield & Butterfield, San Francisco #122/R
$3750	£2604	French village scene. Woman of Finisterre (65x55cm-26x22in) s.verso double-sided. 7-Mar-93 Butterfield & Butterfield, San Francisco #125/R
$5500	£3618	California landscape (66x102cm-26x40in) s. 13-Jun-93 Butterfield & Butterfield, San Francisco #838/R

WARSHAWSKY, Abel George (1883-1962) American-cont.
$5500   £3819   View of village (66x82cm-26x32in) s. 7-Mar-93 Butterfield & Butterfield, San Francisco #124/R

WARSHAWSKY, Alexander (1887-1945) American
$2000   £1316   Hollywood Hills (61x76cm-24x30in) s. 13-Jun-93 Butterfield & Butterfield, San Francisco #888/R

WASHBURN, Cadwallader (1866-1965) American
$600   £417   Flower garden (30x38cm-12x15in) s. W/C. 6-Mar-93 Louisiana Auction Exchange #163/R

WASHBURN, Mary Nightingale (1861-1932) American
$1200   £635   Flora (61x51cm-24x20in) s.d.1917 init.i.verso. 11-Sep-92 Skinner, Bolton #265

WASHINGTON, Elizabeth Fisher (19/20th C) American
$900   £588   Fenced back yards (30x36cm-12x14in) s. board. 22-May-93 Collins, Maine #40/R
$1700   £983   Day at beach (51x61cm-20x24in) s. 27-Sep-92 James Bakker, Cambridge #120/R

WATERMAN, Marcus (1834-1914) American
$825   £543   Clearing in wood (51x76cm-20x30in) s. 5-Jun-93 Louisiana Auction Exchange #91/R
$1600   £1060   High beach, Provincetown (64x76cm-25x30in) s. 13-Nov-92 Skinner, Bolton #90/R

WATERS, Emile (1893-?) American
$850   £556   Autumn afternoon (51x46cm-20x18in) s. 7-Oct-93 Freeman Fine Arts, Philadelphia #954 a

WATERS, George W (1832-1912) American
$2300   £1513   Hudson river landscape (66x107cm-26x42in) s.d.76. 11-Jun-93 Du Mouchelle, Detroit #45

WATERS, Susan (1823-1900) American
$950   £642   Cherries (33x46cm-13x18in) 10-Aug-93 Stonington Fine Arts, Stonington #171/R
$1500   £1049   Sheep in landscape (70x107cm-28x42in) s.verso. 10-Mar-93 Sotheby's, New York #24/R

WATKINS, Franklin Chenault (1894-1972) American
$550   £374   Woman holding her breast (36x28cm-14x11in) init. canvasboard. 14-Apr-94 Freeman Fine Arts, Philadelphia #1027/R
$1700   £1126   Son my son (71x86cm-28x34in) s.d.1946. 13-Nov-92 Du Mouchelle, Detroit #2027/R
$700   £476   Angel (56x61cm-22x24in) pastel needlepoint burlap. 14-Apr-94 Freeman Fine Arts, Philadelphia #1030

WATROUS, Harry W (1857-1940) American
$1500   £1014   Moonlit landscape (41x30cm-16x12in) s. canvasboard. 31-Mar-94 Sotheby's Arcade, New York #256/R
$1800   £1176   Old score (18x16cm-7x6in) s. panel. 4-May-93 Christie's, East, New York #196/R
$5000   £3497   Lady nicotine (48x35cm-19x14in) s.indis.i. 10-Mar-93 Sotheby's, New York #83/R
$5000   £3205   Drawn game (43x55cm-17x22in) s.i. panel. 27-May-93 Sotheby's, New York #178/R
$8000   £5063   Solitaire (60x45cm-24x18in) s. 3-Dec-92 Sotheby's, New York #126/R
$8000   £5405   Still life with golden flowers (69x46cm-27x18in) s. 31-Mar-94 Sotheby's Arcade, New York #339/R

WATSON, Dawson (1864-1939) American
$1000   £529   Elk in a snowy field, twilight (91x56cm-36x22in) s.d.01. 11-Sep-92 Skinner, Bolton #235/R
$1750   £1174   Summer landscape (58x74cm-23x29in) 29-Nov-93 Stonington Fine Arts, Stonington #110/R
$3750   £2534   The Bridge at Avignon (46x55cm-18x22in) s.d.1888. 31-Mar-94 Sotheby's Arcade, New York #164/R

WATSON, Homer Ransford (1855-1936) Canadian
$930   £628   Forest landscape (17x24cm-7x9in) s. board. 3-Nov-93 Sotheby's, Toronto #207/R (C.D 1200)
$1031   £674   Doon Woods (17x24cm-7x9in) s. i.verso board. 19-May-93 Sotheby's, Toronto #29/R (C.D 1300)
$1054   £707   Landscape with river and cattle (25x35cm-10x14in) s. board. 29-Nov-93 Ritchie, Toronto #163/R (C.D 1400)
$1189   £777   Landscape - Hespeler, Ontario (32x42cm-13x17in) s. board. 19-May-93 Sotheby's, Toronto #129/R (C.D 1500)
$1204   £808   Looking from Chicopee Hill (25x35cm-10x14in) s.i. i.verso board. 29-Nov-93 Ritchie, Toronto #193/R (C.D 1600)
$1323   £876   Gravel pit (31x41cm-12x16in) s. board. 24-Nov-92 Joyner Fine Art, Toronto #98/R (C.D 1700)
$1557   £1031   Cattle grazing by river (45x60cm-18x24in) s. board. 24-Nov-92 Joyner Fine Art, Toronto #1/R (C.D 2000)
$1812   £1224   The country road (31x41cm-12x16in) s. board. 23-Nov-93 Joyner Fine Art, Toronto #7/R (C.D 2400)
$1982   £1295   Summer storm (25x38cm-10x15in) s. 19-May-93 Sotheby's, Toronto #276/R (C.D 2500)
$3113   £2062   Riders in a forest (42x39cm-17x15in) s.i.d.verso board. 18-Nov-92 Sotheby's, Toronto #70/R (C.D 4000)
$3964   £2591   Country landscape with sheep (36x46cm-14x18in) s.d.88 s.stretcher. 19-May-93 Sotheby's, Toronto #394/R (C.D 5000)
$4670   £3093   Figures in a forest glade (46x60cm-18x24in) s. 18-Nov-92 Sotheby's, Toronto #168/R (C.D 6000)

WATSON, Walter (19/20th C) American?
$575 £391 At Monterey, California (51x76cm-20x30in) s. i.verso. 16-Apr-94 Young Fine Arts Auctions, Maine #260/R

WATTS, William Clothier (19/20th C) American
$2500 £1645 Haze after storm (76x91cm-30x36in) 13-Jun-93 Butterfield & Butterfield, San Francisco #803/R

WAUD, Alfred Rudolf (1828-1891) American
$1000 £633 Office of the Freedmen's Bureau, Demopolis, Ala. (16x25cm-6x10in) s.i.d.65 pencil htd white. 2-Dec-92 Christie's, East, New York #212 a/R

WAUGH, Frederick J (1861-1940) American
$700 £458 Barbados (30x40cm-12x16in) init. board. 22-May-93 Weschler, Washington #112/R
$700 £461 Crashing waves (58x71cm-23x28in) s. masonite. 5-Jun-93 Louisiana Auction Exchange #30/R
$750 £500 Seascape (30x41cm-12x16in) s. board. 1-Jun-94 Doyle, New York #66
$1000 £662 Morning (28x33cm-11x13in) s. board. 23-Sep-93 Mystic Fine Arts, Connecticut #68 a/R
$1150 £772 Surf and rocks (58x71cm-23x28in) s. masonite. 4-Dec-93 Louisiana Auction Exchange #141/R
$1400 £921 Seascape (66x56cm-26x22in) 4-Jun-93 Dargate Auction Galleries, Pittsburgh #967
$1400 £979 Nocturnal seascape (15x20cm-6x8in) s. panel. 11-Mar-93 Mystic Fine Arts, Connecticut #156
$1600 £1060 Breaking waves (33x51cm-13x20in) s. 15-Jun-94 Butterfield & Butterfield, San Francisco #4449/R
$1800 £1176 Crashing surf (41x51cm-16x20in) s. masonite. 22-May-93 Weschler, Washington #110/R
$2000 £1361 Foster Hall Mill Barbados British West Indies (63x76cm-25x30in) s. 15-Nov-93 Christie's, East, New York #125/R
$2200 £1457 Seagulls (42x91cm-17x36in) s. masonite. 23-Sep-93 Sotheby's, New York #181/R
$2400 £1600 The cove (64x76cm-25x30in) s. i.stretcher. 13-Mar-94 Hindman Galleries, Chicago #775/R
$2600 £1733 Late gleaming (74x93cm-29x37in) s. board. 23-May-94 Christie's, East, New York #162/R
$2750 £1833 Ocean shore scene (76x102cm-30x40in) s. masonite. 20-May-94 Du Mouchelle, Detroit #2016/R
$4000 £2649 Moonlight (63x76cm-25x30in) s. masonite. 22-Sep-93 Christie's, New York #169/R
$4000 £2721 Maine coast (71x91cm-28x36in) s. masonite. 9-Jul-93 Sloan, North Bethesda #2836/R
$4500 £2941 Late gleaming (76x91cm-30x36in) s. board. 30-Jun-94 Mystic Fine Arts, Connecticut #78
$4750 £3210 Late afternoon (63x91cm-25x36in) s. board. 31-Mar-94 Sotheby's Arcade, New York #246/R
$5500 £3618 Lively surf (51x61cm-20x24in) s. masonite. 31-Mar-93 Sotheby's Arcade, New York #174/R
$6000 £3468 Gale from the West (71x91cm-28x36in) s. masonite. 23-Sep-92 Christie's, New York #196/R
$6500 £3757 Coast under heavy surf (63x76cm-25x30in) s. masonite. 24-Sep-92 Sotheby's, New York #106/R
$7000 £4895 Family gathering (46x91cm-18x36in) s.d.1892. 10-Mar-93 Sotheby's, New York #89/R
$7000 £4895 Little harbour, Bailey's Island, Maine (74x91cm-29x36in) s. i.d. 1903verso. 10-Mar-93 Sotheby's, New York #88/R
$8500 £5944 Still life (76x102cm-30x40in) 12-Mar-93 Skinner, Bolton #266/R
$15000 £10490 Breaking seas (77x102cm-30x40in) s. 10-Mar-93 Sotheby's, New York #87/R
$19000 £12667 Yosemite South Fork, looking eastward from King's river (63x127cm-25x50in) init.d.1888. 26-May-94 Christie's, New York #70/R
$35000 £23490 Family resting under tree (46x55cm-18x22in) s.d.1889. 2-Dec-93 Sotheby's, New York #30/R
$800 £537 River landscape (76x49cm-30x19in) s.d.1891 W/C. 11-Dec-93 Weschler, Washington #94/R
$7000 £4430 Looking west, St Ives (36x52cm-14x20in) s. W/C paper on board. 3-Dec-92 Sotheby's, New York #27/R

WAUGH, Frederick J (attrib) (1861-1940) American
$3250 £2138 Playtime in barn (20x25cm-8x10in) i.verso. 31-Mar-93 Sotheby's Arcade, New York #66/R

WAUGH, Ida (1919-) American
$3750 £2517 Bouquet of tulips (48x69cm-19x27in) s. board. 6-Dec-93 Grogan, Massachussetts #488/R

WAY, A J H (1826-1888) American
$5364 £3600 Still life study of grapes, pair. 7-Dec-93 Academy Auctioneers, London #1026

WAY, Andrew John Henry (1826-1888) American
$1800 £1224 Peaches (10x19cm-4x7in) indis.s. 10-Jul-93 Young Fine Arts Auctions, Maine #327/R
$2500 £1678 Still life of cherries and peaches (46x61cm-18x24in) s. 6-Dec-93 Grogan, Massachussetts #469/R
$3200 £2133 Grapes on vine (51x30cm-20x12in) s. 12-Mar-94 Weschler, Washington #146/R
$4992 £3200 Still life of hanging grapes (51x35cm-20x14in) s.d.1879. 15-Dec-92 Phillips, London #51/R
$18000 £12000 Wild grapes (61x46cm-24x18in) s. 16-Mar-94 Christie's, New York #47/R

WAY, Andrew John Henry (attrib) (1826-1888) American
$3000   £1899   Grape vines - still lifes (55x35cm-22x14in) pair. 2-Dec-92 Christie's, East, New York #125/R

WEAVER, William H (19th C) American
$800   £537   Still life with snail on a bunch of grapes (38x25cm-15x10in) s.d.1890. 11-Dec-93 Weschler, Washington #92

WEBB, Thomas (20th C) American
$1300   £861   Last dance (99x46cm-39x18in) s. 13-Nov-92 Skinner, Bolton #181/R

WEBBER, Charles T (1825-1911) American
$5200   £3636   Boy with violin and girl picking flowers in garden (84x41cm-33x16in) s. 14-Mar-93 Hindman Galleries, Chicago #22/R

WEBBER, W (1841-1914) American
$2500   £1773   Figures stranded on raft and approaching angel leading rescue ship (76x127cm-30x50in) s. 12-Feb-93 Du Mouchelle, Detroit #99/R

WEBBER, Wesley (1841-1914) American
$650   £433   Landing party, harbour view (61x46cm-24x18in) s. 20-Aug-93 Skinner, Bolton #75
$700   £473   Still life (46x61cm-18x24in) 10-Aug-93 Stonington Fine Arts, Stonington #129
$850   £450   Indian point Penobscott Bay, Maine (56x91cm-22x36in) s. i.verso. 11-Sep-92 Skinner, Bolton #192 a/R
$875   £572   Water lilies (41x66cm-16x26in) s. 8-May-93 Young Fine Arts Auctions, Maine #298/R
$1000   £578   Sailing by moonlight (66x91cm-26x36in) s. 25-Sep-92 Sotheby's Arcade, New York #58/R
$1000   £654   Ship at moonlight (91x66cm-36x26in) s. 4-May-93 Christie's, East, New York #22/R
$1050   £714   Children at a well (30x51cm-12x20in) mono. 19-Nov-93 Eldred, Massachusetts #911/R
$1300   £657   Moonlight harbour (46x76cm-18x30in) s. 28-Aug-92 Young Fine Arts Auctions, Maine #305/R
$1600   £1074   Sailing at sunset (18x23cm-7x9in) s. board. 6-Dec-93 Grogan, Massachussetts #417
$1700   £1141   Iceberg at sunset (18x28cm-7x11in) s. board. 6-Dec-93 Grogan, Massachussetts #416/R
$3100   £2000   Clipper offshore (56x91cm-22x36in) s.d.79. 15-Jul-94 Christie's, London #67/R
$3750   £2451   Fisherman loading dory, Maine coast (56x91cm-22x36in) s. 18-Sep-93 Young Fine Arts Auctions, Maine #302/R
$5900   £4014   Salvaging from a beached ship (61x114cm-24x45in) s. 19-Nov-93 Eldred, Massachusetts #919/R
$12000   £8392   Near North Head, Grand Manon (76x127cm-30x50in) s. 11-Mar-93 Christie's, New York #69/R

WEBBER, Wesley (attrib) (1841-1914) American
$1700   £885   View of Boston Harbour (61x112cm-24x44in) 4-Aug-92 Richard Bourne, Hyannis #100/R

WEBER, C Phillip (1849-?) American
$900   £588   Wooded stream (32x42cm-13x17in) s. board. 4-May-93 Christie's, East, New York #38
$1200   £779   Rocky landscape (56x91cm-22x36in) s.d.1880. 9-Sep-93 Sotheby's Arcade, New York #51/R
$2400   £1589   Strolling in country wood (54x46cm-21x18in) s.d.1880. 22-Sep-93 Christie's, New York #16/R

WEBER, Carl (1850-1921) American
$617   £420   News of the Day (99x72cm-39x28in) s.d.1878. 6-Apr-94 Bonhams, Chelsea #199/R
$650   £422   Forest stream (48x43cm-19x17in) s. 11-Sep-93 Louisiana Auction Exchange #53/R
$900   £612   Fisherman on the shore (36x74cm-14x29in) s. 14-Apr-94 Freeman Fine Arts, Philadelphia #984/R
$2200   £1392   Hunters and hounds in landscape (51x86cm-20x34in) s.d.1870 canvas on masonite. 3-Dec-92 Freeman Fine Arts, Philadelphia #1888 a
$2895   £1673   Corn harvest in landscape, probably near Dachau (39x63cm-15x25in) s.i.d.1872. 23-Sep-92 Neumeister, Munich #738/R (DM 4200)
$650   £439   *Sheep in a landscape (36x66cm-14x26in) s. W/C. 27-Nov-93 Young Fine Arts Auctions, Maine #339/R*
$650   £411   *Sheep grazing under apple blossoms (58x90cm-23x35in) s. W/C htd white. 2-Dec-92 Christie's, East, New York #90*
$800   £523   *Landscape with cattle (30x61cm-12x24in) s. W/C. 7-Oct-93 Freeman Fine Arts, Philadelphia #950*
$842   £550   *Cattle grazing in orchard by stream (43x69cm-17x27in) s. pencil W/C htd white. 14-Apr-93 Christie's, S. Kensington #7*
$1100   £748   *Pennsylvania landscape at dusk with cattle by brook (33x64cm-13x25in) s. W/C. 8-Apr-94 Sloan, North Bethesda #2350*
$1200   £811   *Springtime in Delaware County (61x91cm-24x36in) s. i.verso W/C. 31-Mar-94 Sotheby's Arcade, New York #120/R*
$1400   £940   *Sheep grazing under apple blossoms (58x89cm-23x35in) s. W/C. 2-Dec-93 Freeman Fine Arts, Philadelphia #787*
$1600   £1074   *Pennsylvania farm scene with grazing sheep (43x66cm-17x26in) s. W/C. 3-Feb-94 Sloan, North Bethesda #2668/R*

WEBER, Max (1881-1961) American
$6500   £4333   The Vigil (41x27cm-16x11in) s. painted c.1915. 17-Mar-94 Sotheby's, New York #169/R
$9000   £6294   Still life (34x27cm-13x11in) s.d.1910 canvasboard. 11-Mar-93 Christie's, New York #193/R
$11000   £7285   Sabbath reading (66x48cm-26x19in) s.d.43. 19-Jun-94 Hindman Galleries, Chicago #708/R

533

WEBER, Max (1881-1961) American-cont.

$13000	£8333	Women in garden (27x21cm-11x8in) s.d.11 tempera board. 26-May-93 Christie's, New York #208/R
$17000	£10897	Primitive head (21x14cm-8x6in) s. board. 26-May-93 Christie's, New York #209/R
$17000	£11565	Moonlit night (53x61cm-21x24in) s. painted 1946. 17-Nov-93 Doyle, New York #62/R
$23000	£16084	Good news (124x97cm-49x38in) s.d.44 board. 10-Mar-93 Sotheby's, New York #159/R
$40000	£25641	Among trees (46x39cm-18x15in) s.d.1911. 27-May-93 Sotheby's, New York #102/R
$90000	£56962	Interior with men (53x45cm-21x18in) s.d.1919 tempera. 3-Dec-92 Sotheby's, New York #132/R
$1500	£987	Drawing class (62x48cm-24x19in) indist.st. chl paper on canvas. 31-Mar-93 Sotheby's Arcade, New York #226/R
$2000	£1325	Tabletop still life with fruit, carafe, glass and aloe plant (28x23cm-11x9in) s.d.10 W/C chl. 2-Oct-93 Weschler, Washington #122/R
$3750	£2622	Resting women (30x23cm-12x9in) s.d.1912 W/C. 10-Mar-93 Sotheby's, New York #145/R
$8000	£5063	Sleep (45x61cm-18x24in) s.d.1938 W/C pastel paper on board. 3-Dec-92 Sotheby's, New York #64/R
$18000	£12000	Six heads (32x20cm-13x8in) W/C graphite paper on board executed 1910. 17-Mar-94 Sotheby's, New York #170/R
$20000	£13333	Landscape with church spires and trees (121x60cm-48x24in) s.d.1911 gouache board. 26-May-94 Christie's, New York #127/R

WEBSTER, Derek (1934-) American

$550	£364	African dancer, init. paint mixed media board. 21-Nov-92 Litchfield Auction Gallery #15

WEBSTER, E Ambrose (1869-1935) American

$5000	£3289	Webster House, Bradford Street (76x51cm-30x20in) s.d.31. 31-Mar-93 Sotheby's Arcade, New York #332/R

WEBSTER, M W (?) American

$725	£487	Troika (76x127cm-30x50in) 5-Mar-94 San Rafael Auction Galleries #201

WEEGEE, William (20th C) American

$950	£601	Untitled (122x122cm-48x48in) s.d.77 handmade paper. 25-Oct-92 Butterfield & Butterfield, San Francisco #2367/R

WEEKS, Edwin Lord (1849-1903) American

$800	£548	The flight into Egypt (28x46cm-11x18in) s. en grisaille board. 10-Feb-94 Skinner, Bolton #209
$1050	£705	Tabreez (25x41cm-10x16in) s. canvasboard. 24-Mar-93 Grogan, Massachussetts #38/R
$1200	£811	Soldiers crossing stream (25x41cm-10x16in) s.i. en grisaille canvas on board. 20-Apr-94 Doyle, New York #88
$2800	£1892	Indian woman sitting on ground (38x51cm-15x20in) st.verso. 31-Mar-94 Sotheby's Arcade, New York #156/R
$3500	£2023	Indian bearers (51x61cm-20x24in) s. 24-Sep-92 Mystic Fine Arts, Connecticut #107/R
$3750	£2517	Elephant and rider (51x36cm-20x14in) s.i. 4-May-94 Doyle, New York #20
$7500	£4967	Study of old shop fronts - Ahmedabad, India (43x33cm-17x13in) s.i.d.82. 23-Sep-93 Sotheby's, New York #128/R
$10000	£6897	Arab scene (46x33cm-18x13in) s. st. i.verso painted between 1884-1889. 18-Feb-93 Christie's, New York #145/R
$17000	£11409	Market place, India (46x34cm-18x13in) s. painted c.1885. 2-Dec-93 Sotheby's, New York #22/R
$20000	£13699	Royal procession with horsemen and draped elephant (105x69cm-41x27in) bears sig.bears i. 16-Feb-94 Sotheby's, New York #80/R
$22000	£14103	Promenade on an Indian Street (61x47cm-24x19in) s. 27-May-93 Christie's, New York #249/R
$24000	£15686	Muttra (51x76cm-20x30in) s.i.d.88. 30-Oct-92 Christie's, New York #30/R
$25000	£16667	A bargain, interior of moorish bazaar (76x51cm-30x20in) s.d.1878 i.verso painted 1878. 25-May-94 Sotheby's, New York #62/R
$30000	£20690	Indian scene (46x33cm-18x13in) s. st. painted between 1884-1889. 18-Feb-93 Christie's, New York #144/R
$32000	£20513	Fete day at Bekanir, Beloochistan, Bekanir (141x187cm-56x74in) s. 27-May-93 Christie's, New York #248/R
$33000	£21154	Before mosque (74x49cm-29x19in) s.indist.i.d.83. 27-May-93 Sotheby's, New York #7/R
$95000	£65068	Horse market, Persian Stables, Bombay (80x100cm-31x39in) s. 15-Feb-94 Christie's, New York #224/R
$100000	£63291	The Buddhist Temple (144x190cm-57x75in) s. 3-Dec-92 Sotheby's, New York #86/R
$120000	£82759	Rajah's favourite (100x80cm-39x31in) s. st. painted between 1884-1889. 18-Feb-93 Christie's, New York #143/R
$120000	£80537	'Ispahan' (142x189cm-56x74in) s. i.verso painted c.1900-01. 13-Oct-93 Sotheby's, New York #46/R

WEEKS, James (1922-) American

$20000	£13514	Girl and dog (140x127cm-55x50in) s.i.d.1959verso. 21-Oct-93 Butterfield & Butterfield, San Francisco #2777/R

WEGMAN, William (1943-) American

$800	£537	Untitled (30x23cm-12x9in) init.d.87 pen. 23-Feb-94 Christie's, East, New York #225
$800	£556	Rene is serving (28x36cm-11x14in) init.d.82 W/C felt tip pen. 22-Feb-93 Christie's, East, New York #261
$2500	£1471	Two untitled drawings (35x28cm-14x11in) init.d.89 brush ink two. 8-Oct-92 Christie's, New York #187/R

WEGMAN, William (1943-) American-cont.
$2600 £1722 Dog paints man (36x28cm-14x11in) init.d.85 brush ink gouache. 17-Nov-92 Christie's, East, New York #56/R

WEIBLING, John (fl.1832-1833) American
$3200 £2133 Gilt-decorated flowers in pitcher, flanked by two birds-of-paradise (23x18cm-9x7in) s. W/C ink. 10-Jun-94 Christie's, New York #507/R

WEILAND, James G (1872-1968) American
$2750 £1821 Woman by a river (61x51cm-24x20in) s. 28-Nov-92 Young Fine Arts Auctions, Maine #398/R

WEIMERSKIRCH, Robert (20th C) American
$900 £566 Landscape (99x127cm-39x50in) s.d.71 acrylic. 23-Apr-93 Hart Gallery, Houston #16

WEINBERG, Emilie Sievert (1882-1958) American
$2500 £1656 The golden cloak, portrait of a lady (81x76cm-32x30in) s.d.1919. 15-Jun-94 Butterfield & Butterfield, San Francisco #4435/R
$3250 £2153 Portrait of artist Gertrude Wall (81x66cm-32x26in) s. s.verso. 20-Sep-93 Butterfield & Butterfield, Los Angeles #101/R

WEINDORF, Paul Friedrich (1887-1965) American
$700 £473 Landscape with farm (58x76cm-23x30in) s. 9-Nov-93 John Moran, Pasadena #885

WEINER, Lawrence (1942-) American
$1119 £741 On one side of the same water (31x40cm-12x16in) mono.i.d.1990 gouache silver paint pencil ink. 20-Nov-92 Lempertz, Cologne #938 (DM 1800)

WEINGARTNER, Pedro (attrib) (1853-1929) Brazilian
$14155 £9500 Hunter by rocky torrent in gorge (81x107cm-32x42in) 16-Jul-93 Christie's, London #148/R

WEINMANN, P (20th C) American
$950 £638 Landscape (71x107cm-28x42in) s. canvas on board. 12-Dec-93 Hindman Galleries, Chicago #307

WEINRICH, Agnes (20th C) American
$1200 £839 Still life with lady slippers (36x28cm-14x11in) s. board. 7-Feb-93 James Bakker, Cambridge #98/R
$550 £369 Landscape (23x33cm-9x13in) s.verso W/C. 5-Dec-93 James Bakker, Cambridge #104
$550 £367 Abstract house (30x48cm-12x19in) s. W/C. 22-May-94 James Bakker, Cambridge #20/R
$600 £403 Still life (20x18cm-8x7in) gouache over graphite. 5-Dec-93 James Bakker, Cambridge #103/R

WEINSTEIN, Matthew (1964-) American
$1400 £940 The Bend (183x229cm-72x90in) init.i.d.1989 verso linen. 23-Feb-94 Christie's, East, New York #305/R

WEIR, J Alden (1852-1919) American
$1200 £789 Portrait of George Piano (99x74cm-39x29in) s.d.1872. 31-Mar-93 Sotheby's Arcade, New York #70/R
$1500 £1000 Dead game (23x41cm-9x16in) s. 1-Jun-94 Doyle, New York #67
$1500 £993 The marsh (51x61cm-20x24in) s. 3-Oct-93 Hanzel Galleries, Chicago #762
$2100 £1409 French village by a river (61x91cm-24x36in) s. 4-Dec-93 Louisiana Auction Exchange #60/R
$4000 £2597 Caroline Clark Marshes (51x61cm-20x24in) s. 15-Jan-93 Du Mouchelle, Detroit #2105/R
$12000 £8054 Portrait of artist's daughter, Caroline Weir (46x36cm-18x14in) s. i.verso. 4-May-94 Doyle, New York #26/R
$13000 £8333 Follower of Grolier (99x79cm-39x31in) s. 27-May-93 Sotheby's, New York #61/R
$15000 £9615 Cora (68x59cm-27x23in) s. 26-May-93 Christie's, New York #122/R
$35000 £22152 The birches (86x69cm-34x27in) s.d.1903. 4-Dec-92 Christie's, New York #13/R
$35000 £22436 Silver chalice, Japanese bronze and red taper (44x29cm-17x11in) s. painted c.1884-89. 27-May-93 Sotheby's, New York #62/R
$1100 £738 Winter woods (53x41cm-21x16in) s.d.88 W/C. 5-Mar-94 Louisiana Auction Exchange #138/R
$8000 £5063 Branchville, Connecticut (15x17cm-6x7in) s. W/C. 3-Dec-92 Sotheby's, New York #33/R

WEIR, J Alden (attrib) (1852-1919) American
$2750 £1809 Woman with mantilla (66x51cm-26x20in) 5-Jun-93 Louisiana Auction Exchange #177/R
$550 £372 Ladies by a stream with apple blossoms (30x41cm-12x16in) s. pastel. 27-Nov-93 Young Fine Arts Auctions, Maine #341/R

WEIR, John Ferguson (1841-1926) American
$1100 £705 Barn at Sugar Loaf (41x43cm-16x17in) board. 13-Dec-92 Litchfield Auction Gallery #24
$5500 £3846 Isola Madre, Lago Maggiore (51x84cm-20x33in) s.d.1885. 11-Mar-93 Christie's, New York #77/R
$11500 £6647 Japanese Iris - six varieties (76x63cm-30x25in) s. 24-Sep-92 Sotheby's, New York #105/R

WEIR, Robert W (1803-1899) American
$4000 £2667 A gentleman caller (56x76cm-22x30in) s.d.1829 i.verso. 1-Jun-94 Doyle, New York #68

WEIR, Robert W (1803-1899) American-cont.
$2600 £1711 Playful new friends (38x51cm-15x20in) s.d.1855 W/C bodycol. 2-Jun-93 Doyle, New York #94

WEIS, John Ellsworth (1892-?) American
$1200 £805 Village street in snow (64x76cm-25x30in) s. 5-Aug-93 Eldred, Massachusetts #672/R

WEISENBORN, Rudolph (1881-?) American
$1000 £654 Portrait of Mrs Kutner (84x51cm-33x20in) s.d.1951. 16-May-93 Hindman Galleries, Chicago #13
$2000 £1307 Kitchen symphony (109x107cm-43x42in) s.d.1928. 19-Sep-93 Hindman Galleries, Chicago #736/R
$950 £621 Abstract head (64x48cm-25x19in) s.d.1948 pastel. 16-May-93 Hindman Galleries, Chicago #11
$3600 £2308 Head (91x58cm-36x23in) s.d.42 gouache board. 13-Dec-92 Hindman Galleries, Chicago #152/R

WEISMAN, Joseph (1907-) American
$650 £430 Boats in marina (38x48cm-15x19in) s. canvasboard. 28-Sep-93 John Moran, Pasadena #322
$600 £397 City street scene (33x48cm-13x19in) s.d.47 W/C. 28-Sep-93 John Moran, Pasadena #276

WELCH, Ludmilla P (1867-1925) American
$1300 £903 Grazing above the bay (30x51cm-12x20in) s. canvas on board. 7-Mar-93 Butterfield & Butterfield, San Francisco #17/R

WELCH, Thaddeus (1844-1919) American
$2000 £1325 Children on a country road (39x58cm-15x23in) s.i.d.1877. 15-Jun-94 Butterfield & Butterfield, San Francisco #469/R
$2250 £1481 Marin County landscape (25x46cm-10x18in) s. 13-Jun-93 Butterfield & Butterfield, San Francisco #774/R
$2500 £1678 The Brook (51x69cm-20x27in) s.d.95. 8-Dec-93 Butterfield & Butterfield, San Francisco #3342/R
$2750 £1821 California valley (33x60cm-13x24in) s. board. 20-Sep-93 Butterfield & Butterfield, Los Angeles #70/R
$6000 £3974 Cows grazing in Marin County (66x117cm-26x46in) s. 15-Jun-94 Butterfield & Butterfield, San Francisco #4625/R
$8500 £5592 Grazing along coast (36x91cm-14x36in) s.d.96. 13-Jun-93 Butterfield & Butterfield, San Francisco #734/R
$13000 £9028 San Geromino Valley (51x91cm-20x36in) s. 7-Mar-93 Butterfield & Butterfield, San Francisco #45/R

WELDON, Charles D (1855-1935) American
$3750 £2622 Interior of fisherman's cottage (76x114cm-30x45in) s. i.verso. 5-Feb-93 Sloan, North Bethesda #2560/R
$950 £634 The Temple courtyard (22x34cm-9x13in) s.d.93 W/C paper on board. 23-May-94 Christie's, East, New York #134/R

WELLER, William (attrib) (20th C) American
$1100 £748 Artist and pupil (76x135cm-30x53in) s.i.d.1914 after R Russler. 17-Apr-94 Schrager Galleries, Milwaukee #454

WELLIVER, Neil (1929-) American
$2500 £1689 Woodland Terry (110x96cm-43x38in) s.i. 8-Nov-93 Christie's, East, New York #231/R
$8500 £5903 Vicky II (152x152cm-60x60in) s.d.73. 22-Feb-93 Christie's, East, New York #168/R
$9000 £5960 Flotsdam, Allagash (61x61cm-24x24in) s. painted 1988. 29-Sep-93 Sotheby's Arcade, New York #337/R

WELSH, Horace Devitt (1888-1942) American
$1000 £505 The gypsies (64x76cm-25x30in) s. 28-Aug-92 Young Fine Arts Auctions, Maine #309/R

WENBAN, Sion Longley (1848-1897) American
$1586 £1004 Wurmtal landscape near Munich (16x28cm-6x11in) mono paper. 30-Nov-92 Wolfgang Ketterer, Munich #371/R (DM 2500)
$1904 £1205 Thunderstorm rising (41x22cm-16x9in) mono.verso W/C gouache. 30-Nov-92 Wolfgang Ketterer, Munich #372/R (DM 3000)

WENDEL, Theodore (1859-1932) American
$4250 £2872 A Venetian street scene (46x20cm-18x8in) s.d.82. 5-Nov-93 Skinner, Bolton #69/R
$11000 £7432 At the north shore (53x76cm-21x30in) s. 10-Aug-93 Stonington Fine Arts, Stonington #150/R
$900 £596 View from boathouse (51x66cm-20x26in) s.d.96 pastel paperboard. 13-Nov-92 Skinner, Bolton #162 a/R
$5000 £3356 Spring landscape with grove of trees (48x64cm-19x25in) s. pastel. 3-Feb-94 Sloan, North Bethesda #2657/R

WENDEROTH, Frederick August (1819-1884) American
$1200 £784 Bay thoroughbred hunter in summer landscape (51x61cm-20x24in) s.d.1878. 15-May-93 Dunning's, Illinois #1048/R

WENDT, William (1865-1946) American
$900 £596 Landscape - sycamore trees and pond (56x71cm-22x28in) 14-Jun-94 John Moran, Pasadena #110 a

WENDT, William (1865-1946) American-cont.

$2400	£1611	Autumn marsh scene (25x36cm-10x14in) s. 16-Dec-93 Mystic Fine Arts, Connecticut #60/R
$5000	£3472	Rocky coast (25x36cm-10x14in) s.d.1918 board. 7-Mar-93 Butterfield & Butterfield, San Francisco #174/R
$5500	£3667	California Hills (64x76cm-25x30in) 23-May-94 Hindman Galleries, Chicago #213/R
$5500	£3667	Valley landscape (64x76cm-25x30in) canvas on masonite. 23-May-94 Hindman Galleries, Chicago #214/R
$7000	£4636	Lights and shadows (46x61cm-18x24in) s. i.verso. 23-Sep-93 Sotheby's, New York #188/R
$10000	£5882	Woman by lake (76x122cm-30x48in) s.d.95. 4-Oct-92 Butterfield & Butterfield, Los Angeles #47/R
$11000	£7051	California landscape (51x91cm-20x36in) s. 17-Dec-92 Mystic Fine Arts, Connecticut #182/R
$14000	£9722	Afternoon's golden light (52x92cm-20x36in) s. 7-Mar-93 Butterfield & Butterfield, San Francisco #200/R
$14000	£9459	The road that leads nowhere (41x51cm-16x20in) s.d.1913. 9-Nov-93 John Moran, Pasadena #939
$14000	£9722	Mountain road (61x51cm-24x20in) s. 7-Mar-93 Butterfield & Butterfield, San Francisco #199/R
$17000	£11724	Atmospheric landscape (71x91cm-28x36in) s. 16-Feb-93 John Moran, Pasadena #48
$18000	£12081	The lone oak (71x91cm-28x36in) s. 8-Dec-93 Butterfield & Butterfield, San Francisco #3385/R
$18000	£12000	Atmospheric seascape with distant boats (61x81cm-24x32in) s.d.1921. 15-Mar-94 John Moran, Pasadena #50
$18000	£10588	Spring (63x76cm-25x30in) s.d.1916. 4-Oct-92 Butterfield & Butterfield, Los Angeles #129/R
$19000	£11176	Midsummer (63x76cm-25x30in) s.d.1928. 4-Oct-92 Butterfield & Butterfield, Los Angeles #151/R
$19000	£12583	Road through the field (71x91cm-28x36in) s.d.1902. 15-Jun-94 Butterfield & Butterfield, San Francisco #4672/R
$19000	£12838	Modjeska Canyon (46x71cm-18x28in) s. 15-Jun-93 John Moran, Pasadena #37
$19000	£13194	View over the trees (62x82cm-24x32in) s.d.1914. 7-Mar-93 Butterfield & Butterfield, San Francisco #149/R
$19000	£12500	Dusk, California (61x91cm-24x36in) s. 13-Jun-93 Butterfield & Butterfield, San Francisco #848/R
$20000	£13423	Malibu Ranch (46x71cm-18x28in) s. 8-Dec-93 Butterfield & Butterfield, San Francisco #3386/R
$22000	£15278	On the heights (81x91cm-32x36in) s.d.1906 i.stretcher. 7-Mar-93 Butterfield & Butterfield, San Francisco #130/R
$23000	£15972	Quiet brook (76x91cm-30x36in) s.d.1923. 7-Mar-93 Butterfield & Butterfield, San Francisco #129/R
$24000	£16667	San Luis Obispo landscape (63x76cm-25x30in) s. 7-Mar-93 Butterfield & Butterfield, San Francisco #151/R
$27500	£16176	Malibu (76x91cm-30x36in) s. 4-Oct-92 Butterfield & Butterfield, Los Angeles #150/R
$35000	£23179	Landscape - cloudland (51x71cm-20x28in) s.d.1919. 14-Jun-94 John Moran, Pasadena #72
$35000	£20588	Ranch in valley (76x102cm-30x40in) s. 4-Oct-92 Butterfield & Butterfield, Los Angeles #128/R
$45000	£26471	Houses along coast (71x91cm-28x36in) s. 4-Oct-92 Butterfield & Butterfield, Los Angeles #136/R
$45000	£31469	Bay Road (63x76cm-25x30in) s.d.1930. 10-Mar-93 Sotheby's, New York #73/R

WENGENROTH, Stow (1906-) American
$700	£470	Floral still life with butterflies (41x30cm-16x12in) s. W/C pencil. 6-Dec-93 Grogan, Massachussetts #542/R

WENGER, John (1891-?) American
$1300	£855	Music room (61x51cm-24x20in) s.indist.d. board. 31-Mar-93 Sotheby's Arcade, New York #150/R

WENTWORTH, D F (1850-?) American
$700	£470	The meadow brook (71x91cm-28x36in) s. 12-Dec-93 Hindman Galleries, Chicago #283

WENTWORTH, Daniel F (1850-?) American
$1200	£805	The meadow brook (74x91cm-29x36in) s. i.verso. 5-Mar-94 Louisiana Auction Exchange #47/R
$1600	£1046	Cows at pond (61x91cm-24x36in) s.d.1890. 1-Nov-92 Hanzel Galleries, Chicago #72

WENZELL, Albert Beck (1864-1917) American
$1100	£724	Couple in outdoor restaurant (66x51cm-26x20in) s. 13-Jun-93 Butterfield & Butterfield, San Francisco #3193/R

WENZLER, Sarah Wilhelmina (school) (fl.1859-1870) American
$8500	£5556	Still life with eggplant, tomatoes and squash on marble topped table (22x30cm-9x12in) indis.s.i. painted c.1860. 31-Oct-92 Skinner, Bolton #198/R

WESCOTT, Paul (1904-1970) American
$1200	£811	Pine trees by the shore (66x117cm-26x46in) s. 20-Mar-93 Weschler, Washington #127/R

WESSELMANN, Tom (1931-) American
$8415	£5500	Untitled (29x34cm-11x13in) s.d.88 acrylic cut paper board. 30-Jun-94 Sotheby's, London #240/R

WESSELMANN, Tom (1931-) American-cont.

$10710	£7000	Rosemary sitting up straight (93x68cm-37x27in) s.d.89verso steel. 30-Jun-94 Sotheby's, London #261/R
$15000	£9804	Studt for smoker - for proposed plastic edition (39x37cm-15x15in) s.d.1975 verso. 4-May-93 Sotheby's, New York #405/R
$18438	£12543	Studio di nudo femminile (37x34cm-15x13in) s.i.d.1984verso. 16-Nov-93 Finarte, Milan #142/R (I.L 31000000)
$19000	£12752	Study for bedroom painting no 2 (20x25cm-8x10in) s.i.d.1967stretcher. 4-May-94 Christie's, New York #187/R
$22000	£14865	Study for Cynthia nude (58x72cm-23x28in) s. i.d.81-53stretcher. 10-Nov-93 Christie's, New York #235 a/R
$36000	£23529	Study for Great American Nude - 6 plus 23 (61x61cm-24x24in) d.84. 4-May-93 Sotheby's, New York #395/R
$38000	£25676	Bedroom painting no.56 (122x230cm-48x91in) s.d.83 verso i.d.1983 stretcher shaped canvas. 11-Nov-93 Sotheby's, New York #392/R
$45000	£30201	Study for nude aquatint (72x81cm-28x32in) s.i.d.80verso. 4-May-94 Christie's, New York #343/R
$50000	£32680	Reclining stockinged nude No.2 (75x130cm-30x51in) canvas on board painted 1982 2/7. 4-May-93 Sotheby's, New York #394/R
$60000	£39216	Fast sketch still life with abstract painting (152x229cm-60x90in) oil cut-out aluminium painted 1989. 4-May-93 Sotheby's, New York #398/R
$1000	£671	Sketch for Smoker No.27 (8x10cm-3x4in) s.d.78 s.i.d.1978 verso crayon col.chk pen board. 23-Feb-94 Christie's, East, New York #333/R
$1900	£1319	Study for 'Claire's Valentine' (28x22cm-11x9in) s.d.69 pencil. 26-Feb-93 Sotheby's Arcade, New York #299/R
$2455	£1659	Reclining nude number 30 (9x12cm-4x5in) s.d.92 crayon dr liquitex board. 18-Jun-93 Francis Briest, Paris #55/R (F.FR 14000)
$2791	£1886	D-32 4 Study for Gan 80 (13x18cm-5x7in) s.d.1966 s.i.d.verso liquitex collage crayon. 24-Nov-93 Watine-Arnault, Paris #60/R (F.FR 16500)
$3000	£2013	Open-ended nude no 7 (9x22cm-4x9in) s.i.d.87 liquitex graphite board. 23-Feb-94 Christie's, New York #44/R
$3500	£2365	Beautiful Kate no.48 (9x22cm-4x9in) s.d.92 liquitex ragboard. 11-Nov-93 Sotheby's, New York #412/R
$3500	£2431	Study for Helen nude (9x9cm-4x4in) d.81 pencil col.pencil. 23-Feb-93 Sotheby's, New York #273/R
$4183	£2789	Embossed nude with still life No.3 (28x35cm-11x14in) s.d.1968 liquitex on embossed paper. 11-Jun-94 Hauswedell & Nolte, Hamburg #389/R (DM 7000)
$4500	£3125	Beautiful Kate (9x22cm-4x9in) s.d.92 gouache pencil paperboard. 23-Feb-93 Sotheby's, New York #278/R
$4698	£3153	Reclining nude with stockings (38x45cm-15x18in) s.d.1967 gouache pencil. 3-Dec-93 Germann, Zurich #50/R (S.FR 7000)
$4800	£3179	Beautiful Kate (9x23cm-4x9in) s.i.d.91 i.verso liquitex graphite board. 19-Nov-92 Christie's, New York #421/R
$4800	£3137	Still life collage (13x18cm-5x7in) s.d.1974 num.56/150 pencil liquitex collage. 11-May-93 Christie's, New York #606/R
$5000	£2941	Long delayed nude (10x14cm-4x6in) s.d.73 pen col.pencil tracing paper. 6-Oct-92 Sotheby's, New York #89/R
$6000	£4167	Study for nude aquatint (12x15cm-5x6in) d.76 and 80 pencil col.pencil. 23-Feb-93 Sotheby's, New York #284/R
$6696	£4464	Claire's Valentine, open ended drawing edition (25x20cm-10x8in) s.i.d.73 thinned liquitex pencil sold with box. 1-Jun-94 Sotheby's, Amsterdam #295/R (D.FL 12500)
$7000	£4730	Beautiful Kate no 7 (9x23cm-4x9in) s.i.d.81 liquitex graphite board. 10-Nov-93 Christie's, New York #138/R
$8000	£5229	Study for woman in green blouse (36x45cm-14x18in) s.d.85 liquitex graphite bristol board. 7-May-93 Christie's, East, New York #170/R
$10000	£6623	Study for blonde on the beach (66x103cm-26x41in) s.d.84 thinned liquitex, graphite paper collage. 19-Nov-92 Christie's, New York #422/R
$16500	£10927	Study for Great American nude no. 70 - D6529 (31x28cm-12x11in) s.d.65 pencil liquitex. 18-Nov-92 Sotheby's, New York #185/R
$20540	£13000	Nude (57x37cm-22x15in) s.d.67 pencil gouache. 3-Dec-92 Sotheby's, London #80/R
$21514	£14343	Study for Great American Nude No.92 (15x25cm-6x10in) s.d.1967 tempera collage. 11-Jun-94 Hauswedell & Nolte, Hamburg #388/R (DM 36000)
$24000	£16107	Portrait collage no 9 (24x35cm-9x14in) s.d.59 i.verso graphite crayons paper collage. 4-May-94 Christie's, New York #186/R
$24480	£16000	Nude with brown and white striped bed (27x40cm-11x16in) s.d.60 gouache pastel pencil fabric paper. 30-Jun-94 Sotheby's, London #172/R
$30000	£20000	Bedroom face with shadow (117x127cm-46x50in) s.d.88 liquitex ragboard. 26-May-94 Christie's, London #87/R
$50000	£29412	Still life with wildflowers, fruit and hat (178x198cm-70x78in) enamel cut-out steel executed 1989. 6-Oct-92 Sotheby's, New York #97/R
$135000	£89404	Still life no.14 (142x142cm-56x56in) s.d.1962 oil paper collage panel mounted panel. 18-Nov-92 Christie's, New York #22/R
$150000	£99338	Great American nude no.89 (112x196cm-44x77in) s. i.d.1967stretcher liquitex oil graphite. 18-Nov-92 Christie's, New York #44/R
$220000	£147651	Great American Nude no 52 (152x122cm-60x48in) s.d.63 acrylic fabric print.paper collage panel. 3-May-94 Christie's, New York #13/R

WESSELS, Glenn (1895-1982) American

$1400	£824	Ferris wheel (48x66cm-19x26in) s. W/C gouache. 4-Oct-92 Butterfield & Butterfield, Los Angeles #254/R

WESSON, Robert (19/20th C) American

$800	£462	Spring farm scene (61x76cm-24x30in) s. 24-Sep-92 Mystic Fine Arts, Connecticut #92/R

WEST, Michael (20th C) American
$1500   £1042   Untitled (43x63cm-17x25in) 26-Feb-93 Sotheby's Arcade, New York #283/R

WESTERMANN, H C (1922-1981) American
$1000   £662   Untitled (28x34cm-11x13in) s.init.d.76 ballpoint pen. 17-Nov-92 Christie's, East, New York #209/R

WESTMACOTT, S (19th C) Canadian
$1300   £855   Niagara Falls (53x66cm-21x26in) s.d.1857. 2-Apr-93 Eldred, Massachusetts #460/R

WESTON, W P (1879-1967) Canadian
$1835   £1162   Trinity Mountain, The Three Sisters, Fernie B.C. (15x18cm-6x7in) s. s.i.d.1957verso board. 21-Oct-92 Maynards, Vancouver #133 (C.D 2300)

WESTON, William Percy (1879-1967) Canadian
$778   £515   Howe Sd. from Copper Cove, 1952 (32x40cm-13x16in) s. panel. 24-Nov-92 Joyner Fine Art, Toronto #149 (C.D 1000)
$1240   £838   Mill Creek Valley Slocan Lake (30x38cm-12x15in) s.i.d.1945verso panel. 1-Nov-93 Levis, Calgary #327/R (C.D 1600)
$973   £644   Three sisters and Elk River (28x41cm-11x16in) st.sig. d.20.9.60 pencil. 24-Nov-92 Joyner Fine Art, Toronto #239 (C.D 1250)
$973   £644   Similkaman Beach (26x42cm-10x17in) st.sig. d.Aug.2.59 pencil. 24-Nov-92 Joyner Fine Art, Toronto #240 (C.D 1250)

WETHERILL, Elisha Kent Kane (1874-1929) American
$1000   £633   Mountainous village (53x56cm-21x22in) 2-Dec-92 Christie's, East, New York #135/R
$1700   £1141   Breton peasant woman with rooster (91x74cm-36x29in) s.d.1905. 5-Mar-94 Louisiana Auction Exchange #133/R

WETMORE, Mary M (19/20th C) American
$650   £448   Dutch girl knitting (20x25cm-8x10in) s. 16-Feb-93 John Moran, Pasadena #28

WEYDEN, Harry van der (1868-?) American
$725   £503   Moonlight in ocean inlet (41x58cm-16x23in) s.d.1922. 5-Mar-93 Skinner, Bolton #724
$814   £546   Southern town scene (43x53cm-17x21in) s. 21-Feb-94 AB Stockholms Auktionsverk (Lilla Kvaliten) #4277 (S.KR 6500)
$962   £650   Storm brewing over coastline (19x30cm-7x12in) s. canvasboard. 17-Jun-93 Christie's, S. Kensington #41
$1700   £1149   Morning labour (16x24cm-6x9in) s.d.April 20th 91 panel. 5-Nov-93 Skinner, Bolton #133/R

WEYL, Max (1837-1914) American
$550   £367   Marsh scene with hills in background (46x61cm-18x24in) s. 20-May-94 Du Mouchelle, Detroit #36/R
$650   £439   Autumn birches (51x25cm-20x10in) s. 4-Nov-93 Sloan, North Bethesda #1568/R
$700   £470   Rock Creek, dusk (51x76cm-20x30in) s. 11-Dec-93 Sloan, North Bethesda #2534/R
$800   £526   Sunrise on forest pond (61x76cm-24x30in) s. 2-Jun-93 Doyle, New York #95
$800   £544   Birches, late autumn (51x38cm-20x15in) s. 9-Jul-93 Sloan, North Bethesda #2635/R
$800   £530   Babbling brook (61x51cm-24x20in) s.d.1890. 2-Oct-93 Weschler, Washington #103/R
$1800   £1224   Spring birches (71x58cm-28x23in) s. 9-Jul-93 Sloan, North Bethesda #2784/R
$2500   £1667   Sunset on the river (51x79cm-20x31in) s. 12-Mar-94 Weschler, Washington #149/R
$5500   £3618   Rock creek park (64x84cm-25x33in) s. 2-Apr-93 Sloan, North Bethesda #2318/R

WHALE, Robert Reginald (1805-1887) Canadian
$707   £448   Landscape with road to river (53x89cm-21x35in) s. 1-Dec-92 Phillips, Toronto #76 (C.D 900)
$4756   £3109   Ferry dock, Grand River (53x89cm-21x35in) s. 19-May-93 Sotheby's, Toronto #388/R (C.D 6000)

WHEATON, Francis (1849-?) American
$2200   £1477   Close Contact (28x41cm-11x16in) s.d.1894 canvas laid down on board. 1-Dec-93 Doyle, New York #80

WHEELOCK, Mabel L (20th C) American
$1000   £654   Group of female artists painting en plein air (46x36cm-18x14in) s.d.1919 gouache. 20-May-93 Boos Gallery, Michigan #456/R

WHISTLER, J A M (1834-1903) American
$894   £600   Shore scene with girl holding large shrimp net (36x28cm-14x11in) s. 5-Aug-93 Russell, Baldwin & Bright, Leominster #764/R

WHISTLER, James Abbott McNeill (1834-1903) American
$3300   £2200   Gwynnes Foundry, Hammersmith (21x29cm-8x11in) s. pencil. 7-Jun-94 Phillips, London #78/R
$4250   £2457   Westpoint cadets (18x11cm-7x4in) rem.s.verso pen. 25-Sep-92 Sotheby's Arcade, New York #74/R
$15000   £9494   Study for 'Mouth of the River' (18x22cm-7x9in) s.with butterfly device W/C board. 4-Dec-92 Christie's, New York #76/R
$45000   £28481   Note in opal - The Sands, Dieppe (21x12cm-8x5in) mono. W/C. 3-Dec-92 Sotheby's, New York #37/R
$47500   £30449   Giudecca - winter - grey and blue (20x30cm-8x12in) mono. chk pastel executed c.1879. 27-May-93 Sotheby's, New York #1/R

WHISTLER, James Abbott McNeill (attrib) (1834-1903) American
$750 £532 Pensive moment (23x23cm-9x9in) mono. pencil. 14-Feb-93 Hanzel Galleries, Chicago #17

WHITAKER, Frederic (1891-?) American
$650 £439 Connecticut harbour (38x53cm-15x21in) s.d.1947 W/C. 9-Nov-93 John Moran, Pasedena #906

WHITAKER, George William (1841-1916) American
$600 £403 Sailboats in bay (41x51cm-16x20in) 27-Mar-94 Myers, Florida #18/R
$715 £467 To hay market - landscape with hay wain crossing bridge (56x71cm-22x28in) s. 14-May-93 Skinner, Bolton #73/R
$1200 £789 Still life with mixed fruit (25x39cm-10x15in) s.d.97. 31-Mar-93 Sotheby's Arcade, New York #42/R
$1200 £784 Figure on path (33x51cm-13x20in) s.d.97. 8-May-93 Young Fine Arts Auctions, Maine #303/R

WHITE, Charles (1918-1980) American
$3200 £2133 Portrait of a man. Portrait of a woman (56x51cm-22x20in) s.d.36 double-sided. 23-May-94 Hindman Galleries, Chicago #244/R
$5400 £3600 Bayou scene and man in chains (46x61cm-18x24in) masonite double-sided. 23-May-94 Hindman Galleries, Chicago #243/R
$9500 £6333 Man with Bible (76x53cm-30x21in) s.d.40 tempera board. 23-May-94 Hindman Galleries, Chicago #242/R

WHITE, Edith (1855-1946) American
$1000 £649 Roses (36x56cm-14x22in) s. 11-Sep-93 Louisiana Auction Exchange #50/R
$1050 £705 Roses (36x56cm-14x22in) s. 4-Dec-93 Louisiana Auction Exchange #188/R
$1600 £1060 Basket of roses (91x69cm-36x27in) s.d.1892. 15-Jun-94 Butterfield & Butterfield, San Francisco #4603/R

WHITE, George Harlow (1817-1888) Canadian/British
$1268 £829 Boy and dog in Sherwood Forest (61x76cm-24x30in) s.d.1863. 19-May-93 Sotheby's, Toronto #31/R (C.D 1600)
$2184 £1456 Burnham Beeches, Buckinghamshire (61x76cm-24x30in) s.d.1863. 11-May-94 Sotheby's, Toronto #16/R (C.D 3000)
$604 £408 Study of children (17x13cm-7x5in) s.d.1879 W/C arched top. 23-Nov-93 Joyner Fine Art, Toronto #262 (C.D 800)

WHITE, Janet (20th C) American
$850 £535 Portrait of girl with crocuses (127x86cm-50x34in) s. 22-Apr-93 Freeman Fine Arts, Philadelphia #1226

WHITE, Joe (20th C) American
$1100 £705 Car headlight (114x102cm-45x40in) acrylic. 10-Dec-92 Sloan, North Bethesda #2680/R

WHITE, Octavius (19th C) Canadian
$1472 £995 Waterfalls (56x89cm-22x35in) s. 3-Nov-93 Sotheby's, Toronto #10/R (C.D 1900)

WHITE, Orrin A (1883-1969) American
$509 £348 A Californian landscape (19x24cm-7x9in) s. i.d.1927 verso board. 8-Feb-94 Christie's, Amsterdam #82/R (D.FL 1000)
$800 £533 Pool Canyon, Santa Barbara (20x25cm-8x10in) s. canvasboard. 15-Mar-94 John Moran, Pasedena #11
$800 £471 California coast (51x61cm-20x24in) s. board. 4-Oct-92 Butterfield & Butterfield, Los Angeles #180/R
$1000 £680 South-western church (51x41cm-20x16in) s. board. 17-Apr-94 Hanzel Galleries, Chicago #950
$1300 £861 Autumn landscape with figures (61x56cm-24x22in) s. 14-Jun-94 John Moran, Pasadena #70
$1300 £872 Market scene (36x51cm-14x20in) s. board. 16-Dec-93 Mystic Fine Arts, Connecticut #61/R
$1500 £1000 California coastal scene (25x30cm-10x12in) s. board. 15-Mar-94 John Moran, Pasedena #159
$1600 £1013 Mission San Miguel de Allende (46x36cm-18x14in) board. 5-Dec-92 San Rafael Auction Galleries #210
$1600 £1081 Fiesta (61x56cm-24x22in) s. 15-Jun-93 John Moran, Pasadena #162
$1600 £1081 Market day in Taxco (64x76cm-25x30in) s. 9-Nov-93 John Moran, Pasadena #945 a
$1600 £1081 Mexico market scene with figures (25x30cm-10x12in) s. board. 9-Nov-93 John Moran, Pasadena #745 b
$3250 £2152 Landscape - sycamores Santa Anita Canyon (61x86cm-24x34in) s. 14-Jun-94 John Moran, Pasadena #115 a
$3250 £2196 Landscape with stream (51x61cm-20x24in) s. canvas on board. 15-Jun-93 John Moran, Pasadena #31
$3250 £2257 Hillside landscape (61x56cm-24x22in) s. 7-Mar-93 Butterfield & Butterfield, San Francisco #177/R
$3250 £2241 Arroyo landscape (30x41cm-12x16in) s. board. 16-Feb-93 John Moran, Pasadena #38
$3500 £2318 Lake Tahoe (58x81cm-23x32in) s. 15-Jun-94 Butterfield & Butterfield, San Francisco #4702/R
$3800 £2484 Brown hillside (63x76cm-25x30in) s. 4-May-93 Christie's, East, New York #127 h/R
$4250 £2931 Sierra stream (61x61cm-24x24in) s. 16-Feb-93 John Moran, Pasadena #124
$8000 £5556 Valley landscape (66x81cm-26x32in) s. 7-Mar-93 Butterfield & Butterfield, San Francisco #181/R
$9000 £6207 Landscape (56x71cm-22x28in) s. 16-Feb-93 John Moran, Pasadena #78

WHITE, R Lee (20th C) American
$3250 £2044 Painted buffalo hide (184x171cm-72x67in) s.d.85 mixed media buffalo hide. 25-Apr-93 Butterfield & Butterfield, San Francisco #2181/R

WHITE, Wade (1909-) American
$3500 £2023 Sun and wind (36x48cm-14x19in) s.d.1936-37. 24-Sep-92 Sotheby's, New York #138/R

WHITE, Willie (c.1905-) American
$1050 £695 Flying creatures (56x71cm-22x28in) s. marker pen. 21-Nov-92 Litchfield Auction Gallery #16

WHITEFIELD, Edwin (1816-1892) American
$1800 £1184 Among Berkshire Hills-Lee, Mass (36x46cm-14x18in) s.verso. 2-Apr-93 Eldred, Massachusetts #549/R

WHITESIDE, Brian (19/20th C) American
$1600 £1053 Polo match, Palm Springs (61x91cm-24x36in) s. 4-Jun-93 Sotheby's, New York #247/R
$1800 £1200 Neck and neck (45x60cm-18x24in) s. 3-Jun-94 Sotheby's, New York #284/R

WHITING, Henry W (19th C) American
$3000 £1961 Mist lifting off the lake (36x61cm-14x24in) s. 5-May-93 Doyle, New York #1/R

WHITMAN, C (19th C) American
$3299 £2229 The Bridal Veil Fall, Yosemite, USA (76x128cm-30x50in) s. 19-Apr-94 Rasmussen, Vejle #942/R (D.KR 22000)

WHITTAKER, J B (1836-?) American
$1000 £680 You angry with me John (76x61cm-30x24in) s. 14-Apr-94 Freeman Fine Arts, Philadelphia #973

WHITTAKER, John Barnard (1836-?) American
$2000 £1361 A powerful embrace (124x89cm-49x35in) s.d.67. 17-Nov-93 Doyle, New York #47/R

WHITTEMORE, William John (1860-1955) American
$2250 £1301 Portrait of young girl (54x43cm-21x17in) s.d.1903 W/C paper on board. 25-Sep-92 Sotheby's Arcade, New York #146/R
$3000 £2000 Young Diana, Goddess of the Hunt (53x43cm-21x17in) s.d.1907 W/C board. 23-May-94 Christie's, East, New York #124/R

WHITTREDGE, W (1820-1910) American
$744 £520 Lake landscape with figures (23x30cm-9x12in) s. 9-Mar-93 Rowland Gorringe, Lewes #1997

WHITTREDGE, Worthington (1820-1910) American
$5750 £3686 Under trees (20x28cm-8x11in) s. 27-May-93 Sotheby's, New York #149/R
$5750 £3834 The old mill (30x38cm-12x15in) s. i.verso. 1-Jun-94 Doyle, New York #69
$7000 £4667 View of Morelia, Mexico (28x41cm-11x16in) d.99 canvas on aluminium. 23-May-94 Christie's, East, New York #69/R
$7600 £5000 View of the Hudson River (25x38cm-10x15in) s. board. 13-Jun-93 Hindman Galleries, Chicago #219
$22000 £14765 Happy as a King (92x122cm-36x48in) s.i.d.1843 before lining. 3-Dec-93 Christie's, New York #127/R
$22500 £15203 Autumn woodland interior with fisherman (71x107cm-28x42in) s.d.1866. 4-Nov-93 Sloan, North Bethesda #2547/R
$27000 £18000 Farm by the shore (29x56cm-11x22in) s. painted 1880's. 17-Mar-94 Sotheby's, New York #9/R
$30000 £18987 Platte River (34x54cm-13x21in) s. 3-Dec-92 Sotheby's, New York #52/R
$45000 £30000 Indian encampment (19x32cm-7x13in) s. 25-May-94 Sotheby's, New York #35/R
$125000 £82781 Indian encampment on Platte River, Colorado (37x56cm-15x22in) s. painted mid 1870's. 23-Sep-93 Sotheby's, New York #88/R
$205000 £136667 Indian encampment on the Platte (37x56cm-15x22in) s. painted c.1870-1872. 25-May-94 Sotheby's, New York #42/R

WHITTREDGE, Worthington (attrib) (1820-1910) American
$1400 £933 Study of a tree (69x51cm-27x20in) bears sig. 23-May-94 Hindman Galleries, Chicago #164/R

WHORF, John (1903-1959) American
$1000 £676 Portrait of Austin Dunham (76x61cm-30x24in) s.d.21 i.verso. 31-Oct-93 Hindman Galleries, Chicago #728/R
$1800 £1208 Moonlit harbour (30x41cm-12x16in) s. canvasboard. 6-Dec-93 Grogan, Massachussetts #547/R
$2750 £1821 Nude standing by a window (76x56cm-30x22in) 28-Nov-92 Young Fine Arts Auctions, Maine #406/R
$600 £403 Forest light (36x51cm-14x20in) s. W/C. 5-Dec-93 James Bakker, Cambridge #37
$850 £574 Boulders (33x48cm-13x19in) s. W/C. 10-Aug-93 Stonington Fine Arts, Stonington #173/R
$900 £600 Lumber yard (41x53cm-16x21in) s. W/C. 22-May-94 James Bakker, Cambridge #181
$1000 £649 Mexican fiesta (46x56cm-18x22in) s. W/C. 11-Sep-93 Louisiana Auction Exchange #42/R
$1100 £738 Coastal view (36x51cm-14x20in) s. W/C. 28-Mar-94 James Bakker, Cambridge #6/R
$1200 £811 Figures in a stormy landscape (38x58cm-15x23in) s. W/C. 27-Nov-93 Young Fine Arts Auctions, Maine #347/R
$1200 £811 By the canal (27x36cm-11x14in) s. W/C board. 31-Mar-94 Sotheby's Arcade, New York #306/R

WHORF, John (1903-1959) American-cont.

$1300	£872	Clipper ship at dock (33x48cm-13x19in) s. W/C. 6-Dec-93 Grogan, Massachussetts #545/R
$1500	£987	Street by night (27x37cm-11x15in) s. W/C paper on board. 31-Mar-93 Sotheby's Arcade, New York #400/R
$1500	£1000	Loggers (37x54cm-15x21in) s. W/C. 23-May-94 Christie's, East, New York #112/R
$1540	£1040	Windy evening (38x56cm-15x22in) s. W/C. 10-Aug-93 Stonington Fine Arts, Stonington #172
$1600	£936	View of a railroad (33x48cm-13x19in) s. W/C. 17-Sep-92 Sloan, North Bethesda #3087
$1800	£1192	Canoeing in the mist (36x53cm-14x21in) s. W/C. 3-Oct-93 Hanzel Galleries, Chicago #43
$1900	£1275	Working boats (36x53cm-14x21in) s. W/C. 6-Dec-93 Grogan, Massachussetts #544/R
$1900	£1267	Duck hunting (37x54cm-15x21in) s. W/C. 23-May-94 Christie's, East, New York #109/R
$2000	£1058	Sunning, view with bathers (36x46cm-14x18in) s. W/C graphite. 11-Sep-92 Skinner, Bolton #243/R
$2500	£1701	Bright morning (14x22cm-6x9in) s. W/C. 10-Jul-93 Young Fine Arts Auctions, Maine #333/R
$2600	£1722	Trout fishing (36x53cm-14x21in) s. W/C. 3-Oct-93 Hanzel Galleries, Chicago #41
$2600	£1699	Spring comes to Parnal Street (37x54cm-15x21in) s. W/C. 4-May-93 Christie's, East, New York #213/R
$2700	£1776	Summer day (36x53cm-14x21in) s.d.38 W/C. 2-Jun-93 Doyle, New York #96
$2800	£1958	Notre Dame (56x76cm-22x30in) s. W/C board. 11-Mar-93 Christie's, New York #201
$2800	£1618	Nude wading (53x36cm-21x14in) s. W/C. 27-Sep-92 James Bakker, Cambridge #93/R
$2900	£1895	The vine (38x53cm-15x21in) s.i. W/C. 18-Sep-93 James Bakker, Cambridge #49/R
$3100	£1640	Returning home from the sleigh ride (51x71cm-20x28in) s. W/C. 11-Sep-92 Skinner, Bolton #237/R
$3300	£2185	A catch in the canoe (36x53cm-14x21in) s. W/C. 3-Oct-93 Hanzel Galleries, Chicago #42
$3400	£2222	Fishing boat in harbour (48x58cm-19x23in) s.d.37 W/C. 16-May-93 Hindman Galleries, Chicago #7/R
$3500	£2365	The hunter (33x50cm-13x20in) s. W/C pencil. 31-Mar-94 Sotheby's Arcade, New York #288/R
$3700	£2450	Breakfast at the campsite (38x53cm-15x21in) s. W/C. 3-Oct-93 Hanzel Galleries, Chicago #45/R
$3750	£2622	Thunderers (56x74cm-22x29in) s. W/C gouache. 12-Mar-93 Dargate Auction Galleries, Pittsburgh #1037
$3800	£2517	Canoeing on a stream (38x53cm-15x21in) s. W/C. 3-Oct-93 Hanzel Galleries, Chicago #44/R
$3944	£2578	Sur le port en Bretagne 24 (76x55cm-30x22in) s. W/C. 16-May-93 Thierry, Brest #142/R (F.FR 21500)
$4500	£2980	Night-time boating scene - fishing boats and schooner 'Island Girl' (76x97cm-30x38in) s. 20-Nov-92 Eldred, Massachusetts #515/R
$4800	£3179	G-Man in attic (38x56cm-15x22in) s. W/C. 22-Sep-93 Christie's, New York #225/R
$9000	£5696	Trap fishermen, foggy morning (57x78cm-22x31in) s.d.53 W/C. 4-Dec-92 Christie's, New York #42/R

WHORF, Richard (20th C) American

$850	£563	Suzannah and the Elders (46x61cm-18x24in) s. i.d.1962verso tempera board. 28-Sep-93 John Moran, Pasadena #334

WICHT, John von (20th C) American

$4500	£3020	Conflict - abstract compostion (51x28cm-20x11in) s. gouache. 4-May-94 Doyle, New York #73/R

WIDFORSS, Gunnar M (1879-1934) American

$13000	£8725	Landscape with cactus (30x41cm-12x16in) s. 2-Dec-93 Sotheby's, New York #85/R
$900	£608	Old houses, Stockholm (33x46cm-13x18in) s.d.1915 W/C. 15-Jun-93 John Moran, Pasadena #51
$3500	£2431	Rocky coastline (32x43cm-13x17in) s.d.1920 W/C. 7-Mar-93 Butterfield & Butterfield, San Francisco #110/R
$4000	£2649	Big trees (55x21cm-22x8in) W/C. 15-Jun-94 Butterfield & Butterfield, San Francisco #4631/R
$5000	£3356	Desert in bloom (21x34cm-8x13in) W/C. 2-Dec-93 Sotheby's, New York #95/R
$6000	£4027	Monterey coastline (36x46cm-14x18in) s.d.1923 W/C. 2-Dec-93 Sotheby's, New York #87/R
$6500	£4362	Temple of Sinawava, Zion National Park (36x43cm-14x17in) s.i.d.1920 W/C. 2-Dec-93 Sotheby's, New York #94/R
$6500	£4514	Merced River, Yosemite (45x35cm-18x14in) s.d.1921 W/C. 7-Mar-93 Butterfield & Butterfield, San Francisco #38/R
$7000	£4698	Monterey cypress (33x43cm-13x17in) s.d.1925 W/C. 2-Dec-93 Sotheby's, New York #86/R
$7500	£5034	Vernal Falls, Yosemite (56x46cm-22x18in) s.d.1926 i.verso W/C. 2-Dec-93 Sotheby's, New York #83/R
$9500	£6643	Grand Canyon (50x44cm-20x17in) s.d.1929 W/C. 10-Mar-93 Sotheby's, New York #50
$10000	£5882	Grand Canyon (43x34cm-17x13in) s. W/C. 4-Oct-92 Butterfield & Butterfield, Los Angeles #139/R
$10000	£6944	Sunlight on the Grand Canyon (39x56cm-15x22in) s.d.1924 W/C. 7-Mar-93 Butterfield & Butterfield, San Francisco #219/R
$19000	£12752	Grand Canyon (38x43cm-15x17in) s. W/C. 2-Dec-93 Sotheby's, New York #84/R

WIDMAN, Bruno (1930-) Uruguayan

$7500	£5068	Circulo y composicion 12, la Sagrada Familia (100x100cm-39x39in) s. s.i.verso acrylic linen. 23-Nov-93 Christie's, New York #200/R

WIEGAND, Charmion von (1899-) American
$2000	£1333	*Knave of Spades (21x16cm-8x6in) init.d.1956 paper collage. 23-May-94 Christie's, East, New York #316/R*

WIEGAND, Gustave (1870-1957) American
$600	£411	Blue Mountain Lake, New York (30x25cm-12x10in) s. board. 19-Feb-94 Young Fine Arts Auctions, Maine #206/R
$600	£403	Landscape with cabin (30x23cm-12x9in) s. 5-Mar-94 Louisiana Auction Exchange #108/R
$700	£470	Landscape with brook (51x41cm-20x16in) s. 4-Dec-93 Louisiana Auction Exchange #119/R
$700	£464	Landscape (51x76cm-20x30in) s. canvas on masonite. 19-Jun-94 Hindman Galleries, Chicago #717 a
$700	£452	View through birches (41x30cm-16x12in) s. 6-Jan-93 Doyle, New York #69
$800	£462	Winter landscape with river (51x61cm-20x24in) s. 25-Sep-92 Sotheby's Arcade, New York #274/R
$800	£544	Blue Mountain Lake, New York (30x25cm-12x10in) s. s.i.verso panel. 8-Apr-94 Sloan, North Bethesda #2103/R
$1200	£811	The Golden Gateway (76x102cm-30x40in) s. i.stretcher. 31-Mar-94 Sotheby's Arcade, New York #267/R
$1300	£872	Man in canoe (61x51cm-24x20in) s. 4-Dec-93 Louisiana Auction Exchange #134/R
$1400	£909	Trout brook. First snow (25x20cm-10x8in) s. s.i.verso panel pair. 9-Sep-93 Sotheby's Arcade, New York #175/R
$1500	£1014	Summer landscape (30x25cm-12x10in) s. board. 31-Mar-94 Sotheby's Arcade, New York #147/R
$1700	£1141	Edge of a birch wood (76x91cm-30x36in) s. 17-Dec-93 Du Mouchelle, Detroit #2193/R
$1800	£1208	Autumn landscape (71x61cm-28x24in) s. 24-Jun-93 Mystic Fine Arts, Connecticut #97
$2100	£1373	Birches on the riverside (76x64cm-30x25in) s. 1-Nov-92 Hanzel Galleries, Chicago #31/R

WIEGHORST, Olaf (1899-1988) American
$650	£425	Equestrian portrait (43x36cm-17x14in) s. 29-Jun-94 Doyle, New York #81
$5000	£3497	On the lookout (76x91cm-30x36in) s. 11-Mar-93 Christie's, New York #125/R
$6250	£4252	Eight seconds a rider on bucking horse (61x51cm-24x20in) s.d.52 s.i.d.verso. 17-Nov-93 Doyle, New York #50/R
$7000	£4636	Montana cowboy (56x61cm-22x24in) s. i.stretcher. 23-Sep-93 Sotheby's, New York #97/R
$16000	£10667	Picking his mount (76x91cm-30x36in) s. 26-May-94 Christie's, New York #60/R
$16000	£10127	Cheyenne sentry (35x30cm-14x12in) s.d.1977. 3-Dec-92 Sotheby's, New York #76/R
$30000	£20134	Government pack train (61x76cm-24x30in) s.d.79 s.i.d.verso. 2-Dec-93 Sotheby's, New York #47/R
$2550	£1678	*Mare and foal (15x20cm-6x8in) s. pencil. 31-Mar-93 Sotheby's Arcade, New York #196/R*
$4000	£2685	*The roper (29x27cm-11x11in) s. pen wash gouache. 2-Dec-93 Sotheby's, New York #74/R*
$5000	£3333	*Snowstorm cowboy (31x25cm-12x10in) s. gouache W/C ink. 17-Mar-94 Sotheby's, New York #71/R*

WIGGINS, Carleton (1848-1932) American
$900	£570	Evening on the farm (73x92cm-29x36in) s. 2-Dec-92 Christie's, East, New York #291/R
$1200	£811	Cow in a field (58x72cm-23x28in) s.d.1881. 31-Mar-94 Sotheby's Arcade, New York #61/R
$1500	£1014	On the farm, Normandy (53x65cm-21x26in) s.d.1881-2. 31-Mar-94 Sotheby's Arcade, New York #63/R
$1800	£1040	Sheep grazing in early spring (51x61cm-20x24in) s.d.1918. 25-Sep-92 Sotheby's Arcade, New York #119/R
$6000	£3529	Ploughing fields (64x91cm-25x36in) s.d.1882. 5-Oct-92 Grogan, Massachussetts #683/R
$7000	£4430	In the Palisades (40x71cm-16x28in) inits.d.1871. 4-Dec-92 Christie's, New York #198/R
$800	£533	*Sheep grazing in a field (28x38cm-11x15in) s. W/C. 1-Jun-94 Doyle, New York #71*

WIGGINS, Guy (1883-1962) American
$600	£411	The twilight hour (30x41cm-12x16in) s. i.verso. 10-Feb-94 Skinner, Bolton #193
$760	£500	Landscape with corn sheafs, church spire beyond (61x61cm-24x24in) s. board. 1-Apr-93 Bonhams, London #29/R
$1500	£1020	Landscape (41x51cm-16x20in) s. board. 16-Apr-94 Young Fine Arts Auctions, Maine #264/R
$3000	£1987	Sunrise at Essex, Conn (30x40cm-12x16in) s. s.i.verso canvasboard. 22-Sep-93 Christie's, New York #168/R
$3000	£2027	Oranges and palms (61x51cm-24x20in) s. s.i.d.1925 verso. 31-Mar-94 Sotheby's Arcade, New York #228/R
$3000	£1987	Life (61x51cm-24x20in) s. s.i.d.1959 verso. 22-Sep-93 Christie's, New York #210/R
$3200	£2025	Broadway in snow (25x20cm-10x8in) s. board. 2-Dec-92 Christie's, East, New York #298/R
$3500	£2333	Winter harmony (30x41cm-12x16in) s. canvasboard. 15-Mar-94 John Moran, Pasadena #130
$3500	£2381	On Dorset Hills Vermont winter (51x61cm-20x24in) s. s.i.verso. 17-Nov-93 Doyle, New York #49/R
$3800	£2222	Golden autumn (61x76cm-24x30in) s. i.verso. 17-Sep-92 Sloan, North Bethesda #3108/R
$4000	£2532	Fifth Avenue blizzard (30x41cm-12x16in) s. 2-Dec-92 Christie's, East, New York #290/R

WIGGINS, Guy (1883-1962) American-cont.

$	£	Description
$4000	£2721	A winter morning in woodland (51x61cm-20x24in) s. s.i.d.1926verso. 17-Nov-93 Doyle, New York #48/R
$4000	£2597	Washington Square (23x30cm-9x12in) s. canvasboard. 9-Sep-93 Sotheby's Arcade, New York #221/R
$5000	£2941	Christmas Eve, New York (30x20cm-12x8in) s. s.i.verso canvasboard. 5-Oct-92 Grogan, Massachussetts #750/R
$5000	£3205	West Side, New York City (25x20cm-10x8in) s. canvasboard. 12-Dec-92 Weschler, Washington #81/R
$5250	£3035	New York skyline (31x40cm-12x16in) s. canvasboard. 24-Sep-92 Sotheby's, New York #158/R
$5500	£3179	Fifth Avenue at 42nd Street (20x25cm-8x10in) s. board. 24-Sep-92 Sotheby's, New York #213/R
$6000	£3947	Quiet day, Essex, Connecticut (63x76cm-25x30in) s. 31-Mar-93 Sotheby's Arcade, New York #173/R
$7000	£4667	Along Central Park in winter (61x51cm-24x20in) s. s.i.verso. 21-May-94 Weschler, Washington #130/R
$7250	£4770	Christmas Eve at Old Trinity (30x20cm-12x8in) s. canvas board. 4-Nov-92 Doyle, New York #40/R
$7500	£5245	Fifth Avenue and 26th Street (12x8cm-5x3in) s. s.i.d.1927verso canvasboard. 11-Mar-93 Christie's, New York #209/R
$7500	£4967	Washington's birthday (30x20cm-12x8in) s. canvasboard. 22-Sep-93 Christie's, New York #147/R
$7750	£5099	City snow storms (41x51cm-16x20in) s. i.d.1934 verso. 31-Mar-93 Sotheby's Arcade, New York #260/R
$8500	£5629	At the library (23x30cm-9x12in) s. canvasboard. 22-Sep-93 Christie's, New York #146/R
$9000	£5202	Central Park skyline (30x40cm-12x16in) s. s.i.d.1936 verso board. 24-Sep-92 Sotheby's, New York #214/R
$9000	£6040	The Great Oak (64x76cm-25x30in) s.d.1922 s.i.d.verso. 3-Dec-93 Christie's, New York #36/R
$10000	£6410	Midtown, New York (30x23cm-12x9in) s. canvasboard. 27-May-93 Sotheby's, New York #105/R
$13000	£8667	Winter's day in Wall Street (63x76cm-25x30in) s. s.i.verso painted late 1950's. 17-Mar-94 Sotheby's, New York #160/R
$14000	£8974	Washington Square in winter (51x61cm-20x24in) s. 26-May-93 Christie's, New York #153/R
$16000	£10667	Snowy day in New York City (55x65cm-22x26in) s. board. 25-May-94 Sotheby's, New York #108/R
$16000	£11189	Red X Week, winter (76x64cm-30x25in) s. i.verso. 11-Mar-93 Christie's, New York #224/R
$16500	£11074	Mid-town storm (71x61cm-28x24in) s. 24-Jun-93 Boos Gallery, Michigan #606/R
$17000	£11111	Washington Arch (63x76cm-25x30in) s.i. s.indis.d.1930verso. 22-May-93 Weschler, Washington #126/R
$20000	£12658	Winter along Central Park (64x76cm-25x30in) s. s.i.verso. 3-Dec-92 Sotheby's, New York #199/R
$20000	£13245	Library in winter (64x76cm-25x30in) s. 23-Sep-93 Mystic Fine Arts, Connecticut #158/R
$22000	£12717	Winter's day at the Library (63x76cm-25x30in) s.i. s.i.verso. 23-Sep-92 Christie's, New York #210/R
$22000	£14765	In the shipyard (61x76cm-24x30in) s. 3-Dec-93 Christie's, New York #50/R
$23000	£13295	Fifth Avenue winter (76x63cm-30x25in) s. 24-Sep-92 Sotheby's, New York #212/R
$2300	*£1544*	*New York City scenes (25x20cm-10x8in) pastels pair. 24-Jun-93 Mystic Fine Arts, Connecticut #100*

WIGGINS, Guy (style) (1883-1962) American

$	£	Description
$1100	£733	Armistice Day in New York (30x41cm-12x16in) bears sig. 1-Jun-94 Doyle, New York #70

WIGGINS, Kim Douglas (20th C) American

$	£	Description
$1300	£872	Practice at San Patricio (51x61cm-20x24in) s.d.87. 5-Mar-94 Louisiana Auction Exchange #17/R

WIGHTMAN, Thomas (attrib) (18/19th C) American

$	£	Description
$6500	£4362	Still life with fruit (61x76cm-24x30in) 1-Dec-93 Doyle, New York #81/R

WILBERT, Robert (1929-) American

$	£	Description
$3300	£2200	Window still life (61x112cm-24x44in) s.d.1982. 12-May-94 Boos Gallery, Michigan #503/R
$850	*£567*	*Sun Glow (33x41cm-13x16in) s.d.82 W/C. 12-May-94 Boos Gallery, Michigan #504/R*

WILBUR, Arthur Rutherford (19/20th C) Canadian?

$	£	Description
$2549	£1699	St.John Harbour (61x99cm-24x39in) s. 11-May-94 Sotheby's, Toronto #215/R (C.D 3500)

WILBUR, Theodore E (19th C) American

$	£	Description
$900	£604	Extensive landscape (61x107cm-24x42in) s. 16-Dec-93 Mystic Fine Arts, Connecticut #145

WILCOX, W S (19th C) American

$	£	Description
$3500	£2318	Violets and copper pot (41x61cm-16x24in) s. i.d.May 1894verso. 15-Jun-94 Butterfield & Butterfield, San Francisco #4604/R

WILDE, John (1919-) American
$3500 £2023 Myself as anatomist (24x30cm-9x12in) s.d.47 i.verso masonite. 23-Sep-92 Christie's, New York #282/R

WILDER, Nicholas (1938-1989) American?
$4800 £3137 Cloud over Sinai (119x196cm-47x77in) linen on panel executed 1987. 22-Dec-92 Christie's, East, New York #82

WILES, Irving Ramsey (1861-1948) American
$800 £537 Actress (97x66cm-38x26in) s.d.1910verso. 2-Dec-93 Freeman Fine Arts, Philadelphia #769
$2750 £1846 Guitar player (66x51cm-26x20in) s. 24-Mar-94 Mystic Fine Arts, Connecticut #218
$14000 £9790 Thoughtful (28x23cm-11x9in) s. 11-Mar-93 Christie's, New York #137/R
$22000 £14667 Haystacks (17x25cm-7x10in) s. panel. 17-Mar-94 Sotheby's, New York #108/R
$28000 £16185 Along shore (24x33cm-9x13in) s. panel. 24-Sep-92 Sotheby's, New York #131/R
$65000 £43333 The little green hat (98x70cm-39x28in) s.d.1916. 25-May-94 Sotheby's, New York #77/R

WILES, Irving Ramsey and CHASE, William Merritt (19th C) American
$25000 £16779 Mrs William Merrit Chase and son Roland Dana Chase (157x128cm-62x50in) s. 2-Dec-93 Sotheby's, New York #125/R

WILES, Lemuel (1826-1905) American
$4250 £2951 Coast of the Pacific near Santa Cruz, California (61x102cm-24x40in) s.d.1881 s.i.d.1881-2verso. 7-Mar-93 Butterfield & Butterfield, San Francisco #74/R
$13000 £8333 St. Helena, Valley of Genesee (23x38cm-9x15in) s.d.1868 s.i.d.verso. 26-May-93 Christie's, New York #8/R
$13000 £7514 Highlands of the Hudson, view near West Point (35x61cm-14x24in) s.d.1872 s.i.d.1872verso. 23-Sep-92 Christie's, New York #57/R

WILEY, William T (1937-) American
$700 *£443* *Untitled (74x58cm-29x23in) s.i. felt-tip pen. 25-Oct-92 Butterfield & Butterfield, San Francisco #2332/R*
$1100 *£696* *Doodle (27x34cm-11x13in) s.d.62 mixed media canvas on board. 25-Oct-92 Butterfield & Butterfield, San Francisco #2303/R*
$1200 *£755* *Open conclusion (45x39cm-18x15in) s.d.1972 W/C ink. 25-Apr-93 Butterfield & Butterfield, San Francisco #2122/R*
$2500 *£1582* *Adore Well Open (35x27cm-14x11in) mono.d.73 W/C pen. 25-Oct-92 Butterfield & Butterfield, San Francisco #2333/R*
$2750 *£1858* *No change like the present (91x110cm-36x43in) graphite W/C painted 1988. 21-Apr-94 Butterfield & Butterfield, San Francisco #1204*

WILKINS, J F (fl.1832-44) American
$1862 *£1267* *Peasant women hanging out their washing. Merrymaking peasants, landscape (9cm-4in circular) min.s.gilt-metal mount rec.wood frame pair. 16-Nov-93 Christie's, Geneva #143 (S.FR 2800)*

WILKINSON, John B (19th C) Canadian
$3459 £2306 Indians shooting the rapids (20x31cm-8x12in) s. 11-May-94 Sotheby's, Toronto #26/R (C.D 4750)

WILLARD, Archibald M (1836-1918) American
$7500 £4967 Pluck I. Pluck II (63x77cm-25x30in) i. pair. 23-Sep-93 Sotheby's, New York #83/R

WILLCOX, W H (c.1831-?) American
$850 £570 The river walk - Philadelphia view (30x25cm-12x10in) s.d.1873 i.verso. 4-Dec-93 Skinner, Bolton #181

WILLIAMS, Dwight (1856-?) American
$2200 £1497 Venice (28x41cm-11x16in) s. i.verso. 15-Nov-93 Christie's, East, New York #147/R

WILLIAMS, Florence White (?-1953) American
$1300 £861 Monhegan landing (61x61cm-24x24in) s. 21-Nov-92 James Bakker, Cambridge #252/R

WILLIAMS, Frederick Ballard (1871-1956) American
$1100 £714 L'allegro (30x38cm-12x15in) s.d.03 panel. 9-Sep-93 Sotheby's Arcade, New York #98/R
$3600 £2338 Happy valley (71x91cm-28x36in) s.d.08. 9-Sep-93 Sotheby's Arcade, New York #97/R

WILLIAMS, Helen (20th C) American
$1500 £987 Summer clouds - North Carolina Mountains (41x51cm-16x20in) s. 31-Mar-93 Sotheby's Arcade, New York #240/R

WILLIAMS, Micah (attrib) (19th C) American
$3300 £2215 Portrait of young woman (58x46cm-23x18in) pastel. 27-Mar-93 Skinner, Bolton #165/R

WILLIAMS, Paul A (1934-) American
$800 £523 Sea shore (20x25cm-8x10in) s. board. 1-Nov-92 Litchfield Auction Gallery #272 a
$800 £513 Summer mood (25x20cm-10x8in) s. i.verso board. 13-Dec-92 Litchfield Auction Gallery #25
$950 £609 Belles femmes (25x20cm-10x8in) s. i.verso board. 13-Dec-92 Litchfield Auction Gallery #26
$1100 £647 Wildflowers (30x23cm-12x9in) s. 3-Oct-92 Weschler, Washington #173/R
$1300 £765 Reve (30x23cm-12x9in) s. 3-Oct-92 Weschler, Washington #174/R

WILLIAMS, Paul A (1934-) American-cont.
$1300	£861	Les fleurs (51x41cm-20x16in) s.i.verso. 28-Nov-92 Young Fine Arts Auctions, Maine #411/R
$1500	£993	Les crossing the bay (30x41cm-12x16in) s. i.verso. 28-Nov-92 Young Fine Arts Auctions, Maine #412/R
$1650	£1146	Summer rapture (51x41cm-20x16in) s. 6-Mar-93 Louisiana Auction Exchange #19/R

WILLIAMS, Robert F (20th C) American
$7250	£4866	Floral gardens at Ditmars Lane (66x91cm-26x36in) s.verso. 24-Mar-94 Mystic Fine Arts, Connecticut #180 b

WILLIAMS, Virgil (1830-1886) American
$510	£333	Italian peasants resting at well with ox-drawn waggon approaching (38x77cm-15x30in) s.d.1865. 28-Oct-92 Christie's, Amsterdam #109 (D.FL 900)
$1400	£972	Shepherd boy (24x32cm-9x13in) s.i.d.65 board. 7-Mar-93 Butterfield & Butterfield, San Francisco #20/R

WILLIAMSON, John (1826-1885) American
$800	£516	Rocky woodland (23x28cm-9x11in) init.i. 13-Jul-94 Doyle, New York #79
$800	£523	River scene (20x28cm-8x11in) mono. 30-Jun-94 Mystic Fine Arts, Connecticut #179
$2200	£1447	Autumn landscape with mountains and river (36x61cm-14x24in) mono. 31-Mar-93 Sotheby's Arcade, New York #46/R
$5000	£3497	Trout brook, Bushkill, New York (56x41cm-22x16in) init.d.82 i.verso i.stretcher. 11-Mar-93 Christie's, New York #44/R
$7000	£4667	View of the Susquehanna near Lanesboro (43x58cm-17x23in) init. s.i.d.1850 verso. 17-Mar-94 Sotheby's, New York #10/R

WILLING, John Thompson (1860-?) American
$650	£442	Daffodils (24x20cm-9x8in) board. 10-Jul-93 Young Fine Arts Auctions, Maine #336/R

WILLIS, Thomas (1850-1912) American
$925	£625	Sailing vessel (56x76cm-22x30in) s. canvas with silk. 30-Jul-93 Eldred, Massachusetts #112
$1800	£1208	Schooner Emma and Hellen (46x71cm-18x28in) s.i. canvas with needlework velvet and silk. 3-Feb-94 Sloan, North Bethesda #2698/R

WILLIS, Thomas (attrib) (1850-1912) American
$3600	£2432	American schooner Vesta (46x81cm-18x32in) silk on canvas. 30-Jul-93 Eldred, Massachusetts #341/R
$2100	*£1409*	*Sandbagger, America - ship portrait -, mg 'H B' on flag (48x74cm-19x29in) mixed media linen on board. 28-Mar-93 James Bakker, Cambridge #143/R*

WILMARTH, Christopher (1943-1987) American
$2000	*£1342*	*Drawing for the New Ninth (30x30cm-12x12in) init.i.d.77 s.i.d.1977 verso W/C graphite. 25-Feb-94 Sotheby's, New York #63/R*
$3500	£2349	*Given image (30x30cm-12x12in) init.d.73 pencil stapled tracing paper on paper. 5-May-94 Sotheby's, New York #248/R*
$6000	£4054	*Black clearing no 4 (20x20cm-8x8in) init.i.d.73 graphite staples paper collage. 10-Nov-93 Christie's, New York #215/R*

WILSON, Ashton (1880-?) American
$750	£521	Peasant girl in twilight (61x51cm-24x20in) s. 27-Feb-93 Young Fine Arts Auctions, Maine #329/R

WILSON, Charles Theller (1855-1920) American
$750	£497	Canyon at sunset (122x81cm-48x32in) indis.s. 28-Nov-92 Dunning's, Illinois #1130

WILSON, Donald Roller (1938-) American
$8000	£5031	Jimmy had been instructed by Mrs. Jenkins... (90x76cm-35x30in) s.i.d.1986. 25-Apr-93 Butterfield & Butterfield, San Francisco #2135/R
$15000	£9804	Full moon (102x81cm-40x32in) s.d.1976. 4-May-93 Sotheby's, New York #416/R

WILSON, J P (20th C) American
$1000	£529	Glimpse of the sea (30x41cm-12x16in) s.d.1940 canvasboard. 11-Sep-92 Skinner, Bolton #214/R

WILSON, Jane (20th C) American
$1600	£1053	Snapdragons and apples (76x102cm-30x40in) 31-Mar-93 Sotheby's Arcade, New York #486/R

WILSON, Ray (1906-1972) American
$550	*£379*	*Houses in landscape (46x61cm-18x24in) s. W/C. 16-Feb-93 John Moran, Pasadena #87*

WILSON, Ronald York (1907-) Canadian
$640	£429	Asiatic fishing fleet (75x101cm-30x40in) s. i.verso. 29-Nov-93 Ritchie, Toronto #203/R (C.D 850)

WILSON, Sol (20th C) American
$550	£367	Fall (30x41cm-12x16in) s. canvasboard. 22-May-94 James Bakker, Cambridge #39
$800	£544	The Upper Floor, Provincetown (46x61cm-18x24in) s. 16-Apr-94 Young Fine Arts Auctions, Maine #268/R
$3080	£1974	Province town pier scene (117x104cm-46x41in) s. 17-Dec-92 Mystic Fine Arts, Connecticut #117/R

WILTZ, Arnold (1889-1937) American/German
$2400   £1611   Figure by a church (71x56cm-28x22in) s. 24-Mar-94 Mystic Fine Arts, Connecticut #75/R

WIMAR, Charles (1828-1862) American
$50000   £32051   On warpath (26x31cm-10x12in) s.d.1856. 27-May-93 Sotheby's, New York #220/R

WIMAR, Charles (attrib) (1828-1862) American
$3750   £2404   Self portrait (18x13cm-7x5in) s.d.1852. 26-Apr-93 Selkirks, St. Louis #306/R

WINFIELD, Rodney (20th C) American
$2700   £1709   Spiritual Marriage (30x23cm-12x9in) W/C gessoed masonite panel. 30-Nov-92 Selkirks, St. Louis #289

WINNER, William E (attrib) (1815-1883) American
$937   £612   Portrait of a gentleman (92x74cm-36x29in) i.d.51verso. 30-Jun-94 Neumeister, Munich #2771 (DM 1500)
$937   £612   Portrait of a lady (92x74cm-36x29in) i.d.51verso. 30-Jun-94 Neumeister, Munich #2772/R (DM 1500)
$1105   £732   Portrait of lady. Portrait of gentleman (92x74cm-36x29in) i.d.1851verso pair. 22-Sep-93 Neumeister, Munich #729/R (DM 1800)

WINTER, Alice Beach (1877-c.1970) American
$750   £472   Pink flowers (41x76cm-16x30in) s. 22-Apr-93 Freeman Fine Arts, Philadelphia #1156

WINTER, Andrew (1893-1958) American
$1400   £909   Little harbour light (64x76cm-25x30in) s.d.39. 9-Sep-93 Sotheby's Arcade, New York #309/R

WINTER, Charles Allan (1869-1942) American
$1100   £724   Summer landscape with distant houses (51x61cm-20x24in) s. 31-Mar-93 Sotheby's Arcade, New York #167/R
$3300   £2157   Diana, portrait of woman (76x66cm-30x26in) s. i.verso. 14-May-93 Skinner, Bolton #148/R
$3750   £2534   Portrait of a young woman wearing a diadem (43x38cm-17x15in) s. 31-Mar-94 Sotheby's Arcade, New York #153/R
$4675   £3056   Woman in red in landscape (66x76cm-26x30in) s. i.verso. 14-May-93 Skinner, Bolton #141/R
$7000   £4667   Sphinx (77x61cm-30x24in) s. 17-Mar-94 Sotheby's, New York #91/R

WINTER, Ezra (1886-1949) American
$1300   £850   The Arts (74x112cm-29x44in) board. 15-May-93 Dunning's, Illinois #1077/R

WINTER, William Arthur (1909-) Canadian
$508   £343   Untitled - girl in chair (25x20cm-10x8in) s. canvas board. 25-Apr-94 Levis, Calgary #348 (C.D 700)
$546   £364   Breakfast table, Venice (40x50cm-16x20in) s. board. 13-May-94 Joyner Fine Art, Toronto #10 (C.D 750)
$583   £388   Children with cat (20x25cm-8x10in) s. board. 13-May-94 Joyner Fine Art, Toronto #167 (C.D 800)
$626   £426   Children with ice cream cones (30x41cm-12x16in) s. board. 7-Jul-93 Maynards, Vancouver #211 (C.D 800)
$634   £415   Rain (30x51cm-12x20in) s. canvasboard. 18-May-93 Joyner Fine Art, Toronto #166 (C.D 800)
$648   £421   Parade (30x41cm-12x16in) s. board. 22-Jun-94 Maynards, Vancouver #695 (C.D 900)
$706   £462   Friends (41x31cm-16x12in) s. s.d.67 verso canvasboard. 10-May-93 Hodgins, Calgary #103/R (C.D 900)
$728   £485   Old Toronto (30x40cm-12x16in) s. board. 13-May-94 Joyner Fine Art, Toronto #139 (C.D 1000)
$755   £510   Girl with baby at the fair (55x40cm-22x16in) s. board. 23-Nov-93 Joyner Fine Art, Toronto #243 (C.D 1000)
$794   £537   Sunbathing (41x51cm-16x20in) s. board. 30-Mar-94 Maynards, Vancouver #9 (C.D 1100)
$856   £567   Street kids (30x41cm-12x16in) s. i.verso canvasboard. 16-Nov-92 Hodgins, Calgary #228/R (C.D 1100)
$865   £547   Summer (30x40cm-12x16in) s. millboard. 30-Nov-92 Ritchie, Toronto #173/R (C.D 1100)
$1077   £718   On the beach (51x41cm-20x16in) s. i.verso artist's board. 30-May-94 Hodgins, Calgary #124/R (C.D 1500)
$1569   £1026   Yellow Veranda (76x91cm-30x36in) s. 10-May-93 Hodgins, Calgary #226/R (C.D 2000)

WINTERS, Terry (1949-) American
$26000   £17568   Rootstock (132x173cm-52x68in) s.i.d.1982stretcher linen. 10-Nov-93 Christie's, New York #230/R
$30000   £19868   Untitled (117x152cm-46x60in) s.i.d.1983verso. 19-Nov-92 Christie's, New York #255/R
$72000   £50000   Theophrastus Garden 1 (221x178cm-87x70in) painted 1982 s.i.stretcher linen. 24-Feb-93 Christie's, New York #91/R
$1700   £1111   Untitled (52x41cm-20x16in) init. s.d.1986 verso W/C graphite. 7-May-93 Christie's, East, New York #70/R
$7000   £4730   Untitled (77x57cm-30x22in) init.d.1989 graphite brush ink. 10-Nov-93 Christie's, New York #365/R
$26000   £17568   Untitled no 3 (105x75cm-41x30in) init.i.d.1984 chl oilstick. 10-Nov-93 Christie's, New York #374/R

WIRSUM, Karl (20th C) American

$1000	£662	Asparagus (69x48cm-27x19in) executed 1965. 30-Jun-93 Sotheby's Arcade, New York #333/R
$600	£400	Untitled, head of man (36x25cm-14x10in) s.d.Nov.1 1966 ink felt pen dr. 13-Mar-94 Hindman Galleries, Chicago #861

WISBY, Jack (1870-1940) American

$800	£503	Bungalow at Stinson (20x30cm-8x12in) board. 24-Apr-93 San Rafael Auction Galleries #263
$900	£592	Yosemite Valley (51x61cm-20x24in) s.i. 13-Jun-93 Butterfield & Butterfield, San Francisco #724/R
$1000	£658	Bolinas landscape (32x55cm-13x22in) s. canvas on board. 13-Jun-93 Butterfield & Butterfield, San Francisco #750/R
$1100	£692	Bungalow at Stinson (36x61cm-14x24in) board. 24-Apr-93 San Rafael Auction Galleries #264
$1100	£692	May morning, Bolinas (36x61cm-14x24in) board. 24-Apr-93 San Rafael Auction Galleries #262
$1600	£1006	Stinson, looking towards Bolinas (36x61cm-14x24in) board. 24-Apr-93 San Rafael Auction Galleries #261
$1800	£1250	Grazing cows (41x71cm-16x28in) s. 7-Mar-93 Butterfield & Butterfield, San Francisco #19/R

WISELBERG, Rose (1908-1992) Canadian

$1311	£874	Still life with roses (66x51cm-26x20in) s. board. 11-May-94 Sotheby's, Toronto #202/R (C.D 1800)

WITKOWSKI, Karl (1860-1910) American

$3000	£1899	Young boy taking a bite (56x35cm-22x14in) s. 2-Dec-92 Christie's, East, New York #118/R
$4000	£2312	Two boys with harmonica (48x61cm-19x24in) s. 23-Sep-92 Christie's, New York #43/R
$7000	£4046	Playing home (53x38cm-21x15in) s. 21-Sep-92 Selkirks, St. Louis #334/R
$7500	£4808	Street urchins (61x51cm-24x20in) s. 26-May-93 Christie's, New York #52 b/R
$7500	£5245	Secrets (61x71cm-24x28in) s. 10-Mar-93 Sotheby's, New York #43/R
$14000	£9272	Flirting (76x63cm-30x25in) s.i.d.1910. 22-Sep-93 Christie's, New York #72/R
$23000	£15436	Stealing apples (74x49cm-29x19in) s. 3-Dec-93 Christie's, New York #93/R

WOELFFER, Emerson (1914-) American

$3000	£2027	Untitled (40x51cm-16x20in) s.d.51 oil collage canvas. 21-Apr-94 Butterfield & Butterfield, San Francisco #1095/R

WOELFLE, Arthur William (1873-1936) American

$1500	£1014	Under the El, New York City (51x61cm-20x24in) s. 31-Mar-94 Sotheby's Arcade, New York #270/R

WOJNAROWICZ, David (1954-1992) American?

$1392	£928	Fish (70x22cm-28x9in) s.d.82 collage oil on stuffed fish. 2-Jun-94 AB Stockholms Auktionsverk, Stockholm #7145/R (S.KR 11000)
$2152	£1435	Myth fragment (122x122cm-48x48in) s.d.1982verso spray varnish collage panel. 2-Jun-94 AB Stockholms Auktionsverk, Stockholm #7145/R (S.KR 17000)
$3165	£2110	Peter Hujar series (101x81cm-40x32in) spray paint acrylic collage six. 2-Jun-94 AB Stockholms Auktionsverk, Stockholm #7178/R (S.KR 25000)
$7000	£4861	Map face (122x122cm-48x48in) s.d.84verso acrylic paper collage masonite. 24-Feb-93 Christie's, New York #143/R
$10000	£6623	Untitled (122x183cm-48x72in) s.d.1983verso spray enamel brush paper collage. 19-Nov-92 Christie's, New York #123/R

WOLCOTT, Harold C (20th C) American?

$600	£403	Rockport village (36x46cm-14x18in) board. 27-Mar-94 Myers, Florida #8/R

WOLF, Hamilton Achille (1883-1967) American

$750	£507	Automation (64x48cm-25x19in) s. board. 15-Jun-93 John Moran, Pasadena #166
$950	£642	Untitled abstract (122x91cm-48x36in) s. masonite. 15-Jun-93 John Moran, Pasadena #167

WOLF, Victoria Fontana (20th C) American

$777	£521	Female nude seated (73x53cm-29x21in) s. pastel. 4-May-94 Galerie Dobiaschofsky, Bern #1650/R (S.FR 1100)

WOLLHEIM, Gert (1894-1974) German/American

$1253	£830	Portrait of young man. Park landscape with three courting couples (45x51cm-18x20in) s.d.1931 panel double-sided. 28-Nov-92 Villa Grisebach, Berlin #842/R (DM 2000)
$1300	£878	Two sleeping labourers (50x76cm-20x30in) s.d.36 panel laid down. 2-Nov-93 Christie's, East, New York #94/R
$2538	£1606	Freunde des Nacht- und Felsendichters (60x81cm-24x32in) s.d.1963 s.i.d.1966verso panel. 30-Nov-92 Wolfgang Ketterer, Munich #981/R (DM 4000)
$3234	£2114	Couple riding in the Grunewald (53x74cm-21x29in) s.d.30 i.d.verso. 8-May-93 Schloss Ahlden, Ahlden #1212/R (DM 5200)
$3538	£2390	Rider in the Grunewald (53x74cm-21x29in) s.d.30 i.verso panel. 23-Apr-94 Kunsthaus am Museum, Cologne #683/R (DM 8000)
$3856	£2520	Model with parrot (60x50cm-24x20in) s.d.30-61 studio st.s.i.d.1930verso panel. 8-May-93 Schloss Ahlden, Ahlden #1213/R (DM 6200)
$15935	£10484	Gymnastique de chambre (39x49cm-15x19in) s.d.1923 W/C chk gouache. 10-Jun-93 Hauswedell & Nolte, Hamburg #983/R (DM 26000)

WONNER, Paul (1920-) American
$2000	£1351	Two yellow roses (24x40cm-9x16in) s. paper painted 1983. 21-Apr-94 Butterfield & Butterfield, San Francisco #1178/R
$5500	£3481	Man in profile (26x30cm-10x12in) s. board. 25-Oct-92 Butterfield & Butterfield, San Francisco #2307/R
$10000	£6289	Model by studio window (56x44cm-22x17in) s. s.i.verso. 25-Apr-93 Butterfield & Butterfield, San Francisco #2112/R
$950	£597	Untitled (57x76cm-22x30in) s. gouache. 25-Apr-93 Butterfield & Butterfield, San Francisco #2114/R
$1100	£692	Oranges and lemons (30x46cm-12x18in) s. i.verso W/C gouache. 25-Apr-93 Butterfield & Butterfield, San Francisco #2102/R
$1500	£949	No 5 View with double rainbow - from 27 studies for view San Francisco (46x43cm-18x17in) s. acrylic pastel. 25-Oct-92 Butterfield & Butterfield, San Francisco #2321/R
$4000	£2516	Model leaning against sofa (43x36cm-17x14in) s. W/C. 25-Apr-93 Butterfield & Butterfield, San Francisco #2110/R
$4500	£3041	Model and black table (46x30cm-18x12in) s. i.d.1964verso graphite W/C. 21-Apr-94 Butterfield & Butterfield, San Francisco #1132/R

WOO, Jade Fon (1911-1983) American
$1600	£1081	Carmel landscape (81x122cm-32x48in) s. 15-Jun-93 John Moran, Pasadena #78
$650	£437	Lake Merritt, Oakland (43x58cm-17x23in) s. W/C. 8-Dec-93 Butterfield & Butterfield, San Francisco #3527/R
$1400	£940	Foggy wharf (55x72cm-22x28in) s. W/C. 8-Dec-93 Butterfield & Butterfield, San Francisco #3530/R
$1500	£1007	Hyde Street (36x53cm-14x21in) s. W/C. 8-Dec-93 Butterfield & Butterfield, San Francisco #3526/R
$1900	£1319	Bay fog (38x53cm-15x21in) s. W/C. 7-Mar-93 Butterfield & Butterfield, San Francisco #253/R

WOOD, Edith (1885-1967) American
$2600	£1769	Abstract village (76x64cm-30x25in) s. 14-Apr-94 Freeman Fine Arts, Philadelphia #1019

WOOD, Edmond (?) American?
$700	£464	Wooded fall landscape with Indian and sheep (61x76cm-24x30in) s. masonite. 28-Sep-93 John Moran, Pasadena #323

WOOD, Grant (1892-1942) American
$9000	£5921	Autumn view (33x38cm-13x15in) s.d.1926 board. 2-Apr-93 Sloan, North Bethesda #2479/R
$18000	£11921	Peter Funcke at Indian Creek, Cedar Rapids, Iowa (61x127cm-24x50in) 15-Jun-94 Butterfield & Butterfield, San Francisco #4466 a/R
$40000	£25641	Tame flowers. Wild flowers (29x38cm-11x15in) s. pencil col.pencil board pair. 26-May-93 Christie's, New York #202/R
$100000	£64103	Booster (61x47cm-24x19in) s.d.1936 chl pencil chk. 26-May-93 Christie's, New York #198/R

WOOD, James Longacre (attrib) (19/20th C) American
$2000	£1333	Woman sewing (68x48cm-27x19in) 16-Mar-94 Christie's, New York #41/R

WOOD, Karl E (1944-1990) Canadian
$701	£464	Winter shadows (61x76cm-24x30in) s. i.stretcher. 16-Nov-92 Hodgins, Calgary #283 (C.D 900)

WOOD, Ogden (1851-1912) American
$4500	£2601	Peasants driving carts with farm animals along road in French landscape (94x124cm-37x49in) s. 21-Sep-92 Selkirks, St. Louis #330/R

WOOD, Robert W (1889-1979) American
$550	£367	California mission (41x51cm-16x20in) s.d.32. 15-Mar-94 John Moran, Pasadena #45
$1600	£847	Mountain stream (64x76cm-25x30in) s. 11-Sep-92 Skinner, Bolton #220/R
$1700	£1141	Wave melody (63x76cm-25x30in) s.d.44. 8-Dec-93 Butterfield & Butterfield, San Francisco #3550/R
$1760	£1128	Mountainous landscape (64x76cm-25x30in) s. 17-Dec-92 Mystic Fine Arts, Connecticut #63/R
$1900	£1258	Texas Bluebonnets (30x41cm-12x16in) s. board. 15-Jun-94 Butterfield & Butterfield, San Francisco #4542/R
$2000	£1325	In the rockies (64x76cm-25x30in) s. 28-Nov-92 Young Fine Arts Auctions, Maine #413/R
$2000	£1299	Sunlight in the mountains (61x74cm-24x29in) s. 15-Jan-93 Du Mouchelle, Detroit #11/R
$2250	£1136	Mountain stream (64x76cm-25x30in) s. 28-Aug-92 Young Fine Arts Auctions, Maine #318/R
$2400	£1558	Vermont spring (46x61cm-18x24in) s. st.sig.verso. 9-Sep-93 Sotheby's Arcade, New York #213/R
$2500	£1582	Mountain landscape (64x76cm-25x30in) s. 5-Dec-92 Louisiana Auction Exchange #35/R
$2750	£1846	Texas spring (30x41cm-12x16in) s. i.verso canvasboard. 8-Dec-93 Butterfield & Butterfield, San Francisco #3549/R
$3000	£1987	Autumn landscape (51x76cm-20x30in) s. canvas on board. 13-Nov-92 Du Mouchelle, Detroit #2018/R
$3200	£2177	Jenny Lake (46x61cm-18x24in) s. 20-Nov-93 Hart Gallery, Houston #8
$3250	£2241	Pacific shores (64x76cm-25x30in) s.d.44 s.i.stretcher. 16-Feb-93 John Moran, Pasadena #41

WOOD, Robert W (1889-1979) American-cont.
$3500	£2381	Summer in the mountains (79x114cm-31x45in) s. 16-Apr-94 Young Fine Arts Auctions, Maine #270/R
$3500	£2381	When the desert blooms in Arizona (63x77cm-25x30in) s. 15-Nov-93 Christie's, East, New York #90/R
$3750	£2484	Monterey Bay (71x91cm-28x36in) s. 15-Jun-94 Butterfield & Butterfield, San Francisco #4748/R
$4000	£2632	San Simeon Coast (51x61cm-20x24in) s.d.54. 13-Jun-93 Butterfield & Butterfield, San Francisco #780/R
$5000	£2646	Mountain landscape (76x91cm-30x36in) s. 12-Sep-92 Louisiana Auction Exchange #69/R
$7500	£5068	High tide (64x76cm-25x30in) s. 15-Jun-93 John Moran, Pasadena #91

WOOD, Stanley L (1860-1940) American
$2200	£1477	Go home (61x91cm-24x36in) 27-Mar-94 Myers, Florida #53/R

WOOD, Thomas Waterman (1823-1903) American
$1900	£1267	In doubt (14x11cm-6x4in) s.i.verso board. 23-May-94 Christie's, East, New York #27
$45000	£31469	Neglecting trade (76x51cm-30x20in) s.d.1883 canvas over panel. 11-Mar-93 Christie's, New York #62/R
$110000	£69620	Fresh eggs (71x51cm-28x20in) s.d.1881. 4-Dec-92 Christie's, New York #200/R
$22000	*£14103*	*Doubtful coin (71x56cm-28x22in) s.d.1881 W/C. 27-May-93 Sotheby's, New York #144/R*

WOOD, William John (1877-1954) Canadian
$2335	£1546	Summer's farewell, Midland, Ontario (69x87cm-27x34in) s.d.1933 i.verso. 18-Nov-92 Sotheby's, Toronto #230/R (C.D 3000)

WOODBURY, Charles (1864-1940) American
$1100	£728	Sunburned girl (20x25cm-8x10in) i.verso board. 28-Nov-92 Young Fine Arts Auctions, Maine #414/R
$1200	£839	Walking in April showers (51x66cm-20x26in) i.verso. 12-Mar-93 Skinner, Bolton #187/R
$1300	£872	Walking in April showers (51x66cm-20x26in) 6-May-94 Skinner, Bolton #74/R
$1600	£1046	Beach scene with striped umbrella (20x25cm-8x10in) s. board. 15-May-93 Dunning's, Illinois #1075/R
$2200	£1477	Maine coastal landscape depicting rolling hills and cottages with ocean view (43x53cm-17x21in) s. 5-Aug-93 Eldred, Massachusetts #986/R
$3500	£2349	Beachedd fishing boat (25x35cm-10x14in) s.d.88. 4-Mar-94 Skinner, Bolton #263/R
$4500	£3041	Maine Coast near Ogunquit (51x76cm-20x30in) s.d.1900. 27-Nov-93 Young Fine Arts Auctions, Maine #350/R
$850	£590	Port de France, Martinique (38x53cm-15x21in) s. W/C. 27-Feb-93 Young Fine Arts Auctions, Maine #332/R
$1800	*£1176*	*The wave (30x56cm-12x22in) W/C. 8-May-93 Young Fine Arts Auctions, Maine #312/R*
$2000	*£1307*	*Gulls (51x41cm-20x16in) s. W/C paperboard. 17-Sep-93 Skinner, Bolton #227/R*

WOODCOCK, Percy Franklin (1855-1936) Canadian
$1168	£773	The willow tree near Chateauguay (19x27cm-7x11in) s. i.verso panel. 18-Nov-92 Sotheby's, Toronto #232/R (C.D 1500)
$1189	£777	Paysage (17x29cm-7x11in) panel. 19-May-93 Sotheby's, Toronto #18/R (C.D 1500)

WOODRUFF, John (1879-?) American
$1982	£1296	Still life of fruit (77x61cm-30x24in) s. 12-May-93 Horhammer, Helsinki #329 (F.M 11000)

WOODSIDE, John Archibald (snr) (1781-1852) American
$2000	£1389	Allegory of bountiful nature (43x36cm-17x14in) s.d.1851. 3-Mar-93 Doyle, New York #67
$28000	£18421	Horse and trainer (63x82cm-25x32in) s. 5-Jun-93 Christie's, New York #107/R

WOODWARD, Ellsworth (1861-1934) American
$800	£523	Granada (51x36cm-20x14in) s.d.1905 W/C. 30-Jun-94 Mystic Fine Arts, Connecticut #47 a

WOODWARD, Mabel (1877-1945) American
$600	£400	Ogunquit, Maine (62x48cm-24x19in) s. canvasboard. 23-May-94 Christie's, East, New York #188/R
$1000	£671	Spring landscape (51x41cm-20x16in) s. masonite. 5-Mar-94 Louisiana Auction Exchange #97/R
$2000	£1325	Venice scene - Grand Canal (20x25cm-8x10in) s. board. 23-Sep-93 Mystic Fine Arts, Connecticut #54 a/R
$3500	£2431	Figures along the beach (20x25cm-8x10in) s. canvasboard. 3-Mar-93 Doyle, New York #68
$6750	£4272	Street scene, autumn (41x51cm-16x20in) s. board. 24-Oct-92 Collins, Maine #49/R
$22000	£13924	The favourite doll (51x41cm-20x16in) s.d.1905 4-Dec-92 Christie's, New York #51/R
$25000	£15823	Afternoon at the playground (63x76cm-25x30in) s. 3-Dec-92 Sotheby's, New York #119/R
$1100	*£636*	*Coastal landscape with figures (36x48cm-14x19in) s. W/C. 27-Sep-92 James Bakker, Cambridge #98/R*

WOODWARD, Mabel (attrib) (1877-1945) American
$850	£559	Sunset at Ogunquit (51x102cm-20x40in) bears sig. 2-Jun-93 Doyle, New York #98

WOODWARD, Robert Strong (1885-1960) American
$1250	£845	New England farmhouse (64x76cm-25x30in) s. 23-Oct-93 Collins, Maine #186/R
$2500	£1634	Grace of age (76x91cm-30x36in) s. 18-Sep-93 Young Fine Arts Auctions, Maine #322/R
$3250	£2211	Sugaring, Buckland, Mass (27x30cm-11x12in) s. 10-Jul-93 Young Fine Arts Auctions, Maine #340/R

WOODWARD, Stanley W (1890-1970) American
$1100	£738	Florida beach scene depicting lone palm tree with seagulls, beach grass (41x51cm-16x20in) s. board. 5-Aug-93 Eldred, Massachusetts #680/R
$1400	£946	Mount Washington snow capped (71x92cm-28x36in) s. 5-Nov-93 Skinner, Bolton #96/R
$2250	£1136	Turn of the road, Vermont (64x76cm-25x30in) s. 28-Aug-92 Young Fine Arts Auctions, Maine #321/R

WOODWARD, William (1859-1939) American
$900	£604	Ebb tide, Pont Croix (66x81cm-26x32in) s. i.stretcher. 11-Dec-93 Weschler, Washington #151/R

WOOL, Christopher (1955-) American
$2400	£1611	Untitled (86x69cm-34x27in) init. alkyd rice paper executed 1989. 23-Feb-94 Christie's, New York #134/R
$3800	£2568	Untitled Bad Dog (51x36cm-20x14in) s.i.d.1992verso alkyd graphite aluminium. 8-Nov-93 Christie's, East, New York #52/R
$4500	£2647	Untitled (102x66cm-40x26in) alkyd painted 1988. 6-Oct-92 Sotheby's, New York #196/R
$9500	£6291	Untitled - study no.14 (122x61cm-48x24in) s.d.87 verso alkyd acrylic aluminium. 18-Nov-92 Sotheby's, New York #315/R
$9500	£5588	Untitled (91x61cm-36x24in) s.d.1989 verso alkyd acrylic aluminium. 6-Oct-92 Sotheby's, New York #194/R
$11000	£6471	Untitled (122x81cm-48x32in) s.d.87 verso alkyd flashe aluminium. 6-Oct-92 Sotheby's, New York #170/R
$12000	£7843	Untitled P 46 (183x122cm-72x48in) s.d.88verso alkyd flashe on aluminum steel. 5-Oct-93 Sotheby's, New York #224/R
$14000	£9396	Untitled, P 76 (244x183cm-96x72in) s.i.d.1988verso alkyd flashe aluminum. 4-May-94 Christie's, New York #262/R
$16000	£10596	Untitled (183x122cm-72x48in) s.d.86verso alkyd aluminum. 19-Nov-92 Christie's, New York #150/R
$16500	£10927	Untitled P.65 (183x122cm-72x48in) s.i.d.1988verso alkyd aluminum. 19-Nov-92 Christie's, New York #106/R
$18000	£12500	Untitled P72 (244x183cm-96x72in) s.i.d.1988verso alkyd aluminum. 24-Feb-93 Christie's, New York #98/R
$20000	£13423	Untitled P.53 (183x122cm-72x48in) s.d.88verso alkyd flashe aluminum. 5-May-94 Sotheby's, New York #321/R
$30000	£19868	Untitled (183x122cm-72x48in) s.d.1989verso alkyd acrylic aluminium. 17-Nov-92 Sotheby's, New York #68/R

WOOLF, Samuel Johnson (1880-1948) American
$3000	£1923	The open doorway (76x56cm-30x22in) s.d.1913. 28-Apr-93 Doyle, New York #70/R
$9500	£6291	Mixing chemicals (159x109cm-63x43in) 23-Sep-93 Sotheby's, New York #160/R
$2700	£1765	Portrait of Chaim Weizmann (45x37cm-18x15in) st.sig. s.by sitter chl htd white. 15-Apr-93 Sotheby's, Tel Aviv #63/R

WOOLFORD, John Elliott (attrib) (19th C) American
$1343	£850	The Governor's residence at Fredericton (23x37cm-9x15in) i. wash over pencil. 21-Oct-92 Sotheby's, London #267/R

WOOLRYCH, F Humphry W (1868-?) American/Australian
$1000	£685	Venetian lagoon and the entrance to the Grand Canal (91x152cm-36x60in) s. masonite. 7-Feb-94 Selkirks, St. Louis #127
$1000	£658	Mother and child (102x76cm-40x30in) s. s.i.verso. 13-Jun-93 Butterfield & Butterfield, San Francisco #3191/R
$1100	£748	Spring forest landscape (81x66cm-32x26in) s. board. 17-Apr-94 Hanzel Galleries, Chicago #9

WOOSTER, Austin C (19/20th C) American
$1350	£794	Still life with apples (36x46cm-14x18in) s.d.1902. 8-Oct-92 Freeman Fine Arts, Philadelphia #1078
$1600	£1081	Basket of apples (30x38cm-12x15in) s.indis.d.'9 s.d.verso. 4-Nov-93 Sloan, North Bethesda #2318/R
$1800	£1216	Basket of peaches and grapes (30x38cm-12x15in) s.d.1902 s.verso. 4-Nov-93 Sloan, North Bethesda #2319/R
$3250	£2196	Still lifes with baskets of fruit (30x38cm-12x15in) one s.d.99 one s.d.1902 pair. 31-Mar-94 Sotheby's Arcade, New York #116/R
$4250	£2972	Still life of lemonade, cake and oranges (33x46cm-13x18in) s.d.1903 i.d.verso. 10-Mar-93 Sotheby's, New York #30/R
$5000	£3378	Still life with water melon (48x64cm-19x25in) s.d.97 s.d.1987 verso. 31-Mar-94 Sotheby's Arcade, New York #74/R

WORES, Theodore (1859-1939) American
$8500	£5629	Children at shrine (38x30cm-15x12in) s. panel. 22-Sep-93 Christie's, New York #76/R
$50000	£31646	Afternoon entertainment with musicians and dancer (182x121cm-72x48in) s.i. 3-Dec-92 Sotheby's, New York #85/R
$850	£559	Harbour scene (28x36cm-11x14in) s. W/C. 5-Jun-93 Louisiana Auction Exchange #34/R

WORES, Theodore (1859-1939) American-cont.
$1550   £1000   Under the blossom tree in a Japanese garden (60x90cm-24x35in) s. pastel. 15-Jul-94 Christie's, London #138/R

WORNER BAZ, Marysole (20th C) Mexican?
$949   £641   Cuatro Vibraciones (80x60cm-31x24in) s. 27-Apr-94 Louis Morton, Mexico #523 (M.P 3200)

WORTH, Thomas (1839-) American
$600   £400   Lady in a horse-drawn sled (28x44cm-11x17in) s. W/C. 10-Jun-94 Christie's, New York #700

WRIGHT, George Hand (1873-1951) American
$9000   £6000   The turning post (49x74cm-19x29in) s.d.1894. 17-Mar-94 Sotheby's, New York #33/R

WRIGHT, James Couper (1906-1969) American
$1000   £658   Hills of New Mexico (35x55cm-14x22in) s.d.1934 W/C pencil. 13-Jun-93 Butterfield & Butterfield, San Francisco #929/R
$1700   £1126   Views of Santa Barbara (46x61cm-18x24in) s. one d.1939 two d.1930 W/C pencil three. 15-Jun-94 Butterfield & Butterfield, San Francisco #4757/R

WRIGHT, John (19th C) American
$596   £400   Italian hillside village (51x57cm-20x22in) s. W/C. 31-Jan-94 Phillips, London #118
$954   £640   Portrait of gentleman wearing dark jacket, shirt and cravat (7x?cm-3x?in) min.exec.c.1810 oval gold frame hair verso. 3-Aug-93 Sotheby's, Billingshurst #1829/R
$1208   £800   St. Mary's Church, Whittall Street, Birmingham (29x39cm-11x15in) s.d.1793 W/C pen. 19-Nov-92 Sotheby's, London #296/R
$1350   £900   Captain Gilbert Heathcote, R.N., wearing blue uniform (8x?cm-3x?in) min.s.i.verso gilt frame painted c.1810 oval. 9-Jun-94 Sotheby's, London #28/R
$1716   £1100   Portrait of lady in low-cut dress with curly hair upswept (13x?cm-5x?in) min.s.i.d.1813verso gilt gesso frame. 26-Apr-93 Christie's, Glasgow #827/R
$2880   £2000   Captain George Scott, in Naval uniform (8x?cm-3x?in) min. s.d.1812 verso gilt-metal mount oval. 3-Mar-93 Christie's, London #15/R

WRIGHT, R Stephens (1903-) American
$1100   £647   Riding along ridge (76x96cm-30x38in) s. 4-Oct-92 Butterfield & Butterfield, Los Angeles #247/R
$1200   £706   Sierra Lake (76x96cm-30x38in) s. 4-Oct-92 Butterfield & Butterfield, Los Angeles #246/R
$2000   £1176   Sailboats along beach (76x96cm-30x38in) s. 4-Oct-92 Butterfield & Butterfield, Los Angeles #245/R

WRIGHT, W Spencer (19/20th C) American
$650   £436   Ship painting 'The J.A. Moffett, Jr' (66x74cm-26x29in) 27-Mar-94 Myers, Florida #52/R

WRINCH, Mary Evelyn (1877-1969) Canadian
$1092   £728   The little stream (24x19cm-9x7in) s. i.verso board. 11-May-94 Sotheby's, Toronto #80/R (C.D 1500)
$1165   £777   Port Hope country (18x23cm-7x9in) s.d.1918 board. 13-May-94 Joyner Fine Art, Toronto #203 (C.D 1600)
$1240   £838   The silver lake (25x29cm-10x11in) s. i.verso panel. 3-Nov-93 Sotheby's, Toronto #18/R (C.D 1600)
$1456   £971   Cape Bromidon (18x23cm-7x9in) s.d.28 board. 13-May-94 Joyner Fine Art, Toronto #263 (C.D 2000)
$1602   £1068   Lowell Lake, Temagami (25x30cm-10x12in) s. board. 13-May-94 Joyner Fine Art, Toronto #226 (C.D 2200)
$1868   £1237   Pond, Wychwood Park (75x85cm-30x33in) s. 24-Nov-92 Joyner Fine Art, Toronto #181/R (C.D 2400)
$2869   £1939   Still life with cinneraria (55x55cm-22x22in) s.d.1924. 23-Nov-93 Joyner Fine Art, Toronto #161/R (C.D 3500)

WUERMER, Carl (1900-1982) American
$1400   £940   Quiet winter day (18x25cm-7x10in) s. board. 24-Jun-93 Mystic Fine Arts, Connecticut #58

WUST, Christoffel (1801-?) American
$5963   £3750   Figures with sledge on frozen river. Children playing on frozen river (28x36cm-11x14in) s.d.1858 pair. 20-Apr-93 Sotheby's, Amsterdam #149 (D.FL 10500)

WYANT, Alexander H (1836-1892) American
$700   £470   Autumnal wooded landscape (30x41cm-12x16in) s. 5-Aug-93 Eldred, Massachusetts #300/R
$900   £588   Figures and cattle in landscape (20x36cm-8x14in) s.d.1884. 1-Nov-92 Hanzel Galleries, Chicago #9
$969   £650   The old schoolhouse (41x61cm-16x24in) s. 16-Jul-93 Christie's, London #161/R
$1100   £719   Landscape with waterfall (51x30cm-20x12in) s.bears d.1892. 7-Oct-93 Freeman Fine Arts, Philadelphia #878
$1700   £1111   Tonal landscape with pond (30x43cm-12x17in) 8-May-93 Young Fine Arts Auctions, Maine #323/R
$2100   £1346   Figures and cattle in landscape (20x36cm-8x14in) s.d.84. 11-Dec-92 Du Mouchelle, Detroit #2034/R

WYANT, Alexander H (1836-1892) American-cont.

$2600	£1757	Adirondack view with deer by mountain stream (61x51cm-24x20in) 5-Nov-93 Skinner, Bolton #43/R
$2800	£1879	Landscape scene (56x72cm-22x28in) s. 4-Mar-94 Skinner, Bolton #236/R
$2800	£1905	Eventide in autumn (31x41cm-12x16in) s. 15-Nov-93 Christie's, East, New York #64/R
$3500	£2288	Wooded landscape (41x51cm-16x20in) s. 4-May-93 Christie's, East, New York #34/R
$3800	£2657	Autumn landscape (25x35cm-10x14in) s. 11-Mar-93 Christie's, New York #45/R
$5250	£3571	Rocky stream in early summer (81x64cm-32x25in) s. 8-Apr-94 Sloan, North Bethesda #2510/R
$19000	£12179	Lake George (51x71cm-20x28in) s.d.1872 i.stretcher. 27-May-93 Sotheby's, New York #145/R
$31000	£19872	Summer haunt (93x123cm-37x48in) canvas backed by panel painted c.1880-82. 27-May-93 Sotheby's, New York #212/R
$1500	*£993*	*Cottage by marsh (43x61cm-17x24in) s. W/C gouache paperboard. 13-Nov-92 Skinner, Bolton #88/R*
$1900	*£1267*	*Stroll through the woods (51x37cm-20x15in) s. W/C. 23-May-94 Christie's, East, New York #95/R*

WYANT, Alexander H (attrib) (1836-1892) American

$1600	£1074	Autumn sunset (94x124cm-37x49in) bears sig. 1-Dec-93 Doyle, New York #84

WYETH, Andrew (1917-) American

$2500	£1582	*Young lady of Maine (32x40cm-13x16in) s. pencil. 2-Dec-92 Christie's, East, New York #354/R*
$4000	£2312	*The trail of the fox, dedication page (23x29cm-9x11in) s.i. W/C gouache pencil. 25-Sep-92 Sotheby's Arcade, New York #324/R*
$8000	£5594	*Winter scene (28x43cm-11x17in) s.i. gouache. 12-Mar-93 Skinner, Bolton #211/R*
$13000	£8609	*First study for Groundhog Day (34x28cm-13x11in) s.i. W/C executed 1959. 23-Sep-93 Sotheby's, New York #288/R*
$22000	£14667	Canoe birch (73x52cm-29x20in) s. W/C. 26-May-94 Christie's, New York #150/R
$24000	£16000	Shore fisherman (46x56cm-18x22in) s. W/C executed 1942. 17-Mar-94 Christie's, New York #180/R
$25000	£16026	White skiff (46x56cm-18x22in) s. W/C executed 1939. 27-May-93 Sotheby's, New York #103/R
$30000	£20134	Lobster boat (30x40cm-12x16in) s. W/C pencil. 3-Dec-93 Christie's, New York #4/R
$30000	£20000	Deer crossing (53x76cm-21x30in) s. W/C painted 1982. 25-May-94 Sotheby's, New York #151/R
$46000	£30065	Wagon blue (46x65cm-18x26in) s. W/C executed 1986. 22-May-93 Weschler, Washington #159/R
$55000	£36667	Isleboro Light (55x75cm-22x30in) s. W/C gouache. 26-May-94 Christie's, New York #151/R
$60000	*£37975*	*Rough pasture (55x75cm-22x30in) s. W/C paper on board. 3-Dec-92 Sotheby's, New York #74/R*
$60000	*£40000*	*Sun and stucco (54x75cm-21x30in) s. W/C. 26-May-94 Christie's, New York #155/R*
$160000	*£101266*	*From my window (54x65cm-21x26in) s. W/C. 3-Dec-92 Sotheby's, New York #72/R*

WYETH, Henriette (1907-) American

$30000	£20000	House at San Patricio (86x107cm-34x42in) s. 26-May-94 Christie's, New York #69/R

WYETH, James (1946-) American

$6000	£3846	*Eagles, London (76x55cm-30x22in) s. mixed media. 27-May-93 Sotheby's, New York #118/R*
$6500	£4333	*House and cow on hill (44x54cm-17x21in) s. W/C painted c.1964. 16-Mar-94 Christie's, New York #139/R*
$9000	£5696	*New calf (44x54cm-17x21in) s. W/C. 4-Dec-92 Christie's, New York #139/R*
$31000	£19620	*Coast guard anchor (55x76cm-22x30in) s. i.d.1982 verso W/C. 3-Dec-92 Sotheby's, New York #197/R*

WYETH, N C (1882-1945) American

$3250	£2153	Red robe (86x63cm-34x25in) s. 23-Sep-93 Sotheby's, New York #296/R

WYETH, Newell Convers (1882-1945) American

$24000	£15385	I ain't through with you yet (61x41cm-24x16in) s. 26-May-93 Christie's, New York #112/R
$26000	£17333	A son of his father (76x81cm-30x32in) s. 26-May-94 Christie's, New York #154/R
$40000	£26490	Arriving home (91x61cm-36x24in) s. 22-Sep-93 Christie's, New York #230/R
$9500	£6643	Memories from Maine, album of sketches (11x13cm-4x5in) s.i.d.W/C ink set of 14 exec.with other artists. 10-Mar-93 Sotheby's, New York #174/R

WYLIE, Alan (1938-) Canadian

$775	£524	Shaded driveway (66x102cm-26x40in) s. i.verso. 3-Nov-93 Sotheby's, Toronto #205/R (C.D 1000)
$1472	£995	March thaw (46x76cm-18x30in) s.d.73 s.i.d.verso board. 3-Nov-93 Sotheby's, Toronto #308/R (C.D 1900)

XCERON, Jean (1890-1967) American/Greek

$8751	£5834	Chateau de Sucinio (50x75cm-20x30in) s.d.1912verso. 15-May-94 Thierry, Brest #189/R (F.FR 50000)
$450	£298	Abstract figures (18x20cm-7x8in) s. W/C. 23-Sep-93 Mystic Fine Arts, Connecticut #289

553

XUL SOLAR, Alejandro (1887-1963) Argentinian
$12000	£6936	Untitled (15x21cm-6x8in) tempera. 23-Sep-92 Roldan & Cia, Buenos Aires #32
$15000	£8671	La Anunciacion (35x22cm-14x9in) tempera. 23-Sep-92 Roldan & Cia, Buenos Aires #33
$14000	£9333	Penso I Miro Calmo (21x8cm-8x3in) init.i.d.1922 W/C graphite. 18-May-94 Sotheby's, New York #222/R
$35000	£23179	Patria B (34x28cm-13x11in) s.d.X 1925 W/C crayon pencil. 24-Nov-92 Christie's, New York #47/R
$45000	£29412	Mundo (28x37cm-11x15in) s.d.1925 W/C ink. 18-May-93 Sotheby's, New York #26/R
$45000	£29412	Paisaje - Cinco Pagodas (38x32cm-15x13in) s.d.1949 W/C paper on board. 17-May-93 Christie's, New York #35/R

YAEGER, Edgar Louis (1904-) American
$700	£470	Porte de Cannet Vallauris France (38x56cm-15x22in) s.i.d.1956 masonite. 15-Dec-93 Boos Gallery, Michigan #431/R
$700	£473	Beaulieu sur Mer (33x46cm-13x18in) s.d.1966. 4-Nov-93 Boos Gallery, Michigan #1276/R
$1200	£811	A church (25x38cm-10x15in) s.d.1963 masonite. 4-Nov-93 Boos Gallery, Michigan #1277/R
$1400	£940	Two young girls bathing in rain shower (81x64cm-32x25in) s. panel. 15-Dec-93 Boos Gallery, Michigan #454/R
$1600	£1046	Seine River, Paris, France (41x53cm-16x21in) s.d.1923. 17-Sep-93 Du Mouchelle, Detroit #2003/R

YAN HSIA (1937-) Chinese/American
$6000	£4000	Flea market (112x168cm-44x66in) s.d.79-80 s.i.d.verso. 23-May-94 Hindman Galleries, Chicago #272/R

YARBER, Robert (1948-) American?
$5000	£3311	Floaters (183x310cm-72x122in) s.i.d.1985verso s.i.d.stretcher acrylic. 17-Nov-92 Christie's, East, New York #57/R

YARD, Sidney Janis (1855-1909) American
$850	£567	Sheep in a landscape (25x41cm-10x16in) s.d.97 W/C. 15-Mar-94 John Moran, Pasedena #27
$1000	£690	Figures by the mill (28x38cm-11x15in) s. W/C. 16-Feb-93 John Moran, Pasadena #20a
$1900	£1319	Grazing sheep (27x39cm-11x15in) s.d.89 W/C pencil. 7-Mar-93 Butterfield & Butterfield, San Francisco #61/R

YATES, Cullen (1866-1945) American
$1100	£692	Off the Maine Coast (30x41cm-12x16in) s. i.verso. 22-Apr-93 Freeman Fine Arts, Philadelphia #1167/R
$2200	£1438	Rocky coastal inlet (30x41cm-12x16in) s. 5-May-93 Doyle, New York #29/R

YATRIDES, Georges (20th C) French/American
$1000	£654	Street scene (65x50cm-26x20in) s.d.60. 10-May-93 Christie's, East, New York #126/R
$2000	£1418	Attentive (74x91cm-29x36in) s.d.62. 11-Feb-93 Boos Gallery, Michigan #378/R

YECKLEY, Norman H (1914-) American
$950	£655	Landscape (64x76cm-25x30in) s. 16-Feb-93 John Moran, Pasadena #20 b

YELLAND, Raymond D (1848-1900) American
$1900	£1275	Landscapes (18x30cm-7x12in) s. board pair. 8-Dec-93 Butterfield & Butterfield, San Francisco #3323/R
$1900	£1111	Autumn landscape (25x41cm-10x16in) s.d.75. 16-Sep-92 Butterfield & Butterfield, San Francisco #759/R
$2000	£1389	Landscape with haystacks (23x30cm-9x12in) s. canvas on board. 7-Mar-93 Butterfield & Butterfield, San Francisco #27/R
$14000	£9333	Cyprus Point, Monterey (56x91cm-22x36in) s. s.i.d.1891 verso. 17-Mar-94 Sotheby's, New York #80/R
$20000	£13263	Half Moon Bay (46x75cm-18x30in) s.d.81. 8-Dec-93 Butterfield & Butterfield, San Francisco #3349/R

YENS, Karl Julius Heinrich (1868-1945) American
$700	£461	In Sierras (46x60cm-18x24in) s.d.1919 canvas on board. 13-Jun-93 Butterfield & Butterfield, San Francisco #723/R
$1400	£946	San Gabriel Mission and in the Mission garden (25x36cm-10x14in) s.d.1912 board. 15-Jun-93 John Moran, Pasadena #34
$1600	£1053	Her Halloween Party (84x91cm-33x36in) s. 13-Jun-93 Butterfield & Butterfield, San Francisco #907/R
$7500	£5208	Finishing touches (96x102cm-38x40in) s.d.1921 s.i.d.verso. 7-Mar-93 Butterfield & Butterfield, San Francisco #163/R
$600	£403	Flower arrangement (30x33cm-12x13in) s.d.1892 W/C. 16-Dec-93 Mystic Fine Arts, Connecticut #235

YIP, Richard (1919-1981) American
$650	£448	San Francsico Bay (36x53cm-14x21in) s.i. W/C. 16-Feb-93 John Moran, Pasadena #81

YOAKUM, Joseph E (1886-1973) American
$1400 £933 Mount Mingo, Thangish Range near Kangting China, East Asia (30x48cm-12x19in) s.i.d.Aug 26 1970 col crayon ink dr. 13-Mar-94 Hindman Galleries, Chicago #823

YONG, Joe de (1894-1975) American
$3750 £2534 The encampment (23x34cm-9x13in) s. 31-Mar-94 Sotheby's Arcade, New York #181/R
$1500 £962 Indians on horseback (24x37cm-9x15in) s.d.1937 W/C gouache pencil paperboard. 9-Dec-92 Butterfield & Butterfield, San Francisco #4000/R

YORKE, William G (19th C) American
$8500 £5705 Wanderer, top sail schooner (46x66cm-18x26in) s.i.d.1872. 6-Feb-94 Skinner, Bolton #77/R
$10000 £6757 Schooner Mary E Douglas of New York (66x91cm-26x36in) s.d.1875. 30-Jul-93 Eldred, Massachusetts #308/R
$12792 £8200 Sailing vessel 'Carrie C.Miles' racing two other vessels (66x92cm-26x36in) s.d.1875. 15-Dec-92 Phillips, London #64/R
$13500 £9122 American two-masted fishing schooner Mary H Dyer (64x91cm-25x36in) s.d.1875. 30-Jul-93 Eldred, Massachusetts #333/R

YOUNG, Charles Morris (1869-1964) American
$1500 £1007 Harbour scene (36x46cm-14x18in) s. 5-Dec-93 James Bakker, Cambridge #13/R
$5000 £2890 Winter landscape (38x46cm-15x18in) s.d.Mar.7.1916. 23-Sep-92 Christie's, New York #151/R

YOUNG, Harvey (1840-1901) American
$750 £497 Landscape with haystacks (30x41cm-12x16in) board. 28-Sep-93 John Moran, Pasadena #246
$1100 £719 View from path (41x61cm-16x24in) s. board. 22-May-93 Weschler, Washington #85 a/R
$1500 £1007 Karveys Pond, Peacham, Vermont (51x76cm-20x30in) s.d.74. 6-Feb-94 Skinner, Bolton #252/R
$1800 £1224 Late autumn, near Colorado Springs, Colorado (51x76cm-20x30in) s.d.1900 artist's board. 9-Jul-93 Sloan, North Bethesda #2779/R
$2200 £1392 Indian encampment (73x98cm-29x39in) s. 2-Dec-92 Christie's, East, New York #180/R
$2250 £1531 Herder with sheep (51x76cm-20x30in) s.i. artist's board. 9-Jul-93 Sloan, North Bethesda #2780/R

YOUNG, Mahonri (1877-1957) American
$700 £476 Ballet dancer (43x30cm-17x12in) s. sepia chk. 9-Jul-93 Sloan, North Bethesda #2664

YOUNG, W S (19th C) American
$3400 £2267 On the Susquehanna (30x46cm-12x18in) s.d. 10-Jun-94 Christie's, New York #741

YOUNGERMAN, Jack (1926-) American
$1200 £805 Untitled (152x96cm-60x38in) s.d.80 acrylic board. 23-Feb-94 Christie's, East, New York #342/R
$1500 £1007 Marine (41x35cm-16x14in) s.i.d.1962verso. 3-May-94 Christie's, East, New York #15/R
$3400 £2282 By the way (183cm-72in circular) s.i.d.1971verso acrylic shaped canvas. 3-May-94 Christie's, East, New York #80/R

YUAN, S C (20th C) American
$1000 £662 Landscape - mountain in desert - Death Valley (38x46cm-15x18in) s. masonite. 14-Jun-94 John Moran, Pasadena #56
$1900 £1284 Monterey Wharf (18x41cm-7x16in) s. i.verso masonite. 9-Nov-93 John Moran, Pasadena #839 a
$3000 £1987 Fishing fleet (30x41cm-12x16in) s. masonite. 28-Sep-93 John Moran, Pasadena #272
$3500 £2349 Still life with orange (41x53cm-16x21in) s. s.i.verso board. 5-Mar-94 Louisiana Auction Exchange #52/R
$3500 £2365 Autumn (43x71cm-17x28in) s. masonite. 15-Jun-93 John Moran, Pasadena #151
$4750 £3146 Figures in landscape (41x51cm-16x20in) s. board. 14-Jun-94 John Moran, Pasadena #31

YUNKERS, Adja (1900-) American
$450 £302 Tortured - four. The sky hides all birds II - print (89x61cm-35x24in) one i.d.75 mixed media string one s.d.1976 two. 26-Mar-94 James Bakker, Cambridge #105

YUZBASIYAN, Arto (1948-) Canadian
$674 £440 White house (15x20cm-6x8in) s. panel. 18-May-93 Joyner Fine Art, Toronto #93/R (C.D 850)
$1323 £876 Victorian Houses, Cabbagetown (30x41cm-12x16in) s. board. 18-Nov-92 Sotheby's, Toronto #74/R (C.D 1700)
$1323 £876 After the storm, Queen St. East (76x102cm-30x40in) s. i.verso. 18-Nov-92 Sotheby's, Toronto #105/R (C.D 1700)
$1383 £922 Winter, Quebec City (85x100cm-33x39in) s. 13-May-94 Joyner Fine Art, Toronto #140/R (C.D 1900)
$1435 £969 Quebec City, summer, 1980 (65x80cm-26x31in) s. 23-Nov-93 Joyner Fine Art, Toronto #129/R (C.D 1900)
$2131 £1440 Houses Gerrard Street East (41x51cm-16x20in) s. i.verso board. 3-Nov-93 Sotheby's, Toronto #35/R (C.D 2750)
$583 £388 Horses and carraiges, Quebec (23x32cm-9x13in) s. W/C. 13-May-94 Joyner Fine Art, Toronto #185 (C.D 800)
$701 £464 Chinatown in winter (56x73cm-22x29in) s. W/C. 24-Nov-92 Joyner Fine Art, Toronto #199 (C.D 900)

YUZBASIYAN, Arto (1948-) Canadian-cont.
$2102 £1392 Queen street West near Bathurst (56x76cm-22x30in) s. i.d.1990verso W/C. 18-Nov-92 Sotheby's, Toronto #103/R (C.D 2700)

ZAKANITCH, Robert (1935-) American
$1500	£1014	Woven Edge Turnips (127x140cm-50x55in) acrylic. 21-Apr-94 Butterfield & Butterfield, San Francisco #1169/R
$2025	£1350	Pink clips (151x127cm-59x50in) s.d.81 acrylic paper. 2-Jun-94 AB Stockholms Auktionsverk, Stockholm #7144/R (S.KR 16000)
$4000	£2685	Follow the Prussian blue road (102x51cm-40x20in) s.i.d.1976verso canvas in three parts. 5-May-94 Sotheby's, New York #331/R
$4200	£2819	Night peepers (168x137cm-66x54in) s.i.d.80-81verso acrylic. 3-May-94 Christie's, East, New York #164/R
$750	£521	Lounger I (153x122cm-60x48in) s.i.d.87 oil graphite. 22-Feb-93 Christie's, East, New York #277/R

ZALCE, Alfredo (1908-) Mexican
$5731	£3673	Mujer en el zaguan (122x84cm-48x33in) s.d.1956 masonite. 29-Apr-93 Louis Morton, Mexico #44 (M.P 18000)
$40000	£26490	Llegando al muelle (62x82cm-24x32in) s.d.1948 gessoed masonite. 24-Nov-92 Christie's, New York #177/R

ZANDT, Thomas Kirby van (19th C) American
$1500	£980	Portrait of bay in landscape (48x66cm-19x26in) s.i.d.Aug.1811. 30-Oct-92 Sloan, North Bethesda #2779/R
$3500	£2318	Erastus Corning II in his Surrey (68x101cm-27x40in) s.d.1864. 22-Sep-93 Christie's, New York #80/R

ZANG, John J (19th C) American
$550	£367	Sunshine of Love Waltz (91x56cm-36x22in) s.d.1882. 23-May-94 Christie's, East, New York #80
$600	£408	River landscape (51x89cm-20x35in) s. 14-Apr-94 Freeman Fine Arts, Philadelphia #1011 a/R
$1200	£816	Winter scene (61x51cm-24x20in) s. 16-Apr-94 Young Fine Arts Auctions, Maine #276/R
$1400	£927	Woods in winter (76x63cm-30x25in) s. 2-Oct-93 Weschler, Washington #108/R

ZANG, John J (attrib) (19th C) American
$1500	£1014	Logging in winter (76x127cm-30x50in) s. 31-Mar-94 Sotheby's Arcade, New York #43/R
$2500	£1667	Hunters in winter landscape (71x127cm-28x50in) s. painted 1880s. 13-Mar-94 Hindman Galleries, Chicago #746

ZAPATA, Marcos (attrib) (fl.1748-1764) Peruvian
$12000 £8000 La Virgen de Loreto (204x143cm-80x56in) painted c.1765. 18-May-94 Christie's, New York #78/R

ZARRAGA, Angel (1886-1946) Mexican
$6198	£4132	Vase de fleurs (41x33cm-16x13in) s. panel. 27-May-94 Ferri, Paris #265 (F.FR 35000)
$12000	£7895	Naturaleza muerta (117x81cm-46x32in) s. 2-Apr-93 Sloan, North Bethesda #2492/R
$13000	£8609	Malabaristas (41x33cm-16x13in) 23-Nov-92 Sotheby's, New York #148/R
$15000	£10000	Nature morte aux coquillages (54x65cm-21x26in) s. painted c.1922. 18-May-94 Sotheby's, New York #209/R
$17000	£11333	Jeune fille au plateau de fruits (46x38cm-18x15in) s. 18-May-94 Sotheby's, New York #305/R
$20000	£13514	Saint Georges terrassant le dragon (160x160cm-63x63in) s.d.1932 canvas on panel three panels shaped top. 22-Nov-93 Sotheby's, New York #184/R
$21000	£13725	Le vieux moyer, biot - a.m (55x38cm-22x15in) s. s.d.1921 verso. 18-May-93 Sotheby's, New York #133/R
$24000	£15894	Bodegon con fruta (36x66cm-14x26in) s. 23-Nov-92 Sotheby's, New York #36/R
$30744	£20773	Le compliment (81x60cm-32x24in) s.i. 19-Mar-93 Delavenne & Lafarge, Paris #71/R (F.FR 172000)
$38000	£25676	Le compliment (81x60cm-32x24in) s.i.d.1918-19 verso. 22-Nov-93 Sotheby's, New York #185/R
$65000	£43333	Femme au bain (65x54cm-26x21in) s.d.1923. 18-May-94 Christie's, New York #96/R
$95000	£62092	Retrato de dama en verde (92x73cm-36x29in) s. painted 1915. 17-May-93 Christie's, New York #9/R
$110000	£73333	Andromede (125x65cm-49x26in) s.d.1937. 17-May-94 Sotheby's, New York #22/R
$507	£341	Portrait de vieille femme (39x31cm-15x12in) s. ch/ col crayon. 2-Dec-93 Francis Briest, Paris #191 (F.FR 3000)
$1133	£713	Tete de femme (26x18cm-10x7in) s.i.d.1922 W/C pastel. 23-Apr-93 Guy Loudmer, Paris #63 (F.FR 6000)
$2500	£1678	Tete de femme (28x19cm-11x7in) s.i.d.1922 W/C pencil. 24-Feb-94 Sotheby's Arcade, New York #311/R

ZARRAGA, Angel (after) (1886-1946) Mexican
$1300 £844 Naturaleza muerta (117x81cm-46x32in) bears sig. 8-Jul-94 Sloan, North Bethesda #2760

ZEFERINO DA COSTA, J (1840-1915) Brazilian
$12000 £7947 Jeanne d'Arc (83x64cm-33x25in) s. i.verso. 24-Nov-92 Christie's, New York #82/R

ZEGRAY, Lucienne (?) Canadian?
$510 £340 Premiere Neige, Rue St Ursule (36x29cm-14x11in) s. col.chk. 13-May-94 Joyner Fine Art, Toronto #266 (C.D 700)
$1165 £777 Le Temps des Fetes Petite Champlain, Quebec (48x63cm-19x25in) s. col.chk. 13-May-94 Joyner Fine Art, Toronto #183/R (C.D 1600)

ZEMSKY, Illya (1892-1961) American
$3000 £2013 Hillside farm scene (41x51cm-16x20in) 27-Mar-94 Myers, Florida #66/R
$2250 £1510 Cubist nudes (38x28cm-15x11in) chl. 27-Mar-94 Myers, Florida #64/R
$3000 £2013 Josephine Baker (58x46cm-23x18in) pastel. 27-Mar-94 Myers, Florida #65/R

ZENDA, Pat (1930-) American
$700 £467 Little girls with bundle of flowers (102x79cm-40x31in) s. 26-May-94 Sloan, North Bethesda #2160

ZENO, Jorge (1956-) Puerto Rican
$9000 £5960 Luna Clara (152x127cm-60x50in) s. s.i.verso linen. 24-Nov-92 Christie's, New York #161/R
$12000 £8054 Europa (94x94cm-37x37in) s. painted 1992-93. 7-Jan-94 Gary Nader, Miami #60/R
$13000 £8497 Agata (121x106cm-48x42in) s. s.i.d.1989 verso. 17-May-93 Christie's, New York #260/R
$15000 £10135 La dama e los girasoles (57x54cm-22x21in) s. i.verso painted 1990. 23-Nov-93 Christie's, New York #264/R
$17000 £11333 La Dama de la Margaritas (81x130cm-32x51in) s. d.1987verso. 18-May-94 Christie's, New York #231/R

ZEPEDA, Marco Antonio (?) Mexican?
$5094 £3265 Vista del Popocatepetl (58x78cm-23x31in) s. 29-Apr-93 Louis Morton, Mexico #175 (M.P 16000)

ZEPHIRIN, Frantz (1963-) Haitian
$626 £415 L'esclavage (51x61cm-20x24in) s. acrylic. 13-Jun-94 Rogeon, Paris #54 (F.FR 3500)
$626 £415 Guerre d'independance (51x61cm-20x24in) s. acrylic. 13-Jun-94 Rogeon, Paris #53 (F.FR 3500)
$1073 £711 Reine des Tainos (76x61cm-30x24in) s. 13-Jun-94 Rogeon, Paris #30 (F.FR 6000)

ZERBE, Karl (1903-1974) German/American
$1016 £677 Southern harbour (34x45cm-13x18in) s.d.25 gouache. 7-Jun-94 Karl & Faber, Munich #1282 (DM 1700)

ZERPA, Carlos (1950-) Latin American
$3250 £2167 Aquella mujer de la Orden del Libertador (64x48cm-25x19in) oil book coins candles collage panel exec.1979. 18-May-94 Sotheby's, New York #241/R

ZIEGLER, Eustace Paul (1881-?) American
$1000 £641 Mt. Blackburn, Alaska (20x25cm-8x10in) s.d.1925 i.verso masonite. 26-Apr-93 Selkirks, St. Louis #291/R
$2000 £1342 The laughing eskimo (25x20cm-10x8in) s. canvasboard. 8-Dec-93 Butterfield & Butterfield, San Francisco #3587/R
$10000 £6623 Mining in the North West (41x52cm-16x20in) s. 15-Jun-94 Butterfield & Butterfield, San Francisco #4458/R
$1000 £658 Climbing the mast (37x27cm-15x11in) s.i.d.1944 W/C. 13-Jun-93 Butterfield & Butterfield, San Francisco #3242/R
$1522 £1014 Cresting a wave (25x33cm-10x13in) s. W/C. 6-Jun-94 Waddingtons, Toronto #1509/R (C.D 2100)
$2000 £1316 Pulling in nets (26x36cm-10x14in) s. W/C. 13-Jun-93 Butterfield & Butterfield, San Francisco #3241/R

ZIMMERMAN, Frederick A (1886-1974) American
$3500 £2365 Summer morning in Old Lyme, Connecticut (63x76cm-25x30in) s. 31-Mar-94 Sotheby's Arcade, New York #219/R

ZOGBAUM, Rufus Fairchild (1849-1925) American
$1000 £676 Sailors and Civil War (45x35cm-18x14in) s. gouache one board one paper on board pair. 31-Mar-94 Sotheby's Arcade, New York #202/R
$1150 £762 Cavalry crossing a river (25x38cm-10x15in) s.d.1885 W/C en grisaille. 28-Nov-92 Young Fine Arts Auctions, Maine #418/R

ZORACH, Marguerite (1887-1968) American
$23000 £15333 Figures walking on a road and landscape (43x55cm-17x22in) s. panel painted c.1910 double-sided. 17-Mar-94 Sotheby's, New York #164/R
$7250 £4678 Birches (25x33cm-10x13in) s.d.1917 i.verso W/C pencil. 13-Jul-94 Doyle, New York #80
$7500 £5034 Deer in the woods (25x20cm-10x8in) s.d.1914 gouache card. 4-May-94 Doyle, New York #48/R

ZORACH, Marguerite and William (20th C) American
$29000 £19728 Whippoorwills. Randolph New Hampshire (51x61cm-20x24in) s.d.1915 s.d.1917verso double-sided. 17-Nov-93 Doyle, New York #55/R

ZORACH, William (1887-1966) American
$27000	£18000	River view, Paris (47x57cm-19x22in) s.d.11 figure study by Marguerite Zorach verso. 16-Mar-94 Christie's, New York #126/R
$750	£524	Coastal landscape with figure (41x51cm-16x20in) s.d.1942 W/C. 7-Feb-93 James Bakker, Cambridge #86/R
$1200	£816	Trees (28x21cm-11x8in) s. W/C. 15-Nov-93 Christie's, East, New York #251/R
$1200	£759	Cottages by lake (26x53cm-10x21in) s. W/C ink. 2-Dec-92 Christie's, East, New York #267/R
$1600	£1067	New Hampshire mountain (24x33cm-9x13in) s.d.1915 W/C pencil. 23-May-94 Christie's, East, New York #215/R
$3100	£2039	Landscape (30x23cm-12x9in) s. W/C graphite executed c.1918. 31-Mar-93 Sotheby's Arcade, New York #331/R
$4200	£2781	Fishboat in harbour (33x42cm-13x17in) s. s.i.verso W/C board. 22-Sep-93 Christie's, New York #201/R

ZORILLA DE SAN MARTIN, Alfredo (20th C) South American
$2500	£1634	Pastores y ovejas (81x100cm-32x39in) init.d.90. 27-Jun-94 Gomensoro, Montevideo #24/R
$3500	£2365	La familia (114x140cm-45x55in) s.d.84 i.verso. 25-Apr-94 Gomensoro, Montevideo #54/R

ZORNES, Milford (1908-) American
$1200	£811	Northern California coastal scene (33x48cm-13x19in) s.d.1947 board. 9-Nov-93 John Moran, Pasadena #913
$650	£451	El Salvador (55x75cm-22x30in) s.d.79 W/C. 7-Mar-93 Butterfield & Butterfield, San Francisco #258/R
$650	£428	Rural landscape with farmhouse (36x53cm-14x21in) s. W/C. 13-Jun-93 Butterfield & Butterfield, San Francisco #973/R
$750	£517	Commercial fishing boat (56x74cm-22x29in) s.d.70 W/C. 16-Feb-93 John Moran, Pasadena #90 b
$900	£596	Paris canal (46x71cm-18x28in) s.i.d.63 W/C. 28-Sep-93 John Moran, Pasadena #239
$900	£621	Mission in southwest landscape (33x53cm-13x21in) s. W/C. 16-Feb-93 John Moran, Pasadena #89
$950	£625	Colorado River, Arizona (55x74cm-22x29in) s.d.40 s.i.verso W/C. 13-Jun-93 Butterfield & Butterfield, San Francisco #974/R
$1500	£993	Valle de Santiago (56x76cm-22x30in) s.d.61 W/C. 15-Jun-94 Butterfield & Butterfield, San Francisco #4761/R
$1600	£1074	Dusk landscape (56x76cm-22x30in) s. W/C. 8-Dec-93 Butterfield & Butterfield, San Francisco #3523/R
$1700	£1181	House in landscape (38x58cm-15x23in) s.d.1939 W/C. 7-Mar-93 Butterfield & Butterfield, San Francisco #259/R
$3000	£1987	Newhall ranch 1937 (53x74cm-21x29in) s. W/C. 14-Jun-94 John Moran, Pasadena #78

ZORTHIAN, Jirayr H (1912-) American
$800	£541	Harvest a mural study (30x41cm-12x16in) oil graphite paperboard. 5-Nov-93 Skinner, Bolton #172/R
$800	£423	At the big game (38x48cm-15x19in) paper watercolour mural on reverse double-sided. 11-Sep-92 Skinner, Bolton #272/R

ZUBIZARRETA, Pedro (1942-) Mexican
$1267	£833	Imaginacion (60x40cm-24x16in) s.d.1989 dr. 4-Nov-92 Mora, Castelltort & Quintana, Juarez #71/R (M.P 4000000)

ZUCKER, Joe (1941-) American
$28310	£19000	Joust (123x490cm-48x193in) s.i.d.10/20/80 acrylic rhoplex cotton panels 2. 25-Mar-93 Christie's, London #201/R
$1600	£1074	2nd '96' Wide Roll (133x132cm-52x52in) s.i.d.31.1.70verso cotton acrylic rhoplex canvas. 3-May-94 Christie's, East, New York #62/R

ZUILL, Abbie Luella (1856-1921) American
$2750	£1389	Strawberries (15x25cm-6x10in) s. s.d.1900verso. 28-Aug-92 Young Fine Arts Auctions, Maine #325/R
$2750	£1389	Cherries (15x18cm-6x7in) s. s.d.1900verso. 28-Aug-92 Young Fine Arts Auctions, Maine #326/R

ZUNIGA, Francisco (1913-) Costa Rican
$1500	£980	Crouching nude (41x64cm-16x25in) s.d.1978 pencil. 1-Nov-92 Hanzel Galleries, Chicago #95/R
$2300	£1544	Sleeping woman (50x65cm-20x26in) s.d.1970 chl. 24-Feb-94 Sotheby's Arcade, New York #312/R
$2500	£1689	Mujer sentada (70x50cm-28x20in) s.d.1977 chl. 21-Apr-94 Butterfield & Butterfield, San Francisco #1121/R
$2700	£1875	Desnudo (50x65cm-20x26in) s.d.1972 brown chk. 26-Feb-93 Sotheby's Arcade, New York #220/R
$3000	£1987	Reclining female nude (46x65cm-18x26in) s.d.1979 chl chk. 29-Sep-93 Sotheby's Arcade, New York #226/R
$3250	£2044	Desnudo (50x65cm-20x26in) s.d.1964 ink board. 25-Apr-93 Butterfield & Butterfield, San Francisco #2089/R
$3500	£2215	Seated female nude (52x67cm-20x26in) s.d.1974 graphite. 25-Oct-92 Butterfield & Butterfield, San Francisco #2259/R
$3500	£2288	Desnudo (49x70cm-19x28in) s.d.1979 pastel. 18-May-93 Sotheby's, New York #221/R
$3750	£2534	Mujer reposando (48x63cm-19x25in) s.d.1965 pastel. 21-Oct-93 Butterfield & Butterfield, San Francisco #2742/R
$4000	£2649	Seated woman (50x65cm-20x26in) s.d.1968 chl pencil ink wash. 29-Sep-93 Sotheby's Arcade, New York #227/R

ZUNIGA, Francisco (1913-) Costa Rican-cont.

$4000	£2649	Mujer dormida (50x64cm-20x25in) s.d.1975 pastel chl sanguine. 24-Nov-92 Christie's, New York #174/R
$4000	£2614	Juventud (49x64cm-19x25in) s.d.1963 chl crayon. 17-May-93 Christie's, New York #269/R
$4250	£2673	Desnudo (46x61cm-18x24in) s.d.1964 pastel chl. 25-Apr-93 Butterfield & Butterfield, San Francisco #2088/R
$4500	£2980	Reclining female nude (50x65cm-20x26in) s.d.59 W/C pencil Indian ink. 30-Jun-93 Sotheby's Arcade, New York #227/R
$5000	£3378	Mujer reposando (48x63cm-19x25in) s.d.1965 pastel. 21-Apr-94 Butterfield & Butterfield, San Francisco #1120/R
$5000	£3356	Mujer sentada (49x65cm-19x26in) s.d.1970 W/C pastel chl. 24-Feb-94 Sotheby's Arcade, New York #309/R
$5000	£3311	Dos Mujeres Reposando (50x70cm-20x28in) s.d.1980 chl pastel. 24-Nov-92 Christie's, New York #171/R
$5500	£3595	Coloquio infantil (48x62cm-19x24in) s.d.1973 pastel chl. 17-May-93 Christie's, New York #268/R
$6000	£4000	Despues del Bano (70x50cm-28x20in) s.d.78 pastel chl chk. 18-May-94 Christie's, New York #103/R
$6200	£4189	Dos mujeres con vela (65x50cm-26x20in) s.d.1964 pastel. 22-Nov-93 Sotheby's, New York #261/R
$6500	£4305	Tres mujeres (28x43cm-11x17in) s.d.1960 W/C crayon. 24-Nov-92 Christie's, New York #172/R
$6500	£4392	Dos mujeres sentadas (55x75cm-22x30in) s.d.1987 chl col.chk. 23-Nov-93 Christie's, New York #211/R
$7000	£4636	Desnudo sentado (64x49cm-25x19in) s.d.1969 W/C graphite. 23-Nov-92 Sotheby's, New York #207/R
$7000	£4730	Mujer desnuda (50x65cm-20x26in) s.d.1970 pastel. 23-Nov-93 Christie's, New York #212/R
$7000	£4667	Rosa en un Pulaque (50x70cm-20x28in) s.d.1982 pastel chl. 18-May-94 Christie's, New York #304/R
$7500	£4967	Mujer sentada (50x70cm-20x28in) s.d.1983 chl pastel Fabriano paper. 24-Nov-92 Christie's, New York #173/R
$8000	£5229	Desnudo sentado (70x49cm-28x19in) s.d.1978 chl pastel. 18-May-93 Sotheby's, New York #222/R
$8000	£5333	Siesta (63x91cm-25x36in) s.d.1976 pastel. 18-May-94 Christie's, New York #102/R
$8000	£5229	Dos mujeres (64x50cm-25x20in) s.d.1963 W/C pen. 17-May-93 Christie's, New York #257/R
$8750	£5872	Adolescente recostada (63x47cm-25x19in) s. pastel executed 1974. 7-Jan-94 Gary Nader, Miami #49/R
$9000	£5882	Grupo de mujeres (50x64cm-20x25in) s.d.62 i.verso W/C pencil. 17-May-93 Christie's, New York #256/R
$10000	£6757	Cuatro mujeres caminando (58x89cm-23x35in) s.d.1980 crayon. 23-Nov-93 Christie's, New York #266/R
$10000	£6536	Tehuanas (51x66cm-20x26in) s.d.1962 W/C chl pencil pen. 17-May-93 Christie's, New York #111/R
$11000	£7432	Dos mujeres con Rebozo (50x65cm-20x26in) s.d.1971 W/C wax crayon. 23-Nov-93 Christie's, New York #267/R
$11000	£7333	Mujer con canasta (69x100cm-27x39in) s.d.1981 pastel. 18-May-94 Christie's, New York #104/R

ZUNIGA, Francisco (attrib) (1913-) Costa Rican

$1500	£1000	Seated woman (48x64cm-19x25in) s.d.1974 chl conte crayon. 26-Aug-93 Skinner, Bolton #204

ZWACK, Michael (1949-) American

$1646	£1097	Untitled (46x35cm-18x14in) s.d.82verso paper canvas. 2-Jun-94 AB Stockholms Auktionsverk, Stockholm #7048/R (S.KR 13000)
$1709	£1139	History of the world (60x95cm-24x37in) oil pigment paper. 2-Jun-94 AB Stockholms Auktionsverk, Stockholm #7209/R (S.KR 13500)
$1899	£1266	Landscape (75x102cm-30x40in) s.d.84verso pigment paper. 2-Jun-94 AB Stockholms Auktionsverk, Stockholm #7049/R (S.KR 15000)
$4800	£3137	History of the world (132x274cm-52x108in) oil raw pigment executed 1987. 22-Dec-92 Christie's, East, New York #83
$750	£504	Pace (93x61cm-37x24in) s.d.82verso pigment paper mounted on canvas. 3-May-94 Christie's, East, New York #161/R

ZWILLINGER, Rhonda (1950-) American

$1000	£694	Bon voyage (138x199cm-54x78in) painted 1985. 22-Feb-93 Christie's, East, New York #284/R

Index

Sculpture, bronzes and three dimensional
works of art sold during the two auction seasons
1992/93 and 1993/94

STARTING PRICES

Sculpture or 3 dimensional works of art
from - $750

AARONS, George (1896-1980) American
$4500   2941   Portrait bust (64cm-25in) s.d.1939 white marble on stone base. 18-Sep-93 James Bakker, Cambridge #84/R

ABDELL, Doug (1947-) American
$2750   1858   Kayefeau, Aekyad (84cm-33in) s.i.d.6.26.79 bronze. 21-Apr-94 Butterfield & Butterfield, San Francisco #1171/R

AGUIRRE ROA, Mario (1940-) Mexican
$2850   1875   Vendedora de jarros (40x36x56cm-16x14x22in) s.d.1990 bronze. 4-Nov-92 Mora, Castelltort & Quintana, Juarez #109/R (M.P 9000000)

AHEARN, John (1951-) American
$1266   844   Cosmic (41x20cm-16x8in) s.d.82 painted plaster. 2-Jun-94 AB Stockholms Auktionsverk, Stockholm #7062/R (S.KR 10000)
$5000   3472   Untitled (53x43x19cm-21x17x7in) executed 1978-83 painted cast plaster. 23-Feb-93 Sotheby's, New York #388/R
$6000   4027   Janice 'Peanut' Harvey (88x53x23cm-35x21x9in) painted cast plaster executed 1983. 25-Feb-94 Sotheby's, New York #162/R

AITKEN, Robert Ingersoll (1878-1949) American
$6000   4196   Tired Mercury (77cm-30in) i.d.1907 green brown pat.bronze F.Rom.Bronze W. 11-Mar-93 Christie's, New York #99/R

AKEEAKTASHUK (1898-1954) North American
$1129   758   Standing Inuit hunter wearing parka and leggings (18cm-7in) marbled dark green serpentine. 29-Nov-93 Waddingtons, Toronto #899/R (C.D 1500)

ALSTINE, John van (1952-) American
$1300   855   The wedge (66x28x33cm-26x11x13in) granite on welded steel base. 2-Apr-93 Sloan, North Bethesda #2334

AMAR, Joseph (1954-) American
$2400   1589   Untitled (61cm-24in) s.d.1987 wood lead. 30-Jun-93 Sotheby's Arcade, New York #357/R

AMBELLAN, Harold (1912-) American
$5853   4009   La sentinelle (43cm-17in) s.num.III/VI bronze. 11-Feb-94 Dumousett-Deburaux, Paris #29/R (F.FR 35000)
$6690   4582   Femme allongee (20x38cm-8x15in) s.num.II/VI bronze. 11-Feb-94 Dumousett-Deburaux, Paris #28/R (F.FR 40000)

AMERICAN SCHOOL, 19th C
$3600   2353   Stove figure of a Muse, neoclassical drapery (145cm-57in) cast iron. 18-Apr-93 Hindman Galleries, Chicago #29/R
$3800   2484   Stove figure of a muse, neoclassical drapery (145cm-57in) cast iron. 18-Apr-93 Hindman Galleries, Chicago #30/R
$4000   2614   Stove figure of George Washington wearing waistcoat, classical drapery (145cm-57in) cast iron. 18-Apr-93 Hindman Galleries, Chicago #28/R
$100000   66667   Seated Dalmatians (63cm-25in) d.1880 carved painted pair. 10-Jun-94 Christie's, New York #522/R

AMERICAN SCHOOL, 19th/20th C
$3761   2524   Model of Negro doorman, life-size wearing frilled shirt and bow-tie (188cm-74in) painted plaster. 24-Mar-94 Stephan Welz, Johannesburg #571/R (SA.R 13000)

AMERICAN SCHOOL, 20th C
$7250   4932   Eve (99cm-39in) s.indist.d. brown pat.bronze st.f.Kunst Fndrs. 8-Apr-94 Sloan, North Bethesda #2825/R

ANDRE, Carl (1935-) American
$2842   1822   13 rectangular long gander (3x76x1cm-1x30x0in) s.i.d.num.85/6 on certificat wood. 27-May-93 Lempertz, Cologne #559 (DM 4500)
$5364   3600   16 Brass Channel Line (2x2x55cm-1x1x22in) sixteen brass channels executed 1977. 3-Dec-93 Sotheby's, London #211/R
$6000   3529   Untitled (7x29x30cm-3x11x12in) red slate sulphur two cement blocks. 8-Oct-92 Christie's, New York #226/R
$6194   3800   28 Rubber rod run (767cm-302in) flexible rubber rod 28 unit line end to end. 15-Oct-92 Sotheby's, London #28/R
$6500   4362   4 zinc rectangle (1x46x35cm-0x18x14in) zinc four unit rectangle executed 1976. 23-Feb-94 Christie's, New York #66/R
$8500   5705   Plumbar (5x10x150cm-2x4x59in) lead 30 unit rectangular solid executed 1982. 23-Feb-94 Christie's, New York #94/R
$9000   6040   Waterbody (5x276cm-2x109in) 24 units col.galvanized steel sheet exec.1973. 4-May-94 Christie's, New York #238/R
$10000   5882   Aluminium-zinc dipole - E-W (1x100x100cm-0x39x39in) aluminium zinc executed 1989. 6-Oct-92 Sotheby's, New York #125/R
$11000   7383   Zinc-zinc dipole - N-S (1x100x100cm-0x39x39in) zinc two units side by side executed 1975. 23-Feb-94 Christie's, New York #87/R
$12000   8000   45-Part Steel Cut (10x278cm-4x109in) transformer core steel 45 parts executed 1972. 26-May-94 Christie's, London #119/R
$16000   10811   Copper-Copper Dipole N/S (100x50cm-39x20in) copper two units executed 1973. 10-Nov-93 Christie's, New York #210/R
$22000   14765   25 steel rectangle (1x18x21cm-0x7x8in) hot rolled steel 25 units executed 1977. 4-May-94 Christie's, New York #307/R

ANDRE, Carl (1935-) American-cont.

$26820	18000	Blue equivalent, 2 header (25x595cm-10x234in) 30 pieces of hot-rolled steel executed 1977. 2-Dec-93 Sotheby's, London #46/R
$30000	19868	Fifth copper cardinal (1x50x250cm-0x20x98in) executed 1973 copper 5 units. 19-Nov-92 Christie's, New York #389/R
$30000	19868	Aluminum triode (3x466x204cm-1x183x80in) executed 1975 aluminum 22 units. 19-Nov-92 Christie's, New York #377/R
$37250	25000	The way south, uncarved blocks (91x61x91cm-36x24x36in) western red cedar timer two units executed 1975. 2-Dec-93 Sotheby's, London #59/R
$37500	25168	Fifth copper cardinal (1x50x250cm-0x20x98in) copper 5-unit line extending from base of wall. 5-May-94 Sotheby's, New York #265 a/R
$50000	33113	45 degrees swipe (1x53x267cm-0x21x105in) seven hot-rolled steel plates. 18-Nov-92 Christie's, New York #28/R
$60000	40541	The way south and west - Uncarved blocks (91x91x122cm-36x36x48in) s.d.30 mar 84 red cedar three units exec.1975. 10-Nov-93 Sotheby's, New York #50/R
$80000	53691	Sixteenth copper cardinal (5x50x50cm-2x20x20in) 16 unit square copper plates executed 1976. 3-May-94 Christie's, New York #23/R
$135000	91216	Aluminium-zinc plain (1x183x183cm-0x72x72in) aluminium zinc squares executed 1969. 10-Nov-93 Sotheby's, New York #26/R
$240000	166667	Aluminum steel plain (8x183x183cm-3x72x72in) exec.1969 aluminum steel plates 36-unit squares. 23-Feb-93 Sotheby's, New York #325/R

ANDREA, John de (1941-) American

$25000	16892	Reclining figure (112x223x109cm-44x88x43in) oil polyester resin upholstered sofa executed 72. 11-Nov-93 Sotheby's, New York #406 a/R
$75000	50676	Arden Anderson and Norma Murphy (61x211x94cm-24x83x37in) oil polyester fibreglass execute 1972. 11-Nov-93 Sotheby's, New York #394/R

ANGHIK, Abraham Apakark (1951-) North American

$870	580	A swimming loon, head turned preening itself (56cm-22in) mottled light green soapstone. 6-Jun-94 Waddingtons, Toronto #1060 (C.D 1200)

AQIGAAQ, Mathew (1940-) North American

$1355	909	Standing Inuit hunter wearing a parka holding large fish (35cm-14in) s. mottled dark grey soapstone. 29-Nov-93 Waddingtons, Toronto #807 (C.D 1800)

ARCHIPENKO, Alexander (1887-1964) American/Russian

$1208	800	Graceful Movement (66cm-26in) polished silvered pat.bronze. 10-Nov-92 Allen & Harris, Bristol #46/R
$2211	1417	Woman combing hair (35cm-14in) s.d.1915 and 1987 num.27/499 bronze marble socle. 25-May-93 Dr Fritz Nagel, Stuttgart #2202/R (DM 3500)
$3000	1948	Flat torso (53x10cm-21x4in) i.d.1914 bronze on marble base. 11-Sep-93 Louisiana Auction Exchange #76/R
$4389	2966	Torso (37cm-15in) s.d.1922 nickel silver alloy marble base. 19-Oct-93 Campo & Campo, Antwerp #2/R (B.FR 160000)
$5795	3915	Cubist female figure with hat (33cm-13in) s.d.1959 green brown pat.bronze. 29-Mar-94 Campo & Campo, Antwerp #2/R (B.FR 200000)
$6574	4382	Woman combing hair (35cm-14in) s.d.1915 red/brown pat. bronze marble socle. 7-Jun-94 Karl & Faber, Munich #464/R (DM 11000)
$7250	4932	Heroica a draped figure (43cm-17in) s. green brown pat.bronze. 17-Nov-93 Doyle, New York #110/R
$8880	6000	White torso (47cm-19in) s.d.1916 bronze. 30-Oct-93 Dr Fritz Nagel, Stuttgart #94/R (DM 15000)
$11000	7383	Frau ihr haar kaemmend (33cm-13in) s.d.1915 num.1/25 brown-black pat bronze. 3-Jan-94 Gordon Galleries, Tel Aviv #437/R
$11700	7905	Woman combing her hair (32cm-13in) i.d.1915 black brown pat.bronze on marble socle. 27-Nov-93 Villa Grisebach, Berlin #264/R (DM 20000)
$13300	7000	Femme nue accroupie (38cm-15in) I. black pat.bronze conceived 1912. 22-Jun-93 Christie's, London #171/R
$13770	9000	White torso (51cm-20in) i. polished terracotta. 29-Jun-94 Sotheby's, London #239/R
$14076	9384	Woman wearing a fur (33cm-13in) s. bronze. 16-May-94 Hotel de Ventes Horta, Brussels #126/R (B.FR 480000)
$17399	11523	Woman combing hair (33cm-13in) i.d.1915/1955 dark brown pat.bronze. 20-Nov-93 Neumeister, Munich #19/R (DM 28000)
$18583	12146	Female standing (68cm-27in) s.d.1914 gold brown pat.bronze on wooden socle. 17-Sep-93 Schloss Ahlden, Ahlden #305/R (DM 30000)
$19000	12838	Small reclining figure (16cm-6in) i.d.1910 num.4/8 F green pat.bronze. 4-Nov-93 Sotheby's, New York #292/R
$20000	13245	Birth of Venus (31cm-12in) s.d.54 num.6/6 polychromed bronze granite. 12-Nov-92 Christie's, New York #224/R
$28000	18667	Torse tournant (47cm-19in) s.d.1921 num.2 black pat.bronze exec.1921. 11-May-94 Christie's, New York #235/R
$38740	26000	Torse - flat torso (38cm-15in) i.d.1914 bronze. 23-Jun-93 Sotheby's, London #318/R
$38740	26000	Torse (38cm-15in) executed 1914 bronze. 24-Mar-93 Sotheby's, London #37/R
$42000	28000	Geometric statuette (68cm-27in) i.d.1914 st.num.5/8 pat. bronze. 4-Jun-94 Lempertz, Cologne #7/R (DM 70000)
$42840	28000	White torso (48cm-19in) i.d.1916 bronze. 29-Jun-94 Sotheby's, London #236/R
$45000	30405	Woman combing her hair (35cm-14in) i.d.1915 num.2/8 brown pat.bronze. 4-Nov-93 Sotheby's, New York #198/R
$47258	31505	Torse de femme (43cm-25in) s.num.1/12 pat.bronze st.f.Modern Art exec.1945. 10-Mar-94 Christian de Quay, Paris #183/R (F.FR 270000)
$47680	32000	Silver torso (98cm-39in) polished silvered pat.bronze executed c.1931. 30-Nov-93 Christie's, London #182/R
$54000	36486	Green concave (49cm-19in) i.d.1913 num.5/6 brown pat.bronze. 4-Nov-93 Sotheby's, New York #258/R

ARCHIPENKO, Alexander (1887-1964) American/Russian-cont.
$56610	37000	Reclining (44cm-17in) i. bronze. 29-Jun-94 Sotheby's, London #237/R
$67500	45000	Standing figure (66cm-26in) i. brown pat.bronze exec.1922 Cast Heinze-Barth. 12-May-94 Sotheby's, New York #336/R
$67500	44118	Green concave (49cm-19in) i. st.4/6 green pat.bronze. 12-May-93 Sotheby's, New York #266/R
$110000	73333	Soldat qui marche (116cm-46in) st.sig.d.1917 num.6/10F brown pat.bronze. 11-May-94 Christie's, New York #181/R
$151980	102000	Gedrehter Torso (48cm-19in) s. marble executed c.1921. 30-Nov-93 Christie's, London #177/R

ARMAN, Fernandez (1928-) American/French
$1101	734	Accumulation of paint brushes (66x45cm-26x18in) s.num.30/100 paintbrushes in plexiglass. 2-Jun-94 AB Stockholms Auktionsverk, Stockholm #6137/R (S.KR 8700)
$1108	749	Long time parking (22cm-9in) s.num.32/100, bronze multiple. 3-Nov-93 Bukowskis, Stockholm #283/R (S.KR 9000)
$1300	850	Nice crime (30x19x4cm-12x7x2in) s.num.5/50 gambling chips in resin. 5-Oct-93 Sotheby's, New York #194/R
$1300	872	Accumulation (47cm-19in) s.num.31/100 mixed media on wood construction. 24-Feb-94 Sotheby's Arcade, New York #451/R
$1303	899	Statue de la liberte (75cm-30in) s. gilded bronze. 15-Feb-93 Hotel de Ventes Horta, Brussels #175/R (B.FR 44000)
$1307	865	Passe-Temps (41x41cm-16x16in) s.num.63/150 metal parts cast in acrylic. 16-Jun-94 Galerie Koller, Zurich #3137 (S.FR 1800)
$1406	944	Crosses de violons (41x8x8cm-16x3x3in) one of 50 gilt bronze Cast.Bocquel. 19-Dec-93 Perrin, Versailles #3 (F.FR 8200)
$1406	944	Crosses de violons (41x8x8cm-16x3x3in) one of 50 gilt bronze Cast.Bocquel. 19-Dec-93 Perrin, Versailles #1 (F.FR 8200)
$1438	978	Cut coffee pot (33x34cm-13x13in) s.num.88/100, gilded bronze marble base. 20-Nov-93 Soderkopings #326/R (S.KR 12000)
$1455	977	Venus (34x12cm-13x5in) s.num.60/100 brown pat.bronze executed 1990. 29-Nov-93 Wolfgang Ketterer, Munich #529/R (DM 2500)
$1457	978	Crosses de violons (41x8x8cm-16x3x3in) one of 50 gilt bronze Cast.Bocquel. 19-Dec-93 Perrin, Versailles #2 (F.FR 8500)
$1529	1019	Camera (31x60x23cm-12x24x9in) painted bronze. 7-Jun-94 Rasmussen, Copenhagen #67 (D.KR 10000)
$1534	1029	Crosses de violons, multiple (41x8x8cm-16x3x3in) s.num.19/50 gilt bronze Cast.Bocquel. 27-Mar-94 Perrin, Versailles #2 (F.FR 8800)
$1560	1040	Poubelle (40x30x7cm-16x12x3in) s.verso num.66/90 crumpled letters in acryl.box. 3-Jun-94 Lempertz, Cologne #467/R (DM 2600)
$1603	1076	Crosses de violons (41x8x8cm-16x3x3in) s.num.13/50 gilt bronze Cast.Bocquel. 27-Mar-94 Perrin, Versailles #4 (F.FR 9200)
$1603	1076	Crosses de violons, multiple (41x8x8cm-16x3x3in) s.num.4/50 gilt bronze Cast.Bocquel. 27-Mar-94 Perrin, Versailles #3 (F.FR 9200)
$1613	1090	Petite victoire de Samothrace (24x16x15cm-9x6x6in) num.2/100 bronze wood Cast.Bocquel exec.1990. 16-Jun-93 Watine-Arnault, Paris #56 (F.FR 9200)
$1673	1116	Saxophone decoupe (23x19x4cm-9x7x2in) s.num.121/150 bronze stone socle. 6-Jun-94 Wolfgang Ketterer, Munich #524/R (DM 2800)
$1677	1118	Putty knives with red paint in acrylic (65x44x4cm-26x17x2in) s.num.38/100. 15-Mar-94 Rasmussen, Copenhagen #71/R (D.KR 11000)
$1677	1118	Paint brushes dipped in blue paint in acrylic (66x44x4cm-26x17x2in) s.num.87/100. 15-Mar-94 Rasmussen, Copenhagen #70/R (D.KR 11000)
$1697	1109	Accumulation of violins (23cm-9in) s.num.12/100, polished bronze Cast.Bocquel. 12-May-93 AB Stockholms Auktionsverk, Stockholm #6123 (S.KR 12500)
$1697	1074	Accumulation of violins (23cm-9in) s.num.2/100, polished bronze Cast.Bocquel. 1-Dec-92 AB Stockholms Auktionsverk, Stockholm #6007 (S.KR 12500)
$1697	1139	Sans titre (90x80cm-35x31in) s. collage panel book boxes. 6-Feb-94 Guy Loudmer, Paris #152 (F.FR 10000)
$1743	1170	Petite Venus Eclosion 1990 (26x16x7cm-10x6x3in) s.num.17/100 gilt pat.bronze Cast.Bocquel. 27-Mar-94 Perrin, Versailles #180 (F.FR 10000)
$1752	1161	Trumpet (55cm-22in) s. num.73/100, brass. 24-Nov-92 Goteborg Auktionsverk #258 (S.KR 12000)
$1793	1195	Violin decoupe (60x20x12cm-24x8x5in) s.num.23/100 white plastic. 6-Jun-94 Wolfgang Ketterer, Munich #523/R (DM 3000)
$1833	1247	Cut Greek female face (51cm-20in) s.num.15/20 gilded bronze marble base. 20-Nov-93 Soderkopings #324/R (S.KR 15300)
$1839	1210	Venus (34x12cm-13x5in) s.i.num.76/100 brown pat.bronze. 7-Jun-93 Wolfgang Ketterer, Munich #526/R (DM 3000)
$1854	1261	Acropolis (24x6x6cm-9x2x3in) s.num.10/20 bronze st.f.Bocquel executed 1986. 8-Jul-93 Guy Loudmer, Paris #137 (F.FR 11000)
$1854	1261	Eclosion de la petite Venus (26cm-10in) s.num.2/100 bronze st.f.Bocquel executed 1990. 8-Jul-93 Guy Loudmer, Paris #138 (F.FR 11000)
$1869	1214	Accumulation of chess pieces (41x18x16cm-16x7in) s. num.20/90 wood plexiglass executed 1973. 24-Jun-94 Germann, Zurich #81/R (S.FR 2500)
$1904	1205	Head (40x16x13cm-16x6x5in) s.num.95/100 gold pat.bronze. 30-Nov-92 Wolfgang Ketterer, Munich #8/R (DM 3000)
$1918	1214	Venus (32cm-13in) s.num.36/100, brown pat bronze Cast.Bocquel. 1-Dec-92 AB Stockholms Auktionsverk, Stockholm #6006/R (S.KR 13000)
$1921	1289	Paint brushes (20x27x24cm-8x11x9in) s.num.41/100 oil brown pat.bronze executed 1989. 3-Dec-93 Lempertz, Cologne #550/R (DM 3300)
$1994	1338	Accumulation of violins (145x115cm-57x45in) s. gold pat.bronze 23/50 executed 1978. 8-Dec-93 Christie's, Amsterdam #396 a (D.FL 3800)
$2015	1371	Untitled (39x28cm-15x11in) s.num.24/65, clog-wheels in plexiglass. 13-Apr-94 Bukowskis, Stockholm #418/R (S.KR 16000)

ARMAN, Fernandez (1928-) American/French-cont.

$2058	1381	Crosses de violon (40x8x8cm-16x3x3in) s.num.11/50 gold pat.bronze Cast.Bocquel. 8-Dec-93 Cornette de St.Cyr, Paris #65/R (F.FR 12000)
$2125	1417	Compressione (60x49x5cm-24x19x2in) s.num.87/99 metal in plexiglass. 23-May-94 Christie's, Milan #8 (I.L 3400000)
$2128	1509	Acropolis (24x6x6cm-9x2x2in) s.num.15/20 yellow pat.bronze Cast.Bocquel. 10-Feb-93 Guy Loudmer, Paris #125 (F.FR 12000)
$2172	1420	Black violin (60cm-24in) s.num.36/100, plastic Cast.R.O.Haligon D'art. 12-May-93 AB Stockholms Auktionsverk, Stockholm #6122 (S.KR 16000)
$2173	1458	Petite Victoire de Samothrace (24x20x10cm-9x8x4in) s.num.46/100 bronze wood st.f.Bocquel. 22-Mar-93 Ader Tajan, Paris #247/R (F.FR 12000)
$2212	1484	Violon decoupe (60x20x12cm-24x8x5in) s.num.42/100 black resin executed 1987. 29-Nov-93 Wolfgang Ketterer, Munich #528/R (DM 3800)
$2213	1401	Split head of Venus (39cm-15in) init.num.8/20, polished bronze. 1-Dec-92 AB Stockholms Auktionsverk, Stockholm #6005/R (S.KR 15000)
$2251	1511	Les Pinceaux (30cm-12in) s. num.27/100, pat bronze incl.marble base. 7-Dec-93 Rasmussen, Copenhagen #21/R (D.KR 15000)
$2256	1514	Cello (27cm-11in) s.num.23/100, brown pat bronze. 29-Nov-93 AB Stockholms Auktionsverk, Stockholm #6162/R (S.KR 19000)
$2280	1540	Acropolis (24x6x6cm-9x2x2in) num.11/20 weld gold bronze cellos Cast.Bocquel. 16-Jun-93 Watine-Arnault, Paris #52 b (F.FR 13000)
$2328	1563	Book (27x22x10cm-11x9x4in) s.num.74/100 oil pat.bronze. 3-Dec-93 Lempertz, Cologne #552/R (DM 4000)
$2354	1580	Acropolis (25x10x10cm-10x4x4in) s.num.3/20 maquette welded bronze st.f.Bocquel. 22-Mar-93 Ader Tajan, Paris #253 (F.FR 13000)
$2399	1632	The Statue of Liberty (75cm-30in) s.num.83/150 bronze. 9-Apr-94 Falkkloos, Malmo #19/R (S.KR 19000)
$2401	1611	Untitled (66x44x4cm-26x17x2in) s. putty knives red colour in plexiglass. 7-Dec-93 Rasmussen, Copenhagen #22/R (D.KR 16000)
$2404	1624	Accumulation de chevalets inclus sous plexiglas (50x25x5cm-20x10x2in) s.num.26/100 wood perspex. 20-Apr-94 Guy Loudmer, Paris #338 (F.FR 14000)
$2435	1613	Chandelier (45cm-18in) num.23/35 executed 1989-90 bronze. 24-Nov-92 Sotheby's, Zurich #373/R (S.FR 3500)
$2518	1690	Venus (33cm-13in) s.i.num.21/100 bronze executed 1990. 8-Dec-93 Christie's, Amsterdam #396/R (D.FL 4800)
$2546	1708	Crosses (41cm-16in) s.num.48/50 gilt bronze st.f.Bocquel. 6-Feb-94 Guy Loudmer, Paris #156/R (F.FR 15000)
$2572	1726	Venus decoupee bronze multiple. 19-Dec-93 Lombrail & Teucquam, Paris #103 b (F.FR 15000)
$2572	1726	Accumulation de chevalets de violon multiple. 19-Dec-93 Lombrail & Teucquam, Paris #103 c (F.FR 15000)
$2584	1700	Echo (115x87cm-45x34in) s.d.64 prisms in polyester. 5-Nov-92 Christie's, S. Kensington #134
$2629	1752	Chevalets de violons, inclusion (50x25x5cm-20x10x2in) s.num.55/100 executed 1971. 1-Jun-94 Marc Kohn, Paris #58/R (F.FR 15000)
$2715	1822	Petite victoire de Samothrace (24x16x15cm-9x6x6in) s.num.35/100 bronze wood st.f.Bocquel. 6-Feb-94 Guy Loudmer, Paris #150/R (F.FR 16000)
$2750	1798	Untitled (66x30x6cm-26x12x2in) s.num.14/20 paint brushes in resin exec.1991. 5-Oct-93 Sotheby's, New York #195/R
$2790	1848	Accumulazione di pennelli (86x48x20cm-34x19x8in) s.num.88/100 enamel paintbrushes in plexiglass. 14-Jun-94 Finarte, Rome #35/R (I.L 4500000)
$2803	1774	Violin (64cm-25in) s.num.67/150, polished bronze incl.black base. 1-Dec-92 AB Stockholms Auktionsverk, Stockholm #6002/R (S.KR 19000)
$2832	1913	Saxophone in three parts (78cm-31in) s.num.P.A. silver metal marble base. 3-Nov-93 Bukowskis, Stockholm #281/R (S.KR 23000)
$2878	1931	The camera (31x60x23cm-12x24x9in) s.num.69/95, painted bronze. 23-Mar-93 Rasmussen, Copenhagen #97/R (D.KR 18000)
$3001	2014	Untitled (66x44x4cm-26x17x2in) s.num.46/100 paintbrushes blue colour plexiglass. 7-Dec-93 Rasmussen, Copenhagen #23/R (D.KR 20000)
$3055	2050	Burned bridges (50x25x5cm-20x10x2in) s.num.8/100 violin bridges plexiglass exec.1971. 6-Feb-94 Guy Loudmer, Paris #151/R (F.FR 15000)
$3151	2115	Cordes Vibrantes (28cm-11in) s.i.num.78/100, pat bronze. 7-Dec-93 Rasmussen, Copenhagen #25/R (D.KR 21000)
$3231	2154	Bather with a violin (34x19cm-13x7in) s. green pat.bronze one of 50 st.f.Bocquel. 28-May-94 Kunstgalerij de Vuyst, Lokeren #544 (B.FR 110000)
$3342	2102	Trumpeter (54cm-21in) s.num.99/100, bronze on marble. 20-Apr-93 Bukowskis, Stockholm #313/R (S.KR 24000)
$3365	2243	Cafetiere (28cm-11in) s.num.E.A.2/10 gold pat.bronze wood executed 28. 30-May-94 Catherine Charbonneaux, Paris #167/R (F.FR 19000)
$3366	2200	Mirror Mirror (79x60cm-31x24in) s. bronze 1 of 8 executed 1984. 30-Jun-94 Sotheby's, London #189/R
$3383	2211	Accumulation de boulons (27x22x5cm-11x9x2in) s.d.1963 metal plexiglass. 28-Oct-92 Guy Loudmer, Paris #80/R (F.FR 18000)
$3411	2186	Book (27x22x10cm-11x9x4in) s.num.50/100 pat.bronze painted with oil. 27-May-93 Lempertz, Cologne #570/R (DM 5400)
$3448	2329	Violons (145x102cm-57x40in) s.num.25/50, brass. 3-Nov-93 Bukowskis, Stockholm #282/R (S.KR 28000)
$3509	2339	Menorah (45cm-18in) s.num.19/50 pat.welded bronze st.f.Bocquel. 8-Jun-94 Guy Loudmer, Paris #270 (F.FR 20000)
$3517	2361	Statue of Liberty (79cm-31in) s.num.69/100, pat. bronze. 23-Mar-93 Rasmussen, Copenhagen #100/R (D.KR 22000)
$3530	2307	Statue of Liberty (75cm-30in) s.num.144/150, green pat bronze incl.stone base. 12-May-93 AB Stockholms Auktionsverk, Stockholm #6121/R (S.KR 26000)
$3682	2488	Violoncelle (70x50x45cm-28x20x18in) s. brown pat.bronze parallelepiped. 18-Jun-93 Claude Boisgirard, Paris #45 (F.FR 21000)

ARMAN, Fernandez (1928-) American/French-cont.

$4063	2673	Menorah (44x47cm-17x19in) s.num.7/50 brown pat.bronze Cast.Bocquel. 4-Apr-93 Guy Loudmer, Paris #76/R (F.FR 22000)
$4131	2700	But not Me (27x16cm-11x6in) s.verso metal plexiglass executed 1964. 30-Jun-94 Sotheby's, London #179/R
$4357	2924	Menorah (44x49cm-17x19in) s.i.num.12/50 brown pat.bronze Cast.Bocquel. 27-Mar-94 Guy Loudmer, Paris #231/R (F.FR 25000)
$4421	2947	Violin dekupation (62x25cm-24x10in) s.nu.77/150 bronze in acrylic. 15-Mar-94 Rasmussen, Copenhagen #73/R (D.KR 29000)
$4430	2954	Goddess of Liberty (80cm-31in) s.num.70/150 green pat bronze incl.stone base. 2-Jun-94 AB Stockholms Auktionsverk, Stockholm #6136/R (S.KR 35000)
$4500	2941	Pizzicato violin (56x19cm-22x7in) s.num.114/150 exec.1972 bronze on marble base. 11-May-93 Christie's, New York #355/R
$4636	3132	Assemblage of razors (40cm-16in) s.d.1972 num.40/40. 29-Mar-94 Campo & Campo, Antwerp #5/R (B.FR 160000)
$4661	3171	Cut violin (59cm-23in) s. gold pat bronze incl.base. 13-Apr-94 Bukowskis, Stockholm #417/R (S.KR 37000)
$4802	3159	Baroquial (36x15x15cm-14x6x6in) s.num.67/100 welded bronze Cast.Bocquel exec.84. 4-Apr-93 Hoebanx, Paris #128/R (F.FR 26000)
$5102	3424	Saxophones (130x92cm-51x36in) s.num.64/99, gilt bronze. 7-Dec-93 Rasmussen, Copenhagen #74/R (D.KR 34000)
$5400	3600	Venus cut in two (33x11cm-13x4in) s.i.num.4/100 bronze. 3-Jun-94 Lempertz, Cologne #468/R (DM 9000)
$5971	3828	Tete vide (28x15x10cm-11x6x4in) s.num.6/8 pat.bronze Cast.Bocquel executed 1986. 28-May-93 Catherine Charbonneaux, Paris #203/R (F.FR 32000)
$6000	4027	Untitled (61x30x12cm-24x12x5in) with sig.d.67 feathers in polyester resin metal. 23-Feb-94 Christie's, New York #20/R
$6120	4000	Untitled (44x54x9cm-17x21x4in) s.num.5/8 bronze executed 1986-87. 30-Jun-94 Sotheby's, London #190/R
$6152	4129	Accumulated red monocrome (65x54cm-26x21in) s.num.1501, collage paint-tubes canvas 1987-89. 7-Dec-93 Rasmussen, Copenhagen #39/R (D.KR 41000)
$6156	4160	Monochrome accumulation No 3008 (92x73cm-36x29in) s.verso paint tubes canvas on panel. 3-Nov-93 Bukowskis, Stockholm #211/R (S.KR 50000)
$6263	4147	Paintbrushes (65x44cm-26x17in) s.num.XV/XXX exec.1990 paintbrushes plexiglass. 24-Nov-92 Sotheby's, Zurich #374/R (S.FR 9000)
$6296	4225	Jaws (62x53x49cm-24x21x19in) s.num.1/1 welded cast bronze pliers executed '78. 8-Dec-93 Christie's, Amsterdam #375/R (D.FL 12000)
$6300	4200	Nu couche (28x76x15cm-11x30x6in) s.st.num.8/8 bronze executed 1983. 26-May-94 Christie's, London #128/R
$6434	3785	Venus (33x9x12cm-13x4x5in) s.num.63/100 brown pat.bronze. 10-Oct-92 Wolfgang Ketterer, Munich #530/R (DM 9500)
$6500	4392	Long term parking (34x19x19cm-13x7x7in) toy cars plaster executed 1982. 10-Nov-93 Christie's, New York #142/R
$6579	4300	Pour ma jolie (100x40x10cm-39x16x4in) s. num.7/8 soldered bronze Cast.1982. 27-Oct-92 Cornette de St.Cyr, Paris #81/R (F.FR 35000)
$6820	4577	Guitare cassee (93x37x12cm-37x15x5in) s.num.1/2 bronze executed c.1985 1/15. 8-Dec-93 Christie's, Amsterdam #346/R (D.FL 13000)
$7001	4667	Oeuvre en laine et brosses (200x150cm-79x59in) s. wool paint brushes panel executed 1989. 8-Mar-94 Marc Kohn, Paris #41/R (F.FR 40000)
$7214	4975	Petite Venus au bain et violon (39x16x11cm-15x6x4in) s.num.EA 3/4 1990 pat.bronze. 31-Jan-93 Hoebanx, Paris #57 (F.FR 40000)
$7307	4745	Canto Rondo (122x100x5cm-48x39x2in) s. paint brushes mixed media canvas executed 91. 24-Jun-94 Francis Briest, Paris #53/R (F.FR 40000)
$7345	4930	Cute cutted cupid (72x49x41cm-28x19x16in) s.i.num.2/2 dark green pat.bronze executed 1986. 8-Dec-93 Christie's, Amsterdam #392/R (D.FL 14000)
$7562	5145	Hommage a Marcel Duchamp (25x25x25cm-10x10x10in) s.d.1966 chess pieces cement. 10-Apr-94 Perrin, Versailles #88/R (F.FR 44500)
$7800	5200	Mars, Veni, Vidi, Vici (63x29x31cm-25x11x12in) s.st.num.2/5 bronze executed 1986. 26-May-94 Christie's, London #121/R
$8354	5254	Statue de la Liberte (71cm-28in) s.num.1/1, green gold pat bronze. 20-Apr-93 Bukowskis, Stockholm #312/R (S.KR 60000)
$8940	6000	Accumulation de tubes de couleurs d'or (80x65cm-31x26in) s. gold paint paint tubes on canvas. 24-Mar-93 Sotheby's, London #330/R
$9198	6300	Proposition simple (130x97cm-51x38in) s.verso paint brushes acrylic canvas exec.1988. 10-Feb-94 Cornette de St.Cyr, Paris #84/R (F.FR 55000)
$9685	6500	Humphrey Bogart's Memorial (58x34x23cm-23x13x9in) s.num.1/2 bronze executed 1989. 25-Mar-93 Christie's, London #24/R
$9697	6422	Accumulation de contrabasses (23cm-9in) s.exec.1928 num.37/100 bronze marble F.Bocquel. 21-Nov-92 Auktionhaus Burkard, Luzern #176/R (S.FR 14000)
$9780	6000	Statue of Liberty (73cm-29in) s.num.1/1 bronze executed c.1985. 14-Oct-92 Sotheby's, London #396/R
$9927	6090	Chorus (66x55x35cm-26x22x14in) s.num.AP 1/2 bronze. 18-Oct-92 Catherine Charbonneaux, Paris #67/R (F.FR 50000)
$10092	6728	Untitled (100x100cm-39x39in) s. paint tubes in plexiglass executed c.1975. 7-Jun-94 Rasmussen, Copenhagen #5/R (D.KR 66000)
$10101	6475	Jupiter rend fous ceux qui vent perdre (97x100x55cm-38x39x22in) s.i.num.2/3 green pat.bronze executed 1986. 26-May-93 Christie's, Amsterdam #397/R (D.FL 18000)
$10329	6932	Spanish guitar (98cm-39in) s.num.6/8, pat bronze. 29-Nov-93 AB Stockholms Auktionsverk, Stockholm #6158/R (S.KR 87000)
$10430	7000	Violon coule (63x28x7cm-25x11x3in) s. violin in polyester. 2-Dec-93 Christie's, London #149/R
$10430	7000	Accumulation de feutres (178x178cm-70x70in) felt-tip pens plexiglass executed 1974. 2-Dec-93 Christie's, London #182/R
$10430	7000	And metal (154x79cm-61x31in) s. paint scrapers acrylic board executed 1987. 25-Mar-93 Christie's, London #77/R

ARMAN, Fernandez (1928-) American/French-cont.

Price	Lot	Description
$10468	7026	Petite Venus au bain et violon (38x14x12cm-15x6x5in) s.num.EA 2/4 brown pat.bronze st.f.Bocquel. 23-Jun-93 Guy Loudmer, Paris #34/R (F.FR 60000)
$10595	6500	Statue of Liberty (73cm-29in) s. bronze executed c.1985. 14-Oct-92 Sotheby's, London #393/R
$10662	6835	Eros inside Eros (89x43x54cm-35x17x21in) s.i.num.3/3 bronze executed 1986. 26-May-93 Christie's, Amsterdam #397 a/R (D.FL 19000)
$10697	7227	Untitled (68cm-27in) s.num.EA 2/2 violin in bronze f.Bocquel c.1986/7. 18-Jun-93 Francis Briest, Paris #49/R (F.FR 61000)
$10728	7200	Untitled (97x89cm-38x35in) acrylic paint tubes canvas on board executed 88. 2-Dec-93 Christie's, London #223/R
$10889	7212	Sculpture with three trombones cut in half (102x62cm-40x24in) s. num.5/8 bronze executed 1986. 16-Jun-94 Galerie Koller, Zurich #3136/R (S.FR 15000)
$11060	7000	Maquette for 'La Descente aux Enfers' (10x125x54cm-4x49x21in) toy motorcycles plaster. 3-Dec-92 Sotheby's, London #92/R
$11175	7500	Untitled (92x73cm-36x29in) s. paint tubes on canvas executed 1986. 25-Mar-93 Christie's, London #32/R
$11250	7500	Accumulation (32x22x6cm-13x9x2in) s.d.1962verso mechanical drives in wood box. 26-May-94 Christie's, London #71/R
$11250	7500	Zeus, god of futurism (97x50x38cm-38x20x15in) s.st.num.3/5 bronze executed 1986. 26-May-94 Christie's, London #122/R
$11410	7000	Tubes couleur Suedois II (100x100cm-39x39in) s. paint tubes in plexiglass. 15-Oct-92 Christie's, London #39/R
$11670	7832	Zeus, God of Futurism (97x50x38cm-38x20x15in) s.num.4/5 pat.bronze Cast.Bocquel executed 1986. 5-Dec-93 Perrin, Versailles #78/R (F.FR 69000)
$11829	7834	Pyraviole (60cm-24in) s.num.EA 1/2 executed c.1983 bronze i.Bocquel F. 24-Nov-92 Sotheby's, Zurich #368/R (S.FR 17000)
$11920	8000	Violin, marbre et Breton (83x30x11cm-33x12x4in) s. broken marble violin concrete in wood box. 25-Mar-93 Christie's, London #25/R
$12600	8400	Untitled - spatulas in red paint (92x73cm-36x29in) s. acrylic spatulas panel. 3-Jun-94 Lempertz, Cologne #465/R (DM 21000)
$12665	8500	Panneau de fourchettes (122x143cm-48x56in) s. welded forks on metal frame executed 1983. 25-Mar-93 Christie's, London #16/R
$12665	8500	Accumulation de violons decoupes (81x50cm-32x20in) s. fragmented violins in plexiglass. 23-Mar-94 Sotheby's, London #341/R
$12665	8500	Untitled (136x102cm-54x40in) acrylic paint tubes canvas on panel executed 89. 2-Dec-93 Christie's, London #221/R
$12689	8134	Violon prisonnier (69x28cm-27x11in) s.num.5/8 gilt bronze wood. 12-Dec-92 Catherine Charbonneaux, Paris #62/R (F.FR 68000)
$12750	8500	Accumulation de tubes de peintures (100x81cm-39x32in) s. paint tubes laid down on canvas exec.1986. 26-May-94 Christie's, London #79/R
$13000	8725	Paradise for Asthmatics (125x160cm-49x63in) oxygen cylinder pressure dials polyester resin. 23-Feb-94 Christie's, New York #21/R
$13005	8500	Untitled (59x39x3cm-23x15x1in) s.d.66 paint tubes plexiglass. 30-Jun-94 Sotheby's, London #125/R
$13116	8803	Object arme (124x84x20cm-49x33x8in) s. sliced violin in concrete plexiglass box. 8-Dec-93 Christie's, Amsterdam #376/R (D.FL 25000)
$13152	8886	Autumn in Connecticut (100x81cm-39x32in) s. tubes of colour on canvas. 18-Jun-93 Francis Briest, Paris #62/R (F.FR 75000)
$13410	9000	Venus (90cm-35in) s.exec.1970 ed.of 20 dollar notes in plexiglass. 24-Mar-93 Sotheby's, London #328/R
$13410	9000	40 Kg de non ferreux (100x50x12cm-39x20x5in) metal polyester executed 1973. 25-Mar-93 Christie's, London #54/R
$13410	9000	Liberte musical (76cm-30in) s.num.EA 2/2 green pat.bronze. 21-Jun-93 Christie's, S. Kensington #185/R
$14079	9324	Heracles divided strength (77x36x26cm-30x14x10in) num.1/5 bronze Cast.Bocquel executed 1986. 29-Sep-93 Cornette de St.Cyr, Paris #42/R (F.FR 80000)
$14155	9500	Demeter (117x58x30cm-46x23x12in) s.num.2/5 brown pat.bronze executed 1986. 25-Mar-93 Christie's, London #84/R
$14155	9500	Violon prisonnier (70cm-28in) s.num.7/8 bronze wood violin bow exec.c.1986-87. 24-Jun-93 Sotheby's, London #117/R
$14160	9255	Colere (61x26cm-24x10in) s. musical instrument in plexiglass. 21-Dec-92 Jean Louis Picard, Paris #7/R (F.FR 77000)
$14211	9474	Strip tease (56x93cm-22x37in) s.d. 1963 coffee pots panel. 9-Jun-94 Christian de Quay, Paris #368/R (F.FR 81000)
$14376	9648	Violons et cadrans (64cm-25in) s.num.5/8 gold pat.bronze st.f.Bocquel. 29-Nov-93 Francis Briest, Paris #74/R (F.FR 85000)
$15000	10000	Acrosage, violon (45x26x13cm-18x10x5in) i. polyester resin executed c.1975. 31-May-94 Christie's, Amsterdam #436/R (D.FL 28000)
$15000	10067	Untitled (25x25x24cm-10x10x9in) gouache paint tubes in polyester resin exec.1967. 4-May-94 Christie's, New York #122/R
$15300	10000	Untitled (120x120cm-47x47in) s.d.71 fragmented accordeon plexiglass. 30-Jun-94 Sotheby's, London #209/R
$15334	10155	Split cello (100x70cm-39x28in) s.num.1/8, bronze wood. 25-Nov-92 Bukowskis, Stockholm #55/R (S.KR 105000)
$15485	9500	Violins (79cm-31in) s.num.EA 2/2 bronze wood executed c.1986. 14-Oct-92 Sotheby's, London #312/R
$15750	10500	Athena como un espada (156x32x40cm-61x13x16in) s. one of five bronze executed 1986. 26-May-94 Christie's, London #62/R
$16000	10738	Long term parking (72x26x27cm-28x10x11in) s. ed.of 8 toy cars in cement executed 1982. 4-May-94 Christie's, New York #77/R
$16273	10432	Tranche de Lagoya (100cm-39in) s.num.2/2 bronze wooden guitar. 27-May-93 Sotheby's, Amsterdam #299/R (D.FL 29000)
$16390	11000	Accumulation of paint tubes (153x212cm-60x83in) s.overlap paint tubes canvas executed c.1973. 25-Mar-93 Christie's, London #85/R

ARMAN, Fernandez (1928-) American/French-cont.

$16730	11228	Accumulation brisee (160x120x12cm-63x47x5in) s. porcelain fragments perspex executed 1989. 21-Mar-94 Guy Loudmer, Paris #97/R (F.FR 96000)
$17000	11409	Monochrome accumulation No.3005 (91x73cm-36x29in) s.verso acrylic paint tubes on canvas exec.c.87. 25-Feb-94 Sotheby's, New York #58/R
$17115	10500	Vacuum, Delire et Orbe (120x120x21cm-47x47x8in) s.d.71 broken vacuum cleaner polyester plexiglas. 15-Oct-92 Christie's, London #42/R
$17503	11669	Les plaintes de l'amour (94x70x60cm-37x28x24in) num.5/8 gold pat.bronze Cast.Bocquel exec.1988. 8-Mar-94 Marc Kohn, Paris #61/R (F.FR 100000)
$17880	12000	Ophicleide (120x60x11cm-47x24x4in) s.d.71 cut ophicleide in polyester. 2-Dec-93 Christie's, London #152/R
$18000	12500	Accumulation of tubes (117x89cm-46x35in) s. executed 1986 paint tubes acrylic canvas. 23-Feb-93 Sotheby's, New York #288/R
$18625	12500	Untitled (115x89x18cm-45x35x7in) s.d.89 acrylic paint tubes broken mandolin. 25-Mar-93 Christie's, London #75/R
$18750	12500	Le tombeau de Paga (93x63cm-37x25in) s. violin carrying case in concrete exec.1973. 26-May-94 Christie's, London #70/R
$18960	12000	Poubelle organique (102x51x12cm-40x20x5in) accumulation of garbage executed 1972. 3-Dec-92 Sotheby's, London #72/R
$19370	13000	Torso, with broken glasses (82cm-32in) s. broken glasses in polyester executed c.1971. 25-Mar-93 Christie's, London #51/R
$19484	12903	Violon prisonnier (63cm-25in) s. executed 1985 bronze wood. 24-Nov-92 Sotheby's, Zurich #37/R (S.FR 28000)
$19560	12000	Tranche de Lagoya (101x80x50cm-40x31x20in) s.num.EA 1/2 sliced guitar brass. 15-Oct-92 Christie's, London #53/R
$19560	1?000	Up (124x75cm-49x30in) s.d.64 metal strainers in polyester. 15-Oct-92 Christie's, London #13/R
$20169	13269	Blanc et or (198x158cm-78x62in) s. gouache bottles plexiglass executed 1968. 6-Apr-93 Guy Loudmer, Paris #37/R (F.FR 110000)
$20371	13672	Untitled, accumulation of paint tubes (100x80x10cm-39x31x4in) s. i.verso acrylic canvas plexiglass exec.1990. 3-Dec-93 Lempertz, Cologne #548/R (DM 35000)
$21324	13669	Sans titre (135x91cm-53x36in) s. brush paint canvas. 26-May-93 Christie's, Amsterdam #396/R (D.FL 38000)
$21809	14637	Orgueil masculin (105cm-41in) s.num.HC 1/2 brown pat.bronze st.f.Bocquel. 23-Jun-93 Guy Loudmer, Paris #41/R (F.FR 125000)
$22350	15000	Venus, Porte Ouverte (180cm-71in) s.num.1/3 sliced bronze Venus f.i. executed 1986. 2-Dec-93 Christie's, London #179/R
$22500	13235	Cello (120x60cm-47x24in) num.4/8 cello brass. 6-Oct-92 Christie's, New York #87/R
$22555	14742	Long term parking (70x26x26cm-28x10x10in) s. cars in concrete. 28-Oct-92 Guy Loudmer, Paris #85/R (F.FR 120000)
$23027	15665	Harmonie dans la Discorde (187x87x90cm-74x34x35in) s.num.IV/V col gold pat.bronze Cast.Immart 89. 10-Apr-94 Perrin, Versailles #83/R (F.FR 135500)
$23250	15500	Accumulation watchbox (35x63x5cm-14x25x2in) boxes Matchbox toy cars in plexiglas exec.1964. 26-May-94 Christie's, London #63/R
$23840	16000	Accumulations of violins (65x69x8cm-26x27x3in) s. burnt violins in plexiglass executed 1969. 25-Mar-93 Christie's, London #52/R
$23840	16000	Cello callipyge (143x103x25cm-56x41x10in) s. broken cello embedded in concrete exec.1973. 25-Mar-93 Christie's, London #14/R
$25669	16888	Proud in despite of, violoncelle decoupe (140x49x20cm-55x19x8in) s.num.3/8 bronze st.f.Bocquel executed 1981. 6-Apr-93 Guy Loudmer, Paris #52/R (F.FR 140000)
$26000	15294	Violin table service (89x56x29cm-35x22x11in) sig.num.34/99 violin plexiglass others. 8-Oct-92 Christie's, New York #143/R
$26080	16000	Accumulation de Feutres (178x178cm-70x70in) s.verso felt-tip pen polyester plexiglass. 15-Oct-92 Christie's, London #35/R
$26285	17523	Resurrection (74x45x25cm-29x18x10in) num.H.C. pat.bronze Cast.Bocquel executed 1984. 1-Jun-94 Marc Kohn, Paris #57/R (F.FR 150000)
$26481	18519	Sans titre (100x100x3cm-39x39x1in) paint tubes plexiglass executed 1968. 10-Mar-93 Watine-Arnault, Paris #59/R (F.FR 150000)
$26820	18000	Floral (152x122x5cm-60x48x2in) welded steel turbine cogs executed 1981. 2-Dec-93 Christie's, London #233/R
$26823	18002	Paint brushes (195x152cm-77x60in) brushes acrylic canvas executed 1987. 14-Oct-93 Guy Loudmer, Paris #102/R (F.FR 155000)
$27710	17000	Athena como una Espada (160x42x39cm-63x17x15in) s.num.Ea 1/2 sliced bronze sculpture. 15-Oct-92 Christie's, London #54/R
$27808	17600	Frank's true colours (123x173x14cm-48x68x6in) jars of paint in polyester painted wood box. 3-Dec-92 Christie's, London #80/R
$29800	20000	Counters from Nice (57x26x16cm-22x10x6in) s. accumulation casino chips in polyester. 2-Dec-93 Christie's, London #160/R
$30012	20988	La fiancee de Casals (132x60x48cm-52x24x19in) s.num.artist's proof bronze Cast.Bocquel. 14-Mar-93 Watine-Arnault, Paris #53/R (F.FR 170000)
$31150	20906	Sans titre (140x101cm-55x40in) collection of violins in plexiglass. 14-Oct-93 Guy Loudmer, Paris #27/R (F.FR 180000)
$33401	22120	Table, sculpten en violoncelle et violin decoupee (45x90cm-18x35in) s. executed 1988 gilded bronze and crystal glass. 24-Nov-92 Sotheby's, Zurich #372/R (S.FR 48000)
$38740	26000	Black Indian invasion (149x192cm-59x76in) s. inkpots acrylic in plexiglass executed 1967. 24-Jun-93 Sotheby's, London #52/R
$41720	28000	Glory (137x236x20cm-54x93x8in) accumulation welded sliced trombones executed 84. 2-Dec-93 Christie's, London #178/R
$42000	24706	Bout de souffle (48x43x46cm-19x17x18in) accumulation clocks glass box. 6-Oct-92 Sotheby's, New York #73/R
$43264	29036	Venus labyrinthe of love (176x82cm-69x32in) s.num.3/5 cut welded pat.bronze st.f.Bocquel 86. 14-Oct-93 Guy Loudmer, Paris #105/R (F.FR 250000)
$44700	30000	Violoncelle brule (195x115x6cm-77x45x2in) s.d.73 burnt violoncell plexiglas. 24-Jun-93 Christie's, London #37/R

ARMAN, Fernandez (1928-) American/French-cont.
$45000	30000	Le grand violoncelle (180x130x25cm-71x51x10in) s. burned cellow in plexi-sheets exec.c.1970. 26-May-94 Christie's, London #43/R
$47680	32000	Accumulation de rouages - Iris d'Octopuss (123x93cm-48x37in) s.d.1964 brass cogs plexiglas. 2-Dec-93 Christie's, London #31/R
$50000	29412	Untitled (68x32x8cm-27x13x3in) burnt violin plexiglass. 6-Oct-92 Sotheby's, New York #81/R
$50560	32000	Accord majeur (160x130cm-63x51in) s.d.62 cello panel. 3-Dec-92 Sotheby's, London #24/R
$50660	34000	Apollo, the offering (218x142x116cm-86x56x46in) s.num.1/1 bronze f.st. executed 1986. 24-Jun-93 Christie's, London #112/R
$77480	52000	DHL (360x150x110cm-142x59x43in) sliced bronze Hermes motorcycles executed 1988. 2-Dec-93 Christie's, London #181/R
$79618	52727	Colere de violoncelle calcine (117x86cm-46x34in) s. scorched cello polyester executed 1964. 22-Nov-92 Perrin, Versailles #50/R (F.FR 435000)

ARNESON, Robert (1930-1992) American
$5000	3165	Squish (107x99x25cm-42x39x10in) s.d.81 verso cast paper. 25-Oct-92 Butterfield & Butterfield, San Francisco #2313/R
$12000	8108	Pollock mask no 2 (41x29x19cm-16x11x7in) s.i.d.1983 num.2 glazed ceramic. 10-Nov-93 Christie's, New York #218/R
$12000	8108	Askance (109x99cm-43x39in) s.i.d.81 cast paper pulp wood. 21-Oct-93 Butterfield & Butterfield, San Francisco #2803/R

ARNOLDI, Charles (1946-) American
$3500	2365	Untitled (40cm-16in) s.d.83 bronze. 21-Apr-94 Butterfield & Butterfield, San Francisco #1197/R

ARTSCHWAGER, Richard (1923-) American
$1200	784	Hairbox (13x26x36cm-5x10x14in) s.num.6/100 paint on rubberized horsehair. 5-Oct-93 Sotheby's, New York #162/R
$1400	915	Door (44x63x13cm-17x25x5in) s.num.15 ed.of 25 formica hardware wood. 5-Oct-93 Sotheby's, New York #161/R
$1400	824	Hair Blip (36x20x2cm-14x8x1in) s.d.89verso rubberised horse hair. 8-Oct-92 Christie's, New York #188/R
$2500	1689	Book (13x51x30cm-5x20x12in) s.num.10/40 formica wood executed 1987. 8-Nov-93 Christie's, East, New York #34/R
$4000	2685	Pregunta III (74x22x2cm-29x9x1in) painted wood two parts executed 1983 5/6. 25-Feb-94 Sotheby's, New York #85/R
$4500	2941	Pregunta III (74x22x2cm-29x9x1in) s.num.ed. of 6 painted wood two parts in case. 5-Oct-93 Sotheby's, New York #85/R
$6000	4054	Table (76x59x5cm-30x23x2in) graphite felt-tip pen formica on wood exec.1977. 10-Nov-93 Christie's, New York #371/R
$8000	5229	File (76x154x24cm-30x61x9in) s.i.d.89verso formica stainless steel. 5-May-93 Christie's, New York #138/R
$11000	7285	Mirror, green (183x92cm-72x36in) s.i.d.88verso formica. 19-Nov-92 Christie's, New York #258/R
$22500	15203	Untitled (99x69x13cm-39x27x5in) s.d.1963-64 verso formica wood. 11-Nov-93 Sotheby's, New York #119/R
$30000	20270	Tree of life (134x89x10cm-53x35x4in) acrylic celotex wood executed 1981. 11-Nov-93 Sotheby's, New York #124/R
$33000	21854	Dugout III (214x69x25cm-84x27x10in) executed 1967 formica wood. 19-Nov-92 Christie's, New York #404/R
$42000	27815	Door/Door (189x343x19cm-74x135x7in) formica acrylic wood. 18-Nov-92 Christie's, New York #63/R
$45000	29801	Instrument (195x96x41cm-77x38x16in) formica wood chrome plated brass executed 1990. 18-Nov-92 Sotheby's, New York #245/R
$100000	66225	Tower III - Confessional (152x119x81cm-60x47x32in) formica oak. 17-Nov-92 Sotheby's, New York #66/R
$155000	104027	Piano III (86x86x330cm-34x34x130in) formica wood rubberized hair executed 1965-79. 4-May-94 Sotheby's, New York #57/R
$160000	104575	Chair (94x56x51cm-37x22x20in) formica wood construction executed 1963. 3-May-93 Sotheby's, New York #65/R
$310000	208054	Sailors (51x66x22cm-20x26x9in) s.i.d.6.20.64verso acrylic celotex. 4-May-94 Sotheby's, New York #26/R

ASAWA, Ruth (1926-) American
$2000	1351	Untitled (193cm-76in) aluminum copper wire mesh. 27-Apr-94 Christie's, New York #17/R

ASHEVAK, Karoo (1940-1974) North American
$2446	1641	Spence Bay - chanting Inuit shaman wearing parka sitting back on haunches (36cm-14in) s. weathered whalebone. 29-Nov-93 Waddingtons, Toronto #920 (C.D 3350)
$6773	4545	Standing Inuit hunter with inset eyes, wearing parka (43cm-17in) s. weathered whalebone. 29-Nov-93 Waddingtons, Toronto #917/R (C.D 9000)
$9354	6154	Carving of standing Inuit woman with her child (71cm-28in) whalebone. 7-Jun-93 Waddingtons, Toronto #998/R (C.D 12000)

ASHEVAK, Kenojuak (1927-) North American
$725	483	Transformation carving of a shaman-animal head (30cm-12in) veined mottled green soapstone. 6-Jun-94 Waddingtons, Toronto #961 (C.D 1000)
$3551	2367	Carving of a hawk standing with swept back wings (52cm-20in) darkly mottled green soapstone. 6-Jun-94 Waddingtons, Toronto #977/R (C.D 4900)

ASHOONA, Kaka (1928-) North American
$1411 905 Kneeling Inuit woman with braided hair, carrying small animal in amaut (38cm-15in) s. marbled dark green serpentine. 7-Dec-92 Waddingtons, Toronto #1009/R (C.D 1800)

ATCHEALAK, Davie (1947-) North American
$1355 909 Inuit hunter wearing a parka, dragging a seal on to ice floe (38cm-15in) s. marbled green soapstone. 29-Nov-93 Waddingtons, Toronto #946 (C.D 1800)
$1377 918 Walrus standing upright on rear flippers (43cm-17in) s.d.79 mottle dark green soapstone. 6-Jun-94 Waddingtons, Toronto #1034/R (C.D 1900)
$1884 1256 Polar bear dancing on its hind leg (47cm-19in) s. marbled light green soapstone. 6-Jun-94 Waddingtons, Toronto #1030/R (C.D 2600)
$3261 2174 Running Inuk wearing hide leggings with spear (56cm-22in) s. marbled dark green serpentine. 6-Jun-94 Waddingtons, Toronto #1025 (C.D 4500)
$3292 2111 Chanting head of shaman's spirit running on stunted legs, carrying antler (41cm-16in) s. mottled dark green soapstone. 7-Dec-92 Waddingtons, Toronto #1019 (C.D 4200)
$4899 3141 Singing Inuit drummer with braided hair, dancing with swirling parka (71cm-28in) s. mottled light green soapstone. 7-Dec-92 Waddingtons, Toronto #1014/R (C.D 6250)

AYCOCK, Alice (1946-) American
$5500 3642 Swirls after Leonardo (71x66x66cm-28x26x26in) galvanized steel executed 1982. 18-Nov-92 Sotheby's, New York #239/R

BAIZERMAN, Saul (1889-1957) Russian/American
$2500 1689 Italian woman. The cement man (16cm-6in) i. one d.1921 brown pat.bronze pair. 31-Mar-94 Sotheby's Arcade, New York #458/R

BAKER, Percy Bryant (1881-1970) American
$16000 10127 The pioneer woman (44cm-17in) i.num.10 red-brown pat.bronze.Cast.Gorham Co. 4-Dec-92 Christie's, New York #259/R

BALL, Thomas (1819-1911) American
$3500 2349 Portrait of Henry Ward Beecher (56cm-22in) s.d.1867 marble. 6-Dec-93 Grogan, Massachussetts #455/R
$4000 2649 Daniel Webster (79cm-31in) i.d.1853 dark brown pat.bronze f.i.Ames,Chicopee. 23-Sep-93 Sotheby's, New York #82/R
$11000 7051 'Love's memories' - figure of seated cupid (78cm-31in) s.d.1875 white marble. 26-May-93 Christie's, New York #88/R

BARTLETT, Paul Wayland (1881-1925) American
$2600 1722 Figure of turtle (24cm-9in) i.d.1921 reddish brown pat.bronze. 22-Sep-93 Christie's, New York #96/R

BASCOM, Earl W (20th C) American
$1500 974 Santa Anita (30cm-12in) s.i.d.c.1982 num.6/30 brown pat.bronze. 11-Sep-93 Louisiana Auction Exchange #99/R

BASKIN, Leonard (1922-) American
$2500 1445 Plaque of raven (30x43cm-12x17in) i. red pat.bronze. 25-Sep-92 Sotheby's Arcade, New York #375/R
$2500 1667 Boy maquette (38cm-15in) s.num.7/15 brown pat.bronze st.f.Bedi Rassy. 26-May-94 Sotheby's, New York #153/R
$5000 3247 Ram (107cm-42in) s. green brown pat.bronze. 9-Sep-93 Sotheby's Arcade, New York #414/R
$6000 4000 The arrival (65cm-26in) s.d.1980 num.1/5 st.f.Bedi Makky. 26-May-94 Sotheby's, New York #156/R
$6000 4000 Mourning woman (109cm-43in) s. red brown pat.bronze st.f.Bedi Makky. 26-May-94 Sotheby's, New York #154/R

BASQUIAT, Jean Michel (1960-1988) American
$160000 107383 Untitled (214x272x30cm-84x107x12in) s.d.85verso oil acrylic three panels. 4-May-94 Christie's, New York #406/R

BATTENBERG, John (1931-) American
$9500 6013 Untitled - two women (178x102x25cm-70x40x10in) s.i.d.77 num.2/3 cast bronze. 25-Oct-92 Butterfield & Butterfield, San Francisco #2335/R

BAUR, Theodore (1835-1898) American
$3500 2273 Portrait of crazy horse (74cm-29in) i.d.1885 brown pat.bronze. 9-Sep-93 Sotheby's Arcade, New York #151/R

BEACH, Chester (1881-1956) American
$15000 10000 Glint of the sea - fountain figure of nymph (122cm-48in) i. green brown pat.bronze wood base. 26-May-94 Christie's, New York #110/R

BEAUJOUR, Jean Sonson (1954-) Haitian
$2420 1551 Ballet (205cm-81in) mahogany. 14-Dec-92 Hoebanx, Paris #143/R (F.FR 13000)

BECKMAN, Ford (1952-) American
$1800   1216   Untitled (177x159x20cm-70x63x8in) s.i.d.1989verso two panels. 8-Nov-93 Christie's, East, New York #69/R
$2532   1688   Untitled black wall painting with steel (172x122x172cm-68x48x68in) d.f.87 acrylic wax furnace wood steel. 2-Jun-94 AB Stockholms Auktionsverk, Stockholm #7064/R (S.KR 20000)

BEELER, Joe Neil (1931-) American
$3600   2416   Dog soldiers (89cm-35in) s.num.3/17 brown pat.bronze. 2-May-94 Selkirks, St. Louis #129/R

BEGG, John Alfred (1903-1974) American
$1864   1235   Owl (22cm-9in) s. green pat.bronze on wooden socle. 20-Nov-92 Schloss Ahlden, Ahlden #408/R (DM 3000)

BELL, Larry (1939-) American
$11000   7383   Glass cube cal no 8 (132x51x51cm-52x20x20in) mirrored cube on plexiglas base executed 1985. 4-May-94 Christie's, New York #314/R

BENDER, Gretchen (1951-) American
$823   549   Return of the living dead (51x56cm-20x22in) steel panel opening film strip light exec.1988. 2-Jun-94 AB Stockholms Auktionsverk, Stockholm #7160/R (S.KR 6500)

BENGLIS, Linda (1941-) American
$2600   1745   Cosworth (33x25x8cm-13x10x3in) silver-plated bronze on steel mesh executed 1989. 23-Feb-94 Christie's, East, New York #270/R
$3200   2148   Curtis Wright (29x23x8cm-11x9x3in) silver-plated bronze on steel mesh. 23-Feb-94 Christie's, East, New York #268/R
$4000   2685   Puppis (43x15x12cm-17x6x5in) bronze copper zinc wall sculpture. 3-May-94 Christie's, East, New York #252/R
$5000   3268   Sparkle knot (44x46x30cm-17x18x12in) wall relief acrylic glitter collage plaster. 7-May-93 Christie's, East, New York #56/R
$6000   4167   Peter, knot (152x43x28cm-60x17x11in) executed 1974 suray paint aluminum and screen. 23-Feb-93 Sotheby's, New York #377/R
$9000   5294   Andromeda (67x60x27cm-26x24x11in) vapourised aluminium. 8-Oct-92 Christie's, New York #160/R
$14000   9150   Lyra (155x43x39cm-61x17x15in) bronze wire mesh zinc nickel copper. 4-May-93 Sotheby's, New York #187/R

BENTON, Fletcher (1931-) American
$2500   1689   Steel water color no.7 (169cm-67in) s.i.d.1984 corten steel. 21-Oct-93 Butterfield & Butterfield, San Francisco #2805/R
$2500   1572   Moving Colour Panels (169x69cm-67x27in) plexiglass aluminium stainless steel wood. 25-Apr-93 Butterfield & Butterfield, San Francisco #2151/R

BENTON, Thomas Hart (1889-1975) American
$7750   5420   Scotch and Soda, ship model (52cm-20in) i.exec.1923 carved wood cloth string. 10-Mar-93 Sotheby's, New York #151/R

BERGE, Edward Henry (1876-1924) American
$2076   1393   'Flora' - young dancing girl (60cm-24in) s. num.10, bronze marble base. 2-Feb-94 Kunsthallen, Copenhagen #234/R (D.KR 14000)
$2500   1689   Wild flower (51cm-20in) i. dark brown green pat.bronze. 31-Mar-94 Sotheby's Arcade, New York #84/R

BERKE, Ernest (1921-) American
$2400   1600   The war signal (71cm-28in) i.d.1978 num.15/20 goldish brown pat.bronze. 22-May-94 Hindman Galleries, Chicago #36/R
$3000   1987   Ceremony of Fastest Horse (47cm-19in) i.num.1/20 greenish brown pat.bronze. 23-Sep-93 Sotheby's, New York #89/R
$4000   2312   Chief Crazy Horse (41cm-16in) s.d.1955 num.15 reddish-brown pat.bronze. 24-Sep-92 Sotheby's, New York #77/R

BERLANT, Tony (1941-) American
$3000   2013   House (23x22x18cm-9x9x7in) printed sheet metal steel brads on wood. 23-Feb-94 Christie's, East, New York #271/R

BERRONE, Juan (20th C) Argentinian
$1492   1001   Suonatore di tamburi (20x30x26cm-8x12x10in) s. exec.c.1930 black pat.bronze Cast Valsuani. 25-Mar-93 Finarte, Rome #215/R (I.L 2400000)

BERTOIA, Harry (1915-1978) American
$2284   1446   Untitled (80x90x90cm-31x35x35in) executed 1969 stainless steel. 30-Nov-92 Wolfgang Ketterer, Munich #541/R (DM 3600)
$2682   1800   Untitled (78cm-31in) stainless steel executed c.1965. 23-Mar-94 Sotheby's, London #376/R
$3000   1987   Untitled (39cm-15in) beryllium copper rods on bronze base. 29-Sep-93 Sotheby's Arcade, New York #320/R
$3725   2500   Untitled (65cm-26in) stainless steel executed c.1967. 23-Mar-94 Sotheby's, London #319/R
$4000   2685   Screen (99cm-39in) gold pat.bronze executed c.1968. 24-Feb-94 Sotheby's Arcade, New York #430/R
$4000   2649   Untitled (99cm-39in) steel wire sculpture. 30-Jun-93 Sotheby's Arcade, New York #307/R

BERTOIA, Harry (1915-1978) American-cont.
$4000	2685	Untitled (112x24x15cm-44x9x6in) beryllium executed c.1962. 23-Feb-94 Christie's, East, New York #350/R
$4500	3041	Bush (20x18x19cm-8x7x7in) bronze. 8-Nov-93 Christie's, East, New York #207/R
$4500	2647	Untitled (75cm-30in) welded bronze. 6-Oct-92 Sotheby's, New York #22/R
$5000	3311	Bush (26x27x27cm-10x11x11in) green pat.bronze. 17-Nov-92 Christie's, East, New York #255/R
$5500	3642	Untitled (51x23x8cm-20x9x3in) st.init.i. steel brass base. 17-Nov-92 Christie's, East, New York #257/R
$5500	3819	Sound sculpture (45x30x9cm-18x12x4in) executed c.1965 berillium copper. 23-Feb-93 Sotheby's, New York #235 a/R
$6400	4183	Wheat (77x99x99cm-30x39x39in) stainless steel wire executed c.1962. 7-May-93 Christie's, East, New York #157/R
$6500	4362	Tree (89x69x46cm-35x27x18in) bronze executed 1972. 23-Feb-94 Christie's, New York #23/R
$7000	4118	Untitled (178cm-70in) stainless steel wires rod brass base. 6-Oct-92 Sotheby's, New York #25/R
$7000	4118	Bush (29cm-11in) bronze brass copper tube. 6-Oct-92 Sotheby's, New York #23/R
$7500	5208	Bush (25x25x25cm-10x10x10in) executed c.1966 bronze. 23-Feb-93 Sotheby's, New York #223/R
$8000	5298	Winds (93cm-37in) beryllium copper rods bronze base executed 1965. 30-Jun-93 Sotheby's Arcade, New York #309 a/R
$9000	6040	Tonal sculpture (66x20x20cm-26x8x8in) berillium copper executed c.1970. 25-Feb-94 Sotheby's, New York #13/R
$9000	6081	Untitled (178cm-70in) stainless steel wires rod brass base exec.c.1968. 11-Nov-93 Sotheby's, New York #312/R
$10000	6944	Sunburst (112x48x48cm-44x19x19in) executed c.1966 stainless steel and rod. 23-Feb-93 Sotheby's, New York #218/R
$11000	7639	Sonambient (94cm-37in) brass bronze executed 1965. 26-Feb-93 Sotheby's Arcade, New York #340/R
$11000	6471	Untitled (156cm-61in) stainless steel bronze. 6-Oct-92 Sotheby's, New York #20/R
$11000	6471	Dandelion (175cm-69in) gilt stainless steel wire rod. 6-Oct-92 Sotheby's, New York #26/R
$13000	8725	Untitled (211cm-83in) gold green red blue pat.bronze. 24-Feb-94 Sotheby's Arcade, New York #431/R
$15000	10067	Untitled (30x46x43cm-12x18x17in) bronze executed 1974. 5-May-94 Sotheby's, New York #111/R
$16000	10811	Untitled (203x94x94cm-80x37x37in) gilded beryllium copper executed c.1965. 11-Nov-93 Sotheby's, New York #291/R
$16000	10738	Dandelion (203x84x84cm-80x33x33in) stainless steel berylium copper executed 1958. 5-May-94 Sotheby's, New York #106/R
$19000	12925	Willow tree (30cm-12in) stainless steel wire executed c.1967-68. 14-Apr-94 Freeman Fine Arts, Philadelphia #933/R
$26000	15294	Bush (102cm-40in) bronze. 6-Oct-92 Sotheby's, New York #21/R

BICKERTON, Ashley (1959-) American
$5500	3691	UGH (76x123x15cm-30x48x6in) s.i.d.85/86 acrylic on plastic aluminum steel. 4-May-94 Christie's, New York #278/R
$10000	6711	Biofragment no 1 (284x213x114cm-112x84x45in) wood aluminum glass rubber nylon coral exec.1989. 4-May-94 Christie's, New York #288/R
$10000	6757	Me portrait no 2, six gun (157x121x107cm-62x48x42in) s. acrylic aluminum plastic steel cables exec.87. 10-Nov-93 Christie's, New York #288/R
$12000	8108	GUH (61x122x16cm-24x48x6in) s.i.d.85/86verso aluminium acrylic panel. 10-Nov-93 Christie's, New York #264/R
$26000	16993	Landscape 3, desert biosphere (245x154x113cm-96x61x44in) anodized aluminum wood glass pulleys fans 1988. 5-Oct-93 Sotheby's, New York #246/R

BITTER, Karl Theodore Francis (1867-1915) American/Austrian
$850	570	Captain John Barry (43cm-17in) brown pat.bronze on marble base. 3-Feb-94 Sloan, North Bethesda #2716/R

BLAKE, Nayland (1960-) American
$3200	2222	Restraint, neck prod (198x28x15cm-78x11x6in) exec.1990 wall sculpture chrome-plated metal. 22-Feb-93 Christie's, East, New York #256/R

BLEVON, Guy (attrib) (20th C) American
$850	578	Male nude (64x20x15cm-25x8x6in) s. bronze. 17-Apr-94 Schrager Galleries, Milwaukee #407

BLOOM, Barbara (1951-) American
$9500	6291	The culture of narcissm, vitrine with books (104x129x52cm-41x51x20in) s.d.1989 num.2/3 vitrine with 38 books. 19-Nov-92 Christie's, New York #118/R

BOGHOSIAN, Varujan (20th C) American?
$8500	5705	Smoking. Sleeping box construction wood boat two exec.1987. 4-May-94 Christie's, New York #118/R

BOLINGER, Truman (1944-) American
$3400	2267	Break in Silence (81cm-32in) i.num.2/10 green brwon pat.bronze f.i. 22-May-94 Hindman Galleries, Chicago #45/R

BOLOTOWSKY, Ilya (1907-1981) American/Russian
$5500	3691	Column (30x9x9cm-12x4x4in) s.d.1962 oil wood. 25-Feb-94 Sotheby's, New York #49/R

BONEVARDI, Marcelo (1929-) Argentinian
$1500 993 Facade (30x25cm-12x10in) s.i.d.69 verso oil on wood construction. 24-Nov-92 Christie's, New York #318/R
$6000 3922 Box with shadows II (127x111cm-50x44in) s.d.69 verso canvas wood construction. 18-May-93 Sotheby's, New York #188/R

BONTECOU, Lee (1931-) American
$40000 27027 Untitled (145x138x56cm-57x54x22in) s. canvas welded steel wire executed 1962. 10-Nov-93 Sotheby's, New York #18/R

BORGLUM, John Gutzon (1867-1941) American
$16000 10256 Indian scouts (33cm-13in) i.d.1892 dark green brown pat.bronze. 27-May-93 Sotheby's, New York #251/R
$23000 16084 Portrait bust of Abraham Lincoln (47cm-19in) i.num.9 pat.bronze on marble base Cast Bedi R. 10-Mar-93 Sotheby's, New York #135/R
$150000 100000 Abraham Lincoln (56x74cm-22x29in) i. st.num.1028 rich brown pat.bronze f.i. 22-May-94 Hindman Galleries, Chicago #16/R

BORGLUM, Solon Hannibal (1868-1922) American
$2000 1282 Buffalo dancer (71cm-28in) s.i.indis.num.5 bronze Cast Young Fine Art. 9-Dec-92 Butterfield & Butterfield, San Francisco #3977/R
$5000 3333 Horse tamed (20cm-8in) i.d.1915 brown pat.bronze Roman bronze works NY. 26-May-94 Christie's, New York #44/R
$10000 6711 Cowboy at rest (32cm-13in) i.d.1906 brown pat.bronze Cast Rom.Bronze Works. 2-Dec-93 Sotheby's, New York #67/R
$13000 8333 'Night hawking' (32cm-13in) i. brown pat.bronze f.i. executed 1898. 26-May-93 Christie's, New York #99/R
$15000 9615 Cowboy at rest (31cm-12in) i.d.1906 brownish black pat.bronze f.i. 27-May-93 Sotheby's, New York #252/R
$80000 51282 Lassoing wild horses wild horses (81cm-32in) i. black brown pat.bronze f.i.Roman Works NY. 27-May-93 Sotheby's, New York #239/R

BORNSTEIN, Eli (20th C) American
$5000 3378 Structural relief No.CLII (60x60x12cm-24x24x5in) s.i.d.1964 wood construction executed 1957. 11-Nov-93 Sotheby's, New York #282/R

BOROFSKY, Jonathan (1942-) American
$15000 10417 Universal groan painting at 2,841,781 (306x201x46cm-120x79x18in) exec.1979-1983 num.2841781 acrylic canvas vase. 24-Feb-93 Christie's, New York #121/R
$27500 18212 Stone head (114x129x182cm-45x51x72in) oil canvas four parts painted 1978-83. 18-Nov-92 Sotheby's, New York #254/R
$40000 27027 Shapes with chattering man num.30000001acrylic wood metal motor three parts. 9-Nov-93 Christie's, New York #62/R

BOTERO, Fernando (1932-) Colombian
$20000 13245 Cabeza de Nina (43cm-17in) s.num.5/6 terracotta. 24-Nov-92 Christie's, New York #130/R
$55000 36424 Naturaleza muerta con Jarra y Botella (54cm-21in) s.num.5/6 brown pat.bronze executed 1985. 24-Nov-92 Christie's, New York #60/R
$75000 49020 Angel (119cm-47in) s.i. num.2/6 brown pat.bronze executed 1981. 17-May-93 Christie's, New York #61/R
$110000 72848 Desnudo reclinado (17x33cm-7x13in) s. num.4/6 dark grey pat.bronze f.st.Tesconi. 24-Nov-92 Christie's, New York #16/R
$135000 90000 Hombre y mujer (40x44x30cm-16x17x12in) s.num.2/6 brown pat.bronze st.f.Fond.M. exec.88. 18-May-94 Christie's, New York #46/R
$160000 108108 Perro (69cm-27in) s.num.4/6 brown pat.bronze. 23-Nov-93 Christie's, New York #53/R
$200000 132450 Man with a cane (201cm-79in) s.num.3/6 bronze brown pat. 23-Nov-92 Sotheby's, New York #54/R
$240000 160000 La poupee (150cm-59in) s.num.4/6 brown pat.bronze st.f.Tesconi exec.77. 18-May-94 Christie's, New York #41/R
$240000 162162 Mujer reclinada fumando (75x135x59cm-30x53x23in) s.num.3/6 brown pat.bronze Cast Fonderia M. 23-Nov-93 Christie's, New York #28/R

BOURGEOIS, Louise (1911-) American/French
$6000 4027 Untitled (10x23x15cm-4x9x6in) init.d.90 bronze num.4/40. 4-May-94 Christie's, New York #311/R
$12000 8054 Janus (20x30x14cm-8x12x6in) ceramic executed 1968 1/7. 25-Feb-94 Sotheby's, New York #24/R
$170000 111111 Untitled (166x55x30cm-65x22x12in) painted wood steel executed 1954. 4-May-93 Christie's, New York #5/R
$180000 117647 Nature study (75x148x71cm-30x58x28in) with sig.d.1986 marble. 4-May-93 Christie's, New York #45/R

BOYLE, John J (1852-1917) American
$16500 10577 Indian capturing eagle (46cm-18in) i.d.05 num.3 dark brown pat.bronze f.i. 27-May-93 Sotheby's, New York #243 a/R

BRACKEN, Julia (1871-1942) American
$2500 1678 Bonjour (8x11cm-3x4in) s.i.d.1923 bronze pat.plaster. 8-Dec-93 Butterfield & Butterfield, San Francisco #3477/R

BRACONY, Leopold (19/20th C) American
$1609 1052 Woman in Arabic costumes with fan (77cm-30in) s. white marble executed c.1890. 13-May-93 Rasmussen, Copenhagen #940 (D.KR 10000)

BRACONY, Leopold (19/20th C) American-cont.
$2345   1553   Woman wearing Arabian outfit with fan (77cm-30in) s. white marble executed c.1890.
                 21-Sep-93 Rasmussen, Vejle #378/R (D.KR 15500)
$15000   9934   Female bather partially draped seated on pedestal (180cm-71in) s. Carrara marble
                 green marble pedestal. 27-Sep-93 Selkirks, St. Louis #276/R

BRADY, Robert David (1946-) American
$3250   2181   Untitled (31x48x16cm-12x19x6in) s.d.86 glazed painted earthenware. 25-Feb-94
                 Sotheby's, New York #172/R

BRESCHI, Karen (1941-) American
$1600   1074   Flower woman with flowers (50x27x30cm-20x11x12in) s.d.1984 painted ceramic wood.
                 25-Feb-94 Sotheby's, New York #174/R

BRINDESI, Olympio (1897-1965) American
$2250   1573   Bust of Indian brave (43cm-17in) i.d.May 28,1920 red brown pat.bronze. 10-Mar-93
                 Sotheby's, New York #66 a/R

BRINGHURST, Robert Porter (1855-1925) American
$3200   2177   Statue of Diana (224cm-88in) s. bronze. 14-Apr-94 Freeman Fine Arts, Philadelphia
                 #930/R

BROOKS, Richard Edwin (1865-1919) American
$1729   1176   Female nude seated with drape (32x37cm-13x15in) s. bronze Cast C.Valsuani.
                 19-Nov-93 Auktionhaus Zofingen, Zofingen #1987/R (S.FR 2600)

BROWN, James (1951-) American
$1800   1216   Stabat mater (204x49x49cm-80x19x19in) glazed ceramic marble base. 10-Nov-93
                 Christie's, New York #387/R
$2235   1500   Untitled (44x28x23cm-17x11x9in) moulded clay. 2-Dec-93 Christie's, London #274/R
$2500   1689   Untitled (138x60x78cm-54x24x30in) s.d.84verso col pencil acrylic wood. 8-Nov-93
                 Christie's, East, New York #121/R
$4000   2649   Untitled (53x43cm-21x17in) s.i.d.1985 glazed terracotta. 17-Nov-92 Christie's,
                 East, New York #123/R
$7500   4967   Untitled (206cm-81in) col.crayo graphite nails wood steel base. 19-Nov-92
                 Christie's, New York #446/R
$12000   8054   Venice (199x98x58cm-78x39x23in) s.i.d.1984 latex acrylic graphite wood nails.
                 3-May-94 Christie's, East, New York #208/R

BROWN, Joe (1909-1985) American
$3500   2333   The punter, figure of athlete (45cm-18in) i.d.1948 black brown pat.bronze on wood
                 base. 16-Mar-94 Christie's, New York #63/R
$4200   2800   Figure of fallen boxer (23cm-9in) brown pat.bronze. 16-Mar-94 Christie's, New York
                 #62/R

BRYANT, Nanna Matthews (1871-1933) American
$2200   1447   Rock (29cm-11in) i. dark brown pat.bronze f.st.Roman Works, N.Y. 31-Mar-93
                 Sotheby's Arcade, New York #246/R

BUKILL, G (19th C) American
$5304   3400   Mare and foal (28cm-11in) s.num.1050 brown pat.bronze. 30-Apr-93 Sotheby's, London
                 #26/R

BURROUGHS, Edith Woodman (1871-1916) American
$8000   5063   L'Arriere Pensee - female nude (52cm-20in) i.red green brown pat.bronze f.Roman
                 Bronze Wks. 4-Dec-92 Christie's, New York #104/R

BURTON, Scott (1939-1989) American
$5500   3235   Concrete tables (24x61cm-9x24in) cast concrete four parts pair executed 1981.
                 6-Oct-92 Sotheby's, New York #137/R
$14000   9396   Hectapod table (52x60x60cm-20x24x24in) nickel-plated steel executed 1982 1/6.
                 25-Feb-94 Sotheby's, New York #89/R
$26000   17568   Blue granite table (73x152x81cm-29x60x32in) init.d.75-78 enamel steel base
                 granite. 10-Nov-93 Christie's, New York #372/R
$65000   43046   Chair (76x60x178cm-30x24x70in) aluminium constructed 1981. 17-Nov-92 Sotheby's,
                 New York #10/R
$130000 86093   Chairs (76x93x102cm-30x37x40in) unpolished Sierra granite. 17-Nov-92 Sotheby's,
                 New York #74/R

BURWELL, Vernon (1916-1990) American
$1400   927   The Last Supper (81x127x53cm-32x50x21in) paint carved wood mixed media. 21-Nov-92
                 Litchfield Auction Gallery #3

BUTENSKY, Jules Leon (1871-?) American/Russian
$1200   811   Exile (33cm-13in) i. dark brown pat.bronze. 31-Mar-94 Sotheby's Arcade, New York
                 #83/R

BUTTER, Tom (1952-) American
$1300   850   G.B (254cm-100in) fibreglass executed 1982. 22-Dec-92 Christie's, East, New York
                 #3
$1800   1176   M.M (183cm-72in) fibreglass executed 1982. 22-Dec-92 Christie's, East, New York #5
$2000   1307   If and then (216x165x81cm-85x65x32in) fibreglass resin wood executed 1986.
                 22-Dec-92 Christie's, East, New York #6

BUTTERFIELD, Deborah (20th C) American
$18000	12162	Laying down horse (81x356x196cm-32x140x77in) chicken wire mud sticks dextrine executed 1977. 11-Nov-93 Sotheby's, New York #173/R
$30000	20134	Whistlejacket (190x277x84cm-75x109x33in) enamel on welded steel executed 1988. 4-May-94 Christie's, New York #327/R
$48000	32432	Jerusalem Horse III (210x279x119cm-83x110x47in) steel rod wire wood executed 1980. 10-Nov-93 Christie's, New York #22/R

BYARS, James Lee (20th C) American
$35000	23649	The table of perfect (102x102x102cm-40x40x40in) gold leaf on cut and polished marble exec.1989. 10-Nov-93 Christie's, New York #214/R

BYRON, Michael (1954-) American
$1100	743	Japanese Industrialist (62x117x6cm-24x46x2in) s.i.d.88verso oil silkscreen graphite panel. 8-Nov-93 Christie's, East, New York #75/R

CALDER, Alexander (1898-1976) American
$3500	2431	Untitled (47cm-19in) s. wood. 26-Feb-93 Sotheby's Arcade, New York #267/R
$3500	2349	Maquette for a 707 (9x47x34cm-4x19x13in) init. gouache moulde plastic. 23-Feb-94 Christie's, East, New York #335/R
$4250	2872	Hair ornament (27x16cm-11x6in) brass executed c.1940. 11-Nov-93 Sotheby's, New York #250/R
$4500	3041	Brooch (15x6cm-6x2in) brass executed c.1945. 11-Nov-93 Sotheby's, New York #251/R
$6500	4392	Belt buckle (13x6cm-5x2in) silver executed c.1945. 11-Nov-93 Sotheby's, New York #322/R
$7964	5381	Animobil yellow and black (33x30cm-13x12in) s.exec.c.1970-72 metal. 18-Jun-93 Galerie Koller, Zurich #3124/R (S.FR 12000)
$8940	6000	Untitled (9x5x5cm-4x2x2in) standing mobile painted sheet metal and rod. 25-Mar-93 Christie's, London #55/R
$13000	8784	Brooch (11x11cm-4x4in) brass executed c.1945. 11-Nov-93 Sotheby's, New York #252/R
$18000	12081	Maquette for Hard to Swallow (20x11x15cm-8x4x6in) init. painted sheet metal stabile exec.1966. 4-May-94 Christie's, New York #171/R
$20000	13423	Untitled (4x8cm-2x3in) with init. painted sheet metal brass wire. 23-Feb-94 Christie's, New York #3/R
$20000	13072	The chicken (63x34x24cm-25x13x9in) s.num.2/6, bronze conceived 1944 Cast.1969. 5-May-93 Christie's, New York #257/R
$26000	17450	Untitled (20x43x14cm-8x17x6in) init. painted standing metal mobile exec.c.1973. 5-May-94 Sotheby's, New York #120/R
$27000	18750	Untitled (14x11x2cm-6x4x1in) exec.c.1940 standing mobile painted sheet metal. 24-Feb-93 Christie's, New York #1/R
$30000	20134	Untitled (40x46cm-16x18in) init. painted sheet metal wire brass exec.c.1963. 4-May-94 Christie's, New York #135/R
$30600	20000	Untitled (33x21x9cm-13x8x4in) init. painted metal executed c.1965. 30-Jun-94 Sotheby's, London #111/R
$32588	21871	Mobile, Stabile (24x39x15cm-9x15x6in) mono.d.1976 painted metal. 23-Mar-93 Cornette de St.Cyr, Paris #116/R (F.FR 180000)
$32780	22000	Untitled (20x38cm-8x15in) mono. painted sheet metal and rod exec.c.1955-60. 25-Mar-93 Christie's, London #13/R
$32780	22000	White and yellow (17x38cm-7x15in) mono. painted metal executed c.1960. 23-Mar-93 Sotheby's, London #333/R
$34611	23229	Le poisson rouge, stabile mobile (18x39x10cm-7x15x4in) init.d.1976 painted metal. 14-Oct-93 Guy Loudmer, Paris #61/R (F.FR 200000)
$38250	25000	La Chauve Souris (53x54x50cm-21x21x20in) init. painted sheet metal. 30-Jun-94 Christie's, London #36/R
$40096	26379	Mobile stabile (39x38cm-15x15in) init. painted sheet metal iron wire exec.c.1960. 11-Jun-93 Poulain & le Fur, Paris #109/R (F.FR 220000)
$41000	27152	Untitled (33x28x25cm-13x11x10in) painted metal stabile executed c.1958. 18-Nov-92 Sotheby's, New York #82/R
$45184	30530	Stabile mobile (37x50cm-15x20in) s.d.73 sculpture. 21-Oct-93 Christian de Quay, Paris #51/R (F.FR 265000)
$47500	32095	B is for Barney (28x39x10cm-11x15x4in) init.i.d.73 painted metal standing mobile. 11-Nov-93 Sotheby's, New York #295/R
$50000	32680	Horizontal Yellow (74x84x28cm-29x33x11in) init.d.72 painted sheet metal rod mobile. 5-May-93 Christie's, New York #280/R
$50490	33000	Untitled (25x29x10cm-10x11x4in) init. painted metal executed c.1950-53. 30-Jun-94 Sotheby's, London #176/R
$53000	34641	Untitled (25x29x10cm-10x11x4in) init. painted metal standing mobile. 4-May-93 Sotheby's, New York #294/R
$54000	36242	Untitled (9x15x6cm-4x6x2in) init. painted metal standing mobile. 5-May-94 Sotheby's, New York #84/R
$56620	38000	Catalan (130x110cm-51x43in) mono.d.72 mobile painted steel metal rod. 25-Mar-93 Christie's, London #60/R
$60000	39735	Blue face (75x148x56cm-30x58x22in) init.d.71 painted sheet metal. 19-Nov-92 Christie's, New York #410/R
$60000	39216	Yellow crinkly (37x33cm-15x13in) init. painted sheet metal wire brass mobile. 5-May-93 Christie's, New York #252/R
$65000	43046	Mobile avec tete humaine (135x74x74cm-53x29x29in) init.d.76 painted metal hanging mobile. 18-Nov-92 Sotheby's, New York #113/R
$65000	42484	Untitled (102x36x36cm-40x14x14in) init. painted metal standing mobile. 4-May-93 Sotheby's, New York #285/R

CALDER, Alexander (1898-1976) American-cont.

Price	Lot	Description
$68921	45643	Stabile (60cm-24in) mono.d.71 painted metal wire. 27-Nov-92 Villa Grisebach, Berlin #60/R (DM 110000)
$80000	54054	Sun and stars (36x41x8cm-14x16x3in) painted metal standing mobile executedd 1949. 11-Nov-93 Sotheby's, New York #278/R
$84760	52000	Beggar's Penny (150x78cm-59x31in) init. standing mobile sheet metal rod. 15-Oct-92 Christie's, London #62/R
$85000	57432	Untitled (43x48x25cm-17x19x10in) painted metal standing mobile executed c.1945. 10-Nov-93 Sotheby's, New York #11/R
$86420	58000	Red bull with blue-red head and blue and white ears (61x88x44cm-24x35x17in) init.d.70 standing mobile sheet metal and rod. 25-Mar-93 Christie's, London #57/R
$90000	58824	Crinkly giraffe (128x53x48cm-50x21x19in) painted steel executed 1971. 4-May-93 Sotheby's, New York #349/R
$90000	60811	Blue wing, black wing (76x81cm-30x32in) init.d.65 painted metal hanging mobile. 11-Nov-93 Sotheby's, New York #302/R
$90000	60811	White in the air (58x112cm-23x44in) init.d.67 painted metal hanging mobile. 11-Nov-93 Sotheby's, New York #248/R
$93852	59400	Great Washers (223x259x121cm-88x102x48in) init.d.68 standing mobile painted metal. 3-Dec-92 Christie's, London #23/R
$100000	66225	Untitled (96x76x66cm-38x30x26in) init.d.71 painted metal standing mobile. 18-Nov-92 Sotheby's, New York #127/R
$105000	70946	Mobile with eight elements (102x119cm-40x47in) painted sheet metal rod hanging mobile exec.48. 9-Nov-93 Christie's, New York #1/R
$105000	70470	Lion marin noir (74x71x36cm-29x28x14in) init.d.70 painted metal standing mobile. 5-May-94 Sotheby's, New York #143/R
$115000	77181	Untitled (66x175x30cm-26x69x12in) init.d.73 painted hanging metal mobile. 5-May-94 Sotheby's, New York #133/R
$120000	78431	Le lys (91x152cm-36x60in) s.d.64 hanging mobile painted sheet metal rod. 4-May-93 Christie's, New York #3/R
$122250	75000	Season (84x167cm-33x66in) init.d.63 painted metal. 14-Oct-92 Sotheby's, London #370/R
$126650	85000	Two fish tails (249x152cm-98x60in) init.d.75 mobile painted sheet metal rod. 24-Jun-93 Christie's, London #73/R
$130000	90278	The black eye (69x173cm-27x68in) s.d.61 painted sheet metal and rod. 24-Feb-93 Christie's, New York #15/R
$130000	87248	L'angle droit (117x142cm-46x56in) init.d.71 paint.sheet metal rod standing mobile. 4-May-94 Christie's, New York #150/R
$140000	94595	Big fat banana (71x109x27cm-28x43x11in) init.d.69 painted metal standing mobile. 11-Nov-93 Sotheby's, New York #274/R
$145000	97973	Long trunk (47x137x47cm-19x54x19in) painted metal standing animobile execute 1971. 11-Nov-93 Sotheby's, New York #323/R
$150000	99338	Untitled (140x145cm-55x57in) init. painted metal hanging mobile. 17-Nov-92 Sotheby's, New York #27/R
$155000	104027	Prelude to the man-eater (146x99cm-57x39in) init. painted shee metal rod standing mobile. 4-May-94 Christie's, New York #127/R
$156060	102000	L'Indien (125x190cm-49x75in) init.d.64 painted sheet metal. 30-Jun-94 Christie's, London #39/R
$158000	100000	Les deux boomerangs (115x190cm-45x75in) init.d.66 painted metal. 3-Dec-92 Sotheby's, London #42/R
$160000	104575	Model for Rosenhof (170x89x62cm-67x35x24in) standing mobile painted sheet metal rod. 4-May-93 Christie's, New York #44/R
$170000	114865	Brazil (71x99x18cm-28x39x7in) painted wood metal string mobile executed 1946. 10-Nov-93 Sotheby's, New York #3/R
$178800	120000	Untitled (250x180cm-98x71in) init.d.61 painted metal. 2-Dec-93 Sotheby's, London #36/R
$180000	120805	Les sept mouettes (43x244cm-17x96in) init.d.63 painted sheet metal wire rod. 23-Feb-94 Christie's, New York #22/R
$180000	119205	Untitled (251cm-99in) init.d.67 mobile black elemment painted metal ro. 18-Nov-92 Christie's, New York #41/R
$190000	128378	Untitled (71x201cm-28x79in) s.d.59 sheet metal wire rod hanging mobile. 10-Nov-93 Christie's, New York #113/R
$190000	124183	Black and red graphs (168x168x105cm-66x66x41in) int.d.74 painted metal standing mobile. 3-May-93 Sotheby's, New York #67/R
$200000	135135	Untitled (122x81x81cm-48x32x32in) painted metal standing mobile executed c.1950. 10-Nov-93 Sotheby's, New York #42/R
$220000	145695	Blue moon (56x236x160cm-22x93x63in) s.d.64 painted metal hanging mobile. 17-Nov-92 Sotheby's, New York #42/R
$230000	150327	Black spray (350x251cm-138x99in) init.d.56 hanging mobile painted sheet metal. 4-May-93 Christie's, New York #29/R
$245000	162252	Oak leaf (124x137x53cm-49x54x21in) init.d.73 painted metal standing mobile. 18-Nov-92 Sotheby's, New York #96/R
$250000	168919	Untitled (90x133cm-35x52in) painted sheet metal rod hanging mobile exec.1948. 9-Nov-93 Christie's, New York #23/R
$260000	172185	Point blanc disque bleu (165cm-65in) init.d.63 mobile painted sheet metal and rod. 18-Nov-92 Christie's, New York #12/R
$270000	181208	Stonymobile (51x91x23cm-20x36x9in) stones wire painted metal rod standing mobile. 4-May-94 Sotheby's, New York #3/R
$290000	189542	Untitled (66x358x142cm-26x141x56in) init.d.56 painted metal hanging mobile. 3-May-93 Sotheby's, New York #11/R
$300674	190300	Crag with petals and yellow cascade (196x202x155cm-77x80x61in) init.d.74 standing mobile painted sheet metal. 3-Dec-92 Christie's, London #41/R
$320000	214765	Untitled (96x178x102cm-38x70x40in) init.d.64 painted metal hanging mobile. 4-May-94 Sotheby's, New York #42/R

CALDER, Alexander (1898-1976) American-cont.

$330000	221477	The orange panel (91x122x23cm-36x48x9in) motorized painted sheet metal wire wood ex.1936. 4-May-94 Sotheby's, New York #4/R
$340000	229730	Fish (38x93cm-15x37in) painted rod wire glass porcelain string mobile. 9-Nov-93 Christie's, New York #5/R
$380000	255034	Untitled (72x279cm-28x110in) init.d.56 painted sheet metal rod hanging mobile. 3-May-94 Christie's, New York #45/R
$596700	390000	Black peacock (150x300cm-59x118in) executed 1950 painted sheet metal. 30-Jun-94 Christie's, London #14/R
$655600	440000	39-50 (117x230cm-46x91in) init. painted sheet metal rod executed 1959. 24-Jun-93 Christie's, London #68/R
$660000	442953	Tower with painting (102x152x41cm-40x60x16in) init. canvas wood painted hanging metal mobile. 4-May-94 Sotheby's, New York #16/R
$775000	513245	Untitled (508x656cm-200x258in) s.d.66 painted metal standing mobile. 17-Nov-92 Sotheby's, New York #38/R
$980000	657718	Haverford Monster (218x330cm-86x130in) black painted steel standing mobile exec.1944. 4-May-94 Sotheby's, New York #7/R
$1650000	1114865	Constellation (442cm-174in) init.d.60 painted metal standing mobile. 10-Nov-93 Sotheby's, New York #38/R

CARBONELL, Manuel (1918-) Cuban

$2750	1797	Des hombres con caballo (124x94cm-49x37in) i. aluminium sold with drawings exec.1961. 15-May-93 Dunning's, Illinois #1062/R

CARDENAS, Augustin (1927-) Cuban

$2030	1362	Forme verticale (40x9x10cm-16x4x4in) s.num.1/8 black pat.bronze Cast.Oceane exec.83. 5-Dec-93 Perrin, Versailles #98/R (F.FR 12000)
$2549	1734	Forme verticale (36x9x10cm-14x4x4in) s.num.3/8 black pat.bronze Cast.Oceane exec.83. 10-Apr-94 Perrin, Versailles #98/R (F.FR 15000)
$3213	2157	On se parle de choses, Patience (27x19x16cm-11x7x6in) s.num.1/8 brown pat.bronze Cast.Oceane. 2-Dec-93 Francis Briest, Paris #212/R (F.FR 19000)
$3463	2278	Untitled (30cm-12in) s.num.1/6 black pat.bronze. 11-Jun-93 Herve Chayette, Paris #175/R (F.FR 19000)
$3661	2424	La fleur dynamique (32x29x16cm-13x11x6in) s.num.2/8 dark pat.bronze executed 1979. 22-Nov-92 Perrin, Versailles #62/R (F.FR 20000)
$4063	2673	On se parle de choses..patience (28x15x16cm-11x6x6in) s.num.2/8 brown pat.bronze executed 1980. 4-Apr-93 Perrin, Versailles #57/R (F.FR 22000)
$4758	3237	La liberte revee (52x23x12cm-20x9x5in) s.num.4/8 black pat.bronze Cast.Oceane. 10-Apr-94 Perrin, Versailles #97/R (F.FR 28000)
$5228	3509	Sans titre (41cm-16in) s.i.num.6/6 brown pat.bronze executed 1971. 21-Mar-94 Guy Loudmer, Paris #35/R (F.FR 30000)
$6000	4027	Tortuga (21x44x20cm-8x17x8in) s.d.1983-85 black pat.bronze. 7-Jan-94 Gary Nader, Miami #90/R
$6016	3906	Papagini (60cm-24in) s.d.1972num.5/6 pat.bronze Cast.Tesconi. 5-Jul-94 Jean Louis Picard, Paris #31/R (F.FR 32500)
$10084	6634	La main, ca.1965 (31x85cm-12x33in) s.num.5/6 pat.bronze st.f.Tesconi bronze base. 6-Apr-93 Guy Loudmer, Paris #34 b/R (F.FR 55000)
$11000	7333	Figure assise (43cm-17in) s.d.83-85 black pat.bronze. 18-May-94 Sotheby's, New York #389/R
$14000	9396	Petit marbre (46cm-18in) s.d.71 Carrara marble. 7-Jan-94 Gary Nader, Miami #121/R
$20860	14000	Science et famille (190x127x93cm-75x50x37in) executed in 1964 marble. 21-Jun-93 Christie's, S. Kensington #200/R
$35518	23214	Porte de l'histoire (198x51cm-78x20in) s.d.1960-61 wood. 29-Jun-94 Guy Loudmer, Paris #231/R (F.FR 195000)

CARLSON, George (1940-) American

$750	503	Approaching death, a Tarahumara mother comforts her child (30cm-12in) s.d.1974 pat.bronze wood base. 2-May-94 Selkirks, St. Louis #116/R
$750	503	Tarahumara Mother (23cm-9in) s.d.1977 pat.bronze wood base. 2-May-94 Selkirks, St. Louis #87
$750	503	Teresa (23cm-9in) s.d.1975 pat.bronze wood base. 2-May-94 Selkirks, St. Louis #88/R
$800	537	Blessing the fields, the Yumari Ceremony (30cm-12in) s.d.1976 pat.bronze wood base. 2-May-94 Selkirks, St. Louis #114/R
$900	604	To the Ceremony (33cm-13in) s.d.1976 pat.bronze wood base. 2-May-94 Selkirks, St. Louis #91/R
$950	638	Ignacio (25cm-10in) s.d.1975 pat.bronze wood base. 2-May-94 Selkirks, St. Louis #92/R
$1000	671	Canyon Winds (41cm-16in) s.d.1974 pat.bronze wood base. 2-May-94 Selkirks, St. Louis #90/R
$1300	872	Day of Guadalupe (46cm-18in) s.d.1975 pat.bronze wood base. 2-May-94 Selkirks, St. Louis #124/R
$1300	872	The hunter (30cm-12in) s.d.1974 pat.bronze wood base. 2-May-94 Selkirks, St. Louis #119/R
$2100	1409	River's edge (48cm-19in) s.d.1975 pat.bronze wood base. 2-May-94 Selkirks, St. Louis #102/R
$4500	3020	I am the drum, Tarahumara figure (91cm-36in) s.d.1976 pat.bronze. 2-May-94 Selkirks, St. Louis #128/R
$26000	17450	Courtship flight, eagle courtship (94cm-37in) s. pat.bronze. 2-May-94 Selkirks, St. Louis #126/R

CARROLL, Lawrence (20th C) American

$3000	1765	Untitled (245x39x30cm-96x15x12in) oil wax staples crayons canvas over wood. 6-Oct-92 Sotheby's, New York #192/R

CARROLL, Lawrence (20th C) American-cont.
$6500	4392	I will try - cry (117x117x63cm-46x46x25in) s.i.d.87-88 verso oil wax canvas staples rubber. 11-Nov-93 Sotheby's, New York #235/R
$7000	4636	Between future and past (275x152x30cm-108x60x12in) s.d.1988/89 verso oil wax canvas on wood 2 part. 18-Nov-92 Sotheby's, New York #305 a/R
$10000	6757	Buoy (221x96x30cm-87x38x12in) s.d.87-88 verso oil wax rubber canvas over wood. 11-Nov-93 Sotheby's, New York #211/R

CASTANEDA, Felipe (1933-) Mexican
$5000	3356	Dos mujeres sentadas (38cm-15in) i.d.1969 white onyx. 24-Feb-94 Sotheby's Arcade, New York #280/R
$5250	3524	Nyade (23cm-9in) i.d.1974 dark blue pat.bronze. 24-Feb-94 Sotheby's Arcade, New York #281/R
$6000	4027	Posando (38cm-15in) i.d.1970 white onyx. 24-Feb-94 Sotheby's Arcade, New York #282/R
$7000	4403	Seated nude female (61cm-24in) s.d.1985 num.II/VII green pat.bronze. 25-Apr-93 Butterfield & Butterfield, San Francisco #2094/R
$7000	4667	Mujer sentada (37cm-15in) s.d.1984 num.V/VII col pat.bronze executed 1984. 18-May-94 Christie's, New York #277/R
$8500	5380	Seated nude (29cm-11in) s.d.1980 blue-green pat.bronze. 25-Oct-92 Butterfield & Butterfield, San Francisco #2261/R
$9000	5882	Desnudo sentado (35cm-14in) s.d.1984 num.IV/VII dark grey pat.bronze. 17-May-93 Christie's, New York #291/R
$12000	7947	Pueblerina (65cm-26in) s.d.1987 num.VI/VII green pat.bronze. 24-Nov-92 Christie's, New York #209/R
$12000	8108	Desnudo (80cm-31in) s.d.1976 alabaster. 22-Nov-93 Sotheby's, New York #262/R
$15000	9804	Mujer sentada (35cm-14in) s.d.1981 white marble. 17-May-93 Christie's, New York #180/R
$15000	10000	Desnudo de pie (146cm-57in) s.i.d.77 num.III/V green pat.bronze. 18-May-94 Christie's, New York #100/R
$15000	10135	Mujer sentada (36cm-14in) s.d.1980 black marble. 23-Nov-93 Christie's, New York #210/R
$17000	11333	Mujer Arrodillada (22x41x22cm-9x16x9in) s.d.1980 marble. 18-May-94 Christie's, New York #278/R

CASTILLO, Sergio (1925-) Chilean
$2152	1435	Phoenix (213cm-84in) s.d.76 pat iron. 2-Jun-94 AB Stockholms Auktionsverk, Stockholm #6142/R (S.KR 17000)

CASTLE, Wendell (1932-) American
$4000	2685	Untitled (199x112x51cm-78x44x20in) laminated carved walnut executed c.1962. 25-Feb-94 Sotheby's, New York #305/R

CEMIN, Saint Clair (1951-) American
$759	506	Windwolf (8cm-3in) s.d.1985 terracotta. 2-Jun-94 AB Stockholms Auktionsverk, Stockholm #6143/R (S.KR 6000)
$1100	738	Untitled (12x13x10cm-5x5x4in) init.d.86 num.3/7 bronze. 23-Feb-94 Christie's, East, New York #247/R
$1100	743	10 Minutes Elephant (6x20x8cm-2x8x3in) s.num.3/9 bronze. 8-Nov-93 Christie's, East, New York #133/R
$1200	833	Girl (10x20x12cm-4x8x5in) s. terracotta. 22-Feb-93 Christie's, East, New York #238/R
$1200	811	Paper Weight (18x10x18cm-7x4x7in) s.d.86 terracotta. 8-Nov-93 Christie's, East, New York #122/R
$4500	3020	Tea bell (20x35x31cm-8x14x12in) s.num.3/5 bronze st.f. executed 1990. 3-May-94 Christie's, East, New York #266/R
$5500	3691	Hommage to Sartre (117x117x79cm-46x46x31in) bronze on steel table ed.3 of 3 exec.1989. 4-May-94 Christie's, New York #258/R
$6962	4641	Car (125cm-49in) marble incl.large varnished socle executed 1990. 2-Jun-94 AB Stockholms Auktionsverk, Stockholm #7080/R (S.KR 55000)
$8195	5500	Untitled Tall Man (256x89cm-101x35in) dark patina bronze executed 1988. 25-Mar-93 Christie's, London #198/R
$11000	7383	Elegy-allergy (150x84x40cm-59x33x16in) s.d.89 plaster burlap tape wood talc on peestal. 23-Feb-94 Christie's, New York #122/R
$12000	8108	Untitled form with reversed jar (79x96x38cm-31x38x15in) bronze num.2/3 executed 1987. 10-Nov-93 Christie's, New York #252/R
$12000	7843	Tripod with statue (183x46x46cm-72x18x18in) cast bronze hydrocal bronze base executed 1987. 4-May-93 Sotheby's, New York #264/R
$12000	7947	Gallo (66x70x25cm-26x28x10in) s.d.88/89 num.1/3 black marble. 19-Nov-92 Christie's, New York #117/R
$16769	10613	Rain Fountain (137x117cm-54x46in) marble bronze. 6-Dec-92 Binoche et Godeau, Paris #21/R (F.FR 90000)
$19000	12583	Untitled (34x110x36cm-13x43x14in) executed 1988 mahogany bronze. 19-Nov-92 Christie's, New York #124/R
$19000	13194	Wheelbarrow (98x103x53cm-39x41x21in) init.exec.1987 num.3/3 bronze hydrocal wheels. 24-Feb-93 Christie's, New York #115/R

CHAMBERLAIN, John (1927-) American
$4890	3000	Polacca (103x113x48cm-41x44x19in) mineral coated synthetic polymer resin. 15-Oct-92 Christie's, London #60/R
$6258	4200	Tonk 11-83 (12x34x9cm-5x13x4in) s.d.83 painted steel. 25-Mar-93 Christie's, London #126/R
$6500	3824	Crash Aluminum series (51cm-20in) crushed aluminium. 8-Oct-92 Christie's, New York #158/R

CHAMBERLAIN, John (1927-) American-cont.
$8000	5369	Untitled (30x30x8cm-12x12x3in) s.d.62 num.100 enamel oil paper sheet metal. 23-Feb-94 Christie's, New York #64/R
$9000	5882	Untitled (63x27x27cm-25x11x11in) enamel chromium-plated steel executed 1983. 7-May-93 Christie's, East, New York #126/R
$12000	8054	Crash series (21x27x20cm-8x11x8in) s. enamel on steel on wood base executed c.1970. 23-Feb-94 Christie's, New York #70/R
$12000	7947	Tonk 12-83 (16x20x14cm-6x8x6in) s.d.83 painted chromium plated steel. 18-Nov-92 Sotheby's, New York #189/R
$14000	9459	Tonk no 7 (16x23x22cm-6x9x9in) s.d.83 enamel on steel. 10-Nov-93 Christie's, New York #154/R
$16000	10458	Tonk - 10-84 (14x102x10cm-6x40x4in) s. painted steel executed 1984. 4-May-93 Sotheby's, New York #228/R
$17000	11486	Zoomette (89x84x27cm-35x33x11in) painte chromium-plated steel executed 1983. 11-Nov-93 Sotheby's, New York #383/R
$20000	13245	Crissum-Kiss (53x46x38cm-21x18x15in) galvanized steel executed 1967. 18-Nov-92 Sotheby's, New York #152/R
$25000	16779	Gennaro (81x69x36cm-32x27x14in) painted chromium-plated steel executed 1976. 5-May-93 Sotheby's, New York #170/R
$26000	18056	Wooten's whisper (39x82x46cm-15x32x18in) executed 1988 enamel chromium plated steel. 24-Feb-93 Christie's, New York #55/R
$37000	24183	Untitled (36x25x13cm-14x10x5in) painted metal construction paper collage board. 4-May-93 Sotheby's, New York #375/R
$37500	24834	Untitled (43x42x25cm-25x17x10in) s.d.60verso painted metal mounted on wood. 17-Nov-92 Sotheby's, New York #12/R
$37500	24834	Spike (71x79x61cm-28x31x24in) painted chromium-plated steel executed 1964. 18-Nov-92 Sotheby's, New York #147/R
$40000	26144	Madam Moon (48x74x53cm-19x29x21in) painted chromium plated steel executed 1964. 3-May-93 Sotheby's, New York #26/R
$40230	27000	Falconer-fitten (85x99x94cm-33x39x37in) painted crushed steel executed 1960. 2-Dec-93 Christie's, London #30/R
$60000	39735	Mountain of no difference (185x210x33cm-73x83x13in) wall relief enamel on chromium-plated steel. 18-Nov-92 Christie's, New York #39/R
$60000	40541	Slapps (162x175x58cm-64x69x23in) s.d.1983 enamel on chromium plate steel. 9-Nov-93 Christie's, New York #50/R
$65000	43046	Tomato poodle (264x127x119cm-104x50x47in) enamel on chromium-plated steel. 18-Nov-92 Christie's, New York #16/R
$70000	47297	Remnant Gardens (279x159x110cm-110x63x43in) enamel chromium-plated steel executed 1986. 9-Nov-93 Christie's, New York #57/R
$70000	46358	Infected eucharist (277x102x91cm-109x40x36in) painted chromium-plated steel. 17-Nov-92 Sotheby's, New York #55/R
$75000	49669	Andrea Floretina Luchezzi (188x97x89cm-74x38x35in) executed 1983 enamel chromium plated steel. 19-Nov-92 Christie's, New York #400/R
$77500	45588	Untitled (152x152cm-60x60in) steel. 6-Oct-92 Sotheby's, New York #77/R

CHAMBERLIN, Frank Tolles (1873-1961) American
$3100	1962	Standing female nude classical figures, holding dish (66cm-26in) s.d.1912 dark brown pat.bronze f.st.Gorham Co. 30-Nov-92 Selkirks, St. Louis #246/R

CHINNI, Peter Anthony (1928-) American
$2100	1458	Genesis IV (62cm-24in) i.d.73 num.1/4, black pat bronze. 26-Feb-93 Sotheby's Arcade, New York #411/R

CHOMENKO, Mary (20th C) American
$4250	2690	Woolley Mammoth (137cm-54in) s.d.1984 2/5 cast bronze. 25-Oct-92 Butterfield & Butterfield, San Francisco #2393/R

CHRISTO (1935-) American/Bulgarian
$2172	1420	Wrapped book (30x28x3cm-12x11x1in) s.num.26/100, original book wrapped with string. 12-May-93 AB Stockholms Auktionsverk, Stockholm #6125/R (S.KR 16000)
$3244	2148	Look 1965 (56x46cm-22x18in) s.num.75/100 tied up bundle of magazines. 3-Jul-93 Dr Fritz Nagel, Leipzig #1277/R (DM 5500)
$17135	11500	Wrapped cushion (80x60x22cm-31x24x9in) fabric string cushion mounted in box. 24-Mar-93 Sotheby's, London #334/R
$19890	13000	Wrapped magazines (55x23cm-22x9in) s.d.62verso magazines rope plastic foil fabric. 30-Jun-94 Sotheby's, London #169/R
$21000	14189	Storefront - project (58x74x5cm-23x29x2in) s.i.d.64 gauze plastic oil panel. 11-Nov-93 Sotheby's, New York #101/R
$23127	16173	Mannequin empaquete (175x60x30cm-69x24x12in) s.i. mannequin executed 1963-71. 10-Mar-93 Watine-Arnault, Paris #22/R (F.FR 131000)
$27000	17881	Wrapped iron (15x22x12cm-6x9x5in) s.d.64 iron plastic rope wood. 18-Nov-92 Sotheby's, New York #141/R

CHRISTO and PAIK, Nam June (20th C) American
$44700	30000	Wrapped television (33x31x29cm-13x12x11in) s.d.67 portabel television in plastic and twine. 24-Jun-93 Sotheby's, London #74/R

CIARLO, Franco (1939-) American?
$1800	1208	Isabelle (212x117x10cm-83x46x4in) s. oil fresco gauze executed 1984. 23-Feb-94 Christie's, East, New York #302/R

CLARK, Allan (c.1897-1950) American
$1600	1026	Oriental woman holding bottle (20cm-8in) s. green pat.bronze st.f.Roman Bronze Works. 28-Apr-93 Doyle, New York #78/R

CLARK, Allan (c.1897-1950) American-cont.
$5000 3311 Temptress of King (52x38cm-20x15in) s.d.1927 polychrome wood painted. 23-Sep-93 Sotheby's, New York #268/R

CLARK, James Lippitt (1883-1957) American
$4500 2980 Rhinoceros foot humidor (25cm-10in) i. bronze f.st.Gorham Co Founders QFU. 22-Sep-93 Christie's, New York #95/R
$5500 3667 White rhino. Black rhino (19x38cm-7x15in) one i.c.24 st.2 one i.c.27 st.3 pat.bronze. 26-May-94 Christie's, New York #45/R

COHEN, Katherine M (1859-1914) American
$3750 2534 Bust of Abraham Lincoln (46cm-18in) i.d.1898 brown pat.bronze f.i.Henry-Bonnard NY. 31-Mar-94 Sotheby's Arcade, New York #79/R

COINS, Raymond (1904-) American
$2000 1325 Horseman (15x36cm-6x14in) c.1980 carved river stone. 21-Nov-92 Litchfield Auction Gallery #6
$2450 1623 AnAngel (30x48cm-12x19in) s.verso carved river stone. 21-Nov-92 Litchfield Auction Gallery #5

COLSON, Greg (1956-) American
$2400 1611 Spray away (37x46x32cm-15x18x13in) s.i.d.1990 steel aluminium iron wood paper. 23-Feb-94 Christie's, East, New York #230/R

CONTWAY, Jay (20th C) American
$2081 1388 Whiskey on the old whoop-up (36x55x38cm-14x22x15in) s.d. painted bronze wood base 3/35. 30-May-94 Hodgins, Calgary #258/R (C.D 2900)

CORNELL, Joseph (1903-1972) American
$30000 20270 Night voyage soap bubble set series (27x46x9cm-11x18x4in) s.verso wood oil lacquer book pages nails glass. 10-Nov-93 Christie's, New York #112/R
$30000 20134 Untitled, dovecote (48x33x11cm-19x13x4in) s. painted wood and glass box executed c.1952. 4-May-94 Christie's, New York #105/R
$37500 26042 Untitled (24x36x2cm-9x14x1in) s.verso exec.c.1954-56 mixed media construction. 23-Feb-93 Sotheby's, New York #210/R
$85000 57432 Untitled - An owl for Gwendoline (24x18x11cm-9x7x4in) s.i.d.1955 box construction. 10-Nov-93 Sotheby's, New York #13/R
$105000 68627 Untitled - Palais de Cristal (33x23x11cm-13x9x4in) s.verso box construction executed c.1953. 3-May-93 Sotheby's, New York #4/R
$170000 114865 Untitled - Palace of the sleeping beauty (22x38x10cm-9x15x4in) s.i.verso twigs mirror paper sparkling chips. 10-Nov-93 Sotheby's, New York #5/R

CORREA MORALES, Lucio (1852-1923) Argentinian
$8500 4913 Bernabe Delgado, El Remero (107cm-42in) marble. 23-Sep-92 Roldan & Cia, Buenos Aires #3

COSTE, Jorge (?) Mexican?
$1545 1044 Don Porfirio y sus toros (54x16cm-21x6in) bronze. 9-Nov-93 Louis Morton, Mexico #25 (M.P 5000)

CRAIG, Charles (1846-1931) American
$2000 1156 Indian brave (29x23cm-11x9in) s.d.1898 W/C paper on board. 25-Sep-92 Sotheby's Arcade, New York #195/R

CRAWFORD, Thomas (1813-1857) American
$6000 3846 Bust of Charles Brooks (64cm-25in) i.d.1843 white marble. 9-Dec-92 Grogan, Massachussetts #18/R
$24000 16000 Bride of Abydos (72cm-28in) i.d.1842 white marble. 25-May-94 Sotheby's, New York #31/R

CREEFT, Jose de (1884-1982) American/Spanish
$1300 751 Female head (17cm-7in) i. stone. 25-Sep-92 Sotheby's Arcade, New York #372/R
$1700 1189 Reclining nude (47x73cm-19x29in) s. painted beaten lead relief. 11-Mar-93 Christie's, New York #177/R

CROZIER, William (1933-) American
$3200 2162 Debbie (76x73x125cm-30x29x49in) s.d.1979-80 num.2/9 bronze wood base. 8-Nov-93 Christie's, East, New York #203/R

CRUZ-DIEZ, Carlos (1923-) Venezuelan
$6316 4049 Physichromie no 336 (61x243x6cm-24x96x2in) s.i.d.1967 optical object in two wooden boxes. 27-May-93 Lempertz, Cologne #669/R (DM 10000)

DALLIN, Cyrus Edwin (1861-1944) American
$2100 1382 Scout (56cm-22in) i. black pat.bronze f.st.Gorham Founders Q49024. 31-Mar-93 Sotheby's Arcade, New York #218/R
$2800 1842 On the alert (53cm-21in) i. black pat.bronze f.st.Gorham Founders. 31-Mar-93 Sotheby's Arcade, New York #220/R
$3500 2303 Protest (52cm-20in) i. black pat.bronze f.st.Gorham Founders. 31-Mar-93 Sotheby's Arcade, New York #219/R

DALLIN, Cyrus Edwin (1861-1944) American-cont.
$5000	3497	Protest (51cm-20in) i.num.5 red brown pat.bronze Cast Gorham Co F. 10-Mar-93 Sotheby's, New York #67/R
$10000	6329	The protest (51cm-20in) i. red-brown pat.bronze.Cast.Roman Bronze Works. 4-Dec-92 Christie's, New York #255/R
$10000	6135	The Scout (58x61cm-23x24in) init.num.19 red brown pat.bronze Cast.Gorham Co. 16-Oct-92 Du Mouchelle, Detroit #2085
$11000	7383	'Archery lesson' - group (46cm-18in) s.d.07 rich greenish brown pat.bronze. 3-Dec-93 Christie's, New York #79/R
$14000	9396	'The Scout' - equestrian group (60cm-24in) s.i.d.1910 num.24 reddish brown pat.bronze f.st. 3-Dec-93 Christie's, New York #80/R
$15000	10000	Paul Revere (91cm-36in) i. dark brown pat.bronze. 22-May-94 Hindman Galleries, Chicago #3/R
$20000	13333	Medicine man (79cm-31in) i.d.1899 brown pat.bronze st. 22-May-94 Hindman Galleries, Chicago #4/R
$20000	13333	The Scout (89cm-35in) i.d.1910 brown pat.bronze f.i.Gorham Co. 22-May-94 Hindman Galleries, Chicago #6/R
$20000	12821	Chief Geronimo (68cm-27in) i. brown pat.bronze f.i.Gorham Co Founders QFQJ. 27-May-93 Sotheby's, New York #245/R
$24000	15385	Chief Joseph - Little Bear (73cm-29in) i. brown pat.bronze f.i.Gorham Co. Foundes QFQH. 27-May-93 Sotheby's, New York #246/R
$24000	15385	Marksman (94cm-37in) i.d.1912 reddish dark brown pat.bronze f.i. 27-May-93 Sotheby's, New York #243/R
$24000	15385	Mystery man (63cm-25in) i.d.1926 brown pat.bronze f.i.Gorham Co. 27-May-93 Sotheby's, New York #247/R
$30000	20000	Pioneer mother (109cm-43in) i.d.1931 green pat.bronze f.st.Gorham Founders. 22-May-94 Hindman Galleries, Chicago #8/R
$36000	24000	Signal of Peace (94cm-37in) i.d.1890 reddish brown pat.bronze f.st.Gorham Co. 22-May-94 Hindman Galleries, Chicago #9/R
$40000	26667	On the war path (107cm-42in) i.d.1914 reddish brown pat.bronze f.i.Gorham Co. 22-May-94 Hindman Galleries, Chicago #7/R
$50000	33333	Appeal to the Great Spirit (99cm-39in) i. brown pat.bronze f.i.Gorham Co Founders. 22-May-94 Hindman Galleries, Chicago #5/R

DALLIN, Cyrus Edwin (after) (1861-1944) American
$9000	6000	Appeal to the Great Spirit (99cm-39in) i.d.1912 brown pat.bronze. 22-May-94 Hindman Galleries, Chicago #10/R

DAVIDSON, Jo (1883-1952) American
$3100	2039	Franklin D Roosevelt (25cm-10in) i. brown pat.bronze. 31-Mar-93 Sotheby's Arcade, New York #251/R

DAVIS, Ron (1937-) American
$4000	2649	Plane slab (127x354cm-50x139in) s.i.d.8-70verso enamel fiberglass resin. 17-Nov-92 Christie's, East, New York #170/R

DEHNER, Dorothy (1908-) American
$950	638	Abstract sculpture (13cm-5in) s.d.59 bronze marble base. 26-Mar-94 James Bakker, Cambridge #30

DELAP, Tony (1927-) American
$2000	1351	Tilted table with arc (34cm-13in) s.d.1986 pat.bronze marble base. 21-Apr-94 Butterfield & Butterfield, San Francisco #1198/R

DELIOTTI, Walter (20th C) Uruguayan?
$1250	817	Puerto (33x40cm-13x16in) s.d.62 wood. 3-May-93 Gomensoro, Montevideo #25

DEMING, Edwin Willard (1860-1942) American
$6000	4027	Buffalo (36x53cm-14x21in) s.d. brown pat.bronze executed 1907. 17-Dec-93 Du Mouchelle, Detroit #2144/R

DERUJINSKY, Gleb W (1888-1975) American/Russian
$2800	1867	Youth with pan pipes (67cm-26in) s. wood. 16-Mar-94 Christie's, New York #72/R
$4100	2628	Adolphe Bolm as Harlequin in Carnaval (36cm-14in) i.num.3 col pat.bronze st.f.Roman marble base. 24-May-93 Grogan, Massachussetts #332/R

DINE, Jim (1935-) American
$24000	16107	Boot bench no 1 (46x182x30cm-18x72x12in) st.sig.i.d.1965 cast aluminum. 4-May-94 Christie's, New York #188/R
$30000	19868	Tallix heart (99x53x23cm-39x21x9in) bronze executed 1988. 18-Nov-92 Sotheby's, New York #174/R
$38000	25503	The heart on the rock (47x45x24cm-19x18x9in) s.d.1983 num.4/6 bronze. 4-May-94 Christie's, New York #211/R
$48000	32215	Trembling for colour (163x46x61cm-64x18x24in) acrylic on bronze ed.2 of six exec.1990. 4-May-94 Christie's, New York #172/R
$80000	52980	White suit no.2 (182x183x9cm-72x72x4in) s.d.1964 oil chl.canvas metal chain others. 18-Nov-92 Christie's, New York #47/R

DOMPE, Hernan (20th C) Argentinian
$11000	7383	Viejo reloj de cobre (107x19x13cm-42x7x5in) wood bronze pigments executed 1992. 7-Jan-94 Gary Nader, Miami #18/R

DOYLE, Alexander (1857-1922) American
$8500	5380	Figure of Robert E. Lee (51cm-20in) i. red-brown pat.bronze.Cast.Henry and Bonnard. 4-Dec-92 Christie's, New York #169/R

DRYER, Moira (1957-1992) American
$1519	1013	Domestic life (183x71x46cm-72x28x18in) s.d.1987 wood metal construction. 2-Jun-94 AB Stockholms Auktionsverk, Stockholm #7116/R (S.KR 12000)
$2200	1438	Portrait no.429 (107x107x20cm-42x42x8in) s.d.1988 verso casein enamel panel. 7-May-93 Christie's, East, New York #158/R
$5500	3691	The Rumour (122x160x8cm-48x63x3in) s.i.d.88 verso casein wood. 25-Feb-94 Sotheby's, New York #117/R

DUFF, Dana (1955-) American
$1300	850	Screen - Rashomon (94x118x10cm-37x46x4in) soot movie screen executed 1988. 22-Dec-92 Christie's, East, New York #12

DUFF, John (1925-) Canadian
$9000	6081	Blue serrated wedge (203x13x8cm-80x5x3in) s.d.1985 fibreglass enamel paint. 11-Nov-93 Sotheby's, New York #170/R

DWYER, Nancy (1954-) American
$1300	850	The me block (34x32x34cm-13x13x13in) s.num.25/40 Honduran mahogany exec.1989. 5-Oct-93 Sotheby's, New York #191/R
$2025	1350	Wild (41x170x84cm-16x67x33in) s.d.1987 laminated wood four pieces. 2-Jun-94 AB Stockholms Auktionsverk, Stockholm #7072/R (S.KR 16000)
$3500	2349	The fourth step (85x127x81cm-33x50x32in) steel executed 1988. 3-May-94 Christie's, East, New York #180/R
$7000	4118	Fate built (41x184x61cm-16x72x24in) formica shaped wood. 8-Oct-92 Christie's, New York #238/R

EBERLE, Abastenia St Leger (1878-1942) American
$8000	5594	Bacchanale (48cm-19in) i.d.1904 brown pat.bronze Cast Gorham Co. 10-Mar-93 Sotheby's, New York #98/R
$46000	30872	'Salome', figure of dancer (59cm-23in) i. medium brown pat.bronze. 3-Dec-93 Christie's, New York #20/R

ECHALOOK, Luccassie (attrib) (1942-) North American
$1400	903	Pulling tooth (23cm-9in) i.d.87 num. dark grey soapstone. 9-Jan-93 Skinner, Bolton #179/R

ELWELL, Robert Farrington (1874-1962) American
$2664	1800	The sun fisher, cowboy buck-jumping unbroken horse (29x45x27cm-11x18x11in) s. bronze. 28-Oct-93 Christie's, London #115/R

ENNUTSIAK (1896-1967) North American
$1806	1212	Inuit hunter and his wife sitting with entwined arms and legs (20cm-8in) s.i. marbled grey soapstone. 29-Nov-93 Waddingtons, Toronto #756/R (C.D 2400)
$3574	2399	Inuit birth scene with crouching Inuit mother and three midwives (16cm-6in) mottled grey soapstone. 29-Nov-93 Waddingtons, Toronto #754 (C.D 4750)

ERHARDY, Joseph (1928-) American
$1803	1244	La Maree (19cm-7in) s.num.2/8 brown pat.bronze Cast.Venturi. 31-Jan-93 Hoebanx, Paris #79 (F.FR 10000)

ERKOK, D (20th C) North American
$1594	1063	Inuit woman, her child in her amaut, fishing with sinew line (38cm-15in) s. dark green grey soapstone. 6-Jun-94 Waddingtons, Toronto #814/R (C.D 2200)

ESTOPINAN, Roberto (1920-) Cuban
$2500	1678	Untitled (30cm-12in) s.i.d.1984 green pat.bronze. 7-Jan-94 Gary Nader, Miami #126/R

ETROG, Sorel (1933-) Canadian/Rumanian
$947	631	Rushman (23cm-9in) s.i.d.1974-76 num.1/10 bronze. 11-May-94 Sotheby's, Toronto #133/R (C.D 1300)
$1200	759	Untitled (16cm-6in) s.num.7/10 black pat.bronze. 25-Oct-92 Butterfield & Butterfield, San Francisco #2371/R
$1274	850	Key Head No.4 (16cm-6in) s.num.5/10 bronze. 11-May-94 Sotheby's, Toronto #131/R (C.D 1750)
$1400	927	Untitled (27cm-11in) st. num.4/10 dark brown pat.bronze. 30-Jun-93 Sotheby's Arcade, New York #289/R
$1401	928	Abstract (22cm-9in) s.num.3/15 bronze marble base. 18-Nov-92 Sotheby's, Toronto #181/R (C.D 1800)
$1800	1192	Untitled (20cm-8in) st. num.2/10 dark brown pat.bronze. 30-Jun-93 Sotheby's Arcade, New York #291/R
$2000	1342	Double Key Head I (24x17x10cm-9x7x4in) st.num.4/10 bronze. 23-Feb-94 Christie's, East, New York #252/R
$3400	2297	Untitled (53cm-21in) st.sig. bronze. 31-Oct-93 Hindman Galleries, Chicago #642/R
$4200	2800	Knotted hand (41cm-16in) st.sig.num.2/7 bronze 1969 sold with etching. 13-Mar-94 Hindman Galleries, Chicago #1022/R
$6199	4188	The Madonna (56cm-22in) s.num.4/7 bronze. 3-Nov-93 Sotheby's, Toronto #237/R (C.D 8000)
$10306	6736	Study for mother and child (81cm-32in) s.num.1/7 red enamelled bronze executed c.1971. 19-May-93 Sotheby's, Toronto #191/R (C.D 13000)

ETROG, Sorel (1933-) Canadian/Rumanian-cont.
$10306   6736   Key head (66cm-26in) pink graphite. 19-May-93 Sotheby's, Toronto #192/R (C.D 13000)
$23351 15464 The large hand (152cm-60in) s.num.1/5 base bronze. 18-Nov-92 Sotheby's, Toronto #217/R (C.D 30000)
$26161 17098 Pieton (145cm-57in) s.num.3/7 bronze. 19-May-93 Sotheby's, Toronto #270/R (C.D 33000)

EVALUARDJUK, Henry (1923-) North American
$2195   1407   Prowling polar bear (41cm-16in) s. light green soapstone. 7-Dec-92 Waddingtons, Toronto #877 (C.D 2800)

EVALUARDJUK, Henry (attrib) (1923-) North American
$1300   839   Seated woman (30cm-12in) s.i.num.CH87 mottled grey-green soapstone. 9-Jan-93 Skinner, Bolton #183/R

FABRO, Luciano (1936-) American
$65000 42484 Efeso (340x236x38cm-134x93x15in) marble steel cable executed 1986. 5-May-93 Christie's, New York #188/R

FAFARD, Joseph (1942-) Canadian
$3020   2041   Ruizdale (36cm-14in) s.d.91 bronze. 23-Nov-93 Joyner Fine Art, Toronto #45/R (C.D 4000)
$4005   2670   Leezan (40cm-16in) s.d.71 num.6/7 bronze. 13-May-94 Joyner Fine Art, Toronto #45/R (C.D 5500)

FARNSWORTH, Shirley (20th C) American
$1200   795   Peter Pan (56cm-22in) s. green pat.bronze f.i.Roman Bronze Works NY. 13-Nov-92 Skinner, Bolton #175/R

FARROW, Al (1943-) American
$4000   2532   Seated dancer (22x41x23cm-9x16x9in) s.d.81 num.1/3 bronze. 25-Oct-92 Butterfield & Butterfield, San Francisco #2337/R

FELGUEREZ, Manuel (20th C) South American
$6500   4333   Gimnasta (67cm-26in) s. painted metal. 18-May-94 Christie's, New York #298/R

FENTON, Beatrice (attrib) (1887-?) American
$5000   3311   Figure of boy (124cm-49in) bronze. 28-Jun-93 Christie's, East, New York #20/R

FERBER, Herbert (1906-1991) American
$2100   1409   Untitled (27cm-11in) i. brown pat.bronze. 24-Feb-94 Sotheby's Arcade, New York #438/R
$2400   1589   Maquette for Chesterwood (38x61x21cm-15x24x8in) st.sig.d.79 welded copper. 17-Nov-92 Christie's, East, New York #226/R
$2600   1745   Pointer (61x25x20cm-24x10x8in) brass executed 1957-1958. 23-Feb-94 Christie's, East, New York #385/R
$4800   3179   Williams 2B (91x91x66cm-36x36x26in) st.sig.d.76 welded brass. 17-Nov-92 Christie's, East, New York #227/R

FERREN, John (1905-1970) American
$2500   1689   Standing form (185cm-73in) painted wood executed 1960's. 31-Mar-94 Sotheby's Arcade, New York #479/R

FINSTER, Howard (1916-) American
$1000   671   Black panther (30x69x9cm-12x27x4in) s.d.1988 verso oil felt-tip pen shaped panel. 23-Feb-94 Christie's, East, New York #266/R
$1100   743   Howard's Hand (19x14x2cm-7x6x1in) s.i. enamel plaster. 8-Nov-93 Christie's, East, New York #37/R

FISCHER, R M (1947-) American
$2800   1854   Flame (142x144x79cm-56x57x31in) executed 1987 brass steel aluminum glass. 17-Nov-92 Christie's, East, New York #129/R

FISCHLI, Peter and WEISS, David (20th C) American?
$3291   2194   The plant (41cm-16in) black rubber. 2-Jun-94 AB Stockholms Auktionsverk, Stockholm #7008/R (S.KR 26000)
$3544   2363   Dog pot No.2 (9x28cm-4x11in) black rubber executed 1987. 2-Jun-94 AB Stockholms Auktionsverk, Stockholm #7123/R (S.KR 28000)
$4200   2819   Untitled - Grosse frau (113x25x18cm-44x10x7in) plaster one of six executed 1989. 3-May-94 Christie's, East, New York #212/R
$7000   4698   Square cushion (38x54x54cm-15x21x21in) black rubber executed 1987. 3-May-94 Christie's, East, New York #211/R
$16000 10458 Stewardess I (113x27x19cm-44x11x7in) ed.of 6 plaster executed 1989. 5-Oct-93 Sotheby's, New York #80/R

FLANNAGAN, John (1897-1942) American
$2600   1733   Long bird II, figure of pelican (45cm-18in) parcel gilt bronze on wood base. 16-Mar-94 Christie's, New York #61/R
$2750   1858   Bear (22cm-9in) mono.num.1/6 cast stone. 31-Mar-94 Sotheby's Arcade, New York #459/R

FLANNAGAN, John (1897-1942) American-cont.
$3500	2303	Rag doll (53cm-21in) golden brown pat.bronze f.st. 31-Mar-93 Sotheby's Arcade, New York #418/R
$4000	2667	Lady with fox (47cm-19in) stone. 16-Mar-94 Christie's, New York #70/R
$5500	3618	Not yet (33cm-13in) dark brown pat.bronze cast 1941. 31-Mar-93 Sotheby's Arcade, New York #417/R

FLAVIN, Dan (1933-) American
$15000	10067	Untitled - to Jean Christophe (122x22x10cm-48x9x4in) pink green blue red fluorescent lights exec.1970. 23-Feb-94 Christie's, New York #86/R
$17000	11111	Untitled - to V Mayakovsky 2 (102x140x10cm-40x55x4in) red fluorescent light 3/5 executed 1987. 4-May-93 Sotheby's, New York #151/R
$17000	11409	Untitled to Rainer 3 (213x18x9cm-84x7x4in) cool and warm white fluorescent lights exec.1987. 4-May-94 Christie's, New York #231/R
$20000	13423	Untitled (18x122x7cm-7x48x3in) blue red fluorescent lights executed c.1970. 23-Feb-94 Christie's, New York #69/R
$21000	13907	Untitled (65x123cm-26x48in) yellow fluorescent lights executed 1968. 18-Nov-92 Sotheby's, New York #216/R
$22000	12941	Untitled (90x91x61cm-35x36x24in) red yellow green blue fluorescent lights. 8-Oct-92 Christie's, New York #195/R
$24000	16216	Untitled to the real Dan Hill (244x13x21cm-96x5x8in) num.3/5 col.fluorescent lights executed 1978. 10-Nov-93 Christie's, New York #221/R
$30000	19868	Untitled - to Pat and Bob Rohm (244cm-96in) red yellow green fluorescent executed 1973. 18-Nov-92 Sotheby's, New York #231/R
$35000	23649	Untitled (244x244x25cm-96x96x10in) pink yellow flourescent light executed 1987 2/3. 11-Nov-93 Sotheby's, New York #139/R
$35000	23490	Untitled, for you Leo in long respect and affection (122x122cm-48x48in) s.i.d.1977 ed.of five fluorescent lights. 5-May-94 Sotheby's, New York #242 a/R
$37500	25338	Monument for V.Tatlin (244x61cm-96x24in) white flourescent light executed 1967 3/5. 11-Nov-93 Sotheby's, New York #122/R
$41000	26797	Untitled - to Donna (244x244x20cm-96x96x8in) blue yellow pink fluorescent lights 1/5. 4-May-94 Christie's, New York #24/R
$45900	30000	Untitled - To Bob and Pat Rohm (244x244x6cm-96x96x2in) red green yellow fluorescent light. 29-Jun-94 Sotheby's, London #49/R

FLORIO, Salvatore Erseny (1890-?) American
$1400	897	America (48cm-19in) s.i.d.1917 black pat.bronze st.f.SEG/STA. 28-Apr-93 Doyle, New York #74/R

FONSECA, Gonzalo (1922-) Uruguayan
$60000	40541	Mueble constructivista (180x90x30cm-71x35x12in) i. painted mother of pearl inlay executed 1950. 22-Nov-93 Sotheby's, New York #44/R
$70000	47297	Untitled (57x66x18cm-22x26x7in) s.d.71 marble. 23-Nov-93 Christie's, New York #34/R
$95000	62092	Columbarium No.1 (218cm-86in) mixed media wood construction executed 1966. 18-May-93 Sotheby's, New York #69/R

FONTAINE, Bruce la (20th C) American
$1500	1007	Hunters sharing secrets (86cm-34in) s.d.1990 alabaster wood stand. 25-Mar-93 Boos Gallery, Michigan #51/R

FORG, Gunther (1952-) American
$7450	5000	Untitled (120x70x6cm-47x28x2in) bronze executed 1987. 25-Mar-93 Christie's, London #199/R
$9000	5960	Untitled (98x59cm-39x23in) executed 1987 cast bronze. 19-Nov-92 Christie's, New York #126/R
$10000	6944	Untitled (120x70cm-47x28in) executed 1987 bronze. 24-Feb-93 Christie's, New York #128/R
$10000	6711	Fenster I (160x140cm-63x55in) s.i.d.27/12/89 panel. 4-May-94 Christie's, New York #386/R

FRASER, James Earle (1876-1953) American
$2000	1282	Head of young woman (23cm-9in) s.d.1916 brown pat.bronze st.f.Grifford. 28-Apr-93 Doyle, New York #80/R
$3000	1765	In wind (13cm-5in) i. greenish-brown pat.bronze. 5-Oct-92 Grogan, Massachussetts #715/R
$18000	12000	Seate Lincoln (74cm-29in) i.num.2 dark brown pat.bronze f.st. 22-May-94 Hindman Galleries, Chicago #14/R
$150000	100671	The end of the trail (88cm-35in) i.d.1918 num.2 green pat.bronze Cast Rom.Bronze. 2-Dec-93 Sotheby's, New York #38/R

FREDERICKS, Marshall Maynard (1908-) American
$1250	833	Suzanna (23x15cm-9x6in) s. bronze. 26-Aug-93 Boos Gallery, Michigan #143/R
$1900	1267	Goldfish (30x20cm-12x8in) s. bronze on marble plinth. 26-Aug-93 Boos Gallery, Michigan #137/R
$2000	1333	Lion and monkey (28x18cm-11x7in) s. bronze. 26-Aug-93 Boos Gallery, Michigan #139/R
$2250	1500	Bookends of seated warriors (15x23cm-6x9in) s. bronze pair. 26-Aug-93 Boos Gallery, Michigan #142/R
$2500	1667	Mandolin player (30cm-12in) s. bronze on marble plinth. 26-Aug-93 Boos Gallery, Michigan #140/R
$3250	2181	Childhood friends (36x8x36cm-14x3x14in) s. bronze. 25-Mar-93 Boos Gallery, Michigan #39/R
$3500	2333	Baby baboon, self portrait (18x25cm-7x10in) s.i. bronze on marble plinth. 26-Aug-93 Boos Gallery, Michigan #141/R

FREDERICKS, Marshall Maynard (1908-) American-cont.
$4250	2833	Don Quixote (51cm-20in) s. exec.c.1939 silvered bronze. 26-Aug-93 Boos Gallery, Michigan #135/R
$7500	5034	Boy on bear (28x28cm-11x11in) s. bronze. 24-Mar-94 Boos Gallery, Michigan #509/R
$10000	6711	Boy on bear (28cm-11in) bronze. 25-Mar-93 Boos Gallery, Michigan #35/R
$12000	8000	Boy on bear (28x28cm-11x11in) s. bronze on marble plinth. 26-Aug-93 Boos Gallery, Michigan #138/R

FRENCH, Daniel Chester (1850-1931) American
| $68000 | 45333 | Abraham Lincoln (97cm-38in) i.d.1911 brown pat.bronze f.i.Gorham Co. 22-May-94 Hindman Galleries, Chicago #1/R |

FRISHMUTH, Harriet Whitney (1880-1980) American
$3000	1987	The vine, a female nude (30cm-12in) st.sig.d.c.1921 green brown pat.bronze. 15-Jun-94 Butterfield & Butterfield, San Francisco #4481/R
$3000	1974	The vine (28cm-11in) s.d.1921 gold brown pat.bronze Cast Gorham Co.F. 4-Nov-92 Doyle, New York #71/R
$3750	2451	The star (48cm-19in) s.d.1918 brown pat.bronze Cast Gorham Co. 5-May-93 Doyle, New York #63/R
$4800	3200	The vine, female figure (30cm-12in) i.d.1921 green brown pat.bronze Cast Gorham Co. 16-Mar-94 Christie's, New York #64/R
$5000	3311	Vine - figure (30cm-12in) i. greenish brown pat.bronze marble base. 22-Sep-93 Christie's, New York #108/R
$5000	3333	The Vine (30cm-12in) i.d.1921 reddish brown pat.bronze marble base. 17-Mar-94 Sotheby's, New York #88/R
$5250	3523	The Star (48cm-19in) s.d.1918 num.261 greenish brown pat.bronze f.st. 6-Dec-93 Grogan, Massachussetts #504 c
$5500	3642	Allegra (30cm-12in) i. greensih brown pat.bronze marble base. 22-Sep-93 Christie's, New York #106/R
$6000	3947	Dancer (48cm-19in) i.d.1918 edition of 20 bronze st.f.Gorham. 5-Jun-93 Louisiana Auction Exchange #101/R
$7000	4895	The vine (26cm-10in) s.d.1921 ed.350 brown pat.bronze on marble base. 10-Mar-93 Sotheby's, New York #105/R
$7000	4698	Desha (36cm-14in) s.d.1927 brown pat.bronze Cast Gorham Co.F. 2-Dec-93 Sotheby's, New York #97/R
$7000	4605	Crest of wave (52cm-20in) s. pat.bronze f.st.Gorham Co Founders OFHL. 13-Jun-93 Butterfield & Butterfield, San Francisco #3184/R
$7500	5245	Eagle (25cm-10in) i. brown pat.bronze Cast Gorham Co Founders Qex. 11-Mar-93 Christie's, New York #100/R
$7500	4747	The Vine (30cm-12in) i.greenish brown pat.bronze on marble base. 4-Dec-92 Christie's, New York #109/R
$8500	5380	Crest of the Wave (53cm-21in) i.greenish brown pat.bronze.Cast.Gorham Co. 4-Dec-92 Christie's, New York #110/R
$9000	6040	Crest of the wave (51cm-20in) s.i.d.1925 green brown pat.bronze Cast Gorham. 3-Feb-94 Sloan, North Bethesda #2713/R
$9000	5960	Extase - figure (50cm-20in) i. rich brown pat.bronze f.i.Gorham QBKE. 22-Sep-93 Christie's, New York #107/R
$9000	5960	Laughing Waters (41cm-16in) i.d.1929 greenish brown pat.bronze f.i.Gorham. 23-Sep-93 Sotheby's, New York #139/R
$10500	7143	Crest of Wave (53cm-21in) s.d.1925 greenish-brown pat.bronze f.st.Gorham. 9-Jul-93 Sloan, North Bethesda #2701/R
$11000	7333	Crest of the wave, figure of water nymph (53cm-21in) i.d.1925 green brown pat.bronze C.Rom.Bronze W. 16-Mar-94 Christie's, New York #65/R
$11000	7383	Crest of the wave (53cm-21in) i.d.1925 green pat.bronze Cast Gorham Co.F. 2-Dec-93 Sotheby's, New York #96/R
$11000	7692	Rhapsody (29cm-11in) i.d.1925 brown pat.bronze Cast Gorham F. 10-Mar-93 Sotheby's, New York #106/R
$14000	8861	Sweet Grapes (48cm-19in) i.green red brown pat.bronze.Cast.Gorham Co. 4-Dec-92 Christie's, New York #111/R
$15000	9494	Laughing Waters (41cm-16in) i.red green brown pat.bronze.Cast.Gorham Co. 4-Dec-92 Christie's, New York #108/R
$16000	10256	Pas de deux - group of two dancers (43cm-17in) i. brown pat.bronze f.st.Gorham Founders. 26-May-93 Christie's, New York #172/R
$20000	12658	Thread of life (68cm-27in) s.d.1918 foundry Gorham Founders bronze. 3-Dec-92 Sotheby's, New York #176/R
$22000	14865	Scherzo, female nude as fountain (58cm-23in) i. bronze st.f.Gorham executed 1929. 4-Nov-93 Boos Gallery, Michigan #501/R
$27500	18212	Joy of the Waters, female nude with leg and arms raised (110cm-43in) st.sig.d.1930 blue green pat.bronze st.f.Roman. 15-Jun-94 Butterfield & Butterfield, San Francisco #4480/R
$55000	36424	Joy of the Waters (161cm-63in) i.d.1920 green pat.bronze f.i.Roman Works NY. 23-Sep-93 Sotheby's, New York #138/R
$65000	41139	Playdays (127cm-50in) i. greenish brown pat.bronze.Cast.Gorham Co. 4-Dec-92 Christie's, New York #107/R

GABO, Naum (1890-1977) American/Russian
| $1655 | 1089 | Composition, multiple as lamp shade (39cm-15in) plexiglass nylon threads. 7-Jun-93 Wolfgang Ketterer, Munich #652 a/R (DM 2700) |
| $10101 | 6475 | Maquette for Bijenkorf Construction (24x6cm-9x2in) wood plexiglass executed c.1954. 26-May-93 Christie's, Amsterdam #300/R (D.FL 18000) |

GABO, Naum (1890-1977) American/Russian-cont.
$120000   81081   Linear construction in space no 2 (82cm-32in) i.d.1961 perspex with nylon monofilament on base. 4-Nov-93 Sotheby's, New York #327/R

GIBBONS, Arthur (20th C) American?
$2500   1656   Untitled (156x137x71cm-61x54x28in) oil varnish welded steel. 17-Nov-92 Christie's, East, New York #127/R

GINNEVER, Charles (1931-) American
$4000   2532   Untitled (19x61x28cm-7x24x11in) corten steel. 25-Oct-92 Butterfield & Butterfield, San Francisco #2372/R

GLEN, Robert (20th C) American
$1200   800   Cheetah heads (20x13cm-8x5in) s.d.1993 num.3/10 bronze on black marble plinth. 3-Jun-94 Christie's, S. Kensington #592/R
$4500   3000   Three impala (28x36cm-11x14in) s.d.1990 num.6/6 bronze on black marble plinth. 3-Jun-94 Christie's, S. Kensington #593/R

GLICENSTEIN, Enoch-Henryk (1870-1942) American
$2100   1409   The lovers (69cm-27in) dark brown pat.bronze. 24-Feb-94 Sotheby's Arcade, New York #30 a/R
$3250   2167   Ruth and Boaz (41x67cm-16x26in) s. green pat.bronze. 26-May-94 Sotheby's, New York #102/R

GOBER, Robert (1954-) American
$100000   67568   Small bathroom sink (30x66x76cm-12x26x30in) s.d.1984 verso enamel plaster wire wood. 9-Nov-93 Christie's, New York #55/R
$105000   68627   Untitled (70x119x56cm-28x47x22in) mixed media executed 1980. 4-May-93 Sotheby's, New York #239/R
$135000   89404   Crib (114x131x82cm-45x52x32in) s.i.d.1986 enamel cotton wood. 18-Nov-92 Christie's, New York #55/R
$171350   115000   Untitled (47x38x23cm-19x15x9in) s.i.d.1990 wax hair paint. 24-Jun-93 Christie's, London #98/R

GOLDSTEIN, Jack (1945-) American
$3725   2500   Untitled (213x182x15cm-84x72x6in) s.i.d.1987verso. 21-Jun-93 Christie's, S. Kensington #213/R

GOODWIN, Betty (20th C) American?
$2258   1515   Steel notes, an unnamable disaster (61x30cm-24x12in) i. steel magnets oil two parts executed 1989. 29-Nov-93 Ritchie, Toronto #155/R (C.D 3000)

GOOR, Ilana (20th C) American
$1800   938   Figural console table base, mounted with cat and bird (89x112x51cm-35x44x20in) steel bronze c.1989. 5-Aug-92 Boos Gallery, Michigan #124/R

GRAHAM, Robert (1938-) American
$5500   3819   Kentucky Derby 1985 (183x77x65cm-72x30x26in) init.num.5/15 bronze zinc relief suspended. 22-Feb-93 Christie's, East, New York #208/R
$11000   7432   Torso II (52cm-20in) mono.i.num.3/12 pat.bronze executed 1976. 21-Apr-94 Butterfield & Butterfield, San Francisco #1155/R

GRAVES, Nancy (1940-) American
$3874   2600   Liq, Shadow Series (229x163x36cm-90x64x14in) s.i.d.84 oil glitter canvas aluminium sculpture. 25-Mar-93 Christie's, London #150/R
$24000   15686   Limn alum (101x84x56cm-40x33x22in) s.i.d.II-28-88 aluminium polycrome pat bronze. 5-May-93 Christie's, New York #314/R
$28000   18919   Colubra (94x74x61cm-37x29x24in) s.i.d.8 '82 oil on bronze. 10-Nov-93 Christie's, New York #246/R
$40000   26846   Whiffle tree, Pendula series (246x152x165cm-97x60x65in) polyurethane bronze stainless steel exec.1985. 5-May-94 Sotheby's, New York #325/R

GREENOUGH, Horatio (1805-1852) American
$4050   2700   Young boy seated on grassy mound with circlet of flowers (69cm-27in) s.i.d.1840 white marble. 20-May-94 Sotheby's, London #173/R

GREGORY, John (1879-1958) American
$5000   3268   Philomena (30cm-12in) s.i.d.1922 pat.bronze Cast Roman Bronze Works. 16-Sep-93 Sloan, North Bethesda #3319/R

GROOMS, Red (1937-) American
$12000   7059   Man in field (90x17cm-35x7in) s. oil wood metal hoe. 6-Oct-92 Sotheby's, New York #96/R
$30000   17647   Muscle beach totem (104x38x25cm-41x15x10in) s.num.4/9 oil bronze. 6-Oct-92 Sotheby's, New York #93/R

GROSS, Chaim (1904-1991) American
$1500   1049   Two acrobats (36cm-14in) s. pat.plaster on wooden plinth. 12-Mar-93 Skinner, Bolton #277/R
$2000   1307   Figure (36cm-14in) mono.i. st.1/6 dark brown pat.bronze wood base. 4-May-93 Christie's, East, New York #130/R
$2300   1494   Unicyclist (25cm-10in) i. wood. 9-Sep-93 Sotheby's Arcade, New York #403/R
$2600   1688   Mother with two children (33x61cm-13x24in) i.d.1957 num.1/6 bronze. 9-Sep-93 Sotheby's Arcade, New York #411/R

GROSS, Chaim (1904-1991) American-cont.
$3000	1987	Acrobats on unicycle (51cm-20in) i. st.num.1/6 and 3 reddish brown pat.bronze. 22-Sep-93 Christie's, New York #115/R
$3000	2027	The acrobat (33cm-13in) i. mahogany. 31-Mar-94 Sotheby's Arcade, New York #462/R
$3250	2111	Two female acrobats (43cm-17in) s.i.d.1945 wood. 9-Sep-93 Sotheby's Arcade, New York #400/R
$3250	1879	Standing woman (30cm-12in) s.i. bronze. 25-Sep-92 Sotheby's Arcade, New York #378/R
$4000	2312	Draped woman (42cm-17in) s.i. lignum vitae. 24-Sep-92 Sotheby's, New York #238/R
$5000	3497	Tourists (36cm-14in) i.d.1959 num.1/6 brown pat.bronze on marble base. 11-Mar-93 Christie's, New York #178/R
$6000	3974	Female figure (49cm-19in) i.d.1955 num.1/6 no.2 reddish brown pat.bronze. 23-Sep-93 Sotheby's, New York #282/R

GROSSMAN, Nancy (1940-) American
$5500	3691	Untitled (42x16x15cm-17x6x6in) s.d.70-71 leather mask over polyester mould. 5-May-94 Sotheby's, New York #204/R
$6500	4514	Untitled (42cm-17in) init.d.69 nails leather rivets metal plastic. 26-Feb-93 Sotheby's Arcade, New York #319/R

GROSVENOR, Robert (1937-) American
$5000	3378	Untitled (22x254x22cm-9x100x9in) creasote wood executed 1975. 10-Nov-93 Christie's, New York #213/R
$21000	14094	Untitled alternative view of Mastaba (86x216x89cm-34x85x35in) creasote painted wood blocks with metal dowel. 5-May-94 Sotheby's, New York #258/R

GRUZALSKI, James A (20th C) American
$1700	1141	Brave wolf (51cm-20in) s.num.10/33 brown pat.bronze on wood base. 17-Jul-93 Dargate Auction Galleries, Pittsburgh #5
$1750	1174	Puma (51cm-20in) s.num.14/30 brown pat.bronze bronze w.wood base. 17-Jul-93 Dargate Auction Galleries, Pittsburgh #3
$3750	2517	Crazy horse (61cm-24in) s.num.12/30 brown pat.bronze on wood base. 17-Jul-93 Dargate Auction Galleries, Pittsburgh #4

GUAYASAMIN, Oswaldo (1919-) Ecuadorian
$9000	5260	Cabeza de Mujer (60cm-24in) s. copper bronze alloy. 23-Nov-92 Sotheby's, New York #245/R
$23000	15541	La Patria Joven (216cm-85in) s.num.2/3 painted hammered copper executed 1971. 22-Nov-93 Sotheby's, New York #234/R

GURTUBAY, Jose Antonio (20th C) Mexican
$1935	1299	Toro marino (86x60cm-34x24in) bronze. 1-Dec-93 Louis Morton, Mexico #205/R (M.P 6000)

HAGUE, Raoul (1905-) American
$14000	9150	Swamp pepperwood (72x160x49cm-28x63x19in) carved pepperwood wooded base executed c.1966. 4-May-93 Sotheby's, New York #333/R

HAMILTON, Juan (20th C) American?
$4500	3041	Abstract form 15 (69x38x43cm-27x15x17in) s.d.79 polychrome clay. 11-Nov-93 Sotheby's, New York #153/R
$6500	4392	Abstract form 14 (69x38x43cm-27x15x17in) s.d.1979 polychrome clay. 11-Nov-93 Sotheby's, New York #152/R

HANSON, Duane (1925-) American
$125000	81699	Photographer polyvinyl polychrom oil accessories lifesize. 3-May-93 Sotheby's, New York #30/R

HARING, Keith (1958-1990) American
$1740	1160	And L A Z (50cm-20in) s.i.d.8 oct 1982 painted plastic. 24-May-94 Norden, Stockholm #209/R (S.KR 13500)
$3500	2288	Untitled (30x38x2cm-12x15x1in) s.d.1984 pen silver ink enamel wood. 7-May-93 Christie's, East, New York #184/R
$7500	5034	Untitled (27x56x5cm-11x22x2in) s.d.1982 marker spray paint on steel. 25-Feb-94 Sotheby's, New York #157/R
$20000	13245	Untitled (84x63x34cm-33x25x13in) s.d.86 polyurethane paint aluminum. 19-Nov-92 Christie's, New York #452/R
$27540	18000	Untitled (79x42cm-31x17in) felt pen terracotta executed 1984. 30-Jun-94 Sotheby's, London #226/R
$29340	18000	Untitled (102x55x33cm-40x22x13in) painted steel. 15-Oct-92 Christie's, London #90/R
$41000	27703	Breakers (113x142x168cm-44x56x66in) polyurethane painted aluminium executed 1987 1/3. 11-Nov-93 Sotheby's, New York #176/R
$55000	32353	Amphora (52cm-20in) s.i.d.22-84 black felt-tip pen terracotta. 8-Oct-92 Christie's, New York #257/R

HARING, Keith and LA2 (20th C) American
$15000	10417	Untitled (103x69x69cm-41x27x27in) s.d.January 18 1981 marker fiberglass. 23-Feb-93 Sotheby's, New York #394/R

HART, Joel Tanner (1810-1877) American
$8250   5537   Portrait of Erastus Brigham Bigelow (64cm-25in) s.d.1853 marble. 6-Dec-93 Grogan, Massachussetts #457/R

HARTLEY, Jonathan Scott (1845-1912) American
$4500   2980   Figure of Indian boy dancing (56cm-22in) i. rich brown pat.bronze f.i. Roman Works NY. 22-Sep-93 Christie's, New York #97/R
$7000   4895   Whirlwind, female figure (77cm-30in) i.red brown pat.bronze with verdigris F.Gorham. 11-Mar-93 Christie's, New York #98/R

HARVEY, Eli (1860-1957) American
$2000   1325   Resting lion (19cm-7in) i.d.1904 brown pat.bronze st.f.Klaber. 15-Jun-94 Butterfield & Butterfield, San Francisco #4484/R
$2500   1656   Lion with cub (19cm-7in) i.d.1903 brown pat.bronze st.f.Zopo Foundries. 15-Jun-94 Butterfield & Butterfield, San Francisco #4483/R

HASELTINE, Herbert (1877-1962) American
$1400   946   Monkey (12cm-5in) i.d.1906 brown pat.bronze f.i.Valsuani. 31-Mar-94 Sotheby's Arcade, New York #173/R
$8000   5128   IV Percheron (18cm-7in) i.d.MCMXXV black green gold mottled pat.bronze. 27-May-93 Sotheby's, New York #113/R
$11000 7333   Carlos Unzue on hunter - equestrian group (74cm-29in) mono.i.d.num. brown pat.bronze f.i.Valsuani. 17-Mar-94 Sotheby's, New York #49/R
$100000 63291 'Percheron' - figure of the stallion Rhum (71cm-28in) i.green/brown pat.bronze onyx on oak plinth. 4-Dec-92 Christie's, New York #115/R
$100000 63291 'Percherons' - the mare Messaline and her foal (55cm-22in) i. green/brown pat.bronze onyx on oak plinth. 4-Dec-92 Christie's, New York #116/R

HAYES, David (20th C) American?
$1700   1126   Woman dressing (173cm-68in) welded steel. 30-Jun-93 Sotheby's Arcade, New York #353/R

HEBALD, Milton (1917-) American
$2000   1299   Head and hand of James Joyce (43x132cm-17x52in) i.d.1966 num.III/6 bronze. 9-Sep-93 Sotheby's Arcade, New York #405/R
$3250   2124   Seated nude (109cm-43in) s. green pat.bronze. 15-Sep-93 Doyle, New York #30 a

HEBERT, Louis Philippe (1850-?) Canadian
$5397   3505   Mademoiselle de Vercheres (48cm-19in) s.i. pat.bronze. 21-Jun-94 Fraser Pinneys, Quebec #67 (C.D 7500)

HEIKKA, Earle E (1910-1941) American
$1077   718   Morning frolic (48x40x13cm-19x16x5in) s.d. bronze wood base. 30-May-94 Hodgins, Calgary #34/R (C.D 1500)

HELMICK, Ralph (20th C) American
$2200   1438   Slit, 1983 (117cm-46in) masonite. 14-May-93 Skinner, Bolton #192/R

HENDRICKS, Geoffrey (1931-) American
$1416   950   Calendar (30x89x13cm-12x35x5in) twigs twine paper collage ink executed 1981. 24-Jun-93 Sotheby's, London #84/R

HENRY, John (1943-) American
$2000   1342   Untitled (175x122x81cm-69x48x32in) enamel on steel. 3-May-94 Christie's, East, New York #182/R

HEROLD, Georg (20th C) American?
$3500   2349   Corpus Delirium (210x44x46cm-83x17x18in) s.d.1989 num.4/5 wood hanger broom stockings. 3-May-94 Christie's, East, New York #255/R
$5570   3713   Brick painting - untitled (170x120cm-67x47in) s.d.90verso stones on velvet. 2-Jun-94 AB Stockholms Auktionsverk, Stockholm #7109/R (S.KR 44000)
$10000 6623   Durerhase (217x185x120cm-85x73x47in) executed 1989 roofing lathe nails. 19-Nov-92 Christie's, New York #159/R

HESSE, Eva (1936-1970) American
$430000 290541 Several (213x28x18cm-84x11x7in) acrylic papier-mache balloon rubber cords 1965. 10-Nov-93 Sotheby's, New York #27/R

HILL, George William (1862-1934) Canadian
$1655   1075   George Etienne Cartier (28cm-11in) s.i. pat.bronze st.f.Cie.des Bronzes. 21-Jun-94 Fraser Pinneys, Quebec #149 (C.D 2300)

HOAR, Steve (20th C) Canadian
$2024   1340   High ridin' (61x40x25cm-24x16x10in) s.i.d.1978 num.4/20 bronze. 16-Nov-92 Hodgins, Calgary #139/R (C.D 2600)

HOFFMAN, Malvina (1885-1966) American
$2400   1509   Bust of young woman reading book (66cm-26in) marble. 22-Apr-93 Freeman Fine Arts, Philadelphia #1088 b
$4800   3038   Hindu Incese burner (27cm-11in) i. black pat.bronze. Cast.Roman Bronze Works. 4-Dec-92 Christie's, New York #114/R
$5000   3333   Bust of Anna Pavlowa (27cm-11in) i.d.1926 brown pat.bronze Cast Valsuani. 16-Mar-94 Christie's, New York #56/R

HOLLAND, Tom (1936-) American
$2000	1307	Mola (45x82x5cm-18x32x2in) s.d.87 oil epoxy felt-tip pen fibreglass. 7-May-93 Christie's, East, New York #151/R
$2500	1689	Duga 194 (69x46cm-27x18in) s.i.d.1984 epoxy fibreglass aluminium. 21-Apr-94 Butterfield & Butterfield, San Francisco #1206

HOLMES, Robert (1891-1930) American
$2831	1900	Dancers (93x202x30cm-37x80x12in) s.i.d.1987 num.4/11 green pat.bronze. 21-Jun-93 Christie's, S. Kensington #191/R

HOLZER, Jenny (1950-) American
$1700	1126	Selection from the survival series (8x25cm-3x10in) executed 1983-1985 1/10 relief cast aluminum. 17-Nov-92 Christie's, East, New York #128/R
$3750	2517	Gifted children, those with an IQ of 125..Selection from the Living Series (20x25cm-8x10in) bronze executed 1980-82 1/3. 25-Feb-94 Sotheby's, New York #114/R
$7000	4698	Selections from the living series (54x59cm-21x23in) num.3 ed.of 5 enamel metal exec.1980-1982. 5-May-94 Sotheby's, New York #355
$15000	10417	Selections from truisms (14x77x10cm-6x30x4in) exec.1984 num.2/5 electr.LED sign one col.diode. 24-Feb-93 Christie's, New York #112/R
$22000	12941	The living series (44x91x46cm-17x36x18in) Bethel white granite bench. 8-Oct-92 Christie's, New York #210/R
$26000	17219	Selection from the survival series (16x154x10cm-6x61x4in) executed 1983 electronic LED sign 1-colour diode. 19-Nov-92 Christie's, New York #129/R
$27000	18121	The Living Series, you can watch people (43x91x46cm-17x36x18in) bethel white granite bench ed.1 of 3 exec.1989. 4-May-94 Christie's, New York #268/R
$31000	20530	Selection from truisms (14x77x15cm-6x30x6in) electronic LED sign red diodes executed 1983. 18-Nov-92 Sotheby's, New York #283/R
$33000	22148	Selection from the Living Series (43x91x46cm-17x36x18in) bethel white granite. 5-May-94 Sotheby's, New York #347/R
$35000	23490	Untitled, selection from Truisms (76x287x30cm-30x113x12in) computerized UNEX electronic display signboard. 4-May-94 Christie's, New York #287/R
$35000	23649	I am a man (284x25x11cm-112x10x4in) electronic LED sign num.2/4 executed 1987. 10-Nov-93 Christie's, New York #263/R
$35000	22876	The Living Series - The smallest thing can make. (42x90x45cm-17x35x18in) 1/3, Bethel white granite bench exec.1989. 5-May-93 Christie's, New York #152/R
$35000	23490	Selection from truisms (16x308x10cm-6x121x4in) electronic L.E.D. red diodes ed.of 5 eec.1983-84. 5-May-94 Sotheby's, New York #299/R

HORN, Roni (1944-) American
$16000	10458	Asphere V (30cm-12in) solid forged copper circular executed 1989. 5-May-93 Christie's, New York #131/R
$16000	10811	Paris object I (38x2cm-15x1in) copper stainl.steel 4 units num.3/3 exec.89-90. 10-Nov-93 Christie's, New York #262/R
$18000	12500	Thicket no 1 (5x163x123cm-2x64x48in) executed 1990 apoxy resin brushed aluminum. 23-Feb-93 Sotheby's, New York #374/R

HUMPHREY, Ralph (1932-1990) American
$15000	9934	Untitled number 4 (161x116x16cm-63x46x6in) s.d.74-75 acrylic modelling paste shaped canvas. 19-Nov-92 Christie's, New York #387/R

HUNT, Bryan (1947-) American
$9000	5882	Ritual II (182x23x23cm-72x9x9in) num.4/6 bronze limestone base executed 1986. 4-May-93 Sotheby's, New York #185/R
$10000	6711	Study for Roebling Monument I (176x25x25cm-69x10x10in) s.d.84 num.4/4 bronze. 23-Feb-94 Christie's, New York #107/R
$12252	8168	Pilgrim (160x50x50cm-63x20x20in) s.num.1/4 green pat.bronze executed 1987. 17-Mar-94 Catherine Charbonneaux, Paris #48/R (F.FR 70000)
$25000	16892	Step falls (278x33x13cm-109x13x5in) bronze executed 1981. 11-Nov-93 Sotheby's, New York #144/R
$33600	22400	Muse and Lake (192x33x33cm-76x13x13in) s.d.90 num.3/3 dark brown pat.bronze marble base. 3-Jun-94 Lempertz, Cologne #706/R (DM 56000)
$40000	26490	Means IV (105cm-41in) gouache silkpaper balsa wood executed 1977. 18-Nov-93 Sotheby's, New York #251/R
$45000	29264	Airship (18x18x150cm-7x7x59in) silver leaf silk paper balsa wood. 5-May-93 Christie's, New York #108/R

HUNTINGTON, Anna Hyatt (1876-1973) American
$2500	1634	Panther perched on rock (23cm-9in) s.i.num.7 green brown pat.bronze Cast Gorham Co. 16-Sep-93 Sloan, North Bethesda #2832/R
$2800	1867	Reaching jaguar on rock (17cm-7in) i.brown pat.bronze Cast Gorham Co Q493. 16-Mar-94 Christie's, New York #58/R
$3000	1765	Yawning tiger (33cm-13in) num.38 greenish-brown pat.bronze f.st.Gorham. 5-Oct-92 Grogan, Massachussetts #716/R
$3000	1987	A pair of mountain goats (17cm-7in) i.one num.75 one num.76 bronze st.f.Gorham two. 15-Jun-94 Butterfield & Butterfield, San Francisco #4676/R
$4500	3000	Yawning tiger (34cm-13in) i.red green brown pat.bronze Cast Gorham Q492. 16-Mar-94 Christie's, New York #59/R

INNERST, Mark (1957-) American
$7500   5034   New Centre (25x61x6cm-10x24x2in) init.verso four panels wood base. 3-May-94 Christie's, East, New York #155/R

INUKPUK, Johnny (1911-) North American
$725   483   Inuk making a mukluk (51cm-20in) mottled grey soapstone. 6-Jun-94 Waddingtons, Toronto #936 (C.D 1000)
$1489   955   Young Inuk carrying baby sister on back (33cm-13in) s. marbled grey/green soapstone. 7-Dec-92 Waddingtons, Toronto #959/R (C.D 1900)

IPEELEE, Osuitok (1923-) North American
$2806   1846   Carving of an owl (28cm-11in) s. soapstone executed c.1955. 7-Jun-93 Waddingtons, Toronto #908/R (C.D 3600)

IRWIN, Robert (1928-) American
$45000 29412 Untitled (286x12x12cm-113x5x5in) polyester resin executed 1971. 5-May-93 Christie's, New York #103/R

JAAR, Alfredo (1956-) American
$8500   5556   Coyote light box gold leaf mirror duratrans. 4-May-93 Sotheby's, New York #269/R
$10000 6623   He ram (124x103x70cm-49x41x28in) transperencies in lightbox with mirror. 19-Nov-92 Christie's, New York #119/R

JACKSON, Harry (1924-) American
$800   533   Lone ballad, figure of cowboy (15cm-6in) i. green brown pat.bronze. 16-Mar-94 Christie's, New York #78/R
$1400   946   One feather - head of Indian (9cm-4in) i.d.71 num.67 brown pat.bronze 67/100. 31-Mar-94 Sotheby's Arcade, New York #208/R
$2250   1510   Silent pardners, cowboy on horseback (30cm-12in) s.d.1973 num.16/40 pat.bronze. 2-May-94 Selkirks, St. Louis #135/R
$2800   1867   Trapper II (39cm-15in) s.thumbprint i.d.1982 bronze Cast Wyoming F. 16-Mar-94 Christie's, New York #75/R
$4000   2685   Sacagawea, Shoshone Indian guide (66cm-26in) s.d.1977 num.17/40 pat.bronze st.f.Wyoming. 2-May-94 Selkirks, St. Louis #140/R
$4250   2853   John Wayne on horseback (61cm-24in) s.d.1981 num.WU22 pat.bronze st.Wyoming Foundry. 4-May-94 Doyle, New York #56/R
$6500   4333   The dog soldier (63cm-25in) i.d.1983 num.DS18 red/brown pat.bronze Wyoming f. 26-May-94 Christie's, New York #50/R
$7000   4698   A lack of slack, cowboy and horse group (41cm-16in) s.d.1973 num.15/40 brown pat.bronze. 2-May-94 Selkirks, St. Louis #139/R
$7000   4667   Algonquin Chief and warrior (76cm-30in) i.num.8/40 brown pat.bronze conceived 1971. 22-May-94 Hindman Galleries, Chicago #39/R
$8000   5369   Bronc stomper (43cm-17in) s.num.11P/17 polychrome bronze. 2-May-94 Selkirks, St. Louis #136/R
$8000   5333   The Marshall II, equestrian group of John Wayne as Rooster Cogburn (42cm-17in) s.thumbprint i.d.1979 bronze C.Wyoming F. 16-Mar-94 Christie's, New York #76/R
$8000   5369   Flag bearer on horseback (69cm-27in) s.d.1983 num.TF15 pat.bronze st.Wyoming Foundry. 4-May-94 Doyle, New York #54/R
$8500   5705   Safe and sound (48cm-19in) s.d.1982 num.SAS36 pat.bronze st.Wyoming Foundry. 4-May-94 Doyle, New York #55/R
$9000   5696   Sacagawea - First working model for monument (67cm-26in) i. brown pat.bronze.Cast.Wyoming Foundry Studios. 4-Dec-92 Christie's, New York #257/R
$9000   6040   Marshall II, John Wayne as Rooster Cogburn in True Grit (43cm-17in) s.i.d.79 1 of 50 polychrome bronze st.f.Wyoming. 2-May-94 Selkirks, St. Louis #137/R
$11000 7383   Indian mother and child (64cm-25in) s.i.d.80 num.2P polychrome bronze st.f.Wyoming. 2-May-94 Selkirks, St. Louis #142/R
$11000 7383   Washakie, Shoshone Indian Chief (89cm-35in) s.i.d.78 1 of 20 polychrome bronze st.f.Wyoming. 2-May-94 Selkirks, St. Louis #141/R
$13000 9091   Pony express (46cm-18in) i.d.1967 num.2 ed.of 40 grren black pat.bronze. 10-Mar-93 Sotheby's, New York #58/R
$13000 9091   Pennsylvania woodsman 1750 (51cm-20in) i.d.1965 num.5.P ed. of 20 polychrome bronze. 10-Mar-93 Sotheby's, New York #59/R
$14000 9272   Sacagawea (69cm-27in) s.i.d.1980 and 1977 painted bronze f.i. 23-Sep-93 Sotheby's, New York #91/R
$18000 12000 Pony Express (155cm-61in) s.i.d.1984 red green blue poylchrome bronze. 22-May-94 Hindman Galleries, Chicago #37/R
$19000 12667 Washakie, equestrian group (89cm-35in) s.thumbprint i.d.1978 cold-painted bronze. 16-Mar-94 Christie's, New York #77/R
$19000 12667 Safe and sound, equestrian group (49cm-19in) s.thumbprint i.d.1982 cold painted bronze. 16-Mar-94 Christie's, New York #79/R
$21000 14094 Dog soldier (64cm-25in) s.d.1983 1 of 20 polychrome bronze st.f.Wyoming. 2-May-94 Selkirks, St. Louis #138/R
$22000 14667 The flagbearer (71cm-28in) i.d.1983 num.TF18 brown pat.bronze Wyoming f. 26-May-94 Christie's, New York #51/R
$22000 14765 Pony Express rider (48cm-19in) i.d.1967 num.21/40 black brown pat.bronze. 2-Dec-93 Sotheby's, New York #77/R
$32000 21333 The marshal (145x165cm-57x65in) i.d.1980 brown pat.bronze st.Wyoming Foundry. 26-May-94 Christie's, New York #48/R
$33000 22148 Two Champs, Clayton Danks on the horse Old Steamboat (76cm-30in) s.d.1974 num.20P polychrome bronze marble base. 2-May-94 Selkirks, St. Louis #143/R

JACKSON, Harry (1924-) American-cont.
$170000   114094   Stampede (152cm-60in) s.d.1958-59 num.1P/5 polychrome bronze. 2-May-94 Selkirks, St. Louis #144/R

JENKINS, Michael (20th C) American
$2000   1351   Cabinet No.2 (185x43x18cm-73x17x7in) s.d.1989 mixed media construction. 11-Nov-93 Sotheby's, New York #222/R

JENNEWEIN, Carl Paul (1890-1978) American
$5000   3378   Figural group of boy and dolphin (30cm-12in) i. brown pat.bronze. 24-Nov-93 Sotheby's Arcade, New York #277/R
$8500   5449   Greek dance - figure of goddess (46cm-18in) i. dark brown pat.bronze. 26-May-93 Christie's, New York #170/R

JENNEY, Neil (1945-) American
$135000   90604   Paint and painted (122x123x9cm-48x48x4in) s.d.70verso acrylic graphite canvas. 4-May-94 Sotheby's, New York #51/R

JEWETT, Maude Sherwood (1873-1953) American
$5000   3165   Flower holder - two dancers (26cm-10in) i. greenish brown pat.bronze.Cast.Gorham Co. 4-Dec-92 Christie's, New York #137/R

JOHNS, Jasper (1930-) American
$240000   161074   Wilderness I (107x66x7cm-42x26x3in) s.d.1963 ruler string and items w.oil on paper. 3-May-94 Christie's, New York #58/R

JOHNSON, Cletus (1941-) American
$1600   1074   Thornapple Theatre (80x49x19cm-31x19x7in) s.i.d.1987 box enamel plastic glass electrical. 3-May-94 Christie's, East, New York #179/R

JOHNSON, Stanley Q (1939-) American
$3200   2133   Taught by the eagle (97cm-38in) i.num.AP 2/50 copper brown pat.bronze f.st. 22-May-94 Hindman Galleries, Chicago #43/R
$4200   2800   Hiawatha (89cm-35in) i.num.11/40 copper brown pat.bronze. 22-May-94 Hindman Galleries, Chicago #40/R
$5500   3667   Taos Navajo (66cm-26in) i.num.2/6 copper brown pat.bronze. 22-May-94 Hindman Galleries, Chicago #42/R
$7000   4667   Eagle boy (114cm-45in) i.num.5/5 copper brown pat.bronze f.st. 22-May-94 Hindman Galleries, Chicago #41/R

JUDD, Donald (1928-1994) American
$2131   1366   Chair (75x50x50cm-30x20x20in) metal. 27-Apr-93 Campo, Vlaamse Kaai #471/R (B.FR 70000)
$2200   1457   Untitled (62x41cm-24x16in) st.sig.i.81-84 10 R 4-82 wood. 17-Nov-92 Christie's, East, New York #117/R
$2250   1562   Untitled (53x40x5cm-21x16x2in) st.sig.num.89-31 17R 4-89 sugar pine wood. 23-Feb-93 Sotheby's, New York #330/R
$2500   1634   Table object (51x61x7cm-20x24x3in) s.i. proof aside from ed.of 200 stainless steel 1968. 5-Oct-93 Sotheby's, New York #12/R
$3060   2000   Untitled (40x53x5cm-16x21x2in) st.sig.num.89.31.18R 4.89 wood. 30-Jun-94 Sotheby's, London #241/R
$3260   2000   Untitled (40x53x5cm-16x21x2in) st. d.89-31 25R 4-89 sugar pine wood. 14-Oct-92 Sotheby's, London #377/R
$3500   2318   Untitled (43x53x5cm-17x21x2in) st.sig. d.81-84 num.11 R 4-82 C.K.verso wood. 18-Nov-92 Sotheby's, New York #233 a/R
$4500   3020   Untitled - chair prototype (76x38x38cm-30x15x15in) s.d.80 yellow pine executed 1982. 25-Feb-94 Sotheby's, New York #86/R
$7000   4575   Untitled (36x50x5cm-14x20x2in) s.d.1991 num.11/20 cadmium oil wood. 4-May-93 Sotheby's, New York #150/R
$9000   5960   Untitled (30x60x30cm-12x24x12in) st.sig.d.89 pulver aluminum i.Lascaux Materials. 19-Nov-92 Christie's, New York #244/R
$10500   7047   Untitled (29x60x29cm-11x24x11in) st.s.d.89-27 pulver on aluminium. 25-Feb-94 Sotheby's, New York #99/R
$13000   8725   Untitled (50x100cm-20x39in) wood executed 1976. 5-May-94 Sotheby's, New York #239/R
$13040   8000   Untitled (90x30x30cm-35x12x12in) painted aluminium executed c.1985. 14-Oct-92 Sotheby's, London #397/R
$15000   10067   Untitled (30x60x30cm-12x24x12in) st.sig.d.89-36 galvanized iron. 4-May-94 Christie's, New York #298/R
$16000   10458   Untitled (50x100x50cm-20x39x20in) st. d.81-5 copper blue plexiglass 5/6. 4-May-93 Sotheby's, New York #140/R
$19000   12838   Untitled (13x101x23cm-5x40x9in) st.sig.d.88-11verso painted aluminum. 10-Nov-93 Christie's, New York #367/R
$21000   13907   Untitled (30x90x30cm-12x35x12in) st.sig.d.89 pulver on aluminum st.Lascaux. 19-Nov-92 Christie's, New York #397/R
$22350   15000   Lippencott wall sculpture (25x114x25cm-10x45x10in) st.sig.d.85-12 anodized aluminium plexiglass. 2-Dec-93 Christie's, London #159/R
$25000   16779   Untitled (37x194x65cm-15x76x26in) st.s.d.87-16 anodized aluminium. 25-Feb-94 Sotheby's, New York #88/R
$26000   16993   Untitled progression (12x64x23cm-5x25x9in) st.sig.d.71-14 one of four stainless steel. 5-May-93 Christie's, New York #120/R
$27000   18243   Untitled (30x180x12cm-12x71x5in) pulver on aluminium executed 1986. 11-Nov-93 Sotheby's, New York #155/R
$27500   16176   Untitled (15x74x61cm-6x29x24in) copper executed 1976. 6-Oct-92 Sotheby's, New York #121/R

JUDD, Donald (1928-1994) American-cont.

$30000	20134	Untitled (50x100x50cm-20x39x20in) st.sig.d.num.88-11A-11B aluminium plexiglas two. 23-Feb-94 Christie's, New York #68/R
$32000	21192	Untitled (50x100x50cm-20x39x20in) st.sig.d.82 steel plexiglass st.Bernstein Bros. 19-Nov-92 Christie's, New York #396/R
$42000	28378	Untitled (12x65x21cm-5x26x8in) galvanized iron executed 1970. 10-Nov-93 Christie's, New York #211/R
$65000	43624	Untitled (86x40x86cm-34x16x34in) aluminum plate tempered glass four units. 5-May-94 Sotheby's, New York #249/R
$80000	54054	Untitled (305x69x61cm-120x27x24in) stainless steel red plexiglass ten units exec.89. 11-Nov-93 Sotheby's, New York #132/R
$98000	64052	Untitled (23x102x79cm-9x40x31in) ten units one st.verso yellow plexiglas steel. 4-May-93 Christie's, New York #20/R
$115000	77181	Untitled (362x100x50cm-143x39x20in) st.sig.d.86 num.7 aluminum blue plexiglas six. 4-May-94 Christie's, New York #309/R
$125000	83893	Untitled (11x194x65cm-4x76x26in) scarlet lacquer on galvanized iron exec.1967. 3-May-94 Christie's, New York #21/R
$210000	137255	Untitled (305x69x61cm-120x27x24in) stainless steel green plexiglas ten units. 3-May-93 Sotheby's, New York #49/R
$230000	155405	Untitled (13x64x22cm-5x25x9in) s.d.1964 red lacquer on wood. 10-Nov-93 Sotheby's, New York #20/R

KADOJUAK (?) North American

$1957	1313	Three standing birds, one with extended wing (61cm-24in) weathered whalebone. 29-Nov-93 Waddingtons, Toronto #921/R (C.D 2600)

KAHANE, Anne (1924-) Canadian

$1820	1214	Emerging figure (147cm-58in) wood. 11-May-94 Sotheby's, Toronto #230/R (C.D 2500)

KALISH, Max (1891-1945) American

$900	596	Female nude (17x38cm-7x15in) i.f.Andro Fondeur Paris bronze marble base. 13-Jun-94 Christie's, East, New York #587/R
$6500	4114	Farmer ploughing (39cm-15in) i. brown pat.bronze on marble base. 4-Dec-92 Christie's, New York #102/R

KAMITAKI, Gerald (20th C) American?

$3000	1987	The 4 ten (214x194x14cm-84x76x6in) graphite plaster nails on wood 55 panels. 17-Nov-92 Christie's, East, New York #31/R

KATZ, Alex (1927-) American

$3750	2484	Untitled (27cm-11in) oil aluminum. 29-Sep-93 Sotheby's Arcade, New York #326/R

KAUBA, Carl (1865-1922) Austrian/American

$1100	744	Indian on a rock (19cm-7in) i. dark green brown pat.bronze. 31-Mar-94 Sotheby's Arcade, New York #195/R
$1110	750	Standing female figure enclosed in hinged cloak opening to reveal naked form beneath (17cm-7in) s. gilt bronze table lamp. 28-Apr-94 Christie's, S. Kensington #248/R
$1332	900	Mechanical figure of lady on couch (14cm-6in) s. gold lacquer brass. 16-Mar-93 Sotheby's Colonnade, London #241
$1696	1131	Amorous couple (22cm-9in) i. gilt bronze white marble base. 8-Mar-94 Dorotheum, Vienna #155/R (A.S 20000)
$2100	1469	Indian eyes (18cm-7in) i. polychrome painted bronze. 10-Mar-93 Sotheby's, New York #62/R
$2200	1538	Reclining Indian smoking pipe (27cm-11in) i. polychrome painted bronze. 10-Mar-93 Sotheby's, New York #63/R
$2300	1503	Taking aim (23cm-9in) s. polychrome bronze. 16-Sep-93 Sloan, North Bethesda #3294/R
$2371	1394	The Cheyenne Indian (31x19cm-12x7in) i. polychrom brnze on wooden socle. 9-Oct-92 Bolland & Marotz, Bremen #1091/R (DM 3500)
$2371	1394	Open sesame, standing young woman opening dress (21cm-8in) s. bronze. 6-Oct-92 Michael Zeller, Lindau #2034/R (DM 3500)
$2500	1689	Man and boy with rifle (38cm-15in) i. golden brown pat.bronze. 31-Mar-94 Sotheby's Arcade, New York #204/R
$2600	1757	Boy with rifle (42cm-17in) i. golden brown pat.bronze. 31-Mar-94 Sotheby's Arcade, New York #205/R
$2600	1818	Running indian (24cm-9in) i. polychrome painted bronze. 10-Mar-93 Sotheby's, New York #64/R
$3250	2124	Indian chief with rifle (61cm-24in) s. num.27/100 brown pat.bronze on marble base. 16-Sep-93 Sloan, North Bethesda #3308/R
$3400	2000	Red Indian chief (46cm-18in) cold painted bronze. 9-Oct-92 Sotheby's, London #202/R
$3500	2448	Tough shot (15cm-6in) i.num.2 red-brown pat.bronze. 10-Mar-93 Sotheby's, New York #61/R
$4500	3147	Indian with eagle (48cm-19in) red-brown pat.bronze. 10-Mar-93 Sotheby's, New York #55/R
$4500	3147	Scout (46cm-18in) i.num.6254 polychrome painted bronze. 10-Mar-93 Sotheby's, New York #56/R
$5000	3378	Indian with pipe (41cm-16in) i.num.6234 brown pat.bronze polychrome. 31-Mar-94 Sotheby's Arcade, New York #206/R
$5624	3800	'Butterfly girl' - butterfly with hinged wings which open to reveal naked figure (22cm-9in) s. silvered gilt bronze. 28-Apr-94 Christie's, S. Kensington #249/R

KAUBA, Carl (1865-1922) Austrian/American-cont.

$6000	3846	Indian attack (70cm-28in) i. painted bronze. 27-May-93 Sotheby's, New York #241/R
$7500	5245	Indian on horseback (57cm-22in) red brown pat.bronze. 10-Mar-93 Sotheby's, New York #60/R
$12000	8000	Chief Wolf Robe (69cm-27in) i. polychrome bronze. 17-Mar-94 Sotheby's, New York #77/R
$16000	10256	Chief Wolf robe (67cm-26in) i. painted bronze. 27-May-93 Sotheby's, New York #240/R
$18000	12587	Friend in need (52cm-20in) i. red brown pat.bronze. 10-Mar-93 Sotheby's, New York #57/R

KAUBA, Carl (attrib) (1865-1922) Austrian/American

$1500	1014	Bucking bronco (29cm-11in) i. red brown pat.bronze. 31-Mar-94 Sotheby's Arcade, New York #194/R
$2371	1394	Wild West rider on rearing horse (24x27cm-9x11in) polychrom bronze on wooden socle. 9-Oct-92 Bolland & Marotz, Bremen #1092/R (DM 3500)
$12000	7595	Indian attack (22x69cm-9x27in) i. red-brown pat.bronze on marble base i.f.Thenn. 4-Dec-92 Christie's, New York #256/R

KAVIK, John (1897-?) North American

$1204	808	Standing Inuit woman carrying her child in her amaut (16cm-6in) mottled dark grey soapstone. 29-Nov-93 Waddingtons, Toronto #822 (C.D 1600)
$1559	1026	Carving of standing Inuit woman (30cm-12in) grey soapstone ebonized base. 7-Jun-93 Waddingtons, Toronto #941/R (C.D 2000)
$2027	1333	Carving of standing Inuit hunter (41cm-16in) grey soapstone ebonized base. 7-Jun-93 Waddingtons, Toronto #946/R (C.D 2600)
$2117	1357	Standing Inuit figure wearing parka (35cm-14in) mottled dark grey soapstone. 7-Dec-92 Waddingtons, Toronto #980/R (C.D 2700)

KELLEY, Mike (1954-) American

$12000	7843	Two frogs-two cats (51x175x18cm-20x69x7in) stuffed animals executed 1990. 4-May-93 Sotheby's, New York #274/R

KELLY, Ellsworth (1923-) American

$24000	16257	Mirrored concorde (131x79x33cm-52x31x13in) s.d.1971 num.1/12 chrome plated steel oak base. 4-May-94 Christie's, New York #235/R
$130000	84967	Black Venus (216x91x6cm-85x36x2in) wall relief painted aluminium executed 1959. 4-May-93 Christie's, New York #14/R

KEMEYS, Edward (1843-1907) American

$2200	1467	Grizzly bear (33cm-13in) i. green brown pat.bronze st.f.Roman Works. 13-Mar-94 Hindman Galleries, Chicago #1016/R
$2200	1467	Wolf (23cm-9in) i. brown pat.bronze st.f.Roman Works. 13-Mar-94 Hindman Galleries, Chicago #1017/R
$2600	1733	Cougar with alligator (33cm-13in) i. brown pat.bronze st.f.Roman Works. 13-Mar-94 Hindman Galleries, Chicago #1018/R
$4750	3167	Wolf at bay (33cm-13in) i.d.1870 dark green pat.bronze. 17-Mar-94 Sotheby's, New York #76/R

KENDRICK, Mel (1949-) American

$1200	805	Untitled (49x21x21cm-19x8x8in) s.d.1983 graphite adhesive wood. 3-May-94 Christie's, East, New York #120/R
$2500	1656	Untitled (32x36x28cm-13x14x11in) s.d.1984 num.5/5 green pat.bronze. 17-Nov-92 Christie's, East, New York #126/R
$2658	1772	Irregular lines (181cm-71in) s.d.1984-86 painted walnut incl.iron pedestal. 2-Jun-94 AB Stockholms Auktionsverk, Stockholm #7201/R (S.KR 21000)
$4200	2819	Birch 4 laminations (193x42x41cm-76x17x16in) s.d.1983 adhesive graphite oil wood steel base. 23-Feb-94 Christie's, New York #103/R
$5000	3356	Poplos, black and green (159x27x25cm-63x11x10in) s.d.83 adhesive oil graphite wood steel base. 4-May-94 Christie's, New York #272/R
$5500	3642	Untitled (68x37x23cm-27x15x9in) s.d.1984 graphite adhesive wood. 19-Nov-92 Christie's, New York #114/R
$6329	4219	Untitled (151cm-59in) cast iron incl.wooden socle executed 1984. 2-Jun-94 AB Stockholms Auktionsverk, Stockholm #7111/R (S.KR 50000)
$6556	4400	Three woods (138x67x74cm-54x26x29in) graphite adhesive wood executed 1986. 25-Mar-93 Christie's, London #195/R
$10000	6623	Untitled (178x30cm-70x12in) s.d.1983 oil resin wood steel base. 19-Nov-92 Christie's, New York #115/R
$15823	10549	Poplar cast graphite (166cm-65in) one of 3, pat bronze executed 1986. 2-Jun-94 AB Stockholms Auktionsverk, Stockholm #7110/R (S.KR 125000)
$21000	14094	Large cast poplar (149x86x71cm-59x34x28in) bronze executed c.1985. 5-May-94 Sotheby's, New York #292/R
$22000	14379	Untitled (185x112x84cm-73x44x33in) num.2/3 bronze executed 1987. 4-May-93 Sotheby's, New York #191/R

KIENHOLZ, Edward (1927-1994) American

$10000	6757	The 6 o'clock News (73x44x23cm-29x17x9in) s.i.d.64 plastic glass resin enamel metal light. 8-Nov-93 Christie's, East, New York #10/R
$40000	26490	The Little Eagle Rock Incident (157x124x51cm-62x49x20in) s. s.i.d.58verso oil trophy head of deer wood. 17-Nov-92 Sotheby's, New York #13/R
$45000	29801	God Tracking Station I (76x136x48cm-30x54x19in) s.d.58 painted wood metal assemblage. 18-Nov-92 Sotheby's, New York #115/R

KIENHOLZ, Edward and Nancy (20th C) American
$2980	2000	Double cross (41x33x33cm-16x13x13in) s.verso steel copper brass oil plastic exec.1987. 3-Dec-93 Sotheby's, London #204/R
$10000	6711	Toten Tanz (114x39x40cm-45x15x16in) s.i.d.89 enamel lacquer steel copper wood fabric. 4-May-94 Christie's, New York #316/R
$35000	22876	Twilight home (216x58x132cm-85x23x52in) wood plastic metal executed 1983. 3-May-93 Sotheby's, New York #55 a/R

KING, William (attrib) (20th C) American
$2000	1361	Standing girl (130cm-51in) brown pat.bronze. 14-Apr-94 Freeman Fine Arts, Philadelphia #932

KONTI, Isidore (1862-1938) Austrian/American
$1600	1067	Kneeling figures, bookends (16cm-6in) s.d.1911 brown pat.bronze. 21-May-94 Weschler, Washington #110/R
$2200	1486	'Youth' and 'Age' (21cm-8in) i.d.1914 green pat.bronze pair. 31-Mar-94 Sotheby's Arcade, New York #85/R
$3200	2119	Allegro - group of two girls and boy (41cm-16in) i. greenish brown pat.bronze f.i.Roman Works NY. 22-Sep-93 Christie's, New York #104/R
$3500	2215	Literature and Drama - Bookends of two Muses (22cm-9in) i. greenish-brown pat.bronze pair. 4-Dec-92 Christie's, New York #100/R
$4000	2797	Two girls and boy (41cm-16in) i. green brown pat.bronze Cast Roman Bronze W.NY. 11-Mar-93 Christie's, New York #173/R

KOONING, Willem de (1904-) American/Dutch
$330000	221477	Cross legged figure (61x46x38cm-24x18x15in) s. num.6/7 bronze exec.1972 Cast Modern Art F. 4-May-94 Sotheby's, New York #43/R

KOONS, Jeff (1955-) American
$18000	11765	Mermaid troll (32x22x22cm-13x9x9in) stainless steel executed 1986. 4-May-93 Sotheby's, New York #257/R
$42000	27815	New shop vac wet dry (71x56x56cm-28x22x22in) ex.1980 vacuum cleaner fluorescent tubes in box. 19-Nov-92 Christie's, New York #151/R
$42000	27451	Basketball (23cm-9in) num.3/3, circular bronze executed 1985. 5-May-93 Christie's, New York #138 a/R
$42000	27815	Soccer ball (20cm-8in) executed 1985 edit.of 3 bronze. 19-Nov-92 Christie's, New York #141/R
$59000	39865	French coach couple (46x36x25cm-18x14x10in) stainless steel executed 1986 3/3. 11-Nov-93 Sotheby's, New York #220/R
$60000	40268	Baccarat crystal set (32x41x41cm-13x16x16in) cast stainless steel executed 1986. 4-May-94 Christie's, New York #289 a/R
$100000	67568	New double Shelton wet dry (109x137x71cm-43x54x28in) two vacuum cleaners fluorescent lights exec.1980. 10-Nov-93 Sotheby's, New York #61/R
$135000	89404	Three ball total equilibrium tank - two Dr.J.Silver Series, Wilson Supershot (154x124x34cm-61x49x13in) executed 1985 glass iron water basketballs. 17-Nov-92 Sotheby's, New York #72/R

KOTKER, David (20th C) American
$1400	946	Grand caisson (163x58x150cm-64x23x59in) bronze lead rifle steel. 31-Oct-93 Hindman Galleries, Chicago #645

KRAJCBERG, Frans (1921-) Brazilian
$6518	4374	Tableau de pierres (40x80cm-16x31in) s.verso pebbles on panel. 23-Mar-93 Cornette de St.Cyr, Paris #143 (F.FR 36000)
$7242	4860	Sans titre (220cm-87in) natural wood executed 1967. 23-Mar-93 Cornette de St.Cyr, Paris #164/R (F.FR 40000)

KUEHNE, Max (1880-c.1968) American
$2500	1678	Coffee table (43x107cm-17x42in) s. carved wood silver leaf. 26-Mar-94 James Bakker, Cambridge #50/R

KUITCA, Guillermo (1961-) Argentinian
$14000	9333	L'Enfance du Christ (114x58x10cm-45x23x4in) s.d.1989 i.verso acrylic fabric matress. 18-May-94 Christie's, New York #258/R

KUNTZ, Roger (1926-1975) American
$2000	1258	Woman in water (14cm-6in) s. brown pat.bronze. 25-Apr-93 Butterfield & Butterfield, San Francisco #2109/R

KWAGULTH, Ellen Neel (20th C) Canadian?
$939	634	Carved and painted pole, Thunderbird and bear (30cm-12in) with copper executed c.1949. 30-Mar-94 Maynards, Vancouver #82 (C.D 1300)

LADD, Anna Coleman (1878-1939) American
$1300	872	The muse (100cm-39in) s. bronze. 6-May-94 Skinner, Bolton #124/R

LALIBERTE, Alfred (1878-1953) Canadian
$2913	1942	Saule pleureur (30cm-12in) s.i. bronze st.f.Andro. 11-May-94 Sotheby's, Toronto #233/R (C.D 4000)
$6189	4126	Jeunes Indiens chassant (38cm-15in) s.i. bronze st.f.Andro. 11-May-94 Sotheby's, Toronto #174/R (C.D 8500)

LAM, Wilfredo (1902-1982) Cuban
$3000	2027	Mayimbe (46x34x6cm-18x13x2in) s.d.77 num.13/50 brown pat.bronze C.Artcurial. 23-Nov-93 Christie's, New York #280/R
$5000	3333	L'Oiseau de Feu, l'Oiseau de Fer 1970 (26cm-10in) s. one num.483/500A one num.483/500B brass pair. 18-May-94 Christie's, New York #178/R
$15000	9934	Osun (99cm-39in) s.d.1977 dark brown pat.bronze. 24-Nov-92 Christie's, New York #122/R

LAURENT, Robert (1890-1970) American
$3750	2534	Female nude (19cm-7in) i. golden pat.bronze. 31-Mar-94 Sotheby's Arcade, New York #468/R

LEEB, M (20th C) American
$2281	1542	Female nude dancers standing on one leg (57x60cm-22x24in) s. brown pat.bronze on marble socle pair. 26-Nov-93 Schloss Ahlden, Ahlden #311/R (DM 3900)

LENTELLI, Leo (1879-1961) American
$1600	1053	Xavier Martinez (47cm-19in) s.d.1916 pat.bronze. 13-Jun-93 Butterfield & Butterfield, San Francisco #834/R

LEVINE, Sherrie (1947-) American
$14000	9150	La Fortune - after Man Ray (84x279x152cm-33x110x60in) felt mahogany wood pool balls 1/6, exec.1990. 5-May-93 Christie's, New York #140/R
$26000	17568	Untitled, the bachelors Larbin (175x51x51cm-69x20x20in) frosted glass and vitrine executed 1989. 10-Nov-93 Christie's, New York #260/R

LEWIS, Edmonia (1843-?) American
$77500	51667	The old Indian arrow maker and his daughter (61cm-24in) i.d.1866 white marble. 17-Mar-94 Sotheby's, New York #28/R

LEWITT, Sol (1928-) American
$2600	1757	Cube construction (28x28x28cm-11x11x11in) st.sig.d.79 num.28/35 aluminium st.f.Gratz. 31-Oct-93 Hindman Galleries, Chicago #641/R
$3000	2013	Pyramid I. Pyramid IV (39cm-15in) s.i.num. cast aluminium painted white two. 23-Feb-94 Christie's, East, New York #320/R
$3200	2119	Pyramid I. Pyramid II (38x99x21cm-15x39x8in) s.i.d.6/12 cast aluminum painted white pair. 17-Nov-92 Christie's, East, New York #122/R
$6394	4152	Pyramid (28x103x57cm-11x41x22in) s.d.1985 wood. 24-Jun-94 Francis Briest, Paris #49/R (F.FR 35000)
$8221	5338	Structure (62x62x62cm-24x24x24in) s. painted wood executed c.1970. 24-Jun-94 Francis Briest, Paris #61/R (F.FR 45000)
$10000	6623	Pyramid number 6 (201x63x121cm-79x25x48in) wood painted white. 19-Nov-92 Christie's, New York #262/R
$12000	7843	Untitled (95x95cm-37x37in) white enamel aluminium executed 1984-85. 4-May-93 Sotheby's, New York #128/R
$13000	9028	Untitled (56x56x56cm-22x22x22in) wood painted white. 24-Feb-93 Christie's, New York #83/R
$14000	9396	Untitled (39x39cm-15x15in) s.d.1978 painted wood. 5-May-94 Sotheby's, New York #246/R
$16000	9412	Serial Project No. 1 - C-1-2-3 (37x107x35cm-15x42x14in) painted wood executed 1966. 6-Oct-92 Sotheby's, New York #112/R
$16595	11605	1,2,3,4,5,4,3,2,1 (33x212x43cm-13x83x17in) wood structure executed 1980. 14-Mar-93 Watine-Arnault, Paris #33/R (F.FR 94000)
$18000	12081	Incomplete cube (105x105x105cm-41x41x41in) aluminium painted white executed 1974. 23-Feb-94 Christie's, New York #74/R
$18000	11765	Untitled (91x91x1cm-36x36x0in) wall sculpture nine parts graphite enamel. 5-May-93 Christie's, New York #117/R
$22000	14379	Modular structure (61x99x62cm-24x39x24in) wood painted white executed 1972. 5-May-93 Christie's, New York #107/R
$22000	14765	Incomplete open cube (105x105x105cm-41x41x41in) aluminum painted white ed.of 122. 4-May-94 Christie's, New York #222/R
$22000	14570	Untitled (48x238x48cm-19x94x19in) executed 1987 wood painted white. 19-Nov-92 Christie's, New York #246/R
$48000	31788	Four part modular cube (320x320x320cm-126x126x126in) executed 1975 baked enamel steel. 19-Nov-92 Christie's, New York #403/R

LIBERMAN, Alexander (1912-) American
$1200	805	Untitled (25x22x17cm-10x9x7in) st. polished aluminium. 3-May-94 Christie's, East, New York #70/R

LICHTENSTEIN, Roy (1923-) American
$3240	2160	Seascape (33x62x9cm-13x24x4in) s. num.91/100 collage in wooden box. 3-Jun-94 Lempertz, Cologne #754/R (DM 5400)
$20000	13072	Brush stroke No.4 (173x76x21cm-68x30x8in) s.i.num.1/10, acrylic epoxy wood. 5-May-93 Christie's, New York #307/R
$20000	13514	Brushstroke no 5 (152x79x34cm-60x31x13in) s.i.num.10/10 epoxy acrylic enamel wood exec.86. 10-Nov-93 Christie's, New York #237/R
$30000	19608	Ceramic sculpture - No.8 (23x23x17cm-9x9x7in) s.d.65 glazed ceramic acrylic. 5-May-93 Christie's, New York #233/R
$30000	17647	Brush stroke (113x163x30cm-44x64x12in) s.verso num.7/10 acrylic epoxy wood. 8-Oct-92 Christie's, New York #146/R

LINDER, Henry (1854-1910) American
$2400	1589	Andiron with bust of child (63cm-25in) green brown pat.bronze st.f.Roman pair. 28-Jun-93 Christie's, East, New York #18/R

LIPSKI, Donald (20th C) American?
$3500   2431   Building steam no 249 (69x18x5cm-27x7x2in) executed 1984 bronze ladle paraffin baseball. 23-Feb-93 Sotheby's, New York #373/R

LIPTON, Seymour (20th C) American
$18000   12162   Untitled (190x66x41cm-75x26x16in) monel metal executed c.1957. 11-Nov-93 Sotheby's, New York #287/R

LIV, Lena (20th C) American
$12500   8170   Kinder des Genua, Genovese children (159x230x27cm-63x91x11in) s.verso mixed media in steel structure. 5-Oct-93 Sotheby's, New York #60/R

LOBE, Robert (20th C) American
$3250   2181   Ecstasy of St Teresa (151x71x99cm-59x28x39in) s.i.d.1981 hammered anodized aluminum. 5-May-94 Sotheby's, New York #359/R

LONGMAN, Evelyn Beatrice (1874-?) American
$1565   1050   Victory, athletic young man holding laurel wreath standing on sphere (74cm-29in) s.d.1908 bronze on slate base Cast Rom.Bronze W. 6-Dec-93 Sotheby's, London #258/R

LONGO, Robert (1953-) American
$2500   1736   Camouflage in heaven (48x117x16cm-19x46x6in) mixed media. 23-Feb-93 Sotheby's, New York #335/R
$2600   1745   Songs of silent running (75x28x9cm-30x11x4in) s.d.81 num.4 cast aluminium bonding. 23-Feb-94 Christie's, East, New York #248/R
$3800   2550   Untitled (96x121x16cm-38x48x6in) mono.verso lacquer on cast aluminum bonding. 4-May-94 Christie's, New York #283/R
$5500   3716   Wall reliefs Songs of Silent Running (66x29x10cm-26x11x4in) s.d.81verso one num.6 one num.7 aluminium two. 8-Nov-93 Christie's, East, New York #135/R
$12000   8054   Untitled - figures from Lenny (172x137x41cm-68x54x16in) bronze steel executed 1986 3/3. 23-Feb-94 Christie's, New York #128/R
$12000   8108   Songs of silent running s.d.81 num.1,2,3verso cast aluminium three. 10-Nov-93 Christie's, New York #278/R
$37000   24183   Strong in love (183x213x18cm-72x84x7in) oil canvas two parts bronze relief. 4-May-93 Sotheby's, New York #253/R

LOVET-LORSKI, Boris (1891-?) Russian/American
$12000   8054   Female torso (47cm-19in) s. marble. 3-Dec-93 Christie's, New York #29/R
$78000   50000   'Polymnia' - torso (60cm-24in) s. black marble. 26-May-93 Christie's, New York #178/R
$135000 90000   Man and woman (43x53cm-17x21in) i. black marble executed c.1928. 25-May-94 Sotheby's, New York #130/R

LUCCHESI, Bruno (1926-) American
$2000   1156   Coffee (33cm-13in) terracotta painted. 25-Sep-92 Sotheby's Arcade, New York #506/R
$2300   1513   Woman reading newspaper (34cm-13in) i. dark brown pat.bronze executed 1964. 31-Mar-93 Sotheby's Arcade, New York #422/R
$2800   1842   Standing woman (71cm-28in) i. dark brown pat.bronze f.st.Luigi Tommasi. 31-Mar-93 Sotheby's Arcade, New York #420/R
$5000   2890   Musing (26cm-10in) i. dark brown pat.bronze. 25-Sep-92 Sotheby's Arcade, New York #507/R

LUE, Donald de (1897-?) American
$5500   3526   Man and horse (51cm-20in) s.d.1960 num.6/12 green pat.bronze. 28-May-93 Sloan, North Bethesda #2580/R

LUNDEEN, George W (1948-) American
$9500   6333   Promise of the Prairie (84cm-33in) i.num.3/21 copper brown pat.bronze. 22-May-94 Hindman Galleries, Chicago #44/R

MACDONALD, Chris (1957-) American
$1000   671   Work truck variation (309x93x183cm-122x37x72in) wood bolts executed 1989. 3-May-94 Christie's, East, New York #210/R
$1000   662   Untitled (38x66x34cm-15x26x13in) wood steel bolts. 17-Nov-92 Christie's, East, New York #25/R

MACLEOD, Yan (20th C) American
$1800   1224   Three geese in flight (147x104cm-58x41in) cast lead. 17-Apr-94 Hindman Galleries, Chicago #982

MACMONNIES, Frederick William (1863-1937) American
$2700   1824   Bacchante (42cm-17in) i.d.1893 green pat.bronze f.i.H.Rouard. 31-Mar-94 Sotheby's Arcade, New York #171/R
$2800   1879   Bacchante and infant faun (41cm-16in) s.d.1890 num.RB5 brown pat.bronze. 12-Jan-94 Doyle, New York #56
$3000   2013   'The Pioneer Mother' - study for the Pioneer Monument (29x39cm-11x15in) plaster. 3-Dec-93 Christie's, New York #78/R
$3500   2333   Pan of Rohallion (38cm-15in) i.d.MDCCCLXL brown pat.bronze. 16-Mar-94 Christie's, New York #53/R

MACMONNIES, Frederick William (1863-1937) American-cont.

$4250	2796	Bacchante and infant faun (85cm-33in) st.sig.d.1894 pat.bronze st.f.Gruet exec.c.1900. 31-Mar-93 Butterfield & Butterfield, Los Angeles #5489/R
$7500	4747	Pan of Rohallion (77cm-30in) i.d.1890 green-brown pat.bronze f.Jabouef Rouard. 4-Dec-92 Christie's, New York #173/R
$8500	4913	Bacchante with infant faun (88cm-35in) s.d.1894 medium brown pat.bronze f.st.Gruet. 24-Sep-92 Sotheby's, New York #101/R
$12000	7947	Bacchante and infant faun (85cm-33in) i.d.1894 brown pat.bronze f.st.Jabouef-Rouard. 23-Sep-93 Sotheby's, New York #140/R
$13000	8667	Pan of Rohallion (76cm-30in) i. greenish-brown pat.bronze. 17-Mar-94 Sotheby's, New York #89/R
$16000	10256	Nathan Hale (86cm-34in) i.d.1890 green pat.bronze f.st.Jaboeuf-Rouard. 27-May-93 Sotheby's, New York #216/R
$40000	25641	Venus and Adonis (71cm-28in) i.d.1895 reddish brown pat.bronze f.st. 26-May-93 Christie's, New York #169/R
$60000	38462	Boy and duck - fountain group (117cm-46in) bronze marble. 26-May-93 Christie's, New York #167/R
$90000	60000	Portrait of girl with goat (173cm-68in) s.d.1912 white marble. 26-May-94 Christie's, New York #35/R

MACNEIL, Hermon Atkins (1866-1947) American

$2300	1474	Early toil (28cm-11in) s.i. brown pat.bronze. 28-Apr-93 Doyle, New York #73/R
$4250	2972	Manuelito (39cm-15in) i.d.1901 black pat.bronze Cast Roman Bronze Work. 10-Mar-93 Sotheby's, New York #66/R
$4250	2891	Primitive chant to the great spirit - figure of American Indian (64cm-25in) with sig.i.num.4 black pat.bronze f.st. 17-Apr-94 Hanzel Galleries, Chicago #137
$26000	17333	The sun vow (86cm-34in) s.i. dark brown pat.bronze. 22-May-94 Hindman Galleries, Chicago #17/R
$27000	18000	The returning of the snakes, the Moqui prayer for rain (57cm-22in) s.i. brown pat.bronze Cast Fond.Nelli Roma. 25-May-94 Sotheby's, New York #40/R
$45000	30000	Chief of the Multnomah Tribe (94cm-37in) i. dark brown pat.bronze. 22-May-94 Hindman Galleries, Chicago #19/R

MAN-RAY (1890-1976) American

$3542	2377	Main et fruits (24x28x24cm-9x11x9in) mono.num. exec.1971 bronze. 25-Mar-93 Finarte, Rome #45/R (I.L 5700000)
$3884	2716	L'hotel meuble de 1921-1969 (20x29cm-8x11in) painted bronze one of 9. 10-Mar-93 Watine-Arnault, Paris #71/R (F.FR 22000)
$4157	2828	Hand in fruit (25x31cm-10x12in) init.num.5/8 brown pat.bronze. 13-Apr-94 Bukowskis, Stockholm #433/R (S.KR 33000)
$5500	3819	Proverbe (32cm-13in) s.num.1/9 exec.1944 silver on wooden base. 22-Feb-93 Christie's, East, New York #109/R
$6656	4379	Autoritratto (29x15x8cm-11x6x3in) mono.num.6/8 exec.1971 bronze. 6-Apr-93 Finarte, Milan #102/R (I.L 10500000)
$7450	5000	Domesticated egg (9x21cm-4x8in) mono.num.8/9 iron wood executed 1973. 1-Dec-93 Sotheby's, London #245/R
$7500	5000	Domesticated egg (32cm-13in) init.num.6/9 wood with painted metal rod. 11-May-94 Christie's, New York #238/R
$12640	8000	It's springtime (31cm-12in) s.i.d.1961-71 num.6/10 bedsprings wood base. 1-Dec-92 Christie's, London #202/R
$15500	10333	Idole du pecheur (41cm-16in) s.i. black pat.bronze. 11-May-94 Christie's, New York #237/R
$18000	12162	New York (25cm-10in) init.i.num.d.1920-1973 41 steel balls in bottle. 3-Nov-93 Christie's, New York #356/R
$18500	12092	Chess set (47x81x54cm-19x32x21in) s.num.13/50 lucite table chess set 1962. 5-Oct-93 Sotheby's, New York #125/R
$21000	12353	Torse tournant (54cm-21in) s.num.9/9 brown pat.bronze. 8-Oct-92 Christie's, New York #64/R
$22000	14865	Featherweight I, poids plume I (22x13x24cm-9x5x9in) s.i.d.1965 num.8/10 painted lead feathers. 3-Nov-93 Christie's, New York #355/R
$24000	16216	Main Ray (20cm-8in) s.i.d.1935-1971 painted bronze plexiglass. 3-Nov-93 Christie's, New York #352/R
$25000	17361	Le torse tournant (56cm-22in) s.num.6/9 exec.1970 brown pat.bronze. 23-Feb-93 Sotheby's, New York #77/R

MANSHIP, Paul Howard (1885-1966) American

$1900	1098	Winston Churchill (18cm-7in) i. green black pat.bronze. 25-Sep-92 Sotheby's Arcade, New York #508/R
$5000	3333	Pegasus (19cm-7in) greenish-brown pat.bronze marble base. 17-Mar-94 Sotheby's, New York #117/R
$6500	4333	The Wrestlers (23x41cm-9x16in) s.d.1915 1 of 8 pat.bronze Cast.Michelucci 1967. 26-May-94 Sotheby's, New York #100/R
$6500	4333	Shoebill Stork (36cm-14in) i.d.1932 gilt-bronze lapis lazuli base. 17-Mar-94 Sotheby's, New York #86/R
$12000	8000	Alfred E Smith memorial flagpole base (23cm-9in) i. ed.of five brown pat.bronze with verdigris. 25-May-94 Sotheby's, New York #32/R
$14000	9333	Venus Anadyomene (20cm-8in) i.d.1924 num.9 brown pat.bronze f.st. 17-Mar-94 Sotheby's, New York #116/R
$15000	9494	Satyr and sleeping nymph (24cm-9in) s.d.1912 foundry Roman Bronze Wks bronze. 3-Dec-92 Sotheby's, New York #175/R
$33000	20886	Figure of fawn (41cm-16in) st. brown pat.bronze black lacquer granite base. 4-Dec-92 Christie's, New York #117/R
$40000	25641	Adam. Eve (45cm-18in) i. greenish brown pat.bronze 1924 f.i. pair. 26-May-93 Christie's, New York #175/R

MANSHIP, Paul Howard (1885-1966) American-cont.
$48000	32000	Flight of night - female figure (36cm-14in) i.d.1916 brown pat.bronze Roman Bronze Works NY. 26-May-94 Christie's, New York #109/R
$50000	33333	Europa and the Bull (23cm-9in) i.d.1924 brown pat.bronze marble base. 17-Mar-94 Sotheby's, New York #85/R
$70000	46358	Briseis, a female nude (112cm-44in) st.sig.d.c.1916 brown pat.bronze st.f.Roman Br. 15-Jun-94 Butterfield & Butterfield, San Francisco #4479/R
$75000	50336	'Flight of Night' - figure (69cm-27in) i. dark greenish black pat.bronze f.i. 3-Dec-93 Christie's, New York #27/R
$220000	146667	Indian and Pronghorn antelope (30cm-12in) i.d.1914 greenish brown pat.bronze f.i.pair. 17-Mar-94 Sotheby's, New York #84/R

MARCA-RELLI, Conrad (1913-) American
$5000	3311	XL-6-64 (114x142x2cm-45x56x1in) s.i.d.64 acrylic aluminum. 17-Nov-92 Christie's, East, New York #259/R

MARISOL (1930-) American/Venezulean
$10000	6667	Figuras (56cm-22in) black pat.bronze executed c.1965. 18-May-94 Sotheby's, New York #325/R
$45000	29412	Portrait of Georgia O'Keefe with antelope (140x140x108cm-55x55x43in) chl wood stone plaster antelope executed 1980. 3-May-93 Christie's, New York #55/R
$60000	40541	Person with poodle (118x60x46cm-46x24x18in) painted wood glass executed 1962. 11-Nov-93 Sotheby's, New York #356/R

MARTIN, Eddie Owens (1908-1986) American
$1400	927	Mythological Head (36cm-14in) hand molded carved concrete. 21-Nov-92 Litchfield Auction Gallery #26

MATTA (1911-) Chilean
$3825	2500	Hiroscemia (210x72x21cm-83x28x8in) st.mono. 1 of 4 aluminium executed 1969. 30-Jun-94 Sotheby's, London #235/R
$4590	3000	Minotando (178x145x25cm-70x57x10in) st.mono.1 of 4 aluminium executed 1969. 30-Jun-94 Sotheby's, London #157/R
$26000	17568	Pareja (70x67x25cm-28x26x10in) s.num.1/6 brown pat.bronze exec.1959 C.Susse F. 23-Nov-93 Christie's, New York #162/R

MATTO, Francisco (1911-) Uruguayan
$5200	2613	Tres Formas (61x87cm-24x34in) s.d.58 wood construction oil. 31-Aug-92 Gomensoro, Montevideo #51/R
$10000	6757	Constructivo (83x48cm-33x19in) s.verso painted wood construction exec.c.1960. 22-Nov-93 Sotheby's, New York #218/R

MAYER, Louis (1869-?) American
$9000	6383	Abraham Lincoln (64cm-25in) bronze. 12-Feb-93 Du Mouchelle, Detroit #65/R

McCARTAN, Edward (1879-1953) American
$8200	5430	Fountain figure of nymph with shell (72cm-28in) i. green brown pat.bronze st.f.Roman. 28-Jun-93 Christie's, East, New York #19/R

McCRACKEN, John (1934-) American
$2500	1656	Untitled (18x18x19cm-7x7x7in) s.d.68 fiberglass. 17-Nov-92 Christie's, East, New York #246/R
$4000	2703	Untitled faceted sculpture (29x37x23cm-11x15x9in) s.d.79 polished fibreglass. 8-Nov-93 Christie's, East, New York #193/R
$8000	5405	Untitled (304x56x6cm-120x22x2in) s.d.10-29-73 polished fiberglass. 10-Nov-93 Christie's, New York #189/R
$10000	6711	Minnesota (244x69x43cm-96x27x17in) s.i.d.1989 fiberglass. 4-May-94 Christie's, New York #313/R
$12000	7843	Untitled (230x39x5cm-91x15x2in) fibreglass wood executed 1979. 4-May-93 Sotheby's, New York #147/R

McELCHERAN, William (1927-) Canadian
$2518	1702	Single business man (39x14cm-15x6in) init.d.87 num.2/3 bronze. 3-Nov-93 Sotheby's, Toronto #258 a (C.D 3250)
$2731	1820	Taxi (38cm-15in) init.num.3/6 bronze marble base. 11-May-94 Sotheby's, Toronto #171/R (C.D 3750)
$5097	3398	Passing by (38cm-15in) init.i.d.88 num.6/9 bronze. 11-May-94 Sotheby's, Toronto #172/R (C.D 7000)
$6199	4188	Businessmen (53x48cm-21x19in) bronze probable Edition of six executed 1973. 3-Nov-93 Sotheby's, Toronto #365/R (C.D 8000)
$7282	4854	Smiling businessman (71cm-28in) init.i.d.91 num.3/9 bronze. 11-May-94 Sotheby's, Toronto #173/R (C.D 10000)

McKENZIE, Carl (1905-) American
$1700	1149	Noahs Ark (64x15x51cm-25x6x20in) s.d.1987 wood. 4-Nov-93 Boos Gallery, Michigan #85/R

McKENZIE, Robert Tait (1867-1938) American
$1360	800	Call (24cm-9in) s.i. mid light brown pat.bronze f.st. 9-Oct-92 Sotheby's, London #185/R
$2000	1307	The call (23x13cm-9x5in) s.i.d.1914 bronze Cast Roman Bronze Works. 17-Sep-93 Du Mouchelle, Detroit #2151/R
$3800	2657	Sprinter (11cm-4in) i. red brown pat.bronze Cast QHCJ Gorham Co. 11-Mar-93 Christie's, New York #104/R

McKENZIE, Robert Tait (1867-1938) American-cont.
$8000	5594	Athlete (43cm-17in) i.d.1903 red brown pat.bronze st.QHJG Gorham Co. 11-Mar-93 Christie's, New York #106/R
$10000	6993	Javelin cast (56x43cm-22x17in) s.d.1923 bronze. 12-Mar-93 Dargate Auction Galleries, Pittsburgh #1039/R

MEAD, Larkin Goldsmith (1835-1910) American
$1300	878	Portrait bust of girl (49x44cm-19x17in) s. marble. 26-Oct-93 Christie's, East, New York #34/R
$12000	8054	Figure of 'Echo' (102cm-40in) s. marble. 14-Jan-94 Du Mouchelle, Detroit #1999/R

MEADMORE, Clement (1929-) American?
$1800	1208	Untitle (28x20x10cm-11x8x4in) s.d.1977 num.8/10 brown pat.bronze f.st.Singer. 23-Feb-94 Christie's, East, New York #352/R
$2600	1745	U Turn (38x72x56cm-15x28x22in) enamel corten steel. 3-May-94 Christie's, East, New York #71/R
$7000	4861	Untitled (86x122x112cm-34x48x44in) painted steel. 22-Feb-93 Christie's, East, New York #176/R

MELLON, Eleanor Mary (1894-1980) American
$1000	658	Guardian angel figure (56cm-22in) shellacked plaster. 13-Jun-93 Butterfield & Butterfield, San Francisco #3185/R

MESTROVIC, Ivan (1883-1962) American/Yugoslavian
$1500	962	Suffer the little children to come unto me (150cm-59in) plaster painted to simulate bronze. 13-Dec-92 Hindman Galleries, Chicago #233/R

MEXICAN SCHOOL
$8000	5405	Figure of San Juan Bautista (79cm-31in) painted wood. 22-Nov-93 Sotheby's, New York #79/R

MEXICAN SCHOOL, 18th C
$8000	5298	Figure of an angel (100cm-39in) painted wood. 23-Nov-92 Sotheby's, New York #80/R
$8000	5333	Figure of an Angel (129cm-51in) gilt painted wood. 18-May-94 Sotheby's, New York #101/R
$9000	5960	Christ enthroned (78cm-31in) gilt painted wood. 23-Nov-92 Sotheby's, New York #83/R
$17000	11333	Figure of an Angel (84cm-33in) gilt painted wood. 18-May-94 Sotheby's, New York #102/R
$24000	16216	Figure of San Rafael (113cm-44in) gilt painted wood. 22-Nov-93 Sotheby's, New York #78/R
$25000	16892	Figure of Inmaculada concepcion (54cm-21in) gilt painted wood. 22-Nov-93 Sotheby's, New York #77/R
$31000	20530	Figure of an angel (100cm-39in) painted wood. 23-Nov-92 Sotheby's, New York #81/R
$34000	22517	Figure of an angel (100cm-39in) painted wood. 23-Nov-92 Sotheby's, New York #82/R

MEYER, Frederick (1872-1960) American
$1600	1081	Tom Mix (109cm-43in) i. painted terracotta. 31-Mar-94 Sotheby's Arcade, New York #199/R

MEYLAN, Pedro (1890-1954) Argentinian
$2264	1509	Bust of the artist H C Forestier (47cm-19in) s.i.f.Pastori bronze. 3-Jun-94 Auktionhaus Zofingen, Zofingen #1907/R (S.FR 3200)
$11308	7589	Portrait bust of Ferdinand Hodler (33x19x26cm-13x7x10in) s.d.17 brown pat.bronze on marble socle. 23-Jun-93 Galerie Kornfeld, Berne #583/R (S.FR 17000)

MILLER, Carol (1933-) American/Mexican
$1935	1299	Jinete (95x35cm-37x14in) s.d.1979 bronze. 1-Dec-93 Louis Morton, Mexico #143/R (M.P 6000)
$4000	2614	Cocai, la luciernaga (75cm-30in) s. green pat.bronze executed 1992 2/10. 17-May-93 Christie's, New York #179/R
$4000	2703	Atanua, Goddess of Dawn (37x106x58cm-15x42x23in) s.num.4/10 green grey pat.bronze executed 1982. 23-Nov-93 Christie's, New York #226/R
$4200	2781	Diana Mother Earth (68cm-27in) s. green pat.bronze executed 1988. 24-Nov-92 Christie's, New York #165/R
$6000	4000	Saraband (62cm-24in) s. green pat.bronze executed 1987. 18-May-94 Christie's, New York #243/R

MILLES, Carl (1875-1955) American
$885	598	Small head of Europa (13cm-5in) s. pat bronze. 26-Apr-94 Goteborg Auktionsverk #303 (S.KR 7000)
$1011	683	Small head of Europa (13cm-5in) s. pat bronze. 26-Apr-94 Goteborg Auktionsverk #302 (S.KR 8000)
$1269	803	Head of girl (14x10x13cm-6x4x5in) i. gold-black pat.bronze on wooden socle. 30-Nov-92 Wolfgang Ketterer, Munich #842/R (DM 2000)
$1302	880	Small head of Europa (13cm-5in) s. pat bronze. 26-Apr-94 Goteborg Auktionsverk #301 (S.KR 10300)
$1737	1182	Europa and the bull (78x66cm-31x26in) pat plaster. 20-Nov-93 Soderkopings #327/R (S.KR 14500)
$1844	1167	The kiss (11cm-4in) s. dark pat bronze Cast. H Bergman. 1-Dec-92 AB Stockholms Auktionsverk, Stockholm #6043 (S.KR 12500)
$1873	1224	Girl with cat (21cm-8in) s. pat bronze. 11-May-93 Goteborg Auktionsverk #199/R (S.KR 13800)
$2337	1547	Girl with apple (33cm-13in) brown pat bronze. 25-Nov-92 Bukowskis, Stockholm #188/R (S.KR 16000)

MILLES, Carl (1875-1955) American-cont.

Price	Lot	Description
$2381	1609	Small head of Europa (13cm-5in) s. pat bronze. 23-Nov-93 Goteborg Auktionsverk #302 (S.KR 20000)
$2951	1867	Small head of Europa (24cm-9in) s. green pat bronze Cast.Rasmussen. 30-Nov-92 Rasmussen, Stockholm #143/R (S.KR 20000)
$2964	1976	Folke Filbyter (36cm-14in) s. green pat bronze Cast. G Pettersson. 25-May-94 Bukowskis, Stockholm #264/R (S.KR 23000)
$3000	2013	Head of boy - study for Faith Fountain (20cm-8in) s.d.1947 num.4 bronze f.st.Herman Bergman. 25-Mar-93 Boos Gallery, Michigan #34/R
$3000	2000	Europa and the Bull (79x61cm-31x24in) gilt plaster. 11-Jun-94 Christie's, New York #93/R
$3250	1879	The sun singer (33cm-13in) i. bronze st.f.Rasmussen Kobenhavn. 25-Sep-92 Sotheby's Arcade, New York #177/R
$3279	2143	Small head of Europa (23cm-9in) s. green pat bronze incl.marble base f.Rasmussen. 17-May-93 Bukowskis, Stockholm #182/R (S.KR 24000)
$3359	2224	Eagle on globe (34cm-13in) s. Cast.E.Pettersson pat bronze. 25-Nov-92 Bukowskis, Stockholm #187/R (S.KR 23000)
$3393	2148	Dutch girl - the water carrier (22cm-9in) s.i. dark pat bronze Cast. H Berman. 1-Dec-92 AB Stockholms Auktionsverk, Stockholm #6042 (S.KR 23000)
$3500	2273	Struggle for life (20cm-8in) s.i. greenish brown pat.bronze. 9-Sep-93 Sotheby's Arcade, New York #167/R
$3562	2390	Dutch girl (25cm-10in) s. green pat bronze Cast AG Bronze. 29-Nov-93 AB Stockholms Auktionsverk, Stockholm #5636/R (S.KR 30000)
$3600	2416	Figure of charging boar (25x23cm-10x9in) sig. pat.bronze. 5-Feb-94 Skinner, Bolton #337/R
$3680	2470	Nude girl on wine carafe (28cm-11in) s.d.97 brown pat bronze Cast Sthlms. 29-Nov-93 AB Stockholms Auktionsverk, Stockholm #5637/R (S.KR 31000)
$4000	2667	Family against the wind (39cm-15in) s. brown pat.bronze executed c.1901. 26-May-94 Sotheby's, New York #121/R
$4089	2708	Elk (39cm-15in) init. pat bronze. 25-Nov-92 Bukowskis, Stockholm #186/R (S.KR 28000)
$4131	2614	Dutch girl (25cm-10in) s. green pat bronze Cast.A G Paris. 1-Dec-92 AB Stockholms Auktionsverk, Stockholm #6041/R (S.KR 28000)
$4381	2921	Beggar woman (30cm-12in) s. green pat bronze. 24-May-94 Norden, Stockholm #214/R (S.KR 34000)
$4430	2954	Wild boar (25cm-10in) st.sig. green pat bronze Cast. L Rasmussen. 31-May-94 AB Stockholms Auktionsverk, Stockholm #5633/R (S.KR 35000)
$4430	2954	The milk maid (22cm-9in) s.i. brown pat bronze Cast.Herman Bergman. 4-Jun-94 AB Stockholms Auktionsverk (Lilla Kvaliten) #4570/R (S.KR 35000)
$4500	3000	At the cafe (33cm-13in) s. brown pat.bronze st.f.DBB. 26-May-94 Sotheby's, New York #123/R
$4500	3000	Women dancing the Tarantella (30cm-12in) s. black pat.bronze executed 1901-2. 26-May-94 Sotheby's, New York #122/R
$5000	2890	Study for Jonah fountain (38cm-15in) s. green pat.bronze st. 24-Sep-92 Sotheby's, New York #233/R
$5000	3333	Hunting dogs chasing (22x49cm-9x19in) s. green pat.bronze st.f.Rasmussen exec.1929. 26-May-94 Sotheby's, New York #120/R
$5100	3000	Struggle for existence (19cm-7in) s. light brown golden pat.bronze. 9-Oct-92 Sotheby's, London #218/R
$5224	3506	Bison oxen (36cm-14in) s. dark pat bronze Cast Bergman. 29-Nov-93 AB Stockholms Auktionsverk, Stockholm #5636/R (S.KR 44000)
$5294	3553	Elk (40cm-16in) s. dark pat bronze Cast.Rasmussen. 23-Mar-94 Norden, Stockholm #241/R (S.KR 42000)
$5500	3691	Figures of lion and orb (23cm-9in) sig. gilt bronze pair. 5-Feb-94 Skinner, Bolton #338/R
$5901	3735	The struggle for life (19cm-7in) s. green brown pat bronze Cast.Andro. 1-Dec-92 AB Stockholms Auktionsverk, Stockholm #6040/R (S.KR 40000)
$6053	3982	Elk (39x27cm-15x11in) init. green pat. bronze. 3-Nov-92 Bukowskis, Stockholm #315/R (S.KR 36000)
$6460	3800	Returning form well (25cm-10in) s. mid brown pat.bronze. 9-Oct-92 Sotheby's, London #186/R
$7000	4575	Ganymede (56cm-22in) s. bronze. 18-May-93 Butterfield & Butterfield, San Francisco #1536/R
$11802	7470	Glistening sun (62x69cm-24x27in) gold pat bronze. 1-Dec-92 AB Stockholms Auktionsverk, Stockholm #6038/R (S.KR 80000)
$15000	10067	Tribute to Genius (43cm-17in) s. bronze f.st.Herman Bergman Foundry. 25-Mar-93 Boos Gallery, Michigan #38/R
$16028	10757	The dancer (38cm-15in) s. bronze Cast.H.Bergman. 1-Dec-93 Norden, Stockholm #229/R (S.KR 135000)
$16028	10757	Folke Filbyter - man on horseback (104cm-41in) s.d.1951 num.1 bronze incl.marble base F.Bergman. 1-Dec-93 Norden, Stockholm #220/R (S.KR 135000)
$22635	14990	Man and Pegasus (64x70cm-25x28in) s. Cast.G.Pettersson green pat bronze. 25-Nov-92 Bukowskis, Stockholm #184/R (S.KR 155000)
$33505	22337	People and Pegasus (231cm-91in) s. dark pat bronze incl.wood socle Cast.Bergman. 25-May-94 Bukowskis, Stockholm #263/R (S.KR 260000)
$47500	31667	The sisters (84cm-33in) s. green pat.bronze st.f.Rasmussen. 26-May-94 Sotheby's, New York #124/R

MILLES, Carl (after) (1875-1955) American

Price	Lot	Description
$4868	3267	'Solsangaren' - sun singer (53cm-21in) s.num.1/2, green pat bronze black wooden base. 29-Nov-93 AB Stockholms Auktionsverk, Stockholm #5641/R (S.KR 41000)

MONTUFAR, Valdimir (1956-) Latin American

Price	Lot	Description
$6500	4333	Colonne II (152cm-60in) black pat.bronze wire executed 1992. 18-May-94 Sotheby's, New York #424/R

MOORMAN, Charlotte (1933-1991) American
$7152   4800   2 bomb cello - performance for John Cage Piece 26'1.1499 for string player (121cm-48in) painted metal executed c.1965 two. 24-Jun-93 Sotheby's, London #76/R

MORALES, Dario (1944-1988) Colombian
$26000   17333   Woman in rocking chair No.2 (28x29x42cm-11x11x17in) s.d.87 num.8/8 gold brown pat.bronze. 18-May-94 Christie's, New York #149/R
$28000   18919   Woman on matress (17x68x62cm-7x27x24in) s.d.80 num.3/6 green brown pat.bronze C.Susse F. 23-Nov-93 Christie's, New York #115/R
$30000   20270   Mujer desvistiendose (56cm-22in) s.d.82 num.II/III brown pat.bronze f.st.Paris. 22-Nov-93 Sotheby's, New York #256/R
$38000   25676   The bed (43x92x74cm-17x36x29in) s.d.86 num.3/8 brown pat.bronze. 23-Nov-93 Christie's, New York #31/R
$45000   29801   Entrando a la Tina de bano (44x50x57cm-17x20x22in) s.d.82 num.2/6 golden brown pat.bronze. 24-Nov-92 Christie's, New York #62/R
$48000   31373   El artista y su modelo (102x80x64cm-40x31x25in) s.d.82 num.3/6 golden pat.bronze f.st.Susse. 17-May-93 Christie's, New York #42/R

MORRIS, Robert (1931-) American
$9685   6500   Plus and minus box (29x54x15cm-11x21x6in) wood box string rubber brass hinges pulls. 2-Dec-93 Christie's, London #29/R
$11000   7285   Dresden, Feb.14, 1945 (210x253x9cm-83x100x4in) st.i.d. col.chk paper on canvas metal frame. 19-Nov-92 Christie's, New York #435/R

MURRAY, Elizabeth (1940-) American
$60000   40541   My Manhattan (211x272x41cm-83x107x16in) s.d.1987 verso oil shaped canvas. 9-Nov-93 Christie's, New York #56/R

NADELMAN, Elie (1885-1946) American
$6500   3757   Standing female nude (38cm-15in) plaster. 25-Sep-92 Sotheby's Arcade, New York #373/R
$10000   6667   Female nude (37cm-15in) white marble marble base. 26-May-94 Christie's, New York #116/R
$18000   11921   Wounded bull. Standing bull (22cm-9in) black-brown pat.bronze cast c.1915 2 of 6. 23-Sep-93 Sotheby's, New York #257/R
$26000   17219   Man's head in top hat (70cm-28in) galvano-plastique brown pat.bronze exec.c.1924. 23-Sep-93 Sotheby's, New York #258/R
$27000   18121   Classical head (41cm-16in) marble executed c.1910. 2-Dec-93 Sotheby's, New York #134/R
$30000   20000   Head of woman (29cm-11in) i. white marble. 25-May-94 Sotheby's, New York #127/R
$38000   25333   Classical female head (41cm-16in) i. brown pat.bronze C.Bingen and Costenoble F. 16-Mar-94 Christie's, New York #67/R
$100000 67114   The hostess (77cm-30in) ed.of 2 brown pat.bronze polychrome eyes. 2-Dec-93 Sotheby's, New York #145/R

NADELMAN, Elie (after) (1885-1946) American
$22000   14966   Tango (86cm-34in) init.num.2/3 brown pat.bronze executed c.1918. 17-Nov-93 Doyle, New York #63/R

NAUMAN, Bruce (1941-) American
$17000   11111   Abstracting the shoe tar wood shoe sold with video tape. 5-May-93 Christie's, New York #116/R
$22500   13235   Double poke in eye II (61x91x28cm-24x36x11in) neon construction executed 1985. 6-Oct-92 Sotheby's, New York #151/R
$24000   16107   Double poke in the eye II (61x91x28cm-24x36x11in) aluminium box neon light executed 1985. 23-Feb-94 Christie's, New York #92/R
$26000   17568   Double poke in the eye II (61x91x28cm-24x36x11in) s.num.5b aluminum box neon light executed 1985. 10-Nov-93 Christie's, New York #222/R
$60000   39735   Malice (18x74x8cm-7x29x3in) green red neon clear glass tubing suspension. 18-Nov-92 Sotheby's, New York #235/R
$80000   52288   Trench, shaft, pit, tunnel and chamber (183x427x244cm-72x168x96in) corten steel two parts executed 1979 2/3. 4-May-93 Sotheby's, New York #158/R
$92380   62000   Eating buggers (61x91x23cm-24x36x9in) neon tubes on white metal box executed 1985. 2-Dec-93 Sotheby's, London #50/R
$130000 84967   Second poem piece (152x152x2cm-60x60x1in) steel plate executed 1969. 4-May-93 Christie's, New York #17/R
$220000 147651 Model for trench and four buried passages (165x914cm-65x360in) plaster fiberglass wire executed 1977. 3-May-94 Christie's, New York #25/R
$420000 274510 South America circle (427cm-168in) s.num.F-36777 steel cast iron executed 1981. 4-May-93 Christie's, New York #35/R
$1750000 1158940 One hundred Live and Die (300x336x53cm-118x132x21in) neon tubing suspension frame mounted on 4 panels. 17-Nov-92 Sotheby's, New York #67/R

NEGRET, Edgar (1920-) Colombian
$2250   1510   Laberinto (25x23x23cm-10x9x9in) num.16/60 executed 1986. 7-Jan-94 Gary Nader, Miami #58/R
$3000   2013   Laberinto (25x23x23cm-10x9x9in) num.6/60 executed 1986. 7-Jan-94 Gary Nader, Miami #59/R
$4000   2614   Untitled (19cm-7in) s. st. silver. 17-May-93 Christie's, New York #246/R

NERI, Manuel (1930-) American

$20000	12658	Untitled - figure 1975 (170cm-67in) cast plaster. 25-Oct-92 Butterfield & Butterfield, San Francisco #2326/R
$20000	13514	Woman emerging (198x142cm-78x56in) plaster wood steel styroform. 21-Oct-93 Butterfield & Butterfield, San Francisco #2786/R
$25000	16892	Rossa (171cm-67in) s.d.1982 num.3/4 enamel paint bronze. 21-Oct-93 Butterfield & Butterfield, San Francisco #2796/R
$27500	17405	Untitled - figure, 1991 (163cm-64in) white pat.bronze. 25-Oct-92 Butterfield & Butterfield, San Francisco #2338/R

NEVELSON, Louise (1899-1988) American

$1700	1181	Figure (43cm-17in) i.indist.d. black stone. 26-Feb-93 Sotheby's Arcade, New York #268/R
$2250	1490	Diminishing reflection XIX (36x25x11cm-14x10x4in) painted wood mirrors plexiglass construction. 30-Jun-93 Sotheby's Arcade, New York #308/R
$2750	1910	Canada series I (48x56x23cm-19x22x9in) st.sig. num.2/3, clear lucite exec.1968. 26-Feb-93 Sotheby's Arcade, New York #338/R
$3000	2083	Untitled (25x34x16cm-10x13x6in) executed c.1955 painted wood construction. 23-Feb-93 Sotheby's, New York #238/R
$3759	2506	Composizione (39x30x7cm-15x12x3in) s.i.verso wood. 10-May-94 Finarte, Firenze #278/R (I.L 6000000)
$5500	3642	America (52cm-20in) painted wood plexiglass construction. 29-Sep-93 Sotheby's Arcade, New York #319/R
$6500	4362	Canada series II (49x56x23cm-19x22x9in) s.num.2-6 plexiglass executed 1967-68. 5-May-94 Sotheby's, New York #117/R
$7600	5101	Cryptic no 61 (18x27x16cm-7x11x6in) painted wood construction executed 1969. 5-May-94 Sotheby's, New York #137/R
$8500	5705	Diminishing reflection XX (150x49x14cm-59x19x6in) with sig.d.65 verso plexiglass wood formica base. 23-Feb-94 Christie's, New York #9/R
$10000	5882	Floating cloud cryptic IX (8x21x15cm-3x8x6in) white painted wood box construction. 6-Oct-92 Sotheby's, New York #53/R
$10000	6623	Untitled (60x51x4cm-24x20x2in) s.d.65 wood on panel. 19-Nov-92 Christie's, New York #306/R
$14000	9272	Queen Anne (114x53x58cm-45x21x23in) s.d.1958 painted wood construction. 18-Nov-92 Sotheby's, New York #91/R
$16000	11111	Dancer (41x33x38cm-16x13x15in) s. executed c.1940-45 bronze on wood base. 23-Feb-93 Sotheby's, New York #205/R
$18500	12092	Atmosphere and environment IX (274x488x274cm-108x192x108in) exec.c.1968 painted aluminum construction. 16-May-93 Hindman Galleries, Chicago #305/R
$20000	13245	Maquette for monumental sculpture (69x25x25cm-27x10x10in) black painted wood construction. 18-Nov-92 Sotheby's, New York #138/R
$22000	14865	End of Day, cryptic IV (37x21x20cm-15x8x8in) wood painted black executed 1972. 10-Nov-93 Christie's, New York #145/R
$30000	20134	Black sun (61x76x25cm-24x30x10in) s.d.1959verso painted wood construction. 5-May-94 Sotheby's, New York #96/R
$30000	20833	Undermarine scape (73x43x43cm-29x17x17in) s. exec.1956 wood in glass and metal case. 23-Feb-93 Sotheby's, New York #215/R
$38000	25503	Untitled (183x123x38cm-72x48x15in) painted wood construction executed 1987. 5-May-94 Sotheby's, New York #134/R
$40000	26846	Night rhythm III (60x45x13cm-24x18x5in) wood painted black in formica frame exec.1968. 4-May-94 Christie's, New York #138/R
$55000	32353	Undermarine scape (73x43x43cm-29x17x17in) s. wood construction glass metal case. 6-Oct-92 Sotheby's, New York #3/R
$80000	52288	Untitled - columns (249x229x124cm-98x90x49in) ten wooded columns on base white executed 1976. 4-May-93 Christie's, New York #13/R
$80000	53691	Sky columns presence (168x15x9cm-66x6x4in) painted wood construction four parts exec.1960. 5-May-94 Sotheby's, New York #104/R
$100000	67114	Moon tide I (221x121x23cm-87x48x9in) painted wood construction executed 1978. 4-May-94 Sotheby's, New York #48/R
$110000	74324	Black light - Zag I (104x178x15cm-41x70x6in) black painted wood construction executed 1970. 11-Nov-93 Sotheby's, New York #300/R
$110000	72848	Exotic landscape (145x328x38cm-57x129x15in) wall relief painted black. 18-Nov-92 Christie's, New York #10/R
$140000	94595	Night personage presence (241x91x23cm-95x36x9in) painted wood construction executed 1968. 10-Nov-93 Sotheby's, New York #36/R
$175000	118243	Royal Tide - dawn (231x160x27cm-91x63x11in) s.d.1960 s.d.1964 wood painted gold. 9-Nov-93 Christie's, New York #13/R

NEWMAN, John (1952-) American

$2025	1350	Rollback (215cm-85in) s. aluminium copper executed 1986. 2-Jun-94 AB Stockholms Auktionsverk, Stockholm #7024/R (S.KR 16000)
$6000	4027	Shelf life (127x157x39cm-50x62x15in) acrylic on cast aluminum executed 1987. 4-May-94 Christie's, New York #271/R

NOGUCHI, Isamu (1904-1988) American

$7296	4800	Portrait head of Joella Levey (30cm-12in) s.d.1929 bronze. 1-Apr-93 Bonhams, London #39/R
$10106	6200	Square coupling (10x25x25cm-4x10x10in) cast iron executed 1966-67 two parts. 14-Oct-92 Sotheby's, London #320/R
$50000	32680	Celebration - holiday (47x53x4cm-19x21x2in) cast iron executed 1952 1/6. 4-May-93 Christie's, New York #1/R
$52000	34437	Okame (33x23x12cm-13x9x5in) executed 1956 edit.of 3 cast iron. 19-Nov-92 Christie's, New York #319/R
$100000	65359	Solitude (192x30x30cm-76x12x12in) bronze executed 1962. 3-May-93 Sotheby's, New York #39/R

NOGUCHI, Isamu (1904-1988) American-cont.
$180000   119205   Solitude (193cm-76in) s.d.62 num.4/6 bronze. 18-Nov-92 Sotheby's, New York #101/R
$390000   258278   Shiva Rock (170x81x56cm-67x32x22in) inits.d.81 basalt wood base. 17-Nov-92 Sotheby's, New York #32/R

NOLAND, Cady (1956-) American
$9000   6081   The mirror device (57x72x10cm-22x28x4in) metal handcuffs gun mirror executed 1987. 10-Nov-93 Christie's, New York #267/R
$19000   12418   Model from Entropy (84x86x23cm-33x34x9in) s.d.1984 hat helmet belt book mounted on wood. 5-May-93 Christie's, New York #144/R

NONAS, Richard (20th C) American
$2000   1342   Light of the East (34x41x3cm-13x16x1in) s.num.7verso oil welded steel executed 1987. 3-May-94 Christie's, East, New York #181/R
$3000   1765   Three part sculpture (4x35x23cm-2x14x9in) s.i.d.80 bronze three parts. 8-Oct-92 Christie's, New York #186/R

NUKTIALUK, Lucassie (1930-1962) North American
$1254   804   Inuit woman carrying child in amaut, bending to collar young son (20cm-8in) s.i. mottled dark grey soapstone. 7-Dec-92 Waddingtons, Toronto #957/R (C.D 1600)

NUNEZ DEL PRADO, Marina (1910-) Bolivian
$5000   3268   Torso (32cm-13in) s. black basalt. 17-May-93 Christie's, New York #247/R

NUNZIO (20th C) American
$4031   2669   Caduta (112x43x8cm-44x17x3in) d.1990 burned wood shaped. 9-Nov-92 Finarte, Milan #116/R (I.L 5500000)

OKULICK, John (1947-) American
$6500   4362   Stake bed (170x135x18cm-67x53x7in) s.i.d.1980 pine birch wall sculpture. 3-May-94 Christie's, East, New York #122/R

OLDENBURG, Claes (1929-) American
$2000   1351   Cigarette butts (9x12x4cm-4x5x2in) s.i.d.67 cigarettes acrylic resin paper wood. 8-Nov-93 Christie's, East, New York #19/R
$2308   1508   Beschmierte Friderick - souvenir of Documenta 7 (19cm-7in) s.num.13, enamel col plaster executed 1982. 12-May-93 AB Stockholms Auktionsverk, Stockholm #6135/R (S.KR 17000)
$3720   2480   Tea bag - multiple (100x71cm-39x28in) s.verso pressed felt string under plexiglass. 3-Jun-94 Lempertz, Cologne #828/R (DM 6200)
$4000   2614   London knees (38cm-15in) flexible latex coated in polyurethane two. 5-Oct-93 Sotheby's, New York #4/R
$9128   5600   Urethane baked potato (23x28cm-9x11in) s.d.1964verso enamel urethane wooden board. 15-Oct-92 Christie's, London #59/R
$25000   16779   Flashlight model (189x52x52cm-74x20x20in) st.sig.i.d.1980 num.4/4 acrylic steel aluminum. 4-May-94 Christie's, New York #336/R
$30000   19608   Flashlight model (190cm-75in) s.st.1980 2/4 steel aluminium electric light. 4-May-93 Sotheby's, New York #402/R
$32000   21622   Model for giant ice bag on corner site - Oberlin (30x86x74cm-12x34x29in) init.i.d.69 4/24 painted cardboard fabric wood. 11-Nov-93 Sotheby's, New York #362/R
$33000   22148   Souvenir of Venice, California (23x34cm-9x13in) enamel found objects muslin burlap exec.1963. 5-May-94 Sotheby's, New York #190/R
$50000   33784   Inverted q prototype (183x163x180cm-72x64x71in) foam epoxy polyurethane enamel executed 1976. 10-Nov-93 Sotheby's, New York #33/R
$66000   44295   Six cream bars (64x53x11cm-25x21x4in) enamel plaster wood on panel executed 1962. 5-May-94 Sotheby's, New York #180/R
$75000   49669   Fagend study (51x179x61cm-20x70x24in) init.base cor-ten steel and lead. 18-Nov-92 Christie's, New York #45/R
$115000   77181   Typewriter eraser (82x63x88cm-32x25x35in) st.sig.i.d.1977 num.3/18 acrylic aluminum. 3-May-94 Christie's, New York #57/R
$150000   101351   Stockinged thighs framed by skirt (88x106cm-35x42in) init.d.1961 enamel plaster wire mesh exec.1961. 9-Nov-93 Christie's, New York #31/R
$160000   108108   Typewriter eraser (81cm-32in) st.sig.num.10/18, cement aluminium steel. 10-Nov-93 Sotheby's, New York #30/R
$370000   248322   7-up (140x94x14cm-55x37x6in) init.d.61 muslin plaster over wire frame enamel. 4-May-94 Sotheby's, New York #25/R

OONARK, Jessie (1906-1985) North American
$1247   821   Eskimo woman, Cape Dorset (57x32cm-22x13in) num.12/50 cut stone executed 1960. 7-Jun-93 Waddingtons, Toronto #800 (C.D 1600)

OQUTAQ, Sheokjuk (1920-1982) North American
$2246   1498   Bird swimming with its head turned (22cm-9in) s. marbled green serpentine. 6-Jun-94 Waddingtons, Toronto #967/R (C.D 3100)

OTTERNESS, Tom (1952-) American
$2532   1688   Bookends (22cm-9in) s.d.1979 num.2/3, black pat bronze pair. 2-Jun-94 AB Stockholms Auktionsverk, Stockholm #7029/R (S.KR 20000)
$4500   2941   Messenger (36x36x8cm-14x14x3in) s.d.1982 num.1/3 graphite cast polyalam. 4-May-93 Sotheby's, New York #218/R

OTTERNESS, Tom (1952-) American-cont.
$24000　15894　Birds and bees (61x53x30cm-24x21x12in) s.d.1985 num.1/3 bronze. 19-Nov-92 Christie's, New York #122/R

OTTERSON, Joel (20th C) American
$3500　2059　Artificial intelligent (176x42x33cm-69x17x13in) init.i.d.1986 copper wood wooden base. 8-Oct-92 Christie's, New York #184/R
$4000　2703　Non-found, un-found (259x51x33cm-102x20x13in) aluminium bats copper brass valve steel wood. 11-Nov-93 Sotheby's, New York #168/R

PACHECO, Ana Maria (1943-) Brazilian
$6705　4500　Head (180cm-71in) carved painted wood glass teeth. 26-Mar-93 Christie's, London #171/R

PAIK, Nam June (1932-) American/Korean
$1570　1054　Metrobots (49x33x10cm-19x13x4in) s.num.17/20 d.88 metal audio cassette. 25-Jun-93 Francis Briest, Paris #219 (F.FR 9000)
$3129　2100　Untitled (22x48cm-9x19in) s.d.3/25/79 metal plastic. 24-Jun-93 Sotheby's, London #82/R
$6556　4400　Heart is in question (49x48x8cm-19x19x3in) s. s.i.d.84 verso oil panel television frame. 2-Dec-93 Christie's, London #240/R
$22350　15000　Hitchcocked (186x134x56cm-73x53x22in) s.d.90 TVcabinet birdcage statue disk player. 24-Mar-93 Sotheby's, London #344/R
$29800　20000　Buda game (147x93x60cm-58x37x24in) s.d.91 antique television set gold leaf antennae. 2-Dec-93 Christie's, London #146/R
$35000　22876　Laurie Anderson (318x136x16cm-125x54x6in) s.d.88 disc players televisions silk metal cable. 5-May-93 Christie's, New York #134/R
$57500　38851　Family of robot - painted metal child (189x97x72cm-74x38x28in) painted televisions executed 1986. 11-Nov-93 Sotheby's, New York #198/R

PAIK, Nam June and CHRISTO (20th C) American
$44700　30000　Wrapped television (33x31x29cm-13x12x11in) s.d.67 portable television in plastic and twine. 24-Jun-93 Sotheby's, London #74/R

PALMER, Erastus Dow (1817-1904) American
$2235　1500　Memory, bust of maiden (46cm-18in) s.i.d.1867 white marble. 15-Jul-93 Christie's, London #238/R
$4000　2532　Bust of child (44cm-17in) s. white marble incl.socle. 4-Dec-92 Christie's, New York #165/R

PANGNARK, John (1920-1980) North American
$725　483　Two embracing figures (20cm-8in) s. mottled grey soapstone. 6-Jun-94 Waddingtons, Toronto #999 (C.D 1000)
$1129　758　Inuit figure (15cm-6in) dark veined green soapstone. 29-Nov-93 Waddingtons, Toronto #887 (C.D 1500)
$1159　773　Seated figure (16cm-6in) s. mottled light grey soapstone. 6-Jun-94 Waddingtons, Toronto #992 (C.D 1600)
$1176　754　Standing Inuit figure wearing parka (17cm-7in) s. mottled dark grey soapstone. 7-Dec-92 Waddingtons, Toronto #969 (C.D 1500)
$1247　821　Carving of seated Inuit figure (25cm-10in) s. grey soapstone. 7-Jun-93 Waddingtons, Toronto #856/R (C.D 1600)

PARDO TAVERA, F (1859-?) South American
$809　550　'C'est mi' (28cm-11in) s.d.1890 num.88 dark brown pat.bronze. 7-Apr-94 Sotheby's Colonnade, London #1195/R

PARKS, Bob (1948-) American
$1100　733　An Ornery cuss (48cm-19in) i.num.5/25 copper brown pat.bronze. 22-May-94 Hindman Galleries, Chicago #47/R
$1200　800　Sioux warrior-buffalo scout (38cm-15in) i.num.17/20 bronze. 22-May-94 Hindman Galleries, Chicago #48/R
$3200　2133　Late for school (69cm-27in) i. greenish brown pat.bronze. 22-May-94 Hindman Galleries, Chicago #46/R

PARSONS, Edith Baretto (1878-1956) American
$2100　1419　Children playing - book-ends (16cm-6in) i. rich brown pat.bronze f.i.Gorham Co pair. 31-Mar-94 Sotheby's Arcade, New York #174/R
$7000　4487　'Duck baby' - fountain figure (104cm-41in) i. greenish brown pat.bronze f.i.Roman Works NY. 26-May-93 Christie's, New York #166/R
$15000　9494　The fish baby (103cm-41in) i. bronze fountain. Cast.Roman Bronze Works. 4-Dec-92 Christie's, New York #106/R

PARTRIDGE, William Ordway (1861-1930) American
$5500　3481　Portrait bust of Alfred, Lord Tennyson (52cm-20in) i. reddish brown pat.bronze. 4-Dec-92 Christie's, New York #167/R

PENALBA, Alicia (1918-1982) Argentinian
$3855　2570　Sans titre (27cm-11in) s.num.5/8 silver pat.bronze. 2-Jun-94 Christian de Quay, Paris #89/R (F.FR 22000)
$8651　6049　Etincelle (41x19x19cm-16x7x7in) s.num.3/6 green pat.bronze st.f.Valsuani. 14-Mar-93 Watine-Arnault, Paris #24/R (F.FR 49000)

PENALBA, Alicia (1918-1982) Argentinian-cont.
$16000   10667   Tropique (55cm-22in) s.num.EdAr black pat.bronze Cast Valsuani. 17-May-94 Sotheby's, New York #38/R
$26000   17333   Le voyageur des nuits (196cm-77in) s.num.5/6 col pat.bronze st.f.Susse executed 57. 18-May-94 Christie's, New York #171/R
$30964   20238   Grande Ailee (105x95x195cm-41x37x77in) s.num.5/5 col pat.bronze Cast.Susse exec.60-63. 29-Jun-94 Guy Loudmer, Paris #233/R (F.FR 170000)

PEPPER, Beverly (1924-) American
$1300   872   Table sculpture (27cm-11in) i. white paint steel. 24-Feb-94 Sotheby's Arcade, New York #399/R
$3000   1987   Santoni Artemus (118cm-46in) painted metal. 30-Jun-93 Sotheby's Arcade, New York #350/R
$5000   3268   Untitled - wedge variation (79x30x17cm-31x12x7in) cast iron steel. 7-May-93 Christie's, East, New York #3/R
$6500   4392   San Marco Plaza (83x35x36cm-33x14x14in) forged painted cast steel cast iron exec.c.1981. 11-Nov-93 Sotheby's, New York #309/R
$24000   16216   Tarquinia Spiral (301x62x62cm-119x24x24in) cast iron executed 1979-1980. 10-Nov-93 Christie's, New York #162/R
$26000   16993   Harmonius triad (259x61x67cm-102x24x26in) cast ductile iron executed 1982-83. 4-May-93 Sotheby's, New York #189/R

PETERLOOSIE, Joansie (20th C) North American
$1739   1159   Walking, alert polar bear (53cm-21in) s. marbled dark green serpentine. 6-Jun-94 Waddingtons, Toronto #984 (C.D 2400)

PETTIBONE, Richard (1938-) American
$2800   1830   The shakers, Brancusi, Ezra Pound (129x48x48cm-51x19x19in) wood executed 1988. 22-Dec-92 Christie's, East, New York #53

PICCIRILLI, Attilio (1868-1945) American
$1400   809   The outcast (16cm-6in) i.d.1904 dark brown pat.bronze. 25-Sep-92 Sotheby's Arcade, New York #178/R
$2500   1623   Spring dream (31cm-12in) i. exec.1918 black pat.bronze. 9-Sep-93 Sotheby's Arcade, New York #162

PIERCE, Elijah (19/20th C) American
$1200   805   Two in One Bird (18x8x25cm-7x3x10in) mixed media on wood. 25-Mar-93 Boos Gallery, Michigan #430/R

PIQTOUKUN, David Ruben (1950-) North American
$1467   985   A shaman dancing on a stone moon (41cm-16in) marbled dark green serpentine stone. 29-Nov-93 Waddingtons, Toronto #939/R (C.D 1950)
$1667   1111   Standing spirit muskox, with face of shaman (38cm-15in) s. mottled light green soapstone. 6-Jun-94 Waddingtons, Toronto #926/R (C.D 2300)

POLEO, Hector (1918-) Venezuelan
$8000   5298   Cabeza de mujer (32cm-13in) s.d.87 num.1/7 brown pat.bronze. 24-Nov-92 Christie's, New York #246/R

POONS, Larry (1937-) American
$8195   5500   Mike and Gustav (215x104x10cm-85x41x4in) s.i.d.1986 verso oil composition canvas. 2-Dec-93 Christie's, London #230/R

POWERS, Hiram (1805-1873) American
$4200   2781   Portrait bust of woman (56cm-22in) s. white marble. 22-Sep-93 Christie's, New York #100/R
$7000   4895   Proserpine (61cm-24in) white marble. 10-Mar-93 Sotheby's, New York #10/R
$8000   5333   Faith (70cm-28in) s. white marble. 16-Mar-94 Christie's, New York #55/R
$17000   11409   'Fisherboy' (49cm-19in) s. white marble incl.socle. 3-Dec-93 Christie's, New York #116/R
$22000   14667   Bust of Diana (76cm-30in) s. white marble incl.marble socle. 26-May-94 Christie's, New York #34/R
$23000   15436   The fisher boy (56cm-22in) s. marble. 3-Feb-94 Sloan, North Bethesda #2897/R
$26000   15029   Proserpine (62cm-24in) s. white marble. 24-Sep-92 Sotheby's, New York #28/R
$30000   20000   Bust of Prosperpine, goddess rising from bed of leaves (62cm-24in) s.d.1846 white marble. 17-Mar-94 Christie's, London #237/R
$37000   23418   Proserpine (63cm-25in) i. marble. 3-Dec-92 Sotheby's, New York #30/R
$41000   27333   Greek slave (55cm-22in) i. white marble. 17-Mar-94 Sotheby's, New York #22/R
$42000   26582   Proserpine (64cm-25in) s. white marble incl.socle with fluted column. 4-Dec-92 Christie's, New York #164/R

PRATT, Bela Lyon (1867-1917) American
$6250   4371   Youth (79cm-31in) i.d.03 brown pat.bronze Cast Roman Bronze Works. 10-Mar-93 Sotheby's, New York #99/R

PRESTINI, James (1908-) American
$6000   4054   Untitled (140cm-55in) nickel plated steel. 21-Apr-94 Butterfield & Butterfield, San Francisco #1142/R

PRICE, Ken (1935-) American
$4600   3007   Untitled - Oriental (7x10x10cm-3x4x4in) acrylic ceramic executed 1984. 7-May-93 Christie's, East, New York #123/R
$10000   6711   Astronauts in the ocean (27x14x10cm-11x6x4in) glazed ceramic painted wood executed c.1960-61. 25-Feb-94 Sotheby's, New York #285/R

PRICE, Ken (1935-) American-cont.
$10000   6711   Rebuncular (33x36x41cm-13x14x16in) acrylic paint ceramic executed c.1988. 25-Feb-94 Sotheby's, New York #193/R
$11000   7432   Hawaiian (14x29x22cm-6x11x9in) glazed ceramic executed 1980. 8-Nov-93 Christie's, East, New York #146/R

PROCTOR, Alexander Phimister (1862-1950) American
$1300   855   Buckaroo (69cm-27in) i.d.1915 brown pat.bronze st.f.Roman Bronze Wks. 13-Jun-93 Hindman Galleries, Chicago #299
$2750   1763   Fawn (17cm-7in) s.i.d.1893 brown pat.bronze. 9-Dec-92 Butterfield & Butterfield, San Francisco #3979/R
$3300   2185   Stalking panther (97cm-38in) s. bronze. 23-Sep-93 Mystic Fine Arts, Connecticut #104
$5500   3642   The buckaroo (69cm-27in) i.d.1915 brown pat.bronze st.f.Roman Bronze. 15-Jun-94 Butterfield & Butterfield, San Francisco #4507/R
$6000   3846   The buckaroo (66cm-26in) s.i.d.1915 num.24 brown pat.bronze F.Rom.Bronze. 9-Dec-92 Butterfield & Butterfield, San Francisco #3981/R
$6250   4252   Stalking panther (99cm-39in) i. pat.bronze. 17-Apr-94 Hanzel Galleries, Chicago #136
$11500   8042   Buffalo (30cm-12in) i.d.1890 red-brown pat.bronze. 10-Mar-93 Sotheby's, New York #65/R
$44000   29333   The Indian warrior (102cm-40in) i. dark brown pat.bronze f.i.Gorham Co. 22-May-94 Hindman Galleries, Chicago #13/R

PUTNAM, Arthur (1873-1930) American
$1400   927   Squirrel (18cm-7in) i.d.1908 brown pat.bronze. 15-Jun-94 Butterfield & Butterfield, San Francisco #4677/R
$6000   4000   Boy with lynx (53x48cm-21x19in) indis.init.i. brown pat.bronze. 3-Jun-94 Sotheby's, New York #140/R

PUTNAM, Brenda (1890-1975) American
$2800   1772   Spear Dance - figure of male nude (55cm-22in) i. red green brown pat.bronze.Cast.Kunst Foundry. 4-Dec-92 Christie's, New York #103/R
$3000   1948   The spear dance (62cm-24in) i.brown pat.bronze Cast Kunst Foundry NY. 9-Sep-93 Sotheby's Arcade, New York #159/R
$5000   3268   Figure of child at pond (51cm-20in) s. brown pat.bronze f.i.Gorham Co. Fondeur. 17-Sep-93 Sotheby's, New York #216/R

QAYUTINNUAQ, Paul (1957-) North American
$725   483   Carving of a loon protecting her hatching young (36cm-14in) s. light green soapstone. 6-Jun-94 Waddingtons, Toronto #759/R (C.D 1000)
$870   580   Carving of an Inuit hunter wearing a parka and leggings, with spear (38cm-15in) s. marbled green soapstone. 6-Jun-94 Waddingtons, Toronto #761 (C.D 1200)

QUIJANO, Alejandro (1957-) Mexican
$1119   756   La huay imix, cocodrila ocultadora del tiempo (17x30x29cm-7x12x11in) bronze. 20-Oct-93 Louis Morton, Mexico #112/R (M.P 3500)

QUINN, Edmond T (1867-1929) American
$3500   2365   Standing female nude (56cm-22in) i.d.1913 black pat.bronze f.st.Gorham Co. 31-Mar-94 Sotheby's Arcade, New York #89/R

RABINOWITCH, David (1943-) Canadian
$8000   5556   Triangular plane in three sections (11x80x65cm-4x31x26in) exec.1976-1978 steel three parts. 24-Feb-93 Christie's, New York #85/R
$13000   8725   Untitled (5x80x71cm-2x31x28in) four units hot rolled steel exec.1969-1974. 4-May-94 Christie's, New York #225/R

RAINEY, Clifford (1950-) American
$3750   2517   Torso (55x20x18cm-22x8x7in) glass bronze wood marble. 25-Feb-94 Sotheby's, New York #312/R

RAMOS, Nelson (1932-) Uruguay
$12000   8000   El coleccionista (110x84cm-43x33in) s.d.92 acrylic paper board gauze plaster constr. 17-May-94 Sotheby's, New York #80/R

RAUSCHENBERG, Robert (1925-) American
$40000   26490   Untitled (122x124x11cm-48x49x4in) s.d.89 oil silkscreen synth.polymer steel grill. 19-Nov-92 Christie's, New York #414/R

RECCHIA, Richard H (1885-?) American
$8500   5556   Young pan playing flute (84cm-33in) s.d.56 green brown pat.bronze. 5-May-93 Doyle, New York #66/R

REMINGTON, F (1861-1909) American
$1293   873   Vaquero a caballo (87x27x107cm-34x11x42in) s. bronze. 27-Oct-93 Fernando Duran, Madrid #777/R (S.P 175000)

REMINGTON, Frederic (1861-1909) American

$2500	1656	The Savage (28cm-11in) i.d.1908 brown pat.bronze st.f.Roman Bronze. 15-Jun-94 Butterfield & Butterfield, San Francisco #4506/R
$3750	2484	Bronco buster (76cm-30in) i. brown pat.bronze. 15-Jun-94 Butterfield & Butterfield, San Francisco #4503/R
$35000	23179	Rattlesnake - equestrian group (61cm-24in) i.num.103 greenish brown pat.bronze f.i. 22-Sep-93 Christie's, New York #99/R
$57500	36859	Savage (28cm-11in) i.d.1905 num.13 greenish black pat.bronze f.i. 27-May-93 Sotheby's, New York #237/R
$57500	38333	The bronco buster (57cm-22in) i.num.265 brown pat.bronze C.Roman Bronze Works. 25-May-94 Sotheby's, New York #41/R
$60000	40000	The savage (27cm-11in) i.d.1908 st.num.7 green/brown pat.bronze. 26-May-94 Christie's, New York #43/R
$68000	45333	The Cheyenne - figure on horseback (51cm-20in) i.st.num.70 green/brown pat.bronze f.Roman NY. 26-May-94 Christie's, New York #40/R
$70000	46667	The bronco buster (57cm-22in) i. num.149 brown pat.bronze Roman bronze works. 26-May-94 Christie's, New York #47/R
$70000	44304	The rattlesnake (60cm-24in) s.i.num.74 f.Roman Bronze Wks bronze br.pat. 3-Dec-92 Sotheby's, New York #66/R
$80000	53333	The Cheyenne (50cm-20in) i. num.31 brown pat.bronze Roman bronze works NY. 26-May-94 Christie's, New York #46/R
$90000	60403	The bronco buster (60cm-24in) i.num.77 brown pat.bronze Cast Roman Bronze W. 2-Dec-93 Sotheby's, New York #45/R
$140000	89744	Bronco buster (60cm-24in) i. dark black-brown pat.bronze f.i. 27-May-93 Sotheby's, New York #242/R
$200000	134258	'Mountain Man' - equestrian group (72cm-28in) i.num.27 rich brown pat.bronze f.i.New York. 3-Dec-93 Christie's, New York #81/R
$205000	135762	Bronco buster (61cm-24in) i.d.1896 brown pat.bronze st.f.Henry Bonnard. 15-Jun-94 Butterfield & Butterfield, San Francisco #4510/R
$260000	174497	'The Scalp' - equestrian group (67cm-26in) i.num.8 reddish brown pat.bronze f.st. 3-Dec-93 Christie's, New York #82/R
$280000	186667	Mountain man - figure on horseback (72cm-28in) i. green/brown pat.bronze Roman bronze works NY. 26-May-94 Christie's, New York #41/R
$300000	198676	The Cheyenne (52cm-20in) i.d.1901 brown pat.bronze st.f.Roman Bronze. 15-Jun-94 Butterfield & Butterfield, San Francisco #4502/R
$400000	268256	Trooper of the plains (67cm-26in) i.num.5 green black pat.bronze C.Roman Bronze W. 2-Dec-93 Sotheby's, New York #56/R
$460000	291139	The bronco buster (83cm-33in) s.i.num.12 bronze green brown pat. 3-Dec-92 Sotheby's, New York #65/R
$500000	335570	'The Cheyenne' - equestrian group (51cm-20in) i.d.1901 rich reddish brown pat.bronze f.i. 3-Dec-93 Christie's, New York #77/R
$1100000	738255	Coming through the rye (73cm-29in) i.d.1908-1913 brown pat.bronze on marble base. 2-Dec-93 Sotheby's, New York #66/R
$1800000	1153846	'Wounded bunkie' - equestrian group (53cm-21in) i. reddish brown pat.bronze f.i.H Bonnard 1896. 26-May-93 Christie's, New York #98/R

REMINGTON, Frederic (after) (1861-1909) American

$1979	1244	The mountain man (68cm-27in) i. bronze. 21-Apr-93 Germann, Zurich #120/R (S.FR 2800)
$2200	1486	A sergeant (26cm-10in) i. brown pat.bronze. 31-Mar-94 Sotheby's Arcade, New York #196/R
$4000	2667	Coming through the rye (69cm-27in) i. dark brown pat.bronze. 22-May-94 Hindman Galleries, Chicago #11/R

RHIND, John Massey (1860-1936) American

$6000	4000	The Lookout (61cm-24in) s.i.d.1919 copper brown pat.bronze f.st. 22-May-94 Hindman Galleries, Chicago #2/R

RICKEY, George (1907-) American

$1400	940	Untitled (15cm-6in) num. steel plane on base. 24-Feb-94 Sotheby's Arcade, New York #400/R
$4500	3000	Five triangles (41x53x11cm-16x21x4in) s.d.68 steel object in two parts wooden base. 3-Jun-94 Lempertz, Cologne #881/R (DM 7500)
$5500	3642	Untitled (53cm-21in) steel marble. 30-Jun-93 Sotheby's Arcade, New York #306/R
$7000	4698	Two circles one cube (30x16x16cm-12x6x6in) s.d.1978 num.1/3 stainless steel marble base. 25-Feb-94 Sotheby's, New York #50/R
$8500	5743	Untitle (53x18x15cm-21x7x6in) s.d.1987 num.3/3 stainless steel marble base. 11-Nov-93 Sotheby's, New York #326/R
$9500	6597	Untitled (127x45x61cm-50x18x24in) s.d.66 stainless steel. 24-Feb-93 Christie's, New York #4/R
$10000	6711	Unstable square (74x48x8cm-29x19x3in) s.d.5 7 71 num.3/8 stainless steel lead ex.1971. 4-May-94 Christie's, New York #166/R
$10040	6693	A theme (38x50cm-15x20in) s.i.d.1986 num.2/3 steel metal base. 11-Jun-94 Hauswedell & Nolte, Hamburg #317/R (DM 16800)
$11000	7190	Four rectangles oblique (127x127cm-50x50in) s.d.1972-73 stainless steel 1/3. 4-May-93 Sotheby's, New York #366/R
$11475	7500	Untitled (99cm-39in) s.d.1990 num.3/3 stainless steel. 30-Jun-94 Sotheby's, London #161/R
$12000	8054	Broken lines oblique (66x66x6cm-26x26x2in) s.d.1977 num.1/3 stainless steel. 25-Feb-94 Sotheby's, New York #45/R
$13000	9028	Wall sculpture four square diagonal (133x133x43cm-52x52x17in) s.d.1982 num.1/3 stainless steel. 24-Feb-93 Christie's, New York #49/R
$14000	9396	Two fixed - three moving lines (224x254cm-88x100in) s.d.1970 num.2 stainless steel lead. 23-Feb-94 Christie's, New York #37/R

RICKEY, George (1907-) American-cont.
$16000	10596	Untitled (80x109x15cm-31x43x6in) s.d.1982 num.1/3 stainless steel. 19-Nov-92 Christie's, New York #370/R
$17000	11409	One up two down (137x69x10cm-54x27x4in) s.d.1990 num.2/3 stainless steel. 5-May-94 Sotheby's, New York #151/R
$20000	13889	Two line eccentric (335cm-132in) s.d.1983-86 num.3/3 stainless steel. 23-Feb-93 Sotheby's, New York #255/R
$22000	14765	Three lines (246x150x23cm-97x59x9in) s.d.70 num.59 stainless steel. 5-May-94 Sotheby's, New York #140/R
$22350	15000	Six triangles hexagon V (174x63cm-69x25in) s.d.1979 polished steel triangles 1/3. 2-Dec-92 Christie's, London #169/R
$24000	16216	Summer IV (88x46x33cm-35x18x13in) brass lead stainl.steel marble base exec.1962-63. 10-Nov-93 Christie's, New York #148/R
$25000	16892	Open triangle one up one down (138x76x15cm-54x30x6in) s.d.1983 num.1/3 stainless steel. 11-Nov-93 Sotheby's, New York #276/R
$25000	16556	One up, one down, eccentric (325x333x348cm-128x131x137in) s.d.1977 stainless steel. 19-Nov-92 Christie's, New York #416/R
$25000	16556	One up, two down (188cm-74in) s.d.89 stainless steel number 3/3. 18-Nov-92 Sotheby's, New York #137/R
$26000	15294	Two open triangles up (305cm-120in) s.num.1/3 d.1983 stainless steel. 6-Oct-92 Sotheby's, New York #69/R
$34000	20000	Four rectangles oblique II (259cm-102in) s.num.3/3 d.1978 stainless steel. 6-Oct-92 Sotheby's, New York #60/R
$42000	28188	One Up, One Down, Eccentric (325x333x348cm-128x131x137in) s.d.1977 stainless steel. 23-Feb-94 Christie's, New York #32/R
$45000	30201	Two slender lines eccentric (670x853cm-264x336in) s.d.1980 num.2/3 stainless steel lead. 4-May-94 Christie's, New York #147/R
$62000	41892	Four lines oblique V (422x472x46cm-166x186x18in) s.i.d.1978 num.2/3 stainless steel lead. 10-Nov-93 Christie's, New York #164/R

RIOPELLE (1923-) Canadian
$8573	5754	Composition abstraite (34cm-13in) s. brown pat.bronze st.f.Clementi. 10-Dec-93 Poulain & le Fur, Paris #322/R (F.FR 50000)

RIOS, Miguel Angel (1943-) Argentinian
$6000	3922	Icono (76x49x6cm-30x19x2in) s.d.1988 s.i.d.1988 verso clay tempera panel. 17-May-93 Christie's, New York #161/R
$7000	4730	The devil making jokes in Times Square (112x154cm-44x61in) s.d.1990 aluminium ceramic mica on wood. 22-Nov-93 Sotheby's, New York #272/R
$8000	5229	Retrato del cielo (141x87x9cm-56x34x4in) i. s.d.1988 verso clay mica wire panel steel. 17-May-93 Christie's, New York #162/R
$12000	8108	Sin titulo (115x128cm-45x50in) s.d.1987 terracotta stone painted wood. 23-Nov-93 Christie's, New York #166/R
$16000	10458	El metro del D.F. - San Jose Norte (140x192cm-55x76in) s. s.d.1988 verso ceramic burlap wood. 18-May-93 Sotheby's, New York #71/R

RIVERA, Jose de (1904-) American
$2308	1550	Untitled, no.147 (31cm-12in) st.d.64 forged bronze wood base electric motor. 25-Mar-93 Christie's, London #107/R
$2750	1846	Untitled (46cm-18in) brass. 24-Feb-94 Sotheby's Arcade, New York #455/R
$12000	7843	Untitled (159cm-63in) st.d.1983 num.196, bronze wood base motorized. 5-May-93 Christie's, New York #316/R

RIVERS, Larry (1923-) American
$2400	1611	Boxed head of woman (31x30x23cm-12x12x9in) s.d.68 wood Plexiglas light bulb fabric oil. 23-Feb-94 Christie's, East, New York #329/R
$28000	18792	Big Webster, parts distributed (140x169x8cm-55x67x3in) s.d.89 canvas on foamcore collage panel. 4-May-94 Christie's, New York #342/R

ROBUS, Hugo (1885-1964) American
$2000	1351	Meditating girl (20cm-8in) i. polished bronze f.st.Fonderia Battaglia. 31-Mar-94 Sotheby's Arcade, New York #466/R
$8000	5063	Cradle song (27cm-11in) i. natural pat.bronze on wood base i.f.Battaglia. 4-Dec-92 Christie's, New York #121/R

ROCKWELL, Robert Henry (1885-?) American
$1300	878	Chestnut horse (41cm-16in) i.d.1948 num.3/10 brown pat.bronze. 31-Mar-94 Sotheby's Arcade, New York #464/R

ROGERS, John (1829-1904) American
$1900	1293	Fetching the doctor on horseback (38cm-15in) i.d.1881 brown pat.bronze. 14-Apr-94 Freeman Fine Arts, Philadelphia #928/R

ROGERS, Randolph (1825-1892) American
$1360	800	Female bust (74cm-29in) s. white marble. 9-Oct-92 Sotheby's, London #114/R
$3000	1974	Figure of woman in flowing drapery (129cm-51in) s. marble. 13-Jun-93 Butterfield & Butterfield, San Francisco #3186/R

ROONEY, Anne (20th C) American
$3200	2148	Veiled woman (61cm-24in) i.num.1/15 teal pat.bronze. 14-Oct-93 Christie's, New York #393/R

ROSENTHAL, Tony (1914-) American
$3600	2500	Hi-jack (279cm-110in) init.d.76 corten steel. 26-Feb-93 Sotheby's Arcade, New York #405/R

RUPPERSBERG, Allen (1944-) American
$4000   2685   Play on words/Collection of rare books - Jonathan Swift (72x55x70cm-28x22x28in) wood box ink book card satin plexiglas exec. 1979. 3-May-94 Christie's, East, New York #95/R

RUSSELL, Charles M (1865-1926) American
$2203   1469   Coach and six (40x105cm-16x41in) s. brown pat.bronze. 28-May-94 Kunstgalerij de Vuyst, Lokeren #298 (B.FR 75000)
$2373   1551   Cowboy on horseback with steer (28x35cm-11x14in) s. brown pat.bronze. 29-Jun-94 Auktionhaus Schopmann, Hamburg #615/R (DM 3800)
$6000   4027   The Texas Steer (9x16cm-4x6in) init. brown pat.bronze sold with letter. 8-Dec-93 Butterfield & Butterfield, San Francisco #3592/R
$11500 7718   The snake priest (10cm-4in) i. brown pat.bronze. 2-Dec-93 Sotheby's, New York #72/R
$21000 13462 Enemy tracks (30cm-12in) i. dark brown pat.bronze executed 1920 f.i. 27-May-93 Sotheby's, New York #238/R
$23000 15436 The medicine man (18cm-7in) i. bronze. 2-Dec-93 Sotheby's, New York #69/R
$25000 16779 Weapons of the weak (15cm-6in) i. bronze. 2-Dec-93 Sotheby's, New York #71/R
$28000 18792 Enemy that warns (13cm-5in) i. brown pat.bronze Cast Roman Bronze Works. 2-Dec-93 Sotheby's, New York #70/R

RUSSELL, Charles M (after) (1865-1926) American
$1200   774   Lunch hour (18cm-7in) i. bronze. 6-Jan-93 Doyle, New York #607
$1300   839   Monarch of forest (23cm-9in) i. bronze. 6-Jan-93 Doyle, New York #612
$1600   1006   Stagecoach (38x79cm-15x31in) s. brown pat.bronze. 22-Apr-93 Freeman Fine Arts, Philadelphia #1170 a/R
$1900   1226   Standing horse (30cm-12in) i. bronze. 6-Jan-93 Doyle, New York #615
$2800   1806   Weaver - bucker and buckeroo (36cm-14in) i. bronze. 6-Jan-93 Doyle, New York #616

SAILA, Pauta (1916-) North American
$861   574   Roaring polar bear (20cm-8in) s.i. grey stone. 30-May-94 Ritchie, Toronto #92/R (C.D 1200)

SAINT-GAUDEN, Augustus (1848-1907) American
$7887   5293   Buste de femme (50cm-20in) s.i. marble. 8-Dec-93 Francis Briest, Paris #63 (F.FR 46000)
$8500   5944   Portrait of Robert Louis Stevenson (44cm-17in) i.st.MDCCC XCV tondo green brown pat.bronze. 11-Mar-93 Christie's, New York #97/R
$12000 8000   Jules Bastien Lepage - portrait relief (37x26cm-15x10in) i. golden brown pat.bronze. 17-Mar-94 Sotheby's, New York #37/R
$30000 20134 'Nikh-Eiphnh' - head of victory (20cm-8in) s. medium brown pat.bronze white marble base. 3-Dec-93 Christie's, New York #114/R
$50000 33333 The Puritan (79cm-31in) i.d.MDCCCXCIX black pat.bronze Cast Aubry Br.F. 25-May-94 Sotheby's, New York #33/R
$90000 56962 Amor Caritas (102cm-40in) i. greenish brown pat.bronze relief. 4-Dec-92 Christie's, New York #172/R

SAINT-GAUDEN, Augustus and VOLK, Leonard Wells (19th C) American
$1500   867   Bust of Abraham Lincoln (53cm-21in) i.d.1860 gold painted plaster st.foundry seal. 25-Sep-92 Sotheby's Arcade, New York #173/R

SALLE, David (1952-) American
$95000 62914 Poverty is no disgrace (249x521cm-98x205in) acrylic oil chair canvas three panels. 17-Nov-92 Sotheby's, New York #65/R

SAMARAS, Lucas (1936-) American
$10000 6757   Stiff box no 8 (46x35x46cm-18x14x18in) cor-ten steel executed 1971. 10-Nov-93 Christie's, New York #203/R
$12000 7843   Box No.57 (30x63x15cm-12x25x6in) yarn over painted wood executed 1966. 4-May-93 Sotheby's, New York #388/R
$15000 9804   Box - No.71 (35x37x20cm-14x15x8in) acrylic wood executed 1968. 5-May-93 Christie's, New York #229/R
$25000 16779 Jewel box (11x16x16cm-4x6x6in) wood box glass plastic jewels steel pins tape. 5-May-94 Sotheby's, New York #197/R
$40000 27027 Shoe box (27x39x27cm-11x15x11in) wood wool yarn shoe steel pins cotton paint. 11-Nov-93 Sotheby's, New York #376/R

SANDBACK, Fred (1943-) American
$1500   993   Untitled (51x41x19cm-20x16x7in) executed 1990 acrylic on yarn. 17-Nov-92 Christie's, East, New York #7/R
$7500   4967   Untitled (183x15x5cm-72x6x2in) orange elastic cord painted rod. 18-Nov-92 Sotheby's, New York #230 a/R

SANFORD, Marion (1904-1988) American
$3500   2023   Diana (56cm-22in) i.d.1937 green pat.bronze i.f.Basky N.Y. 25-Sep-92 Sotheby's Arcade, New York #179/R

SARET, Alan (1944-) American
$4200   2819   Green wave of air (137x152x122cm-54x60x48in) painted galvanized hexagonal wire netting. 23-Feb-94 Christie's, New York #109/R

SARTORE, Hugo (1935-) Uruguayan
$10000 6536 Construccion (82x61cm-32x24in) s.d.1976 verso painted wood construction. 18-May-93 Sotheby's, New York #189/R

SAXE, Adrian (1943-) American
$8000 5369 Gold bowl on stand (34x47x25cm-13x19x10in) s.d.1988 porcelain raku. 25-Feb-94 Sotheby's, New York #177/R

SCANGA, Italo (1932-) American
$1937 1300 Monte Cassino, the view (293x114x81cm-115x45x32in) s.d.1983 executed 1983 oil on wood. 21-Jun-93 Christie's, S. Kensington #207/R
$2533 1700 Untitled (325x149x79cm-128x59x31in) s.d.1983 acrylic on wood. 21-Jun-93 Christie's, S. Kensington #206/R
$4000 2703 Fear of nature (76cm-30in) s.d.1980 painted wood metal. 21-Oct-93 Butterfield & Butterfield, San Francisco #2807/R

SCARPITTA, Salvatore (1919-) American
$10740 7112 Core (157x122x15cm-62x48x6in) oil mixed media collage on panel. 24-Nov-92 Sotheby's, Milan #196/R (I.L 15000000)

SCHARF, Kenny (1958-) American
$1139 759 Radio (30x50x12cm-12x20x5in) painted radio-cassette player. 2-Jun-94 AB Stockholms Auktionsverk, Stockholm #6154/R (S.KR 9000)
$6000 4167 Vomidingbugerano (79x102x11cm-31x40x4in) executed 1985 oil foam plastic toys canvas. 23-Feb-93 Sotheby's, New York #395/R

SCHEURICH, Paul (1883-1945) American/German
$1253 830 Trotting horse (34cm-13in) s. brown pat.bronze on wooden socle. 28-Nov-92 Phillips, Dusseldorf #49 (DM 2000)
$1486 1004 Venus (35cm-14in) s.i. porcelain executed c.1920. 18-Apr-94 Hotel de Ventes Horta, Brussels #436 (B.FR 52000)

SCHIMMEL, Wilhelm (attrib) (1817-1890) American
$3500 2333 Pine rooster (16cm-6in) carved painted pine. 10-Jun-94 Christie's, New York #552/R
$5500 3667 Eaglet perched on mound (18cm-7in) carved painted. 10-Jun-94 Christie's, New York #554/R
$17000 11333 Eagle (32cm-13in) carved painted. 10-Jun-94 Christie's, New York #553/R

SCHIWETZ, Berthold (1909-1971) American
$2750 1846 Wedding couple (13cm-5in) s. bronze. 25-Mar-93 Boos Gallery, Michigan #37/R
$5500 3691 Jonah in mouth of whale (46cm-18in) bronze. 25-Mar-93 Boos Gallery, Michigan #36/R
$10000 6711 Taming of unicorn (178x28x69cm-70x11x27in) bronze. 25-Mar-93 Boos Gallery, Michigan #47/R

SCHNABEL, Julian (1951-) American
$30000 20270 George Washington crossing the Delaware (236x234x89cm-93x92x35in) init.d.1989 num.AP II acrylic bronze steel. 10-Nov-93 Christie's, New York #360/R
$50000 32680 Portrait of Patrick (213x142x20cm-84x56x8in) oil plates bondo epoxy wood executed 1989. 4-May-93 Sotheby's, New York #256/R
$55000 35948 T.D.A. (152x122x25cm-60x48x10in) oil ceramic bondo wood. 5-May-93 Christie's, New York #171/R
$125000 81699 Affection for surfing (274x579x61cm-108x228x24in) plates bondo oil wood executed 1983. 4-May-93 Sotheby's, New York #193/R
$150000 99338 Nightime Rhonda (275x214x49cm-108x84x19in) diptych oil plates deer antlers bondo on wood. 18-Nov-92 Christie's, New York #35/R

SCHREYVOGEL, Charles (1861-1912) American
$18000 11538 Man watering horse (30cm-12in) s.i.d.1903 num.47 pat.bronze F.Roman Bronze Work. 9-Dec-92 Butterfield & Butterfield, San Francisco #3980/R
$26000 16667 White Eagle (49cm-19in) i.d.1899 dark brown pat.bronze f.i. 27-May-93 Sotheby's, New York #248/R
$33000 22148 The last drop (30cm-12in) i.d.1903 brown pat.bronze Cast Rom.Bronze Works. 2-Dec-93 Sotheby's, New York #68/R

SCRIVER, Robert Macfie (1914-) American
$2153 1435 Sky climbers (51x66x38cm-20x26x15in) s.i.d. bronze. 30-May-94 Hodgins, Calgary #33/R (C.D 3000)

SCULLY, Sean (1946-) American/Irish
$85000 56291 Dark face (283x236x19cm-111x93x7in) s.i.d.86verso oil canvas on 3 panels. 18-Nov-92 Christie's, New York #59/R

SEARS, Philip Shelton (1867-1953) American
$1800 1208 Figure of a hunter with a spear (140cm-55in) s.d.1927 bronze st.f.McBain. 2-May-94 Selkirks, St. Louis #109/R

SEGAL, George (1924-) American
$1679 1077 Girl on a chair (92x61cm-36x24in) num.120/150 white plaster red chair exec.1970. 28-May-93 Catherine Charbonneaux, Paris #208 (F.FR 9000)
$3833 2590 Girl meditating (48x26cm-19x10in) s. exec.1975 num.41/47 polyester. 20-Mar-93 Kunstgalerij de Vuyst, Lokeren #434/R (B.FR 130000)
$5500 3642 Untitled (32x29x13cm-13x11x5in) s.d.78 num.HF7 acrylic plaster gauze. 17-Nov-92 Christie's, East, New York #228/R
$32000 21477 Bas-relief, the bather (102x80x24cm-40x31x9in) s.d.1972verso cast plaster in wood frame. 4-May-94 Christie's, New York #198/R

SEGAL, George (1924-) American-cont.

$44000	29730	Oriental woman (83x43x27cm-33x17x11in) plaster ceramic tiles executed 1981. 11-Nov-93 Sotheby's, New York #391/R
$60000	40268	Girl looking out of window (127x57x74cm-50x22x29in) wall relief oil plaster with wood support. 3-May-94 Christie's, New York #59/R
$80000	52288	Woman washing leg on stepladder (137x48x114cm-54x19x45in) plaster metal executed 1984. 4-May-93 Sotheby's, New York #396/R
$130000	87248	Women on bench with sunglasses (127x102x48cm-50x40x19in) bronze wood edition of five executed 1984. 5-May-94 Sotheby's, New York #234/R
$170000	112583	Girl washing her foot on chair (122x117x61cm-48x46x24in) plaster wood chair. 17-Nov-92 Sotheby's, New York #18/R
$180000	117647	Girl on green kitchen chair (104x76x96cm-41x30x38in) plaster painted wood executed 1964. 4-May-93 Christie's, New York #8/R
$190000	127517	Seated girl, hands clasped (131x53x91cm-52x21x36in) plaster wood executed 1969. 4-May-94 Sotheby's, New York #27/R

SEGUI, Antonio (1934-) Argentinian

$3994	2717	Triangle, assemblage (54x60cm-21x24in) s.d.1967 cut painted wood. 10-Apr-94 Perrin, Versailles #62/R (F.FR 23500)
$6155	3776	Sans titre (58x64x10cm-23x25x4in) s. cut painted wood plexiglass. 18-Oct-92 Catherine Charbonneaux, Paris #69/R (F.FR 31000)

SEIDEL, Emory P (?) American

$1700	1149	Boy and girl reading - book-ends (23cm-9in) i.d.1918 light brown pat.bronze pair. 31-Mar-94 Sotheby's Arcade, New York #175/R
$1800	1169	Mother and child (37cm-15in) i.brown pat.bronze. 9-Sep-93 Sotheby's Arcade, New York #154 b/R
$2000	1299	Female dancer (48cm-19in) i.d.1926 brown pat.bronze Cast Am-Art Bronze F. 9-Sep-93 Sotheby's Arcade, New York #156/R

SELIGMANN, Kurt (1900-1962) American/Swiss

$32000	21622	Deux tetes (53cm-21in) painted wood construction executed 1925. 3-Nov-93 Christie's, New York #252/R

SERRA, Richard (1939-) American

$38740	26260	Model for three plate piece (76x58x58cm-30x23x23in) i. iron concrete executed 1980. 2-Dec-93 Christie's, London #203/R
$65000	43046	La defense (113x61x61cm-44x24x24in) executed 1979 hot-rolled steel. 19-Nov-92 Christie's, New York #238/R
$100000	67568	Flats (388x164x8cm-153x65x3in) hot-rolled steel in 2 plates, executed 1986. 10-Nov-93 Sotheby's, New York #54/R
$155000	102649	Square level forged (175x19x19cm-69x7x7in) forged steel two blocks. 17-Nov-92 Sotheby's, New York #63 a/R

SERVULO, Esmeraldo (1929-) Brazilian

$1200	795	Untitled (120x19cm-47x7in) varnished steel. 24-Nov-92 Christie's, New York #326/R

SHAFER, L E Gus (1907-) American

$3200	2133	Trouble i.num2/6 light brown pat.bronze. 22-May-94 Hindman Galleries, Chicago #30/R

SHAPIRO, Joel (1941-) American

$12000	8054	Untitled (18x20x15cm-7x8x6in) s.d.1987-1988 num.6/6 bronze. 25-Feb-94 Sotheby's, New York #98/R
$14000	9396	Untitled (22x39x6cm-9x15x2in) bronze executed 1983. 5-May-94 Sotheby's, New York #340/R
$18000	11921	Untitled (15x18x14cm-6x7x6in) s.d.85-86 oil on bronze. 18-Nov-92 Sotheby's, New York #285/R
$21000	12353	Untitled (29x17x13cm-11x7x5in) bronze number 4/6. 6-Oct-92 Sotheby's, New York #145/R
$21000	14189	Untitled (60x33x21cm-24x13x8in) cast bronze executed 1980-82. 11-Nov-93 Sotheby's, New York #142/R
$21000	13907	Untitled (9x18x20cm-4x7x8in) st. d.75 num.1/1 cast iron. 18-Nov-92 Sotheby's, New York #247/R
$25000	16779	Untitled (19x22x33cm-7x9x13in) s.d.80 num.3/3 bronze. 5-May-94 Sotheby's, New York #332/R
$26000	17568	Untitled (22x19x33cm-9x7x13in) s.d.80 num.3/3 cast bronze. 11-Nov-93 Sotheby's, New York #151/R
$35000	23649	Untitled - House (16x14x11cm-6x6x4in) d.1974 bronze. 10-Nov-93 Sotheby's, New York #47/R
$45000	26471	Untitled (11x89x6cm-4x35x2in) cast iron wood base executed 1974. 6-Oct-92 Sotheby's, New York #140/R
$60000	39735	Untitled JS 712 (138x32x25cm-54x13x10in) executed 1986 wood. 19-Nov-92 Christie's, New York #237/R
$70000	46358	Untitled (28x43x27cm-11x17x11in) s.d.1981-82 bronze. 18-Nov-92 Sotheby's, New York #252/R
$75000	50676	Untitled (69x137x113cm-27x54x44in) one of three, bronze executed 1986-87. 10-Nov-93 Sotheby's, New York #56/R
$75000	50676	Fall (68x137x112cm-27x54x44in) sig.d.86/87 num.3/3 bronze. 9-Nov-93 Christie's, New York #39/R
$95000	63758	Untitled (122x130x80cm-48x51x31in) s.d.82-83 num.3/3 bronze. 4-May-94 Christie's, New York #306/R
$120000	81081	Untitled (124x38x112cm-49x15x44in) bronze executed 1986-87. 11-Nov-93 Sotheby's, New York #129/R

SHAPIRO, Joel (1941-) American-cont.
$150000 100671 Untitled JS 625 (298x338x183cm-117x133x72in) bronze num.1 ed.of 3 executed 1985. 5-May-94 Sotheby's, New York #279/R
$150000 98039   Untitled (165x201x127cm-65x79x50in) bronze executed 1989 2/4. 4-May-93 Christie's, New York #50/R
$210000 137255 Untitled (229x170x56cm-90x67x22in) cast bronze 1/4 executed 1989. 3-May-93 Sotheby's, New York #78/R
$240000 158940 Untitled (135x163x115cm-53x64x45in) bronze. 17-Nov-92 Sotheby's, New York #54/R

SHEPHERD, J Clinton (1888-?) American
$2000   1227   Cowboy on rearing horse (51x41cm-20x16in) s. bronze Cast.Roman Bronze works. 16-Oct-92 Du Mouchelle, Detroit #27/R
$4250   2872   The bulldogger (30cm-12in) i.num.5 greenish brown pat.bronze f.i. 31-Mar-94 Sotheby's Arcade, New York #197/R

SHIRE, Peter (1947-) American
$2000   1342   Vase project (31x55x36cm-12x22x14in) s.d.1990 painted metal. 25-Feb-94 Sotheby's, New York #189/R

SHRADY, Henry M (1871-1922) American
$12000   8054   The empty saddle (28cm-11in) i.d.1900 green brown pat.bronze Cast R.B.W.N.Y. 2-Dec-93 Sotheby's, New York #78/R
$15000   10000   Equestrian of George Washington (66cm-26in) i. brown pat.bronze f.i. 22-May-94 Hindman Galleries, Chicago #15/R
$20000   12821   'Monarch of the Plains' - figure of elk buffalo (35cm-14in) i.d.1899 brown pat.bronze. 26-May-93 Christie's, New York #101/R

SIBELLINO, Antonio Silvestre (1891-1960) Argentinian
$4200   2781   Muchacho (40cm-16in) cement executed 1929. 11-Nov-92 VerBo, Buenos Aires #99
$17000   10000   La rebelde (46cm-18in) bronze. Cast.R.Buchhass. 29-Sep-92 VerBo, Buenos Aires #119

SIMEONIE (20th C) North American
$978   652   Kneeling Inuit hunter wearing a parka (23cm-9in) s. mottled dark grey soapstone. 6-Jun-94 Waddingtons, Toronto #937/R (C.D 1350)

SIQUEIROS, David (1896-1974) Mexican
$2044   1294   Don Quixote (20x15cm-8x6in) executed 1950 welded steel. 1-Dec-92 Ritchie, Toronto #150/R (C.D 2600)

SIVURAQ, Thomas (1941-) North American
$906   604   Kneeling Inuit woman carrying her child in her amaut (28cm-11in) s. mottled dark soapstone. 6-Jun-94 Waddingtons, Toronto #910 (C.D 1250)

SKOGLUND, Sandy (20th C) American
$2750   1846   Untitled (29x51x46cm-11x20x18in) painted bronze executed 1988. 25-Feb-94 Sotheby's, New York #159/R
$2750   1798   A breeze at work (36x41x41cm-14x16x16in) painted telephone and leaves on wood base. 5-Oct-93 Sotheby's, New York #253/R
$2750   1846   Typewriter No.1 (39x71x39cm-15x28x15in) painted bronze executed 1988. 25-Feb-94 Sotheby's, New York #154/R

SLIVKA, David (1913-) American
$1000   671   Maternity alabaster executed 1951. 24-Feb-94 Sotheby's Arcade, New York #452/R

SMILER, Isa (1921-1986) North American
$1169   769   Carving of muskox with inset carved horns (35cm-14in) s. grey soapstone. 7-Jun-93 Waddingtons, Toronto #885/R (C.D 1500)

SMITH, David (1906-1965) American
$36000   23841   Untitled (19x15x5cm-7x6x2in) s.d.1938 welded steel wood base. 18-Nov-92 Sotheby's, New York #81/R
$50000   33557   Classic figure II, sedate figure (31x8x15cm-12x3x6in) s.d.45 bronze. 4-May-94 Sotheby's, New York #1/R
$52500   34314   Construction no.35 (16x29x8cm-6x11x3in) s.verso steel executed c.1939. 3-May-93 Sotheby's, New York #1/R
$85000   56291   Untitled (42x20x13cm-17x8x5in) s.d.37 welded iron. 17-Nov-92 Sotheby's, New York #35/R
$190000 127517 Forging X (199x28x28cm-78x11x11in) st.sig.i.d.1956 stainless steel. 3-May-94 Christie's, New York #38/R
$200000 135135 Spectre of mother (59x60x24cm-23x24x9in) st.sig.d.1946 welded steel bronze wood base. 9-Nov-93 Christie's, New York #2/R
$210000 137255 Voltri IX (199x81x30cm-78x32x12in) s.d.6/62 steel. 3-May-93 Sotheby's, New York #36/R
$740000 500000 Land coaster (238x85x66cm-94x33x26in) with sig.d.2/10/60 painted steel. 9-Nov-93 Christie's, New York #24/R
$3700000 2483222 Cubi V (248x185x56cm-98x73x22in) s.i.d.June 16,1963 polished stainless steel. 4-May-94 Sotheby's, New York #15/R

SMITH, Ray (1959-) American
$2278   1519   Untitled (112cm-44in) painted wood wool executed 1989. 2-Jun-94 AB Stockholms Auktionsverk, Stockholm #7047/R (S.KR 18000)

SMITH, Tony (1912-1980) American
$7000   4487   Untitled (30x33x36cm-12x13x14in) s.d.61 black pat.bronze. 11-Dec-92 Du Mouchelle, Detroit #2143/R

SMITH, Tony (1912-1980) American-cont.
$12000	7843	Duck (28x34x20cm-11x13x8in) st.sig.d.1963 2/9, bronze. 5-May-93 Christie's, New York #119/R
$13000	8784	Spitball (30x35x35cm-12x14x14in) s.d.61 num.10/50 black marble. 10-Nov-93 Christie's, New York #178/R
$15000	10417	We lost (46x46x46cm-18x18x18in) st.sig.d.1962 num.2/9 bronze. 24-Feb-93 Christie's, New York #30/R
$25000	16779	Moses (86x112x61cm-34x44x24in) cut welded steel executed 1975. 5-May-94 Sotheby's, New York #268/R
$26000	17568	Moses (57x80x33cm-22x31x13in) s.d.1968 num.5/9 bronze. 11-Nov-93 Sotheby's, New York #126/R
$28000	18301	For V.T (74x102x102cm-29x40x40in) bronze executed c.1969 2/6. 4-May-93 Sotheby's, New York #154/R
$55000	37162	Trap (25x140x140cm-10x55x55in) bronze executed 1968 1/9. 11-Nov-93 Sotheby's, New York #105/R
$75000	50336	Tau (114x178x109cm-45x70x43in) ed.of 6 painted aluminum executed 1965. 5-May-94 Sotheby's, New York #255/R
$75000	50676	Throne (71x112x81cm-28x44x32in) welded steel executed 1969. 9-Nov-93 Christie's, New York #19/R

SMITHSON, Robert (1938-1973) American
$32000	21477	Four sided vortex (90x71x71cm-35x28x28in) stainless steel and mirror executed 1967. 4-May-94 Christie's, New York #240/R

SMYTH, Ned (20th C) American?
$2086	1400	Palm tree (173cm-68in) slate glass concrete. 21-Jun-93 Christie's, S. Kensington #163/R

SNELSON, Kenneth (1927-) American
$3000	1961	Untitled (37x37x37cm-15x15x15in) init.st.d.67 aluminium tubes wire. 7-May-93 Christie's, East, New York #121/R
$14000	9459	Bee tree II (81x96x96cm-32x38x38in) aluminium stainless steel execute 1980 2/4. 11-Nov-93 Sotheby's, New York #336/R

SONNIER, Keith (1941-) American
$16000	9412	Fa - reconstruction (190x180cm-75x71in) neon sculpture executed 1969-1974. 6-Oct-92 Sotheby's, New York #131/R

SORIANO, Juan (1920-) Mexican
$10000	6623	Toro (28cm-11in) s.i.d.1990 num.3/6 green pat. bronze. 23-Nov-92 Sotheby's, New York #195 a/R

SOTO, Jesus Rafael (1923-) Venezuelan
$1016	677	Wall piece (50x66x12cm-20x26x5in) s.num.41/175 wood metal. 6-Jun-94 Wolfgang Ketterer, Munich #1265/R (DM 1700)
$6000	4000	Vibration Black, White and Brown (35cm-14in) s.d.1967 painted wood metal nylon wire circular. 18-May-94 Christie's, New York #167/R
$8940	6000	Untitle construction (35x30x9cm-14x12x4in) s.d.61 gouache paper collage metal relief board. 2-Dec-93 Christie's, London #207/R
$11920	8000	Untitled (55x95x15cm-22x37x6in) gouache paper collage painted metal relief board. 2-Dec-93 Christie's, London #130/R
$13049	8642	Azul al centro (52x52x6cm-20x20x2in) s.i.d.1988verso object acrylic wood. 20-Nov-92 Lempertz, Cologne #865/R (DM 21000)
$14900	10000	Untitled (106x106x33cm-42x42x13in) oil wood metal nylon cord executed 1965. 2-Dec-93 Christie's, London #151/R
$16300	10000	Volume sur le losange (112x112x53cm-44x44x21in) s.i.d.1963verso oil on wood painted metal nylon. 15-Oct-92 Christie's, London #28/R
$26000	17568	Modulation en bleu et noir (107x107cm-42x42in) s.i.d.1966 oil panel wire nylon cord. 23-Nov-93 Christie's, New York #170/R
$28000	18667	Barras Negras y Plata (124x60cm-49x24in) s.i.d.1968 painted wood nylon cord metal. 18-May-94 Christie's, New York #169/R
$28000	18301	Escultura en azul y negro (175x106x66cm-69x42x26in) s.d.1966 painted wood nylon cord metal wires. 17-May-93 Christie's, New York #170/R
$30000	19868	Nucleo Central (211x108cm-83x43in) s.d.1969 verso painted metal construction. 23-Nov-92 Sotheby's, New York #75/R
$32000	21622	Vibration III (150x61cm-59x24in) oil canvas wire masonite executed c.1960-61. 23-Nov-93 Christie's, New York #170/R
$44000	29253	AMB.38 (118x107cm-46x42in) s.d.1983 i.verso painted wood metal. 18-May-94 Christie's, New York #134/R

SPAMPINATO, Clemente (1912-) American
$1500	1000	Saddle bronc rider (58cm-23in) i.d.1955 greenish brown pat.bronze f.st. 22-May-94 Hindman Galleries, Chicago #33/R
$1900	1267	You crazy bay (71cm-28in) i.d.1973 greenish brown pat.bronze f.st. 22-May-94 Hindman Galleries, Chicago #32/R

STANKIEWICZ, Richard (1922-) American
$2000	1351	Untitled wall relief (42x29x6cm-17x11x2in) st.init.d.1976 oxidized steel. 8-Nov-93 Christie's, East, New York #206/R
$5000	3356	Untitled (41x41x18cm-16x16x7in) welded steel executed 1964. 5-May-94 Sotheby's, New York #127/R
$8000	5369	Composition (32x41x23cm-13x16x9in) steel executed 1959. 25-Feb-94 Sotheby's, New York #30 a/R
$17000	11409	Untitled (79x80x48cm-31x31x19in) welded steel executed 1981. 5-May-94 Sotheby's, New York #153/R

STANKIEWICZ, Richard (1922-) American-cont.
$24000	16107	Untitled no RS69 (112x61x46cm-44x24x18in) welded steel executed 1959. 5-May-94 Sotheby's, New York #87 a/R

STARN TWINS (1961-) American
$1165	776	Yellow strip (31x340cm-12x134in) silver print tape wood glass executed 1986. 2-Jun-94 AB Stockholms Auktionsverk, Stockholm #7092/R (S.KR 9200)
$8000	5369	Untitled (130x119x39cm-51x47x15in) s.d.89 num.544 photo emulsion mylar wood steel. 4-May-94 Christie's, New York #284/R

STEINBACH, Haim (1944-) American
$2800	1892	Shelf with Lifetime Cutlery (57x53x48cm-22x21x19in) s.d.83 painted wood nails screws knives. 8-Nov-93 Christie's, East, New York #148/R
$7000	4730	Together naturally, tri-part Scandinavian ash (62x104x37cm-24x41x15in) ceramic vase ten wood trays formica shelf. 10-Nov-93 Christie's, New York #256/R
$8000	5369	Flavour (63x131x27cm-25x52x11in) s.d.89 glass decanters on mirrored formica shelf. 4-May-94 Christie's, New York #289/R
$8000	5405	Dramatic yet neutral (96x119x44cm-38x47x17in) s.d.84 verso wood formica wicker baskets balls. 11-Nov-93 Sotheby's, New York #238/R
$12000	8108	Together naturally - doubled (61x140x37cm-24x55x15in) mixed media construction executed 1984. 11-Nov-93 Sotheby's, New York #229/R
$13000	8725	One minute managers V-2 (68x445x35cm-27x175x14in) s.d.90 verso caphalon pots medicine balls shelf. 23-Feb-94 Christie's, New York #127/R
$22000	14379	No wires no power cord (155x287x55cm-61x113x22in) s.d.1989 metal trash cans lava lamps on formica. 5-Oct-93 Sotheby's, New York #247/R

STELLA, Frank (1936-) American
$15000	10067	Playskool screen (102x119x74cm-40x47x29in) sig.d.num.'83 3/5 acrylic enamel aluminium steel. 23-Feb-94 Christie's, New York #31/R
$16000	10738	The bonny bunch of roses (56x41x23cm-22x16x9in) s.d.85 num.1/3 shoe polish enamel welded steel. 5-May-94 Sotheby's, New York #288/R
$16000	10738	In the pit from Sin Set Free (63x41x34cm-25x16x13in) s.d.85 num.1/3 liquid encaustic sealed on steel. 25-Feb-94 Sotheby's, New York #93/R
$32000	20915	Virginia's bloody soul (89x66x46cm-35x26x18in) num.2/3 liquid encaustic beeswax steel. 4-May-93 Sotheby's, New York #186 a/R
$100000	67114	Corpo senza l'anima no 12, 4X (419x329x56cm-165x130x22in) mixed media canvas magnesium aluminum fiberglas. 4-May-94 Sotheby's, New York #49/R
$100000	67114	Western holdings (305x284x249cm-120x112x98in) mixed media honeycombed aluminium executed 1983. 25-Feb-94 Sotheby's, New York #92/R

SULTAN, Donald (1951-) American
$4000	2703	Oct. 1 (30x30x5cm-12x12x2in) init.i.d.1978 graphite lino tile wood. 8-Nov-93 Christie's, East, New York #172/R
$8000	5229	April 27, 1979 (30x30x4cm-12x12x2in) init. init.i.verso linoleum tile graphite wood. 7-May-93 Christie's, East, New York #127/R
$30000	20833	Migs, June 18, 1984 (245x244x4cm-96x96x2in) s.i.d.num.1-4 latex tar vinyl tiles on masonite. 24-Feb-93 Christie's, New York #89/R

SURLS, James (1943-) American
$5600	3758	Night dancing (178x127x102cm-70x50x40in) hanging wood sculpture executed 1985-86. 25-Feb-94 Sotheby's, New York #130/R

SUVERO, Mark di (1933-) American
$1000	667	Untitled (25cm-10in) init.d.1972 st.num.100/250 steel five pieces. 23-May-94 Hindman Galleries, Chicago #403
$1200	805	Untitled (39x66x41cm-15x26x16in) i.st.7/20 steel. 23-Feb-94 Christie's, New York #71/R
$1400	946	Untitled (11x10x3cm-4x4x1in) welded steel. 8-Nov-93 Christie's, East, New York #138/R
$1500	1000	Untitled (38x33cm-15x13in) i.num.5/50 steel sculpture five pieces. 23-May-94 Hindman Galleries, Chicago #404
$7500	4717	Untitled (22x23cm-9x9in) mono. welded steel two parts. 25-Apr-93 Butterfield & Butterfield, San Francisco #2155/R
$15000	10067	Untitled (28x44x28cm-11x17x11in) painted steel in two parts executed 1962. 5-May-94 Sotheby's, New York #124/R
$18000	11765	Untitled (41x66x30cm-16x26x12in) s. steel executed c.1970. 4-May-93 Sotheby's, New York #362/R
$20000	13423	Unchained (46x47x46cm-18x19x18in) welded steel in two parts executed 1969. 5-May-94 Sotheby's, New York #147/R
$22000	14865	Untitled (46x36x30cm-18x14x12in) s. steel two parts executed c.1970. 11-Nov-93 Sotheby's, New York #297/R
$24000	16107	Untitled (27x28x29cm-11x11x11in) welded steel executed 1965. 4-May-94 Christie's, New York #129/R
$25000	16892	Elke (43cm-17in) steel in two parts executed 1992-93. 21-Apr-94 Butterfield & Butterfield, San Francisco #1205
$45000	29412	Untitled (262x119x119cm-103x47x47in) welded steel executed 1980. 4-May-93 Christie's, New York #7/R
$85000	57432	Spirit of Southpaw (159x284x286cm-63x112x113in) steel executed 1981-85. 11-Nov-93 Sotheby's, New York #13/R
$425000	277778	Che Faro Senza Eurydice (213x264x231cm-84x104x91in) weathered timber rope nails executed 1959-60. 3-May-93 Sotheby's, New York #13/R

SUZOR-COTE, Marc-Aurele de Foy (1867-1937) Canadian
$1550	1047	The Scotsman (45cm-18in) s.i. bronze. 3-Nov-93 Sotheby's, Toronto #84/R (C.D 2000)

SUZOR-COTE, Marc-Aurele de Foy (1867-1937) Canadian-cont.
$1888	1276	L'Iroquois (48cm-19in) s.i.d.1907 num.13/24 pat.bronze i.Rom.Bronze W. 23-Nov-93 Fraser Pinneys, Quebec #388 (C.D 2500)
$1965	1244	Le faucheur (28x22cm-11x9in) s.d.1907 num.5 bronze f.i.Roman Bronze Works NY. 30-Nov-92 Ritchie, Toronto #285/R (C.D 2500)
$3641	2427	Jeune Canadienne (18cm-7in) s.i.d.1922 bronze wood base. 11-May-94 Sotheby's, Toronto #175/R (C.D 5000)
$3892	2577	L'Appel a l'orignal (53cm-21in) s.i.num.3/25base bronze. 18-Nov-92 Sotheby's, Toronto #293 (C.D 5000)
$4650	3142	Le vieux pionnier canadien (39cm-15in) s.i.d.1912 num.8/25 bronze st.f.Roman Br.Works. 3-Nov-93 Sotheby's, Toronto #271/R (C.D 6000)
$5663	3827	La compagne du vieux pionnier (40cm-16in) s.i.d.1912 pat.bronze Cast Roman Bronze Works. 23-Nov-93 Fraser Pinneys, Quebec #385/R (C.D 7500)
$6418	4337	Le modele (39cm-15in) s.i.d.1925 pat.bronze Cast Roman Bronze Works. 23-Nov-93 Fraser Pinneys, Quebec #382/R (C.D 8500)
$7005	4639	La Compagne du vieux pionnier (37cm-15in) s.i.d.1912 bronze Cast.Roman Bronze Works N.Y. 18-Nov-92 Sotheby's, Toronto #132/R (C.D 9000)
$7282	4854	Le pionnier (56cm-22in) s.num.11 bronze st.f.Roman Bronze Works. 11-May-94 Sotheby's, Toronto #176/R (C.D 10000)
$8636	5607	Le halage du bois (37x152cm-15x60in) s. pat.bronze st.f.Roman Bronze Works. 21-Jun-94 Fraser Pinneys, Quebec #160 (C.D 12000)
$8720	5699	Le vieux pionnier Canadien (39cm-15in) s.i.d.1912 bronze f.i.Roman Bronze Works NY. 19-May-93 Sotheby's, Toronto #293/R (C.D 11000)
$12064	7990	Le vieux pionnier Canadien (39cm-15in) s.i.d.1912 bronze Cast.Roman Bronze Works N.Y. 18-Nov-92 Sotheby's, Toronto #131/R (C.D 15500)
$13477	8808	La compagne du vieux pionnier (38cm-15in) s.i.d.1912 bronze f.i.Roman Bronze Works NY. 19-May-93 Sotheby's, Toronto #292/R (C.D 17000)

TAKKIRUQ, Nelson (1930-) North American
$861	574	Two Inuit facing each other singing (22x29cm-9x11in) s. green stone. 30-May-94 Ritchie, Toronto #93/R (C.D 1200)
$1481	974	Carving of seated Inuit fisherman landing fish (41cm-16in) green serpentine ivory stone ebonized base. 7-Jun-94 Waddingtons, Toronto #905/R (C.D 1900)

TALIRUNILI, Joe (1906-1976) North American
$870	580	Standing owl (13cm-5in) mottled dark grey soapstone. 6-Jun-94 Waddingtons, Toronto #1004 (C.D 1200)
$2408	1616	Standing Inuit hunter, pack on back, carrying bow and arrow (18cm-7in) mottled grey soapstone wood string ivory. 29-Nov-93 Waddingtons, Toronto #928/R (C.D 3200)

TATANIQ, George (1910-) North American
$1254	804	Standing Inuit drummer wearing parka, holding carved antler drum in hand (28cm-11in) s. mottled dark grey soapstone. 7-Dec-92 Waddingtons, Toronto #978/R (C.D 1600)

THERRIEN, Robert (1947-) American
$8000	5405	Keyhole (13x4x2cm-5x2x1in) bronze executed 1983. 10-Nov-93 Christie's, New York #375/R
$10000	6536	Untitled (13x4x1cm-5x2x0in) init.d.1981 bronze. 5-May-93 Christie's, New York #124/R
$12000	8054	Yellow seagull (249x290x20cm-98x114x8in) init.verso enamel steel executed 1990. 23-Feb-94 Christie's, New York #98/R
$35000	23649	Untitled (152x74cm-60x29in) tin on bronze executed 1985. 10-Nov-93 Christie's, New York #225/R

THOMPSON, L (19/20th C) American
$1848	1200	Bull elephant (36cm-14in) s.num.1/12 oxidised metal green marble base. 14-Jan-93 Sotheby's, London #500

TIKTAK, John (1916-1981) North American
$2174	1449	Inuit woman carrying her child in her amaut (15cm-6in) s. mottled light grey soapstone. 6-Jun-94 Waddingtons, Toronto #1036/R (C.D 3000)
$3085	2071	Kneeling Inuit woman carrying child in her amaut (18cm-7in) s. mottled grey soapstone. 29-Nov-93 Waddingtons, Toronto #823/R (C.D 4100)
$4872	3205	Family group, carved with four faces (27cm-11in) s. green soapstone. 7-Jun-93 Waddingtons, Toronto #951/R (C.D 6250)

TINGUELY, Jean and SAINT PHALLE, Niki de (20th C) Swiss/American
$53640	36000	Pallus Athenee ou le chariot (79x208x71cm-31x82x28in) num.2/10 iron steel motor polyester figure table. 24-Jun-93 Christie's, London #71/R

TOLEDO, Francisco (1940-) Mexican
$6000	4000	El Toro (25cm-10in) s.num.II/V brown pat.bronze. 18-May-94 Christie's, New York #198/R

TOLSON, Edgar (1904-1984) American
$7600	5033	Adam and Eve Exec.1973 carved poplar paint. 21-Nov-92 Litchfield Auction Gallery #11

TOMASELLO, Luis (1915-) Argentinian
$1049	704	Chromopastique no.496 (50x60x1cm-20x24x0in) s.d.1981 moving cut out. 8-May-94 Jonquet, Paris #127 (F.FR 6000)
$4019	2610	Atmosphere Chromoplastique (143x98cm-56x39in) painted wood relief panel painted 1970. 24-Jun-94 Francis Briest, Paris #42 (F.FR 22000)

TORRALVA, Luis (20th C) Chilean
$8000	5298	El beso (56cm-22in) bronze. 18-Nov-92 Roldan & Cia, Buenos Aires #23

TORRES-GARCIA, Joaquin (1874-1949) Uruguayan
$22500	15203	Grafismo con caracol (37x24cm-15x9in) i. panel executed c.1930. 22-Nov-93 Sotheby's, New York #34/R
$32000	20915	Cinco juguetes (21cm-8in) 17 painted wooden toys executed c.1920. 18-May-93 Sotheby's, New York #43/R
$42000	27815	Pez A A C (19x35cm-7x14in) init.d.39 verso oil on incised wood. 23-Nov-92 Sotheby's, New York #5/R
$42500	28146	Madera en Forma de T Roja con Signos (31x17cm-12x7in) incised painted wood construction. 23-Nov-92 Sotheby's, New York #9/R
$45000	30405	Constuctivo (50x22cm-20x9in) painted wood construction executed c.1928. 22-Nov-93 Sotheby's, New York #36/R
$47500	32095	Hombre abstracto (72x25cm-28x10in) painted wood construction. 22-Nov-93 Sotheby's, New York #39/R
$57500	38079	Madera Planos de Color (43x20cm-17x8in) s.d.29 verso oil on incised wood. 23-Nov-92 Sotheby's, New York #13/R
$60000	39735	Sin titulo (20x29cm-8x11in) s.d.1927 verso painted wood construction. 23-Nov-92 Sotheby's, New York #6/R
$95000	62914	Estructura en blanco y negro (48x35cm-19x14in) s.d.30 verso painted wood construction. 23-Nov-92 Sotheby's, New York #10/R
$97500	64570	Construccion (43x19cm-17x7in) init.d.35 verso painted wood construction. 23-Nov-92 Sotheby's, New York #3/R
$100000	66225	Forma Policromada (40x40cm-16x16in) s.d.31 painted wood construction. 23-Nov-92 Sotheby's, New York #16/R

TROIANI, Troiano (1885-1963) Argentinian
$1200	795	Heroe legendario (38cm-15in) i.num.1/10 black bronze. 29-Sep-93 Sotheby's Arcade, New York #58/R
$1600	1074	Female nude (34cm-13in) i.num.1/10 dark brown-black pat.bronze. 24-Feb-94 Sotheby's Arcade, New York #277/R
$2600	1745	The labourer (38cm-15in) i.num.1/10 black pat.bronze. 24-Feb-94 Sotheby's Arcade, New York #278/R

TROVA, Ernest (1927-) American
$1300	861	Untitled (61x60cm-24x24in) enamel steel. 17-Nov-92 Christie's, East, New York #229/R
$2500	1736	Etrog (29cm-11in) i.num.4/7, brown pat bronze. 26-Feb-93 Sotheby's Arcade, New York #320/R
$10000	6711	FM/24 New Cut Figure No.3 (77x35x13cm-30x14x5in) st.sig.d.num.3-8 1986 stainless steel. 23-Feb-94 Christie's, New York #42/R
$20000	13889	AWF no 3FM 24 (81x18x29cm-32x7x11in) st.sig.d.1986 num.4-8 stainless steel. 23-Feb-93 Sotheby's, New York #290/R

TUCKER, William (1935-) American
$2010	1350	Union of Opposites (104cm-41in) painted wood. 26-Mar-93 Christie's, London #165/R

TUDLIK (1890-1966) North American
$1413	942	Carving of an owl standing with outstretched wings (13cm-5in) marbled green serpentine. 6-Jun-94 Waddingtons, Toronto #957 (C.D 1950)

TUNNILLIE, Ashevak (1956-) North American
$1325	872	Carving of Inuit hunter fighting with polar bear (51cm-20in) s. green soapstone. 7-Jun-93 Waddingtons, Toronto #936 (C.D 1700)

TUTTLE, Richard (1941-) American
$4500	3020	Lamp (120x90x30cm-47x35x12in) s.i.d.1985 acrylic graphite collage wire. 23-Feb-94 Christie's, New York #93/R
$4750	3188	XI (21x15x8cm-8x6x3in) acrylic string aluminum foil wood cardboard wire. 5-May-94 Sotheby's, New York #256/R
$10430	7000	Monkey's recovery I-No.5 (82x101x9cm-32x40x4in) wood wire oil linen cotton executed 1983. 2-Dec-93 Christie's, London #161/R
$11000	7190	Sentences 1 (117x160x14cm-46x63x6in) wood acrylic ceramic light fixtures bulbs -1989. 5-May-93 Christie's, New York #192/R
$85000	55556	Green triptych (68x171x6cm-27x67x2in) three elements s.d.1965 verso oil on wood. 4-May-93 Christie's, New York #25/R

VAISMAN, Meyer (1960-) American
$6500	4362	Untitled (115x94x24cm-45x37x9in) acrylic silkscr.canvas on wood construction. 5-May-94 Sotheby's, New York #356/R
$10000	6623	Pollute the fool (181x130x43cm-71x51x17in) s.i.d.1986 ink canvas over panel glass resin. 19-Nov-92 Christie's, New York #107/R
$30000	20270	Untitled (184x175x17cm-72x69x7in) acrylic silkscreened canvas over wood exec.1990. 11-Nov-93 Sotheby's, New York #219/R

VARELA, Abigail (1948-) Venezuelan
$13000	8667	Mujer recostada (47x65x28cm-19x26x11in) s.num.6/6 brown pat.bronze executed 1990. 18-May-94 Christie's, New York #235/R
$16000	10811	Mujer vertical Mirando al horizonte (93x64x52cm-37x25x20in) s.num.6/6 brown pat.bronze executed 1990. 23-Nov-93 Christie's, New York #114/R
$18000	11765	Mujer sentada con brazos abiertos (62cm-24in) s.num.1/8 brown pat.bronze f.st. 17-May-93 Christie's, New York #235/R
$50000	33113	Caminadora con Nino Volador (185cm-73in) s.d.num.1 brown pat.bronze. 24-Nov-92 Christie's, New York #29/R

VILLAREAL (1944-) Mexican
$1200	800	Ballerina in arabesque position (71cm-28in) bronze. 21-May-94 Dargate Auction Galleries, Pittsburgh #2

VITAL, Not (1948-) American
$2500	1656	Einhorn, Zweihorn, Dreihorn (299x66x14cm-118x26x6in) s.d.1985verso wood hydrocal and horns. 17-Nov-92 Christie's, East, New York #23/R
$5000	3311	Untitled, wheel (284x256x8cm-112x101x3in) executed 1988 bronze. 17-Nov-92 Christie's, East, New York #30/R

VIVOLO, John (20th C) American
$1300	861	Chicken slaughter weathervane whirligig carved painted wood tin. 21-Nov-92 Litchfield Auction Gallery #12

VOLK, Leonard Wells (1828-1895) American
$950	638	Bust of Abraham Lincoln (76cm-30in) s. 5-Mar-94 San Rafael Auction Galleries #53

VOLK, Leonard Wells and SAINT-GAUDEN, Augustus (19th C) American
$1500	867	Bust of Abraham Lincoln (53cm-21in) i.d.1860 gold painted plaster st.foundry seal. 25-Sep-92 Sotheby's Arcade, New York #173/R

VONNOH, Bessie Potter (1872-1955) American
$3000	1987	Standing woman in classical dress (49cm-19in) i.num.2/9 medium brown pat.bronze. 23-Sep-93 Sotheby's, New York #136/R
$4000	2597	The intruder (32cm-13in) i.brown pat.bronze Cast Roman Bronze Works. 9-Sep-93 Sotheby's Arcade, New York #154 a
$5250	3548	Dancing girl (27cm-11in) num.A10 brown pat.bronze f.i.Roman Works NY. 31-Mar-94 Sotheby's Arcade, New York #92/R
$6500	4221	Motherhood, a group (46cm-18in) polychrome plaster executed 1903. 8-Jul-94 Sloan, North Bethesda #2726/R
$8500	5629	Girl dancing (36cm-14in) s.i. brown pat.bronze f.i.Roman Bronze Works NY. 13-Nov-92 Skinner, Bolton #167/R
$16000	10667	In Arcadia (72cm-28in) i. greenish-brown pat.bronze f.i.Roman Works NY. 17-Mar-94 Sotheby's, New York #87/R
$28000	18543	Water lilies (74cm-29in) i.num.11 golden pat.bronze f.i.Roman Works NY. 23-Sep-93 Sotheby's, New York #137/R

VOULKOS, Peter (1924-) American
$9000	5696	Philadelphia story (42x152x51cm-17x60x20in) s.num.3/5 bronze. 25-Oct-92 Butterfield & Butterfield, San Francisco #2328/R
$13000	8228	Vessel (71cm-28in) s.d.68 black gas-fired ceramic. 25-Oct-92 Butterfield & Butterfield, San Francisco #2295/R

WALT DISNEY STUDIOS (20th C) American
$2000	1342	Model of Broom and Buckets for 'Fantasia' wood straw wire frame animation model exec.1940. 12-Dec-93 Butterfield & Butterfield, Los Angeles #1149/R
$5500	3595	Abu. Sultan. Iago (x9999cm-in) 6 of 18, 9 of 16, 15 of 15, painted figures. 9-Oct-93 Sotheby's, New York #260/R
$6000	3922	Aladdin. Lamp 34 of 38, 5 of 16, painted model statues two. 9-Oct-93 Sotheby's, New York #257/R
$7000	4575	Genie (38cm-15in) 6 of 25 hand painted statue. 9-Oct-93 Sotheby's, New York #258/R
$7500	4902	Jafar with staff. Staff head 8 of 21, 4 of 8 painted figures two. 9-Oct-93 Sotheby's, New York #259/R
$8500	5556	Rajah. Jasmine 7 of 14, 20 of 20, painted figures two. 9-Oct-93 Sotheby's, New York #256/R

WALTER, Valerie Harrisse (1892-?) American
$1000	676	Bamboo the gorilla (19cm-7in) i.d.1926 black pat.bronze f.st.Roman Works Inc. 31-Mar-94 Sotheby's Arcade, New York #176/R

WARD, John Quincy Adams (1830-1910) American
$2000	1299	Henry B. Hyde, founder Equitable Life Assurance Society (53cm-21in) s.i. brown pat.bronze st.f.Bonnard exec.1901. 8-Jul-94 Sloan, North Bethesda #2727/R

WARHOL, Andy (1928-1986) American
$1861	1257	Brillo (16x13x6cm-6x5x2in) s. box board. 24-Nov-93 Watine-Arnault, Paris #64/R (F.FR 11000)
$5412	3632	Campbells (11cm-4in) s. tins two sold with signed photograph. 29-Nov-93 Francis Briest, Paris #51/R (F.FR 32000)
$9198	6132	Times / 5. New York - five watches on one strap (22x2cm-9x1in) s.num.169/250 executed 1987/1988. 4-Jun-94 Aucktionhaus Burkard, Luzern #100/R (S.FR 13000)

WARHOL, Andy (1928-1986) American-cont.
$15000	9804	Campbell's Tomato Juice (25x48x24cm-10x19x9in) silkscreen inks synthetic polymer wood exec.1964. 5-May-93 Christie's, New York #295/R
$22000	14570	Campbell's tomato juice (25x48x24cm-10x19x9in) s.executed 1964 synth.polymer silkscreen wood. 19-Nov-92 Christie's, New York #335/R
$33000	21569	White Brillo box (43x43x36cm-17x17x14in) s. synthetic polymer paint silkscreened wood. 4-May-93 Sotheby's, New York #381 a/R
$38000	24837	Brillo Box (33x41x33cm-13x16x13in) s. silkscreen inks synthetic polymer wood. 5-May-93 Christie's, New York #232/R

WARNEKE, Heinz (1895-?) American/German
$2500	1645	Royal Minstrel (43x51cm-17x20in) i. silver plated bronze f.st.Valsuani. 4-Jun-93 Sotheby's, New York #90/R

WARNER BROS STUDIOS (20th C) American
$800	537	Figure of 'Joker' from 'Batman' (44cm-17in) bronze hollow wood base executed 1989. 12-Dec-93 Butterfield & Butterfield, Los Angeles #965/R

WEAVER, John (1920-) Canadian
$1077	718	Bear claws III (46x51x24cm-18x20x9in) init. bronze 1/25. 30-May-94 Hodgins, Calgary #50/R (C.D 1500)

WEBSTER, Meg (20th C) American
$4000	2649	Contained pond water (124x46x46cm-49x18x18in) glass water algae executed 1987 edition of 3. 18-Nov-92 Sotheby's, New York #292/R

WEIN, Albert W (1915-) American
$3250	2196	Naomi (52cm-20in) i.num.3/9 green pat.bronze f.st. 31-Mar-94 Sotheby's Arcade, New York #90/R

WEINMAN, Adolph Alexander (1870-1952) American
$24000	15385	'Chief Blackbird - Ogalalla sioux' (40cm-16in) i. reddish brown pat.bronze f.i.Roman Works NY. 26-May-93 Christie's, New York #102/R
$26000	16456	Chief Blackbird-Ogalalla Sioux (47cm-19in) s.i.foundry Roman Bronze Wks bronze. 3-Dec-92 Sotheby's, New York #77/R

WEISS, David and FISCHLI, Peter (20th C) American?
$3291	2194	The plant (41cm-16in) black rubber. 2-Jun-94 AB Stockholms Auktionsverk, Stockholm #7008/R (S.KR 26000)
$3544	2363	Dog pot No.2 (9x28cm-4x11in) black rubber executed 1987. 2-Jun-94 AB Stockholms Auktionsverk, Stockholm #7123/R (S.KR 28000)
$4200	2819	Untitled - Grosse frau (113x25x18cm-44x10x7in) plaster one of six executed 1989. 3-May-94 Christie's, East, New York #212/R
$7000	4698	Square cushion (38x54x54cm-15x21x21in) black rubber executed 1987. 3-May-94 Christie's, East, New York #211/R

WESSELMANN, Tom (1931-) American
$5800	3791	Tiny dropped bra no.16 (8x13x6cm-3x5x2in) s.d.1981 num.16 liquitex board plexiglas box. 7-May-93 Christie's, East, New York #191/R
$6500	4362	Maquette for smoking cigar (18x23x5cm-7x9x2in) s.i.d.1983 verso liquitex bristol board wood. 25-Feb-94 Sotheby's, New York #70/R
$8046	5400	Maquette for Bedroom Blonde Doodle with photo - 3D (33x38x4cm-13x15x2in) s.d.88 liquitex bristol board on card. 2-Dec-93 Christie's, London #122/R
$95000	64189	Tulip and smoking cigarette (208x307x188cm-82x121x74in) st.sig.num.d.83 1/3 enamel aluminium. 9-Nov-93 Christie's, New York #53/R

WESTERMANN, H C (1922-1981) American
$18000	12162	Strong man's chair (107x56x52cm-42x22x20in) st.sig.d.1970 wood metal screws faux leather. 10-Nov-93 Christie's, New York #220/R
$31000	20530	The pig house (138x99x45cm-54x39x18in) s.i.d.72 pine copper rubber wood base. 19-Nov-92 Christie's, New York #429/R
$47000	31757	Clean air (40x58x37cm-16x23x15in) st.sig.i.d.1964 wood glass caulk. 10-Nov-93 Christie's, New York #224/R

WHARTON, Margaret (1943-) American
$6000	4054	Book ends (309x40x5cm-122x16x2in) book fragments glue wood executed 1981. 8-Nov-93 Christie's, East, New York #33/R

WHEELER, Hughlette (1901-1954) American
$2100	1214	Cowboy (39cm-15in) i. dark brown pat.bronze st.f.Gorham Co. 25-Sep-92 Sotheby's Arcade, New York #200/R

WHITNEY, Gertrude (c.1876-1942) American
$1500	993	Figure of nurse (44cm-17in) i. brown pat.bronze f.st.Roman Bronze Works NY. 22-Sep-93 Christie's, New York #112/R
$4250	2796	Chinoise (36cm-14in) greenish pat.bronze f.st.Gorham Co Founders. 31-Mar-93 Sotheby's Arcade, New York #245/R
$6000	4196	Spirit of the Red Cross (46cm-18in) i.d.1920 black pat.bronze Cast Roman Bronze Work. 10-Mar-93 Sotheby's, New York #100/R
$8000	5298	Wallflower - portrait of Barbara Whitney (52cm-20in) i. medium brown pat.bronze f.st.C Valsuani. 22-Sep-93 Christie's, New York #110/R

WIEGAND, Don (20th C) American
$1400	897	Bust of Mark Twain (41cm-16in) s.num.47/110 bronze. 26-Apr-93 Selkirks, St. Louis #152/R

WILEY, William T (1937-) American
$3000   2027   Fresh start for Pandora (114x28x15cm-45x11x6in) init.d.1985 wood canvas graphite metal plastic. 8-Nov-93 Christie's, East, New York #26/R

WILMARTH, Christopher (1943-1987) American
$15000   10135   Long leavers gate in steps (51x41x51cm-20x16x20in) s.d.1980 num.sc06 steel glass. 11-Nov-93 Sotheby's, New York #149/R
$45000   30405   Schottland's second slope (216x30x8cm-85x12x3in) etched glass wire executed 1970. 10-Nov-93 Sotheby's, New York #52/R
$50000   33784   Stray (107x107x8cm-42x42x3in) s.i.d.1977 etched glass steel wire steel plate. 10-Nov-93 Christie's, New York #217/R

WITKIN, Isaac (20th C) American
$2250   1324   Untitled (39cm-15in) init.num.IV/VI welded steel paint. 6-Oct-92 Sotheby's, New York #51/R

WOODBURY, Lloyd (1917-) American
$1900   1267   Range Boss (84cm-33in) i. brown green pat.bronze. 22-May-94 Hindman Galleries, Chicago #29/R

WYLAND (1956-) American
$2315   1553   Celebration of the sea (16cm-6in) s.d.1990 num.7/300 bronze. 21-Mar-94 Stephan Welz, Johannesburg #83/R (SA.R 8000)

WYLE, Florence (1881-1968) Canadian
$1712   1134   Spring (28cm-11in) s.i. bronze. 18-Nov-92 Sotheby's, Toronto #180/R (C.D 2200)

YOKO ONO (1933-) American
$1100   738   A box of smile (6x6x6cm-2x2x2in) st.init.i.d.67 stainless steel mirror one of 150. 3-May-94 Christie's, East, New York #94/R
$2400   1611   Painting to hammer a nail in (113x22x6cm-44x9x2in) with sig.d.1961 num.6/9 bronze metal chain nails. 23-Feb-94 Christie's, East, New York #319/R
$2800   1879   Keys to Open the Skies (18x26x4cm-7x10x2in) st.init.i.88 bronze. 23-Feb-94 Christie's, East, New York #321/R
$3874   2600   Box of smile (6x6x6cm-2x2x2in) st.init.d.67 stainless steel box mirror. 24-Jun-93 Sotheby's, London #73/R
$9000   5882   Painting to Hammer a Nail in (113x22x6cm-44x9x2in) sig.st.num.d.6/9 61-68 bronze nails chain hammer. 7-May-93 Christie's, East, New York #64/R

YOUNG, Mahonri (1877-1957) American
$4000   2532   Bookends of elephants (14cm-6in) i. greenish-brown pat.bronze pair. 4-Dec-92 Christie's, New York #99/R
$17000   11409   'Right to the Jaw' - group of boxers (36x50cm-14x20in) i. reddish brown pat.bronze f.st.Valsuani. 3-Dec-93 Christie's, New York #25/R
$18000   12081   'On the Button' - group of boxers (36x59cm-14x23in) i. medium brown pat.bronze f.st.Valsuani. 3-Dec-93 Christie's, New York #24/R

YOUNGBLOOD, Daisy (1945-) American
$4800   3179   Two headed horse (52x74x12cm-20x29x5in) terracotta hair mounted on stone. 17-Nov-92 Christie's, East, New York #121/R

ZOGBAUM, Wilfrid M (1915-1965) American
$800   537   Clockwork (23x22x13cm-9x9x5in) sig.d.num.62 6 brass. 23-Feb-94 Christie's, East, New York #383/R
$3400   2282   Rabbit (101x57x25cm-40x22x10in) sig. spray enamel steel granite executed 1960. 23-Feb-94 Christie's, East, New York #382/R

ZORACH, William (1887-1966) American
$850   567   Nude (18cm-7in) s. brownish-gold pat.bronze. 22-May-94 James Bakker, Cambridge #85/R
$2000   1299   Pegasus (41cm-16in) cast pink stone. 9-Sep-93 Sotheby's Arcade, New York #409/R
$2400   1558   Couple (44cm-17in) i. gold pat.bronze. 9-Sep-93 Sotheby's Arcade, New York #410/R
$3800   2500   Sleeping cat (29cm-11in) i. terracotta. 31-Mar-93 Sotheby's Arcade, New York #419/R
$5000   3333   Figure of child (58cm-23in) i.indis.d. green brown pat.bronze. 16-Mar-94 Christie's, New York #69/R
$5000   3333   Affection, girl and dog (37cm-15in) i. brown pat.bronze. 16-Mar-94 Christie's, New York #68/R
$21000   14094   Floating figure (84cm-33in) i.d.1922 gilt pat.bronze. 2-Dec-93 Sotheby's, New York #146/R
$22000   14103   'Young woman' (57cm-22in) s. pink marble. 26-May-93 Christie's, New York #179/R
$28000   18667   Pioneer family group (244x132cm-96x52in) i.d.1964 num.1 brown pat.bronze. 26-May-94 Christie's, New York #117/R

ZUNIGA, Francisco (1913-) Costa Rican
$5870   3939   Mujer reclinada (28cm-11in) terracotta. 1-Dec-93 Louis Morton, Mexico #150/R (M.P 18200)

ZUNIGA, Francisco (1913-) Costa Rican-cont.

$8000	5333	Mujer de pie, from Mexican Masters Suite (37cm-15in) s.d.1970 num.13/25 brown pat.bronze. 18-May-94 Sotheby's, New York #366/R
$8000	5298	Mother and child (29cm-11in) i.d.1974 num.IX/XXVIII green pat.bronze. 29-Sep-93 Sotheby's Arcade, New York #231/R
$10000	6711	Mujer con rebozo (22cm-9in) s.d.1965 black pat.bronze. 7-Jan-94 Gary Nader, Miami #91/R
$10000	6623	Desnudo sentado (41cm-16in) i.d.1971 num.V/VI dark brown pat.bronze. 30-Jun-93 Sotheby's Arcade, New York #225/R
$12000	8000	Mujer de Pie con Rebozo (41cm-16in) s. one of three brown pat.bronze executed 1960. 18-May-94 Christie's, New York #305/R
$12000	7947	Mujer de Pie (40cm-16in) s.num.I/IV green pat.bronze. 24-Nov-92 Christie's, New York #116/R
$14000	9396	Mujer Agachada (20x22x19cm-8x9x7in) s.d.1966 brown pat.bronze executed 1969. 7-Jan-94 Gary Nader, Miami #37/R
$14000	9333	Mujer sentada (31cm-12in) s.d.1978 num.IV/V black pat.bronze. 18-May-94 Sotheby's, New York #336/R
$16000	10596	Juchiteca sentada (23cm-9in) s.d.1967 num.I/III brown pat.bronze. 24-Nov-92 Christie's, New York #175/R
$16000	10596	pareja (34cm-13in) s.d.1971 num.II/III brown pat.bronze. 24-Nov-92 Christie's, New York #166/R
$16000	10667	Mujer en cuclillas (16cm-6in) s. green pat.bronze executed c.1965. 18-May-94 Sotheby's, New York #372/R
$16000	10667	Pescadores (47cm-19in) s.d.1981 num.II/VI black pat.bronze. 18-May-94 Sotheby's, New York #335/R
$16000	10458	Evelia (27cm-11in) s.d.1969 num.I/III green pat.bronze. 18-May-93 Sotheby's, New York #226/R
$18000	12162	Mujer sentada (29cm-11in) s.d.1980 num.VI/VI grey brown pat.bronze. 23-Nov-93 Christie's, New York #118/R
$21000	14189	Mujer agachada (26cm-10in) s.d.1967 num.VI/VI brown pat.bronze. 22-Nov-93 Sotheby's, New York #253/R
$25000	16340	Reclining woman (25cm-10in) s. carved onyx executed 1965. 14-May-93 Du Mouchelle, Detroit #2041/R
$27000	18243	Maternidad (31cm-12in) s.d.1971 num.II/VI brown pat.bronze. 23-Nov-93 Christie's, New York #119/R
$27000	17647	Tres mujeres sentadas (25cm-10in) num.IV/VI black pat.bronze executed 1980. 18-May-93 Sotheby's, New York #209/R
$28000	18301	Virginia de Pie (61cm-24in) s.d.1980 num.V/VI dark brown pat.bronze. 17-May-93 Christie's, New York #255/R
$28000	18301	Tres mujeres paradas (42cm-17in) s.d.1980 num.III/VI black pat.bronze. 18-May-93 Sotheby's, New York #210/R
$29000	18954	Madre e Hijo (56cm-22in) s.d.1965 num.III/V green pat.bronze. 18-May-93 Sotheby's, New York #59/R
$35000	23333	Juchitecas conversando (41cm-16in) s.d.1985 num.VI/VI pat.bronze executed 1985. 18-May-94 Christie's, New York #106/R
$35000	23179	Virginia con Ropaje (48cm-19in) s.d.1977 num.I/V green pat.bronze. 24-Nov-92 Christie's, New York #107/R
$35000	23649	Madre e Hijo Parados (76cm-30in) s.d.1960 num.II brown pat.bronze. 22-Nov-93 Sotheby's, New York #49/R
$40000	26490	Virginia desnuda (29x50x48cm-11x20x19in) s.d.1973 num.IV/VI greenish-brown pat.bronze. 24-Nov-92 Christie's, New York #108/R
$40000	26490	Reclining couple (43x62x26cm-17x24x10in) s.d.1977 alabaster. 23-Nov-92 Sotheby's, New York #205/R
$42000	28378	Maternidad (115x56x35cm-45x22x14in) s.d.1982 num.I/IV brown pat.bronze. 23-Nov-93 Christie's, New York #21/R
$45000	30405	Evelia sentada en una silla (46cm-18in) s.d.1980 num.IV/VI black pat.bronze. 22-Nov-93 Sotheby's, New York #260/R
$50000	33113	Mujer Hacha (49cm-19in) s.d. black marble. 24-Nov-92 Christie's, New York #54/R
$60000	39216	Rosa sobre una silla (123x75x68cm-48x30x27in) s.i.d.1980 num.II/V dark brown pat.bronze 1980. 17-May-93 Christie's, New York #13/R
$60000	39735	Dos mujeres (43x43x38cm-17x17x15in) s.d.1978 black marble. 24-Nov-92 Christie's, New York #18/R
$65000	43333	Mujer sentada (59cm-23in) black marble executed 1980. 18-May-94 Christie's, New York #35/R
$70000	47297	Mujer con rebozo sentada (64cm-25in) s.d.1978 black marble. 22-Nov-93 Sotheby's, New York #60/R
$80000	53333	Dos mujeres (47cm-19in) s.d.1959 basalt. 17-May-94 Sotheby's, New York #66/R
$105000	70946	Mujer en cuclillas (86cm-34in) s.d.1969 green pat.bronze f.st. 22-Nov-93 Sotheby's, New York #26/R
$110000	73333	Amelia sentada (74x105x79cm-29x41x31in) s.d.1972 num.IV/V green pat.bronze executed 72. 18-May-94 Christie's, New York #58/R
$135000	88235	Juchiteca sentada (107cm-42in) s.d.1973 num.I/IV green pat.bronze f.st. 18-May-93 Sotheby's, New York #40/R
$135000	88235	Coloquio (117cm-46in) s.d.1979 num.IV/V black pat.bronze f.st. 18-May-93 Sotheby's, New York #64/R
$160000	106667	Juchiteca de Pie (194cm-76in) s.d.1968 num.III/III st.Cast F.Moises del Aguila. 17-May-94 Sotheby's, New York #46/R

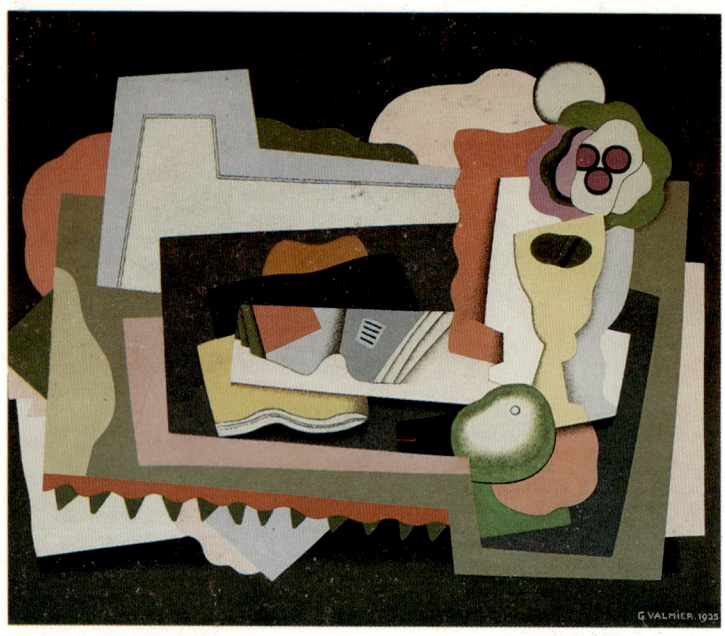

Georges Valmier *Fruits et Fleurs* 1925

Largest gallery in western America specializing in:

French Impressionists and Post Impressionists
European 19th century • Barbizon School
American 19th century • California Impressionism
Western • Old Masters • Modernists

Serving an international clientele of
private collectors, museums and institutions

Peter M. Fairbanks, Director
Ellen M. Storck, European Art • Elisabeth T. Peters, American Art

MONTGOMERY GALLERY

250 Sutter Street, San Francisco, CA 94108 USA
Phone: 415.788.8300 Fax: 415.788.5469